The Cosmos Reader

The

Cosmos Reader

THE EDITORS

EDGAR Z. FRIEDENBERG
Dalhousie University

MAX BLACK
Institute for Advanced Studies

RICHARD POIRIER
Rutgers University

RENÉ DUBOS
Rockefeller University

STANLEY KAUFFMANN

IRVING HOWE
Hunter College

HARVEY COX
Harvard University

ROBERT COLES
Harvard University

ROBERT DAVIS
The Everdale Place

LESLIE FIEDLER
State University of New York at Buffalo

HENRY NASH SMITH
University of California, Berkeley

Harcourt Brace Jovanovich, Inc.

NEW YORK   CHICAGO   SAN FRANCISCO   ATLANTA

ISBN: 0-15-514173-2

Library of Congress Catalog Card Number: 70-141608

Printed in the United States of America

PREFACE

The turbulent years since the Second World War have produced a torrent of new and renewed ideas. The more than one hundred selections in this reader express some of these ideas and examine their antecedents and origins.

The selections for each of the eleven subject areas were chosen by a contributing editor with special qualifications in that area. Each editor introduces his section with an essay that offers a succinct orientation to the subject and is a seminal contribution in its own right.

The selections were chosen to treat subjects of current concern and to place them in historical context: The aim is to define what is new, disclose its past, and probe how the two are related. The selections embrace a broad range of view, style, tone, and approach. There are a measured, reflective piece by Alfred North Whitehead and a passionate, undisciplined statement by a member of Weatherman; Dietrich Bonhoeffer's very personal thoughts on latter-day theology, and accounts of religious experience at once new and old from Timothy Leary and Alan Watts. Martin Luther King, Jr., speaks from Birmingham Jail of the prison of race, and Bruno Bettelheim of another kind of prison. Abbie Hoffman clowns revolution, and Noam Chomsky introduces a quietly revolutionary approach to the idea of language; Eldridge Cleaver and Norman Mailer examine the white–black equation from inside and out; Norman O. Brown sees in an old idea a potential for a new kind of brother- and sisterhood. Harry Stack Sullivan sees little virtue in adversity;

W. R. Robinson postulates a world of difference between literature and the new cinema; Marshall McLuhan envisions the electronic explosion as the truly decentralizing force in education; and James Agee briefly examines the paradox of man's individuality and mankind's integrity.

Taken together, these and the dozens of other selections make a lively but not always regular pattern that reflects the disorder, ferment, and potential of our times. It is a pattern that we feel will challenge the ingenuity of the instructor and engage the interests of today's students.

Making this book has occupied the talents of many whose contributions cannot be individually acknowledged, and those we thank en masse; the suggestions, comments, and analyses by Gerald Levin, however, compel special recognition, and we here reaffirm our gratitude for his invaluable help in this project.

THE PUBLISHER

CONTENTS

Language   EDITED BY MAX BLACK

Style   EDITED BY RICHARD POIRIER

Science   EDITED BY RENÉ DUBOS

Film   EDITED BY STANLEY KAUFFMANN

Liberty, Toleration, and Dissent   EDITED BY IRVING HOWE

The Changing Face of Religion   EDITED BY HARVEY COX

The Cultural Revolution and Its Prophets
EDITED BY LESLIE FIEDLER

The Idea of a Humane Tradition   EDITED BY HENRY NASH SMITH

The Cosmos Reader

The Self

EDITED BY EDGAR Z. FRIEDENBERG

INTRODUCTION

Although not a recent invention, selfhood remains, even today, an ambiguous resource that is very unevenly distributed through time and space. Though Socrates exhorted: "Know thyself," and Polonius, ironically, urged his son Laertes "To thine own self be true"—both admonitions having since become fundamental clichés of Western morality—there have been many millions of people since antiquity who would not really have understood either phrase; and there have been and are languages into which these simple imperatives could not be translated. The conviction that each person is a separate individual, with a particular personality distinguishable from all others and a distinctive view of reality derived from his unique experience, is the basis of the Western view of human dignity. Our moral sense derives from the assumption that each individual possesses the means to judge for himself what—in view of his particular place in the universe, as he sees it—he is obliged to do; to know what is best for him and what he really wants, as we say, *out of life* and *from other* people.

To note that Western morality is based on a sense of self, and particularly on self-consciousness and self-determination, is not necessarily to praise it. Self-awareness is not a state of grace. The Book of Genesis—one of the earliest and still perhaps the soundest of publications to deal clinically with the problem of self-consciousness—treats the condition as a form of

3

pathology and ascribes its onset to improper diet. The sense of individuality is also, ineluctably, a sense of alienation from others; the skin becomes a frontier both in the new-world sense of a boundary beyond which the savage and the unknown lurk, and in the old-world sense of a barrier between potentially hostile entities. Selfhood implies not only separation from others, but a situation in which to exploit them through selfishness or self-interest.

The sense of self is the basis of individuality and individualism, both of which are prized in the Western system of values. True, both are continuously threatened by social forces that may extinguish them; yet the very fact that conformity and invasion of privacy are regarded as threats in our society is enough to establish the value of individualism, though not to ensure its survival. Since our conception of morality depends on the assumption of individual free will, our complex economic arrangements on the mythic ideal of individual freedom of contract, and our self-esteem on individual, usually competitive, achievement, the self is clearly a key concept for contemporary Americans; at the same time the social conditions that increasingly limit and threaten the possibility of self-determination are major sources of anxiety and frustration in modern life and account for its prevailing flavor of alienation.

Yet it may be argued that Western culture is not so much devoted to individualism as addicted to it. We apply its moral canons in situations and through institutions that make it destructive. Historically, the self concept emerged and developed as part of the ideological system which facilitated technical mastery of man over nature and other men. Whether one chooses to think of this as the rise of Protestantism, of capitalism, of the bourgeoisie over feudalism, or of modern technology, it is clear that what has been basic is the growth of our conviction that the individual could and should dominate his environment and impose his will and his moral judgment on weaker, less technologically competent social groups and their members. If our peculiar conception of human dignity derives from our attitude toward the individual self, so does our use of technology to treat everybody and everything as objects to be manipulated by the freestanding, mobile, detached individual.

Both the moral and psychological roles of the self remain highly ambiguous. To ourselves, in our culture, the most intolerable assaults are those directed against the self, whether physically or in its social role; and the noblest human acts are those of self-assertion against serious and threatening opposition, physical or political. But this does not imply that societies in which selfhood is less clearly defined and human beings less individualized will be more brutal and less noble, though they will certainly appear to a modern bourgeois to have a lower standard of living. American society today can hardly be called morally superior to that of relatively rural, peasant Vietnam; or the Puritans less oppressive than the Indians they destroyed. Children, especially, are treated more respectfully and less manipulatively in most "primitive" societies than in individualistic, developed societies, which instill the motivations needed to maintain themselves by pitting children competitively against one another in school and by rewarding success in school with more love at home. Societies in which individuals develop a strong sense of separate selfhood have their own forms of bondage and brutality. Marshall McLuhan, most familiarly, sees modern, print-oriented man, with his highly individualized point of view, as the epitome of alienation: alone, with his family, in their very own tract house separated from its neighbors but not distinguished from them except by superficial forms of personalization, which are themselves mass produced. He also sees this situation being rapidly resolved in favor of the "global village," in which the effort to achieve, or simulate, unique selfhood by mass-production methods has been abandoned and replaced by more communal relationships among persons who are less self-conscious, competitive, and uptight. The emergence of the hippie life-style in the late 1960's and the fascinated hostility it has evoked from older persons with more rigid self systems suggest that he may well be right. At a higher level of abstraction, Marxian thought would treat the self-consciousness of modern Western man as merely the special form of false-consciousness required by and appropriate to his ideology of competitive self-advancement perpetually challenged in the marketplace. The self *is* important; particularly, in America, if you have nothing else to sell.

Although, meanwhile, life goes on, the prospect of living happy ever after in the marketplace does seem to be rapidly declining. In mass industrial societies—whether basically socialist or capitalist—institutions inimical to individuality and a strong sense of self evolve in closely parallel ways, while fascism appears less as a dreadful alternative to democracy than as a condition toward which mass democracies evolve and as the peculiar form of tyranny to which they are subject. Both here and in the Soviet Union, devotion to technological mastery as the most socially approved form of self-expression seems linked to imperialist ambition and an egregious contempt for private personality and more primitive local institutions. These are perhaps more closely linked in the United States, where success is conceived wholly in terms of individual mastery and where the temptation to gain it by using others ruthlessly is correspondingly great. The Chinese "struggle-session"—much abhorred by us as brainwashing—turns out in practice to be virtually indistinguishable in quality and tone from the more extreme, and extremely fashionable, forms of the "encounter group" or "T-group" sessions, especially those designed to eradicate behavior and character structure deemed antisocial in our society—drug addiction, for example. It is even more discouraging to find that a liberal, democratic society which assumes that its devotion to individualism will put at its disposal the moral resources of the free self is actually as little capable of responding to any moral challenge as a totalitarian regime (perhaps less capable, since it is impossible to find out who is to be held responsible) and can be dissuaded from evil only by failure, never by pity or even shame. In this century, what American official or executive—public or private—has laid his career on the line by publicly opposing a policy he thought to be wrong or resigning in protest against it? Who supposes that such an act would have any influence? Luther lived a long time ago.

The idea of the self, and of personal autonomy, may have achieved its highest relevance, like the railway and the conscript army, as part of the apparatus of industrialization and mass democracy—as an essential component of the ideology needed to effect the modernization of feudal societies by breaking the communal bonds that interfered with progress. In doing so, it appears to have destroyed the conditions that gave rise to it: the existence of a middle class secure enough to defend its independence, yet not so well ensconced as to be able to take itself for granted.

No author in the century and a half since Alexis de Tocqueville wrote his classic *Democracy in America* has shown as much insight as he did into the relationship between democratic institutions and the character structure, sense of values, and selfhood of the people who maintain and are molded by them. Himself the grandson of a French nobleman executed in the terror of the French Revolution, Tocqueville—who visited America in 1831 to study its prisons—became a sympathetic and perceptive critic of democracy, which he saw as affording mankind generally a better chance of a decent life than any other social system. Its deficiencies, as the excerpts in this book make clear, were perfectly apparent to Tocqueville; but, having firmly grasped the inevitability of a mass society and accepted the loss of aristocratic qualities from daily life, he turned to democracy as likely to sustain the least oppressive form of egalitarianism. In the sections included here, he discusses specifically the kind of person he found dominant in American society and the social conditions in which such people flourish.

Tocqueville's observations of American life are still so fitting that most readers may find it hard to recognize the subtle but sometimes crucial ways in which they have ceased to fit. Tocqueville was quite aware that his work depended for its validity on certain conditions of American life that were quite likely to change, and he identified them explicitly: a class of yeomen farmers, independent in their small but securely held landholdings; "the fact that America has no great capital city, whose direct or indirect influence is felt over the whole extent of the country"; and a poor system of communications. "If," he observed,

a democratic republic, similar to that of the United States were ever founded in a country where the power of one man had previously established a centralized administration, and had sunk it deep into the habits and laws of the people, I do not hesitate to assert that, in such a republic, a more insufferable despotism would prevail than in any of the absolute monarchies of Europe; or, indeed, than any which could be found this side of Asia.

Today, therefore, Tocqueville's readers must bear in mind that he is not quite as modern as he sounds; American society has, as he envisaged, become much more a mass society than it was in his day. The self that each individual develops in the process of coping with such a society has taken on characteristics that he would probably have disliked. The greater fragmentation of relationships in a highly urban, mobile society in which people seldom get to know their friends, neighbors, or enemies in their full personalities, and the bureaucratization of most interpersonal relationships

(What, indeed, would one of Tocqueville's American acquaintances have made of the phrase "interpersonal relationship"?) has greatly encouraged the kind of role-playing so brilliantly discussed by Erving Goffman in his classic *Presentation of Self in Everyday Life.* Although Goffman's initial observations were made not on city-dwellers but on rural innkeepers on a remote Scottish island who were trying both to please and to control urban guests who tended to romanticize the life of the crofter, his inferences apply to the behavior of any individual or social group whose ability to satisfy a clientele depends, in substantial part, on encouraging the client's illusions— especially those about himself. There is nothing very modern about this problem, which has always been basic to the practice of the world's oldest profession. What *is* modern is the plight of the individual who has never been confirmed in his identity by a set of deep and lasting relationships and who comes to feel, perhaps quite accurately, that his whole life consists of a series of such roles and that the actor does not exist apart from them. Even this is not truly new: Ibsen, in *Peer Gynt,* published in 1867, dealt precisely and exhaustively with this theme, and in a format more like that of the contemporary theater of the absurd than the realism of his other works. Peer Gynt's tragic destiny marks a fundamental division point in man's relationship to the social forces with which he interacts; in every era, the results of that interaction have been tragic more often than not. But the tragedy has traditionally contained elements of the heroic, the essence of the tragedy lying in the hero's being trapped or forced by circumstances into situations wholly inappropriate to his identity and character—like Oedipus or Marat— and hence tormented or destroyed precisely because he was who he was. In contemporary life, as in contemporary fiction, the tragedy—or the nightmare —lies in the fact that people are crushed or reduced to absurdity by circumstances to which their personalities, if they have any, seem totally irrelevant; at most, they are interesting case studies, overwhelmed by reality or simply cut to pieces by jagged fragments of their own experience, which even if intact would show no coherent pattern. "A tense and peculiar family, the Oedipuses, were they not?" Max Beerbohm mused elegantly a few decades ago, thus ushering in as best he could the age of the selfless anti-hero. Only the Sphinx that riddled Oedipus remains, asking, with deceptive simplicity, merely, "Who's in charge here?"

To select from contemporary literature writings illustrative of the problems of the emerging self is therefore already to introduce a bias; to have such problems today is already a little luxurious and old-fashioned, as if this were still the heyday of the novel or of psychoanalysis—these having been the two most highly developed art forms devoted to the reification of personality. This is undoubtedly one reason why the pieces included in this section, which were selected for the vividness and depth of their self-portraiture, are about quite extraordinary people, and sometimes from extraordinary periods in those lives. Michael Rossman, surely the most brilliant of the original group of Berkeley students whose dissent in the Free Speech Movement of 1965 first cracked the smug façade of the American university system, wrote the selection included here while serving a term in the Santa

Rita Prison Farm in California, having been convicted of trespass on the complaint of university officials. At the time, this was still a rather unusual experience for a middle-class graduate student; Rossman's reflections on it tell us, as it did him, much that is new about the ways in which the self responds to insight into the nature of a hostile social system. The experience of Malcolm X recounted here complements that of Rossman, for it was on his journey to Mecca that Malcolm first fully experienced unqualified respect—as a Muslim and a human being—without regard to race. From this belated grace he gained a wholeness that transcended the hatreds and parochialism of his previous experience—and that may have led to his murder as a person who had become an intolerable threat to the iniquitous politics of race in America. It is odd that the first deep draft of humiliation affected Rossman so nearly the same way Malcolm's deepest experience of human acceptance affected him; each, perhaps, was delivered from the exhaustion of trying to come to terms with a social system that stood finally revealed as destructive, and, therefore, as devoid of moral authority. Both men grew in stature as they came to realize that their society could no longer add insult to the injury it had already done them and would continue to do.

Ned Rorem, by contrast, sounds like a gilded youth from another era; as, indeed, Paris in the summer of 1951 was to a young American composer whose extraordinary personal beauty—which he coolly and shamelessly exploited—gave him entrée to any society he wished. Yet his dry and somber wit and unpitying self-awareness make him what few men are—an unsparing witness to his own human condition. The very first sentence of his *Paris Diary,* included in this anthology, is a charming lie. He *is* Ned Rorem, all right, and he knows who he is, though he is not always pleased by the knowledge. Rorem's sensitivity and candor would, in any case, make his diary an exceptionally valuable account of his selfhood. But his homosexual preferences make it more valuable still, not as a set of notes from underground, but because they lead him to discuss very fully the ways in which his body affected his sense of self both through his awareness of it and through the response it evoked from other people. Had he been an ugly or graceless youth he could not, despite his musical talents, have become at all the person he did; and this is a factor we tend to overlook in men and overstate in women as we assess the course of their development. Yet the self is indistinguishable from its embodiment.

The response of American males to one another in a social relationship that defines their bodies as salient is likely to be awkward and embarrassed, even if their roles are defined as unimpeachably masculine and aggressive. What makes most military humor insufferably strained and embarrassing is not its obscenity but its stereotypy in a system of conventions that denies the existence of certain aspects of the self. Thus, even *Lysistrata* tends to strike modern audiences not as an outspoken play but as one whose lewdness is evasive and cute; erotic interest may be expressed in the absent women *only* —and that must be shouted. In this way, society seems to hope, sexually unconventional aspects of the self will remain unconfirmed and will atrophy. The repressive function of myth and play, which mold the self by resolutely ignoring unmentionables or by putting them cutely in quotes, is less familiar than their expressive function; but both denial and confirmation are involved in the process by which society molds the self. This process is discernible, with just these limitations, in George Plimpton's account of the hackneyed ritual of the annual party by which the Detroit Lions initiate and welcome the rookies who have survived the first season's testing. The celebration, which follows immediately upon the day when failed rookies are cut off the team and slink away from their former buddies and competitors as unobtrusively as they can, is meant to be an occasion of Dionysian revelry. Some such *rite de passage* is universal among social groups as a way of recording and emphasizing important stages in self-development. But this festival is mixed and awkward. The triumphant young Lions do celebrate the satisfaction of making it and their relief from the anxieties of probation, but any human relationships that may have developed in the training camp—and in other sections of *Paper Lion* Plimpton conveys its atmosphere of brooding intensity very skillfully—are dissipated in clowning at the party, and the clowning itself is stereotyped and empty. After the weeks of shared ordeal and enforced intimacy, the party seems almost designed to deny what Norman Mailer justly observed in his short essay "T-Formation and Single Wing" more than a decade ago:

> Now, of course, football was always oriented around the ass—any game which uses up the power of the male hormone must find a way to counteract the passivities of fatigue. The quick and simple solution of athletes has always been to pat each other on the butt, and it is a practical solution so far as that goes and seems to do its biochemical work. . . . This act of fraternity can be offered as easily in the Single Wing as the T, but since the pat on the bottom is a personal expression, it lacks the formal sanction and so greater unconscious pleasure of an institutionalized ritual. Here is where the T-formation satisfies society and self.[1]

To some extent the conventionality of the young Lions at play, and their blank lack of sensuality, are social-class characteristics, for they—except Plimpton—are working class, while self-elaboration and preoccupation with the varieties of personal experience are primarily middle-class characteristics.

The refinement and precision of E. M. Forster's sense of self, and of the obligations imposed by his selfhood, as recorded in "What I Believe," are really sufficient to define the work as what it is: the statement of a Cambridge don, novelist, and literary critic, made during World War II, when he was already sixty. Probably none of us, and no social class, will ever again be so certain what it or we are skeptical about or committed to. This was the very heyday of the Self, and the great British universities were, in a sense, its true home. Of course, social classes differ in the institutional forms and language available to them for expressing the claims of their selfhood—though not in their common humanity.

It would be hard to imagine a more moving statement about the way experience affects personality—or a more self-conscious one—than Oscar

[1] From *Advertisements for Myself* (New York: Putnam, 1959), pp. 429-30.

Lewis' transcription of the account of Roberto, a poor boy from a Mexico City slum. Deprivation and suffering do not arrest the development of the self. They certainly distort it; but each of us, after all, is distinguished by his scars and by the twists and turns he took in order to avoid the obstacles that would have blocked growth. This is what makes us who we are, just as it keeps us from being what we might have been:

> You know what you could be.
> Tell me, my friend,
> Why you worry all the time
> What you should be.[2]

But cultural deprivation can deny its victims the symbols and the minimum degree of detachment needed in order to tell their story coherently. Without Oscar Lewis's intervention, Roberto would have remained mute and inglorious; so would the young girls Miss Dunn met *Up the Junction* and movingly portrayed. A clear sense of personal identity is least common in those social groups or classes whose members are constantly taught by bitter experience that their wishes and feelings will not be seriously considered by those who make demands upon them, and who acquiesce to or even identify with their oppressors. Still, as Herbert Marcuse and many less celebrated critics of our society have noted: These days, one way or another, that means most of us.

The readings so far discussed all deal with social influences on the self, and the response of certain individuals to such influences. I have avoided the rather more conventional approach, which begins with psychological theory, because it is associated in my mind with a form of social and political reaction that I find profoundly distasteful. To put psychology first seems to many people to imply that whenever social conflict arises it is the feelings and personalities of the doubtless poorly adjusted and improperly socialized members of the trouble-making groups that are the real problem. This has been especially true of commentators on recent protest and disruption by high school and college students.

Both conflict and selfhood are psychosocial; but if the society is to be taken as given, then it is the psychic processes that are expected to give and that are subjected to manipulation and control in the interests of social stability. This position is equally indefensible scientifically and morally; in order to avoid it I have literally and figuratively put the social factors first. But this is not meant to minimize the importance of psychological theory to an understanding of selfhood and its operations, and the selections from Bettelheim, Sullivan, and, finally—and in a quite different way—Norman O. Brown are intended to restore the emphasis I have thus far withheld from the psychological bases of the self.

As indicated above, several of my selections illustrate how the body and the

[2] From "You Know What You Could Be" by Mike Heron. Copyright © 1967 by Paradox Music, a division of the Dyna Corporation. All rights reserved.

responses it elicits from others—which are themselves greatly affected by custom—are involved in the process of self-development. No scholar has dealt with this issue more fundamentally than Bruno Bettelheim in the passages on "Body Language" and "Mutuality" in communication between mother and infant, taken from the chapter called "Where the Self Begins" in his book *The Empty Fortress*. Neither has any author been more cavalier than has Bettelheim in his treatment of student protest (in his more recent popular writings) as a psychological phenomenon with minimal social meaning, to be dealt with by firm discipline, as one deals—perhaps, indeed, with no more basic right—with a child's temper tantrum. But where, as in the passages presently cited, Bettelheim addresses himself exclusively to the psychology of selfhood rather than to its social consequences, few men speak with greater insight.

One of those who did is Harry Stack Sullivan, whose death twenty years ago deprived psychoanalytic thought of its most original contributor since Freud and of the only native American to have achieved major stature as an innovative theoretician in that subtle field. It is really an impertinence to excerpt Sullivan on the self—a subject that his entire work elucidates. But doing so may serve to interest readers in his work, particularly *The Interpersonal Theory of Psychiatry,* from which the remarks included here are taken.

The Sullivanian *self,* though comparable to the Freudian *ego,* is a less imperious and perhaps today more relevant concept. Sullivan is, on the whole, less confident than Freud of the potentialities of the human will to contest, by its rationality, the cruel demands of reality and of the unconscious. The human will, in fact, is even better than Freud thought at avoiding probate. The self system is the instrument—or rather, the set of psychic processes—by which it does so, thereby limiting anxiety to bearable intensity but at great cost in personal potential. Sullivan therefore makes it very clear that self-development is a peculiarly intaglio process; we recognize our image from what has been relinquished and cut away from our original endowment, sensual and intellectual—though the duality implied by the latter distinction is itself evidence that serious psychic injury has already been sustained. In the healthy creature, mind, body, and feeling are one.

In Sullivan's terms, the *self system* is what we use to cope with our premonitions of increased anxiety, which are the most painful feelings possible. But since reality, and not anxiety, is the source of any real danger that may exist, responses of the self system that relieve anxiety tend to be maladaptive. An ostrich that complains that the sand is dirtier than it used to be and likely to cause conjunctivitis does not thereby protect its tail. Anxiety encourages sentimentality; and sentimentality insulates the self further from encounter with the realities of experience through which it might grow.

Growth and wisdom, or maturation, are processes encouraged by acceptance of feeling, even of anxiety, as the best clues we have to the nature of our relationship to reality. The process has nowhere been better expressed than in this passage from Rebecca West's classic *Black Lamb and Grey Falcon,* in which she relates an encounter with an old Montenegrin peasant woman wandering in the hills and trying to come to terms with the tragedy that has befallen her—her family killed in war, her second husband mad and senile:

It is doubtful whether, walk as she would on these heights, she would arrive at any conclusion that was of value even to herself. She was, however, the answer to my doubts. She took her destiny not as the beasts take it, nor as the plants and trees; she not only suffered it, she examined it. As the sword swept down on her through the darkness she threw out her hand and caught the blade as it fell, not caring if she cut her fingers so long as she could question its substance, where it had been forged, and who the wielder. She wanted to understand the secret which Gerda denied, the mystery of process. I knew that art and science were the instruments of this desire, and this was their sole justification, though in the Western world where I lived I had seen art debauched to ornament and science prostituted to the mul- tiplication of gadgets. I knew that they were descended from man's primitive neces- sities, that the cave man who had to hunt the aurochs drew him on the rock-face that he might better understand the aurochs and have fuller fortune in hunting and was the ancestor of all artists, that the nomad who had to watch the length of shadows to know when he should move his herd to the summer pasture was the ancestor of all scientists. But I did not know these things thoroughly with my bowels as well as my mind. I knew them now, when I saw the desire for understand- ing move this woman. It might have been far otherwise with her, for she had been confined by her people's past and present to a kind of destiny that might have stunned its victims into an inability to examine it. Nevertheless, she desired neither peace nor gold, but simply knowledge of what her life might mean. The instru- ment used by the hunter and the nomad was not too blunt to turn to finer uses; it was not dismayed by complexity, and it could regard the more stupendous au- rochs that range within the mind and measure the diffuse shadows cast by history. And what was more, the human will did not forget its appetite for using it.[3]

This may be taken as a definitive description of ego function at its best, unhampered, as nearly as possible, by the constrictions of the self system, which so often stuns its victims into an inability, or an invincible reluctance, to examine the meaning of their lives. This Montenegrin woman, one might say, is truly self-conscious and striving to become more so. Yet even Miss West does not quite deal with the ultimate issues affecting the nature of selfhood. Hers is as fine a statement of the rationalist position as I have ever read; but it is classical in its dependence on mind as what is quintessentially human, as distinct from the thoughtlessness of animal nature. "Where id was, there shall ego be" is probably Freud's most frequently quoted statement of the purpose of psychoanalysis; and by it he meant that man might achieve a state of enlightenment and thus a measure of control over his own destiny quite like that which Miss West believed her Montenegrin acquaintance to be seeking. But this kind of enlightenment is indeed akin to science; it is very different from the enlightenment implied in the Eastern concept of *satori,* in which the self is no longer held willfully distinct from others and from nature. The hunter and the nomad, moreover, were, like many

[3] From *Black Lamb and Grey Falcon* by Rebecca West. Copyright 1940, 1941, Copyright © renewed 1968 by Rebecca West. Reprinted by permission of The Viking Press, Inc.

scientists today, not even fundamentally interested in science, but in technology; they sought to control and not merely, or even primarily, to understand those aspects of nature that they saw as affecting their lives.

So we have returned to the issue we started with. Does self-consciousness *inherently* imply a predisposition to manipulate that which is not-self, and thus to treat other people as things? Is self-awareness rooted—in principle, and hence inevitably—in alienation? Norman O. Brown, the final contributor to this section, holds that it is. The brief passages from *Love's Body* included here may be regarded as the culmination of a brilliant analysis of the processes, historical and individual, by which Western man has lost his self in the process of seeking to control himself and everything else in nature. I say "may be regarded" because Brown, especially in his later work, eschews linearity of organization as itself a form of overcontrol and excessively constrictive rationality, and chooses to present his reflections in the form of aphorisms that are left to the reader to organize if he wishes. To Brown, then, psychoanalysis becomes a way of reducing the id to the service of the ego, and oneself to the status of an object. Even definitively masculine or feminine sexuality is explained by Brown as the consequence of traumatic self-discipline which extinguishes the diffuse—in Freud's term "polymorphous-perverse"—sexuality of childhood, with its attendant rich possibilities for diversity in pleasure and in love relationships, in favor of the firm self-definition as a he-man or dependent woman that our society supports and often demands.

Only man (and a few higher anthropoids) possesses this possibility of polymorphous-perverse development because other animals, whose infancy is shorter, must cope with reality on their own at an earlier stage of development and therefore abandon those sensual possibilities which, though pleasurable, would prolong their dependency. In this connection it is suggestive, too, that the hippie trip, with its blurring of sex distinctions and its strongly developed sensuality, which is cultivated at the expense of competitive achievement, is primarily a phenomenon of affluence and the protection affluence affords. Readers who wish to follow Brown's discussion on these topics are referred to his books, *Life Against Death* and *Love's Body*; the selections from Brown's work included here present only its culminating implications for selfhood and for the idea of personality. But with Brown, the argument has come full circle. Self-seeking, in Brown's construction, becomes a slow but thorough form of suicide—and suicide, surely, is a consummate act of self-assertion though also, for most people, probably a waste of time.

From DEMOCRACY IN AMERICA

Alexis de Tocqueville

I have shown how it is that in ages of equality every man seeks for his opinions within himself; I am now to show how it is that in the same ages all his feelings are turned towards himself alone. *Individualism* is a novel expression, to which a novel idea has given birth. Our fathers were only acquainted with *égoïsme* (selfishness). Selfishness is a passionate and exaggerated love of self, which leads a man to connect everything with himself and to prefer himself to everything in the world. Individualism is a mature and calm feeling, which disposes each member of the community to sever himself from the mass of his fellows and to draw apart with his family and his friends, so that after he has thus formed a little circle of his own, he willingly leaves society at large to itself. Selfishness originates in blind instinct; individualism proceeds from erroneous judgment more than from depraved feelings; it originates as much in deficiencies of mind as in perversity of heart.

Selfishness blights the germ of all virtue; individualism, at first, only saps the virtues of public life; but in the long run it attacks and destroys all others and is at length absorbed in downright selfishness. Selfishness is a vice as old as the world, which does not belong to one form of society more than to another; individualism is of democratic origin, and it threatens to spread in the same ratio as the equality of condition.

Among aristocratic nations, as families remain for centuries in the same condition, often on the same spot, all generations become, as it were, contemporaneous. A man almost always knows his forefathers and respects them; he thinks he already sees his remote descendants and he loves them. He willingly imposes duties on himself towards the former and the latter, and he will frequently sacrifice his personal gratifications to those who went before and to those who will come after him. Aristocratic institutions, moreover, have the effect of closely binding every man to several of his fellow citizens. As the classes of an aristocratic people are strongly marked and permanent, each of them is regarded by its own members as a sort of lesser country, more tangible and more cherished than the country at large. As in aristocratic communities all the citizens occupy fixed positions, one above another, the result is that each of them always sees a man above himself whose patronage is necessary to him, and below himself another man whose co-operation he may claim. Men living in aristocratic ages are therefore almost always closely attached to something placed out of their own sphere, and they are often disposed to forget themselves. It is true that in these ages the notion of human fellowship is faint and that men seldom think of sacrificing themselves for mankind; but they often sacrifice themselves for other men. In democratic times, on the contrary, when the duties of each individual to the race are much more clear, devoted service to any one man becomes more rare; the bond of human affection is extended, but it is relaxed.

Among democratic nations new families are constantly springing up, others are constantly falling away, and all that remain change their condition; the woof of time is every instant broken and the track of generations effaced. Those who went before are soon forgotten; of those who will come after, no one has any idea: the interest of man is confined to those in close propinquity to himself. As each class gradually approaches others and mingles with them, its members become undifferentiated and lose their class identity for each other. Aristocracy had made a chain of all the members of the community, from the peasant to the king; democracy breaks that chain and severs every link of it.

As social conditions become more equal, the number of persons increases who, although they are neither rich nor powerful enough to exercise any great influence over their fellows, have nevertheless acquired or retained sufficient education and fortune to satisfy their own wants. They owe nothing to any man, they expect nothing from any man; they acquire the habit of always considering themselves as standing alone, and they are apt to imagine that their whole destiny is in their own hands.

Thus not only does democracy make every man forget his ancestors, but it hides his descendants and separates his contemporaries from him; it throws him back forever upon himself alone and threatens in the end to confine him entirely within the solitude of his own heart.

.   .   .   .   .

THAT THE AMERICANS COMBAT THE EFFECTS OF INDIVIDUALISM BY FREE INSTITUTIONS

Despotism, which by its nature is suspicious, sees in the separation among men the surest guarantee of its continuance, and it usually makes every effort to keep them separate. No vice of the human heart is so acceptable to it as selfishness: a despot easily forgives his subjects for not loving him, provided they do not love one another. He does not ask them to assist him in governing the state; it is enough that they do not aspire to govern it themselves. He stigmatizes as turbulent and unruly spirits those who would combine their exertions to promote the prosperity of the community; and, perverting the natural meaning of words, he applauds as good citizens those who have no sympathy for any but themselves.

Thus the vices which despotism produces are precisely those which equality fosters. These two things perniciously complete and assist each other. Equality places men side by side, unconnected by any common tie; despotism raises barriers to keep them asunder; the former predisposes them not to consider their fellow creatures, the latter makes general indifference a sort of public virtue.

Despotism, then, which is at all times dangerous, is more particularly to be feared in democratic ages. It is easy to see that in those same ages men stand most in need of freedom. When the members of a community are forced to attend to public affairs, they are necessarily drawn from the circle of their own interests and snatched at times from self-observation. As soon as a man begins to treat of public affairs in public, he begins to perceive that he is not so independent of his fellow men as he had at first imagined, and that in order to obtain their support he must often lend them his co-operation.

When the public govern, there is no man who does not feel the value of public goodwill or who does not endeavor to court it by drawing to himself the esteem and affection of those among whom he is to live. Many of the passions which congeal and keep asunder human hearts are then obliged to retire and hide below the surface. Pride must be dissembled; disdain dares not break out; selfishness fears its own self. Under a free government, as most public offices are elective, the men whose elevated minds or aspiring hopes are too closely circumscribed in private life constantly feel that they cannot do without the people who surround them. Men learn at such times to think of their fellow men from ambitious motives; and they frequently find it, in a manner, their interest to forget themselves.

I may here be met by an objection derived from electioneering, intrigues, the meanness of candidates, and the calumnies of their opponents. These are occasions of enmity which occur the oftener the more frequent elections become. Such evils are doubtless great, but they are transient; whereas the benefits that attend them remain. The desire of being elected may lead some men for a time to violent hostility; but this same desire leads all men in the long run to support each other; and if it happens that an election accidentally severs two friends, the electoral system brings a multitude of citizens permanently together who would otherwise always have remained unknown to one another. Freedom produces private animosities, but despotism gives birth to general indifference.

The Americans have combated by free institutions the tendency of equality to keep men asunder, and they have subdued it. The legislators of America did not suppose that a general representation of the whole nation would suffice to ward off a disorder at once so natural to the frame of democratic society and so fatal; they also thought that it would be well to infuse political life into each portion of the territory in order to multiply to an infinite extent opportunities of acting in concert for all the members of the community and to make them constantly feel their mutual dependence. The plan was a wise one. The general affairs of a country engage the attention only of leading politicians, who assemble from time to time in the same places; and as they often lose sight of each other afterwards, no lasting ties are established between them. But if the object be to have the local affairs of a district conducted by the men who reside there, the same persons are always in contact, and they are, in a manner, forced to be acquainted and to adapt themselves to one another.

It is difficult to draw a man out of his own circle to interest him in the destiny of the state, because he does not clearly understand what influence the destiny of the state can have upon his own lot. But if it is proposed to make a road cross the end of his estate, he will see at a glance that there is a connection between this small public affair and his greatest private affairs; and he will discover, without its being shown to him, the close tie that unites private to general interest. Thus far more may be done by entrusting to the citizens the administration of minor affairs than by surrendering to them in the control of important ones, towards interesting them in the public welfare and convincing them that they constantly stand in need of one another in order to provide for it. A brilliant achievement may win for you the favor of a people at one stroke; but to earn the love and respect of the population that surrounds you, a long succession of little services rendered and of obscure good deeds, a constant habit of kindness, and an established reputation for disinterestedness will be required. Local freedom, then, which leads a great number of citizens to value the affection of their neighbors and of their kindred, perpetually brings men together and forces them to help one another in spite of the propensities that sever them.

In the United States the more opulent citizens take great care not to stand aloof from the people; on the contrary, they constantly keep on easy terms with the lower classes: they listen to them, they speak to them every day. They know that the rich in democracies always stand in need of the poor, and that in democratic times you attach a poor man to you more by your manner than by benefits conferred. The magnitude of such benefits, which sets off the difference of condition, causes a secret irritation to those who reap advantage from them, but the charm of simplicity of manners is almost irresistible; affability carries men away, and even want of polish is not always displeasing. This truth does not take root at once in the minds of the rich. They generally resist it as long as the democratic revolution lasts, and they do not acknowledge it immediately after that revolution is accomplished. They are very ready to do good to the people, but they still choose to keep them at arm's length; they think that is sufficient, but they are mistaken. They might spend fortunes thus without warming the hearts of the population around them; that population does not ask them for the sacrifice of their money, but of their pride.

It would seem as if every imagination in the United States were upon the stretch to invent means of increasing the wealth and satisfying the wants of the public. The best-informed inhabitants of each district constantly use their information to discover new truths that may augment the general prosperity; and if they have made any such discoveries, they eagerly surrender them to the mass of the people.

When the vices and weaknesses frequently exhibited by those who govern in America are closely examined, the prosperity of the people occasions, but improperly occasions, surprise. Elected magistrates do not make the American democracy flourish; it flourishes because the magistrates are elective.

It would be unjust to suppose that the patriotism and the zeal that every

American displays for the welfare of his fellow citizens are wholly insin-
cere. Although private interest directs the greater part of human actions
in the United States as well as elsewhere, it does not regulate them all. I
must say that I have often seen Americans make great and real sacrifices
to the public welfare; and I have noticed a hundred instances in which
they hardly ever failed to lend faithful support to one another. The free
institutions which the inhabitants of the United States possess, and the
political rights of which they make so much use, remind every citizen, and
in a thousand ways, that he lives in society. They every instant impress
upon his mind the notion that it is the duty as well as the interest of men
to make themselves useful to their fellow creatures; and as he sees no
particular ground of animosity to them, since he is never either their master
or their slave, his heart readily leans to the side of kindness. Men attend
to the interests of the public, first by necessity, afterwards by choice; what
was intentional becomes an instinct, and by dint of working for the good
of one's fellow citizens, the habit and the taste for serving them are at length
acquired.

Many people in France consider equality of condition as one evil and
political freedom as a second. When they are obliged to yield to the former,
they strive at least to escape from the latter. But I contend that in order
to combat the evils which equality may produce, there is only one effectual
remedy: namely, political freedom.

.   .   .   .   .

HOW THE AMERICANS COMBAT INDIVIDUALISM BY THE PRINCIPLE OF SELF-INTEREST RIGHTLY UNDERSTOOD

When the world was managed by a few rich and powerful individuals, these
persons loved to entertain a lofty idea of the duties of man. They were fond
of professing that it is praiseworthy to forget oneself and that good should
be done without hope of reward, as it is by the Deity himself. Such were
the standard opinions of that time in morals.

I doubt whether men were more virtuous in aristocratic ages than in
others, but they were incessantly talking of the beauties of virtue, and its
utility was only studied in secret. But since the imagination takes less lofty
flights, and every man's thoughts are centered in himself, moralists are
alarmed by this idea of self-sacrifice and they no longer venture to present
it to the human mind. They therefore content themselves with inquiring
whether the personal advantage of each member of the community does
not consist in working for the good of all; and when they have hit upon
some point on which private interest and public interest meet and amal-
gamate, they are eager to bring it into notice. Observations of this kind
are gradually multiplied; what was only a single remark becomes a general
principle, and it is held as a truth that man serves himself in serving his
fellow creatures and that his private interest is to do good.

I have already shown, in several parts of this work, by what means the inhabitants of the United States almost always manage to combine their own advantage with that of their fellow citizens; my present purpose is to point out the general rule that enables them to do so. In the United States hardly anybody talks of the beauty of virtue, but they maintain that virtue is useful and prove it every day. The American moralists do not profess that men ought to sacrifice themselves for their fellow creatures *because* it is noble to make such sacrifices, but they boldly aver that such sacrifices are as necessary to him who imposes them upon himself as to him for whose sake they are made.

They have found out that, in their country and their age, man is brought home to himself by an irresistible force; and, losing all hope of stopping that force, they turn all their thoughts to the direction of it. They therefore do not deny that every man may follow his own interest, but they endeavor to prove that it is the interest of every man to be virtuous. I shall not here enter into the reasons they allege, which would divert me from my subject; suffice it to say that they have convinced their fellow countrymen.

Montaigne said long ago: "Were I not to follow the straight road for its straightness, I should follow it for having found by experience that in the end it is commonly the happiest and most useful track." The doctrine of interest rightly understood is not then new, but among the Americans of our time it finds universal acceptance; it has become popular there; you may trace it at the bottom of all their actions, you will remark it in all they say. It is as often asserted by the poor man as by the rich. In Europe the principle of interest is much grosser than it is in America, but it is also less common and especially it is less avowed; among us, men still constantly feign great abnegation which they no longer feel.

The Americans, on the other hand, are fond of explaining almost all the actions of their lives by the principle of self-interest rightly understood; they show with complacency how an enlightened regard for themselves constantly prompts them to assist one another and inclines them willingly to sacrifice a portion of their time and property to the welfare of the state. In this respect I think they frequently fail to do themselves justice; for in the United States as well as elsewhere people are sometimes seen to give way to those disinterested and spontaneous impulses that are natural to man; but the Americans seldom admit that they yield to emotions of this kind; they are more anxious to do honor to their philosophy than to themselves.

I might here pause without attempting to pass a judgment on what I have described. The extreme difficulty of the subject would be my excuse, but I shall not avail myself of it; and I had rather that my readers, clearly perceiving my object, would refuse to follow me than that I should leave them in suspense.

The principle of self-interest rightly understood is not a lofty one, but it is clear and sure. It does not aim at mighty objects, but it attains without excessive exertion all those at which it aims. As it lies within the reach of

all capacities, everyone can without difficulty learn and retain it. By its
admirable conformity to human weaknesses it easily obtains great dominion;
nor is that dominion precarious, since the principle checks one personal
interest by another, and uses, to direct the passions, the very same instrument that excites them.

The principle of self-interest rightly understood produces no great acts
of self-sacrifice, but it suggests daily small acts of self-denial. By itself it
cannot suffice to make a man virtuous; but it disciplines a number of persons in habits of regularity, temperance, moderation, foresight, self-com-
mand; and if it does not lead men straight to virtue by the will, it gradually draws them in that direction by their habits. If the principle of
interest rightly understood were to sway the whole moral world, extraordinary virtues would doubtless be more rare; but I think that gross depravity would then also be less common. The principle of interest rightly
understood perhaps prevents men from rising far above the level of mankind, but a great number of other men, who were falling far below it, are
caught and restrained by it. Observe some few individuals, they are lowered
by it; survey mankind, they are raised.

I am not afraid to say that the principle of self-interest rightly understood appears to me the best suited of all philosophical theories to the
wants of the men of our time, and that I regard it as their chief remaining
security against themselves. Towards it, therefore, the minds of the moralists of our age should turn; even should they judge it to be incomplete, it
must nevertheless be adopted as necessary.

I do not think, on the whole, that there is more selfishness among us than
in America; the only difference is that there it is enlightened, here it is not.
Each American knows when to sacrifice some of his private interests to
save the rest; we want to save everything, and often we lose it all. Everybody I see about me seems bent on teaching his contemporaries, by precept
and example, that what is useful is never wrong. Will nobody undertake
to make them understand how what is right may be useful?

No power on earth can prevent the increasing equality of conditions
from inclining the human mind to seek out what is useful or from leading
every member of the community to be wrapped up in himself. It must
therefore be expected that personal interest will become more than ever
the principal if not the sole spring of men's actions; but it remains to be
seen how each man will understand his personal interest. If the members
of a community, as they become more equal, become more ignorant and
coarse, it is difficult to foresee to what pitch of stupid excesses their selfishness may lead them; and no one can foretell into what disgrace and wretchedness they would plunge themselves lest they should have to sacrifice
something of their own well-being to the prosperity of their fellow creatures.

I do not think that the system of self-interest as it is professed in America
is in all its parts self-evident, but it contains a great number of truths so
evident that men, if they are only educated, cannot fail to see them. Educate, then, at any rate, for the age of implicit self-sacrifice and instinctive
virtues is already flitting far away from us, and the time is fast approaching

when freedom, public peace, and social order itself will not be able to exist without education.

.   .   .   .   .

OF THE TASTE FOR PHYSICAL WELL-BEING IN AMERICA

In America the passion for physical well-being is not always exclusive, but it is general; and if all do not feel it in the same manner, yet it is felt by all. The effort to satisfy even the least wants of the body and to provide the little conveniences of life is uppermost in every mind. Something of an analogous character is more and more apparent in Europe. Among the causes that produce these similar consequences in both hemispheres, several are so connected with my subject as to deserve notice.

When riches are hereditarily fixed in families, a great number of men enjoy the comforts of life without feeling an exclusive taste for those comforts. The heart of man is not so much caught by the undisturbed possession of anything valuable as by the desire, as yet imperfectly satisfied, of possessing it and by the incessant dread of losing it. In aristocratic communities the wealthy, never having experienced a condition different from their own, entertain no fear of changing it; the existence of such conditions hardly occurs to them. The comforts of life are not to them the end of life, but simply a way of living; they regard them as existence itself, enjoyed but scarcely thought of. As the natural and instinctive taste that all men feel for being well off is thus satisfied without trouble and without apprehension, their faculties are turned elsewhere and applied to more arduous and lofty undertakings, which excite and engross their minds.

Hence it is that in the very midst of physical gratifications the members of an aristocracy often display a haughty contempt of these very enjoyments and exhibit singular powers of endurance under the privation of them. All the revolutions which have ever shaken or destroyed aristocracies have shown how easily men accustomed to superfluous luxuries can do without the necessaries of life; whereas men who have toiled to acquire a competency can hardly live after they have lost it.

If I turn my observation from the upper to the lower classes, I find analogous effects produced by opposite causes. Among a nation where aristocracy predominates in society and keeps it stationary, the people in the end get as much accustomed to poverty as the rich to their opulence. The latter bestow no anxiety on their physical comforts because they enjoy them without an effort; the former do not think of things which they despair of obtaining and which they hardly know enough of to desire. In communities of this kind the imagination of the poor is driven to seek another world; the miseries of real life enclose it, but it escapes from their control and flies to seek its pleasures far beyond.

When, on the contrary, the distinctions of ranks are obliterated and privileges are destroyed, when hereditary property is subdivided and education and freedom are widely diffused, the desire of acquiring the comforts of the world haunts the imagination of the poor, and the dread of losing them that of the rich. Many scanty fortunes spring up; those who possess them have a sufficient share of physical gratifications to conceive a taste for these pleasures, not enough to satisfy it. They never procure them without exertion, and they never indulge in them without apprehension. They are therefore always straining to pursue or to retain gratifications so delightful, so imperfect, so fugitive.

If I were to inquire what passion is most natural to men who are stimulated and circumscribed by the obscurity of their birth or the mediocrity of their fortune, I could discover none more peculiarly appropriate to their condition than this love of physical prosperity. The passion for physical comforts is essentially a passion of the middle classes; with those classes it grows and spreads, with them it is preponderant. From them it mounts into the higher orders of society and descends into the mass of the people.

I never met in America any citizen so poor as not to cast a glance of hope and envy on the enjoyments of the rich or whose imagination did not possess itself by anticipation of those good things that fate still obstinately withheld from him.

On the other hand, I never perceived among the wealthier inhabitants of the United States that proud contempt of physical gratifications which is sometimes to be met with even in the most opulent and dissolute aristocracies. Most of these wealthy persons were once poor; they have felt the sting of want; they were long a prey to adverse fortunes; and now that the victory is won, the passions which accompanied the contest have survived it; their minds are, as it were, intoxicated by the small enjoyments which they have pursued for forty years.

Not but that in the United States, as elsewhere, there is a certain number of wealthy persons who, having come into their property by inheritance, possess without exertion an opulence they have not earned. But even these men are not less devotedly attached to the pleasures of material life. The love of well-being has now become the predominant taste of the nation; the great current of human passions runs in that channel and sweeps everything along in its course.

PECULIAR EFFECTS OF THE LOVE OF PHYSICAL GRATIFICATIONS IN DEMOCRATIC TIMES

It may be supposed, from what has just been said, that the love of physical gratifications must constantly urge the Americans to irregularities in morals, disturb the peace of families, and threaten the security of society at large. But it is not so: the passion for physical gratifications produces in democracies effects very different from those which it occasions in aristocratic nations.

It sometimes happens that, wearied with public affairs and sated with opulence, amid the ruin of religious belief and the decline of the state, the heart of an aristocracy may by degrees be seduced to the pursuit of sensual enjoyments alone. At other times the power of the monarch or the weakness of the people, without stripping the nobility of their fortune, compels them to stand aloof from the administration of affairs and, while the road to mighty enterprise is closed, abandons them to the disquietude of their own desires; they fall back heavily upon themselves and seek in the pleasures of the body oblivion of their former greatness.

When the members of an aristocratic body are thus exclusively devoted to the pursuit of physical gratifications, they commonly turn in that direction all the energy which they derive from their long experience of power. Such men are not satisfied with the pursuit of comfort; they require sumptuous depravity and splendid corruption. The worship they pay the senses is a gorgeous one, and they seem to vie with one another in the art of degrading their own natures. The stronger, the more famous, and the more free an aristocracy has been, the more depraved will it then become; and however brilliant may have been the luster of its virtues, I dare predict that they will always be surpassed by the splendor of its vices.

The taste for physical gratifications leads a democratic people into no such excesses. The love of well-being is there displayed as a tenacious, exclusive, universal passion, but its range is confined. To build enormous palaces, to conquer or to mimic nature, to ransack the world in order to gratify the passions of a man, is not thought of, but to add a few yards of land to your field, to plant an orchard, to enlarge a dwelling, to be always making life more comfortable and convenient, to avoid trouble, and to satisfy the smallest wants without effort and almost without cost. These are small objects, but the soul clings to them; it dwells upon them closely and day by day, till they at last shut out the rest of the world and sometimes intervene between itself and heaven.

This, it may be said, can be applicable only to those members of the community who are in humble circumstances; wealthier individuals will display tastes akin to those which belonged to them in aristocratic ages. I contest the proposition: in point of physical gratifications, the most opulent members of a democracy will not display tastes very different from those of the people; whether it be that, springing from the people, they really share those tastes or that they esteem it a duty to submit to them. In democratic society the sensuality of the public has taken a moderate and tranquil course, to which all are bound to conform: it is as difficult to depart from the common rule by one's vices as by one's virtues. Rich men who live amid democratic nations are therefore more intent on providing for their smallest wants than for their extraordinary enjoyments; they gratify a number of petty desires without indulging in any great irregularities of passion; thus they are more apt to become enervated than debauched.

The special taste that the men of democratic times entertain for physical enjoyments is not naturally opposed to the principles of public order; nay, it often stands in need of order that it may be gratified. Nor is it adverse to regularity of morals, for good morals contribute to public tranquillity and are favorable to industry. It may even be frequently combined with a species of religious morality; men wish to be as well off as they can in this world without forgoing their chance of another. Some physical gratifications cannot be indulged in without crime; from such they strictly abstain. The enjoyment of others is sanctioned by religion and morality; to these the heart, the imagination, and life itself are unreservedly given up, till, in snatching at these lesser gifts, men lose sight of those more precious possessions which constitute the glory and the greatness of mankind.

The reproach I address to the principle of equality is not that it leads men away in the pursuit of forbidden enjoyments, but that it absorbs them wholly in quest of those which are allowed. By these means a kind of virtuous materialism may ultimately be established in the world, which would not corrupt, but enervate, the soul and noiselessly unbend its springs of action.

·   ·   ·   ·   ·

WHAT CAUSES ALMOST ALL AMERICANS TO FOLLOW INDUSTRIAL CALLINGS

Agriculture is perhaps, of all the useful arts, that which improves most slowly among democratic nations. Frequently, indeed, it would seem to be stationary, because other arts are making rapid strides towards perfection. On the other hand, almost all the tastes and habits that the equality of condition produces naturally lead men to commercial and industrial occupations.

Suppose an active, enlightened, and free man, enjoying a competency, but full of desires; he is too poor to live in idleness, he is rich enough to feel himself protected from the immediate fear of want, and he thinks how he can better his condition. This man has conceived a taste for physical gratifications, which thousands of his fellow men around him indulge in; he has himself begun to enjoy these pleasures, and he is eager to increase his means of satisfying these tastes more completely. But life is slipping away, time is urgent; to what is he to turn? The cultivation of the ground promises an almost certain result to his exertions, but a slow one; men are not enriched by it without patience and toil. Agriculture is therefore only suited to those who already have great superfluous wealth or to those whose penury bids them seek only a bare subsistence. The choice of such a man as we have supposed is soon made; he sells his plot of ground, leaves his dwelling, and embarks on some hazardous but lucrative calling.

Democratic communities abound in men of this kind; and in proportion as the equality of conditions becomes greater, their multitude increases. Thus, democracy not only swells the number of working-men, but leads men to prefer one kind of labor to another; and while it diverts them from agriculture, it encourages their taste for commerce and manufactures.[1]

[1] It has often been remarked that manufacturers and merchants are inordinately addicted to physical gratifications, and this has been attributed to commerce and manufactures; but that, I apprehend, is to take the effect for the cause. The taste for physical gratifications is not imparted to men by commerce or manufactures, but it is rather this taste that leads men to engage in commerce and manufactures, as a means by which they hope to satisfy themselves more promptly and more completely. If commerce and manufactures increase the desire of well-being, it is because every passion gathers strength in proportion as it is cultivated, and is increased by all the efforts made to satiate it. All the causes that

This spirit may be observed even among the richest members of the community. In democratic countries, however opulent a man is supposed to be, he is almost always discontented with his fortune because he finds that he is less rich than his father was, and he fears that his sons will be less rich than himself. Most rich men in democracies are therefore constantly haunted by the desire of obtaining wealth, and they naturally turn their attention to trade and manufactures, which appear to offer the readiest and most efficient means of success. In this respect they share the instincts of the poor without feeling the same necessities; say, rather, they feel the most imperious of all necessities, that of not sinking in the world.

In aristocracies the rich are at the same time the governing power. The attention that they unceasingly devote to important public affairs diverts them from the lesser cares that trade and manufactures demand. But if an individual happens to turn his attention to business, the will of the body to which he belongs will immediately prevent him from pursuing it; for, however men may declaim against the rule of numbers, they cannot wholly escape it; and even among those aristocratic bodies that most obstinately refuse to acknowledge the rights of the national majority, a private majority is formed which governs the rest.

In democratic countries, where money does not lead those who possess it to political power, but often removes them from it, the rich do not know how to spend their leisure. They are driven into active life by the disquietude and the greatness of their desires, by the extent of their resources, and by the taste for what is extraordinary, which is almost always felt by those who rise, by whatever means, above the crowd. Trade is the only road open to them. In democracies nothing is greater or more brilliant than commerce; it attracts the attention of the public and fills the imagination of the multitude; all energetic passions are directed towards it. Neither their own prejudices nor those of anybody else can prevent the rich from devoting themselves to it. The wealthy members of democracies never form a body which has manners and regulations of its own; the opinions peculiar to their class do not restrain them, and the common opinions of their country urge them on. Moreover, as all the large fortunes that are found in a democratic community are of commercial growth, many generations must succeed one another before their possessors can have entirely laid aside their habits of business.

Circumscribed within the narrow space that politics leaves them, rich men in democracies eagerly embark in commercial enterprise; there they can extend and employ their natural advantages, and, indeed, it is even by the boldness and the magnitude of their industrial speculations that we may measure the slight esteem in which productive industry would have been held by them if they had been born in an aristocracy.

A similar observation is likewise applicable to all men living in democ-

make the love of worldly welfare predominate in the heart of man are favorable to the growth of commerce and manufactures. Equality of conditions is one of those causes; it encourages trade, not directly, by giving men a taste for business, but indirectly, by strengthening and expanding in their minds a taste for well-being.

racies, whether they are poor or rich. Those who live in the midst of demo-cratic fluctuations have always before their eyes the image of chance; and they end by liking all undertakings in which chance plays a part. They are therefore all led to engage in commerce, not only for the sake of the profit it holds out to them, but for the love of the constant excitement occasioned by that pursuit.

The United States of America has only been emancipated for half a cen-tury from the state of colonial dependence in which it stood to Great Britain; the number of large fortunes there is small, and capital is still scarce. Yet no people in the world have made such rapid progress in trade and manu-factures as the Americans; they constitute at the present day the second maritime nation in the world, and although their manufactures have to struggle with almost insurmountable natural impediments, they are not prevented from making great and daily advances.

In the United States the greatest undertakings and speculations are exe-cuted without difficulty, because the whole population are engaged in pro-ductive industry, and because the poorest as well as the most opulent mem-bers of the commonwealth are ready to combine their efforts for these purposes. The consequence is that a stranger is constantly amazed by the im-mense public works executed by a nation which contains, so to speak, no rich men. The Americans arrived but as yesterday on the territory which they inhabit, and they have already changed the whole order of nature for their own advantage. They have joined the Hudson to the Mississippi and made the Atlantic Ocean communicate with the Gulf of Mexico, across a conti-nent of more than five hundred leagues in extent which separates the two seas. The longest railroads that have been constructed up to the present time are in America.

But what most astonishes me in the United States is not so much the marvelous grandeur of some undertakings as the innumerable multitude of small ones. Almost all the farmers of the United States combine some trade with agriculture; most of them make agriculture itself a trade. It seldom happens that an American farmer settles for good upon the land which he occupies; especially in the districts of the Far West, he brings land into tillage in order to sell it again, and not to farm it: he builds a farmhouse on the speculation that, as the state of the country will soon be changed by the in-crease of population, a good price may be obtained for it.

Every year a swarm of people from the North arrive in the Southern states and settle in the parts where the cotton plant and the sugar-cane grow. These men cultivate the soil in order to make it produce in a few years enough to enrich them; and they already look forward to the time when they may re-turn home to enjoy the competency thus acquired. Thus the Americans carry their businesslike qualities into agriculture, and their trading passions are displayed in that as in their other pursuits.

The Americans make immense progress in productive industry, because they all devote themselves to it at once; and for this same reason they are exposed to unexpected and formidable embarrassments. As they are all en-gaged in commerce, their commercial affairs are affected by such various and complex causes that it is impossible to foresee what difficulties may arise. As they are all more or less engaged in productive industry, at the least shock given to business all private fortunes are put in jeopardy at the same time, and the state is shaken. I believe that the return of these commercial panics is an endemic disease of the democratic nations of our age. It may be rendered less dangerous, but it cannot be cured, because it does not originate in accidental circumstances, but in the temperament of these nations.

.   .   .   .   .

HOW THE ASPECT OF SOCIETY IN THE UNITED STATES IS AT ONCE EXCITED AND MONOTONOUS

It would seem that nothing could be more adapted to stimulate and to feed curiosity than the aspect of the United States. Fortunes, opinions, and laws are there in ceaseless variation; it is as if immutable Nature herself were mutable, such are the changes worked upon her by the hand of man. Yet in the end the spectacle of this excited community becomes monotonous, and after having watched the moving pageant for a time, the spectator is tired of it.

Among aristocratic nations every man is pretty nearly stationary in his own sphere, but men are astonishingly unlike each other; their passions, their notions, their habits, and their tastes are essentially different: nothing changes, but everything differs. In democracies, on the contrary, all men are alike and do things pretty nearly alike. It is true that they are subject to great and frequent vicissitudes, but as the same events of good or adverse fortune are continually recurring, only the name of the actors is changed, the piece is always the same. The aspect of American society is animated because men and things are always changing, but it is monotonous because all these changes are alike.

Men living in democratic times have many passions, but most of their passions either end in the love of riches or proceed from it. The cause of this is not that their souls are narrower, but that the importance of money is really greater at such times. When all the members of a community are independent of or indifferent to each other, the co-operation of each of them can be obtained only by paying for it: this infinitely multiplies the purposes to which wealth may be applied and increases its value. When the reverence that belonged to what is old has vanished, birth, condition, and profession no longer distinguish men, or scarcely distinguish them; hardly anything but money remains to create strongly marked differences between them and to raise some of them above the common level. The distinction originating in wealth is increased by the disappearance or diminution of all other distinctions. Among aristocratic nations money reaches only to a few points on the vast circle of man's desires; in democracies it seems to lead to all.

The love of wealth is therefore to be traced, as either a principal or an accessory motive, at the bottom of all that the Americans do; this gives to all their passions a sort of family likeness and soon renders the survey of them exceedingly wearisome. This perpetual recurrence of the same passion is

monotonous; the peculiar methods by which this passion seeks its own gratification are no less so.

In an orderly and peaceable democracy like the United States, where men
cannot enrich themselves by war, by public office, or by political confiscation,
the love of wealth mainly drives them into business and manufactures. Although these pursuits often bring about great commotions and disasters, they
cannot prosper without strictly regular habits and a long routine of petty
uniform acts. The stronger the passion is, the more regular are these habits
and the more uniform are these acts. It may be said that it is the vehemence
of their desires that makes the Americans so methodical; it perturbs their
minds, but it disciplines their lives.

The remark I here apply to America may indeed be addressed to almost
all our contemporaries. Variety is disappearing from the human race; the
same ways of acting, thinking, and feeling are to be met with all over the
world. This is not only because nations work more upon each other and
copy each other more faithfully, but as the men of each country relinquish
more and more the peculiar opinions and feelings of a caste, a profession,
or a family, they simultaneously arrive at something nearer to the constitution of man, which is everywhere the same. Thus they become more alike,
even without having imitated each other. Like travelers scattered about some
large wood, intersected by paths converging to one point, if all of them
keep their eyes fixed upon that point and advance towards it, they insensibly
draw nearer together, though they do not seek, though they do not see and
know each other; and they will be surprised at length to find themselves all
collected at the same spot. All the nations which take, not any particular
man, but Man himself as the object of their researches and their imitations
are tending in the end to a similar state of society, like these travelers converging at the central spot of the forest.

.   .   .   .   .

WHY SO MANY AMBITIOUS MEN AND SO LITTLE LOFTY AMBITION ARE TO BE FOUND IN THE UNITED STATES

The first thing that strikes a traveler in the United States is the innumerable
multitude of those who seek to emerge from their original condition; and
the second is the rarity of lofty ambition to be observed in the midst of the
universally ambitious stir of society. No Americans are devoid of a yearning
desire to rise, but hardly any appear to entertain hopes of great magnitude
or to pursue very lofty aims. All are constantly seeking to acquire property,
power, and reputation; few contemplate these things upon a great scale; and
this is the more surprising as nothing is to be discerned in the manners or laws
of America to limit desire or to prevent it from spreading its impulses in every
direction. It seems difficult to attribute this singular state of things to the
equality of social conditions, for as soon as that same equality was established
in France, the flight of ambition became unbounded. Nevertheless, I think
that we may find the principal cause of this fact in the social condition and
democratic manners of the Americans.

All revolutions enlarge the ambition of men. This is more peculiarly true of those revolutions which overthrow an aristocracy. When the former barriers that kept back the multitude from fame and power are suddenly thrown down, a violent and universal movement takes place towards that eminence so long coveted and at length to be enjoyed. In this first burst of triumph nothing seems impossible to anyone: not only are desires boundless, but the power of satisfying them seems almost boundless too. Amid the general and sudden change of laws and customs, in this vast confusion of all men and all ordinances, the various members of the community rise and sink again with excessive rapidity, and power passes so quickly from hand to hand that none need despair of catching it in turn.

It must be recollected, moreover, that the people who destroy an aristocracy have lived under its laws; they have witnessed its splendor, and they have unconsciously imbibed the feelings and notions which it entertained. Thus, at the moment when an aristocracy is dissolved, its spirit still pervades the mass of the community, and its tendencies are retained long after it has been defeated. Ambition is therefore always extremely great as long as a democratic revolution lasts, and it will remain so for some time after the revolution is consummated.

The recollection of the extraordinary events which men have witnessed is not obliterated from their memory in a day. The passions that a revolution has roused do not disappear at its close. A sense of instability remains in the midst of re-established order; a notion of easy success survives the strange vicissitudes which gave it birth; desires still remain extremely enlarged, while the means of satisfying them are diminished day by day. The taste for large fortunes persists, though large fortunes are rare; and on every side we trace the ravages of inordinate and unsuccessful ambition kindled in hearts which it consumes in secret and in vain.

At length, however, the last vestiges of the struggle are effaced; the remains of aristocracy completely disappear; the great events by which its fall was attended are forgotten; peace succeeds to war, and the sway of order is restored in the new realm; desires are again adapted to the means by which they may be fulfilled; the wants, the opinions, and the feelings of men cohere once more; the level of the community is permanently determined, and democratic society established.

A democratic nation, arrived at this permanent and regular state of things, will present a very different spectacle from that which I have just described, and we may readily conclude that if ambition becomes great while the conditions of society are growing equal, it loses that quality when they have grown so.

As wealth is subdivided and knowledge diffused, no one is entirely destitute of education or of property; the privileges and disqualifications of caste being abolished, and men having shattered the bonds that once held them fixed, the notion of advancement suggests itself to every mind, the desire to rise swells in every heart, and all men want to mount above their station; ambition is the universal feeling.

But if the equality of conditions gives some resources to all the members of the community, it also prevents any of them from having resources of great extent, which necessarily circumscribes their desires within somewhat narrow limits. Thus, among democratic nations, ambition is ardent and continual, but its aim is not habitually lofty; and life is generally spent in eagerly coveting small objects that are within reach.

What chiefly diverts the men of democracies from lofty ambition is not the scantiness of their fortunes, but the vehemence of the exertions they daily make to improve them. They strain their faculties to the utmost to achieve paltry results, and this cannot fail speedily to limit their range of view and to circumscribe their powers. They might be much poorer and still be greater.

The small number of opulent citizens who are to be found in a democracy do not constitute an exception to this rule. A man who raises himself by degrees to wealth and power contracts, in the course of this protracted labor, habits of prudence and restraint which he cannot afterwards shake off. A man cannot gradually enlarge his mind as he does his house.

The same observation is applicable to the sons of such a man: they are born, it is true, in a lofty position, but their parents were humble; they have grown up amid feelings and notions which they cannot afterwards easily get rid of; and it may be presumed that they will inherit the propensities of their father, as well as his wealth.

It may happen, on the contrary, that the poorest scion of a powerful aristocracy may display vast ambition, because the traditional opinions of his race and the general spirit of his order still buoy him up for some time above his fortune.

Another thing that prevents the men of democratic periods from easily indulging in the pursuit of lofty objects is the lapse of time which they foresee must take place before they can be ready to struggle for them. "It is a great advantage," says Pascal, "to be a man of quality, since it brings one man as forward at eighteen or twenty as another man would be at fifty, which is a clear gain of thirty years." Those thirty years are commonly wanting to the ambitious characters of democracies. The principle of equality, which allows every man to arrive at everything, prevents all men from rapid advancement.

In a democratic society, as well as elsewhere, there is only a certain number of great fortunes to be made; and as the paths that lead to them are indiscriminately open to all, the progress of all must necessarily be slackened. As the candidates appear to be nearly alike, and as it is difficult to make a selection without infringing the principle of equality, which is the supreme law of democratic societies, the first idea which suggests itself is to make them all advance at the same rate and submit to the same trials. Thus, in proportion as men become more alike and the principle of equality is more peaceably and deeply infused into the institutions and manners of the country, the rules for advancement become more inflexible, advancement itself slower, the difficulty of arriving quickly at a certain height far greater. From hatred of privilege and from the embarrassment of choosing, all men are at last forced, whatever may be their standard, to pass the same ordeal; all are indiscriminately subjected to a multitude of petty preliminary exercises, in which their youth is wasted and their imagination quenched, so that they despair of ever fully attaining what is held out to them; and when at length they are in a condition to perform any extraordinary acts, the taste for such things has forsaken them.

In China, where the equality of conditions is very great and very ancient, no man passes from one public office to another without undergoing a competitive trial. This probation occurs afresh at every stage of his career; and the notion is now so rooted in the manners of the people that I remember to have read a Chinese novel in which the hero, after numberless vicissitudes, succeeds at length in touching the heart of his mistress by doing well on an examination. A lofty ambition breathes with difficulty in such an atmosphere.

The remark I apply to politics extends to everything: equality everywhere produces the same effects; where the laws of a country do not regulate and retard the advancement of men by positive enactment, competition attains the same end.

In a well-established democratic community great and rapid elevation is therefore rare; it forms an exception to the common rule; and it is the singularity of such occurrences that makes men forget how rarely they happen.

Men living in democracies ultimately discover these things; they find out at last that the laws of their country open a boundless field of action before them, but that no one can hope to hasten across it. Between them and the final object of their desires they perceive a multitude of small intermediate impediments, which must be slowly surmounted; this prospect wearies and discourages their ambition at once. They therefore give up hopes so doubtful and remote, to search nearer to themselves for less lofty and more easy enjoyments. Their horizon is not bounded by the laws, but narrowed by themselves.

I have remarked that lofty ambitions are more rare in the ages of democracy than in times of aristocracy; I may add that when, in spite of these natural obstacles, they do spring into existence, their character is different. In aristocracies the career of ambition is often wide, but its boundaries are determined. In democracies ambition commonly ranges in a narrower field, but if once it gets beyond that, hardly any limits can be assigned to it. As men are individually weak, as they live asunder and in constant motion, as precedents are of little authority and laws but of short duration, resistance to novelty is languid and the fabric of society never appears perfectly erect or firmly consolidated. So that, when once an ambitious man has the power in his grasp, there is nothing he may not dare; and when it is gone from him, he meditates the overthrow of the state to regain it. This gives to great political ambition a character of revolutionary violence, which it seldom exhibits to an equal degree in aristocratic communities. The common aspect of democratic nations will present a great number of small and very rational objects of ambition, from among which a few ill-controlled desires of a larger growth will at intervals break out; but no such thing as ambition conceived and regulated on a vast scale is to be met with there.

I have shown elsewhere by what secret influence the principle of equality makes the passion for physical gratification and the exclusive love of the present predominate in the human heart. These different propensities mingle with the sentiment of ambition and tinge it, as it were, with their hues.

I believe that ambitious men in democracies are less engrossed than any others with the interests and the judgment of posterity; the present moment alone engages and absorbs them. They are more apt to complete a number of undertakings with rapidity than to raise lasting monuments of their achievements, and they care much more for success than for fame. What they most ask of men is obedience, what they most covet is empire. Their manners, in almost all cases, have remained below their station; the consequence is that they frequently carry very low tastes into their extraordinary fortunes and that they seem to have acquired the supreme power only to minister to their coarse or paltry pleasures.

I think that in our time it is very necessary to purify, to regulate, and to proportion the feeling of ambition, but that it would be extremely dangerous to seek to impoverish and to repress it overmuch. We should attempt to lay down certain extreme limits which it should never be allowed to outstep; but its range within those established limits should not be too much checked.

I confess that I apprehend much less for democratic society from the boldness than from the mediocrity of desires. What appears to me most to be dreaded is that in the midst of the small, incessant occupations of private life, ambition should lose its vigor and its greatness; that the passions of man should abate, but at the same time be lowered; so that the march of society should every day become more tranquil and less aspiring.

I think, then, that the leaders of modern society would be wrong to seek to lull the community by a state of too uniform and too peaceful happiness, and that it is well to expose it from time to time to matters of difficulty and danger in order to raise ambition and to give it a field of action.

Moralists are constantly complaining that the ruling vice of the present time is pride. This is true in one sense, for indeed everyone thinks that he is better than his neighbor or refuses to obey his superior; but it is extremely false in another, for the same man who cannot endure subordination or equality has so contemptible an opinion of himself that he thinks he is born only to indulge in vulgar pleasures. He willingly takes up with low desires without daring to embark on lofty enterprises, of which he scarcely dreams.

Thus, far from thinking that humility ought to be preached to our contemporaries, I would have endeavors made to give them a more enlarged idea of themselves and of their kind. Humility is unwholesome to them; what they most want is, in my opinion, pride. I would willingly exchange several of our small virtues for this one vice.

THE ROLE OF EXPRESSION
IS CONVEYING IMPRESSIONS OF SELF

Erving Goffman

Perhaps a moral note can be permitted at the end. In this report the expressive component of social life has been treated as a source of impressions given to or taken by others. Impression, in turn, has been treated as a source of information about unapparent facts and as a means by which the recipients can guide their response to the informant without having to wait for the full consequences of the informant's actions to be felt. Expression, then, has been treated in terms of the communicative role it plays during social interaction and not, for example, in terms of consummatory or tension-release function it might have for the expresser.[1]

Underlying all social interaction there seems to be a fundamental dialectic. When one individual enters the presence of others, he will want to discover the facts of the situation. Were he to possess this information, he could know, and make allowances for, what will come to happen and he could give the others present as much of their due as is consistent with his enlightened self-interest. To uncover fully the factual nature of the situation, it would be necessary for the individual to know all the relevant social data about the others. It would also be necessary for the individual to know the actual outcome or end product of the activity of the others during the interaction, as well as their innermost feelings concerning him. Full information of this order is rarely available; in its absence, the individual tends to employ substitutes—cues, tests, hints, expressive gestures, status symbols, etc.—as predictive devices. In short, since the reality that the individual is concerned with is unperceivable at the moment, appearances must be relied upon in its stead. And, paradoxically, the more the individual is concerned with the reality that is not available to perception, the more must he concentrate his attention on appearances.

The individual tends to treat the others present on the basis of the impression they give now about the past and the future. It is here that communicative acts are translated into moral ones. The impressions that the others give tend to be treated as claims and promises they have implicitly made, and claims and promises tend to have a moral character. In his mind the individual says: "I am using these impressions of you as a way of checking up on you and your activity, and you ought not to lead me astray."

[1] A recent treatment of this kind may be found in Talcott Parsons, Robert F. Bales, and Edward A. Shils, *Working Papers in the Theory of Action* (Glencoe, Ill.: The Free Press, 1953), Chap. II, "The Theory of Symbolism in Relation to Action."

The peculiar thing about this is that the individual tends to take this stand even though he expects the others to be unconscious of many of their expressive behaviors and even though he may expect to exploit the others on the basis of the information he gleans about them. Since the sources of impression used by the observing individual involve a multitude of standards pertaining to politeness and decorum, pertaining both to social intercourse and task-performance, we can appreciate afresh how daily life is enmeshed in moral lines of discrimination.

Let us shift now to the point of view of the others. If they are to be gentlemanly, and play the individual's game, they will give little conscious heed to the fact that impressions are being formed about them but rather act without guile or contrivance, enabling the individual to receive valid impressions about them and their efforts. And if they happen to give thought to the fact that they are being observed, they will not allow this to influence them unduly, content in the belief that the individual will obtain a correct impression and give them their due because of it. Should they be concerned with influencing the treatment that the individual gives them, and this is properly to be expected, then a gentlemanly means will be available to them. They need only guide their action in the present so that its future consequences will be the kind that would lead a just individual to treat them now in a way they want to be treated; once this is done, they have only to rely on the perceptiveness and justness of the individual who observes them.

Sometimes those who are observed do, of course, employ these proper means of influencing the way in which the observer treats them. But there is another way, a shorter and more efficient way, in which the observed can influence the observer. Instead of allowing an impression of their activity to arise as an incidental by-product of their activity, they can reorient their frame of reference and devote their efforts to the creation of desired impressions. Instead of attempting to achieve certain ends by acceptable means, they can attempt to achieve the impression that they are achieving certain ends by acceptable means. It is always possible to manipulate the impression the observer uses as a substitute for reality because a sign for the presence of a thing, not being that thing, can be employed in the absence of it. The observer's need to rely on representations of things itself creates the possibility of misrepresentation.

There are many sets of persons who feel they could not stay in business, whatever their business, if they limited themselves to the gentlemanly means of influencing the individual who observes them. At some point or other in the round of their activity they feel it is necessary to band together and directly manipulate the impression that they give. The observed become a performing team and the observers become the audience. Actions which appear to be done on objects become gestures addressed to the audience. The round of activity becomes dramatized.

We come now to the basic dialectic. In their capacity as performers, individuals will be concerned with maintaining the impression that they are living up to the many standards by which they and their products are judged. Because these standards are so numerous and so pervasive, the individuals who are performers dwell more than we might think in a moral world. But, *qua* performers, individuals are concerned not with the moral issue of realizing these standards, but with the amoral issue of engineering a convincing impression that these standards are being realized. Our activity, then, is largely concerned with moral matters, but as performers we do not have a moral concern with them. As performers we are merchants of morality. Our day is given over to intimate contact with the goods we display and our minds are filled with intimate understandings of them; but it may well be that the more attention we give to these goods, then the more distant we feel from them and from those who are believing enough to buy them. To use a different imagery, the very obligation and profitability of appearing always in a steady moral light, of being a socialized character, forces one to be the sort of person who is practiced in the ways of the stage.

STAGING AND THE SELF

The general notion that we make a presentation of ourselves to others is hardly novel; what ought to be stressed in conclusion is that the very structure of the self can be seen in terms of how we arrange for such performances in our Anglo-American society.

In this report, the individual was divided by implication into two basic parts: he was viewed as a *performer,* a harried fabricator of impressions involved in the all-too-human task of staging a performance; he was viewed as a *character,* a figure, typically a fine one, whose spirit, strength, and other sterling qualities the performance was designed to evoke. The attributes of a performer and the attributes of a character are of a different order, quite basically so, yet both sets have their meaning in terms of the show that must go on.

First, character. In our society the character one performs and one's self are somewhat equated, and this self-as-character is usually seen as something housed within the body of its possessor, especially the upper parts thereof, being a nodule, somehow, in the psychobiology of personality. I suggest that this view is an implied part of what we are all trying to present, but provides, just because of this, a bad analysis of the presentation. In this report the performed self was seen as some kind of image, usually creditable, which the individual on stage and in character effectively attempts to induce others to hold in regard to him. While this image is entertained *concerning* the individual, so that a self is imputed to him, this self itself does not derive from its possessor, but from the whole scene of his action, being generated by that attribute of local events which renders them interpretable by witnesses. A correctly staged and performed scene leads the audience to impute a self to a performed character, but this imputation—this self—is a *product* of a scene that comes off, and is not a *cause* of it. The self, then, as a performed character, is not an organic thing that has a specific location, whose fundamental fate is to be born, to mature, and to die; it is a dramatic effect arising diffusely from a scene that is presented, and the characteristic issue, the crucial concern, is whether it will be credited or discredited.

In analyzing the self then we are drawn from its possessor, from the person who will profit or lose most by it, for he and his body merely provide the peg on which something of collaborative manufacture will be hung for a time. And the means for producing and maintaining selves do not reside inside the peg; in fact these means are often bolted down in social establishments. There will be a back region with its tools for shaping the body, and a front region with its fixed props. There will be a team of persons whose activity on stage in conjunction with available props will constitute the scene from which the performed character's self will emerge, and another team, the audience, whose interpretive activity will be necessary for this emergence. The self is a product of all of these arrangements, and in all of its parts bears the marks of this genesis.

The whole machinery of self-production is cumbersome, of course, and sometimes breaks down, exposing its separate components: back region control; team collusion; audience tact; and so forth. But, well oiled, impressions will flow from it fast enough to put us in the grips of one of our types of reality—the performance will come off and the firm self accorded each performed character will appear to emanate intrinsically from its performer.

Let us turn now from the individual as character performed to the individual as performer. He has a capacity to learn, this being exercised in the task of training for a part. He is given to having fantasies and dreams, some that pleasurably unfold a triumphant performance, others full of anxiety and dread that nervously deal with vital discreditings in a public front region. He often manifests a gregarious desire for teammates and audiences, a tactful considerateness for their concerns; and he has a capacity for deeply felt shame, leading him to minimize the chances he takes of exposure.

These attributes of the individual *qua* performer are not merely a depicted effect of particular performances; they are psychobiological in nature, and yet they seem to arise out of intimate interaction with the contingencies of staging performances.

And now a final comment. In developing the conceptual framework employed in this report, some language of the stage was used. I spoke of performers and audiences; of routines and parts; of performances coming off or falling flat; of cues, stage settings and backstage; of dramaturgical needs, dramaturgical skills, and dramaturgical strategies. Now it should be admitted that this attempt to press a mere analogy so far was in part a rhetoric and a maneuver.

The claim that all the world's a stage is sufficiently commonplace for readers to be familiar with its limitations and tolerant of its presentation, knowing that at any time they will easily be able to demonstrate to themselves that it is not to be taken too seriously. An action staged in a theater is a relatively contrived illusion and an admitted one; unlike ordinary life, nothing real or actual can happen to the performed characters—although at another level of course something real and actual can happen to the reputation of performers *qua* professionals whose everyday job is to put on theatrical performances.

And so here the language and mask of the stage will be dropped. Scaffolds, after all, are to build other things with, and should be erected with an eye to taking them down. This report is not concerned with aspects of theater that creep into everyday life. It is concerned with the structure of social encounters—the structure of those entities in social life that come into being whenever persons enter one another's immediate physical presence. The key factor in this structure is the maintenance of a single definition of the situation, this definition having to be expressed, and this expression sustained in the face of a multitude of potential disruptions.

A character staged in a theater is not in some ways real, nor does it have the same kind of real consequences as does the thoroughly contrived character performed by a confidence man; but the *successful* staging of either of these types of false figures involves use of *real* techniques—the same techniques by which everyday persons sustain their real social situations. Those who conduct face to face interaction on a theater's stage must meet the key requirement of real situations; they must expressively sustain a definition of the situation: but this they do in circumstances that have facilitated their developing an apt terminology for the interactional tasks that all of us share.

NOTES FROM THE COUNTY JAIL

Michael Rossman

On December 2, 1964, 800 Berkeley students were arrested in the big sit-in that climaxed the Free Speech Movement. Two and a half years later, the Supreme Court refused to review our case. So a number of us went to the county jail, for having (successfully) fought the university's attempt to prohibit our advocacy on campus of actions—like burning draft cards or trying to shut down the Induction Centers or signing complicity statements or smoking pot or being black, though at the time we were thinking more of Civil Rights sit-ins—which might prove to be illegal.

These notes were written, then, during last year's summer vacation, nine weeks in the Santa Rita Rehabilitation Center. They were written to my friends, who know their longer original form as "The Adventures of Garbageman Under the Gentle Thumb of the Authority Complex." I wish I were certain of their relevance to the many more who are going in soon, and for far longer.

They locked us in messhall again, to wait through a recount and a recount and a recount outside. Shadowboxing; the black kids singing. "Hey, sport,

NOTES FROM THE COUNTY JAIL From *The New York Review of Books*, Vol. 2, No. 4 (September 22, 1966). Copyright © 1966 by Michael Rossman. Reprinted by permission of Cyrilly Abels.

you're kinda crazy," said my new sidekick on the garbage crew. A Mexican kid with a sour expression, he pulled his toothbrush out and combed his mustache. You see it on most of them, that bent-over plastic handle hooked over their shirt pocket. Sideburns and beards are verboten, a mustache is all you can nurse. "Grows out all kinky if you don't keep after it," explained the kid who married a virgin. It really gave me a start, the first time I saw someone pull out his toothbrush and use it, casual as a comb through greaser hair.

"You're kinda crazy, sport," said my partner—he does the kitchen head, I keep after the cans. "I know," I said, idly. "No . . . you act kinda crazy, most of the time." "Yeah, I know." "No, I really mean it, you do." "Man, *I know*," I said, "it's cool." "You like acid, dontcha," he stated. I cracked up and eyed him for a moment, doing that little widening motion so the pupil floats like a blue yolk in its innocent white. "Man, I was crazy *before* I took acid," I said, "but yeah, I do." He was the fourth one to tell me I liked acid; they all say it with the positive relief of a bird-watcher hitting the right page in his manual. No one asks about grass. It's taken for granted: everyone here smokes shit on the outside. But—even though a number of the spades have tried acid and dig it, and some of us haven't—LSD is taken as a kind of dividing line. We are the hippies. Even though we stalk around with books in our hands all the time, that's our identification: not college kids, or "professor" (as it was when I used to dig ditches, that traditional tag), but hippies. No question about it. The other inmates are friendly, curious, josh us. There's a goodly amount of respect for us as a group: we have status, an identity. Hippies.

"They don't understand you guys," said the wiseacre kid who tools the messhall truck around and jokes with the guards. "Whaddaya mean?" I asked him. "Like, what went on between you'n the officer inside, it really put him up tight. He was about ready to roll you up and send you off to Greystone, thought you were some kinda fruit." We were sitting behind the messhall, waiting for the count-clear siren. Earlier I'd walked into the little glassed-off office in the kitchen, to get the duty officer to clear my work so I could go. Four of the mess crew were clustered around his desk. "Whaddaya want?" An antic impulse: I answered, "Love." "What?" "Love, man, and I'm happy. Also you could check my work." He gave me a very odd look, and said to wait a bit; cleared me later without mentioning the incident, which I thought no more of till the kid brought it up.

He went on. "A lot of the officers, they don't like you guys. I mean, they're cops, you know, and you guys fought City Hall, and got away with it. Now with us, that's cool, we understand and dig you, know what I mean? But you made the cops look foolish then, and a lot still have it in for you even if it was a couple years ago. They look for you to be troublemakers, and when you aren't, well, that bugs 'em too. You gotta be careful with them, because they don't understand you."

But aside from not letting our books through, there's been remarkably little hard-timing. Partly this is because, almost to a man, we're easy with being here. (Today at lunch I remembered how bristling with hostility we'd been on our first visit, the night of the arrest, and we all had a good laugh at the contrast. "But," said Mario, "there were reasons then, you know, like getting dragged down stairs and all that.") But also it's because we've violated their expectations. We're open and friendly and curious, and we work hard. That counts for a lot. Garson, Lustig, and Saslow are on Bakery crew, up at 4:00 in the morning; now Mario has joined them. At first the ex-service guy who runs that show was down on them, riding them. Now he treats them with open friendliness, so much so that it's getting to be a bit of a distraction. "He keeps trying to father me," says Mario. Word has leaked back from the Booking Office, Santa Rita's nerve center: he keeps talking about us. "Get me nine more like them . . . hell, I'll have this place so changed. . . ." There has been a bit of trouble: a couple of kids have wound up in the Hole for four days, for refusing to work. But the work was painting Army barracks, the objection moral rather than lazy. All in all, our stock is sound and rising. But still no books.

Everyone's curious about Mario. "Which one he, where he, he you leader? Say man, point him out to me." Sitting around behind Mess-Hall, waiting for the count siren to sound all-clear: a dozen of us, all but two black. They talked about Mohammed Ali, about the fighters he admires, then about us. "Mario, he the leader of them hippies." "Shit, he had like a million people following him, that dude. And why? Man, because he spoke *freely* what he thought, that why. . . ."

.   .   .   .   .

A bird flew into the garbage compound. Some wanted to kill it; three of us went in. One heaved a brush as it flew, missed. I climbed the mountain of boxed empty tins, retrieved it, jumped down. Outside someone took it gently from my hand. "Look here"—to no one—"here's how you hold it, see so he free in you hand." Then chucked it into the sky, underhand and up. *Away.* The tension broke, and suddenly a tall black kid did a spot routine. "Ho, when he get home. . . ." The circle acted it out: the girl birds hanging around twittering, testing his muscles. "There they was, hundreds of them, two of 'em had me by the wings and one by the legs, oh, but I faked 'em all out. Shit, they was *all* over me, man, they was gonna roast me . . . you got any idea what they smell like?" "Tell it, man, tell it. . . ."

Rehabilitation—with a vengeance. This place is so middle class I can't believe it. Dig: we get up at 6:15 every morning; our lights are out by 9:30, though we get till 10 on Saturdays (that's our big day). Make your bed, sweep up, keep your area clean. Or Else. I shave and shower every other day, and change clothes on the day in between. Three square meals a day, perforce, nutritionally adequate and sometimes even good (with respect to regularity, bulk, and nutrition, I eat better than I do at home. Karen's mad at my spreading that about). We work five or seven days a week. No beards permitted, hair to be kept neatly trimmed. My mother would love it.

Me, I'm the Garbageman: three times a day I keep after the mess in the messhall, so to speak, cleaning and jerking 150-lb. cans full of slop, again so to speak. "You gonna have some muscles when you get out of here I bet, man." (The slop goes to the hog farm, where Jack is working.) "How long you in for?" asked the messguard when I reported. "90 days." "What for?" "Sit-in." "Garbage!" I still don't know if he was for or against me: I dig the job. My hidden advantage, of course, is that I can't smell: but if I keep after the stuff, even that doesn't make much of a difference.

My day is criss-crossed by counts, meals at the odd hours of Messmen's Schedule, and having to sling garbage after each regular meal (which runs me two to three hours a day of welcome work). I am left with seven clear segments of one to two hours. Mornings and afternoons I read or write; evenings now, volleyball, or an occasional game of chess or dominoes. That's an idyllic picture, actually; unless I go off and hide to write, people are constantly falling on to me, and I into conversations with them—or, more often, listening and watching. I've begun mild calisthenics morning and evening (many of us, and a few of the regulars, go through some such counting ritual). All in all, there's much more freedom than I'd expected.

Taking a page from Cassius Clay, when he still used that name, I cultivate a somewhat antic air: careening down the tile corridors with an endlessly varied wail of "Gaaaaarbage, make way for de gaaahbudge . . . ," like a London street-cry. And at other times, endlessly with a book and writing pad in my hand. "I'm conditioning the guards," I told the kid who asked why. If they think you're slightly mad, you can get away with a lot.

Many of us are looking on this imprisonment as our only possible live rehearsal for what draft-resistance might bring. A county jail isn't much like a federal prison, nor is a month or two like three to five years, but that's the best we can do. I have been cheered both because I adapt easily to the life and people here, and also because I've had no trouble at all in launching and sustaining a mind-project: the essay I'm working on, about the generation gap. For the month before I came in, I was working my ass off to finish another manuscript; I expected to need an (involuntary) vacation. Instead, my desires to talk with people and to plug away on the essay are constantly fighting each other.

Paradoxically, even as maintaining an independent mental and emotional life here is much more practical than I'd expected, the idea of spending a long time in jail becomes even less appealing. I'm not sure why. Weinberg points out that Santa Rita is oppressive precisely because it's relatively humane, a model county jail (he likens it to the ideal socialist state). I dig what he means; it confuses me even more about doing federal time, behind bars. S———, W———, a couple of others have already decided to split for Canada; their stay here has had little impact on that decision. I have begun thinking about it seriously, for the first time. Barely.

Visiting days are a mixed blessing, mail call also. "You have to be where you are to make it," points out Steve, "and news or touch of the outside pulls you back, between two worlds." There are other reminders, besides the papers, to keep our thoughts ambivalent. Last Sunday's flick was a World

War II romance, set in S.E. Asia: jungle warfare, the whole bit. We have been well-conditioned: we cheered when Sinatra and his faithful handful of natives wiped out the Jap jungle airstrip with its planes near the end, in a sneak attack, and then penetrated the Chinese border and executed a couple of hundred captives taken there, in retaliation for their attack on the supply convoy that was supposed to support our boys. Back in the barracks, the papers describe Westmoreland's request for 140,000 more men. How many of us lay awake that night, trying to pick apart that snarl of feelings generated by the flick: exhilaration, regret, detachment, anger, and fear?

Saslow has built a microscope: an improvement on the Leeuwenhoek model, with a carefully formed drop of Karo syrup held in a pierced thin metal plate for its optics. A rock, string, twigs, glue, paper, pencil pulleys for focusing, tongue-depressor slide platforms, the chrome blade from fingernail clippers as reflector, etc. The prisoners have been very attentive and helpful, scrounging things he needs. They all agree on the one ground rule: no contraband material to be used in its construction. His first slide is onion-skin tissue, stained with beet-juice to bring out cell walls and nuclei. I overheard some of them discussing it—they use "telescope," "microscope" and "magnifying-glass" indiscriminately, but no confusion results. "Mario showed him how," said one, "he smart, that dude, he the leader."

College kids in jail. We learn quickly the patient shuffle that the random cloddy shoes enforce, the perfect complement to the floppy prison blues we wear. "Too fast to be standing still," as one inmate put it, or to be yelled at by The Man; slow enough not to raise a sweat in the sky-covered roaster of Valley summer. For those of us who have lived in dormitories, this *in loco parentis* scene is basically familiar, and—save for the frequent recall-to-barracks-and-count, which I imagine the girls recognize—scarcely exaggerated. The food, in fact, is better than that at most college dorms. The barracks scene may look like Army: but the pace of our lives and the general atmosphere are much closer to the Academy.

.   .   .   .   .

At night, after lights-out, we visit other bunks and swap stories about backgrounds and travels, and—again like a college dorm—talk a great deal about our past sexual exploits, in boastful detail, and how we wish we were getting some pussy, and what we'll do when we get it. Under the constant glare of the blue bulbs in the tall ceiling, the young spades in their corner chatter like jaybirds for hours, punctuating it occasionally with horseplay yelps. The quiet longtimer from the end of the barracks sits on the john with the light on, fighting a compound interest problem. The old drunk blows silent insomnia smoke, as Al and I crouch at the foot of Dennis's bunk listening to him tell of burglaries in Berkeley: a life of smashed windows, snatched TV sets and suits, and careening 3 A.M. chases down the quiet streets of the city we know so differently.

Still slightly sweaty from pushups—the silent spade across the way looked up from Richard Wright, said not to do them just before bed, didn't do no good—we listen to the lanky kid from Tennessee dissect the lives and loves of the small California town where he was sent up for moonshining. Al, knowing the town and some of its citizens—yeah, I remember her, tall skinny girl well-hung, she was half Piyute Indian and half Scandinavian—is particularly tickled. "So there they was, going at it on the mountain, and him sitting down there with his fifty-power sniper scope, everyone in town come have a looksee. Whooee!" Vern, the gentle old alky who taught me to tap out the mop deftly in the morning, allowed as how if they legalized pot it would be the salvation of him and a lot of others. But Tennessee's never touched grass, "no, nor bennies nor H nor none of that stuff." We try to straighten him out on drug categories, tell him of hiking on acid at 11,000 feet and swimming on grass, balling on both; invite him to Berkeley. The door to the barracks slams open and an officer lurches through with flashlight waving—"Bull session, uh?" We swallow our start of guilt and fear. He's looking for someone to butcher a deer just brought in, leaves for another barracks. This morning the carcass hangs behind the messhall, someone is at it. The meat will grace officer's mess, we'll never see it.

Bananas for lunch. Their fragments will reappear the next day, encased in jello as the beans turn to soup: the principles of cooking here are few and predictable. They saunter out of the messhall, sly pockets full of peels: "mellow-yellow" they whisper, with a knowing wink. Later that afternoon: "hey, hippie, what you guys know about how to fix these? there a special way or sumpin?" We are in demand for certain minor specialized functions: "hey, what kind of complex you call it when a guy keeps coming on like he knows everything?" Since we haven't been singled out for any special kind of treatment—good or bad—by the guards (or inmates), we are left to define our own identity as a group. We aren't overly clannish, though a few stick to their own devices and with most the book or writing-pad in hand has become a near trademark. Except among ourselves, we listen much more than we talk—though sometimes art or politics will flare in a tight knot for an hour on the street in front of the library, and some of our new friends or strangers will hang around the edges, curious to hear us at our own game.

The dormitory atmosphere of the place is partly due to the age-distribution: a good half of the inmates are twenty-five or under (many of the rest are old alkies: their numbers rise after the weekend, you can tell them in messline Monday morning by their shaking hands). Most of them are here for trivia: driving with a suspended license, dodging child support, burglary. A few for heavier things: manslaughter, slugging a cop, and so on: the county jail. "Shit, most of them are just kids, nothing serious," said the officer who confessed to having read *Walden* five times, after I complained to him that we were disappointed because we'd expected to be locked up with criminals.

.   .   .   .   .

There is very little sense of being among criminals here. The kids in the kitchen constantly mimic the "crank" (methedrine) rituals, going through the motions of tying up and shooting—but with exactly the same good humor with which we noisily inhale the last drag on a handrolled cigarette ("square"), holding the roach delicately between thumb and forefinger. To have a candybar and a pack disappear from my drawer came as a surprise. "Hide your stuff in your pillow," advised the queen trusty, "remember, you among thieves here."

It's hard to believe, as I lie here stripped to the waist on the beach of the volleyball court (five days in the Hole for stripping to shorts). Sounds of argument drift from the open doors of the barracks. There are always arguments going—most discussions get there quickly, on any subject—but they seldom flare into real anger. Al points out the high aggressive quotient, the many overlapping pecking orders: everything becomes a vehicle for proof, in this arena of constant enforced contact. Yet strangely, there is no pressure: and much of that appearance is deceptive. You are in the pecking order only if you choose to be. (None of us does.) To opt out is simple, and nobody bugs you to get in. And so organized or permanent competition is totally absent. There is no barracks chess champ, no constant volleyball team, scant interest in the ping-pong table.

Low key and easy is the word. Almost everyone's out to do easy time—those who aren't soon get on the guards' wrong side and wind up in Greystone. (But generally, hostility between guards and inmates is almost completely absent; and there has been only one fight that I know of in our first three weeks, plus a few punches quickly concealed after a flick.) Such action as takes place is lined with good humor, mostly: the eternal games of men-against-the-System. Two kids come furtive, zip! out of the messhall, with a twenty-pound tin of coffee under an army blanket. Guard at the barracks gate, they split it up in the john into paper bags to stash it, and crushed the can's carcass, hid it in the garbage. They boosted it on commission, so to speak: for packs (of cigarettes, the standard currency) plus grass if it came through. (There *is* grass here, but it's pretty far under the surface.) Needles zip out of messhall clothing, to be embedded in toothbrush handles and wound with black thread, as a tattooing device. Slippers disappear from Little Greystone, to be hidden under mattresses, worn at night, and turned up among protestations of innocence in occasional shakedowns. All things considered, the atmosphere is pretty familiar. As Mario points out, this place is no great shucks as a deterrent. If they'd let our women in on the weekend—as they do in Mexico and Russia—pass through our books and make a decent cup of coffee now and then, I'd be nearly contented.

Most of the people here are black; and of the remainder, most are Mexican. There seems to be no active discrimination, though colors have a way of hanging together to chatter. The reading room, with its stock of tattered journals, has no black magazines like *Ebony* or *Jet,* nor any in Spanish; the library has a handful of books in Spanish and a double handful of

black books—Malcolm X's autobiography being conspicuously absent—
balanced by a magnificent collection of mysteries, a fair one of science-fiction
and westerns, a lot of old novels, and little else. (Our boys are rediscovering
the classics—Zola, Dostoevsky, Flaubert—mainly because the books are old
and worn enough to have found their way here.) As in the Haight-A., there
is much tolerance for deviant behavior. Nobody comes on—or, rather, coming on is so clearly that, that it makes no difference.

A week ago, a dozen of our thirty clustered rapping after every meal.
Now more than four in a knot is unusual. One by one they are leaving;
after this weekend, almost all of the short-timers will be gone, and a week
later we'll be down to five, two of whom I dislike. It'll be a bit lonely.
Partly for this reason, I've kept more to myself than I usually would, not
wanting to build a dependence. Aside from talking with Mario—we fall into
instant intricate dialogue on any trivial or major detail—I've spent time
only with S——— and W———, neither of whom I knew before and both
of whom I dig immensely. (Within a few months both will probably be out
of the country to begin the long exile.) Today the mess officers offered me
a new job, leaderman of the mop crew. I blew their minds by refusing—
they kept coming back out to make sure I understood. "No, man, I'm comfortable at it," I told them—not sure that *they* understood how one programs even days full of life into a mechanical pattern, so as to make the
time pass quickly and unnoticed, without disturbance.

Behind messhall, gathered waiting for the all-clear, a gem of a scene.
Dennis is jiving, and somehow this other kid brings in pimping, and they
build a contrast. You got to have a hustle, says Dennis. Don't got one, the
kid says; can shoot a little pool, but got beat out of $20 last time I tried
so can't really do that; but you really gotta work at a hustle like pimping.
Big money in it, says Dennis. I pimp too, says the kid, for Ford. It bring me
$127 a week, she do; I drive to work and back with the heater on, don't have
to get out in the rain and make them broads work. Same thing every day,
says Dennis, today and tomorrow, you get home and go to bed, too tired to
do anything: you hustle, you c'n work when you choose. Got a car but not
one of them fine, fine Caddies, says the kid, and a little in the bank, about
to get married, save up for a down payment on a house. A stoniness invades
Dennis's face; the kid goes on, sure would like some of that money, though,
but I'm too strung out behind my woman to put her on the street. Get home
too tired to do anything, repeats Dennis. That's right; this here's my vacation, two weeks, that 127 keep coming in; if I had the kinda money you make
hustling I'd sure use it to bail out. How much? I asked. $59 or 9 days he gave
me, tickets, didn't have the money so here I am; I'd say to one of them
broads, hey, go out and get me the money. I c'n dig it, Dennis keeps repeating, meaning I understand or you're right or I'm cool with what I'm doing
or I'm hurting, depending on how you read the look in his voice; and against
this background the kid goes on. "Where I made my mistake, I learned to
do something"—he's a welder for Ford—"got stuck in it, went in the army,
took two years at school, got an Associate of Arts degree in Criminology; sure

wish I had a hustle, still owe $300 on 5 suits that've almost wore out now; but when I want I can go down to the bank and say, 'give me some bread. . . .' " "And they'll suck your blood," chime in Al and me, enthusiastically. We've been listening with total absorption, providing a running third voice about not digging work or the things money can buy; fill in the antiphony yourself. Abruptly, at some point—precisely when doesn't matter—Dennis gets up without a word, takes his milk box, moves it twenty feet away into the sun, sits down on it. The circle reforms, talk shifts to unfaithful lovers (wives). "I didn't know whether to cry or beat the shit out of the dude or beat the shit out of her." "So she asked him for five dollars." "Cheap." "Wait, you ain't heard what he did. He nailed the bill over the doorway. Whenever anyone came over he'd take out his .38 and say: 'Honey, tell 'em what that five dollars for.' And she knew he meant it, and she'd say, 'my husband caught me fucking with another man.' "

Scarlatti this morning, over the barracks radio that shakes us from sleep each 6:15. Like fresh water, that crystal streamflow of melody. I have forgotten what real water tastes like, I no longer notice the flat mineral-thick taste of the hydrant and bathroom streams. Only the coffee reminds me. Once a week I try a sip, recoil. And the Beatles and Stones tonight, just before lights-out. Real music: what a treat!

Usually the mornings are breakfast-club chatter and song, bright and false as yellow formica in an LA motel; and at evening either a talk-back program or cocktail-music, denatured mush to drown us to sleep. All too loud, you never quite get used to it. And even when the radio's silent the speaker is still live, so that the morse machinegun of the mad telegraphist, frantically punching his key somewhere beyond the hills in Pleasanton (we presume), can catch your soul at any moment: unaware, floating free of your body.

For a time it was KJAZ—good jazz—twice a week, rock once, some rhythm and blues. The spades and everyone else dug it. Then mush. No explanation. Eventually they got up a petition: can we have our music back? No— the answer came down from the Olympia of the Detail Office—because the petition was a demand, an attempt to pressure.

Well, Mood control, that's the secret to making it here. At first I was genuinely, perpetually cheerful, because I'd imagined a constant boot-camp attempt to grind us down that didn't materialize. So I made the mistake of relaxing, of letting my guard down—and all of a sudden it looks like a jail with cops, and I feel somehow reassured, vigilant again. Like the food: initial hosannahs because it was edible; but now that the menu begins to repeat its weekly cycle for the fourth time, we realize that you don't need teeth for any of it, that everything is full of pepper for a reason; that. . . .

A chorus of groans goes up from outside, in the dark main room. The radio has just snapped off for the night, after the first bars of a good song. An inflexible rule: if the last song is slop, it plays through to the end; good songs get cut in the middle. That's how this place is, no kidding. Seeing that I wasn't dismayed by the garbage detail, the mess officer started also putting me on the short line to serve in the mornings. Innocent, I asked why. "Standard practice." And suddenly I found myself promoted to long line: an hour and a half sometimes serving food, before I can eat. I got the message. Then, gratuitously or to make sure, he sent me to get my second haircut in three weeks, at the butcher-barber's. I now have the shortest hair of any Anglo or Mex in the whole Mess Barracks. That was the guard who'd read *Walden* five times; I don't smile at him any more.

·   ·   ·   ·   ·

The blond, sallow one with the big ears and the hard voice did the pre-mail call count last night. (Our main recreation is getting counted, at least six times a day.) He caught me with a book in my hand, Dennis with a paper, Fast Black slouching; pulled us outside; gave us what-for, with words that slapped like dominoes. You will *stand* up *straight,* having *nothing* in your *hands,* five *days* in the *Hole.* Our faces were rock. I wanted to kill him. Literally. We blew it off inside, horseplay, yelling. Dennis slugged the wall. Most of the guards just whiz through, counting; but you can never tell who'll play ego-games like that, or who will get the two bakery men up at 4 A.M. for the early shift by standing in the middle of the barracks and yelling their names until they dress (though their names and bunk numbers hang together on the wall by the door).

So mood control is the word. The cheap bit with the second haircut cost me two days of rage; my head was sheerly scrambled, I couldn't write a word, all those intricate lovely thoughts scattered like trout when the wind rises. I read science-fiction furiously, five books, a drug. Finally I pulled up to a real smile, by thinking what a joke it was to have let the *Walden* bit shape my expectations so deeply. The sallow-faced guard only cost me three hours; I'm learning. Mood control.

And you've got to make *genuine* changes. There's no burying anger, not here: it builds up and blows at any unforeseen order—and the place, oddly enough, is full of orders, many with no point. The kids who can't work the magic of transmutation on their emotions wind up in the Hole, almost to a man.

All yesterday the Beatles were singing, "All you need is love." I think maybe we also need fewer cops, no cops . . . I am not sure if it comes to the same thing. But people who enjoy having power over others are a stone drag; and the matter is worse when it is cloaked in a social sanction. They offered me leaderman of the mop-crew, the guards who still seem sympathetic did. No, I said, I'm cool with being garbageman—no one knows I can't smell —"and besides, I don't like to be nobody's boss." Nor, but this silent, to have nobody boss over me. Benevolent or not. Not even the Beatles.

Reading this last rap, Mario is worried lest I give an unbalanced view of the guards. I don't mean to: the place is not vicious, just erratically petty. Yesterday I actually got some books, after three weeks trying. There's one compound officer who's overtly friendly to us—and hides out most of the time, seems completely ineffectual in the officer pecking-order. He has a good reputation with the inmates; such is the fate of good guys here, his goodness has become an ego-crutch in a losing battle: how lovely, how common, how sad. He felt guilty because I'd searched all over for him for six days running, asked him each time to get a paper from my box so I could revise it; took my name each time, forgot. So when I bumped into him with a note from the history teacher okaying my getting books, he escorted me up to the front office, glaring around with a bluff protectiveness made safe by the note, and let me take out Keniston's *The Uncommitted*, Friedenberg's *Coming of Age in America*, and *Ulysses*. "*Ulysses*," he mused, "I flunked that book once. . . ." His voice trailed off. "Tough book," I responded glibly, "my chick's flippy about it, been after me three years to read it, promised her I'd get through it while I was in. You know . . . Gee, thanksamillion for helping me to get these," enthusiastically, scrammed. Not daring to meet his eyes or ask through the excuse of literature what lies beneath his lonely and passionless decency.

The history etcetera teacher was most obliging when I showed him the book list, even though he didn't understand quite why I wanted them; wrote me a note only the second time I saw him. "Hey, Mac," he called over to the accounting etcetera teacher, in his high, piping voice, "how do you spell 'taking'? T-a-k-e-i-n-g or . . . ?" Mac told him, while I stood respectfully by, and as he finished the note in his childish scrawl I looked down on his bald head, worn as the once-linen backing on the ancient texts, and thanked him very much and honestly; left him to his two occasional students, wandered toward the front office thinking of model jails. "It's a model jail," said the guard in the office, "known all over the state." "It's a model jail," said the old-timer in the Mess-Hall, "why, at San Bruno you can get a steak out of the officer's mess for a pack, and pussy now and then. And they don't hardly have no commissary."

.   .   .   .   .

Commissary here is run by an old codger named Dyke, who is subject to unpredictable fits of temper in which he imagines he hears talking in the line and closes it down for the day; those outside are out of luck, for he's an officer and can do what he wants to, right? He also arbitrarily decides what and how much may be bought each day. Not surprisingly, the regulars here speculate endlessly and cynically about where the commissary take goes. But he has his kind side. The twenty-seven-sheet tablet I'm writing on *says* 25 cents on its cover, but he lets the prisoners have it for 20 cents. All in all, it seems to be a much straighter operation than the one the old junkie doctor runs.

I was thinking about the haircut incident, which happened well over a week ago, while hustling garbage after dinner today. It was probably not malicious, but gratuitous, I decided: meant as a sort of benign amusement. And so my account of my reactions probably says a lot about my hairtrigger feelings about authority, pun intended.

That being so, and me being in jail, I've decided there's a definite advantage to my college background, despite the way the high-school dropouts in the officers' mess tease me, with their oranges and corned beef. For what is jail but a primitive form of the Authority Complex, cast in locks, alarms, and barbed wire? And what sort of problem does *that* present to a young man trained for nine years in the most Prestigious Multiversity in the land? Despite my touchiness about personal integrity, my dislike of stupid orders, and so on, I get along just fine: doing easy time, an exemplary prisoner: *my* suntan will never pale from days spent in the Hole, and if they gave Extra-Good Time I'd get that too and be out of here the sooner. For if there's anything being in college teaches you, it's how to relate to authority: even more than being black does, though the techniques are similar.

For here I am, the friendly Garbageman. With an antic smile and an off-key wail of "Gaaarbaaage . . . ," like a London street-cry. (Establish a distinct but non-threatening identity.) My cleaned cans upside-down on the cart, so the imprisoned steam can *puff!* impressively as I upend them back in their places. (Pick a symbol of excellence in your subject; accentuate it.) Clanging the cans with great zeal, even risking an occasional caution about too much noise when the officers are eating. (Be passionately dedicated to the pursuit of Truth; venture a daringly unorthodox hypothesis whose subtle flaw the instructor can point out.) Candidly confessing—when nothing could be proved—that the carbon paper found among the empty cans was mine, hastily thrust there after someone I'd asked idly for a sheet brought me a sheaf, swiped from the office. (Admit an evident mistake gracefully; show yourself open to instruction and able to profit by it.) Wheeling the cart like a madman past others leaning indolently on their mops; cleaning up someone else's mess silently and for free—but in public—once in a while. (Invite favorable comparison, but let others provide it.) Changing clothes at best every other day, and not trying too hard to keep clean—it goes with the role. (Be a bit of an eccentric—you *must* be bright.) Hosing the whole garbage-room down on Mondays; asking innocently if this wasn't standard practice before. (Establish a minor but admirable innovation in the System's procedure; undervalue it.)

I could go on, but fuck it. The truth of the matter is that I *do* hustle—partly because I simply dig hustling and doing a good job, partly because being a political prisoner is or seems to be like what being a Jew and short was for my old man *in situ* thirty years ago: "You've got to be twice as good as anyone else to come out even," he reasoned or felt, and he may have been right, who knows? But over all this, as a surface gilding long since learned into instinct (Woodrow Wilson Fellowship, '63), is the complex of little actions, attitudes, and details that constitute my way of relating to—of "handling"—the Authority Complex. They are as involuntary as the deep anger, whose possible consequences they so nicely avert, even as they disguise and are fueled by that anger. I learned my lesson well, in a thorough school.

Strolling through the litter of pork-chop bones that graces the barracks yard—which is always decorated on the rare morning-after something decent and portable appears for dinner—a puzzle came clear to me. Before I came here I phoned all over the country to get quotes for an article I was writing. This gave me a chance to hear some dear voices again and apologize for my absence and silence. But there was an awkward air about some of the conversations, which I only now understand.

One friend confessed shyly—to my complete surprise, though I knew him for a long and ardent student and admirer of Gandhi and King—that he envied me deeply and would take my place if he could: that he felt keenly, as a lack in his own life, never having gone to jail for his beliefs. Another friend was terribly agitated because no one was making a fuss over our finally going in, or seemed even to remember why. Somehow a proper response was absent: we, and what we meant, were unheralded, unsung. "Surely someone must say something publicly," he cried to me over the phone.

I was taken off-balance and touched by their real concern, and responded to both with the embarrassed careless callousness I so often face emotion with: toss it off, downplay it, trying badly to be gentle. And my own closure is so familiar that I didn't realize till now that something else confused my response—and what it was. One of these men is a college president; the other—generally one of the two most perceptive observers of my generation I know—was offered a presidency and refused it. I love them both; but neither can afford such romantic innocence about the contemporary young. For it is dangerous to lose track of which revolution you're watching—especially if you'd like to help it—or you'll find yourself responding inappropriately.

My grandfather, whose eyes were also blue, was a Bolshevik: prison and exile. I too had certain time-honored feelings when my friends and unknown beloved peers were beaten and bailless in Southern jails. But we are freedom *trippers,* not riders. And there is nothing romantic, nor inspiring, nor unduly grubby, about being this kind of political prisoner. It is a dull and practical necessity, and will not be emulated or repeated. For FSM was a signal beacon which started much, both locally and nationally; but its message was sounded and heard, and there's no need to do certain parts of it again. Eight hundred kids should never again need to choose arrest to spite a college administration that doesn't deserve so much respect. The small price of our current jailing (and the $100,000 in fines) is not even a symbol: merely the tangible mark of a learning experience, a necessary experiment. And so our own kids know better than to waste inappropriate or sloppy sentiment on us. Though FSM and our jailings are in some senses inseparable, their warm feelings about the one and their indifferent practicality about the nuisance of the other are the best indication that the connection is only operational. Being here accrues me no capital save the (considerable) writing I'm doing and some insight. Grandfather or not, if I could buy out, I would.

. . . . .

Granted, I had those nice warm feelings too when we were busted, as much as anyone did; and the martyr's pride did not entirely evaporate in the disgusting tedium of that hot spring's trial. I have traded on it since, for which

I somewhat dislike myself, and will again; and a residue accompanies me here, probably making jail a bit more bearable, spice in the stew of my feelings. But by far my main emotion is simple and sheer irritation: *What a drag!* I've better things to do with my time—not only making love, but building what I was arrested for and have pursued since, in forms which have changed with my understanding. For FSM, in retrospect, was the first clear signal that America was involved in not one but two revolutions; and the rapid events since have brought the newer one out from under the shadow of the Civil Rights Movement and an old politics. Our problem now, and mine, is to learn, by doing, what feelings and actions are proper to being observers and shapers of this other revolution, of which we have no choice but to be a part even as it outdistances our understanding of it. The emotions of the older one, which include familiar forms of martyrdom, gives us no clue. But, though I struggle uncertainly with their residue, I don't mean to put them down: they are simply inappropriate.

For us, that is. The spades who are going to jail for the flaming cities are quite a different story, as it will be if—no, when—they try to frame Stokely and Rap Brown for that. And those brave kids who are choosing, quietly, calmly and without hope, four years in a federal pen rather than play the System's death-games or run out on what they know of their souls—they are also a different story, partly because Vietnam and the spades are slices off the same overdue hunk of my grandfather's flesh. But the steadily growing pool of kids in jail across the country for grass and acid and "street-blocking" are political prisoners just as surely as we are—I think of beautiful Michael Solomon with his black flame halo, busted in the Haight on a trumped-up charge: forty-five days in San Bruno, off light compared to the kids here doing six or nine months—and, because they are movers in the same other revolution as we are, as little deserve to be romanticized. (Though that is not meant to inveigh against feeling or action for the human cost involved in their imprisonment, which is considerable.)

No, a new trip demands new guideposts; and jail simply is not our thing. Not that we too are not romantic—though I think we will ultimately prove less so than our elders, because we are more willing to abandon our foothold on what we have known. But the voices on the telephone wished me well with the expectations of my own past, which will no longer serve. We cannot inherit even the form of our symbols now: which leaves us nothing but trial-and-error to find or build them.

MECCA

Malcolm X

The pilgrimage to Mecca, known as Hajj, is a religious obligation that every orthodox Muslim fulfills, if humanly able, at least once in his or her lifetime.

The Holy Quran says it, "Pilgrimage to the Ka'ba is a duty men owe to God; those who are able, make the journey."

Allah said: "And proclaim the pilgrimage among men; they will come to you on foot and upon each lean camel, they will come from every deep ravine."

At one or another college or university, usually in the informal gatherings after I had spoken, perhaps a dozen generally white-complexioned people would come up to me, identifying themselves as Arabian, Middle Eastern or North African Muslims who happened to be visiting, studying, or living in the United States. They had said to me that, my white-indicting statements notwithstanding, they felt that I was sincere in considering myself a Muslim —and they felt if I was exposed to what they always called "true Islam," I would "understand it, and embrace it." Automatically, as a follower of Elijah Muhammad, I had bridled whenever this was said.

But in the privacy of my own thoughts after several of these experiences, I did question myself: if one was sincere in professing a religion, why should he balk at broadening his knowledge of that religion?

Once in a conversation I broached this with Wallace Muhammad, Elijah Muhammad's son. He said that yes, certainly, a Muslim should seek to learn all that he could about Islam. I had always had a high opinion of Wallace Muhammad's opinion.

Those orthodox Muslims whom I had met, one after another, had urged me to meet and talk with a Dr. Mahmoud Youssef Shawarbi. He was described to me as an eminent, learned Muslim, a University of Cairo graduate, a University of London Ph.D., a lecturer on Islam, a United Nations advisor and the author of many books. He was a full professor of the University of Cairo, on leave from there to be in New York as the Director of the Federation of Islamic Associations in the United States and Canada. Several times, driving in that part of town, I had resisted the impulse to drop in at the F.I.A. building, a brownstone at 1 Riverside Drive. Then one day Dr. Shawarbi and I were introduced by a newspaperman.

He was cordial. He said he had followed me in the press; I said I had been told of him, and we talked for fifteen or twenty minutes. We both had to leave to make appointments we had, when he dropped on me something whose logic never would get out of my head. He said, "No man has believed perfectly until he wishes for his brother what he wishes for himself."

Then, there was my sister Ella herself. I couldn't get over what she had done. I've said before, this is a *strong* big, black, Georgia-born woman. Her domineering ways had gotten her put out of the Nation of Islam's Boston Mosque Eleven; they took her back, then she left on her own. Ella had started studying under Boston orthodox Muslims, then she founded a school where Arabic was taught! *She* couldn't speak it, she hired teachers who did. That's Ella! She deals in real estate, and *she* was saving up to make the pilgrimage. Nearly all night, we talked in her living room. She told me there was no question about it; it was more important that I go. I thought about Ella the whole flight back to New York. A *strong* woman. She had broken the spirits of three husbands, more driving and dynamic than all of them combined. She had played a very significant role in my life. No other woman ever was strong enough to point me in directions; I pointed women in directions. I had brought Ella into Islam, and now she was financing me to Mecca.

Allah always gives you signs, when you are with Him, that He is with you.

When I applied for a visa to Mecca at the Saudi Arabian Consulate, the Saudi Ambassador told me that no Muslim converted in America could have a visa for the Hajj pilgrimage without the signed approval of Dr. Mahmoud Shawarbi. But that was only the beginning of the sign from Allah. When I telephoned Dr. Shawarbi, he registered astonishment. "I was just going to get in touch with you," he said, "by all means come right over."

When I got to his office, Dr. Shawarbi handed me the signed letter approving me to make the Hajj in Mecca, and then a book. It was *The Eternal Message of Muhammad* by Abd ar-Rahman Azzam.

The author had just sent the copy of the book to be given to me, Dr. Shawarbi said, and he explained that this author was an Egyptian-born Saudi citizen, an international statesman, and one of the closest advisors of Prince Faisal, the ruler of Arabia. "He has followed you in the press very closely." It was hard for me to believe.

Dr. Shawarbi gave me the telephone number of his son, Muhammad Shawarbi, a student in Cairo, and also the number of the author's son, Omar Azzam, who lived in Jedda, "your last stop before Mecca. Call them both, by all means."

I left New York quietly (little realizing that I was going to return noisily). Few people were told I was leaving at all. I didn't want some State Department or other roadblocks put in my path at the last minute. Only my wife, Betty, and my three girls and a few close associates came with me to Kennedy International Airport. When the Lufthansa Airlines jet had taken off, my two seatrow mates and I introduced ourselves. Another sign! Both were Muslims, one was bound for Cairo, as I was, and the other was bound for Jedda, where I would be in a few days.

All the way to Frankfurt, Germany, my seatmates and I talked, or I read the book I had been given. When we landed in Frankfurt, the brother bound for Jedda said his warm good-bye to me and the Cairo-bound brother.

We had a few hours layover before we would take another plane to Cairo. We decided to go sightseeing in Frankfurt.

In the men's room there at the airport, I met the first American abroad who recognized me, a white student from Rhode Island. He kept eyeing me, then he came over. "Are you X?" I laughed and said I was, I hadn't ever heard it that way. He exclaimed, "You can't be! Boy, I know no one will believe me when I tell them this!" He was attending school, he said, in France.

The brother Muslim and I both were struck by the cordial hospitality of the people in Frankfurt. We went into a lot of shops and stores, looking more than intending to buy anything. We'd walk in, any store, every store, and it would be Hello! People who never saw you before, and knew you were strangers. And the same cordiality when we left, without buying anything. In America, you walk in a store and spend a hundred dollars, and leave, and you're still a stranger. Both you and the clerks act as though you're doing each other a favor. Europeans act more human, or humane, whichever the right word is. My brother Muslim, who could speak enough German to get by, would explain that we were Muslims, and I saw something I had already experienced when I was looked upon as a Muslim and not as a Negro, right in America. People seeing you as a Muslim saw you as a human being and they had a different look, different talk, everything. In one Frankfurt store —a little shop, actually—the storekeeper leaned over his counter to us and waved his hand, indicating the German people passing by: "This way one day, that way another day—" My Muslim brother explained to me that what he meant was that the Germans would rise again.

Back at the Frankfurt airport, we took a United Arab Airlines plane on to Cairo. Throngs of people, obviously Muslims from everywhere, bound on the pilgrimage, were hugging and embracing. They were of all complexions, the whole atmosphere was of warmth and friendliness. The feeling hit me that there really wasn't any color problem here. The effect was as though I had just stepped out of a prison.

I had told my brother Muslim friend that I wanted to be a tourist in Cairo for a couple of days before continuing to Jedda. He gave me his number and asked me to call him, as he wanted to put me with a party of his friends, who could speak English, and would be going on the pilgrimage, and would be happy to look out for me.

So I spent two happy days sightseeing in Cairo. I was impressed by the modern schools, housing developments for the masses, and the highways and the industrialization that I saw. I had read and heard that President Nasser's administration had built up one of the most highly industrialized countries on the African continent. I believe what most surprised me was that in Cairo, automobiles were being manufactured, and also buses.

I had a good visit with Dr. Shawarbi's son, Muhammad Shawarbi, a nineteen-year-old, who was studying economics and political science at Cairo University. He told me that his father's dream was to build a University of Islam in the United States.

The friendly people I met were astounded when they learned I was a

Muslim—from America! They included an Egyptian scientist and his wife, also on their way to Mecca for the Hajj, who insisted I go with them to dinner in a restaurant in Heliopolis, a suburb of Cairo. They were an extremely well-informed and intelligent couple. Egypt's rising industrialization was one of the reasons why the Western powers were so anti-Egypt, it was showing other African countries what they should do, the scientist said. His wife asked me, "Why are people in the world starving when America has so much surplus food? What do they do, dump it in the ocean?" I told her, "Yes, but they put some of it in the holds of surplus ships, and in subsidized granaries and refrigerated space and let it stay there, with a small army of caretakers, until it's unfit to eat. Then another army of disposal people get rid of it to make space for the next surplus batch." She looked at me in something like disbelief. Probably she thought I was kidding. But the American taxpayer knows it's the truth. I didn't go on to tell her that right in the United States, there are hungry people.

I telephoned my Muslim friend, as he had asked, and the Hajj party of his friends was waiting for me. I made it eight of us, and they included a judge and an official of the Ministry of Education. They spoke English beautifully, and accepted me like a brother. I considered it another of Allah's signs, that wherever I turned, someone was there to help me, to guide me.

The literal meaning of Hajj in Arabic is to set out toward a definite objective. In Islamic law, it means to set out for Ka'ba, the Sacred House, and to fulfill the pilgrimage rites. The Cairo airport was where scores of Hajj groups were becoming *Muhrim,* pilgrims, upon entering the state of Ihram, the assumption of a spiritual and physical state of consecration. Upon advice, I arranged to leave in Cairo all of my luggage and four cameras, one a movie camera. I had bought in Cairo a small valise, just big enough to carry one suit, shirt, a pair of underwear sets and a pair of shoes into Arabia. Driving to the airport with our Hajj group, I began to get nervous, knowing that from there in, it was going to be watching others who knew what they were doing, and trying to do what they did.

Entering the state of Ihram, we took off our clothes and put on two white towels. One, the *Izar,* was folded around the loins. The other, the *Rida,* was thrown over the neck and shoulders, leaving the right shoulder and arm bare. A pair of simple sandals, the *na'l,* left the ankle-bones bare. Over the *Izar* waist-wrapper, a money belt was worn, and a bag, something like a woman's big handbag, with a long strap, was for carrying the passport and other valuable papers, such as the letter I had from Dr. Shawarbi.

Every one of the thousands at the airport, about to leave for Jedda, was dressed this way. You could be a king or a peasant and no one would know. Some powerful personages, who were discreetly pointed out to me, had on the same thing I had on. Once thus dressed, we all had begun intermittently calling out *"Labbayka! Labbayka!"* (Here I come, O Lord!) The airport sounded with the din of *Muhrim* expressing their intention to perform the journey of the Hajj.

Planeloads of pilgrims were taking off every few minutes, but the airport was jammed with more, and their friends and relatives waiting to see them off. Those not going were asking others to pray for them at Mecca. We were on our plane, in the air, when I learned for the first time that with the crush, there was not supposed to have been space for me, but strings had been pulled, and someone had been put off because they didn't want to disappoint an American Muslim. I felt mingled emotions of regret that I had inconvenienced and discomfited whoever was bumped off the plane for me, and, with that, an utter humility and gratefulness that I had been paid such an honor and respect.

Packed in the plane were white, black, brown, red, and yellow people, blue eyes and blond hair, and my kinky red hair—all together, brothers! All honoring the same God Allah, all in turn giving equal honor to each other.

From some in our group, the word was spreading from seat to seat that I was a Muslim from America. Faces turned, smiling toward me in greeting. A box lunch was passed out and as we ate that, the word that a Muslim from America was aboard got up into the cockpit.

The captain of the plane came back to meet me. He was an Egyptian, his complexion was darker than mine; he could have walked in Harlem and no one would have given him a second glance. He was delighted to meet an American Muslim. When he invited me to visit the cockpit, I jumped at the chance.

The co-pilot was darker than he was. I can't tell you the feeling it gave me. I had never seen a black man flying a jet. That instrument panel: no one ever could know what all of those dials meant! Both of the pilots were smiling at me, treating me with the same honor and respect I had received ever since I left America. I stood there looking through the glass at the sky ahead of us. In America, I had ridden in more planes than probably any other Negro, and I never had been invited up into the cockpit. And there I was, with two Muslim seatmates, one from Egypt, the other from Arabia, all of us bound for Mecca, with me up in the pilots' cabin. Brother, I *knew* Allah was with me.

I got back to my seat. All of the way, about an hour's flight, we pilgrims were loudly crying out, *"Labbayka! Labbayka!"* The plane landed at Jedda. It's a seaport town on the Red Sea, the arrival or disembarkation point for all pilgrims who come to Arabia to go to Mecca. Mecca is about forty miles to the east, inland.

The Jedda airport seemed even more crowded than Cairo's had been. Our party became another shuffling unit in the shifting mass with every race on earth represented. Each party was making its way toward the long line waiting to go through Customs. Before reaching Customs, each Hajj party was assigned a *Mutawaf*, who would be responsible for transferring that party from Jedda to Mecca. Some pilgrims cried *"Labbayka!"* Others, sometimes large groups, were chanting in unison a prayer that I will translate, "I submit to no one but Thee, O Allah, I submit to no one but Thee. I submit to Thee because Thou hast no partner. All praise and blessings come from Thee, and Thou art alone in Thy kingdom." The essence of the prayer is the Oneness of God.

Only officials were not wearing the *Ihram* garb, or the white skull caps, long, white, nightshirt-looking gown and the little slippers of the *Mutawaf,* those who guided each pilgrim party, and their helpers. In Arabic, an *mmmm* sound before a verb makes a verbal noun, so "*Mutawaf*" meant "the one who guides" the pilgrims on the "*Tawaf,*" which is the circumambulation of the Ka'ba in Mecca.

I was nervous, shuffling in the center of our group in the line waiting to have our passports inspected. I had an apprehensive feeling. Look what I'm handing them. I'm in the Muslim world, right at The Fountain. I'm handing them the American passport which signifies the exact opposite of what Islam stands for.

The judge in our group sensed my strain. He patted my shoulder. Love, humility, and true brotherhood was almost a physical feeling wherever I turned. Then our group reached the clerks who examined each passport and suitcase carefully and nodded to the pilgrim to move on.

I was so nervous that when I turned the key in my bag, and it didn't work, I broke open the bag, fearing that they might think I had something in the bag that I shouldn't have. Then the clerk saw that I was handing him an American passport. He held it, he looked at me and said something in Arabic. My friends around me began speaking rapid Arabic, gesturing and pointing, trying to intercede for me. The judge asked me in English for my letter from Dr. Shawarbi, and he thrust it at the clerk, who read it. He gave the letter back, protesting—I could tell that. An argument was going on, *about* me. I felt like a stupid fool, unable to say a word, I couldn't even understand what was being said. But, finally, sadly, the judge turned to me.

I had to go before the *Mahgama Sharia,* he explained. It was the Muslim high court which examined all possibly nonauthentic converts to the Islamic religion seeking to enter Mecca. It was absolute that no non-Muslim could enter Mecca.

My friends were going to have to go on to Mecca without me. They seemed stricken with concern for me. And *I* was stricken. I found the words to tell them, "Don't worry, I'll be fine. Allah guides me." They said they would pray hourly in my behalf. The white-garbed *Mutawaf* was urging them on, to keep schedule in the airport's human crush. With all of us waving, I watched them go.

It was then about three in the morning, a Friday morning. I never had been in such a jammed mass of people, but I never had felt more alone, and helpless, since I was a baby. Worse, Friday in the Muslim world is a rough counterpart of Sunday in the Christian world. On Friday, all the members of a Muslim community gather, to pray together. The event is called *yaum al-jumu'a*—"the day of gathering." It meant that no courts were held on Friday. I would have to wait until Saturday, at least.

An official beckoned a young Arab *Mutawaf's* aide. In broken English, the official explained that I would be taken to a place right at the airport. My passport was kept at Customs. I wanted to object, because it is a traveler's first law never to get separated from his passport, but I didn't. In my wrapped towels and sandals, I followed the aide in his skull cap, long white gown, and slippers. I guess we were quite a sight. People passing us were speaking all kinds of languages. I couldn't speak anybody's language. I was in bad shape.

Right outside the airport was a mosque, and above the airport was a huge, dormitory-like building, four tiers high. It was semi-dark, not long before dawn, and planes were regularly taking off and landing, their landing lights sweeping the runways, or their wing and tail lights blinking in the sky. Pilgrims from Ghana, Indonesia, Japan, and Russia, to mention some, were moving to and from the dormitory where I was being taken. I don't believe that motion picture cameras ever have filmed a human spectacle more colorful than my eyes took in. We reached the dormitory and began climbing, up to the fourth, top, tier, passing members of every race on earth. Chinese, Indonesians, Afghanistanians. Many, not yet changed into the *Ihram* garb, still wore their national dress. It was like pages out of the *National Geographic* magazine.

My guide, on the fourth tier, gestured me into a compartment that contained about fifteen people. Most lay curled up on their rugs asleep. I could tell that some were women, covered head and foot. An old Russian Muslim and his wife were not asleep. They stared frankly at me. Two Egyptian Muslims and a Persian roused and also stared as my guide moved us over into a corner. With gestures, he indicated that he would demonstrate to me the proper prayer ritual postures. Imagine, being a Muslim minister, a leader in Elijah Muhammad's Nation of Islam, and not knowing the prayer ritual.

I tried to do what he did. I knew I wasn't doing it right. I could feel the other Muslims' eyes on me. Western ankles won't do what Muslim ankles have done for a lifetime. Asians squat when they sit, Westerners sit upright in chairs. When my guide was down in a posture, I tried everything I could to get down as he was, but there I was, sticking up. After about an hour, my guide left, indicating that he would return later.

I never even thought about sleeping. Watched by the Muslims, I kept practicing prayer posture. I refused to let myself think how ridiculous I must have looked to them. After a while, though, I learned a little trick that would let me get down closer to the floor. But after two or three days, my ankle was going to swell.

As the sleeping Muslims woke up, when dawn had broken, they almost instantly became aware of me, and we watched each other while they went about their business. I began to see what an important role the rug played in the overall cultural life of the Muslims. Each individual had a small prayer rug, and each man and wife, or large group, had a larger communal rug. These Muslims prayed on their rugs there in the compartment. Then they spread a tablecloth over the rug and ate, so the rug became the dining room. Removing the dishes and cloth, they sat on the rug—a living room. Then they curl up and sleep on the rug—a bedroom. In that compartment, before I was to leave it, it dawned on me for the first time why the fence had paid such a high price for Oriental rugs when I had been a burglar in Boston. It was because so much intricate care was taken to weave fine rugs in countries where rugs were so culturally versatile. Later, in Mecca, I would see yet another use of the rug. When any kind of a dispute arose, someone who was respected highly and who was not involved would sit on a rug with the disputers around him, which made the rug a courtroom. In other instances it was a classroom.

One of the Egyptian Muslims, particularly, kept watching me out of the corner of his eye. I smiled at him. He got up and came over to me. "Hel-lo—" he said. It sounded like the Gettysburg Address. I beamed at him. "Hello!" I asked his name. "Name? Name?" He was trying hard, but he didn't get it. We tried some words on each other. I'd guess his English vocabulary spanned maybe twenty words. Just enough to frustrate me. I was trying to get him to comprehend anything. "Sky." I'd point. He'd smile. "Sky," I'd say again, gesturing for him to repeat it after me. He would. "Airplane . . . rug . . . foot . . . sandal . . . eyes. . . ." Like that. Then an amazing thing happened. I was so glad I had some communication with a human being, I was just saying whatever came to mind. I said "Muhammad Ali Clay—" All of the Muslims listening lighted up like a Christmas tree. "You? You?" My friend was pointing at me. I shook my head, "No, no. Muhammad Ali Clay my friend—*friend!*" They half understood me. Some of them didn't understand, and that's how it began to get around that I was Cassius Clay, world heavyweight champion. I was later to learn that apparently every man, woman and child in the Muslim world had heard how Sonny Liston (who in the Muslim world had the image of a man-eating ogre) had been beaten in Goliath-David fashion by Cassius Clay, who then had told the world that his name was Muhammad Ali and his religion was Islam and Allah had given him his victory.

Establishing the rapport was the best thing that could have happened in the compartment. My being an American Muslim changed the attitudes from merely watching me to wanting to look out for me. Now, the others began smiling steadily. They came closer, they were frankly looking me up and down. Inspecting me. Very friendly. I was like a man from Mars.

The *Mutawaf's* aide returned, indicating that I should go with him. He pointed from our tier down at the mosque and I knew that he had come to take me to make the morning prayer, *El Sobh,* always before sunrise. I followed him down, and we passed pilgrims by the thousands, babbling languages, everything but English. I was angry with myself for not having taken the time to learn more of the orthodox prayer rituals before leaving America. In Elijah Muhammad's Nation of Islam, we hadn't prayed in Arabic. About a dozen or more years before, when I was in prison, a member of the orthodox Muslim movement in Boston, named Abdul Hameed, had visited me and had later sent me prayers in Arabic. At that time, I had learned those prayers phonetically. But I hadn't used them since.

I made up my mind to let the guide do everything first and I would watch him. It wasn't hard to get him to do things first. He wanted to anyway. Just outside the mosque there was a long trough with rows of faucets. Ablutions had to precede praying. I knew that. Even watching the *Mutawaf's* helper, I didn't get it right. There's an exact way that an orthodox Muslim washes, and the exact way is very important.

I followed him into the mosque, just a step behind, watching. He did his prostration, his head to the ground. I did mine. *"Bi-smi-llahi-r-Rahmain-r-Rahim—"* ("In the name of Allah, the Beneficent, the Merciful—") All Muslim prayers began that way. After that, I may not have been mumbling the right thing, but I was mumbling.

I don't mean to have any of this sound joking. It was far from a joke with me. No one who happened to be watching could tell that I wasn't saying what the others said.

After that Sunrise Prayer, my guide accompanied me back up to the fourth tier. By sign language, he said he would return within three hours, then he left.

Our tier gave an excellent daylight view of the whole airport area. I stood at the railing, watching. Planes were landing and taking off like clockwork. Thousands upon thousands of people from all over the world made colorful patterns of movement. I saw groups leaving for Mecca, in buses, trucks, cars. I saw some setting out to walk the forty miles. I wished that I could start walking. At least, I knew how to do that.

I was afraid to think what might lie ahead. Would I be rejected as a Mecca pilgrim? I wondered what the test would consist of, and when I would face the Muslim high court.

The Persian Muslim in our compartment came up to me at the rail. He greeted me, hesitantly, "Amer . . . American?" He indicated that he wanted me to come and have breakfast with him and his wife, on their rug. I knew that it was an immense offer he was making. You don't have tea with a Muslim's wife. I didn't want to impose, I don't know if the Persian understood or not when I shook my head and smiled, meaning "No, thanks." He brought me some tea and cookies, anyway. Until then, I hadn't even thought about eating.

Others made gestures. They would just come up and smile and nod at me. My first friend, the one who had spoken a little English, was gone. I didn't know it, but he was spreading the word of an American Muslim on the fourth tier. Traffic had begun to pick up, going past our compartment. Muslims in the *Ihram* garb, or still in their national dress, walked slowly past, smiling. It would go on for as long as I was there to be seen. But I hadn't yet learned that I was the attraction.

I have always been restless, and curious. The *Mutawaf's* aide didn't return in the three hours he had said, and that made me nervous. I feared that he had given up on me as beyond help. By then, too, I was really getting hungry. All of the Muslims in the compartment had offered me food, and I had refused. The trouble was, I have to admit it, at that point I didn't know if I could go for their manner of eating. Everything was in one pot on the dining-room rug, and I saw them just fall right in, using their hands.

I kept standing at the tier railing observing the courtyard below, and I decided to explore a bit on my own. I went down to the first tier. I thought, then, that maybe I shouldn't get too far, someone might come for me. So I went back up to our compartment. In about forty-five minutes, I went back down. I went further this time, feeling my way. I saw a little restaurant in the courtyard. I went straight in there. It was jammed, and babbling with languages. Using gestures, I bought a whole roasted chicken and something like thick potato chips. I got back out in the courtyard and I tore up that chicken, using my hands. Muslims were doing the same thing all around me. I saw men at least seventy years old bringing both legs up under them, until they made a human knot of themselves, eating with as much aplomb and satisfaction as though they had been in a fine restaurant with waiters all over the place. All ate as One, and slept as One. Everything about the pilgrimage atmosphere accented the Oneness of Man under One God.

I made, during the day, several trips up to the compartment and back out in the courtyard, each time exploring a little further than before. Once, I nodded at two black men standing together. I nearly shouted when one spoke to me in British-accented English. Before their party approached, ready to leave for Mecca, we were able to talk enough to exchange that I was American and they were Ethiopians. I was heartsick. I had found two English-speaking Muslims at last—and they were leaving. The Ethiopians had both been schooled in Cairo, and they were living in Ryadh, the political capital of Arabia. I was later going to learn to my surprise that in Ethiopia, with eighteen million people, ten million are Muslims. Most people think Ethiopia is Christian. But only its government is Christian. The West has always helped to keep the Christian government in power.

I had just said my Sunset Prayer, *El Maghrib;* I was lying on my cot in the fourth-tier compartment, feeling blue and alone, when out of the darkness came a sudden light!

It was actually a sudden thought. On one of my venturings in the yard full of activity below, I had noticed four men, officials, seated at a table with a telephone. Now, I thought about seeing them there, and with *telephone,* my mind flashed to the connection that Dr. Shawarbi in New York had given me, the telephone number of the son of the author of the book which had been given to me. Omar Azzam lived right there in Jedda!

In a matter of a few minutes, I was downstairs and rushing to where I had seen the four officials. One of them spoke functional English. I excitedly showed him the letter from Dr. Shawarbi. He read it. Then he read it aloud to the other three officials. "A Muslim from America!" I could almost see it capture their imaginations and curiosity. They were very impressed. I asked the English-speaking one if he would please do me the favor of telephoning Dr. Omar Azzam at the number I had. He was glad to do it. He got someone on the phone and conversed in Arabic.

Dr. Omar Azzam came straight to the airport. With the four officials beaming, he wrung my hand in welcome, a young, tall, powerfully built man. I'd say he was six foot three. He had an extremely polished manner. In America, he would have been called a white man, but—it struck me, hard and instantly—from the way he acted. I had no *feeling* of him being a white man. "Why didn't you call before?" he demanded of me. He showed some identification to the four officials, and he used their phone. Speaking in Arabic, he was talking with some airport officials. "Come!" he said.

In something less than half an hour, he had gotten me released, my suitcase and passport had been retrieved from Customs, and we were in Dr. Azzam's car, driving through the city of Jedda, with me dressed in the *Ihram* two towels and sandals. I was speechless at the man's attitude, and at my own physical feeling of no difference between us as human beings. I had heard for years of Muslim hospitality, but one couldn't quite imagine such warmth. I asked questions. Dr. Azzam was a Swiss-trained engineer. His field was city planning. The Saudi Arabian government had borrowed him from the United Nations to direct all of the reconstruction work being done on Arabian holy places. And Dr. Azzam's sister was the wife of Prince Faisal's son. I was in a car with the brother-in-law of the son of the ruler of Arabia. Nor was that all that Allah had done. "My father will be so happy to meet you," said Dr. Azzam. The author who had sent me the book!

I asked questions about his father. Abd ir-Rahman Azzam was known as Azzam Pasha, or Lord Azzam, until the Egyptian revolution, when President Nasser eliminated all "Lord" and "Noble" titles. "He should be at my home when we get there," Dr. Azzam said. "He spends much time in New York with his United Nations work, and he has followed you with great interest."

I was speechless.

It was early in the morning when we reached Dr. Azzam's home. His father was there, his father's brother, a chemist, and another friend—all up that early, waiting. Each of them embraced me as though I were a long-lost child. I had never seen these men before in my life, and they treated me so good! I am going to tell you that I had never been so honored in my life, nor had I ever received such true hospitality.

A servant brought tea and coffee, and disappeared. I was urged to make myself comfortable. No women were anywhere in view. In Arabia, you could easily think there were no females.

Dr. Abd ir-Rahman Azzam dominated the conversation. Why hadn't I called before? They couldn't understand why I hadn't. Was I comfortable? They seemed embarrassed that I had spent the time at the airport; that I had been delayed in getting to Mecca. No matter how I protested that I felt no inconvenience, that I was fine, they would not hear it. "You must rest," Dr. Azzam said. He went to use the telephone.

I didn't know what this distinguished man was doing. I had no dream. When I was told that I would be brought back for dinner that evening, and that, meanwhile, I should get back in the car, how could I have realized that I was about to see the epitome of Muslim hospitality?

Abd ir-Rahman Azzam, when at home, lived in a suite at the Jedda Palace Hotel. Because I had come to them with a letter from a friend, he was going to stay at his son's home, and let me use his suite, until I could get on to Mecca.

When I found out, there was no use protesting: I was in the suite; young Dr. Azzam was gone; there was no one to protest to. The three-room suite had a bathroom that was as big as a double at the New York Hilton. It was suite number 214. There was even a porch outside, affording a beautiful view of the ancient Red Sea city.

There had never before been in my emotions such an impulse to pray— and I did, prostrating myself on the livingroom rug.

Nothing in either of my two careers as a black man in America had served to give me any idealistic tendencies. My instincts automatically examined the reasons, the motives, of anyone who did anything they didn't have to do for me. Always in my life, if it was any white person, I could see a selfish motive.

But there in that hotel that morning, a telephone call and a few hours away from the cot on the fourth-floor tier of the dormitory, was one of the few times I had been so awed that I was totally without resistance. That white man—at least he would have been considered "white" in America— related to Arabia's ruler, to whom he was a close advisor, truly an international man, with nothing in the world to gain, had given up his suite to me, for my transient comfort. He had *nothing* to gain. He didn't need me. He had everything. In fact, he had more to lose than gain. He had followed the American press about me. If he did that, he knew there was only stigma attached to me. I was supposed to have horns. I was a "racist." I was "anti-white"—and he from all appearances was white. I was supposed to be a criminal; not only that, but everyone was even accusing me of using his religion of Islam as a cloak for my criminal practices and philosophies. Even if he had had some motive to use me, he knew that I was separated from Elijah Muhammad and the Nation of Islam, my "power base," according to the press in America. The only organization that I had was just a few weeks old. I had no job. I had no money. Just to get over there, I had had to borrow money from my sister.

That morning was when I first began to reappraise the "white man." It was when I first began to perceive that "white man," as commonly used, means complexion only secondarily; primarily it described attitudes and actions. In America, "white man" meant specific attitudes and actions toward the black man, and toward all other non-white men. But in the Muslim world, I had seen that men with white complexions were more genuinely brotherly than anyone else had ever been.

That morning was the start of a radical alteration in my whole outlook about "white" men.

I should quote from my notebook here. I wrote this about noon, in the hotel: "My excitement, sitting here, waiting to go before the Hajj Committee, is indescribable. My window faces to the sea westward. The streets are filled with the incoming pilgrims from all over the world. The prayers are to Allah and verses from the Quran are on the lips of everyone. Never have I seen such a beautiful sight, nor witnessed such a scene, nor felt such an atmosphere. Although I am excited, I feel safe and secure, thousands of miles from the totally different life that I have known. Imagine that twenty-four hours ago, I was in the fourth-floor room over the airport, surrounded by people with whom I could not communicate, feeling uncertain about the future, and very lonely, and then *one* phone call, following

Dr. Shawarbi's instructions. I have met one of the most powerful men in the Muslim world. I will soon sleep in his bed at the Jedda Palace. I know that I am surrounded by friends whose sincerity and religious zeal I can feel. I must pray again to thank Allah for this blessing, and I must pray again that my wife and children back in America will always be blessed for their sacrifices, too."

I did pray, two more prayers, as I had told my notebook. Then I slept for about four hours, until the telephone rang. It was young Dr. Azzam. In another hour, he would pick me up to return me there for dinner. I tumbled words over one another, trying to express some of the thanks I felt for all of their actions. He cut me off. "Ma sha'a-llah"—which means, "It is as Allah has pleased."

I seized the opportunity to run down into the lobby, to see it again before Dr. Azzam arrived. When I opened my door, just across the hall from me a man in some ceremonial dress, who obviously lived there, was also headed downstairs, surrounded by attendants. I followed them down, then through the lobby. Outside, a small caravan of automobiles was waiting. My neighbor appeared through the Jedda Palace Hotel's front entrance and people rushed and crowded him, kissing his hand. I found out who he was: the Grand Mufti of Jerusalem. Later, in the hotel, I would have the opportunity to talk with him for about a half-hour. He was a cordial man of great dignity. He was well up on world affairs, and even the latest events in America.

I will never forget the dinner at the Azzam home. I quote my notebook again: "I couldn't say in my mind that these were 'white' men. Why, the men acted as if they were brothers of mine, the elder Dr. Azzam as if he were my father. His fatherly, scholarly speech. I *felt* like he was my father. He was, you could tell, a highly skilled diplomat, with a broad range of mind. His knowledge was so worldly. He was as current on world affairs as some people are to what's going on in their living room.

"The more we talked, the more his vast reservoir of knowledge and its variety seemed unlimited. He spoke of the racial lineage of the descendants of Muhammad the Prophet, and he showed how they were both black and white. He also pointed out how color, the complexities of color, and the problems of color which exist in the Muslim world, exist only where, and to the extent that, that area of the Muslim world has been influenced by the West. He said that if one encountered any differences based on attitude toward color, this directly reflected the degree of Western influence."

I learned during dinner that while I was at the hotel, the Hajj Committee Court had been notified about my case, and that in the morning I should be there. And I was.

The Judge was Sheikh Muhammad Harkon. The Court was empty except for me and a sister from India, formerly a Protestant, who had converted to Islam, and was, like me, trying to make the Hajj. She was brown-skinned, with a small face that was mostly covered. Judge Harkon was a kind, impressive man. We talked. He asked me some questions, having to do with my sincerity. I answered him as truly as I could. He not only recognized me as a true Muslim, but he gave me two books, one in English, the other in Arabic. He recorded my name in the Holy Register of true Muslims, and we were ready to part. He told me, "I hope you will become a great preacher of Islam in America." I said that I shared that hope, and I would try to fulfill it.

The Azzam family were very elated that I was qualified and accepted to go to Mecca. I had lunch at the Jedda Palace. Then I slept again for several hours, until the telephone awakened me.

It was Muhammad Abdul Azziz Maged, the Deputy Chief of Protocol for Prince Faisal. "A special car will be waiting to take you to Mecca, right after your dinner," he told me. He advised me to eat heartily, as the Hajj rituals require plenty of strength.

I was beyond astonishment by then.

Two young Arabs accompanied me to Mecca. A well-lighted, modern turnpike highway made the trip easy. Guards at intervals along the way took one look at the car, and the driver made a sign, and we were passed through, never even having to slow down. I was, all at once, thrilled, important, humble, and thankful.

Mecca, when we entered, seemed as ancient as time itself. Our car slowed through the winding streets, lined by shops on both sides and with buses, cars, and trucks, and tens of thousands of pilgrims from all over the earth were everywhere.

The car halted briefly at a place where a *Mutawaf* was waiting for me. He wore the white skullcap and long nightshirt garb that I had seen at the airport. He was a short, dark-skinned Arab, named Muhammad. He spoke no English whatever.

We parked near the Great Mosque. We performed our ablution and entered. Pilgrims seemed to be on top of each other, there were so many, lying, sitting, sleeping, praying, walking.

My vocabulary cannot describe the new mosque that was being built around the Ka'ba. I was thrilled to realize that it was only one of the tremendous rebuilding tasks under the direction of young Dr. Azzam, who had just been my host. The Great Mosque of Mecca, when it is finished, will surpass the architectural beauty of India's Taj Mahal.

Carrying my sandals, I followed the *Mutawaf*. Then I saw the Ka'ba, a huge black stone house in the middle of the Great Mosque. It was being circumambulated by thousands upon thousands of praying pilgrims, both sexes, and every size, shape, color, and race in the world. I knew the prayer to be uttered when the pilgrim's eyes first perceive the Ka'ba. Translated, it is "O God, You are peace, and peace derives from You. So greet us, O Lord, with peace." Upon entering the Mosque, the pilgrim should try to kiss the Ka'ba if possible, but if the crowds prevent him getting that close, he touches it, and if the crowds prevent that, he raises his hand and cries out "Takbir!" ("God is great!") I could not get within yards. "Takbir!"

My feeling there in the House of God was a numbness. My *Mutawaf* led me in the crowd of praying, chanting pilgrims, moving seven times around the Ka'ba. Some were bent and wizened with age; it was a sight that stamped itself on the brain. I saw incapacitated pilgrims being carried by others. Faces were enraptured in their faith. The seventh time around, I prayed two *Rak'a,* prostrating myself, my head on the floor. The first prostration, I prayed the Quran verse "Say He is God, the one and only"; the second prostration: "Say O you who are unbelievers, I worship not that which you worship. . . ."

As I prostrated, the *Mutawaf* fended pilgrims off to keep me from being trampled.

The *Mutawaf* and I next drank water from the well of Zem Zem. Then we ran between the two hills, Safa and Marwa, where Hajar wandered over the same earth searching for water for her child Ishmael.

Three separate times, after that, I visited the Great Mosque and circumambulated the Ka'ba. The next day we sat out after sunrise toward Mount Arafat, thousands of us, crying in unison: "Labbayka! Labbayka!" and "Allah Akbar!" Mecca is surrounded by the crudest-looking mountains I have ever seen; they seem to be made of the slag from a blast furnace. No vegetation is on them at all. Arriving about noon, we prayed and chanted from noon until sunset, and the *asr* (afternoon) and *Maghrib* (sunset) special prayers were performed.

Finally, we lifted our hands in prayer and thanksgiving, repeating Allah's words: "There is no God but Allah. He has no partner. His are authority and praise. Good emanates from Him, and He has power over all things."

Standing on Mount Arafat had concluded the essential rites of being a pilgrim to Mecca. No one who missed it could consider himself a pilgrim.

The *Ihram* had ended. We cast the traditional seven stones at the devil. Some had their hair and beards cut. I decided that I was going to let my beard remain. I wondered what my wife Betty, and our little daughters, were going to say when they saw me with a beard, when I got back to New York. New York seemed a million miles away. I hadn't seen a newspaper that I could read since I left New York. I had no idea what was happening there. A Negro rifle club that had been in existence for over twelve years in Harlem had been "discovered" by the police; it was being trumpeted that I was "behind it." Elijah Muhammad's Nation of Islam had a lawsuit going against me, to force me and my family to vacate the house in which we lived on Long Island.

The major press, radio, and television media in America had representatives in Cairo hunting all over, trying to locate me, to interview me about the furor in New York that I had allegedly caused—when I knew nothing about any of it.

I only knew what I had left in America, and how it contrasted with what I had found in the Muslim world. About twenty of us Muslims who had finished the Hajj were sitting in a huge tent on Mount Arafat. As a Muslim from America, I was the center of attention. They asked me what about the Hajj had impressed me the most. One of the several who spoke English asked; they translated my answers for the others. My answer to that question was not the one they expected, but it drove home my point.

I said, "The *brotherhood!* The people of all races, colors, from all over the world coming together as *one!* It has proved to me the power of the One God."

It may have been out of taste, but that gave me an opportunity, and I used it, to preach them a quick little sermon on America's racism, and its evils.

I could tell the impact of this upon them. They had been aware that the plight of the black man in America was "bad," but they had not been aware that it was inhuman, that it was a psychological castration. These people from elsewhere around the world were shocked. As Muslims, they had a very tender heart for all unfortunates, and very sensitive feelings for truth and justice. And in everything I said to them, as long as we talked, they were aware of the yardstick that I was using to measure everything—that to me the earth's most explosive and pernicious evil is racism, the inability of God's creatures to live as One, especially in the Western world.

I have reflected since that the letter I finally sat down to compose had been subconsciously shaping itself in my mind.

The *color-blindness* of the Muslim world's religious society and the *color-blindness* of the Muslim world's human society: these two influences had each day been making a greater impact, and an increasing persuasion against my previous way of thinking.

The first letter was, of course, to my wife, Betty. I never had a moment's question that Betty, after initial amazement, would change her thinking to join mine. I had known a thousand reassurances that Betty's faith in me was total. I knew that she would see what I had seen—that in the land of Muhammad and the land of Abraham, I had been blessed by Allah with a new insight into the true religion of Islam, and a better understanding of America's entire racial dilemma.

After the letter to my wife, I wrote next essentially the same letter to my sister Ella. And I knew where Ella would stand. She had been saving to make the pilgrimage to Mecca herself.

I wrote to Dr. Shawarbi, whose belief in my sincerity had enabled me to get a passport to Mecca.

All through the night, I copied similar long letters for others who were very close to me. Among them was Elijah Muhammad's son Wallace Muhammad, who had expressed to me his conviction that the only possible salvation for the Nation of Islam would be its accepting and projecting a better understanding of Orthodox Islam.

And I wrote to my loyal assistants at my newly formed Muslim Mosque, Inc. in Harlem, with a note appended, asking that my letter be duplicated and distributed to the press.

I knew that when my letter became public knowledge back in America, many would be astounded—loved ones, friends, and enemies alike. And no less astounded would be millions whom I did not know—who had gained during my twelve years with Elijah Muhammad a "hate" image of Malcolm X.

Even I was myself astounded. But there was precedent in my life for this letter. My whole life had been a chronology of—*changes.*

Here is what I wrote . . . from my heart:

"Never have I witnessed such sincere hospitality and the overwhelming spirit of true brotherhood as is practiced by people of all colors and races here in this Ancient Holy Land, the home of Abraham, Muhammad, and all the other prophets of the Holy Scriptures. For the past week, I have been utterly speechless and spellbound by the graciousness I see displayed all around me by people *of all colors.*

"I have been blessed to visit the Holy City of Mecca. I have made my seven circuits around the Ka'ba, led by a young *Mutawaf* named Muhammad. I drank water from the well of Zem Zem. I ran seven times back and forth between the hills of Mt. Al-Safa and Al-Marwah. I have prayed in the ancient city of Mina, and I have prayed on Mt. Arafat.

"There were tens of thousands of pilgrims, from all over the world. They were of all colors, from blue-eyed blonds to black-skinned Africans. But we were all participating in the same ritual, displaying a spirit of unity and brotherhood that my experiences in America had led me to believe never could exist between the white and the non-white.

"America needs to understand Islam, because this is the one religion that erases from its society the race problem. Throughout my travels in the Muslim world, I have met, talked to, and even eaten with people who in America would have been considered 'white'—but the 'white' attitude was removed from their minds by the religion of Islam. I have never before seen *sincere* and *true* brotherhood practiced by all colors together, irrespective of their color.

"You may be shocked by these words coming from me. But on this pilgrimage, what I have seen, and experienced, has forced me to *re-arrange* much of my thought-patterns previously held, and to *toss aside* some of my previous conclusions. This was not too difficult for me. Despite my firm convictions, I have been always a man who tries to face facts, and to accept the reality of life as new experience and new knowledge unfolds it. I have always kept an open mind, which is necessary to the flexibility that must go hand in hand with every form of intelligent search for truth.

"During the past eleven days here in the Muslim world, I have eaten from the same plate, drunk from the same glass, and slept in the same bed (or on the same rug)—while praying to the *same* God—with fellow Muslims, whose eyes were the bluest of blue, whose hair was the blondest of blond, and whose skin was the whitest of white. And in the *words* and in the *actions* and in the *deeds* of the 'white' Muslims, I felt the same sincerity that I felt among the black African Muslims of Nigeria, Sudan, and Ghana.

"We were *truly* all the same (brothers)—because their belief in one God had removed the 'white' from their *minds,* the 'white' from their *behavior,* and the 'white' from their *attitude.*

"I could see from this, that perhaps if white Americans could accept the Oneness of God, then perhaps, too, they could accept *in reality* the Oneness of Man—and cease to measure, and hinder, and harm others in terms of their 'differences' in color.

"With racism plaguing America like an incurable cancer, the so-called 'Christian' white American heart should be more receptive to a proven solution to such a destructive problem. Perhaps it could be in time to save America from imminent disaster—the same destruction brought upon Germany by racism that eventually destroyed the Germans themselves.

"Each hour here in the Holy Land enables me to have greater spiritual insights into what is happening in America between black and white. The American Negro never can be blamed for his racial animosities—he is only reacting to four hundred years of the conscious racism of the American whites. But as racism leads America up the suicide path, I do believe, from the experiences that I have had with them, that the whites of the younger generation, in the colleges and universities, will see the handwriting on the wall and many of them will turn to the *spiritual* path of *truth*—the *only* way left to America to ward off the disaster that racism inevitably must lead to.

"Never have I been so highly honored. Never have I been made to feel more humble and unworthy. Who would believe the blessings that have been heaped upon an *American Negro?* A few nights ago, a man who would be called in America a 'white' man, a United Nations diplomat, an ambassador, a companion of kings, gave me *his* hotel suite, *his* bed. By this man, His Excellency Prince Faisal, who rules this Holy Land, was made aware of my presence here in Jedda. The very next morning, Prince Faisal's son, in person, informed me that by the will and decree of his esteemed father, I was to be a State Guest.

"The Deputy Chief of Protocol himself took me before the Hajj Court. His Holiness Sheikh Muhammad Harkon himself okayed my visit to Mecca. His Holiness gave me two books on Islam, with his personal seal and autograph, and he told me that he prayed that I would be a successful preacher of Islam in America. A car, a driver, and a guide, have been placed at my disposal, making it possible for me to travel about this Holy Land almost at will. The government provides air-conditioned quarters and servants in each city that I visit. Never would I have even thought of dreaming that I would ever be a recipient of such honors—honors that in America would be bestowed upon a King—not a Negro.

"All praise is due to Allah, the Lord of all the Worlds.

"Sincerely,

"El-Hajj Malik El-Shabazz
"(Malcolm X)"

From THE PARIS DIARY OF NED ROREM

Ned Rorem

A stranger asks, "Are you Ned Rorem?" I answer, "No," adding, however, that I've heard of and would like to meet him.

· · · · ·

It is *conscious* plagiarism that demonstrates invention: we are so taken with what someone else did that we set out to do likewise. Yet prospects of shameful exposure are such that we disguise to a point of opposition; then the song becomes ours. No one suspects. It's *unconscious* stealing that's dangerous.

Yesterday I met Man Ray. I'd always mistakenly thought he was French. For twelve years I've admired his pictures of the French Great, of sadness or sadism (women chained in a courtyard living among their own excrement), pictures of people. These things nourished the legend we Americans are raised on, that celebrities are of different flesh than others. Yet Man Ray himself is a meek little man, not particularly interesting despite his myriad contacts. In fact all the great I've met have disappointed me: they are too concerned with their work to be personally fabulous. They are like anyone, they are like me. Well, then where *are* the myths that, as an American, I craved in my youth? They must, of course, be the movie stars (I have never known one). Gloria Swanson is great through her person and not through her work. It is she, then, whose clothes we rip off in the street to see if she exists (would we do the same for Gide, for Einstein?). Therefore I must know a movie star: Lana Turner or Dietrich. (The men don't count, they don't wear make-up.)

· · · · ·

The night before leaving Paris it seemed as if I had already gone. This was Friday. As always before quitting the great city I took a long walk, this time going far up by *l'Observatoire*. Of course I knew something would happen, since Experiences on the eve of a departure are inevitable (and become more meaningful than similar occurrences at other times, when one can reject or postpone them. Love is Resignation, which means an incident one does not know how to postpone). So, almost to Boulevard Montparnasse, I hear feet and then a bespectacled young man stops me. Would I like to visit his home and *"bavarder un peu"*? He lives on the third story of a house on the darkest street in Paris. I find myself in a

FROM THE PARIS DIARY OF NED ROREM George Braziller, Inc. From *The Paris Diary of Ned Rorem*; reprinted with the permission of the publisher. Copyright © 1966 by Ned Rorem.

huge room lined with books, at least ten thousand books, and all in Russian. My host is a professor of that language, and I eat two small oranges and drink a cup of very good coffee (as I have walked a great deal). It is midnight. Then the guessing game begins; it is always the same. "You have a slight accent; may I ask if you are of foreign origin?" (This question inevitably followed by: "You must be a student *aux Beaux Arts!*") I hate these interrogations which give me a personality when I would prefer to remain anonymous; anonymity and lack of profession make the game more exciting (not to mention getting it over quicker, which is convenient if one has things to do early next day. In strictly anonymous encounters I generally play a role as far removed from my "natural" one as I can manage: this stimulates me). I almost say I am Dutch (that is what I'm most often taken for), then decide this is too revolting, and admit to being American, his Russian books notwithstanding. He says that although he's an accomplished linguist, English is the one language he could never learn—which gives me a feeling of superiority. I decide to tell him I have read *Stavrogin's Confession* and also Gogol, and that Prokofiev made an opera out of *The Nose* (though it may have been Schostakovitch who made it a ballet, but in any case my host wouldn't have known). He falls out of his seat, since until then I have said almost nothing and he has taken me for the anonymous nonprofessional . . . I tell him I am deeply fond of Russian literature; that I feel I have a French soul; that, although I read much less now than when I was fourteen, my taste has not changed and probably never will; that I feel that people whose taste changes have no taste; that I am twenty-seven (he had obviously taken me for younger).

Now he no longer finds me a stray cat ("stray cat" is what he said) and I feel he is drawn to me, and as I consider this a weakness, I become bored. Therefore I use his phone to call Marie Laure and speak in English to increase the mystery. Marie Laure advises me to go to bed soon as we're leaving early. On hanging up I tell the Russian teacher that the woman with whom I've spoken has told me to retire early and that I must therefore leave. This is dangerous, since there is nothing sadder than the parting of a brand new friend, and had he been a maniac or something (they never are) he would have killed me on the spot. I say I am a composer, and he gives me a green leather edition of *Anna Karenina* as I have never read it (on reaching home I inscribe it myself). I leave, but to my aggravation he decides to accompany me as far as Boulevard St. Germain. There we say goodby . . . It is a beautiful summer night of the kind that only happen in big cities . . .

On the rue de Rennes I come across Bel-Amich, who says where did I get that book at such an hour, as he had seen me walking by earlier and I wasn't carrying any book. We go for hot milk on a café terrace and, as I am telling him where I got the book, a man at the next table asks me for a light, and while I am giving it to him he strokes my hand and whispers can he see me tomorrow. His face is pleasing, but I answer that alas I cannot as I'm leaving town (forgetting the danger once again, that the parting

of a brand new friend, etc.). He says he has never seen eyes like mine, gives
me an address, asks me to write. Marie Laure thinks I should.

.   .   .   .   .

In my new canary-yellow shirt (from Chez Vachon in St. Tropez), my
golden legs in khaki shorts, my tan sandals, and orange hair, I look like a jar
of honey.

.   .   .   .   .

Being myself a coward, a cheat, a weak-kneed opportunist, stingy and
dishonest—I despise these things. Yet I have scant respect for courage and
find that nine times out of ten it's the result of dullness or vanity. Not to
cheat is to ignore love. I must admit that strong legs are exciting to behold,
but I always walk swiftly, and besides I could strangle you if I so desired
(still I've always been afraid, nearly ashamed of my strength. I know
why.) . . . Creative men have always known where to look; this is what
makes them seem selfish on the first level, but on the second (and on all
the following rungs as far as the sky) they are the most generous of all.
Sincerity is the virtue of tiny folk; I prefer a many-faceted personality . . .
Yet how long can this go on, since I continue to detest myself because my
motives are irreconcilable.

From PAPER LION

George Plimpton

The day after the night of the Squeaky Shoes, George Wilson called me
over on the practice field and asked me if I would mind overseeing the
rookie show. "You can produce it," he said.

"You cut our best man, Imperiale," I said, "a bona-fide night-club performer."

"He played football like one," said Wilson bluntly.

I said that I would do what I could.

"You're expendable," Wilson explained. "The other rookies have got
their minds occupied."

"I'm supposed to be worrying about Cleveland," I said.

"Worrying isn't going to help you against Cleveland," Wilson said. He
was being very cryptic that morning. "You might as well worry about the
rookie show."

FROM PAPER LION From pp. 264–279 (Chapter 25) in *Paper Lion* by George Plimpton.
Copyright © 1964, 1965, 1966 by George Plimpton. By permission of Harper & Row,
Publishers.

He explained the purpose of the show—which was to give the rookies a chance to have fun at the expense of the coaches and veterans. Afterward, the veterans would entertain the rookies at a party. "Anything goes in the show," he said. "There's no rule book. Make it bawdy. That goes down well. There won't be any dames watching. Put together some skits. You can be as rough on the coaches and the veterans as you want. Then there'll be rookies who play kazoos and harmonicas and crap like that. They can play and fill up the time."

"When are you going to schedule it?" I asked.

"You've got two days. We'll have the rookie night the day after tomorrow." He saw my dismay. "You'll get help," he said. "Barr and Gordy and Schmidt will give you a hand. Most all the Lions are goddamn frustrated actors."

That evening at the team meeting Wilson requested that the rookies stay behind and take over the classroom to discuss their show. Barr, Schmidt, and Gordy stayed on as advisers, and so did LeBeau and Maher. It developed that none of the rookies—there were about ten of them left after the previous night's cut—had musical skills. So LeBeau and Maher volunteered to play their guitars. Wilson was right about the veterans. They had many ideas for skits, and they all wanted to act in them. But the only rookie who seemed enthusiastic was Lucien Reeberg. He began to outline a complex skit he had in mind, but the veterans told him to calm down. "You can do a soft-shoe, Loosh . . ." they said.

Later that night, after our session was over, I wandered around the dormitory and talked to the veterans to find out something about rookie shows. Almost all the teams in the league had them, and afterward the veterans entertained the rookies at a party—a type of initiation ceremonial that took place usually a day or so after the last big squad cut. Some of the shows were especially lavish, I was told, particularly those put on by the two teams on the Coast. Often there were memorable acts. John Gonzaga told me that when he played for the Washington Redskins a rookie appeared on stage who was a whistler, a great whistler, who came on with a paper bag over his head, his navel outlined in red lipstick, and he had control of the muscles around the navel so he could make it work like a mouth. Gonzaga said it was the damnedest thing he had even seen, it killed the audience, and they kept at him to keep it up until the guy's lips got dry, his whistle faded (it was hard enough to hear it through the bag), and his stomach muscles got tired, so that he stood there quietly—a paper bag over his head, and a lipsticked navel which wouldn't work any more—tuckered out, and they finally let him go.

The next day I skipped practice and spent the day in the cellar of Page Hall, where the school dramatic department had a roomful of costumes and props. I picked through the costumes for inspiration. I was not very hopeful.

My experience in the theatre was limited, and what little there had been often seemed tainted with disaster. In one memorable early production of *Macbeth,* truncated for schoolboys, I appeared at the last moments of the play in a procession accompanying Macduff, who came on stage bearing Macbeth's head on a spike. The head was artfully done, cut in profile from the side of a cardboard packing box, painted, and attached to a long pole. Macduff stumbled coming on stage, over a cable, I suppose, and the pole got turned in his hand so that what was displayed to the audience was not Macbeth's head but whatever was on the reverse of the cardboard box, the letters BRILLO, I think, or LUX, quite distinguishable—in fact the announcement soared above Macduff's procession as noticeable as an advertising blimp.

The Earl of Northumberland has the line that greets Macduff. He says: *"Here comes newer comfort."* This unbearable line (under the circumstances) was delivered by the Earl (an eleven-year-old classmate of mine) in a high soprano which was only slightly muffled by his spirit-gummed beard, and out across the footlights a fitful murmur rose from an audience trying to contain itself. It was unsuccessful. Suddenly, as sharp as a scream, a single high piercing bray burst from someone in the back of the theatre, one of the fathers—probably the hardest that man had ever laughed— absolutely uncontrollable it was, catching up the rest of the audience with it so that our mournful procession moved through a storm of laughter so threatening that some of us, in spite of ourselves, looked out nervously across the footlights toward that dark wall of sound. No one knew what had gone wrong. There was a tendency to huddle together, eyes wide over the beards.

Malcolm, hailed as the new king, has the last speech in the play, and, as I recall, he got through it with great speed, his voice high and nervous, so that he seemed terrified to be crowned the king at Scone. On the uncertain note that Scotland has lost its tyrant, Macbeth, to gain a weakling, the curtain came mercifully down.

I did not mention my theatrical career to Barr, Gordy, and Schmidt. We met that evening and put the show together. I showed them the props I had found in the dramatic department, and it took us two or three hours to work out some skits.

The next day after supper Wilson led his coaches and the veterans across the school grounds to the gym. The basketball court had a stage set back from the sidelines. It was well-appointed, with a big curtain and flies and other accoutrements, including a big switchboard with levers which no one was anxious to fool with. We looked out through the part in the curtain and watched the audience seat itself in a big semicircle of foldup chairs set out on the basketball court. Wilson sat in the middle with his coaches on either side.

Traditionally, throughout the National Football League, the rookie shows open on a chorus of big first-year linemen, wearing only jock straps, high-kicking in a thunderous can-can.

We stayed with tradition in our opening number, though some of our people wore additional props—some women's hats along with the jocks, and Lucien Reeberg, the big three-hundred-pounder, wore a bell-shaped wire hoop used under Victorian ball gowns, and he spun a large beach umbrella above his head. He danced with such abandon to a full-volume record of *Gaîté Parisienne* that he nearly collapsed and brought down the can-can line with him. The others danced perfunctorily and self-consciously in their jock straps, looking bleakly out over the footlights at the audience, which gaped at them and cat-called.

When the laughter died away, the curtain came down, and LeBeau went out in front with his guitar to hold the audience while the scenery was set up for the first skit. From out front we could hear the thump of strings as he sang his mournful songs.

The first skit was supposed to be a spoof of Commissioner Peter Rozelle's league headquarters and the goings-on there. I played the part of Rozelle. The part fell to me by default, since no one else had time to learn the lines, such as they were. I wore a Napoleon hat, a cloak, a wooden sword, three cap pistols, and a rubber dirk; and I carried a pair of handcuffs, a tack hammer, and a frying pan. These artifacts, collected from the prop room in Page Hall, were supposed to suggest the inquisitorial aspects of Rozelle's office. He was not popular with the Lions because of the heavy fines he had levied on five of them for gambling, and for the excommunication of Alex Karras, and when I clanked toward the footlights and said, "Howdy, I'm Petesy Rozelle," the audience delivered up a stiff barrage of invective.

The most ingenious device in Rozelle's "office" was a truth machine which spoke its answers—a role performed by four rookies seated bunched in close together on foldup chairs and facing the audience. The "machine" was rigged in Rozelle's favor, toadying to him, and when I put a question to it such as "What's to be said about those who don't think I—Pete Rozelle—am a grand fellow?" the rookie halfback from Iowa, Larry Ferguson, a Negro of dark blue hue, with birthmarks that crossed his face like tribal scars, would tap his foot three times, and at the third beat, he and the other rookies would reply in sharp unison:

"!"

a sharp obscenity, like a bomb going off.

Or I would ask: "What's my feeling about the Detroit Lions?"

"! 'em"

I put a number of questions to the "machine" during the skit, and I wondered afterward—because the volume the four rookies put to their epithets was considerable—what anybody strolling out on the school grounds would have thought, a couple perhaps, one of the Episcopal bishops and his wife, out under the first stars of the dusk, strolling past the fountains, and then, across the lawn, suddenly hearing from the gym,

"!"

"My God, Ellen, did you hear that?"

"What? —I didn't hear anything."

"Well, I don't know . . . a whole congregation shouting . . . well . . . in unison . . . in the gym over there."

"The African delegates, do you think?" she said. "In the gym?" She could see the loom of the building against the evening. "The bishops from

Kenya and Ghana and Sierra Leone, and the other places—how *nice*. It makes you think, doesn't it, Geoffrey?"

"Well, I don't know . . . *listen.*"

In the warm jasmine smell of the evening they waited motionless on the gravel walk, high above them the thin whistles of the nighthawks still hunting, and then out of the darkness of the gym, distinct as a trumpet bray, rose a chorus of male voices:

"!"

She clung to him. "Geoffrey. There's something odd going on in the gym."

My imagination was never able to determine what happened then— whether the couple went and reported to some higher authority that "something odd" was going on in the gym. Or whether they continued their stroll undaunted through the school grounds, as if everything, even the crudities from the gym, was natural and to be endured, as if the nighthawks wheeling in the darkness above had abruptly changed their calls to:

"! ! !"

and nothing was to be done but accept it.

After the Rozelle take-off was done, LeBeau filled in with his guitar while the stage was set for the following skit, which was based on the idea that the coaches were letting the veterans go in favor of a youth movement—each veteran being called by turn and dismissed by George Wilson. I played Wilson—still wearing the Napoleon hat, the cap pistols, the wooden sword, and the dirk. I sat at a table with a teacher's school bell in front of me, and when I banged at it, Pat Studstill, playing the Hawk, would bring in a veteran (played by a rookie) and I would deliver a sharp address and order him cut from the squad. Studstill carried out the order quite literally: he was got up in a knight's helmet he'd found some-where and he carried an executioner's axe made of cardboard on which he had made a suggestive smear of red paint. After my harangue, Studstill led the veteran behind a low curtain and the audience would then see the axe rise and fall above the curtain—a bit of imaginative theatre that was Studstill's own contribution—followed by a sharp squawk and the thud of a body hitting the floor. The sound effects varied—the squawks produced by different rookies Studstill had lined up behind the curtain, and the decapitation was usually indicated by the iron clang of a wrench. A folding chair was dropped once or twice back there, by the sound of it, and so was a tool box.

The sketches gave a chance to divulge the peccadilloes of individual veterans; the players would turn in their seats to grin at the one of their number being lampooned, and he would scrunch down a bit, his chair complaining shrilly under him, and when it was finished he would perk up and twist around to jaw at the victim of the next characterization, loud in the relief that he himself had been done.

I had been supplied with an item or so about each Lion player who was lampooned in the skits. Barr, Schmidt, and Gordy had furnished most of the material, sitting around the previous night. Some of the items made little sense to me at the time, but they were effective enough when presented. For instance, they suggested that I explain to Danny Lewis, the big full-back, that he was being cut from the squad because he spent too much time in the bathroom. That did not seem particularly funny, but I said it anyway when the time came. "Besides, Lewis," I said, finishing up my diatribe against him, "you're getting axed because you spend too much time in the crapper. Take him away, Hawk." It was some legend about him brought to light (I never discovered what it was) and the players brayed with delight to have it recalled.

The lampoons were mild enough. Gail Cogdill was spoofed for his over-concern with his health: "You've let your body go," I remember shouting at the rookie playing the Cogdill role. He was teetering slightly, bent forward awkwardly on a pair of children's crutches. "Cheating your body . . . you're finished here," I cried. The same phrase turned up in the spoof of Harley Sewell, in which his determination was mocked, and also his weight, which was light for his position. "Harley!" I shouted at the rookie, who was wearing a doll's cowboy hat high on the crown of his head, "we ask you to get your weight up—to eat like an elephant and crap like a bird. Harley, you've been cheating your body!" I yelled. "You been eating like a bird, crapping like an elephant . . . etc. etc."

Milt Plum's personal appearance was made fun of: he was invariably fastidious, his hair neatly combed, long for a football player's, every strand of it straight, even in the rigor of a scrimmage, as if it were pasted down with an invisible lacquer. It was always a surprise to see him arrive at the sidelines and wrench off his helmet; no matter how hard he had been knocked around in the scrimmage, even if his nose dripped blood, he would display hair groomed smooth as a banister's newel. In the skit about him (he was played by Lucien Reeberg, still wearing his hoop, who in his eagerness to perform played a number of veterans) I cried out to him: "I'm sorry, Plum, but we're got to let you go. Ever since you came here from the Cleveland Browns, the coaches and I have been trying to do something about your personal appearance, you know, to get your hair *cut* and combed neatly. Scooter McLean even showed you how to hold the comb and apply the hair set. We showed you how to work a pair of nail scissors, clip, clip, clip, and we tried to show you that you can't brush your teeth without opening your mouth. Well, you haven't done it, Milt, and you look like a sheepdog out there . . . etc. etc."

After twenty veterans had been cut, the curtain came down, a piano was wheeled out and I thumped at it for a while. The show was concluded with a few short skits based on the filming of television commercials. One of them had George Wilson trying to record the line of a television commercial without including an obscenity. I played the part of a harried television producer. John Gordy played Wilson. The line he was trying to get straight was: "I like Marlboro, a man's cigarette."

I would say, "Let's try it again, Mr. Wilson," pointing a shoebox at him and turning an imaginary handle to indicate a camera.

Gordy would furrow his brow and announce, "I like Marlboro, a ! cigarette."

"No, Mr. Wilson," I would say. "We haven't got that quite right. We've let that word creep in there. Let's give it another try."

So Gordy would say: "I like Marlboro, a man's !"

"No, not quite right."

"I like !, a man's cigarette."

"No . . ."

"!"

There was a merciful blackout at the skit's close, somewhat delayed since Dennis Gaubatz, the big rookie linebacker, who had refused to dance in the can-can line and had been relegated to "lights," was slow at the switch—the actors stood poised like wax figures as the laughter died at their last lines, and Joe Schmidt, standing in the wings, hissed, *"Lights,* Gaubatz, for Chrissake."

The last skit of the evening was a toothpaste commercial. I said, "Crest toothpaste is proud to bring you the result of one of its surveys. We have two schoolchildren here—on the left little Roger Brown, who is one of two hundred children who for the last six years has been using toothpaste with fluoristan. On my right is John Gordy, who is one of two hundred children using Crest toothpaste with hydrochlorophlexiphil. Now, Roger, will you tell the viewing audience the results of the survey of *your* group."

Lucien Reeberg, who was playing Brown, hammed it up, simpering and carrying on and getting as much into his meager line as he could, which was considerable, considering the line, which was brief: "We had twenty percent less cavities."

After Reeberg was done, I asked, "And now, John Gordy, what about your group?" cranking the imaginary wheel on the shoebox.

Gordy was playing himself. He had removed his bridgework—all his front teeth had been knocked out in some past football war—and at my question he opened his mouth in a cavernous grin, not a tooth to be seen in the front of his head, and he reported loudly: *"No cavities at all!"*

He kept his mouth ajar, leaning forward slightly, motionless, as I was, and from the wings we finally heard Joe Schmidt say, "Lights, Gaubatz, for Chrissakes, *lights."*

They were doused, the curtain was drawn, and when the lights went up again Gordy slipped his teeth back in, and we all went out in front and took awkward bows.

The veterans and coaches came up and crowded around. John Gonzaga said there were things about the show to be remembered, which was high praise considering the number of rookie shows he had seen, and the acts he remembered, such as the player who wore the paper bag and had the lipsticked navel.

Afterward, we piled into cars and the veterans took the rookies out. The coaches told us to watch ourselves. In the past, a number of bars and restaurants in the vicinity had been decimated on rookie night, so the veterans had hired an empty hall on the top floor of the Veterans of Foreign Wars building on the main road to Pontiac. Joe Schmidt was in the car. He said how important the rookie night was—how it made you feel you belonged. After his weeks of ostracization because of the veterans' love for the linebacker, Flanagan, whom he replaced, Schmidt was finally accepted in a drinking bout, out on the town, exactly like rookie night. He was plied with liquor. He tried to fake being drunk by reeling around tossing down ginger ale from a shot glass, but they caught him at it, and at two A.M. he was just barely conscious that he was playing the drums in a Salvation Army band. But it was a great night for him.

A tremendous racket was going on when we arrived. We could hear it as we parked the car out in the back lot. Our group, arriving late, hurried up the stairs. Everything had been prepared up there—a large galvanized garbage pail, with a mop handy, was in the middle of an open enclosure of long tables. Within, the rookies sat. In front of them, on the tables, were the big mugs, and the pitchers of beer ready, and around the perimeter the veterans leaned across, shouting at them to stand and drink up. Toasts were ordered—to Bruce Maher's son, born that afternoon, to the President's son, Patrick Bouvier Kennedy, also born that day, and to die the next—the big men standing up on their chairs, the beer soaking the shirt fronts, as they shouted the children's names, and drank to them—and then more names to toast, the coaches, Alex Karras, Dean Rusk, Dinah Washington, Jean Seberg, Pete Rozelle's grandmother, and as the lists went on the rookies began to weave.

Harley Sewell drank down an entire pitcher to show the rookies the proper way to drink—the beer sliding down his open throat as if poured into an open drain. Roger Brown also gave some drinking lessons—pouring the beer from the pitcher into a mouth cupped wide as a hippo's, it seemed, his throat barely working as the beer, like Sewell's, ran unencumbered to his stomach.

For their final toasts, the rookies were subjected to Cardinal Puff—the familiar fraternity drinking game in which the initiate must follow a prescribed ritual, in exact order; if he makes a mistake in word or gesture, or gets the order wrong in the toasting sequence, he must drink his mug down and start again from the beginning. The veterans were strict judges, quick to penalize, and after a while some of the rookies were barely able to get out the first line, which is, "Here's to Cardinal Puff for the first time."

Harley Sewell came by and caught me looking on.

"What you doin' out here, rook? Git on in there."

I got in the rookie enclosure. Bob Whitlow, the first-line center, sat across from me. He had me drink some warmup toasts—to his home town; to the high school there, and its football coach; and then Sewell leaned across and I drank a toast to *his* home town.

"Saint Jo, Texas!" I called out.

When Gail Cogdill stopped by, I drank a toast to his home town without being asked.

"Worland, Wyoming!" I shouted, "population: fourteen."

It took me almost five mugs to get through the Cardinal Puff exercise. Whitlow was easy on me the last time. When I stood up and left the enclosure, the room was reeling slightly. I went up and concentrated on the wording of an enlarged copy of the Constitution framed on the wall. I went and stood at a window, pulling the rattan shade aside to get some air. Outside the neon lights along the main street beat steadily. The noise behind me was deafening.

I launched myself back into it. At the far end of the hall, a number of the local people were peering in, standing at the head of the stairwell. They crowded the door, quite a few of them; in the back was a row of craning faces, with one in the far back that bobbed up and down, as if the fellow, short of stature, were bouncing on a trampoline to see.

"Wha' you suppose those folks think?" I shouted happily in the uproar. "They look confused and concerned." I went slowly up to them. "Ladies an' gen'l'm'n, the Detroit *Lions,*" I announced. "A grand, finely tuned, superbly con-conditioned football aggre-aggregation who *here,* in this grand hall of yours, for your eyes *alone,* are doing their daily con-conditioning exercises." I swept a hand behind me. "Gym work," I said bluntly.

Their attention remained caught by the goings-on. I turned. It seemed, at sudden glance, a shipboard scene—a promenade deck, storm-lashed, with an occasional scud of beer flying, the footing difficult as the big men, their shirt fronts soaked, swayed and skidded, shouting, gripping each other for support. A number had succumbed to malaise, two at the garbage pail, a third at the window, the rattan window shade askew across his shoulders as he bent out over the parking lot.

"Boats! To the boats!" I shouted—an alarum that went unnoticed in the confusion.

After a while, the veterans began guiding the rookies down to the cars, supporting some of them, one or two being carried, Reeberg for one, the veterans shoulder to shoulder under him calling out directions, "A little down on your side," as they moved down the narrow stairs like furniture movers.

I drove back to camp with Terry Barr and John Gordy.

"Tonight was a picnic," Barr said. "Some of those rookies were *walking.*" He seemed incredulous.

"Oh," I said weakly.

"In Bobby Layne's time, a rookie was never able to get home on his own pins. That was the rule."

They talked about their first rookie night. Both of them had arrived in camp late—from the All-Star game in Chicago in which they'd played—missing a week or so of training, coming in on the day of the rookie night, it turned out, and after a long practice they were taken out on the town with the others. Barr was returned to his room barely conscious. He was put under a shower, briefly, fully clothed, then laid out on his bed, still clothed. They dropped him there as if they were discarding him.

He was there a half hour or so, too miserable to move, though he was conscious of the water squelching in his shoes when he moved his toes. The door to his room swung ajar and he saw the coaches watching him, head coach Buddy Parker with a clipboard. A bedcheck, apparently. He managed a weak smile. "That's Barr," one of the coaches whispered to Parker.

Down the hall, when Parker and his staff looked in, John Gordy was being sick into a pail as the door opened. He also managed a smile. He recognized Parker. He tried to say, "Hi, coach." He raised himself off the bed, but the coach slapped the door shut before he could get the words out.

Gordy and Barr described the considerable consequences of what Parker saw that night, and its effect on him. The rookie night was on a Saturday. On Monday in Detroit there was a "meet the Lions" banquet, to which over five hundred Lion boosters paid ten dollars apiece to eat a chicken-and-peas dinner; they were to be entertained by introductions to players and coaches, then listen to speeches from club officials, and a guest speaker, Otto Graham, the ex-Cleveland quarterback. Parker, the main speaker, sat at the end of the dais. He sent his chicken and peas away, and sat staring out across the room. Otto Graham got up when his turn came and made a number of jokes about the after-hours deportment of the Lion players, which was a surefire cause for merriment. He said, among other things, "They have an early bedcheck at Cranbrook so the players can duck on out the windows and get into town for the parties." Everybody laughed hard, and the players looked into their coffee cups with self-conscious grins.

The Detroit sportscaster, Bob Reynolds, who was the master of ceremonies, then introduced Parker, cuing the applause for him by referring to abilities which made him the "best coach in the league." The applause *was* heavy, the big crowd rising along with Parker as he moved for the lectern, tearing a paper he held in his hand into tiny scraps. He seemed somewhat grim, but that was his manner. Everybody settled in his seat, belts were loosened, smoke rose in clouds from cigars tilted in contentment, and ears were tuned for soothing words about the coming season, perhaps a wry joke or two which would be applauded as much for his attempting it as for its efficacy, Parker not being a man at ease in public.

When it was absolutely quiet, Parker said in a low monotone, "I quit." He did not pause for emphasis, but continued straight on: "I got a situation here I can't handle. These ballplayers have gotten too big for me, or something. I'm getting out of Detroit football—and I'm getting out tonight. So long," he said, and moving laterally along the dais to his seat he sat down.

There was what the press referred to the next day, according to Barr and Gordy, as a "huge silence," finally broken by some incredulous, somewhat tentative, shouts of "What? what?" The master of ceremonies, Reynolds, rose stiffly—his mind apparently set on getting on with the program no matter what—and asked Parker, in that case, if he minded if George Wilson would tell the audience what could be expected of the 1957 Lions. Parker made a resigned gesture, and Wilson, confused and startled, moved to the microphone and mumbled a few words about the team, his mind obviously distracted by Parker's statement, until his feelings got the better of him and he said sharply: "This is serious. I hope Buddy stays and we win the championship. I don't want to get mixed up in any crap, and that's *it!*"

The audience jumped up and began shouting. Reynolds came back on the microphone, still confused, to say that he had never faced such a situation and didn't know what to do. "If I was a newspaperman though," he said, "I'd know enough to start running for the door."

Some of the newsmen did just that, and others stayed around, rushing from group to group of boosters, players, and coaches, trying to find out what was going on, and hearing in the background the voice of General Manager Anderson booming over the ballroom. "Good old Andy," said Barr. "He took over the microphone and was trying to calm everyone down. But it didn't work out, and he finally gave up." Barr remembered Anderson leaning into the microphone and concluding the evening with just what he would have said had the proceedings sailed along smoothly. "That finishes up tonight's program," he called out to the storming, confused crowd. "Thank you."

"So that was how George Wilson became head coach," I said.

"They gave him the team when Buddy Parker quit," Barr said, "and he went on and won the championship with it."

He turned the car through the gates and into the school grounds.

"There's no telling," he said, "if it was the rookie night and seeing all those players boozed up that *did it*. I mean the guy could have had some tea leaves turn up wrong. He was awful superstitious."

"Listen," Gordy said as Barr parked the car.

Out across the lawns drifted snatches of song, bursts of ribaldry, and occasionally distant hallooing, like the cries of campers lost in a forest.

"From the sound of it, some of them are in the fountains," Gordy said. "Best way to get them sobered up."

Barr said, "Pietrosante spent his rookie night in one of those fountains. He got in there, and the water was warm, like lying in moss, he said, and he dozed off. Somebody came along the gravel walk just before daylight and the sound of the steps woke him up. This guy sees him and stops. A gardener, Nick thinks he was. He looked in at Nick, his face like he's seen a corpse in his fountain, a guy drowned in there, naturally, because it *looks* like that. But then Nick jumps up, big, you know, with the water rushing off him, and I guess he was flailing around because he didn't know where he was, of course, and this gardener or mailman, whatever he was, seeing this in the darkness give a squawk and he *lit out,* I mean to tell you."

A distant splash and a high-pitched yell drifted out at us.

"I wonder if they're up in the Milles fountain—" I said—"in there with those nine-foot stick-like nudes."

"Horrible," Gordy said, thinking about the statues. "Of course the rookies might go for those stone gals; or maybe that's Brettschneider up there, giving them the old club rush. A little rough handling by the Badger might improve those statues."

We walked past the gym. "What about George Wilson?" I asked. "What's he make of the rookie night?"

"He doesn't pay this any heed," Barr said. "He shuts his door good and tight. He knows it'll be a better team for it. The rookies are part of it now, they've been initiated—you too," he said, looking over. "Can't you feel it?"

"I feel soused," I said. We went along the gravel walks. "But I know about the other thing too," I said.

WHAT I BELIEVE

E. M. Forster

I do not believe in Belief. But this is an age of faith, and there are so many militant creeds that, in self-defence, one has to formulate a creed of one's own. Tolerance, good temper and sympathy are no longer enough in a world which is rent by religious and racial persecution, in a world where ignorance rules, and science, who ought to have ruled, plays the subservient pimp. Tolerance, good temper and sympathy—they are what matter really, and if the human race is not to collapse they must come to the front before long. But for the moment they are not enough, their action is no stronger than a flower, battered beneath a military jack-boot. They want stiffening, even if the process coarsens them. Faith, to my mind, is a stiffening process, a sort of mental starch, which ought to be applied as sparingly as possible. I dislike the stuff. I do not believe in it, for its own sake, at all. Herein I probably differ from most people, who believe in Belief, and are only sorry they cannot swallow even more than they do. My law-givers are Erasmus and Montaigne, not Moses and St. Paul. My temple stands not upon Mount Moriah but in that Elysian Field where even the immoral are admitted. My motto is: "Lord, I disbelieve—help thou my unbelief."

I have, however, to live in an Age of Faith—the sort of epoch I used to hear praised when I was a boy. It is extremely unpleasant really. It is bloody in every sense of the word. And I have to keep my end up in it. Where do I start?

With personal relationships. Here is something comparatively solid in a world full of violence and cruelty. Not absolutely solid, for Psychology has split and shattered the idea of a "Person," and has shown that there is something incalculable in each of us, which may at any moment rise to the surface and destroy our normal balance. We don't know what we are like. We can't know what other people are like. How, then, can we put any trust in personal relationships, or cling to them in the gathering political storm? In theory we cannot. But in practice we can and do. Though A is not unchangeably A or B unchangeably B, there can still be love and loyalty between the two. For the purpose of living one has to assume that the per-

WHAT I BELIEVE Copyright, 1939, renewed, 1967, by E. M. Forster. Reprinted from his volume, *Two Cheers for Democracy*, by permission of Harcourt Brace Jovanovich, Inc. Published in Canada by Edward Arnold (Publishers) Ltd.

sonality is solid, and the "self" is an entity, and to ignore all contrary evidence. And since to ignore evidence is one of the characteristics of faith, I certainly can proclaim that I believe in personal relationships.

Starting from them, I get a little order into the contemporary chaos. One must be fond of people and trust them if one is not to make a mess of life, and it is therefore essential that they should not let one down. They often do. The moral of which is that I must, myself, be as reliable as possible, and this I try to be. But reliability is not a matter of contract—that is the main difference between the world of personal relationships and the world of business relationships. It is a matter for the heart, which signs no documents. In other words, reliability is impossible unless there is a natural warmth. Most men possess this warmth, though they often have bad luck and get chilled. Most of them, even when they are politicians, *want* to keep faith. And one can, at all events, show one's own little light here, one's own poor little trembling flame, with the knowledge that it is not the only light that is shining in the darkness, and not the only one which the darkness does not comprehend. Personal relations are despised today. They are regarded as bourgeois luxuries, as products of a time of fair weather which is now past, and we are urged to get rid of them, and to dedicate ourselves to some movement or cause instead. I hate the idea of causes, and if I had to choose between betraying my country and betraying my friend, I hope I should have the guts to betray my country. Such a choice may scandalize the modern reader, and he may stretch out his patriotic hand to the telephone at once and ring up the police. It would not have shocked Dante, though. Dante places Brutus and Cassius in the lowest circle of Hell because they had chosen to betray their friend Julius Caesar rather than their country Rome. Probably one will not be asked to make such an agonizing choice. Still, there lies at the back of every creed something terrible and hard for which the worshipper may one day be required to suffer, and there is even a terror and a hardness in this creed of personal relationships, urbane and mild though it sounds. Love and loyalty to an individual can run counter to the claims of the State. When they do—down with the State, say I, which means that the State would down me.

This brings me along to Democracy, "even Love, the Beloved Republic, which feeds upon Freedom and lives." Democracy is not a Beloved Republic really, and never will be. But it is less hateful than other contemporary forms of government, and to that extent it deserves our support. It does start from the assumption that the individual is important, and that all types are needed to make a civilization. It does not divide its citizens into the bossers and the bossed—as an efficiency-regime tends to do. The people I admire most are those who are sensitive and want to create something or discover something, and do not see life in terms of power, and such people get more of a chance under a democracy than elsewhere. They found religions, great or small, or they produce literature and art, or they do disinterested scientific research, or they may be what is called "ordinary people," who are creative in their private lives, bring up their children decently, for instance, or help their neighbors. All these people need to express themselves; they cannot do so unless society allows them liberty to do so, and the society which allows them most liberty is a democracy.

Democracy has another merit. It allows criticism, and if there is not public criticism there are bound to be hushed-up scandals. That is why I believe in the Press, despite all its lies and vulgarity, and why I believe in Parliament. Parliament is often sneered at because it is a Talking Shop. I believe in it *because* it is a talking shop. I believe in the Private Member who makes himself a nuisance. He gets snubbed and is told that he is cranky or ill-informed, but he does expose abuses which would otherwise never have been mentioned, and very often an abuse gets put right just by being mentioned. Occasionally, too, a well-meaning public official starts losing his head in the cause of efficiency, and thinks himself God Almighty. Such officials are particularly frequent in the Home Office. Well, there will be questions about them in Parliament sooner or later, and then they will have to mind their steps. Whether Parliament is either a representative body or an efficient one is questionable, but I value it because it criticizes and talks, and because its chatter gets widely reported.

So Two Cheers for Democracy: one because it admits variety and two because it permits criticism. Two cheers are quite enough: there is no occasion to give three. Only Love the Beloved Republic deserves that.

What about Force, though? While we are trying to be sensitive and advanced and affectionate and tolerant, an unpleasant question pops up: does not all society rest upon force? If a government cannot count upon the police and the army, how can it hope to rule? And if an individual gets knocked on the head or sent to a labor camp, of what significance are his opinions?

This dilemma does not worry me as much as it does some. I realize that all society rests upon force. But all the great creative actions, all the decent human relations, occur during the intervals when force has not managed to come to the front. These intervals are what matter. I want them to be as frequent and as lengthy as possible, and I call them "civilization." Some people idealize force and pull it into the foreground and worship it, instead of keeping it in the background as long as possible. I think they make a mistake, and I think that their opposites, the mystics, err even more when they declare that force does not exist. I believe that it exists, and that one of our jobs is to prevent it from getting out of its box. It gets out sooner or later, and then it destroys us and all the lovely things which we have made. But it is not out all the time, for the fortunate reason that the strong are so stupid. Consider their conduct for a moment in the Niebelung's Ring. The giants there have the guns, or in other words the gold; but they do nothing with it, they do not realize that they are all-powerful, with the result that the catastrophe is delayed and the castle of Walhalla, insecure but glorious, fronts the storms. Fafnir, coiled round his hoard, grumbles and grunts; we can hear him under Europe today; the leaves of the wood already tremble, and the Bird calls its warnings uselessly. Fafnir will destroy us, but by a blessed dispensation he is stupid and slow, and creation goes on just outside the poisonous blast of his breath. The Nietzschean would hurry the monster up, the mystic would say he did not exist, but Wotan, wiser than either, hastens to create warriors before doom declares itself. The Valkyries are symbols not only of courage but of intelligence; they represent the human spirit snatching its opportunity while the going is good, and one of them even finds time to love. Brünnhilde's last song hymns the recurrence of love, and since it is the privilege of art to exaggerate, she goes even further, and proclaims the love which is eternally triumphant and feeds upon freedom, and lives.

So that is what I feel about force and violence. It is, alas! the ultimate reality on this earth, but it does not always get to the front. Some people call its absences "decadence"; I call them "civilization" and find in such interludes the chief justification for the human experiment. I look the other way until fate strikes me. Whether this is due to courage or to cowardice in my own case I cannot be sure. But I know that if men had not looked the other way in the past, nothing of any value would survive. The people I respect most behave as if they were immortal and as if society was eternal. Both assumptions are false: both of them must be accepted as true if we are to go on eating and working and loving, and are to keep open a few breathing holes for the human spirit. No millennium seems likely to descend upon humanity; no better and stronger League of Nations will be instituted; no form of Christianity and no alternative to Christianity will bring peace to the world or integrity to the individual: no "change of heart" will occur. And yet we need not despair, indeed, we cannot despair; the evidence of history shows us that men have always insisted on behaving creatively under the shadow of the sword; that they have done their artistic and scientific and domestic stuff for the sake of doing it, and that we had better follow their example under the shadow of the airplanes. Others, with more vision or courage than myself, see the salvation of humanity ahead, and will dismiss my conception of civilization as paltry, a sort of tip-and-run game. Certainly it is presumptuous to say that we *cannot* improve, and that Man, who has only been in power for a few thousand years, will never learn to make use of his power. All I mean is that, if people continue to kill one another as they do, the world cannot get better than it is, and that since there are more people than formerly, and their means for destroying one another superior, the world may well get worse. What is good in people—and consequently in the world—is their insistence on creation, their belief in friendship and loyalty for their own sakes; and though Violence remains and is, indeed, the major partner in this muddled establishment, I believe that creativeness remains too, and will always assume direction when violence sleeps. So, though I am not an optimist, I cannot agree with Sophocles that it were better never to have been born. And although, like Horace, I see no evidence that each batch of births is superior to the last, I leave the field open for the more complacent view. This is such a difficult moment to live in, one cannot help getting gloomy and also a bit rattled, and perhaps short-sighted.

In search of a refuge, we may perhaps turn to hero-worship. But here we shall get no help, in my opinion. Hero-worship is a dangerous vice, and one of the minor merits of a democracy is that it does not encourage it, or produce that unmanageable type of citizen known as the Great Man. It produces instead different kinds of small men—a much finer achievement. But people who cannot get interested in the variety of life, and cannot make up their own minds, get discontented over this, and they long for a hero to bow down before and to follow blindly. It is significant that a hero is an integral part of the authoritarian stock-in-trade today. An efficiency-regime cannot be run without a few heroes stuck about it to carry off the dullness—much as plums have to be put into a bad pudding to make it palatable. One hero at the top and a smaller one each side of him is a favorite arrangement, and the timid and the bored are comforted by the trinity, and, bowing down, feel exalted and strengthened.

No, I distrust Great Men. They produce a desert of uniformity around them and often a pool of blood too, and I always feel a little man's pleasure when they come a cropper. Every now and then one reads in the newspapers some such statement as: "The coup d'état appears to have failed, and Admiral Toma's whereabouts is at present unknown." Admiral Toma had probably every qualification for being a Great Man—an iron will, personal magnetism, dash, flair, sexlessness—but fate was against him, so he retires to unknown whereabouts instead of parading history with his peers. He fails with a completeness which no artist and no lover can experience, because with them the process of creation is itself an achievement, whereas with him the only possible achievement is success.

I believe in aristocracy, though—if that is the right word, and if a democrat may use it. Not an aristocracy of power, based upon rank and influence, but an aristocracy of the sensitive, the considerate and the plucky. Its members are to be found in all nations and classes, and all through the ages, and there is a secret understanding between them when they meet. They represent the true human tradition, the one permanent victory of our queer race over cruelty and chaos. Thousands of them perish in obscurity, a few are great names. They are sensitive for others as well as for themselves, they are considerate without being fussy, their pluck is not swankiness but the power to endure, and they can take a joke. I give no examples—it is risky to do that—but the reader may as well consider whether this is the type of person he would like to meet and to be, and whether (going farther with me) he would prefer that this type should *not* be an ascetic one. I am against asceticism myself. I am with the old Scotsman who wanted less chastity and more delicacy. I do not feel that my aristocrats are a real aristocracy if they thwart their bodies, since bodies are the instruments through which we register and enjoy the world. Still, I do not insist. This is not a major point. It is clearly possible to be sensitive, considerate and plucky and yet be an ascetic too, if anyone possesses the first three qualities, I will let him in! On they go—an invincible army, yet not a victorious one. The aristocrats, the elect, the chosen, the Best People—all the words that describe them are false, and all attempts to organize them fail. Again and again Authority, seeing their value, has tried to net them and to utilize them as the Egyptian Priesthood or the Christian Church or the Chinese Civil Service or the Group Movement, or some other worthy stunt. But they slip through the net and are gone; when the door is shut, they are no longer in the room; their temple, as one of them remarked, is the Holiness of the Heart's Affection, and their kingdom, though they never possess it, is the wide-open world.

With this type of person knocking about, and constantly crossing one's path if one has eyes to see or hands to feel, the experiment of earthly life cannot be dismissed as a failure. But it may well be hailed as a tragedy, the tragedy being that no device has been found by which these private decencies can be transmitted to public affairs. As soon as people have power they go crooked and sometimes dotty as well, because the possession of power lifts them into a region where normal honesty never pays. For instance, the man who is selling newspapers outside the Houses of Parliament can safely leave his papers to go for a drink and his cap beside them: anyone who takes a paper is sure to drop a copper into the cap. But the men who are inside the Houses of Parliament—they cannot trust one another like that, still less can the Government they compose trust other governments. No caps upon the pavement here, but suspicion, treachery and armaments. The more highly public life is organized the lower does its morality sink; the nations of today behave to each other worse than they ever did in the past, they cheat, rob, bully and bluff, make war without notice, and kill as many women and children as possible; whereas primitive tribes were at all events restrained by taboos. It is a humiliating outlook—though the greater the darkness, the brighter shine the little lights, reassuring one another, signalling: "Well, at all events, I'm still here. I don't like it very much, but how are you?" Unquenchable lights of my aristocracy! Signals of the invincible army! "Come along—anyway, let's have a good time while we can." I think they signal that too.

The Savior of the future—if ever he comes—will not preach a new Gospel. He will merely utilize my aristocracy, he will make effective the good will and the good temper which are already existing. In other words, he will introduce a new technique. In economics, we are told that if there was a new technique of distribution, there need be no poverty, and people would not starve in one place while crops were being ploughed under in another. A similar change is needed in the sphere of morals and politics. The desire for it is by no means new; it was expressed, for example, in theological terms by Jacopone da Todi over six hundred years ago. "Ordina questo amore, O tu che m'ami," he said; "O thou who lovest me—set this love in order." His prayer was not granted, and I do not myself believe that it ever will be, but here, and not through a change of heart, is our probable route. Not by becoming better, but by ordering and distributing his native goodness, will Man shut up Force into its box, and so gain time to explore the universe and to set his mark upon it worthily. At present he only explores it at odd moments, when Force is looking the other way, and his divine creativeness appears as a trivial by-product, to be scrapped as soon as the drums beat and the bombers hum.

Such a change, claim the orthodox, can only be made by Christianity, and will be made by it in God's good time: man always has failed and always will fail to organize his own goodness, and it is presumptuous of him to try. This claim—solemn as it is—leaves me cold. I cannot believe that Christianity will ever cope with the present world-wide mess, and I think that such influence as it retains in modern society is due to the money behind it, rather than to its spiritual appeal. It was a spiritual force once, but the indwelling spirit will have to be restated if it is to calm the waters again, and probably restated in a non-Christian form. Naturally a lot of people, and people who are not only good but able and intelligent, will disagree here; they will vehemently deny that Christianity has failed, or they will argue that its failure proceeds from the wickedness of men, and really proves its ultimate success. They have Faith, with a large F. My faith has a very small one, and I only intrude it because these are strenuous and serious days, and one likes to say what one thinks while speech is comparatively free: it may not be free much longer.

The above are the reflections of an individualist and a liberal who has found liberalism crumbling beneath him and at first felt ashamed. Then, looking around, he decided there was no special reason for shame, since other people, whatever they felt, were equally insecure. And as for individualism—there seems no way of getting off this, even if one wanted to. The dictator-hero can grind down his citizens till they are all alike, but he cannot melt them into a single man. That is beyond his power. He can order them to merge, he can incite them to mass-antics, but they are obliged to be born separately, and to die separately, and, owing to these unavoidable termini, will always be running off the totalitarian rails. The memory of birth and the expectation of death always lurk within the human being, making him separate from his fellows and consequently capable of intercourse with them. Naked I came into the world, naked I shall go out of it! And a very good thing too, for it reminds me that I am naked under my shirt, whatever its color.

[1939]

From THE CHILDREN OF SANCHEZ

Oscar Lewis

I was about six when my mother died in my father's arms early one morning. Her death was a shock and a torment to me all my life, because I feel I was to blame. The day before she died, we all had gone to the Basilica with my aunt and my uncles, Alfredo and José. We were very happy. My blessed mother was always celebrating our Saint's Day and we ate pork and stuff like that, which you know are not good for you. They bring on attacks, and my mother came down with an attack on account of me.

Actually, what happened was that later that day she asked me to bring the bird cages down from the roof. My mother was very fond of birds, understand? She kept the walls covered with bird cages, just because she loved the little creatures. So I climbed on the roof and some dirt dropped over to our neighbor's side and the woman there began to throw water on me.

"You brat, why don't you watch what you're doing?"

My mother ran out to defend me and had an argument with the neighbor. If she hadn't had the argument, my *mamá* would not have died. Anyway, whether I feel guilty or not, that's what happened.

They woke us up at about 2:00 A.M. I didn't want to get up because I had wet the bed and was afraid they would punish me. But we saw my father crying and we got up frightened. I knew something bad was happening because my father had my mother in his arms. We were all crying at the head of the bed when the doctor came. Our relatives tried to get us out of the house but I fought to stay.

I didn't want to believe that my mother was dead. They laid her out and that night I secretly got into bed with her. They were looking for me, and I was sleeping next to my mother under the sheet they had covered her with. At that age I already knew that dying meant the person left this world forever, though I told my brother and sister, "Don't cry, *mamá* is just sleeping." And I went close to my mother and said, "*Mamá, mamá*, you're sleeping, aren't you?" I touched her face, but I knew she would never wake up again.

I missed my mother then, and I still miss her. Since her death I felt I could never be happy again. Some people feel relieved when they talk about their troubles, but I've told this to many people and it has never helped. I feel calm only when I run away, when I go off as a vagabond, when I am alone in the country or up in the mountains. I believe if my mother were still alive I'd be very different. Or perhaps I'd be worse.

When my mother died, my grandmother was a second mother to me. I followed her around all the time. I called her little grandmother with the same love that I had called my mother, *mamá*. She was always good to us, but was very strict and stern in character. After all, she was old and had been brought up in the old style. They were more upright in everything.

She came to live with us and took good care of us. She sold cake crumbs in the plaza and I used to visit her all the time. I felt an urge to be with her because she understood me and used to give me lots of advice. The rest of the family, even my aunt Guadalupe who was closest to us, used to call me "*negro cambujo*" and "devil face." I never knew what "black *cambujo*" meant but it hurt me just the same. So I always stuck close to my grandmother.

Manuel never wanted to go with her to buy the cake crumbs or the bread. I was the one who liked to go with her. I don't know why, I was only a kid, but I felt that if I went along with her early in the morning, nothing could possibly happen to her, and thank God, we never came to any harm. One time Manuel went with us and he made my grandmother very angry. A vendor was selling sugared crab apples on a stick, shouting, *"Tejocotes, tejocotes* one *centavo."* Manuel, who was always teasing my grandmother, began to yell, "Grandmothers, one *centavo . . .* a *centavo* a grandmother . . ." Well, she scolded him and tried to grab him, but, of course, she could never catch him. He was a fast runner. He was only fooling, but he made her cry that time, and it hurt me very much.

We were living on Cuba Street at the time, yes, on Cuba Street, because my *papá* had just gotten to know Elena, and my grandmother left our house and went to live with my aunt Guadalupe. I felt even more lonely and really missed my mother then, because as long as my grandmother was there, I didn't feel as though my mother was gone.

When Elena came to be my stepmother I went to my granny Pachita to complain, telling her Elena this and Elena that. My grandmother was my crying towel in those days. I really unburdened myself with her. I even stole the plants and, well, I didn't steal them, they were my mother's and I didn't want Elena to touch them, so I would bring them to my grandmother or to my aunt. But I lost my poor little grandmother too, for she died soon after.

From the beginning, my stepmother didn't like me and I didn't like her. We did not get along very well, my young stepmother and I. For me there was only one mother in all the world, and even though a hundred others came along and wanted to act like my mother, it was not the same thing. Besides, I had learned from my friends that stepmothers were bad.

Elena was about eighteen years old, I think, or less. Anyway, she was too young and lacked experience to take care of a widower with four children. She didn't know how to get us to obey her, especially me, for I was the wildest. If she had spoken to me nicely, I would have been putty in her hands, but she always wanted to control me, to order me around, to dominate my life. Ever since I was small, I didn't like to have anyone but my mother or father order me around. If Elena laid a hand on me I would fight back. I always defended myself physically, I never knew how to defend myself with words.

One of the reasons I fought so much with Elena was because on account of her Manuel and I had to sleep on the floor. Once I heard my *papá* and Elena talking. She was saying that we had had the bed long enough and that the girls were growing up. So my father ordered Manuel and me to sleep on the floor—not exactly on the floor, because my *papá* bought straw mats for us. I guess at that time he couldn't buy a bed.

I cried a few times but never said a word to my father. It hurt and I had a feeling of anguish around my heart. I felt sad, like a dog sleeping on the floor. I missed my *mamá* very much then. When she was alive we slept on beds and were better off. Even after she died . . . before Elena came . . . we slept in a bed, with my *papá,* in the place that Elena took.

I was very happy sleeping next to my father. What fights Manuel and I had when he took my place next to my *papá!* We would argue until my *papá* said, "Everybody shut up and go to sleep." Wham! Out would go the light, off would come his shoes, his pants would be put on the chair, and then everything was quiet.

From the beginning, one of the things that I didn't like was that Elena had been living with another man. I was very much afraid for my father, because her ex-husband might take revenge or something.

My father gave me many scoldings and beatings on account of the ideas my stepmother put into his head. She was not entirely wrong but she embroidered the truth and twisted things. And many times she provoked me into being bad. If I jumped on the bed and got it dirty, she said, "Get off, *negro cambujo!*" That would hurt me and I answered, "You filthy old bag, why do you call me black? If I am black it is because God made me that way." Then she would hit me and I would hit her back and make her cry.

When my father came home, instead of saying "hello," she heaped it all up on him. So my father, who was all worn out from the day's work, would become exasperated and wouldn't even listen to me. He just beat me. The next day I tangled with Elena again.

My poor father! How much money my quarrels with that woman cost him! How many fifty's, hundred's, three hundred's of *pesos,* how many coats, shoes and dresses, to content the *señora.* How mad it made me! She saved the money and I sometimes stole it from her because of the way she got it from my *papá.*

Although I haven't been able to show it, I not only love my father, I idolize him. I used to be his pride and joy when I was a kid. He liked me more than my brother, because when he'd go anywhere, he took me first. Many times just the two of us would go to the Basilica or to the movies or just take a walk in the evening. He still loves me with the same deep love, except that he doesn't show it any more because I don't deserve it.

My father was always very dry with us; he didn't talk much and we could never discuss our problems with him. I tried to be close to him. I wanted him to treat us in a special way, like other *papás,* to talk with us, to fuss over us. I liked so much the way we used to kiss his hand when he came home, or hug him. I felt my father understood me better in those days, although even then I missed a sign of affection, a word of encouragement.

Only twice in my life did my father speak intimately to me. He asked me, "Son, what troubles you? What is the matter? Tell me your troubles." I felt the most important and happy person in the world to hear him call me "son" so affectionately. Usually he called me Roberto or "you," and scolded me with bad words.

I have always disliked it when a son raises his voice to his father. Whenever my father scolded us or even just talked to us, it was impossible to look him in the eye, because he had a fierce expression. When I wanted to explain myself or at least clear up the truth a bit, he would not let me speak. "You, shut your mouth," and, "The only thing you are good for is this or that." I have never answered him back when he bawled me out. Instead I reproached myself. I told my brother and sisters that if my father was not good with us it was our fault. A father is sacred, especially mine. He is a good, fine person. There isn't another like him.

My father never beat us unless there was a good reason. He hit us with a broad belt he still wears. It was double thick and he'd hit us hard, especially me. He whacked us so much we sort of got hardened and didn't feel it any more, even though when he was angry he laid it on. Unfortunately for me, I had the damnedest habit. When I was being whipped, I'd knock my head against the wall or the wardrobe or something else. I kept whacking myself on the head, without knowing why.

Then when I was about ten years old, my father took to using an electric cord, a very thick one, two meters long. He folded it in four parts and tied a knot in it. Wow! then we could feel the punishment. Every time he gave us a lash, it raised a welt. And my father wasn't the type who stopped with the one who did it, he went after both of us alike. He was impartial that way.

My father always urged me to go to school. How stupid I was not to have listened to him! I could never explain to myself why I didn't like school. When my classmates were sent to the blackboard they did their exercises quickly and were sure of themselves, but when I was called up, I felt a weight on my back because I knew everybody's eyes were on me. I thought they were whispering about me. I wanted to be way ahead of them and because of this I couldn't concentrate and it took me longer.

My mother, my aunt, or my grandmother would take me to school; sometimes they had to drag me there. I had a feeling of desperation about them leaving me alone with all those boys and girls. I felt inferior compared to so many people.

I was in the first grade for four years, not because I was stupid but because I played hooky. I did second grade in one year but when I passed to the third grade I attended only two or three months and never returned. Because of my friends and perhaps because I had so little liberty in my home, I enjoyed playing hooky and often went to Chapultepec Park. My father was notified when I missed school and would be waiting for me with the strap when I got home.

When we were children, my brother and I were closer to each other. He always protected me; for years Manuel was the handkerchief I dried my tears on. I used to be quite a coward and a crybaby, very *rajón,* as we say in Mexico, because if somebody would just shout at me, I'd start crying. I was afraid of the older boys. They'd threaten me and I'd cry; if anyone touched me, I'd scream. Right off I'd go running to my brother and he, poor fellow, had a lot of fighting to do on account of me.

I was in the third grade when Manuel graduated. I didn't have the courage to face all those boys without him and that is why I quit school.

I don't know why but I have always felt less than a nobody. Never in my whole life did I feel that there was anyone who paid attention to me. I have always been sneered at . . . belittled. I always wanted to be something in life, to do whatever I felt like and not have to take orders from anyone. I wanted to make a kite of my life and fly it in any field.

I wanted to be somebody in athletics, to be a great automobile driver or motorcyclist and compete in races. I have always wanted to be an aviator. One day my *papá* took me to the Lagunilla Market to buy me a cap. He said, "Which cap do you want?" I immediately asked for one with goggles, the kind aviators use.

When I played with my friends, the game was always aviation. To make it more real, I would lower my goggles and go up on the roof to run there like a plane. Or I would go running around the courtyard. I'd tie ropes to the water pipes and make a swing. That was my airplane and I really felt as if I were flying. That was one of my dreams. Whenever a plane flew by, even to this day, I keep watching it, longing to fly one some day.

My head was cracked open because I wanted to fly. My cousin Salvador, my aunt Guadalupe's son, may he rest in peace, was very playful and liked to fool around with us. One time I asked him to give me an airplane ride, that is, to swing me around and around. He always did whatever we wanted and so he took hold of my wrist and ankle and began to whirl me around. He suddenly lost control, and wham! I was dashed against the wall. My head was opened and when I came to, my *mamá* and *papá* and everybody were very alarmed. I was covered with blood but I didn't get scared. Actually, I enjoyed the fact that I was bleeding. It left a scar here on my head.

I am full of scars. I was always getting banged up. My head was opened other times, by falling off the roof or getting hit in stone fights, in wars, with my friends. Once I nearly lost an eye and I bled so much I thought I was going to die. I was running and fell on a sharp little toy shovel I was carrying. It went right into my left eye, but they took me to a doctor and I can still see out of it pretty well. The worst scar and one of the worst frights of my life was when I was bitten on the arm by a dog.

I learned to swim before my brother did even though he had gone often with his friends. I sort of hung around them hoping they would take me. I used to play hooky to go swimming in a pool not far from my house. There was an attendant there, Josué, whom I admired very much because he was a good swimmer and a nice guy. He was tall, strong and very husky. I don't mind telling you, he had some body. I wanted to be like him, nice, big, strong, and able to get some recognition. He used to talk to us about how he had been all over the Republic.

Once, when I was eight years old, I didn't have money for a ticket to the pool. Manuel, his friend Alberto, the Donkey, and I were standing outside the gate trying to scrape together money, when a drunk came by. This man gave Manuel and the Donkey the money they needed. So I said, "What about me? Aren't you going to give me some, too?" He just started off, and I said, "Listen, *señor,* won't you give me what I need for a ticket?"

"Who are you?" he says.

"I'm the brother of one of the boys you just gave some money to." And I told him how many *centavos* I needed to get in.

"No, you little son-of-a-bitch. Get out of here. You're too black."

That hurt me very much. My brother and Alberto went in without me, leaving me feeling desperate and humiliated.

When I played hooky, or when my father sent me to the Lagunilla Market to carry home the things he bought, I got into the habit of taking my little sister Marta with me. I have always liked her better than the others. I don't know whether it was because she had never known our mother or because she followed me wherever I went.

I taught Marta how to hitch rides by jumping on to the bumper of the trolley and holding tight. I used to take a little white dog from the Casa Grande too, because he followed me everywhere. There we would be, comfortable and happy, sticking like flies to the back of the trolley, with the dog running after us. Everybody would stop to look at us, people would put their heads out of the cars and buses to see the spectacle. I though they were admiring us and I enjoyed it.

I liked to jump while the trolley went at full speed. Marta was very brave and learned to do it too. I not only risked my life, I risked hers, but she enjoyed it so much that it made quite an impression on me. I believe that's why I preferred her to Consuelo and Manuel.

I used to take her with me to Chapultepec Park and to the Villa where we would climb the steepest hills. I would braid three cords together to make a strong rope and I tied one end around my waist and the other around hers. I picked out the most dangerous cliffs and would climb up first, and pull her after me. She loved it and never complained.

I want to make it clear that I always respected Marta as a sister. Contact with a woman aroused my natural feelings, right? But it's very different with my sisters. It pained me that sometimes my father would act suspicious when he found out we went here or there. He would ask, "And why did you go? And what did you do?" and he would question Marta to see if we had done anything bad. I had worked once in a bakery at the Military Hospital where they paid me with bread and rolls. Later, it occurred to me to take Marta there to see if they would give us some rolls to eat. The hospital was very far out and when my father learned that I took her there, he gave me a terrific beating.

There was a big difference between Marta and Consuelo. Consuelo was more intelligent and persistent and liked to study. When she decided to do something she stuck to it. She never played with boys like Marta and was very reserved even with girls. She was nice and quiet, and very thin and frightened-looking.

When we were little, I got along well with Consuelo. Later, I was surprised at how my sister changed. She blew up at practically nothing and would create a tempest in a glass of water. She had an uneven temperament and seemed to me to be unsociable, secretive and irritable. She was very dry and didn't have much to do with people. But apart from that, she was good, all good.

The trouble between Consuelo and me began after my stepmother came to live with my father. I ate breakfast late, after the others, because, I don't know why but ever since I was little, I was ashamed to sit at the table without doing some chore. I always did work around the house, like lighting the charcoal fire, putting up the coffee, cleaning the bird cages and feeding the birds. No one told me to, but it pained me not to do something before I ate.

After the family had eaten, I'd hunt around the kitchen for food. Many times, right in front of me, Consuelo or Elena would pour the leftover coffee down the drain, or crush up my bread. I would say, "Ha, ha! you make me laugh! I'm not even hungry." I would grab one of the bananas we fed the birds and would go out. I'd send them to the devil, not out of anger but out of hurt feelings. The truth is that when they destroyed my breakfast like that, I felt great anxiety in my heart and a lump in my throat. I would cry, not in front of them, but in one of the little shower rooms in the courtyard. I tried to keep quiet about these things because I knew if I told my father, he'd scold them and maybe even punish them with the strap. He did scold Consuelo at times, but she didn't change.

But I have always been a brother to my sisters. I have never punished them without a reason, like if they didn't obey me, or because they talked back to my *papá,* or called me "lousy black." I am heartbroken at the thought of how many times I have beaten them. I want to ask their pardon, but when I see them I lose my courage. It makes me suffer, because a man shouldn't beat a woman. But I only slapped them with the palm or the back of my hand. And when I slapped, it was only on the arm or the back, or the head.

But when my father came home Consuelo would tell him that I had kicked her or hit her on the lung. *Ay!* my God! Those weren't caresses my father gave me because of those lies! On my word! I speak from the heart, that I never hit her like that. She was a little liar then, and it was Elena's fault that, well, the blessed woman is now at peace, God has her in heaven, but when she and my sister accused me and exaggerated, my *papá* thrashed me with that doubled electric cable that had a copper wire inside and a knot on the end.

How difficult Consuelo and Elena made life for me! I felt that they were against me and that I constantly had to be on guard. And my father favored the women. He had always taken better care of them and it seemed to me that he loved my sisters more. Rather, he loved us all equally, but only they had the privilege of having him demonstrate it to them. He had always preferred women. I never paid attention to it, it never bothered me. On the contrary, I liked it because that way I was more sure of my sisters, that is, the way I see it, they could never say as an excuse that they had missed their father's love . . .

I'll tell you why I hit my sisters. It wasn't because I felt any hatred or bitterness toward them. It was that I never liked my sisters to play with boys. But they didn't pay any attention to me and it's logical, isn't it? because, well, little girls naturally have to play with little boys.

I had this feeling because ever since I was small I've been very mean toward little girls, as mean as they make them. I was full of malice. Sometimes I would take a little girl to the toilet when nobody was home. I always tried to find a way so that we wouldn't be seen, and then I'd begin to feel her up, with her consent, of course. I was only about five or six, and even after my mother died, when I was eight or nine, I still did it. That's why I didn't want my sisters to play with boys, because I figured the boys could do the same thing to them. Just feel them up, as we say, that's all I ever did to the little girls.

When we were older, Manuel, my cousin Matilde, my cousin Julia, and I began to play. My brother went off with Julia in one direction, and I went off in another with Matilde. She was the stepdaughter of my uncle Alfredo, so she was not actually related to me. Unfortunately, ever since I was little and even now that I am grown-up just the slightest contact with a woman, if I would just touch a woman or shake hands with her, stimulates my natural feelings so that I cannot control myself. It's the same with all men, I suppose.

So I had the idea of going to the bathroom with Matilde. There were no inside toilets in the *vecindad* where she lived; they were out in the courtyard, so it was convenient for what I wanted to do.

I convinced her and we went. I told her to lie down in the corner. I lifted up her dress and pulled down her panties, and at that time I couldn't call what I had a member, it was just barely sprouting, but I put it between her legs. I really couldn't do anything and I didn't even know where it should go, but with her consent, there were the two of us, trying to do it this way and that, playing *papá* and *mamá*.

So I did this shameful thing with my cousin and that's why I was always trying to watch over my sisters.

THE GOLD BLOUSE

Nell Dunn

"Anyone lend me their husband for the week-end?"

"Yeah, you can 'ave mine, he's a dirty sod on the quiet."

"I'd lend you mine, only he wouldn't be much good to yer!"

"Send them all up. You know where I live—just by the church."

"Do you like 'em fair or dark?"

"It's not their 'air I'm interested in!"

We laugh, twenty-five women hunched over three long tables, packing cheap sweets for Christmas. Thick red fingers, swollen with the cold, flash from tray to box. In a matter of seconds it's neatly packed, a little circle of sweets with three pink mice in the middle.

The factory only has two rooms; the one I am in is where we wrap and pack, twisting the bright paper around each sweet, licking labels and sticking them on top—*Cognac, Cointreau, Dolcis et Forte*—pretend liqueurs tasting of sickly sweet cordials. And the other one where the sweets are made;

and a rickety conveyor belt moves the colored centers under dripping chocolate.

"I started me diet today," hunch-back Sheila shouts to me, her voice mingling with the music pouring out from high on the damp wall: "I remember you, you're the one who made my dreams come true . . . Yes I do . . ." Dirt hangs in loops around the loudspeaker, ". . . When my life is through, and the angels ask me to recall the thrill of them all . . ." Sheila moves her head in eight-bar time. Her neck is thickly swaddled in a dirty yellow scarf and her hair sticks out stiff over the collar of her coat.

"Are you allowed to eat any?"

"You are if you don't get caught."

Behind me Lily and Rube, the sorters slinging the sweets skilfully into the boxes, twist and talk alternately.

"She don't really care. I'd do meself in!"

"So would I. Do me nutter in."

"Let's hope the baby don't inherit her hunch."

"It's one thing when it's the bloke you're going to marry, but when you don't even know who it is . . ."

"Perhaps he done it in the dark."

"I wouldn't be surprised—she's that daft!"

On my other side an old woman spits into a rag and wipes her hands over —"Got the guitar, get it every winter. Used to be a laundry you know— that's why it's so damp. Can't heat it, it would melt the chocolates. I nearly married a soldier. I was going with him two years, but then he showed me this letter from a girl in the ATS, said it was just playing about. But if they do it before marriage they do it after so I said I was through with him. He cried like a baby. I saw him once in Woolworth's when I was carrying me last child and I had such a lump in me throat I couldn't say nothing. I had to run out. My name would be Mrs. Stacey now instead of Mrs. Smith."

My eyes began to ache in the cold electric light. There are no windows in the room where we have been sitting since eight in the morning earning our two-and-fivepence an hour—tenpence an hour for the under eighteens. The siren hoots. "Tea's up. Go and get some sugar, Bent Sheil!"

"I'll come with you." Bent Sheila and I go up the broken staircase to the loft and turn on the light. Mice scuttle. She dips the chipped mug into an open sack.

"Got any brothers and sisters, Sheila?"

"No, there's just me and me mum. You might think I was spoilt, being the only one, but I'm not really, you know."

"Do you ever go dancing, Sheila?"

"No, but I go up the caff. The boys take me upstairs where it's dark."

I thrust my cup under the urn and watch it fill with grey tea, then follow Rube and Lily into the cloakroom. There are no chairs. We sit on the concrete floor among bicycles, leaning our heads against the coats that hang from the walls. Joyce, a girl with long auburn hair caught back with two pink slides, cuddles in a corner eating some cold chips out of a bit of newspaper.

"When are you getting married, Joyce?"

"Next month, when I'm sixteen."

"Bit young, ain't yer?"

"No use waiting till yer an old crab is there?"

"Have you got yer trousseau ready yet?"

"No."

"Are yer going to wear yer pink pyjamas?"

"No, me birthday suit."

"Hear that? Joyce's going to have a naked ball."

"Don't be filthy."

"It's nice filth though."

"Never mind Joyce, it's smashing!" said old Mrs. Gordon, her arthritic fingers sticking stiffly out from black mitts.

Over the lavatories next door hangs a notice. WASH YOUR HANDS AFTER USING THE TOILETS. THIS IS A FOOD FACTORY. I call Rube. "Could you come over here a minute please?"

"Listen to that. We've got to take her in hand—teach her how to speak. You say, 'Rube, fuck you, get over here, mate!'"

"Know where I can find a towel?"

"There ain't one. Don't wash yer hands love, it'll take them five minutes to thaw out. Anyways, what the eye don't see the heart don't grieve."

"Give us a hand with the urn."

Two of the girls empty the tea-urn down the lavatory. "Look at this! A packet of Weights at the bottom."

"I thought it tasted sour."

Lily is fooling with a bicycle.

"Wait for me, love." Rube climbs on in front of Lily, holds her round the waist and pokes her with the point of the saddle. Sheila giggles. "Like a sandwich?" I take one and bite into the thick bread smeared with lemon curd.

"Me dad sleeps downstairs and I sleep upstairs with me mum. Me mum hasn't slept with me dad for ten years—she's had seven children and the doctor says it would kill her to have any more. Anyways she doesn't want to sleep with me dad now—he's a bad-tempered old sod."

"Here they have a lot of fun . . . twistin' the night away . . ." the music swings out.

"Come on, Rube!" Lily throws the bike against the wall. Rube draws in her stomach, making the CANDY embroidered on her pocket stand out.

"See the man in evening clothes . . . How he got hit right on the nose . . ." Lily bends back and Rube, shaking her violent shoulders, leans over her, thrusting a slinky leg between her twisting thighs.

"Come on, Sheil, let's see you!"

Grinning, Sheila clambers to her feet and sways her heavy body to the beat, clutching her coat at the stomach. "Oh man, there ain't nothing like . . . Twistin' the night away."

"Well done, Sheila!" The women crowd around, shouting encouragement. "Learn it in the ATS, Sheil?"

Excited by the sudden rush of attention, she sticks out her stiff hands and waves her plump leg, purplish from the cold.

"Take yer overcoat off, Sheil, and let yerself go!" Rube and Lily stop dancing and join the onlookers. The room is thick with the smell of fresh sweat. The music blares on . . . "See the fella in blue jeans, dancing with the older queen, who's dolled up in a diamond ring . . . Twistin', twistin', twistin' the night away."

Sheila opens her mouth, swaying desperately. As the music reaches its climax she flings off her coat revealing a gold damask blouse. "Oh man, you oughta see him go . . . Twistin', twistin', twistin' the night away." It's over and she stands still in the hot circle of women, a laconic grin wide over her face, her richly embroidered Victorian blouse pushed into her old tweed skirt.

"Hey, look at that!"

"Wow, what a blouse!"

"Where did you get that Sheil, off the barrows?"

"Life's so drab you've got to wear something bright, ain't you, Sheil?"

"Me mum bought it for me." Her scrawny arms stick out from the delicately puffed sleeves.

"Don't fib—one of yer boy-friends up the café gave it you."

"Go and join the ATS in that!"

"Pity they've cleaned up the streets."

Sheila giggled with coy pleasure, thrusting her chin down into the yellow scarf still wound about her neck.

"Tell you what, Sheila, we'll cut the sleeves off for you, that'll look better!" With a giant pair of scissors amidst a great deal of cat calls, Rube did it.

"There you are, love, all set for the Jazz Band Ball."

The blouse had large arm-holes, and now Sheila's grubby bra was exposed.

"I can see the scruff under your arms, Sheil!" There were howls of laughter.

"Here, Lily, let's give her a low back." Rube grabbed the scissors and cut a V. The blouse slid sideways revealing a torn vest. The door opened. "Back to work you women."

Sheila, still grinning, sat down hugging her arms to her chest till someone threw her a worn cardigan. On the brown lino, amid discarded sweet papers and cigarette ends, the gold sleeves lay gleaming in the raw electric light.

From WHERE THE SELF BEGINS

Bruno Bettelheim

How the infant's activity and the mutual give and take between mother and infant can be furthered or squelched becomes readily observable during the supplementary feedings that infants are given nowadays, as early as the second or third week of life. As the mother spoon-feeds her baby, he can be encouraged in his spontaneous efforts to be active in the feeding process. At first he may merely try to finger her moving arm. Later on he may attempt to get his fingers in the food, and eventually make a grab for the spoon.

In this last situation, the mother may prematurely coax him not only to help, but to do it all by himself, a tendency not unusual with the present widespread push to make children independent as early as possible. While activity is thus encouraged, it is done at the expense of mutuality, because the infant is expected too soon to manage on his own. I do not say such a child will become autistic. But his pattern of relating to others may become constricted; again, not by this single experience, but by a totality of parallels that flow from the same manner of rearing.

In other cases the mother inhibits her baby's efforts to do things on his own. Here, too, mutuality is blocked, though in different ways. Since not only mutuality but activity are inhibited, the consequences may be more serious. And if here too the same pattern extends over all or most inter- actions between mother and child, then infantile autism is a possible out- come.

For example, in later infancy the child may try to grab the spoon his mother feeds him with and experience how she firmly—perhaps even gently —returns his hands to his sides so that food will not spill or the feeding process go on for too long. Not only is he frustrated in trying to do for himself, but also in attempting to make the feeding a mutual process. And if, in addition, the mother carefully wipes his mouth after every spoonful— however gently—the disapproval of how he eats will again not be lost on the child.

I use this example because it has also been observed how the mother of a blind or deaf child will let her infant grab the spoon and hold it with her; will enjoy his clumsy and ineffective efforts at helping her feed him and at feeding himself; will share his enjoyment of food though it gets messy around the mouth. In this way they establish mutuality around spoon- feeding although the blind child cannot see the pleasure on her face, nor the deaf child hear the pleasure in her voice.

A film produced by Mittelman, Malkenson, and Munro [1959] records the expressive movements (or affectomotor patterns) of infancy. In one sequence centering around a feeding situation the child points definitely to the morsel he wants and the mother then feeds it to him. It is fascinating to watch the back-and-forth in the infant's desire to feed himself. It is still much more comfortable to be fed by the mother. Yet her visible delight at the baby's expression of his desire to feed himself leads to a social game around the feeding that makes it more pleasurable to both. It is a perfect example of how good relations between mother and infant permit both of them to find a solution that implies respect for the child's autonomous decisions while still assuring him of dependent care.

Despite all this, the infant does not become active through the experience of mutuality alone. Life is certainly with others. But from the very beginning it is also lived for and with our own selves.

Where, then, does the human personality begin? Normal development happens so smoothly that we take little note of the natural sequence of events. For example, I have suggested that while the infant is active from the start, he is not trying to communicate anything by his action. While he may box himself off from the breast, it is not at all his intention to communicate, "I am suffocating." He is not aware of any listener and intends only to fight free in order to breathe. But if all goes well, things are not this way with the mother.

Whether consciously or not, she senses that she communicates her feelings to the baby by the very way she responds. Though the infant cannot read her message in all its complexity, he may soon react to whether her emotions are mainly positive, negative, or ambivalent. Thus while communication starts from the moment of birth, it begins as a one-sided action. There is no two-way communication as yet.

This is hard to demonstrate for humans from our present knowledge of earliest infant development, but it can be demonstrated for other mammals. The animal mother does something for the newborn baby: for example, she licks it and thus cleans it. The young of some species cannot survive if she fails to do that, and many mammals, if they are separated from the mother for those few hours after birth, will grow up but will not mate, will remain indifferent to others of their kind. Thus in meeting some need of the infant, the animal mother must also communicate something of greatest importance to the baby who obviously receives it, but may not respond yet with a message of his own.

It may be that the baby also begins to relate. For in this action by the mother (or this interaction, if it is such) the infant animal seems to receive the seeds of relatedness from the mother's licking him clean right after birth, though it may be months or years before the hidden seed blossoms as the animal matures.

Typically for the human infant, relating and communicating have their roots in his cooing or crying, and the mother's appropriate and positive response. As she helps him sort out pain from hunger through her different responses, and as different ministrations relieve different forms of discomfort, the infant learns to distinguish between his own feelings of discomfort. As the sense of discomfort becomes less diffuse, becomes located by which part of the body senses it most keenly, the feeling of self (or the body ego) begins to develop.

Once an expression of feelings (crying or smiling) has been accepted as the signal for a specific event by mother and child—and this can be a particular movement or wail of the child responded to by a special reassuring action or noise from the mother—communication has been established. One has left solipsism then, and can join in the experience of another.

Again in normal development, the smooth manner in which a mother cares for her infant in ways that best suit his development often obscures the many separate steps in the process. Only some of these steps have by now become apparent, and of these I will sketch only a few.

For example, the mother's good care—the consistent manner in which she responds to the baby's at first random expressions of vague inner pressures—slowly induces him to shape the expression of his needs, and later also his feelings. This he does first through typical expressions which soon become particular signals that both understand. The connections he then makes between inner pressures and the various signals he gives bring them into some order. They become more concrete, lead to a differentiated awareness of the body. The infant also becomes interested in that part of reality which meets his now more specific needs, and provides comfort.

But even all this is still akin to a conditioning process, although it is an inner signal from the self (cry, smile) that evokes an action from the external world—as opposed to conditioned responses where an outside signal evokes an inner response. There is by no means self-awareness as yet. There is still not a person, aware of trying to get something from another person who is recognized as such. All there is at this point is a striving to gain comfort and avoid discomfort, to observe and take note.

By now the infant has repeatedly experienced that his needs are not always or immediately met. And the manageable frustration that follows is what makes him aware that an outer world even exists. The emphasis here is on the *manageable*. Because otherwise the child is so flooded by unpleasant emotions that nothing else seems to exist. Blotted out is the barely emerging awareness of a world that responds. Thus the child's expectation that something outside of him will satisfy his needs is what powerfully increases his interest in the world and his impulse to learn more about it.

In a next and crucial step he fathoms that he, through his own efforts, through signals or the giving of signs, has been able to influence the external world—and this is the point at which he begins to become a social being. If his efforts keep succeeding, then eventually he wants to make the advantage a permanent one by coming to terms with this something outside him that has the power to satisfy or frustrate. This coming to terms requires a liminal notion of a self evoking, manipulating, influencing a nonself. The wish, on the child's part, to manipulate the nonself is expressed first through efforts at one-sided control. Only when this does not work does he slowly develop a sense of the advantage of mutuality and with it a first conscious responsiveness to others.

Thus while the infant can feel, can observe and give expression to sensations—can in some fashion respond to other persons and objects long before language or some equivalent develops, there is no self as yet, nor can he relate. This happens only after the following sequence: First his own efforts to make contact with others, must have given him some minimal distinction between himself and the nonself. Second, this vague distinction must have been verified by some kind of repeated communication.

Appropriate responses to these expressions of the infant's will soon validate them enough so that crying and smiling become signals for specific events both to him and to others. The damage suffered, if the infant's expression of emotions is not met with validation from the outside, have been described by Spitz and others [Spitz, 1945, Spitz and Wolf, 1949].

This is why artificial feeding times, arranged according to the clock, can dehumanize the infant. The reason is not just that time-clock feeding is contrary to the natural rhythms of the body, or that it signifies a mechanical ordering of time and of the mother-child relation. More important here is that it prevents the infant from feeling that *his* actions (crying, smiling) have a significant effect on this important life experience of being fed.

What humanizes the infant is not being fed, changed, or picked up when he feels the need for it, though they add greatly to his comfort and feeling of well-being. Nor does irregular care necessarily dehumanize, though it will tend to make him dissatisfied with life or may cause poor development or sickness. It is rather the experience that *his* crying for food brings about *his* satiation by others according to *his* timing that makes it a socializing and humanizing experience. It is that *his* smile, or facial grimacing, evokes a parallel or otherwise appropriate response in the mother.

Conversely, the experience that his own actions (cry or smile) make no difference is what stops him from becoming a human being, for it discourages him from interacting with others and hence from forming a personality through which to deal with the environment.

Smile and cry remain crucial examples because through both an emotion is communicated while at the same time an influence is exerted which together bring about the intended result. To act on the environment is hence not enough for developing a human personality. To it must be added the ability to communicate emotions and to experience an appropriate emotional reply. It is an extremely debilitating experience if our emotions fail to meet with a fitting reply. The joke that fails to amuse, the loving gesture that goes unanswered, are some of the most painful experiences. And if we consistently and from an early age fail to meet the appropriate response to our expression of emotions, we stop communicating with others and eventually lose interest in the world.

But even this is not all. Unless we can also influence reality, things are just as destructive for our efforts to develop a personality. If the child's hungry cry met with only deep sympathy for the pain he expressed, and not also with food, the results would be as bad as if there had been no emotional response. This is an unlikely example, since the child must be fed, to survive. But should his smile, inviting to play, be met with even the tenderest smile from the parent but lead to no playing, then too, both environment and the wish to communicate one's feeling lose all interest.

One could argue, of course, that many infants were fed by the clock and eventually grew up to be fine human beings. But this only means that for them the conviction of being able to affect significant aspects of their environment was not acquired around feeding but around other situations. No one situation excludes all others in equipping the infant with the conviction that he can, through his own actions, change the conditions of his life. And so long as we do not have much more knowledge about which experiences are specially pregnant here, compared to others, we must assume that any situation permitting the child to feel "master of his fate" is as good as any other to help him develop into a full human being.

The importance of this entire process for the development of a self can hardly be overrated. With it, the ego expands from one that only acts into one that interacts, that responds to others and becomes slowly aware that it can modify their responses. This is different from the self-contained activity of observing, or paying attention, though the one depends deeply on the other. But first must have come the emotional experience of having something of a self that can act, and of its connection to something outside that responds.

In order for this to happen, the mother must have wished all along to relate to the child in mutuality. But for some time she must not expect the child to contribute, and later must not expect him to do that except in step by small step. If the child has all along known the experience of mutuality, as in nursing, it then helps him to develop it in his personal relations.

Winnicott [1953], among others, recognized the importance of the mother's meeting the child's needs through her own adaptive responses. He writes:

The good enough mother . . . starts off with an almost complete adaptation to her infant's needs, and as time proceeds she adapts less and less completely, gradually, according to the infant's growing ability to deal with her failure. . . . If all goes well the infant can actually come to gain from the experience of frustration, since incomplete adaptation to need makes objects real. . . . Nevertheless at the start adaptation needs to be almost exact, and unless this is so it is not possible for the infant to begin to develop a capacity to experience a relationship. . . . The mother, at the beginning, by almost 100 per cent adaptation affords the infant the opportunity for the illusion that her breast is part of the infant.

Despite the above I feel that Winnicott views the infant as much too passive in this process of adaptation. True, most of the adaptation must come from the mother; at first nearly all of it. But the infant too is active from the start and adapts from the very beginning. The issue here is that mother and infant adapt in radically different ways. The mother adapts to the infant, and ideally her adaptation will end in the satisfaction of his and her needs. The infant, on the other hand, adapts only for his own ends, with only the most limited means, and without any regard for the mother's needs. For the rest Winnicott is correct: growth occurs as the infant, too, slowly begins to adapt to the mother.

Let me cite a typical example of how an instinctive action, based on one-sided need, can lead to an experience of mutuality: the young child extends his arms, and this is interpreted as a signal that he wishes to be picked up. In terms of evolution this is a very old instinctive reaction of the primate baby who feels lost, and would indeed soon get lost, did it not cling to the animal mother. When primate infants cling to their mothers they do so with arms and legs extended, clutching the mother's flank.

Similarly, human infants from a certain age on extend both arms and legs when an adult appears [Bowlby, 1958]. If picked up, the child increases the closeness to the mother on his own, through his clinging. But when the response to him is positive he learns that reaching out to gain closeness increases his well-being. He learns also that whether this happens or not depends on the response of another person, and that his own actions could and did evoke that response. Here the essence of what is communicated is the value of combined action, where one's solitary action might fail.

Later on, communication through spoken language and even more so in silent thought is how we normally grasp and make contact with reality. Even nursing becomes far more effective with language. For out of the one signal of the cry come the separate language symbols for "hurt" (where nutrition would bring no relief) and for "hunger" (where nutrition *would* bring relief).

MUTUALITY

All this and much more happens smoothly where the mother's desire for mutuality does not make her expect it too soon. If she expects her child to relate before enough experience with need satisfaction has led him to recognize that some part of reality (the mother) has positive value for him, she may be too disappointed. If her disappointment is severe her responses will reflect it, and the child may not only fail to develop any wish to relate, he may even lose interest in reality, or at least in trying to influence it. The same may happen if the mother expects too little. If she assumes the infant cannot adapt, she may stymie his efforts in that direction. By not encouraging or responding to his actions she may force him to exist only or mainly as an extension of herself, as the passive object of her care.

Having said all this, it should be stated emphatically that no mother can, even at the start of her baby's life, adapt entirely to his needs, nor later adapt perfectly as he adjusts to her and the world. There will always be times when even the best and most responsive of mothers will expect too much of her infant, and at other times, or in other respects, too little. In the end she is a human being, variable and fallible. Were she not, her child would have little chance to test his adaptive capacities against reality, nor would her behavior ever challenge these to develop. Even the best of mothers is tired after childbirth, is sleepy during night feedings, sometimes picks up the infant too quickly, too forcefully, too gingerly.

Much as I have cautioned against the myth of the blissful infant, so I would caution here against the correlate myth of the perfect, all-giving mother we all wish we had had. Saints may be needed in heaven, but they rarely make good parents. At least we hear little of their having had children or having raised them successfully.

What I am trying to suggest is that since the infant is only capable of small adaptations, what he thrives on are the mother's small adaptations to him. The mother who picks up her infant too vigorously, but quickly relaxes her hold as she senses an unhappy response—she is the mother who provides him with examples of how a very small adaptation can make a great deal of difference. And this he will try to emulate. Conversely, a mother may sense in her infant a small negative reaction to the way she holds him and tense up in fear. She is afraid she is a bad mother who does not know how to hold her baby. Or else she decides that his negative response is directed against her; that he is a bad child who does not love being held in her arms. So she is the mother who is likely to firm up her grip, and in doing so prove to the child that his efforts at bettering his lot, at adapting to how she holds him, have no such results and are better given up.

It seems so unjust, but in regard to motherhood, too, it appears that to those who have will be given, and from those who have not will be taken away. The mother who feels secure as a mother is readily able to adapt her reactions to the tiny cues of her infant, and in doing so support his growing adaptation to her and her ways. The anxious mother, on the other hand, responds defensively to her baby's efforts to adapt to her because for one reason or another they make her anxious. As she stymies his responses and they become fewer, or disappear, she is ever more at sea about how best to care for his needs.

Here, as everywhere in life, fate plays a great and at times decisive role. Infants are born with differing endowments, intelligence, temperaments. However great the influence of our earliest experience, and all later ones that build on them, they can only modify the endowment we are born with. Inheritance is fate in this respect. A very fast mother will find it difficult to gear her rhythm to her very slow child even if she tries, because to move that slowly demands too large an adaptation of her.

Similarly, a hyperactive baby may be too much for a slow-moving mother who cannot speed up her reactions, even if she wants to. Thus the mother and infant whose patterns of reacting are too far apart may have to start from a common base line that is much harder for each of them to reach and maintain than is true for the mother and infant whose temperament, rhythm, and sensitivity mesh together much better. Again life can be very unjust in that mutuality and the rewards for adaptation are so much easier to come by for some than for others.

Normally, however, the infant's reactions will not differ too radically from his mother's, or she will be able to make the needed adjustments. So from the very beginning he will not only seek and respond to body comfort, but will soon interact with his environment. The sooner his actions leave the realm of chance or of random behavior the better. First he has learned to gear them to the environment, however minutely, and to expect certain responses from it. And second, if things go well, he has learned that some consequences of his actions are predictable. These are the basic preconditions for personality development. With it a vague feeling of selfness develops into a self. Or to put it differently, the ego that begins by reacting to inner and outer stimuli slowly engages in goal-directed actions that presuppose some awareness of a goal and how to reach it.

Being active, if this trait is to flourish in the child, must be tested for its value in gaining specific, anticipated results. That there is a critical age when this happens is a decided possibility for some birds and animals, and a well-documented fact for others.

But if this were all I would not be discussing bird behavior. What counts is that the decisive factor is whether, and to what degree, the little bird is active on his own during this time. As Hess [1959] observes of the mallard duck, for example, the more effort he must expend in following the mother (or some experimental substitute), the more successful the imprinting. So even for this comparatively lower species, the infant's acting on his own toward a goal is of crucial importance, above and beyond what was once called instinctive behavior.

Among primates, so much closer to us, parental reaction to the infant's spontaneous activity is also crucial. Carpenter [1934] describes how the howler monkeys care for their very young. At the beginning, their concern goes so far as to react to the mere breaking of a tree limb because it might have been caused by an infant's fall. "The cracking of a limb under the weight of an animal may set the males roaring" and the females rush to pick up the fallen child. This is the early phase of development during which little initiative is expected of the infant. But the next stage of development is one he calls "a transition stage between complete dependence of the infant on the mother . . . and complete independence." During this period "Howler mothers control and condition their infants by facilitating their 'spontaneous' activity at times, and on other occasions by restricting it." [1]

Thus spontaneous action within a social context, and the encourage-

---

[1] Sander [1962] is aware of what mutuality and adaptation require on the part of the mother. He recognizes five distinct stages which he calls "period of initial adaptation, of reciprocal exchange, of early directed activity, of focalization on mother, and of self-assertion." Crucial in each of them is "to what degree . . . will the mother's behavior be specifically appropriate to the baby's state and to the cues he gives of it?"

ment toward it, seem crucial to the development of independence, not only in humans but also in primates; while being active in the learning process seems of crucial importance even for the subprimate species.

As I have indicated before, the literature on mother-child relations has in my opinion overstressed the child's need to passively receive. By comparison it has neglected the fact that from the very beginning the infant needs not only to be cuddled and held, but to actively cling. I believe that the need of many young children to cling to a transitional object (a stuffed animal, a baby blanket, etc.) so vividly described by Winnicott [1953] represents spontaneous efforts to provide themselves with the experience of active clinging which was too little present in their relations to their mothers.

Among primates, it is enough that the baby's cry brings the mother's presence. Once he can cling to any part of her body, he can find the nipple on his own. But for the human infant clinging is not so useful a tool because he cannot get at the breast on his own, even if the mother is in reach. And in Western society, with the prevalence of non-nursing mothers, even if the human infant could get at the breast it would not help much. He would still have to cry for his food.

I believe there is another reason why clinging in the human infant cannot affect his development as it seems to in the animal where clinging appears essential for the later mating of many mammals and for the socialization of primates. The reason is that the primate baby clings actively to the mother's fur. This being active in the interchange may be as crucial for the monkey as it is for the imprinting of birds. Much as the human baby may wish to be active in holding on to his mother, he has little chance, short of fingering the breast or her face as he nurses, or holding on to her finger in his grasping reflex. Nor is the holding on likely to go with much body or skin contact between them. In this area of experience the human infant seems disadvantaged from the start.

Unfortunately the mutuality of clinging is all too little studied in human infants. Perhaps the nursing experience would be vastly more satisfying if the mother could respond with emotional freedom to feeling large areas of her skin against her baby's skin. Then being held to the mother's body might be as important for the human infant as it seems to be in the animal. Certainly in those societies I have any knowledge about the mother's bodily responses are inhibited enough to rule out a total sharing of the experience of holding on and being clung to.

As the infant grows, he learns that crying is not the only way he can bring about the mother's presence in order to cling. Bowlby [1958], in reviewing the literature, discusses how the infant who tries, through his crying, to bring the mother to his side later becomes very active in seeking out her presence on his own.

The tendency to remain within sight or earshot of their mothers . . . is particularly easily evoked if the child is tired, hungry, or in pain; it is also immediately activated if the child is afraid. . . . In many, a zenith seems to be reached in the period eighteen to thirty months. This late dating may come as a surprise, especially to those who, equating psychological attachment with physiological dependence, presume that attachment must be at its maximum soon after birth.

Bowlby then adds that on the basis of his experience, "fully as many psychological disturbances, including the most severe, can date from the second year of life when clinging and following are at their peak as from the early months when they are rudimentary."

We too have been astonished at how often the history of autistic children showed no obvious deviation or traumatization at the earliest age, though it may have occurred. Instead the children were reported as developing more or less normally up to about eighteen or twenty-four months, matching the ages in Bowlby's report. This is an age when the infant still has many needs he cannot fill by himself, but through walking and talking is beginning to try to get what he wants on his own.

Again and again in the history of our mute autistic children we find the statement, often fully verified, that they began to speak normally. Then after the rudiments of speech were acquired—that is, after they could say a few words—they slowly gave up talking, or dropped it suddenly. That is, speech was developed in an effort to influence the environment, but was given up when it failed in this purpose. The child does not withdraw from all efforts at relating because his needs are not adequately met—though this too will scar the personality. He withdraws when these efforts find him less able to modify the environment than before.

Here, the parental observations of their autistic children are significant. Most of their accounts of the child's first year indicate that the autistic child was quiet, a good child; that in the second year he amused himself on his own, often with stereotyped, empty activity, such as humming to music or turning the pages of a book. But that their behavior was strange, out of the ordinary, did not catch the attention of parents or pediatrician until the second year of life.

Isn't it possible that what these children showed, during the first year of life, was only a lowered level of activity? That they only became autistic at the age when spontaneous goal-directed activity is part of normal development, in addition to the earlier behavior that is no less spontaneous but not consciously purposeful? That is: quiet and isolated children they were, even before their second year; but autistic children they became only when their reaching out to relations led to what they viewed as destructive responses. This, in my opinion, is why they gave up all initiative.

Certainly things happened this way for Marcia. The first activity that brought her out of her total isolation was a chasing game where the important thing was that she initiated all action and we had to passively, but with enjoyment, follow her lead. Above all we were not permitted to touch her.

Just as the primate infant who has fallen from a tree or is momentarily lost must be recaptured, and just as his clinging precedes his nursing, so we had to play at recapturing Marcia for several years before she would deal with any feeding or nursing experience. Our willingness to seek her out so that eventually she could cling to us, and her wish to do that actively on her own, all this had to be regained before she let us nurse her. As with primate babies, mutuality in the clinging response certainly preceded by far any mutuality in nursing for this human child.

The Harlows' experiments, on the other hand [Harlow, 1959; Harlow and Harlow, 1962], show that activity without response can be fatal. Monkey babies raised with terrycloth mothers could do all the clinging they wished. They grew, they gained weight, seemed to be doing all right, until such time in development as they would normally have socialized and mated. This they could not or would not do.

Thus the child's active grasping for mutuality will not do, if the reaching out is not met by a parallel enjoyment in the mother at being clung to; if the result is not a process of mutual interaction. For the human infant, it seems that feeding, cuddling, diapering, bathing, humming, singing, and talking to him will have to achieve what clinging and being held, feeding and being fed does for the baby monkey.

Bottle feeding, for example, can support mutuality nearly as completely as nursing from the breast, provided the culture favors mutuality. Pavenstedt [1965] observed five Japanese mothers of children from thirteen to seventeen months of age, four of whom were still breast feeding and the fifth not. The fifth mother was unable to nurse because of a breast abscess that developed at six weeks. "She was almost tearful about it and hastened to assure me that she tried to make up to the child for the loss." But the way she bottle-fed her child is described as follows:

Mother . . . gives him the bottle . . . She lays him down, drinking, and proceeds to lie down beside him. . . . While he drinks, she holds the bottle and looks directly into his eye—it looks almost hypnotic. She smiles at him tenderly and he smiles back. Very soon he rolls over on his side, facing her, and the tender interchange continues. When he tries to kick, she undoes the blanket around his feet to give him more freedom and does not interfere with his sucking his thumb. She shows no impatience and for an hour continues to try to lull him by stroking his head and face. He begins to explore her face and she allows him to. Eventually he just rolls away from her, off his mattress, and so she takes him downstairs again.

Pavenstedt adds, "I felt I had been a witness of a tender love scene."

In short, how active the baby will be in his early experience with mutuality, to what degree his own contributions are allowed to make it more satisfying—these are apt to greatly influence what autonomy he will later achieve.

LEARNING:
THE ORGANIZATION OF EXPERIENCE

Harry Stack Sullivan

I now want to take up an area of very great importance which I have never gotten very well under control. It is undoubtedly a field which requires multidisciplined thinking, and some of the people who could perhaps add most valuably to such a multiple approach are, unhappily, people who feel that psychiatrists have no business in this neighborhood—a form of craft-union antagonism which, I trust, will gradually fade into history. The topic I now wish to discuss is learning—that is, the organization of experience.

So far, the processes of maturation of the underlying animal have not yet included any of the more or less epoch-marking developments which will later concern us—such as the acquisition of language, in contrast to the very few sounds that are identified by others as words; the need for compeers with whom to interact; and the other maturations that mark off the eras of personality development. But still there has been a truly astounding series of maturations of the underlying capabilities, and by the end of the ninth month the infant is manifesting pretty unmistakable evidence of processes which are of the pattern of, or are rudimentary instances of, a very great deal of that which is peculiarly the human way of life. Maturation has progressed, thereby bringing into being capabilities of the underlying human animal for becoming a human being, and experience has been organized in the opportunities which are provided both by the cooperation with the mothering one, and by the rather incidental physical environment of objects and the like.

Thus by the end of the ninth month of infancy there are organizations of experience which are manifested in recall and foresight in many of the categories of behavior that make up the fully human type of living. Needless to say, these organizations are imperfectly developed. But the point is that they are manifested in patterns which make it highly probable that the rudiments of a large area of human living are already organized by the end of the ninth month. These organizations appear as growth of the dynamisms concerned, both with respect to the integration and maintenance of suitable situations, and with respect to the vector quality (the appropriateness and adequacy) of behavior in the resolution of the various situations—that is, with respect to the achievement of satisfaction as a goal. To say this a little differently, the close observation of situations, as early as the end of the ninth month, shows that there is considerable organization of experience which can be called the development of the appropriate dynamisms for integrating and main-

LEARNING: THE ORGANIZATION OF EXPERIENCE Reprinted from *The Interpersonal Theory of Psychiatry* by Harry Stack Sullivan, M.D. By permission of W. W. Norton & Company, Inc. Copyright 1953 by The William Alanson White Psychiatric Foundation.

taining situations, and for the choice—and I am using that word very broadly —of the appropriate and adequate energy transformations or activities for the achievement of the resolution of the situation—that is, for the satisfaction of the need which is involved.

This growth may be considered to result from sundry learning processes which rest on the necessary basis of serial maturation of capacities of the underlying animal, coupled with the opportunity for manifesting the ability concerned; in most cases the opportunity still involves an element of cooperation with the mothering one—that is, it is interpersonal. First, one always has to have the maturation of the capability; and secondly, one must have appropriate and useful experience, so that the ability, the actually demonstrable transformations of energy in activity addressed to the goal, appears; and experience of the type that we can call learning processes has a very great deal to do with the latter.

LEARNING BY ANXIETY

I am now going to set up a heuristic classification of the processes of learning. The first of all learning is, I think, beyond doubt in immediate connection with *anxiety*. I have already tried to suggest, and will again and again suggest, that severe anxiety probably contributes no information. The effect of severe anxiety reminds one in some ways of a blow on the head, in that it simply wipes out what is immediately proximal to its occurrence. If you have a severe blow on the head, you are quite apt later to have an incurable, absolute amnesia covering the few moments before your head was struck. Anxiety has a similar effect of producing useless confusion, and a useless disturbance of the factors of sentience which immediately preceded its onset, a phenomenon which is so striking that in later life the great problem of psychotherapy is very often centered on this very matter of getting the patient to see just when anxiety intervened, because that area is disturbed in such a way that it is almost as if it had not been.

Less severe anxiety does permit gradual realization of the situation in which it occurs, and there is unquestionably, even from very early in life, some learning of an inhibitory nature; that is, the transfer of attributes of "my body" to the "not-me" aspect of the universe. But regardless of all these refinements, the first greatly educative influence in living is doubtless anxiety, unqualified.

Vastly more important, in fact perhaps astoundingly important in its relation to our coming to be human beings acceptable to the particular society which we inhabit, is the next process of learning, which is learning on the basis of the *anxiety gradient*—that is, learning to discriminate increasing from diminishing anxiety and to alter activity in the direction of the latter. As I have said before, this notion of gradients can perhaps be illustrated by the distribution of amoebae in the water near, let us say, a hot spring. The conduction of heat in the water will result in a temperature gradient from extremely high, utterly beyond the temperature limits of life, down to a temperature lower than that in which the amoebae live most successfully. There is a certain optimum temperature for the growth of the amoebae, and at that point the concentration of amoebae will be very high. But because of peculiarities in the amoebae, or peculiarities in physical space which can hold only a certain number of amoebae, the concentration of amoebae will grade off both ways. There will be some amoebae in a rapidly declining triangle, we might say, toward the hotter water, and there will be some, perhaps the more underprivileged amoebae, trailing off as a tail into the colder water. What attenuates the concentration of amoebae, particularly in the direction of the hot water, is their avoidance of temperatures which are intolerable to their processes, which is no more mysterious than anything else that goes on in any of the living. Since these amoebae are influenced by that particular manifestation of energy called heat, they rise to a maximum very rapidly at a certain distance from the hot water, and decline to a minimum rather more slowly in the direction of the cold water.

Very early in human life there begins to be discrimination as to when euphoria is diminishing—that is, when one is getting more anxious; and this is really the discrimination of a gradient. The all-or-nothing character of anxiety and euphoria has disappeared very early in life—in fact, I doubt that it ever existed—and an immense amount of what is human behavior in any society is learned simply on the basis of this gradient from anxiety to euphoria. For example, the satisfaction of rubbing the anal region with the finger, let us say, might carry such rapidly increasing anxiety under certain circumstances—namely, in the presence of the mothering one, the social censor—that really quite early in life there might be learning about this. The infant might learn, first, that this is not to occur when the mothering one is around, which is, more or less, learning by pure anxiety; and secondly, that the peculiar circumstance of fiddling with this area through a blanket— even though the infant does not recognize the blanket as such—seems much less strikingly characterized by very rapidly mounting anxiety. And so, presently, direct manipulation of the anus may be restricted to periods of somnolence; or, if the impulse is quite strong, some mediate performance may be engaged in.

Now, if I make myself at all clear, you will realize that I am indicating here the formulation for a type of process of really staggering importance; I have never found a satisfactory name for this process, and therefore still use the good old term of the most traditional psychoanalytic standing—*sublimation,* the long-circuiting of the resolution of situations, chiefly those pertaining to zonal needs—a long-circuiting which proves to be socially acceptable. However, in considering this stage of infancy, one should not think in terms of impulses, social acceptability, and so on, but should realize that the actually describable and intelligible factor is the anxiety gradient, and that learning by the anxiety gradient often includes irrational tricks that permit satisfaction without encouraging notable anxiety. Needless to say, this begins at a time when anything like consensually valid formulation is simply inconceivable.

[Thus the infant] learns to chart a course by the anxiety gradient. Simple performances which would relax the tension of some needs have to be made more complicated in order that one may avoid becoming more anxious. Before he is very many months of age, the child will be showing full-fledged *sublimation,* in the sense of quite unwittingly having adopted some pattern of activity in the partial, and somewhat incomplete, satisfaction of a need which, however, avoids anxiety that stands in the way of the simplest completely satisfactory activity. . . . Whether it recurs in the second or the fifty-second year of chronological age, sublimation is, unwittingly, not a matter of conscious thought of a communicable sort, but rather the outcome of referential processes in the parataxic mode, in the service of avoiding or minimizing anxiety. . . .[1]

This unwitting development, which is the pattern of sublimation, becomes an important element in learning to be human—that is, in learning to behave as one should behave in a given society.

OTHER LEARNING PROCESSES

The next important learning process is learning by *trial and success* of techniques for the relief of the tensions of needs. For example, in order to satisfy the zonal need to suck, the infant learns how to get the thumb into the proper position in the mouth. That is literally done by trial movements of the extremities, aided by a certain amount of visual sentience and a good deal of kinesthetic sentience. There are quite a number of misses and some hits, the hits being successes in getting the thumb into the mouth; and it is these successes that become stamped in as "habits"—although "habit" has many unfortunate connotations. In other words, the successes are the patterns of sentience and effector impulse which work.

Thus while unnumbered of the manipulative attempts of the infant's hands, for example, fail—which is, perhaps, in infancy not too astounding—some of them succeed. And again, diligent study of the infant shows that a success has a really remarkable fixing power. In other words, that which works, however wrongly designed, is very apt to become part of the activity resources of the person, which is true even in adult life. And so, second only to learning by the anxiety gradient is the learning of how to do things by trial and success.

In late infancy and from then on through life, an important process of learning is by *rewards and punishments.* Probably this kind of learning exists earlier in infancy, but this is more difficult to be sure of, since there it would have to depend on empathic factors.

The rewards which encourage learning in the very young probably begin with *fondling,* pleasure-giving manipulation of the child. They take in general the pattern of a change from relative indifference to the child to more or less active

[1] [*Editors' note:* All the quotations in this chapter, including this one, are from Sullivan's "Tensions Interpersonal and International: A Psychiatrist's View," in *Tensions That Cause Wars,* edited by Hadley Cantril; Urbana, Ill.: Univ. of Ill. Press, 1950, pp. 95–98.]

interest in and approval of whatever he seems to be doing. The need for "audience response" becomes conspicuous remarkably early in human life.

The punishments are commonly the inflicting of *pain,* the refusal of contact or of attention, and of course, the inducing of anxiety—a very special punishment. I know of no reason why punishment should be undesirable as an educative influence excepting it be anxiety-ladened. Pain has a very useful function in life and loneliness and the foresight of enforced isolation, the "fear of ostracism," is bound to be an important influence from early in the third stage of development.

The next very important learning process is *trial-and-error learning by human example,* or from human example. I have already mentioned this in discussing facial postures; smiling, as I have said, appears pretty early, while a number of other instances of this kind of learning can invariably be observed in late infancy—that is, very definitely under the age of eighteen months, and probably by the age of twelve months. In this kind of learning, unlike the manipulative learning, the error is important. The success is, you might say, just too good to be important. When success is achieved, the problem is finished. Success in manipulation, on the other hand, has the effect of immediately stamping in a pattern of behavior. But the error in this particular way of learning—learning from human example—is to be kept clearly in mind. It is what one observes as part of the content of consciousness, in those who are mature enough to communicate clearly their experience.

[Not only is this kind of learning probably exemplified in the patterning of facial expressions, but] it is certainly the chief agency in the acquisition of *language.* The phonemes of any system of speech have simply nothing to do with any but cultural necessity. The child learns to approximate from among an indeterminately great variety of vocal sounds that he utters, the particular sound-areas that are used by the significant people around him. In the same way, he picks up the patterns of tonal melody in their speech; often being able to reproduce the tonal, melodic, progressions of speaking well in advance of his "use" of any word.

The only other very important process in learning that I know of is the very refined process which Spearman called the *eduction*—more or less the pulling out—of relations. This comes to be a highly complex capacity, rather strikingly, but by no means exclusively, restricted to the human. It is a capacity—of the most infinite complexity—of our nervous systems which enables us to get more and more to see relations which endure in nature and therefore are to a truly remarkable degree dependable. Spearman built up tests for superior intelligence which depended practically entirely on the capacity to educe, or to grasp, an increasingly complex series of relations which characterize the world as known.

The first instances of this sort of learning to live are purely matters of inference, but it is entirely reasonable to believe that some of the elementary mechanical-geometric relations pertaining to "parts" of a very important preconceptual "object," presently to be named *my body;* are prehended quite soon after birth.

And this process of educing relations can be observed in the infant in certain rudimentary aspects of his interpersonal relation with the mothering one before the use of words.

Every important process in learning which I have been able to formulate is illustrated, at least in rudiment, before speech. I would like to emphasize again the fact that beyond any perchance, as early as or before the end of the tenth month in many instances, so much learning of sounds by trial and error, or from human example, appears that the baby sounds to a person at a little distance as if he were talking to himself. This is a truly amazing instance of human ability. I would like to remind you that in your dealings with friend and foe, stranger and intimate acquaintance, modifications and stresses in the tonal patterns of your remarks can do things which no words qua words could do. When you see how very early and how extremely important this form of learning is, and how basically important are the things which are learned, oh, so long before communicable thought can take place, you may perhaps feel a little more impressed with the importance of the phase of infancy.

BEGINNINGS OF THE SELF-SYSTEM

Harry Stack Sullivan

We have got our human animal as far, in the process of becoming a person, as the latter part of infancy, and we find him being subjected more and more to the social responsibilities of the parent. As the infant comes to be recognized as educable, capable of learning, the mothering one modifies more and more the exhibition of tenderness, or the giving of tenderness, to the infant. The earlier feeling that the infant must have unqualified cooperation is now modified to the feeling that the infant should be learning certain things, and this implies a restriction, on the part of the mothering one, of her tender cooperation under certain circumstances.

Successful training of the functional activity of the anal zone of interaction accentuates a new aspect of tenderness—namely, the additive role of tenderness as a sequel to what the mothering one regards as good behavior. Now this is, in effect—however it may be prehended by the infant—a *reward*, which, once the approved social ritual connected with defecating has worked out well, is added to the satisfaction of the anal zone. Here is tenderness taking on the attribute of a reward for having learned something, or for behaving right.

Thus the mother, or the parent responsible for acculturation or socializa-

BEGINNINGS OF THE SELF-SYSTEM Reprinted from *The Interpersonal Theory of Psychiatry* by Harry Stack Sullivan, M.D. By permission of W. W. Norton & Company, Inc. Copyright 1953 by The William Alanson White Psychiatric Foundation.

tion, now adds tenderness to her increasingly neutral behavior in a way that can be called rewarding. I think that very, very often the parent does this with no thought of rewarding the infant. Very often the rewarding tenderness merely arises from the pleasure of the mothering one in the skill which the infant has learned—the success which has attended a venture on the toilet chair, or something of that kind. But since tenderness in general is becoming more restricted by the parental necessity to train, these incidents of straightforward tenderness, following the satisfaction of a need like that to defecate, are really an addition—a case of getting something extra for good behavior—and this is, in its generic pattern, a reward. This type of learning can take place when the training procedure has been well adjusted to the learning capacity of the infant. The friendly response, the pleasure which the mother takes in something having worked out well, comes more and more to be something special in the very last months of infancy, whereas earlier, tenderness was universal when the mothering one was around, if she was a comfortable mothering one. Thus, to a certain extent, this type of learning can be called learning under the influence of reward—the reward being nothing more or less than tender behavior on the part of the acculturating or socializing mothering one.

Training in the functional activity of the oral-manual behavior—that is, conveying things by the hand to the mouth and so on—begins to accentuate the differentiation of anxiety-colored situations in contrast to approved situations. The training in this particular field is probably, in almost all cases, the area in which *grades of anxiety* first become of great importance in learning; as I have already stressed, behavior of a certain unsatisfactory type provokes increasing anxiety, and the infant learns to keep a distance from, or to veer away from, activities which are attended by increasing anxiety, just as the amoebae avoid high temperatures.

This is the great way of learning in infancy, and later in childhood—by the grading of anxiety, so that the infant learns to chart his course by mild forbidding gestures, or by mild states of worry, concern, or disapproval mixed with some degree of anxiety on the part of the mothering one. The infant plays, one might say, the old game of getting hotter or colder, in charting a selection of behavioral units which are not attended by an increase in anxiety. Anxiety in its most severe form is a rare experience after infancy, in the more fortunate courses of personality development, and anxiety as it is a function in chronologically adult life, in a highly civilized community confronted by no particular crisis, is never very severe for most people. And yet it is necessary to appreciate that it is anxiety which is responsible for a great part of the inadequate, inefficient, unduly rigid, or otherwise unfortunate performances of people; that anxiety is responsible in a basic sense for a great deal of what comes to a psychiatrist for attention. Only when this is understood, can one realize that this business of whether one is getting more or less anxious is in a large sense the basic influence which determines interpersonal relations—that is, it is not the motor, it does not call interpersonal relations into being, but it more or less directs the course of their development. And even in late infancy there is a good deal of learning by the anxiety gradient, particularly where there is a mothering one who is untroubled, but still intensely interested in producing the right kind of child; and this learning is apt to first manifest itself when the baby is discouraged from putting the wrong things in the mouth, and the like. This kind of learning applies over a vast area of behavior. But in this discussion I am looking for where things are apt to start.

Training of the manual-exploratory function—which I have discussed in connection with the infant's getting his hands near the anus, or into the feces, or, perhaps, in contact with the external genitals—almost always begins the discrimination of situations which are marked by what we shall later discuss as *uncanny emotion*. This uncanny feeling can be described as the abrupt supervention of *severe anxiety,* with the arrest of anything like the learning process, and with only gradual informative recall of the noted circumstances which preceded the extremely unpleasant incident.

Early in infancy, when situations approach the "all-or-nothing" character, the induction of anxiety is apt to be the sudden translation from a condition of moderate euphoria to one of very severe anxiety. And this severe anxiety, as I have said before, has a little bit the effect of a blow on the head, in that later one is not clear at all as to just what was going on at the time anxiety became intense. The educative effect is not by any means as simple and useful as is the educative effect in the other two situations which we have discussed, because the sudden occurrence of severe anxiety practically prohibits any clear prehension, or understanding, of the immediate situation. It does not, however, preclude recall, and as recall develops sufficiently so that one recalls what was about to occur when severe anxiety intervened— in other words, when one has a sense of what one's action was addressed to at the time when everything was disorganized by severe anxiety—then there comes to be in all of us certain areas of "uncanny taboo," which I think is a perfectly good way of characterizing those things which one stops doing, once one has caught himself doing them. This type of training is much less immediately useful, and, shall I say, is productive of much less healthy acquaintance with reality, than are the other two.

GOOD-ME, BAD-ME, AND NOT-ME

Now here I have set up three aspects of interpersonal cooperation which are necessary for the infant's survival, and which dictate learning. That is, these aspects of interpersonal cooperation require acculturation or socialization of the infant. Infants are customarily exposed to all of these before the era of infancy is finished. From experience of these three sorts—with rewards, with the anxiety gradient, and with practically obliterative sudden severe anxiety—there comes an initial personification of three phases of what presently will be *me,* that which is invariably connected with the sentience of *my body*—and you will remember that *my body* as an organization of experience has come to be distinguished from everything else by its self-sentient character. These beginning personifications of three different kinds, which have in common elements of the prehended body, are organized in about mid-infancy

—I can't say exactly when. I have already spoken of the infant's very early double personification of the actual mothering one as the good mother and the bad mother. Now, at this time, the beginning personifications of *me* are *good-me, bad-me,* and *not-me.* So far as I can see, in practically every instance of being trained for life, in this or another culture, it is rather inevitable that there shall be this tripartite cleavage in personifications, which have as their central tie—the thing that binds them ultimately into one, that always keeps them in very close relation—their relatedness to the growing conception of "my body."

Good-me is the beginning personification which organizes experience in which satisfactions have been enhanced by rewarding increments of tenderness, which come to the infant because the mothering one is pleased with the way things are going; therefore, and to that extent, she is free, and moves toward expressing tender appreciation of the infant. Good-me, as it ultimately develops, is the ordinary topic of discussion about "I."

Bad-me, on the other hand, is the beginning personification which organizes experience in which increasing degrees of anxiety are associated with behavior involving the mothering one in its more-or-less clearly prehended interpersonal setting. That is to say, bad-me is based on this increasing gradient of anxiety and that, in turn, is dependent, at this stage of life, on the observation, if misinterpretation, of the infant's behavior by someone who can induce anxiety.[1] The frequent coincidence of certain behavior on the part of the infant with increasing tenseness and increasingly evident forbidding on the part of the mother is the source of the type of experience which is organized as a rudimentary personification to which we may apply the term bad-me.

So far, the two personifications I have mentioned may sound like a sort of laboring of reality. However, these personifications are a part of the communicated thinking of the child, a year or so later, and therefore it is not an unwarranted use of inference to presume that they exist at this earlier stage. When we come to the third of these beginning personifications, *not-me,* we are in a different field—one which we know about only through certain very special circumstances. And these special circumstances are not outside the experience of any of us. The personification of not-me is most conspicuously encountered by most of us in an occasional dream while we are asleep; but it is very emphatically encountered by people who are having a severe schizophrenic episode, in aspects that are to them most spectacularly real. As a matter of fact, it is always manifest—not every minute, but every day, in every life—in certain peculiar absences of phenomena where there should be phenomena; and in a good many people—I know not what proportion—it is very striking in its indirect manifestations (dissociated behavior), in which people do and say things of which they do not and could

---

[1] Incidentally, for all I know, anybody can induce anxiety in an infant, but there is no use cluttering up our thought by considering that, because frequency of events is of very considerable significance in all learning processes; and at this stage of life, when the infant is perhaps nine or ten months old, it is likely to be the mother who is frequently involved in interpersonal situations with the infant.

not have knowledge, things which may be quite meaningful to other people but are unknown to them. The special circumstances which we encounter in grave mental disorders may be, so far as you know, outside your experience; but they were not once upon a time. It is from the evidence of these special circumstances—including both those encountered in everybody and those encountered in grave disturbances of personality, all of which we shall presently touch upon—that I choose to set up this third beginning personification which is tangled up with the growing acquaintance of "my body," the personification of *not-me*. This is a very gradually evolving personification of an always relatively primitive character—that is, organized in unusually simple signs in the parataxic mode of experience, and made up of poorly grasped aspects of living which will presently be regarded as "dreadful," and which still later, will be differentiated into incidents which are attended by awe, horror, loathing, or dread.

This rudimentary personification of not-me evolves very gradually, since it comes from the experience of intense anxiety—a very poor method of education. Such a complex and relatively inefficient method of getting acquainted with reality would naturally lead to relatively slow evolution of an organization of experiences; furthermore, these experiences are largely truncated, so that what they are really about is not clearly known. Thus organizations of these experiences marked by uncanny emotion—which means experiences which, when observed, have led to intense forbidding gestures on the part of the mother, and induced intense anxiety in the infant—are not nearly as clear and useful guides to anything as the other two types of organizations have been. Because experiences marked by uncanny emotion, which are organized in the personification of not-me, cannot be clearly connected with cause and effect—cannot be dealt with in all the impressive ways by which we explain our referential processes later—they persist throughout life as relatively primitive, unelaborated, parataxic symbols. Now that does not mean that the not-me component in adults is infantile; but it does mean that the not-me component is, in all essential respects, practically beyond discussion in communicative terms. Not-me is part of the very "private mode" of living. But, as I have said, it manifests itself at various times in the life of everyone after childhood—or of nearly everyone, I can't swear to the statistics—by the eruption of certain exceedingly unpleasant emotions in what are called nightmares.

These three rudimentary personifications of *me* are, I believe, just as distinct as the two personifications of the objectively same mother were earlier. But while the personifications of me are getting under way, there is some change going on with respect to the personification of mother. In the latter part of infancy, there is some evidence that the rudimentary personality, as it were, is already fusing the previously disparate personifications of the good and the bad mother; and within a year and a half after the end of infancy we find evidence of this duplex personification of the mothering one as the good mother and the bad mother clearly manifested only in relatively obscure mental processes, such as these dreamings while asleep. But, as I have suggested, when we come to consider the question of the peculiarly inefficient and inappropriate interpersonal relations which constitute problems of mental disorder, there again we discover that the trend in organizing experience which began with this duplex affair has not in any sense utterly disappeared.

THE DYNAMISM OF THE SELF-SYSTEM

From the essential desirability of being good-me, and from the increasing ability to be warned by slight increases of anxiety—that is, slight diminutions in euphoria—in situations involving the increasingly significant other person, there comes into being the start of an exceedingly important, as it were, secondary dynamism, which is purely the product of interpersonal experience arising from anxiety encountered in the pursuit of the satisfaction of general and zonal needs. This secondary dynamism I call the *self-system*. As a dynamism it is secondary in that it does not have any particular zones of interaction, any particular physiological apparatus, behind it; but it literally uses all zones of interaction and all physiological apparatus which is integrative and meaningful from the interpersonal standpoint. And we ordinarily find its ramifications spreading throughout interpersonal relations in every area where there is any chance that anxiety may be encountered.

The essential desirability of being good-me is just another way of commenting on the essential undesirability of being anxious. Since the beginning personification of good-me is based on experience in which satisfactions are enhanced by tenderness, then naturally there is an essential desirability of living good-me. And since sensory and other abilities of the infant are well matured by now—perhaps even space perception, one of the slowest to come along, is a little in evidence—it is only natural that along with this essential desirability there goes increasing ability to be warned by slight forbidding—in other words, by slight anxiety. Both these situations, for the purpose now under discussion, are situations involving another person—the mothering one, or the congeries of mothering ones—and she is becoming increasingly significant because, as I have already said, the manifestation of tender cooperation by her is now complicated by her attempting to teach, to socialize the infant; and this makes the relationship more complex, so that it requires better, more effective differentiation by the infant of forbidding gestures, and so on. For all these reasons, there comes into being in late infancy an organization of experience which will ultimately be of nothing less than stupendous importance in personality, and which comes entirely from the interpersonal relations in which the infant is now involved—and these interpersonal relations have their motives (or their motors, to use a less troublesome word) in the infant's general and zonal needs for satisfaction. But out of the social responsibility of the mothering one, which gets involved in the satisfaction of the infant's needs, there comes the organization in the infant of what might be said to be a dynamism directed at how to live with this significant other person. The self-system thus is an organization of educative experience called into being by the necessity to avoid or to minimize incidents of anxiety.[2] The functional activity of the self-system—I am now speaking of it from the general standpoint of a dynamism—is primarily directed to avoiding and minimizing this disjunctive tension of anxiety, and thus indirectly to protecting the infant from this evil eventuality in connection with the pursuit of satisfactions—the relief of general or of zonal tensions.

Thus we may expect, at least until well along in life, that the components of the self-system will exist and manifest functional activity in relation to every general need that a person has, and to every zonal need that the excess supply of energy to the various zones of interaction give rise to. How conspicuous the "sector" of the self-system connected with any particular general need or zonal need will be, or how frequent its manifestations, is purely a function of the past experience of the person concerned.

I have said that the self-system begins in the organizing of experience with the mothering one's forbidding gestures, and that these forbidding gestures are refinements in the personification of the bad mother; this might seem to suggest that the self-system comes into being by the *incorporation* or *introjection* of the bad mother, or simply by the introjection of the mother. These terms, incorporation or introjection, have been used in this way, not in speaking of the self-system, but in speaking of the psychoanalytic superego, which is quite different from my conception of the self-system. But, if I have been at all adequate in discussing even what I have presented thus far, it will be clear that the use of such terms in connection with the development of the self-system is a rather reckless oversimplification, if not also a great magic verbal gesture the meaning of which cannot be made explicit. I have said that the self-system comes into being because the pursuit of general and zonal needs for satisfaction is increasingly interfered with by the good offices of the mothering one in attempting to train the young. And so the self-system, far from being anything like a function of or an identity with the mothering one, is an organization of experience for avoiding increasing degrees of anxiety which are connected with the educative process. But these degrees of anxiety cannot conceivably, in late infancy (and the situation is similar in most instances at any time in life), mean to the infant what the mothering one, the socializing person, believes she means, or what she actually represents, from the standpoint of the culture being inculcated in the infant. This idea that one can, in some way, take in another person to become a part of one's personality is one of the evils that comes from overlooking the fact that between a doubtless real "external object" and a doubtless real "my mind" there is a group of processes—the act of perceiving, understanding, and what not—which is intercalated, which is highly subject to past experience and increasingly subject to foresight of the neighboring future.

---

[2] Since *minimize* in this sense can be ambiguous, I should make it clear that I refer, by minimizing, to moving, in behavior, in the direction which is marked by diminishing anxiety. I do not mean, by minimize, to "make little of," because so far as I know, human ingenuity cannot make little of anxiety.

Therefore, it would in fact be one of the great miracles of all time if our perception of another person were, in any greatly significant number of respects, accurate or exact. Thus I take some pains at this point to urge you to keep your mind free from the notion that I am dealing with something like the taking over of standards of value and the like from another person. Instead, I am talking about the organization of experience connected with relatively successful education in becoming a human being, which begins to be manifest late in infancy.

When I talk about the self-system, I want it clearly understood that I am talking about a *dynamism* which comes to be enormously important in understanding interpersonal relations. This dynamism is an explanatory conception; it is not a thing, a region, or what not, such as superegos, egos, ids, and so on.[3] Among the things this conception explains is something that can be described as a quasi-entity, the personification of the self. The personification of the self is what you are talking about when you talk about yourself as "I," and what you are often, if not invariably, referring to when you talk about "me" and "my." But I would like to make it forever clear that *the relation of personifications to that which is personified is always complex and sometimes multiple;* and that *personifications are not adequate descriptions of that which is personified.* In my effort to make that clear, I have gradually been compelled, in my teaching, to push the beginnings of things further and further back in the history of the development of the person, to try to reach the point where the critical deviations from convenient ideas become more apparent. Thus I am now discussing the beginning of the terrifically important self-dynamism as the time when—far from there being a personification of the self—there are only rudimentary personifications of good-me and bad-me, and the much more rudimentary personification of not-me. These rudimentary personifications constitute anything but a personification of the self such as you all believe you manifest, and which you believe serves its purpose, when you talk about yourselves one to another in adult life.

THE NECESSARY AND UNFORTUNATE ASPECTS
OF THE SELF-SYSTEM

The origin of the self-system can be said to rest on the irrational character of culture or, more specifically, society. Were it not for the fact that a great many prescribed ways of doing things have to be lived up to, in order that one shall maintain workable, profitable, satisfactory relations with his fellows; or, were the prescriptions for the types of behavior in carrying on rela-

---

[3] Please do not bog down unnecessarily on the problem of whether my self-system ought to be called the superego or the ego. I surmise that there is some noticeable relationship, perhaps in the realm of cousins or closer, between what I describe as the personification of the self and what is often considered to be the psychoanalytic ego. But if you are wise, you will dismiss that as facetious, because I am not at all sure of it; it has been so many years since I found anything but headaches in trying to discover parallels between various theoretical systems that I have left that for the diligent and scholarly, neither of which includes me.

tions with one's fellows perfectly rational—then, for all I know, there would not be evolved, in the course of becoming a person, anything like the sort of self-system that we always encounter. If the cultural prescriptions which characterize any particular society were better adapted to human life, the notions that have grown up about incorporating or introjecting a punitive, critical person would not have arisen.

But even at that, I believe that a human being without a self-system is beyond imagination. It is highly probable that the type of education which we have discussed, even probably the inclusion of certain uncanny experience that tends to organize in the personification of not-me, would be inevitable in the process of the human animal's becoming a human being. I say this because the enormous capacity of the human animal which underlies human personality is bound to lead to exceedingly intricate specializations—differentiations of living, function, and one thing and another, to maintain a workable, profitable, appropriate, and adequate type of relationship among the great numbers of people that can become involved in a growing society, the young have to be taught a vast amount before they begin to be significantly involved in society outside the home group. Therefore, the special secondary elaboration of the sundry types of learning—which I call the self-system— would, I believe, be a ubiquitous aspect of all really human beings in any case. But in an ideal culture, which has never been approximated and at the present moment looks as if it never will be, the proper function of the self-system would be conspicuously different from its actual function in the denizens of our civilization. In our civilization, no parental group actually reflects the essence of the social organization for which the young are being trained in living; and after childhood, when the family influence in acculturation and socialization begins to be attenuated and augmented by other influences, the discrete excerpts, you might say, of the culture which each family has produced as its children come into collision with other discrete excerpts of the culture—all of them more or less belonging to the same cultural system, but having very different accents and importances mixed up in them. As a result of this, the self-system in its actual functioning in life in civilized societies, as they now exist, is often very unfortunate. But do not overlook the fact that the self-system comes into being because of, and can be said to have as its goal, the securing of necessary satisfaction without incurring much anxiety. And however unfortunate the manifestations of the self-system in many contexts may seem, always keep in mind that, if one had no protection against very severe anxiety, one would do practically nothing—or, if one still had to do something, it would take an intolerably long time to get it done.

So you see, however truly the self-system is the principal stumbling block to favorable changes in personality—a point which I shall develop later on —that does not alter the fact that it is also the principal influence that stands in the way of unfavorable changes in personality. And while the psychiatrist is skillful, in large measure, in his ability to formulate the self-system of another person with whom he is integrated, and to, shall I say, "intuit" the self-system aspects of his patient which tend to perpetuate the type of morbid living that the patient is showing, that still, in no sense, makes the self-system something merely to be regretted. In any event, it is always before us, whether we regret or praise it. This idea of the self-system is simply tremendously important in understanding the vicissitudes of interpersonal relations from here on. If we understand how the self-system begins, then perhaps we will be able to follow even the most difficult idea connected with its function.

The self-system is a product of educative experience, part of which is of the character of reward, and a very important part of which has the graded anxiety element that we have spoken of. But quite early in life, anxiety is also a very conspicuous aspect of the self-dynamism *function*. This is another way of saying that experience functions in both recall and foresight. Since troublesome experience, organized in the self-system, has been experience connected with increasing grades of anxiety, it is not astounding that this element of recall, functioning on a broad scale, makes the intervention of the self-dynamism in living tantamount to the warning, or foresight, of anxiety. And warning of anxiety means noticeable anxiety, really a warning that anxiety will get worse.

There are two things which I would like to mention briefly at this point. One is the infant's discovery of the unobtainable, his discovery of situations in which he is powerless, regardless of all the cooperation of the mothering one. The infant's crying for the full moon is an illustration of this. Now even before the end of infancy, it is observable that these unattainable objects gradually come to be treated *as if* they did not exist; that is, they do not call out the expression of zonal needs. This is possibly the simplest example of a very important process manifested in living which I call *selective inattention*.

The other thing I would like to mention is this: Where the parental influence is peculiarly incongruous to the actual possibilities and needs of the infant—before speech has become anything except a source of marvel in the family, before it has any communicative function whatever, before alleged words have any meaning—there can be inculcated in this growing personification of bad-me and not-me disastrous distortions which will manifest themselves, barring very fortunate experience, in the whole subsequent development of personality. I shall soon discuss some typical distortions, one of the most vicious of which occurs in late infancy as the outcome of the mothering one's conviction that infants have *wills* which have to be guided, governed, broken, or shaped. And when, finally, we come to discuss concepts of mental disorders we will have to pick up the manifestations of a few particularly typical distortions, in each subsequent stage from the time that they first occur.

From LOVE'S BODY

Norman O. Brown

Some capital texts in the New Testament tell us that God is no respecter of persons—οὐ προσωπολήπτης; "not taken by masks"; not captivated, not crazy about them; not taken in, not deceived by them. This is the God in whom "there is neither Jew nor Greek, there is neither bond nor free, there is neither male nor female, for ye all are one in Christ Jesus." This God cares not for visible distinctions; or visible achievements, outer works. The faith that saves is internal and invisible. Christian virtue, St. Augustine says, is of a kind that "cannot be displayed before men's eyes"; "take heed that ye do not your alms before men, to be seen of them." Here is the deeper root of the Augustinian and Puritanical opposition to the theater. But the theatrical is the political; this Christianity is subversive of the public realm. Hannah Arendt quotes Tertullian: *nec ulla magis res aliena quam publica,* no concern is more alien to us than the public concern or republic. My kingdom is not of this world: not of this world of outward appearance, this vain show. It is a real kingdom, not a spectral theatrical show.

Acts X, 34; Romans II, 11; Galatians III, 28; Ephesians VI, 9; Colossians III, 25; Matthew VI, 1. Arendt, *The Human Condition,* 65–66. Augustine, *De Civitate Dei,* I, 28.

God does not go for personalities; nor does the Last Judgment consist in the award of prizes to personalities for the performance of their parts. The performance principle must go; the show must not go on. The parts are not real: for ye are all one in Christ Jesus; he is not your personal Saviour. In the Last Judgment the apocalyptic fire will burn up the masks, and the theater, leaving not a rack behind. Freud came to give the show away; the outcome of psychoanalysis is not "ego psychology" but the doctrine of "anatta" or no-self: the ego is a "me-fabrication" (*ahamkara*), a piece of illusion (*Maya*), which disintegrates at the moment of illumination: "the self has been completely understood, and so ceases to be." And with the doctrine of no-self goes the doctrine of non-action: action is proper only to an ignorant person, and doing nothing is, if rightly understood, the supreme action.

Cf. Powell, *Zen and Reality,* 49, 69. Nikhilananda, *Bhagavad Gita,* 15. Durckheim, *The Japanese Cult of Tranquillity,* 88–89. Marcuse, *Eros and Civilization,* 44, 75, 89. Mauss, "La notion de personne," 348.

But I Samuel XVI, 7: "For Jehovah seeth not as man seeth; for man looketh on the outward appearance, but Jehovah looketh on the heart." Christian virtue is displayed to an even more exacting audience than the Stoic conscience. Jeremiah XVII, 10: "I, Jehovah, search the heart, I try the reins, even to give every man according to his ways, and according to the fruit of his doings." Christian personality remains a self-dramatization of the son enacted before the eyes of the heavenly father. In the sight of this spectator, personality ceases to be a social or political role (we take from our earthly fathers to give to our heavenly father); all performers are immediate and unique; the distinction between public and private disappears; we are on stage all the time. Christianity will not be rid of the performance principle, will not become a pure principle of invisible grace, until it gets rid of the spectre of the Father, Old Noboddady, the watching institution.

The God who is no respecter of persons is yet himself God in three Persons. The Athanasian Creed says that we worship One God in Trinity, and Trinity in Unity; neither confounding the Persons, nor dividing the Substance. God is three Persons: the Father is God, the Son is God, and the Holy Ghost is God. For like as we are compelled by the Christian verity to acknowledge every Person by himself to be God and Lord; So are we forbidden by the Catholic religion to say, There be three Gods, or three Lords. And of Christ it says that he is God and Man: God, of the Substance of the Father, begotten before the worlds; and Man, of the Substance of his Mother, born in the world; Who although he be God and Man—yet he is not two, but one Christ; One; not by conversion of the Godhead into flesh, but by the taking of the Manhood into God; One altogether: not by confusion of Substance, but by unity of Person.

Cf. Schlossmann, *Persona und πρόσωπον im Recht und im Christlichen Dogma.*

The Athanasian Creed is a doctrine of representation, or impersonation. Hobbes: "A Person, (as I have shewn before, chapt. 13) is he that is Represented, as often as hee [sic] is Represented; and therefore God, who has been Represented (that is, Personated) thrice, may properly enough be said to be three Persons; though neither the word *Person,* nor *Trinity* be ascribed to him in the Bible. . . . For so God the father, as Represented by Moses, is one Person; and as Represented by his Sonne, another Person; and as Represented by the Apostles, and by the Doctors that taught by authority from them derived, is a third Person, and yet every Person here, is the Person of one and the same God." The Trinity is a doctrine of the masks of God. In this play God is one, but three actors take his part; and yet it is not a part but the whole of God that they represent.

Hobbes, *Leviathan,* 430.

The complicated dramaturgy of the Athanasian Creed is a new interpretation of the old story—the drama of the incarnation (or reincarnation) of God in Man. What it seems to assert is the mystical transformation of the actor into the part—the absorption of the Manhood into the Godhead; the Son into the Father (I and my Father are one); and the mystical transformation of the part into the whole. But if the actor is really transformed into the part, and the part is the whole; then mask is reality, and persona finally acquires the modern sense of the personality as the real self. *Persona est substantia rationalis individua:* "a person is a rational individual substance." Substance, Latin *substantia,* is what stands underneath (the mask); but also that which stands by itself or in itself and not in another. A person is a mask which has grown into the body, grown one with the body; which became permanent when the drama was internalized: which became indivisible from the body when it became invisible; a part which is a whole: "some things can exist apart and some cannot, and it is the former that are substances" (Aristotle); an individual, a part which is a whole; that finite substance which Spinoza exposed as a nonentity.

John X, 30. Cassiodorus cited in Mauss, "La notion de personne," 358. Cf. Wolfson, *The Philosophy of Spinoza,* I, 63.

The black fellows of Australia, the rudest savages we know, make themselves a temporary personality by the simple application of "make-up," paint; and the mask is gone as quickly as it is made. Permanent masks, preserved as heirlooms, represent a deeper occupation of the individual by ghosts, a deeper investment of the present by the past; but the mask is worn only on ritual occasions. The juristic personality never dies, and, incorporated in the property, never disappears. The invisible internal drama of conscience never ceases; and, finally, the mystery of Christianity is its abolition of the distinction between person and substance.

The incomprehensibility of the Athanasian Creed corresponds to our unconsciousness of the magic in personality. "Where primitives have magic, we have the unconscious magic which is personality." "What we fail to recognize is that all symptoms, defense mechanisms, in fact, personality itself, are a form of magic. . . . Primitives have magic in a conscious form, whereas with us it can function only (except in certain forms of neurosis or psychosis) if it is unconscious." Except in certain forms of neurosis and psychosis: the insane are closer to the truth.

Roheim, *Magic and Schizophrenia,* 84; *Gates of the Dream,* 132.

D _a_	R _e_	T _i_	_o_	O _u_	i _v_
S _ga_ O _ka_	F _ge_	y _gi_	A _go_	J _gu_	E _gv_
_ha_	P _he_	_hi_	F _ho_	_hu_	_hv_
W _la_	_le_	P _li_	G _lo_	M _lu_	_lv_
_ma_	O _me_	H _mi_	5 _mo_	Y _mu_	
_na_ t _hna_ G _nah_	A _ne_	h _ni_	Z _no_	_nu_	O _nv_
T _qua_	_que_	P _qui_	V _quo_	_quu_	E _quv_
U _sa_ _s_	4 _se_	b _si_	_so_	_su_	R _sv_
L _da_ W _ta_	S _de_ _te_	_di_ _ti_	_do_	S _du_	_dv_
dla L _tla_	L _tle_	C _tti_	_tlo_	_tlu_	P _tlv_
G _tsa_	V _tse_	h _tsi_	K _tso_	J _tsu_	C _tsv_
G _wa_	_we_	_wi_	_wo_	_wu_	6 _wv_
_ya_	B _ve_	_yi_	_yo_	G _yu_	B _yv_

Language

EDITED BY MAX BLACK

INTRODUCTION

A word to the wise is not sufficient if it doesn't make sense.
—James Thurber

Language is, in a number of ways, man's most remarkable achievement. Without words, even the most rudimentary human community would be inconceivable: the societies we patronizingly call "primitive" use languages of baffling grammatical and semantic complexity.

Consider the following illustration:

The Fuegians have a word or rather holophrase *mamiklapinatapai* which means "looking-at-each-other-hoping-that-either-will-offer-to-do-something-which-both-parties-desire-but-are-unwilling-to-do!" This holophrase is quite unanalyzable, it contains no nouns and verbs, it simply expresses an intense relation not unknown to some of us.[1]

What a useful idea. How convenient it would be to be able to speak of diplomats and politicians *mamiklaping* one another.

[1] Jane Ellen Harrison, *Aspects, Aorists, and the Classical Tripos* (Cambridge, Eng.: Cambridge University Press, 1919), p. 16.

Such concentration of meaning in a single verbal unit is characteristic of so-called primitive languages (which are typically "agglutinative" in structure) and remains a precious resource for poetic uses of even as "synthetic" a language as the English spoken in the 1960's. But increasing complexity of a culture and its technology demand progressive differentiation of human activity, which is reflected in language, that supreme instrument of cooperation, expression, and thought. "As civilization advances, the holophrase, overcharged, disintegrates and bit by bit subject, object, verb and the other Parts of Speech are abstracted from the stream of warm, full, human, consciousness—in which they were at first submerged." [2]

But some skepticism is in order. No competent linguist in the 1960's would accord the traditional "Parts of Speech" the respect implied by capitalization: Indeed one of the best-learned lessons of a half-century's intensive study of exotic languages like those of American Indians is the folly of imposing a set of grammatical categories originally invented to fit Latin. The grammatical structure of even the Romance languages, Latin's own descendants, is too complicated to be adequately captured by means of the distinctions between "subject," "object," and the like that we learned in elementary school. In linguistics, as in anthropology, its close relative, the ablest investigators are reluctant (because it might be misleading) to transfer to one culture notions and categories applicable to another. Such cautious pluralism, still compatible with a keen search for "linguistic universals" underlying *all* language, is characteristic of modern linguistic science.

Nor should we fall into the trap of supposing that emergence of explicit linguistic analysis—the breaking of wholes into parts, controlled by precisely formulated rules—is the same as an advance in abstraction. To be sure, the most successful sciences, notably physics and mathematics, rely strongly upon such analysis and codification, and the admirable technical symbolisms they use are paragons of clarity and efficiency. But the abstractness essential to all thought is present, to a degree, even in the first stirrings of language. (Think of the baby indiscriminately calling all men "Dada.") Jane Harrison herself makes the point effectively when she says that "All language is in a sense an abstraction; it is a feeling after class, it is the putting of a shiftable adjustable label for a live uninterchangeable thing." [3]

Many a romantic has thought of the step from the "live uninterchangeable thing" to its abstract verbal substitute as a kind of degradation—or, at best, as an unavoidable necessity, fraught with danger and the likelihood of deception. The literature of talk about talk, from Plato to Wittgenstein, abounds to an astonishing degree in laments about the inadequacy of language. Our verbal counters, discrete packets of sound crudely fashioned for everyday commerce, seem feeble surrogates for what Gerard Manley Hopkins called nature's "million-fuelèd" bonfire. And if a picture is worth a thousand words, as the old cliché has it, how pitiful our plight must be in communicating thoughts, which cannot be literally pictured at all. The great philoso-

[2] *Ibid., loc. cit.*
[3] *Ibid.*, p. 15.

pher John Locke, who made penetrating observations about language, lamented that words "interpose themselves so much between our understanding, and the truth which it would contemplate and apprehend, that, like the medium through which visible objects pass, the obscurity and disorder do not seldom cast a mist before our eyes and impose upon our understanding." [4] A modern writer, himself a virtuoso of verbal fireworks, asks rhetorically, "Why should philosophers drag a toy-net of words, fit to catch butterflies, through the sea of being, and expect to land all the fish in it?" [5] To which a sufficient answer might be that to catch even a few "fish" or "butterflies" might be reward enough. Need a philosophical hunter be as rapacious as Santayana depicts him? (And is figurative zoology in Santayana's vein genuinely conducive to clear thinking about such radical issues as the adequacy of language to reality?)

The warning of *caveat auditor* (let the hearer beware) implicit in admonitions like those of Locke and Santayana is too important and timely to be shrugged off as platitudinous. Any author wanting satisfactory expression for a thought struggling to be born, any reader who has had his mind muffled by vagueness, equivocation, senseless sound, and self-indulgent jargon, will know about the distance between words and understanding. The price of clarity, whether in formulation or understanding, is constant vigilance. But there is, alas, no mental eye that "sees" ideas directly, without intervening symbolism. Embryonic ideas that we are prone to consider fully formed and lacking merely a verbal dress ("I know what I mean; I just don't know how to say it!") are already expressed in some symbolism, however defective, of images, gestures, and truncated words. Thoughts are essentially meaningful—that is to say, they are understood, so far as they are clear, at least by the man who thinks them. A "meaningless thought" is a chimera. And if understood by the thinker himself, then they are intelligible in principle to *any* competent interpreter. Nothing about the scraps of symbolism that we use in "inner thought," which is so hard to distinguish from "inner speech," has a logically privileged position: Nothing that can be thought—or, for that matter felt, intended, and so on—cannot be said, cannot in principle (tiresome but necessary qualification) be expressed. Or, to put the point in another way, any of the some two to four thousand languages now spoken in the world is competent to express anything whatever, from the croonings of the latest pop singer to the meditations of Spinoza and the sublime theories of Einstein. The expressive resources of *any* language are potentially infinite. If a word is lacking (like "schlimazel" or "charisma" or "implosion") it can be borrowed or invented. The point is that nothing about the basic design of a language, however peculiar it may look in its stock of elementary sounds (phonemes) and the rules for combining them into meaningful higher units (morphemes) or the higher-level rules for ordering those morphemes into full messages, restricts its expressive power.

[4] *An Essay Concerning Human Understanding*, Bk. 3, Chap. 9, Sec. 21.
[5] George Santayana, *Character and Opinion in the United States* (New York: Scribner's, 1920), p. 20.

This is not to imply that different languages adapt with equal ease to new complexity of subject matter. In each language, some things can be said concisely and efficiently, others only with tiresome circumlocution—and the patterns of constraint vary from one language to another, as every translator knows to his cost. One translator from Japanese into English complains: "There is in life no fixed subject and predicate, cause and effect. . . . Things do not begin with a capital letter and end with a full stop; there is simply ceaseless becoming. The English language does not recognize this; hence the chief difficulty of the translator." [6] To be sure, the suggestion that Japanese—or, for that matter, any other language—is closer to "life" or reality than English will not stand inspection. Polite evasion, endemic in Japan, is hardly conducive to objectivity. It has been said that "Ambiguity interests the Japanese a good deal more than does logic, and in the pursuit thereof they exhibit an impressive ingenuity." [7] Another expert says: "Japanese sentences are apt to trail off into thin smoke, their whole meaning tinged with doubt by the use of little particles at the end, such as 'perhaps,' 'may it not be so?' " [8] But vagueness and hesitancy, however important for the style and feel of Japanese speech, characterize reality no better than the alleged precision of English does. And as for the latter, it is sobering to learn that "The fluid and ambiguous English sentence makes all white men seem liars to Navahos, whose language is so literal and precise." [9] One shudders to imagine what a Navaho would make of a Japanese speaker, if he could manage to understand him. The truth is that no discourse—whether of someone manifesting "the modest Japanese compulsion to avoid a straightforward statement" [10] in a positively Jamesian fashion, or of an Englishman, to himself so satisfyingly forthright, but to foreigners deceptively "fluid and ambiguous," or of a Navaho, constrained to fine-scale specifications of the character of events and the source of the speaker's claims—is any "nearer to reality" than any other. For users of language are not in the business of imitating or reproducing reality: A sentence resembles a state of affairs as little as a map resembles a terrain. To reproach speech for being a distortion of reality is about as silly as complaining that one cannot float on a nautical chart. The influential idea of a "gap" between speech and "reality" is a myth begotten by muddle.

The proper business of speech is to talk *about*, to refer to, to represent, to symbolize "reality"—and not only reality, but the realm of the possible, where imagination roams freely. (Of course, these are far from being the only uses of speech.) This cannot be done except by means of conventions, as can plainly be seen by considering the symbolism of maps and charts. Language is necessarily artificial, through and through. And the choice of

[6] R. H. Blyth, *Haiku*, Vol. I (Tokyo: Hokuseido, 1950), p. 360.
[7] D. J. Enright, *The World of Dew: Aspects of Living Japan* (London: Secker & Warburg, 1955), p. 80.
[8] Donald Lawrence Keene, *Japanese Literature* (London: John Murray, 1953), introduction, p. 7.
[9] Clyde Kluckhohn and Dorothea Leighton, *The Navaho* (Cambridge, Mass.: Harvard University Press, 1947), p. 117.
[10] Enright, *op. cit.*, p. 81.

conventions, precisely because it is logically arbitrary, shows *something* about those who abide by them:

Each language has its special euphony, as every string or wind instrument has; and its peculiar genius casts over the whole world, which men survey and conceive chiefly through verbal description, a distinctive grammatical and poetic colour, a mode of vibrating and rhyming which only those who use that language can discern in things.[11]

This is a basic justification for mastery of at least one other than a single native language. To see the world through new linguistic spectacles can be intensely illuminating, if only by showing in vivid contrast the unsuspected (because thoroughly internalized) constraints of one's native medium of expression. To parody Kipling, "What do they know of English, who only English know?"

Muddled thinkers who misconstrue language as an abortive instrument for imitating "reality" are easily tempted to lapse into a mysticism that finds more value in silence than in articulate speech. Brigham Young once complained that "The English language, in its written and printed form, is one of the most prominent now in use for absurdity" and proceeded to "long for a time that a point of the finger, or motion of the hand, will express ideas without utterance." He could foresee a time when "I can converse with this people, and not speak to them, but the expression of my countenance will tell the congregation what I wish to convey, without opening my mouth."[12] I am reminded of the caustic apothegm of a Chinese sage: "Without speaking, he can speak; and he can speak and say nothing. And so he roams beyond the limits of this dusty world. These, added Confucius, are wild words."[13]

Of course, silence can be eloquent and very often is: the pauses in a melody are part of the tune. The informational content of even the simplest utterance depends on what is *not* said as well as on what is. If "Pass the butter, please" did not imply "*not* the bread, jam, salt, and so on" the hearer could not know what was expected of him. (By the same token, an all-purpose word like "thing" that applies to almost anything, without exclusions, means practically nothing, but functions merely as a convenient filler.) So the art of writing is partly one of shrewd omission, and the art of intelligent reading, as the following selections repeatedly illustrate, requires sensitive detection of what lies between the lines and behind the words. Unspoken implications, suggestions, presuppositions, are trailed by even the most forthright and literal utterance.

Silence charged with implication has indeed an essential role in communication, which skillful writers exploit to good advantage. A playwright says, memorably:

[11] George Santayana, *Dominations and Powers* (New York: Scribner's, 1951), p. 142.
[12] *Journal of Discourses by Brigham Young*, Vol. I (Liverpool: 1854), p. 170.
[13] *Chuang Tzu—Mystic, Moralist and Social Reformer*, trans. from the Chinese by Herbert A. Giles (Shanghai: 1926), p. 28.

There are two silences. One when no word is spoken. The other when perhaps a torrent of language is being employed. This speech is speaking of a language locked beneath it. That is its continual reference. The speech we hear is an indication of that we don't hear. It is a necessary avoidance, a violent, sly, anguished or mocking smokescreen which keeps the other in its place. When true silence falls we are still left with echo but are nearer nakedness. One way of looking at speech is to say it is a constant stratagem to cover nakedness.[14]

The dialogue of Pinter's own plays admirably illustrates his doctrine.

The individual speaker's stratagems and tactics, whether in the choice of words, their suppression or their arrangement, calls for second thoughts about the dictum that language is "through and through artificial." This is as true as any general remark about so complex a topic can be—that is to say, subject to eventual reservations about deep-seated constraints of the mind that may ultimately reveal universal design features necessarily present in *any* language that humans can use. But if true, it is so only for a *language* abstractly conceived as a system of rules for the assignment of standard meaning to regular combinations and arrangements of sounds. If we think instead of *speech,* the countless episodes and transactions in which words are actually used, we must recognize a generous leeway for individual initiative and choice. There are no instructions for *what* to say: Language dictates only what to say when one means such-and-such *and wishes to speak correctly.* But whether a speaker wishes to be taken by convention as meaning such-and-such, and whether and to what degree he wishes to speak "correctly" are largely up to him. (This basic distinction between the language *system* and the speech *acts* has been carefully heeded by linguists ever since De Saussure made his famous contrast between *langue* and *parole.*)

Some students of language, including many who most aspire to be "scientific" in approach, reject the conception of linguistic "correctness" as delusion or humbug, serving only to mask the pretensions of schoolmarms or other obscurantist defenders of "good English." Good English, it is claimed, is no more than the enshrined prejudices of an elite trying to impose their own mode of speech upon the vulgar. The "good" here, it is said, can only be the effective, and whatever is understood, however expressed, is as "good" as it can be. (*Webster's Third New International Dictionary* of 1966 infuriated linguistic conservatives by recording colloquialisms and vulgarisms without disparaging annotations.) Such reaction against authoritarianism is a salutary antidote to dogmatism: "It's me," for instance, is intrinsically as acceptable as "It is I"—and a good deal easier to say. (But is it mere affectation to prefer "This is he" to "This is him"? Perhaps that depends on the situation: To sound like a mandarin rather than "plain folks" may impede reception of the intended message.) Nevertheless, any utterance, no matter how informal, relaxed, or imaginatively eccentric, strongly depends for its contextual meaning upon a shared understanding of the background linguistic system. Baby talk, Pidgin English, adolescent slang, the jargon of literary critics or bureaucrats, all have their supporting patterns of rules and

[14] Harold Pinter in the *London Sunday Times,* 1962.

conventions awaiting exhibition by resourceful theorists. All "speaker's meaning" is, up to a point, a function of "standard meaning." This is as true of deviations and violations as of conformities: When Gertrude Stein or James Joyce play tricks with English, what they do is intelligible only against a knowledge of the standard that is being modified or transformed. (Cheating in speech, as in other "rule-governed" activities, is possible only for those who know the rules.)

The inevitable interlocking of the background conventions—what the language system demands, on pain of appearing eccentric or maladroit—and the speaker's specific intentions in a given situation creates an eternal and perennially fascinating tension. Only in stereotyped social situations such as greeting, swearing oaths, making formal promises, or the like do "speaker's meaning" and "standard meaning" fully coincide. In a stereotyped role, a man needs only stereotyped words. But inside every mouther of set formulas, there is a poet, an authentic "maker" of words, trying to emerge. How pedestrian the threadbare formulas sound when a man really has something to say. "I love you!"—but is that all? Do those words suffice for what the lover takes to be some unique attitude? (There are as many styles of loving as of talking nonsense.) But when words or other symbolic gestures fail us, there is nothing better to do than to find more effective symbols. So speech, in its inexhaustible variety and complexity, illustrates the continual opposition between tradition and freedom, between the constraints of received authority and the insistent thrust for personal autonomy. It is remarkable that the tensions and conflicts thus engendered, in so fragile a realm as the linguistic, should after all be so well resolved. That we do on the whole make ourselves understood—perhaps all too well at times—is something of a recurrent miracle, though one that hardly invites complacency.

The selections that follow illustrate a few of the many different scholarly approaches to problems of speech and language. The essays by Hockett and Chomsky, both linguists of great distinction, reveal from different standpoints something of the methodology that has led to the great achievements of scientific linguistics. Readers wishing further initiation into the subject might consult such excellent textbooks as H. A. Gleason, *An Introduction to Descriptive Linguistics,* rev. ed. (New York: Holt, Rinehart and Winston, 1961) or Charles F. Hockett, *A Course in Modern Linguistics* (New York: Macmillan, 1958). Noam Chomsky's *Language and Mind* (New York: Harcourt Brace Jovanovich, 1968) is a stimulating introduction to problems of "transformational grammar."

J. B. S. Haldane's provocative and partly speculative essay turns upon the relations between fully formed language and its analogues among "lower" organisms. Faced by such highly organized signaling systems as the "dances" of honeybees (for which see Karl von Frisch's fascinating *Bees: Their Vision, Chemical Senses, and Language* [Ithaca, N.Y.: Cornell University Press, 1950] or Martin Lindauer, *Communication Among Social Bees* [Cambridge, Mass.: Harvard University Press, 1961])—theorists have talked freely about "animal languages." (A useful and relatively nontechnical introduction is H. and M. Frings, *Animal Communication* [New York: Blaisdell, 1964].)

But the cries and gestures by which cicadas, frogs, baboons, dolphins, and many other animals "communicate" are tied to immediate stimuli in a manner uncharacteristic of a full-blown language. Animals cannot refer to the past, though they can signal a prospective future. History needs language.

George Orwell's famous parable *1984* convincingly illustrates the stultifying influence of an official terminology designed to inhibit independent criticism. Anyone who thinks the satire far-fetched should look at the official pronouncements of authoritarian political parties.

The essay by William F. Whyte and Robert R. Braun, based upon extensive experience of Peruvian society, provides some suggestive illustrations of interplay between language and culture. Had space permitted, it would have been pleasant to include some discussion of the controversial "Sapir-Whorf Hypothesis" that a speaker's native language shapes and guides his mental activity. Further information may be had in John B. Carroll, ed., *Language, Thought and Reality: Selected Writings of Benjamin Lee Whorf* (Cambridge, Mass.: The M.I.T. Press, 1956) or Patrick Gleeson and Nancy Wakefield, eds., *Language and Culture: A Reader* (Columbus, Ohio: Charles E. Merrill, 1968).

The pieces by Nemerov and Frost provide tantalizing glimpses of how some poets think about the craft of fashioning words into objects interesting in their own right. Nemerov's provocative juxtaposition of poems and jokes is only one of many analogies that have helped literary critics and estheticians to grasp the elusive essence of poetry. Perhaps nobody has written more stimulatingly about such topics than the distinguished critic I. A. Richards, whose lecture on the interaction of words is a healthy antidote to the somewhat atomistic approach of linguistic scientists.

Finally, the late John Austin's famous work on "performatives," here presented in his own superb popularization, is a small sample of many contributions to insight into language, that have resulted from intensive work by twentieth-century philosophers of language. Full documentation of this movement can be found in Richard Rorty, ed., *The Linguistic Turn* (Chicago: The University of Chicago Press, 1967).

ANIMAL RITUAL AND HUMAN LANGUAGE

J. B. S. Haldane

Ma come d'animal divegna fante
Non vedi tu ancor
Dante's *Purgatorio,* CANTO 25, 61.

Von Frisch's discovery of the methods by which bees communicate is a land-mark in human achievement comparable with Champollion's elucidation of hieroglyphics. . . . Nevertheless the very importance of the facts discovered makes it desirable to discuss their interpretation from a somewhat different standpoint.

Bees in a hive carry out various movements which evoke responses in other bees. For example a peculiar shivering, which a human observer after an hour or so's observation can distinguish from other movements, evokes grooming movements by other bees which clean areas of the shiverer, for example, under the wings, which she cannot reach with her own jaws or legs. Several "dances" are performed when plentiful food has been found, or in dry weather when water is brought back. We will confine ourselves to one of these, the dance performed when honey or pollen has been found at a distance exceeding about seventy-five metres. Different races of bees use somewhat different movements in similar situations, but the comparative philology of bee "languages" is still in an embryonic stage.

If we were to employ the terminology of the logic of Peano and Russell, we should say that the "dance" was a propositional function with four variables, translated as follows. "There is a source of food smelling of A, requiring an effort B to reach it, in direction C, of economic value D." A is indicated by demonstration. Other bees smell the communicatrix, or receive small draughts of scented liquid from her, and then search for food sources with the appropriate scent. B is indicated symbolically by the rhythm of the dance. The number of abdominal oscillations in each straight run of the figure is about three for a flight of 125 metres, and one more oscillation for every additional 75 metres. The rhythm also slows down with the distance. As, however, it slows down when the wind on the outward journey is con-trary, when the journey is uphill, or when a detour must be made, B is probably effort or time taken in reaching the food, rather than distance. The direction C of the flight is indicated by the direction of the straight part of the dance on the comb. The vertical direction indicates the direction of the sun. A deviation to the right or left of it indicates a deviation of the same

ANIMAL RITUAL AND HUMAN LANGUAGE From *Diogenes,* No. 4 (Autumn 1953).

angle to the west or east of the sun. The symbolism may be compared with that of a clock. The angle between the hour hand and the vertical is approximately twice the angle between the direction of the sun and the south. Finally the duration of the dance, which may vary from one second to several minutes, indicates the richness of the food source and therefore the labor force required there. If, however, we wished to use the terminology of human logic, we should have to note that items B, C, and D are quantitative, and not susceptible of a sharp dichotomy into true or false, as a verbal statement may be. The many-valued logic of Tarski and Lukasiewič would be more appropriate than any of the systems which derive from Aristotle in which the principle of the excluded middle holds. . . .

Clearly we could equally well translate the dance into an imperative "You D workers are to go to a food source smelling of A, you are to fly for B seconds in direction C." We shall find reason later to think that this interpretation is a little truer than our first, that the "dance" refers to the future rather than the past, but that it is not necessarily to be interpreted as a command.

Any translation of the dance into words is an anthropomorphism. But if we are to be anthropomorphic, let us be thoroughly so, first however noting a fundamental fact on which Benveniste laid little stress. The bees which fly out in response to a dance have always followed the dancer in her movements, at least for a short distance. They are not merely observers, but participants. Now if an anthropologist observes that before some important communal activity, such as harvest or war, members of a primitive human community imitate the bodily movements of another member, he will say that he is witnessing a ritual dance. If the participants, when questioned, say that this ritual is essential to the success of their undertaking, he will be tempted to add the word "magical." He will not, however, be surprised if, in the course of this ritual, some details regarding the future activity, for example, the direction of the enemy or the method of gathering a crop, are communicated. In Western European cultures he will find the nearest analogues to the dances of bees in country dances, many of which are believed to be vestiges of pre-Christian ritual, and in the close-order drill of soldiers, which is intended to prepare them psychologically for fighting.

The comparison of a large group of animal communications to human ritual rather than human language, has been made in great detail by E. A. Armstrong[1] (a priest of the Church of England). He has successfully avoided the anthropomorphism of attempting to translate them into human sentences in the indicative mood. . . .

If we are to go further we must survey our problem historically, that is to say, from the point of view of evolution, and consider other forms of animal communication, of which the bees' ritual represents one summit, and human language another and higher one. To do so we shall need some definitions.

I say that an activity is carried out for a purpose if it is intended to bring about a future state of affairs which can be imagined or envisaged by its

[1] Edward A. Armstrong, *Bird Display and Behaviour*, London: Lindsay Drummond, 1947.

performer, or to prevent such a state of affairs. Whether animals other than men have purpose is a question which can legitimately be asked. I say that an activity is carried out under the influence of a drive if it is not a mere reflex carried out by a small part of the nervous system, but involves the nervous system as a whole, its details being adapted to the circumstances; and if it would, were it performed by a human being, be accompanied by emotion. Reflex, drive, and purpose, of course, shade into one another in men. Breathing is normally a reflex. If it is seriously impeded, its performance occupies the consciousness and the will to a greater or less degree. The drive becomes compulsive. But it is hardly purposive. We do not breathe, unless perhaps we are physiologists, in order to add oxygen to our blood and remove carbon dioxide from it. We may drink because we are thirsty, because we look forward to enjoying the after-effects of wine, or because we think that a medicine will cure us. In the latter two cases we have a purpose. Purpose implies memory. Even our most sophisticated purposive actions are based on memories. It would be useless to use the fear of hell as a deterrent to a man who had never seen a flame or felt a pain. In making a will, one cannot avoid imagining the legatee using one's property, even if one does not expect to watch this process from another world.

I use the term "prelude" for a movement, sometimes causing a sound, which is usually or often carried out before another more important movement. This term includes what students of animal behavior call intention movements, which are often feeble versions of the principal movement. Thus a newt resting on the ground under water commonly raises its head a few seconds before it swims up to the surface for a breath of air. Displacement activities occur as preludes when a drive is frustrated, and a movement usually evoked by another drive is carried out; or when, as the result of a conflict of two drives, a movement originally appropriate to neither of them, but to a third, is carried out. For example, a seagull, under the simultaneous influences of the drives to attack and escape, or, in human terms, of anger and fear, plucks grass as if to build a nest. Tinbergen[2] has shown the importance of such prelude movements for animal communication, and their tendency to be exaggerated and ritualized so as to serve this purpose.

I shall not discuss here the question of whether a prelude originally learned can become instinctive in the descendants of those who learned it. . . .

In man the commonest displacement activities are termed "fidgeting." These, with other prelude movements, particularly of the facial muscles, are signs of the emotions. Moreover a characteristic intention movement generates its appropriate emotion, at least in man. It is difficult to smile at a person without feeling at least some affection for him. Shakespeare's King Henry V orders his soldiers, before an attack, to make appropriate intention movements.

[2] N. Tinbergen, "Derived Activities, Their Causation, Biological Significance, Origin, and Emancipation during Evolution." *Quarterly Review of Biology*, 27, pp. 1–32, 1952.

Stiffen the sinews, summon up the blood,
Disguise fair nature with hard-favoured rage;
Then lend the eye a terrible aspect.

.   .   .   .   .

Now set the teeth, and stretch the nostril wide,
Hold hard the breath and bend up every spirit
To his full height.

A survey of human literature would, I think, show that the description of animal prelude movements was more effective emotionally than that of the actions which they foreshadow. . . . Thucydides often devoted more space to the speeches before battles than to the battles themselves.

Finally by a communication from animal X to animal Y I mean an action by X involving a moderate expenditure of energy, which evokes a change in the behaviour of Y involving much larger quantities of energy. There is, of course, no sharp line between communication and more intense action. A gentle tap on another man's shoulder is a communication, a violent blow is an assault, even though it communicates to him that I am angry with him.

In many animal communications, X evokes in Y an activity very different from its own. Thus the "hunger call" and gaping of the mouth by a young bird evokes feeding by a parent, the "courting" activities of one sex evoke mating activity in the other, whose final stage, at least, is usually different in the two sexes. We shall not be much further concerned with such activities.

On the other hand, in social animals it is often biologically advantageous either that Y should perform an activity simultaneously with X, or that it should perform an activity like that of X though not necessarily simultaneously. Pavlov showed that an originally neutral stimulus, such as the sounding of a particular note, can release an activity (a conditioned reflex) if it is repeatedly presented shortly before, or even simultaneously with, a stimulus such as the giving of food, which releases an unconditioned reflex. If the originally neutral stimulus is given after the principal stimulus, it has no such effect. The conditioned stimulus is only effective if it points forward in time. Thus animals come to recognize intention movements of other members of their species or of men, and to respond to them. The more such intention movements can be ritualized, the more certain will be this response.

The various movements, including movements causing vocalization, involved in courting, may be regarded as ritualized intention movements for the actual process of mating. They are forward-pointing in time in so far as observable events are concerned, though of course they are determined by the animal's physiological or psychological state in the immediate past. When, however, it is biologically advantageous that Y should carry out a similar activity to X, Y will be brought into the appropriate mood if it imitates X's intention movements or other preludes. True imitation in animals is much rarer than is usually thought, as Tinbergen[3] points out. A fish

---

[3] N. Tinbergen, *Social Behaviour in Animals,* London: Methuen, 1953.

can hardly see itself swimming. It keeps its position in a shoal largely by moving so as to keep the visual images of its fellows in a nearly constant position, as it keeps those of weeds when swimming against a current while remaining in the same place. There are two conspicuous exceptions to this generalization. It is relatively easy to imitate sounds, because a sound made by X produces similar sensations in X to a sound made by Y. We shall return to this later. In the case of bees, if bee Y has already been conditioned to the odour carried by bee X, and more rarely when it has not, it follows X in the dance, and thus automatically imitates it.

Haldane and Spurway have discussed in some detail the reasons for considering the bee's dance as an intention movement, that is to say, as a prediction of her future movements rather than a description of her past movements. The simplest of these reasons is the following. When a bee which has been wandering about for some time in search of food discovers a rich source, she fills her stomach or the "baskets" for pollen on her hind legs. She then returns to the hive and dances, indicating the distance and direction of the food. This is not a report of her last outward journey; for if so she would report a much longer flight than is necessary. It is not a report of her last homeward journey; for if the wind has helped her homewards, she dances more slowly, indicating a greater effort, than if the wind has been against her, but will help her on her next outward journey. Her dance is a prediction of her next outward flight, and not a report of any past events. A number of other arguments lead to the same conclusion, that the dance ritual points forward in time, not backward.

We must remember that simple human beings describe a location in terms of imperatives. If I ask "Where is the Town Hall?" I expect to get such an answer as "Follow the tram lines, turn right beyond the cathedral, and go on till you see a park on your left," rather than "750 metres to the north-west," or "300 metres north of the cathedral," which would be a more "objective" answer.

It therefore seems best to regard the bees' dances as highly ritualized intention movements before a flight, which lead any bee Y, which imitates X, to perform a similar flight. I believe it to be an unjustifiable anthropomorphism to assume either that X has a purpose of informing Y, or that Y has a purpose to fly to a certain locality. When I yawn, I have not necessarily the purpose to go to sleep. It is much more legitimate to speak of drives in such a connection.

Some birds are notoriously gifted in imitating sounds, whether made by other birds, men, or even machines. This capacity is most developed in birds which, at some stage in their life cycle, live in fairly large flocks, such as parrots and starlings. If a particular pattern of sound, whether as the result of learning or otherwise, is habitually produced before a certain activity, its production, whether spontaneous or imitative, will lead to that activity, or at least induce a mood favorable to it. Lorenz points out that geese, when at rest, produce polysyllabic phrases. When moving forward, the number of syllables is reduced. As a preliminary to flight it is reduced still more. In the air the "honk" is monosyllabic. He remarks that the phrase most commonly used by domestic geese could be translated "We are not going to fly"! This language may be complex. Promptov and Lukina can distinguish about twenty different phrases used by the great tit *Parus Major,* most of which have to be learned, and some of which are different in different communities. A single phrase, particularly an alarm call, may be enough to induce communal action in a flock of birds. But preparation for communal flight often involves a good deal of "conversation" before anything like unanimity is reached. I suggest, then, that the function of vocal mimesis in birds is to bring about unanimity. In large flocks, for example flocks of several hundred Indian Whistling Ducks, *Dendrocygnus javanicus,* the "debate" before a communal flight may last for some minutes, during which birds may be seen stretching their wings.

In terms of human grammar, the prelude by itself is a statement in the first person singular of the future, such as "I shall fly." By mimesis it becomes a statement in the first person plural of the future, or even the imperative, such as "Let us fly."

This interpretation is strongly supported by Lindauer's observations on the choice of a new home by a bee swarm. Bees which have found possible sites return to the swarm and indicate their directions and distances by the same symbolism as is used for food sources, save that the dance, being a call to the whole swarm, usually lasts for over five minutes, and may continue for an hour. Other bees follow their direction, explore the sites indicated, and may dance on returning to the swarm. At first a dozen different sites may be indicated. Lindauer gives the history of a "debate" in which bees, to use Lenin's phrase, voted with their feet during five summer days. A site which had at first received only two out of twelve "votes" gradually gained support. During the penultimate day, the dances favoring it rose from seven out of twenty-two to sixty-one out of sixty-three. On the next day, unanimity was reached, and the swarm set off.

In a bird flock most individuals seem to make cries. But only a few of the bees in a swarm take the trouble to fly out and to dance. Their decision sways the community. But they enjoy none of the economic or other privileges of human oligarchs, though their method of decision seems to be that of the eighteenth-century Polish nobility. Lindauer's discovery, if confirmed, may give us considerably more insight into the origin of human political systems than did Hobbes' theory of *Bellum omnium contra omnes,* or Rousseau's of the *Contrat social,* to mention two only.

It is at least plausible to believe with Engels that human language began in a similar way, as a preparation for communal activity. This evocative, forward-pointing character of human language is still very important. . . .

As a vocabulary used before different types of activity develops, some phrases must refer to activities only performed in certain situations. It is just these which are most often learned rather than inborn. Promptov and Lukina state that "young *Paridae,* when brought up without parents, fail to develop such calls as are specifically connected with definite situations and are typical of the species, save for shrieks accompanying fright, fighting, or calls at a large distance." Nor do they react to such calls by other birds. Here we have beginning of language. But a phrase inciting to eat can only point backwards in time, that is to say, mean "Food is present," if the birds in question have a memory. We must, I think, distinguish between memory and recognition. Recognition merely implies a specific activity in the presence of a stimulus, and may be quite unconscious in men. In any skilled activity we react to a considerable range of stimuli unconsciously, and indeed an activity such as cycling or typing is not fully skilled until it has largely ceased to be conscious. Memory implies a revival in consciousness of past experience.

The use of a word or any other symbol as a description implies memory. The transition from evocative speech, pointing forward in time, to descriptive speech, pointing backward in time, must have been extremely difficult, and in my belief only man has made it. It seems probable that just as language made coherent, or logical, thought possible, it also made anything like coherent memory possible. Perhaps a mental image of a nut occasionally flits through a small bird's mind. It is even likely that the phrases calling to eat may evoke such images. But to proceed from the recall of such an image to a vocalization such as "I saw nuts on that tree last year" was one of man's greatest achievements. In its early stages any attempt to describe the past must often have been actively misleading.

If this view of man's intellectual development is anywhere near correct, the recognition of long-enduring objects, to which names could be given, was a great and difficult step. The reconstruction of an intellectually ordered picture of the past, even if it only extended over events in one's own lifetime, was a still greater one. History, palaeontology, and geology seem not only to be some of man's greatest achievements, but his most humanistic.

They are, of course, pragmatically justified because we cannot plan the future without knowledge of the past.

An interest in the past for its own sake is a more human attribute than most of those to which our moral mentors urge us. Many animals are more monogamous than most human beings. Others display a greater degree of altruism, and devote more of their time to securing the welfare of future generations, even if they cannot envisage it in images drawn from the past.

We can perhaps trace the exact point in history at which a human interest in the past for its own sake was first consciously expressed. Kings had recorded their deeds for their own glory. Myths had been created embodying a certain measure of historical truth. It was left for Herodotus in his opening sentence to proclaim the historical ideal . . . "So that neither should human happenings be canceled by time, nor the great and wonderful deeds, both of the Greeks and barbarians, become without fame."

Dante's Ulisse is perhaps the first literary figure in whom curiosity,

> L'ardore
> ch'i' ebbi a divenir del mondo esperto

was an obsessive passion. Dante located him in hell, but it is arguable that the lines which he wrote about him are the greatest in literature. For adumbrations of such a character we must look to some of the Norse Sagas rather than to Graeco-Roman or Asiatic writings.

For a brief period including much of the eighteenth century and perhaps all the nineteenth, curiosity and the dissemination of knowledge were almost respectable throughout Western Europe and North America. States are now beginning to exercise the control over these activities which churches did in the past.

The Aryan or Indo-European languages are still somewhat animalistic in that the simplest forms of their verbs are usually the imperative singular. In the Semitic languages the simplest form is the third person singular of the aorist, the most objective of the verb's forms. Perhaps this is one reason why Moses, Jesus, Mohammed, and Spinoza achieved, on certain matters, an appalling clarity of thought, even though Spinoza wrote, and Jesus' words only survive in, an Aryan language. I do not know whether human languages exist in which the simplest form of the verb is the first person singular of the future indicative tense, or the first person plural of the imperative mood. The example of the Marseillaise, which begins with the word *allons,* suggests that the latter is the most effective of all verbal formulæ whose repetition secures human unanimity. If languages exist with this characteristic they are, at least in that respect, closest to animal communication.

It is noteworthy that conquerors, when learning a language, first learn the imperative forms of the verbs in the language of the conquered, and may then use these as stems which are subsequently inflected. Thus the British soldiers in India learned the second person plural of the imperative of Urdu verbs, which ends in -o and is generally used, rather than the singular form, which is the naked verbal stem, as in Latin and French. They then provided it with English inflections, as "He pukkeroed," from the imperative *pakro*, "catch," rather than learn the periphrasis which does duty for an active past in Urdu. It may be that the coincidence of the imperative with the verb stem in Indo-European languages reflects the conquests of the "Battle axe" peoples, while the Arabs have never been conquered.

The discovery of the past has immense practical advantages in that it enables us to plan the future. But we can only plan the future on the hypothesis that it will resemble the past in most respects. If this is so, we can hope to change a few of them.

If my thesis is correct, man differs very greatly from all other animals in his relation to time; and communications between men, which include all the arts, must be judged, among other things, by their relationship to time. A large fraction of human communication is purely evocative. It incites its recipients to certain activities, whether it is advertising, religious ritual, political oratory, or martial music. Such communications are not specifically human. Others are mere catalogues of past events. The greatest passages in literature could be said to be eddies in the stream of time.

·   ·   ·   ·   ·

The dances of bees are philosophically important just because of their temporal ambiguity. They are at once prophecies and histories. Or shall we say that they are prophecies on their way to becoming histories? It is conceivable that in a bee's consciousness the specious present, which in a man occupies a second or less, extends over five or ten minutes. If so the dance and the flight are simultaneously present to its consciousness, as the whole of a linguistic or musical phrase is simultaneously present to a human mind. A bee's eyes and other sense organs convey so much less information per second than our own that this greater temporal extension would not imply an experience as rich as ours. Such a speculation can certainly not be verified at present. Perhaps it can never be verified.

In spite of von Frisch's magnificent work, almost everything remains to be discovered about the communication of bees. I believe that this discovery, and similar discoveries in other fields, will have very considerable effects on human thought and on human emotion. But, if my thesis is correct, they will reveal differences between men and other animals quite as striking as the similarities. They will also perhaps throw some doubt on Benveniste's statement that everything can be said in human language. The mystics at least have denied this. It seems possible that an analysis of animal communication may show that language and ritual are to some extent complementary in Bohr's sense, that we cannot, in many cases, describe what we perform, or perform what we describe. However that may be, our successors, in so far as they know more about animals, will know more about themselves.

HOW TO LEARN MARTIAN

Charles F. Hockett

An agent of the Galactic Federation, sent to Earth to case the joint secretly for either friendly or inimical purposes, could do a good deal worse than to make a survey of the scientific terms that appear, quite casually, in contemporary science fiction. True enough, there would be some discrepancy between the state of scientific development suggested by such a survey and the actual state of development in laboratory and industry—atomic energy was spoken of quite freely in our type of fiction for decades before technology caught up with imagination, and, in reverse, real recent developments in some fields are only now beginning to find their way into science fiction. If the agent's sole aim were to measure our technological potential, science fiction would be of no great help. But if he also wanted to determine the *degree of general technological readiness* of the whole population—at least in so-called "civilized" parts of the world—then the suggested survey would be of considerable value.

HOW TO LEARN MARTIAN From *Astounding Science Fiction,* published by Street and Smith. Reprinted by permission of the author.

One score on which, as a measure of real technological development, our agent's study of science fiction might badly mislead him, is in the matter of communication, particularly the basic form of human communication, *language*. An occasional term of modern linguistics turns up from time to time in science fiction: "phoneme," in particular, is a word to conjure with just as much as is "transistor" or "cybernetics." The effect sought by the use of such a word is spoiled if the story-writer pauses to explain: the use must be casual, implying that the reader knows all about such things. And, because many of our magazines regularly run factual articles or departments, and we addicts regularly read them, this assumption of the story-writer is very often true.

If we can pride ourselves on the number of modern developments which were anticipated by the lively imaginations of an earlier generation of authors, I think perhaps we should temper this pride with a bit of shame that we have been such Johnny-come-latelies about phonemes, morphemes, intonations, constructions, immediate constituents, the impact of language on culture, and the like. Do you know when the fundamental principle of phonemics was first expounded?

It was explained rather clearly—though of course without the word "phoneme"—by a twelfth-century Icelander who was annoyed by the inaccuracy with which his compatriots put down written marks to represent Icelandic speech. We can probably forgive ourselves for not having known about this particular early episode, especially since modern linguists had forgotten all about it and had to rediscover the principle for themselves. But even in modern times the phonemic principle was stated, in one way or another, as early as about 1910: the earliest mention I have been able to track down in science fiction postdates World War II.

Maybe we should catch up. If our authors would like to follow their usual custom of being ahead of the times instead of lagging behind, they must at least know what the times have to offer. If we readers insist that they should do this, they will.

We are going along on the first voyage to Mars, and very conveniently we shall find intelligent oxygen-breathing beings with respiratory and digestive tracts shaped very much like our own. (Later on we can point out why this last assumption is so convenient.) Our ship lands; we make the first hesitant contact with the Martians; and before long our xenologist, Ferdinand Edward Leonard, B.A., M.A., Ph.D., M.D., X.D.—who is about as chock full of modern anthropological, linguistic, communicative, engineering, psychiatric, and biologic training as one skin can be stuffed with—sits down with a Martian to try to find out something about the latter's language.[1] (Hidden assumption: Martians can sit down.) For short, we shall call

---

[1] Roger Williams, of Rhode Island and Providence Plantations fame, wrote a little book called *Key Into the Language of America*—a grammar of a language spoken by a few hundred Indians in his vicinity, which was but one of *several hundred* distinct languages spoken in aboriginal North America. Some of our exploring science-fiction heroes fall into this same error. If there are millions of intelligent beings on Mars, there may be thousands of Martian languages.

these two "Ferdie" and "Marty"—the latter because even Ferdie won't be able to learn, or to pronounce, Marty's real name for quite a while. (Query: Do Martians have personal names?)

Ferdie points to the Martian's foot and says, of course in English, "What do you call that in your language?" Marty certainly does not understand, but at this moment he makes a bit of vocal sound, something like *GAHdjik*. Ferdie puts this down in his little notebook, and writes the English word "foot" by it. What Ferdie puts down to represent the Martian "word"—if it really is a word, and not just Marty clearing his throat in the typical Martian manner—doesn't look quite like what we have written above, because Ferdie has a special set of written marks which he can use more efficiently and accurately for the purpose (a "phonetic alphabet"); but we needn't bother with this, because it is merely a convenience, not an essential. Now Ferdie is not being a fool and jumping to conclusions when he makes his notebook entry. He knows perfectly well that the sound Marty has made may not only not mean "foot," but may not even be a word at all. Ferdie makes his entry only as a memory aid: it will be easy enough to scratch it out when and if necessary.

Ferdie also says *GAHdjik* himself—or tries to—and observes Marty's reaction. Just for fun, we shall pretend that Marty does not react, so that this time Ferdie has gained nothing.

Next Ferdie points to something else, gets another reaction from Marty which may be a "word," writes it down, and tries to imitate it. Then he points to a third thing. After a while, having elicited a number of such bits of what may be speech, Ferdie returns to Marty's foot. This time what Marty says doesn't sound like *GAHdjik,* but more like *KAHchuk.*

Right at this point, Ferdie comes face to face with the most ticklish and crucial problem which can be encountered by a xenologist or by an Earth linguist. (We except, of course, the task of working with the dragonlike inhabitants of Antares II, whose languages make use not of sound but of heat-waves.) Has friend Marty given two different "words" for two different meanings? Has he given two distinct "words" for a single meaning? Or has he simply said the same "word" twice, with slight differences in pronunciation which are clear to Ferdie but which would be entirely overlooked by Marty's fellows?

Since this problem lies at the very heart of phonemics, we had better return to Earth momentarily and look at some more homely examples of what is involved.

Suppose that your name is Paul Revere and that you want to arrange for me, over in Boston, to send you some sort of a signal across the Charles River so that you can know whether the British are coming by land or by sea. This is all you want to know—it is already clear that they are going to be coming one way or the other, but you need to know which way. What we have to do is to establish a code containing just two signals. One of the signals will mean "they're coming by land," and the other will mean "they're coming by sea." The physical circumstances have something to do with what kinds of signals we can choose. They must both be something that you, over on the Cambridge side of the river, can easily detect, so that a shout or halloo wouldn't do very well. Since it will be night, some sort of arrangement of lights—up in a high place—would be a good idea.

Another consideration is that there must be no possible danger of my sending one signal and you receiving what is apparently the other. That is, we want to keep the two signals physically distinct, so that there will be no danger of misunderstanding. Shall we use a red lantern for "by sea" and a green one for "by land"? No—green might not show up too well, and what's more, we haven't got a green lantern. But I know there are two lanterns over in the basement of the Old North Church: suppose I put just one of them up in the tower for one of the signals, but both of them, at opposite sides, for the other. "One, if by land, and two, if by sea?" Agreed! Good luck on your ride! Hope a fog doesn't come up.

People can make signals out of anything they can *control* and can *observe,* and they can make the signals mean anything they wish. We constantly establish little short-term signaling systems, use them, and then discard them. A wave of the hand, a drop of a handkerchief, a wink of the eye, the raising of a window blind, the toot of an auto horn—such events are assigned special meaning over and over again. Some signaling systems are a little more elaborate and a bit more enduring—for example, the pattern of lights, stable or winking, shown at night by a plane for takeoff, for landing, or during flight. The really elaborate systems are hardly "invented," but merely passed down from generation to generation, with gradual changes; among these, of course, belongs language itself. Now, however varied these different systems may be, they all conform to certain fundamental principles. One of these —the one in which we are concerned here—is that the users of the signals must be able to tell them apart. This sounds simple and obvious enough, but it has some pretty complicated results.

Paul Revere and his side-kick had no trouble on this score, because they needed only two signals—all Paul had to have was one item of information of the either-this-or-that sort. But suppose you had to work out a signaling-system which will include hundreds or thousands of distinct signals. Keeping them physically apart and easily distinguished is in this case much more difficult.

One technique that anybody confronted with such a design-problem is bound to hit on is to set up some fairly small repertory of basic elements, each of them quite different physically from any of the others, and then arrange for the actual signals to consist of some sort of arrangement or combination of the fundamental elements. Suppose Paul and his henchmen had needed a couple of hundred different signals. They could have arranged, for example, for a row of five lights to be put up in the Old North Church tower, each light either red or green or amber: this yields two hundred and forty-three distinct combinations, yet calls for only fifteen lanterns to be available—one of each color for each of the five positions.

It is pretty obvious that this set of two hundred and forty-three signals would be much easier for Paul to read from across the river than, say, the same number of signals consisting each of a lantern of a different shade. The human eye, true enough, can distinguish several thousand shades of color, but finer distinctions are not easy to detect, and for rapid and efficient use ought not to be involved. Even as it is, if Paul's assistant is only able to find four really red lamps and has to fill in with one which is rather orange, there will be the possibility that the orange lamp, intended as functionally "red," will be interpreted by Paul as "amber." This danger can be avoided if Paul knows in advance that the "red" lamps will in actual transmission vary somewhat in precise shade, without making any significant difference in the signal.

This sort of thing has actually happened in every known case of a really complicated signaling system, including language. When a linguist goes to work on a language he has never heard before, he can count on certain things along this line. The colored lanterns in this case are different motions of lips, tongue, throat, and lungs, which produce kinds of sound which can be heard, and told apart, by human ears.

The investigator knows that the people who speak the language will make *distinctive* use only of certain differences of articulatory motion—that is, maybe they will use relatively red, relatively green, and relatively amber lanterns, but not also orange or blue. He knows that if an articulatory motion of an ambiguous sort occurs, it will count as a "mistake" and will be allowed for by the speakers of the language—since orange is not functional, the actual appearance of an orange lantern must be a mistake for red or for amber. But he does not know in advance just what differences of articulatory motion will be thus used.

After all, a lantern-code could make use of any number of different ranges of spectral colors, providing that no two of the significantly different shades were so close together as to give rise to serious danger of confusion. In just the same way, there are any number of ways in which a selection can be made, from the "spectrum" of all possible speech-sound, of shades to be used distinctively. The only way to find out what selection is actually made by the speakers of a given language is—but let's watch Ferdie and Marty again and see if we can find out.

We left Ferdie confronting the problem of *GAHdjik* and *KAHchuk*. Assuming that each of these is really speech, not just Martian throat-clearing, then there are three possibilities:

1. They are two different words with two different meanings. If we were in the position of Marty, the first time a xenologist pointed to our ear we might say *ear*, and at a subsequent time we might think he was asking what the organ is used for, and so say *hear*. *Ear* and *hear* are pretty similar: a Frenchman or Italian who knew no English might easily wonder whether they were two words or just one.

2. They are two different words, but for essentially one and the same meaning. When we pronounce *room* with the vowel sound of *cooed* we are using one word; when we pronounce it with the vowel sound of *could*

we are really using a different word. But it would be hard to find any difference in the meaning of the two.

3. Marty has simply said the same word twice: the apparent variation in pronunciation would not be noticed by his fellow Martians. A speaker of Hindustani, hearing us say *pie* or *tie* or *cow* several times, might be convinced that we were pronouncing the initial *p-* (or *t-* or *k-*) now in one way, now in another, since Hindustani breaks up the "spectrum" of possible speech sound a little more finely in this particular region.

There are several things Ferdie can do to try to solve this problem. First, he points to Marty's foot again and says *KAHchuk,* to observe the response; a little while later, he makes the same gesture and says *GAHdjik.* For good measure, he also tries *GAHdjuk* and *KAHchik,* and even *gahDJIK* and *kahCHIK,* making the second syllable louder than the first. The hope is that he can manage to get something out of Marty's reactions which will indicate acceptance or rejection of the various pronunciations. If Marty accepts all the pronunciations except the last two, then Ferdie has fairly good indication that the answer is the second or third of the possibilities, rather than the first. Of course he can't yet be absolutely certain; perhaps Martians are too polite to criticize, or perhaps we simply haven't yet learned to read their gestures of acceptance and rejection.

Another procedure is available. Ferdie looks through his notebook and notices an entry *GOOpit,* apparently meaning "small tuft of green hair sprouting from the back of a Martian's neck," and an entry *KOOsahng,* which seems to refer to a low-growing yellowish shrub that is plentiful in the vicinity. This what Ferdie does and how Marty reacts:

FERDIE (pointing to the tuft of hair): *"GOOpit."*
MARTY (closing his middle eye—apparently the gesture of assent): *"Fum."*
FERDIE (pointing to the bush): *"KOOsahng."*
MARTY: *"FUM."*
FERDIE (the tuft of hair): *"KOOpit."*
MARTY: *"FUM. NAHboo GOOpit."*
FERDIE (the bush): *"GOOsahng."*
MARTY: *"FUM. NAHboo KOOsahng."*
FERDIE (pointing to the spaceship in which we arrived): *"GOOpit."*
MARTY (popping all three eyes out on their stalks): *"HLA - HLA - HLA - HLA! EEkup SAHCH bah-KEENdut!"*

This last response, whatever it actually means, is certainly different enough from the others to be indicative. Ferdie concludes that he can probably work on the theory that the last response was rejection, the others all acceptance. But what does this tell him? It tells him the following:

1. *GOOpit* (or *KOOpit*) does *not* mean "spaceship."

2. The pronunciations *GOOpit* and *KOOpit* may sound different to us English-speaking Earthlings, but to Marty they are all the same.

3. The pronunciations *KOOsahng* and *GOOsahng* are also all the same for Marty.

4. The pronunciations *GAHdjik, GAHdjuk, KAHchik, KAHchuk* sound

quite varied to us, with our English-speaking habits, but the differences are irrelevant for Marty's language.

Or, in short, for the last three points, the difference between an initial *k*-sound and an initial *g*-sound, which is distinctive for us, is not functional in Marty's language. Ferdie has reached one conclusion about the phonemic system of Marty's language: in the region of the spectrum where English distinguishes between two phonemes, *k* and *g*, Marty's language has only one.

It is entertaining to follow the hard step-by-step field-work of a xenologist or a linguist this far, but after this it quickly becomes boring, at least for everyone but the investigator himself—and, often enough, for him, too. Because what he has to do is simply more of the same—over and over and over again, eliciting, recording, checking, correcting, reaching an occasional tentative conclusion, finding out he was wrong and revising. It is a routine sort of task, before long, but fortunately it is not one which can be assigned to any sort of machine. (At least, a machine that could perform the task would have to have all the logic *and illogic,* all the strengths *and weaknesses,* of human beings.)

Ferdie's aim can be stated rather easily. He wants to reach the point where he can supply an accurate description of all the *differences in pronunciation* which are *distinctive* in the linguistic signaling of Marty and his fellows. He wants to be able to state what shades of lanterns are used, in what sequences the different colors are allowed to occur, and just what range of spectral shades counts as an instance of each color. All of this constitutes the *phonemic system* of Marty's language.

Maybe you think it need not take Ferdie very long to achieve this aim. Well, if Earth languages are any guide, there is a good chance that our ship hasn't brought along enough food to supply Ferdie while he finishes the job; unless he can get along on Martian lizard-weed, the native staple, he is out of luck. In a day or so, a well-trained Earth linguist, working with a completely new language, can get the cultural wax out of his ears and begin to hear something that sounds like it might really be a language. Before that, everything is a mumbling buzz. In another ten or so days of hard work, the linguist can get perhaps ninety per cent of what counts in the sound-making and sound-recognizing habits of the language, though his own hearing may not yet be too well trained for the new system. In another hundred days he can get perhaps ninety per cent *of the remainder.* Sometimes it is years before he gets it all.

However, this rather long program shouldn't discourage us, since Ferdie can be making effective practical use of the local Martian dialect long before the full cycle is up. Ninety per cent is actually pretty good, though so long as, in his own attempts at speaking Martian, Ferdie uses only ninety per cent, he will impress Marty as having a pretty un-Martian accent. Let us see what "ninety per cent" means and why it is effective.

The phonemic system of Marty's language—or of any other—is a set of distinctive *differences* between pronunciations. The units which we call "phonemes" are in themselves of no importance: it is the differences between them that count. A given phoneme, in terms of its use in communication, is nothing except something which is different from all the other phonemes in the system. In Morse code, a "dot" is a "dot" and a "dash" is a "dash" whether the former is a short voltage pulse and the latter a long one, or the former is a wave of a flag in one direction and the latter a wave in the other direction. This is why we will irritate Ferdie no end if we ask him after his first day's work, "Well, do they have a phoneme *K*?" or "Well, is *K* a phoneme in Martian?" If you want to compare languages with each other, the sort of question which must be asked—the sort that will be meaningful to Ferdie even if he can't yet answer it—is "Does Marty have a phonemic contrast between *K* and *G*?"

The difference between *K* and *G* is distinctive in English, so that we have two phonemes rather than just one in this general region of the spectrum, because a great many pairs of words are kept apart by the difference and by nothing else: *good*: *could, gap*: *cap, glue*: *clue, bag*: *back, bigger*: *bicker*, and so on. In Marty's language there are no pairs of words kept apart in just this way. On the other hand, the difference between *EE* and *AH* is distinctive in Marty's language—as in ours—because *KEEtah* means "eye-stalk" while *KAHtah* means "setting of Deimos."

The sole function of phonemes, then, is to be different from each other, and, in being so, to keep words and utterances—whole signals—apart. But some differences between phonemes do a lot more of this work than do others. The difference between *K* and *G* in English carries, relatively speaking, a fairly large share of the total load, as you can easily see by looking for more pairs of words like those which we gave above—it is easy to list hundreds. The difference between the *sh*-sound of *she* or *hush* and the *zh*-sound in the middle of *pleasure* is also functional, but this distinction doesn't carry very much of the total load. If you look hard, you may be able to find three or four pairs of words in which this difference is the only one—one example is *measure* and *mesher*—but there are very few.

Actually, a technique deriving from information theory makes it theoretically possible to express the "functional load" of different phonemic contrasts in a language in quantitative terms, to any desired degree of accuracy. But the amount of counting and computing which is involved is enormous, and would hardly be undertaken without a properly designed computing machine—and then it costs lots of money instead of lots of time, which for linguists is even worse. But we don't need such figures here; the general principle is, we hope, clear enough.

It is because of this that Ferdie can begin making effective use of Martian long before he has ferreted out and pinned down every last vestige of distinctive difference in articulation of which the language makes some use. It is obvious on the face of it that the differences which he discovers first are bound to be, by and large, the differences of greatest functional importance. Working just with these in his own attempts to speak Martian, he will sometimes be misunderstood—but we misunderstand each other from time to time even under the best of circumstances. If you want further empirical evidence, you need only think of the German or the Frenchman who makes you understand him with imperfect English—or of you, yourself, managing to communicate in imperfect French or German.

If there *are* Martians, and they *are* intelligent and have a language, and if they *do* have upper respiratory and alimentary tracts shaped much like our own, and ears much like ours, and finally, if they *do* make use of these organs in speech communication—given all these ifs, then the procedures of Ferdinand Edward Leonard will work, and he will be able to "break" the phonemic system of the language.

But suppose that the Martians fail on just one of the above ifs. Suppose that they have two tongues and no nose. How, then, is Ferdinand Edward Leonard to imitate and to learn to recognize their speech sounds?

Suppose something even more drastic. Suppose that the Martians communicate with a system just as complex as human language and with much the same essential structure, but that instead of modulating sound they modulate a carrier at frequencies above the reach of human ears—or radio waves, or a light beam, or odors, or electrical flows, or some kind of energy transmitted through the "sub-ether." What kind of equipment and training shall we give our xenologists to handle situations of this sort? There are still certain fundamental design-features which any such language-like communications system is bound to include, but the problem of observation and analysis is tremendously harder.

LANGUAGE AND THE MIND

Noam Chomsky

How does the mind work? To answer this question we must look at some of the work performed by the mind. One of its main functions is the acquisition of knowledge. The two major factors in acquisition of knowledge, perception and learning, have been the subject of study and speculation for centuries. It would not, I think, be misleading to characterize the major positions that have developed as outgrowths of classical rationalism and empiricism. The rationalist theories are marked by the importance they assign to *intrinsic* structures in mental operations—to central processes and organizing principles in perception, and to innate ideas and principles in learning. The empiricist approach, in contrast, has stressed the role of experience and control by environmental factors.

LANGUAGE AND THE MIND From "Language and the Mind," by Noam Chomsky, *Psychology Today* Magazine, February, 1968. Copyright © Communications/Research/Machines/Inc.

   The classical empiricist view is that sensory images are transmitted to the brain as impressions. They remain as ideas that will be associated in various ways, depending on the fortuitous character of experience. In this view a language is merely a collection of words, phrases, and sentences, a habit system, acquired accidentally and extrinsically. In the formulation of Willard Quine, knowledge of a language (and, in fact, knowledge in general) can be represented as "a fabric of sentences variously associated to one another and to nonverbal stimuli by the mechanism of conditioned response." Acquisition of knowledge is only a matter of the gradual construction of this fabric. When sensory experience is interpreted, the already established network may be activated in some fashion. In its essentials, this view has been predominant in modern behavioral science, and it has been accepted with little question by many philosophers as well.

   The classical rationalist view is quite different. In this view the mind contains a system of "common notions" that enable it to interpret the scattered and incoherent data of sense in terms of objects and their relations, cause and effect, whole and part, symmetry, gestalt properties, functions, and so on. Sensation, providing only fleeting and meaningless images, is degenerate and particular. Knowledge, much of it beyond immediate awareness, is rich in structure, involves universals, and is highly organized. The innate general principles that underlie and organize this knowledge, according to Leibniz, "enter into our thoughts, of which they form the soul and the connection . . . although we do not at all think of them."

   This "active" rationalist view of the acquisition of knowledge persisted through the romantic period in its essentials. With respect to language, it achieves its most illuminating expression in the profound investigations of Wilhelm von Humboldt. His theory of speech perception supposes a generative system of rules that underlies speech production as well as its interpretation. The system is generative in that it makes infinite use of finite means. He regards a language as a structure of forms and concepts based on a system of rules that determine their interrelations, arrangement, and organization. But these finite materials can be combined to make a never-ending product.

   In the rationalist and romantic tradition of linguistic theory, the normal use of language is regarded as characteristically innovative. We construct sentences that are entirely new to us. There is no substantive notion of "analogy" or "generalization" that accounts for this creative aspect of language use. It is equally erroneous to describe language as a "habit structure" or as a network of associated responses. The innovative element in normal use of language quickly exceeds the bounds of such marginal principles as analogy or generalization (under any substantive interpretation of these notions). It is important to emphasize this fact because the insight has been lost under the impact of the behaviorist assumptions that have dominated speculation and research in the twentieth century.

   In Humboldt's view, acquisition of language is largely a matter of maturation of an innate language capacity. The maturation is guided by internal factors, by an innate "form of language" that is sharpened, differentiated, and given its specific realization through experience. Language is thus a kind of latent structure in the human mind, developed and fixed by exposure to specific linguistic experience. Humboldt believes that all languages will be found to be very similar in their grammatical form, similar not on the surface but in their deeper inner structures. The innate organizing principles severely limit the class of possible languages, and these principles determine the properties of the language that is learned in the normal way.

The active and passive views of perception and learning have elaborated with varying degrees of clarity since the seventeenth century. These views can be confronted with empirical evidence in a variety of ways. Some recent work in psychology and neurophysiology is highly suggestive in this regard. There is evidence for the existence of central processes in perception, specifically for control over the functioning of sensory neurons by the brain-stem reticular system. Behavioral counterparts of this central control have been under investigation for several years. Furthermore, there is evidence for innate organization of the perceptual system of a highly specific sort at every level of biological organization. Studies of the visual system of the frog, the discovery of specialized cells responding to angle and motion in the lower cortical centers of cats and rabbits, and the somewhat comparable investigations of the auditory system of frogs—all are relevant to the classical questions of intrinsic structure mentioned earlier. These studies suggest that there are highly organized, innately determined perceptual systems that are adapted closely to the animal's "life space" and that provide the basis for what we might call "acquisition of knowledge." Also relevant are certain behavioral studies of human infants, for example those showing the preference for faces over other complex stimuli.

These and other studies make it reasonable to inquire into the possibility that complex intellectual structures are determined narrowly by innate mental organization. What is perceived may be determined by mental processes of considerable depth. As far as language learning is concerned, it seems to me that a rather convincing argument can be made for the view that certain principles intrinsic to the mind provide invariant structures that are a precondition for linguistic experience. In the course of this article I would like to sketch some of the ways such conclusions might be clarified and firmly established.

There are several ways linguistic evidence can be used to reveal properties of human perception and learning. In this section we consider one research strategy that might take us nearer to this goal.

Let us say that in interpreting a certain physical stimulus a person constructs a "percept." This percept represents some of his conclusions (in general, unconscious) about the stimulus. To the extent that we can characterize such percepts, we can go on to investigate the mechanisms that relate stimulus and percept. Imagine a model of perception that takes stimuli as inputs and arrives at percepts as "outputs." The model might contain a system of beliefs, strategies for interpreting stimuli, and other factors, such as the organization of memory. We would then have a perceptual model that might be represented graphically.

Consider next the system of beliefs that is a component of the perceptual model. How was this acquired? To study this problem, we must investigate a second model, which takes certain data as input and gives as "output" (again, internally represented) the system of beliefs operating in the perceptual model. This second model, a model of learning, would have its own intrinsic structure, as did the first. This structure might consist of conditions on the nature of the system of beliefs that can be acquired, of innate inductive strategies, and again, of other factors such as the organization of memory.

Under further conditions, which are interesting but not relevant here, we can take these perceptual and learning models as theories of the acquisition of knowledge, rather than of belief. How then would the models apply to language? The input stimulus to the perceptual model is a speech signal, and the percept is a representation of the utterance that the hearer takes the signal to be and of the interpretation he assigns to it. We can think of the percept as the structural description of a linguistic expression which contains certain phonetic, semantic, and syntactic information. Most interesting is the syntactic information, which best can be discussed by examining a few typical cases.

The three sentences in the example

(1) I told John to leave
(2) I expected John to leave
(3) I persuaded John to leave

seem to be the same syntactic structure. Each contains the subject *I,* and the predicate of each consists of a verb (*told, expected, persuaded*), a noun phrase (*John*), and an embedded predicate phrase (*to leave*). This similarity is only superficial, however—a similarity in what we may call the "surface structure" of these sentences, which differ in important ways when we consider them with somewhat greater care.

The differences can be seen when the sentences are paraphrased or subjected to certain grammatical operations, such as the conversion from active to passive forms. For example, in normal conversation the sentence "I told John to leave" can be roughly paraphrased as "What I told John was to leave." But the other two sentences cannot be paraphrased as "What I persuaded John was to leave" or "What I expected John was to leave." Sentence 2 can be paraphrased as: "It was expected by me that John would leave." But the other two sentences cannot undergo a corresponding formal operation, yielding: "It was persuaded by me that John would leave" or "It was told by me that John should leave."

Sentences 2 and 3 differ more subtly. In Sentence 3 *John* is the direct object of *persuade,* but in Sentence 2 *John* is not the direct object of *expect.* We can show this by using these verbs in slightly more complex sentences: "I persuaded the doctor to examine John" and "I expected the doctor to examine John." If we replace the embedded proposition *the doctor to examine John* with its passive form *John to be examined by the doctor,* the change to the passive does not, in itself, change the meaning. We can accept as paraphrases "I expected the doctor to examine John" and "I expected John to be examined by the doctor." But we cannot accept as paraphrases "I persuaded the doctor to examine John" and "I persuaded John to be examined by the doctor."

The parts of these sentences differ in their grammatical functions. In "I persuaded John to leave" *John* is both the object of *persuade* and the subject of *leave*. These facts must be represented in the percept since they are known, intuitively, to the hearer of the speech signal. No special training or instruction is necessary to enable the native speaker to understand these examples, to know which are "wrong" and which "right," although they may all be quite new to him. They are interpreted by the native speaker instantaneously and uniformly, in accordance with structural principles that are known tacitly, intuitively, and unconsciously.

These examples illustrate two significant points. First, the surface structure of a sentence, its organization into various phrases, may not reveal or immediately reflect its deep syntactic structure. The deep structure is not represented directly in the form of the speech signal; it is abstract. Second, the rules that determine deep and surface structure and their interrelation in particular cases must themselves be highly abstract. They are surely remote from consciousness, and in all likelihood they cannot be brought to consciousness.

A study of such examples, examples characteristic of all human languages that have been carefully studied, constitutes the first stage of the linguistic investigation outlined above, namely the study of the percept. The percept contains phonetic and semantic information related through the medium of syntactic structure. There are two aspects to this syntactic structure. It consists of a surface directly related to the phonetic form, and a deep structure that underlies the semantic interpretation. The deep structure is represented in the mind and rarely is indicated directly in the physical signal.

A language, then, involves a set of semantic-phonetic percepts, of sound-meaning correlations, the correlations being determined by the kind of intervening syntactic structure just illustrated. The English language correlates sound and meaning in one way, Japanese in another, and so on. But the general properties of percepts, their forms and mechanisms, are remarkably similar for all languages that have been carefully studied.

Returning to our models of perception and learning, we can now take up the problem of formulating the system of beliefs that is a central component in perceptual processes. In the case of language, the "system of beliefs" would now be called the "generative grammar," the system of rules that specifies the sound-meaning correlation and generates the class of structural descriptions (percepts) that constitute the language in question. The generative grammar, then, represents the speaker-hearer's knowledge of his language. We can use the term *grammar of a language* ambiguously, as referring not only to the speaker's internalized, subconscious knowledge but to the professional linguist's representation of this internalized and intuitive system of rules as well.

How is this generative grammar acquired? Or, using our learning model, what is the internal structure of the device that could develop a generative grammar?

We can think of every normal human's internalized grammar as, in effect, a theory of his language. This theory provides a sound-meaning correlation for an infinite number of sentences. It provides an infinite set of structural descriptions; each contains a surface structure that determines phonetic form and a deep structure that determines semantic content.

In formal terms, then, we can describe the child's acquisition of language as a kind of theory construction. The child discovers the theory of his language with only small amounts of data from that language. Not only does his "theory of the language" have an enormous predictive scope, but it also enables the child to reject a great deal of the very data on which the theory has been constructed. Normal speech consists, in large part, of fragments, false starts, blends, and other distortions of the underlying idealized forms. Nevertheless, as is evident from a study of the mature use of language, what the child learns is the underlying ideal theory. This is a remarkable fact. We must also bear in mind that the child constructs this ideal theory without explicit instruction, that he acquires this knowledge at a time when he is not capable of complex intellectual achievements in many other domains, and that this achievement is relatively independent of intelligence or the particular course of experience. These are facts that a theory of learning must face.

A scientist who approaches phenomena of this sort without prejudice or dogma would conclude that the acquired knowledge must be determined in a rather specific way by intrinsic properties of mental organization. He would then set himself the task of discovering the innate ideas and principles that make such acquisition of knowledge possible.

It is unimaginable that a highly specific, abstract, and tightly organized language comes by accident into the mind of every four-year-old child. If there were not an innate restriction on the form of grammar, then the child could employ innumerable theories to account for his linguistic experience, and no one system, or even small class of systems, would be found exclusively acceptable or even preferable. The child could not possibly acquire knowledge of a language. This restriction on the form of grammar is a precondition for linguistic experience, and it is surely the critical factor in determining the course and result of language learning. The child cannot know at birth which language he is going to learn. But he must "know" that its grammar must be of a predetermined form that excludes many imaginable languages.

The child's task is to select the appropriate hypothesis from this restricted class. Having selected it, he can confirm his choice with the evidence further available to him. But neither the evidence nor any process of induction (in any well-defined sense) could in themselves have led to this choice. Once the hypothesis is sufficiently well confirmed, the child knows the language defined by this hypothesis; consequently, his knowledge extends vastly beyond his linguistic experience, and he can reject much of this experience as imperfect, as resulting from the interaction of many factors, only one of which is the ideal grammar that determines a sound-meaning connection for an infinite class of linguistic expressions. Along such lines as these one might outline a theory to explain the acquisition of language.

As has been pointed out, both the form and meaning of a sentence are determined by syntactic structures that are not represented directly in the signal and that are related to the signal only at a distance, through a long sequence of interpretive rules. This property of abstractness in grammatical structure is of primary importance, and it is on this property that our inferences about mental processes are based. Let us examine this abstractness a little more closely.

Not many years ago, the process of sentence interpretation might have been described approximately along the following lines. A speech signal is received and segmented into successive units (overlapping at the borders). These units are analyzed in terms of their invariant phonetic properties and assigned to "phonemes." The sequence of phonemes, so constructed, is then segmented into minimal grammatically functioning units (morphemes and words). These are again categorized. Successive operations of segmentation and classification will lead to what I have called "surface structure"—an analysis of a sentence into phrases, which can be represented as a proper bracketing of the sentence, with the bracketed units assigned to various categories. Each segment—phonetic, syntactic or semantic—would be identified in terms of certain invariant properties. This would be an exhaustive analysis of the structure of the sentence.

With such a conception of language structure, it made good sense to look forward hopefully to certain engineering applications of linguistics—for example, to voice-operated typewriters capable of segmenting an expression into its successive phonetic units and identifying these, so that speech could be converted to some form of phonetic writing in a mechanical way; to mechanical analysis of sentence structure by fairly straightforward and well-understood computational techniques; and perhaps even beyond to such projects as machine translation. But these hopes have by now been largely abandoned with the realization that this conception of grammatical structure is inadequate at every level, semantic, phonetic, and syntactic. Most important, at the level of syntactic organization, the surface structure indicates semantically significant relations only in extremely simple cases. In general, the deeper aspects of syntactic organization are representable by labeled bracketing, but of a very different sort from that seen in surface structure.

There is evidence of various sorts, both from phonetics and from experimental psychology, that labeled bracketing is an adequate representation of surface structure. It would go beyond the bounds of this paper to survey the phonetic evidence. A good deal of it is presented in a forthcoming book, *Sound Pattern of English,* by myself and Morris Halle. Similarly, very interesting experimental work by Jerry Fodor and his colleagues, based on earlier observations by D. E. Broadbent and Peter Ladefoged, has shown that the disruption of a speech signal (for example, by a superimposed click) tends to be perceived at the boundaries of phrases rather than at the point where the disruption actually occurred, and that in many cases the bracketing of surface structure can be read directly from the data on perceptual displacement. I think the evidence is rather good that labeled bracketing serves to represent the surface structure that is related to the perceived form of physical signals.

Deep structures are related to surface structures by a sequence of certain formal operations, operations now generally called "grammatical transformations." At the levels of sound, meaning, and syntax, the significant structural features of sentences are highly abstract. For this reason they cannot be recovered by elementary data-processing techniques. This fact lies behind the search for central processes in speech perception and the search for intrinsic, innate structure as the basis for language learning.

How can we represent deep structure? To answer this question we must consider the grammatical transformations that link surface structure to the underlying deep structure that is not always apparent.

Consider, for example, the operations of passivization and interrogation. In the sentences (1) John was examined by the doctor, and (2) did the doctor examine John, both have a deep structure similar to the paraphrase of Sentence 1, (3) the doctor examined John. The same network of grammatical relations determines the semantic interpretation in each case. Thus two of the grammatical transformations of English must be the operations of passivization and interrogation that form such surface structures as Sentences 1 and 2 from a deeper structure which in its essentials also underlies Sentence 3. Since the transformations ultimately produce surface structures, they must produce labeled bracketings. But notice that these operations can apply in sequence: we can form the passive question "was John examined by the doctor" by passivization followed by interrogation. Since the result of passivization is a labeled bracketing, it follows that the interrogative transformation operates on a labeled bracketing and forms a new labeled bracketing. Thus a transformation such as interrogation maps a labeled bracketing into a labeled bracketing.

By similar argument, we can show that all grammatical transformations are structure-dependent mappings of this sort and that the deep structures which underlie all sentences must themselves be labeled bracketings. Of course, the labeled bracketing that constitutes deep structure will in general be quite different from that representing the surface structure of a sentence. Our argument is somewhat oversimplified, but it is roughly correct. When made precise and fully accurate it strongly supports the view that deep structures, like surface structures, are formally to be taken as labeled bracketings, and that grammatical transformations are mappings of such structures onto other similar structures.

Recent studies have sought to explore the ways in which grammatical structure of the sort just described enters into mental operations. Much of this work has been based on a proposal formulated by George Miller as a first approximation, namely, that the amount of memory used to store a sentence should reflect the number of transformations used in deriving it.

For example, H. B. Savin and E. Perchonock investigated this assumption in the following way: they presented to subjects a sentence followed by a sequence of unrelated words. They then determined the number of these unrelated words recalled when the subject attempted to repeat the sentence and the sequence of words. The more words recalled, the less memory used to store the sentence. The fewer words recalled, the more memory used to store the sentence. The results showed a remarkable correlation of amount of memory and number of transformations in certain simple cases. In fact, in their experimental material, shorter sentences with more transformations took up more "space in memory" than longer sentences that involved fewer transformations.

Savin has extended this work and has shown that the effects of deep structure and surface structure can be differentiated by a similar technique. He considered paired sentences with approximately the same deep structure but with one of the pair being more complex in surface structure. He showed that, under the experimental conditions just described, the paired sentences were indistinguishable. But if the sequence of unrelated words precedes, rather than follows, the sentence being tested, then the more complex (in surface structure) of the pair is more difficult to repeat correctly than the simpler member. Savin's very plausible inference is that sentences are coded in memory in terms of deep structure. When the unrelated words precede the test sentence, these words use up a certain amount of short-term memory, and the sentence that is more complex in surface structure cannot be analyzed with the amount of memory remaining. But if the test sentence precedes the unrelated words, it is, once understood, stored in terms of deep structure, which is about the same in both cases. Therefore the same amount of memory remains, in the paired cases, for recall of the following words. This is a beautiful example of the way creative experimental studies can interweave with theoretical work in the study of language and of mental processes.

In speaking of mental processes we have returned to our original problem. We can now see why it is reasonable to maintain that the linguistic evidence supports an "active" theory of acquisition of knowledge. The study of sentences and of speech perception, it seems to me, leads to a perceptual theory of a classical rationalist sort. Representative of this school, among others, were the seventeenth-century Cambridge Platonists, who developed the idea that our perception is guided by notions that originate from the mind and that provide the framework for the interpretation of sensory stimuli. It is not sufficient to suggest that this framework is a store of "neural models" or "schemata" which are in some manner applied to perception (as is postulated in some current theories of perception). We must go well beyond this assumption and return to the view of Wilhelm von Humboldt, who attributed to the mind a system of rules that generates such models and schemata under the stimulation of the senses. The system of rules itself determine the content of the percept that is formed.

We can offer more than this vague and metaphoric account. A generative grammar and an associated theory of speech perception provide a concrete example of the rules that operate and of the mental objects that they construct and manipulate. Physiology cannot yet explain the physical mechanisms that affect these abstract functions. But neither physiology nor psychology provides evidence that calls this account into question or that suggests an alternative. As mentioned earlier, the most exciting current work in the physiology of perception shows that even the peripheral systems analyze stimuli into the complex properties of objects, and that central processes may significantly affect the information transmitted by the receptor organs.

The study of language, it seems to me, offers strong empirical evidence that empiricist theories of learning are quite inadequate. Serious efforts have been made in recent years to develop principles of induction, generalization, and data analysis that would account for knowledge of a language. These efforts have been a total failure. The methods and principles fail not for any superficial reason such as lack of time or data. They fail because they are intrinsically incapable of giving rise to the system of rules that underlies the normal use of language. What evidence is now available supports the view that all human languages share deep-seated properties of organization and structure. These properties—these linguistic universals—can be plausibly assumed to be an innate mental endowment rather than the result of learning. If this is true, then the study of language sheds light on certain long-standing issues in the theory of knowledge. Once again, I see little reason to doubt that what is true of language is true of other forms of human knowledge as well.

There is one further question that might be raised at this point. How does the human mind come to have the innate properties that underlie acquisition of knowledge? Here linguistic evidence obviously provides no information at all. The process by which the human mind has achieved its present state of complexity and its particular form of innate organization are a complete mystery, as much of a mystery as the analogous questions that can be asked about the processes leading to the physical and mental organization of any other complex organism. It is perfectly safe to attribute this to evolution, so long as we bear in mind that there is no substance to this assertion—it amounts to nothing more than the belief that there is surely some naturalistic explanation for these phenomena.

There are, however, important aspects of the problem of language and mind that can be studied sensibly within the limitations of present understanding and technique. I think that, for the moment, the most productive investigations are those dealing with the nature of particular grammars and with the universal conditions met by all human languages. I have tried to suggest how one can move, in successive steps of increasing abstractness, from the study of percepts to the study of grammar and perceptual mechanisms, and from the study of grammar to the study of universal grammar and the mechanisms of learning.

In this area of convergence of linguistics, psychology, and philosophy, we can look forward to much exciting work in coming years.

NEWSPEAK

George Orwell

Newspeak was the official language of Oceania and had been devised to meet the ideological needs of Ingsoc, or English Socialism. In the year 1984 there was not as yet anyone who used Newspeak as his sole means of communication, either in speech or writing. The leading articles in the *Times* were written in it, but this was a tour de force which could only be carried out by a specialist. It was expected that Newspeak would have finally superseded Oldspeak (or Standard English, as we should call it) by about the year 2050. Meanwhile it gained ground steadily, all Party members tending to use Newspeak words and grammatical constructions more and more in their everyday speech. The version in use in 1984, and embodied in the Ninth and Tenth Editions of the Newspeak dictionary, was a provisional one, and contained many superfluous words and archaic formations which were due to be suppressed later. It is with the final, perfected version, as embodied in the Eleventh Edition of the dictionary, that we are concerned here.

The purpose of Newspeak was not only to provide a medium of expression for the world-view and mental habits proper to the devotees of Ingsoc, but to make all other modes of thought impossible. It was intended that when Newspeak had been adopted once and for all and Oldspeak forgotten, a heretical thought—that is, a thought diverging from the principles of Ingsoc—should be literally unthinkable, at least so far as thought is dependent on words. Its vocabulary was so constructed as to give exact and often very subtle expression to every meaning that a Party member could properly wish to express, while excluding all other meanings and also the possibility of arriving at them by indirect methods. This was done partly by the invention of new words, but chiefly by eliminating undesirable words and by stripping such words as remained of unorthodox meanings, and so far as possible of all secondary meanings whatever. To give a single example. The word *free* still existed in Newspeak, but it could only be used in such statements as "This dog is free from lice" or "This field is free from weeds." It could not be used in its old sense of "politically free" or "intellectually free," since political and intellectual freedom no longer existed even as concepts, and were therefore of necessity nameless. Quite apart from the suppression of definitely heretical words, reduction of vocabulary was regarded as an end in itself, and no word that could be dispensed with was allowed to survive. Newspeak was designed not to extend

NEWSPEAK From *Nineteen Eighty-Four* by George Orwell. Copyright, 1949 by Harcourt Brace Jovanovich, Inc. Reprinted by permission of Brandt & Brandt, Miss Sonia Brownell, and Martin Secker & Warburg Ltd.

but to *diminish* the range of thought, and this purpose was indirectly assisted by cutting the choice of words down to a minimum.

Newspeak was founded on the English language as we now know it, though many Newspeak sentences, even when not containing newly created words, would be barely intelligible to an English-speaker of our own day. Newspeak words were divided into three distinct classes, known as the A vocabulary, the B vocabulary (also called compound words), and the C vocabulary. It will be simpler to discuss each class separately, but the grammatical peculiarities of the language can be dealt with in the section devoted to the A vocabulary, since the same rules held good for all three categories.

THE A VOCABULARY

The A vocabulary consisted of the words needed for the business of everyday life—for such things as eating, drinking, working, putting on one's clothes, going up and down stairs, riding in vehicles, gardening, cooking, and the like. It was composed almost entirely of words that we already possess—words like *hit, run, dog, tree, sugar, house, field*—but in comparison with the present-day English vocabulary, their number was extremely small, while their meanings were far more rigidly defined. All ambiguities and shades of meaning had been purged out of them. So far as it could be achieved, a Newspeak word of this class was simply a staccato sound expressing *one* clearly understood concept. It would have been quite impossible to use the A vocabulary for literary purposes or for political or philosophical discussion. It was intended only to express simple, purposive thoughts, usually involving concrete objects or physical actions.

The grammar of Newspeak had two outstanding peculiarities. The first of these was an almost complete interchangeability between different parts of speech. Any word in the language (in principle this applied even to very abstract words such as *if* or *when*) could be used either as verb, noun, adjective, or adverb. Between the verb and the noun form, when they were of the same root, there was never any variation, this rule of itself involving the destruction of many archaic forms. The word *thought,* for example, did not exist in Newspeak. Its place was taken by *think,* which did duty for both noun and verb. No etymological principle was followed here; in some cases it was the original noun that was chosen for retention, in other cases the verb. Even where a noun and verb of kindred meaning were not etymologically connected, one or other of them was frequently suppressed. There was, for example, no such word as *cut,* its meaning being sufficiently covered by the noun-verb *knife.* Adjectives were formed by adding the suffix *-ful* to the noun-verb, and adverbs by adding *-wise.* Thus, for example, *speedful* meant "rapid" and *speedwise* meant "quickly." Certain of our present-day adjectives, such as *good, strong, big, black, soft,* were retained, but their total number was very small. There was little need for them, since almost any adjectival meaning could be arrived at by adding *-ful* to a noun-verb. None of the now-existing adverbs was retained, except for a very few already ending in *-wise;* the *-wise* termination was invariable. The word *well,* for example, was replaced by *goodwise.*

In addition, any word—this again applied in principle to every word in the language—could be negatived by adding the affix *un-,* or could be strengthened by the affix *plus-,* or, for still greater emphasis, *doubleplus-.* Thus, for example, *uncold* meant "warm," while *pluscold* and *double- pluscold* meant, respectively, "very cold" and "superlatively cold." It was also possible, as in present-day English, to modify the meaning of almost any word by prepositional affixes such as *ante-, post-, up-, down-,* etc. By such methods it was found possible to bring about an enormous diminu- tion of vocabulary. Given, for instance, the word *good,* there was no need for such a word as *bad,* since the required meaning was equally well— indeed, better—expressed by *ungood.* All that was necessary, in any case where two words formed a natural pair of opposites, was to decide which of them to suppress. *Dark,* for example, could be replaced by *unlight,* or *light* by *undark,* according to preference.

The second distinguishing mark of Newspeak grammar was its regularity. Subject to a few exceptions which are mentioned below, all inflections followed the same rules. Thus, in all verbs the preterite and the past participle were the same and ended in *-ed.* The preterite of *steal* was *stealed,* the preterite of *think* was *thinked,* and so on throughout the lan- guage, all such forms as *swam, gave, brought, spoke, taken,* etc., being abolished. All plurals were made by adding *-s* or *-es* as the case might be. The plurals of *man, ox, life* were *mans, oxes, lifes.* Comparison of adjec- tives was invariably made by adding *-er, -est* (*good, gooder, goodest*), irregu- lar forms and the *more, most* formation being suppressed.

The only classes of words that were still allowed to inflect irregularly were the pronouns, the relatives, the demonstrative adjectives, and the auxiliary verbs. All of these followed their ancient usage, except that *whom* had been scrapped as unnecessary, and the *shall, should* tenses had been dropped, all their uses being covered by *will* and *would.* There were also certain irregularities in word-formation arising out of the need for rapid and easy speech. A word which was difficult to utter, or was liable to be incorrectly heard, was held to be ipso facto a bad word; occasionally therefore, for the sake of euphony, extra letters were inserted into a word or an archaic formation was retained. But this need made itself felt chiefly in connection with the B vocabulary. *Why* so great an importance was attached to ease of pronunciation will be made clear later in this essay.

THE B VOCABULARY

The B vocabulary consisted of words which had been deliberately con- structed for political purposes: words, that is to say, which not only had in every case a political implication, but were intended to impose a desira- ble mental attitude upon the person using them. Without a full under- standing of the principles of Ingsoc it was difficult to use these words correctly. In some cases they could be translated into Oldspeak, or even into words taken from the A vocabulary, but this usually demanded a long paraphrase and always involved the loss of certain overtones. The B words were a sort of verbal shorthand, often packing whole ranges of ideas into a few syllables, and at the same time more accurate and forcible than ordinary language.

The B words were in all cases compound words.[1] They consisted of two or more words, or portions of words, welded together in an easily pronounceable form. The resulting amalgam was always a noun-verb, and inflected according to the ordinary rules. To take a single example: the word *goodthink*, meaning, very roughly, "orthodoxy," or, if one chose to regard it as a verb, "to think in an orthodox manner." This inflected as follows: noun-verb, *goodthink;* past tense and past participle, *goodthinked;* present participle, *goodthinking;* adjective, *goodthinkful;* adverb, *goodthinkwise;* verbal noun, *goodthinker.*

The B words were not constructed on any etymological plan. The words of which they were made up could be any parts of speech, and could be placed in any order and mutilated in any way which made them easy to pronounce while indicating their derivation. In the word *crimethink* (thoughtcrime), for instance, the *think* came second, whereas in *thinkpol* (Thought Police) it came first, and in the latter word *police* had lost its second syllable. Because of the greater difficulty in securing euphony, irregular formations were commoner in the B vocabulary than in the A vocabulary. For example, the adjectival forms of *Minitrue, Minipax,* and *Miniluv* were, respectively, *Minitruthful, Minipeaceful,* and *Minilovely,* simply because *-trueful, -paxful,* and *-loveful* were slightly awkward to pronounce. In principle, however, all B words could inflect, and all inflected in exactly the same way.

Some of the B words had highly subtilized meanings, barely intelligible to anyone who had not mastered the language as a whole. Consider, for example, such a typical sentence from a *Times* leading article as *Oldthinkers unbellyfeel Ingsoc.* The shortest rendering that one could make of this in Oldspeak would be: "Those whose ideas were formed before the Revolution cannot have a full emotional understanding of the principles of English Socialism." But this is not an adequate translation. To begin with, in order to grasp the full meaning of the Newspeak sentence quoted above, one would have to have a clear idea of what is meant by *Ingsoc.* And, in addition, only a person thoroughly grounded in Ingsoc could appreciate the full force of the word *bellyfeel,* which implied a blind, enthusiastic acceptance difficult to imagine today; or of the word *oldthink,* which was inextricably mixed up with the idea of wickedness and decadence. But the special function of certain Newspeak words, of which *oldthink* was one, was not so much to express meanings as to destroy them. These words, necessarily few in number, had had their meanings extended until they contained within themselves whole batteries of words which, as they were sufficiently covered by a single comprehensive term, could now be scrapped

---

[1] Compound words, such as *speakwrite,* were of course to be found in the A vocabulary, but these were merely convenient abbreviations and had no special ideological color.

and forgotten. The greatest difficulty facing the compilers of the Newspeak dictionary was not to invent new words, but, having invented them, to make sure what they meant: to make sure, that is to say, what ranges of words they canceled by their existence.

As we have already seen in the case of the word *free*, words which had once borne a heretical meaning were sometimes retained for the sake of convenience, but only with the undesirable meanings purged out of them. Countless other words such as *honor, justice, morality, internationalism, democracy, science,* and *religion* had simply ceased to exist. A few blanket words covered them, and, in covering them, abolished them. All words grouping themselves round the concepts of liberty and equality, for instance, were contained in the single word *crimethink*, while all words grouping themselves round the concepts of objectivity and rationalism were contained in the single word *oldthink*. Greater precision would have been dangerous. What was required in a Party member was an outlook similar to that of the ancient Hebrew who knew, without knowing much else, that all nations other than his own worshiped "false gods." He did not need to know that these gods were called Baal, Osiris, Moloch, Ashtaroth, and the like; probably the less he knew about them the better for his orthodoxy. He knew Jehovah and the commandments of Jehovah; he knew, therefore, that all gods with other names or other attributes were false gods. In somewhat the same way, the Party member knew what constituted right conduct, and in exceedingly vague, generalized terms he knew what kinds of departure from it were possible. His sexual life, for example, was entirely regulated by the two Newspeak words *sexcrime* (sexual immortality) and *goodsex* (chastity). *Sexcrime* covered all sexual misdeeds whatever. It covered fornication, adultery, homosexuality, and other perversions, and, in addition, normal intercourse practiced for its own sake. There was no need to enumerate them separately, since they were all equally culpable, and, in principle, all punishable by death. In the C vocabulary, which consisted of scientific and technical words, it might be necessary to give specialized names to certain sexual aberrations, but the ordinary citizen had no need of them. He knew what was meant by *goodsex*—that is to say, normal intercourse between man and wife, for the sole purpose of begetting children, and without physical pleasure on the part of the woman; all else was *sexcrime*. In Newspeak it was seldom possible to follow a heretical thought further than the perception that it *was* heretical; beyond that point the necessary words were nonexistent.

No word in the B vocabulary was ideologically neutral. A great many were euphemisms. Such words, for instance, as *joycamp* (forced-labor camp) or *Minipax* (Ministry of Peace, i.e., Ministry of War) meant almost the exact opposite of what they appeared to mean. Some words, on the other hand, displayed a frank and contemptuous understanding of the real nature of Oceanic society. An example was *prolefeed*, meaning the rubbishy entertainment and spurious news which the Party handed out to the masses. Other words, again, were ambivalent, having the connotation "good" when applied to the Party and "bad" when applied to its enemies. But in addition there were great numbers of words which at first sight appeared to be mere abbreviations and which derived their ideological color not from their meaning but from their structure.

So far as it could be contrived, everything that had or might have political significance of any kind was fitted into the B vocabulary. The name of every organization, or body of people, or doctrine, or country, or institution, or public building, was invariably cut down into the familiar shape; that is, a single easily pronounced word with the smallest number of syllables that would preserve the original derivation. In the Ministry of Truth, for example, the Records Department, in which Winston Smith worked, was called *Recdep,* the Fiction Department was called *Ficdep,* the Teleprograms Department was called *Teledep,* and so on. This was not done solely with the object of saving time. Even in the early decades of the twentieth century, telescoped words and phrases had been one of the characteristic features of political language; and it had been noticed that the tendency to use abbreviations of this kind was most marked in totalitarian countries and totalitarian organizations. Examples were such words as *Nazi, Gestapo, Comintern, Inprecorr, Agitprop.* In the beginning the practice had been adopted as it were instinctively, but in Newspeak it was used with a conscious purpose. It was perceived that in thus abbreviating a name one narrowed and subtly altered its meaning, by cutting out most of the associations that would otherwise cling to it. The words *Communist International,* for instance, call up a composite picture of universal human brotherhood, red flags, barricades, Karl Marx, and the Paris Commune. The word *Comintern,* on the other hand, suggests merely a tightly knit organization and a well-defined body of doctrine. It refers to something almost as easily recognized, and as limited in purpose, as a chair or a table. *Comintern* is a word that can be uttered almost without taking thought, whereas *Communist International* is a phrase over which one is obliged to linger at least momentarily. In the same way, the associations called up by a word like *Minitrue* are fewer and more controllable than those called up by *Ministry of Truth.* This accounted not only for the habit of abbreviating whenever possible, but also for the almost exaggerated care that was taken to make every word easily pronounceable.

In Newspeak, euphony outweighed every consideration other than exactitude of meaning. Regularity of grammar was always sacrificed to it when it seemed necessary. And rightly so, since what was required, above all for political purposes, were short clipped words of unmistakable meaning which could be uttered rapidly and which roused the minimum of echoes in the speaker's mind. The words of the B vocabulary even gained in force from the fact that nearly all of them were very much alike. Almost invariably these words—*goodthink, Minipax, prolefeed, sexcrime, joycamp, Ingsoc, bellyfeel, thinkpol,* and countless others—were words of two or three syllables, with the stress distributed equally between the first syllable and the last. The use of them encouraged a gabbling style of speech, at once staccato and monotonous. And this was exactly what was aimed at. The intention was to make speech, and especially speech on any subject

not ideologically neutral, as nearly as possible independent of consciousness. For the purposes of everyday life it was no doubt necessary, or sometimes necessary, to reflect before speaking, but a Party member called upon
to make a political or ethical judgment should be able to spray forth the
correct opinions as automatically as a machine gun spraying forth bullets.
His training fitted him to do this, the language gave him an almost fool-
proof instrument, and the texture of the words, with their harsh sound
and a certain willful ugliness which was in accord with the spirit of Ingsoc,
assisted the process still further.

So did the fact of having very few words to choose from. Relative to our
own, the Newspeak vocabulary was tiny, and new ways of reducing it were
constantly being devised. Newspeak, indeed, differed from almost all other
languages in that its vocabulary grew smaller instead of larger every year.
Each reduction was a gain, since the smaller the area of choice, the smaller
the temptation to take thought. Ultimately it was hoped to make articulate
speech issue from the larynx without involving the higher brain centers
at all. This aim was frankly admitted in the Newspeak word *duckspeak*,
meaning "to quack like a duck." Like various other words in the B vocabulary, *duckspeak* was ambivalent in meaning. Provided that the opinions
which were quacked out were orthodox ones, it implied nothing but praise,
and when the *Times* referred to one of the orators of the Party as a *double-
plusgood duckspeaker* it was paying a warm and valued compliment.

THE C VOCABULARY

The C vocabulary was supplementary to the others and consisted entirely
of scientific and technical terms. These resembled the scientific terms in
use today, and were constructed from the same roots, but the usual care
was taken to define them rigidly and strip them of undesirable meanings.
They followed the same grammatical rules as the words in the other two
vocabularies. Very few of the C words had any currency either in everyday
speech or in political speech. Any scientific worker or technician could
find all the words he needed in the list devoted to his own speciality, but
he seldom had more than a smattering of the words occurring in the other
lists. Only a very few words were common to all lists, and there was no
vocabulary expressing the function of Science as a habit of mind, or a
method of thought, irrespective of its particular branches. There was,
indeed, no word for "Science," any meaning that it could possibly bear
being already sufficiently covered by the word *Ingsoc*.

From the foregoing account it will be seen that in Newspeak the expression of unorthodox opinions, above a very low level, was well-nigh impossible. It was of course possible to utter heresies of a very crude kind, a
species of blasphemy. It would have been possible, for example, to say
Big Brother is ungood. But this statement, which to an orthodox ear
merely conveyed a self-evident absurdity, could not have been sustained
by reasoned argument, because the necessary words were not available.

Ideas inimical to Ingsoc could only be entertained in a vague wordless form, and could only be named in very broad terms which lumped together and condemned whole groups of heresies without defining them in doing so. One could, in fact, only use Newspeak for unorthodox purposes by illegitimately translating some of the words back into Oldspeak. For example, *All mans are equal* was a possible Newspeak sentence, but only in the same sense in which *All men are redhaired* is a possible Oldspeak sentence. It did not contain a grammatical error, but it expressed a palpable untruth, i.e., that all men are of equal size, weight, or strength. The concept of political equality no longer existed, and this secondary meaning had accordingly been purged out of the word *equal*. In 1984, when Oldspeak was still the normal means of communication, the danger theoretically existed that in using Newspeak words one might remember their original meanings. In practice it was not difficult for any person well grounded in *doublethink* to avoid doing this, but within a couple of generations even the possibility of such a lapse would have vanished. A person growing up with Newspeak as his sole language would no more know that *equal* had once had the secondary meaning of "politically equal," or that *free* had once meant "intellectually free," than, for instance, a person who had never heard of chess would be aware of the secondary meanings attaching to *queen* and *rook*. There would be many crimes and errors which it would be beyond his power to commit, simply because they were nameless and therefore unimaginable. And it was to be foreseen that with the passage of time the distinguishing characteristics of Newspeak would become more and more pronounced—its words growing fewer and fewer, their meanings more and more rigid, and the chance of putting them to improper uses always diminishing.

When Oldspeak had been once and for all superseded, the last link with the past would have been severed. History had already been rewritten, but fragments of the literature of the past survived here and there, imperfectly censored, and so long as one retained one's knowledge of Oldspeak it was possible to read them. In the future such fragments, even if they chanced to survive, would be unintelligible and untranslatable. It was impossible to translate any passage of Oldspeak into Newspeak unless it either referred to some technical process or some very simple everyday action, or was already orthodox (*goodthinkful* would be the Newspeak expression) in tendency. In practice this meant that no book written before approximately 1960 could be translated as a whole. Prerevolutionary literature could only be subjected to ideological translation—that is, alteration in sense as well as language. Take for example the well-known passage from the Declaration of Independence:

We hold these truths to be self-evident, that all men are created equal, that they are endowed by their Creator with certain inalienable rights, that among these are life, liberty and the pursuit of happiness. That to secure these rights, Governments are instituted among men, deriving their powers from the consent of the governed.

That whenever any form of Government becomes destructive of those ends, it is the right of the People to alter or abolish it, and to institute new Government . . .

It would have been quite impossible to render this into Newspeak while keeping to the sense of the original. The nearest one could come to doing so would be to swallow the whole passage up in the single word *crimethink*. A full translation could only be an ideological translation, whereby Jefferson's words would be changed into a panegyric on absolute government.

A good deal of the literature of the past was, indeed, already being transformed in this way. Considerations of prestige made it desirable to preserve the memory of certain historical figures, while at the same time bringing their achievements into line with the philosophy of Ingsoc. Various writers, such as Shakespeare, Milton, Swift, Byron, Dickens, and some others were therefore in process of translation; when the task had been completed, their original writings, with all else that survived of the literature of the past, would be destroyed. These translations were a slow and difficult business, and it was not expected that they would be finished before the first or second decade of the twenty-first century. There were also large quantities of merely utilitarian literature—indispensable technical manuals and the like—that had to be treated in the same way. It was chiefly in order to allow time for the preliminary work of translation that the final adoption of Newspeak had been fixed for so late a date as 2050.

ON LANGUAGE AND CULTURE

William F. Whyte
and Robert R. Braun

Our introduction to this study came about through an apparent mistranslation of an item in a questionnaire. The English statement was, "Some are born to lead and others to follow." The bilingual secretary had given this translation: *Unos han nacido para mandar y otros para obedecer.*

Whyte objected, "That means, 'Some are born to command and others to obey.'" She agreed that he was right but insisted that she was right also. In other words, "lead" or "command" can both be rendered by the verb *mandar,* and, likewise, "follow" and "obey" can both be rendered by *obedecer.*

There is an important difference between the words in each pair in

ON LANGUAGE AND CULTURE Reprinted from Howard S. Becker, Blanche Geer, David Riesman, and Robert S. Weiss, editors, *Institutions and the Person* (Chicago: Aldine Publishing Company, 1968); copyright © 1968 by Howard S. Becker, Blanche Geer, David Riesman, and Robert S. Weiss. This selection has been slightly changed from the original with permission of the authors.

English: one suggests voluntarism; the other suggests coercion. It is significant that Spanish provides no neat and economical way for making
this distinction.

In Spanish culture, *mandar* conveys the sense of sending someone somewhere to do something while the commander stays behind. An indication
of this meaning is that *mandar* is also used for sending physical objects:
El manda un paquete a su esposa (He is sending a package to his wife).
In consequence, the counterpart of *mandar* is necessarily *obedecer,* with
the original meaning being "to obey." If the commander stays behind, it
is awkward to think of his people following him.

In Spanish a politician *arrastra a la muchedumbre* (carries away the
crowds) and *lleva a su partido a la victoria* (takes his party to victory).
Guiar (to guide) cannot be used in this sense, since it is an unheroic word
that does not touch the imagination. *Guiar* is only used in connection with
school children, blind people, tourists, and vehicles.

While origins of new words must remain speculative, we think we can
trace the beginning of change to the era of *Il Duce* and *Der Führer,* which
dramatized the need to have a way to refer to "the leader." In this period,
newspapermen began to use the term *líder,* which is clearly a translitera-
tion and is pronounced approximately the same as "leader." Under the
post–World War II impact of North American culture, with its emphasis
upon enlightened leadership, conference leadership seminars, and the exercise of managerial leadership, the word *liderazgo* (leadership) was added.

Thus the gap for "voluntaristic leadership" in Spanish has been partly
filled in through the borrowing of nouns (but not verbs) from English.
However, the adoption of the word *líder* often leads to a confusion with
the older Spanish words *lidia* (struggle—but mainly used for bullfights)
and *lidiar* (to struggle). We hear an executive say, *"Estoy lidiando con mi
sindicato"* (I am struggling with the union in my company). The similarity
between *líder* and *lidiar,* added to the difficulties the inexperienced executive faces in coping with labor relations and production, banking, financial,
or sales problems, seems to have given rise to the revealing mental attitude
according to which a *líder* is supposed to *lidiar*—whether with the union
or with other problems. This seems to reflect the difference between the
two cultures. "To lead" conveys the impression of voluntary cooperation,
whereas *lidiar* suggests a long drawn out contest of opposing wills and skills.

Let us approach the problem through the Spanish word *caudillo,* which
has been attached to many political leaders, most especially to those who
have taken power by force. One dictionary (Williams) gives these meanings: "chief, leader; military leader, chieftain, *caudillo,* head of state." Another (Velázquez) gives a briefer definition: "commander of an armed
troop; chief, leader or director of a company." Neither of these sets of definitions seems to get at the essence of the word.

How would we express the concept in English? "Charismatic leader"?
But that term is more sociologese than English, and, furthermore, it leaves
out an important element. The word *caudillo* conveys a sense of highly
personal power: the individual gives off some kind of aura that convinces

his followers that he possesses the mystical element of power. He *imposes* his will on his followers, and they feel compelled to follow him. If that seems like a clumsy and long winded definition, we can only plead that the problem is inherent in *caudillo,* which defies translation into English.

The English-speaking student of management first becomes aware of another language-culture problem when he hears references to *el Chairman.* The dictionary translates "chairman" as *presidente.* But *presidente* is, of course, also used to mean "president." In other words, Spanish provides no economical way of distinguishing between a chief executive officer and a person who, while holding a position of prestige and being responsible for the performance of the group, is not able to give orders. In the U. S. world of industry, the chairman of the board does indeed enjoy a much more powerful position in relation to his board members than does the chairman of some civic committee. However, if the chairman is indeed expected to run the show, he is generally given the title "Chairman of the Board and Chief Executive Officer."

Let us also consider the word *patrón.* If we limit ourselves only to words referring to human beings, we find in the dictionary the following meanings: "sponsor, protector; patron saint, patron; landlord; owner, master; boss, foreman; host, skipper (of a boat)." Here we find a linking of a religious symbol (the patron saint) and authority symbols, with a single word expressing what are in English a number of quite different positions. The paternalistic attitude that characterized Latin American employers' associations in their beginnings is still reflected, for example, in the official title of the *Confederación Patronal de la Republica Mexicana.*

Let us seek to put these fragments in some sort of coherent pattern. The difficulty we have in Spanish in distinguishing between voluntaristic and coercive leadership suggests the much greater emphasis upon formal authority that we observe in Spanish and Latin American societies. Our problem with *caudillo* reflects the greater Latin American preoccupation with power —with the "strong man." The problems we have with *patrón* and with *presidente* also reflect this pre-occupation with formal authority, but there is an additional element involved. In Latin American culture, reflecting a society that has been more rigidly stratified than ours, there tends to be less role differentiation in leadership terminology. Thus we can link together concepts so distinct (to us) as an executive officer and a discussion leader, or a top-management man and a low-level supervisor.

THE LANGUAGE OF CONFLICT RESOLUTION

In industrial relations in the United States, union and management are supposed to reach agreement by "discussing" their differences and by "negotiating." In the process, they are expected to manifest sentiments of "mutual respect." In the Peruvian context, the words in quotation marks in the last two sentences all present problems. In the first place, *respeto* does not convey a sense of mutuality. It is generally used to describe the feelings of a subordinate toward someone of superior status.

The student of Spanish must learn not to invite Latin Americans to *discutir* something with him. While *discutir* does mean "to discuss," it can also mean "to debate." The foreigner can avoid unfriendly implications if he simply invites people to "talk about" a given subject with him. The dictionary translates "to negotiate" as *negociar*, but in Peru *negociar* conveys the implication of a stronger individual or organization taking advantage of a weaker one. Furthermore, the past participle, *negociado*, has the definite connotation of a shady deal, involving graft or other illicit procedures. No such meanings are implied in U. S. usage. These differences suggest that a U. S. diplomat may unwittingly project the wrong images when he proposes to *negociar* with Latin Americans.

It is noteworthy that Peruvian newspapers rarely use the words *negociar* or *negociaciones* to refer to collective bargaining. Instead, they refer to *trato directo*: literally, "direct dealings" between the parties. In speech, we find the word *directo* emphasized, which tells us that in the past it has been customary to resolve conflicts through recourse to a third party more powerful than union or management—a point which we shall explore more fully later.

WORK ACTIVITIES

Let us now turn to the world of work.

We first note that types of work are more sharply categorized in Spanish than in English. An *obrero* is a man who works with his hands. An *empleado* is a man who does the cleaner work with papers and with the use of his mind. The clear implication is that the *obrero* does not use his brains.

This linguistic distinction is paralleled in the social structure of work. The distinctions go well beyond the work place. Peru has one social security system for *obreros*, a different one for *empleados*. The social security system for *empleados* has its hospital, the social security system for *obreros* has a different hospital.

In English, we find it much more difficult to make the distinctions that are so neatly and sharply made in Spanish. "Employees" sounds like a more refined term than "workers," and yet either term can be used to refer to the total body of non-supervisory personnel of an organization. Furthermore, we never hear anyone speak of "our employees and our workers," to express the *empleado-obrero* distinction.

The most common way of making the social distinction is to speak of "white-collar workers" and "blue-collar workers." There are two points to be made about this way of expressing the difference. In the first place, it is far more cumbersome than the Spanish, using six words, while the Spanish can put the idea into two. In the second place, we find a contrast between the apparently superficial and the assumedly intrinsic aspects of these distinctions. The American phraseology suggests a social distinction that is subject to change if people put on different clothes. The implication in Spanish is that there is a basic distinction in the quality of the human beings involved.

This is not to say that in the United States there are no social distinctions involved in categories such as "blue-collar worker" and "white-collar worker." Any textbook in industrial sociology will devote at least a few paragraphs to the status symbols surrounding the work place. The point is that the distinction is not nearly as sharp nor as clearly defined as it is in Latin American culture. Nor do we find attached to manual labor the stigma that is so evident in Peru. This is observed not only in the work place; it becomes particularly evident in the things men do away from the job. A college professor in the United States who has painted his house or has worked in the garden to raise vegetables for the family table would not hesitate to acknowledge these activities. In fact, he might even boast about them to friends and acquaintances. Such behavior just could not be expected to occur in Peru. Nor do Peruvian stores feature the "do-it-yourself" kits so common in the United States. If a Peruvian had enough money to buy such a kit, he would be middle-class and would not do it himself.

On reading a Lima newspaper one day, we came across the statement that there is no exact Spanish equivalent for the German word *gründlichkeit*. Is there an exact English equivalent for this word? "Thoroughness" seems to fit perfectly. The word involves three ideas: (1) attention to detail, (2) high standards, and (3) the capacity for getting things done. Why no such word in Spanish? Is "thoroughness" not an important virtue in Latin culture?

Another reflection of this underlying problem is found in the words *serio* and *seriedad*. The dictionary provides no clue to the problem; we find the straightforward translations are "serious" and "seriousness." The student may be puzzled when he hears that so-and-so is *un hombre serio*. "A serious man"? The phrase tells nothing about a man's sense of humor or the expression on his face. What is being said is that the man is not fooling around; he is working in concentrated fashion at whatever he is engaged in.

We recently asked a Peruvian friend why he preferred one internal Peruvian airline to the other. He replied, *"Más seriedad."* "More seriousness"? That hardly makes sense in English. What he was saying was that the airline of his preference tended to its business more effectively.

Can we express these concepts economically in English? The word "businesslike" seems close to this meaning of *serio,* but its use tends to be limited to commercial, industrial, and bureaucratic activities. Furthermore, it refers to the impression that a man gives in going about his work, whereas *serio* tells us something important about his motivation. There is the same difficulty with the words "efficient" and "efficiency": they tell about the quality of the performer or the performance, but not about the attitude of the individual toward his work.

We can say that Jones is "a serious artist" to distinguish him from Smith, who is a "Sunday painter," but if we say, "Jones is a serious man," we will only confuse our listeners. Why do we have such a problem with this idea? We suggest that the explanation involves the implicit assumptions of U. S. culture. We assume that a man is just naturally serious about his work, and a business organization is obviously serious about its activities, so why state the obvious? No such presumption is made in Peru. We often hear about people in positions both high and low in the society who are not giving very serious attention to the jobs they are supposed to be carrying out. Therefore it seems important to state not only what activity a man is carrying out but whether or not he is *serio* about it.

In Peru the seriousness of a man's demeanor is thought to be related to the seriousness of his purpose. There is no such presumption in the United States. In fact, we often find men talking in a light and casual manner about matters that are obviously of deep concern to them. (Perhaps this facility for mixing the light with the heavy makes it easier for North Americans to take criticism and confront critics than it is for our Latin American colleagues.)

Peruvians are puzzled, if not offended, when the speaker prefaces his remarks with a joke, as is customary in the United States. To appear *serio* in demeanor is not necessarily accepted as the equivalent of being *serio* in thoughts and actions, but to speak in a light manner on a heavy topic raises questions about a man's *seriedad*.

WORDS: INSTRUMENTAL OR EXPRESSIVE?

We have concentrated so far upon problems of meaning of particular words. We should also recognize that words *in general* are used in rather different ways in our two cultures. Peruvians and Spanish speakers generally have much more of a feeling about the importance of their language itself and of the particular words they use than do North American English-speakers.

In the United States, words are looked upon as instrumental, of value insofar as they enable one to get things done. We say, "Actions speak louder than words." We celebrate the "strong, silent man" and speak approvingly of the "man of few words," as if there were some necessary connection between strength and silence. We tell people, "Don't waste words" or "Save your breath," suggesting that there is no point in speaking unless it advances us toward some practical objective.

Children learn to say, "Sticks and stones can break my bones, but names can never hurt me." Of course, words do hurt in the United States, but, except under the most extreme provocation, it is expected that the man who is injured by the words will simply disregard the incident.

In Peru words are not considered simply instruments toward reaching practical objectives, nor can they be taken lightly on any other grounds. It is significant that the sticks-and-stones saying has no counterpart in Latin America. Words carry more weight and are fraught with more perils.

Offensive words cannot simply be ignored. A gentleman must rise to defend his honor. Although duels were outlawed in Peru many years ago, the papers still occasionally report a challenge to a duel. In case of such a challenge, both parties appoint seconds who seek to negotiate in the hope of being able to show that the incident was based on some kind of misunderstanding. In this way, most challenges are resolved without a duel, but duels sometimes do take place. Several years ago, Fernando Belaúnde Terry (now President) fought a duel with sabers against a prominent politician of an opposing party. We have the impression that the duel contributed to the favorable public image of each man. Certainly the political fortunes of both of them have prospered impressively since that event.

An incident in a factory illustrates the weight of words in Peru. The factory manager said that he had for some time been wanting to get rid of a certain local union leader. How was he finally successful? He provoked an argument with the man so that the union leader lost his temper and accused the manager of a *falta de dignidad* (lack of honor). The manager immediately replied that the union leader with these words had committed what the law considers a *falta grave* (serious offense) and was therefore discharged.

In another Peruvian case, the North American owner of a small factory told about the problems he was having with a union officer in his plant. His troubles with the man had culminated in the following incident: before a crowd of workers, the union leader pulled a *management* notice from the *management* bulletin board, ripped it into pieces, threw the pieces on the floor, and stamped on them. Earlier, when the owner's pregnant wife was walking through the plant, the union leader had made an indelicate joke about her to the other workers. When the owner heard of this from his wife and from one of the workers, he said, "Now, if only one or two of those workers would be willing to testify in the Ministry as to what that union man said, I would have no problem. I could fire him in a minute."

How would these two cases be regarded by a U. S. arbitrator? The *words* concerning the owner's wife would be regarded as an unfortunate breach of etiquette that has nothing to do with the collective bargaining relationship and therefore does not justify institutional sanctions. The *actions* of the union leader in publicly defying management authority would call for the imposition of heavy penalties.

Such differences in the weight of words provide one clue as to why it has proved easier to maintain free speech in the United States and Britain than in Latin America. Those who regard words as relatively light and inconsequential should find it easier to maintain free expression than those who see words as heavy and potentially punishing.

If words are indeed such dangerous elements, how can Peruvians avoid getting into conflicts all the time? The answer seems to be that the culture favors the avoidance of direct face-to-face expressions of disagreement. North Americans have the rather naive idea that almost any conflict can be resolved if the parties will just come together and thrash things out, face-to-face. Peruvians have no such idea of the value of personal confrontation. In their culture, the emphasis is on avoiding direct expressions of interpersonal conflict.

This same tendency to avoid open disagreement is found in cases when one Peruvian asks another to do something for him. It somehow does not seem quite appropriate to refuse outright. The appropriate response is one or another form of "yes"—but then often the thing does not get done.

In Peru the word is used so seldom that we are startled when we hear somebody say "no." One attuned to the culture learns not to take "yes" seriously. You cannot judge by the words alone; you must learn to listen for the melody. In other words, you look and listen for cues surrounding the word "yes" in the current situation and in the past behavior of the speaker in order to predict what he is likely to do. While a well attuned Peruvian is far better at divining the meaning of "yes" than an outsider, even Peruvians have a good deal of trouble judging what a man will do on the basis of what he says. In part, this grows out of the cultural inhibition against saying "no." If a man cannot say "no," then the word "yes" loses its meaning. Under these circumstances the predictability that is so important for organizational life is difficult to achieve.

ON THE RELATIONSHIP BETWEEN LANGUAGE AND CULTURE

We have been illustrating various aspects of the relationship between language and culture. Can we put our conclusions in more general form?

While words referring to physical objects may be said to have an absolute meaning, in the sense that all speakers would identify a given word with the same object, such is not the case with words and phrases referring to the interactions and activities of men. The pattern of these interactions and activities will tend to shape the meaning of the words used to describe them.

If two cultures show marked differences at certain points, then we can expect to have difficulty in finding exact translations at these points. Cultures, of course, also influence the types of discourse that are used and found acceptable.

From this it follows that as a culture changes we can expect to find changes in the meanings of words and phrases and changes in the style of discourse. Looking backward, we can note such changes. Looking forward, if we can predict the course of cultural change, we should also be able to predict the adaptations that will take place in language meanings and usage.

While we can expect cultural changes to produce changes in meanings of words, the differential weight of words may be a matter that rests at a deeper cultural level, where adjustments will not come so rapidly.

To get along in a foreign country, it is generally recognized that one must learn the language *and* the culture. This way of putting it suggests that these are two separate tasks. Our experience indicates that it is more profitable to consider this one task. As one learns the language, he should be viewing the culture through his observations of language usage. As he learns the culture, he should develop a framework that enables him to communicate more effectively to native speakers and to interpret more skillfully what they are saying to him.

BOTTOM'S DREAM:
The Likeness of Poems and Jokes

Howard Nemerov

The poetic attempt to say the world, to name it rightly, is perhaps a matter altogether too mysterious to be talked about. When someone, behaving "poetically," looks into the landscape and tries to speak it, this mystery turns inward and takes the form of an anxious searching and striving, until (sometimes) the mind by some wild reach having an evident relation with insanity produces a phrase, and this phrase—somehow—*expresses* . . . whereupon some quiet click of accurate conjunction tells us that what has happened is somehow reasonable.

Yet this moment of expressiveness itself occurs at a crossing point, and tells us that something in language is not linguistic, that something in reason is not reasonable. It speaks of a relation between inside and outside, an identity between inside and outside, but this relation, this identity, is itself unspeakable:

> Suddenly I saw the cold and rook-delighting heaven. . . .

That has no meaning, strictly, that can be expressed otherwise, or translated. How, then, to someone who for a long time entertains the phrase as a sort of empty and objectless talisman, a piece of jade turned over in the hand, does it—suddenly, as the poet says—come to identify one alone sort of weather, one alone sort of poetry, that quality the poet wanted, he said elsewhere, of "cold light and tumbling clouds"?

Echo answers. Which is not to say that nothing answers, for it may be by a species of radar that intelligence moves through the world. We might say of expressiveness itself, of the irreducible phrase, that first it is, and then it finds a meaning in the world. Or else: Whatever the mind invents, it also discovers. Or again: Whatever is revealed, in poetry, plays at being revealed.

It is that element of play that I wish to talk about as an essentially poetic quality. This quality, I think, somehow exists in all language, in language considered as an unstable fusion of practicality and dream, in language which is in so large part an instrument for repeating, but in some small part an instrument for inventing and discovering what is invented—which is

BOTTOM'S DREAM: THE LIKENESS OF POEMS AND JOKES From *The Virginia Quarterly Review*, Vol. 42, No. 4 (Autumn 1966); Reprinted by permission of the author.

only to say, perhaps, that epic poems and systems of theology are all written by people who, whatever their talents, could not have been the first to say "cat," because it had already been said for them.

Though this poetic quality exists in all language, it will most often and most easily be visible in expressions which time or custom has set free from the urgencies of exhortation and the immediate claims of life: inscriptions on tombs, the proud dominations of antiquity, Ozymandias in his desert—surely the superfluity I mean has its relations equally with the ideal and the idea of death. Yet it may as certainly be identified in the most trival examples. If you remove, say, the headline from an advertisement and let it dry in the sun until it shrivels out of context, it will grow other and rather surprising relations:

> . . . new shades of youth. . . .

Its valency, standing thus alone, is other than what it is when you put it back in its intentional place as an incitement to buy something called Ogilvie Creme Hair Color Foam. The tonality of *shades,* for instance, is more Stygian.

So in seeking to identify, if possible, something of the quality of expressiveness called "poetic" you might start, not with the sublime, but down at the humble end of the scale, with such things as that, with appearances of this quality in misprints, newspaper items, jokes . . . working your way up in Horatio Alger style to see how far your descriptions will take you (whether in the end you will marry Sophia, holy wisdom, the boss's daughter). In doing this we shall rely on the help of Freud—in some particulars on his fine joke book, *Wit and Its Relation to the Unconscious,* and in general on his attempt to demonstrate systematically how mental life is continuous with itself in all its manifestations, from slips of the tongue to systems of philosophy and the visions of religion.

Also of Shakespeare, who in giving a title to these remarks gives also an instance of the quality we are trying to say something about. When Nick Bottom wakes in the forest from the true dream in which he wore an ass's head and was adored by Titania, he speaks of what has happened in language whose comic effect has much to do with its tone of reverence, its being so full of garbles from scripture, and so on; and he says:

> It shall be called Bottom's Dream, because it hath no bottom.

Probably there can be no better definition of poetry—no better definition, I am tempted to say, of anything that matters to us—though all the same it is clearly better for Bottom than for the rest of us.

Something of the quality I mean may be discovered in misprints. The mathematical probability must be quite large that any misprint, such as the omission or addition or substitution of a single letter, will produce merely a moment of nonsense in the result, and indeed that happens often enough. But given this preponderant possibility it is surprising to notice how often misprints make a curious other sense, and surprising, too, how economically such transformations may be effected. Here are a few examples:

a. The Russians dredging what will be "the largest man-maid lake in the world." Nearly nonsense, and not quite; though not quite witty, either. Between man and lake the idea of mixed bathing has intervened to pervert the spelling by the nicest economy so that it gives another sense which hovers between the appropriate and the absurd; perhaps this secondary sense is not quite strong enough, and that may have to do with the fact that we cannot hear the difference but have to see it or spell it.

b. A reviewer of one of Kinsey's reports was made to say, "The sexual urge in females is demonstarted by". . . . Who would bother reading the rest of the sentence? Not only does "demonstarted" make sense instead of nonsense; it makes a sense which is as it were subversively appropriate to the serious discussion which was supposed to be going on.

c. A girl escaping from East Berlin "swam the icy river to be with her finance in the West." One imagines a Communist reading this with deepest satisfaction, since it confirms what he has always believed about love and money in the West. And the compositor was so taken with his invention that he used it again in the next sentence, while giving the finance's name. One observes, too, that the pertness of the criticism is enhanced by the somewhat ballad-like romance of the subject.

The effect common to all three examples is that one reality gives place to another, and a tension is revealed between them: the world of information and, we might say, the symbolic world, reflect one another in this tension. Moreover, the reality revealed by inadvertence is in each instance subversive of the reality intended; this is not so surprising in the first example, since we generally expect the sexual to be the hidden reality in statements, as it is in the second and third, where sexual and marital concerns themselves give way to themes of deeper mystery and deeper obsession still, theology of sorts, and money.

As to the relation of all this with the quality of the poetic, which many have called "vision," it is the first effect of Freud's demonstrations, on errors, dreams, jokes, to show that vision begins with a fault in this world's smooth façade.

The examination now of a few rather more complicated and elaborated examples will perhaps enable us to go further in our description of this quality and its mechanisms.

In *A Handbook of Arms and Armor,* by Bashford Dean, I read that Japanese feudal warfare was especially rough on horses because they were not armored; there followed this sentence: "Not until the Tokugawa period, when warfare disappeared, was the horse given adequate armor."

This statement takes the mind away from arms and armor, but not entirely away. It combines with the subject another subject, of symbolic reflexions and resonances, in which the sentence bears a sadly ironic truth (everything is always too late) without in any way losing its pleasant and somehow Oriental flavor of bland paradox calmly mastered (as in the report of an English-language Japanese newspaper, that "the entire aircrew climbed out on the wing of the burning plane and parachuted safely to their death"). It would be possible, no doubt, to appreciate intellectually the wit of the proposition alone, dismissing all that was abstract as irrelevant; but that would be to lose the nice particularity of "the Tokugawa period," the elegant *coup de grâce* given in "adequate," and the fine intricate play of sounds (*r* and *w* especially) and internal rimes (like that between "period" and "disappeared") which stitches the words together and gives decisive character to the entire statement.

The second example is an AP dispatch reporting that a former lawyer of Al Capone's is convicted of income tax evasion. "I have in mind that you've suffered enough," said the judge, who also said, "Ten years ago . . . you were a well-to-do man. Now you're a man without means because of the debts you incurred in paying off the taxes. You've lost your law practice. This is a strong reminder that the power to tax is the power to destroy."

Something here, maybe the biblical austerity of the last sentence especially, strikes me as bearing the quality of expressiveness I am after; something both tragic and funny, featured by the judge's deadpan style—is he aware, right there, of the comparison implied between gangsters and governments?—and the whole rather complicated situation of the feelings wants only a touch of arrangement, a little bit of pointing, to be brought out. I imagine the former lawyer brooding on what has been said to him:

> Ten years ago, I was a well-to-do man,
> Now I am a man without means.
> I have received
> The strong reminder.
> The power to tax is the power to destroy.

> The lesson of the State's Do What You Can,
> That is what the law means
> Though we are deceived,
> O strong reminder
> Of Alcatraz, my master, my joy.

> Out here beyond the average life span
> The end no longer means
> What it did. Reprieved
> By the strong reminder,
> I get up the ante and go to destroy.

My last example is also a news item, reporting that a jet plane was shot down by its own gunfire. It is probably interesting enough to know that we live in a world in which this has become possible, but the thing sticks in the mind as well as the throat. An admiral and what the *Times* called "other Navy experts" explain: "The shells left the cannon traveling 1,500 feet a second faster than the airplane. After entering their trajectory they immediately began to slow down and fall because of air resistance and gravity. Meanwhile, [the pilot], going into a steeper dive, began a short cut across the shells' curved course. About two or three miles from the point at which the shells were fired, they reached the same point the plane had achieved. . . ."

This may already be a poem, finished and impossible to meddle with, though the newspaper's account is a little dispersed on the page for my entire satisfaction, and stuffed with irrelevant details. All the same, the relations expressed between murder and suicide are splendidly and as it were secretly there: "a short cut across the shells' curved course" is in itself a fine piece of virtuosity, giving the truth of the human situation with a decisiveness not so easily matched in poetry, though surpassed in this of John Webster: "Like diamonds we are cut with our own dust."

So it seems that this episode of the jet shot down by its own gunfire may be only the last playable variation on a theme poets have constantly handled; the particular comparison which comes to mind is with Hardy's "The Convergence of the Twain (Lines on the loss of the *Titanic*)" where the likeness and prospective identity of ship with iceberg are guaranteed at last by their literally coming together: the point of the joke, which Hardy calls "consummation."

Not trying for the moment to demonstrate the relation of such things to poetry, I shall say instead what characteristics my examples have in common.

Each is a thing in itself, a something decisive which the mind easily recognizes and detaches from the context in which it occurs. To say almost the same thing in another way, each example has the intention of giving information, but is received by the mind as giving something else; the statement, as it is made, crosses over from the practical realm into another, the realm of the superfluous and ideal, where it becomes a focus for meditations on the human condition under the figure of armored horses, aged lawyers, jet pilots who shoot themselves down.

This crossing over, this relation between two realms and the process of moving between them, is perhaps comparable with the relation, in poetry, between letter and allegory, between the picturesque and the symbolic.

The examples have, though in varying degrees, a reflexive character, or one in which contradictions resolve; they are, again in varying degrees, increasingly from first to last, about retributive justice, and it may be this which gives them their quality of decisiveness and finish. This reflexive character could be put another way, as a principle of economy: they use their materials twice. And they all three, rather unexpectedly, exhibit the pathos of the obsolete, or obsolescent; they are all about something's being caught up with, something's being over.

Our next step will be to see if the mechanism of a joke in any way illuminates that of a lyric poem; we shall limit ourselves to brief examples.

One critical resemblance between the two will be clear to anyone who has ever tried to make up either—(by the way, how do jokes get made? I do not know that anyone has seriously studied this question)—and this is the problem of the ending. Anyone can begin a poem, anyone can begin a joke (the pointlessness of doing that is very clear, it seems, but many people begin poems). As Plato says in the Laws, "The beginning is like a god, who while he lives among men redeems all." There is a grand feeling of liberty about beginning anything, for it looks as though any gesture in the whole world will do. But, in the difficult world of forms, the gesture you elect will entail consequences good and bad, seen and unseen. Sooner or later, you have to ask yourself how to stop, what it means to stop, what it is that has finished. This is the question we will now examine, first with reference to a few jokes.

a. A riddle. How do you catch the lions in the desert? Answer: you strain off the sand, and the remainder will be lions.

b. From Shipley, *Dictionary of Word Origins,* s.v. Strategy. A Chinese general sent his advance guard up to the edge of a forest. To find out if the enemy were in ambush there, he ordered each man to throw a stone into the forest, and if birds flew up there were no men there, so that it would be safe to advance. All this was done, birds flew, the army marched forward— and was captured. For the opposing general, also as it happened Chinese, had said to *his* soldiers: Men, I want each of you to grab a bird, and let it go when they throw those stones.

These instances are perhaps directed against the intellect's characteristic wish to simplify situations so as reductively to bring out logical structure at the expense of everything else in experience, the wit being that this same essentializing structure is employed to bring out the absurdity of logic in this world. Both jokes make use of the same almost absolute economy, using as much as possible in the response what was given in the stimulus, merely revising the elements of the relation in an "impossible" way.

The pleasure we get must come from the fulfillment of an expectation that the resolution in both instances will make use very purely, indeed exclusively, of the given materials, plus our surprise at the use made, which as straight men for the occasion we should not have thought of. But note that although we should not have thought of the reply, the very fact of its employing *only* terms already used gave us a not quite explicit sense that we might have thought of it in another instant; that though we did not in fact think of it, our minds were playing with the possibilities of lions-deserts, stones-birds, so that the answer, as a matter of timing, seemed "right," or "inevitable," responsive to a wish on our part for symmetry and economy together with a certain shock, the compounded fulfillment of fairly definite formal expectations with a material surprise. We might compare what happens with what happens in music, eighteenth-century music, say, where to a strict and relatively narrow canon of harmonic possibility, including certain clichés of cadence, is added the composer's originality at handling his materials within the convention.

c. From Freud, "Thoughts for the Times on War and Death" (1915). A husband to his wife, "If one of us should die, I would go and live in Paris."

Here we observe, as with so many jokes, and especially those bearing on sex and marriage, that the sentiment itself is about as unfunny as it could be, setting the death of one partner against the pleasure of the other and leaving no doubt of the choice that would be made. The wit, we suppose, the element which allows us to laugh, comes from two circumstances: first, that the wish expressed is one very widely entertained but usually concealed; second, that it breaks from its concealment so economically, using as its means a very slight grammatical displacement of the solemn, "objective" statement, with its air of entertaining the worst contingencies, which the husband must have consciously intended.

Thus, like our misprints earlier, this remark makes a revelation of sorts. A revelation can be only of that which is hidden, what is hidden is secret, what is secret is so because it is, or is thought to be, evil, shameful, taboo (sacred); finally, this evil represents something we believe to be true. So that the revelation is subversive of the usual order of appearances, beneath which it shows another order, one that gains its reality from the comparison of the two.

d. A last example, not a joke, but from Freud's analysis of one of his own dreams. He dreamt of a place called Mödling. No amount of personal association gave any reason for its presence in the dream, until he went through the following process of dream etymology or even archeology: Mödling, from early Mödelitz, from the Latin Mea Delicia (my joy) = *mein Freud.*

Though not strictly a joke, this instance purely illuminates a vital quality of wit, which takes the longest way round only as the shortest way home, whose beginnings and endings seem to be disposed upon a circle, not a straight line. This quality has to do with that economy we mentioned earlier in connection with our first two examples, to which it adds, however, the further consideration that this economy may tend to be reflexive, to turn back on itself and use itself again in a new sense (here quite literally a translation into another language and back). This is in itself a very poetical idea about the nature of forms, that they are like human beings who in seeking the world find themselves, like Odysseus who encompassed a vast world simply by trying to get home (this aspect of the journey is finely brought out in a beautiful poem by Cavafy, "Ithaka"). So also Donne: "Thy firmness makes my circle just, And makes me end where I begunne." (The example suggests another and more recondite possibility, that dreamer, poet, and wit are somehow endeavoring to say the world as a form of their own name. "When Thou hast done, Thou hast not Donne." This would only rarely, if ever, be demonstrable, though I have observed my own name, only slightly concealed, in my contention that the poet is a "namer of" the world. But it is in this sense that Shakespeare, with a "profound" or "abysmal" pun, has Bottom say of his night in the enchanted wood, "It shall be called Bottom's Dream, because it hath no bottom.")

Summing up what we have so far: our examples tell us about the effect and mechanism of jokes that they depend on a strictly limited material, which they resolve surprisingly in terms of itself. Freud would remark that this economy is itself a source of our pleasure, and adduce such terms as remembering, recognition, recurrence, as analogous; and would add, what we discovered from one of our examples, that hostility may also be a

pleasure-bearing part of wit. For, after all, a smile, physiologically speaking,
is a step on the road to a snarl and a bite (cf. "sarcasm," a "biting remark").
So we have:
    economy of materials.
    sudden reversal of the relations of the elements.
    introduction of absurdity, but
    the apparent absurdity, introduced into the context of the former
       sense, makes a new and deeper sense;
    the hidden is revealed.

We may suspect that makers of jokes and smart remarks resemble poets
at least in this, that they too would be excluded from Plato's Republic; for
it is of the nature of Utopia and the Crystal Palace, as Dostoevsky said,
that you can't stick your tongue out at it. A joke expresses tension, which
it releases in laughter; it is a sort of permissible rebellion against things as
they are—permissible, perhaps, because this rebellion is at the same time
stoically resigned, it acknowledges that things are as they are, and that they
will, after the moment of laughter, continue to be that way. That is why
jokes concentrate on the most sensitive areas of human concern: sex, death,
religion, and the most powerful institutions of society; and poems do the
same. We might consider in this connection how grave a business civilization must be, to require professional comedians. Or, as Mr. Empson said
(in a poem), "The safety valve alone knows the worst truth about the
engine."

THE FIGURE A POEM MAKES

Robert Frost

Abstraction is an old story with the philosophers, but it has been like a new
toy in the hands of the artists of our day. Why can't we have any one
quality of poetry we choose by itself? We can have in thought. Then it
will go hard if we can't in practice. Our lives for it.

Granted no one but a humanist much cares how sound a poem is if it is
only *a* sound. The sound is the gold in the ore. Then we will have the
sound out alone and dispense with the inessential. We do till we make the
discovery that the object in writing poetry is to make all poems sound as
different as possible from each other, and the resources for that of vowels,
consonants, punctuation, syntax, words, sentences, meter are not enough.
We need the help of context—meaning—subject matter. That is the greatest
help towards variety. All that can be done with words is soon told. So also

with meters—particularly in our language where there are virtually but two, strict iambic and loose iambic. The ancients with many were still poor if they depended on meters for all tune. It is painful to watch our sprung-rhythmists straining at the point of omitting one short from a foot for relief from monotony. The possibilities for tune from the dramatic tones of meaning struck across the rigidity of a limited meter are endless. And we are back in poetry as merely one more art of having something to say, sound or unsound. Probably better if sound, because deeper and from wider experience.

Then there is this wildness whereof it is spoken. Granted again that it has an equal claim with sound to being a poem's better half. If it is a wild tune, it is a poem. Our problem then is, as modern abstractionists, to have the wildness pure; to be wild with nothing to be wild about. We bring up as aberrationists, giving way to undirected associations and kicking ourselves from one chance suggestion to another in all directions as of a hot afternoon in the life of a grasshopper. Theme alone can steady us down. Just as the first mystery was how a poem could have a tune in such a straightness as meter, so the second mystery is how a poem can have wildness and at the same time a subject that shall be fulfilled.

It should be of the pleasure of a poem itself to tell how it can. The figure a poem makes. It begins in delight and ends in wisdom. The figure is the same as for love. No one can really hold that the ecstasy should be static and stand still in one place. It begins in delight, it inclines to the impulse, it assumes direction with the first line laid down, it runs a course of lucky events, and ends in a clarification of life—not necessarily a great clarification, such as sects and cults are founded on, but in a momentary stay against confusion. It has denouement. It has an outcome that though unforeseen was predestined from the first image of the original mood—and indeed from the very mood. It is but a trick poem and no poem at all if the best of it was thought of first and saved for the last. It finds its own name as it goes and discovers the best waiting for it in some final phrase at once wise and sad—the happy-sad blend of the drinking song.

No tears in the writer, no tears in the reader. No surprise for the writer, no surprise for the reader. For me the initial delight is in the surprise of remembering something I didn't know I knew. I am in a place, in a situation, as if I had materialized from cloud or risen out of the ground. There is a glad recognition of the long lost and the rest follows. Step by step the wonder of unexpected supply keeps growing. The impressions most useful to my purpose seem always those I was unaware of and so made no note of at the time when taken, and the conclusion is come to that like giants we are always hurling experience ahead of us to pave the future with against the day when we may want to strike a line of purpose across it for somewhere. The line will have the more charm for not being mechanically straight. We enjoy the straight crookedness of a good walking stick. Modern instruments of precision are being used to make things crooked as if by eye and hand in the old days.

I tell how there may be a better wildness of logic than of inconsequence.

But the logic is backward, in retrospect, after the act. It must be more felt than seen ahead like prophecy. It must be a revelation, or a series of revelations, as much for the poet as for the reader. For it to be that there must have been the greatest freedom of the material to move about in it and to establish relations in it regardless of time and space, previous relation, and everything but affinity. We prate of freedom. We call our schools free because we are not free to stay away from them till we are sixteen years of age. I have given up my democratic prejudices and now willingly set the lower classes free to be completely taken care of by the upper classes. Political freedom is nothing to me. I bestow it right and left. All I would keep for myself is the freedom of my material—the condition of body and mind now and then to summons aptly from the vast chaos of all I have lived through.

Scholars and artists thrown together are often annoyed at the puzzle of where they differ. Both work from knowledge; but I suspect they differ most importantly in the way their knowledge is come by. Scholars get theirs with conscientious thoroughness along projected lines of logic; poets theirs cavalierly and as it happens in and out of books. They stick to nothing deliberately, but let what will stick to them like burrs where they walk in the fields. No acquirement is on assignment, or even self-assignment. Knowledge of the second kind is much more available in the wild free ways of wit and art. A schoolboy may be defined as one who can tell you what he knows in the order in which he learned it. The artist must value himself as he snatches a thing from some previous order in time and space into a new order with not so much as a ligature clinging to it of the old place where it was organic.

More than once I should have lost my soul to radicalism if it had been the originality it was mistaken for by its young converts. Originality and initiative are what I ask for my country. For myself the originality need be no more than the freshness of a poem run in the way I have described: from delight to wisdom. The figure is the same as for love. Like a piece of ice on a hot stove the poem must ride on its own melting. A poem may be worked over once it is in being, but may not be worried into being. Its most precious quality will remain its having run itself and carried away the poet with it. Read it a hundred times: It will forever keep its freshness as a metal keeps its fragrance. It can never lose its sense of a meaning that once unfolded by surprise as it went.

THE INTERINANIMATION OF WORDS

I. A. Richards

I turn now to that other sense of "context"—the literary context—which I distinguished last time from the technical sense of "context," as a recurrent group of events, that is convenient for the theorem of meaning. Let us consider some of the effects on words of their combination in sentences, and how their meaning depends upon the other words before and after them in the sentence. What happens when we try with a sentence to decide what single words in it mean?

The sentence, of course, as Aristotle taught, is the unit of discourse. We can hardly give too much importance here to the influence of our modern way of separating words in writing. In conversation we do not ordinarily separate them so—unless we are asking questions about words. With languages which have not been used in writing and thus subjected to a special kind of grammatical analysis—it is worth recalling that grammar takes its name from writing—there is often very great uncertainty as to where one word ends and another begins. The written form gives words far more independence than they possess as units of sound in speech and we derive thence a habit of supposing that they have far more independence as regards their meanings than they usually have in either written or spoken discourse.

The mutual dependence of words varies evidently with the type of discourse. At one end of the scale, in the strict exposition of some highly criticized and settled science through technicalized and rigid speech, a large proportion of them are independent. They mean the same whatever other words they are put with; or if a word fluctuates, it moves only into a small number of stable positions, which can be recorded and are anchored to definitions. That is the ideal limit towards which we aim in exposition. Unfortunately we tend—increasingly since the 17th Century—to take rigid discourse as the norm, and impose its standards upon the rest of speech. This is much as if we thought that water, for all its virtues, in canals, baths and turbines, were really a weak form of ice. The other end of the scale is in poetry—in some forms of poetry rather. We know very much less about the behavior of words in these cases—when their virtue is to have no fixed and settled meaning separable from those of the other words they occur with. There are many more possibilities here than the theory of language has yet tried to think out. Often the whole utterance in which the co-operating meanings of the component words hang on one another is not itself stable in meaning. It utters not one meaning but a *movement* among meanings. Of course, even in the strictest prose we always have one thing that may be described as a movement of meaning. We have change as the sentence develops. In "The cat is on the mat" we begin with the cat and end with the mat. There is a progression of some sort in every explicit sentence. But in the strictest prose the meanings of the separate words theoretically stay put and thought passes from one to another of them. At the other end of the scale the whole meaning of the sentence shifts, and with it any meanings we may try to ascribe to the individual words. In the extreme case it will go on moving as long as we bring fresh wits to study it. When Octavius Cæsar is gazing down at Cleopatra dead, he says,

> She looks like sleep,
> As she would catch another Antony
> In her strong toil of grace.

"Her strong toil of grace." Where, in terms of what entries in what possible dictionary, do the meanings here of *toil* and *grace* come to rest?

But my subject is Rhetoric rather than Poetics and I want to keep to prose which is not too far from the strict scientific or "rigid" end of this scale of dependent variabilities. In the kind of prose I am talking now, you have usually to wait till I have gone on a bit before you can decide how you will understand the opening parts of the sentences. If, instead, I were reading you the first few theorems of Euclid, that would not be so. You would understand, as soon as I said "a triangle," what the word meant, and though what I went on to say might qualify the meaning ("having two sides equal"), it would not destroy or completely change the meaning that you had so far given to the word. But in most prose, and more than we ordinarily suppose, the opening words have to wait for those that follow to settle what they shall mean—if indeed that ever gets settled.

All this holds good not only as to the *sense* of the waiting words but as regards all the other functions of language which we can distinguish and set over against the mere sense. It holds for the *feeling* if any towards what I am talking about, for *the relation towards my audience* I want to establish or maintain with the remark, and for the *confidence* I have in the soundness of the remark—to mention three main sorts of these other language functions. In speech, of course, I have the aid of intonation for these purposes. But, as with the meanings of words, so with the intonation structure. The intonation of the opening words is likely to be ambiguous; it waits till the utterance is completed for its full interpretation.

In writing we have to replace intonation as far as we can. Most of the more recondite virtues of prose style come from the skill with which the rival claims of these various language functions are reconciled and combined. And many of the rather mysterious terms that are usually employed in discussing these matters, *harmony, rhythm, grace, texture, smoothness, suppleness, impressiveness,* and so on are best taken up for analysis from this point of view. Or rather the passages which seem to exemplify these qualities (or fail to) are best examined with the multiplicity of the language functions in mind. For we can obviously do nothing with such words as these by themselves, in the blue. They may mean all sorts of different things in different literary contexts.

I have been leading up—or down, if you like—to an extremely simple and obvious but fundamental remark: that no word can be judged as to whether it is good or bad, correct or incorrect, beautiful or ugly, or anything else that matters to a writer, in isolation. That seems so evident that I am almost ashamed to say it, and yet it flies straight in the face of the only doctrine that for two hundred years has been officially inculcated—when any doctrine is inculcated in these matters. I mean the doctrine of Usage. The doctrine that there is a right or a good use for every word and that literary virtue consists in making that good use of it.

There are several bones that can be picked with that doctrine—as it has been expounded in many epochs and, in particular for us, from the middle of the 18th Century onwards. . . . It asserts that "Good use is the general, present-day practice of the best writers." One bone we could pick would be with that "best." How are they the best writers except by using the words in the best ways? We settle that they *are* the best writers because we find them using their words successfully. We do not settle that theirs is the right, the "good usage" of the words because *they* use them so. Never was there a crazier case of putting the cart before the horse. It is as though we were to maintain that apples are healthy because[1] wise people eat them, instead of recognizing that it is the other way about—that it is what the food will do for us which makes us eat it, not the fact that we eat it which makes it good food.

But that is not the main bone I have to pick with the doctrine, which is that it blanks out and hides the interinanimation between words. I had better cite you a sentence or two in evidence, or you may think I am inventing a ghost to exorcize. I will take them from a *Manual of Rhetoric* which carries the names of three authors: Messrs. Gardiner, Kittredge and Arnold. And I choose this book because the regard which I have for Mr. Kittredge's name makes a doctrine which has that sanction seem the better worth refuting. The authors write: "Usage governs language. There is no other standard. By usage, however, is meant the practice of the best writers and speakers." (I have already asked what standard is supposed to settle which are the best.) They go on to consider "four great general principles of choice: *correctness, precision, appropriateness* and *expressiveness*," which, they say, "within the limits of good usage and in every case controlled by it . . . should guide us in the choice of words." And this is what they say of correctness: "Correctness is the most elementary of all requirements. The meanings of words are settled by usage. If we use a word incorrectly—that is in a sense which does not customarily belong to it—our readers will miss our thought, or, at best, they must arrive at it by inference and guesswork."

[1] "Because" is offering to play one of its most troublesome tricks here, of course, in the shift from "cause" to "reason."

Inference and guesswork! What else is interpretation? How, apart from inference and skilled guesswork, can we be supposed ever to understand a writer or speaker's thought? This is, I think, a fine case of poking the fire from the top. But I have still my main bit of evidence to give you. My authors say: "In studying the four great principles of choice, we observe that only the first (correctness) involves the question of right and wrong. The others deal with questions of discrimination between better and worse —that is with the closer adaptation of words to the thoughts and feelings which we undertake to express. Further, it is only in dealing with the first principle (correctness) that we can keep our attention entirely on the single word."

There! that is the view I wished to illustrate. Let us not boggle about the oddities of its expression: "right and wrong," "better and worse"; or worry as to how by keeping "our attention entirely on a single word" we could settle anything at all about it—except perhaps about its spelling! The important point is that words are here supposed just sheerly to possess their sense, as men have their names in the reverse case, and to carry this meaning with them into sentences regardless of the neighbor words. That is the assumption I am attacking, because, if we follow up its practical consequences in writing and reading and trace its effects upon interpretation, we shall find among them no small proportion of the total of our verbal misunderstandings.

I am anxious not to seem to be illustrating this sort of misunderstanding myself here, unwittingly, in my interpretation of this passage. I know well enough that the authors probably had in mind such incorrectness as occurs when people say "ingenious" when they mean "ingenuous"; and I know that the Usage Doctrine can be interpreted in several ways which make it true and innocuous.

It can say and truly, for example, that we learn how to use words from responding to them and noting how other people use them. Just how we do so learn is a deep but explorable question. It can say equally truly, that a general conformity between users is a condition of communication. *That* no one would dream of disputing. But if we consider conformity we see that there are two kinds of conformity. Conformity in the general process of interpretation, and conformity in the specific products. We all know how the duller critics of the 18th Century (the century that gave us the current Doctrine of Usage) the people Wordsworth was thinking of when he wrote his Preface, confused the poetic product with the poetic process and thought a poem good because it used poetic diction—the words that former good poets had used—and used them in the same ways. The Usage Doctrine, in the noxious interpretation of it, is just that blunder in a more pervasive and more dangerous incidence. The noxious interpretation is the common one. Its evil is that it takes the senses of an author's words to be things we know before we read him, fixed factors with which he has to build up the meaning of his sentences as a mosaic is put together of discrete independent tesserae. Instead, they are resultants which we arrive at only through the interplay of the interpretative possibilities of the whole utterance. In brief, we have to guess them and we guess much better when we realize we are guessing, and watch out for indications, than when we think we know.

There are as many morals for the writer as for the reader in all this, but I will keep to interpretation. A word or phrase when isolated momentarily from its controlling neighbors is free to develop irrelevant senses which may then beguile half the other words to follow it. And this is at least equally true with the language functions *other than sense,* with *feeling,* say.

·   ·   ·   ·   ·

Let me go on to some further types of the mutual control and interinanimation between words. So far I have considered only the influence of words actually present in the passage, but we have to include words which are not actually being uttered and are only in the background. Take the case of what are variously called expressive, symbolic, or simulative words— words which "somehow illustrate the meaning more immediately than do ordinary speech forms," to quote Leonard Bloomfield. Examples are *flip, flap, flop, flitter, flimmer, flicker, flutter, flash, flush, flare, glare, glitter, glow, gloat, glimmer, bang, bump, lump, thump, thwack, whack, sniff, sniffle, snuff.* . . . Why should these seem so peculiarly appropriate, or fitting, to the meanings we use them for? The popular view is that these words just simply imitate, are copies of, what they mean. But that is a short-cut theory which often does not work, and we can, I think, go further and do better. As Bloomfield, in his excellent book, *Language,* says, "the explanation is a matter of grammatical structure, to the speaker it seems as if the sounds were especially suited to the meaning." The speaker usually thinks moreover that the word seems suited because in some way it resembles the meaning, or, if this seems unplausible, that there must be *some* direct connection between them. If it is not the sound of the word which resembles the meaning then perhaps the tongue and lip movements instead imitate something to do with the meaning and so on. Sir Richard Paget's theories of imitative gestures are likely to be appealed to nowadays.

The most that the modern linguist—who compares the very different words which are used in different languages for their meanings—is prepared to allow towards this resemblance of sound and sense is that "we can distinguish, with various degrees of clearness and with doubtful cases on the border line, a system of initial and final root-forming morphemes of vague signification." Note how guarded Bloomfield is over such a point.

I must explain what a morpheme is. Two or more words are said to share a morpheme when they have, at the same time, something in common in their meaning and something in common in their sound. The joint semantic-phonetic unit which distinguishes them is what is called a morpheme. It is the togetherness of a peculiar sound and a peculiar meaning for a number of words.

Thus *flash, flare, flame, flicker, flimmer* have in common the sound (fl-) and a suggestion of a "moving light"—and this joint possession is the morpheme. Similarly *blare, flare, glare, stare* have the sound (-ɛə) in common

and also the meaning "big light or noise" shall we say, and this couple—
sound and meaning is the morpheme. So with "smoothly wet" and (sl-) in
slime, slip, slush, slobber, slide, slither. But *pare, pear, pair,* though they
have a sound in common, have no meaning in common, so have no common
morpheme.

Of course, the existence of a group of words with a common morpheme
has an influence on the formation of other words, and on the pronunciation
of other words—assimilating them to the group. Thus, given *skid* and *skate,*
that is a strong additional reason, against an English convention, for saying
skee rather than *shee.*

This pedantic looking term, *morpheme,* is useful because with its help
we manage to avoid saying that the sound (sl-) somehow itself means something like "smoothly wet or slippery" and gain a way of saying no more than
that a group of words which share that sound also share a peculiar meaning.
And that is all we are entitled to say. To go further and say that the words
share the meaning *because* they contain this sound and because this sound
has that meaning is to bring in more than we know—an explanation or
theory to account for what we do know. And actually it is a bad explanation.
For this sound, by itself, means nothing. It is not the shared sound but each
of the words which has the meaning. The sound by itself either means
nothing at all—as with (fl) in *flame, flare, flash, flicker*—or as with (-εə) in
blare, flare, glare, stare it has by itself only an irrelevant meaning, namely,
that of *air,* "what we breathe."

The theoretical position here is worth close study because it is typical of
a very large group of positions in which we tend, too boldly and too innocently, to go beyond our evidence and to assume, as the obvious explanation, as almost a datum, what is really the conclusion of a vague and
quick and unchecked inductive argument, often a bad and unwarrantable
argument. Why should a group of words with a sound in common have
similar meanings unless there was a correspondence of some kind between
the sound and the meaning? That seems plausible. But state the argument
more explicitly, look over the evidence carefully, and it becomes unplausible, for then we have to notice the other words which share the sound but
do not share the meaning and the other words which share the meaning
without the sound. Then we see that we have been applying to words the
sort of argument which would represent a fashion as a spontaneous expression of original taste on the part of all who follow it. We find in fact that
we have been looking at the problem upside down. That so far from a perceived correspondence between sound and meaning being the explanation
of the sharing, the existence of a group of words with a common sound and
meaning is the explanation of our belief in a correspondence.

This situation, I said a moment ago, is typical. We can hardly, I think,
exaggerate in an estimate of the number of literary and rhetorical problems
which, as usually formulated, are upside down in this fashion. For example, our common assumption that when a word such as *beautiful* or *art* or
religion or *good,* is used in a great variety of ways, there will be found something in common to all the uses, something which is the fundamental or

essential meaning of the word and the explanation of its use. So we spend our wits trying to discover this common essential meaning, without considering that we are looking for it, most often, only as a result of a weak and hasty inductive argument. This assumption that the same word ought to have or must have the same meaning, in an important respect, is one of those bullying assumptions that the context theorem of meanings would defend us from . . .

But to come back to this parallel assumption that some words, apart from other words, and in their own right in virtue of their sound must mean certain things. It was Aristotle who said that there can be no natural connection between the sound of any language and the things signified, and, if we set the problem right side up and remember the other words before examining it, we shall have to agree with him. Indeed, if we ask the question fairly it becomes—when we get it clear—nearly senseless. What resemblance or natural connection can there be between the semantic and phonetic elements in the morpheme? One is a sound, the other a reference. "Is (fl-) really like 'moving light' in any way in which (sl-) or (gl-) is not?" Is that not like asking whether the taste of turkey is like growing in some way that the taste of mint is not?

I conclude then that these expressive or symbolic words get their feeling of being peculiarly fitting from the other words sharing the morpheme which support them in the background of the mind. If that is so, all sorts of consequences are at once evident. In translation, for example, the expressive word in another language will not necessarily sound at all like the original word. It will be a word that is backed up by other words in a somewhat analogous fashion. Evidently again, a proper appreciation of the expressiveness of a word in a foreign language will be no matter of merely knowing its meaning and relishing its sound. It is a matter of having, in the background of the mind, the other words in the language which share morphemes with it. Thus no one can appreciate these expressive features of foreign words justly without a really wide familiarity with the language. Without that our estimates are merely whimsical.

We can, and I think should, extend this notion of a word as being backed up by other words that are not uttered or thought of. A first extension is to words that sound alike but do not share a morpheme, do not have a common meaning but only some relevant meaning. Thus *blare, scare* and *dare* do not share a morpheme, but on occasion the peculiar force of *blare* may well come to it in part from the others. This, of course, is only recognizing on a larger, wider scale the principle that Lewis Carroll was using in Jabberwocky. Its relevance to the theory of rhymes and assonances is obvious.

Another and a wider extension would include not only influences from words which in part sound alike, but from other words which in part overlap in meaning. Words, for example, which we might have used instead, and, together with these, the reasons why we did not use them. Another such extension looks to the other uses, in other contexts, of what we, too simply, call "the same word." The meaning of a word on some occasions is quite as much in what it keeps out, or at a distance, as in what it brings in. And, on other occasions, the meaning comes from other partly parallel uses whose relevance we can feel, without necessarily being able to state it explicitly. But with these last leaps I may seem in danger of making the force of a word, the feeling that no other word could possibly do so well or take its place, a matter whose explanation will drag in the whole of the rest of the language. I am not sure, though, that we need be shy of something very like this as a conclusion. A really masterly use of a language—in free or fluid, not technical discourse—Shakespeare's use of English for example, goes a long way towards using the language as a whole.

Cleopatra, taking up the asp, says to it:

> Come, thou mortal wretch,
> With thy sharp teeth this knot intrinsicate
> Of life at once untie; poor venomous fool,
> Be angry, and despatch!

Consider how many senses of *mortal*, besides "death-dealing" come in; compare: "I have immortal longings in me." Consider *knot:* "This knot intrinsicate of life": "Something to be undone," "Something that troubles us until it is undone," "Something by which all holding-together hangs," "The nexus of all meaning." Whether the homophone *not* enters in here may be thought a doubtful matter. I feel it does. But consider *intrinsicate* along with *knot.* Edward Dowden, following the fashion of his time in making Shakespeare as simple as possible, gives "intricate" as the meaning here of *intrinsicate.* And the Oxford Dictionary, sad to say, does likewise. But Shakespeare is bringing together half a dozen meanings from *intrinsic* and *intrinse:* "Familiar," "intimate," "secret," "private," "innermost," "essential," "that which constitutes the very nature and being of a thing"—all the medical and philosophic meanings of his time as well as "intricate" and "involved." What the word does is exhausted by no one of these meanings and its force comes from all of them and more. As the movement of my hand uses nearly the whole skeletal system of the muscles and is supported by them, so a phrase may take its powers from an immense system of supporting uses of other words in other contexts.

PERFORMATIVE UTTERANCES

John L. Austin

You are more than entitled not to know what the word "performative" means. It is a new word and an ugly word, and perhaps it does not mean anything very much. But at any rate there is one thing in its favour, it is not a profound word. I remember once when I had been talking on this subject that somebody afterwards said: "You know, I haven't the least idea what he means, unless it could be that he simply means what he says." Well, that is what I should like to mean.

Let us consider first how this affair arises. We have not got to go very far back in the history of philosophy to find philosophers assuming more or less as a matter of course that the sole business, the sole interesting business, of any utterance—that is, of anything we say—is to be true or at least false. Of course they had always known that there are other kinds of things which we say—things like imperatives, the expressions of wishes, and exclamations —some of which had even been classified by grammarians, though it wasn't perhaps too easy to tell always which was which. But still philosophers have assumed that the only things that they are interested in are utterances which report facts or which describe situations truly or falsely. In recent times this kind of approach has been questioned—in two stages, I think. First of all people began to say: "Well, if these things are true or false it ought to be possible to decide which they are, and if we can't decide which they are they aren't any good but are, in short, nonsense." And this new approach did a great deal of good; a great many things which probably are nonsense were found to be such. It is not the case, I think, that all kinds of nonsense have been adequately classified yet, and perhaps some things have been dismissed as nonsense which really are not; but still this movement, the verification movement, was, in its way, excellent.

However, we then come to the second stage. After all, we set some limits to the amount of nonsense that we talk, or at least the amount of nonsense that we are prepared to admit we talk; and so people began to ask whether after all some of those things which, treated as statements, were in danger of being dismissed as nonsense did after all really set out to be statements at all. Mightn't they perhaps be intended not to report facts but to influence people in this way or that, or to let off steam in this way or that? Or perhaps at any rate some elements in these utterances performed such functions, or, for example, drew attention in some way (without actually reporting it) to some important feature of the circumstances in which the utterance was being made. On these lines people have now adapted a new slogan,

PERFORMATIVE UTTERANCES From *Philosophical Papers of J. L. Austin* by John L. Austin, edited by J. O. Urmson. By permission of the Clarendon Press, Oxford.

the slogan of the "different uses of language." The old approach, the old statemental approach, is sometimes called even a fallacy, the descriptive fallacy.

Certainly there are a great many uses of language. It's rather a pity that people are apt to invoke a new use of language whenever they feel so inclined, to help them out of this, that, or the other well-known philosophical tangle; we need more of a framework in which to discuss these uses of language; and also I think we should not despair too easily and talk, as people are apt to do, about the *infinite* uses of language. Philosophers will do this when they have listed as many, let us say, as seventeen; but even if there were something like ten thousand uses of language, surely we could list them all in time. This, after all, is no larger than the number of species of beetle that entomologists have taken the pains to list. But whatever the defects of either of these movements—the "verification" movement or the "use of language" movement—at any rate they have effected, nobody could deny, a great revolution in philosophy and, many would say, the most salutary in its history. (Not, if you come to think of it, a very immodest claim.)

Now it is one such sort of use of language that I want to examine here. I want to discuss a kind of utterance which looks like a statement and grammatically, I suppose, would be classed as a statement, which is not nonsensical, and yet is not true or false. These are not going to be utterances which contain curious verbs like "could" or "might," or curious words like "good," which many philosophers regard nowadays simply as danger signals. They will be perfectly straightforward utterances, with ordinary verbs in the first person singular present indicative active, and yet we shall see at once that they couldn't possibly be true or false. Furthermore, if a person makes an utterance of this sort we should say that he is *doing* something rather than merely *saying* something. This may sound a little odd, but the examples I shall give will in fact not be odd at all, and may even seem decidedly dull. Here are three or four. Suppose, for example, that in the course of a marriage ceremony I say, as people will, "I do"—(sc. take this woman to be my lawful wedded wife). Or again, suppose that I tread on your toe and say "I apologize." Or again, suppose that I have the bottle of champagne in my hand and say "I name this ship the *Queen Elizabeth*." Or suppose I say "I bet you sixpence it will rain tomorrow." In all these cases it would be absurd to regard the thing that I say as a report of the performance of the action which is undoubtedly done—the action of betting, or christening, or apologizing. We should say rather that, in saying what I do, I actually perform that action. When I say "I name this ship the *Queen Elizabeth*" I do not describe the christening ceremony, I actually perform the christening; and when I say "I do" (sc. take this woman to be my lawful wedded wife), I am not reporting on a marriage, I am indulging in it.

Now these kinds of utterance are the ones that we call *performative* utterances. This is rather an ugly word, and a new word, but there seems to be no word already in existence to do the job. The nearest approach that I can think of is the word "operative," as used by lawyers. Lawyers when talking about legal instruments will distinguish between the preamble, which recites the circumstances in which a transaction is effected, and on the other hand the operative part—the part of it which actually performs the legal act which it is the purpose of the instrument to perform. So the word "operative" is very near to what we want. "I give and bequeath my watch to my brother" would be an operative clause and is a performative utterance. However, the word "operative" has other uses, and it seems preferable to have a word specially designed for the use we want.

Now at this point one might protest, perhaps even with some alarm, that I seem to be suggesting that marrying is simply saying a few words, that just saying a few words *is* marrying. Well, that certainly is not the case. The words have to be said in the appropriate circumstances, and this is a matter that will come up again later. But the one thing we must not suppose is that what is needed in addition to the saying of the words in such cases is the performance of some internal spiritual act, of which the words then are to be the report. It's very easy to slip into this view at least in difficult, portentous cases, though perhaps not so easy in simple cases like apologizing. In the case of promising—for example, "I promise to be there tomorrow"—it's very easy to think that the utterance is simply the outward and visible (that is, verbal) sign of the performance of some inward spiritual act of promising, and this view has certainly been expressed in many classic places. There is the case of Euripides' Hippolytus, who said "My tongue swore to, but my heart did not"—pehaps it should be "mind" or "spirit" rather than "heart," but at any rate some kind of backstage artiste. Now it is clear from this sort of example that, if we slip into thinking that such utterances are reports, true or false, of the performance of inward and spiritual acts, we open a loophole to perjurers and welshers and bigamists and so on, so that there are disadvantages in being excessively solemn in this way. It is better, perhaps, to stick to the old saying that our word is our bond.

However, although these utterances do not themselves report facts and are not themselves true or false, saying these things does very often *imply* that certain things are true and not false, in some sense at least of that rather woolly word "imply." For example, when I say "I do take this woman to be my lawful wedded wife," or some other formula in the marriage ceremony, I do imply that I'm not already married, with wife living, sane, undivorced, and the rest of it. But still it is very important to realize that to imply that something or other is true, is not at all the same as saying something which is true itself.

These performative utterances are not true or false, then. But they do suffer from certain disabilities of their own. They can fail to come off in special ways, and that is what I want to consider next. The various ways in which a performative utterance may be unsatisfactory we call, for the sake of a name, the infelicities; and an infelicity arises—that is to say, the utterance is unhappy—if certain rules, transparently simple rules, are broken. I will mention some of these rules and then give examples of some infringements.

First of all, it is obvious that the conventional procedure which by our utterance we are purporting to use must actually exist. In the examples given here this procedure will be a verbal one, a verbal procedure for marrying or giving or whatever it may be; but it should be borne in mind that there are many non-verbal procedures by which we can perform exactly the same acts as we perform by these verbal means. It's worth remembering too that a great many of the things we do are at least in part of this conventional kind. Philosophers at least are too apt to assume that an action is always in the last resort the making of a physical movement, whereas it's usually, at least in part, a matter of convention.

The first rule is, then, that the convention invoked must exist and be accepted. And the second rule, also a very obvious one, is that the circumstances in which we purport to invoke this procedure must be appropriate for its invocation. If this is not observed, then the act that we purport to perform would not come off—it will be, one might say, a misfire. This will also be the case if, for example, we do not carry through the procedure—whatever it may be—correctly and completely, without a flaw and without a hitch. If any of these rules are not observed, we say that the act which we purported to perform is void, without effect. If, for example, the purported act was an act of marrying, then we should say that we "went through a form" of marriage, but we did not actually succeed in marrying.

Here are some examples of this kind of misfire. Suppose that, living in a country like our own, we wish to divorce our wife. We may try standing her in front of us squarely in the room and saying, in a voice loud enough for all to hear, "I divorce you." Now this procedure is not accepted. We shall not thereby have succeeded in divorcing our wife, at least in this country and others like it. This is a case where the convention, we should say, does not exist or is not accepted. Again, suppose that, picking sides at a children's party, I say "I pick George." But George turns red in the face and says "Not playing." In that case I plainly, for some reason or another, have not picked George—whether because there is no convention that you can pick people who aren't playing, or because George in the circumstances is an inappropriate object for the procedure of picking. Or consider the case in which I say "I appoint you Consul," and it turns out that you have been appointed already—or perhaps it may even transpire that you are a horse; here again we have the infelicity of inappropriate circumstances, inappropriate objects, or what not. Examples of flaws and hitches are perhaps scarcely necessary—one party in the marriage ceremony says "I will," the other says "I won't"; I say "I bet sixpence," but nobody says, "Done," nobody takes up the offer. In all these and other such cases, the act which we purport to perform, or set out to perform, is not achieved.

But there is another and a rather different way in which this kind of utterance may go wrong. A good many of these verbal procedures are designed for use by people who hold certain beliefs or have certain feelings or intentions. And if you use one of these formulae when you do not have the requisite thoughts or feelings or intentions then there is an abuse of the procedure, there is insincerity. Take, for example, the expression, "I congratulate you." This is designed for use by people who are glad that the per-

son addressed has achieved a certain feat, believe that he was personally responsible for the success, and so on. If I say "I congratulate you" when I'm
not pleased or when I don't believe that the credit was yours, then there is
insincerity. Likewise if I say I promise to do something, without having the
least intention of doing it or without believing it feasible. In these cases
there is something wrong certainly, but it is not like a misfire. We should
not say that I didn't in fact promise, but rather that I did promise but
promised insincerely; I did congratulate you but the congratulations were
hollow. And there may be an infelicity of a somewhat similar kind when the
performative utterance commits the speaker to future conduct of a certain
description and then in the future he does not in fact behave in the expected way. This is very obvious, of course, if I promise to do something
and then break my promise, but there are many kinds of commitment of a
rather less tangible form than that in the case of promising. For instance, I
may say "I welcome you," bidding you welcome to my home or wherever
it may be, but then I proceed to treat you as though you were exceedingly
unwelcome. In this case the procedure of saying "I welcome you" has been
abused in a way rather different from that of simple insincerity.

Now we might ask whether this list of infelicities is complete, whether the
kinds of infelicity are mutually exclusive, and so forth. Well, it is not complete, and they are not mutually exclusive; they never are. Suppose that you
are just about to name the ship, you have been appointed to name it, and
you are just about to bang the bottle against the stem; but at that very
moment some low type comes up, snatches the bottle out of your hand,
breaks it on the stem, shouts out "I name this ship the *Generalissimo
Stalin,*" and then for good measure kicks away the chocks. Well, we agree
of course on several things. We agree that the ship certainly isn't now named
the *Generalissimo Stalin,* and we agree that it's an infernal shame and so on
and so forth. But we may not agree as to how we should classify the particular infelicity in this case. We might say that here is a case of a perfectly
legitimate and agreed procedure which, however, has been invoked in the
wrong circumstances, namely by the wrong person, this low type instead of
the person appointed to do it. But on the other hand we might look at it
differently and say that this is a case where the procedure has not as a whole
been gone through correctly, because part of the procedure for naming a
ship is that you should first of all get yourself appointed as the person to do
the naming and that's what this fellow did not do. Thus the way we
should classify infelicities in different cases will be perhaps rather a difficult
matter, and may even in the last resort be a bit arbitrary. But of course
lawyers, who have to deal very much with this kind of thing, have invented
all kinds of technical terms and have made numerous rules about different
kinds of cases, which enable them to classify fairly rapidly what in particular
is wrong in any given case.

As for whether this list is complete, it certainly is not. One further way in
which things may go wrong is, for example, through what in general may
be called misunderstanding. You may not hear what I say, or you may
understand me to refer to something different from what I intended to

refer to, and so on. And apart from further additions which we might make to the list, there is the general over-riding consideration that, as we are performing an act when we issue these performative utterances, we may of course be doing so under duress or in some other circumstances which make us not entirely responsible for doing what we are doing. That would certainly be an unhappiness of a kind—any kind of nonresponsibility might be called an unhappiness; but of course it is a quite different kind of thing from what we have been talking about. And I might mention that, quite differently again, we could be issuing any of these utterances, as we can issue an utterance of any kind whatsoever, in the course, for example, of acting a play or making a joke or writing a poem—in which case of course it would not be seriously meant and we shall not be able to say that we seriously performed the act concerned. If the poet says "Go and catch a falling star" or whatever it may be, he doesn't seriously issue an order. Considerations of this kind apply to any utterance at all, not merely to performatives.

That, then, is perhaps enough to be going on with. We have discussed the performative utterance and its infelicities. That equips us, we may suppose, with two shining new tools to crack the crib of reality maybe. It also equips us—it always does—with two shining new skids under our metaphysical feet. The question is how we use them.

2.

So far we have been going firmly ahead, feeling the firm ground of prejudice glide away beneath our feet which is always rather exhilarating, but what next? You will be waiting for the bit when we bog down, the bit where we take it all back, and sure enough that's going to come but it will take time. First of all let us ask a rather simple question. How can we be sure, how can we tell, whether any utterance is to be classed as a performative or not? Surely, we feel, we ought to be able to do that. And we should obviously very much like to be able to say that there is a grammatical criterion for this, some grammatical means of deciding whether an utterance is performative. All the examples I have given hitherto do in fact have the same grammatical form; they all of them begin with the verb in the first person singular present indicative active—not just any kind of verb of course, but still they all are in fact of that form. Furthermore, with these verbs that I have used there is a typical asymmetry between the use of this person and tense of the verb and the use of the same verb in other persons and other tenses, and this asymmetry is rather an important clue.

For example, when we say "I promise that . . . ," the case is very different from when we say "He promises that . . . ," or in the past tense "I promised that . . . ." For when we say "I promise that . . ." we do perform an act of promising—we give a promise. What we do *not* do is to report on somebody's performing an act of promising—in particular, we do not report on somebody's use of the expression "I promise." We actually do use it and do the promising. But if I say "He promises," or in the past tense "I promised," I precisely do report on an act of promising, that is to say an act of using this formula "I promise"—I report on a present act of promising by him, or on a past act of my own. There is thus a clear difference between our first person singular present indicative active, and other persons and tenses. This is brought out by the typical incident of little Willie whose uncle says he'll give him half-a-crown if he promises never to smoke till he's 55. Little Willie's anxious parent will say "Of course he promises, don't you, Willie?" giving him a nudge, and little Willie just doesn't vouchsafe. The point here is that he must do the promising himself by saying "I promise," and his parent is going too fast in saying he promises.

That, then, is a bit of a test for whether an utterance is performative or not, but it would not do to suppose that every performative utterance has to take this standard form. There is at least one other standard form, every bit as common as this one, where the verb is in the passive voice and in the second or third person, not in the first. The sort of case I mean is that of a notice inscribed "Passengers are warned to cross the line by the bridge only," or of a document reading "You are hereby authorized" to do so-and-so. These are undoubtedly performative, and in fact a signature is often required in order to show who it is that is doing the act of warning, or authorizing, or whatever it may be. Very typical of this kind of performative—especially liable to occur in written documents of course —is that the little word "hereby" either actually occurs or might naturally be inserted.

Unfortunately, however, we still can't possibly suggest that every utterance which is to be classed as a performative has to take one or another of these two, as we might call them, standard forms. After all it would be a very typical performative utterance to say "I order you to shut the door." This satisfies all the criteria. It is performing the act of ordering you to shut the door, and it is not true or false. But in the appropriate circumstances surely we could perform exactly the same act by simply saying "Shut the door," in the imperative. Or again, suppose that somebody sticks up a notice "This bull is dangerous," or simply "Dangerous bull," or simply "Bull." Does this necessarily differ from sticking up a notice, appropriately signed, saying "You are hereby warned that this bull is dangerous?" It seems that the simple notice "Bull" can do just the same job as the more elaborate formula. Of course the difference is that if we just stick up "Bull" it would not be quite clear that it is a warning; it might be there just for interest or information, like "Wallaby" on the cage at the zoo, or "Ancient Monument." No doubt we should know from the nature of the case that it was a warning, but it would not be explicit.

Well, in view of this break-down of grammatical criteria, what we should like to suppose—and there is a good deal in this—is that any utterance which is performative could be reduced or expanded or analysed into one of these two standard forms beginning "I . . ." so and so or beginning "You (or he) hereby . . ." so and so. If there was any justification for this hope, as to some extent there is, then we might hope to make a list of all the verbs which can appear in these standard forms, and then we might classify the kinds of acts that can be performed by performative utterances. We might do this with the aid of a dictionary, using such a test as that already mentioned—whether there is the characteristic asymmetry between the first person singular present indicative active and the other persons and tenses—in order to decide whether a verb is to go into our list or not. Now if we make such a list of verbs we do in fact find that they fall into certain fairly well-marked classes. There is the class of cases where we deliver verdicts and make estimates and appraisals of various kinds. There is the class where we give undertakings, commit ourselves in various ways by saying something. There is the class where by saying something we exercise various rights and powers, such as appointing and voting and so on. And there are one or two other fairly well-marked classes.

Suppose this task accomplished. Then we could call these verbs in our list explicit performative verbs, and any utterance that was reduced to one or the other of our standard forms we could call an explicit performative utterance. "I order you to shut the door" would be an explicit performative utterance, whereas "Shut the door" would not—that is simply a "primary" performative utterance or whatever we like to call it. In using the imperative we may be ordering you to shut the door, but it just isn't made clear whether we are ordering you or entreating you or imploring you or beseeching you or inciting you or tempting you, or one or another of many other subtly different acts which, in an unsophisticated primitive language, are very likely not yet discriminated. But we need not overestimate the unsophistication of primitive languages. There are a great many devices that can be used for making clear, even at the primitive level, what act it is we are performing when we say something—the tone of voice, cadence, gesture—and above all we can rely upon the nature of the circumstances, the context in which the utterance is issued. This very often makes it quite unmistakable whether it is an order that is being given or whether, say, I am simply urging you or entreating you. We may, for instance, say something like this: "Coming from him I was bound to take it as an order." Still, in spite of all these devices, there is an unfortunate amount of ambiguity and lack of discrimination in default of our explicit performative verbs. If I say something like "I shall be there," it may not be certain whether it is a promise, or an expression of intention, or perhaps even a forecast of my future behavior, of what is going to happen to me; and it may matter a good deal, at least in developed societies, precisely which of these things it is. And that is why the explicit performative verb is evolved—to make clear exactly which it is, how far it commits me and in what way, and so forth.

This is just one way in which language develops in tune with the society of which it is the language. The social habits of the society may considerably affect the question of which performative verbs are evolved and which, sometimes for rather irrelevant reasons, are not. For example, if I say "You are a poltroon," it might be that I am censuring you or it might be that I am insulting you. Now since apparently society approves of censuring or reprimanding, we have here evolved a formula "I reprimand you," or "I censure you," which enables us expeditiously to get this desirable business over. But on the other hand, since apparently we don't approve of insulting, we have not evolved a simple formula "I insult you," which might have done just as well.

By means of these explicit performative verbs and some other devices, then, we make explicit what precise act it is that we are performing when we issue our utterance. But here I would like to put in a word of warning. We must distinguish between the function of making explicit what act it is we are performing, and the quite different matter of *stating* what act it is we are performing. In issuing an explicit performative utterance we are not stating what act it is, we are showing or making explicit what act it is. We can draw a helpful parallel here with another case in which the act, the conventional act that we perform, is not a speech-act but a physical performance. Suppose I appear before you one day and bow deeply from the waist. Well, this is ambiguous. I may be simply observing the local flora, tying my shoe-lace, something of that kind; on the other hand, conceivably I might be doing obeisance to you. Well, to clear up this ambiguity we have some device such as raising the hat, saying "Salaam," or something of that kind, to make it quite plain that the act being performed is the conventional one of doing obeisance rather than some other act. Now nobody would want to say that lifting your hat was stating that you were performing an act of obeisance; it certainly is not, but it does make it quite plain that you are. And so in the same way to say "I warn you that . . ." or "I order you to . . ." or "I promise that . . ." is not to state that you are doing something, but makes it plain that you are—it does constitute your verbal performance, a performance of a particular kind.

So far we have been going along as though there was a quite clear difference between our performative utterances and what we have contrasted them with, statements or reports or descriptions. But now we begin to find that this distinction is not as clear as it might be. It's now that we begin to sink in a little. In the first place, of course, we may feel doubts as to how widely our performatives extend. If we think up some odd kinds of expression we use in odd cases, we might very well wonder whether or not they satisfy our rather vague criteria for being performative utterances. Suppose, for example, somebody says "Hurrah." Well, not true or false; he is performing the act of cheering. Does that make it a performative utterance in our sense or not? Or suppose he says "Damn"; he is performing the act of swearing, and it is not true or false. Does that make it performative? We feel that in a way it does and yet it's rather different. Again, consider cases of "suiting the action to the words"; these too may make us wonder whether perhaps the utterance should be classed as performative. Or sometimes, if somebody says "I am sorry," we wonder whether this is just the same as "I apologize"—in which case of course we have said it's a performative utterance—or whether perhaps it's to be taken as a description, true or false, of the state of his feelings. If he had said "I feel perfectly awful about it," then we should think it must be meant to be a description of the state of his feelings. If he had said "I apologize," we should feel this was clearly a performative utterance, going through the ritual of apologizing. But if he says "I am sorry" there is an unfortunate hovering between the two. This phenomenon is quite common. We often find cases in which there is an obvious pure performative utterance and obvious other utterances connected with it which are not performative but descriptive, but on the other hand a good many in between where we're not quite sure which they are. On some occasions of course they are obviously used the one way, on some occasions the other way, but on some occasions they seem positively to revel in ambiguity.

Again, consider the case of the umpire when he says "Out" or "Over," or the jury's utterance when they say that they find the prisoner guilty. Of course, we say, these are cases of giving verdicts, performing the act of appraising and so forth, but still in a way they have some connexion with the facts. They seem to have something like the duty to be true or false, and seem not to be so very remote from statements. If the umpire says "Over," this surely has at least something to do with six balls in fact having been delivered rather than seven, and so on. In fact in general we may remind ourselves that "I state that . . ." does not look so very different from "I warn you that . . ." or "I promise to . . . ." It makes clear surely that the act that we are performing is an act of stating, and so functions just like "I warn" or "I order." So isn't "I state that . . ." a performative utterance? But then one may feel that utterances beginning "I state that . . ." do have to be true or false, that they *are* statements.

Considerations of this sort, then, may well make us feel pretty unhappy. If we look back for a moment at our contrast between statements and performative utterances, we realize that we were taking statements very much on trust from, as we said, the traditional treatment. Statements, we had it, were to be true or false; performative utterances on the other hand were to be felicitous or infelicitous. They were the doing of something, whereas for all we said making statements was not doing something. Now this contrast surely, if we look back at it, is unsatisfactory. Of course statements are liable to be assessed in this matter of their correspondence or failure to correspond with the facts, that is, being true or false. But they are also liable to infelicity every bit as much as are performative utterances. In fact some troubles that have arisen in the study of statements recently can be shown to be simply troubles of infelicity. For example, it has been pointed out that there is something very odd about saying something like this: "The cat is on the mat but I don't believe it is." Now this is an outrageous thing to say, but it is not self-contradictory. There is no reason why the cat shouldn't be on the mat without my believing that it is. So how are we to classify what's wrong with this peculiar statement? If we remember now the doctrine of infelicity we shall see that the person who makes this remark about the cat is in much the same position as somebody who says something like this: "I promise that I shall be there, but I haven't the least intention of being there." Once again you can of course perfectly well promise to be there without having the least intention of being there, but there is something outrageous about saying it, about actually avowing the insincerity of the promise you give. In the same way there is insincerity in the case of the person who says "The cat is on the mat but I don't believe it is," and he is actually avowing that insincerity—which makes a peculiar kind of nonsense.

A second case that has come to light is the one about John's children— the case where somebody is supposed to say "All John's children are bald but John hasn't got any children." Or perhaps somebody says "All John's children are bald," when as a matter of fact—he doesn't say so—John has no children. Now those who study statements have worried about this; ought they to say that the statement "All John's children are bald" is meaningless in this case? Well, if it is, it is not a bit like a great many other more standard kinds of meaninglessness; and we see, if we look back at our list of infelicities, that what is going wrong here is much the same as what goes wrong in, say, the case of a contract for the sale of a piece of land when the piece of land referred to does not exist. Now what we say in the case of this sale of land, which of course would be effected by a performative utterance, is that the sale is void—void for lack of reference or ambiguity of reference; and so we can see that the statement about all John's children is likewise void for lack of reference. And if the man actually says that John has no children in the same breath as saying they're all bald, he is making the same kind of outrageous utterance as the man who says "The cat is on the mat and I don't believe it is," or the man who says "I promise to but I don't intend to."

In this way, then, ills that have been found to afflict statements can be precisely paralleled with ills that are characteristic of performative utterances. And after all when we state something or describe something or report something, we do perform an act which is every bit as much an act as an act of ordering or warning. There seems no good reason why stating should be given a specially unique position. Of course philosophers have been wont to talk as though you or I or anybody could just go round stating anything about anything and that would be perfectly in order, only there's just a little question: is it true or false? But besides the little question, is it true or false, there is surely the question: *is* it in order? Can you go round just making statements about anything? Suppose for example you say to me "I'm feeling pretty moldy this morning." Well, I say to you "You're not"; and you say "What the devil do you mean, I'm not?" I say "Oh nothing—I'm just stating you're not, is it true or false?" And you say "Wait a bit about whether it's true or false, the question is what did you mean by making statements about somebody else's feelings? I told you I'm feeling pretty moldly. You're just not in a position to say, to state that I'm not." This brings out that you can't just make statements about other people's feelings (though you can make guesses if you like); and there are very many things which, having no knowledge of, not being in a position to pronounce about, you just can't state. What we need to do for the case of stating, and by the same token describing and reporting, is to take them a bit off their pedestal, to realize that they are speech-acts no less than all these other speech-acts that we have been mentioning and talking about as performative.

Then let us look for a moment at our original contrast between the performative and the statement from the other side. In handling performatives we have been putting it all the time as though the only thing that a performative utterance had to do was to be felicitous, to come off, not to be a misfire, not to be an abuse. Yes, but that's not the end of the matter. At least in the case of many utterances which, on what we have said, we should have to class as performative—cases where we say "I warn you to . . . ," "I advise you to . . ." and so on—there will be other questions besides simply: was it in order, was it all right, as a piece of advice or a warning, did it come off? After that surely there will be the question: was it good or sound advice? Was it a justified warning? Or in the case, let us say, of a verdict or an estimate: was it a good estimate, or a sound verdict? And these are questions that can only be decided by considering how the content of the verdict or estimate is related in some way to fact, or to evidence available about the facts. This is to say that we do require to assess at least a great many performative utterances in a general dimension of correspondence with fact. It may still be said, of course, that this does not make them *very* like statements because still they are not true or false, and that's a little black and white speciality that distinguishes statements as a class apart. But actually—though it would take too long to go on about this—the more you think about truth and falsity the more you find that very few statements that we ever utter are just true or just false. Usually there is the question are they fair or are they not fair, are they adequate or not adequate, are they exaggerated or not exaggerated? Are they too rough, or are they perfectly precise, accurate, and so on? "True" and "false" are just general labels for a whole dimension of different appraisals which have something or other to do with the relation between what we say and the facts. If, then, we loosen up our ideas of truth and falsity we shall see that statements, when assessed in relation to the facts, are not so very different after all from pieces of advice, warnings, verdicts, and so on.

We see then that stating something is performing an act just as much as is giving an order or giving a warning; and we see, on the other hand, that, when we give an order or a warning or a piece of advice, there is a question about how this is related to fact which is not perhaps so very different from the kind of question that arises when we discuss how a statement is related to fact. Well, this seems to mean that in its original form our distinction between the performative and the statement is considerably weakened, and indeed breaks down. I will just make a suggestion as to how to handle this matter. We need to go very much farther back, to consider all the ways and senses in which saying anything at all is doing this or that—because of course it is always doing a good many different things. And one thing that emerges when we do do this is that, besides the question that has been very much studied in the past as to what a certain utterance *means,* there is a further question distinct from this as to what was the *force,* as we may call it, of the utterance. We may be quite clear what "Shut the door" means, but not yet at all clear on the further point as to whether as uttered at a certain time it was an order, an entreaty or whatnot. What we need besides the old doctrine about meanings is a new doctrine about all the possible forces of utterances, towards the discovery of which our proposed list of explicit performative verbs would be a very great help; and then, going on from there, an investigation of the various terms of appraisal that we use in discussing speech-acts of this, that, or the other precise kind—orders, warnings, and the like.

The notions that we have considered then, are the performative, the infelicity, the explicit performative, and lastly, rather hurriedly, the notion of the forces of utterances. I dare say that all this seems a little unremunerative, a little complicated. Well, I suppose in some ways it is unremunerative, and I suppose it ought to be remunerative. At least, though, I think that if we pay attention to these matters we can clear up some mistakes in philosophy; and after all philosophy is used as a scapegoat, it parades mistakes which are really the mistakes of everybody. We might even clear up some mistakes in grammar, which perhaps is a little more respectable.

And is it complicated? Well, it is complicated a bit; but life and truth and things do tend to be complicated. It's not things, it's philosophers that are simple. You will have heard it said, I expect, that over-simplification is the occupational disease of philosophers, and in a way one might agree with that. But for a sneaking suspicion that it's their occupation.

OVERLEAF PHOTO: Bob Fitch; courtesy of Black Star →

Style

EDITED BY RICHARD POIRIER

INTRODUCTION

It is unlikely that many people today, young or old, would want to be bound by the aphorism, eighteenth-century and French in its origins, that "style is the man himself." Criticizing the notion in 1924 in a letter to Louis Untermeyer, Robert Frost points out that this would mean that a "man's ideas would be some element then of his style. So would his deeds. But I would narrow the definition. His deeds are his deeds; his ideas are his ideas. His style is the way he carries himself toward his ideas and deeds." Frost was insisting on a distinction essential to the dramatic life in literature: that no situation ever dictates the responses to it, no posture is ever predictably funny or necessarily sad, even grief can be expressed by gaiety. There can be no determinism about style in Frost's sense of that term. Essentially, it is the presence of the writer as it emanates from his performance. He performs *about* ideas and happenings and can be located less in his opinions than in his stance—in every modulation of phrase and punctuation. Frost himself performs not so much through but in relation to his own language, as if it were a kind of teasing antagonist.

With that sense of style in mind we can better see what Norman Mailer means in his discussion of style in the selection reprinted here from *The Armies of the Night*. We learn that his use of "obscene" words in *Why Are We In Vietnam?* does not express him any more than do the "concepts" that can be located in that novel. Mailer exists rather in the effort to bring the one into play with the other. More exactly, he lets "his sense of language play on obscenity as freely as it wished, so discovering that everything he knew about the American language (with its incommensurable resources) went flying in and out of the line of his prose with the happiest beating of wings—it was the first time his style seemed at once very American to him and very literary in the best way." He asks here and elsewhere to be imagined as a writer fully alive in the *act* of writing, so much so that the Mailer who is doing the writing refers to the Mailer of the earlier time, the Mailer of the march on the Pentagon, in the third person. The Mailer who acted, that is, is a different Mailer from the one who is writing about it. Style in Mailer, as in Frost, tends to exude a kind of rough sportiveness which works against the very terrors and outrages that are the ostensible subject of the writing. Not many people in the activity of writing or in any other kind of activity have so strong a sense of the power of self or of personal style.

In a variety of ways, our selections are concerned with a problem as old as style itself, as old probably as the transmission, in whatever form, of human expression: Is this style mine (the speaker, writer, painter, dancer, musician might ask), or is it someone else's? Am I seeing or hearing without any interference, or is that impossible and am I not looking or listening through what Harold Rosenberg calls a "gridiron of style"?

Harold Rosenberg, art critic for the *New Yorker,* proposes that stylistic newness is less a condition that can be attained than an elusive hope always to be pursued. It is a tradition of effort and of labor. Through the arts, or through other agencies of persuasion, including the style of daily life— about which Edwin Denby, the ballet critic, writes so charmingly—we learn to see, to listen, and thus to respond in some ways and not in others. We learn in fact to see or hear only certain things as being of importance and to pay little or even no attention to other things. Thus our perceptions are to some extent predetermined by the style we have learned even before we begin to create what we like to think of as a style of our own.

This problem has always been of central concern to the arts and to criticism of the arts. It has been discussed under such headings as "convention and originality," or "imitation and sincerity." Is one being sincere, for example, if he expresses himself through conventions that are the shared property of all those who choose to use or adapt them? If so, to what extent, and how do we locate that sincerity? The essays by Rosenberg and Denby address themselves to this issue, and the reader can decide which offers the more optimistic view of the possibilities of escaping inherited or imposed style in the creation of art and in the act of looking at it or at the world around us. For Rosenberg, "the dream world of style always moves ahead of the actual world and overlays it," while Denby, who echoes Rosenberg's remarks in what he says about the photographs of New York done by Rudolf Burckhardt, encourages his class of ballet dancers to think that they can see more, not less, of the wonderful peculiarity that is in familiar things if they watch daily life with some of the

intensity that they bring to dancing, if they look for what he calls "dancing in daily life"—the way people walk, the way they loll, the way, finally,
they fill space. His argument, like Rosenberg's, is a complicated one in
which the relation between life and art, and especially between seeing one
with the powers developed by the discipline of the other, is forever alive
and reciprocal. Both authors share a strong conviction of the great power
of style in art. So much are they convinced that they are concerned about
the possible limitations imposed on anyone trained in an art—and that can
include even the military arts—when he looks out on life.

I now want to make a transition which some readers will already have
made for themselves but which some others might not want to make, since
it implies that what goes on with style in the arts, such as painting or
dancing, music or writing, goes on also in activities which, with only a bit
of elasticity, we can call the arts of politics, of advertising, or even of
military tactics. It is significant in this regard that Denby ends with a suggestion that these different kinds of art might compete for our sense of
wonder and for the inquisitiveness that wonder excites. "Art," he says,
"is certainly even more mysterious and nonsensical than daily life. But
what a pleasure it can be. A pleasure much more extraordinary than a
hydrogen bomb is extraordinary." The style of his talk—open, rambling,
as if disavowing the authoritarian role of lecturer—is much like the style
of seeing that his piece recommends. It is equally open and expectant
about the possibilities of discovering the strange wonders lurking in the
obvious: "the violent paint on cars, signs, houses, lips." Denby's style, as
well as the style of seeing that he hopes to propagate, is meant to cherish
life in the free and exploratory way that is the antithesis of the flattening,
dread force of the bomb.

To borrow the title of the book from which Herbert Marcuse's essay
is taken, the bomb is the ultimate force of one-dimensionality. If the political hints at the end of the Denby piece are leading us to the overt political
discussions of Marcuse, the opening of Rosenberg's piece does so even more
emphatically. He describes the defeat of the British under General Braddock by the American insurgents during the Revolution, and points out
that the latter were wholly unlearned in the European military arts while
the British were perhaps the best-trained army in Europe. What defeated
the British, he says, was nothing less than their skill. He writes very sympa-
thetically about their dilemma, and with a critical tolerance (of their
commitment to a style and of their inability to adapt that style to changed
environmental conditions) that also informs the tone of his criticism of
painting. "They were such extreme European professionals," he writes,

even the Colonials among them, they did not *see* the American trees. Their too
highly perfected technique forbade them to acknowledge such chance topographical
phenomena. According to the assumptions of their military art, by which their
senses were controlled, a battlefield had to have a certain appearance and structure, that is to say, a style. Failing to qualify, these American trees and rocks from
which come such deadly but meaningless stings are overlooked. The Redcoats fall,

expecting at any moment to enter upon the true battlefield, the soft rolling greenswards prescribed by the canons of their craft and presupposed by every principle
that makes warfare intelligible to the soldier of the 18th century.

Not just the style of painting, then, but the style of wars, and not just
that alone but the very outcome of wars can be decided by what Rosenberg
calls the "hallucination of the displaced terrain, originating in style." One
in fact knows too painfully of more recent colonial wars that also have
been initiated and directed by such hallucinations. Thus the selections that
have to do with art refer us to those having to do more specifically with
politics, and in all of them is the same recognition: Style can and does
create states of mind, modes of perception, structures of reality, that are
of central consequence to the political and cultural shaping of society. And
just as there can be some differences between Denby and Rosenberg about
the degree to which one's consciousness is constrained as well as expanded
by style, so there are differences among those who, like Herbert Marcuse
and Robert Lifton, are concerned with what the latter calls the "flooding
of imagery produced by the extraordinary flow of post-modern cultural
influences over man's communication networks."

Marcuse, the German philosopher who now teaches in this country (and
who is also discussed in the section "The Cultural Revolution and Its
Prophets") is concerned with the control over the mind that results from
such a "flooding of imagery," though the images he considers are mostly the
result of verbal and grammatical structurings. What in Lifton might be
taken as yet another stylistic option that can be absorbed into the style of
his "protean man" is in Marcuse merely another technique of manipulation
designed to produce "one-dimensional man." He writes of the "abridgment of the concept in fixed images; arrested development in self-validating,
hypnotic formulas; immunity against contradictions; identification of the
thing (and of the person) with its function—these tendencies reveal the
one-dimensional mind in the languages it speaks."

As this brief quotation alone will indicate, Marcuse's own style can on
occasion be as claustrophobic as the public ones he is criticizing. The reasons
have to do in part with his continuing attachment to the German academic
and Hegelian philosophical traditions even while becoming a figure of
paternal consequence to many younger radical dissidents in the universities.
But it can also be explained by the extraordinary difficulty of his attempt
to transcend those forces of "one-dimensionality" which he also wants to
show to be in nearly complete control of discourse. He thus has to resort to
the near paradox of saying that "the power over man which this society has
acquired is daily absolved by its efficacy and productiveness." It is not its
failure to satisfy certain needs but its enormous success in doing so that
makes modern industrial-technological society—either of the Soviet Union
or the United States—so overwhelming. There is no essential difference,
Marcuse says, between the modes of life offered by the two superpowers;
there are merely different techniques of manipulation and control. Their

"power over man" is the harder to combat because man can even be made to have a "Happy Consciousness," though Marcuse refuses to believe that he is truly happy; he can have his needs satisfied without realizing that his needs have themselves been created by manipulation and are therefore false.

These are difficult arguments to conduct, and the convoluted abstractness of Marcuse's style shows the strain. And yet there is something perhaps less commendable to be said about it. Possibly it is a symptom of his imagining a world that is populated by nothing but his own abstractions. Most certainly it is not populated with those erratic and saving human presences that are acknowledged in Lifton's illustrations of what he means by "protean man," though Lifton himself is guilty of occasional dehumanizing cant phrases like "symbolic impairments" and "counterfeit nurturants." Is Marcuse's view—that style can have a "magical and hypnotic" power over contemporary man—the only one that can follow from a conviction that man cannot resist a system that suppresses or simply coopts the individual into a corporate style? Or might one imagine instead, and much less flatteringly to the author, that the view results from his not having given sufficient attention to, from his not really being able even to see, the daily assertions of individual and personal style that indicate freedom from one-dimensionality? While the question probably cannot be answered, it is essential that it be asked.

In any case, the conditions that Marcuse finds so desperate are, in Lifton's essay, disposed of as something of a rear-guard action in the face of what he takes to be an inevitable and mostly healthful proliferation of styles in contemporary life. "Where this kind of constricted or 'one-dimensional' self-process exists," he writes, "it has an essentially reactive and compensatory quality. . . . a constricted self-process requires continuous 'psychological work' to fend off protean influences which are always abroad." Part of Lifton's optimism is possibly a result of his having worked intimately with some victims of one-dimensional thinking as research professor of psychiatry at Yale and author of a remarkable book, *Death in Life,* about the survivors of Hiroshima. Individual variations, individual heroisms, individual capacities to survive and suffer no matter what the distressing conditions of survival, tend to call into question not simply the power of any political or rhetorical style over the mind but the pessimism of those who think that the mind is necessarily a helpless victim of that power.

Lifton feels that there are far more stylistic opportunities open to men now than ever before. "The protean style of self-process," he observes, " . . . is characterized by an interminable series of experiments and explorations—some shallow, some profound—each of which may be readily abandoned in favor of still new psychological quests." And he goes on to talk about the implications of this new "protean style" in ways that suggest why he doesn't appear to fear "one-dimensionality": "Just as elements of the self can be experimented with and readily altered, so can idea systems and ideologies be embraced, modified, let go of and reembraced, all with a new ease that stands in sharp contrast to the inner struggle we have in the past associated with these shifts." Apparently it is easy to decide, at least for those who are so fortunate as to have this "new ease," that traditional and institutionalized styles are so inflexible, that they account for so little of the flux of reality, as to be absurd, and Lifton remarks on the fact that nowadays "in American life, absurdity and mockery are everywhere." Being fully aware of possible styles, the "protean man" necessarily refuses to endow any one of them with total sanctity; everything becomes some form of theater, a "caper," a "game," a "scenario." What is "reality" for one-dimensional man is a "scene" for protean man.

Jerry Rubin's "demonstration theater" as described in his "Yippie Manifesto" is an expression of a nearly bombastic proteanism. "The mind is programmed," he asserts in chorus with some of the other writers in this section, but he is alone in the unmodified vigor with which he tells us to "get in there and break that bloody program!" Acting on his own instructions, he performs not one but various parts of himself. When refused entrance to the New York Stock Exchange by an official who tells him that "You can't come in. You are hippies and you are coming to demonstrate," he simply changes identities, or rather calls upon one of his other identities, and thereby gains admission: "Hippies? Demonstrate? We're Jews," he retorts. "And we're coming to see the stock market." But he does more than perform parts of himself; he also performs those parts of the culture which others do not want to see "demonstrated." Knowing with Denby that there is a distinction between art and life, he goes even further in believing that art or performance can be a distillation, a concentration of the images of life. He thus disrupts the stock exchange not by "demonstrating" himself, as it were, but by demonstrating the nature of the stock exchange and by forcing some of its habitués to "demonstrate" those parts of themselves which they hide under the style of decorum. He and his friends drop dollar bills from the top of the exchange and watch "these guys [who] deal in millions of dollars as a game. . . . chasing and fighting each other for dollar bills thrown by the hippies."

In a curious way unknown to him, Rubin resembles an earlier American dissident, Henry Thoreau. Using punning and role-playing, Thoreau's style was designed to subvert the meaning in his society of such capitalistic concepts as "ownership" just as Rubin catches a number of social absurdities in his pun "subpoenas envy"; and Rubin believes, even more than did Thoreau, in the possibilities of creating new myths and a new man. "We are a new generation, species, race," he asserts, and seems little concerned with the problem that if contemporary man really is as programmed as he says, then he (Rubin) ought to agree with Rosenberg, who, with a similarly acute sense of the power of style on men's minds, remarks that "To be a new man is not a condition but an effort." Rubin's confidence is derived in some part from his conviction that the power of television "telescopes the revolution by centuries." This may be true, but whose revolution? There is evidence that the styles given preferential room on the screen are more likely to induce one-dimensional than protean men or Yippies.

One can go further. Even when the young do succeed in inventing themselves and a community for themselves, they seem to be quickly conventionalized not simply by the media but, as we see in Tom Wolfe's sympathetic piece about "The Pump House Gang," by the very people—the young—who want to preserve it. The process of cooption and the sad fact that the styles invented by the "gang" tend ultimately to exclude its inventors as they reach and pass the magic age of twenty-five, then twenty-six . . . these factors don't prevent Wolfe from offering a rather elegiacally affectionate portrait of a group style in speech and dress designed to exclude the world of oldsters and the speech and dress that go with it. Wolfe's own style registers both the destiny of the gang and his own desire to extend them as much of his own imagination as he can. Thus the piece begins with some language intended to make many readers, especially older ones, feel that indeed they do not understand the young, or even the language of the young. Yet as the account continues, Wolfe becomes more and more in his voice one of the oldsters himself, the difference being, as he lets us know, that he is an informed one, someone who has "been there" and can report back. By the middle, the strange words have all been defined, the strange conduct explicated in terms any reader of the middle-aged and middle-class magazines for which Wolfe writes can understand. The stylistic development of the essay is in a way an image of the career of the styles of the young being described: from uniqueness and freedom to homogenization.

Norman Mailer was discussed at the beginning of this introduction but it is proper that he should also receive concluding attention. He is, of all the writers here, the one most concerned with finding a style that will bring into dialectical and life-giving tension the many and often conflicting styles that he finds not only in America but in himself as an image of America. That is why it is important that he chooses to address those assembled for the march on the Pentagon in a Southern accent, which they would associate not only with the class and geography of some of their opponents, including the soldiers against whom they are going to march the next day, but with the President, Lyndon Baines Johnson, against whose policies they are demonstrating. Married at the time to a Southern woman whose father is a sergeant in the professional army stationed in the South, himself a veteran of World War II in the Pacific theater, where many of his buddies were Southern (like the "Southern cracker" about whom he talks admiringly in his discussion of obscenity), Mailer isn't playing an alien role when he says that "ever since seeing *All the King's Men* years ago he wanted to come on in public as a Southern demagogue." He is instead playing a true part of himself that enlivens and agitates other parts of himself, and this beautifully unmoralistic self-awareness comes into play most poignantly when he calls himself in public "Lyndon Johnson's little old *dwarf* alter ego," and immediately thinks to himself, standing there on stage a little like Jerry Rubin during some bit of his "demonstration theater," "My God, that is probably exactly what you are at this moment, Lyndon Johnson with all his sores, sorrows, and vanity, squeezed down to five foot eight." It is of crucial importance, however, that Jerry Rubin would *not* have had such a thought standing there on stage.

To him there is no *self*-discovery in the imitation of another man's style but only the exposure of the other man's hidden freakishness—be it of Governor Wallace or Presidential candidates—as "pigs." In Mailer, the "happy play"—a phrase worth pondering—of "obscenity upon concept" is designed not to destroy the concept but rather to "enable one to go back to concept again." It might be said that Mailer solves the problem of one-dimensionality not merely by being protean but by going beyond that in his insistence, as a stylistic enterprise, that the various parts of himself and his writing give renewed and organic life to one another. His is the prose not of revolution but of the effort to hold in some kind of solution all the constituent styles that belong to America and to check, by evoking the power of any given style, the possible dominance of some other. Finding a style of one's own that won't exclude some living element of the social and political environment of which one is a part, a style that will yet remain flexible, tender, and contentious is under the best conditions a nearly impossible job. Now, assaulted on every side by the conflicting blandishments of images and sounds, it is at once a more difficult achievement than ever before and a more necessary one. The essays that follow illustrate the dilemma and show some ways of contending with it. Style may not be the man, but we must try to make man the style.

A TRANSFER OF POWER

Norman Mailer

The evening went on. It was in fact far from climax. Lowell, resting in the wing on the floor of the stage, Lowell recuperating from the crack he had given his head, was a dreamy figure of peace in the corner of the proscenium, a reclining shepherd contemplating his flute, although a Washington newspaper was to condemn him on Saturday in company with Mailer for "slobbish behavior" at this unseemly lounging.

Now Macdonald finished. What with the delays, the unmanageable public address system, and the choppy waters of the audience at his commencement, for Mailer had obviously done him no good, Macdonald had been somewhat less impressive than ever. A few people had shown audible boredom with him. (Old-line Communists perhaps. Dwight was now one of the oldest anti-Communists in America.)

> Take up the White Man's burden—
>   Ye dare not stoop to less—
> Nor call too loud on Freedom
>   To cloak your weariness;
> By all ye cry or whisper,
>   By all ye leave or do,
> The silent, sullen peoples
>   Shall weigh your Gods and you.

read Macdonald from Kipling's poem, and the wit was in the selection, never the presentation.

He was done. He walked back to the wings with an air of no great satisfaction in himself, at most the sense of an obligation accomplished. Lowell's turn had arrived. Mailer stood up to introduce him.

The novelist gave a fulsome welcome to the poet. He did not speak of his poetry (with which he was not conspicuously familiar) nor of his prose which he thought excellent—Mailer told instead of why he had respect for Lowell as a man. A couple of years ago, the poet had refused an invitation from President Johnson to attend a garden party for artists and intellectuals, and it had attracted much attention at the time for it was one of the first dramatic acts of protest against the war in Vietnam, and Lowell was the only invited artist of first rank who had refused. Saul Bellow, for example, had attended the garden party. Lowell's refusal could not have been easy, the novelist suggested, because artists were attracted to formal afternoons of such elevated kind since that kind of experience was often stimulating to new perception and new work. So, an honorific occasion in full panoply was not easy for the mature artist to eschew. Capital! Lowell had therefore bypassed the most direct sort of literary capital. Ergo, Mailer respected him —he could not be certain he would have done the same himself, although, of course, he assured the audience he would not probably have ever had the opportunity to refuse. (Hints of merriment in the crowd at the thought of Mailer on the White House lawn.)

If the presentation had been formal up to here, it had also been somewhat graceless. On the consequence, our audience's amusement tipped the slumbering Beast. Mailer now cranked up a vaudeville clown for finale to Lowell's introduction. "Ladies and gentlemen, if novelists come from the middle class, poets tend to derive from the bottom and the top. We all know good poets at the bot'—ladies and gentlemen, here is a poet from the top, Mr. Robert Lowell." A large and vigorous hand of applause, genuine enthusiasm for Lowell, some standing ovation.

But Mailer was depressed. He had betrayed himself again. The end of the introduction belonged in a burlesque house—he worked his own worst veins, like a man on the edge of bankruptcy trying to collect hopeless debts. He was fatally vulgar! Lowell passing him on the stage had recovered sufficiently to cast him a nullifying look. At this moment, they were obviously far from friends.

Lowell's shoulders had a slump, his modest stomach was pushed forward a hint, his chin was dropped to his chest as he stood at the microphone, pondering for a moment. One did not achieve the languid grandeurs of that slouch in one generation—the grandsons of the first sons had best go through the best troughs in the best eating clubs at Harvard before anyone in the family could try for such elegant note. It was now apparent to Mailer that Lowell would move by instinct, ability, and certainly by choice, in the direction most opposite from himself.

"Well," said Lowell, softly to the audience, his voice dry and gentle as any New England executioner might ever hope to be, "this has been a zany evening." Laughter came back, perhaps a little too much. It was as if Lowell wished to reprove Mailer, not humiliate him. So he shifted, and talked a bit uneasily for perhaps a minute about very little. Perhaps it was too little. Some of the audience, encouraged by earlier examples, now whistled. "We can't hear you," they shouted, "speak louder."

Lowell was annoyed. "I'll bellow," he said, "but it won't do any good." His firmness, his distaste for the occasion, communicated some subtle but impressive sense of his superiority. Audiences are moved by many cues but the most satisfactory of them is probably the voice of their abdomen. There are speakers who give a sense of security to the abdomen, and they always elicit the warmest kind of applause. Mailer was not this sort of speaker; Lowell was. The hand of applause which followed this remark was fortifying. Lowell now proceeded to read some poetry.

He was not a splendid reader, merely decent to his own lines, and he read

from that slouch, that personification of ivy climbing a column, he was even
diffident, he looked a trifle helpless under the lights. Still, he made no effort
to win the audience, seduce them, dominate them, bully them, amuse them,
no, they were there for him, to please *him,* a sounding board for the plucked
string of his poetic line, and so he endeared himself to them. They adored
him—for his talent, his modesty, his superiority, his melancholy, his petu-
lance, his weakness, his painful, almost stammering shyness, his noble
strength—*there* was the string behind other strings.

> O to break loose, like the chinook
> salmon jumping and falling back,
> nosing up to the impossible
> stone and bone-crushing waterfall—
> raw-jawed, weak-fleshed there, stopped by ten
> steps of the roaring ladder, and then
> to clear the top on the last try,
> alive enough to spawn and die.

Mailer discovered he was jealous. Not of the talent. Lowell's talent was
very large, but then Mailer was a bulldog about the value of his own talent.
No, Mailer was jealous because he had worked for this audience, and Lowell
without effort seemed to have stolen them: Mailer did not know if he was
contemptuous of Lowell for playing *grand maître,* or admiring of his ability
to do it. Mailer knew his own version of *grand maître* did not compare. Of
course no one would be there to accept his version either. The pain of bad
reviews was not in the sting, but in the subsequent pressure which, like
water on a joint, collected over the decade. People who had not read your
books in fifteen years were certain they were missing nothing of merit. A
buried sorrow, not very attractive (for bile was in it and the bitterness of
unrequited literary injustice) released itself from some ducts of the heart,
and Mailer felt hot anger at how Lowell was loved and he was not, a pure
and surprising recognition of how much emotion, how much simple and
childlike bitter sorrowing emotion had been concealed from himself for
years under the manhole cover of his contempt for bad reviews.

> Pity the planet, all joy gone
> from this sweet volcanic cone;
> peace to our children when they fall
> in small war on the heels of small
> war—until the end of time
> to police the earth, a ghost
> orbiting forever lost
> in our monotonous sublime.

They gave Lowell a good standing ovation, much heartiness in it, much
obvious pleasure that they were there on a night in Washington when
Robert Lowell had read from his work—it was as nice as that—and then

Lowell walked back to the wings, and Mailer walked forward. Lowell did not seem particularly triumphant. He looked still modest, still depressed, as if he had been applauded too much for too little and so the reservoir of guilt was still untapped.

Nonetheless, to Mailer it was now *mano a mano*. Once, on a vastly larger scale of applause, perhaps people had reacted to Manolete not unlike the way they reacted to Lowell, so stirred by the deeps of sorrow in the man, that the smallest move produced the largest emotion. If there was any value to the comparison then Mailer was kin to the young Dominguin, taking raucous chances, spitting in the eye of the bull, an excess of variety in his passes. But probably there was no parallel at all. He may have felt like a matador in the flush of full competition, going out to do his work after the other torero has had a triumph, but for fact he was probably less close in essence now to the bullfighter than the bull. We must not forget the Beast. He had been sipping the last of the bourbon out of the mug. He had been delayed, piqued, twisted from his purpose and without anything to eat in close to ten hours. He was on the hunt. For what, he hardly knew. It is possible the hunt existed long before the victim was ever conceived.

"Now, you may wonder who I am," he said to the audience, or bellowed to them, for again he was not using the mike, "and you may wonder why I'm talking in a Southern accent which is phony"—the Southern accent as it sounded to him in his throat, was actually not too bad at this moment—"and the reason is that I want to make a presentation to you." He did not have a notion of what he would say next, but it never occurred to him something would not come. His impatience, his sorrow, his jealousy were gone, he just wanted to live on the edge of that rhetorical sword he would soon try to run through the heart of the audience. "We are gathered here"—shades of Lincoln in hippieland—"to make a move on Saturday to invest the Pentagon and halt and slow down its workings, and this will be at once a symbolic act and a real act"—he was roaring—"for real heads may possibly get hurt, and soldiers will be there to hold us back, and some of us may be arrested"—how, wondered the wise voice at the rear of this roaring voice, could one ever leave Washington now without going to jail?—"some blood conceivably will be shed. If I were the man in the government responsible for controlling this March, I would not know what to do." Sonorously—"I would not wish to arrest too many or hurt anyone for fear the repercussions in the world would be too large for my bureaucrat's heart to bear—it's so full of shit." Roars and chills from the audience again. He was off into obscenity. It gave a heartiness like the blood of beef tea to his associations. There was no villainy in obscenity for him, just—paradoxically, characteristically—his love for America: he had first come to love America when he served in the U. S. Army, not the America of course of the flag, the patriotic unendurable fix of the television programs and the newspapers, no, long before he was ever aware of the institutional oleo of the most suffocating American ideas he had come to love what editorial writers were fond of calling the democratic principle with its faith in the common man. He found that principle and that man in the Army, but what none of the editorial writers ever mentioned was that that noble common man was obscene as an old goat, and his obscenity was what saved him. The sanity of said common democratic man was in his humor, his humor was in his obscenity. And his philosophy as well—a reductive philosophy which looked to restore the hard edge of proportion to the overblown values overhanging each small military existence—viz: being forced to salute an overconscientious officer with your back stiffened into an exaggerated posture. "That Lieutenant is chicken-shit," would be the platoon verdict, and a blow had somehow been struck for democracy and the sanity of good temper. Mailer once heard a private end an argument about the merits of a general by saying, "his spit don't smell like ice cream either," only the private was not speaking of spit. Mailer thought enough of the line to put it into *The Naked and the Dead,* along with a good many other such lines the characters in his mind and his memory of the Army had begun to offer him. The common discovery of America was probably that Americans were the first people on earth to live for their humor; nothing was so important to Americans as humor. In Brooklyn, he had taken this for granted, at Harvard he had thought it was a by-product of being at Harvard, but in the Army he discovered that the humor was probably in the veins and the roots of the local history of every state and county in America—the truth of the way it really felt over the years passed on a river of obscenity from small-town storyteller to storyteller there down below the bankers and the books and the educators and the legislators—so Mailer never felt more like an American than when he was naturally obscene—all the gifts of the American language came out in the happy play of obscenity upon concept, which enabled one to go back to concept again. What was magnificent about the word shit is that it enabled you to use the word noble: a skinny Southern cracker with a beatific smile on his face saying in the dawn in a Filipino rice paddy, "Man, I just managed to take me a noble shit." Yeah, that was Mailer's America. If he was going to love something in the country, he would love that. So after years of keeping obscene language off to one corner of his work, as if to prove after *The Naked and the Dead* that he had many an arrow in his literary quiver, he had come back to obscenity again in the last year—he had kicked goodbye in his novel *Why Are We In Vietnam?* to the old literary corset of good taste, letting his sense of language play on obscenity as freely as it wished, so discovering that everything he knew about the American language (with its incommensurable resources) went flying in and out of the line of his prose with the happiest beating of wings—it was the first time his style seemed at once very American to him and very literary in the best way, at least as he saw the best way. But the reception of the book had been disappointing. Not because many of the reviews were bad (he had learned, despite all sudden discoveries of sorrow, to live with that as one lived with smog) no, what was disappointing was the crankiness across the country. Where fusty conservative old critics had once defended the obscenity in *The Naked and the Dead,* they, or their sons, now condemned it in the new book, and that *was* disappointing. The country was not growing up so much as getting a premature case of arthritis.

At any rate, he had come to the point where he liked to use a little obscenity in his public speaking. Once people got over the shock, they were sometimes able to discover that the humor it provided was not less powerful than the damage of the pain. Of course he did not do it often and he tried not to do it unless he was in good voice—Mailer was under no illusion that public speaking was equal to candid conversation; an obscenity uttered in a voice too weak for its freight was obscene, since obscenity probably resides in the quick conversion of excitement to nausea—which is why Lyndon Johnson's speeches are called obscene by some. The excitement of listening to the American President alters abruptly into the nausea of wandering down the blind alleys of his voice.

This has been a considerable defense of the point, but then the point was at the center of his argument and it could be put thus: the American corporation executive, who was after all the foremost representative of Man in the world today, was perfectly capable of burning unseen women and children in the Vietnamese jungles, yet felt a large displeasure and fairly final disapproval at the generous use of obscenity in literature and in public.

The apology may now be well taken, but what in fact did Mailer say on the stage of the Ambassador before the evening was out? Well, not so very much, just about enough to be the stuff of which footnotes are made, for he did his best to imitate a most high and executive voice.

"I had an experience as I came to the theater to speak to all of you, which is that before appearing on this stage I went upstairs to the men's room as a prelude to beginning this oratory so beneficial to all"—laughs and catcalls —"and it was dark, so—ahem—I missed the bowl—all men will know what I mean. Forgiveness might reign. But tomorrow, they will blame that puddle of water on Communists which is the way we do things here in Amurrica, anyone of you pinko poos want to object, lemme tell ya, the reason nobody was in the men's room, and it so dark, is that if there been a light they'd had to put a CIA man in there and the hippies would grope him silly, see here, you know who I am, why it just came to me, ah'm so phony, I'm as full of shit as Lyndon Johnson. Why, man, I'm nothing but his little old alter ego. That's what you got right here working for you, Lyndon Johnson's little old *dwarf* alter ego. How you like him? How you like him?" (Shades of Cassius Clay again.)

And in the privacy of his brain, quiet in the glare of all that sound and spotlight, Mailer thought quietly, "My God, that is probably exactly what you are at this moment, Lyndon Johnson with all his sores, sorrows, and vanity, squeezed down to five foot eight," and Mailer felt for the instant possessed, as if he had seized some of the President's secret soul, or the President seized some of his—the bourbon was as luminous as moonshine to the spores of insanity in the flesh of his brain, a smoke of menace swished in the air, and something felt real, almost as if he had caught Lyndon Johnson by the toe and now indeed, bugger the rhyme, should never let him go.

"Publicity hound," shouted someone from the upper balcony.

"Fuck you," cried Mailer back with absolute delight, all the force of the Texas presidency in his being. Or was it Lucifer's fire? But let us use asterisks for these obscenities to emphasize how happily he used the words, they went off like fireworks in his orator's heart, and asterisks look like rocketbursts and the orbs from Roman candles ***. F*ck you he said to the heckler but with such gusto the vowel was doubled. F*-*ck you! was more like it. So, doubtless, had the President disposed of all opposition in private session. Well, Mailer was here to bring the presidency to the public.

"This yere dwarf alter ego has been telling you about his imbroglio with the p*ssarooney up on the top floor, and will all the reporters please note that I did not talk about defecation commonly known as sheeee-it!"—full imitation of LBJ was attempted there—"but to the contrary, speak of you-rye-nation! I p*ssed on the floor. Hoo-ee! Hoo-ee! How's that for Black Power full of white p*ss? You just know all those reporters are going to say it was sh*t tomorrow. F*ck them. F*ck all of them. Reporters, will you stand up and be counted?"

A wail of delight from the students in the audience. What would the reporters do? Would they stand?

One lone figure arose.

"Where are *you* from?" asked Mailer.

"Washington *Free Press.*" A roar of delight from the crowd. It was obviously some student or hippie paper.

"Ah want *The Washington Post,*" said Mailer in his best Texas tones, "and the *Star.* Ah know there's a *Time* magazine man here for one, and twenty more like him no doubt." But no one stood. So Mailer went into a diatribe. "Yeah, people," he said, "watch the reporting which follows. Yeah, these reporters will kiss Lyndon Johnson's *ss and Dean Rusk's *ss and Man Mountain McNamara's *ss, they will rush to kiss it, but will they stand up in public? No! Because they are the silent assassins of the Republic. They alone have done more to destroy this nation than any force in it." They will certainly destroy me in the morning, he was thinking. But it was for this moment worth it, as if two very different rivers, one external, one subjective, had come together; the frustrated bile, piss, pus, and poison he had felt at the progressive contamination of all American life in the abscess of Vietnam, all of that, all heaped in lighted coals of brimstone on the press' collective ear, represented one river, and the other was the frustrated actor in Mailer—ever since seeing *All the King's Men* years ago he had wanted to come on in public as a Southern demagogue.

The speech went on, and a few fine things possibly were said next to a few equally obscene words, and then Mailer thought in passing of reading a passage from *Why Are We In Vietnam?* but the passage was full of plays of repetition on the most famous four-letter word of them all, and Mailer thought that was conceivably redundant now and so he ended modestly with a final, "See you on Saturday!"

The applause was fair. Not weak, but empty of large demonstration. No standing ovation for certain. He felt cool, and in a quiet, pleasant, slightly depressed mood. Since there was not much conversation between Macdonald, Lowell, and himself, he turned after a moment, left the stage, and walked along the floor where the audience had sat. A few people gathered about him, thanked him, shook his hand. He was quiet and reserved now, with genial slightly muted attempts to be cordial. He had noticed this shift in mood before, even after readings or lectures which had been less eventful. There was a mutual embarrassment between speaker and audience once the speaker had left the stage and walked through the crowd. It was due no doubt to the intimacy—that most special intimacy—which can live between a speaker and the people he has addressed, yes they had been so intimate then, that the encounter now, afterward, was like the eye-to-the-side maneuvers of client and whore once the act is over and dressing is done.

Mailer went on from there to a party of more liberal academics, and drank a good bit more and joked with Macdonald about the superiority of the introduction he had given to Lowell over the introduction Dwight had received.

"Next time don't interrupt me," he teased Macdonald, "and I'll give you a better introduction."

"Goodness, I couldn't hear a word you said," said Macdonald, "you just sounded awful. Do you know, Norman, the acoustics were terrible on the wing. I don't think any of us heard anything anyone else said."

Some time in the early morning, or not so early, Mailer got to bed at the Hay-Adams and fell asleep to dream no doubt of fancy parties in Georgetown when the Federal period in architecture was young. Of course if this were a novel, Mailer would spend the rest of the night with a lady. But it is history, and so the Novelist is for once blissfully removed from any description of the hump-your-backs of sex. Rather he can leave such matters to the happy or unhappy imagination of the reader.

PARABLE OF AMERICAN PAINTING

Harold Rosenberg

"The American is a new man who acts on new principles: he must therefore entertain new ideas and form new opinions."
                                        J. Hector St. John de Crèvecoeur

"Cursed be that mortal inter-debtedness . . . I would be as free as air: and I'm down in the whole world's books."
                                        Herman Melville

People carry their landscapes with them, the way travelers used to cart along their porcelain chamber pots. The stronger their sense of form the more reluctant they are to part with either.

Since the eye sees through a gridiron of style and memory, it is not so easy for a man to be "new" as Crèvecoeur implies.

BRADDOCK'S DEFEAT

For me the most dramatic example of the newcomer's illusion of being else-where is Braddock's Defeat. I recall in my grammar-school history book a linecut illustration which shows the Redcoats marching abreast through the woods, while from behind trees and rocks naked Indians and coonskinned trappers pick them off with musket balls. Maybe it wasn't Braddock's de-feat but some ambush of the Revolutionary War. In any case, the Redcoats march in file through the New World wilderness, with its disorder of rocks, underbrush and sharpshooters, as if they were on a parade ground or on the meadows of a classical European battlefield and one by one they fall and die.

I was never satisfied with the explanation that the Redcoats were simply stupid or stubborn, wooden copies of King George III. In my opinion what defeated them was their skill. They were such extreme European profes-sionals, even the Colonials among them, they did not *see* the American trees. Their too highly perfected technique forbade them to acknowledge such chance topographical phenomena. According to the assumptions of their military art, by which their senses were controlled, a battlefield had to have a certain appearance and structure, that is to say, a style. Failing to qualify, these American trees and rocks from which come such deadly but meaningless stings are overlooked. The Redcoats fall, expecting at any moment to enter upon the true battlefield, the soft rolling greenswards prescribed by the canons of their craft and presupposed by every principle that makes warfare intelligible to the soldier of the eighteenth century.

The difficulty of the Redcoats was that they were in the wrong place. The dream-world of a style always moves ahead of the actual world and over-lays it; unless one is of the unblinking wilderness like those Coonskinners behind the trees.

In honor of the dream-defeated Braddock, I call the hallucination of the displaced terrain, originating in style, Redcoatism. In America it is an ex-perience of the first importance. If Crèvecoeur were right and the American were a "new man acting on new principles," Redcoatism as a mental condi-tion should have ceased to exist with the departure of Cornwallis. The fact is, however, that the art-entranced Redcoat, in a succession of different na-tional uniforms, dominates the history of American art. Like Braddock, painting in this country has behaved as if it were elsewhere—to the point where artists have often emigrated physically in order to join their minds in some foreign country. What has counted with the art corps has been the Look, from the British Look of Colonial portraiture, through the Düssel-dorf Look, the Neo-Classic Look, down to the Last-Word Look of abstract art today. The uniforms change, Redcoatism endures.

Of course the sharpshooting individuals—we shall speak of them later—have the last word. But granted that what counts in the art of any nation, since the Renaissance, at any rate, is primarily the works of its individual masters, American art has differed in this respect: that the triumphs of individuals have been achieved against the prevailing style or apart from it, rather than within it or through it.

The issue is not that American painting is influenced by Europe; the painting of all European countries has also been influenced. The issue is Redcoatism, the difficulty for the artist of finding here a spot on which to begin. But a starting point in experience is indispensable if the artist is to prevail against the image of Great Painting that slides between him and the canvas he is working on.

The first American playwrights could think of nothing less to compose than Shakespearean tragedies in blank verse. Had it not been for a will to bad art in order to satisfy the appetites of the street, the American theatre would never have come into being.

What marks the paintings of America's past as provincial is not their inferior general level—the low quality of Dutch poetry or British music in a given period does not make it provincial—but the absence in them of any continuing visual experience that demands recognition. Copley's later canvases did enter as a force into the continuity of *British* historical painting. But until very recently no American painter, or assumption put into practice about painting, has had the power of emanating into world art as Whitman or Poe did into literature, so that it became possible to say that Nietszche or Tolstoy was a Whitmanite, that Gide and Lorca Whitmanize and that through Baudelaire the cue to modern poetry was given by Poe.

To be legitimate, a style in art must connect itself with a style outside of art, whether in palaces or dance halls or in the dreams of saints and courtesans. Physically, America has been moving away from style (more exactly, from styles). Eighteenth-century Boston, Philadelphia, Richmond, are "works of art" in the British mode, L'Enfant's Washington in the mode of the incredible. The frontier, however, is not a "landscape"—Gainsborough could not have painted it. Nor are the later cities. They are raw *scene*.

No wonder that the edges of the canvas meant nothing to the Hudson River panoramists. Geography (history, too) becomes in America an endless roll of uncomposed appearances, as in the cycloramas depicting famous Indian battles and the Civil War. Or if an attempt at composition is made, it is by arbitrary means, with the result that the form becomes mechanical, as in the Currier & Ives street scenes whose parts are articulated like a fire engine of those days.

America's steady backing away from style explains why British portrait painting in Colonial Philadelphia is better painting than German Expressionism in twentieth-century Texas, which does not justify any style.

The discovery of *modern* art by Americans in the first decades of this century did not rid them of their old habit of misplacing themselves; in the mirror of post-Impressionism they mistook their cultural environment instead of their physical one. By the 'twenties, under the banner of Experiment, everyone had learned how to manipulate a Look, sometimes three or four, developed out of the crisis of French, German or Italian painting.

The profusion of codes to obey gave rise to an illusion of self-liberation: instead of the Redcoat, single Uhlans, Hussars, Swiss Guards marching in step to distant rhythms. Yet American art was no closer than before to a reality of its own.

COONSKINISM—OR THE MADE-UP

What could Braddock do among those sudden trees? One thing only: call for straighter ranks, a more measured step, louder banging on the drums. In Europe an art could be slowly modified and still keep its form; here, it either had to stand fast on its principles or risk becoming no art at all.

"I, for my poems—What have I?" exclaimed Walt Whitman, taking that risk. "I have all to *make*."

Crèvecoeur's mistake lay in assuming that every American was aware that he had to begin anew. His determinism took it for granted that if a man is in a given situation his consciousness will be there with him. Crèvecoeur should have reflected more deeply on the fact that the Dutch superimposed a small Amsterdam on the tip of Manhattan and that the Pilgrims built not a New World but a New England. In art there have been few examples of the "American" in Crèvecoeur's sense of a psyche designed by history for the constant production of novelties. What's more, the "new men" have tended not to stay new but to settle into a self-repeating pattern.

To be a new man is not a condition but an effort—an effort that follows a revelation in behalf of which existing forms are discarded as irrelevant or are radically revised. The genuine accomplishments of American art spring from the tension of such singular experiences. In honor of Braddock's foes I call this anti-formal or trans-formal effort Coonskinism. The fellows behind the trees are "men without art," to use Wyndham Lewis' label for Faulkner and Hemingway. This does not mean that they do not know how to fight. They have studied manoeuvers among squirrels and grizzly bears and they trust their knowledge against the tradition of Caesar and Frederick. Their principle is simple: watch the object—if it's red, shoot!

Obviously, this proposition can be valid only in a particular situation. The Coonskinners win, but their method can hardly be considered a contribution to military culture. It has a closer tie with primitive art, which also learns from its subject and which, like Whitman, *has* nothing but has all *to make*.

Creation by a mind devoid of background, or deliberately cleansed of it, results in primitive art. The best painting in America is related to the primitives in its methods of overcoming ignorance through the particular problem to be solved. Copley contrives his New England style through carefully studying his models during unusually numerous sittings. His American portraits owe more to the British style of his sitters than to the contemporaneous British manner in painting. When he goes to England, he can no longer paint in the same way and his portraiture declines. Perhaps Copley missed in the Britons in Britain the conflict of style with non-style which had stimulated him in their American imitators. Waterhouse, in his

Painting in Britain, points out that Copley's best British portraits are of children, who are made to look "unEnglish."

Coonskinism is the search for the principle that applies, even if it applies only once. For it, each situation has its own exclusive key. Hence general knowledge of his art does not abate the Coonskinner's ignorance nor relieve him of the need to improvise. Melville's masterpiece begins by being a novel and becomes in turn some fragments of a play, a scientific and historical treatise, an eye-witness report. Out of the Bible, Homer, the newspapers, opera, Whitman puts together poetry from which the appearance of poetry has managed to depart. Art is similarly subsumed in the intense prose of Eakins' paintings which find their problems in the manner in which a pair of well-worn feet hold on to the floor or in the shine of the skin on the back of an old man's hand. If Eakins' realism tends towards the nonLook, Ryder's romance of being privately in a cosmos tends in the same direction. It is not, as the academicians say of artists like Copley or Eakins, that in them Truth conquers over Beauty, it is that both Truth and Beauty are for them the result of a specific encounter.

As made-up art, folk painting in America is the mass-product of Coonskinism, as academic painting is the continuing output of Redcoatism. American artists have moved in both directions between these two extremes, self-taught limners turning into august Redcoats, learned academicians—from Allston to Edwin Dickinson—shedding their red coats, hopping behind trees and aiming with the stubborn concentration of Coonskinners.

Under these circumstances American folk painting cannot be separated from its fine art, as it makes sense to do in other countries. Folk art has no development; its successes are a sum of individual pot shots; in sum, it lacks history. But in the United States, fine art also lacks history and its best examples consist of individual inventions which do not carry over into the future. Nor does any of its imported styles reach a culmination; it ends by being replaced. An historical exhibition of American painting is not complete unless it presents the Coonskin antithesis to the prevailing Redcoatism. Audubon, for instance, is very close to folk art, being largely a self-taught peerer through trees who derived his style from absorption in his subject matter; yet he is, without doubt, a much superior painter to, say, Bierstadt —in fact, Audubon is the first important painter who belongs thoroughly to the United States. Nor can many American painters and sculptors be found who equal as artists the draftsmen of Currier and Ives. (I have seen enlarged details of their New York scenes that are a match for Seurat.)

Coonskin doggedness is a major characteristic of America's most meaningful painters. Not one—Copley, Audubon, Eakins, Ryder, Homer, Marin, Stuart Davis, de Kooning—in whom this quality is not predominant. To make one's own art, one must be able to overcome an enormous amount of doubt and waste of time.

Coonskinism as a principle won ascendancy in American painting for the first time during World War II. With no new styles coming from Europe— and for deeper reasons than transportation difficulties—American artists became willing to take a chance on unStyle or antiStyle. Statements in interviews and catalogues emphasized the creative bearing of such elements of creation as the mistake, the accident, the spontaneous, the incomplete, the absent. The esthetic watchword of the new American painting might almost have been adapted from Melville's: "So far as I am individually concerned and independent of my pocket, it is my earnest desire to write those sorts of books which are said to fail."

At the same time Redcoatism, no longer overfed, reached new degrees of refinement. The American practitioners of Cubism, Neo-Romanticism, Neo-Plasticism, highly conscious of their debt, were able to accumulate a balance of their own.

Today, Coonskinism itself in the form of "free" abstract expression is in danger of becoming a style—as I reminded Crèvecoeur, the new man does not automatically stay that way. With most of the pioneers of 1946, the transformation of the Coonskinner into a Redcoat has already taken place.

What is historically unique is that American Coonskinism has become the prevalent Style of Europe's newest paintings. The Europeans of the '50's have captured the look of the made-up in American art, though their pictures fail to achieve the reality and the feeling of being made-up. The uneasy insistence and individual self-consciousness that go with discovery and give the new American painting its vitality and point are lacking in the Europeans.

Coonskinism has become the Redcoatism of Europe. Once again, the hallucination of the displaced terrain. But this time everything in reverse—Art copying non-Art, rocks and trees carefully laid out as an obstacle-run on the parade ground. It is the setting of a comedy.

DANCERS, BUILDINGS
AND PEOPLE IN THE STREETS

Edwin Denby

On the subject of dance criticism, I should like to make clear a distinction that I believe is very valuable, to keep the question from getting confused. And that is that there are two quite different aspects to it. One part of dance criticism is seeing what is happening on stage. The other is describing clearly what it is you saw. Seeing something happen is always fun for everybody, until they get exhausted. It is very exhausting to keep looking, of course, just as it is to keep doing anything else; and from an instinct of self-preservation many people look only a little. One can get along in life perfectly well without looking much. You all know how very little one is

likely to see happening on the street—a familiar street at a familiar time of
day while one is using the street to get somewhere. So much is happening
inside one, one's private excitements and responsibilities, one can't find the
energy to watch the strangers passing by, or the architecture or the weather
around; one feels there is a use in getting to the place one is headed for and
doing something or other there, getting a book or succeeding in a job or
discussing a situation with a friend, all that has a use, but what use is there
in looking at the momentary look of the street, of 106th and Broadway. No
use at all. Looking at a dance performance has some use, presumably. And
certainly it is a great deal less exhausting than looking at the disjointed
fragments of impression that one can see in traffic. Not only that the performance is arranged so that it is convenient to look at, easy to pay continuous attention to, and attractive, but also that the excitement in it seems
to have points of contact with the excitement of one's own personal life,
with the curiosity that makes one want to go get a special book, or the
exciting self-importance that makes one want to succeed, or even the absorbing drama of talking and listening to someone of one's own age with
whom one is on the verge of being in love. When you feel that the emotion
that is coming toward you from the performance is like a part of your own
at some moment when you were very excited, it is easy to be interested. And
of course if you feel the audience thrilled all around you just when you are
thrilled too, that is very peculiar and agreeable. Instead of those people and
houses on the street that are only vaguely related to you in the sense that
they are Americans and contemporary, here in the theatre, you are almost
like in some imaginary family, where everybody is talking about something
that concerns you intimately and everybody is interested and to a certain
extent understands your own viewpoint and the irrational convictions you
have that are even more urgent than your viewpoint. The amplitude that
you feel you see with at your most intelligent moments, this amplitude seems
in the theatre to be naturally understood on stage and in the audience, in
a way it isn't often appreciated while you are with the people you know
outside the theatre. At a show you can tell perfectly well when it is happening to you, this experience of an enlarged view of what is really so and
true, or when it isn't happening to you. When you talk to your friends about
it after the curtain goes down, they sometimes agree, and sometimes they
don't. And it is strange how whether they do or don't, it is very hard usually
to specify what the excitement was about, or the precise point at which it
gave you the feeling of being really beautiful. Brilliant, magnificent, stupendous, no doubt all these things are true of the performance, but even if
you and your friends agree that it was all those things, it is likely that there
was some particular moment that made a special impression which you are
not talking about. Maybe you are afraid that that particular moment
wasn't really the most important, that it didn't express the idea or that
it didn't get special applause or wasn't the climax. You were really excited
by the performance and now you are afraid you can't show you understand
it. Meanwhile while you hesitate to talk about it, a friend in the crowd who
talks more readily is delivering a brilliant criticism specifying technical

dance details, moral implications, musicological or iconographic finesses; or else maybe he is sailing off into a wild nonsensical camp that has nothing to do with the piece but which is fun to listen to, even though it's a familiar trick of his. So the evening slips out of your awareness like many others. Did you really see anything? Did you see any more than you saw in the morning on the street? Was it a real excitement you felt? What is left over of the wonderful moment you had, or didn't you really have any wonderful moment at all, where you actually saw on stage a real person moving and you felt the relation to your real private life with a sudden poignancy as if for that second you were drunk. Dance criticism has two different aspects: one is being made drunk for a second by seeing something happen; the other is expressing lucidly what you saw when you were drunk. I suppose I should add quite stuffily that it is the performance you should get drunk on, not anything else. But I am sure you have understood me anyway.

Now the second part of criticism, that of expressing lucidly what happened, is of course what makes criticism criticism. If you are going in for criticism you must have the gift in the first place, and in the second place you must cultivate it, you must practice and try. Writing criticism is a subject of interest to those who do it, but it is a separate process from that of seeing what happens. And seeing what happens is of course of much more general interest. This is what you presumably have a gift for, since you have chosen dancing as a subject of special study, and no doubt you have already cultivated this gift. I am sure you would all of you have something interesting and personal to say about what one can see and perhaps too about what one can't see.

Seeing is at any rate the subject I would like to talk about today. I can well imagine that for some of you this is not a subject of prime interest. Some of you are much more occupied with creating or inventing dances, than with seeing them; when you look at them you look at them from the point of view of an artist who is concerned with his own, with her own, creating. Creating, of course, is very exciting, and it is very exciting whether you are good at it or not; you must have noticed that already in watching other people create, whose work looks silly to you, but whose excitement, even if you think it ought not to be, is just as serious to them as that of a creator whose creating isn't silly. But creating dancing and seeing dancing are not the same excitement. And it is not about creating that I mean to speak; I am telling you this, so you won't sit here unless you can spare the time for considering in a disinterested way what seeing is like; please don't feel embarrassed about leaving now, though I agree it would be rude of you to leave later. And it is not very likely either that I shall tell you any facts that you had better write down. I rather think you know all the same facts I do about dancing, and certainly you know some I don't; I have forgotten some I used to know. About facts, too, what interests me just now is how differently they can look, one sees them one way and one sees them another way another time, and yet one is still seeing the same fact. Facts have a way of dancing about, now performing a solo then reappearing in the chorus, linking themselves now with facts of one kind, now with facts of another, and quite changing their style as they do. Of course you have to know the facts so you can recognize them, or you can't appreciate how they move, how they keep dancing. We are supposed to discuss dance history sometime in this seminar and I hope we will. But not today.

At the beginning of what I said today I talked about one sort of seeing, namely a kind that leads to recognizing on stage and inside yourself an echo of some personal, original excitement you already know. I call it an echo because I am supposing that the event which originally caused the excitement in one's self is not literally the same as the event you see happen on stage. I myself, for instance, have never been a Prince or fallen in love with a creature that was half girl and half swan, nor have I myself been an enchanted Swan Princess, but I have been really moved, and transported by some performances of *Swan Lake,* and by both sides of that story. In fact, it is much more exciting if I can feel both sides happening to me, and not just one. But I am sure you have already jumped ahead of me to the next step of the argument, and you can see that not only have I never been such people or been in their situation, but besides that I don't look like either of them, nor could I, even if I were inspired, dance the steps the way they do. Nor even the steps of the other dancers, the soloists or the chorus.

You don't seem to have taken these remarks of mine as a joke. But I hope you realized that I was pointing out that the kind of identification one feels at a dance performance with the performers is not a literal kind. On the other hand, it is very probable that you yourselves watch a dance performance with a certain professional awareness of what is going on.

A professional sees quite clearly "I could do that better, I couldn't do that nearly so well." A professional sees the finesse or the awkwardness of a performer very distinctly, at least in a field of dance execution he or she is accustomed to working in; and a choreographer sees similarly how a piece is put together, or as the phrase is, how the material has been handled. But this is evidently a very special way of looking at a performance. One may go further and say that a theatre performance is not intended to be seen from this special viewpoint. Craftsmanship is a matter of professional ethics; a surgeon is not bound to explain to you what he is doing while he is operating on you, and similarly no art form, no theatre form is meant to succeed in creating its magic with the professionals scattered in the audience. Other doctors seeing a cure, may say, your doctor was a quack but he was lucky; and similarly professionals may say after a performance, Yes, the ballerina was stupendous, she didn't fake a thing—or else say, she may not have thrilled you, but there aren't four girls in the world who can do a something or other the way she did—and this is all to the good, it is honorable and it is real seeing. But I am interested just now to bring to your attention or recall to your experience not that professional way of seeing, but a more general way. I am interested at the moment in recalling to you how it looks when one sees dancing as non-professionals do, in the way you yourselves I suppose look at pictures, at buildings, at political history or at landscapes or at strangers you pass on the street. Or as you read poetry.

In other words the way you look at daily life or at art for the mere pleasure of seeing, without trying to put yourself actively in it, without meaning to do anything about it. I am talking about seeing what happens when people are dancing, seeing how they look. Watching them and appreciating the beauty they show. Appreciating the ugliness they show if that's what you see. Seeing this is beautiful, this ugly, this is nothing as far as I can see. As long as you pay attention there is always something going on, either attractive or unattractive, but nobody can always pay attention, so sometimes there is nothing as far as you can see, because you have really had enough of seeing; and quite often there is very little, but anyway you are looking at people dancing, and you are seeing them while they dance.

Speaking personally, I think there is quite a difference between seeing people dance as part of daily life, and seeing them dance in a theatre performance. Seeing them dance as part of daily life is seeing people dance in a living room or a ballroom or a nightclub, or seeing them dance folk dances either naturally or artificially in a folk dance group. For that matter classroom dancing and even rehearsal dancing seems to me a part of daily life, though it is as special as seeing a surgeon operate, or hearing the boss blow up in his office. Dancing in daily life is also seeing the pretty movements and gestures people make. In the Caribbean, for instance, the walk of Negroes is often, well, miraculous. Both the feminine stroll and the masculine one, each entirely different. In Italy you see another beautiful way of strolling, that of shorter muscles, more complex in their plasticity, with girls deliciously turning their breast very slightly, deliciously pointing their feet. You should see how harmoniously the young men can loll. American young men loll quite differently, resting on a peripheral point, Italians loll resting on a more central one. Italians on the street, boys and girls, both have an extraordinary sense of the space they really occupy, and of filling that space harmoniously as they rest or move; Americans occupy a much larger space than their actual bodies do; I mean, to follow the harmony of their movement or of their lolling you have to include a much larger area in space than they are actually occupying. This annoys many Europeans; it annoys their instinct of modesty. But it has a beauty of its own, that a few of them appreciate. It has so to speak an intellectual appeal; it has because it refers to an imaginary space, an imaginary volume, not to a real and visible one. Europeans sense the intellectual volume but they fail to see how it is filled by intellectual concepts—so they suppose that the American they see lolling and assuming to himself too much space, more space than he actually needs, is a kind of a conqueror, is a kind of nonintellectual or merely material occupying power. In Italy I have watched American sailors, soldiers and tourists, all with the same expansive instinct in their movements and their repose, looking like people from another planet among Italians with their self-contained and traditionally centered movements. To me these Americans looked quite uncomfortable, and embarrassed, quite willing to look smaller if they only knew how. Here in New York where everybody expects them to look the way they do, Americans look unselfconscious and modest despite their traditional expansivity of movement. There is room enough. Not because there is actually more—there isn't in New York—but because people expect it, they like it if people move that way. Europeans who arrive here look peculiarly circumspect and tight to us. Foreign sailors in Times Square look completely swamped in the big imaginary masses surging around and over them.

Well, this is what I mean by dancing in daily life. For myself I think the walk of New Yorkers is amazingly beautiful, so large and clear. But when I go inland, or out West, it is much sweeter. On the other hand, it has very little either of Caribbean lusciousness or of Italian *contraposto*. It hasn't much savor, to roll on your tongue, that it hasn't. Or at least you have to be quite subtle, or very much in love to distinguish so delicate a perfume.

That, of course, is supposed to be another joke, but naturally you would rather travel yourself than hear about it. I can't expect you to see my point without having been to countries where the way of walking is quite different from what ours is here. However, if you were observant, and you ought to be as dance majors, you would have long ago enjoyed the many kinds of walking you can see right in this city, boys and girls, Negro and white, Puerto Rican and Western American and Eastern, foreigners, professors and dancers, mechanics and businessmen, ladies entering a theatre with half a drink too much, and shoppers at Macy's. You can see everything in the world here in isolated examples at least, peculiar characters or people who are for the moment you see them peculiar. And everybody is quite peculiar now and then. Not to mention how peculiar anybody can be at home.

Daily life is wonderfully full of things to see. Not only people's movements, but the objects around them, the shape of the rooms they live in, the ornaments architects make around windows and doors, the peculiar ways buildings end in the air, the watertanks, the fantastic differences in their street façades on the first floor. A French composer who was here said to me, "I had expected the streets of New York to be monotonous, after looking at a map of all those rectangles; but now I see the differences in height between buildings, I find I have never seen streets so diverse one from another." But if you start looking at New York architecture, you will notice not only the sometimes extraordinary delicacy of the window framings, but also the standpipes, the grandiose plaques of granite and marble on ground floors of office buildings, the windowless side walls, the careful, though senseless, marble ornaments. And then the masses, the way the office and factory buildings pile up together in perspective. And under them the drive of traffic, those brilliantly colored trucks with their fanciful lettering, the violent paint on cars, signs, houses, as well as lips. Sunsets turn the red-painted houses in the cross-streets to the flush of live rose petals. And the summer sky of New York for that matter is as magnificent as the sky of Venice. Do you see all this? Do you see what a forty- or sixty-story building looks like from straight below? And do you see how it comes up from the sidewalk as if it intended to go up no more than five stories?

Do you see the bluish haze on the city as if you were in a forest? As for myself, I wouldn't have seen such things if I hadn't seen them first in the photographs of Rudolph Burckhardt. But after seeing them in his photographs, I went out to look if it were true. And it was. There is no excuse for you as dance majors not to discover them for yourselves. Go and see them. There is no point in living here, if you don't see the city you are living in. And after you have seen Manhattan, you can discover other grandeurs out in Queens, in Brooklyn, and in those stinking marshes of Jersey.

All that is here. And it is worth seeing. When you get to Rome, or to Fez in Morocco, or to Paris, or to Constantinople, or to Peking, I hope you will get there, I have always wanted to, you will see other things beautiful in another way, but meanwhile since you are dance majors and are interested and gifted in seeing, look around here. If you cut my talks and bring me instead a report of what you saw in the city. I will certainly mark you present, and if you can report something interesting I will give you a good mark. It is absurd to sit here in four walls while all that extraordinary interest is going on around us. But then education is a lazy, a dull way of learning, and you seem to have chosen it; forget it.

However, if you will insist on listening to me instead of going out and looking for yourselves, I will have to go on with this nonsense. Since you are here I have to go on talking and you listening, instead of you and me walking around and seeing things. And I have to go on logically, which we both realize is nonsense. Logically having talked about what you can see in daily life, I have to go on that very different way of seeing, which you use in seeing art.

For myself, I make a distinction between seeing daily life and seeing art. Not that seeing is different. Seeing is the same. But seeing art is seeing an ordered and imaginary world, subjective, and concentrated. Seeing in the theatre is seeing what you don't see quite that way in life. In fact, it's nothing like that way. You sit all evening in one place and look at an illuminated stage, and music is going on, and people are performing who have been trained in some peculiar way for years, and since we are talking about a dance performance, nobody is expected to say a word, either on stage or in the house. It is all very peculiar. But there are quite a lot of people, ordinary enough citizens watching the stage along with you. All these people in the audience are used to having information conveyed to them by words spoken or written, but here they are just looking at young people dancing to music. And they expect to have something interesting conveyed to them. It is certainly peculiar.

But then, art is peculiar. I won't speak of concert music, which is obviously peculiar, and which thousands every evening listen to, and evidently get satisfaction out of. But even painting is a strange thing. That people will look at some dirt on a canvas, just a little rectangle on a wall, and get all sorts of exalted feelings and ideas from it is not at all natural, it is not at all obvious. Why do they prefer one picture so much to another one? They will tell you and get very eloquent, but it does seem unreasonable. It seems unreasonable if you don't see it. And for all the other arts it's the same. The difference between the "Ode on a Grecian Urn" and a letter on the editorial page of the *Daily News* isn't so great if you look at both of them without reading them. Art is certainly even more mysterious and nonsensical than daily life. But what a pleasure it can be. A pleasure much more extraordinary than a hydrogen bomb is extraordinary.

There is nothing everyday about art. There is nothing everyday about dancing as an art. And that is the extraordinary pleasure of seeing it. I think that is enough for today.

THE CLOSING
OF THE UNIVERSE OF DISCOURSE

Herbert Marcuse

"Dans l'état présent de l'Histoire, toute écriture politique ne peut que confirmer un univers policier, de même toute écriture intellectuelle ne peut qu'instituer une para-littérature, qui n'ose plus dire son nom."

"In the present state of history, all political writing can only confirm a police-universe, just as all intellectual writing can only produce para-literature which does not dare any longer to tell its name."
                                                                    Roland Barthes

The Happy Consciousness—the belief that the real is rational and that the system delivers the goods—reflects the new conformism which is a facet of technological rationality translated into social behavior. It is new because it is rational to an unprecedented degree. It sustains a society which has reduced—and in its most advanced areas eliminated—the more primitive irrationality of the preceding stages, which prolongs and improves life more regularly than before. The war of annihilation has not yet occurred; the Nazi extermination camps have been abolished. The Happy Consciousness repels the connection. Torture has been reintroduced as a normal affair, but in a colonial war which takes place at the margin of the civilized world. And there it is practiced with good conscience for war is war. And this war, too, is at the margin—it ravages only the "underdeveloped" countries. Otherwise, peace reigns.

The power over man which this society has acquired is daily absolved by its efficacy and productiveness. If it assimilates everything it touches, if it absorbs the opposition, if it plays with the contradiction, it demonstrates its cultural superiority. And in the same way the destruction of

THE CLOSING OF THE UNIVERSE OF DISCOURSE From *One-Dimensional Man* by Herbert Marcuse. Reprinted by permission of the Beacon Press, copyright © 1964 by Herbert Marcuse.

resources and the proliferation of waste demonstrate its opulence and the "high levels of well-being"; "the Community is too well off to care!" [1]

THE LANGUAGE OF TOTAL ADMINISTRATION

This sort of well-being, the productive superstructure over the unhappy base of society, permeates the "media" which mediate between the masters and their dependents. Its publicity agents shape the universe of communication in which the one-dimensional behavior expresses itself. Its language testifies to identification and unification, to the systematic promotion of positive thinking and doing, to the concerted attack on transcendent, critical notions. In the prevailing modes of speech, the contrast appears between two-dimensional, dialectical modes of thought and technological behavior or social "habits of thought."

In the expression of these habits of thought, the tension between appearance and reality, fact and factor, substance and attribute tend to disappear. The elements of autonomy, discovery, demonstration, and critique recede before designation, assertion, and imitation. Magical, authoritarian and ritual elements permeate speech and language. Discourse is deprived of the mediations which are the stages of the process of cognition and cognitive evaluation. The concepts which comprehend the facts and thereby transcend the facts are losing their authentic linguistic representation. Without these mediations, language tends to express and promote the immediate identification of reason and fact, truth and established truth, essence and existence, the thing and its function.

These identifications, which appeared as a feature of operationalism, reappear as features of discourse in social behavior. Here functionalization of language helps to repel non-conformist elements from the structure and movement of speech. Vocabulary and syntax are equally affected. Society expresses its requirements directly in the linguistic material but not without opposition; the popular language strikes with spiteful and defiant humor at the official and semi-official discourse. Slang and colloquial speech have rarely been so creative. It is as if the common man (or his anonymous spokesman) would in his speech assert his humanity against the powers that be, as if the rejection and revolt, subdued in the political sphere, would burst out in the vocabulary that calls things by their names: "head-shrinker" and "egghead," "boob tube," "think tank," "beat it" and "dig it," and "gone, man, gone."

However, the defense laboratories and the executive offices, the governments and the machines, the time-keepers and managers, the efficiency experts and the political beauty parlors (which provide the leaders with the appropriate make-up) speak a different language and, for the time being, they seem to have the last word. It is the word that orders and organizes, that induces people to do, to buy, and to accept. It is transmitted in a style which is a veritable linguistic creation; a syntax in which the structure of the sentence is abridged and condensed in such a way that no tension, no

[1] John K. Galbraith, *American Capitalism* (Boston, Houghton Mifflin, 1956), p. 96.

"space" is left between the parts of the sentence. This linguistic form militates against a development of meaning. I shall presently try to illustrate this style.

The feature of operationalism—to make the concept synonymous with the corresponding set of operations—recurs in the linguistic tendency "to consider the names of things as being indicative at the same time of their manner of functioning, and the names of properties and processes as symbolical of the apparatus used to detect or produce them." [2] This is technological reasoning, which tends "to identify things and their functions." [3]

As a habit of thought outside the scientific and technical language, such reasoning shapes the expression of a specific social and political behaviorism. In this behavioral universe, words and concepts tend to coincide, or rather the concept tends to be absorbed by the word. The former has no other content than that designated by the word in the publicized and standardized usage, and the word is expected to have no other response than the publicized and standardized behavior (reaction). The word becomes *cliché* and, as cliché, governs the speech or the writing; the communication thus precludes genuine development of meaning.

To be sure, any language contains innumerable terms which do not require development of their meaning, such as the terms designating the objects and implements of daily life, visible nature, vital needs and wants. These terms are generally understood so that their mere appearance produces a response (linguistic or operational) adequate to the pragmatic context in which they are spoken.

The situation is very different with respect to terms which denote things or occurrences beyond this noncontroversial context. Here, the functionalization of language expresses an abridgment of meaning which has a political connotation. The names of things are not only "indicative of their manner of functioning," but their (actual) manner of functioning also defines and "closes" the meaning of the thing, excluding other manners of functioning. The noun governs the sentence in an authoritarian and totalitarian fashion, and the sentence becomes a declaration to be accepted —it repels demonstration, qualification, negation of its codified and declared meaning.

At the nodal points of the universe of public discourse, self-validating, analytical propositions appear which function like magic-ritual formulas. Hammered and re-hammered into the recipient's mind, they produce the effect of enclosing it within the circle of the conditions prescribed by the formula.

I have already referred to the self-validating hypothesis as propositional form in the universe of political discourse. Such nouns as "freedom," "equality," "democracy," and "peace" imply, analytically, a specific set of attributes which occur invariably when the noun is spoken or written. In the West, the analytic predication is in such terms as free enterprise, initia-

---

[2] Stanley Gerr, "Language and Science," in: *Philosophy of Science,* April 1942, p. 156.
[3] *Ibid.*

tive, elections, individual; in the East in terms of workers and peasants, building communism or socialism, abolition of hostile classes. On either side, transgression of the discourse beyond the closed analytical structure is incorrect or propaganda, although the means of enforcing the truth and the degree of punishment are very different. In this universe of public discourse, speech moves in synonyms and tautologies; actually, it never moves toward the qualitative difference. The analytic structure insulates the governing noun from those of its contents which would invalidate or at least disturb the accepted use of the noun in statements of policy and public opinion. The ritualized concept is made immune against contradiction.

Thus, the fact that the prevailing mode of freedom is servitude, and that the prevailing mode of equality is superimposed inequality is barred from expression by the closed definition of these concepts in terms of the powers which shape the respective universe of discourse. The result is the familiar Orwellian language ("peace is war" and "war is peace," etc.), which is by no means that of terroristic totalitarianism only. Nor is it any less Orwellian if the contradiction is not made explicit in the sentence but is enclosed in the noun. That a political party which works for the defense and growth of capitalism is called "Socialist," and a despotic government "democratic," and a rigged election "free" are familiar linguistic—and political—features which long predate Orwell.

Relatively new is the general acceptance of these lies by public and private opinion, the suppression of their monstrous content. The spread and the effectiveness of this language testify to the triumph of society over the contradictions which it contains; they are reproduced without exploding the social system. And it is the outspoken, blatant contradiction which is made into a device of speech and publicity. The syntax of abridgment proclaims the reconciliation of opposites by welding them together in a firm and familiar structure. I shall attempt to show that the "clean bomb" and the "harmless fall-out" are only the extreme creations of a normal style. Once considered the principal offense against logic, the contradiction now appears as a principle of the logic of manipulation—realistic caricature of dialectics. It is the logic of a society which can afford to dispense with logic and play with destruction, a society with technological mastery of mind and matter.

The universe of discourse in which the opposites are reconciled has a firm basis for such unification—its beneficial destructiveness. Total commercialization joins formerly antagonistic spheres of life, and this union expresses itself in the smooth linguistic conjunction of conflicting parts of speech. To a mind not yet sufficiently conditioned, much of the public speaking and printing appears utterly surrealistic. Captions such as "Labor is Seeking Missile Harmony," [4] and advertisements such as a "Luxury Fall-Out Shelter" [5] may still evoke the naïve reaction that "Labor," "Missile,"

[4] New York Times, December 1, 1960.
[5] Ibid., November 2, 1960.

and "Harmony" are irreconcilable contradictions, and that no logic and no language should be capable of correctly joining luxury and fall-out. However, the logic and the language become perfectly rational when we learn that a "nuclear-powered, ballistic-missile-firing submarine" "carries a price tag of $120,000,000" and that "carpeting, scrabble and TV" are provided in the $1,000 model of the shelter. The validation is not primarily in the fact that this language sells (it seems that the fall-out business was not so good) but rather that it promotes the immediate identification of the particular with the general interest, Business with National Power, prosperity with the annihilation potential. It is only a slip of the truth if a theater announces as a "Special Election Eve Perf., Strindberg's *Dance of Death*." [6] The announcement reveals the connection in a less ideological form than is normally admitted.

The unification of opposites which characterizes the commercial and political style is one of the many ways in which discourse and communication make themselves immune against the expression of protest and refusal. How can such protest and refusal find the right word when the organs of the established order admit and advertise that peace is really the brink of war, that the ultimate weapons carry their profitable price tags, and that the bomb shelter may spell coziness? In exhibiting its contradictions as the token of its truth, this universe of discourse closes itself against any other discourse which is not on its own terms. And, by its capacity to assimilate all other terms to its own, it offers the prospect of combining the greatest possible tolerance with the greatest possible unity. Nevertheless its language testifies to the repressive character of this unity. This language speaks in constructions which impose upon the recipient the slanted and abridged meaning, the blocked development of content, the acceptance of that which is offered in the form in which it is offered.

The analytic predication is such a repressive construction. The fact that a specific noun is almost always coupled with the same "explicatory" adjectives and attributes makes the sentence into a hypnotic formula which, endlessly repeated, fixes the meaning in the recipient's mind. He does not think of essentially different (and possibly true) explications of the noun. Later we shall examine other constructions in which the authoritarian character of this language reveals itself. They have in common a telescoping and abridgment of syntax which cuts off development of meaning by creating fixed images which impose themselves with an overwhelming and petrified concreteness. It is the well-known technique of the advertisement industry, where it is methodically used for "establishing an image" which sticks to the mind and to the product, and helps to sell the men and the goods. Speech and writing are grouped around "impact lines" and "audience rousers" which convey the image. This image may be "freedom" or "peace," or the "nice guy" or the "communist" or "Miss Rheingold." The reader or listener is expected to associate (and does associate) with them a

[6] *Ibid.*, November 7, 1960.

fixated structure of institutions, attitudes, aspirations, and he is expected to react in a fixated, specific manner.

Beyond the relatively harmless sphere of merchandising, the consequences are rather serious, for such language is at one and the same time "intimidation and glorification." [7] Propositions assume the form of suggestive commands—they are evocative rather than demonstrative. Predication becomes prescription; the whole communication has a hypnotic character. At the same time it is tinged with a false familiarity—the result of constant repetition, and of the skillfully managed popular directness of the communication. This relates itself to the recipient immediately—without distance of status, education, and office—and hits him or her in the informal atmosphere of the living room, kitchen, and bedroom.

The same familiarity is established through personalized language, which plays a considerable role in advanced communication.[8] It is "your" congressman, "your" highway, "your" favorite drugstore, "your" newspaper; it is brought "to you," it invites "you," etc. In this manner, superimposed, standardized, and general things and functions are presented as "especially for you." It makes little difference whether or not the individuals thus addressed believe it. Its success indicates that it promotes the self-identification of the individuals with the functions which they and the others perform.

In the most advanced sectors of functional and manipulated communication, language imposes in truly striking constructions the authoritarian identification of person and function. *Time* magazine may serve as an extreme example of this trend. Its use of the inflectional genitive makes individuals appear to be mere appendices or properties of their place, their job, their employer, or enterprise. They are introduced as Virginia's Byrd, U. S. Steel's Blough, Egypt's Nasser. A hyphenated attributive construction creates a fixed syndrome:

"Georgia's high-handed, low-browed governor . . . had the stage all set for one of his wild political rallies last week."

The governor,[9] his function, his physical features, and his political practices are fused together into one indivisible and immutable structure which, in its natural innocence and immediacy, overwhelms the reader's mind. The structure leaves no space for distinction, development, differentiation of meaning: it moves and lives only as a whole. Dominated by such personalized and hypnotic images, the article can then proceed to give even essential information. The narrative remains safely within the well-edited framework of a more or less human interest story as defined by the publisher's policy.

[7] Roland Barthes, *Le Degré zéro de l'écriture* (Paris, Editions du Seuil, 1953), p. 33.
[8] See Leo Lowenthal, *Literature, Popular Culture, and Society* (Prentice-Hall, 1961), p. 109 ff. and Richard Hoggart, *The Uses of Literacy* (Boston, Beacon Press, 1961), p. 161 ff.
[9] The statement refers, not to the present Governor, but to Mr. Talmadge.

Use of the hyphenized abridgment is widespread. For example, "brush-browed" Teller, the "father of the H-bomb," "bull-shouldered missileman von Braun," "science-military dinner" [10] and the "nuclear-powered, ballistic-missile-firing" submarine. Such constructions are, perhaps not accidentally, particularly frequent in phrases joining technology, politics, and the military. Terms designating quite different spheres or qualities are forced together into a solid, overpowering whole.

The effect is again a magical and hypnotic one—the projection of images which convey irresistible unity, harmony of contradictions. Thus the loved and feared Father, the spender of life, generates the H-bomb for the annihilation of life; "science-military" joins the efforts to reduce anxiety and suffering with the job of creating anxiety and suffering. Or, without the hyphen, the Freedom Academy of cold war specialists,[11] and the "clean bomb"—attributing to destruction moral and physical integrity. People who speak and accept such language seem to be immune to everything— and susceptible to everything. Hyphenation (explicit or not) does not always reconcile the irreconcilable; frequently, the combine is quite gentle—as in the case of the "bull-shouldered missileman"—or it conveys a threat, or an inspiring dynamic. But the effect is similar. The imposing structure unites the actors and actions of violence, power, protection, and propaganda in one lightning flash. We see the man or the thing in operation and only in operation—it cannot be otherwise.

Note on abridgment. NATO, SEATO, UN, AFL-CIO, AEC, but also USSR, DDR, etc. Most of these abbreviations are perfectly reasonable and justified by the length of the unabbreviated designata. However, one might venture to see in some of them a "cunning of Reason"—the abbreviation may help to repress undesired questions. NATO does not suggest what North Atlantic Treaty Organization says, namely, a treaty among the nations on the North-Atlantic—in which case one might ask questions about the membership of Greece and Turkey. USSR abbreviates Socialism and Soviet; DDR: democratic. UN dispenses with undue emphasis on "united"; SEATO with those Southeast-Asian countries which do not belong to it. AFL-CIO entombs the radical political differences which once separated the two organizations, and AEC is just one administrative agency among many others. The abbreviations denote that and only that which is institutionalized in such a way that the transcending connotation is cut off. The meaning is fixed, doctored, loaded. Once it has become an official vocable, constantly repeated in general usage, "sanctioned" by the intellectuals, it has lost all cognitive value and serves merely for recognition of an unquestionable fact.

---

[10] The last three items quoted in *The Nation,* Feb. 22, 1958.

[11] A suggestion of *Life* magazine, quoted in *The Nation,* August 20, 1960. According to David Sarnoff, a bill to establish such an Academy is before Congress. See John K. Jessup, Adlai Stevenson, and others, *The National Purpose* (produced under the supervision and with the help of the editorial staff of *Life* magazine, New York, Holt, Rinehart and Winston, 1960), p. 58.

This style is of an overwhelming *concreteness*. The "thing identified with its function" is more real than the thing distinguished from its function, and the linguistic expression of this identification (in the functional noun, and in the many forms of syntactical abridgment) creates a basic vocabulary and syntax which stand in the way of differentiation, separation, and distinction. This language, which constantly imposes *images,* militates against the development and expression of *concepts*. In its immediacy and directness, it impedes conceptual thinking; thus, it impedes thinking. For the concept does *not* identify the thing and its function. Such identification may well be the legitimate and perhaps even the only meaning of the operational and technological concept, but operational and technological definitions are specific usages of concepts for specific purposes. Moreover, they dissolve concepts in operations and exclude the conceptual intent which is opposed to such dissolution. Prior to its operational usage, the concept *denies* the identification of the thing with its function; it distinguishes that which the thing *is* from the contingent functions of the thing in the established reality.

The prevalent tendencies of speech, which repulse these distinctions, are expressive of the changes in the modes of thought discussed in the earlier chapters—the functionalized, abridged and unified language is the language of one-dimensional thought. In order to illustrate its novelty, I shall contrast it briefly with a classical philosophy of grammar which transcends the behavioral universe and relates linguistic to ontological categories.

According to this philosophy, the grammatical subject of a sentence is first a "substance" and remains such in the various states, functions, and qualities which the sentence predicates of the subject. It is actively or passively related to its predicates but remains different from them. If it is not a proper noun, the subject is more than a noun: it names the *concept* of a thing, a universal which the sentence defines as in a particular state or function. The grammatical subject thus carries a meaning in *excess* of that expressed in the sentence.

In the words of Wilhelm von Humboldt: the noun as grammatical subject denotes something that "can enter into certain relationships," [12] but is not identical with these relationships. Moreover, it remains what it is in and "against" these relationships; it is their "universal" and substantive core. The propositional synthesis links the action (or state) with the subject in such a manner that the subject is designated as the actor (or bearer) and thus is distinguished from the state or function in which it happens to be. In saying: "lightning strikes," one "thinks not merely of the striking lightning, but of the lightning itself which strikes," of a subject which "passed into action." And if a sentence gives a definition of its subject, it does not dissolve the subject in its states and functions, but defines it as being in this state, or exercising this function. Neither disappearing in its predicates nor existing as an entity before and outside its

---

[12] W. V. Humboldt, *Über die Verschiedenheit des menschlichen Sprachbaues,* reprint Berlin 1936, p. 254.

predicates, the subject constitutes itself in its predicates—the result of a process of mediation which is expressed in the sentence.[13]

I have alluded to the philosophy of grammar in order to illuminate the extent to which the linguistic abridgments indicate an abridgment of thought which they in turn fortify and promote. Insistence on the philosophical elements in grammar, on the link between the grammatical, logical, and ontological "subject," points up the contents which are suppressed in the functional language, barred from expression and communication. Abridgment of the concept in fixed images; arrested development in self-validating, hypnotic formulas; immunity against contradiction; identification of the thing (and of the person) with its function—these tendencies reveal the one-dimensional mind in the language it speaks.

If the linguistic behavior blocks conceptual development, if it militates against abstraction and mediation, if it surrenders to the immediate facts, it repels recognition of the factors behind the facts, and thus repels recognition of the facts, and of their historical content. In and for the society, this organization of functional discourse is of vital importance; it serves as a vehicle of coordination and subordination. The unified, functional language is an irreconcilably anti-critical and anti-dialectical language. In it, operational and behavioral rationality absorbs the transcendent, negative, oppositional elements of Reason.

I shall discuss these elements in terms of the tension between the "is" and the "ought," between essence and appearance, potentiality and actuality—ingression of the negative in the positive determinations of logic. This sustained tension permeates the two-dimensional universe of discourse which is the universe of critical, abstract thought. The two dimensions are antagonistic to each other; the reality partakes of both of them, and the dialectical concepts develop the real contradictions. In its own development, dialectical thought came to comprehend the historical character of the contradictions and the process of their mediation as historical process. Thus the "other" dimension of thought appeared to be *historical* dimension—the potentiality as historical possibility, its realization as historical event.

The suppression of this dimension in the societal universe of operational rationality is a *suppression of history,* and this is not an academic but a political affair. It is suppression of the society's own past—and of its future, inasmuch as this future invokes the qualitative change, the negation of the present. A universe of discourse in which the categories of freedom have become interchangeable and even identical with their opposites is not only practicing Orwellian or Aesopian language but is repulsing and forgetting the historical reality—the horror of fascism; the idea of socialism; the preconditions of democracy; the content of freedom. If a bureaucratic dictatorship rules and defines communist society, if fascist regimes are functioning as partners of the Free World, if the welfare program of enlightened

[13] See for this philosophy of grammar in dialectical logic Hegel's concept of the "substance as subject" and of the "speculative sentence" in the Preface to the *Phaenomenology of the Spirit.*

capitalism is successfully defeated by labeling it "socialism," if the foundations of democracy are harmoniously abrogated in democracy, then the old historical concepts are invalidated by up-to-date operational redefinitions. The redefinitions are falsifications which, imposed by the powers that be and the powers of fact, serve to transform falsehood into truth.

The functional language is a radically anti-historical language: operational rationality has little room and little use for historical reason.[14] Is this fight against history part of the fight against a dimension of the mind in which centrifugal faculties and forces might develop—faculties and forces that might hinder the total coordination of the individual with the society? Remembrance of the past may give rise to dangerous insights, and the established society seems to be apprehensive of the subversive contents of memory. Remembrance is a mode of dissociation from the given facts, a mode of "mediation" which breaks, for short moments, the omnipresent power of the given facts. Memory recalls the terror and the hope that passed. Both come to life again, but whereas in reality, the former recurs in ever new forms, the latter remains hope. And in the personal events which reappear in the individual memory, the fears and aspirations of mankind assert themselves—the universal in the particular. It is history which memory preserves. It succumbs to the totalitarian power of the behavioral universe:

Das "Schreckbild einer Menschheit ohne Erinnerung . . . ist kein blosses Verfallsprodukt . . . sondern es ist mit der Fortschrittlichkeit des bürgerlichen Prinzips notwendig verknüpft." "Oekonomen und Soziologen wie Werner Sombart und Max Weber haben das Prinzip des Traditionalismus den feudalen Gesellschaftsformen zugeordnet und das der Rationalität den bürgerlichen. Das sagt aber nicht weniger, als dass Erinnerung, Zeit, Gedächtnis von der fortschreitenden bürgerlichen Gesellschaft selber als eine Art irrationaler Rest liquidiert wird . . ."[15]

If the progressing rationality of advanced industrial society tends to liquidate, as an "irrational rest," the disturbing elements of Time and Memory, it also tends to liquidate the disturbing rationality contained in this irrational rest. Recognition and relation to the past as present counteracts the functionalization of thought by and in the established reality.

[14] This does not mean that history, private or general, disappears from the universe of discourse. The past is evoked often enough: be it as the Founding Fathers, or Marx-Engels-Lenin, or as the humble origins of a presidential candidate. However these too, are ritualized invocations which do not allow development of the content recalled; frequently, the mere invocation serves to block such development, which would show its historical impropriety.

[15] "The spectre of man without memory . . . is more than an aspect of decline—it is necessarily linked with the principle of progress in bourgeois society." "Economists and sociologists such as Werner Sombart and Max Weber correlated the principle of tradition to feudal, and that of rationality to bourgeois, forms of society. This means no less than that the advancing bourgeois society liquidates Memory, Time, Recollection as irrational leftovers of the past . . ." Th. W. Adorno, "Wes bedeutet Aufarbeitung der Vergangenheit?", in: Bericht über die Erzieherkonferenz am 6 und 7. November in Wiesbaden; Frankfurt 1960, p. 14.

It militates against the closing of the universe of discourse and behavior; it renders possible the development of concepts which de-stabilize and transcend the closed universe by comprehending it as historical universe. Confronted with the given society as object of its reflection, critical thought becomes historical consciousness; as such, it is essentially judgment. Far from necessitating an indifferent relativism, it searches in the real history of man for the criteria of truth and falsehood, progress and regression. The mediation of the past with the present discovers the factors which made the facts, which determined the way of life, which established the masters and the servants; it projects the limits and the alternatives. When this critical consciousness speaks, it speaks "le langage de la connaissance" (Roland Barthes) which breaks open a closed universe of discourse and its petrified structure. The key terms of this language are not hypnotic nouns which evoke endlessly the same frozen predicates. They rather allow of an open development; they even unfold their content in contradictory predicates.

The Communist Manifesto provides a classical example. Here the two key terms, Bourgeoisie and Proletariat, each "govern" contrary predicates. The "bourgeoisie" is the subject of technical progress, liberation, conquest of nature, creation of social wealth, *and* of the perversion and destruction of these achievements. Similarly, the "proletariat" carries the attributes of total oppression *and* of the total defeat of oppression.

Such dialectical relation of opposites in and by the proposition is rendered possible by the recognition of the subject as an historical agent whose identity constitutes itself in *and against* its historical practice, in *and against* its social reality. The discourse develops and states the conflict between the thing and its function, and this conflict finds linguistic expression in sentences which join contradictory predicates in a logical unit— conceptual counterpart of the objective reality. In contrast to all Orwellian language, the contradiction is demonstrated, made explicit, explained, and denounced.

I have illustrated the contrast between the two languages by referring to the style of Marxian theory, but the critical, cognitive qualities are not the exclusive characteristics of the Marxian style. They can also be found (though in different modes) in the style of the great conservative and liberal critique of the unfolding bourgeois society. For example, the language of Burke and Tocqueville on the one side, of John Stuart Mill on the other is a highly demonstrative, conceptual, "open" language, which has not yet succumbed to the hypnotic-ritual formulas of present-day neo-conservatism and neo-liberalism.

However, the authoritarian ritualization of discourse is more striking where it affects the dialectical language itself. The requirements of competitive industrialization, and the total subjection of man to the productive apparatus appears in the authoritarian transformation of the Marxist into the Stalinist and post-Stalinist language. These requirements, as interpreted by the leadership which controls the apparatus, define what is right and wrong, true and false. They leave no time and no space for a discussion which would project disruptive alternatives. This language no longer lends itself to "discourse" at all. It pronounces and, by virtue of the power of the apparatus, establishes facts—it is self-validating enunciation. Here,[16] it must suffice to quote and paraphrase the passage in which Roland Barthes describes its magic-authoritarian features: "il n'y a plus aucun sursis entre la dénomination et le jugement, et la clôture du langage est parfaite . . ." [17]

The closed language does not demonstrate and explain—it communicates decision, dictum, command. Where it defines, the definition becomes "separation of good from evil"; it establishes unquestionable rights and wrongs, and one value as justification of another value. It moves in tautologies, but the tautologies are terribly effective "sentences." They pass judgment in a "prejudged form"; they pronounce condemnation. For example, the "objective content," that is, the definition of such terms as "deviationist," "revisionist," is that of the penal code, and this sort of validation promotes a consciousness for which the language of the powers that be is the language of truth.[18]

Unfortunately, this is not all. The productive growth of the established communist society also condemns the libertarian communist opposition; the language which tries to recall and preserve the original truth succumbs to its ritualization. The orientation of discourse (and action) on terms such as "the proletariat," "workers' councils," the "dictatorship of the Stalinist apparatus," becomes orientation on ritual formulas where the "proletariat" no longer or not yet exists, where direct control "from below" would interfere with the progress of mass production, and where the fight against the bureaucracy would weaken the efficacy of the only real force that can be mobilized against capitalism on an international scale. Here the past is rigidly retained but not mediated with the present. One opposes the concepts which comprehended a historical situation without developing them into the present situation—one blocks their dialectic.

The ritual-authoritarian language spreads over the contemporary world, through democratic and non-democratic, capitalist and non-capitalist countries.[19] According to Roland Barthes, it is the language "propre à tous les régimes d'autorité," and is there today, in the orbit of advanced industrial civilization, a society which is not under an authoritarian regime? As the substance of the various regimes no longer appears in alternative modes of life, it comes to rest in alternative techniques of manipulation and control. Language not only reflects these controls but becomes itself an instrument of control even where it does not transmit orders but information; where it demands, not obedience but choice, not submission but freedom.

[16] See my Soviet Marxism.
[17] "there is no longer any delay between the naming and the judgment, and the closing of the language is complete."
[18] Roland Barthes, loc. cit., pp. 37–40.
[19] For West Germany see the intensive studies undertaken by the Institut für Sozialforschung, Frankfurt am Main, in 1950–1951: Gruppen Experiment, ed. F. Pollock (Frankfurt, Europaeische Verlagsanstalt, 1955) esp. p. 545 f. Also Karl Korn, Sprache in der verwalteten Welt (Frankfurt, Heinrich Scheffler, 1958), for both parts of Germany.

This language controls by reducing the linguistic forms and symbols of reflection, abstraction, development, contradiction; by substituting images for concepts. It denies or absorbs the transcendent vocabulary; it does not search for but establishes and imposes truth and falsehood. But this kind of discourse is not terroristic. It seems unwarranted to assume that the recipients believe, or are made to believe, what they are being told. The new touch of the magic-ritual language rather is that people don't believe it, or don't care, and yet act accordingly. One does not "believe" the statement of an operational concept but it justifies itself in action—in getting the job done, in selling and buying, in refusal to listen to others, etc.

If the language of politics tends to become that of advertising, thereby bridging the gap between two formerly very different realms of society, then this tendency seems to express the degree to which domination and administration have ceased to be a separate and independent function in the technological society. This does not mean that the power of the professional politicians has decreased. The contrary is the case. The more global the challenge they build up in order to meet it, the more normal the vicinity of total destruction, the greater their freedom from effective popular sovereignty. But their domination has been incorporated into the daily performances and relaxation of the citizens, and the "symbols" of politics are also those of business, commerce, and fun.

The vicissitudes of the language have their parallel in the vicissitudes of political behavior. In the sale of equipment for relaxing entertainment in bomb shelters, in the television show of competing candidates for national leadership, the juncture between politics, business, and fun is complete. But the juncture is fraudulent and fatally premature—business and fun are still the politics of domination. This is not the satire-play after the tragedy; it is not *finis tragoediae*—the tragedy may just begin. And again, it will not be the hero but the people who will be the ritual victims.

PROTEAN MAN

Robert Jay Lifton

I should like to examine a set of psychological patterns characteristic of contemporary life, which are creating a new kind of man—a "protean man." As my stress is upon change and flux, I shall not speak much of "character" and "personality," both of which suggest fixity and permanence. Erikson's concept of identity has been, among other things, an effort to get away from this principle of fixity; and I have been using the term self-

PROTEAN MAN Copyright © 1968 by Robert Jay Lifton. Reprinted from *History and Human Survival,* by Robert Jay Lifton, by permission of Random House, Inc. Originally published in *Partisan Review,* Vol. 35, No. 1 (Winter 1968).

process to convey still more specifically the idea of flow. For it is quite possible that even the image of personal identity, in so far as it suggests inner stability and sameness, is derived from a vision of a traditional culture in which man's relationship to his institutions and symbols are still relatively intact—which is hardly the case today. If we understand the self to be the person's symbol of his own organism, then self-process refers to the continuous psychic recreation of that symbol.

I came to this emphasis through work in cultures far removed from my own, studies of young (and not so young) Chinese and Japanese. Observations I was able to make in America also led me to the conviction that a very general process was taking place. I do not mean to suggest that everybody is becoming the same, or that a totally new "world-self" is taking shape. But I am convinced that a new style of self-process is emerging everywhere. It derives from the interplay of three factors responsible for human behavior: the psychobiological potential common to all mankind at any moment in time; those traits given special emphasis in a particular cultural tradition; and those related to modern (and particularly contemporary) historical forces. My thesis is that this third factor plays an increasingly important part in shaping self-process.

My work with Chinese was done in Hong Kong, in connection with a study of the process of "thought reform" (or "brainwashing") as conducted on the mainland. I found that Chinese intellectuals of varying ages, whatever their experience with thought reform itself, had gone through an extraordinary set of what I at that time called identity fragments—of combinations of belief and emotional involvement—each of which they could readily abandon in favor of another. I remember particularly the profound impression made upon me by the extraordinary history of one young man in particular: beginning as a "filial son" or "young master," that elite status of an only son in an upper-class Chinese family; then feeling himself an abandoned and betrayed victim, as traditional forms collapsed during civil war and general chaos, and his father, for whom he was to long all his life, was separated from him by political and military duties; then a "student activist" in rebellion against the traditional culture in which he had been so recently immersed (as well as against a Nationalist Regime whose abuses he had personally experienced); leading him to Marxism and to strong emotional involvement in the Communist movement; then, because of remaining "imperfections," becoming a participant in a thought reform program for a more complete ideological conversion; but which, in his case, had the opposite effect, alienating him, so he came into conflict with the reformers and fled the country; then, in Hong Kong, struggling to establish himself as an "anti-Communist writer"; after a variety of difficulties, finding solace and meaning in becoming a Protestant convert; and following that, still just thirty, apparently poised for some new internal (and perhaps external) move.

Even more dramatic were the shifts in self-process of a young Japanese whom I interviewed in Tokyo and Kyoto from 1960 to 1962. I shall mention one in particular as an extreme example of this protean pattern,

though there were many others who in various ways resembled him. Before
the age of twenty-five he had been all of the following: a proper middle-
class Japanese boy, brought up in a professional family within a well-
established framework of dependency and obligation; then, due to extensive
contact with farmers' and fishermen's sons brought about by wartime evacuation, a "country boy" who was to retain what he described as a life-long
attraction to the tastes of the common man; then, a fiery young patriot who
"hated the Americans" and whose older brother, a kamikaze pilot, was
saved from death only by the war's end; then a youngster confused in his
beliefs after Japan's surrender, but curious about rather than hostile toward
American soldiers; soon an eager young exponent of democracy, caught
up in the "democracy boom" which swept Japan; at the same time a youthful devotee of traditional Japanese arts—old novels, Chinese poems, kabuki
and flower arrangement; during junior high and high school, an all-round
leader, outstanding in studies, student self-government and general social
and athletic activities; almost simultaneously, an outspoken critic of society
at large and of fellow students in particular for their narrow careerism,
on the basis of Marxist ideas current in Japanese intellectual circles; yet
also an English-speaking student, which meant, in effect, being in still
another vanguard and having strong interest in things American; then,
midway through high school, experiencing what he called a "kind of
neurosis" in which he lost interest in everything he was doing and, in quest
of a "change in mood," took advantage of an opportunity to become an
exchange student for one year at an American high school; became a convert to many aspects of American life, including actually being baptized
as a Christian under the influence of a minister he admired who was also
his American "father," and returned to Japan only reluctantly; as a "re-
turnee," found himself in many ways at odds with his friends and was
accused by one of "smelling like butter" (a traditional Japanese phrase for
Westerners); therefore reimmersed himself in "Japanese" experience—sitting on *tatami,* indulging in quiet, melancholy moods, drinking tea and
so on; then became a *ronin*—in feudal days, a samurai without a master,
now a student without a university—because of failing his examinations
for Tokyo University (a sort of Harvard, Yale, Columbia and Berkeley
rolled into one), and as is the custom, spending the following year preparing for the next round rather than attend a lesser institution; once
admitted, found little to interest him until becoming an enthusiastic
Zengakuren activist, with full embrace of its ideal of "pure Communism"
and a profound sense of fulfillment in taking part in the planning and
carrying out of student demonstrations; but when offered a high position
in the organization during his junior year, abruptly became an ex-*Zengakuren* activist by resigning, because he felt he was not suited for "the life
of a revolutionary"; then an aimless dissipator, as he drifted into a pattern
of heavy drinking, marathon mah-jongg games and affairs with bargirls;
but when the time came, had no difficulty gaining employment with one
of Japan's mammoth industrial organizations (and one of the *bêtes noires*

of his Marxist days) and embarking upon the life of a young executive or *sarariman* (salaried man)—in fact doing so with eagerness, careful preparation and relief, but at the same time having fantasies and dreams of kicking over the traces, sometimes violently, and embarking upon a world tour (largely Hollywood-inspired) of exotic and sophisticated pleasure-seeking.

There are, of course, important differences between the protean life styles of the two young men, and between them and their American counterparts—differences which have to do with cultural emphases and which contribute to what is generally called national character. But such is the intensity of the shared aspects of historical experience that contemporary Chinese, Japanese and American self-process turn out to have striking points of convergence.

I would stress two historical developments as having special importance for creating protean man. The first is the world-wide sense of what I have called *historical* (or *psychohistorical*) *dislocation,* the break in the sense of connection which men have long felt with the vital and nourishing symbols of their cultural tradition—symbols revolving around family, idea systems, religions, and the life cycle in general. In our contemporary world one perceives these traditional symbols (as I have suggested elsewhere, using the Japanese as a paradigm) as irrelevant, burdensome or inactivating, and yet one cannot avoid carrying them within or having one's self-process profoundly affected by them. The second large historical tendency is the *flooding of imagery* produced by the extraordinary flow of post-modern cultural influences over mass communication networks. These cross readily over local and national boundaries, and permit each individual to be touched by everything, but at the same time cause him to be overwhelmed by superficial messages and undigested cultural elements, by headlines and by endless partial alternatives in every sphere of life. These alternatives, moreover, are universally and simultaneously shared—if not as courses of action, at least in the form of significant inner imagery.

We know from Greek mythology that Proteus was able to change his shape with relative ease—from wild boar to lion to dragon to fire to flood. But what he did find difficult, and would not do unless seized and chained, was to commit himself to a single form, the form most his own, and carry out his function of prophecy. We can say the same of protean man, but we must keep in mind his possibilities as well as his difficulties.

The protean style of self-process, then, is characterized by an interminable series of experiments and explorations—some shallow, some profound—each of which may be readily abandoned in favor of still new psychological quests. The pattern in many ways resembles what Erik Erikson has called "identity diffusion" or "identity confusion," and the impaired psychological functioning which those terms suggest can be very much present. But I would stress that the protean style is by no means pathological as such, and, in fact, may well be one of the functional patterns of our day. It extends to all areas of human experience—to political as well as sexual behavior, to the holding and promulgating of ideas and to the general organization of lives.

I would like to suggest a few illustrations of the protean style, as expressed in America and Europe, drawn both from psychotherapeutic work with patients and from observations on various forms of literature and art.

One patient of mine, a gifted young teacher, spoke of himself in this way:

I have an extraordinary number of masks I can put on or take off. The question is: is there, or should there be, one face which should be authentic? I'm not sure that there is one for me. I can think of other parallels to this, especially in literature. There are representations of every kind of crime, every kind of sin. For me, there is not a single act I cannot imagine myself committing.

He went on to compare himself to an actor on the stage who "performs with a certain kind of polymorphous versatility"—and here he was referring, slightly mockingly, to Freud's term, "polymorphous perversity," for diffusely inclusive (also protean) infantile sexuality. And he asked:

Which is the real person, so far as an actor is concerned? Is he more real when performing on the stage—or when he is at home? I tend to think that for people who have these many, many masks, there is no home. Is it a futile gesture for the actor to try to find his real face?

My patient was by no means a happy man, but neither was he incapacitated. And although we can see the strain with which he carries his "polymorphous versatility," it could also be said that, as a teacher and a thinker, and in some ways as a man, it served him well.

In contemporary American literature, Saul Bellow is notable for the protean men he has created. In *The Adventures of Augie March,* one of his earlier novels, we meet a picaresque hero with a notable talent for adapting himself to divergent social worlds. Augie himself says: "I touched all sides, and nobody knew where I belonged. I had no good idea of that myself." And a perceptive young English critic, Tony Tanner, tells us: "Augie indeed celebrates the self, but he can find nothing to do with it." Tanner goes on to describe Bellow's more recent protean hero, Herzog, as "a representative modern intelligence, swamped with ideas, metaphysics, and values, and surrounded by messy facts. It labours to cope with them all."

A distinguished French literary spokesman for the protean style—in his life and in his work—is, of course, Jean-Paul Sartre. Indeed, I believe that it is precisely because of these protean traits that Sartre strikes us as such an embodiment of twentieth-century man. An American critic, Theodore Solotaroff, speaks of Sartre's fundamental assumption that "there is no such thing as even a relatively fixed sense of self, ego, or identity—rather there is only the subjective mind in motion in relationship to that which it confronts." And Sartre himself refers to human consciousness as "a sheer activity transcending toward objects," and "a great emptiness, a wind blowing toward objects." These might be overstatements, but I doubt that they could have been written thirty years ago. Solotaroff further characterizes Sartre as

constantly on the go, hurrying from point to point, subject to subject: fiercely intentional, his thought occupies, fills, and distends its material as he endeavors to lose and find himself in his encounters with other lives, disciplines, books, and situations.

This image of repeated, autonomously willed death and rebirth of the self, so central to the protean style, becomes associated with the themes of father-lessness—as Sartre goes on to tell us in his autobiography with his character-istic tone of serious self-mockery:

There is no good father, that's the rule. Don't lay the blame on men but on the bond of paternity, which is rotten. To beget children, nothing better; *to have* them, what iniquity! Had my father lived, he would have lain on me at full length and would have crushed me. . . . Amidst Aeneas and his fellows who carry their Anchises on their backs, I move from shore to shore, alone and hating those invisible begetters who bestraddle their sons all their life long. I left behind me a young man who did not have time to be my father and who could now be my son. Was it a good thing or bad? I don't know. But I readily subscribed to the verdict of an eminent psychoanalyst: I have no Superego.

We note Sartre's image of interchangeability of father and son, of "a young man who did not have time to be my father and who could now be my son" —which, in a literal sense refers to the age at which his father died, but symbolically suggests an extension of the protean style to intimate family relationships. And such reversals indeed become necessary in a rapidly changing world in which the sons must constantly "carry their fathers on their backs," teach them new things which they, as older people, cannot possibly know. The judgment of the absent superego, however, may be mis-leading, especially if we equate superego with susceptibitily to guilt. What has actually disappeared—in Sartre and in protean man in general—is the *classic* superego, the internalization of clearly defined criteria of right and wrong transmitted within a particular culture by parents to their children. Protean man requires freedom from precisely that kind of superego—he requires a symbolic fatherlessness—in order to carry out his explorations. But rather than being free of guilt, we shall see that his guilt takes on a different form from that of his predecessors.

There are many other representations of protean man among contempo-rary novelists: in the constant internal and external motion of "beat genera-tion" writings, such as Jack Kerouac's *On the Road*; in the novels of a gifted successor to that generation, J. P. Donleavy, particularly *The Ginger Man*; and of course in the work of European novelists such as Günter Grass, whose *The Tin Drum* is a breathtaking evocation of prewar Polish-German, war-time German and postwar German environments, in which the protagonist combines protean adaptability with a kind of perpetual physical-mental "strike" against any change at all.

In the visual arts, one of the most important postwar movements has been aptly named "action painting" to convey its stress upon process rather than fixed completion. And a more recent and related movement in sculpture, called Kinetic Art, goes further. According to Jean Tinguely, one of its leading practitioners, "artists are putting themselves in rhythm with their time, in contact with their epic, especially with permanent and perpetual movement." As revolutionary as any style or approach is the stress upon innovation per se which now dominates painting. I have frequently heard artists, themselves considered radical innovators, complain bitterly of the current standards dictating that "innovation is all," and of a turnover in art movements so rapid as to discourage the idea of holding still long enough to develop a particular style.

We also learn much from film stars. Marcello Mastroianni, when asked whether he agreed with *Time* magazine's characterization of him as "the neo-capitalist hero," gave the following answer:

In many ways, yes. But I don't think I'm any kind of hero, neo-capitalist or otherwise. If anything I am an *anti*-hero or at most a *non*-hero. *Time* said I had the frightened, characteristically 20th-century look, with a spine made of plastic napkin rings. I accepted this—because modern man is that way; and being a product of my time and an artist, I can represent him. If humanity were all one piece, I would be considered a weakling.

Mastroianni accepts his destiny as protean man; he seems to realize that there are certain advantages to having a spine made of plastic napkin rings, or at least that it is an appropriate kind of spine to have these days.

John Cage, the composer, is an extreme exponent of the protean style, both in his music and in his sense of all of us as listeners. He concluded a recent letter to the *Village Voice* with the sentence: "Nowadays, everything happens at once and our souls are conveniently electronic, omniattentive." The comment is McLuhan-like, but what I wish to stress particularly is the idea of omniattention—the sense of contemporary man as having the possibility of "receiving" and "taking in" everything. In attending, as in being, nothing is "off limits."

To be sure, one can observe in contemporary man a tendency which seems to be precisely the opposite of the protean style. I refer to the closing off of identity or constriction of self-process, to a straight-and-narrow specialization in psychological as well as in intellectual life, and to reluctance to let in any "extraneous" influences. But I would emphasize that where this kind of constricted or "one-dimensional" self-process exists, it has an essentially reactive and compensatory quality. In this it differs from earlier characterological styles it may seem to resemble (such as the "inner-directed" man described by Riesman, and still earlier patterns in traditional society). For these were direct outgrowths of societies which then existed, and in harmony with those societies, while at the present time a constricted self-process requires continuous "psychological work" to fend off protean influences which are always abroad.

Protean man has a particular relationship to the holding of ideas which has, I believe, great significance for the politics, religion, and general intellectual life of the future. For just as elements of the self can be experimented with and readily altered, so can idea systems and ideologies be embraced, modified, let go of and reembraced, all with a new ease that stands in sharp contrast to the inner struggle we have in the past associated with these shifts. Until relatively recently, no more than one major ideological shift was likely to occur in a lifetime, and that one would be long remembered as a significant individual turning-point accompanied by profound soul-searching and conflict. But today it is not unusual to encounter several such shifts, accomplished relatively painlessly, within a year or even a month; and among many groups, the rarity is a man who has gone through life holding firmly to a single ideological vision.

In one sense, this tendency is related to "the end of ideology" spoken of by Daniel Bell, since protean man is incapable of enduring an unquestioning allegiance to the large ideologies and utopian thought of the nineteenth and early twentieth centuries. One must be cautious about speaking of the end of anything, however, especially ideology, and one also encounters in protean man what I would call strong ideological hunger. He is starved for ideas and feelings that can give coherence to his world, but here too his taste is toward new combinations. While he is by no means without yearning for the absolute, what he finds most acceptable are images of a more fragmentary nature than those of the ideologies of the past; and these images, although limited and often fleeting, can have great influence upon his psychological life. Thus political and religious movements, as they confront protean man, are likely to experience less difficulty convincing him to alter previous convictions than they do providing him a set of beliefs which can command his allegiance for more than a brief experimental interlude.

Intimately bound up with his flux in emotions and beliefs is a profound inner sense of absurdity, which finds expression in a tone of mockery. The sense and the tone are related to a perception of surrounding activities and belief as profoundly strange and inappropriate. They stem from a breakdown in the relationship between inner and outer worlds—that is, in the sense of symbolic integrity—and are part of the pattern of psychohistorical dislocation I mentioned earlier. For if we view man as primarily a symbol-forming organism, we must recognize that he has constant need of a meaningful inner formulation of self and world in which his own actions, and even his impulses, have some kind of "fit" with the "outside" as he perceives it.

The sense of absurdity, of course, has a considerable modern tradition, and has been discussed by such writers as Camus as a function of man's spiritual homelessness and inability to find any meaning in traditional belief systems. But absurdity and mockery have taken much more extreme form in the post-World War II world, and have in fact become a prominent part of a universal life style.

In American life, absurdity and mockery are everywhere. Perhaps their most vivid expression can be found in such areas as Pop Art and the more general burgeoning of "pop culture." Important here is the complex stance of the pop artist toward the objects he depicts. On the one hand he embraces the materials of the everyday world, celebrates and even exalts them—boldly asserting his creative return to representational art (in active rebellion against the previously reigning nonobjective school), and his psychological return to the "real world" of *things*. On the other hand, everything he touches he mocks. "Thingness" is pressed to the point of caricature. He is indeed artistically reborn as he moves freely among the physical and symbolic materials of his environment, but mockery is his birth certificate and his passport. This kind of duality of approach is formalized in the stated "duplicity" of Camp, a poorly-defined aesthetic in which (among other things) all varieties of mockery converge under the guiding influence of the homosexual's subversion of a heterosexual world.

Also relevant are a group of expressions in current slang, some of them derived originally from jazz. The "dry mock" has replaced the dry wit; one refers to a segment of life experience as a "bit," "bag," "caper," "game," (or "con game"), "scene," "show" or "scenario"; and one seeks to "make the scene" (or "make it"), "beat the system" or "pull it off"—or else one "cools it" ("plays it cool") or "cops out." The thing to be experienced, in other words, is too absurd to be taken at its face value; one must either keep most of the self aloof from it, or if not one must lubricate the encounter with mockery.

A similar spirit seems to pervade literature and social action alike. What is best termed a "literature of mockery" has come to dominate fiction and other forms of writing on an international scale. Again Günter Grass's *The Tin Drum* comes to mind, and is probably the greatest single example of this literature—a work, I believe, which will eventually be appreciated as much as a general evocation of contemporary man as of the particular German experience with Nazism. In this country the divergent group of novelists known as "black humorists" also fit into the general category—related as they are to a trend in the American literary consciousness which R. W. B. Lewis has called a "savagely comical apocalypse" or a "new kind of ironic literary form and disturbing vision, the joining of the dark thread of apocalypse with the nervous detonations of satiric laughter." For it is precisely death itself, and particularly threats of the contemporary apocalypse, that protean man ultimately mocks.

The relationship of mockery to political and social action has been less apparent, but is, I would claim, equally significant. There is more than coincidence in the fact that the largest American student uprising of recent decades, the Berkeley Free Speech Movement of 1965, was followed immediately by a "Dirty Speech Movement." While the object of the Dirty Speech Movement—achieving free expression of forbidden language, particularly of four-letter words—can be viewed as a serious one, the predominant effect, even in the matter of names, was that of a mocking caricature of the movement which preceded it. But if mockery can undermine protest, it can also enliven it. There have been signs of craving for it in major American expressions of protest such as the Negro movement and the opposition to the war in Vietnam. In the former a certain chord can be struck by the comedian Dick Gregory, and in the latter by the use of satirical skits and parodies, that revives the flagging attention of protestors becoming gradually bored with the repetition of their "straight" slogans and goals. And on an international scale, I would say that, during the past decade, Russian intellectual life has been enriched by a leavening spirit of mockery—against which the Chinese leaders are now, in the extremes of their "Cultural Revolution," fighting a vigorous but ultimately losing battle.

Closely related to the sense of absurdity and the spirit of mockery is another characteristic of protean man which can be called "suspicion of counterfeit nurturance." Involved here is a severe conflict of dependency, a core problem of protean man. I first began to think of the concept several years ago while working with survivors of the atomic bomb in Hiroshima. I found that these survivors both felt themselves in need of special help, and resented whatever help was offered them because they equated it with weakness and inferiority. In considering the matter more generally, I found this equation of nurturance with a threat to autonomy a major theme of contemporary life. The increased dependency needs resulting from the breakdown of traditional institutions lead protean man to seek out replacements wherever he can find them. The large organizations (government, business, academic, etc.) to which he turns, and which contemporary society more and more holds out as a substitute for traditional institutions, present an ambivalent threat to his autonomy in one way; and the intense individual relationships in which he seeks to anchor himself in another. Both are therefore likely to be perceived as counterfeit. But the obverse side of this tendency is an expanding sensitivity to the unauthentic, which may be just beginning to exert its general creative force on man's behalf.

Technology (and technique in general), together with science, have special significance for protean man. Technical achievement of any kind can be strongly embraced to combat inner tendencies toward diffusion, and to transcend feelings of absurdity and conflicts over counterfeit nurturance. The image of science itself, however, as the ultimate power behind technology and, to a considerable extent, behind contemporary thought in general, becomes much more difficult to cope with. Only in certain underdeveloped countries can one find, in relatively pure form, those expectations of scientific-utopian deliverance from all human want and conflict which were characteristic of eighteenth- and nineteenth-century Western thought. Protean man retains much of this utopian imagery, but he finds it increasingly undermined by massive disillusionment. More and more he calls forth the other side of the God-devil polarity generally applied to science, and sees it as a purveyor of total destructiveness. This kind of profound ambivalence creates for him the most extreme psychic paradox: the very force he still feels to be his liberator from the heavy burdens of past irrationality also threatens him with absolute annihilation, even extinction. But this paradox may well be—in fact, I believe, already has been—the source of imaginative efforts to achieve new relationships between science and man, and indeed, new visions of science itself.

I suggested before that protean man was not free of guilt. He indeed suffers from it considerably, but often without awareness of what is causing his suffering. For his is a form of hidden guilt: a vague but persistent kind of self-condemnation related to the symbolic disharmonies I have described, a sense of having no outlet for his loyalties and no symbolic structure for his achievements. This is the guilt of social breakdown, and it includes various forms of historical and racial guilt experienced by whole nations and peoples, both by the privileged and the abused. Rather than a clear feeling of evil or sinfulness, it takes the form of a nagging sense of unworthiness all the more troublesome for its lack of clear origin.

Protean man experiences similarly vague constellations of anxiety and resentment. These too have origin in symbolic impairments and are particularly tied-in with suspicion of counterfeit nurturance. Often feeling himself uncared for, even abandoned, protean man responds with diffuse fear and anger. But he can neither find a good cause for the former, nor a consistent target for the latter. He nonetheless cultivates his anger because he finds it more serviceable than anxiety, because there are plenty of targets of one kind or another beckoning, and because even moving targets are better than none. His difficulty is that focused indignation is as hard for him to sustain as is any single identification or conviction.

Involved in all of these patterns is a profound psychic struggle with the idea of change itself. For here too protean man finds himself ambivalent in the extreme. He is profoundly attracted to the idea of making all things, including himself, totally new—to the "mode of transformation." But he is equally drawn to an image of a mythical past of perfect harmony and prescientific wholeness, to the "mode of restoration." Moreover, beneath his transformationism is nostalgia, and beneath his restorationism is his fascinated attraction to contemporary forms and symbols. Constantly balancing these elements midst the extraordinarily rapid change surrounding his own life, the nostalgia is pervasive, and can be one of his most explosive and dangerous emotions. This longing for a "Golden Age" of absolute oneness, prior to individual and cultural separation or delineation, not only sets the tone for the restorationism of the politically Rightist antagonists of history: the still-extant Emperor-worshiping assassins in Japan, the Colons in France and the John Birchites and Ku Klux Klanners in this country. It also, in more disguised form, energizes that transformationist totalism of the Left which courts violence, and is even willing to risk nuclear violence, in a similarly elusive quest.

Following upon all that I have said are radical impairments to the symbolism of transition within the life cycle—the *rites de passage* surrounding birth, entry into adulthood, marriage and death. Whatever rites remain seem shallow, inappropriate, fragmentary. Protean man cannot take them seriously, and often seeks to improvise new ones with whatever contemporary materials he has available, including cars and drugs. Perhaps the central impairment here is that of symbolic immortality—of the universal need for imagery of connection predating and extending beyond the individual life span, whether the idiom of this immortality is biological (living on through children and grandchildren), theological (through a life after death), natural (*in* nature itself which outlasts all) or creative (through what man makes and does). I have suggested elsewhere that this sense of immortality is a fundamental component of ordinary psychic life, and that it is now being profoundly threatened: by simple historical velocity, which subverts the idioms (notably the theological) in which it has traditionally been maintained; and, of particular importance to protean man, by the existence of nuclear weapons, which, even without being used, call into question all modes of immortality. (Who can be certain of living on through children and grandchildren, through teachings or kindnesses?)

Protean man is left with two paths to symbolic immortality which he tries to cultivate, sometimes pleasurably and sometimes desperately. One is the natural mode we have mentioned. His attraction to nature and concern at its desecration has to do with an unconscious sense that, in whatever holocaust, at least nature will endure—though such are the dimensions of our present weapons that he cannot be absolutely certain even of this. His second path may be termed that of "experiential transcendence"—of seeking a sense of immortality in the way that mystics always have, through psychic experience of such great intensity that time and death are, in effect, eliminated. This, I believe, is the larger meaning of the "drug revolution," of protean man's hunger for chemical aids to "expanded consciousness." And indeed all revolutions may be thought of, at bottom, as innovations in the struggle for immortality, as new combinations of old modes.

We have seen that young adults individually, and youth movements collectively, express most vividly the psychological themes of protean man. And although it is true that these themes make contact with what we sometimes call the "psychology of adolescence," we err badly if we overlook their expression in all age groups and dismiss them as "mere adolescent phenomena." Rather, protean man's affinity for the young—his being metaphorically and psychologically so young in spirit—has to do with his never-ceasing quest for imagery of rebirth. He seeks such imagery from all sources: from ideas, techniques, religious and political systems, mass movements and drugs; or from special individuals of his own kind whom he sees as possessing that problematic gift of his namesake, the gift of prophecy. The dangers inherent in the quest seem hardly to require emphasis. What perhaps needs most to be kept in mind is the general principle that renewal on a large scale is impossible to achieve without forays into danger, destruction and negativity. The principle of "death and rebirth" is as valid psychohistorically as it is mythologically. However misguided many of his forays may be, protean man also carries with him an extraordinary range of possibility for man's betterment, or more important, for his survival.

A YIPPIE MANIFESTO

Jerry Rubin

This is a Viet Cong flag on my back. During the recent hearings of the House UnAmerican Activities Committee in Washington, a friend and I are walking down the street en route to Congress—he's wearing an American flag and I'm wearing this VC flag.

The cops mass, and boom! all of a sudden they come toward us. I think: Oh, man, curtains. I am going to be arrested for treason, for supporting the enemy.

And who do the cops grab and throw in the paddy wagon?

My friend with the American flag!

And I'm left all alone in the VC flag.

"What kind of a country is this?" I shout at the cops. "YOU COMMU-NISTS!"

Everything is cool en route to Canada until the border. An official motions me into a small room and pulls out a five-page questionnaire.

"Do you use drugs?" he asks quite seriously.

"Yeah," I say.

"Which?"

"Coca Cola."

"I mean DRUGS!" he shouts.

"Coca Cola is more dangerous for you than marijuana," I say. "Fucks up your body, and it's addictive."

"Have you ever advocated the overthrow of the Canadian government?" he asks.

"Not until I get into Canada."

"Have you ever been arrested for inciting to riot?"

I reply no, and it is true. In August I was arrested in Chicago for something similar, "solicitation to mob action," a violation of a sex statute.

Finally I ask the border official to drop out. "Man, your job is irrelevant," I say. "The Canadian-American border does not exist. There are no such things as borders. The border exists only in your head.

"No state has the right to ask me these questions. The answers are mine. Next thing I know you guys will be tapping my brain!"

I try to get the cat to take off his uniform right there. But he refuses, saying, "I've got a job to do and a family to support."

So goes the cancer of the Western world: everyone just doing his "job." Nobody learned the lesson of Eichmann. Everyone still points the finger elsewhere.

America and the West suffer from a great spiritual crisis. And so the yippies are a revolutionary religious movement.

We do not advocate political solutions that you can vote for. You are never going to be able to *vote* for the revolution. Get that hope out of your mind.

And you are not going to be able to buy the revolution in a supermarket, in the tradition of our consumer society. The revolution is not a can of goods.

Revolution only comes through personal transformation: finding God and changing your life. Then millions of converts will create a massive social upheaval.

The religion of the yippies is: "RISE UP AND ABANDON THE CREEPING MEATBALL!!"

That means anything you want it to mean. Which is why it is so powerful a revolutionary slogan. The best picket sign I ever saw was blank. Next best was: "We Protest ————!"

Slogans like "Get out of Vietnam" are informative, but they do not create myths. They don't ask you to do anything but carry them.

Political demonstrations should make people dream and fantasize. A religious-political movement is concerned with people's souls, with the creation of a magic world which we make real.

When the national media first heard our slogan, they reported that the "creeping meatball" was Lyndon Johnson. Which was weird and unfair, because we liked Lyndon Johnson.

We cried when LBJ dropped out. "LBJ, you took us too literally! We didn't mean YOU should drop out! Where would WE be if it weren't for you, LBJ?"

Is there any kid in America, or anywhere in the world, who wants to be like LBJ when he grows up?

As a society falls apart, its children reject their parents. The elders offer us Johnsons, Agnews, and Nixons, dead symbols of a dying past.

The war between THEM and US will be decided by the seven-year-olds.

We offer: sex, drugs, rebellion, heroism, brotherhood.

They offer: responsibility, fear, puritanism, repression.

Dig the movie *Wild in the Streets*! A teenage rock-and-roll singer campaigns for a Bobby Kennedy-type politician.

Suddenly he realizes: "We're all young! Let's run the country ourselves!"

"Lower the voting age to 14!"

"14 or FIGHT!"

They put LSD in the water fountains of Congress and the Congressmen have a beautiful trip. Congress votes to lower the voting age to 14.

The rock-and-roll singer is elected President, but the CIA and military refuse to recognize the vote. Thousands of longhairs storm the White House, and six die in the siege. Finally the kids take power, and they put all people over 30 into camps and give them LSD every day. (Some movies are even stranger than OUR fantasies.)

"Don't trust anyone over 30!" say the yippies—a much-quoted warning. I am four years old.

We are born twice. My first birth was in 1938, but I was reborn in Berkeley in 1964 in the Free Speech Movement.

When we say "Don't trust anyone over 30," we're talking about the second birth. I got 26 more years.

When people 40 years old come up to me and say, "Well, I guess I can't be part of your movement," I say, "What do you mean? You could have been born yesterday. Age exists in your head."

Bertrand Russell is our leader. He's 90 years old.

Another yippie saying is: "THE GROUND YOU STAND ON IS LIBERATED TERRITORY!"

Everybody in this society is a policeman. We all police ourselves. When we free ourselves, the real cops take over.

I don't smoke pot in public often, although I love to. I don't want to be arrested: that's the only reason.

I police myself.

We do not own our own bodies.

We fight to regain our bodies—to make love in the parks, say "fuck" on television, do what we want to do whenever we want to do it.

Prohibitions should be prohibited.

Rules are made to be broken.

Never say "no."

The yippies say: "PROPERTY IS THEFT."

What America got, she stole.

How was this country built? By the forced labor of slaves. America owes black people billions in compensation.

"Capitalism" is just a polite schoolbook way of saying: "Stealing."

Who deserves what they get in America? Do the Rockefellers deserve their wealth? HELL NO!

Do the poor deserve their poverty? HELL NO!!

America says that people work only for money. But check it out: those who don't have money work the hardest, and those who have money take very long lunch hours.

When I was born I had food on my table and a roof over my head. Most babies born in the world face hunger and cold. What is the difference between them and me?

Every well-off white American better ask himself that question or he will never understand why people hate America.

The enemy is this dollar bill right here in my hand.

Now if I get a match, I'll show you what I think of it.

This burning gets some political radicals very uptight. I don't know exactly why. They burn a lot of money putting out leaflets nobody reads.

I think it is more important today to burn a dollar bill than it is to burn a draft card.

(Hmmm, pretty resilient. Hard to burn. Anybody got a lighter?)

We go to the New York Stock Exchange, about 20 of us, our pockets stuffed with dollar bills. We want to throw real dollars down at all those people on the floor playing monopoly games with numbers.

An official stops us at the door and says, "You can't come in. You are hippies and you are coming to demonstrate."

With TV cameras flying away, we reply: "Hippies? Demonstrate? We're Jews. And we're coming to see the stock market."

Well, that gets the guy uptight, and he lets us in. We get to the top, and the dollars start raining down on the floor below.

These guys deal in millions of dollars as a game, never connecting it to people starving. Have they ever seen a real dollar bill?

"This is what it is all about, you sonavabitches!!"

Look at them: wild animals chasing and fighting each other for the dollar bills thrown by the hippies!

And then the cops come. The cops are a necessary part of any demonstration theater. When you are planning a demonstration, always include a role for the cops. Cops legitimize demonstrations.

The cops throw us out.

It is noon. Wall Street. Businessmen with briefcases and suits and ties. Money freaks going to lunch. Important business deals. Time. Appointments.

And there we are in the middle of it, burning five-dollar bills. Burning their world. Burning their Christ.

"Don't! Don't!" some scream, grasping for the sacred paper. Several near fist-fights break out.

We escape with our lives.

Weeks later *The New York Times* publishes a short item revealing that the New York Stock Exchange is installing a bulletproof glass window between the visitors' platform and the floor, so that "nobody can shoot a stockbroker."

(In Chicago 5,000 yippies come, armed only with our skin. The cops bring tanks, dogs, guns, gas, long-range rifles, missiles. Is it South Vietnam or Chicago? America always overreacts.)

The American economy is doomed to collapse because it has no soul. Its stability is war and preparation for war. Consumer products are built to break, and advertising brainwashes us to consume new ones.

The rich feel guilty. The poor are taught to hate themselves. The guilty and the wretched are on a collision course.

If the men who control the technology used it for human needs and not profit and murder, every human being on the planet could be free from starvation. Machines could do most of the work: people would be free to do what they want.

We should be very realistic and demand the impossible. Food, housing, clothing, medicine, and color TV free for all!!

People would work because of love, creativity, and brotherhood. A new economic structure would produce a new man.

That new structure will be created by new men.

American society, because of its Western-Christian-Capitalist bag, is organized on the fundamental premise that man is bad, society evil, and that: People must be motivated and forced by external reward and punishment.

We are a new generation, species, race. We are bred on affluence, turned on by drugs, at home in our bodies, and excited by the future and its possibilities.

Everything for us is an experience, done for love or not done at all.

We live off the fat of society. Our fathers worked all-year-round for a two-week vacation. Our entire life is a vacation!

Every moment, every day we decide what we are going to do.

We do not groove with Christianity, the idea that people go to heaven after they are dead. We want HEAVEN NOW!

We do not believe in studying to obtain degrees in school. Degrees and grades are like money and credit, good only for burning.

There is a war going on in the Western world: a war of genocide by the old against the young.

The economy is closed. It does not need us. Everything is built.

So the purpose of universities is: to get us off the streets. Schools are baby-sitting agencies.

The purpose of the Vietnam war is: to get rid of blacks. They are a nuisance. America got the work she needed out of blacks, but now she has no use for them.

It is a psychological war. The old say, "We want you to die for us." The old send the young to die for the old.

Our response? Draft-card burning and draft dodging! We won't die for you.

Young whites are dropping out of white society. We are getting our heads straight, creating new identities. We're dropping out of middle-class institutions, leaving their schools, running away from their homes, and forming our own communities.

We are becoming the new niggers.

I'm getting on a plane en route to Washington. An airline official comes up to me and says, "You can't go on this airplane."

"Why not?" I ask.

"Because you smell."

That's what they used to say about black people, remember?

They don't say that about black people anymore. They'd get punched in their fucking mouths.

Our long hair communicates disrespect to America. A racist, short-hair society gets freaked by long hair. It blinds people. In Vietnam, America bombs the Vietnamese, but cannot see them because they are brown.

Long hair is vital to us because it enables us to recognize each other. We have white skin like our oppressors. Long hair ties us together into a visible counter-community.

A car drives down the street, parents in front, and 15-year-old longhair kid in back. The kid gives me the "V" sign! That's the kind of communication taking place.

Within our community we have the seeds of a new society. We have our own communications network, the underground press. We have the beginnings of a new family structure in communes. We have our own stimulants.

When the cops broke into my home on the Lower East Side to arrest me for possession of pot, it was like American soldiers invading a Vietnamese village. They experienced cultural shock.

Fidel Castro was on the wall. They couldn't believe it! Beads! They played with my beads for 20 minutes.

When the cops kidnapped me in Chicago, they interviewed me as if I had just landed from Mars.

"Do you fuck each other?"

"What is it like on LSD?"

"Do you talk directly with the Viet Cong?"

The two generations cannot communicate with one another because of our different historical experiences.

Our parents suffered through the Depression and World War II. We experience the consumer economy and the U.S.A. as a military bully in Vietnam.

From 1964 to 1968 the movement has been involved in the destruction of the old symbols of America. Through our actions we have redefined those symbols for the youth.

Kids growing up today expect school to be a place to demonstrate, sit-in, fight authority, and maybe get arrested.

Demonstrations become the initiation rites, rituals, and social celebrations of a new generation.

Remember the Pentagon, center of the military ego? We urinated on it. Thousands of stoned freaks stormed the place, carrying Che's picture and stuffing flowers in the rifles of the 82nd Airborne.

Remember the Democratic Convention? Who, after Chicago, can read schoolbook descriptions of national political conventions with a straight face anymore? The farce within the convention became clear because of the war between the yippies and the cops in the streets.

We are calling the bluff on the myths of America. Once the myth is exposed, the structure behind it crumbles like sand. Chaos results. People must create new realities.

In the process we create new myths, and these new myths forecast the future.

In America in 1969 old myths can be destroyed overnight, and new ones created overnight because of the power of television. By making communications instantaneous, television telescopes the revolution by centuries. What might have taken 100 years will now take 20. What used to happen in 10 years now happens in two. In a dying society, television becomes a revolutionary instrument.

For her own protection, the government is soon going to have to suppress freedom of the press and take direct control over what goes on television, especially the news.

TV has dramatized the longhair drop-out movement so well that virtually every young kid in the country wants to grow up and be a demonstrator.

What do you want to be when you grow up? A fireman? A cop? A professor?

"I want to grow up and make history."

Young kids watch TV's thrill-packed coverage of demonstrations—including the violence and excitement—and dream about being in them. They look like fun.

Mayor Daley put out this television film about Chicago. It had cops beating up young longhairs. In one scene, the cops threw a tear-gas canister into the crowd, and one demonstrator picked it up and heaved it right back.

Who do you think every kid in the country identified with?

Then the announcer said the chiller: "These demonstrations are Communist led! . . ."

Communism? Who the hell knows from Communism? We never lived through Stalin. We read about it, but it doesn't affect us emotionally. Our emotional reaction to Communism is Fidel marching into Havana in 1959.

There is NO WORD that the Man has to turn off your youth, no scare word.

"They're for ANARCHY!"

Damn right, we're for anarchy! This country is fucking over-organized anyway.

"DON'T DO THIS, DON'T DO THAT, DON'T!"

Growing up in America is learning what NOT to do.

We say: "DO IT, DO IT. DO WHATEVER YOU WANT TO DO."

Our battlegrounds are the campuses of America. White middle-class youth are strategically located in the high schools and colleges of this country. They are our power bases.

If one day 100 campuses were closed in a nationally coordinated rebellion, we could force the President of the United States to sue for peace at the conference table.

As long as we are in school we are prisoners. Schools are voluntary jails. We must liberate ourselves.

Dig the geography of a university. You can always tell what the rulers have up their sleeves when you check out the physical environment they create. The buildings tell you how to behave. Then there is less need for burdensome rules and cops. They designed classrooms so that students sit in rows, one after the other, hierarchically, facing the professor who stands up front talking to all of them.

Classrooms say:
"Listen to the Professor.
"He teaches you.
"Keep your place.
"Don't stretch out.
"Don't lie on the floor.
"Don't relax.
"Don't speak out of turn.
"Don't take off your clothes.
"Don't get emotional.
"Let the mind rule the body.
"Let the needs of the classroom rule the mind."

Classrooms are totalitarian environments. The main purpose of school and education in America is to force you to accept and love authority, and to distrust your own spontaneity and emotions.

How can you grow in such an over-structured environment? You can't. Schools aren't for learning.

Classrooms should be organized in circles, with the professor one part of the circle. A circle is a democratic environment.

Try breaking up the environment. Scream "Fuck" in the middle of your prof's lecture.

So, we organize a University of the Flesh. Four of us go into a classroom. We sit in the middle of the class. The lecture is on "Thinking."

Thinking!

We take off our shirts, smoke joints, and start French kissing. A lot of students get nervous. This goes on for 10–15 minutes, and the professor goes on with his lecture like nothing is happening.

Finally a girl says, "The people there are causing a distraction, and could they either put their shirts back on or could they please leave."

And the prof says, "Well, I agree with that. I think that if you're not here to hear what I'm saying . . ."

We shout: "You can't separate thinking from loving! We are hard in thought!!"

And the prof says, "Well, in my classroom I give the lessons."

Scratch a professor deep and you find a cop!

Fucking milquetoast! Didn't have the guts to throw us out, but in his classroom, HE GIVES the lesson. So he sends his teaching assistant to get the cops, and we split.

We must bring psychological guerrilla war to the university.

The mind is programmed. Get in there and break that bloody program!

Can you imagine what a feeling a professor has standing in front of a class and looking at a room full of bright faces taking down every word he says, raising their hands and asking him questions? It really makes someone think he is God. And to top it off, he has the power to reward and punish you, to decide whether or not you are fit to advance in the academic rat race.

Is this environment the right one for teacher and student?

Socrates is turning in his grave.

I was telling a professor of philosophy at Berkeley that many of his students were wiser men than he, even though he may have read more books and memorized more theories.

He replied, "Well, I must take the lead in the transfer of knowledge."

Transfer of knowledge! What is knowledge?

How to Live.

How to Legalize Marijuana.

How to Make a Revolution.

How to Free People from Jail.

How to Organize Against the CIA.

When a professor takes off his suit and tie, and joins us in the streets, then I say, "Hey man, what's your first name? You're my brother. Let's go. We're together."

I don't dig the "professor" bullshit. I am more interested in a 15-year-old stoned dope freak living on street corners than I am in a Ph.D.

There is anti-intellectualism in America because professors have created an artificial environment. That is why the average working guy does not respect professors.

The university is a protective and plastic scene, shielding people from the reality of life, the reality of suffering, of ecstasy, of struggle. The university converts the agony of life into the security of words and books.

You can't learn anything in school. Spend one hour in a jail or a courtroom and you will learn more than in five years spent in a university.

All I learned in school was how to beat the system, how to fake answers. But there are no answers. There are only more questions. Life is a long journey of questions, answered through the challenge of living. You would never know that, living in a university ruled by the "right" answers to the wrong questions.

Graffiti in school bathrooms tells you more about what's on people's minds than all the books in the library.

We must liberate ourselves. I dropped out. The shit got up to my neck and I stopped eating. I said: NO. NO. NO!! I'm dropping out.

People at Columbia found out what it felt like to learn when they seized buildings and lived in communes for days.

We have to redesign the environment and remake human relationships. But if you try it, you will be kicked out.

You know what professors and deans will say? "If you don't like it here, why don't you go back to Russia!"

A lot is demanded of white, middle-class youth in 1969. The whole thing about technological and bureaucratic society is that it is not made for heroes. We must become heroes.

The young kids living in the streets as new niggers are the pioneers of tomorrow, living dangerously and existentially.

The yippies went to Chicago to have our own counter-festival, a "Festival of Life" in the parks of Chicago, as a human contrast to the "Convention of Death" of the Democrats.

I get a phone call on Christmas Day, 1967 from Marvin Garson, the editor of the *San Francisco Express-Times,* and he says, "Hey, it looks like the Peace and Freedom Party is not going to get on the ballot."

I say, "I don't care. I'm not interested in electoral politics anyway."

And he says, "Let's run a pig for President."

An arrow shoots through my brain. Yeah! A pig, with buttons, posters, bumper stickers.

"America, why take half a hog, when you can have the whole hog?"

At the Democratic convention, the pigs nominate the President and he eats the people.

At the yippie convention, we nominate our pig and after he makes his nominating speech, we eat him. The contrast is clear: Should the President eat the people or the people eat the President?

Well, we didn't kill our pig. If there is one issue that could split the yippies, it is the issue of vegetarianism. A lot of yippies don't believe in killing and eating animals, so I had to be less militant on that point.

We bring Pigasus to Chicago, and he is arrested in Civic Center. The cops grab him. They grab seven of us, and they throw us in the paddy wagon with Pigasus.

The thing about running a pig for President is that it cuts through the shit. People's minds are full of things like, "You may elect a greater evil." We must break through their logic. Once we get caught in their logic, we're trapped in it.

Just freak it all out and proclaim: "This country is run on the principles of garbage. The Democratic and Republican parties have nominated a pig. So have we. We're honest about it."

In Chicago, Pigasus was a hell of a lot more effective than all those lackeys running around getting votes for the politicians. It turned out that the pig was more relevant to the current American political scene than Senator Eugene McCarthy. I never thought McCarthy could reform the Democratic party. Hell, McCarthy barely got into the convention himself. He had to have a ticket. That's how controlled the damn thing was. Finally, we forced McCarthy out into the streets with the people.

The election was not fair because every time we brought the pig out to give a campaign speech, they arrested him. It happened in Chicago, in New York, in San Francisco, even in London.

The yippies asked that the presidential elections be canceled until the rules of the game were changed. We said that everyone in the world should vote in the American election because America controls the world.

Free elections are elections in which the people who vote are the people affected by the results. The Vietnamese have more right to vote in the American elections than some 80-year-old grandmother in Omaha. They're being bombed by America! They should have at least some choice about if, how, and by whom they are going to be bombed.

I have nothing in particular against 80-year-old grandmothers, but I am in favor of lowering the voting age to 12 or 14 years. And I am not sure whether people over 50 should vote.

It is the young kids who are going to live in this world in the next 50 years. They should choose what they want for themselves.

Most people over 50 don't think about the potentialities of the future: they are preoccupied with justifying their past.

The only people who can choose change without suffering blows to their egos are the young, and change is the rhythm of the universe.

Many older people are constantly warning: "The right wing will get you." "George Wallace will get your momma."

I am so scared of George Wallace that I wore his fucking campaign button. I went to his campaign rally—all old ladies.

There are six Nazis who come with black gloves and mouthpieces, looking for a fight. And two fights break out. Two guys with long hair beat the shit out of them.

I am not afraid of the right wing because the right wing does not have the youth behind it.

"Straight" people get very freaked by Wallace. "Freaks" know the best way to fuck Wallace up. We support him.

At Wallace's rally in the Cow Palace in San Francisco, we come with signs saying "CUT THEIR HAIR!" "SEND THEM BACK TO AFRICA!" "BOMB THE VIETNAMESE BACK TO THE STONE AGE!"

When we arrive there is a picket line going on in front of the rally. I recognize it is the Communist Party picketing.

What? Picketing Wallace?

I walk up to my friend Bettina Aptheker and say, "Bettina, you're legitimizing him. You're legitimizing him by picketing. Instead, support him, kiss him. When he says the next hippie in front of his car will be the last hippie, cheer! Loudly!"

We have about two hundred people there, and we are the loudest people at the rally. Every five seconds we are jumping up and swearing, "Heil! Hitler! Heil! Hitler!"

Wallace is a sick man. America is the loony bin. The only way to cure her is through theatrical shock. Wallace is necessary because he brings to the surface the racism and hate that is deep within the country.

The yippie Fugs spearheaded the anti-war movement of the past five years by touring theaters and dance halls shouting into a microphone: "KILL, KILL, KILL FOR PEACE! KILL, KILL, KILL FOR PEACE!"

Wallace says aloud what most people say privately. He exposes the beast within liberal America. He embarrasses the liberal who says in one breath, "Oh, I like Negroes," and then in another breath, "We must eliminate crime in the streets."

Remember what Huey Long said: "When fascism comes to America, it will come as Americanism."

Wallace may be the best thing for those of us who are fighting him. You can only fight a disease after you recognize and diagnose it. America does not suffer from a cold: she has cancer.

The liberals who run this country agree with Wallace more than they disagree with him. George tells tales out of school. The liberals are going to have to shut that honest motherfucker up.

Do you dig that most cops support Wallace? Cops—the people who make and enforce the law in the streets! Wallace speaks FOR them.

Isn't that scary? Can't you see why blacks are getting guns and organizing into small self-defense units? Wouldn't you, if you were in *their* situation? Shouldn't *you* be?

Make America see her vampire face in the mirror. Destroy that gap between public talk and private behavior. Only when people see what's happening can they hear our screams, and feel our passion.

The Vietnam war is an education for America. It is an expensive teaching experience, but the American people are the most brainwashed people in the world.

At least the youth are learning that this country is no paradise—America kills infants and children in Vietnam without blinking. Only professional killers can be so cool.

If you become hip to America in Vietnam, you can understand the reaction against the red-white-and-blue in Latin America, and you can feel why China hates us.

They are not irrational—America is.

Wallace is a left-wing agitator. Dig him. He speaks to the same anxiety and powerlessness that the New Left and yippies talk about.

Do you feel overwhelmed by bigness, including Big Government?

Do you lack control over your own life?

Are you distrustful of the politicians and bureaucrats in Washington?

Are you part of the "little people"?

Wallace stirs the masses. Revolutions should do that too.

When is the left going to produce an inflammatory and authentic voice of the people? A guy who reaches people's emotions? Who talks about revolution the way some of those nuts rap about Christ?

Wallace says: "We're against niggers, intellectuals, liberals, hippies."

Everybody! He puts us all together. He organizes us for us.

We must analyze how America keeps people down. Not by physical force, but by fear. From the second kids are hatched, we are taught fear. If we can overcome fear, we will discover that we are Davids fighting Goliath.

In late September a friend calls and says, "Hey, I just got a subpoena from HUAC."

I say, "Yeah? I didn't. What's going on here? I'm angry. I want a subpoena too."

It's called subpoenas envy.

So I telephone a confidante to the Red Squad, a fascist creep who works for the *San Francisco Examiner,* and I say, "Hey, Ed, baby, what about HUAC? Are they having hearings?"

He answers, "Well, I don't know. Are they?"

"Well, my friend just got a subpoena," I say. "I'd like one, too. If you can manage it."

He says, "Call me back in a few hours."

I call him back that afternoon and he says, "Well, I just talked to HUAC in Washington, and you are right. They are having hearings, and they are looking for you in New York."

"In NEW YORK? I've been in Berkeley a week! You guys are sure doing a shitty job trying to save this country!"

We exaggerate the surveillance powers of cops. We shouldn't. They are lazy. Their laziness may be the one reason why America doesn't yet have a totally efficient police state.

The cops were not lazy in Chicago. They followed "the leaders" continuously, 24 hours a day. If you are trailed by four cops just six steps behind you, you can't do very much.

But the people really doing things—why, the cops didn't even know who they were!

Pigs cannot relate to anarchy. They do not understand a movement based on personal freedom. When they look at our movement, they look for a hierarchy: leaders, lieutenants, followers.

The pigs think that we are organized like their pig department. We are not, and that's why we are going to win. A hierarchical, top-down organization is no match for the free and loose energy of the people.

As the pigs check with their higher-ups to find out what to do next, we have already switched the tactics and scene of the battle. They are watching one guy over there, and it is happening over here!

I come to the HUAC hearings wearing a bandolero of real bullets and carrying a toy M-16 rifle on my shoulder. The rifle was a model of the rifles the Viet Cong steal and then use to kill American soldiers in Vietnam.

The pigs stop me at the door of the hearings. They grab the bullets and the gun. It is a dramatic moment. Press and yippies pack us in tightly. The pigs drag me down three flights of stairs and remove the bullets, leaving the gun, Viet Cong pajamas, Eldridge Cleaver buttons, Black Panther beret, war paint, earrings, bandolero, and the bells which ring every time I move my body. My costume carried a nonverbal message: "We must all become stoned guerrillas."

The secret to the costume was the painted tits. Guerrilla war in America is going to come in psychedelic colors. We are hippie-guerrillas.

In HUAC's chambers Abbie Hoffman jumps up and yells out, "May I go to the bathroom?" Young kids reading that in their hometown papers giggle because they have to ask permission every time they want to go to the bathroom in school.

The message of my costume flipped across the country in one day: an example of our use of the enemy's institutions—her mass media—to turn on and communicate with one another.

I wore a Santa Claus costume to HUAC two months later in a direct attempt to reach the head of every child in the country.

Our victories are catching up with us: America isn't ready to napalm us yet, but the future doesn't look easy.

From June to November 1968, when I was helping to organize the demonstrations against the Democratic convention in Chicago, I experienced the following example of Americana:

New York pigs use a phony search warrant to bust into my apartment, question me, beat me, search the apartment, and arrest me for alleged felonious possession of marijuana; a pig in Chicago disguises himself as a biker to "infiltrate" the yippies as an agent provocateur and spy; he busts me on a frame-up, "solicitation to mob action," a felony punishable by five years in the pen; the judge imposes $25,000 bail and restricts my travel to Illinois; then the Justice Department in a document to a Virginia court admits that it maintains "electronic surveillance . . . of Jerry Rubin . . . in the interests of national security."

To try to suppress youth, Nixon will have to destroy the Constitution.

We will be presumed guilty until proven innocent.

Our privacy will vanish. Big Brother will spy on all of us and dominate our lives.

Every cop will become a law unto himself.

The courts will become automatic transmission belts sending us to detention camps and prisons.

People will be arrested for what they write and say.

Congress will impose censorship on the mass media, unless the media first censors itself, which is more likely.

To be young will be a crime.

In response, we must never become cynical, or lose our capacity for anger. We must stay on the offensive and be aggressive:

AMERICA: IF YOU INJURE ONE, YOU MUST FIGHT ALL.

If our opposition is united, the repression may backfire and fail. The government may find the costs too heavy.

Don't think, "They can never get ME."

They can.

You are either on the side of the cops or on the side of human beings.

YIPPIE!

THE PUMP HOUSE GANG

Tom Wolfe

Our boys never hair out. The black panther has black feet. Black feet on the crumbling black panther. Pan-thuh. Mee-dah. Pam Stacy, 16 years old, a cute girl here in La Jolla, California, with a pair of orange bell-bottom hip-huggers on, sits on a step about four steps down the stairway to the beach and she can see a pair of revolting black feet without lifting her head. So she says it out loud, "The black panther."

Somebody farther down the stairs, one of the boys with the *major* hair and khaki shorts, says, "The black feet of the black panther."

"Mee-dah," says another kid. This happens to be the cry of a, well, *underground* society known as the Mac Meda Destruction Company.

"The pan-thuh."

"The poon-thuh."

All these kids, seventeen of them, members of the Pump House crowd, are lollygagging around the stairs down to Windansea Beach, La Jolla, California, about 11 a.m., and they all look at the black feet, which are a woman's pair of black street shoes, out of which stick a pair of old veiny white ankles, which lead up like a senile cone to a fudge of tallowy, edematous flesh, her thighs, squeezing out of her bathing suit, with old faded yellow bruises on them, which she probably got from running eight feet to catch a bus or something. She is standing with her old work-a-hubby, who has on *san*dals: you know, a pair of navy-blue anklet socks and these sandals with big, wide, new-smelling tan straps going this way and that, *for keeps*. Man, they look like orthopedic sandals, if one can imagine that. Obviously, these people come from Tucson or Albuquerque or one of those hincty adobe towns. All these hincty, crumbling black feet come to La Jolla-by-the-sea from the adobe towns for the weekend. They even drive in cars all full of thermos bottles and mayonnaisey sandwiches and some kind of latticework wooden-back support for the old crock who drives and Venetian blinds on the back window.

"The black panther."

"Pan-thuh."

"Poon-thuh."

"Mee-dah."

Nobody says it to the two old crocks directly. God, they must be practically 50 years old. Naturally, they're carrying every piece of garbage imaginable: the folding aluminum chairs, the newspapers, the lending-library book with the clear plastic wrapper on it, the sunglasses, the sun ointment, about a vat of goo—

It is a Mexican standoff. In a Mexican standoff, both parties narrow their eyes and glare but nobody throws a punch. Of course, nobody in the Pump House crowd would ever even jostle these people or say anything right to them; they are too cool for that.

Everybody in the Pump House crowd looks over, even Tom Coman, who is a cool person. Tom Coman, 16 years old, got thrown out of his garage last night. He is sitting up on top of the railing, near the stairs, up over the beach, with his legs apart. Some nice long willowy girl in yellow slacks is standing on the sidewalk but leaning into him with her arms around his body, just resting. Neale Jones, 16, a boy with great lank perfect surfer's hair, is standing nearby with a Band-Aid on his upper lip, where the sun has burnt it raw. Little Vicki Ballard is up on the sidewalk. Her older sister, Liz, is down the stairs by the Pump House itself, a concrete block, 15 feet high, full of machinery for the La Jolla water system. Liz is wearing her great "Liz" styles, a hulking rabbit-fur vest and black-leather boots over her Levis, even though it is about 85 out here and the sun is plugged in up there like God's own dentist lamp and the Pacific is heaving in with some fair-to-middling surf. Kit Tilden is lollygagging around, and Tom Jones, Connie Carter, Roger Johnson, Sharon Sandquist, Mary Beth White, Rupert Fellows, Glenn Jackson, Dan Watson from San Diego, they are all out here, and everybody takes a look at the panthers.

The old guy, one means, you know, he must be practically 50 years old, he says to his wife, "Come on, let's go farther up," and he takes her by her fat upper arm as if to wheel her around and aim her away from here.

But she says, "No! We have just as much right to be here as they do."

"That's *not the point*—"

"Are you going to—"

"*Mrs. Roberts*," the work-a-hubby says, calling his own wife by her official married name, as if to say she took a vow once and his word is law, even if he is not testing it with the blond kids here—"farther up, *Mrs. Roberts*."

They start to walk up the sidewalk, but one kid won't move his feet, and, oh, god, her work-a-hubby breaks into a terrible shaking Jello smile as she steps over them, as if to say, Excuse me, sir, I don't mean to make trouble, please, and don't you and your colleagues rise up and jump me, screaming *Gotcha*—

Mee-dah!

But exactly! This beach *is* verboten for people practically 50 years old. This is a segregated beach. They can look down on Windansea Beach and see nothing but lean tan kids. It is posted "no swimming" (for safety reasons), meaning surfing only. In effect, it is segregated by age. From Los Angeles on down the California coast, this is an era of age segregation. People have always tended to segregate themselves by age, teenagers hanging around with teenagers, old people with old people, like the old men who sit on the benches up near the Bronx Zoo and smoke black cigars. But before, age segregation has gone on within a larger community. Sooner or later during the day everybody has melted back into the old community network that embraces practically everyone, all ages.

But in California today surfers, not to mention rock 'n' roll kids and the hot-rodders or Hair Boys, named for their fanciful pompadours—all sorts of sets of kids—they don't merely hang around together. They establish whole little societies for themselves. In some cases they live with one another for months at a time. The "Sunset Strip" on Sunset Boulevard used to be a kind of Times Square for Hollywood hot dogs of all ages, anyone who wanted to promenade in his version of the high life. Today "The Strip" is almost completely the preserve of kids from about 16 to 25. It is lined with go-go clubs. One of them, a place called It's Boss, is set up for people 16 to 25 and won't let in anybody over 25, and there are some terrible I'm-dying-a-thousand-deaths scenes when a girl comes up with her boyfriend and the guy at the door at It's Boss doesn't think she looks under 25 and tells her she will have to produce some identification proving she is young enough to come in here and live The Strip kind of life and— she's *had* it, because she can't get up the I.D. and nothing in the world is going to make a woman look stupider than to stand around trying to argue *I'm younger than I look, I'm younger than I look*. So she practically shrivels up like a Peruvian shrunken head in front of her boyfriend and he trundles her off, looking for some place you can get an old doll like this into. One of the few remaining clubs for "older people," curiously, is the Playboy Club. There are apartment houses for people 20 to 30 only, such as the Sheri Plaza in Hollywood and the E'Questre Inn in Burbank. There are whole suburban housing developments, mostly private develop- ments, where only people over 45 or 50 can buy a house. Whole towns, meantime, have become identified as "young": Venice, Newport Beach, Balboa—or "old": Pasadena, Riverside, Coronado Island.

Behind much of it—especially something like a whole nightclub district of a major city, "The Strip," going teenage—is, simply, money. World War II and the prosperity that followed pumped incredible amounts of money into the population, the white population at least, at every class level. All of a sudden here is an area with thousands of people from 16 to 25 who can get their hands on enough money to support a whole nightclub belt and to have the cars to get there and to set up autonomous worlds of their own in a fairly posh resort community like La Jolla—

—Tom Coman's garage. Some old bastard took Tom Coman's garage away from him, and that means eight or nine surfers are out of a place to stay.

"I went by there this morning, you ought to see the guy," Tom Coman says. Yellow Stretch Pants doesn't move. She has him around the waist. "He was out there painting and he had this brush and about a thousand gallons of ammonia. He was really going to scrub me out of there."

"What did he do with the furniture?"

"I don't know. He threw it out."

"What are you going to do?"

"I don't know."

"Where are you going to stay?"

"I don't know. I'll stay on the beach. It wouldn't be the first time. I haven't had a place to stay for three years, so I'm not going to start worry- ing now."

Everybody thinks that over awhile. Yellow Stretch just hangs on and smiles. Tom Coman, 16 years old, piping fate again. One of the girls says, "You can stay at my place, Tom."

"Um. Who's got a cigarette?"

Pam Stacy says, "You can have these."

Tom Coman lights a cigarette and says, "Let's have a destructo." A destructo is what can happen in a garage after eight or 10 surfers are kicked out of it.

"Mee-dah!"

"Wouldn't that be bitchen?" says Tom Coman. Bitchen is a surfer's term that means "great," usually.

"Bitchen!"

"Mee-dah!"

It's incredible—that old guy out there trying to scour the whole surfing life out of that garage. He's a pathetic figure. His shoulders are hunched over and he's dousing and scrubbing away and the sun doesn't give him a tan, it gives him these . . . *mottles* on the back of his neck. But never mind! The hell with destructo. One only has a destructo spontaneously, a Dionysian . . . *bursting out,* like those holes through the wall during the Mac Meda Destruction Company Convention at Manhattan Beach—Mee-dah!

Something will pan out. It's a magic economy—yes!—all up and down the coast from Los Angeles to Baja California kids can go to one of these beach towns and live the complete surfing life. They take off from home and get to the beach, and if they need a place to stay, well, somebody rents a garage for twenty bucks a month and everybody moves in, girls and boys. Furniture—it's like, one means, you know, one *appropriates* furniture from here and there. It's like the Volkswagen buses a lot of kids now use as beach wagons instead of woodies. Woodies are old station wagons, usually Fords, with wooden bodies, from back before 1953. One of the great things about a Volkswagen bus is that one can . . . *exchange* motors in about three minutes. A good VW motor exchanger can go up to a parked Volkswagen, and a few ratchets of the old wrench here and it's up and out and he has a new motor. There must be a few nice old black panthers around wondering why their nice hubby-mommy VWs don't run so good anymore—but—then—they—are—probably—puzzled—about —a—lot of things. Yes.

Cash—it's practically in the air. Around the beach in La Jolla a guy can walk right out in the street and stand there, stop cars and make the candid move. Mister, I've got a quarter, how about 50 cents so I can get a *large* draft. Or, I need some after-ski boots. And the panthers give one a Jello smile and hand it over. Or a guy who knows how to do it can get $40 from a single night digging clams, and it's nice out there. Or he can go around and take up a collection for a keg party, a keg of beer. Man, anybody who won't kick in a quarter for a keg is a jerk. A couple of good keg collections—that's a trip to Hawaii, which is the surfer's version of a trip to Europe: there is a great surf and great everything there. Neale spent three weeks in Hawaii last year. He got $30 from a girl friend, he scrounged a little here and there and got $70 more and he headed off for Hawaii with $100.02, that being the exact plane fare, and borrowed 25 cents when he got there to . . . blast the place up. He spent the 25 cents in a photo booth, showed the photos to the people on the set of *Hawaii* and got a job in the movie. What's the big orgy about money? It's warm, nobody even wears shoes, nobody is starving.

All right, Mother gets worried about all this, but it is limited worry, as John Shine says. Mainly, Mother says, *Sayonara*, you all, and you head off for the beach.

The thing is, everybody, practically everybody, comes from a good family. Everyone has been . . . *reared well*, as they say. Everybody is very upper-middle, if you want to bring it down to that. It's just that this is a new order. Why hang around in the hubby-mommy household with everybody getting neurotic hang-ups with each other and slamming doors and saying, Why can't they have some privacy? Or, it doesn't mean anything that I have to work for a living, does it? It doesn't mean a thing to you. All of you just lie around here sitting in the big orange easy chair smoking cigarettes. I'd hate for you to have to smoke standing up, you'd probably get phlebitis from it—Listen to me, Sarah—

—why go through all that? It's a good life out here. Nobody is mugging everybody for money and affection. There are a lot of bright people out here, and there are a lot of interesting things. One night there was a toga party in a garage, and everybody dressed in sheets, like togas, boys and girls and they put on the appropriated television set to an old Deanna Durbin movie and turned off the sound and put on Rolling Stones records, and you should have seen Deanna Durbin opening her puckered kumquat mouth with Mick Jagger's voice bawling out, *I ain't got no satisfaction.* Of course, finally everybody started pulling the togas off each other, but that is another thing. And one time they had a keg party down on the beach in Mission Bay and the lights from the amusement park were reflected all over the water and that, the whole design of the thing, those nutty lights, that was part of the party. Liz put out the fire throwing a "sand potion" or something on it. One can laugh at Liz and her potions, her necromancy and everything, but there is a lot of thought going into it, a lot of, well, mysticism.

You can even laugh at mysticism if you want to, but there is a kid like Larry Alderson, who spent two years with a monk, and he learned a lot of stuff, and Artie Nelander is going to spend next summer with some Outer Mongolian tribe; he really means to do that. Maybe the "mysterioso" stuff is a lot of garbage, but still, it is interesting. The surfers around the Pump House use that word, mysterioso, quite a lot. It refers to the mystery of the Oh Mighty Hulking Pacific Ocean and everything. Sometimes a guy will stare at the surf and say, "Mysterioso." They keep telling the story of Bob Simmons' wipeout, and somebody will say "mysterioso."

Simmons was a fantastic surfer. He was fantastic even though he had a bad leg. He rode the really big waves. One day he got wiped out at Windansea. When a big wave overtakes a surfer, it drives him right to the bottom. The board came in but he never came up and they never found his body. Very mysterioso. The black panthers all talked about what happened to "the Simmons boy." But the mysterioso thing was how he could have died at all. If he had been one of the old pan-thuhs, hell, sure he could have got killed. But Simmons was, well, one's own age, he was the kind of guy who could have been in the Pump House gang, he was . . .

immune, he was plugged into the whole pattern, he could feel the whole Oh Mighty Hulking Sea, he didn't have to think it out step by step. But he got wiped out and killed. Very mysterioso.

Immune! If one is in the Pump House gang and really keyed in to this whole thing, it's—well, one is . . . *immune,* one is not full of black panthuh panic. Two kids, a 14-year-old girl and a 16-year-old boy, go out to Windansea at dawn, in the middle of winter, cold as hell, and take on 12-foot waves all by themselves. The girl, Jackie Haddad, daughter of a certified public accountant, wrote a composition about it, just for herself, called "My Ultimate Journey":

"It was six o'clock in the morning, damp, foggy and cold. We could feel the bitter air biting at our cheeks. The night before, my friend Tommy and I had seen one of the greatest surf films, *Surf Classics.* The film had excited us so much we made up our minds to go surfing the following morning. That is what brought us down on the cold, wet, soggy sand of Windansea early on a December morning.

"We were the first surfers on the beach. The sets were rolling in at eight to 10, filled with occasional 12-footers. We waxed up and waited for a break in the waves. The break came, neither of us said a word, but instantly grabbed our boards and ran into the water. The paddle out was difficult, not being used to the freezing water.

"We barely made it over the first wave of the set, a large set. Suddenly Tommy put on a burst of speed and shot past me. He cleared the biggest wave of the set. It didn't hit me hard as I rolled under it. It dragged me almost 20 yards before exhausting its strength. I climbed on my board gasping for air. I paddled out to where Tommy was resting. He laughed at me for being wet already. I almost hit him but I began laughing, too. We rested a few minutes and then lined up our position with a well known spot on the shore.

"I took off first. I bottom-turned hard and started climbing up the wave. A radical cut-back caught me off balance and I fell, barely hanging onto my board. I recovered in time to see Tommy go straight over the falls on a 10-footer. His board shot nearly 30 feet in the air. Luckily, I could get it before the next set came in, so Tommy didn't have to make the long swim in. I pushed it to him and then laughed. All of a sudden Tommy yelled, 'Outside!'

"Both of us paddled furiously. We barely made it up to the last wave, it was a monster. In precision timing we wheeled around and I took off. I cut left in reverse stance, then cut back, driving hard toward the famous Windansea bowl. As I crouched, a huge wall of energy came down over me, covering me up. I moved toward the nose to gain more speed and shot out of the fast-flowing suction just in time to kick out as the wave closed out.

"As I turned around I saw Tommy make a beautiful drop-in, then the wave peaked and fell all at once. Miraculously he beat the suction. He cut back and did a spinner, which followed with a reverse kick-up.

"Our last wave was the biggest. When we got to shore, we rested, neither of us saying a word, but each lost in his own private world of thoughts. After we had rested, we began to walk home. We were about half way and the rain came pouring down. That night we both had bad colds, but we agreed it was worth having them after the thrill and satisfaction of an extra good day of surfing."

John Shine and Artie Nelander are out there right now. They are just "outside," about one fifth of a mile out from the shore, beyond where the waves start breaking. They are straddling their surfboards with their backs to the shore, looking out toward the horizon, waiting for a good set. Their backs look like some kind of salmon-colored porcelain shells, a couple of tiny shells bobbing up and down as the swells roll under them, staring out to sea like Phrygian sacristans looking for a sign.

John and Artie! They are—they are what one means when one talks about the surfing life. It's like, you know, one means, they have this life all of their own; it's like a glass-bottom boat, and it floats over the "real" world, or the square world or whatever one wants to call it. They are not exactly off in a world of their own, they are and they aren't. What it is, they float right through the real world, but it can't touch them. They do these things, like the time they went to Malibu, and there was this party in some guy's apartment, and there wasn't enough *legal* parking space for everybody, and so somebody went out and painted the red curbs white and everybody parked. Then the cops came. Everybody ran out. Artie and John took an airport bus to the Los Angeles Airport, just like they were going to take a plane, in khaki shorts and T-shirts with Mac Meda Destruction Company stenciled on them. Then they took a helicopter to Disneyland. At Disneyland crazy Ditch had his big raincoat on and a lot of flasks strapped onto his body underneath, Scotch, bourbon, all kinds of stuff. He had plastic tubes from the flasks sticking out of the flyfront of his raincoat and everybody was sipping whiskey through the tubes—

—Ooooo-eeee—Mee-dah! They chant this chant, Mee-dah, in a real fakey deep voice, and it *really bugs people*. They don't know what the hell it is. It is the cry of the Mac Meda Destruction Company. The Mac Meda Destruction Company is . . . an *underground* society that started in La Jolla about three years ago. Nobody can remember exactly how; they have arguments about it. Anyhow, it is mainly something to *bug* people with and organize huge beer orgies with. They have their own complete, bogus phone number in La Jolla. They have Mac Meda Destruction Company decals. They stick them on phone booths, on cars, any place. Some mommy-hubby will come out of the shopping plaza and walk up to his Mustang, which is supposed to make him a hell of a tiger now, and he'll see a sticker on the side of it saying, "Mac Meda Destruction Company," and for about two days or something he'll think the sky is going to fall in.

But the big thing is the parties, the "conventions." Anybody can join, any kid, anybody can come, as long as they've heard about it, and they can only hear about it by word of mouth. One was in the Sorrento Valley, in the gulches and arroyos, and the fuzz came, and so the older guys put the young ones and the basket cases, the ones just too stoned out of their gourds, into the tule grass, and the cops shined their searchlights and all they saw was tule grass, while the basket cases moaned scarlet and oozed on their bellies like reptiles and everybody else ran down the arroyos, yelling Mee-dah.

The last one was at Manhattan Beach, inside somebody's poor hulking house. The party got *very Dionysian* that night and somebody put a hole through one wall, and everybody else decided to see if they could make it bigger. Everybody was stoned out of their hulking gourds, and it got to be about 3:30 a.m. and everybody decided to go see the riots. These were the riots in Watts. The Los Angeles *Times* and the San Diego *Union* were all saying, WATTS NO-MAN'S LAND and STAY WAY FROM WATTS YOU GET YO' SE'F KILLED, but naturally nobody believed that. Watts was a blast, and the Pump House gang was immune to the trembling gourd panic rattles of the L. A. *Times* black pan-thuhs. Immune!

So John Shine, Artie Nelander and Jerry Sterncorb got in John's VW bus, known as the Hog of Steel, and they went to Watts. Gary Wickham and some other guys ran into an old man at a bar who said he owned a house in Watts and had been driven out by the drunk niggers. So they drove in a car to save the old guy's house from the drunk niggers. Artie and John had a tape recorder and decided they were going to make a record called "Random Sounds from the Watts Riots." They drove right into Watts in the Hog of Steel and there was blood on the streets and roofs blowing off the stores and all these apricot flames and drunk Negroes falling through the busted plate glass of the liquor stores. Artie got a nice recording of a lot of Negroes chanting "Burn, baby, burn." They all got out and talked to some Negro kids in a gang going into a furniture store, and the Negro kids didn't say Kill Whitey or Geed'um or any of that. They just said, Come on, man, it's a party and it's free. After they had been in there for about three hours talking to Negroes and watching drunks collapse in the liquor stores, some cop with a helmet on came roaring up and said, "Get the hell out of here, you kids, we cannot and will not provide protection."

Meantime, Gary Wickham and his friends drove in in a car with the old guy, and a car full of Negroes *did* stop them and say, Whitey, Geed'um, and all that stuff, but one of the guys in Gary's car just draped a pistol he had out the window and the colored guys drove off. Gary and everybody drove the old guy to his house and they all walked in and had a great raunchy time drinking beer and raising hell. A couple of Negroes, the old guy's neighbors, came over and told the old guy to cut out the racket. There were flames in the sky and ashes coming down with little rims of fire on them, like apricot crescents. The old guy got very cocky about all his "protection" and went out on the front porch about dawn and started yelling at some Negroes across the street, telling them "No more drunk niggers in Watts" and a lot of other unwise slogans. So Gary Wickham got up and everybody left. They were there about four hours altogether and when they drove out, they had to go through a National Guard checkpoint, and a lieutenant from the San Fernando Valley told them he could not and would not provide protection.

But exactly! Watts just happened to be what was going on at the time, as far as the netherworld of La Jolla surfing was concerned, and so one goes there and sees what is happening and comes back and tells everybody about it and laughs at the L. A. *Times*. That is what makes it so weird when all these black pan-thuhs come around to pick up "surfing styles," like the clothing manufacturers. They don't know what any of it means. It's like archaeologists discovering hieroglyphics or something, and they say, god, that's neat—Egypt!—but they don't know what the hell it is. They don't know anything about . . . *The Life*. It's great to think of a lot of old emphysematous pan-thuhs in the Garment District in New York City struggling in off the street against a gummy 15-mile-an-hour wind full of soot and coffee-brown snow and gasping in the elevator to clear their old nicotine-phlegm tubes on the way upstairs to make out the invoices on a lot of surfer stuff for 1966, the big nylon windbreakers with the wide, white horizontal competition stripes, nylon swimming trunks with competition stripes, bell-bottom slacks for girls, the big hairy sleeveless jackets, vests, the blue "tennies," meaning tennis shoes, and the . . . *look,* the Major Hair, all this long lank blond hair, the plain face kind of tanned and bleached out at the same time, but with big eyes. It all starts in a few places, a few strategic groups, the Pump House gang being one of them, and then it moves up the beach, to places like Newport Beach and as far up as Malibu.

Well, actually there is a kind of back-and-forth thing with some of the older guys, the old heroes of surfing, like Bruce Brown, John Severson, Hobie Alter and Phil Edwards. Bruce Brown will do one of those incredible surfing movies and he is out in the surf himself filming Phil Edwards coming down a 20-footer in Hawaii, and Phil has on a pair of nylon swimming trunks, which he has had made in Hawaii, because they dry out fast— and it is like a grapevine. Everybody's got to have a pair of nylon swimming trunks, and then the manufacturers move in, and everybody's making nylon swimming trunks, boxer trunk style, and pretty soon every kid in Utica, N. Y., is buying a pair of them, with the competition stripe and the whole thing, and they never heard of Phil Edwards. So it works back and forth— but so what? Phil Edwards is part of it. He may be an old guy, he is 28 years old, but he and Bruce Brown, who is even older, 30, and John Severson, 32, and Hobie Alter, 29, never haired out to the square world even though they make thousands. Hair refers to courage. A guy who "has a lot of hair" is courageous; a guy who "hairs out" is yellow.

Bruce Brown and Severson and Alter are known as the "surfing millionaires." They are not millionaires, actually, but they must be among the top businessmen south of Los Angeles. Brown grossed something around

$500,000 in 1965 even before his movie *Endless Summer* became a hit
nationally; and he has only about three people working for him. He goes
out on a surfboard with a camera encased in a plastic shell and takes his
own movies and edits them himself and goes around showing them himself
and narrating them at places like the Santa Monica Civic Auditorium,
where 24,000 came in eight days once, at $1.50 a person, and all he has to
pay is for developing the film and hiring the hall. John Severson has the
big surfing magazine, *Surfer*. Hobie Alter is the biggest surfboard manufacturer, all hand-made boards. He made 5,000 boards in 1965 at $140 a board.
He also designed the "Hobie" skate boards and gets 25 cents for every one
sold. He grossed between $900,000 and $1 million in 1964.

God, if only everybody could grow up like these guys and know that
crossing the horror dividing line, 25 years old, won't be the end of everything. One means, keep on living *The Life* and not get sucked into the
ticky-tacky life with some insurance salesman sitting forward in your stuffed
chair on your wall-to-wall telling you that life is like a football game and
you sit there and take that stuff. The hell with that! Bruce Brown has
the money and *The Life*. He has a great house on a cliff about 60 feet
above the beach at Dana Point. He is married and has two children, but
it is not that hubby-mommy you're-breaking-my-gourd scene. His office is
only two blocks from his house and he doesn't even have to go on the
streets to get there. He gets on his Triumph scrambling motorcycle and
cuts straight across a couple of vacant lots and one can see him . . . *bounding* to work over the vacant lots. The Triumph hits ruts and hummocks
and things and Bruce Brown bounces into the air with the motor—
thraggggh—moaning away, and when he gets to the curbing in front of
his office, he just leans back and pulls up the front wheel and hops it and
gets off and walks into the office barefooted. *Barefooted;* why not? He wears
the same things now that he did when he was doing nothing but surfing.
He has on a faded gray sweatshirt with the sleeves cut off just above the
elbows and a pair of faded corduroys. His hair is the lightest corn yellow
imaginable, towheaded, practically white, from the sun. Even his eyes seem
to be bleached. He has a rain-barrel old-apple-tree Tom-Sawyer little-boy
roughneck look about him, like Bobby Kennedy.

Sometimes he carries on his business right there at the house. He has a
dugout room built into the side of the cliff, about 15 feet down from the
level of the house. It is like a big pale green box set into the side of the
cliff, and inside is a kind of upholstered bench or settee you can lie down
on if you want to and look out at the Pacific. The surf is crashing like a
maniac on the rocks down below. He has a telephone in there. Sometimes
it will ring, and Bruce Brown says hello, and the surf is crashing away
down below, roaring like mad, and the guy on the other end, maybe one
of the TV networks calling from New York or some movie hair-out from
Los Angeles, says:

"What is all that noise? It sounds like you're sitting out in the surf."

"That's right," says Bruce Brown, "I have my desk out on the beach now.
It's nice out here."

The guy on the other end doesn't know what to think. He is another Mr. Efficiency who just got back from bloating his colon up at a three-hour executive lunch somewhere and now he is Mr.-Big-Time-Let's-Get-This-Show-on-the-Road.

"On the beach?"

"Yeah. It's cooler down here. And it's good for you, but it's not so great for the desk. You know what I have now? A warped leg."

"A warped leg?"

"Yeah, and this is an $800 desk."

Those nutball California kids—and he will still be muttering that five days after Bruce Brown delivers his film, on time, and Mr. Efficiency is still going through memo thickets or heaving his way into the bar car to Darien—in the very moment that Bruce Brown and Hobie Alter are both on their motorcycles out on the vacant lot in Dana Point. Hobie Alter left his surfboard plant about two in the afternoon because the wind was up and it would be good catamaranning and he wanted to go out and see how far he could tip his new catamaran without going over, and he did tip it over, about half a mile out in high swells and it was hell getting the thing right side up again. But he did, and he got back in time to go scrambling on the lot with Bruce Brown. They are out there, roaring over the ruts, bouncing up in the air, and every now and then they roar up the embankment so they can . . . fly, going up in the air about six feet off the ground as they come up off the embankment—*thraaagggggh*—all these people in the houses around there come to the door and look out. These two . . . nuts are at it again. Well, they can only fool around there for 20 minutes, because that is about how long it takes the cops to get there if anybody gets burned up enough and calls, and what efficient business magnate wants to get hauled off by the Dana Point cops for scrambling on his motorcycle in a vacant lot.

Bruce Brown has it figured out so no one in the whole rubber-bloated black pan-thuh world can trap him, though. He bought a forest in the Sierras. There is nothing on it but trees. His own wilds: no house; no nothing, just Bruce Brown's forest. Beautiful things happen up there. One day, right after he bought it, he was on the edge of his forest, where the road comes into it, and one of these big rancher king motheroos with the broad belly and the $70 lisle Safari shirt comes tooling up in a Pontiac convertible with a funnel of dust pouring out behind. He gravels it to a great flashy stop and yells:

"Hey! You!"

Of course, what he sees is some towheaded barefooted kid in a torn-off sweatshirt fooling around the edge of the road.

"Hey! You!"

"Yeah?" says Bruce Brown.

"Don't you know this is private property?"

"Yeah," says Bruce Brown.

"Well, then, why don't you get your ass off it?"

"Because it's mine, it's my private property," says Bruce Brown. "Now you get *yours* off it."

And Safari gets a few rays from that old apple-tree rain-barrel don't-cross-that-line look and doesn't say anything and roars off, slipping gravel, the dumb crumbling pan-thuh.

But . . . perfect! It is like, one means, you know, poetic justice for all the nights Bruce Brown slept out on the beach at San Onofre and such places in the old surfing days and would wake up with some old crock's black feet standing beside his head and some phlegmy black rubber voice saying:

"All right, kid, don't you know this is private property?"

And he would prop his head up and out there would be the Pacific Ocean, a kind of shadowy magenta-mauve, and one thing, *that* was nobody's private property—

But how many Bruce Browns can there be? There is a built-in trouble with age segregation. Eventually one *does* reach the horror age of 25, the horror dividing line. Surfing and the surfing life have been going big since 1958, and already there are kids who—well, who aren't kids anymore, they are pushing 30, and they are stagnating on the beach. Pretty soon the California littoral will be littered with these guys, stroked out on the beach like beached white whales, and girls, too, who can't give up the mystique, the mysterioso mystique, Oh Mighty Hulking Sea, who can't *conceive* of living any other life. It is pathetic when they are edged out of groups like the Pump House gang. Already there are some guys who hang around with the older crowd around the Shack who are stagnating on the beach. Some of the older guys, like Gary Wickham, who is 24, are still in *The Life,* they still have it, but even Gary Wickham will be 25 one day and then 26 and then. . . . and then even pan-thuh age. Is one really going to be pan-thuh age one day? Watch those black feet go. And Tom Coman still snuggles with Yellow Slacks, and Liz still roosts moodily in her rabbit fur at the bottom of the Pump House and Pam still sits on the steps contemplating the mysterioso mysteries of Pump House ascension and John and Artie still bob, tiny pink porcelain shells, way out there waiting for godsown bitchen *set,* and godsown sun is still turned on like a dentist's lamp and so far—

—the panthers scrape on up the sidewalk. They are at just about the point Leonard Anderson and Donna Blanchard got that day, December 6, 1964, when Leonard said, Pipe it, and fired two shots, one at her and one at himself. Leonard was 18 and Donna was 21—21!—god, for a girl in the Pump House gang that is almost the horror line right there. But it was all so mysterioso. Leonard was just lying down on the beach at the foot of the Pump House, near the stairs, just talking to John K. Weldon down there, and then Donna appeared at the top of the stairs and Leonard got up and went up the stairs to meet her, and they didn't say anything, they weren't *angry* over anything, they never had been, although the police said they had, they just turned and went a few feet down the sidewalk, away

from the Pump House and—blam blam!—these two shots. Leonard fell
dead on the sidewalk and Donna died that afternoon in Scripps Memorial
Hospital. Nobody knew what to think. But one thing it seemed like—well,
it seemed like Donna and Leonard thought they had lived *The Life* as far
as it would go and now it was running out. All that was left to do was—
but that is an *insane* idea. It can't be like that, *The Life* can't run out,
people can't change all that much just because godsown chronometer runs
on and the body packing starts deteriorating and the fudgy tallow shows
up at the thighs where they squeeze out of the bathing suit—

Tom, boy! John, boy! Gary, boy! Neale, boy! Artie, boy! Pam, Liz, Vicki,
Jackie Haddad! After all this—just a pair of bitchen black panther bunions
inching down the sidewalk away from the old Pump House stairs?

Science

EDITED BY RENÉ DUBOS

INTRODUCTION

Charles Darwin was at the height of his fame and intellectual powers when he wrote, in 1868, that the demands of his scientific work had made him lose interest in music, literature, and painting: "The loss of these tastes is a loss of happiness. My mind seems to have become a machine for grinding general laws out of a large collection of facts. It sometimes makes me hate Science."

This astounding statement, written a century ago, has a contemporary ring. It provides support for those who believe that scientists are insensitive to the values that are most meaningful to ordinary human beings. Humanists find further evidence of the scientists' estrangement from their concerns in Lord Snow's celebrated essay on "The Two Cultures." C. P. Snow is now best known as a novelist but was trained as a scientist and functioned for many years as scientific adviser to industry and government. In "The Two Cultures" he asserts that there is an increasing loss of contact between science and the humanities and that this disjunction impoverishes our societies. He claims in particular that humanists will become socially ineffective unless they acquire knowledge of the fundamental facts and principles of science. Humanists have reacted violently to Lord Snow's thesis; they, in turn, have accused scientists of becoming a class apart by creating a culture and a language meaningless to the rest of mankind.

Throughout history, however, scientists have found it possible to participate in the arts and in public affairs while continuing their scientific work. Many in particular have applied their professional knowledge to philosophical problems. Witness the flurry of speculative books by scientists as soon as a new discovery provides them with the opportunity to express opinions about parascientific subjects. The theory of evolution, for example, has been used as a platform for the advocacy of religious and political doctrines; abstract concepts of theoretical physics have been made the basis of speculations not only about the structure of the cosmos but also about the origin of life and the existence of free will.

The possibility of integrating humanistic and scientific knowledge is beautifully illustrated in the writings of Alfred North Whitehead, a famous English mathematician who elected to spend the second half of his immensely productive life as a philosopher in America. His classic *Science and the Modern World* makes it clear that although some of the most important human values are at present outside the scope of scientific investigation, this fact does not imply a schism between science and the humanities; it provides instead material for an enriching complementarity.

Whitehead's *Science and the Modern World* was published in 1925; its mood still pervades the essay by Warren Weaver, who also was trained as a mathematician. He did not become a professional philosopher, but his philosophical wisdom has been embodied in the policies of several American institutions for which he has acted as executive officer and intellectual guide. His presidential address before the American Association for the Advancement of Science in 1954, reproduced here, shows what science can and should do in the modern world and defines the aspects of man's nature that appear at present to be outside the scientific domain. Furthermore, it urges scientists to move out of their ivory towers and become directly involved in public life because science now plays a dominant role in human affairs. Weaver charges scientists in particular with the responsibility to educate the public regarding the social relevance of scientific activities.

In the portion of his article reproduced here, Dr. Alvin Weinberg ponders whether science can provide a basis for human values, taking up such questions as whether the underlying ethic of the "republic of science" can serve as a model for a human ethic.

During the seventeenth century, Europeans became convinced that science could solve all practical problems. Francis Bacon, eloquent exponent of the new scientific faith, based his advocacy on the Christian dogma of Original Sin and on the belief that man could recover dominion over the external world by cultivating knowledge, not for its own sake but for the benefit of human life: "Knowledge, that tendeth but to satisfaction is but a courtesan, which is for pleasure and not for fruit or generation. . . . The sure and lawful goal of the sciences is none other than this: that human life be endowed with new discoveries and power. . . ."

From Bacon's time until the past few decades, scientists and technologists did not have to be concerned about the value of their role in society; each advance resulted in some positive contribution to human health and hap-

piness. This situation, however, is rapidly changing, because most technological achievements now create dangers that often outweigh the blessings
they bring. The threats of nuclear warfare, the pressure of increasing population, the multifarious forms of environmental pollution, the creeping destruction of privacy, are but a few of the consequences of modern knowledge
that pose ethical dilemmas to the scientific community. As part of contemporary culture, science and technology must be related to other human
interests and especially to the future.

The question of *how* to do things is a technical one that can be decided
according to scientific criteria; but the choice of *what* to do, among all the
things that could and should be done, implies awareness of social consequences and involves value judgments. There is now an immense amount
of soul-searching within the scientific community over the directions most
likely to lead to desirable achievements, but great difficulties arise from the
fact that the criteria of objectivity used in the natural sciences are inadequate when the discussion turns to the social impact of these sciences.

The articles by Elmer Engstrom, W. O. Roberts, and Harvey Brooks—
three illustrious American scientists—were published within a few months
of each other. I have selected them to illustrate the complexity of the problems posed by the encounter between science, scientific technology, and
human affairs and to suggest that awareness of the interrelatedness of things
is as important as technical knowledge in formulating a balanced judgment
on the social applications of science.

While it is useful that the facts of scientific progress be reported in the
lay press as accurately as possible, this is not enough to help the public
pass judgment on their social value. For a meaningful assessment of the
effects of science on man it is essential that the implications of scientific
findings be discussed with regard not only to their practical applications but
also to their larger meaning for man's place in the order of things. The
philosophical and social uncertainties that are emerging from scientific
advances must be emphasized just as strongly as the technological break-
throughs. Our communities can make responsible choices only if up-to-date
information concerning scientific developments is supplemented by awareness of consequences.

Most human activities have fostered the development of sophisticated
professions concerned with the criticism of their values, achievements,
trends, and potentialities. ("Criticism" is used here in the more creative
spirit of its Greek etymology, *kritikos,* referring to discernment or judgment.) In our societies, the professional critics of art, music, literature, economics, government, and so on play a creative role even when they do not
themselves contribute directly to the activities they evaluate. Science would
similarly benefit from this kind of evaluation. A society that blindly accepts
the decisions of experts is a sick society. We must produce, alongside specialists, another class of scholars and citizens, who have broad familiarity with
the methods and objectives of science and thus are capable of making critical judgments about scientific policies. In the words of Warren Weaver:

The relations of science to society, to our total culture, and incidentally to our government are now quite unlike what they were even twenty-five years ago.

In addition to the great innovators of new theories, the penetrators of nature's deep secrets, it is essential that we today have individuals who are capable of understanding science, and who are willing to live their lives partly within science but also partly within the world of affairs.

These may be persons who have the capacity to make science intelligible to all of the citizens, who must have a better understanding of the scientific aspect of public decisions. These may be individuals who can bear the steadily increasing burden of administrative responsibility in activities involving science. These persons, working at the interface of science and society, are more than useful—they have become essential.[1]

As the applications of science penetrate more and more deeply into practical human affairs, there is an increasing tendency to neglect the broader values that used to be associated with the term "natural philosophy." But these values are indirectly reflected in ethics and religion because these disciplines continuously evolve to integrate scientific knowledge. The answers to questions concerning the structure of the cosmos, the nature of life, and human destiny must be consistent with scientific facts.

Science is more than accumulation of techniques for achieving mastery over nature; at its best, it is the symbol of man's endless effort to achieve understanding of his condition. As Aristotle wrote more than two thousand years ago: "The search for Truth is in one way hard and in another easy. For it is evident that no one can master it fully nor miss it wholly. But each adds a little to our knowledge of Nature, and from all the facts assembled there arises a certain grandeur."

By opening new vistas and uncovering some of the hidden mechanisms of appearances, science acts as a new revelation that enriches and sharpens the intuitive awareness from which philosophy originated. Hopefully its abstractions may help in penetrating the complexities of direct experience and recognizing the fundamental patterns that define man's relation to the cosmic order. We can understand our real being only by discovering how we relate organically to the rest of the world.

[1] From the response by Dr. Weaver to the announcement of his receipt of the 1965 Arches of Science Award of the Pacific Science Center Foundation.

THE ORIGINS OF MODERN SCIENCE

Alfred North Whitehead

The progress of civilization is not wholly a uniform drift towards better things. It may perhaps wear this aspect if we map it on a scale which is large enough. But such broad views obscure the details on which rests our whole understanding of the process. New epochs emerge with comparative suddenness, if we have regard to the scores of thousands of years throughout which the complete history extends. Secluded races suddenly take their places in the main stream of events: technological discoveries transform the mechanism of human life: a primitive art quickly flowers into full satisfaction of some aesthetic craving: great religions in their crusading youth spread through the nations the peace of Heaven and the sword of the Lord.

The sixteenth century of our era saw the disruption of Western Christianity and the rise of modern science. It was an age of ferment. Nothing was settled, though much was opened—new worlds and new ideas. In science, Copernicus and Vesalius may be chosen as representative figures: they typify the new cosmology and the scientific emphasis on direct observation. Giordano Bruno was the martyr; though the cause for which he suffered was not that of science, but that of free imaginative speculation. His death in the year 1600 ushered in the first century of modern science in the strict sense of the term. In his execution there was an unconscious symbolism: for the subsequent tone of scientific thought has contained distrust of his type of general speculativeness. The Reformation, for all its importance, may be considered as a domestic affair of the European races. Even the Christianity of the East viewed it with profound disengagement. Furthermore, such disruptions are no new phenomena in the history of Christianity or of other religions. When we project this great revolution upon the whole history of the Christian Church, we cannot look upon it as introducing a new principle into human life. For good or for evil, it was a great transformation of religion; but it was not the coming of religion. It did not itself claim to be so. Reformers maintained that they were only restoring what had been forgotten.

It is quite otherwise with the rise of modern science. In every way it contrasts with the contemporary religious movement. The Reformation was a popular uprising, and for a century and a half drenched Europe in blood. The beginnings of the scientific movement were confined to a minority among the intellectual élite. In a generation which saw the Thirty Years' War and remembered Alva in the Netherlands, the worst that happened to men of science was that Galileo suffered an honorable detention and a mild reproof, before dying peacefully in his bed. The way in which the persecution of Galileo has been remembered is a tribute to the quiet commencement of the most intimate change in outlook which the human race had yet encountered. Since a babe was born in a manger, it may be doubted whether so great a thing has happened with so little stir.

The thesis which these lectures will illustrate is that this quiet growth of science has practically recolored our mentality so that modes of thought which in former times were exceptional are now broadly spread through the educated world. This new coloring of ways of thought had been proceeding slowly for many ages in the European peoples. At last it issued in the rapid development of science; and has thereby strengthened itself by its most obvious application. The new mentality is more important even than the new science and the new technology. It has altered the metaphysical presuppositions and the imaginative contents of our minds; so that now the old stimuli provoke a new response. Perhaps my metaphor of a new color is too strong. What I mean is just that slightest change of tone which yet makes all the difference. This is exactly illustrated by a sentence from a published letter of that adorable genius, William James. When he was finishing his great treatise on the *Principles of Psychology,* he wrote to his brother Henry James, "I have to forge every sentence in the teeth of irreducible and stubborn facts."

This new tinge to modern minds is a vehement and passionate interest in the relation of general principles to irreducible and stubborn facts. All the world over and at all times there have been practical men, absorbed in "irreducible and stubborn facts": all the world over and at all times there have been men of philosophic temperament who have been absorbed in the weaving of general principles. It is this union of passionate interest in the detailed facts with equal devotion to abstract generalization which forms the novelty in our present society. Previously it had appeared sporadically and as if by chance. This balance of mind has now become part of the tradition which infects cultivated thought. It is the salt which keeps life sweet. The main business of universities is to transmit this tradition as a widespread inheritance from generation to generation.

Another contrast which singles out science from among the European movements of the sixteenth and seventeenth centuries is its universality. Modern science was born in Europe, but its home is the whole world. In the last two centuries there has been a long and confused impact of western modes upon the civilization of Asia. The wise men of the East have been puzzling, and are puzzling, as to what may be the regulative secret of life which can be passed from West to East without the wanton destruction of their own inheritance which they so rightly prize. More and more it is becoming evident that what the West can most readily give to the East is its science and its scientific outlook. This is transferable from country to country, and from race to race, wherever there is a rational society.

In this course of lectures I shall not discuss the details of scientific discovery. My theme is the energizing of a state of mind in the modern world, its broad generalizations, and its impact upon other spiritual forces. There are two ways of reading history, forwards and backwards. In the history of thought, we require both methods. A climate of opinion—to use the happy phrase of a seventeenth century writer—requires for its understanding the consideration of its antecedents and its issues. Accordingly in this lecture I shall consider some of the antecedents of our modern approach to the investigation of nature.

In the first place, there can be no living science unless there is a widespread instinctive conviction in the existence of an *Order of Things,* and, in particular, of an *Order of Nature.* I have used the word *instinctive* advisedly. It does not matter what men say in words, so long as their activities are controlled by settled instincts. The words may ultimately destroy the instincts. But until this has occurred, words do not count. This remark is important in respect to the history of scientific thought. For we shall find that since the time of Hume, the fashionable scientific philosophy has been such as to deny the rationality of science. This conclusion lies upon the surface of Hume's philosophy. Take for example, the following passage from Section IV of his *Inquiry Concerning Human Understanding*:

> In a word, then, every effect is a distinct event from its cause. It could not, therefore, be discovered in the cause; and the first invention or conception of it, *a priori,* must be entirely arbitrary.

If the cause in itself discloses no information as to the effect, so that the first invention of it must be *entirely* arbitrary, it follows at once that science is impossible, except in the sense of establishing *entirely arbitrary* connections which are not warranted by anything intrinsic to the natures either of causes or effects. Some variant of Hume's philosophy has generally prevailed among men of science. But scientific faith has risen to the occasion, and has tacitly removed the philosophic mountain.

In view of this strange contradiction in scientific thought, it is of the first importance to consider the antecedents of a faith which is impervious to the demand for a consistent rationality. We have therefore to trace the rise of the instinctive faith that there is an Order of Nature which can be traced in every detailed occurrence.

Of course we all share in this faith, and we therefore believe that the reason for the faith is our apprehension of its truth. But the formation of a general idea—such as the idea of the Order of Nature—and the grasp of its importance, and the observation of its exemplification in a variety of occasions are by no means the necessary consequences of the truth of the idea in question. Familiar things happen, and mankind does not bother about them. It requires a very unusual mind to undertake the analysis of the obvious. Accordingly I wish to consider the stages in which this analysis became explicit, and finally became unalterably impressed upon the educated minds of Western Europe.

Obviously, the main recurrences of life are too insistent to escape the notice of the least rational of humans; and even before the dawn of rationality, they have impressed themselves upon the instincts of animals. It is unnecessary to labor the point, that in broad outline certain general states of nature recur, and that our very natures have adapted themselves to such repetitions.

But there is a complementary fact which is equally true and equally obvious:—nothing ever really recurs in exact detail. No two days are identical, no two winters. What has gone, has gone forever. Accordingly the practical philosophy of mankind has been to expect the broad recurrences, and to accept the details as emanating from the inscrutable womb of things beyond the ken of rationality. Men expected the sun to rise, but the wind bloweth where it listeth.

Certainly from the classical Greek civilization onwards there have been men, and indeed groups of men, who have placed themselves beyond this acceptance of an ultimate irrationality. Such men have endeavoured to explain all phenomena as the outcome of an order of things which extends to every detail. Geniuses such as Aristotle, or Archimedes, or Roger Bacon, must have been endowed with the full scientific mentality, which instinctively holds that all things great and small are conceivable as exemplifications of general principles which reign throughout the natural order.

But until the close of the Middle Ages the general educated public did not feel that intimate conviction, and that detailed interest, in such an idea, so as to lead to an unceasing supply of men, with ability and opportunity adequate to maintain a coordinated search for the discovery of these hypothetical principles. Either people were doubtful about the existence of such principles, or were doubtful about any success in finding them, or took no interest in thinking about them, or were oblivious to their practical importance when found. For whatever reason, search was languid, if we have regard to the opportunities of a high civilization and the length of time concerned. Why did the pace suddenly quicken in the sixteenth and seventeenth centuries? At the close of the Middle Ages a new mentality discloses itself. Invention stimulated thought, thought quickened physical speculation, Greek manuscripts disclosed what the ancients had discovered. Finally although in the year 1500 Europe knew less than Archimedes who died in the year 212 B. C., yet in the year 1700, Newton's *Principia* had been written and the world was well started on the modern epoch.

There have been great civilizations in which the peculiar balance of mind required for science has only fitfully appeared and has produced the feeblest result. For example, the more we know of Chinese art, of Chinese literature, and of the Chinese philosophy of life, the more we admire the heights to which that civilization attained. For thousands of years, there have been in China acute and learned men patiently devoting their lives to study. Having regard to the span of time, and to the population concerned, China forms the largest volume of civilization which the world has seen. There is no reason to doubt the intrinsic capacity of individual Chinamen for the pursuit of science. And yet Chinese science is practically negligible. There is no reason to believe that China if left to itself would have ever produced any progress in science. The same may be said of India. Furthermore, if the Persians had enslaved the Greeks, there is no definite ground for belief that science would have flourished in Europe. The Romans showed no particular originality in that line. Even as it was, the Greeks, though they founded the movement, did not sustain it with the concentrated interest which modern Europe has shown. I am not alluding to the last few generations of the European peoples on both sides of the ocean; I mean the smaller Europe of the Reformation period, distracted as it was with wars and religious disputes. Consider the world of the eastern Mediterranean, from Sicily to western Asia, during the period of about 1400 years from the death of Archimedes [in 212 B. C.] to the irruption of the Tartars. There were wars and revolutions and large changes of religion: but nothing much worse than the wars of the sixteenth and seventeenth centuries throughout Europe. There was a great and wealthy civilization, Pagan, Christian, Mahometan. In that period a great deal was added to science. But on the whole the progress was slow and wavering; and, except in mathematics, the men of the Renaissance practically started from the position which Archimedes had reached. There had been some progress in medicine and some progress in astronomy. But the total advance was very little compared to the marvellous success of the seventeenth century. For example, compare the progress of scientific knowledge from the year 1560, just before the births of Galileo and of Kepler, up to the year 1700, when Newton was in the height of his fame, with the progress in the ancient period, already mentioned, exactly ten times as long.

Nevertheless, Greece was the mother of Europe; and it is to Greece that we must look in order to find the origin of our modern ideas. We all know that on the eastern shores of the Mediterranean there was a very flourishing school of Ionian philosophers, deeply interested in theories concerning nature. Their ideas have been transmitted to us, enriched by the genius of Plato and Aristotle. But, with the exception of Aristotle, and it is a large exception, this school of thought had not attained to the complete scientific mentality. In some ways, it was better. The Greek genius was philosophical, lucid and logical. The men of this group were primarily asking philosophical questions. What is the substratum of nature? Is it fire, or earth, or water, or some combination of any two, or of all three? Or is it a mere flux, not reducible to some static material? Mathematics interested them mightily. They invented its generality, analyzed its premises, and made notable discoveries of theorems by a rigid adherence to deductive reasoning. Their minds were infected with an eager generality. They demanded clear, bold ideas, and strict reasoning from them. All this was excellent; it was genius; it was ideal preparatory work. But it was not science as we understand it. The patience of minute observation was not nearly so prominent. Their genius was not so apt for the state of imaginative muddled suspense which precedes successful inductive generalization. They were lucid thinkers and bold reasoners.

Of course there were exceptions, and at the very top: for example, Aris-

totle and Archimedes. Also for patient observation, there were the astronomers. There was a mathematical lucidity about the stars, and a fascination
about the small numerable band of run-away planets.

Every philosophy is tinged with the coloring of some secret imaginative
background, which never emerges explicitly into its trains of reasoning.
The Greek view of nature, at least that cosmology transmitted from them
to later ages, was essentially dramatic. It is not necessarily wrong for this
reason: but it was overwhelmingly dramatic. It thus conceived nature as
articulated in the way of a work of dramatic art, for the exemplification of
general ideas converging to an end. Nature was differentiated so as to
provide its proper end for each thing. There was the center of the universe
as the end of motion for those things which are heavy, and the celestial
spheres as the end of motion for those things whose natures lead them
upwards. The celestial spheres were for things which are impassible and
ingenerable, the lower regions for things passible and generable. Nature
was a drama in which each thing played its part.

I do not say that this is a view to which Aristotle would have subscribed
without severe reservations, in fact without the sort of reservations which
we ourselves would make. But it was the view which subsequent Greek
thought extracted from Aristotle and passed on to the Middle Ages. The
effect of such an imaginative setting for nature was to damp down the
historical spirit. For it was the end which seemed illuminating, so why
bother about the beginning? The Reformation and the scientific movement
were two aspects of the revolt which was the dominant intellectual movement of the later Renaissance. The appeal to the origins of Christianity,
and Francis Bacon's appeal to efficient causes as against final causes, were
two sides of one movement of thought. Also for this reason Galileo and
his adversaries were at hopeless cross purposes, as can be seen from his
Dialogues on the Two Systems of the World.

Galileo keeps harping on how things happen, whereas his adversaries
had a complete theory as to why things happen. Unfortunately the two
theories did not bring out the same results. Galileo insists upon "irreducible and stubborn facts," and Simplicius, his opponent, brings forward
reasons, completely satisfactory, at least to himself. It is a great mistake to
conceive this historical revolt as an appeal to reason. On the contrary, it
was through and through an anti-intellectualist movement. It was the return to the contemplation of brute fact; and it was based on a recoil from
the inflexible rationality of medieval thought. In making this statement I
am merely summarizing what at the time the adherents of the old régime
themselves asserted. For example, in the fourth book of Father Paul Sarpi's
History of the Council of Trent, you will find that in the year 1551 the
Papal Legates who presided over the Council ordered: "That the Divines
ought to confirm their opinions with the holy Scripture, Traditions of the
Apostles, sacred and approved Councils, and by the Constitutions and Authorities of the holy Fathers; that they ought to use brevity, and avoid
superfluous and unprofitable questions, and perverse contentions. . . . This
order did not please the Italian Divines; who said it was a novity, and a

condemning of School-Divinity, which, in all difficulties, *useth reason, and* because it was not lawful [*i.e.,* by this decree] to treat as St. Thomas [Aquinas], St. Bonaventure, and other famous men did."

It is impossible not to feel sympathy with these Italian divines, maintaining the lost cause of unbridled rationalism. They were deserted on all hands. The Protestants were in full revolt against them. The Papacy failed to support them, and the Bishops of the Council could not even understand them. For a few sentences below the foregoing quotation, we read: "Though many complained here-of [*i.e.,* of the Decree], yet it prevailed but little, because generally the Fathers [*i.e.,* the Bishops] desired to hear men speak with intelligible terms, not abstrusely, as in the matter of Justification, and others already handled."

Poor belated medievalists! When they used reason they were not even intelligible to the ruling powers of their epoch. It will take centuries before stubborn facts are reducible by reason, and meanwhile the pendulum swings slowly and heavily to the extreme of the historical method.

Forty-three years after the Italian divines had written this memorial, Richard Hooker in his famous *Laws of Ecclesiastical Polity* makes exactly the same complaint of his Puritan adversaries.[1] Hooker's balanced thought —from which the appellation "The Judicious Hooker" is derived—and his diffuse style, which is the vehicle of such thought, make his writings singularly unfit for the process of summarizing by a short, pointed quotation. But, in the section referred to, he reproaches his opponents with *Their Disparagement of Reason*; and in support of his own position definitely refers to "The greatest amongst the school-divines" by which designation I presume that he refers to St. Thomas Aquinas.

Hooker's *Ecclesiastical Polity* was published just before Sarpi's *Council of Trent*. Accordingly there was complete independence between the two works. But both the Italian divines of 1551, and Hooker at the end of that century testify to the anti-rationalist trend of thought at that epoch, and in this respect contrast their own age with the epoch of scholasticism.

This reaction was undoubtedly a very necessary corrective to the unguarded rationalism of the Middle Ages. But reactions run to extremes. Accordingly, although one outcome of this reaction was the birth of modern science, yet we must remember that science thereby inherited the bias of thought to which it owes its origin.

The effect of Greek dramatic literature was many-sided so far as concerns the various ways in which it indirectly affected medieval thought. The pilgrim fathers of the scientific imagination as it exists today are the great tragedians of ancient Athens, Aeschylus, Sophocles, Euripides. Their vision of fate, remorseless and indifferent, urging a tragic incident to its inevitable issue, is the vision possessed by science. Fate in Greek Tragedy becomes the order of nature in modern thought. The absorbing interest in the particular heroic incidents, as an example and a verification of the workings of fate, reappears in our epoch as concentration of interest on the crucial experiments. It was my good fortune to be present at the meeting of the

[1] *Cf.* Book III, Section viii.

Royal Society in London when the Astronomer Royal for England announced that the photographic plates of the famous eclipse, as measured by his colleagues in Greenwich Observatory, had verified the prediction of Einstein that rays of light are bent as they pass in the neighborhood of the sun. The whole atmosphere of tense interest was exactly that of the Greek drama: we were the chorus commenting on the decree of destiny as disclosed in the development of a supreme incident. There was dramatic quality in the very staging:—the traditional ceremonial, and in the background the picture of Newton to remind us that the greatest of scientific generalizations was now, after more than two centuries, to receive its first modification. Nor was the personal interest wanting: a great adventure in thought had at length come safe to shore.

Let me here remind you that the essence of dramatic tragedy is not unhappiness. It resides in the solemnity of the remorseless working of things. This inevitableness of destiny can only be illustrated in terms of human life by incidents which in fact involve unhappiness. For it is only by them that the futility of escape can be made evident in the drama. This remorseless inevitableness is what pervades scientific thought. The laws of physics are the decrees of fate.

The conception of the moral order in the Greek plays was certainly not a discovery of the dramatists. It must have passed into the literary tradition from the general serious opinion of the times. But in finding this magnificent expression, it thereby deepened the stream of thought from which it arose. The spectacle of a moral order was impressed upon the imagination of a classical civilization.

The time came when that great society decayed, and Europe passed into the Middle Ages. The direct influence of Greek literature vanished. But the concept of the moral order and of the order of nature had enshrined itself in the Stoic philosophy. For example, Lecky in his *History of European Morals* tell us "Seneca maintains that the Divinity has determined all things by an inexorable law of destiny, which He has decreed, but which He Himself obeys." But the most effective way in which the Stoics influenced the mentality of the Middle Ages was by the diffused sense of order which arose from Roman law. Again to quote Lecky, "The Roman legislation was in a twofold manner the child of philosophy. It was in the first place formed upon the philosophical model, for, instead of being a mere empirical system adjusted to the existing requirements of society, it laid down abstract principles of right to which it endeavoured to conform; and, in the next place, these principles were borrowed directly from Stoicism." In spite of the actual anarchy throughout large regions in Europe after the collapse of the Empire, the sense of legal order always haunted the racial memories of the Imperial populations. Also the Western Church was always there as a living embodiment of the traditions of Imperial rule.

It is important to notice that this legal impress upon medieval civilization was not in the form of a few wise precepts which should permeate conduct. It was the conception of a definite articulated system which defines the legality of the detailed structure of social organism, and of the detailed way in which it should function. There was nothing vague. It was not a question of admirable maxims, but of definite procedure to put things right and to keep them there. The Middle Ages formed one long training of the intellect of Western Europe in the sense of order. There may have been some deficiency in respect to practice. But the idea never for a moment lost its grip. It was preeminently an epoch of orderly thought, rationalist through and through. The very anarchy quickened the sense for coherent system; just as the modern anarchy of Europe has stimulated the intellectual vision of a League of Nations.

But for science something more is wanted than a general sense of the order in things. It needs but a sentence to point out how the habit of definite exact thought was implanted in the European mind by the long dominance of scholastic logic and scholastic divinity. The habit remained after the philosophy had been repudiated, the priceless habit of looking for an exact point and of sticking to it when found. Galileo owes more to Aristotle than appears on the surface of his *Dialogues*: he owes to him his clear head and his analytic mind.

I do not think, however, that I have even yet brought out the greatest contribution of medievalism to the formation of the scientific movement. I mean the inexpugnable belief that every detailed occurrence can be correlated with its antecedents in a perfectly definite manner, exemplifying general principles. Without this belief the incredible labors of scientists would be without hope. It is this instinctive conviction, vividly poised before the imagination, which is the motive power of research:—that there is a secret, a secret which can be unveiled. How has this conviction been so vividly implanted on the European mind?

When we compare this tone of thought in Europe with the attitude of other civilizations when left to themselves, there seems but one source for its origin. It must come from the medieval insistence on the rationality of God, conceived as with the personal energy of Jehovah and with the rationality of a Greek philosopher. Every detail was supervised and ordered: the search into nature could only result in the vindication of the faith in rationality. Remember that I am not talking of the explicit beliefs of a few individuals. What I mean is the impress on the European mind arising from the unquestioned faith of centuries. By this I mean the instinctive tone of thought and not a mere creed of words.

In Asia, the conceptions of God were of a being who was either too arbitrary or too impersonal for such ideas to have much effect on instinctive habits of mind. Any definite occurrence might be due to the fiat of an irrational despot, or might issue from some impersonal, inscrutable origin of things. There was not the same confidence as in the intelligible rationality of a personal being. I am not arguing that the European trust in the scrutability of nature was logically justified even by its own theology. My only point is to understand how it arose. My explanation is that the faith in the possibility of science, generated antecedently to the development of modern scientific theory, is an unconscious derivative from medieval theology.

But science is not merely the outcome of instinctive faith. It also requires an active interest in the simple occurrences of life for their own sake.

This qualification "for their own sake" is important. The first phase of the Middle Ages was an age of symbolism. It was an age of vast ideas, and of primitive technique. There was little to be done with nature, except to coin a hard living from it. But there were realms of thought to be explored, realms of philosophy and realms of theology. Primitive art could symbolize those ideas which filled all thoughtful minds. The first phase of medieval art has a haunting charm beyond compare: its own intrinsic quality is enhanced by the fact that its message, which stretched beyond art's own self-justification of aesthetic achievement, was the symbolism of things lying behind nature itself. In this symbolic phase, medieval art energized in nature as its medium, but pointed to another world.

In order to understand the contrast between these early Middle Ages and the atmosphere required by the scientific mentality, we should compare the sixth century in Italy with the sixteenth century. In both centuries the Italian genius was laying the foundations of a new epoch. The history of the three centuries preceding the earlier period, despite the promise for the future introduced by the rise of Christianity, is overwhelmingly infected by the sense of the decline of civilization. In each generation something has been lost. As we read the records, we are haunted by the shadow of the coming barbarism. There are great men, with fine achievements in action or in thought. But their total effect is merely for some short time to arrest the general decline. In the sixth century we are, so far as Italy is concerned, at the lowest point of the curve. But in that century every action is laying the foundation for the tremendous rise of the new European civilization. In the background the Byzantine Empire, under Justinian, in three ways determined the character of the early Middle Ages in Western Europe. In the first place, its armies, under Belisarius and Narses, cleared Italy from the Gothic domination. In this way, the stage was freed for the exercise of the old Italian genius for creating organizations which shall be protective of ideals of cultural activity. It is impossible not to sympathize with the Goths: yet there can be no doubt but that a thousand years of the Papacy were infinitely more valuable for Europe than any effects derivable from a well-established Gothic kingdom of Italy.

In the second place, the codification of the Roman law established the ideal of legality which dominated the sociological thought of Europe in the succeeding centuries. Law is both an engine for government and a condition restraining government. The canon law of the Church, and the civil law of the State, owe to Justinian's lawyers their influence on the development of Europe. They established in the Western mind the ideal that an authority should be at once lawful, and law-enforcing, and should in itself exhibit a rationally adjusted system of organization. The sixth century in Italy gave the initial exhibition of the way in which the impress of these ideas was fostered by contact with the Byzantine Empire.

Thirdly, in the non-political spheres of art and learning Constantinople exhibited a standard of realised achievement which, partly by the impulse to direct imitation, and partly by the indirect inspiration arising from the mere knowledge that such things existed, acted as a perpetual spur to Western culture. The wisdom of the Byzantines, as it stood in the imagination of the first phase of medieval mentality, and the wisdom of the Egyptians as it stood in the imagination of the early Greeks, played analogous rôles. Probably the actual knowledge of these respective wisdoms was, in either case, about as much as was good for the recipients. They knew enough to know the sort of standards which are attainable, and not enough to be fettered by static and traditional ways of thought. Accordingly, in both cases men went ahead on their own and did better. No account of the rise of the European scientific mentality can omit some notice of this influence of the Byzantine civilization in the background. In the sixth century there is a crisis in the history of the relations between the Byzantines and the West; and this crisis is to be contrasted with the influence of Greek literature on European thought in the fifteenth and sixteenth centuries. The two outstanding men, who in the Italy of the sixth century laid the foundations of the future, were St. Benedict and Gregory the Great. By reference to them, we can at once see how absolutely in ruins was the approach to the scientific mentality which had been attained by the Greeks. We are at the zero point of scientific temperature. But the life-work of Gregory and of Benedict contributed elements to the reconstruction of Europe which secured that this reconstruction, when it arrived, should include a more effective scientific mentality than that of the ancient world. The Greeks were over-theoretical. For them science was an offshoot of philosophy. Gregory and Benedict were practical men, with an eye for the importance of ordinary things; and they combined this practical temperament with their religious and cultural activities. In particular, we owe it to St. Benedict that the monasteries were the homes of practical agriculturalists, as well as of saints and of artists and men of learning. The alliance of science with technology, by which learning is kept in contact with irreducible and stubborn facts, owes much to the practical bent of the early Benedictines. Modern science derives from Rome as well as from Greece, and this Roman strain explains its gain in an energy of thought kept closely in contact with the world of facts.

But the influence of this contact between the monasteries and the facts of nature showed itself first in art. The rise of Naturalism in the later Middle Ages was the entry into the European mind of the final ingredient necessary for the rise of science. It was the rise of interest in natural objects and in natural occurrences, for their own sakes. The natural foliage of a district was sculptured in out-of-the-way spots of the later buildings, merely as exhibiting delight in those familiar objects. The whole atmosphere of every art exhibited a direct joy in the apprehension of the things which lie around us. The craftsmen who executed the late medieval decorative sculpture, Giotto, Chaucer, Wordsworth, Walt Whitman, and, at the present day, the New England poet Robert Frost, are all akin to each other in this respect. The simple immediate facts are the topics of interest, and these reappear in the thought of science as the "irreducible stubborn facts."

The mind of Europe was now prepared for its new venture of thought. It is unnecessary to tell in detail the various incidents which marked the rise of science: the growth of wealth and leisure; the expansion of universities; the invention of printing; the taking of Constantinople; Copernicus; Vasco da Gama; Columbus; the telescope. The soil, the climate, the seeds, were there, and the forest grew. Science has never shaken off the impress of its origin in the historical revolt of the later Renaissance. It has remained predominantly an anti-rationalistic movement, based upon a naïve faith. What reasoning it has wanted, has been borrowed from mathematics which is a surviving relic of Greek rationalism, following the deductive method. Science repudiates philosophy. In other words, it has never cared to justify its faith or to explain its meanings; and has remained blandly indifferent to its refutation by Hume.

Of course the historical revolt was fully justified. It was wanted. It was more than wanted: it was an absolute necessity for healthy progress. The world required centuries of contemplation of irreducible and stubborn facts. It is difficult for men to do more than one thing at a time, and that was the sort of thing they had to do after the rationalistic orgy of the Middle Ages. It was a very sensible reaction; but it was not a protest on behalf of reason.

There is, however, a Nemesis which waits upon those who deliberately avoid avenues of knowledge. Oliver Cromwell's cry echoes down the ages, "My brethren, by the bowels of Christ I beseech you, bethink you that you may be mistaken."

The progress of science has now reached a turning point. The stable foundations of physics have broken up: also for the first time physiology is asserting itself as an effective body of knowledge, as distinct from a scrap-heap. The old foundations of scientific thought are becoming unintelligible. Time, space, matter, material, ether, electricity, mechanism, organism, configuration, structure, pattern, function, all require reinterpretation. What is the sense of talking about a mechanical explanation when you do not know what you mean by mechanics?

The truth is that science started its modern career by taking over ideas derived from the weakest side of the philosophies of Aristotle's successors. In some respects it was a happy choice. It enabled the knowledge of the seventeenth century to be formularized so far as physics and chemistry were concerned, with a completeness which has lasted to the present time. But the progress of biology and psychology has probably been checked by the uncritical assumption of half-truths. If science is not to degenerate into a medley of *ad hoc* hypotheses, it must become philosophical and must enter upon a thorough criticism of its own foundations.

In the succeeding lectures of this course, I shall trace the success and the failures of the particular conceptions of cosmology with which the European intellect has clothed itself in the last three centuries. General climates of opinion persist for periods of about two to three generations, that is to say, for periods of sixty to a hundred years. There are also shorter waves of thought, which play on the surface of the tidal movement. We shall find, therefore, transformations in the European outlook, slowly modifying the successive centuries. There persists, however, throughout the whole period the fixed scientific cosmology which presupposes the ultimate fact of an irreducible brute matter, or material, spread throughout space in a flux of configurations. In itself such a material is senseless, valueless, purposeless. It just does what it does do, following a fixed routine imposed by external relations which do not spring from the nature of its being. It is this assumption that I call "scientific materialism." Also it is an assumption which I shall challenge as being entirely unsuited to the scientific situation at which we have now arrived. It is not wrong, if properly construed. If we confine ourselves to certain types of facts, abstracted from the complete circumstances in which they occur, the materialistic assumption expresses these facts to perfection. But when we pass beyond the abstraction, either by more subtle employment of our senses, or by the request for meanings and for coherence of thoughts, the scheme breaks down at once. The narrow efficiency of the scheme was the very cause of its supreme methodological success. For it directed attention to just those groups of facts which, in the state of knowledge then existing, required investigation.

The success of the scheme has adversely affected the various currents of European thought. The historical revolt was anti-rationalistic, because the rationalism of the scholastics required a sharp correction by contact with brute fact. But the revival of philosophy in the hands of Descartes and his successors was entirely colored in its development by the acceptance of the scientific cosmology at its face value. The success of their ultimate ideas confirmed scientists in their refusal to modify them as the result of an inquiry into their rationality. Every philosophy was bound in some way or other to swallow them whole. Also the example of science affected other regions of thought. The historical revolt has thus been exaggerated into the exclusion of philosophy from its proper role of harmonizing the various abstractions of methodological thought. Thought is abstract; and the intolerant use of abstractions is the major vice of the intellect. This vice is not wholly corrected by the recurrence to concrete experience. For after all, you need only attend to those aspects of your concrete experience which lie within some limited scheme. There are two methods for the purification of ideas. One of them is dispassionate observation by means of the bodily senses. But observation is selection. Accordingly, it is difficult to transcend a scheme of abstraction whose success is sufficiently wide. The other method is by comparing the various schemes of abstraction which are well founded in our various types of experience. This comparison takes the form of satisfying the demands of the Italian scholastic divines whom Paul Sarpi mentioned. They asked that *reason* should be used. Faith in reason is the trust that the ultimate natures of things lie together in a harmony which excludes mere arbitrariness. It is the faith that at the base of things we shall not find mere arbitrary mystery. The faith in the order of nature which has made possible the growth of science is a particular example of a deeper faith. This faith cannot be justified by any inductive generalization. It springs from direct inspection of the nature of things as disclosed in our own immediate present experience. There is no parting from your own shadow. To experience this faith is to know that in being ourselves we are more than ourselves: to know that our experience, dim and fragmentary as it is, yet sounds the utmost depths of reality: to know that detached details merely in order to be themselves demand that they should find themselves in a system of things: to know that this system includes the harmony of logical rationality, and the harmony of aesthetic achievement: to know that, while the harmony of logic lies upon the universe as an iron necessity, the aesthetic harmony stands before it as a living ideal molding the general flux in its broken progress towards finer, subtler issues.

RELIGION AND SCIENCE

Alfred North Whitehead

The difficulty in approaching the question of the relations between Religion and Science is, that its elucidation requires that we have in our minds some clear idea of what we mean by either of the terms, "religion" and "science." Also I wish to speak in the most general way possible, and to keep in the background any comparison of particular creeds, scientific or religious. We have got to understand the type of connection which exists between the two spheres, and then to draw some definite conclusions respecting the existing situation which at present confronts the world.

The *conflict* between religion and science is what naturally occurs to our minds when we think of this subject. It seems as though, during the last half-century, the results of science and the beliefs of religion had come into a position of frank disagreement, from which there can be no escape, except by abandoning either the clear teaching of science, or the clear teaching of religion. This conclusion has been urged by controversialists on either side. Not by all controversialists, of course, but by those trenchant intellects which every controversy calls out into the open.

The distress of sensitive minds, and the zeal for truth, and the sense of the importance of the issues, must command our sincerest sympathy. When we consider what religion is for mankind, and what science is, it is no exaggeration to say that the future course of history depends upon the decision of this generation as to the relations between them. We have here the two strongest general forces (apart from the mere impulse of the various senses) which influence men, and they seem to be set one against the other—the force of our religious intuitions, and the force of our impulse to accurate observation and logical deduction.

RELIGION AND SCIENCE Reprinted with permission of The Macmillan Company from *Science and the Modern World* by Alfred North Whitehead. Copyright 1925 by The Macmillan Company, renewed 1953 by Evelyn Whitehead.

A great English statesman once advised his countrymen to use large-scale maps, as a preservative against alarms, panics, and general misunderstanding of the true relations between nations. In the same way in dealing with the clash between permanent elements of human nature, it is well to map our history on a large scale, and to disengage ourselves from our immediate absorption in the present conflicts. When we do this, we immediately discover two great facts. In the first place, there has always been a conflict between religion and science; and in the second place, both religion and science have always been in a state of continual development. In the early days of Christianity, there was a general belief among Christians that the world was coming to an end in the lifetime of people then living. We can make only indirect inferences as to how far this belief was authoritatively proclaimed; but it is certain that it was widely held, and that it formed an impressive part of the popular religious doctrine. The belief proved itself to be mistaken, and Christian doctrine adjusted itself to the change. Again in the early Church individual theologians very confidently deduced from the Bible opinions concerning the nature of the physical universe. In the year A. D. 535, a monk named Cosmas[1] wrote a book which he entitled, *Christian Topography*. He was a traveled man who had visited India and Ethiopia; and finally he lived in a monastery at Alexandria, which was then a great center of culture. In this book, basing himself upon the direct meaning of Biblical texts as construed by him in a literal fashion, he denied the existence of the antipodes, and asserted that the world is a flat parallelogram whose length is double its breadth.

In the seventeenth century the doctrine of the motion of the earth was condemned by a Catholic tribunal. A hundred years ago the extension of time demanded by geological science distressed religious people, Protestant and Catholic. And to-day the doctrine of evolution is an equal stumbling-block. These are only a few instances illustrating a general fact.

But all our ideas will be in a wrong perspective if we think that this recurring perplexity was confined to contradictions between religion and science; and that in these controversies religion was always wrong, and that science was always right. The true facts of the case are very much more complex, and refuse to be summarized in these simple terms.

Theology itself exhibits exactly the same character of gradual development, arising from an aspect of conflict between its own proper ideas. This fact is a commonplace to theologians, but is often obscured in the stress of controversy. I do not wish to overstate my case; so I will confine myself to Roman Catholic writers. In the seventeenth century a learned Jesuit, Father Petavius, showed that the theologians of the first three centuries of Christianity made use of phrases and statements which since the fifth century would be condemned as heretical. Also Cardinal Newman devoted a treatise to the discussion of the development of doctrine. He wrote it before he became a great Roman Catholic ecclesiastic; but throughout his life, it was never retracted and continually reissued.

Science is even more changeable than theology. No man of science could

[1] *Cf.* Lecky's *The Rise and Influence of Rationalism in Europe*, Ch. III.

subscribe without qualification to Galileo's beliefs, or to Newton's beliefs, or to all his own scientific beliefs of ten years ago.

In both regions of thought, additions, distinctions, and modifications have been introduced. So that now, even when the same assertion is made to-day as was made a thousand, or fifteen hundred years ago, it is made subject to limitations or expansions of meaning, which were not contemplated at the earlier epoch. We are told by logicians that a proposition must be either true or false, and that there is no middle term. But in practice, we may know that a proposition expresses an important truth, but that it is subject to limitations and qualifications which at present remain undiscovered. It is a general feature of our knowledge, that we are insistently aware of important truths; and yet that the only formulations of these truths which we are able to make presuppose a general standpoint of conceptions which may have to be modified. I will give you two illustrations, both from science: Galileo said that the earth moves and that the sun is fixed; the Inquisition said that the earth is fixed and the sun moves; and Newtonian astronomers, adopting an absolute theory of space, said that both the sun and the earth move. But now we say that any one of these three statements is equally true, provided that you have fixed your sense of "rest" and "motion" in the way required by the statement adopted. At the date of Galileo's controversy with the Inquisition, Galileo's way of stating the facts was, beyond question, the fruitful procedure for the sake of scientific research. But in itself it was not more true than the formulation of the Inquisition. But at that time the modern concepts of relative motion were in nobody's mind; so that the statements were made in ignorance of the qualifications required for their more perfect truth. Yet this question of the motions of the earth and the sun expresses a real fact in the universe; and all sides had got hold of important truths concerning it. But with the knowledge of those times, the truths appeared to be inconsistent.

Again I will give you another example taken from the state of modern physical science. Since the time of Newton and Huyghens in the seventeenth century there have been two theories as to the physical nature of light. Newton's theory was that a beam of light consists of a stream of very minute particles, or corpuscles, and that we have the sensation of light when these corpuscles strike the retinas of our eyes. Huyghens' theory was that light consists of very minute waves of trembling in an all-pervading ether, and that these waves are traveling along a beam of light. The two theories are contradictory. In the eighteenth century Newton's theory was believed, in the nineteenth century Huyghens' theory was believed. To-day there is one large group of phenomena which can be explained only on the wave theory, and another large group which can be explained only on the corpuscular theory. Scientists have to leave it at that, and wait for the future, in the hope of attaining some wider vision which reconciles both.

We should apply these same principles to the questions in which there is a variance between science and religion. We would believe nothing in either sphere of thought which does not appear to us to be certified by solid reasons based upon the critical research either of ourselves or of competent authorities. But granting that we have honestly taken this precaution, a clash between the two on points of detail where they overlap should not lead us hastily to abandon doctrines for which we have solid evidence. It may be that we are more interested in one set of doctrines than in the other. But, if we have any sense of perspective and of the history of thought, we shall wait and refrain from mutual anathemas.

We should wait: but we should not wait passively, or in despair. The clash is a sign that there are wider truths and finer perspectives within which a reconciliation of a deeper religion and a more subtle science will be found.

In one sense, therefore, the conflict between science and religion is a slight matter which has been unduly emphasized. A mere logical contradiction cannot in itself point to more than the necessity of some readjustments, possibly of a very minor character on both sides. Remember the widely different aspects of events which are dealt with in science and in religion respectively. Science is concerned with the general conditions which are observed to regulate physical phenomena; whereas religion is wholly wrapped up in the contemplation of moral and aesthetic values. On the one side there is the law of gravitation, and on the other the contemplation of the beauty of holiness. What one side sees, the other misses; and vice versa.

Consider, for example, the lives of John Wesley and of Saint Francis of Assisi. For physical science you have in these lives merely ordinary examples of the operation of the principles of physiological chemistry, and of the dynamics of nervous reactions: for religion you have lives of the most profound significance in the history of the world. Can you be surprised that, in the absence of a perfect and complete phrasing of the principles of science and of the principles of religion which apply to these specific cases, the accounts of these lives from these divergent standpoints should involve discrepancies? It would be a miracle if it were not so.

It would, however, be missing the point to think that we need not trouble ourselves about the conflict between science and religion. In an intellectual age there can be no active interest which puts aside all hope of a vision of the harmony of truth. To acquiesce in discrepancy is destructive of candor, and of moral cleanliness. It belongs to the self-respect of intellect to pursue every tangle of thought to its final unravelment. If you check that impulse, you will get no religion and no science from an awakened thoughtfulness. The important question is, In what spirit are we going to face the issue? There we come to something absolutely vital.

A clash of doctrines is not a disaster—it is an opportunity. I will explain my meaning by some illustrations from science. The weight of an atom of nitrogen was well known. Also it was an established scientific doctrine that the average weight of such atoms in any considerable mass will be always the same. Two experimenters, the late Lord Rayleigh and the late Sir William Ramsay, found that if they obtained nitrogen by two different methods, each equally effective for that purpose, they always observed a persistent slight difference between the average weights of the atoms in

the two cases. Now I ask you, would it have been rational of these men
to have despaired because of this conflict between chemical theory and scientific observation? Suppose that for some reason the chemical doctrine
had been highly prized throughout some district as the foundation of its
social order:—would it have been wise, would it have been candid, would
it have been moral, to forbid the disclosure of the fact that the experiments
produced discordant results? Or, on the other hand, should Sir William
Ramsay and Lord Rayleigh have proclaimed that chemical theory was now
a detected delusion? We see at once that either of these ways would have
been a method of facing the issue in an entirely wrong spirit. What Rayleigh
and Ramsay did was this: They at once perceived that they had hit upon
a line of investigation which would disclose some subtlety of chemical
theory that had hitherto eluded observation. The discrepancy was not a
disaster: it was an opportunity to increase the sweep of chemical knowledge.
You all know the end of the story: finally argon was discovered, a new
chemical element which had lurked undetected, mixed with the nitrogen.
But the story has a sequel which forms my second illustration. This discovery drew attention to the importance of observing accurately minute
differences in chemical substances as obtained by different methods. Further
researches of the most careful accuracy were undertaken. Finally another
physicist, F. W. Aston, working in the Cavendish Laboratory at Cambridge
in England, discovered that even the same element might assume two or
more distinct forms, termed *isotopes,* and that the law of the constancy
of average atomic weight holds for each of these forms, but as between the
different isotopes differs slightly. The research has effected a great stride in
the power of chemical theory, far transcending in importance the discovery
of argon from which it originated. The moral of these stories lies on the
surface, and I will leave to you their application to the case of religion and
science.

In formal logic, a contradiction is the signal of a defeat: but in the evolution of real knowledge it marks the first step in progress towards a victory.
This is one great reason for the utmost toleration of variety of opinion.
Once and forever, this duty of toleration has been summed up in the words,
"Let both grow together until the harvest." The failure of Christians to
act up to this precept, of the highest authority, is one of the curiosities of
religious history. But we have not yet exhausted the discussion of the moral
temper required for the pursuit of truth. There are short cuts leading
merely to an illusory success. It is easy enough to find a theory, logically
harmonious and with important applications in the region of fact, provided that you are content to disregard half your evidence. Every age
produces people with clear logical intellects, and with the most praiseworthy
grasp of the importance of some sphere of human experience, who have
elaborated, or inherited, a scheme of thought which exactly fits those experiences which claim their interest. Such people are apt resolutely to ignore,
or to explain away, all evidence which confuses their scheme with contradictory instances. What they cannot fit in is for them nonsense. An unflinch-
ing determination to take the whole evidence into account is the only

method of preservation against the fluctuating extremes of fashionable opinion. This advice seems so easy, and is in fact so difficult to follow.

One reason for this difficulty is that we cannot think first and act afterwards. From the moment of birth we are immersed in action, and can only fitfully guide it by taking thought. We have, therefore, in various spheres of experience to adopt those ideas which seem to work within those spheres. It is absolutely necessary to trust to ideas which are generally adequate, even though we know that there are subtleties and distinctions beyond our ken. Also apart from the necessities of action, we cannot even keep before our minds the whole evidence except under the guise of doctrines which are incompletely harmonized. We cannot think in terms of an indefinite multiplicity of detail; our evidence can acquire its proper importance only if it comes before us marshalled by general ideas. These ideas we inherit—they form the tradition of our civilization. Such traditional ideas are never static. They are either fading into meaningless formulae, or are gaining power by the new lights thrown by a more delicate apprehension. They are transformed by the urge of critical reason, by the vivid evidence of emotional experience, and by the cold certainties of scientific perception. One fact is certain, you cannot keep them still. No generation can merely reproduce its ancestors. You may preserve the life in a flux of form, or preserve the form amid an ebb of life. But you cannot permanently enclose the same life in the same mold.

The present state of religion among the European races illustrates the statements which I have been making. The phenomena are mixed. There have been reactions and revivals. But on the whole, during many generations, there has been a gradual decay of religious influence in European civilization. Each revival touches a lower peak than its predecessor, and each period of slackness a lower depth. The average curve marks a steady fall in religious tone. In some countries the interest in religion is higher than in others. But in those countries where the interest is relatively high, it still falls as the generations pass. Religion is tending to degenerate into a decent formula wherewith to embellish a comfortable life. A great historical movement on this scale results from the convergence of many causes. I wish to suggest two of them which lie within the scope of this chapter for consideration.

In the first place for over two centuries religion has been on the defensive, and on a weak defensive. The period has been one of unprecedented intellectual progress. In this way a series of novel situations have been produced for thought. Each such occasion has found the religious thinkers unprepared. Something, which has been proclaimed to be vital, has finally, after struggle, distress, and anathema, been modified and otherwise interpreted. The next generation of religious apologists then congratulates the religious world on the deeper insight which has been gained. The result of the continued repetition of this undignified retreat, during many generations, has at last almost entirely destroyed the intellectual authority of religious thinkers. Consider this contrast: when Darwin or Einstein proclaim theories which modify our ideas, it is a triumph for science. We do not go about saying that there is another defeat for science, because its old ideas have been abandoned. We know that another step of scientific insight has been gained.

Religion will not regain its old power until it can face change in the same spirit as does science. Its principles may be eternal, but the expression of those principles requires continual development. This evolution of religion is in the main a disengagement of its own proper ideas from the adventitious notions which have crept into it by reason of the expression of its own ideas in terms of the imaginative picture of the world entertained in previous ages. Such a release of religion from the bonds of imperfect science is all to the good. It stresses its own genuine message. The great point to be kept in mind is that normally an advance in science will show that statements of various religious beliefs require some sort of modification. It may be that they have to be expanded or explained, or indeed entirely restated. If the religion is a sound expression of truth, this modification will only exhibit more adequately the exact point which is of importance. This process is a gain. In so far, therefore, as any religion has any contact with physical facts, it is to be expected that the point of view of those facts must be continually modified as scientific knowledge advances. In this way, the exact relevance of these facts for religious thought will grow more and more clear. The progress of science must result in the unceasing codification of religious thought, to the great advantage of religion.

The religious controversies of the sixteenth and seventeenth centuries put theologians into a most unfortunate state of mind. They were always attacking and defending. They pictured themselves as the garrison of a fort surrounded by hostile forces. All such pictures express half-truths. That is why they are so popular. But they are dangerous. This particular picture fostered a pugnacious party spirit which really expresses an ultimate lack of faith. They dared not modify, because they shirked the task of disengaging their spiritual message from the associations of a particular imagery.

Let me explain myself by an example. In the early medieval times, Heaven was in the sky, and Hell was underground; volcanoes were the jaws of Hell. I do not assert that these beliefs entered into the official formulations: but they did enter into the popular understanding of the general doctrines of Heaven and Hell. These notions were what everyone thought to be implied by the doctrine of the future state. They entered into the explanations of the influential exponents of Christian belief. For example, they occur in the *Dialogues* of Pope Gregory,[2] the Great, a man whose high official position is surpassed only by the magnitude of his services to humanity. I am not saying what we ought to believe about the future state. But whatever be the right doctrine, in this instance the clash between religion and science, which has relegated the earth to the position of a second-rate planet attached to a second-rate sun, has been greatly to the benefit of the spirituality of religion by dispersing these medieval fancies.

Another way of looking at this question of the evolution of religious

---

[2] *Cf.* Gregorovius' *History of Rome in the Middle Ages,* Book III, Ch. III, Vol. II, English Trans.

thought is to note that any verbal form of statement which has been before the world for some time discloses ambiguities; and that often such ambiguities strike at the very heart of the meaning. The effective sense in which a doctrine has been held in the past cannot be determined by the mere logical analysis of verbal statements, made in ignorance of the logical trap. You have to take into account the whole reaction of human nature to the scheme of thought. This reaction is of a mixed character, including elements of emotion derived from our lower natures. It is here that the impersonal criticism of science and of philosophy comes to the aid of religious evolution. Example after example can be given of this motive force in development. For example, the logical difficulties inherent in the doctrine of the moral cleansing of human nature by the power of religion rent Christianity in the days of Pelagius and Augustine—that is to say, at the beginning of the fifth century. Echoes of that controversy still linger in theology.

So far, my point has been this: that religion is the expression of one type of fundamental experiences of mankind: that religious thought develops into an increasing accuracy of expression, disengaged from adventitious imagery: that the interaction between religion and science is one great factor in promoting this development.

I now come to my second reason for the modern fading of interest in religion. This involves the ultimate question which I stated in my opening sentences. We have to know what we mean by religion. The churches, in their presentation of their answers to this query, have put forward aspects of religion which are expressed in terms either suited to the emotional reactions of bygone times or directed to excite modern emotional interests of non-religious character. What I mean under the first heading is that religious appeal is directed partly to excite that instinctive fear of the wrath of a tyrant which was inbred in the unhappy populations of the arbitrary empires of the ancient world, and in particular to excite that fear of an all-powerful arbitrary tyrant behind the unknown forces of nature. This appeal to the ready instinct of brute fear is losing its force. It lacks any directness of response, because modern science and modern conditions of life have taught us to meet occasions of apprehension by a critical analysis of their causes and conditions. Religion is the reaction of human nature to its search for God. The presentation of God under the aspect of power awakens every modern instinct of critical reaction. This is fatal; for religion collapses unless its main positions command immediacy of assent. In this respect the old phraseology is at variance with the psychology of modern civilizations. This change in psychology is largely due to science, and is one of the chief ways in which the advance of science has weakened the hold of the old religious forms of expression. The nonreligious motive which has entered into modern religious thought is the desire for a comfortable organization of modern society. Religion has been presented as valuable for the ordering of life. Its claims have been rested upon its function as a sanction to right conduct. Also the purpose of right conduct quickly degenerates into the formation of pleasing social relations. We have here a subtle degradation of religious ideas, following upon their gradual purification under the influence of keener ethical intuitions. Conduct is a by-product of religion—an inevitable by-product, but not the main point. Every great religious teacher has revolted against the presentation of religion as a mere sanction of rules of conduct. Saint Paul denounced the Law, and Puritan divines spoke of the filthy rags of righteousness. The insistence upon rules of conduct marks the ebb of religious fervor. Above and beyond all things, the religious life is not a research after comfort. I must now state, in all diffidence, what I conceive to be the essential character of the religious spirit.

Religion is the vision of something which stands beyond, behind, and within, the passing flux of immediate things; something which is real, and yet waiting to be realized; something which is a remote possibility, and yet the greatest of present facts; something that gives meaning to all that passes, and yet eludes apprehension; something whose possession is the final good, and yet is beyond all reach; something which is the ultimate ideal, and the hopeless quest.

The immediate reaction of human nature to the religious vision is worship. Religion has emerged into human experience mixed with the crudest fancies of barbaric imagination. Gradually, slowly, steadily the vision recurs in history under nobler form and with clearer expression. It is the one element in human experience which persistently shows an upward trend. It fades and then recurs. But when it renews its force, it recurs with an added richness and purity of content. The fact of the religious vision, and its history of persistent expansion, is our one ground for optimism. Apart from it, human life is a flash of occasional enjoyments lighting up a mass of pain and misery, a bagatelle of transient experience.

The vision claims nothing but worship; and worship is a surrender to the claim for assimilation, urged with the motive force of mutual love. The vision never overrules. It is always there, and it has the power of love presenting the one purpose whose fulfilment is eternal harmony. Such order as we find in nature is never force—it presents itself as the one harmonious adjustment of complex detail. Evil is the brute motive force of fragmentary purpose, disregarding the eternal vision. Evil is overruling, retarding, hurting. The power of God is the worship He inspires. That religion is strong which in its ritual and its modes of thought evokes an apprehension of the commanding vision. The worship of God is not a rule of safety—it is an adventure of the spirit, a flight after the unattainable. The death of religion comes with the repression of the high hope of adventure.

SCIENCE AND PEOPLE

Warren Weaver

Because I feel so deeply and so strongly concerning what I have to say on the subject of science and people, I shall run the risk of being dully pedagogical and state my plan at once. First, I am going to ask what successes man has had in his various endeavors and inquire why science seems to bulk so large among these successes. I am going to recount some foolish ideas concerning science that have arisen partly because of its successes. I am going to contrast these with a series of statements that seem to me more accurately to describe science and its relation to life. The main conclusion will be that science belongs to all the people, and that this fact presents the American Association for the Advancement of Science with a great opportunity and a great duty.

MAN'S MAJOR SUCCESSES

Think of the various major tasks to which men have, over the ages, addressed themselves. They have sought food, warmth, shelter, and other guards against the physical assaults of nature. Each individual or group has also sought protection against attack from the rest of mankind.

Men have tried to understand the physical universe. They have striven to apply this body of understanding to attain control of and to exploit this power over physical nature.

Men have tried to understand organic nature—how it evolved, and how individual organisms reproduce, grow, and function. They have sought health of body. They have tried to understand the nature of mind, of consciousness, of memory, of the learning process. They have endeavored to manage personal relationships within family groups, the village, the tribe, the state, the nation, and the world at large. They have attempted social and eventually political organization at all levels of inclusiveness and complexity, and they have tried to understand human behavior as it affects all these interrelationships.

Men have created methods for ownership of property and have elaborated systems of customs and laws in an attempt to protect individuals and serve society. They have recorded history and have attempted to understand it. They have, at great cost and with high dedication, tried to strike a balance between regulation and liberty.

SCIENCE AND PEOPLE From *Science* Magazine, Vol. 122, No. 3883 (December 30, 1955), pp. 1255–59. Reprinted with permission. Based on Mr. Weaver's presidential address to the American Association for the Advancement of Science, given in Atlanta on December 28, 1955.

Men have sought to enrich life through development of the pictorial arts, literature, music, drama, and the dance. They have created systems of logic and metaphysics and have tried to analyze the nature of knowledge and reality. They have formulated codes of esthetics and morals and have contemplated the purpose and meaning of life.

In this vast and interrelated range of concerns and activities, where do the successes lie? What things have men really done well?

Each man is entitled to his own answer, but my own reply would go as follows. Probably the most conspicuous, the most universally recognized, and the most widely applied success lies in the understanding and control of the forces of physical nature. Coupled with this, I would place the progress that has been made—even though it is but a start—in the understanding of organic nature.

But along with these two I would want to bracket, without attempting to suggest an order of importance, two other major successes. The first of this second pair of successes is to be found in the grandeur and practicality of the principles of personal conduct that have been enunciated by the great religious leaders. I would suggest, for example, that the Ten Commandments, the Golden Rule, and the rest of Sermon on the Mount have the generality within their realms that Newton's laws of motion have in theirs, plus the fact that no religious Einstein has found it necessary to insert correction terms of higher order.

The second further success that seems of major proportion is to be found in the degree to which life can be and has been enriched by the arts. Thus it is my own conviction that the poet has done a job that science must thoroughly respect, and perhaps should envy.

In listing only these four major successes, some real unfairness may have been done to our social advances. Granting all the confusions and troubles that greet us with each issue of the newspapers, it remains true that man has made great progress in sorting out his human relationships. The cry "Who goes home?" which still adjourns the House of Commons, reminds us that not too long ago members required armed escort to protect them from the brigands who lurked between Westminster and the City. The constitutional experience of the American republic is impressive evidence that society does not always blunder. His Majesty's loyal opposition—the difference between political opposition and treason—is the basic treaty of political life in widening areas of the world. If science has made great contributions to man's wellbeing, the institution of contract has, in an unobtrusive way, made it possible. And it is deeply satisying to recall that the daily lives of most people are saved from Hobbes' jungle by the presumption of good faith that infuses our relationships with one another.

To return to the four major successes, it seems interesting to note certain features that show how disparate they are. The first success—that of the physical sciences—is in a field where logic and quantitative measurement are dominant. The second—the dawning light of understanding of animate nature—is far less advanced, and it involves factors that are certainly nonquantitative and may well prove alogical. The third—the perfection of the code of personal conduct—is curiously and unhappily more a matter of theory than of practice. I believe it was Chesterton who remarked that no one knows whether Christianity will work because no one has ever tried it. As an ex-mathematician, I would point out that one single clear exception proves that a presumptive general rule is incorrect, and I would therefore say that Chesterton's remark is characteristically vivid and interesting, but that it is false. The fourth success—man's enrichment of his life through the arts—presents features that are baffling to a scientist. Indeed, I am not sure that the word *success* really applies here, for success connotes a bad start and good progress. But the arts, as a previous AAAS president has pointed out, seem to constitute an almost completely nonaccumulative part of experience. Rutherford had a great natural advantage over Faraday, and he over Gilbert; with respect to electric phenomena, both theory and the techniques of experimentation kept advancing, and each step was built on top of the preceding one. But Emily Dickinson had no advantage over Sappho. Each simply had words, the challenge of beauty, and the ineffable genius to condense, purify, and universalize experience.

SUCCESS OF PHYSICAL SCIENCE

Of these four major successes, I believe it is rather clear that the most tangible and obvious is the success of physical science. And this is an instance in which success and danger are close companions, as they often are. I do not refer here to the danger—ominous as it is—that science has unleashed forces that can physically destroy us. I refer to the more subtle danger that this success may mislead us concerning the real nature of science and its relationship to the rest of life and thus destroy something that is in the long run more important than a factory or a city, namely, our sense of value.

What made possible the great success that the physical sciences have experienced, particularly during the last century and a half? The explanation appears actually to be rather simple. *Physical* nature, first of all, seems to be on the whole very *loosely coupled.* That is to say, excellently workable approximations result from studying physical nature bit by bit, two or three variables at a time, and treating these bits as isolated. Furthermore, a large number of the broadly applicable laws are, to useful approximation, *linear,* if not directly in the relevant variables, then in nothing worse than their second time derivatives. And finally, a large fraction of physical phenomena (meteorology is sometimes an important exception) exhibit *stability:* perturbations tend to fade out, and great consequences do not result from very small causes.

These three extremely convenient characteristics of physical nature bring it about that vast ranges of phenomena can be satisfactorily handled by linear algebraic or differential equations, often involving only one or two dependent variables; they also make the handling *safe* in the sense that small errors are unlikely to propagate, go wild, and prove disastrous. Animate nature, on the other hand, presents highly complex and highly coupled systems —these are, in fact, dominant characteristics of what we call organisms. It takes a lot of variables to describe a man, or for that matter a virus; and you cannot often usefully study these variables two at a time. Animate nature also exhibits very confusing instabilities, as students of history, the stock market, or genetics are well aware.

If the successes of physical theory had remained limited to those highly useful but none the less essentially simple situations covered by two variable equations such as Ohm's law in electricity, or Hook's law for elastic deformation, or Boyle's law for volume and pressure of gases, or even to the vastly greater range of dynamic phenomena that are so superbly summarized in Newton's second law of motion, then it seems likely that mankind would have preserved a reasonable, take-it-or-leave-it attitude toward science. But two further things occurred.

Physical science pushed on to much more subtle and more complicated realms of phenomena, particularly in astrophysics and in atomic and then nuclear physics. And it kept on having successes. Second, physical science (and remember that nowadays it is not really useful to discriminate between physics and chemistry) began to be applied more and more to certain limited sorts of problems of animate nature. Biochemistry, to take a very conspicuous example, began to deal successfully with phase after phase of the happenings within the individual cells of living creatures.

At the same time, of course, scientific theories kept getting more and more complicated and technical. Not only were they generally formidable to the public at large—scientific experts themselves had increasing difficulty in understanding anything outside their own specialties.

SUPERSTITIONS

All this has tended to create a set of superstitions about science. These seem to be rather widely adopted by the public, and some of them even have adherents among scientists! These superstitions go something like this:

Science is all-powerful. It can just do anything. If you doubt this, just look around and see what it has done. A procedure known as "the scientific method" would in fact, if we only used it, solve all the problems of economics, sociology, political science, esthetics, philosophy, and religion. And the reason why science has been so successful, and the basis of confidence that it can go on to do anything whatsoever, is that science has somehow got the real low-down on nature and life. It has found out how to capture absolute truth, exact fact, incontrovertible evidence. Its statements are just "mathematically true," and in the face of that, you had better be confident and respectful, even if you are confused.

But science (to continue the superstitions) cannot be understood by ordinary folk. It is too technical, too abstruse, too special, and too different from ordinary thinking and ordinary experience. There is a special small priesthood of scientific practitioners; they know the secrets and they hold the power.

The scientific priests themselves are wonderful but strange creatures. They admittedly possess mysterious mental abilities; they are motivated by a strange and powerful code known as "the spirit of science," one feature of which seems to be that scientists consider that they deserve very special treatment by society.

Now these are dangerous misconceptions about science. If they were wholly untrue, if they were total and complete nonsense, then one could confidently await the general recognition of their fraudulent nature. But there is just enough apparent and illusive evidence in favor of these statements to give them an unfortunate vitality.

ALTERNATIVE STATEMENTS

Let me list as briefly as I can a set of alternative statements which I believe to be more reasonable and accurate.

1. Science has impressively proved itself to be a powerful way of dealing with certain aspects of our experience. These are, in general, the logical and quantitative aspects, and the method works superbly for linear and stable physical problems in two or three variables. The physical universe seems to be put together in such a way that this scientific approach is exceedingly successful in producing a good, workable, initial description. And with that kind of solid start, physical science can then safely proceed to elaborate more sophisticated theories.

2. We simply do not yet know how far these methods, which have worked so well with physical nature, will be successful in the world of living things. The successes to date are very impressive. One feature after another that previously seemed to fall in a special "vital" category has usefully yielded to biochemical or biophysical attack. But it is also the case that we have as yet made only a beginning. How far the logical-quantitative method will succeed here, one would be rash to forecast, although the prospects do indeed seem extremely promising.

3. We have made small beginnings at extending the scientific method into the social sciences. Insofar as these fields can be dealt with in terms of measurable quantities, they seem to present closely intercoupled situations that can very seldom usefully be handled with two or three variables and that often require a whole hatful—for example, W. Leontief's input-output analysis of the U.S. economy deals with some 50 variables and regrets that it does not handle more. Science has, as yet, no really good way of coping with these multivariable but nonstatistical problems, although it is possible that ultrahigh-speed computers will inspire new sorts of mathematical procedures that will be successful in cases where the effects are too numerous to handle easily but not numerous enough or of suitable character to permit statistical treatment. If we try to avoid the many-variable aspect of the social sciences by using highly simplified models of few variables, then these models are often too artificial and oversimplified to be useful. The statistical approach, on the other hand, has recently exhibited—for example, in the stochastic models for learning—new potentialities in the field of human behavior.

4. It is, incidentally, not at all necessary that the particular analytic tech-

niques of the physical sciences be forced upon biological or social problems
with the arrogant assumption that they can and should make unnecessary
other types of insight and experience. During the recent war, an extremely
useful collaboration was developed, known often as operations analysis, in
which reasoning of a mathematical type was applied to certain aspects of
very complicated situations, but with no expectation that judgment, experience, intuition, or a vague sort of general wisdom would be displaced
or superseded—rather only that these would be aided by whatever partial
light could be furnished by quantitative analysis.

5. An important characteristic of science, which we must note in passing,
is its incapacity to be impractical. The most far-reaching discoveries and the
most widespread useful applications flow regularly out of ideas that initially
seem abstract and even esoteric. These ideas arise out of the unguided and
free activity of men who are motivated by curiosity or who, even more
generally, are thinking about scientific problems simply because they like
to. The way in which apparently aimless curiosity stubbornly refuses to be
foolish and leads to important goals doubtless seems strange or even incredible to some persons. The eventual usefulness of the initially impractical is widely held to be a very special feature of science, but I am not so sure
of this. I think that apparent impracticality is more generally important
than we are inclined to suppose.

6. Science presents the kind of challenge that attracts to it young men and
women who tend to have a rather high degree of a certain kind of intelligence. Since this particular kind of intelligence is relatively easy to recognize
and measure, and since many other types are subtle and illusive, even though
perhaps more important, we tend to adopt this one type as the norm. In
addition, this particular type of intelligence leads rather promptly to tangible results. These circumstances lead to the conclusion, which is then
something of a tautology, that scientists are more intelligent than other people. This may or may not be true; more important, however, it may be
neither true nor untrue in the sense that the attempted comparison is meaningless.

7. However, despite their appearing to be so bright, scientists are not
special creatures: they are people. Like lots of other people, they are good
at their own tasks. Off their jobs they seem, as Shylock remarked in another
connection, "to be fed with the same food, hurt with the same weapons, subject to the same diseases, healed by the same means, warmed and cooled by
the same winter and summer" as other men are. When you prick them, they
do indeed bleed.

A. V. Hill, while he was president of the British Association for the Advancement of Science, stated: "Most scientists are quite ordinary folk, with
ordinary human virtues, weaknesses, and emotions. A few of the most eminent ones indeed are people of superlative general ability, who could have
done many things well; a few are freaks, with a freakish capacity and intuition in their special fields, but an extreme naiveté in general affairs. . . .
The great majority of scientists are between these groups, with much the

same distribution of moral and intellectual characteristics as other educated people."

8. One rather accidental fact has led many to think that scientists are strange and special, and this is the fact that scientists often use a strange and special language. Science does find it desirable to use very many technical words, and it has indeed developed, as a matter of saving time, a sort of language of its own. This gives to science an external appearance of incomprehensibility that is very unfortunate. The public need not think itself stupid for failing intuitively to grasp all this technicality. Indeed, what has developed is not so much a language as a series of very specialized dialects, each really understood only by its inventors. "On faithful rings" is not a sociological discussion of marriage but an article in modern algebra. The "Two-body problem for triton" is not mythology but physics: a "folded tree" is not a botanical accident but a term in telephone switching theory.

9. If scientists are human, so also is science itself. For example, science does not deserve the reputation it has so widely gained of being based on absolute fact (whatever that is supposed to mean), of being wholly objective, of being infinitely precise, of being unchangeably permanent, of being philosophically inescapable and unchallengeable. There seem still to be persons who think that science deals with certainty, whereas it is the case, of course, that it deals with probabilities. There seem still to be persons who think that science is the one activity that deals with truth, whereas it is the case, of course, that—to take a very simple example—"the true length of a rod" is so clearly not obtainable by any scientific procedure that, insofar as science is concerned, this "true length" remains a pleasant fiction.

I could document this particular point at length, but will restrict myself to three quotations from the relatively mature fields of physics, astronomy, and mathematics.

Edmund Whittaker said of theoretical physics: ". . . it is built around conceptions; and the progress of the subject consists very largely in replacing these conceptions by other conceptions, which transcend or even contradict them."

Herbert Dingle, in his retiring address as president of the Royal Astronomical Society, said: "The universe . . . is a hypothetical entity of which what we observe is an almost negligible part. . . . In cosmology we are again, like the philosophers of the Middle Ages, facing a world almost entirely unknown."

Alfred North Whitehead has stated: "While mathematics is a convenience in relating certain types of order to our comprehension, it does not . . . give us any account of their activity. . . . When I was a young man, . . . I was taught science and mathematics by brilliant men; . . . since the turn of the century I have lived to see every one of the basic assumptions of both set aside."

10. These quotations indicate that the ablest scientists themselves realize the postulational and provisional character of science. Perhaps not so widely recognized or accepted is the extent to which the development of Western

science, rather than constituting a uniquely inevitable pattern, has been influenced by the general nature of Greco-Judaic culture, including especially the standards, arising within that tradition, of what is interesting and important.

Confronted by the totality of experience, men select the features that seem interesting and important—and the criteria for interest and importance arise not just or even primarily within scientific thought, but rather within the entire cultural complex. One then seeks to find a way of ordering this selected experience so that the end result is acclaimed as satisfying and useful—again as judged within the total culture. This process has different possible beginnings and different possible procedures; so, of course, it has different possible end results. Clyde Kluckhohn has remarked, "What people perceive, and how they conceptualize their perceptions is overwhelmingly influenced by culture." H. M. Tomlinson said, "We see things not as they are, but as we are."

If, for example, a culture almost wholly disregards physical suffering, considers the present life an unimportant episode, and places a very high premium on prolonged mystic contemplation, then this viewpoint regarding values does more than, for example, underemphasize modern scientific medicine (using all these words in the Western sense). It produces something that is different *in kind;* I know of no criteria that justify calling one kind good and intelligent, and the other poor and ignorant.

Chang Tung-San, a Chinese philosopher, has said: "Take Aristotelian logic, for example, which is evidently based on Greek grammar. The differences between Latin, French, English, and German grammatical form do not result in any difference between Aristotelian logic and their respective rules of reasoning, because they belong to the same Indo-European linguistic family. Should this logic be applied to Chinese thought, however, it will prove inappropriate. This fact shows that Aristotelian logic is based on the Western system of language. Therefore we should not follow Western logicians in taking for granted that their logic is the universal rule of human reasoning."

If this general line of thought seems to you either interesting or improbable, I urge you to read some of the fascinating papers of Benjamin Lee Whorf and of Dorothy D. Lee on the value systems and the conceptual implications of the languages of various American Indian tribes. Whorf, for example, points out that the Hopi Indian language "is seen to contain no words, grammatical forms, constructions or expressions that refer directly to what we call *time,* or to past, present, or future, or to enduring or lasting, or to motion as kinematic rather than dynamic. . . . At the same time the Hopi language is capable of accounting for and describing correctly, in a pragmatic or operational sense, all observable phenomena of the universe."

11. The ten preceding numbered comments concerning certain general characteristics of science all contribute, I believe, to a major conclusion—that science is a very human enterprise, colored by our general ideas, changeable as any human activity must be, various in its possible forms, and a common part of the lives of all men.

Indeed, even the impressive methods that science has developed—methods which sometimes seem so formidable—are in no sense superhuman. They involve only improvement—great, to be sure—of procedures of observation and analysis that the human race has always used. In the appeal to evidence, science has taught us a great deal about objectivity and relevance, but, again, this is refinement of procedure, not invention of wholly new procedure.

In short, every man is to some degree a scientist. It is misleading that a tiny fraction of the population is composed of individuals who possess a high degree of scientific skill, while most of the rest are indifferent or poor scientists. This creates the false impression that there is a difference in kind, when it is actually only one of degree.

If, when a window sticks, you pound it unreasonably, or jerk so hard that you hurt your back, or just give up in ignorant disgust, then you are being a poor scientist. If you look the situation over carefully to see what is really the matter—paint on the outside that needs cutting through, or a crooked position in the frame—then you are being a good scientist.

Even primitive men were scientists, and in certain aspects of accurate and subtle observation and deduction it would probably be hard to beat the ancient skilled hunter.

Indeed, one important contrast between the savage and the professor is simply that modern scientific methods make it possible to crystallize our experience rapidly and reliably, whereas primitive science does this clumsily, slowly, and with much attendant error. But it is, after all, well to remember that ephedrine is the active principle in an herb, Ma Huang, that has been empirically employed by native Chinese physicians for some 5000 years. Certain African savages when they moved their villages did take with them to the new location some dirt from the floor of the old hut. Moreover, it is true that they said that they did this to avoid the anger of their gods who might not wish them to move, fooling them by continuing to live on some of the same ground. But the fact remains that by this process they brought to the new location the soil microorganisms that continued to give some degree of protection from certain ailments. We quite properly honor Fleming and Florey, but Johannes de Sancto Paulo, a medical writer of the 12th century, did prescribe moldy bread for an inflamed abscess. "We are all scientists," Thomas Huxley said, because "the method of scientific investigation is nothing but the expression of the necessary mode of working of the human mind."

SCIENCE AS A HUMAN ACTIVITY

Let us now back away from the trees and look at the forest. Where have we arrived in this discussion?

I have just listed 11 points that, in my judgment at least, fairly characterize science as a universal human activity. These comments do not support the concept of science as some sort of super creed, magical and mysterious as it is all-powerful, arrogant from its successes, and avid to invade and conquer, one after another, all the fields of human activity and thought. This viewpoint does not justify the notion that science is so special as to be unique, as well as so curious as to be incomprehensible. This does not depict scientists as strange creatures who are in one sense so objective, judicial, and precise as to be incredible, and in another sense so apart from life as to be selfish and sinister. This does not set up quantitative analytic Western science as the only valid way in which man may approach and interpret experience.

On the contrary, these descriptive comments picture science as the servant of man, not his master; and as a friendly companion of art and of moral philosophy. This is a science that is the way it is because man wants it to be that way. It is a natural expression of both his curiosity and his faith.

If the public could be brought to understand and appreciate this position concerning science and scientists, I do not think that so many persons would harm this great enterprise of ours with a combination of mistrust, fear, and overestimation. I do not think that so many would treat scientists one-third of the time as amusing but beneficial eccentrics, one-third of the time as sorcerers, and one-third of the time as irresponsible rascals. I do not think that so many would view scientists as careless dabblers with danger, or as a selfish minority that, to quote a nationally syndicated columnist, "hold they are an extra special group not tied down by the obligations and rules under which the rest of us work. Hundreds of them are now bellyaching about the Oppenheimer verdict and saying it ruins their morale and makes them hard to get. What goes with those birds?" Or consider another newspaper writer who opened one of his columns with the sentence, "We Americans have been confronted with an arrogant proposition that persons presuming to call themselves intellectuals, and particularly those who claim the title of scientist, are a superior cult entitled to deference or even homage from the common man." One of our greatest universities takes a sound and courageous stand, and a newspaper writer complains, "Harvard has a peculiar fondness nowadays for putting security and the safety of the nation second to their fancy ideas of importance." If some speak out against the climate of fear resulting from the stupidities and iniquities of what is misnamed as the security system—doubly misnamed since it is not a system and does not achieve security—then their protest is labeled, as it was by Eugene Lyons in the *Saturday Evening Post*, as "the mock-heroic posture of this close-knit band of Cassandras"; he insultingly adds that these protesters do not themselves seem to have suffered, for "not one of them has as yet been muzzled, lynched, or denied his due royalties."

Anti-intellectual views such as these are widely expressed in those newspapers that combine a wide circulation with a narrow intellectual viewpoint, in some very popular national magazines, and even, one reports with shame, by highly placed persons in Washington.

It is hardly necessary to argue, these days, that science is essential to the public. It is becoming equally true, as the support of science moves more and more to state and national sources, that the public is essential to science. The lack of general comprehension of science is thus dangerous both to science and to the public, these being interlocked aspects of the common danger that scientists will not be given the freedom, the understanding, and the support that are necessary for vigorous and imaginative development. It is, moreover, of equally grave importance that science understand itself.

There are persons who are pessimistic concerning the prospects of materially improving the public understanding of science, and even the understanding that one branch of science has of the other branches. If one subscribes to the falsities and exaggerations that I stated in the first part of this article, then he could properly be pessimistic. If, on the other hand, he accepts the broader, more liberal, more human and humane view that I have advanced here, then—or at least so it seems to me—he can be very optimistic.

When David Brewster, a century and a quarter ago, was one of the prime movers in founding the British Association for the Advancement of Science, he said, "The principal objects of the Society would be to make the cultivators of science acquainted with each other, to stimulate one another to new exertions—to bring the objects of science more before the public eye and to take measures for advancing its interests and accelerating its progress."

This is a challenge which our own Association has always sought to meet. It is a challenge which, at this moment in history, requires renewed zeal and ever-renewed patience. Speaking of the present-day scientist, J. Bronowski has said, "Outside his laboratory, his task is to educate us in what goes on inside it, and to give it a meaning for us. In a world in which statesmen as much as voters are ignorant of the simplest implications in science, this is a formidable responsibility . . . [the scientist] has no other choice today but patiently to become a teacher, in a world in which distrust and prejudice are free. . . . There is no alternative to an informed public opinion: and that can exist only where scientists speak to voters and voters accept their responsibility, which is to listen, to weigh, and then to make their own choice."

If, as I believe, the sciences and the arts are lively and noncompetitive partners in the business of life, it is appropriate that we close, not with a scientist, but with a great artist. "Our privacy," Faulkner says, "has been slowly and steadily and increasingly invaded until now our very dream of civilization is in danger. Who will save us but the scientist and the humanitarian. Yes, the humanitarian in science, and the scientist in the humanity of man."

From SCIENCE, CHOICE,
AND HUMAN VALUES

Alvin M. Weinberg

The main philosophic principle that emerges from the very practical question: How should we cut the scientific pie? is a reaffirmation of the imbeddedness of scientific values. This is so, in the sense, first, that value judgments are to be made from a neighboring vantage point; and second, that such judgments are to depend on the extent to which the activity being judged enlarges or furthers the neighboring universes.

Can the calculus of scientific values and its underlying idea of imbeddedness be applied in any useful or meaningful sense to human values generally? In short, can science, or at least our attempt to construct an ethic for science, provide us with clues as to how to order human conduct and create a pattern of human value? This is an old question which is usually answered in the negative: most writers argue that science, concerned with a nature which is morally neutral, is itself bereft of any capacity to make value judgments, to moralize. But there have been contrary views, and I shall review two.

The first, put forward by Jacob Bronowski, Anatol Rapoport, and Michael Polanyi, argues that, because science and its practitioners are so strongly dedicated to truth, the entire enterprise of science—the "republic of science" as Polanyi calls it, or the "society of scientists" as Bronowski calls it—is the most perfect republic conceived by man. It is a social order, as described by Rapoport, ". . . in which investigation, criticism, intellectual cross-fertilization, and intellectual revolution are always possible and always welcome" (*Science and the Goals of Man*, New York, Harper, 1950, p. 232). In it truth reigns supreme. The style of scientific interaction, that is, the habit of self-criticism of the scientific community, keeps the quest for truth straight and narrow. The charlatan is ruthlessly exposed; the "right" collective path to follow emerges as the result of innumerable interplays between individuals, each playing the game according to rules that each understands and that keep everyone honest. Bronowski and Rapoport in effect propose that we devise a human ethic by copying the underlying ethic of the "republic of science": in this sense science provides a basis for human values and a human system of ethics.

I find this vision of an almost perfect republic of science and of the correspondingly perfect republic of man to be very appealing. Yet, aside from the practical question of actually making the supposedly isomorphic transi-

FROM SCIENCE, CHOICE, AND HUMAN VALUES From *Bulletin of the Atomic Scientists*, Vol. 26, No. 4 (April 1966). Reprinted by permission of Science and Public Affairs, the Bulletin of the Atomic Scientists. Copyright © 1970 by the Educational Foundation for Nuclear Science.

tion from one republic to the other, I see grave questions. These have mainly to do with the corruption of the republic of science caused by the advent of "big science." In this age of big money for science it is harder to find the scientist dedicated solely to truth; he is responsible for spending "big money," and his pursuit of science is sometimes distorted by his method of funding. But more important is the blunting of science's instrument of self-criticism, the scientific literature, simply because science has become so big. The fragmentation of science tends to make scientific criticism parochial and even self-serving, a situation that is aggravated by the vastness of the scientific literature that hardly gets read. If the republic of science is to be kept honest by the traditional interplay of scientific critics, mediated by the scientific journals, what does the republic do when there are too many journals to read? Thus, appealing though the republic of science may be, I hardly think it is as perfect as Polanyi or Bronowski make it out to be and it can therefore serve only as a partial basis for a human ethic.

THE IMPERATIVE TOWARD ORDER

Another attempt to find within science a basis for a human ethic was put forward by Bruce Lindsay of Brown University in 1959 ("Entropy Consumption and Values in Physical Science," *The American Scientist*, 47, 1959, p. 376). Lindsay points out that the living biological organism tends to reduce its local entropy, i.e., to produce order out of disorder locally, although, of course, the total entropy of the universe continues to increase. As Lindsay views it, it is inherent in the biological organism, simply because it is a biological organism, to increase the order of what it incorporates. This in a way can be extended into an ethical principle: whatever increases order is natural in the sense of being biological. Ethics, insofar as it implies that the good is that which increases order, is not so much a philosophical principle as it is a biological fact. I find Lindsay's idea attractive, but the issue obviously revolves around what we mean by "order." A clue is suggested by a remark Eugene Wigner once made to me about his motivation in creating the majestic principles of symmetry which now dominate so much of physics: "I hope that I leave this world a little more orderly than I found it." By order here he means not a lock-step Hitlerism devoid of human dignity, but rather that he hopes to increase the relatedness of things, to show how the existence of the Ω^- follows from a fairly natural extension of the symmetry principles which underlie much of atomic quantum mechanics.

Thus insofar as Lindsay's imperative toward order can be paraphrased into a quest for relatedness, for showing the connections between things and thus striving for a unity, I would be glad to accept his entropy principle as a basis for human ethical systems.

But this seems to me to be a manifestation of the "principle of the imbeddedness of values" which I believe underlies the proper analysis of our debate on scientific values. In deciding what science is good, we have invoked the notion that scientific merit is to be measured by the degree to which that science illuminates and deepens our understanding of the neighboring sciences. We have based our scientific value system, our scientific ethic so to speak, on the notion that truth is whole, that the purpose of science is not merely to unearth the facts but also to show the relatedness of facts. We have elevated the principle of "scientific parsimony," i.e., the idea that the aim of science is to unify our picture of the world and thus enable us to explain the world with the fewest ad hoc postulates, to an ethical or moral principle. Science in striving for better relatedness between its segments seeks more order; or perhaps more accurately, Lindsay's imperative toward order is interpreted as an imperative toward relatedness.

I suppose I should pause at this point to impress you with the danger of falling in love with a tricky philosophic principle, in this case the principle of the imbeddedness of values and the notion of the merit of relatedness. I put forward this idea of the virtue of relatedness even as I batten the hatches awaiting the outcries from the professionals.

Yet there are some outside of science who seem to hold rather a similar view. Sir Kenneth Clark, in his beautiful Smithsonian Bicentennial talk on artistic criticism, after saying "as science has become more specialized and more abstract, so art has felt the need to make its own realism purer and more inaccessible, . . ." goes on to say ". . . the notion that this universal sense of form must be unconnected with other human experience was in error." In other words, Sir Kenneth seems to come to the same position with respect to artistic criticism as I have with respect to scientific criticism: that some of the criteria of merit for judging art, no less than for judging science, must be sought outside art or outside science—and indeed, in the human life and human spirit of which these two seemingly unrelated human activities are manifestations.

And I would go further: I would argue that human value systems, not only in art and science but in the broadest human experiences—our sense of justice, our idea of morality, our criteria of virtue—involve the kind of ethical relativism implicit in our calculus of scientific value. Certainly everything that the social sciences have learned, particularly cultural anthropology, points to the idea that what is good can hardly be decided ultimately: what is good in one society may be bad in another and vice versa. That a similar principle underlies our judgment of scientific merit is not surprising. But our scientific calculus, combined with Lindsay's ethical imperative, allows us to move beyond a neutral and austere ethical relativism—that everything is a matter of taste, a matter of fashion. For we argue that things, scientific activities or human activities, are themselves imbedded in a total human matrix, and that merit is to be judged by the degree to which the activity, scientific or human, contributes to the unity and illumination and, ultimately, to the harmony of the many activities with which it interacts. Thus, there is a kind of ethical reciprocity: we decide on the good from the standpoint of the neighboring universes; in making the judgment, we ask if the activity or attitude we are judging helps create a unity, a harmony in the universes doing the judging. What we are judging is good to the extent to which the answer is yes.

I recognize that my foray into the sticky country of human ethics is at best awkward. Yet I am encouraged by two separate points. First, that with the weakening of religion as a basis for modern ethical behavior, it would be nice to have a substitute. We scientists are naturally attracted toward attempts to find such substitutes in our professional business. And second, I am encouraged that my views are not original. As Bronowski put it, "When Coleridge tried to define beauty, he turned always to one deep thought: beauty, he said, is 'unity in variety.' Science is nothing else than the search to discover unity in the wild variety of nature—or more exactly, in the variety of our experience."

Perhaps to use this same principle of unity in diversity as a meaningful ethical principle is asking too much. Yet, the analogy between our problem of scientific choice and the problem of human choice—that is, between the ethics of science and the ethics of man—is too tantalizing to be ignored. Perhaps such reckless forays will encourage others to think about these issues—and will encourage them to bring forth a logical ethics for science and a credible ethics for man.

SCIENCE, TECHNOLOGY,
AND STATESMANSHIP

Elmer W. Engstrom

Your choice for the William Proctor Prize has, in a sense, placed you in double jeopardy. Fifteen years ago, when the Prize was awarded to Ernest O. Lawrence, your program committee honored me with the invitation to provide the address. Thus I have won today not only a valued award, but also a rare opportunity for a second try at the speech. For those with long memories, I shall make every effort not to repeat myself.

Fortunately, the risk of repetition is minimal. The world of 1966 is substantially different from the world of 1951 in any subject area that we are apt to consider at such a gathering as this. Among the most remarkable achievements of modern science and technology are the acceleration of human experience and the compression of historical time. In terms of material progress and change, the past fifteen years are equivalent to a century or more by earlier standards.

The benefits have been immense and far-reaching, and the professions which we represent are surely entitled to a substantial share of the credit. Yet we cannot overlook dangers which have become increasingly evident in

SCIENCE, TECHNOLOGY, AND STATESMANSHIP From *American Scientist* Magazine, Vol. 55, No. 1 (March 1967). Reprinted with permission. Based on The Procter Prize Address, 1966, RESA–Sigma Xi Luncheon, Washington, D.C., December 29, 1966.

recent years. There is new urgency today to the question as to whether our society can maintain effective control of a technology that continues to multiply in speed and power.

It is necessary for us here to ask whether we, as scientists and engineers, are prepared to do all we must to help prevent our creations from getting entirely out of hand. While I cannot pretend to have a definitive answer, I believe that it may be useful to take this opportunity for a fresh look at certain aspects of the problem.

To establish the perspective, consider how short a journey backward in time is needed in order to arrive at the infancy of the principal technologies that are now transforming our environment.

THE ELECTRONICS TECHNOLOGIES

As an example, my own career of forty-three years has run parallel in time and experience to the growth of electronics and mass communications from the early days of radio broadcasting. In 1923, when I joined General Electric as a young engineering graduate, an individual could comprehend the bulk of available knowledge about electronic theory and application. The outer limits of the technology were clearly visible, and the most advanced apparatus held no mysteries for anyone who had completed a basic course in electrical engineering. None of us, in fact, would have recognized that we were engaged in electronics, because the term itself had not been coined. We were in radio, and that offered glamour enough.

We now know, of course, that we were helping to breed a revolution. Through the following two decades, research and development in a few university and industry laboratories provided new insight into the character of electrons and the means for controlling their behavior. This knowledge was applied increasingly to practical ends. Impressive results were achieved through innovations in the structure and material of electron tubes and through variations in circuit design. Using the tube as its building block, electronic technology broadened to encompass microwave and FM radio, television, radar, automation and control systems, microscopy, and rudimentary computing functions.

Yet there were basic limitations to further progress. Tubes were relatively large and delicate. They required substantial power to operate, and they emitted significant amounts of heat. Obviously, there was a point beyond which electronic systems employing tubes could not be built or operated economically. By the late 1940's, the technology was pushing against these limits.

At this point, the results of basic research were translated dramatically into a series of achievements that led to a wholly new technology whose limits are not yet apparent. The symbol of this new era is the transistor, which emerged in 1948 as the first solid-state device capable of performing the basic functions of the electron tube.

The initial result was a revolution in conventional electronic circuitry. Using the transistor as a new building block, the technology began to provide miniaturized and rugged equipment that required only a small fraction of the power needed to operate tube circuits. Even more significantly, research and application began to advance across a widening spectrum of electronically active solids to achieve entirely new effects.

This advance continues unabated today. It has already moved electronics far beyond the technology of the 1940's to pervade nearly all significant areas of human activity. It has transformed the earlier functions of electronics into more versatile and sophisticated operations. It has engendered countless new functions that had been either technically or economically impossible to achieve. This new technology is the genesis of our present-day high-speed computers, color television, satellite communications, space technology, missile guidance, and a host of advanced techniques and systems. Now it is moving on to new generations of equipment based on such devices as integrated circuits, lasers, and superconductive magnets.

More technological progress has been made in electronics during the past decade than in all of the four decades preceding.

THE ERA OF MATERIAL CHANGE

I cite the example of electronics because of my own experience, and because the recent impact of electronics has perhaps been felt more widely than that of any other aspect of technology. Yet the story has its counterpart in virtually all of the physical sciences and the technologies that stem from them. The past two decades have seen historic advances in all principal branches of chemistry, biology, and physics. The effects have been profound not only in electronics, but also in medicine and public health, nucleonics, agriculture, and electrical technology.

It is generally recognized that we are living in an era of material change unprecedented in swiftness and scope. It is perhaps less generally recognized, however, that the rate of change continues to accelerate and is likely to continue to do so.

The groundwork for this era was laid over a period of many years. In the modern sense, its direct ancestry lies in the growing relationship between science and engineering during the nineteenth century and the astonishing outburst of fundamental discovery in physics during the two decades from 1890 to 1910. In our own time a critical new element has been added by the spectacular narrowing of the time gap between discovery and application.

The great scientific achievements of the past occurred in a leisurely environment. Many years ordinarily elapsed between original discovery and practical use, or between invention and mass production. Only during the present era, for example, have the discoveries of Hertz and Marconi been effectively converted into mass communications in sight and sound. Only during the present era has the invention of the Wright brothers in 1906 developed into a means of worldwide mass transportation. And only during the present era have the fundamental studies of Becquerel, the Curies, Planck, and Einstein at the turn of the century been translated into new sources of energy and weapons of mass destruction.

Today, in contrast to any earlier time, we seek to convert scientific knowledge as rapidly as possible into new technology. Only a decade, or in some cases five years or even less, may now elapse from the prediction or first observation of a new phenomenon to its employment in a practical device. The results are added more or less indiscriminately to our environment in the form of new or improved products and services. Moreover, economic, social, and political forces continue to generate new pressures that tend to accelerate the process.

These forces began to appear in some strength during the first World War. This was the catalyst that transformed the airplane, the submarine, and radio communications virtually overnight from experimental status to full-fledged technology.

However, it was the concerted drive for technological superiority in World War II that gave greatest impetus to the present dynamic trend. Between 1940 and 1945, massive efforts were undertaken to expand the nation's research and development facilities in response to military needs.

GOVERNMENT SUPPORT

Government funds were poured into laboratories, engineering facilities, and pilot plants. These were staffed by industrial or university contractors, or, in some cases, by the government itself. By the end of the war, an immense new reservoir of technological resources had been created. In the realm of private industry, hundreds of enterprises had been drawn for the first time into research and development—and they remained.

The acceleration of technology has continued ever since. Government support has expanded steadily in a post-war environment of increasingly complex weapons, sustained international tension, competition in space, and mounting social needs at home. Research and development activities within industry have multiplied in the heated competition to provide new products and services for an affluent and growing population.

Today, research and development expenditures in the nation amount to nearly $20 billion a year—five times greater than a decade ago, and at least 200 times greater than the total spent in 1940. An estimated two million scientists and engineers are engaged in public and private programs ranging from theoretical studies to the development of operating products and systems.

CONSEQUENCES OF CHANGES IN SCIENCE AND TECHNOLOGY

The consequence in this country—and to some degree in all advanced nations—has been described as a social system imploding with change.

The immense impact of technology can be measured in many ways, but perhaps most easily in terms of the material wealth that is generated. The gross national product has risen from $285 billion in 1950 to approximately $750 billion this year. It is expected to pass the level of $1 thousand billion by 1975 and to double that amount by the end of this century. Average family personal income is expected to exceed $10,000 annually by 1975, even with the continued growth of population to an estimated 225 million.

Shifting patterns of employment continue to offer increasing opportunity in white collar occupations. It is significant that the fastest growing occupational categories today are in the systems analysis and programming activities associated with computer technology. By 1975, it is estimated that 54 per cent of employed Americans will hold white collar jobs, and only 33 per cent will be engaged in the blue collar tasks associated largely with factory employment.

DOUBTS AND DANGERS

The material prospects are exceedingly bright, but we must balance against them the doubts and dangers that arise in so dynamic a situation. Several years ago, the late Norbert Wiener concluded that it had become possible to build systems that could escape from the control of the men who made them. We must ask today whether it is not equally possible for entire areas of technology to escape from human control.

This is no longer a theoretical question. Apparent overconfidence in a technical system recently permitted a catastrophic breakdown to occur in the power supply to a major concentration of the nation's industry and population. Misjudgment of the possible effects of an atomic explosion has disturbed the structure of the Van Allen belts, apparently for many years to come. The proliferation of motor vehicles, jet aircraft, and other exhaust-producing machines has contributed to massive pollution of the atmosphere. Uncontrolled disposal of industrial waste and the widespread use of chemical pesticides and weed killers have tainted water supplies and affected marine life.

In short, the introduction of new technology without regard to *all* of the possible effects can amount to setting a time bomb that will explode in the face of society anywhere from a month to a generation in the future.

Lack of foresight in the past has forced us to create countertechnologies that can alleviate or reverse the harmful effects of earlier technology. To curb environmental pollution, for example, immense expenditures of talent and money must now be made for the systematic development and application of new techniques for exhaust control, waste disposal, and water purification.

The triumph of automotive technology has led inexorably to massive congestion throughout our metropolitan and urban areas. This, too, is generating a costly countertechnology of traffic control employing computers, electronic detectors, and other new instruments. A similar situation is developing in air transportation as jet aircraft continue to multiply more rapidly than our facilities for handling them at airports.

Such hazards as these will continue to arise and to call for counteraction as long as there is a failure to take account of relationships among all elements of the environment in which new technology must function.

I believe that the harmful effects which we observe in some aspects of technology might have been minimized by more effective communication in the past within the scientific and technical community and between this community and those who determine public policy.

IMPROVEMENT IN COMMUNICATIONS

Much has been done to improve and expand communications through these channels in recent years. There is unquestionably greater exchange now than in the past among the various disciplines. In the realm of public policy, some fifty qualified professionals provide continuing counsel to the President on science matters. Hundreds of scientists and engineers are involved in the formulation of policy at various levels of national government. There is no reliable census of the many thousands more who participate in state and local government affairs.

Against these gains, however, must be placed an exponential rise in the inventory of knowledge to be communicated in every field of science. This in turn leads to greater specialization and to diminished opportunity or incentive for the individual to gain knowledge outside of his immediate field. It then becomes more likely that a chemist, for example, might promote in good faith the use of a substance whose harmful effect somewhere in the environment could be anticipated only by a worker in some specialized branch of biology.

Under these conditions, we could surely benefit from the application to broad areas of technology of the philosophy that we now employ on an *ad hoc* basis in the conception, design, and development of specific systems.

A typical system project begins with examination of a particular need and of alternative proposals for meeting the need. A choice of method follows, and the required talents are enlisted from the various disciplines that can contribute to the end result. Each task is pursued and evaluated in the light of its role in the complete system. Moreover, the entire project is constantly under review to take account of actual and prospective changes in the environment in which it is expected to function.

Obviously, the analogy cannot be exact. The original source of knowledge that leads eventually to technology is the research worker who can seldom be guided by the statement of a practical need. As Fred Seitz remarked in a recent issue of AMERICAN SCIENTIST, "the most certain way to limit the usefulness of science is to insist that only those studies which have immediate and obvious practical meaning are carried through."

However, it is possible to ensure through initial education and continued communication that the basic researcher is aware of society and its needs. He will then be likely, when faced with a choice of directions, to follow that which relates more closely to the interests of society.

As we proceed further toward the development and application of technology, the analogy becomes more relevant. Just as many disciplines are called into cooperative action to evaluate and pursue the specific goal, so can they be enlisted in matters that relate to broad technological advances and the possible effects.

Modern electronics can help substantially in achieving this end. As scientific and technical activities and information grow in volume, electronic systems offer a facility for transmitting, receiving, and processing data more effectively than ever before.

Already, computers have been coupled with communications networks to serve as electronic data classification and reference centers in limited areas of research and other technical activity. As we gain further insight into problems of system organization and programming, highly versatile regional electronic libraries can eventually be established. Within their memory banks, the bulk of scientific knowledge can be kept up-to-date and available for instant retrieval.

Even in their present stage, these methods of communication and data processing provide useful means for obtaining and weighing the views of specialists in many disciplines before an irrevocable commitment is made to widespread use of a new technology. By extension, the same facilities permit us to seek the views and guidance of those best qualified to assess the possible political and social consequences.

But means alone are not enough: the will must also exist to ask the right questions before final commitments are made.

For example, will efforts to reduce pollution created by earlier technology bring new dangers? Do we know what possible effects may result from the use of a hundred million or more fuel cells or batteries for electric motors to replace internal combustion engines? Is systematic attention being given to the possible physical and psychological consequences when travelers are rushed by the thousands each day between widely separated time zones by supersonic mass transportation?

There are many such questions to be asked about impending results of research and development and their potential effects not only tomorrow, but ten, twenty, or fifty years hence. With the growing complexity of all technology, miscalculations of any type will become even more costly and potentially catastrophic.

THE NEED FOR STATESMANSHIP

There are stirrings today of a trend toward more concerted action by the technical community to seek the answers that are so urgently needed. A number of significant discussion and study programs, for example, are under way or projected by the National Academies of Science and Engineering in cooperation with governmental agencies and with other professional groups.

Yet the total effort today can be considered only a beginning in proportion to the need. I believe that more aggressive action is required now to undertake the comprehensive systems approach and action in the broad areas that I have cited. I believe, too, that the scientific and engineering community should take the initiative in summoning all of the disciplines and the social sciences to cooperate in determining how technology can be applied to maximum benefit with minimum risk of future harm.

There is urgent need of scientific and engineering as well as political statesmanship in this new environment. Through education, through planning, through use of the systems philosophy, and through new techniques of information processing, we can exercise such statesmanship to maintain control of our technology.

For those of us who choose to listen, the voice of history in this era seems to be saying, "T minus X and counting." It is our task to assure that X represents sufficient time to respond to the challenge.

SCIENCE, A WELLSPRING
OF OUR DISCONTENT

Walter Orr Roberts

Science has many images; and it has many spokesmen. A century and a half ago, Goethe said of science, "To one man it is the highest thing, a heavenly goddess; to another it is a productive and proficient cow, who supplies him with butter." On TV, a scientist may be a mad genius, or a man in a white lab coat, or an iron-willed and hard-driving researcher without time for, or interest in, his wife or children. On TV, science is space rockets, computers, and miracle coatings that make razor blades last longer, cut closer.

But I believe that, in searching for a spokesman for science, I could scarcely find a wiser man to quote before an AAAS audience than a past president, Warren Weaver, who wrote in 1960:

Science is not technology, it is not gadgetry, it is not some mysterious cult, it is not a great mechanical monster. Science is an adventure of the human spirit. It is essentially an artistic enterprise, stimulated largely by curiosity, served largely by disciplined imagination, and based largely on faith in the reasonableness, order, and beauty of the universe of which man is part.

In other words, science, like music or fine art, is a wellspring of the divine discontent that stirs man to seek more of life than merely to eat and to sleep; and that discontent is flamed higher by the partner of science, advancing technology, through which we can realistically contemplate the practical achievement of the highest of ideals for the condition of man.

SCIENCE, A WELLSPRING OF OUR DISCONTENT From *American Scientist* Magazine, Vol. 55, No. 1 (March 1967). Reprinted with permission. Based on the Sigma Xi–Phi Beta Kappa address at the meeting of the American Association for the Advancement of Science, Washington, D.C., December 29, 1966.

SIGNIFICANCE OF THE SPACE AGE

To me, the true significance of the space age, this accelerating age of science and technology in which we now live, is that it is beginning to lead us to wonder, once again, about the nature and purpose of man, about what constitutes the good life and the good society. It is bringing philosophy, once more, to the center of the scene, making it as important as ever it was in the Golden Age of Greece; and, it is doing so because the products of science and technology offer us the prospect, at last, of satisfying the material needs of all of the people of earth, if we but have the wit, and the will, to organize and to share our resources.

Moreover, in today's world, concern over the nature and purpose of man no longer need occupy the attention solely of a small elite with the leisure and the interest. Today it can become the domain of an ever-growing class of people who have the free time, the education, and the material resources that are the inevitable products of space-age control of nature by reasonable men.

Today science is a matter of concern to everybody. It is a large and growing part of our national effort. The flowering of science seems suddenly to have burst upon us. But, to be truthful, the progress of science has not been sudden, nor has it very often been made in big jumps. Rather it has come, by and large, in steady and persistent small steps. Events sometimes do dramatize for us, suddenly, the heights to which our steps have brought us. So, on the afternoon of October 4, 1957, Sputnik I made us realize that we were living in the age of man's conquest of space.

I shall never forget that Friday evening! It gives me chills to relive the frenzy of excitement that a man-made earth satellite, launched far away in Russia, would pass over Boulder. The phone became hopelessly jammed with radio and newspaper queries, and with calls from other scientists planning to organize cooperative observations. Janet had just started supper hamburgers, which I never ate. My little boy, Jonny, then six, had to go over to the Observatory with me at 7:00 P.M. because we didn't have time to get a baby-sitter, and Janet had a meeting. Next day Jonny told us with pride that he was the first one in his class to hear Sputnik, real, not just on the radio. Indeed, he was probably one of the first people in the country to hear its radio transmitter "real" or otherwise!

SPACE AGE ORIGINS IN HISTORY

Few events have so dramatically heralded an advance of science-technology; but, of course, the space age really didn't begin that evening, nor even have any sharp date of onset. Its origins go back to Robert Goddard in the twenties, and to Hermann Oberth, still earlier. In a kind of poetic way they go back, perhaps, all the way to Jules Verne or Jonathan Swift, or even to 1650, to Cyrano de Bergerac's wild concept of a flying machine powered by the lift of the morning dew. Certainly it can be traced to the young Russian, Nicholas Kibaltchitch, jailed nearly a century ago in Saint Petersburg for revolutionary activities, who wrote from his cell of a jet-propelled rocket designed for cosmic travel.

The force of science has always, in modern times, been a major factor shaping social and cultural patterns in the more highly developed countries. Back at the time of the pilgrims, Francis Bacon, for example, stated that "knowledge and power are synonymous." Slightly over 100 years later Benjamin Franklin urged his countrymen to note that:

the first drudgery for settling new colonies, which confines the attentions of people to mere necessaries, is now pretty well over; and there are many in every province in circumstances that set them at ease, and afford leisure to cultivate the finer arts and improve the common stock of knowledge.

And he went on to exhort them, through scientific activities, to increase their power over matter and to multiply the conveniences or pleasures of life.

Franklin's appreciation of the dream of science was shared by many of his revolutionary associates. The people of America developed cultural patterns that fostered vigorous science and invention, and promoted its prompt exploitation. The Pennsylvania Assembly, for example, long before the creation of the National Science Foundation, voted 450 pounds to a basic research program, namely, to observe the 1769 transit of Venus; and, after it was all over, William Smith, speaking on the floor of the Assembly, stated, "It hath done a credit to our Country which would have been cheaply purchased for 20 times the sum."

Appreciation of the importance and impact of science was at the heart of the philosophical thought of the intellectual leaders of Revolutionary times, who did indeed understand the spirit of the Enlightenment. Many of them had faith that they could demonstrate that freedom has a favorable influence on the growth of useful sciences and arts. And many understood and sought to realize David Hume's concept of the "science of man" and had confidence in their ability to govern themselves rationally and with justice.

Subsequent history has seen, here and elsewhere, the steady growth of the influence of science on social organization and thought. As Julian Huxley has been so eloquent to point out, the prime fact of today's world is the fantastically accelerating pace of scientific progress. We are indeed living in a revolution. Within the very lifetimes of some of us have come:

1. The evolution of manned flight.

2. The rise of the automobile from a curiosity that sometimes worked, to the sleek and highly reliable product of a multibillion dollar industry.

3. The development of fantastic new tools like automated lathes, computer-programmed manufacturing units controlled by servo systems, continuous-flow food processing equipment, transistor and integrated circuit electronic components, micro-miniaturized information storage that can print the Holy Bible on a 2 × 2 inch-slide and retrieve an image of any page in a fraction of a second.

4. The perfection of many aspects of environmental control such as air conditioning, pest management, outdoor nighttime illumination for sports, etc.

5. The establishment of huge and profitable industries, like television, where a mere 30 years ago there were only experiments and prototypes.

Perhaps even closer to the heart of what science is all about, history has unfolded, for us who live in this revolution, the superb beauty of discovery of the molecular patterns in a crystal, the organization in a single living cell, the functioning of the ruby that generates a laser beam. In our most powerful telescopes we have glimpsed the concept-shaking mysteries of the enigmatic red-shifted quasars. Are these objects the most fantastically brilliant and distant objects in man's ken, dwarfing whole galaxies by their light—which calls for revisions of our notions of the origins of the Universe? Or are they much nearer objects, unique in experience in being so red-shifted as to radiate their light in a manner and from a source of previously unsuspected character—which calls for substantial revisions of our ideas of stellar energy generation? Either way, we have before us one of nature's most majestic enigmas. Such is the pace of progress, moreover, that few astronomers doubt that a decade will see the sweeping consequences of its solution, just as few scientists today ridicule our serious search to listen, in the signals of deep space, for intelligible messages from vastly more advanced civilizations than our own.

Before us lie the known riddles, and the even more challenging mysteries still unknown. James B. Conant said it well: "As the beam of the spotlight on the dark stage broadens to show the characters and the settings, the circumference of the circle of darkness grows." It is indeed a time of wonder and of excitement!

SCIENCE HAS TWO FACES

There is another side to the growing power of control over nature afforded us by science and the associated technology. Nearly every advance of science has two faces. One smiles on us and lifts the aspirations of man; the other scowls sternly on all future hopes. For the miracle of the modern automobile there is the rising scourge of car-born air pollution that threatens to choke our Bosnywashes, our giant Boston-N.Y.-Washington megalopoli. The advance of urbanism, made possible by the miracle of air conditioning and food transportation, brings us befouled rivers, vanishing privacy, and lives of strain and tension. For the miracles that atomic energy has wrought in medicine, industry, power generation, there hangs over us the spectre of nuclear war.

For, as Glenn Seaborg has pointed out, "knowledge is born without moral properties. It is man who applies it according to his acquired patterns of behavior . . . . Man, not knowledge, is the cause of violence." And the power of science magnifies man's ability to achieve utopia or to destroy all that is civilized, or free, or beautiful. The examples are legion, and familiar to all of us.

Molecular biology, for example, offers exciting new prospects and, at the same time, serious moral problems. We can now begin to unfold something of the incredible workings of the purveyors of our genetic heritage; we also sense new hopes for cancer control, defective organ replacement, control of mongolism. But we can also see the shadowy portent of Aldous Huxley's *Brave New World* of man-made, docile, semimorons for labor in semimoronic tasks, or of the replication of Einsteins or Von Neumanns of the future, numberlessly and at will; but will it be for good or ill?

In my own field, the atmospheric sciences, we foresee bringing the entire globe under continuous weather observation by the mid-1970's—and at reasonable cost. We envision, from this, vastly improved forecasting of storms, freezes, droughts, smog episodes—with attendant opportunities to avert disaster. We can also see lurking in the beyond-knowledge of today an awesome potential weapon of war—the deliberate manipulation of weather for the benefit of the few and the powerful, to the detriment of the enemy, and perhaps the bystanders as well. If such powers of weather control emerge—and this is not at all certain to be so—imagine the conflicts of purpose and interest even within a single nation, when the rains and the clouds and the clear days are influenced deliberately. Future work may even show us that, unwittingly, we have already begun affecting weather— with our jet-airplane-induced cirrus blankets and our persistent continental hazes of man's making. How many ways we must be wise!

Perhaps the most exciting still-dream-stage prospect involves the burgeoning of computer science. Our nation's largest and probably most rapidly growing industry is education. To my mind the greatest prospect for personalizing the educational process to meet the individual needs of every student lies in developments looming in the computer field, in related information storage, retrieval, and processing developments for education. I suspect, however, that nowhere in our whole science-based advance is there greater public fear and distrust than over the threat of the loss of human freedom to mechanization and regimentation through "do not spindle, fold or mutilate." Like it or not, there will be giant strides in command and decision-making—automated and semiautomated—in war, economics, and other walks of life. We will likely know when the first intercontinental missile of World War III comes, should that happen, in a routine computerized check, on millisecond time scale, of the inventory of space debris; and the decision to retaliate, to enter total war, will probably be made on computer-based advice.

My list of examples could be enlarged to the field of work of every scientist.

TRAITS OF SCIENCE

Principally, however, I want to discuss something else having to do with the impact of science. I want to make a few observations about the way science is done, at least as I see it. I want to do so because it seems to me to be relevant to any discussion of the cultural impact of science or of the public understanding of science.

Let me list, one after another, some of the salient traits of science and of the people who practice science. I'm sure that one could add to my list, or criticize the balance of emphasis of my listing. But I think it a worthwhile enterprise to talk for a few minutes about this.

1. First, science is constantly, systematically, and inexorably revisionary. Science, by the rules of the game, is a self-correcting process and one that is self-destroying of its own errors. Moreover, the rules of the game are essentially the same in every nation. It is the essence of the scientific way that none of the laws of science is sacred, but stands or falls by the degree to which it works, and the effectiveness with which it simplifies the apparent complexity of what we see in the natural world about us. The instances of this are legion. One can trace, for example, the evolution of the notion of gravitation and of falling bodies through the work of Aristotle, who believed that heavier bodies have stronger force and fall faster—to the more general and illuminating discoveries of Galileo, formulated in his early notions of acceleration, that causes light and heavy bodies to fall at the same rate, if irrelevant effects of air are discounted—down to the views of Newton, who quantified and developed general laws of motion and of forces acting at a distance—down to Einstein with the magnificently general relativistic laws of falling bodies.

Here is the working of a self-revising science, which progressed over many, many years, steadily improving our ability to describe and to predict, with a minimum of ad hoc assumptions, what happens when bodies fall in space or in the atmosphere near the earth. Moreover, it is characteristic of science that it pushes constantly into new and unfamiliar realms of experience, and that when it does so our older laws often prove inadequate and their predictions fail, requiring revisions. One of the prime joys of a scientist's life is to discover these inadequacies, and to develop the improvements that lead to more general laws.

It is because of this eternally revisionary nature that science is disruptive of the status quo. And the accelerating pace of science hasn't made this any easier for society to absorb. Every year, the time from the development of a new basic principle to its working application grows shorter.

2. A related trait of science is its destruction of idols, destruction of the gods that men live by. Science, being self-revising, has no absolute right or absolute justice. It is not concerned with ultimate truths, but with useful, or simple, or aesthetically beautiful interrelationships among things apparently unconnected.

One example that comes to my mind is the notion in pre-Galilean times of the divinity and the perfection of the sun. This notion, much to the distress of the Church and of Galileo, could not be held on an absolute basis, and when the dogma of perfection of the sun was apparently contradicted by observations of sunspots and in the obvious interpretation of those observations, something had to give. Galileo and the Church both suffered. But the new concept was far more useful, and ultimately simpler.

To live comfortably with science, it is necessary to live with a dynamically changing system of concepts. It is necessary to live with enough conservatism to resist the easy abandonment of concepts, but enough flexibility to be able, when necessary, to switch rather than fight.

In this same way science forces us—through geology, astronomy, meteorology, and physics—to resign ourselves to making poetic or allegorical interpretations of the literal statements of our most respected cultural authorities—as, for example, the statements about the origin of the earth that are found in the Bible. There are so many examples of this—the genesis, the day the sun stood still, the parting of the Red Sea, and many others.

Similarly, science has a way of weakening old and respected bonds, like the bonds of family in Japanese and Chinese culture, teacher-student relationships when machines begin to teach, or the relationship of the boss and the employee in automated plants. Science tends to destroy witchcraft in Salem and white supremacy in Mississippi.

3. Not only are the tenets of science constantly subject to challenge and to revision, but its prophets are under challenge too. For example, we have, many of us, observed and enjoyed the stimulating intellectual exchanges between George Gamow with his "big bang theory" and Fred Hoyle with his continuous creation theory of the origin of the universe. To a non-scientist this disagreement, however, can be a source of great distress. How can these two experts disagree on matters of exact science?

And we have seen how the law of conservation of mass had to be modified and become the law of conservation of mass-energy when the relativistic physics of Einstein emerged. But such revision of scientific "laws" often confuses the layman, who has been taught to think that scientific laws are of nature and not the whim of man. He can't understand why scientists should disagree; and, I suspect that one of our big jobs is to make understandable to the general public the reasons why and the limits within which the prophets of science can disagree, argue, and take sides—and what is meant when a "law" is refined or abandoned.

4. Moreover, the findings of science have an embarrassing way of turning out to be relevant to the customs and to the civil laws of men—and of requiring these customs and laws also to be revised. For example, the growing knowledge of psychology has forced changes in the laws governing insanity, and the rules regarding confinement of patients in mental hospitals. The development of tranquilizers and other drug therapy has even affected the customs of business management and the pulling power of the image of the uncompromisingly tough business executive. Likewise, our rules of punishment and control for alcoholism, or the use of marijuana, tobacco, or LSD sometimes require changes as a result of new scientific findings about the use of these substances. The advance of medical science can also bring us real embarrassment in these fields, because penal codes are often geared to a system far slower to adapt to change than fits the pace of science.

We are called upon to change even our notions about what is proper or best in the education and the discipline of our children, as we face new findings regarding the nature of intellectual growth, or the tender age of most productive personality development.

5. Certainly we have seen spectacular changes in the concept of private property and of national borders as we have moved into the space age. For example, at what height above a country is it perfectly all right to fly a satellite without consulting the country it flies over? At what height does it become an invasion to fly an airplane or a balloon? Camera-equipped military or civil satellites do not violate the territory of nations, but U-2 airplanes are quite another matter.

Who needs to be consulted, for example, before a single nation tests globe-circling "needles" put into the atmosphere to reflect radio signals? Very strong feelings arose about this matter, just a few years ago, in the International Astronomical Union.

How do we deal with the conflicts between the State of California and the State of Colorado over the water of the Colorado River? Colorado designed its contracts with California in the absence of secure knowledge about the science of hydrology and of river run-off. What are its obligations to live up to its prior contracts, if future science shows that they were based on very bad scientific reasoning and evidence?

Or cloud seeding—whose water has been wrung out of a cloud on the western slope of Colorado's continental divide? Who assures the rancher of the Great Plains that he has not thereby faced a drier summer? Whose air is it that the mainland Chinese contaminate when they test A-bombs? Whose radio quiet is shattered by the generation of artificial Van Allen radiation belts? Whose right is it to fluoridate the water of a major city, or to generate radio-iodine in the atmosphere?

6. Moreover, the pace of technological advance gravely threatens the bountiful and restorative power of nature to resist modification. It takes just so many years for a tin can to rust away or for a sand-born glass beer bottle to go again to sand. Polluted air from gigantic super-cities can spread beyond the borders of whole states and cannot be rapidly enough cleansed by the rains and the winds and the curative breathing of plants. Fouled rivers, harbors, beaches contaminate our food supplies, spread disease, violate the beauty of the out-of-doors which the space age gives us ever more leisure to enjoy, could we but find it.

For these reasons many non-scientists would like moratoria placed on science for awhile—but this is almost certainly impossible. What are the alternatives?

7. Another trait of science that leads to much hostility or misunderstanding by the non-scientist is the fact that science is practiced by a small elite. Worse yet, the scientists who make up this elite are hard for others to understand. They are obscure, if not threatening. These scientists have a special language, verbal and mathematical, all their own. They use common words in unfamiliar ways, and in strangely strait-jacketed senses. When they speak about truth they are not speaking about absolute truth. And their language of mathematics is mixed up in ordinary sentences so that it often becomes difficult, abbreviated, and abstract for others to understand.

Moreover, this small scientific elite has cultural patterns discernibly different from those of the rest of society. For example, a good many scientists do their science for fun—while to much of the rest of the world, it seems like expensive or almost capricious fun. It looks like fun with other people's money and lives.

Moreover, within this scientific elite, uncertainty is a daily actuality, and sometimes they don't seem to others to be sufficiently worried by this uncertainty. To the outsider, they often look irresponsible. Their strange and inconstantly held concepts are to them matters of interest, like the plays of a chess game. Knocking down sacred principles is a matter of challenge and of satisfaction. They often deny familiar concepts for the sake of argument, without even believing the denial. Moreover, their reasons for rejecting concepts are often hard to explain to non-scientists. They seem frivolous, or authoritarian—as witness the great uproar about the almost universal scientific repudiation, a few years ago, of the popularly-appealing concepts of Emmanuel Velikovsky and his "Worlds in Collision."

This whole business tends to breed among laymen suspicion and distrust of scientists. It sometimes leads to fears that the scientists are "mad," irresponsible, "Red," or "far-out."

All of this would be a problem even if it were not also painfully true that scientists, in addition to being members of an intellectual elite, are also people. They have, alas, all of the foibles, jealousies, ambitions, and weaknesses of other people.

It is particularly unfortunate that an air of distrust of science and its practitioners occurs just at this juncture in time, when the universality of the language of science—the ability to communicate with each other possessed by scientists of all countries—offers the hope of bridging the deep political abysses between the East and the West.

It is still worse because if ever in history we needed optimism, we today need the optimism of science. We need it to give us the courage to tackle creatively and forcefully the awesome problems pushed on us by the pace of science-based progress. Think, for example, of the world population explosion that will bring the population of the United States by the year 2000 to 400 million, and that half of the Earth's people will be of Oriental race in the not so distant future when world population reaches 10 billion.

The problem is still further compounded by the fact that progress and optimism are desperately needed in the social sciences. But the social sciences are under even deeper suspicion than the physical sciences, even though they are identical with these in formal construction. Maybe the problem here is that they deal with our pocketbooks. Certainly, they are like other aspects of science, revisionary and revolutionary;—and, this means that in economic, social, and behavioral science fields there are big revolutions and revisions ahead. Moreover, in these fields of science we are much closer to our Dark Ages and the changes may be sweeping. In the sciences that deal with men's interactions, we still have unburned witches to deal with. There are many wrong turns ahead, in these sciences— but it is an essential of science to blunder down some of these wrong turns, to develop and to test wrong hypotheses. That is the way we get ahead. The social sciences must not be thrown down the drain because of some of the essential blundering that will make real progress possible.

We have somehow to surmount the quaint, almost anachronistic misconception—not only in the general public but often within the ranks of the physical scientists that the social sciences differ essentially from the physical because here we are dealing with *man*.

8. The trait that, to me, seems the most socially important, about science, however, is that it is a major source of man's dissatisfaction with the world as it is. It is a wellspring of man's discontent with the status quo. The implicit promises of science and technology are the heart of the present rebellion of the underfed and the underclothed. They give clear, achievable prospect of food and comfort for all, if only all the people of earth become sufficiently determined to use science and technology to this end. Moreover, our Telstars, and our radios, our color movies, and our magazines give the poor nations a way to know how poor they really are.

Surely 50 years will see a harvest of the major fruits of science and engineering in the underdeveloped regions of the earth, whether we in America like it or not. If we stand in the way of this irresistible impact of science on the developing cultural patterns, we will be destroyed. If we ignore the approaching tides of progress, we may find ourselves a small island isolated in a vast hostile sea.

IT IS HERE

But above all else, the thing for us to realize about the scientific revolution is simply that *it is here*. We are now deep into the age of science. It cannot be ignored. Jet airplanes circle the globe in hours. Images of wealth or poverty, or of particular political ideology flash into millions of homes everywhere, instantly. Weapons systems can eradicate hundreds of millions of lives in minutes, and we have not been the only nation diligently applying technological skills to the problem of how to design and manage such weapons systems.

My voice can be embossed for my great-grandchildren, yet unborn, on thin mylar and ferrous oxide tape. I can listen, as I did a few nights ago, to Sviatoslav Richter's magnificent playing of Moussorgsky's *Pictures at an Exhibition* recorded on February 25, 1958, at Sofia, Bulgaria. In the background of this music I can hear the coughs of men I shall never know, whose language I cannot speak, but who are my brothers listening with me in my living room.

I can strip a tiny fleck of skin from my body, and have it preserved, intact, alive and growing indefinitely in a laboratory test tube, so that a curious inquisitor can examine microscopically the genetic code that makes me most of what I am, even long after I am through being it.

I can place my eye to the viewing screen of a giant telescope and peer into the silent depths of the Virgo Cluster of island universes, noting the soft glow of the 1000 billion suns that there generate the strange life processes of a hundred million planets, where thinking creatures think out their days, forever beyond communication with us.

It is here, this age of science, and with it some of the most compelling ideas of mankind: The magnificent structure of the relativity theory of Einstein, a notion that has stirred the very foundations of our thought, a creation of beauty that ranks with the greatest of Beethoven. Or the incredible principle of indeterminacy of Heisenberg, with its idea of the unavoidable uncertainty of definite knowledge about particular events in nature. This is a challenging notion that sets limits on the knowable.

Or the thrilling concept of the continuous creation of the universe, with its picture of stars and men coming and going through an infinite span of time—yet living always in a place in space that appears to its inhabitants but a few billion years old.

It is here, this age of science, and with it comes its promise of what the life of man can be, with food for all, with education, with human freedom, with a stable population. With this age of technology comes the realistic expectation that even the added billions can live in harmonious equilibrium with a natural environment of quality, and one that man can appreciate the more because he knows what a rare thing it is in the universe. For man, life need not be nasty, brutish, short—but a life rich with peace of mind and rewarding leisure tasks, with comfort and health, and with a language that transcends political ideology.

But to bring to substance this great dream for humanity we must know that this is what we really want and be willing to work to achieve it. To a tragic degree we in the West have drifted, not so much for lack of willingness to pay the price, but for lack of knowing what it is that we have really wanted—aside from factories, and a rise in the standard of living.

In our explosively changing world it is no longer sufficient to live with philosophies or religions simply handed down from an older generation. We must take up a vital, flexible, and ever-evolving concern about the nature and purpose of man, and about what constitutes a good life and a good society in the light of today's communications, population growth, races, political systems, weapons. We must exhibit a concern with philosophy that is geared to the chain-reacting growth of science, and that is consonant with the impact of science on man's changing conception of himself and his world.

Rather than simply fight for the preservation of the old things that are good, we must plan creatively also to shape the new. We must commit ourselves to dare to build the world we want, knowing that it is possible if we but demand it—and if we use intelligently all the potent forces of science, the arts and the humanities that are at our disposal.

There will always be dangers. But I hold with Thornton Wilder, who said, "Every good and excellent thing stands moment by moment at the razor edge of danger, and must be fought for." To be what we can be, we must be unafraid to place ourselves, our ways of life, our economic systems, in the microscope of science; and, we must have the courage to put into practice the findings that come out, no matter how hard they hit at the patterns of our folkways. To be what we can be, we must first and foremost know what we want to be.

From TOWARD THE YEAR 2000:
Work in Progress

Harvey Brooks

An assumption of the Commission is that we are moving into a postindustrial society in which the codification and institutionalization of knowledge, particularly in science and technology, become increasingly important bases of innovation.

The first task of this group will be to identify the social trends implicit in this development and to explore its implications for various social sectors, such as the industrial, governmental, professional, intellectual, and cultural.

Second, the group will devote explicit attention not only to the opportunities inherent in new technology, but also to the ways in which technology generates new problems for society. Until the present, technical innovations have generally been accepted as inherently good and progressive by definition, and the scientific community has tended to think of itself as the major agent of desirable change and social progress. Currently, however, scientists and others who think about science and technology are becoming increasingly aware that decisions about science and technology must be made in the light of their possible second-order consequences—even when these cannot be anticipated—since the disadvantageous consequences of introducing a new technology can at times outweigh the primary expected benefits.

The scientific community may thus become a much more conservative force in society than it has been, or it may adopt an ambivalent attitude toward change, as its institutions, methods, and assumptions become matters of public concern and are altered and controlled to suit the changing social role of science and technology. The third task of the working party will be to investigate this reciprocal effect of society on science and to gauge its implications for the forms of organization and operational procedures internal to the institutions of science.

In the context of these explorations, the group will seek to understand and assess the problems that are raised as society tries to anticipate the effects and direction of technological change.

FROM TOWARD THE YEAR 2000: WORK IN PROGRESS Reprinted by permission from *Daedalus,* Journal of the American Academy of Arts and Sciences, Boston, Massachusetts, Volume 96, Number 3 (Fall 1967).

OVERLEAF: Hewitt–Micolupo →

Film

EDITED BY STANLEY KAUFFMANN

INTRODUCTION

In terms of interest and effect, film is the preeminent art of this century. Not everyone is overjoyed by that fact, but few would dispute it. Other twentieth-century inventions have also changed our lives profoundly: technologies that altered transportation and communication and, above all, the computer, whose fantastic territories we are just beginning to enter; but in art, the prime mover has been film. There is only one other invention of the century that has had a remotely comparable esthetic effect: not television (which in these terms is only another form of film) but radio, which has real and unique links with the poetic faculty. But film, born of this century and the humanist flower of its technology, is strongest in immediacy and appeal, in stimulation of social myth and of private fantasy. Jean Cocteau, poet and novelist, said of his work in films: "I am not a writer to order. I write when I cannot not write. . . . But to move this great machine of dreams, to do battle with the angel of light, with the angel of machines, with the angels of space and time, this is work to my measure!"

It is the only art where we all meet. Passions for painting or dance or theater or architecture or fiction vary sharply from one person to another, and many devotees of one art have little response to others; but film is the one art which, to some degree, we all need.

And yet, in this world of busy coexistence with the powers of film, there is a paradox, a great overarching paradox. This is the art where esthetics is least coherent. The esthetics of all the arts is in flux, but the situation is at its least clarified in film. The study of film at the collegiate level is increasing rapidly, high-school students are making films, grammar-school children are also involved, and yet this is the field where organized esthetic thought is scarcest. Part of this is the defect of film's virtue—its youth. (We have all met people who were born before this world-dominating medium was even invented.) There simply has not been time, compared with other arts, to evolve comparable critical theory. Part of the reason also is the fact that film arrived in an era of drastic social, religious, and political turbulence, to all of which esthetics is closely knit. But the quest for critical values in film continues, and it is not an academic imposition; it is generated out of audiences and has existed since film began. In 1916, comparing film and theater, Ezra Pound wrote:

Whether the violet-tinted aesthete like it or not, [film] is developing an art sense. The minute the spectator begins to wonder why Charles Chaplin amuses him, the minute he comes to the conclusion that Chaplin is better than X———, Y——— and Z———, because he, Chaplin, gets the maximum effect with the minimum effort, minimum expenditure, etc., etc., the said spectator is infinitely near a conception of art and infinitely more fit to watch creditable drama than when he, or she, is entranced by Mrs. So-and-So's gown or by the color of Mr. So-and-So's eyes.

And the matter has long been of special concern to the young audience. In 1922, when the American poet Vachel Lindsay published the second edition of his *Art of the Moving Picture,* our first important book on the subject, he noted that, since the first edition had appeared—seven years before—"the world of the college and the university," where he had been active, "while at a loss for policy, were not only willing but eager to take the films with seriousness."

That seriousness and that appetite for policy (in esthetics) are today stronger than ever. "What standards shall I use to judge films?" The question is very familiar to anyone who has ever spoken or written about films, and it cannot be dismissed simply because it is sometimes like asking Consumers Union's advice on buying an automobile. Generally, the impulse behind that question is, at its base, a moral one, as is the case with so many questions that concern young people today.

My principle of choice for the selections that follow has been one of response to that persistent question. *These selections do not constitute an answer.* There is no "answer." But I have chosen material by critics who address the question with commitment; and I have supplemented it with technical insights to help make the question more intelligent, and I have included something of credo and intent from important film artists. Deliberately omitted is extensive "proof" that film is important in our society, which seems to me about as necessary as proof that the airplane has arrived. This little anthology is intended as a conspectus, not a canon, from which the reader can draw stimulation on the subject of film esthetics and on which he can base value judgments of film.

First, a brief prelude, to set forth some general propositions (a few of which are expanded in the following selections). To begin with, film is an art with a popular base. It is made for groups of people, for audiences, not for individuals. It is possible to enjoy a film when seeing it alone (I have done it many times), but that is not the nature of the art, as it is the nature of the novel to be enjoyed alone. If an art has a popular base, it means that most of the work in that art is intended to appeal to a lot of people. This is also true of the theater, but in a real sense it is even more true of the film, because *all* of film coexists simultaneously, both the popular elements and the highest reaches, in a unique way. When Samuel Beckett writes a play, he assumes that his audience has very little interest in routine Broadway comedies or sentimental dramas. But when Ingmar Bergman makes a film, he knows very well that his audience may have seen a historical spectacular the night before and may see a sci-fi thriller the night after, and he relies on that knowledge in ways that are specific to film.

It is not simply that Bergman employs the same cinema vocabulary and technology. After all, Beckett uses the same dictionary as any hack. Outside the identical basic means of all films, Bergman relies on certain powers of film—in amplification of reality, in articulation of time, in penetration of the subconscious—that are present in the least ambitious film as well; and, in a certain healthy sense, the least ambitious film has helped to prepare the filmgoer for Bergman. In his essay André Bazin says that by "image" he means "anything that can be added to a depicted object by its being depicted on the screen." That power of making images, in Bazin's sense, is absolutely central to film, and it creates a consanguinity between Bergman and a routine director that does not exist comparably between the pinnacle and the valley in other arts. The best film blossoms out of all film.

But this unique consanguinity has led to some vulgarization of film judgment—a vulgarization which, in certain quarters, has been inflated into complicated theories. Some have concluded that, because there is this consanguinity between the best film artist and the film entertainer, there is no substantive difference between them; that, say, a fine Western like *Stagecoach* is the artistic equivalent of *Citizen Kane* because, in the exercise of film technique and film mystique, both are proficient. But this attempt to equate *Stagecoach* and *Citizen Kane* neglects two factors: intent in the use of technique, and the quality of the materials, the *content*. To this critical approach, a clever—even beautiful—piece of editing in a private-eye chase is not less, substantively, than the editing in the beautiful love scene between the hero and the barmaid in Truffaut's *Shoot the Piano Player*. This is to reduce technique to an absolute, devoid of commitment, and to confuse style, a term inseparably weighted with moral resonance, with sheer technique. It is a commonplace that style transforms material: *Macbeth* in lesser hands would be a melodrama. But style cannot easily make the trivial into the serious. What is more relevant, style applied to good material produces better results than style applied to inferior material. There is an old adage in sports: A good big man is better than a good little man. Style applied to serious content is better than style applied to trivia.

What is worse, the critical attitude toward film that says that film style is virtually all—and it is a relatively widespread attitude—seems to me reductive of film's potential. It thinks to aggrandize film by saying that good cinematic execution is the highest criterion, but this approach seems to me to do the opposite: to relegate the film to second-class status by saying that if a film is well made we must make no further demands on it. In the theater no serious person has ever said that because *Guys and Dolls* is excellent of its kind, its kind is all we need expect of the theater. The theater has popular forms in which excellence is possible and desirable, but no one equates those popular forms with *Oedipus Rex.* Yet that equation is often made with regard to film.

In short, the film seems to me an art with as great a capability and at least as great a responsibility as any art. If there is yet no film equivalent of *Hamlet* or *Paradise Lost,* that is possibly the result of the era in which the film has been extant rather than an intrinsic limitation of the medium. (Twentieth-century drama and poetry have not given us another *Hamlet* or *Paradise Lost,* for that matter.) The film's limitations are, in intrinsic terms, only the limitations of spirit and faith in human survival that attend all the arts. Film's popular base and its unique internal consanguinity are not shackles but assets, which give it a foundation of universality on which to build. Nothing that is still possible to man is impossible of expression in film; and because of its consonance with psychological complexity, its apotheosis of technology, its enhancement of sensory perception, it may prove to be the one art best suited to be companion and solace, even sire, of *all* psychical and imaginative enterprise.

There are other factors that affect the judgment of film. It is a collaborative art. We take the director to be the central and controlling artist nowadays, but that is often more wish than fact. Dozens of people, beginning with the producer, have a substantive effect on the resultant film, sometimes with the director's knowledge, sometimes not. (Very few American directors have final control over their work.) Sometimes the contributions of others are harmful, sometimes not. I once remarked to a film professional that Director X's new film was disappointing compared with his previous one, and the film man replied, "But on the last one his cameraman was James Wong Howe." Some ability to judge the different artistic and technical contributions is essential—and some of the selections following should be helpful in that regard.

The conditions of filmmaking, the *business* conditions around the world, have an effect, ultimately, on esthetics. We talk about a painter passing from one period to another, following one bent or another, and then make easy analogies with a filmmaker as if choices were as available to one as the other. They are not. Everyone who works in films spends part—sometimes a large part—of his life just looking for the chance to work and must often settle for less than optimum conditions. (See Orson Welles's letter.) In the judgment of films, not the slightest concession should be made because of these facts, else we would quickly end up with lopsided patronizing standards or sheer economic-sociological history; but neither should analogies with other, "individual" arts be facile.

An imminent technological development that may well affect the film esthetically is the electronic cassette that will make possible the viewing of films through one's television set. One will simply slip a cassette into an aperture and watch a film as neatly as one now plays a tape recording. The film industry will probably be affected by this development in the way it produces and in the quantity and quality of what it produces. Surely the social patterns that have grown up in American life around the film theater and moviegoing will be affected. But, I would guess, there will be intrinsic esthetic effects as well. When we watch a television show now, or a film on television, there is an unconscious comparison in our minds with the movie screen; we know that we are watching the film in one of two possible ways. If the television screen becomes the most prevalent size, possibly the only one except for special events, that unconscious comparison (as a constant) will disappear—and motion, gestures, spatial and temporal relationships, even a certain quality of awe, will be altered.

All the factors mentioned above, and others to be mentioned below, indicate that the options for film esthetics remain open—perhaps more widely, even more lastingly, than for any other art. Yet, as the options persist, the appetite for guidance grows stronger. "What standards shall I use to judge films?" There is in the film world no Aristotle, no Dryden, no Hegel, and it is possible, given the general state of all the arts, that the film is blessed by having less of a canon to wrestle with and to depart from. But the search for values is very strong and very persistent. St. Augustine is supposed to have said, "I know what God is if you don't ask me." Well, I—and many others—know what a good film is if I don't absolutely have to define an ideal Good Film in anything like canonical terms.

This is true of the writers whose work I have selected for this anthology. The critics among them are not dogmatic, they are analytic out of experience and insight. I do not agree with all their judgments, but I shall not harass them by specifying our differences, for I obviously respect their views in general. I have by no means represented all the directors I admire, but those I have chosen speak of their lives and works in ways that illuminate other lives and works.

David Thomson provides a contextual overture. W. R. Robinson presents a large critical-philosophical overview. Vernon Young and André Bazin deal with the film lexicon and its modern development. George Orwell speculates on the film's semantic possibilities. This is followed by discussion of the development of two major film techniques: lighting (Josef von Sternberg) and editing (Jean-Luc Godard). Ingmar Bergman states his personal views in an essay; those of Federico Fellini, Michelangelo Antonioni, and Akira Kurosawa come through interviews. Orson Welles's letter throws grim light on the realities of film directing. (When we praise a film artist, we are always to some extent praising his triumph over the conditions of filmmaking.) Penelope Houston looks rigorously but hopefully ahead, and at the last, John Hollander reminds us why we all got into moviegoing in the first place: because we like it.

Sureties are rare in our century, and no sureties follow here. But these selections show—to me and I hope to the reader—that it is still wonderfully possible to profit by the intellectual and artistic experience of others.

BACKGROUND TO A VISUAL SOCIETY

David Thomson

The association of "movie" and "man" in the title of this book is intended to evoke a variety of meanings. There are four ways one could interpret "movie man": a man who makes films—the director, perhaps; a man who appears in a film—the actor; a man who is presented in a film—a character; and a man who may watch a film or only live in a society that employs film. These roles are generally thought of as being distinct but I believe the phrase is capable of sustaining the merger of all the roles into one concept that we might compare with Stone Age man or Renaissance man. Movie man is the unit in a society that has so assimilated the methods and effects of moving film that they are determining his understanding of the present and his discovery of the future.

Movie is an invention of the twentieth century, though like the potential of the atom its possibility had always existed. It is not sufficient to accept its discovery as chance; why was movie brought to fruition in the years after 1890? I want to show to what extent it was a necessity for industrial man, the logical consequence of the development of society and communication. It cannot be isolated from the processes of urbanization and mechanization which had been set in motion over a hundred years before Lumière and Méliès, and which had themselves been the consequence of the previous stages of society. This evolution is concerned not only with methods of production and increases in population but with the sort of terms in which man thinks of himself. It is only in comparatively recent times, for instance, that terms like "means of production," "demography," "urbanization" and "equality" have become exchangeable between men.

THE NEW CITY

There was no day, or year even, in which Birmingham, Manchester or Chicago arose, but from our hindsight we can see and feel the change from parochial assortments of buildings to vigorous centers of industry and organization. There was no watershed, although now the time-charts seem littered with them. The inventions, like Crompton's mule or Bessemer's steel process, were observed as quietly by their contemporaries as real innovations are today.

Within a hundred years there were so many more people; the graph of population turns almost a right angle between 1770 and 1870. We are more able to note the increase in production and population than to distinguish exactly which caused which. But the new urban consciousness was not entirely economic. Both John Stuart Mill and Karl Marx refused to separate economic from moral welfare. They recognized that the new city gave to its inhabitants a new conception of themselves. Once a society functioned through its economy, rather than through its basic inequality of class, the common index had attained an equality man had never experienced in the pastoral existence of previous ages.

No slogan embodies Marx's unity of morality and economics more than the American colonists': "No taxation without representation." The fact that the idealism of neither the American nor the Russian revolutions has been fulfilled *in toto* by the present power blocs does not invalidate the original excitement of individual validity or the bitterness of the grievance that stimulated the revolutions. In both cases the socio-economic consciousness of a people was directed against the aristocratic rulers. Just as the population level had risen slowly, without dramatic alterations, in the years before 1700, so aristocratic oligarchy, whether secular or religious, had continued to shape peoples' conceptions of themselves; the only change had been in the primitiveness of the subject awe and fear. The same pattern of subjugate population and the concentration of power, riches and refinement in an *élite* existed throughout Europe. "The divine right of kings" demonstrated the comprehensive sway of the *élite;* the last English king to make that claim credible, Charles I, was, significantly, forced to flee his own capital. By 1640 the balance of power in London had shifted from the Tower and the royal palaces to the City and the Houses of Parliament.

In concentrating population, the city generated the phenomenon of "society." The technological and mechanical advance has intensified a basic psychological predicament, for the development of building has deprived man of Crusoe's experience in providing his own shelter. The juxtaposition of people highlighted contrasts of behavior and heightened the conflict between reactions in the human subconscious towards buildings: both shelter and prison, security and threat.

As shelter has expanded beyond the home and the town to the metropolis, escape has been made more difficult. We are increasingly deprived of natural landscape and more and more subject to urban claustrophobia. Long before cottage industry converged to form urban industrialization, the city, its keep and its high thick walls were resorted to for defense against enemies. In time of war, the city offers company, distraction, organization and community. It also offers to the enemy the most inviting target for his most powerful weapons.

A similar ambiguity runs through our whole experience of the city now, for at the same time as its organization assists the efficiency of our lives it threatens to dehumanize them. Fritz Lang's and Joseph Losey's films, particularly their versions of *M*, show how the same methods of authority and networks of power exist above and below normal society—the one representing law and the other the underworld; the psychopathy of Losey's murderer in *M* is thus an anguished version of the surrounded individual. Man's encounter with mechanisms cannot stop short with the benefits of the water-closet, electricity and the motor car; he has to face their more destructive effects. The ideal city of prosperity, welfare and the exercise of human talents—such as stimulates the pioneers in some of Anthony Mann's films— may become the Poisonville in Dashiell Hammett's *Red Harvest* or even Jean-Luc Godard's Alphaville.

ARCHITECTURE

The gap between the ethos of aristocracy and the response of a slave populace is expressed in the scale and soaring points of Gothic architecture. It is significant that, with very few exceptions, the Gothic buildings that remain are castles or cathedrals. Their amplitude was believed to be filled by the authority of the nobles and the Church, and in a comparatively underpopulated country the difference in riches and power that the size manifested could be accepted. The peasant dwellings were so primitive that most of them have long since collapsed.

Ironically, at a time when such social differences were becoming intolerable, a bastard Gothic style was still being employed in architecture. The 1832 Reform Act and the destruction of the old buildings by fire demanded a new parliamentary chamber that would implement the new desire for political expression. The competition for designs stipulated the Gothic or Elizabethan styles and the accepted building, as planned by Barry and Pugin, was a part of the Gothic revival. It was more functional than Strawberry Hill or Beckford's Fonthill, which were still aristocratic self-indulgence, but it did not seem to approve of the reformed political structure and even the original efficiency of its lay-out had degenerated within a hundred years into a legislative chamber that imposed absurd privations on its elected members.

The English Gothic revival was one element in the eclecticism of Victorian architecture. For although the cities and their purposes were palpably novel there was no successful new architectural form to assist them. In England the innovation of the Crystal Palace was ridiculed and potentially exciting railway stations were covered with the unnecessary decoration that makes them today so dismally filthy and archaic. It was not until the end of the nineteenth century, in Germany and America, that an urban architecture was realized by Behrens, Gropius, Sullivan and Wright that was stripped to fit need.

Frank Lloyd Wright's position is ambiguous, for while many of his buildings were revolutionary, and many of his statements enlightened, his whole career fits a nineteenth rather than a twentieth century pattern. Wright was a Middle West romantic who loved the horizontal form because, rather like Wordsworth, he believed it helped the building to share the strength and naturalness of the earth. Yet he was the victim of a twentieth century temptation; believing himself right when so many criticized him, he felt justified in dramatizing his own inventiveness and its effect of shock upon the "mobocracy": thus he demanded, "Genius must dominate." King Vidor's film *The Fountainhead,* which is loosely based on Wright's life, takes up this issue.

The very size of the most revolutionary new buildings and the need for drastic innovation in the face of so many years' waste made it necessary for the patrons of the architect to be men of great power. In *The Fountainhead* the physical detail of a man quarrying rock is an image of primitive strength that Vidor's romanticism associates with the more sophisticated power of a commercial tycoon. The houses Wright built were for rich men and, because of the increased density of society, their magnificence seems more out of proportion than that of the Elizabethan or Augustan houses built for political or mercantilist leaders.

Such houses, built by the Victorians, had resorted to precedent styles because, as social buildings, they were not new. The new sort of domestic unit was the urban worker's house. In row after row in the new cities it comprised not only the slum but a fact of political implication. It is from the slums created by speculative building that we derive the credo that "form is the function of purpose." The conclusion to be drawn from degrading housing was that it indicated an opinion that the lower classes had only a depressed purpose; this provoked them to political consciousness. Through form people became more aware that they might have a purpose.

Out of this consciousness a sense of modernity was born. In the 1830s Barry could not have conceived of a "modern" architecture because his society lacked a contemporary sense of itself. Instead its yardsticks were the monuments of past styles: the image of the Parthenon recurs in innumerable Victorian public buildings. Barry's Houses of Parliament was envisaged as being permanent because of a universally felt security. Its present redundancy, on the other hand, would make it impossible for any successful new legislative assembly to be built without the recognition that it served only for a limited time. It is, of course, contrary to conventional "artistic" conceptions of the architect that his work should be only temporary: Lloyd Wright's Taliesin West Buildings were based on a stone superstructure of such durability that its monumentality as a ruin in years to come might be its finest, if Ozymandian, effect.

Against this idea there is now posed the practicality of kinetic architecture: buildings of steel, glass and plastic that can alter their shapes to suit the various functions of the inhabitants. Such an architectural form corresponds with the conditions of a film soundstage, the hangar-like building in which a large part of a film is shot. The controlling factor on a soundstage is the need of "now." All lights, all technical abilities, all recording equipment, the energy and creativity of actors, director and crew are concentrated in a small corner of the building and a small area of emotion and action within the larger context of a film's script. The localization of this intensity will be transferred as soon as one shot has been completed. Then another set, previously struts, paint and cardboard, will be made to take on cinematic life, and the used one broken down and parts of it employed in making another set. National architecture may yet have to acquire a similar ability to focus its materials and skills, and landscape may even become as fluctuating as skyscape.

LITERATURE

We may see two sorts of sequence in writing: the first is that of the narrative or the author's uncovering process, and the novels of Dickens, Eliot, James and Conrad are examples of it; the second is the inevitable one of words succeeding words. Every book illustrates this category but those of Burroughs, which deliberately shuffle words out of grammatical and narrative sequence into new and possibly more liberating patterns, and of Nabokov, which parody narrative with grotesque coincidence, have shifted the emphasis and in so doing have blurred fiction and fact.

In earlier ages that were confirmed in their faith, and socially static, the sequence in writing was one of enactment or of allegory. Character lacked psychological detail in such a context and was expressed in an emblematic or poetic sense. By the nineteenth century this confidence had been undermined; at the same time the rationalism of the previous century could not confront the new consciousness of inchoate masses. If the picaresque novels of Fielding or Diderot are satires on prejudice, the sort of credible naturalistic narrative of the nineteenth century, whatever its moral resources, is possible only as faith subsides. Its detail indicates a step-by-step discovery and description of a new world. Actions were no longer divinely supervised but could be measured against a social index. As Henry James said in *The Last of the Valerii,* people were, or were not, "susceptible of a moral life."

James is the classic discriminator of this morality, upholding a sense of personal independence and guarding against trespass on it without invoking the full Christian doctrine as support. His agnosticism is sharper because it recognizes how much its values are threatened by superficiality and selfishness. The intelligence that observes these encounters is noble, the more so because a half-century in which its standards have been overthrown has not made the stand seem foolish or pathetic. Rather, the difference that has been set up seems as poignant as that which Nanda, in *The Awkward Age,* is made to feel between herself and her grandmother.

The viciousness James sees is discreet because his world has not allowed its outward appearance to be overcome by it. It is an interior malaise made worse by the circle being so intent on itself. For is not James's society quite as enclosed as Jane Austen's? It is true that it is close to the centers of influence and cultivation as they existed in James's time, but there is so little effort to take up this responsibility. One has only to think of the cursory appearances in doorways to announce entrances of James's servants, and compare them with Renoir's recurrent theme of servants carrying on a complete duplicated life beneath, and finally among, their masters, to see that James did not appreciate servants as human beings, let alone moral beings, for all the respect with which he regarded every human potential at the level of "possible" people. Together, the elevated social circumstances and the moral exclusiveness constitute an aristocracy that showed no presentiment of the great shadow of people that would never read a word the novelist wrote.

An aura of academism settled on the novel, in its way as romantic as the Victorian idealization of the Shelleyan poets. In neither James's prefaces nor even in Leavis's elevation of James as a moral arbiter to *The Great Tradition* is there any note of the anguish or chaos that might disturb the order within which novels could be written. Instead, in the preface to *The Awkward Age*, James says that "though the relations of a human figure or a social occurrence are what make such objects interesting, they also make them, to the same tune, difficult to isolate, to surround with the sharp black line, to frame in the square, the circle, the charming oval that helps any arrangement of objects to become a picture." And yet for the writer or the reader is there an essential difference if material shifts from the consciously contrived to the knowingly random, when the words have effects more chance than their selection and more schematic than their fortuitousness?

The intermingling of factual and imaginative content is nowhere clearer than in the native American novel. Herman Melville's dramatization of his own experiences culminates in the practical and mystical treatise on whale-hunting, *Moby Dick.* John Dos Passos has continued to alternate the actual events of his lifetime with fictional accounts of archetypal projections with an energy that is comparable with Melville's. But with Ernest Hemingway and Norman Mailer the duality forces itself into the writer's consciousness, and Hemingway's belief that it is first necessary to be a good man before being a good writer identifies the difficulties of the characters in leading honest lives with the difficulties of the author in making an unbiased account.

It is in Hemingway's prose solution to this problem that we can see an association with the film-camera. Hemingway was intent on seeing the things that a bourgeoisie would rather not look at. *Death in the Afternoon* is a constant adjuration to observe the process closely and report the detail exactly. It was his wish to achieve a style that described action without including intention. Undoubtedly there was too much of the romantic in Hemingway for intention not sometimes to infect the account. At the ending of *A Farewell to Arms* the factual account is free of every interpretative nuance except that it is raining, and we recall how much Catherine Barkley feared the rain.

Even so, Hemingway was at pains to reject this sort of novelistic device because he believed a man could only use words honestly if he was committed to believing them. He thought a man might see an event and describe it accurately but that if emotion and subjectivity were once explored the only honest response was to collapse in doubt. The fact that he attempted to do what the camera does automatically places him at the end of a narrative tradition, and his reliance on a mechanical effect denotes the dissolution of the efficacy of the omniscient narrative. The world has passed out of the novelist's control and the terse telegram that Colonel Cantwell leaves at the end of *Across the River and into the Trees* is a last unblinking message, its factual content ready for a computer.

It is possible that Dashiell Hammett, because he was a more cynical man, went further in the process. In *The Glass Key,* for instance, the level of reportage is so devoid of interior or justifying versions from the characters, and the pressure of society so great, that a profound uncertainty surrounds Ned Beaumont's character. Perhaps more than any modern fictional character he has been observed in reality, the nature of such a process being that it is consistent to only one level. The doubt we are made to feel about him is a just equivalent of the doubt he might feel about himself. A situation has been reached whereby any attempt to discover meaning through prose will appear as an experiment: the writer has been forced to make the reader more conscious of writing than story.

THE SCIENTIFIC PERSONALITY

"Science" is a concept that still provides an obstacle. Not only Lord Snow sees our culture as divided between the artists and scientists. Even Jean-Luc Godard falls at the obstacle in *Alphaville*. After a succession of films that treated contemporary life in an exemplarily scientific way he approaches the subject with a crude directness, turning Paris into a "scientific city" as outmoded as the versions of H. G. Wells and George Orwell, and can only combat it with the strip-cartoon certainty of Lemmy Caution. That Caution wins is incredible, for the longer "Alpha 60," the controlling machine, speaks the more essentially Godardian it sounds, even though the temptation to humanize the brain, by adding breathing sounds to the electronic voice, has not been avoided.

Science is not, as our schooling tries to suggest, one subject among many. It is everything; because, as J. B. S. Haldane defined it, it is simply "a body of general statements about a set of natural events which can be verified in practice." Man is in a scientific age not because he is surrounded by machines like computers but because he realizes that computers operate in the way that he does. A scientific personality is the fitting result of the changes in experience and self-consciousness that I have already described in this chapter.

Time chastens the scientist, just as it does the artist. Atoms and electrons, for instance, existed in Galileo's time but were not identified for several hundred years. A general scientific statement on the nature of matter would be that it does not, in the scale of reasonable human experience, alter, but that man's sense of it extends. John Dalton conceived of the atom as being like a marble. His concept is the simplest and thus still the most general of atomic theories. From his solid object we derive the difficulty of "particle"— the only suitable word we have, which evokes the corners of a crumb between our fingertips. The linguistic barrier is reached with "particle" but the process of re-definition goes on. It became necessary to invoke an electronic nature for the atom and to suppose a duality of nature—of wave and particle—that directly contradicts a dictionary's confidence.

In the 1920s Werner Heisenberg announced his uncertainty principle. Briefly, this says that it is not possible to fix both the velocity and the position of a particle, and that the attempt at both is made impossible by the very act of measurement. Hemingway may not have known about Heisenberg but his prose solution has taken account of his findings. The real significance of Heisenberg's work lies in the admissions it makes about the reflexivity of our recording instruments. In his philosophical predicament as the definer of our nature and our knowledge of ourselves, the scientist finds himself in the position we once allotted to the artist.

The branch of science closest to the artistic end is psychology because, like narrative, it attempts to interpret events and, like morality, it hopes to improve them in the future. Freud was its pioneering genius and his own consciousness of that status reveals how far his findings were influenced by a classical culture and essentially in support of established ideals. Freud and his immediate colleagues and rivals were all, in some form or other, doctors and their function was to treat the sick. They realized a new dimension of sickness and to define it had to posit the phenomenon of "normality." Freud grasped his own theory not methodically but intuitively, composing a vast palace of dogma from a comparatively few cases rather in the way contemporary novels were written.

The absence of measurements in Freud's work is concomitant with the conviction that the people he is dealing with are sick victims of an alien diversion from the whole and natural life. Looking back on Freud's work one is aware of the greater social and cultural confidence he had, even though he ended his life being chased from Vienna by Hitler. Its subsequent undermining has borne down on all Western society as the distinction by which it recognized the sane and insane seemed less credible. In Vincente Minnelli's movie *The Cobweb,* which is set in a psychiatric clinic, one character sums up the film when he says you can't tell the doctors from the patients. Acknowledgement of this is increasingly appealing to analysts; there is now less conception of a sick minority than an acceptance of common patterns of character that break down the old barriers which were social in the sense that a man was termed mad when his actions isolated him socially. The new terms of reference equate the doctor and the patient, as Professor G. A. Kelly, the originator of Personal Construct Theory, points out:

"Thus the psychology of personality is not simply a matter of disinterested psychologists assessing a disinterested organism but of psychologists, who happen to be professionally and casually interested in their chosen subject matter, assessing a nonprofessional psychologist, who, on his part, is intimately and urgently involved with the job of making sense out of the life upon which his existence depends." [1]

As a result, the scientist does not measure symptoms of confirmation but the phenomena of behaviour. The implication of whatever social power he holds over a patient may even be painful to realize. The institution in which strict distinctions were once observed between the sick and the healthy seems to the analyst an unsatisfactory microcosm of the society he inhabits outside. It becomes harder for him to offer stable ideals to the patient from that external world and, like contemporary politicians, he becomes sceptical of presenting principle and can only suggest the most pragmatic treatment

[1] G. A. Kelly, *Proceedings 14th International Congress on Psychology,* quoted by D. Bannister in *New Horizons in Psychology,* Penguin, 1966.

of every problem. He wonders if the patient's view of reality may not be as plausible as his own as their dialogues become divergent definitions of the same word.

The blurring of distinctions between artist, scientist and layman reflects the possibility of uniting the various interpretations of "movie man." We have arrived at a state in which man's most engrossing occupation is epistemological. The increasing necessity for practitioners in either the arts or the sciences to adopt a style or a form of research that is modern is the result of an acceleration in all the means by which a society develops. Events move so swiftly that it is not possible to note every stage in development as a stable unit; instead one is conscious of the fact of process. Just as an eye scanning a landscape—from a railway carriage perhaps—jumps from one point of focus to another, so from a fixed emotional vantage an intelligence scans events in the same way, constructing narrative out of incidents. But a camera in the carriage passes smoothly over the panorama offering less a version of events than a record.

The American soldier who discovered a concentration camp is supposed to have said, "The English language does not have the words to describe what I saw." The newsreel compensated for his difficulty, and in doing so defined a human neutrality towards such events. Hitler was passed off by a humane culture as mad and the camps as evil, although the facts of Nazism made the integrity of any code that might condemn them precarious.

The age of moving film is one that can forget nothing. The miles of newsreel footage will be shown repeatedly until, like a feedback process, they pass into the collective consciousness. The plasticity of moving film makes all its content information until there is no real distinction between its personal and public significance. As Norbert Wiener put it, "To live effectively is to live with adequate information. Thus, communication and control belong to the essence of man's inner life, even as they belong to his life in society." [2]

[2] *The Human Use of Human Beings*, Eyre & Spottiswoode, 1955.

THE MOVIES, TOO, WILL MAKE YOU FREE

W. R. Robinson

Not too long ago there was no film theory. Today—as exemplified by the recent flood of paperbacks on the subject—it has reached the saturation point. Yet most of what passes for film theory is not, strictly speaking,

THE MOVIES, TOO, WILL MAKE YOU FREE From *Man and the Movies: Essays on the Art of Our Time,* edited by W. R. Robinson. Reprinted by permission of Louisiana State University Press.

theory at all; or, rather, it is applied, not pure, theory, for in it the theorizing faculty is made to defend personal causes or taste. When employed for special pleading, such theory contributes little toward identifying the necessary and sufficient properties of the movies as art.

In an argument waged at one time on the nature of cinema, for example, Sergei Eisenstein insisted that montage is the essence of film. And it may be the essence of an Eisenstein film—certainly, without his total dedication to it the intellectual cinema would have missed some of its supreme achievements. His purpose, he rightly sensed, made this device absolutely necessary to his art. But from a truly theoretical perspective, montage is, as Eisenstein himself eventually admitted, just one device in the film-maker's repertoire, useful for some purposes, not for others. What his films and theory actually prove is that montage can be used for certain effects—sensations of speed, power, hostility, alienation, disorder, violence (impressions that the world threatens to overwhelm the perceiver).

In the same vein is Alfred Hitchcock's insistence on using a shot of a glass of champagne gone flat as a metaphor for a finished love affair. Though more simple-minded than Eisenstein's theorizing, Hitchcock's attempt at defining something essential to films is actually an assertion of taste—a preference for wit, an intellectual delight in clever analogy instead of the thing itself directly seen. (This literary quality in Hitchcock's work is one reason why, despite the slightness of his films, he is a favorite among intellectuals.) The same holds true for the purist, realist, surrealist, and other sectarian definitions of the movies; these, like those of Eisenstein and Hitchcock, are rhetorical supports for a value espoused independently of the movies as an aesthetic phenomenon. In every case one aspect of the movies is singled out as definitive and assigned ontological dominance.

At work in film theory and responsible for much of the confusion that reigns in it, as the above instances illustrate, is a careless mental habit, a variation on what philosophers call the naturalistic fallacy. For a quality in art or life to be truly valuable, film theorists almost invariably assume (and they differ from no one else, including philosophers, in this respect) that it must be supported by a theory which attributes reality to it—indeed, proclaims it to be the "realest." In other words, their theorizing stems from a hunger for substance or weightiness, and their theory serves to anchor an airy moral entity to solid intellectual earth. Deeper yet, underlying this hunger, is man's most adamant presupposition: that only what endures can be really valuable—only if our souls are immortal does life have meaning and therefore value; only if love is forever is it true and good. Disguised as ontological definition but actually support for a value, the normal adaptations of theory for determining the nature of film attempt to put intellectual muscle into the ethereal in the hope of justifying it on the intellect's terms, thereby capturing intelligence for moral ends. A difference in taste is mistaken for a difference in reality, and, whether or not overtly, "reality" performs a service decidedly normative, functioning as the ultimate honorific epithet.

The principle, "the more transitory the less valuable," probably is responsible for much of the resistance against recognition of the movies as serious art, since they reek of temporality. They come and go at the theaters with great frequency and in great haste, never to return, and they are not possessable like books or paintings or records. We cannot live and grow in their immediate company or display them as status symbols. Above all, they take the transient—from Plato on, the lowliest aspect of life—as their subject. Western culture has been predominantly intellective, and so its art and criticism, following the natural propensity of the intellect, have been heavily biased toward permanence. They have always proclaimed plenitude and imperishability the summum bonum. Thus it comes as no surprise that early movie directors, especially European ones, sought a cinematic means to give body to the universal truths underlying the appearance of things or to evolve a style by which to elevate human consciousness out of time. Today that object is not so strenuously pursued, although its absence, nostalgically lamented, is still profoundly felt in the latest European films— particularly in the solemn movies of Antonioni, Visconti, Truffaut, and Resnais, but also in the more joyous ones of Bergman and Fellini.

From this traditional distaste for the ephemeral emerges the most persistent theme in Western art—the problem of appearance and reality— and the artist's most enduring challenge—to counterbalance transitoriness by formal strategies capable of articulating the truths behind the mask, a realm beyond change. Now every art or work of art with any pretensions to seriousness at least tacitly solves these problems and is to be judged by the intelligence with which it does so. Yet the movies appear to be attached to the physical and particular much more than any other art and so seem to resist cooperating quietly with the old values and the old aesthetic. For this reason they ought to be more at ease in the hands of Americans, for whom traditionally process is reality. But the American director, when he isn't a European, looks to the Old World for guidance. As American literature did, the American movie will probably come of age when it looks to other sources, native and abroad, for its inspiration and guiding principles. Its major indigenous form to date has been the western, and probably its greatest achievement is also to be found there, not because the cowboy is a mythic hero but because the western, to a large extent a drama of the solitary figure against the wilderness, combines the two main traditions in American visual art.

A bad mental habit and an aesthetic bias issuing from it, then, vitiate the art, criticism, and theory of the film. The immense quantity of "theory," contradictory and confined to a movie's obvious or accidental features, is more an obstacle to accurately understanding the movies as art than anything else. Consequently, to arrive at a true theory it is necessary to begin at the beginning, with the aesthetic phenomenon itself. What can be said in the way of theory without making a value commitment and turning theory into propaganda is decidedly limited: something like, the movies are an art of light produced by mechanical means. Beyond that you're in trouble. But you're already in trouble anyway—for the definition provokes the question: Yes, but what is art? That's obviously a moot matter. In fact, the confusion in film theory results largely from confusions in the theory of art, which in turn result from deeply imbedded fallacies in moral reasoning. So it is necessary at this juncture to enter into questions of aesthetics in order to free film theory from its many false entanglements.

As art a movie is a complex phenomenon, a multifaceted diamond whose glitter can be muted or magnified depending upon the intensity and angle of the light. This is because, as the end result of a deliberate human act, it is imbued with all the intangible emotional, intellectual, and moral attitudes man necessarily expresses in everything he does. Its material base is different from man's—one inorganic, the other organic; but, allowing for that, a movie as art is almost an incarnation of man, standing in relation to him as he has been conceived of standing in relation to his Maker. As such, it invites nearly every question that can be asked of life and even seems to promise an answer to most.

Since a movie reflects human nature, the key to its aesthetic being must be found there. Indeed, as soon as one asks any other than a technical question of it, the inquiry is about man. But man is a complex phenomenon, too. Traditionally, he has conceived of himself as a tripartite creature, with the parts variously designated as reason, passion, and desire in Plato's view; the religious, the moral, and the aesthetic in Kierkegaard's; the id, ego, and superego in Freud's, etc. And each of these three facets has its corresponding ideal, formulated by classical thought as the True, the Beautiful, and the Good. The product of human will, a movie is inevitably a composite of all three facets and so can be said to reflect the organization of man's being—the degree of his wholeness or fragmentation, his balance or madness. Moreover, the movie is expected to incorporate all three ideals simultaneously. To pass critical judgment with a perfect score it must be simultaneously Beautiful, Truthful, and Good. That is, it has to excite the senses with striking forms, satisfy what William James called "the sentiment of rationality," and confirm the imagination's intuitive sense of what is right for man.

Perfection will always elude the moviemaker. His work cannot be fully realized in every respect simply because, though all three facets are inescapably present in his art, he must emphasize one at the expense of another. His work will necessarily favor Truth over Beauty and the Good, or Beauty over the Good and Truth, and so on. None of the three ideals has a determinable priority; each opens out upon a unique vista; all, from a theoretical standpoint, are equally real and valuable. A work will always be just *a* view, never *the* view; it will always be an art of Truth or of Beauty or of the Good, never of all to the same degree. Similarly, a film "theory," and movie criticism as well, will inescapably lean toward either an aesthetic of Truth, an aesthetic of Beauty, or an aesthetic of Value, as has happened historically, with the classical era favoring an aesthetic of Beauty and the modern era an aesthetic of Truth.

A movie, it follows, is a pluralistic phenomenon of such a complexity it is undefinable. For this reason there is no such thing as "the movies," no one essential quality common to all movies; there are only movies. All essentialists—whether moviemakers, theorists, or critics—are necessarily moralists. The numerous schools and styles already on the books demonstrate beyond a doubt that as a medium the movies are alive with possibilities. Some things, to be sure, come more easily to them than others—action, comedy, and spectacle more easily than analysis, tragedy, and verbal theme. Nevertheless, the argument that good cinema can be produced by doing only what comes naturally with the camera makes a neat deduction but a poor observation. As the Modern novel illustrates—in its case a descriptive, temporal genre gets sharply wrenched in order to render an essential, atemporal reality—the most exciting artistic achievements may be generated from a tension between the medium and a view of things unnatural for it.

Movies are certainly recognizable as a distinct phenomenon, but their identity lies not in what they are but in what they do—or, more accurately, in what one chooses to do with them. Film per se is just celluloid strips, as useful for decorating posters, starting fires, or recording information as for making visual narratives. It becomes art when a choice is made to employ it for aesthetic ends. When those ends, not rhetoric, profit, or propaganda, are regarded as worth trying for, a movie becomes an end in itself, a vehicle by which the human spirit becomes free. Indeed, to choose to use the movies for the purposes of art is to make freedom the supreme value.

The most persistent and unjust criticism leveled at the movies has been that they are *sui generis* "escapist." But this critical term, the nastiest epithet conceivable within a very narrow-minded aesthetic of truth which sprung up alongside realism, absurdly distorts our sense of what art is or should be. It implies that only an art as grim and dour as the realist thought life to be under the aegis of materialism can qualify as serious aesthetic achievement. It is easy to understand why the realist would think this; inhabiting a cold, indifferent, inhospitable universe, nothing remained for him except to endure stoically the ruthless pushing about to which man seemed subjected. Yet even in the dourest realistic view truth is a human triumph; through it man transcends suffering and determinism. Nikolai Berdyaev saw this clearly when he argued that all art is a victory over heaviness. It is always escape. When a movie is called "escapist," therefore, all that can legitimately be meant is that it wins its battle too easily. Take, for instance, the simple examples of *From Russia with Love* and *Thunderball*. Every sophisticated Bond fan unquestionably preferred the former because, while still a hero, Bond fought as a human being reliant upon his human wits and strength against a formidable but vulnerable enemy. In *Thunderball*, on the other hand, he is a superhuman creature beyond being ruffled by normally overwhelming adversaries and extreme circumstances. A good movie, like a good athletic contest, offers a true test against a worthy opponent. It wins its victory after genuine struggle, with honor and dignity. And this applies to the movie itself, not just to the characters in it; the movie as art, as the result of a battle between imagination and reality, persuades us that its escape, the victory of the human spirit over the material medium, has been duly earned. If the triumph for the protagonist or the artist comes

too easily, if little wit or courage is expended by them, then the human
spirit has not been tried to its depths and so is not profoundly entertained
and refreshed. Winning is inevitable—the existence of the work bears witness to that—but what is defeated and how the victory is won is the heart
of the aesthetic matter.

The desire to escape from heaviness is so fundamental and universal a
passion that it pervades everything man does and may even be the major
moving force behind his culture and history. Certainly, he has cultivated
the various intellectual disciplines in order to transcend his necessity, in
the hope that he could "choose himself." Religion has always been devoted
to making man free through liberating the soul from spiritual ignorance
or guilt, while science has been employed to equip man with a powerful
knowledge capable of freeing him from nature. The arts in general, the
movies included, are a part of man's intellectual armament in this war to
liberate himself from heaviness, but they serve in a distinctive capacity.
Like religion and science, art frees man's consciousness from the pragmatic
pressures of living for a moment's respite to meditate upon isolated qualities
before he plunges again into the stream of life. But whereas religious dogma
focuses upon the conceptual truths of the spirit and science upon those of
nature, art, a conjunction of spirit and nature, takes moral truth as its
province. In effect, it discovers or creates values; by incarnating the Good,
a spiritual entity, in a concrete form, art frees it to be.

The primordial truth about a movie as art, then, is that it confronts its
viewer with moral fact and engages him in a moral dialogue. Though
ignored by theorists, the moral power of art is so evident as to have made
it the center of a vociferous, protracted quarrel from Classical Greece to
the present. The movies simply stepped into the middle of a centuries-old
row when, as soon as they appeared on the scene, censors and critics attacked them for distracting people from their proper moral development
by stirring up their lower depths. The record clearly testifies that moral
reaction to the movies—and to art in general over the ages—has seldom,
if ever, been free of specific moral biases, so that the true moral character
of the movies has remained obscured by parochial passions. This impasse
can be skirted with the observation that the most likely remarks made or
heard after a movie are: "I liked it. Did you?" "That was a good movie,
don't you think so?" "It was awful; it wasn't any good at all; it's worthless."
Although they use more formal language, the reviewer and critic concern
themselves with the same matters. In short, everyone instinctively recognizes
that a movie—all art, in fact—invites him to exercise his taste in making
a value judgment. He senses that a value assertion has been made and that
a reply is demanded of him. And, except for the most diffident, everybody
also senses that he is qualified to reply, for, despite the scholar's defense
of his hard-earned learning, no special knowledge is required and no greater
moral authority exists than the individual's own conscience—which must
be defended at all costs, since his identity is inseparable from it.

What transpires in the moral dialogue becomes clear when the movies
are contrasted with science, a companion empirical discipline. Science—

pure science, that is, not applied science—clarifies phenomena. It opens our eyes to the facts of nature by concentrating our attention on objects, events, and relations not immediately obvious. What was hidden before, presto, we now behold. Its terminology literally discriminates what has been beyond our power to see. To record what he has seen for public and perhaps personal benefit, a scientist molds language (whether mathematical or verbal) into a proposition which accurately represents the state of affairs he has observed. Or, if working with models, he makes a visual metaphor to perform that task. But he has seen something—call it a fact—which acts as a criterion in molding his proposition or model. The moviemaker, a storyteller, has to have a similar principle of selection to tell him when he has got his tale right, when what he is making accurately embodies what he has perceived. That principle is not a fact, however, but a quality, for his subject is man, not nature. This moral fact, even if vague initially and clear only when his story receives its final touches, has precedence over and determines the devices he selects from the cinematic bag of tricks or creates on the spot to serve his unique purposes. The finished product is imbued in every part by the quality which it is constructed to embody, and as the scientist invites his reader to view the reality he has seen, so the moviemaker invites his audience to behold the moral fact he has discovered. A "pure" movie, like pure science, enhances awareness by bringing a hidden or vague quality out into the open.

We cannot overlook the power of a movie to strike and pierce the senses and thereby arouse passion and emotion and even awaken the soul. With its vigorously impersonal method science cools us off emotionally and morally to receive a dispassionate truth about objective matters. Its icy illuminations may be a great delight for the intellect, but they are not intended to bring joy to the heart or conscience. Perhaps the most evident thing about a movie is its power to excite; but like a church service it does so of necessity, for we can receive its insight, actually a state of being, only if it elevates us into exalted consciousness. Similarly, the demand that a movie be exciting, engaging, alive, that its moral truth be felt and feelable, springs from the intuition that a value is a vital existence, something worth living for and caring about. For a value is a sensation, or a feeling, as Susanne Langer calls it, given an objective state before consciousness. Art fixes sensations in form and thereby allows them to become objects of knowledge and desiderata, states of being to be achieved and returned to as a vital creature's good.

When properly employing his craft, the moviemaker does not imitate, refer to, or symbolically represent a value but gives body to it there in the movie. All he therefore has to do to become a serious artist is to dedicate himself to making "objects of value"—not of meaning or for communication, nor of social or historical or psychological import, nor as vehicles for avoiding greater moral clarity. A movie which depends primarily upon a topical subject, a fashion in taste, or rhetoric for its appeal, although considerable artistry may be expended for these purposes, has a short life span. When these lose their interest the movie is dead. If, however, it primarily, accurately, and vividly embodies a quality which, despite changes in taste, is an eternal good, the movie has what used to be called universality: it is always alive and relevant; it remains a living option.

To carry out his serious intentions the moviemaker ideally has to have complete control over his medium, which means that as a storyteller he must master not only the narrative denotations but also the moral connotations of the images with which he works. All the implications of character, plot, pace, lighting, camera angle, cutting, and such highlighting elements as dialogue and music have to be within his control. These are determined by traditional usage and are public for the most part, although in a young art like the movies many of the connotations are not yet clearly fixed. Thus the preview. Because most defects in craftsmanship are immediately apparent, nobody gets damned simply for being a poor craftsman; he is just ignored. A certain level of seriousness and craftsmanship has to be self-evident for a movie to attract attention in the first place. No one gets excited over the worthless; and craftsmanship, except in someone like Hitchcock, where it is all there is, receives only a passing comment. Our central concern is values. Confronted with a certain pretension to seriousness, as in a Jules Dassin film, we test for authenticity by looking for intellectual blindness and for moral crudity owing to viciousness or insensitivity. We mean by sensitivity, in fact, the capacity for subtle moral discriminations. Correspondingly, the sensitive moviemaker, if truly an artist, via his imagination-conscience feels and thinks his way in and through his medium, making an ironic, romantic, realistic, or surrealistic movie, not one which abstractedly asserts the desirability of those qualities. He creates these values; he gives them flesh; he brings them to life.

The moviemaker as artist, it should now be clear, is a moral educator. Like every artist, he forges, in James Joyce's phrase, the conscience of his race. Take as an example Richard Brooks's recent movie *The Professionals*, not likely to be a classic but still a good film. This is an especially handy movie to illustrate the moral role of art because its title specifies the quality the movie is constructed to define. Professionalism as a value comes naturally to an era dominated by technology and technicians and prone to a taste for craft, camp, and the cool. But the movie is not a sociological tract, nor is it a treatise on the virtues of professionalism. Instead, it is a professional work, or at least it aspires to be. Not only are the major characters professionals in skill and temperament but the movie itself exemplifies complete knowledge and know-how. In effect, defining its value structurally, stylistically, and tonally as well as narratively, it not only identifies the good of professionalism but in doing so establishes a criterion by which the movie itself is to be judged. The movie insists that its viewers clearly perceive what professionalism is, then turn it back upon the movie, asking, "Does it measure up to the criterion it affirms? Has the director met and mastered every problem that came up in his professional bailiwick, moviemaking? Has he been cool and calm, always on top of the situation?" If art is creative, if it does add something to matter which wasn't there previously, it is this moral illumination inherent in form. Moreover, since the movie brings new qualities into existence, established criteria are irrelevant for judging it. Movie criticism and theory, always waiting upon art to educate them, stand disarmed before moral truth while the movies dig out within and bring to light in objective form new dimensions of moral reality.

The normative logic inherent in the sort of persuasion the movie attempts forces the viewer to ask whether the movie fulfills itself on its own terms. Intuitively sensed from man's first encounter with art this has always been the question art poses—does it pass the test of unity and coherence? In deciding if a movie is coherent or unified, we ask first whether it is being true to itself as art—does it embody value?—and then whether the quality has been so treated as to include everything necessary to its embodiment and nothing extraneous. In other words, we ask if it does what art is supposed to do in the way art must do it. The movie succeeds as art, it successfully embodies a value, when both conditions are fulfilled.

This role the movies play in our moral education is tacitly recognized by our educational practices. In the sciences students are not asked to read the original authors but a textbook or one authoritative work stating a commonly acknowledged public truth. And the same is true for religion, although it is not formally taught in the school system—unless students are old enough to become comparativists, they study the one true doctrine. But in the arts the original artists, and many of them, are studied, since the human-moral reality they serve as texts for is too complex to be exhaustively treated by one man. Even in school systems where one literary figure, such as Dante or Goethe, is looked upon as a natural institution, that writer is not taught exclusively. Every writer is limited to construing the truth available within the purview of one moral perspective. Although within some schematic approaches the possible perspectives on moral reality may be reduced to a few categories, the wide variety of conservative and liberal, romantic and classical, middle-class and working-class perspectives, for example, is so great that an accurate sense of man's moral predicament can be arrived at only through reading widely. The fact that just a small part of the moral spectrum can be relevant to any individual's purpose is no argument against extensive reading, for to be able to choose what our own temperaments, equally committed to a specific value, need to clarify and strengthen their impulsions, we have to weigh the pros and cons of the whole moral truth.

We study the value spectrum so that we may become more precise about our specific good, with tolerance, it is hoped, as a side effect. Because the arts are habitually used to teach history, it is customary to emphasize their temporal aspect, whereas science, a body of constantly verifiable knowledge about nature, is taught independently of history. Yet the movies no less than science are devoted to the discovery and establishment of timeless truth. The movies, like the other art works created in the past and accumulated as our heritage, pass on moral knowledge from one generation to another; they thereby allow us to possess now the possibilities of good discovered by our forebears. As a body of work on the books, they, like the sciences, constitute an encyclopedia of knowledge. That heritage is not sufficient, however. Movies must be constantly in the making; old stories must be forever told anew; to remain living options, values must be continually validated within ever-changing reality—every moment requiring a new synthesis of Beauty, Truth, and the Good. Thus the movies, when art, explore on the frontiers of knowledge, refurbishing old values, refining discrimination in areas already charted, and producing new insight in areas of the moral spectrum previously ignored.

Because the movies play such a crucial role in our education, they must be free to follow moral truth wherever it may lead. This means they have to be as free from censorship as political thought and the other intellectual disciplines are. Censorship, long a bugaboo for the movies, defends the moral status quo, prohibiting search and discovery where they are most needed. Freedom of taste clearly is as important as freedom of speech. For the quality of our private and public lives depends upon their being nourished by living values, and only constant reassessment and refinement of the values we live by, through aesthetic meditation, can assure that. The complexity, nuances, and consequences of a value must be aired if the naive and pretentious ones are to be unmasked, the invidious exposed, and the confused clarified. Satirical movies, for example, quite overtly seek to demonstrate that a value cherished by some individual or the public is phony, a sham supported by nothing better than fear, ignorance, or malice. The genuine, of course, bear up under scrutiny and survive.

The moral dialogue a movie invites us to participate in, ideally a free field without favor, can, if it leads to the conclusion that taste is not disputable, beget disabling doubt about the profitableness of discussion or the trustworthiness of our own values. Cynicism arises from diffidence or from a failure to impress our reality cogently upon others—if we cannot intellectually establish what we value, then nothing is valuable; all is meaningless. Because our consciences cannot ultimately tolerate one another, critical dialogues quickly turn into ego contests leading nowhere but to ever louder shouting. The aim of the dialogue is not, and should not be, conversion, however, but clarification. Even if a moviemaker wanted to, he could not force his viewers to believe or act as he wished. As art a movie persuades by its power to illuminate. Most often, as with education in general, it facilitates rational defense of what otherwise would be called prejudice. Instead of converting, it brings into lucid focus a good that has been wrongly understood or obscured, correcting an error in reason or awareness. The dialogue initiated by the movie, whether directly or indirectly and regardless at what remove from the work itself, leads in its most aesthetically profitable instances to an understanding of what one's good truly is and wherein it truly lies. It does not incite to action; it clarifies for action, should the individual be so inclined.

Thus a movie as art objectively and vividly displays man's good. It brings moral truth into the world. Psychologically, by being out there, it confirms us, assuring us that our good is real. We go to a movie, certainly in our most serious moods, but probably on all occasions, in search of our moral truth; and when we find it, for the moment we dwell spiritually or meditatively in it, it is our fulfillment, our fullness of being. And if we don't like the movie, still, through the friction of an imperfect meeting of consciences, we become clear about moral alternatives.

Taste may not be disputable in the sense that differences can be arbitrated by logic, but nevertheless disputing it is our means to personal and public wisdom. When the logical positivists and their disciples legislated that what cannot be empirically verified is meaningless, their logic was sound but their common sense was asleep. From a scientific perspective all cinematic or aesthetic utterances are nonsense, and all but descriptive propositions about a movie are sales pitches designed to persuade others to buy our way of packaging life. The trouble here is that movies are not utterances; they make no claim—nor does any art, as architecture and music illustrate glaringly—to propositional truth or falsity. Their province is taste; and taste, not truth, at least not truth independent of taste, is our preeminent concern as living creatures. To live is to act, and efficient action requires clear goals. By contributing to the enhancement of moral awareness, the movies as art help free man to know and pursue his true good. Whereas our scientific education equips us to use the world more effectively, the movies, assisting in our moral education, help prepare us to act more wisely.

And not just movies themselves but their criticism and theory, part of the moral dialogue they stimulate, contribute to the clarification of ends. In the final analysis, despite some impurities that creep in, applied theory magnifies and thereby facilitates examination of the values which particular schools, movements, directors, and critics have espoused. Their commitment and its resultant distortions, perhaps misleading to the unsuspecting mind, function as a necessary agency in our moral illumination. Thus that mental atavism of justifying taste with ontological argument, for all its logical absurdity, turns out to be the heart of the aesthetic matter. It is an instrument, as the movie itself is, to confirm man's being by giving substance and permanence to his supreme good. Although his commitment keeps him from being cool and therefore a reliable pure theorist, the applied theorist's intellectual power issues from his belief in himself, in what he has seen, and in his pressing need to justify himself and make living room for his moral kind.

The movies, via the moral dialogue they initiate and participate in, open our eyes to values. At their best they excite and refresh not simply the ordinary emotions but the profoundest feeling in our deepest moral reaches as well. To reiterate, they are one means by which man, through the powers of his imagination, perceives for himself possibilities without precedent in nature. Incarnations of the Good, providing opportunities to contemplate imaginatively concrete moral truth, they enhance and enrich consciousness. They are instruments helpful in lifting man up literally by his own bootstraps to contemplate the ideal and perhaps eventually to direct his effort towards its realization. When properly charged, their images empower men to behold and enjoy their finest life. No art does any more, and on the contemporary scene none surpasses them in scope and power, none more "realistically" confirms man's truth, none liberates or is liberated more completely.

That the movies possess the depth and breadth necessary for articulating contemporary moral reality, or the aesthetic means to bring it into vivid relief, is borne out by the difference between them and literature. Both are predominantly narrative arts employing images—one directly, the other indirectly—as vehicles for storytelling. Because of that slight difference, however, they are worlds apart. Literature and the literary imagination are metaphorical; they seek to make explicit a reality hidden to the senses. From one point of view literature, an art of words, duplicates the acts of creation by the Greek Logos or the Christian God: through it the Word, the primordial ontological power in Greek and Christian metaphysics, brings order into the world by imposing itself upon chaos. Since words are not natural or material entities, literature is inherently deductive—words issuing from the Word—both alienated from the physical and constituting a self-enclosed system which locates the source of the Good outside the physical world, within the Word, an a priori realm which validates particular words. But from another, a human, point of view, literature, originating within a worldly predicament, arises either from the longing of words to be themselves or from man's hunger to dwell in the realm of ideas or reason. Not inherently inclined to be denotative, words much prefer to consort among their own kind and, indeed, ardently long to return to their source. In any case, the literary imagination works from a fallen state and, nostalgically lamenting its paradise lost, aspires to regain verbal heaven.

Drama nicely illustrates the bias of literature and one of the ways in which it functions. In drama, at least when it is authentic art, words turn characters inside out, manifesting their inner being with language. For this reason the dialogue, in, say, *Who's Afraid of Virginia Woolf?* can be heard from a recording and still be aesthetically effective. With neither the theatrical nor cinematic spectacle distracting attention from the words, they intensively activate the hearer's imagination and turn him, too, inside out. Characters serve as the metaphorical vehicles by which the Word is made manifest. In a verbal medium such as drama the visual element complements the words and is eventually dispensable. Poetry—lyric poetry in particular—reigns supreme among the literary arts because the words are relatively unencumbered by the sensory, although in poetry, too, imagery is indispensable as metaphorical agency. Its object is, of course, to let the human spirit sing out. Verbal narrative on the other hand relies more heavily on the referential dimension of language, and words as a consequence tend to function analytically, pointing to underlying patterns, causes, or essences. Not by accident fiction favors temporal and historical explanations. Read in solitude, it cultivates the mind, and whatever the circumstances it proffers the intellectual satisfaction attained through comprehending the abstractions governing life. Nevertheless, despite being more abstract than drama or poetry, verbal narrative is also governed by the principle that literature be concrete and specific or "make sense"; and with drama and poetry it paradoxically employs words as the instrument by which man can penetrate through the mask of phenomena to the Word beyond it and transcend his finite condition. Literature and the literary imagination are bound by the laws of language, which is always metaphorical; through postulating likenesses, they put the mind in contact with intangible intellectual essences not directly perceptible.

In contrast to literature, the movies and the cinematic imagination are literal. A visual medium in which the word is complementary and dispensable, the movies illuminate sensory reality or outer form. They are empirical revelations lighting the thing itself and revealing change as nothing more than it appears to be. In their world there is no becoming, only being, or pointless change, no innate potential to be realized in time, no essence to be released from original darkness, no law to be learned and obeyed. For this reason analysis is rarely successful in the movies, *Citizen Kane* being the most famous of the very few exceptions. Even the Russian intellectual cinema, which on first impression seems analytical, at its best is hortatory—it inspires the viewer to be. Or, more specifically, in individual frames, by composition and photographic style, it endows the lowly and exploited with splendid being. Whatever a movie illuminates it has already celebrated, saying, in effect, "So be it." Its atomic constituents seem to have a greater life than the enclosing forms, while order, causality, and pattern appear arbitrarily imposed. And, with the atomistic quality so pronounced in them, the movies evoke an emotional rather than an intellectual response—the thing directly perceived is directly felt, and intellectual reflection follows upon the emotion, whereas in literature the emotion follows upon the word after the mind has made the initial encounter. Understandably, movies more perfectly satisfy Tolstoy's requirement that art appeal to the universal innate feelings in man. Consequently, they tend to be egalitarian, and literature elitist—only those who know how to read and think are admitted to its domain, while anyone with eyes qualifies as a citizen of the movie world. From these differences it is clear that literature testifies, while the movies witness. As a verbal medium, literature gives voice to the mind's lust for meaning. In seeking to commit the mind to what is not at once evident to the senses, literature demands belief; it insists that its report, always an interpretation, be trusted. The movies, on the other hand, a visual art, are immersed in the sensory, physical world, viewing it from within as a passing parade ceaselessly coming and going. They have no way, except for words, to gain a vantage point outside it. In this respect they are the archetype for the contemporary intellectual predicament characterized by the twilight of absolutes—they have no revealed word or a priori ideas, nor any criterion within experience itself, by which to ascertain reality or value; they are face to face with what is in its full multiplicity and glory. They dwell in the present, in a world all surface. Lacking a second level of reality, they are without complexity—without irony, meaning, or necessity. On the face of things appear process, activity, energy, and behind this mask is nothingness. Whereas the word is mysterious, the image is evident; everything it has is showing. Thus for movies the created world is good, not fallen; they offer no salvation through belief, as Christianity and rationalism do, but instead regard the given world as redeemed. They are existentialist, valuing the concrete, existence, or what is.

Little wonder, then, that the literary sensibility is not at home in the cinematic world and suspects movies of being superficial—without soul, intellectually impotent, and morally frivolous. One devoted to ideas, the other to particulars, one committed to transcendent truth, the other to ever-present reality, the verbal and visual modes are fated to eternal hostility. Yet despite this inherent hostility, the movies have their inevitable literary aspect—in their title and dialogue, and in the property or scenario from which they are derived. (Perhaps this literary origin raises major obstacles to successful film-making, since the film is in effect a translation and the viewer is invited—or does so out of habit—to translate it back into its original, and truer, literary prototype. The film functions, in this case, as literature did in classical theory, as a decorative illustration for a truth known through a prior and more authoritative faculty.)

There are those who lament the fact that movies must have a literary aspect; purists of a sort, they long for a return to the era of the silent film, when movies were movies and that's all there was to them. That nostalgia is understandable, for the pure movie demands a less complex response and poses less complex critical problems. The fact is, however, that the movies, allowing for the proper dominance, are an image-word medium, as is literature, and all for the better. For, despite the invidious criticism which can arise from a bias favoring either the intellect or the senses, the presence of the antagonistic elements reflects the human predicament. The tension generated between images and words in an impure movie and our ambivalent response to their interaction beget a truth that would otherwise be lost. As literature is enriched by the tension between word and image, so are the movies. The beneficent effects of this tension can be readily observed in many movies, but it has become consciously explicit in such recent ones as *Alfie,* in which a narrator terrified of death tries unsuccessfully, through directly addressing the audience or from a verbal point of view, to determine what his life comes to within a cinematic context; and *Fahrenheit 451,* in which a French director flatly and ludicrously repudiates his own art in lamenting the demise of book man.

The tension in these movies also appears, reversed, in recent literature, perhaps most notably in the work of Alain Robbe-Grillet. Words are being adapted to cinematic reality, with the result that they no longer mean anything. Readers trained in the traditional ways of words, predictably, are deeply frustrated by the literature of nothingness. Paradoxically, the impurity of the movies makes them a more perfect art, capable of more extensively exploring its own possibilities and limitations, and thereby of more profoundly and more precisely giving body to man's truth.

Once the movies are acknowledged to be art and what they unveil is taken seriously, we have to face the fact, extensively argued by Existentialists, that the word has been superseded by sensation. The movies define better than any other art what we feel today to be the relation between the intellect and the senses. Among other things they make it quite clear, to the verbalist's distress, that the word is an adjunct of the image. In their version of the play between the eye's truth and the mind's, the ancient theme of appearance versus reality is reversed. In contrast to, say, Elizabethan poetry, in which images decorate a rational framework, in the movies reason rides on the tiger back of images in motion.

This new relation between the senses and the mind is the contemporary form assumed by an ancient and enduring antagonism. For at stake ultimately in the difference between literature and the movies are the prerogatives of two moral universes, two cultures, and two ideas of creation. Both art forms, just by existing, pay tribute to their source, the power which makes them possible—literature to the Word, the movies to the Light. But beyond that, by implication when not directly, literature celebrates a God transcendent, the movies a god immanent; one affirms creation by fiat, the other creation by emanation. These inevitably hostile alternatives, if Joseph Campbell's account in *The Masks of God* is correct, led to the division of East from West some eight thousand years ago—the East following the way of the Light and the West the way of the Word—and has been the source of their mutual suspicion ever since. But the Light and the Word have also vied with one another for supremacy within Christendom. The Old and New Testament offer conflicting accounts of the instrument responsible for creation, and St. John indiscriminately mixes creation by the Word with creation by the Light. St. John's confusion, a careless mixture of Judaic and Greek attitudes, may well be the source of the traditional friction in Western culture between the Light and the Word. At any rate Judaism's existential, worldly faith has persistently contended with Greek rationalistic idealism for dominance in Western culture. The Word has been clearly dominant until recently, but as a result of science's corrosive effect upon Christianity, the Light is now in the ascendant. So the difference between the movies and literature is rooted in a fundamental antithesis in man's being, and the rise of the movies as an art is one sign of a profound change taking place in Western culture—a transformation begetting what pundits have been variously calling a post-Christian, post-rationalistic, post-typographical, or post-literary period.

The movies derive their aesthetic stature, obviously, from being a closer analogue to reality than is literature. For the alert film-maker and his audience today a movie can and should be a microcosm of life. All the world's a movie screen. Thus the director's medium is inherently closer than any other to life, and he is the most advantageously equipped artist for adventuring in moral reality.

The movies at their best have always performed the task of art, even when film-makers, critics, and theorists claimed that, paradoxically, the movies could be art only if the imagination was weighed down by materiality. Accepting this condition in *Greed,* Erich Von Stroheim created serious art in spite of the inherent bias against the medium. Nonetheless this assumption hurt the movies in the pressure it exerted on moviemakers to honor piously the dominion of the mechanical, material, and casual over their art. And theorists, including such sophisticated ones as Erwin Panofsky and Susanne Langer, in their turn were impaled on a dichotomy which forced them to choose between conceptions of the movie as dream or as bound to physical reality.

The movie of the last decade, along with developments elsewhere in thought and the arts, has put this realistic assumption to rest. It was a period's taste, time has made evident—a corruption of reality. Today the movie is explicitly and confidently committed to freedom as the supreme value and truth, and the moral dialogue it is now participating in is probing the career of man's good in that direction—whether in great, good, bad or indifferent films, in parts of films or in their entirety; in the character of the emancipated female: Mrs. Waters in *Tom Jones,* Jeanne Moreau or Brigitte Bardot in *Viva Maria,* Jean Seberg in *Breathless,* or the various roles played by Natalie Wood; or the cool, resilient male: Belmondo in *Breathless* and elsewhere, Anthony Quinn in *Zorba the Greek,* or Vittorio Gassman in *The Easy Life*; or as a theme in the work of Bergman and Fellini.

The free camera, moreover, supports the free character. It has always been understood that the camera used with skill is a projection of an individual's sensibility, not a mechanical eye; foreign films especially, coming out of visual traditions different from our own, have been constant reminders of this fact. Today there is not even a shadow of a doubt that the movies, instead of being by nature or moral precept enslaved to physical reality, are a technological vehicle by which the human spirit can escape material limitations once thought to be narrowly restrictive. Not too long ago regarded as man's nemesis, technology, in the movies as well as in the airplane, enlarges his power of flight. The movies, consequently, need no longer be an illusion of the "real" but are at liberty to be artifice and even to call attention to their fictional character, as Tony Richardson does in *Tom Jones* and as Richard Lester does in *A Hard Day's Night.* A still more striking example is Mario Monicelli's *The Organizer,* in which, although the movie is ostensibly a realistic treatment of capitalistic inhumanity, the artistry draws attention to itself, contradictorily and ironically proclaiming the dominion of the imagination over substance.

But the movies' greatest contribution to today's moral dialogue over freedom does not lie in characters or camera technique. It lies, rather, in the emancipation of the image. Not long ago it was excitedly argued that the camera gave painting a new life by freeing it from photographic representation, but the camera has done even more than that: it has freed itself, too, at least from all debilitating forms of representation. This child of empiricism, repudiating its parent, has liberated form from the physical world. Marilyn Monroe, never a physical actuality for moviegoers, lives on every time the camera projects her image on the screen, and so, although physically dead, she has gained immortality. She has been released, as has the moviemaker and the viewer, and, indeed, man's mind everywhere, to dance in the imagination's heaven. Actually physics is mainly responsible for destroying the idea of substance, but the movies have done more to set the imagination free to dream upon human moral possibilities within a substanceless universe. By conclusively demonstrating that an image does not necessarily signify substance, they have destroyed the last vestige of our materialistic mental habits. Unburdening us of the hunger for and anxiety about meaning, the free movie teaches us that to be is enough; existence needs no justification. Ironically, in the new intimacy between the senses and the mind which the movie achieves, Plato's realm of forms is realized through physical vision.

Once regarded as a puerile, cowardly escape from life because they begot and simulated dreaming, the movies are now recognizable as an extension of the supreme power inherent in a universe of energy, chance, evolution, explosiveness, and creativity. In such a youthful, exuberant universe the movies' kind of dreaming gives concrete probability and direction to the ongoing drive of energy, and as a consequence what at one time was thought to be a vitiating defect is now their greatest virtue. The new freedom they reflect and extend is freedom within the world, contingent and not absolute, a heightened vision of existence through concrete form beyond abstraction. In a world of light and a light world—unanalyzable, uninterpretable, without substance or essence, meaning or direction—being and non-being magically breed existence. Out of the darkness and chaos of the theater beams a light; out of nothingness is generated brilliant form, existence suspended somewhere between the extremes of total darkness and total light. Performing its rhythmic dance to energy's tune, the movie of the imagination proves, should there be any doubt, that cinema, an art of light, contributes more than any other art today to fleshing out the possibilities for good within an imaginative universe.

THE WITNESS POINT

Vernon Young

While the Hollywood motion picture is continually under fire from a variety of fronts for not being sufficiently radical in its social interpretation or for being too radical, for appealing to the twelve-year-old mind or for not appealing to a larger number of twelve-year-old minds, for not filming the classics or for filming too many bad classics (or for filming good ones badly), for being sexually evasive or for being sexually self-conscious, one might well abandon the area of civic criticism for the amoral and simple question: Just what *is* a movie?

The expense of spirit in a waste of shameful moralizing over content has

THE WITNESS POINT From *New World Writing*, No. 4 (1953), a Mentor Book. Published by New American Library, Inc.

ignored the fundamental identity of the motion picture as an art—or shall we say as a synthesis of science and of various art forms?—since it is with some such temporization that we must begin. And before we can conclude with high-minded resolutions as to the motion picture's public obligations, we should come to some agreement on its intrinsic endowments. Means determine, or at least qualify, ends; syntax precedes argument.

The instigator of a form should certainly be listened to and remembered when he coins its definition, even if the form thereafter undergoes mutations which modify the original defining. In the late 1870s an American named Edward Muybridge performed an experiment with twelve still cameras in order to record the motions of a trotting horse for Leland Stanford. This is the first known experiment in the development of what later became "moving pictures." Subsequently, Muybridge defined the movie as "an apparatus for synthetically demonstrating movements analytically photographed from life." No purer definition of the movie as a process has been evolved; all extensions of definition derive from this one, since they have had to derive from the nature of the thing in itself.

Later, when the film as a vehicle of aesthetically organized content was being more widely recognized and more intensively urged, Sergei Eisenstein, one of the most voluble theorists working in the film medium, declared that film form was "a question of creating a series of images in such a way that it provokes an effective movement which in turn awakens a series of ideas. From image to sentiment, from sentiment to thesis." Here is a dialectical description rather than a mechanistic analysis. Between Muybridge and Eisenstein we find the essence and the limits of our definition. All elaborations of statement on this subject must assume the premise that the movie begins with *the art of photographed motion*. The movie is the art of making motion meaningful; it is a dynamic of visual relationships, assisted, generally, by the arts of the scenarist and the actor and by the incorporation of selected sound. Within the framework of the pictorialized problem, the director and editor may augment, distill, or diffuse; increase or decrease tempo by mechanical means, compound images after the event and otherwise arbitrarily complicate, simplify, or intensify the continuity originally devised.

Self-evident, it would seem; yet the commercial movie perennially abdicates its own potential in favor of the lazier chronology of the legitimate theater and the novel of the Fielding tradition, using an unimaginative succession of medium, distance, and close shots, little more dynamic than the magic lantern. The great pioneers of the film art, such as Meliès, D. W. Griffith, Abel Gance, and Pudovkin, empirically established the simple fact that a movie *must be kept moving*, and over the years this principle has been fortified by continuing implementations: moving the camera instead of merely moving the object, and moving it from a variety of positions; employing many brief shots to indicate simultaneity or rapid sequence; balancing "dissolves," "irises," and "fade-outs" with direct cuts; flashing rapidly from detail to larger scene and utilizing music in direct or in counterpoint relation with the photographed images.

Between the experience of watching a play and that of watching a movie the distinction should be elementary, but, from the reactions of the layman and of all but a very few critics, it would appear to be still incompletely understood. Since their modes of presentation materially differ from each other, the stage and the movie, pursuing different formal ends, will arouse qualitatively different perceptions. When the film and the play appear to overlap, they have seceded from their native means. The movie is basically different from the staged play in kind—aside from the patent fact of its being a *recorded* performance—by virtue of its powers of mobility. The stage is three-dimensional, the movie multi-dimensional (even without the amplifications of the new "Cineramic" techniques). The stage play can create epic, for example, only by borrowing movie methods. The movie, likewise, can debate ideas only by imitating the relative stasis of theater and, in pursuit of ideas or not, it unnaturally limits its prowess by containing action within one room or other closely confined area (this constriction is frequently achieved, just to show that it can be done: e.g., *Rope* and *Detective Story*). The imperative of movie motion makes any concession to the working principles of theater a retrograde act, for the form of a play must be violated in order to be converted; if this violation is shirked, the movie's integrity will be sacrificed for that of the play. One cannot possibly imagine a fluid movie adapted from a play by Molière, Chekhov, Sternheim, or Pirandello, unless the original content were disastrously modified. Nor can the social dramas of Ibsen and the discursive comedies of Shaw profit from the movie medium. Their action, in the literal sense, is not going anywhere; their moods and theses can only be dissipated by a compulsively mobile camera.

In this order of playwriting, drama is impelled by people facing each other and exchanging opinions or combatting each other's being in modes dependent upon emotional and intellectual forces irrelevant to or beyond the wiles of the motion-picture apparatus. The inappropriateness of any three-wall play which is screened, retaining its original structure and dialogue, demonstrates functional abuse. Only an ill-educated movie public could have swallowed the uncomfortable versions of Shaw's plays to which we have been exposed, and it is amusing to note that it has been the best educated (in literary ideas only) who have swallowed them whole. But almost any filmed play—*All My Sons, Born Yesterday, Another Part of the Forest, Cyrano de Bergerac*—suffers from the necessity of keeping scenes within limited precincts for long periods, from the superfluous motion resorted to in order to keep not the *idea* but the *scene* moving, and from the tyranny of stage dialogue, highly absolute, rigidly constructed within the otherwise flowing context. (Film dialogue is often less artificial than even the most naturalistic theater talk, seeming to arise more spontaneously from contingencies in the development of action. The privilege of latitude is imposed on it by the interjectional nature of the screen play: sharper than life yet more casual than theater.) That the moral "point" of a play can still be made after its metamorphosis on celluloid need not be disputed, but what we have a right to demand is an almost total translation of aesthetic experience. *A Streetcar Named Desire* was a brilliantly manipulated adaptation. It was still a *screened play.* The producers of *The Importance of Being Earnest* found themselves with a stylized theater product and were forced by honesty to open and close the film with a theater program, pretending whimsically that they had not really made a movie at all! (Shakespeare's multi-ordinal drama, constructed along more serpentine lines of action and form, is the best conceivable exception to this general incompatibility of genre. The Expressionist drama of the first quarter of our century was in many ways a half-cinematic measure, which may largely account for its demise.)

For the modern sensibility, the moviegoing experience is rightly a manifold one. The agents of a play's action move across one's field of vision at an unvarying distance; those of a movie's travel in a stranger sense. With increased ratio to the degree of directorial sophistication, *you* move into the field of vision. You have the illusion of leaving normal dimensions; you are inescapably involved, mute witness and participator as well; not restricted to a set distance from the drama, you may approach it from in front, from above, even from underneath—see it *in toto, in medias res,* or agonizingly from its peripheral inceptions. The helpless filmgoer is a Gulliver, subject to extraordinary and shaking changes of perspective. More unbearably than Gulliver, he inhabits Lilliput and Brobdingnag simultaneously, or at least within shattering accelerations of time, and may find himself transported in the flutter of an eyelid (a change of lens) from a mountaintop to a dark alleyway, from thence to beneath a table, behind a curtain, or within palpitating distance of the heroine's bosom.

In view (and one means just that) of this superior kaleidoscope of momentum, it is surprising how the inveterate filmgoer has taken this wonder for granted, how unaware he is that its artisans have confected an art-science organically expressive of an age that successively finds itself characterized in terms of such process fields as engineering, thermodynamics, psychology, or physics. For the motion picture, so understood, is *the* art of our time analogous with these subjects—mobile, divisive, atomic if you like: a form-breaker, disintegrator, working from specialized and defined mechanical methods toward frequently undetermined ends, incorporating as it goes the ruins of our historical arts of painting, music, and poetry, creating a new whole, plastic, beautiful perhaps, irregularly conditioned by the confused tone of journalism, by the multiple kinesthetic appetites of the driven masses, by our now universal mania for disregarding privacy, for annihilating distance and identity. The movie reflects the inquisitive lust for the panoramic vision indulged by the aviator but present in us all, *malgré nous;* reflects, from each of us, the amateur psychoanalyst, the arrogant sociologist, the latent violator, the cold *voyeur.* (Wouldn't we all rather see Audrey Hepburn than Botticelli's Venus, rising from the foam?) And because it is dedicated to our collateral retinizing, to what Morris Ernst has justly called "the Esperanto of the eye," it is often colossally vulgar. Yet is it more so than Broadway's musical comedies or the average fiction best-seller?

The French, who care pertinently for this subject, have produced, as might be expected, a spokesman with a flair for definition. René Guillère, in an essay primarily concerned with jazz, has provided us with an elegantly exact defense of that world of form in which the cinema finds its justification.

Formerly the science of aesthetics rested content on the principle of fused elements. In music—on the continuous melodic line threaded through harmonic chords; in literature—on the fusion of a sentence's elements through conjunctions and transitions; in art—on a continuity of plastic forms and structures of combinations of these forms. Modern aesthetics is built upon the disunion of elements, heightening the contrast of each other: repetition of identical elements, which serves to strengthen the identity of contrast. . . .

Allowing with a shrug for M. Guillère's cavalier appropriation of the entire scope of modern art, we must concede that he has herein precisely described the qualitative nature of the motion picture. "The disunion of elements, heightening the contrast of each other" is the basis of film assembly: union through disunion, a somewhat more dynamic modification of terms than Eisenstein's Hegelian "from image to sentiment, from sentiment to thesis."

For all these reasons it is significantly the contemporary world that has, by Hollywood, been most fittingly translated into usable movie terms. We live in a fragmented, motile environment, and in the motion picture the seemingly futile activity of daily American urban life acquires, by reason of its decoction into meaningful rhythms and patterns of sound and image, excitement and acceptability. The modern temper, exasperated and energetic, yet passive under bombardment by accessories to nature, receives, in this visual drama of multiplicity, its most authentic revelation. You may beg this question by supporting Yvor Winters' objection to mimetic poetry as "the fallacy of expressive form," or you may defer to the subtler justice in George Williamson's approval of John Donne: "To be contemporary in the right sense means to find the peculiar emotional tension of the time and to mold language to its expression." In what other medium can one find a language so rhythmically molded to express the peculiar emotional tension of *our* time (no irony avoided) as the language of the movie camera? European moviemakers are not so historically restricted; they have an intimate sense of the past. American producers see the past as no less in mindless frenzy than the present; therefore, the strange hollow sound of our Westerns and our costume epics. During the last decade, certainly, the most expertly made American films have been almost all contemporary in subject matter.

(It is noteworthy to observe, in passing, that largely because the writers are permitted more honesty in this direction, the direct subject has been either the underworld of society or the underside of the mind: cf. *The Strange Love of Martha Ivers, The Killers, The Lady in the Lake, Cross Fire, Act of Violence, Champion, Criss Cross, They Live by Night, Caught, The Sniper.*) This phase of the art, if regrettably obsessive, has not been without imaginative value. It has stimulated imagistic reprisal from the greatest among our poets of metamorphosis, Dylan Thomas:

In this our age the gunman and his moll,
Two one-dimensioned ghosts, love on a reel,
Strange to our solid eye,
And speak their midnight nothings as they swell. . . .

We watch the show of shadows kiss or kill,
Flavoured of celluloid give love the lie.[1]

From the literary bias, one could insist that the movie is the art of the novel reduced to absurdity. Like the novel in respect of flexibility, shifts of viewpoint, the ability intimately to dissect or comprehensively to mass, the movie takes the novel one step further, the last, often the disastrous step. It literalizes the novel. (All movie literalism is of course relative; once beyond newsreel immediacy, the artistry is created by a consistent intention and a host of tributary services. And artistry does not necessarily increase with the degree of expressionism, impressionism, surrealism, or plotless vagary the movie may serve. The important fantasists, from Meliès to Cocteau, have sought to transcend all modes of cinematic realism. Their achievements have often been prodigious. But for purposes of easier reference, I am not attempting, in the ensuing notations, to research the extremist adventure on film.)

On its own naked account, the motion picture cannot take you into the articulated content of thought but it can suggest the content by showing objects so related as to mirror the associations of thought. (Like symbolist poetry it may conceal and delay meaning until its images are completed.) The film version of your literary world banishes ambiguity and alternative renderings. The spectator's private mind is made up for him; the intermediate reaction of the reader is eliminated, his imagination circumscribed, his initiative preëmpted. There is substituted instead this particular image or sequence, dictatorially composed: not any street lined with poplars, vanishing to a distant sky of one's own impalpable painting but this street, these poplars here, this house-front so, this demarcated horizon with no other arrangement than this embodied-in-Technicolor one, no more, no less, and no time to ask or to wonder what is around this exactly measured corner; not any heroine you might individually have imagined from the subtle clues of a prose writer who would allow you, despite his precise order of coloration and anatomy, freedom to wander by yourself with the creature of your own nocturnal imagination, but *this* actress, vivid and irrevocable, her hairline gliding around the tangible curve of an ear you might never have included, hands scorning the poverty of your tactile invention, mouth promising, perhaps, variations you had not yet arrived at. With a recklessness unavailable to the legitimate theater, the movie teases one into an even greater illusion of spontaneity and volition which is the satisfying and some-

times sinister secret of its power. It is a form of literalism which, if insuffi-
ciently transformed, will indeed be "strange to our solid eye." It will stupefy,
instead of releasing, the imagination of the spectator.

The foregoing character of the motion picture, always leading us into
psychological and sociological territory, has been generalized from the sum
of its effects as it reaches the observer's subjective and synthetic view. But
this sum or "grammar" of cinematography, to risk an academic figure, is
evolved from parts of speech usually unidentified by even the more attentive
moviegoer who still too often fails to recognize that the foundation of a
movie's vital existence is the right relationship of its *details.* Snobbery toward
"mere technique" in a movie is untenable. Every inch of a movie *is* technique, under, over, and above all felicities of paraphrasable content and of
personality. Just as a poem is, by Mallarmé's sane correction, "written not
with ideas but with words," so a movie's totality is made up of concrete syntax, built from experience with the medium, a syntax primarily visual, or
today *audio-visual* (tomorrow the 3-D world?). Makers of movies have by
now developed a number of refinements instrumental to the greater effectiveness of their art; some of these have been raised into inviolable principles, some are by-products of a particular context and have not been mar-
shaled into a rationale. A few of the more creative of these refinements may
be pointed out, in the hope that moviegoers will recall and then re-look, to
the greater glory of their cinema experience:

The device of *moving into a scene from the part to the whole,* rather than
the other way around: "From image to sentiment." An easily available example is a fight in *Treasure of the Sierra Madre,* ending with a closeup, floor-
level, of the loser's battered face. Scene is "dissolved" into close-up of bloody
hands being washed at the plaza fountain. Moving up from the hands to
the faces of the victorious combatants discussing their next move, the
camera gradually frames a more complete view of the fountain. The older
method would have moved us from the bar, probably "fading" instead of
dissolving (thereby breaking momentum), out to the entire plaza, then
moved us in to the fountain, then out again before picking up the action.
By this time, any close-up of the hands would be anti-climactic. The later
method obviously saves footage, besides gaining emphasis by concentrating
our attention sharply on the transitional detail.

The dissolve through parallel compositional structures: a continuity-
design especially gratifying if not overworked. In *Body and Soul,* the shot
of a triangulated section of a prize-fight ring is dissolved rapidly into a
dressing-room scene where the immediate arrangement of massage table and
group of characters repeats the triangle, with a shaded ceiling light as apex.
A more poetic illustration can be elicited from *Letter from an Unknown
Woman;* an arched railway station in which the woman has just said a
strained goodbye to her lover recedes into the similar construction of a hospital corridor among cries from the maternity ward. Here the device was
expository, not merely formal. Even without the dissolve in sequence, the

repetition of a structure at just the right moment, or the introduction of an element which resembles another, can be a compelling reminder or a premonitory announcement. The elevator gates which close on Mary Astor at the end of *The Maltese Falcon* clearly suggest a jail, and in *Madeline* the attorney's feet pacing behind the wicket recall to the woman on trial her poisoned lover, who paced nightly behind the railings of her house.

The transitional caesura, a kind of *delaying* action, is uniquely effective when managed with tact. This process occurs when a fade-out or dissolve leads into an *aftermath* of the next scene logically expected. In *They Won't Believe Me,* Robert Young is shown packing to leave his wife for another woman; she pleads, apparently without success. Dissolve from close-up of Young's suitcase in the bedroom to the same suitcase in a train compartment. As this scene enlarges, we discover that Young is on the train with his wife, having been persuaded by means we discover much later in the film. (This is a shrewd use of anticlimax.) The *symbolic* or *oblique cut* serves a related purpose, as climax to a *suspended* action: an image is abruptly substituted for the deed. In *They Won't Forget,* the cut, from a lynch mob dragging its victim from a train, to a mailbag being jerked from its hook, made a particularly brutal impact. And in the film version of Graham Greene's *The Man Within* (retitled in America *The Smugglers*), the camera boom suddenly left the boy being flogged at the mast to travel swiftly upward and catch a flock of seagulls screaming against a bright sky.

Among the most valuable assets of movie composition, one has to isolate the judicious use of the *closeup* in relation to the larger continuity. A sure knowledge of when to employ closeup so as to emphasize rather than retard action, and to focus instead of dispelling a mood, is one of the cardinal factors. Since Eisenstein's terrifying, and over-prolonged, closeups in the Odessa Steps sequence (*Potemkin*), the management of closeup has come a long and subtle way, even if in the California commodity glamor, not dramatic necessity, seems to be the foremost aim. Anatole Litvak (*The Snake Pit*), Alexander Mackendrick (*Tight Little Island*), and Carol Reed come to mind as having an unfailing sense of the right moment for the appropriate style of closeup. The final cross-examination of the boy, on the stairs of the embassy, in Carol Reed's *The Fallen Idol,* was a superlative example of camera position as the decisive control. It is impossible to imagine the scene being maneuvered, shot for shot, with any better combination of angles. Reed saved his strongest closeup for the moment when the boy's web of prevarication threatened to break.

The use of closeup is governed by another aid to integration, by what I should like to call *the witness point:* this is to say, the camera's coign of vantage not simply within the action of a scene but throughout the entire film. *Whose eye* is the camera, at any moment, intended to represent? Is the strategy to be omnivisual, like Tolstoi's in *War and Peace,* so that the point of view is ricocheted from one participant to another? Is one actor to be concentrated on to the exclusion of others and always seen through another's eyes or is the angle of vision to proceed *from* him? The question of witness point must be initial in the plans of scenarist and director. One remembers

Olivier's conspicuous violation of this principle in *Hamlet*, when we saw not only the Ghost but also Hamlet, himself, becoming dim! *Who* is supposed to be looking at Hamlet at this point? Long before the inflated adulation of Olivier's directorial ability, Edward Dmytryk, working with far less elevated material, made no such mistake in *Murder, My Sweet*, where the drugged detective concentrated on clearing his vision; in this case, we saw *him* with *our* eyes open and only blurred *with* him as the stairs, door, and so forth wavered in his focus.

The distinguishing feature of Alfred Hitchcock's early pictures was this working close to a single protagonist, never including more of an incident than could logically be observed by one implicated witness. Since his arrival in Hollywood, he has disowned the method as a controlling style. It found its most extensive assimilation in Robert Montgomery's production, advertised as You *and Robert Montgomery in* THE LADY IN THE LAKE; here the action was seen *exclusively* through the eyes of one narrator. (We never saw *him* except for a brief confrontation by a mirror.) Closeup acting received an extra share of attention and dramatic intimacy was thereby furthered. There are many who find such concentration of means visually monotonous but its possibilities, as Montgomery suggested them, are all in the direction of disciplining the ubiquitous method which, properly handled, does make for greater speed and variety but, if abused, corrupts its privileges by the vice of inordinate maneuvering. (The first-person-singular narration in a novel offers comparative grounds for studying the advantages and the limitations of the restrictive view.)

Deployable view is a startling addition to film narrative: not the mere flashback which is now a Hollywood cliché of storytelling, but a richer extension—the recapitulation of a key action from more than a single viewpoint, a multiple dramatization, as in the Japanese *Rashomon*. Its most intelligent Hollywood employment to date was in Dmytryk's *Cross Fire*, where three G.I.'s told their separate versions of a sadistic and fatal beating, and it was also used to astute psychological advantage in one involved sequence of *The Smugglers*, wherein we first saw a flashback of what had *actually* taken place, followed immediately by another flashback of the same incident deliberately misrepresented by the narrator, under duress of torture.

Musical scoring is a lengthy subject which cannot be more than honored here; its relevance to cinematic success can surely no longer be questioned. If there are any critics remaining who puristically believe that the movie is or should be essentially, or only, visual, and that sound, musical or other, is a gratuitous addition, let them re-view, as test cases, the two worthies, *Treasure of the Sierra Madre* and *The Third Man*, and try subtracting the musical contours from the visual ones. A great deal of the total cinematic thrill will be lost to them, I believe, without Anton Karas's zither and Carlos Chávez' adaptation of the Yaqui Indian theme. A good piece of cinematography will have, of course, a visual logic of its own but a movie, as finished product, is now a *sight and sound* experience. The emotional fruitfulness of thematic music or of orchestrated sounds-in-themselves is indisputable. One needs only to remember the scraping club foot in *Act of Violence*, the harpsichord theme of *Ivy*, the bell in *Day of Wrath*, the Varsovienne of *A Streetcar Named Desire*, the tapping stick and dragging skirts of the Countess' ghost in *Queen of Spades*, the relentless feet stomping and clattering through *Oliver Twist*, or for that matter the syncopated machine of *The Man in the White Suit* or the unearthly laughter of those girls in the Eiffel Tower elevator sequence of *The Lavender Hill Mob*. *The Thief*, a "silent movie" made in 1952, is the best proof by default we could have. Nobody in it *talked*, sure enough, but sound was carefully retained and the best bit in the film (the *only* one worth remembering) was the covering of a woman's scream by car brakes—an artful, if passé, contrivance!

In the last analysis or, speaking by the card, in the last synthesis, the determining factor of a film's structural purity is *the proportioning of its connective sequences*—no news to the student of the novel or the symphony. In the motion picture, one solid scene following upon another of about equal length, no matter how flexibly directed each of the scenes may be, will be dangerously contrapuntal; whereas a running narrative with brief but punctuating expository shots cut into the more prolonged and fully dramatized sections will "strengthen the identity of contrast" and more fittingly serve that "affective movement" for the recording of which the movie camera was invented. The final responsibility for integrating these elements so that a structure becomes a style falls to the editor (ideally, in collaboration with the director), and it is this vitalizing organization of scene and fragment which is known as *montage*.

It should not be necessary to conclude that a film ought finally to be something better than its most ingenious moments, and something more than the sum of meticulous parts. But the form-and-content dichotomy in the evaluation of movies has been aggravated by the plain fact that American producers rarely know *what* they are doing at the primary creative level: taking pretty pictures, telling a story as eclectically as possible, reproducing the sensations of another form of entertainment, or imitating life.

Carol Reed has claimed that he makes a movie to please himself, hoping that it will also please the public, and that so far he has been lucky. Mr. Reed's honesty is instructive, but obviously he has been more than lucky. He has been artistic—which is to say he has kept his eye on his subject. *And* he has been left alone! Under the Hollywood dispensation, few directors are given such freedom of authority. The usual result is an irresolution of all but commercial purposes, which has fostered an equal irresolution of critical approach from the audience. *Portrait of Jenny* and *Duel in the Sun* included fabulous experiments with color and photography but their substantial trashiness was unredeemable. *Ivy*, produced by William Cameron Menzies in 1947, remains as perfect a specimen of controlled montage as ever came out of Hollywood; the critics failed to observe its formal perfection and one moral snob, without pausing to look and listen for its exceptional charms of texture and pattern, dismissed it as having a shallow sense of evil. So it had, of course; yet it deserved a less puritanical concession for its consistent and exciting elaboration of cinematic means.

No doubt there has never been a film from Hollywood which has surpassed *Les Enfants du Paradis* or *Panique* in ethical force and poetic conception, and it must be confessed that neither of these films is notable for technical brilliance. Faced with such contradictions, many critics jump to the easy conclusion that the techniques of film are therefore subordinate to the "story" or the "acting." The answer is not quite so simple as it may demonstrably appear by making invidious comparisons. . . . *Day of Wrath,* the Danish tragedy of witch-burning, had all the necessary ingredients for a great movie: a story of considerable dramatic and moral cogency, responsive actors, and a careful audio-visual scheme of symbolism and accent. Nonetheless, Carl Dreyer, who directed the picture, failed in his total operation. His elements simply did not fuse. It is my opinion that this film could have been radically improved by correction of certain faults in the montage (which I will also assert for even *Les Enfants* and *Panique*). The conceptual values would not have been disturbed; in fact, they would have been enhanced. *Rashomon* is perhaps closer to the perfect union than any film yet produced; it is captivatingly all of a piece, cinema and dialectic.

The subtle uncertainty which belies critical conviction on the subject of what constitutes form is one reason for my having avoided the "final" questions in favor of the less exalted matters of the craft. For I think we are in a safer position to raise the old dilemma of content determining form or form determining content *after* we have acknowledged that movie appreciation should begin with understanding the idiosyncratic contributions of the form, and not by passing judgment, derived from extrinsic standards, on the paraphrasable content. The motion picture in America will not greatly improve in any of the directions demanded of it by the civic intelligentsia until it is at least honored as a potentially independent art, in spite of its derivative composition. The synthesis which we call a *motion picture* is finally something quite different from the media which combine to supply its elements (still photography, the theater, the novel, music). And its peculiar autonomy cannot be respected until the nature of its dependence upon these elements has been clearly defined.

THE EVOLUTION OF FILM LANGUAGE

André Bazin

By 1928, the art of the silent film was at its height. Many of the best directors were understandably, though not justifiably, sorry to witness the disappearance of this perfect world of images. They felt that the cinema, having taken a certain aesthetic direction, had become an art that was supremely suited to

THE EVOLUTION OF FILM LANGUAGE From *The New Wave* edited by Peter Graham, copyright © 1968 by Peter Graham. Reprinted by permission of Doubleday & Company, Inc.

what was known as the "exquisite unnaturalness" of silence. The realism of sound was bound to upset matters.

In fact, now that the use of sound has satisfactorily proved that far from annihilating the Old Testament of the cinema it has brought it to fulfillment, one might well ask oneself if the technical revolution that resulted from the introduction of sound could really be called an aesthetic revolution. In other words, did the years 1928–30 really witness the birth of a new cinema? As far as the way a film is put together is concerned, the history of the cinema does not in fact reveal as marked a difference as one might expect between the silent and sound cinema. There are many affinities to be found between certain directors of the twenties and others of the thirties and especially the forties—between, for instance, Erich von Stroheim and Jean Renoir or Orson Welles, Carl Theodor Dreyer and Robert Bresson. These more or less marked affinities prove first of all that the dividing line of 1930 was no barrier, that certain qualities of the silent cinema were carried over into the sound era, but above all that instead of contrasting "sound" with "silent" films we should examine in what ways they differed from *and* resembled each other in conception and style.

I am quite aware that the brevity of this essay will oblige me to make some critical simplifications, and I shall regard what I put forward more as a working hypothesis than an objective truth. With this in mind, I would say that by and large there were two opposing schools in the cinema from 1920 to 1940: directors who believed in the image and those who believed in reality.

By "image," I mean in a general sense anything that can be added to a depicted object by its being depicted on the screen. This addition is complex, but it can be traced back to two factors: the plasticity of the image and the resources of editing (in other words, the organisation of images in time). By plasticity I mean the style of the sets and the make-up, to a certain extent even the acting, and of course the lighting and framing which complete the composition. As for the editing, which, as is well known, had its source in Griffith's masterpieces, André Malraux wrote in *The Psychology of the Cinema* that it constitutes the birth of the film as an art: editing is what truly distinguishes it from simple animated photography and makes it a language.

The use of editing can be "invisible"; and this was most frequently the case in the classical pre-war American film. The only purpose of breaking down the shots is to analyze an event according to the physical and dramatic logic of a scene. This analysis is rendered imperceptible by its very logicality. The spectator's mind naturally accepts the camera angles that the director offers him because they are justified by the disposition of the action or the shifting of dramatic interest.

But the neutrality of this "invisible" breakdown of sequences does not take into account the full possibilities of editing. These are to be found in three devices generally known as "parallel editing," "accelerated editing," and "editing by attraction." In creating parallel editing, Griffith managed to evoke the simultaneity of two widely separately actions, by a succession of shots of first one, then the other. In *La Roue*, Abel Gance creates the illusion of an accelerating locomotive without having recourse to any real images of speed (for all we know, the wheels might as well be revolving on the spot), simply by an accumulation of shorter and shorter shots. Finally, editing by attraction, conceived by Eisenstein and more difficult to describe, might be broadly defined as the reinforcement of the meaning of one image by another image which does not necessarily belong to the same action: for instance, the cascade of light, in *The General Line*, which follows the shot of the bull. In this extreme form, editing by attraction has not been used very frequently, even by its originator, but the much more general practice of ellipse, comparison, or metaphor is basically very similar: for instance, stockings thrown on to the chair at the foot of the bed, or even spilt milk (in Clouzot's *Quai des Orfèvres*).

Naturally there exist various combinations of these three devices. But whatever they are, they have a common recognizable feature (which could serve as the very definition of editing): the creation of a meaning which is not contained objectively in the individual images themselves, but which arises from their collocation. Kuleshov's famous experiment with the same shot of Moszhukhin, whose smile seemed to change in implication according to the shot that preceded it, is a perfect summary of the properties of editing.

Kuleshov, Eisenstein, and Gance do not show the event through their editing; they allude to it. True, they take most of their elements from the reality they are supposed to be describing, but the final meaning of the film lies much more in the organisation of these elements than in their objective content. The substance of the narrative, whatever the realism of the individual shots, arises essentially from these relationships (Moszhukhin smiling plus dead child = pity); that is to say there is an abstract result whose origins are not to be found in any of the concrete elements. In the same way, one could imagine that young girls plus apple trees in blossom = hope. The combinations are innumerable. But they all have one thing in common: they suggest an idea by means of a metaphor or an association of ideas. And so between the scenario proper—the ultimate object of the narrative—and the raw image, a supplementary link is inserted, a kind of aesthetic "transformer." The meaning is not *in* the image, but is merely a shadow of it, projected by the editing on the consciousness of the spectator.

To sum up: both the plastic content of the image and the possibilities of editing mean that the cinema disposes of a whole arsenal of devices with which it can impose its own interpretation of a depicted event on the spectator. By the end of the silent era, one can consider this arsenal to have been complete. The Soviet cinema took the theory and practice of editing to their ultimate conclusions, whereas the German expressionist school subjected the plasticity of the image (sets and lighting) to every possible distortion. The German and Soviet cinemas were certainly not the only important schools at the time, and one could hardly claim that in France, Sweden, or America film language lacked the means to say what it had to say. If the essence of cinematic art is to be found in all that plasticity and editing can add to a given reality, then the silent cinema was a complete art. Sound could have played only a subordinate and complementary role, as a counterpoint to the visual image. But this kind of potential enrichment (which at the best of times could only have been minor) would have paled beside the whole range of supplementary reality that was in fact introduced by sound.

What we have done is to suppose that expressionism in the editing and the image is the essential part of film art. It is precisely this generally accepted notion that is implicitly challenged, as early as the silent era, by directors such as Erich von Stroheim, F. W. Murnau, or Robert Flaherty. Editing plays practically no role at all in their films, except in the purely negative sense of eliminating what is superfluous. The camera cannot see everything at once, but at least it tries not to miss anything of what it has chosen to see. For Flaherty, the important thing to show when Nanook hunts the seal is the relationship between the man and the animal and the true proportions of Nanook's lying in wait. Editing could have suggested the passage of time; Flaherty is content to *show* the waiting, and the duration of the hunt becomes the very substance and object of the image. In the film this episode consists of a single shot. Can anyone deny that it is in this way much more moving than "editing by attraction" would have been?

Murnau is less interested in time than in the reality of dramatic space: in neither *Nosferatu* nor *Sunrise* does editing play a decisive part. One might perhaps suppose that the plasticity of Murnau's images has an affinity with a certain kind of expressionism; but this would be a superficial view. The way Murnau composes his images is not at all pictorial, it adds nothing to reality, it does not deform it; rather it strives to bring out the deeper structure of reality, to reveal pre-existent relationships which become the constituents of the drama. Thus, in *Tabu,* the entry of a ship into the left of the screen makes the spectator see it as a metaphor of fate, without Murnau in any way distorting the strict realism of the film, shot entirely on location.

But it was without doubt Stroheim who was the most reluctant to use visual expressionism and editing devices. In his work, reality admits its meaning like a suspect who is being grilled by an indefatigable police inspector. The principle of his direction, a simple one, is to look at the world from so close and with such insistence that it ends up by revealing its cruelty and its ugliness. One can well imagine, in theory, a Stroheim film composed of a single shot, which would be as long and as close up as one liked.

I do not want to limit my case to these three directors. We shall certainly find others, here and there, who reject expressionist elements and do not rely on editing to play a large part. Even Griffith is one of them, for example. But perhaps these examples will suffice to show that in the middle of the silent period there existed a film art that was diametrically opposed to what is normally thought to be true cinema, a language whose syntactic and semantic components are not at all the individual shots: the images are important not for what they add to reality but for what they reveal in it. The silent cinema could only counteract this tendency. Both

Greed and *La Passion de Jeanne d'Arc* are virtually sound films. Once editing and visual composition cease to be considered as the very essence of film language, it can be seen that the arrival of sound was not an aesthetic watershed dividing two radically different aspects of the medium. Some people saw that sound was bringing a certain kind of cinema to an end; but this was not at all *the* cinema. The true cleavage plane was elsewhere; it was, and still is, cutting clean across thirty-five years of the history of cinematic expression.

Now that the aesthetic unity of the silent cinema is not as solid as it seemed, caught as it is between two strongly contrasting tendencies, we should perhaps take another look at the history of the last twenty years.

From 1930 to 1940, a certain kinship of expression in the cinema grew up throughout the world, originating in particular from America. Hollywood was riding high with five or six well-tried types of film which gave it overwhelming superiority: the American comedy (*Mr. Smith Goes to Washington*, 1939), the burlesque film (the Marx Brothers), the song and dance musical (Fred Astaire and Ginger Rogers, *Ziegfeld Follies*, 1945), the gangster film (*Scarface*, 1932, *I Was a Fugitive from a Chain Gang*, 1932, *The Informer*, 1935), the psychological and social drama (*Back Street*, 1932, *Jezebel*, 1938), the horror film (*Dr. Jekyll and Mr. Hyde*, 1931, *The Invisible Man*, 1933, *Frankenstein*, 1931), the Western (*Stagecoach*, 1939). During the same period, the French cinema was undoubtedly the next best after the American: its quality gradually emerged in the trend which might broadly be termed "black realism" or "poetic realism," and which was dominated by four directors: Jacques Feyder, Jean Renoir, Marcel Carné, and Julien Duvivier. As it is not my purpose to award prizes, there would not be much point in lingering on the Soviet, British, German, and Italian films of this period, which were relatively less important than they were to be during the following ten years. In any case, the American and French films will suffice to demonstrate clearly that the pre-war sound cinema was an art that had visibly reached well-balanced maturity.

A word about content first of all: there were the well-tried genres, governed by carefully worked-out laws, capable of entertaining the largest possible international public, and also of attracting a cultivated élite, as long as these felt no *a priori* hostility towards the cinema.

As for form, the photographic and narrative styles were perfectly clear and they conformed with their subject: a total reconciliation of sound and image. When one re-sees films like William Wyler's *Jezebel*, John Ford's *Stagecoach*, or Marcel Carné's *Le Jour se Lève* today, one senses an art that has attained a perfect balance, an ideal form of expression. Conversely, one admires dramatic and moral themes which, although not entirely creations of the cinema, were raised to a certain nobility, to an artistic effectiveness that they would not have achieved without it. In short, these were all characteristics of "classic" art in full flower.

I am perfectly aware that there is a case for maintaining that the originality of the post-war cinema, compared with that of 1939, lies in the emergence of certain individual countries as film-producers, especially in the dazzling explosion of the Italian cinema and the appearance of a British cinema that was original and free from influences from Hollywood; that the truly important phenomenon of the forties was the infusion of new blood, the opening up of unexplored regions; that the real revolution took place more on the level of subject-matter than of style, and concerned what the cinema had to say to the world rather than the way of saying it. Is not neorealism above all a kind of humanism rather than a style of direction? And is not the essential feature of this style self-effacement before reality?

It is certainly not my intention to champion some supposed superiority of form over content. "Art for art's sake" is just as heretical in the cinema as it is elsewhere, perhaps even more so! But new wine should not be put into old bottles! And one way of understanding better what a film is trying to say is to know how it is saying it.

In 1938 or 1939, then, the sound cinema had, especially in France and America, reached a degree of classical perfection that was based both on the maturity of the dramatic genres that had been developed over ten years or inherited from the silent cinema, and on the stabilization of technical progress. The thirties saw the arrival of panchromatic film as well as sound. Of course, the studios never stopped trying to improve their equipment, but these improvements were only incidental—none of them opened up radically new possibilities in film direction. Moreover this situation has not changed since 1940, except possibly in the field of photography, thanks to an increase in the sensitivity of film. Panchromatic film upset the balance of values in the image, and ultra-sensitive emulsions allowed modifications to be made in the composition. Now that the director of photography was free to shoot in a studio with a much smaller lens aperture, he could, if necessary, eliminate the blurred backgrounds that used to be the rule. But one can find plenty of examples of depth of focus being employed well before then (by Jean Renoir, for instance); it had always been possible in exteriors and even in the studio with a little ingenuity. It was there to be resorted to if the director so desired. And so what is important here is not so much the technical problem, although the solution of this was considerably facilitated, as the stylistic effect (which I will come back to). In short, ever since the use of panchromatic film and the possibilities offered by the microphone and the crane became general in studios, the technical conditions necessary and sufficient for the creation of film art had been achieved by 1930.

As technical requirements played practically no part in this, the signs and the principles of the evolution in language must be sought elsewhere: in the renewal of subject-matter and, in consequence, of the styles that were needed to express it. In 1939, the sound cinema had reached a point which geographers call the line of equilibrium of a river, i.e. that ideal mathematical curve that is the result of sufficient erosion. Once a river attains its line of equilibrium, it flows effortlessly from its source to its mouth without hollowing out its bed further. But if any geological shift occurs which raises the peneplain or alters the altitude of the source, the water becomes active again, penetrating the underlying land, sinking in, undermining, and hollowing out. Occasionally, if there is a bed of lime-stone, a whole new network of hollows forms on the plateau; it is scarcely perceptible, but is complex and contorted if one follows the way the water takes.

THE EVOLUTION OF THE SHOOTING SCRIPT SINCE SOUND

In 1938, the way shots were broken down in a shooting script was the same almost everywhere. If, to be conventional, we call the type of silent film based on visual and editing devices "expressionist" or "symbolic," we might dub the new form of narrative "analytic" and "dramatic." Suppose, to go back to one of the elements in Kuleshov's experiment, we have a table laden with food and a poor famished beggar. In 1936, the breakdown might have been as follows:

1. General shot taking in both the actor and the table.
2. Tracking shot forward ending in a close-up of his face which expresses a mixture of wonder and desire.
3. A series of close-ups of the food.
4. Back to the character (in medium shot) who walks slowly towards the camera.
5. Slight track back to take in the actor from the knees up, seizing a chicken's wing.

There could be many variations on this breakdown, but they would all still have several things in common:

1. Spatial verisimilitude, whereby the position of the character is always determined, even when a close-up cuts out the décor.
2. The intention and effect of this breakdown are exclusively dramatic or psychological.

In other words, if this scene were acted on stage and seen from a seat in the stalls, it would have exactly the same meaning; the event would still have an objective existence. The change in camera angles does not add anything, it simply presents reality in the most effective manner. First of all by allowing one to see it better, and then by emphasizing what needs emphasizing.

True, the film director, just like the theatre producer, has a margin of interpretation within which he can inflect the meaning of the action. But this is only a margin, and it cannot modify the formal logic of what takes place. By way of contrast, take the editing of the stone lions in *Battleship Potemkin*; skillfully put together, a series of shots of different pieces of sculpture give the impression that one lion (like the people) is getting to its feet. This admirable editing device was unthinkable after 1932. In *Fury*, Fritz Lang inserted, as late as 1935, a shot of clucking chickens in a farm-yard after a series of shots of tittle-tattling women. This was a survival from the age of editing by attraction which brought people up in their seats even at the time and now seems totally out of place in the context of the rest of the film. However marked the art of a director like Carné may be, for instance in his enhancement of the scenarios of *Quai des Brumes* and *Le Jour se Lève*, his breakdown of shots remains on the same level as the events it is analyzing. It is just a good way of looking at them. This is why we are witnessing the almost complete disappearance of special visual effects, such as superimposition, and even, especially in America, the close-up, which has such a violent physical effect that it makes one aware the director has cut from one shot to another. In the typical American comedy, the director returns as often as he can to a shot of the characters from the knees up (the so-called *plan américain*), which accords best with the spontaneous attentiveness of the spectator—it is a point of natural equilibrium for his mental accommodation.

In fact, this use of editing has its origins in the silent cinema. This is more or less the part it plays in Griffith's work, in *Broken Blossoms* for example; but with *Intolerance*, Griffith was already beginning to introduce the synthetic conception of editing which the Soviet cinema was to take to its ultimate conclusions and which can be found, less exclusively, in several films at the end of the silent period. Besides, it is understandable that the sound image, being much less malleable than the visual image, made editing more realistic again and to an ever-increasing extent eliminated both plastic expressionism and symbolic relationships between images.

And so in about 1938, films were almost always put together according to the same principles. The story was told by a succession of shots, which varied very little in number (around six hundred per film). The characteristic technique of this type of narrative was cross-cutting, which, in a dialogue for instance, consists of alternate shots of either speaker according to the logic of the text. This type of shooting script, which perfectly suited the best films of 1930–39, was strongly challenged by the technique of composition in depth used by Orson Welles and William Wyler.

The reputation of *Citizen Kane* is no exaggeration. Thanks to composition in depth, whole scenes are filmed in a single shot (a device known as the sequence-shot), sometimes even without the camera moving. The dramatic effects which used to depend on the editing are all obtained here by the movements of the actors within a chosen framing. Welles did not of course "invent" composition in depth, any more than Griffith did the close-up; all the early pioneers of the cinema used it, and with good reason. The partially blurred image, which came in only with editing, was not simply due to technical subservience resulting from the use of close shots; it was the logical consequence of editing, its plastic equivalent. If at a certain point in the action the director takes for example, as in the imaginary sequence already mentioned, a close-up of a fruit-bowl, it is normal for him also to isolate it in space by the focusing of the lens. A blurred background confirms an editing effect. Whereas it is only an accessory part of the style of photography, it is an essential part of the style of the narrative. Jean Renoir understood this perfectly when he wrote in 1938, i.e. after *La Bête Humaine* and *La Grande Illusion* and before *La Règle du Jeu*:

"The longer I work in my profession, the more I am drawn to *mise-en-scène* in depth in relation to the screen; the more I do that, the more I am able to avoid the confrontation of two actors who stand like good boys in front of the camera as though they were at the photographer's." And in fact if one looks for a precursor to Orson Welles, it is not Louis Lumière or Zecca but Jean Renoir. In Renoir's work, the tendency to compose the image in depth goes hand in hand with a partial suppression of editing, which is replaced by frequent panning shots and entries into frame. It implies a respect for the continuity of dramatic space and also, of course, for its duration.

Anyone who can use his eyes must realize that Welles's sequence-shots in *The Magnificent Ambersons* are by no means the passive "recording" of an action photographed within a single frame, but that on the contrary this reluctance to break up an event or analyze its dramatic reverberations within time is a positive technique which produces better results than a classical breakdown of shots could ever have done.

One needs only to compare two stills which are composed in depth, one from a film of 1910, the other from a film by Welles or Wyler, and one will see just from looking at each still, detached from the film, that their functions are diametrically opposed. The 1910 framing more or less takes up the position of the absent fourth wall of a theatre stage or, out of doors anyway, of the best viewpoint of the action, whereas the sets, the camera angle, and the lighting in the second composition have to be looked at with different eyes. Over the surface of the screen, the director and the director of photography have managed to organize a dramatic chessboard from which no detail is excluded. The most obvious, if not the most original, examples of this are to be found in *The Little Foxes*, where the *mise-en-scène* has the precision of a blueprint (with Welles, the baroque overtones make analysis more complicated). The placing of objects in relation to the characters is such that their meaning *cannot* escape the spectator, a meaning which editing would have built up in a series of successive shots.

Take, for instance, a dramatic construction pivoted on three characters in Wyler's *The Best Years of Our Lives* (the scene where Dana Andrews and Teresa Wright break off their engagement). The sequence takes place in a bar. Fredric March has just persuaded his friend to break off with his daughter and urges him to go and telephone her immediately. Dana Andrews gets up and goes towards the call box which is by the door at the far end of the room. Fredric March puts his elbows on the piano in the foreground and pretends to be engrossed in the musical exercises of the disabled sergeant who is learning to play with the hooks he has instead of hands. The frame contains the keyboard in close shot, takes in Fredric March in close medium shot, includes the whole room, and leaves Dana Andrews quite visible, though small, right at the back in the call box. This shot is clearly governed by two points of dramatic interest and three characters. The action taking place in the foreground is of secondary importance, although interesting and unusual enough to demand our close attention, especially as it occupies a privileged position on the screen and a considerable amount of its surface. The real action, however, the one that at this point constitutes a decisive turning-point in the plot, is taking place almost secretly in a tiny rectangle at the back of the room, i.e. on the very left of the screen.

The link between these two dramatic zones is Fredric March, who is the only person, apart from the spectator, to know what is going on in the call box, and who, as is logical in such a situation, is also moved by the prowess of his disabled friend. From time to time, Fredric March turns his head slightly, and casts an anxious glance diagonally across the screen at Dana Andrews's gesticulations. The latter finally rings off and without looking round abruptly disappears into the street. If we reduce the real action to its elements, it consists basically of a telephone call made by Dana Andrews. The only thing which interests us at this moment is the telephone conversation. The only actor whose face we want to see in close-up is precisely the one whom we cannot distinguish clearly because he is so far away from the camera and behind the glass window of the call box. His words of course cannot be heard. The real drama is taking place in the distance in a kind of small aquarium which lets us see only the banal and ritual gestures of someone telephoning.

This idea of the call box at the back of the room which forces the spectator to imagine what is going on inside it, i.e. to share Fredric March's anxiety, was in itself an excellent brainwave on the part of the director. But Wyler knew very well that alone it would destroy the spatial and temporal equilibrium of the shot. It had to be both counterbalanced and reinforced. Whence the idea of a diverting action *in the foreground,* secondary in itself, but whose visual prominence would be in inverse proportion to its dramatic importance. Although a secondary action, it is not an insignificant one; the spectator is also concerned about what will happen to the disabled sergeant and so is interested in what he is doing. And anyway it is certainly not every day that one sees someone play the piano with hooks! Held in suspense and unable really to see at what point the hero finishes telephoning, the spectator is also obliged to divide his attention between the hooks and the call box. In this way, Wyler kills two birds with one stone: the diversion of the piano first of all allows him to hold for as long as necessary a shot which alone would have been interminable and inevitably monotonous, but it is above all the introduction of this pivot of subsidiary action which gives the image its dramatic organization and quite literally its very construction. The real action is overlaid with the action of the *mise-en-scène* itself, which consists of dividing the attention of the spectator against his will, of guiding it in the right direction, and thus of making him participate in his own right in the drama created by the director.

To be more precise, I should point out that this scene is cut twice by a close shot of Fredric March looking at the call box. No doubt Wyler was afraid that the spectator would be too fascinated by the piano exercises and might gradually lose interest in the main action, i.e. the dramatic interplay between Fredric March and Dana Andrews. The editing probably showed that the two interpolated shots were necessary to recharge the flagging attention of the audience. Such foresight is incidentally very characteristic of Wyler's technique. Orson Welles would have managed to make the call box stand out by its very remoteness and would have held the shot for as long as necessary. For Orson Welles, composition in depth is an aesthetic end in itself; for Wyler, it remains subordinate to the dramatic needs of the *mise-en-scène* and especially the clarity of the narrative. The two interpolated shots have the same effect as bold type or a heavily penciled line.

Wyler especially likes to construct his *mise-en-scène* around the tension created in a shot by the simultaneity of two actions of disparate importance. This can be clearly seen in the still taken from the final sequence of the film.

The characters grouped on the right, in the middle ground, seem to form the main dramatic point of interest, as everyone has gathered in this room to attend the wedding of the disabled sergeant. In fact, since this action is a foregone conclusion and, in a sense, already over, the spectator's interest is focused on Teresa Wright (in white in the background) and Dana Andrews (on the left in the foreground), who are meeting for the first time since they broke off their engagement. Throughout the whole sequence of the wedding, Wyler manipulates his actors with consummate skill so as gradually to bring to the fore the two protagonists, who, the spectator is sure, are continually thinking of each other. [In a still of an intermediate stage of this scene, one sees that] the two centers of interest, Dana Andrews and Teresa Wright, have not yet come together, but the natural though carefully calculated movements of the other actors throw their relationship into clear relief. Teresa Wright's white dress, standing out almost in the center of the frame, makes a kind of dramatic fissure, so that if one were to cut the image in half at the point where the walls meet the action would also be bisected into its two elements. The two lovers are visually and logically thrust into the left part of the frame.

The importance of the direction in which people look should also be noticed in this still. The look always forms the skeleton of Wyler's *mise-en-scène*. As well as the actual look of the characters, Wyler also excels at getting across to us the virtual look of the camera, with which our own eyes identify themselves. Jean Mitry has drawn attention to the low angle shot in *Jezebel* which places the lens right in line with Bette Davis's gaze as she sees the walking-stick that Henry Fonda has in his hand and intends to use. In this way we can follow the gaze of the characters better than if the camera, as in an ordinary shooting script, showed us the stick from above as if through Bette Davis's own eyes.

There is a variant of the same principles in *The Little Foxes*: in order to make us understand the thoughts of the character who notices the small steel box which used to contain some stolen shares (their absence is going to reveal his theft), Wyler puts the object in the foreground, this time with the camera at the same height as the man, but still symmetrically placed in relation to the actor and to what he is looking at. Our gaze does not meet that of the actor directly through the regarded object, but, as through the interplay of a mirror, the angle of incidence of our own gaze on the box is somehow equivalent to the angle of reflection which leads us to the eyes of the actor. In every case, Wyler guides our mental outlook by means of the strict laws of an invisible dramatic perspective.

The spectator has only to follow the gaze of the characters like a pointing finger and he will have an exact understanding of all the intentions of the director. If these could be made tangible on the image by a pencil line, we would see, as clearly as we see the ghost of a magnet in iron filings, the dramatic forces which are crossing the screen. All Wyler's preparatory work consists of simplifying the mechanics of *mise-en-scène* as far as possible by making it as efficient and as clear as he can. In *The Best Years of Our Lives,* he attains an almost abstract purity. Every point of dramatic articulation is so sensitive that a shift of a few degrees in the angle of somebody's gaze is not only quite obvious to the most obtuse spectator, but is also capable, through a kind of leverage, of turning a whole scene upside-down.

The modern director, in using the sequence-shot with composition in depth, is not rejecting editing—how could he do so without reverting to a kind of rudimentary gibberish? He is integrating it into his visual style. The narrative of Welles and Wyler is no less explicit than that of John Ford, but it has the advantage of not having to forfeit the special effects that can be obtained from the unity of the image in time and space. It matters a great deal (at least in a work that has some style) whether an event is analyzed fragment by fragment or shown in its physical unity. It would of course be absurd to deny the marked progress in film language that has been brought about by the use of editing, but it has been gained at the expense of other qualities that are no less specifically cinematic.

This is why composition in depth is not just another cameraman's device like the use of filters or of a certain type of lighting; it is a vital contribution to direction: a dialectical advance in the history of film language.

And this advance is not merely a formal one. Composition in depth, well used, is not just a more economic, subtle, and simple way of heightening an event; it affects not only the structure of film language but also the intellectual relationship between the spectator and the image, thus actually modifying the meaning of the film.

It would be beyond the scope of this article to analyze the psychological repercussions of this relationship, let alone its aesthetic consequences, but perhaps it will suffice to make the following general remarks:

1. Composition in depth means that the spectator's relationship with the image is nearer to that which he has with reality. It is then true to say that quite independently of the actual content of the image its structure is more realistic.

2. Consequently, composition in depth demands a more active mental attitude on the part of the spectator and even a positive contribution to the direction. Whereas with analytic editing he has only to follow his guide and let his attention focus on whatever the director has chosen for him to see, a certain minimum of personal choice is required here. The fact that the image has a meaning depends partly on his attention and his will.

3. From the two preceding propositions, which are of a psychological

nature, there follows a third one which might be defined as metaphysical.

By analyzing reality, the very nature of editing assumes the dramatic event to have a unity of meaning. Another analytical process might be possible, but the result would be a different film. In short, the nature and essence of editing is such that it stands in the way of the expression of ambiguity. And it was precisely this that was proved by Kuleshov's *reductio ad absurdum*: each time, an exact meaning was given to the face whose ambiguity made possible these three alternately exclusive interpretations.

Composition in depth, on the other hand, brings ambiguity back into the structure of the image; this is not automatic (Wyler's films are hardly ambiguous at all), but it is certainly a possibility. That is why it is no exaggeration to say that *Citizen Kane* is conceived entirely in terms of composition in depth. One's uncertainty about the spiritual key or interpretation of the film hangs on the very composition of the image.

It is not that Welles purposely refrains from using expressionist editing techniques. In fact, their episodic use, in between sequence-shots with composition in depth, gives them new meaning. Editing had once been the very stuff of cinema, the tissue of a scenario. In *Citizen Kane*, a series of superimpositions stands in contrast to the continuity of a scene taken in a single shot; it is a different, explicitly abstract register of the narrative. Accelerated editing used to distort time and space; Welles's editing, far from attempting to deceive us, offers us a temporal résumé—the equivalent, for example, of the French imperfect tense or the English frequentative. And so "quick editing," "editing by attraction," and the superimpositions which the sound cinema had not resorted to for ten years, found a possible use in conjunction with the temporal realism of cinema without editing. I have dwelt on the case of Orson Welles because the date of his appearance in the cinematic firmament marks the beginning of a new period, and also because his case is the most spectacular and significant in its very excesses. But *Citizen Kane* fits into a general movement, into a vast geological shift of strata which, in one way and another, confirms this revolution in expression.

Confirmation along different lines can be found in the Italian cinema. In Rossellini's *Paisan* and *Germania, Anno Zero* and De Sica's *Bicycle Thieves*, Italian neo-realism stands in contrast to previous forms of cinematic realism by its elimination of any expressionism and especially by the total absence of effects obtained by editing. Just as in Welles's work (and despite their very different styles), neo-realism tends to give a film the feeling of the ambiguity of reality. The way Rossellini looks at the child's face in *Germania, Anno Zero* is at opposite poles to Kuleshov's attitude to the close-up of Moszhukhin; he wants to preserve its mystery. One should not be put on the wrong track by the fact that the evolution of neo-realism does not at first sight seem, as in America, to consist of some revolution in the technique of breaking down shots in a shooting script. There are various means of achieving the same end. Rossellini's and De Sica's are not so very spectacular, but they too aim at eliminating editing and transferring on to the screen the true continuity of reality. It is Zavattini's dream simply to film ninety consecutive minutes in the life of a man to whom nothing important happens! Luchino Visconti, the "aesthete" of the neo-realists, revealed just as clearly as Welles the fundamental aim of his art in *La Terra Trema*, a film that is almost entirely composed of sequence-shots where the desire to take in the totality of an event can be seen in the composition in depth and the endless panning shots.

But we could not possibly examine all the films which have contributed to this linguistic evolution since 1940. It is time to draw some conclusions from what I have said. The last ten years have, I think, shown a marked progress in the field of cinematic expression. I intentionally neglected, from 1930 on, the tendency of the silent cinema that was particularly evident in Erich von Stroheim, F. W. Murnau, R. Flaherty, and Dreyer; but I do not think it died out with the coming of sound. On the contrary, I am sure it was the most fertile aspect of the so-called silent cinema, and the only one which, precisely because the essence of its aesthetic conception was not bound up with editing, called for the realism of sound as its natural extension. But it is true that the sound cinema from 1930 to 1940 owes almost nothing to it, apart from the notable and, in retrospect, prophetic exception of Jean Renoir, the only director who consistently attempted in his films up to *La Règle du Jeu* to rise above facile editing effects and seize the secret of a cinematic style which was capable of expressing everything without fragmenting the world, of revealing the hidden meaning of human beings and their environment without destroying their natural unity.

However, it would be out of the question to throw discredit on the cinema of the thirties (in any case, this would not stand up to the evidence of several masterpieces). My purpose is simply to suggest a notion of dialectical progress, the turning-point of which took place in the forties. It is true that the arrival of sound proved fatal to a certain aesthetic approach to film language, but this was an approach that was leading it farthest away from its vocation for realism. The sound cinema did however retain the essential function of editing: discontinuous description and dramatic analysis of an event. It rejected the metaphor and the symbol, and aimed instead at an illusion of objective representation. Expressionist editing almost completely disappeared, but the relative realism of that narrative style which was the general rule in 1937 contained a congenital limitation of which we could not at that time have been aware, so perfectly appropriate to it were the subjects that were treated. This was true in the case of American comedy, which reached perfection within the framework of a narrative where temporal realism played no part. Essentially logical, like vaudeville and punning, perfectly conventional in its moral and sociological content, American comedy had nothing to gain from descriptive and linear precision or from the rhythmic resources of the classical narrative style.

It is above all in the direction taken by Stroheim and Murnau, almost entirely neglected in the thirties, that the cinema has been veering more or less consciously for the last ten years. But directors are not confining themselves to prolonging it, they are deriving from it the secret of a realistic regeneration of the narrative. This narrative is again becoming capable of reintegrating the temporal truth of things, the actual duration of an event which the classical narrative insidiously replaced with intellectual and abstract time. But far from eliminating the achievements of editing once and for all, modern film-makers are giving them a relativity and a meaning. It is only when related to an increased realism in the image that extra abstraction becomes possible. The stylistic repertory of a director such as Hitchcock for example stretches from the powers of the documentary image to superimpositions and extreme close-ups. But Hitchcock's close-ups are not the same as those of Cecil B. de Mille in *The Cheat*. They are just one stylistic device among others. In other words, in the silent era, the editing *evoked* what the director wanted to say, in 1938 the narrative *described,* and today one can say that the director *writes* directly in film. The image—its plastic structure and its organization within time—because it can now draw on greater realism, has more means at its disposal of inflecting and modifying reality from within. The film-maker is no longer simply the competitor of the painter or the playwright; he is at last the equal of the novelist.

From NEW WORDS

George Orwell

Everyone must have noticed the extraordinary powers that are latent in the film—the powers of distortion, of fantasy, in general of escaping the restrictions of the physical world. I suppose it is only from commercial necessity that the film has been used chiefly for silly imitations of stage plays, instead of concentrating as it ought on things that are beyond the stage. Properly used, the film is the one possible medium for conveying mental processes. A dream, for instance, as I said above, is totally indescribable in words, but it can quite well be represented on the screen. Years ago I saw a film of Douglas Fairbanks', part of which was a representation of a dream. Most of it, of course, was silly joking about the dream where you have no clothes on in public, but for a few minutes it really was like a dream, in a manner that would have been impossible in words, or even in a picture, or, I imagine, in music. I have seen the same kind of thing by flashes in other films. For instance in *Dr. Caligari*—a film, however, which was for the most part merely silly, the fantastic element being exploited for its own sake and not to convey any definite meaning. If one thinks of it, there is very little in the mind that could not *somehow* be represented by the strange distorting powers of the film. A millionaire with a private cinematograph, all the necessary props and a troupe of intelligent actors could, if he wished, make

FROM NEW WORDS From "New Words" in *The Collected Essays, Journalism and Letters of George Orwell,* Volume 2, copyright © 1968 by Sonia Brownell Orwell. Reprinted by permission of Harcourt Brace Jovanovich, Inc.

practically all of his inner life known. He could explain the real reasons of his actions instead of telling rationalized lies, point out the things that seemed to him beautiful, pathetic, funny, etc.—things that an ordinary man has to keep locked up because there are no words to express them. In general, he could make other people understand him. Of course, it is not desirable that any one man, short of a genius, should make a show of his inner life. What is wanted is to discover the now nameless feelings that men have *in common*. All the powerful motives which will not go into words and which are a cause of constant lying and misunderstanding, could be tracked down, given visible form, agreed upon, and named. I am sure that the film, with its almost limitless powers of representation, could accomplish this in the hands of the right investigators, though putting thoughts into visible shape would not always be easy—in fact, at first it might be as difficult as any other art.

From THE PARADE'S GONE BY

Kevin Brownlow

In answer to my questions about his photographic technique, von Sternberg offered to demonstrate. "Give me a camera and some lights, and I will show you," he said. With BBC producer Barrie Gavin, who was planning a program on von Sternberg, I arranged for a studio to be available the following Sunday.

Isleworth Studios, in a suburb of London, are generally shut on Sundays. This Sunday, however, especially for von Sternberg, they had been opened by the owner of the studios, Ralph Solomons.

Von Sternberg climbed out of the taxi and walked into the studio. "This will take five minutes," he said, "if everything is ready."

Everything was not ready. A full staff was not available, and several people were doubling up. A two-man television camera crew shadowed von Sternberg's every move.

"Where is the floor light?" Von Sternberg's customarily soft voice now had a commanding ring about it.

The electrician brought up a heavy lamp, known as a 5k. Without removing his coat or scarf, von Sternberg set to work. He pushed the lamp forward, until it stood a few feet from the girl who was acting as model. He asked the electrician to raise the lamp to its fullest extent. Then he produced a chair for the girl to lean against; it also marked her position.

He ordered the camera to be set up with a two-inch lens. The assistant did so, and von Sternberg saw him peering through the finder. "You don't mind me looking through it, do you?" von Sternberg asked. The assistant grinned sheepishly.

Von Sternberg removed his glasses and looked at the shot. He straightened up from the camera and appraised it with the naked eye.

"Would you take this bench away and move your light closer? Now get up there and put the back light on." The electrician clambered up the ladder to the lighting gantry.

"Not so fast, it is dangerous," said von Sternberg, with concern.

The light clicked, but did not come on. The second electrician fiddled with the junction box. No result.

"When I work I use a light bridge over my camera, so I don't have to reorganize my lighting each time," said von Sternberg, ignoring the delay.

"Does this apply to traveling shots as well?" I asked.

Von Sternberg was silent for some time. Then he said, "Well, you ask extraordinary questions. How could it apply to traveling shots?"

"If the light bridge moved, the light would remain constant with the camera."

"The trick is not to make the light constant." At last the lamp came on. "Now get me one of those little baby spots." A second backlight came on. "Take that off, will you? Just this one. Throw it down on the girl's hair, and make it hot—as hot as you can."

He altered the position of the girl's head and aimed the spotlight behind her at the wall, then gazed at the result for a few moments.

"I want a black gauze," he announced.

"What does he want the black gauze for?" asked the electrician from among the lights.

"Who said that?" demanded von Sternberg. There was a momentary silence.

"Er—me—up here."

"You want to know what I want it for?"

"Which lamp—"

"Huh?"

"Which lamp?"

"Get a gauze down here. You don't want to know what I want it for." Von Sternberg returned to the camera and looked through the viewfinder.

"You have moved," he said to the girl. He went up to alter her position and decided she should remove her jacket. He was not pleased with her black sweater.

The gauze was put over the 5k, and a wooden board, known as a flag, placed in front.

"That's it. Now raise it up. See if you can cut across her forehead. Move that clock on the mantelpiece, will you? More. Hold it. Take this light and turn it, easy—easy—whoa!"

He looked up at the flag. "This thing is wrong. Have you got such a thing as what we call a cookalourus?"

The English technicians knew it as an "ulcer," and one was soon produced.

"That's better. Take the flag off and put that on. That light is not on her head. That light is on her shoulders. Put it up on her head. Put it on *her!*"

Suddenly a transformation took place. The backlight moved, and an authentic von Sternberg close-up began to appear.

"My God," whispered the electrician, "look at that! He's making a Dietrich out of her. She looks really *beautiful!*"

Von Sternberg looked at his shot through the viewfinder, then straightened up. "This damn thing isn't right," he muttered. The television camera, constantly aimed at his face, began to irritate him. "I wish you'd stop. I mean you've taken enough, haven't you?" The cameraman hurriedly switched off and backed away. Von Sternberg went up to the model and put his hand gently on her chin. He brought the face down fractionally.

"Now, if you want you can shoot this, but this is not the right unit here," he said, including the cookalourus. "You need one that hasn't got such straight lines, one that is made of cellulose. A regulation broken line. You haven't got one here." He turned back to the girl. "Now move from right to left. Your face should be reasonably pleasant—reasonably. Just relax and move. All right, it's not perfect but take it."

The assistant switched on the camera. The 5k, directly above the girl, produced a very short nose shadow and a soft modeling to the cheekbones. The cookalourus protected the forehead; the backlight lit up the hair.

"As you see," explained von Sternberg, "the forehead must be slightly shaded. The hot light should be on the chin. The background should be broken; you see what the spotlight did for the background. She should not wear a black dress. I would take a spray gun and spray that with aluminum. It is not photographic. She should wear a light dress. But in general, there's your scene. Now let's go home, huh?"

Von Sternberg signed a few more copies of his book, said good-bye to everyone, and was driven back to his hotel. The studio staff began to relax. They came to the conclusion that this use of two heavy lamps and one small spotlight was "the simplicity of genius." The electrician was particularly interested. For the record, I asked his name.

"Ralph Solomons," he said—the man who owned the studio. . . .

MONTAGE, MON BEAU SOUCI

Jean-Luc Godard

. . . We'll save it in editing . . . Though true of James Cruze, Griffith, Stroheim, this maxim was hardly any longer true of Murnau, Chaplin, and becomes irretrievably untrue with sound film. Why? Because in a film such as *October* (and still more so with *Que Viva Mexico*) editing is above all the supreme touch of direction. The two cannot be separated without rhythm and melody. *Elena,* just as *Mr. Arkadin,* is a model of editing because each in its class is a model of directing . . .

"We will save it all in editing," is, then, a typical producer's statement. The most that good editing will bring to a film otherwise devoid of all interest is precisely, first, the impression of having been directed. It will restore to the lifelike the ephemeral grace which the snob and amateur disregard; or it will transform chance into destiny. Is there greater praise than that the public rightly confuses editing with cutting?

If to direct is a glance, to edit is a beating of the heart. To anticipate is the characteristic of both. But what one seeks to foresee in space, the other seeks in time. Suppose you see an attractive girl in the street. You hesitate to follow her. A quarter of a second. How to convey this hesitation? The question: "How to approach her?" will be answered for you by directing. But in order to make explicit this other question, "Am I going to love her?" you will have to grant importance to the quarter of a second during which both arise. It is possible, then, that it is no longer up to the direction of an idea, or its abrupt bursting forth in the course of narration, but to the editing. When? Each time that the *situation* calls for it; be it in the middle of a scene, when a shock effect demands an arabesque; or be it that the basic continuity of the film requires, as the scene changes, superimposing the description of a character upon that of the plot. The above exemplifies the fact that to speak of directing is automatically to speak, yet and again, of editing. When the effects of editing carry it off in effectiveness over the effects of the direction, the beauty of the latter will find itself redoubled; its charm will consist in disclosing the unforeseen by an operation analogous to that in mathematics which makes an unknown entity evident.

Those who yield to the temptations of editing also yield to the appeal of the short scene. How? By making the glance the major part of his game. To splice on a look, this is practically the definition of editing, its supreme ambition at the same time as its subjugation to directing. It is in fact to bring

MONTAGE, MON BEAU SOUCI From *Jean-Luc Godard,* edited by Toby Mussman, published by E. P. Dutton & Co., Inc. Originally published in *Cahiers du Cinema,* December 1956; English translation by Nell Cox originally published in *Film Culture,* Summer 1961. Reprinted by permission.

out the soul under the mind, the passion behind the scheme, to make the heart prevail over intelligence through destroying the notion of space in favor of that of time. The renowned sequence of the cymbals in the new version of *The Man Who Knew Too Much* is the best proof of it. To know how long one can make a scene last is already a part of the problems of shooting. A very cleverly directed film gives the impression of having disposed entirely of directing. Cinematographically speaking, on the same subject, the battle in *Alexander Nevsky* yields none of it to *La Croisière du Navigator*. On the whole to give the impression of duration through movement, of a close-up through long shot would be one of the aims of directing and the reverse one of the aims of editing. One improvises, one invents in front of the moviola just as one does on the set. Cutting a movement of the camera in quarters can reveal itself more effective than keeping it as it has been filmed. An exchange of glances, to take the same example as above, can only be expressed with enough pungency, when necessary, through clever editing. When in Balzac's *Une Ténébreuse Affaire* Peyrade and Corentin break open the door to the Saint-Cygne living room, their first notice is of Laurence: "We'll have you, my little one"—"You won't know a thing." The proud young woman and the spies of Fouché guessed at first glance that this was their most deadly enemy. This extraordinary exchange of looks, a simple reversed shot, by its very restraint, is more powerfully expressive than any premeditated zoom or pan. What it is trying to convey is how long the struggle will last—then, on what grounds it will unfold. Editing, therefore, at the same time that it denies, announces and prepares the way for directing; they are interdependent on each other. To direct is to plot, and one speaks of a plot as well- or poorly-knit.

This is why to say that a director owes it to himself to supervise closely the editing of his film is the equivalent of saying the editor owes it to himself to forsake the odor of glue and film for the heat of spotlights. Wandering on the set he will see exactly where the interest of a scene lies, what the strong or weak moments of it are, what the motives for changing scenes are and therefore he won't be tempted to cut them solely on the basis of harmonizing movement, the ABC of editing, I admit, but on the strict condition that it is not used in too mechanical a fashion—as for example Marguerite Renoir, who often gives the impression of cutting a scene at the moment when it was going to become interesting. And on the way, he will make the first steps from editor to filmmaker.

WHAT IS "FILM MAKING"?

Ingmar Bergman

"Film-making" is for me a necessity of nature, a need comparable to hunger and thirst. For some, self-expression involves writing books, climbing mountains, beating one's children or dancing the samba. In my case, I express myself in making films.

In *The Blood of a Poet,* the great Jean Cocteau shows us his alter ego stumbling down the corridors of a nightmare hotel and gives us a glimpse, behind each one of the doors, of one of the factors of which he is composed and which form his ego.

Without attempting here to equate my personality with Cocteau's, I thought I would take you on a guided tour of my internal studios where, invisibly, my films take form. This visit, I am afraid, will disappoint you; the equipment is always in disorder because the owner is too absorbed in his affairs to have time to straighten it up. Furthermore, the lighting is rather bad in certain spots, and on the door of certain rooms, you will find the word "Private" written in large letters. Finally, the guide himself is not always sure of what is worth the trouble of showing.

Whatever the case may be, we will open a few doors a crack. I won't guarantee that you will find precisely the answer to the questions you are wondering about, but perhaps, in spite of everything, you will be able to put together a few pieces of the complicated puzzle that the forming of a film represents.

If we consider the most fundamental element of the cinematographic art, the perforated film, we note that it is composed of a number of small, rectangular images—fifty-two per meter—each of which is separated from the other by a thick, black line. Looking more closely, we discover that these tiny rectangles, which at first glance seem to contain exactly the same picture, differ from each other by an almost imperceptible modification of this picture. And when the feeding mechanism of the projector causes the images in question to succeed each other on the screen so that each one is seen only for a twentieth of a second, we have the illusion of movement.

Between each of these small rectangles the shutter closes and plunges us into total darkness, only to return us to full light with the next rectangle. When I was ten years old and working with my first apparatus, a shaky lantern made of sheet metal—with its chimney, its gas lamp and its perpetual films which repeated themselves indefinitely—I used to find the above-mentioned phenomenon exciting and full of mystery. Even today, I feel myself quiver as I did when I was a child when I think of the fact that, in reality, I

WHAT IS "FILM MAKING"? From *Film Makers on Film Making* edited by Harry M. Geduld. Translated by Royal Brown. Copyright © 1967 by Indiana University Press. Reprinted by permission.

am creating illusion; for the cinema would not exist but for an imperfection of the human eye, namely its inability to perceive separately a series of images which follow each other rapidly and which are essentially identical.

I have calculated that if I see a film that lasts an hour, I am in fact plunged for twenty minutes in total darkness. In making a film, therefore, I am making myself guilty of a fraud; I am using a device designed to take advantage of a physical imperfection of man, a device by means of which I can transport my audience from a given feeling to the feeling that is diametrically opposed to it, as if each spectator were on a pendulum; I can make an audience laugh, scream with terror, smile, believe in legends, become indignant, take offense, become enthusiastic, lower itself or yawn from boredom. I am, then, either a deceiver or—when the audience is aware of the fraud—an illusionist. I am able to mystify, and I have at my disposal the most precious and the most astounding magical device that has ever, since history began, been put into the hands of a juggler.

There is in all this, or at least there should be, the source of an insoluble moral conflict for all those who create films or work on them.

As for our commercial partners, this is not the place to bring out the mistakes they have made from year to year, but it would certainly be worthwhile someday for a scientist to discover some unit of weight or measure which one could use to "calculate" the quantity of natural gifts, initiatives, genius and creative forces that the film industry has ground through its formidable mills. Obviously, anyone entering into the game must accept the rules in advance, and there is no reason why work in the cinematographic branch should be more respected than anywhere else. The difference is due to the fact that, in our specialty, brutality is manifested more overtly, but this is actually rather an advantage.

Loss of balance offers consequences that are even more grave for the film-maker than for a tightrope walker or an acrobat who performs his tricks beneath a circus tent and without a net. For the film-maker as well as for the equilibrist, the danger is of the same order: falling and being killed. No doubt you think I am exaggerating; making a film isn't as dangerous as all that! I maintain my point, however; the risk is the same. Even if, as I mentioned, one is a bit of a magician, no one can mystify the producers, the bank directors, the movie-theatre owners or the critics when the public abstains from going to see a film and from paying out the obol from which producers, bank directors, movie-theatre owners, critics and magicians must draw their subsistence!

I can give you as an example a very recent experience, the memory of which still makes me shudder—an experience in which I myself risked losing my balance. A singularly bold producer invested money in one of my films which, after a year of intense activity, appeared under the title of *The Naked Night* (*Gycklarnas afton*). The reviews were, in general, destructive, the public stayed away, the producer added up his losses, and I had to wait several years before trying again.

If I make two or three more films which fail financially, the producer will quite justifiably consider it a good idea not to bet on my talents.

At that point, I will become, suddenly, a suspect individual, a squanderer, and I will be able to reflect at my leisure on the usefulness of my artistic gifts, for the magician will be deprived of his apparatus.

When I was younger, I didn't have these fears. Work for me was an exciting game and, whether the results succeeded or failed, I was delighted with my work like a child with his castles of sand or clay. The equilibrist was dancing on his rope, oblivious and therefore unconcerned about the abyss beneath him and the hardness of the ground of the circus-ring.

The game has changed into a bitter combat. The walk on the rope is now performed in full awareness of the danger, and the two points where the rope is attached are now called "fear" and "incertitude." Each work to be materialized mobilizes all of the resources of one's energy. The act of creation has become, under the effect of causes that are as much interior as they are exterior and economic, an exacting duty. Failure, criticism, coldness on the part of the public today cause more sensitive wounds. These wounds take longer to heal and their scars are deeper and more lasting.

Before undertaking a work or after having begun it, Jean Anouilh has the habit of playing a little mental game in order to exorcise his fear. He says to himself, "My father is a tailor. He intimately enjoys creating with his hands, and the result is a beautiful pair of pants or an elegant overcoat. This is the joy and the satisfaction of the artisan, the pride of a man who knows his profession."

This is the same practice I follow. I recognize the game, I play it often and I succeed in duping myself—and a few others—even if this game is in fact nothing but a rather poor sedative: "My films are fine pieces of work, I am enthusiastic, conscientious and extremely attentive of details. I create for my contemporaries and not for eternity; my pride is the pride of an artisan."

I know however that, if I speak this way, it is in order to deceive myself, and an irrepressible anxiety cries out to me, "What have you done that can last? Is there in any of your movies a single foot of film worthy of being passed on to posterity, a single line of dialogue, a single situation which is really and indisputably true?"

And to this question I am forced to answer—perhaps still under the effect of a disloyalty which is ineradicable even in the most sincere people—"I don't know, I hope so."

You must excuse me for having described at such length and with so much commentary the dilemma which those who create films are forced to confront. I wanted to try to explain to you why so many of those who are devoted to the realization of cinematographic works give in to a temptation which cannot really be expressed and which is invisible; why we are afraid; why we sometimes lose our enthusiasm for the works we are doing; why we become fools and allow ourselves to be annihilated by colorless and vile compromises.

I would still, however, like to dwell a bit longer on one of the aspects of the problem, the aspect that is the most important and difficult to comprehend—the public.

The creator of films is involved in a means of expression which concerns not only himself but also millions of other people, and more often than not he feels the same desire as other artists: "I want to succeed today. I want celebrity now. I want to please, to delight, to move people immediately."

Midway between this desire and its realization is found the public, who demands but one thing of the film: "I've paid, I want to be distracted, swept off my feet, involved; I want to forget my troubles, my family, my work, I want to get away from myself. Here I am, seated in the darkness, and, like a woman about to give birth, I want deliverance."

The film-maker who is aware of these demands and who lives on the money of the public is placed in a situation which is difficult and which creates obligations for him. In making his film, he must always take the reaction of the public into account. On my part, personally, I am forever asking myself this question: "Can I express myself more simply, more purely, more briefly? Will everybody understand what I want to say now? Will the simplest mind be able to follow the course of these events? And, even more importantly, this question: up to what point do I have the right to admit compromise and where do my obligations to myself begin?"

Any experimentation necessarily involves a great risk, for it always keeps the public at a distance, and keeping the public at a distance can lead to sterility and to isolation in an ivory tower.

It would be quite desirable, then, for producers and other technical directors of the cinema to put laboratories at the disposition of the creators. But this is scarcely the case today. The producers have confidence only in the engineers and stupidly imagine that the salvation of the film industry depends on inventions and technical complications.

Nothing is easier than frightening a spectator. One can literally terrify him, for most people have in some part of their bearing a fear that is all ready to blossom. It is much more difficult to make people laugh, and to *make them laugh* in the right way. It is easy to put a spectator in a state worse than the one he was in when he entered the theater; it is difficult to put him in a better state; it is precisely this, however, that he desires each time he sits down in the darkness of a movie-theater. Now, how many times and by what means do we give him this satisfaction?

This is the way I reason; but at the same time I know with an absolute evidence that this reasoning is dangerous, since it involves the risk of condemning all failures, of confusing the ideal with pride, and of considering as absolute the frontiers that the public and the critics establish, whereas you neither recognize these frontiers nor consider them your own, since your personality is perpetually in the process of becoming. On the one hand, I am tempted to adapt myself and to make myself what the public wants me to be; but on the other hand, I feel that this would be the end of everything, and that this would imply a total indifference on my part. Thus, I am delighted to have not been born with exactly as many brains as feelings, and it has never been written anywhere that a film-maker must be contented, happy, or satisfied. Who says you can't make noise, cross frontiers, battle against windmills, send robots to the moon, have visions, play with dynamite or tear pieces of flesh from one's self or others? Why not frighten film producers? It is their job to be afraid, and they are paid to have stomach ulcers!

But *"film-making"* is not always confronting problems, dilemmas, economic worries, responsibilities and fear. There are also games, dreams, secret memories.

Often it begins with an image: a face which is suddenly and strongly illuminated; a hand which rises; a square at dawn where a few old ladies are seated on a bench, separated from each other by sacks of apples. Or it may be a few words that are exchanged; two people who, suddenly, say something to each other in a completely personal tone of voice—their backs are perhaps turned from me, I can't even see their faces, and yet I am forced to listen to them, to wait for them to repeat the same words which are without any particular meaning but which are pregnant with a secret tension, with a tension of which I am not yet even fully conscious but which acts like a crafty potion. The illuminated face, the hand raised as if for an incantation, the old ladies at the square, the few banal words, all of these images come and attach themselves like silvery fish to my net, or more precisely, I myself am trapped in a net, the texture of which I am not aware of—fortunately!

Quite rapidly, even before the motive has been entirely designed in my mind, I submit the game of my imagination to the test of reality. I place, as if I'm playing a game, my sketch, which is still very rough and fragile, on an easel in order to judge it from the point of view of all the technical resources of the studios. This imaginary test of "viability" constitutes for the motive an effective ferruginous bath. Will it suffice? Will the motive keep its value when it is plunged into the daily, murderous routine of the studios, far from the shadows of sunrises, which are quite propitious for the games of the imagination?

A few of my films mature very quickly and are finished rapidly. These are the ones that meet the general expectations, like children that are still undisciplined but in good health and about whom one can predict immediately: "They are the ones who will support the family."

And then there are other films, films which come slowly, which take years, which refuse to be imprisoned in a formal or technical solution, and which, in general, refuse any concrete solution. They remain in a shadowy zone; if I want to find them, I have to follow them there and find a context, characters and situation. There, faces that are turned aside begin to speak, the streets are strange, a few, scattered people glance out through window-panes, an eye glistens at dusk or changes into a carbuncle and then bursts with a noise of breaking crystal. The square, this autumn morning, is a sea; the old ladies are transformed into ancient trees and the apples are children building cities of sand and stone near the foam of the waves.

The tension is there, ever present, and it appears again, either in the written word, or in the visions, or in the excess of energy, which bends like the arch of a bridge, ready to rise up by its own forces, by these forces which are the most important element, once the manuscript is finished, in setting in motion the immense wheel which the work required in shooting a film represents.

What is "shooting a film," then? If I were to ask this question of every-body, I would no doubt obtain quite different responses, but perhaps you would all agree on one point: shooting a film is doing what is necessary in order to transport the contents of the manuscript onto a piece of film. In doing so, you would be saying quite a lot and yet not nearly enough. For me, shooting a film represents days of inhumanly relentless work, stiffness of the joints, eyes full of dust, the odors of make-up, sweat and lamps, an indefinite series of tensions and relaxations, an uninterrupted battle between volition and duty, between vision and reality, conscience and laziness. I think of early risings, of nights without sleep, of a feeling keener than life, of a sort of fanaticism centered about a single task, by which I myself become, finally, an integral part of the film, a ridiculously tiny piece of apparatus whose only fault is requiring food and drink.

It sometimes happens—in the middle of all this excitement, when the studios are humming with a life and a labor that seem as if they should make the studios explode—that, suddenly, I find the idea for my next film. You would be wrong, however, if you thought that the activity of a film-maker supposes, at this moment, a kind of ecstatic vertigo, an uncontrolled excitement and a frightening disorganization. To shoot a film is to undertake the taming of a wild beast that is difficult to handle and very valuable; you need a clear mind, meticulousness, stiff and exact calculations. Add to this a temper that is always even and a patience that is not of this world.

Shooting a film is organizing an entire universe, but the essential elements are industry, money, construction, shooting, developing and copying, a schedule to follow but which is rarely followed, a battle plan minutely prepared where the irrational factors occur the most often. The star has too much black around her eyes—a thousand dollars to start the scene over again. One day, the water in the pipes has too much chlorine in it and the negatives got spotted—let's start again! Another day, death plays a dirty trick on you by taking away an actor—let's start with another—and there are several thousand more dollars swallowed up. It starts to thunder, the electric trans-former breaks down, and there we are, all made up and waiting in the pale light of the day, the hours flying by and money with them.

Idiotic examples, chosen at random. But they have to be idiotic, since they touch that great and sublime idiocy, the transforming of dreams into shadows, the chopping up of a tragedy into five hundred small pieces, the experimentation with each of these pieces, and finally the putting back to-gether of these pieces so that they constitute again a unity which will once more be the tragedy. It is the idiocy of fabricating a tapeworm 8,000 feet long which will nourish itself on the life and mind of the actors, producers, and creators. Shooting a film is all that, but it is still something else, and it is much worse.

Film-making is also plunging with one's deepest roots back into the world of childhood. Let's descend, if you wish, into this interior studio, located in the most intimate recesses of the life of the creator. Let's open up for a moment the most secret of these rooms so that we can look at a painting of Venice, an old window-blind, and a first apparatus for showing "action films."

At Upsala, my grandmother had a very old apartment. While I was there, I once slipped beneath the dining-room table; I was wearing an apron with a pocket in front of it; from my vantage point I listened to the voice of the sunbeams which entered through the immensely high windows. The rays moved continually; the bells of the cathedral chimed out; the rays moved, and their movement generated a sort of special sound. It was one of those days between winter and spring; I had the measles and I was five years old. In the neighboring apartment, somebody was playing the piano—it was always waltzes—and on the wall hung a big painting of Venice. While the rays of sun and the shadows were passing like waves across the painting, the water of the canal began to flow, the pigeons flew up from the pavement of the square, people spoke to each other noiselessly, making movements with their hands and heads. The sound of the bells wasn't coming from the cathedral but rather from the painting, as were the strains from the piano. There was something very strange about this painting of Venice. Almost as strange as the fact that the sunbeams in my grandmother's living-room were not silent but had a sound. Perhaps it was all those bells—or perhaps the enormous pieces of furniture which were conversing uninterruptedly.

I seem to remember, however, an experience even more distant than the one of the year I had measles: the perception—impossible to date—of the movement of a window-blind.

It was a black window-blind of the most modern variety, which I could see, in my nursery, at dawn or at dusk, when everything becomes living and a bit frightening, when even toys transform into things that are either hostile or simply indifferent and curious. At that moment the world would no longer be the everyday world with my mother present, but a vertiginous and silent solitude. It wasn't that the blind moved; no shadow at all appeared on it. The forms were on the surface itself; they were neither little men, nor animals, nor heads, nor faces, but *things for which no name exists!* In the darkness, which was interrupted here and there by faint rays of light, these forms freed themselves from the blind and moved toward the green folding-screen or toward the bureau, with its pitcher of water. They were pitiless, impassive and terrifying; they disappeared only after it became completely dark or light, or when I fell asleep.

Anyone who, like myself, was born in the family of a pastor, learns at an early age to look behind the scenes in life and death. Whenever Father has a burial, a marriage, a baptism, a mediation, he writes a sermon. You make an early acquaintance with the devil and, like all children, you need to give him a concrete form. Here is where the magic lantern comes in, a little sheet-metal box with a gas lamp (I can still smell the odor of the heated metal) and which projected colored pictures. Among others, there was Little Red

Ridinghood and the wolf. The wolf was the devil, a devil without horns but with a tail and vivid red mouth, a curiously palpable and yet elusive devil, the emissary of evil and persecution on the flowered wallpaper of the nursery.

The first film I ever owned was about ten feet long and brown. It pictured a young girl asleep in a prairie; she woke up, stretched, arose and, with outstretched arms, disappeared at the right side of the picture. That was all. Drawn on the box the film was kept in was a glowing picture with the words, "Frau Holle." Nobody around me knew who Frau Holle was, but that didn't matter; the film was quite successful, and we showed it every evening until it got torn so badly we couldn't repair it.

This shaky bit of cinema was my first sorcerer's bag, and, in fact, it was pretty strange. It was a mechanical plaything; the people and things never changed, and I have often wondered what could have fascinated me so much and what, even today, still fascinates me in exactly the same way. This thought comes to me sometimes in the studio, or in the semidarkness of the editing room, while I am holding the tiny picture before my eyes and while the film is passing through my hands; or else during that fantastic childbirth that takes place during the recomposition as the finished film slowly finds its own face. I can't help thinking that I am working with an instrument so refined that with it, it would be possible for us to illuminate the human soul with an infinitely more vivid light, to unmask it even more brutally and to annex to our field of knowledge new domains of reality. Perhaps we would even discover a crack that would allow us to penetrate into the *chiaroscuro* of surreality, to tell tales in a new and overwhelming manner. At the risk of affirming once more something I cannot prove, let me say that, the way I see it, we film-makers utilize only a minute part of a frightening power—we are moving only the little finger of a giant, a giant who is far from not being dangerous.

But it is equally possible that I am wrong. It might be that the cinema has attained the high point of its evolution, that this instrument, by its very nature, can no longer conquer new territory, that we are stuck with our noses to the wall, since the road ends in a dead end. Many people are of this opinion, and it is true that we are treading water in a marsh, our noses just rising above the surface of the water, and paralyzed by economic problems, conventions, stupidity, fear, incertitude and disorder.

I am asked sometimes what I am trying to attain in my films, what my *goal* is. The question is difficult and dangerous, and I usually answer it by lying or hedging: "I am trying to tell the truth about the condition of men, the truth as I see it." This answer always satisfies people, and I often wonder how it happens that nobody notices my bluff, because the true response should be, "I feel an incoercible need to express through film that which, in a completely subjective way, takes form some place in my consciousness. This being the case, I have no other goal but myself, my daily bread, the amusement and respect of the public, a kind of truth that I feel precisely at that moment. And if I try to sum up my second answer, the formula I end up with is not terribly exciting: 'An activity without much meaning.' "

I am not saying that this conclusion doesn't distress me inordinately. I am in the same situation as most artists of my generation; the activity of each one of us doesn't have much meaning. Art for art's sake. My personal truth, or three-quarters of a truth, or no truth at all, except that it has a value for me.

I realize that this way of looking at things is quite unpopular, particularly today. Let me hasten, then, to form the question in a different way: "What would be your goal in making your films?"

The story is told that, a long time ago, the cathedral of Chartres was struck by lightning and burned from top to bottom. It is said that thousands of people rushed there from the four corners of the world, people of all conditions; they crossed Europe like lemmings in migration; together, they began to rebuild the cathedral upon its old foundations. They stayed there until the immense edifice was completed, all of them, architects, workers, artists, jugglers, nobles, priests and the bourgeoisie, but their names were unknown, and, even today, nobody knows the names of those who built the cathedral of Chartres.

Without letting that give you any preconceived ideas about my beliefs or doubts—which, furthermore, have nothing to do with what we are discussing here—I think that any art loses its essential potency the moment it becomes separated from the "cult." It has cut the umbilical cord and it lives its own separate life, a life that is astonishingly sterile, dim, and degenerate. Creative collectivity, humble anonymity are forgotten and buried relics, deprived of any value. Little wounds of the ego and moral colics are examined under a microscope *sub specie aeternitatis*. The fear of the dark which characterizes subjectivism and scrupulous consciences has become quite stylish, and ultimately we are all running around in a big enclosure where we argue with one another about our solitude without listening to each other or even noticing that we are pushing ourselves mutually to the point of dying of suffocation from all this. It is in such a way that individualists look each other in the eye, deny the existence of those they see and invoke omnipotent obscurity without ever having once felt the saving force of the joys of community. We are so poisoned by our own vicious circles, so closed in by our own anguish that we are becoming incapable of distinguishing true from false, the ideality of gangsters and sincere unaffectedness.

To the question concerning the goal of my films, I could therefore answer: "I want to be one of the artists of the cathedral that stands above the plains. I want to occupy myself making from stone a dragon's head, an angel or a devil, or perhaps a saint, it doesn't really matter; I feel the same enjoyment in each case. Whether I am a believer or an unbeliever, a Christian or a pagan, I am working along with everybody else to construct a cathedral, because I am an artist and an artisan, and because I have learned to extract faces, limbs, and bodies from stone. I never have to worry about the judgment of posterity or of my contemporaries; my first and last names are engraved nowhere, and they will disappear with me. But a small part of my self will survive in the anonymous and triumphant totality. A dragon or a devil, or perhaps a saint, what does it matter!"

FEDERICO FELLINI: An Interview

Gideon Bachmann

BACHMANN: I do not want to talk to you about one or another specific film, but rather more generally—about your attitudes toward filmmaking, your reasons for making certain films, and your philosophical and sociological approach to what you use as film material. For example, many critics have said that there is a deep symbolism in your work, that there are recurring motifs in all your films. Like the image of the piazza at night with a fountain, of the seashore, and others. Is there a conscious intention on your part in repeating these images?

FELLINI: It is not intentional. In choosing a location, I do not choose it for its symbolic content. Things happen. If they happen well, they convey my meaning. Concerning the specific examples you mention, I'd like to say that all my films to date are concerned with people looking for themselves. Night and the loneliness of empty streets, as shown in the shots of piazzas you mention, is perhaps the best atmosphere in which I see these people. Also, it is quite possible that the associations which make me choose these locations are based on autobiographical experiences, for I cannot remove myself from the content of my films. Possibly what is in my mind when I shoot these scenes is the memory of my first impression of Rome—when I had left my hometown of Rimini and was in Rome alone. I was sixteen; I had no job, no idea of what I wanted to do. Often I was out of work, often I didn't have the money to stay in a hotel or eat properly. Or I would work at night. In any case, it is quite possible that the image of the town at night, empty and lonely, has remained in my soul from those days.

BACHMANN: Did you intend to go into films when you first came to Rome?

FELLINI: No, I didn't really know what I wanted to do. Still, my coming to Rome did have something to do with films: I had seen so many American films in which newspapermen were glamorous figures—I don't remember the titles, that was 25 years ago—but I was so impressed with the lives of newspapermen, that I decided to become one too. I liked the coats they wore and the way they wore their hats on the back of their heads. Unfortunately, the job I found was very different from my dream—I became a cub reporter who was sent by the editor to hospitals and to the police to get the obvious news. Later I began to write for the radio—sketches, mostly. After that I was tempted by the stage; and I toured Italy with a small traveling musical show. That period was one of the richest in my life, and I still draw on many of my experiences from those days.

BACHMANN: Certainly touring musical shows are one of the recurring motifs in your films. By the way, how did you finally begin working in films?

FELLINI: First, I was a rewrite man—I used to add gags to the scripts of dull comedies. My first original screenplay was called *Avanti c'è posto,* and it was the story of a bus conductor. Freely translated the title would be "Please Move to the Rear." It was directed by Bonnard, who had taken to directing pictures when his fame as a matinee idol had faded. That was 1940. After that, I wrote many scripts. Too many. All were produced. They were comedies, mostly, in a pathetic vein. After the war, I met Rossellini, and for him I worked on *Open City* and *Paisan.* That's when I began to understand—or at least to suspect—that one could express deep things too in films. So I continued for two or three years writing scripts for the postwar Italian directors. After that, though, I became . . . I don't want to say disappointed, but when one really loves films, one cannot stop at the written page. I decided to direct. My first film was called *Luci del varietà* ("Footlights").

BACHMANN: You directed this yourself?

FELLINI: Yes, I wrote and directed it. It was the story of the small troupe with whom I had spent a year on the road.

BACHMANN: When did you write and appear in *The Miracle?*

FELLINI: When I worked for Rossellini. Before I began to direct.

BACHMANN: Your serious film career, then, began during the period of the flowering of Italian neo-realism. The relation between your films and "classical" neo-realism has been much debated by the critics. Do you feel that your work in any way derives from, or was influenced by the neo-realist directors with whom you have worked, like deSica, Rossellini, Lattuada, etc.?

FELLINI: Well, I was one of the first to write scripts for neo-realist films. I think all my work is definitely in the neo-realist style, even if in Italy today some people don't think so. But this is a long story. For me, neo-realism is a way of seeing reality without prejudice, without the interference of conventions—just parking yourself in front of reality without any preconceived ideas.

BACHMANN: You don't mean simply to put the camera in front of "life" and photograph what's there?

FELLINI: No, it's a question of having the feeling for reality. Naturally, there is always the need for an interpretation. What has happened in Italy is that after the war everything for us was completely new. Italy was in ruins; you could say everything you felt by just looking around. Later, the leftist press capitalized on this inadvertent one-sidedness by saying that the only valid thing to do in films is to show what happens around you. But this has no value from an artistic point of view, because always the important thing is to know *who* sees the reality. Then it becomes a question of the power to condense, to show the essence of things. After all, why are the films we make so much better than newsreels?

BACHMANN: Though, of course, even newsreels are already one step removed from reality, through the selectivity of the cameraman who took them.

FELLINI: Right. . . . But why should people go to the movies, if films only show reality through a very cold, objective eye? It would be much better just to walk around in the street. For me, neo-realism means looking at reality with an honest eye—but any kind of reality: not just social reality, but also spiritual reality, metaphysical reality, anything man has inside him.

BACHMANN: You mean anything that has reality for the director?

FELLINI: Yes.

BACHMANN: Then the completed film is really *two* steps removed from nature: first the personal *view* of it by the director, and then his *interpretation* of that personal view.

FELLINI: Yes, yes. For me, neo-realism is not a question of *what* you show —its real spirit is in *how* you show it. It's just a way of looking around, without convention or prejudice. Certain people still think neo-realism is fit to show only certain kinds of reality; and they insist that this is social reality. But in this way, it becomes mere propaganda. It is a program; to show only certain aspects of life. People have written that I am a traitor to the cause of neo-realism, that I am too much of an individualist, too much of an individual. My own personal conviction, however, is that the films I have done so far are in the same style as the first neo-realist films, simply telling the story of people. And always, in telling the story of some people, I try to show some truth.

BACHMANN: Is there any underlying philosophy in your films? I mean besides the depiction of what is truth for you.

FELLINI: Well, I could tell you what for me is one of the most pressing problems, one which provides part of the theme for all my films. It's the terrible difficulty people have in talking to each other—the old problem of communication, the desperate anguish to be *with,* the desire to have a real, authentic relationship with another person. You'll find this in *I Vitelloni,*[1] in *La Strada,* in *Il Bidone,*[2] and also in *Notti di Cabiria.*[3] It may be that I'll change, but for now I'm completely absorbed in this problem—maybe because I have not yet solved it in my private life.

BACHMANN: Do you feel that the reason for this difficulty in interpersonal communication is that we have created a kind of society which makes it hard for people to have true relationships?

FELLINI: It is the fault of society only because society is made up of men. I believe that everyone has to find truth by himself. It is completely useless to prepare a statement for a crowd, or make a film with a message for everyone. I don't believe in talking to a crowd. Because what is a crowd? It is a

[1] Released in the U.S. as *The Young and the Passionate.*
[2] Still not released in the U.S. at the time of writing.
[3] Released in the U.S. as *Cabiria.*

collection of many individuals, each with his own reality. That is also the reason why my pictures never end. They never have a simple solution. I think it is immoral (in the true sense of the word) to tell a story that has a conclusion. Because you cut out your audience the moment you present a solution on the screen. Because there are no "solutions" in their lives. I think it is more moral—and more important—to show, let's say, the story of one man. Then everyone, with his own sensibility and on the basis of his own inner development, can try to find his own solution.

BACHMANN: You mean to say that by "ending" a problem, the filmmaker takes away from the audience the feeling that what they are seeing is the truth?

FELLINI: Yes, or even worse. For when you show a true problem and then resolve it, the spectator is beguiled into feeling that the problems in his own life, too, will solve themselves, and he can stop working on them for himself. By giving happy endings to films, you goad your audience into going on living in a trite, bland manner, because they are now sure that sometime, somewhere, something happy is going to happen to them, too, and without their having to do anything about it. Conversely, by not serving them the happy ending on a platter, you can make them think; you can re-move some of that smug security. Then they'll *have* to find their own answers.

BACHMANN: This would seem to indicate that you're not just making pic-tures to make pictures, but because there are certain things you want to say.

FELLINI: Well, I don't start that way. What usually starts me on a film idea is that something happens to me which I think has some bearing on other people's experiences. And the feeling is usually the same: to try, first of all, to tell something about myself; and in doing so, to try to find a salva-tion, to try to find a road toward some meaning, some truth, something that will be important to others, too. And when, as often happens, people who have seen my films come to visit me—not to discuss my films, but to talk to me about their personal problems—I feel I have achieved something. It is always a great satisfaction for me. Of course, I can't help them clarify their problems, but it means the picture has done some good.

BACHMANN: When you say you don't start that way, do you mean to say that the real "message" of your films develops out of the material?

FELLINI: Well, a picture is a mixture of things. It changes. That is one of the reasons why making films is such a wonderful thing.

BACHMANN: Could you tell me about the process in your film work? A kind of step-by-step description of your work on any given film?

FELLINI: First, I have to be moved by a feeling. I have to be interested in one character or one problem. Once I have that, I don't really need a very well-written story or a very detailed script. I need to begin without knowing that everything is in perfect order; otherwise I lose all the fun of it. If I knew everything from the start, I would no longer be interested in doing it. So that when I begin a picture, I am not yet sure of the location or the actors. Because for me, to make a picture is like leaving for a trip. And the most interesting part of a trip is what you discover on the way. I am very open to suggestions when I start a film. I am not rigid about what I do. I like the people with me on the film to share this new adventure. Certainly, I do remember that I am shooting, sometimes.

When the picture is finished, I would, if possible, like not to see it. I often say to my producer, joking: "Let's not cut this one; let's make a new one instead." But I cut all my own films. Cutting is one of the most emotional aspects of film-making. It is the most exciting thing to see the picture begin to breathe; it is like seeing your child grow up. The rhythm is not yet well identified, the sequence not established. But I never reshoot. I believe that a good picture has to have defects. It has to have mistakes in it, like life, like people. I don't believe that beauty, in the sense of perfection, exists—except maybe for the angels. A beautiful woman is only attractive if she is not perfect. The most important thing is to see to it that the picture is alive. This is the most rewarding moment in making films: when the picture begins to live. And I never go back to look at what I have already done—I edit the whole film right through. When it's finished, and I go into the projection room to see it for the first time, I like to be alone. I can't express exactly what happens. I look at the picture; the picture looks at me. A lot of things happen. Some ideas are born; some die. Later I begin to "clean" the picture. In Italy we do not use the sound we shoot on location, but redo the whole track in the studio. But the first answer print still has the location sound on it. Once that is removed, something happens again. The answer print still has the flavor of the adventure of making the film—a train that passed, a baby that cried, a window that opened. I remember the people who were with me on location. I remember the trip. I would like to retain these memories. Once they put the clean, new track on it, it's like a father seeing his little girl wear lipstick for the first time. You have to get to know this new creature that is emerging; you have to try to like it. Then when you add the music, again something is added and something is lost. Every time you see it again, there is some new feeling. When it is completely finished, you have lost the objective point of view. Then, when others see it, I react personally—I feel they have no right to say anything about *my* picture. But I listen carefully, nevertheless—I am trying to find out whether for them the picture is alive.

BACHMANN: Do you feel that in all the films you have made you have always remained faithful to what you were trying to say when you started the picture?

FELLINI: Yes, I do.

BACHMANN: Do you feel there is a relation between your work and that of the current crop of Italian writers, like, for example, Carlo Levi and Ennio Flaiano?

FELLINI: Yes, I think this core of neo-realism in films has influenced all the arts.

BACHMANN: Have you, yourself, done any writing except scripts?

FELLINI: No. Just some short stories when I worked for newspapers. But not since I've worked in films. It's a different medium. A writer can do everything by himself—but he needs discipline. He has to get up at seven in the morning, and be alone in a room with a white sheet of paper. I am too much of a *vitellone* to do that. I think I have chosen the best medium of expression for myself. I love the very precious combination of work and of living-together that filmmaking offers. I approach filmmaking in a very personal way. That's why I consider myself a neo-realist. Any research that a man does about himself, about his relationships with others and with the mystery of life, is a spiritual and—in the true sense—religious search. I suppose that is the extent of my formal philosophy. I make movies in the same way that I talk to people—whether it's a friend, a girl, a priest, or anyone: to seek some clarification. That is what neo-realism means to me, in the original, pure sense. A search into oneself, and into others. In any direction, any direction where there is life. All the formal philosophy you could possibly apply to my work is that there is no formal philosophy. In filmmaking, as in living, you must take the experiences that life presents, those which apply to yourself and to others. Except that in filmmaking only the absolute truth will work. In life I may be a swindler or a crook, but that wouldn't work in a film. A man's film is like a naked man—nothing can be hidden. I must be truthful in my films.

MICHELANGELO ANTONIONI

Jean-Luc Godard

GODARD: Your three previous films, *L'Avventura, La Notte, L'Eclisse*, gave us the impression of being in a straight line, going ahead, searching; and now, you arrived in a new area, which is called, perhaps, the *Red Desert*, which is perhaps a desert for this woman, but which, for you, is, on the contrary, a film about the entire world, and not only about some fuller and more complete world or other: it's a film about the entire world, and not only about today's world. . . .
ANTONIONI: It is very difficult for me to talk about this film now. It's too recent. I am still too tied up with the "intentions" that pushed me to make it; I have neither the lucidity nor the detachment necessary in order to be able to judge it. I believe I can say, however, that this time it's not a question of a film about sentiments. The results (whether they be good or bad, beautiful or ugly) obtained in my previous films are here out-dated, null and void. This is another matter altogether. Before, it was the relationship of one character to another that interested me. Here, the central character is confronted with a social milieu as well, and this means I must treat my story in a completely different way. It simplifies things too much (as many have done)

MICHELANGELO ANTONIONI From *Interviews with Film Directors*, edited by Andrew Sarris. Originally published in *Cahiers du Cinema*, No. 160 (November 1964); English translation by Rose Kaplin originally published in *Cahiers du Cinema in England*, No. 1 (January 1966). © 1966 by Cahiers Publishing Company. Reprinted by permission of Grove Press, Inc.

to say that I accuse this inhuman, industrialized world in which the individual is crushed and led to neurosis. My intention, on the contrary (moreover, we may know very well where we start but not at all where we'll end up), was to translate the beauty of this world, in which even the factories can be very beautiful. . . . The line, the curves of factories and their smoke-stacks, are perhaps more beautiful than a row of trees—which every eye has already seen to the point of monotony. It's a rich world—living, useful. As for me, I hold that the sort of neurosis seen in *Red Desert* is above all a question of adaptation. There are people who adapt themselves, and others who haven't yet done this, for they are too tied to structures, or life rhythms, that are now out of date. This is the case with Giuliana. The violence of the variation, the wedge between her sensitivity, intelligence and psychology and the cadence that is imposed on her, provoke the character's breakdown. It is a breakdown concerning not only her epidermic contacts with the world, her perception of the noises, colors, cold personalities surrounding her, but also her system of value (education, morality, faith), which are no longer valuable and no longer sustain her. She finds herself, thus, in the position of needing to renew herself completely, as a woman. This is what the doctors advise and this is what she strives to do.

GODARD: What is the explanation for the insert of the episode of the story she tells the little boy?

ANTONIONI: There is a woman and a sick child. The mother must tell the child a story, but he has already heard all the ones she knows. She must therefore invent one. Giuliana's psychology being given, it seems natural to me that this story become, for her—unconsciously—an evasion of the reality surrounding her, towards a world where the colors belong to nature: the blue sea, the pink sand. The rocks themselves take on human form, embrace her and sing sweetly.

Do you remember the scene in the room, with Corrado? She says, leaning against the wall, "Do you know what I'd like? . . . Everyone who ever loved me . . . to have them here, around me, like a wall." She needs them, in fact, to help her to live, because she is afraid she won't be able to arrive at it alone.

GODARD: The modern world is therefore only the revealer of an older and more profound neurosis?

ANTONIONI: The milieu in which Giuliana lives accelerates the personality's breakdown, but, naturally, the personality must carry within itself a favorable terrain for this breakdown. It isn't easy to determine the causes and origins of neurosis; it is manifested in such different forms, at times going as far as schizophrenia, whose symptoms often resemble neurotic symptoms. But it is by means of a like exasperation that one arrives at encompassing a situation. I have been reproached for having chosen a pathological case. But, if I had chosen a normally adapted woman, there would no longer be a drama; the drama concerns those who do not adapt.

GODARD: Aren't there already traces of this character in the one in *L'Eclisse*?

ANTONIONI: The character of Vittoria in *L'Eclisse* is the opposite of that of Giuliana. In *L'Eclisse*, Vittoria is a calm and well-balanced girl, who thinks about what she does. There isn't a single neurotic element in her. The crisis, in *L'Eclisse*, is a crisis of the sentiments. In *Red Desert*, the sentiments are a ready-made fact. Moreover, the relationship between Giuliana and her husband is normal. If you were to ask her, "Do you love your husband?," she would answer yes. Until her attempt at suicide, the crisis is underground, it is not visible.

I want to underline the fact that it isn't the milieu that gives birth to the breakdown: it only makes it show. One may think that outside of this milieu, there is no breakdown. But that's not true. Our life, even if we don't take account of it, is dominated by "industry." And "industry" shouldn't be understood to mean factories only, but also and above all, products. These products are everywhere, they enter our homes, made of plastics and other materials unknown barely a few years ago; they overtake us wherever we may be. With the help of publicity, which considers our psychology and our subconscious more and more carefully, they obsess us. I can say this: by situating the story of *Red Desert* in the world of factories, I have gone back to the source of that sort of crisis which, like a torrential river, swelled a thousand tributaries, divides in a thousand arms in order, finally, to submerge everything and spread everywhere.

GODARD: But isn't this beauty of the modern world also the resolution of the characters' psychological difficulties, doesn't it show vanity?

ANTONIONI: One must not underestimate the drama of man thus conditioned. Without drama, there are perhaps no longer men. Furthermore, I do not believe that the beauty of the modern world in itself can resolve our dramas. I believe, on the contrary, that once adapted to new life-techniques we will perhaps find new solutions to our problems.

But why have me speak of these things? I am not a philosopher and all these observations have nothing to do with the "invention" of the film.

GODARD: Was the presence of the robot in the little boy's room benevolent or malevolent?

ANTONIONI: In my opinion, benevolent. Because the child, by playing with this genre of toy, will adapt very well to the life waiting for him. But here we come back to what we were just talking about. The toys are produced by industry, which in this way even influences the education of children.

I am still stupefied by a conversation I had with a cybernetics professor from the University of Milan, Silvio Ceccato, considered by the Americans to be another Einstein. A formidable type, who has invented a machine that looks and describes, a machine that can drive a car, make a report from an aesthetic point of view—or ethical or journalistic, etc. And it's not a matter of television: it's an electronic brain. This man, who, moreover, proved to be extraordinarily lucid, never spoke one technical word in the course of a conversation I didn't understand. Well, I went crazy. At the end of each minute, I longer understood anything of what he had just said to me. He forced himself to use my language, but he was in another world. With him was a young girl, 24 or 25 years old, pretty, of *petit bourgeois* origin—his secretary. Now she understood it perfectly. In Italy, these are generally very young and very simple girls, who have only a modest diploma, who work at programming electronic brains: for them, it's very simple and very easy to program an electronic brain—while it isn't easy at all for me.

Another savant, Robert M. Stewart, came to see me, six months ago, in Rome. He had invented a chemical brain and presented himself at a cybernetics congress in Naples to give an account of his discovery, which is one of the most extraordinary discoveries in the world. It's a very small box, mounted on tubes: it's a matter of cells, into whose composition gold enters, mixed with other substances. The cells are alive in a liquid chemical and they live an autonomous life; they have reactions: if you come into the room, the cell takes on a certain form; and if I come in, it takes on another form, etc. In this little box there are only a few million cells, but starting from that, one can arrive at remaking the human brain. This savant feeds them, puts them to sleep . . . he talked to me about all that, which was very clear but so unbelievable that at a certain point I was no longer following him. By contrast, when he gets a little older, the little boy who plays with the robot from earliest childhood will understand very well; he will have no trouble at all in going, if he wants to, out to space in a rocket.

I look at all that with a great deal of envy, and would like to be already in this new world. Unfortunately, we aren't there yet; it's a drama that will last several generations—mine, yours and the generation of those born right after WW II. I think that, in the years to come, there are going to be very violent transformations, both in the world and in the individual's interior. Today's crisis comes from this spiritual confusion, from this confusion of conscience, of faith and of politics; there are so many symptoms of the transformations to come. Then I said to myself, "What does one say, today, in the cinema?" And I wanted to tell a story based on these motivations I was talking about before.

GODARD: However, the heroes of this film are integrated with this mentality, these are engineers, they're part of this world. . . .

ANTONIONI: Not all of them. The character played by Richard Harris is almost a romantic, who thinks about fleeing to Patagonia and has no idea at all about what he must do. He is taking flight and believes he is resolving, in this way, the problems of his life. But this problem is inside, not outside, of him. All the more true that it is enough for him to meet a woman in order to provoke a crisis, and he no longer knows whether he will leave or not; the whole thing turns him around. I would like to point out a moment in the film which is an accusation of the old world: when, at the breaking point, this woman needs someone to help her, she finds a man who profits from her and from that crisis. She finds herself face-to-face with old things, and it is the old things that shake her and sweep her off her feet. If she had met someone like her husband, he would have acted differently; he would have, first of all, tried to take care of her, then, after that, perhaps. . . . When there, it's her own world that betrays her.

GODARD: At the end of the film is she going to become like her husband?

ANTONIONI: I believe that, following the efforts she makes to find a link with reality, she ends by finding a compromise. Neurotics have crises, but also moments of lucidity which may last all their lives. Perhaps she finds a compromise, but the neurosis stays with her. I believe I have given the idea of this continuity of illness by means of the slightly soft image: she is in a static phase. What is she going to become? Another film would have to be made in order to know that.

GODARD: Do you think that this new world's heightened consciousness may have repercussions on aesthetics, on the conception of the artist?

ANTONIONI: Yes, I believe so. That changes the way of seeing, of thinking: everything changes. Pop Art demonstrated that something else is sought. One must not underestimate Pop Art. It is an "ironic" movement, and this conscious irony is very important. The Pop Art painters know very well that they are making things whose aesthetic value is not yet ripe—except for Rauschenberg, who is more of a painter than the others . . . even though Oldenburg's "soft typewriter" is very fine. . . . I like it very much. It believes it is good that all that is coming out. That can only accelerate the transformation process in question.

GODARD: But does the savant have the conscience we do? Does he reason as we do, in respect to the world?

ANTONIONI: I asked that of Stewart, the inventor of the chemical brain. He answered that his very specialized work, without a doubt, had reverberations in his private life, even including his relationship with his family.

GODARD: And must the sentiments be preserved?

ANTONIONI: What a question! Do you think it is easy to answer that? All I can say about sentiments is that they must change. "Must" isn't what I mean to say. They are changing. They have already changed.

GODARD: In the science-fiction novels, there are never artists, poets. . . .

ANTONIONI: Yes, it's curious. Perhaps they think that one can do without art. Perhaps we are the last to produce things so apparently gratuitous as are works of art.

GODARD: Does *Red Desert* also help you to settle personal problems?

ANTONIONI: While making a film, we live, and nevertheless, we are always settling personal problems. Problems which concern our work, but also our private life. If the things we talk about are not those we were talking about right after the war, it is because the world around us has, in fact, changed and, also, we ourselves have changed. Our requirements have changed, our purposes, our themes.

Right after the war, there were numerous things to be said; it was interesting to show social reality, the social condition of the individual. Today, all that has already been seen and done. The new themes we can treat of today are those about which we were just speaking. I don't know yet how we can approach them, present them. I have tried to develop one of these themes in *Red Desert* and I don't think I exhausted it. It is only the beginning of a series of problems and aspects of our modern society and of the way of life that is ours. Moreover, you too, Godard, you make very modern films, your way of treating subjects reveals an intense need to break with the past.

GODARD: When you begin or end certain sequences with quasi-abstract forms of objects or details, do you do it in a pictorial spirit?

ANTONIONI: I feel the need to express reality in terms that are not completely realistic. The abstract white line that enters the picture at the beginning of the sequence of the little gray street interests me much more than the car that arrives: it's a way of approaching the character in terms of things rather than by means of her life. Her life, basically, interests me only relatively. It is a character that participates in the story as a function of her femininity; her feminine aspect and character are the essential things for me. It is exactly for that reason that I had this role played a bit statically.

GODARD: Thus, there is also on this point a break with your previous films.

ANTONIONI: Yes, it is a less realistic film, from a figurative point of view. That is to say, it is realistic in a different way. For example, I used the telescopic lens a great deal in order not to have deep-focus, which is for good reason an indispensable element of realism. What interests me now is to place the character in contact with things, for it is things, objects and materials that have weight today. I do not consider *Red Desert* a result: it is a research. I want to tell different stories with different means. Everything that's been done, everything I've done until now no longer interests me, it bores me. Perhaps you, too, feel the same thing?

GODARD: Was filming in color an important change?

ANTONIONI: Very important. I had to change my technique because of it, but not only because of it. I already had a need to change my technique, for the reasons we've spoken about. My requirements were no longer the same. The fact of using color accelerated this change. With color, you don't use the same lenses. Also, I perceived that certain camera movements didn't always jell with it: a rapid panoramic sweep is efficacious on brilliant red, but it does nothing for a sour green, unless you're looking for a new contrast. I believe there is a relationship between camera movement and color. A single film is not sufficient for studying the problem in depth, but it's a problem that must be examined. I made, for this reason, some 16mm tests. They were very interesting, but I was unable to achieve, in the film itself, certain effects I had found by this means. Up to this point, I've been in too much of a corner.

You know that a psycho-physiology of color exists; studies, experiments have been done on this subject. The interior of the factory seen in the film was painted red; two weeks later the workers were fighting amongst one another. It was re-painted in pale green and everyone was peaceful. The workers' eyes must have a rest.

GODARD: How did you choose the colors for the store?

ANTONIONI: It was necessary to choose between warm colors and cool colors. Giuliana wants cool colors for her store. These are colors that are less discordant with the objects displayed. If you paint a wall orange, this color will kill any object nearby, while sky-blue or pale green will set the objects off without overwhelming them. I wanted this contrast between warm colors and cool colors: there is an orange, a yellow, a maroon ceiling, and my character discovers that, for her, they don't go well together.

GODARD: The film's title was *Celeste E Verde* (Heavenly Blue And Green).
ANTONIONI: I abandoned it, because it didn't seem to be a virile enough title; it was too directly linked to the color. Moreover, I had never thought about color in itself. The film was born in colors, but I always thought, first of all, of the thing to be said—this is natural—and thus aided the expression by means of the color. I never thought: I'm going to put a blue next to a maroon. I dyed the grass around the shed on the edge of the marsh in order to reinforce the sense of desolation, of death. The landscape had to be rendered truthfully: when trees are dead, they have that color.
GODARD: The drama is thus no longer psychological, but plastic. . . .
ANTONIONI: It's the same thing.
GODARD: Thus, all those shots of objects during the conversation about Patagonia? . . .
ANTONIONI: It's sort of "distraction" on the character's part. He is tired of listening to all these conversations. He is thinking of Giuliana.
GODARD: The dialogue is simpler, more functional than that of your previous films; isn't their traditional role of "commentary" taken by the color?
ANTONIONI: Yes, I believe that is true. Let us say that, here, the dialogue is reduced to an indispensable minimum and that, in this sense, it is linked to the color. For example, I would never have done the scene in the shack where they talk about drugs, aphrodisiacs, without using red. I would never have done it in black and white. The red puts the spectator in a state of mind that permits him to accept this dialogue. The color is correct for the characters (who are justified by it) and also for the spectator.
GODARD: Do you feel yourself to be closer to the researches of painters than to those of novelists?
ANTONIONI: I don't feel too distant from the researches of the New Novel, but they help me less than the others: painting and scientific research interest me more. I don't believe they influence me directly. There is, in this film, no pictorial research at all; we are far from painting, it seems to me. And, naturally, the requirements of painting have nothing to do with narrative content, where one is found in the cinema: this is where the novel's researches join those of painting.
GODARD: Did you re-work the color in the laboratory, as is permitted with Technicolor?
ANTONIONI: I placed no confidence at all in the laboratory, during the shooting. That is to say, I tried, during the shooting, to put the colors I wanted on the things themselves, on the landscapes. I painted directly, instead of trafficking with color in the laboratory. After that, what I demanded from the laboratory was a faithful reproduction of the effects I had obtained. It wasn't easy, for Technicolor, as you know, requires numerous operations involving the master print: the job was very long and delicate.
GODARD: You verified things during the shooting, as you went along. . . .
ANTONIONI: Exactly. I believe one mustn't place too much trust in the work that can be done in the laboratory. It's not their fault. It's just that technically, color is still a long way behind.

GODARD: In your opinion, does Giuliana see the color as you show it?

ANTONIONI: You know, there are neurotics who see color differently. Doctors have done experiments on this subject, with mescaline for example, in order to try to know what they see. At a certain point, I had the intention of having some effects of this nature. But now there is no longer anything of this but one single moment, when you see stains on a wall. I also thought of modifying the color of certain objects, and then the fact of using all those "tricks" very quickly seemed to me to become artificial; it was an artificial way of saying things which could be said in a much more simple way. Well, I eliminated these effects. But we may think that she sees color differently.

It's amusing: at this moment, I am speaking with Godard, one of the most modern talented *cinéastes* of today, and just a little while ago, I lunched with René Clair, one of the greatest directors of the past: it wasn't at all the same genre of conversation . . . he is preoccupied with the future of the cinema. We, on the contrary (you agree, I believe), have confidence in the future of the cinema.

GODARD: And what are you going to do now?

ANTONIONI: I am going to do a sketch with Soraya. . . . This sketch interests me because I am going to pursue my researches with color, push ahead the experiments I did with *Red Desert*. After that, I am going to make a film that interests me more. If I find a producer who will let me do it. . . .

AKIRA KUROSAWA: An Interview

James R. Silke
and Shinbi Iida

INTERVIEWER: There has been much speculation as to the content of your films, particularly those not adapted from another source. *Time* magazine went so far as to describe the conflict in "Yojimbo" as a symbol of the current East-West struggle. *Cinema* has seen a continuing emphasis on the combat between good and evil during an age which, in its struggle to see both sides of every issue, often cannot tell which is which. Can you give us a brief idea of your viewpoint on film content—are there any basic philosophic questions you ask or answer, or are you simply engrossed with telling stories full of the drama and passion of life? If this question seems to imply that we haven't understood your films in the United States, we have been greatly moved and entertained by them and are a little more in love with life because of them.

KUROSAWA: I view the affairs of life as a natural, ordinary man, and I

AKIRA KUROSAWA: AN INTERVIEW From *Cinema* Magazine, Vol. 1, No. 2 (August/September 1963). Translated by Yoshio Kamii. Reprinted by permission.

simply put my feeling into a motion picture. Looking back upon the various ages in Japan or, for that matter, the world, how man is repeating the same thing all the time!

INTERVIEWER: Having no knowledge of the earlier Japanese masters of cinema, we tend to compare your style with the earlier American directors like Ford, Hawks and Stevens. Are you aware of their films and have you been at all influenced by them?

KUROSAWA: I have respected John Ford from the beginning. Needless to say, I pay close attention to his productions, and I think I am influenced by them. The productions of Howard Hawks and George Stevens may have influenced me similarly, though unconsciously. American pictures are superior to ours in every respect.

INTERVIEWER: Can you name ten favorite American directors, or more?

KUROSAWA: If ten names were called for, everyone might presumably raise almost the same ten names invariably. If I may mention just three names, I can readily point out John Ford, Frank Capra and William Wyler.

INTERVIEWER: A comparison has frequently been drawn between your Samurai pictures, "Seven Samurai," "Yojimbo," "Sanjuro" and others, and the Western films of our country. Have you consciously borrowed or learned anything from the latter?

KUROSAWA: Good Westerns are unquestionably liked by all people, regardless of nationality. As human beings are weak, they wish to dream of the good people and great heroes who lived in olden times. Western dramas have been filmed over and over again for a very long time, have been kneaded, pounded and polished, and in the process have evolved a kind of "grammar" of cinema. And I have learned from this grammar.

INTERVIEWER: We have heard that you want to make a Western. Is this true? If so, what is planned?

KUROSAWA: I am a Japanese. I do not think I can make a Western picture.

INTERVIEWER: Can you define your style? What cinematic approaches do you most often use that might constitute a recognizable style?

KUROSAWA: Nothing could be more difficult for me than to define my own style. I simply make a picture as I wish it to be or as nearly as it is within my power to do so. I have never thought of defining my style. If I tried such a thing, I would be caught within my own trap.

INTERVIEWER: We'd like to discuss for a moment your use of talent. Your performers seem, for example, to perform cinematically rather than theatrically. In "Yojimbo" Mifune's walk makes him seem at least twice as big a man as he actually is. Did you develop this with him?

KUROSAWA: Mifune's walk is his own invention. In order to stress it, I carefully selected camera framings and lenses.

INTERVIEWER: The "Yojimbo" walk of Mifune was a radical change from his erratic gestures in "Seven Samurai." Did you help devise these?

KUROSAWA: Mifune's performances in both pictures reveal his acting gifts and talents. But between "Seven Samurai" and "Yojimbo" there was a lapse of ten years, and during this period both Mifune and I probably matured. The more or less unusual overacting in "Samurai" calmed down noticeably in "Yojimbo," I think.

INTERVIEWER: Your use of crowd movements in both these films (where the two opposing forces face each other) had an almost dance-like effect. Was this stylization deliberately developed?

KUROSAWA: I did not try to stylize the movement of the crowd in either "Seven Samurai" or "Yojimbo." Is it possible that the effect of the music created such an impression? Of course, there is a style of bodily movement resulting from the training in swordsmanship of both the Samurai or the hooligan. This may be what caught your attention.

INTERVIEWER: Your use of sound (not speaking now of dialogue) seems to be another distinguishing feature of your films. Miss Yamada's swishing kimona, in "Throne of Blood" for example, as she proceeded to assassinate the feudal lord was most ominous. Can you discuss the integration of sound with picture?

KUROSAWA: Since the silent film gave way to the talkie, sound appears to have overshadowed image. At the same time, the flood of sound has made sound itself meaningless. In motion pictures both image and sound must be treated with special care. In my view, a motion picture stands or falls on the effective combination of these two factors. Truly cinematic sound is neither merely accompanying sound (easy and explanatory) nor the natural sounds captured at the time of simultaneous recording. In other words cinematic sound is that which does not simply add to, but multiplies, two or three times, the effect of the image. I wish to be excused from going into more detail. I have tried to state simply my view about motion picture sound.

INTERVIEWER: Your cutting for continuous action seems to make pronounced use of nature. In "Rashomon" your bandit kept passing behind the bushes of the forest. In "Seven Samurai" the young warrior chases the farm girl, and while the camera covers this action it also glides between the delicate beauty of the trees and the flower patch the warrior and girl are in. In "Throne of Blood" the feudal lords race through the forest to the witches' hut on horseback, and the camera races with them amid frantic shapes of thorn bushes, losing and finding the riders. Each of these seemed to be a series of long takes, cut together for one continuous motion. Is this true?

KUROSAWA: I make use of two or three cameras almost all the time. I cut the film freely and splice together the pieces which have caught the action most forcefully, as if flying from one piece to another.

INTERVIEWER: Each of those three films had a movement of camera which seemed to imitate the movement of the characters: "Rashomon" jaunty. "Seven Samurai" lyric and sweeping. "Throne of Blood" swift, erratic, fierce. Is this true? Is this style?

KUROSAWA: Before thinking how to photograph an object, I think first how to improve the object to be photographed. When that object is perfected, I study how and from what point the picture is to be shot to get the best results. And the condition and movement of the camera must differ according to the nature and spirit of a production.

INTERVIEWER: Each of those films used the device of having objects between the camera and the subject. Was this a stylistic device? Why was it done?

KUROSAWA: This is because I want to produce in the audience the same feeling the characters have of being trapped.

INTERVIEWER: How much is the cinematographer responsible for the graphic look of a Kurosawa film?

KUROSAWA: I explain the desired image in detail not only to the cameraman but also to every member of the staff, and have them do their utmost to produce the best possible likeness to it. This is my responsibility. Speaking of the cameraman alone, the volume of responsibility borne by him should differ in ratio to his caliber as a cameraman.

INTERVIEWER: Do you employ a production designer on your films? Do you design, or frame your shots, in advance of actual shooting?

KUROSAWA: No, I do not employ one. It is I who make the frame and design of a shot. But I gladly take the idea of anyone if it is better than mine.

INTERVIEWER: Do you make use of professionals—Tateshi, I think they're called—who teach or design patterns of sword fighting for the stage or cinema?

KUROSAWA: I make use of Tateshi. But instead of using the pattern of Tateshi as it is, I endeavor to break the conventional patterns and invent new ones as much as possible.

A LETTER TO THE *NEW STATESMAN*

Orson Welles

Sir,—Without being quite so foolish as to set my name to that odious thing, a "reply to the critic," perhaps I may add a few oddments of information to Mr. Whitebait's brief reference to my picture *Touch of Evil* (what a silly title, by the way; it's the first time I've heard it). Most serious film reviewers appear to be quite without knowledge of the hard facts involved in manufacturing and, especially, merchandising a motion picture. Such innocence, I'm sure, is very proper to their position; it is, therefore, not your critic I venture to set straight, but my own record. As author-director I was not— and normally would not be—consulted on the matter of the "release" of my film without a press showing. That this is an "odd subterfuge," I agree; but there can be no speculation as to the responsibility for such a decision. As to the reason, one can only assume that the distributor was so terrified of what the critics might write about it that a rash attempt was made to evade them altogether and smuggle *Touch of Evil* directly to the public. This is under-

A LETTER TO THE NEW STATESMAN From the *New Statesman*, May 24, 1958. Reprinted by permission.

standable in the light of the wholesale re-editing of the film by the executive producer, a process of re-hashing in which I was forbidden to participate. Confusion was further confounded by several added scenes which I did not write and was not invited to direct. No wonder Mr. Whitebait speaks of muddle.

He is kind enough to say that "like Graham Greene" I have "two levels." To his charge that I have "let the higher slip" I plead not guilty. When Mr. Greene finishes one of his "entertainments" he is immediately free to set his hand to more challenging enterprises. His typewriter is always available; my camera is not. A typewriter needs only paper; a camera uses film, requires subsidiary equipment by the truck-load and several hundreds of technicians. That is always the central fact about the film-maker as opposed to any other artist: he can never afford to own his own tools. The minimum kit is incredibly expensive; and one's opportunities to work with it are rather less numerous than might be supposed. In my case, I've been given the use of my tools exactly eight times in 20 years. Just once my own editing of the film has been the version put into release; and (excepting the Shakespearean experiments) I have only twice been given any voice at all as to the "level" of my subject matter. In my trunks stuffed with unproduced film scripts, there are no thrillers. When I make this sort of picture—for which I can pretend to no special interest or aptitude—it is not "for the money" (I support myself as an actor) but because of a greedy need to exercise, in some way, the function of my choice: the function of director. Quite baldly, this is my only choice. I have to take whatever comes along from time to time, or accept the alternative, which is not working at all.

Mr. Whitebait revives my own distress at the shapeless poverty of Macbeth's castle. That papier mâché stagy effect in my film was dictated by a "B-Minus" budget with a "quickie" shooting schedule of 20 days. Returning to the current picture, since he comments on the richness of "the urban scenery of the Mexican border" perhaps Mr. Whitebait will be amused to learn that all shooting was in Hollywood. There was no attempt to approximate reality; the film's entire "world" being the director's invention.

Finally, while the style of *Touch of Evil* may be somewhat overly baroque, there are positively no "camera tricks." Nowadays the eye is tamed, I think, by the new wide screens. These "systems" with their rigid technical limitations are in such monopoly that any vigorous use of the old black-and-white, normal aperture camera runs the risk of seeming "tricky" by comparison. The old camera permits of a range of visual conventions as removed from "realism" as grand opera. This is a language, not a bag of tricks. If it is now a dead language, as a candid partisan of the old eloquence, I must face the likelihood that I shall not again be able to put it to the service of any theme of my own choosing.

ROME   Orson Welles

TOWARDS A NEW CINEMA

Penelope Houston

New cinema, new wave, new American cinema, Italian renaissance: the phrases crop up, forming a convenient kind of critical shorthand, which like most shorthand can only be effectively read back by the writer. Of course nothing is really new, so that antecedents can always be traced, ancestors run to earth; and of course new waves all too soon begin to look like tired conventions. One thing, however, seems certain. In the doldrums of the middle fifties, it would have been difficult to write a survey of this kind without casting sneaking glances over one's shoulder towards the supposed golden ages of film-making. Neo-realism was dying with the whimper of an *Il Tetto,* British cinema somnolent, the French industry given over to a professionalism that masked an absence of original thought, Hollywood still narcissistically enchanted by the size of its own screens. Lethargy seemed to be creeping up, as though the cinema felt television closing up on it and had half-hearted ideas of conceding the race. Now, looking back, the period around 1956 seems a watershed: between the neo-realists and the *nouvelle vague,* or (and this is not simply another way of saying the same thing) between a middle-aged cinema and a young one.

It was certainly time some of the rules were broken, technically as well as aesthetically. Raoul Coutard, the brilliant French cameraman, shoots straight into the light in *Lola;* the ubiquitous hand-held camera gets close in among the crowds; *Hiroshima mon Amour* obliterates the flashback; Antonioni takes over a golf club to shoot part of *La Notte;* Woodfall rents a house for *A Taste of Honey;* everyone, everywhere, discovers the advantage of making films outside studios, so avoiding that systematization which manages to impose the same kind of technical stamp on each and every subject. What the cinema of the middle fifties needed, to shake it up, was some artists prepared to have a go, to smash up a few conventions just to see what the pieces looked like. The fact that it found them, in France, spurred on other people. Everyone wanted a *nouvelle vague,* even if the French decided, as soon as they had it, that they were not entirely sure what they had got hold of. As a result, and to an extent unthinkable only a few years ago, we are living in the age of the first film. Godard, Truffaut, Varda, Demy, Pasolini, Olmi, Patroni Griffi, Polanski, Reisz, Schlesinger, Cassavetes: none of these have had to serve an apprenticeship in B-features, to await the moment of critical recognition. Festival entries tend to be divided between the films of the cinema's great and now aging artists (Renoir, Buñuel, Ozu), of its post-

TOWARDS A NEW CINEMA From *The Contemporary Cinema* by Penelope Houston by kind permission of Penguin Books Limited.

war generation (Antonioni, Wajda, Torre Nilsson, Bergman) and of its established and unestablished newcomers. Missing, on the whole, is the generation from the first decade of sound.

As always, the reaction is against the recent past. But although there is something just tangible enough to be called a new way of looking at the cinema, there certainly is no such thing as a collective spirit. Any generalization based on one group of films can be smartly canceled out on the evidence of another. If there is no common ground between, say, Godard and Antonioni, there is not much more between Godard and Resnais, his fellow-countryman. But *some* movies, it can be said, are more spontaneous than they used to be, more inclined to snatch at the fleeting moment; they relish ambiguity, the kind of Pirandellian situations in which characters are always going in search of their own identities, are not even entirely sure where life ends and film begins; they are based on a knowledge of the cinema's past which enables them to use quotation and allusion, to work within a frame of reference necessary to the creators if sometimes perplexing to the audience; they look as though the people making them enjoyed what they were doing; and they admit their own imperfections.

Should one [to quote Truffaut] continue to pretend to be telling a story which is controlled and authoritative, weighted with the same meaning and interest for the film-maker and for the spectator? Or ought one rather to admit that one is throwing on the market a kind of rough draft of one's ideal film, hoping that it will help one advance in the practice of this terribly difficult art?

Any number of young artists are engaged in this exploration; and are assuming, as directors have not been able to do on this scale since the twenties, that they have a right of discovery, that the whole industrial framework of studios and big companies ought not to stand in their way. In America, inevitably, the problem comes most clearly into focus. From a round-table discussion published in the Californian magazine *Film Quarterly,* one extracts two quotations. According to the producer John Houseman:

Think how very few American films, even among the good ones, have a signature. This has something to do with the organization of the studios and the releasing companies, but it also has a lot to do with the audience. There is a very strong resistance to individual statements in American pictures, while among the worst European film-makers there is nearly always some kind of personal statement.

From Irvin Kershner, one of the younger American directors:

How do you make a film which is entertaining, which has ideas, which is let's say adult, which doesn't depend on violence for its shock, doesn't depend on sex for its excitement—how do you create this kind of drama for $200,000 when there's no time to play, to waste, to take a chance, to do all the things that an artist has to do to make a film?

The director is talking practically, in terms of the low-budget film made within the industrial system, and the producer theoretically. But both are preoccupied with this question of a "signature," of the stamp of personality as something which ought to be burnt into a film. A few years ago, in a Hollywood more easily confident of its own considerable assets, the distinction between one kind of movie and another might have been taken for granted, or at least accepted as a fact of cinema life. Now it has to be argued out, with the implication, which by no means all Europeans would subscribe to, that Europe has got the upper hand.

An answer, of a sort, is to work outside the studios; and within the last few years there has been a good deal of talk about a new American cinema, New York based, independent, radically minded. Some critics have resolutely battled to extract evidence of a "movement" from films made in half a dozen styles: from Lionel Rogosin's dramatized documentary of Skid Row, *On the Bowery,* to John Cassavetes's improvised actors' exercise, *Shadows*; from Shirley Clarke's *The Connection,* which wraps its study of junkies waiting for a fix within the elaborate protective cocoon of a film within a film, to Richard Leacock's television documentaries, where a remorseless camera moves close in on a football match or an election meeting; from the short-film work of numerous *avant-garde* experimentalists to the low-budget features with a toe-hold in the commercial market.

Jonas Mekas, a New York critic and one of the most energetic propagandists for this whole elusive idea of a new American cinema, sees it as

an ethical movement, a human act. . . . It was in his quest for inner freedom that the new artist came to improvisation. The young American film-maker, like the young painter, musician, actor, resists his society. . . . He cannot arrive at any true creation by reworking and rehashing ideas, images and feelings that are dead and inflated—he has to descend much deeper, below all that clutter. His spontaneity, his anarchy, even his passivity, are his acts of freedom. [Further, argues Mekas] . . . If we study the modern film poetry, we find that even the mistakes, the out-of-focus shots, the shaky shots, the unsure steps, the hesitant movements, the over-exposed, the under-exposed bits, have become part of the new cinema vocabulary, *being part of the psychological and visual reality of modern man* [my italics].

Part of the vocabulary these things certainly are, though in employing resounding theory in defence of practical inadequacy, Jonas Mekas hardly makes the out-of-focus shots seem any less blurred. A shaky camera is much more likely to be evidence of financial stringency or practical inexperience than of sincerity. But it becomes very easy to get into a state of mind in which roughness is equated with honesty, in which the more raw and unfinished and obviously unprofessional a film looks, the more fervently it will be held to be asserting its independence. (Then, unfairly, Hollywood strikes back by trying to give some of its movies the fashionable grainy look of hard actuality.)

Resistance to Hollywood's pluperfect technique, precisely because it is Hollywood, and professional, and expensive, goes with the kind of unfocused protest against society and its works which turns a film such as Mekas's own *Guns of the Trees* into a tirade of outrage. Here the Americans part company with the markedly unpolitical French. But they come together again in their feelings about improvisation, the value of the film which evolves its own sense of direction as it goes along. In itself, improvisation can hold a different meaning for almost any film-maker who experiments with it. Jean Rouch, in a film such as *Chronique d'un Été,* uses the camera as a kind of psychiatric tool, allowing it to form a third in conversations in the belief that in its admonitory presence people are closer to revealing the truth about themselves. But he also shoots hours of footage, and it is in the editing of this that the film emerges. Truffaut and Godard improvise when it suits them. John Cassavetes, in *Shadows,* made a film which announced itself proudly as a work of total improvisation, in which the validity of any given moment depended on the degree of response the actor managed to bring to it. Improvisation may achieve that spontaneity many filmmakers long for. But few directors, after all, arrive at their results through a single take, and what was spontaneous at the beginning of the day's shooting may by the end of it have become something quite different.

Advocates of improvisation, though, are much more concerned with the idea of release: the freeing of the actor to make contributions going beyond the range of his part, as the script records it, the freeing of the camera from any rigidly preconceived plan: the freedom, in fact, to invent at the moment of shooting, to send the film off at a tangent if it seems a good idea. Many of these semi-improvised films inevitably look embarrassing naive: a bad actor speaking good lines is probably a happier sight than a bad actor struggling to communicate some ill-defined, ineffable inner something or other. Even when the improvised film works, as *Shadows* mostly did, it seems to do so as a once-for-all experiment, a stage in a director's career which he could not revisit if he tried, and where others follow him at their own risk. The film-maker probably has to go through technique to emerge safely on the other side, needs to know exactly what effect he's after before he sets other people loose to achieve it for him. Directors of greater *naïveté* are liable to waste as much footage on pursuing their players aimlessly around, waiting for the elusive and significant truth to hit them like a thunderbolt, as Hollywood does on tracking its stars through romantic locations. And, of course, the conventions pile up: the dead-into-camera monologues, the shots of rubbish heaps, stretches of wasteland, all the well-worn symbols of city squalor which creep like so much ivy over experimental films.

Essentially, these improvised and semi-improvised works see their function not as a controlling and shaping of experience, the discovery of a pattern or logic in a series of events, but as a baring of immediate emotion, and the shattering of expected patterns through the intervention of the haphazard and the unplanned. Art itself is a word such film-makers might not care to accept too readily, because of its connotations of tradition and discipline. A moment of direct emotional truth can bite deep beneath the surface. *Shadows* pulls off such a moment, for instance, in the needling dialogue between the white boy who has come to take the colored girl out for the evening, the girl resentful of his color and her own, and her two brothers. And although such piercing insights may be few and far between, and the film-maker may not always be able to regulate their coming, or to sort out the absolutely genuine from the just-off-the-mark, they are the justification of his method. Film-making, like bird-watching, creeps up on the truth.

Improvisation is a technique and a tool, and one which many contemporary film-makers reject. It is an interesting exercise to compare the published texts of such films as *L'Année dernière à Marienbad* or *L'Avventura* with the pictures themselves, to see the extent to which two films very precise in their structure had a prior existence on paper, and also to note the points at which the director has moved away from the original text. Film-making is not an exact science: areas for improvisation always remain open. The creative process is continuous, from the thinking that goes on before the film actually goes into production, to the changes in the original conception effected at the shooting stage, to the final shaping of the picture during the editing.

"I go away by myself for half an hour or so before we begin shooting," says Antonioni, and "you might say I was inventing a little bit of film."

"I arrive in the morning knowing what I intend to do during the day, but not how I intend to do it," says Bresson.

"I have an idea at the back of my mind, and I develop it with my actors; although we work from a written text, the dialogue may only be put down on paper a few minutes before we start filming," says Godard.

Use of actual locations, for interior as well as exterior scenes, has also cut down on some of the elaborate pre-planning customary where sets have to be constructed to order in the studio.

Another pointer for the new cinema, and one which links directors who otherwise have little in common, is the kind of relationship the film-maker assumes with his audience. Increasingly, he tells them as much as he cares to, and they take it from there. When one talks of the film as moving closer to the novel, this is to some extent what one means: that it addresses itself to each of us as an individual, that it deals in ambiguities of motivation and relationship which it is for us to elucidate, that it assumes our familiarity with the grammar of the screen. What does it mean? It means what you think it means. "Am I to sympathize with this character or not?"—"I've shown him to you as I see him, now it's for you to make up your mind." This is the sort of dialogue set up between spectator and director. Why does Anna disappear in *L'Avventura,* and what has happened to her? Have the man and the woman in *L'Année dernière* met last year, or this year, or never? Why does Patricia betray Michel in *À Bout de Souffle,* and what are we to make of her last enigmatic close-up? Why does Jeanne Moreau drive her car off the broken bridge in *Jules et Jim?* Are the various women we encounter in *Lola* meant to express aspects of Lola herself—Lola as she was, as she will be, as she might have been? Audiences may ask the questions, and critics speculate, at enormous length, about the answers. The directors concerned know that they have made the questions irrelevant, or have answered them to their own satisfaction.

It would not do to make too much of this: the cinema is in no danger of becoming as esoteric as all that. But it is, on a previously unprecedented scale, testing out some of its own powers, its ability to move freely in time as well as space, its ability to withhold as well as to deliver information, to surprise, and confuse. In Roger Leenhardt's *Rendezvous de Minuit* there is a café episode in which the conversation turns on the possibility that one of the new film-makers, from the shelter of a newspaper kiosk, is at that moment turning a hidden camera on the scene. A joke; a critic's conceit (Leenhardt is critic as well as film-maker); an affectation; and also a comment by the cinema on the cinema, on its determination that we should take it on its own terms, remember that we are sitting in a theatre watching a film, and adjust our conception of reality to admit that in the present-tense grammar of the movies there is only the reality of what is *now* on the screen.

Whether all this should be regarded as merely fashionable, or as symptomatic of the way art reacts to a disordered and confused society, a world in which areas of certainty contract, and judgments become relative, it certainly relates to another trend in contemporary film-making. A reaction has set in against the cinema of straightforward social purpose, and a *Grapes of Wrath* or a *Bicycle Thieves,* a *Stars Look Down* or a *Terra Trema,* is not very likely to be made today by any of the major film-makers in the West. Underlying many of the really significant films of the last few years is an unspoken sense that the public context, the social scene in all its complexity, is something too big to grasp and too unwieldy to be susceptible to change. We have a cinema of personal relationships, private worlds, with anti-heroes engaged in splicing together the broken and rough ends of personality, or in pursuing illusions half-recognized as such; an amoral cinema, or one endeavoring to construct its morality through a series of *ad hoc* judgments. *Hiroshima mon Amour* is not about peace or the Bomb, as much as it is about a woman trying to live with her past; *Shadows* is not about the color question, as much as it is about a colored family whose attitudes to each other are at least as relevant as their feelings about the way the world treats them; *A Bout de Souffle* is not about crime, but about Jean-Paul Belmondo and Jean Seberg; *La Notte* is not a tract on modern marriage. Within their context, these films are not uncommitted or disengaged works, but their commitments remain essentially to individuals. Any generalizations we care to make really become our own affair; and the films accept no responsibility (as did *The Grapes of Wrath* or *Bicycle Thieves*) to offer them on our behalf.

In an essay on the novel, Mary McCarthy has complained that what modern fiction lacks is the factual context: the calm, detailed, *interested* description of how factories are run, how a town is put together as a social organism, the accumulation of facts about freemasonry or whaling or the Chancery Courts, which characterized the nineteenth-century novel. Elsewhere she has written:

The writer must be first of all a listener and observer, who can pay attention to reality, like an obedient pupil, and who is willing, always, to be surprised by the messages reality is sending through to him. And if he gets the messages correctly he will not have to go back and put in the symbols; he will find that the symbols are there, staring at him significantly from the commonplace.

Such comments could be applied with almost equal relevance (which is hardly surprising) to the contemporary cinema. The artist's passion for putting in the symbols, like so many currants in a cake, and the critic's for pulling them out again, rapidly enough become a bore. And the film, as well as the novel, seems to be moving away from the period when information, the assembly of facts, engaged its major artists. If the cinema robbed the novel of much of its journalism and factual reporting, television has done the same thing to the cinema.

A cinema preoccupied with personal relationships and subjective landscapes may find itself losing contact with this hard, limiting, disciplinary, and necessary world of fact. But the cinema is also a more objective medium than the novel, in the most simple sense of the novelist being able to move so exclusively into areas of subjectivity that he no longer feels any need to tell us what his people and places look like, while the film must always, and by its nature, surround its characters with the clutter of their material existence. Even if we see events through the eyes of a central character, we also remain outside him, evaluating his actions as we watch them on the screen. Even a *L'Année dernière,* with its open invitation to a subjective response, is filmed objectively. The novelist may describe a scene, and forget it: the movie can hardly get away from its own scenery.

In so much as there is a new cinema worth talking about, it is because a number of directors are very consciously thinking in terms of how screen language can be made to work for them. They are more interested in the way things look and feel and sound than in what they signify in general terms; more interested in mood than in narrative; more concerned with how people behave and give themselves away in action than with how they might choose to see themselves. They are asking from their actors not the great neon-blazing star turns but performances which break through the hard professional surface: at the worst, an emotional strip-tease; at the best, a revelation. In players such as Jeanne Moreau and Monica Vitti, Jean-Paul Belmondo and Marcello Mastroianni, they have acquired willing accomplices. Above all, they give us the sense of the film itself as a risky and unique creative adventure.

Any amount of nonsense has been produced during the last few years by directors whose main creative activity consists in taking over other people's mannerisms. Entertainment-film clichés may afford restful and tranquilizing evidence that the conventions are still in working order. New-wave clichés are deadly because they come from directors trying to pass them off as new currency. But all this was to be expected. The cinema moves a few steps closer to the minority arts: its passion for allusion and quotation, for instance, is not really very far distant from the point reached by poetry almost forty years ago; and its emphasis on the immediate can not too implausibly be related to action painting. And as it moves, so it acquires the affectations along with the advantages. Antonioni occupies the painter's traditional position: far enough back from his subject to give us our sense of dramatic distance. Some of the young French directors keep our noses pressed up against it: we can distinguish a brilliant blob of color here, some dashing brushwork there, but if we stand a few yards back all we can see is a blurred image, with a signature scrawled boldly across the corner.

Yet the exhibitionism and self-display and dandyish conceits have been symptoms of a necessary bravado. Whatever comes out of all this restless activity of the late fifties and early sixties, in the way of durable reputations and positive advances, we are still in the middle of a whole series of uncommonly difficult transitions, as the minority film-makers move in to fill part of the gap left by the decline of the big production empires. If iconoclasm and a certain optimistic anarchy were necessary three or four years ago, a period of consolidation and sorting out now looks equally important. Can the new film-makers take enough of the audience with them? Are we likely to have, by 1970 or so, a cinema split between the mass-entertainment movies, made at huge cost for huge audiences, and the small-scale films which have left the majority audience lagging behind? It has happened in the novel, in painting, in music, and it is not inconceivable that it could happen in the cinema. Certainly one could no more expect a mass public to go every step of the way with Antonioni or Resnais or Godard, or even Truffaut despite his sensitivity to audience response, than one could have asked them to go along with Proust or Henry James or Virginia Woolf.

If the cinema had held itself down, at any given moment, to the kind of subtleties and complexities it assumed people would be able unquestioningly to follow, we would still be back with *The Great Train Robbery* and *Rescued by Rover*. But a creative cinema which leaves too much of its audience too far behind would be running a clear risk of widening the gap, already quite wide enough, between one kind of audience and another. A snobbery of the specialized cinemas can be much more debilitating and depressing than the free-for-all in which each film takes its chance with the rest. The artist who wants to put his own vision into his work is never likely to find the going entirely smooth: imagine even a Picasso who had to beg £100,000 or so before he could put paint to canvas. And the cinema enthusiasts will always be on the side of such an artist: they will look also to the takers of chances who help to keep this immensely difficult medium alive. But the showmen who found the sun shining in Los Angeles and settled down there half a century ago to make the movies were not thinking like this. They wanted the biggest audience in the world, and they got it; and along with the audience they built an art form not quite like any other.

The impulse which leads me to a Humphrey Bogart movie has little in common with the impulse which leads me to the novels of Henry James or the poetry of T. S. Eliot [wrote the American critic Robert Warshow]. That there is a connection between the two impulses I do not doubt, but the connection is not adequately summed up in the statement that the Bogart movie and the Eliot poem are both forms of art.

The new film-makers may be taking us that much closer to the James novel or the Eliot poem; but no one concerned about the future of the cinema, much less its past, would jettison the Bogart movie in the process. If the cinema ever goes out of business as a mass entertainment, then the fact that certain areas of experiment still remain open would be small consolation for anyone. We need the lot: films and movies, James and Bogart, minority art and mass medium. In spite of all the hazards of the last decade, which have produced so many dismal forecasts, so many pronouncements of commercial decline, it seems tolerably certain that the cinema will continue to give them to us. During the worst of its troubles, Hollywood adopted the defiant and appealing slogan "movies are better than ever." Oddly enough, in the long run and on a world view, the publicists may have got it about right.

MOVIE-GOING

John Hollander

Drive-ins are out, to start with. One must always be
Able to see the overpainted Moorish ceiling
Whose pinchbeck jazz gleams even in the darkness, calling
The straying eye to feast on it, and glut, then fall
Back to the sterling screen again. One needs to feel
That the two empty, huddled, dark stage-boxes keep
Empty for kings. And having frequently to cope
With the abominable goodies, overflow
Bulk and (finally) exploring hands of flushed
Close neighbors gazing beadily out across glum
Distances is, after all, to keep the gleam
Alive of something rather serious, to keep
Faith, perhaps, with the City. When as children our cup
Of joys ran over the special section, and we clutched
Our ticket stubs and followed the bouncing ball, no clash
Of cymbals at the start of the stage-show could abash
Our third untiring time around. When we came back,
Older, to cop an endless series of feels, we sat
Unashamed beneath the bare art-nouveau bodies, set
High on the golden, after-glowing proscenium when
The break had come. And still, now as always, once
The show is over and we creep into the dull
Blaze of mid-afternoon sunshine, the hollow dole
Of the real descends on everything and we can know
That we have been in some place wholly elsewhere, a night
At noonday, not without dreams, whose portals shine
Peculiarly, being made, in ever-changing shapes,
Of some translucent substance, not often used for gates.

MOVIE-GOING From the book *Movie-Going and Other Poems* by John Hollander, published by Atheneum. Copyright © 1960, 1962 by John Hollander. Reprinted by permission of Atheneum.

Stay for the second feature on a double bill
Always: it will teach you how to love, how not to live,
And how to leave the theater for that unlit, aloof
And empty world again. "B"-pictures showed us: shooting
More real than singing or making love; the shifting
Ashtray upon the mantel, moved by some idiot
Between takes, helping us learn beyond a trace of doubt
How fragile are imagined scenes; the dimming-out
Of all the brightness of the clear and highly-lit
Interior of the hero's cockpit, when the stock shot
Of ancient dive-bombers peeling off cuts in, reshapes
Our sense of what is, finally, plausible; the grays
Of interiors, the blacks of cars whose window glass
At night allows the strips of fake Times Square to pass
Jerkily by on the last ride; even the patch
Of sudden white, and inverted letters dashing
Up during the projectionist's daydream, dying
Quickly—these are the colors of our inner life.

Never ignore the stars, of course. But above all,
Follow the asteroids as well: though dark, they're more
Intense for never glittering; anyone can admire
Sparklings against a night sky, but against a bright
Background of prominence, to feel the Presences burnt
Into no fiery fame should be a more common virtue.
For, just as Vesta has no atmosphere, no verdure
Burgeons on barren Ceres, bit-players never surge
Into the rhythms of expansion and collapse, such
As all the flaming bodies live and move among.
But there, more steadfast than stars are, loved for their being,
Not for their burning, move the great Characters: see
Thin Donald Meek, that shuffling essence ever so
Affronting to Eros and to Pride; the pair of bloated
Capitalists, Walter Connolly and Eugene Pallette, seated
High in their offices above New York; the evil,
Blackening eyes of Sheldon Leonard, and the awful
Stare of Eduardo Cianelli. Remember those who have gone—
(Where's bat-squeaking Butterfly McQueen? Will we see again
That ever-anonymous drunk, waxed-moustached, rubber-legged
Caught in revolving doors?) and think of the light-years logged
Up in those humbly noble orbits, where no hot
Spotlight of solar grace consumes some blazing hearts,
Bestowing the flimsy immortality of stars
For some great distant instant. Out of the darkness stares
Venus, who seems to be what once we were, the fair
Form of emerging love, her nitrous atmosphere

Hiding her prizes. Into the black expanses peers
Mars, whom we in time will come to resemble: parched,
Xanthine desolations, dead Cimmerian seas, the far
Distant past preserved in the blood-colored crusts; fire
And water both remembered only. Having shined
Means having died. But having been real only, and shunned
Stardom, the planetoids are what we now are, humming
With us, above us, ever into the future, seeming
Ever to take the shapes of the world we wake to from dreams.

Always go in the morning if you can; it will
Be something more than habit if you do. Keep well
Away from most French farces. Try to see a set
Of old blue movies every so often, that the sight
Of animal doings out of the clothes of 'thirty-five
May remind you that even the natural act is phrased
In the terms and shapes of particular times and places.

Finally, remember always to honor the martyred dead.
The forces of darkness spread everywhere now, and the best
And brightest screens fade out, while many-antennaed beasts
Perch on the housetops, and along the grandest streets
Palaces crumble, one by one. The dimming starts
Slowly at first; the signs are few, as "Movies are
Better than Ever," "Get More out of Life. See a Movie" Or
Else there's no warning at all and, Whoosh! the theatre falls,
Alas, transmogrified: no double-feature fills
A gleaming marquee with promises, now only lit
With "Pike and Whitefish Fresh Today" "Drano" and "Light
Or Dark Brown Sugar, Special" Try never to patronize
Such places (or pass them by one day a year). The noise
Of movie mansions changing form, caught in the toils
Of our lives' withering, rumbles, resounds and tolls
The knell of neighborhoods. Do not forget the old
Places, for everyone's home has been a battlefield.

I remember: the RKO COLONIAL; the cheap
ARDEN and ALDEN both;
LOEW'S LINCOLN SQUARE'S bright shape;
The NEWSREEL; the mandarin BEACON, resplendently arrayed;
The tiny SEVENTY-SEVENTH STREET, whose demise I rued
So long ago; the eighty-first street, sunrise-hued,
RKO; and then LOEW'S at eighty-third which had
The colder pinks of sunset on it; and then, back
Across Broadway again, and up, you disembarked
At the YORKTOWN and then the STODDARD, with their dark
Marquees; the SYMPHONY had a decorative disk

With elongated 'twenties nudes whirling in it;
(Around the corner the THALIA, daughter of memory! owed
Her life to Foreign Hits, in days when you piled your coat
High on your lap and sat, sweating and cramped, to catch
La Kermesse Héroïque every third week, and watched
Fritz Lang from among an audience of refugees, bewitched
By the sense of Crisis on and off that tiny bit
Of screen) Then north again: the RIVERSIDE, the bright
RIVIERA rubbing elbows with it; and right
Smack on a hundredth street, the MIDTOWN; and the rest
Of them: the CARLTON, EDISON, LOEW'S OLYMPIA, and best
Because, of course, the last of all, its final burst
Anonymous, the NEMO! These were once the pearls
Of two-and-a-half miles of Broadway! How many have paled
Into a supermarket's failure of the imagination?

Honor them all. Remember how once their splendor blazed
In sparkling necklaces across America's blasted
Distances and deserts: think how, at night, the fastest
Train might stop for water somewhere, waiting, faced
Westward, in deepening dusk, till ruby illuminations
Of something different from Everything Here, Now, shine
Out from the local Bijou, truest gem, the most bright
Because the most believed in, staving off the night
Perhaps, for a while longer with its flickering light.

These fade. All fade. Let us honor them with our own fading sight.

Liberty, Toleration, and Dissent

EDITED BY IRVING HOWE

INTRODUCTION

Perhaps the one certainty we can hold about democracy is that it is inherently precarious. We may believe, as I do, that a democratic society is a precondition, though certainly not a guarantee, of human progress; we may believe that life without the kind of freedoms embodied in the Bill of Rights would be intolerable; but we must also acknowledge that democracy is a political system always in danger of decay from within and assault from without. Of all known arrangements for political rule, democracy makes the greatest demands upon human intelligence, activity, cooperation, and restraint. It depends on a high level of civilization and probably a certain degree of economic well-being. Only in a few Western countries has the historical experience of modern democracy, as it began with the French and American revolutions, been sustained for any length of time or with any notable success. And even in these countries—as the ghastly surrender of German society to Nazi totalitarianism showed—there can never be an easy assurance that democracy will be preserved. Whatever else, it won't work automatically.

It is a political system that creates for itself a range of severe problems. Some of these can't be "solved" (though they may be alleviated), since they seem to be part of the price we must pay for liberties. Some are likely to become especially severe when the delicate mechanism of political democracy starts to break down; others have to do with the economic substructure of society, which may create unbearable injustices or intolerable conflicts that threaten the survival of democratic institutions.

Let me list, briefly and without much elaboration, a few of the questions and criticisms raised concerning a democratic society:

Is there a conflict between the passional and perhaps irrational nature of man and the kinds of order and restraint required by democracy? Some social thinkers have felt that while democracy may be attractive in the abstract it is not realizable for any length of time in the concrete. Given the fallen and corrupted nature of man, they say, democracy must sooner or later degenerate into rule by financial oligarchy, or into manipulation by demagogues, or into the corruption of party machines.

Modern democracies seem often to function according to the principle of "countervailing powers"—that is, a balance of competing social, economic, and political groups. These groups clash, they have conflicting interests, but the struggle among them is held within more or less peaceful limits by the democratic rules of the game. What happens, however, to the larger, overall interests of society during this interplay of group interests? Is there not a tendency for the more powerful groups to bend the society to their own interests and thereby to neglect the needs of the people as a whole? Such questions have frequently been raised by theorists of both the Left and the Right.

One premise of democracy, seldom stated but clearly present, is that the interplay of competing ideas and parties will eventually lead to a clarification of political policy. In this view, a political opposition is essential for checking the tendencies of those in office toward concentrating too much power in their own hands or succumbing to the temptations of corruption. But at the same time there are tendencies within modern society that make for passivity, cynicism, and indifference among large segments of the population. The problem then arises: Can ways be found to stimulate adequate participation in the political process by large numbers of citizens, not merely once every few years in the voting booth but steadily, through parties, communities, discussions, and protests? Without such participation, democracy is certain to wither away or become a mechanism in the hands of one or another elite.

One powerful criticism made of democracy, especially in recent decades, is that it fails to deal with the urgent and immediate needs of large numbers of people—in America the blacks and the poor especially. Still trapped in the struggle for survival, such people, it is said, can't afford the "luxury" of political involvement. Sometimes this criticism is extended to embrace the question: How "real" or "meaningful" can democracy be when it coincides with an economic system (in our country the critic may point to capitalism, in others to communism) that deprives most people of economic power and concentrates it in the hands of a privileged few? Doesn't the imbalance of economic power necessarily create an imbalance of political power?

What, in a democracy, are the legitimate rights and limits of a political opposition? So long as an opposition movement confines itself to "working within the system"—that is, to sanctioned public criticism of those in power, running candidates in elections, and so on—there is not likely to be an insoluble problem. But suppose the opposition feels that the party in power is so unjust or, in a particular instance (say, the Vietnam war), is pursuing a policy so outrageous that it is necessary to turn to extraparliamentary or extrapolitical methods of struggle. It goes into the streets, it tries to rally the people against the government. Now, demonstrations are an entirely legitimate part of political life in a democracy, and their use should, in principle, cause no difficulties. But suppose the opposition then takes a still more radical step. Let us say that it has come to feel that the injustice against which it protests is intolerable and that to wait upon the slow, uncertain workings of the democratic process is to allow that injustice to flourish. Therefore it decides to disrupt public life, trying to prevent the carrying-out of the government's policy, even if that means the use of violent methods by a minority. Does it then have a right still to enjoy the privileges of democracy? Some would argue that the precedent established in suppressing such an opposition is usually more dangerous to democracy than the risks involved in allowing it to continue, though there clearly are situations —as in Germany during the early 1930's—when this was not true. Others would argue that an opposition has the right to advocate revolutionary methods, such advocacy coming under the rubric of free speech, but that it should be suppressed if and when it actually tries to put them into effect. Still others would say that, since preserving the general rules and institutions of democracy is more important than any particular policy, even a bad one, it is necessary to suppress oppositions that go beyond agreed-upon procedures for legal dissent. The problem is knotty.

In recent years, tacit arrangements have been worked out in this country that allow serious oppositional movements to register their revulsion against policies they regard as immoral, even if that means breaking a particular law. According to the gradually developing concept of "civil disobedience," men of conscience may, under certain conditions, break a law they believe to be seriously unjust. The conditions are these: They must challenge the law openly, in public, so as to assume full responsibility for their conduct; they must offer this challenge only as a last resort, after having tried to change the law through the usual ways of political persuasion; they must be peaceful in their violation of the law, so as to indicate that they are not engaged in a revolutionary act; and they must be prepared to accept an appropriate punishment for breaking the law, first because they wish thereby to indicate their respect for law in general, and second because they hope, by their act of sacrifice, to move their fellow citizens to reconsider the validity of the law in question. (In the sentence above, one may substitute "policy" for "law"—that is, an act of civil disobedience can be undertaken against, say, a policy such as the Vietnam war as well as against a law requiring racial segregation.)

So far, all this can occur within the confines of, though it may cause a strain upon, a democratic society. Yet an opposition movement may come to feel that a particular policy, even though arrived at through democratic means, is so antipathetic to humane or democratic values, it must—reluctantly—choose between the two. It may then, in effect, move from civil to uncivil disobedience. It may declare itself a kind of outlaw, no longer playing by the rules of democratic society, because adherence to those rules has, in its judgment, led to a policy that must conscientiously be opposed completely and immediately. Of all the dilemmas that can occur in a democratic society, this is probably the most tragic.

Now it would be foolish to claim that all of these problems are fully treated in the selections that follow: Such a treatment would require, and can indeed be found in, entire volumes. But an effort has been made here to bring together a group of writings that grapple with the problems I have outlined.

The first essay, by the distinguished French novelist and thinker Albert Camus, deals with a question that goes a little beyond, or deeper than, the explicit political issues of liberty, toleration, and dissent. Camus asks whether we can find in man some "inherent" element, some impulse to dignity and self-assertion, that can lead him to risk comfort, freedom, and even life in order to rebel against tyranny. The rise of totalitarian despotism in the twentieth century sooner or later forced its opponents to consider the problem of "human nature." Is there something indestructible within us that forms a kind of biological basis for rebellion, or are we endlessly malleable through force and propaganda? Is there some substratum in our nature upon which those of us believing in liberty can depend? In its own vivid way, the poem by e. e. cummings that follows Camus's essay raises similar kinds of questions.

The classical case for democratic liberties was made by the great nineteenth-century English philosopher John Stuart Mill in his book *On Liberty*. We reprint here a portion of the second chapter of that book, entitled "Of the Liberty of Thought and Discussion." Writing with characteristic reasonableness and nobility of tone, Mill considers and refutes some of the arguments traditionally advanced against freedom of thought. He is especially cogent in arguing against those restrictions upon freedom of thought and speech that a government feels able or even justified in undertaking because it believes they meet with the approval of a majority of its citizens. A characteristic theme, indeed a characteristic worry, of twentieth-century political thought—how to cope with a tyranny supported and enforced by a majority of the people—is already present in Mill. And in the selection from the American political commentator Walter Lippmann, which can be read as a footnote to Mill's argument, the idea is further developed that a political opposition in a democratic society should not merely be tolerated but should be actively encouraged. Lippmann argues that a stream of criticism by an opposition is essential for the health of a society and the sanity of its government; criticism keeps things lively, helps ideas to circulate, and prevents the political life of a nation from becoming complacent and stagnant.

In the few pages excerpted from George Orwell's antiutopian novel *1984* there is condensed a veritable library of description and analysis concerning the horrible ways in which a totalitarian state breaks the spirit of a dissident. Not only must the dissident acquiesce to the power of the state, he must be broken to the point where he sincerely believes that power to be good. In an episode of incomparable vividness, the outlook of antiliberalism here finds complete depiction.

There follows a group of writings that deal with problems of dissent, tolerance, and civil disobedience in a democratic society. The selection from Mark Twain's *Huckleberry Finn* poses, with a fine blend of irony and tenderness, one of the central problems of the individual living in a society he has not made. Huck, living by the conventional views of the slave society in which he has been raised, believes that his "conscience" requires him to turn in the escaped slave, Nigger Jim; but his feelings as a human being who has become Jim's friend tell him that he must help the slave to escape.

Problems of this kind are discussed, though in more narrowly legal terms, in the next item, an opinion by Supreme Court Justice Hugo Black, *Wilkinson v. United States,* February 27, 1961. Frank Wilkinson had been called before the House Committee on Un-American Activities and had refused to testify on the ground that it was probing into his personal beliefs, which were legally beyond its purview. He was found guilty of contempt of Congress, and his conviction was then upheld by the U.S. Court of Appeals. Before the Supreme Court his conviction was again upheld, five to four, but Justice Black's dissenting opinion has since come to be recognized as a notable statement in behalf of individual liberty.

Many of the issues touched upon in this introduction and in the selections themselves are discussed with brilliant wit by Leszek Kolakowski, a dissident Polish Marxist philosopher who has found himself in repeated conflict with the Communist regime of his country. Kolakowski argues for a kind of humaneness of spirit incompatible with rigid ideologies, a commitment to an "inconsistency" that is "a consciously sustained reserve of uncertainty, a permanent feeling of possible personal error," and which he sets in opposition to that "total consistency [which] is tantamount in practice to fanaticism." Kolakowski's essay stands in the sharpest possible contrast to that of another thinker calling himself a Marxist, Herbert Marcuse, who has become a favorite among radical students and who has the view that the notion of tolerance as advanced by liberals has become a device for subtly acclimatizing people into acceptance of the status quo.

The classic statement in behalf of civil disobedience is the famous essay by Henry David Thoreau, written in the rural quiet of nineteenth-century Concord but since become a major political document of our time. Thoreau argues in terms of an absolutist devotion to individual conscience, and barely considers the problems that must arise when the individual conscience finds itself in conflict with the democratic majority, or the problem of how a democracy could survive if each of its citizens were to act uncompromisingly in accordance with his conscience. Brilliantly written and stirring in its insistence that there are crucial moments when men must follow their own convictions regardless of the costs or consequences, Thoreau's essay raises difficulties for the theory and practice of a democratic society that are explored in Sidney Hook's essay, "Intelligence, Conscience and the Right to Revolution." And finally, this section concludes with a trenchant essay by Sir Isaiah Berlin, the British philosopher, which makes out a strong case for political liberty, despite the disadvantages and failures that often attend it.

In the nearly two hundred years since the French and American revolutions, democracy has been the strongest revolutionary force transforming masses of previously mute human beings into active, or potentially active, citizens determining their own fate. The "long revolution" begun in France and America at the end of the eighteenth century is by no means complete; it has numerous weaknesses; yet nothing but democracy seems able to achieve a fulfillment of the ideals of freedom, liberty, equality.

For human beings raised on the values of personal independence, candor of speech, and forthright expression of disagreements, democracy has by now become a necessity of existence, quite (or almost) as much as food and shelter. The freedom to speak and write as one pleases, without threat of penalty; the freedom to organize parties in behalf of one's political views; the freedom to denounce men in power without having to worry that the secret police will be knocking on the door in the early hours of the morning; the freedom to read the books one wants to read—these are indispensable rights of civilized men.

Any society that destroys democracy is a reactionary society, no matter what professions of idealism its leaders indulge. Once men can no longer form legal parties of opposition in order to contest through free elections the parties and men wielding power, a condition of slavery exists.

Democracy has signified not merely a system of political arrangements, but also a cluster of social values; in the long run, the political mechanisms of democracy can take on full meaning only if accompanied by social justice. The presence of democracy does not guarantee social justice, but the struggle for social justice is best conducted under conditions of democracy.

Tolerance is an essential norm of a free society. To be tolerant, however, does not mean to be indifferent or lukewarm; it does not mean to suppose that all opinions are more or less equally good or bad. Without tolerance for conflicting opinions, there cannot be that ventilation of ideas and that interplay of opposing political commitments by means of which we can change our own and other minds.

It is sometimes true that changing public policy in a democracy can be a slow and cumbersome process. But what, we must ask ourselves, is the alternative? In a dictatorship the mass of men have no choice but to obey; they cannot influence policy, let alone oppose it, unless they happen to be among the tiny handful close to the ruling power. To oppose an unjust policy in a democratic society can often be frustrating and difficult; the only tolerable solution for such difficulties is freedom of opinion.

The weaknesses and failures of democracy require sharp correction, but that correction is possible in only one way—through more democracy.

THE REBEL

Albert Camus

What is a rebel? A man who says no, but whose refusal does not imply a renunciation. He is also a man who says yes, from the moment he makes his first gesture of rebellion. A slave who has taken orders all his life suddenly decides that he cannot obey some new command. What does he mean by saying "no"?

He means, for example, that "this has been going on too long," "up to this point yes, beyond it no," "you are going too far," or, again, "there is a limit beyond which you shall not go." In other words, his no affirms the existence of a borderline. The same concept is to be found in the rebel's feeling that the other person "is exaggerating," that he is exerting his authority beyond a limit where he begins to infringe on the rights of others. Thus the movement of rebellion is founded simultaneously on the categorical rejection of an intrusion that is considered intolerable and on the confused conviction of an absolute right which, in the rebel's mind, is more precisely the impression that he "has the right to . . ." Rebellion cannot exist without the feeling that, somewhere and somehow, one is right. It is in this way that the rebel slave says yes and no simultaneously. He affirms that there are limits and also that he suspects—and wishes to preserve—the existence of certain things on this side of the borderline. He demonstrates, with obstinacy, that there is something in him which "is worth while . . ." and which must be taken into consideration. In a certain way, he confronts an order of things which oppresses him with the insistence on a kind of right not to be oppressed beyond the limit that he can tolerate.

In every act of rebellion, the rebel simultaneously experiences a feeling of revulsion at the infringement of his rights and a complete and spontaneous loyalty to certain aspects of himself. Thus he implicitly brings into play a standard of values so far from being gratuitous that he is prepared to support it no matter what the risks. Up to this point he has at least remained silent and has abandoned himself to the form of despair in which a condition is accepted even though it is considered unjust. To remain silent is to give the impression that one has no opinions, that one wants nothing, and in certain cases it really amounts to wanting nothing. Despair, like the absurd, has opinions and desires about everything in general and nothing in particular. Silence expresses this attitude very well. But from the moment that the rebel finds his voice—even though he says nothing but "no"—he begins to desire and to judge. The rebel, in the etymological sense, does a complete turnabout. He acted under the lash of his master's whip. Suddenly he turns and faces him. He opposes what is preferable to what is not. Not every value entails rebellion, but every act of rebellion tacitly invokes a value. Or is it really a question of values?

Awareness, no matter how confused it may be, develops from every act of rebellion: the sudden, dazzling perception that there is something in man with which he can identify himself, even if only for a moment. Up to now this identification was never really experienced. Before he rebelled, the slave accepted all the demands made upon him. Very often he even took orders, without reacting against them, which were far more conducive to insurrection than the one at which he balks. He accepted them patiently, though he may have protested inwardly, but in that he remained silent he was more concerned with his own immediate interests than as yet aware of his own rights. But with loss of patience—with impatience—a reaction begins which can extend to everything that he previously accepted, and which is almost always retroactive. The very moment the slave refuses to obey the humiliating orders of his master, he simultaneously rejects the condition of slavery. The act of rebellion carries him far beyond the point he had reached by simply refusing. He exceeds the bounds that he fixed for his antagonist, and now demands to be treated as an equal. What was at first the man's obstinate resistance now becomes the whole man, who is identified with and summed up in this resistance. The part of himself that he wanted to be respected he proceeds to place above everything else and proclaim it preferable to everything, even to life itself. It becomes for him the supreme good. Having up to now been willing to compromise, the slave suddenly adopts ("because this is how it must be . . .") an attitude of All or Nothing. With rebellion, awareness is born.

But we can see that the knowledge gained is, at the same time, of an "all" that is still rather obscure and of a "nothing" that proclaims the possibility of sacrificing the rebel to this "All." The rebel himself wants to be "all"—to identify himself completely with this good of which he has suddenly become aware and by which he wants to be personally recognized and acknowledged —or "nothing"; in other words, to be completely destroyed by the force that dominates him. As a last resort, he is willing to accept the final defeat, which is death, rather than be deprived of the personal sacrament that he would call, for example, freedom. Better to die on one's feet than to live on one's knees.

Values, according to good authorities, "most often represent a transition from facts to rights, from what is desired to what is desirable (usually through the intermediary of what is generally considered desirable)." [1] The transition from facts to rights is manifest, as we have seen, in rebellion. So is the transition from "this must be" to "this is how I should like things to be," and even more so, perhaps, the idea of the sublimation of the individual in a henceforth universal good. The sudden appearance of the concept of "All or Nothing" demonstrates that rebellion, contrary to current opinion, and though it springs from everything that is most strictly individualistic in

[1] Lalande: *Vocabulaire philosophique.*

man, questions the very idea of the individual. If the individual, in fact, accepts death and happens to die as a consequence of his act of rebellion, he demonstrates by doing so that he is willing to sacrifice himself for the sake of a common good which he considers more important than his own destiny. If he prefers the risk of death to the negation of the rights that he defends, it is because he considers these rights more important than himself. Therefore he is acting in the name of certain values which are still indeterminate but which he feels are common to himself and to all men. We see that the affirmation implicit in every act of rebellion is extended to something that transcends the individual in so far as it withdraws him from his supposed solitude and provides him with a reason to act. But it is already worth noting that this concept of values as pre-existent to any kind of action contradicts the purely historical philosophies, in which values are acquired (if they are ever acquired) after the action has been completed. Analysis of rebellion leads at least to the suspicion that, contrary to the postulates of contemporary thought, a human nature does exist, as the Greeks believed. Why rebel if there is nothing permanent in oneself worth preserving? It is for the sake of everyone in the world that the slave asserts himself when he comes to the conclusion that a command has infringed on something in him which does not belong to him alone, but which is common ground where all men—even the man who insults and oppresses him—have a natural community.[2]

Two observations will support this argument. First, we can see that an act of rebellion is not, essentially, an egoistic act. Of course, it can have egoistic motives. But one can rebel equally well against lies as against oppression. Moreover, the rebel—once he has accepted the motives and at the moment of his greatest impetus—preserves nothing in that he risks everything. He demands respect for himself, of course, but only in so far as he identifies himself with a natural community.

Then we note that rebellion does not arise only, and necessarily, among the oppressed, but that it can also be caused by the mere spectacle of oppression of which someone else is the victim. In such cases there is a feeling of identification with another individual. And it must be pointed out that this is not a question of psychological identification—a mere subterfuge by which the individual imagines that it is he himself who has been offended. On the contrary, it can often happen that we cannot bear to see offenses done to others which we ourselves have accepted without rebelling. The suicides of the Russian terrorists in Siberia as a protest against their comrades' being whipped is a case in point. Nor is it a question of the feeling of a community of interests. Injustices done to men whom we consider enemies can, actually, be profoundly repugnant to us. There is only identification of one's destiny with that of others and a choice of sides. Therefore the individual is not, in himself alone, the embodiment of the values he wishes to defend. It needs all humanity, at least, to comprise them. When he rebels, a man identifies himself with other men and so surpasses himself, and from this point of view

---

[2] The community of victims is the same as that which unites victim and executioner. But the executioner does not know this.

human solidarity is metaphysical. But for the moment we are only talking of the kind of solidarity that is born in chains.

It would be possible for us to define the positive aspect of the values implicit in every act of rebellion by comparing them with a completely negative concept like that of resentment as defined by Scheler. Rebellion is, in fact, much more than pursuit of a claim, in the strongest sense of the word. Resentment is very well defined by Scheler as an autointoxication—the evil secretion, in a sealed vessel, of prolonged impotence. Rebellion, on the contrary, breaks the seal and allows the whole being to come into play. It liberates stagnant waters and turns them into a raging torrent. Scheler himself emphasizes the passive aspect of resentment and remarks on the prominent place it occupies in the psychology of women who are dedicated to desire and possession. The fountainhead of rebellion, on the contrary, is the principle of superabundant activity and energy. Scheler is also right in saying that resentment is always highly colored by envy. But one envies what one does not have, while the rebel's aim is to defend what he is. He does not merely claim some good that he does not possess or of which he was deprived. His aim is to claim recognition for something which he has and which has already been recognized by him, in almost every case, as more important than anything of which he could be envious. Rebellion is not realistic. According to Scheler, resentment always turns into either unscrupulous ambition or bitterness, depending on whether it is implanted in a strong person or a weak one. But in both cases it is a question of wanting to be something other than what one is. Resentment is always resentment against oneself. The rebel, on the contrary, from his very first step, refuses to allow anyone to touch what he is. He is fighting for the integrity of one part of his being. He does not try, primarily, to conquer, but simply to impose.

Finally, it would seem that resentment takes delight, in advance, in the pain that it would like the object of its envy to feel. Nietzsche and Scheler are right in seeing an excellent example of this in the passage where Tertullian informs his readers that one of the greatest sources of happiness among the blessed will be the spectacle of the Roman emperors consumed in the fires of hell. This kind of happiness is also experienced by the decent people who go to watch executions. The rebel, on the contrary, limits himself, as a matter of principle, to refusing to be humiliated without asking that others should be. He will even accept pain provided his integrity is respected.

It is therefore hard to understand why Scheler completely identifies the spirit of rebellion with resentment. His criticism of the resentment to be found in humanitarianism (which he treats as the non-Christian form of love for mankind) could perhaps be applied to certain indeterminate forms of humanitarian idealism, or to the techniques of terror. But it rings false in relation to man's rebellion against his condition—the movement that enlists the individual in the defense of a dignity common to all men. Scheler wants to demonstrate that humanitarian feelings are always accompanied by a hatred of the world. Humanity is loved in general in order to avoid having to love anybody in particular. This is correct, in some cases, and it is easier to understand Scheler when we realize that for him humanitarianism is represented by Bentham and Rousseau. But man's love for man can be born of other things than a mathematical calculation of the resultant rewards or a theoretical confidence in human nature. In face of the utilitarians, and of Émile's preceptor, there is, for example, the kind of logic, embodied by Dostoievsky in Ivan Karamazov, which progresses from an act of rebellion to metaphysical insurrection. Scheler is aware of this and sums up the concept in the following manner: "There is not enough love in the world to squander it on anything but human beings." Even if this proposition were true, the appalling despair that it implies would merit anything but contempt. In fact, it misunderstands the tortured character of Karamazov's rebellion. Ivan's drama, on the contrary, arises from the fact that there is too much love without an object. This love finding no outlet and God being denied, it is then decided to lavish it on human beings as a generous act of complicity.

Nevertheless, in the act of rebellion as we have envisaged it up to now, an abstract ideal is not chosen through lack of feeling and in pursuit of a sterile demand. We insist that the part of man which cannot be reduced to mere ideas should be taken into consideration—the passionate side of his nature that serves no other purpose than to be part of the act of living. Does this imply that no rebellion is motivated by resentment? No, and we know it only too well in this age of malice. But we must consider the idea of rebellion in its widest sense on pain of betraying it; and in its widest sense rebellion goes far beyond resentment. When Heathcliff, in *Wuthering Heights,* says that he puts his love above God and would willingly go to hell in order to be reunited with the woman he loves, he is prompted not only by youth and humiliation but by the consuming experience of a whole lifetime. The same emotion causes Eckart, in a surprising fit of heresy, to say that he prefers hell with Jesus to heaven without Him. This is the very essence of love. Contrary to Scheler, it would therefore be impossible to overemphasize the passionate affirmation that underlies the act of rebellion and distinguishes it from resentment. Rebellion, though apparently negative, since it creates nothing, is profoundly positive in that it reveals the part of man which must always be defended.

But, to sum up, are not rebellion and the values that it implies relative? Reasons for rebellion do seem to change, in fact, with periods and civilizations. It is obvious that a Hindu pariah, an Inca warrior, a primitive native of central Africa, and a member of one of the first Christian communities had not at all the same ideas about rebellion. We could even assert, with considerable assurance, that the idea of rebellion has no meaning in these particular cases. However, a Greek slave, a serf, a *condottiere* of the Renaissance, a Parisian bourgeois during the Regency, a Russian intellectual at the beginning of the twentieth century, and a contemporary worker would undoubtedly agree that rebellion is legitimate, even if they differed about the reasons for it. In other words, the problem of rebellion seems to assume a precise meaning only within the confines of Western thought. It is possible to be even more explicit by remarking, like Scheler, that the spirit of rebellion finds few means of expression in societies where inequalities are very great (the Hindu caste system) or, again, in those where there is absolute equality (certain primitive societies). The spirit of rebellion can exist only in a society where a theoretical equality conceals great factual inequalities. The problem of rebellion, therefore, has no meaning except within our own Western society. One might be tempted to affirm that it is relative to the development of individualism if the preceding remarks had not put us on our guard against this conclusion.

On the basis of the evidence, the only conclusion that can be drawn from Scheler's remark is that, thanks to the theory of political freedom, there is, in the very heart of our society, an increasing awareness in man of the idea of man and, thanks to the application of this theory of freedom, a corresponding dissatisfaction. Actual freedom has not increased in proportion to man's awareness of it. We can only deduce from this observation that rebellion is the act of an educated man who is aware of his own rights. But there is nothing which justifies us in saying that it is only a question of individual rights. Because of the sense of solidarity we have already pointed out, it would rather seem that what is at stake is humanity's gradually increasing self-awareness as it pursues its course. In fact, for the Inca and the pariah the problem never arises, because for them it had been solved by a tradition, even before they had had time to raise it—the answer being that tradition is sacred. If in a world where things are held sacred the problem of rebellion does not arise, it is because no real problems are to be found in such a world, all the answers having been given simultaneously. Metaphysic is replaced by myth. There are no more questions, only eternal answers and commentaries, which may be metaphysical. But before man accepts the sacred world and in order that he should be able to accept it—or before he escapes from it and in order that he should be able to escape from it—there is always a period of soul-searching and rebellion. The rebel is a man who is on the point of accepting or rejecting the sacred and determined on laying claim to a human situation in which all the answers are human—in other words, formulated in reasonable terms. From this moment every question, every word, is an act of rebellion while in the sacred world every word is an act of grace. It would be possible to demonstrate in this manner that only two possible worlds can exist for the human mind: the sacred (or, to speak in Christian terms, the world of grace[3]) and the world of rebellion. The disappearance of one is equivalent to the appearance of the other, despite the fact that this appearance can take place in disconcerting forms. There again we rediscover the *All or Nothing*. The present interest of the problem of rebellion only springs from the fact that nowadays whole societies have wanted to discard the sacred. We live in an unsacrosanct moment in history. Insurrection is certainly not the sum total of human experience. But history today, with all its storm and strife, compels us to say that rebellion is one of

[3] There is, of course, an act of metaphysical rebellion at the beginning of Christianity, but the resurrection of Christ and the annunciation of the kingdom of heaven interpreted as a promise of eternal life are the answers that render it futile.

the essential dimensions of man. It is our historic reality. Unless we choose to ignore reality, we must find our values in it. Is it possible to find a rule of conduct outside the realm of religion and its absolute values? That is the question raised by rebellion.

We have already noted the confused values that are called into play by incipient rebellion. Now we must inquire if these values are to be found again in contemporary forms of rebellious thought and action, and if they are, we must specify their content. But, before going any farther, let us note that the basis of these values is rebellion itself. Man's solidarity is founded upon rebellion, and rebellion, in its turn, can only find its justification in this solidarity. We have, then, the right to say that any rebellion which claims the right to deny or destroy this solidarity loses simultaneously its right to be called rebellion and becomes in reality an acquiescence in murder. In the same way, this solidarity, except in so far as religion is concerned, comes to life only on the level of rebellion. And so the real drama of revolutionary thought is announced. In order to exist, man must rebel, but rebellion must respect the limit it discovers in itself—a limit where minds meet and, in meeting, begin to exist. Rebellious thought, therefore, cannot dispense with memory: it is a perpetual state of tension. In studying its actions and its results, we shall have to say, each time, whether it remains faithful to its first noble promise or if, through indolence or folly, it forgets its original purpose and plunges into a mire of tyranny or servitude.

Meanwhile, we can sum up the initial progress that the spirit of rebellion provokes in a mind that is originally imbued with the absurdity and apparent sterility of the world. In absurdist experience, suffering is individual. But from the moment when a movement of rebellion begins, suffering is seen as a collective experience. Therefore the first progressive step for a mind overwhelmed by the strangeness of things is to realize that this feeling of strangeness is shared with all men and that human reality, in its entirety, suffers from the distance which separates it from the rest of the universe. The malady experienced by a single man becomes a mass plague. In our daily trials rebellion plays the same role as does the *"cogito"* in the realm of thought: it is the first piece of evidence. But this evidence lures the individual from his solitude. It founds its first value on the whole human race. I rebel—therefore we exist.

I SING OF OLAF GLAD AND BIG

e. e. cummings

i sing of Olaf glad and big
whose warmest heart recoiled at war:
a conscientious object-or

his wellbelovéd colonel(trig
westpointer most succinctly bred)
took erring Olaf soon in hand;
but—though an host of overjoyed
noncoms(first knocking on the head
him)do through icy waters roll
that helplessness which others stroke
with brushes recently employed
anent this muddy toiletbowl,
while kindred intellects evoke
allegiance per blunt instruments—
Olaf(being to all intents
a corpse and wanting any rag
upon what God unto him gave)
responds,without getting annoyed
"I will not kiss your f.ing flag"

straightway the silver bird looked grave
(departing hurriedly to shave)

but—though all kinds of officers
(a yearning nation's blueeyed pride)
their passive prey did kick and curse
until for wear their clarion
voices and boots were much the worse,
and egged the firstclassprivates on
his rectum wickedly to tease
by means of skilfully applied
bayonets roasted hot with heat—
Olaf(upon what were once knees)
does almost ceaselessly repeat
"there is some s. I will not eat"

> our president,being of which
> assertions duly notified
> threw the yellowsonofabitch
> into a dungeon,where he died
>
> Christ(of His mercy infinite)
> i pray to see;and Olaf,too
>
> preponderatingly because
> unless statistics lie he was
> more brave than me:more blond than you.

OF THE LIBERTY OF THOUGHT
AND DISCUSSION

John Stuart Mill

The time, it is to be hoped, is gone by when any defence would be necessary of the "liberty of the press" as one of the securities against corrupt or tyrannical government. No argument, we may suppose, can now be needed, against permitting a legislature or an executive, not identified in interest with the people, to prescribe opinions to them, and determine what doctrines or what arguments they shall be allowed to hear. This aspect of the question, besides, has been so often and so triumphantly enforced by preceding writers, that it needs not be specially insisted on in this place. Though the law of England, on the subject of the press, is as servile to this day as it was in the time of the Tudors, there is little danger of its being actually put in force against political discussion, except during some temporary panic, when fear of insurrection drives ministers and judges from their propriety; and, speaking generally, it is not, in constitutional countries, to be apprehended that the government, whether completely responsible to the people or not, will often attempt to control the expression of opinion, except when in doing so it makes itself the organ of the general intolerance of the public. Let us suppose, therefore, that the government is entirely at one with the people, and never thinks of exerting any power of coercion unless in agreement with what it conceives to be their voice. But I deny the right of the people to exercise such coercion, either by themselves or by their government. The power itself is illegitimate. The best government has no more title to it than the worst. It is as noxious, or more noxious, when exerted in accordance with public opinion, than when in opposition to it. If all mankind minus one, were of one opinion, and only one person were of the contrary opinion, mankind would be no more justified in silencing that one person, than he, if he had the power, would be justified in silencing mankind. Were an opinion a personal possession of no value except to the owner; if to be obstructed in the enjoyment of it were simply a private injury, it would make some difference whether the injury was inflicted only on a few persons or on many. But the peculiar evil of silencing the expression of an opinion is, that it is robbing the human race; posterity as well as the existing generation; those who dissent from the opinion, still more than those who hold it. If the opinion is right, they are deprived of the opportunity of exchanging error for truth: if wrong, they lose, what is almost as great a benefit, the clearer perception and livelier impression of truth, produced by its collision with error.

It is necessary to consider separately these two hypotheses, each of which has a distinct branch of the argument corresponding to it. We can never be sure that the opinion we are endeavoring to stifle is a false opinion; and if we were sure, stifling it would be an evil still.

First: the opinion which it is attempted to suppress by authority may possibly be true. Those who desire to suppress it, of course deny its truth; but they are not infallible. They have no authority to decide the question for all mankind, and exclude every other person from the means of judging. To refuse a hearing to an opinion, because they are sure that it is false, is to assume that *their* certainty is the same thing as *absolute* certainty. All silencing of discussion is an assumption of infallibility. Its condemnation may be allowed to rest on this common argument, not the worse for being common.

Unfortunately for the good sense of mankind, the fact of their fallibility is far from carrying the weight in their practical judgment, which is always allowed to it in theory; for while every one well knows himself to be fallible, few think it necessary to take any precautions against their own fallibility, or admit the supposition that any opinion of which they feel very certain, may be one of the examples of the error to which they acknowledge themselves to be liable. Absolute princes, or others who are accustomed to unlimited deference, usually feel this complete confidence in their own opinions on nearly all subjects. People more happily situated, who sometimes hear their opinions disputed, and are not wholly unused to be set right when they are wrong, place the same unbounded reliance only on such of their opinions as are shared by all who surround them, or to whom they habitually defer: for in proportion to a man's want of confidence in his own solitary judgment, does he usually repose, with implicit trust, on the infallibility of "the world" in general. And the world, to each individual, means the part of it with which he comes in contact; his party, his sect, his church, his class of society: the man may be called, by comparison, almost liberal and large-minded to whom it means anything so comprehensive as his own country or his own age. Nor is his faith in this collective authority at all shaken by his being aware that other ages, countries, sects, churches, classes, and parties have thought, and even now think, the exact reverse. He devolves upon his own world the responsibility of being in the right against the dissentient worlds of other people; and it never troubles him that mere accident has decided which of these numerous worlds is the object of his reliance, and that the same causes which make him a Churchman in London, would have made him a Buddhist or a Confucian in Pekin. Yet it is as evident in itself as any amount of argument can make it, that ages are no more infallible than individuals; every age having held many opinions which subsequent ages have deemed not only false but absurd; and it is as certain that many opinions, now general, will be rejected by future ages, as it is that many, once general, are rejected by the present.

The objection likely to be made to this argument, would probably take some such form as the following. There is no greater assumption of infallibility in forbidding the propagation of error, than in any other thing which is done by public authority on its own judgment and responsibility. Judgment is given to men that they may use it. Because it may be used erroneously, are men to be told that they ought not to use it at all? To prohibit what they think pernicious, is not claiming exemption from error, but fulfilling the duty incumbent on them, although fallible, of acting on their conscientious conviction. If we were never to act on our opinions, because those opinions may be wrong, we should leave all our interests uncared for, and all our duties unperformed. An objection which applies to all conduct can be no valid objection to any conduct in particular.

It is the duty of governments, and of individuals, to form the truest opinions they can; to form them carefully, and never impose them upon others unless they are quite sure of being right. But when they are sure (such reasoners may say), it is not conscientiousness but cowardice to shrink from acting on their opinions, and allow doctrines which they honestly think dangerous to the welfare of mankind, either in this life or in another, to be scattered abroad without restraint, because other people, in less enlightened times, have persecuted opinions now believed to be true. Let us take care, it may be said, not to make the same mistake: but governments and nations have made mistakes in other things, which are not denied to be fit subjects for the exercise of authority: they have laid on bad taxes, made unjust wars. Ought we therefore to lay on no taxes, and, under whatever provocation, make no wars? Men, and governments, must act to the best of their ability. There is no such thing as absolute certainty, but there is assurance sufficient for the purposes of human life. We may, and must, assume our opinion to be true for the guidance of our own conduct: and it is assuming no more when we forbid bad men to pervert society by the propagation of opinions which we regard as false and pernicious.

I answer, that it is assuming very much more. There is the greatest difference between presuming an opinion to be true, because, with every opportunity for contesting it, it has not been refuted, and assuming its truth for the purpose of not permitting its refutation. Complete liberty of contradicting and disproving our opinion, is the very condition which justifies us in assuming its truth for purposes of action; and on no other terms can a being with human faculties have any rational assurance of being right.

When we consider either the history of opinion, or the ordinary conduct of human life, to what is it to be ascribed that the one and the other are no worse than they are? Not certainly to the inherent force of the human understanding; for, on any matter not self-evident, there are ninety-nine persons totally incapable of judging of it, for one who is capable; and the capacity of the hundredth person is only comparative; for the majority of the eminent men of every past generation held many opinions now known to be erroneous, and did or approved numerous things which no one will now justify. Why is it, then, that there is on the whole a preponderance among mankind of rational opinions and rational conduct? If there really is this preponderance—which there must be, unless human affairs are, and have always been, in an almost desperate state—it is owing to a quality of the human mind, the source of everything respectable in man, either as an intellectual or as a moral being, namely, that his errors are corrigible. He is capable of rectifying his mistakes by discussion and experience. Not by experience alone. There must be discussion, to show how experience is to be interpreted. Wrong opinions and practices gradually yield to fact and argument: but facts and arguments, to produce any effect on the mind, must be brought before it. Very few facts are able to tell their own story, without comments to bring out their meaning. The whole strength and value, then, of human judgment, depending on the one property, that it can be set right when it is wrong, reliance can be placed on it only when the means of setting it right are kept constantly at hand. In the case of any person whose judgment is really deserving of confidence, how has it become so? Because he has kept his mind open to criticism of his opinions and conduct. Because it has been his practice to listen to all that could be said against him; to profit by as much of it as was just, and expound to himself, and upon occasion to others, the fallacy of what was fallacious. Because he has felt, that the only way in which a human being can make some approach to knowing the whole of a subject, is by hearing what can be said about it by persons of every variety of opinion, and studying all modes in which it can be looked at by every character of mind. No wise man ever acquired his wisdom in any mode but this; nor is it in the nature of human intellect to become wise in any other manner. The steady habit of correcting and completing his own opinion by collating it with those of others, so far from causing doubt and hesitation in carrying it into practice, is the only stable foundation for a just reliance on it: for, being cognizant of all that can, at least obviously, be said against him, and having taken up his position against all gainsayers knowing that he has sought for objections and difficulties, instead of avoiding them, and has shut out no light which can be thrown upon the subject from any quarter—he has a right to think his judgment better than that of any person, or any multitude, who have not gone through a similar process.

It is not too much to require that what the wisest of mankind, those who are best entitled to trust their own judgment, find necessary to warrant their relying on it, should be submitted to by that miscellaneous collection of a few wise and many foolish individuals, called the public. The most intolerant of churches, the Roman Catholic Church, even at the canonization of a saint, admits, and listens patiently to, a "devil's advocate." The holiest of men, it appears, cannot be admitted to posthumous honors, until all that the devil could say against him is known and weighed. If even the Newtonian philosophy were not permitted to be questioned, mankind could not feel as complete assurance of its truth as they now do. The beliefs which we have most warrant for, have no safeguard to rest on, but a standing invitation to the whole world to prove them unfounded. If the challenge is not accepted, or is accepted and the attempt fails, we are far enough from certainty still; but we have done the best that the existing state of human reason admits of; we have neglected nothing that could give the truth a chance of reaching us: if the lists are kept open, we may hope that if there be a better truth, it will be found when the human mind is capable of receiving it; and in the meantime we may rely on having attained such approach to truth, as is possible in our own day. This is the amount of certainty attainable by a fallible being, and this the sole way of attaining it.

Strange it is, that men should admit the validity of the arguments for free discussion, but object to their being "pushed to an extreme"; not seeing that unless the reasons are good for an extreme case, they are not good for any case. Strange that they should imagine that they are not assuming infallibility when they acknowledge that there should be free discussion on all subjects which can possibly be *doubtful,* but think that some particular principle or doctrine should be forbidden to be questioned because it is *so certain,* that is, because *they are certain* that it is certain. To call any proposition certain, while there is any one who would deny its certainty if permitted, but who is not permitted, is to assume that we ourselves, and those who agree with us, are the judges of certainty, and judges without hearing the other side.

In the present age—which has been described as "destitute of faith, but terrified at scepticism,"—in which people feel sure, not so much that their opinions are true, as that they should not know what to do without them—the claims of an opinion to be protected from public attack are rested not so much on its truth, as on its importance to society. There are, it is alleged, certain beliefs, so useful, not to say indispensable to well-being, that it is as much the duty of governments to uphold those beliefs, as to protect any other of the interests of society. In a case of such necessity, and so directly in the line of their duty, something less than infallibility may, it is maintained, warrant, and even bind, governments, to act on their own opinion, confirmed by the general opinion of mankind. It is also often argued, and still oftener thought, that none but bad men would desire to weaken these salutary beliefs; and there can be nothing wrong, it is thought, in restraining bad men, and prohibiting what only such men would wish to practice. This mode of thinking makes the justification of restraints on discussion not a question of the truth of doctrines, but of their usefulness; and flatters itself by that means to escape the responsibility of claiming to be an infallible judge of opinions. But those who thus satisfy themselves, do not perceive that the assumption of infallibility is merely shifted from one point to another. The usefulness of an opinion is itself matter of opinion: as disputable, as open to discussion and requiring discussion as much, as the opinion itself. There is the same need of an infallible judge of opinions to decide an opinion to be noxious, as to decide it to be false, unless the opinion condemned has full opportunity of defending itself. And it will not do to say that the heretic may be allowed to maintain the utility or harmlessness of his opinion, though forbidden to maintain its truth. The truth of an opinion is part of its utility. If we would know whether or not it is desirable that a proposition should be believed, is it possible to exclude the consideration of whether or not it is true? In the opinion, not of bad men, but of the best men, no belief which is contrary to truth can be really useful: and can you prevent such men from urging that plea, when they are charged with culpability for denying some doctrine which they are told is useful, but which they believe to be false? Those who are on the side of received opinions, never fail to take all possible advantage of this plea; you do not find *them* handling the question of utility as if it could be completely abstracted from that of truth: on the contrary, it is, above all, because their doctrine is "the truth," that the knowledge or the belief of it is held to be so indispensable. There can be no fair discussion of the question of usefulness, when an argument so vital may be employed on one side, but not on the other. And in point of fact, when law or public feeling do not permit the truth of an opinion to be disputed, they are just as little tolerant of a denial of its usefulness. The utmost they allow is an extenuation of its absolute necessity or of the positive guilt of rejecting it.

In order more fully to illustrate the mischief of denying a hearing to opinions because we, in our own judgment, have condemned them, it will be desirable to fix down the discussion to a concrete case; and I choose, by preference, the cases which are least favorable to me—in which the argument against freedom of opinion, both on the score of truth and on that of utility, is considered the strongest. Let the opinions impugned be the belief in a God and in a future state, or any of the commonly received doctrines of morality. To fight the battle on such ground, gives a great advantage to an unfair antagonist; since he will be sure to say (and many who have no desire to be unfair will say it internally), Are these the doctrines which you do not deem sufficiently certain to be taken under the protection of law? Is the belief in a God one of the opinions, to feel sure of which, you hold to be assuming infallibility? But I must be permitted to observe, that it is not the feeling sure of a doctrine (be it what it may) which I call an assumption of infallibility. It is the undertaking to decide that question *for others,* without allowing them to hear what can be said on the contrary side. And I denounce and reprobate this pretension not the less, if put forth on the side of my most solemn convictions. However positive any one's persuasion may be, not only of the falsity, but of the pernicious consequences—not only of the pernicious consequences, but (to adopt expressions which I altogether condemn) the immorality and impiety of an opinion; yet if, in pursuance of that private judgment, though backed by the public judgment of his country or his contemporaries, he prevents the opinion from being heard in its defense, he assumes infallibility. And so far from the assumption being less objectionable or less dangerous because the opinion is called immoral or impious, this is the case of all others in which it is most fatal. These are exactly the occasions on which the men of one generation commit those dreadful mistakes which excite the astonishment and horror of posterity. It is among such that we find the instances memorable in history, when the arm of the law has been employed to root out the best men and the noblest doctrines; with deplorable success as to the men, though some of the doctrines have survived to be (as if in mockery) invoked, in defense of similar conduct towards those who dissent from *them,* or from their received interpretation.

Mankind can hardly be too often reminded, that there was once a man named Socrates, between whom and the legal authorities and public opinion of his time, there took place a memorable collision. Born in an age and country abounding in individual greatness, this man has been handed down to us by those who best knew both him and the age, as the most virtuous man in it; while *we* know him as the head and prototype of all subsequent teachers of virtue, the source equally of the lofty inspiration of Plato and the judicious utilitarianism of Aristotle, *"i maëstri di color che sanno,"* the two headsprings of ethical as of all other philosophy. This acknowledged master of all the eminent thinkers who have since lived—whose fame, still growing after more than two thousand years, all but outweighs the whole remainder of the names which make his native city illustrious—was put to death by his countrymen, after a judicial conviction, for impiety and immorality. Impiety, in denying the gods recognized by the State; indeed his accuser asserted (see the "Apologia") that he believed in no gods at all. Immorality, in being, by his doctrines and instructions, a "corrupter of youth." Of these charges the tribunal, there is every ground for believing, honestly found him guilty, and condemned the man who probably of all then born had deserved best of mankind, to be put to death as a criminal.

To pass from this to the only other instance of judicial iniquity, the mention of which, after the condemnation of Socrates, would not be an anti-climax: the event which took place on Calvary rather more than eighteen hundred years ago. The man who left on the memory of those who witnessed his life and conversation, such an impression of his moral grandeur, that eighteen subsequent centuries have done homage to him as the Almighty in person, was ignominiously put to death, as what? As a blasphemer. Men did not merely mistake their benefactor; they mistook him for the exact contrary of what he was, and treated him as that prodigy of impiety, which they themselves are now held to be, for their treatment of him. The feelings with which mankind now regard these lamentable transactions, especially the latter of the two, render them extremely unjust in their judgment of the unhappy actors. These were, to all appearance, not bad men—not worse than men most commonly are, but rather the contrary; men who possessed in a full, or somewhat more than a full measure, the religious, moral, and patriotic feelings of their time and people: the very kind of men who, in all times, our own included, have every chance of passing through life blameless and respected. The high-priest who rent his garments when the words were pronounced, which, according to all the ideas of his country, constituted the blackest guilt, was in all probability quite as sincere in his horror and indignation, as the generality of respectable and pious men now are in the religious and moral sentiments they profess; and most of those who now shudder at his conduct, if they had lived in his time and been born Jews, would have acted precisely as he did. Orthodox Christians who are tempted to think that those who stoned to death the first martyrs must have been worse men than they themselves are, ought to remember that one of those persecutors was Saint Paul.

Let us add one more example, the most striking of all, if the impressiveness of an error is measured by the wisdom and virtue of him who falls into it. If ever any one, possessed of power, had grounds for thinking himself the best and most enlightened among his cotemporaries, it was the Emperor Marcus Aurelius. Absolute monarch of the whole civilized world, he preserved through life not only the most unblemished justice, but what was less to be expected from his Stoical breeding, the tenderest heart. The few failings which are attributed to him, were all on the side of indulgence: while his writings, the highest ethical product of the ancient mind, differ scarcely perceptibly, if they differ at all, from the most characteristic teachings of Christ. This man, a better Christian in all but the dogmatic sense of the word, than almost any of the ostensibly Christian sovereigns who have since reigned, persecuted Christianity. Placed at the summit of all the previous attainments of humanity, with an open, unfettered intellect, and a character which led him of himself to embody in his moral writings the Christian ideal, he yet failed to see that Christianity was to be a good and not an evil to the world, with his duties to which he was so deeply penetrated. Existing society he knew to be in a deplorable state. But such as it was, he saw or thought he saw, that it was held together and prevented from being worse, by belief and reverence of the received divinities. As a ruler of mankind, he deemed it his duty not to suffer society to fall in pieces; and saw not how, if its existing ties were removed, any others could be formed which could again knit it together. The new religion openly aimed at dissolving these ties: unless, therefore, it was his duty to adopt that religion, it seemed to be his duty to put it down. Inasmuch then as the theology of Christianity did not appear to him true or of divine origin; inasmuch as this strange history of a crucified God was not credible to him, and a system which purported to rest entirely upon a foundation to him so wholly unbelievable, could not be foreseen by him to be that renovating agency which, after all abatements, it has in fact proved to be; the gentlest and most amiable of philosophers and rulers, under a solemn sense of duty, authorized the persecution of Christianity. To my mind this is one of the most tragical facts in all history. It is a bitter thought, how different a thing the Christianity of the world might have been, if the Christian faith had been adopted as the religion of the empire under the auspices of Marcus Aurelius instead of those of Constantine. But it would be equally unjust to him and false to truth, to deny, that no one plea which can be urged for punishing anti-Christian teaching, was wanting to Marcus Aurelius for punishing, as he did, the propagation of Christianity. No Christian more firmly believes that Atheism is false, and tends to the dissolution of society, than Marcus Aurelius believed the same things of Christianity; he who, of all men then living, might have been thought the most capable of appreciating it. Unless any one who approves of punishment for the promulgation of opinions, flatters himself that he is a wiser and better man than Marcus Aurelius—more deeply versed in the wisdom of his time, more elevated in his intellect above it—more earnest in his search for truth, or more single-minded in his devotion to it when found; —let him abstain from that assumption of the joint infallibility of himself and the multitude, which the great Antoninus made with so unfortunate a result.

Aware of the impossibility of defending the use of punishment for restraining irreligious opinions, by any argument which will not justify Marcus Antoninus, the enemies of religious freedom, when hard pressed, occasionally accept this consequence, and say, with Dr. Johnson, that the persecutors of Christianity were in the right; that persecution is an ordeal through which truth ought to pass, and always passes successfully, legal penalties being, in the end, powerless against truth, though sometimes beneficially effective against mischievous errors. This is a form of the argument for religious intolerance, sufficiently remarkable not to be passed without notice.

A theory which maintains that truth may justifiably be persecuted because persecution cannot possibly do it any harm, cannot be charged with being intentionally hostile to the reception of new truths; but we cannot commend the generosity of its dealing with the persons to whom mankind are indebted for them. To discover to the world something which deeply concerns it, and of which it was previously ignorant; to prove to it that it had been mistaken on some vital point of temporal or spiritual interest, is as important a service as a human being can render to his fellow-creatures, and in certain cases, as in those of the early Christians and of the Reformers, those who think with Dr. Johnson believe it to have been the most precious gift which could be bestowed on mankind. That the authors of such splendid benefits should be requited by martyrdom; that their reward should be to be dealt with as the vilest of criminals, is not, upon this theory, a deplorable error and misfortune, for which humanity should mourn in sackcloth and ashes, but the normal and justifiable state of things. The propounder of a new truth, according to this doctrine, should stand, as stood, in the legislation of the Locrians, the proposer of a new law, with a halter round his neck, to be instantly tightened if the public assembly did not, on hearing his reasons, then and there adopt his proposition. People who defend this mode of treating benefactors, can not be supposed to set much value on the benefit; and I believe this view of the subject is mostly confined to the sort of persons who think that new truths may have been desirable once, but that we have had enough of them now.

But, indeed, the dictum that truth always triumphs over persecution, is one of those pleasant falsehoods which men repeat after one another till they pass into commonplaces, but which all experience refutes. History teems with instances of truth put down by persecution. If not suppressed forever, it may be thrown back for centuries. To speak only of religious opinions: the Reformation broke out at least twenty times before Luther, and was put down. Arnold of Brescia was put down. Fra Dolcino was put down. Savonarola was put down. The Albigeois were put down. The Vaudois were put down. The Lollards were put down. The Hussites were put down. Even after the era of Luther, wherever persecution was persisted in, it was successful. In Spain, Italy, Flanders, the Austrian empire, Protestantism was rooted out; and, most likely, would have been so in England, had Queen Mary lived, or Queen Elizabeth died. Persecution has always succeeded, save where the heretics were too strong a party to be effectually persecuted. No reasonable person can doubt that Christianity might have been extirpated in the Roman empire. It spread, and became predominant, because the persecutions were only occasional, lasting but a short time, and separated by long intervals of almost undisturbed propagandism. It is a piece of idle sentimentality that truth, merely as truth, has any inherent power denied to error, of prevailing against the dungeon and the stake. Men are not more zealous for truth than they often are for error, and a sufficient application of legal or even of social penalties will generally succeed in stopping the propagation of either. The real advantage which truth has, consists in this, that when an opinion is true, it may be extinguished once, twice, or many times, but in the course of ages there will generally be found persons to rediscover it, until some one of its reappearances falls on a time when from favorable circumstances it escapes persecution until it has made such head as to withstand all subsequent attempts to suppress it.

THE INDISPENSABLE OPPOSITION

Walter Lippmann

Were they pressed hard enough, most men would probably confess that political freedom—that is to say, the right to speak freely and to act in opposition—is a noble ideal rather than a practical necessity. As the case for freedom is generally put today, the argument lends itself to this feeling. It is made to appear that, whereas each man claims his freedom as a matter of right, the freedom he accords to other men is a matter of toleration. Thus, the defense of freedom of opinion tends to rest not on its substantial, beneficial, and indispensable consequences, but on a somewhat eccentric, a rather vaguely benevolent, attachment to an abstraction.

It is all very well to say with Voltaire, "I wholly disapprove of what you say, but will defend to the death your right to say it," but as a matter of fact most men will not defend to the death the rights of other men: if they disapprove sufficiently what other men say, they will somehow suppress those men if they can.

So, if this is the best that can be said for liberty of opinion, that a man must tolerate his opponents because every one has a "right" to say what he pleases, then we shall find that liberty of opinion is a luxury, safe only in pleasant times when men can be tolerant because they are not deeply and vitally concerned.

Yet actually, as a matter of historic fact, there is a much stronger foundation for the great constitutional right of freedom of speech, and as a matter of practical human experience there is a much more compelling reason for cultivating the habits of free men. We take, it seems to me, a naïvely self-righteous view when we argue as if the right of our opponents to speak were something that we protect because we are magnanimous, noble, and unselfish. The compelling reason why, if liberty of opinion did not exist, we should have to invent it, why it will eventually have to be restored in all civilized countries where it is now suppressed, is that we must protect the right of our opponents to speak because we must hear what they have to say.

We miss the whole point when we imagine that we tolerate the freedom of our political opponents as we tolerate a howling baby next door, as we put up with the blasts from our neighbor's radio because we are too peaceable to heave a brick through the window. If this were all there is to freedom of opinion, that we are too good-natured or too timid to do anything about our opponents and our critics except to let them talk, it would be difficult to say whether we are tolerant because we are magnanimous or because we are lazy, because we have strong principles or because we lack serious convictions, whether we have the hospitality of an inquiring mind or the indifference of an empty mind. And so, if we truly wish to understand why freedom is necessary in a civilized society, we must begin by realizing that, because freedom of discussion improves our own opinions, the liberties of other men are our own vital necessity.

We are much closer to the essence of the matter, not when we quote Voltaire, but when we go to the doctor and pay him to ask us the most embarrassing questions and to prescribe the most disagreeable diet. When we pay the doctor to exercise complete freedom of speech about the cause and cure of our stomachache, we do not look upon ourselves as tolerant and magnanimous, and worthy to be admired by ourselves. We have enough common sense to know that if we threaten to put the doctor in jail because we do not like the diagnosis and the prescription it will be unpleasant for the doctor, to be sure, but equally unpleasant for our own stomachache. That is why even the most ferocious dictator would rather be treated by a doctor who was free to think and speak the truth than by his own Minister of Propaganda. For there is a point, the point at which things really matter, where the freedom of others is no longer a question of their right but of our own need.

The point at which we recognize this need is much higher in some men than in others. The totalitarian rulers think they do not need the freedom of an opposition: they exile, imprison, or shoot their opponents. We have concluded on the basis of practical experience, which goes back to Magna Carta and beyond, that we need the opposition. We pay the opposition salaries out of the public treasury.

In so far as the usual apology for freedom of speech ignores this experience, it becomes abstract and eccentric rather than concrete and human. The emphasis is generally put on the right to speak, as if all that mattered were that the doctor should be free to go out into the park and explain to the vacant air why I have a stomachache. Surely that is a miserable caricature of the great civic right which men have bled and died for. What really matters is that the doctor should tell *me* what ails me, that I should listen to him; that if I do not like what he says I should be free to call in another doctor; and that then the first doctor should have to listen to the second doctor; and that out of all the speaking and listening, the give-and-take of opinions, the truth should be arrived at.

This is the creative principle of freedom of speech, not that it is a system for the tolerating of error, but that it is a system for finding the truth. It may not produce the truth, or the whole truth all the time, or often, or in some cases ever. But if the truth can be found, there is no other system which will normally and habitually find so much truth. Until we have thoroughly understood this principle, we shall not know why we must value our liberty, or how we can protect and develop it. . . .

The only reason for dwelling on all this is that if we are to preserve democracy we must understand its principles. And the principle which distinguishes it from all other forms of government is that in a democracy the opposition not only is tolerated as constitutional but must be maintained because it is in fact indispensable.

The democratic system cannot be operated without effective opposition. For, in making the great experiment of governing people by consent rather than by coercion, it is not sufficient that the party in power should have a majority. It is just as necessary that the party in power should never outrage the minority. That means that it must listen to the minority and be moved by the criticisms of the minority. That means that its measures must take account of the minority's objections, and that in administering measures it must remember that the minority may become the majority.

The opposition is indispensable. A good statesman, like any other sensible human being, always learns more from his opponents than from his fervent supporters. For his supporters will push him to disaster unless his opponents show him where the dangers are. So if he is wise he will often pray to be delivered from his friends, because they will ruin him. But, though it hurts, he ought also to pray never to be left without opponents; for they keep him on the path of reason and good sense.

The national unity of a free people depends upon a sufficiently even balance of political power to make it impracticable for the administration to be arbitrary and for the opposition to be revolutionary and irreconcilable. Where that balance no longer exists, democracy perishes. For unless all the citizens of a state are forced by circumstances to compromise, unless they feel that they can affect policy but that no one can wholly dominate it, unless by habit and necessity they have to give and take, freedom cannot be maintained.

From NINETEEN EIGHTY-FOUR

George Orwell

"There are three stages in your reintegration," said O'Brien. "There is learning, there is understanding, and there is acceptance. It is time for you to enter upon the second stage."

As always, Winston was lying flat on his back. But of late his bonds were looser. They still held him to the bed, but he could move his knees a little and could turn his head from side to side and raise his arms from the elbow. The dial, also, had grown to be less of a terror. He could evade its pangs if he was quick-witted enough; it was chiefly when he showed stupidity that O'Brien pulled the lever. Sometimes they got through a whole session without use of the dial. He could not remember how many sessions there had been. The whole process seemed to stretch out over a long, indefinite time—weeks, possibly—and the intervals between the sessions might sometimes have been days, sometimes only an hour or two.

"As you lie there," said O'Brien, "you have often wondered—you have even asked me—why the Ministry of Love should expend so much time and trouble on you. And when you were free you were puzzled by what was essentially the same question. You could grasp the mechanics of the society you lived in, but not its underlying motives. Do you remember writing in your diary, 'I understand *how;* I do not understand *why*'? It was when you thought about 'why' that you doubted your own sanity. You have read *the book,* Goldstein's book, or parts of it, at least. Did it tell you anything that you did not know already?"

"You have read it?" said Winston.

"I wrote it. That is to say, I collaborated in writing it. No book is produced individually, as you know."

"Is it true, what it says?"

"As description, yes. The program it sets forth is nonsense. The secret accumulation of knowledge—a gradual spread of enlightenment—ultimately a proletarian rebellion—the overthrow of the Party. You foresaw yourself that that was what it would say. It is all nonsense. The proletarians will never revolt, not in a thousand years or a million. They cannot. I do not have to tell you the reason; you know it already. If you have ever cherished any dreams of violent insurrection, you must abandon them. There is no way in which the Party can be overthrown. The rule of the Party is forever. Make that the starting point of your thoughts."

He came closer to the bed. "Forever!" he repeated. "And now let us get back to the question of 'how' and 'why.' You understand well enough *how* the Party maintains itself in power. Now tell me *why* we cling to power. What is our motive? Why should we want power? Go on, speak," he added as Winston remained silent.

Nevertheless Winston did not speak for another moment or two. A feeling of weariness had overwhelmed him. The faint, mad gleam of enthusiasm had come back into O'Brien's face. He knew in advance what O'Brien would say: that the Party did not seek power for its own ends, but only for the good of the majority. That it sought power because men in the mass were frail, cowardly creatures who could not endure liberty or face the truth, and must be ruled over and systematically deceived by others who were stronger than themselves. That the choice for mankind lay between freedom and happiness, and that, for the great bulk of mankind, happiness was better. That the Party was the eternal guardian of the weak, a dedicated sect doing evil that good might come, sacrificing its own happiness to that of others. The terrible thing, thought Winston, the terrible thing was that when O'Brien said this he would believe it. You could see it in his face. O'Brien knew everything. A thousand times better than Winston, he knew what the world was really like, in what degradation the mass of human beings lived and by what lies and barbarities the Party kept them there. He had understood it all, weighed it all, and it made no difference: all was justified by the ultimate purpose. What can you do, thought Winston, against the lunatic who is more intelligent than yourself, who gives your arguments a fair hearing and then simply persists in his lunacy?

"You are ruling over us for our own good," he said feebly. "You believe that human beings are not fit to govern themselves, and therefore—"

He started and almost cried out. A pang of pain had shot through his body. O'Brien had pushed the lever of the dial up to thirty-five.

"That was stupid, Winston, stupid!" he said. "You should know better than to say a thing like that."

He pulled the lever back and continued:

"Now I will tell you the answer to my question. It is this. The Party seeks power entirely for its own sake. We are not interested in the good of others; we are interested solely in power. Not wealth or luxury or long life or happiness; only power, pure power. What pure power means you will understand presently. We are different from all the oligarchies of the past in that we know what we are doing. All the others, even those who resembled ourselves, were cowards and hypocrites. The German Nazis and the Russian Communists came very close to us in their methods, but they never had the courage to recognize their own motives. They pretended, perhaps they even believed, that they had seized power unwillingly and for a limited time, and that just round the corner there lay a paradise where human beings would be free and equal. We are not like that. We know that no one ever seizes power with the intention of relinquishing it. Power is not a means; it is an end. One does not establish a dictatorship in order to safeguard a revolution; one makes the revolution in order to establish the dictatorship. The object of persecution is persecution. The object of torture is torture. The object of power is power. Now do you begin to understand me?"

Winston was struck as he had been struck before, by the tiredness of O'Brien's face. It was strong and fleshy and brutal, it was full of intelligence and a sort of controlled passion before which he felt himself helpless; but it was tired. There were pouches under the eyes, the skin sagged from the cheekbones. O'Brien leaned over him, deliberately bringing the worn face nearer.

"You are thinking," he said, "that my face is old and tired. You are thinking that I talk of power, and yet I am not even able to prevent the decay of my own body. Can you not understand, Winston, that the individual is only a cell? The weariness of the cell is the vigor of the organism. Do you die when you cut your fingernails?"

He turned away from the bed and began strolling up and down again, one hand in his pocket.

"We are the priests of power," he said. "God is power. But at present power is only a word so far as you are concerned. It is time for you to gather some idea of what power means. The first thing you must realize is that power is collective. The individual only has power in so far as he ceases to be an individual. You know the Party slogan 'Freedom is Slavery.' Has it ever occurred to you that it is reversible? Slavery is freedom. Alone— free—the human being is always defeated. It must be so, because every human being is doomed to die, which is the greatest of all failures. But if he can make complete, utter submission, if he can escape from his identity, if he can merge himself in the Party so that he *is* the Party, then he is all-powerful and immortal. The second thing for you to realize is that power is power over human beings. Over the body—but, above all, over the mind. Power over matter—external reality, as you would call it—is not important. Already our control over matter is absolute."

For a moment Winston ignored the dial. He made a violent effort to raise himself into a sitting position, and merely succeeded in wrenching his body painfully.

"But how can you control matter?" he burst out. "You don't even control the climate or the law of gravity. And there are disease, pain, death—"

O'Brien silenced him by a movement of the hand. "We control matter because we control the mind. Reality is inside the skull. You will learn by degrees, Winston. There is nothing that we could not do. Invisibility, levitation—anything. I could float off this floor like a soap bubble if I wished to. I do not wish to, because the Party does not wish it. You must get rid of those nineteenth-century ideas about the laws of nature. We make the laws of nature."

"But you do not! You are not even masters of this planet. What about Eurasia and Eastasia? You have not conquered them yet."

"Unimportant. We shall conquer them when it suits us. And if we did not, what difference would it make? We can shut them out of existence. Oceania is the world."

"But the world itself is only a speck of dust. And man is tiny—helpless! How long has he been in existence? For millions of years the earth was uninhabited."

"Nonsense. The earth is as old as we are, no older. How could it be older? Nothing exists except through human consciousness."

"But the rocks are full of the bones of extinct animals—mammoths and mastodons and enormous reptiles which lived here long before man was ever heard of."

"Have you ever seen those bones, Winston? Of course not. Nineteenth-century biologists invented them. Before man there was nothing. After man, if he could come to an end, there would be nothing. Outside man there is nothing."

"But the whole universe is outside us. Look at the stars! Some of them are a million light-years away. They are out of our reach forever."

"What are the stars?" said O'Brien indifferently. "They are bits of fire a few kilometers away. We could reach them if we wanted to. Or we could blot them out. The earth is the center of the universe. The sun and the stars go round it."

Winston made another convulsive movement. This time he did not say anything. O'Brien continued as though answering a spoken objection:

"For certain purposes, of course, that is not true. When we navigate the ocean, or when we predict an eclipse, we often find it convenient to assume that the earth goes round the sun and that the stars are millions upon millions of kilometers away. But what of it? Do you suppose it is beyond us to produce a dual system of astronomy? The stars can be near or distant, according as we need them. Do you suppose our mathematicians are unequal to that? Have you forgotten doublethink?"

Winston shrank back upon the bed. Whatever he said, the swift answer crushed him like a bludgeon. And yet he knew, he *knew,* that he was in the right. The belief that nothing exists outside your own mind—surely there must be some way of demonstrating that it was false. Had it not been exposed long ago as a fallacy? There was even a name for it, which he had forgotten. A faint smile twitched the corners of O'Brien's mouth as he looked down at him.

"I told you, Winston," he said, "that metaphysics is not your strong point. The word you are trying to think of is solipsism. But you are mistaken. This is not solipsism. Collective solipsism, if you like. But that is a different thing; in fact, the opposite thing. All this is a digression," he added in a different tone. "The real power, the power we have to fight for night and day, is not power over things, but over men." He paused, and for a moment assumed again his air of a schoolmaster questioning a promising pupil: "How does one man assert his power over another, Winston?"

Winston thought. "By making him suffer," he said.

"Exactly. By making him suffer. Obedience is not enough. Unless he is suffering, how can you be sure that he is obeying your will and not his own? Power is in inflicting pain and humiliation. Power is in tearing human minds to pieces and putting them together again in new shapes of your own choosing. Do you begin to see, then, what kind of world we are creating? It is the exact opposite of the stupid hedonistic Utopias that the old reformers imagined. A world of fear and treachery and torment, a world of trampling and being trampled upon, a world which will grow not less but *more* merciless as it refines itself. Progress in our world will be progress toward more pain. The old civilizations claimed that they were founded on love and justice. Ours is founded upon hatred. In our world there will be no emotions except fear, rage, triumph, and self-abasement. Everything else we shall destroy—everything. Already we are breaking down the habits of thought which have survived from before the Revolution. We have cut the links between child and parent, and between man and man, and between man and woman. No one dares trust a wife or a child or a friend any longer. But in the future there will be no wives and no friends. Children will be taken from their mothers at birth, as one takes eggs from a hen. The sex instinct will be eradicated. Procreation will be an annual formality like the renewal of a ration card. We shall abolish the orgasm. Our neurologists are at work upon it now. There will be no loyalty, except loyalty toward the Party. There will be no love, except the love of Big Brother. There will be no laughter, except the laugh of triumph over a defeated enemy. There will be no art, no literature, no science. When we are omnipotent we shall have no more need of science. There will be no distinction between beauty and ugliness. There will be no curiosity, no employment of the process of life. All competing pleasures will be destroyed. But always—do not forget this, Winston—always there will be the intoxication of power, constantly increasing and constantly growing subtler. Always, at every moment, there will be the thrill of victory, the sensation of trampling on an enemy who is helpless. If you want a picture of the future, imagine a boot stamping on a human face—forever."

He paused as though he expected Winston to speak. Winston had tried to shrink back into the surface of the bed again. He could not say anything. His heart seemed to be frozen. O'Brien went on:

"And remember that it is forever. The face will always be there to be stamped upon. The heretic, the enemy of society, will always be there, so that he can be defeated and humiliated over again. Everything that you have undergone since you have been in our hands—all that will continue and worse. The espionage, the betrayals, the arrests, the tortures, the executions, the disappearances will never cease. It will be a world of terror as much as a world of triumph. The more the Party is powerful, the less it will be tolerant; the weaker the opposition, the tighter the despotism. Goldstein and his heresies will live forever. Every day, at every moment, they will be defeated, discredited, ridiculed, spat upon—and yet they will always survive. This drama that I have played out with you during seven years will be played out over and over again, generation after generation, always in subtler forms. Always we shall have the heretic here at our mercy, screaming with pain, broken up, contemptible—and in the end utterly penitent, saved from himself, crawling to our feet of his own accord. That is the world that we are preparing, Winston. A world of victory after victory, triumph after triumph after triumph: an endless pressing, pressing, pressing upon the nerve of power. You are beginning, I can see, to realize what that world will be like. But in the end you will do more than understand it. You will accept it, welcome it, become part of it."

Winston had recovered himself sufficiently to speak. "You can't!" he said weakly.

"What do you mean by that remark, Winston?"

"You could not create such a world as you have just described. It is a dream. It is impossible."

"Why?"

"It is impossible to found a civilization on fear and hatred and cruelty. It would never endure."

"Why not?"

"It would have no vitality. It would disintegrate. It would commit suicide."

"Nonsense. You are under the impression that hatred is more exhausting than love. Why should it be? And if it were, what difference would that make? Suppose that we choose to wear ourselves out faster. Suppose that we quicken the tempo of human life till men are senile at thirty. Still what difference would it make? Can you not understand that the death of the individual is not death? The Party is immortal."

As usual, the voice had battered Winston into helplessness. Moreover he was in dread that if he persisted in his disagreement O'Brien would twist the dial again. And yet he could not keep silent. Feebly, without arguments, with nothing to support him except his inarticulate horror of what O'Brien had said, he returned to the attack.

"I don't know—I don't care. Somehow you will fail. Something will defeat you. Life will defeat you."

"We control life, Winston, at all its levels. You are imagining that there is something called human nature which will be outraged by what we do and will turn against us. But we create human nature. Men are infinitely malleable. Or perhaps you have returned to your old idea that the proletarians or the slaves will arise and overthrow us. Put it out of your mind. They are helpless, like the animals. Humanity is the Party. The others are outside—irrelevant."

"I don't care. In the end they will beat you. Sooner or later they will see you for what you are, and then they will tear you to pieces."

"Do you see any evidence that this is happening? Or any reason why it should?"

"No. I believe it. I *know* that you will fail. There is something in the universe—I don't know, some spirit, some principle—that you will never overcome."

"Do you believe in God, Winston?"

"No."

"Then what is it, this principle that will defeat us?"

"I don't know. The spirit of Man."

"And do you consider yourself a man?"

"Yes."

"If you are a man, Winston, you are the last man. Your kind is extinct; we are the inheritors. Do you understand that you are *alone?* You are outside history, you are nonexistent." His manner changed and he said more harshly: "And you consider yourself morally superior to us, with our lies and our cruelty?"

"Yes, I consider myself superior."

O'Brien did not speak. Two other voices were speaking. After a moment Winston recognized one of them as his own. It was a sound track of the conversation he had had with O'Brien, on the night when he had enrolled himself in the Brotherhood. He heard himself promising to lie, to steal, to forge, to murder, to encourage drug taking and prostitution, to disseminate venereal diseases, to throw vitriol in a child's face. O'Brien made a small impatient gesture, as though to say that the demonstration was hardly worth making. Then he turned a switch and the voices stopped.

"Get up from that bed," he said.

The bonds had loosened themselves. Winston lowered himself to the floor and stood up unsteadily.

"You are the last man," said O'Brien. "You are the guardian of the human spirit. You shall see yourself as you are. Take off your clothes."

Winston undid the bit of string that held his overalls together. The zip fastener had long since been wrenched out of them. He could not remember whether at any time since his arrest he had taken off all his clothes at one time. Beneath the overalls his body was looped with filthy yellowish rags, just recognizable as the remnants of underclothes. As he slid them to the ground he saw that there was a three-sided mirror at the far end of the room. He approached it, then stopped short. An involuntary cry had broken out of him.

"Go on," said O'Brien. "Stand between the wings of the mirror. You shall see the side view as well."

He had stopped because he was frightened. A bowed, gray-colored, skeletonlike thing was coming toward him. Its actual appearance was frightening, and not merely the fact that he knew it to be himself. He moved closer to the glass. The creature's face seemed to be protruded, because of its bent carriage. A forlorn, jailbird's face with a nobby forehead running back into a bald scalp, a crooked nose and battered-looking cheekbones above which the eyes were fierce and watchful. The cheeks were seamed, the mouth had a drawn-in look. Certainly it was his own face, but it seemed to him that it had changed more than he had changed inside. The emotions it registered would be different from the ones he felt. He had gone partially bald. For the first moment he had thought that he had gone gray as well, but it was only the scalp that was gray. Except for his hands and a circle of his face, his body was gray all over with ancient, ingrained dirt. Here and there under the dirt there were the red scars of wounds, and near the ankle the varicose ulcer was an inflamed mass with flakes of skin peeling off it. But the truly frightening thing was the emaciation of his body. The barrel of the ribs was as narrow as that of a skeleton; the legs had shrunk so that the knees were thicker than the thighs. He saw now what O'Brien had meant about seeing the side view. The curvature of the spine was astonishing. The thin shoulders were hunched forward so as to make a cavity of the chest, the scraggy neck seemed to be bending double under the weight of the skull. At a guess he would have said that it was the body of a man of sixty, suffering from some malignant disease.

"You have thought sometimes," said O'Brien, "that my face—the face of a member of the Inner Party—looks old and worn. What do you think of your own face?"

He seized Winston's shoulder and spun him round so that he was facing him.

"Look at the condition you are in!" he said. "Look at this filthy grime all over your body. Look at the dirt between your toes. Look at that disgusting running sore on your leg. Do you know that you stink like a goat? Probably you have ceased to notice it. Look at your emaciation. Do you see? I can make my thumb and forefinger meet around your bicep. I could snap your neck like a carrot. Do you know that you have lost twenty-five kilograms since you have been in our hands? Even your hair is coming out in handfuls. Look!" He plucked at Winston's head and brought away a tuft of hair. "Open your mouth. Nine, ten, eleven teeth left. How many had you when you came to us? And the few you have left are dropping out of your head. Look here!"

He seized one of Winston's remaining front teeth between his powerful thumb and forefinger. A twinge of pain shot through Winston's jaw. O'Brien had wrenched the loose tooth out by the roots. He tossed it across the cell.

"You are rotting away," he said; "you are falling to pieces. What are you? A bag of filth. Now turn round and look into that mirror again. Do you see that thing facing you? That is the last man. If you are human, that is humanity. Now put your clothes on again."

Winston began to dress himself with slow stiff movements. Until now he had not seemed to notice how thin and weak he was. Only one thought stirred in his mind: that he must have been in this place longer than he had imagined. Then suddenly as he fixed the miserable rags round himself a feeling of pity for his ruined body overcame him. Before he knew what he was doing he had collapsed onto a small stool that stood beside the bed and burst into tears. He was aware of his ugliness, his gracelessness, a bundle of bones in filthy underclothes sitting weeping in the harsh white light; but he could not stop himself. O'Brien laid a hand on his shoulder, almost kindly.

"It will not last forever," he said. "You can escape from it whenever you choose. Everything depends on yourself."

"You did it!" sobbed Winston. "You reduced me to this state."

"No, Winston, you reduced yourself to it. This is what you accepted when you set yourself up against the Party. It was all contained in that first act. Nothing has happened that you did not foresee."

He paused, and then went on:

"We have beaten you, Winston. We have broken you up. You have seen what your body is like. Your mind is in the same state. I do not think there can be much pride left in you. You have been kicked and flogged and insulted, you have screamed with pain, you have rolled on the floor in your own blood and vomit. You have whimpered for mercy, you have betrayed everybody and everything. Can you think of a single degradation that has not happened to you?"

Winston had stopped weeping, though the tears were still oozing out of his eyes. He looked up at O'Brien.

"I have not betrayed Julia," he said.

O'Brien looked down at him thoughtfully. "No," he said, "no; that is perfectly true. You have not betrayed Julia."

The peculiar reverence for O'Brien, which nothing seemed able to destroy, flooded Winston's heart again. How intelligent, he thought, how intelligent! Never did O'Brien fail to understand what was said to him. Anyone else on earth would have answered promptly that he *had* betrayed Julia. For what was there that they had not screwed out of him under the torture? He had told them everything he knew about her, her habits, her character, her past life; he had confessed in the most trivial detail everything that had happened at their meetings, all that he had said to her and she to him, their black-market meals, their adulteries, their vague plottings against the Party—everything. And yet, in the sense in which he intended the word, he had not betrayed her. He had not stopped loving her; his feeling toward her had remained the same. O'Brien had seen what he meant without the need for explanation.

"Tell me," he said, "how soon will they shoot me?"

From THE ADVENTURES OF HUCKLEBERRY FINN

Mark Twain

We went drifting down into a big bend, and the night clouded up and got hot. The river was very wide, and was walled with solid timber on both sides; you couldn't see a break in it hardly ever, or a light. We talked about Cairo, and wondered whether we would know it when we got to it. I said likely we wouldn't, because I had heard say there warn't but about a dozen houses there, and if they didn't happen to have them lit up, how was we going to know we was passing a town? Jim said if the two big rivers joined together there, that would show. But I said maybe we might think we was passing the foot of an island and coming into the same old river again. That disturbed Jim—and me too. So the question was, what to do? I said, paddle ashore the first time a light showed, and tell them pap was behind, coming along with a trading-scow, and was a green hand at the business, and wanted to know how far it was to Cairo. Jim thought it was a good idea, so we took a smoke on it and waited.

There warn't nothing to do now but to look out sharp for the town, and not pass it without seeing it. He said he'd be mighty sure to see it, because he'd be a free man the minute he seen it, but if he missed it he'd be in a slave country again and no more show for freedom. Every little while he jumps up and says:

"Dah she is?"

But it warn't. It was Jack-o'-lanterns, or lightning-bugs; so he set down again, and went to watching, same as before. Jim said it made him all over trembly and feverish to be so close to freedom. Well, I can tell you it made me all over trembly and feverish, too, to hear him, because I begun to get it through my head that he *was* most free—and who was to blame for it? Why, *me*. I couldn't get that out of my conscience, no how nor no way. It got to troubling me so I couldn't rest; I couldn't stay still in one place. It hadn't ever come home to me before, what this thing was that I was doing. But now it did; and it stayed with me, and scorched me more and more. I tried to make out to myself that *I* warn't to blame, because *I* didn't run Jim off from his rightful owner; but it warn't no use, conscience up and says, every time, "But you knowed he was running for his freedom, and you could 'a' paddled ashore and told somebody." That was so—I couldn't get around that no way. That was where it pinched. Conscience say to me, "What had poor Miss Watson done to you that you could see her nigger go off right under your eyes and never say one single word? What did that poor old woman do to you that you could treat her so mean? Why, she tried to learn you your book, she tried to learn you your manners, she tried to be good to you every way she knowed how. *That's* what she done."

I got to feeling so mean and so miserable I most wished I was dead. I fidgeted up and down the raft, abusing myself to myself, and Jim was fidgeting up and down past me. We neither of us could keep still. Every time he danced around and says, "Dah's Cairo!" it went through me like a shot, and I thought if it *was* Cairo I reckoned I would die of miserableness.

Jim talked out loud all the time while I was talking to myself. He was saying how the first thing he would do when he got to a free state he would go to saving up money and never spend a single cent, and when he got enough he would buy his wife, which was owned on a farm close to where Miss Watson lived; and then they would both work to buy the two children, and if their master wouldn't sell them, they'd get an Ab'litionist to go and steal them.

It most froze me to hear such talk. He wouldn't ever dared to talk such talk in his life before. Just see what a difference it made in him the minute he judged he was about free. It was according to the old saying, "Give a nigger an inch and he'll take an ell." Thinks I, this is what comes of my not thinking. Here was this nigger, which I had as good as helped to run away, coming right out flat-footed and saying he would steal his children—children that belonged to a man I didn't even know; a man that hadn't ever done me no harm.

I was sorry to hear Jim say that, it was such a lowering of him. My conscience got to stirring me up hotter than ever, until at last I says to it, "Let up on me—it ain't too late yet—I'll paddle ashore at the first light and tell." I felt easy and happy and light as a feather right off. All my troubles was gone. I went to looking out sharp for a light, and sort of singing to myself. By and by one showed. Jim sings out:

"We's safe, Huck, we's safe! Jump up and crack yo' heels! Dat's de good ole Cairo at las', I jis knows it!"

I says:

"I'll take the canoe and go and see, Jim. It mightn't be, you know."

He jumped and got the canoe ready, and put his old coat in the bottom for me to set on, and give me the paddle; and as I shoved off, he says:

"Pooty soon I'll be a-shoutin' for joy, en I'll say, it's all on accounts o' Huck; I's a free man, en I couldn't ever ben free ef it hadn't ben for Huck; Huck done it. Jim won't ever forgit you, Huck; you's de bes' fren' Jim's ever had, en you's de *only* fren' ole Jim's got now."

I was paddling off, all in a sweat to tell on him; but when he says this, it seemed to kind of take the tuck all out of me. I went along slow then, and I warn't right down certain whether I was glad I started or whether I warn't. When I was fifty yards off, Jim says:

"Dah you goes, de ole true Huck; de on'y white genlman dat ever kep' his promise to ole Jim."

Well, I just felt sick. But I says, I *got* to do it—I can't get *out* of it. Right then along comes a skiff with two men in it with guns, and they stopped and I stopped. One of them says:

"What's that yonder?"

"A piece of raft," I says.

"Do you belong on it?"

"Yes, sir."

"Any men on it?"

"Only one, sir."

"Well, there's five niggers run off to-night up yonder, above the head of the bend. Is your man white or black?"

I didn't answer up promptly. I tried to, but the words wouldn't come. I tried for a second or two to brace up and out with it, but I warn't man enough—hadn't the spunk of a rabbit. I see I was weakening; so I just give up trying, and up and says:

"He's white."

"I reckon we'll go and see for ourselves."

"I wish you would," says I, "because it's pap that's there, and maybe you'd help me tow the raft ashore where the light is. He's sick—and so is mam and Mary Ann."

"Oh, the devil! we're in a hurry, boy. But I s'pose we've got to. Come, buckle to your paddle, and let's get along."

I buckled to my paddle and they laid to their oars. When we had made a stroke or two, I says:

"Pap'll be mighty much obleeged to you, I can tell you. Everybody goes away when I want them to help me tow the raft ashore, and I can't do it by myself."

"Well, that's infernal mean. Odd, too. Say, boy, what's the matter with your father?"

"It's the—a—the—well, it ain't anything much."

They stopped pulling. It warn't but a mighty little ways to the raft now. One says:

"Boy, that's a lie. What *is* the matter with your pap? Answer up square now, and it'll be the better for you."

"I will, sir, I will, honest—but don't leave us, please. It's the—the— Gentlemen, if you'll only pull ahead, and let me heave you the head-line, you won't have to come a-near the raft—please do."

"Set her back, John, set her back!" says one. They backed water. "Keep away, boy—keep to looard. Confound it, I just expect the wind has blowed it to us. Your pap's got the smallpox, and you know it precious well. Why didn't you come out and say so? Do you want to spread it all over?"

"Well," says I, a-blubbering, "I've told everybody before, and they just went away and left us."

"Poor devil, there's something in that. We are right down sorry for you, but we—well, hang it, we don't want the smallpox, you see. Look here, I'll tell you what to do. Don't you try to land by yourself, or you'll smash everything to pieces. You float along down about twenty miles, and you'll come to a town on the left-hand side of the river. It will be long after sun-up then, and when you ask for help you tell them your folks are all down with chills and fever. Don't be a fool again, and let people guess what is the matter. Now we're trying to do you a kindness; so you just put twenty miles between us, that's a good boy. It wouldn't do any good to land yonder where the light is—it's only a wood-yard. Say, I reckon your father's poor, and I'm bound to say he's in pretty hard luck. Here, I'll put a twenty-dollar gold piece on this board, and you get it when it floats by. I feel mighty mean to leave you; but my kingdom! it won't do to fool with smallpox, don't you see?"

"Hold on, Parker," says the man, "here's a twenty to put on the board for me. Good-by, boy; you do as Mr. Parker told you, and you'll be all right."

"That's so, my boy—good-by, good-by. If you see any runaway niggers you get help and nab them, and you can make some money by it."

"Good-by, sir," says I; "I won't let no runaway niggers get by me if I can help it."

They went off and I got aboard the raft, feeling bad and low, because I knowed very well I had done wrong, and I see it warn't no use for me to try to learn to do right; a body that don't get *started* right when he's little ain't got no show—when the pinch comes there ain't nothing to back him up and keep him to his work, and so he gets beat. Then I thought a minute, and says to myself, hold on; s'pose you'd 'a' done right and give Jim up, would you felt better than what you do now? No, says I, I'd feel bad—I'd feel just the same way I do now. Well, then, says I, what's the use you learning to do right when it's troublesome to do right and ain't no trouble to do wrong, and the wages is just the same? I was stuck. I couldn't answer that. So I reckoned I wouldn't bother no more about it, but after this always do whichever come handiest at the time.

I went into the wigwam; Jim warn't there. I looked all around; he warn't anywhere. I says:

"Jim!"

"Here I is, Huck. Is dey out o' sight yit? Don't talk loud."

He was in the river under the stern oar, with just his nose out. I told him they were out of sight, so he come aboard. He says:

"I was a-listenin' to all de talk, en I slips into de river en was gwyne to shove for sho' if dey come aboard. Den I was gwyne to swim to de raf' agin when dey was gone. But lawsy, how you did fool 'em, Huck! Dat *wuz* de smartes' dodge! I tell you, chile, I 'spec it save' ole Jim—ole Jim ain't going to forgit you for dat, honey."

Then we talked about the money. It was a pretty good raise—twenty dollars apiece. Jim said we could take deck passage on a steamboat now, and the money would last us as far as we wanted to go in the free states. He said twenty mile more warn't far for the raft to go, but he wished we was already there.

WILKINSON v. UNITED STATES

Hugo Black

MR. JUSTICE BLACK, WITH WHOM THE CHIEF JUSTICE AND MR. JUSTICE DOUGLAS CONCUR, DISSENTING

In July 1958 the House Un-American Activities Committee announced its intention to conduct a series of hearings in Atlanta, Georgia, ostensibly to obtain information in aid of the legislative function of the House of Representatives. Petitioner, a long-time opponent of the Committee, decided to go to Atlanta for the purpose of lending his support to those who were fighting against the hearings. He arrived in Atlanta and registered in a hotel there on July 23 as a representative of the Emergency Civil Liberties Committee, a New York organization which was working for the abolition of the Un-American Activities Committee. Within an hour of his registration, petitioner was served with a subpoena requiring his appearance before the Committee. When he appeared in response to this subpoena, petitioner was told that he had been subpoenaed because the Committee was informed that "you were sent to this area by the Communist Party for the purpose of developing a hostile sentiment to this Committee and to its work for the purpose of undertaking to bring pressure upon the United States Congress to preclude these particular hearings." A number of questions were then put to petitioner all of which related to his personal beliefs and associations, but petitioner refused to answer any of these questions on the ground that they violated his rights under the First Amendment. For this, he was convicted under 2 U.S.C. Section 192 and sentenced to jail for twelve months.

On these facts, which are undisputed in the record, the majority upholds petitioner's conviction as "indistinguishable" from that upheld in *Barenblatt* v. *United States*. On this point, I find myself only partially in disagreement with the majority. I think this case could and should be distinguished from *Barenblatt* on the ground urged by Mr. Justice Douglas—that the resolution authorizing the Un-American Activities Committee does not authorize that Committee to interrogate a person for criticizing it. I therefore join in the dissent filed by Mr. Justice Douglas on that ground. On the other hand, I must agree with the majority that so far as petitioner's constitutional claims are concerned, *Barenblatt* is "indistinguishable." Unlike the majority, however, I regard this recognition of the unlimited sweep of the decision in the *Barenblatt Case* a compelling reason, not to reaffirm that case, but to overrule it.

In my view, the majority by its decision today places the stamp of constitutional approval upon a practice as clearly inconsistent with the Constitution, and indeed with every ideal of individual freedom for which this country has so long stood, as any that has ever come before this Court. For, like Mr. Justice Douglas, I think it clear that this case involves nothing more nor less than an attempt by the Un-American Activities Committee to use the contempt power of the House of Representatives as a weapon against those who dare to criticize it. The majority does not and, in reason, could not deny this for the conclusion is all but inescapable for anyone who will take the time to read the record. They say instead that it makes no difference whether the Committee was harassing petitioner solely by reason of his opposition to it or not because "it is not for us to speculate as to the motivations that may have prompted the decision of individual members of the subcommittee to summon the petitioner." The clear thrust of this sweeping abdication of judicial power is that the Committee may continue to harass its opponents with absolute impunity so long as the "protections" of *Barenblatt* are observed. Since this is to be the rule under which the Committee will be permitted to operate, I think it necessary in the interest of fairness to those who may in the future wish to exercise their constitutional right to criticize the Committee that the true nature of those "protections" be clearly set forth.

The first such "protection" relates to the question of whom the Committee may call before it. Is there any limitation upon the power of the Committee to subpoena and compel testimony from anyone who attacks it? On this point, the majority, relying upon the fact that at a previous hearing the Committee was told by a paid informant that petitioner was a Communist and upon statements by the Committee's counsel to the effect that the

Committee had information that petitioner had been sent to Atlanta by the Communist Party, says simply: "It is to be emphasized that the petitioner was not summoned to appear as the result of an indiscriminate dragnet procedure, lacking in probable cause for belief that he possessed information which might be helpful to the subcommittee." Significantly, the majority does not say just how much its "emphasis" on this point is worth, if anything. Thus, for all that appears in the majority opinion, there is no assurance that the Committee will be required to produce any information at all as a prerequisite to the exercise of its subpoena and contempt powers. Assuming for the sake of argument, however, that such a requirement will be imposed, it then becomes relevant to inquire as to just how much this requirement will mean in terms of genuine protection for those who in good faith wish to criticize the Committee.

That inquiry is, to my mind, satisfactorily settled by a look at the facts of this case. So far as appears from this record, the only information the Committee had with regard to petitioner was the testimony of a paid informant at a previous Committee hearing. The only evidence to the effect that petitioner was in fact a member of the Communist Party that emerges from that testimony is a flat conclusory statement by the informant that it was so. No testimony as to particular happenings upon which such a conclusion could rationally be based was given at that hearing. When this fact is considered in conjunction that the fact that petitioner was not accorded the opportunity to cross-examine the informant or the protection of the statute permitting inspection of statements given to the FBI by paid informants, it seems obvious to me that such testimony is almost totally worthless for the purpose of establishing probable cause. For all we know, the informant may have had no basis at all for her conclusion and, indeed, the possibility of perjury cannot, in view of its frequent recurrence in these sorts of cases, be entirely discounted. Thus, in my view, the "protection" afforded by a requirement of some sort of probable cause, even if imposed, is almost totally worthless. In the atmosphere existing in this country today, the charge that someone is a Communist is so common that hardly anyone active in public life escapes it. Every member of this Court has, on one occasion or another, been so designated. And a vast majority of the members of the other two branches of Government have fared no better. If the mere fact that someone has been called a Communist is to be permitted to satisfy a requirement of probable cause, I think it plain that such a requirement is wholly without value. To impose it would only give apparent respectability to a practice which is inherently in conflict with our concepts of justice and due process.

The other such "protection" afforded to critics of the Un-American Activities Committee under these decisions is included in the majority's so-called balancing test. Under that test, we are told, this Court will permit only those abridgments of personal beliefs and associations by Committee inquiry that the Court believes so important in terms of the need of the Committee for information that such need outweighs the First Amendment rights of the witness and the public. For my part, I need look no further than this very case to see how little protection this high-sounding slogan really affords. For in this case the majority is holding that the interest of the Committee in the information sought outweighs that of the witness and the public in free discussion, while, at the same time, it disclaims any power to determine whether the Committee is in fact interested in the information at all. The truth of the matter is that the balancing test, at least as applied to date, means that the Committee may engage in *any* inquiry a majority of this Court happens to think could possibly be for a legitimate purpose whether that "purpose" be the true reason for the inquiry or not. And under the tests of legitimacy that are used in this area, any first-year law school student worth his salt could construct a rationalization to justify almost any question put to any witness at any time.

Thus, in my view, the conclusion is inescapable that the only real limitation upon the Committee's power to harass its opponents is the Committee's own self-restraint, a characteristic which probably has not been predominant in the Committee's work over the past few years. The result of all this is that from now on anyone who takes a public position contrary to that being urged by the House Un-American Activities Committee should realize that he runs the risk of being subpoenaed to appear at a hearing in some far off place, of being questioned with regard to every minute detail of his past life, of being asked to repeat all the gossip he may have heard about any of his friends and acquaintances, of being accused by the Committee of membership in the Communist Party, of being held up to the public as a subversive and a traitor, of being jailed for contempt if he refuses to co-operate with the Committee in its probe of his mind and associations, and of being branded by his neighbors, employer, and erstwhile friends as a menace to society *regardless of the outcome of that hearing*. With such a powerful weapon in his hands, it seems quite likely that the Committee will weather all criticism, even though justifiable, that may be directed toward it. For there are not many people in our society who will have the courage to speak out against such a formidable opponent. If the present trend continues, this already small number will necessarily dwindle as their ranks are thinned by the jails. Government by consent will disappear to be replaced by government by intimidation because some people are afraid that this country cannot survive unless Congress has the power to set aside the freedoms of the First Amendment at will.

I can only reiterate my firm conviction that these people are tragically wrong. This country was not built by men who were afraid and it cannot be preserved by such men. Our Constitution, in unequivocal terms, gives the right to each of us to say what we think without fear of the power of the Government. That principle has served us so well for so long that I cannot believe it necessary to allow any governmental group to reject it in order to preserve its own existence. Least of all do I believe that such a privilege should be accorded the House Un-American Activities Committee. For I believe that true Americanism is to be protected, not by committees that persecute unorthodox minorities, but by strict adherence to basic principles of freedom that are responsible for this Nation's greatness. Those principles are embodied for all who care to see in our Bill of Rights. They were put there for the specific purpose of preventing just the sort of governmental suppression of criticism that the majority upholds here. Their ineffectiveness to that end stems, not from any lack of precision in the statement of the principles, but from the refusal of the majority to apply those principles as precisely stated. For the principles of the First Amendment are stated in precise and mandatory terms, and unless they are applied in those terms, the freedoms of religion, speech, press, assembly and petition will have no effective protection. Where these freedoms are left to depend upon a balance to be struck by this Court in each particular case, liberty cannot survive. For under such a rule, there are no constitutional rights that cannot be "balanced" away.

IN PRAISE OF INCONSISTENCY

Leszek Kolakowski

I speak of consistency in one sense only, limited to the correspondence between behavior and thought, to the inner harmony between general principles and their application. Therefore I consider a consistent man to be simply one who, possessing a certain number of general, absolute concepts, strives earnestly in all he does, and in all his opinions about what should be done, to remain in the fullest possible accord with those concepts. A consistent man is one who considers killing evil and refuses to enter military service; one who is convinced of the superiority of monogamy over other forms of family life and so does not deceive his wife. Consistent, too, is the policeman who believes regulations must be observed and therefore gives out summonses to jaywalkers and the like.

There exists in the history of culture a rare race of highly talented authors of the extreme Right, whose works provide invaluable material for reflection upon consistency. In France this is the breed of Bossuet, De Maistre, and Maurras. Men of considerable intellectual courage, they have not been afraid to carry their assumptions to their logical conclusions and loudly voice their judgments on every matter in which their principles were engaged.

Joseph de Maistre knows exactly what is the best order of the world, as ordained by God. He knows, too, what is most precious in this order and what is subordinate. Next, he demonstrates his amazing consistency by applying these general assumptions to all concrete questions: The world is so fashioned that evil must exist; given the existence of evil, there must be punishment. This being so, someone must inflict punishment, and that "someone" is an indispensable element in the social order, worthy of respect for that reason. De Maistre then writes in praise of the hangman: "All greatness, all power, the hierarchy as a whole rest upon the hangman: he is the terror and the mainstay of human society. Remove this misconstrued factor from the world and instantly order will yield to chaos, thrones will shake, and society perish. God, who created authority, also created punishment." It follows that the hangman, because his profession is shrouded in dread, "is an anomalous being and to include him in the family of man requires a special dispensation, a *fiat* of creative power. He was created just as the world was."

Similarly: Spiritual crimes are worse than those of the flesh because the good of the spirit carries more weight. Spiritual crimes are also more odious because they offend against God's majesty, which is greater than that of terrestrial sovereigns; and this leads De Maistre to praise the Spanish Inquisition. In like fashion, Galileo was himself responsible for his trial because he could not refrain from writing despite his promise, because he defended the compatibility between Copernicus and the Bible, because he wrote in the vernacular and not in Latin. De Maistre concludes by lauding the tribunal that found Galileo guilty.

We may salute this fine example of consistency, of strict application of principle. On the other hand, we must note that humanity has survived only thanks to inconsistency.

What is required of a soldier going off to war? Uniquely that he be consistent in his righteous duty to defend his country. (I say "defend" because, as we know, all that seems to exist in wartime is "defense," and always "righteous," at that.) Battles fought by consistent soldiers can end only when the last man on one of the sides gives up the ghost. What is required of a citizen? Consistent loyalty to the state or government. Therefore a consistent citizen will always be proud to cooperate with the secret police, knowing it to be necessary to the existence of the state, to its glory and growth. To prove this is so is the easiest thing in the world, and every citizen who hesitates to write systematically to the secret police informing on his neighbors is surely inconsistent. Let us assume that we consider a certain matter to be the most important in the world; for example, a universal obligation to wear a top hat. Why, then, should we object to imposing our idea by means of war, aggression, provocation, blackmail, assassination, intimidation, terror, murder, or torture?

The race of those who vacillate and are soft, the inconsistent people, precisely those who happily eat steak for dinner but are totally incapable of slaughtering a chicken; those who do not wish to contravene the laws of the land yet do not denounce others to the secret police; those who go to war but in a hopeless situation surrender as prisoners rather than die in a last-ditch fight; those who prize frankness but cannot bring themselves to tell a famous painter that his work is terrible, nervously uttering words of praise which they do not mean—in short, the race of inconsistent people—continues to be one of the greatest sources of hope that possibly the human species will somehow manage to survive. For this is the race of which part believes in God and the superiority of eternal salvation over temporal well-being, yet does not demand that heretics be converted at the stake; while the other part, not believing in God, espouses revolutionary changes in social conditions yet rejects methods purporting to bring about these changes which openly contradict a certain moral tradition in which these people were raised.

In other words, total consistency is tantamount in practice to fanaticism, while inconsistency is the source of tolerance. Why should anyone inflexibly convinced of the exclusive truth of his concepts regarding any and all questions be willing to tolerate opposing ideas? What good can he expect of a situation in which everyone is free to express opinions that to his mind are patently false and therefore harmful to society? By what right should he abstain from using any means whatsoever to attain the goal he regards as correct?

We could say at this point that tolerance is extorted, that the only things tolerated are those which, for lack of ammunition, cannot be destroyed. And as a rule the only people are those who are so strong that their opponents cannot eliminate them with impunity. This observation is certainly well documented by history, but it does not explain everything. If a power relationship were the sole basis of tolerance, and if in addition fanatical consistency ruled the minds of the antagonists, the two groups would be permanently involved in trying to eradicate each other. Since this does not occur, or at least not always, it is only as the blessed result of inconsistency, an inconsistency which does not necessarily spring from conscious acceptance of the principle of tolerance, but merely manifests itself as if that principle were accepted to some degree.

Inconsistency is simply a secret awareness of the contradictions of this world. By contradictions I mean the various values that are, notoriously throughout history, introduced into society by mutually antagonistic forces. If convictions of the absolute and exclusive superiority of a given value to which all else is subordinate were to spread and be practiced widely, they would of necessity transform the world into an ever-larger battleground— which indeed does occur from time to time. The lack of consistency checks this tendency.

Inconsistency as an individual attitude is merely a consciously sustained reserve of uncertainty, a permanent feeling of possible personal error, or if not that, then of the possibility that one's antagonist is right. We have been speaking all this time about the relationship between thinking and the bases of practical action. Now, all thought that can in any way manifest itself as a causative factor in practical conduct is the affirmation of a value. In turn—and this is one of the most important principles we wish to formulate —*the world of values is not logically dualistic,* as opposed to the world of theoretical thought. In other words, there are values that exclude each other without ceasing to be values (although there are no mutually exclusive truths that still remain truths). Daily life shows at every step what a truism this statement is.

Inconsistency, in the sense we use it here, is simply *a refusal once and for all to choose beforehand between any values whatever which mutually exclude each other*. A clear awareness of the eternal and incurable antinomy in the world of values is nothing but conscious inconsistency, though inconsistency is more often practiced than proclaimed. Inconsistency is a constant effort to cheat life, which incessantly tries to place us before alternative doors, each of which is an entrance but through neither of which we can return. Once we have entered we are compelled to fight to the end, to the last bullet, for life or death, with him who entered through the other door. Thus we try to dodge, to maneuver, to use all the tricks and traps, all the suspect manipulations and stratagems, subterfuges and evasions, the chicanery, half-truths, hints, and circumspection—anything to keep from being pushed through either of the doors that opens upon a single direction.

These attempts to deceive life, to conciliate implacable antagonists—these efforts to evade the fatal "either-or" between contradictory values—all this is not the result of a temporary derangement in people's lives that will be removed with the advent of the new era. It is the result of human nature, whose antinomies are always with us. Accepting them as part of man's universal lot, we can elude these antinomies through inconsistency, in order not to reject permanently something we value just because something else we esteem is eternally contradictory to it. So we try to postpone final decisions until the end of life overtakes us, the sole situation in which there is no longer any possibility of choice.

At this point someone may ask: Is this any different from the common-sense wisdom Aristotle set forth in his Nicomachean Ethic? Indeed, his idea is based on the premise that there exist virtues and antivirtues, as well as corresponding vices and antivices. Thrift is a virtue and parsimony a vice; but generosity is also a virtue, while extravagance is wrong. We can—so taught the father of Europe's intellectual tradition—reconcile contradictory virtues without falling prey to the opposite vices. Let us be at once frugal and open-handed, but neither miserly nor prodigal. Let us hold that middle ground between recklessness and cowardice which harmoniously combines valor and prudence. As between a feverish lust for fame and timorous humility, let us seek to maintain a position which unites healthy ambition with modesty. Equally removed from brutal vengefulness and abject submissiveness, let us be both firm and gentle. For the truly generous man is not wasteful but thrifty; just as the courageous man is not reckless but cautious. And so forth.

Have we, in praising inconsistency, come to the point of merely repeating the age-old dictum of the golden mean? Let me confess at once that my idea does not pretend to the slightest consanguinity with this middle-of-the-road theory; it is, in fact, the exact opposite. Aristotle's ethic! Aristotle's ethic was clearly earthly, but his earth was flat. He expounded a novel concept that unified the Hellenistic world. He conquered the world because he was the embodiment of the spirit of universal conciliation at a time when unity was needed most. In metaphysics, politics, and moral doctrine he personified this unity. But Aristotle's genius is alien to us because we live in a world of extremes.

If we look more closely at this Aristotelian ethic we see that its main current is a longing for synthesis and a belief that between any two extremes one can find a mean that will preserve the best of each and reject what is harmful. It is assumed that a reasonable mind can harmonize what to the immoderate one appear to be contradictions. In other words, Aristotle believes that the contradictions in human attitudes that erupt into social antagonisms are not inherent in the world but are caused by lack of reasonableness. Thus antinomies are created by man, who in one way or another misuses the good in the world.

My praise of inconsistency, however, springs from a completely different source. It posits that contradictions in values do not stem from their abuse and therefore are not merely appearances that can be overcome by intelligent moderation. These contradictions inhere in the world of values and cannot be reconciled in any synthesis. Reasonable inconsistency does not seek to forge a synthesis between extremes, knowing it does not exist, since values as such exclude each other integrally. The real world of values is inconsistent; that is to say, it is made up of antagonistic elements. To grant them full recognition simultaneously is impossible, yet each demands total acceptance. This is not a matter of logical contradictions, because values are not theoretical theses. It is a contradiction which lies at the heart of human behavior.

Inconsistency is thus a certain attitude which, having realized that this is the situation, knows the extremes to be irreconcilable yet refuses to reject either because it recognizes each as valid. Naturally, I do not mean that no concrete conflict of two values clashing in a given situation can ever be reconciled. My thesis is not concerned with any pair of contradictions within a defined context, but with the condition of contradiction as such. In other words, I believe it is possible to synthesize or surmount actual contradictions, but at the same time I am convinced—in accordance with the experience of history as a whole—that one contradiction disappears only to give way to another; that therefore, no universal synthesis is possible. In the world we live in, contradictions cannot be reconciled; once resolved, they pertain no longer to this world but to a dead one, regarding which we need no longer take a practical stand. Contradictions pursue us as long as we act in a world of values, which simply means for as long as we live.

Let us take an example from everyday political life. We believe that nations have the right to decide their own fate. This belief affirms a certain value. We also believe that certain important social institutions preserved in the life of our nation are detrimental to its development. Yet we see unmistakably that our people prize these very institutions highly and obviously have no intention of listening to our arguments on the subject. For instance, we are not only immune to the benefits of religious consolation but deeply convinced, besides, that the continuing influence of religious institutions upon public life is damaging. Nonetheless, this influence not only manifests itself, but undoubtedly does so in accordance with the will of the people. How should we behave? We do not want to renounce either of the opposing principles involved. We do not want to destroy by force and against the people's will an institution manifestly supported by the majority. Nor do we wish to abandon the fight to abolish this institution.

Some might call this a trite situation, one that in no way excludes a synthesis. That synthesis will come about in the course of history. We expect that as people grow sufficiently enlightened the present conflict will cease to exist. Meanwhile, though, we must—with total consistency—strive to educate people so that in the future they will be disposed to accept our concepts and choose of their own free will to extirpate institutions that, in our opinion, hamper the nation's growth.

Unfortunately, this sage advice does not dispel our doubts. Certainly nothing prevents us from believing that in the course of history, measured by the yardstick of generations, the will of the people will undergo such a change, and that their level of maturity will rise to the point where this particular conflict will disappear. Nevertheless, this hope is of fleeting value in practical daily behavior. Let us suppose that in this country I have to vote on whether the teaching of religion should be introduced in public schools, when heretofore there was none; or, on the contrary, whether to discontinue existing religious education. Then I have no other choice: I vote either in agreement with the will of the people, or else in accordance with what I consider their good. I must vote—this obligation has been forced upon me by circumstances beyond my control. I cannot remain consistent toward both my principles at once, but I do not want to forsake either. This example is neither contrived nor exceptional. How many deputies in any number of parliaments vote one way while secretly hoping the opposition will win?

The problem of the antinomy inherent in the principle of tolerance is eternal and eternally unresolved: how to preach and practice tolerance toward ideas and movements which are intolerant. We act against our basic tenet if we silence these ideas and movements by force; we also act against our principle if we tolerate them, for we thus enable them to triumph and destroy the principle of tolerance in social practice. And it is cold comfort under the circumstances to hope that this contradiction will be solved in the process of historical development, either because, having slaughtered all the enemies of tolerance, we shall be able to apply it boundlessly; or else because these movements will in the course of time discard their intolerance. In practical everyday actions and in our daily participation in society, such perspectives help us minimally in making decisions.

These examples are not fictitious. Our lives are bound up in conflicting loyalties that we must choose between in concrete situations. We must break one bond in favor of another, while still not questioning the first. Loyalty to the individual, to one's own outlook on the world, to human communities in which we find ourselves either accidentally or of free choice, loyalty to nations, parties, governments, friends, to ourselves and those close to us, to our own nature and our convictions, to the present and the future, to concrete things and universalities—there are as many insurmountable contradictions as there are loyalties. An authentic synthesis resolving chronic conflicts rarely occurs; most often the supposed synthesis is superficial and fraudulent. We deceive ourselves with it in order to appear consistent, for one of the values instilled in us since childhood is consistency. Our proposition, aimed at making us realize that in these conditions consistency is an ideological fiction, is thus also intended to remove at least one kind of conflict: that which results from a belief in consistency as a value. So, proclaiming the contradictory nature of the world, we strive to attenuate it at least at one point, for, as we see, conflicts multiply because they are misunderstood. In other words, praise of inconsistency is at the same time the rejection of a specific value, that of the consistent life. The contradiction between the value of a consistent life and that of a basically reasonable one belongs to the species of conflict which may perhaps be removed unilaterally—not by synthesis, but by the repudiation of one of the sides to the dispute.

And immediately the question arises: Can we really proclaim the principle of inconsistency in a perfect formulation, which means, in essence, consistently? Is there no sphere of human events for which we can postulate total consistency, thus falling in turn into conflict with the above-mentioned repudiation? We must answer this question affirmatively. Such a sphere does exist. We call such events elementary situations.

Elementary situations are those in which tactics perish; that is, those human situations in which our moral attitude is unchanged regardless of the way these situations arrive at their culmination. If a man is dying of hunger and I can feed him, then there is no confluence of circumstances in which it would be right to say "It is, nevertheless, tactically better to let him die"; or, if I cannot help him, to say "Tactically it is better to hush up the fact that he died of hunger." Open aggression, genocide, torture, mistreatment of the defenseless—all these are elementary situations. In such situations the values of inconsistency cease to play a role, and here we suddenly confront a dual-valued world. In this way our praise of inconsistency is also inconsistent. Inconsistency has certain limits within which it is valid: the limits wherein reality is contradictory. But reality is contradictory only up to a certain point. (We are speaking at all times about the reality of values and not about the reality which is the subject of theoretical speculation.) For let us also carefully bear in mind that to be consistent in inconsistency means to contradict by an act (the application of a certain consistency) something the affirmation of which (the affirmation of inconsistency) is the substance of that act; in short, to fall into an impossible situation, into an antinomy.

Let us therefore also be inconsistent in our inconsistency, and apply the principle of inconsistency to itself. But, someone may reproach us, only then do we practice strict inconsistency, only then do we attain total consistency in the practice of inconsistency—for if we were always inconsistent, but our very inconsistency were completely consistent, then by that very fact we would not always be inconsistent. When, however, we limit our inconsistency, that is, when we are not always inconsistent, only then do we become absolutely inconsistent. In other words, we have arrived at the most classical antinomy of terms: consistent inconsistency is not consistent inconsistency (for it excludes inconsistency itself from the principle of inconsistency); inconsistent inconsistency, on the other hand, is actually consistent inconsistency. To this extent, therefore, we propose to preserve the principle of consistency as a value, by practicing the principle of inconsistency inconsistently. To this extent we mold our praise of inconsistency to a perfect form, protesting against the practice of inconsistency in its perfect form.

So much for praise of inconsistency. The rest cannot be verbalized. The rest must be done.

CIVIL DISOBEDIENCE [1]

Henry David Thoreau

I heartily accept the motto,—"That government is best which governs least"; and I should like to see it acted up to more rapidly and systematically. Carried out, it finally amounts to this, which also I believe,—"That government is best which governs not at all"; and when men are prepared for it, that will be the kind of government which they will have. Government is at best but an expedient; but most governments are usually, and all governments are sometimes, inexpedient. The objections which have been brought against a standing army, and they are many and weighty, and deserve to prevail, may also at last be brought against a standing government. The standing army is only an arm of the standing government. The government itself, which is only the mode which the people have chosen to execute their will, is equally liable to be abused and perverted before the people can act through it. Witness the present Mexican war, the work of comparatively a few individuals using the standing government as their tool; for, in the outset, the people would not have consented to this measure.

This American government,—what is it but a tradition, though a recent one, endeavoring to transmit itself unimpaired to posterity, but each instant losing some of its integrity? It has not the vitality and force of a single living man; for a single man can bend it to his will. It is a sort of wooden gun to the people themselves. But it is not the less necessary for this; for the people must have some complicated machinery or other, and hear its din, to satisfy that idea of government which they have. Governments show thus how successfully men can be imposed on, even impose on themselves, for their own advantage. It is excellent, we must all allow. Yet this government never of itself furthered any enterprise, but by the alacrity with which it got out of its way. *It* does not keep the country free. *It* does not settle the West. *It* does not educate. The character inherent in the American people has done all that has been accomplished; and it would have done somewhat more, if the government had not sometimes got in its way. For government is an expedient by which men would fain succeed in letting one another alone; and, as has been said, when it is most expedient, the governed are most let alone by it. Trade and commerce, if they were not made of India-rubber, would never manage to bounce over the obstacles which legislators are continually putting in their way; and, if one were to judge these men wholly by the effects of their actions and not partly by their intentions, they

[1] Aesthetic Papers, No. I. Boston, 1849.

would deserve to be classed and punished with those mischievous persons who put obstructions on the railroads.

But, to speak practically and as a citizen, unlike those who call themselves no-government men, I ask for, not at once no government, but *at once* a better government. Let every man make known what kind of government would command his respect, and that will be one step toward obtaining it.

After all, the practical reason why, when the power is once in the hands of the people, a majority are permitted, and for a long period continue, to rule, is not because they are most likely to be in the right, nor because this seems fairest to the minority, but because they are physically the strongest. But a government in which the majority rule in all cases cannot be based on justice, even as far as men understand it. Can there not be a government in which majorities do not virtually decide right and wrong, but conscience?— in which majorities decide only those questions to which the rule of expediency is applicable? Must the citizen ever for a moment, or in the least degree, resign his conscience to the legislator? Why has every man a conscience, then? I think that we should be men first, and subjects afterward. It is not desirable to cultivate a respect for the law, so much as for the right. The only obligation which I have a right to assume, is to do at any time what I think right. It is truly enough said, that a corporation has no conscience; but a corporation of conscientious men is a corporation *with* a conscience. Law never made men a whit more just; and, by means of their respect for it, even the well-disposed are daily made the agents of injustice. A common and natural result of an undue respect for law is, that you may see a file of soldiers, colonel, captain, corporal, privates, powder-monkeys, and all, marching in admirable order over hill and dale to the wars, against their wills, ay, against their common sense and consciences, which makes it very steep marching indeed, and produces a palpitation of the heart. They have no doubt that it is a damnable business in which they are concerned; they are all peaceably inclined. Now, what are they? Men at all? or small movable forts and magazines, at the service of some unscrupulous man in power? Visit the Navy-Yard, and behold a marine, such a man as an American government can make, or such as it can make a man with its black arts,—a mere shadow and reminiscence of humanity, a man laid out alive and standing, and already, as one may say, buried under arms with funeral accompaniments, though it may be,—

> "Not a drum was heard, not a funeral note,
>   As his corse to the rampart we hurried;
> Not a soldier discharged his farewell shot
>   O'er the grave where our hero we buried."

The mass of men serve the state thus, not as men mainly, but as machines, with their bodies. They are the standing army, and the militia, jailers, constables, posse comitatus, &c. In most cases there is no free exercise whatever of the judgment or of the moral sense; but they put themselves on a level with wood and earth and stones; and wooden men can perhaps be manufactured that will serve the purpose as well. Such command no more respect than men of straw or a lump of dirt. They have the same sort of worth only as horses and dogs. Yet such as these even are commonly esteemed good citizens. Others,—as most legislators, politicians, lawyers, ministers, and office-holders,—serve the state chiefly with their heads; and, as they rarely make any moral distinctions, they are as likely to serve the Devil, without *intending* it, as God. A very few, as heroes, patriots, martyrs, reformers in the great sense, and *men,* serve the state with their consciences also, and so necessarily resist it for the most part; and they are commonly treated as enemies by it. A wise man will only be useful as a man, and will not submit to be "clay," and "stop a hole to keep the wind away," but leave that office to his dust at least:—

> "I am too high-born to be propertied,
> To be a secondary at control,
> Or useful serving-man and instrument
> To any sovereign state throughout the world."

He who gives himself entirely to his fellow-men appears to them useless and selfish; but he who gives himself partially to them is pronounced a benefactor and philanthropist.

How does it become a man to behave toward this American government to-day? I answer, that he cannot without disgrace be associated with it. I cannot for an instant recognize that political organization as *my* government which is the *slave's* government also.

All men recognize the right of revolution; that is, the right to refuse allegiance to, and to resist, the government, when its tyranny or its inefficiency are great and unendurable. But almost all say that such is not the case now. But such was the case, they think, in the Revolution of '75. If one were to tell me that this was a bad government because it taxed certain foreign commodities brought to its ports, it is most probable that I should not make an ado about it, for I can do without them. All machines have their friction; and possibly this does enough good to counterbalance the evil. At any rate, it is a great evil to make a stir about it. But when the friction comes to have its machine, and oppression and robbery are organized, I say, let us not have such a machine any longer. In other words, when a sixth of the population of a nation which has undertaken to be the refuge of liberty are slaves, and a whole country is unjustly overrun and conquered by a foreign army, and subjected to military law, I think that it is not too soon for honest men to rebel and revolutionize. What makes this duty the more urgent is the fact, that the country so overrun is not our own, but ours is the invading army.

. . . . .

Practically speaking, the opponents to a reform in Massachusetts are not a hundred thousand politicians at the South, but a hundred thousand merchants and farmers here, who are more interested in commerce and agriculture than they are in humanity, and are not prepared to do justice to the slave and to Mexico, *cost what it may.* I quarrel not with far-off foes, but with those who, near at home, co-operate with, and do the bidding of, those far away, and without whom the latter would be harmless. We are accustomed to say, that the mass of men are unprepared; but improvement is slow, because the few are not materially wiser or better than the many. It is not so important that many should be as good as you, as that there be some absolute goodness somewhere; for that will leaven the whole lump. There are thousands who are *in opinion* opposed to slavery and to the war, who yet in effect do nothing to put an end to them; who, esteeming themselves children of Washington and Franklin, sit down with their hands in their pockets, and say that they know not what to do, and do nothing; who even postpone the question of freedom to the question of free-trade, and quietly read the prices-current along with the latest advices from Mexico, after dinner, and, it may be, fall asleep over them both. What is the price-current of an honest man and patriot to-day? They hesitate, and they regret, and sometimes they petition; but they do nothing in earnest and with effect. They will wait, well disposed, for others to remedy the evil, that they may no longer have it to regret. At most, they give only a cheap vote, and a feeble countenance and God-speed, to the right, as it goes by them. There are nine hundred and ninety-nine patrons of virtue to one virtuous man. But it is easier to deal with the real possessor of a thing than with the temporary guardian of it.

All voting is a sort of gaming, like checkers or backgammon, with a slight moral tinge to it, a playing with right and wrong, with moral questions; and betting naturally accompanies it. The character of the voters is not staked. I cast my vote, perchance, as I think right; but I am not vitally concerned that that right should prevail. I am willing to leave it to the majority. Its obligation, therefore, never exceeds that of expediency. Even voting *for the right* is *doing* nothing for it. It is only expressing to men feebly your desire that it should prevail. A wise man will not leave the right to the mercy of chance, nor wish it to prevail through the power of the majority. There is but little virtue in the action of masses of men. When the majority shall at length vote for the abolition of slavery, it will be because they are indifferent to slavery, or because there is but little slavery left to be abolished by their vote. *They* will then be the only slaves. Only *his* vote can hasten the abolition of slavery who asserts his own freedom by his vote.

I hear of a convention to be held at Baltimore, or elsewhere, for the selection of a candidate for the Presidency, made up chiefly of editors, and men who are politicians by profession; but I think, what is it to any independent, intelligent, and respectable man what decision they may come to? Shall we not have the advantage of his wisdom and honesty, nevertheless? Can we not count upon some independent votes? Are there not many individuals in the country who do not attend conventions? But no: I find that the respectable man, so called, has immediately drifted from his position, and despairs of his country, when his country has more reason to despair of him. He forthwith adopts one of the candidates thus selected as the only *available* one, thus proving that he is himself *available* for any purposes of the demagogue. His vote is of no more worth than that of any unprincipled foreigner or hireling native, who may have been bought. O for a man who is a *man,* and, as my neighbor says, has a bone in his back which you cannot pass your hand through! Our statistics are at fault: the population has been returned too large. How many *men* are there to a square thousand miles in this country? Hardly one. Does not America offer any inducement for men to settle here? The American has dwindled into an Odd Fellow,—one who may be known by the development of his organ of gregariousness, and a manifest lack of intellect and cheerful self-reliance; whose first and chief concern, on coming into the world, is to see that the Almshouses are in good repair; and, before yet he has lawfully donned the virile garb, to collect a fund for the support of the widows and orphans that may be; who, in short, ventures to live only by the aid of the Mutual Insurance company, which has promised to bury him decently.

It is not a man's duty, as a matter of course, to devote himself to the eradication of any, even the most enormous wrong; he may still properly have other concerns to engage him; but it is his duty, at least, to wash his hands of it, and, if he gives it no thought longer, not to give it practically his support. If I devote myself to other pursuits and contemplations, I must first see, at least, that I do not pursue them sitting upon another man's shoulders. I must get off him first, that he may pursue his contemplations too. See what gross inconsistency is tolerated. I have heard some of my townsmen say, "I should like to have them order me out to help put down an insurrection of the slaves, or to march to Mexico;—see if I would go"; and yet these very men have each, directly by their allegiance, and so indirectly, at least, by their money, furnished a substitute. The soldier is applauded who refuses to serve in an unjust war by those who do not refuse to sustain the unjust government which makes the war; is applauded by those whose own act and authority he disregards and sets at naught; as if the State were penitent to that degree that it hired one to scourge it while it sinned, but not to that degree that it left off sinning for a moment. Thus, under the name of Order and Civil Government, we are all made at last to pay homage to and support our own meanness. After the first blush of sin comes its indifference; and from immoral it becomes, as it were, *un*moral, and not quite unnecessary to that life which we have made.

The broadest and most prevalent error requires the most disinterested virtue to sustain it. The slight reproach to which the virtue of patriotism is commonly liable, the noble are most likely to incur. Those who, while they disapprove of the character and measures of a government, yield to it their allegiance and support, are undoubtedly its most conscientious supporters, and so frequently the most serious obstacles to reform. Some are petitioning the State to dissolve the Union, to disregard the requisitions of the President. Why do they not dissolve it themselves,—the union between themselves and the State,—and refuse to pay their quota into its treasury? Do not they stand in the same relation to the State, that the State does to the Union? And have not the same reasons prevented the State from resisting the Union, which have prevented them from resisting the State?

How can a man be satisfied to entertain an opinion merely, and enjoy *it?* Is there any enjoyment in it, if his opinion is that he is aggrieved? If you are

cheated out of a single dollar by your neighbor, you do not rest satisfied with
knowing that you are cheated, or with saying that you are cheated, or even
with petitioning him to pay you your due; but you take effectual steps at
once to obtain the full amount, and see that you are never cheated again.
Action from principle, the perception and the performance of right, changes
things and relations; it is essentially revolutionary, and does not consist
wholly with anything which was. It not only divides states and churches, it
divides families; ay, it divides the *individual,* separating the diabolical in
him from the divine.

Unjust laws exist: shall we be content to obey them, or shall we endeavor
to amend them, and obey them until we have succeeded, or shall we trans-
gress them at once? Men generally, under such a government as this, think
that they ought to wait until they have persuaded the majority to alter them.
They think that, if they should resist, the remedy would be worse than the
evil. But it is the fault of the government itself that the remedy *is* worse
than the evil. *It* makes it worse. Why is it not more apt to anticipate and
provide for reform? Why does it not cherish its wise minority? Why does it
cry and resist before it is hurt? Why does it not encourage its citizens to be
on the alert to point out its faults, and *do* better than it would have them?
Why does it always crucify Christ, and excommunicate Copernicus and
Luther, and pronounce Washington and Franklin rebels?

One would think, that a deliberate and practical denial of its authority
was the only offence never contemplated by government; else, why has it
not assigned its definite, its suitable and proportionate penalty? If a man
who has no property refuses but once to earn nine shillings for the State, he
is put in prison for a period unlimited by any law that I know, and determined only by the discretion of those who placed him there; but if he should
steal ninety times nine shillings from the State, he is soon permitted to go at
large again.

If the injustice is part of the necessary friction of the machine of government, let it go, let it go: perchance it will wear smooth,—certainly the machine will wear out. If the injustice has a spring, or a pulley, or a rope, or a
crank, exclusively for itself, then perhaps you may consider whether the
remedy will not be worse than the evil; but if it is of such a nature that it
requires you to be the agent of injustice to another, then, I say, break the
law. Let your life be a counter friction to stop the machine. What I have to
do is to see, at any rate, that I do not lend myself to the wrong which I condemn.

As for adopting the ways which the State has provided for remedying the
evil, I know not of such ways. They take too much time, and a man's life
will be gone. I have other affairs to attend to. I came into this world, not
chiefly to make this a good place to live in, but to live in it, be it good or
bad. A man has not everything to do, but something; and because he cannot
do *everything,* it is not necessary that he should do *something* wrong. It is
not my business to be petitioning the Governor or the Legislature any more
than it is theirs to petition me; and, if they should not hear my petition,

what should I do then? But in this case the State has provided no way: its very Constitution is the evil. This may seem to be harsh and stubborn and unconciliatory; but it is to treat with the utmost kindness and consideration the only spirit that can appreciate or deserves it. So is all change for the better, like birth and death, which convulse the body.

I do not hesitate to say, that those who call themselves Abolitionists should at once effectually withdraw their support, both in person and property, from the government of Massachusetts, and not wait till they constitute a majority of one, before they suffer the right to prevail through them. I think that it is enough if they have God on their side, without waiting for that other one. Moreover, any man more right than his neighbors constitutes a majority of one already.

I meet this American government, or its representative, the State government, directly, and face to face, once a year—no more—in the person of its tax-gatherer; this is the only mode in which a man situated as I am necessarily meets it; and it then says distinctly, Recognize me; and the simplest, the most effectual, and, in the present posture of affairs, the indispensablest mode of treating with it on this head, of expressing your little satisfaction with and love for it, is to deny it then. My civil neighbor, the tax-gatherer, is the very man I have to deal with,—for it is, after all, with men and not with parchment that I quarrel,—and he has voluntarily chosen to be an agent of the government. How shall he ever know well what he is and does as an officer of the government, or as a man, until he is obliged to consider whether he shall treat me, his neighbor, for whom he has respect, as a neighbor and well-disposed man, or as a maniac and disturber of the peace, and see if he can get over this obstruction to his neighborliness without a ruder and more impetuous thought or speech corresponding with his action. I know this well, that if one thousand, if one hundred, if ten men whom I could name,—if ten *honest* men only,—ay, if *one* HONEST man, in this State of Massachusetts, *ceasing to hold slaves,* were actually to withdraw from this copartnership, and be locked up in the county jail therefor, it would be the abolition of slavery in America. For it matters not how small the beginning may seem to be: what is once well done is done forever. But we love better to talk about it: that we say is our mission. Reform keeps many scores of newspapers in its service, but not one man. If my esteemed neighbor, the State's ambassador, who will devote his days to the settlement of the question of human rights in the Council Chamber, instead of being threatened with the prisons of Carolina, were to sit down the prisoner of Massachusetts, that State which is so anxious to foist the sin of slavery upon her sister,—though at present she can discover only an act of inhospitality to be the ground of a quarrel with her,—the Legislature would not wholly waive the subject the following winter.

Under a government which imprisons any unjustly, the true place for a just man is also a prison. The proper place to-day, the only place which Massachusetts has provided for her freer and less desponding spirits, is in her prisons, to be put out and locked out of the State by her own act, as they have already put themselves out by their principles. It is there that the fugitive slave, and the Mexican prisoner on parole, and the Indian come to plead the wrongs of his race, should find them; on that separate, but more free and honorable ground, where the State places those who are not *with* her, but *against* her,—the only house in a slave State in which a free man can abide with honor. If any think that their influence would be lost there, and their voices no longer afflict the ear of the State, that they would not be as an enemy within its walls, they do not know by how much truth is stronger than error, nor how much more eloquently and effectively he can combat injustice who has experienced a little in his own person. Cast your whole vote, not a strip of paper merely, but your whole influence. A minority is powerless while it conforms to the majority; it is not even a minority then; but it is irresistible when it clogs by its whole weight. If the alternative is to keep all just men in prison, or give up war and slavery, the State will not hesitate which to choose. If a thousand men were not to pay their tax-bills this year, that would not be a violent and bloody measure, as it would be to pay them, and enable the State to commit violence and shed innocent blood. This is, in fact, the definition of a peaceable revolution, if any such is possible. If the tax-gatherer, or any other public officer, asks me, as one has done, "But what shall I do?" my answer is, "If you really wish to do anything, resign your office." When the subject has refused allegiance, and the officer has resigned his office, then the revolution is accomplished. But even suppose blood should flow. Is there not a sort of blood shed when the conscience is wounded? Through this wound a man's real manhood and immortality flow out, and he bleeds to an everlasting death. I see this blood flowing now.

I have contemplated the imprisonment of the offender, rather than the seizure of his goods,—though both will serve the same purpose,—because they who assert the purest right, and consequently are most dangerous to a corrupt State, commonly have not spent much time in accumulating property. To such the State renders comparatively small service, and a slight tax is wont to appear exorbitant, particularly if they are obliged to earn it by special labor with their hands. If there were one who lived wholly without the use of money, the State itself would hesitate to demand it of him. But the rich man,—not to make any invidious comparison,—is always sold to the institution which makes him rich. Absolutely speaking, the more money, the less virtue; for money comes between a man and his objects, and obtains them for him; and it was certainly no great virtue to obtain it. It puts to rest many questions which he would otherwise be taxed to answer; while the only new question which it puts is the hard but superfluous one, how to spend it. Thus his moral ground is taken from under his feet. The opportunities of living are diminished in proportion as what are called the "means" are increased. The best thing a man can do for his culture when he is rich is to endeavor to carry out those schemes which he entertained when he was poor. Christ answered the Herodians according to their condition. "Show me the tribute-money," said he;—and one took a penny out of his pocket;—if you use money which has the image of Caesar on it, and which he has made current and valuable, that is, *if you are men of the State,* and gladly enjoy the advantages of Caesar's government, then pay him back some of his own when he demands it; "Render therefore to Caesar that which is Caesar's, and to God those things which are God's,"—leaving them no wiser than before as to which was which; for they did not wish to know.

When I converse with the freest of my neighbors, I perceive that, whatever they may say about the magnitude and seriousness of the question, and their regard for the public tranquillity, the long and the short of the matter is, that they cannot spare the protection of the existing government, and they dread the consequences to their property and families of disobedience to it. For my own part, I should not like to think that I ever rely on the protection of the State. But, if I deny the authority of the State when it presents its tax-bill, it will soon take and waste all my property, and so harass me and my children without end. This is hard. This makes it impossible for a man to live honestly, and at the same time comfortably, in outward respects. It will not be worth the while to accumulate property; that would be sure to go again. You must hire or squat somewhere, and raise but a small crop, and eat that soon. You must live within yourself, and depend upon yourself always tucked up and ready for a start, and not have many affairs. A man may grow rich in Turkey even, if he will be in all respects a good subject of the Turkish government. Confucius said: "If a state is governed by the principles of reason, poverty and misery are subjects of shame; if a state is not governed by the principles of reason, riches and honors are the subjects of shame." No: until I want the protection of Massachusetts to be extended to me in some distant Southern port, where my liberty is endangered, or until I am bent solely on building up an estate at home by peaceful enterprise, I can afford to refuse allegiance to Massachusetts, and her right to my property and life. It costs me less in every sense to incur the penalty of disobedience to the State, than it would to obey. I should feel as if I were worth less in that case.

Some years ago, the State met me in behalf of the Church, and commanded me to pay a certain sum toward the support of a clergyman whose preaching my father attended, but never I myself. "Pay," it said, "or be locked up in the jail." I declined to pay. But, unfortunately, another man saw fit to pay it. I did not see why the schoolmaster should be taxed to support the priest, and not the priest the schoolmaster; for I was not the State's schoolmaster, but I supported myself by voluntary subscription. I did not see why the lyceum should not present its tax-bill, and have the State to back its demand, as well as the Church. However, at the request of the selectmen, I condescended to make some such statement as this in writing:—"Know all men by these presents, that I, Henry Thoreau, do not wish to be regarded as a member of any incorporated society which I have not joined." This I gave to the town clerk; and he has it. The State, having thus learned that I did not wish to be regarded as a member of that church, has never made a like demand on me since; though it said that it must adhere to its original presumption that time. If I had known how to name them, I should then have signed off in detail from all the societies which I never signed on to; but I did not know where to find a complete list.

I have paid no poll-tax for six years. I was put into a jail once on this account, for one night; and, as I stood considering the walls of solid stone, two or three feet thick, the door of wood and iron, a foot thick, and the iron grating which strained the light, I could not help being struck with the foolishness of that institution which treated me as if I were mere flesh and blood and bones, to be locked up. I wondered that it should have concluded at length that this was the best use it could put me to, and had never thought to avail itself of my services in some way. I saw that, if there was a wall of stone between me and my townsmen, there was a still more difficult one to climb or break through, before they could get to be as free as I was. I did not for a moment feel confined, and the walls seemed a great waste of stone and mortar. I felt as if I alone of all my townsmen had paid my tax. They plainly did not know how to treat me, but behaved like persons who are underbred. In every threat and in every compliment there was a blunder; for they thought that my chief desire was to stand the other side of that stone wall. I could not but smile to see how industriously they locked the door on my meditations, which followed them out again without let or hindrance, and *they* were really all that was dangerous. As they could not reach me, they had resolved to punish my body; just as boys, if they cannot come at some person against whom they have a spite, will abuse his dog. I saw that the State was half-witted, that it was timid as a lone woman with her silver spoons, and that it did not know its friends from its foes, and I lost all my remaining respect for it, and pitied it.

Thus the State never intentionally confronts a man's sense, intellectual or moral, but only his body, his senses. It is not armed with superior wit or honesty, but with superior physical strength. I was not born to be forced. I will breathe after my own fashion. Let us see who is the strongest. What force has a multitude? They only can force me who obey a higher law than I. They force me to become like themselves. I do not hear of *men* being *forced* to live this way or that by masses of men. What sort of life were that to live? When I meet a government which says to me, "Your money or your life," why should I be in haste to give it my money? It may be in a great strait, and not know what to do: I cannot help that. It must help itself; do as I do. It is not worth the while to snivel about it. I am not responsible for the successful working of the machinery of society. I am not the son of the engineer. I perceive that, when an acorn and a chestnut fall side by side, the one does not remain inert to make way for the other, but both obey their own laws, and spring and grow and flourish as best they can, till one, perchance, overshadows and destroys the other. If a plant cannot live according to its nature, it dies; and so a man.

.   .   .   .   .

When I came out of prison,—for some one interfered, and paid that tax, —I did not perceive that great changes had taken place on the common, such as he observed who went in a youth, and emerged a tottering and gray-headed man; and yet a change had to my eyes come over the scene,—the town, and State, and country,—greater than any that mere time could effect. I saw yet more distinctly the State in which I lived. I saw to what extent the people among whom I lived could be trusted as good neighbors and friends; that their friendship was for summer weather only; that they did not greatly propose to do right; that they were a distinct race from me by their prejudices and superstitions, as the Chinamen and Malays are; that, in their sacrifices to humanity, they ran no risks, not even to their property; that, after all, they were not so noble but they treated the thief as he had treated them, and hoped, by a certain outward observance and a few prayers, and by walking in a particular straight though useless path from time to time, to save their souls. This may be to judge my neighbors harshly; for I believe that many of them are not aware that they have such an institution as the jail in their village.

It was formerly the custom in our village, when a poor debtor came out of jail, for his acquaintances to salute him, looking through their fingers, which were crossed to represent the grating of a jail window, "How do ye do?" My neighbors did not thus salute me, but first looked at me, and then at one another, as if I had returned from a long journey. I was put into jail as I was going to the shoemaker's to get a shoe which was mended. When I was let out the next morning, I proceeded to finish my erand, and having put on my mended shoe, joined a huckleberry party, who were impatient to put themselves under my conduct; and in half an hour,—for the horse was soon tackled,—was in the midst of a huckleberry field, on one of our highest hills, two miles off, and then the State was nowhere to be seen.

This is the whole history of "My Prisons."

I have never declined paying the highway tax, because I am as desirous of being a good neighbor as I am of being a bad subject; and, as for supporting schools, I am doing my part to educate my fellow-countrymen now. It is for no particular item in the tax-bill that I refuse to pay it. I simply wish to refuse allegiance to the State, to withdraw and stand aloof from it effectually. I do not care to trace the course of my dollar, if I could, till it buys a man or a musket to shoot one with,—the dollar is innocent,—but I am concerned to trace the effects of my allegiance. In fact, I quietly declare war with the State, after my fashion, though I will still make what use and get what advantage of her I can, as is usual in such cases.

If others pay the tax which is demanded of me, from a sympathy with the State, they do but what they have already done in their own case, or rather they abet injustice to a greater extent than the State requires. If they pay the tax from a mistaken interest in the individual taxed, to save his property, or prevent his going to jail, it is because they have not considered wisely how far they let their private feelings interfere with the public good.

This, then, is my position at present. But one cannot be too much on his guard in such a case, lest his action be biased by obstinacy, or an undue regard for the opinions of men. Let him see that he does only what belongs to himself and to the hour.

I think sometimes, Why, this people mean well; they are only ignorant; they would do better if they knew how: why give your neighbors this pain to treat you as they are not inclined to? But I think again, this is no reason why I should do as they do, or permit others to suffer much greater pain of a different kind. Again, I sometimes say to myself, When many millions of men, without heat, without ill will, without personal feeling of any kind, demand of you a few shillings only, without the possibility, such is their constitution, of retracting or altering their present demand, and without the possibility, on your side, of appeal to any other millions, why expose yourself to this overwhelming brute force? You do not resist cold and hunger, the winds and the waves, thus obstinately; you quietly submit to a thousand similar necessities. You do not put your head into the fire. But just in proportion as I regard this as not wholly a brute force, but partly a human force, and consider that I have relations to those millons as to so many millions of men, and not of mere brute or inanimate things, I see that appeal is possible, first and instantaneously, from them to the Maker of them, and, secondly, from them to themselves. But, if I put my head deliberately into the fire, there is no appeal to fire or to the Maker of fire, and I have only myself to blame. If I could convince myself that I have any right to be satisfied with men as they are, and to treat them accordingly, and not according, in some respects, to my requisitions and expectations of what they and I ought to be, then, like a good Mussulman and fatalist, I should endeavor to be satisfied with things as they are, and say it is the will of God. And, above all, there is this difference between resisting this and a purely brute or natural force, that I can resist this with some effect; but I cannot expect, like Orpheus, to change the nature of the rocks and trees and beasts.

I do not wish to quarrel with any man or nation. I do not wish to split hairs, to make fine distinctions, or set myself up as better than my neighbors. I seek rather, I may say, even an excuse for conforming to the laws of the land. I am but too ready to conform to them. Indeed, I have reason to suspect myself on this head; and each year, as the tax-gatherer comes round, I find myself disposed to review the acts and position of the general and State governments, and the spirit of the people, to discover a pretext for conformity.

> "We must affect our country as our parents;
> And if at any time we alienate
> Our love or industry from doing it honor,
> We must respect effects and teach the soul
> Matter of conscience and religion,
> And not desire of rule or benefit."

I believe that the State will soon be able to take all my work of this sort out of my hands, and then I shall be no better a patriot than my fellow-countrymen. Seen from a lower point of view, the Constitution, with all its faults, is very good; the law and the courts are very respectable; even this State and this American government are, in many respects, very admirable and rare things, to be thankful for, such as a great many have described them; but seen from a point of view a little higher, they are what I have described them; seen from a higher still, and the highest, who shall say what they are, or that they are worth looking at or thinking of at all?

However, the government does not concern me much, and I shall bestow the fewest possible thoughts on it. It is not many moments that I live under a government, even in this world. If a man is thought-free, fancy-free, imagination-free, that which *is not* never for a long time appearing *to be* to him, unwise rulers or reformers cannot fatally interrupt him.

I know that most men think differently from myself; but those whose lives are by profession devoted to the study of these or kindred subjects, content me as little as any. Statesmen and legislators, standing so completely within the institution, never distinctly and nakedly behold it. They speak of moving society, but have no resting-place without it. They may be men of a certain experience and discrimination, and have no doubt invented ingenious and even useful systems, for which we sincerely thank them; but all their wit and usefulness lie within certain not very wide limits. They are wont to forget that the world is not governed by policy and expediency. Webster never goes behind government, and so cannot speak with authority about it. His words are wisdom to those legislators who contemplate no essential reform in the existing government; but for thinkers, and those who legislate for all time, he never once glances at the subject. I know of those whose serene and wise speculations on this theme would soon reveal the limits of his mind's range and hospitality. Yet, compared with the cheap professions of most reformers, and the still cheaper wisdom and eloquence of politicians in general, his are almost the only sensible and valuable words, and we thank Heaven for him. Comparatively, he is always strong, original, and, above all, practical. Still his quality is not wisdom, but prudence. The lawyer's truth is not Truth, but consistency, or a consistent expediency. Truth is always in harmony with herself, and is not concerned chiefly to reveal the justice that may consist with wrong-doing. He well deserves to be called, as he has been called, the Defender of the Constitution. There are really no blows to be given by him but defensive ones. He is not a leader, but a follower. His leaders are the men of '87. "I have never made an effort," he says, "and never propose to make an effort; I have never countenanced an effort, and never mean to countenance an effort, to disturb the arrangement as originally made, by which the various States came into the Union." Still thinking of the sanction which the Constitution gives to slavery, he says, "Because it was a part of the original compact,—let it stand." Notwithstanding his special acuteness and ability, he is unable to take a fact out of its merely political relations, and behold it as it lies absolutely to be disposed of by the intellect,—what, for instance, it behooves a man to do here in America today with regard to slavery, but ventures, or is driven, to make some such desperate answer as the following, while professing to speak absolutely, and as a private man,—from which what new and singular code of social duties might be inferred? "The manner," says he, "in which the governments of those States where slavery exists are to regulate it, is for their own consideration, under their responsibility to their constituents, to the general laws of propriety, humanity, and justice, and to God. Associations formed elsewhere, springing from a feeling of humanity, or any other cause, have nothing whatever to do with it. They have never received any encouragement from me, and they never will." [2]

They who know of no purer sources of truth, who have traced up its stream no higher, stand, and wisely stand, by the Bible and the Constitution, and drink at it there with reverence and humility; but they who behold where it comes trickling into this lake or that pool, gird up their loins once more, and continue their pilgrimage towards its fountainhead.

No man with a genius for legislation has appeared in America. They are rare in the history of the world. There are orators, politicians, and eloquent men, by the thousand; but the speaker has not yet opened his mouth to speak, who is capable of settling the much-vexed questions of the day. We love eloquence for its own sake, and not for any truth which it may utter, or any heroism it may inspire. Our legislators have not yet learned the comparative value of free-trade and of freedom, of union, and of rectitude, to a nation. They have no genius or talent for comparatively humble questions of taxation and finance, commerce and manufactures and agriculture. If we were left solely to the wordy wit of legislators in Congress for our guidance, uncorrected by the seasonable experience and the effectual complaints of the people, America would not long retain her rank among the nations. For eighteen hundred years, though perchance I have no right to say it, the New Testament has been written; yet where is the legislator who has wisdom and practical talent enough to avail himself of the light which it sheds on the science of legislation?

The authority of government, even such as I am willing to submit to,— for I will cheerfully obey those who know and can do better than I, and in many things even those who neither know nor can do so well,—is still an impure one: to be strictly just, it must have the sanction and consent of the governed. It can have no pure right over my person and property but what I concede to it. The progress from an absolute to a limited monarchy, from a limited monarchy to a democracy, is a progress toward a true respect for the individual. Even the Chinese philosopher was wise enough to regard the individual as the basis of the empire. Is a democracy, such as we know it, the last improvement possible in government? Is it not possible to take a step further towards recognizing and organizing the rights of man? There will never be a really free and enlightened State, until the State comes to recognize the individual as a higher and independent power, from which all its own power and authority are derived, and treats him accordingly. I please myself with imagining a State at last which can afford to be just to all men, and to treat the individual with respect as a neighbor; which even

---

[2] These extracts have been inserted since the Lecture was read.

would not think it inconsistent with its own repose, if a few were to live aloof from it, not meddling with it, nor embraced by it, who fulfilled all the duties of neighbors and fellow-men. A State which bore this kind of fruit, and suffered it to drop off as fast as it ripened, would prepare the way for a still more perfect and glorious State, which also I have imagined, but not yet anywhere seen.

INTELLIGENCE, CONSCIENCE, AND THE RIGHT TO REVOLUTION

Sidney Hook

In this . . . chapter, I shall discuss a cluster of problems which may be called variations on a Jeffersonian theme. The theme is the nature and limits of democratic resistance to democratic authority. My conclusions will not be startling—originality in this sphere is almost always a sign of error—but I hope they will be of interest. At any rate, I console myself with Justice Holmes's observation that sometimes the vindication of the obvious is more important than the elucidation of the obscure—especially when the obvious is challenged. Even tautologies have their uses when counterposed to absurdities.

In the summer of 1960, a Declaration concerning the Right of Insubordination in the Algerian War was signed and circulated in France by 121 intellectuals headed by Jean Paul Sartre. It came to the defense of Frenchmen, in the army and without, who were being imprisoned, tried, and condemned for refusing to participate in the war and for having given direct aid to the Algerian rebels. It asked and answered affirmatively the questions whether "civic responsibility in certain circumstances becomes shameful submission" and whether or not there are "instances when the refusal to serve is a sacred duty, when 'treason' means the courageous respect of the truth." The government responded by taking certain measures against some of the signers, ranging from indictment of a few to banning some literary and dramatic personalities from state-controlled radio, television, and theater. The Declaration of the 121 set off a series of manifestos and counter-manifestos, some denouncing the signers as "professors of treason" and some denouncing the government for proceeding against them. It was more than the usual Parisian brouhaha, because some asserted that soldiers and recruits had been induced by the Declaration to desert. The repercussions of the Declaration were felt abroad, and some intellectuals in Italy and the United States expressed their solidarity with the signers.

Shortly thereafter in Great Britain, Bertrand Russell and some other lead-

INTELLIGENCE, CONSCIENCE, AND THE RIGHT TO REVOLUTION From *The Paradoxes of Freedom* by Sidney Hook. Reprinted by permission of The Regents of the University of California.

ers of the Aldermaston marchers called for a civil disobedience movement in protest against the decision of the Tory government to continue the policy of nuclear defense armament, originally introduced by the Labour government.

In our own country, in several parts of the South, in consequence of the desegregation decision, agitators abetted by some local officials called for both active and passive resistance to the legal directives of the courts to integrate the schools. Some of them made use of the same kind of language and type of argument which Northerners who violated the Fugitive Slave Laws a century ago had invoked to denounce the Constitution as "a compact with Hell." At the same time, Negro and white students carried out widespread sit-ins and sit-downs, violating local ordinances with the widely expressed approval of principled democrats who felt they were articulating the democratic conscience of the country.

Considered as a moral problem, the question of justification of revolution is comparatively simple, once we disentangle it from the mystical notion that submission to the will of a divine ruler requires submission to the will of the political rulers on earth. Indeed, such a notion is incompatible with a moral position on the generic question of political obedience. In principle a moral position must allow for the desirability of political revolution under certain conditions, even if on prudential grounds some practical decisions are left open. This is true even for those moral positions which regard the use of force or violence as intrinsically evil and wish to reduce it to a minimum. They cannot consistently condemn revolutionary action against oppressive government if there is good reason to believe that the costs in violence and human suffering of such action, broadly viewed, are less than the costs of the continued existence of the government. The problem is complicated by the fact that not all resistance to the specific evils of a government are intended to be revolutionary. The evil, however grave, may be episodic rather than systematic.

There are certain kinds of situation in which resistance to government, even when felt justified, is not intended to be an act, or part of an act, of total revolutionary overthrow. Antigone disobeyed the law without wishing to destroy the rule of Creon in behalf of another political order. She may have even felt some interest in preserving his rule. Analogously, the problem faced by a democrat in violating laws of a genuinely functioning democracy is much more difficult to resolve than when the problem is posed as an abstract ethical one independently of the individual's own political allegiance. Tyranny is tyranny, whether exercised by one man or by many, whether expressed through the arbitrary decision of a power-crazed maniac or through the considered decision of a majority pursuing some notion of the public good. But the *limits* of tyranny—the point at which disobedience is undertaken, the point of no return when disobedience turns to open resistance—cannot be laid down without reference to one's own political commitment. That is why it seems to me to be unrewarding to seek some general or universally valid answer to the *political* question concerning the justification of revolution on abstract ethical grounds alone.

Our own government was born in revolution, and the right to revolutionary overthrow of oppressive governments is enshrined as a natural right in the Declaration of Independence. Almost every line of this document assumes the validity of the democratic premises of a self-governing community. Its language could hardly be used by those who accepted absolute monarchy or benevolent despotism or the rule of an hereditary aristocracy as legitimate. It is axiomatic that anyone who takes as his point of departure its commitment to self-government cannot *in principle* be opposed to the revolutionary overthrow of an oppressive and tyrannical minority government anywhere, although he may conclude in specific cases that the occasion and times may make such action unwise. That is why democrats can hail and even encourage revolutions in Fascist, Communist, and other dictatorial countries, and, without the slightest inconsistency, take vigorous measures to prevent totalitarians of any variety from overthrowing genuinely functioning democracies wherever they exist.

Why do I say that although a democrat *in principle* is justified in overthrowing a dictatorial regime, he may forgo advocating it? There are a number of obvious reasons, some of which may be made apparent by considering different types of situation. (1) Democrats may not be sure that they have sufficient strength and popular support to triumph; they may wish to avoid a *Putsch* which, even if successful, would require that they impose democracy in a country from above—as in some South American revolutions. Since such governments, established by a *Putsch* or by minority groups which declare themselves democratic, are usually unstable unless they transform themselves into dictatorships, democrats may wish to postpone action until they have built sufficient strength or sentiment to provide a majority consensus for the act of revolutionary overthrow. (2) But even when democrats are convinced that they have the majority of the population behind them, they may have reason to believe that the outcome is problematic because of the potential power of repression from internal or external mercenaries, better armed and more ruthless than the supporters of the revolution. Some of my Polish democratic friends, with poignant memories of what happened in Hungary when the West stood idly by as the Soviet soldiers, on direct orders from Khrushchev, slaughtered the freedom fighters, say that although the overwhelming majority of the Polish people oppose the minority Communist regime, few would ever dream of launching a revolution. Coming from gallant Poles, this is highly significant. (3) Even if the outcome is unproblematic, and there is good reason to believe that the democratic revolution against tyranny will triumph, democrats may regard the cost of victory as too heavy and wait for a more favorable course while continuing an outer and inner resistance.

None of these situations in any way affects the validity in principle of democratic revolutions in oppressive nondemocratic countries. But the question we are now concerned with is whether they have any bearing on the right to revolution or disobedience in *democratic* countries. Is there any implicit answer in the considerations so far offered? What does traditional political theory say? When we differentiate the problem of resistance to democratic authority by believers in democracy from the problem of resistance to undemocratic government, we cannot find much of a guide in the traditional solution offered in political theory to the question of the nature and limits of obedience to government.

The traditional solution was one in which the processes of democratic self-government were offered as the only reasonable alternative between unacceptable evils. We may recapitulate the argument as follows: there is a truth about revolutions in history, recognized not only by ancient thinkers but by the authors of the Declaration of Independence, that men "are more disposed to suffer, while evils are sufferable, than to right themselves by abolishing the forms to which they are accustomed." They knew that revolutions and civil wars are often terrible events in history—until recently they produced more terror and suffering than most wars. Our own Civil War, in which comparatively humane conventions of conflict were followed, was the bloodiest of all wars until that time. Ernest Renan once observed: "Happy is a people which inherits a revolution: woe to those who make it." This wisdom is as old as the human race. Hobbes was wrong in believing that a state of nature is usually marked by a war of all against all: it is only after law has been established and then breaks down, fragmenting the center of authority, that something approaching a war of all against all is likely to result. It was this realization which accounts for Aristotle's view that it is better for a bad law to be obeyed than by disobeying it to have all law brought into disrepute.

But how bad must a bad law be before Aristotle's counsel of prudence becomes a support of insufferable tyranny? Suppose a people accept a bad law in hopes of being able to change it by petition or the appeal to reason, but find "a long train of abuses and usurpations, pursuing invariably the same object, evinces a design to reduce them under absolute despotism"— what then? Here we must answer, as did the authors of the Declaration: "It is their right" to overthrow such governments. There is a limit to the blessings of law and order if they become the law of the hangman and the order of the grave.

How can we tell what laws of duly constituted authority to obey or to disobey? The second traditional position, sometimes evoked by the first, is that we should obey laws which conform with our conscience and disobey those which violate our conscience. This would be a wonderfully simple solution if only the conscience of the people spoke with one voice. But conscience, of all things, is an individual matter. One man's conscience is another man's abomination. There is hardly any important law to which some man's conscience has not taken and may not take exception. If it is conscience, and only conscience, which justifies a man in refusing to bear arms in defense of his country, why does not another man's conscience justify *him* in ridding the country of the first conscientious objector? If a man's conscience is the sole or sufficient authority for *his* action, how can it serve as an authority for *my* action, by what right can it deny, suppress, or ignore my conscience? The history of the deliverance of human conscience has shown that an indefinite multiplicity of actions, varying from the pitiless slaughter of harmless old women as witches to the odd refusal to wear bone buttons, has been justified in its name. On the other hand, some of our cruelest actions—and especially our neighbors' actions—seem to be accompanied by no twinge of conscience whatever. Some Biblical incidents, which outrage our moral sensibilities when we read about them today, seem to have left unmoved the conscience of even contemporary prophets. At any rate, if the law were to be obeyed only when it is authorized by our conscience, the result would be anarchy. And not the anarchy of the philosophical anarchists! Most philosophical anarchists quietly assume that there will always be a policeman on the corner protecting them from the ordinary varieties of anarchy, including unphilosophical larceny and worse.

How do we escape the dilemma between the acceptance of tyranny, on the one hand, and anarchy, on the other?

The traditional argument in favor of democracy is that it is a political system which enables us to avoid both horns of the dilemma. In a democracy the major policies of government rest directly or indirectly upon the freely given consent of the majority of the governed or their representatives. Every citizen who meets certain standard qualifications has a right to participate in the political process and to convince his neighbors of the justice and wisdom of the deliverance of his conscience. The hope is that in the course of the political process consciences would submit themselves *conscientiously* to public criticism and debate, and finally work out the reasonable compromises which permit those with different consciences to live and let live, if not to live and help live. Tyranny is avoided by virtue of the fact that when a law is considered unwise or unjust by a dissenter or nonconformist, and the means of inducing consent remain unimpaired, he is free to agitate for its amendment or repeal. Anarchy is avoided in that after the discussion is over, and the votes are counted, the decision of the majority is accepted and obeyed as law. To the question, then, whether anybody who accepts the principle of democratic self-government can believe in the right to a revolution in a democracy, the answer is obviously, "No."

I am saying something more, I believe, than what Justice Hand said when he wrote: "Revolutions are often 'right' but 'right to revolution' is a contradiction in terms, for a society which acknowledged it could not stop at tolerating conspiracies to overthrow it, but must include their execution." [1] In this *legal* sense of "right," there can be no "right to revolution" in any system. What I am saying is that in the moral and political sense of "right," democratic theory and practice would be self-stultifying if they admitted a right to revolution in a democracy because the *faith* of the democrat is that all morally legitimate demands can sooner or later be realized through democratic processes without recourse to revolutionary violence. To a democrat there is a presumption of validity in any law passed by democratic process, in the sense that it commands a prima facie justified

---

[1] *Federal Reporter*, Second Series, 183, F2d at 213 (1950).

obedience. Its validity is comparable to the claim upon the assent of an individual who accepts scientific methods as the most reliable way of reaching truth, of any conclusion reached by these methods, even if later in the light of additional evidence the conclusion is modified or abandoned.

But this faith in the democratic process may be strained to the breaking point. It may be strained in two ways: by extremely unwise or oppressive substantive action, and by procedural violation. By substantive action, I mean that a democratic community may by due legal process adopt a measure so morally outrageous that some individuals say: "No matter how constitutional, we refuse to submit to this piece of legislation and will fight with *any* means to overthrow it." This was the position of the extreme abolitionists in the North who were prepared to approve even of secession from the Union to bring an end to slavery. At a great public meeting in the 1850's in Boston's Faneuil Hall in which the Constitution was called "a compact with Hell," a resolution was offered which declared: "Constitution or no Constitution, law or no law, we will not allow a fugitive slave to be taken in Massachusetts." [2]

By procedural violations, I mean a situation in which the democratic rules of political process are so abridged that doubt arises whether the outcome does represent the democratic consensus. Here the objection to the procedural action usually follows hard on the disapproval of some substantive measure which was adopted or imposed by breaching democratic rules. We shall find this kind of situation the most difficult.

Positions polarize with respect to the morally legitimate mode of behavior incumbent upon the citizen of a self-governing community when its representative assembly, by due process, adopts a measure that seems violative of basic human values. One of these positions may be characterized as the position of absolutist democracy which holds that obedience to democratic law, good or bad, must be unqualified. It obviously differs from the position of Bill of Rights' absolutism which asserts that any law which violates any right in the Bill of Rights has no legitimacy. This is the position which Abraham Lincoln took in a famous address on "The Perpetuation of our Political Institutions."

Let every American, every lover of liberty, every well wisher to his posterity swear by the blood of the Revolution, never to violate in the least particular, the laws of the country; and never to tolerate their violation by others. . . . Let every man remember that to violate the law, is to trample on the blood of his father, and to tear the charter of his own, and his children's liberty. Let reverence for the laws be breathed by every American mother to the lisping baby that prattles on her lap —let it be taught in schools, in seminaries and in colleges; let it be written in primers, spelling books and Almanacs; let it be preached from the pulpit, proclaimed in legislative halls, and enforced in courts of justice. And, in short, let it become *the political religion* of the nation; and let the old and the young, the rich

---

[2] See the interesting account of the events and the spirit of the times in Massachusetts during the 1850's, *The Life and Writings of B. R. Curtis: A Memoir by George Tichnor Curtis*, edited by B. R. Curtis, Jr. (Boston: Little, Brown, 1879), Vol. I.

and the poor, the grave and the gay, of all sexes and tongues and colors and conditions, sacrifice unceasingly upon its altars. . . .

When I so pressingly urge a strict observance of all the laws, let me not be understood as saying there are no bad laws, nor that grievances may not arise, for the redress of which, no legal provisions have been made. I mean to say no such thing. But I do mean to say, that, although bad laws, if they exist, should be repealed as soon as possible, still while they continue in force, for the sake of example, they should be religiously observed. So also in unprovided cases. If such arise, let proper legal provisions be made for them with the least possible delay; but, till then, let them if not too intolerable, be borne with.[3]

This is a very strong statement; it denies almost without qualification the primacy of moral principle over any political or legal decision made by duly constituted democratic authority. It does not distinguish between degree or occasion. For most laws which come from legislative chambers and governmental commissions, much can be said for this attitude, despite the needless extremism of the language. The consequences of the widespread violation of the Prohibition Amendment, by making crime a way of life and encouraging a cynical attitude towards law enforcement, were far more harmful to the community than the arbitrary and unjust restrictions which this ill-considered amendment placed upon the sumptuary habits of American citizens. A foolish traffic law usually works less hardship than would its widespread flouting. An unjust tax is to be deplored less than a tax strike. But suppose it is a matter which touches deeply not merely one's conscience but one's *reflective* conscience. What then? The law may command an action which outrages the strong feelings of a minority whose reasoned arguments and protests have been ignored. It was a situation of this kind which confronted those citizens of the North who, although opposed to slavery, were willing to suffer it so long as they were permitted to agitate against it, but who refused to obey the Fugitive Slave Act of September, 1850.

Here is a characteristic passage from Theodore Parker which expresses a not uncommon response by a man of religion to Lincoln's demand that all laws on the statute books be religiously obeyed and enforced.

Let me suppose a case which may happen here, and before long. A woman flies from South Carolina to Massachusetts to escape from bondage. Mr. Greatheart aids her in her escape, harbors and conceals her, and is brought to trial for it. The punishment is a fine of one thousand dollars and imprisonment for six months. I am drawn to serve as a juror and pass upon this offence. I may refuse to serve and be punished for that, leaving men with no scruples to take my place, or I

---

[3] *The Collected Works of Abraham Lincoln* (Basler edition), Vol. I, p. 112. (New Brunswick: Rutgers University Press, 1953.) Lincoln's speech was delivered in 1838. In this connection, it is pertinent to observe that Jefferson in listing the essential principles of the American government emphasizes "absolute acquiescence in the decisions of the majority—the vital principle of republics, from which there is no appeal but to force, the vital principle and immediate parent of despotism." "First Inaugural Address," March 4, 1801. Commager, H., *Documents of American History*, Vol. I, p. 188.

may take the juror's oath to give a verdict according to the law and the testimony. The law is plain, let us suppose and the testimony conclusive. Greatheart himself confesses that he did the deed alleged, saving one ready to perish. The judge charges that, if the jurors are satisfied of that fact, then they must return that he is guilty. This is a nice matter. Here are two questions. The one put to me in my official capacity as juror is this,—"Did Greatheart aid the woman?" The other put to me in my natural character as man is this,—"Will you help to punish Greatheart with fine and imprisonment for helping a woman to obtain her unalienable rights?" If I have extinguished my manhood by my juror's oath, then I shall do my official business and find Greatheart guilty, and I shall seem to be a true man; but if I value my manhood, I shall answer after my natural duty to love a man and not hate him, to do him justice, not injustice, to allow him the natural rights he has not alienated, and shall say, "Not guilty." Then men will call me forsworn and a liar, but I think human nature will justify the verdict. . . .[4]

This position was strongly condemned by a great many believers in constitutional democracy, especially by Justice Curtis, who was to write the dissenting opinion in the Dred Scott decision. And yet there is moral heroism in refusing to do the things which Parker describes which we would not like to see disappear from life. But how can a *democrat* defend such unlawful action? It seems to me he can defend it *only* if he willingly accepts the punishment entailed by his defiance of the law, only if he does not seek to escape or subvert or physically resist it. If he engages in any kind of resistance to the punitive processes of the law which follows upon his sentence of legal guilt, he has in principle embarked upon a policy of revolutionary overthrow. If he insists upon his moral right to overthrow the government because of its infamous laws, then he has abandoned the position of the principled democrat and must stand on God's law as he interprets it or on the moral right as he sees it. We may agree with him on the ground that we are both "God's angry men" come to bring his erring children to their senses, or we may, as secular humanists, speak up for human liberty against democratic power, but we cannot consistently do so on democratic grounds. Were the democratic process to result in laws which we regard as so morally iniquitous as to justify overt or implicit rebellion, we would have to conclude that men were incapable of self-government, that good government could not be achieved by democratic processes. To seek to overthrow a democratic government whose deliberative processes, attended by all the procedural safeguards of civil and political rights, results in a reign of terror against an innocent and helpless minority may certainly be morally justifiable. To do so in the name of democracy is usually a piece of suave hypocrisy or self-deception, and is to shift the meaning of democracy from a set of political procedures to a set of goals which might very well be achieved by other than democratic political procedures.

John Brown and others like him had the honesty of their fanaticism. They never pretended that they were violating and destroying the fabric of democracy in the name of democracy. For the history of democracy had

[4] Quoted by Curtis, *op. cit.,* Vol. I, p. 127.

shown them that justice, freedom, God's will—however they conceived it, mistakenly, as I believe, or not—could not be achieved by the democratic political process. They would have felt at home in a theocracy administered by their favorite sectarian luminaries. Thoreau, on the other hand, never saw the issue clearly. His theoretical position as expressed in his *Essay on Civil Disobedience* is thoroughly confused and muddled because it implies both that one can accept democracy as a political system and also believe that every citizen has a right to overthrow it if any law passed by a democracy violates his obligation to the right. Thoreau's practice was, however, compatible with the democratic position in that, refusing to pay taxes to be used to enforce laws he regarded as evil, he did not take to the hills but gladly and proudly went to jail. Under certain circumstances, if the penalty for the violation of a law were extreme enough, one can conceive a democrat violating the law and at the same time willingly forfeiting his life rather than weakening or betraying the structure of democratic law by flight or resistance. The argument which Socrates makes in the *Crito* is unanswerable and is binding on anyone who, despite his differences with the democratic community, still feels that he is a loyal member of that community and not at war with it. In war—national, civil or class war—one expects prisoners to attempt to escape. In Socrates' case, he carried matters a little far, not by his willingness to accept punishment, but by his insistence upon it. One gets the impression that he thought he was punishing the Athenians. And perhaps he was.

The situation is more complicated with respect to the violation of procedural principles of a democracy by its legislative or executive organs. For in such instances one may claim that beyond a *certain point* a democracy in violating its own democratic laws is moving into a condition of despotism which emboldens the democratic dissenter or rebel to proceed against it as he would against any despotism. According to some democrats, Lincoln violated the laws of democracy in suspending the writ of habeas corpus in states which were outside the immediate theater of war. One can conceive of many situations in which an unwise or corrupted democracy destroys its own institutional presuppositions. But so long as one still regards the community, despite its procedural lapses, as still functioning under a democratic political system, revolutionary opposition to it cannot be justified on democratic grounds.

It is at this point that we must recognize a distinction in principle between revolutionary violence and nonviolent civil disobedience, even though situations may arise which make it difficult *in practice* to draw the precise line. Although a democrat must condemn any kind of revolutionary violence, no matter how nobly motivated, he may condone, within certain narrowly prescribed limits, some forms of civil disobedience, Lincoln to the contrary notwithstanding. A situation may arise in which a democrat believes that a municipal or state law violates the fundamental law of the land. In a desire to test the local law—and it is a law because it is currently being enforced—a democrat may defy it in the way in which Norman Thomas defied the decrees laid down by "I-am-the-Law" Mayor Hague of

Jersey City. Such situations are clear and simple. One may, however, go further. Even when such laws are upheld by the courts of highest instance, even in cases where federal laws have been held constitutionally valid, a democratic dissenter may, without inconsistency to his principles, disobey them provided he is prepared to accept the consequences. His justification lies in his hope that his act, and the acts of others, will serve as moral challenge and educational reinfluence on the attitudes of the majority. His very willingness to endure all sorts of hardships and their attendant deprivations normally arouses, when not compassion, second thoughts about the wisdom and justice of the law in question. That is why a sincere democrat who disobeys the law cannot whine or dodge or evade or fall back on the Fifth Amendment. Indeed, the very effectiveness of the violation of the law, in the intent of the dissenter, depends upon his being punished. Much worse than the punishment is to be ignored. I recall that during the war against Hitler, a group of conscientious objectors all crowding the age of sixty-five, led by Reverend A. J. Muste, publicly proclaimed their intention to defy the Registration Act. They gave up their valuable apartments, put their furniture in storage, made their farewells to their families, notified the newspapers—and awaited the federal marshal. But someone in Washington with a sense of humor or proportion completely ignored them. The expectant martyrs were furious, and spoke about the deception of the government in shockingly un-Christian terms.

Of course no one can lay down in advance at what precise point civil disobedience, especially mass civil disobedience, by disorganizing essential services, may lead to the destruction of the entire democratic process. This is something which cannot be settled by principled formulations. But any democrat who advocates or undertakes a policy of civil disobedience must take note of considerations of this order and, as a democrat, must always stop short this side of the line.

We must also qualify, in the interests of clarity, what was said above about the nonviolent character of civil disobedience. The absence of violence is normally evidence of the bona fides of those who publicly disobey a law, since it reveals the absence of revolutionary intention. But the judgment of the character and legitimacy of acts of civil disobedience must, in the end, depend not so much on whether the acts are nonviolent or not but on the consequences of those acts on the community. A nonviolent or passive act of disobedience which will result in starving a city or in deprivation of essential care may be much worse and less tolerable, from a democratic point of view, than a flurry of transient violence.

We are now in a position to apply some of the distinctions we have made to the situations from which we took our point of departure. On the assumption that Sartre and his group are democrats, and on the assumption that they are not merely expressing an opinion, the incitement to French soldiers to desert is incompatible with the existence of a democratic state if the Fifth Republic is considered democratic as most of the signers, but not Sartre, seem to believe. It is sometimes said that no government can tolerate incitement to desertion and insubordination among its military forces. This is an incipient revolutionary act. True, but that is not the point here. As democrats, we can see nothing wrong in inciting the soldiers of totalitarian states to come over to the camp of freedom. The question is restricted only to soldiers of a democratic state. Some of the signers have made loud protests against the halfhearted measures taken against them, and some of the extralegal sanctions invoked have, indeed, the touch of a French farce and an uncharacteristic logical inconsistency about them. There is also an air of *opéra bouffe* about the protests of some individuals against government sanctions on the ground that, although the government may have a right to shoot the signers, it has no right to prevent them from singing over the state-owned radio. Nonetheless, an important point is involved here. If the signers are guilty of incitement to desertion, they should be charged and proceeded against under due legal process. But *until* this is done, the imposition of other extralegal discriminatory sanctions against them cannot be justified, if they are not state officials bound by a code of professional conduct, for they have not yet been adjudged guilty.

One thing should be clear. If it is established that the declaration was an incitement to desertion and disobedience, I can see no democratic justification for protesting or refusing to accept the consequences of the violation of the law. One cannot with integrity—especially if one is a democrat—both defy a law of the democratic community, take bows and plaudits for a stand widely heralded as "heroic," and then run from the consequences of one's heroism. After all, a soldier who deserted on the strength of the appeal of these intellectuals might be court-martialed and shot. How can those who issued the appeal to him responsibly claim immunity for actions which their appeal brought about?

The discussion precipitated by the case of the French intellectuals revealed some curious—even startling—misconceptions about the nature of democracy by individuals who regard themselves as committed to democratic principles. In a supporting statement drawn up by some Italian intellectuals, which was endorsed by some of their American confreres, it was asserted that "The right to disobedience . . . is the essence of democracy. It is an extreme right, to be exercised only in extreme circumstances." [5] The inadequacy of this radical political innocence is apparent on its face. A strange essence, this right to disobedience! The essence of anything is found, not in extreme circumstances, where it is difficult to tell whether we are dealing with a phenomenon which belongs to the class whose essence we are defining, but in its normal and ordinary state. As well say that the essence of humanity is to be found in the extreme, borderline cases in which we do not know whether to classify an animal as belonging to Homo sapiens or to the lower primates. To make the right to disobedience "essential" to democracy is to conceive of democracy as a state of permanent civil war, except possibly on the assumption that men have angelic natures, so that their disagreement with the decisions of the majority never goes beyond the limits of philosophic discourse. But not even the "real" angels of sacred theology, judging by the story of Lucifer, are that angelic!

[5] *Yale Review* (Spring, 1961), p. 463.

In explaining what he means by this peculiar concept of the essence of democracy, the author of the supporting Declaration, Nicola Chiaromonte, writes: "The principle of disobedience . . . is implicit in the very essence of democracy in the sense that, if democracy rests on an ever renewed act of *spontaneous* obedience to law, the moment the act becomes in all conscience impossible, is also the moment both of revolt and of the end of democracy." [6]

This is false and horrendous doctrine. It logically implies that a democracy is impossible unless it rests on unanimous and spontaneous obedience to law. If such a situation existed, we should have no need of the state or of laws with any penal sanction whatsoever. A democracy rests upon the freely given consent of the majority of the governed, after full, fair, and free discussion and criticism. The obedience to the laws of a democracy by a democrat need not be spontaneous in the least. It can be as reluctant as one pleases, so long as they are obeyed—with the exception of the carefully circumscribed acts of civil disobedience. The Spanish Loyalist government was no less democratic because Franco regarded revolt against it as a matter of conscience. Signor Chiaromonte, like so many other well-intentioned persons—whether Christian or humanist, anarchist or pacifist—assumes that only men of good faith have consciences, and that by definition the conscience of all men of good faith is at least compatible with, if not the same as, his own.

The instance of the conscientious objector to war is more familiar to us. Those who oppose *any* kind of war on religious grounds do not feel bound by any overriding commitment to the values of democracy, even in situations where democracy can survive only by means of a defensive war. They feel about war—any war—the way John Brown felt about slavery, but happily, unlike John Brown, they cannot consistently engage in any violent action in behalf of their cause. Modern democracies try to accommodate these religious dissenters as much as possible by giving them an opportunity to perform nonmilitary service. Where any kind of service is refused, they *may* be held accountable if their refusals are too widespread and dangerous to be ignored and the prospects of democratic survival weakened. It is—or should be—one of the great merits of democratic government that it respects and tries to accommodate *as far as possible* the scruples of those who believe that their relation to God "involves duties superior to those arising from any human relation," but, as we have seen, we cannot absolutize this belief. As democrats we cannot suffer it to go beyond the line set by reflective morality and the necessity of safeguarding the whole structure of other democratic freedoms.

The instances of nonreligious violators of laws and obligations relating to military defense should be treated no differently, if their moral convictions against any war are sincere. To the extent that they are principled democrats, we can rely on their setting limits on the scale of their own civil disobedience. This may not be true for some groups who are engaging in the practice of civil disobedience in behalf of unilateral disarmament and

[6] *Ibid.*, p. 478.

who are prepared, however reluctantly, to sacrifice free institutions to the risk of a nuclear war in their defense. Since, in the extreme situation posed by the threat of war, they are disposed to surrender democracy, they may be tempted to encourage the transformation of a movement of civil disobedience into one of revolution if this were the only means which seemed available to prevent war. For this reason nonpacifist civil disobedience movements are as a rule far more dangerous than purely pacifist ones.

Those who are currently engaged in violating the federal laws relating to desegregation in education are probably not very much concerned whether their behavior is consistent with democratic principles or not. To the extent that this opposition is articulate, one gathers that some Southern editors and political figures believe that in resisting the law they are upholding the Constitution against the Supreme Court. The ruffians who have been threatening parents willing to send their children to desegregated schools are something else again. The law must be enforced against them. But enforcement, although necessary, is not enough. If disorders continue, they cannot be attributed exclusively to agitators but to principled resentment against the law. The task of the over-all democratic community is to convince those who feel that they are fighting *for* democracy in fighting *against* the law, that they are mistaken in this belief and that the spirit of democratic community, whose basic principle is equality of concern for all individuals to develop themselves as persons, requires the abandonment of unjust and arbitrary discriminations against any group of citizens.

The sit-in and sit-down strikes of students, since they have not been accompanied by violence and since they have ended happily in some Southern towns and cities, are the best illustrations of a kind of civil disobedience undertaken in the name of democracy to reëducate a community to the significance of the democratic way of political life. It may be that those who yielded did so out of convenience or business considerations. No matter. Habit, use, and wont will gradually put down taproots to nourish the frail blossoms of social equality which until now have withered in the climate of hate and fear. Nonetheless, it must be acknowledged that civil disobedience is at best a danger to a democracy, even when in small doses it may have some healthy medicinal effect. It can be legitimately undertaken only when the action is sustained by a great moral principle implicit in the democratic process, and only when there is no great danger it will be a preface to riot and civil war, or imperil the functioning of democratic political life.

There is such a thing as social timing in human affairs. Properly regarded, it enables one to strike a blow for human liberation which will echo in the hearts and minds of even those against whom it is directed. If social timing is disregarded, then, no matter how exalted the motive behind the action, it may shatter all bonds of community and have disastrous effects upon the cause of freedom. A half-century ago, the Southern sit-ins and sit-downs would have resulted in a series of bloody disasters. What Gandhi accomplished against the British could not have had the same effect at the time against a Nazi or Communist or Japanese military regime, because British democracy had already reached a point where its colonial possessions troubled the sensibilities and conscience of its citizens.

One may contrast the civil disobedience of the sit-in and sit-down strikes against racial segregation in the United States with the kind of sit-in and sit-down strikes conducted by the left-wing Socialist party of Japan in recent years. Seizing upon the phrase "the dictatorship of the majority," from some misremembered context in the lessons of their American teachers of the Occupation, and fearful of the fancied consequences of legislation proposed by the majority party in the Japanese Diet, they mobilized their partisans time and again to prevent the speaker from opening the session and by locked-arm tactics prevented the ministers and leading members of the opposing party from attending to their legislative functions. Even if their grievances had been legitimate, and their fears of unwise legislation justified, by their tactics they did far more damage to the faltering, uncertain traditions of democratic process in Japan than what would have resulted from the enactment of the measures they proposed. We must therefore distinguish between the tactic of civil disobedience as part of a calculated strategy to destroy the political democratic process—Communists too pose as pacifists and civil libertarian absolutists!—and civil disobedience undertaken with a kind of religious veneration for the values of democracy and which inspires by its openness and self-sacrifice community rethinking of the issues involved.

All this may strike enthusiasts, who identify good causes only with their own causes, as hedging the right to civil disobedience about with too many restrictions and cautions to make it a powerful means of social protest and change. But I submit that democratic theory requires that these limitations be put upon it, whereas common sense tells us that the effectiveness of civil disobedience in raising the standards of democratic practice is, beyond a certain point, inversely proportional to its frequency.

Lest I be misunderstood, I should like to repeat that nothing I have written about civil disobedience implies that there is an obligation on the moral and religious dissenter to accept the authority of the political system of democracy blindly, to forgo his moral claims to defy the entire structure of the democratic ethos on the grounds that it imperils some sacred value or some assurance of salvation which for him is beyond price and commands an *unpostponable* allegiance. In other words, if individuals refuse to play within the rules of the democratic game on the ground that these rules are too frivolous for the great stakes at issue, they are free to act as if they are at war with the democratic community. By the same token, democrats are just as free to crush them if they resort to war instead of argument. Despite Lincoln's words in praise of democracy as a political religion, his moral sensibilities rejected the absolutism which makes a fetish of any set of political institutions independently of their fruits. Facing the grim threat of rebellion which he believed both politically and morally unjustified, he nonetheless acknowledged in his First Inaugural, "If by the mere force of numbers a majority should deprive a minority of any clearly written constitutional right, it might in a moral point of view justify revolution—certainly would if such a right were a vital one."

I am not asserting that in such historical situations of conflict, when conscience is arrayed against conscience, both sides are equally justified merely because they stake their lives on the outcome. One or another side may be hasty, partial, or mistaken about what their needs and interests are, and the consequences of the different methods of gratifying them. The faith of the democrat in this juncture of disagreement is one with the faith of all liberal civilization. It is that so long as the processes of reflective inquiry are kept open, what seems to be an ultimate or inarbitrable conflict of interest and value may prove to be negotiable—at the very least, that mutual agreement can be established that there are some lesser evils in the situation which are preferable to the risks of mutual destruction. If and when such conflicts are not negotiable, if it is true that the reflective good of one side is incompatible with the reflective good of the other, what is shown is *not* that the moral values at issue are devoid of objectivity but that they lack universality, not that they are relativistic, in the sense that they are arbitrary and subjective, but that they are relational—that is to say, related to the kind of creatures we are or may become.

At any rate, whether the alleged antinomies of "ultimate" moral conflict can be resolved by this theory of objective relativism, the freedom or liberty which is inherent in the theory and practice of democracy is not the liberty to do anything one's conscience dictates. A surprisingly large number of generous spirits have been misled by this notion. No less a thinker than Lord Acton, in his *History of Freedom,* gives currency to this illusion of noble but naïve minds. He writes: "Liberty is the assurance that every man shall be protected in doing what he believes his duty, against the influence of authority and majorities, custom and opinion." [7] This would entail our protecting the actions of madmen and fools, and invite perpetual war between conflicting fanaticisms. The only duty which can make a legitimate claim to overarching authority in a democratic community is the duty to accept the test of all the rational methods that can be brought to bear on our value claims.

These value claims may be legion, and when intelligence tests them, it can only do so in the light of commonly shared values which grow out of common interests. Although these too may be questioned at any given time they possess the working authority of experience. None is final. A democratic society is more congenial than other societies to the recognition of a plurality of values. It is also more vulnerable than other societies in virtue of the potential conflicts latent in such plurality. That is why the perpetuation of the rationale of the democratic process becomes of primary importance to all who cherish the ideal of an open society with plural values, even when they differ among themselves concerning the order and hierarchy of values. Religious freedom was originally born as a consequence of

[7] *The History of Freedom and Other Essays,* edited by Lawrence and Figgis (London, 1907), p. 3.

the impotence of religious persecution. But, once having tasted the fruits of religious toleration, even the believer in the "true" religion—whatever it may be—is likely to accept religious freedom as intrinsically justified and not merely as a hedge against possible persecution or as a means of converting unbelievers.

There is a corresponding moral extension—not displacement—from individuals and individual values to society when it is considered as a set of arrangements which nurtures and cherishes individuals and individual values. The good life cannot be pursued independently of the good society because a bad society can make the good life impossible. Failure to recognize this sometimes leads to very strange pronouncements. Consider, for example, the avowal of E. M. Forster that "if I had to choose between betraying my country and betraying my friend, I hope I should have the guts to betray my country." [8]

This paradoxical remark is Forster's way of saying that personal relations should come first in the order of our moral allegiances, and that social and political systems are ultimately to be tested by the character of the personal relations they make possible and not by production figures, rates of economic growth, and the mythologies of progress. To the extent that a democracy is truly committed to an equality of concern for all human beings to develop themselves to the fullest reach of their personalities, it is the faces which men turn to their neighbors in everyday life which carry the message of their faith rather than the cold and remote promises of their ideology.

Taken unqualifiedly, however, Forster's remark violates the very spirit which he strove to articulate. Surely his dictum does not apply to any country, any friend. Suppose the country a democracy, worthy of the two cheers which is top score for Forster for anything short of the City of God or brotherly love. Suppose the country a democracy which regards the individual as possessing intrinsic worth, and which views the quality of personal relations as the test of all social institutions. Suppose the country a democracy which encourages variety and permits criticism. Does this not make an enormous difference to the decision of which to betray—country or friend? And suppose one's friend—something hard to imagine but conceivable— turns out to be a Quisling, a Fuchs, a Hiss, prepared to open the gates of the open society to its deadly foes—foes of every value Forster holds dear. Would Forster still pray to have the guts to betray his country rather than his friend? I very much doubt it. In betraying his country he would be betraying many more friends, who are no less deserving of his concern, than the one who creates the dilemma. Nor is it necessary to paint countries in black-and-white contrasts to recognize that it is the direction in which they are moving which counts.

The days of Epicurus, who could cultivate his friendships and his garden in independence of the world, are gone forever. There is no longer any distinction between Greek and barbarian. We are all Greeks, and underlying all other differences is whether we are to live in a free society or a

[8] E. M. Forster, *Two Cheers for Democracy* (New York: Harcourt, Brace, 1951), p. 78.

totalitarian one. To profess an indifference to the good society in behalf of the pursuit of the good life for ourselves and our friends indicates an indifference to the lives of others which is sure to be revenged upon us and our descendants. It is not necessary, even if it were possible, to love all men, but in a democracy it is necessary to respect every man until he forfeits our respect.

This poses for us the last great problem. Its theoretical roots are as tangled and deep as its practical sweep is troublesome and wide. What attitude should the democratic community take toward political groups which invoke democratic rights and privileges in order to destroy the entire system that makes these rights and privileges possible? What action, if any, should a democratic community take toward any minority that proposes, if and when it comes to power, to make forever impossible the opportunity of any other minority to become a majority through peaceful and orderly means, by destroying all the rights of the Bill of Rights and instituting a reign of terror?

. . . . .

Is it permissible for a majority to alienate the freedom of a minority together with its own? No, not if one believes in freedom. But if the majority does not believe in freedom, even though as a minority we may fiercely complain and forcibly resist it, we cannot charge it with inconsistency. If the majority does believe in freedom, and prevents the minority which wishes to alienate its own and others' freedom from doing so, the minority in this instance has the same formal right to complaint and can take the same risk of action. There is no logical inconsistency here either.

Every majority decision in a democracy decides something, good or bad, to which by definition the minority is opposed. But we are not discussing what is specifically good or bad, but only the legitimacy of the majority action, under the democratic rules, in voting into office those who will destroy democracy. If a democracy behaves this way, it would establish, for those who believe in personal freedom, sufficient evidence of the inadequacy of a democratic system to preserve human freedom and a decent social order. It does not justify them in asserting that a true democracy consists in preventing the majority from doing what is foolish or unwise. If this were to be construed as democracy, we should have to regard Plato as a democrat-something, which would be dismissed as absurd in the light of customary usage.

The same considerations hold in considering the argument that the surrender of democracy by any majority is "undemocratic" because it binds future generations. No decision irrevocably binds future generations. The decision to uphold a democratic system does not obligate future generations to preserve it; the decision to surrender it does not prevent future generations from restoring it.

Any political system which accepts the premise that a people must be forced to be free seems to me to be psychologically defective. Freedom—like loyalty, like love—by the very nature of the human emotions involved, cannot be commanded. Those who are prevented from expressing their wish to challenge democracy will not thereby cease wishing and feeling. They will be driven to express their determination to transform the system of democracy by hypocritical professions of strengthening it.

Despite asseverations to the contrary, the danger that a people which has once enjoyed democracy will voluntarily vote a totalitarian regime into power, although always present, seen in the perspective of history has rarely been acute. Historically, there is no clear example in which the majority of a self-governing people entrusted its destiny to a dictator who declared that he would end their liberties in the future. Neither Bolshevism nor Fascism came to power through the vicissitudes of the free political process. Although Hitler reached the chancellorship by constitutional means, the Nazi party received a majority only after a campaign in which it unloosened a reign of terror against its political opponents. Nonetheless, instances can be cited of communities living in comparative freedom which voluntarily voted to place themselves under the heel of dictatorships. The plebiscite by which the Saar voted to rejoin a Nazi Germany rather than affiliate with a democratic France or remain independent shows that the spirit of nationalism may be stronger than allegiance to democracy. Today in Italy and France a complex pattern of fear, hate, and myth may prove stronger than both the spirit of nationalism and the love of freedom. Although improbable, the situation is not inconceivable.

Nonetheless, it is not necessary to make a religious absolute out of any set of political institutions and place them beyond the reach of criticism and change. The greatness, the nobility of the American Revolution lies in the fact that it was conceived as an experiment in liberty. Until the thought of the American Enlightenment challenged the view, it was assumed, on the basis of the record of human ignorance, folly, and cruelty in history, that men were born either to rule or to be ruled. It was the daring hypothesis of the philosopher-statesmen of the American Republic that if given an opportunity, under conditions in which they had free access to information and in which traditions of free speech and press prevailed, men could be trusted to govern themselves. "I have no fear," wrote Jefferson, "but that the result of our experiment will be, that men may be trusted to govern themselves without a master. Could the contrary of this be proved, I should conclude either that there is no God, or that He is a malevolent being." [9]

Events have so far confirmed this faith, although it has come near to failing. But it cannot be finally confirmed, because self-government is a *continuing experiment* facing new challenges which are created by the very successes of the past, challenges which require more and more resourcefulness, more and better education, and a commitment as deep and sustained as that which inspired those who left us our heritage of freedom.

Jefferson and those who fought to make the American experiment in freedom succeed staked not only their faith in God and human intelligence,

[9] Letter of July 2, 1787, *The Living Thoughts of Thomas Jefferson*, presented by John Dewey (New York: Longmans, Green, 1940), p. 67.

they staked their very lives. Creative intelligence, courage to think and act on a world scale, and a passion for human freedom cannot guarantee the survival of liberal civilization today, but they are our best hope.

The world we live in is far removed from Jefferson's. The dangers to peace and to freedom are more massive and dreadful than he ever conceived them. Only those who refuse to see can deny that the threatening tides of Communist totalitarianism threaten to engulf the remaining islands of freedom—West Berlin, West Germany, Western Europe. They are already lapping at the shores of the Western Hemisphere, not far from the North American mainland. The prospects of conflict are so fearful that one can observe in Europe and in Great Britain, and even in the United States, a growing mood which defines our choice as limited to universal destruction, if we resist Communist aggression, or surrender to Communism if we do not resist. These alternatives are neither exclusive nor exhaustive—not exclusive, because surrender does not guarantee survival; not exhaustive, because there is an entire gamut of possibilities that remain to be explored which, without sacrificing human freedom, can preserve peace.

In moments of crisis, however, there are those who are prepared to abandon the experiment of freedom and self-government for the sake of survival at any price and at all costs in human infamy. They say that if the defense of freedom imperils peace, then better life under Communist despotism, with all its evils, than the risk of destruction. To which, I reply, invoking in all humility the values of the Jeffersonian tradition: Those who will never risk their lives for freedom will surely lose their freedom without surely saving their lives; that unless we prize something in life which is more precious than mere life, we have renounced the human estate, that in our precarious world, intelligence and courage have proved to have greater survival value than hysterical fear; and that if we continue to place our trust in them, we are justified, in Jefferson's words, "to disdain despair, encourage trial, and nourish hope."

TWO CONCEPTS OF LIBERTY

Isaiah Berlin

To coerce a man is to deprive him of freedom—freedom from what? Almost every moralist in human history has praised freedom. Like happiness and goodness, like nature and reality, the meaning of this term is so porous that there is little interpretation that it seems able to resist. I do not propose to discuss either the history or the more than two hundred senses of this protean word recorded by historians of ideas. I propose to examine no more

TWO CONCEPTS OF LIBERTY   From *Four Essays on Liberty* by Sir Isaiah Berlin, published by Oxford University Press.

than two of these senses—but those central ones, with a great deal of human history behind them, and, I dare say, still to come. The first of these political senses of freedom or liberty (I shall use both words to mean the same), which (following much precedent) I shall call the "negative" sense, is involved in the answer to the question "What is the area within which the subject—a person or group of persons—is or should be left to do or be what he is able to do or be, without interference by other persons?" The second, which I shall call the positive sense, is involved in the answer to the question "What, or who, is the source of control or interference that can determine someone to do, or be, this rather than that?" The two questions are clearly different, even though the answers to them may overlap.

THE NOTION OF "NEGATIVE" FREEDOM

I am normally said to be free to the degree to which no man or body of men interferes with my activity. Political liberty in this sense is simply the area within which a man can act unobstructed by others. If I am prevented by others from doing what I could otherwise do, I am to that degree unfree; and if this area is contracted by other men beyond a certain minimum, I can be described as being coerced, or, it may be, enslaved. Coercion is not, however, a term that covers every form of inability. If I say that I am unable to jump more than ten feet in the air, or cannot read because I am blind, or cannot understand the darker pages of Hegel, it would be eccentric to say that I am to that degree enslaved or coerced. Coercion implies the deliberate interference of other human beings within the area in which I could otherwise act. You lack political liberty or freedom only if you are prevented from attaining a goal by human beings.[1] Mere incapacity to attain a goal is not lack of political freedom.[2] This is brought out by the use of such modern expressions as "economic freedom" and its counterpart, "economic slavery." It is argued, very plausibly, that if a man is too poor to afford something on which there is no legal ban—a loaf of bread, a journey round the world, recourse to the law courts—he is as little free to have it as he would be if it were forbidden him by law. If my poverty were a kind of disease, which prevented me from buying bread, or paying for the journey round the world or getting my case heard, as lameness prevents me from running, this inability would not naturally be described as a lack of freedom, least of all political freedom. It is only because I believe that my inability to get a given thing is due to the fact that other human beings have made arrangements whereby I am, whereas others are not, prevented from having enough money with which to pay for it, that I think myself a victim of coercion or slavery. In other words, this use of the term depends on a particular social and economic theory about the causes of my poverty or weakness. If my lack of material means is due to my lack of mental or physical capacity, then I begin to

[1] I do not, of course, mean to imply the truth of the converse.
[2] Helvétius made this point very clearly: "The free man is the man who is not in irons, nor imprisoned in a gaol, nor terrorized like a slave by the fear of punishment . . . it is not lack of freedom not to fly like an eagle or swim like a whale."

speak of being deprived of freedom (and not simply about poverty) only if I accept the theory.[3] If, in addition, I believe that I am being kept in want by a specific arrangement which I consider unjust or unfair, I speak of economic slavery or oppression. "The nature of things does not madden us, only ill will does," said Rousseau. The criterion of oppression is the part that I believe to be played by other human beings, directly or indirectly, with or without the intention of doing so, in frustrating my wishes. By being free in this sense I mean not being interfered with by others. The wider the area of non-interference the wider my freedom.

This is what the classical English political philosophers meant when they used this word.[4] They disagreed about how wide the area could or should be. They supposed that it could not, as things were, be unlimited, because if it were, it would entail a state in which all men could boundlessly interfere with all other men; and this kind of "natural" freedom would lead to social chaos in which men's minimum needs would not be satisfied; or else the liberties of the weak would be suppressed by the strong. Because they perceived that human purposes and activities do not automatically harmonize with one another, and because (whatever their official doctrines) they put high value on other goals, such as justice, or happiness, or culture, or security, or varying degrees of equality, they were prepared to curtail freedom in the interests of other values and, indeed, of freedom itself. For, without this, it was impossible to create the kind of association that they thought desirable. Consequently, it is assumed by these thinkers that the area of men's free action must be limited by law. But equally it is assumed, especially by such libertarians as Locke and Mill in England, and Constant and Tocqueville in France, that there ought to exist a certain minimum area of personal freedom which must on no account be violated; for if it is overstepped, the individual will find himself in an area too narrow for even that minimum development of his natural faculties which alone makes it possible to pursue, and even to conceive, the various ends which men hold good or right or sacred. It follows that a frontier must be drawn between the area of private life and that of public authority. Where it is to be drawn is a matter of argument, indeed of haggling. Men are largely interdependent, and no man's activity is so completely private as never to obstruct the lives of others in any way. "Freedom for the pike is death for the minnows"; the liberty of some must depend on the restraint of others. "Freedom for an Oxford don," others have been known to add, "is a very different thing from freedom for an Egyptian peasant."

This proposition derives its force from something that is both true and important, but the phrase itself remains a piece of political claptrap. It is true that to offer political rights, or safeguards against intervention by the

---

[3] The Marxist conception of social laws is, of course, the best-known version of this theory, but it forms a large element in some Christian and utilitarian, and all socialist, doctrines.
[4] "A free man," said Hobbes, "is he that . . . is not hindered to do what he hath the will to do." Law is always a "fetter," even if it protects you from being bound in chains that are heavier than those of the law, say, some more repressive law or custom, or arbitrary despotism or chaos. Bentham says much the same.

state, to men who are half-naked, illiterate, underfed, and diseased is to mock their condition; they need medical help or education before they can understand, or make use of, an increase in their freedom. What is freedom to those who cannot make use of it? Without adequate conditions for the use of freedom, what is the value of freedom? First things come first: there are situations, as a nineteenth-century Russian radical writer declared, in which boots are superior to the works of Shakespeare; individual freedom is not everyone's primary need. For freedom is not the mere absence of frustration of whatever kind; this would inflate the meaning of the word until it meant too much or too little. The Egyptian peasant needs clothes or medicine before, and more than, personal liberty, but the minimum freedom that he needs today, and the greater degree of freedom that he may need tomorrow, is not some species of freedom peculiar to him, but identical with that of professors, artists, and millionaires.

What troubles the consciences of Western liberals is not, I think, the belief that the freedom that men seek differs according to their social or economic conditions, but that the minority who possess it have gained it by exploiting, or, at least, averting their gaze from, the vast majority who do not. They believe, with good reason, that if individual liberty is an ultimate end for human beings, none should be deprived of it by others; least of all that some should enjoy it at the expense of others. Equality of liberty; not to treat others as I should not wish them to treat me; repayment of my debt to those who alone have made possible my liberty or prosperity or enlightenment; justice, in its simplest and most universal sense—these are the foundations of liberal morality. Liberty is not the only goal of men. I can, like the Russian critic Belinsky, say that if others are to be deprived of it—if my brothers are to remain in poverty, squalor, and chains—then I do not want it for myself, I reject it with both hands and infinitely prefer to share their fate. But nothing is gained by a confusion of terms. To avoid glaring inequality or widespread misery I am ready to sacrifice some, or all, of my freedom: I may do so willingly and freely: but it is freedom that I am giving up for the sake of justice or equality or the love of my fellow men. I should be guilt-stricken, and rightly so, if I were not, in some circumstances, ready to make this sacrifice. But a sacrifice is not an increase in what is being sacrificed, namely freedom, however great the moral need or the compensation for it. Everything is what it is: liberty is liberty, not equality or fairness or justice or culture, or human happiness or a quiet conscience. If the liberty of myself or my class or nation depends on the misery of a number of other human beings, the system which promotes this is unjust and immoral. But if I curtail or lose my freedom, in order to lessen the shame of such inequality, and do not thereby materially increase the individual liberty of others, an absolute loss of liberty occurs. This may be compensated for by a gain in justice or in happiness or in peace, but the loss remains, and it is a confusion of values to say that although my "liberal," individual freedom may go by the board, some other kind of freedom—"social" or "economic" —is increased. Yet it remains true that the freedom of some must at times be curtailed to secure the freedom of others. Upon what principle should this be done? If freedom is a sacred, untouchable value, there can be no such principle. One or other of these conflicting rules or principles must, at any rate in practice, yield: not always for reasons which can be clearly stated, let alone generalized into rules or universal maxims. Still, a practical compromise has to be found.

Philosophers with an optimistic view of human nature and a belief in the possibility of harmonizing human interests, such as Locke or Adam Smith and, some moods, Mill, believed that social harmony and progress were compatible with reserving a large area for private life over which neither the state nor any other authority must be allowed to trespass. Hobbes, and those who agreed with him, especially conservative or reactionary thinkers, argued that if men were to be prevented from destroying one another and making social life a jungle or a wilderness, greater safeguards must be instituted to keep them in their places; he wished correspondingly to increase the area of centralized control and decrease that of the individual. But both sides agreed that some portion of human existence must remain independent of the sphere of social control. To invade that preserve, however small, would be despotism. The most eloquent of all defenders of freedom and privacy, Benjamin Constant, who had not forgotten the Jacobin dictatorship, declared that at the very least the liberty of religion, opinion, expression, property, must be guaranteed against arbitrary invasion. Jefferson, Burke, Paine, Mill, compiled different catalogues of individual liberties, but the argument for keeping authority at bay is always substantially the same. We must preserve a minimum area of personal freedom if we are not to "degrade or deny our nature." We cannot remain absolutely free, and must give up some of our liberty to preserve the rest. But total self-surrender is self-defeating. What then must the minimum be? That which a man cannot give up without offending against the essence of his human nature. What is this essence? What are the standards which it entails? This has been, and perhaps always will be, a matter of infinite debate. But whatever the principle in terms of which the area of noninterference is to be drawn, whether it is that of natural law or natural rights, or of utility or the pronouncements of a categorical imperative, or the sanctity of the social contract, or any other concept with which men have sought to clarify and justify their convictions, liberty in this sense means liberty *from*; absence of interference beyond the shifting, but always recognizable, frontier. "The only freedom which deserves the name is that of pursuing our own good in our own way," said the most celebrated of its champions. If this is so, is compulsion ever justified? Mill had no doubt that it was. Since justice demands that all individuals be entitled to a minimum of freedom, all other individuals were of necessity to be restrained, if need be by force, from depriving anyone of it. Indeed, the whole function of law was the prevention of just such collisions: the state was reduced to what Lassalle contemptuously described as the functions of a night-watchman or traffic policeman.

What made the protection of individual liberty so sacred to Mill? In his famous essay he declares that, unless men are left to live as they wish "in the path which merely concerns themselves," civilization cannot advance; the truth will not, for lack of a free market in ideas, come to light; there will be no scope for spontaneity, originality, genius, for mental energy, for moral courage. Society will be crushed by the weight of "collective mediocrity." Whatever is rich and diversified will be crushed by the weight of custom, by men's constant tendency to conformity, which breeds only "withered capacities," "pinched and hidebound," "cramped and warped" human beings. "Pagan self-assertion is as worthy as Christian self-denial." "All the errors which a man is likely to commit against advice and warning are far outweighed by the evil of allowing others to constrain him to what they deem is good." The defense of liberty consists in the "negative" goal of warding off interference. To threaten a man with persecution unless he submits to a life in which he exercises no choices of his goals; to block before him every door but one, no matter how noble the prospect upon which it opens, or how benevolent the motives of those who arrange this, is to sin against the truth that he is a man, a being with a life of his own to live. This is liberty as it has been conceived by liberals in the modern world from the days of Erasmus (some would say of Occam) to our own. Every plea for civil liberties and individual rights, every protest against exploitation and humiliation, against the encroachment of public authority, or the mass hypnosis of custom or organized propaganda, springs from this individualistic, and much disputed, conception of man.

Three facts about this position may be noted. In the first place Mill confuses two distinct notions. One is that all coercion is, in so far as it frustrates human desires, bad as such, although it may have to be applied to prevent other, greater evils; while noninterference, which is the opposite of coercion, is good as such, although it is not the only good. This is the "negative" conception of liberty in its classical form. The other is that men should seek to discover the truth, or to develop a certain type of character of which Mill approved—critical, original, imaginative, independent, non-conforming to the point of eccentricity, and so on—and that truth can be found, and such character can be bred, only in conditions of freedom. Both these are liberal views, but they are not identical, and the connection between them is, at best, empirical. No one would argue that truth or freedom of self-expression could flourish where dogma crushes all thought. But the evidence of history tends to show (as, indeed, was argued by James Stephen in his formidable attack on Mill in his *Liberty, Equality, Fraternity*) that integrity, love of truth, and fiery individualism grow at least as often in severely disciplined communities among, for example, the puritan Calvinists of Scotland or New England, or under military discipline, as in more tolerant or indifferent societies; and if this is so, Mill's argument for liberty as a necessary condition for the growth of human genius falls to the ground. If his two goals proved incompatible, Mill would be faced with a cruel dilemma, quite apart from the further difficulties created by the inconsistency of his doctrines with strict utilitarianism, even in his own humane version of it.[5]

[5] This is but another illustration of the natural tendency of all but a very few thinkers to believe that all the things they hold good must be intimately connected, or at least compatible, with one another. The history of thought, like the history of nations, is strewn

In the second place, the doctrine is comparatively modern. There seems to be scarcely any discussion of individual liberty as a conscious political ideal (as opposed to its actual existence) in the ancient world. Condorcet had already remarked that the notion of individual rights was absent from the legal conceptions of the Romans and Greeks; this seems to hold equally of the Jewish, Chinese, and all other ancient civilizations that have since come to light.[6] The domination of this ideal has been the exception rather than the rule, even in the recent history of the West. Nor has liberty in this sense often formed a rallying cry for the great masses of mankind. The desire not to be impinged upon, to be left to oneself, has been a mark of high civilization both on the part of individuals and communities. The sense of privacy itself, of the area of personal relationships as something sacred in its own right, derives from a conception of freedom which, for all its religious roots, is scarcely older, in its developed state, than the Renaissance or the Reformation.[7] Yet its decline would mark the death of a civilization, of an entire moral outlook.

The third characteristic of this notion of liberty is of greater importance. It is that liberty in this sense is not incompatible with some kinds of autocracy, or at any rate with the absence of self-government. Liberty in this sense is principally concerned with the area of control, not with its source. Just as a democracy may, in fact, deprive the individual citizen of a great many liberties which he might have in some other form of society, so it is perfectly conceivable that a liberal-minded despot would allow his subjects a large measure of personal freedom. The despot who leaves his subjects a wide area of liberty may be unjust, or encourage the wildest inequalities, care little for order, or virtue, or knowledge; but provided he does not curb their liberty, or at least curbs it less than many other régimes, he meets with Mill's specification.[8] Freedom in this sense is not, at any rate logically, connected with democracy or self-government. Self-government may, on the whole, provide a better guarantee of the preservation of civil liberties than other régimes, and has been defended as such by libertarians. But there is no necessary connection between individual liberty and democratic rule. The answer to the question "Who governs me?" is logically distinct from the question "How far does government interfere with me?" It is in this difference that the great contrast between the two concepts of negative and posi-

---

with examples of inconsistent, or at least disparate, elements artificially yoked together in a despotic system, or held together by the danger of some common enemy. In due course the danger passes, and conflicts between the allies arise, which often disrupt the system, sometimes to the great benefit of mankind.

[6] See the valuable discussion of this in Michel Villey, *Leçons d'histoire de la philosophie du droit*, who traces the embryo of the notion of subjective rights to Occam.

[7] Christian (and Jewish or Moslem) belief in the absolute authority of divine or natural laws, or in the equality of all men in the sight of God, is very different from belief in freedom to live as one prefers.

[8] Indeed, it is arguable that in the Prussia of Frederick the Great or in the Austria of Josef II men of imagination, originality, and creative genius, and, indeed, minorities of all kinds, were less persecuted and felt the pressure, both of institutions and custom, less heavy upon them than in many an earlier or later democracy.

tive liberty, in the end, consists.[9] For the "positive" sense of liberty comes to light if we try to answer the question, not "What am I free to do or be?", but "By whom am I ruled?" or "Who is to say what I am, and what I am not, to be or do?" The connection between democracy and individual liberty is a good deal more tenuous than it seemed to many advocates of both. The desire to be governed by myself, or at any rate to participate in the process by which my life is to be controlled, may be as deep a wish as that of a free area for action, and perhaps historically older. But it is not a desire for the same thing. So different is it, indeed, as to have led in the end to the great clash of ideologies that dominates our world. For it is this—the "positive" conception of liberty: not freedom from, but freedom to—to lead one prescribed form of life—which the adherents of the "negative" notion represent as being, at times, no better than a specious disguise for brutal tyranny.

[9] "Negative liberty" is something the extent of which, in a given case, it is difficult to estimate. It might, prima facie, seem to depend simply on the power to choose between at any rate two alternatives. Nevertheless, not all choices are equally free, or free at all. If in a totalitarian state I betray my friend under threat of torture, perhaps even if I act from fear of losing my job, I can reasonably say that I did not act freely. Nevertheless, I did, of course, make a choice, and could, at any rate in theory, have chosen to be killed or tortured or imprisoned. The mere existence of alternatives is not, therefore, enough to make my action free (although it may be voluntary) in the normal sense of the word. The extent of my freedom seems to depend on (a) how many possibilities are open to me (although the method of counting these can never be more than impressionistic. Possibilities of action are not discrete entities like apples, which can be exhaustively enumerated); (b) how easy or difficult each of these possibilities is to actualize; (c) how important in my plan of life, given my character and circumstances, these possibilities are when compared with each other; (d) how far they are closed and opened by deliberate human acts; (e) what value not merely the agent, but the general sentiment of the society in which he lives, puts on the various possibilities. All these magnitudes must be "integrated," and a conclusion, necessarily never precise, or indisputable, drawn from this process. It may well be that there are many incommensurable kinds and degrees of freedom, and that they cannot be drawn up on any single scale of magnitude. Moreover, in the case of societies, we are faced by such (logically absurd) questions as "Would arrangement X increase the liberty of Mr. A more than it would that of Messrs. B, C, and D between them, added together?" The same difficulties arise in applying utilitarian criteria. Nevertheless, provided we do not demand precise measurement, we can give valid reasons for saying that the average subject of the King of Sweden is, on the whole, a good deal freer today than the average citizen of Spain or Albania. Total patterns of life must be compared directly as wholes, although the method by which we make the comparison, and the truth of the conclusions, are difficult or impossible to demonstrate. But the vagueness of the concepts, and the multiplicity of the criteria involved, is an attribute of the subject-matter itself, not of our imperfect methods of measurement, or incapacity for precise thought.

OVERLEAF PHOTO: Don Snyder →

ON THIS SITE IN FEDERAL HALL
APRIL 30 1789
GEORGE WASHINGTON
TOOK THE OATH AS THE FIRST PRESIDENT
OF THE UNITED STATES

The Changing Face
of Religion

EDITED BY HARVEY COX

INTRODUCTION

What is happening to religion today? What will happen to it in the next fifty years? Priests, pundits, prophets, and ordinary people are posing this question to themselves during the closing decades of the twentieth century—and giving themselves a wide variety of answers. Although there are some who still argue that religion remains changeless and eternal, most honest observers have to concede that religion does change.

Some think religion as such is slowly disappearing, that man is on the verge of an entirely rational, functional, and nonreligious epoch. This is not a new idea. It was articulated by the French philosopher Auguste Comte as long ago as 1830. Comte taught that a society moves through a "theological" to a "metaphysical" stage and then to what he called a stage of "positivism," in which all explanations are made on the basis of scientific experimentation. Comte invented the term "sociology" to refer to the ultimate science of society that would emerge during this final stage.

But even with the spread of the scientific mentality and the development of social science, would all religion really disappear? Here Comte faltered a bit. Twenty years after predicting the disappearance of the theological and metaphysical stages of society Comte wrote a book entitled *System of Positive*

Polity in which he once again assigned religion a prominent place in society, above even sociology. It was, admittedly, a strange kind of religion, a religion in which humanity rather than God became the object of worship. Still Comte wrote a catechism for his novel faith and developed a new kind of mass to be used in its cultus. The story of Comte reminds us of the fact that religion has a stubborn way of reappearing, albeit in strange disguises, even in the courts of those who try most assiduously to banish it.

Others in the past, including Karl Marx, have confidently predicted the disappearance of religion. Today, however, one hears fewer such predictions. One reason is that previous analyses of religion often marked it down as nothing more than a superstitious holdover. Religion was viewed as "primitive science," something mankind would eventually outgrow. These analyses, however, have been challenged in recent years not just by theologians but by anthropologists and sociologists. The great Polish anthropologist Bronislaw Malinowski, for example, showed that religion serves a purpose in society different from science. Émile Durkheim demonstrated that the religious system of a society provides a base of meaning without which social life would be impossible. Recent writers have emphasized that religion includes much more than whatever it is that churches teach and do. "Religion" refers to the basic symbols and patterns of meaning that hold a society together. Therefore, although the churches no longer exert a monopolistic control over religious symbols and values in modern society, this is something very different from the disappearance of religion as such. Religion is changing, not disappearing.

But then *how* is it changing? Some claim we are moving toward a new, unified, world religion, a creative synthesis of the main tenets of all the great religious traditions of the world. As evidence of the coming new world religion they point to the ecumenical movement among the Christian churches, the Pope's creation of a permanent secretariat for relations with non-Christian faiths, and the generally improved atmosphere of increased tolerance among Christians, Jews, Hindus, Buddhists, and Moslems.

Another group holds that the ancient pre-Biblical religious traditions of the world are fated for extinction, but that Christianity and related religions —Judaism and Islam—are not. And they see a broadened and transmuted form of Christianity becoming the world faith of the future. At first this prophecy sounds narrow and provincial. In some cases it is. Some, however, base such a prediction not on a theological claim of the truth of Christianity, but on the fact that, since virtually the whole world is modernizing and industrializing itself, a "Western mentality" will soon emerge all over the planet. For these thinkers it follows that, since Christianity is "Western" and has had longer experience in coping with the hopes and anxieties of industrial man, it is the religious alternative best suited for such a Westernized world.

This prediction foresees in effect the spread of a Christian-influenced form of Western humanism throughout the globe. What members of this school often overlook is that Christianity has not recently had notable success in addressing itself to the moral and spiritual dilemmas of the West. Auschwitz and Hiroshima were perpetrated, after all, by Western nations. It is true that Christianity, more than other faiths, has facilitated the growth of technology, but is this really enough? Many today are beginning to wonder. Has technology come to the point where it must be challenged and, at places, opposed by radically different ways of understanding life, ways that emphasize contemplative and unitive attitudes toward nature rather than attitudes of control and manipulation? If so, certain Oriental religions may be better suited than Christianity to carry out this task.

Still another school foresees neither the disappearance of religion nor its transformation into a single world faith, Christian or syncretistic, but the intensification of pluralism in religion, the multiplication of the faith options open to any man. These observers see the churches' loss of monopolistic control and the shrinking of the world through high-speed travel and communication as the most significant factors shaping the future of religion. In a resultant world of bewildering religious heterogeneity, they argue, the synthesizing will be done more and more not by churches and denominations but by the individual. Each person will become his own center of selection from among the various religious signals that pour in on him. Each man will construct his own configuration of beliefs and values in order to make sense of his own world. Though many people may continue to "belong" to this or that church or religious group, the meaning of such belonging will change; people will simply drop from their belief patterns whatever "official" elements are unacceptable, the way many Roman Catholics have already shelved their church's traditional position on contraception. They will also include elements that seem meaningful in other faiths. Since each person will ultimately construct his own configuration of belief, the basic unit of religion will be not the church or the congregation but the religious person himself—the individual. As Thomas Jefferson said, "I am a sect myself."

This individualization of the responsibility for religious belief does not mean that churches will disappear. Groups of people whose patterns of belief display common motifs will certainly gather for worship, celebration, study, and fellowship. Man is an irreducibly social animal and so long as this remains the case most people will look for some social expression of religion. But even in such groups there will be a good deal of selective appropriation of the symbols and beliefs. Few people will be able to say, as St. Augustine did, "My faith is the faith of the church." If heresy means, as its etymology implies, the choosing of one's own belief, then heresy will become a way of life for most religious people. This is beginning to happen.

One of the hopes underlying my selection of the following essays is that they will illustrate the rich variety of religious styles and perspectives available in the world today. For this reason a variety of forms has been used— poems, sermons, letters, theological and sociological writings, a short story. No single theological perspective is being promoted, unless it is an undisguised appreciation for the dazzling variety of religious commitments abroad in the land. If there is a theme common to these articles, it is that contemporary man, unlike his parents, is unwilling to settle for either uncritical belief or uncritical atheism. He asks religious questions and reaches for some kind of faith, if often in novel or eccentric forms. He revels in the long history and enormous variety of religions as a storehouse of ideas and practices from which he can choose the components of an authentically personal mode of life. He has not stopped asking about God, but he asks this ultimate religious question by asking about man and his place in history and in the cosmos. He thinks of religion as a resource for coping with the question: What does it mean to be fully human?

This section of the reader opens with a few of the letters written from prison by Dietrich Bonhoeffer, the German theologian-martyr of World War II, during the final months of his life. Bonhoeffer had once been an avid pacifist. His earlier theological writings reveal his somewhat pietistic inclinations and his often rather narrow view of religious life. Though there are indications of the later startling developments, the "early Bonhoeffer" is of interest to us now mainly because of his later writings. Returning to Germany from the United States at the beginning of World War II, Bonhoeffer quickly joined the resistance to the Nazi regime and later took part in the now famous plot to assassinate Hitler that has come to be called the "July 20th Movement." Arrested even before the plot could be carried out, Bonhoeffer spent the last two years of his life in prison.

While in prison, Bonhoeffer wrote a series of letters in which it became quite evident that his theological ideas were changing rapidly. Unlike what one might expect, however, Bonhoeffer did not become morose and otherworldly in the face of death. On the contrary, he developed a much more life-affirming theology and ethic. He greeted the emergence of a new world in which the power of the church would be severely reduced, and he chided those who held that Christianity should deal mainly with the "borderline" areas of life—suffering, death, sin. He insisted that the Gospel should speak to man "in his strength not just in his weakness." He affirmed the process of secularization. Using a phrase that has beguiled and bewildered people ever since, he called for a "nonreligious interpretation" of Biblical concepts. Though he suggested that he wanted to go on and explore this idea more, history intervened. Bonhoeffer was executed by the Gestapo just a few hours before his prison was captured by advancing American troops.

Bonhoeffer never had the chance to spell out what he meant, but his ideas have tantalized us ever since. How do we "speak . . . in secular fashion of God?" How do we serve God *etsi deus non daretur*" (as though He did not exist)? There is probably no theologian who has been as influential in the last twenty years as this enigmatic man and lover of life who died at thirty-nine and left mainly a jumble of elliptical ideas and sketchy letters for succeeding generations to ponder.

Philip Larkin's poem congeals in a set of emotional images some of the very things Bonhoeffer anticipated. Here is the secular man, alone, a bit embarrassed by a church building, yet somehow strangely drawn to it. In fact Larkin's poem suggests another dimension that some writers feel is seriously missing in Bonhoeffer—the idea that even in the most secularized man there are ineradicable moments of religious feeling, moments when life's defeats and victories evoke a sense of awe and some effort to comprehend them in a larger symbolic universe. The poem is especially apt in its skillful combination of figures that evoke both the skepticism and the hunger for belief, the doubt and the spiritual quest—all of which inhabit the soul of contemporary man. Like T. S. Eliot's "children at the gate" (in his poem "Ash Wednesday") who "will not go away and cannot pray . . . ," the modern mentality seems to include simultaneously both belief and unbelief, both faith and doubt. No longer are believers and unbelievers sorted out between church and world. The boundary now runs through the spirit of every person.

There is still more dramatic evidence, however, that even if some feel God is dead, religion is not. In his lively description of the "new-time religion," Andrew Greeley, a Catholic priest and sociologist, shows that the quest for the sacred, the mysterious, the occult, and even the bizarre is very much alive. Greeley examines the current interest in astrology, I Ching, witchcraft, and sorcery. He notes its mixture of fun and seriousness and interprets it as having in many cases a really important religious significance as a new quest for the sacred.

In very recent years, industrial man has begun to rediscover the festive and the fanciful dimensions of life. A centuries-long process may be reversing itself. Our recent increased exposure both to non-Western cultures and to those sectors of our own civilization that have escaped complete integration into the industrialization process have made us aware that we are missing something. Technologically produced leisure has forced us to ask ourselves some hard questions about our traditional worship of work. Young people in industrial societies everywhere are demonstrating that expressive play and artistic creation belong in the center of life, not at its far periphery. A theater of the body, replete with mime, dance, and acrobatics, is upstaging our inherited theater of the mind. Street festivals, once disappearing as fast as the whooping crane, are coming back. Psychiatrists and educators are beginning to reject their traditional roles as the punishers of fantasy. Some are even searching for ways to encourage it. The awakened interest of white people in the black experience has enhanced our appreciation for a more festive and feeling-oriented approach to life. We call it "soul." Films, novels, and plays explore the world of dreams and even some philosophers are rediscovering the significance of fantasy. Even in the churches, dance, color, movement, and new kinds of music dramatize the recovery of celebration. In short, we may be witnessing the overture to a sweeping cultural renaissance, a revolution of human sensibilities in which the faculties we have starved and repressed during the centuries of industrialization will be nourished and appreciated again.

Religion for many people is the ultimate source of their ethical values. Because traditional sexual ethics have been challenged so vigorously in recent years, the importance of what a particular faith teaches in this area has grown. Although Christianity has rarely based its sexual ethic on imitating Jesus, still the question of how Jesus dealt with sex does come up from time to time. Usually such a question is ruled out of bounds by theologians either because it appears unseemly or because the evidence is so scanty. In Tom Driver's essay "Sexuality and Jesus" the issue is confronted in a forthright way. Driver's essay also has the advantage of illustrating another trend in contemporary theological writing—the analysis and explication of literary treatments of religious themes.

Another interesting facet of the modern American religious scene is the growing awareness of non-Christian religious traditions. Some black Americans have turned to a form of Islam, in part as a protest against the role Christianity played in the sanctioning of slavery and segregation. Increasing numbers of young people have found in Zen Buddhism a religious way of life that seems more satisfactory than that offered by Christianity. Two essays illustrate this tendency. In the first, Malcolm X, a brilliant and charismatic black leader, tells of his pilgrimage to Mecca and of his discovery of the racially inclusive power of the Islamic faith; in the other, the late D. T. Suzuki, a noted Zen sage, describes *satori*, the Buddhist goal of spiritual enlightenment.

For twentieth-century Jews, the problem of sorting out the religious, ethnic, and cultural aspects of being Jewish has provided a poignant challenge. The unspeakable crime of Auschwitz had strengthened a sense of Jewish identity as, for some, had the creation of the state of Israel. But for many young Jews, all that seems somehow very remote. How to discover Jewish identity in suburban America has become a crucial question. In his short story "Eli, the Fanatic" the American Jewish writer Philip Roth uncovers the tortured psychic depths of this problem for many young Jews.

But how have modern religious thinkers sought to answer the more pervasive skepticism and spiritual hunger of modern man? Four examples of efforts to articulate such a response have been included here. The first is a sermon by the late Paul Tillich, one of the twentieth century's most influential Protestant theologians. In "You Are Accepted," Tillich tries to communicate the basic essence of Biblical faith without using traditional religious concepts. He recognizes that man's hunger for faith remains but that he often cannot satisfy that hunger with symbols that have lost their power. In trying to restate the Christian message Tillich was not afraid to make use of existentialist and psychoanalytic categories. In this sermon he explicitly goes beyond the claims of any one church and tries to distill from them a Word of God for men of today. Some people feel that, in his effort to restate the Gospel in contemporary idiom, Tillich lost sight of its original content. Others claim that in his sermons they heard for the first time a voice that permitted them to say yes to the claims of religion without saying no to their intellects.

As a Protestant Christian, Tillich nevertheless put a great emphasis on the preaching of the word, on the articulation of religion through speech. For Martin Buber, the most widely known Jewish philosopher of the century, there was an essential element in religion that words could never touch. Buber was impressed with the silence and hiddenness of the divine, with what he called the "eclipse of God." Still Buber was confident that in the deepest relationships of human life there is something that transcends those relationships and opens us to a deeper dimension of existence. In his essay Buber touches on a perennial issue in religion: Do we meet God because of or in spite of our enmeshment in the lives of other men? The essay is an answer to Søren Kierkegaard, the nineteenth-century religious philosopher who broke his betrothal because he felt his relationship to God demanded a single-minded dedication from which a woman could only be a serious distraction. Buber disagreed. He saw man's relationship to God coming only in and through relationships to fellow human beings. God, for Buber, is not one who calls us away from deep involvement with each other in the pain and pleasure of life but is the one whom we meet in life's depths. It was Buber who made famous the idea of the "I-Thou" relationship as utterly constitutive of human existence. His thought has been just as influential in Christian theology as in Jewish thought, perhaps even more so.

Buber's insistence on the relationship between man and man as the primary place of God's self-disclosure illustrates the man-centered orientation of much modern theology. One of the difficulties of this approach, however, is its conflict with the tendency in the history of Western thought to thrust man more and more to the periphery of things. Galileo, by showing that the sun is the center of the solar system, destroyed the notion that man stands at the center of the physical cosmos. Darwin linked man to the animal kingdom more closely than many felt was comfortable, undermining another fictive human distinction. The religious consequence of this process was that man began to feel less significant. If God had a special relationship to man, the religious question was how this puny creature could be reinstated in the immensity of the cosmos and in the towering sweep of historical time. One answer to this puzzle has been given by the Roman Catholic philosopher and paleontologist Pierre Teilhard de Chardin. Chardin was a practicing scientist who was especially interested in the evolution of man from lower forms of life. At the same time he was a Jesuit priest. He spent his life trying to reconcile these two ways of thinking and, although many people believe he never quite succeeded, his brilliant efforts to do so have inspired widespread admiration. He is beyond doubt the most widely read and influential Roman Catholic theologian of the century.

Chardin attempted the task of reconciling religious and evolutionary thinking by suggesting that evolution does not move in a steady stream but occasionally displays a sudden spurt. After such a nodal point the next stage of evolution moves on a wholly new level. Such a spurt, claims Teilhard, came when living tissue first burst out of the inorganic matrix. Another occurred when consciousness first came into being. Teilhard believes that man's spiritual life marks the next major nodal point and that man is the bearer of this new dimension. With the coming of man, "the stuff of the universe began to think." Chardin calls the new reality brought about by consciousness the "noosphere." The self-conscious human spirit signals the highest possible development of the universe. For Teilhard, the whole cosmos was really moving toward what he called "hominization";

dependency on and direction by man. Thus reinstated, man becomes the spearpoint of evolution, the precursor of its next stage. In all of this, Teilhard believes, there is a divine purpose at work. Though he sees the emergence of more and more collective forms of human life he feels that the result will be the development of a highly conscious, hyperpersonal reality. He relates all this closely to his ideas of God and of the incarnation of God in Jesus Christ, an incarnation that continues to operate in all men and in all history.

I close this section with a poem by W. H. Auden, one of the great poets of our era. In his work he grapples constantly with nearly all the themes we have raised in this introduction—the erosion of symbol, the absence of God, the quest for identity and meaning. In this excerpt from his long poem entitled "For the Time Being—A Christmas Oratorio" Auden charts the trek of the modern soul through skepticism and sophistication to a possible new affirmation of faith. For Auden it must be a faith that turns man toward the earthly world of his neighbor, not away from it. Such a faith, says Auden, transforms our normal experience into a vehicle of the divine.

Ironically, the contemporary religious views of man, whether those of Paul Tillich or of Martin Buber, now face a criticism that is nearly the opposite of the one theologians faced two centuries ago. At that time the typical enlightened critique alleged that Christianity belittled man, called him a "despicable worm" or a "worthless sinner," when it was clear, at least to the critics, that man was really a noble and elevated being. A certain type of humanism emerged in conscious opposition to Christianity. Today the shoe is often on the other foot. Secular critics of Christianity find religion unreasonably affirmative in its estimate of man's place. Against what seems to be Christianity's groundlessly grandiose view of human destiny, the secularist frequently reminds us that we are, after all, only a transient eczema on a small planet in a third-rate galaxy. Its critics now often deride Christianity not for making man paranoid but for giving him what seem to be illusions of grandeur.

The fact that the continuing debate between religious and nonreligious intellectuals has recently taken this turn is a significant one. It means that the stature and significance of man rather than the existence of the deity is now the main focus of discussion.

From LETTERS AND PAPERS FROM PRISON

Dietrich Bonhoeffer

30 April 1944

. . . . . .

You would be surprised, and perhaps even worried, by my theological thoughts and the conclusions that they lead to; and this is where I miss you most of all, because I don't know whom else I could so well discuss them with, so as to have my thinking clarified. What is bothering me incessantly is the question what Christianity really is, or indeed who Christ really is, for us today. The time when people could be told everything by means of words, whether theological or pious, is over, and so is the time of inwardness and conscience—and that means the time of religion in general. We are moving toward a completely religionless time; people as they are now simply cannot be religious any more. Even those who honestly describe themselves as "religious" do not in the least act up to it, and so they presumably mean something quite different by "religious." Our whole nineteen-hundred-year-old Christian preaching and theology rest on the "religious *a priori*" of mankind. "Christianity" has always been a form—perhaps the true form—of "religion." But if one day it becomes clear that this *a priori* does not exist at all, but was a historically conditioned and transient form of human self-expression, and if therefore man becomes radically religionless—and I think that that is already more or less the case (how else is it, for example, that this war, in contrast to all previous ones, is not calling forth any "religious" reaction?)—what does that mean for "Christianity?"

It means that the foundation is taken away from the whole of what has up to now been our "Christianity," and that there remain only a few "last survivors of the age of chivalry," or a few intellectually dishonest people, on whom we can descend as "religious." Are they to be the chosen few? Is it on this dubious group of people that we are to pounce in fervor, pique, or indignation, in order to sell them our goods? Are we to fall upon a few unfortunate people in their hour of need and exercise a sort of religious compulsion on them?

If we do not want to do all that, if our final judgment must be that the western form of Christianity, too, was only a preliminary stage to a complete absence of religion, what kind of situation emerges for us, for the Church? How can Christ become the Lord of the religionless as well? Are there religionless Christians? If religion is only a garment of Christianity—and even this garment has looked very different at different times—then

FROM LETTERS AND PAPERS FROM PRISON Reprinted with permission of The Macmillan Company from *Letters and Papers from Prison* by Dietrich Bonhoeffer. Copyright by The Macmillan Company, 1953. © SCM Press Ltd. 1953, 1967.

what is a religionless Christianity? Barth, who is the only one to have started along this line of thought, did not carry it to completion, but arrived at a positivism of revelation, which in the last analysis is essentially a restoration. For the religionless working man (or any other man) nothing decisive is gained here. The questions to be answered would surely be: What do a church, a community, a sermon, a liturgy, a Christian life mean in a religionless world? How do we speak of God—without religion, i.e., without the temporally conditioned presuppositions of metaphysics, inwardness, and so on? How do we speak (or perhaps we cannot now even "speak" as we used to) in a "secular" way about "God?" In what way are we "religionless-secular" Christians, in what way are we the ἐκκλησία, those who are called forth, not regarding ourselves from a religious point of view as specially favored, but rather as belonging wholly to the world? In that case Christ is no longer an object of religion, but something quite different, really the Lord of the world. But what does that mean? What is the place of worship and prayer in a religionless situation? Does the secret discipline, or alternatively the difference (which I have suggested to you before) between penultimate and ultimate take on a new importance here?

.   .   .   .   .

The Pauline question whether περιτομή [circumcision] is a condition of justification seems to me in present-day terms to be whether religion is a condition of salvation. Freedom from περιτομή is also freedom from religion. I often ask myself why a "Christian instinct" often draws me more to the religionless people than to the religious, by which I do not in the least mean with any evangelizing intention, but, I might almost say, "in brotherhood." While I am often reluctant to mention God by name to religious people—because that name somehow seems to me here not to ring true, and I feel myself to be slightly dishonest (it is particularly bad when others start to talk in religious jargon; I then dry up almost completely and feel awkward and uncomfortable)—to people with no religion I can on occasion mention him by name quite calmly and as a matter of course. Religious people speak of God when human knowledge (perhaps simply because they are too lazy to think) has come to an end, or when human resources fail—in fact it is always the *deus ex machina* that they bring on to the scene, either for the apparent solution of insoluble problems, or as strength in human failure—always, that is to say, exploiting human weakness or human boundaries. Of necessity, that can go on only till people can by their own strength push these boundaries somewhat further out, so that God becomes superfluous as a *deus ex machina*. I have come to be doubtful of talking about any human boundaries (is even death, which people now hardly fear, and is sin, which they now hardly understand, still a genuine boundary today?). It always seems to me that we are trying anxiously in this way to reserve some space for God; I should like to speak of God not on the boundaries but at the center, not in weakness but in strength; and therefore not in death and guilt but in man's life and goodness. As to the boundaries, it seems to me better to be silent and leave the insoluble unsolved. Belief in the resurrection is *not* the "solution" of the problem of death. God's "beyond" is not the beyond of our cognitive faculties. The transcendence of epistemological theory has nothing to do with the transcendence of God. God is beyond in the midst of our life. The church stands, not at the boundaries where human powers give out, but in the middle of the village. That is how it is in the Old Testament, and in this sense we still read the New Testament far too little in the light of the Old.

.   .   .   .   .

5 May 1944

.   .   .   .   .

A few more words about "religionlessness." I expect you remember Bultmann's essay on the "demythologizing" of the New Testament? My view of it today would be, not that he went "too far," as most people thought, but that he did not go far enough. It is not only the "mythological" concepts, such as miracle, ascension, and so on (which are not in principle separable from the concepts of God, faith, etc.), but "religious" concepts generally, which are problematic. You cannot, as Bultmann supposes, separate God and miracle, but you must be able to interpret and proclaim both in a "nonreligious" sense. Bultmann's approach is fundamentally still a liberal one (i.e., abridging the gospel), whereas I am trying to think theologically.

What does it mean to "interpret in a religious sense?" I think it means to speak on the one hand metaphysically, and on the other hand individualistically. Neither of these is relevant to the Bible message or to the man of today. Has not the individualistic question about personal salvation almost completely left us all? Are we not really under the impression that there are more important things than that question (perhaps not more important than the *matter* itself, but more important than the *question!*)? I know it sounds pretty monstrous to say that. But, fundamentally, is it not actually biblical? Does the question about saving one's soul appear in the Old Testament at all? Are not righteousness and the Kingdom of God on earth the focus of everything, and is it not true that Rom. 3.24ff. is not an individualistic doctrine of salvation, but the culmination of the view that God alone is righteous? It is not with the beyond that we are concerned, but with this world as created and preserved, subjected to laws, reconciled, and restored. What is above this world is, in the gospel, intended to exist *for* this world; I mean that, not in the anthropocentric sense of liberal, mystic, pietistic, ethical theology, but in the biblical sense of the creation and of the incarnation, crucifixion, and resurrection of Jesus Christ.

Barth was the first theologian to begin the criticism of religion, and that remains his really great merit; but he put in its place a positivist doctrine of revelation which says, in effect, "Like it or lump it": virgin birth, Trinity, or anything else; each is an equally significant and necessary part of the whole, which must simply be swallowed as a whole or not at all. That is not biblical. There are degrees of knowledge and degrees of significance; that means that a secret discipline must be restored whereby the *mysteries* of the Christian faith are protected against profanation. The positivism of revelation makes it too easy for itself, by setting up, as it does in the last analysis, a law of faith, and so mutilates what is—by Christ's incarnation!—a gift for us. In the place of religion there now stands the Church—that is in itself biblical—but the world is in some degree made to depend on itself and left to its own devices, and that is the mistake.

．　．　．　．　．

25 May 1944

. . . We have to get people out of their one-track minds; that is a kind of "preparation" for faith, or something that makes faith possible, although really it is only faith itself that can make possible a multi-dimensional life.

．　．　．　．　．

Weizsäcker's book *Das Weltbild der Physik* is still keeping me very busy. It has again brought home to me quite clearly how wrong it is to use God as a stop-gap for the incompleteness of our knowledge. If in fact the frontiers of knowledge are being pushed further and further back (and that is bound to be the case), then God is being pushed back with them, and is therefore continually in retreat. We are to find God in what we know, not in what we do not know; God wants us to realize his presence, not in unsolved problems but in those that are solved. That is true of the relationship between God and scientific knowledge, but it is also true of the wider human problems of death, suffering, and guilt. It is now possible to find, even for these questions, human answers that take no account whatever of God. In point of fact, people deal with these questions without God (it has always been so), and it is simply not true to say that only Christianity has the answers to them. As to the idea of "solving" problems, it may be that the Christian answers are just as unconvincing—or convincing —as any others. Here again, God is no stop-gap; he must be recognized at the center of life, not when we are at the end of our resources; it is his will to be recognized in life, and not only when death comes; in health and vigor, and not only in suffering; in our activities, and not only in sin. The ground for this lies in the revelation of God in Jesus Christ. He is the center of life, and he certainly did not "come" to answer our unsolved problems. From the center of life certain questions, and their answers, are seen to be wholly irrelevant (I am thinking of the judgment pronounced on Job's friends). In Christ there are no "Christian problems." . . .

．　．　．　．　．

8 June 1944

．　．　．　．　．

The movement that began about the thirteenth century (I am not going to get involved in any argument about the exact date) toward the autonomy of man (in which I should include the discovery of the laws by which the world lives and deals with itself in science, social and political matters, art, ethics, and religion) has in our time reached an undoubted completion. Man has learned to deal with himself in all questions of importance without recourse to the "working hypothesis" called "God." In questions of science, art, and ethics this has become an understood thing at which one now hardly dares to tilt. But for the last hundred years or so it has also become increasingly true of religious questions; it is becoming evident that everything gets along without "God"—and, in fact, just as well as before. As in the scientific field, so in human affairs generally, "God" is being pushed more and more out of life, losing more and more ground.

Roman Catholic and Protestant historians agree that it is in this development that the great defection from God, from Christ, is to be seen; and the more they claim and play off God and Christ against it, the more the development considers itself to be anti-Christian. The world that has become conscious of itself and the laws that govern its own existence has grown self-confident in what seems to us to be an uncanny way. False developments and failures do not make the world doubt the necessity of the course that it is taking, or of its development; they are accepted with fortitude and detachment as part of the bargain, and even an event like the present war is no exception. Christian apologetic has taken the most varied forms of opposition to this self-assurance. Efforts are made to prove to a world thus come of age that it cannot live without the tutelage of "God." Even though there has been surrender on all secular problems, there still remain the so-called "ultimate questions"—death, guilt—to which only "God" can give an answer, and because of which we need God and the Church and the pastor. So we live, in some degree, on these so-called ultimate questions of humanity. But what if one day they no longer exist as such, if they too can be answered "without God?" Of course, we now have the secularized offshoots of Christian theology, namely existentialist philosophy and the psychotherapists, who demonstrate to secure, contented, and happy mankind that it is really unhappy and desperate and simply unwilling to admit that it is in a predicament about which it knows nothing, and from which only they can rescue it. Wherever there is health, strength, security, simplicity, they sent luscious fruit to gnaw at or to lay their pernicious eggs in. They set themselves to drive people to inward despair, and then the game is in their hands. That is secularized methodism. And whom does it touch? A small number of intellectuals, of degenerates, of people who regard themselves as the most important thing in the world, and who therefore like to busy themselves with themselves. The ordinary man, who spends his everyday life at work and with his family, and of course with all kinds of diversions, is not affected. He has neither the time nor the inclination to concern himself with his existential despair, or to regard his perhaps modest share of happiness as a trial, a trouble, or a calamity.

The attack by Christian apologetic on the adulthood of the world I consider to be in the first place pointless, in the second place ignoble, and in the third place unchristian. Pointless, because it seems to me like an attempt to put a grown-up man back into adolescence, i.e., to make him dependent on things on which he is, in fact, no longer dependent, and thrusting him into problems that are, in fact, no longer problems to him.

Ignoble, because it amounts to an attempt to exploit man's weakness for purposes that are alien to him and to which he has not freely assented. Unchristian, because it confuses Christ with one particular stage in man's religiousness; i.e., with a human law. More about this later.

But first, a little more about the historical position. The question is: Christ and the world that has come of age. The weakness of liberal theology was that it conceded to the world the right to determine Christ's place in the world; in the conflict between the Church and the world it accepted the comparatively easy terms of peace that the world dictated. Its strength was that it did not try to put the clock back, and that it genuinely accepted the battle (Troeltsch), even though this ended with its defeat.

Defeat was followed by surrender, and by an attempt to make a completely fresh start based on the fundamentals of the Bible and the Reformation. Heim sought, along pietist and methodist lines, to convince the individual man that he was faced with the alternative "despair or Jesus." He gained "hearts." Althaus (carrying forward the modern and positive line with a strong confessional emphasis) tried to wring from the world a place for Lutheran teaching (ministry) and Lutheran worship, and otherwise left the world to its own devices. Tillich set out to interpret the evolution of the world (against its will) in a religious sense—to give it its shape through religion. That was very brave of him, but the world unseated him and went on by itself; he, too, sought to understand the world better than it understood itself; but it felt that it was completely misunderstood, and rejected the imputation. (Of course, the world *must* be understood better than it understands itself, but not "religiously" as the religious socialists wanted.) Barth was the first to realize the mistake that all these attempts (which were all, in fact, still sailing, though unintentionally, in the channel of liberal theology) were making in leaving clear a space for religion in the world or against the world.

He brought in against religion the God of Jesus Christ, "*pneuma* against *sarx*." That remains his greatest service (his *Epistle to the Romans,* second edition, in spite of all the neo-Kantian egg-shells). Through his later dogmatics, he enabled the Church to effect this distinction, in principle, all along the line. It was not in ethics, as is often said, that he subsequently failed—his ethical observations, as far as they exist, are just as important as his dogmatic ones—; it was that in the nonreligious interpretation of theological concepts he gave no concrete guidance, either in dogmatics or in ethics. There lies his limitation, and because of it his theology of revelation has become positivist, a "positivism of revelation," as I put it.

The Confessing Church has now largely forgotten all about the Barthian approach, and has lapsed from positivism into conservative restoration. The important thing about that Church is that it carries on the great concepts of Christian theology; but it seems as if doing this is gradually just about exhausting it. It is true that there are in those concepts the elements of genuine prophecy (among them two things that you mention: the claim to truth, and mercy) and of genuine worship; and to that extent the Confessing Church gets only attention, hearing, and rejection. But both of them remain undeveloped and remote, because there is no interpretation of them.

Those who, like E.G. Schütz or the Oxford Group or the Berneucheners, miss the "movement" and the "life," are dangerous reactionaries; they are reactionary because they go right back behind the approach of the theology of revelation and seek for "religious" renewal. They simply have not yet understood the problem at all, and their talk is entirely beside the point. There is no future for them (though the Oxford Group would have the best chance if they were not so completely without biblical substance).

Bultmann seems to have somehow felt Barth's limitations, but he misconstrues them in the sense of liberal theology, and so goes off into the typical liberal process of reduction—the "mythological" elements of Christianity are dropped, and Christianity is reduced to its "essence."—My view is that the full content, including the "mythological" concepts, must be kept—the New Testament is not a mythological clothing of a universal truth; this mythology (resurrection, etc.) is the thing itself—but the concepts must be interpreted in such a way as not to make religion a precondition of faith (cf. Paul and circumcision). Only in that way, I think, will liberal theology be overcome (and even Barth is still influenced by it, though negatively) and at the same time its question be genuinely taken up and answered (as is *not* the case in the Confessing Church's positivism of revelation!).

Thus the world's coming of age is no longer an occasion for polemics and apologetics, but is now really better understood than it understands itself, namely on the basis of the gospel and in the light of Christ.

.   .   .   .   .

30 June 1944

.   .   .   .   .

I had been saying that God is being increasingly pushed out of a world that has come of age, out of the spheres of our knowledge and life, and that since Kant he has been relegated to a realm beyond the world of experience.

Theology has on the one hand resisted this development with apologetics, and has taken up arms—in vain—against Darwinism, etc. On the other hand, it has accommodated itself to the development by restricting God to the so-called ultimate questions as a *deux ex machina;* that means that he becomes the answer to life's problems, and the solution of its needs and conflicts. So if anyone has no such difficulties, or if he refuses to go into these things, to allow others to pity him, then either he cannot be open to God; or else he must be shown that he is, in fact, deeply involved in such problems, needs, and conflicts, without admitting or knowing it. If that can be done—and existentialist philosophy and psychotherapy have worked out some quite ingenious methods in that direction—then this man can now be claimed for God, and methodism can celebrate its triumph. But if he cannot be brought to see and admit that his happiness is really an evil, his health sickness, and his vigor despair, the theologian is at his wits' end. It is a case of having to do either with a hardened sinner of a particularly ugly type, or with a man of "bourgeois complacency," and the one is as far from salvation as the other.

You see, that is the attitude that I am contending against. When Jesus blessed sinners, they were real sinners, but Jesus did not make everyone a sinner first. He called them away from their sin, not into their sin. It is true that encounter with Jesus meant the reversal of all human values. So it was in the conversion of Paul, though in his case the encounter with Jesus preceded the realization of sin. It is true that Jesus cared about people on the fringe of human society, such as harlots and tax-collectors, but never about them alone, for he sought to care about man as such. Never did he question a man's health, vigor, or happiness, regarded in themselves, or regard them as evil fruits; else why should he heal the sick and restore strength to the weak? Jesus claims for himself and the Kingdom of God the whole of human life in all its manifestations.

. . . Let me just summarize briefly what I am concerned about—how to claim for Jesus Christ a world that has come of age.

.   .   .   .   .

8 July 1944

.   .   .   .   .

The displacement of God from the world, and from the public part of human life, led to the attempt to keep his place secure at least in the sphere of the "personal," the "inner," and the "private." And as every man still has a private sphere somewhere, that is where he was thought to be the most vulnerable. The secrets known to a man's valet—that is, to put it crudely, the range of his intimate life, from prayer to his sexual life—have become the hunting-ground of modern pastoral workers. In that way they resemble (though with quite different intentions) the dirtiest gutter journalists—do you remember the *Wahrheit* and the *Glocke,* which made public the most intimate details about prominent people? In the one case it is social, financial, or political blackmail, and in the other, religious blackmail. Forgive me, but I cannot put it more mildly.

From the sociological point of view this is a revolution from below, a revolt of inferiority. Just as the vulgar mind is not satisfied till it has seen some highly placed personage "in his bath," or in other embarrassing situations, so it is here. There is a kind of evil satisfaction in knowing that everyone has his failings and weak spots. In my contacts with the "outcasts" of society, its "pariahs," I have noticed repeatedly that mistrust is the dominant motive in their judgment of other people. Every action, even the most unselfish, of a person of high repute is suspected from the outset. These "outcasts" are to be found in all grades of society. In a flower-garden they grub around only for the dung on which the flowers grow. The more isolated a man's life, the more easily he falls a victim to this attitude.

There is also a parallel isolation among the clergy, in what one might call the "clerical" sniffing-around-after-people's-sins in order to catch them out. It is as if you could not know a fine house till you had found a cobweb in the furthest cellar, or as if you could not adequately appreciate a good play till you had seen how the actors behave offstage. It is the same kind of thing that you find in the novels of the last fifty years, which do not think they have depicted their characters properly till they have described them in their marriage-bed, or in films where undressing scenes are thought necessary. Anything clothed, veiled, pure, and chaste is presumed to be deceitful, disguised, and impure; people here simply show their own impurity. A basic antisocial attitude of mistrust and suspicion is the revolt of inferiority.

Regarded theologically, the error is twofold. First, it is thought that a man can be addressed as a sinner only after his weaknesses and meannesses have been spied out. Secondly, it is thought that a man's essential nature consists of his inmost and most intimate background; that is defined as his "inner life," and it is precisely in those secret human places that God is to have his domain!

On the first point it is to be said that man is certainly a sinner, but is far from being mean or common on that account. To put it rather tritely, were Goethe and Napoleon sinners because they were not always faithful husbands? It is not the sins of weakness, but the sins of strength, which matter here. It is not in the least necessary to spy out things; the Bible never does so. (Sins of strength: in the genius, *hubris;* in the peasant, the breaking of the order of life—is the decalogue a peasant ethic?—; in the bourgeois, fear of free responsibility. Is this correct?)

On the second point: the Bible does not recognize our distinction between the outward and the inward. Why should it? It is always concerned with *anthrōpos teleios,* the *whole* man, even where, as in the Sermon on the Mount, the decalogue is pressed home to refer to "inward disposition." That a good "disposition" can take the place of the total goodness is quite unbiblical. The discovery of the so-called inner life dates from the Renaissance, probably from Petrarch. The "heart" in the biblical sense is not the inner life, but the whole man in relation to God. But as a man lives just as much from "outwards" to "inwards" as from "inwards" to "outwards," the view that his essential nature can be understood only from his intimate spiritual background is wholly erroneous.

I therefore want to start from the premise that God should not be smuggled into some last secret place, but that we should frankly recognize that the world, and people, have come of age, that we should not run man down in his worldliness, but confront him with God at his strongest point, that we should give up all our clerical tricks, and not regard psychotherapy and existentialist philosophy as God's pioneers. The importunity of all these people is far too unaristocratic for the Word of God to ally itself with them. The Word of God is far removed from this revolt of mistrust, this revolt from below. On the contrary, it reigns.

.   .   .   .   .

16 July 1944

.   .   .   .   .

Now for a few more thoughts on our theme. I am only gradually working my way to the non-religious interpretation of biblical concepts; the job is too big for me to finish just yet.

On the historical side: There is one great development that leads to the world's autonomy. In theology one sees it first in Lord Herbert of Cherbury, who maintains that reason is sufficient for religious knowledge. In ethics it appears in Montaigne and Bodin with their substitution of rules of life for the commandments. In politics Machiavelli detaches politics from morality in general and founds the doctrine of "reasons of State." Later, and very differently from Machiavelli, but tending like him toward the autonomy of human society, comes Grotius, setting up his natural law as international law, which is valid *etsi deus non daretur,* "even if there were no God." The philosophers provide the finishing touches: on the one hand we have the deism of Descartes, who holds that the world is a mechanism, running by itself with no interference from God; and on the other hand the pantheism of Spinoza, who says that God is nature. In the last resort, Kant is a deist, and Fichte and Hegel are pantheists. Everywhere the thinking is directed toward the autonomy of man and the world.

(It seems that in the natural sciences the process begins with Nicolas of Cusa and Giordano Bruno and their "heretical" doctrine of the infinity of the universe. The classical *cosmos* was finite, like the created world of the Middle Ages. An infinite universe, however it may be conceived, is self-subsisting, *etsi deus non daretur.* It is true that modern physics is not as sure as it was about the infinity of the universe, but it has not gone back to the earlier conceptions of its finitude.)

God as a working hypothesis in morals, politics, or science, has been surmounted and abolished; and the same thing has happened in philosophy and religion (Feuerbach!). For the sake of intellectual honesty, that working hypothesis should be dropped, or as far as possible eliminated. A scientist or physician who sets out to edify is a hybrid.

Anxious souls will ask what room there is left for God now; and as they know of no answer to the question, they condemn the whole development that has brought them to such straits. I wrote to you before about the various emergency exits that have been contrived; and we ought to add to them the *salto mortale* (death-leap) back into the Middle Ages. But the principle of the Middle Ages is heteronomy in the form of clericalism; a return to that can only be a counsel of despair, and it would be at the cost of intellectual honesty. It is a dream that reminds one of the song *O wüsst ich doch den Weg zurück, den weiten Weg ins Kinderland.*[1] There is no such way—at any rate not if it means deliberately abandoning our mental integrity; the only way is that of Matt. 18.3, i.e., through repentance, through *ultimate* honesty.

And we cannot be honest unless we recognize that we have to live in

---

[1] "Oh if only I knew the way back, the long way back to the land of childhood."

the world *etsi deus non daretur*. And this is just what we do recognize—before God! God himself compels us to recognize it. So our coming of age leads us to a true recognition of our situation before God. God would have us know that we must live as men who manage our lives without him. The God who is with us is the God who forsakes us (Mark 15.34). The God who lets us live in the world without the working hypothesis of God is the God before whom we stand continually. Before God and with God we live without God. God lets himself be pushed out of the world on to the cross. He is weak and powerless in the world, and that is precisely the way; the only way, in which he is with us and helps us. Matt. 8.17 makes it quite clear that Christ helps us, not by virtue of his omnipotence, but by virtue of his weakness and suffering.

Here is the decisive difference between Christianity and all religions. Man's religiosity makes him look in his distress to the power of God in the world: God is the *deus ex machina*. The Bible directs man to God's power-lessness and suffering; only the suffering God can help. To that extent we may say that the development toward the world's coming of age outlined above, which has done away with a false conception of God, opens up a way of seeing the God of the Bible, who wins power and space in the world by his weakness. This will probably be the starting-point for our "secular interpretation."

. . . . .

18 July 1944

. . . "Christians stand by God in his hour of grieving"; that is what distinguishes Christians from pagans. Jesus asked in Gethsemane, "Could you not watch with me one hour?" [2] That is a reversal of what the religious man expects from God. Man is summoned to share in God's sufferings at the hands of a godless world.

He must therefore really live in the godless world, without attempting to gloss over or explain its ungodliness in some religious way or other. He must live a "secular" life, and thereby share in God's sufferings. He *may* live a "secular" life: i.e., he is freed (as one who has been liberated from false religious obligation inhibitions). To be a Christian does not mean to be religious in a particular way, to make something of oneself (a sinner, a penitent, or a saint) on the basis of some method or other, but to be a man—not a type of man, but the man that Christ creates in us. It is not the religious act that makes the Christian, but participation in the sufferings of God in the secular life.

That is *metanoia:* not in the first place thinking about one's own needs, problems, sins, and fears, but allowing oneself to be caught up into the way of Jesus Christ, into the messianic event, thus fulfilling Isa. 53. Therefore "believe in the gospel," [3] or, in the words of John the Baptist, "Behold, the Lamb of God, who takes away the sin of the world" (John 1.29). (By the way, Jeremias has recently asserted that the Aramaic word for

[2] Matt. 26.40.   [3] Mark 1.15.

"lamb" may also be translated "servant"; this is very appropriate in view of Isa. 53.)

This being caught up into the messianic suffering of God in Jesus Christ takes a variety of forms in the New Testament. It appears in the call to discipleship, in Jesus' table-fellowship with sinners, in "conversions" in the narrower sense of the word (e.g., Zacchaeus), in the act of the woman who was a sinner (Luke 7)—an act that she performed without any confession of sin, in the healing of the sick (Matt. 8.17; see above), in Jesus' acceptance of children. The shepherds, like the wise men from the East, stand at the crib, not as "converted sinners," but simply because they are drawn to the crib by the star just as they are. The centurion of Capernaum (who makes no confession of sin) is held up as a model of faith[4] (cf. Jairus).[5] Jesus "loved" the rich young man.[6] The eunuch (Acts 8) and Cornelius (Acts 10) are not standing at the edge of an abyss. Nathaniel is "an Israelite indeed, in whom there is no guile" (John 1.47). Finally, Joseph·of Arimathea and the women at the tomb.[7] The only thing that is common to all these is their sharing in the suffering of God in Christ. That is their "faith."

There is nothing of religious method here. The "religious act" is always something partial; "faith" is something whole, involving the whole of one's life. Jesus calls men, not to a new religion, but to life. But what does this life look like, this participation in the powerlessness of God in the world? I will write about that next time, I hope.

Just one more point for today. When we speak of God in a "non-religious" way, we must speak of him in such a way that the godlessness of the world is not in some way concealed but for that very reason revealed rather in, and thus exposed to, an unexpected light. The world that has come of age is more godless, and perhaps its coming of age is nearer to God than before.

·   ·   ·   ·   ·

21 July 1944[8]

·   ·   ·   ·   ·

During the last year or so I have come to know and understand more and more the profound this-worldliness of Christianity. The Christian is not a *homo religiosus,* but simply a man, as Jesus was a man—in contrast, shall we say, to John the Baptist. I don't mean the shallow and banal this-worldliness of the enlightened, the busy, the comfortable, or the lascivious, but the profound this-worldliness, characterized by discipline and the constant knowledge of death and resurrection. I think Luther live a this-worldly life in this sense.

I remember a conversation that I had in A.[9] thirteen years ago with a young French pastor.[10] We were asking ourselves quite simply what we wanted to do with our lives. He said he would like to become a saint (and

---

[4] Matt. 8.   [5] Mark 5.   [6] Mark 10.   [7] Mark 15–16.
[8] The day after the unsuccessful attempt to assassinate Hitler.
[9] America.   [10] Jean Lasserre.

I think it is quite likely that he did become one). At the time I was very impressed, but I disagreed with him, and said, in effect, that I should like to learn to have faith. For a long time I did not realize the depth of the contrast. I thought I could acquire faith by trying to live a holy life, or something like it. I suppose I wrote *The Cost of Discipleship* as the end of that path. Today I can see the dangers of that book, though I still stand by what I wrote.

I discovered later, and I am still discovering right up to this moment, that it is only by living completely in this world that one learns to have faith. One must completely abandon any attempt to make something of oneself, whether it be a saint, or a converted sinner, or a churchman (a so-called priestly type!), a righteous man or an unrighteous one, a sick man or a healthy one. By this-worldliness I mean living unreservedly in life's duties, problems, successes and failures, experiences and perplexities. In so doing we throw ourselves completely into the arms of God, taking seriously, not our own sufferings, but those of God in the world—watching with Christ in Gethsemane. That I think is faith, that is *metanoia;* and that is how one becomes a man and a Christian (cf. Jer. 45!). How can success make us arrogant, or failure lead us astray, when we share in God's sufferings through a life of this kind?

· · · · ·

OUTLINE FOR A BOOK

I should like to write a book of not more than 100 pages, divided into three chapters:
1. A Stocktaking of Christianity.
2. The Real Meaning of Christian Faith.
3. Conclusions.

Chapter 1 to deal with:
   a. The coming of age of mankind (as already indicated). The safeguarding of life against "accidents" and "blows of fate"; even if these cannot be eliminated, the danger can be reduced. Insurance (which, although it lives on "accidents," seeks to mitigate their effects) as a western phenomenon. The aim: to be independent of nature. Nature was formerly conquered by spiritual means, with us by technical organization of all kinds. Our immediate environment is not nature, as formerly, but organization. But with this protection from nature's menace there arises a new one—through organization itself.

   But the spiritual force is lacking. The question is: What protects us against the menace of organization? Man is again thrown back on himself. He has managed to deal with everything, only not with himself. He can insure against everything, only not against man. In the last resort it all turns on man.
   b. The religionlessness of man who has come of age. "God" as a work-

ing hypothesis, as a stop-gap for our embarrassments, has become superfluous (as already indicated).

c. The Protestant Church: Pietism as a last attempt to maintain evangelical Christianity as a religion; Lutheran orthodoxy, the attempt to rescue the Church as an institution for salvation; the Confessing Church: the theology of revelation; a δὸς μοὶ ποῦ στῶ over against the world, involving a "factual" interest in Christianity; art and science searching for their origin. Generally in the Confessing Church: standing up for the Church's "cause," but little personal faith in Christ. "Jesus" is disappearing from sight. Sociologically: no effect on the masses—interest confined to the upper and lower middle classes. A heavy incubus of difficult traditional ideas. The decisive factor: the Church on the defensive. No taking risks for others.

d. Public morals—as shown by sexual behavior.

Chapter 2.
   a. God and the secular.
   b. Who is God? Not in the first place an abstract belief in God, in his ominpotence, etc. That is not a genuine experience of God, but a partial extension of the world. Encounter with Jesus Christ. The experience that a transformation of all human life is given in the fact that "Jesus is there only for others." His "being there for others" is the experience of transcendence. It is only this "being there for others," maintained till death, that is the ground of his omnipotence, omniscience, and omnipresence. Faith is participation in this being of Jesus (incarnation, cross, and resurrection). Our relation to God is not a "religious" relationship to the highest, most powerful, and best Being imaginable—that is not authentic transcendence—but our relation to God is a new life in "existence for others," through participation in the being of Jesus. The transcendental is not infinite and unattainable tasks, but the neighbor who is within reach in any given situation. God in human form—not, as in oriental religions, in animal form, monstrous, chaotic, remote, and terrifying, nor in the conceptual forms of the absolute, metaphysical, infinite, etc., nor yet in the Greek divine-human form of "man in himself," but "the man for others," and therefore the Crucified, the man who lives out of the transcendent.
   c. Interpretation of biblical concepts on this basis. (Creation, fall, atonement, repentance, faith, the new life, the last things.)
   d. Cultus. (Details to follow later, in particular on cultus and "religion.")
   e. What do we really believe? I mean, believe in such a way that we stake our lives on it? The problem of the Apostles' Creed? "What *must* I believe?" is the wrong question; antiquated controversies, especially those between the different sects; the Lutheran versus Reformed, and to some extent the Roman Catholic versus Protestant, are now unreal. They may at any time be revived with passion, but they no longer carry conviction. There is no proof of this, and we must simply take it that it is so. All that we can prove is that faith of the Bible and Christianity does not stand or fall by these issues. Karl Barth and the Confessing Church have en-

couraged us to entrench ourselves persistently behind the "faith of the Church," and evade the honest question as to what we ourselves really believe. That is why the air is not quite fresh, even in the Confessing Church. To say that it is the Church's business, not mine, may be a clerical evasion, and outsiders always regard it as such. It is much the same with the dialectical assertion that I do not control my own faith, and that it is therefore not for me to say what my faith is. There may be a place for all these considerations, but they do not absolve us from the duty of being honest with ourselves. We cannot, like the Roman Catholics, simply identify ourselves with the Church. (This, incidentally, explains the popular opinion about Roman Catholics' insincerity.) Well then, what do we really believe? Answer: see (b), (c), and (d).

Chapter 3.
Conclusions:
The Church is the Church only when it exists for others. To make a start, it should give away all its property to those in need. The clergy must live solely on the free-will offerings of their congregations, or possibly engage in some secular calling. The Church must share in the secular problems of ordinary human life, not dominating, but helping and serving. It must tell men of every calling what it means to live in Christ, to exist for others. In particular, our own Church will have to take the field against the vices of *hubris,* power-worship, envy, and humbug, as the roots of all evil. It will have to speak of moderation, purity, trust, loyalty, constancy, patience, discipline, humility, contentment, and modesty. It must not underestimate the importance of human example (which has its origin in the humanity of Jesus and is so important in Paul's teaching); it is not abstract argument, but example, that gives its word emphasis and power. (I hope to take up later this subject of "example" and its place in the New Testament; it is something that we have almost entirely forgotten.) Further: the question of revising the creeds (the Apostles' Creed); revision of Christian apologetics; reform of the training for the ministry and the pattern of clerical life.

All this is very crude and condensed, but there are certain things that I am anxious to say simply and clearly—things that we so often like to shirk. Whether I shall succeed is another matter, especially if I cannot discuss it with you. I hope it may be of some help for the Church's future.

CHURCH GOING

Philip Larkin

Once I am sure there's nothing going on
I step inside, letting the door thud shut.
Another church: matting, seats, and stone,
And little books; sprawlings of flowers, cut
For Sunday, brownish now; some brass and stuff
Up at the holy end; the small neat organ;
And a tense, musty, unignorable silence,
Brewed God knows how long. Hatless, I take off
My cycle-clips in awkward reverence,

Move forward, run my hand around the font.
From where I stand, the roof looks almost new—
Cleaned or restored? Someone would know: I don't.
Mounting the lectern, I peruse a few
Hectoring large-scale verses, and pronounce
"Here endeth" much more loudly than I'd meant.
The echoes snigger briefly. Back at the door
I sign the book, donate an Irish sixpence,
Reflect the place was not worth stopping for.

Yet stop I did: in fact I often do,
And always end much at a loss like this,
Wondering what to look for; wondering, too,
When churches fall completely out of use
What we shall turn them into, if we shall keep
A few cathedrals chronically on show,
Their parchment, plate and pyx in locked cases,
And let the rest rent-free to rain and sheep.
Shall we avoid them as unlucky places?

Or, after dark, will dubious women come
To make their children touch a particular stone;
Pick simples for a cancer; or in some
Advised night see walking a dead one?
Power of some sort or other will go on
In games, in riddles, seemingly at random;

But superstition, like belief, must die,
And what remains when disbelief has gone?
Grass, weedy pavement, brambles, buttress, sky,

A shape less recognizable each week,
A purpose more obscure. I wonder who
Will be the last, the very last, to seek
This place for what it was; one of the crew
That tap and jot and know what rood-lofts were?
Some ruin-bibber, randy for antique,
Or Christmas-addict, counting on a whiff
Of gown-and-bands and organ-pipes and myrrh?
Or will he be my representative,

Bored, uninformed, knowing the ghostly silt
Dispersed, yet tending to this cross of ground
Through suburb scrub because it held unspilt
So long and equably what since is found
Only in separation—marriage, and birth,
And deaths, and thoughts of these—for whom was built
This special shell? For, though I've no idea
What this accoutred frowsty barn is worth,
It pleases me to stand in silence here;

A serious house on serious earth it is,
In whose blent air all our compulsions meet,
Are recognized, and robed as destinies.
And that much never can be obsolete,
Since someone will forever be surprising
A hunger in himself to be more serious,
And gravitating with it to this ground,
Which, he once heard, was proper to grow wise in,
If only that so many dead lie round.

THERE'S A NEW-TIME RELIGION
ON CAMPUS

Andrew M. Greeley

During a recent unpleasantness between the University of Chicago and its Students for a Democratic Society the normal, decorous quiet of the Social Science Building was rent one fine afternoon by ear-piercing sounds. Secretaries, research assistants and even a few faculty members dashed to their office doors to discover who was being murdered. Three young women dressed in shabby and tattered garments were standing in front of the Sociology Department office shrieking, "Fie on thee, Morris Janowitz! A hex on thy strategy!" WITCH (Women's International Terrorists Corps from Hell) had come to put a curse on the Sociology Department.

So far, nothing seems to have happened to Professor Janowitz or the Sociology Department. But if it does, there's going to be an awful lot of frightened people along the Midway. (I offered to sprinkle holy water on the departmental office; but, while social science seems ready for witchcraft, it is not yet ready for exorcism.)

WITCH is only one manifestation—though a spectacular one—of a resurgence of interest in the occult on the college campuses of the country. Although some observers of WITCH's "hexing" dismiss it as a form of "guerrilla theater," the WITCHes themselves elaborate a quasi-scholarly explanation of how they continue a neolithic religion that worshipped the great earth mother goddess until it was replaced by Christianity. One suspects that the WITCHes are but first cousins of the California Druids who also claim to be carrying on a tradition from the neolithic underground— thus confounding those of us who thought that the only Druids left in the world were Irish Monsignors.

WITCH is a combination of the put-on and the serious, the deliberately comic and the profoundly agonized, of the bizarre and the holy. The same is true of the other manifestations of the neo-sacred now observable around the country:

> Prof. Huston Smith of M.I.T. describes an experience with a seminar of some of the best students in the institution. "I cannot recall the exact progression of topics, but it went something like this: Beginning with Asian philosophy, it moved on to meditation, then yoga, then Zen, then Tibet, then successively to the 'Bardo Thodol,' tantra, the kundalini, the chakras, the *I Ching* [*ee-ching,* a book presenting an ancient Chinese

THERE'S A NEW-TIME RELIGION ON CAMPUS From *The New York Times Magazine,* June 1, 1969. © 1969 by The New York Times Company. Reprinted by permission.

divination device which enables one to make decisions—a sort of pre-I.B.M. computer], karate and aikido, the yang-yin macrobiotic (brown rice) diet, Gurdjieff, Maher Baba, astrology, astral bodies, auras, U.F.O.'s, tarot cards, parapsychology, witchcraft and magic. And, underlying everything, of course, the psychedelic drugs. Nor were the students dallying with these subjects. They were *on* the drugs; they were eating brown rice; they were meditating hours on end; they were making their decisions by *I Ching* divination, which one student designated the most important discovery of his life; they were constructing complicated electronic experiments to prove that their thoughts, via psychokinesis, could affect matter directly.

"And they weren't plebeians. Intellectually they were aristocrats with the highest average math scores in the land, Ivy League verbal scores, and two to three years of saturation in M.I.T. science."

A certain Catholic university discovered that it had a coven of warlocks on campus (warlocks, for the uninitiated, are male witches). As the dean of the institution put it, "We've really become progressive around here. A couple of hundred years ago we would have burned them at the stake. Twenty-five years ago I would have expelled them. Now we simply sent them all to psychiatrists."

At a Canadian university, the student body was given a chance to recommend courses of its own choosing to be included in the curriculum. The majority of the courses chosen had to do with astrology, Zen, sorcery and witchcraft.

In most of the élite universities in the country, horoscopes and the prediction of the future by the use of tarot cards are widespread. Not all the students, not even a majority, are engaging in such divination. But a minority is and the majority does not ridicule their efforts. On the contrary, one has the impression that the majority reacts the same way it reacts to the S.D.S.: "We understand why they want to do it, even if we are not yet ready to do it ourselves."

Catholic girls' colleges seem to be particularly disposed to producing groups of young women who make decisions by use of the *I Ching*.

In a number of colleges, particularly in California, semi-monastic cults have arisen composed of young people who subsist on vegetarian diets, take vows not to cut their hair and spend long hours in contemplation.

A thin network of students has formed a loose "community" to support one another through the stresses of graduate school, a community which does not take spatial separation to be a very serious problem in the providing of mutual support. One leader of the "community" describes quite bluntly what the "community" is about: "You might say we're forming a new religious order."

In the hills of Sonoma, Calif., there flourishes an institution called the "Six-Day School," composed largely of Berkeley dropouts, who learn about political pacifism, astrology, vegetarian dieting, mysticism and magic, during the course of their stay at the school—which usually exceeds six days. One group last year left Sonoma to proceed to Mount Shasta, there to await the end of the world.

A bookstore just off Harvard Square, clearly doing an excellent business, announces itself as "The Sphinx—Occult Books."

The White Brotherhood, a medieval Catharist sect made up of those in direct contact with "the spirit" (who has revealed to them that they are among the 144,000 white-robed martyrs of the Book of Revelation) is spreading at West Coast universities from Seattle to San Diego. Interestingly enough, the brotherhood is being spread by the same messengers who propagated it in the 13th century—wandering poets and minstrels, or, as they used to be called, troubadours and meistersingers.

I remarked in one of my classes that I had been able to locate almost every kind of offbeat religious behavior on our campus save for spiritualistic seances and wondered why someone hadn't thought of hunting up a medium. Several members of the class promptly assured their confreres that I hadn't looked very far; spiritualism was alive and well in Hyde Park.

Perhaps the most puzzling aspect of the new pursuit of the sacred is that it is so funny and yet so serious. Students cannot talk about it without laughing and yet they must interrupt their laughter to protest that they respect the goals of new devotees of the sacred. However, the puzzle is less difficult when one understands that the cultists are engaging in a form of *drama*—partly, one suspects, under the influence of their cousins, the hippies. Drama about the sacred is *liturgy*; and liturgy, as J. Huizinga pointed out in his famous book, "Homo Ludens," is sacred play.

The sacred by its very nature has large components of the playful and the comic close to its core. Only with the Reformation did the idea that the sacred was grimly serious finally triumph in the Western world. Catholic clerics will probably admit, now that the venerable Solemn High Mass has fallen into disuse, that they frequently found it hard to keep a straight face during its complex ceremonies. The new manifestations of the sacred, like the Solemn High Mass, are simultaneously much in earnest and a hilarious put-on. To put a hex on the Sociology Department is comic; but it is also a tentative assertion that there are powers in heaven and on earth which may transcend sociology departments.

Let us, first of all, make all the proper qualifications. Only a minority of students is engaged in the pursuit of the bizarrely sacred. Such a pursuit is not new among young people but is a continuation of the interest in the occult and the mystical which has persisted for some time. It is a form of romanticism which has recurred in one fashion or another periodically in years gone by. It is experimental and does not indicate any return to the organized churches; as one student said to me, "Who in the world would expect to find anything sacred in the churches?"

The evidence for this resurgence of interest in the sacred is "impressionistic" and not yet based on the kind of "hard" empirical data that so delight the heart of the social scientist. Nevertheless, with all these qualifications, it still does seem there has been a very notable increase, however temporary, in interest in the sacred and particularly the bizarrely sacred among students on the college and university campuses in the last few years. Furthermore, the "return of the sacred" has happened exactly where one would least expect it—among the élite students at the best colleges and universities in the land, precisely those places where secularization would presumably have been most effective and most complete.

What the hell is going on? God is dead, but the devil lives?

One of the things that strikes an interviewer who talks to students about the "return of the sacred"—even though they may themselves not be involved in witchcraft, astrology, or the *I Ching*—is that they resolutely refuse to dismiss as foolish those who are so involved. The first reason that young people give for the "return of the sacred" is the failure of science. One graduate student said to me, "Let's face it, science is dead. While the newspapers and magazines were giving all the attention to the death of God, science was really the one that was dying."

The extent and the depth of the revolts against positivism come as a considerable shock to those like myself whose training in the positive sciences took place in a time when they were totally unquestioned at the great universities. During the last winter quarter I put a statistical table on the blackboard and proceeded to explain the implications. One of my students respectfully but pointedly observed, "Mr. Greeley, I think you're an empiricist. In fact, at times I even think you are a *naive* empiricist." The accusation didn't surprise me because I guess I am an empiricist, but the tone of it did, for it was a tone of voice that used to be reserved for the accusation of being a "clerical Fascist."

The student then went on to deliver a fierce harangue against "the epistemology of science," and to assert that the "imperialism" of science by which it claimed to be the only valid form of human knowledge and the only valid rationale for organizing society was completely unsatisfactory to his generation. A number of other students rose to offer vigorous support to this position.

After class I pondered the matter in some confusion and returned the following session to ask if there was anyone who disagreed. Would no one rise with the appropriate quote from Kaspar Naegele to defend empiricism, positivism and rationality? The class was completely silent, until one young woman remarked, "I think we all agree with what was said in the last class." At the beginning of the nineteen-sixties when I was in graduate school, such thoughts would have been "thinking the unthinkable."

The young people seem to be angry at science for its failures. A coed observed, "Science hasn't ended war, it hasn't ended injustices, and it doesn't respond to most of man's needs. Why should we take it seriously?" And another joined in: "Pure rationalism just isn't rational because man is more than reason and religion knows that even if positive science doesn't." And a third coed concluded, "Science was something that we had to work through our system. It only started with people like Darwin and it's not surprising that for a while everybody thought it was the only thing that mattered. It's just now that we've come to know better."

Other students explained the return to the sacred as a reaction to the failure of the university administrations and faculties to live up to their own rhetoric of the radical political movements. Words like "honesty," integrity," we see the utter incapacity of the rationalists to engage in rational discourse with us, we begin to rediscover the legitimacy of emotions. From these it is just a short step to the legitimacy of the sacred."

The rhetoric of the return to the sacred is not so very different from the rhetoric of the radical political movements. Words like "honesty," "integrity," "fidelity," "love," "openness" and "community" abound. The hippy culture with its emphasis on drugs stands midway between the two, bridging the gap between and pervading both other movements with its influence. Yet the movements are distinct. The hippies and the radicals may frequently use religious terminology and even respond to "religious needs," but their concerns still tend to be this-worldly. The neo-sacralists, on the other hand, are willing to accept as a working possibility a world which, if it does not completely transcend the present world, at least to some extent stands beyond it.

It is precisely this "standing beyond" which young people relate to the second reason for the return to the sacred: The sacred seems to provide an avenue for personal efficacy. As a male undergraduate described it, "Why use the *I Ching* in a world where you have the I.B.M. 360? The answer is easy. You can't understand the 360 and you don't have much control over it. The *I Ching* says that there are powers that stand beyond and are more powerful than the 360, powers with which in some way you can enter into a meaningful relationship when you can't do it with the 360." And one of his friends added, "Most of us realize that other people make our decisions for us quite arbitrarily. Whether I go to Vietnam or not, whether I get killed there or not doesn't depend at all on who I am or what I think. I'd sooner feel that my future was being shaped by the stars or by the turn of the cards because these would represent powers that would be more concerned about me than would either my draft board or the Pentagon."

I pressed these two young men to question whether they really did think that there was something beyond that made itself known through the movements of the stars or the turn of the cards. One of them shrugged uncomfortably. "I'm not sure," he said, "but I like to think so." And the other commented, "It's like the conclusion of Arthur Miller's 'Death of a Salesman.' In death, somebody did 'notice' Willy Loman. When someone turns the cards for you, you feel at least here you are being noticed."

The theme that religion is a response to alienation and to a feeling of unimportance against the larger society is widespread in the students' comments. "Religion makes you feel like you're a *person.*" A woman undergraduate told me, "It makes you feel that you are important and that what you do does matter and you can have influence on others." Students are further impressed by the enthusiasm and confidence of the cultists. "They really believe that what they say is *true,*" observed one young man to me. "They really believe that they do have the answer and that they do know what is ethically right and ethically wrong. It's hard to avoid being affected by their enthusiasm after you've been in a school that really isn't sure what is true or what is right or wrong."

Like the radicals and the hippies, the neo-sacralists are in desperate search for something to belong to. The religious groups are *communities,* places where you are more than just an I.B.M. file card. A young woman put it this way: "If you get into a group like that, you at least know that somebody will notice the difference if you're murdered. Around this university, you could be dead in your room for days and nobody would ever know the difference." And another commented, "We don't have to worry anymore, at least not very much, about where our food and housing is going to come from so we worry about ourselves and about finding ourselves. The only place where we are going to find ourselves is in deep relationships with others and that means either religion or sex and maybe both." The religious communities that grew up around the various cults of the sacred are felt to provide opportunities for meaningful intimate relationships over against the depersonalizing formalism of the academic and governmental bureaucracies. "You're a *person* in the group even if you don't want to be. You're forced to face yourself and discover who you are."

The quest for community in small groups makes the neosacralists quite conscious of the relevance to their quest of T-groups (T stands for training), encounter groups, and the whole bag of group-dynamics tricks. Just as for some students group dynamics or sensitivity training become almost a religion, so for others already involved in quasi-religious behavior, sensitivity training and its cousins become an important means of religious growth. One girl told me how delighted she was to be part of a T-group which included two people who were on drugs and two others who were making their major decisions by means of horoscopes. It was, she noted, a fascinating experience.

Underlying the other three explanations the young people offer for the return to the sacred is a fourth: the sacred provides meaning. "In one way," a charming young woman said to me, "the sacred is even better than drugs, because when you're on drugs the world looks beautiful to you only if you're on a trip and ugly when you're not on a trip. But religion has persuaded some people that the world is beautiful most of the time despite the ugliness we see. That's terribly important."

One of her male classmates chimed in, "What we're really concerned about is whether anything is real, I mean, whether it is *really real.* Is there something that is so powerful that it can even make *us* real?" And an older graduate student (a clergyman, I suspect, but nowadays it's hard to tell) pointed out, "And Mircea Eliade [professor of history of religions at the University of Chicago and one of the world's most distinguished experts on the sacred] tells us that this is exactly what the sacred is, the *really real*."

Some of those who have kept an eye on WITCH argue that its principal contribution is to give its members some sense of what it means to be a woman, even if it is a bizarre concept of womanhood. Full meaning involves not only understanding what the world is all about or at least understanding whether the world has anything in it that is "really real," but it also involves having some sense of what you are all about and whether there is a possibility that you are "really real." The religious experience in the final analysis is seen as "ecstatic," that is to say, that it, like sex, takes a person out of himself and brings him into contact not only with other human beings but with the "creative powers" which presumably underpin the cosmos.

My very unsystematic survey of student opinion on the neo-sacred leads me to conclude that what is going on is authentically, if perhaps transiently and bizarrely, religious. Personal efficacy, meaning, community, encounter with the ecstatic and the transcendental, and the refusal to believe that mere reason can explain either life or personhood—all of these have traditionally been considered religious postures. An anthropologist visiting the secular university campus from another planet could not help but conclude that there was a lot of very interesting religious behavior going on and he would probably feel that it was very primal and primordial, if not indeed primitive religious behavior.

Do these students believe in God? I have the impression that most of the young neosacralists would not understand the question or at least would find it premature. They don't believe in the God they left behind in their parish congregations. But they are frankly experimenting—as a part of a self-conscious "psychosocial moratorium"—with the "experience of the sacred" to see whether there is anything there which could add depth and richness to their lives. Most of them seem to hope, at times rather forlornly, that they will be able to find something or Something. But they are not ready to give it or It a name just yet.

The new religious enthusiasts clearly owe a major debt of gratitude to the hippies. Indeed, one might even consider them to be merely one wing of the hippie movement. Both emphasize the prerational if not the antirational. The quest for the spontaneous and the "natural" in the two dissenting groups is a protest against the "hang-ups" of a society that is viewed as over-organized and overrationalized but less than human. Both are a search for "experience"—and for a specific kind of experience—one that "takes one out of oneself." Both have, as noted, a strong comic element about them—an irresistible urge to "put on" the rational society.

Both the neo-sacralists and the hippies are communitarian, seeking experience and vitality from intimate friendships, friendships which in many instances are strongly at odds with the conventions of the large society. The two groups are further linked by their longing for the mystical and the reflective, again because these activities are seen as a means of standing apart from the rest of society, which has so little time for anything else but activity. The ceremonies, the rituals, even the *vestments* of the two groups also represent a common revolt against the sober and somber garb of the suburban businessman and his daily schedule. (Long hair used to be important but now that even the suburban executive is wearing sideburns and maybe a goatee, we might expect the deviants to imitate Buddhist monks and shave their heads.)

So the new search for the sacred shares with the hippies an "acted out" rejection of the rationalized bourgeois society, a rejection that is also a put-on of that society. The hippies were the first to become concerned with the mystical and the occult. But many of the new religious enthusiasts are not hippies in the ordinary sense and most of them are not willing to go the "drug route" with the hippies. Some say quite frankly that they view religion as a substitute for drugs and one that is much less dangerous. One hesitates to say it, but the neo-sacralists appear to be much more "respectable" than the hippies.

But the important difference, I think, is that the religious cultists are seeking for something that hippies refuse to be hung up on; they seem to be looking for what the sociologists would call a "meaning system" or an "interpretative scheme." The hippies put on life because they think life is a put-on and ought not to be taken seriously. Those who are engaging in the quest for the sacred are, with a greater or lesser amount of explicit acknowledgment of the fact, looking for an explanation for life and for themselves. They're not sure they'll find it; they're not even sure that the search is anything more than a joke. But they'd like to think it just might be.

It might be pertinent to ask why we are so surprised about the return of the sacred. The non-rational has been with man a long time and so has the supernatural and even the superstitious. Was it not unduly naive of us to assume that it would disappear so quickly? Astrology has always been a rather successful industry. Superstition is widespread in the general population. More than two-fifths of the American population go to church every week as do almost half the college students in the country. The limited amount of longitudinal research done on religious beliefs and behavior shows very little change in the last two decades. If the sacred and the superstitious still permeate the larger society, why are we so surprised that they have been tenacious enough to reassert themselves on the college campus?

Students themselves will cheerfully admit that their lives are not at all free from superstitious behavior even if they don't take the sacred or the supernatural very seriously. As one girl said to me, "I always wear the same sweatshirt every time I take an exam and I know other people who simply refuse to go into an exam unless they've had a shower beforehand. When you ask us why we do these things, the only response we can come up with is, why not? Sure, it might not make any difference, but then again it might, and there's no point in taking any chances." One is reminded of the famous agnostic prayer which is addressed "To Whom it may concern."

My friend, Peter H. Rossi, chairman of the Department of Social Relations at Johns Hopkins University, summarized only half-facetiously the relationship between agnosticism and superstition: "I'm not sure that I believe in good spirits but I have the uncanny feeling that there might be evil spirits."

Will the interest in the sacred on the college campus survive? For some individual students, it is clearly nothing more than an experiment which is part of their youthful "psychosocial moratorium," a part of their quest for personal identity. If the data on graduate student church attendance are to be believed, the moratorium will end not so much with agnosticism or even a new form of religion for most students, but rather with a return to some form of traditional religion. (A recent survey of graduate students showed that about 40 per cent of the students at the 12 major arts and science graduate schools in the country were regular church-attenders.) Witchcraft, astrology and divination, if they lose at all, are likely to lose to the traditional religions.

Yet some of the present concern about the sacred is likely to continue influencing the traditional church system within—perhaps even leading to the formation of new religious sects. Like most everything else on campus, the return to the sacred, while it is communitarian, is profoundly anti-organizational. Whatever of the present commitment to the sacred survives is likely to be informal and casual but such groups as the Druids and WITCH could conceivably grow much larger.

The students, in any event, have little doubt that the sacred will continue to interest them and that it will continue to fascinate their successors on campus. As one undergraduate male argued, "The interest in the sacred is rooted in a kind of existentialist dissatisfaction with the way things are and since the way things are is not likely to change for a while, there is no reason to think the sacred is going to go away either."

Certainly the dissatisfaction with the failures of positive science does not seem to be reversible and one is inclined to suspect that it will be a fairly long time before the argument that religion or the supernatural or the sacred are not "scientific" will be persuasive. Not everybody will be religious; but neither will religion be in full retreat, and some of the more bizarre, primitive, and superstitious forms of the religious are likely to enjoy a respectability for a number of years to come.

Max Weber, the founder of modern social theory, anticipated the rise of new prophecy (or the resurgence of old ones) as long ago as the first decade of the present century and anticipated it precisely as a revolt against the rationalism of the "spirit of capitalism." He wrote: "In the field of its highest development, in the United States, the pursuit of wealth, stripped of its religious and ethical meaning, tends to become associated with purely mundane passions, which often actually give it the character of sport. No one knows who will live in this cage in the future, or whether at the end of this tremendous development entirely new prophets will arise, or there will be a great rebirth of old ideas and ideals, or, if neither, mechanized petrification, embellished with a sort of convulsive self-importance. For of the last stage of this cultural development, it might well be truly said: 'Specialists without spirit, sensualists without heart; this nullity imagines that it has attained a level of civilization never before achieved.' "

Most of the contemporary manifestations of the sacred on the college and university campus are a form of withdrawal from the larger society—if not positively destructive in their view of said society. Yet the constructive element is not completely absent. I remarked a few weeks ago to my seminar on the sociology of religion that I thought most of the new religious forms offered personal redemption but despaired of social redemption. One young woman raised her hand. "Mr. Greeley," she asked, "have you ever heard of a book called 'The Phenomenon of Man' by a man named Teilhard de Chardin?" I admitted that I had. "Well," she said, "I was deeply impressed by that book because even though there is so much wrong with the world right now, I think Teilhard is right when he says that we're on the verge of a great leap into a much better form of human life, that we are moving into the noosphere and that we are traveling toward an omega point. I think there's a lot of us that feel that we can have a faith in the sacred which will help us to create a better world."

I admitted to being something of a Teilhardist myself and conceded that there might be some of what she described in the student quest for the sacred, but insisted that I didn't see much of it and that I felt the "return of the sacred" assumed largely that the world was unredeemable and discriminating.

That was a mistake, for all kinds of hands rose up in the seminar room and all kinds of students rose up to assert their faith in the possibility of a Teilhardist-like vision of evolution toward the omega point.

I still can't quite figure out the meaning of that experience, but I must say I never expected to encounter a classroom of Teilhardists at the University of Chicago. Such people are necessarily a minority—a very small minority —of the whole student population, or indeed of the whole population of the world. There are not very many Teilhardists around. But it wouldn't take very many . . .

SEXUALITY AND JESUS

Tom F. Driver

Nothing, it has been said, frightens the Church as much as sex.

We might be inclined, in this day of frankness, to doubt the truth of such an observation and to point, by way of proof, to the spate of Christian literature in recent years that has addressed itself to sexual ethics in a positive frame of mind. Examination of the literature, however, reveals a curious fact. In almost every case sexuality is linked, by one argument or another, with love. Then, implicitly or explicitly, the two are equated, and the discussion of sexual ethics turns into a discussion of the ethics of love. This persistent tendency among Christian writers cannot but leave the impression that Christianity shies from sex as a horse will shy at danger. The argument turns aside into a "safer" subject, leaving the impression that sexuality is to be redeemed by love.

In one sense, of course, love *does* redeem sexuality, but this is the same sense in which it redeems *all* human activity. Hence, to speak of love as the fulfillment of sex, however true, is not to say anything unique or informative about sex itself. It is of no more help than to say that love redeems politics.

The situation is not improved very much if, in addition to love, the author speaks also of "responsibility." To urge that the sexual life be made responsible or that responsibility be the criterion of its rightness is at once to say too much and too little. It is counsel of perfection. The more seriously one takes it, the more likely is he to delude himself. To tell a person to be responsible is like telling a clown to be funny. He knows that's his business, but he may not know how to go about it, and he may think he's most funny when he's really boring us with his self regard.

The accent is placed so strongly on love and responsibility in Christian writing about sex because the mood of the times is so strongly anti-legalistic. The Protestant theologian who concerns himself with the law nowadays is a rare bird. As long as this is the case, the Church will not be able to shed much light on the subject of sexual ethics.

However, the question of law and gospel is one I shall not open at present. I shall merely observe that law is never taken seriously where the given phenomena of life are slighted, where there is a disposition to subordinate pragmatic decisions to general statements of value. As long as we prefer to speak of love and responsibility rather than of sexual acts and desires we shall not understand the wisdom of societies that have dealt with sexuality by confronting it with rules that are, or appear to be, partly arbitrary. Sex is a force, and like all other forces it dissipates itself unless it is, by some extraneous power, contained.

To see this, however, requires that sexuality be accepted and examined in its own right without being transmuted into a mere instance of an absolute value such as love. We must therefore ask why the Church refuses to do this in its present state of mind. I suggest it is because there is a very touchy spot in what might be called the "sexual imagination" of the Church. This spot appears in its thinking about Jesus and sexuality. It is there I shall probe to see if a pocket of infection may not be lanced.

MODERN SEXUALITY

It was a matter of some disappointment to D. H. Lawrence that the Gospels say nothing about the sex-life of Jesus. Lawrence was more than disappointed by this silence: he was outraged, and I suppose that many Christians will in their turn be outraged if I choose to speak of that whereof the Gospels are mute. Nevertheless I do it, not only because others have preceded me but also because the Church's doctrine of the humanity of Christ is at stake. This doctrine, which might seem the least problematic of all Christian assertions —that Jesus was a human being—has actually proved to be one of the most troublesome. Almost every age has its own kind of Docetism, which is the theological name for a view of Christ that makes him no real man of flesh and blood but instead a being who appears human but is in fact something else. Docetism was early condemned as a heresy, but it has never disappeared. In our day it may be suggested that a Docetism lingers with regard to Jesus' sexuality. This means, if it is true, that Christians are not sure about the humanity of Him whom they call True Man. And this uncertainty results in a confusion about what it means for *us* to be human. One of the signs of this confusion is the chaos in sexual mores at the present time, which the Church has not been able to overcome and which it has actually helped to bring about because it had no adequate teaching with regard to the relation between sex and humanity.

D. H. Lawrence's dissatisfaction with the Gospels' picture of Jesus was most boldly stated in the famous short story, "The Man Who Died." [1] In it, Jesus' resurrection is pictured as an awakening to sensual love. The resurrection from the tomb is treated by Lawrence as a curse for Jesus until it is eventually followed by an awakening to the desires and consummations of the flesh. Lawrence equates Jesus' true resurrection with erection:

He crouched to her, and he felt the blaze of his manhood and his power rise up in his loins, magnificent.
"I am risen!" [2]

[1] Most readily available in *St. Mawr* and *The Man Who Died.* Vintage Books, 1959.
[2] *Ibid.*, p. 207.

"The Man Who Died" has been regarded as blasphemous because Lawrence suggested that Jesus had, or should have had, sexual feelings and because Lawrence punned with holy phrases. The story, however, is less blasphemous than heretical, and this for the reason that Lawrence took it upon himself to reinterpret the total meaning of the Resurrection. He reduced the full mystery of God's victory over death to the age-old, pagan view that the victory of the gods is nothing but a transcendent version of the fertility principle. Thus Lawrence would have returned Christianity to a pre-Christian state in which natural sexuality is elevated into a religious and sacramental act. But sexuality will not bear this burden. Whenever it has been forced to carry it, a reaction has followed in which sexuality, and then all human relatedness, has been drained of meaning. That is the circumstance now. Our post-Lawrentian generation lives on an empty plain of sexual license and the collapse of human meanings. It is the opposite of what Lawrence intended, but he is in large part responsible for it. Yet Christianity is also responsible, because its inadequate teaching helped to call forth the equally inadequate teaching of Lawrence. In some quarters, the Church turns completely around and identifies its own message with what Lawrence was trying to say.

Lawrence was a sort of prophet *manqué,* and the prophet in him deserves to be taken by us more seriously, if less flamboyantly, than he took it himself. Underneath the Lawrentian manner there lies a genuine, although distorted, impulse. It is the urge to declare that sexuality belongs to the goodness of man's created nature and that if it does not find suitable expression and release, it turns man into something not more but less than human.

For Lawrence, modern rationalism and industrialism are both false at the core because they exclude on principle the formative power of the sexual drive. Rationalism does so because it regards sexuality as irrational—necessary perhaps, but ever to be regarded as an enemy of reason. One could say that rationalism assigns to sexuality only a "secondary citizenship" in the mind-body kingdom. Industrialism is also anti-sexual because its methods are determined by the machine, and its methods shape its values. Hence industrialism gives rise to a way of life that is ruthlessly un-organic. In industrial Nottinghamshire where he grew up Lawrence observed the enervating effects that industrialism had upon sexuality as well as upon the spirits of men.

That an age of rationalism and industrialism is also an age of sexual license does not destroy Lawrence's point; it corroborates it. Under the sway of rationalism, sex becomes a subject of dispassionate study by the specialist and a topic of conversation in the parlor. People get what Lawrence called "sex in the head." If we sometimes feel that Lawrence himself had more than a touch of this disease, at least it is to his everlasting credit that he preferred and advocated sex in the loins.

As rationalism tends to put sex in the head, industrialism tends to turn sex into a machine. A manufacturing and commercial society deliberately amplifies sexual desire, then distributes and sells at a profit the gratifications for it. In industrial societies man lives amid huckstered and huckstering sex.

What Lawrence wanted was to combat sexiness with sexuality. He intended to be a champion of what we nowadays call "the whole man." He saw standing squarely in his way not only rationalism and industrialism but also a religious tradition that seemed to give aid and comfort to those twin pervertors of human nature. For Christianity itself seemed to have said that sex was best managed by denying it. "Christian man" seemed to be something other than sexual man. Therefore Christianity led to a double standard and to an artificial sex life.

During the past fifty years, a number of Christian spokesmen have been very busy trying to repair the damage done by Victorian hypocrisy and, more serious, the damage done by Platonic elements in the Christian view of man. Biblical scholars have shown that Paul's word "flesh," which for Paul is the domain of sin, does not mean the sexual desires of the body, or at least not these alone. They have shown that the Bible does not, in the main, teach that the soul can be saved while the body belongs to the Devil. They have shown that marital sex is a positive good in both the Old and New Testaments. Karl Barth has even suggested that the best clue to the meaning of the *imago Dei* in man is to be found in the man-woman relationship. Christian ethicists have insisted that there is to be no condemnation of sex as such. Certainly the climate has begun to change.

Lawrence, however, saw with a clear instinct where the problem lay, as far as Christianity is concerned. Though he did not solve the problem well, he did locate it precisely. The problem lies in the New Testament picture of Jesus.

THE SEXUALITY OF JESUS

Exegesis might go on forever proving that sex is not necessarily sin. Ethics might echo the tune. But if The Man for Men was conceived to be without sexuality—was never, unlike the saints, even tempted by sex—then all would labor in vain who strove to prove that the Christian God looks favorably upon the sexual life of humanity. Hunger Jesus knew, and thirst. Death He endured. Pride, sloth, envy, desire for power, idolatry—all came close to Him and were overcome in favor of the virtues of which they are the perversions. But where do we find Jesus taking our sexuality upon Him? Human love, yes. Love extended liberally even to those who, in a sexual way, have "loved much." But never, so far as we are told, a man stirred in himself by that desire which for the rest of us is part of our created nature.

To put it bluntly, a sexless Jesus can hardly be conceived to be fully human. As long as Jesus is somehow above masculinity or femininity, the drift toward a Docetic Christ is inevitable. I do not know why this has not been more often observed. Lacking such a pervasively human element, the humanity of Christ tends to become a mere affirmation, a matter of pure dogma. Jesus is then man in principle but not in fact. If to this is added the belief that He was conceived in the womb of a virgin, His separation from our sexuality becomes complete. "Veiled in flesh," He is not flesh. He has the appearance of humanity but not its limiting substance, however much might be said in the abstract about "finitude." It is an inherent part of my finitude, and yours, that our lives are shaped in many decisive ways by our sexual histories.

Anti-docetism has become a recurring motif in modern imaginative literature about the Christ. Its presence should cause some theological reflection. It provides the motivation for Lawrence's story. We may object that Lawrence is "dragging Christ down" to our level, but there remains the biblical testimony that He *was* on our level, save only indulging in our sin. If sex is not inherently sinful, did He not share our sexuality also? Thus we find Nikos Kazantzakis representing Jesus as one whose spiritual struggle was in large part defined by his desire for woman, embodied in Mary Magdalene.[3] G. Wilson Knight, in *The Christian Renaissance*,[4] pictures Christ as androgynous, filled with both masculinity and femininity, thus "transcending" our sexuality while he yet shares it. Ronald Duncan, in his poem *Judas*,[5] pictures Jesus in an encounter with a prostitute:

> Remembering the brothel we'd passed outside the city
> Where an old whore had lifted her skirts in the doorway
>   And challenged Jesus to prove He was a man
> And how He had surprised us by going up to the woman
> And had drawn the sore from her lips, the years from her eyes
>   and,—it was this that shocked Peter—
> How He had then kissed her, and pulled her hair in a tease as she
>   repeated her challenge
> Not realizing that He had proved much more.

If we try to reach some understanding of Jesus' sexuality and ours, we must be careful to avoid both the whore's challenge and also the too-facile resolution in the last line quoted from Ronald Duncan. The mistake of the whore's challenge lies in the opinion that "unproven" sex is not sex. Its taunt is, "Prove to *me* that you are a man," which is not only self-regarding but is also a temptation to what we would today call "inauthentic existence," since it requires to deliver over to another person the power to judge one's own nature. He who yields to this temptation enters that Hell that Sartre has described in *No Exit*, wherein all suffer because none has the courage to be his own judge. Jesus' refusal to "prove himself a man"—taken in both the colloquial and the generalized senses of the word "man"—is but the other side of the coin of His refusal to offer on demand proofs of His divinity. He

---

[3] *The Last Temptation of Christ*, trans. P. A. Bien, Simon and Schuster 1960. Departing from the Gospels' accounts of the temptations (*cf.* Mt. 4:1–11 and Luke 4:1–13), Kazantzakis depicts one of the temptations as that of carnal love and marriage. Indeed, the fight between a spiritual vocation and a life of domestic love is the central motif of this book, and Kazantzakis apparently intended to say that this is not only Jesus' choice but that of every man. In this respect he takes an opposite stance from that of Lawrence, one more in keeping with Catholic and Orthodox traditions. But the anti-docetic intention is clear and results in numerous descriptions of Jesus' amorous stirrings.
[4] The Macmillan Co., 1933. Reprinted by W. W. Norton Co., 1962.
[5] Anthony Blond, Ltd., 1960.

will not be authenticated by "signs," and this is a strong reason to believe in His authenticity.

Here we touch upon what is the actual offense created by literature that attempts to "prove" the humanity of Jesus. It is not shocking, to me at least, to imagine Jesus moved to love according to the flesh. I cannot imagine a *human* tenderness, which the Gospels show to be characteristic of Jesus, that is not fed in some degree by the springs of passion. The human alternative to sexual tenderness is not a-sexual tenderness but sexual fear. Jesus lived in His body, as other men do. But as He is The Authentic Man, we are not to be shown a proof of this, neither by Him on our demand nor by a writer on his behalf.

Proofs of manhood never prove anything except that we desire proof. In this respect, stories written about the sexuality of Jesus are on the same footing as those popular novels (of Lloyd C. Douglas, for instance) that go out of their way to convince us that Jesus ate and breathed like other people. Such essays in the humanizing of Jesus have interest only in so far as their readers are already Docetists at heart and therefore want reassurance that The Man was man. That which is already human has no need of being humanized. I am always offended by a writer, be it Lawrence, Lloyd Douglas, or Dorothy Sayers, who urges me to believe what I never doubted—that Jesus was of my own race. Methinks the writer doth protest too much.

Ronald Duncan's Judas says that although the whore was disappointed that Jesus did not prove His manhood to her, actually "He had proved much more." One feels as he reads this line that the whore's question has received a rhetorical answer. I would prefer Duncan to say that it was precisely His manhood that Jesus had proved or, better, that He had denied her the inauthentic sign she had demanded. For it is not good theology to suppose that the question of Jesus' manhood can be answered by an appeal to His divinity. This can no more be the case than that the question of His divinity could be answered by an appeal to His manhood. Christian orthodoxy has always steered clear of making either affirmation dependent upon the other. That is why the Church has never enunciated the doctrine of the two natures with satisfactory logic. Logic demands that a relation of dependency be established, so that either the divinity follows upon the perfect manhood or else the perfect manhood is called forth by the divinity. Orthodoxy, to the chagrin of all theologians, has eschewed both these formulations, rendering the Incarnation, as Paul Tillich says, the only absolute paradox in Christian faith. Jesus was not man because He is God, neither is He God because He was man. But doctrine holds that He is both, an assertion that cannot be proved since it cannot even be explained.

We cannot, then, render Jesus more adequate as man by rendering Him the redemptive Son of God. That is why the line of Ronald Duncan I have cited falls short of its mark. In fairness to Duncan I should add that the main burden of his remarkable poem seems to me to lie in quite the other direction. It is about the too-late awakening of a very religious Judas to the fact that Jesus was very human.

Similarly, we cannot render Jesus more clearly or decisively as Son of God by rendering Him more fully human. That is why stories about His alleged sexual encounters miss their mark. As proofs of humanity, they are superfluous and out of line with that authenticity that cannot be subjected to proof. As concerns His divinity, they neither add nor subtract, unless of course we take the *a priori* position that all sex is sin.

THE SIGNIFICANCE OF THE GOSPELS' SILENCE

I mentioned earlier the curious silence of the Gospels regarding the sexuality of Jesus. Let us now ask what bearing that phenomenon has upon the New Testament picture of Jesus as the Christ.

There are only three conceivable ways of dealing with the Gospels' silence on this matter. The first is easily disposed of. We may quickly rule out the possibility that the silence about Jesus' sexuality is due merely to the historical situation in which Jesus lived and in which the Gospels were written. On that ground we can plausibly explain silences about many things, such as the relation of faith to science or the evils of slavery, since the human mind and conscience were not sensitized to these problems until later periods. But sexuality as a matter of conscience and as a reality of importance to the gods is as old as religion, is basic to the natural man's conception of himself, and is therefore in another class. A different reason must be sought for the Gospels' failure to speak of Jesus' sexuality.[6]

The traditional explanation is that since Jesus was without sin, it follows that He did not engage in any sexual activity. A sinless man who loved sexually would, in this view, be a contradiction in terms, since sex belongs only to fallen man. Merely to think of Jesus as having sexual desire is to offend against His purity.

The first objection to this view, however much it be supported by traditions of theology and piety, is that it does not account for the fact that Jesus in the Gospels is specifically tempted by other sins, which He resists, but seems to have been spared this particular temptation. I submit that not to engage in sexual activity is one thing but that to be without temptation to do so is quite another. The significant fact is that the Gospels are silent on both counts.

The traditional view can therefore be maintained only if sex itself is held to be no part of the original goodness of created man, if it is made to be the very sign and seal of the Fall, so that the Sinless One is He who does not encounter it even as temptation. Sexuality, however, is so pervasive a reality in organic nature that one cannot assign it *in toto* to the Fall without coming eventually to Manichaeism: that is, absolving the Lord and Father of

[6] My reasoning throughout this section omits one further possibility: that the sexuality of Jesus is not mentioned by the Gospel writers because the early Church's selective memory of Him screened it out, and this because its consciousness was shaped by Judaic traditions of the time rather than, as I suggest, by confrontation with other Near Eastern religious attitudes. Lacking sufficient knowledge of first-century Judaism, I cannot evaluate this possibility. Even if true, it would seem to me a factor contributory to the reason I shall state below as the decisive one.

Jesus Christ of responsibility for the created structures of living things. For sexuality is not only, or even primarily, a human phenomenon but belongs to the created structure of all animal life.

If historic Christianity has failed in its dealings with sexuality, which is not far from the truth, a principal reason may be that its equation of sex and the Fall has fostered a Manichaeism that now informs the view of sex held by the majority of people in the "Christian" world. The equation, however, is not biblical. It is to be found in the early Church Fathers, but it is never clearly stated in Scripture.

In Protestant theology any "necessary" link between sex and sin has been broken in modern times. This has been due to the biblical research fostered by Protestantism in the last two centuries. It is no longer held (outside Fundamentalism, and not always inside it) that Adam's sin was sexual desire. The prevailing view is that sex is part of man's created goodness and therefore participates in sin only when man lives in disobedience to God and in lack of faith. It would appear that theology, guided by biblical exegesis, has now gone so far in this direction that it cannot turn back, for to do so would undercut not only the results of biblical study but also the entire effort so valiantly and wisely made to bring the life of "the whole man" under the Lordship of Christ.

If one moves in the prevailing direction, however, a consequence must be faced: namely, that the traditional view of the Gospels' silence about sexuality in Jesus himself must be abandoned and a new interpretation put on the facts. What may the outline of such an interpretation be?

If we take it that the Gospels do not intend to present a Docetic Christ, if this may be true even of the Fourth Gospel, which in any case speaks most about Jesus' love for particular individuals, then the absence of all comment in them about Jesus' sexuality cannot be taken to imply that He had no sexual feelings. That would land us back into the traditional view, according to which the Christ redeems us *from* sexuality, it being the part of our nature He did not share. If the Christian, who is a member of the Body of Christ, is to grow up into a psychologically healthy and morally right sexual life, then the God-Man cannot be totally apart from the sexual realm.

Let us go a step further. If the Gospels do not speak of Jesus' sexuality, this silence may occur for a positive reason.

Few characteristics of the Gospels separate them more sharply from the literature of other savior figures and religious heroes than their abstention from representing their protagonist *either* as a champion of sexual renewal *or* as a warrior against the "demonic" sexual force. This is astonishing. Almost all religions make sexuality a principal concern. Either they regard it as a sign of power that must be replenished from on high, or they regard it as a pollution of which man must be purged. From the point of view of comparative religion, it is not surprising at all that Christianity as a religion brought forth monasticism, made a cult of virginity, and elevated its God-man above all sexual feeling. What is surprising is that the Gospels show in Jesus himself no sufficient basis for these attitudes.

It is true that the Gospels include a few very sharp statements from the "teachings" of Jesus that are apparently negative about sex. The most severe of these is Matthew 5:27–28:

> You have heard that it was said, "You shall not commit adultery." But I say to you that every one who looks at a woman lustfully has already committed adultery with her in his heart.

This verse is peculiar to Matthew. Luke and Mark do not have it. The next two verses seem to take on an anti-sexual meaning when read in this context:

> If your right eye causes you to sin, pluck it out and throw it away; it is better that you lose one of your members than that your whole body be thrown into hell. And if your right hand causes you to sin, cut it off and throw it away; it is better that you lose one of your members than that your whole body go into hell.

However, the words may not be in their proper context here. With slight variation they turn up again in Matthew 18:8–9 in a very different context, at which point they are paralleled by Mark.

Matthew 5:31–32 goes on to the absolute proscription of divorce, and *that* passage not only appears also in Mark and Luke but is repeated later in all three synoptics. We are also told that "in the resurrection they neither marry nor are given in marriage" (Matthew 22:30, *cf.* Mark 12:25 and Luke 20:35) and so on in a few other passages.

It is not my purpose here to examine these passages in detail. It is sufficient to point out that the ascetic passages all come from the so-called "teachings," that they are not nearly as strong in the canonical Gospels as in the apocryphal, and that there is *no* passage that speaks one way or the other about any sexuality of Jesus, not even in the temptations.

THE RELIGIOUS NEUTRALITY OF SEX

Over against the pagan gods and the pagan religions we may say that Jesus appears as the great neutralizer of the religious meaning of sex. He does not, it is clear, regard sexuality as a mystical force emanating from the God-head. Jesus is no Dionysus. But contrary to what many Christians have assumed, the Jesus of the Gospels is not plainly "anti-Dionysian" either. That is, he does not, as far as we can tell, regard sexuality as a force emanating from Satan. This opinion was left to the Gnostics to develop, who found some remarks of St. Paul to encourage them, and who have had a profound influence on the history of Christianity. Our modern ambivalence about sex, according to which it is either the best or the worst of all things, is Gnostic in origin and Manichaean in character.[7]

Most of so-called Christendom, not to mention other parts of the world, still labors under the assumption that, for a Christian, sexuality stands as a barrier in the way of salvation. Nowadays we meet this mainly in its inverted (actually its older) form: namely, the exaltation of sex into a

---

[7] Cf. Denis de Rougemont, *Love in the Western World*, Pantheon Books, rev. ed., 1956.

condition of spiritual blessedness. D. H. Lawrence would blast Jesus out of His neutrality regarding sex. He would make Jesus a sensual lover in order to make Him a savior. Norman Mailer and others make the quest for the "good orgasm" into a religious quest. William Inge, like Hollywood in its heyday, makes the reconciliations of the bed the end-all in human relationships. Aphrodite and Priapus have as many worshippers among us as ever they did at Corinth and Rome.

In combating these apostasies, the task is not to show that Aphrodite and Priapus are forms of the Devil. To do so would only ratify their religious power. The task is rather to proclaim what the Gospels show—that as far as Jesus is concerned these gods have lost their power. They are facts dressed up as numinous beings.

The reader will not assume that I am making any case for unbridled license in sexual behavior. Man may sin with sex, as he may with money or in politics. But if so, it is *man* who sins; it is not an exterior force sinning in him. Man is a debtor to Original Sin not because of his physical nature but because of the proclivities of his total self acting in his total world. He is the more prone to sin when he absolutizes (even in a negative way) any one part of himself and any one part of his world.

It may be thought that the position I urge puts too much emphasis on the Gospels, to the neglect of the Old Testament and the rest of the New. That may be so, but in any search for a Christian opinion, we should start in the Gospels, however much we may yet have to learn from the rest of Scripture. I am simply urging that we see the Jesus of the Gospels not as isolated from sexuality, even in His own person, but as refusing to sanction its religious status.

It may also be thought that I make too much of an "argument from silence" in the Gospels. Perhaps, but there is support for my view in the Gospels' accounts of Jesus' dealings with persons whose sexual life is "impure." Their "impurity" seems never to have been what concerned Him.

Finally, I have not attempted to frame, even in outline, a sexual ethic. My reflections belong only among the prolegomena to such ethics. I believe that the construction of a Christian ethic of sex cannot be properly attempted as long as one retains the mythology of sex that grew up in the ancient religions, is perpetuated in new ones, and from which Jesus as the Christ would liberate us.

I am arguing, then, for the de-mythologization of sex. Contrary to what some recent theologians seem to think, Christianity itself cannot be demythologized. But the world of our everyday experience can be. The task of theology is not to de-mythologize the Christ, but to share in His work of de-mythologizing the world. This is a labor that helps to realize "the glorious liberty of the Sons of God."

MECCA, *by Malcolm X,*

appears on pages 51–68 of the section "The Self."

SATORI, OR ENLIGHTENMENT

D. T. Suzuki

The essence of Zen Buddhism consists in acquiring a new viewpoint on life and things generally. By this I mean that if we want to get into the inmost life of Zen, we must forgo all our ordinary habits of thinking which control our everyday life, we must try to see if there is any other way of judging things, or rather if our ordinary way is always sufficient to give us the ultimate satisfaction of our spiritual needs. If we feel dissatisfied somehow with this life, if there is something in our ordinary way of living that deprives us of freedom in its most sanctified sense, we must endeavour to find a way somewhere which gives us a sense of finality and contentment. Zen proposes to do this for us and assures us of the acquirement of a new point of view in which life assumes a fresher, deeper, and more satisfying aspect. This acquirement, however, is really and naturally the greatest mental cataclysm one can go through with in life. It is no easy task, it is a kind of fiery baptism, and one has to go through the storm, the earthquake, the overthrowing of the mountains, and the breaking in pieces of the rocks.

This acquiring of a new point of view in our dealings with life and the world is popularly called by Japanese Zen students "satori" (*wu* in Chinese). It is really another name for Enlightenment (*anuttara-samyak-sambodhi*), which is the word used by the Buddha and his Indian followers ever since his realization under the Bodhi-tree by the River Nairanjana. There are several other phrases in Chinese designating this spiritual experience, each of which has a special connotation, showing tentatively how this phenomenon is interpreted. At all events there is no Zen without satori, which is indeed the Alpha and Omega of Zen Buddhism. Zen devoid of satori is like a sun without its light and heat. Zen may lose all its literature, all its monasteries, and all its paraphernalia; but as long as there is satori in it

SATORI, OR ENLIGHTENMENT From *Zen Buddhism* by D. T. Suzuki. Reprinted by permission of the Hutchinson Publishing Group Ltd.

it will survive to eternity. I want to emphasize this most fundamental fact concerning the very life of Zen; for there are some even among the students of Zen themselves who are blind to this central fact and are apt to think when Zen has been explained away logically or psychologically, or as one of the Buddhist philosophies which can be summed up by using highly technical and conceptual Buddhist phrases, Zen is exhausted, and there remains nothing in it that makes it what it is. But my contention is, the life of Zen begins with the opening of satori (*kai wu* in Chinese).

Satori may be defined as an intuitive looking into the nature of things in contradistinction to the analytical or logical understanding of it. Practically, it means the unfolding of a new world hitherto unperceived in the confusion of a dualistically-trained mind. Or we may say that with satori our entire surroundings are viewed from quite an unexpected angle of perception. Whatever this is, the world for those who have gained a satori is no more the old world as it used to be; even with all its flowing streams and burning fires, it is never the same one again. Logically stated, all its opposites and contradictions are united and harmonized into a consistent organic whole. This is a mystery and a miracle, but according to the Zen masters such is being performed every day. Satori can thus be had only through our once personally experiencing it.

Its semblance or analogy in a more or less feeble and fragmentary way is gained when a difficult mathematical problem is solved, or when a great discovery is made, or when a sudden means of escape is realized in the midst of most desperate complications; in short, when one exclaims "Eureka! Eureka!" But this refers only to the intellectual aspect of satori, which is therefore necessarily partial and incomplete and does not touch the very foundations of life considered one indivisible whole. Satori as the Zen experience must be concerned with the entirety of life. For what Zen proposes to do is the revolution, and the revaluation as well, of oneself as a spiritual unity. The solving of a mathematical problem ends with the solution, it does not affect one's whole life. So with all other particular questions, practical or scientific, they do not enter the basic life-tone of the individual concerned. But the opening of satori is the remaking of life itself. When it is genuine—for there are many simulacra of it—its effects on one's moral and spiritual life are revolutionary, and they are so enhancing, purifying, as well as exacting. When a master was asked what constituted Buddhahood, he answered, "The bottom of a pail is broken through." From this we can see what a complete revolution is produced by this spiritual experience. The birth of a new man is really cataclysmic.

In the psychology of religion this spiritual enhancement of one's whole life is called "conversion." But as the term is generally used by Christian converts, it cannot be applied in its strict sense to the Buddhist experience, especially to that of the Zen followers; the term has too affective or emotional a shade to take the place of satori, which is above all noetic. The general tendency of Buddhism is, as we know, more intellectual than emotional, and its doctrine of Enlightenment distinguishes it sharply from the

Christian view of salvation; Zen as one of the Mahayana schools naturally shares a large amount of what we may call transcendental intellectualism, which does not issue in logical dualism. When poetically or figuratively expressed, satori is "the opening of the mind-flower," or "the removing of the bar," or "the brightening up of the mind-works."

II

The coming of Bodhi-Dharma (Bodai-daruma in Japanese, P'u-ti Ta-mo in Chinese) to China early in the sixth century was simply to introduce this satori element into the body of Buddhism, whose advocates were then so engrossed in subtleties of philosophical discussion or in the mere literary observance of rituals and disciplinary rules. By the "absolute transmission of the spiritual seal," which was claimed by the first patriarch, is meant the opening of satori, obtaining an eye to see into the spirit of the Buddhist teaching.

The sixth patriarch, Yeno (Hui-neng), was distinguished because of his upholding the satori aspect of dhyana against the mere mental tranquilliza-tion of the Northern school of Zen under the leadership of Jinshu (Shen-hsiu). Baso (Ma-tsu), Obaku (Huan-po), Rinzai (Lin-chi), and all the other stars illuminating the early days of Zen in the T'ang dynasty were advocates of satori. Their life-activities were unceasingly directed towards the ad-vancement of this; and as one can readily recognize, they so differed from those merely absorbed in contemplation or the practising of dhyana so called. They were strongly against quietism, declaring its adherents to be purblind and living in the cave of darkness. Before we go on it is advisable, therefore, to have this point clearly understood so that we leave no doubt as to the ultimate purport of Zen, which is by no means wasting one's life away in a trance-inducing practice, but consists in seeing into the life of one's being or opening an eye of satori.

There is in Japan a book going under the title of *Six Essays by Shoshitsu* (that is, by Bodhi-Dharma, the first patriarch of Zen); the book contains no doubt some of the sayings of Dharma, but most of the Essays are not his; they were probably composed during the T'ang dynasty when Zen Bud-dhism began to make its influence more generally felt among the Chinese Buddhists. The spirit, however, pervading the book is in perfect accord with the principle of Zen. One of the Essays entitled "Kechimyakuron," or "Treatise on the Lineage of Faith," discusses the question of *Chien-hsing*,[1]

[1] *Hsing* means nature, character, essence, soul, or what is innate to one. "Seeing into one's Nature" is one of the set phrases used by the Zen masters, and is in fact the avowed ob-ject of all Zen discipline. Satori is its more popular expression. When one gets into the inwardness of things, there is satori. This latter, however, being a broad term, can be used to designate any kind of a thorough understanding, and it is only in Zen that it has a restricted meaning. In this article I have used the term as the most essential thing in the study of Zen; for "seeing into one's Nature" suggests the idea that Zen has something concrete and substantial which requires being seen into by us. This is misleading, though satori too I admit is a vague and naturally ambiguous word. For ordinary purposes, not too strictly philosophical, satori will answer, and whenever *chien-hsing* is referred to it means this: the opening of the mental eye.

or satori, which, according to the author, constitutes the essence of Zen Buddhism. The following passages are extracts.

"If you wish to seek the Buddha, you ought to see into your own Nature (*hsing*); for this Nature is the Buddha himself. If you have not seen into your own Nature, what is the use of thinking of the Buddha, reciting the Sutras, observing a fast, or keeping the precepts? By thinking of the Buddha, your cause [i.e. meritorious deed] may bear fruit; by reciting the Sutras your intelligence may grow brighter; by keeping the precepts you may be born in the heavens; by practising charity you may be rewarded abundantly; but as to seeking the Buddha, you are far away from him. If your Self is not yet clearly comprehended, you ought to see a wise teacher and get a thorough understanding as to the root of birth-and-death. One who has not seen into one's own Nature is not to be called a wise teacher.

"When this [seeing into one's own Nature] is not attained, one cannot escape from the transmigration of birth-and-death, however well one may be versed in the study of the sacred scriptures in twelve divisions. No time will ever come to one to get out of the sufferings of the triple world. Anciently there was a Bhikshu Zensho (Shan-hsing[2]) who was capable of reciting all the twelve divisions of scriptures, yet he could not save himself from transmigration, because he had no insight into his own Nature. If this was the case even with Zensho, how about those moderners who, being able to discourse only on a few Sutras and Sastras, regard themselves as exponents of Buddhism? They are truly simple-minded ones. When Mind is not understood it is absolutely of no avail to recite and discourse on idle literature. If you want to seek the Buddha, you ought to see into your own Nature, which is the Buddha himself. The Buddha is a free man—a man who neither works nor achieves.

"If, instead of seeing into your own Nature, you turn away and seek the Buddha in external things, you will never get at him.

"The Buddha is your own Mind, make no mistake to bow [to external objects]. 'Buddha' is a Western word, and in this country it means 'enlightened nature'; and by 'enlightened' is meant 'spiritually enlightened.' It is one's own spiritual Nature in enlightenment that responds to the external world, comes in contact with objects, raises the eyebrows, winks the eyelids, and moves the hands and legs. This Nature is the Mind, and the Mind is the Buddha, and the Buddha is the Way, and the Way is Zen. This simple word, Zen, is beyond the comprehension both of the wise and the ignorant. To see directly into one's original Nature, this is Zen. Even if you are well learned in hundreds of the Sutras and Sastras, you still remain an ignoramus in Buddhism when you have not yet seen into your original Nature. Buddhism is not there [in mere learning]. The highest truth is unfathomably deep, is not an object of talk or discussion, and even the canonical texts have no way to bring it within our reach. Let us once see into our own

[2] According to the *Mahaparinirvana-sutra*, translated into Chinese by Dharmaraksha, A.D. 423, Vol. XXXIII, he was one of the three sons of the Buddha while he was still a Bodhisattava. He was most learned in all Buddhist lore, but his views tended to be nihilistic and he finally fell into hell.

original Nature and we have the truth, even when we are quite illiterate, not knowing a word. . . .

"Those who have not seen into their own Nature may read the Sutras, think of the Buddha, study long, work hard, practise religion throughout the six periods of the day, sit for a long time and never lie down for sleep, and may be wide in learning and well informed in all things; and they may believe that all this is Buddhism. All the Buddhas in successive ages only talk of seeing into one's Nature. All things are impermanent; until you get an insight into your Nature, do not say 'I have perfect knowledge.' Such is really committing a very grave crime. Ananda, one of the ten great disciples of the Buddha was known for his wide information, but did not have any insight into Buddhahood, because he was so bent on gaining information only. . . ."

The sixth patriarch, Hui-neng (Yeno), insists on this in a most unmistakable way when he answers the question: "As to your commission from the fifth patriarch of Huang-mei, how do you direct and instruct others in it?" The answer was, "No direction, no instruction there is; we speak only of seeing into one's Nature and not of practising dhyana and seeking deliverance thereby."

Elsewhere they are designated as the "confused" and "not worth consulting with"; they that are empty-minded and sit quietly, having no thoughts whatever; whereas "even ignorant ones, if they all of a sudden realize the truth and open their mental eyes, are, after all, wise men and may attain even to Buddhahood."

Again, when the patriarch was told of the method of instruction adopted by the masters of the Northern school of Zen, which consisted in stopping all mental activities, quietly absorbed in contemplation, and in sitting cross-legged for the longest while at a stretch, he declared such practices to be abnormal and not at all to the point, being far from the truth of Zen, and added this stanza which was quoted elsewhere:

> "While living one sits up and lies not,
> When dead, one lies and sits not;
> A set of ill-smelling skeleton!
> What is the use of toiling and moiling so?"

When at Demboin, Baso used to sit cross-legged all day and meditating. His master, Nangaku Yejo (Nan-yueh Huai-jang, 677–744), saw him and asked:

"What seekest thou here thus sitting cross-legged?"

"My desire is to become a Buddha."

Thereupon the master took up a piece of brick and began to polish it hard on the stone near by.

"What workest thou on so, my master?" asked Baso.

"I am trying to turn this into a mirror."

"No amount of polishing will make a mirror of the brick, sir."

"If so, no amount of sitting cross-legged as thou doest will make of thee a Buddha," said the master.

"What shall I have to do then?"

"It is like driving a cart; when it moveth not, wilt thou whip the cart or the ox?"

Baso made no answer.

The master continued: "Wilt thou practice this sitting cross-legged in order to attain dhyana or to attain Buddhahood? If it is dhyana, dhyana does not consist in sitting or lying; if it is Buddhahood, the Buddha has no fixed forms. As he has no abiding place anywhere, no one can take hold of him, nor can he be let go. If thou seekest Buddhahood by thus sitting cross-legged, thou murderest him. So long as thou freest thyself not from sitting so,[3] thou never comest to the truth."

These are all plain statements, and no doubts are left as to the ultimate end of Zen, which is not sinking oneself into a state of torpidity by sitting quietly after the fashion of a Hindu saint and trying to exclude all the mental ripplings that seem to come up from nowhere, and after a while pass away—where nobody knows. The Zen masters, as we see below, are always found trying to avail themselves of every apparently trivial incident of life in order to make the disciples' minds flow into a channel hitherto altogether unperceived. It is like picking a hidden lock, the flood of new experiences gushes forth from the opening. It is again like the clock's striking the hours; when the appointed time comes it clicks, and the whole percussion of sounds is released. The mind seems to have something of this mechanism; when a certain moment is reached, a hitherto closed screen is lifted, an entirely new vista opens up, and the tone of one's whole life thereafter changes. This mental clicking or opening is called satori by the Zen masters and is insisted upon as the main object of their discipline.

In this connection the reader will find the following words of Meister Eckhart quite illuminative: "Upon this matter a heathen sage hath a fine saying in speech with another sage: 'I become aware of something in me which flashes upon my reason. I perceive of it that it is something, but what it is I cannot perceive. Only meseems that, could I conceive it, I should comprehend all truth.' "[4]

III

Here are some examples to show that the whole Zen discipline gains meaning when there takes place this turning of the mental hinge to a wider and

[3] That is, from the idea that this sitting cross-legged leads to Buddhahood. From the earliest periods of Zen in China, the quietist tendency has been running along the whole history with the intellectual tendency which emphasizes the satori element. Even today these currents are represented to a certain extent by the Soto on the one hand and the Rinzai on the other, while each has its characteristic features of excellence. My own standpoint is that of the intuitionalist and not that of the quietist; for the essence of Zen lies in the attainment of satori.

[4] W. Lehmann, *Meister Eckhart*. Gottingen, 1917, p. 243. Quoted by Professor Rudolf Otto in his *The Idea of the Holy*, p. 201.

deeper world. For when this wise and deeper world opens, everyday life, even the most trivial thing of it, grows loaded with the truths of Zen. On the one hand, therefore, satori is a most prosaic and matter-of-fact thing; on the other hand, a mystery. But after all, is not life itself filled with wonders, mysteries, and unfathomabilities, far beyond our discursive understanding?

A monk asked Joshu (Chao-chou Tsung-shen, 778–897) to be instructed in Zen. Said the master, "Have you had your breakfast or not?" "Yes, master, I have," answered the monk. "If so, have your dishes washed," was an immediate response, which, it is said, at once opened the monk's mind to the truth of Zen.

Tokusan (Teh-shan Hsuan-chien, 779–865) was a great scholar of the *Diamond Sutra (Vajracchedika)*. Learning that there was such a thing as Zen ignoring all the written scriptures and directly laying hands on one's soul, he came to Ryutan (Lung-t'an) to be instructed in the doctrine. One day Tokusan was sitting outside trying to see into the mystery of Zen. Ryutan said, "Why don't you come in?" Replied Tokusan, "It is pitch dark." A candle was lighted and handed over to Tokusan. When the latter was at the point of taking it, Ryutan suddenly blew the light out, whereupon the mind of Tokusan was opened.[5]

Hyakujo (Pai-chang Huai-hai, 724–814) one day went out attending his master Baso (Ma-tsu). A flock of wild geese was seen flying and Baso asked:

"What are they?"

"They are wild geese, sir."

"Whither are they flying?"

"They have flown away, sir."

Baso abruptly taking hold of Hyakujo's nose gave it a twist. Overcome with pain, Hyakujo cried aloud: "Oh! Oh!"

"You say they have flown away," Baso said, "but all the same they have been here from the very beginning."

This made Hyakujo's back wet with cold perspiration. He had satori.

Is there any connection in any possible way between the washing of the dishes and the blowing out of a candle and the twisting of the nose? We must say with Ummon: If there is none, how could they all come to the realization of the truth of Zen? If there is, what inner relationship is there? What is this satori? What new point of viewing things is this? So long as our observation is limited to those conditions which preceded the opening of a disciple's eye we cannot perhaps fully comprehend where lies the ultimate issue. They are matters of everyday occurrence, and if Zen lies objectively among them, every one of us is a master before we are told of it. This is partly true inasmuch as there is nothing artificially constructed in Zen,

---

[5] In Claud Field's *Mystics and Saints of Islam*, p. 25, we read under Hasan Basri: "Another time I saw a child coming toward me holding a lighted torch in his hand. 'Where have you brought the light from?' I asked him. He immediately blew it out, and said to me, 'O Hasan, tell me where it is gone, and I will tell you whence I fetched it.'" Of course the parallel is here only apparent, for Tokusan got his enlightenment from quite a different source than the mere blowing out of the candle. Still the parallel in itself is interesting enough to be quoted here.

but if the nose is to be really twisted or the candle blown out in order to take the scale off the eye, our attention must be directed inwardly to the working of our minds, and it will be there where we are to take hold of the hidden relation existing between the flying geese and the washed dishes and the blown-out candle and any other happenings that weave our infinitely variegated patterns of human life.

Under Daiye (Tai-hui, 1089–1163), the great Zen teacher of the Sung dynasty, there was a monk named Doken (Tao-ch'ien) who had spent many years in the study of Zen, but who had not yet delved into its secrets, if there were any. He was discouraged when he was sent on an errand to a distant city. A trip requiring half a year to finish would surely be a hindrance rather than a help to his study. Sogen (Tsung-yuan), one of his fellow-monks, took pity on him and said: "I will accompany you on this trip and do all that I can for you. There is no reason why you cannot go on with your meditation even while traveling." They started together.

One evening Doken despairingly implored his friend to assist him in the solution of the mystery of life. The friend said: "I am willing to help you in every way, but there are five things in which I cannot be of any help to you. These you must look after yourself." Doken expressed the desire to know what they were. "For instance," said the friend, "when you are hungry or thirsty, my eating of food or drinking does not fill your stomach. You must drink and eat yourself. When you want to respond to the calls of nature, you must take care of them yourself, for I cannot be of any use to you. And then it will be nobody else but yourself that will carry this corpse of yours [i.e. the body] along this highway." This remark at once opened the mind of the truth-seeking monk, who, transported with his discovery, did not know how to express his joy.

Sogen now told him that his work was done and that his further companionship would have no meaning after this. So they parted company and Doken was left alone to continue the trip. After the half-year, Doken came back to his own monastery. Daiye, his teacher, happened to meet him on his way down the mountain, and made the following remark, "This time he knows it all." What was it, one may remark, that flashed through Doken's mind when his friend Sogen gave him such matter-of-fact advice?

Kyogen (Hsian-yen) was a disciple of Hyakujo. After the master's death he went to Yisan (Wei-shan, 771–853), who was a senior disciple of Hyakujo. Yisan asked him: "I am told that you have been under my late master Hyakujo, and also that you have remarkable intelligence; but the understanding of Zen through this medium necessarily ends in intellectual and analytical comprehension, which is not of much use. Yet you may have had an insight into the truth of Zen. Let me have your view as to the reason of birth-and-death; that is, as to your own being before your parents gave birth to you."

Thus asked, Kyogen did not know how to reply. He retired into his own room and assiduously made research among his notes which he had taken of the sermons given by his late master. He failed to come across a suitable passage he might present as his own view. He returned to Yisan and implored him to teach in the faith of Zen. But Yisan said: "I really have nothing to impart to you, and if I tried to do so you may have occasion to make me an object of ridicule later on. Besides, whatever I can instruct you is my own and will never be yours." Kyogen was disappointed and considered his senior disciple unkind. Finally he came to the decision to burn up all his notes and memorandums which were of no help to his spiritual welfare, and, retiring altogether from the world, to spend the rest of his life in solitude and simplicity in accordance with the Buddhist rules. He reasoned: "What is the use of studying Buddhism, so difficult to comprehend and too subtle to receive instructions from another? I shall be a plain homeless monk, troubled with no desire to master things too deep for thought." He left Yisan and built a hut near the tomb of Chu (Huichung), the National Master, at Nan-yang. One day he was weeding and sweeping the ground, and when a piece of rock brushed away struck a bamboo, the sound produced by the percussion unexpectedly elevated his mind to a state of satori. The question proposed by Yisan became transparent; his joy was boundless, he felt as if meeting again his lost parent. Besides, he came to realize the kindness of his abandoned senior brother monk who refused him instruction. For he now knew that this would not have happened to him if Yisan had been unkind enough to explain things for him.

Below is the verse he composed soon after his achievement, from which we may get an idea of his satori:

> One stroke has made me forget all my previous knowledge,
> No artificial discipline is at all needed;
> In every movement I uphold the ancient way,
> And never fall into the rut of mere quietism;
> Wherever I walk no traces are left,
> And my senses are not fettered by rules of conduct;
> Everywhere those who have attained to the truth,
> All declare this to be of the highest order.

IV

There is something, we must admit, in Zen that defies explanation, and to which no master however ingenious can lead his disciples through intellectual analysis. Kyogen or Tokusan had enough knowledge of the canonical teachings or of the master's expository discourses; but when the real thing was demanded of them they significantly failed to produce it either to their inner satisfaction or for the master's approval. The satori, after all, is not a thing to be gained through the understanding. But once the key is within one's grasp, everything seems to be laid bare before him; the entire world assumes then a different aspect. By those who know, this inner change is recognized. The Doken before he started on his mission and the Doken after the realization were apparently the same person; but as soon as Daiye saw him he knew what had taken place in him, even when he uttered not a word.

Baso twisted Hyakujo's nose, and the latter turned into such a wild soul as to have the audacity to roll up the matting before his master's discourse had hardly begun (see below). The experience they have gone through within themselves is not a very elaborate, complicated, and intellectually demonstrable thing; for none of them ever try to expound it by a series of learned discourses; they do just this thing or that, or utter a single phrase unintelligible to outsiders, and the whole affair proves most satisfactory both to the master and to the disciple. The satori cannot be a phantasm, empty and contentless, and lacking in real value, but the simplest possible experience perhaps because it is the very foundation of all experiences.

As to the opening of satori, all that Zen can do is to indicate the way and leave the rest all to one's own experience; that is to say, following up the indication and arriving at the goal—this is to be done by oneself and without another's help. With all that the master can do, he is helpless to make the disciple take hold of the thing unless the latter is inwardly fully prepared for it. Just as we cannot make a horse drink against his will, the taking hold of the ultimate reality is to be done by oneself. Just as the flower blooms out of its inner necessity, the looking into one's own nature must be the outcome of one's own inner overflowing. This is where Zen is so personal and subjective, in the sense of being inner and creative.

Zen does not give us any intellectual assistance, nor does it waste time in arguing the point with us; but it merely suggests or indicates, not because it wants to be indefinite, but because that is really the only thing it can do for us. If it could, it would do anything to help us come to an understanding. In fact Zen is exhausting every possible means to do that, as we can see in all the great masters' attitudes towards their disciples. When they are actually knocking them down, their kindheartedness is never to be doubted. They are just waiting for the time when their pupils' minds get all ripened for the final moment. When this is come, the opportunity of opening an eye to the truth of Zen lies everywhere. One can pick it up in the hearing of an inarticulate sound, or listening to an unintelligible remark, or in the observation of a flower blooming, or in the encountering of any trivial everyday incident such as stumbling, rolling up a screen, using a fan, etc. These are all sufficient conditions that will awaken one's inner sense. Evidently a most insignificant happening, and yet its effect on the mind infinitely surpasses all that one could expect of it. A light touch of an ignited wire, and an explosion shaking the very foundations of the earth. In fact, all the causes of satori are in the mind. That is why when the clock clicks, all that has been lying there bursts up like a volcanic eruption or flashes out like a bolt of lightning.[6] Zen calls this "returning to one's

[6] The lightning simile in the *Kena-Upanishad* (IV, 30), as is supposed by some scholars, is not to depict the feeling of inexpressive awe as regards the nature of Brahman, but it illustrates the bursting out of enlightenment upon consciousness. "A—a—ah" is most significant here.

own home"; for its followers will declare: "You have now found yourself; from the very beginning nothing has been kept away from you. It was yourself that closed the eye to the fact. In Zen there is nothing to explain, nothing to teach, that will add to your knowledge. Unless it grows out of yourself, no knowledge is really of value to you, a borrowed plumage never grows."

As satori strikes at the primary fact of existence, its attainment marks a turning-point in one's life. The attainment, however, must be thoroughgoing and clear-cut in order to produce a satisfactory result. To deserve the name "satori" the mental revolution must be so complete as to make one really and sincerely feel that there took place a fiery baptism of the spirit. The intensity of this feeling is proportional to the amount of effort the opener of satori has put into the achievement. For there is a gradation in satori as to its intensity, as in all our mental activity. The possessor of a lukewarm satori may suffer no such spiritual revolution as Rinzai, or Bukko (Fo-kuang), whose case is quoted below. Zen is a matter of character and not of the intellect, which means that Zen grows out of the will as the first principle of life. A brilliant intellect may fail to unravel all the mysteries of Zen, but a strong soul will drink deep of the inexhaustible fountain. I do not know if the intellect is superficial and touches only the fringe of one's personality, but the fact is that the will is the man himself, and Zen appeals to it. When one becomes penetratingly conscious of the working of this agency, there is the opening of satori and the understanding of Zen. As they say, the snake has now grown into the dragon; or, more graphically, a common cur—a most miserable creature wagging its tail for food and sympathy, and kicked about by the street boys so mercilessly—has now turned into a golden-haired lion whose roar frightens to death all the feeble-minded.

Therefore, when Rinzai was meekly submitting to the "thirty blows" of Obaku, he was a pitiable sight; as soon as he attained satori he was quite a different personage, and his first exclamation was, "There is not much after all in the Buddhism of Obaku." And when he saw the reproachful Obaku again, he returned his favor by giving him a slap on the face. "What an arrogance, what an impudence!" Obaku exclaimed; but there was reason in Rinzai's rudeness, and the old master could not but be pleased with this treatment from his former tearful Rinzai.

When Tokusan gained an insight into the truth of Zen he immediately took up all his commentaries on the *Diamond Sutra,* once so valued and considered indispensable that he had to carry them wherever he went; he now set fire to them, reducing all the manuscripts to nothingness. He exclaimed, "However deep your knowledge of abstruse philosophy, it is like a piece of hair placed in the vastness of space; and however important your experience in things worldly, it is like a drop of water thrown into an unfathomable abyss."

On the day following the incident of the flying geese, to which reference is made elsewhere, Baso appeared in the preaching-hall, and was about to speak before a congregation, when Hyakujo came forward and began to roll up the matting.[7] Baso without protesting came down from his seat and returned to his own room. He then called Hyakujo and asked him why he rolled up the matting before he had uttered a word.

"Yesterday you twisted my nose," replied Hyakujo, "and it was quite painful."

"Where," said Baso, "was your thought wandering then?"

"It is not painful any more today, master."

How differently he behaves now! When his nose was pinched, he was quite an ignoramus in the secrets of Zen. He is now a golden-haired lion, he is master of himself, and acts as freely as if he owned the world, pushing away even his own master far into the background.

There is no doubt that satori goes deep into the very root of individuality. The change achieved thereby is quite remarkable, as we see in the examples above cited.

When our consideration is limited to the objective side of satori as illustrated so far, it does not appear to be a very extraordinary thing—this opening an eye to the truth of Zen. The master makes some remarks, and if they happen to be opportune enough, the disciple will come at once to a realization and see into a mystery hitherto undreamed of. It seems all to depend upon what kind of mood or what state of mental preparedness one is in at the moment. Zen is after all a haphazard affair, one may be tempted to think; but when we know that it took Nangaku (Nan-yueh) eight long years to answer the question "Who is he that thus cometh towards me?" we shall realize the fact that there was in him a great deal of mental anguish and tribulation which he had to go through before he could come to the final solution and declare, "Even when one asserts that it is a somewhat, one misses it altogether." We must try to look into the psychological aspect of satori, where is revealed the inner mechanism of opening the door to the eternal secrets of the human soul. This is done best by quoting some of the masters themselves whose introspective statements are on record.

Koho (Kao-feng, 1238–1285) was one of the great masters in the latter part of the Sung dynasty. When his master first let him attend to the "Joshu's Mu," [8] he exerted himself hard on the problem. One day his master, Setsugan (Hsueh-yen), suddenly asked him, "Who is it that carries for you this lifeless corpse of yours?" The poor fellow did not know what to make of the question, for the master was merciless and it was usually followed

---

[7] This is spread before the Buddha and on it the master performs his bowing ceremony, and its rolling up naturally means the end of a sermon.

[8] This is one of the most noted ko-an and generally given to the uninitiated as an eye-opener. When Joshu was asked by a monk whether there was Buddha-Nature in the dog, the master answered "Mu!" (*wu* in Chinese), which literally means "no." But as it is nowadays understood by the followers of Rinzai, it does not mean anything negative as the term may suggest to us ordinarily, it refers to something most assuredly positive, and the novice is told to find it out by himself, not depending upon others (*aparapaccaya*), as no explanation will be given nor is any possible. This ko-an is popularly known as "Joshu's Mu or Muji." A ko-an is a theme or statement or question given to the Zen student for solution, which will lead him to a spiritual insight. The subject will be fully treated in the Second Series of the *Essays in Zen Buddhism*.

by a hard knocking down. Later, in the midst of his sleep one night, he recalled the fact that once when he was under another master he was told to find out the ultimate signification of the statement "All things return to one," [9] and this kept him up the rest of that night and through the several days and nights that succeeded. While in this state of an extreme mental tension he found himself one day looking at Goso Hoyen's verse on his own portrait, which partly read:

> One hundred years—thirty-six thousand morns,
> This same old fellow moveth on for ever!

This at once made him dissolve his eternal doubt as to "Who's carrying around this lifeless body of yours?" He was baptized and became an altogether new man.

He leaves us in his *Goroku* ("Sayings Recorded") an account of those days of the mental strain in the following narrative: "In olden days when I was at Sokei (Shuang-ching), and before one month was over after my return to the Meditation Hall there, one night while deep in sleep I suddenly found myself fixing my attention on the question 'All things return to the One, but where does this One return?' My attention was so rigidly fixed on this that I neglected sleeping, forgot to eat, and did not distinguish east from west, nor morning from night. While spreading the napkin, producing the bowls, or attending to my natural wants, whether I moved or rested, whether I talked or kept silent, my whole existence was wrapped up with the question 'where does this One return?' No other thoughts ever disturbed my consciousness; no, even if I wanted to stir up the least bit of thought irrelevant to the central one, I could not do so. It was like being screwed up or glued; however much I tried to shake myself off, it refused to move. Though I was in the midst of a crowd or congregation, I felt as if I were all by myself. From morning till evening, from evening till morning, so transparent, so tranquil, so majestically above all things were my feelings! Absolutely pure and not a particle of dust! My one thought covered eternity; so calm was the outside world, so oblivious of the existence of other people I was. Like an idiot, like an imbecile, six days and nights thus elapsed when I entered the Shrine with the rest, reciting the Sutras, and happened to raise my head and looked at the verse by Goso. This made me all of a sudden awake from the spell, and the meaning of 'Who carries this lifeless corpse of yours?' burst upon me—the question once given by my old master. I felt as if this boundless space itself were broken up into pieces, and the great earth were altogether leveled away. I forgot myself, I forgot the world, it was like one mirror reflecting another. I tried several ko-an in my mind and found them so transparently clear! I was no more deceived as to the wonderful working of Prajna (transcendental wisdom)." When Koho

[9] Another ko-an for beginners. A monk once asked Joshu, "All things return to the One, but where does the One return?" To which the master answered, "When I was in the province of Seiju (Ts'ing-chou) I had a monkish garment made which weighed seven kin (*chin*).

saw his old master later, the latter lost no time in asking him, "Who is it that carries this lifeless corpse of yours?" Koho burst out a "Kwats!" Thereupon the master took up a stick ready to give him a blow, but the disciple held it back, saying, "You cannot give me a blow today." "Why can't I?" was the master's demand. Instead of replying to him, however, Koho left the room briskly. The following day the master asked him, "All things return to the One, and where does the One return to?" "The dog is lapping the boiling water in the cauldron." "Where did you get this nonsense?" reprimanded the master. "You had better ask yourself," promptly came the response. The master rested well satisfied.

These cases show what mental process one has to go through before the opening of satori takes place. Of course these are prominent examples and highly accentuated, and every satori is not preceded by such an extraordinary degree of concentration. But an experience more or less like these must be the necessary antecedent to all satori, especially to that which is to be gone through at the outset of the study. The mirror of mind or the field of consciousness then seems to be so thoroughly swept clean as not to leave a particle of dust on it.

When thus all mentation is temporarily suspended, even the consciousness of an effort to keep an idea focused at the center of attention is gone—that is, when, as the Zen followers say, the mind is so completely possessed or identified with its object of thought that even the consciousness of identity is lost as when one mirror reflects another, the subject feels as if living in a crystal palace, all transparent, refreshing, buoyant, and royal. But the end has not yet been reached, this being merely the preliminary condition leading to the consummation called satori. If the mind remains in this state of fixation, there will be no occasion for its being awakened to the truth of Zen. The state of "Great Doubt" (tai-gi), as it is technically known, is the antecedent. It must be broken up and exploded into the next stage, which is looking into one's nature or the opening of satori.

The explosion, as it is nothing else, generally takes place when this finely balanced equilibrium tilts for one reason or another. A stone is thrown into a sheet of water in perfect stillness, and the disturbance at once spreads all over the surface. It is somewhat like this. A sound knocks at the gate of consciousness so tightly closed, and it at once reverberates through the entire being of the individual. He is awakened in the most vivid sense of the word. He comes out baptized in the fire of creation. He has seen the work of God in his very workshop. The occasion may not necessarily be the hearing of a temple bell, it may be reading a stanza, or seeing something moving, or the sense of touch irritated, when a most highly accentuated state of concentration bursts out into a satori.

V. CHIEF CHARACTERISTICS OF SATORI

1. *Irrationality*. By this I mean that satori is not a conclusion to be reached by reasoning, and defies all intellectual determination. Those who have ex-

perienced it are always at a loss to explain it coherently or logically. When it is explained at all, either in words or gestures, its content more or less undergoes a mutilation. The uninitiated are thus unable to grasp it by what is outwardly visible, while those who have had the experience discern what is genuine from what is not. The satori experience is thus always characterized by irrationality, inexplicability, and incommunicability.

Listen to Tai-hui once more: "This matter [i.e. Zen] is like a great mass of fire; when you approach it your face is sure to be scorched. It is again like a sword about to be drawn; when it is once out of the scabbard, someone is sure to lose his life. But if you neither fling away the scabbard nor approach the fire, you are no better than a piece of rock or of wood. Coming to this pass, one has to be quite a resolute character full of spirit." [10] There is nothing here suggestive of cool reasoning and quiet metaphysical or epistemological analysis, but of a certain desperate will to break through an insurmountable barrier, of the will impelled by some irrational or unconscious power behind it. Therefore, the outcome also defies intellection or conceptualization.

2. *Intuitive insight.* That there is noetic quality in mystic experiences has been pointed out by James in his *Varieties of Religious Experience,* and this applies also to the Zen experience known as satori. Another name for satori is "ken-sho" (*chien-hsing* in Chinese) meaning "to see essence or nature," which apparently proves that there is "seeing" or "perceiving" in satori. That this seeing is of quite a different quality from what is ordinarily designated as knowledge need not be specifically noticed. Hui-k'e is reported to have made this statement concerning his satori which was confirmed by Bodhidharma himself: "[As to my satori], it is not a total annihilation; it is knowledge of the most adequate kind; only it cannot be expressed in words." In this respect Shen-hui was more explicit, for he says that "the one character *chih* (knowledge) is the source of all mysteries." [11]

Without this noetic quality satori will lose all its pungency, for it is really the reason of satori itself. It is noteworthy that the knowledge contained in satori is concerned with something universal and at the same time with the individual aspect of existence. When a finger is lifted, the lifting means, from the viewpoint of satori, far more than the act of lifting. Some may call it symbolic, but satori does not point to anything beyond itself, being final as it is. Satori is the knowledge of an individual object and also that of Reality which is, if I may say so, at the back of it.

3. *Authoritativeness.* By this I mean that the knowledge realized by satori is final, that no amount of logical argument can refute it. Being direct and personal it is sufficient unto itself. All that logic can do here is to explain it, to interpret it in connection with other kinds of knowledge with which our minds are filled. Satori is thus a form of perception, an inner perception, which takes place in the most interior part of consciousness. Hence the

[10] Tai-hui's sermon at the request of Li Hsuan-chiao.
[11] *Miao* is a difficult term to translate; it often means "exquisiteness," "indefinable subtlety." In this case *miao* is the mysterious way in which things are presented to this ultimate knowledge. Tsung-mi on *Zen Masters and Disciples.*

sense of authoritativeness, which means finality. So, it is generally said that Zen is like drinking water, for it is by one's self that one knows whether it is warm or cold. The Zen perception being the last term of experience, it cannot be denied by outsiders who have no such experience.

4. *Affirmation.* What is authoritative and final can never be negative. For negation has no value for our life, it leads us nowhere; it is not a power that urges, nor does it give one a place to rest. Though the satori experience is sometimes expressed in negative terms, it is essentially an affirmative attitude towards all things that exist; it accepts them as they come along regardless of their moral values. Buddhists call this *kshanti,* "patience," or more properly "acceptance," that is, acceptance of things in their suprarelative or transcendental aspect where no dualism of whatever sort avails.

Some may say that this is pantheistic. The term, however, has a definite philosophic meaning and I would not see it used in this connection. When so interpreted the Zen experience exposes itself to endless misunderstandings and "defilements." Tai-hui says in his letter to Miao-tsung: "An ancient sage says that the Tao itself does not require special disciplining, only let it not be defiled. I would say: To talk about mind or nature is defiling; to talk about the unfathomable or the mysterious is defiling; to practise meditation or tranquilization is defiling; to direct one's attention to it, to think about it is defiling; to be writing about it thus on paper with a brush is especially defiling. What then shall we have to do in order to get ourselves oriented, and properly apply ourselves to it? The precious vajra sword is right here and its purpose is to cut off the head. Do not be concerned with human questions of right and wrong. All is Zen just as it is, and right here you are to apply yourself." Zen is Suchness—a grand affirmation.

5. *Sense of the Beyond.* Terminology may differ in different religions, and in satori there is always what we may call a sense of the Beyond; the experience indeed is my own but I feel it to be rooted elsewhere. The individual shell in which my personality is so solidly encased explodes at the moment of satori. Not, necessarily, that I get unified with a being greater than myself or absorbed in it, but that my individuality, which I found rigidly held together and definitely kept separate from other individual existences, becomes loosened somehow from its tightening grip and melts away into something indescribable, something which is of quite a different order from what I am accustomed to. The feeling that follows is that of a complete release or a complete rest—the feeling that one has arrived finally at the destination. "Coming home and quietly resting" is the expression generally used by Zen followers. The story of the prodigal son in the *Saddharmapundarika,* in the *Vajra-samadhi,* and also in the New Testament points to the same feeling one has at the moment of a satori experience.

As far as the psychology of satori is considered, a sense of the Beyond is all we can say about it; to call this the Beyond, the Absolute, or God, or a Person is to go further than the experience itself and to plunge into a theology or metaphysics. Even the "Beyond" is saying a little too much. When a Zen master says, "There is not a fragment of a tile above my head, there is not an inch of earth beneath my feet," the expression seems to be an appropriate one. I have called it elsewhere the Unconscious, though this has a psychological taint.

6. *Impersonal Tone.* Perhaps the most remarkable aspect of the Zen experience is that it has no personal note in it as is observable in Christian mystic experiences. There is no reference whatever in Buddhist satori to such personal and frequently sexual feelings and relationships as are to be gleaned from these terms: flame of love, a wonderful love shed in the heart, embrace, the beloved, bride, bridegroom, spiritual matrimony, Father, God, the Son of God, God's child, etc. We may say that all these terms are interpretations based on a definite system of thought and really have nothing to do with the experience itself. At any rate, alike in India, China, and Japan, satori has remained thoroughly impersonal, or rather highly intellectual.

Is this owing to the peculiar character of Buddhist philosophy? Does the experience itself take its colors from the philosophy or theology? Whatever this is, there is no doubt that in spite of its having some points of similitude to the Christian mystic experience, the Zen experience is singularly devoid of personal or human colorings. Chao-pien, a great government officer of the Sung dynasty, was a lay-disciple of Fach'uan of Chiang-shan. One day after his official duties were over, he found himself leisurely sitting in his office, when all of a sudden a clash of thunder burst on his ear, and he realized a state of satori. The poem he then composed depicts one aspect of the Zen experience:

> Devoid of thought, I sat quietly by the desk in my official room,
> With my fountain-mind undisturbed, as serene as water;
> A sudden clash of thunder, the mind-doors burst open,
> And lo, there sitteth the old man in all his homeliness.

This is perhaps all the personal tone one can find in the Zen experience, and what a distance between "the old man in his homeliness" and "God in all his glory," not to say anything about such feelings as "the heavenly sweetness of Christ's excellent love," etc.! How barren, how unromantic satori is when compared with the Christian mystic experiences!

Not only satori itself is such a prosaic and non-glorious event, but the occasion that inspires it also seems to be unromantic and altogether lacking in supersensuality. Satori is experienced in connection with any ordinary occurrence in one's daily life. It does not appear to be an extraordinary phenomenon as is recorded in Christian books of mysticism. Someone takes hold of you, or slaps you, or brings you a cup of tea, or makes some most commonplace remark, or recites some passage from a sutra or from a book of poetry, and when your mind is ripe for its outburst, you come at once to satori. There is no romance of love-making, no voice of the Holy Ghost, no plenitude of Divine Grace, no glorification of any sort. Here is nothing painted in high colors, all is gray and extremely unobtrusive and unattractive.

7. *Feeling of Exaltation.* That this feeling inevitably accompanies satori is

due to the fact that it is the breaking-up of the restriction imposed on one as an individual being, and this breaking up is not a mere negative incident but quite a positive one fraught with signification because it means an infinite expansion of the individual. The general feeling, though we are not always conscious of it, which characterizes all our functions of consciousness, is that of restriction and dependence, because consciousness itself is the outcome of two forces conditioning or restricting each other. Satori, on the contrary, essentially consists in doing away with the opposition of two terms in whatsoever sense—and this opposition is the principle of consciousness as before mentioned, while satori is to realize the Unconscious which goes beyond the opposition.

To be released of this, therefore, must make one feel above all things intensely exalted. A wandering outcast maltreated everywhere not only by others but by himself finds that he is the possessor of all the wealth and power that is ever attainable in this world by a mortal being—if this does not give him a high feeling of self-glorification, what could? Says a Zen master, "When you have satori you are able to reveal a palatial mansion made of precious stones on a single blade of grass; but when you have no satori, a palatial mansion itself is concealed behind a simple blade of grass."

Another Zen master, evidently alluding to the *Avatamsaka,* declares: "O monks, lo and behold! A most auspicious light is shining with the utmost brilliancy all over the great chiliocosm, simultaneously revealing all the countries, all the oceans, all the Sumerus, all the suns and moons, all the heavens, all the lands—each of which number as many as hundreds of thousands of kotis. O monks, do you not see the light?" But the Zen feeling of exaltation is rather a quiet feeling of self-contentment; it is not at all demonstrative, when the first glow of it passes away. The Unconscious does not proclaim itself so boisterously in the Zen consciousness.

8. *Momentariness.* Satori comes upon one abruptly and is a momentary experience. In fact, if it is not abrupt and momentary, it is not satori. This abruptness (*tun*) is what characterizes the Hui-neng school of Zen ever since its proclamation late in the seventh century. His opponent Shen-hsiu was insistent on a gradual unfoldment of Zen consciousness. Hui-neng's followers were thus distinguished as strong upholders of the doctrine of abruptness. This abrupt experience of satori, then, opens up in one moment (*ekamuhurtena*) an altogether new vista, and the whole existence is appraised from quite a new angle of observation.

ELI, THE FANATIC

Philip Roth

Leo Tzuref stepped out from back of a white column to welcome Eli Peck. Eli jumped back, surprised; then they shook hands and Tzuref gestured him into the sagging old mansion. At the door Eli turned, and down the slope of lawn, past the jungle of hedges, beyond the dark, untrampled horse path, he saw the street lights blink on in Woodenton. The stores along Coach House Road tossed up a burst of yellow—it came to Eli as a secret signal from his townsmen: "Tell this Tzuref where we stand, Eli. This is a modern community, Eli, we have our families, we pay taxes . . ." Eli, burdened by the message, gave Tzuref a dumb, weary stare.

"You must work a full day," Tzuref said, steering the attorney and his briefcase into the chilly hall.

Eli's heels made a racket on the cracked marble floor, and he spoke above it. "It's the commuting that's killing," he said, and entered the dim room Tzuref waved open for him. "Three hours a day . . . I came right from the train." He dwindled down into a harp-backed chair. He expected it would be deeper than it was and consequently jarred himself on the sharp bones of his seat. It woke him, this shiver of the behind, to his business. Tzuref, a bald shaggy-browed man who looked as if he'd once been very fat, sat back of an empty desk, halfway hidden, as though he were settled on the floor. Everything around him was empty. There were no books in the bookshelves, no rugs on the floor, no draperies in the big casement windows. As Eli began to speak Tzuref got up and swung a window back on one noisy hinge. "May and it's like August," he said, and with his back to Eli, he revealed the black circle on the back of his head. The crown of his head was missing! He returned through the dimness—the lamps had no bulbs—and Eli realized all he'd seen was a skullcap. Tzuref struck a match and lit a candle, just as the half-dying shouts of children at play rolled in through the open window. It was as though Tzuref had opened it so Eli could hear them.

"Aah, now," he said. "I received your letter."

Eli poised, waiting for Tzuref to swish open a drawer and remove the letter from his file. Instead the old man leaned forward onto his stomach, worked his hand into his pants pocket, and withdrew what appeared to be a week-old handkerchief. He uncrumpled it; he unfolded it; he ironed it on the desk with the side of his hand. "So," he said.

Eli pointed to the grimy sheet which he'd gone over word-by-word with

ELI, THE FANATIC From *Goodbye Columbus*. Copyright © 1959 by Philip Roth. Reprinted by permission of the publisher, Houghton Mifflin Company.

his partners, Lewis and McDonnell. "I expected an answer," Eli said. "It's a week."

"It was so important, Mr. Peck, I knew you would come."

Some children ran under the open window and their mysterious babble— not mysterious to Tzuref, who smiled—entered the room like a third person. Their noise caught up against Eli's flesh and he was unable to restrain a shudder. He wished he had gone home, showered and eaten dinner, before calling on Tzuref. He was not feeling as professional as usual—the place was too dim, it was too late. But down in Woodenton they would be waiting, his clients and neighbors. He spoke for the Jews of Woodenton, not just himself and his wife.

"You understood?" Eli said.

"It's not hard."

"It's a matter of zoning . . ." and when Tzuref did not answer, but only drummed his fingers on his lips, Eli said, "We didn't make the laws . . ."

"You respect them."

"They protect us . . . the community."

"The law is the law," Tzuref said.

"Exactly!" Eli had the urge to rise and walk about the room.

"And then of course"—Tzuref made a pair of scales in the air with his hands—"the law is not the law. When is the law that is the law not the law?" He jiggled the scales. "And vice versa."

"Simply," Eli said sharply. "You can't have a boarding school in a residential area." He would not allow Tzuref to cloud the issue with issues. "We thought it better to tell you before any action is undertaken."

"But a house in a residential area?"

"Yes. That's what residential means." The DP's English was perhaps not as good as it seemed at first. Tzuref spoke slowly, but till then Eli had mistaken it for craft—or even wisdom. "Residence means home," he added.

"So this is my residence."

"But the children?"

"It is their residence."

"*Seventeen* children?"

"Eighteen," Tzuref said.

"But you *teach* them here."

"The Talmud. That's illegal?"

"That makes it school."

Tzuref hung the scales again, tipping slowly the balance.

"Look, Mr. Tzuref, in America we call such a place a boarding school."

"Where they teach the Talmud?"

"Where they teach period. You are the headmaster, they are the students."

Tzuref placed his scales on the desk. "Mr. Peck," he said, "I don't believe it . . ." but he did not seem to be referring to anything Eli had said.

"Mr. Tzuref, that is the law. I came to ask what you intend to do."

"What I *must* do?"

"I hope they are the same."

"They are." Tzuref brought his stomach into the desk. "We stay." He smiled. "We are tired. The headmaster is tired. The students are tired."

Eli rose and lifted his briefcase. It felt so heavy packed with the grievances, vengeances, and schemes of his clients. There were days when he carried it like a feather—in Tzuref's office it weighed a ton.

"Goodbye, Mr. Tzuref."

"Sholom," Tzuref said.

Eli opened the door to the office and walked carefully down the dark tomb of a corridor to the door. He stepped out on the porch and, leaning against a pillar, looked down across the lawn to the children at play. Their voices whooped and rose and dropped as they chased each other round the old house. The dusk made the children's game look like a tribal dance. Eli straightened up, started off the porch, and suddenly the dance was ended. A long piercing scream trailed after. It was the first time in his life anyone had run at the sight of him. Keeping his eyes on the lights of Woodenton, he headed down the path.

And then, seated on a bench beneath a tree, Eli saw him. At first it seemed only a deep hollow of blackness—then the figure emerged. Eli recognized him from the description. There he was, wearing the hat, that hat which was the very cause of Eli's mission, the source of Woodenton's upset. The town's lights flashed their message once again: "Get the one with the hat. What a nerve, what a nerve . . ."

Eli started towards the man. Perhaps he was less stubborn than Tzuref, more reasonable. After all, it was the law. But when he was close enough to call out, he didn't. He was stopped by the sight of the black coat that fell down below the man's knees, and the hands which held each other in his lap. By the round-topped, wide-brimmed Talmudic hat, pushed onto the back of his head. And by the beard, which hid his neck and was so soft and thin it fluttered away and back again with each heavy breath he took. He was asleep, his sidelocks curled loose on his cheeks. His face was no older than Eli's.

Eli hurried towards the lights.

The note on the kitchen table unsettled him. Scribblings on bits of paper had made history this past week. This one, however, was unsigned. "Sweetie," it said, "I went to sleep. I had a sort of Oedipal experience with the baby to-day. Call Ted Heller."

She had left him a cold soggy dinner in the refrigerator. He hated cold soggy dinners, but would take one gladly in place of Miriam's presence. He was ruffled, and she never helped that, not with her infernal analytic powers. He loved her when life was proceeding smoothly—and that was when she loved him. But sometimes Eli found being a lawyer surrounded him like quicksand—he couldn't get his breath. Too often he wished he were pleading for the other side; though if he were on the other side, then he'd wish he were on the side he was. The trouble was that sometimes the law didn't seem to be the answer, *law* didn't seem to have anything to do with what was aggravating everybody. And that, of course, made him feel foolish and unnecessary . . . Though that was not the situation here—the townsmen had a case. But not *exactly,* and if Miriam were awake to see Eli's upset, she would set about explaining his distress to him, understanding him, forgiving him, so as to get things back to Normal, for Normal was where they loved one another. The difficulty with Miriam's efforts was they only upset him more; not only did they explain little to him about himself or his predicament, but they convinced him of *her* weakness. Neither Eli nor Miriam, it turned out, was terribly strong. Twice before he'd faced this fact, and on both occasions had found solace in what his neighbors forgivingly referred to as "a nervous breakdown."

Eli ate his dinner with his briefcase beside him. Halfway through, he gave in to himself, removed Tzuref's notes, and put them on the table, beside Miriam's. From time to time he flipped through the notes, which had been carried into town by the one in the black hat. The first note, the incendiary:

To whom it may concern:

Please give this gentleman the following: Boys shoes with rubber heels and soles.

> 5 prs size 6c
> 3 prs size 5c
> 3 prs size 5b
> 2 prs size 4a
> 3 prs size 4c
> 1 pr size 7b
> 1 pr size 7c

Total 18 prs. boys shoes. This gentleman has a check already signed. Please fill in correct amount.

> L. Tzuref
> Director, Yeshivah of
> Woodenton, N.Y.
> (5/8/48)

"Eli, a regular greenhorn," Ted Heller had said. "He didn't say a word. Just handed me the note and stood there, like in the Bronx the old guys who used to come around selling Hebrew trinkets."

"A Yeshivah!" Artie Berg had said. "Eli, in Woodenton, a Yeshivah! If I want to live in Brownsville, Eli, I'll live in Brownsville."

"Eli," Harry Shaw speaking now, "the old Puddington place. Old man Puddington'll roll over in his grave. Eli, when I left the city, Eli, I didn't plan the city should come to me."

Note number two:

Dear Grocer:

Please give this gentleman ten pounds of sugar. Charge it to our account,

Yeshivah of Woodenton, NY—which we will now open with you and expect a bill each month. The gentleman will be in to see you once or twice a week.

L. Tzuref, Director
(5/10/48)

P.S. Do you carry kosher meat?

"He walked right by my window, the greenie," Ted had said, "and he nodded, Eli. He's my *friend* now."

"Eli," Artie Berg had said, "he handed the damn thing to a *clerk* at Stop N' Shop—and in that hat yet!"

"Eli," Harry Shaw again, "it's not funny. Someday, Eli, it's going to be a hundred little kids with little *yamalkahs* chanting their Hebrew lessons on Coach House Road, and then it's not going to strike you funny."

"Eli, what goes on up there—my kids hear strange sounds."

"Eli, this is a modern community."

"Eli, we pay taxes."

"Eli."

"Eli!"

"*Eli!*"

At first it was only another townsman crying in his ear; but when he turned he saw Miriam, standing in the doorway, behind her belly.

"Eli, sweetheart, how was it?"

"He said no."

"Did you see the other one?" she asked.

"Sleeping, under a tree."

"Did you let him know how people feel?"

"He was sleeping."

"Why didn't you wake him up? Eli, this isn't an everyday thing."

"He was tired!"

"Don't shout, please," Miriam said.

" 'Don't shout. I'm pregnant. The baby is heavy.' " Eli found he was getting angry at nothing she'd said yet; it was what she was going to say.

"He's a very heavy baby the doctor says," Miriam told him.

"Then sit *down* and make my dinner." Now he found himself angry about her not being present at the dinner which he'd just been relieved that she wasn't present at. It was as though he had a raw nerve for a tail, that he kept stepping on. At last Miriam herself stepped on it.

"Eli, you're upset. I understand."

"You *don't* understand."

She left the room. From the stairs she called, "I do, sweetheart."

It was a trap! He would grow angry knowing she would be "understanding." She would in turn grow more understanding seeing his anger. He would in turn grow angrier . . . The phone rang.

"Hello," Eli said.

"Eli, Ted. So?"

"So nothing."

"Who is Tzuref? He's an American guy?"

"No. A DP. German."

"And the kids?"

"DP's too. He teaches them."

"What? What subjects?" Ted asked.

"I don't know."

"And the guy with the hat, you saw the guy with the hat?"

"Yes. He was sleeping."

"Eli, he sleeps with the *hat*?"

"He sleeps with the hat."

"Goddam fanatics," Ted said. "This is the twentieth century, Eli. Now it's the guy with the hat. Pretty soon all the little Yeshivah boys'll be spilling down into town."

"Next thing they'll be after our daughters."

"Michele and Debbie wouldn't look at them."

"Then," Eli mumbled, "you've got nothing to worry about, Teddie," and he hung up.

In a moment the phone rang. "Eli? We got cut off. We've got nothing to worry about? You worked it out?"

"I have to see him again tomorrow. We can work something out."

"That's fine, Eli. I'll call Artie and Harry."

Eli hung up.

"I thought you said *nothing* worked out." It was Miriam.

"I did."

"Then why did you tell Ted *something* worked out?"

"It did."

"Eli, maybe you should get a little more therapy."

"That's enough of that, Miriam."

"You can't function as a lawyer by being neurotic. That's no answer."

"You're ingenious, Miriam."

She turned, frowning, and took her heavy baby to bed.

The phone rang.

"Eli, Artie. Ted called. You worked it out? No trouble?"

"Yes."

"When are they going?"

"Leave it to me, will you, Artie? I'm tired. I'm going to sleep."

In bed Eli kissed his wife's belly and laid his head upon it to think. He laid it lightly, for she was that day entering the second week of her ninth month. Still, when she slept, it was a good place to rest, to rise and fall with her breathing and figure things out. "If that guy would take off that crazy hat. I know it, what eats them. If he'd take off that crazy hat everything would be all right."

"What?" Miriam said.

"I'm talking to the baby."

Miriam pushed herself up in bed. "Eli, please, baby, shouldn't you maybe stop in to see Dr. Eckman, just for a little conversation?"

"I'm fine."

"Oh, sweetie!" she said, and put her head back on the pillow.

"You know what your mother brought to this marriage—a sling chair and a goddam New School enthusiasm for Sigmund Freud."

Miriam feigned sleep, he could tell by the breathing.

"I'm telling the kid the truth, aren't I, Miriam? A sling chair, three months to go on a *New Yorker* subscription, and *An Introduction to Psychoanalysis*. Isn't that right?"

"Eli, must you be aggressive?"

"That's all you worry about, is your insides. You stand in front of the mirror all day and look at yourself being pregnant."

"Pregnant mothers have a relationship with the fetus that fathers can't understand."

"Relationship my ass. What is my liver doing now? What is my small intestine doing now? Is my island of Langerhans on the blink?"

"Don't be jealous of a little fetus, Eli."

"I'm jealous of your island of Langerhans!"

"Eli, I can't argue with you when I know it's not me you're really angry with. Don't you see, sweetie, you're angry with yourself."

"You and Eckman."

"Maybe he could help, Eli."

"Maybe he could help you. You're practically lovers as it is."

"You're being hostile again," Miriam said.

"What do you care—it's only *me* I'm being hostile towards."

"Eli, we're going to have a beautiful baby, and I'm going to have a perfectly simple delivery, and you're going to make a fine father, and there's absolutely no reason to be obsessed with whatever is on your mind. All we have to worry about—" she smiled at him "—is a name."

Eli got out of bed and slid into his slippers. "We'll name the kid Eckman if it's a boy and Eckman if it's a girl."

"Eckman Peck sounds terrible."

"He'll have to live with it," Eli said, and he went down to his study where the latch on his briefcase glinted in the moonlight that came through the window.

He removed the Tzuref notes and read through them all again. It unnerved him to think of all the flashy reasons his wife could come up with for his reading and rereading the notes. "Eli, why are you so *preoccupied* with Tzuref?" "Eli, stop getting *involved*. Why do you think you're getting *involved*, Eli?" Sooner or later, everybody's wife finds their weak spot. His goddam luck he had to be neurotic! Why couldn't he have been born with a short leg.

He removed the cover from his typewriter, hating Miriam for the edge she had. All the time he wrote the letter, he could hear what she would be saying about his not being *able* to let the matter drop. Well, her trouble was that she wasn't *able* to face the matter. But he could hear her answer already: clearly, he was guilty of "a reaction formation." Still, all the fancy phrases didn't fool Eli: all she wanted really was for Eli to send Tzuref and family on their way, so that the community's temper would quiet, and the calm circumstances of their domestic happiness return. All she wanted were order and love in her private world. Was she so wrong? Let the world bat its brains out—in Woodenton there should be peace. He wrote the letter anyway:

Dear Mr. Tzuref:

Our meeting this evening seems to me inconclusive. I don't think there's any reason for us not to be able to come up with some sort of compromise that will satisfy the Jewish community of Woodenton and the Yeshivah and yourself. It seems to me that what most disturbs my neighbors are the visits to town by the gentleman in the black hat, suit, etc. Woodenton is a progressive suburban community whose members, both Jewish and Gentile, are anxious that their families live in comfort and beauty and serenity. This is, after all, the twentieth century, and we do not think it too much to ask that the members of our community dress in a manner appropriate to the time and place.

Woodenton, as you may not know, has long been the home of well-to-do Protestants. It is only since the war that Jews have been able to buy property here, and for Jews and Gentiles to live beside each other in amity. For this adjustment to be made, both Jews and Gentiles alike have had to give up some of their more extreme practices in order not to threaten or offend the other. Certainly such amity is to be desired. Perhaps if such conditions had existed in prewar Europe, the persecution of the Jewish people, of which you and those 18 children have been victims, could not have been carried out with such success—in fact, might not have been carried out at all.

Therefore, Mr. Tzuref, will you accept the following conditions? If you can, we will see fit not to carry out legal action against the Yeshivah for failure to comply with township Zoning ordinances No. 18 and No. 23. The conditions are simply:

1. The religious, educational, and social activities of the Yeshivah of Woodenton will be confined to the Yeshivah grounds.

2. Yeshivah personnel are welcomed in the streets and stores of Woodenton provided they are attired in clothing usually associated with American life in the 20th century.

If these conditions are met, we see no reason why the Yeshivah of Woodenton cannot live peacefully and satisfactorily with the Jews of Woodenton—as the Jews of Woodenton have come to live with the Gentiles of Woodenton. I would appreciate an immediate reply.

Sincerely,
ELI PECK, Attorney

Two days later Eli received his immediate reply:

Mr. Peck:

The suit the gentleman wears is all he's got.

Sincerely,
LEO TZUREF, Headmaster

Once again, as Eli swung around the dark trees and onto the lawn, the children fled. He reached out with his briefcase as if to stop them, but they were gone so fast all he saw moving was a flock of skullcaps.

"Come, come . . ." a voice called from the porch. Tzuref appeared from behind a pillar. Did he *live* behind those pillars? Was he just watching the children at play? Either way, when Eli appeared, Tzuref was ready, with no forewarning.

"Hello," Eli said.

"Sholom."

"I didn't mean to frighten them."

"They're scared, so they run."

"I didn't do anything."

Tzuref shrugged. The little movement seemed to Eli strong as an accusation. What he didn't get at home, he got here.

Inside the house they took their seats. Though it was lighter than a few evenings before, a bulb or two would have helped. Eli had to hold his briefcase towards the window for the last gleamings. He removed Tzuref's letter from a manila folder. Tzuref removed Eli's letter from his pants pocket. Eli removed the carbon of his own letter from another manila folder. Tzuref removed Eli's first letter from his back pocket. Eli removed the carbon from his briefcase. Tzuref raised his palms. ". . . It's all I've got . . ."

Those upraised palms, the mocking tone—another accusation. It was a crime to keep carbons! Everybody had an edge on him—Eli could do no right.

"I offered a compromise, Mr. Tzuref. You refused."

"Refused, Mr. Peck? What is, is."

"The man could get a new suit."

"That's all he's got."

"So you told me," Eli said.

"So I told you, so you know."

"It's not an insurmountable obstacle, Mr. Tzuref. We have stores."

"For that too?"

"On Route 12, a Robert Hall—"

"To take away the one thing a man's got?"

"Not take away, *replace*."

"But I tell you he has nothing. *Nothing*. You have that word in English? *Nicht? Gornisht?*"

"Yes, Mr. Tzuref, we have the word."

"A mother and a father?" Tzuref said. "No. A wife? No. A baby? A little ten-month-old baby? No! A village full of friends? A synagogue where you knew the feel of every seat under your pants? Where with your eyes closed you could smell the cloth of the Torah?" Tzuref pushed out of his chair, stirring a breeze that swept Eli's letter to the floor. At the window he leaned out, and looked, beyond Woodenton. When he turned he was shaking a finger at Eli. "And a medical experiment they performed on him yet! That leaves nothing, Mr. Peck. Absolutely nothing!"

"I misunderstood."

"No news reached Woodenton?"

"About the suit, Mr. Tzuref. I thought he couldn't afford another."

"He can't."

They were right where they'd begun. "Mr. Tzuref!" Eli demanded. "*Here?*" He smacked his hand to his billfold.

"Exactly!" Tzuref said, smacking his own breast.

"Then we'll buy him one!" Eli crossed to the window and taking Tzuref by the shoulders, pronounced each word slowly. "We-will-pay-for-it. All right?"

"Pay? What, diamonds!"

Eli raised a hand to his inside pocket, then let it drop. Oh stupid! Tzuref, father to eighteen, had smacked not what lay under his coat, but deeper, under the ribs.

"Oh . . ." Eli said. He moved away along the wall. "The suit is all he's got then."

"You got my letter," Tzuref said.

Eli stayed back in the shadow, and Tzuref turned to his chair. He swished Eli's letter from the floor, and held it up. "You say too much . . . all this reasoning . . . all these conditions . . ."

"What can I do?"

"You have the word 'suffer' in English?"

"We have the word suffer. We have the word law too."

"Stop with the law! You have the word suffer. Then try it. It's a little thing."

"They won't," Eli said.

"But you, Mr. Peck, how about you?"

"I am them, they are me, Mr. Tzuref."

"Aach! You are us, we are you!"

Eli shook and shook his head. In the dark he suddenly felt that Tzuref might put him under a spell. "Mr. Tzuref, a little light?"

Tzuref lit what tallow was left in the holders. Eli was afraid to ask if they couldn't afford electricity. Maybe candles were all they had left.

"Mr. Peck, who made the law, may I ask you that?"

"The people."

"No."

"Yes."

"Before the people."

"No one. Before the people there was no law." Eli didn't care for the conversation, but with only candlelight, he was being lulled into it.

"Wrong," Tzuref said.

"We make the law, Mr. Tzuref. It is our community. These are my neighbors. I am their attorney. They pay me. Without law there is chaos."

"What you call law, I call shame. The heart, Mr. Peck, the heart is law! God!" he announced.

"Look, Mr. Tzuref, I didn't come here to talk metaphysics. People use the law, it's a flexible thing. They protect what they value, their property, their well-being, their happiness—"

"Happiness? They hide their shame. And you, Mr. Peck, you are shameless?"

"We do it," Eli said, wearily, "for our children. This is the twentieth century . . ."

"For the goyim maybe. For me the Fifty-eighth." He pointed at Eli. "That is too old for shame."

Eli felt squashed. Everybody in the world had evil reasons for his actions. Everybody! With reasons so cheap, who buys bulbs. "Enough wisdom, Mr. Tzuref. Please. I'm exhausted."

"Who isn't?" Tzuref said.

He picked Eli's papers from his desk and reached up with them. "What do you intend for us to do?"

"What you must," Eli said. "I made the offer."

"So he must give up his suit?"

"Tzuref, Tzuref, leave me be with that suit! I'm not the only lawyer in the world. I'll drop the case, and you'll get somebody who won't talk compromise. Then you'll have no home, no children, nothing. Only a lousy black suit! Sacrifice what you want. I know what I would do."

To that Tzuref made no answer, but only handed Eli his letters.

"It's not me, Mr. Tzuref, it's them."

"They are you."

"No," Eli intoned, "I am me. They are them. You are you."

"You talk about leaves and branches. I'm dealing with under the dirt."

"Mr. Tzuref, you're driving me crazy with Talmudic wisdom. This is that, that is the other thing. Give me a straight answer."

"Only for straight questions."

"Oh, God!"

Eli returned to his chair and plunged his belongings into his case. "Then, that's all," he said angrily.

Tzuref gave him the shrug.

"Remember, Tzuref, you called this down on yourself."

"*I* did?"

Eli refused to be his victim again. Double-talk proved nothing.

"Goodbye," he said.

But as he opened the door leading to the hall, he heard Tzuref.

"And your wife, how is she?"

"Fine, just fine." Eli kept going.

"And the baby is due when, any day?"

Eli turned. "That's right."

"Well," Tzuref said, rising. "Good luck."

"You know?"

Tzuref pointed out the window—then, with his hands, he drew upon himself a beard, a hat, a long, long coat. When his fingers formed the hem they touched the floor. "He shops two, three times a week, he gets to know them."

"He *talks* to them?"

"He sees them."

"And he can tell which is my wife?"

"They shop at the same stores. He says she is beautiful. She has a kind face. A woman capable of love . . . though who can be sure."

"He talks about *us,* to *you?"* demanded Eli.

"You talk about us, to her?"

"Goodbye, Mr. Tzuref."

Tzuref said, "Sholom. And good luck—I know what it is to have children. Sholom," Tzuref whispered, and with the whisper the candles went out. But the instant before, the flames leaped into Tzuref's eyes, and Eli saw it was not luck Tzuref wished him at all.

Outside the door, Eli waited. Down the lawn the children were holding hands and whirling around in a circle. At first he did not move. But he could not hide in the shadows all night. Slowly he began to slip along the front of the house. Under his hands he felt where bricks were out. He moved in the shadows until he reached the side. And then, clutching his briefcase to his chest, he broke across the darkest spots of the lawn. He aimed for a distant glade of woods, and when he reached it he did not stop, but ran through until he was so dizzied that the trees seemed to be running beside him, fleeing not towards Woodenton but away. His lungs were nearly ripping their seams as he burst into the yellow glow of the Gulf station at the edge of town.

"Eli, I had pains today. Where were you?"

"I went to Tzuref."

"Why didn't you call? I was worried."

He tossed his hat past the sofa and onto the floor. "Where are my winter suits?"

"In the hall closet. Eli, it's May."

"I need a strong suit." He left the room, Miriam behind him.

"Eli, talk to me. Sit down. Have dinner. Eli, what are you doing? You're going to get moth balls all over the carpet."

He peered out from the hall closet. Then he peered in again—there was a zipping noise, and suddenly he swept a greenish tweed suit before his wife's eyes.

"Eli, I love you in that suit. But not now. Have something to eat. I made dinner tonight—I'll warm it."

"You've got a box big enough for this suit?"

"I got a Bonwit's box, the other day. Eli, *why?"*

"Miriam, you see me doing something, let me do it."

"You haven't eaten."

"I'm *doing* something." He started up the stairs to the bedroom.

"Eli, would you please tell me what it is you want, and why?"

He turned and looked down at her. "Suppose this time you give me the reasons *before* I tell you what I'm doing. It'll probably work out the same anyway."

"Eli, I want to help."

"It doesn't concern you."

"But I want to help *you*," Miriam said.

"Just be quiet, then."

"But you're upset," she said, and she followed him up the stairs, heavily, breathing for two.

"Eli, what now?"

"A shirt." He yanked open all the drawers of their new teak dresser. He extracted a shirt.

"Eli, batiste? With a tweed suit?" she inquired.

He was at the closet now, on his knees. "Where are my cordovans?"

"Eli, why are you doing this so compulsively? You look like you *have* to do something."

"Oh, Miriam, you're supersubtle."

"Eli, stop this and talk to me. Stop it or I'll call Dr. Eckman."

Eli was kicking off the shoes he was wearing. "Where's the Bonwit box?"

"Eli, do you want me to have the baby right *here!*"

Eli walked over and sat down on the bed. He was draped not only with his own clothing, but also with the greenish tweed suit, the batiste shirt, and under each arm a shoe. He raised his arms and let the shoes drop onto the bed. Then he undid his necktie with one hand and his teeth and added that to the booty.

"Underwear," he said. "He'll need underwear."

"Who!"

He was slipping out of his socks.

Miriam kneeled down and helped him ease his left foot out of the sock. She sat with it on the floor. "Eli, just lie back. Please."

"Plaza 9-3103."

"What?"

"Eckman's number," he said. "It'll save you the trouble."

"Eli—"

"You've got that goddam tender 'You need help' look in your eyes, Miriam, don't tell me you don't."

"I don't."

"I'm not flipping," Eli said.

"I know, Eli."

"Last time I sat in the bottom of the closet and chewed on my bedroom slippers. That's what I did."

"I know."

"And I'm not doing that. This is not a nervous breakdown, Miriam, let's get that straight."

"Okay," Miriam said. She kissed the foot she held. Then, softly, she asked, "What *are* you doing?"

"Getting clothes for the guy in the hat. Don't tell me why, Miriam. Just let me do it."

"That's all?" she asked.

"That's all."

"You're not leaving?"

"No."

"Sometimes I think it gets too much for you, and you'll just leave."

"What gets too much?"

"I don't *know,* Eli. Something gets too much. Whenever everything's peaceful for a long time, and things are nice and pleasant, and we're expecting to be even happier. Like now. It's as if you don't think we *deserve* to be happy."

"Damn it, Miriam! I'm giving this guy a new suit, is that all right? From now on he comes into Woodenton like everybody else, is that all right with you?"

"And Tzuref moves?"

"I don't even know if he'll take the suit, Miriam! What do you have to bring up moving!"

"Eli, I didn't bring up moving. Everybody did. That's what everybody wants. Why make everybody un*happy*. It's even a law, Eli."

"Don't tell me what's the law."

"All right, sweetie. I'll get the box."

"*I'll* get the box. Where is it?"

"In the basement."

When he came up from the basement, he found all the clothes neatly folded and squared away on the sofa: shirt, tie, shoes, socks, underwear, belt, and an old gray flannel suit. His wife sat on the end of the sofa, looking like an anchored balloon.

"Where's the green suit?" he said.

"Eli, it's your loveliest suit. It's my favorite suit. Whenever I think of you, Eli, it's in that suit."

"Get it out."

"Eli, it's a Brooks Brothers suit. You say yourself how much you love it."

"Get it out."

"But the gray flannel's more practical. For shopping."

"Get it out."

"You go overboard, Eli. That's your trouble. You won't do anything in moderation. That's how people destroy themselves."

"I do *everything* in moderation. That's my trouble. The suit's in the closet again?"

She nodded, and began to fill up with tears. "Why does it have to be *your* suit? Who are you even to decide to give a suit? What about the others?" She was crying openly, and holding her belly. "Eli, I'm going to have a baby. Do we need all *this?*" and she swept the clothes off the sofa to the floor.

At the closet Eli removed the green suit. "It's a J. Press," he said, looking at the lining.

"I hope to hell he's happy with it!" Miriam said, sobbing.

A half hour later the box was packed. The cord he'd found in the kitchen cabinet couldn't keep the outfit from popping through. The trouble was there was too much: the gray suit *and* the green suit, an oxford shirt as well as the batiste. But let him have two suits! Let him have three, four, if only this damn silliness would stop! And a hat—of course! God, he'd almost forgotten the hat. He took the stairs two at a time and in Miriam's closet yanked a hatbox from the top shelf. Scattering hat and tissue paper to the floor, he returned downstairs, where he packed away the hat he'd worn that day. Then he looked at his wife, who lay outstretched on the floor before the fireplace. For the third time in as many minutes she was saying, "Eli, this is the real thing."

"Where?"

"Right under the baby's head, like somebody's squeezing oranges."

Now that he'd stopped to listen he was stupefied. He said, "But you have two more weeks . . ." Somehow he'd really been expecting it was to go on not just another two weeks, but another nine months. This led him to suspect, suddenly, that his wife was feigning pain so as to get his mind off delivering the suit. And just as suddenly he resented himself for having such a thought. God, what had he become! He'd been an unending bastard towards her since this Tzuref business had come up—just when her pregnancy must have been most burdensome. He'd allowed her no access to him, but still, he was sure, for good reasons: she might tempt him out of his confusion with her easy answers. He could be tempted all right, it was why he fought so hard. But now a sweep of love came over him at the thought of her contracting womb, and his child. And yet he would not indicate it to her. Under such splendid marital conditions, who knows but she might extract some promise from him about his concern with the school on the hill.

Having packed his second bag of the evening, Eli sped his wife to Woodenton Memorial. There she proceeded not to have her baby, but to lie hour after hour through the night having at first oranges, then bowling balls, then basketballs, squeezed back of her pelvis. Eli sat in the waiting room, under the shattering African glare of a dozen rows of fluorescent bulbs, composing a letter to Tzuref.

Dear Mr. Tzuref:

The clothes in this box are for the gentleman in the hat. In a life of sacrifice what is one more? But in a life of no sacrifices even one is impossible. Do you see what I'm saying, Mr. Tzuref? I am not a Nazi who would drive eighteen children, who are probably frightened at the sight of a firefly, into homelessness. But if you want a home here, you must accept what we have to offer. The world is the world, Mr. Tzuref. As you would say, what is, is. All we say to this man is change your clothes. Enclosed are two suits and two shirts, and everything else he'll need, including a new hat. When he needs new clothes let me know.

We await his appearance in Woodenton, as we await friendly relations with the Yeshivah of Woodenton.

He signed his name and slid the note under a bursting flap and into the box. Then he went to the phone at the end of the room and dialed Ted Heller's number.

"Hello."

"Shirley, it's Eli."

"Eli, we've been calling all night. The lights are on in your place, but nobody answers. We thought it was burglars."

"Miriam's having the baby."

"At home?" Shirley said. "Oh, Eli, what a fun-idea!"

"Shirley, let me speak to Ted."

After the ear-shaking clatter of the phone whacking the floor, Eli heard footsteps, breathing, throat-clearing, then Ted. "A boy or a girl?"

"Nothing yet."

"You've given Shirley the bug, Eli. Now she's going to have *our* next one at home."

"Good."

"That's a terrific way to bring the family together, Eli."

"Look, Ted, I've settled with Tzuref."

"When are they going?"

"They're not exactly going, Teddie. I settled it—you won't even know they're there."

"A guy dressed like 1000 B.C. and I won't know it? What are you thinking about, pal?"

"He's changing his clothes."

"Yeah, to what? Another funeral suit?"

"Tzuref promised me, Ted. Next time he comes to town, he comes dressed like you and me."

"What! Somebody's kidding somebody, Eli."

Eli's voice shot up. "If he says he'll do it, he'll do it!"

"And, Eli," Ted asked, "he said it?"

"He said it." It cost him a sudden headache, this invention.

"And suppose he doesn't change, Eli. Just suppose. I mean that *might* happen, Eli. This might just be some kind of stall or something."

"No," Eli assured him.

The other end was quiet a moment. "Look, Eli," Ted said, finally, "he changes. Okay? All right? But they're still up there, aren't they? *That* doesn't change."

"The point is you won't know it."

Patiently Ted said, "Is this what we asked of you, Eli? When we put our faith and trust in you, is that what we were asking? We weren't concerned that this guy should become a Beau Brummel, Eli, believe me. We just don't think this is the community for them. And, Eli, we isn't me. The Jewish members of the community appointed me, Artie, and Harry to see what could be done. And we appointed you. And what's happened?"

Eli heard himself say, "What happened, happened."

"Eli, you're talking in crossword puzzles."

"My wife's having a baby," Eli explained, defensively.

"I realize that, Eli. But this is a matter of zoning, isn't it? Isn't that what we discovered? You don't abide by the ordinance, you go. I mean I can't raise mountain goats, say, in my backyard—"

"This isn't so simple, Ted. People are involved—"

"People? Eli, we've been through this and through this. We're not just dealing with people—these are religious fanatics is what they are. Dressing like that. What I'd really like to find out is what goes on up there. I'm getting more and more skeptical, Eli, and I'm not afraid to admit it. It smells like a lot of hocus-pocus abracadabra stuff to me. Guys like Harry, you know, they think and they think and they're afraid to admit what they're thinking. I'll tell you. Look, I don't even know about this Sunday school business. Sundays I drive my oldest kid all the way to Scarsdale to learn Bible stories . . . and you know what she comes up with? This Abraham in the Bible was going to kill his own *kid* for a sacrifice. She gets nightmares from it, for God's sake! You call that religion? Today a guy like that they'd lock him up. This is an age of science, Eli. I size people's feet with an X-ray machine, for God's sake. They've disproved all that stuff, Eli, and I refuse to sit by and watch it happening on my own front lawn."

"Nothing's happening on your front lawn, Teddie. You're exaggerating, nobody's sacrificing their kid."

"You're damn right, Eli—I'm not sacrificing mine. You'll see when you have your own what it's like. All the place is, is a hideaway for people who can't face life. It's a matter of *needs*. They have all these superstitions, and why do you think? Because they can't face the world, because they can't take their place in society. That's no environment to bring kids up in, Eli."

"Look, Ted, see it from another angle. We can convert them," Eli said, with half a heart.

"What, make a bunch of Catholics out of them? Look, Eli—pal, there's a good healthy relationship in this town because it's modern Jews and Protestants. That's the point, isn't it, Eli? Let's not kid each other, I'm not Harry. The way things are now are fine—like human beings. There's going to be no pogroms in Woodenton. Right? 'Cause there's no fanatics, no crazy people—" Eli winced, and closed his eyes a second—"just people who respect each other, and leave each other be. Common sense is the ruling thing, Eli. I'm for common sense. Moderation."

"Exactly, exactly, Ted. I agree, but common sense, maybe, says make this guy change his clothes. Then maybe—"

"Common sense says that? Common sense says to me they go and find a nice place somewhere else, Eli. New York is the biggest city in the world, it's only 30 miles away—why don't they go there?"

"Ted, give them a chance. Introduce them to common sense."

"Eli, you're dealing with *fanatics*. Do they display common sense? Talking a dead language, that makes sense? Making a big thing out of suffering, so you're going oy-oy-oy all your life, that's common sense? Look, Eli, we've been through all this. I don't know if you know—but there's talk that *Life* magazine is sending a guy out to the Yeshivah for a story. With pictures."

"Look, Teddie, you're letting your imagination get inflamed. I don't think *Life*'s interested."

"But I'm interested, Eli. And we thought you were supposed to be."

"I am," Eli said, "I am. Let him just change the clothes, Ted. Let's see what happens."

"They live in the medieval ages, Eli—it's some superstition, some *rule*."

"Let's just *see*," Eli pleaded.

"Eli, every day—"

"One more day," Eli said. "If he doesn't change in one more day . . ."

"What?"

"Then I get an injunction first thing Monday. That's that."

"Look, Eli—it's not up to me. Let me call Harry—"

"You're the spokesman, Teddie. I'm all wrapped up here with Miriam having a baby. Just give me the day—them the day."

"All right, Eli. I want to be fair. But tomorrow, that's all. Tomorrow's the judgment day, Eli, I'm telling you."

"I hear trumpets," Eli said, and hung up. He was shaking inside—Teddie's voice seemed to have separated his bones at the joints. He was still in the phone booth when the nurse came to tell him that Mrs. Peck would positively not be delivered of a child until the morning. He was to go home and get some rest, he looked like *he* was having the baby. The nurse winked and left.

But Eli did not go home. He carried the Bonwit box out into the street with him and put it in the car. The night was soft and starry, and he began to drive the streets of Woodenton. Square cool windows, apricot-colored, were all one could see beyond the long lawns that fronted the homes of the townsmen. The stars polished the permanent baggage carrier atop the station wagons in the driveways. He drove slowly, up, down, around. Only his tires could be heard taking the gentle curves in the road.

What peace. What incredible peace. Have children ever been so safe in their beds? Parents—Eli wondered—so full in their stomachs? Water so warm in its boilers? Never. Never in Rome, never in Greece. Never even did walled cities have it so good! No wonder then they would keep things just as they were. Here, after all, were peace and safety—what civilization had been working toward for centuries. For all his jerkiness, that was all Ted Heller was asking for, peace and safety. It was what his parents had asked for in the Bronx, and his grandparents in Poland, and theirs in Russia or Austria, or wherever else they'd fled to or from. It was what Miriam was asking for. And now they had it—the world was at last a place for families, even Jewish families. After all these centuries, maybe there just had to be this communal toughness—or numbness—to protect such a blessing. Maybe that was the trouble with the Jews all along—too soft. Sure, to live takes guts . . . Eli was thinking as he drove on beyond the train station, and parked his car at the darkened Gulf station. He stepped out, carrying the box.

At the top of the hill one window trembled with light. What *was* Tzuref doing up there in that office? Killing babies—probably not. But studying a language no one understood? Practicing customs with origins long forgotten? Suffering sufferings already suffered once too often? Teddie was right—why keep it up! However, if a man chose to be stubborn, then he couldn't expect to survive. The world is give-and-take. What sense to sit and brood over a suit. Eli would give him one last chance.

He stopped at the top. No one was around. He walked slowly up the lawn, setting each foot into the grass, listening to the shh shhh shhhh his shoes made as they bent the wetness into the sod. He looked around. Here there was nothing. Nothing! An old decaying house—and a suit.

On the porch he slid behind a pillar. He felt someone was watching him. But only the stars gleamed down. And at his feet, off and away, Woodenton glowed up. He set his package on the step of the great front door. Inside the cover of the box he felt to see if his letter was still there. When he touched it, he pushed it deeper into the green suit, which his fingers still remembered from winter. He should have included some light bulbs. Then he slid back by the pillar again, and this time there was something on the lawn. It was the second sight he had of him. He was facing Woodenton and barely moving across the open space towards the trees. His right fist was beating his chest. And then Eli heard a sound rising with each knock on the chest. What a moan! It could raise hair, stop hearts, water eyes. And it did all three to Eli, plus more. Some feeling crept into him for whose deepness he could find no word. It was strange. He listened—it did not hurt to hear this moan. But he wondered if it hurt to make it. And so, with only stars to hear, he tried. And it did hurt. Not the bumble-bee of noise that turned at the back of his throat and winged out his nostrils. What hurt buzzed down. It stung and stung inside him, and in turn the moan sharpened. It became a scream, louder, a song, a crazy song that whined through the pillars and blew out to the grass, until the strange hatted creature on the lawn turned and threw his arms wide, and looked in the night like a scarecrow.

Eli ran, and when he reached the car the pain was only a bloody scratch across his neck where a branch had whipped back as he fled the greenie's arms.

The following day his son was born. But not till one in the afternoon, and by then a great deal had happened.

First, at nine-thirty the phone rang. Eli leaped from the sofa—where he'd dropped the night before—and picked it screaming from the cradle. He could practically smell the hospital as he shouted into the phone, "Hello, yes!"

"Eli, it's Ted. Eli, he *did* it. He just walked by the store. I was opening the door, Eli, and I turned around and I swear I thought it was you. But it was him. He still walks like he did, but the clothes, Eli, the clothes."

"Who?"

"The greenie. He has on man's regular clothes. And the suit, it's a beauty."

The suit barreled back into Eli's consciousness, pushing all else aside. "What color suit?"

"Green. He's just strolling in the green suit like it's a holiday. Eli . . . is it a Jewish holiday?"

"Where is he now?"

"He's walking straight up Coach House Road, in this damn tweed job. Eli, it worked. You were right."

"We'll see."

"What next?"

"We'll see."

He took off the underwear in which he'd slept and went into the kitchen where he turned the light under the coffee. When it began to perk he held his head over the pot so it would steam loose the knot back of his eyes. It still hadn't when the phone rang.

"Eli, Ted again. Eli, the guy's walking up and down every street in town. Really, he's on a tour or something. Artie called me, Herb called me. Now Shirley calls that he just walked by our house. Eli, go out on the porch you'll see."

Eli went to the window and peered out. He couldn't see past the bend in the road, and there was no one in sight.

"Eli?" He heard Ted from where he dangled over the telephone table. He dropped the phone into the hook, as a few last words floated up to him— "Eliyousawhim . . . ?" He threw on the pants and shirt he'd worn the night before and walked barefoot on to his front lawn. And sure enough, his apparition appeared around the bend: in a brown hat a little too far down on his head, a green suit too far back on the shoulders, an unbuttoned-down button-down shirt, a tie knotted so as to leave a two-inch tail, trousers that cascaded onto his shoes—he was shorter than that black hat had made him seem. And moving the clothes was that walk that was not a walk, the tiny-stepped shlumpy gait. He came round the bend, and for all his strangeness— it clung to his whiskers, signaled itself in his locomotion—he looked as if he belonged. Eccentric, maybe, but he belonged. He made no moan, nor did he invite Eli with wide-flung arms. But he did stop when he saw him. He stopped and put a hand on his hat. When he felt for its top, his hand went up too high. Then it found the level and fiddled with the brim. The fingers fiddled, fumbled, and when they'd finally made their greeting, they traveled down the fellow's face and in an instant seemed to have touched each one of his features. They dabbed the eyes, ran the length of the nose, swept over the hairy lip, until they found their home in the hair that hid a little of his collar. To Eli the fingers said, *I have a face, I have a face at least.* Then his hand came through the beard and when it stopped at his chest it was like a pointer—and the eyes asked a question as tides of water shifted over them. *The face is all right, I can keep it?* Such a look was in those eyes that Eli was still seeing them when he turned his head away. They were the hearts of his jonquils, that only last week had appeared—they were the leaves on his birch, the bulbs in his coach lamp, the droppings on his lawn: those eyes were the eyes in his head. They were his, he had made them. He turned and went into his house and when he peeked out the side of the window, between shade and molding, the green suit was gone.

The phone.

"Eli, Shirley."

"I saw him, Shirley," and he hung up.

He sat frozen for a long time. The sun moved around the windows. The coffee steam smelled up the house. The phone began to ring, stopped, began again. The mailman came, the cleaner, the bakery man, the gardener, the ice cream man, the League of Women Voters lady. A Negro woman spreading some strange gospel calling for the revision of the Food and Drug Act knocked at the front, rapped the windows, and finally scraped a half-dozen pamphlets under the back door. But Eli only sat, without underwear, in last night's suit. He answered no one.

Given his condition, it was strange that the trip and crash at the back door reached his inner ear. But in an instant he seemed to melt down into the crevices of the chair, then to splash up and out to where the clatter had been. At the door he waited. It was silent, but for a fluttering of damp little leaves on the trees. When he finally opened the door, there was no one there. He'd expected to see green, green, green, big as the doorway, topped by his hat, waiting for him with those eyes. But there was no one out there, except for the Bonwit's box which lay bulging at his feet. No string tied it and the top rode high on the bottom.

The coward! He couldn't do it! He couldn't!

The very glee of that idea pumped fuel to his legs. He tore out across his back lawn, past his new spray of forsythia, to catch a glimpse of the bearded one fleeing naked through yards, over hedges and fences, to the safety of his hermitage. In the distance a pile of pink and white stones—which Harriet Knudson had painted the previous day—tricked him. "Run," he shouted to the rocks, "run, you . . ." but he caught his error before anyone else did, and though he peered and craned there was no hint anywhere of a man about his own size, with white, white, terribly white skin (how white must be the skin of his body!) in cowardly retreat. He came slowly, curiously, back to the door. And while the trees shimmered in the light wind, he removed the top from the box. The shock at first was the shock of having daylight turned off all at once. Inside the box was an eclipse. But black soon sorted from black, and shortly there was the glassy black of lining, the coarse black of trousers, the dead black of fraying threads, and in the center the mountain of black: the hat. He picked the box from the doorstep and carried it inside. For the first time in his life he *smelled* the color of blackness: a little stale, a little sour, a little old, but nothing that could overwhelm you. Still, he held the package at arm's length and deposited it on the dining room table.

Twenty rooms on a hill and they store their old clothes with me! What am I supposed to do with them? Give them to charity? That's where they came from. He picked up the hat by the edges and looked inside. The crown was smooth as an egg, the brim practically threadbare. There is nothing else to do with a hat in one's hands but put it on, so Eli dropped the thing on his head. He opened the door to the hall closet and looked at himself in the full-length mirror. The hat gave him bags under the eyes. Or perhaps he had not slept well. He pushed the brim lower till a shadow touched his lips. Now the bags under his eyes had inflated to become his face. Before the mirror he unbuttoned his shirt, unzipped his trousers, and then, shedding his clothes, he studied what he was. What a silly disappointment to see yourself naked in a hat. Especially in that hat. He sighed, but could not rid himself of the great weakness that suddenly set on his muscles and joints, beneath the terrible weight of the stranger's strange hat.

He returned to the dining room table and emptied the box of its contents: jacket, trousers, and vest (*it* smelled deeper than blackness). And under it all, sticking between the shoes that looked chopped and bitten, came the first gleam of white. A little fringed serape, a gray piece of semiunderwear, was crumpled at the bottom, its thready border twisted into itself. Eli removed it and let it hang free. What is it? For warmth? To wear beneath underwear in the event of a chest cold? He held it to his nose but it did not smell from Vick's or mustard plaster. It was something special, some Jewish thing. Special food, special language, special prayers, why not special BVD's? So fearful was he that he would be tempted back into wearing his traditional clothes—reasoned Eli—that he had carried and buried in Woodenton everything, including the special underwear. For that was how Eli now understood the box of clothes. The greenie was saying, Here, I give up. I refuse even to be tempted. We surrender. And that was how Eli continued to understand it until he found he'd slipped the white fringy surrender flag over his hat and felt it clinging to his chest. And now, looking at himself in the mirror, he was momentarily uncertain as to who was tempting who into what. Why *did* the greenie leave his clothes? Was it even the greenie? Then who was it? And why? But, Eli, for Christ's sake, in an age of science things don't happen like that. Even the goddam pigs take drugs . . .

Regardless of who was the source of the temptation, what was its end, not to mention its beginning, Eli, some moments later, stood draped in black, with a little white underneath, before the full-length mirror. He had to pull down on the trousers so they would not show the hollow of his ankle. The greenie, didn't he wear socks? Or had he forgotten them? The mystery was solved when Eli mustered enough courage to investigate the trouser pockets. He had expected some damp awful thing to happen to his fingers should he slip them down and out of sight—but when at last he jammed bravely down he came up with a khaki army sock in each hand. As he slipped them over his toes, he invented a genesis: a G.I.'s present in 1945. Plus everything else lost between 1938 and 1945, he had also lost his socks. Not that he had lost the socks, but that he'd had to stoop to accepting these, made Eli almost cry. To calm himself he walked out the back door and stood looking at his lawn.

On the Knudson back lawn, Harriet Knudson was giving her stones a second coat of pink. She looked up just as Eli stepped out. Eli shot back in again and pressed himself against the back door. When he peeked between the curtains all he saw were paint bucket, brush, and rocks scattered on the Knudsons' pink-spattered grass. The phone rang. Who was it—Harriet Knudson? Eli, there's a Jew at your door. *That's me.* Nonsense, Eli, I saw him with my own eyes. *That's me, I saw you too, painting your rocks pink.* Eli, you're having a nervous breakdown again. Jimmy, Eli's having a nervous breakdown again. Eli, this is Jimmy, hear you're having a little breakdown, anything I can do, boy? Eli, this is Ted, Shirley says you need help. Eli, this is Artie, you need help. Eli, Harry, you need help you need help . . . The phone rattled its last and died.

"God helps them who help themselves," intoned Eli, and once again he stepped out the door. This time he walked to the center of his lawn and in full sight of the trees, the grass, the birds, and the sun, revealed that it was he, Eli, in the costume. But nature had nothing to say to him, and so stealthily he made his way to the hedge separating his property from the field beyond and he cut his way through, losing his hat twice in the under-brush. Then, clamping the hat to his head, he began to run, the threaded tassels jumping across his heart. He ran through the weeds and wild flowers, until on the old road that skirted the town he slowed up. He was walking when he approached the Gulf station from the back. He supported himself on a huge tireless truck rim, and among tubes, rusted engines, dozens of topless oil cans, he rested. With a kind of brainless cunning, he readied himself for the last mile of his journey.

"How are you, Pop?" It was the garage attendant, rubbing his greasy hands on his overalls, and hunting among the cans.

Eli's stomach lurched and he pulled the big black coat round his neck.

"Nice day," the attendant said and started around to the front.

"Sholom," Eli whispered and zoomed off towards the hill.

The sun was directly overhead when Eli reached the top. He had come by way of the woods, where it was cooler, but still he was perspiring beneath his new suit. The hat had no sweatband and the cloth clutched his head. The children were playing. The children were always playing, as if it was that alone that Tzuref had to teach them. In their shorts, they revealed such thin legs that beneath one could see the joints swiveling as they ran. Eli waited for them to disappear around a corner before he came into the open. But something would not let him wait—his green suit. It was on the porch, wrapped around the bearded fellow, who was painting the base of a pillar. His arm went up and down, up and down, and the pillar glowed like white fire. The very sight of him popped Eli out of the woods onto the lawn. He did not turn back, though his insides did. He walked up the lawn, but the children played on; tipping the black hat, he mumbled, "Shhh . . . shhhh," and they hardly seemed to notice.

At last he smelled paint.

He waited for the man to turn to him. He only painted. Eli felt suddenly that if he could pull the black hat down over his eyes, over his chest and belly and legs, if he could shut out all light, then a moment later he would be home in bed. But the hat wouldn't go past his forehead. He couldn't kid himself—he was there. No one he could think of had forced him to do this.

The greenie's arm flailed up and down on the pillar. Eli breathed loudly, cleared his throat, but the greenie wouldn't make life easier for him. At last, Eli had to say "Hello."

The arm swished up and down; it stopped—two fingers went out after a brush hair stuck to the pillar.

"Good day," Eli said.

The hair came away; the swishing resumed.

"Sholom," Eli whispered and the fellow turned.

The recognition took some time. He looked at what Eli wore. Up close, Eli looked at what he wore. And then Eli had the strange notion that he was two people. Or that he was one person wearing two suits. The greenie looked to be suffering from a similar confusion. They stared long at one another. Eli's heart shivered, and his brain was momentarily in such a mixed-up condition that his hands went out to button down the collar of his shirt that somebody else was wearing. What a mess! The greenie flung his arms over his face.

"What's the matter . . ." Eli said. The fellow had picked up his bucket and brush and was running away. Eli ran after him.

"I wasn't going to hit . . ." Eli called. "Stop . . ." Eli caught up and grabbed his sleeve. Once again, the greenie's hands flew up to his face. This time, in the violence, white paint spattered both of them.

"I only want to . . ." But in that outfit Eli didn't really know what he wanted. "To talk . . ." he said finally. "For you to look at me. Please, just *look* at me . . ."

The hands stayed put, as paint rolled off the brush onto the cuff of Eli's green suit.

"Please . . . please," Eli said, but he did not know what to do. "Say something, speak *English*," he pleaded.

The fellow pulled back against the wall, back, back, as though some arm would finally reach out and yank him to safety. He refused to uncover his face.

"Look," Eli said, pointing to himself. "It's your suit. I'll take care of it."

No answer—only a little shaking under the hands, which led Eli to speak as gently as he knew how.

"We'll . . . we'll moth-proof it. There's a button missing"—Eli pointed —"I'll have it fixed. I'll have a zipper put in . . . Please, please—just look at me . . ." He was talking to himself, and yet how could he stop? Nothing he said made any sense—that alone made his heart swell. Yet somehow babbling on, he might babble something that would make things easier between them. "Look . . ." He reached inside his shirt to pull the frills of underwear into the light. "I'm wearing the special underwear, even . . . Please," he said, *"please, please, please"* he sang, as if it were some sacred word. "Oh, *please* . . ."

Nothing twitched under the tweed suit—and if the eyes watered, or twinkled, or hated, he couldn't tell. It was driving him crazy. He had dressed like a fool, and for what? For this? He reached up and yanked the hands away.

"There!" he said—and in that first instant all he saw of the greenie's face were two white droplets stuck to each cheek.

"Tell me—" Eli clutched his hands down to his sides—"Tell me, what can I do for you, I'll do it . . ."

Stiffly, the greenie stood there, sporting his two white tears.

"Whatever I can do . . . Look, look, what I've done *already*." He grabbed his black hat and shook it in the man's face.

And in exchange, the greenie gave him an answer. He raised one hand to his chest, and then jammed it, finger first, towards the horizon. And with what a pained look! As though the air were full of razors! Eli followed the finger and saw beyond the knuckle, out past the nail, Woodenton.

"What do you want?" Eli said. "I'll bring it!"

Suddenly the greenie made a run for it. But then he stopped, wheeled, and jabbed that finger at the air again. It pointed the same way. Then he was gone.

And then, all alone, Eli had the revelation. He did not question his understanding, the substance or the source. But with a strange, dreamy elation, he started away.

On Coach House Road, they were double-parked. The Mayor's wife pushed a grocery cart full of dog food from Stop N' Shop to her station wagon. The President of the Lions Club, a napkin around his neck, was jamming pennies into the meter in front of the Bit-in-Teeth Restaurant. Ted Heller caught the sun as it glazed off the new Byzantine mosaic entrance to his shoe shop. In pinkened jeans, Mrs. Jimmy Knudson was leaving Halloway's Hardware, a paint bucket in each hand. Roger's Beauty Shoppe had its doors open—women's heads in silver bullets far as the eye could see. Over by the barbershop the pole spun, and Artie Berg's youngest sat on a red horse, having his hair cut; his mother flipped through *Look*, smiling: the greenie had changed his clothes.

And into this street, which seemed paved with chromium, came Eli Peck. It was not enough, he knew, to walk up one side of the street. That was not enough. Instead he walked ten paces up one side, then on an angle, crossed to the other side, where he walked ten more paces, and crossed back. Horns blew, traffic jerked, as Eli made his way up Coach House Road. He spun a moan high up in his nose as he walked. Outside no one could hear him, but he felt it vibrate the cartilage at the bridge of his nose.

Things slowed around him. The sun stopped rippling on spokes and hubcaps. It glowed steadily as everyone put on brakes to look at the man in black. They always paused and gaped, whenever he entered the town. Then in a minute, or two, or three, a light would change, a baby squawk, and the flow continue. Now, though lights changed, no one moved.

"He shaved his beard," Eric the barber said.

"Who?" asked Linda Berg.

"The . . . the guy in the suit. From the place there."

Linda looked out the window.

"It's Uncle Eli," little Kevin Berg said, spitting hair.

"Oh, God," Linda said, "Eli's having a nervous breakdown."

"A nervous breakdown!" Ted Heller said, but not immediately. Immediately he had said "Hoooly . . ."

Shortly, everybody in Coach House Road was aware that Eli Peck, the nervous young attorney with the pretty wife, was having a breakdown.

Everybody except Eli Peck. He knew what he did was not insane, though he felt every inch of its strangeness. He felt those black clothes as if they were the skin of his skin—the give and pull as they got used to where he bulged and buckled. And he felt eyes, every eye on Coach House Road. He saw headlights screech to within an inch of him, and stop. He saw mouths: first the bottom jaw slides forward, then the tongue hits the teeth, the lips explode, a little thunder in the throat, and they've said it: Eli Peck Eli Peck Eli Peck Eli Peck. He began to walk slowly, shifting his weight down and forward with each syllable: E–li–Peck–E–li–Peck–E–li–Peck. Heavily he trod, and as his neighbors uttered each syllable of his name, he felt each syllable shaking all his bones. He knew who he was down to his marrow— they were telling him. Eli Peck. He wanted them to say it a thousand times, a million times, he would walk forever in that black suit, as adults whispered of his strangeness and children made "Shame . . . shame" with their fingers.

"It's going to be all right, pal . . ." Ted Heller was motioning to Eli from his doorway. "C'mon, pal, it's going to be all right . . ."

Eli saw him, past the brim of his hat. Ted did not move from his doorway, but leaned forward and spoke with his hand over his mouth. Behind him, three customers peered through the doorway. "Eli, it's Ted, remember Ted . . ."

Eli crossed the street and found he was heading directly towards Harriet Knudson. He lifted his neck so she could see his whole face.

He saw her forehead melt down to her lashes. "Good morning, Mr. Peck."

"Sholom," Eli said, and crossed the street where he saw the President of the Lions.

"Twice before . . ." he heard someone say, and then he crossed again, mounted the curb, and was before the bakery, where a delivery man charged past with a tray of powdered cakes twirling above him. "Pardon me, Father," he said, and scooted into his truck. But he could not move it. Eli Peck had stopped traffic.

He passed the Rivoli Theater, Beekman Cleaners, Harris' Westinghouse, the Unitarian Church, and soon he was passing only trees. At Ireland Road he turned right and started through Woodenton's winding streets. Baby carriages stopped whizzing and creaked—"Isn't that . . ." Gardeners held their clipping. Children stepped from the sidewalk and tried the curb. And Eli greeted no one, but raised his face to all. He wished passionately that he had white tears to show them . . . And not till he reached his own front lawn, saw his house, his shutters, his new jonquils, did he remember his wife. And the child that must have been born to him. And it was then and there he had the awful moment. He could go inside and put on his clothes and go to his wife in the hospital. It was not irrevocable, even the walk wasn't. In Woodenton memories are long but fury short. Apathy works like forgiveness. Besides, when you've flipped, you've flipped—it's Mother Nature.

What gave Eli the awful moment was that he turned away. He knew exactly what he could do but he chose not to. To go inside would be to go halfway. There was more . . . So he turned and walked towards the hospital and all the time he quaked an eighth of an inch beneath his skin to think that perhaps he'd chosen the crazy way. To think that he'd *chosen* to be crazy! But if you chose to be crazy, then you weren't crazy. It's when you didn't choose. No, he wasn't flipping. He had a child to see.

"Name?"

"Peck."

"Fourth floor." He was given a little blue card.

In the elevator everybody stared. Eli watched his black shoes rise four floors.

"Four."

He tipped his hat, but knew he couldn't take it off.

"Peck," he said. He showed the card.

"Congratulations," the nurse said, ". . . the grandfather?"

"The father. Which room?"

She led him to 412. "A joke on the Mrs.?" she said, but he slipped in the door without her.

"Miriam?"

"Yes?"

"Eli."

She rolled her white face towards her husband. "Oh, Eli . . . Oh, Eli." He raised his arms. "What could I do?"

"You have a son. They called all morning."

"I came to see him."

"Like *that!*" she whispered harshly. "Eli, you can't go around like that."

"I have a son. I want to see him."

"Eli, why are you doing this to me!" Red seeped back into her lips. "*He's* not your fault," she explained. "Oh, Eli, sweetheart, why do you feel guilty about everything? Eli, change your clothes. I forgive you."

"Stop forgiving me. Stop understanding me."

"But I love you."

"That's something else."

"But, sweetie, you *don't* have to dress like that. You didn't do anything. You don't have to feel guilty because . . . because everything's all right. Eli, can't you see that?"

"Miriam, enough reasons. Where's my son?"

"Oh, please, Eli, don't flip now. I need you now. Is that why you're flipping—because I need you?"

"In your selfish way, Miriam, you're very generous. I want my son."

"Don't flip now. I'm afraid, now that he's out." She was beginning to whimper. "I don't know if I love him, now that he's out. When I look in the mirror, Eli, he won't be there . . . Eli, Eli, you look like you're going to your own funeral. Please, can't you leave well enough *alone?* Can't we just have a family?"

"No."

In the corridor he asked the nurse to lead him to his son. The nurse walked on one side of him, Ted Heller on the other.

"Eli, do you want some help? I thought you might want some help."

"No."

Ted whispered something to the nurse; then to Eli he whispered, "Should you be walking around like this?"

"Yes."

In his ear Ted said, "You'll . . . frighten the kid . . ."

"There," the nurse said. She pointed to a bassinet in the second row and looked, puzzled, to Ted. "Do I go in?" Eli said.

"No," the nurse said. "She'll roll him over." She rapped on the enclosure full of babies. "Peck," she mouthed to the nurse on the inside.

Ted tapped Eli's arm. "You're not thinking of doing something you'll be sorry for . . . are you, Eli? Eli—I mean you know you're still Eli, don't you?"

In the enclosure, Eli saw a bassinet had been wheeled before the square window.

"Oh, Christ. . . ." Ted said. "You don't have this Bible stuff on the brain—" And suddenly he said, "You wait, pal." He started down the corridor, his heels tapping rapidly.

Eli felt relieved—he leaned forward. In the basket was what he'd come to see. Well, now that he was here, what did he think he was going to say to it? I'm your father, Eli, the Flipper? I am wearing a black hat, suit, and fancy underwear, all borrowed from a friend? How could he admit to this reddened ball—*his* reddened ball—the worst of all: that Eckman would shortly convince him he wanted to take off the whole business. He couldn't admit it! He wouldn't do it!

Past his hat brim, from the corner of his eye, he saw Ted had stopped in a doorway at the end of the corridor. Two interns stood there smoking, listening to Ted. Eli ignored it.

No, even Eckman wouldn't make him take it off! No! He'd wear it, if he chose to. He'd make the kid wear it! Sure! Cut it down when the time came. A smelly hand-me-down, whether the kid liked it or not!

Only Teddie's heels clacked; the interns wore rubber soles—for they were there, beside him, unexpectedly. Their white suits smelled, but not like Eli's.

"Eli," Ted said, softly, "visiting time's up, pal."

"How are you feeling, Mr. Peck? First child upsets everyone. . . ."

He'd just pay no attention; nevertheless, he began to perspire, thickly, and his hat crown clutched his hair.

"Excuse me—Mr. Peck. . . ." It was a new rich bass voice. "Excuse me, rabbi, but you're wanted . . . in the temple." A hand took his elbow, firmly; then another hand, the other elbow. Where they grabbed, his tendons went taut.

"Okay, rabbi. Okay okay okay okay okay okay. . . ." He listened; it was a very soothing word, that okay. "Okay okay everything's going to be okay." His feet seemed to have left the ground some, as he glided away from the window, the bassinet, the babies. "Okay easy does it everything's all right all right—"

But he rose, suddenly, as though up out of a dream, and flailing his arms, screamed: *"I'm the father!"*

But the window disappeared. In a moment they tore off his jacket—it gave so easily, in one yank. Then a needle slid under his skin. The drug calmed his soul, but did not touch it down where the blackness had reached.

YOU ARE ACCEPTED

Paul Tillich

> Moreover the law entered, that the offence might abound. But where sin abounded, grace did much more abound.
>
> Romans 5:20.

These words of Paul summarize his apostolic experience, his religious message as a whole, and the Christian understanding of life. To discuss these words, or to make them the text of even several sermons, has always seemed impossible to me. I have never dared to use them before. But something has driven me to consider them during the past few months, a desire to give witness to the two facts which appeared to me, in hours of retrospection, as the all-determining facts of our life: the abounding of sin and the greater abounding of grace.

There are few words more strange to most of us than "sin" and "grace." They are strange, just because they are so well-known. During the centuries they have received distorting connotations, and have lost so much of their genuine power that we must seriously ask ourselves whether we should use them at all, or whether we should discard them as useless tools. But there is a mysterious fact about the great words of our religious tradition: they cannot be replaced. All attempts to make substitutions, including those I have tried myself, have failed to convey the reality that was to be expressed; they have led to shallow and impotent talk. There are no substitutes for words like "sin" and "grace." But there *is* a way of rediscovering their meaning, the same way that leads us down into the depth of our human existence. In that depth these words were conceived; and *there* they gained power for all ages; *there* they must be found again by each generation, and by each of us for himself. Let us therefore try to penetrate the deeper levels of our life, in order to see whether we can discover in them the realities of which our text speaks.

Have the men of our time still a feeling of the meaning of sin? Do they, and do we, still realize that sin does *not* mean an immoral act, that "sin" should never be used in the plural, and that not our sins, but rather our *sin* is the great, all-pervading problem of our life? Do we still know that it is arrogant and erroneous to divide men by calling some "sinners" and others "righteous"? For by way of such a division, we can usually discover that we ourselves do not *quite* belong to the "sinners," since we have avoided heavy sins, have made some progress in the control of this or that sin, and have been even humble enough not to call ourselves "righteous." Are we still able to realize that this kind of thinking and feeling about sin is far removed from what the great religious tradition, both within and outside the Bible, has meant when it speaks of sin?

I should like to suggest another word to you, not as a substitute for the word "sin," but as a useful clue in the interpretation of the word "sin": "separation." Separation is an aspect of the experience of everyone. Perhaps the word "sin" has the same root as the word "asunder." In any case, *sin is separation*. To be in the state of sin is to be in the state of separation. And separation is threefold: there is separation among individual lives, separation of a man from himself, and separation of all men from the Ground of Being. This three-fold separation constitutes the state of everything that exists; it is a universal fact; it is the fate of every life. And it is our human fate in a very special sense. For *we* as men know that we are separated. We not only suffer with all other creatures because of the self-destructive consequences of our separation, but also know *why* we suffer. We know that we are estranged from something to which we really belong, and with which we *should* be united. We know that the fate of separation is not merely a natural event like a flash of sudden lightning, but that it is an experience in which we actively participate, in which our whole personality is involved, and that, as fate, it is also *guilt*. Separation which is fate *and* guilt constitutes the meaning of the word "sin." It is *this* which is the state of our entire existence, from its very beginning to its very end. Such separation is prepared in the mother's womb, and before that time, in every preceding generation. It is manifest in the special actions of our conscious life. It reaches beyond our graves into all the succeeding generations. It is our existence itself. *Existence is separation!* Before sin is an act, it is a state.

We can say the same things about grace. For sin and grace are bound to each other. We do not even have a knowledge of sin unless we have already experienced the unity of life, which is grace. And conversely, we could not grasp the meaning of grace without having experienced the separation of life, which is sin. Grace is just as difficult to describe as sin. For some people, grace is the willingness of a divine king and father to forgive over and again the foolishness and weakness of his subjects and children. We must reject such a concept of grace; for it is a merely childish destruction of a human dignity. For others, grace is a magic power in the dark places of the soul, but a power without any significance for practical life, a quickly vanishing and useless idea. For others, grace is the benevolence that we may find beside the cruelty and destructiveness in life. But then, it does not matter whether we say "life goes on," or whether we say "there is grace in life"; if grace means no more than this, the word should, and will, disappear. For other people, grace indicates the gifts that one has received from nature or society, and the power to do good things with the help of those gifts. But grace is more than gifts. In grace something is overcome; grace occurs "in spite of" something; grace occurs in spite of separation and estrangement. Grace is the *re*union of life with life, the *re*conciliation of the self with itself. Grace is the acceptance of that which is rejected. Grace transforms fate into a meaningful destiny; it changes guilt into confidence and courage. There is something triumphant in the word "grace": in spite of the abounding of sin grace abounds much more.

And now let us look down into ourselves to discover there the struggle between separation and reunion, between sin and grace, in our relation to others, in our relation to ourselves, and in our relation to the Ground and aim of our being. If our souls respond to the description that I intend to give, words like "sin" and "separation," "grace" and "reunion," may have a new meaning for us. But the words themselves are not important. It is the response of the deepest levels of our being that is important. If such a response were to occur among us this moment, we could say that we have known grace.

Who has not, at some time, been lonely in the midst of a social event? The feeling of our separation from the rest of life is most acute when we are surrounded by it in noise and talk. We realize then much more than in moments of solitude how strange we are to each other, how estranged life is from life. Each one of us draws back into himself. We cannot penetrate the hidden center of another individual; nor can that individual pass beyond the shroud that covers our own being. Even the greatest love cannot break through the walls of the self. Who has not experienced that disillusionment of all great love? If one were to hurl away his self in complete self-surrender, he would become a nothing, without form or strength, a self without self, merely an object of contempt and abuse. Our generation knows more than the generation of our fathers about the hidden hostility in the ground of our souls. Today we know much about the profusive aggressiveness in every being. Today we can confirm what Immanuel Kant, the prophet of human reason and dignity, was honest enough to say: there is something in the misfortune of our best friends which does not displease us. Who amongst us is dishonest enough to deny that this is true also of him? Are we not almost always ready to abuse everybody and everything, although often in a very refined way, for the pleasure of self-elevation, for an occasion for boasting, for a moment of lust? To know that we are ready is to know the meaning of the separation of life from life, and of "sin abounding."

The most irrevocable expression of the separation of life from life today is the attitude of social groups within nations towards each other, and the attitude of nations themselves towards other nations. The walls of distance, in time and space, have been removed by technical progress; but the walls of estrangement between heart and heart have been incredibly strengthened. The madness of the German Nazis and the cruelty of the lynching mobs in the South provide too easy an excuse for us to turn our thoughts from our own selves. But let us just consider ourselves and what we feel, when we read, this morning and tonight, that in some sections of Europe all children under the age of three are sick and dying, or that in some sections of Asia millions without homes are freezing and starving to death. The strangeness of life to life is evident in the strange fact that we can know all this, and yet can live today, this morning, tonight, as though we were completely ignorant. And I refer to the most sensitive people amongst us. In both mankind and nature, life is separated from life. Estrangement prevails among all things that live. Sin abounds.

It is important to remember that we are not merely separated from each other. For we are also separated from ourselves. *Man Against Himself* is not merely the title of a book, but rather also indicates the rediscovery of an age-old insight. Man is split within himself. Life moves against itself through aggression, hate, and despair. We are wont to condemn self-love; but what we really mean to condemn is contrary to self-love. It is that mixture of selfishness and self-hate that permanently pursues us, that prevents us from loving others, and that prohibits us from losing ourselves in the love with which we are loved eternally. He who is able to love himself is able to love others also; he who has learned to overcome self-contempt has overcome his contempt for others. But the depth of our separation lies in just the fact that we are not capable of a great and merciful divine love towards ourselves. On the contrary, in each of us there is an instinct of self-destruction, which is as strong as our instinct of self-preservation. In our tendency to abuse and destroy others, there is an open or hidden tendency to abuse and to destroy ourselves. Cruelty towards others is always also cruelty towards ourselves. Nothing is more obvious than the split in both our unconscious life and conscious personality. Without the help of modern psychology, Paul expressed the fact in his famous words, "For I do not do the good I desire, but rather the evil that I do not desire." And then he continued in words that might well be the motto of all depth psychology: "Now if I should do what I do not wish to do, it is not I that do it, but rather sin which dwells within me." The apostle sensed a split between his conscious will and his real will, between himself and something strange within and alien to him. He was estranged from himself; and that estrangement he called "sin." He also called it a strange "law in his limbs," an irresistible compulsion. How often we commit certain acts in perfect consciousness, yet with the shocking sense that we are being controlled by an alien power! That is the experience of the separation of ourselves from ourselves, which is to say "sin," whether or not we like to use that word.

Thus, the state of our whole life is estrangement from others and ourselves, because we are estranged from the Ground of our being, because we are estranged from the origin and aim of our life. And we do not know where we have come from, or where we are going. We are separated from the mystery, the depth, and the greatness of our existence. We hear the voice of that depth; but our ears are closed. We feel that something radical, total, and unconditioned is demanded of us; but we rebel against it, try to escape its urgency, and will not accept its promise.

We cannot escape, however. If that something is the Ground of our being, we are bound to it for all eternity, just as we are bound to ourselves and to all other life. We always remain in the power of that from which we are estranged. That fact brings us to the ultimate depth of sin: separated and yet bound, estranged and yet belonging, destroyed and yet preserved, the state which is called despair. Despair means that there is no escape. Despair is "the sickness unto death." But the terrible thing about the sickness of despair is that we cannot be released, not even through open or hidden suicide. For we all know that we are bound eternally and inescapably to the Ground of our being. The abyss of separation is not always visible. But it has become more visible to our generation than to the preceding generations, because of our feeling of meaninglessness, emptiness, doubt, and cynicism—all expressions of despair, of our separation from the roots and the meaning of our life. Sin in its most profound sense, sin, as despair, abounds amongst us.

"Where sin abounded, grace did much more abound," says Paul in the same letter in which he describes the unimaginable power of separation and self-destruction within society and the individual soul. He does not say these words because sentimental interests demand a happy ending for everything tragic. He says them because they describe the most overwhelming and determining experience of his life. In the picture of Jesus as the Christ, which appeared to him at the moment of his greatest separation from other men, from himself and God, he found himself accepted in spite of his being rejected. And when he found that he was accepted, he was able to accept himself and to be reconciled to others. The moment in which grace struck him and overwhelmed him, he was reunited with that to which he belonged, and from which he was estranged in utter strangeness. Do we know what it means to be struck by grace? It does *not* mean that we suddenly believe that God exists, or that Jesus is the Saviour, or that the Bible contains the truth. To believe that something *is,* is almost contrary to the meaning of grace. Furthermore, grace does not mean simply that we are making progress in our moral self-control, in our fight against special faults, and in our relationships to men and to society. Moral progress may be a fruit of grace; but it is not grace itself, and it can even prevent us from receiving grace. For there is too often a graceless acceptance of Christian doctrines and a graceless battle against the structures of evil in our personalities. Such a graceless relation to God may lead us by necessity either to arrogance or to despair. It would be better to refuse God and the Christ and the Bible than to accept Them without grace. For if we accept without grace, we do so in the state of separation, and can only succeed in deepening the separation. We cannot transform our lives, unless we allow them to be transformed by that stroke of grace. It happens; or it does not happen. And certainly it does *not* happen if we try to force it upon ourselves, just as it shall not happen so long as we think, in our self-complacency, that we have no need of it. Grace strikes us when we are in great pain and restlessness. It strikes us when we walk through the dark valley of a meaningless and empty life. It strikes us when we feel that our separation is deeper than usual, because we have violated another life, a life which we loved, or from which we were estranged. It strikes us when our disgust for our own being, our indifference, our weakness, our hostility, and our lack of direction and composure have become intolerable to us. It strikes us when, year after year, the longed-for perfection of life does not appear, when the old compulsions reign within us as they have for decades, when despair destroys all joy and courage. Sometimes at that moment a wave of light breaks into our darkness, and it is as though a voice were saying: "You are accepted. *You are accepted,* accepted by that which is greater than you, and the name of which you do not know. Do not ask for the name now; perhaps you will find it later. Do not try to do anything now; perhaps later you will do much. Do not seek for anything; do not perform anything; do not intend anything. *Simply accept the fact that you are accepted!*" If that happens to us, we experience grace. After such an experience we may not be better than before, and we may not believe more than before. But everything is transformed. In that moment, grace conquers sin, and reconciliation bridges the gulf of estrangement. And nothing is demanded of this experience, no religious or moral or intellectual presupposition, nothing but *acceptance.*

In the light of this grace we perceive the power of grace in our relation to others and to ourselves. We experience the grace of being able to look frankly into the eyes of another, the miraculous grace of reunion of life with life. We experience the grace of understanding each other's words. We understand not merely the literal meaning of the words, but also that which lies behind them, even when they are harsh or angry. For even then there is a longing to break through the walls of separation. We experience the grace of being able to accept the life of another, even if it be hostile and harmful to us, for, through grace, we know that it belongs to the same Ground to which we belong, and by which we have been accepted. We experience the grace which is able to overcome the tragic separation of the sexes, of the generations, of the nations, of the races, and even the utter strangeness between man and nature. Sometimes grace appears in all these separations to reunite us with those to whom we belong. For life belongs to life.

And in the light of this grace we perceive the power of grace in our relation to ourselves. We experience moments in which we accept ourselves, because we feel that we have been accepted by that which is greater than we. If only more such moments were given to us! For it is such moments that make us love our life, that make us accept ourselves, not in our goodness and self-complacency, but in our certainty of the eternal meaning of our life. We cannot force ourselves to accept ourselves. We cannot compel anyone to accept himself. But sometimes it happens that we receive the power to say "yes" to ourselves, that peace enters into us and makes us whole, that self-hate and self-contempt disappear, and that our self is reunited with itself. Then we can say that grace has come upon us.

"Sin" and "grace" are strange words; but they are not strange things.

We find them whenever we look into ourselves with searching eyes and longing hearts. They determine our life. They abound within us and in all of life. May grace more abound within us!

THE QUESTION TO THE SINGLE ONE [1]

Martin Buber

THE SINGLE ONE AND HIS THOU

Kierkegaard's "to become a Single One" is, as we have seen, not meant Socratically. The goal of this becoming is not the "right" life, but entry into a relation. "To become" here means to become *for* something—"for" in the strict sense in which the circle of the person himself is transcended. It means to be made ready for the one relation which can be entered into only as the Single One, the one, the relation for whose sake man exists.

This relation is an exclusive one, the exclusive one, and this, according to Kierkegaard, means that it is the excluding relation, excluding all others; more precisely, that it is the relation which in virtue of its unique, essential life drives all other relations into the realm of the unessential.

"Everyone should be chary about having to do with 'the others,' and should essentially speak only with God and with himself," Kierkegaard says in his exposition of the category. Everyone, so it is to be understood, because everyone can be the one.

This joining of the "with God" with the "with himself" is a serious incompatibility that nothing can mitigate. All the enthusiasm of the philosophers for monologue, from Plato to Nietzsche, hardly touches the simple experience of faith that speaking with God is something *toto genere* different from "speaking with oneself," whereas, remarkably enough, it is not something *toto genere* different from speaking with another human being. For in the latter case, there is in common the fact of being approached, grasped, addressed, which cannot be anticipated in any depth of the soul;

THE QUESTION TO THE SINGLE ONE Reprinted with permission of The Macmillan Company from *Between Man and Man* by Martin Buber. Copyright © 1965 by The Macmillan Company. Reprinted with permission of Routledge & Kegan Paul Ltd.

[1] *The Question to the Single One*. The German which I have rendered by the cumbrous and none too clear phrase "the Single One" is *der Einzelne,* which is a fairly precise rendering of Kierkegaard's *hiin Enkelte*. It is a pity that in the English translations of Kierkegaard no effort seems to have been made by the translators to avoid the use of the word "individual," which is highly misleading. For every man is *individuum,* but not everyone is an *Einzelner* or *Enkelte*. In fact, the whole course of Kierkegaard's life, and the whole force of his teaching, is directed toward "becoming a Single One," and this is not a natural or biological category, but, as Kierkegaard reiterates, it is "the spirit's category," and a rare thing. The reader's complaisance is invited, therefore, as it was decided better to make the English a little odd rather than customary and misleading. [Translator]

but in the former, there is no such common fact in spite of all the soul's adventures in doubling roles—games, intoxications, dreams, visions, surprises, overwhelmings, overpowerings—in spite of all tensions and divisions, and in spite of all the noble and powerful images for traffic with oneself. "Then one became two": that can never be *ontically* true, just as the reverse "one and one in one" of mysticism can never be ontically true. Only when I have to do with another essentially—that is, in such a way that he is no longer a phenomenon of my *I*, but instead is my *Thou*—do I experience the reality of speech with another, in the irrefragable genuineness of mutuality. *Abyssus abyssum clamat:* what that means the soul first experiences when it reaches its frontier and finds itself faced by one that is simply not the soul itself and yet is a self.

But on this point Kierkegaard seems to correct himself. In the passage in his Journals where he asks the question, "And how does one become a Single One?", the answer begins with the formulation, obviously more valid for the problem there under discussion, that one should be, "regarding the highest concerns, related solely to God."

If, in this statement, the word "highest" is understood as limiting in its content, then this is self-evident: the highest concerns can be put only to the highest. But it cannot be meant this way; that is clear from the other statement. "Everyone should. . . ." If both are taken together, then Kierkegaard's meaning is evident: the Single One has to do *essentially*—is not to be "chary"—only with God.

But thereby the category of the Single One, scarcely properly discovered, is already fatefully misunderstood.

Kierkegaard, the Christian concerned with "contemporaneity" with Jesus, here contradicts his master.

To the question—which was not merely directed at "tempting" him, but was rather a current and significant controversial question of the time—as to which was the all-inclusive and fundamental commandment, the "great" commandment, Jesus replied by connecting the two Old Testament commandments between which the choice lay: "Love God with all your might" and "Love your neighbor as one like yourself." [2] Both are to be "loved," God and the "neighbor" (that is, not man in general, but the man who meets me time and again in the context of life), but in different ways. The neighbor is to be loved "as one like myself" (not "as I love myself"; in the final reality, one does not love oneself, but one should rather learn to love oneself through love of one's neighbor); to him I should show love as I wish it shown to me. But God is to be loved with all my soul and all my might. By connecting the two, Jesus brings to light the Old Testament truth that God and man are not rivals. Exclusive love of God ("with *all* your heart") is, *because he is God,* inclusive love, ready to accept and in-

[2] "Love your neighbor as one like yourself": this departure from the customary rendering of the Authorized Version is again an effort to render the original more precisely (in this case the Hebrew of Lev. 19:18) in order to keep before the reader the stark objectivity of the command—the other whom you are required to "love" being one with a real life of his own, and not one whom you are invited to "acquire." [Translator]

clude all love. It is not himself that God creates, not himself he redeems; even when he "reveals himself," it is not himself he reveals: his revelation does not have himself as object. He limits himself in all his limitlessness; he makes room for creatures, and so, in the love of him, he makes room for love to creatures.

"In order to come to love," says Kierkegaard about his renunciation of Regina Olsen, "I had to remove the object." That is sublimely to misunderstand God. Creation is not a hurdle on the road to God; it is the road itself. We are created along with one another and directed to a life with one another. Creatures are placed in my way so that I, their fellow creature, by means of them and with them, may find the way to God. A God reached by excluding them would not be the God of all beings in whom all being is fulfilled. A God in whom only the parallel lines of single approaches intersect is more akin to the "God of the philosophers" than to the "God of Abraham, Isaac, and Jacob." God wants us to come to him by means of the Reginas he has created, and not by renunciation of them. If we remove the object, then—we remove the object altogether. Without an object, artificially producing the object from the abundance of the human spirit and calling it God, this kind of love has its being in the void.

"The matter must be brought back to the monastery from which Luther broke out." So Kierkegaard defines the task of the time. "Monastery" can here mean only the institutional safeguarding of man from an essential relation—inclusive of his whole being—to any others but God. And certainly, to one so safeguarded, the orientation toward the point called God is made possible with a precision not to be attained otherwise. But what "God" means in this case is, in fact, only the end point of a human line of orientation. The real God is hardly to be reached by a line shorter than each man's longest, which is the line embracing the world that is accessible to him. For the real God is the Creator, and all beings stand before him in relation to one another in his creation, becoming useful for his creative purpose in living with one another. To teach an acosmic relation to God is not to know the Creator. Acosmic worship of a God of whom one knows, as does Kierkegaard, that it is of his grace "that he wills to be a person in relation to you," is Marcionism, and not even consistent Marcionism; for this worship does not separate the creator and the redeemer, as it would have to do were it consistent.

But one must not overlook the fact that Kierkegaard is not at all concerned to put Luther breaking out of the monastery in the wrong. On one occasion, he treats Luther's marriage as something removed from all natural personal life, from all directness between man and wife, as a symbolic action, a deed representing and expressing the turning point of the spiritual history of the West. "The most important thing," he makes Luther say, "is that it becomes notorious that I am married." But behind Luther's marrying Katharina, there emerges, unnamed but clear, Kierkegaard's not marrying Regina. "Put the other way round, one could say . . . in defiance of the whole nineteenth century, I cannot marry." Here there is added as a new perspective the qualitative difference between historical epochs. Certainly, on Kierkegaard's view, it is true for both ages that the Single One should not have to do essentially with any others but God; according to him, then, Luther speaks not essentially but only symbolically with Katharina: though bound to the world, he remains essentially worldless and "alone before God." But the symbolic actions are opposed: by the one, the word of a new bond with the world—even if, perhaps, in the end, a bond that is not binding—is spoken to the one century; by the other, the word of a new, and in any event binding, renunciation is spoken to the other century. What is the reason? Because the nineteenth century has given itself up to the "crowd," and "the crowd is untruth."

But now two things are possible. Either the bond with the world preached with his life by Luther is in Kierkegaard's view neither binding, nor "essential," nor necessary for the leading of Luther's age to God. But that would make Luther one who permits what is not binding to be effective as something that is binding; it would make him one who has a different thing to say for men than he has for God, who treats the sacrament as though it were fulfilled outside God; it would make Luther one whose symbolic action possessed no authority. Or else, on the other hand, the bond with the world preached with his life by Luther is in Kierkegaard's view binding, and essential, and necessary for leading to God. Then the difference between the two epochs, which is indubitably a qualitative one, would enter in what is basically independent of history, more so than birth and death—the relation of the Single One to God. For the essential quality of this relation cannot be of one kind in the former century and of another in the latter; it cannot in the one go right through the world, and in the other go over and beyond the world. Human representations of the relation change, the truth of the relation is unchangeable because it stands in eternal mutuality; it is not man who defines his approach to it, but the Creator who, in the unambiguity of his creation of man, has instituted the approach.

It is certainly not possible to speak of God other than dialectically, for he does not come under the principle of contradiction. Yet there is a limit to dialectic where assertion ceases, but where there is knowledge. Who is there who confesses the God whom Kierkegaard and I confess who could suppose in decisive insight that God wants Thou to be truly said only to him, but to all others merely an unessential and fundamentally invalid word—that God demands of us to choose between him and his creation? The objection is raised that the world as a fallen world is not to be identified with the creation. But what fall of the world could be so mighty that it could *for him* break it away from being his creation? That would be to make the action of the world into something more powerful than God's action, into something compelling him.

The essential is not that we should see things as standing out from God, nor as being absorbed in him, but that we should "see things in God," the things themselves. To apply this to our relations with creatures: only when all relations, uncurtailed, are taken into the one relation, do we set the circle of our life's world round the sun of our being.

Certainly that is the most difficult thing, and in order to be able to do it, man must let himself be helped from time to time by an inner-worldly "monastery." Our relations to creatures are always threatening to become incapsulated. As the world itself is sustained in its independence as the world through striving to be closed against God, though as creation it is open to him, so every great bond of man—though in it he perceives his connection with the infinite—protects itself vigorously against continually debouching into the infinite. Here the monastic forms of life in the world, the loneliness in the midst of life into which we turn as into hostelries, help us prevent the connection between the conditioned bonds and the one unconditioned bond from slackening. This, too, if we do not wish to see our participation in the Present Being die off, is an indispensable interchange, the systole of the soul to its diastole. The loneliness must know the quality of strictness, of a monastery's strictness, in order to do its work. But it must never wish to tear us away from creatures, never refuse to send us off to them. If it failed to do that, it would act contrary to its own law and would close us up, instead of enabling us, as is its function, to keep open the gates of finitude.

Kierkegaard does not conceal from us for a moment that his resistance to a bond with the world, his religious doctrine of loneliness, is based on personal nature and personal destiny. He confesses that he "ceased to have common speech" with men. He notes that the finest moment in his life is in the bath house, before he dives into the water: "I have nothing more to do with the world." He exposes before our eyes some of the roots of his "melancholy." He knows precisely what has brought him to the point of being chary about having to do with others, and of essentially speaking only with God and with himself. And yet, as soon as he begins with the "direct" language, he expresses it as an imperative: let *everyone* do so. Continually he points to his own shadow—and wants to leap across it. He is a being excepted and exposed, and certainly so are we all, for so is man as man. But Kierkegaard has moved to the fringe of being excepted and exposed, and maintains equilibrium only by means of the extraordinary balance of his "author's" reticently communicative existence with all the complicated safeguards of the "pseudonyms"; whereas we are not on the fringe, and that is no "not yet" nor any sort of compromising, no shirking of melancholy; it is organic continuance and grace of preservation, and it is significant for the future of the spirit. Kierkegaard behaves in our sight like a schizophrenic, who tries to win over the beloved individual into "his" world as if it were the true one. But it is not the true one. We, ourselves wandering on the narrow ridge, must not shrink from the sight of the jutting rock on which he stands over the abyss; nor may we step on it. We have much to learn from him, but not the final lesson.

Our rejection can be supported by Kierkegaard's own teaching. He describes "the ethical" as "the only means by which God communicates with 'man'" (1853). The context of the teaching naturally prevents us from understanding this in the sense of an absolutizing of the ethical. But it must be understood in such a way that not merely an autarchic ethic, but also an autarchic religion, is inadmissible, so that as the ethical cannot be freed from the religious neither can the religious be freed from the ethical without ceasing to do justice to the present truth. The ethical no longer appears here, as in Kierkegaard's earlier thought, as a "stage" from which a "leap" leads to the religious, a leap by which a level is reached that is quite different and has a different meaning; here it dwells in the religious, in faith and service. This ethical can no longer mean a morality belonging to a realm of relativity, time and again overtaken and invalidated by the religious; it means *essential* acting and suffering in relation to men, coordinated with the essential relation to God. But only he who has to do with men essentially can essentially act and suffer in relation to them. If the ethical is the only means by which God communicates with man, then I am forbidden to speak essentially only with God and myself. And so indeed it is. I do not say that it is forbidden to Kierkegaard on his rock, along with the mercy of the Merciful. I say only that it is forbidden to you and to me.

Kierkegaard is deeply conscious of the dubiousness which arises from the negativizing extension of the category of the Single One. "The frightful thing," he writes in his Journal, and we read it, as he wrote it, with fear and trembling, "is that precisely the highest form of piety, to let everything earthly go, can be the highest egoism." Here obviously a distinction is made according to motive, and the idea of egoism used here is an idea of motivation. If we put in its place an objective idea, an idea of a state of affairs, the statement is changed to a still more frightful one: "Precisely what appears to us as the highest form of piety—to let everything earthly go—is the highest egoism."

Is it true that the Single One "corresponds" to God? Does he realize the "image" of God solely by having become a Single One? One thing is lacking for that—and it is the decisive thing.

"Certainly," says Kierkegaard, "God is no egoist, but he is the infinite Ego." Yet thereby too little is said of the God whom we confess—if one dares to say anything at all. He hovers over his creation not as over a chaos; he embraces it. He is the infinite *I* that makes every *It* into his *Thou*.

The Single One corresponds to God when he, in his human way, embraces the bit of the world offered to him as God embraces his creation in his divine way. He realizes the image when, as much as he can in a personal way, he says *Thou* with his being to the beings living round about him.

No one can refute Kierkegaard as well as Kierkegaard himself. Reasoning with and judging himself, he corrects his own spirit from its depths, often before it has uttered its word. In 1843, Kierkegaard enters this unforgettable confession in his Journal: "Had I had faith, I would have remained with Regina." By this he means: "Had I really believed that 'with God all things are possible,' hence also the resolution of this—my melancholy, my powerlessness, my fear, my fateful alienation from woman and from the world— then I would have remained with Regina." But while he means this, he says something else too, namely, that the Single One, if he really believes, and that means if he is really a Single One (which, as we saw, he has become for the one relation of faith), can and may have to do essentially with another. And behind this there lurks the extreme that he who can and may also *ought* to do this. "The only means by which God communicates with man is the ethical." But the ethical in its plain truth means to help God by loving his creation in his creatures, by loving it towards him. For this, to be sure, one must let oneself be helped by him.

"The Single One is the category through which, from the religious standpoint, time and history and the race must pass." What is this "religious standpoint"? One beside others? The standpoint toward God, gained by standing aside from all others? God one object beside other objects, the chosen one beside the rejected ones? God as Regina's successful rival? Is that still God? Is that not merely an object adapted to the religious genius? (Note that I am not speaking of true holiness, for which, as it hallows *everything*, there is no "religious standpoint.") Religious genius? Can there be religious geniuses? Is that not a *contradictio in adjecto?* Can the religious be a specification? "Religious geniuses" are theological geniuses. Their God is the God of the theologians. Admittedly, that is not the God of the philosophers, but neither is it the God of Abraham, Isaac, and Jacob. The God of the theologians, too, is a logicized God, and so is the God even of a theology which will speak only dialectically and makes light of the principle of contradiction. So long as they practise theology, they do not get away from religion as a specification. When Pascal, in a volcanic hour, made that stammering distinction between God and God, he was no genius but a man experiencing the primal glow of faith; at other times, however, he was a theological genius, and dwelt in a specifying religion, out of which the happening of that hour had lifted him.

Religion as a specification misses its mark. God is not an object beside objects, and hence cannot be reached by renunciation of objects. God is, indeed, not the cosmos, but even less is he being *minus* cosmos. He is not to be found by subtraction, and not to be loved by reduction.

THE SINGLE ONE AND THE BODY POLITIC

Kierkegaard's thought circles round the fact that he essentially renounced an essential relation to a definite person. He did not resign this casually, or in the relativity of the many experiences and decisions of life, or with the soul alone, but essentially. The essential nature of his renunciation, its downright positive essentiality, is what he wants to express by saying: "In defiance of the whole nineteenth century, I cannot marry." The renunciation becomes essential through its representing in concrete biography the renunciation of an essential relation to the world as that which hinders being alone before God. Moreover, as I have already said, this does not happen just once, as when a man enters a monastery and thereby cuts himself off from the world and lives outside it; it is peculiarly enduring: the renunciation becomes the center of a spiritual coordinate system whose every point is determined in relation to this point. It is in this way that the system receives its true existential character, by means of which it has given the impulse to a new philosophy and a new theology. And certainly, there belongs to this secularly significant concreteness of biography the curiously manifold motivation—

which is undoubtedly legitimate, and is to be found piecemeal in the sound-ings of inwardness—of the renunciation which Kierkegaard expresses di-rectly and indirectly, by suggestion and by concealment. But beyond that, on a closer consideration, it is to be noted that there arises, between the renunciation and an increasingly strong point of view an attitude which is finally expressed with penetrating clarity in the "Two Notes" to the "Report to History," a secret and unexpressed connection important for Kierkegaard and for us.

"The crowd is untruth." "This consideration of life, the Single One, is the truth." "No one is excluded from becoming a Single One except he who excludes himself by wanting to be crowd." And again: " 'The Single One' is the category of the spirit, of spiritual awakening and revival, and is as sharply as possible opposed to politics." The Single One and the crowd, the "spirit" and "politics": this opposition is not to be separated from that in which Kierkegaard enters the world, expressing it symbolically by means of his renunciation.

Kierkegaard does not marry "in defiance of the whole nineteenth century." What he describes as the nineteenth century is the "age of dissolution," the age of which he says that a single man "cannot help it or save it"; he can "only express that it is going under"—going under, if it cannot reach God through the "narrow pass." And Kierkegaard does not marry. In a symbolic action of negation, in defiance of this age, because it is the age of the "crowd" and the age of "politics." Luther married in symbolic action, because he wanted to lead the believing man of his age out of a rigid religious separa-tion—which finally separated him from grace itself—to a life with God in the world. Kierkegaard does not marry (this, of course, is not part of the manifold subjective motivation, but is the objective meaning of the symbol) because he wants to lead the unbelieving man of his age, who is entangled in the crowd, to become single, to the solitary life of faith, to be alone before God. Certainly, "to marry or not to marry" is the representative question when the monastery is in view. If the Single One really must be, as Kierke-gaard thinks, a man who does not have to do essentially with others, then marriage hinders him if he takes it seriously—and if he does not take it seriously, then, in spite of Kierkegaard's remark about Luther, it cannot be understood how he, as an existing person, can be "the truth." For man, with whom alone Kierkegaard is fundamentally concerned, there is the additional factor that in his view woman stands "quite differently from man in a dangerous rapport to finitude." But there is still something special to be made clear at this point.

If one makes a fairly comprehensive survey of the whole labyrinthine structure of Kierkegaard's thought about renunciation, it will be recognized that he is speaking not solely of a hard, hard-won renunciation of life with a person; but in addition, he is speaking of the positively valued renuncia-tion of life with an impersonal being, conditioned by life with a person—an impersonal being, which in the foreground of the happening is called "people," and in the background, "the crowd." This being, however, in its essence—of which Kierkegaard knows or wants to know nothing—rejects these descriptions as caricatures and acknowledges as its true name only that of *res publica,* in English the "body politic." When Kierkegaard says the category of the "Single One" is "as sharply as possible opposed to politics," he obviously means an activity that has essentially lost touch with its origin, the *polis.* But this activity. however degenerate, is one of the decisive manifestations of the body politic. Every degeneration indicates its genus, and in such a way that the degeneration is never related to the genus simply as present to past, but as in a distorted face, the distortion is related to the form persisting beneath it. The body politic, which is sometimes also called the "world," that is, the human world, seeks, knowingly or unknowingly, to realize in its genuine formations the togetherness of men according to creation. The false formations distort, but they cannot eliminate, the eternal origin. Kierkegaard, in his horror of malformation, turns away; but the man who has not ceased to love the human world in all its abasement sees genuine form even today. Supposing that the crowd is untruth, it is only a state of affairs in the body politic; how truth is here related to untruth must be part and parcel of the true question to the Single One, and the warning against the crowd can be only its preface.

From this standpoint, that special matter can be made clear of which I said that it is an additional reason for Kierkegaard's considering marriage to be an impediment. Marriage, essentially understood, brings one into an essential relation to the "world"; more precisely, to the body politic, to its malformation and its genuine form, to its sickness and its health. Marriage, as the decisive union of one with another, confronts one with the body politic and its destiny—man can no longer shirk that confrontation in marriage; he can only prove himself in it or fail. The isolated person, who is unmarried or whose marriage is merely a fiction, can maintain himself in isolation; the "community" of marriage is part of the great community, contributing its own problems to the general problems, bound up with its hope of salvation to the hope of the great being that in its most miserable state is called the crowd. He who "has entered on marriage," who has entered into marriage, has taken in earnest, in the intention of the sacrament, the fact that the other *is,* the fact that I cannot legitimately share in the Present Being without sharing in the being of the other, the fact that I cannot answer the lifelong address of God to me without answering at the same time for the other, the fact that I cannot be answerable without being at the same time answerable for the other as one who is entrusted to me. But in this way, he has decisively entered into relation with otherness; and the basic structure of otherness, in many ways uncanny, but never quite unholy or incapable of being hallowed, in which I and the others who meet me in my life are inwoven, is the body politic. It is to this, into this, that marriage intends to lead us. Kierkegaard himself makes one of his pseudonyms, the "married man" of the *Stages,* express this, though in the style of a lower point of view which is meant to be overcome by a higher. But it is a lower point of view only when trivialized; there is no higher, because to be raised above the situation in which we are set never yields in truth a higher point of view. Marriage is the exemplary bond; it carries us as does no other into the greater bondage, and only as those who are bound can we reach the freedom of the children of God. Expressed with reference to the man: woman certainly stands "in a dangerous rapport to finitude," and finitude is certainly the danger, for nothing threatens us so sharply as the danger that we remain clinging to it. But our hope of salvation is forged on this very danger, for our human way to the infinite leads only through fulfilled finitude.

The Single One is not the man who has to do with God essentially, and only unessentially with others, who is unconditionally concerned with God, and conditionally with the body politic. The Single One is the man for whom the reality of relation with God as an exclusive relation includes and encompasses the possibility of relation with all otherness, and for whom the whole body politic, the reservoir of otherness, offers just enough otherness for him to pass his life with it.

THE SINGLE ONE IN RESPONSIBILITY

I say, therefore, that the Single One, that is, the man living in responsibility, can make even his political decisions properly only from that ground of his being where he is aware of the event as divine speech to him; if he lets the awareness of this ground be choked off by his group, he is refusing to give God an actual reply.

What I am speaking of has nothing to do with "individualism." I do not consider the individual to be either the starting point or the goal of the human world. But I consider the human person to be the irremovable central place of the struggle between the world's movement away from God and its movement toward God. This struggle takes place today to a very great extent in the realm of public life, not between group and group, but within each group. Yet the decisive battles in this realm as well are fought in the depth, in the ground or the groundlessness, of the person.

Our age is intent on escaping from the demanding "ever anew" of such an obligation of responsibility by a flight into a protective "once for all." The last generation's intoxication with freedom has been followed by the present generation's passion for bondage; the untruth of intoxication has been followed by the untruth of hysteria. He alone is true to the one Present Being who knows he is bound to his place—and precisely there free for his proper responsibility. Only those who are bound and free in this way can still produce what can be truly called community. Yet even today, the believing man, if he adheres to something that is presented in a group, may do right to join it. But belonging to it, he must remain submissive with his whole life, therefore with his group life as well, to the One who is his Lord. His responsible decision will thus at times be opposed to, say, a tactical decision of his group. At times, he will be moved to carry the fight for the truth, the human, uncertain-certain truth which is brought forward by the depth of his conscience, into the group itself, and thereby establish or strengthen an inner front within it. This can prove more important for the future of our world than all fronts that are drawn today between groups or between associations of groups; for this front, if it is everywhere upright and strong, may run as a secret unity across all groups.

What the right is none of the groups of today can come to know except through men who belong to them staking their own souls to discover and then reveal it, however bitter, to their companions—charitably if possible, cruelly if must be. Into this fiery furnace, the group plunges time and again, or it dies an inward death.

And if one still asks if one may be certain of finding what is right on this steep path, once again the answer is *no;* there is no certainty. There is only a chance; but there is no other chance but this. The risk does not ensure the truth for us; but it, and it alone, leads us to where the breath of truth is to be felt.

PSYCHEDELICS
AND RELIGIOUS EXPERIENCE

Alan W. Watts

The experiences resulting from the use of psychedelic drugs are often described in religious terms. They are therefore of interest to those like myself who, in the tradition of William James, are concerned with the psychology of religion.[1] For more than thirty years I have been studying the causes, the consequences, and the conditions of those peculiar states of consciousness in which the individual discovers himself to be one continuous process with God, with the Universe, with the Ground of Being, or with whatever name he may use by cultural conditioning or personal preference for the ultimate and eternal reality. We have no satisfactory and definitive name for experiences of this kind. The terms "religious experience," "mystical experience," and "cosmic consciousness" are all too vague and comprehensive to denote that specific mode of consciousness which, to those who have known it, is as real and overwhelming as falling in love. This article describes such states of consciousness as and when induced by psychedelic drugs, although they are virtually indistinguishable from genuine mystical experiences. It then discusses objections to the use of psychedelic drugs which arise mainly from the opposition between mystical values and the traditional religious and secular values of western society.

PSYCHEDELICS AND RELIGIOUS EXPERIENCE From the *California Law Review*, Vol. 56, No. 100. Copyright, ©, 1968, California Law Review, Inc. Reprinted by permission.
[1] James, William: *The Varieties of Religious Experience: A Study of Human Nature* (Longmans, Green & Co., New York, New York) 1911.

THE PSYCHEDELIC EXPERIENCE

The idea of mystical experiences resulting from drug use is not readily accepted in western societies. Western culture has, historically, a particular fascination with the value and virtue of man as an individual, self-determining, responsible ego, controlling himself and his world by the power of conscious effort and will. Nothing, then, could be more repugnant to this cultural tradition than the notion of spiritual or psychological growth through the use of drugs. A "drugged" person is by definition dimmed in consciousness, fogged in judgment, and deprived of will. But not all psychotropic (consciousness-changing) chemicals are narcotic and soporific, as are alcohol, opiates, and barbiturates. The effects of what are now called psychedelic (mind-manifesting) chemicals differ from those of alcohol as laughter differs from rage or delight from depression. There is really no analogy between being "high" on LSD and "drunk" on bourbon. True, no one in either state should drive a car, but neither should one drive while reading a book, playing a violin, or making love. Certain creative activities and states of mind demand a concentration and devotion which are simply incompatible with piloting a death-dealing engine along a highway.

I myself have experimented with five of the principal psychedelics: LSD-25, mescaline, psilocybin, dimethyl-tryptamine (DMT), and cannabis. I have done so, as William James tried nitrous oxide, to see if they could help me in identifying what might be called the "essential" or "active" ingredients of the mystical experience. For almost all the classical literature on mysticism is vague, not only in describing the experience, but also in showing rational connections between the experience itself and the various traditional methods recommended to induce it—fasting, concentration, breathing exercises, prayers, incantations, and dances. A traditional master of Zen or Yoga, when asked why such-and-such practices lead or predispose one to the mystical experience, always responds, "This is the way my teacher gave it to me. This is the way I found out. If you're seriously interested, try it for yourself." This answer hardly satisfies an impertinent, scientifically minded, and intellectually curious westerner. It reminds him of archaic medical prescriptions compounding five salamanders, powdered gallowsrope, three boiled bats, a scruple of phosphorus, three pinches of henbane, and a dollop of dragon dung dropped when the moon was in Pisces. Maybe it worked, but what was the essential ingredient?

It struck me, therefore, that if any of the psychedelic chemicals would in fact predispose my consciousness to the mystical experience, I could use them as instruments for studying and describing that experience as one uses a microscope for bacteriology, even though the microscope is an "artificial" and "unnatural" contrivance which might be said to "distort" the vision of the naked eye. However, when I was first invited to test the mystical qualities of LSD-25 by Dr. Keith Ditman of the Neuropsychiatric Clinic at the UCLA Medical School, I was unwilling to believe that any mere chemical could induce a genuine mystical experience. At most it might bring about a state of spiritual insight analogous to swimming with water wings. Indeed, my first experiment with LSD-25 was not mystical. It was an intensely interesting aesthetic and intellectual experience which challenged my powers of analysis and careful description to the utmost.

Some months later, in 1959, I tried LSD-25 again with Dr. Sterling Bunnell and Dr. Michael Agron, who were then associated with the Langley-Porter Clinic in San Francisco. In the course of two experiments I was amazed and somewhat embarrassed to find myself going through states of consciousness which corresponded precisely with every description of major mystical experiences that I had ever read.[2] Furthermore, they exceeded both in depth and in a peculiar quality of unexpectedness the three "natural and spontaneous" experiences of this kind which had happened to me in previous years.

Through subsequent experimentation with LSD-25 and the other chemicals named above (with the exception of DMT, which I find amusing but relatively uninteresting) I found I could move with ease into the state of "cosmic consciousness," and in due course became less and less dependent on the chemicals themselves for "tuning-in" to this particular wave length of experience. Of the five psychedelics tried, I found that LSD-25 and cannabis suited my purposes best. Of these two, the latter, which I had to use abroad in countries where it is not outlawed, proved to be the better. It does not induce bizarre alterations of sensory perception, and medical studies indicate that it may not, save in great excess, have the dangerous side effects of LSD, namely chromosomal damage and possible psychotic episodes.

For the purposes of this study, in describing my experiences with psychedelic drugs, I avoid the occasional and incidental bizarre alterations of sense perception which psychedelic chemicals may induce. I am concerned, rather, with the fundamental alterations of the normal, socially induced consciousness of one's own existence and relation to the external world. I am trying to delineate the basic principles of psychedelic awareness. But I must add that I can speak only for myself. The quality of these experiences depends considerably upon one's prior orientation and attitude to life, although the now voluminous descriptive literature of these experiences accords quite remarkably with my own.

Almost invariably, my experiments with psychedelics have had four dominant characteristics. I shall try to explain them—in the expectation that the reader will say, at least of the second and third, "Why, that's obvious! No one needs a drug to see that." Quite so, but every insight has degrees of intensity. There can be obvious$_1$ and obvious$_2$—and the latter comes on with shattering clarity, manifesting its implications in every sphere and dimension of our existence.

The first characteristic is a slowing down of time, a *concentration in the present*. One's normally compulsive concern for the future decreases, and one becomes aware of the enormous importance and interest of what is happening at the moment. Other people, going about their business on the

[2] Johnson, Raynor Carey: *Watcher on the Hills* (Hodder & Stoughton, Ltd, London, England) 1959. An excellent anthology of mystical experiences.

streets, seem to be slightly crazy, failing to realize that the whole point of life is to be fully aware of it as it happens. One therefore relaxes, almost luxuriously, into studying the colors in a glass of water, or in listening to the now highly articulate vibration of every note played on an oboe or sung by voice.

From the pragmatic standpoint of our culture, such an attitude is very bad for business. It might lead to improvidence, lack of foresight, diminished sales of insurance policies, and abandoned savings accounts. Yet this is just the corrective that our culture needs. No one is more fatuously impractical than the "successful" executive who spends his whole life absorbed in frantic paperwork with the objective of retiring in comfort at sixty-five, when it will all be too late. Only those who have cultivated the art of living completely in the present have any use for making plans for the future, for when the plans mature they will be able to enjoy the results. "Tomorrow never comes." I have never yet heard a preacher urging his congregation to practice that section of the Sermon on the Mount which begins, "Be not anxious for the morrow. . . ." The truth is that people who live for the future are, as we say of the insane, "not quite all there"—or here; by overeagerness they are perpetually missing the point. Foresight is bought at the price of anxiety, and, when overused it destroys all its own advantages.

The second characteristic I will call *awareness of polarity*. This is the vivid realization that states, things, and events which we ordinarily call opposite are interdependent, like back and front or the poles of a magnet. By polar awareness one sees that things which are explicitly different are implicitly one: self and other, subject and object, left and right, male and female—and then, a little more surprisingly, solid and space, figure and background, pulse and interval, saints and sinners, police and criminals, and in-groups and out-groups. Each is definable only in terms of the other, and they go together transactionally, like buying and selling, for there is no sale without a purchase, and no purchase without a sale. As this awareness becomes increasingly intense, you feel that you yourself are polarized with the external universe in such a way that you imply each other. Your push is its pull, and its push is your pull, as when you move the steering wheel of a car. Are you pushing it or pulling it?

At first, this is a very odd sensation, not unlike hearing your own voice played back to you on an electronic system immediately after you have spoken. You become confused, and wait for it to go on! Similarly, you feel that you are something being done by the universe, yet that the universe is equally something being done by you, which is true, at least in the neurological sense that the peculiar structure of our brains translates the sun into light and air vibrations into sound. Our normal sensation of relationship to the outside world is that sometimes I push it, and sometimes it pushes me. But if the two are actually one, where does action begin and responsibility rest? If the universe is doing me, how can I be sure that, two seconds hence, I will still remember the English language? If I am doing it, how can I be sure that, two seconds hence, my brain will know how to turn the sun into light? From such unfamiliar sensations as these the psychedelic experience can generate confusion, paranoia, and terror, even though the individual is feeling his relationship to the world exactly as it would be described by a biologist, ecologist, or physicist, for he is feeling himself as the unified field of organism and environment.

The third characteristic, arising from the second, is *awareness of relativity.* I see that I am a link in an infinite hierarchy of processes and beings, ranging from molecules through bacteria and insects to human beings, and, maybe, to angels and gods—a hierarchy in which every level is in effect the same situation. For example, the poor man worries about money while the rich man worries about his health; the worry is the same, but the difference is in its substance or dimension. I realize that fruit flies must think of themselves as people, because, like ourselves, they find themselves in the middle of their own world, with immeasurably greater things above and smaller things below. To us, they all look alike and seem to have no personality—as do the Chinese when we have not lived among them. Yet fruit flies must see just as many subtle distinctions among themselves as we among ourselves.

From this it is but a short step to the realization that all forms of life and being are simply variations on a single theme; we are all in fact one being doing the same thing in as many different ways as possible. As the French proverb goes, *plus ça change, plus c'est la même chose*—"the more it varies, the more it is one." I see, further, that feeling threatened by the inevitability of death is really the same experience as feeling alive, and that as all beings are feeling this everywhere, they are all just as much "I" as myself. Yet the "I" feeling, to be felt at all, must always be a sensation relative to the "other" —to something beyond its control and experience. To be at all, it must begin and end. But the intellectual jump which mystical and psychedelic experience makes here is in enabling you to see that all these myriad I-centers are yourself—not, indeed, your personal and superficially conscious ego, but what Hindus call the *paramatman,* the Self of all selves.

[Thus Hinduism regards the universe, not as an artifact, but as an immense drama in which the One Actor (the *paramatman* or *brahman*) plays all the parts, which are his (or "its") masks or *personae.* The sensation of being only this one particular self, John Doe, is due to the Actor's total absorption in playing this and every other part. For fuller exposition, see [6; 10:355–463; 8].]

As the retina enables us to see countless pulses of energy as a single light, so the mystical experience shows us innumerable individuals as a single Self.

The fourth characteristic is *awareness of eternal energy,* often in the form of intense white light, which seems to be both the current in your nerves and that mysterious *e* which equals mc^2. This may sound like megalomania or delusion of grandeur, but one sees quite clearly that all existence is a single energy, and that this energy is one's own being. Of course there is death as well as life, because energy is a pulsation, and just as waves must have both crests and troughs the experience of existing must go on and off. Basically, therefore, there is simply nothing to worry about, because you yourself are the eternal energy of the universe playing hide-and-seek (off-and-on) with itself. At root, you are the Godhead, for God is all that there is. Quoting

Isaiah just a little out of context: "I am the Lord, and there is none else. I form the light and create the darkness: I make peace, and create evil. I, the Lord, do all these things." [3] This is the sense of the fundamental tenet of Hinduism: *Tat tvam asi*—"THAT (i.e., "that subtle Being of which this whole universe is composed") art thou." [4] A classical case of this experience from the west is in Tennyson's *Memoirs*:

A kind of waking trance I have frequently had, quite up from boyhood, when I have been all alone. This has generally come upon me thro' repeating my own name two or three times to myself silently, till all at once, as it were out of the intensity of the consciousness of individuality, the individuality itself seemed to dissolve and fade away into boundless being, and this not a confused state, but the clearest of the clearest, the surest of the surest, the weirdest of the weirdest, utterly beyond words, where death was an almost laughable impossibility, the loss of personality (if so it were) seeming no extinction but the only true life [7:320].

Obviously, these characteristics of the psychedelic experience, as I have known it, are aspects of a single state of consciousness, for I have been describing the same thing from different angles. The descriptions attempt to convey the reality of the experience, but in doing so they also suggest some of the inconsistencies between such experience and the current values of society.

OPPOSITION TO PSYCHEDELIC DRUGS

Resistance to allowing use of psychedelic drugs originates in both religious and secular values. The difficulty in describing psychedelic experiences in traditional religious terms suggests one ground of opposition. The westerner must borrow such words as *samadhi* or *moksha* from the Hindus, or *satori* or *kensho* from the Japanese, to describe the experience of oneness with the universe. We have no appropriate word because our own Jewish and Christian theologies will not accept the idea that man's inmost self can be identical with the Godhead, even though Christians may insist that this was true in the unique instance of Jesus Christ. Jews and Christians think of God in political and monarchical terms, as the supreme governor of the universe, the ultimate boss. Obviously, it is both socially unacceptable and logically preposterous for a particular individual to claim that he, in person, is the omnipotent and omniscient ruler of the world, to be accorded suitable recognition and honor.

Such an imperial and kingly concept of the ultimate reality, however, is neither necessary nor universal. The Hindus and the Chinese have no difficulty in conceiving of an identity of the self and the Godhead. For most Asians, other than Muslims, the Godhead moves and manifests the world in much the same way that a centipede manipulates a hundred legs—spontaneously, without deliberation or calculation. In other words, they

[3] Isaiah 45:6, 7.
[4] *Chandogya Upanishad* 6.15.3.

conceive the universe by analogy with an organism as distinct from a mecha-nism. They do not see it as an artifact or construct under the conscious di-rection of some supreme technician, engineer, or achitect.

If, however, in the context of Christian or Jewish tradition an individual declares himself to be one with God, he must be dubbed blasphemous (sub-versive) or insane. Such a mystical experience is a clear threat to traditional religious concepts. The Judaeo-Christian tradition has a monarchical image of God, and monarchs, who rule by force, fear nothing more than insubordi-nation. The church has therefore always been highly suspicious of mystics because they seem to be insubordinate and to claim equality or, worse, identity with God. For this reason John Scotus Erigena and Meister Eckhart were condemned as heretics. This was also why the Quakers faced opposition for their doctrine of the Inward Light, and for their refusal to remove hats in church and in court. A few occasional mystics may be all right so long as they watch their language, like St. Teresa of Avila and St. John of the Cross, who maintained, shall we say, a meta-physical distance of respect between themselves and their heavenly King. Nothing, however, could be more alarm-ing to the ecclesiastical hierarchy than a popular outbreak of mysticism, for this might well amount to setting up a democracy in the kingdom of heaven —and such alarm would be shared equally by Catholics, Jews, and funda-mentalist Protestants.

The monarchical image of God with its implicit distaste for religious in-subordination has a more pervasive impact than many Christians might admit. The thrones of kings have walls immediately behind them, and all who present themselves at court must prostrate themselves or kneel because this is an awkward position from which to make a sudden attack. It has per-haps never occurred to Christians that when they design a church on the model of a royal court (basilica) and prescribe church ritual, they are imply-ing that God, like a human monarch, is afraid. This is also implied by flattery in prayers:

O Lord our heavenly Father, high and mighty, King of kings, Lord of lords, the only Ruler of princes, who dost from thy throne behold all the dwellers upon earth: most heartily we beseech thee with thy favor to behold . . .[5]

The western man who claims consciousness of oneness with God or the universe thus clashes with his society's concept of religion. In most Asian cultures, however, such a man will be congratulated as having penetrated the true secret of life. He has arrived, by chance, or by some such discipline as Yoga or Zen meditation, at a state of consciousness in which he experiences directly and vividly what our own scientists know to be true in theory. For the ecologist, the biologist, and the physicist know (but seldom feel) that every organism constitutes a single field of behavior, or process, with its en-vironment. There is no way of separating what any given organism is doing from what its environment is doing, for which reason ecologists speak not

[5] *Book of Common Prayer*, Order for Morning Prayer, A Prayer for the King's Majesty (Church of England) 1904.

of organisms in environments but of organism-environments. Thus the words "I" or "self" should properly mean what the whole universe is doing at this particular "here-and-now" called John Doe.

The kingly concept of God makes identity of self and God or self and universe inconceivable in western religious terms. The difference between Eastern and Western concepts of man and his universe, however, extends beyond strictly religious concepts. The western scientist may rationally perceive the idea of organism-environment, but he does not ordinarily *feel* this to be true. By cultural and social conditioning, he has been hypnotized into experiencing himself as an ego—as an isolated center of consciousness and will inside a bag of skin, confronting an external and alien world. We say, "I came into this world." But we did nothing of the kind. We came *out* of it in just the same way that fruit comes out of trees. Our galaxy, our cosmos, "peoples" in the same way that an apple tree "apples."

Such a vision of the universe clashes with the idea of a monarchical God, with the concept of the separate ego, and even with the secular, atheist-agnostic mentality, which derives its common sense from the mythology of nineteenth century scientism. According to this view, the universe is a mindless mechanism and man a sort of accidental micro-organism infesting a minute globular rock which revolves about an unimportant star on the outer fringe of one of the minor galaxies. This "put-down" theory of man is extremely common among such quasi-scientists as sociologists, psychologists, and psychiatrists, most of whom are still thinking of the world in terms of Newtonian mechanics, and have never really caught up with the ideas of Einstein and Bohr, Oppenheimer and Schrödinger. Thus to the ordinary institutional-type psychiatrist, any patient who gives the least hint of mystical or religious experience is automatically diagnosed as deranged. From the standpoint of the mechanistic religion he is a heretic and is given electroshock therapy as an up-to-date form of the thumbscrew and rack. And, incidentally, it is just this kind of quasi-scientist who, as a consultant to government and law enforcement agencies, dictates official policies on the use of psychedelic chemicals.

Inability to accept the mystical experience is more than an intellectual handicap. Lack of awareness of the basic unity of organism and environment is a serious and dangerous hallucination. For in a civilization equipped with immense technological power, the sense of alienation between man and nature leads to the use of technology in a hostile spirit—to the "conquest" of nature instead of intelligent cooperation with nature. The result is that we are eroding and destroying our environment, spreading Los Angelization instead of civilization. This is the major threat overhanging western, technological culture, and no amount of reasoning or doom-preaching seems to help. We simply do not respond to the prophetic and moralizing techniques of conversion upon which Jews and Christians have always relied. But people have an obscure sense of what is good for them—call it "unconscious self-healing," "survival instinct," "positive growth potential," or what you will. Among the educated young there is therefore a startling and unprecedented interest in the transformation of human consciousness. All over the western world publishers are selling millions of books dealing with Yoga, Vedanta, Zen Buddhism, and the chemical mysticism of psychedelic drugs, and I have come to believe that the whole "hip" subculture, however misguided in some of its manifestations, is the earnest and responsible effort of young people to correct the self-destroying course of industrial civilization.

The content of the mystical experience is thus inconsistent with both the religious and secular concepts of traditional western thought. Moreover, mystical experiences often result in attitudes which threaten the authority not only of established churches, but also of secular society. Unafraid of death and deficient in worldly ambition, those who have undergone mystical experiences are impervious to threats and promises. In addition, their sense of the relativity of good and evil arouses the suspicion that they lack both conscience and respect for law. Use of psychedelics in the United States by a literate bourgeoisie means that an important segment of the population is indifferent to society's traditional rewards and sanctions.

In theory, the existence within our secular society of a group which does not accept conventional values is consistent with our political vision. But one of the great problems of the United States, legally and politically, is that we have never quite had the courage of our convictions. The Republic is founded on the marvelously sane principle that a human community can exist and prosper only on a basis of mutual trust. Metaphysically, the American Revolution was a rejection of the dogma of original sin, which is the notion that because you cannot trust yourself or other people, there must be some superior authority to keep us all in order. The dogma was rejected because if it is true that we cannot trust ourselves and others, it follows that we cannot trust the superior authority which we ourselves conceive and obey and that the very idea of our own untrustworthiness is unreliable!

Citizens of the United States believe, or are supposed to believe, that a republic is the best form of government. Yet vast confusion arises from trying to be republican in politics and monarchist in religion. How can a republic be the best form of government if the universe, heaven, and hell are a monarchy?

[Thus, until quite recently, belief in a Supreme Being was a legal test of valid conscientious objection to military service. The implication was that the individual objector found hmself bound to obey a higher echelon of command than the President and Congress. The analogy is military and monarchical, and therefore objectors who, as Buddhists or naturalists, held an organic theory of the universe often had difficulty in obtaining recognition.]

Thus, despite the theory of government by consent, based upon mutual trust, the peoples of the United States retain, from the authoritarian backgrounds of their religions or national origins, an utterly naive faith in law as some sort of supernatural and paternalistic power. "There ought to be a law against it!" Our law enforcement officers are therefore confused, hindered, and bewildered—not to mention corrupted—by being asked to enforce sumptuary laws, often of ecclesiastical origin, which vast numbers of people have no intention of obeying and which, in any case, are immensely difficult or simply impossible to enforce—for example, the barring of anything so un-detectable as LSD-25 from international and interstate commerce.

Finally, there are two specific objections to the use of psychedelic drugs. First, this use may be dangerous. However, every worthwhile exploration is dangerous—climbing mountains, testing aircraft, rocketing into outer space, skin-diving, or collecting botanical specimens in jungles. But if you value knowledge and the actual delight of exploration more than mere duration of uneventful life, you are willing to take the risks. It is not really healthy for monks to practice fasting, and it was hardly hygienic for Jesus to get himself crucified, but these are risks taken in the course of spiritual adventures. To-day the adventurous young are taking risks in exploring the psyche, testing their mettle at the task just as, in times past, they have tested it—more vio-lently—in hunting, dueling, hot-rod racing, and playing football. What they need is not prohibitions and policemen but the most intelligent encourage-ment and advice that can be found.

Second, drug use may be criticized as an escape from reality. However this criticism assumes unjustly that the mystical experiences themselves are escapist or unreal. LSD, in particular, is by no means a soft and cushy escape from reality. It can very easily be an experience in which you have to test your soul against all the devils in hell. For me, it has been at times an ex-perience in which I was at once completely lost in the corridors of the mind and yet relating that very lostness to the exact order of logic and language, simultaneously very mad and very sane. But beyond these occasional lost and insane episodes, there are the experiences of the world as a system of total harmony and glory, and the discipline of relating these to the order of logic and language must somehow explain how what William Blake called that "energy which is eternal delight" can consist with the misery and suffering of everyday life.[6]

The undoubted mystical and religious intent of most users of the psyche-delic drugs, even if some of these substances should be proved injurious to physical health, requires that their free and responsible use be exempt from legal restraint in any republic which maintains a constitutional separation of church and state.

["Responsible" in the sense that such substances be taken by or administered to consenting adults only. The user of cannabis, in particular, is apt to have peculiar difficulties in establishing his "undoubted mystical and religious intent" in court. Having committed so loathsome and serious a felony, his chances of clemency are better if he assumes a repentant demeanor, which is quite inconsistent with the sin-cere belief that his use of cannabis was religious. On the other hand, if he insists unrepentantly that he looks upon such use as a religious sacrament, many judges will declare that they "dislike his attitude," finding it truculent and lacking in appreciation of the gravity of the crime, and the sentence will be that much harsher. The accused is therefore put in a "double-bind" situation in which he is "damned if he does, and damned if he doesn't." Furthermore, religious integrity—as in con-scientious objection—is generally tested and established by membership in some

[6] Watts, Alan: The Joyous Cosmology: Adventures in the Chemistry of Consciousness (Pantheon Books, New York, New York) 1962.

church or religious organization with a substantial following. But the felonious status of cannabis is such that grave suspicion would be cast upon all individuals forming such an organization, and the test cannot therefore be fulfilled. It is generally forgotten that our guarantees of religious freedom were designed to protect precisely those who were *not* members of established denominations, but rather such screwball and (then) subversive individuals as Quakers, Shakers, Levellers, and Anabaptists. There is little question that those who use cannabis, or other psychedelics, with religious intent are now members of a persecuted religion which appears to the rest of society as a grave menace to "mental health," as distinct from the old-fashioned "immortal soul." But it's the same old story.]

To the extent that mystical experience conforms with the tradition of genuine religious involvement, and to the extent that psychedelics induce that experience, users are entitled to some constitutional protection. Also, to the extent that research in the psychology of religion can utilize such drugs, students of the human mind must be free to use them. Under the present laws, I, as an experienced student of the psychology of religion, can no longer pursue research in the field. This is a barbarous restriction of spiritual and intellectual freedom, suggesting that the legal system of the United States is, after all, in tacit alliance with the monarchical theory of the universe, and will, therefore, prohibit and persecute religious ideas and practices based on an organic and unitary vision of the universe.

[Amerindians belonging to the Native American Church, who employ the psychedelic peyote cactus in their rituals, are firmly opposed to any government control of this plant, even if they should be guaranteed the right to its use. They feel that peyote is a natural gift of God to mankind, and especially to natives of the land where it grows, and that no government has a right to interfere with its use. The same argument might be made on behalf of cannabis, or the mushroom *psilocybe mexicana Heim*. All these things are natural plants, not processed or synthesized drugs, and by what authority can individuals be prevented from eating them? There is no law against eating or growing the mushroom *amanita pantherina*, even though it is fatally poisonous and only experts can distinguish it from a common edible mushroom. This case can be made even from the standpoint of believers in the monarchical universe of Judaism and Christianity, for it is a basic principle of both religions, derived from Genesis, that all natural substances created by God are inherently good, and that evil can arise only in their misuse. Thus laws against mere possession, or even cultivation, of these plants are in basic conflict with Biblical principles. Criminal conviction of those who employ these plants should be based on proven misuse. "And God said, 'Behold, I have given you *every* herb bearing seed, which is upon the face of all the earth, and every tree, in the which is the fruit of a tree yielding seed; to you it shall be for meat.' . . . And God saw every thing that he had made, and, behold, it was very good" [Genesis 1:29, 31].]

From FOR THE TIME BEING
A Christmas Oratorio

W. H. Auden

IV

RECITATIVE

If the muscle can feel repugnance, there is still a false move to be made;
If the mind can imagine tomorrow, there is still a defeat to remember;
As long as the self can say "I," it is impossible not to rebel;
As long as there is an accidental virtue, there is a necessary vice:
And the garden cannot exist, the miracle cannot occur.

For the garden is the only place there is, but you will not find it
Until you have looked for it everywhere and found nowhere that is not a
    desert;
The miracle is the only thing that happens, but to you it will not be
    apparent,
Until all events have been studied and nothing happens that you cannot
    explain;
And life is the destiny you are bound to refuse until you have consented to
    die.

Therefore, see without looking, hear without listening, breathe without ask-
    ing:
The Inevitable is what will seem to happen to you purely by chance;
The Real is what will strike you as really absurd;
Unless you are certain you are dreaming, it is certainly a dream of your own;
Unless you exclaim—"There must be some mistake"—you must be mistaken.

.   .   .   .   .   .

III

FUGAL-CHORUS

Great is Caesar: He has conquered Seven Kingdoms.
The First was the Kingdom of Abstract Idea:
Last night it was Tom, Dick and Harry; tonight it is S's with P's;
Instead of inflexions and accents
There are prepositions and word-order;

Instead of aboriginal objects excluding each other
There are specimens reiterating a type;
Instead of wood-nymphs and river-demons,
There is one unconditioned ground of Being.
Great is Caesar: God must be with Him.

Great is Caesar: He has conquered Seven Kingdoms.
The Second was the Kingdom of Natural Cause:
Last night it was Sixes and Sevens; tonight it is One and Two;
Instead of saying, "Strange are the whims of the Strong,"
We say, "Harsh is the Law but it is certain";
Instead of building temples, we build laboratories;
Instead of offering sacrifices, we perform experiments;
Instead of reciting prayers, we note pointer-readings;
Our lives are no longer erratic but efficient.
Great is Caesar: God must be with Him.

Great is Caesar; He has conquered Seven Kingdoms.
The Third was the Kingdom of Infinite Number:
Last night it was Rule-of-Thumb, tonight it is To-a-T;
Instead of Quite-a-lot, there is Exactly-so-many;
Instead of Only-a-few, there is Just-these;
Instead of saying, "You must wait until I have counted,"
We say, "Here you are. You will find this answer correct";
Instead of a nodding acquaintance with a few integers
The Transcendentals are our personal friends.
Great is Caesar: God must be with Him.

Great is Caesar: He has conquered Seven Kingdoms.
The Fourth was the Kingdom of Credit Exchange:
Last night it was Tit-for-Tat, tonight it is C.O.D.;
When we have a surplus, we need not meet someone with a deficit;
When we have a deficit, we need not meet someone with a surplus;
Instead of heavy treasures, there are paper symbols of value;
Instead of Pay at Once, there is Pay when you can;
Instead of My Neighbor, there is Our Customers;
Instead of Country Fair, there is World Market.
Great is Caesar: God must be with Him.

Great is Caesar; He has conquered Seven Kingdoms.
The Fifth was the Kingdom of Inorganic Giants:
Last night it was Heave-Ho, tonight it is Whee-Spree;
When we want anything, They make it;
When we dislike anything, They change it;
When we want to go anywhere, They carry us;
When the Barbarian invades us, They raise immovable shields:
When we invade the Barbarian, They brandish irresistible swords;

Fate is no longer a fiat of Matter, but a freedom of Mind.
Great is Caesar: God must be with Him.

Great is Caesar: He has conquered Seven Kingdoms.
The Sixth was the Kingdom of Organic Dwarfs:
Last night it was Ouch-Ouch, tonight it is Yum-Yum;
When diseases waylay us, They strike them dead;
When worries intrude on us, They throw them out;
When pain accosts us, They save us from embarrassment;
When we feel like sheep, They make us lions;
When we feel like geldings, They make us stallions;
Spirit is no longer under Flesh, but on top.
Great is Caesar: God must be with Him.

Great is Caesar: He has conquered Seven Kingdoms.
The Seventh was the Kingdom of Popular Soul:
Last night it was Order-Order, tonight it is Hear-Hear;
When he says, You are happy, we laugh;
When he says, You are wretched, we cry;
When he says, It is true, everyone believes it;
When he says, It is false, no one believes it;
When he says, This is good, this is loved;
When he says, That is bad, that is hated.
Great is Caesar: God must be with Him.

.   .   .   .   .

III

NARRATOR

Well, so that is that. Now we must dismantle the tree,
Putting the decorations back into their cardboard boxes—
Some have got broken—and carrying them up to the attic.
The holly and the mistletoe must be taken down and burnt,
And the children got ready for school. There are enough
Left-overs to do, warmed-up, for the rest of the week—
Not that we have much appetite, having drunk such a lot,
Stayed up so late, attempted—quite unsuccessfully—
To love all of our relatives, and in general
Grossly overestimated our powers. Once again
As in previous years we have seen the actual Vision and failed
To do more than entertain it as an agreeable
Possibility, once again we have sent Him away,
Begging though to remain His disobedient servant,
The promising child who cannot keep His word for long.
The Christmas Feast is already a fading memory,
And already the mind begins to be vaguely aware

Of an unpleasant whiff of apprehension at the thought
Of Lent and Good Friday which cannot, after all, now
Be very far off. But, for the time being, here we all are,
Back in the moderate Aristotelian city
Of darning and the Eight-Fifteen, where Euclid's geometry
And Newton's mechanics would account for our experience,
And the kitchen table exists because I scrub it.
It seems to have shrunk during the holidays. The streets
Are much narrower than we remembered; we had forgotten
The office was as depressing as this. To those who have seen
The Child, however dimly, however incredulously,
The Time Being is, in a sense, the most trying time of all.
For the innocent children who whispered so excitedly
Outside the locked door where they knew the presents to be
Grew up when it opened. Now, recollecting that moment
We can repress the joy, but the guilt remains conscious;
Remembering the stable where for once in our lives
Everything became a You and nothing was an It.
And craving the sensation but ignoring the cause,
We look round for something, no matter what, to inhibit
Our self-reflection, and the obvious thing for that purpose
Would be some great suffering. So, once we have met the Son,
We are tempted ever after to pray to the Father;
"Lead us into temptation and evil for our sake."
They will come, all right, don't worry; probably in a form
That we do not expect, and certainly with a force
More dreadful than we can imagine. In the meantime
There are bills to be paid, machines to keep in repair,
Irregular verbs to learn, the Time Being to redeem
From insignificance. The happy morning is over,
The night of agony still to come; the time is noon:
When the Spirit must practice his scales of rejoicing
Without even a hostile audience, and the Soul endure
A silence that is neither for nor against her faith
That God's Will will be done, that, in spite of her prayers,
God will cheat no one, not even the world of its triumph.

Outsiders

EDITED BY ROBERT COLES

INTRODUCTION

As Dante knew so well, there are many kinds of hell, something that ought to be stated right off in an introduction to selections that generally aim to describe what it is like to be different, to be an outsider, to be scorned and refused and ignored and badly treated. One does not have to be poor or black to feel bad about things, about life, about oneself. A child who has everything—at least everything that rich, well-born and well-educated parents have to offer—can in fact feel bewildered, lost, sad, and badly out of sorts even if not the kind of outsider Dr. Martin Luther King, Jr., or Harry Caudill describe in the following essays.

So suffering knows no barriers; suffering crosses the color line, and transcends man-made distinctions of class, caste, and nation. On the other hand, there is no point in only saying that we all are outside some circle and inside another, or that each of us has his memories, in Thomas Mann's phrase, of "disorder and early sorrow." The point is to recognize what all men share and at the same time to come to understand those special hells that men inflict arbitrarily on other men—whose skin is this color rather than that, whose home is here and not there, whose tongue is foreign and not native. And the point is also to make that recognition without losing sight of something else: how poor men, ailing men, insulted men, also persist, make do, cling tenaciously to life, and, as much as possible, endure if not prevail. The moral strength that Faulkner claimed for all humble but decent men, and particularly for his black neighbors, has to be remembered whenever abstractions like "racism" or "prejudice" are discussed—because it is all too easy to lose all perspective and demonstrate an outrageous kind of arrogance and condescension under cover of sympathy, pity, analysis, scholarship, whatever.

"We're more than some of those people say we are," I once heard a Southern tenant farmer insist. He was not talking about segregationists, about Klansmen and racist politicians, but about some students who had just arrived on the scene and, at a meeting in a church, had taken it upon themselves to say (in a worldly, oh so knowing way) this, that, and, it seemed, everything: "We are down here to help you become free. It's time you became citizens—with the right to vote and have a job and be accepted by people. For too long you've had nothing while everyone else in America has a lot. We're here to work for you, and keep on working until you have the dignity you deserve—and a lot of other things you don't have now. We're here to make your lives better, to help you move from nothing to something, to overcome, to *be* someone."

All well and good, and yet that tenant farmer and others there felt vaguely (and not so vaguely) troubled: "It's true, we don't have a whole lot of things," he said, "but I don't like it said that we're so bad that we're the lowest on the whole earth. We have our life here, and it may be hard, but we do the best we can, and we can say when we're getting ready to die that we've tried, every day we've tried; and we've had our good times, too—yes, sir, we have, no matter what they tell you, the outside people."

How ironic—that "outside people," desperately intent on helping that man and others like him, should be seen as confused and a bit wrong-headed by people who have everything to gain and very little to lose from any intervention, any protest, whether awkward and graceless or not. The fact is, though, that such encounters—between the outsider and his would-be benefactors, between victims and those who would join them to fight the oppressor—are not uncommon.

On the pages that follow, the millions who are outsiders here in the United States are summoned forth by writers who have known them and tried to tell what their fate is—as American citizens alive in the twentieth century, which is the second century of the world's most powerful democracy. More than poverty binds together sharecroppers and migrant farmers and Appalachian families and Mexican-Americans by the thousands and Indians all over the country. Such people lack not only money but probably too a sense of participation (of the most elementary and unself-conscious kind) in the nation's day-to-day life. Most "insiders" forget how very involved they are—involved in all sorts of issues and problems. They read newspapers and magazines and books, worry over a wide assortment of problems, favor some developments and oppose others, have opinions and ideas and hopes that are tied not only to their concrete, immediate lives, but to the wider world of a city, a state, a region, a nation, and even (particularly in this century) the entire world. For the people who come alive in the following essays, life is far different. Time becomes a matter of the next meal rather than so-and-so's Presidency or the future after college. Space has to do with getting water (in the country) or dodging rats in alleys (in city ghettos) rather than taking relaxed walks or finding a new and enjoyable restaurant. As children it is not hard for them to see how they are treated—by sheriffs or policemen or teachers—and after a while it is all too easy to stop asking questions and to simply try to do all they can to stay alive, keep going, manage to make it to the next crisis, the next trial, the next day.

About a fifth of the nation is poor or significantly exiled. At the same time the rest—the comfortable majority—are intimately affected by the problems and tensions, the social strife that racism and poverty generate. Today murder in Mississippi or demonstrations in New York or Chicago (not to mention the battles in faraway wars) enter the living rooms of the nation; and today, riots and demonstrations, as never before, make the alternatives manifest: Crush the outsider or open the doors to him, however difficult that offer may be for all. In the essays on Mexican-Americans and migrant farmers and Appalachian folk and sharecroppers something besides the extreme poverty can be sensed: By the many millions, outsiders want "in." They may not at the present time know how to get in. They may seem hopelessly out of it, so far as a complicated technological society goes, but they emphatically are not middle-class radical critics, fed up with the cheapness and rot in society—however much some consider them as just that: allies in a larger social and cultural struggle. Young idealists should not attribute their thoroughly reasonable purposes to hungry, penniless men and women who have the next minute, the next meal, to worry about rather than large-scale reconstructions of society. All of which is not to say that alliances cannot be formed between different classes and groups of citizens; but it is certainly best that different hopes and goals be acknowledged right off. Over and over again sharecroppers or migrant farmers or mountain people in Appalachia or those who live in urban ghettos have spoken words like these of a West Virginian become a Chicagoan: "I'm going to get me a job, I hope I will, and later go back home. I don't care about all those 'larger things' they keep on telling you about, the kids. That's for them to figure out. I get dizzy listening to them, even though they ask me if I can understand, and I say yes. It's not that I don't see their point; it's just that people like us, we're not sure there'll be supper, you know, and that's what's on our mind, yes sir, all the time—and going home, I'll admit."

It is an old story, the stubborn, fearful desire to survive that observers note among the poor and exiled—a desire that contrasts with the sharp, intelligent, far-sighted critiques heard among would-be leaders of various proletariats. The poor are outsiders by fate; their organizers and advocates are often enough outsiders by choice, and in the clutch even the choice is not binding, because a return to the "compact majority" (which, of course, is not so compact) can always take place, something poor people very definitely know, at *some* psychological level.

In a sense there are many outsiders besides the "insulted and injured," who may be black or Indian or white but share the common experience of pitiless exclusion from a rich nation's social and economic life: There are also those who choose to forgo much in order to champion unpopular causes, or simply (and of course not so simply) choose the private life of the mind. That interior world can be irresponsibly fussy and frivolous or in every way illuminating and ennobling to the rest of us, who need the vision and coherence that those peculiar outsiders like Michelangelo and Tolstoy and Faulkner and Van Gogh provide to men of all nations and eras. The remote, lonely, abstracted poet, seemingly uninterested in the social and political heat of the day, may have much to say about the very heart of life; yes, even something to say about the heart of life as it is lived by desperately hungry, jobless people who are looked down on and kept apart. If there is anything an outsider feels, it is loneliness and a sense of despair, not only about the future but about *himself* as an individual. Is there, then, something a writer, even a rather "aristocratic" poet, such as T. S. Eliot, can have to say to the social activists, the aroused critics of this and that in the Establishment? And can writers like Walker Percy and Flannery O'Connor, novelists and white Southerners, tell us much about the steps America will have to take if things are to be different for millions of its poor citizens, white and black?

I think the answers to questions like these will come clear once a few of James Agee's words (from his long, extraordinary, and haunting prose-poem *Let Us Now Praise Famous Men*) are allowed to cast their powerful spell. Even in the name of widespread and necessary social change, can we possibly afford to deny the existence of a shared experience—however rigid and cruel the lines of class and caste may be? What I like about Robert Penn Warren's piece, *Segregation* (and about books such as George Orwell's *The Road to Wigan Pier,* George Bernanos' *The Diary of a Country Priest,* and Simone Weil's *The Need for Roots*—not dealt with here, but recommended), has to do with the compassionate artist's vision that they all offer: Yes, it is a hellish world, an unjust one; yes, men and women by the millions suffer because they have no bread, no work, no sense of authority over the ordinary details of life; but yes, so do others suffer, the rich and the well bred and the powerful.

So I hope these selections will cause trouble. I hope all will feel the pain that most of these essays describe, the pain that pervades so many lives, in American citizens who are—well, everywhere, it seems. But I also hope there will be another kind of pain, the pain that truth generates and the pain that is deliberately invoked by artists like Warren and Percy and Agee and others just mentioned. Perhaps one day we will, most of us, know that every man is somehow, in some way, an outsider. With that recognition we will learn to respect one another, to share ourselves and what matters to us, or we will die together in one terrible apocalyptic moment, when evil and injustice combine with incredible technology to banish mankind altogether.

NIGHT COMES TO THE CUMBERLANDS:
INTRODUCTION

Harry M. Caudill

The Cumberland Plateau region of Kentucky is a serrated upland in the eastern and southeastern part of the state. Its jagged hills and narrow winding valleys cover some ten thousand square miles. It embraces nineteen counties and portions of a dozen others. These units of government were created by the caprice of governors and legislators and, with one exception, were named for the state's heroes of statecraft and battlefield: Bell, Breathitt, Clay, Floyd, Harlan, Knott, Knox, Laurel, Lee, Leslie, Letcher, McCreary, Magoffin, Martin, Owsley, Perry, Pike, Whitley and Wolfe. Few of the heroes deserved so high an honor and few of the counties were worthy of creation. Only Pike County has proved to be sufficiently large and wealthy to discharge even fairly well the responsibilities inherent in local government.

The plateau's half million inhabitants are among the earth's most interesting folk. Their European ancestry and American adventures constitute a remarkable page in the history of mankind. The American public is prone to think of them as quaint hillbillies, a concept sociologists have neglected to explain or explore. In truth, the Kentucky mountaineer is drawn from some of the oldest white stock to be found north of Florida. His forebears had dwelt in or on the edge of the Southern Appalachians for generations before the Declaration of Independence was penned. In their long residence on this continent they left behind a unique, checkered and violent history. Their past created the modern mountaineers and the communities in which they live, and resulted in a land of economic, social and political blight without parallel in the nation. The purpose of this work is to trace the social, economic and political forces which produced the vast "depressed area" of eastern Kentucky.

Much of the region's story is the story of coal. Geologists tell us that two hundred million years ago it was a plain that had risen from the floor of a long-dry inland sea. Then the tortured crust of the earth cracked and "faulted," rearing the Pine Mountain. This long, steep, ragged ridge now stretches from the Breaks of the Big Sandy River on the Virginia line some hundred and thirty miles southwesterly into northern Tennessee. It parallels the Cumberland (or Big Black) Mountain, the southern boundary of the plateau. Water flowing away from its base over a great fan-shaped territory carved the channels of three of the state's major streams and chiseled thousands of narrow valleys—the creeks and hollows of today.

After the shallow sea receded it left a vast bog where vegetation flourished, died, piled up in deep beds, turned to peat and finally, aeons later, to coal. When the streams carved out the mountains and ridges of today they sliced through magnificent seams of coal, a mineral the steel age would esteem more highly than rubies.

Coal has always cursed the land in which it lies. When men begin to wrest it from the earth it leaves a legacy of foul streams, hideous slag heaps and polluted air. It peoples this transformed land with blind and crippled men and with widows and orphans. It is an extractive industry which takes all away and restores nothing. It mars but never beautifies. It corrupts but never purifies.

But the tragedy of the Kentucky mountains transcends the tragedy of coal. It is compounded of Indian wars, civil war and intestine feuds, of layered hatreds and of violent death. To its sad blend, history has added the curse of coal as a crown of sorrow.

What I have written is drawn from experience—from seeing, hearing and working with mountaineers. In a land with few books and pens many tales are transmitted from father and mother to son and daughter. Such tales and legends breathe out a rich past to anyone patient enough to hear them. From my grandmothers and scores of other ancient storytellers were acquired many of the incidents and impressions I have related. After all, people of my blood and name have lived in the plateau from the beginning. My grandfather's grandfather, James Caudill, was the first white man to call what is now Letcher County his home. He built his cabin in 1792. Another of my forebears was scalped by an Indian raiding party when he was two years old. The redskins killed his parents, brothers and sisters and left him for dead in the corner of a rail fence a few yards from their burned cabin. A hunter found him, nursed him back to health, reared him with his own children and gave him his name. My grandfather, Henry Caudill, served four years as a lieutenant in the Confederate Army, was wounded and totally pauperized in the process. My mother's grandfather fought on the other side, a fact which caused me to be indoctrinated from both directions. In more recent times, my father lost an arm in a mining accident. Still later my only brother was seriously disabled in a similar mishap. Since 1948 I have practiced law in mountain courthouses. Three times I have been elected to represent my county in the Kentucky Legislature. This personal background is mentioned, pardonably I hope, as evidence that my narrative is not founded on hasty first impresssions.

In the 1960 preferential primary, Senator—now President—John F. Kennedy campaigned across West Virginia and saw at first hand the conditions existing in the coalfields of that state. The spectacle of mass misery and of mass surrender to it appears to have deeply impressed him, because in the general election campaign he repeatedly referred to the hunger and depression he had seen there. West Virginia is not far from the great population centers of the eastern seaboard where Mr. Kennedy grew up, and it may be cause for wonder that this inquisitive and well-educated young man could have been unaware of the deplorable situation in which the West Virginia highlander finds himself in the seventh decade of the twentieth century. However, the fact is that a million Americans in the Southern Appalachians live today in conditions of squalor, ignorance and ill health which could scarcely be equaled in Europe or Japan or, perhaps, in parts of mainland Asia. For example, the 1960 census disclosed that 19 per cent of the adult population of the Southern mountain region can neither read nor write. Bell County, Kentucky, with a total population of 35,336, was found to contain 17,213 citizens twenty-five years of age or older. Of these adults 1018 had never attended school at all. In addition, 3884 had attended school four years or less. Thus, 4902 persons—substantially more than 25 per cent—were classified, for all practical purposes, as functional illiterates.

A plethora of articles and feature stories have been written in national magazines and metropolitan newspapers about this paradox of medieval stagnation in the midst of twentieth-century prosperity and progress, but none of them has traced the long road over which the Southern mountaineer has traveled to the helplessness and hopelessness which so frequently marks him today.

The people of the Southern mountains share a similar history and background and, with local variations, they have journeyed together into the tragedy which now enfolds them. The same geologic processes which culminated in the Kentucky coal seams produced similar deposits in a small corner of Maryland, and in Virginia, West Virginia, Alabama and Tennessee. The mining industry developed in each of these states along the same general lines though during somewhat different periods of time. Few of the deep social and economic forces which afflict a people stop at lines drawn on political maps, and the pressures which have undermined the character and independence of the Kentucky coalfield mountaineer have been at work with similar results in other states. What I shall say about the Kentucky coal miner applies, with local modifications, to the entire coal-producing area of the Southern highlands.

The mountaineer can present no enigma to a world which is interested enough to look with sympathy into the forces which have made him. And look we must, because with his fruitful wife and brood of untamed children he presents a problem to the nation which is many-faceted and which will deepen in complexity during the ensuing decades. As the nation moves toward the challenges of a new century and a world ringing with change, it cannot afford to leave huge islands of its own population behind, stranded and ignored. Idleness and waste are antipathetic to progress and growth, and, unless the Cumberland Plateau is to remain an anchor dragging behind the rest of America, it—and the rest of the Southern Appalachians—must be rescued while there is yet time.

In the spring of 1960 I was invited to serve as commencement speaker at an eighth-grade graduation in a coal camp school. The seven graduates received their diplomas in the dilapidated two-room building which had sheltered two generations of their forebears. A shower sent a little torrent of water through the ancient roof onto one of the scarred desks. The worn windows rattled in their frames and the paper decorations which had been prepared by the seventh-graders fluttered in drafts admitted by the long-unpainted walls. Outside, the grassless playground lay in the shadow of an immense slate dump and was fringed by a cluster of ramshackle houses. One of the graduates had been orphaned by a mining accident, and the father of another wheezed and gasped with silicosis. The fathers of three others were jobless.

The little ceremony was opened with the singing of "America the Beautiful," our most stirring patriotic hymn. The irony of the words, sung so lustily in such a setting, inspired the writing of this book. Perhaps it may help a little to bring the sad reality and the splendid dream a little closer together, for my friends, my kinsmen, my fellow mountaineers.

LETTER FROM BIRMINGHAM JAIL

Martin Luther King, Jr.

April 16, 1963

My Dear Fellow Clergymen:

While confined here in the Birmingham city jail, I came across your recent statement calling my present activities "unwise and untimely." Seldom do I pause to answer criticism of my work and ideas. If I sought to answer all the criticisms that cross my desk, my secretaries would have little time for anything other than such correspondence in the course of the day, and I would have no time for constructive work. But since I feel that you are men of genuine good will and that your criticisms are sincerely set forth, I want to

LETTER FROM BIRMINGHAM JAIL From *Why We Can't Wait* by Martin Luther King, Jr. Copyright © 1963 by Martin Luther King, Jr. By permission of Harper & Row, Publishers, Inc.

AUTHOR'S NOTE: This response to a published statement by eight fellow clergymen from Alabama (Bishop C. C. J. Carpenter, Bishop Joseph A. Durick, Rabbi Hilton L. Grafman, Bishop Paul Hardin, Bishop Holan B. Harmon, the Reverend George M. Murray, the Reverend Edward V. Ramage and the Reverend Earl Stallings) was composed under somewhat constricting circumstances. Begun on the margins of the newspaper in which the statement appeared while I was in jail, the letter was continued on scraps of writing paper supplied by a friendly Negro trusty, and concluded on a pad my attorneys were eventually permitted to leave me. Although the text remains in substance unaltered, I have indulged in the author's prerogative of polishing it for publication.

try to answer your statement in what I hope will be patient and reasonable terms.

I think I should indicate why I am here in Birmingham, since you have been influenced by the view which argues against "outsiders coming in." I have the honor of serving as president of the Southern Christian Leadership Conference, an organization operating in every southern state, with headquarters in Atlanta, Georgia. We have some eighty-five affiliated organizations across the South, and one of them is the Alabama Christian Movement for Human Rights. Frequently we share staff, educational and financial resources with our affiliates. Several months ago the affiliate here in Birmingham asked us to be on call to engage in a nonviolent direct-action program if such were deemed necessary. We readily consented, and when the hour came we lived up to our promise. So I, along with several members of my staff, am here because I was invited here. I am here because I have organizational ties here.

But more basically, I am in Birmingham because injustice is here. Just as the prophets of the eighth century B.C. left their villages and carried their "thus saith the Lord" far beyond the boundaries of their home towns, and just as the Apostle Paul left his village of Tarsus and carried the gospel of Jesus Christ to the far corners of the Greco-Roman world, so am I compelled to carry the gospel of freedom beyond my own home town. Like Paul, I must constantly respond to the Macedonian call for aid.

Moreover, I am cognizant of the interrelatedness of all communities and states. I cannot sit idly by in Atlanta and not be concerned about what happens in Birmingham. Injustice anywhere is a threat to justice everywhere. We are caught in an inescapable network of mutuality, tied in a single garment of destiny. Whatever affects one directly, affects all indirectly. Never again can we afford to live with the narrow, provincial "outside agitator" idea. Anyone who lives inside the United States can never be considered an outsider anywhere within its bounds.

You deplore the demonstrations taking place in Birmingham. But your statement, I am sorry to say, fails to express a similar concern for the conditions that brought about the demonstrations. I am sure that none of you would want to rest content with the superficial kind of social analysis that deals merely with effects and does not grapple with underlying causes. It is unfortunate that demonstrations are taking place in Birmingham, but it is even more unfortunate that the city's white power structure left the Negro community with no alternative.

In any nonviolent campaign there are four basic steps: collection of the facts to determine whether injustices exist; negotiation; self-purification; and direct action. We have gone through all these steps in Birmingham. There can be no gainsaying the fact that racial injustice engulfs this community. Birmingham is probably the most thoroughly segregated city in the United States. Its ugly record of brutality is widely known. Negroes have experienced grossly unjust treatment in the courts. There have been more unsolved bombings of Negro homes and churches in Birmingham than in any other city in the nation. These are the hard, brutal facts of the case. On the basis of these conditions, Negro leaders sought to negotiate with the city fathers. But the latter consistently refused to engage in good-faith negotiation.

Then, last September, came the opportunity to talk with leaders of Birmingham's economic community. In the course of the negotiations, certain promises were made by the merchants—for example, to remove the stores' humiliating racial signs. On the basis of these promises, the Reverend Fred Shuttlesworth and the leaders of the Alabama Christian Movement for Human Rights agreed to a moratorium on all demonstrations. As the weeks and months went by, we realized that we were the victims of a broken promise. A few signs, briefly removed, returned; the others remained.

As in so many past experiences, our hopes had been blasted, and the shadow of deep disappointment settled upon us. We had no alternative except to prepare for direct action, whereby we would present our very bodies as a means of laying our case before the conscience of the local and the national community. Mindful of the difficulties involved, we decided to undertake a process of self-purification. We began a series of workshops on nonviolence, and we repeatedly asked ourselves: "Are you able to accept blows without retaliating?" "Are you able to endure the ordeal of jail?" We decided to schedule our direct-action program for the Easter season, realizing that except for Christmas, this is the main shopping period of the year. Knowing that a strong economic-withdrawal program would be the by-product of direct action, we felt that this would be the best time to bring pressure to bear on the merchants for the needed change.

Then it occurred to us that Birmingham's mayoralty election was coming up in March, and we speedily decided to postpone action until after election day. When we discovered that the Commissioner of Public Safety, Eugene "Bull" Connor, had piled up enough votes to be in the run-off, we decided again to postpone action until the day after the run-off so that the demonstrations could not be used to cloud the issues. Like many others, we waited to see Mr. Connor defeated, and to this end we endured post-ponement after postponement. Having aided in this community need, we felt that our direct-action program could be delayed no longer.

You may well ask: "Why direct action? Why sit-ins, marches and so forth? Isn't negotiation a better path?" You are quite right in calling for negotia-tion. Indeed, this is the very purpose of direct action. Nonviolent direct action seeks to create such a crisis and foster such a tension that a commu-nity which has constantly refused to negotiate is forced to confront the issue. It seeks so to dramatize the issue that it can no longer be ignored. My citing the creation of tension as part of the work of the nonviolent-resister may sound rather shocking. But I must confess that I am not afraid of the word "tension." I have earnestly opposed violent tension, but there is a type of constructive, nonviolent tension which is necessary for growth. Just as Socrates felt that it was necessary to create a tension in the mind so that individuals could rise from the bondage of myths and half-truths to the unfettered realm of creative analysis and objective appraisal, so must we see the need for nonviolent gadflies to create the kind of tension in society that will help men rise from the dark depths of prejudice and racism to the majestic heights of understanding and brotherhood.

The purpose of our direct-action program is to create a situation so crisis-packed that it will inevitably open the door to negotiation. I therefore concur with you in your call for negotiation. Too long has our beloved Southland been bogged down in a tragic effort to live in monologue rather than dialogue.

One of the basic points in your statement is that the action that I and my associates have taken in Birmingham is untimely. Some have asked: "Why didn't you give the new city administration time to act?" The only answer that I can give to this query is that the new Birmingham administration must be prodded about as much as the outgoing one, before it will act. We are sadly mistaken if we feel that the election of Albert Boutwell as mayor will bring the millennium to Birmingham. While Mr. Boutwell is a much more gentle person than Mr. Connor, they are both segregationists, dedicated to maintenance of the status quo. I have hope that Mr. Boutwell will be reasonable enough to see the futility of massive resistance to deseg-regation. But he will not see this without pressure from devotees of civil rights. My friends, I must say to you that we have not made a single gain in civil rights without determined legal and nonviolent pressure. Lamenta-bly, it is an historical fact that privileged groups seldom give up their privileges voluntarily. Individuals may see the moral light and voluntarily give up their unjust posture; but, as Reinhold Niebuhr has reminded us, groups tend to be more immoral than individuals.

We know through painful experience that freedom is never voluntarily given by the oppressor; it must be demanded by the oppressed. Frankly, I have yet to engage in a direct-action campaign that was "well timed" in the view of those who have not suffered unduly from the disease of segre-gation. For years now I have heard the word "Wait!" It rings in the ear of every Negro with piercing familiarity. This "Wait" has almost always meant "Never." We must come to see, with one of our distinguished jurists, that "justice too long delayed is justice denied."

We have waited for more than 340 years for our constitutional and God-given rights. The nations of Asia and Africa are moving with jetlike speed toward gaining political independence, but we still creep at horse-and-buggy pace toward gaining a cup of coffee at a lunch counter. Perhaps it is easy for those who have never felt the stinging darts of segregation to say, "Wait." But when you have seen vicious mobs lynch your mothers and fathers at will and drown your sisters and brothers at whim; when you have seen hate-filled policemen curse, kick and even kill your black brothers and sisters; when you see the vast majority of your twenty million Negro brothers smothering in an airtight cage of poverty in the midst of an affluent society; when you suddenly find your tongue twisted and your speech stam-mering as you seek to explain to your six-year-old daughter why she can't go to the public amusement park that has just been advertised on television, and see tears welling up in her eyes when she is told that Funtown is closed to colored children, and see ominous clouds of inferiority beginning to form in her little mental sky, and see her beginning to distort her personality by developing an unconscious bitterness toward white people; when you have to concoct an answer for a five-year-old son who is asking: "Daddy, why do white people treat colored people so mean?"; when you take a cross-country drive and find it necessary to sleep night after night in the uncomfortable corners of your automobile because no motel will accept you; when you are humiliated day in and day out by nagging signs reading "white" and "colored"; when your first name becomes "nigger," your middle name becomes "boy" (however old you are) and your last name becomes "John," and your wife and mother are never given the respected title "Mrs."; when you are harried by day and haunted by night by the fact that you are a Negro, living constantly at tiptoe stance, never quite knowing what to expect next, and are plagued with inner fears and outer resentments; when you are forever fighting a degenerating sense of "nobodiness" —then you will understand why we find it difficult to wait. There comes a time when the cup of endurance runs over, and men are no longer willing to be plunged into the abyss of despair. I hope, sirs, you can understand our legitimate and unavoidable impatience.

You express a great deal of anxiety over our willingness to break laws. This is certainly a legitimate concern. Since we so diligently urge people to obey the Supreme Court's decision of 1954 outlawing segregation in the public schools, at first glance it may seem rather paradoxical for us consciously to break laws. One may well ask: "How can you advocate breaking some laws and obeying others?" The answer lies in the fact that there are two types of laws: just and unjust. I would be the first to advocate obeying just laws. One has not only a legal but a moral responsibility to obey just laws. Conversely, one has a moral responsibility to disobey unjust laws. I would agree with St. Augustine that "an unjust law is no law at all."

Now, what is the difference between the two? How does one determine whether a law is just or unjust? A just law is a man-made code that squares with the moral law or the law of God. An unjust law is a code that is out of harmony with the moral law. To put it in the terms of St. Thomas Aquinas: An unjust law is a human law that is not rooted in eternal law and natural law. Any law that uplifts human personality is just. Any law that degrades human personality is unjust. All segregation statutes are unjust because segregation distorts the soul and damages the personality. It gives the segregator a false sense of superiority and the segregated a false sense of inferiority. Segregation, to use the terminology of the Jewish philosopher Martin Buber, substitutes an "I—it" relationship for an "I—thou" relationship and ends up relegating persons to the status of things. Hence segregation is not only politically, economically and sociologically unsound, it is morally wrong and sinful. Paul Tillich has said that sin is separation. Is not segregation an existential expression of man's tragic separation, his awful estrangement, his terrible sinfulness? Thus it is that I can urge men to obey the 1954 decision of the Supreme Court, for it is morally right; and

I can urge them to disobey segregation ordinances, for they are morally wrong.

Let us consider a more concrete example of just and unjust laws. An unjust law is a code that a numerical or power majority group compels a minority group to obey but does not make binding on itself. This is *difference* made legal. By the same token, a just law is a code that a majority compels a minority to follow and that it is willing to follow itself. This is *sameness* made legal.

Let me give another explanation. A law is unjust if it is inflicted on a minority that, as a result of being denied the right to vote, had no part in enacting or devising the law. Who can say that the legislature of Alabama which set up that state's segregation laws was democratically elected? Throughout Alabama all sorts of devious methods are used to prevent Negroes from becoming registered voters, and there are some counties in which, even though Negroes constitute a majority of the population, not a single Negro is registered. Can any law enacted under such circumstances be considered democratically structured?

Sometimes a law is just on its face and unjust in its application. For instance, I have been arrested on a charge of parading without a permit. Now, there is nothing wrong in having an ordinance which requires a permit for a parade. But such an ordinance becomes unjust when it is used to maintain segregation and to deny citizens the First-Amendment privilege of peaceful assembly and protest.

I hope you are able to see the distinction I am trying to point out. In no sense do I advocate evading or defying the law, as would the rabid segregationist. That would lead to anarchy. One who breaks an unjust law must do so openly, lovingly, and with a willingness to accept the penalty. I submit that an individual who breaks a law that conscience tells him is unjust, and who willingly accepts the penalty of imprisonment in order to arouse the conscience of the community over its injustice, is in reality expressing the highest respect for law.

Of course, there is nothing new about this kind of civil disobedience. It was evidenced sublimely in the refusal of Shadrach, Meshach and Abednego to obey the laws of Nebuchadnezzar, on the ground that a higher moral law was at stake. It was practiced superbly by the early Christians, who were willing to face hungry lions and the excruciating pain of chopping blocks rather than submit to certain unjust laws of the Roman Empire. To a degree, academic freedom is a reality today because Socrates practiced civil disobedience. In our own nation, the Boston Tea Party represented a massive act of civil disobedience.

We should never forget that everything Adolf Hitler did in Germany was "legal" and everything the Hungarian freedom fighters did in Hungary was "illegal." It was "illegal" to aid and comfort a Jew in Hitler's Germany. Even so, I am sure that, had I lived in Germany at the time, I would have aided and comforted my Jewish brothers. If today I lived in a Communist country where certain principles dear to the Christian faith are suppressed, I would openly advocate disobeying that country's antireligious laws.

I must make two honest confessions to you, my Christian and Jewish brothers. First, I must confess that over the past few years I have been gravely disappointed with the white moderate. I have almost reached the regrettable conclusion that the Negro's great stumbling block in his stride toward freedom is not the White Citizen's Counciler or the Ku Klux Klanner, but the white moderate, who is more devoted to "order" than to justice; who prefers a negative peace which is the absence of tension to a positive peace which is the presence of justice; who constantly says: "I agree with you in the goal you seek, but I cannot agree with your methods of direct action"; who paternalistically believes he can set the timetable for another man's freedom; who lives by a mythical concept of time and who constantly advises the Negro to wait for a "more convenient season." Shallow understanding from people of good will is more frustrating than absolute misunderstanding from people of ill will. Lukewarm acceptance is much more bewildering than outright rejection.

I had hoped that the white moderate would understand that law and order exist for the purpose of establishing justice and that when they fail in this purpose they become the dangerously structured dams that block the flow of social progress. I had hoped that the white moderate would understand that the present tension in the South is a necessary phase of the transition from an obnoxious negative peace, in which the Negro passively accepted his unjust plight, to a substantive and positive peace, in which all men will respect the dignity and worth of human personality. Actually, we who engage in nonviolent direct action are not the creators of tension. We merely bring to the surface the hidden tension that is already alive. We bring it out in the open, where it can be seen and dealt with. Like a boil that can never be cured so long as it is covered up but must be opened with all its ugliness to the natural medicines of air and light, injustice must be exposed, with all the tension its exposure creates, to the light of human conscience and the air of national opinion before it can be cured.

In your statement you assert that our actions, even though peaceful, must be condemned because they precipitate violence. But is this a logical assertion? Isn't this like condemning a robbed man because his possession of money precipitated the evil act of robbery? Isn't this like condemning Socrates because his unswerving commitment to truth and his philosophical inquiries precipitated the act by the misguided populace in which they made him drink hemlock? Isn't this like condemning Jesus because his unique God-consciousness and never-ceasing devotion to God's will precipitated the evil act of crucifixion? We must come to see that, as the federal courts have consistently affirmed, it is wrong to urge an individual to cease his efforts to gain his basic constitutional rights because the quest may precipitate violence. Society must protect the robbed and punish the robber.

I had also hoped that the white moderate would reject the myth concerning time in relation to the struggle for freedom. I have just received a letter from a white brother in Texas. He writes: "All Christians know that the colored people will receive equal rights eventually, but it is possible that you are in too great a religious hurry. It has taken Christianity almost two thousand years to accomplish what it has. The teachings of Christ take time to come to earth." Such an attitude stems from a tragic misconception of time, from the strangely irrational notion that there is something in the very flow of time that will inevitably cure all ills. Actually, time itself is neutral; it can be used either destructively or constructively. More and more I feel that the people of ill will have used time much more effectively than have the people of good will. We will have to repent in this generation not merely for the hateful words and actions of the bad people but for the appalling silence of the good people. Human progress never rolls in on wheels of inevitability; it comes through the tireless efforts of men willing to be co-workers with God, and without this hard work, time itself becomes an ally of the forces of social stagnation. We must use time creatively, in the knowledge that the time is always ripe to do right. Now is the time to make real the promise of democracy and transform our pending national elegy into a creative psalm of brotherhood. Now is the time to lift our national policy from the quicksand of racial injustice to the solid rock of human dignity.

You speak of our activity in Birmingham as extreme. At first I was rather disappointed that fellow clergymen would see my nonviolent efforts as those of an extremist. I began thinking about the fact that I stand in the middle of two opposing forces in the Negro community. One is a force of complacency, made up in part of Negroes who, as a result of long years of oppression, are so drained of self-respect and a sense of "somebodiness" that they have adjusted to segregation; and in part of a few middleclass Negroes who, because of a degree of academic and economic security and because in some ways they profit by segregation, have become insensitive to the problems of the masses. The other force is one of bitterness and hatred, and it comes perilously close to advocating violence. It is expressed in the various black nationalist groups that are springing up across the nation, the largest and best-known being Elijah Muhammad's Muslim movement. Nourished by the Negro's frustration over the continued existence of racial discrimination, this movement is made up of people who have lost faith in America, who have absolutely repudiated Christianity, and who have concluded that the white man is an incorrigible "devil."

I have tried to stand between these two forces, saying that we need emulate neither the "do-nothingism" of the complacent nor the hatred and despair of the black nationalist. For there is the more excellent way of love and nonviolent protest. I am grateful to God that, through the influence of the Negro church, the way of nonviolence became an integral part of our struggle.

If this philosophy had not emerged, by now many streets of the South would, I am convinced, be flowing with blood. And I am further convinced that if our white brothers dismiss as "rabble-rousers" and "outside agitators" those of us who employ nonviolent direct action, and if they refuse to support our nonviolent efforts, millions of Negroes will, out of frustration and despair, seek solace and security in black-nationalist ideologies—a development that would inevitably lead to a frightening racial nightmare.

Oppressed people cannot remain oppressed forever. The yearning for freedom eventually manifests itself, and that is what has happened to the American Negro. Something within has reminded him of his birthright of freedom, and something without has reminded him that it can be gained. Consciously or unconsciously, he has been caught up by the *Zeitgeist,* and with his black brothers of Africa and his brown and yellow brothers of Asia, South America and the Caribbean, the United States Negro is moving with a sense of great urgency toward the promised land of racial justice. If one recognizes this vital urge that has engulfed the Negro community, one should readily understand why public demonstrations are taking place. The Negro has many pent-up resentments and latent frustrations, and he must release them. So let him march; let him make prayer pilgrimages to the city hall; let him go on freedom rides—and try to understand why he must do so. If his repressed emotions are not released in nonviolent ways, they will seek expression through violence; this is not a threat but a fact of history. So I have not said to my people: "Get rid of your discontent." Rather, I have tried to say that this normal and healthy discontent can be channeled into the creative outlet of nonviolent direct action. And now this approach is being termed extremist.

But though I was initially disappointed at being categorized as an extremist, as I continued to think about the matter I gradually gained a measure of satisfaction from the label. Was not Jesus an extremist for love: "Love your enemies, bless them that curse you, do good to them that hate you, and pray for them which despitefully use you, and persecute you." Was not Amos an extremist for justice: "Let justice roll down like waters and righteousness like an ever-flowing stream." Was not Paul an extremist for the Christian gospel: "I bear in my body the marks of the Lord Jesus." Was not Martin Luther an extremist: "Here I stand; I cannot do otherwise, so help me God." And John Bunyan: "I will stay in jail to the end of my days before I make a butchery of my conscience." And Abraham Lincoln: "This nation cannot survive half slave and half free." And Thomas Jefferson: "We hold these truths to be self-evident, that all men are created equal . . ." So the question is not whether we will be extremists, but what kind of extremists we will be. Will we be extremists for hate or for love? Will we be extremists for the preservation of injustice or for the extension of justice? In that dramatic scene on Calvary's hill three men were crucified. We must never forget that all three were crucified for the same crime—the crime of extremism. Two were extremists for immorality, and thus fell below their environment. The other, Jesus Christ, was an extremist for love, truth and goodness, and thereby rose above his environment. Perhaps the South, the nation and the world are in dire need of creative extremists.

I had hoped that the white moderate would see this need. Perhaps I was too optimistic; perhaps I expected too much. I suppose I should have realized that few members of the oppressor race can understand the deep groans and passionate yearnings of the oppressed race, and still fewer have the vision to see that injustice must be rooted out by strong, persistent and determined action. I am thankful, however, that some of our white brothers in the South have grasped the meaning of this social revolution and committed themselves to it. They are still all too few in quantity, but they are big in quality. Some—such as Ralph McGill, Lillian Smith, Harry Golden, James McBride Dabbs, Ann Braden and Sarah Patton Boyle —have written about our struggle in eloquent and prophetic terms. Others have marched with us down nameless streets of the South. They have languished in filthy, roach-infested jails, suffering the abuse and brutality of policemen who view them as "dirty nigger-lovers." Unlike so many of their moderate brothers and sisters, they have recognized the urgency of the moment and sensed the need for powerful "action" antidotes to combat the disease of segregation.

Let me take note of my other major disappointment. I have been so greatly disappointed with the white church and its leadership. Of course, there are some notable exceptions. I am not unmindful of the fact that each of you has taken some significant stands on this issue. I commend you, Reverend Stallings, for your Christian stand on this past Sunday, in welcoming Negroes to your worship service on a nonsegregated basis. I commend the Catholic leaders of this state for integrating Spring Hill College several years ago.

But despite these notable exceptions, I must honestly reiterate that I have been disappointed with the church. I do not say this as one of those negative critics who can always find something wrong with the church. I say this as a minister of the gospel, who loves the church; who was nurtured in its bosom; who has been sustained by its spiritual blessings and who will remain true to it as long as the cord of life shall lengthen.

When I was suddenly catapulted into the leadership of the bus protest in Montgomery, Alabama, a few years ago, I felt we would be supported by the white church. I felt that the white ministers, priests and rabbis of the South would be among our strongest allies. Instead, some have been outright opponents, refusing to understand the freedom movement and misrepresenting its leaders; all too many others have been more cautious than courageous and have remained silent behind the anesthetizing security of stained-glass windows.

In spite of my shattered dreams, I came to Birmingham with the hope that the white religious leadership of this community would see the justice of our cause and, with deep moral concern, would serve as the channel through which our just grievances could reach the power structure. I had hoped that each of you would understand. But again I have been disappointed.

I have heard numerous southern religious leaders admonish their worshipers to comply with a desegregation decision because it is the law, but I have longed to hear white ministers declare: "Follow this decree because integration is morally right and because the Negro is your brother." In the midst of blatant injustices inflicted upon the Negro, I have watched white churchmen stand on the sideline and mouth pious irrelevancies and sanctimonious trivialities. In the midst of a mighty struggle to rid our nation of racial and economic injustice, I have heard many ministers say: "Those are social issues, with which the gospel has no real concern." And I have watched many churches commit themselves to a completely other-worldly religion which makes a strange, un-Biblical distinction between body and soul, between the sacred and the secular.

I have traveled the length and breadth of Alabama, Mississippi and all the other southern states. On sweltering summer days and crisp autumn mornings I have looked at the South's beautiful churches with their lofty spires pointing heavenward. I have beheld the impressive outlines of her massive religious-education buildings. Over and over I have found myself asking: "What kind of people worship here? Who is their God? Where were their voices when the lips of Governor Barnett dripped with words of interposition and nullification? Where were they when Governor Wallace gave a clarion call for defiance and hatred? Where were their voices of support when bruised and weary Negro men and women decided to rise from the dark dungeons of complacency to the bright hills of creative protest?"

Yes, these questions are still in my mind. In deep disappointment I have wept over the laxity of the church. But be assured that my tears have been tears of love. There can be no deep disappointment where there is not deep love. Yes, I love the church. How could I do otherwise? I am in the rather unique position of being the son, the grandson and the great-grandson of preachers. Yes, I see the church as the body of Christ. But, oh! How we have blemished and scarred that body through social neglect and through fear of being nonconformists.

There was a time when the church was very powerful—in the time when the early Christians rejoiced at being deemed worthy to suffer for what they believed. In those days the church was not merely a thermometer that recorded the ideas and principles of popular opinion; it was a thermostat that transformed the mores of society. Whenever the early Christians entered a town, the people in power became disturbed and immediately sought to convict the Christians for being "disturbers of the peace" and "outside agitators." But the Christians pressed on, in the conviction that they were "a colony of heaven," called to obey God rather than man. Small in number, they were big in commitment. They were too God-intoxicated to be "astronomically intimidated." By their effort and example they brought an end to such ancient evils as infanticide and gladiatorial contests.

Things are different now. So often the contemporary church is a weak, ineffectual voice with an uncertain sound. So often it is an archdefender of the status quo. Far from being disturbed by the presence of the church, the power structure of the average community is consoled by the church's silent—and often even vocal—sanction of things as they are.

But the judgment of God is upon the church as never before. If today's church does not recapture the sacrificial spirit of the early church, it will lose its authenticity, forfeit the loyalty of millions, and be dismissed as an irrelevant social club with no meaning for the twentieth century. Every day I meet young people whose disappointment with the church has turned into outright disgust.

Perhaps I have once again been too optimistic. Is organized religion too inextricably bound to the status quo to save our nation and the world? Perhaps I must turn my faith to the inner spiritual church, the church within the church, as the true *ekklesia* and the hope of the world. But again I am thankful to God that some noble souls from the ranks of organized religion have broken loose from the paralyzing chains of conformity and joined us as active partners in the struggle for freedom. They have left their secure congregations and walked the streets of Albany, Georgia, with us. They have gone down the highways of the South on tortuous rides for freedom. Yes, they have gone to jail with us. Some have been dismissed from their churches, have lost the support of their bishops and fellow ministers. But they have acted in the faith that right defeated is stronger than evil triumphant. Their witness has been the spiritual salt that has preserved the true meaning of the gospel in these troubled times. They have carved a tunnel of hope through the dark mountain of disappointment.

I hope the church as a whole will meet the challenge of this decisive hour. But even if the church does not come to the aid of justice, I have no despair about the future. I have no fear about the outcome of our struggle in Birmingham, even if our motives are at present misunderstood. We will reach the goal of freedom in Birmingham and all over the nation, because the goal of America is freedom. Abused and scorned though we may be, our destiny is tied up with America's destiny. Before the pilgrims landed at Plymouth, we were here. Before the pen of Jefferson etched the majestic words of the Declaration of Independence across the pages of history, we were here. For more than two centuries our forebears labored in this country without wages; they made cotton king; they built the homes of their masters while suffering gross injustice and shameful humiliation—and yet out of a bottomless vitality they continued to thrive and develop. If the inexpressible cruelties of slavery could not stop us, the opposition we now face will surely fail. We will win our freedom because the sacred heritage of our nation and the eternal will of God are embodied in our echoing demands.

Before closing I feel impelled to mention one other point in your statement that has troubled me profoundly. You warmly commended the Birmingham police force for keeping "order" and "preventing violence." I doubt that you would have so warmly commended the police force if you had seen its dogs sinking their teeth into unarmed, nonviolent Negroes. I doubt that you would so quickly commend the policemen if you were to observe their ugly and inhumane treatment of Negroes here in the city jail; if you were to watch them push and curse old Negro women and young Negro girls; if you were to see them slap and kick old Negro men and young boys; if you were to observe them, as they did on two occasions, refuse to give us food because we wanted to sing our grace together.

I cannot join you in your praise of the Birmingham police department.

It is true that the police have exercised a degree of discipline in handling the demonstrators. In this sense they have conducted themselves rather "nonviolently" in public. But for what purpose? To preserve the evil system of segregation. Over the past few years I have consistently preached that nonviolence demands that the means we use must be as pure as the ends we seek. I have tried to make clear that it is wrong to use immoral means to attain moral ends. But now I must affirm that it is just as wrong, or perhaps even more so, to use moral means to preserve immoral ends. Perhaps Mr. Connor and his policemen have been rather nonviolent in public, as was Chief Pritchett in Albany, Georgia, but they have used the moral means of nonviolence to maintain the immoral end of racial injustice. As T. S. Eliot has said: "The last temptation is the greatest treason: To do the right deed for the wrong reason."

I wish you had commended the Negro sit-inners and demonstrators of Birmingham for their sublime courage, their willingness to suffer and their amazing discipline in the midst of great provocation. One day the South will recognize its real heroes. They will be the James Merediths, with the noble sense of purpose that enables them to face jeering and hostile mobs, and with the agonizing loneliness that characterizes the life of the pioneer. They will be old, oppressed, battered Negro women, symbolized in a seventy-two-year-old woman in Montgomery, Alabama, who rose up with a sense of dignity and with her people decided not to ride segregated buses, and who responded with ungrammatical profundity to one who inquired about her weariness: "My feets is tired, but my soul is at rest." They will be the young high school and college students, the young ministers of the gospel and a host of their elders, courageously and nonviolently sitting in at lunch counters and willingly going to jail for conscience' sake. One day the South will know that when these disinherited children of God sat down at lunch counters, they were in reality standing up for what is best in the American dream and for the most sacred values in our Judaeo-Christian heritage, thereby bringing our nation back to those great wells of democracy which were dug deep by the founding fathers in their formulation of the Constitution and the Declaration of Independence.

Never before have I written so long a letter. I'm afraid it is much too long to take your precious time. I can assure you that it would have been much shorter if I had been writing from a comfortable desk, but what else can one do when he is alone in a narrow jail cell, other than write long letters, think long thoughts and pray long prayers?

If I have said anything in this letter that overstates the truth and indicates an unreasonable impatience, I beg you to forgive me. If I have said anything that understates the truth and indicates my having a patience that allows me to settle for anything less than brotherhood, I beg God to forgive me.

I hope this letter finds you strong in the faith. I also hope that circumstances will soon make it possible for me to meet each of you, not as an integrationist or a civil rights leader but as a fellow clergyman and a Christian brother. Let us all hope that the dark clouds of racial prejudice will soon pass away and the deep fog of misunderstanding will be lifted from our fear-drenched communities, and in some not too distant tomorrow the radiant stars of love and brotherhood will shine over our great nation with all their scintillating beauty.

Yours for the cause of Peace and Brotherhood,

Martin Luther King, Jr.

FISH ARE JUMPING AN' THE COTTON IS HIGH:
Notes from the Mississippi Delta
Mike Thelwell

There is an immense mural in the Hinds County Courthouse in Jackson, Mississippi. On the wall behind the judge's bench is this mansion. White, gracefully colonnaded in a vaguely classical style, it overlooks vast fields, white with cotton which rows of darkies are busily (and no doubt, happily) picking. In the foreground to the left stands a family. The man is tall, well-proportioned with a kind of benevolent nobility shining from his handsome Anglo-Saxon face. He is immaculate in white linen and a planter's stetson as he gallantly supports his wife, who is the spirit of demure grace and elegance in her lace-trimmed gown. To the right, somewhat in the background to be sure, stands a buxom, grinning handkerchief-headed Aunt Jemima, everyone's good-humored black Mammy. In this mural, progress is represented by a work-gang of Negroes, building under the direction of a white overseer what appears to be an addition to the great house. Although this painting is not wired for sound—a concession, one imagines, to the dignity of the court—it requires little imagination to hear the soothing, homey sound of a spiritual wafting on the gentle wind from the cotton fields. The general tone is certainly one of orderly industry, stability and a general contentment. "Take a good look at them," a Negro lawyer said to me, "because they are the last happy darkies you are likely to see here."

Actually, this mural is so inept in technique and execution, that at first flush one is inclined to mistake it for parody. But Mississippians, especially the politicians, have never demonstrated the sense of security or humor that would permit them consciously to parody themselves, although they seem incapable of escaping this in their public utterances. That this mural,

FISH ARE JUMPING AN' THE COTTON IS HIGH: NOTES FROM THE MISSISSIPPI DELTA Reprinted from *The Massachusetts Review*, Vol. 7, No. 2 (Spring 1966). © 1966 The Massachusetts Review, Inc.

consciously or not, is a burlesque of a parody of a stereotype which has never had historical or social reality goes without saying, but the mere fact that the mural exists and is intended to be taken seriously, or at least with a straight face, is equally important. Because, despite the fact that the Deep South is an area of as vast geographic, economic, and even sociological differentiation as any region in the nation, it is this plantation image of the South that persists in the sentimental subconscious of the American popular imagination. It is this image, or some derivative of it, that people tend to see when the Deep South is mentioned.

In point of fact the area in which huge cotton plantations of "Gone With The Wind" popular fame existed, and to an extent still do, is limited to a relatively small, specific geographic area. This is a narrow land of very level, fertile black earth which runs erratically south, then west from the bottom of Virginia through parts of the Carolinas, central Alabama, picks up in south-west Georgia, and runs through northwestern Mississippi and into Arkansas. This very generally describes the region known as the "Black-belt," where the institutional replacements of the huge ante-bellum plantations exist, and where the descendants of the slaves still greatly outnumber the descendants of their masters, and where the relationship between these two groups shows only a superficial formal change. In Mississippi, this area is called the Delta, a term which, in its precise geographic meaning, refers only to the wedge of land between the Mississippi and Yazoo rivers, but which extends in popular usage to most of the northwestern quarter of the state. The area of the Delta coincides almost exactly with the Second Congressional District of Mississippi, the home of Senator Eastland, the Citizen's Council, and of the densest population of Negroes in the state. It is here, were it to exist anywhere, that one would find the image of the mural translated into reality.

What can be said about this place that will express the impact of a land so surrealistic and monotonous in its flatness that it appears unnatural, even menacing? Faulkner comes close to expressing the physical impact of the region: ". . . *Crossing the last hill, at the foot of which the rich unbroken alluvial flatness began as the sea began, at the base of its cliffs, dissolving away in the unhurried rain as the sea itself would dissolve away.*"

This description suggests the dominant quality: a flatness like an ocean of land, but within that vast flatness, a sense of confinement, a negation of distance and space that the sea does not have. And there are the rivers— in the east the headwaters of the river called Big Black, and sluggish tributaries, the Skuna, Yalabusha, and Yacona which flow into the Tallahatchie, which in turn meets the Sunflower to become the Yazoo which was called by the Indians the river of the dead. The Yazoo flows south and west until it meets the Mississippi at the city of Vicksburg. These rivers are, in Faulkner's words, ". . . *thick, black, slow, unsunned streams almost without current, which once each year ceased to flow at all, then reversed, spreading, drowning the rich land and subsiding again leaving it even richer.*"

I once entered the Delta from the west, from Arkansas, over a long, narrow old bridge that seemed to go for miles over the wide and uncertain Mississippi. It was mid-summer and a heat that seemed independent of the sun rose from the land. The slightest indentation in the road's surface became a shimmering sheet of water that disappeared as you approached it. The numbing repetition of cotton-fields blurring in the distance wore on one's nerves and perceptions. This has been called the richest agricultural soil in the world. So it may have been, but it also is tough and demanding— no longer boundlessly fecund, it now yields its fruits only after exacting disproportionate prices in human sweat and effort. An old man told me, "for every man it enriches it kills fifty," and some folks joke that "the Delta will wear out a mule in five years, a white man in ten, and a nigger in fifteen."

For long stretches of highway where the fields are unbroken by any structure or sign of habitation, one might be in another century, except that a few things serve to place you in time. Even if tractors are not visible they are suggested by the certainty that there could not be, no, not in all the Southland, enough Negroes and mules to have planted all this. And there are the planes. On smooth strips next to the cotton these toylike little craft, fragile and buoyant as children's kites, are tethered to the ground. The gentlest wind causes them to rear and buck against their moorings like colts. At times they are seen at absurdly low heights, skimming the top of the crops they are "dusting" against the boll weevil. They are used increasingly on the large plantations. One pilot, unnecessarily reckless, you think, crosses the highway *underneath* the telegraph wires and directly over your car. You remember, in that moment, the outdoor rally in Indianola that was bombed from one of these planes one night.

The billboards along the highway are also indices, not only of time but of place. They exhort you to support your Citizens' Council, to save America by impeaching Earl Warren, and challenge you to deny that "In Your Heart, You Know He Is Right." "KILLS 'EM FAST, KEEPS 'EM DYING," is the message of another, and it is only when you are nearly abreast of the sign that the small print reveals that an insecticide is being advertised, and nothing larger than a boll weevil is the proposed victim.

But the combination of plane and grisly advertisement reminds you of a report from Panola County, in the heart of the Delta. The SNCC worker who wrote the report is distressed by the fact that many small Negro children in that area are plagued by running, chancre-like sores on their faces or limbs. These lingering and persistent ulcers are attributed by the community to a side-effect of the "pizen" sprayed on the cotton. Children of all ages pick cotton in the Delta, and apparently this insecticide enters any exposed break in the skin and eats away at the flesh like an acid. "What can we do," the report asks, "isn't there some law. . . ." Perhaps, you think, it may be this particular brand of pesticide that "keeps 'em dying."

This is "The Heart of Dixie"—as numerous signs proclaim—the very center of the myth and the image, but what is its reality? For you right now its only reality is heat, and an almost unbearable cumulative discomfort, sweat burning your eyes, oven blasts of dusty air when you open the window, the metal edge of the window that keeps scorching your arm, and all around a punitive white glare that is painful to look into.

For the SNCC workers who are your companions the reality seems to be a certain tense caution. They work the Delta and know the road, but in curious terms. Their knowledge is of the condition of the jail, idiosyncrasies of the lawmen, and the make, model and color of the cars they drive. They chose a route, not necessarily the most direct, but one that avoids certain towns and the jurisdictions of certain local officers. They watch the back-road intently for the car that may be the sheriff, the Highway Patrol, or one of the new radio-equipped prowl cars of the Klan. A car or pick-up truck filled with youngish white men, stripped of license tags, is always ominous, especially if they keep passing and inspecting your car. Often, because it is legal to carry openly displayed weapons here, the cars will be fitted with racks on which rifles and shotguns are conspicuous. This should not suggest that violence is an inevitable consequence of using the highways. But the tension is always present, for when a car follows you a few miles, passes you a number of times then streaks off down the highway, you have no way of knowing their intentions. "Man, watch for a '63 Chevvy, light grey, no plate on front an' a long aerial. See anything that look like it shout."

The tension in the car draws to a fine edge. All know the car, and the reputation of the patrolman who polices the next fifty or so miles of highway. Two of the young men in the car have been "busted"—arrested by him—and as one says, "Once is enough. That man would rather whup yore head than eat shrimp . . . an' he's a sea-food lover."

This trooper is regarded with a mixture of fear and contempt by the Negroes in the County. He is reputed to stop every Negro he encounters, driving or on foot, to check their licenses and to find out where they are going and why. He is particularly fond of "interrogating" adolescent girls. As your companions talk about him a sort of grim, parodic humor attaches to him. His first statement, they say, is invariably, "All right Nigger, pull to the side, take off your hat, spit out your gum an' lemme see your license." It makes no difference if you are hatless and have never chewed gum. And because, for SNCC workers anyway, the response is either silent compliance or a denial that their name is Nigger, his next utterance is usually "Dammit Nigger, don't you know to say Sir?" But this day he does not appear.

On another occasion I saw him making an arrest. Like most things in the Delta, he verges on being a caricature, drawn with too heavy a hand. He is not tall, but blocky and heavy. His hair is thinning, his face is round, full-cheeked, cherubic save for small pale-blue eyes behind absolutely innocuous gold-rimmed glasses. In the heat his complexion could not be called merely florid, it was red, deeply and truly red. His khaki-colored military-style uniform was too tight and stained with damp circles at the armpits and the seat of his pants. His ponderous, hard-looking belly sags over the belt which slopes down almost to the junction of his thighs. Most striking are his hands:

blunt, stubby, very wide—with the skin of the fingers stretched tight, like so many plump, freckled and hairy link sausages. Two images stay with me: one of a boneless, formless, shapeless face; another of the chunky figure, standing spraddle-legged and tugging at the cloth of his trousers where it bunched in tight wrinkles between his thighs. I often wonder about this man. From all accounts he is a sadist, and one with entirely too much opportunity to indulge his impulses, but there is also present a pathetic, somehow pitiable banality about him. Besides, he represents the most easily solved of the problems in the Delta.

Driving along the highways in the Delta you occasionally pass people walking—a single man, two, or sometimes what appears to be an entire family. Usually the man is in front in overalls, or blue denim pants and jacket and with a wide-brimmed straw hat against the sun. The children follow behind in single file, with the woman usually at the end. They often carry tools, but more often cardboard boxes and newspaper-wrapped bundles tied with string. These little caravans become visible while you are some distance down the highway. If they have shoes then they walk on the hot but smooth asphalt, if they are barefoot they take to the weeds. When they hear your car approaching they step off the highway and face the road, motionless, waiting with a quality of dogged, expressionless patience to resume their plodding journey. Sometimes, but rarely, a child will wave, a vague and tentative motion of the arm somewhere between greeting and dismissal, and that is the only sign. No smiles. Often you find such a group miles from any house, village, side road, or anything that might be called a town. One wonders where they sprang from, where they hope to go, and why. They are almost always—I cannot remember seeing any white families walking—Negroes.

Indianola is the capital of Sunflower County, a county distinguished because it contains the 4,800-acre plantation of U.S. Senator James O. Eastland, the state prison farm at Parchman, and is the home of Mrs. Fannie Lou Hamer, the ex-plantation worker who has become the symbol of the resistance.

Although this is your first time there, you recognize when you have come home. When the pavement runs out—the streetlights become fewer or nonexistent and the rows of weather-textured, grey-grained clapboard shacks begin—you experience feelings of relief, almost love. This chaotic, dilapidated shanty-town represents community, safety in numbers, friendship, and some degree of security after the exposed vulnerability of the highway.

Even if you wanted to, you could not escape the children of all sizes and shades who abandon their games in the dusty streets or weed-filled lots for the excitement of a new arrival. Noisy with impatient curiosity and quick vitality they surround you, shooting questions. "Is yo' a freedom fighter? Yo' come for the Meeting? Is yo' start up the school? Have any money?" Or proudly, "We does leafletting, yo' want us to give out any?" Big-eyed and solemn they await the answers, ignoring their elders' warnings, shouted from the porches, "Yo' all don't be botherin' that man now, heah?" They must have some bit of information so that they can go scampering importantly up the porches to inform the old people. The community grapevine.

And on the porches, the people are almost always old, at least no longer young. Frequently they are the grandparents of the children because the true parents, the generation in between, are at work, or have left the state in search of work. This gap between generations lies like a blight on every Negro community, and especially in the Delta. You see it in any kind of meeting, in the churches—any gathering of Negroes in Mississippi consists predominantly of teenagers and older people.

So the old people on the porch rock and fan and listen politely, perhaps too politely, expressing a cautious, noncommittal agreement that is somehow too glib and practised. And their eyes flick over your shoulder to see who may be watching. It may be the Man. The quiescent, easy agreement is another aspect of the mask, and one has no right to judge the only practical response that they have fashioned, the only defense they had. For if they survived yessing the white man to death, why not you? "Thou seest this man's fall, but thou knowest not his wrasslin'."

The motion and energy, the openness and thirst to know of the children in the road forms a tragic counterpoint to the neutral caution of the porches. So short a journey and symbolically so final. The problem comes clear: to create within the community those new forms, new relationships, new alternatives that will preserve this new generation from the paralysis of fear and hopelessness.

In all the shanty-towns that cluster on the edge of every Delta city and town the population steadily increases as increasing numbers of Negroes are driven off the plantations and off the land. Everywhere you get the impression of hopelessness and waiting. Large numbers of human beings in a kind of limbo, physically present and *waiting*. And what they wait for is the cotton. At planting time, chopping time, and picking time, busses and trucks come into the shanty-towns before the sun is well up. The people—men, women and children—file on in the numbers needed and are taken to the plantations where they work a twelve-hour day for $2.50, or 30 cents an hour. Each year 'fewer and fewer people are needed for less and less work. If the fall is unusually wet, then it is a little better. The dust becomes a black and adhesive mud miring down the ponderous cotton-picking machines. Then, for a few hectic weeks almost the entire community can find work getting the crop in before it rots. Still, denied education and the skills that would give them mobility, these waiting people are superfluous, the obsolete victims of a vicious system that depended on large numbers of human beings being kept available in case they were needed. One plantation owner in the county is quoted as saying, "Niggers went out like the mule."

One way to understand this primitive and haunting place and the gratuitous human misery that it breeds, is to figure out who is in charge. Two forces rule the Delta: racism and cotton. Though the whitefolks put up a great show of control and dominance they are at the mercy of both. It is

Cotton—not even Anglo-Saxon, but an immigrant from Egypt that determines how the society is organized. And as a ruler, he is as ruthless, capricious and sickly as the final issue of some inbred and decadent European
House. Delicate, it must be protected from more vigorous hybrid weeds, and
from a small beetle from Mexico. Drought will burn it out, water will rot it.
Extravagant and demanding, it has—in alliance with human cupidity—all
but exhausted a land of once incredible fertility which must now be
pampered and fertilized excessively before it will produce. This process is so
expensive that the final, grudging yield must be bought by the U.S. government which alone can afford it. The federal government has a surplus at
present of some 14,000,000 bales. This spring the federal cotton allotment
has been reduced by one-third in the Delta. Even fewer Negroes will have
work of any kind. The millionaire planter Eastland and other landlords,
however, will still profit handsomely from their federal subsidy. While
awaiting a federal check that runs into hundreds of thousands of dollars, the
Senator will, if he maintains his average, make three speeches deploring the
immorality of government handouts and creeping socialism, by which he
must mean the distribution of food surpluses to starving families in his
county.

At suppertime the "freedom house" is full of bustle, the local kids pass
in and out, a couple of carloads of SNCC workers from other parts of the
state have stopped by on their way through. The shouted laughter and
greetings are loud, the exchange of news marked by a wry humor. A young
man from the southwest corner around Natchez tells stories about a local
judge, nicknamed by the lawyers "Necessity," because in Horace's observation "necessity knows no law." But this judge is a favorite, because his
records invariably contain so much error that although he never fails to convict, the higher court hardly ever fails to reverse him. Frequently, they say,
his mind wanders, and he interrupts the proceedings of his own court with,
"Your Honor, I object."
    Another worker just down from Sharkey County, which is very rural and
contains no city of any size, complains loudly about conditions. "Even the
mosquitoes threatening to leave the county. They organized and sent Johnson a telegram saying that if the Red Cross didn't come down and distribute
blood, they weren't staying." He wouldn't be surprised, he adds, to find
when he returned that they had gotten relief.
    The meeting is called for eight, but will not really get started much before
nine, as the women must feed their white folks their suppers before going
home to feed their own families. But folks start gathering from seven. They
use the time to "testify"; to talk about whatever troubles their mind—mostly
the absence of food, money, work, and the oppressiveness of the police. They
talk about loss of credit, eviction and voting, three things which form an
inseparable unity in the Delta. Some young men are there from Washington
County. They say the peoples over there got together and told the owners
that they wouldn't work anymore for thirty cents. After the evictions they

started a tent city, have a "strike fund" collected in the community, and are planting a "freedom garden" for winter food. Everyone cheers. What they want is cooperation. "If they sen' busses from Washington County don't go. Be workin' gainst us if you do."

"Thass right. Nevah. Freedom."

In the clapping, shouting, stomping excitement there is brief release from tension and fear. But over it all hovers an unease, the desperation of the unanswered question, "Whut *is* we gon' do." Winter is coming. *"Whut is we gon' do?"*

A lady wants to know. She is from "out in the rural" she says and two nights ago was awakened by what sounded like people crying. A man, his wife and seven children were coming down the road carrying bundles. The children were crying and tears were in the man's eyes. They had no shoes. He said that that evening the owner had given him twenty dollars and told him to find someplace else. He had worked that plantation all his life, had less than three years of school and had never been outside the county. "Ah tell yo' that man was *shock,* he wuz *confused.* I want to know, what is we gon' do."

A portly, middle-aged lady answers her. This lady is known for a tough nerviness, insouciant streak of daring best characterized by the Yiddish word *chutzpah,* or by the sheriff in the term "smart nigger." She also has a heart condition of some fame and strategic value. (As she gets up, you recall the time she was in jail and convinced the jailor, after two minor attacks and a constant and indignant harangue, that she was quite likely to die, and that he was certain to be held responsible, if she were not allowed to have her "heart prescription." And she got it, too. You remember her, dramatically clutching her ailing heart, breathing laboriously, and accepting with a quick wink the druggist's bottle of sour mash bourbon.) There were two little boys walking down the road, she says. They were throwing stones at everything they met. They came upon a chicken which the larger boy sent off with a well-placed stone. He does the same for a pig, a cow and a mule. Then, they come to a hornets' nest. When the bigger boy makes no effort to hit that target the other asks, "Ain't you' gonna pop that nes'?" "Nope, sho' ain't." "Why ain't yo' gonna hit thet nes'," the smaller asks. "Well, Ah ain't gonna hit thet nes',"—she pauses, looks at the audience, winks, shakes her head—"I ain't gonna hit thet nes' *because dey's organized."*

They like that story, even if it is only a partial answer, saying *what,* but not *how.* So they nod agreement and murmur that "we'uns gotta be *together,* an' we gotta keep on, keeping on, no matter how mean times git." There is in these Delta communities a great spirit of closeness and cooperation. When a family is evicted, the children may be absorbed into the community, two here, one there. Or an entire family that finds itself suddenly homeless (landlords aren't required by any law to give notice) may be taken in by another family whose home is already too small. Without these traditions the folks could not have endured.

In the meetings, everything—uncertainty, fear, even desperation—finds expression, and there is comfort and sustenance in "talkin' bout hit." A

Preacher picks the theme up with a story of his own. "Wunst times wuz very bad fer the rabbits."

"Fo' the *Whut?*" comes a chorus. The old man smiles, "Fer the *rabbits.* Yes Sir, Ah tells yo' they wuz bein' hard *pressed.* Them ol' houn's wuz runnin' them *ragged.* Got so bad it seem like they couldn't git down to the fiel's to nibble a little grass. It looked like they wasn't gonna be able to make it."

"*Yeah, Yeah, Tellit,*" the people shake their heads in sympathy. "They wuz *hard pressed* fo' a fack. So fin'lly, not knowin' what else to do, they calls a meetin'. Yessir, they call a *mass meetin'.*"

"*Ahuh, Freedom.*"

"So they talked an' talked, discussed it back an' fo'th, how the houn's wasn't givin' them space even to live."

"*Thass right, tell it.*"

"But they couldn't meet with no solution. It jes' didn't seem like hit was nothin' they could do." The speaker shakes his head. "No, it didn't seem like they could make it. So fin'lly thisyer ol' rabbit, he wuz ol' anyways an' fixin' to die anyhow, he sugges' that since they wuzn't making it *nohow,* they should all jes' join together an' run down to the *river an' drown theyself.*"

Everyone in the church is listening very closely. There is the beginning of a low murmur of rejection.

"But since nobody said any better, they put hit in the form of a motion, an' someone secon' hit an' they take a vote. It passed [pause] *unanimous.* So on the nex' moonlight night, they all git together jes' as the motion call fer, link they arms and start fer the river, fo' to drown theyself. Hit wuz *a-a-l* the rabbits in the county, an' thet wuz a long line, jes' hoppin' along in the moonlight to go drown theyse'f. It wuz somethin' to see, chillun, it sho' wuz. An, yo' know, they hadn't gon far befo' they come upon the houn's, out looking fo' rabbits to chase. Them ol' houn's be so surprise at seein' all them rabbits commin' towards them steady, *they thought they time had come.* They be so surprised they turn roun' an' run so fas' they was outen the county, befo' sun come up. Rabbits had no mo' trouble."

"*Talk 'bout Freedom.*"

There is little of subtlety or delicacy here, it is a region of extremes and nothing occurs in small measure. All is blatant, even the passing of time. Night in the Delta is sudden and intense, an almost tangible curtain of blue-purple darkness that comes abruptly, softening and muting the starkness of the day. The moon and stars seem close, shining with a bright yellow haziness like ripe fruit squashed against a black-board. The wind is warm, very physical and furry as it moves with suggestive intimacy over your face and body. Like the sea, the Delta is at its most haunting and mysterious in the dark. The air is heavy with the ripe smell of honeysuckle and night-blooming jasmine, at once cloying and aphrodisiac. A woman's voice deep-timbered, husky, and *negro* is singing an old plaintive song of constant sorrow with new words. The song becomes part of the rich-textured night, like the tracings of the fireflies. In the restless and erotic night you believe. For the first time you can believe the blues, tales of furtive and shameful passions, madness, incest, rape and violence. Half-intoxicated by the night, by its sensuous, textured restlessness, it is possible to believe all the secret, shameful history that everyone seems to know and none will admit except in whispers. It is easy to believe that the land is finally and irrevocably cursed. That faceless voice singing to the darkness an old song with new words, *"They say that freedom . . . is a constant sorrow."*

Just off the road stands the shack. There is a quality of wildness to the scrubby bush around it, and because it is set on short wood piles it appears to have been suddenly set down on the very top of the carpet of weeds around it. The greyed wood siding has long since warped, so that a fine line shows between each plank, giving the shack the appearance of a cage. Crossing the porch you step carefully, avoiding the rotted holes. The woman inside turns dull eyes towards where you stand in the doorway. She is sharing out a pot of greens onto tin plates. The cabin is windowless and dim but is crisscrossed by rays of light beaming through the cracks in the siding and from gaps in the roof where the shingles have rotted and blown away. This light creates patterns of light and shadow on everything in the room. As the woman watches you, at least inclines her head in your direction, her children sidle around her so that she is between them and the door. You see that there are only five—at first it seemed as though the cabin was full. None of them is dressed fully, and the two smallest are completely nude. As the mother gives you the directions back to the highway, she ladles out the greens and each child seizes a plate but stands looking at you. They are all eyes, and these eyes in thin tight faces blaze at you. The full, distended bellies of the children contrasts with the emaciated limbs, big prominent joints, narrow chests in which each rib stands out, the black skin shiny, almost luminous. You cannot leave, so you stand gently talking with the mother, who answers your questions with an unnatural candor. She seems beyond pride. As you talk, she sits on a box and gives her breast to the smallest child even though he seems to be about five. This doesn't surprise you unduly for you have learned that in the Delta Negro mothers frequently do not wean their children until the next one arrives. What will substitute when there is not enough food?

You find out that she is twenty-four, was married at fifteen, had seven children but two died, the father is in Louisiana chopping pulpwood, the nearest work he could find. He sends money when he works. She lives in this abandoned cabin because it was the only rent-free house she could find after they were put off the plantation. As you leave, you see them framed in the doorway, the mother in unlaced man's shoes, one brown, the other black, holding her smallest child with the unnaturally big head and eyes.

You wonder how they are to survive the winter in a cabin with walls that cannot even keep the dust out. But this is Tallahatchie county, where 33 percent of all Negro babies die in the first year of life, where Negroes live, grow old and die without ever being properly examined by a doctor, and children die of cold and hunger in the winter. One reason given for the high infant mortality rate—you meet women who admit to having birthed 10 children of which three or four survived—is that in this completely agricultural county, families survive the winter, when there is no work for the men, on the ten or twelve dollars the mother makes working as a cook or maid. When her time of labor approaches she dares not stop working.

But, all of this was some time ago. All I know of the Delta now is what I hear. I am told that snow blanketed it in January and I am glad I was not there to see it. I am told that in December 250 families were given notice to be off the plantations by January 1st. This means that some 2,200 human beings are without home or livelihood, and none of the programs of the federal government—social security, unemployment compensation, or job retraining—affects them. By spring, they say, some 12,000 people will be homeless. I am glad I was not there to see the ghostly silent caravans trudging through the snow at the side of the highway. A lady in Sunflower County told me on the phone that families were at the tent city asking to be taken in.

Throughout the Delta the plantations are automating, driven by the dual pressure of cutting costs and the potential effect of the 1965 voting rights bill in a region with a Negro majority. The state of Mississippi wants its Negro population thinned out. They make no secret of it. Gov. Johnson has said in praise of his predecessor that under Ross Barnett's regime "116,000 Negroes fled the state." And the state has still not been able to find any way to use the 1.6 million dollars appropriated by the Office of Economic Opportunity to be used to finance the distribution of surplus food in the Delta. Before this grant, it had been Mississippi's position that they simply could not afford the cost of *distributing* the free food. I am just cowardly enough to be glad I am not there to see.

WHAT WE WANT

Stokely Carmichael

One of the tragedies of the struggle against racism is that up to now there has been no national organization which could speak to the growing militancy of young black people in the urban ghetto. There has been only a civil rights movement, whose tone of voice was adapted to an audience of liberal whites. It served as a sort of buffer zone between them and angry young blacks. None of its so-called leaders could go into a rioting community and be listened to. In a sense, I blame ourselves—together with the mass media —for what has happened in Watts, Harlem, Chicago, Cleveland, Omaha.

WHAT WE WANT From *The New York Review of Books*, September 22, 1966. Reprinted by permission of the Student National Coordinating Committee.

Each time the people in those cities saw Martin Luther King get slapped, they became angry; when they saw four little black girls bombed to death, they were angrier; and when nothing happened, they were steaming. We had nothing to offer that they could see, except to go out and be beaten again. We helped to build their frustration.

For too many years, black Americans marched and had their heads broken and got shot. They were saying to the country, "Look, you guys are supposed to be nice guys and we are only going to do what we are supposed to do—why do you beat us up, why don't you give us what we ask, why don't you straighten yourselves out?" After years of this, we are at almost the same point—because we demonstrated from a position of weakness. We cannot be expected any longer to march and have our heads broken in order to say to whites: come on, you're nice guys. For you are not nice guys. We have found you out.

An organization which claims to speak for the needs of a community—as does the Student Nonviolent Coordinating Committee—must speak in the tone of that community, not as somebody else's buffer zone. This is the significance of black power as a slogan. For once, black people are going to use the words they want to use—not just the words whites want to hear. And they will do this no matter how often the press tries to stop the use of the slogan by equating it with racism or separatism.

An organization which claims to be working for the needs of a community —as SNCC does—must work to provide that community with a position of strength from which to make its voice heard. This is the significance of black power beyond the slogan.

Black power can be clearly defined for those who do not attach the fears of white America to their questions about it. We should begin with the basic fact that black Americans have two problems: they are poor and they are black. All other problems arise from this two-sided reality: lack of education, the so-called apathy of black men. Any program to end racism must address itself to that double reality.

Almost from its beginning, SNCC sought to address itself to both conditions with a program aimed at winning political power for impoverished Southern blacks. We had to begin with politics because black Americans are a propertyless people in a country where property is valued above all. We had to work for power, because this country does not function by morality, love, and nonviolence, but by power. Thus we determined to win political power, with the idea of moving on from there into activity that would have economic effects. With power, the masses could *make or participate in making* the decisions which govern their destinies, and thus create basic change in their day-to-day lives.

But if political power seemed to be the key to self-determination, it was also obvious that the key had been thrown down a deep well many years earlier. Disenfranchisement, maintained by racist terror, made it impossible to talk about organizing for political power in 1960. The right to vote had to be won, and SNCC workers devoted their energies to this from 1961 to

1965. They set up voter registration drives in the Deep South. They created pressure for the vote by holding mock elections in Mississippi in 1963 and by helping to establish the Mississippi Freedom Democratic Party (MFDP) in 1964. That struggle was eased, though not won, with the passage of the 1965 Voting Rights Act. SNCC workers could then address themselves to the question: "Who can we vote for, to have our needs met—how do we make our vote meaningful?"

SNCC had already gone to Atlantic City for recognition of the Mississippi Freedom Democratic Party by the Democratic convention and been rejected; it had gone with the MFDP to Washington for recognition by Congress and been rejected. In Arkansas, SNCC helped thirty Negroes to run for School Board elections; all but one were defeated, and there was evidence of fraud and intimidation sufficient to cause their defeat. In Atlanta, Julian Bond ran for the state legislature and was elected—twice—and unseated—twice. In several states, black farmers ran in elections for agricultural committees which make crucial decisions concerning land use, loans, etc. Although they won places on a number of committees, they never gained the majorities needed to control them.

All of the efforts were attempts to win black power. Then, in Alabama, the opportunity came to see how blacks could be organized on an independent party basis. An unusual Alabama law provides that any group of citizens can nominate candidates for county office and, if they win 20 per cent of the vote, may be recognized as a county political party. The same then applies on a state level. SNCC went to organize in several counties such as Lowndes, where black people—who form 80 per cent of the population and have an average annual income of $943—felt they could accomplish nothing within the framework of the Alabama Democratic Party because of its racism and because the qualifying fee for this year's elections was raised from $40 to $500 in order to prevent most Negroes from becoming candidates. On May 3, five new county "freedom organizations" convened and nominated candidates for the offices of sheriff, tax assessor, members of the school boards. These men and women are up for election in November—if they live until then. Their ballot symbol is the black panther: a bold, beautiful animal, representing the strength and dignity of black demands today. A man needs a black panther on his side when he and his family must endure—as hundreds of Alabamians have endured—loss of job, eviction, starvation, and sometimes death, for political activity. He may also need a gun and SNCC reaffirms the right of black men everywhere to defend themselves when threatened or attacked. As for initiating the use of violence, we hope that such programs as ours will make that unnecessary; but it is not for us to tell black communities whether they can or cannot use any particular form of action to resolve their problems. Responsibility for the use of violence by black men, whether in self defense or initiated by them, lies with the white community.

This is the specific historical experience from which SNCC's call for "black power" emerged on the Mississippi march last July. But the concept of "black power" is not a recent or isolated phenomenon: It has grown out of the ferment of agitation and activity by different people and organizations in many black communities over the years. Our last year of work in Alabama added a new concrete possibility. In Lowndes County, for example, black power will mean that if a Negro is elected sheriff, he can end police brutality. If a black man is elected tax assessor, he can collect and channel funds for the building of better roads and schools serving black people—thus advancing the move from political power into the economic arena. In such areas as Lowndes, where black men have a majority, they will attempt to use it to exercise control. This is what they seek: control. Where Negroes lack a majority, black power means proper representation and sharing of control. It means the creation of power bases from which black people can work to change statewide or nationwide patterns of oppression through pressure from strength—instead of weakness. Politically, black power means what it has always meant to SNCC: the coming-together of black people to elect representatives and *to force those representatives to speak to their needs*. It does not mean merely putting black faces into office. A man or woman who is black and from the slums cannot be automatically expected to speak to the needs of black people. Most of the black politicians we see around the country today are not what SNCC means by black power. The power must be that of a community, and emanate from there.

SNCC today is working in both North and South on programs of voter registration and independent political organizing. In some places, such as Alabama, Los Angeles, New York, Philadelphia, and New Jersey, independent organizing under the black panther symbol is in progress. The creation of a national "black panther party" must come about; it will take time to build, and it is much too early to predict its success. We have no infallible master plan and we make no claim to exclusive knowledge of how to end racism; different groups will work in their own different ways. SNCC cannot spell out the full logistics of self-determination but it can address itself to the problem by helping black communities define their needs, realize their strength, and go into action along a variety of lines which they must choose for themselves. Without knowing all the answers, it can address itself to the basic problem of poverty; to the fact that in Lowndes County, 86 white families own 90 per cent of the land. What are black people in that county going to do for jobs, where are they going to get money? There must be real-location of land, of money.

Ultimately, the economic foundations of this country must be shaken if black people are to control their lives. The colonies of the United States—and this includes the black ghettoes within its borders, north and south—must be liberated. For a century, this nation has been like an octopus of exploitation, its tentacles stretching from Mississippi and Harlem to South America, the Middle East, southern Africa, and Vietnam; the form of exploitation varies from area to area but the essential result has been the same—a powerful few have been maintained and enriched at the expense of the poor and voiceless colored masses. This pattern must be broken. As its grip loosens here and there around the world, the hopes of black Americans become more realistic. For racism to die, a totally different America must be born.

This is what the white society does not wish to face; this is why that society prefers to talk about integration. But integration speaks not at all to the problem of poverty, only to the problem of blackness. Integration today means the man who "makes it," leaving his black brothers behind in the ghetto as fast as his new sports car will take him. It has no relevance to the Harlem wino or to the cottonpicker making three dollars a day. As a lady I know in Alabama once said, "the food that Ralph Bunche eats doesn't fill my stomach."

Integration, moreover, speaks to the problem of blackness in a despicable way. As a goal, it has been based on complete acceptance of the fact that *in order to have* a decent house or education, blacks must move into a white neighborhood or send their children to a white school. This reinforces, among both black and white, the idea that "white" is automatically better and "black" is by definition inferior. This is why integration is a subterfuge for the maintenance of white supremacy. It allows the nation to focus on a handful of Southern children who get into white schools, at great price, and to ignore the 94 per cent who are left behind in unimproved all black schools. Such situations will not change until black people have power—to control their own school boards, in this case. Then Negroes become equal in a way that means something, and integration ceases to be a one-way street. Then integration doesn't mean draining skills and energies from the ghetto into white neighborhoods; then it can mean white people moving from Beverly Hills into Watts, white people joining the Lowndes County Freedom Organization. Then integration becomes relevant.

Last April, before the furor over black power, Christopher Jencks wrote in a *New Republic* article on white Mississippi's manipulation of the anti-poverty program:

The war on poverty has been predicated on the notion that there is such a thing as *a community* which can be defined geographically and mobilized for a collective effort to help the poor. This theory has no relationship to reality in the Deep South. In every Mississippi county there are *two* communities. Despite all the pious platitudes of the moderates on both sides, these two communities habitually see their interests in terms of conflict rather than cooperation. Only when the Negro community can muster enough political, economic and professional strength to compete on somewhat equal terms, will Negroes believe in the possibility of true co-operation and whites accept its necessity. En route to integration, the Negro community needs to develop greater independence—a chance to run its own affairs and not cave in whenever "the man" barks . . . Or so it seems to me, and to most of the knowledgeable people with whom I talked in Mississippi. To OEO, this judgment may sound like black nationalism . . .

Mr. Jencks, a white reporter, perceived the reason why America's anti-poverty program has been a sick farce in both North and South. In the South, it is clearly racism which prevents the poor from running their own programs; in the North, it more often seems to be politicking and bureaucracy. But the results are not so different: In the North, non-whites make up 42 per cent of all families in metropolitan "poverty areas" and only 6 per cent of families in areas classified as not poor. SNCC has been working with local residents in Arkansas, Alabama, and Mississippi to achieve control by the poor of the program and its funds; it has also been working with groups in the North, and the struggle is no less difficult. Behind it all is a federal government which cares far more about winning the war on the Vietnamese than the war on poverty; which has put the poverty program in the hands of self-serving politicians and bureaucrats rather than the poor themselves; which is unwilling to curb the misuse of white power but quick to condemn black power.

To most whites, black power seems to mean that the Mau Mau are coming to the suburbs at night. The Mau Mau are coming, and whites must stop them. Articles appear about plots to "get Whitey," creating an atmosphere in which "law and order must be maintained." Once again, responsibility is shifted from the oppressor to the oppressed. Other whites chide, "Don't forget—you're only 10 per cent of the population; if you get too smart, we'll wipe you out." If they are liberals, they complain, "what about me?— don't you want my help any more?" These are people supposedly concerned about black Americans; but today they think first of themselves, of their feelings of rejection. Or they admonish, "you can't get anywhere without coalitions," without considering the problems of coalition with whom?; on what terms? (coalescing from weakness can mean absorption, betrayal); when? Or they accuse us of "polarizing the races" by our calls for black unity, when the true responsibility for polarization lies with whites who will not accept their responsibility as the majority power for making the democratic process work.

White America will not face the problem of color, the reality of it. The well-intended say: "We're all human, everybody is really decent, we must forget color." But color cannot be "forgotten" until its weight is recognized and dealt with. White America will not acknowledge that the ways in which this country sees itself are contradicted by being black—and always have been. Whereas most of the people who settled this country came here for freedom or for economic opportunity, blacks were brought here to be slaves. When the Lowndes County Freedom Organization chose the black panther as its symbol, it was christened by the press "the Black Panther Party"—but the Alabama Democratic Party, whose symbol is a rooster, has never been called the White Cock Party. No one ever talked about "white power" because power in this country *is* white. All this adds up to more than merely identifying a group phenomenon by some catchy name or adjective. The furor over that black panther reveals the problems that white America has with color and sex; the furor over "black power" reveals how deep racism runs and the great fear which is attached to it.

Whites will not see that I, for example, as a person oppressed because of my blackness, have common cause with other blacks who are oppressed because of blackness. This is not to say that there are no white people who see things as I do, but that it is black people I must speak to first. It must be the oppressed to whom SNCC addresses itself primarily, not to friends from the oppressing group.

From birth, black people are told a set of lies about themselves. We are told that we are lazy—yet I drive through the Delta area of Mississippi and watch black people picking cotton in the hot sun for fourteen hours. We are told, "If you work hard, you'll succeed"—but if that were true, black people would own this country. We are oppressed because we are black—not because we are ignorant, not because we are lazy, not because we're stupid (and got good rhythm), but because we're black.

I remember that when I was a boy, I used to go to see Tarzan movies on Saturday. White Tarzan used to beat up the black natives. I would sit there yelling, "Kill the beasts, kill the savages, kill 'em!" I was saying: Kill *me*. It was as if a Jewish boy watched Nazis taking Jews off to concentration camps and cheered them on. Today, I want the chief to beat hell out of Tarzan and send him back to Europe. But it takes time to become free of the lies and their shaming effect on black minds. It takes time to reject the most important lie: that black people inherently can't do the same things white people can do, unless white people help them.

The need for psychological equality is the reason why SNCC today believes that blacks must organize in the black community. Only black people can convey the revolutionary idea that black people are able to do things themselves. Only they can help create in the community an aroused and continuing black consciousness that will provide the basis for political strength. In the past, white allies have furthered white supremacy without the whites involved realizing it—or wanting it, I think. Black people must do things for themselves; they must get poverty money they will control and spend themselves, they must conduct tutorial programs themselves so that black children can identify with black people. This is one reason Africa has such importance: The reality of black men ruling their own nations gives blacks elsewhere a sense of possibility, of power, which they do not now have.

This does not mean we don't welcome help, or friends. But we want the right to decide whether anyone is, in fact, our friend. In the past, black Americans have been almost the only people whom everybody and his momma could jump up and call their friends. We have been tokens, symbols, objects—as I was in high school to many young whites, who liked having "a Negro friend." We want to decide who is our friend, and we will not accept someone who comes to us and says: "If you do X, Y, and Z, then I'll help you." We will not be told whom we should choose as allies. We will not be isolated from any group or nation except by our own choice. We cannot have the oppressors telling the oppressed how to rid themselves of the oppressor.

I have said that most liberal whites react to "black power" with the question, What about me?, rather than saying: Tell me what you want me to do and I'll see if I can do it. There are answers to the right question. One of the most disturbing things about almost all white supporters of the movement has been that they are afraid to go into their own communities—which is where the racism exists—and work to get rid of it. They want to run from Berkeley to tell us what to do in Mississippi; let them look instead at Berkeley. They admonish blacks to be nonviolent; let them preach nonviolence in the white community. They come to teach me Negro history; let them go to the suburbs and open up freedom schools for whites. Let them work to stop America's racist foreign policy; let them press this government to cease supporting the economy of South Africa.

There is a vital job to be done among poor whites. We hope to see, eventually, a coalition between poor blacks and poor whites. That is the only coalition which seems acceptable to us, and we see such a coalition as the major internal instrument of change in American society. SNCC has tried several times to organize poor whites; we are trying again now, with an initial training program in Tennessee. It is purely academic today to talk about bringing poor blacks and whites together, but the job of creating a poor-white power bloc must be attempted. The main responsibility for it falls upon whites. Black and white can work together in the white community where possible; it is not possible, however, to go into a poor Southern town and talk about integration. Poor whites everywhere are becoming more hostile—not less—partly because they see the nation's attention focused on black poverty and nobody coming to them. Too many young middle-class Americans, like some sort of Pepsi generation, have wanted to come alive through the black community; they've wanted to be where the action is—and the action has been in the black community.

Black people do not want to "take over" this country. They don't want to "get Whitey"; they just want to get him off their backs, as the saying goes. It was for example the exploitation by Jewish landlords and merchants which first created black resentment toward Jews—not Judaism. The white man is irrelevant to blacks, except as an oppressive force. Blacks want to be in his place, yes, but not in order to terrorize and lynch and starve him. They want to be in his place because that is where a decent life can be had.

But our vision is not merely of a society in which all black men have enough to buy the good things of life. When we urge that black money go into black pockets, we mean the communal pocket. We want to see money go back into the community and used to benefit it. We want to see the cooperative concept applied in business and banking. We want to see black ghetto residents demand that an exploiting landlord or storekeeper sell them, at minimal cost, a building or a shop that they will own and improve cooperatively; they can back their demand with a rent strike, or a boycott, and a community so unified behind them that no one else will move into the building or buy at the store. The society we seek to build among black people, then, is not a capitalist one. It is a society in which the spirit of community and humanistic love prevail. The word love is suspect; black expectations of what it might produce have been betrayed too often. But those were expectations of a response from the white community, which failed us. The love we seek to encourage is within the black community, the only American community where men call each other "brother" when they meet. We can build a community of love only where we have the ability and power to do so: among blacks.

As for white America, perhaps it can stop crying out against "black supremacy," "black nationalism," "racism in reverse," and begin facing reality. The reality is that this nation, from top to bottom, is racist; that racism is not primarily a problem of "human relations" but of an exploitation maintained—either actively or through silence—by the society as a whole. Camus and Sartre have asked, can a man condemn himself? Can whites, particularly liberal whites, condemn themselves? Can they stop blaming us, and blame their own system? Are they capable of the shame which might become a revolutionary emotion?

We have found that they usually cannot condemn themselves, and so we have done it. But the rebuilding of this society, if at all possible, is basically the responsibility of whites—not blacks. We won't fight to save the present society, in Vietnam or anywhere else. We are just going to work, in the way *we* see fit, and on goals *we* define, not for civil rights but for all our human rights.

WHAT KIND OF PEOPLE?

Louisa R. Shotwell

> I believe in aristocracy . . . Not an aristocracy of power, based upon rank and influence, but an aristocracy of the sensitive, the considerate and the plucky. Its members are to be found in all nations and classes, and all through the ages, and there is a secret understanding between them when they meet . . . They represent the true human tradition, the one permanent victory of our queer race over cruelty and chaos. Thousands of them perish in obscurity . . .
>
> —E. M. Forster.

As a facet of American life, agricultural migrancy has characteristics peculiarly its own.

The migrant is a minority within a minority. The components of the general migrant population belong to racial or ethnic minorities. In addition, each in turn within his own ethnic group occupies a place at the very bottom of the social and economic hierarchy. He meets the most discrimination, does the hardest work, earns the least money; he has the least job security, the least formal schooling, the lowest status. His migrancy separates him from the larger community; his minority status aggravates the separation.

Migrancy is unobtrusive. It lacks the visibility of large-scale housing developments or city slums. Neither its erstwhile barns and hen houses nor its barrack compounds nor yet its newer cinder-block housing units stand near the superhighways. In its trekking migrancy does not frequent toll roads. Unlike suburbia, it imposes no patterns of living on the national culture; its way of life does not invite imitation.

The migrant works in a labor market that, in spite of years of well-intentioned and zealous effort of public and private agencies and individuals, can only be described as chaotic. He is a necessary cog in an agricultural machine that differs from the traditional family farm in just about the same degree that the shop of the village blacksmith differs from a General Motors assembly line. The urban influences that tend to lift the material level of living of the rest of the American community have been slow to penetrate his rural folk culture. He has little or no education. He is unorganized and inarticulate; there is no indigenous leadership to speak in his behalf. The stoop labor he performs makes the most severe demands on his physical stamina, yet he is not regarded as belonging to labor with a capital "L." If the cotton he picks is deliberately weighed short, he has no legal recourse. His grievance does not fall within the jurisdiction of a labor relations board. The protections of the Fair Labor Standards Act do not extend to him. The forces of industrial labor have tried to organize migrant farm workers; the results have been negligible. If labor legislation and academic treatises on labor mention farm workers at all, they do so only to specify that agriculture is excluded from consideration. Sensing exploitation, the migrant may bite back, but his bite is sporadic, illogical, and futile. And his teeth are weak. In an industrial economy he stands as a lonely anachronism.

Migrancy engenders community resentment, puts in peril such practical aspects of normal family living as regular schooling for children, housing that is sanitary and convenient and conducive to wholesome family relationships, voting privileges, stable income, health and welfare services available to residents. Migrancy reduces to zero the chance to develop the feeling of belonging to a stable community.

Time and again the cumulative negatives surrounding migrancy break through to fascinate and appall the public conscience; but as they haunt it, they also confound it. The public does not know what to do about them. The thorny questions they raise generate strong feelings, but they neither win nor lose elections. Faced with pressures from powerful farm groups and dwarfed by larger issues, they simply stay lost.

What kind of people choose a way of life with so many disadvantages? And why do they do it? Are they just too happy-go-lucky to hold down a steady job in one locale? Or are they too lazy? How accurate is the stereotype of itchy feet?

If it is difficult to make definitive pronouncements about numbers of migrant workers and their migration patterns, it is even more hazardous to generalize about the motivations, the habits, the values, the behavior and culture patterns either of migrants across the board or of the individual groups that make up this fluid, massive, leaderless army. It is an easy pitfall to blunder into accepting the caricature of the irresponsible Mexican, the volatile Puerto Rican, the razor-carrying Negro, the feud-holding mountaineer, the lazy Indian, the drunken stumblebum and to forget that individual differences of temperament and talent exist within all groups.

The truth is that all sorts of people turn up as migrants: people frail and solid, perceptive and dull, industrious and indolent, sensitive and stoic, crusty and charming, honest and crooked, clean and dirty. To attribute particular motivations to them and to predict their behavior in special situations is just as inaccurate as it is with businessmen or schoolteachers or lawyers or politicians or farmers.

At the same time, along with disposition and native ability, group mores and the limitations of environment do operate to determine how individuals respond to recurring situations. Annunciata Fontanez is governed by standards of behavior traditional for Mexican women. Negroes with generations of plantation culture behind them share a casual attitude toward time not found among Negroes with long-time urban experience. Reservation Indian people exhibit tribal loyalties difficult for Anglos to comprehend.

Apart from ethnic differences, the very nature of migrancy makes it possible to isolate certain values and social characteristics commonly found among migrants: a spirit of resignation; a sense of being trapped; an astonishing lack of bitterness; a fierce family loyalty; a buoyant, often subtle wit; a tendency to spend money, when they have it, to meet not only immediate needs but immediate desires; a longing to be somebody, manifested sometimes as a blatant groping for status, more often as a craving for recognition as a human being; a longing for a better life for their children; a quick and generous sympathy for neighbors in trouble; a high incidence of stamina and courage.

In all the migrating groups there are a few who like the freedom to move about; there are a few who simply like to work outdoors; there are some who enjoy the independence of working at a piece rate and stopping when they feel inclined. Especially with the southwestern Latin workers the element of excitement at the prospect of a trip north plays a part. The fact that crops give opportunity for every member of the family to earn money figures as a strongly persuasive factor.

But with due allowance for the part played by all these motivations, for overwhelming numbers migration offers the only visible alternative to unemployment. There is at the heart of the "why" question one categorical answer. Unlike restlessness or improvidence or sloth, its key is neither a native characteristic nor an acquired mode of behavior. It is an external factor, a pressure from environment. It is primitive and it is stark.

Asked where he secured his seasonal workers, the personnel director of an industrial farm on the eastern seaboard said:

"I tell you, I've been in this business for twenty-eight years. Back in the thirties we used day hauls from the cities; you know, Italians and Polocks and Hunkies and people like that. In the early forties we had prisoners of war, and sometimes we've contracted for British West Indians. These past years we've had Negro families from the South and some Puerto Ricans, sugar-cane workers off the Island. They change as the years go by, but I'll tell you one thing for sure. When spring comes, whoever they are, they're the people who are the hungriest. Who else wants to work that hard for that little money?"

Well, who does?

Like the southern Negroes, most of the migrating Anglo families come from a hand-to-mouth existence, either as displaced tenants or sharecroppers or as marginal farm owners unable to meet the competition of mechanized agriculture. Some have made abortive attempts to work in industry, but with little education and few skills, they are the inevitable first victims of layoffs.

Jim Vinson worked in a score of states after the summer ten years back when he first took his child-wife and their baby girl Lucy from their Kentucky hill farm to pick blueberries in Michigan.

Two thirds of Jim's eighty Kentucky acres were untillable wooded upland, and his cash intake in a good year never came to more than a thousand dollars. When Lucy was born, Ellie Vinson was fifteen; she had a difficult confinement. Jim's meager savings stretched to cover only a fifth of the hospital bill. Ellie's brother lent money to pay the rest. Jim Vinson had been bred to a horror of debt even within the family, and migration to a place where he and Ellie both could work for cash looked like a good, and indeed the only, way to pay off the loan.

As she picked, Ellie would park Lucy at the end of each blueberry row. By the close of the second summer in Michigan, Jim was able to pay off his brother-in-law's loan. But the following spring Kentucky floods wiped out all his crops. It was too late to replant, and this time they went to Arkansas. From there to Oklahoma. Then to Idaho.

They never did get back to Kentucky, and Ellie never did grow up. Each year brought a new baby, and with each addition to the family Ellie receded further into childhood. She grew physically robust; she was docile, and she worked in the fields without complaint, but she seldom spoke and she made no attempt to cope with her family. By the time Lucy was ten, it was not her mother but Lucy who cooked the eternal grits and hot dogs and macaroni and Jello, did the washing, and more or less looked after her seven brothers and sisters, rounding them up and counting them when Jim said it was time to move on.

As for Jim, he worked doggedly whenever and wherever there was work to be had. A few times he tried to get work at something besides picking. He was strong, but he had no experience at anything but farming and he had no facility for selling himself. Once they found out that he was a migrant, employers of day labor shook their heads. For five days in Indiana he did get work replacing railroad ties, and then the job folded. After that he stopped trying for any kind of work but crops. Every time he was paid, the first three dollars went into his right shoe. No matter if crops were running good or bad, and even when the picking kept him working ten hours a day for seven days in the week, each Saturday night he religiously took the three dollars out of his right shoe, found a tavern in the nearest town, and quietly and systematically got drunk.

DISPATCH FROM WOUNDED KNEE

Calvin Kentfield

WOUNDED KNEE, S.D.

From time to time over the years, since long before the frigid Plains winter of 1890 when United States forces armed with Hotchkiss machine guns mowed down men, women, children and some of their own soldiers in the final slaughter at Wounded Knee, the Congress of the United States has become guiltily concerned about the condition and fate of the native American Indian. The most recent manifestation of that concern is the House of Representatives Bill 10560, also known as the Indian Resources Development Act of 1967, sponsored by Representative James Haley, a Florida Democrat, and a fellow Democrat, Representative Wayne N. Aspinall of Colorado, chairman of the Committee on Interior and Insular Affairs with which the bill now resides.

If enacted, the bill would allow the Indians greater freedom in selling, mortgaging, and developing what lands they still possess, encourage them through Government loans to bring industry to the reservations, and enable them with the approval of the Interior Department's Bureau of Indian Affairs to obtain loans from private sources. Indians in general, after years of bitter experience with Congressional maneuvers and of watching the depletion of their lands despite Federal largesse, are wary of the bill's benevolence, but most of their tribal councils have chosen to go along with it, chiefly because they hope that this time around the economic provisions will really work and because they figure that this is as good a bill as they can get at this time.

Out where the battle of Wounded Knee took place, however, the tribal elders are decidedly unenthusiastic about the bill and its Government backers. "We know they mean well," says Johnson Holy Rock, the chairman of the Tribal Council of the Oglala Sioux at Pine Ridge Reservation in South Dakota. "Their intentions in putting forth this bill are undoubtedly of the best, but they don't understand the Indian mind, and we here at Pine Ridge

DISPATCH FROM WOUNDED KNEE From *The New York Times Magazine,* October 15, 1967. © 1967 by The New York Times Company. Reprinted by permission.

have simply said we won't accept it, we want to be left out, we're not ready for it, we know we'd lose more than we'd gain and we've lost too much already."

And Brice Lay, the chief of the Pine Ridge Agency of the Bureau of Indian Affairs to which an Indian must apply in order to sell or lease his land, says, "We here at the bureau know, and the council knows, that if a piece of land comes up for bids, a non-Indian's going to get it." He pointed to a chart of the reservation that showed 42 per cent of the land already in white hands. "The Indians have first choice," he went on, "but very few of them can afford it, not even the council acting for the tribe as a whole. It's simply going to go out of Indian hands, and there's nothing on earth we can do about it."

The ever-diminishing land is almost the sole source of subsistence for the inhabitants of the Pine Ridge Reservation—or, more colorfully, the Land of Red Cloud—which is the seventh largest of the 300-odd reservations in the United States. It stretches for 90 miles east from the Black Hills and about 50 miles from the northern Badlands south to the Nebraska line.

In the eastern part some of the land is fertile enough to bear wheat, oats, safflower and the like, but 99 per cent of this farm land is now and forever in the hands of the white man. The rest of the reservation consists of rolling short-grass prairie land, an enormous landscape divided into four parts: endless green grass, tall blue sky, low ridges of ponderosa pine, and a constant rustling, sighing wind. Through these great plains wander cottonwood-shaded creeks such as Bear In the Lodge, Potato, Wounded Knee, and the twisted White and Cheyenne Rivers. In the summer, thunderclouds build up towers on the far horizons and the uninhibited sun may produce temperatures of 120 degrees; in the winter, the creeks become ice and blizzard winds such as those that froze the bodies at the massacre of Wounded Knee into such baroque and unusual shapes can bring the thermometer down to 40 below.

U.S. Highway 18 passes east-west through the southern edge of the reservation. There are miles and miles of good black-top roads kept in repair by Indians working for the Interior Department road service; and there are miles and miles of roads that are no good at all. There are modern boarding schools exclusively for Indian children as well as local public schools and a Catholic mission school, outlying clinics and a good free hospital with doctors, surgeons, dentists and a psychiatrist. There are churches of all kinds (40 per cent of the Indians profess to be Catholics and more to be Protestants, but the old beliefs still lie heavily in their souls). There is an American Legion Post, a Lions Club, a Ladies' Aid, a P.-T.A. and a Boy Scout troop. Nearly all of the Sioux (or Dakotas, their own pre-reservation name for themselves) speak English as well as their native Lakota dialect, and there are still a few medicine men around, like old Frank Fools Crow who usually presides over the annual Sun Dance. The center of nearly everything—government, society, law and order, education—is Pine Ridge, a town of 1,256 people close enough to the state line to have a "suburb" in Nebraska, Whiteclay, center of shopping (three supermarkets) and entertainment (bars and dance halls).

On this reservation live, in one fashion or another, nearly 10,000 Teton Sioux of the Oglala tribe. They are not the poorest nor the richest of the country's Indians. The Hopis and some of the Apaches of the Southwest are poorer, and the inhabitants of the Aguacaliente reservation in Southern California, who more or less own Palm Springs, are richer, to say nothing of those few tribes that have oil wells. But the Oglalas range from a state of imminent starvation to fair affluence.

On the reservation itself, unemployment is 43 per cent, so some of the younger people go elsewhere for summer work. There is a new factory at Pine Ridge that employs about a hundred people to make "handmade" moccasins. A fishhook factory near Wounded Knee employs nearly 200 more, and a few more work for the Bureau of Indian Affairs. Most of the businesses —filling stations, grocery stores—are owned by whites, and the rest of the Indians work for white ranchers or live off the land which they work themselves or lease to white ranchers. The land, though it belongs to the Indians, is held in trust by the Department of the Interior, which takes care of all the leasing arrangements and issues checks to the owners each month from a computer in Aberdeen.

Aside from Interior Department employees and a few Indian ranchers, the average annual income per family is less than $900. The 34 members of the Tribal Council, however, have voted themselves a yearly salary of $7,500, paid out of proceeds from tribal lands under grazing leases. "Those earnings are supposed to be divided up amongst us all," one man told me, "but we ain't none of us seen a pinny of it for years." Most of the money, of course, goes into the operation of the tribal government, which has charge of all municipal services—police, fire and courts—as well as the maintenance of lawyers in Rapid City and Washington to represent the tribe in all higher dealings with the Government, such as House Bill 10560. Though technically wards of the Federal Government under the guiding thumb of the Bureau of Indian Affairs, the Indians, since 1924, have enjoyed the rights and privileges of full American citizenship, including the right to fight in Vietnam and the privilege of paying income taxes. They enjoy some extra privileges as well, such as untaxed land.

"We try to help them," said Brice Lay in his office in the new air-conditioned bureau headquarters in Pine Ridge, "to make the best possible use of the land they have, but it's very hard." Like most of the non-Indian (the bureau does not use the term "white man") employees of the bureau, he is intensely sincere in his desire to help the Indian become a white man. "Here in Pine Ridge most of the people live fairly well, but you go out on the reservation—the way some of those people live!" He made a gesture of despair. "*No* one should have to live that way."

And, indeed, out on the windy treeless tracts of the reservation, at the end of two dirt ruts across the prairie, will be a one-room shack, possibly a log cabin, possibly a frame house walled in tarpaper, for a family of six, eight, ten people and surrounded by a circle of old car bodies that, like the bodies of U.S. soldiers killed in a battle of olden times, have been stripped and mutilated and left to rot where they lay. An outhouse nearby. No electricity, no running water. A monthly ration of rice, flour, powdered milk, peanut butter, margarine, lard, raisins, oatmeal, cornmeal, potted meat, dried beans, dried peas, bulgur and rolled wheat, plus $50 in cash from Welfare. This kind of poverty engenders horror, pity and disgust in the Anglo-Saxon breast, but all the Oglalas are not that badly off, and many of them simply don't want some of the amenities that the Great White Father insists they must have, if possible, for their own good.

"We had one old woman out on the reservation," Brice Lay said, "that was all by herself and living in a tent, so we found a house for her, but she wouldn't move in. She said she'd die if she lived in a house, that the air in a house was bad air. Oh, she was stubborn. But finally," he concluded with a tone of great satisfaction, "we got her in there."

Out at Wounded Knee about two miles from the general store and post office lives a man in his late 50's, his wife, two married sons, six grandchildren, three dogs, two cats, some hens and a rooster. He is a full blood, very dark, though his wife is not. He owns a section of land (640 acres) through which runs Wounded Knee Creek and on which graze about 200 head of cattle and 60 or 70 horses. He has a field of alfalfa which, this year, because of the late rains, is exceptionally rich and high and, when I visited him, was ready for cutting. There are tall shade trees along the creek, plenty of water, and a small field of sweet corn nearby.

He and his wife and one orphaned grandchild live in a very old, one-room log cabin with a shade, or "squaw cooler" (though "squaw" is an insulting word these days), a kind of summer house made of poles and pine boughs that keep off the sun but let the breeze come through, making it a comfortable outdoor kitchen and sleeping place during the hot months. His sons and their families live in small asphalt-shingled houses on either side of the parental house. One son is a cowboy and works the section, the other works at the fishhook factory over the hill. Standing to one side at the edge of the alfalfa is a two-hole outhouse.

They carry their water from the creek, build their fire with wood and light their lamps with kerosene. They walk to the store and back, as they have no car. They are well and presumably happy. They are members of the Native American Church who use peyote, the hallucinatory cactus, in their services, during which, under the spell of the drug, they chant and sing and pray to God that the day will come when all men will be at peace and all men will be brothers. Not half a mile from this man's house reside the bones in a mass hilltop grave of the victims of the massacre of Wounded Knee.

Though a Peace Sacrifice was the climax of this year's Sun Dance—"Richard 'Buddy' Red Bow," the posters read, "17 years old, member of the Oglala Sioux tribe, will pray for worldwide peace by performing the traditional

Sun Dance worship. Red Bow will pierce his flesh and offer his blood, praying for the safety of American Servicemen and a peaceful speedy end to war in Vietnam"—the Sioux were not always a peaceable people.

"Sioux" is short for "Nadowessioux," which is French for "Nadowessi," which is Chippewa meaning "little snakes" or, in other words, treacherous enemies. The Sioux fought everybody—the Chippewa, the Crow, the Cheyenne, the Kiowa and the white man after he came pushing onto the plains, stealing, pushing, lying, slaughtering the buffalo, always pushing. In 1866, Red Cloud, "the first and only Indian leader in the West to win a war with the United States," said to a Colonel Carrington, come to open a road to the Montana goldfields, "You are the White Eagle who has come to steal the road! The Great Father sends us presents and wants us to sell him the road, but the White Chief comes with soldiers to steal it before the Indian says yes or no! I will talk with you no more. As long as I live I will fight you for the last hunting grounds of my people."

Red Cloud and Crazy Horse, Custer's Last Stand, Sitting Bull and Big Foot, and the final slaughter at Wounded Knee! After all that misery, bravery, and bloodshed, the Sioux, romanticized by the white man, became the Ideal Indian, the Mounted Warrior in War Bonnet, the End of the Trail, the Indian at the Medicine Show, the All-American Buffalo-Nickel Indian.

The last treaty the Sioux made with the United States Government (1868–69) set aside nearly half of South Dakota, including the sacred Black Hills, and part of North Dakota as the "Great Sioux Reserve." But white men discovered gold in the Black Hills (as Johnson Holy Rock said to me, "The Indians still don't understand gold, it's a white man's concept and the white man just can't understand that"), so an Act of Congress in 1877 removed the Black Hills from the Indians' reserve. Later, another act divided what was left of the "Great Sioux Reserve" into five reservations with still more loss of land, settling the Oglalas at Pine Ridge. It is no wonder, indeed, that the Indian leaders look twice and twice again at Acts of Congress.

The Indian Bureau demands at least one-quarter Indian blood as a prerequisite for donating its paternalistic blessings—but the Pine Ridge Tribal Council has *never* been able to decide upon who is and who is not an Indian.

"The Tribal Council is ridiculous," said a man I shall call Edgar Running Bear because he has asked me not to use his real name. "Two of them are stupid women who have not even had a sixth-grade education, one of them is a hopeless alcoholic, and they're all prejudiced."

We were sitting in Edgar Running Bear's house in one of the several new Pine Ridge subdivisions financed by the Public Housing Authority and built by Indian labor against the fierce objections of half-a-dozen union leaders. It is a two-bedroom house, pink and white, with a carport and a front lawn like millions of others all over America. In the living room were two modernistic armchairs, a huge radio-phonograph-television combination set in the corner. On top of the TV stood a vase of plastic flowers and on the wall opposite the picture window hung a small imitation tapestry of a roaring tiger printed in lurid colors on black velvet.

It was a hot day and through the open windows we could hear the drumming and amplified chanting of one of the bands, the Oglala Juniors or the Sioux Travelers, who had gathered at the nearby campground for the four-day Sun Dance celebration, a kind of county fair, carnival and tribal get-together combined with ancient ritual which was just then beginning. The celebration is an annual rite that Edgar, at one point in our conversation, referred to scornfully as a reversion to primitivism, though he later took his children over to the campground to ride the Space-Mobile.

"Why do you say they're prejudiced?" I asked. "Against whom?"

"Against the mixed bloods."

Both Edgar and his wife, and indeed most of the population of the reservation, are mixed bloods. The classic face of Red Cloud is seldom seen. Johnson Holy Rock himself is three-quarter Oglala and one-quarter Scotch-Irish. I mentioned this fact and elicited only a shrug from Edgar.

"Do you find," I asked, "that white people on the reservation or off it show prejudice toward you because you're Indians?"

"Oh, yes," Edgar's wife said quickly. "They move onto our land, look down their noses at us, and complain about our laws and our dogs and—"

"When I go off the reservation," Edgar broke in, "I expect to abide by the ways of the people there. It doesn't bother me, if we don't get served one place, we'll go someplace else, but *you* could go staggering drunk down the main street of Rushville [Rushville, Neb., the nearest town of any size] and nobody'd look at you, but if *I* did—well, not me because being a policeman they know me—but if an ordinary Innun did the same thing he'd be in jail so fast. . . ."

I related an incident I had witnessed in a restaurant-bar in Rushville. The television had been giving news of the aftermath of the Negro riots in Detroit and the waitress had said, "I know it's a funny attitude to take, but if one of them come in here, I just couldn't serve him. I don't know what it is, but—" Then she had given a little laugh and said, "But nobody kin accuse me of racial prejudice because I feel the same damn way about the dirty Indians."

There was a moment of silence while the drums beat at the Sun Dance grounds.

"Well," Edgar said, "that's the kind of thing you run into."

"Well, us Innuns aren't prejudiced against the niggers," Edgar's wife said. "Of course, I wouldn't want my daughter to marry one any more than I'd want her to marry a full blood."

Edgar, slouching deeply in his armchair, gave the living room wall a kick with the side of his foot. "Look at this damn house," he said. "It's coming apart already."

"That's why we send our kids to public school instead of the B.I.A. Innun school," his wife went on, "because we don't want them to grow up with nothing but Innuns."

"To live here, to live this life we live here," Edgar said, shaking his head, "you have to be half-drunk all the time."

Until 1953, it was, as a Klamath Indian friend of mine once explained, "against the law to feed liquor to Indians." It's still against the law on Pine Ridge because the members of the tribe voted for a dry reservation, though in the "suburb" of Whiteclay there are bars and dance halls that get quite lively on a Saturday night or just after the computer has issued the Mother's Aid or Welfare check.

In those resorts, there is, as well as drunkenness, a great deal of laughter and joking and horseplay; the Oglala is a friendly and, at times, very witty creature. He loves athletic games and plays them well, and his manual deftness makes him an excellent carpenter, machinist or technician if he takes the trouble to develop his talents and possesses the courage to go into the outside world and exercise his skills. One of the commonest reasons, of course, for Indian apathy toward Government training programs is that once an Indian learns a white man's trade there is no place on the reservation where he can exercise it. He has to leave his home and relatives and work in some foreign place, and he doesn't want to. The sponsors of H.R. 10560 eagerly point out that the bill will help relieve that condition.

In one Whiteclay bar, I met a fat jolly Oglala lady who, although she has an excellent secretarial job with the bureau, also creates fine tomahawks for the ever so slightly increasing tourist trade. She has three daughters who are or are becoming registered nurses, one son who has a Ph.D. in sociology and is working with other Indians in Nebraska, and a young son who is a good-for-nothing drunk. She knows Edgar Running Bear very well.

"Pooh! You can't believe a word Ed says," she said, although she allowed that the council was, in fact, incompetent and overpaid and that Johnson Holy Rock was unfair in his recommendations for loans. In general, she felt, the Innuns on the reservation were a passably contented lot and pretty much satisfied with the way the Bureau was handling their affairs.

"This is our place," she said. "Some of us go away, but an awful lot of us come back. See those two boys over there in the ball caps? They've been in Oakland, California, making good money, but they've come back."

I asked them why they had come back. One of them laughed and said, "Hell, *I* don't know. I guess to play baseball."

Johnson Holy Rock told me that he had been to Washington and explained to the Interior Department people that the chief complaints they have against the Government were that the Government treated them like digits instead of human beings, that it didn't understand the Indians' attachment to their people and their land, and that the Indians themselves didn't yet understand the white man's notion of business and money and private property. "We're not ready to be let out on our own," he had told them, "but treat us like people instead of numbers."

I remarked that all of us, not just the Indians, were victims of the official digital computer, that we were all cards full of little holes. "'*We've* given up," I said, but this time he didn't understand, because he means to go right on trying to keep his people what they are, more so than any other Americans I know—human beings. But I'm sure that one day he, too, will give up just as Red Cloud, in spite of his vow to fight for his lands forever, gave up, finally telling his people in tones of scornful irony:

"You must begin anew and put away the wisdom of your fathers. You must lay up food and forget the hungry. When your house is built, your storeroom filled, then look around for a neighbor whom you can take advantage of and seize all he has."

That was the way, he said, to get rich like a white man.

THE MEXICAN-AMERICAN LABORERS:
A Different Drummer?

Marjorie Fallows

Since Mexican-Americans have seldom inspired public interest outside the Southwest, it was an occasion for wonder when, in the spring of 1966, major reports appeared in news media ranging from *The Wall Street Journal* to *Life* magazine, describing this group as one of America's most overlooked, neglected and poverty-stricken minorities, now finally on the move. The image that triggered public sympathy was of a straggling band of Mexican-American grape pickers making the dogged two hundred and fifty mile march on foot from Delano, California to the state capitol in Sacramento, climaxing an eight month strike to protest their right to organize and bargain for better wages. The "grape picker's movement," started from within the ranks of the Mexican-American migrant laborers by their own Cesar Chavez, not only caught the sympathy of liberal church, student, and civil rights groups in California but made its impact on the national consciousness when Schenley, the leading grape grower in the region, finally recognized the right of the predominantly Mexican-American farm workers to bargain through their new National Farm Workers Association.

That this breakthrough in organizing and establishing the right to bargain among the depressed migratory farm workers should have occurred at all was remarkable enough, for these have been workers generally characterized as both unorganized and unorganizable. That the impetus should have come from within the Mexican-American group itself has seemed doubly unexpected, for by tradition and inclination these have been people more willing to accept fate than to challenge it. Yet it is not as unintelligible as we might suppose if we investigate the framework within which Mexican-American acculturation is taking place in the Southwest, and if we place the "grape picker's movement" in the context of the larger society to which it has appealed and to which it responds. Ultimately the Mexican-Americans

THE MEXICAN-AMERICAN LABORERS: A DIFFERENT DRUMMER? Reprinted from *The Massachusetts Review*, Vol. 8, No. 1 (Winter 1967). © 1967 The Massachusetts Review, Inc.

face the need to find a place within this larger society—highly organized, predominantly urban and industrial—for which they have been grossly unprepared by anything in their past experience. The success of the "grape picker's movement" may offer some clues to how such a place may be found.

If we recall the characteristics of the rural folk society from which these people were thrust by gradual loss of the means to support themselves, and picture then the *colonias* and *pueblitas* of the Southwest where they gathered for psychological support, or the migratory labor camps where they worked in predominantly ethnic gangs, it is not hard to see why the nearly four million Mexican-Americans in the Southwest have clung to their Spanish language so long, have retained their Mexican cultural values so long, have failed to make what we have come to regard as normal steps toward acculturation. They have never really emerged from isolation. If they have not rejected the past to the extent that other immigrant groups have, it has been largely because they have not come into significant contact with an intelligible and accessible substitute. The psychological costs of culture abandonment may be heavy, even when one sees an adequate substitute. When one does not, the costs may be so great that life no longer has dignity and purpose. Yet a reality of the Mexican peasant heritage least understood by Americans is that life may have dignity and purpose, that prestige may be won and the good life lived, in terms quite different from ours.

Our assumption has usually been that our terms must be accepted by the incoming immigrant before he could begin to share the fruits of American affluence. It was the price immigrants paid, and the majority have seemed content with the bargain. But the Mexican-American has been more wary, and until ten years ago it was logical to predict that, because of this wariness, he would suffer semi-permanent exclusion from American society. Has it really been he who has changed so much in a decade that we can alter this prediction? Probably not. It may be instead the climate of opinion, the level of self-awareness, the sense of direction in the United States that have been changing. There are at least enough tentative signs of change to suggest that the Mexican-American may emerge from his ethnic isolation into a climate more understanding of his own values.

The lowest social and economic levels, of which this group is clearly a part, are suddenly of considerable concern to Americans at large. They are being "understood" as never before, and in this surge of "understanding" the Mexican-Americans emerge from anonymity with a rather favorable image—unobtrusively hugging the Mexican border, caught by the rhythm of a different drummer. That they have been out of step they have sensed, and we have reminded them. But as we take stock of ourselves in a flush of self-consciousness we are reminded by those like William Madsen who know them well that we could learn much from our Mexican-American citizens about family solidarity, child rearing, respect patterns and religious values. These words touch the quick of our own fears, for in precisely these areas we feel ourselves most insecure. The question we put to ourselves in candid moments is whether we can have the best of a material abundance and still retain the spiritual values to give it meaning. And if so, how? This is precisely the dilemma many Mexican-Americans have been facing, and for want of an answer they have moved slowly and have accepted the second-class citizenship that was the price. It is only recently that national concern has discovered them and begun to ask questions about their future.

Just what have we been expecting of immigrant groups as they move toward assimilation? The loss of any identifying ethnic differences that might set them apart from the "average" American? If so, the Mexican-American has little to hope for, since he is marked off from the dominant American pattern by his own unique blend of Spanish and Indian in racial type as well as in culture, religion and language. He cannot easily merge into the white, Protestant, English-speaking group of Anglo-Americans with whom he comes in contact in the Southwest. Yet should merging even be the goal? Are we perhaps ready to recognize that the "melting pot" described an assumption rather than a reality in American social life? That there are immigrant groups of long residence in this country who have neither melted nor merged in the areas of their personal and private social lives, yet have still found a secure place in the economic and political sphere? And is this not a legitimate alternative to our earlier assumption that there is something wrong with any group that does not merge on all levels? It is the rigidity of the demand for either total assimilation or subordination that the Mexican-American questions when he says "This country should be big enough to allow us the freedom to be different without being oppressed."

But just how different can a minority group be without inviting oppression? Can its value system be diametrically opposed to that of the host culture, a mirror-image of it? Observers of Mexican-American life in the Southwest point out that the demands of an urban industrial economy will require significant shifts in traditional values for these people, if they would make even nominal headway in America, for the Mexican-American characteristically values the present in contrast to planning for a better future; he values "being," with its spontaneous expression of impulses, in contrast to "doing" for the sake of accomplishing something; he values a dignified acceptance of life rather than efforts to change and control it; he looks for guidance and support from someone in authority in contrast to coveting individualistic independence. Even where individuals may have adopted American values, the group as a whole has clung to the security offered by traditional ways—ways which have seemed hopelessly backward to the majority of Americans in the Southwest.

Stereotyping comes easily in response to such stark contrasts in outlook. Nor has the Anglo been the only one to criticize those undesirable "foreign" qualities which he believes to be virtually bred in and unalterable. If he sees the typical Mexican-American as lazy, dirty, unpredictable and childishly willing to enjoy himself when there is little to enjoy, the Mexican-American in turn has viewed the typical Anglo as exploitive, willing to sacrifice his family and his honesty for money, and as having little regard for spiritual values. The stereotypes sound surprisingly familiar, for they reflect the images the successful middle classes and the unsuccessful lower classes often have of each other. In the Southwest, where the majority in the lower class are indeed Mexican-American, it has been easy to equate the culture of the poor with the culture of Mexico, and to regard the defense mechanisms of the group as part of their unalterable racial and cultural inheritance. Yet even supposing we are willing to recognize that poverty develops its own rationale which undergirds and makes bearable the life of the poor wherever they may be, is there any reason to suppose that the culture of poverty could be assimilated more easily than the culture of Mexico? Perhaps there is. The Mexican-American may not have changed from the person he was, but our viewpoint about him is altered when we see him as a product of more or less permanent poverty, rather than as a product of racial or cultural inadequacy.

Inchoate and lacking in focus as our current war on poverty may be in many areas, it has provided for many the first awareness that the poor are not necessarily poor because they deserve to be poor. For a group like the Mexican-American it may also have provided a first awareness that poverty is not inevitable. But if not inevitable, what alternative do we offer? Money and influence through which to acquire the social status he is now denied? He would quickly admit the desirability of enough money to share in the fallout of American technological progress, for in this area he clearly sees America as superior, but his own definition of wealth is something to use and enjoy, not something to invest or convert into prestige or make an end in itself. As for power and influence, these are to be distrusted in one's self as much as in others. One does not seek power; one is occasionally awarded it or entrusted with it as a mark of high esteem, but it is a byproduct. As for social status—status in whose terms? The Mexican-American sees status in the Anglo world as something to bought or seized. In his own world it is something to be won through adherence to the ideals of the group: loyalty to one's own, devotion to the family, a dignified acceptance and appreciation of things as they are because this is the way God has planned it. He who achieves status and respect in his own group virtually cuts himself off from achieving it in Anglo terms.

Yet there are some who have wanted it in Anglo terms and who have achieved enough wealth, or power, or prestige to illustrate to the rest that they too can dream a different dream. The reaction toward this mobile group may be to reject them as having gone *inglisado*, but evidence of success does not go unnoticed, even when it is denigrated. There are even some, like Cesar Chavez with his "grape picker's movement," who have managed to achieve power and status in both Mexican-American and Anglo terms at the same time.

It becomes a matter of significance, then, to ask why so few leaders of Chavez' stature have emerged within the Mexican-American group. Here we find, throughout the Southwest, that those who have advanced themselves have tended to forsake their identity with the Mexican-American group. Some have dispersed to Midwestern industrial centers like St. Paul, Chicago and Detroit, where relatively small clusters of Mexican-Americans suffer little of the special discrimination produced by their denser concentration in the Southwest. Still others have moved out of the group socially, rather than spatially, a movement made possible by the existence of an old established upper class, dating back to the days of Spanish conquest, which identifies itself as Spanish-American, and which has traditionally remained aloof from both the Mexican peasantry and the Anglo upper class. A Mexican-American whose racial characteristics are Castilian enough and whose educational level is high enough, can identify with this respected group, whether or not he actually joins it socially. Of importance to the Mexican-American community is the fact that both these forms of movement away from the group represent serious losses, both in potential leadership and in models for successful adaptation to American life. As for an emerging middle class which may have improved its lot while remaining within the Mexican-American group, we find little evidence that such a class has reached significant numbers or status to assume effective leadership.

Indeed, since leadership is difficult to assume in a group which is traditionally resistant to, and suspicious of, any attempts at organization, it has been lack of leaders which has consistently been the greatest obstacle to effective improvement of the Mexican-American's lot. The form of leadership the Mexican peon best understood was lost with the breakdown of the patrón-peon relationship, familiar throughout rural Mexico and in those nothern reaches of the colonial empire which later became the American Southwest. The land-owning patrón had been expected to take responsibility for the entire well-being of the peons and their families, providing employment, social and economic security, and leadership for those who did the manual work. The peons, in return, had been expected to give complete loyalty and cooperation, often to get necessary communal tasks done. Stripped of this secure and dependent position, the Mexican-American still often reflects the values and attitudes appropriate to the lost relationship, for he prefers to leave major decisions to those with the prominence or wealth or political power equivalent to a patrón's, feeling that such a person is best equipped to take the responsibility involved. He still prefers friendly person-to-person relationships in a stable hierarchical social system, where mutual obligations and statuses are clearly spelled out. He resists those social and cultural changes which require personal initiative in a competitive world.

In terms of these values and attitudes, Cesar Chavez' success in organizing the grape pickers in Delano, California becomes intelligible and significant, for where other leaders and organizers, working within the American value system, failed to inspire interest or action among the clearly exploited migratory group, he achieved unexpected success by operating within their value system and providing a form of leadership they understood. It was no easy task, given both the militant resistance of the large growers in Southern California to any efforts to organize the farm workers and the suspicion with which the workers themselves viewed such efforts. Nor was there any guarantee of success, even as the group staged its last-ditch march to Sacramento. Father Vizzard, Chairman of the National Council on Agricultural Life and Labor, who had been in close touch with Chavez and the work he was doing, told a group of students on April 1st that the strikers were near the end of their resources then, and if the march failed to bring results he didn't know what they would do. Chavez had been slowly developing the National Farm Workers Association since 1962, leading to this cooperative action, but much of the success of the eight month strike stemmed from the quality of his leadership. Father Vizzard described him as "one of only two really charismatic leaders I have ever met," suggesting that the devotion of the workers was so great that even though Chavez had been developing leadership among others in the group and had several potential leaders who might replace him, "if anything happened to Cesar, I'm not sure the men would give their loyalty to anyone else. The whole thing might collapse." As it turned out the strikers won their significant victory nine days later when Schenley recognized their union's right to bargain.

What, if anything, did this strike actually accomplish for the Mexican-Americans in the Southwest? At the very least, it illustrated that these people are not unorganizable and that they are capable of enormous massed strength if they find leadership they can trust and to which they can give their loyalty. Of primary importance, perhaps, in understanding the conditions that led to the organization of this "unorganizable" group is the fact that the grape pickers had established a home base in Delano, where they put down tenuous roots. Their social organization was not one of the migratory camps but one of the town and valley. Cesar Chavez had a relatively stable group with that same potential for cooperative community action that would have existed in the Mexican village under the leadership of a patrón. He operated, in fact, within the patrón-peon pattern, but in a way curiously adapted to the American environment. The patrón, it must be understood, does not win the loyalty of the group simply because he is well-liked. He fills an institutionalized role, and the success of the patrón-peon relationship depends on how well each fulfills the reciprocal obligations involved. Yet Chavez was not an established patrón, nor could he personally provide any of the social or economic securities attendant on this role. He could only help to build the organization which would do it in his place. Such was the character of the National Farm Workers Association which he founded. We need hardly be reminded that he could not initially have won the respect of the migrants had he not shown those qualities by which status is measured in Mexican-American eyes and for which loyalty is given: unwillingness to seek self-aggrandizement, and devotion to the group. His personal charisma and his training under Saul Alinsky were vital assets too, but his National Farm Workers Association won the support of the migrants because he was the "right" kind of leader and it was the "right" kind of organization.

To understand what kind of patrón the migrants of Delano needed requires a glimpse of the conditions under which they worked. For the 500,000 agricultural workers in California's largest industry, the average yearly income has been one sixth that of other industrial workers. They have had no minimum wage, no holidays, paid vacations, sick leave, unemployment insurance or pension plan. The large growers who hired them frequently violated child labor laws and consistently denied them the right to collective bargaining. They have been the only industry in America exempt from the Taft-Hartley Act and from the jurisdiction of the National Labor Relations Board. It was no mere literary fancy that dubbed this "the 'grapes of wrath' strike," for the massive social legislation passed since the Depression had never touched this group.

The National Farm Workers Association, in response to the migrants' desperate need, operated more as a welfare cooperative than as a labor union. It provided a credit union, cooperative food store, drug store and service station; ran a newspaper; provided legal help, a burial insurance program and a grievance committee to investigate job misrepresentation. The Association itself, as far as it could, provided social and economic security within the social and economic insecurity of the occupation, filling the institutionalized role of the patrón. But to Cesar Chavez as its symbol went the loyalty due the patrón as a man, for here was no outside organizer but one of the group. It was not, then, so much that the Mexican-American migrants were unorganizable as that the right vehicle for cooperative action had not been offered under the right leadership.

Still another, if seemingly less spectacular, gain emerged from the events that led to the march on Sacramento. The cooperation required to put the National Farm Workers Association on its feet and to survive an eight month strike brought an awareness that social and economic gains need not be solely in terms of mobility out of and away from the group. We have seen that both spatial and social distance have tended to separate those who "succeeded" from those who did not, but the National Farm Workers Association represented a group effort requiring minimal change of established patterns. The members, far from having to strike out on their own with all the attendant personal risks, made their bid for the right to bargain within the security of the group. Once this right was won, other gains might follow.

That this sequence of events—from group effort to collective gains which would have expanding and beneficial repercussions for the group—did not seem self-evident to the Mexican-Americans shows clearly in the reluctance with which they entered the strike. The Mexican peasant has had little personal experience with the successful operation of any revolutionary action. He has lived under one authoritarian rule after another, and even the gains in the Revolution of 1910–20 left many of the peasants untouched. The large landowners of California, enjoying much the same monopolistic control as the wealthy landowners with whom the Mexicans had been familiar, represented a formidable adversary. Like other agriculturists in the Southwest, they had for years employed *braceros* brought up from Mexico under government auspices to work for less than the resident Mexican-Americans. The official ending of the *bracero* program in the fall of 1964 had given the local workers that first leverage which was a prerequisite for action, but the National Farm Workers Association still might not have made the decision to strike had it not been pushed. On September 8, 1965, the AFL-CIO farm labor organizers called a strike in Delano for the predominantly Filipino agricultural workers they had been able to organize, and rather than let this strike fail, as it seemed almost certain to do, Chavez formed a joint committee with the AFL-CIO leadership and joined the strike. From that time on, the character of the strike was molded almost entirely by Cesar Chavez.

Father Vizzard described the reluctance with which this decision was reached: "He didn't want the strike then. He didn't think they were ready to risk it. It was a forced choice." It is not hard to understand the hesitancy, if we recall the Mexican-American's desire for stability and his dislike of aggressive competition, if we recall the strength of his opponent and the loss of morale that might follow a failure. For such modest demands as a minimum wage of $1.40 an hour, as opposed to the old average of $1.20, "standard" working conditions, and the right to negotiate, the risks were great. There was danger of losing what small security the National Farm Workers Association had been able to provide.

In recognition of these risks, a frank appeal went out to the wider community for support of the strikers. This is vital for understanding what the strike accomplished, for the accomplishment would have been significant for the Mexican-Americans whether their immediate demands had been met by the growers or not. Had the growers provided the economic and social security needed by the migrants they could have counted on the loyalty of their workers, for the dependent position is not onerous for the Mexican-American provided the reciprocal obligations are met by both parties. But clearly the growers neither understood nor took any interest in this type of relationship. It was to others in California that the strikers appealed for support: church and Civil Rights groups, students at Berkeley, labor unions, SNCC. From these groups came picketers, funds, speakers, cooperation in establishing an effective boycott of the growers' products, and ultimately those volunteers who swelled the ranks of the Mexican-Americans as they marched on Sacramento.

Protestant, Catholic, and Jewish clergymen joined to issue a strong statement calling for the same kind of "active support that . . . Christians and Jews have given to the basic demands for justice for Negroes in the South." The Mexican-Americans had finally tied into the growing public awareness that the South does not have a monopoly on discrimination! In the support of those liberal forces already mobilized in defense of Civil Rights, they found a more effective patrón than the growers could ever have been. The big growers like Schenley and DiGiorgio, cast in the role of villains, found themselves facing more than a pitiful group of protesting Mexican-American migrant workers, for their land monopolies came under fire in the press and in Congress.

Now, along with the growers, it may be that others of us in America face a need to answer some questions about ourselves. We have seen ourselves described as having values that are diametrically opposed to those of the Mexican-Americans. We take the initiative in planning for a better future, we are told. Yet we have a Social Security program that has ironically covered almost everyone in the nation *except* groups like the migrant workers. We value "doing" for the sake of accomplishing something, we are told. Yet we are facing the economic necessity of entering the job market late and retiring from it early in order to make the available jobs go around. (How well equipped are we to appreciate "being"—to use our increasing leisure?) We value efforts to change and control life, we are told. Yet we are now in the process of relinquishing control to the federal government in such areas as health, education and welfare. We value individualism and independence, we are told. Yet our economic affairs have become so massive and complex that businessmen are more than ever dependent on the federal government to manipulate the economy for continued prosperity.

The burden of this comparison is not to suggest that our self-image has been wrong, but merely to suggest that these values which we have held up to the Mexican-American as characteristic may be values we are moving away from. David Riesman has spoken of the Mexican-Americans as examples of those vanishing remnants of tradition-directed peoples whose resentment and resistance to the demands of the host culture often drain them of emotional energy and make them appear lazy or apathetic. Since the official culture of schools, businesses, and public agencies is still inner-directed, the contrast in values appears to them extreme, and the requirements of such radical adjustment produce strain and confusion. In a society which has always valued individual initiative and autonomy, hard work and thrift, as well as freedom from government interference, the growing need to adjust to a more leisure-oriented consumption economy produces strain and confusion for the very people Mexican-Americans are urged to emulate. The big growers may well fall in this category.

It is those whom Riesman describes as other-directed who have taken up the cause of the poor, for they have shed much of the scarcity psychology of the inner-directed group. Being themselves in search of values consistent with what they feel to be a new time, they may think they have found in the culture of poverty some attitudes and values with which they can be in sympathy. For in the poor's defense against the desolation of never winning, they may feel they have found a defense against the desolation of having won. Having heard a different drummer themselves, they may be more in sympathy with the right of others to step to the music which they hear.

Today, in spite of recent publicity, the Mexican-Americans in the Southwest still remain a group little known in the United States, and still without champions of the stature of those who have spoken out for the Negro. Yet it may well be that they will never need champions in quite the same way, for we have begun to recognize the injustice in the kinds of demands we have made of these remnant groups that are largely unacculturated and chronically poor. We have demanded proof of their ability to succeed in our terms, without having provided them with the economic and social supports with which to achieve success—supports on which the rest of the nation has come to depend. The "grape picker's movement" reminded us that the Mexican-Americans sense this injustice and are ready to band together to ask that something be done. The response to the strike indicates that we within the nation sense that such injustice must be dealt with—not just because we see the Mexican-Americans as a group in need of special protection, but because we see them as citizens in need of equal protection.

HUGHES AT COLUMBIA

Charlayne Hunter

On a miserably wet evening seven months after the death of Langston Hughes, we sat, almost comfortably (except for our damp feet), in the cavernous Wollman Auditorium, at Columbia University, and listened to the low, bemused voice of Hughes on tape as, against a taped musical background, it sent his "Weary Blues" floating over a group of people who had assembled to pay tribute to him. The program, "A Langston Hughes Memorial Evening," was sponsored by The Forum, which is, in the words of its nineteen-year-old president, Bruce Kanze, "a student organization that brings to the University interesting people whom the University itself would never consider bringing, to discuss issues and topics that are important."

A few minutes after eight, when nearly every seat was filled, three men walked onto the stage: Leon Bibb, the actor and singer; Jonathan Kozol, author of "Death at an Early Age"; and Professor James P. Shenton, of Columbia. ("He teaches a course on Reconstruction—the closest thing to a course on Negro history at Columbia," Mr. Kanze told us later.) They were soon joined by Miss Viveca Lindfors, the actress, who was wearing a pale-gray fur coat but removed it as she was sitting down, and gracefully placed it over her mini-exposed knees.

Professor Shenton, who had to leave early, was introduced, and hurried to the microphone. "I am here partly as a way of saying for Columbia that we owe some apologies," he said solemnly. "For a while, there lived a poet down the street from Columbia, and Columbia never took the time to find out what he was about." The Professor paused for a few seconds, and then continued, "For a while, there lived a poet down the street from Columbia, who even attended Columbia for a while, and yet he never received an honorary degree from here. When we buried him, *then* we gave him a memorial. But, after all, that's the experience of the black man down the street from Columbia."

Professor Shenton left the platform, and Mr. Kozol, a slim young man wearing rimless glasses, came to the microphone. In 1965, he was discharged from a ghetto school in Boston, in part because he read Langston Hughes' poem "Ballad of the Landlord" to his class:

HUGHES AT COLUMBIA From *The New Yorker*, December 30, 1967. Reprinted by permission; © 1967 The New Yorker Magazine, Inc.

Landlord, landlord,
My roof has sprung a leak.
Don't you 'member I told you about it
Way last week?

Landlord, landlord,
These steps is broken down.
When you come up yourself
It's a wonder you don't fall down.

Ten bucks you say I owe you?
Ten bucks you say is due?
Well, that's ten bucks more'n I'll pay you
Till you fix this house up new.

What? You gonna get eviction orders?
You gonna cut off my heat?
You gonna take my furniture and
Throw it in the street?

Um-huh! You talking high and mighty.
Talk on—till you get through.
You ain't gonna be able to say a word
If I land my fist on you.

Police! Police!
Come and get this man!
He's trying to ruin the government
And overturn the land!

Copper's whistle!
Patrol bell!
Arrest.

Precinct station.
Iron cell.
Headlines in press:

MAN THREATENS LANDLORD

TENANT HELD NO BAIL

JUDGE GIVES NEGRO 90 DAYS IN COUNTY JAIL

Mr. Kozol said that he might have avoided some of the trouble that
eventually led to his firing if he had chosen to "restrict his reading and
reference materials to the list of approved publications"—poetry, for in-

stance, to be read from officially approved selections called "Memory Gems." He gave the Hughes audience a sample:

> Dare to be right! Dare to be true:
> The failings of others can never save you.
> Stand by your conscience, your honor, your faith;
> Stand like a hero, and battle till death.

And another:

> There is beauty in the sunshine
> An' clouds that roam the sky;
> There is beauty in the Heavens,
> An' the stars that shine on high.

Later, Mr. Kozol read from a paper that had been handed in by one of his fourth-grade students after he had asked the class to write about the kinds of things *they* saw around them:

> In my school I see dirty boards and I see papers on the floor. I see an old browken window with a sign on it saying, Do not unlock this window are browken. And I see cracks in the walls and I see old books with ink poured all over them and I see old painting hanging on the walls. I see old alfurbet letter hanging on one nail on the wall. I see a dirty fire exit, I see a old closet with supplys for the class. I see pigons flying all over the school. I see old freght trains throgh the fence of the school yard. . . .

The young teacher spoke at length about his experiences in this school, and then read a few paragraphs from a description of Africa in a book called "Our Neighbors Near and Far":

> Yumbu and Minko are a black boy and a black girl who live in this jungle village. Their skins are of so dark a brown color that they look almost black. Their noses are large and flat. Their lips are thick. Their eyes are black and shining, and their hair is so curly that it seems like wool. They are Negroes and they belong to the black race.

Two children in another area of the world were described this way:

> Two Swiss children live in a farmhouse on the edge of town. . . . These children are handsome. Their eyes are blue. Their hair is golden yellow. Their white skins are clear, and their cheeks are as red as ripe, red apples.

Mr. Kozol said that he had never met Langston Hughes but that a short while after his much publicized firing he had received a new collection of some of Hughes' "Simple" stories from the poet, with these words written on the flyleaf: "I wish the rent / Was heaven sent."

Leon Bibb, in his turn, rose and thanked Mr. Hughes, whom he called Lang, first by reading the James Weldon Johnson poem "O Black and Unknown Bards" and then by giving a poignant rendering of Mr. Hughes' poem "The Negro Speaks of Rivers" and the spiritual "I've Been 'Buked and I've Been Scorned." He wound up by saying, "Lang had the foresight to stand on his own words."

Soon Hughes' own words were being read by Miss Lindfors, who remained seated, and whose Swedish accent was lost in translation as she read from "The Panther and the Lash," a recent Hughes collection, brought out by Knopf. She read about the "Junior Addict":

> . . . Yes, easier to get dope
> than to get a job—
> daytime or nighttime job,
> teen-age, pre-draft,
> pre-lifetime job.
>
> Quick, sunrise, come!
> Sunrise out of Africa,
> Quick, come!
> Sunrise, please come!
> Come! Come!

And she read about the "Dream Deferred." And she read "Impasse":

> I could tell you,
> If I wanted to,
> What makes me
> What I am.
>
> But I don't
> Really want to—
> And you don't
> Give a damn.

Miss Lindfors also read the poem whose first line is "That Justice is a blind goddess" and the poem about "Birmingham Sunday"—September 15, 1963, when four little Negro girls were killed in Sunday school by a bomb thrown from outside the church. Miss Lindfors read several more poems—some bitterly humorous ones, and the one that asks, "What color/ Is the face/Of war?," and one called "Peace," and, finally, "Down Where I Am":

> Too many years
> Beatin' at the door—
> I done beat my
> Both fists sore.
>
> Too many years
> Tryin' to get up there—

Done broke my ankles down,
Got nowhere.

Too many years
Climbin' that hill,
'Bout out of breath.
I got my fill.

I'm gonna plant my feet
On solid ground.
If you want to see me,
Come down.

The memorial to Langston Hughes ended as it had begun, with Langston Hughes' low, bemused voice—this time telling about how he came from the Midwest to Columbia to go to school, and caused great consternation when he presented himself at Hartley Hall. That was in 1921, and no one of African descent, he says, had ever lived in a dormitory at Columbia. "There are many barriers people try to break down," he told an audience (which had also been a Columbia audience) when the tape was made, in 1964. "I try to do it with poetry."

WALKER PERCY,
THE MAN AND THE NOVELIST:
An Interview

Carlton Cremeens

Q: In October, 1965, *The Atlantic* published an article by Eudora Welty entitled "Must The Novelist Crusade?" In the article Miss Welty took issue with some journalist who had written that Faulkner would have to be reassessed because "he was only a white Mississippian." This statement by the journalist, of course, followed several murders in the Mississippi racial conflict. Miss Welty gave the journalist a good verbal spanking and then took the position that the novelist and the crusader both have their own place, separate and apart, with a different function to perform. How do you feel about this?

PERCY: I read the article. I think she wrote that someone called her up in the middle of the night and demanded to know what she was going to do about all the trouble there in Mississippi, which meant that the caller

WALKER PERCY, THE MAN AND THE NOVELIST: AN INTERVIEW From *The Southern Review*, Vol. 4, No. 2 (Spring 1968). Reprinted by permission of the author.

thought Eudora Welty, as the leading writer of Mississippi, should at least have taken a stand on it.

Actually, this is a question that bothers me a great deal. I can't say whether I think Eudora Welty is wrong and that I know what the right answer is because I think it would be a mistake for a creative artist of any kind to get so embroiled in a local political or social issue that he stopped his creative work. But, on the other hand, I don't quite agree with her. I think her point in the article was that a creative writer ought to tend to his knitting, that if he does his work well, if he studies the human heart and the motions of the human heart, he is still doing what he is supposed to do, and the political and social issues are not his concern. I can see what she means, but I still think a writer, with his peculiar position of being a communicator, and particularly a prominent writer like Eudora Welty, who is influential, highly respected, can do a great deal of good, can have a great deal of influence without compromising her creative endeavors. My own feeling is: I don't mind saying or writing what I think on the social issues or the race issue in the South.

Q : Within the framework of a novel?

PERCY : Anywhere. In a novel. In an article. In this interview. I'm not an activist, a racial activist. I don't march in picket lines, but I am completely convinced of the rightness of the Negro struggle for civil rights. My writings I think reflect this, and I don't mind saying so. I don't see how anybody, any serious writer living in the South, or in America, for that matter, who is writing novels, can avoid the social issue of race because, particularly in the South and recently in the whole country, it is the number one issue of this society. In the South it always was. And when any writer in the South pretends he can write a novel and ignore the social issue of the Negro, something is wrong.

Q : But, at the same time, don't you agree the journalist was wrong when he suggested a reassessment of Faulkner simply because, as he put it, "Faulkner was, after all, only a white Mississippian?"

PERCY : Yes, of course.

Q : I presume the statement was made because Faulkner hadn't, in the opinion of the journalist, dealt squarely with the race problem. I think Faulkner was very conscious of the race problem in the South and that it was reflected in the body of his work.

PERCY : Well, I agree that he certainly was conscious of the issue. But the interesting thing was Faulkner's ambivalence about it. For instance, in those days it was a case of the Southerners having the problem and the Northerners criticizing the Southerners. And Faulkner, when he was criticized, or when he was approached from the wrong angle on this, would react in an old-fashioned, Southern way. I'm sure you remember when he made that famous remark about not pushing the South too far or the whole thing would end up with the whites shooting Negroes in the streets? Or maybe he said it would end with Southerners shooting Northerners. I don't remember which. And then later, during the last years of his life when he was at the University of Virginia, he came out squarely against the whole social institution of segregation, unequivocally against the whole thing. But he *was* ambivalent about it before that.

Q: I think one point of disagreement among writers who take a stand on social issues and those who don't is whether there's a danger of becoming so involved that it can affect the quality of a creative work. For instance, it appears the later works of James Baldwin are taken less seriously by a large number of people because, they say, he has become too embittered.

PERCY: Yes, I see what you mean. And I think that's true. But I want to get something straight. Now, I often feel that a good deal of energy in my writing comes from a passion or strong feeling on something, for or against. And there is a good precedent for this. Dostoyevsky began several of his best novels after having read a news story in the paper, of some incident, of a murder, for instance, and he would become enflamed on ideological grounds. He was usually a conservative as against the liberals, you know. Anyway, he would write a tract, a piece of propaganda, which if anyone else had written it, would have remained a piece of propaganda. But with him, something happened, some miraculous transformation, and what began as some anti-liberal, anti-nihilist propaganda turned into a work of art. That's the way *The Possessed* started out. It was written in a rage about a certain incident that happened in Russia. And I think it works both ways. A man has to have some sort of passion, either a dislike for something or a like for something—love or malice—to have enough energy to write about it.

But, on the other hand, there has to be a fine balance, because if he is too consumed with his likes or dislikes, then his art will be overwhelmed by his own predilections. For instance, if I get extremely angry about some racial thing it often produces very bad writing. You cannot translate this anger immediately into writing. It has to undergo a transformation, it has to be sublimated into some other form.

I'll tell you a strange thing that happened to me in connection with the creative process. It was the Kennedy assassination, which happened right in the middle of my last book, *The Last Gentleman*. The assassination affected me so strongly it caused me to lose a year of work. It changed the whole direction of the book. I got off on the wrong track, wrote a long thing about Kennedy, brought Kennedy into the book, and I actually wasted a year. It was no good. I had to back up. And it took me a year. It really threw me. I ended up with about four lines referring to Kennedy in the book. He was mentioned once. And that was the residue of about three hundred pages.

Q: Do you think your effort was entirely wasted?

PERCY: I don't know. But it goes to show you how rage, outrage, or shock cannot be transmuted raw into a viable art form. But, presumably, it can be transformed if you can maintain the fine balance required to do it.

Q: Are there any other inherent dangers for the creative writer who gets involved with social problems?

PERCY: I suppose another danger, as Ralph Ellison pointed out in an interview with three young Negro writers, is the temptation to understand the issues of the times in terms of sociology, in terms of abstractions. Perhaps the danger here is greater than that of becoming embroiled, or getting caught up in an issue, or getting embittered. Young writers, even young Negro writers, tend too often to understand themselves in terms of what the sociologists say: that they are victims of slavery, of broken homes, of a matriarchal society, and of various other things. They begin to feel themselves as exemplars of this or that sociological theory, forgetting many of the riches of their own lives. And so, when you start writing novels to illustrate sociology you are going to write bad novels, because sociology is a simplification, an abstraction from what is the case. A novelist should be concerned with what is the case in the world, the facts, the richness, the intricacy and the variety of the way things are. And God help you if you ever start writing sociology, because it might be good sociology, but it's going to be a bad novel.

Q : Short lived, too?

PERCY : Yes.

Q : Do you think we have any outstanding Negro writers in America today?

PERCY : Well, I think of Ralph Ellison. And of course, there was Wright. But, as Ellison says, there seem to be fewer good Negro writers around now than there were several years ago. I don't know why that is.

Q : Perhaps we're back to what was just said about the tendency among many Negro writers to look into the sociologist's looking glass and to see an image created by the sociologists. And that, according to the thinking of some people, also brings us back to James Baldwin.

PERCY : Yes, there *is* Baldwin. He was certainly first class when he was at his best. I think his first novel and then his *The Fire Next Time* were very eloquent things. But I think his last things have been simply consumed with hatred and obscenity. His last novel is a very unhappy business.

Q : Do you think discrimination is something innate in the human being? It seems to have been with us in one form or another throughout the history of the world.

PERCY : Well, I guess it is. It has certainly been true in this country. Given any two cultural ethnic groups you are going to have prejudice and discrimination and a degree of oppression, depending on which one is first in the pecking order, which got to the country first and which came later. But the big problem the Negro faces is the fact that he is black. With the Irish, Italians, Jews, the Catholics—name any one—it was different. After the initial period of oppression, the second and third generations were able to break out of the pattern, and there was rather little discrimination after that. But the Negro has not been able to do that, even now, of course, because after the second, third, or fourth generation he is still black. You see him. There he is. And he's something different. Assuming that the recent discrimination takes place because of differences, that there is something innate in the human being that tends to find a scapegoat in the person who is different, then other cultural groups can overcome their differences simply by becoming acculturated. But the Negro cannot lose his blackness. He can become totally assimilated in all the other respects. In fact, if you have known many middle-class Negroes, nobody in the world is more middle-class or conventional than the middle-class Negro. But he is still black. And he still has difficulties. He has the worst of both worlds. He has his blackness which he despises and he cleaves to the more fatuous of white middle-class values. That is the trouble.

Q: There was one particular passage in your novel, *The Last Gentleman*, which said a Southerner sees a Negro twice in his life. I think you wrote that he sees the Negro for the first time when he looks up from his cradle at his Negro nurse. And then he sees the Negro for the second and last time when he looks up from his death bed and there is the Negro folding the bed clothes around him. Perhaps you were thinking of a certain type of Southerner when you wrote that, but do you think the Southerner's awareness of the Negro is so limited? That he doesn't understand the Negro?

PERCY: I feel two ways about that. The passage in my book is an exaggeration, of course; it was a bit of satire on the universal feeling among Southerners that they do *completely* understand the Negro. I have seldom met one in my life who didn't claim that he knew all there was to know about them. I don't. But that is the Southerner's main argument.

Now, having said that the Southerner has this exaggerated opinion of his own knowledge and insight into the Negro I think, as a matter of fact, that both Negroes and white Southerners know a lot more about each other than white and colored people do anywhere else. They have been living together in the most intimate household relations for two or three hundred years, and there is an accumulated certain wisdom there. But I couldn't resist poking fun at this omniscient attitude Southerners have about their knowledge of Negroes.

Q: Do you think the Negroes understand us?

PERCY: I think they had developed—until recently—the most exquisite intuition and natural radar, a most extraordinary courtesy, a natural intuition and manners as far as white people were concerned. And so had the white people, the best of the white people. As James Dabbs says, the knowledgeable white Southerner tried to make up in courtesy and personal kindness for the dreadful injustice he helped inflict upon the Negro. Of course, it has been the Negro's business in the past to understand and anticipate, and I think he has been very good at it. They are a people with a most wonderful grace, not that there is anything new about that. This is a traditional item in literature. But the pity of it is, in the Negro revolution of the past ten years, this grace, which has been so long in cultivation by the Negro, has been kicked out the window. There has been a tendency to kick it out the window in the Negro's general rebellion against his subservient place in the American society. He's kicking out everything from the past. I don't blame him. But I think he's kicking out a lot of the good, too. And I believe, even now at this late date, here in the South there is still a reservoir of good will and a natural grace in the relationship between the white and colored people. I would go further than that. I would hope, and maybe even to a degree believe, that the South still, in spite of all, may ultimately have the genius in human relations to show the way to the rest of the country in solving the whole race situation. That would be my hope and dream for the South. And the tragedy would be if, in the era of bad feeling, both in the Negro revolution, the Negro rebellion, and the white right-wing reaction, the whole tradition of manners and grace and good feeling were simply kicked out, everything lost. I think we are going to need all the grace we can get.

Q: Since your feelings about the racial problem are very evident in your books, do you ever have any trouble with the racists?

PERCY: No. Racists don't read novels.

Now, a writer living here does find himself in a rather curious position, which reminds me of something I've been thinking about in the last few days. I get several journals in the mail. I get one Southern journal, a rabid racist rag. I also get another journal from New York and, although it's on a lofty intellectual level, there is a peculiar parallel between it and the Southern publication. On the one hand, in this part of the country as you well know, there is so much absolutely irrational, downright political hatred and abuse of President Johnson and our foreign policy. These are the people who want to go in there and end the war by bombing Hanoi, dropping the hydrogen bomb on North Vietnam or China, whatever it takes. This is the radical right wing which has corrupted the whole conservative tradition. They use the words *conservative* and *constitutional*. They have appropriated these words and they have prostituted the whole tradition. They are not conservatives. They are radicals. All of this is reflected in the journal that comes out of the South.

Now, on the other hand, you will find that many intellectuals of New York, of California, the American intellectual community, are almost as uniform and conformist—and irrational—in their hatred of President Johnson as the Southern right wingers. This you will find in my journal that comes out of New York. It reflects the thinking of the people who want to pull out of Vietnam and who ignore the systematic atrocities of the Viet Cong. It's a well-written journal, very lively, but it's very close to the Southern racist paper in its same abuse and hatred of President Johnson. There's not much difference. And it's almost as scurrilous in its distortion of the war.

So, you have two extremes, two radical groups, and the extremes have got so far apart they have almost met again. They are remarkably alike in their distortions and hatreds and fantasies. I think it's a change, this converging of the Northern intellectual and the Southern right winger. It's an unprecedented position for a Southern writer to be in. Twenty years ago my natural sympathies would have been with the liberal tradition in the North and against any resurgence of hatred and violence. But the recent changes are complicated by how close the wild-eyed have come to the highbrowed. The Southern writer now finds himself in the middle of somewhere and not quite knowing where. He's caught between the right in the South and this intellectual herd in the North who profess to be free creative spirits, and yet, all conforming to the same lines, the same hatred and abuse of the things they oppose. So where *does* the Southern writer stand? It may be an advantage—living in the South. I don't know. Most writers in the North seem to be caught up in this intellectual community, while most Southern writers, who are any good, simply won't have anything to do with this business of hatred and abuse.

From LET US NOW PRAISE FAMOUS MEN

James Agee
and Walker Evans

Each is intimately connected with the bottom and the extremest reach of time:

Each is composed of substances identical with the substance of all that surrounds him, both the common objects of his disregard, and the hot centers of stars:

All that each person is, and experiences, and shall never experience, in body and in mind, all these things are differing expressions of himself and of one root, and are identical: and not one of these things nor one of these persons is ever quite to be duplicated, nor replaced, nor has it ever quite had precedent: but each is a new and incommunicably tender life, wounded in every breath, and almost as hardly killed as easily wounded: sustaining, for a while, without defense, the enormous assaults of the universe:

So that how it can be that a stone, a plant, a star, can take on the burden of being; and how it is that a child can take on the burden of breathing; and how through so long a continuation and cumulation of the burden of each moment one on another, does any creature bear to exist, and not break utterly to fragments of nothing: these are matters too dreadful and fortitudes too gigantic to meditate long and not forever to worship.

FROM LET US NOW PRAISE FAMOUS MEN From *Let Us Now Praise Famous Men* by James Agee and Walker Evans. Reprinted by permission of the publisher, Houghton Mifflin Company.

From SEGREGATION

Robert Penn Warren

"I'm glad it's you going," my friend, a Southerner, long resident in New York, said, "and not me." But I went back, for going back this time, like all the other times, was a necessary part of my life. I was going back to look at the landscapes and streets I had known—Kentucky, Tennessee, Arkansas, Mississippi, Louisiana—to look at the faces, to hear the voices, to hear, in fact, the voices in my own blood. A girl from Mississippi had said to me: "I feel it's all happening inside of me, every bit of it. It's all there."

I know what she meant.

To the right, the sun, cold and pale, is westering. Far off, a little yellow plane scuttles down a runway, steps awkwardly into the air, then climbs busily, learning grace. Our big plane trundles ponderously forward, feeling its weight like a fat man, hesitates, shudders with an access of sudden, building power; and with a new roar in my ears, I see the ground slide past, then drop away, like a dream. I had not been aware of the instant we had lost that natural contact.

Memphis is behind me, and I cannot see it, but yonder is the river, glittering coldly, and beyond, the tree-sprigged flats of Arkansas. Still climbing, we tilt eastward now, the land pivoting away below us, the tidy toy farms, white houses, silos the size of a spool of white thread, or smaller, the stock ponds bright like little pieces of gum wrapper dropped in brown grass, but that brown grass is really trees, the toy groves with shadows precise and long in the leveling light.

Arkansas has pivoted away. It is Mississippi I now see down there, the land slipping away in the long light, and in my mind I see, idly, the ruined, gaunt, classic clay hills, with the creek bottoms throttled long since in pink sand, or the white houses of Holly Springs, some of them severe and beautiful, or Highway 61 striking south from Memphis, straight as a knife edge through the sad and baleful beauty of the Delta country, south toward Vicksburg and the Federal cemeteries, toward the fantasia of Natchez.

It seems like a thousand years since I first drove that road, more than twenty-five years ago, a new concrete slab then, dizzily glittering in the August sun-blaze, driving past the rows of tenant shacks, Negro shacks set in the infinite cotton fields, and it seems like a hundred years since I last drove it, last week, in the rain, then toward sunset the sky clearing a little, but clouds solid and low on the west like a black range of mountains frilled upward with an edge of bloody gold light, quickly extinguished. Last week, I noticed that more of the shacks were ruinous, apparently abandoned. More, but not many, had an electric wire running back from the road. But when I caught a glimpse, in the dusk, of the interior of a lighted shack, I usually saw the coal-oil lamp. Most shacks were not lighted. I wondered if it was too early in the evening. Then it was early no longer. Were that many of the shacks abandoned?

Then we would pass in the dark some old truck grudging and clanking down the concrete, and catch, in the split-second flick of our headlamps, a glimpse of the black faces and the staring eyes. Or the figure, sudden in our headlight, would rise from the roadside, dark and shapeless against the soaked blackness of the cotton land: the man humping along with the croker sack on his shoulders (containing what?), the woman with a piece of sacking or paper over her head against the drizzle now, at her bosom a bundle that must be a small child, the big children following with the same slow, mud-lifting stride in the darkness. The light of the car snatches past, and I think of them behind us in the darkness, moving up the track beside the concrete, seeing another car light far yonder toward Memphis, staring at it perhaps, watching it grow, plunge at them, strike them, flick past. They will move on, at their pace. Yes, they are still here.

I see a river below us. It must be the Tennessee. I wonder on which side of us Shiloh is, and guess the right, for we must have swung far enough north for that. I had two grandfathers at Shiloh, that morning of April 6, 1862, young men with the other young men in gray uniforms stepping toward the lethal spring thickets of dogwood and redbud, to the sound of bird song. "One hundred and sixty men we took in the first morning, son. Muster the next night, and it was sixteen answered." They had fallen back on Corinth, into Mississippi.

The man in the seat beside me on the plane is offering me a newspaper. I see the thumb of the hand clutching the paper. The nail is nearly as big as a quarter, split at the edges, grooved and horny, yellowish, with irrevocable coal-black grime deep under the nail and into the cuticle. I took at the man. He is a big man, very big, bulging over the seat, bulging inside his blue serge. He is fiftyish, hair graying. His face is large and raw-looking, heavy-jowled, thick gray eyebrows over small, deep-set, appraising eyes. His name, which he tells me, sounds Russian or Polish, something ending in -ski.

I begin to read the paper, an article about the riots at the University of Alabama. He notices what I am reading. "Bet you thought I was from down here," he said. "From the way I talk. But I ain't. I was born and raised in New York City, but I been in the scrap business down here ten years. Didn't you think I was from down here?"

"Yes," I say, for that seems the sociable thing to say.

He twists his bulk in the blue serge and reaches and stabs a finger at the headline about Alabama. "Folks could be more gen'rous and fair-thinking," he says. "Like affable, you might say, and things would work out. If folks get affable and contig'ous, you might say, things sort of get worked out in time, but you get folks not being affable-like and stirring things up and it won't work out. Folks on both sides the question."

He asks me if I don't agree, and I say, sure, I agree. Sure, if folks were just affable-like.

I am thinking of what a taxi driver had said to me in Memphis: "Looks like the Lucy girl wouldn't want to go no place where people throwed eggs at her and sich. But if they'd jist let her alone, them Goodrich plant fellers and all, it would blow over. What few niggers come would not have stayed no duration. Not when they found she couldn't git the social stuff, and all."

And what the school superintendent, in middle Tennessee, had said: "You take a good many people around here that I know, segregationists all right, but when they read about a thousand to one, it sort of makes them sick. It is the unfairness in that way that gets them."

And an organizer of one of the important segregation groups, a lawyer, when I asked him if Autherine Lucy wasn't acting under law, he creaked his swivel chair, moved his shoulders under his coat, and touched a pencil on his desk, before saying: "Yes—yes—but it was just the Federal Court ruled it."

And a taxi driver in Nashville, a back-country man come to the city, a hard, lean, spare face, his lean, strong shoulders humped forward over the wheel so that the clavicles show through the coat: "A black-type person and a white-type person, they ain't alike. Now the black-type person, all they think about is fighting and having a good time and you know what. Now the white-type person is more American-type, he don't mind fighting but he don't fight to kill for fun. It's that cannibal blood you caint git out."

Now, on the plane, my companion observes me scribbling something in a notebook.

"You a writer or something?" he asks. "A newspaper fellow, maybe?"

I say yes.

"You interested in that stuff?" he asks, and points to the article. "Somebody ought to tell 'em not to blame no state, not even Alabam' or Mississippi, for what the bad folks do. Like stuff in New York or Chicago. Folks in Mississippi got good hearts as any place. They always been nice and goodhearted to me, for I go up to a man affable. The folks down here is just in trouble and can't claw out. Don't blame 'em, got good hearts but can't claw out of their trouble. It is hard to claw out from under the past and the past way."

He asks me if I have been talking to a lot of people.

I had been talking to a lot of people.

I had come to the shack at dusk, by the brimming bayou, in the sea of mud where cotton had been. The cold drizzle was still falling. In the shack, on the hickory chair, the yellow girl, thin but well made, wearing a salmon sweater and salmon denim slacks, holds the baby on her knee and leans toward the iron stove. On the table beyond her is an ivory-colored portable radio and a half-full bottle of Castoria. On the other side of the stove are her three other children, the oldest seven. Behind me, in the shadowy background, I know there are faces peering in from the other room of the shack, black faces, the half-grown boys, another girl I had seen on entering. The girl in the salmon sweater is telling how she heard her husband had been killed. "Livin in town then, and my sister, she come that night and tole me he was shot. They had done shot him dead. So I up and taken out fer heah, back to the plantation. Later, my sister got my chillen and brought 'em. I ain't gonna lie, mister. I tell you, I was scairt. No tellin if that man what done it was in jail or no. Even if they had arrest him, they might bon' him out and he come and do it to me. Be mad because they 'rest him. You caint never tell. And they try him and 'quit him, doan know as I kin stay heah. Even they convick him, maybe I leave. Some good folks round heah and they helping me, and I try to appreciate and be a prayin chile, but you git so bore down on and nigh ruint and sort of brain-washed, you don't know what. Things git to goin round in yore head. I could run out or somethin, but you caint leave yore chillen. But look like I might up and leave. He git 'quitted, that man, and maybe I die, but I die goin."

This is the cliché. It is the thing the uninitiate would expect. It is the cliché of fear. It is the cliché come fresh, and alive.

There is another image. It is morning in Nashville. I walk down Union Street, past the Negro barber shops, past the ruinous buildings plastered over with placards of old circuses and rodeos, buildings being wrecked now to make way for progress, going into the square where the big white stone boxlike, ugly and expensive Davidson County Court House now stands on the spot where the old brawling market once was. Otherwise, the square hasn't changed much, the same buildings, wholesale houses, liquor stores, pawn shops, quick lunches, and the same kind of people stand on the corners, countrymen, in khaki pants and mackinaw coats, weathered faces and hard, withdrawn eyes, usually pale eyes, lean-hipped men ("narrow-assted" in the country phrase) like the men who rode with Forrest, the farm wives, young with a baby in arms, or middle-aged and work-worn, with colored cloths over the head, glasses, false teeth, always the shopping bag.

I walk down toward the river, past the Darling Display Distribution show window, where a wax figure stands in skirt and silk blouse, the fingers spread on one uplifted hand, the thin face lifted with lips lightly parted as though in eternal, tubercular expectation of a kiss. I see the power pylons rising above the river mist. A tug is hooting up-river in the mist.

I go on down to the right, First Street, to the replica of Fort Nashborough, the original settlement, which stands on the river bank under the shadow of warehouses. The stockade looks so child-flimsy and jerry-built jammed against the massive, soot-stained warehouses. How could the settlers have ever taken such protection seriously? But it was enough, that and their will and the long rifles and the hunting knives and the bear-dogs they unleashed to help them when they broke the Indians at the Battle of the Bluffs. They took the land, and remain.

I am standing in the middle of the empty stockade when a boy enters and approaches me. He is about fifteen, strongly built, wearing a scruffed and tattered brown leather jacket, blue jeans, a faded blue stocking cap on the back of his head, with a mop of yellow hair hanging over his forehead. He is a fine-looking boy, erect, manly in the face, with a direct, blue-eyed glance. "Mister," he said to me, "is this foh't the way it was, or they done remodeled it?"

I tell him it is a replica, smaller than the original and not on the right spot, exactly.

"I'm glad I seen it, anyway," he says. "I like to go round seeing things that got history, and such. It gives you something to think about. Helps you in a quiz sometimes, too."

I ask him where he goes to school.

"Atlanta," he says. "Just come hitch-hiking up this away, looking at things for interest. Like this here foh't."

"You all been having a little trouble down your way," I ask, "haven't you?"

He looks sharply at me, hesitates, then says: "Niggers—you mean niggers?"

"Yes."

"I hate them bastards," he says, with a shuddering, automatic violence, and averts his face and spits through his teeth, a quick, viperish, cut-off expectoration.

I say nothing, and he looks at me, stares into my face with a dawning belligerence, sullen and challenging, and suddenly demands: "Don't you?"

"I can't say that I do," I reply. "I like some and I don't like some others."

He utters the sudden obscenity, and removes himself a couple of paces from me. He stops and looks back over his shoulder. "I'm hitching on back to Atlanta," he declares in a flat voice, "this afternoon," and goes on out of the fort.

This, too, is a cliché. The boy, standing on the ground of history and heroism, his intellect and imagination stirred by the fact, shudders with that other, automatic emotion which my question had evoked. The cliché had come true: the cliché of hate. And somehow the hallowedness of the ground he stood on had vindicated, as it were, that hate.

Education

EDITED BY ROBERT DAVIS

INTRODUCTION

America's Dewey eyes are bloodshot. It was such a lovely vision: the school melting down all the immigrants; the kids of the nation learning by all those classroom meetings how to go out and vote intelligently, how to form lots of little pressure groups for the enrichment of this best of all possible industrial democracies; all that manual training and phys. ed. instead of the useless Latin and Greek that we had been hanging onto from Europe; all the baths for kids with lice, and the health classes, the guidance and the child-centered psychology; the mood that said that farm schools should be different from slum schools, which should be different from rich kids' schools; the spectacle of some universities, like Wisconsin and St. Francis Xavier, actually offering their scholars and research facilities to the farmers and to union groups instead of just to the powerful; the adult educators stumping the countryside, telling everyone that you never stopped learning even if you learned bad things, and that education should have an impact on one's life, and so on. White Americans and English Canadians embraced Dewey as part of their conviction that, on this continent of plenty, liberal free-enterprise democracy, with its pluralist balance of power, could achieve better than anywhere else the greatest good for the greatest number. And the schools were obviously the place to train people for this style, this mode of operating.

By now it all looks like a Thornton Wilder play—sentimental, chummy, and completely out of sight. So Dewey is bad news these days because he saw industrial, liberal democracy working, and right now it's not working at all. He saw the school in a beautiful relationship with that democracy: The student who graduated and took his place as a citizen was for Dewey not a glass filled with water, but a tadpole that had become a frog. But today tadpoles are turning into pigs and panthers, hawks and astrobirds, birds of inner space and angels from hell. And since this American freak show is no hallucination, about all that most sensitive people can muster is a kind of psychotic stare.

The dream has been smashed domestically in the ghettos and on campuses, and internationally in Vietnam. It's obvious that this liberal society, if it ever did exist, exists no longer. What is less obvious to many people is that the disintegration of liberal society means the disintegration of the school system as well, for in Dewey's view the two were very closely wed.

Dewey is quaint, but in education he's all we have. That's why we have to get him out of our systems before we can look ahead to any new coherence. Of course the old, shallow criticisms of Dewey are not enough. In the 1950's a number of conservative critics—notably Admiral Rickover and Robert Hutchins and, in Canada, Hilda Neatby—attacked America's Dewey-dominated schools, but they did so from such naively conservative positions that their voices are heard no more. As an indication of how well Dewey survived his 1950's critics, in the early 1960's Paul Goodman took the position that the problem was that we just didn't understand Dewey, or, more often, that we hadn't really tried him. It was tempting to believe this, especially when it was expressed so righteously and simply and by America's most popular education critic. Especially too when one went back and read the details of Dewey's pedagogy and a history of the Progressive movement like Lawrence Cremin's *The Transformation of the School*. It was a shock to find how beautiful and how largely untried were all those methods of integrating subjects, those visions of getting out into the world to learn, of teachers learning from students, of learning that can actually be pleasant, of learning in which you design the process as you go along.

And so, many of us started getting optimistic again in the early 1960's; we devoured all the popular education books of the decade—books by John Holt, Jonathan Kozol, Herbert Kohl, James Herndon, A. S. Neill, Sylvia Ashton-Warner, and Bel Kaufman. And we said, Hey, things *can* be done; the school system is all buggered up, but sensitive people are surviving in it and some are starting beautiful experimental schools. What's needed is not any big new analysis; what we should be doing is all there in Dewey, or it's all there in Rousseau, for Christ's sake. Besides, Marshall McLuhan is giving us this poetic vision that technology is inevitably transforming the schools for the better anyway. . . .

And then we started to act. And soon the problems started. If you're working within the public system, you find that all these beautiful things you're trying are winning you enemies. People keep telling you to be patient. You see the society around you disintegrating and you're told to be patient if you try to introduce a few good novels into an English course. Or you find that changes are fine until you start organizing students or teachers to win changes through power.

Or maybe you start an experimental school. But you find that we're all so freaked out right now that a lot of people in one place, each doing his own thing, doesn't necessarily add up to a group that can function together. And the more radical the project, the more difficulty you have getting money for it.

And soon, unless you are happy just bouncing from experience to experience, or unless you drift back disillusioned to the fold, you end up advocating one of the four programs of action described below (which is roughly where I think North American education is at this writing):

1. *Abolish schools, especially high schools*   You say with Ivan Illich, Paul Goodman, John Holt, and other sensitive souls that school itself is obsolete, that compulsory education should be abolished, that kids will learn better by being let go free in the world.

With schools the way they are right now, these people sound right. And their writing and speaking gain great power by concentrating on the many beautiful alternatives to school that we could all be enjoying. The problem enters when one asks whether the authorities could be persuaded to abolish schools or whether revolutionaries and reformers have as part of their program this worthy cause. "No" is the answer to both questions, and the voluntary-school supporters know it. The established powers do not want millions more young people wandering the streets and highways of this continent, and revolutionaries and reformers don't want to abolish compulsory schooling because it would disperse the troops.

And so this suggestion is romantic. Since the program will not be instituted it gives young people a dream that removes their fight. Its advocates tell young people they are cannon fodder for the elite, but evade the question of how one gets out of this oppressed position. On a more complex level, it is not even honest about the very real camaraderie and tribal needs (see the selection by Peter Marin) that even the present fucked-up school system provides. In a way, this view suggests that young people, who at least as an oppressed group are now congregated, should disperse and start over like bands of lonely gypsies.

Those who recommend abolishing compulsory education, it should be noted, are quite different from that great company of people who want to clear the school of all functions not strictly related to intellectual and technical learning. Those in this latter group are largely politically conservative, but it is important to describe their views at this point, since they share with Illich *et al.* one very important passion—a reverence for civil liberties—which is, finally, both the strength and the limitation of the original group.

The conservative dissenters complain that the school is doing everything these days. Families, churches, private agencies, and clubs ought to get busy, they say, before the school takes over the entire lives of our children. There are all sorts in this category: Jews and Unitarians who object to Christian prayers in school, teachers whose professional security is shaken when they have to help kindergarten kids with their overshoes, those who oppose sex education in school, those who dislike compulsory physical education.

If one argues within the premises of present liberal society, there are certainly some interesting questions of civil liberties raised by this enormous expansion of school functions. Dr. Thomas Szasz of Syracuse University has expounded on this point better than anyone. To him, the increasing presence of psychiatrists, social workers and guidance counselors in schools is evil (and he means this literally) because what poses as help for students is really a sophisticated kind of control. The school decides what the sane, normal student is and plants its agents to engineer this normality. Szasz believes this gives the schools unconstitutional powers. At this point Szasz comes very close to the main group of critics I have been discussing—especially Edgar Friedenberg and Ivan Illich—since all tend to link their analysis of schools to civil liberties and the Constitution.

This view, which concentrates on the schools' abrogation of civil liberties, has achieved its most beautiful expression in the writings and speeches of Edgar Friedenberg. It is a beauty that is both elegant and elegiac. But finally it is too fragile. Friedenberg talks almost as if compulsory education is unconstitutional and concentrates almost entirely on what the schools should *not* do.

This viewpoint seldom mentions the *work* of society and the preparation for it. And it implies (Goodman's version more than Friedenberg's) a nostalgia for a society in which, though the schools take a very precise but limited role, there are, miraculously, other social groups or institutions—families (?), networks of stable friendships (?), little towns (?), Jane Jacobs' little New York or Toronto neighborhoods (?), churches (?)—those that would give kids their social cohesion, would fulfill their tribal needs. Or more miraculously still, in this vision we would all be strong, autonomous individuals traveling, learning from each other, watching educational television maybe, doing manly work, seeing friends, coming together betimes as communities of scholars, participating in group action only by improvisation and free choice.

Just where job training fits into such a revised liberal or revolutionized society is not clear. For some of these critics it appears that the topic is too mundane for them to soil their minds with it. For some, like Goodman, it seems that a revised version of the apprenticeship scheme is the answer. He seems to forget that it does not profit a business to gain a whole bunch of apprentices and lose its profits. (This was the message of an Ontario Government Commission Report on Manpower released in 1960, which said that the money the federal and provincial governments were spending on huge programs of technical and commercial training in schools would be much better spent improving apprenticeship programs so that business and industry itself could do the training. It went on to say, however, that business and industry could not be expected to support this proposal since, in a period when layoffs are more and more common, the apprentices are the first to go.)

If a big new apprenticeship scheme is not profitable and indeed not needed by business, what would happen to job training under a voluntary school system? What is much more possible is the direct entry of private business into the school business, with its own courses, its own fees, its own teachers.

Quite beyond the problem of job training, those who want to abolish compulsory schooling are, by their theories, implicated in the move in many liberal quarters to put the schools totally into the private sector of the economy. Give the tax money directly to parents and/or students and let them choose their own school, this view goes. I mention this scheme only to point out to those who want to see kids doing their own thing that the powerful economic interests will have several very profitable work and learning solutions to this. The present establishment will welcome any schemes that keep the young separated.

But the young do not show signs of leaving their schools en masse. Why this should be when the schools are doing such a bad job is surely a baffling question. I find the answer partly in the tribal value of the school, to which I have alluded. Institutions that supposedly looked after nonacademic needs in an earlier time no longer do so. The family, the church, the town, and the neighborhood are shattered, and young people themselves—not just some sinister totalitarian group at the top—are forcing the schools to be all-encompassing institutions. For better or for worse, the schools are becoming therapy centers, families, recreation centers, churches, travel agencies, information bureaus, motels, drop-in centers, housing authorities, rest homes, theaters, and sensoria. If they were closed, the students would soon reopen them. Many Neanderthal authority hierarchies would be gone, but all the problems of creating communal superinstitutions and all the problems of job training would still be there.

2. *Work within or outside the school system but devote most of your energy to a serious analysis of education and society that digs deeper than Dewey's* All over this continent there are scores of men and women in their twenties and thirties who, fifteen years ago, would have passed through the normal university channels and become university professors, reporters for leading newspapers, editors in major publishing houses, and civil servants. In 1970 they are concealed and wandering scholars, some writing for leftist and underground newspapers and news services, most of them former leftist activists who have decided that the forms of upheaval in this society will not cohere into serious opposition without serious, new analyses on which to base action.

This consuming interest in vast new analyses of schools and society has led people back to the nineteenth century, to Marx and Freud, and across to the East to the religions of ancient India, China, and Japan. This strange trip in time and space had a brief stop in the early 1960's within American history with Jefferson and Thoreau. The disintegration of American culture and political economy has suggested to the most perceptive of thinkers that American thought has never pierced deeply enough into the primordial roots of human experience. The perceptive have now moved to modern bearers of the older wisdom, people like Herbert Marcuse, Norman O.

Brown, Ernest Mandel, the looming figure of Mao Tse-tung, and, of course, Marshall McLuhan.

Educated, middle-aged Americans and Canadians who feel themselves part of that noble Anglo-Saxon tradition that deplores all dogmatism, all extremes of thought and action, cannot understand why all these fine young kids have embraced these old systems with such strident certainty. Isn't the truth found by keeping your cool, by compromise, by acting in the patient evolutionary way, and by thinking like a good Humean skeptic? Maybe black people have some excuse for being impatient, irrational, dogmatic, and freaked out. But all these good white North American boys and girls becoming Marxists or trailing after the Maharishi—there's got to be a good psychological explanation, surely it's a paranoid reaction, an escape mechanism, etc.

Wrong. Or right only insofar as a social and political disintegration has its psychological face. The fact that clues and answers are coming so considerably from the nineteenth century and from the East is a measure of both the wisdom of those times and places and of the recentness of the search. We have not had time to digest the last ten years, and this accounts in part for our obsession with ideas from other places, other times. When time has passed—if there *is* time—solutions and philosophies less rigidly attached to older theories and modes of being will emerge.

My digression away from schools to look at the current intellectual climate is intentional. It is an important feature of the education scene that many of the continent's best minds that were formerly devoted to education are now being applied to understanding the whole society. For such theorists schools will end up where intellectual honesty takes them. Some Marxists suggest that students and youth may occupy a new role in postindustrial society, one akin to that held by workers in earlier societies. The most compelling evidence for this view has been gathered and analyzed by John and Margaret Rowntree in "Youth as Class" (*Our Generation,* Vol. 6, Nos. 1–2 [May–July 1968]). For some McLuhan enthusiasts like George Leonard (*Education and Ecstasy*), the new technology and new therapies from places like Esalen suggest that schools can now pass beyond their concentration on the intellect and be new centers of sense liberation. For some of those fascinated by Eastern religion, schools should now be places of meditation where skills are learned the way Zen masters learned archery and judo.

If these examples seem sketchy and whimsical it is because the new insights about the whole of society are green and the insights about the school's place in it are even greener. Take the case of Marshall McLuhan as a prime case in point: Among the seers, only McLuhan has presented a vision that seems genuinely in touch with much of the basic novelty of our situation. He is a figure for our century as Nietzsche was for the nineteenth, a poet-philosopher of monumental insight accused by one side of giving wicked ideas to revolutionaries like Abbie Hoffman and Jerry Rubin and by the other side of giving smug comfort to tyrants in swinger's clothing like John Kennedy and Pierre Elliot Trudeau. When I was in college—the late 1950's—we were still being fed books that said that the entire justification for Hitler could be found in Nietzsche and even Hegel. I suspect that if this continent goes fascist historians will blame it on McLuhan's philosophy.

The weakness of McLuhan is that he's a Hegel in need of a Marx. Someone must stand him on his head. His brilliant insights about electronic technology and human existence must be wedded to an analysis of the actual struggles that working people, the colonized, students, and youth are going through. Without this, McLuhan is rather like a Marx who might have said that once the Industrial Revolution took place, so had the socialist revolution.

A "global village" with any dignity and justice for black, brown, and yellow people will not come with television and relay satellites alone, but with the organization, struggle, and death of thousands in the third world and within the United States. And though the transformation of the schools may already have happened in the mind of McLuhan—and even in the consciousness of many North American kids—it is starting to be *enacted* only with the organization, struggle, and death of these same kids.

3. *Organize and disrupt the school system and try to link this disruption to things like the war in Southeast Asia, corruption of the environment, and the economy*   Of those who believe the North American school system is rotten at its core, only a few are advocating the abolition of compulsory schooling. Very few are capable of the intellectual demands of rethinking the entire basis of modern society. More are ending up in this third category.

It is almost impossible to present a coherent picture of current disruption in the schools. Things are changing too quickly and the movements organizing confrontation and disruption are badly divided because of repression and internal disagreement. The 1960's have seen many strategies and movements involving students rise and fall, or stumble badly: civil rights, black liberation, war on poverty, war resistance, community organization and community schools, student power, free universities and schools, and hippies as radicals. Methods of confrontation have been tried and found wanting: nonviolent resistance, mass marches, sit-ins and occupations. Finally, adding to the confusion of school disruption is the unresolved question of whether there is any viable way to combine left radicalism with the cultural revolution of drugs, music, free sex, and communal living.

My personal symbol for the speed with which radicalism has changed recently is the story of two of my friends, Diana Oughton and Bill Ayers. In 1968 they were teachers at a small free elementary school for children in Ann Arbor. That fall they moved into SDS organizing in Ohio and Michigan. In 1969 both became members of Weatherman, and now Diana has blown her head off making explosives and Bill is underground and wanted for his part in organizing and participating in the Chicago action of October 1969.

But certain things have been learned from the experience of the 1960's that are shared by all disrupters, whether radical or liberal, whether veterans of earlier struggles or students new to the cause.

First, the feeling of passivity, the sense that nothing can be done, is fast passing from the student population. The talk is not always of oppression and alienation any more, but also of mobilizing to win victories.

Second, since the Democratic Convention in Chicago, the election of Nixon, and the unprovoked shooting of the four students at Kent, it is increasingly obvious to more and more students that the power and policies they want will not be coaxed and persuaded out of the Establishment. A resulting militance and willingness to organize to use violent and disruptive tactics contrasts strongly with a civil rights movement moving nonviolently under the protection of the federal Attorney General's office. It contrasts even more with the delusion—common at the faddish height of the hippie phenomenon—that the kids would love us all into the new age.

Third, nobody who wants significant change in the school system questions any more that this can come without constantly linking school issues to the broader issues of the war, the economy, the power structure, and the environment.

Because of these commonly held beliefs, because those in the student, the black, and the youth movements increasingly realize they must develop ways of encouraging and working with labor, and above all because the American empire is on the defensive internationally for the first time in its history, it seems increasingly unlikely that the American power elite will be able to repress, buy off, and soothe its youth as it has other oppressed peoples in revolt.

It should be obvious that the number of students involved in the category I have just been discussing is still a small percentage of the total student population. Teachers are mostly not in this category, since they have so far engaged in militant action only for particular professional and union rights. Some parent groups, like those in certain New York City school districts, have been militant, it is true, but it is not yet clear whether they want local control for anything other than the perfectly reasonable demand that their children be taught to read as well as white kids—and in a way that does not insult black culture.

4. *Focus everything on one new education scheme*   Most people who have given up on the general philosophy and practice of the public schools end up in this final category. This passionate espousal of one scheme as the answer to the entire school mess runs the complete spectrum from liberal schemes like nongrading and the open-plan school to the free university, the decentralized black school district, and certain features of student disruption. Of course it's not rare in history to have lots of particular education schemes being proposed as the final solution. The difference comes when these schemes are proposed in a period when the vastest empire in history is beginning to crack, when the philosophical basis of that empire has given schooling so prominent and sacred a place, and when the very people that sacred place has been created for are increasingly defiant and resistant.

In such a period it is very difficult to feel that you're working with anyone, on anything serious, that's going anywhere. So if you like action, and you haven't retired to a library to think, and you aren't part of a group that's moving somewhere, you invent or take over some new theory of learning and try to practice it (you're probably a teacher) inside or outside the system, usually being convinced at the same time that it represents *the* new way for schools generally. In order to believe more firmly in what you're doing, you ritually claim that you have only part of the truth, but you don't really believe this because you don't have the energy to be that broad-minded, and you proceed as if you were doing the only serious work in education. For most of us in this bag there's little sense of brotherhood, of camaraderie. We're even prone, like many political radicals, to reserve our most devastating attacks for those closest to us. As a free school founder and teacher, for example, if I talk to an elementary-school principal who's trying, say, an open-plan school, we usually get involved in just this kind of ritual mutual congratulation across a chasm of mistrust.

We have lots of company, we single-bag people. There are the people like Jerome Bruner, whose bag is the psychology of teaching complicated college physics and mathematics to small children. There are the Carl Bereiter people—whom the Panthers copied in training some young blacks, back when they had a little more peace. Bereiter can prepare ghetto kids under five with a high-pressure, rapid-fire method to compete with their middle-class classmates in grade one. When asked whether middle-class schools weren't a rather pathetic thing to prepare for, Bereiter answered with the basic single-bag argument: "Let's be modest. Let's at least do one thing well."

And then there are the people who have discovered that one can build buildings with movable walls so that pressing a button turns one room into eight. They're especially proud of one feature of their work: telling the big electrical, heating, and building materials companies what components they want. "We're calling the tune on industry now," they say, and this new architecture will be the panacea.

The list is endless: the people gung-ho on sensitivity training ("Get all those teachers into group therapy and we would transform the school system."); those who say that thematic treatment of material is the way; the school-trips trip; the course-content nuts; the "get a few students on the board" approach; Glasser's reality therapy; those who want kids to stay at home with educational TV; those who believe that when the choice of curriculum is individualized the problem is licked; the creativity people, whose work centers entirely on getting kids to write their own poems, make their own movies, perform their own plays.

I mock us, but I'm glad that most of these things are going on. What it amounts to is that students who have been to a school with the open plan and with teachers proud to be part of an experiment have some pleasant memories of school, which puts them in a very small minority.

With North American education so disrupted and yet so productive of schemes and ideas, it is difficult to center on *the* key essays, as one could have in the 1950's. Few pieces of enduring analysis are emerging. Only the piece by McLuhan looks into the future at the whole picture and that from his chirpy, poetic perch. John McDermott's brilliant essay on the kind of culture that colleges try to pass on is the kind of careful analysis of the details of the school experience that is rare, especially from radicals.

For some picture of the schools as they presently function, I include two pieces: Miriam Wasserman's "Miss White's Second Grade" and Eric Mann's "A Thing Called Berkeley." Mann is now in jail for radical activity in Boston, so this might be considered another of those letters from prison. He includes a postscript from Cell 274 containing the international revolutionary perspective from which he now sees schools and United States society. For a picture of schooling as it can relate to active political participation I have chosen, in addition to Eric Mann, Florence Howe's description of *Mississippi's Freedom Schools* and Miriam Wasserman's account of the speech class taught by Stokely Carmichael. Peter Marin's *Fiery Vehemence of Youth* came partly out of his experiences at Pacific High School in Palo Alto, California, a place which George Leonard described several years ago as the only truly experimental school in the United States. (The fact that the school may no longer be in existence when this book comes out does not invalidate the writing and would be a nice illustration of the state of experimental schooling at this blessed moment.)

The piece that may seem strangest is the selection from A. S. Makarenko's *The Road to Life.* I include it as much as anything because I hope many readers will read the entire three volumes of this magnificent work. Makarenko is the most renowned education theorist in Soviet history, and his book is about his work in a school for delinquent boys who roamed Russia after the revolution. The selection I include seems right to illustrate the kind of passionate relationships that must exist between teacher and learner, particularly in areas of violence like the ghetto. I confess I'm partial to the book because Makarenko's school, like ours, was a commune.

ELECTRONICS
& THE PSYCHIC DROP-OUT

Marshall McLuhan

The movement in education during the past 50 years or so has been a movement towards specialization, each expert burrowing in depth into a particular segment of knowledge. Today all this has changed. Specialization won't work any more as a means of learning. The only technique today for obtaining depth is by interrelating knowledge, whether it be in physics or anthropology or anything else. When a man attempts to study anything, he crosses the boundaries of that field almost as soon as he begins to look into it. For example, in physics in the last decade big discoveries have all taken place by benefit of biology and the models of structure borrowed from other areas altogether different from physics.

INFORMATION NOT HARDWARE

Under present-day electronic conditions the total human environment becomes made of information. The electronic bomb, for example, is almost pure information. In terms of hardware it only weighs a few ounces, but the whole power of the thing and its whole relation to mankind is informational circuitry. They represent the real strength and the real power of our time. The moving of information has become the task and the occupation of almost all of mankind, whereas a scant 50 years ago most men were engaged in making and conveying hardware hither and thither or across national boundaries. At the same time, information levels have risen spectacularly and the amount of information needed to conduct oneself in the most ordinary jobs has risen tremendously. It is that that causes education to become appreciated and enormously stepped up in its scope. One way of testing this is simply to look into the matter of how much research and higher education is considered normal in the business world today or in the military establishment. Ten times the money is being spent on higher education inside the business and military establishments compared to the community at large. And there's no ideal behind this, no educational goals whatever, simply a pressure of daily need and urgency.

SMALL CHILDREN CAN NOW DO TOP LEVEL RESEARCH

Now this has some strange implications for the community at large. One of them is that higher education is going to be forced downward into the

ELECTRONICS & THE PSYCHIC DROP-OUT From *This Magazine is About Schools*, Vol. 1, Issue 1 (April 1966). Reprinted by permission.

elementary schools. In other words, we're going to have to re-program the whole of our educational establishment for discovery rather than for instruction. Instruction is something that will have to be taken for granted under the new conditions of electronic information and movement. We have to realize that more instruction is going on outside the classroom, many times more every minute of the day than goes on inside the classroom. That is, the amount of information that is embedded in young minds per minute outside the classroom far exceeds anything that happens inside the classroom in just quantitative terms now. And this is going to increase enormously. In the future basic skills will no longer be taught in classrooms. They can be taught by gramophone records or by tape records or video tape playback machines. When video tape becomes available to the ordinary household as it will shortly, there will be a revolution in education comparable with that which took place with the coming of the printed book. As long as education depended upon access to manuscripts, it was a very slow and painful process. With the coming of the portable privately-owned printed book, the whole educational process took on a new character. This is going to happen with video tape machines, because it means then that anybody can have top-level surgeons, biologists, physicists, philosophers, poets—anything for his own private use on all subjects and at his own time, his own leisure and in his own space.

That is why all the talk about instructional aids in the classroom from electronic means is nonsense. You cannot introduce electronic forms into the classroom without rescheduling the whole process of instruction, and this is impossible under our unwieldy, fragmented conditions of classroom use. But we're on the verge of a complete decentralization of instruction.

CHILDREN AND ADOLESCENTS A BACKWARD COUNTRY OF THE MIND

As the levels of information rise in the total community, it means that very small children have access to very high learning indeed. And as the whole community becomes structured environmentally by information and knowledge and circuitry, it means that quite small children can do top level research by team methods co-operatively. Robert Oppenheimer has been saying for years that there are small children playing here on this street who could solve some of his top problems in physics because they have modes of perception which an adult has lost a long time ago. This awareness of the perceptual modes that enable people to participate in various types of high level research as much as anything they could be taught or anything they could learn instructionally, is only beginning to filter through. Edmund Bacon, for example, the head of the Town Planning commission in Philadelphia, a few years ago became world-famous overnight when he enlisted the aid of the elementary schools in solving some of his top problems in Town Planning. He got children in the early grades to study the plans for Philadelphia and to discuss them among themselves and their parents and neighbors, and to study their communities physically and geographically, and they came up with some of the top solutions to the whole problem. It is clear that we are just beginning to recognize that children and adolescents are a kind of backward country of the mind that's been deliberately suppressed for centuries in our Western world. They are now an under-developed country that have to be brought into the picture. It means educationally, of course, that our whole system of grading is useless in the schools. Because if you live in a community where the information levels are very high—just in the sense of the amount of data moving on the radio and TV and movies and so on—then the idea that you should use your school system as a means of eliminating half or three quarters of the community from higher education is ludicrous.

MERE LITERACY WON'T DO ANY MORE

The task of community education ought to be to lift the entire community up to the level of the technology the community is using. Otherwise the whole society collapses. The only reason that we ever had universal literacy was quite simply that the industrial tycoons demanded that the labour market be flooded with people who could read and write. And the military likewise demanded that the entire population be able to read and write so that they could be available for military service.

What we still call a backward country is an area where most of the population is illiterate. That means that we cannot lay our industrial hands on them: they are immune to our manipulations. As soon as they can read and write they are completely in our grasp. We can do anything with a literate population that we want whereas an illiterate population is relatively immune to our type of operations. On the other hand it is not free from the atom bomb, which is pure information that has become environmental—and can affect any area and culture on the globe.

But in our world where our typical environments are now made of information, and high level information, mere literacy won't do any more. We now have to teach literacy on many levels; pictorial and electronic forms of knowledge have to be imparted in order to enable people to live and work. Automation will wipe out the narrow specialist: a machine will be more effective in storing information and making deductive calculation on the basis of it. And this will have a profound impact on the educational system.

THE PSYCHIC DROPOUT IS PROBABLY 100%

Canada is still almost entirely a 19th-century country. It has very little relation to the 20th century. Its educational system is anachronistic: students are still being processed through the old fragmented specialist chopper and they might as well be on a carousel or a merry-go-round in some entertainment park. Our youngsters at school are reacting to this, and dropping out of school is one response. The youngsters coming out of a highly integral electronic environment go to school and are confronted by a fragmented, specialist environment of subjects and hours and instructions which baffle them. They know that this form of fragmentation does not correspond in any way to the world they're living in. They've already been deeply imbued with this new electronic world from the cradle, from the time they begin to look at TV. When the school fails to make sense of their environment, they drop out, either physically or psychologically. The psychic dropout far outnumbers the physical dropout which also is on the increase. The psychic dropout is probably about 100%.

The failure to relate one's needs and one's actual environmental structure to any educational procedures is something that can happen only during periods of very rapid change. And we live in a period of such a rapid change that change itself has become the only form of stability we know. We relate everything to the fixed point of change. An educational system that tries to hold a line is making the Maginot Line mistake. What happens to Maginot Lines is that people ignore them and go around them. The dropouts are just people who are going around the Maginot Line of our educational system, looking for some other source of entry into the territory of their times.

AN AGE OF FEED-BACK . . . AN AGE OF INVOLVEMENT

We have to become aware of the fact that the whole effect of electronic technology is to bypass our older mechanical, fragmented ways of organizing society. We have moved suddenly from the age of the wheel to the age of the circuit. Whereas the wheel merely conveyed materials and data, the circuit inter-relates and is a thing of feed-back. From an era of transmission we move into an age of feed-back which is also an age of involvement.

Now, when I'm talking about involvement, I'm not talking about ideals. I think that sort of visualizing of distant goals belongs to a much earlier period. When you are deeply involved and participate in the life of your time, you don't have goals. The man who is involved doesn't have ideals. A mother does not have a job; she has a role, she has about forty jobs at once and she doesn't have any ideals whatever. She is thoroughly involved. It's like a man and his hobby; he doesn't have any ideals about his hobby; he is involved in it. Anybody who is involved in what he's doing doesn't have any goals or ideals whatever; he's just with it. He's doing something that takes every ounce of his energy.

Instead of a specialist job, people now have to go back to roles in depth in all levels of work and employment and study and knowledge.

A PROBE, NOT A PACKAGE

Education on all levels has to move from packaging to probing, from the mere conveying of data to the experimental discovering of new dimensions of experience. The search will have to be for patterns of experience and discovery of principles of organization which have universal application, not for facts. An example of this, if you like, is the psychopathology of everyday life: every child now understands the patterns of the Freudian slip—this is a probe, not a package. In some circles this is called "mature learning", a learning for discovery rather than mechanical learning. This kind of learning, in the end, has nothing to do with an age level: there is nothing to stop small children from becoming very adept experimenters, graduate probers, explorers. It is the orientation of the society that matters, and our whole world, in shifting from the old mechanical forms to the new electronic feed-back forms, has already shifted from data packaging to probing of patterns.

THE LAYING ON OF CULTURE

John McDermott

About a year ago I accepted an invitation to speak "against the war," at, let's call it, the University of Dexter. It is located in the city of that name, one of the major manufacturing towns of the Midwestern industrial belt. Since Dexter is somewhat off the main circuit for anti-war speech-making, I read up on the university and the town, and what I found made me look forward to my visit.

The university tended to draw most of its students from the town itself. They came heavily from working-class families and were often the first in their families to attend college. Frequently English was not the only language spoken at home. More significant was the fact that the city itself had at one time considerable fame for working-class militancy. One of the great early strikes of the depression was fought in Dexter, and the issue was not settled in the workers' favor until they had fought the National Guard to a draw in pitched street battles. Before that the city had been a center of Socialist Party activity, and still earlier, a stronghold of IWW sentiment. Thus I looked forward to my visit as an opportunity to talk to the kind of students seldom reached by Movement speakers.

It wasn't. Attendance at the well-publicized meeting was spotty; those who came tended to be about evenly divided between faculty and graduate students, almost all of whom were from outside the state. And there were no students at the party to which I was taken later in the evening, though they had helped plan the meeting, for student segregation is the campus rule at Dexter, no less within the Movement than outside it. Perhaps it was that or perhaps my disappointment at the absence of "normal" students at the evening's meeting; anyhow, I deliberately forced the party to become a meeting. It had taken no great powers of observation to note that the anti-war movement at Dexter, and, by extension, its Left, was largely a preserve of the faculty and some fellow-traveling graduate students, and I was inter-

THE LAYING ON OF CULTURE From *The Nation*, March 10, 1969. Reprinted by permission.

ested to discover why that was so. In particular, I wanted to explore the role these teachers had adopted to their "normal" students and to examine with them the contradiction between that professional role and their wider political aspirations. I have taught in several universities, I've suffered the same contradiction and was unable to overcome it.

The most prominent feature of the discussion which followed, and of all the subsequent ones I've started on the same subject in similar situations, was that the faculty, to a man, still aspired to teach in elite schools. Dexter, after all, is what is popularly known as a "cow" college. A state school, it gets those students who, for lack of skill or money or interest, don't go to the main state university and couldn't "make" the liberal arts colleges in the area, even if they wanted to. Its students are very much vocationally oriented and still tied to their families. Most of them live at home.

Dexter is frequently under nuisance attack by some right-wing faction or other. It pays rather badly and is not in an attractive metropolitan area. Its library is inferior, it provides little research money, and the teaching loads are heavy. The administration is fusty and conservative, as is much of the faculty.

My faculty friends, obviously talented men and women, had not reconciled themselves to this exile. They depreciated the region, the town, the university and, especially, the students, even the graduate students. Loyalty and affection they reserved for the graduate schools from which they had come, and they reflected this feeling in their teaching and counseling by relating only to that one student in a hundred who might go on to one of those prestigious graduate schools. Those were the students who shared with them the culture of books and civility—and scorn for Dexter; who might by their success at a "good" graduate school justify the faculty's exile in Dexter.

Of course they didn't put it that way, and neither did I when I taught in similar places. They saw themselves as embattled missionaries to the culturally Philistine. They worked hard and creatively with the students who merited hope. As for the others, these men and women, in spite of their expressed scorn, nourished a vision, hesitantly expressed, of a society in which no student would be oppressed by cultural bondage to ignorance, vocationalism, anti-intellectualism and provincialism. In fact, that attitude and hope gave rise to and was expressed in their left-wing politics.

The guests at the party were woefully ignorant of the background of their "normal" students. They were vaguely aware that most of them came from working-class families, though what that might mean aside from greater resistance to formal education they had no idea. They had no knowledge either of Dexter's militant labor traditions. This was sad, for it penalized the faculty in a number of ways. To cite an apparently trivial instance, most of the faculty present were concerned over attacks made on the university by the right wingers in town. Respect for free speech and expression had an important place in their scale of values, and they tried to convey it to their classes, using all the familiar academic examples, from HUAC witch hunting and Joe McCarthy, to Stuart Mill, Milton and Sophocles.

Yet that they might relate the principle of free expression to the problems of Wobbly agitators in the 1910s or of CIO organizers in the 1930s (or of white-collar workers in the 1970s)—in short, relate it to the actual cultural history (or future) of their own students—never occurred to them. Instead, they were put off when the students responded to the alien and seemingly irrelevant world of HUAC and Milton and academic freedom with either passive unconcern or active hostility.

I believe this example successfully characterizes how the great majority of faculty behave in schools like Dexter, including, especially, the left wing of the faculty. Socialized like all their fellows into a rigid professional role by their university, graduate school and early professional experiences, they have neither the information nor the inclination to break out of that role and relate openly and positively to the majority of their students who cannot accept the culture of the university world as their own.

University professors as a group seem exceptionally uncritical of the limited value—and values—of a university education and the acculturation it represents. In their view, a student who is really open to his classroom and other cultural experiences at the university will, as a rule, turn out to be more sophisticated, more interested in good literature, more sensitive morally than one who is less open or who has not had the benefit of college. The student will also be free of the more provincial ties of home, home town, region and class. In short, most academics take it as an article of faith that a student benefits by exchanging his own culture for that of the university. It is by far the most common campus prejudice.

And it would be harmless enough if it were limited in its sanction to those students who allow their university education to "take," who do well at university work and will go on to graduate school and then to a place within the university world or, perhaps, into some other related profession. University attitudes and values are appropriate to that world. But what about the others, the cultural red-necks, the "normal" boy and girl at a place like Dexter? Do they really profit from acquiring the attitudes, values, life style, and so forth of the peculiar culture whose institutional base is the university? One way of attacking this question is to ask to what extent those values, attitudes and life style may be usefully transferred to other institutional settings—to little towns and big cities, to industrial or agricultural life, to life in a corporation or in government.

That was about as far as we went at that party a year ago. We agreed that we were part of a university system which was actively engaged at its Dexters in destroying whatever indigenous culture might remain among the American working class. We recognized that, consciously or not, we had assumed an invidious clerical relationship to our student laity. Like medieval priests or missionaries to the heathen, we dispensed a culture to all our students, despite the fact that a scant few could participate in it. For the others, the language of that culture, like Latin to the colloquial, was grasped largely in rote phrases, its symbols and doctrines recognized but only dimly understood. To the extent that this majority of students acquired the external trappings of the university, they seemed both culturally pacified and made culturally passive. Pacified because they were acculturated away from their own historical values and traditions; passive because they could at best be spectators of a culture whose home remained an alien institution.

II

In the year that has passed since my visit to Dexter my views of the relationship of general culture to political culture have very much developed under the influence of Edward Thompson's *The Making of the English Working Class*. I find particularly persuasive and suggestive Thompson's demonstration of how certain aspects of the general culture of the English working class, over a period of time and under the stress of events, came to support a specifically political culture—that is, to enlarge its capacity to define its social interests and to struggle successfully in their behalf. I shall cite several instances of this, for I want later to use them to illuminate the problem at Dexter from a new and, I think, hopeful standpoint.

Thompson shows that the movement into the factories in England of the late 18th and early 19th centuries was made up of two distinct streams. One was the movement of poor, dispossessed rural persons to the city and the factory in search of opportunity; the other of highly skilled, often literate craftsmen being pushed down the social and economic ladder by the new forces of industrialism and technology. The former, abruptly torn from their rural poverty, had some reason to view the change as an improvement. The cultural shock of the transition, the traditional passivity to authority, the stimulus of urban life, and the novelty of cash wages might easily have disguised for a time the exploitative nature of their place in the new factory system. The urban craftsmen, however, having a sense of their own skill and worth, with still lively guild traditions, and a strong sense of declining status and economic position, were most unlikely to think of the factory experience as a road to opportunity. They knew it for the oppression it really was. It was the meeting of these two groups that proved so creative for the future of the working-class movement. The skilled printers, weavers and mechanics recognized that their lot was cast with the unskilled rural migrants, and they became a creative element among the larger mass. Their literacy, their talent for organization, their family and folk memories that working people had once lived secure in their homes, livelihoods and craftsmanship, were transferred over the years to the mass of working people. But they were transferred with a radical difference. By contributing them to the cause of the entire working class, what might otherwise have been merely a narrow defense of guild interests was instead universalized into a struggle for the rights of all Englishmen, a struggle for the rights of man.

Thompson also shows how important for the new working-class movement was the experience so many workers had in the Dissenting Churches. Men and women who, over the years, had learned to contend with the problems of maintaining a minister's salary, keeping up the church and parsonage, administering an active religious and social program, and organizing regional church activities were able to apply these skills to nascent working-class organizations. Of particular importance was their long experience of persecution at the hands of the Church of England. Both ministers and congregations had learned how to preserve their churches and beliefs in the face of official hostility and repression. Thus when Pitt, Burke and their successors attempted to destroy the new workingmen's organizations, these were able to go underground, preserving their organizations, maintaining their programs and extending their networks throughout the country.

Still another general cultural factor cited by Thompson as a primary support for the growing working-class movement was the belief among the English lower classes that they were "freeborn Englishmen." The phrase had no precise meaning, but it was habitually called into play to criticize or resist any arbitrary act against the populace and its organizations, any claim to special place by the upper classes, any innovation in government control over the speech, writing, travels or associations of the common people. It was a useful and eminently flexible weapon in the hands of the working-class movement against the power of the capitalists and the wiles of Edmund Burke.

What makes Thompson's work of more than antiquarian interest is the suggestive analogy it offers to situations such as that at Dexter. There is a double movement into such universities today, somewhat as there was a double movement into the factories of England two centuries ago. On the one hand, a flood of lower-class young people is moving into these universities, seeking entrée into the old independent professional middle class which university attendance supposedly affords. It is necessary to add "supposedly," for passage through a non-elite university no longer qualifies one for that kind of life. The jobs for which the Dexters and the junior colleges prepare students are elementary and secondary teaching, the lower levels of social work, white-collar hire, petty management—that is, employments which were once semiprofessional, but which now are being rapidly industrialized by bureaucracy, managerial science and the IBM machine. Thus the lower-class boys or girls who go to Dexter only appear to escape from the world of industry; they are really taking the first vocational step into a new kind of industrial life.

The second movement into such institutions as Dexter is of a gifted minority of educated persons, who identify with the values, accomplishments and prestige of elite professions, but are forced by the economics of academic employment to take positions they consider beneath their skills, their sense of worth and accomplishment, their lively memories of the recent past.

But here the analogy with Thompson's English working class begins to break down, for these latter specifically and pointedly refuse to make common cause with the lower-class students with whom they share daily existence. This gifted Left minority does not help the students to develop an effective and vital popular political culture. On the contrary, it often occupies the vanguard of a university culture which, as I suggested above and now wish to argue more fully, pacifies lower-class students.

III

The most obvious political characterization of university culture is that it lives by, and presents to its students, the values and attitudes appropriate to its own upper-middle-class life style—a style that is part of the older, now declining, professional middle classes. As indicated above, a university education did once promise membership in the professional classes. This meant that university graduates could ordinarily expect a life of considerable social and economic independence, some measure of personal influence in local business and political communities, significant autonomy and initiative in carrying out their daily work, and thus the possibility of enjoying the pride that follows from personal accomplishment and craftsmanship.

Could it be clearer that no such life awaits the graduates of the nation's Dexters? Today a degree from a second- or third-line institution is a passport to a life style of high consumption and of reasonable job security. But it will probably be an industrial life style, characterized by social and economic dependence on a large institution, by little or no political or social influence, and by participation in rationalized work processes wherein one must try merely "to get by and not step on anybody's toes." Consider, therefore, how the professionally oriented values of the university's culture might function in such an industrial environment. High on the scale of university values, now and in the past, stands the virtue of tolerance—not only personal tolerance in the face of new or differing ideas, attitudes and values but the belief that tolerance itself is of greater personal and social value than the substance of almost any set of creeds. Such a value was useful in the professional worlds of the past, for it would normally help diminish conflict in a middle class made up of highly autonomous individuals. And in elite circles even today it diminishes the weight assigned to ideological differences and helps to harmonize the social and political relations of our pluralistic, semi-autonomous industrial, educational, government and other managers. It carries the advantage, too, that it opens managers to the merits of technological and organizational novelty in a political economy strongly oriented to such innovations.

But how does this belief function for the young men and women of Dexter, who will normally occupy the lower and middle levels of great institutional bureaucracies, and who may have reason to resist those very same innovations: speed-up, compulsory overtime, more and more alienating work processes, forced transfer to another city or region, institutional propaganda, Muzak and the other normal tyrannies of personnel managers? Is it a value that helps them to initiate or continue those collective struggles which are necessary to defend or enhance their interests; or does it rob them of the moral and ideological assurance which must support the beliefs of people who challenge the social legitimacy and retributive power of authority?

A second political aspect of university culture is its almost uniform hostility to the institutions of local and community life. Many churches, fraternities, veterans' associations, councils and boards upon which local and community life in America is built are havens of the narrowest sorts of provincialism, racism, intellectual baiting, babbittry and jingoism. For these reasons, and for reasons having to do with the demands of the national economy for college-trained persons, the tendency of university experience is to propel the young away from local and community life and toward national life and its institutions. A result of the university's liberalism, cosmopolitanism and technologism, this tendency is supported by the national culture, by the students themselves, and by their parents.

But it should be combated by those, like my friends at Dexter, who are interested in building mass resistance to the prevailing currents of American life. A young person from Dexter, unless extraordinarily gifted or fortunate, has almost no means of gaining influence in national politics. And to the extent that university culture directs great masses of lower- and lower-middle-class young people into the institutions of national rather than local and community life, it assists in disenfranchising them from political influence. Of course, the conventional representatives of university culture argue that the decline of local politics and local institutions is inevitable, given the institional needs of 20th-century industry and government, the gradual nationalization of American life, and the march of technology—i.e., liberalism, cosmopolitanism and technologism. But we should begin to question whether this inevitability amounts to more than advantageous prejudice. For the kind of society which these university spokesmen describe as inevitable appears to be coincidentally one in which the Ph.D. takes its place with property and birth as a means to political influence and social status.

Similarly, the ignorance, racism and the like which characterize so much of local life should not put us off. Given the preoccupation of the Left, over the past epoch, with national rather than local concerns and institutions, it is not surprising that local America has become a playpen of unchallenged right-wing attitudes, persons and organizations. Of course, one could not expect, even under the best conditions, that the life style of local America will rival the faculty club in gentility, civility, humanist learning and other caricatures of university life. But that is not its test, any more than the theological elegance of the Dissenting Churches was the test of their usefulness to a struggling movement of ordinary Englishmen. Those who are today concerned about a different kind of economic barbarism and a similar kind of world-wide crusade should draw the appropriate lessons.

A third political aspect of university culture is its latent hostility to two of the more valuable and humane realities in current popular culture. One cannot move around this country without being impressed by its egalitarianism, that is the depth and vitality of the ordinary American's feeling that he is as good as the next fellow. And the other reality so important in our popular culture is the well-nigh universal belief among our people that they possess an extraordinary range and variety of substantive rights. Like the belief in "the freeborn Englishmen," the belief in substantive rights is often vague and contradictory. Nevertheless, the history of popular political movements is the history of ordinary people acting in behalf of what they believe to be their substantive rights.

It would be too much to say that the university's culture is uniformly hostile to these popular realities, for the situation is ambiguous. However, it is not difficult to identify important hostile tendencies. Thus in contrast to the normal American acceptance of the principle of equality, the professoriat strongly values formalized differences of age, academic rank, scholarly reputation and, it may even be, accomplishment. The effect of this sort of deference is somewhat difficult to gauge and it may be tendentious on my part to believe that it influences student attitudes on legitimacy, authority and equality. Perhaps the issue is instead that university men and women, by failing to provide a living example of egalitarian relationships, merely fail to make common cause with the American people in their resistance to the hierarchic tendencies implicit in the social and economic system.

A more secure case can be made against the disposition in the university world to identify right not with substantive but with procedural matters. Peter Gay expressed this position in the Summer 1968 issue of *Partisan Review*: ". . . democracy is essentially procedural and what matters is not so much (important though it may be) what a given policy is as how it is arrived at. . . ." Persons as fortunately placed as Professor Gay, whose substantive rights are well established in easily available procedures, have an understandable tendency to overlook the fact that, for example, tenure, sabbaticals, choice of hours, and freedom of expression on the job—are virtually unknown outside the academic world. Obviously there are other, important and thorny issues here as well. Without going into them at any length, note that the test of Professor Gay's remark is its fidelity to historical fact. From that point of view, it tends to obscure the fact that the great libertarian and democratic turning point in postwar American political history, a turning point with great promise still, came not from the narrow defense of procedural rights by academic and other liberals against Joe McCarthy in the 1950s but from the assertion of substantive rights in the 1960s by mass movements of students, blacks, professors and ordinary Americans.

The students at Dexter, and a great part of their countrymen, rightly view the liberal and academic preference for procedural right as a defense of privileges which they themselves are denied. Many view the principle of academic freedom, for example, as they view some of the laws of property. It is a tricky device which enables professors to do things, like criticize the dean or the country, for which ordinary people can be fired; just as the law of property is a tricky device which enables installment houses and loan companies to do things for which ordinary people can be sent to jail. The goal is not to do away with academic freedom, or any other hard-won libertarian procedure. A better approach would be to shape a university culture which would help to extend Professor Gay's tenure, sabbaticals, and freedom of expression on the job to everyone, on campus and off.

The existence of hostile tendencies toward egalitarianism and the primacy of substantive right is very much related to still a fourth political aspect of university culture. Even though the university is the home and source of much of the libertarian ideology within our culture, it is often the source of authoritarian ideology as well. I have two cases in mind. The first has to do with the extensive commitment to technologism found among many faculty members. A considerable body of university opinion believes with Zbigniew Brzezinski that the promises of modern technology demand for their social realization a society characterized by "equal opportunity for all but . . . special opportunity for the singularly talented few." The evasiveness of the formula should not be allowed to obscure the authoritarian social and political processes which are envisioned and justified by it—processes today best exemplified in the area of national security, where the equal voting opportunities of all are nullified by the special bureaucratic opportunities open to a singularly talented few. The second of the university's authoritarian ideologies I call clericism. To borrow from Brzezinski's formula, it is the claim to "equal cultural rights for all, but special cultural authority for a singularly scholarly few." I refer to the still widespread (but declining) academic belief that, whatever else culture may include, it also includes the Western Heritage, the Western Tradition, the Literary Tradition, the traditions of reason and civility, etc., and that these are most fully embodied in the profession of academe and the written treasures of which academe is priestly custodian and inspired interpreter.

This principle underlies faculty sovereignty over curricular matters, justifies any and every required course, oppresses first-year graduate students, and received its most prosaic formulation in the observation by Columbia's vice dean of the graduate facilities that ". . . whether students vote 'yes' or 'no' on an issue is like telling me they like strawberries." Clericism and technologism have their good points; no one wishes seriously to derogate either the social or the moral value of good scholarship or competent technology. But as principles under which to organize cultural or political life they are distinctly hostile to the interests of great numbers of non-elite students, the social classes from which they are drawn, and especially the social classes they will constitute when they leave the university. For clericism and technologism, like the doctrines of apostolic succession and of property which they tend to replace, transpose major areas of social concern from the purview of all to the treasure house of the few. Culture, no less than politics, is a critical factor in the nature of social organization; in the distribution of power, reward and status; in the infliction of powerlessness, oppression and despair. This is becoming increasingly understood with regard to politics, where ten years of war, urban decay and increasing social chaos seem to have been the fruit of the same decade's obeisance to technology's claims. But I am not persuaded that clericist depredations on culture are similarly recognized.

As I think was made clear at the start of this essay, the faculty at Dexter did not feel called upon to know the specific cultural history and experiences of the students they taught. Neither they nor anyone in the academic profession consider it their task to use their own superior symbolic gifts and wider historical perspective to identify the specific historical culture of their students, to clarify its ambiguities, to criticize it, purging it of its moral (not geographical) provincialism, and thus to assist the students to develop a culture which is at once personally ennobling and politically self-conscious. On the contrary, at Dexter and elsewhere the faculty assume that it is their duty to replace the students' actual culture with an alien culture. Missionaries from these graduate schools, like clergy from colonial empires everywhere and in every time, feel confident that what they bring is good for the natives and will improve them in the long run. In culture, as elsewhere, this is manifestly not so.

Consider the matter of historical traditions. No acculturation worth the name should be permitted to block the transmission of Dexter's militant working-class traditions. Even granting, as is probably the case, that only a small minority of the Dexter students are children of depression workers or the earlier Wobblies, to assist, even if only negatively, in destroying these traditions is to minimize for most of the students the opportunity to discover the reasons for their attitudes on a score of moral and social questions, the reality of their social lives, and the possibility of rebuilding a more humane culture in Dexter for their own advantage. White intelligentsia recognize this danger when they peer across cultural lines at blacks or Vietnamese; why are they so blinded by the class lines of their own society? It should come as no surprise, therefore, that the anti-intellectualism of the students is often as deep and as bitter as the hatred exhibited by other colonial peoples toward foreigners and their works.

A university culture which related positively and creatively to the traditions and history of the working classes, blue collar and white collar, would find allies not only among the hippies and the leftists of Smith and Williams but from the squares of Dexter as well.

What is particularly disturbing about cultural pacification in the university is that it is not entirely an accidental phenomenon. At least since Herbert Croly's *Promise of American Life* (1909), America's dominant historians have been strongly nationalist, more interested in discovering and celebrating the American essence or character, the national mainstream, consensus or moral epic, or the peculiar quality of our national integration, than in emphasizing its divisions, especially those based on class. It has often crossed my mind that when liberal historians two decades hence write the chronicle of the Southern freedom movement of the early 1960s or of the anti-Vietnamese War movement of today, they will find imaginative and persuasive reasons to show that the first was really part of the New Frontier and the second of the Great Society. It was thus that their predecessors have managed to reduce the richness and variety of popular revolt in the 1930s to the bureaucratic dimensions of a Washington-based "New Deal."

Fortunately, some of the younger historians, such as Staughton Lynd and Jesse Lemisch, have begun to undermine the epic poetry of the Crolyites by reviving interest in the history of popular insurgency in America. Thus they have created the possibility that at least at some universities young people will be reacquainted with the real diversity and conflict of their past. More than that, and without exaggerating its importance or extent, this new scholarship provides a point of departure for a fundamentally different university culture than the one I have been describing.

IV

Faced with the vast social diversity of America and in opposition to the variety and strength of its Populist traditions, the thrust of university culture is to pacify its working-class "natives" and thus, I believe, to help preclude any fundamental change in national politics and priorities. Because of the surge of rebellion on campus since last spring, it is likely that this is understood better now among faculty than it was at the time I visited Dexter. But many university men and women, comparing the university's cultural values to those of industry, the mass media and the military, or to the restless hostility of lower- and working-class America, remain partisans and priests of academe, convinced that for all its faults it is, at least minimally, a humane alternative to its rivals.

The analogy I began earlier to the work of Edward Thompson points in a more hopeful and, I think, more realistic direction. A survey of recent campus rebellions would show that it is no longer only the Harvards and the Berkeleys which suffer serious student unrest; some of the most interesting and militant activity occurs at the non-elite schools. In addition, scores of young men and women continue to be exiled by their elite graduate schools into a lifetime of work in the non-elite universities. The narrowest interests of these teachers and their most lofty professional and political aspirations lie in the same direction. It is to take up the task, in common with their students, of rebuilding the vitality of a popular resistance culture —that is, of a culture which will "enhance the capacity of ordinary Americans to identify their social interests and to struggle successfully in their behalf."

This is not a task which individuals can successfully undertake in isolation, nor one whose champions will be free of serious reprisal at the hands of university and political authorities. Nevertheless, there are already a handful of campuses where the work has begun, in critical universities, liberation courses, seminars in local and working-class history, student-taught courses for faculty, and research projects on local and campus decision making. It remains for others to add to these hopeful beginnings.

MISS WHITE'S SECOND GRADE

Miriam Wasserman

Inside the classroom the interaction between the teacher and the children continues the process that began for each child with his assignment to a top, middle, or bottom class—the process of teaching the children their relative place in the world. For all children in conventional schools, regardless of class and race, schooling is learning to submit to authority, procedures, rituals as much as it is learning skills and acquiring information. Also, schooling is learning that many of their natural social, physical, and emotional impulses are either nasty or irrelevant to the teacher's needs and so must be denied, repressed, or perverted. For non-middle-class children and nonwhite children sitting under middle-class or would-be middle-class teachers, whether white or nonwhite, such lessons are likely to be even more pronounced. The teacher's anxieties about the children's strange or despised family origins, their low-status speech habits, and their unfamiliarity with typical middle-class physical and emotional repressions—anxieties often related to vague, implicit sexual fears—may lead her to concentrate almost one hundred percent of her teaching energies on trying to socialize her pupils according to middle-class criteria rather than on simply imparting the academic skills and information that are supposed to comprise the curriculum. And as she concentrates on socializing, she is likely to convey to the children, perhaps even without so intending, the inappropriateness of their group and individual life styles. Depending on the teacher's personality, her degree of distaste for the attitudes, speech, and habits of which she is seeking to cure her pupils, and her sensitivity to the children's reactions to her, she may also convey quite explicitly her disapproval of her pupils as representatives of a low-status social group.

This kind of communication, where nonwhite children are involved, is called racism by those of the children's advocates who disapprove of it. It is, in fact, a complex cultural and social process, in which white pupils may sometimes be the objects or Negro teachers the actors. So, although the phenomenon overlaps racism, it is not identical with the kind of racism that derives from a conscious belief in the inferiority of nonwhites and an explicit wish to keep them unequal and inferior. Indeed, it often parades under a sentiment that is quite the opposite of conventional racism. Thus: "These are poor children who have none of the advantages children ought to have—not even parents who can teach them right from wrong. And I am doing everything I can to make up for some of these terrible deficiencies in their sad little lives."

Miss White's second grade is an illustration of the way in which classroom organization and teacher messages convey a sense of the children's worth and interfere with teaching the academic skills. The teacher and the events are a composite of several elementary school classes that I visited in predominantly nonwhite areas. But all the incidents and behavior patterns actually occurred. I should record that I also observed a number of classes in which there was much more teaching of skills and subject matter and much less teaching of manners and place. On the other hand, as permission to observe had always to be obtained both from the principal and the teacher herself, I did not observe at the elementary school level classes in which the teachers' naked racism, extreme hostility, or utter indifference set the tone—classes that student and parent informants frequently report. I believe, while the style may vary from teacher to teacher, the kinds of messages conveyed by Miss White, described here, represent a very common experience for nonwhite (perhaps also white) lower-class children in New York City elementary schools.

In rereading my own notes on my visits, I am most struck by the way in which the teacher (the classroom situation), in teaching the child how to be a pupil, alienates him from his fellows, from his body, from his feelings and impulses, from his immediate physical surroundings, from his opinions, from his language and thoughts, from his community and daily experiences —in other words, from all that he is as a human organism living and growing in a nourishing, sustaining environment. He is denied access to the very biologic and human wellsprings whose flow is necessary to learning and growing, and converted into a little automaton who makes gestures and repeats answers to please an adult to whose signals of pleasure and displeasure he must become almost pathologically sensitized. So he sustains her status as the central figure in the social situation and gratifies her ego's demand for attention, while she downgrades his status by remaining more or less insensitive to his satisfactions or dissatisfactions except insofar as they interfere with the classroom routine (her needs).

The whole school is assembled in the great dreary inside yard. The children in straight lines by size places, the teacher at the head of each line sh-sh-shing, frowning, prodding. One alert young teacher walks up and down her line arranging her children. She pulls a boy's hands out of his pockets, grabs a hand that is scratching a head and sets it down neatly along the side of the body, mutters a scold at a girl whose finger is near a nostril. Another, looking hardly more than a college girl, with twitching mouth and haunted eyes, can't manage her line at all; as fast as she pops two in, squeezing and hissing, three more pop out. What is going to happen among these thirty people when they are alone behind the closed classroom doors? The principal never once looks in her direction. I think she must be among the already condemned. The principal is walking about like Elizabeth reviewing the troops; where a line is crooked or whispering, she frowns at the teacher, who jabs a word or a hand at a child. Finally she dismisses the lines to their rooms in the order of the quietest and straightest. On the way up the stairs the teachers recite sharply, "Don't run, you'll fall." "Which way are you walking? Then LOOK that way." "One step at a time, Roger, one step at a time, you'll trip." "Sh-sh-sh. Sh-sh-sh. Sh-sh-sh."

I come to Miss White's room where the principal has arranged that I am to visit.

Miss White is fortyish, tall, thin, pale, stiff in her movements, very hard-working, very energetic. Indeed, she seems to me to expend at each turn an amount of energy quite out of proportion to the task being performed. At lunch she told me that she uses herself up trying to help those children but that their home backgrounds are so poor she feels she is hardly making a dent. I suspect that if she were able to relax and forget about their un-favorable home backgrounds, both she and the children would accomplish a hundred times more than they do. She seems to be fighting herself and the children every moment.

Her room, like her person, is aseptic. It is a small class, and the children's movable chairs and desks are spread about the room as far from one another as possible, as if some centrifugal force had flung them apart, each child to be suspended alone in his allotted space. On the side bulletin board, ar-ranged with infinite precision under a frill of yellow and green construction paper, are arithmetic and spelling exercises, with the examples and the words identically positioned on each paper. On the back bulletin board, under a frill of red and blue construction paper, are the results of an art lesson, rexographed outlines of an Easter bunny bearing a basket of flowers colored in with crayons. The bunnies are all white and the baskets all blue, but there is some variation in the colors of the flowers. The children must have spent hours producing these pictures in which the colors remain so obediently within the bounding outlines. Only the irregularly printed names announce them to be products of individual, real-life children.

Miss White introduces me to the children. "This is Mrs. Wasserman, children, a very distinguished writer. Say 'Good morning, Mrs. Wasser-man.'" "Good morning, Mrs. Wasserman." "Good morning, children." "This is a very s-l-o-w class, h-o-l-d-o-v-e-r-s," she spells, trying to enlist my gaze in an understanding complicity. I look away, ashamed.

The well-trained children stand neatly behind their chairs. At a signal, first the girls sit, then the boys. Miss White says, "Feet flat on the floor, heads up, sit straight, hands clasped on desk." I think that some kind of posture exercise is about to begin, but it turns out to be the required position of the morning except when the class or a child is ordered to stand, go to the board, etc. If occasionally a child slumps, scratches, bends down to retrieve an object he has cleverly managed to drop, or turns his head to look at another child, the whole lesson comes to a grinding halt as Miss White announces, "Just one minute, Alette [or whoever is reciting], Julio isn't listening." Or, really angered, "Franklin, you look at ME! You listen to ME!" During the hours of tutelage, the children must give over to her keeping their bodies as well as their souls. One ingenious boy, held im-mobile, has learned to ripple his abdominal muscles behind the desk. He does this on and off throughout the morning, looking down surreptitiously at his jiggling belt buckle.

Only Beryl is excepted. Small, light-brown, quiet, almost always faintly smiling, Beryl comes in late, sits when and as she wishes, picks up a book from the book table and reads if she wishes, plays with her fingers if she wishes. She is quiet and alone with herself. She is never called on in the way the other children are. When the homework assignment is to be copied, Beryl and Alonzo turn out to have left their notebooks home. Miss White gives Alonzo a sheet of paper, but ignores Beryl. She later explained to me that it would have been pointless to have had Beryl copy the assignment as she wouldn't have done the homework anyway, why waste a sheet of paper. One example of a teacher's expectations reinforcing a child's deviant ways. While the children are writing, Beryl helps herself to a book and reads. I invite her to my back corner to read to me, which she does willingly and well. Although the other children ignore her, and she them, every twenty minutes or so, with no external stimulus that I can see, Miss White turns on Beryl her own and the entire class's disapproving attention. "Beryl, don't you *want* to learn? Do you want to be left back? If you don't pay attention, you won't go on to third grade. Don't you *want* to go on to third grade with the other children?" Beryl only sustains her thin smile. But Jewell manages to catch my eye in a gaze of disapproving complicity that is a replica of Miss White's.

To the extent that they respond overtly to one another at all, the children do so entirely in accordance with the teacher's needs. So, when Miss White has three or four times downgraded one boy for giving a series of wrong answers, the children finally all laugh aloud at him. Then she transmits a signal quite opposite to the one she had been transmitting, saying, "You mustn't make fun of Collins. That's unkind."

The opening lesson is to read from the blackboard a list of twenty words. It seems to me that the children already know these words (i.e., can read them), but with scoldings about hands beneath the desk and Beryl's diversions, frequent reminders that these words "might, ju-u-ust might" turn up on next week's Metropolitan Reading Tests, and somewhat meandering discussions after each word, the lesson takes thirty-five minutes. The discussions, which Miss White later explained to me are a way of lightening the lesson by letting the children tell about "their own little experiences," are actually explicit reminders of the rules of middle-class morality and the irrelevance and unworthiness of their own impulses, opinions, and experiences, for which reminders the bodily regimentation serves as unremitting practice.

A child is called on, and reads, "Sling shot." Miss White, "That's right, 'sling shot.' Does anyone know what a sling shot is?" A chorus of responses, "When you take a rubber band. . . ." "You go like this with a paperclip." Etc. "Hands, hands." Silence. Hands are raised. A child is called on and explains. Miss White, "Do you think it's a good idea to use a sling shot?" Chorus of disapproving "No-o-o's," and one unwary, "Yes." Miss White is very angry. "Who said 'yes'?" "Not me . . ." "It was Josie." "Josie did." "Josie, you ought to know better than that. Don't you know somebody can get hurt? You could hit a person's eye and blind him." She enlists the whole class's dismay and disapproval of naughty (too honest) Josie.

A hand is raised, "My uncle he blind, and . . ."

"My uncle *is* blind."

"My uncle he *is* blind, and one day when I be walking with him . . ."

"One day when I *was* walking with him."

A few tales of the blind and the halt are told. Miss White sometimes but not always interrupts to correct the storyteller's speech. The child dutifully parrots the revised sentence, and then like a rubber band, his tongue snaps back into the speech he first heard from his mother's lips and hears (and uses) all his waking hours except from his alien teachers or TV. He will be corrected five or ten times a day every day he is in school, for ten or twelve years, but will remain loyal all that time to his mother tongue.

Miss White points to the next word and calls on a child. It is "plow," which the child pronounces to rhyme with "snow." A chorus of spontaneous corrections. Miss White draws herself up menacingly, scolding, *"Excuse me!"* Silence. *She* corrects the mispronunciation. As in every instance when the children move or call out, they are required to suppress their natural impulse to set aright what is wrong, to respond verbally to the written symbol, to essay an answer and see if it goes ("If you don't know, don't guess.")—in other words to learn.

If the children cannot (or do not) adopt the teacher's speech as their own, she sometimes does not even understand theirs, or the ideas they seek to convey by means of it.

"What is a plow?" she asks.

"Like a trapter," Alonzo responds confidently.

"Like a *what?*" less confused than angry.

"Like a trapter," somewhat less confidently.

"Speak up, Alonzo. What are you trying to say? Talk more carefully. Now once more. What is a plow?"

"Trapter?"

Miss White is by now very annoyed and disapproving. "Trapter? Trapter? I don't know what you're saying." She makes a kind of shrug of hopelessness. Alonzo is expressionless.

"Now, somebody else. What is a plow?"

"A snowplow?" Jewell asks hopefully.

"Well. Not exactly. Look." Miss White gets out a book, and shows a picture of a farmer in overalls and straw hat walking behind a plow being pulled by a drayhorse. "That's a plow. Now I want you to remember what a plow is. You might, you just might, meet it on the reading test." She sighs.

Now Miss White points to "flower." A child reads it. Then, "Who sees a flower in the room?" Josie, straining out of his seat and grunting as if he were on the toilet, is called on and rushes toward the Easter baskets. "JOSIE! Did I tell you to get up? Go Back To Your Seat. . . . Now, can someone tell me where there is a flower, without getting out of your seat." (Ah, Josie, Josie, you have a lot to learn.)

"Flower" is followed by a long hassle in which the children describe a "trunk" (also from the Metropolitan Reading Tests, where it is illustrated by a picture of a footlocker) as "where you put the suitcases."

"Why in the world"—trying to imagine perhaps the homes they come from—"would you want to put a suitcase in a trunk? Unless," speculating, "there isn't room in the closet."

"You know, like to go on a picnic."

Outraged, "Who would take a *trunk* on a picnic?"

All of them, teacher and children, are now utterly bewildered, caught in a kind of entanglement of confusion, and helpless to extricate themselves. I think if a visitor were not present someone would have some kind of a temper tantrum, out of the fury of impotence. I violate a cardinal rule for observers and break in to say that maybe the children are referring to the trunk of a car. I shouldn't have done it; of course Miss White is embarrassed. "Oh," explaining, "it is some years since I've had a car." Then disapprovingly, "You know *they* all have cars"—one-upping after having been one-upped.

Alonzo meanwhile has fallen out of position and is languishing. "Alonzo, sit up. What did you have for breakfast, Alonzo?"

"Crackles and peanut butter-and-jelly sandwich."

"Who gave you your breakfast, Alonzo?"

"Me myself."

"Tell your grandmother *she* should give you breakfast." To me, "He's terribly n-e-g-l-e-c-t-e-d." To Alonzo, "You make sure your grandmother gives you supper tonight, Alonzo."

"She always do."

To me, "You can see what the trouble is. . . ." Then, "Alonzo draws very well. Show Mrs. Wasserman your picture, Alonzo." I tell Alonzo it is a beautiful picture. (It is not a coloring in, but a genuine creation.) "But that's all he wants to do," she says, negating the effects of her and my praise.

Now a relief teacher comes in and Miss White sits down with me at the back of the room to perform some clerical chores and brief me on what I have observed. *This one hasn't even seen* Mary Poppins *because his mother won't take him to the movies, and that one has had three "fathers" already. What can you expect when they come from homes like that? They don't even know how to talk in sentences. They have to be stimulated to think, they don't have an idea in their heads. They look around them and they don't know what they see.* But they know that a snowplow is a kind of plow, that a plow is related to a tractor, and that you put the picnic things in the trunk. And one too-brave soul knows that he likes to use a sling shot. But what they see is declared to be not there and what they think to be wicked. "Beryl just came to us from Ocean Hill-Brownsville. It's no wonder she's so bad and doesn't know anything." I said I thought she read very well. "Yes," sighing, "but that's all she wants to do."

The relief teacher is distributing some construction paper buckets that the children had made on a previous day. They are different colors and on each is written the name of the child who made it. But they are passed out at random, and the children begin to demand to receive their own with their own names. The teacher says it doesn't matter who gets which one. (That is, it doesn't matter to her.) The children have had empty hands and empty desks since the morning began and many grasp at the little pieces of colored paper like a hungry infant at the breast. The teacher says they mustn't touch them until she tells them what to do with them, they are only paper and they can tear, if they tear then they won't have them for what they need them for, and on and on. Miss White several times nervously interrupts her conversation with me to jump up and remove one child's hands from the paper or rearrange another's limbs. Most of the children refrain from touching and content themselves with looking. It is said that slum children are not good learners because they are incapable of delayed gratification. I find my stomach in knots until finally the signal is given that the pathetic little papers may be touched. I suspect that slum children are bad learners because they are denied the gratification of being allowed to learn.

The buckets are finally employed in a mass enactment of Jack and Jill. Miss White explains that this way the children have an opportunity to "experience some freedom and new experiences" and the teacher can "get into the children's world." Next comes Humpty Dumpty, which is an occasion for some cultural background. It is elicited that Humpty Dumpty is an egg. "What happens when you drop an egg?" "It breaks." "What comes out when an egg breaks?" There is some hesitation. Finally a girl who has learned to read the teacher's mind faster than I says, "The yolk." No one asks what happens to the white, but "yolk" is written on the board. Then they go on to Little Miss Muffet. One boy, enacting the spider, so far departs from the script as to snarl at Miss Muffet with clawed hands and bared teeth. The class cracks up, in the first spontaneous interaction among themselves I have seen. Miss White drops her pen and hurries to the front of the room, saying, "No, no, you must do it on the word 'frighten,' not before. Like this. Now class, recite it again and watch how I do it."

Dutifully, they recite it again, and Miss White acts the spider, while the boy spider returns quietly to his seat.

Now they copy their homework assignment and finish just in time before the bell rings for lunch.

This is a holdover class of slow readers. Except for Beryl, who will certainly get a bad report card, during the entire morning's instruction, they have read all of twenty words, plus "yolk." And the educators are trying to understand why year by year the children of the poor show progressive reading retardation.

STOKELY'S SPEECH CLASS

Miriam Wasserman

The difference between Miss White's dialect ("good English") and her pupils' dialect ("bad English") constituted perhaps the greatest source of friction between them. The dialect problem was not idiosyncratic but is endemic to our society.

In the lesson which follows a group of serious students explore with their serious teacher the meaning and consequences of dialect differences in America. The lesson was one in a work-study institute for high-school–age SNCC workers conducted in 1965 in Waveland, Mississippi. The teacher was Stokely Carmichael, then a SNCC field worker in Lowndes County, Alabama, and the recorder was Jane Stembridge, another SNCC worker and a poet.

Stokely put eight sentences on the blackboard, with a line between, like this:

I digs wine.	I enjoy drinking cocktails.
The peoples wants freedom.	The people want freedom.
Whereinsoever the policemens goes they causes troubles.	Anywhere the officers of the law go, they cause trouble.
I wants to reddish to vote.	I want to register to vote.

STOKELY: What do you think about these sentences? Such as, "The peoples wants freedom"?
ZELMA: It doesn't sound right.
STOKELY: What do you mean?
ZELMA: "Peoples" isn't right.
STOKELY: Does it mean anything?
MILTON: "People" means everybody. "Peoples" means everybody in the world.
ALMA: Both sentences are right as long as you understand them.
HENRY: They're both okay, but in a speech class you have to use correct English.
(Stokely writes "correct English" in corner of blackboard.)
ZELMA: I was taught at least to use the sentences on the right side.

STOKELY'S SPEECH CLASS Reprinted by permission from *The School Fix, NYC, USA*, by Miriam Wasserman, Copyright © 1970 by Outerbridge & Dienstfrey.

STOKELY: Does anybody you know use the sentences on the left?

CLASS: Yes.

STOKELY: Are they wrong?

ZELMA: In terms of English, they are wrong.

STOKELY: Who decides what is correct English and what is incorrect English?

MILTON: People made rules. People in England, I guess.

STOKELY: You all say some people speak like on the left side of the board. Could they go anywhere and speak that way? Could they go to Harvard?

CLASS: Yes. No. (disagreement)

STOKELY: Does Mr. Turnbow[1] speak like on the left side?

CLASS: Yes.

STOKELY: Could Mr. Turnbow go to Harvard and speak like that? "I wants to reddish to vote."

CLASS: Yes.

STOKELY: Would he be embarrassed?

CLASS: Yes! No!

ZELMA: He wouldn't be, but I would. It doesn't sound right.

STOKELY: Suppose someone from Harvard came to Holmes County and said, "I want to register to vote?" Would they be embarrassed?

ZELMA: No.

STOKELY: Is it embarrassing at Harvard but not in Holmes County? The way you speak?

MILTON: It's inherited. It's depending on where you come from. The people at Harvard would understand.

STOKELY: Do you think the people at Harvard should forgive you?

MILTON: The people at Harvard should help teach us correct English.

ALMA: Why should we change if we understand what we mean?

SHIRLEY: It is embarrassing.

STOKELY: Which way do most people talk?

CLASS: Like on the left.

(He asks each student. All but two say "left." One says that southerners speak like on the left, northerners on the right. Another said that southerners speak like on the left, but the majority of people speak like on the right.)

STOKELY: Which way do television and radio people speak?

CLASS: Left.

(There was a distinction made by the class between northern commentators and local programs. Most programs were local and spoke like on the left, they said.)

STOKELY: Which way do teachers speak?

CLASS: On the left, except in class.

STOKELY: If most people speak on the left, why are they trying to change these people?

---

[1] Hartman Turnbow, a black farmer from Mileston, Mississippi, the first black man to attempt to register to vote in the Holmes County registration campaign of that decade. A popular indigenous leader of extraordinary poise, charm, and courage, he used the common "reddish" for "register."

GLADYS: If you don't talk right, society rejects you. It embarrasses other people if you don't talk right.

HANK: But Mississippi society, ours, isn't embarrassed by it.

SHIRLEY: But the middle class wouldn't class us with them.

HANK: They won't accept "reddish." What is "reddish"? It's Negro dialect and it's something you eat.

STOKELY: Will society reject you if you don't speak like on the right side of the board? Gladys said society would reject you.

GLADYS: You might as well face it, man! What we gotta do is go out and become middle class. If you can't speak good English, you don't have a car, a job, or anything.

STOKELY: If society rejects you because you don't speak good English, should you learn to speak good English?

CLASS: No!

ALMA: I'm tired of doing what society say. Let society say "reddish" for a while. People ought to just accept each other.

ZELMA: I think we should be speaking just like we always have.

ALMA: If I change for society, I wouldn't be free anyway.

ERNESTINE: I'd like to learn correct English for my own sake.

SHIRLEY: I would too.

ALMA: If the majority speaks on the left, then a minority must rule society. Why do we have to change to be accepted by the minority group? (lunchtime)

STOKELY: Let's think about two questions for next time: What is society? Who makes the rules for society?

In her summing up, Miss Stembridge commented on both the manner and the substance of the lesson. She pointed out that the lesson concentrated on one theme which was significant to the students and that the students made the connections and developed the ideas themselves. She also said, "People learn from someone they trust who trusts them. This trust included Stokely's self-trust and trust, or seriousness, about the subject matter."

The substance of the lesson involved the significance of "good English." Having arrived at the insights as they did, some students might decide to learn to speak "good English"; others might decide to be like Mr. Turnbow and not be embarrassed by their "bad English."

All the qualities that made Stokely's lesson successful were absent from Miss White's lesson: trust all around, including trust in the students' ability to learn; sensible recognition of the world outside the classroom; concentration on subject matter. Her compulsive admonishing about her pupils' speech (like all such adult behavior) could not possibly change their speech, but only make them ashamed of it. The one teacher was an amateur and the students' presence voluntary, the other a professional and the students' presence coerced. Some people are beginning to say there is no hope for public education in America. I don't know.

A THING CALLED BERKELEY

Eric Mann

Eric Mann is a communist, a member of Weatherman, and a political prisoner. He is also, I think, one of the few authentic heroes of the New Left.

Eric has lived an extraordinary life; in many ways his experience reads like a history of the young Left in America: After he graduated from Cornell, in the days when we believed in the Integrationist Solution, Eric was a member of CORE and organized a boycott of Trailways buses to protest segregation in their Southern terminals. In 1965, he began his active opposition to America's war in Southeast Asia by starting the first teach-ins in Washington, D.C. In the fall of that year, Eric joined Tom Hayden in creating the Newark (New Jersey) Community Union Project, which was the first major attempt by Students for a Democratic Society to organize a radical constituency off campus. In 1967 he went to Boston as an S.D.S. organizer at Boston University. At the time he was also a national campus traveler for S.D.S. and a member of its national council. In June 1969, the Progressive Labor faction was expelled from S.D.S. and Weatherman was born; Eric was part of it.

As a Weatherman he organized a demonstration in Cambridge against the Harvard Center for International Affairs, which has done research for the Defense Department. It is because of his participation in that protest, and probably because he is a communist and a Weatherman, that he is now serving two years of his life at the prison at Deer Island, Massachusetts.

Eric is twenty-seven years old.

—DOTSON RADER

I'm very happy to be here, but also in some ways I'm very sad. I'm sad because I'm looking at you, thinking back to when I was a freshman, and I'm thinking that a lot of the things I would like to say to you would be cruel platitudes. I could say things like, "Welcome," "I'm sure you'll have four happy years at the University of Windsor," or, "These are going to be the four happiest years of your life"—the usual things people say when you come in as a freshman. I won't say it, though, because I don't believe it. It was said to me and it wasn't true. And so I start out with a certain amount of trepidation.

There is another reason I am worried about speaking to a large group of people: Many of you won't agree with a word I say. Now, in one way I

A THING CALLED BERKELEY   Based on a speech given in 1968 during Orientation at the University of Windsor, Ontario, and revised in 1970 by the author. Reprinted by permission.

guess that's a little O.K. because some of you probably won't agree with anything they tell you in the next four years, and you'll have about as much choice in the matter as you do this evening. At least tonight there are no grades being given, so if you walk out, try to walk out quietly. I'll begin by talking about what happened to me, and try to explain what I think may happen to you.

My parents never went to college. They spent a lot of time, probably from the time I was twelve or thirteen, talking to me about college. Now, they'd never even seen the inside of a college, but they had absorbed so much propaganda they talked like a college recruiting office. They told me that if I went to college, it would be a place where I would really meet people who are getting together in quest of knowledge, people who are interested in developing skills to help the people; a place where I would really broaden myself, where I would learn a lot about the world, where I would make the kind of friendships that I could not make in high school, where, though I didn't like the work in high school, it would be different: "You're really going to like your work in college." Essentially, college life was described to me as being very different from the lives that my parents were leading, and very different from the kind of life I was leading. College was being held up as a very practical utopia. And so I went. I remember being very happy, and walking into a dormitory, at Cornell.

Cornell is built on some hills and valleys, and I remember standing at the top of a hill feeling very much alone, looking down at the freshman dorms in the valley. I said to myself, "I'm going to really make it at this place. This is going to be the place where I'm going to find myself." That old expression. What an expression! "Finding yourself."

Well, I don't know where it started to go downhill. Six weeks after the school year started, some of the people got midterm grades. A small percentage of the people were asked to leave. And so the dormitory I was in became, in some way, a very scary kind of place; in some way, maybe, like a jail. Ed Hogue, class of '64, left after six weeks to go back to Kingston, New York. I thought, "Well, somebody else will fill that room. We don't need him. We've got a lot of students here. He couldn't cut the mustard. Maybe somebody else can. Good-by Ed, have a nice life."

I remember the first months, grabbing my books and running into the library. Man, was I studying—five, six, maybe seven hours a day, taking so many notes. I would read seven pages of work and take ten or eleven pages of notes. I remember trying very, very hard to do well, and having the sense that this was the place where I would prove that I was an "intellectual"—if not superior, at least talented.

But many problems started to develop. Six or eight weeks into the school year, I found out something; something that took me four years to acknowledge. What I found out was that I didn't like to read and write too much. Now, for those of you coming here, I hope you like to read a lot, and I hope you like to write a lot, because that's what college is, stripped of all the rhetoric. You get your books, you read a lot, you listen, and you write. You get some more books, you read them, you listen, and you write. Once in a while, you're even allowed to talk. But the main thing is that you'd better like books a lot. You'd better be committed to the idea that reality is found in books, *their* books, because the whole university system revolves around that concept. If you like to sing, if you like to speak, if you like to organize, you can do that. But it's called extracurricular. Those are things you do in your spare time. They're not essentially valuable, you see, they're something they give you to keep you busy and interested enough to go back to that essential task of more reading and more writing.

Now, to start with, I think a lot of us wouldn't want to be here if that were the definition of four years of our lives. If you went up to a person on the street and said, "Hey, I've got a really good deal for you. Wanna come to a place where you spend four or five hours a day reading and writing? Sounds great, doesn't it?" how many people would spontaneously say, "Wow, that's exactly what I've been looking forward to doing for four years. How do I join?"

"Oh, you don't join, you have to pay."

"Oh, that sounds out of sight; I pay to read and write for five or six hours a day."

Clearly, the university is not based on a voluntary system. We aren't there because we find it rewarding. We are there for a whole series of different reasons. But very few of those reasons come from inside ourselves. At Cornell, the reason you went there was pretty clear: When you got out you could say you had gone to Cornell. It really didn't matter what the hell you did for four years. You were paying to say you had gone there. And people competed to see how they could go there with the least amount of effort. Cornell, you see, is a big fraternity school. And I remember sitting with one of my friends in the dormitory, saying, "We don't want to join a fraternity because fraternities limit your individuality. Fraternities cut you off from other people. Fraternities are racially selective, economically selective. They're against everything we stand for." My friend said, "You're absolutely right."

We walked home together arm in arm and two days later we were both in fraternities. There were fifty-three fraternities. Most guys joined fraternities, and so you joined. You joined for a very basic reason: Joining a fraternity protected you from the job of being a person. Instead of hearing, "Who's Eric Mann?" and saying, "Well, I'm a lot of different things, I'm pretty complicated—you'll have to get to know me," by joining I could just reply, "Tau Delta Phi." Now Tau Delta Phi may not mean anything to you, University of Windsor may not mean anything, I.B.M. may not mean anything, and yet when you think about it, these are the ways we define ourselves. They allow us to avoid the problem of being somebody. In fact, they say, "Don't you want to know who I am? I drive that car. Don't you want to know who I am? I wear silk ties. Don't you want to know who I am? I wear work shirts." The main point is that these labels allow people to avoid having to be somebody. And in a certain way this makes it easier, because we don't have to worry about really getting to know people. Like, "I know who you are. You're the blond preppie with the expensive silk ties in Sigma Chi. You're the fat chick in history honors who drives a Chevy. You're the good-looking woman whose name I forget, but whom the guys just call 'Jerry's chick.' " And of course, looks are very important, because we all know we are living in a society where what things look like is considered more important than what things really are.

And so we see how certain things begin to be built in—how we look at people, how we look at ourselves.

O.K. I went back second semester. I started making little charts. "Well, if I get a ninety in this—no, a ninety-five—then I can afford a seventy in this; no, a ninety in this and I can afford seventy-five in this. That will give me an average of eighty-five. Boy, that sounds good. I think I'll get an eighty-five this semester." So I would work out my projected goal, and I had the fantasy that this time things were going to be different. I remember that my first average was seventy-nine-point-eight. Now, at Cornell, seventy-nine-point-eight was a very dangerous average to have, because eighty was the lowest possible grade to have and still be *sort of smart*. With anything below eighty you were *run of the mill*. At eighty they would say, "Hey, he's pretty smart." Now I went through a big identity crisis, wondering if I should tell people that my average was really seventy-nine-point-eight, because seventy-nine-point-eight was very different from eighty. Eighty is smart and seventy-nine-point-eight is, "Oh, I see."

So sometimes I would say to people, very bravely, "I got seventy-nine-point-eight" and imagine that they were looking at me very differently. Sometimes I would say "eighty" and then feel cheap. Either way I felt that I had lost. Either way a set of numbers had been developed to define who I was. I was now Eric Mann, Tau Delta Phi, seventy-nine-point-eight.

The second semester was worse than the first. In the second semester it was warm, and somehow I couldn't get into those five or six hours a day. You see, I really loved the springtime. Once in a while the days were so beautiful I was able to be even a little happy. But there is a problem with that five or six hours if you like to walk around in the springtime. There's no such thing as real leisure. The week is just one big treadmill. There's no such thing as being finished with your work. There are always additional books to read, additional course material, and usually the course material is more than you can read in one week. You're always ahead in this and behind in that. You finally get caught up in biology and you find out that you're behind in government, and when you get caught up in sociology, you're behind in lit. You have to figure out, "Well, let's see. If I don't show up for lit, and I say I'm having emotional problems, then I can have the time to catch up on bio," and the process continues. And if you don't work, which usually is the case, you find that you can't enjoy your leisure. You find that when you take an afternoon off, there's this cloud hanging over your head: *I am three weeks behind in Ec-101.* "Well, that's O.K. If you're not going to do your work, at least enjoy your afternoon. Sure. But I'm three weeks behind in Ec-101. What am I going to do?" So I never enjoyed either work or leisure.

So I did the only logical thing. I went to sleep. I found myself sleeping eight, then eight and a half, and then ten hours. Then ten hours plus a nice two-hour nap in the afternoon. I found myself so tired that I was tired when I woke up. You know, I would wake up in the morning after having ten hours sleep; I would think about my work, think about what was ahead of me, and plan on having my afternoon nap. It was really very scary. I was beginning to hate myself.

While I was thinking less and less of myself, I discovered that there were only two basic options. One was more sleep and the other was finding out ways to think more and more of myself. And so, in my sophomore year, because I had been president of my freshman dorm, my fraternity told me that it was good for the house for me to run for Treasurer of the Inter-Fraternity Council. Now Treasurer of the I.F.C. is a very important position. What the Treasurer actually does . . . well, I forget actually, but I remember it was very important because I was told to run for it. I think, in fact, what's important about being Treasurer of the I.F.C. is that you go up to people and say, "I'm Treasurer of the I.F.C." In fact, that's the only thing important about it. Again, it's a substitution for being a person. I was now Eric Mann, Tau Delta Phi, seventy-nine-point-eight, Treasurer of the I.F.C. With all those numbers and all those titles I still didn't like myself very much. In fact, I began to like myself even less.

After Treasurer of the I.F.C. I ran for President of the I.F.C. I lost, but luckily enough I won Vice-President. Vice-President is not as good as President, but it's better than Treasurer. The most important thing about being Vice-President of the I.F.C. is that it gets you into Quill and Dagger. A lot of you don't know what Quill and Dagger is. Quill and Dagger results when the Vice-President of the I.F.C., football players, and other people who do meaningless work all get together and create an honorary society. Now, you may ask, "Why did you need an honorary?" It should be obvious. Without an honorary, how do you know who's cool?

And so I found myself going to these parties. We all walked around with quills and daggers in our ties and went with girls we tried to make into extensions of Quill and Dagger. We all walked around saying, "I'm cool, you're cool, how's it going?" You know? Now about this time, I got pretty proficient at sleeping—I had it worked out to a science. But every once in a while I would have little academic spurts. I remember going to some professor who would say to me stuff like, "Look, you're doing good work, you just showed up for two straight classes. Why don't you start coming more often? I mean like it's not too late. You still have five weeks left in the semester. I'd really like to help you. Why don't you do your work? I mean if you'd start doing your work, I think you could come out with good grades. And if you pulled good grades I think you could get into a good graduate school."

And I remember, on one of those rare instances when I was talked to by a faculty person, feeling fantastically exhilarated, running home—I mean literally *running*—back to the fraternity, picking up a book, saying, "Man, I'm really gonna do it this time." I'd read the first five or six pages and then read the next nine. "This is really fantastic!" Then about the thirty-seventh page I'd start getting sleepy again. And I couldn't figure out what it was.

You know? Well, after a couple of those starts it became clear that it was the same basic theme that I couldn't face—I didn't like school.

Now, I had a sociology professor who considered himself a radical, but who was a radical in a very interesting way. His course was about alienation. The basic theme of the course was that in a capitalist society people hate their work. They make products for war and for waste. They cheat their friends and themselves by making useless and defective products. They have no voice in what is produced or how it is produced. They hate themselves and their work; they don't have any sense of being a whole person. I said, "What a beautiful guy to say things like that. What a very sensitive person. He's really great. He really understands what's wrong with the country. He's gonna teach me a lot." Except for one problem: He didn't believe that alienation extended to his course. He didn't believe that his course was work. He couldn't believe that for me, reading his nineteen books on alienation was very alienating. He thought the rest of society was terrible except for his course. You could rebel any way you wanted against capitalist corporations, because they were evil. You could rebel all you wanted against the public schools, because they were evil. You could rebel all you wanted against racism, because it was evil. But if you rebelled against his course, you were subversive and ungrateful. So what I found out was that many radicals, or people who call themselves radicals, can't be judged radicals until you see what they do with their own lives, until you see what they do when they have real power. Are they willing to use that power to serve the people? If they're not, then they're no different from anybody else.

So not only was I unhappy, but slowly I came to feel that I wasn't really very smart after all—that most of the people in college were better than me. The people I respected were the people who could work eight, nine, ten hours a day. There were premeds in my fraternity who would go off at one o'clock in the morning. We'd call them "the Goldwyn Smith Boys," because they'd go to this building called Goldwyn Smith in ten-below-zero weather with these big clodhoppers on at one o'clock in the morning, to study, after having studied all day. I mean, they were just very serious guys. Like it's late at night and you'd say, "Where ya going?" and they would solemnly say, "I'm going to study." And they would trudge off in the middle of the night to find this old building. And I remember not just feeling that it was O.K. for them, but feeling very much too, "Why can't I be like them? Why can't I be one of the Goldwyn Smith Boys? Why can't I have that concern for knowledge?"

Well, I got out of college, graduated, I think as a mutual favor. They wanted me out and I wanted to be out, and when it came down to some last-minute credits, they gave me some government credits toward my biology requirement, we were all happy, and I left. My basic conclusion about college was that it was a pretty good place, but it just wasn't for me. And I remember I left Cornell the day of my last final. I didn't go to graduation; I literally left Ithaca three minutes after I put down that pen. I shut my eyes to the past and drove straight to New York; I didn't want to come back. But a very funny thing happened the next year.

It was a thing called Berkeley. Now, thousands of students at Berkeley went around protesting on the issue of free speech and civil rights for black people. But they also began to talk about something called the multiversity. The students began to say, "Maybe"—they didn't say it to me, but I knew they were talking to me—"Maybe college wasn't your fault. Maybe it's because that place stinks. Maybe that place wasn't built for human beings. Maybe you weren't the only person sleeping. Maybe you weren't the only person that hated that work. Maybe you weren't the only person who wanted to leave in his freshman year but stayed three more years because 'you need that piece of paper,' as we are so often told." What Berkeley did was to say to me for the first time, "You're a person and you count, and if an institution makes you feel like shit, you should lose *it*, not yourself." That changed a whole lot of my feelings about myself and society, and I began to feel a lot of different things from then on. I began to think maybe it wasn't just the university that didn't care about me. Maybe I could look around and see other things.

For years we had been telling black people that all they had to do was get integrated into our world, because we had the good life. But all of a sudden some of us discovered that the good life wasn't as good as we thought it was. Now what I want to talk about to finish up is college as an extension of the kind of life that it's preparing us for. College in many ways is a very bad place. But it's a very logical place. I remember being told by a teacher once, "You're doing very good work, keep it up, keep it up." Keep what up? Sitting at that desk for three hours—you know, sitting in a system of their rewards and punishments. Of course, there's the sympathetic principal who tells your parents, "Joan is a very promising student. But she just can't seem to apply herself. She has no span of attention. Why don't you work with her?" Having been deputized, the parents begin their campaign of psychological warfare. "Joan, why are you such a discipline problem? We know the rules aren't always right, but getting ahead involves learning to do things you don't agree with. Do you think your father agrees with everything his company does? Of course not, but . . . . Don't you want to get ahead? Don't you love us?" Not ready to bolt her family and school at age ten, Joan goes along with the program—temporarily.

I remember writing a paper on Balboa in third grade. Why did I do it? Because my teacher was going to put it up on the wall. I did one on Balboa, one on Da Gama and one on Cabeza de Vaca. Now, if you were to ask me who Balboa is, who Da Gama is, or who Cabeza de Vaca is, I couldn't tell you. But I can tell you that all three papers were put up on the wall for Open School Night, and that's why I wrote them. I didn't write them because I cared about those three names; in fact, Cabeza de Vaca could have discovered Balboa for all I know. And it's interesting to know that the teacher placed them so high up on the board that you couldn't read them even if you wanted to. We all understood how the system worked.

So we can talk about what it's like to work in a school that produces people who do things not because it is important to do them, but because the more paper you have on the wall the better it looks, no matter what's on them.

Now isn't this the same thing as working in a factory that produces televisions that are made to last two or three years, even though we have a technology that could make them work for fifteen? Why do we make a television last for three years if we can make it last for fifteen? Because we want to sell a lot of televisions. Now you may ask, "Who's we? *We* don't want to sell more televisions. *They* want to sell more televisions." But you see, they have a way of talking to us that makes it seem that we're all working together. Their argument goes like this: "Look, if our TV lasts for fifteen years, then we won't sell a lot of TV's. And if we don't sell a lot of TV's, then you'll be out of work. So you have a vested interest in selling a TV that lasts for three years, because that fifteen-year TV will knock you out of a job."

Now what kind of relationship is that to work? We've all been given that American myth about American craftsmanship. Can you imagine making a pair of shoes for a friend and staying up nights trying to figure out how to get them to wear out quickly? But capitalists don't make things for friends—they make things to get rich. That's what I mean by things being logical. If you want to earn a pretty high wage as a factory worker, you usually have to work for a highly automated, high-profit company. A highly automated company usually makes its money by breaking the job down into a lot of very small parts and using a lot of technology. I met a woman who said to me, "That's a very nice doll." I said, "Thanks. I bought it for my daughter." She said, "Yeah, I used to make them." I said, "Oh, you used to make this doll? It must have been a good job." She said, "Well, not really. I used to work in the inspection department. You see, when you push the button in little Annie-Fanny's back, her right arm goes up and down like this. And my job was pressing the button four times. If it worked four times in a row, it passed inspection. If the arm stuck, it didn't."

That was her job. Eight hours a day, five days a week, forty-eight to fifty weeks a year: pushing that fucking button, watching that arm go up and down, up and down. That's what we call "craftsmanship" in America. We have butchers who don't cut meat; they cut fat, pour blood on it, and call it chopped meat. We have farmers who somehow get rich by not producing and by not selling what they do produce. And another example: walking by an escalator, I look down at a guy fixing the escalator, and just to make small talk, I say to him, "Boy, these escalators are breaking a lot, aren't they?" And he turns on me angrily: "You're damn right, and they better keep breaking, because if they don't I'm out of a job." Now in a capitalist society that guy's job pits him against me. It means that I want escalators that work and he wants escalators that break. The capitalist system guarantees that work will be dangerous and monotonous.

Some of you may say, "Well, yeah, that's true, but you know how workers are." You say, "Yes sir, that's why I'm going to college, I don't wanna pour blood on meat, I don't wanna push that button, I want a job with real responsibility. I want a job that's going to make me somebody. I want a job with great insight and creativity. That's why you go to college." For the women here you should know that there are powerful forces working to crush those hopes. You see, our system of male domination says that it's your job to have children. Now, I don't mean for nine months. I mean for your life. You see, men don't like children too much. Men? They have more important things to do with their lives. They have to go out and win the bread and butter.

Now you may say, "I'll get a college degree. I can win the bread and butter." Yeah, but what man with a B.A. is going to sit home and take care of a baby? But you're expected to do it. Your job now is to be the college-educated wife, the good conversationalist, the person who is brought to parties and occasionally given some babysitting time off in the evenings. But basically, when you have a child, your relationship with that child is one that you're going to have for at least those first six years before he goes off to school. And if you have two or three children it's going to continue for at least six, nine, ten years.

Now, I have a child. I find it very hard to bring up a child. I find it very hard to be a real loving person, because my child—her name is Lisa—takes up a lot of my time, sometimes even when I don't really want to be with her, times when I want to be alone. She demands things of me that sometimes I don't want to give. Sometimes I'm really freaked out and I'm very lonely and upset. But she's only a year and nine months old and she says to me, "I want you to pay attention to me," and all I can feel is, "I want you to go away." But then I realize that she can't go away. A lot of times I have to take care of her alone. Then I have to say to myself, "O.K. You can't freak out. You have to deal with her." So I deal with her. I deal with her mechanically. I give her a bottle and hope that she will go to sleep, even though she's passed the age when she wants to sleep all the time. I do other mechanical things, but basically I'm not with her.

Now, women face this all the time. You've been told that it's an evil thing not to want to be with your kids all the time. What do you mean you don't want to be? Didn't you ever see *Ozzie and Harriet?* When did you ever see Harriet not want to be with her kids? After all, every mother you've seen on television loves her kids all the time. She loves every minute of it. O.K., models are held up for us, models that are destructive, models that are unreal, models that we can't possibly meet and that force us to feel lousy because we just think, "Man, I'm just not as good as old Harriet," instead of saying, "Goddam Harriet. You're a liar. You're a fraud. Ricky and David were probably smoking grass when they were three."

When my daughter was about four or five months old, my wife and I were separated, which meant that I didn't have any option. I had to learn to take care of a child. For the first four or five months of the marriage, I just felt, "It's her kid; it's her job to do a lot of those things." Then all of a sudden I had to learn to stay up in the middle of the night when I wanted to sleep. I had to take the psychological responsibility of being alone with a helpless person; helpless because five- or six-month-old kids are pretty helpless. And it was pretty scary.

But like I've been saying, it all makes sense. The American family, like the society it's part of, is incredibly sick. Daddy spends all day at work feeling like shit. Sexually insecure, beaten down, all his creative energies frustrated, Daddy comes home to be King in his apathetic kingdom. It is taboo for Mommy to be strong—little men want even littler women. If she persists in asserting herself she is subjected to verbal and physical abuse. Mommy is the great listener. Daddy rambles on with his fiftieth rendition of his famous stories, all of which have the same moral—he was right, he was terrific, he was powerful. His condescending question, "And how was *your* day?" is a veiled insult. They both know how her day was. How often can she recite stories about neighborhood gossip, anecdotes about the children, and play-by-play descriptions of grocery shopping?

At night the two strangers go through a painful sexual ritual in which the woman—defeated, stripped of her power, resentful—exerts her strength in the only way open to her: sexual rejection. Real and imagined headaches, claims of frigidity, or totally passive fucking tell her husband what she is afraid to say directly: "I don't like you. I don't respect you or myself. How did I ever get trapped like this? I'm suffocating!"

We are all choking to death in Amerika. Women's Liberation is an important part of the people's revolution that is beginning to take place, to really change this country. We need day-care centers to free women from the sole responsibility of child rearing and to provide a place where women, men, and children can get a chance to love each other. We need new living arrangements—collective families, common-law marriages, acceptance of having several close friends with whom we make love, and unharassed homosexual relationships—to provide the minimum situational stability that children and adults do need without duplicating the unbearable oppression of the nuclear family. We need equal job opportunity for men and women. And we need a whole new way of dealing between men and women.

The fight is starting now, but it won't fully succeed until we've crushed the brutal system that is intent upon destroying the planet and the people on it. Full equality for women would be an important victory. But as the women make clear, they're not fighting for equal oppression and exploitation. They want full liberation for themselves—and for men too.

Now let's talk about men and the few women who will take careers. The kind of careers that people take in business are being advertised today as very dramatic, very exciting, dynamic. But let's talk about it. You are a personnel director. You are told you have a lot of responsibility, a lot of freedom. But what kind of real responsibility do you have? You have the responsibility to tell people what to do. Your job is to get them to work harder. Why? Because working harder makes more profits. You ought to read *Business Week* to see what the businessmen have in store for you. For example, *Business Week* advertises that Fedders air conditioners should be used in the factory. Why? Because the days of the sweatshop are over. Now that's a really great idea. Maybe the bosses are getting a little more humane. But wait—why do they want Fedders air conditioners? Because cooler workers are happier workers. And happier workers produce more. And workers who produce more make a higher profit for the company. So, in fact, the only way you can sell a Fedders air conditioner to a capitalist is to tell him that he'll have cooler, happier workers who will make more money for him by their increased production. That's a hell of a reason to protect workers from the misery of overcrowded, hot, sweaty working conditions. And if a whip company can convince the boss that its product will insure even greater productivity, then he will try like hell to use it.

There's a new magazine called *Careers Today*. You ought to look at it, because it's geared to the youth market. *Careers Today* is psychedelic oppression. What it says is, "Turn on, tune in, and do what we say." What it says is, "Work for the big companies and we'll give you everything you want." This guy comes up to me and says, "Hey, I'm working for this great company. You can do anything you want. They let me wear sideburns."

"Oh, that's really great. What do you do?"

"Well, I do what they tell me."

"Then what do you mean, you do what you want?"

"Well, that's a great step. A lot of companies won't let you wear sideburns."

What corporations are trying to do through *Careers Today* is to avoid the essence of the student rebellion by offering the periphery. What they say is, "Do what we want and we'll give you an air conditioner, an expense account, and sideburns." But your job still is to do what the guy on top says and then tell the people under you what to do.

Now I imagine what a lot of you are saying is, "He's interesting and kind of funny, but man, he's so sick. He is so depressing. He's painting a distorted picture. In fact a lot of people aren't really that unhappy. I know a lot of people who beat the system. He's one of these professional revolutionaries who's trying to stir me up. He's probably some kind of misfit. I'm going to handle it. Some people don't make it. But I'm going to make it."

Now I'll just say that some of you *will* make it for a while. But I think you'll make it in very limited terms. I think the only way you can make it under the imperialist system that we all live under is to sell yourself short.

I have, you see, talked tonight about *our* problems, those of young white college students. But the world is a lot more than just us. There are revolutionaries in prisons in Vietnam, peasants on U.S. sugar plantations in the Dominican Republic, slaves in U.S. diamond mines in South Africa, and blacks in ghettos in Watts and Harlem who can't really get very upset about our problems. And despite our humanitarian rhetoric, we have had great difficulty in relating to theirs. But our fates are being linked by history. A worldwide revolutionary alliance is emerging from North Korea to Brazil, from Vietnam to Newark, from Red China to Kent State. This alliance centers on a common interest: U.S. imperialism is oppressing all of us.

The white student rebellion is a protest against the *quality* of life in Amerika. That is not surprising. Despite some important exceptions, most white people should have few complaints with the quantity of goods available to them. The Amerikan Empire has accumulated 60 percent of the world's wealth and 50 percent of the world's resources for 6 percent of the world's people. The corporate rich take most of this wealth for their personal savings, investment, and consumption. But they realize it is in their interest to distribute a tolerable amount to the large white middle class and white working class. During the prosperous years since World War II, white Amerikans have further developed a barren, racist culture and a conservative political ideology—the admission requirements for the silent majority. But the postwar reign of the silent generation was a period of intense revolutionary action by oppressed people all over the world.

You see, all that wealth didn't just *happen* to end up in the United States. Our government calls it "commercial ingenuity" when it is able to rip off Bolivian tin, South African diamonds, Chilean copper, and Saudi Arabian oil while the people of those countries live in misery and squalor. I call it piracy, rape, and murder. More importantly, that's what the people of those countries call it.

U.S. imperialism is the most successful blood-sucking operation in the world. But you can't keep over a billion people in misery and expect them to accept it voluntarily. To meet that problem our government has put together an elaborate network of alliances, treaties, and puppet governments to prevent revolution and protect its investments. NATO, SEATO, OAS, three and one-half million American soldiers, the World Bank, bank loans to South Africa, free surplus military equipment, foreign aid, and military dictatorships from Argentina to Greece are all designed to hold the empire together.

But the Empire *isn't* holding together. In the past twenty years U.S. imperialism has suffered a series of political and military defeats that have shaken the foundation of the whole operation.

In 1949 the Chinese people finally overthrew Chiang Kai-shek and the Amerikans. They took control of their country and began building a prosperous and democratic life for seven hundred million people. Our government went around screaming that communists at home had led to the "loss" of China. Now that's really incredible. Seven hundred million people thousands of miles away overthrow a dictatorial government, and they tell us "we" lost China. *I* didn't lose China. I never owned it in the first place. *They* lost China, and the Chinese people found themselves.

In 1951 the Chinese and Koreans forced the U.S. Army into a long retreat and abandonment of the plan to "roll back" North Korea.

In 1954 the Vietnamese people won half their country from the French and Amerikans. After almost deciding to drop nuclear weapons to prevent the loss of the North, the U.S. chose not to risk a world war and to set up a military dictatorship in the south to preserve what was left of their holdings.

In 1959 some bearded commies overthrew the Batista regime and began developing a society that, despite Amerikan blockades and invasions, has become an inspiring model of economic progress and cooperation among people.

In 1965 most of Vietnam was in the hands of the Viet Cong. The United States moved in with an impressive show of military brutality. Five years later most of Vietnam is still under Viet Cong control, the U.S.-controlled cities are rife with anti-U.S. demonstrations, and the revolution has spread to Laos and Cambodia.

Unity at home is impossible. The fire of black liberation has grown brighter and hotter on the kindling wood of a system that is so inherently racist that it couldn't change itself even if it wanted to—and it doesn't really want to. The political awareness of black people today is very high. Despite the state apparatus of pigs, guardsmen, and troopers arrayed against them, black people are developing a revolutionary culture, an impressive number of new leaders who keep coming forward despite the imprisonments and murders, and a growing sense of power from allying themselves with oppressed people all over the world.

We young whites are living in the middle of a revolutionary torrent. We have been shielded from violence all our lives. We have not been brutalized, assaulted, or murdered. We are suffocating slowly. We are not the stuff of which good revolutionaries are made.

But though we are not anxious to be revolutionaries, we are determined not to be pigs. Young white teachers are refusing to be policemen in colonial ghetto schools and are siding with the black parents and kids who are demanding that the schools serve the people or be shut down altogether.

Young white social workers are taking the advice of their "clients," who are telling them that the best service they can provide is to quit their jobs and organize themselves and their people for a revolution that will provide jobs, housing, and good schools for everyone.

G.I.'s are refusing to fight in Vietnam. Stockade rebellions, desertions, insubordination in combat, and sabotage aren't fantasies from war flicks. They are happening now!

Many whites in college—the old heartland of upwardly mobile flunkies—consider Huey P. Newton the President and the Viet Cong flag their banner.

The growth of white middle-class insubordination has led the government to say to us, "O.K. You want to march around like Viet Cong. You want to act like Black Panthers. We'll show you how we treat them! That should end your revolutionary fantasies and bring you back into the system." Kent State will not bring us back into the system.

We have been shielded from violence all our lives. The shield is gone. We haven't been brutalized, assaulted, or murdered. They are brutalizing us. They are assaulting us. They are murdering us.

We are not the material of which good revolutionaries are made. But we are learning.

MISSISSIPPI'S FREEDOM SCHOOLS:
The Politics of Education

Florence Howe

All education is political. In Mississippi, at least, it is impossible to find this trite. There, it is inescapable that the educational system furthers the political, that the kind of learning the individual gets depends completely upon the role he is supposed to live.

A thirteen year old Jackson, Mississippi girl, sitting within a Freedom School circle this summer, described the events of the last day, the previous year, in her public (segregated) junior high school. Students in a high school nearby had asked the students in "Shirley's" school to join them in a protest-demonstration against local school conditions and procedures. "Shirley's" (Negro) teacher had threatened the class with failure for the year, should they walk out to join the demonstrators. Most of the class was intimidated, but not "Shirley" and several of her friends. She left, she said, because she knew that she had not failed for the year, she knew she had earned good grades, and she knew that it was right to join the demonstrators. As she and her friends reached the downstairs floor, they met, head on, the (Negro) principal "who was coming at us with a board." They turned, fled, backtracked through the cafeteria and out the back way to join the demonstrators.

The Negro school child in Mississippi, like "Shirley," associates the school he attends, in spite of the color of his teachers and principal, with the white world outside him—the police, the White Citizens' Council, the mayor or sheriff, the governor of his state. And the school child's instinctive vision is perfectly correct. His teachers are either timid and quiescently part of the system or they are actively extra-punitive, dictatorial, hostile, vengeful, or worse. Sometimes his teachers are badly-trained, misinformed, but even when they know just that, they remain fearfully bound to the system that made them. The teacher with the ruler or iron chain or whip is himself caught in a power structure that allows him to teach only by rote to rote-learners. You learn this, he says, and you too can learn to get along. Get used to the violence, get used to being struck, get used to taking orders, for that is the way life is on the outside. You too can learn to follow the rules and get to sit up here, ruler in hand, ready to strike out at anything out of line.

It is possible to sympathize with the middle-class Negro teacher caught between his own desire to rise from the poverty around him and his fear of the white power structure that controls his ability to rise. For the Negro

MISSISSIPPI'S FREEDOM SCHOOLS: THE POLITICS OF EDUCATION From the *Harvard Educational Review*, Vol. 35, No. 2 (Spring 1965). Copyright © 1967 by President and Fellows of Harvard College. Reprinted by permission.

teacher and his Negro principal are directed by white school superintendents, themselves under the direction of other white political forces. In Negro schools, the intercom is used by the principal to intimidate and harass the teacher. The principal, in turn, is harassed by others. And only the "Shirley," finally, is able to stand up and sing, with her friends and associates in Freedom Schools:

> Before I'll be a slave
> I'll be buried in my grave
> And go home to my Lord and be free.

If the official public school system of Mississippi is geared and oiled to operate efficiently for the status quo, it is no wonder, then, that the civil rights movement should have conceived of the Freedom School. But would children for whom a school was an unpleasant training ground for a repressive society come, voluntarily, even to a "Freedom" school? Of course, voluntarily was the first cue. No one had to come, and once there, no "attendance" was taken. You came if you wanted to and you stayed if you were interested and you left if you felt like leaving. Your teacher, moreover, was "Tom" or "Leo" or "Gene," who shook your hand, called you by your first name, and said how glad he was to meet you. In your "class," your teacher sat with you in a circle, and soon you got the idea that you could say what you thought and that no one, least of all the teacher, would laugh at you or strike you. Soon, too, you got the idea that you might disagree with your teacher, white or black, and get a respectful hearing, that your teacher was really interested in what *you* thought or felt. Soon you were forgetting about skin colors altogether and thinking about ideas or feelings, about people and events.

As educators, we live in a fool's paradise, or worse in a knave's, if we are unaware that when we are teaching *something* to anyone we are also teaching *everything* to that same anyone. When we say we are teaching mathematics to Freddy, we also must admit that we are teaching Freddy what kind of person we are, how we live in the kind of world we control (or the kind of world that controls us), and how he can grow up to be one of the controllers or controlled. Teaching, we become, as so many people have said, a model for Freddy to learn from, quite apart from the mathematics or French or history we may be teaching him. And sometimes we are very "good" models. Sometimes, like "good" parents or "good" political leaders, we teach Freddy to love his neighbors, to honor honesty and integrity, to value the means as well as the ends, to abstain from using and controlling and killing human life. But sometimes we are not so inclined. Sometimes, at our worst, we educators resemble tyrants.

The idea of the Freedom School turns upside down particularly effectively the conventions of many public school systems that have to do with the role of the teacher. The teacher is not to be an omnipotent, aristocratic dictator, a substitute for the domineering parent or the paternalistic state. He is not to stand before rows of students, simply pouring pre-digested, pre-censored information into their brains. The Freedom School teacher is, in fact, to be present not simply to teach, but rather *to learn with* the students. In the democratic and creative sense that Wordsworth understood when he described the poet as "a man among men," the Freedom School teacher is a student among students. He does not have all the answers; his creativity is his ability to communicate with his students, to listen to them as much as they listen to him. The vitality of the teacher, as Freedom Schools would have it, lies in the student's and the teacher's mutual apprehension of life. A Freedom School teacher knows that education is the *drawing out* not of blood from stones, but rather of experience and observation from human beings. He knows that a thirteen year old who has survived his years in Mississippi understands, however fearfully or inarticulately, a great deal about the world he has survived in. The Freedom School teacher is there not as professional manipulator, but as concerned questioner—who really wants to hear what his companions will say, who really wants, himself, to be led by it. And thus he can turn the key to help the student break through the door that confines him—and all without recourse to the same means, authoritarianism, repression, violence, that have kept him locked in.

For much of the month of August, I coordinated and taught in one of Jackson, Mississippi's nine Freedom Schools. Opened on the fifth of August, these were in addition to the more than forty others that functioned through the summer in more than twenty different towns. Like most of the schools around the state, mine was located in the basement of a church. The basement room was acoustically difficult for a single voice and yet many voices together filled it uncomfortably. How to get attention, even briefly for announcements or for the start of some activity, perhaps the breaking up of the group into small discussion units? On the second day, when my voice had begun to hurt and when clapping my hands had begun to seem ineffectual, I hit accidentally upon the Quakerly method of raising your right hand. The children saw me standing before them, my right hand raised, and for communication's sake, my left index finger against my lips. They began to nudge one another, to raise their own hands, and to place their own fingers on their lips. And very quickly, the room grew quiet. I said, "All hands down," and delighted that the method had worked, added, "Isn't this a lovely way to get silence?" Of course the children responded all together to me and to each other, and we had to begin all over again, right hands raised. But the method did work.

Also on one of the very first days, in the hot afternoon, with the teachers uncomfortable because they had had no lunch, and the children restless because we had not yet solved the problem of outdoor play space, two little boys began to fight. They were small enough so that I could forcibly separate them, but even in the midst of my hot, hungry exasperation, I had a vision of other fights and bigger boys whom I would be unable to pull apart. And from somewhere came the words: "Now, look here, we have few rules in this school, but we do have one important one and that is we do not hit each other—we talk. Understand? We talk here. This is a school for talking. Whenever you feel like hitting someone, remember to talk instead." The children looked puzzled and I said it all again. And then I sat down—in the midst of chaos—to talk with the two little boys about their fight. There were more fights in the next several days, but my words had begun to spread so that some of the older children were repeating them to the younger ones. And while we were never entirely free from an occasional blow—it was virtually impossible, for example, to keep older brothers from "punishing" their younger siblings—there were few or no fights after the first week.

The Greater Blair Street AME Zion Church, under the direction of Reverend R. M. Richmond, gave us not only shelter and equipment but most of all moral support and friendly protection. We drew our students, regardless of church membership, from the neighborhood. The families in a·six to ten block radius ranged from lower-middle class to very poor (incomes from close to nothing to four thousand). The people in the neighborhood, like most of Jackson, were nervous about the arriving Freedom School teachers and were especially loath to give us housing, for that would signify open support. Reverend Richmond convinced the people next door to give their empty room to the two male teachers. They, Gene Gogol and Tom Timberg, in the company of friendly students-to-be, had been canvassing the neighborhood during the time I was spending getting acquainted with the minister. When they reported back that they had had several offers of spare cots that could be moved elsewhere as well as of food—signs, of course, of a desire to help but without the attendant danger of housing a summer volunteer—we were able to make arrangements to move the beds into the empty room in the house next door to the church.

Our first impressions of the community were not incorrect: the parents continued to be cautious. With few exceptions, we had no contact with parents. But the children, of course, were different. They turned up, they turned out, they were willing to do anything, to go anywhere with us.

As Staughton Lynd, professor of history at Yale and summer director of all Freedom Schools in Mississippi, said, it was "a political decision for any parent to let his child come to a Freedom School." And many parents, in Jackson at least, avoided making that decision. I had assumed that parents knew that their children were attending Freedom School—until the day when I took up the question of sending a representative from our school to the state-wide Freedom School convention in Meridian. Expenses would be paid and the weekend program would be entertaining; I felt certain, that morning, that it would be difficult choosing the one delegate we were allowed to represent us. But to my surprise no one was willing to make a nomination—it was as if they all understood something I did not. I asked for volunteers and got no response again. Then I asked a thirteen year old girl, who had been particularly articulate the day before in a discussion, whether she would like to go. She said, first, only an abrupt "No," but when questioned in disbelieving tones, she admitted to, "Yes, but I can't."

"But why not, then? All your expenses would be paid, and you know you'd enjoy it."

She finally said that her father would not allow her to go, that he disapproved of her association with "the movement" in general, and that he did not approve even of her attending Freedom School. She was deliberately vague about whether or not he knew she was attending. When I asked whether it would help if I went to see him, she first laughed and then urged me most seriously not to. The story repeated itself, with certain variations, around the room.

Two young mothers, both of them relatively new to the neighborhood, were sympathetic enough to the movement and interested enough to issue invitations to us. The mother of a six year old, who sent her daughter to Freedom School, sent word also that she would like to see "the teachers" after school, at which point she invited all of us to a hot dinner the following afternoon at three. Later, she asked to be included in our evening activities. Another mother of a teen-ager, whose own family disapproved of the student's attending Freedom School, also sent for the teachers, whom she then invited to accompany her to a jazz concert. Later, this mother held a party for the departing teachers and announced her willingness to be of service to Freedom Schools in the future.

Freedom Schools were planned originally with high school students in mind. In most places around the state, when Freedom School opened, *all* children turned up, regardless of publicity about high school students. Eventually, around the state, community centers were founded, first to take care of the younger children, later to function in ways that Freedom School could not or would not. When we opened our Blair Street doors on Wednesday, August 5, at eight a.m., "children," ages three to twenty-three, began to arrive. And of course we turned no one away. They came in twos and threes, sometimes several from a family, the teen-agers holding the hands of their younger brothers and sisters. Fifty-one students arrived throughout that first day and fifty more during the next several days. Some stayed awhile and left, never to appear again. Others stayed that day and came every day thereafter. Some came and disappeared, and then came again to stay to the end.

Nearly half of any total number of children present at the Blair Street School were under the age of ten. For these children we ran a combined school and community center in one of the two basement rooms of the church. Luckily, on the day before school had opened, I had met Leo Reese, a magically personable reading specialist from Gary, Indiana, the father of eleven children, who had volunteered to spend one week in Jackson. Leo, a native Mississippian and a Negro, had been born and raised in Pascagoula, on the Gulf. In the few days that Leo was present, he organized a program for the younger children, and because of his skills, freed three of the four assigned teachers for work with the older students. Later, after Leo had gone, two young women, Shirley Logan, a Jacksonian and a recent college graduate, and her cousin from Chicago, Superior Walker, came to the Blair Street School for a visit and stayed for two weeks to carry on the program with the younger children.

Mornings at Freedom School began slowly without opening bells. On some days we sang freedom songs until the group collected. On one day, August 6, Hiroshima Day, I told the students about what had happened nineteen years ago. On another day, I read from Langston Hughes' poems and then listened to reactions from the students. By nine-thirty, we were usually numerous enough to break into smaller discussion groups. Those children under ten went off to their room, generally for the rest of the day, unless there was to be a special activity in the afternoon. The older students separated sometimes into several age groups for a discussion that occupied most of the morning. The Citizenship Curriculum, about which I shall have more to say later, is the core of the program shared by all Freedom Schools in Mississippi. There was usually time, an hour before lunch and one after, for two hours of "electives." Negro history, chemistry, biology, English, French, and typing were the subjects settled on by the groups' desires and their teachers' abilities.

The afternoons were particularly hot, and more and more frequent were the noisy visits to the drinking fountain and the lavatories at the back of the church. There was no outdoor play space, but, eventually, teachers began to take groups of students to the playground of a nearby Catholic school that the sisters allowed us to use. One of the older boys organized a softball team and both boys and girls were eager to play ball regardless of the heat. Late in the afternoon (called "evening" in Mississippi) some of the teachers and students joined the regular COFO precinct workers for voter registration work.

The best afternoons at Blair Street were those filled with special events. On opening day, for example, Pete Seeger arrived at one-thirty in the afternoon to give us a private concert. With the whole school present, the very littlest ones asleep in any arms that would hold them, Pete talked first of his recent visit to twenty-seven countries around the world. He told us that all children were the same the world over and that music was a language that flew easily over even the highest walls. He demonstrated his statements by playing and singing Indian, African, Chinese, and Polynesian songs, in each instance allowing the rhythms to illustrate the emotion before offering a translation of the words. "Isn't this a happy song," he said, after singing, in African dialect, "Everybody Loves Saturday Night." He taught the children to sing the foreign words of several songs, and though we didn't know it then, that was the high moment for them. The Blair Street students had no idea that Pete was a famous man, but they wanted to hear more of him and happily turned up that evening to be transported across town to Anderson Chapel where Pete Seeger sang for a packed and overflowing house until his voice gave out.

Films were also a good afternoon activity. On the day we showed the full-length *Oliver Twist* to an audience of more than one hundred, I heard one boy of ten mutter to himself about Oliver, "He sho' is white, but he's a slave just the same." The film ran too late in the afternoon for discussion, but the following morning was filled with questions and talk about child labor. Another group of films were part of a special, state-wide program arranged by Paul Lauter, a professor of English at Smith College. All bearing upon the connections among the struggle for civil rights, non-violence, and the need for world peace, the four films were used by Paul to spark discussions. Two of these films were documentaries, one about Gandhi, the other about the Montgomery, Alabama, bus strike. The students were more interested in talking, however, about the other pair of films. One was a recent Polish film, *The Magician*. The other, an animated cartoon, *The Hat*, consisted of a dialogue between two soldiers (Dizzy Gillespie—whose music also filled the film— and the British comedian, Dudley Moore) who guard either side of a line, the hat of one falling onto the side of the other as they march. The students were quick to compare lines that divided nations with lines that divided people within nations. They remembered, during the discussion that followed, relevant details through which the film attempted to show that talking, in human terms, helps to erase lines.

Evening activities provided still other kinds of experience for the Freedom School student. Apart from concerts, there were mass meetings, at one of which, for example, A. Philip Randolph spoke along with leading Jackson ministers. Best of all was the Free Southern Theatre's production of *In White America*, which toured the state as part of a continuing program of special entertainment for Freedom Schools. Most of these students had never seen live theatre, and certainly not a play about themselves in history. Their response as audience was continuously energetic, especially since, as they reported the next day, they enjoyed recognizing incidents they had been reading of or discussing. One student, Kaaren Robinson, age fifteen, wrote the following as part of a review published in the *Blair Street Freedom Bugle*:

It portrayed the brutal transportation of the Negro from his native Africa to a new country, the inhuman treatment upon his arrival, the confusing position of the political-minded white man with regard to his stand on the slave question and the continuous struggle of the Negro against overwhelming odds.
. . . Because of his up-bringing, the new freedom put the Negro in a confusing state which naturally led him back into another kind of slavery. This slavery has lasted until now.
The author achieved these points through narration and conversation. Through this medium the Negro of today can better understand why the white man feels as he does toward him. However, this does not justify his feelings nor his actions. *In White America* is a great and moving drama which should be seen by black and white alike.

Though questioned, Kaaren resisted any attempt to enlarge upon the play's effect. From her point of view, the play allowed her to understand the white man's confusion; it told her nothing about the Negro she did not already know.

Charles Cobb, a student at Howard University before he joined the SNCC staff, was responsible late in 1963 for suggesting the idea of Freedom Schools. He has written cogently of their *raison d'être*, in a piece called "This is the Situation":

Repression is the law; oppression, a way of life—regimented by the judicial and executive branches of the state government, rigidly enforced by state police machinery, with veering from the path of "our way of life" not tolerated at all. Here, an idea of your own is a subversion that must be squelched; for each bit of intellectual initiative represents the threat of a probe into the why of denial.

Learning here means only learning to stay in your place. Your place is to be satisfied—a "good nigger."

They have learned the learning necessary for immediate survival: that silence is safest, so volunteer nothing: that the teacher is the state, and tell them only what they want to hear; that the law and learning are white man's law and learning.

There is hope and there is dissatisfaction—feebly articulated—both born out of the desperation of needed alternatives not given. This is the generation that has silently made the vow of no more raped mothers—no more castrated fathers; that looks for an alternative to a lifetime of bent, burnt, and broken backs, minds, and souls. Their creativity must be molded from the rhythm of a muttered "white son-of-a-bitch"; from the roar of a hunger bloated belly; and from the stench of rain and mud washed shacks.

There is the waiting, not to be taught, but to be, to reach out and meet and join together, and to change. The tiredness of being told it must be, "cause that's white folks' business," must be met with the insistence that it's their business. They know that anyway. It's because their parents didn't make it their business that they're being so systematically destroyed. What they must see is the link between a rotting shack and a rotting America.

The Citizenship Curriculum, the discussion of which filled most of our mornings, is frankly a response to the repressive society Charles Cobb has described. It is aimed at meeting two basic needs of students: first, a need for information; second, a need for identity and hence activity. The "facts" of history; in terms of dates, people's names, places, events, as well as the interpretations of history—all this has been denied to them, and denied particularly in relation to their own situation as American Negroes. Not only is Negro history unknown to them, but even the history of the current Negro revolution is known only in bits and pieces, largely through television, since their newspapers are notoriously uninformative. The second need, the need for identity and activity, is organically one with the need for facts. It has to do with what happens when an individual begins to know himself as part of history, with a past and a potential future as well as a present. What happens when an individual begins to assess himself as a human being? The aim of the Citizenship Curriculum here is to assist the growth of self-respect, through self-awareness, both of which lead to self-help. In this way, the curriculum at the center of the Freedom Schools is frankly and avowedly a program for leadership development.

In many different ways, the mimeographed curriculum makes clear the Freedom Schools' purpose: "to provide an educational experience for students which will make it possible for them to challenge the myths of our society, to perceive more clearly its realities, and to find alternatives, and ultimately, new directions for action." Or more briefly, "to train people to be active agents in bringing about social change." The curriculum itself, however, declares that "It is not our purpose to impose a particular set of conclusions. Our purpose is to encourage the asking of questions, and hope that society can be improved."

Because the chief tool is the question, the curriculum is hopefully "developmental," that is, one that "begins on the level of the students' everyday lives and those things in their environment that they have either already experienced or can readily perceive, and builds up to a more realistic perception of American society, themselves, the conditions of their oppression, and alternatives offered by the Freedom Movement." The seven units are as follows:

1. Comparison of students' reality with others (the way the students live and the way others live)
2. North to Freedom? (The Negro in the north)
3. Examining the apparent reality (the "better lives" that whites live)
4. Introducing the power structure
5. The poor Negro and the poor white
6. Material things versus soul things
7. The Movement

In addition, two sets of questions are to be constantly in the minds of the teachers and frequently introduced to the students:

The Basic Set of Questions:

1. Why are we (teachers and students) in Freedom Schools?
2. What is the Freedom Movement?
3. What alternatives does the Freedom Movement offer us?

The Secondary Set of Questions:

1. What does the majority culture have that we want?
2. What does the majority culture have that we don't want?
3. What do we have that we want to keep?

Some of my own experience was with a relatively young group—eleven to fourteen-year-olds. After describing their own houses, they went on to describe the houses of whites in Jackson that they had seen, either because they had themselves worked as domestics, or because their mothers did. When asked what changes they would like made in their own houses, while their answers varied from additional rooms to more yard space, no one thought in terms as grandiose as the "white" houses they had described, and most of them thought of their houses as "comfortable." On the other hand, they were certain that their (segregated) schools were inferior, even when they admitted that the buildings were new. They resented their hand-me-down textbooks, they suspected the inadequacy of their teachers, and they complained particularly bitterly about the repressive atmosphere. In their schools, they reported that no questioning or discussion was allowed, except in rare instances when they and a particular teacher knew they were "taking a chance." Of course, they knew little or nothing of conditions in white schools, either in Mississippi or elsewhere, beyond their impression that these, somehow, were "better."

High school juniors and seniors were especially interested in the subject of going north to freedom. On the one hand, many of them expressed a wish to go north to college, in part because they suspected that Negro colleges in Mississippi were as inadequate as their public schools, but also because they wanted the experience of learning in an integrated group. They were articulate about the need for communication between black and white. The freedom songs they sang each day—"Black and white together/ We shall overcome," for example—were not simply words to be mouthed. On the other hand, some of them had been reading with us from the works of Richard Wright and James Baldwin of the Negro in Chicago or Harlem; and they knew they were living through a summer which had brought riots to northern cities, though not to Jackson, Mississippi. They questioned the condition of Negroes everywhere, and many of them concluded that it was probably better to stay in Mississippi and work to improve things there than to imagine that things were better in another place.

The Freedom School curriculum's most substantial statement about values, "Material Things and Soul Things," takes as its central idea the society that is "humane" because it is "nonviolent." Negroes, of course, are no more naturally violent or nonviolent than any other group. But these students, brought up on the edge of a volcano, named as their heroes Martin Luther King and Medgar Evers, and, when they knew of him, Gandhi as well. At Blair Street, I asked the question about heroes because Paul Lauter had reported that when he asked the question at Freedom Schools throughout the state, those very three names occurred. It was also Paul's impression that as SNCC people became veterans at their jobs, nonviolence for them became not strategic manner but genuine conviction. For the veteran SNCC worker, Matt Suarez, who dropped in one afternoon at Blair Street for a visit and stayed for a discussion, nonviolence had become essential to life. Some of the students who listened to him had also experienced organized demonstrations within the discipline of the nonviolent movement. But their minds were far from decided. They questioned the theory; they suspected themselves of "violent feelings"; they talked about "strategy"; they asked for a "speaker"—and got more discussion!

Because the student needs to learn not only about the world he lives in, but also how to be free enough to live in it, the chief tool of Freedom Schools always was discussion. Ideally, discussion began with the question, "How do you feel about . . . ?" or "How would you feel if . . . ?" and moved on to questions about motivation ("Why do you feel this way?" or "Why would anyone feel this way?"). Once the discussion had begun, the questions could move on to students' reactions to each other's ideas. At first, of course, students were distrustful of the situation generally. Some were also shy before their peers as well as frightened of their teacher. But of course they all had feelings and they all had some words with which to describe them. And eventually the moment came, unnoticed and passed over, when a student could say easily to his (white) teacher or to a fellow student, "I disagree," and explain why.

The teacher's main problem was to learn to keep quiet, to learn how to listen and to question creatively rather than to talk at the students. He had to discard whatever formal classroom procedures he had ever learned and respond with feeling and imagination as well as with intelligence and good humor to the moods and needs of the group. Above all, the students challenged his honesty: he could not sidestep unpleasantness; he could not afford to miss any opportunity for discussing differences.

I have no crystal ball, but I can submit two aspects of my own experience that suggest that the Freedom Schools of '64 spread more than transitory ripples in a huge Mississippi sea. The first was a discussion that led directly to social action independently instigated by the students themselves. The second was an experiment that led directly to the students writing poetry.

The third week of Freedom Schools in Jackson was also the week of school registration for those Negro first-graders who were to attend previously white schools. Registration was scheduled for early Thursday morning; a mass meeting for interested parents had been called by thirty-six Negro ministers of Jackson for Tuesday night. This was Monday morning, and the group at the Blair Street School had begun, for some reason, to talk about the "myth" of Negro inferiority. At one point, when there was silence, I asked how many of the twenty students present (ages fourteen to twenty) knew some first-grader who was about to start school. Everyone did. Did anyone know any who were going to a white school? No one did. When I asked why, I got many different responses:

My sister thinks her son would be unhappy with white children.
My brother hasn't gone to kindergarten.
The white school is too far away.
My mother wants my brother to be with his friends.
My father says he doesn't like the idea.

None of the students had mentioned the word fear. They all looked uncomfortable and I felt my anger rise: "What am I going to say to my friends back North when they ask me why Negro mothers haven't registered their children in white schools? That they like things the way they are?" I could see the consternation on the face of Gene Gogol, my fellow teacher, who began, "I disagree, Florence, you just don't understand the situation." I felt that his rebuke was probably a just one, but then the students began to smile wryly and, one by one, they began to talk of the various fears that "perhaps" these parents were feeling. Personal safety. Economic security—the loss of jobs because they weren't being "good niggers." Failure in the white school—either because of social ostracism or because of poor training and possibly the alleged intellectual inferiority. But then suddenly, I don't know exactly what shifted the discussion, perhaps something about the white faces that Gene and I wore in the midst of the black ones, suddenly the students were talking about *positive* reasons for sending children into integrated schools. Then one of the sixteen-year-old girls suggested that perhaps we—meaning those of us in the discussion group—ought to go out into the neighborhood and talk with parents who were reluctant to send their children to white schools, that perhaps we were most suited for this job since we knew the value of good education and we knew there was really nothing to fear. When I suggested that we try one of the school's favorite procedures, role-playing, there were volunteers immediately for mother, father, child, and for two visitors from the Freedom School. The players were evenly matched so that the play-discussion rehearsed all the arguments we had heard. The role-playing father remained essentially unconvinced, but his wife assured the visitors that she had really changed her mind and that, after they had gone, she would "work on" her husband.

Gene and a crew of student-volunteers worked all the rest of Monday, Monday night, and all of Tuesday. They talked to more than seventy families and received from twenty-seven of these assurances that at least the mother would attend Tuesday night's mass meeting, perhaps would take advantage of the transportation we would provide. Disappointingly, only one mother kept her promise. But on Wednesday morning, Gene and some students began their visits again, and by Thursday noon, all of Blair Street's Freedom School were boasting that eleven of the forty-three Negro children in Jackson who actually registered to attend previously white schools had done so as a direct result of Gene's and the students' talks with parents.

Thus the students had direct evidence that their school experience had led them to create something that was lasting and profound. Additional evidence —this of a more personal nature—followed their reading and discussion of poetry.

We had begun with poems by Langston Hughes. They knew immediately that when Hughes, in a poem called "As I Grew Older," mentioned a "thick wall" and a "shadow" growing between him and his childhood "dream," he was talking about walls and shadows they knew every day in Jackson: the barbed wire around the parks, for example, or the hate in white men's faces when they tried to go to a movie downtown. I didn't need to be a teacher showing the difference between literal meaning and what was "symbolized." There *was* curiosity about forms. Do all poems rhyme? What is rhyme, anyway? Can poets use any words they like? The students, who had never heard of Langston Hughes, were surprised by his slang, by his use of jazz expressions. They listened to the occasional irregularity that made rhythms interesting, especially in a Hughes song-poem like "The Weary Blues"—which they never tired of.

One day, when discussion had flagged, I suggested a "game." Let's divide into four groups of five and try writing a "group" poem. I even offered a subject: try writing about yourselves and Jackson—we had just been reading about Hughes and Harlem. When I returned, half an hour later, cries of "Listen to this" greeted me. With one exception, the poems were not group products—the groups had stayed to watch individual members create. The best poem came from a sixteen-year-old girl, a visitor to Jackson from Pascagoula, who had just come for the first time to Freedom School, and who was to continue attending thenceforth. This is Alice Jackson's poem called "Mine":

> I want to walk the streets of a town,
> Turn into any restaurant and sit down,
> And be served the food of my choice,
> And not be met by a hostile voice.
> I want to live in the best hotel for a week,

Or go for a swim at a public beach.
I want to go to the best university
And not be met with violence or uncertainty.
I want the things my ancestors
Thought we'd never have.
They are mine as a Negro, an American;
I shall have them or be dead.

In the days that followed, we read poems by Sandburg and Frost, two poets the students had heard of, but the greatest excitement came from their introduction to e. e. cummings, especially to the poem "Anyone Lived in a Pretty How Town." One day, after two hours of a discussion of cummings' poems, I asked the eight or nine students present—ages fourteen to seventeen—whether they wanted to try writing again. When I asked whether they wanted a suggested subject, I heard an overwhelming series of no's. No subject . . . let us write what we feel like writing.

Within twenty minutes, Shirley Ballard, age seventeen, was reading aloud to me a poem called "Time." She read it slowly, emphasizing the individuality of certain words and phrases. Its feeling was clearly fragmentary. But then she showed me the page on which she had written the poem: four long lines, resembling her reading not at all. She had read it in a manner that suggested something else, and I showed her cummings' page. She caught on instantly, took her page, and returned in several minutes with the following version:

Time goes by so slowly
my mind reacts so lowly
    how faint
how moody
    I feel,
             I love not
    I care not.
Don't love me.
Let me live.
  Die
  Cry
  Sigh
All alone
    Maybe someday I'll go home.

Another seventeen year old, Sandra Ann Harris, quickly produced a cummings-like poem—even to the elimination of all capitalization:

why did i my don'ts
why did i my dids
what's my didn'ts' purpose
is it to fulfill my dids

what isn'ts have i proclaimed
what ises have i pronounced
why can't i do my doings
my couldn'ts do renounce

my wouldn'ts are excuses
my couldn'ts couldn't be helped
my weren'ts were all willful
my words of little help

the haven'ts were just there
my didn'ts did believe
that all my won'ts are daring
my wills to receive

If it is startling to consider how much these students learned so quickly, it is also instructive to consider that in Freedom Schools all over Mississippi this summer students were becoming both social activists and poets. An impressive volume of poetry (which may soon be published) appeared in Freedom School newspapers. And a Mississippi Student Union has been formed. The connection between poetry and politics should surprise no one who has read the Romantics or, more recently, the poets of the Irish Renaissance. What is surprising is that, in some ways, it took *so little* to accomplish so much in the Mississippi Freedom Schools.

Consider the discussion circle, the union of teachers and students in a status-free ring. Consider too the position of these students—blacks in a white culture—as outsiders who were now, in 1964, *conscious* outsiders, youngsters seeing new possibilities ahead of them and, at the same time, young adults with the wisdom to see what Negro slavery has been. Under these special new conditions, one could talk and think about what it was like to be a slave and what it might be like to be free. One could even try *being* free. Under these special conditions—the consciousness of being suppressed combined with the proffered opportunity to base education on that consciousness—creativity was the natural response.

What have we to learn from Freedom Schools? The politics of education. That our schools are political grounds in which our students begin to learn about society's rules. That, therefore, if we wish to alter our students and our society, we must alter our schools. That if we would have strong and creative minds we must remove chains both from bodies and spirits. That we as adults and educators have to listen and respond rather than preach. That we need to share with our students a sense of being open to what each uniquely experienced companion can reveal. That this perspective of equality is itself a revolution that goes far beyond the surface movement of Negroes into white society. And that if Freedom School teachers in Mississippi society know themselves as unwelcome and harassed outsiders, not unlike the Negro students, then authentic teachers anywhere must face a similar knowledge.

The Freedom School students and teachers who heard Langston Hughes'

"As I Grew Older" understood that Hughes' prayer was theirs too—for strength and wisdom to break through all spiritual prisons of self and society and so to reach freedom:

> My hands!
> My dark hands!
> Break through the wall!
> Find my dream!
> Help me to shatter this darkness,
> To smash this night,
> To break this shadow
> Into a thousand lights of sun,
> Into a thousand whirling dreams
> Of sun!

THE OPEN TRUTH
AND FIERY VEHEMENCE OF YOUTH

A Sort of Soliloquy

Peter Marin

It is midnight and I am sitting here with my notes, enough of them to make two books and a half and a volume of posthumous fragments, trying to make some smaller sense of them than the grand maniacal design I have in my mind. I don't know where to begin. Once, traveling in summer across the country with a friend from Hollywood and my young son in a battered green Porsche, I stopped for lunch somewhere in Kansas on a Sunday morning. As we walked into the restaurant, bearded, wearing dark glasses and strange hats, and followed by my long-haired boy, one Kansas matron bent toward another and whispered: "I bet those two men have kidnapped that little girl." I took a deep breath and started to speak, but I did not know where to begin or how to explain just how many ways she was mistaken. Now, trying to write clearly about education and adolescence, I feel the same way.

For that reason I have chosen an eccentric method of composition, one that may seem fragmentary, jumpy, and broken. This article will be more like a letter, and the letter itself is an accumulation of impressions and ideas, a sampling of thoughts at once disconnected but related. There is a method to it that may disappear in its mild madness, but I do not know at this juncture how else to proceed. Shuffling through my notes I feel like an archeologist with a mass of uncatalogued shards. There is a pattern to all

THE OPEN TRUTH AND FIERY VEHEMENCE OF YOUTH: A SORT OF SOLILOQUY Reprinted, by permission, from the January 1969 issue of *The Center Magazine,* a publication of the Center for the Study of Democratic Institutions in Santa Barbara, California.

this, a coherence of thought, but all I can do here is assemble the bits and pieces and lay them out for you and hope that you can sense how I get from one place to another.

An entire system is hiding behind this, just beginning to take form, and these notes are like a drawing, a preliminary sketch. I feel comfortable with that notion, more comfortable than with the idea of forcing them together, cutting and pasting, to make a more conventional essay. I can perceive in myself at this moment what I also see in the young: I am reluctant to deal in sequence with my ideas and experience, I am impatient with transition, the habitual ways of getting "from here to there." I think restlessly; my mind, like the minds of my students, works in flashes, in sudden perceptions and brief extended clusters of intuition and abstraction—and I have stuck stubbornly to that method of composition. There is still in me the ghost of an apocalyptic adolescent, and I am trying to move it a few steps toward the future.

One theme, as you will see, runs through what I have written or thought: we must rethink our ideas of childhood and schooling. We must dismantle them and start again from scratch. Nothing else will do. Our visions of adolescence and education confine us to habit, rule perception out. We make do at the moment with a set of ideas inherited from the nineteenth century, from an industrial, relatively puritanical, repressive, and "localized" culture; we try to gum them like labels to new kinds of experience. But that won't do. Everything has changed. The notions with which I began my job as a high-school director have been discarded one by one. They make no sense. What emerges through these children as the psyche of this culture is post-industrial, relatively unrepressed, less literate and local: a new combination of elements, almost a new strain. Adolescents are, each one of them, an arena in which the culture transforms itself or is torn between contrary impulses; they are the victims of a culture raging within itself like man and wife, a schizoid culture—and these children are the unfinished and grotesque products of that schism.

They are grotesque because we give them no help. They are forced to make among themselves adjustments to a tension that must be unbearable. They do the best they can, trying, in increasingly eccentric fashions, to make sense of things. But we adults seem to have withdrawn in defeat from that same struggle, to have given up. We are enamored, fascinated, and deluded by adolescence precisely because it is the last life left to us; only the young rebel with any real passion against media, machines, the press of circumstance itself. Their elders seem to have no options, no sense of alternative or growth. Adult existence is bled of life and we turn in that vacuum toward children with the mixed repulsion and desire of wanton Puritans toward life itself.

As for me, an adult, I think of myself as I write as an observer at a tribal war—an anthropologist, a combination of Gulliver and a correspondent sending home news by mule and boat. By the time you hear of it, things will have changed. And that isn't enough, not enough at all. Somebody must step past the children, must move into his own psyche or two steps past his own limits into the absolute landscape of fear and potential these children inhabit. That is where I am headed. So these ideas, in effect, are something like a last message tacked to a tree in a thicket or tucked under a stone. I mean: we cannot *follow* the children any longer, we have to step ahead of them. Somebody has to mark a trail.

Adolescence: a few preliminary fragments . . .

(FROM MY STUDENT, v): yr whole body moves in a trained way & you know that youve moved this way before & it contains all youve been taught its all rusty & slow something is pushing under that rusted mesh but STILL YOU CANNOT MOVE you are caught between 2 doors & the old one is much closer & you can grab it all the time but the other door it disappears that door you cant even scratch & kick (like the early settlers were stung by the new land) but this new land doesnt even touch you & you wonder if youre doing the right thing to get in

(FROM FRANZ KAFKA): He feels imprisoned on this earth, he feels constricted; the melancholy, the impotence, the sicknesses, the feverish fancies of the captive afflict him; no comfort can comfort him, since it is merely comfort, gentle headsplitting comfort glazing the brutal fact of imprisonment. *But if he is asked what he wants he cannot reply. . . . He has no conception of freedom.*

(FROM TAPES RECORDED IN PACIFIC PALISADES, 1966, SEVERAL BOYS AND GIRLS AGED 12–14):—Things are getting younger and younger. Girls twelve will do it now. One guy said I fuck a girl every Friday night. What sexual pleasure do you get out of this (he's very immature you know) and he would say, I don't know I'm just going to fuck.

or

—*How old are you?* —Twelve. —*Will you tell us your first experience with drugs, how you got into it?* —Well, the people I hung around with were big acid-heads. So one day my friend asked me if I wanted to get stoned and I said yes. That was about five months ago and I've been getting on it ever since. Started taking LSD about one month ago. Took it eleven times in one month. I consider it a good thing. For getting high, smoking grass is better, or hashish—it's about six times stronger than marijuana.

(FROM PAUL RADIN: *Primitive Man As Philosopher*): It is conceivably demanding too much of a man to whom the pleasures of life are largely bound up with the life of contemplation and to whom analysis and introspection are the self-understood prerequisites for a proper understanding of the world, that he appreciate . . . expressions which are largely non-intellectual—where life seems, predominatingly, a discharge of physical vitality, a simple and naive release of emotions or an enjoyment of sensations for their own sake. Yet . . . it is just such an absorption in a life of sensations that is the outward characteristic of primitive peoples.

Can you see where my thought leads? It is precisely at this point, adolescence, when the rush of energies, that sea-sex, gravitation, the thrust of the ego up through layers of childhood, makes itself felt, that the person is once more like an infant, is swept once more by energies that are tidal, unfamiliar, and unyielding. He is in a sense born again, a fresh identity beset inside and out by the rush of new experience. It is at this point, too—when we seem compelled by a persistent lunacy to isolate him—that what is growing within the adolescent demands expression, requires it, and must, in addition, be received by the world and given form—or it will wither or turn to rage. Adolescence is a second infancy. It is then that a man desires solitude and at the same time contact with the vivid world; must test within social reality the new power within himself; needs above all to discover himself for the first time as a bridge between inner and outer, a maker of value, a vehicle through which culture perceives and transforms itself. It is now, ideally, that he begins to understand the complex and delicate nature of the ego itself as a thin skin between living worlds, a synaptic jump, the self-conscious point at which nature and culture combine.

In this condition, with these needs, the adolescent is like a primitive man, an apocalyptic primitive; he exists for the moment in that stage of single vision in which myth is still the raw stuff of being, he knows at first hand through his own energies the possibilities of life—but he knows these in muddled, sporadic, contradictory ways. The rush of his pubescent and raw energy seems at odds with public behavior, the *order* of things, the tenor of life around him, especially in a culture just emerging—as is ours—from a tradition of evasion, repression, and fear.

The contradictions within the culture itself intensify his individual confusion. We are at the moment torn between future and past: in the midst of a process of transformation we barely understand. The development of adolescent energy and ego—difficult at any time—is complicated in our own by the increase in early sexuality, the complicated messages of the media, and the effects of strong and unfamiliar drugs. These three elements are, in themselves, the salient features of a culture that is growing more permissive, less repressive. They are profound, complex, and strong: heavy doses of experience demanding changes in attitude, changes in behavior. The direction and depth of feeling responds accordingly; the adolescent tries—even as a form of self-defense against the pressure of his own energies—to move more freely, to change his styles of life, to "grow." But it is then that he finds he is locked into culture, trapped in a web of ideas, law, and rituals that keep him a child, deprive him of a chance to test and assimilate his newer self. It is now that the culture turns suddenly repressive. His gestures are evaded or denied; at best he is "tolerated," but even then his gestures, lacking the social support of acknowledgment and reward, must seem to him lacking in authenticity—more like forms of neurosis or selfishness than the natural stages in growth.

He is thrust back upon himself. The insistent natural press within him toward becoming whole is met perpetually by unbudging resistance. Schools, rooted as they are in a Victorian century and seemingly suspicious of life itself, are his natural enemies. They don't help, as they might, to make that bridge between his private and the social worlds; they insist, instead, upon their separation. Indeed, family, community, and school all combine—especially in the suburbs—to isolate and "protect" him from the adventure, risk, and participation he needs; the same energies that relate him at this crucial point to nature result in a kind of exile from the social environment.

Thus the young, in that vivid confrontation with the thrust of nature unfolding in themselves, are denied adult assistance. I once wrote that education through its limits denied the gods, and that they would return in the young in one form or another to haunt us. That is happening now. You can sense it as the students gather, with their simplistic moral certainty, at the gates of the universities. It is almost as if the young were once more possessed by Bacchanalian gods, were once again inhabited by divinities whose honor we have neglected. Those marvelous and threatening energies! What disturbs me most about them is that we lack rituals for their use and balance, and the young—and perhaps we ourselves—now seem at their mercy. The young have moved, bag and baggage, into areas where adults cannot help them, and it is a scary landscape they face, it is crowded with strange forms and faces, and if they return from it raddled, without balance and pitched toward excess, who can pretend to be surprised—or blameless?

At times they seem almost shell-shocked, survivors of a holocaust in which the past has been destroyed and all the bridges to it bombed. I cannot describe with any certainty what occurs in their minds, but I do know that most adults must seem to the young like shrill critics speaking to them in an alien language about a Greek tragedy in which they may lose their lives. The words we use, our dress, our tones of voice, the styles of adult lives—all of these are so foreign to that dramatic crisis that as we approach them we seem to increase the distance we are trying to cross. Even our attention drives them further away, as if adolescents perceived that adults, coming closer, diminish in sense and size.

The inner events in an adolescent demand from what surrounds him life on a large scale, in a grand style. This is the impulse to apocalypse in the young, as if they were in exile from a nation that does not exist—and yet they can sense it, they know it is there—if only because their belief itself demands its presence. Their demand is absolute and unanswerable, but it exists and we seem unable at this point in time to suppress or evade it. For one reason or another, massive shifts in cultural balances, the lessening of repression for whatever reasons—economic, technological, evolutionary— those energies, like gods, have appeared among us again. But what can we make of them? The simple problem is that our institutions are geared to another century, another set of social necessities, and cannot change quickly enough to contain, receive, or direct them—and as we suppress or refuse them they turn to rage.

Primitive cultures dealt with this problem, I think, through their initiation rites, the rites of passage; they legitimized and accepted these energies and turned them toward collective aims; they were merged with the life of the tribe and in this way acknowledged, honored, and domesticated—but not destroyed. In most initiation rites the participant is led through the mythical or sacred world (or a symbolic version) and is then returned, transformed, to the secular one as a new person, with a new role. He is introduced through the rites to a dramatic reality coexistent with the visible or social one and at its root; he is put in direct touch with the sources of energy, the divinities of the tribe. In many cultures the symbolic figures in the rites are unmasked at the end, as if to reveal to the initiate the interpenetration of the secular and sacred worlds. Occasionally the initiate is asked at some point to don the ritual mask himself—joining, as he does, one world with another and assuming the responsibility for their connection. This shift in status, in *relation*, is the heart of the rite; a liturgized merging of the individual with shared sources of power.

Do you see what I am driving at? The rites are in a sense a social contract, a binding up; one occurring specifically, profoundly, on a deep psychic level. The individual is redefined in the culture by his new relation to its mysteries, its gods, to one form or another of nature. His experience of that hidden and omnipotent mythical world is the basis for his relation to the culture and his fellows, each of whom has a similar bond—deep, personal, and unique, but somehow shared, invisibly but deeply. These ritualized relationships of each man to the shared gods bind the group together; they form the substance of culture: an invisible landscape that is real and felt, commonly held, a landscape which resides in each man and in which, in turn, each man resides.

I hope that makes sense. That is the structure of the kaleidoscopic turning of culture that Blake makes in "The Crystal Cabinet," and it makes sense too, in America, in relation to adolescents. What fascinates me is that our public schools, designed for adolescents—who seem, as apocalyptic men, to demand this kind of drama, release, and support—educate and "socialize" their students by depriving them of everything the rites bestow. They manipulate them through the repression of energies; they isolate them and close off most parts of the community; they categorically refuse to make use of the individual's private experience. The direction of all these tendencies is toward a cultural schizophrenia in which the student is forced to choose between his own relation to reality or the one demanded by the institution. The schools are organized to weaken the student so that he is forced, in the absence of his own energies, to accept the values and demands of the institution. To this end we deprive the student of mobility and experience; through law and custom we make the only legal place for him the school, and then, to make sure he remains dependent, manipulable, we empty the school of all vivid life.

We appear to have forgotten in our schools what every primitive tribe with its functional psychology knows: allegiance to the tribe can be forged only at the deepest levels of the psyche and in extreme circumstance demanding endurance, daring, and awe; that the participant must be given *direct* access to the sources of cultural continuity—by and in himself; and that only a place in a coherent community can be exchanged for a man's allegiance.

I believe that it is precisely this world that drugs replace; adolescents provide for themselves what we deny them: a confrontation with some kind of power within an unfamiliar landscape involving sensation and risk. It is there, I suppose, that they hope to find, by some hurried magic, a new way of seeing, a new relation to things, to discard one identity and assume another. They mean to find through their adventures the *ground* of reality, the resonance of life we deny them, as if they might come upon their golden city and return still inside it: at home. You can see the real veterans sometimes on the street in strange costumes they have stolen from dreams: American versions of the Tupi of Brazil, who traveled thousands of miles each year in search of the land where death and evil do not exist. Theirs is a world totally alien to the one we discuss in schools; it is dramatic, it enchants them; its existence forms a strange brotherhood among them and they cling to it—as though they alone had been to a fierce land and back. It is that which draws them together and makes of them a loose tribe. It is, after all, some sort of shared experience, some kind of foray into the risky dark; it is the best that they can do.

When you begin to think about adolescence in this way, what sense can you make of our schools? None of the proposed changes makes sense to me: revision of curriculum, teaching machines, smaller classes, encounter groups, redistributions of power—all of these are stopgap measures, desperate attempts to keep the young in schools that are hopelessly outdated. The changes suggested and debated don't go deeply enough; they don't question or change enough. For what needs changing are not the methods of the school system but its aims, and what is troubling the young and forcing upon their teachers an intolerable burden is the *idea* of childhood itself; the ways we think about adolescents, their place in the culture itself. More and more one comes to see that changes in the schools won't be enough; the crisis of the young cuts across the culture in all its areas and includes the family and the community. The young are displaced; there seems no other word for it. They are trapped in a prolonged childhood almost unique.

In few other cultures have persons of fifteen or eighteen been so uselessly isolated from participation in the community, or been deemed so unnecessary (in their elders' eyes), or so limited by law. Our ideas of responsibility, our parental feelings of anxiety, blame, and guilt, all of these follow from our curious vision of the young; in turn, they concretize it, legitimize it so that we are no longer even conscious of the ways we see childhood or the strain that our vision puts upon us. That is what needs changing: the definitions we make socially and legally of the role of the young. They are trapped in the ways we see them, and the school is simply one function, one aspect, of the whole problem. What makes real change so difficult in the schools is only in part their natural unwieldiness; it is more often the difficulty we have in escaping our preconceptions about things.

In general the school system we have inherited seems to me based upon three particular things:

1. What Paul Goodman calls the idea of "natural depravity": our puritanical vision of human nature in which children are perceived as sinners or "savages" and in which human impulse or desire is not to be trusted and must therefore be constrained or "trained."

2. The necessity during the mid-nineteenth century of "Americanizing" great masses of immigrant children from diverse backgrounds and creating, through the schools, a common experience and character.

3. The need in an industrialized state for energy and labor to run the machines: the state, needing workers, educates persons to be technically capable but relatively dependent and responsive to authority so that their energies will be available when needed.

These elements combine with others—the labor laws that make childhood a "legal" state, and a population explosion that makes it necessary now to keep adolescents off both the labor market and the idle street—to "freeze" into a school system that resists change even as the culture itself and its needs shift radically. But teachers can't usually see that, for they themselves have been educated in this system and are committed to ideas that they have never clearly understood. Time and again, speaking to them, one hears the same questions and anguish:

"But what will happen to the students if they don't go to school?" "How will they learn?" "What will they do without adults?"

What never comes clear, of course, is that such questions are, at bottom, statement. Even while asking them teachers reveal their unconscious and contaminating attitudes. They can no longer imagine what children will do "outside" schools. They regard them as young monsters who will, if released from adult authority or help, disrupt the order of things. What is more, adults no longer are capable of imagining learning or child-adult relationships outside the schools. But mass schooling is a recent innovation. Most learning—especially the process of socialization or acculturation—has gone on outside schools, more naturally, in the fabric of the culture. In most cultures the passage from childhood to maturity occurs because of social necessity, the need for responsible adults, and is marked by clear changes in role. Children in the past seem to have learned the ways of the community or tribe through constant contact and interchange with adults, and it was taken for granted that the young learned continually through their place close to the heart of the community.

We seem to have lost all sense of that. The school is expected to do what the community cannot do and that is impossible. In the end, we will have to change far more than the schools if we expect to create a new coherence between the experiences of the child and the needs of the community. We will have to rethink the meaning of childhood; we will begin to grant greater freedom *and* responsibility to the young; we will drop the compulsory-schooling age to fourteen, perhaps less; we will take for granted the "independence" of adolescents and provide them with the chance to live alone, away from parents and with peers; we will discover jobs they can or want to do in the community—anything from mail delivery to the teaching of smaller children and the counseling of other adolescents. At some point, perhaps, we will even find that the community itself—in return for a minimum of work or continued schooling—will provide a minimal income to young people that will allow them to assume the responsibility for their own lives at an earlier age, and learn the ways of the community outside the school: finally, having lowered the level of compulsory schooling, we will find it necessary to provide different *kinds* of schools, a wider choice, so that students will be willing voluntarily to continue the schooling that suits their needs and aims.

All these changes, of course, are aimed at two things: the restoration of the child's "natural" place in the community and lowering the age at which a person is considered an independent member of the community. Some of them, to be sure, can be made in the schools, but my sense of things, after having talked to teachers and visited the schools, is that trying to make the changes in schools *alone* will be impossible.

One problem, put simply, is that in every school I have visited, public or private, traditional or "innovational," the students have only these two choices: to drop out (either physically or mentally) or to make themselves smaller and smaller until they can act in ways their elders expect. One of my students picked up a phrase I once used, "the larger and smaller worlds." The schools we visit together, he says, are always the smaller world: smaller at least than his imagination, smaller than the potential of the young. The students are asked to put aside the best things about themselves—their own desires, impulses, and ideas—in order to "adjust" to an environment constructed for children who existed one hundred years ago, if at all. I wonder sometimes if this condition is simply the result of poor schooling; I am more inclined to believe that it is the inevitable result of mass compulsory schooling and the fabrication of artificial environments by adults for children. Is it possible at all for adults to understand what children need and to change their institutions fast enough to keep up with changes in culture and experience? Is it possible for children to grow to their full size, to feel their full strength, if they are deprived of individual volition all along the line and forced to school? I don't know. I know only that during the Middle Ages they sometimes "created" jesters by putting young children in boxes and force-feeding them so that, as they grew, their bones would warp in unusual shapes. That is often how the schools seem to me. Students are trapped in the boxes of pedagogic ideas, and I am tempted to say to teachers again and again: more, much more, you must go further, create more space in the schools, you must go deeper in thought, create more resonance, a different feeling, a different and more human, more daring style.

Even the best teachers, with the best intentions, seem to diminish their students as they work through the public-school system. For that system is, at bottom, designed to produce what we sometimes call good citizens but what more often than not turn out to be good soldiers; it is through the schools of the state, after all, that we produce our armies. I remember how struck I was while teaching at a state college by the number of boys who wanted to oppose the draft but lacked the courage or strength to simply say no. They were trapped; they had always been taught, had always tried, to be "good." Now that they wanted to refuse to go, they could not, for they weren't sure they could bear the consequences they had been taught would follow such refusal: jail, social disgrace, loss of jobs, parental despair. They could not believe in institutions, but they could not trust themselves and their impulse and they were caught in their own impotence: depressed and resentful, filled with self-hatred and a sense of shame.

That is a condition bred in the schools. In one way or another our methods produce in the young a condition of pain that seems very close to a mass neurosis: a lack of faith in oneself, a vacuum of spirit into which authority or institutions can move, a dependency they feed on. Students are encouraged to relinquish their own wills, their freedom of volition; they are taught that value and culture reside outside oneself and must be acquired from the institution, and almost everything in their education is designed to discourage them from activity, from the wedding of idea and act. It is almost as if we hoped to discourage them from thought itself by making ideas so lifeless, so hopeless, that their despair would be enough to make them manipulable and obedient.

The system breeds obedience, frustration, dependence, and fear: a kind of gentle violence that is usually turned against oneself, one that is sorrowful and full of guilt, but a violence nonetheless, and one realizes that what is done in the schools to persons is deeply connected to what we did to the blacks or are doing now in Vietnam. That is: we don't teach hate in the schools, or murder, but we do isolate the individual; we empty him of life by ignoring or suppressing his impulse toward life; we breed in him a lack of respect for it, a loss of love—and thus we produce gently "good" but threatened men, men who will kill without passion, out of duty and obedience, men who have in themselves little sense of the vivid life being lost nor the moral strength to refuse.

From first to twelfth grade we acclimatize students to a fundamental deadness and teach them to restrain themselves for the sake of "order." The net result is a kind of pervasive cultural inversion in which they are asked to separate at the most profound levels their own experience from institutional reality, self from society, objective from subjective, energy from order— though these various polarities are precisely those which must be made coherent during adolescence.

I remember a talk I had with a college student.

"You know what I love to do," he said. "I love to go into the woods and run among the trees."

"Very nice," I said.

"But it worries me. We shouldn't do it."

"Why not?" I asked.

"Because we get excited. It isn't *orderly*."

"Not orderly?"

"Not orderly."

"Do you run into the trees?" I asked.

"Of course not."

"Then it's orderly," I said.

In a small way this exchange indicates the kind of thinking we encourage in the schools: the mistaking of rigidity and stillness for order, of order as the absence of life. We try to create and preserve an order which depends upon the destruction of life both inside and out and which all life, when expressed, must necessarily threaten or weaken.

The natural process of learning seems to move naturally from experience through perception to abstraction in a fluid continuous process that cannot be clearly divided into stages. It is in that process that energy is somehow articulated in coherent and meaningful form as an act or thought or a made object. The end of learning is wisdom and wisdom to me, falling back as I do on a Jewish tradition, is, in its simplest sense, "intelligent activity" or, more completely, the suffusion of activity with knowledge, a wedding of the two. For the Hassidic Jews every gesture was potentially holy, a form of prayer, when it was made with a reverence for God. In the same way a gesture is always a form of wisdom—an act is wisdom—when it is suffused with knowledge, made with a reverence for the truth.

Does that sound rhetorical? I suppose it does. But I mean it. The end of education is intelligent activity, *wisdom,* and that demands a merging of opposites, a sense of process. Instead we produce the opposite: immobility, insecurity, an inability to act without institutional blessing or direction, or, at the opposite pole, a headlong rush toward motion without balance or thought. We cut into the natural movement of learning and try to force upon the students the end product, abstraction, while eliminating experience and ignoring their perception. The beginning of thought is in the experience through one's self of a particular environment—school, community, culture. When this is ignored, as it is in schools, the natural relation of self and knowledge is broken, the parts of the process become polar opposites, antitheses, and the young are forced to choose between them: objectivity, order, and obedience as against subjectivity, chaos, and energy. It doesn't really matter which they choose; as long as the two sets seem irreconcilable their learning remains incomplete. Caught between the two, they suffer our intellectual schizophrenia until it occupies them, too. They wait. They sit. They listen. They learn to "behave" at the expense of themselves. Or else—and you can see it happening now—they turn against it with a vengeance and may shout, as they did at Columbia, "Kill all adults," for they have allied themselves with raw energy against reason and balance—our delicate, hard-won virtues—and we should not be surprised. We set up the choices ourselves, and it is simply that they have chosen what we hold to be the Devil's side.

If this is the case, what are the alternatives? I thought at one time that changes in schooling could be made, that the school itself could become at least a microcosm of the community outside, a kind of halfway house, a preparatory arena in which students, in semi-protective surroundings, would develop not only the skill but the character that would be needed in the world. But more and more, as I have said, it seems to me impossible to do that job in a setting as isolated and restrictive as our schools. Students don't need the artificiality of schools; they respond more fully and more intelligently when they make direct contact with the community and are allowed to choose roles that have some utility for the community and themselves. What is at stake here, I suppose, is the freedom of volition, for this is the basic condition with which people must learn to deal, and the sooner they achieve within that condition wit, daring, and responsibility the stronger they will be. It seems absurd to postpone the assumption of that condition as long as we do. In most other cultures, and even in our own past, young people have taken upon themselves the responsibility of adults and have dealt with it as successfully as most adults do now. The students I have seen can do that, too, when given the chance. What a strain it must be to have that capacity, to sense in one's self a talent for adventure or growth or meaning, and have that sense continually stifled or undercut by the role one is supposed to play.

Thus, it seems inescapably clear that our first obligation to the young is to create a place in the community for them to act with volition and freedom. They are ready for it, certainly, even if we aren't. Adolescents seem to need at least some sense of risk and gain "out there" in the world: an existential sense of themselves that is vivid to the extent that the dangers faced are "real." The students I have worked with seem strongest and most alive when they are in the mountains of Mexico or the Oakland ghetto or out in the desert or simply hitchhiking or riding freights to see what's happening. They thrive on distance and motion—and the right to solitude when they want it. Many of them want jobs; they themselves arrange to be teachers in day-care centers, political canvassers, tutors, poolroom attendants, actors, governesses, gardeners. They returned from these experiences immeasurably brightened and more sure of themselves, more willing, in that new assurance, to learn many of the abstract ideas we had been straining to teach them. It was not simply the experience in itself that brought this about. It was also the feeling of freedom they had, the sense that they could come and go at will and make any choice they wanted—no matter how absurd—if they were willing to suffer what real consequences followed. Many wanted to work and travel and others did not; they wanted to sit and think or read or live alone or swim or, as one student scrawled on my office wall, "ball and goof." What they finally came to understand, of course, was that the school made no pretense at either limiting or judging their activities; we considered them free agents and limited our own activities to advice, to what "teaching" they requested, and to support when they needed it in facing community, parents, or law.

What we were after was a *feeling* to the place: a sense of intensity and space. We discarded the idea of the microcosm and replaced it with an increased openness and access to the larger community. The campus itself became a place to come back to for rest or discussion or thought; but we turned things inside out to the extent that we came to accept that learning took place more naturally elsewhere, in any of the activities that our students chose, and that the school was in actuality wherever they were, whatever they did. What students learned at the school was simply the feel of things; the sense of themselves as makers of value; the realization that the environment is at best an extension of men and that it can be transformed by them into what they vitally need.

What we tried to create was a flexible environment, what a designer I know has called permissive space. It was meant to be in a sense a model for the condition in which men find themselves, in which the responsibility of a man was to make connections, value, and sense. We eliminated from the school all preconceptions about what was proper, best, or useful; we gave up rules and penalties; we refused at all levels to resort to coercive force and students were free to come and go at will, to do anything. What we were after was a "guilt-free" environment, one in which the students might become or discover what they were without having to worry about preconceived ideas of what they had to be.

What we found was that our students seemed to need, most of all, relief from their own "childhood"—what was expected of them. Some of them needed merely to rest, to withdraw from the strange grid of adult expectation and demand for lengthy periods of introspection in which they appeared to grow mysteriously, almost like plants. But an even greater number seemed to need independent commerce with the world outside the school: new sorts of social existence. Nothing could replace that. The simple fact seemed to be that our students grew when they were allowed to move freely into and around the adult community; when they were not, they languished.

We came to see that learning is natural, yes, but it results naturally from most things adolescents do. By associating learning with one particular form of intellection and insisting upon that in school we make a grave error. When students shy away from that kind of intellection it doesn't mean they are turning away forever from learning or abstractions; it means simply that they are seeking another kind of learning momentarily more natural to themselves. That may be anything from physical adventure or experimental community work to withdrawn introspection and an exploration of their fantasies and dreams.

Indeed, it is hard for them to do anything without some kind of learning, but that may be what we secretly fear—that those other forms of learning will make them less manageable or less like ourselves. That, after all, may be one reason we use all those books. Levi-Strauss insists on the relation of increased literacy and the power of the state over the individual. It may well be that dependence on print and abstraction is one of the devices we use to make students manipulable, as if we meant to teach them that ideas exist in talk or on the page but rarely in activity. We tried to avoid that. When we permitted students the freedom of choice and gave them easy access to the community, we found that ideas acquired weight and value to the extent that students were allowed to try them out in action. It was in practical and social situations that their own strength increased, and the merging of the two—strengthened self and tested knowledge—moved them more quickly toward manhood than anything else I have seen.

One might make a formula of it: to the extent that students had freedom of volition and access to experience knowledge became important. But volition and access were of absolute value; they took precedence over books or parental anxiety; without them, nothing worked. So we had to trust the students to make their own choices, no matter what we thought of them. We learned to take their risks with them—and to survive. In that sense we became equals, and that equality may in the end be more educational for students than anything else. That, in fact, may be the most important thing we learned. New ways in seeing them were more effective than changes in curriculum, and without them nothing made much difference. But we must understand too that the old way of seeing things—the traditional idea of childhood—is in some way baked into the whole public-school system at almost every level and also hidden in most pedagogy.

In some ways it is compulsory schooling itself which is the problem, for without real choice students will remain locked in childhood and schools, away from whatever is vivid in life. But real choice, as we know, includes dominion over one's own time and energies, and the right to come and go on the basis of what has actual importance. And I wonder if we will ever get round, given all our fears, to granting that privilege to students.

One thing alone of all I have read has made recent sense to me concerning adolescents. That is the implicit suggestion in Erik Erikson's *Young Man Luther* that every sensitive man experiences in himself the conflicts and contradictions of his age. The great man, he suggests, is the man who articulates and resolves these conflicts in a way that has meaning for his time; that is, he is himself, as was Luther, a victim of his time and its vehicle and, finally, a kind of resolution. But all men, not only the great, have in some measure the capacity to experience in themselves what is happening in the culture around them. I am talking here about what is really shared among the members of a particular culture is a condition, a kind of internal "landscape," the psychic shape that a particular time and place assumes within a man as the extent and limit of his perceptions, dreams, and pleasure and pain.

If there is such a shared condition it seems to me a crucial point, for it means that there is never any real distance between a man and his culture, no real isolation or alienation from society. It means that adolescents are not in their untutored state cut off from culture nor outside it. It means instead that each adolescent is an arena in which the contradictions and currents sweeping through the culture must somehow be resolved, must be resolved by the person himself, and that those individual resolutions are, ideally, the means by which the culture advances itself.

Do you see where this leads? I am straining here to get past the idea of the adolescent as an isolate and deviant creature who must be joined—as if glued and clamped—to the culture. For we ordinarily think of schools, though not quite consciously, as the "culture" itself, little models of society. We try to fit the student into the model, believing that if he will adjust to it he will in some way have been "civilized." That approach is connected to the needs of the early century, when the schools were the means by which the children of immigrant parents were acculturated and moved from the

European values of their parents toward more prevalent American ones. But all of that has changed now. The children in our schools, all of them, are little fragments of *this* culture; they no longer need to be "socialized" in the same ways. The specific experiences of every adolescent—his fears, his family crises, his dreams and hallucinations, his habits, his sexuality—all these are points at which the general culture reveals itself in some way. There is no longer any real question of getting the adolescent to "adjust" to things.

The problem is a different one: What kind of setting will enable him to discover and accept what is already within him; to articulate it and perceive the extent to which it is shared with others; and, finally, to learn to change it within and outside himself? For that is what I mean when I call the adolescent a "maker of value." He is a trustee, a trustee of a world that already exists in some form within himself—and we must both learn, the adolescent and his teachers, to respect it.

In a sense, then, I am calling for a reversal of most educational thought. The individual is central; the individual, in the deepest sense, *is* the culture, not the institution. His culture resides in him, in experience and memory, and what is needed is an education that has at its base the sanctity of the individual's experience and leaves it intact.

What keeps running through my mind is a line I read twelve years ago in a friend's first published story: *The Idea in that idea is: there is no one over you.* I like that line: *There is no one over you.* Perhaps that signifies the gap between these children and their parents. For the children it is true, they sense it: there is no one over them; believable authority has disappeared; it has been replaced by experience. As Thomas Altizer says, God is dead; he is experienced now not as someone above or omnipotent or omniscient or "outside," but inwardly, as conscience or vision or even the unconscious or Tillich's "ground of being." This is all too familiar to bother with here, but this particular generation is a collective dividing point. The parents of these children, the fathers, still believe in "someone" over them, insist upon it; in fact, demand it for and from their children. The children themselves cannot believe it; the idea means nothing to them. It is almost as if they are the first real Americans—suddenly free of Europe and somehow fatherless, confused, forced back on their own experience, their own sense of things, even though, at the same time, they are forced to defy their families and schools in order to keep it.

This is, then, a kind of Reformation. Arnold was wrong when he said that art would replace religion; education replaced it. Church became School, the principal vehicle for value, for "culture," and just as men once rebelled against the established Church as the mediator between God and man, students now rebel against the *public* school (and its version of things) as the intermediary between themselves and experience, between themselves and experience and the making of value. Students are expected to reach "reality" (whether of knowledge or society) through their teachers and school. No one, it is said, can participate in the culture effectively without having at one time passed through their hands, proven his allegiance to them, and been blessed. This is the authority exercised by priests or the

Church. Just as men once moved to shorten the approach to God, they are moved now to do the same thing in relation to learning and to the community. For just as God was argued to appear within a man—unique, private, and yet shared—so culture is, in some way, grounded in the individual; it inhabits him. The schools, like the Church, must be the expression of that habitation, not its exclusive medium. This is the same reformative shift that occurred in religion, a shift from the institutional (the external) to the individual (the internal), and it demands, when it occurs, an agony, an apocalyptic frenzy, a destruction of the past itself. I believe it is happening now. One sees and feels it everywhere: a violent fissure, a kind of quake.

I remember one moment in the streets of Oakland during the draft demonstrations. The students had sealed off the street with overturned cars and there were no police; the gutters were empty and the students moved into them from the sidewalks, first walking, then running, and finally almost dancing in the street. You could almost see the idea coalesce on their faces: The street is ours! It was as if a weight had been lifted from them, a fog; there was not at that moment any fury in them, any vengefulness or even politics; rather, a lightness, delight, an exhilaration at the sudden inexplicable sense of being free. George Orwell describes something similar in *Homage to Catalonia*: that brief period in Barcelona when the anarchists had apparently succeeded and men shared what power there was. I don't know how to describe it, except to say that one's inexplicable sense of invisible authority had vanished: the oppressive father, who is not really there, was gone.

That sudden feeling is familiar to us all. We have all had it from time to time in our own lives, that sense of "being at home," that ease, that feeling of a Paradise which is neither behind us nor deferred but is around us, a natural household. It is the hint and beginning of Manhood: a promise, a clue. One's attention turns to the immediate landscape and to one's fellows: toward what is there, toward what can be felt as a part of oneself. I have seen the same thing as I watched Stokely Carmichael speaking to a black audience and telling them that they must stop begging the white man, like children, for their rights. They were, he said, neither children nor slaves, no, they were—and here they chanted, almost cried, in unison—a beautiful people: *yes our noses are broad and our lips are thick and our hair is kinky . . . but we are beautiful, we are beautiful, we are black and beautiful.* Watching, you could sense in that released joy an emergence, a surfacing of pride, a refusal to accept shame or the white man's dominance —and a turning to one another, to their own inherent value.

But there is a kind of pain in being white and watching that, for there is no one to say the same things to white children; no "fathers" or brothers to give them that sense of manhood or pride. The adolescents I have seen —white, middle-class—are a long way from those words *we are beautiful, we are beautiful.* I cannot imagine how they will reach them, deprived as they are of all individual strength. For the schools exist to deprive one of strength. That is why one's own worth must be proven again and again by the satisfaction of external requirements with no inherent value or importance; it is why one must satisfy a set of inexplicable demands; it is why there is a continual separation of self and worth and the intrusion of a kind of institutional guilt: failure not of God but of *the system,* the nameless "others," the authority that one can never quite see; and it explains the oppressive sense of some nameless transgression, almost a shame at Being itself.

It is this feeling that pervades both high schools and college, this Kafkaesque sense of faceless authority that drives one to rebellion or withdrawal, and we are all, for that reason, enchanted by the idea of the Trial, that ancient Socratic dream of confrontation and vindication or martyrdom. It is then, of course, that Authority shows its face. In the mid-fifties I once watched Jack Kerouac on a television show and when the interviewer asked him what he wanted he said: to see the face of God. How arrogant and childish and direct! And yet, I suppose, it is what we all want as children: to have the masks of authority, all its disguises, removed and to see it plain. That is what lies in large part behind the riots in the schools. Their specific grievances are incidental; their real purpose is to make God show his face, to have whatever pervasive and oppressive force makes us perpetual children reveal itself, declare itself, commit itself at last. It is Biblical; it is Freudian; it reminds me in some way of the initiation rites, the need to unmask the gods and assume their power, to become an equal—and to find in that the manhood one has been denied.

The schools seem to enforce the idea that there *is* someone over you; and the methods by which they do it are ritualized, pervasive. The intrusion of guilt, shame, alienation from oneself, dependence, insecurity—all these feelings are not the accidental results of schools; they are intentional, and they are used in an attempt to make children manipulable, obedient, "good citizens" we call it, and useful to the state. The schools are the means by which we deprive the young of manhood—that is what I mean to say—and we must not be surprised when they seek that manhood in ways that must of necessity be childish and violent.

But I must admit this troubles me, for there is little choice between mindless violence and mindless authority, and I am just enough of an academic, an intellectual, to want to preserve much of what will be lost in the kind of rebellion or apocalypse that is approaching. And yet, and yet . . . the rapidity of events leaves me with no clear idea, no solution, no sense of what will be an adequate change. It may be that all of this chaos is a way of breaking with the old world and that from it some kind of native American will emerge. There is no way of knowing, there no longer seems any way of estimating what is necessary or what will work. I know only that the problem now seems to be that our response to crisis is to move away or back rather than forward, and that we will surely, for the sake of some imagined order, increase in number and pressure the very approaches that have brought us to this confusion. I don't know. I believe that the young must have values, of course, be responsible, care, but I know too that most of the violence I have seen done to the young has been done in the name of value, and that the well-meaning people who have been so dead set on making things right have had a hand in bringing us to where we are now. The paradox is a deep and troubling one for me. I no longer know if change can be accomplished—for the young, for any of us, without the apocalyptic fury that seems almost upon us. The crisis of youth and education is symptomatic of some larger, deeper fault in our cities and minds, and perhaps nothing can be done consciously in those areas until the air itself is violently cleared one way or another.

So I have no easy conclusions, no startling synthesis with which to close. I have only a change in mood, a softening, a kind of sadness. It may be, given that, that the best thing is simply to close with an unfinished fragment in which I catch for myself the hint of an alternative:

. . . I am trying to surround you, I see that, I am trying to make with these words a kind of city so natural, so familiar, that the other world, the one that appears to be, will look by comparison absurd and flat, limited, unnecessary. What I am after is liberation, not my own, which comes often enough these days in solitude or sex, but yours, and that is arrogant, isn't it, that is presumptuous, and yet that is the function of art: to set you free. It is that too which is the end of education: a liberation from childhood and what holds us there, a kind of midwifery, as if the nation itself were in labor and one wanted to save both the future and the past—for we *are* both, we are, we are the thin bridge swaying between them, and to tear one from the other means a tearing of ourselves, a partial death.

And yet it may be that death is inevitable, useful. It may be. Perhaps, as in the myth, Aphrodite can rise only where Cronos' testicles have fallen into the sea. It may be that way with us. The death of the Father who is in us, the death of the old authority which is part of us, the death of the past which is also our death; it may all be necessary: a rending and purgation. And yet one still seeks another way, something less (or is it more) apocalyptic, a way in which the past becomes the future *in ourselves,* in which *we* become the bridges between: makers of culture.

Unless from us the future takes place, we are Death only, said Lawrence, meaning what the Chassids do: that the world and time reside within, not outside, men; that there is no distance, no "alienation," only a perpetual wedding to the world. It is that—the presence in oneself of Time—that makes things interesting, is more gravid and interesting than guilt. I don't want to lose it, don't want to relinquish that sense in the body of another dimension, a distance, the depth of the body as it extends backward into the past and forward, as it contains and extends and transforms.

What I am after is an alternative to separation and rage, some kind of connection to things to replace the system of dependence and submission— the loss of the self—that now holds sway, slanted toward violence. I am trying to articulate a way of seeing, of feeling, that will restore to the young a sense of manhood and potency without at the same time destroying the past. That same theme runs through whatever I write: the necessity for each man to experience himself as an extension and maker of culture, and to feel the whole force of the world within himself, not as an enemy—but as himself:

> . . . An act of learning is a meeting, and every meeting is simply the discovery in the world of a part of oneself that had previously been unacknowledged by the self. It is the recovery of the extent of one's being. It is the embrace of an eternal but elusive companion, the shadowy "other" in which one truly resides and which blazes, when embraced, like the sun.

From THE ROAD TO LIFE

A. S. Makarenko

Six kilometres from Poltava, springing out of sandy hillocks, there is a pine forest of some 200 hectares, bordered by the smooth, endlessly gleaming cobblestones of the highroad to Kharkov. In a corner of a 40-hectare clearing in the forest, a perfect square is formed by a group of uncompromisingly symmetrical brick buildings. This is to be the new colony for juvenile delinquents.

The sandy, sloping courtyard merges in a wide glade extending towards a reed-fringed lake, on the opposite bank of which may be discerned the dwellings and wattle fences of a kulak farmstead. Beyond these, etched against the sky, is a straight line of ancient birch trees and a huddle of thatched roofs.

Before the Revolution there had been a colony for juvenile delinquents in this place, but in 1917 its inmates all ran away, leaving behind them extremely faint vestiges of an educational system. Judging by the contents of the dilapidated registers, the educational staff had been chiefly recruited from retired noncommissioned officers, whose main duty it was never to take their eyes off their charges, either during work or recreation, and at night to sleep next to them in an adjoining room.

According to the local peasantry, the educational methods of these tutors were not very subtle, being in practice limited to that simplest of all pedagogical apparatus—the rod.

Material traces of the former colony were still further to seek, its neighbours having carried and carted away to their own barns and outhouses everything in the way of furniture, stores, and workshop equipment on which they could lay their hands. Among other valuables they even removed the orchard. But there was not the slightest indication of a spirit of vandalism in all this. The fruit trees had not been cut down, but simply uprooted and replanted elsewhere, the windowpanes not broken, but taken

FROM THE ROAD TO LIFE From *The Road to Life (An Epic of Education)* by A. S. Makarenko. Translated by Ivy and Tatiana Litvinov. Published by Foreign Languages Publishing House, Moscow.

carefully out of their frames, the doors hacked by no ruthless axe, but gently lifted off their hinges, the stoves removed brick by brick. The only article of furniture left was a sideboard in the apartment of the former director.

"How is it that the sideboard was left behind?" I asked Luka Semyonovich Verkhola, a neighbour who had come from the farmstead to have a look at the new bosses.

"Well, you see, *our* people had no use for this cupboard. It wouldn't have gone through their doors—too high, and too wide. And there would be no point in taking it to pieces."

The sheds were crammed with odd articles, but there was nothing of any practical use in them. Following a hot scent I managed to retrieve a few things which had been stolen quite recently. Thus I recovered an old seed-drill, eight rickety joiners' benches, a brass bell, and a thirty-year-old cob, an erstwhile fiery Kirghiz steed.

Kalina Ivanovich, manager of supplies, who was already on the spot when I arrived, greeted me with the question:

"Are you the pedagogical director?"

I was soon to learn that Kalina Ivanovich spoke with a Ukrainian accent, although he refused, on principle, to recognize the Ukrainian language. There were many Ukrainian words in his lexicon, and he pronounced his g's in the southern manner.

"Are you the pedagogical director?"

"Me? I'm the director of the colony."

"No, you're not!" said he, taking his pipe out of his mouth. "You're the pedagogical director, and I'm the supply manager."

Picture to yourself Vrubel's "Pan," but Pan gone quite bald, with only a tuft of hair over each ear. Shave off Pan's goatee, trim his moustache in the episcopal manner, stick a pipestem between his teeth, and Pan becomes Kalina Ivanovich Serdyuk. He was a remarkably versatile individual for so modest a post as that of manager of supplies in a children's colony. Of his fifty-odd years, which had been spent in the most varied activities, he was proud to recall only two phases—his youth, when he had been a private in the Keksholm Infantry Regiment of the Guards, and his superintendence, in 1918, of the evacuation of Mirgorod during the German offensive.

Kalina Ivanovich became the first object of my educational zeal. It was the very abundance and variety of his views which constituted my greatest difficulty. With impartial fervour, he damned the bourgeoisie and the Bolsheviks, the Russians and the Jews, Russian slackness and German punctiliousness. But out of his blue eyes there shone such a zest for living, and he seemed so responsive and so full of life, that I did not grudge expending a little of my pedagogical energy on him. I started on his education the very first day, beginning with our very first encounter.

"Comrade Serdyuk, surely you don't imagine a colony can get on without a director! After all, somebody has to be responsible for everything!"

Kalina Ivanovich again removed his pipe, and said, with a courteous inclination of the head in my direction:

"So you want to be the director! And you want me to be so-to-speak your subordinate!"

"Not necessarily! I could be your subordinate if you prefer it that way."

"Well, I've never been taught pedagogics. I don't claim what isn't mine by rights! Still, you're only a young man and you want an old man like me to be at your beck and call. And that's not right, either. But I haven't got enough book learning to be the director—besides, I don't want to be!"

Kalina Ivanovich stalked away in a huff. All day he seemed dejected, and in the evening he came into my room quite heartbroken.

"I've moved a bed and a table in here. They're the best I could find," he said.

"Thanks."

"I've been thinking and thinking what we're to do about this here colony. And I've decided that you'd better be the director and I'll be so-to-speak your subordinate."

"We'll get on all right, Kalina Ivanovich!"

"I think so, too. After all, it doesn't take a genius to put a sole on a boot. We'll manage. And you, since you're an educated man, will be so-to-speak the director."

We set about our work. The thirty-year-old cob was raised to its feet by the judicious use of props. Kalina Ivanovich clambered into a sort of phaeton, kindly provided by one of our neighbours, and the whole remarkable contraption set out for the town at the rate of two kilometres an hour.

The organizational period had begun.

The task set for the organizational period was a most appropriate one— to wit, the accumulation of the material values required for the creation of the new man. Kalina Ivanovich and I spent whole days in town during the first two months, he driving there, I going on foot. He considered it beneath his dignity to walk, and I could not stand the languid pace of our Kirghiz steed.

During these two months we managed, with the help of experts from the villages, to get one of the barracks of the old colony into some sort of shape, putting in windowpanes, repairing stoves, hanging new doors.

We had only one victory on the "external front," but it was a notable one: we succeeded in wangling 150 poods of rye flour out of the Food Commissariat of the First Reserve Army. And this was all we managed to "accumulate" in the way of material values.

But when I came to compare what had actually been done with my ideals in the sphere of material culture, I realized that even if I had achieved a hundred times as much, I should have fallen just as short of my aim. And so, bowing to the inevitable, I declared the organizational period concluded. Kalina Ivanovich was quite of my way of thinking.

"What can we expect to find here," he exclaimed, "when those parasites produce nothing but cigarette lighters? First they lay the land waste, and then they ask us to 'organize'! We'll have to do as Ilya Muromets did!"

"Ilya Muromets?"

"Yes, Ilya Muromets! Maybe you've heard of him! They've made a hero of him—a bogatyr—the parasites! But *I* say he was just a tramp—a loafer, going sleigh riding in the summer!"

"All right, then! Let's be like Muromets. We could do worse! But who'll be Solovei, the highwayman?"

"There'll be no lack of them—don't you worry!"

Two teachers arrived at the colony—Ekaterina Grigoryevna, and Lydia Petrovna. I had by that time almost despaired of finding teachers; no one seemed anxious to devote himself to the task of creating the new man in our forest—everyone was afraid of our "tramps," and no one believed our plans would come to any good. And then one day at a conference of village schoolteachers, in response to my efforts at persuasive eloquence, two real live people came forward. I was glad they were women. It seemed to me that the "elevating feminine influence" was just what was needed to round out our system.

Lydia Petrovna was extremely young, hardly more than a schoolgirl. She had only just graduated from high school, and was fresh from the maternal nest. The Chief of the Gubernia Department of Public Education, while putting his signature to her appointment, asked me:

"What do you want with a girl like that? She doesn't know a thing!"

"She's just what I was looking for. D'you know I sometimes think book learning is not the chief thing just now. This Lydochka is an unspoiled little thing, and I regard her as a kind of yeast to leaven our dough."

"Aren't you being a bit farfetched? All right, here you are!"

Ekaterina Grigoryevna, on the other hand, was a seasoned pedagogue. She wasn't so very much older than Lydochka, but Lydochka clung to her as a child clings to its mother. Ekaterina Grigoryevna had a grave beauty of countenance, emphasized by black eyebrows almost masculine in their straightness. She was always neat, in clothes that had been preserved as by a miracle, and Kalina Ivanovich justly observed, after making her acquaintance:

"You've got to watch your step with a girl like that!"

Now everything was in readiness.

On the fourth of December our first six charges arrived at the colony, presenting me with a fantastic packet bearing five huge seals. This packet contained their "records." Four of them had been sent to us for housebreaking while bearing arms. These were about eighteen years old. The other two, who were a little younger, had been accused of theft. Our new charges were splendidly attired, in the smartest of riding breeches and cavalry boots. They wore their hair in the height of fashion. These were no mere street arabs. Their names were Zadorov, Burun, Volokhov, Bendyuk, Gud, and Taranets.

We received them with the utmost cordiality. The whole morning went in preparations for a gala dinner; the cook bound her hair with a fillet of dazzling whiteness; in the dormitory, festive tables were spread in the space unoccupied by the beds; we had no tablecloths, but brand-new sheets provided effective substitutes. All the members of our incipient colony were gathered there. Kalina Ivanovich turned up in honour of the occasion in a green velvet jacket instead of his usual stained grey coat.

I made a speech about the new life of toil, and the need for forgetting the past and pressing ever onward. The newcomers paid scant attention to my words, whispering to one another and allowing their sardonic glances to rove over the camp beds with their worn quilts, and the unpainted window frames and doors. While I was in the middle of my speech, Zadorov suddenly exclaimed loudly to another boy:

"You're the one who let us in for all this!"

We devoted the rest of the day to drawing up plans for our future life. The newcomers, however, listened to my proposals with courteous indifference, eager to get the whole thing over.

And the next morning a much-perturbed Lydia Petrovna came to me with the complaint:

"I can't manage them! When I told them to fetch water from the lake, one of them—the one with his hair done so smartly—started tugging on his boot, letting the toe swing right up to my face, and all he said was: 'Look how tight the bootmaker has made them!' "

The first days they weren't even rude, they merely ignored us. Towards evening they would saunter away, returning only in the morning and acknowledging my pathetic expostulations with discreet smiles. And then, a week later, Bendyuk was arrested by a detective from the Gubernia Criminal Investigation Department for robbery with murder the previous night. Lydochka, frightened out of her wits by this event, retreated to her room for a good cry, only emerging every now and then to ask of all and sundry: "What does it mean? I don't understand! Did he just go out and kill somebody?"

Ekaterina Grigoryevna, smiling gravely and knitting her brows, exclaimed:

"I don't know, Anton Semyonovich, I really don't know! Perhaps we'd better just go away! I don't seem to be able to find the right approach."

The lonely forest surrounding the colony, the empty shells of our buildings, our dozen camp beds, the axes and spades which were almost our only tools, the half-dozen boys who were in frank opposition not only to our pedagogical system, but to the very principles of human culture itself—all this was as unlike as possible to any scholastic experience any of us had ever had.

The long winter evenings in the colony were distinctly uncanny. Two oil lamps, one in the dormitory, the other in my room, afforded our only illumination. The teachers and Kalina Ivanovich were reduced to the time-honoured system of our forebears—a wick floating in a saucer of oil. The chimney of my lamp glass was broken at the top, and the lower part was always grimy with soot, owing to Kalina Ivanovich's habit of poking nearly half a newspaper down it to light his pipe.

The snowstorms started early that year, and the yard was soon blocked with drifting snow, through which it was nobody's business to clear paths. I asked the boys to do this, but Zadorov said:

"That's easy enough, but wouldn't it be better to wait till the end of the winter? What's the good of us clearing it away when it's sure to snow again? See?"

Bestowing a smile of angelic sweetness upon me, he joined a friend, as if oblivious of my very existence. It could be seen at a glance that Zadorov was the child of educated parents. He spoke correctly, and his face had that youthful refinement only found among those who have had a well-nurtured childhood. Volokhov belonged to quite another category. His wide mouth, spreading nose, and wide-set eyes, composed, with the puffy mobility of his features, the physiognomy of a typical "tough." Volokhov, his hands as always deep in the pockets of his riding breeches, sauntered up to me:

"Well, you've had your answer," he drawled.

I went out of the dormitory, my rage congealing into a hard lump in my chest. But paths had to be cleared, and my suppressed fury called imperatively for the outlet of action.

"Let's go and clear away the snow!" I said, having sought out Kalina Ivanovich.

"What? Have I come here to be a navvy? And those chaps?"

He motioned in the direction of the dormitory. "The highwaymen?"

"They won't!"

"The parasites! Come on, then!"

Kalina Ivanovich and I had almost finished the first path, when Volokhov and Taranets came along it for their nightly sally townwards.

"Atta boy!" cried Taranets gaily.

"And high time, too!" added Volokhov.

Kalina Ivanovich blocked their way.

"What d'you mean 'high time'?" he spluttered. "Just because you, you blighters, don't want to work, you think I'm going to do it for you! You shan't use this path, you parasites! You go through the snow, or I'll bash your head in with this shovel!"

Kalina Ivanovich brandished the spade fiercely, but the next moment it had flown into a distant snowdrift, while his pipe catapulted in another direction, and the astonished Kalina Ivanovich stood there, blinking at the departing youths.

"You can go and get the shovel yourself!" they shouted, proceeding on their way with gales of laughter.

"I'll quit, hang me if I don't! I'm not going to work here any more!" said Kalina Ivanovich, and he went back to his room, leaving the spade in the snowdrift.

Life at the colony became melancholy and gruesome. Cries of "Help, help!" were heard on the Kharkov road night after night, and the plundered villagers were always begging for succour in the most tragic accents. I procured myself a revolver from the Chief of the Gubernia Department of Public Education, by way of protection from our own particular knights of the road, but concealed from him the situation at our colony. I had not as yet given up hope of coming to some sort of an understanding with my charges.

These first months of the existence of the colony, as well as being a time of despair and futile effort for myself and my colleagues, were also a time of ardent research. In the whole of my previous existence I had not read so many books on education as I did that winter of 1920.

It was the time of Wrangel and the Polish war. Wrangel was quite near, just outside Novomirgorod; and quite near to us, in Cherkassy, was the Polish army, while all over the Ukraine roamed the "atamans," and many of those around us were still going about under the blue-and-yellow spell of Petlyura's banners. But in our wilderness we endeavoured, our chins propped on our hands, to shut out the thunder of great events, and devoted ourselves to the study of pedagogics.

The chief outcome of all this reading was a firm, well-founded conviction that the books had yielded me very little in the way of science or theory, and that I should have to wring my own theories out of the sum total of the actual phenomena, as displayed in everyday life.

At first I felt, rather than understood, that what I needed was not a set of abstract formulae, which I should anyhow have been unable to apply, but immediate analysis of the situation, followed by immediate action.

I was well aware that I should have to hurry, that I could not afford to lose a single day. The colony was becoming more and more like a den of thieves and cutthroats. The attitude of the boys to their teachers was rapidly crystallizing into habitual insolence and frank hooliganism. By now they were bandying dirty stories in front of the women teachers, rudely demanding their dinner, throwing plates about the dining room, making open play with their Finnish knives, and inquiring facetiously into the extent of everybody's possessions, with jeering remarks such as: "You never know what might come in handy!"

They flatly refused to cut down trees for firewood, breaking up the wooden roof of a shed under the very nose of Kalina Ivanovich, joking and laughing good-humouredly the while.

"It'll last our time!" they cried gaily.

Kalina Ivanovich, scattering constellations of sparks from his pipe, threw out his arms in despair:

"What's the good of talking to them, the parasites!" he cried. "Who taught them to break up what other people have built? Their parents, the parasites, ought to go to quod for it!"

And then, one day, the storm broke. I suddenly lost my footing on the tight-rope of pedagogical practice. One wintry morning I asked Zadorov to chop some wood for the kitchen stove, receiving the usual cheerfully insolent reply: "Do it thyself! God knows there are plenty of you here!"

It was the first time any of the boys addressed me with the familiar "thou." Desperate with rage and indignation, driven to utter exasperation by the experiences of the previous months, I raised my hand and dealt

Zadorov a blow full in the face. I hit him so hard that he lost his balance and fell against the stove. Again I struck him, seizing him by the collar and actually lifting him off his feet. And then I struck him the third time.

I saw to my astonishment that he was simply aghast. Pale as death, he kept putting on and taking off his cap with trembling hands. Perhaps I would have gone on hitting him, if he had not begun to whimper out: "Forgive me, Anton Semyonovich!"

My rage was so wild and unbridled that a word of resistance would have set me rushing at the whole pack of them, ready for murder, ready to wipe out this gang of thugs. An iron poker had somehow found its way into my hand. The other five huddled speechless around their beds. Burun was nervously adjusting his clothes.

Turning towards them, I rapped with the poker against the foot of one of the beds.

"Either you all go this minute to work in the woods, or you leave the colony, and to hell with you!"

With this I left the room.

Going to the shed in which our tools were kept, I took up an axe, and grimly watched the boys, who had trooped after me, select axes and saws. It did pass through my mind that it might be as well not to put axes into the boys' hands on such a day, but it was too late—they had taken everything they needed. But I was at the end of my tether. I was ready for anything, resolving only that I would not sell my life cheap. Besides, there was a revolver in my pocket.

We set out for the forest. Kalina Ivanovich, overtaking me, whispered in profound excitement: "What's up? For God's sake what has made them so obliging all of a sudden?"

I looked abstractly into Pan's blue eyes and replied:

"A bad business, old man! For the first time in my life I've struck my fellow man."

"God almighty!" exclaimed Kalina Ivanovich, "and what if they complain?"

"If that were all!"

To my astonishment, however, everything went off swimmingly. The boys and I worked away till dinner-time, cutting down the more stunted pine trees. They were a bit sulky, but the bracing frosty air, the splendid, snow-crowned pines, and the fellowship of toil, mingling with the rhythm of axe and saw, did their work.

When a halt was called, all self-consciously dipped into my proffered store of coarse tobacco, and Zadorov, sending a puff of smoke towards the pine tops, suddenly burst out laughing:

"That was a good one!"

It was quite a pleasure to look at his rosy, laughing visage, and I couldn't help smiling back at him.

"What? The work?" I asked.

"The work's all right. I meant the way you licked me!"

He was a strong, strapping lad, and could certainly afford to laugh. I was astonished at myself for having dared to lay hands on such a Hercules.

With another peal of laughter, he picked up his axe and went up to a tree:

"What a joke! Oh, what a joke!"

We had dinner all together, with good appetites, bandying jokes, and nobody mentioned the occurrence of the morning.

Still feeling slightly embarrassed, but determined not to relax my authority, I firmly issued orders after dinner.

Volokhov grinned, but Zadorov came up to me and said, with a grave look: "We're not such bad chaps, Anton Semyonovich! Everything will be all right! We understand. . . ."

A DESCRIPTION OF OUR PRIMARY NEEDS

The next day I said to the boys: "The dormitory must be kept clean! You must appoint a dormitory monitor. You can only go to town with my permission. If anyone goes without it, he needn't trouble to come back, for I won't let him in."

"I say!" exclaimed Volokhov, "couldn't you let us down a little more lightly?"

"Well, boys, you can choose for yourselves," I said. "That's all I can do! There's got to be discipline in the colony. If you don't like it, find somewhere else to go to. But those who stay will submit to discipline. Whatever you think, we're not going to run a thieves' den here."

"Shake!" said Zadorov, extending his hand towards me. "You're right! You, Volokhov, shut up! You're a fool about this sort of thing. Anyhow we have to stay here for a while. And it's better than quod, isn't it?"

"And is attending school compulsory?" asked Volokhov.

"Certainly!"

"And if I don't wish to study? What good'll it do me?"

"School is compulsory. You've got to attend whether you like it, or not. Zadorov called you a fool just now. You must learn and grow wise."

Volokhov shook his head comically, exclaiming:

"We're in for it now!"

The incident with Zadorov proved to be a turning point in discipline. I have to admit that I was beset by no qualms of conscience. Very well—I had struck one of my pupils. Keenly as I felt the pedagogical impropriety, the illegality of my action, at the same time I realized that the purity of our pedagogical conscience would have to be subordinated to the immediate task before me. I firmly decided to be a dictator if other methods failed. Not long after I came to loggerheads with Volokhov, who, while monitor, had failed to clean up the dormitory, and refused to do so on being reprimanded.

"Don't drive me to extremes," I said, looking sternly at him. "Do the room!"

"And if I don't you'll give me one in the eye, will you? You have no right to!"

I seized him by the collar, dragged him towards me, and, with the fullest sincerity, hissed into his face:

"Listen! I give you fair warning! I shan't give you one in the eye—I'll mark you for life! Then you can complain. If I go to prison for it, it's no business of yours."

Volokhov wriggled out of my grasp, exclaiming plaintively:

"No sense in going to prison for a little thing like that! I'll tidy the room, damn you!"

"Don't you dare to talk to me like that!" I roared at him.

"Well, how d'you want to be talked to? Go to————"

"Go on! Swear!"

Suddenly he burst out laughing, with a baffled gesture.

"What a fellow!" he cried. "All right, I'll tidy the room, don't shout at me!"

It should not be thought that I believed, even for a moment, that I had discovered a sovereign disciplinary method in the use of physical force. The Zadorov incident had cost me more than it had cost Zadorov himself. I was in constant fear of falling into the habit of taking the line of least resistance. Lydia Petrovna criticized me with frank severity:

"So you've discovered a method at last? Just like in the old seminary, isn't it?"

"Leave me alone, Lydochka!"

"No, but really! Are we to beat them up? May I, too? Or is it your monopoly?"

"I'll let you know a little later, Lydochka. I don't yet know myself. Give me time!"

"All right! I can wait."

Ekaterina Grigoryevna went about with a frown on her brows for some days, addressing me with distant politeness. Five days passed before she asked me, with her grave smile:

"Well, how are you feeling?"

"Thanks! I'm all right."

"D'you know what's the most distressing feature of this affair?"

"Distressing?"

"Yes. It is that the boys speak of your exploit with enthusiasm. They are all but in love with you, especially Zadorov. What does it mean—I don't understand! Could it come from a habit of servitude?"

I thought for a while before answering, and then said:

"No, it isn't that. It has nothing to do with servitude. It must be something else. Let's look deeper: after all, Zadorov is stronger than I am, he could have crippled me with a single blow. And he fears nothing, any more than Burun and the rest do. In this whole affair it's not the beating they remember, it's the passion, the fury of a human being. They know very well I needn't have beaten them, I could easily have sent Zadorov back to the Commission as incorrigible, and made things unpleasant for them in all sorts of ways. But I didn't do any of this; instead I chose a way which was dangerous for myself, but it was a human, not a bureaucratic way. And after all they do really need our colony. Things are not so simple. And they see how we work for them. They're human beings, too. And this is a most important factor."

OVERLEAF PHOTO: Jean Marie Guyaux ➔

The Cultural Revolution and Its Prophets

EDITED BY LESLIE FIEDLER

INTRODUCTION

The following essays are all prophecies of the cultural revolution through which we are now living; and, appropriately enough, they are all written by Americans, some of whom were born here, some of whom came here precisely in search of the Future which it is the prophet's task to define. Prophecy is not an exclusively American talent, but it has always flourished in this country, which began by thinking of itself as a model for things to come and has not ceased to project new utopian fantasies just because it has conspicuously failed to achieve the older ones. Yet we have seemed to need in the twentieth century new immigrants to dream our new dreams—recent refugees from worlds with a longer history of failure and a tradition of cynicism or stoicism to which we remain somehow profoundly alien.

D. H. Lawrence came to the United States just after World War I, in quest of what he had already called "The Spirit of Place," after having caught a glimpse of it in the classic fiction of our nineteenth century. It was *The Leatherstocking Tales* that chiefly moved him, so that "kindled by Fenimore Cooper" he headed directly for the Southwest, where he could live among the Indians whom he thought of as providing a model for the new kind of men that Americans might, under favorable circumstances, become. At the close of the 1960's, when the Indian has returned to the center of our imagination and has become once more a central character in American art on all levels, Lawrence seems a prophet justified. Had he lived long enough to see young people returning to the land, organizing themselves into "tribes," and dressing themselves in the garb of the red man, he would surely have believed that the total transformation of the European in the New World, which he foresaw five decades ago, is now an accomplished fact. Lawrence did not stay in America, to be sure, returning to Europe to die; but he had, in his years of residence here, and even more perhaps in those years during which he prepared for emigration from England, become the first imaginary American of the world—which is to say, the first true man of the Future we all now live.

Lawrence's name is still known to young people, though it is somewhat doubtful how much of him they read except on assignment in class. Wilhelm Reich, however, who is in some ways even closer to what is happening in our sex lives, and who anticipated our need to turn science back into magic, is considerably less well known, despite the fact that his work was most favorably received in the 1950's, which is to say, only yesterday. He had fled Hitler and arrived here in time to live through World War II, to achieve temporarily a modicum of success, and, in 1957, to die a martyr to his faith in his own vision—a prisoner in a federal penitentiary, under psychiatric care and deserted by his colleagues in psychiatry. A political prisoner really —a sexual revolutionary ahead of his time—he was ostensibly convicted of violating the "pure food and drug laws" by manufacturing and advertising a "quack device": that is, for developing the theory of the orgasm and producing for therapeutic use orgone accumulators; or, as they were more familiarly called by the very few who then believed in and used them, "orgone boxes."

Reich believed that he had discovered the life force that gives strength to the libido and to the workings of the universe in general. Not content to treat this force as a metaphor or even a state, he tried all of his life with various techniques to discover it in the physical world, in the genitals and in the air about him; and eventually he began to believe he could see it. Yet all he had initially wanted to prove was that the power released by the orgasm, the power Freud had been content to treat as a figure of speech, was "real." In the end, he became more and more nearly psychotic, obsessed by the conviction that he was being watched and hunted down by "red fascists" and other enemies fearful that his discovery would end the universal plague that repression and bad politics had visited on the world. Baffled and weary, he finally convinced himself that he had solved the secret of flying saucers and was about to control the weather and cure cancer.

Nonetheless, his theories about the good orgasm and character armoring, as well as his new methods of psychiatric therapy, represent a permanent contribution to our culture and an opening-up of new possibilities for the survivors of the Age of Gentility. He had begun as a favorite student of Freud, but had soon parted company with his master, chiefly on political grounds, since at an early point in his career he had become a Communist, committed to combining the teachings of Freud with those of his other guru,

Karl Marx. In the name of the latter, as well as in terms of his own irrepressible optimism, he resisted the skepticism and pessimism of Freud, battling valiantly against the notion of "sublimation" as necessary and desirable.

For Freud's essentially tragic vision, he tried hard to substitute a joyous view of human life, holding out to his disciples the hope of endless satisfaction and unlimited self-fulfillment. And he attracted, therefore, the naturally or theoretically ebullient; one of his lifelong friends and followers, for instance, was A. S. Neill, the founder of the Summerhill School. But his influence was even more important on certain American writers of the 1950's brought up, like him (though a generation later), on Freud and Marx: Isaac Rosenfeld, Paul Goodman, Saul Bellow, and Norman Mailer, through whom certain readers, ignorant of Reich's own writing, have got his message. He was, at any rate, guru-in-chief to the 1950's—which is why, in the midst of darkest Africa, Henderson the Rain King reads his views of characterological armoring, and, in the midst of grayest New York, Norman Mailer has been reinventing him over and over in his own language.

D. H. Lawrence was also interested in crossing into the unknown, frankly committed to the occult as an admirer of Madame Blavatsky and Annie Besant; and consequently he, too, appeals to a time in which the "secret" sciences—astrology, chirography, all forms of fortune-telling—are once again being celebrated. Reich, however, is even closer to the contemporary temper in that he wants to have it both ways at once; that is to say, to embrace ancient magic and prove its claims in the modern laboratory. He did not merely write, but lived what tends to become our favorite literary form—science fiction.

Compared with Reich, Herbert Marcuse seems a rather conventional academic, unwilling and unable to escape the influence of the German university and that Hegelian philosophy which once and for all endowed it with a characteristic tone and an obsessive vocabulary. Like Marcuse, Reich came from German-speaking Europe; but, fortunately for him, his birthplace was at its easternmost limits—in Galicia, homeland of the *Chassidim,* miracle-workers and mystics. Yet, ironically, it is Marcuse whose name is on the lips of the dissenting and radical young these days, and in his pages they look for—even claim to find—the perfect mating of Marx and Freud, Revolution and Eros, which exists, in fact, more extravagantly and disturbingly imagined in Reich. But perhaps it is to be expected that, being for the most part in universities themselves, the leaders of the New Left should prefer to follow one who expresses their own ambivalence toward academic life—though in the language of an older generation and another country.

It is from their dissident professors that dissident students most easily learn, and Marcuse seems to provide a link between immigrant prophets like Lawrence and Reich and those American mantic academics more recently in the spotlight, like Buckminster Fuller, Marshall McLuhan, Norman O. Brown, and Timothy Leary. Leary is presently outside of the university and Fuller came to it relatively late in life, but all four members of the group have made their influence felt basically in and through the academy. Brown and McLuhan, as a matter of fact, continue to teach, functioning day by day in the classroom, at the same time that they experiment with ways of reaching a wider audience through their books. Despite their university attachments, or perhaps because of them, all of these prophetic figures have gone on record as distrusting print. The only one of them who is not essentially a word man, committed by temperament and training to the Gutenberg tradition, is Buckminster Fuller.

"Bucky" Fuller has, as a matter of fact, never quite written a book, most of the volumes which appear under his name being transcriptions from tapes of the almost endless speeches which he so loves to give. Half-blind in fact, he is a talking man, who comes alive in his own mouth and in the ears of his auditors, and what he talks is once more the language of science fiction, the language of the Future. Fuller was to begin with an engineer and an inventor, his greatest technological success being the geodesic dome and his most touching failure the three-wheeled automobile. He began, that is to say, with the point of view of a technician, impatient with the whole body of politics and religion invented by those who never built or repaired a machine; during the early part of his career, he fell, therefore, under the influence of Howard Scott, the founder of the Technocratic movement, which advocated making engineers the rulers of society.

In style and approach, Fuller seems more like such inspired tinkerers as Benjamin Franklin or Thomas Alva Edison or, at best, Frank Lloyd Wright, rather than the three antiliterary literary prophets with whom he is associated in this collection. Yet Fuller is the man who speaks with most authority to the moment on the subject of what education can and must become in an age of computers and automation. Moreover, he began teaching us as long ago as 1938, long before the university had invited him in out of the cold, how it is possible to live with machines without becoming their victims: how, in fact, the machine can be humanized, incorporated, by being thought of not as a sibling rival or possible substitute for man, but as an extension and refinement of that primary machine with which we have lived during the whole course of human evolution, the body.

Moreover, it was inevitable that Fuller came to be thought of as one of the pioneers in the attempt to turn ecology from a science into an art, from a rationalistic way of understanding the world to a passionate way of living in it. Picking up a copy of the *Whole Earth Catalogue,* that new Bible of young people determined to live in a creative rather than destructive relationship with their environment, one discovers the name of Fuller evoked everywhere in its pages as a prophet and almost as a saint.

Fuller must find his election to sainthood rather embarrassing, however, for though he has apparently thought of himself as a kind of visionary, he has never had any religious aspirations at all. He is, in fact, the most eminently *sane* of American prophets, uncharacteristically at home in the world of reason. The same cannot be said of Brown or McLuhan or Leary, in whom a touch of Celtic blood seems to create an affinity for madness not shared by so pure a descendant of New England, Harvard-educated Anglo-Saxons as Fuller. Whatever capacity for insanity there was in the family line seems to have been used up once and for all by Margaret Fuller, his eccentric great-aunt.

Marshall McLuhan began, quite like Fuller, with an investigation of the effect of machines on modern society, and in particular with the way in which technology determines the Future that politicians pretend is in their control—or in that of the electorate to whom they appeal. But McLuhan has been interested in only one kind of machine, the kind that makes possible ever broader and faster mass communication. His interest, that is, begins with Gutenberg's printing press, first means of mass production in the Western world, and continues on to the post-Gutenberg media— radio, television, etc., which have changed the very nature of communication by substituting for the linear messages transmitted by words on the page more primordial images, oral and visual, transmitted by electronic circuitry.

It seems natural that McLuhan's concern be limited to the technology of transmission, since he began and has continued to function as a professor of literature, which is to say, of story and song as reproduced in that elementary teaching machine, the book. Early in his career, he wrote essays on Shakespeare, Gerard Manley Hopkins, and James Joyce, and first attracted wide attention with a long study of certain Southern writers and their tradition. Despite his later objections to a print-oriented culture, his own ideas have continued to come to him from books, and books have always seemed to him the natural mode of expressing his vision of the end of the Age of Gutenberg. There is a certain irony implicit in all this, and, even more perhaps, an implicit tension that tends to divide his head in two, to pit him against himself. These contradictions are further aggravated by the split in him between a prophetic vision that compels him to penetrate the future and a set of political principles that draws him back toward the Medieval past.

A Catholic, a Thomist, and a sympathizer with the Southern Agrarians, McLuhan seems the most improbable of men to have foreseen, and by foreseeing to have helped create, the cultural revolution which threatens much that is dearest to him. At first glance, indeed, it seems a comic error, a bad joke that he has been found so sympathetic by the new mass audience, the youth audience which is profoundly hostile to his religious and political commitments. In the end, however, what Fuller has long been telling us proves to be truer than we can ever quite believe: traditional politics *is* irrelevant to the world in which we live, and it therefore scarcely matters whether one starts as a Right Wing reactionary like McLuhan or an orthodox Stalinist like Norman O. Brown or a Technocrat like Buckminster Fuller. The Future lies at the end of each of these avenues in a shape utterly different from what those entering any of them foresaw. Indeed, one of the things that the prophets of our age have been telling us all along is that the traditional distinctions between Right and Left are no longer viable. Such familiar dichotomies die hard, to be sure, and there continue to be exponents of the New Left and the New New Left, as well as of the New Right and the New New Right, but they so qualify the traditional meanings of the labels to which they cling that such labels serve the purposes of sentiment more than those of definition.

To say what Timothy Leary's politics is, for instance, would be very difficult indeed, since what he advocates is a kind of mystical experience in which the "realities," the actual social conditions on which political positions are based, totally dissolve. His solutions are interior and personal solutions, personal conversions that change the outer world only, or at least primarily, by changing inward consciousness. Yet, like Fuller and McLuhan, Leary, too, began with an interest in technology and a commitment as well to the university—with "real" links to the "real" world. His area of investigation, however, was from the start neither engineering nor the media but pharmacology and psychochemistry—a technology aimed at making the "mystical experience" as broadly available as canned foods or pop art. He is, finally, one of the first prophets of a religion based on technology, a religion that advocates a kind of conversion based not on unaided contemplation or faith, but on a series of changes in the mind induced by the use of chemical compounds, in particular, LSD. And LSD, we remember, was synthesized by no religious devotee or spiritually dedicated monk, but by a white-coated experimenter in a laboratory in Switzerland.

Unlike Fuller and McLuhan, who have been rewarded by their society with degrees, high lecture fees and recognition by the captains of industry themselves, Leary has tended to become more and more of an outcast, even an outlaw. He will probably not, like Reich, end in jail, but the series of punitive sanctions against him which began with his being forced out of the Psychology Department at Harvard University has ended with his being charged and convicted in court of breaking the laws of the land.[1] The actual charges are merely subterfuges, however; what is at stake is the new creed of liberation through drugs that he preaches, and it would, therefore, be immensely satisfying if one could defend Leary without any reservations. He has, however, come to seem a less and less trustworthy apostle of his own cause as the years have gone by; he has, on the one hand, turned into a kind of professional crowd-pleasing evangelist like Billy Graham, and, on the other, his mind seems to have been corroded by his own experiments. Nonetheless, even though his public performances these days are likely to be less than coherent, he remains important as the first distinguished spokesman for a movement that has everywhere triumphed, though not quite along the lines that he foresaw. If we do, in fact, young and old alike, live these days in a drug culture rather than a whiskey culture, it is in part because Leary had the courage to take his vision out of the uncongenial university onto the public platform.

One has a sense that what is disorderly and even mad in the writings of Leary and McLuhan is more accidental than willed. If McLuhan, for instance, sounds sometimes like the body fluids man in *Dr. Strangelove,* this is not because he considers it strategic to do so. Norman O. Brown, on the

---

[1] Since this writing Leary has been jailed and has escaped and gone into exile.

other hand, has deliberately worked toward a style not only more and more mantic, but more and more dissociated and irrational. In his latest book, *Love's Body,* he has carried his war against logic and syntax to a point where he seems to be speaking not merely on behalf of those "out of their minds," but as if he himself were in that blessed state.

Brown began as a conventional enough classicist, writing a scholarly book on Hermes the Trickster; but once he had become liberated enough from doctrinaire Marxism to read Sigmund Freud, his interests became more wide and his approach more and more psychoanalytic. Reich and Marcuse before him had tried to qualify the insights of Marx with those of Freud and vice-versa, but neither had been quite willing to grant that the total synthesis of the two would have to be on a religious and even mystical level. The formulation that best describes the work of Brown is Marx plus Freud plus Jacob Boehme; which is to say, he has two allies rather than one in his war against Freudian theories of sublimation and his campaign to replace the ideal of "full genitality" with that of "polymorphous perverse" sexuality preserved from cradle to grave.

Unlike Fuller, Brown, McLuhan, and Leary, the last three writers with selections included in this group have chosen to make their lives outside of the university in the realm of practical politics. Norman Mailer, to be sure, has attempted to live in two worlds at once, as a novelist, poet, and even on occasion a literary critic, as well as a journalist and an active contender in the political arena. From time to time he remembers that he was properly educated at Harvard and even ventures among the academics to say some reasonably academic things. Most of Mailer's efforts, however, are directed at a larger and more varied audience and fall in the area of agitprop rather than that of the reflective essay. He was closely associated with John F. Kennedy just before and after his election to the Presidency, and has recently run vigorously, if unsuccessfully and even somewhat absurdly, for mayor of New York. Mailer, that is to say, has chosen for himself a kind of engagement very different, not only from that of the academic prophets, but even from the role played by the three immigrant visionaries with whom this group of essays begins.

It is hard to say, perhaps even to know, exactly where Mailer's primary importance lies, and perhaps it is best to think of him as one who has not merely commented on but lived, acted out, the major new movements of our time—in the realm of drugs and sex and radical dissent. His most popular writing at the moment seems to be that in which, with a certain amount of ironical detachment, he describes his own involvement in Left Wing protest movements, as well as those reports in which he brings alive such different spectacles as a boxing match and a major political convention.

Nonetheless, the passage of time seems to indicate that if a single essay of his will survive for its aptness and prophetic insight, it is the essay on "The White Negro," which remains still the most illuminating examination of the movement among the young to really possess the future and create an ethos appropriate to it. Mailer catches only a single moment in the rapidly changing process in the course of which the truly new men of the truly new world have called themselves or have been called by various names: beats, beatniks, hipsters, hippies, longhairs, heads, freaks, etc., etc. Yet the moment he describes seems an ideal one from which to understand both what comes immediately before and immediately after.

Finally, however, Mailer remains in an odd way detached from what he describes, having both feet firmly in the world of an older generation, and only his nose, as it were, poked into that of the newer ones. In his latest writings, one begins to feel that he more and more identifies himself with the fathers of those most at home in the present world rather than with the unruly sons themselves. Eldridge Cleaver and Abbie Hoffman, on the other hand, though no longer kids, are clearly and unequivocally such sons.

Mailer's political commitments, though they have occasionally brought him into head-on conflict with the forces of law and order, have, by and large, enabled him to function inside the establishment. His basic commitment, that is to say, has been with the liberal wing of the Democratic party, and his ideas have come to seem even to the ordinary electorate more eccentric than truly revolutionary. Eldridge Cleaver and Abbie Hoffman, on the other hand, have moved toward more and more extreme dissent, a kind of total opposition not only to things as they are, but to the illusion of possible change within the system; and therefore, the former is, at the moment, an exile from the United States, and the latter is, at the time of this writing, on trial for conspiracy against the city of Chicago and its police.[2]

Nonetheless, Cleaver has some ties with Mailer, and through Mailer, with the whole prophetic modern tradition. His public life may have begun with a jail sentence for a crime neither intellectual nor political; but he was from the start in some sense always an intellectual as well as an activist. His mind, consequently, like that of all the others represented here, has been made largely by books—and what is especially odd in his case, since he is black and committed to the black liberation movement—by white men's books. In the end, like most other prophets, now or ever, he seems curiously traditional as well as radically original. And it is doubtless some deep sense of his roots in the tradition of the white man's world that has helped persuade him to espouse an alliance between white and black revolutionaries rather than the sort of separatist black movement sponsored by such leaders as Stokely Carmichael.

Cleaver is represented here by an essay dealing with the problem of women in our society rather than with a more specifically black issue—in part because there is no greater authority on white females in the United States than black males, and in part because it seems impossible to deal with the cultural revolution without coming to terms with the changing status of women in a time of sexual liberation and the advocacy (by men) of "polymorphous perverse" love. Unfortunately, no woman has emerged on the scene who speaks for the members of her sex with real authority and freshness of vision. Until such a figure appears, the kind of identification of the

[2] Hoffman was convicted of intent to incite to riot and is appealing the verdict.

ethically and sexually oppressed possible to someone in Cleaver's position will have to do.

Youngest of the writers here is Abbie Hoffman, who is in his early thirties, but has already lived a long life in the public eye, beginning with the march on the Pentagon in October 1967 and participation in the Columbia University student demonstrations, and culminating in the founding of the Yippie movement and the protest organized in and around the 1968 Democratic Presidential convention in Chicago. To certain young Americans under twenty or twenty-five, to whom last year's events tend always to appear ancient history, even Abbie Hoffman may already seem an elder statesman, merely the youngest of the elder statesmen represented here. He is, nevertheless, one of the first to have defined the kind of metapolitics appropriate to a time when almost everyone has begun to suspect that traditional politics are as obsolete as Buckminster Fuller long ago suggested.

Abbie Hoffman begins with the conviction that political meetings are bullshit and most political leaders solemn frauds; but this has not kept him from engaging in a kind of activity involving public issues in which the momentary demonstration replaces the long-lived political party, and crowds are led not by buttoned-down, crew-cut gentlemen in well-tailored suits, but by longhaired kids in Halloween costumes. No one understands better than he the sense in which what remains of politics has become theater and the uniform has been replaced by the costume; and no one is better able to manage the kind of language—obscene, jocular, self-mocking—in which such insights can best be expressed. This group of essays appropriately stops with his, since beyond that point, we pass from the future we all now inhabit, which is to say, the present future, into another realm of time for which we do not yet have a mythological name.

THE SPIRIT OF PLACE

D. H. Lawrence

It is natural that we should regard American literature as a small branch or province of English literature. None the less there is another view to be taken. The American art-speech contains a quality that we have not calculated. It has a suggestive force which is not relative to us, not inherent in the English race. This alien quality belongs to the American continent itself.

All art partakes of the Spirit of Place in which it is produced. The provincial Latin literature ferments with a foreign stimulus. It is Africa, and the mysterious religious passion of Libya, which, voicing itself in Latin, utters the infant cry of Tertullian, Augustine, Athanasius, the great saints of the African Church. These are not Romans. They are the prelude to a new era. It is not only that they utter the *ideas* which made Europe. Chiefly in them is felt the first throb of the great mystic passion of mediaeval life. And in Apuleius, decadent and sensuous, we feel the last throb of the old way of sensuality, Babylon, Tyre, Carthage. Africa, seething in Roman veins, produces these strange pulses of new experience, incipient newness within the old decadence.

In the same way America, the new continent, seething in English veins, has produced us the familiar American classics, of Hawthorne, Poe, Whitman, or Fenimore Cooper, for example. We read the English utterance without getting the alien American implication. We listen to our own speech in American mouths, but our ears have been shut to the strange reverberation of that speech. We have not wanted to hear the undertone, the curious foreign, uncouth suggestion, which is in the over-cultured Hawthorne or Poe or Whitman. Augustine and Apuleius are both writers of the Roman decadence. The orthodox Romans, no doubt, saw mainly the decadence, and objected to it. They could not see that the qualities which *they* called decadence, judging from the standards of Virgil and Cicero and Tacitus, were perhaps the incipient realities of a whole new era of experience.

It is time now, for us, who have always looked with indulgence on the decadent or uncouth or provincial American literature, to open new eyes, and look with respect, if not with fear. It is time for us now to see that our great race experience is surpassed and exceeded. Our race *idea* may apparently hold good in the American mind. What we have to realize is that our way of feeling is superseded, just as Cicero's way of feeling was superseded in Apuleius. It is the quality of life-experience, of emotion and passion and desire, which has changed in the Romans of Africa, and in the English-speaking Americans. Life itself takes on a new reality, a new motion, even while the idea remains ostensibly the same.

And it is this change in the way of experience, a change in being, which we should now study in the American books. We have thought and spoken till now in terms of likeness and oneness. Now we must learn to think in terms of difference and otherness. There is a stranger on the face of the earth, and it is no use our trying any further to gull ourselves that he is one of us, and just as we are. There is an unthinkable gulf between us and America, and across the space we see, not our own folk signalling to us, but strangers, incomprehensible beings, simulacra perhaps of ourselves, but *other,* creatures of an other-world. The connection holds good historically, for the past. In the pure present and in futurity it is not valid. The present reality is a reality of untranslatable otherness, parallel to that which lay between St. Augustine and an orthodox senator in Rome of the same day. The oneness is historic only.

The knowledge that we are no longer one, that there is this inconceivable difference in *being* between us, the difference of an epoch, is difficult and painful to acquiesce in. Yet our only hope of freedom lies in acquiescing. The change has taken place in reality. And unless it take place also in our consciousness, we maintain ourselves all the time in a state of confusion. We must get clear of the old oneness that imprisons our real divergence.

It is the genuine American literature which affords the best approach to the knowledge of this othering. Only art-utterance reveals the whole truth of a people. And the American art-speech reveals what the American plain speech almost deliberately conceals. What Hawthorne deliberately says in *The Scarlet Letter* is on the whole a falsification of what he unconsciously says in his art-language. And this, again, is one of the outstanding qualities of American literature: that the deliberate ideas of the man veil, conceal, obscure that which the artist has to reveal. This quality of duplicity which runs through so much of the art of the modern world is almost inevitable in an American book. The author is unconscious of it himself. He is sincere in his own intention. And yet, all the time, the artist, who writes as a somnambulist, in the spell of pure truth as in a dream, is contravened and contradicted by the wakeful man and moralist who sits at the desk.

The occultists say that once there was a universal mystic language, known to the initiated, or to the adept, or to the priesthood of the whole world, whether Chinese or Atlantean or Maya or Druid—a language that was universal over the globe at some period, perhaps before the Flood. This must have been a written rather than a spoken language, and must have consisted in symbols or ideographs. It is conceivable, perhaps even probable, that at one time the priesthoods of all the world—Asiatic, African, European, American, Polynesian—held some common idea of the creation of the Cosmic universe, and expressed this idea in the same symbols or graphs. It is quite easy to conceive that the circle should be a universal symbol for the All, and the rosy cross, and the ankh, the Egyptian so-called symbol of life, may have been used by all the wise men on the earth to express certain cosmological ideas. And it may be possible, as the scientists of the subtler psychic activities desire and need to do, to discover a universal system of symbology: for practically the whole of psychometry and psycho-analysis depends on the understanding of symbols.

But art-speech, art-utterance, is, and always will be, the greatest universal language of mankind, greater than any esoteric symbolism. Art-speech is also a language of pure symbols. But whereas the authorized symbol stands always for a thought or an idea, some mental *concept,* the art-symbol or art-term stands for a pure experience, emotional and passional, spiritual and perceptual, all at once. The intellectual idea remains implicit, latent and nascent. Art communicates a state of being—whereas the symbol at best only communicates a whole thought, an emotional idea. Art-speech is a use of symbols which are pulsations on the blood and seizures upon the nerves, and at the same time pure percepts of the mind and pure terms of spiritual aspiration.

Therefore, when we reduce and diminish any work of art to its didactic capacity—as we reduce a man to his mere physical-functional capacity in the science of medicine—then we find that that work of art is a subtle and complex *idea* expressed in symbols. It is more or less necessary to view man as a thing of various functions and organs. And in the same way, for certain purposes, it is necessary to degrade a work of art into a thing of meanings and reasoned exposition. This process of reduction is part of the science of criticism.

But before we can undertake to criticize American books, to discover their symbolic meaning, we must first trace the development of the orthodox European idea on American soil; because there is always a dual import in these works of art: first, the didactic import given by the author from his own moral consciousness; and then the profound symbolic import which proceeds from his unconscious or subconscious soul, as he works in a state of creation which is something like somnambulism or dreaming. Also we must wake and sharpen in ourselves the subtle faculty for perceiving the greater inhuman forces that control us. It is our fatal limitation, at the present time, that we can only understand in terms of personal and conscious choice. We cannot see that great motions carry us and bring us to our place before we can even begin to know. We cannot see that invisible great winds carry us unwitting, as they carry the locust swarms, and direct us before our knowledge, as they direct the migrating birds.

We ask ourselves, How was it that America became peopled by white men at all? How, in the first place, did Europeans ever get across the great blank ocean? The Greeks and Romans turned their backs on space, and kept their breasts landwards as if magnetized. How was it, then, that fifteenth-century Europe looked spacewards? Was it just the attraction of space? Or was it that Spanish and Venetian sailors were determined to fill in the great blank on the Atlantic Ocean which confronted them?

It was something more positive. Every people is polarized in some particular locality, some home or homeland. And every great era of civilization seems to be the expression of a particular continent or continent region, as well as of the people concerned. There is, no doubt, some peculiar potentiality attaching to every distinct region of the earth's surface, over and above the indisputable facts of climate and geological condition. There is some subtle magnetic or vital influence inherent in every specific locality, and it is this influence which keeps the inhabitant stable. Thus race is ultimately as much a question of place as of heredity. It is the island of Great Britain which has really determined the English race, the genius of Place has made us one people. The place attracts its own human element, and the race drifts inevitably to its own psychic geographical pole.

We see this in Roman history. We see the city of Rome gradually losing its psychic-magnetic polarity, the Roman individuals gradually loosed from the old stay, and drifting like particles absolved from the original influence, falling imperceptibly into two currents—one setting northwards towards Milan and Gaul, one setting east towards Constantinople and Asia. Africa had always been connected with Rome herself—Rome and Carthage were the positive and negative poles of a stable, vital current, as were Athens and Sardis or Ecbatana.

After the removal of the Empire to the east a new circuit began, the circuit of Rome and Treves, or, better, of Italy and Germany. There is, and has been, since the break of the old Roman-African circuit, a natural and inevitable balance between Rome and Germany.

England, France, and even Spain lay within the great German-Italian circuit of vital magnetism, which subsisted all through the Middle Ages. We can see Spain caught in another influence, from Africa again, and Germany influenced from the great Slavonic field. But the main polarity of Europe, from the time of Diocletian to the Renaissance, lay between Italy and Germany.

About the time of the Renaissance, however, this circuit exhausted itself, as the Italian-African circuit had been exhausted a thousand years before. Italy suddenly scintillated, and was finished in her polar potentiality. The old stability of Europe was gone, the old circle of vital flow was broken. It was then that Europe fell directly into polar unison with America. Europe and America became the great poles of negative and positive vitalism.

And it was on the wings of this new attraction that Europe discovered America. When the great magnetic sway of the mediaeval polarity broke, then those units which were liberated fell under the sway of new vital currents in the air, and they were borne helplessly as birds migrate, without knowing or willing, down the great magnetic wind towards America, towards the centrality in the New World. So the first individuals were caught up and swept overseas in the setting of the great current. They had no choice, because the influence which was upon them was prior to all knowledge and all option.

Some races of Europe, moreover, seem never to have been included in the great Latin-Germanic circuit of cultural vitalism. Among these are the Iberian and the Celtic. The strange early flowering of Celtic Christianity would be found, on examination, to be quite apart from the whole Italian-Germanic Christianity which has prevailed in Europe. Its first principle was individualistic, separatist, almost anti-social, a recoil of the individual into mystic isolation, quite the contrary of the European religious principle, which was the fusing into a whole.

And these separate races located themselves on the sea-board, under the influence of the Atlantic Ocean; Spain, Ireland, Scotland, England, Brittany, these have lain from the beginning under the spell of the great western sea. And the people of Spain, dissociated from the circle of Italian-German culture, felt most distinctly the pull of the American magnetism. And they answered the pull as the needle answers the pull of the magnetic north. Spain moved across-seas in one great blind impulse, which was not primarily a desire for wealth. Desire for wealth never shifted a nation which was attached to its home, or vital in its own home-life.

If we are to understand the Celtic and Iberian races at all, we must realize that they have always remained outside of the European circuit of life—that they have always been excluded and subjected, never incorporated; and that their principle has been one of mystic opposition, even hatred, of the civilizing principle of the rest of Europe. These races have remained true to some principle which was contained in the African and the Druid realities, but which has had no place in the European Christian-social scheme. Therefore they placed themselves in a polarity with the great invisible force of America, they looked to their positive pole into the west, the land of the setting sun, over the great sea to the unknown America. Their heaven was the land under the western wave, the Celtic Tir na Og.

They knew of no America. And yet, in the most immediate sense, they knew America. They existed in the spell of the vital magnetism of the unknown continent. The same is more or less true of Spain and of Scandinavia. These great sea-board countries are inevitably controlled by the pull of America. It is inevitable that the Vikings should sail to Greenland and Labrador.

This unconscious reaction to the vital magnetism of the far-off unknown world is perhaps sufficient to have given rise to the Atlantis myth. If it gave rise to the land of Tir na Og, which lies under the western wave, why not to Atlantis? If the great magnetic pole of the Celtic and Iberian psyche was away in the west, would it not follow that, as in a dream, the myth should interpret the unconscious experience? The same would be true of the Norse myths—their polarity is westwards, towards America.

It follows, also, that if the Atlantic sea-board of Europe lies under the spell of the far-off American vital magnetism, the Atlantic sea-board of America must lie under the spell of Europe. And so, when Cortes lands in Mexico, he finds the subtle and pathetic Montezuma, the priest-emperor, who receives him with mystic sympathy, mystic desire. In America a similar break in the circuit of vitalism, a similar shifting of the great mystic-magnetic polarity must have taken place, in the fifteenth century, as it took place in Europe. And as Europe fell under the spell of America, America fell under the spell of Europe. So Montezuma embraced the Spanish as the fulfilment of the legend of the white, bearded strangers, who would come as gods across the east. Legend is supposed to be race-memory. But surely it is just as likely to be a kind of race-clairvoyance. Montezuma, a priest, a decadent and sensitive character, was filled with mystic apprehension. The Aztecs, subject to the fine vibrations in the ether, given off by vital Europe, highly religious and mystical in their natures, only expressed in their legend of the coming of the white stranger that which their innermost, sensitized souls knew beforehand as a fact. If we can understand the sending of wireless messages from continent to continent, can we not much more readily understand that the unthinkably sensitive substance of the human intelligence could receive the fine waves of vital effluence transmitted across the intervening space, could receive, and, as in a dream, plainly comprehend? It was not even in symbols that the Aztecs knew the future; but in plain, direct prescience. They knew the white, bearded strangers hundreds of years before they could see them. And they knew so perfectly because, in their semi-barbaric state, their consciousness was fluid, not mechanically fixed, and the rarest impressions upon the physical soul, from the invisible ether, could pass on occasionally into uninterrupted consciousness.

Prophecy, the mystery of prophecy, is no absurdity. It is no more absurd than the sending of a wireless message. A people, or an individual, need only most delicately submit to the message which is being received all the time upon its own finest tissue, and it will be able to prophesy. But it is easier for us to invent sensitive machines than to avail ourselves of our own extreme and marvelous sensibilities.

We may see, then, how Spain was called across the Atlantic, in the spell of the positive magnetism of the great western continent. And we may understand better the departure of the Pilgrim Fathers. It is not enough, it is never enough, upon an important occasion to accept the plausible explanation offered by the protagonist. The protagonist will always assert that he moves of his own intention. The Pilgrim Fathers sailed off in an enthusiastic, stern vigor of desire for religious freedom. They sailed to find freedom of worship—so they say. But it is a palpable fiction. Because at once they instigated the most cruel religious tyranny in America, equivalent to the Spanish-American Inquisition. Nay, it even seems as if the impulse to religious cruelty *came* to the Spaniards from America, and was exercised secondarily by them in Europe.

The Pilgrim Fathers did not sail to America in search of religious freedom. The Pilgrim Fathers, if they had wanted this freedom, would have stayed and fought for it, with Cromwell. Religious liberty was with them a phrase that covered complex motives. For the deepest human soul all the while offers specious reasons for her own movement, covering beyond all knowledge the true motive. The Pilgrim Fathers sternly believed themselves that they sailed in search of purer Christian worship and the liberty to that worship. It was the innermost soul offering a sufficient pretext to their stubborn, self-righteous minds.

For, if we consider the early American colonies, the Pilgrim Fathers were not Christians at all—not in any reasonable sense of the word. They were no more Christians than the dark and violent Spaniards of the Inquisition were Christian. At the close of the fifteenth century Spain fell back from Christian Europe and became a thing apart. In the same way the first Americans departed from the Christian and the European vital mystery. They became dark, sinister, repellent. They seemed to seek, not liberty, but a gloomy and tyrannical sense of power. They wanted to have power over all immediate life. They had a gloomy passion, similar to that of some of the African sects of the Early Christian Church, to destroy or mutilate life at its very quick, lusting in their dark power to annihilate all living impulses, both their own and those of their neighbor. For all of which the Christian religion served as a word, a weapon, an instrument: the instrument of their dark lust for power over the immediate life itself, as it stirred to motion in the breasts and bowels of the living.

This lust is latent in all religious passion. So long as a people is living and generous, it fulfils its religious passion in setting free the deep desires which are latent in all human souls. Bernard of Clairvaux, St. Francis of Assisi, Martin Luther, these were liberators. They made it possible for every man to be more himself, more whole, more full and spontaneous than ever man had been before.

But into Puritanism and Calvinism had already entered the dangerous *negative* religious passion of repression, this passion which so easily becomes a lust, a deep lust for vindictive power over the life-issue. It was on the hard recoil of this destructive religious passion that the Pilgrim Fathers left Europe. America, dark, violent, aboriginal, would lend them force to satisfy their lust of anti-life.

It is absolutely necessary to realize once and for all that every enthusiasm, every passion, has a dual motion: first a motion of liberation, of setting free; and secondly a motion of vindictive repression of the living impulse, the utter subjection of the living, spontaneous being to the fixed, mechanical, ultimately insane *will*.

When at the Renaissance the great religious impulse of Europe broke, these two motions became separate. We see the Calvinists, the Puritans, the Spaniards of the Inquisition, all filled with a wild lust for cruelty, the lust for the power to torture, to dominate and destroy the mysterious body of life. It is the will of man rising frenzied against the mystery of life itself, and struggling insanely to *dominate,* to have the life-issue in unutterable control, to squeeze the mystic thing, life, within the violent hands of possession, grasp it, squeeze it, have it, have unspeakable power over it.

Whereas, if we have one spark of sanity, we know that we can never possess and direct the life-mystery. The utmost of our power is to possess and destroy. The life-mystery precedes us. Our simplest spontaneous movement *precedes* all knowing and willing. Secondly, and afterwards, we are conscious, we have voluntary control. Our knowing is always secondary and subsequent to our being, which is an issue of the creative unknown. And our volition is always subsidiary to our spontaneous arrival.

But there lies latent in the soul of man, at all times, the desire to reverse this order. In every man lies latent the passion to control and compel the issue of creation, by force of the self-conscious will. We have a latent craving to control from our deliberate will the very springing and welling-up of the life-impulse itself. This craving, once admitted, becomes a lust. This lust, once established and dominant, carries mankind to unthinkable lengths in the frenzied, insane purpose of having the life-issue utterly under human compulsion.

The Jews of old became established in this lust: hence their endless purifications, their assertion of control over the natural functions; hence also the rite of circumcision, the setting of the seal of self-conscious will upon the very quick of bodily impulse. The frenzied, self-mutilating Christians, the fakir-like saints, such as St. Simeon Stylites, the St. Anthony frenzied in celibacy, these men do but assert the utter tyranny of deliberate will over every spontaneous, uncontrollable motion. There must be a measure of control, that every deep desire may be fulfilled in its own fullness and proportion. But there must never be control for control's sake.

The great field for the lust of control in the modern world is America. Whether we read the history of Spanish America or of English-speaking America, it is the same, a disheartening, painful record of the lusting triumph of the deliberate will. On the one hand, the Spaniards in America, following the Spaniards of the Inquisition, lusted in the overweening sensual desire for repression of freedom in the spiritual self, whereas the North Americans lusted spiritually for utter repression in the sensual or passional self.

The New Englanders, wielding the sword of the spirit backwards, struck down the primal impulsive being in every man, leaving only a mechanical, automatic unit. In so doing they cut and destroyed the living bond between men, the rich passional contact. And for this passional contact gradually was substituted the mechanical bond of purposive utility. The spontaneous passion of social union once destroyed, then it was possible to establish the perfect mechanical concord, the concord of a number of parts to a vast whole, a stupendous productive mechanism. And this, this vast mechanical concord of innumerable machine-parts, each performing its own motion in the intricate complexity of material production, this is the clue to the western democracy.

It has taken more than three hundred years to build this vast living machine. It has taken just as long to produce the modern Mexican, a creature of incomprehensible sensual reactions, barely human any longer.

But North America has proceeded in one line wonderfully. After only two generations in New England the first Yankees noticed that their stock had changed. The sturdy, ruddy, lusty English yeoman had disappeared, the long-jawed, sallow American took his place, with a pale, nervous women-folk such as England has only lately begun to reckon with.

Uprooted from the native soil, planted in strong aboriginal earth, this thing happened to the English stock. The natural impulsive being withered, the deliberate, self-determined being appeared in his place. There was soon no more need to militate directly against the impulsive body. This once dispatched, man could attend to the deliberate perfection in mechanized existence. This is what makes good business men. And in this the American is like the Jew: in that, having conquered and destroyed the instinctive, impulsive being in himself, he is free to be always deliberate, always calculated, rapid, swift, and single in practical execution as a machine. The perfection of machine triumph, of deliberate self-determined motion, is to be found in the Americans and the Jews. Hence the race talent for acting. In other races the impulsive mystery of being interferes with the deliberate intention of the individual. In these not. Only, Americans and Jews suffer from a torturing frictional unease, an incapacity to rest. They must run on, like machines, or go mad. The only difference between a human machine and an iron machine is that the latter can come to an utter state of rest, the former cannot. No living thing can lapse into static inertia, as a machine at rest lapses. And this is where life is indomitable. It will be mechanized, but it will never allow mechanical inertia. Hence the Orestes-like flight of unrest of Americans and Jews.

And yet it cannot be for this alone that the millions have crossed the Ocean. This thing, this mechanical democracy, new and monstrous on the face of the earth, cannot be an end in itself. It is only a vast intervention, a marking-time, a mechanical life-pause. It is the tremendous statement in negation of our European being.

This sheer and monstrous reflection of Europe, Europe in negative reality, reflected to enormity on the American continent, will surely vanish swiftly, like one of the horrifying dreams. This is not the reality of America. It is only the reality of our own negation that the vast aboriginal continent re-flects back at us. There will come an America which we cannot foretell, a new creation on the face of the earth, a world beyond us. The early Chris-tianity produced monstrous growths, monstrous reflections of the world then dying, distorted and made huge by the new spirit. These monstrosities, like enormous horrifying phantoms that men do not care to remember, dis-appeared, leaving the new era to roll slowly on to the European summer. So the mechanical monstrosity of the west will presently disappear.

It was not for this that myriads crossed the seas, magnetically carried like birds in migration, without knowing why or whither, yet conducted along lines of pure magnetic attraction, to a goal. Spaniards, Puritans, Jews, Celts, they went in recoil of negation from Europe. They went in the lust for deliberate control of the living issues: lust for sensual gratification in pride or power or slave-tyranny on the part of the Spaniards and perhaps the Celts; lust for spiritual gratification on the ethical control of all life on the part of Jews and Puritans. But this was not the final motive for departure. This was the negative impulse. The positive is more unsearchable.

They went like birds down the great electric direction of the west, lifted like migrating birds on a magnetic current. They went in subtle vibration of response to the new earth, as animals travel far distances vibrating to the salt-licks.

They walked a new earth, were seized by a new electricity, and laid in line differently. Their bones, their nerves, their sinews took on a new molecular disposition in the new vibration.

They breathed a savage air, and their blood was suffused and burnt. A new fierce salt of the earth, in their mouths, penetrated and altered the substance of their bones. Meat of wild creatures, corn of the aboriginal earth, filled and impregnated them with the unknown America. Their subtlest plasm was changed under the radiation of new skies, new influence of light, their first and rarest life-stuff transmuted.

Thus, through hundreds of years, new races are made, people slowly smelted down and re-cast. There is the slow and terrible process of transubstantiation. Who can tell what will come at the negative crisis of this reduction? What monstrosity? And, much more, who can tell what will come when the new world sets in?

For every great locality has its own pure daimon, and is conveyed at last into perfected life. We have seen Asia, and North Africa, and a good deal of Europe. We know the white abstraction of the Arctic and Antarctic continents, the unspeakable immortality of the ice, where existence is and being is not. There remains America, and, beyond, the even farther-off Australia.

Every great locality expresses itself perfectly, in its own flowers, its own birds and beasts, lastly its own men, with their perfected works. Mountains convey themselves in unutterable expressed perfection in the blue gentian flower and in the edelweiss flower, so soft, yet shaped like snow-crystals. The very strata of the earth come to a point of perfect, unutterable concentration in the inherent sapphires and emeralds. It is so with all worlds and all places of the world. We may take it as a law.

So now we wait for the fulfillment of the law in the west, the inception of a new era of living. At present there is a vast myriad-branched human engine, the very thought of which is death. But in the winter even a tree looks like iron. Seeing the great trunk of dark iron and the swaying steel flails of boughs, we cannot help being afraid. What we see of buds looks like sharp bronze stud-points. The whole thing hums elastic and sinister and fatally metallic, like some confused scourge of swinging steel thongs. Yet the lovely cloud of green and summer luster is within it.

We wait for the miracle, for the new soft wind. Even the buds of iron break into soft little flames of issue. So will people change. So will the machine-parts open like buds and the great machines break into leaf. Even we can expect our iron ships to put forth vine and tendril and bunches of grapes, like the ship of Dionysos in full sail upon the ocean.

It only wants the miracle, the new, soft, creative wind: which does not blow yet. Meanwhile we can only stand and wait, knowing that what is, is not. And we can listen to the sad, weird utterance of this classic America, watch the transmutation from men into machines and ghosts, hear the last metallic sounds. Perhaps we can see as well glimpses of the mystic transubstantiation.

A BIOLOGICAL REVOLUTION
THAT MISCARRIED

Wilhelm Reich

Where are the sources of neurotic plague?

First of all, in the authoritarian, sex-suppressing *family upbringing* with its inevitable sexual child-parent conflict and sexual anxiety. Just because Freud's clinical observations were correct, it was inevitable to draw the consequences which I drew. Furthermore, I had solved a problem which previously had remained obscure: the relationship between the sexual child-parent attachment and the general social suppression of sexuality. The realization that sex repression is a fact characteristic of *education as a whole* made the problem appear in a different light.

It was easy to see that the majority of people became neurotic. The question was rather how people—under present conditions of education—could remain *healthy!* This much more interesting question called for an examination of the relationship between authoritarian family upbringing and sex repression.

Parents—unconsciously at the behest of authoritarian, mechanized society—repress the sexuality of infants and adolescents. Since the children find their way to vital activity blocked by asceticism and in part by unemployment, they develop a sticky kind of parent fixation characterized by helplessness and guilt feelings. This in turn prevents their growing out of the infantile situation with all its sexual anxieties and inhibitions. Children thus brought up become character-neurotic adults and re-create their illness in their own children. And so it goes on from generation to generation. In this way, conservative tradition, a tradition which is afraid of life, is perpetuated. How can humans grow up to be healthy, and remain healthy, in spite of this?

The orgasm theory provided the answer: accidental or socially conditioned circumstances sometimes make possible the attainment of genital gratification; this in turn eliminates the energy source of the neurosis and alleviates the fixation in the infantile situation. Thus there can be healthy individuals in spite of the family situation. The sexual life of the youth of 1940 is, fundamentally, freer than that of the youth of 1900, but it is also more burdened with conflicts. The difference between the healthy and the sick individual is not that the former did not experience the typical family conflicts or sex repression. Rather, a peculiar and, in this society, unusual combination of circumstances, particularly the industrial collectivation of work, makes it possible for him to escape the clutches of both with the aid of a sex-economic way of living. There remains the question as to the later fate of such individuals. Certainly, they do not have an easy life. At any rate, the *"spontaneous organotherapy of the neurosis,"* as I termed the orgastic release of tension, enables them to overcome the pathological family ties as well as the effects of social sex repression. There are human beings of a certain kind, living and working here and there, unobtrusively, who are equipped with *natural* sexuality; they are the *genital characters.* They are found frequently among the industrial workers.

The plague of the neuroses is bred during three principal phases of life: in *early infancy* through the atmosphere of the neurotic parental home; in *puberty;* and finally, in *compulsive marriage* based on strictly moralistic standards.

In the first phase, much harm is done by strict and premature training for excremental cleanliness, and the demand to be "good," to show absolute self-restraint and quiet good behavior. These measures prepare the ground for the most important prohibition of the following period, the *prohibition of masturbation.* Other restrictions of infantile development may vary, but these are typical. The inhibition of infantile sexuality is the basis for the fixation to the parental home and its atmosphere, the "family." This is the origin of the typical lack of independence in thought and action. Psychic mobility and strength go with sexual mobility and cannot exist without it. Conversely, psychic inhibition and awkwardness presupposes sexual inhibition.

In *puberty,* the same harmful educational principle that leads to psychic impoverishment and character armoring is repeated. This repetition takes place on the solid basis of the previously established inhibition of infantile impulses. *The basis of the puberty problem is sociological, not biological.* Nor does it lie in the child-parent conflict, as is assumed by psychoanalysis. For, those adolescents who find their way into a real sexual and working life, outgrow their infantile fixation to their parents. The others, hard hit by the actual sex suppression, are pushed back all the more into the infantile situation. This is the reason why most neuroses and psychoses develop at puberty. Barasch's statistics regarding the relationship of the duration of marriages to the age at which genital sexual life is taken up, confirms the close connection between the demands of abstinence and those of marriage: the earlier an adolescent takes up satisfactory sexual intercourse, the less capable does he become of conforming to the strict demand of "only *one* partner, and that one for life." Whatsoever attitude one may take toward this finding, the fact remains and cannot be denied. It means: the purpose of the demand for sexual abstinence is that of *making the adolescent submissive and capable of marriage.* That it does do. But in doing so it creates the very sexual impotence which in turn destroys marriage and accentuates the problem of marriage.

It is sheer hypocrisy to give a youth the legal right to marry, say, on the eve of his sixteenth birthday, thus inferring that in this case sexual intercourse does *no* harm, if at the same time one demands "continence until marriage," even if such marriage cannot take place until the age of, say, thirty. In the latter case, one finds all of a sudden that "sexual intercourse at an early age is harmful or immoral." No thinking person could tolerate such reasoning any more than he could tolerate the resulting neuroses and perversions. To mitigate the severity with which masturbation is penalized is merely a convenient subterfuge. *What is at stake is the gratification of the physical needs of ripening youth. Puberty signifies coming into sexual maturity,* and primarily nothing else. What esthetic philosophies call "cultural puberty," is, to put it mildly, just so much talk. *Sexual happiness of maturing youth is a central issue in the prevention of the neuroses.*

The function of youth at any given time is that of representing the *next* step of civilization. The parent generation at any given time tries to restrain youth to their own cultural level. Their motives for doing so are predominantly of an irrational nature: they have had to yield, and become irritated when youth reminds them of what they have been unable to achieve. The typical rebellion of adolescent youth against the parental home is, therefore, not a neurotic manifestation of puberty; it is, rather, the preparation for the social function which this youth will have to fulfill as adults. Youth has to *fight* for its capability for progress. Whatever the cultural tasks confronting any new generation may be, the inhibiting factor is always the older generation's fear of youth's sexuality and fighting spirit.

I have been accused of harboring the Utopian idea of a world in which I would eliminate unpleasure and have nothing but pleasure. This is contradicted by my repeated statement that education, as it is, makes the human incapable of pleasure, *by armoring him against unpleasure. Pleasure and joie de vivre are inconceivable without fight, without painful experiences and without unpleasurable struggling with oneself.* Not the Yogies' and Buddhists' theories of Nirvana, not the hedonistic philosophy of Epicurus,[1] not the renunciation of monasticism—are what characterizes psychic health, but the alternation of painful struggle and happiness, of error and truth, of mistake and reflection upon it, of rational hatred and rational love, in brief, full vitality in all possible situations of life. The capacity of tolerating unpleasure and pain without fleeing disillusioned into a state of rigidity goes hand in hand with the capacity to take happiness and to give love. To use Nietzsche's words: he who wants to learn to "jubilate to high heaven" must be prepared to be "dejected unto death." In contrast to this, our European social concepts and education have turned the young—depending on their social position—either into dolls wrapped in cotton wool or into dried-up, chronically morose machines of industry or "business," incapable of pleasure.

---

[1] This term is used here in the sense of everyday parlance. In reality, Epicurus and his school have nothing in common with the so-called "Epicurean philosophy of life" but the name. The earnest natural philosophy of Epicurus was interpreted by the half-educated and uneducated masses of people in a specific way: it came to mean the gratification of the *secondary* impulses. There are no means of defending oneself against such corruption of correct thoughts. Sex-economy is threatened by the same fate at the hands of human beings who suffer from pleasure anxiety and of science which is afraid of the subject of sexuality.

The *problem of marriage* calls for clear thinking. Marriage is neither merely a matter of love, as claimed by some, nor merely an economic institution, as claimed by others. It is the form into which sexual needs were forced by socio-economic processes.[2] Sexual and economic needs, especially on the part of the woman, merge into the desire for marriage, apart from the ideology acquired in early childhood, and the moral pressure of society. Every marriage sickens as a result of an ever increasing conflict between *sexual* and *economic* needs. The sexual needs can be satisfied with one and the same partner only for a limited period of time. Economic dependence, moral demands and habituation, on the other hand, work towards permanence of the relationship. This conflict is the basis of marital misery. *Premarital* continence is supposed to prepare for marriage. But the very same continence creates sexual disturbances and thus undermines marriage. Full sexual capacity can make a marriage happy. But the same capacity is at variance with every aspect of the moralistic demand for a life-long monogamous marriage. This is a fact, and nothing but a fact. Again, we may take whatever attitude we care to toward this. But we should not be hypocritical about it. These contradictions—under unfavorable external and internal circumstances—lead to resignation. This requires far-reaching inhibition of the vegetative impulses. This in turn brings forth all possible neurotic mechanisms. Sexual partnership and human companionship in marriage then become replaced by a child-parent relationship and mutual slavery, in brief, by masked incest. These things have been described so often and are so well known today as almost to be platitudinous; they remain unknown only to a great many clergymen, psychiatrists, social reformers and politicians.

Such inner obstacles to mass mental hygiene, serious enough in themselves, are made far more serious by the *external* social conditions which produce them. Psychic misery is not purposed by the sexual chaos of today: it is rather an inseparable part of it. For, *compulsive marriage and the compulsive family go on re-creating the human structure of this economically and psychically mechanized age.* From the sexual hygiene point of view, simply everything is wrong in this order. Biologically speaking, the healthy human organism calls for three to four thousand sexual acts in the course of a genital life of, say, 30 to 40 years. The wish for offspring is satisfied with two to four children. Moralistic and ascetic ideologies condone sexual pleasure even in marriage only for the purpose of procreation; carried to its logical conclusion, that would mean at the most *four* sexual acts in a life-time. And with such a principle, medical authorities agree; and people suffer in silence, or they cheat on it and become hypocrites. But nobody makes any forceful attempt to do away with such an absurdity. This absurdity expresses itself in the official or moral prohibition of the use of contraceptives or information about them. This results in sexual disturbances and fear of pregnancy, which in turn arouses infantile sexual anxieties and undermines marriage. In an inevitable manner, the elements of the chaos combine in their effect. The prohibition of masturbation encountered in

[2] Cf. L. Morgan, "Ancient Society."

childhood creates a fear of any manipulation of the vagina. Thus, women come to be afraid of using contraceptives, and resort to "criminal abortion," which in turn is a starting point for innumerable neurotic manifestations. Fear of pregnancy precludes satisfaction in both man and woman. About 60 per cent of the adult male population practice withdrawal. This practice produces sexual stasis and nervousness *en masse*.

About all this, science and the medical profession say nothing. More than that, they impede, with evasions, academisms, erroneous theories and direct obstruction, every serious scientific, social or medical attempt to remedy the situation. When one hears all the talk about the "moral necessity" and the "harmlessness" of abstinence and withdrawal, propounded in the most dignified and authoritative manner, one has every reason for indignation. I did not say this in the meeting at Freud's, but the facts themselves did of necessity evoke this feeling of indignation.

Another, largely overlooked problem is the *housing problem*. According to statistics of Vienna in 1927, more than 80 per cent of the population lived four or more in one room. That means, that in over 80 per cent of the population a physiological sexual gratification is impossible, even under the best inner conditions. Neither medicine nor sociology even mention this fact.

Mental and sexual hygiene presuppose a regulated, economically secure existence. An individual who worries about where the next meal is coming from cannot enjoy pleasure and easily becomes a sexual psychopath. That is, if we hope for the prevention of the neuroses, we must count on a radical change in *everything* that causes the neuroses. This is why the question of the prevention of the neuroses never came up for discussion, why it was not even thought of. My statements could not help being provocative, whether I wanted it or not. The facts alone contained a good deal of provocativeness. I did not even mention such legal concepts as "marital duty" or "obedience to parents even to the extent of tolerating being beaten." Mention of such things was not customary in academic circles and was considered "unscientific." Yet, although nobody was inclined to listen to the facts presented, nobody could deny them either. For, everyone knew that individual therapy was socially unimportant, that education was in a hopeless state, and that ideas and lectures about sexual enlightenment were not sufficient. This situation led with inescapable logic to the *problem of culture* in general.

Up to 1929, the relationship of psychoanalysis and "culture" had not been discussed. Not only did the psychoanalysts see no contradiction between the two, but, quite generally, they considered Freud's theory to be "promoting culture" and not at all as critical of it. Between 1905 and 1925, the opponents of psychoanalysis had continually pointed to the "cultural danger" which was to be expected from psychoanalysis. The opponents and a listening world had imputed to psychoanalytic theory more than psychoanalysis had intended. This was due to the deep need felt by everybody for clarity in sexual matters, and to the fear of sexual chaos felt by the "bearers of culture." Freud believed that his theory of sublimation and renunciation of the instinct had abolished the danger. Gradually, the rumblings subsided, particularly with the flourishing of the theory of the death instinct and after the repudiation of the theory of stasis anxiety. The theory of a biological will to suffer saved embarrassment. These theories proved that psychoanalysis was not in conflict with culture. This equanimity was now threatened by my publications. In order not to be compromised by them, one called my views either "old stuff," or erroneous. But I had not made things easy for myself by any means. I had not simply come out with the contention that psychoanalysis was at variance with culture, and that it was "revolutionary." Things were much more complicated than many think today.

My views could not simply be disregarded. More and more clinicians were working with the genital theory of therapy. These views could not be denied either, only minimized at best. They confirmed the revolutionary character of a scientific theory of sex. Had it not been proclaimed that Freud had opened a new cultural era? But neither could they be openly concurred in. That would have conflicted with the material security of the psychoanalysts as well as with their contention that psychoanalysis was *only* "promoting culture." *Nobody asked what it was in this "culture" that was being promoted and what it was that was being endangered.* It was overlooked that, by its very development, that which is "new" criticizes and negates that which is old.

The leading circles in social science in Austria and Germany rejected psychoanalysis and tried to compete with it in the attempt to understand human nature. It was far from easy to find the right way through this difficulty. It is surprising how I was able to keep from making some really big blunders at that time. The temptation was great to take some short-cut, to make some compromise, to try to find a quick practical solution. One might have said, for example, that sociology and psychoanalysis could be united without any difficulty; or, that psychoanalysis, though correct as a psychology of the individual, was culturally unimportant. This is, in fact, what was said by Marxists with psychoanalytic leanings. But that was no solution. I was too much of a psychoanalyst to be superficial, and too much interested in a development of the world toward freedom to be content with a banal answer. For the moment I was content with having been able to coordinate psychoanalysis and sociology, even if only methodologically for the time being.[3] My friends' and enemies' unceasing accusations that I was jumping to conclusions did not disquiet me, though they often annoyed me. I knew that none of them was making as much of a theoretical or practical effort, and my finished manuscripts were kept in the desk drawer for years before I would decide to publish them. I was willing to leave being "smart" to others.

The relationship of psychoanalysis and culture began to clarify itself when a young psychiatrist read a paper on *"Psychoanalyse und Weltanschauung"* at Freud's. Only a very few know that Freud's *"Unbehagen in der Kultur"* originated from these discussions on culture, which took place in order to refute my maturing work and the "danger" which was supposed

[3] Cf. Wilhelm Reich, Dialektischer Materialismus und Psychoanalyse, 1929.

to arise from it. The book contains sentences which Freud used in our discussion to oppose my views.

In this book, which did not appear until 1931, Freud, though acknowledging natural sexual pleasure to be the goal of human striving, at the same time attempted to demonstrate the untenability of this principle. His theoretical and practical basic formula was always: The human—normally and of necessity—progresses from the "pleasure principle" to the "reality principle." *He must renounce pleasure and adjust himself.* Freud neither questioned the irrational in this "reality," nor did he ask *which kind of pleasure is compatible with sociality and which kind is not.* Today I consider it a fortunate thing for real mental hygiene that this problem was brought to light. It made for clarity and made it impossible to consider psychoanalysis any longer a force for reshaping culture, without a *practical criticism* of the conditions of education and without any attempt to *change* them. Otherwise, what is the meaning of that often abused word "progress"?

The following concept corresponded to the academic attitude at that time. Science, they said, has to do with problems of what *is,* social pragmatism with problems of what *should be.* "What is" (*science*) and "what should be" (*social pragmatism*) are two different things which have no common ground. The finding of a fact does not involve a "should be," that is, the indication of a goal which should be striven toward. With a scientific finding, every ideological or political group could do what it pleased. I took issue with these ethical logicians who took refuge from reality in an abstract formula. If I find that an adolescent is made neurotic and incapable of work by the sexual abstinence which is demanded of him, that is "science." From the point of view of "abstract logic," one may conclude that he should continue to live in abstinence, as well as that he should give it up. Such a conclusion is "Weltanschauung" and its realization social pragmatism. But, I said, *there are scientific findings from which, in practice, only one thing follows, and never the other.* What is logically correct may be practically wrong. If today somebody would come out with the finding that abstinence is harmful to the adolescent, without drawing the conclusion that abstinence should be given up, he would be simply laughed at. This is why it is so important to formulate problems in terms of practice. A physician cannot allow himself to take an abstract point of view. Whoever refuses to draw the practical conclusions from the above finding must of necessity make erroneous statements of a "purely scientific" nature. He will have to contend with "scientific authority" that abstinence is *not* harmful to the adolescent; in short, he will have to camouflage the truth and play the hypocrite, in order to defend his demand for abstinence. *Every scientific finding has a basis in Weltanschauung and a practical consequence in social life.*

For the first time, I saw clearly the abyss between abstract logical thinking and functional thinking in terms of natural science. Abstract logic has often the function of admitting scientific facts without letting them have any practical consequences. Thus, practical functionalism, which postulates unity of theory and practice, appealed more to me.

Freud's point of view was this: the attitude of the average man toward religion is understandable. A famous poet once said,

> Wer Wissenschaft und Kunst besitzt,
> *hat* auch Religion,
> Wer jene beiden nicht besitzt,
> der *habe* Religion! [4]

The statement is correct for our times, like everything that is contended by a conservative ideology. The right of the conservatives is identical with the right to attack it with scientific and medical knowledge so deeply that the source of conservative arrogance, ignorance, is destroyed. The fact that the question is unanswered as to the pathological spirit of toleration on the part of the working multitudes, as to their pathological renunciation of the knowledge and the cultural fruits of this world of "science and art," as to their helplessness, fear of responsibility and their craving for authority— the fact that this question is unanswered is bringing the world towards an abyss in the form of the pestilence of Fascism. What is the sense of science anyhow, if it taboos such questions? What kind of a conscience can a scientist have who is, or might be, able to work out an answer and who wilfully fails to fight against this psychic plague? Today, in the face of danger to life, that becomes clear to all the world which twelve years ago could scarcely be mentioned. Social life has placed in sharp focus problems which at that time were considered to be merely the concern of individual physicians.

Freud was able to justify the renunciation of happiness on the part of humanity as splendidly as he had defended the fact of infantile sexuality. A few years later, a pathological genius—making the best of human ignorance and fear of happiness—brought Europe to the verge of destruction *with the slogan of "heroic renunciation."*

"Life as it is imposed on us," writes Freud, "is too hard for us, too full of pain, disillusionments and impossible tasks. In order to bear it, we cannot do without palliatives. . . . There are perhaps three of these; powerful diversions of interest which make us think little of our own misery; substitute gratifications which lessen it; and narcotics which make us insensitive to it. Something of this kind is indispensable."

At the same time (in *"Die Zukunft einer Illusion"*) Freud rejected the most dangerous of the illusions, religion.

The ordinary man cannot imagine this Providence otherwise than in the person of a greatly exalted father. Only such a one could understand man's needs, could be softened by his prayers and placated by the signs of his remorse. The whole thing

He who has Science and has Art, Religion, too, has he;
Who has not Science, has not Art, Let him religious be!
(From the translation of *"Das Unbehagen in der Kultur"* by Joan Riviere).

is so obviously infantile, so incongruous wtih reality that to one whose attitude to humanity is friendly it is painful to think that the great majority of mortals will never be able to rise above this view of life.

Thus, Freud's correct findings concerning religious mysticism ended in resignation. And on the outside, life was seething with the struggle for *a rational Weltanschauung and a scientifically regulated social order*. In principle, there was no disagreement. Freud did not declare himself as having no Weltanschauung. He refuted the pragmatic Weltanschauung in favor of the scientific. He felt himself in opposition to social pragmatism as represented by the European political parties. I tried to show that the striving for a democratization of the work process is and must be *scientifically rational*. At that time, the destruction of Lenin's social democracy and the development of dictatorship in the Soviet Union, and the relinquishing of all principles of truth in sociological thinking had already begun. There was no denying that. I rejected the unpragmatic standpoint of Freud which evaded the social consequences of scientific discoveries. I had only a faint inkling of the fact that Freud's point of view as well as the dogmatic attitude of the Soviet government, each in its own way, had their good reasons: *Scientific, rational regulation of humanity is the supreme goal. However, the acquired irrational structure of the masses of people, that is, those who participate in the making of history, makes dictatorship through utilization of the irrational possible.* It depends on *who* exerts power, to what *purpose,* and *against what*. At any rate, the original social democracy in Russia was at the outset the most human solution possible under existing conditions of history and human structure. That, Freud had explicitly admitted. The degeneration of Lenin's social democracy into the dictatorial Stalinism of today is an undeniable fact and is grist in the mill of the opponents of democracy. Freud's pessimism seemed to be cruelly justified during the ensuing years: "there is nothing that can be done." After what had happened in Russia, the development of true democracy appeared to be a Utopia. It really looked now as if "he who does not have art and science, had better have" the "socialist religion" to which an enormous world of scientific thought had degenerated. The fact has to be stressed that Freud's attitude was only an expression of the general fundamental attitude of academic scientists: they had no confidence in democratic self-education and the intellectual productivity of the masses of people; for that reason, they did nothing to stem the tide of dictatorship.

Ever since the beginning of my activity in the field of sexual hygiene I had been convinced that cultural happiness in general and sexual happiness in particular are the very content of life and should be the goal of practical social endeavor. I was contradicted on all sides, but my findings were more important than all objections and difficulties. The whole of literature, from the dime novel to the best of poetry, proved me correct. All cultural interest (movies, the novel, poetry, etc.) revolves around sexuality, thrives on the affirmation of the ideal and the negation of the actual. Cosmetic industries, fashion trades and business advertising make their living by this. If all humanity dreams and writes of happiness in love, why could not this dream of life be realized? The goal was clear. The facts found in the biological depths called for medical action. Why did the striving for happiness continue to remain a phantastic something, at war with hard reality? Freud gave up hope, in the following manner.

What does human behavior itself disclose as the goal of life? What do humans expect of life, what do they want to get out of it? Such were the questions in Freud's mind in 1930 after those discussions which had brought the sexual demands of the masses right into the scientist's peaceful study and had brought about a sharp clash of opinions.

Freud had to admit: *"The answer can hardly be missed. They strive for happiness; they want to become happy and remain so."* They want to experience strong sensations of pleasure. It is simply the pleasure principle which sets up the goal of life. This principle governs the operation of the psychic apparatus from the very beginning.

There can be no doubt about its purpose, and yet its program is in conflict with the whole world, with the macrocosm as well as with the microcosm. It simply cannot be put into execution; the whole constitution of things runs counter to it. One might say that the intention that man should be "happy" is not included in the scheme of "Creation." What is called happiness in its narrowest sense comes from the gratification—most often instantaneous—of highly pent-up needs, and by its very nature can only be a transitory experience.

In saying so, Freud expressed a feeling which is part of the human *incapacity* for happiness. The argument sounds well, but it is erroneous. According to this argument, it would seem as if asceticism were a necessary prerequisite for happiness. In so arguing, the fact is overlooked that the damming-up of a need is itself experienced as pleasure, *provided it has a prospect of gratification and does not last too long.* Also the fact that this damming-up makes the organism rigid and incapable of pleasure if this prospect does not exist or if pleasure is constantly threatened with punishment. The supreme experience of happiness, the sexual orgasm, characteristically presupposes a damming-up of energy. From that, one cannot draw Freud's conclusion that the pleasure principle "simply cannot be put into execution." Today I have experimental proof of the incorrectness of this contention. At that time I only felt that Freud was hiding a reality behind a phrase. To admit the possibility of human happiness would have meant scrapping the theories of the repetition-compulsion and of the death instinct. It would have meant a criticism of the social institutions which destroy happiness in life. To maintain his position of resignation, Freud adduced arguments which he borrowed from the existing situation, without asking, however, whether this situation was of its nature inevitable and unchangeable. I could not see how Freud could believe that the discovery of infantile sexuality could have no effect whatsoever in bringing about changes in the world. He seemed to be doing a cruel injustice to his own work, and to feel the tragedy of this contradiction. For, when I set forth my arguments against him, he said that I was either totally wrong or "I would have one day to carry the heavy lot of psychoanalysis all alone." Since I was not wrong, his prophecy proved correct.

Freud, in the discussion as well as in his book, escaped into the theory of biological *suffering*. He was looking for a way out of the cultural catastrophe in an "effort of the Eros." In a private conversation in 1926, Freud had expressed the hope that the revolutionary "experiment" in Soviet Russia might succeed. Nobody had as yet any idea of the catastrophic failure of Lenin's attempt for a social democracy. Freud knew, and he said so in writing, that humanity is sick. The connection between this general illness and the catastrophe that took place in Russia and later in Germany was as alien to the thinking of the psychiatrist as to that of the statesman or political scientist. Three years later, conditions in Germany and Austria were already so disturbed as to affect any professional activity. Irrationalism in political life became plainly evident; analytical psychology penetrated more and more into sociological problems. In my work, "man" as patient and "man" as social being merged more and more into one. I saw that neurotic and hungry masses were falling prey to political pirates. Freud, in spite of his knowledge of the psychic plague, was afraid of the inclusion of psychoanalysis in the political chaos. His conflict made him seem all the more human to me, for it was so intense. Today I also understand the necessity of his resignation. For fifteen years, he had been fighting for the recognition of simple facts. The world of his colleagues had besmeared him, called him a charlatan, had even called the sincerity of his motives into question. He was not a social pragmatist, only a "pure scientist," but as such strict and honest. The world could no longer deny the facts of unconscious psychic life. So it began anew its old accustomed game of debasing what it cannot otherwise destroy. It gave him a great many pupils, who came to a table all set for them and who did not have to work hard for what they got. They had only *one* interest: to make psychoanalysis socially acceptable as quickly as possible. They carried the conservative traditions of this world into their organization, and without an organization, Freud's work could not exist. One after the other, they sacrificed the libido theory or diluted it. Freud knew how difficult it is to continue to advocate the libido theory. But the interest of self-preservation and of safeguarding the psychoanalytic movement prevented him from saying what in a more honest world he certainly would have fought for. He had with his science far transcended the narrow intellectual horizon of his contemporaries. His school pulled him back into it. He knew in 1929 that in my youthful scientific enthusiasm I was right. But to admit this would have meant to sacrifice half of the organization.

That psychic disturbances are the result of sexual repression was an established fact. Analytic pedagogy and therapy attempted to eliminate the repression of the sexual instincts. *What happens,* was the question, *to the instincts once they are liberated from repression?* The answer of psychoanalysis was: the instincts are *rejected* or *sublimated*. Of actual satisfaction there was no mention; there could not be, because the unconscious was thought of as the inferno of antisocial and perverse impulses alone.

For a long time, I tried to obtain an answer to the question as to *what happens to the natural genitality of children and adolescents after it is liberated from repression.* Should it, too, be "rejected or sublimated"? It was never answered by the psychoanalysts. And yet, it constitutes the central problem of character formation.

The whole process of education suffers from the fact that social adjustment demands repression of natural sexuality, and that this repression makes people ill and antisocial. What had to be questioned, therefore, was whether the demands of education were justified. They were based on a fundamental misconception of sexuality.

Freud's great tragedy was that he escaped into biologistic theories; he might have kept silent or let people do as they pleased. And so he came to contradict himself:

Happiness, he said, is an illusion; for, suffering threatens inexorably from three sides. "From one's *own body* which is destined to disintegration and decay." *Why then,* one must ask, *does science keep dreaming of the prolongation of life?* "From the *outer world* which is capable of attacking us with overpowering inexorable destructive forces." *Why then,* one must ask, *did great thinkers spend their lives thinking about liberty? Why then, did millions of fighters for liberty shed their blood in the struggle against this threatening outer world?* Had not pestilence been finally vanquished? And had not physical and social slavery been at least diminished? Should it not be possible to vanquish the disease of cancer? Or possible to vanquish wars as it had been possible to vanquish pestilence? Should it never be possible to vanquish the moralistic hypocrisy which makes cripples out of our children and adolescents?

More serious and difficult was the *third* argument against the human longing for happiness: the suffering which springs from relations with other people, said Freud, is more painful than any other. One might be inclined to consider it as some superficial and accidental intrusion, but at the same time it is no less fatefully inescapable than the suffering from other sources. Here spoke Freud's own bitter experiences with the human species. Here he touched upon our problem of structure, in other words, the irrationalism which determines people's behavior. Some of this I had come to feel painfully in the psychoanalytic society; an organization the very task of which consisted in the medical mastery of irrational behavior. Now Freud said that this was fateful and inescapable.

But how? Why then did one assume the lofty viewpoint of rational science? Why then did one proclaim the education of the human towards rational, realistic behavior? For a reason which I could not understand, Freud did not see the contradiction in his attitude. On the one hand, he had—correctly —reduced human thinking and behavior to unconscious irrational motives. On the other hand, there could exist for him a Weltanschauung in which the very law he had found should *not* be valid. A science beyond its own principles! Freud's resignation was nothing but a shunning of the gigantic difficulties presented by the pathological in human behavior, the malicious. *He was disillusioned.* Originally he believed that he had discovered the radical therapy of the neuroses. In reality, he had made no more than a beginning. Things were much more complicated than the formula of the making conscious of the unconscious would lead one to believe. He had claimed that psychoanalysis could comprehend general problems of human existence, not merely medical problems. But he did not find his way into sociology. In *"Jenseits des Lustprinzips"* he had touched upon important biological questions in a hypothetical way, and thus arrived at the theory of the death instinct. It proved a misleading theory. Freud himself viewed it very skeptically at first. But the psychologizing of sociology as well as of biology took away every prospect for a practical solution of these enormous problems.

In addition, Freud had, in his practice as well as from their reactions to his teachings, come to know his fellow humans as highly unreliable, malicious beings. For decades he had now been living in seclusion from the world, for the protection of his own peace of mind. Had he entered upon all the irrational objections that were raised, he would have lost himself in petty destructive struggles. In order to seclude himself, he needed a skeptical attitude toward human "values"; more than that, a certain contempt for the human of his day. Knowledge came to mean more to him than human happiness. This all the more as the humans did not seem able to manage their happiness if ever it presented itself. This attitude corresponded completely to the academic superiority of the time, and had its substantiation in facts. But it did not seem admissible to judge general problems of human existence from the point of view of a scientific pioneer.

Although I understood Freud's motives, two important facts kept me from following him here. One was the steadily increasing demand on the part of uneducated, mistreated, psychically ruined people for a revision of the social order in terms of earthly happiness. Not to see this, or to fail to take it into account, would have been a ridiculous ostrich policy. I had come to know this mass awakening too well to be able to deny it or to underestimate it as a social force. Freud's motives were correct. But so were those of the awakening masses of people. To disregard them meant inescapably to take the side of the non-working parasites of society.

The other fact was that I had learned to see people *in two ways*. They were often corrupt, incapable of thinking, faithless, full of meaningless slogans, treacherous, or simply empty. *But that was not natural. They had been made that way by the existing conditions of life.* In principle, then, they could also be made *different:* decent, straightforward, capable of love, sociable, cooperative, truly and without compulsion social. More and more I had to realize that what is called "bad" or "antisocial" is really neurotic. For example, a child plays in a natural fashion. The environment puts on the brakes. At first the child fights back, then it succumbs; it loses its capacity for pleasure while keeping up the fight against the inhibition of pleasure in the form of pathological, aimless, irrational spite reactions. In the same way, human behavior in general was only a reflection of the affirmation and the negation of life in the social process. Was it conceivable that the conflict between the striving for pleasure and its social frustration could some day be solved? Psychoanalytic investigation of sexuality seemed to be the first step in the direction of such a change. But this first beginning did not make good the promise it seemed to hold out. It turned first into an abstract, then into a conservative doctrine of "cultural adaptation" with a great many insoluble contradictions.

The conclusion was irrefutable: *The human longing for life and pleasure cannot be banished. But the social regulation of sexual life can be changed.*

At this point, Freud began to create justifications for an ascetic ideology. "Unrestricted gratification" of all needs, he said, would seem to be the most tempting mode of life, but that would mean putting enjoyment before caution, and would bring swift punishment. To that I could reply even at that time that we have to distinguish the *natural* strivings for happiness from the secondary, *antisocial* strivings which are the result of compulsive education. The secondary, unnatural drives can be kept in bounds only by moral inhibition; that will always be so. To the natural pleasure needs, on the other hand, the principle of freedom applies, if you will, the "living out." One only has to know what the word "drive" means in each case.

"The efficiency of narcotics in the struggle for happiness and in warding off misery ranks so highly as a benefit that both individuals and races have given them an established position in their libido economy," writes Freud. But he does not add one word of medical opposition to this substitute gratification which ruins the organism! Not a word about the cause of narcotic addiction, namely the denial of sexual happiness! Not a word about the connection between addiction and lack of genital satisfaction in the whole psychoanalytic literature!

Freud's proposition was hopeless. True, he said, the striving for pleasure could not be eradicated. But what should be changed was not the social chaos, but the striving for pleasure itself. The complicated structure of the psychic apparatus admitted of a number of modes of influence. Just as instinctual gratification is happiness, so it becomes the source of grave suffering if the outer world denies gratification. It was to be hoped, therefore, that by influencing the instinctual impulses (*i.e., not by influencing the frustrating world!*) we would be able to free ourselves from part of the suffering. This influencing would seek to master the inner sources of the needs. To an extreme degree this is done by killing the instincts, as taught by oriental philosophy and put into practice by Yoga. This from Freud, the same man who had presented to the world the incontrovertible facts of infantile sexuality and of sexual repression!

Here, one no longer could and should follow Freud. More than that, one had to muster all forces to fight against the consequences of such concepts, coming, as they did, from such an authority. It was to be foreseen that in the days to come all the evil spirits representing the fear of living would call Freud to witness. This was no way of dealing with a human problem of the first order. One could not defend the resignation of the Chinese coolie or the infant mortality of a cruel East Indian patriarchy which was just suffering its first defeats. The most burning problem of the misery of childhood and adolescence was the killing of spontaneous vital impulses by the process of education in the interest of a dubious refinement. This, science should not condone; it could not take such a convenient way out. The less so, as Freud himself did not question the role of the human striving for happiness and its basic correctness.

As he admitted, the striving for a positive fulfillment of happiness, that orientation of life which revolves around love and expects all satisfaction from loving and being loved, would seem to be the most natural to everyone; sexual love provided the most intense sensations of pleasure and thus became the prototype of all striving for happiness. But, he said, this concept had a weak point, or else it would not have occurred to anybody to abandon this way of living for another. One is never more unprotected against suffering, he said, than when one loves, never more helpless and unhappy than upon the loss of love or a love object. The program of the pleasure principle, the attainment of happiness, he concluded, could not be put into practice. Again and again Freud maintained the unchangeability of human structure as well as of the conditions of human existence. Freud had in mind here attitudes like the neurotic reactions of disappointment of emotionally and economically dependent women.

The overcoming of these points of view of Freud, and the working out of the sex-economic solution of this problem took place in two parts. First, the striving for happiness had to be clearly comprehended in its *biological* nature. Thus it could be separated from the secondary distortions of human nature. Secondly, there was the great question as to the social practicability of that which humans most deeply long for and at the same time are so much afraid of.

Life, and with it, the striving for pleasure, does not take place in a vacuum, but under definite natural and social conditions. The first part was *biological* uncharted territory. Nobody had as yet investigated the pleasure mechanism from the point of view of biology. The second part was *sociological,* or rather, uncharted territory of social sexual policy. If it is generally recognized that people have a natural striving, and social conditions prevent them from attaining their goal, then the question naturally arises as to what ways and means might make this goal attainable. This applies to sexual happiness no less than to economic goals. It takes a particular mentality characterized by the use of cliché, to deny for sexuality what otherwise (e.g. with regard to making money or preparing for war) one would not hesitate to admit. The safeguarding of the distribution of goods requires a rational economic policy. A rational sexual policy is not different if the same obvious principles are applied to the sexual instead of the economic needs. It did not take much to recognize sexual hygiene as the focal point of mental hygiene in general, to differentiate it from the shallow attempts at sexual reform and from the pornographic mentality, and to advocate its basic scientific principles.

The entire cultural production, as expressed in literature, poetry, art, dance, movies, folklore, etc., is characterized by its interest in sex.

There is no interest with a stronger influence on man than the sexual interest.

Patriarchal laws pertaining to culture, religion and marriage are essentially laws *against* sex.

Freud's psychology had found the libido, the energy of the sexual instinct, to be the central motor of psychic activity.

Human pre-history and mythology are—in the strict sense of the word—reproductions of the sexual economy of humanity.

There was no escaping the question: *Is sexual repression an indispensable part of the cultural process in general?* If scientific investigation could answer this question unequivocally in the affirmative, then any attempt at a positive social program was hopeless. Then, also, any psychotherapeutic endeavor was hopeless.

This *could not* be correct. It ran counter to all human endeavor, all scientific findings and intellectual productions. As my clinical work had given me the unshakeable conviction that the sexually complete person is also culturally the more productive one, the acceptance of Freud's solution was out of the question. The question as to whether sexual repression is necessary or not was replaced by a much more important question: What are the human motives for evading a clear answer to this question consistently and —so far—so successfully? I searched for the motives of a man like Freud, who placed his authority at the disposal of a conservative ideology, who, through his theory of culture, threw overboard what he had elaborated as a scientist and physician. Surely, he did it neither because of intellectual cowardice nor for conservative political motives. He did it in the framework of a science which, like all others, was dependent on society. The social barrier made itself felt not only in the therapy of the neuroses, but also in the investigation of the origin of sexual repression.

In my sex hygiene clinics, the fact became clear to me that *the function of the suppression of infantile and adolescent sexuality is that of facilitating for the parents the authoritarian submissiveness of the children.*

In the very beginnings of the economic patriarchy, the sexuality of children and adolescents used to be fought by direct castration or genital mutilation of one kind or another. Later, psychic castration by way of implanting sexual anxiety and guilt feeling became the accepted method. Sex repression serves the function of keeping humans more easily in a state of submissiveness, just as the castration of stallions and bulls serves that of securing willing beasts of burden. However, nobody had thought of the devastating results of this *psychic castration,* and nobody can predict how human society will be able to cope with them. Later, after I had forced the issue in print,[5] Freud confirmed the connection between sexual repression and submissiveness:

"Fear of revolt among the oppressed," he writes, "then becomes a motive for ever stricter regulations. A high-water mark in this type of development has been reached in our Western European civilization. Psychologically, it is fully justified in beginning by censoring any manifestations of the sexual life of children, for there would be no prospect of curbing the sexual desires of adults if the ground

[5] Wilhelm Reich, *"Geschlechtsreife, Enthaltsamkeit, Ehemoral,"* 1930.

had not been prepared for it in childhood. Nevertheless there is no sort of justification for the lengths beyond this to which civilized society goes in actually denying the existence of these manifestations."

The formation of the sex-negative character structure, then, was the real, though unconscious, goal of education. Consequently, psychoanalytic pedagogy could no longer be discussed without discussing the problem of structure; neither could the latter be discussed without defining the *goal* of education. Education serves the purposes of the social order of any given time. If this social order contradicts the interest of the child, then education must leave the child out of consideration, and must do one of two things: either openly relinquish its set goal, "the welfare of the child," or else *pretend* to advocate it. This kind of education failed to distinguish between the *compulsive family* which suppresses the children, from the *family* which is built upon the deep natural love relationship between parents and children, and which is constantly being destroyed by the compulsive family relationships. Education, furthermore, failed to take cognizance of the gigantic revolution which had been taking place since the turn of the century in human sex life as well as in family life. With its "ideas" and "reforms" it was—and still is—hobbling far behind the actual changes. In short, it was caught in its own irrational motives of which it did not know nor dared to know.

Nevertheless, the plague of the neuroses is comparable to a pestilence. It disintegrates everything that human effort, thinking and work creates. Pestilence was attacked without hindrance, because such attack did not encroach either on profit or on mystical emotional interests. To fight against the plague of the neuroses is far more difficult. Everything that thrives on human mysticism clings to it and possesses power. Who would accept the argument that the psychic plague should not be attacked because the necessary measures of mental hygiene would be asking too much of the people? Blaming it on lack of funds is a poor excuse. The sums that go up in smoke in one week of the war would be enough to provide for the hygienic needs of millions and millions. We are also apt to underestimate the gigantic forces that lie fallow in people and press towards expression and action.

Sex-economy had comprehended the biological goal of human striving, which was at variance with human *structure* and certain institutions of our social order. Freud sacrificed the goal of happiness to the existing human structure and the existing sexual chaos. There was nothing left for me to do but to retain the goal and to study the laws according to which this human structure *develops* and can be *altered.* I had no idea of the extent of the problem, let alone of the fact that neurotic psychic structure becomes *somatic innervation,* a "second nature," as it were.

For all his pessimism, Freud could not let matters rest in such a state of hopelessness. His final statement was:

The fateful question of the human species seems to me to be whether and to what extent its cultural development will succeed in mastering the derangements of communal life caused by the human instinct of aggression and self-destruction. . . . And now it may be expected that the other of the two "heavenly forces," eternal

Eros, will put forth his strength so as to maintain himself against his equally immortal adversary.

This statement was much more than the turn of phrase for which it was taken by the psychoanalysts, certainly more than just a brilliant remark. *"Eros" presupposes full sexual capacity.* Full sexual capacity, in turn, presupposes a general affirmation of life, and a fostering of it on the part of society. Freud seemed secretly to wish me luck in my undertaking. He expressed himself obscurely, but the very material ways had indeed been found which would one day fulfill his hope: *Only the liberation of the natural capacity for love in human beings can master their sadistic destructiveness.*

THE IMAGES OF ORPHEUS
AND NARCISSUS

Herbert Marcuse

The attempt to draft a theoretical construct of culture beyond the performance principle is in a strict sense "unreasonable." Reason is the rationality of the performance principle. Even at the beginning of Western civilization, long before this principle was institutionalized, reason was defined as an instrument of constraint, of instinctual suppression; the domain of the instincts, sensuousness, was considered as eternally hostile and detrimental to reason. The categories in which philosophy has comprehended the human existence have retained the connection between reason and suppression: whatever belongs to the sphere of sensuousness, pleasure, impulse has the connotation of being antagonistic to reason—something that has to be subjugated, constrained. Every-day language has preserved this evaluation: the words which apply to this sphere carry the sound of the sermon or of obscenity. From Plato to the *"Schund und Schmutz"* laws of the modern world,[1] the defamation of the pleasure principle has proved its irresistible power; opposition to such defamation easily succumbs to ridicule.

Still, the dominion of repressive reason (theoretical and practical) was never complete: its monopoly of cognition was never uncontested. When Freud emphasized the fundamental fact that phantasy (imagination) retains a truth that is incompatible with reason, he was following in a long historical

THE IMAGES OF ORPHEUS AND NARCISSUS   From *Eros and Civilization* by Herbert Marcuse. Reprinted by permission of the Beacon Press, copyright 1955, © 1966 by the Beacon Press.
[1] A bill proposed by the New York Joint Legislative Committee on Comic Books would prohibit the sale and distribution of books portraying "nudity, sex or lust in a manner which reasonably tends to excite lustful or lecherous desires . . ." (*New York Times,* February 17, 1954).

tradition. Phantasy is cognitive in so far as it preserves the truth of the Great Refusal, or, positively, in so far as it protects, against all reason, the aspirations for the integral fulfillment of man and nature which are repressed by reason. In the realm of phantasy, the unreasonable images of freedom become rational, and the "lower depth" of instinctual gratification assumes a new dignity. The culture of the performance principle makes its bow before the strange truths which imagination keeps alive in folklore and fairy tale, in literature and art; they have been aptly interpreted and have found their place in the popular and academic world. However, the effort to derive from these truths the content of a valid reality principle surpassing the prevailing one has been entirely inconsequential. Novalis' statement that "all internal faculties and forces, and all external faculties and forces, must be deduced from productive imagination" [2] has remained a curiosity—as has the surrealist program *de pratiquer la poésie*. The insistence that imagination provide standards for existential attitudes, for practice, and for historical possibilities appears as childish fantasy. Only the archetypes, only the symbols have been accepted, and their meaning is usually interpreted in terms of phylogenetic or ontogenetic stages, long since surpassed, rather than in terms of an individual and cultural maturity. We shall now try to identify some of these symbols and examine their historical truth value.

More specifically, we look for the "culture-heroes" who have persisted in imagination as symbolizing the attitude and the deeds that have determined the fate of mankind. And here at the outset we are confronted with the fact that the predominant culture-hero is the trickster and (suffering) rebel against the gods, who creates culture at the price of perpetual pain. He symbolizes productiveness, the unceasing effort to master life; but, in his productivity, blessing and curse, progress and toil are inextricably intertwined. Prometheus is the archetype-hero of the performance principle. And in the world of Prometheus, Pandora, the female principle, sexuality and pleasure, appear as curse—disruptive, destructive. "Why are women such a curse? The denunciation of the sex with which the section [on Prometheus in Hesiod] concludes emphasizes above all else their economic unproductivity; they are useless drones; a luxury item in a poor man's budget." [3] The beauty of the woman, and the happiness she promises are fatal in the work-world of civilization.

If Prometheus is the culture-hero of toil, productivity, and progress through repression, then the symbols of another reality principle must be sought at the opposite pole. Orpheus and Narcissus (like Dionysus to whom they are akin: the antagonist of the god who sanctions the logic of domination, the realm of reason) stand for a very different reality.[4] They have not become the culture-heroes of the Western world: theirs is the image of joy

---

[2] *Schriften*, ed. J. Minor (Jena: Eugen Diederichs, 1923), III, 375. See Gaston Bachelard, *La Terre et les Rêveries de la Volonté* (Paris: José Corti, 1948), pp. 4–5.

[3] See Norman O. Brown, *Hesiod's Theogony* (New York: Liberal Arts Press, 1953), pp. 18–19, 33; and *Hermes the Thief* (University of Wisconsin Press, 1947), pp. 23ff.

[4] The symbol of Narcissus and the term "Narcissistic" as used here do not imply the meaning given to them in Freud's theory.

and fulfillment; the voice which does not command but sings; the gesture which offers and receives; the deed which is peace and ends the labor of conquest; the liberation from time which unites man with god, man with nature. Literature has preserved their image. In the *Sonnets to Orpheus*:

> Und fast ein Mädchen wars und ging hervor
> aus diesem einigen Glück von Sang und Leier
> und glänzte klar durch ihre Frühlingsschleier
> und machte sich ein Bett in meinem Ohr.
>
> Und schlief in mir. Und alles war ihr Schlaf.
> Die Bäume, die ich je bewundert, diese
> fühlbare Ferne, die gefühlte Wiese
> und jedes Staunen, das mich selbst betraf.
>
> Sie schlief die Welt. Singender Gott, wie hast
> du sie vollendet, dass sie nicht begehrte,
> erst wach zu sein? Sieh, sie erstand und schlief.
> Wo ist ihr Tod? [5]

Or Narcissus, who, in the mirror of the water, tries to grasp his own beauty. Bent over the river of time, in which all forms pass and flee, he dreams:

Narcisse rêve au paradis . . .

Quand donc le temps, cessant sa fuite, laissera-t-il que cet écoulement se repose? Formes, formes divines et pérennelles! qui n'attendez que le repos pour reparaître, oh! quand, dans quelle nuit, dans quel silence, vous recristalliserez-vous?

Le Paradis est toujours à refaire; il n'est point en quelque lointaine Thulé. Il demeure sous l'apparence. Chaque chose détient, virtuelle, l'intime harmonie de son être, comme chaque sel, en lui, l'archétype de son cristal;—et vienne un temps de nuit tacite, où les eaux plus denses descendent: dans les abîmes imperturbés fleuriront les tremies secrètes . . .

Tout s'efforce vers sa forme perdue . . .[6]

[5]
> "Almost a maid, she came forth shimmering
> From the high happiness of song and lyre,
> And shining clearly through her veils of spring
> She made herself a bed within my ear
> And slept in me. All things were in her sleep:
> The trees I marvelled at, the enchanting spell
> Of farthest distances, the meadows deep,
> And all the magic that myself befell.
> Within her slept the world. You singing god, o how
> Did you perfect her so she did not long
> To be awake? She rose and slept.
> Where is her death?"

Rainer Maria Rilke, *Sonnets to Orpheus: Duino Elegies*, transl. Jessie Lemont (New York: Fine Editions Press, 1945), p. 3 (with minor changes in translation). Reprinted by permission of Columbia University Press.

[6] "Alas, when will Time cease its flight and allow this flow to rest? Forms, divine and perennial forms which only wait for rest in order to reappear! O when, in what night, will you crystallize again?

Un grand calme m'écoute, où j'écoute l'espoir.
La voix des sources change et me parle du soir;
J'entends l'herbe d'argent grandir dans l'ombre sainte,
Et la lune perfide élève son miroir
Jusque dans les secrets de la fontaine éteinte.[7]

Admire dans Narcisse un éternel retour
Vers l'onde où son image offerte à son amour
Propose à sa beauté toute sa connaissance:
    Tout mon sort n'est qu'obéissance
    A la force de mon amour.

Cher CORPS, je m'abandonne à ta seule puissance;
L'eau tranquille m'attire où je me tends mes bras:
A ce vertige pur je ne résiste pas.
Que puis-je, ô ma Beauté, faire que tu ne veuilles? [8]

The climate of this language is that of the *"diminution des traces du péché originel,"*—the revolt against culture based on toil, domination, and renunciation. The images of Orpheus and Narcissus reconcile Eros and Thanatos. They recall the experience of a world that is not to be mastered and controlled but to be liberated—a freedom that will release the powers of Eros now bound in the repressed and petrified forms of man and nature. These powers are conceived not as destruction but as peace, not as terror but as beauty. It is sufficient to enumerate the assembled images in order to circumscribe the dimension to which they are committed: the redemption of pleasure, the halt of time, the absorption of death; silence, sleep, night, paradise—the Nirvana principle not as death but as life. Baudelaire gives the image of such a world in two lines:

Lá, tout n'est qu'ordre et beauté,
Luxe, calme, et volupté.[9]

"Paradise must always be re-created. It is not in some remote Thule; it lingers under the appearance. Everything holds within itself, as potentiality, the intimate harmony of its being—just as every salt holds within itself the archetype of its crystal. And a time of silent night will come when the waters will descend, more dense; then, in the unperturbed abysses, the secret crystals will bloom . . . Everything strives toward its lost form . . ." André Gide, *Le Traité du Narcisse*.

[7] "A great calm hears me, where I hear Hope. The voice of the wells changes and speaks of the night; in the holy shade I hear the silver herb grow, and the treacherous moon raises its mirror deep into the secrets of the extinguished fountain." Paul Valéry, *Narcisse Parle*.

[8] "Admire in Narcissus the eternal return toward the mirror of the water which offers his image to his love, and to his beauty all his knowledge. All my fate is obedience to the force of my love. *Body,* I surrender to your sole power; the tranquil water awaits me where I extend my arms: I do not resist this pure madness. What, O my Beauty, can I do that thou dost not will?" Paul Valéry, *Cantate du Narcisse*, Scène II.

[9] "There all is order and beauty, luxury, calm, and sensuousness."

This is perhaps the only context in which the word *order* loses its repressive connotation: here, it is the order of gratification which the free Eros creates. Static triumphs over dynamic; but it is a static that moves in its own fullness —a productivity that is sensuousness, play, and song. Any attempt to elaborate the images thus conveyed must be self-defeating, because outside the language of art they change their meaning and merge with the connotations they received under the repressive reality principle. But one must try to trace the road back to the realities to which they refer.

In contrast to the images of the Promethean culture-heroes, those of the Orphic and Narcissistic world are essentially unreal and unrealistic. They designate an "impossible" attitude and existence. The deeds of the culture-heroes also are "impossible," in that they are miraculous, incredible, super-human. However, their objective and their "meaning" are not alien to the reality; on the contrary, they are useful. They promote and strengthen this reality; they do not explode it. But the Orphic-Narcissistic images do explode it; they do not convey a "mode of living"; they are committed to the under-world and to death. At best, they are poetic, something for the soul and the heart. But they do not teach any "message"—except perhaps the negative one that one cannot defeat death or forget and reject the call of life in the admiration of beauty.

Such moral messages are superimposed upon a very different content. Orpheus and Narcissus symbolize realities just as do Prometheus and Hermes. Trees and animals respond to Orpheus' language; the spring and the forest respond to Narcissus' desire. The Orphic and Narcissistic Eros awakens and liberates potentialities that are real in things animate and inanimate, in organic and inorganic nature—real but in the un-erotic reality suppressed. These potentialities circumscribe the *telos* inherent in them as: "just to be what they are," "being-there," existing.

The Orphic and Narcissistic experience of the world negates that which sustains the world of the performance principle. The opposition between man and nature, subject and object, is overcome. Being is experienced as gratification, which unites man and nature so that the fulfillment of man is at the same time the fulfillment, without violence, of nature. In being spoken to, loved, and cared for, flowers and springs and animals appear as what they are—beautiful, not only for those who address and regard them, but for themselves, "objectively." "Le monde tend à la beauté." [10] In the Orphic and Narcissistic Eros, this tendency is released: the things of nature become free to be what they are. But to be what they are they *depend* on the erotic attitude: they receive their *telos* only in it. The song of Orpheus pacifies the animal world, reconciles the lion with the lamb and the lion with man. The world of nature is a world of oppression, cruelty, and pain, as is the human world; like the latter, it awaits its liberation. This liberation

---

[10] Gaston Bachelard, *L'Eau et les Rêves* (Paris: José Corti, 1942), p. 38. See also (p. 36) Joachim Gasquet's formulation: "Le monde est un immense Narcisse en train de se penser."

is the work of Eros. The song of Orpheus breaks the petrification, moves the forests and the rocks—but moves them to partake in joy.

The love of Narcissus is answered by the echo of nature. To be sure, Narcissus appears as the *antagonist* of Eros: he spurns love, the love that unites with other human beings, and for that he is punished by Eros.[11] As the antagonist of Eros, Narcissus symbolizes sleep and death, silence and rest.[12] In Thracia, he stands in close relation to Dionysus.[13] But it is not coldness, asceticism, and self-love that color the images of Narcissus; it is not these gestures of Narcissus that are preserved in art and literature. His silence is not that of dead rigidity; and when he is contemptuous of the love of hunters and nymphs he rejects one Eros for another. He lives by an Eros of his own,[14] and he does not love only himself. (He does not know that the image he admires is his own.) If his erotic attitude is akin to death and brings death, then rest and sleep and death are not painfully separated and distinguished: the Nirvana principle rules throughout all these stages. And when he dies he continues to live as the flower that bears his name.

In associating Narcissus with Orpheus and interpreting both as symbols of a non-repressive erotic attitude toward reality, we took the image of Narcissus from the mythological-artistic tradition rather than from Freud's libido theory. We may now be able to find some support for our interpretation in Freud's concept of *primary narcissism*. It is significant that the introduction of narcissism into psychoanalysis marked a turning point in the development of the instinct theory: the assumption of independent ego instincts (self-preservation instincts) was shaken and replaced by the notion of an undifferentiated, unified libido prior to the division into ego and external objects. Indeed, the discovery of primary narcissism meant more than the addition of just another phase to the development of the libido; with it there came in sight the archetype of another existential relation to *reality*. Primary narcissism is more than autoeroticism; it engulfs the "environment," integrating the narcissistic ego with the objective world. The normal antagonistic relation between ego and external reality is only a later form and stage of the relation between ego and reality:

[11] Friedrich Wieseler, *Narkissos: Eine kunstmythologische Abhandlung* (Göttingen, 1856), pp. 90, 94.

[12] *Ibid.*, pp. 76, 80–83, 93–94.

[13] *Ibid.*, p. 89. Narcissus and Dionysus are closely assimilated (if not identified) in the Orphic mythology. The Titans seize Zagreus-Dionysus while he contemplates his image in the mirror which they gave him. An ancient tradition (Plotinus, Proclus) interprets the mirror-duplication as the beginning of the god's self-manifestation in the multitude of the phenomena of the world—a process which finds its final symbol in the tearing asunder of the god by the Titans and his rebirth by Zeus. The myth would thus express the reunification of that which was separated, of God and world, man and nature—identity of the one and the many. See Erwin Rhode, *Psyche* (Freiburg, 1898), II, 117 note; Otto Kern, *Orpheus* (Berlin, 1920), pp. 22–23; Ivan M. Linforth, *The Arts of Orpheus* (University of California Press, 1941), pp. 307ff.

[14] In most pictorial representations, Narcissus is in the company of an Amor, who is sad but not hostile. See Wieseler, *Narkissos*, pp. 16–17.

Originally the ego includes everything, later it detaches from itself the external world. The ego-feeling we are aware of now is thus only a shrunken vestige of a far more extensive feeling—a feeling which *embraced the universe* and expressed an *inseparable connection of the ego with the external world.*[15]

The concept of primary narcissism implies what is made explicit in the opening chapter of *Civilization and Its Discontents*—that narcissism survives not only as a neurotic symptom but also as a constitutive element in the construction of the reality, coexisting with the mature reality ego. Freud describes the "ideational content" of the surviving primary ego-feeling as "limitless extension and oneness with the universe" (oceanic feeling).[16] And, later in the same chapter, he suggests that the oceanic feeling seeks to reinstate "limitless narcissisms." [17] The striking paradox that narcissism, usually understood as egotistic withdrawal from reality, here is connected with oneness with the universe, reveals the new depth of the conception: beyond all immature autoeroticism, narcissism denotes a fundamental relatedness to reality which may generate a comprehensive existential order.[18] In other words, narcissism may contain the germ of a different reality principle: the libidinal cathexis of the ego (one's own body) may become the source and reservoir for a new libidinal cathexis of the objective world—transforming this world into a new mode of being. This interpretation is corroborated by the decisive role which narcissistic libido plays, according to Freud, in sublimation. In *The Ego and the Id,* he asks "whether all sublimation does not take place through the agency of the ego, which begins by changing sexual object-libido into narcissistic libido and then, perhaps, goes on to give it another aim." [19] If this is the case, then all sublimation would begin with the reactivation of narcissistic libido, which somehow overflows and extends to objects. The hypothesis all but revolutionizes the idea of sublimation: it hints at a non-repressive mode of sublimation which results from an extension rather than from a constraining deflection of the libido. We shall subsequently resume the discussion of this idea.

The Orphic-Narcissistic images are those of the Great Refusal: refusal to accept separation from the libidinous object (or subject). The refusal aims at liberation—at the reunion of what has become separated. Orpheus is the

---

[15] *Civilization and Its Discontents* (London: Hogarth Press, 1949), p. 13. Italics added.
[16] *Ibid.,* p. 14.
[17] *Ibid.,* p. 21.
[18] In his paper on "The Delay of the Machine Age," Hanns Sachs made an interesting attempt to demonstrate narcissism as a constitutive element of the reality principle in Greek civilization. He discussed the problem of why the Greeks did not develop a machine technology although they possessed the skill and knowledge which would have enabled them to do so. He was not satisfied with the usual explanations on economic and sociological grounds. Instead, he proposed that the predominant narcissistic element in Greek culture prevented technological progress: the libidinal cathexis of the body was so strong that it militated against mechanization and automatization. Sachs' paper appeared in the *Psychoanalytic Quarterly,* II (1933), 420ff.
[19] *The Ego and the Id* (London: Hogarth Press, 1950), p. 38.

archetype of the poet as *liberator* and *creator*:[20] he establishes a higher order in the world—an order without repression. In his person, art, freedom, and culture are eternally combined. He is the poet of redemption, the god who brings peace and salvation by pacifying man and nature, not through force but through song:

> Orpheus, the priest, the mouthpiece of the gods,
> Deterred wild men from murders and foul foods,
> And hence was said to tame the raging moods
> Of tigers and of lions . . .
> In times of yore it was the poet's part—
> The part of sapience—to distinguish plain
> Between the public and the private things,
> Between the sacred things and things profane,
> To check the ills that sexual straying brings,
> To show how laws for married people stood,
> To build the towns, to carve the laws in wood.[21]

But the "culture-hero" Orpheus is also credited with the establishment of a very different order—and he pays for it with his life:

> . . . Orpheus had shunned all love of womankind, whether because of his ill success in love, or whether he had given his troth once for all. Still, many women felt a passion for the bard; many grieved for their love repulsed. He set the example for the people of Thrace of giving his love to tender boys, and enjoying the springtime and first flower of their growth.[22]

He was torn to pieces by the crazed Thracian women.[23]

The classical tradition associates Orpheus with the introduction of homosexuality. Like Narcissus, he rejects the normal Eros, not for an ascetic ideal, but for a fuller Eros. Like Narcissus, he protests against the repressive order of procreative sexuality. The Orphic and Narcissistic Eros is to the end the negation of this order—the Great Refusal. In the world symbolized by the culture-hero Prometheus, it is the negation of *all* order; but in this negation Orpheus and Narcissus reveal a new reality, with an order of its own, governed by different principles. The Orphic Eros transforms being: he masters cruelty and death through liberation. His language is *song,* and his work is *play.* Narcissus' life is that of *beauty,* and his existence is *contemplation.* These images refer to the *aesthetic dimension* as the one in which their reality principle must be sought and validated.

[20] See Walther Rehm, *Orpheus* (Düsseldorf: L. Schwann, 1950), pp. 63ff. On Orpheus as culture-hero, see Linforth, *The Arts of Orpheus,* p. 69.
[21] Horace, *The Art of Poetry,* transl. Alexander Falconer Murison, in *Horace Rendered in English Verse* (London and New York: Longmans, Green, 1931) , p. 426. Reprinted by permission of the publisher.
[22] Ovid, *Metamorphoses,* X, 79–85, transl. Frank Justus Miller (Loeb Classical Library), Vol. II, p. 71. See Linforth, *The Arts of Orpheus,* p. 57.
[23] Ovid, *Metamorphoses,* XL, 1ff; Vol. II, pp. 121–122.

THE PHANTOM CAPTAIN

R. Buckminster Fuller

What is that, mother?"
"It's a man, darling."
"What's a man?"

Man?

A self-balancing, 28-jointed adapter-base biped; an electrochemical reduction-plant, integral with segregated stowages of special energy extracts in storage batteries, for subsequent actuation of thousands of hydraulic and pneumatic pumps, with motors attached; 62,000 miles of capillaries; millions of warning signal railroad and conveyor systems; crushers and cranes (of which the arms are magnificent 23-jointed affairs with self-surfacing and lubricating systems, and a universally distributed telephone system needing no service for 70 years if well managed); the whole, extraordinarily complex mechanism guided with exquisite precision from a turret in which are located telescopic and microscopic self-registering and recording range finders, a spectroscope, *et cetera,* the turret control being closely allied with an air conditioning intake-and-exhaust, and a main fuel intake.

Within the few cubic inches housing the turret mechanisms, there is room, also, for two sound-wave and sound-direction-finder recording diaphragms, a filing and instant reference system, and an expertly devised analytical laboratory large enough not only to contain minute records of every last and continual event of up to 70 years' experience, or more, but to extend, by computation and abstract fabrication, this experience with relative accuracy into all corners of the observed universe. There is, also, a forecasting and tactical plotting department for the reduction of future possibilities and probabilities to generally successful specific choice.

Finally, the whole structure is not only directly and simply mobile on land and in water, but, indirectly and by exquisite precision of complexity, mobile in air, and, even in the intangible, mathematically sensed electrical "world," by means of the extension of the primary integral mechanism to secondary mechanical compositions of its own devising, operable either by a direct mechanical hook-up with the device, or by indirect control through wired or wire-less electrical impulses.

"A man," indeed! Dismissed with the appellation Mr. "Jones"!

Common to all such "human" mechanisms—and without which they are imbecile contraptions—is their guidance by a phantom captain.

This phantom captain has neither weight nor sensorial tangibility, as has often been scientifically proven by careful weighing operations at the moment of abandonment of the ship by the phantom captain, i.e., at the instant of "death." He may be likened to the variant of polarity dominance in our bipolar electric world which, when balanced and unit, vanishes as abstract unity I or O. With the phantom captain's departure, the mechanism becomes inoperative and very quickly disintegrates into basic chemical elements.

This captain has not only an infinite self-identity characteristic but, also, an infinite understanding. He has, furthermore, infinite sympathy with all captains of mechanisms similar to his.

What is this UNDERSTANDING? It consists in an intuitive, non-graphable awareness of perfection, or of unity, or of eternity, or of infinity, or of truth. This awareness of perfection serves as a universal yardstick relative to which any sense experience may be measured, and by virtue of which CONSCIOUS SELECTION may be made.

("This is a better pair of shoes." How does one know? Because it the more closely approximates a "perfect" pair—the "perfect" pair that will *never* hurt, wear out, become dirty, or have weight. "Perfect," though impossible of demonstration, is nonetheless the criterion of selection. "Perfect" is not only a *direction,* but a *time direction,* "perfection" being *never* in "reality" attainable. There is herein to be discerned the meaning of *Never, Never Land.* Children dream truly.)

By the process of conscious selection relative to sense of perfect, the segregation of such phenomena as sounds has developed, followed by the selective recomposition of the segregated sounds into specific sound-continuities, or "words" (sound symbols) provocative of basic understanding in others, adequate for the *moment.* No matter how relatively imperfect the articulation, or the receiver-conception, there is nonetheless some characteristic of "uniformity," though not of "identity," of understanding between sender and receiver. For instance, the word "cow" ("black-white," "daisy" or "bossy" are inconsequential) conveys the concept of a mechanical process which is substantially understood as a composite "cow"—the milk factory. Each phantom captain for himself, however, associates "cow" with the most vividly impressive cow of his particular experience, the speakers a Jersey, the listeners a Guernsey.

This infinite communicating code, based on processes and continuities and not on static fixation identities, enables the phantom captain to signal, via the complicated visual, aural and oral, tactile and olfactory systems of his machine, to captains of other machines, who receive the message through complementary mechanical systems of reception. The success of the transmission depends upon the relative degree of communicated understanding, i.e., upon how "time"-rationalizing vs. statically-reflexing the receiving captain may be.

Curiously, each captain is so impressed by the command of such an elaborate mechanism and one so excellently attuned to operation that it readily yields to his un-self-conscious guidance of its processes and instruments, that he feels himself thrillingly and virtually a part of it. Only when the parts are abused is there awareness of a seemingly separate presence of parts; for instance, when the tongue has been bitten or burned its motions are painful whereas normally it wags merrily, carelessly and unnoted.

Inevitably, the captain's habitual association of his infinite self with his subconsciously subservient mechanisms has inclined him to a dual "presumption": (1) that this mechanism is an ACTUAL (by extension) part of his phantom self, whereas it is purely an electro-chemical combination of inanimate energy molecules that are intrinsically the ship the phantom captain commands, and (2) an attitude of ownership: the mechanism of ordination for his will is "his" permanent "possession," whereas in reality it is only temporarily in his custody. This illusion of "possession" of the mechanism has been further extended, through accustomed relationship, to include "possession" of one's clothes, pencils, house in general, land, friends, wife and children, business, state, nation, world, and, finally, "God"—the last named quite naturally being "pictured" in the exclusively original form of his "own" egotistically important, special mechanistic and chemical process arrangement.

As the "possessor" of all of his extensions, the phantom captain automatically evolves a myriad of illusory necessities for which he assumes a vain, egotistical responsibility. This false-possession and always innocuous myth (which is consumptive of the complete lifetime, from four years onward, of the vast majority of people) stone-blinds the possessor to the simple, delightful truth-trends that are everywhere and at all times about us. For unspoilt children and happily debunked, emancipated grown-ups, these trends make life's courses as evident as a highway through a meadow. Ironically, the non-possession-blinded person's citation of evident trends has always been fearfully hailed as witchcraft, mysticism and quackery by the still mystified, self-be-quackeried majority.

The phantom captain is but mildly shaken in his preoccupation, or possession obsession, by the intermittent necessity of replacement of "his" parts, or by the dissection from, or application to, his mechanism by other phantom-captained mechanisms of such service parts as crude gold inlays inserted in "his" raw fuel crushers, additional lenses or color-filters for "his" rangefinders, or an enema bag douching nozzle temporarily passed into "his" clogged canal. The inlay or the douche bag is, temporarily at least, as factually connected to self as a toenail, tooth, hair, or eyeball.

This continual arrogation of "his" mechanisms is closely allied with the captain's habitual assumption that all objects are "seen" at locations outside the phantom captain's mechanism, whereas actually the captain "sees" them inside his turret through his peritelescopic range finders. A long history of mechanical reliability—attested by frequent accurate measurements of the deduced range of, and direction to, an object's external location with the ability to move a crane grappler into an assumed location so that contact with the discovered object is provided, and further attested by the receipt in the turret of affirmative telephone reports, from several of the myriad contact alarms in the crane grappler—seems to justify the captain's habit of thinking "I SEE IT OVER THERE."

The phantom captain's habitual notion not only that he is part of "his" mechanisms but that the mechanisms are himself, is extended still further. He frequently confuses the surface characteristics of other "observed" mechanisms, similar to those he controls, with the identities of the phantom captains controlling them. Forgetting the true, infinite *phantom* character of the other captains, he "logically" evolves two additional illusions: One of these is that the commanded mechanism of the other captain is all that there is to that other phantom captain; the other is that the *surface* is all there is to that mechanism. In other words, he assumes that the tangible surface of the "other" "person" *is* that person's phantom captain, and that this *surface alone* is "reality." (This is the "reality" of the "practical" minded or materialism-dominated personality.) So he customarily interprets the behavior characteristics of the whole of another's mechanism by surface clues only; there has actually developed a language in terms of surface reflexing.

To illustrate: If Mr. and Mrs. Murphy, out for a walk with baby Tim, were to see a plane flying overhead, they might readily exclaim to "darling," "See that aviator!" They might easily be wrong. Planes are being ably controlled by radio without a human pilot on board.

An illuminating rationalization indicates that *captains*—being phantom, abstract, infinite, and bound to other captains by a bond of understanding as proven by their recognition of each other's signals and the meaning thereof by reference to a common direction (toward "perfect")—*are not only all related, but are one and the same captain.* Mathematically, since characteristics of unity exist, they cannot be non-identical.

The phantom captain's *executive officer*, yclept "brain," is a mechanistic device similar to the metal "mike" of the Sperry gyroscope, whose gyroscopic directional-insistence, useful though it is while the captain is absent from the bridge is nonetheless provocative, if unwatched, of habit grooves of motion.

When the complexity of the metal "mike" currently used in aeroplanes and aboard ship in hands-off navigation is compared with that of the "mike" or "brain" of the human phantom-captained mechanism, it is as though one contrasted an Ingersoll watch and a battleship, in the matter of number of parts and precision of operation, except that the human "mike" is as small in relation to the metal "mike" as are the new complex seven-element, glass-lined metal radio tubes "small" in relation to their crude, large three-element forerunners.

The "mike" of the human ship may be "set" by the phantom captain to detect the slightest lack of balance, not only in every one of the ship's external relationships but in all of its interior synchronizing mechanisms. So many settings does "mike" carry, at most times, that he seems ALIVE, and he is so satisfactory to the captain that the latter flies the human ship "hands-off" much of the time. This possibility of hands-off flying encourages the phantom captain to regard the "mikes" of other phantom captains, also, as almost alive—that is, animate rather than animated.

Such a mistaken assumption of surface clues for reality must inevitably lead to a myriad of misunderstanding and erroneous conclusions, into "blind alleys" and "dead end" streets. This is just what happens when (rationalization of an illusion being *ipso facto* impossible and illusion being no further extensible, on the occasion of "death" or the abandonment of a mechanism) those "individuals" whose captains are still at their posts and who are still confusing themselves with the mechanism they are directing, ceremoniously "bury" the abandoned, now disintegrating mechanism under the impression that it is the captain whom they "honor." They might as well bury the can opener that "he" customarily used and which he regarded as "his." Indeed, it would honor the phantom captain more to bury his can opener, since it is a device rationally objectivized by him and is, therefore, more directly creditable to him than the involuntary custody and management of the unit mechanism he had under "his" control. The cans he opened might, also, be honored by burial in dirt.

There are two main types of phantom-captained mechanisms, differing only in their machinery for the reproduction of miniature replicas of themselves (a manufacturing process). The union of these complementary types, or "plants," allows the electrochemical processing of raw materials into infinitely elaborate, replica structures and instrument ensembles.

There are, of course, innumerable subtypes of the male and female main types, varying widely in external color, size, smell and textural characteristics. In fact, no two are physically identical, although they are miraculously *uniform* from a mechanical, chemical, structural, and process characteristic viewpoint, even to the maintenance of an identical thermal characteristic which, when the machine is in proper running order, is 98.6° F. under most highly diversified exterior environment conditions.

When one of the phantom captains seeks a mechanism of the complementary type to join with his in the manufacture of an improved model replica of their mutual custody mechanisms, he misinterprets his un-self-conscious appraisal of the adequacy of the observed complement to his "own" half-plant as constituting suitable hook-up conditions in the terms of superficial or sensorial-surface-satisfactions. The result is often the peculiarly amusing selective sound-wave emission, through the major exit-entrance aperture of the turret, "BEAUTIFUL!"

Phantom captains have fallen into such a careless mythology of surface words and nicknames, to excuse slothfulness in telegraphing accurately the observed external phenomena to the turret laboratories, that, although Murphy's phantom captain meant by "beautiful" that he had noted in Julia a mechanism that was highly uniform, i.e., not deformed, and, therefore, so far as he was concerned one that was favorable for plant hook-up, he probably further elaborated inaccurately and meaninglessly, "Julia is the MOST BEAUTIFUL girl in the world!" (The writer does not mean to infer that he does not say "beautiful," and believes that he means it, over and over again.) Murphy also probably would say, "My Julia is a PEARL!" and send her a "rose," the latter being a broken-off portion of another highly intricate, phantom-captained mechanism, but of so relatively wide non-identity with the "Julia" mechanism as to allow of its becoming a "living" sacrifice on the altar of the Julia manufacturing-plant worship.

Had Murphy failed at first to convince Julia of favorable conditions for plant hook-up, through surface clues observable by her, he would not have ceased his campaign. No, he would have sought to impose on Julia an *illusion* of satisfactory surface clues, by altering his surface conditions—such as adding to the size of his turret with a new "fedora," or subtracting from its size by cutting off part of his hair—just as Julia, were the situation reversed, would have "dressed ship" in velvet "washed down" with attar of roses.

It has been but a step from false adornment and artificial surface extensions of the human body, in the matter of clothing, to shelter; and from shelter to the myriad tools and instruments that were rationally evolved at an earlier time by the phantom captain in the extension of his own mechanism. The tools were born of the necessity to perform a specific function either with greater precision or with greater leverage than could be effected by the integral mechanism of the primary machine,—a tooth-pick, for instance, is better than a fingernail for tooth-picking and is more expeditiously replaceable.

The Murphys are not content, as their "wealth" (mechanical extensions) increases, with simple tooth-picks. Unless completely bereft of "hook-up" potentials, they will probably go in for gold tooth-picks, even gold filagreed tooth-picks, "individualistic" tooth-picks; embroidered roofs and arches; tattooed everythings.

So pleased are human beings by the artifices with which they constantly attain *self*-satisfaction, *despite* bad hook-up conditions, that they experience a constant urge to evolve codes of morals, ethics and laws for the purpose of making permanent the conditions of self-satisfaction that they have attained by artificiality. Out of these morals, ethics, artifices and vanities have been evolved so many "mike" sayings or brainistic words, that, although they are utterly meaningless from the viewpoint of the true phantom captain, they constitute 99% of today's broadcast, printed and person-to-person communication.

The artificial illusion extensions provided by the momentum of the gyroscopic "mike" display a wide range in various races variously located. For instance, when Doctor Jung, able student of psychology, made an extensive visit to Africa for the purpose of carrying on basic psychologic studies, he discovered that the primitive people there demonstrated a most interesting seemingly factual illusion extension from their simple experience memory storage. What had been regarded as purely ghost or demon fabrications, inherited through mythical tradition, proved to be none other than vivid memory concepts. When a leader or a parent died, the people had such simple, clear, visual memory pictures of the deceased that they were able satisfactorily to objectivize him as though still in bodily presence. In other words, they simply reversed our particular civilization's assumption that we SEE objects at a point EXTERNAL to our self-mechanism, although, in fact, the seeing is done, not even in the eye but in the brain or reception end of the nervous system that records the exterior light reflections.

Jung found, also, that African primitives, in common with others throughout the world, have such a simple cosmic problem that they have only two categories of numbers, *viz., "one"* or *"many."* Because they "SEE" either "one" or "many," they have evolved fabulous legendary stories. They recognize that one stranger may be readily matched in physical combat, whereas two or more may be overpowering. So two or three or more strangers are "seen" as hordes, the fear instinct warning the beholder of the risk of being overcome. Combining this "seeing" of either "one" or "many" with the extension of a SEEN factual memory form of a father or leader calls forth the illusion of the close proximity of multitudes of fathers, leaders, demons, *et cetera.*

There is, also, a tracery of the simple number sense limitation in certain old cultures. In Chinese, for example, one carriage is a carriage, many carriages are "noise." The Chinese symbol of "tree" is one tree; "two trees" equals "woods," and "three trees" constitute a "forest"—one, few, many.

Jung had the strange experience of noticing that, while he was endeavoring to understand primitive illusions, his own particular modern civilization's illusion broke down to such an extent that he, too, began to "see" partially in terms of the primitive illusion and partially in his own earlier illusion, with the result that he seemed to himself almost to be crazy, for there was no reliability in any illusion.

In connection with the phantom captain's illusion that the mechanisms of his survival are an intrinsic part of his abstract self, it is to be noted that every physical extension has been a matter of survival adequacy in the phantom captain's command of specific animal and vegetable species. It might almost be said that a new "type" of human animal has developed in the United States and that this type is by way of being an advance demonstration of a world-wide type, inasmuch as the evidences are all in terms of scientific world trends. When a sufficient number of members of a species has become characterized by relatively identical extensions, these extensions may properly be called part and parcel of the "being"-entity of that species.

If we will admit that a section of Julia's hair is just as much Julia's hair after it is cut off as it was when on her head—and it certainly is as much Julia as is the name "Julia," which is a most arbitrary appendage—we must admit, also, that if Julia's cut-off hair were woven into a fabric and worn on her head in the form of a hat, everything in the ensemble would still be "Julia." This would apply equally to any other hat that Julia might don or to the pigment which, for improved hook-up allure, she might apply to her lips and cheeks. Everything that Julia uses in her sometimes by-seeming selection, and again by-inadvertence choice, is "Julia."

The phantom captain of the butterfly has a great variety of mechanical externals for survival, but the apparently different stages of moth-caterpillar-chrysalis-butterfly in no way alter the identity of the phantom captain, which persists as unity throughout. Similarly, at sea, the various ships that Captain "Smith" commands are known to his contemporary skippers simply as "Smith." As Smith's ship, the *Mary,* appears on the horizon they exclaim, "Here comes Smith!" Smith may change commands but the other skippers will continue to say, "Here comes Smith!" whenever they recognize the externals of the ship he happens currently to be commanding.

In the United States passenger automobiles number approximately one per family, and the head of the family is usually the driver thereof. So accelerated are the time-space characteristics of the auto in comparison to the time-space covering ability of the man on legs that every reflex characteristic of the phantom captain of the driver is amplified in direct proportion to the time-space differential between the car's and the unmounted driver's tactical maneuvering ability. People who are not recognized as nervous or physically unbalanced while walking and talking are often seen to be distinctly so in their operation of an automobile. The traffic manners and ethics of people while driving reveal their character as a whole far more readily than would their cultivated mannerisms and behavior while walking.

Holding the full significance of this thought in mind, one can suddenly comprehend, while driving along a heavy traffic artery, that the automobiles seen are extensions of their drivers, just as are the "drivers'" hats, coats, shoes and faces; it is the progression of boxes within boxes of childhood play. Accepting this rationalization of man's unity extending into his automobile, it may be said that the average young working American man now weighs better than a ton, since the average automobile weighs 2800 lbs., and that the composite American extensible into his group mechanisms (aeroplane, railroad train, the *Normandie,* and Boulder Dam) is larger by millions of times than any historical animate organism. It is quite possible that Lewis Carroll was writing the poetry of this concept in *Alice Through the Looking-Glass.*

There is another interesting phase of the phantom captain phenomenon. There is to be distinguished in the current era—as differentiated from the early crafts period of individual survival without the aid of mechanical extensions—a set of mechanisms, such as the power dynamo in the city, mutually commanded by phantom captains. When either Julia or Murph' pushes a certain button, the act serves to bring about a mechanical extension of the visual ability of both, although "seeing," let us remember, occurs within the turret and not externally to the mechanism of the phantom captain. This introduces an extraordinary rationalization, namely: Industrial mechanisms so gargantuan as to be without warrant as an extension of any one person are justifiable as extensions of multitudes of persons, proving to mathematical satisfaction that all people, of a species characterized by participation in the use of such mutual extension mechanisms, are one and the same person at the time of such utilization.

This conception of the phantom captain leads to a viewpoint quite the opposite of the "mechanistic" bogey so fearfully heralded and decried in recent years because of an apprehension that the man-created machine will overpower man somewhat as would a Frankenstein monster.

The thrilling inference of the phantom captaincy conception is that it not only precludes the possibility of the operation of extended machinery without the volition of inner man, but that the unit mechanisms are doing for man what politics has consistently failed to accomplish.

Industrial man, being unit, can only be effective in the direction of his own best survival interest.

THE GALAXY RECONFIGURED
or the Plight of Mass Man in an Individualist Society

Marshall McLuhan

The present volume has employed a mosaic pattern of perception and observation up till now. William Blake can provide the explanation and justification of this procedure. *Jerusalem,* like so much of his other poetry, is concerned with the changing patterns of human perception. Book II, chapter 34, of the poem contains the pervasive theme:

> If Perceptive organs vary, Objects of Perception seem to vary:
> If the Perceptive Organs close, their Objects seem to close also.

Determined as he was to explain the causes and effects of psychic change, both personal and social, he arrived long ago at the theme of *The Gutenberg Galaxy*:

> The Seven Nations fled before him: they became what they beheld.

Blake makes quite explicit that when sense ratios change, men change. Sense ratios change when any one sense or bodily or mental function is externalized in technological form:

> The Spectre is the Reasoning Power in Man, & when separated
> From Imagination and closing itself as in steel in a Ratio
> Of the Things of Memory, It thence frames Laws & Moralities
> To destroy Imagination, the Divine Body, by Martyrdoms & Wars.[1]

Imagination is that ratio among the perceptions and faculties which exists when they are not embedded or outered in material technologies. When so

THE GALAXY RECONFIGURED OR THE PLIGHT OF MASS MAN IN AN INDIVIDUALIST SOCIETY Reprinted from *The Gutenberg Galaxy,* by Marshall McLuhan, by permission of University of Toronto Press, © University of Toronto Press 1962.
[1] *Jerusalem,* III, 74.

outered, each sense and faculty becomes a closed system. Prior to such outering there is entire interplay among experiences. This interplay or synesthesia is a kind of tactility such as Blake sought in the bounding line of sculptural form and in engraving.

When the perverse ingenuity of man has outered some part of his being in material technology, his entire sense ratio is altered. He is then compelled to behold this fragment of himself "closing itself as in steel." In beholding this new thing, man is compelled to become it. Such was the origin of lineal, fragmented analysis with its remorseless power of homogenization:

> The Reasoning Spectre
> Stands between the Vegetative Man & his Immortal Imagination.[2]

Blake's diagnosis of the problem of his age was, like Pope's in *The Dunciad,* a direct confrontation of the forces shaping human perception. That he sought mythical form by which to render his vision was both necessary and ineffectual. For myth is the mode of simultaneous awareness of a complex group of causes and effects. In an age of fragmented, lineal awareness, such as produced and was in turn greatly exaggerated by Gutenberg technology, mythological vision remains quite opaque. The Romantic poets fell far short of Blake's mythical or simultaneous vision. They were faithful to Newton's single vision and perfected the picturesque outer landscape as a means of isolating single states of the inner life.[3]

It is instructive for the history of human sensibility to note how the popular vogue of the Gothic romance in Blake's time later unfolded into a serious esthetic with Ruskin and the French symbolists. This Gothic taste, trite and ridiculous as it first appeared to serious people, was yet a confirmation of Blake's diagnosis of the defects and needs of his age. It was itself a pre-Raphael or pre-Gutenberg quest for a unified mode of perception. In *Modern Painters* (vol. III, p. 91) Ruskin states the matter in a way which entirely dissociates Gothic medievalism from any historical concern about the Middle Ages. He states the matter in a way that won him the serious interest of Rimbaud and Proust:

A fine grotesque is the expression, in a moment, by a series of symbols thrown together in bold and fearless connection, of truths which it would have taken a long time to express in any verbal way, and of which the connection is left for the beholder to work out for himself; the gaps, left or overleaped by the haste of the imagination, forming the grotesque character.

For Ruskin, Gothic appeared as an indispensable means of breaking open the closed system of perception that Blake spent his life describing and fighting. Ruskin proceeds (p. 96) to explain Gothic grotesque as the best way of ending the regime of Renaissance perspective and single vision or realism:

[2] *Ibid.,* II, 36.
[3] This Newtonian theme is developed by myself apropos "Tennyson and Picturesque Poetry" in John Killham, ed., *Critical Essays on the Poetry of Tennyson,* pp. 67–85.

It is with a view (not the least important among many others bearing upon art) to the reopening of this great field of human intelligence, long entirely closed, that I am striving to introduce Gothic architecture into daily domestic use; and to revive the art of illumination, properly so called; not the art of miniature-painting in books, or on vellum, which has ridiculously been confused with it; but of making *writing*, simple writing, beautiful to the eye, by investing it with the great chord of perfect colour, blue, purple, scarlet, white, and gold, and in that chord of colour, permitting the continual play of the fancy of the writer in every species of grotesque imagination, carefully excluding shadow; the distinctive difference between illumination and painting proper, being, that illumination admits *no* shadows, but only gradations of pure colour.

The student of Rimbaud will find that it was while reading this part of Ruskin that Rimbaud found his title for *Illuminations*. The technique of vision in the *Illuminations* or "painted slides" (as Rimbaud called them, in English, on his title page) is exactly as Ruskin delineates the grotesque. But even Joyce's *Ulysses* finds anticipatory designation in the same context:

Hence it is an infinite good to mankind when there is full acceptance of the grotesque, slightly sketched or expressed; and, if field for such expression be frankly granted, an enormous mass of intellectual power is turned to everlasting use, which, in this present century of ours, evaporates in street gibing or vain revelling; all the good wit and satire expiring in daily talk, (like foam on wine,) which in the thirteenth and fourteenth centuries had a permitted and useful expression in the arts of sculpture and illumination, like foam fixed into chalcedony.[4]

Joyce, that is to say, also accepted the grotesque as a mode of broken or syncopated manipulation to permit *inclusive* or simultaneous perception of a total and diversified field. Such, indeed, is symbolism by definition—a collocation, a *parataxis* of components representing insight by carefully established ratios, but without a point of view or lineal connection or sequential order.

Nothing, therefore, could be more remote from Joyce's ratios than the aim of pictorial realism. Indeed, he uses such realism and such Gutenberg technology as part of his symbolism. For example, in the seventh or Aeolus episode of *Ulysses* the technology of the newspaper is made the occasion for introducing all of the nine hundred and more rhetorical figures specified by Quintilian in his *Institutes of Oratory*. The figures of classical rhetoric are archetypes or postures of individual minds. Joyce by means of the modern press translates them into archetypes or postures of collective consciousness. He breaks open the closed system of classical rhetoric at the same time that he cuts into the closed system of newspaper somnambulism. Symbolism is a kind of witty jazz, a consummation of Ruskin's aspirations for the grotesque that would have shocked him a good deal. But it proved to be the only way out of "single vision and Newton's sleep."

Blake had the insights but not the technical resources for rendering his

---

[4] John Ruskin, *Modern Painters,* vol. III, p. 96.

vision. Paradoxically, it was not through the book but through the development of the mass press, especially the telegraph press, that poets found the artistic keys to the world of simultaneity, or of modern myth. It was in the format of the daily press that Rimbaud and Mallarmé discovered the means of rendering the interplay of all the functions of what Coleridge called the "esemplastic" imagination.[5] For the popular press offers no single vision, no point of view, but a mosaic of the postures of the collective consciousness, as Mallarmé proclaimed. Yet these modes of collective or tribal consciousness proliferating in the telegraphic (simultaneous) press, remain uncongenial and opaque to the bookmen locked in "single vision and Newton's sleep."

The principal ideas of the eighteenth century were so crude as to seem risible to the wits of the time. The great chain of Being was in its way as comical as the chains which Rousseau proclaimed in his *Social Contract*. Equally inadequate as an idea of order was the merely visual notion of goodness as a *plenum:* "The best of all possible worlds" was merely a quantitative idea of a bag crammed to the utmost with goodies—an idea which lurked still in the nursery world of R. L. Stevenson. ("The world is so full of a number of things.") But in J. S. Mill's *Liberty* the quantitative idea of truth as an ideal container packed with every possible opinion and point of view created mental anguish. For the suppression of any possible aspect of truth, any valid angle, might weaken the whole structure. In fact, the stress on the abstract visual evoked as standards of truth the mere matching of object with object. So unconscious were people of this matching theory as being dominant, that when a Pope or a Blake pointed out that truth is a ratio between the mind and things, a ratio made by the shaping imagination, there was nobody to note or comprehend. Mechanical matching, not imaginative making, will rule in the arts and sciences, in politics and education, until our own time.

Earlier, in presenting Pope's prophetic vision of the return of tribal or collective consciousness, the relation to Joyce's *Finnegans Wake* had been indicated. Joyce had devised for Western man individual pass-keys to the collective consciousness, as he declared on the last page of the *Wake*. He knew that he had solved the dilemma of Western individual man faced with the collective or tribal consequences of first his Gutenberg, and next his Marconi, technologies. Pope had seen the tribal consciousness latent in the new mass culture of the book-trade. Language and the arts would cease to be prime agents of critical perception and become mere packaging devices for releasing a spate of verbal commodities. Blake and the Romantics and the Victorians alike became obsessed with the actualization of Pope's vision in the new organization of an industrial economy embedded in a self-regulating system of land, labor, and capital. The Newtonian laws of mechanics, latent in Gutenberg typography, were translated by Adam Smith to govern the laws of production and consumption. In accordance with Pope's prediction of automatic trance or "robo-centrism," Smith declared that the mechanical laws of the economy applied equally to the things of the mind: "In opulent

[5] See H. M. McLuhan, "Joyce, Mallarmé and the Press," *Sewanee Review,* winter, 1954, pp. 38–55.

and commercial societies to think or to reason comes to be, like every other employment, a particular business, which is carried on by a very few people, who furnish the public with all the thought and reason possessed by the vast multitudes that labour." [6]

Adam Smith is always faithful to the fixed visual point of view and its consequent separation of faculties and functions. But in this passage Smith does seem to sense that the new role of the intellectual is to tap the collective consciousness of "the vast multitudes that labour." That is to say, the intellectual is no longer to direct individual perception and judgment but to explore and to communicate the massive unconsciousness of collective man. The intellectual is newly cast in the role of a primitive seer, *vates*, or hero incongruously peddling his discoveries in a commercial market. If Adam Smith was reluctant to push his view to this point of the transcendental imagination, Blake and the Romantics felt no qualms but turned literature over to the transcendental arm. Henceforth, literature will be at war with itself and with the social mechanics of conscious goals and motivations. For the matter of literary vision will be collective and mythic, while the forms of literary expression and communication will be individualist, segmental, and mechanical. The vision will be tribal and collective, the expression private and marketable. This dilemma continues to the present to rend the individual Western consciousness. Western man knows that his values and modalities are the product of literacy. Yet the very means of extending those values, technologically, seem to deny and reverse them. Whereas Pope fully faced up to this dilemma in *The Dunciad,* Blake and the Romantics tended to devote themselves to one side of it, the mythic and collective. J. S. Mill, Matthew Arnold, and a great many others devoted themselves to the other side of the dilemma, the problem of individual culture and liberty in an age of mass-culture. But neither side has its meaning alone, nor can the causes of the dilemma be found anywhere but in the total galaxy of events that constitute literacy and Gutenberg technology. Our liberation from the dilemma may, as Joyce felt, come from the new electric technology, with its profound organic character. For the electric puts the mythic or collective dimension of human experience fully into the conscious wake-a-day world. Such is the meaning of the title *Finnegans Wake.* While the old Finn cycles had been tribally entranced in the collective night of the unconscious, the new Finn cycle of totally interdependent man must be lived in the daylight of consciousness.

At this point, *The Great Transformation* by Karl Polanyi, on "the political and economic origins of our time," assumes complete relevance in the mosaic of *The Gutenberg Galaxy.* Polanyi is concerned with the stages by which the Newtonian mechanics invaded and transformed society in the eighteenth and nineteenth centuries, only to encounter a reverse dynamic from within. His analysis of how prior to the eighteenth century "the economic system was absorbed in the social system" is exactly parallel to the situation of literature and the arts up till that time. This was true till the time of Dryden, Pope, and Swift, who lived to detect the great transforma-

[6] Cited by Raymond Williams, *Culture and Society, 1780–1850,* p. 38.

tion. Polanyi enables us (p. 68) to face the familiar Gutenberg principle of practical advance and utility by separation of forms and functions:

As a rule, the economic system was absorbed in the social system, and whatever principle of behavior predominated in the economy, the presence of the market pattern was found to be compatible with it. The principle of barter or exchange, which underlies this pattern, revealed no tendency to expand at the expense of the rest. Where markets were most highly developed, as under the mercantile system, they throve under the control of a centralized administration which fostered autarchy both in the households of the peasantry and in respect to national life. Regulation and markets, in effect, grew up together. The self-regulating market was unknown; indeed the emergence of the idea of self-regulation was a complete reversal of the trend of development.

The principle of self-regulation repeating by reverberation from the Newtonian sphere swiftly entered all the social spheres. It is the principle that Pope mocked in "whatever is is right" and that Swift ridiculed in "the mechanickal operation of the Spirit." It derives from a merely vision image of an uninterrupted chain of Being or a visual *plenum* of the good as "the best of all possible worlds." Granted the merely visual assumptions of lineal continuity or of sequential dependence, the principle of non-interference in the natural order becomes the paradoxical conclusion of applied knowledge.

Through the sixteenth and seventeenth centuries the transformation of mechanization of crafts by the application of visual *method* had proceeded slowly. But it was a procedure of maximal interference with existing non-visual modes. By the eighteenth century the process of applied knowledge had reached such a momentum that it became accepted as a natural process which must not be impeded save at the peril of greater evil: "all partial evil universal good." Polanyi notes (p. 69) this automation of consciousness as follows:

A further group of assumptions follows in respect to the state and its policy. Nothing must be allowed to inhibit the formation of markets, nor must incomes be permitted to be formed otherwise than through sales. Neither must there be any interference with the adjustment of prices to changed market conditions—whether the prices are those of goods, labor, land, or money. Hence there must not only be markets for all elements of industry, but no measure of policy must be countenanced that would influence the action of these markets. Neither price, nor supply, nor demand must be fixed or regulated; only such policies and measures are in order which help to ensure the self-regulation of the market by creating conditions which make the market the only organizing power in the economic sphere.

The assumptions latent in typographic segmentation, and in applied knowledge by the method of fragmenting of crafts and the specializing of social tasks, these assumptions were the more acceptable in the degree that typography enlarged its markets. The same assumptions presided over the formation of Newtonian space and time and mechanics. So literature, industry, and economics were easily accommodated within the Newtonian sphere. Those who questioned these assumptions were simply denying the facts of science. Now that Newton is no longer synonymous with science, we can meditate on the dilemmas of the self-regulating economy and the hedonistic calculus with light hearts and clear heads. But eighteenth century man was locked into a closed visual system that had enveloped him he knew not how. So he proceeded, robo-centered, to carry out the behests of the new vision.

However, in 1709 Bishop Berkeley had published *A New Theory of Vision,* which revealed the lop-sided assumptions of Newtonian optics. Blake, at least, had understood the Berkeleyan critique and had restored tactility to its prime role as agent of unified perception. Today artists and scientists alike concur in praising Berkeley. But his wisdom was lost on his age that was wrapped in "single vision and Newton's sleep." The hypnotized patient carried out the behests of the abstract visual control. Polanyi observes (p. 71):

A self-regulating market demands nothing less than the institutional separation of society into an economic and political sphere. Such a dichotomy is, in effect, merely the restatement, from the point of view of society as a whole, of the existence of a self-regulating market. It might be argued that the separateness of the two spheres obtains in every type of society at all times. Such an inference, however, would be based on a fallacy. True, no society can exist without a system of some kind which ensures order in the production and distribution of goods. But that does not imply the existence of separate economic institutions; normally, the economic order is merely a function of the social, in which it is contained. Neither under tribal, nor feudal, nor mercantile conditions was there, as we have shown, a separate economic system in society. Nineteenth century society, in which economic activity was isolated and imputed to a distinctive economic motive, was, indeed, a singular departure.

Such an institutional pattern could not function unless society was somehow subordinated to its requirements. A market economy can exist only in a market society. We reached this conclusion on general grounds in our analysis of the market pattern. We can now specify the reasons for this assertion. A market economy must comprise all elements of industry, including labor, land, and money. (In a market economy the last also is an essential element of industrial life and its inclusion in the market mechanism has, as we will see, far-reaching institutional consequences.) But labor and land are no other than the human beings themselves of which every society consists and the natural surroundings in which it exists. To include them in the market mechanism means to subordinate the substance of society itself to the laws of the market.

A market economy "can exist only in a market society." But to exist, a market society requires centuries of transformation by Gutenberg technology; hence, the absurdity in the present time of trying to institute market economies in countries like Russia or Hungary, where feudal conditions obtained until the twentieth century. It is possible to set up modern production in such areas, but to create a market economy that can handle what comes off the assembly lines presupposes a long period of psychic transformation, which is to say, a period of altering perception and sense ratios.

When a society is enclosed within a particular fixed sense ratio, it is quite unable to envisage another state of affairs. Thus, the advent of nationalism was quite unforeseen in the Renaissance, although its causes arrived earlier.

The Industrial Revolution was well on the way in 1795, yet, as Polanyi points out (p. 89):

> . . . the generation of Speenhamland was unconscious of what was on its way. On the eve of the greatest industrial revolution in history, no signs and portents were forthcoming. Capitalism arrived unannounced. No one had forecast the development of a machine industry; it came as a complete surprise. For some time England had been actually expecting a permanent recession of foreign trade when the dam burst, and the old world was swept away in one indomitable surge towards a planetary economy.

That every generation poised on the edge of massive change should later seem oblivious of the issues and the imminent event would seem to be natural enough. But it is necessary to understand the power and thrust of technologies to isolate the senses and thus to hypnotize society. The formula for hypnosis is "one sense at a time." And new technology possesses the power to hypnotize because it isolates the senses. Then, as Blake's formula has it: "They became what they beheld." Every new technology thus diminishes sense interplay and consciousness, precisely in the new area of novelty where a kind of identification of viewer and object occurs. This somnambulist conforming of beholder to the new form or structure renders those most deeply immersed in a revolution the least aware of its dynamic. What Polanyi observes about the insentience of those involved in the expediting of the new machine industry is typical of all the local and contemporary attitudes to revolution. It is felt, at those times, that the future will be a larger or greatly improved version of the *immediate past.* Just before revolutions the image of the immediate past is stark and firm, perhaps because it is the only area of sense interplay free from obsessional identification with new technological form.

No more extreme instance of this delusion could be mentioned than our present image of TV as a current variation on the mechanical, movie pattern of processing experience by repetition. A few decades hence it will be easy to describe the revolution in human perception and motivation that resulted from beholding the new mosaic mesh of the TV image. Today it is futile to discuss it at all.

Looking back to the revolution in literary forms in the later eighteenth century, Raymond Williams writes in *Culture and Society, 1780–1850* (p. 42) that "changes in convention only occur when there are radical changes in the general structure of feeling." Again, "while in one sense the market was specializing the artist, artists themselves were seeking to generalize their skills into the common property of imaginative truth" (p. 43). This can be seen in the Romantics who, discovering their inability to talk to conscious men, began by myth and symbol to address the unconscious levels of dream life. The imaginative reunion with tribal man was scarcely a voluntary strategy of culture.

One of the most radical of new literary conventions of the market society of the eighteenth century was the novel. It had been preceded by the discovery of "equitone prose." Addison and Steele, as much as anybody else, had devised this novelty of maintaining a single consistent tone to the reader. It was the auditory equivalent of the mechanically fixed view in vision. Mysteriously, it is this break-through into equitone prose which suddenly enabled the mere author to become a "man of letters." He could abandon his patron and approach the large homogenized public of a market society in a consistent and complacent role. So that with both sight and sound given homogeneous treatment, the writer was able to approach the mass public. What he had to offer the public was equally a homogenized body of common experience such as the movie finally took over from the novel. Dr. Johnson devoted his *Rambler no. 4* (March 31, 1750) to this theme:

The works of fiction, with which the present generation seems more particularly delighted, are such as exhibit life in its true state, diversified only by accidents that daily happen in the world, and influenced by passions and qualities which are really to be found in conversing with mankind.

Johnson shrewdly notes the consequences of this new form of social realism, indicating its basic deviation from the forms of book learning:

The task of our present writers is very different; it requires, together with that learning which is to be gained from books, that experience which can never be attained by solitary diligence, but must arise from general converse and accurate observation of the living world. Their performances have, as Horace expresses it, *plus oneris quantum veniae minus,* little indulgence, and therefore more difficulty. They are engaged in portraits of which every one knows the original, and can detect any deviation from exactness of resemblance. Other writings are safe, except from the malice of learning, but these are in danger from every common reader; as the slipper ill executed was censured by a shoemaker who happened to stop in his way at the Venus of Apelles.

Johnson continues in this vein, pointing out further rivalries between the new novel and the older modes of book learning:

In the romances formerly written, every transaction and sentiment was so remote from all that passes among men, that the reader was in very little danger of making any applications to himself; the virtues and crimes were equally beyond his sphere of activity; and he amused himself with heroes and with traitors, deliverers and persecutors, as with beings of another species, whose actions were regulated upon motives of their own, and who had neither faults nor excellencies in common with himself.
But when an adventurer is levelled with the rest of the world, and acts in such scenes of the universal drama, as may be the lot of any other man; young spectators fix their eyes upon him with closer attention, and hope, by observing his behaviour and success, to regulate their own practices, when they shall be engaged in the like part.
For this reason these familiar histories may perhaps be made of greater use than the solemnities of professed morality, and convey the knowledge of vice and virtue with more efficacy than axioms and definitions.

Quite parallel with this extension of the book page into the form of a talking picture of ordinary life, was what Leo Lowenthal mentions in *Popular Culture and Society* (p. 75) as "the crucial shift from Patron to Public," citing the testimony of Oliver Goldsmith's 1759 *Enquiry into the Present State of Polite Learning in Europe*:

At present the few poets of England no longer depend on the Great for subsistence, they have now no other patrons but the public, and *the public*, collectively considered, *is a good and generous master.* . . . A writer of real merit now may easily be rich if his heart be set only on fortune: and for those who have no merit, it is but fit that such should remain in merited obscurity.

Leo Lowenthal's new study of popular literary culture is not only concerned with the eighteenth century and after, but studies the dilemmas of diversion *v.* salvation through art from Montaigne and Pascal to modern magazine iconology. In pointing out how Goldsmith made a great change in criticism by shifting attention to the *experience* of the reader, Lowenthal has broken rich new ground (pp. 107–8):

But perhaps the most far-reaching change which took place in the concept of the critic was that a two-way function was premised for him. Not only was he to reveal the beauties of literary works to the general public by means of which, in Goldsmith's terms, "even the philosopher may acquire popular applause"; he must also interpret the public back to the writer. In brief, the critic not only "teaches the vulgar on what part of a character to lay the emphasis of praise," he must also show "the scholar where to point his application so as to deserve it." Goldsmith believed that the absence of such critical mediators explained why wealth rather than true literary fame was the goal of so many writers. The result, he feared, might be that nothing would be remembered of the literary works of his time.

We have observed that Goldsmith, in his endeavor to come to grips with the dilemma of the writer, represented a variety of sometimes conflicting views. We have seen, however, that it was likely to be Goldsmith in his optimistic rather than in his pessimistic vein who set the tone for what was to come. So, too, his view of the "ideal" critic, of his function as one of mediation between the audience and the writer, was to prevail. Critics, writers, and philosophers—Johnson, Burke, Hume, Reynolds, Kames, and the Whartons—all adopted Goldsmith's premise as they began to analyze the experience of the reader.

As the market society defined itself, literature moved into the role of consumer commodity. The public became patron. Art reversed its role from guide for perception into convenient amenity or package. But the producer or artist was compelled, as never before, to study the effect of his art. This in turn revealed to human attention new dimensions of the function of art. As manipulators of the mass market tyrannized over the artist, the artist in isolation achieved new clairvoyance concerning the crucial role of design and of art as a means to human order and fulfilment. Art has become as total in its mandate for human order as the mass markets that created the plateau from which all can now share the awareness of new scope and potential for everyday beauty and order in all aspects of life at once. Retrospectively, it may well prove necessary to concede to the period of mass marketing the creation of the means of a world order in beauty as much as in commodities.

It is quite easy to establish the fact that the same means that served to create the world of consumer abundance by mass production served also to put the highest levels of artistic production on a more assured and consciously controlled basis. And, as usual, when some previously opaque area becomes translucent, it is because we have moved into another phase from which we can contemplate the contours of the preceding situation with ease and clarity. It is this fact that makes it feasible to write *The Gutenberg Galaxy* at all. As we experience the new electronic and organic age with ever stronger indications of its main outlines, the preceding mechanical age becomes quite intelligible. Now that the assembly line recedes before the new patterns of information, synchronized by electric tape, the miracles of mass-production assume entire intelligibility. But the novelties of automation, creating workless and propertyless communities, envelop us in new uncertainties.

A most luminous passage of A. N. Whitehead's classic *Science and the Modern World* (p. 141) is one that was discussed previously in another connection.

The greatest invention of the nineteenth century was the invention of the method of invention. A new method entered into life. In order to understand our epoch, we can neglect all the details of change, such as railways, telegraphs, radios, spinning machines, synthetic dyes. We must concentrate on the method in itself; that is the real novelty, which has broken up the foundations of the old civilisation. The prophecy of Francis Bacon has now been fulfilled; and man, who at times dreamt of himself as a little lower than the angels, has submitted to become the servant and the minister of nature. It still remains to be seen whether the same actor can play both parts.

Whitehead is right in insisting that "we must concentrate on the method itself." It was the Gutenberg method of homogeneous segmentation, for which centuries of phonetic literacy had prepared the psychological ground, that evoked the traits of the modern world. The numerous galaxy of events and products of that method of mechanization of handicrafts, are merely incidental to the method itself. It is the method of the fixed or specialist point of view that insists on repetition as the criterion of truth and practicality. Today our science and method strive not towards a point of view but to discover how not to have a point of view, the method not of closure and perspective but of the open "field" and the suspended judgment. Such is now the only viable method under electric conditions of simultaneous information movement and total human interdependence.

Whitehead does not elaborate on the great nineteenth century discovery of the method of invention. But it is, quite simply, the technique of beginning at the end of any operation whatever, and of working backwards from that point to the beginning. It is the method inherent in the Gutenberg technique of homogeneous segmentation, but not until the nineteenth century was the method extended from production to consumption. Planned production means that the total process must be worked out in exact stages, backwards, like a detective story. In the first great age of mass production of commodities, and of literature as a commodity for the market, it became necessary to study the consumer's experience. In a word it became necessary to examine the *effect* of art and literature before producing anything at all. This is the *literal* entrance to the world of myth.

It was Edgar Allan Poe who first worked out the rationale of this ultimate awareness of the poetic process and who saw that instead of directing the work to the reader, it was necessary to incorporate the reader in the work. Such was his plan in "the philosophy of composition." And Baudelaire and Valéry, at least, recognized in Poe a man of the Leonardo da Vinci stature. Poe saw plainly that the anticipation of effect was the only way to achieve organic control for the creative process. T. S. Eliot, like Baudelaire and Valéry, gives his entire sanction to Poe's discovery. In a celebrated passage of his essay on *Hamlet*,[7] he writes:

> The only way of expressing emotion in the form of art is by finding an "objective correlative"; in other words, a set of objects, a situation, a chain of events which shall be the formula of that *particular* emotion; such that when the external facts, which must terminate in sensory experience, are given, the emotion is immediately evoked. If you examine any of Shakespeare's more successful tragedies, you will find this exact equivalence; you will find that the state of mind of Lady Macbeth walking in her sleep has been communicated to you by a skillful accumulation of imagined sensory impressions; the words of Macbeth on hearing of his wife's death strike us as if, given the sequence of events, these words were automatically released by the last event in the series.

Poe set this method to work in many of his poems and stories. But it is most obvious in his invention of the detective story in which Dupin, his sleuth, is an artist-esthete who solves crimes by a method of artistic perception. Not only is the detective story the great popular instance of working backwards from effect to cause, it is also the form in which the reader is deeply involved as co-author. Such is also the case in symbolist poetry whose completion of effect from moment to moment requires the reader to participate in the poetic process itself.

It is a characteristic chiasmus that waits upon the utmost development of any process that the last phase shall show characteristics opposite to the early phases. A typical example of massive psychic chiasmus or reversal occurred when Western man fought the harder for individuality as he surrendered the idea of unique personal existence. The nineteenth century artists made a mass-surrender of that unique selfhood, that had been taken for granted in the eighteenth century, as the new mass pressures made the burdens of selfhood too heavy. Just as Mill fought for individuality even though he had given up the self, the poets and artists moved towards the idea of impersonal process in art production in proportion as they berated the new masses for impersonal process in the consumption of art products.

[7] In *Selected Essays*, p. 145.

A similar and related reversal or chiasmus occurred when the consumer of popular art was invited by new art forms to become participant in the art process itself.

This was the moment of transcendence of the Gutenberg technology. The centuries-old separation of senses and functions ended in a quite unexpected unity.

The reversal by which the presence of the new markets and the new masses encouraged the artist to surrender the unique self might have seemed a final consummation for art and technology alike. It was a surrender made almost inevitable when the symbolist began to work backwards from effect to cause in the shaping of the art product. Yet it was just at this extreme moment that a new reversal occurred. The art process had no sooner approached the rigorous, impersonal rationale of the industrial process, in the period from Poe to Valéry, than the assembly line of symbolist art was transformed into the new "stream of consciousness" mode of presentation. And the stream of consciousness is an open "field" perception that reverses all aspects of the nineteenth century discovery of the assembly-line or of the "technique of invention." As G. H. Bantock writes of it:

in a world of increasing socialization, standardization, and uniformity, the aim was to stress uniqueness, the purely personal in experience; in one of "mechanical" rationality, to assert other modes through which human beings can express themselves, to see life as a series of emotional intensities involving a logic different from that of the rational world and capturable only in dissociated images or stream of consciousness musings.[8]

Thus the technique of the suspended judgment, the great discovery of the twentieth century in art and physics alike, is a recoil and transformation of the impersonal assembly-line of nineteenth century art and science. And to speak of the stream of consciousness as unlike the rational world is merely to insist upon visual sequence as the rational norm, handing art over to the unconscious quite gratuitously. For what is meant by the irrational and the non-logical in much modern discussion is merely the rediscovery of the ordinary transactions between the self and the world, or between subject and object. Such transactions had seemed to end with the effects of phonetic literacy in the Greek world. Literacy had made of the enlightened individual a closed system, and set up a gap between appearance and reality which ended with such discoveries as the stream of consciousness.

As Joyce expressed it in the *Wake*, "My consumers are they not my producers?" Consistently, the twentieth century has worked to free itself from the conditions of passivity, which is to say, from the Gutenberg heritage itself. And this dramatic struggle of unlike modes of human insight and outlook has resulted in the greatest of all human ages, whether in the arts or in the sciences. We are living in a period richer and more terrible than the "Shakespearean Moment" so well described by Patrick Cruttwell in his book of the same title. But it has been the business of *The Gutenberg Galaxy*

---

[8] "The Social and Intellectual Background" in *The Modern Age* (The Pelican Guide to English Literature), p. 47.

to examine only the mechanical technology emergent from our alphabet and the printing press. What will be the new configurations of mechanisms and of literacy as these older forms of perception and judgment are interpenetrated by the new electric age? The new electric galaxy of events has already moved deeply into the Gutenberg galaxy. Even without collision, such co-existence of technologies and awareness brings trauma and tension to every living person. Our most ordinary and conventional attitudes seem suddenly twisted into gargoyles and grotesques. Familiar institutions and associations seem at times menacing and malignant. These multiple transformations, which are the normal consequence of introducing new media into any society whatever, need special study and will be the subject of another volume on *Understanding Media* in the world of our time.

TRIP 6

Timothy Leary

ALLEN GINSBERG
DECEMBER 1960:

Here is a statement for Sandoz. Is it okay?

By this time there was in existence an informal international network of scientists and scholars who had taken the trip and who foresaw the powerful effect that the new alkaloids would have on human culture. The members of this group differed in age, temperament, and had widely differing ideas about tactics, but the basic vision was common to all—these wondrous plants and drugs could free man's consciousness and bring about a new conception of man, his psychology, and philosophy.

Have had experience with mescaline, LSD-25, and psilocybin. The mushroom synthetic seems to me the easiest on the body physically, and the most controllable in dosage.

There was Albert Hoffman, who had invented LSD, who dreamed the utopian dream, but who was limited by the cautious politics of Sandoz Pharmaceuticals. What a frustrating web his genius had woven for Sandoz. How could a medical-drug house make a profit on a revelation pill?

The effects are generally similar, subjectively. Psilocybin seems to me to be some sort of psychic godsend.

Sandoz knew they had patented the most powerful mind-changing substance known to man. They spent millions to promote research on LSD. They righteously expected to make millions when the psychiatric profession learned how to use LSD, and they were continually disappointed to discover that human society didn't want to have

TRIP 6 Reprinted by permission of The World Publishing Company from *High Priest* by Timothy Leary. An NAL book. Copyright © 1968 by League for Spiritual Discovery, Inc.

its mind changed, didn't want to touch a love-ecstasy potion.

In 1961 a top executive of Sandoz leaned across the conference table and said to me, LSD isn't a drug at all. It's a food. Let's bottle it in Coca-Cola and let the world have it. And his legal counsel frowned and said, foods still come under the jurisdiction of the Food and Drug Administration.

By 1966, when LSD was crowding Vietnam for the headlines, officials of Sandoz Pharmaceuticals were groaning, we wish we had never heard of LSD.

I do really wish to destroy it! cried Frodo. Or well, to have it destroyed. I am not made for perilous quests. I wish I had never seen the Ring! Why did it come to me? Why was I chosen? (*The Lord of the Rings*)

The story of Albert Hoffman, the secret behind his wise silence, has yet to be told. But for the moment he was uneasily forced to play the drug-company researcher game.

There were the detached philosophers—Aldous Huxley, Father Murray, Gerald Heard, Alan Watts, Harry Murray, Robert Gordon Wasson—who knew that the new drugs were re-introducing the platonic-gnostic vision. These men had read their theological history and understood both the glorious possibility and the angered reaction of the priestly establishment. They were not activists but sage observers.

Then there were the turned-on doctors—psychiatrists who had taken the trip, and came back hoping to fit the new potions into the medical game. Humphrey Osmond, witty, wise, cultured, had invented the name psychedelic and tolerantly wondered how to introduce a harmony-ecstasy drug into an aggressive-puritanical social order. Sidney Cohen and Keith Ditman and Jim Watt and Abram Hofer and Nick Chewelos hoped to bring about a psychiatric renaissance and a new era of mental health with the new alchemicals.

And there was that strange, intriguing, delightful cosmic magician called Al Hubbard, the rum-drinking, swashbuckling, Roman Catholic frontier salesman who promoted uranium ore during the 40's and who took the trip and recog-

It offers unparalleled opportunity to catalyze awareness of otherwise unconscious psychic processes. To widen the area of human consciousness.

To deepen reification of ideas and identification of real objects. To perceive the inner organization of natural objects and human art-works.

To enter the significance and aesthetic organization of music, painting, poetry, architecture.

It seems to make philosophy make sense. It aids consciousness to contemplate itself and serve some of the most delightful functions of the mind.

As if, turning up the volume on a receiving set, background and FM stations can be heard. The effects are not unnatural.

I have experienced similar things without use of chemical catalysts, and correspond to what I, as a poet, have called previously aesthetic, poetic, transcendental or mystical awareness.

A kind of useful, practical cosmic consciousness. I think it will help mankind to grow.

∞

ALLEN GINSBERG
JANUARY 1961:

I spoke to Wilhelm De Kooning yesterday and he was ready to turn on, so please drop him an invitation too.

I figure Kline, De Kooning, Monk and Gillespie are the most impressive quartet imaginable for you to turn-on at the moment, so will leave it at that for awhile, till they can be taken care of.

I won't send you new names and work-trouble for awhile. Hope you can get these four letters off.

I also wrote Osmond and Huxley asking them to connect Burroughs with Heim, or anyone in Paris. None of my business actually, but Koestler always struck me as a little *hard*-hearted somehow.

nized that LSD was the fissionable material of the mind and who turned on Osmond and Hofer to the religious mystical meaning of their psychotomimetic drug. Al Hubbard set out to turn-on the world and flew from country to country with his leather bag full of drugs and claimed to have turned-on bishops and obtained *nihil obstat* from Pope John, and when the medical society complained that only doctors could give drugs, bought himself a doctor's degree from a Kentucky diploma mill and swept through northern California turning-on scientists and professors and God-seekers.

And when the day of Pentecost was fully come, they were all with one accord in one place. And suddenly there came a sound from heaven as of a rushing mighty wind, and it filled all the house where they were sitting. And there appeared unto them cloven tongues like as of fire, and it sat upon each of them. And they were all filled with the Holy Ghost, and began to speak with other tongues, as the spirit gave them utterance. And they were all amazed, and were in doubt, saying one to another, what meaneth this? Others mocking said, these men are full of new wine.

Right from the beginning this dedicated group of ring-bearers was rent with a basic disagreement. There were those who said work within the system. Society has assigned the administration of drugs to the medical profession. Any non-doctor who gives or takes drugs is a dope fiend. Play ball with the system. Medicine must be the vanguard of the psychedelic movement. Capture the medical profession. Cohen and Ditman and Al Hubbard and his two loyal, gifted lieutenants, Willis Harman and Myron Stolaroff, warned that any non-medical use of psychedelic drugs would create a new marijuana mess and set back research into the new utopia.

The medical point of view made little sense to religious philosophers. Aldous Huxley called the psychedelic experience a gratuitous grace. His vibrant flame-colored wife, Laura, agreed. So, in gentle tones, did Huston Smith and Alan Watts and Gerald Heard.

And so did Allen Ginsberg, who had discovered

the Buddha nature of drugs with Jack Kerouac and Gary Snyder and Bill Burroughs.

I had been visited by most of the psychedelic eminences by this time and was under steady pressure to make the Harvard psychedelic research a kosher-medically-approved project. Everyone was aware of the potency of Harvard's name. Timothy, you are the key figure, said Dr. Al Hubbard; I'm just old deputy-dog Al at your service. But the message was clear: keep it respectable and medical.

And now here was Allen Ginsberg, secretary general of the world's poets, beatniks, anarchists, socialists, free-sex/love cultists.

The sunny Sunday afternoon that we gave Allen Ginsberg the mushrooms started slowly. Rhona and Charlie were down in the kitchen by nine to start a cycle of breakfasts. First there were Jack Leary and his friend Bobbie who had spent the night. Bobbie went off to Mass. When I came down I found Donald, an uninvited raccoon hipster-painter from New York solemnly squatting at the table gnawing at toast and bacon. Frank Barron and the poets, Allen Ginsberg and Peter and Lafcadio Orlovsky remained upstairs and we moved around the kitchen with that Sunday morning hush not wanting to wake the sleepers. Lafcadio, Peter's brother, was on leave from a mental hospital.

About twelve-thirty the quiet exploded into family noise. Bobbie was back from church where he excitedly had told his father about the party we had given the night before for the Harvard football team and how I had given the boys, Bobbie and Jack, a dollar each for being bartenders.

I toted up the political profit and loss from this development. The Harvard football team rang up a sale. But the boys bartending? Bobbie's father is Irish so that's all right. All okay.

Then wham, the door opened and in flooded Susan Leary with three teen-age girls, through the kitchen, upstairs to get clothes, down to make a picnic lunch, up again for records, out and then back for the ginger ale.

By now the noise had filtered upstairs and we

Hate myself to have him as a final *curandero*. That is, being an intellectual, he tends to organize a polemic-dogmatic-mental system around experience.

As in his essay on Zen, which is very intelligent, but not so magnanimous. But by all means send him batches to hand out.

So H.S. fears the peril of mind let loose. Well I agree with you generally. But I have had that experience of absolute fear.

Suppose it decides not to keep the body going?—In Peru. It never recurred, but I can't guarantee it won't recur to me.

That is, there was something mysterious happening beyond what I know and later experienced. Each incarnation is *different*.

But at the time I was *sure* that if I really let go I would literally die, and that it might be a *good idea*. To get another dimension.

But I wasn't so positive it was a good idea. Really fearfully confused. Maybe you *could* die, like a yoga or Buddha or something worse or better? Who knows?

I mean who knows how deep the soul goes into the universe and what outright magic it can work? Like maybe leaving this body and going to a God-world maybe leaving this body Literally.

At least I haven't myself surmounted that superstition, if it is superstition, not uncanny awareness. So, I tend to feel mentally a hands-off policy, as far as making final judgment of what is actually psychologically happening to H.S.

But I wasn't there. I generally agree with your reaction, or I also tend to have your reaction—as to Barney or H.S.

Nonetheless, my knowledge of fact is not final. I've been operating as much on faith and hope in a way.

Send me a bill for the mescaline. No need for you to pay.

could hear the late sleepers moving around and the bathroom waters running, and down came Frank Barron, half-awake, to fry codfish cakes for his breakfast. And then, Allen Ginsberg and Peter. Allen hopped around the room with near-sighted crow motions cooking eggs, and Peter sat silent watching.

After breakfast the poets fell to reading the *Times* and Frank moved upstairs to Susan's room to watch a pro football game on TV and I told Allen to make himself at home and got beers and went up to join Frank. Donald the painter had been padding softly around the house watching with his big, soft creature eyes and sniffing in corners and at the bookcase and the record cabinets. He had asked to take mushrooms in the evening and was looking for records of Indian peyote drum music. We told him to phone around to the local libraries. A friend of his, an anthropology student, could possibly locate some Indian records, and could he borrow the car and go to Cambridge? All his words came up halting, labored, serious, and I said sure go ahead.

During the game, Jack Leary and his pals came in dressed in their football uniforms and watched the action for a while and then got bored and went up to the third-floor playroom. We kidded them about getting suited up like pigskin warriors and then sitting around inside and not playing. After the game Frank Barron rounded up Charlie and the boys and we went out behind the garage and had a game of touch football. The poets declined to play. At dusk we came in and started a long kitchen Sunday supper scene, cold ham and meat pies, highballs (but not for the poets). It was an agreeable kitchen chaos with everyone puttering around. Rhona and Charlie were sick with stomach flu and headed upstairs early. Lafcadio had stayed in bed most of the afternoon until Allen had gone up to tell him to come down and he sat in the corner quiet, impassive, eerie, probably thinking wonderful thoughts about the Martians landing on earth. He nodded every time we offered him food, and Allen would tell him to put his plates away and he would obey silently and mechanically. After the meal we asked Jack and Bobbie if they wanted

to play catch in the upstairs hallway with Lafcadio and they said sure and ran off with Lafcadio
lumbering after them. There are ball marks on
the white ceiling to this day and the wall lamp
has never quite worked the same, but Allen said
that the weekend was tremendous therapy for
Lafcadio. He started talking more and it kept up
for several weeks after they left.

Allen Ginsberg, hunched over a teacup, peering out through his black-rimmed glasses, the left
lens bisected by a break, started telling of his
experiences with Ayahuasca, the fabled visionary
vine of the Peruvian jungles. He had followed the
quest of Bill Burroughs, sailing south for new
realms of consciousness, looking for the elixir of
wisdom. Sitting, sweating with heat, lonely in a
cheap hotel in Lima, holding a wad of ether-
soaked cotton to his nose with his left hand and
getting high and making poetry with his right
hand and then traveling by second-class bus with
Indians up through the Cordillera de los Andes
and then more buses and hitchhiking into the
Montana jungles and shining rivers, wandering
through steaming equatorial forests. Then the
village Pucalpa, and the negotiations to find the
curandero, paying him with *aguardiente,* and the
ritual itself, swallowing the bitter stuff, and the
nausea and the colors and the drums beating and
sinking down into thingless void, into the great
eye that brings it all together, and the terror of
the great snake coming, lying on the earth floor
helpless and the great snake coming. The old
curandero, wrinkled face bending over him and
Allen telling him, *culebra,* and the *curandero*
nodding clinically and blowing a puff of smoke
to make the great snake disappear and it did.

The fate of fire depends on wood; as long as there is
wood below, the fire burns above. It is the same in
human life; there is in man likewise a fate that lends
power to his life. (*I Ching L*)

I kept asking Allen questions about the *curandero.* I wanted to learn the rituals, to find out
how other cultures (older and wiser than ours)
had handled the visionary business. I was fascinated by the ritual thing. Ritual is to the science
of consciousness what experiment is to external

No news yet from Cuba, so
I think it safe to send
psilocybin here. I'll call you
before I leave, which may
yet be another week—if at
all at this rate.

Burroughs is in Paris. I
wrote Huxley his address
today with an explanatory
note—but if you have any
means of connecting him
with Heim or anyone there
—could you do so.

Perhaps send him an
academic letter of
introduction which he could
deliver to Heim? This got
to be done soon, as
Burroughs is on way East
in a few weeks I think—
not sure.

He writes he had some LSD
in London, as well as an
injection of another drug—
what, I dunno. He writes
Don't flip pops is all. One
must be careful of altitude
sickness and depth madness
and the bends. Hazards of
the silent world. Space is
silent remember, etc.

Anyway, I'll let you know before I leave to Cuba. Send me what you can, if you can, when you can. Been finished with proofs of my book this week and doing some writing.

∞

ALLEN GINSBERG FEBRUARY 1961:

Been paralyzed making decisions, so forgive me not writing last week till I figured out what I wanted to do. Got letter and telegram from Corso in Athens summoning me to hurry up or he sez he'll take a boat to here.

I replied I'd stand on Acropolis with him in a month if the gods please and he replied he'd wait then. Meanwhile, been running around in frenzy.

Huncke now cured and taking rest in Jacobi hospital for a few weeks in psycho ward with friendly doctors. He's free to come or go.

science. I was convinced that none of our American rituals fit the mushroom experience. Not the cocktail party. Not the psychiatrist. Not the teacher-minister role. I was impressed by what Allen said about his own fear and sickness whenever he took drugs and about the solace and comforting strength of the *curandero,* about how good it was to have someone there who knew, who had been to those far regions of the mind and could tell you by a look, by a touch, by a puff of smoke that it was all right, go ahead, explore the strange world, it's all right, you'll come back, it's all right, I'm here back on familiar old human earth when you need me, to bring you back.

Allen told me about the training of *curanderos.* The old witch doctor going off in the mountain for weeks with the young candidate and having him take the drug day after day, night after night, exploring all the corners and caves and hidden inlets of the visionary world—the terrain of heaven and hell, the joy, the horror, the orgiastic peaks, the black burning swamps, the angels and the devil snakes—until he had been there, all the way to the far reaches of awareness. Then he was equipped to act as *curandero,* to take care of visionary travelers, to understand the words and behavior which confuse and frighten the unprepared observer.

Allen told of the therapeutic impact of the kind village doctor as he went through the age-old rituals of caring-for—the hand on the shoulder, and cup of hot tea and the covering with blankets. I remembered back to a session when a lonely graduate student fell to the carpet in anguished panic, and how Frank Barron the veteran front-line medic took over with cold compresses and kind words, and how the student never forgot his being there, doing the right thing at exactly the right time.

Allen was going to take the mushrooms later that night and he was shaping me up to help him. Allen was weaving a word spell, dark eyes gleaming through the glasses, chain-smoking, moving his hands, intense, chanting trance poetry. Frank Barron was in the study now, and with him Lafcadio Orlovsky.

Then a car came up the driveway and in a minute the door opened, and Donald, furry and moist, ambled in. He had brought his friend, an anthropology student from Harvard, to be with him when he tripped. Donald asked if his friend could be there during the mushroom session. I liked the idea of having a friend present for the mushrooms, someone to whom you could turn at those moments when you needed support, so I said sure, but he couldn't take the pills because he was a University student. Everyone was warning us to keep our research away from Harvard to avoid complications with the University Health Bureau and to avoid the rumors. He wasn't hungry so I mixed him a drink and then I got the little round bottle and pulled out the cotton topping and gave Donald 30 mg. and Allen Ginsberg 36. SEVERAL NIGHTS LATER AT LEARY'S HOUSE, I TOOK A LARGE DOSE OF 18 (36 MG.) AND WENT UPSTAIRS WITH ORLOVSKY TO A SEPARATE ROOM.

Allen started bustling around getting his cave ready. I brought Susan's record player up to his room and he took some Beethoven and Wagner from the study and he turned out the lights so that there was just a glow in the room. TOOK OFF ALL MY CLOTHES AND LAY IN BED LISTENING TO MUSIC. I told him we'd be checking back every fifteen minutes and he should tell me if he wanted anything.

By the time I got downstairs Donald was already high, strolling around the house on dainty raccoon feet with his hands clasped behind his back, thinking and digging deep things. AS MY AWARENESS EXPANDED I SAW MYSELF LYING IN BED, WITH THE ALTERNATIVE OF WITHDRAWING INTO MYSTIC INTROSPECTION, AND VOMIT, OR SWALLOWING BACK MY VOMIT, OPENING MY EYES, AND LIVING IN THE PRESENT UNIVERSE. I stayed in the study writing letters, reading the *Times*. I had forgotten about the anthropology student. He was waiting in the kitchen. I FELT INTIMIDATED BY THE KNOWLEDGE THAT I HAD NOT REACHED YET A PERFECT UNDERSTANDING WITH MY CREATOR, WHOEVER HE BE, GOD, CHRIST, OR BUDDHA—THE FIGURE OF OCTOPUS AS BEFORE.

After about thirty minutes I found Donald in the hallway. He called me over earnestly and

Yvonne I've seen a number of times, took her out one night to LeRoi Jones and got drunk. She can't make up her mind what to do with her life—wants someone to depend on—also wants independence, but she's spoiled and beautiful.

Barney is polite too. I had talk with him—mollified him by saying in sum, I thought it was a mistake to turn him and her on.

Otherwise he'll get into a big battle over the word mistake. So I guess they'll just go on as before and work out their fate.

Only way I can see otherwise is taking over Yvonne entirely, me marrying her or something. (Don't think she didn't suggest it.) She still wants *him*.

We just barged in on the middle of some insoluble modern romance. I dunno, how to resolve the mushroom politics of this, without their resolving their own politics.

So far it all seems quieted down. I really want to get out of U.S. and go to Greece and begin Orient voyages, etc. A lot of things keep me here now, the mushroom work, people who depend on me, like Huncke.

(Or people who I *think* depend on me, etc.) But I'd like to be alone and start a new phase, awhile.

I can write, either way, here or there, it's not so much a problem of having solitude for poetry, it's just I feel like taking off, boop-boop-a-doop.

Meanwhile I've been conspiring with everyone I can reach in N.Y. the last weeks to do something about the general dope problem.

Various other people working on other different angles. Yesterday got on TV with N. Mailer and Ashley Montagu and gave big speech attacking Narco Dept and recommending everybody get high—be on locally in N.Y. Sunday after this, if they don't suppress the program.

Montagu is an old woman, but he cooperated a bit. Maybe I'll go on Mike Wallace show. They asked me to.

Also making an appointment with Eleanor Roosevelt to try to interest her in the social problem. Met her and Martin Luther King at Dorothy Norman's last night.

began talking about the artificiality of civilization. He was thinking hard about basic issues and it was obvious what was going on with him— clearing his mind of abstractions, trying to get back behind the words and concepts. SUDDENLY, HOWEVER, REALIZED THEY WERE ALL IMAGINARY BEINGS I WAS INVENTING TO SUBSTITUTE FOR THE FEAR OF BEING MYSELF—THAT ONE WHICH I HAD DREAMED OF.

And if he succeeds in assigning the right place to life and to fate, thus bringing the two into harmony, he puts his fate on a firm footing. These words contain hints about the fastening of life as handed on by oral tradition in the secret teachings of Chinese yoga. (*I Ching L*)

The anthropology student was standing by, watching curiously and Donald asked if he minded leaving so that he could talk to me privately. Anthro went back to the kitchen and Donald continued talking about the falseness of houses and machines and deploring the way man cut himself off from the vital stuff with his engines and structures. I was trying to be polite and be a good *curandero* and support him and tell him, great boy, stay with it and work it out.

Susan came back from her friend's about this time and went upstairs to her homework, and I followed her up to check on Allen. He was lying on top of the blanket. His glasses were off and his black eyes, pupils completely dilated, looked up at me. Looking down into them they seemed like two deep, black, wet wells and you could look down them way through the man Ginsberg to something human beyond. The eye is such a defenseless, naïve, trusting thing. PROFESSOR LEARY CAME INTO MY ROOM, LOOKED IN MY EYES, AND SAID I WAS A GREAT MAN. THAT DETERMINED ME TO MAKE AN EFFORT TO LIVE HERE AND NOW.

Allen was scared and unhappy and sick. And still he was lying there voluntarily, patiently searching, pushing himself into panics and fears, into nausea, trying to learn something, trying to find meaning. Shamelessly weak and shamelessly human and greatly classic. Peter was lying next to him, eyes closed, sleeping or listening to the record. I GOT NAUSEOUS SOON AFTER—SAT UP IN BED

NAKED AND SWALLOWED DOWN THE VOMIT THAT
BESIEGED FROM MY STOMACH AS IF AN INDEPENDENT
BEING DOWN THERE WAS REBELLING AT BEING
DRAGGED INTO EXISTENCE.

Allen asked me what I thought of him and his
situation. I leaned over and looked down into the
black liquid eyes, fawn's eyes, man's eyes, and told
him that he was a great man and that it was good
to know him. He reached up his hand. Can I get
you anything, Allen? No thanks. I'll be back in a
while. He nodded. ORLOVSKY WAS NAKED IN BED
WITH ME AND HIS EROTIC GESTURES LOOKED REP-
TILIAN, AS IF OUT OF HINDU-DEVA STATUARY—HIS
LIDDED EYES AND HOOKED NOSE ALMOST LIKE BLUE
KRISHNA STATUE FROM THE WRONG PLANE OF EXIST-
ENCE NOT CONSONANT WITH 1960 USA.

On the way downstairs I checked by Susan's
room. She was curled up on the carpet, with her
books scattered around her and reading in the
shadows. I scolded her about ruining her eyes and
flicked on the two wall bulbs. Downstairs Frank
was still at the study desk. SUDDENLY OUT OF THE
WINDOW SAW IMAGE AS OF A BETHLEHEM STAR,
HEARD GREAT HORNS OF GOTTERDAMMERUNG-WAG-
NER ON THE PHONOGRAPH I'D ARRANGED TO HEAR
IN THE ROOM. Anthro was wandering in the living
room and told me that Donald had gone outside.
The rule we set up was that no one would leave
the house and the idea of Donald padding down
Beacon Street in a mystic state chilled me. LIKE
THE HORNS OF JUDGMENT CALLING FROM THE ENDS
OF THE COSMOS—CALLED ON ALL HUMAN CON-
SCIOUSNESS TO DECLARE ITSELF THE CONSCIOUSNESS.
Out on the front porch I turned on the two rows
of spotlights that flooded the long winding stone
stairs and started down, shielding my eyes and
shouting Donald. Halfway down I heard him
answering back and saw him standing under an
oak tree on the lower lawn. I asked him how he
was but he didn't talk, just stood there looking
wise and deep. SEEMED AS IF ALL THE WORLDS OF
HUMAN CONSCIOUSNESS WERE WAITING FOR A MES-
SIAH, SOMEONE TO TAKE ON THE RESPONSIBILITY OF
BEING THE CREATIVE GOD AND SEIZE POWER OVER
THE UNIVERSE. He was barefoot and higher than
Picard's balloon. I want to talk to you, but first
you must take off your shoes. Okay, why not? I

Got lunch date with Rev.
Norman Eddy of East
Harlem Protestant parish
this Tuesday. He's the big
dope do-gooder.

Didn't mention mushrooms
in all of this, for tactful
reasons. Best keep that on
its own high level.

Otherwise might get mixed
up with beatnikism. You
sure got a lot of energy.

I dunno, but I think it
would help the mushroom
atmosphere lots if there
were a general U.S.
rethinking (as the N.Y.
Times friend says) on the
dope social problem.

Lindesmith and Indiana U
Press are putting out this
joint report of interim
committee of AMA and
Amer. Bar Assn. So I got in
touch with all the liberal
pro-dope people I know to
have it publicized and
circulated and have all of
them interconnect to
exchange information.

I wrote a five-page summary of situation to this friend Kenny Love on the N.Y. *Times* and he said he'd perhaps do a story (newswise) on the book, which could then be picked up by UP friend on national wire.

Also gave copy to Al Aronowitz on N.Y. *Post* and Rosalind Constable at *Time* and Bob Silvers on *Harpers* magazine and informed *Yugen, Evergreen, Big Table, Metronome.*

Meanwhile Indiana U people are working on *Commentary, The Nation*, etc. Regular network. Also got a copy of La Guardia Report to Grove Press.

They will republish it with additional stronger material. Maybe Dan Wakefield edit a book.

. . . just got your Feb. 1 letter. Glad you heard the *Howl* record. That never got circulated.

So, I also got to work this month arranging advertisements for that Fantasy Record Co. Is very inert unless I prod them.

If that begins selling something this year, with *Kaddish* out in a month, I'll have plenty loot for Europe and Asia and Lafcadio too.

sat down to unlace my shoes and he squatted alongside and told about how the machines complicate our lives and how cold and hot were abstractions and how we didn't really need houses and shoes and clothes because it was just our concepts that made us think we needed these things. I agreed with him and followed what his mind was doing, suspending for a moment the clutch of the abstract but at the same time shivering from the November wind and wanting to get back behind the warm glow of the windows. MILTON'S LUCIFER FLASHED THROUGH MY MIND. The young anthropology student was standing in the hallway. I told him that Donald was doing fine, great mystical stuff, philosophizing without concepts. He looked puzzled. He didn't want a drink or food. I walked upstairs and found the door to Allen's room closed. I waited for a while, not knowing what to do and then knocked softly and said softly, Allen I'm here now and will be back in a few minutes. *Paradise Lost*, A BOOK I'D NEVER UNDERSTOOD BEFORE—WHY MILTON SIDED WITH LUCIFER THE REBEL IN HEAVEN.

I GOT UP OUT OF BED AND WALKED DOWNSTAIRS NAKED, ORLOVSKY FOLLOWING ME CURIOUS WHAT I WOULD DO AND WILLING TO GO ALONG IN CASE I DID ANYTHING INTERESTINGLY EXTRAVAGANT.

Susan was sitting cross-legged on her bed brushing her hair when there came a patter of bare feet on the hallway carpet. I got to the door just in time to see naked buttocks disappearing down the stairway. It was Peter. I was grinning when I went back to Susan. Peter is running around without any clothes on. Susan picked up her paraphernalia—curlers, brush, pins, and trotted up to the third floor. I headed downstairs.

URGING ME ON IN FACT, THANK GOD. When I got to the study Frank was leaning back in his chair behind the desk grinning quizzically. In front of the desk looking like medieval hermits were Allen and Peter both stark naked. I WENT IN AMONG THE PSYCHOLOGISTS IN STUDY AND SAW THEY TOO WERE WAITING FOR SOMETHING VAST TO HAPPEN, ONLY IT REQUIRED SOMEONE AND THE MOMENT TO MAKE IT HAPPEN—ACTION, REVOLUTION. No, Allen had on his glasses and as I came in he peered out at me and raised his finger in the air. Hey, Allen, what goes on? Allen had a holy gleam in his eye and he waved his finger. I'm the Messiah. I've come down to preach love to the world. We're going to walk through the streets and teach people to stop hating. I DECIDED I MIGHT AS WELL BE THE ONE TO DO SO—PRONOUNCED MY NAKEDNESS AS THE FIRST ACT OF REVOLUTION AGAINST THE DESTROYERS OF THE HUMAN IMAGE.

Well, Allen, that sounds like a pretty good idea. Listen, said Allen, do you believe that I'm the Messiah. THE NAKED BODY BEING THE HIDDEN SIGN. Look, I can prove it. I'm going to cure your hearing. Take off your hearing machine. Your ears are cured. Come on, take it off, you don't need it. AND GRABBED THE TELEPHONE TO COMMUNICATE MY DECISION—WANTED TO HOOK UP KHRUSHCHEV, KEROUAC, BURROUGHS, IKE, KENNEDY, MAO TSE-TUNG, MAILER IN BELLEVUE, ETC.

Frank was still smiling. Peter was standing by watching seriously. The hearing aid was dumped on the desk. That's right. And now your glasses, I'll heal your vision too. The glasses were laid on the desk too. ALL IN ONE TELEPHONE LINE AND GET THEM ALL TO COME IMMEDIATELY TO HARVARD TO HAVE SPECTRAL CONFERENCE OVER THE FUTURE OF THE UNIVERSE.

Allen was peering around with approval at his healing. But Allen, one thing. What? Your glasses. You're still wearing them. Why don't you cure your own vision. Allen looked surprised. Yes, you're right. I will. He took off his glasses and laid them on the desk. TAKE OVER FROM THE COSMIC POLICE AND TAKE THE WORLD FOR OUR OWN INSTEAD OF BEING AT THE MERCY OF INTERCONNECTED NETWORK OF ECONOMIC POWER AND ELECTRONIC COMMUNICATION THAT WAS THREATENING US WITH DESTRUCTION.

Now Allen was a blind messiah squinting around to find his followers. ATOM BOMB APOCALYPSES. Come on. We're going down to the city streets to tell the people about peace and love. And then we'll get lots of great people onto a big telephone network to settle all this warfare bit. GOT AS FAR AS TELLING THE PHONE OPERATOR I WAS GOD AND WANTED TO TALK WITH KEROUAC IMMEDIATELY.

Fine, said Frank, but why not do the telephone

I won't, therefore, be able to make the Harvard mushroom seminar week— I'm sorry—don't let it bug you.

I don't know exactly when I'm leaving yet—but it's *got* to be around the first week in March. Peter and I will come up to Harvard for weekend before we leave tho.

Please don't be mad at me for taking off and leaving you holding the bag with so much on your mind. In the long run I do much better in anonymous goofing and writing than being Allen Ginsberg politicking.

I get the impression that the general psychic fog in the U.S. may be lifting. Also wrote a stern appeal for drugs into the GAP conference report, which'll be published by them.

Said they should invite some Amazon *curanderos* for their next conference. Do you want or need, or does the situation actually need, that I stay longer here and make the Harvard conference?

I feel that if I stay I'll just keep staying—and Gregory is calling, etc. If he comes here it'll be a ball, but it'll be a year or half-year before we can go again.

Prison sounds great. Don't give mushrooms to junkies who are just in physiological process (first weeks) of kicking. Burroughs says in an article it would be pure hell.
Physical pains, maybe get magnified. Kaufman said he'd already sent you material—didn't it arrive? I told him you'd not received it.

Which Osmond handbook on LSD? On giving LSD? Was that one of the papers I had?

In confusion I gave all papers to a Dr. Joe Gibbs, young psychiatrist who's had mescaline—including your poem-paper, before I had read it. Can you send me another?

Who's the Boston poet? I wound up imitating Kerouac too, for a week. He sounds fine on phone. I think that weekend did him permanent good, sort of made him more resolved and peaceful.

bit first, right here in the house. Frank was heading off the pilgrimage down the avenue naked. REMEMBERED TO RUN UPSTAIRS AND GIVE HER HIS PHONE NUMBER IN CASE IT DELAYED MY SCHEME WHILE SHE SEARCHED IT OUT.

Who we gonna call, said Peter. Well, we'll call Kerouac on Long Island, and Kennedy and Khrushchev and Bill Burroughs in Paris and Norman Mailer in the psycho ward in Bellevue. We'll get them all hooked up in a big cosmic electronic love talk. War is just a hang-up. We'll get the love-thing flowing on the electric Bell telephone network. REACHED HIM AND HAD A VERY EXPRESSIVE CONVERSATION—ONE OF THE FRANKEST I'VE HAD WITH HIM IN LAST FIVE YEARS. Who we gonna call first, said Peter. Let's start with Khrushchev, said Allen.

Look, why don't we start with Kerouac on Long Island. EXPLAINED ALL THE ABOVE AND DEMANDED HE JOIN ME IMMEDIATELY. In the meantime, let's pull the curtains, said Frank. There's enough going on in here so I don't care about looking outside. HE SAID HE HAS HIS MOTHER— "BRING YOUR MOTHER"—THE FIRST TIME I'D HAD THE NERVE TO CHALLENGE HIS MOTHER'S PSYCHIC PRIMACY OVER HIS FATE. Allen picked up the white telephone and dialed Operator. The two thin figures leaned forward wrapped up in a holy fervor trying to spread peace. The dear noble innocent helplessness of the naked body. They looked as though they had stepped out of a quatrocento canvas, apostles, martyrs, dear fanatic holy men. Allen said, Hello, operator, this is God, I want to talk to Kerouac. FELT EQUAL TO INCLUDING HER IN ON THE REBELLION IN HEAVEN. To whom do I want to talk? Kerouac. What's my name? This is God. G.O.D. Okay. We'll try Capitol 7-0563. Where? Northport, Long Island. There was a pause. We were all listening hard. Oh. Yes. That's right. That's the number of the house where I was born. Look, operator, I'll have to go upstairs to get the number. Then I'll call back. HE SAID, I DON'T WANT TO DIE.

Allen hung up the receiver. What was all that about, Allen? Well, the operator asked me my name and I said I was God and I wanted to speak to Kerouac and she said, I'll try to do my best, sir, but you'll have to give me his number and then I gave her the number of my mother's house. I've got Kerouac's number upstairs in my book. Just a minute and I'll get it.

Allen hopped out of the room, and Peter the Hermit lit a cigarette. I took advantage of the time out to check on the third floor. Susan was sitting on the floor of the TV room sticking bobby pins in her curlers. Rhona was lying on the couch watching a program. Charlie said, Hey, what's going on down there? Allen says he is God and he and Peter are naked and are phoning around to Kennedy and Kerouac. Naked? Both of them? Rhona and Charlie giggled. Rhona had been troubled by the poets' old clothes and felt that they hadn't been bathing. Hey, said Rhona, if they're really naked why don't you get them to jump under a shower. Good God, Rhona, with all this celestial business breaking out how can you get hung up on personal hygiene. Charlie got up from the easy chair. Naked, huh? This is something I can't miss. Dad-burn-it. I'm going down to catch this show.

Charlie followed down to the study. The two saints were standing gaunt and biblical by the desk. Allen was shouting in the telephone to Jack, I SAID, WHAZZAMATTER YOU AFRAID! ! ? HE GIGGLED—CONVERSATION SOON ENDED. He wanted Jack to come up to Cambridge and then he wanted Jack's mother to come too. Jack had a lot to say because Allen held the phone listening for long spaces. I HEARD HE WENT INTO NY AND DIDN'T DRINK FOR A WEEK AS A RESULT. Charlie was standing with his feet apart watching. Frank was still sitting behind the desk smiling. Donald and the anthro student were standing in the hallway looking in curiously. I walked over to explain. I HAD FEELING IF I WEAKENED IN ENERGY THE SCHEME WOULD FAIL. Allen says he is the Messiah and he's calling Kerouac to start a peace and love movement. Donald wasn't interested. He went on telling me about the foolishness of believing in hot and cold. It occurred to me that Allen and Peter were proving his point. IF I ATE OR SHIT AGAIN I WOULD TURN BACK TO MERE NON-MESSIAH HUMAN. The phone call continued and

Your letter very lovely, makes me feel like a messiah —running out on the cross part. I was always a little ashamed of the love poem for being so schmaltzy and schwarmerai and vague and abstract.

The *America* reading is a combination of different readings pieced on tape— I wanted to get campy tones into it, burlesque horror and goo-goo eyes.

Can you send me copy of Amer Psych Assn Speech? I been typing all day and also on junk—want to lie down and rest and think— so sign off.

Peter working 12 hours a day as messenger in snow to get up some more Europe loot.

If we're starving in India, we'll send you big demanding telegrams taking you up on your offer.

I gave 15 mushrooms to Thelonious Monk and he wanted to be alone with family in his house. I spoke to him on phone 5 hours later and he was fine.

No report from him yet, I'll send that as soon as possible. David Solomon is a good guy, but he is long-winded, an ex-political Red intellectual who's got humane.

He's given mescaline out, so I guess he can do it safely. I don't know if formal center need can be set up in N.Y. till the fungus spreads from Cambridge academy to N.Y. academy.

You have all the equipment for working with security there, that's the best—it will spread on its own once some N.Y. psychiatrist meets up with you.

Glad Schultes is friendly. Never did meet him. I've got to lie down awhile—write me a note—I hope my departure won't bring you down—is it alright if I go? Tell me.

Janine not taken mushrooms yet. I have 23 left—I gave 8 to a painter friend. All the young kids lately are shooting (needle) a drug called methedrine . . .

finally I walked back in and said, Hey Allen, for the cost of this phone call we could pay his way up here by plane. Allen shot an apologetic look and then I heard him telling Jack, Okay Jack, I have to go now, but you've got to take the mushrooms and let's settle this quarrel between Kennedy and Khrushchev. BUT NEEDED MY GLASSES —THOUGH HAD YELLED AT LEARY THAT HE DIDN'T NEED HIS EARPIECE TO HEAR THE REAL VIBRATIONS OF THE COSMOS.

HE WENT ALONG WITH ME AGREEABLY. Allen and Peter were sitting on the big couch in the living room and Allen was telling us about his visions, cosmic electronic networks, and how much it meant to him that I told him he was a great man and how this mushroom episode had opened the door to women and heterosexuality and how he could see new womanly body visions and family life ahead. BUT THEN I BEGAN BREATHING AND WANTING TO LIE DOWN AND REST. Peter's hand was moving back and forth on Allen's shoulder. It was the first time that he had stood up to Jack and he was sorry about the phone bill but wasn't it too bad that Khrushchev and Kennedy couldn't have been on the line and, hey, what about Norman Mailer in that psychiatric ward in Bellevue, shouldn't we call him. AND SAW THE CONTROL OF THE UNIVERSE SLIPPING OUT OF MY HANDS.

I don't think they'd let a call go through to him, Allen. Well, it all depends on how we come on. I don't think coming on as Allen Ginsberg would help in that league. I don't think coming on as the Messiah would either. Well, you could come on as big psychologists and make big demanding noises about the patient. It was finally decided that it was too much trouble.

Still *curandero,* I asked if they wanted anything to eat or drink. Well, how about some hot milk. FROM PHYSICAL FEAR AND FEELINGS OF WANTING TO FORGET IT ALL AND DIE, SLEEP, EAT, SHIT, BE BACK HUMAN. Allen and Peter went upstairs to put on robes and I put some cold milk in a pan and turned on the stove. Donald was still moving around softly with his hands behind his back. Thinking. Watching. He was too deep and Buddha for us to swing with and I later realized that I hadn't been a very attentive *curandero* for him and that there was a gulf between Allen and him never closed and that the geographic arrangement was too scattered to make a close loving session. Of course, both of them were old drug hands and ready to go off on their own private journeys and both wanted to make something deep and their own.

Anthro's role in all of this was never clear. He stood in the hallway watching curiously but for the most part we ignored him, treated him as an object just there but not involved and that, of course, was a mistake. Any time you treat someone as an object rest assured he'll do the same and that was the way that score was going to be tallied.

We ended up with a great scene in the kitchen. I bustled around pouring the hot milk into cups, and the poets sat around the table looking like Giotto martyrs in checkered robes. Lafcadio came down and we got him some food and he nodded yes when I asked him about ice cream and Allen started to talk about his visions and about the drug scene in New York and, becoming eloquent, wound up preaching with passion about the junkies, helpless, hooked, lost, thin, confused creatures, sick and the police and the informers. I SAW THE BEST MINDS OF MY GENERATION DE-STROYED BY MADNESS, STARVING HYSTERICAL NAKED, DRAGGING THEMSELVES THROUGH THE NEGRO STREETS AT DAWN LOOKING FOR AN ANGRY FIX. And then we started planning the psychedelic revolution. Allen wanted everyone to have the mushrooms. Who has the right to keep them from someone else? And there should be freedom for all sorts of rituals, too. ANGELHEADED HIPSTERS BURNING FOR THE ANCIENT HEAVENLY CONNECTION TO THE STARRY DYNAMO IN THE MACHINERY OF NIGHT. The doctors could have them and there should be *curanderos,* and all sorts of good new holy rituals that could be developed and ministers have to be involved. Although the church is naturally and automatically opposed to mushroom visions, still the experience is basically religious and some ministers would see it and start using them. But with all these groups and organizations and new rituals, there still had to be

. . . an amphetamine semihallucinogen—haven't tried it yet. It's all the vogue.

See—I don't know if I should stay here and rave and scream politically and give big Carnegie Hall readings and Harvard readings—but I think a quiet silly trip to Greece would be better in the long run. ∞

ALLEN GINSBERG
MARCH 1961:

Still hoping to come up, but can't figure it till I settle other things—leaving arrangements, filing all papers, etc. Glad Burroughs will be back at Harvard.

It's hard trying to turn off faucet of correspondence. The FCC complained to John Crosby about my TV speech and after network pressure Crosby let them play a 7-minute rebuttal last weekend, lots of crap.

I also hear Paul Goodman and N. Podhoretz are forming some kind of committee for intelligent action which has as program various things such as sex freedom and drug freedom.

A young girl approached me and transmitted a suggestion from Goodman that I go to jail in passive resistance action on marijuana. Sounds like a good deal, actually.

I told her I was going to Greece tho, so couldn't. They're having a meeting tonight at Debs Hall—just like the 20's

The Times refused to run a series on Fed Narco Bureau but Harrison Salisbury is now lobbying to find why; and they did agree to run the Lindesmith-Ploscowe report in summary when it does come out and various Chicago and SF papers are now interested too.

I think people at Living Theater and Goodman and others soon will prepare some sort of intellectual's prohibition.

I'll write Dr. Spiegel. Rev. John Snow of Gould Farm asked for your address, says he been reading up on subject and now wants to try LSD or mushrooms. I'll send it to him.

room for the single, lone, unattached, non-groupy individual to take the mushrooms and go off and follow his own rituals—brood big cosmic thoughts by the sea or roam through the streets of New York, high and restless, thinking poetry, and writers and poets and artists to work out whatever they were working out. WHO WERE EXPELLED FROM THE ACADEMIES FOR CRAZY AND PUBLISHING OBSCENE ODES ON THE WINDOWS OF THE SKULL.

But all this was going to be hard to bring about. What a political struggle! Think of all the big powerful forces lined up ready to crush anything wonderful and holy and free—the big fascist businessmen and the people who wanted to start a war against Russia and crush Castro. WHO COWERED IN UNSHAVEN ROOMS IN UNDERWEAR, BURNING THEIR MONEY IN WASTEBASKETS AND LISTENING TO THE TERROR THROUGH THE WALL. And all the sadistic little men who get together in groups like the American Legion and the white supremacy councils, and of course all the people who had their own little autocratic empires going who would be threatened if people really began to see with mushroom honesty, and finally and always there the police ready to investigate and arrest and indict and bully and keep people in jail because they want to live quiet lives of freedom and poetry. WHO REAPPEARED ON THE WEST COAST INVESTIGATING THE F.B.I. IN BEARDS AND SHORTS WITH BIG PACIFIST EYE SEXY IN THEIR DARK SKIN PASSING OUT INCOMPREHENSIBLE LEAFLETS.

As Allen talked nearsighted Marx-Trotsky-Paine poetry, there was always the Terror just back there a bit. Terror of Moloch. MOLOCH! MOLOCH! ROBOT APARTMENTS! INVISIBLE SUBURBS! SKELETON TREASURES! BLIND CAPITALS! DEMONIC INDUSTRIES! SPECTRAL NATIONS! INVINCIBLE MADHOUSES! GRANITE COCKS! MONSTROUS BOMBS! Terror of the Nazi national Golgotha. Terror of the void. Terror of death. Terror of Rockland State Hospital madness. Terror of the void. Terror of the long coiled snake of Peru slithering up closer with the slit-eye of destruction. WHO BURNED CIGARETTE HOLES IN THEIR ARMS PROTESTING THE NARCOTIC TOBACCO HAZE OF CAPITALISM.

The present hexagram refers to the cultural super-structure of society. Here it is the wood that serves as nourishment for the flame, the spirit. (*I Ching L*)

WHO DISTRIBUTED SUPERCOMMUNIST PAMPHLETS IN UNION SQUARE WEEPING AND UNDRESSING WHILE THE SIRENS OF LOS ALAMOS WAILED THEM DOWN. Allen Ginsberg hunched over the kitchen table, shabby robe hiding his thin white nakedness, cosmic politician. Give them the mystic vision. They'll see it's good and honest and they'll say so publicly and then no one from the police or the narcotics bureau can put them down. And you're the perfect persons to do it. Big serious scientist professors from Harvard. That's right. I can't do it. I'm too easy to put down. Crazy beatnik poet. Let me get my address book. I've got lots of connections in New York and we'll go right down the list and turn them all on. AND WAILED DOWN WALL, AND THE STATEN ISLAND FERRY ALSO WAILED, WHO BROKE DOWN CRYING IN WHITE GYMNASIUMS NAKED AND TREMBLING BEFORE THE MACHINERY OF OTHER SKELETONS.

AMERICA I'VE GIVEN YOU ALL AND NOW I'M NOTHING. Allen Ginsberg, cosmic crusader, running a worldwide campaign out of a small Lower East Side cold-water flat, helping a man in Scotland start a literary magazine by sending him poems from a dozen undiscovered youngsters in blue jeans, anxious but irrepressible, protected only by the honest nakedness. Allen Ginsberg, Zen master politician. AMERICA AFTER ALL IT IS YOU AND I WHO ARE PERFECT NOT THE NEXT WORLD. YOUR MACHINERY IS TOO MUCH FOR ME. YOU MADE ME WANT TO BE A SAINT.

Allen explaining his nakedness. When men set out to kill and bully they dress up. Suit of armor. Combat boots. Uniforms. I'M TRYING TO COME TO THE POINT. I REFUSE TO GIVE UP MY OBSESSION.

Allen Ginsberg the social-worker politician explaining the sex-drug-freedom-ecstasy movement. AMERICA STOP PUSHING I KNOW WHAT I'M DOING. Junk gives peace, relief from pain and a shattering cosmic detachment. But the relief is so brief and detachment so ruthlessly physical that the very weak and the very selfish get hooked. Junkies are the confused and helpless victims of

Looks like your own area is very sunny and I think it will remain so.

La Barre is lovely guy—hope you meet him somewhere. Jack moved his mama to Florida, so's out of town.

Harry Smith and Phipps are negotiating and I've now dropped out since they seem to be able to handle it all between them O.K. Haven't heard results.

Lafcadio is taking *dancing* lessons—great—twice a week—turns out pretty graceful and light on his feet.

I'm reading Wilhelm Reich and I think he's really great. You ever pick up on him?

. . . to translate in your terms, says the formation of abstractions sets in after crippling of *the* primary non-abstract body function, genital communication . . .

. . . the genital embrace being total annihilation of individuation and formation of a new third being of two separate identities . . .

. . . if the individual is blocked from experience of that communism all other reactions (and mental life) will be screwed up, and he describes thus, the origin of the worldwide emotional plague.

Farrar Straus stocks all his previously banned books— see the *Murder of Christ*. Dave Solomon gave LeRoi Jones the mushrooms finally —very good results too.

∞

ALLEN GINSBERG
APRIL 1961:

Got your letter—all sounds smashing good show there. Saw Monk play beautifully in Olympia theater in Paris, but didn't see him except on stage—a monk.

I receive mail safely at American Express, 11 Rue Scribe, Paris, France. If you have a sufficient supply, I would like to have some mushrooms or LSD.

I am looking for French connection, no success yet but have not looked intensively. Can use all you can send.

a one-sided game they started with the police. MY MIND IS MADE UP THERE IS GOING TO BE TROUBLE. Who wants the thankless task of helping the tormented egocentricity of the junkie? Long subway rides around Manhattan to borrow money to get the junkie to a doctor. AMERICA I AM ADDRESSING YOU. Endless calls on the delicatessen pay phone to arrange help. Locking yourself in a dingy hotel room to spend the next two days helping the sweating, writhing body kick its sickness. And the ceaseless politicking. Lining up all the little magazines and the friendly reporters to give a favorable review to the Indiana University book which shows the cruelty and futility of our drug laws. AMERICA THIS IS QUITE SERIOUS. Rushing uptown to the television show where you tell the American public they should get high on pot. I'D BETTER GET RIGHT DOWN TO THE JOB. In the thirties the fight to save the poor. In the forties the fight to save the Jews. In the fifties the fight to save the junkie. In the sixties we'll save the world. IT'S TRUE I DON'T WANT TO JOIN THE ARMY OR TURN LATHES IN PRECISION PARTS FACTORIES.

Now Allen Ginsberg, stooping over the kitchen table peering at his address book. There's Robert Lowell and Muriel Rukeyser. And Kerouac, of course, and LeRoi Jones. And Dizzy Gillespie and Thelonious Monk. And the painters. And the publishers. He was chanting out names of the famous and the talented. He was completely serious, dedicated, wound up in the crusade. I'M NEARSIGHTED AND PSYCHOPATHIC ANYWAY. AMERICA I'M PUTTING MY QUEER SHOULDER TO THE WHEEL.

And so Allen spun out the cosmic campaign. He was to line up influentials and each weekend I would come down to New York and we'd run mushroom sessions. This fit our Harvard research plans perfectly. Our aim there was to learn how people reacted, to test the limits of the drug, to get creative and thoughtful people to take them and tell us what they saw and what we should do with the mushrooms. Allen's political plan was appealing, too. I had seen enough and read enough in Spanish of the anti-vision crowd, the power-holders with guns, and the bigger and better men we got on our team the stronger our position. And then too, the big-name bit was intriguing. Meeting and sharing visions with the famous.

The ritual was to be the *curandero* sequence. These people will have more confidence in you than in me, said Allen. The wise-guide ritual sounded good. The cause was right and the contract beneficial to all concerned. We were after all offering a free round-trip ticket for the greatest journey known to man. From this moment on my days as a respectable establishment scientist were numbered. I just couldn't see the new society given birth by medical hands. Or psychedelic sacraments as psychiatric tools. From this evening on my energies were offered to the ancient underground society of alchemists, artists, mystics, alienated visionaries, drop-outs and the disenchanted young, the sons arising.

For a while the hobbits continued to talk and think of the past journey and of the perils that lay ahead; but such was the virtue of the land of Rivendell that soon all fear and anxiety was lifted from their minds. The future, good or ill, was not forgotten, but ceased to have any power over the present. (*The Lord of the Rings*)

It was around midnight. Donald still seemed high and would walk in and out of the room, silently, hands behind his back, Talmudic raccoon, studying the kitchen crowd seriously, and then padding out. The anthropology student had joined us around the table. We had given him something to drink and he was listening to the conversation and saying nothing. He made some comment about schedules back to Cambridge and it was time for him to make the last train so I drove him down to the station. He asked some questions about the scientific meaning of the mushroom research and it was clear that he didn't understand what had happened and what we were doing. There wasn't time to explain and I felt badly that he had been dragged into a strange situation. We had made the rule that people could bring their friends when they took the mushrooms and this seemed like a good idea for the person taking the mushrooms but it was just beginning to dawn on me that the problem

Burroughs is in Tangier, c/o U.S. Consulate. He or Brian Gysin et my mushrooms. I'll go down to visit Burroughs as soon as financially able.

. . . All three of us down to $80.00, but there will be loot coming in. We got offer from Gerodias of Olympia to be editors of a big time sexual magazine, free hand with vast salaries and print anything *mad* we want.

Gregory wants to, I'm hesitating, Peter still wants India directly. If I accept it means being tied down here in Europe a year or two, but also weirdest century literary mag yet. I dunno.

I'll probably be around here when you came in June. Send me forms to fill out as I gave mushrooms to Gregory. Gysin has filled out and will send you his.

I don't know him well, and no intimate contact with him emotionally, tho Burroughs thinks we should dig each other.

Gysin has invented a *great* flicker machine. Dig this— cut out 10 apertures on a stovepipe hat or piece of cardboard and set it revolving on phonograph at 33 speed.

It flickers and is homemade strobe. I looked in it—it sets up optical fields as religious and mandalic as the hallucinogenic drugs—literally.

. . . (look in with eyes closed)—it's like being able to have jewelled biblical designs and landscapes without taking chemicals. Amazing.

It *works*. Gysin says the apertures have to be measured and adjusted right to get 16 flickers a second or something.

He also paints the inside of the stovepipe-cardboard Of course, you have to drop an electric bulb, I forgot it, in the center of it to flicker thru apertures.

I'll try to connect him with a toy manufacturer—homemade optic movies possible.

Burroughs' present cut up operates—in theory—on similar flicker principle—trying to play his words over and over flashing in different combos to perhaps set up a 3-D field in imagination or some other practical level.

never was with the person taking the drug but rather the people who didn't. Like Brother Toriblo the Spanish monk, who talked about cruelty and drunkenness caused by the Sacred Mushrooms. It's okay to bring a friend, but he should take the mushrooms with you. And poor anthro, it turned out, wasn't even a friend of Donald's and as it turned out didn't like him and he was clearly bewildered by and critical of what he had seen and heard and the nakedness of the poets. His train was about due and I was too preoccupied by what Allen had been saying to feel like explaining to anthro. The uneasy feeling persisted and I suggested that he not tell people about the mystic visions and the naked crusaders because this might be misunderstood and he said he wouldn't talk about it and we shook hands and he left.

That was Sunday night.

By Monday afternoon the rumors were spreading around the Harvard yard.

Beatniks. Orgies. Naked poets. Junkies. Homosexuality. Drug parties. Tried to lure a decent naive graduate student into sin. Wild parties masquerading as research. Queers. Beards. Criminal types.

The chairman of my department called me. What the hell is going on, Tim? Two graduate students have come to me indignant—demanding that your work be stopped.

I laughed. I'll send you the reports from the session as soon as they are typed. It was a good session. God would approve. We're learning a lot.

The disapproving gaze of the establishment was on us. You should fear the wary eyes of the servants of Sauron were the words of Elrond. I do not doubt that news . . . has already reached him, and he will be filled with wrath. Naked poets, indeed!

From this time on we saw ourselves as unwitting agents of a social process that was far too powerful for us to control or to more than dimly understand. An historical movement that would inevitably change man at the very center of his nature, his consciousness.

We did sense that we were not alone. The quest for internal freedom, for the elixir of life, for the drought of immortal revelation was not new. We were part of an ancient and honorable fellowship which had pursued this journey since the dawn of recorded history. We began to read the accounts of earlier trippers—Dante, Hesse, Rene Daumal, Tolkien, Homer, Blake, George Fox, Swedenborg, Bosch, and the explorers from the Orient—tantrics, Sufis, Bauls, Gnostics, hermetics, Sivites, saddhus. No, we were not alone.

Nor were we isolated in the twentieth century. The three groups who always await and accept the revelation which comes in every historical time were present in full and goodly numbers. The young (who always want more and have no game to protect), the artists (who always hunger for the ecstatic moment), and the alienated (the wise slaves and noble minority groups watching from the periphery of the society).

The success of the psychedelic movement was guaranteed. The energies released by the sacred drugs were too great to suppress.

We began to see it as a question of time. The movement would grow like everything organic grows, cell by cell. Friend turning-on friends. Husbands turning-on wives. Teachers turning-on students. The contagion of contiguity. The tissue underground.

Shortly after Allen Ginsberg left, we made statistical predictions about the growth of the psychedelic movement. We drew a cumulative percentage graph and hung it on the wall. The rapidly ascending curve spelled out our forecast.

In 1961, we estimated that 25,000 Americans had turned-on to the strong psychedelics—LSD, mescaline, peyote. (Marijuana we stayed away from.) This figure did not include the 125,000 American Indians who use peyote as their sacrament and who were there as an inestimable psychic asset when we were ready to use it. (It is no accident that the psychedelic movement by 1967 was a tribal phenomenon.)

At the rate of cellular growth we expected that by 1967 a million Americans would be using LSD. We calculated that the critical figure for blowing the mind of the American society would be four million LSD users and this would happen by 1969.

Interesting experiment and more grounded in practical constructive purpose than I had grasped—thought before it was just a negative thing to cut up life or recombine words artistically.

Can you send me a pack of psilocybin?—and also send the forms, they'll be filled out. Here is Peter, who a half-hour ago shot 250 of mescaline into his vein with a needle.

First, yes, also, I saw Michaux who has just finished a book on his experiments with mushroom pills too—nice old man—says it's all in *you* and no outside forces or gods too . . .

Peter Orlovski: Yes, it's all an inward force, we are all God, so being God it feels very nice to shoot up mescaline in the vein which I just did two hours ago—got laid last night—so many girls here. Now that I am high, would like to see this flicker

. . . but it's being fixed—so at the moment the world seems very physical and all the physicalness going somewhere—soup on the stove—it all boils down to ass and roses on the table—you been able to turn-on Kennedy's brother yet? Kennedy real mean to Castro and acting so stupid . . .

. . . instead of making friends—he's giving me a bad name—help—hey Kennedy, why don't you get laid instead of fucking around with politics? So Tim, I've been studying French here and going to gym with a funny hard-on.

Allen Ginsberg: That was Peter, half-hour sitting at typewriter—totally high. Lots happening here, a great shade (Negro) painter in town who tells me he stayed high on mescaline 3 months last year. . . .

Magnificent imaginist painter (new school we named)— i.e. visionary literal dream vision or waking visionary imagery as subject, breaktḣru from abstract— *Gregory* a great book— *American Express* the last word on cosmic politics—

A dreamy comedy writ like *Candide* and *Alice in Wonderland,* pix by author, we'll send you a copy—Burroughs one of the goofy conspirers.

∞

We were wrong in our estimates. We were too conservative. By 1966 *Life* magazine announced that a million Americans were using LSD. In the spring of 1966, a million doses a month were being distributed by a messianic underground in California alone. By 1967 four million Americans had taken the trip. In June of 1967, an album by the Beatles which openly celebrated the psychedelic experience sold a million copies the first week of its release.

Our forecast was off because, as middle-aged professors, we counted on the artists and the minorities and the college youth, but we failed to anticipate the use of LSD by high-school kids. In our academic isolation we forgot that for thousands of years the psychedelic vision has been the rite of passage of the teen-ager—the Dakota Indian boy who sits on the mountaintop fasting and sleepless, waiting for the revelation. The threshold of adult game life is the ancient and natural time for the rebirth experience, the flip-out trip from which you come back as a man. A healthy society provides and protects the sacredness of the teen-age psychedelic voyage. A sick, static society fears and forbids the revelation.

The psychedelic movement was to develop without organization, without leaders, without dogmatic doctrines and become a full-blown religious renaissance of the young.

It moved quickly, always shocking, continually shattering structures. You either surrendered to the flow and went with that full tide of two billion years, or you were thrown to the bank where you shouted stop! danger! medical control! evil! scientific respectability! and despaired that your words couldn't slow the relentless current.

Allen Ginsberg came to Harvard and shook us loose from our academic fears and strengthened our courage and faith in the process.

THE CALDRON. *Supreme good fortune. Success.*
(I Ching)

THE RESURRECTION OF THE BODY

Norman O. Brown

The path of sublimation, which mankind has religiously followed at least since the foundation of the first cities, is no way out of the human neurosis, but, on the contrary, leads to its aggravation. Psychoanalytical theory and the bitter facts of contemporary history suggest that mankind is reaching the end of this road. Psychoanalytical theory declares that the end of the road is the dominion of death-in-life. History has brought mankind to that pinnacle on which the total obliteration of mankind is at last a practical possibility. At this moment of history the friends of the life instinct must warn that the victory of death is by no means impossible; the malignant death instinct can unleash those hydrogen bombs. For if we discard our fond illusion that the human race has a privileged or providential status in the life of the universe, it seems plain that the malignant death instinct is a built-in guarantee that the human experiment, if it fails to attain its possible perfection, will cancel itself out, as the dinosaur experiment canceled itself out. But jeremiads are useless unless we can point to a better way. Therefore the question confronting mankind is the abolition of repression —in traditional Christian language, the resurrection of the body.

We have already done what we could to extract from psychoanalytical theory a model of what the resurrected body would be like. The life instinct, or sexual instinct, demands activity of a kind that, in contrast to our current mode of activity, can only be called play. The life instinct also demands a union with others and with the world around us based not on anxiety and aggression but on narcissism and erotic exuberance.

But the death instinct also demands satisfaction; as Hegel says in the *Phenomenology,* "The life and knowledge of God may doubtless be described as love playing with itself; but this idea sinks into triviality, if the seriousness, the pain, the patience and the labor of the Negative are omitted." [1] The death instinct is reconciled with the life instinct only in a life which is not repressed, which leaves no "unlived lines" in the human body, the death instinct then being affirmed in a body which is willing to die. And, because the body is satisfied, the death instinct no longer drives it to change itself and make history, and therefore, as Christian theology divined, its activity is in eternity.

At the same time—and here again Christian theology and psychoanalysis agree—the resurrected body is the transfigured body. The abolition of repression would abolish the unnatural concentrations of libido in certain particular bodily organs—concentrations engineered by the negativity of

[1] Hegel, *Phenomenology of Mind,* p. 81.

the morbid death instinct, and constituting the bodily base of the neurotic character disorders in the human ego. In the words of Thoreau: "We need pray for no higher heaven than the pure senses can furnish, a purely sensuous life. Our present senses are but rudiments of what they are destined to become." [2] The human body would become polymorphously perverse, delighting in that full life of all the body which it now fears. The consciousness strong enough to endure full life would be no longer Apollonian but Dionysian—consciousness which does not observe the limit, but overflows; consciousness which *does not negate any more.*

If the question facing mankind is the abolition of repression, psychoanalysis is not the only point of view from which the question can and should be raised. We have already indicated that the question is intrinsic to Christian theology. The time has come to ask Christian theologians, especially the neo-orthodox, what they mean by the resurrection of the body and by eternal life. Is this a promise of immortality after death? In other words, is the psychological premise of Christianity the impossibility of reconciling life and death either in "this" world or the "next," so that flight from death—with all its morbid consequences—is our eternal fate in "this world" and in "the next"? For we have seen that the perfect body, promised by Christian theology, enjoying that perfect felicity promised by Christian theology, is a body reconciled with death.

In the last analysis Christian theology must either accept death as part of life or abandon the body. For two thousand years Christianity has kept alive the mystical hope of an ultimate victory of Life over Death, during a phase of human history when Life was at war with Death and hope could only be mystical. But if we are approaching the last days, Christian theology might ask itself whether it is only the religion of fallen humanity, or whether it might be asleep when the bridegroom comes. Certain it is that if Christianity wishes to help mankind toward that erasure of the traces of original sin which Baudelaire said was the true definition of progress,[3] there are priceless insights in its tradition—insights which have to be transformed into a system of practical therapy, something like psychoanalysis, before they are useful or even meaningful.

The specialty of Christian eschatology lies precisely in its rejection of the Platonic hostility to the human body and to "matter," its refusal to identify the Platonic path of sublimation with ultimate salvation, and its affirmation that eternal life can only be life in a body. Christian asceticism can carry punishment of the fallen body to heights inconceivable to Plato; but Christian hope is for the redemption of that fallen body. Hence the affirmation of Tertullian: *Resurget igitur caro, et quidem omnis, et quidem ipsa, et quidem integra*—The body will rise again, all of the body, the identical body, the entire body.[4] The medieval Catholic synthesis between Christianity

---

[2] Thoreau, *A Week on the Concord and Merrimack Rivers*; cf. Read, *Icon and Idea*, p. 139.
[3] Baudelaire, *Mon coeur mis a nu*. Cf. Marcuse, *Eros and Civilization*, p. 153.
[4] Tertullian, *De Carnis Resurrectione*, p. 63. Cf. Mead, *The Doctrine of the Subtle Body in Western Tradition*, p. 111.

and Greek philosophy, with its notion of an immortal soul, compromised and confused the issue; only Protestantism carries the full burden of the peculiar Christian faith. Luther's break with the doctrine of sublimation (good works) is decisive; but the theologian of the resurrected body is the cobbler of Görlitz, Jacob Boehme. When Tillich and Barth finally get round to the substance of things hoped for, their eschatology, they will have to reckon with Boehme. Meanwhile, as neoorthodox theology plunges deeper into the nature of sin and death, Boehme's *theologia ex idea vitae deducta* is neglected except by the lonely mystic and revolutionary Berdyaev.

Whatever the Christian churches do with him, Boehme's position in the Western tradition of mystic hope of better things is central and assured. Backward he is linked, through Paracelsus and alchemy, to the tradition of Christian gnosticism and Jewish cabalism; forward he is linked, through his influence on the romantics Blake, Novalis, and Hegel, with Freud. We have argued that psychoanalysis has not psychoanalyzed itself until it places itself inside the history of Western thought—inside the general neurosis of mankind. So seen, psychoanalysis is the heir to a mystical tradition which it must affirm.

Mysticism, in the mind of the general public, is identified with that flight from the material world and from life preached by such popularizers as Evelyn Underhill and Aldous Huxley[5]—which, from the psychoanalytical point of view, may be termed Apollonian or sublimation mysticism. But there is in the Western tradition another kind of mysticism, which can be called Dionysian or body mysticism, which stays with life, which is the body, and seeks to transform and perfect it. Western body mysticism—a tradition which urgently needs re-examination—contains three main strands: the Christian (Pauline) notion of the "spiritual" body, the Jewish (cabalistic) notion of Adam's perfect body before the Fall, and the alchemical notion of the subtle body.[6] All of these strands unite in Boehme, and even a little knowledge of the real Boehme—for example Ernst Benz' first-rate book, not available in English[7]—makes it plain that Boehme and Freud have too much in common to be able to dispense with each other.

Boehme, like Freud, understands death not as a mere nothing but as a positive force either in dialectical conflict with life (in fallen man), or dialectically unified with life (in God's perfection). Thus, says Benz, "Our life remains a struggle between life and death, and as long as this conflict lasts, anxiety lasts also." [8] In Boehme's concept of life, the concept of play, or love-play, is as central as it is in Freud's; and his concept of the spiritual or paradisaical body of Adam before the Fall recognizes the potent demand in our unconscious both for an androgynous mode of being and for a

---

[5] Underhill, *Mysticism*; Huxley, *The Perennial Philosophy*.
[6] Mead, *The Doctrine of the Subtle Body in Western Tradition*; Scholem, *Major Trends in Jewish Mysticism*; Gray, *Goethe the Alchemist*. Cf. Savage, "Jung, Alchemy and Self," pp. 14–37.
[7] Benz, *Der vollkommene Mensch nach Jacob Boehme*.
[8] Benz, *op. cit.*, p. 138.

narcissistic mode of self-expression, as well as the corruption in our current use of the oral, anal, and genital functions. It is true that Boehme does not yet accept the brutal death of the individual physical body, and therefore makes his paradisaical body ambiguously immaterial, without oral, anal, and genital organs; and yet he clings obstinately to the body and to bodily pleasure, and therefore says that Adam was "magically" able to eat and enjoy the "essence" of things, and "magically" able to reproduce and to have sexual pleasure in the act of reproduction. Boehme is caught in these dilemmas because of his insight into the corruption of the human body, his insight that all life is life in the body, and, on the other hand, his inability to accept a body which dies. No Protestant theologian has gone further; or rather, later Protestantism has preferred to repress the problem and to repress Boehme.

Oriental mysticism also, to judge from Needham's survey of Taoism or Eliade's study of Yoga,[9] has reached the same point. Needham (quoting Maspéro) is right in stressing that the Taoist quest for a more perfect body transcends the Platonic dualism of soul and matter. But Needham's enthusiasm for Taoism as a human and organismic response to life in the world must be qualified by recognizing that the Taoist perfect body is immortal: Taoism does not accept death as part of life. (In an earlier chapter we argued that there is the same defect in Needham's other enthusiasm, Whitehead's philosophy of nature.)

Psychoanalysis accepts the death of the body; but psychoanalysis has something to learn from body mysticism, occidental and oriental, over and above the wealth of psychoanalytical insights contained in it. For these mystics take seriously, and traditional psychoanalysis does not, the possibility of human perfectibility and the hope of finding a way out of the human neurosis into that simple health that animals enjoy, but not man.

As Protestantism degenerated from Luther and Boehme, it abandoned its religious function of criticizing the existing order and keeping alive the mystical hope of better things; in psychoanalytical terminology, it lost contact with the unconscious and with the immortal repressed desires of the unconscious. The torch passed to the poets and philosophers of the romantic movement. The heirs of Boehme are Blake, Novalis, Hegel, and, as Professor Gray has recently shown, Goethe.[10] These are the poets whom Freud credited with being the real discoverers of the unconscious.

Not only toward the mystics but also toward the poets psychoanalysis must quit its pretension of supramundane superiority. Instead of exposing the neuroses of the poets, the psychoanalysts might learn from them, and abandon the naive idea that there is an immense gap, in mental health and intellectual objectivity, between themselves and the rest of the world. In the world's opinion, in the eyes of common sense, Novalis is crazy, and Ferenczi also: the world will find it easier to believe that we are all mad

[9] Needham, *Science and Civilization in China*, II, 139–54. Needham seems to underestimate Occidental body mysticism; cf. *op. cit.*, p. 464, the only reference to Boehme. See also Watts, "Asian Psychology and Modern Psychiatry," pp. 25–30.
[10] Gray, *Goethe the Alchemist*.

than to believe that the psychoanalysts are not. And further, it does not seem to be the case that the psychoanalytical mode of reaching the unconscious has superannuated the poetic, or artistic, mode of attaining the same objective. Anyone conversant both with modern literature and with psychoanalysis knows that modern literature is full of psychoanalytical insights not yet grasped, or not so clearly grasped, by "scientific" psychoanalysis. And anyone who loves art knows that psychoanalysis has no monopoly on the power to heal. What the times call for is an end to the war between psychoanalysis and art—a war kept alive by the sterile "debunking" approach of psychoanalysis to art—and the beginning of cooperation between the two in the work of therapy and in the task of making the unconscious conscious. A little more Eros and less strife.

Modern poetry, like psychoanalysis and Protestant theology, faces the problem of the resurrection of the body. Art and poetry have always been altering our ways of sensing and feeling—that is to say, altering the human body. And Whitehead rightly discerns as the essence of the "Romantic Reaction" a revulsion against abstraction (in psychoanalytical terms, sublimation) in favor of the concrete sensual organism, the human body.[11] "Energy is the only life, and is from the Body. . . . Energy is Eternal Delight," says Blake.

A young critic, whose first book represents a new mode of criticism—a criticism for which poetry is an experience both mystical and bodily—has traced the persistent quest in modern poetry for the resurrection of the body and the perfection of the body.[12] Wordsworth, in contrast with the sublime (and sublimating) tendency of Milton, "considers that his revelation can be expressed in the forms and symbols of daily life" and "sees Paradise possible in any sweet though bare nook of the earth." Hopkins "is engaged on a theodicy, and has taken for his province the stubborn senses and the neglected physical world"; "no one has gone further than Hopkins in presenting Christ as the direct and omnipresent object of perception, so deeply ingrained in the eyes, the flesh, and the bone (and the personal sense of having eyes, flesh, and bone), that the sense of self and the sense of being in Christ can no longer be distinguished." Rilke's plaint throughout his career is that "we do not know the body any more than we know nature": Rilke believes (in his own words) that "the qualities are to be taken away from God, the no longer utterable, and returned to creation, to love and death"; so that the outcome of his poetry is that "for Rilke, the body becomes a spiritual fact." Valéry's poetry "may be considered as the Odyssey of Consciousness in search of its true body"; and "the intellectual pursuit of Valéry is to this end, that the body may be seen as what it virtually is, a magnificent revelation and instrument of the soul. Could it be viewed as such, the eyes would not be symbol, but reality." [13]

The "magical" body which the poet seeks is the "subtle" or "spiritual" or "translucent" body of occidental mysticism, and the "diamond" body of

[11] Whitehead, *Science and the Modern World*, pp. 93–118.
[12] Hartman, *The Unmediated Vision*.
[13] Hartman, *op. cit.*, pp. 27–28, 57, 64, 94, 96, 107, 109.

oriental mysticism, and, in psychoanalysis, the polymorphously perverse body of childhood. Thus, for example, psychoanalysis declares the fundamentally bisexual character of human nature; Boehme insists on the androgynous character of human perfection; Taoist mysticism invokes feminine passivity to counteract masculine aggressivity; and Rilke's poetic quest is a quest for a hermaphroditic body. There is an urgent need for elucidation of the interrelations between these disparate modes of articulating the desires of the unconscious. Jung is aware of these interrelations, and orthodox psychoanalysts have not been aware of them. But no elucidation results from incorporation of the data into the Jungian system, not so much because of the intellectual disorder in the system, but rather because of the fundamental orientation of Jung, which is flight from the problem of the body, flight from the concept of repression, and a return to the path of sublimation. Freudianism must face the issue, and Freud himself said: "Certain practices of the mystics may succeed in upsetting the normal relations between the different regions of the mind, so that, for example, the perceptual system becomes able to grasp relations in the deeper layers of the ego and in the id which would otherwise be inaccessible to it." [14]

Joseph Needham's interest in what we have called body mysticism, an interest which underlies his epoch-making work *Science and Civilization in China,* reminds us that the resurrection of the body has been placed on the agenda not only by psychoanalysis, mysticism, and poetry, but also by the philosophical criticism of modern science. Whitehead's criticism of scientific abstraction is, in psychoanalytical terms, a criticism of sublimation. His protest against "The Fallacy of Misplaced Concreteness" is a protest on behalf of the living body as a whole: "But the living organ of experience is the living body as a whole"; and his protest "on behalf of value" insists that the real structure of the human body, of human cognition, and of the events cognized is both sensuous and erotic, "self-enjoyment." Whitehead himself recognized the affinity between himself and the romantic poets; and Needham of course recognizes the affinity between the philosophy of organism and mysticism. Actually Needham may be exaggerating the uniqueness of Taoism. The whole Western alchemical tradition, which urgently needs re-examination, is surely "Whiteheadian" in spirit, and Goethe, the last of the alchemists, in his "Essay on the Metamorphosis of Plants" produced the last, or the first, Whiteheadian scientific treatise. Goethe, says a modern biologist, "reached out to the reconciliation of the antithesis between the senses and the intellect, an antithesis with which traditional science does not attempt to cope." [15]

Needham has recognized the crucial role of psychology in the philosophy of science. The refutation of Descartes, he has said, will come from psychology, not biology.[16] And yet he seems to be unaware of the profound

---

[14] Sigmund Freud, *New Introductory Lectures on Psychoanalysis,* trans. N. J. H. Sprott, International Psycho-Analytical Library, no. 24 (London: Hogarth Press and Institute of Psycho-Analysis, 1933), p. 106.
[15] Cf. Gray, *Goethe the Alchemist,* pp. 98–99.
[16] Needham, "Mechanistic Biology," in *Science, Religion and Reality,* p. 257.

affinities between the Tao, which he so much admires, and psychoanalysis. He seems to be unaware of Ferenczi's brilliant essay attempting to reorganize the whole theory of biological evolution in the light of psychoanalysis.[17] But the function of psychoanalysis in relation to Whitehead and Needham's critique of science is not that of supplementing their ideology with sympathetic support; rather it is indispensable if their critique of science is to amount to more than mere ideology. For what they are calling in question is the subjective attitude of the scientist, and if their critique is to amount to more than mere dislike, it must be supplemented by a psychoanalysis of the subject. In fact a psychoanalysis of the subject (the "observer") seems necessary if science is to remain "objective." The essential point has been seen by Ferenczi, who coined the term "utraquism" to indicate the required combination of analysis of the subject and analysis of the object: "If science is really to remain objective, it must work alternately as pure psychology and pure natural science, and must verify both our inner and outer experience by analogies taken from both points of view. . . . I called this the 'utraquism' of all true scientific work." [18]

Ferenczi's formulations date from 1923–1926: today we would presumably think of "integration" rather than alternation. Ferenczi saw psychoanalysis as marking a significant step forward in general scientific methodology, a step which he defined as "a return to a certain extent to the methods of ancient animistic science" and "the re-establishment of an animism no longer anthropomorphic." [19] But the re-establishment of an animism is precisely the outcome of Whitehead and Needham's line of thought. And Ferenczi argues that psychoanalysis is necessary in order to differentiate the new "purified" animism from the old naive animism:[20]

Insofar as Freud attempts to solve problems of biology as well as of sexual activity by means of psychoanalytic experience, he returns to a certain extent to the methods of ancient animistic science. There is a safeguard, however, against the psychoanalyst falling into the error of such naïve animism. Naïve animism transferred human psychic life *en bloc* without analysis onto natural objects. Psychoanalysis, however, dissected human psychic activity, pursued it to the limit where psychic and physical came into contact, down to the instincts, and thus freed psychology from anthropprocentrism, and only then did it trust itself to evaluate this purified animism in terms of biology. To have been the first in the history of science to make this attempt is the achievement of Freud.

We therefore conclude with a plea for "utraquistic" integration between psychoanalysis and the philosophy of science. Ferenczi, in his important analysis of Ernst Mach entitled "The Psychogenesis of Mechanism," put it this way: "When will the physicist, who finds the soul in the mechanism, and the psychoanalyst, who perceives mechanisms in the soul, join hands

[17] Ferenczi, *Thalassa.*
[18] Ferenczi, *Further Contributions,* p. 373.
[19] Ferenczi, *Further Contributions,* p. 256; *Thalassa,* p. 2.
[20] Ferenczi, *Further Contributions,* p. 256.

and work with united forces at a *Weltanschauung* free from one-sidedness and 'idealizations'?" [21]

Perhaps there are even deeper issues raised by the confrontation between psychoanalysis and the philosophy of organism. Whitehead and Needham are protesting against the inhuman attitude of modern science; in psychoanalytical terms, they are calling for a science based on an erotic sense of reality, rather than an aggressive dominating attitude toward reality. From this point of view alchemy (and Goethe's essay on plants) might be said to be the last effort of Western man to produce a science based on an erotic sense of reality. And conversely, modern science, as criticized by Whitehead, is one aspect of a total cultural situation which may be described as the dominion of death-in-life. The mentality which was able to reduce nature to "a dull affair, soundless, scentless, colorless; merely the hurrying of material endlessly, meaninglessly"—Whitehead's description[22]—is lethal. It is an awe-inspiring attack on the life of the universe; in more technical psychoanalytical terms, its anal-sadistic intent is plain. And further, the only historian of science who uses psychoanalysis, Gaston Bachelard, concludes that it is of the essence of the scientific spirit to be mercilessly ascetic, to eliminate human enjoyment from our relation to nature, to eliminate the human senses, and finally to eliminate the human brain:[23]

It does indeed seem that with the twentieth century there begins a kind of scientific thought in opposition to the senses, and that it is necessary to construct a theory of objectivity *in opposition to* the object. . . . It follows that the entire use of the brain is being called into question. From now on the brain is strictly no longer adequate as an instrument for scientific thought; that is to say, the brain is the *obstacle* to scientific thought. It is an obstacle in the sense that it is the coordinating center for human movements and appetites. It is necessary to think *in opposition to* the brain.

Thus modern science confirms Ferenczi's aphorism: *"Pure intelligence* is thus a product of dying, or at least of becoming mentally insensitive, and is therefore *in principle madness."* [24]

What Whitehead and Needham are combating is not an error but a disease in consciousness. In more technical psychoanalytical terms, the issue is not the conscious structure of science, but the unconscious premises of science; the trouble is in the unconscious strata of the scientific ego, in the scientific character-structure. Whitehead called the modern scientific point of view, in spite of its world-conquering successes, "quite unbelievable." [25] Psychoanalysis adds the crucial point: it is insane. Hence there is unlikely to be any smooth transition from the "mechanistic" point of view to the "organismic" point of view. It is unlikely that problems generated in the

[21] Ferenczi, *Further Contributions*, p. 393.
[22] Whitehead, *Science and the Modern World*, p. 69.
[23] Bachelard, *La formation de l'esprit scientifique*, pp. 250–51.
[24] Ferenczi, *Final Contributions*, p. 246.
[25] Whitehead, *Science and the Modern World*, p. 69.

mechanistic system will lead to organismic solutions. The two points of view represent different instinctual orientations, different fusions of life and death. It is even doubtful that the adoption of an organismic point of view under present conditions would be a gain; it might be a relapse into naive animism. Thus the kind of thinking which Needham hails as Taoist wisdom (alchemy, etc.), is attacked by Bachelard as unconscious projection, dreaming, and naive mythologizing; he sees science (and psychoanalysis) as sternly committed to the task of demythologizing our view of nature. It would seem, therefore, in line with Ferenczi's argument, that Taoist ideology without psychoanalytical consciousness could be a relapse into naive animism. And psychoanalytical consciousness means psychoanalytical therapy also. Psychoanalytical therapy involves a solution to the problem of repression; what is needed is not an organismic ideology, but to change the human body so that it can become for the first time an organism—the resurrection of the body. An organism whose own sexual life is as disordered as man's is in no position to construct objective theories about the Yin and the Yang and the sex life of the universe.

The resurrection of the body is a social project facing mankind as a whole, and it will become a practical political problem when the statesmen of the world are called upon to deliver happiness instead of power, when political economy becomes a science of use-values instead of exchange-values —a science of enjoyment instead of a science of accumulation. In the face of this tremendous human problem, contemporary social theory, both capitalist and socialist, has nothing to say. Contemporary social theory (again we must honor Veblen as an exception) has been completely taken in by the inhuman abstractions of the path of sublimation, and has no contact with concrete human beings, with their concrete bodies, their concrete though repressed desires, and their concrete neuroses.

To find social theorists who are thinking about the real problem of our age, we have to go back to the Marx of 1844, or even to the philosophers influencing Marx in 1844, Fourier and Feuerbach. From Fourier's psychological analysis of the antithesis of work and pleasure Marx obtained the concept of play, and used it, in a halfhearted way to be sure, in some of his early utopian speculations. From Feuerbach Marx learned the necessity of moving from Hegelian abstractions to the concrete senses and the concrete human body. Marx' "philosophic-economic manuscripts" of 1844 contain remarkable formulations calling for the resurrection of human nature, the appropriation of the human body, the transformation of the human senses, and the realization of a state of self-enjoyment. Thus, for example, "Man appropriates himself as an all-sided being in an all-sided way, hence as total man. [This appropriation lies in] every one of his human relationships to the world—seeing, hearing, smell, taste, feeling, thought, perception, experience, wishing, activity, loving, in short, all organs of his individuality." [26] The human physical senses must be emancipated from the sense of possession, and then the humanity of the senses and the human enjoyment

[26] Marx, Engels, *Kleine ökonomische Schriften*, p. 131; cf. pp. 127-37.

of the senses will be achieved for the first time. Here is the point of contact between Marx and Freud: I do not see how the profundities and obscurities of the "philosophic-economic manuscripts" can be elucidated except with the aid of psychoanalysis.

Psychoanalysis, mysticism, poetry, the philosophy of organism, Feuerbach, and Marx—this is a miscellaneous assemblage; but, as Heraclitus said, the unseen harmony is stronger than the seen. Common to all of them is a mode of consciousness that can be called—although the term causes fresh difficulties—the dialectical imagination. By "dialectical" I mean an activity of consciousness struggling to circumvent the limitations imposed by the formal-logical law of contradiction. Marxism, of course, has no monopoly on "dialectics." Needham has shown the dialectical character of Whitehead's philosophy, and he constantly draws attention to dialectical patterns in mystical thought.[27] The goal of Indian body mysticism, according to Eliade, is the "conjunction of contrarieties" (*coincidentia oppositorum*). Scholem, in his survey of Jewish mysticism, says, "Mysticism, intent on formulating the paradoxes of religious experience, uses the instrument of dialectics to express its meaning. The Kabbalists are by no means the only witnesses to this affinity between mystical and dialectical thinking." [28]

As for poetry, are not those basic poetic devices emphasized by recent criticism—paradox, ambiguity, irony, tension—devices whereby the poetic imagination subverts the "reasonableness" of language, the chains it imposes? (Compare Valéry's theory of poetry; see chapter VI.) And from the psychoanalytical point of view, if we, with Trilling (see above, chapter V), accept the substantial identity between poetic logic (with its symbolism, condensation of meaning, and displacement of accent) and dream logic, then the connection between poetry and dialectics, as defined, is more substantially grounded. Dreams are certainly an activity of the mind struggling to circumvent the formal-logical law of contradiction.[29]

Psychoanalytical thinking has a double relation to the dialectical imagination. It is, on the one hand (actually or potentially), a mode of dialectical consciousness; on the other hand, it contains, or ought to contain, a theory about the nature of the dialectical imagination. I say "actually or potentially" because psychoanalysis, either as a body of doctrine or an experience of the analysand, is no total revelation of the unconscious repressed. The struggle of consciousness to circumvent the limitations of formal logic, of language, and of "common sense" is under conditions of general repression never ending (see Freud's essay, "Analysis Terminable and Interminable").[30] "Dialectical" are those psychoanalysts who continue this struggle; for the rest, psychoanalytical terminology can be a prison house of Byzantine scholas-

[27] Needham, "A Biologist's View of Whitehead's Philosophy," in Schilpp (ed.), *The Philosophy of Alfred North Whitehead*, pp. 241–72; Needham, *Science and Civilization in China*, II, 75–77, 291, 454, 467.

[28] Eliade, *Le Yoga*, pp. 110, 258, 269; Scholem, *Major Trends in Jewish Mysticism*, p. 218.

[29] Cf. the role of paradox in philosophy: Wisdom, *Philosophy and Psycho-Analysis*, pp. 169–81, 248–82.

[30] Sigmund Freud, *Collected Papers*, ed. J. Riviere and J. Strachey, International Psycho-Analytical Library, no. 7–10, 37, 5 vols. (New York, London: International Psycho-Analytical Press, 1924–50), vol. V, pp. 316–57.

ticism in which "word-consciousness" is substituting for consciousness of the unconscious.

And even if we take Freud as the model of psychoanalytical consciousness, we have argued that at such crucial points as the relation between the two instincts and the relation between humanity and animality, Freud is trapped because he is not sufficiently "dialectical." Nevertheless, the basic structure of Freud's thought is committed to dialectics, because it is committed to the vision of mental life as basically an arena of conflict; and his finest insights (for example, that when the patient denies something, he affirms it[31]) are incurably "dialectical." Hence the attempt to make psychoanalysis out to be "scientific" (in the positivist sense) is not only vain but destructive.[32] Empirical verification, the positivist test of science, can apply only to that which is fully in consciousness; but psychoanalysis is a mode of contacting the unconscious under conditions of general repression, when the unconscious remains in some sense repressed. To put the matter another way, the "poetry" in Freud's thought cannot be purged away, or rather such an expurgation is exactly what is accomplished in "scientific" textbooks of psychology; but Freud's writings remain unexpurgatable. The same "poetical" imagination marks the work of Róheim and Ferenczi as superior, and explains why they are neglected by "scientific" anthropologists and psychoanalysts. The whole nature of the "dialectical" or "poetical" imagination is another problem urgently needing examination; and there is a particular need for psychoanalysis, as part of the psychoanalysis of psychoanalysis, to become conscious of the dialectical, poetical, mystical stream that runs in its blood.

The key to the nature of dialectical thinking may lie in psychoanalysis, more specifically in Freud's psychoanalysis of negation. There is first the theorem that "there is nothing in the id which can be compared to negation," and that the law of contradiction does not hold in the id. Similarly, the dream does not seem to recognize the word "no." [33] Instead of the law of contradiction we find a unity of opposites: "Dreams show a special tendency to reduce two opposites to a unity"; "Any thing in a dream may mean its opposite." [34] We must therefore entertain the hypothesis that there is an important connection between being "dialectical" and dreaming, just as there is between dreaming and poetry or mysticism. Furthermore, in his essay "The Antithetical Sense of Primal Words" [35] Freud compares the linguistic phenomenon of a hidden (in the etymological root) identity between words with antithetical meanings, he reveals the significant fact that it was the linguistic phenomenon that give him the clue to the dream phenomenon, and not vice versa. It is plain that both psychoanalysis and

[31] Freud, *Collected Papers*, vol. V, pp. 181–82.
[32] For the positivist approach to psychoanalysis, see Kris, "The Nature of Psychoanalytical Propositions and Their Validation," pp. 239–59; Frenkel-Brunswik, "Psychoanalysis and the Unity of Science," pp. 273–347; Pumpian-Mindlin (ed.), *Psychoanalysis and Science*.
[33] Sigmund Freud, *The Basic Writings of Sigmund Freud*, trans. and ed. A. A. Brill (New York: Modern Library, 1938), pp. 345–46; Freud, *New Introductory Lectures*, p. 99; Freud, *Collected Papers*, vol. III, p. 559n., vol. IV, pp. 119, 184, vol. V, p. 185.
[34] Freud, *Collected Papers*, vol. IV, p. 184; Freud, *Basic Writings*, p. 346.
[35] Freud, *Collected Papers*, vol. IV, pp. 184–91. Cf. *Basic Writings*, p. 346n.

the study of language (philosophical and philological) need a marriage or at least a meeting.

And, on the other hand, Freud's essay "On Negation" [36] may throw light on the nature of the "dialectical" dissatisfaction with formal logic. Negation is the primal act of repression; but it at the same time liberates the mind to think about the repressed under the general condition that it is denied and thus remains essentially repressed. With Spinoza's formula *omnis determinatio est negatio* in mind, examine the following formulations of Freud: "A negative judgment is the intellectual substitute for repression; the 'No' in which it is expressed is the hall-mark of repression. . . . By the help of the symbol of negation, the thinking process frees itself from the limitations of repression and enriches itself with the subject-matter without which it could not work efficiently." But: "Negation only assists in undoing one of the consequences of repression—the fact that the subject-matter of the image in question is unable to enter consciousness. The result is a kind of intellectual acceptance of what is repressed, though in all essentials the repression persists." [37]

We may therefore entertain the hypothesis that formal logic and the law of contradiction are the rules whereby the mind submits to operate under general conditions of repression. As with the concept of time, Kant's categories of rationality would then turn out to be the categories of repression. And conversely, "dialectical" would be the struggle of the mind to circumvent repression and make the unconscious conscious. But by the same token, it would be the struggle of the mind to overcome the split and conflict within itself. It could then be identified with that "synthesizing" tendency in the ego of which Freud spoke, and with that attempt to cure, inside the neurosis itself, on which Freud came finally to place his hope for therapy.[38] As an attempt to unify and to cure, the "dialectical" consciousness would be a manifestation of Eros. And, as consciousness trying to throw off the fetters of negation, the "dialectical" consciousness would be a step toward that Dionysian ego which does not negate any more.

What the great world needs, of course, is a little more Eros and less strife; but the intellectual world needs it just as much. A little more Eros would make conscious the unconscious harmony between "dialectical" dreamers of all kinds—psychoanalysts, political idealists, mystics, poets, philosophers— and abate the sterile and ignorant polemics. Since the ignorance seems to be mostly a matter of self-ignorance, a little more psychoanalytical consciousness on all sides (including the psychoanalysts) might help—a little more self-knowledge, humility, humanity, and Eros. We may therefore conclude with the concluding words of Freud's *Civilization and Its Discontents:*[39]

Men have brought their powers of subduing the forces of nature to such a pitch that by using them they could now very easily exterminate one another to the last

[36] Freud, *Collected Papers*, vol. V, pp. 181–85.
[37] Freud, *Collected Papers*, vol. V, p. 182. Cf. vol. III, p. 559n., vol. IV, p. 119.
[38] Freud, *Collected Papers*, vol. V, pp. 369–71.
[39] Sigmund Freud, *Civilization and Its Discontents*, trans. J. Riviere, ed. E. Jones, International Psycho-Analytical Library, no. 17 (London: Hogarth Press, 1930), p. 144.

man. They know this—hence arises a great part of their current unrest, their dejection, their mood of apprehension. And now it may be expected that the other of the two "heavenly forces," eternal Eros, will put forth his strength so as to maintain himself alongside of his equally immortal adversary.

And perhaps our children will live to live a full life, and so see what Freud could not see—in the old adversary, a friend.

THE WHITE NEGRO
Superficial Reflections
on the Hipster

Norman Mailer

Our search for the rebels of the generation led us to the hipster. The hipster is an *enfant terrible* turned inside out. In character with his time, he is trying to get back at the conformists by lying low . . . You can't interview a hipster because his main goal is to keep out of a society which, he thinks, is trying to make everyone over in its own image. He takes marijuana because it supplies him with experiences that can't be shared with "squares." He may affect a broad-brimmed hat or a zoot suit, but usually he prefers to skulk unmarked. The hipster may be a jazz musician; he is rarely an artist, almost never a writer. He may earn his living as a petty criminal, a hobo, a carnival roustabout or a free-lance moving man in Greenwich Village, but some hipsters have found a safe refuge in the upper income brackets as television comics or movie actors. (The late James Dean, for one, was a hipster hero.) . . . It is tempting to describe the hipster in psychiatric terms as infantile, but the style of his infantilism is a sign of the times. He does not try to enforce his will on others, Napoleon-fashion, but contents himself with a magical omnipotence never disproved because never tested. . . . As the only extreme nonconformist of his generation, he exercises a powerful if underground appeal for conformists, through newspaper accounts of his delinquencies, his structureless jazz, and his emotive grunt words.

> —*"Born 1930: The Unlost Generation"*
> by Caroline Bird
> HARPER'S BAZAAR, Feb. 1957

Probably, we will never be able to determine the psychic havoc of the concentration camps and the atom bomb upon the unconscious mind of almost everyone alive in these years. For the first time in civilized history, perhaps for the first time in all of history, we have been forced to live with the suppressed knowledge that the smallest facets of our personality or the most minor projection of our ideas, or indeed the absence of ideas and the absence of personality could mean equally well that we might still be doomed to die as a cipher in some vast statistical operation in which our teeth would be counted, and our hair would be saved, but our death itself would be unknown, unhonored, and unremarked, a death which could not follow with dignity as a possible consequence to serious actions we had chosen, but rather a death by *deus ex machina* in a gas chamber or a radioactive city; and so if in the midst of civilization—that civilization founded upon the Faustian urge to dominate nature by mastering time, mastering the links of social cause and effect—in the middle of an economic civilization founded upon the confidence that time could indeed be subjected to our will, our psyche was subjected itself to the intolerable anxiety that death being causeless, life was causeless as well, and time deprived of cause and effect had come to a stop.

The Second World War presented a mirror to the human condition which blinded anyone who looked into it. For if tens of millions were killed in concentration camps out of the inexorable agonies and contractions of superstates founded upon the always insoluble contradictions of injustice, one was then obliged also to see that no matter how crippled and perverted an image of man was the society he had created, it was nonetheless his creation, his collective creation (at least his collective creation from the past) and if society was so murderous, then who could ignore the most hideous of questions about his own nature?

Worse. One could hardly maintain the courage to be individual, to speak with one's own voice, for the years in which one could complacently accept oneself as part of an elite by being a radical were forever gone. A man knew that when he dissented, he gave a note upon his life which could be called in any year of overt crisis. No wonder then that these have been the years of conformity and depression. A stench of fear has come out of every pore of American life, and we suffer from a collective failure of nerve. The only courage, with rare exceptions, that we have been witness to, has been the isolated courage of isolated people.

2.

It is on this bleak scene that a phenomenon has appeared: the American existentialist—the hipster, the man who knows that if our collective condition is to live with instant death by atomic war, relatively quick death by the State as *l'univers concentrationnaire,* or with a slow death by conformity with every creative and rebellious instinct stifled (at what damage to the mind and the heart and the liver and the nerves no research foundation for cancer will discover in a hurry), if the fate of twentieth-century man is to live with death from adolescence to premature senescence, why then the only life-giving answer is to accept the terms of death, to live with death as immediate danger, to divorce oneself from society, to exist without roots, to set out on that uncharted journey into the rebellious imperatives of the self. In short, whether the life is criminal or not, the decision is to encourage the psychopath in oneself, to explore that domain of experience where security is boredom and therefore sickness, and one exists in the present, in that enormous present which is without past or future, memory or planned intention, the life where a man must go until he is beat, where he must gamble with his energies through all those small or large crises of courage and unforeseen situations which beset his day, where he must be with it or doomed not to swing. The unstated essence of Hip, its psychopathic brilliance, quivers with the knowledge that new kinds of victories increase one's power for new kinds of perception; and defeats, the wrong kind of defeats, attack the body and imprison one's energy until one is jailed in the prison air of other people's habits, other people's defeats, boredom, quiet desperation, and muted icy self-destroying rage. One is Hip or one is Square (the alternative which each new generation coming into American life is beginning to feel), one is a rebel or one conforms, one is a frontiersman in the Wild West of American night life, or else a Square cell, trapped in the totalitarian tissues of American society, doomed willy-nilly to conform if one is to succeed.

A totalitarian society makes enormous demands on the courage of men, and a partially totalitarian society makes even greater demands, for the general anxiety is greater. Indeed if one is to be a man, almost any kind of unconventional action often takes disproportionate courage. So it is no accident that the source of Hip is the Negro for he has been living on the margin between totalitarianism and democracy for two centuries. But the presence of Hip as a working philosophy in the sub-worlds of American life is probably due to jazz, and its knifelike entrance into culture, its subtle but so penetrating influence on an avant-garde generation—that postwar generation of adventurers who (some consciously, some by osmosis) had absorbed the lessons of disillusionment and disgust of the twenties, the depression, and the war. Sharing a collective disbelief in the words of men who had too much money and controlled too many things, they knew almost as powerful a disbelief in the socially monolithic ideas of the single mate, the solid family and the respectable love life. If the intellectual antecedents of this generation can be traced to such separate influences as D. H. Lawrence, Henry Miller, and Wilhelm Reich, the viable philosophy of Hemingway fit most of their facts: in a bad world, as he was to say over and over again (while taking time out from his parvenu snobbery and dedicated gourmandise), in a bad world there is no love nor mercy nor charity nor justice unless a man can keep his courage, and this indeed fitted some of the facts. What fitted the need of the adventurer even more precisely was Hemingway's categorical imperative that what made him feel good became therefore The Good.

So no wonder that in certain cities of America, in New York of course, and New Orleans, in Chicago and San Francisco and Los Angeles, in such American cities as Paris and Mexico, D.F., this particular part of a generation was attracted to what the Negro had to offer. In such places as Greenwich Village, a ménage-à-trois was completed—the bohemian and the juvenile delinquent came face-to-face with the Negro, and the hipster was a fact in American life. If marijuana was the wedding ring, the child was the language of Hip for its argot gave expression to abstract states of feeling which all could share, at least all who were Hip. And in this wedding of the white and the black it was the Negro who brought the cultural dowry. Any Negro who wishes to live must live with danger from his first day, and no experience can ever be casual to him, no Negro can saunter down a street with any real certainty that violence will not visit him on his walk. The cameos of security for the average white: mother and the home, job and the family, are not even a mockery to millions of Negroes; they are impossible. The Negro has the simplest of alternatives: live a life of constant humility or ever-threatening danger. In such a pass where paranoia is as vital to survival as blood, the Negro had stayed alive and begun to grow by following the need of his body where he could. Knowing in the cells of his existence that life was war, nothing but war, the Negro (all exceptions admitted) could rarely afford the sophisticated inhibitions of civilization, and so he kept for his survival the art of the primitive, he lived in the enormous present, he subsisted for his Saturday night kicks, relinquishing the pleasures of the mind for the more obligatory pleasures of the body, and in his music he gave voice to the character and quality of his existence, to his rage and the infinite variations of joy, lust, languor, growl, cramp, pinch, scream and despair of his orgasm. For jazz is orgasm, it is the music of orgasm, good orgasm and bad, and so it spoke across a nation, it had the communication of art even where it was watered, perverted, corrupted, and almost killed, it spoke in no matter what laundered popular way of instantaneous existential states to which some whites could respond, it was indeed a communication by art because it said, "I feel this, and now you do too."

So there was a new breed of adventurers, urban adventurers who drifted out at night looking for action with a black man's code to fit their facts. The hipster had absorbed the existentialist synapses of the Negro, and for practical purposes could be considered a white Negro.

To be an existentialist, one must be able to feel oneself—one must know one's desires, one's rages, one's anguish, one must be aware of the character of one's frustration and know what would satisfy it. The overcivilized man can be an existentialist only if it is chic, and deserts it quickly for the next chic. To be a real existentialist (Sartre admittedly to the contrary) one must be religious, one must have one's sense of the "purpose"—whatever the purpose may be—but a life which is directed by one's faith in the necessity of action is a life committed to the notion that the substratum of existence is the search, the end meaningful but mysterious; it is impossible to live such a life unless one's emotions provide their profound conviction. Only the French, alienated beyond alienation from their unconscious could welcome an existential philosophy without ever feeling it at all; indeed only a Frenchman by declaring that the unconscious did not exist could then proceed to explore the delicate involutions of consciousness, the microscopically sensuous and all but ineffable *frissons* of mental becoming, in order finally to create the theology of atheism and so submit that in a world of absurdities the existential absurdity is most coherent.

In the dialogue between the atheist and the mystic, the atheist is on the side of life, rational life, undialectical life—since he conceives of death as emptiness, he can, no matter how weary or despairing, wish for nothing but more life; his pride is that he does not transpose his weakness and spiritual fatigue into a romantic longing for death, for such appreciation of death is then all too capable of being elaborated by his imagination into a universe of meaningful structure and moral orchestration.

Yet this masculine argument can mean very little for the mystic. The mystic can accept the atheist's description of his weakness, he can agree that his mysticism was a response to despair. And yet . . . and yet his argument is that he, the mystic, is the one finally who has chosen to live with death, and so death is his experience and not the atheist's, and the atheist by eschewing the limitless dimensions of profound despair has rendered himself incapable to judge the experience. The real argument which the mystic must always advance is the very intensity of his private vision—his argument depends from the vision precisely because what was felt in the vision is so extraordinary that no rational argument, no hypotheses of "oceanic feelings" and certainly no skeptical reductions can explain away what has become for him the reality more real than the reality of closely reasoned logic. His inner experience of the possibilities within death is his logic. So, too, for the existentialist. And the psychopath. And the saint and the bullfighter and the lover. The common denominator for all of them is their burning consciousness of the present, exactly that incandescent consciousness which the possibilities within death has opened for them. There is a depth of desperation to the condition which enables one to remain in life only by engaging death, but the reward is their knowledge that what is happening at each instant of the electric present is good or bad for them, good or bad for their cause, their love, their action, their need.

It is this knowledge which provides the curious community of feeling in the world of the hipster, a muted cool religious revival to be sure, but the element which is exciting, disturbing, nightmarish perhaps, is that incompatibles have come to bed, the inner life and the violent life, the orgy and the dream of love, the desire to murder and the desire to create, a dialectical conception of existence with a lust for power, a dark, romantic, and yet undeniably dynamic view of existence for it sees every man and woman as moving individually through each moment of life forward into growth or backward into death.

3.

It may be fruitful to consider the hipster a philosophical psychopath, a man interested not only in the dangerous imperatives of his psychopathy but in codifying, at least for himself, the suppositions on which his inner universe is constructed. By this premise the hipster is a psychopath, and yet not a psychopath but the negation of the psychopath, for he possesses the narcissistic detachment of the philosopher, that absorption in the recessive nuances of one's own motive which is so alien to the unreasoning drive of the psychopath. In this country where new millions of psychopaths are developed each year, stamped with the mint of our contradictory popular culture (where sex is sin and yet sex is paradise), it is as if there has been room already for the development of the antithetical psychopath who extrapolates from his own condition, from the inner certainty that his rebellion is just, a radical vision of the universe which thus separates him from the general ignorance, reactionary prejudice, and self-doubt of the more conventional psychopath. Having converted his unconscious experience into much conscious knowledge, the hipster has shifted the focus of his desire from immediate gratification toward that wider passion for future power which is the mark of civilized man. Yet with an irreducible difference. For Hip is the sophistication of the wise primitive in a giant jungle, and so its appeal is still beyond the civilized man. If there are ten million Americans who are more or less psychopathic (and the figure is most modest), there are probably not more than one hundred thousand men and women who consciously see themselves as hipsters, but their importance is that they are an elite with the potential ruthlessness of an elite, and a language most adolescents can understand instinctively, for the hipster's intense view of existence matches their experience and their desire to rebel.

Before one can say more about the hipster, there is obviously much to be said about the psychic state of the psychopath—or, clinically, the psychopathic personality. Now, for reasons which may be more curious than the similarity of the words, even many people with a psychoanalytical orientation often confuse the psychopath with the psychotic. Yet the terms are polar. The psychotic is legally insane, the psychopath is not; the psychotic is almost always incapable of discharging in physical acts the rage of his frustration, while the psychopath at his extreme is virtually as incapable of restraining his violence. The psychotic lives in so misty a world that what is happening at each moment of his life is not very real to him whereas the psychopath seldom knows any reality greater than the face, the voice, the being of the particular people among whom he may find himself at any moment. Sheldon and Eleanor Glueck describe him as follows:

The psychopath . . . can be distinguished from the person sliding into or clambering out of a "true psychotic" state by the long tough persistence of his anti-social attitude and behaviour and the absence of hallucinations, delusions, manic flight of ideas, confusion, disorientation, and other dramatic signs of psychosis.

The late Robert Lindner, one of the few experts on the subject, in his book *Rebel Without a Cause—The Hypnoanalysis of a Criminal Psychopath* presented part of his definition in this way:

. . . the psychopath is a rebel without a cause, an agitator without a slogan, a revolutionary without a program: in other words, his rebelliousness is aimed to achieve goals satisfactory to himself alone; he is incapable of exertions for the sake of others. All his efforts, hidden under no matter what disguise, represent

investments designed to satisfy his immediate wishes and desires. . . . The psychopath, like the child, cannot delay the pleasures of gratification; and this trait is one
of his underlying, universal characteristics. He cannot wait upon erotic gratification
which convention demands should be preceded by the chase before the kill: he must
rape. He cannot wait upon the development of prestige in society: his egoistic
ambitions lead him to leap into headlines by daring performances. Like a red
thread the predominance of this mechanism for immediate satisfaction runs through
the history of every psychopath. It explains not only his behaviour but also the
violent nature of his acts.

Yet even Lindner who was the most imaginative and most sympathetic of
the psychoanalysts who have studied the psychopathic personality was not
ready to project himself into the essential sympathy—which is that the
psychopath may indeed be the perverted and dangerous front-runner of a
new kind of personality which could become the central expression of
human nature before the twentieth century is over. For the psychopath is
better adapted to dominate those mutually contradictory inhibitions upon
violence and love which civilization has exacted of us, and if it be remembered that not every psychopath is an extreme case, and that the condition
of psychopathy is present in a host of people including many politicians,
professional soldiers, newspaper columnists, entertainers, artists, jazz musicians, call-girls, promiscuous homosexuals and half the executives of Hollywood, television, and advertising, it can be seen that there are aspects of
psychopathy which already exert considerable cultural influence.

What characterizes almost every psychopath and part-psychopath is that
they are trying to create a new nervous system for themselves. Generally we
are obliged to act with a nervous system which has been formed from infancy, and which carries in the style of its circuits the very contradictions
of our parents and our early milieu. Therefore, we are obliged, most of us,
to meet the tempo of the present and the future with reflexes and rhythms
which come from the past. It is not only the "dead weight of the institutions
of the past" but indeed the inefficient and often antiquated nervous circuits
of the past which strangle our potentiality for responding to new possibilities which might be exciting for our individual growth.

Through most of modern history, "sublimation" was possible: at the
expense of expressing only a small portion of oneself, that small portion
could be expressed intensely. But sublimation depends on a reasonable
tempo to history. If the collective life of a generation has moved too quickly,
the "past" by which particular men and women of that generation may
function is not, let us say, thirty years old, but relatively a hundred or two
hundred years old. And so the nervous system is overstressed beyond the
possibility of such compromises as sublimation, especially since the stable
middle-class values so prerequisite to sublimation have been virtually destroyed in our time, at least as nourishing values free of confusion or doubt.
In such a crisis of accelerated historical tempo and deteriorated values,
neurosis tends to be replaced by psychopathy, and the success of psychoanalysis (which even ten years ago gave promise of becoming a direct major
force) diminishes because of its inbuilt and characteristic incapacity to

handle patients more complex, more experienced, or more adventurous than the analyst himself. In practice, psychoanalysis has by now become all too often no more than a psychic blood-letting. The patient is not so much changed as aged, and the infantile fantasies which he is encouraged to express are condemned to exhaust themselves against the analyst's non-responsive reactions. The result for all too many patients is a diminution, a "tranquilizing" of their most interesting qualities and vices. The patient is indeed not so much altered as worn out—less bad, less good, less bright, less willful, less destructive, less creative. He is thus able to conform to that contradictory and unbearable society which first created his neurosis. He can conform to what he loathes because he no longer has the passion to feel loathing so intensely.

The psychopath is notoriously difficult to analyze because the fundamental decision of his nature is to try to live the infantile fantasy, and in this decision (given the dreary alternative of psychoanalysis) there may be a certain instinctive wisdom. For there is a dialectic to changing one's nature, the dialectic which underlies all psychoanalytic method: it is the knowledge that if one is to change one's habits, one must go back to the source of their creation, and so the psychopath exploring backward along the road of the homosexual, the orgiast, the drug-addict, the rapist, the robber and the murderer seeks to find those violent parallels to the violent and often hopeless contradictions he knew as an infant and as a child. For if he has the courage to meet the parallel situation at the moment when he is ready, then he has a chance to act as he has never acted before, and in satisfying the frustration—if he can succeed—he may then pass by symbolic substitute through the locks of incest. In thus giving expression to the buried infant in himself, he can lessen the tension of those infantile desires and so free himself to remake a bit of his nervous system. Like the neurotic he is looking for the opportunity to grow up a second time, but the psychopath knows instinctively that to express a forbidden impulse actively is far more beneficial to him than merely to confess the desire in the safety of a doctor's room. The psychopath is inordinately ambitious, too ambitious ever to trade his warped brilliant conception of his possible victories in life for the grim if peaceful attrition of the analyst's couch. So his associational journey into the past is lived out in the theatre of the present, and he exists for those charged situations where his senses are so alive that he can be aware actively (as the analysand is aware passively) of what his habits are, and how he can change them. The strength of the psychopath is that he knows (where most of us can only guess) what is good for him and what is bad for him at exactly those instants when an old crippling habit has become so attacked by experience that the potentiality exists to change it, to replace a negative and empty fear with an outward action, even if—and here I obey the logic of the extreme psychopath—even if the fear is of himself, and the action is to murder. The psychopath murders—if he has the courage—out of the necessity to purge his violence, for if he cannot empty his hatred then he cannot love, his being is frozen with implacable self-hatred for his cowardice. (It can of course be suggested that it takes little courage for two strong eighteen-year-old hoodlums, let us say, to beat in the brains of a candy-store keeper, and indeed the act—even by the logic of the psychopath—is not likely to prove very therapeutic, for the victim is not an immediate equal. Still, courage of a sort is necessary, for one murders not only a weak fifty-year-old man but an institution as well, one violates private property, one enters into a new relation with the police and introduces a dangerous element into one's life. The hoodlum is therefore daring the unknown, and so no matter how brutal the act, it is not altogether cowardly.)

At bottom, the drama of the psychopath is that he seeks love. Not love as the search for a mate, but love as the search for an orgasm more apocalyptic than the one which preceded it. Orgasm is his therapy—he knows at the seed of his being that good orgasm opens his possibilities and bad orgasm imprisons him. But in this search, the psychopath becomes an embodiment of the extreme contradictions of the society which formed his character, and the apocalyptic orgasm often remains as remote as the Holy Grail, for there are clusters and nests and ambushes of violence in his own necessities and in the imperatives and retaliations of the men and women among whom he lives his life, so that even as he drains his hatred in one act or another, so the conditions of his life create it anew in him until the drama of his movements bears a sardonic resemblance to the frog who climbed a few feet in the well only to drop back again.

Yet there is this to be said for the search after the good orgasm: when one lives in a civilized world, and still can enjoy none of the cultural nectar of such a world because the paradoxes on which civilization is built demand that there remain a cultureless and alienated bottom of exploitable human material, then the logic of becoming a sexual outlaw (if one's psychological roots are bedded in the bottom) is that one has at least a running competitive chance to be physically healthy so long as one stays alive. It is therefore no accident that psychopathy is most prevalent with the Negro. Hated from outside and therefore hating himself, the Negro was forced into the position of exploring all those moral wildernesses of civilized life which the Square automatically condemns as delinquent or evil or immature or morbid or self-destructive or corrupt. (Actually the terms have equal weight. Depending on the telescope of the cultural clique from which the Square surveys the universe, "evil" or "immature" are equally strong terms of condemnation.) But the Negro, not being privileged to gratify his self-esteem with the heady satisfactions of categorical condemnation, chose to move instead in that other direction where all situations are equally valid, and in the worst of perversion, promiscuity, pimpery, drug addiction, rape, razorslash, bottle-break, what-have-you, the Negro discovered and elaborated a morality of the bottom, an ethical differentiation between the good and the bad in every human activity from the go-getter pimp (as opposed to the lazy one) to the relatively dependable pusher or prostitute. Add to this, the cunning of their language, the abstract ambiguous alternatives in which from the danger of their oppression they learned to speak ("Well, now, man, like I'm looking for a cat to turn me on . . ."), add even more the profound sensitivity of the Negro jazzman who was the cultural mentor of a people, and it is not too difficult to believe that the language of Hip which evolved was an artful language, tested and shaped by an intense experience and therefore different in kind from white slang, as different as the special obscenity of the soldier, which in its emphasis upon "ass" as the soul and "shit" as circumstance, was able to express the existential states of the enlisted man. What makes Hip a special language is that it cannot really be taught—if one shares none of the experiences of elation and exhaustion which it is equipped to describe, then it seems merely arch or vulgar or irritating. It is a pictorial language, but pictorial like nonobjective art, imbued with the dialectic of small but intense change, a language for the microcosm, in this case, man, for it takes the immediate experiences of any passing man and magnifies the dynamic of his movements, not specifically but abstractly so that he is seen more as a vector in a network of forces than as a static character in a crystallized field. (Which latter is the practical view of the snob.) For example, there is real difficulty in trying to find a Hip substitute for "stubborn." The best possibility I can come up with is: "That cat will never come off his groove, dad." But groove implies movement, narrow movement but motion nonetheless. There is really no way to describe someone who does not move at all. Even a creep does move— if at a pace exasperatingly more slow than the pace of the cool cats.

4.

Like children, hipsters are fighting for the sweet, and their language is a set of subtle indications of their success or failure in the competition for pleasure. Unstated but obvious is the social sense that there is not nearly enough sweet for everyone. And so the sweet goes only to the victor, the best, the most, the man who knows the most about how to find his energy and how not to lose it. The emphasis is on energy because the psychopath and the hipster are nothing without it since they do not have the protection of a position or a class to rely on when they have overextended themselves. So the language of Hip is a language of energy, how it is found, how it is lost.

But let us see. I have jotted down perhaps a dozen words, the Hip perhaps most in use and most likely to last with the minimum of variation. The words are man, go, put down, make, beat, cool, swing, with it, crazy, dig, flip, creep, hip, square. They serve a variety of purposes and the nuance of the voice uses the nuance of the situation to convey the subtle contextual difference. If the hipster moves through his life on a constant search with glimpses of Mecca in many a turn of his experience (Mecca being the apocalyptic orgasm) and if everyone in the civilized world is at least in some small degree a sexual cripple, the hipster lives with the knowledge of how he is sexually crippled and where he is sexually alive, and the faces of experience which life presents to him each day are engaged, dismissed or avoided as his need directs and his lifemanship makes possible. For life is a contest between people in which the victor generally recuperates quickly and the loser takes long to mend, a perpetual competition of colliding explorers in which one must grow or else pay more for remaining the same (pay in sickness, or depression, or anguish for the lost opportunity), but pay or grow.

Therefore one finds words like go, and make it, and with it, and swing: "Go" with its sense that after hours or days or months or years of monotony, boredom, and depression one has finally had one's chance, one has amassed enough energy to meet an exciting opportunity with all one's present talents for the flip (up or down) and so one is ready to go, ready to gamble. Movement is always to be preferred to inaction. In motion a man has a chance, his body is warm, his instincts are quick, and when the crisis comes, whether of love or violence, he can make it, he can win, he can release a little more energy for himself since he hates himself a little less, he can make a little better nervous system, make it a little more possible to go again, to go faster next time and so make more and thus find more people with whom he can swing. For to swing is to communicate, is to convey the rhythms of one's own being to a lover, a friend, or an audience, and—equally necessary—be able to feel the rhythms of their response. To swing with the rhythms of another is to enrich oneself—the conception of the learning process as dug by Hip is that one cannot really learn until one contains within oneself the implicit rhythm of the subject or the person. As an example, I remember once hearing a Negro friend have an intellectual discussion at a party for half an hour with a white girl who was a few years out of college. The Negro literally could not read or write, but he had an extraordinary ear and a fine sense of mimicry. So as the girl spoke, he would detect the particular formal uncertainties in her argument, and in a pleasant (if slightly Southern) English accent, he would respond to one or another facet of her doubts. When she would finish what she felt was a particularly well-articulated idea, he would smile privately and say, "Other-direction . . . do you really believe in that?"

"Well . . . No," the girl would stammer, "now that you get down to it, there is something disgusting about it to me," and she would be off again for five more minutes.

Of course the Negro was not learning anything about the merits and demerits of the argument, but he was learning a great deal about a type of girl he had never met before, and that was what he wanted. Being unable to read or write, he could hardly be interested in ideas nearly as much as in lifemanship, and so he eschewed any attempt to obey the precision or lack of precision in the girl's language, and instead sensed her character (and the values of her social type) by swinging with the nuances of her voice.

So to swing is to be able to learn, and by learning take a step toward making it, toward creating. What is to be created is not nearly so important as the hipster's belief that when he really makes it, he will be able to turn his hand to anything, even to self-discipline. What he must do before that is find his courage at the moment of violence, or equally make it in the act of love, find a little more between his woman and himself, or indeed between his mate and himself (since many hipsters are bisexual), but paramount, imperative, is the necessity to make it because in making it, one is making the new habit, unearthing the new talent which the old frustration denied.

Whereas if you goof (the ugliest word in Hip), if you lapse back into being a frightened stupid child, or if you flip, if you lose your control, reveal the buried weaker more feminine part of your nature, then it is more difficult to swing the next time, your ear is less alive, your bad and energy-wasting habits are further confirmed, you are farther away from being with it. But to be with it is to have grace, is to be closer to the secrets of that inner unconscious life which will nourish you if you can hear it, for you are then nearer to that God which every hipster believes is located in the senses of his body, that trapped, mutilated and nonetheless megalomaniacal God who is It, who is energy, life, sex, force, the Yoga's *prana*, the Reichian's orgone, Lawrence's "blood," Hemingway's "good," the Shavian life-force; "It"; God; not the God of the churches but the unachievable whisper of mystery within the sex, the paradise of limitless energy and perception just beyond the next wave of the next orgasm.

To which a cool cat might reply, "Crazy, man!"

Because, after all, what I have offered above is an hypothesis, no more, and there is not the hipster alive who is not absorbed in his own tumultuous hypotheses. Mine is interesting, mine is way out (on the avenue of the mystery along the road to "It") but still I am just one cat in a world of cool cats, and everything interesting is crazy, or at least so the Squares who do not know how to swing would say.

(And yet crazy is also the self-protective irony of the hipster. Living with questions and not with answers, he is so different in his isolation and in the far reach of his imagination from almost everyone with whom he deals in the outer world of the Square, and meets generally so much enmity, competition, and hatred in the world of Hip, that his isolation is always in danger of turning upon itself, and leaving him indeed just that, crazy.)

If, however, you agree with my hypothesis, if you as a cat are way out too, and we are in the same groove (the universe now being glimpsed as a series of ever-extending radii from the center), why then you say simply, "I dig," because neither knowledge nor imagination comes easily, it is buried in the pain of one's forgotten experience, and so one must work to find it, one must occasionally exhaust oneself by digging into the self in order to perceive the outside. And indeed it is essential to dig the most, for if you do not dig you lose your superiority over the Square, and so you are less likely to be cool (to be in control of a situation because you have swung where the Square has not, or because you have allowed to come to consciousness a pain, a guilt, a shame or a desire which the other has not had the courage to face). To be cool is to be equipped, and if you are equipped it is more difficult for the next cat who comes along to put you down. And of course one can hardly afford to be put down too often, or one is beat, one has lost one's confidence, one has lost one's will, one is impotent in the world of action and so closer to the demeaning flip of becoming a queer, or indeed closer to dying, and therefore it is even more difficult to recover enough energy to try to make it again, because once a cat is beat he has nothing to give, and no one is interested any longer in making it with him. This is the terror of the hipster—to be beat—because once the sweet of sex has deserted him, he still cannot give up the search. It is not granted to the hipster to grow old gracefully—he has been captured too early by the oldest dream of power, the gold fountain of Ponce de León, the fountain of youth where the gold is in the orgasm.

To be beat is therefore a flip, it is a situation beyond one's experience, impossible to anticipate—which indeed in the circular vocabulary of Hip is still another meaning for flip, but then I have given just a few of the connotations of these words. Like most primitive vocabularies each word is a prime symbol and serves a dozen or a hundred functions of communication in the instinctive dialectic through which the hipster perceives his experience, that dialectic of the instantaneous differentials of existence in which one is forever moving forward into more or retreating into less.

5.

It is impossible to conceive a new philosophy until one creates a new language, but a new popular language (while it must implicitly contain a new philosophy) does not necessarily present its philosophy overtly. It can be asked then what really is unique in the life-view of Hip which raises its argot above the passing verbal whimsies of the bohemian or the lumpenproletariat.

The answer would be in the psychopathic element of Hip which has almost no interest in viewing human nature, or better, in judging human nature, from a set of standards conceived a priori to the experience, standards inherited from the past. Since Hip sees every answer as posing immediately a new alternative, a new question, its emphasis is on complexity rather than simplicity (such complexity that its language without the illumination of the voice and the articulation of the face and body remains hopelessly incommunicative). Given its emphasis on complexity, Hip abdicates from any conventional moral responsibility because it would argue that the result of our actions are unforeseeable, and so we cannot know if we do good or bad, we cannot even know (in the Joycean sense of the good and the bad) whether we have given energy to another, and indeed if we could, there would still be no idea of what ultimately the other would do with it.

Therefore, men are not seen as good or bad (that they are good-and-bad is taken for granted) but rather each man is glimpsed as a collection of possibilities, some more possible than others (the view of character implicit in Hip) and some humans are considered more capable than others of reaching more possibilities within themselves in less time, provided, and this is the dynamic, provided the particular character can swing at the right time. And here arises the sense of context which differentiates Hip from a Square view of character. Hip sees the context as generally dominating the man, dominating him because his character is less significant than the context in which he must function. Since it is arbitrarily five times more demanding of one's energy to accomplish even an inconsequential action in an unfavorable context than a favorable one, man is then not only his character but his context, since the success or failure of an action in a given context reacts upon the character and therefore affects what the character will be in the next context. What dominates both character and context is the energy available at the moment of intense context.

Character being thus seen as perpetually ambivalent and dynamic enters then into an absolute relativity where there are no truths other than the isolated truths of what each observer feels at each instant of his existence. To take a perhaps unjustified metaphysical extrapolation, it is as if the universe which has usually existed conceptually as a Fact (even if the Fact were Berkeley's God) but a Fact which it was the aim of all science and philosophy to reveal, becomes instead a changing reality whose laws are remade at each instant by everything living, but most particularly man, man raised to a neo-medieval summit where the truth is not what one has felt yesterday or what one expects to feel tomorrow but rather truth is no more nor less than what one feels at each instant in the perpetual climax of the present.

What is consequent therefore is the divorce of man from his values, the liberation of the self from the Super-Ego of society. The only Hip morality (but of course it is an ever-present morality) is to do what one feels whenever and wherever it is possible, and—this is how the war of the Hip and the Square begins—to be engaged in one primal battle: to open the limits of the possible for oneself, for oneself alone, because that is one's need. Yet in widening the arena of the possible, one widens it reciprocally for others as well, so that the nihilistic fulfillment of each man's desire contains its antithesis of human co-operation.

If the ethic reduces to Know Thyself and Be Thyself, what makes it radically different from Socratic moderation with its stern conservative respect for the experience of the past is that the Hip ethic is immoderation, childlike in its adoration of the present (and indeed to respect the past means that one must also respect such ugly consequences of the past as the collective murders of the State). It is this adoration of the present which contains the affirmation of Hip, because its ultimate logic surpasses even the unforgettable solution of the Marquis de Sade to sex, private property, and the family, that all men and women have absolute but temporary rights over the bodies of all other men and women—the nihilism of Hip proposes as its final tendency that every social restraint and category be removed, and the affirmation implicit in the proposal is that man would then prove to be more creative than murderous and so would not destroy himself. Which is exactly what separates Hip from the authoritarian philosophies which now appeal to the conservative and liberal temper—what haunts the middle of the twentieth century is that faith in man has been lost, and the appeal of authority has been that it would restrain us from ourselves. Hip, which would return us to ourselves, at no matter what price in individual violence, is the affirmation of the barbarian, for it requires a primitive passion about human nature to believe that individual acts of violence are always to be preferred to the collective violence of the State; it takes literal faith in the creative possibilities of the human being to envisage acts of violence as the catharsis which prepares growth.

Whether the hipster's desire for absolute sexual freedom contains any genuinely radical conception of a different world is of course another matter, and it is possible, since the hipster lives with his hatred, that many of them are the material for an elite of storm troopers ready to follow the first truly magnetic leader whose view of mass murder is phrased in a language which reaches their emotions. But given the desperation of his condition as a psychic outlaw, the hipster is equally a candidate for the most reactionary and most radical of movements, and so it is just as possible that many hipsters will come—if the crisis deepens—to a radical comprehension of the horror of society, for even as the radical has had his incommunicable dissent confirmed in his experience by precisely the frustration, the denied opportunities, and the bitter years which his ideas have cost him, so the sexual adventurer deflected from his goal by the implacable animosity of a society constructed to deny the sexual radical as well, may yet come to an equally bitter comprehension of the slow relentless inhumanity of the conservative power which controls him from without and from within. And in being so controlled, denied, and starved into the attrition of conformity, indeed the hipster may come to see that his condition is no more than an exaggeration of the human condition, and if he would be free, then everyone must be free. Yes, this is possible too, for the heart of Hip is its emphasis upon courage at the moment of crisis, and it is pleasant to think that courage contains within itself (as the explanation of its existence) some glimpse of the necessity of life to become more than it has been.

It is obviously not very possible to speculate with sharp focus on the future of the hipster. Certain possibilities must be evident, however, and the most central is that the organic growth of Hip depends on whether the Negro emerges as a dominating force in American life. Since the Negro knows more about the ugliness and danger of life than the white, it is probable that if the Negro can win his equality, he will possess a potential superiority, a superiority so feared that the fear itself has become the underground drama of domestic politics. Like all conservative political fear it is the fear of unforeseeable consequences, for the Negro's equality would tear a profound shift into the psychology, the sexuality, and the moral imagination of every white alive.

With this possible emergence of the Negro, Hip may erupt as a psychically armed rebellion whose sexual impetus may rebound against the antisexual foundation of every organized power in America, and bring into the air such animosities, antipathies, and new conflicts of interest that the mean empty hypocrisies of mass conformity will no longer work. A time of violence, new hysteria, confusion and rebellion will then be likely to replace the time of conformity. At that time, if the liberal should prove realistic in his belief that there is peaceful room for every tendency in American life, then Hip would end by being absorbed as a colorful figure in the tapestry. But if this is not the reality, and the economic, the social, the psychological, and finally the moral crises accompanying the rise of the Negro should prove insupportable, then a time is coming when every political guidepost will be gone, and millions of liberals will be faced with political dilemmas they have so far succeeded in evading, and with a view of human nature they do not wish to accept. To take the desegregation of the schools in the South as an example, it is quite likely that the reactionary sees the reality more closely than the liberal when he argues that the deeper issue is not desegregation but miscegenation. (As a radical I am of course facing in the opposite direction from the White Citizen's Councils—obviously I believe it is the absolute human right of the Negro to mate with the white, and matings there will undoubtedly be, for there will be Negro high school boys brave enough to chance their lives.) But for the average liberal whose mind has been dulled by the committee-ish cant of the professional liberal, miscegenation is not an issue because he has been told that the Negro does not desire it. So, when it comes, miscegenation will be a terror, comparable perhaps to the derangement of the American Communists when the icons to Stalin came tumbling down. The average American Communist held to the myth of Stalin for reasons which had little to do with the political evidence and everything to do with their psychic necessities. In this sense it is equally a psychic necessity for the liberal to believe that the Negro and even the reactionary Southern white are eventually and fundamentally people like himself, capable of becoming good liberals too if only they can be reached by good liberal reason. What the liberal cannot bear to admit is the hatred beneath the skin of a society so unjust that the amount of collective violence buried in the people is perhaps incapable of being contained, and therefore if one wants a better world one does well to hold one's breath, for a worse world is bound to come first, and the dilemma may well be this: given such hatred, it must either vent itself nihilistically or become turned into the cold murderous liquidations of the totalitarian state.

6.

No matter what its horrors the twentieth century is a vastly exciting century for its tendency is to reduce all of life to its ultimate alternatives. One can well wonder if the last war of them all will be between the blacks and the whites, or between the women and the men, or between the beautiful and ugly, the pillagers and managers, or the rebels and the regulators. Which of course is carrying speculation beyond the point where speculation is still serious, and yet despair at the monotony and bleakness of the future have become so engrained in the radical temper that the radical is in danger of abdicating from all imagination. What a man feels is the impulse for his creative effort, and if an alien but nonetheless passionate instinct about the meaning of life has come so unexpectedly from a virtually illiterate people, come out of the most intense conditions of exploitation, cruelty, violence, frustration, and lust, and yet has succeeded as an instinct in keeping this tortured people alive, then it is perhaps possible that the Negro holds more of the tail of the expanding elephant of truth than the radical, and if this is so, the radical humanist could do worse than to brood upon the phenomenon. For if a revolutionary time should come again, there would be a crucial difference if someone had already delineated a neo-Marxian calculus aimed at comprehending every circuit and process of society from ukase to kiss as the communications of human energy—a caculus capable of translating the economic relations of man into his psychological relations and then back again, his productive relations thereby embracing his sexual relations as well, until the crises of capitalism in the twentieth century would yet be understood as the unconscious adaptations of a society to solve its economic imbalance at the expense of a new mass psychological imbalance. It is almost beyond the imagination to conceive of a work in which the drama of human energy is engaged, and a theory of its social currents and dissipations, its imprisonments, expressions, and tragic wastes are fitted into some gigantic synthesis of human action where the body of Marxist thought, and particularly the epic grandeur of *Das Kapital* (that first of the major *psychologies* to approach the mystery of social cruelty so simply and practically as to say that we are a collective body of humans whose life-energy is wasted, displaced, and procedurally stolen as it passes from one of us to another)— where particularly the epic grandeur of *Das Kapital* would find its place in an even more God-like view of human justice and injustice, in some more excruciating vision of those intimate and institutional processes which lead to our creations and disasters, our growth, our attrition, and our rebellion.

1957

Note to "Reflections on Hip"

A prime virtue of The White Negro may be in the number of heresies it commits. Here, on this exchange with Jean Malaquais and Ned Polsky two such heresies are engaged: that a modern revolution can arise out of some other condition than an organized militant movement of the proletariat, and that there are other cures to neurosis than the couch of the analyst. For readers who are indifferent to these subjects, the exchange will be of doubtful interest; for those who would like a little more of The White Negro, the matter may be worth the difficulty.

I have taken one liberty. The exchange was called "Reflections on Hipsterism," when it appeared in Dissent. *I did not choose the title, and so I have altered the name of the piece.*

Reflections on Hip

1. JEAN MALAQUAIS

Once upon a time there was a myth named *le prolétariat*. Though obviously a male, the myth was believed to be pregnant with child—a well conformed socialistic baby true to the Scriptures. Baby being long overdue, the congregation of the faithful first became skeptical, then frankly disgusted. Feeling cheated, never allowing that they may have misread the Book, they repudiated *le prolétariat,* sued for divorce, and being an idealistically inclined flock, started to shop around for a better, less sterile myth. Great schisms followed, yet few of the flock turned cynical. Quite the contrary. Prompted by their thirst for eternal values, many made dangerous inroads into heretofore uncharted lands. There, as in a secret Eden happily rediscovered, amazingly new and refreshing reasons to live awaited the bold myth hunter: Liberalism, Democracy, Free World, Peace, Stop-the-AH-Experiments, etc., and—honor to whom honor is due—the long neglected bastard-brother of *le prolétariat:* marijuana soaked Hip.

That Hip found in Norman Mailer its most outstanding and original theologist (I don't say apologist), seems quite clear in the light of his essay [*Dissent,* Summer 1957]. He may be correct in stating that Hip and psychopathology follow two parallel paths, but he has still to persuade this reader that the American Negro bohemian and his white imitator embody a special brand of the human species. Starting with the fact that the Negro's status within the American community is a marginal one, Mailer is not content to allow him his particular or characteristic psychological bent; he bestows upon him a Messianic mission.

He seems to forget that the American hipster has his counterparts and equivalents in countries with no Negro population: Sweden, England, Russia, Poland, France, to name only a few places. The Swedish youth runs properly amok. The British Teddy, the Russian *besprizornyé,* the Polish hooligans, the French psuedo-existentialist fauna, don't behave differently toward life than the hipster. All are the product of an identical social phenomenon prevailing in highly industrialized and more or less paternalistically ruled countries: extreme inner insecurity dipped in a State-sponsored "welfare" at the price of a terrific loss to the individual's self. That's one reason why, as a rule, they react on the level of a purely personal idea of "recovery"—but from what and toward what none of them really knows.

When Mailer says of the hipster that he has "converted his unconscious experience into much conscious knowledge," he may speak of the hipster's knowledge in a very narrow practical way, as for instance knowledge on how to survive momentarily in a back alley; but he is mistaken if he takes it for more than it is: an instinctive and empirical know-how. The remarkable thing about hipsters of all kinds and variety (and they vary indeed in many aspects) is that, except for a case or two in a generation, as a body they are sooner or later swallowed up by the most conforming routine ever.

Hip is but another name for lumpen, and lumpen make excellent conformists and the best of potential hangmen for "order's" sake. Even before they fall into rank and file, rather than raping and murdering they blabber of rape and murder; they dream of rape and murder in idiotic clichés, vicariously, with a hand from the tabloids and other such literature. Yet if a handful among the tens of thousands, as Mailer numbers them, do go through rape and murder, it is mostly by accident, by a tragic mistake, almost never by deliberate clear choice, and then only once, for they are ambushed as soon as they have zipped up their pants.

One other reason why lumpen of all kind are but a myth in terms of social action, except possibly a small home-made pogrom with the implicit or explicit blessing of State and municipality, is that they do not form any coherent social body. Negro shopkeepers and white shopkeepers, should their shops be endangered, would dismiss all color lines and slaughter hand in hand Negro and white lumpen. There is more real solidarity (class solidarity) between white and Negro "law abiding citizens" than between people of "Caucasian" or "African" complexion.

Moreover, there is hardly a hipster alive who doesn't long to conform (like his extreme representative, the pyschopath, he is always a case of a frustrated conformist), and there is hardly a conformist alive, white or Negro, who doesn't long to rape and murder (like his extreme representative, the pulpit moralist, he is always a case of a frustrated rebel). The difference is that the conformist hardly ever becomes a lumpen, that the lumpen almost always becomes a conformist (all exceptions granted). In turn, the difference is due to the only real relationship in modern society: property relationship. For the conformist to become a lumpen means to give up his actual or virtual property, which he cannot do by free choice; for the lumpen to become a conformist means to acquire property, which he always wills by free choice —however strong his overt denial. (As a matter of fact, lumpen *is* a way of making a living.)

On the other hand, the rebel who outgrew the romantic stage of his rebellion, who knows himself to be a grown up rebel—which is quite different from being a "radical," for after all a McCarthy too was a "radical"— knows also that *he conforms,* that he moves within the bonds of social and cultural institutions whose weight he cannot shake off in his private way, but who keeps within his conformity a lucid mind and a clear heart as to what conforming and what rebellion means in terms not of his subjective immediate I, but in terms of man as such, of man as a social creature. To make an image: the lumpen yells sh . . to the cop on the street-corner and feels purged, the conformist lifts his cap to the same cop and feels reassured in his pants, the grown up rebel ignores the cop (though he may summon his help in an emergency) and applies his energy to fell the tree that breeds cops, conformists and lumpen.

The amusing thing is that one can read into Mailer's essay precisely the proposition that the hipster is nothing but a conformist in reverse. "If," says Hip in Mailer's words, "if the fate of 20th century man is to live with death . . . why then the only life-giving answer is to accept the terms of death, to live with death as immediate danger, to divorce oneself from society," etc. Now if man's fate is to live with death, how does the hipster manage to divorce himself from society since he does accept "the terms of death"? If the terms are death, and if he accepts the terms—nay, if he so to speak naturalizes the terms generally prevailing for his private use, why he conforms nice and clean, he is at the avant-garde of conformity.

"Death you want?" says Hip to society. "Good, death there'll be!" And there he goes, the small entrepreneur in death competing with industrial death. One Mr. Verdoux once made a superb parody of our death-bent hipster. But no. Hip, says Mailer truly, Hip wants love, wants peace in a nice kitchenette with a white apron around his girl's waist. All the "mysticism," all the "dialectical conception of existence" Mailer so generously bestows upon Hip is, as far as I am concerned, a gorgeous flower of Mailer's romantic idealism.

Paris   September 4, 1957

MAILER'S REPLY

In his search for a sexual life which will suit his orgiastic needs, the hipster willy-nilly attacks conventional sexual morality, and to some degree succeeds in disturbing the balance. If capitalist society is grounded upon property relations, these relations are wed to monogamy, family, and the sexual strictures which maintain them. It is yet to be established that sexual life can be promiscuously altered without affecting the psychic real estate of capitalism. Since Malaquais seems to be indirectly arguing the affirmative, I would suggest that there are obstructions to his proof which the poetic excellences of his style cannot storm by metaphor.

Man is a flux of possibilities and energies long before and perhaps long after he is a manipulator of land, properties, and productions. A civilization from now, the vast chapter of Western expansion which was built on property and such inhuman abstractions of human energy as money, credit, and surplus value, may be seen as an ice-age of cruel and brutally slow liberations of productive, purposive, creative and sexual energies which the contradictions of inequity and exploitation congealed not only into the working habits of men, elaborated not only into the institutional hypocrisies of society, but indeed drove as cancerous ambivalences and frustrations into the texture of being itself.

The growth of human consciousness in this century demanded—for its expanding vitality—that a revolution be made, that a mankind be liberated, and since the attempt failed in its frontal revolutionary attack, failed precisely to change the exploitative character of our productive relations, it may well be that the rise of the hipster represents the first wind of a second revolution in this century, moving not forward toward action and more rational equitable distribution, but backward toward being and the secrets of human energy, not forward to the collectivity which was totalitarian in the proof but backward to the nihilism of creative adventurers, a revolution admittedly impossible to conceive even in its outlines, for unlike that first revolution which was conscious, Faustian, and vain, enacted in the name of the proletariat but more likely an expression of the scientific narcissism we inherited from the nineteenth century, a revolution motivated by the rational mania that consciousness could stifle instinct and marshal it into productive formations, the second revolution, if it is to come, would come indeed as antithesis to the "Great Experiment":—its desire would be to turn materialism on its head, have consciousness subjugated to instinct. The hipster, rebel cell in our social body, lives out, acts out, follows the close call of his instinct as far as he dares, and so points to possibilities and consequences in what have hitherto been chartless jungles of moral nihilism. The essence of his expression, his faith if you will, is that the real desire to make a better world exists at the heart of our instinct (that instinctual vision of a human epic which gave birth to consciousness itself), that man is therefore roughly more good than evil, that beneath his violence there is finally love and the nuances of justice, and that the removal therefore of all social restraints while it would open us to an era of incomparable individual violence would still spare us the collective violence of rational totalitarian liquidations (which we must accept was grossly a pyschic index of the buried, voiceless, and ineradicable violences of whole nations of people), and would—and here is the difference—by expending the violence directly, open the possibility of working with that human creativity which is violence's opposite.

But of course this may be no more than the sword dance of my "romantic idealism." Immediately, the charge by Malaquais is that the hipster is our old black sheep, our discontented nephew of the proletariat, the impotent lumpen no more than a thousand dollars away from kissing the penny-calloused hands of the petit-bourgeoisie. I wonder. Is it so very lumpen to be able to influence American culture? The mass audience may turn in for the night to the chest-out, stomach-in, pinch-buttocks of the Star-Spangled Banner, with perhaps a five-minute sermonette to speed them to churchly sleep, but their waking hours were vibrated by that now déclassé (so fast does it change) Holy Shaker, that ex-apostle of small-town Southern orgasm, Elvis Presley.

Malaquais says the hipster has his opposite number in the British Teddy, the *besprizornyé* (still untamed?—how unlumpen!), the Polish hooligans, the French existentialists, all Hip, and not a drop of Negro blood in a thousand of their black masses. But Malaquais would be hard-put to find the taint of Hip without the blood of jazz. The Negro's experience appears to be the most universal communication of the West, and the authority of their tortured senses may indeed be passing by the musical states of their artistic expression, *without language, without conscious communication,* into the no doubt equally tortured senses of the wild sensitive spawn of two vast wars. But to Malaquais the lumpen is the lumpen. If Marx did not find it necessary to take them seriously, how dare we?

I wonder, however, if it would not be more "Marxist" to recognize that the superstructure of society has attained vast autonomies outside productive relations, psychological undercurrents which often clash with material economic realities—as, for example, the swoop of the stockmarket in response to the Sputnik. There may even be ineradicable conflicts of interest between the superstructure and the base of productive relations. At the least, is it not reasonable to assume that society has reached a point of such complexity, such "organismishness," that it is capable of adapting itself to avoid economic crisis by unwillingly (owing to the contradictions of mass manipulation) communicating mass psychological crises via the mass communications?

The contemporary contradictions from which America has been suffering (given the virtually self-regulating economic valves of war finance) have been almost insupportable psychological contradictions, virtually perfect Orwellian ambivalences—(War is Peace, Love is Hate, Ignorance is Knowledge); if these psychic contradictions should eventually introduce an apathy sufficient to turn our country back into economic contradictions and economic depression, which is indeed far from impossible, it will not mean that the process was a simple dialectic whose breath moved only through the circuits of productive relations. What one may fumble toward is a dialectic which can bridge the material and the ideal—which can infuse material notions of energy into that philosophical country of the ideal (read: the individual unconscious) which psychoanalysis now occupies with a middle-class mechanistic *weltanschauung*. If we socialists, radicals, anarchists, rebels, nihilists, and dissenters are to become more than the dried twigs of an old family tree, the shabby genteel clerks who end the line of a warrior family, it can at least be recognized that until the radical bridge from Marx to Freud is built, and our view of man embraces more facts, contradictions, and illuminations than any conservative view, and stares into such terrifying alternatives as totalitarianism or barbarism, we are doing no more than scolding ourselves, and ignoring that revolutionary indictment which every human alive can respond to in some part of himself: that an unjust society wreaks cruel if subtle imprisonments and destructions of personal energy, wreaks them not only upon an individual class or race, but upon the being of each of us. For, ultimately, unjust societies must, out of the nature of their contradictions, stifle the best part of each creativity, and so starve into neglect and atrophy that future we hear raging to be born.

2. NED POLSKY

Although Norman Mailer, in "The White Negro," shows ample awareness of some drawbacks of hipster life, others he romanticizes away or ignores. Mailer is right in seeing the hipsters as the only significant new group of rebels in America. He is also right to recognize the new Bohemia, extend it his "essential sympathy," and where he cannot find much of merit, perhaps yet encourage it by praising with faint damns. But it is equally legitimate and desirable to recognize that there are qualitative differences among Bohemias and that the current Bohemia is greatly inferior to its predecessors of at least the past four decades.

1.

The new Bohemia's inferiority shows up clearly in its lack of intellectual content. Most hipsters scarcely read at all, not because they can't (nearly all of them have finished high school, and a surprising number of the whites have attended our better universities) but because they won't. The closest thing to an intellectual discussion is their chatter about the pseudo-profundities of contemporary jazz; they don't even know—worse, don't want to know —that the things they praise were achieved by art-music composers years ago. As for the few who can be said to read with any regularity: they turn their backs not only on the horrors but the grandeurs of the past, restrict their horizon to contemporary literature, and from this area select what is in large part tripe—a compound of Rexroth and Rimbaud, Henry Miller and *Mad Comics,* Sartre and science fiction, jazz magazines and jerkoff magazines.

Their own literary productions are few, and what there are of them—with the exception of some poems by Robert Duncan and parts of his unpublished play, *Faust Foutu*—have almost no literary merit whatever. (Buy *Evergreen Review No. 2* and back issues of *Origin* and see for yourself.) The reason is not far to seek: even if we grant Mailer's dubious claim that the American existentialists feel their existentialism more than the French do, it is still true that for art something more is required than the raw recital of raw emotion. Thus the American hipsters' writings cannot begin to compare with the work of the arch-hipsters of modern European literature, Céline and Genêt, to say nothing of any number of nonhipsters.

2.

Hipster hedonism takes many forms. Some hipster groups, for example, have everything to do with motorcycles, whereas others have nothing to do with them. But not significant in any of these groups, Mailer to the contrary, is a sexual revolution. Of course hipsters are willing to try a variety of partners and positions, have no objection to interracial intercourse, etc.—but this is merely to say that they are "liberated" in the superficial ways that many "liberals" are. For all its probings of hipster pathology, Mailer's rhetoric covers up the fact that hipsters are not only more "psychologically" crippled than most people but sexually likewise—that they are not sexually free and have no chance to become so, and that this means they are not actual or potential sexual revolutionaries in the profound sense that Mailer is talking about. Two examples: many male hipsters (if I am to believe the testimony of several Hip men and women) are extremely sadistic in their sexual relationships, and many others are so narcissistic that inevitably their orgasms are premature and puny. No amount of plain or fancy screwing is going to change this. When Mailer glamorizes the hipsters' "search after the good orgasm" he is simply accepting at face value their rationalization for what is in truth a pathetic, driven sex life in which the same failures are repeated again and again. On this matter as on others, Mailer confuses the life of action with the life of acting out.

I imagine that Mailer really knows all this but that he cannot state it baldly because it would then be obvious that "bad orgasm" is one habit the hipster will never kick without the "dreary alternative" of psychoanalysis. Of course now that psychoanalysis has become a respectable part of psychiatry and the old-style European analysts, who were mostly rebels by definition, are being rapidly replaced by bourgeois young American M.D.'s, it is undeniable that the patient runs a much greater risk of encountering the analyst for whom "cure" necessarily includes "adjustment" to the present social structure. And not a few pioneer analysts now devote all their energies to making rich men's children content with their lot in life. But it is equally undeniable that psychoanalysis—whatever the brand—still provides greater sexual benefits than does the dreary alternative that Mailer glorifies. Psychoanalysis has been domesticated but not castrated.

3.

The world of the hipster is commonly held to break down racial barriers, and indeed it does. If we accept the usual ultimate test (and Mailer's)—whether whites and Negroes sleep together—hipsters undoubtedly meet it much more often than squares do. Nevertheless there is a built-in barrier to full acceptance of black hipsters by white ones (and to a lesser extent vice versa), which stems from the fact that hipsters are marginal in a very special way.

The white Negro, as Mailer aptly calls him, is of course a marginal man. He puts down the white world from which he came. And he can never fully make it in, or be accepted by, the Negro world; so with rare exceptions (notably Mezz Mezzrow) he doesn't even try to live within the Negro community, and if he does he is put down by Negroes a lot. He exists, then, between the two worlds, where he meets his obverse: the Negro hipster, who puts down the Negro community at large (one reason, though not the main one, being that most Negroes are also squares, Mailer's stereotype of the Negro notwithstanding) and can never fully make it in the white world.

The first thing to notice about these marginal men—white or black—is that they are not the utterly isolated, atomized individuals whom sociologists assume all marginal men to be. They come together and create a little world of their own which elaborates its own worldview, code of behavior, institutions, argot, and so on. They create what to sociologists is a contradiction in terms: a subculture of marginal men.[1]

Now, the inner tragedy of the hipster subculture is this: the white member is attracted to the Negro member because of the latter's Negro-ness, whereas the Negro—and this Mailer ignores—is attracted to the white precisely because of his whiteness. Although the interracial groups which constitute the hipster subculture are "primary" groups in sociological terms, since in them whites and Negroes meet in "intimate, face-to-face relationships," this does not automatically imply the deepest kind of social bond; sociological theory is too gross at this point because it neglects the fact that "face to face" occasionally means, among other things, "looking in opposite directions." Many a time I have heard white hipsters, when no Negro members were present, put down one of the absent Negroes with "The trouble with X is that he's too fay-oriented," or "Y is a drag; all he's interested in is laying white chicks." And I'd bet my bottom dollar that Negro hipsters, among themselves, often put down the whites with something like "Man, those fay cats are pretty cool and don't want us to be Uncle Toms,

---

[1] A good index of the subculture's strength is provided by that most pervasive of hipster activities, marijuana-smoking and its attendant exploration of exotic states of consciousness, for the reactions of one under the influence of marijuana are determined not nearly so much by his individual psychology or physiology as by subcultural norms. For a related point of view, and much concrete evidence, cf. Howard S. Becker, "On Becoming a Marihuana Smoker," *American Journal of Sociology*, LIX (November 1953), pp. 235-242.

but they still want us to be spooks. They don't really dig us as people; they just dig us for our music and our pot." Which is true. Even in the world of the hipster the Negro remains essentially what Ralph Ellison called him —an invisible man. The white Negro accepts the real Negro not as a human being in his totality, but as the bringer of a highly specified and restricted "cultural dowry," to use Mailer's phrase. In so doing he creates an inverted form of keeping the nigger in his place.

MAILER'S REPLY

As a cool critical view of the affectations, vanities, and hypocrisies of the hipster, I have little quarrel with Ned Polsky's remarks. They were written with a keen eye. But I believe he overrides a most complex question when he declares that many male hipsters have orgasms premature and puny. Since he can hardly have had the requisite personal experience—"Uncle," said a bisexual Negro to me once, "I couldn't have more charge for that chick if I'd gone down on a platoon of Marines"—I wonder if Polsky isn't really just passing on a tyrannical assumption which is one of the cement blocks of the Square throne of psychoanalysis.

In the Western sexual literature with which I am familiar, classical, technical, and pornographic, I can remember—with the harsh radical exception of Wilhelm Reich—almost no incisive discussion of male orgasm. The very notion of "good orgasm" (which indeed I used superficially in "The White Negro," DISSENT, Summer '57) betrays the lack of examination we bring to it, for it assumes there are two domains, good orgasm and bad, each clearly set apart by a defense line of psychic dragon teeth. But the Hip argument, if one is to dredge it forth, would claim that even in an orgasm which is *the most* there is always the vision of an outer wider wilder orgasm which is even more *with it*. The nature of orgasm is a spectrum, perhaps an infinite spectrum, perhaps intimately dialectical: in the worst of orgasm there are nips of pleasure, in the best of orgasms some mannered containments denying pleasure beyond high pleasure, restraining the rarer liberations of energy for the next day.

I am sure that the average psychoanalyst would now say, "The fact that the advocate of this thesis wants more of orgasm, is an indication of dissatisfaction with his narcissistic involvements. The adjusted social person knows better than to worry about his orgasm. It has been improved by psychoanalytical therapy." Of course one could walk through a mile of analysand-type persons to find one who really believed that his orgasm had been sexually improved.

But to argue this way is to stalk one's opponent about a circle, each a safe diameter apart. Finally, one cannot enter another being's orgasm and measure its scope (especially since many people's frustrated theatrical talents are brought resolutely to bed), one can only guess from the spectrum of one's own what the possibilities may be for others. And the line I would prefer to engage is to call into account the psychoanalyst's self-interest in believing that almost all sexual rebels are sick sexually. Indeed, he is right.

But almost everyone is sick sexually in more or less degree, and so the indictment by the psychoanalyst should come forth no more maternally than to claim: better you should be sick as a Square than sick as a Hip.

Still the impolite question remains to be asked: does the direct experience of the analyst's own life prepare him to judge the inner states of Hip? Sedentary, middle-class, in fief to fifteen years of training, living among the absurd magpie scrutinies of wife, children, colleagues, patients, and hostile strangers, most analysts are obliged to be more proper than proper, and their characters, impulses and value judgments become shaped to satisfy the social necessities of their work. The social necessities of their work? The analyst is Gibraltar in a pathless middle-class sea, his guiding torch is lit by money, his triumphs are invariably with plain and miserable patients squashed too early by life, ruined permanently for pleasure, and so burgeoning under the stern authority and human comfort that an expensive person listens to them for two and a half hours a week. But the analyst, this middle-class and usually pampered son, is he the one to make the imaginative journey into the tortured marijuana-racked mind and genitalia of a hipster daring to live on the edge of the most dangerous of the Negro worlds? Or is it not finally a matter of courage, courage not necessarily nor uniquely before violence, but courage to accept telling blows to the ego? For what would the analyst do, and what would become of his tidy, narrow, other-directed little world if he were to discover, and may God help him, that the hipster way out by the lip of danger may conceivably know more of the savor and swing in the damn dialectic of the orgasm than he, the doctor, the educated ball-shrinker who diagnoses all joys not his own as too puny.

THE PRIMEVAL MITOSIS

Eldridge Cleaver

And the Lord God caused a deep sleep to fall upon Adam, and he slept: and he took one of his ribs, and closed up the flesh instead thereof; And the rib, which the Lord God had taken from man, made he a woman, and brought her unto the man. And Adam said, This is now bone of my bones, and flesh of my flesh: she shall be called Woman, because she was taken out of Man.

—Genesis 2:21–23

It is as if in the evolution of sex a particle one day broke away from an X-chromosome, and thereafter in relation to X-chromosomes could produce only an incomplete female—the creature we now call the male! It is to this original chromosomal deficiency that all the various troubles to which the male falls heir can be traced.

Ashley Montagu,
The Natural Superiority of Women

I think that *any* submerged class is going to be more accustomed to sexuality than a leisure class. A leisure class may be more *preoccupied* with sexuality; but a submerged class is going to be more drenched in it.

You see, the upper classes are obsessed with sex, but they contain very little of it themselves. They use up much too much sex in their manipulations of power. In effect, they exchange sex for power. So they restrict themselves in their sexuality—wheras the submerged classes have to take their desires for power and plow them back into sex.

Norman Mailer,
The Presidential Papers

The roots of heterosexuality are buried in that evolutionary choice made long ago in some misty past—but not so remote that it can't be reached with the long arm of the mind—by some unknown forerunner of Homo sapiens. Struggling up from some murky swamp, some stagnant mudhole, some peaceful meadow, that unknown ancestor of Man/Woman, by some weird mitosis of the essence, divided its Unitary Self in half—into the male and female hemispheres of the Primeval Sphere. These hemispheres evolved into what we know today as man and woman.

When the Primeval Sphere divided itself, it established a basic tension of attraction, a dynamic magnetism of opposites—the Primeval Urge—which exerts an irresistible attraction between the male and female hemispheres, ever tending to fuse them back together into a unity in which the male and female realize their true nature—the lost unity of the Primeval Sphere. This is the eternal and unwavering motivation of the male and female hemispheres, of man and woman, to transcend the Primeval Mitosis and achieve supreme identity in the Apocalyptic Fusion.

Each half of the human equation, the male and female hemispheres of the Primeval Sphere, must prepare themselves for the fusion by achieving a Unitary Sexual Image, i.e., a heterosexual identity free from the mutually exclusive, antagonistic, antipodal impediments of homosexuality (the product of the fissure of society into antagonistic classes and a dying culture and civilization alienated from its biology).

Man's continual striving for a Unitary Sexual Image, which can only be achieved in a Unitary Society, becomes a basic driving force of the Class Struggle, which is, in turn, the dynamic of history. The quest for the Apocalyptic Fusion will find optimal conditions only in a Classless Society, the absence of classes being the *sine qua non* for the existence of a Unitary Society in which the Unitary Sexual Image can be achieved.

Each social structure projects onto the screen of possibility the images of the highest type of male and female sexual identities realizable within the limits of that society. The people within that society are motivated and driven, by the perennial quest for Apocalyptic Fusion, to achieve this highest identity, or as close as they can come to the perfection of the Unitary

Sexual Image. All impediments to realization of this image become sources of alienation, obstacles in the way of the Self seeking to realize its ultimate identity.

Since each society projects its own sexual image, the Unitary Society will project a Unitary Sexual Image. We can thus postulate, following the model of Marx, that in ancient communal society, which was not cleft into antagonistic classes, there existed a Unitary Society in which a Unitary Sexual Image was in natural coincidence with the way of life of the people. This is the lost innocence of the Garden of Eden.

The Class Society projects a fragmented sexual image. Each class projects a sexual image coinciding with its class-function in society. And since its class-function will differ from that of other classes, its sexual image will differ also and in the same proportion. The source of the fragmentation of the Self in Class Society lies in the alienation between the function of man's Mind and the function of his Body. Man as thinker performs an Administrative Function in society. Man as doer performs a Brute Power Function. These two basic functions I symbolize, when they are embodied in living men functioning in society, as the Omnipotent Administrator and the Supermasculine Menial.

Since all men are created equal, when the Self is fragmented by the operation of the laws and forces of Class Society, men in the elite classes usurp the controlling and Administrative Function of the society as a whole —i.e., they usurp the administrative component in the nature and biology of the men in the classes below them. Administrative power is concentrated at the apex of society, in the Godhead of the society (pharaoh, king, president, chairman). Administrative power beneath the apex is delegated. Those in classes to which no administrative power has been delegated have the administrative component in their personalities suppressed, alienated, denied expression. Those who have usurped the Administrative Function we shall call the Omnipotent Administrators. Struggling among themselves for higher positions in the administrative hierarchy, they repudiate the component of Brute Power in themselves, claim no kinship with it, and project it onto the men in the classes below them.

All the males in the classes beneath *the* Omnipotent Administrator, or Godhead of the society, are alienated from the administrative component in themselves in proportion to their distance from the apex. That is, they perceive their alienation in terms of their distance from the apex. This perception of their alienation, in terms of the apex, is an illusion. In fact, their alienation must be measured by their distance from the attainment of a Unitary Sexual Image, the take-off stage for the Apocalyptic Fusion. Generally, in a fragmented Class Society, the basic impulse of Omnipotent Administrators is to despise their bodies and glorify their minds.

Those who have been assigned the Brute Power Function we shall call the Supermasculine Menials. They are alienated from their minds. For them the mind counts only insofar as it enables them to receive, understand, and carry out the will of the Omnipotent Administrators.

The Class Society has a built-in bias, which tends to perpetuate the social system. The Omnipotent Administrators, wishing to preserve what they perceive as their superior position and way of life, have, from a class point of view and also on an individual level, a negative reaction toward any influence in the society that tends to increase the number of males qualified to fulfill the functions of administration. When it comes to anything that will better the lot of those beneath him, the Omnipotent Administrator starts with a basic "anti" reflex. Any liberality he might show is an indication of the extent to which he has suppressed his "anti" reflex, and is itself a part of his lust for omnipotence. His liberality is, in fact, charity.

The Supermasculine Menial clearly realizes that the superiority of the Omnipotent Administrators over him is based upon the development of their minds and the power they command as a result. Hence, he starts with a "pro" reflex. He is, for example, pro-universal education at public expense.

Weakness, frailty, cowardice, and effeminacy are, among other attributes, associated with the Mind. Strength, brute power, force, virility, and physical beauty are associated with the Body. Thus the upper classes, or Omnipotent Administrators, are perennially associated with physical weakness, decay, underdeveloped bodies, effeminacy, sexual impotence, and frigidity. Virility, strength, and power are associated with the lower classes, the Supermasculine Menials.

In feudal society, the men of the nobility, who were Omnipotent Administrators by Divine Right, are generally considered to have been weak, delicate, and effeminate, with the affectations of demonstrative homosexuals. The serfs and peasants are considered to have been physically strong, sturdy, hearty, fecund—"supermasculine."

The image of the Omnipotent Administrator, that he is markedly effeminate and delicate by reason of his explicit repudiation and abdication of his body in preference for his mind, is decisive for the image of the woman of the elite classes. *Even though her man is effeminate, she is required to possess and project an image that is in sharp contrast to his, more sharply feminine than his, so that the effeminate image of her man can still, by virtue of the sharp contrast in degrees of femininity, be perceived as masculine.* Therefore, she becomes "Ultrafeminine."

In order to project an image of Ultrafemininity, the women of the elite repudiate and abdicate the Domestic Function of the female (which is, in the female, the counterpart of the function of Brute Power in the male). To enhance her image and to increase her femininity, the domestic component of her nature is projected onto the women in the classes beneath her, and the femininity of the women below is correspondingly decreased. In effect, a switch is made: the woman of the elite absorbs into her being the femininity of the woman below her, and she extirpates her domestic component; the woman below absorbs the elite woman's cast-off domestic component and relinquishes her own femininity. The elite woman thus becomes *Ultrafeminine* while the woman below becomes *Subfeminine*. For the purposes of social imagery, the woman below becomes an Amazon.

Thus, a most weird and complex dialectic of inversion is established in

Class Society. The Omnipotent Administrator is launched on a perpetual search for his alienated body, for affirmation of his unstable masculinity. He becomes a worshiper of physical prowess, or he may come to despise the body and everything associated with it. Fearing impotence, impotence being implicit in his negation and abdication of his Body, his profoundest need is for evidence of his virility. His opposite, the Body, the Supermasculine Menial, is a threat to his self-concept (and to compound it all, this perceived threat and resultant fear is reinforced decisively by the fact that the men beneath him are a threat to him *in reality,* because their life goal is to destroy his Omnipotence over them). He views them as his enemies and inferiors, men of a lesser breed than himself and his kind. He despises, hates them. Yet, because of the infirmity in his image and being which moves him to worship masculinity and physical prowess, the Omnipotent Administrator cannot help but covertly, and perhaps in an extremely sublimated guise, envy the bodies and strength of the most alienated men beneath him—those furthest from the apex of administration—because the men most alienated from the mind, least diluted by admixture of the Mind, will be perceived as the most masculine manifestations of the Body: the Supermasculine Menials. (This is precisely the root, the fountainhead, of the homosexuality that is perennially associated with the Omnipotent Administrator.) The dialectic of the Supermasculine Menial is the converse of that of the Omnipotent Administrator. The Supermasculine Menial has an infirmity of the brain because of his alienation from his mind.

Because he despises weakness of the body in himself, the Omnipotent Administrator will have a secret or subconscious aversion to the women of his own class, because of the Ultrafemininity which they have developed to counterbalance his effeminacy. At the same time, he will surpass himself in his efforts to conceal his aversion and make believe that the very opposite is true. He thus makes an icon of his woman and, literally, worships her. He pays obeisance to Her ritualistically while in the chapel of Her presence. Enshrining Her on a pedestal, he goes off seeking confirmation of his insecure masculinity elsewhere. Since the women of the elite tend to become the same, i.e., to project a homogeneous image of Ultrafemininity, they cannot, in the end, satisfy his psychic need—the confirmation of his masculinity. Strength gauges its own potency through a confrontation with other strength. To test it, he must go where it is. He may become addicted to a masculine-imaged sport, become a big-game hunter, outdoorsman, mountain climber. He may find satisfaction enough from some outlet as to have no problem at all which he is aware of as a sexual infirmity. He may be unaware of his impotence because he is blinded by his dazzling success and superiority in another field.

But in his quest for confirmation of his masculinity, a quest which he usually perceives as a search for sexual satisfaction and new conquests, his attention is attracted, with the force of the pull of gravity, to the potent Bodies in the classes beneath him, to the strength. He may sexually exploit the white-collar Bodies at the office; then, on his descent toward the Power Source, he may be drawn to the blue-collar Bodies in the plant. If these

Bodies leave him still in the clutches of his lust and insecurity, he will bore deeper and deeper into the lower strata until he finds his sexual Balm of Gilead. There is a Pandora's box of sexual aberrations here.

The Body is tropical, warm, hot: Fire! It is soft, pleasing to the touch, luscious to the kiss. The blood is hot. Muscles are strength. *The basic motion of the women of the elite is flight from their bodies.* The weakness of the female body when contrasted to the strength of the male body is an obvious attribute of femininity as manifested in social imagery. Thus, to enhance and emphasize the femininity of her image—which is mandatory in order that she present a sharp feminine contrast to the effeminate image of her man, the Omnipotent Administrator—she seeks to increase the weakness of her body and stamp out all traces of strength, to differentiate it further from the effeminate form of her man. An appearance of strength in her body is called *ugly*.

Having projected her strength, her domestic component, onto the women beneath her, she achieves an image of frailty, weakness, helplessness, delicacy, daintiness. Silks, ruffles, frills, bangles, and laces are her element. In the realm of sex, because the act of sexual intercourse is both a physical and mental process, a joint venture between the Mind and the Body, her basic contradiction is that she is physically inadequate while mentally voracious, with her mind in extreme conflict with her body. The mechanism of her orgasm, which begins in her body and ends in the psychic depths of her mind, becomes short-circuited in the struggle between her mind and her body.

Sitting at the foot of her bed, like the mute Sphinx on the bank of the Nile, is the Ogre of Frigidity. She is terrified, because of the quality of her life, by the prospect of becoming a life-termer in the prison of frigidity. Her basic fear is frigidity, the state in which her frantic search for Ultrafemininity collides with an icepack death of the soul: where the fire in her body is extinguished by the ice in her mind. The psychic core of her sensuality, the male-seeking pole of her Female Principle, the trigger of the mechanism of her orgasm, moves beyond the reach or range of the effeminate clitoris of her man. Frigid, cold, icy, ice. Arctic. Antarctic. At the end of her flight from her body is a sky-high wall of ice. (If a lesbian is anything she is a frigid woman, a frozen cunt, with a warp and a crack in the wall of her ice.)

In proportion to the intensity of the Ultrafeminine's fear and feel of the ice is her psychic lust for the flame, for the heat of the fire: the Body. The Ultrafeminine, seeking sexual satisfaction, finds only physical exhaustion in the bed of the Omnipotent Administrator, and the odds are against her finding psychic satisfaction there. Her "psychic bridegroom" is the Supermasculine Menial. The Omnipotent Administrator, having repudiated and abdicated his body, his masculine component which he has projected onto the men beneath him, cannot present his woman, the Ultrafeminine, with an image of masculinity capable of penetrating into the psychic depths where the treasure of her orgasm is buried. The sexual act being a joint venture of the Mind and Body, though he satisfy her body and sap its strength, he cannot touch that magic spot in her mind which triggers the mechanism of her orgasm. Bereft of psychic satisfaction, and inhibited by social conventions and mores from embarking on a quest for her sexual fulfillment, yet performing her function as a mother and wife to the Omnipotent Administrator, the Ultrafeminine becomes a psychic celibate.

At the nth degree of the Ultrafeminine's scale of psychic lust (the contours of which few men or women throughout their entire lives ever in fact explore, resort being had to the forms of sublimation) stands the walking phallus symbol of the Supermasculine Menial. Though she may never have had a sexual encounter with a Supermasculine Menial, she is fully convinced that he can fulfill her physical need. It will be no big thing for him to do since he can handle those Amazons down there with him, with his strong body, rippling muscles, his strength and fire, the driving force of his spine, the thrust of his hips and the fiery steel of his rod. But what wets the Ultrafeminine's juice is that she is allured and tortured by the secret, intuitive knowledge that he, her psychic bridegroom, can blaze through the wall of her ice, plumb her psychic depths, test the oil of her soul, melt the iceberg in her brain, touch her inner sanctum, detonate the bomb of her orgasm, and bring her sweet release.

The chip on the Supermasculine Menial's shoulder is the fact that he has been robbed of his mind. In an uncannily effective manner, the society in which he lives has assumed in its very structure that he, minus a mind, is the embodiment of Brute Power. The bias and reflex of the society are against the cultivation or even the functioning of his mind, and it is borne in upon him from all sides that the society is actually deaf, dumb, and blind to his mind. The products of his mind, unless they are very closely associated with his social function of Brute Power, are resented and held in contempt by society as a whole. The further away from Brute Power his mental productions stand, the more emphatically will they be rejected and scorned by society, and treated as upstart invasions of the realm of the Omnipotent Administrator. His thoughts count for nothing. He doesn't run, regulate, control, or administer anything. Indeed, he is himself regulated, manipulated, and controlled by the Omnipotent Administrators. The struggle of his life is for the emancipation of his mind, to receive recognition for the products of his mind, and official recognition of the fact that he has a mind.

In his society, the Mind has been adjudged superior to the Body, and he knows that he is the Body and the Omnipotent Administrator is the Mind. It's Mind over matter, and the Body is matter. He may despise the Omnipotent Administrator for his physical weakness and envy him for his mind; or he may despise his own body and idolize the weak body of the Omnipotent Administrator. He may even strive to attain a weak physical image himself in order to identify with the image of the Omnipotent Administrator. The people at the base of society, where the Supermasculine Menial is, are well known for their reflex of attempting to conform to the style, pattern, manners, and habits of the upper classes, of the Omnipotent Administrators and Ultrafeminines. Just how this works itself out is a problem for analysis by sociologists and social psychologists on the mass level, and the headshrinkers and nutcrackers on the individual level. What we are outlining here is a perspective from which such analysis might best be approached.

The psychic bride of the Supermasculine Menial is the Ultrafeminine. She is his "dream girl." She, the delicate, weak, helpless Ultrafeminine, exerts a magnetic attraction upon him. When he compares her with his own woman, the strong, self-reliant Amazon, lust for her burns in his brain. He recoils from the excess of strength injected into the Amazon by the Domestic Function she performs. Also, since standards of beauty are set by the elite, the Ultrafeminine personifies the official standard of feminine beauty of society as a whole. Influenced by and imbued with this official standard of beauty, while at the same time surrounded by Amazons who do not embody this standard and who are in fact clashing with it, the Supermasculine Menial develops an obsessive yearning and lust for sexual contact with the Ultrafeminine. These yearnings are compounded by the fact that on the whole they are foredoomed to remain unfulfilled. The society has arranged things so that the Supermasculine Menial and the Ultrafeminine are not likely to have access or propinquity to each other conducive to stimulating sexual involvement. In fact, it has not been rare for the Supermasculine Menial and the Ultrafeminine to be severely persecuted, if not put to death, for such sexual contact.

The Amazon is in a peculiar position. Just as her man has been deprived of his manhood, so she has been deprived of her full womanhood. Society has decreed that the Ultrafeminine, the woman of the elite, is the goddess on the pedestal. The Amazon is the personification of the rejected domestic component, the woman on whom "dishpan hands" seem not out of character. The worship and respect which both the Omnipotent Administrator and the Supermasculine Menial lavish upon the image of the Ultrafeminine is a source of deep vexation to the Amazon. She envies the pampered, powderpuff existence of the Ultrafeminine and longs to incorporate these elements into her own life. Alienated from the feminine component of her nature, her reinforced domestic component is an awesome burden and shame of which she longs to be free.

The Amazon finds it difficult to respect the Supermasculine Menial. She sees him essentially as only half a man, an incomplete man. Having no sovereignty over himself, he hasn't that sovereignty over her which our traditional patriarchal myths lead her to believe he should have. On a still deeper level, the urges and needs of the Amazon's psyche move her toward the source of power, toward the receptacle of sovereignty—an attraction motivated by the Primeval Urge to transcend the Primeval Mitosis. When the Primeval Sphere split into the male and female hemispheres, the attribute of sovereignty was reposited in the male hemisphere, and this attribute exercises a magnetic attraction upon the female hemisphere. Usurping the Supermasculine Menial's mind, the Omnipotent Administrator usurped all sovereignty; and because of his monopoly on sovereignty, he is the psychic bridegroom of the Amazon. In another sense, however, being also attracted to the body of the Supermasculine Menial, the Amazon is lost between two worlds.

In net effect, then, there will exist in Class Society two sets of competing images. Contending for the crown of masculinity is one image based on the Body and another based on the Mind; contending for the crown of femininity is one image based on weak, helpless Ultrafemininity and another based on the strong, self-reliant attributes of the Amazon. In a society with a racially homogeneous population, in which the people at the top are racially the same as the ones at the bottom, the competing images are not mutually exclusive. A Supermasculine Menial, for instance, who acquires the training of an Omnipotent Administrator, can become a member of the elite and function accordingly—assuming the existence of some vertical social mobility, which is not, of course, always the case. But even if he is prevented from ascending the social ladder in fact, a Supermasculine Menial can at least imagine himself doing so without first having to transcend any biological barriers. Likewise, an Omnipotent Administrator can descend the social ladder, develop his muscles, and hoe the row with the coolest serf on the manor. The women, too, can descend or ascend, depending on the merits, without having to breach a biological chain.

But in a society where there exists a racial caste system, where the people at the top are sharply distinguished from those at the bottom by race as well as social image, then the two sets of competing images can come to be considered mutually exclusive. The gulf between the Mind and the Body will seem to coincide with the gulf between the two races. At that point, the fear of biological miscegenation is transposed into social imagery; and since the distinction between the two races is founded in biology, the social distinction between Mind and Body is made sacred. Any attempt by the Supermasculine Menial to heal his wound and reclaim his mind will be viewed as a malignant desire to transcend the laws of nature by mixing, "mongrelizing," miscegenating. Coming from the other side, if a member of the elite should attempt to bridge the gulf, it will be conceived as the rankest form of degeneracy and treason to caste. Deep-seated fears and emotions, which are in fact connected with biological traits and are part of a mechanism to aid racial and ethnic survival, are harnessed to social images and thereby transformed into weapons of the Class Struggle. Race fears are weapons in the struggle between the Omnipotent Administrator and the Supermasculine Menial for control of sexual sovereignty.

The Supermasculine Menial and the Amazon are the least alienated from the biological chain, although their minds—especially the Supermasculine Menials'!—are in a general state of underdevelopment. Still, they are the wealth of a nation, an abundant supply of unexhausted, undeessenced human raw material upon which the future of the society depends and with which, through the implacable march of history to an ever broader base of democracy and equality, the society will renew and transform itself.

TALKING IN MY SLEEP—
AN EXERCISE IN SELF-CRITICISM

Abbie Hoffman

A mythical interview of questions that are asked and answers that are given. Interviews are always going on. Here's one with myself.

Do you have an ideology?
No. Ideology is a brain disease.

Do you have a movement?
Yes. It's called Dancing.

Isn't that a put-on?
No.

Can you explain that?
Suppose we start the questions again.

OK. Do you have an ideology?
We are for peace, equal rights, and brotherhood.

Now I understand.
I don't. That was a put-on. I don't understand what I said.

I'm getting confused.
Well, let's go on.

Are you for anything? Do you have a vision of this new society you talk of?
Yes. We are for a free society.

Could you spell that out?
F-R-E-E.

What do you mean free?
You know what that means. America: the land of the free. Free means you don't pay, doesn't it?

Yes, I guess so. Do you mean all the goods and services would be free?
Precisely. That's what the technological revolution would produce if we let it run unchecked. If we stopped trying to control it.

What controls it?
The profit incentive, I guess. Property hang-ups. One task we have is to separate the concept of productivity from work. Work is money. Work is postponement of pleasure. Work is always done for someone else: the boss,

TALKING IN MY SLEEP—AN EXERCISE IN SELF-CRITICISM Reprinted from *Revolution for the Hell of It* by Abbie Hoffman. Copyright © 1968 by The Dial Press, Inc. and used by permission of the publisher.

the kids, the guy next door. Work is competition. Work was linked to productivity to serve the Industrial Revolution. We must separate the two. We must abolish work and all the drudgery it represents.

Who will do what we now call dirty work, like picking up the garbage?
Well, there are a lot of possibilities. There won't be any dirty work. If you're involved in a revolution you have a different attitude toward work. It is not separate from your vision . . . All work now is dirty work. Lots of people might dig dealing with garbage. Maybe there won't be any garbage. Maybe we'll just let it pile up. Maybe everybody will have a garbage disposal. There are numerous possibilities.

Don't you think competition leads to productivity?
Well, I think it did during the Industrial Revolution but it won't do for the future. Competition also leads to war. Cooperation will be the motivating factor in a free society. I think cooperation is more akin to the human spirit. Competition is grafted on by institutions, by a capitalist economy, by religion, by schools. Every institution I can think of in this country promotes competition.

Are you a communist?
Are you an anti-communist?

Does it matter?
Well, I'm tempted to say Yes if I sense you are. I remember when I was young I would only say I was Jewish if I thought the person asking the question was anti-Semitic.

What do you think of Russia?
Ugh! Same as here. Dull, bureaucratic-sterile-puritanical. Do you remember when Kosygin came here and met with Johnson in New Jersey? They looked the same. They think the same. Neither way the wave of the future. Johnson is a communist.

What is the wave of the future?
The National Liberation Front, the Cuban Revolution, the young here and around the world.

Doesn't everybody always place great hope in the young?
Yes, I think so. But young people today are very different from previous generations. I think generational revolt has gone on throughout history. Ortega y Gasset in *Man and Crisis* shows that very dramatically. But there are significant differences. The hydrogen bomb, TV, satellites, jet planes— everything is more immediate, more involving. We are the first internationalists. Vietnam rice paddies are as real to me as the Empire State Building. If you don't live in New York, maybe they are more real. We live in a global village.

Do you like McLuhan?
Let's say I think he is more relevant than Marx. Quentin Fiore, his assistant, is more McLuhan than McLuhan. He's the one who puts the ideas into action. McLuhan still struggles with the printed word. But he is an explorer. He experiments. For an old guy he does well. He understands how

to communicate information. It's just that his living style—Catholic, university life, grants, the risks that he takes—is merely academic. Let's say I respect him, but don't love him. What we seek are new living styles. We don't want to talk about them. We want to live them.

Do you consider what you are doing politically relevant?
No.

Is that the best answer you can think of?
Well, when you ask a question like that you trigger off umpteen responses in my head. I believe in the politics of ecstasy.

Can you explain that a little more?
No, but I can touch it, I can smell it, I can even dance it. I can even fight it. Politics to me is the way somebody lives his life. Not what they vote for or support or even believe in. I'm more interested in art than politics but, well, see, we are all caught in a word box. I find it difficult to make these kinds of divisions. Northrop, in *Meeting of East and West,* said, "Life is an undifferentiated aesthetic continuum." Let me say that the Vietcong attacking the U.S. Embassy in Saigon is a work of art. I guess I like revolutionary art.

This word game, as you call it. Doesn't that present problems in conveying what you want to say?
Yes, but not in what I want to do. Let me say . . . Did you ever hear Andy Warhol talk?

Yes, or at least I think it was him.
Well, I would like to combine his style and that of Castro's. Warhol understands modern media. Castro has the passion for social change. It's not easy. One's a fag and the other is the epitome of virility. If I was forced to make the choice I would choose Castro, but right now in this period of change in the country the styles of the two can be blended. It's not guerrilla warfare but, well, maybe a good term is monkey warfare. If the country becomes more repressive we must become Castros. If it becomes more tolerant we must become Warhols.

Do you see the country becoming more repressive?
Well, it's very hard to be objective about that. The cops around here are certainly a bunch of bastards. It's winter now and traditionally that's a time of paranoia because it's a time of less action than the summer. Everything has always been geared to the summer. School's out. People in the streets. More action. When you are involved you don't get paranoid. It's when you sit back and try to figure out what's going on, or what you should do. The winter is the hardest time for revolutionists in this country. We probably should hibernate. Everything builds toward the summer. This year it seems more so. Everyday we talk of Chicago and the Festival. Everyday the news carries a prediction of the "long hot summer." The other day I saw a report from Detroit. People, one white line, one black line, lining up at a gun shop. Meanwhile the mayor is trying to cool things with a nice friendly speech on brotherhood. It was some contrast. Every day has a new report on some new police weapon system. Then there is uncertainty and the

tendency to re-examine your tactics. Right now I feel like Dwight Eisenhower on an acid trip. "On the one hand this—on the other hand that." I think it's a case of information overload. See, I am conditioned to perform well in chaos—actual chaos. Say a riot. In a riot I know exactly what to do. I'm not good for the winter. This is my last winter in the North. I have to live in total summer if I am to survive.

Will the summer action bring on more repression?
Oh, I suppose so. I see this country as getting simultaneously more repressive and more tolerant. People run off to Hanoi to collaborate with the enemy. Everybody's smoking pot on the streets. People go on TV and radio shows and spell out in detail plans of sabotage. And simultaneously there is repression. The combination of the two is going to produce highly volatile conditions and that's why many different tactics are needed. Right now revolution is anything you can get away with. It has to be that way because of the nature of the opposition.

What is going to accelerate that process?
Well, Vietnam, the black revolution, and most importantly, WE ARE! All three present this system with more unsolvable problems than it can deal with. You see, there is no solution to the Vietnam war. To leave or to stay is a defeat. No matter what the government does in the ghettos it loses. More aid programs increase the appetite for more demands. More repression produces more anger and defensive violence. The same with the young. I know a girl, Peggy Dobbins, who was a teacher at Brooklyn College. She let the students determine the curriculum; before you knew it, the students wanted to grade themselves. She agreed to go along and of course got the ax from the administration. The more you get, the more you want. The more you are prevented from getting what you want, the more you fight to get it. These are trends that are irreversible, because the government cannot deal with these problems—I mean, the government "deals" with problems rather than solving them.

That's pretty political in its analysis. It's New Left in its wording.
Ah, well, it's a regression. I haven't presented any new ideas. But, well, that's the point. All the ideas are in and have been for some time. I guess I just rap on that from force of habit. I was once in the New Left but I outgrew it. Or perhaps it outgrew me. We differ on many things.

Like what?
Fun. I think fun and leisure are great. I don't like the concept of a movement built on sacrifice, dedication, responsibility, anger, frustration and guilt. All those down things. I would say, Look, you want to have more fun, you want to get laid more, you want to turn on with friends, you want an outlet for your creativity, then get out of school, quit your job. Come on out and help build and defend the society you want. Stop trying to organize everybody but yourself. Begin to live your vision. For example, the other night I was at a benefit for a peace group. Great music, light shows, friends all over the place. It was a good time. Some of the money raised goes to arrange rallies at which speakers give boring political speeches.

People think it's a drag but that's the sacrifice to get out the politically relevant statement. The point is, nobody listens to politically relevant statements. In Chicago we'll have a huge free music festival. Everyone already knows our feelings on the issues because we are there. It will have a tremendous impact if we can also project the image that we are having all the fun too. When I say fun, I mean an experience so intense that you actualize your full potential. You become LIFE. LIFE IS FUN. Political irrelevance is more effective than political relevance.

I notice as we get further into the interview that your answers get more linear and longer.
You're observant. I'm getting tired.

A few more: I hear you're writing a book. What's it about?
Well, it's called *Revolution for the Hell of It.* Sometimes I think I'm writing it just to see that title on a book jacket. Actually, if I have my way, the book jacket won't have the title on it. The book jacket will have two sleeves, a collar, buttons down the front, and the word BOOK on the back.

Why are you writing it?
Well, 'cause I have no idea how to make a movie. It has some parts I like but the book form is difficult and I write on the run. There is also the time gap. You know, months of delay before it comes out. By then it's a whole new ball game. As far as the medium of print is concerned, I would say I like free street leaflets the best.

Which medium do you like the best of all?
Making love.

Anything else?
Well, I like to experience pleasure, to have fun. I enjoy blowing people's minds. You know, walking up to somebody and saying, "Would you hold this dollar for me while I go in that store and steal something?" The crazier the better. I like being crazy. Letting go. Losing control. Just doing what pops into my mind. I trust my impulses. I find the less I try to think through a situation, the better it comes off.

I've seen things you've written under other names. Is that part of the put-on?
I do that a lot. It is fun because I really get pleasure in doing the act or helping to see it come off. Using false names or other people's makes sense to me. I'm not so sure about it now. You get known. As soon as you do anything in this country you become a celebrity. It's not really the same as being a leader. You can only stimulate actions. Stopping them or controlling them is something leaders can do. I'm not a leader. Nobody is under my command. I haven't the vaguest idea how to stop a demonstration, say, except to go home. I'm really not interested in stopping anything, so I'm not a leader. But this celebrity thing has certain problems. Using false names just tends to increase the myth after a while. Sometimes I do now, and sometimes I don't. If I can get away with it, I do.

Will you use a false name on the book?
If I can get away with it.

Isn't this celebrity or star system alien to your visions of a new society?
Most definitely. I find as you get more and more well known you get less
personal freedom. You spend more time doing other people's things than
your own. You know, people calling in the middle of the night with their
problems. Imagine this scene: You are trying to steal some groceries and
some old lady comes up and says how much she likes what you're doing.
That's why I use disguises, so I can keep in shape by having to hustle without the myth. The day I can't shoplift, panhandle, or pass out leaflets on
my own is the day I'll retire. The myth, like everything else, is free. Anybody can claim he is it and use it to hustle.

What's the solution? Is there any to the celebrity game?
I don't know. I envision a new life after Chicago. I don't intend to deal with
symbolic confrontations. I'm interested in just living with a few friends and
building a community. If there is to be confrontation, let it be with the
local sheriff rather than LBJ. Maybe this is just a fantasy, though. Maybe it
won't happen. I guess everyone dreams of a peaceful life in the country.
Especially in the winter.

You're planning to drop out?
Well, dropping out is a continual process. I don't see anything really
definite in the future. I just don't want to get boxed-in to playing a predetermined role. Let's say, so much of what we do is theater—in life I just
don't want to get caught in a Broadway show that lasts five years, even if
it is a success. The celebrity bag is another form of careerism. But you see,
celebrity status is very helpful in working with media. It's my problem and
I'll deal with it just like any other problem. I'll do the best I can.

Is that why the Yippies were created? To manipulate the media?
Exactly. You see, we are faced with this task of getting huge numbers of
people to come to Chicago along with hundreds of performers, artists,
theater groups, engineers. Essentially, people involved in trying to work
out a new society. How do you do this starting from scratch, with no organization, no money, nothing? Well, the answer is that you create a myth.
Something that people can play a role in, can relate to. This is especially
true of media people. I'll give you an example. A reporter was interviewing
us once and he liked what we were doing. He said "I'm going to tell what
good ideas you guys really have. I'm going to tell the truth about the
Yippies." We said, "That won't help a bit. Lie about us." It doesn't matter
as long as he gets Yippie! and Chicago linked together in a magical way.
The myth is about LIFE vs. DEATH. That's why we are headed for a
powerful clash.

You don't want the truth told?
Well, I don't want to get philosophical but there is really no such animal.
Especially when one talks of creating a myth. How can you have a true
myth? When newspapers distort a story they become participants in the
creation of the myth. We love distortions. Those papers that claim to be
accurate, *i.e.,* the New York *Times, Village Voice, Ramparts, The Nation,
Commentary,* that whole academic word scene is a total bore. In the end

they probably distort things more than the *Daily News*. The New York *Times* is the American Establishment, not the *Daily News*. The *Daily News* creates a living style. You know: "Pot-smoking, dirty, beatnik, pinko, sex-crazy, Vietnik, so-called Yippies." Compare that to the New York *Times*: "Members of the newly formed Youth International Party (YIP)." The New York *Times* is death. The *Daily News* is the closest thing to TV. Look at its front page, always a big picture. It looks like a TV set. I could go on and on about this. It's a very important point. Distortion is essential to myth-making.

Are you saying that you actually like the Daily News?
Not exactly, but I don't consider it the enemy, in the same way that I don't consider George Wallace the enemy. Corporate liberalism, Robert Kennedy, Xerox, David Susskind, the New York *Times,* Harvard University—that is where the real power in America lies, and it is the rejection of those institutions and symbols that distinguishes radicals. That is not to say that I love the *Daily News* but that I consider it more honest than the New York *Times*. I once wanted to start a newspaper called the New York *Liar*. It would be the most honest paper in the country. I would sit in a dark closet and write all the news. The paper would be printed with lemon juice, which is invisible until you heat it with an iron, hence involving the reader. I would write about events without ever leaving the closet. The point is, we all live in dark closets. We all see things through a closet darkly.

That's some fantasy.
Of course. It'll come true, though. Fantasy is the only truth. Once we had a demonstration at the *Daily News* Building. About three hundred people smoked pot, danced, sprayed the reporters with body deodorant, burned money, handed out leaflets to all the employees that began: "Dear fellow member of the Communist conspiracy . . ." We called it an "Alternative Fantasy." It worked great.

What do you mean, it worked great?
Nobody understood it. That is, nobody could explain what it all meant yet everyone was fascinated. It was pure information, pure imagery, which in the end is truth. You see, the New York *Times* can get into very theoretical discussions on the critical level of what we are doing. The *Daily News* responds on a gut level. That's it. The New York *Times* has no guts.

Then being understood is not your goal?
Of course not. The only way you can understand is to join, to become involved. Our goal is to remain a mystery. Pure theater. Free, with no boundaries except your own. Throwing money onto the floor of the Stock Exchange is pure information. It needs no explanation. It says more than thousands of anticapitalist tracts and essays. It's so obvious that I hesitate to discuss it, since everyone reading this already has an image of what happened there. I respect their images. Anything I said would come on like expertise. "Now, this is what *really* happened." In point of fact nothing happened. Neither we nor the Stock Exchange exist. We are both rumors. That's it. That's what happened that day. Two different rumors collided.

Can you think of any people in theater that influence you?
W. C. Fields, Ernie Kovacs, Ché Guevara, Antonin Artaud, Alfred Hitchcock, Lenny Bruce, the Marx Brothers—probably the Beatles have the most influence. I think they have the perfect model for the new family. They have unlimited creativity. They are a continual process, always changing, always burying the old Beatles, always dropping out.

Can you pursue that a little?
Well, the Beatles are a new family group. They are organized around the way they create. They are communal art. They are brothers and, along with their wives and girl friends, form a family unit that is horizontal rather than vertical, in that it extends across a peer group rather than descending vertically like grandparents–parents–children. More than horizontal, it's circular with the four Beatles the inner circle, then their wives and kids and friends. The Beatles are a small circle of friends, a tribe. They are far more than simply a musical band. Let's say, if you want to begin to understand our culture, you can start by comparing Frank Sinatra and the Beatles. It wouldn't be perfect but it would be a good beginning. Music is always a good place to start.

Why is that?
Well, a revolution always has rhythm. Whether it's songs of the Lincoln Brigade, black soul music, Cuban love songs by José Martí, or white psychedelic rock. I once heard songs of the Algerian rebels that consisted mostly of people beating guns on wooden cases. It was fantastic. What is the music of the system? Kate Smith singing the National Anthem. Maybe that's Camp, but it's not Soul.

What about dancing?
There too. Arthur Murray. Dance lessons. What a joke. If you need lessons you haven't got the message. Dancing for us is doing anything you want. You have to see a huge throbbing light-rock show. Especially one that is free, because the free-est people only go to free events. You will see people doing all sorts of fantastic dances. Frenzied and smooth. Butterflies and antelopes. Indians and spiders. Swimming and jumping. Lots of people just sit or lie on the floor, which is a nice step too. Nobody takes lessons. In fact, if you liked the way somebody danced and asked them where they learned to do it, they would laugh. Dance schools are about as outmoded as public schools, which really are archaic. In fact, I wouldn't be surprised to find out that Arthur Murray was U.S. Commissioner of Education, and high school was just a training ground for millions of fox-trotters. You can see the difference if you look at one of those silly dance books with the shoe prints. One-Two-Three, One-Two-Three. You know. It would be funny to make one for the new dances, which, by the way, don't have names anymore. I think about two years ago dances stopped having names. Anyway, one of those books would have shoe-prints all over the walls and ceilings. A possible title for this book I'm working on could be *The Three Basic Steps in Modern Dance*. One–Two–FREE . . . One–Three–T . . . O . . .

net wo . . . 10–9–8–7–6–5–4–3–2–1 NOW! That's it. Now you've got it. Turn your motor on and fly. You can go forever.

Forever?
Haven't you heard of nuclear energy? Yes, you can dance forever. That's the Beatles' message. That's why I said before that our movement was called Dancing.

Doesn't all this dancing present a problem for society?
Not for ours, but for the parent culture, the one decaying, most definitely. The cops hate us.

How do you feel about cops?
Cops are our enemy. Not each one as a person, naked, say. We're all brothers when we are naked. Did you ever see a fight in a steam bath? But cops in uniform are a different story. Actually, all uniforms are enemies. Just another extension of machine living. The way we dress—in costumes—is in direct opposition to a uniform culture. Costumes are the opposite of uniforms. Since the cops' uniforms also include clubs, handcuffs, guns, etc., they are particularly hated uniforms. I should also add that I've been arrested seventeen times and beaten by police on at least five occasions. I would no more think of asking a cop for help than shooting arsenic to get high.

Who would you ask for help?
My brothers. None of my brothers are cops. You see a cop's principal role is to protect private property. Our goal is the abolition of property. How could I ever call a cop?

Don't they do more than protect property?
Yeah, they kick the shit out of people who have none. Listen. You should have seen Grand Central Station last week during the YIP-IN. Picture this, thousands, maybe ten thousand people, dancing, singing, throwing balloons in the air. Some people decided to climb on top of the information booth; while they were up there they pulled the hands off the clock. This triggered a police riot, with maybe two hundred cops swinging nightsticks charging into people. No warning. No order to clear. About one hundred people were hospitalized, including my wife and me, and over sixty people arrested. There were the police lined up around the clock, guarding it while others smashed skulls. One kid, Ron Shea, tried to come to my rescue while I was being beaten. He was thrown through a glass door and had both hands broken. He may never be able to use one again. Which hands do you think the cops cared more about, the hands on the clock or Ron Shea's hands?

Why did the kids rip the hands off the clock?
I don't know. Maybe they hate time and schedules. Maybe they thought the clock was ugly. They also decorated the clock with sketches. Maybe they were having fun. When we put on a large celebration the aim is to create a liberated area. People can do whatever they want. They can begin to live the revolution even if only within a confined area. We will learn how to govern ourselves. By the way, this goes on in every revolution. Take Viet-

nam. In liberated zones the National Liberation Front has schools and theater troupes and hospitals and building programs. The revolutionary experience is far more than just the fighting units.

Do you read revolutionary writings?
Yes, Guevara, Debray, Mao, Giap, McLuhan. I find Giap and McLuhan the most interesting. But of course I am totally caught up with Ché as a hero. His death moved me far more than, say, that of Martin Luther King. Although King's was a shock also.

What do you think of death?
Well, I must say I have no fear of death. I faced it once about two years ago on an internal level. This is hard to explain. I've actually faced the risk of death a number of times but this one time I actually became paranoid. I was overcome with anxiety. It was unclear what was going on. I overcame that state purely on a mind level and realized that I had the power in me not to become paranoid. It's the paranoia, the living in constant fear of death, that is the real bad trip, not the death itself. I will be surprised if I get a chance to live out my life. Gleefully surprised, but surprised none the less.

Isn't that sort of gloomy?
No! Not really. You can't deny there is a tremendous amount of violence in this country. People who are engaged daily in radical social change are always exposed to that violence. I would rather die fighting for change than surrender. Death in a physical sense is just not seen as the worst of all possible things.

What is?
I don't know. Going to jail. Surrendering. . . . Maybe nothing is really bad, since I am so convinced that we will win the future.

The Idea of a Humane Tradition

EDITED BY HENRY NASH SMITH

INTRODUCTION

The surge of student protest during the past five years in universities throughout the world has called into question the very bases of the educational systems of advanced industrial societies. The challenge has been directed with special energy toward education in the humanities—that is, in history, philosophy, literature, and the arts—and, as might be expected in such verbal fields, it has called forth a flood of eloquence and logical analysis, of lyrical self-expression and statistics. Since the debate is still in full cry, neither the issues nor the arguments have fallen into a coherent pattern. The brief selection of documents presented here cannot do justice to a corpus of polemic writings that numbers thousands of items, even if we limit the count to those in English. But these materials do represent the more conspicuous positions along a wide spectrum (except the nihilism of the extreme Left), and convey some of the flavor and texture of the controversy.

The idea of a humane tradition is implied in the very existence of a human society. In his *Preface to Plato* Eric Havelock points out that all civilizations rely on a sort of cultural "book," that is, on the capacity to put information in storage in order to reuse it. . . . Such a linguistic statement or paradigm, telling us what we are and how we should behave . . . is formed to be drilled into the successive generations as they grow up within the family or clan system. It provides the content of the educational apparatus of the group.[1]

In pre-Socratic Greece this "book" was oral: It took the form of poems (the Homeric epics, Hesiod's *Works and Days*) that could be held in memory with the aid of metrical patterning. Although one function of such poems was to transmit technical information (the description of a voyage in the first book of the *Iliad,* for example, is the nearest approximation to a textbook of seamanship available in that society[2]), the inculcation of ethical principles and proper forms of behavior was even more important. In our society, of course, the educational process has been organized into curricula that in turn imply the existence of distinct fields of learning. The ethical functions of the Greek *paideia,* which were subsequently carried on for centuries by the churches in Europe and in this country, are now in large part assigned to courses in the humanities. Thus an ostensibly secular educational system has been given a heavy share of a responsibility it was not primarily designed to bear. This is one of the reasons why the teaching of the humanities has become so controversial: It is a central part of the process by which our society modifies its system of values in response to social change.

The idea of a humane tradition in American education has long been closely connected with the name of Matthew Arnold—who was during much of his life an inspector of schools and, ultimately, a professor of poetry at Oxford. Often in a diluted and vulgarized version, Arnold's doctrines have exerted a controlling influence on the teaching of literature in American schools and colleges since the later nineteenth century, when education began to lose its explicitly religious commitment. The Arnoldian ideas that have proved most influential are, first, that our society has its cultural "book" (in Havelock's sense) in "the best that has been thought and said in the world"—an identifiable and acknowledged corpus of great literature; and, second, that this corpus has the power to form the character of those exposed to it. The implications for a democratic educational system are obvious: It is to the interest both of the society as a whole and of the individual that everyone have this redeeming experience. Therefore the educational system must not only meet the demands of industry for technically trained workers, but must also provide for all pupils at least a minimal exposure to great literature.

Such a program reaches its apex in the colleges and universities. Stuart P. Sherman, perhaps the most enthusiastic exponent of this educational conception in American academic life of the past generation, used to teach a course in Arnold at the University of Illinois that became an institution. According to Jacob Zeitlin, a colleague, Sherman told his students that "the

---

[1] Eric Havelock, *Preface to Plato* (Cambridge, Mass.: Harvard University Press, 1963), pp. vii, 41–42.
[2] *Ibid.,* pp. 81–84.

highest aim which education could propose was to make good citizens of the world, to bring the entire body of humanity into a harmonious civil life." At the same time, he pointed out "how badly we in America stood in need of 'fineness, elevation, distinction, high and intelligent seriousness, the grand style (less jazz and razz), the sense for exquisite workmanship, philosophical depth, the romantic note, glamour, the English sense for the delights of homes and gardens and flowers, permanence and solidity . . .'" Sherman held that, fortunately, "these defects could be corrected by reaching out in spirit to the great writings of other lands and other apostles."[3] Sherman was unabashedly moralistic. He conceived of his function as a teacher to be that of "shaping men and women," and he said that the purpose of his course in Arnold was to lead the students "to imitate the Arnoldian personality." More concretely, he believed with Arnold that "the grand style in poetry" is "a power that will form our emotions, shape our character."[4]

These once familiar phrases embody assumptions about the moral authority of the teacher that seem now to belong to an almost prehistoric epoch —the age of American innocence. Actually, they were already anachronistic when Sherman uttered them in the 1920's. As early as 1911, George Santayana had put into circulation that devastating phrase, "the genteel tradition," which summed up the resentment felt by young writers and critics for the timidities and evasions of high culture inherited from the previous century. Van Wyck Brooks had taken an iconoclastic stand in *America's Coming of Age* in 1916. From the 1920's onward, all the major forces in American culture have operated to undermine and discredit the conception of an unchanging humane tradition as a source of esthetic and moral values. The disillusionment of the "Lost Generation" caused by the failure of Wilsonian idealism after World War I fostered a widespread alienation among writers and intellectuals that is expressed in, for example, Hemingway's *The Sun Also Rises* (1926). The American fascination with Freudian psychology, which dates from the opening decade of the twentieth century, has produced similar results. Freud's concept of rationalization has undercut all the ideals that had seemed to be the solid foundation of cultural and especially moral values. Once we recognize that men are seldom conscious of their own deepest motives, then no asserted doctrine or principle, however seriously and sincerely meant, is likely to be taken at face value. When subjected to this kind of scrutiny, in the words of a recent critic, "The humanism that purports to defend classical and Judaeo-Christian values by cherishing the texts in which those values supposedly reside . . . amounts to little more than the confusion of a book list with an education, and its practical results are hardly worth preserving."[5]

Arnold had taken over the model of the psyche that was prevalent in Vic-

---

[3] Jacob Zeitlin and Homer Woodbridge, *Life and Letters of Stuart P. Sherman,* Vol. II (New York: Farrar, Straus & Giroux, 1929), p. 416.
[4] Stuart Sherman, *Shaping Men and Women: Essays on Literature and Life,* ed. by Jacob Zeitlin (Garden City, N.Y.: Doubleday, 1928), pp. 8, 269, 275.
[5] Frederick Crews, "Anaesthetic Criticism: II," *New York Review of Books,* March 12, 1970, p. 49.

torian England. He shrank from the exploration of subconscious or precon-
scious mental processes, which seemed to him quite simply a "darkness"
against which an endless war must be waged in the name of reason. In 1865
he wrote:

No one has a stronger and more abiding sense than I have of the "daemonic"
element—as Goethe called it—which underlies and encompasses our life; but I
think, as Goethe thought, that the right thing is, while conscious of this element,
and of all that there is inexplicable round one, to keep pushing on one's posts into
the darkness, and to establish no post that is not perfectly in light and firm. One
gains nothing on the darkness by being, like Shelley, as incoherent as the darkness
itself.[6]

To be sure, Freud also wanted to bring the light of consciousness into the
darker regions of repressed experience. But his view of art was really quite
unlike the Arnoldian view that makes it a repository of man's triumphs of
reason and self-control. From a Freudian perspective, a work of art is not
primarily a monument to the victory of order over chaos, but an often precarious compromise between repressed feelings and the restraints of intelligible form. And the provisional weakening of the forces of repression that
allows unconscious impulses to achieve indirect expression is more important
than the relatively superficial cognitive elements in the work.

Applied to society as a whole, the dynamic model of the psyche can lead to
an even more drastic repudiation of the Victorian elements in the idea of a
literary tradition. Whereas Arnold virtually identified the past with its surviving works of art and saw these works as a reservoir of power available for
man's use in his unending struggle against his own lower nature, Norman O.
Brown derives from Freudian postulates, as well as from modern imaginative
literature, the notion that the past is a disease of which mankind must struggle to cure itself. Just as the psychoanalyst helps the patient to free himself
from the neurotic product of his childhood traumas, Brown maintains, so
must the entire community struggle to free itself from the crippling repressions that have shaped the history of the race. The revolt against rationality
that this process entails, especially the "resurrection of the body" and the
casting off of sexual inhibitions, is particularly offensive to the social decorum implicit in the Arnoldian tradition.

During the first two or three decades of the twentieth century the revolt
of American intellectuals against the dominant values of the society was expressed in cultural rather than political terms. It is true that the idea of a
humane tradition was upheld mainly within the universities and was often
attacked by nonacademic critics such as H. L. Mencken, who derided the
professors of literature as "native, white, Protestant *gelehrten*." [7] Yet

[6] Matthew Arnold, *Letters*, Vol. I, p. 329 (Vol. XIII in *Works*, London, 1903–04). Quoted in
John H. Raleigh, *Matthew Arnold and American Culture* (Berkeley: University of California Press, 1957), p. 143.
[7] H. L. Mencken, *Prejudices: Fourth Series* (New York: Knopf, 1924), p. 9. Quoted in
Raleigh, *op. cit.*, p. 141.

Mencken was notoriously conservative in politics, and it was not until the vogue of Marxism during the Depression years of the 1930's that the debate between attackers and defenders of the Arnoldian tradition took on an avowed political cast.

The New Criticism, which gained currency in the universities with the waning of literary Marxism during and after World War II, had conservative overtones, but literary discussion was seldom overtly political during the 1940's and 1950's. It is the New Left of recent years that has brought political controversy back into the academy. The current attack on established procedures is clearly indebted to Marxism for its charge that conventional scholarship is condemned to impotence because it fails to transcend the false consciousness propagated by the existing economic and political order. There is, however, a tendency to revise the Marxism of former decades by accepting Herbert Marcuse's contention that the enemy is not capitalism but technocracy (since the Soviet Union is caught in the same trap) and also by professing now to speak not in the name of an industrial proletariat but in the name of nonwhite colonial peoples throughout the world—including with special emphasis the blacks and other ethnic minorities within the United States. From this doctrinal platform, a literary curriculum based on great books of the past is denounced as elitist (because Shakespeare is less accessible to young people from the ghetto than to those from the middle- and upper-class suburbs) and racist (because the Western European cultural tradition is foreign to ethnic minorities, again particularly the blacks). James F. Goldberg, who deserves close attention as an unusually articulate spokesman for the young radicals, argues that the elitism of the academic literary establishment and its blindness to the repressive character of the capitalist regime have deep roots in history. He maintains that Arnold was profoundly hostile to stirrings of democratic protest in nineteenth-century Britain, and that his program for making reason and the will of God prevail gave law and order precedence over freedom and justice. The case for repudiating the conception of a humane tradition thus rests on the recognition of a latent authoritarianism in it.

In the many varieties of current radical theory there is a recurrent tendency to reject all forms of hierarchy or control. The tendency resembles theoretical anarchism as much as it resembles anything else in the array of inherited political ideas. In this respect the radical rejection of a humane tradition is in harmony with the dominant tendency of the arts in our day. For a century or more, Western culture has been moving toward the view that the universe is basically absurd. Nietzsche's proclamation that "God is dead" (dating from 1885) has proved to be an expression of the deepest intuition of three or four generations of writers and artists on both sides of the Atlantic. The most impressive formulations of the doctrine have been those of the Existentialists, particularly Albert Camus and Jean Paul Sartre. We have a theater of the absurd and a "new novel" concerned with the burden of moral responsibility which falls upon the individual when he realizes that he is absolutely alone in the universe, that he must create himself moment by moment in the act of making choices without being able to rely on any stable principles or general ideas.

Sartre describes the kind of novel that would represent this existential view of reality. It would contain no privileged, omniscient narrator. On the contrary, the novelist would be obliged

> to present creatures whose reality would be the tangled and contradictory tissue of each one's evaluations of all the other characters—himself included—and the evaluation by all the others of himself, and who could never decide from within whether the changes of their destinies came from their own efforts, from their own faults, or from the course of the universe.[8]

May we not find here the epistemological equivalent of participatory democracy? The omniscient narrator has been expelled from the fictive universe just as God had been expelled from the intellectual world of nineteenth-century Europe; and the professor of literature who considers himself guardian of a stable and orderly humane tradition is perhaps about to be supplanted by a more Dionysian figure in the educational system.[9]

Are there any signs of an accommodation between the academic establishment and its radical critics? Although few Americans have adopted the extreme position that the university must be destroyed,[10] the dissidents have not been very clear about what methods of literary study and teaching they advocate in place of the traditional approach, and defenders of the status quo have done little more than acknowledge the need for cautious reforms. No twentieth-century Matthew Arnold has appeared, although he is long overdue. The response of the academy to challenge is represented here by Father Walter J. Ong's robust ecumenical optimism, which welcomes the transformation of literary scholarship by technology as a new release of human energies; by G. Jon Roush's hopeful recommendation of more collaboration between teachers and students; and by James S. Ackerman's acute remarks about the possibility of adopting an engaged style in place of the sterile style of objective analysis that has dominated humanistic scholarship and teaching during recent decades.

[8] Jean Paul Sartre, "Situation of the Writer in 1947," in *What Is Literature?* trans. by Bernard Frechtman (New York: Harper & Row, 1965), p. 218.
[9] The following observation by Geoffrey Hartman is relevant ("Toward Literary History," *Daedalus*, Spring 1970, p. 364):

> The [contemporary] artist has a bad conscience because of the idea that forms, structures, and so on always reconcile or integrate, that they are conservative despite themselves. To create a truly iconoclastic art, a structure-breaking art, to change the function of form from reconciliation and conservation to rebellion, and so to participate in the enormity of present experience—this is the one Promethean aim still fiery enough to inspire. It is the psychic state of art today.

[10] This slogan occurs occasionally in the oratory and the manifestoes of left-wing student groups but in the United States it seems to be taken literally only by the Weatherman faction of Students for a Democratic Society. In France it has more status as a principled position: See, for example, André Gorz, "Détruire l'Université," *Les Temps Modernes*, 26ᵉ année, No. 285 (April 1970), pp. 1558 ff.

The basic affirmations that underlie most such proposals for reform are summarized in an eloquent statement by Eric Weil that may conclude this introduction:

It may well be that youth exacts from us an education instead of mere instruction. Even a superficial analysis shows that all the muddle-headed *pronunciamentos* of today express a *moral* revolt against a society whose only values belong to the order of technique, organization, and material progress. It is the humanist's task to bring to consciousness and clarity what lurks behind these dumb reactions and confused cries. Nobody else can do it. The humanist alone can establish humanity's dialogue with its own unconscious or semiconscious drives, because he alone considers man a free being, a being who has to do with himself before and after he has to do with conditions and results.[11]

[11] Eric Weil, "Humanistic Studies: Their Objects, Methods, and Meaning," *Daedalus*, Spring 1970, p. 254.

DO LITERARY STUDIES HAVE
AN IDEOLOGY? [1]

Frederick Crews

Our common task this afternoon is, I suppose, to define what literary education should be and explain why the real thing differs so markedly from the ideal; to inquire whether scholarship, in its present condition, shall be suffered to live; to characterize the emerging social crisis in America and decide who caused it; to take a stand on student violence and institutional violence; to decide whether it is all right to use the term "academic freedom" without a sneer; to determine a teacher's political responsibility to his students; and of course to judge whether the MLA is more to be pitied than censured, or *vice versa.* Fortunately, two whole hours have been set aside for this inquiry. My title, however, is meant to convey a hope that some of the burden will fall on other speakers; I only intend to provoke some thought about the possibility that our literary studies have been significantly affected by an ideological bias.

The temptation to self-righteousness on this issue is strong, and after a few precautionary paragraphs I am going to succumb to it. Our debate today will be pointless, however, unless we keep in mind the plight we share as well as the differences that make us distrust and accuse one another. Trading slogans of "repressive tolerance" and "irrelevance" on one side with "scholarly neutrality" and "professionalism" on the other will gain us nothing beyond a superfluous confirmation that "they," the ones with the wrong shibboleths, are a menace to learning.

Our real situation is more ironical than such Manichean gestures would suggest. Those among us who grumble about repressive tolerance are exercising it as they complain, and would pine for it again if it were supplanted by repression pure and simple. Those who uphold the neutrality of the academy scarcely seem to have noticed that most of this neutrality has been bought out over the past twenty-five years, so that the ideal they are defending is just that—an ideal, not a fact. Cold-War America seems to have played a joke on all of us. Whether we have tigerish dreams of revolution or pastoral yearnings for the vanished academic cloister, we all inhabit a mixed world, as comfortable as it is corrupt. Perhaps because America is still very much a Protestant country, what we have most in common seems to be our unwillingness to accept this compromised reality and work within it knowingly. We can be fairly well divided into people who disclaim any taint of the system's abominations (meanwhile punctually collecting salary checks) and people

DO LITERARY STUDIES HAVE AN IDEOLOGY? Reprinted by permission of the Modern Language Association of America from *PMLA*, Vol. 85 (May 1970).

[1] A shorter version of this paper was read at the 1969 MLA Annual Meeting.

who see nothing amiss that a little discipline and conventional study couldn't rectify. The latter group is, of course, less puritanical, but this is only what you would expect from the anti-revolutionary faction in any dispute.

I happen to have affinities with both groups, one by background and one by the recent trauma of the Vietnam war, which has made me attentive to arguments about the long-range tendencies of the American system. Once those tendencies are even dimly understood, and one has grasped the almost total acquiescence of the universities in the expansionist schemes of business and government, it becomes hard to retain a moderate argumentative style. One feels like shouting at one's fellow professors, begging them to drop the scales from their eyes and see what one has only lately seen oneself: the perversion of scholarly research to purposes of exploitation and conquest, and the more pervasive influence of a socially manipulative style of thinking on the evolution of various academic fields. One is awestruck by the unimpaired capacity of scholars to sermonize about the value-free university when their daily walk from parking lot to office may take them past guarded institutes where the best-paid of their colleagues are learning how ten cities can be destroyed by one missile, how botulism can be suspended in an aerosol spray, or how a whole peasantry can be bombed and starved off its land and into relocation camps. One suspects a disingenuousness in literary intellectuals who choose not to comprehend what they could read in their morning newspaper.

But such cynicism is inappropriate. I think it can be assumed that all of us are primarily concerned with truth, not power, and that we cherish our mental independence. Though it would be worthwhile to look into the effect of agencies like the CIA and USIA on literary studies, I am sure one would find nothing comparable either in magnitude or serviceability to, say, Project Camelot or the Michigan State field trip to arm Ngo Dien Diem against his own citizenry. Our normal enterprises, after all, seem well outside the most urgent pragmatic interests of the state; as C. Wright Mills once said, there can be no sellout where there is nothing to be sold. The famous ratio for successful counter-insurgency, ten anthropologists for each guerrilla, has no literary equivalent. What bears investigating is our remarkable political innocence rather than our guilt.

Even those of us who take up the government's invitation to lecture abroad about the spiritual strivings of Cooper and Sims while napalm and phosphorus continue to rain on Vietnamese villages would deny any imputation of compromised principles, and they would be right. The whole field of American Literature and American Studies is taciturn about such themes as racism, imperialism, and monopoly, but eloquent about myths, motifs, and morals—the Fulbrighter's stock-in-trade. Given this situation, it would be absurd to maintain that the government had subverted a few men's minds by dangling some opportunities for fun and travel. We are dealing rather with a congruency between ideologically useful attitudes and what scholars already believe, and the question to be asked is whether ideology has helped to shape those beliefs without the scholars' conscious awareness. This would be a relatively undramatic but quite serious politicization of learning, for someone who does not even know that he is thinking propagandistically is farther from objectivity than one who decides to suppress his real views.

I believe that our literary studies generally do have an ideological cast, less in what they say than in what they refuse to consider. Plausible lines of investigation that might lead to disquieting conclusions, or that would employ politically alien categories of thought are not pursued, while dubious but politically reinforced assumptions are elevated into articles of faith. There is no way of proving absolutely that these irrationalities must be explained as the result of an unconscious ideological consensus, but one can observe that the same biases characterize the social sciences, whose answerability to the current political order is undeniable.

I hope I needn't insist that we are living under a capitalistic set of arrangements, and that our regnant ideology is therefore bound to be a capitalist one. Capitalism is a system operated by and for large investors, and when it runs into trouble, the state, which is answerable to those same investors, intervenes to safeguard their profits regardless of the social cost. I cannot pause to defend this proposition, but it is consistent with all known evidence, and it is particularly appropriate to the present period, when the government has propped the domestic economy with enormous subsidies to the corporate rich, mostly under the pretext of national defense. The ideology surrounding this inverted welfarism is no less capitalistic than Jeremy Bentham's belief in free trade. When capitalism moves from underdevelopment to overdevelopment, from acquiring basic industries within a home nation to imposing an international order in which the desired flow of raw materials and sales is encouraged by armed force, an advanced school of thought arises favoring state regulation, foreign aid, placation of the unemployed, and similar measures to help things go smoothly. Thus, for example, Nelson Rockefeller is as much a capitalist ideologue as Barry Goldwater; being a Rockefeller, he just happens to have a broader understanding of the system's needs.

Though it may be bad taste to say so, capitalism rests on exploitation and social inequality; these are not its casual by-products but in large part its *raison d'être*. The main task of capitalist ideology is to disguise this fact, whether through the fantasy of steady social progress or that of equal opportunity or that of saving the world from all sorts of evils, from pestilence and paganism through Bolshevism. The deception, however, is usually not Machiavellian but sentimental: those who acquiesce in the order want to believe that it has a human face, and to a limited extent they succeed in lending it one.

This is especially true of academics, who are mostly decent, tolerant, socially conscious people with an obsessive scrupulosity about the correctness of their words and deeds. Scholars are grateful for the genuine intellectual freedom they enjoy under capitalism in its confident periods, and they would like to think that this freedom is guaranteed by the general commitment to constitutional ideals. Some scholars have, in addition, a special patriotism based on their self-image as public advisers who will lead the ignorant politicians into enlightened paths, but many others are temperate and unquestioning for a humbler reason: they see themselves as economically unproductive, easily dispensable drones who could be tossed out of their universities into the distasteful commercial world. For whatever reason, fundamental critical perceptions tend to be muted or diverted into a reformist vein. In any crisis, foreign or domestic or intramural, the typical scholar can be counted on to welcome a speedy restoration of order and routine, no matter who is in the right.

This is to say that most scholars are liberals, and that liberalism, for all its amiable intentions and good works, is somewhat handicapped for political understanding. Liberalism takes the most recent phase of capitalism to be reality itself in all its mysterious complexity, and then improvises *ad hominem* explanations for whatever social dysfunctions it perceives. (Conservatism, not minding the dysfunctions so long as the profits are coming in, goes through fewer mental gymnastics and has a simpler, sterner vision.) The morally overwrought quality of much liberal thinking derives, I believe, not merely from indignation but from the strain of trying not to perceive that capitalism's logical tendency is to preserve inequality, deplete resources, pollute the elements, keep an underclass out of work, and tyrannize over the economies of other nations. The attempt to address such problems without calling attention to property relations yields a confused, symbolic, and hortatory thinking which seizes on immediate occasions for outrage or sympathy while neglecting structural factors. Each new military intervention, if not quickly and successfully concluded, is a tragic blunder that "we" can never make again, for "we" have learned better—as if it had been our decision in the first place. Each new welfare program is an all-out war on injustice, definitive proof that "we care." Each new articulate candidate with good manners and a patrician distaste for politics will surely save our country from its real internal enemies, the uncouth rednecks and crazy generals who lack all humor and compassion.

Inevitably, a social scientist who holds these shallow expectations in private life will carry them into his academic studies. American social science is united in its lack of serious interest in American power. It willingly follows what Martin Nicolaus has called "the one and only general sociological law that has ever been discovered, namely that the oppressors research the oppressed." [2] Thus, though the U. S. has an overseas network of more than 3,000 military bases, a formidable array of client states, and direct foreign investments of over $60 billion—in effect the world's third largest economy —this major force in the contemporary world is not considered a proper subject of academic study, and there is not a single funded research project looking into it. [3] That we have positively stunted the development of some of the world's most abused countries, extracting their minerals, bribing and arming their feudal oligarchies, and preventing the economic diversification that might make them independent of us, is apparently unknown not only

[2] Martin Nicolaus, "The Professional Organization of Sociology: A View from Below," *Antioch Review*, XXIX (Fall 1969), 381.
[3] See David Horowitz, "Sinews of Empire," *Ramparts* (Oct. 1969), p. 42, and Harry Magdoff, *The Age of Imperialism* (New York, 1969).

to a specialist in development like Walt Rostow, but also to a more authentic liberal like John Kenneth Galbraith, whose urbane 418-page apology for monopoly, *The New Industrial State,* gives no hint that our corporations do any business abroad at all.[4] Naturally, then, there can be no study of how the government takes military steps to protect and expand the forgotten investments. On the contrary: by restricting his attention only to that part of the order that is already monopolized while ignoring its more classical rapaciousness elsewhere, Galbraith is able to compose a veritable ode to the giant post-competitive corporation, only reminding us that "we" must keep trying to improve our cultural tone.

When a whole academic field such as economics refuses to set up any perspective outside our own Keynesian order and devotes its major energies not to understanding the economy's history and consequences but to tinkering with its seemingly eternal "business cycles" so as to prevent catastrophe, not much can be expected by way of value-neutral objectivity. The very categories of accepted economic thinking, such as gross national product, aggregate demand, and structural unemployment, assume the profit values of capitalism as objectively given, and help to reconcile us uncritically to the government's preference for socially wasteful over socially useful spending and to the forced idleness of large numbers of people. Similarly, a political science that dwells fondly on polls and elections without considering new centers of unreviewable power; a sociology that studies belief systems and attitude dispositions apart from historical process; an anthropology that examines "natives" in the wake of colonial conquest but shows no interest either in colonialism or in the culture of the putatively neutral investigators; and a psychology that imprisons and debases its objects of study while counseling businessmen and advertisers on the most efficient means of inducing compliant behavior—all have been appreciably shaped by a single ideology. The requirements and predilections of the ruling order are not only left unexamined, they are casually accepted as guidelines for the choice of projects, methods, and assumptions.

Capitalist scholarship that deals with the contemporary world is distinguished by its mistaking of an ideological consensus for neutrality, its reluctance to question capitalism itself, its preference for short views and abstracted statistics over dynamic historical understanding, its embarrassment about recognizing power, and its penchant for isolating phenomena from their structural causes. On the last of these points, one is reminded of Marx's and Engel's critique of Hegel, who had elevated ideas to a state of autonomy, mystifying their origin in the defense of specific property arrangements and treating them as the principal agents of history. American social science is

---

[4] See Rostow, *The United States in the World Arena: An Essay in Recent History* (New York, 1960), and *The Stages of Economic Growth: A Non-Communist Manifesto* (Cambridge, Eng., 1961); and Galbraith, *The New Industrial State* (Boston, 1967). Whether Galbraith is truly naive in this omission and in some of his assertions, such as that the corporations are now run by their middle-level bureaucrats and engineers and are no longer interested in profit, is hard to ascertain; what is striking is that his book is taken seriously by intelligent liberals.

impatient with ideas, preferring easily disposable constructs such as opinion samples, voting patterns, and consumer preferences, but it treats these trivialities as if they conveyed the broadest truth, and in so doing it obscures class dominance. The proliferation of bland, narrowly defined research acts as a filibuster against questions about the order as a whole, while each gainfully employed scholar comforts himself with the thought that he is adding a grain to the gross world product of objective knowledge.

For several reasons, this relatively clear picture of ideologically influenced study becomes clouded when we turn to literary criticism and scholarship. Rational understanding is not the sole aim of our discipline, and for many of us it is a poor second to the cultivation of taste. Flagrant departures from rationality are more easily indulged in our field, and one is never sure whether a given instance should be laid to political prejudice, emotive fervor, or sheer preciosity. The fact that our work generally avoids discussion of capitalism is not much of a scandal, though capitalism is reflected in most of the literature we study. The escape clause is that we conceive our task to be the study of end-products rather than of raw social forces. Even historians, who resemble us in some of their conventional thought patterns, are worse off in this respect, for they are often expected to come up with explanatory formulations. By contrast, we try to establish rapport with certain objects as objects, and some of our weightiest theorists even argue that we have no business explaining anything, for explanation would diminish our respect for art. Though it is only a short step from this state of mind to the virgin anti-intellectualism of our freshmen who regard all discourse as a profanation of selfhood, we believe our lack of curiosity to be more sophisticated and high-principled than theirs.

As soon as we look a little more closely at the imperative to prostrate ourselves before literature's autonomous emanations of meaning, we begin to see that here, too, ideology has been at work. It can hardly be coincidental that in socialist countries an exactly opposite attitude prevails. A revolutionary society or one that still feels its existence imperiled by class enemies finds the meaning of literary works in the social dynamics they express or promote. To be sure, officially sanctioned socialist criticism is almost always simpleminded and venal, like any other mental effort that must flatter a bureaucracy and meet a doctrinal test; our criticism seems to do better if only because it is less closely supervised. Yet the root assumption that literature conveys class meaning is, as a Georg Lukács can show, both true and important. A criticism neglecting the historical struggles behind art's genesis and stressing the formal harmonies, resolved differences, and sententious wisdom that emerge at the other end of artistic process is well suited to a prosperous and entrenched society. Such a criticism is certainly less ideological than one that makes political correctness the touchstone of esthetic value, but it does have an ideological aspect in its very neglect of social forces. It rests upon, and helps to foster, the illusion of present classlessness—an illusion whose effective function is to ensure compliance with disguised class governance.

Capitalism in general seems to promote a style of humanistic discourse that errs on the side of vagueness and false transcendence rather than on that of dogmatic simplicity; there is little need for militant moralism when one is reaping the profits of an imperial order. But capitalism is by nature unstable; not only does it expand absolutely over time, it suffers periodic convulsions which shake the faith of intelligent people. Americans today are still living in the aftermath of capitalism's worst crash so far, which was ended not by the negligible efforts of the New Deal but by the industrial spurt of World War II, which has been artificially prolonged through a militarization of the peacetime economy. Whether this militarization can be stemmed is a matter of dispute; meanwhile, "defense" has poisoned our lives in many ways,[5] not least in its heightening of the dissociated mentality normally required for self-respect under capitalism. While most intellectuals are resistant to Cold-War paranoia, we find other, equally timely, ways of channeling anxiety about the destructive and insecure basis of our "security."

American literary criticism has many conflicting strands, but over several decades one can make out approximate shifts in spirit that correspond to the vicissitudes of the economy. No one would dispute that the thirties were a time of ideological debate among critics and that from the forties until very recently that debate has seemed increasingly quaint and embarrassing. Many of us, like our social science colleagues, have been ready to believe that the end of ideology has arrived and that the leftist squabbles of the past were pointless and immature. Those squabbles were indeed strident, and the current revival of their excommunicative hairsplitting gives one cause to doubt that history teaches anything at all. Yet it could be argued that the very best American discussions of literature were generated by the political ferment preceding World War II. Critics like Wilson, Trilling, Burke, Kazin, and Howe had to ask themselves where ideology ended and art began. Their urgently personal efforts to accommodate their sense of esthetic complexity to their politics, which seemed to be falling in ruins at the end of the thirties, yielded apprehensions of literature that were full of a clarifying passion. One need not agree with the accommodations themselves in order to grant the importance of the effort and the excitement it generated for others. When we compare such criticism with the formalism and static didacticism that have characterized much of the intervening period, we may wonder whether a certain political anguish may not be essential to good criticism. Perhaps our most challenging criticism is more indebted to the Depression and the shock of Stalinism than to the theoretical efforts of Eliot and Richards.

It is widely acknowledged that much recent criticism has been characterized by a primness of tone, a spirit of dry routine, and a preoccupation with abstracted formal patterns. The New Critics, with their generally nostalgic politics and their ostentatious piety, are usually blamed for this arid development, but the accusation is unfair, for most of the men who have been called New Critics were artists and thinkers with a clear sense of their commitments. The hallmark of most criticism produced today is precisely its low

[5] See Seymour Melman, *Our Depleted Society* (New York, 1965). Ironically, even the war contractors have suffered; see George E. Berkley, "The Myth of War Profiteering," *New Republic* (20 Dec. 1969), pp. 15–18.

degree of commitment, its air of occupying a niche rather than of claiming some territory. The niche is the one where most of us reside—the affluent and multifarious university, the crowning ornament of a credit-card civilization whose basis cannot be examined with a clear conscience. Our obvious difference from the liveliest critics of thirty years ago is that we are completely at home in academe. And if the most general trait of recent criticism is its absence of worry over what the business and loyalty of the critic should be, this is because the answer is intuitively known: he should enter the academic hierarchy and do whatever it asks of him.

A history of postwar criticism might begin by setting aside the various contending factions and examining the university itself, with its haven for both upward mobility and snobbery, its trials and perquisites and sinecures —in short, its capacity to become a substitute world. With tenure for wafer and the assistant professorship for circumcision, nothing further is needed to account for the submissive and ritualistic aspect of most published work. Perhaps the most eloquent fact about contemporary schools of criticism is how alike they sound. All of them, even those that affect familiarity with terrible Dionysian powers, have a cautious politeness and orderliness, an air of going through predetermined motions. Even the more original spirits seem loyal to the temper of the times. One notices, for example, that young critics are now likely to invent an entire terminological system with which to overwhelm a single text, and one is startled at such a squandering of ingenuity. Reflecting, however, that conventional methods have pretty much picked over the modest harvest of English and American literature, one can grasp the need for novelty. Constant revolution in the means of promotion is now the emergent law.

Yet even insincerity expresses certain values, and predictably enough, recent criticism usually expresses the values of capitalism in its monopoly phase. Not justice and passion, but order and sophistication are implicitly treasured. The critic's relation to his text is manipulative rather than involved. Instead of accepting and examining the temperamental affinity that led him to treat a certain author, he displays his capacity to perform correct and efficient operations that will give him total possession of the work. Writers who may have been scarcely able to contain their sensuality or savage indignation are thus transmuted into masters of cunning who have subliminally engineered our responses. Their seeming disunities are secret unities after all—indeed, are devices to trip us up.[6] And if it is often hard for us to accept such a depiction of the writer, we at least know that the critic has succeeded in replacing *his* vulnerable feelings with cold and subtle strategy. It is like the computerized pacification of a province.

In the oddly segregated portion of our field known as "scholarship," things have changed much less over the past four decades than one could

---

[6] The alleged unities are often religious, even in some instances where the writer was a notorious scoffer. Such misperception might be traced not only to the critic's personal background, which may have been quite secular, but also to our society's reduction of all problems to questions of personal morality and to its interest in higher rationales for earthly injustice. The heyday of crypto-religious criticism was, naturally enough, the Eisenhower period.

gather from following the "critics." For most literary scholars there has been no end of ideology because there was never any ideology in the first place; as in the social sciences, a posture of neutrality before facts has obviated questions of political value. Yet this very unconcern has ensured a hospitality to the assumptions ingrained in our system, and in some cases those assumptions can be blamed for shallow thinking about literature. It is, for instance, an absence of feeling for historical dynamics that allows some scholars to account for one author's work merely by the "influence" of another's, as if his life-situation did not contain features that readied him for one sort of guidance. Much history-of-ideas scholarship commits the same error; it is Hegel's error of taking the verbal precipitates of power relations to be power itself, so that material circumstances can be altogether discounted. Or again, note the political up-to-dateness of commentaries that mistake an era's dominant value system for its whole play of social forces. If "the Renaissance" believed in holy kingship or the Great Chain of Being, the problem of any single case has been settled in advance. The scholar, occupying a post in an institution whose purposes and values are by now sensitively attuned to those of the state, perhaps even having sworn his ideological loyalty on pain of firing and blacklisting, is undisposed to imagine that a writer might have questioned the myths by whose means the ruling families stayed in power.

If we can discern such a thing as capitalist scholarship and begin to see its blind spots, this is possible only because capitalism itself is once again in trouble. The suffocation of dialogue under present-day socialism might suggest that the very chaos of capitalism, cruel and dangerous though it is, is the best guarantee of intellectual ferment. But such reasoning forgets that capitalism favors democratic procedures only to the extent that they enhance trade; there are no known instances in which values of free inquiry have won out over the imperatives of profit when profit has decided to cast its lot with totalitarianism. The increasing centralization of American power, policy, and communications, the persecution of dissidents, and the forceful maintaining of imperial outposts ought to inspire some scholarly caution about investing faith in modern capitalism's libertarian avowals.

For the moment, however, the strains that became visible in the 1960's have begun to yield a fundamental debate about intellectual values and methods. While the challenges to obscurantist scholarship are sometimes uninformed and even anti-intellectual, it is becoming possible in several fields, including literary study, to perceive that the old legitimations for conventional work—objectivity, neutrality, humanistic values, "culture"—are not what they once seemed.[7] Whereas many critics of thirty years ago were prompted by political disillusion to seek a truer order within art, I suspect that the best critics in the immediate future will reject such escapism and demand that works be understood, not as transcendent icons and refuges

---

[7] I have amplified this point in an essay, "Anaesthetic Criticism," which will form the opening chapter of *Psychoanalysis and Literary Process*, ed. Crews (Cambridge, Mass., 1970). Further pertinent critiques by others are mentioned in the notes to that essay. See, in addition, James F. Goldberg, " 'Culture' and 'Anarchy' and the Present Time," *Kenyon Review*, XXXI (1969), 583–611 [reprinted in this book on pp. 1004–23—ED.].

from the world, but as contingent, imperfect expressions of social and mental forces. Without necessarily having any political end in view, such an understanding will have political determinants and political effects, for it will share in the awakening from Cold-War mystification. I would like to think that this awakening will be welcomed by everyone who respects scholarship's ideal of shedding prejudice and discovering principles that make the world accessible to reason.

NEUROSIS AND HISTORY

Norman O. Brown

The doctrine that all men are mad appears to conflict with a historical perspective on the nature and destiny of man: it appears to swallow all cultural variety, all historical change, into a darkness in which all cats are gray. But this objection neglects the richness and complexity of the Freudian theory of neurosis.

In the first place there are several distinct kinds of neurosis, each with a different set of symptoms, a different structure in the relations between the repressed, the ego, and reality. We are therefore in a position to return to the varieties and complexities of individual cultures if we entertain, as Freud does in *Civilization and Its Discontents,* the hypothesis that the varieties of culture can be correlated with the varieties of neurosis: "If the evolution of civilization has such a far-reaching similarity with the development of an individual, and if the same methods are employed in both, would not the diagnosis be justified that many systems of civilization—or epochs of it—possibly even the whole of humanity—have become 'neurotic' under the pressure of civilizing trends? To analytic dissection of these neuroses therapeutic recommendations might follow which could claim a great practical interest." [1]

And furthermore, it is a Freudian theorem that each individual neurosis is not static but dynamic. It is a historical process with its own internal logic. Because of the basically unsatisfactory nature of the neurotic compromise, tension between the repressed and repressing factors persists and produces a constant series of new symptom-formations. And the series of symptom-formations is not a shapeless series of mere changes; it exhibits a regressive pattern, which Freud calls the slow return of the repressed. It is a law of

[1] Sigmund Freud, *Civilization and Its Discontents,* trans. J. Riviere, International Psycho-Analytical Library, ed. E. Jones, no. 17 (London: Hogarth Press, 1930), p. 141.

neurotic diseases, he says, that these obsessive acts increasingly come closer to the original impulse and to the original forbidden act itself.[2] The doctrine of the universal neurosis of mankind, if we take it seriously, therefore compels us to entertain the hypothesis that the pattern of history exhibits a dialectic not hitherto recognized by historians, the dialectic of neurosis.

A reinterpretation of human history is not an appendage to psychoanalysis but an integral part of it. The empirical fact which compelled Freud to comprehend the whole of human history in the area of psychoanalysis is the appearance in dreams and in neurotic symptoms of themes substantially identical with major themes—both ritualistic and mythical—in the religious history of mankind. The link between the theory of neurosis and the theory of history is the theory of religion, as is made perfectly clear in *Totem and Taboo* and *Moses and Monotheism*.

And the link affects both ends linked. Freud not only maintains that human history can be understood only as a neurosis but also that the neuroses of individuals can be understood only in the context of human history as a whole. From the time when he wrote *Totem and Taboo* (1913), Freud says in *Moses and Monotheism* (1937), "I have never doubted that religious phenomena are to be understood only on the model of the neurotic symptoms of the individual." [3] According to the analogy elaborated in *Moses and Monotheism,* "In the history of the species something happened similar to the events in the life of the individual. That is to say, mankind as a whole passed through conflicts of a sexual-aggressive nature, which left permanent traces, but which were for the most part warded off and forgotten; later, after a long period of latency, they came to life again and created phenomena similar in structure and tendency to neurotic symptoms." [4]

This analogy supplies Freud with his notion of the "archaic heritage"; mankind is a prisoner of the past in the same sense as "our hysterical patients are suffering from reminiscences" and neurotics "cannot escape from the past." [5] Thus the bondage of all cultures to their cultural heritage is a neurotic constriction. And conversely, Freud came to recognize that the core of the neuroses of individuals lay in the same "archaic heritage," "memory-traces of the experiences of former generations," which "can only be understood phylogenetically." [6] The repressed unconscious which produces neurosis is not an individual unconscious but a collective one. Freud abstains

---

[2] Sigmund Freud, *Totem and Taboo* in *The Basic Writings of Sigmund Freud*, trans. and ed. A. A. Brill (New York: Modern Library, 1938), pp. 831, 875; Sigmund Freud, *Collected Papers*, ed. J. Riviere and J. Strachey, International Psycho-Analytical Library, no. 7–10, 37, 5 vols. (New York, London: International Psycho-Analytical Press, 1924–50), III:454; IV:93; Sigmund Freud, *Inhibitions, Symptoms and Anxiety*, trans. A. Strachey, International Psycho-Analytical Library, no. 28 (London: Hogarth Press and Institute of Psycho-Analysis, 1936), pp. 61, 71; Sigmund Freud, *Moses and Monotheism*, trans. K. Jones, International Psycho-Analytical Library, no. 33 (London: Hogarth Press and Institute of Psycho-Analysis, 1939; New York, Alfred A. Knopf, 1939), pp. 122–29, 201.

[3] Freud, *Moses and Monotheism*, p. 94.

[4] Freud, *Moses and Monotheism*, p. 129.

[5] These passages, and their importance, were first drawn to my attention by P. Rieff, "The Meaning of History and Religion in Freud's Thought," *Journal of Religion*, XXXI (1951), p. 115.

[6] Freud, *Collected Papers*, V:343; Freud, *Moses and Monotheism*, pp. 159, 204–05.

from adopting Jung's term but says, "The content of the unconscious is collective anyhow." [7] Ontogeny recapitulates phylogeny (each individual recapitulates the history of the race): in the few years of childhood "we have to cover the enormous distance of development from primitive man of the Stone Age to civilized man of today." [8] From this it follows that the theory of neurosis must embrace a theory of history; and conversely a theory of history must embrace a theory of neurosis.

Psychoanalysis must view religion both as neurosis and as that attempt to become conscious and to cure, inside the neurosis itself, on which Freud came at the end of his life to pin his hopes for therapy. Psychoanalysis is vulgarly interpreted as dismissing religion as an erroneous system of wishful thinking. In *The Future of an Illusion,* Freud does speak of religion as a "substitute-gratification"—the Freudian analogue to the Marxian formula, "opiate of the people." But according to the whole doctrine of repression, "substitute-gratifications"—a term which applies not only to poetry and religion but also to dreams and neurotic symptoms—contain truth: they are expressions, distorted by repression, of the immortal desires of the human heart.

The proper psychoanalytical perspective on religion is that taken in *Moses and Monotheism,* where Freud set out to find the fragment of historic and psychological truth in Judaism and Christianity. Even Marx—in the same passage in which the notorious formula "opiate of the people" occurs —speaks of religion as "the sigh of the oppressed creature, the heart of a heartless world." [9] But Marx, lacking the concept of repression and the unconscious—that is to say, not being prepared to recognize the mystery of the human heart—could not pursue the line of thought implied in his own epigram. Psychoanalysis is equipped to study the mystery of the human heart, and must recognize religion to be the heart of the mystery. But psychoanalysis can go beyond religion only if it sees itself as completing what religion tries to do, namely, make the unconscious conscious; then psychoanalysis would be the science of original sin. Psychoanalysis is in a position to define the error in religion only after it has recognized the truth.

It is not to be denied that Freud's earlier writings, especially *Totem and Taboo,* contain, besides much that looks forward to *Moses and Monotheism,* another line of thought on the relation between psychoanalysis and history. This other line of thought works out the notion that ontogeny recapitulates phylogeny in a different way. The psychoanalytical model for understanding history is not neurosis but the process of growing up; or rather, maturity is envisaged not as a return of the repressed infantile neurosis but as the overcoming of it. In effect, Freud correlates his own psycho-sexual stages of the individual with the stages of the history postulated by nineteenth-century evolutionary-minded thinkers of the type of Comte and Frazer. Thus in *Totem and Taboo* he says that the animistic phase corresponds to narcissism, in both time and substance; the religious phase corresponds to

[7] Freud, *Moses and Monotheism,* p. 208.
[8] Sigmund Freud, *Questions of Lay Analysis,* p. 167, quoted by Rieff, "The Authority of the Past," p. 430.
[9] K. Marx, *Der historische Materialismus, die Frühschriften,* ed. S. Landshut and J. P. Mayer (Leipzig: A. Kröner, 1932), p. 264.

the stage of object-finding in which dependence on the parents is paramount; while the scientific phase corresponds to maturity, in which the individual, who by now has renounced the pleasure-principle and has accepted reality, seeks his object in the outer world.[10]

This line of thought is a residue of eighteenth-century optimism and rationalism in Freud; in it history is not a process of becoming sicker but a process of becoming wiser. The early Freud—if we forget the later Freud—thus justifies the quite naive and traditionalist view of history held by most psychoanalysts. But this line of thought is not simply inadequate as history; it is inadequate as psychoanalysis. It belongs with Freud's early system of psychoanalysis, with his early theory of the instincts, and with his early (and traditionalist) theory of the human ego.

It is true that the implementation of the approach to history adumbrated in Freud's later writings involves great difficulties. Freud himself, in the passage suggesting a correlation between cultures and neurosis, put his finger on the heart of the problem when he pointed out the need to develop a concept of a "normal" or healthy culture by which to measure the neurotic cultures recorded by history.[11] From the point of view taken in this book, the development of such a concept is the central problem confronting both psychoanalysis and history. And the lack of such a concept explains the failure of both historians and psychoanalysts (with the exception of Róheim) to pursue Freud's pioneering efforts.

But if historians have failed to follow Freud, poets have characteristically anticipated him. Is there not, for example, a still unexplored truth in the statement of the German poet Hebbel: "Is it so hard to recognize that the German nation has up till now no life history to show for itself, but only the history of a disease (*Krankheitsgeschichte*)?" [12] And not just the German nation—which is or used to be the scapegoat carrying all the sins of the Western world. According to James Joyce, "History is a nightmare from which I am trying to awaken." [13] The poets, and Nietzsche—Nietzsche's *Genealogy of Morals* is the first attempt to grasp world history as the history of an ever increasing neurosis. And both Nietzsche and Freud find the same dynamic in the neurosis of history, an ever increasing sense of guilt caused by repression. Nietzsche's climax—"Too long has the world been a madhouse" [14]—compares with the dark conclusion of *Civilization and Its Discontents*: "If civilization is an inevitable course of development from the group of the family to the group of humanity as a whole, then an intensification of the sense of guilt . . . will be inextricably bound up with it, until perhaps the sense of guilt may swell to a magnitude that individuals can hardly support." [15]

The necessity of a psychoanalytical approach to history is pressed upon the historian by one question: Why does man, alone of all animals, have

[10] Freud, *Totem and Taboo* in *Basic Writings*, pp. 876–77.
[11] Freud, *Civilization and Its Discontents*, p. 142.
[12] Cf. G. Lukács, *Goethe und seine Zeit* (Bern: A. Francke, 1947), p. 131.
[13] J. Joyce, *Ulysses* (New York: Modern Library, 1934), p. 35.
[14] F. W. Nietzsche, *The Philosophy of Nietzsche* (New York: Modern Library, 1927), p. 712.
[15] Freud, *Civilization and Its Discontents*, pp. 121–22.

a history? For man is distinguished from animals not simply by the possession and transmission from generation to generation of that suprabiological
apparatus which is culture, but also, if history and changes in time are
essential characteristics of human culture and therefore of man, by a desire
to change his culture and so to change himself. In making history "man
makes himself," to use the suggestive title of Gordon Childe's book. Then
the historical process is sustained by man's desire to become other than what
he is. And man's desire to become something different is essentially an unconscious desire. The actual changes in history neither result from nor
correspond to the conscious desires of the human agents who bring them
about. Every historian knows this, and the philosopher of history, Hegel,
in his doctrine of the "cunning of Reason," made it a fundamental point
in his structural analysis of history. Mankind today is still making history
without having any conscious idea of what it really wants or under what
conditions it would stop being unhappy; in fact what it is doing seems to
be making itself more unhappy and calling that unhappiness progress.

Christian theology, or at least Augustinian theology, recognizes human
restlessness and discontent, the *cor irrequietum,* as the psychological source
of the historical process. But Christian theology, to account for the origin
of human discontent and to indicate a solution, has to take man out of this
real world, out of the animal kingdom, and inculcate into him delusions of
grandeur. And thus Christian theology commits its own worst sin, the sin of
pride.

Freud's real critique of religion in *The Future of an Illusion* is the contention (also Spinoza's) that true humility lies in science. True humility, he
says, requires that we learn from Copernicus that the human world is not
the purpose or the center of the universe; that we learn from Darwin that
man is a member of the animal kingdom; and that we learn from Freud
that the human ego is not even master in its own house.[16] Apart from
psychoanalysis there are no secular or scientific theories as to why man is
the restless and discontented animal. The discontented animal is the neurotic animal, the animal with desires given in his nature which are not
satisfied by culture. From the psychoanalytical point of view, these unsat-
isfied and repressed but immortal desires sustain the historical process.
History is shaped, beyond our conscious wills, not by the cunning of Reason
but by the cunning of Desire.

The riddle of history is not in Reason but in Desire; not in labor, but
in love. A confrontation with Marx will clarify Freud. It is axiomatic in
Marxism to define the essence of man as labor. Freud has no quarrel with
the Marxist emphasis on the importance of the "economic factor" in history: he formally praises Marxism for "its clear insight into the determining
influence which is exerted by the economic conditions of man upon his
intellectual, ethical, and artistic reactions." [17] For Freud, work and eco-

---

[16] Freud, *Collected Papers,* IV:350–55.
[17] Sigmund Freud, *New Introductory Lectures on Psychoanalysis,* trans. W. J. H. Sprott,
International Psycho-Analytical Library, no. 24 (London: Hogarth Press and Institute of
Psycho-Analysis, 1933), p. 228.

nomic necessity are the essence of the reality-principle: but the essence of man lies not in the reality-principle but in repressed unconscious desires. No matter how stringently economic necessities press down on him, he is not in his essence *Homo economicus* or *Homo laborans;* no matter how bitter the struggle for bread, man does not live by bread alone.

Thus Freud becomes relevant when history raises this question: What does man want over and beyond "economic welfare" and "mastery over nature"? Marx defines the essence of man as labor and traces the dialectic of labor in history till labor abolishes itself. There is then a vacuum in the Marxist utopia. Unless there is no utopia, unless history is never abolished, unless labor continues to be, like Faust, driven to ever greater achievements, some other and truer definition of the essence of man must be found. Freud suggests that beyond labor there is love. And if beyond labor at the end of history there is love, love must have always been there from the beginning of history, and it must have been the hidden force supplying the energy devoted to labor and to making history. From this point of view, repressed Eros is the energy of history and labor must be seen as sublimated Eros. In this way a problem not faced by Marx can be faced with the aid of Freud.

Marxism is a system of sociology; the importance of the "economic factor" is a sociological question to be settled by sociologists; Freud himself, speaking as a sociologist, can say that in imposing repression "at bottom society's motive is economic." [18] The quarrel between psychoanalysis and "economic determinism" arises in the tacit psychological assumptions behind economic determinism, and therefore arises only when we pass from sociology to psychology, from the abstraction of "society" to the concrete human individual. The issue is not the importance of economics but its psychology. Marx himself, though always complicated, is not free from the tacit assumption, held generally by economic determinists, that the concrete human needs and drives sustaining economic activity are just what they appear to be and are fully in consciousness: "self-preservation" and "pleasure," as understood by the utilitarians, summarize the psychological theory implied by the ingenuous invocation of categories like "economic necessity" and "human needs."

But the proof that human needs are not what they seem to be lies precisely in the fact of human history. The Faustian restlessness of man in history shows that men are not satisfied by the satisfaction of their conscious desires; men are unconscious of their real desires. Thus a psychology of history must be psychoanalytical.

In so far as Marx faced this question at all, lacking the concept of repressed unconscious desires he could only come up with a psychology of history which condemns man to be eternally Faustian and precludes any possibility of happiness. Marx needs a psychological premise to explain the unceasing bent for technological progress sustaining the dialectic of labor

[18] Sigmund Freud, *A General Introduction to Psycho-Analysis,* trans. J. Riviere (New York: Liveright, 1953), p. 321. (Copyright 1935 by Edward L. Bernays. Quotation by permission of Liveright Publishers, New York, and G. Allen & Unwin Ltd., London.)

in history. Lacking the doctrine of repression—or rather not being able to see man as a psychological riddle—Marx, as a sympathetic critic has shown, turns to biology and postulates an absolute law of human biology that the satisfaction of human needs always generates new needs.[19] If human discontent is thus biologically given, it is incurable. Quite specifically, not only "the abolition of history" but also an "economy of abundance," as envisioned in Marx's utopian phase, are out of the question. Hence the dark clouds of pessimism in the third volume of *Capital,* where he says:[20]

Just as the savage must wrestle with nature, in order to satisfy his wants, in order to maintain his life and to reproduce it, so the civilized man has to do it in all forms of society and under all modes of production. With his development the realm of natural necessity expands, because his wants increase; but at the same time the forces of production increase, by which these wants are satisfied.

But Marx's assumption of a biological basis for "progress" in history really amounts to a confession that he is unable to explain it psychologically.

Psychoanalysis can provide a theory of "progress," but only by viewing history as a neurosis. By defining man as the neurotic animal, psychoanalysis not merely assumes man's Faustian character but also explains why man is so. To quote Freud:[21]

What appears . . . as an untiring impulsion toward further perfection can easily be understood as a result of the instinctual repression upon which is based all that is most precious in human civilization. The repressed instinct never ceases to strive for complete satisfaction, which would consist in the repetition of a primary experience of satisfaction. No substitutive or reactive formations and no sublimations will suffice to remove the repressed instinct's persisting tension.

By the same token, psychoanalysis offers a theoretical framework for exploring the possibility of a way out of the nightmare of endless "progress" and endless Faustian discontent, a way out of the human neurosis, a way out of history. In the case of the neurotic individual, the goal of psycho-analytical therapy is to free him from the burden of his past, from the burden of his history, the burden which compels him to go on having (and being) a case history. And the method of psychoanalytical therapy is to deepen the historical consciousness of the individual ("fill up the memory-gaps") till he awakens from his own history as from a nightmare. Psycho-analytical consciousness, as a higher stage in the general consciousness of mankind, may be likewise the fulfillment of the historical consciousness, that ever widening and deepening search for origins which has obsessed Western thought ever since the Renaissance. If historical consciousness is finally transformed into psychoanalytical consciousness, the grip of the dead

[19] Cf. H. Popitz, *Der entfremdete Mensch: Zeitkritik und Geschichtsphilosophie des jungen Marx* (Basel: Verlag für Recht und Gesellschaft, 1953), pp. 151–52.
[20] K. Marx, *Capital,* trans. E. Untermann, 3 vols. (Chicago: C. H. Kerr, 1906–1909), III:954.
[21] Sigmund Freud, *Beyond the Pleasure Principle,* trans. J. Strachey, International Psycho-Analytical Library, ed. E. Jones, no. 4 (London: Hogarth Press, 1950), p. 56.

hand of the past on life in the present would be loosened, and man would be ready to live instead of making history, to enjoy instead of paying back old scores and debts, and to enter that state of Being which was the goal of his Becoming.

"CULTURE" AND "ANARCHY" AND THE PRESENT TIME

James F. Goldberg

Talking to people I know, around Columbia and elsewhere, I found that I am not alone in my unreadiness to teach this year. Granted the hangover from the spring of '68, if not from the action of this past spring, is more severe at Columbia than at many other places, still the number of people I know suggests that there may have been many who were making or wrestling with the same decision. I do not think a mass exodus is in prospect, only that there are enough people involved to make it possible to speak publicly, to try to describe a social phenomenon instead of confessing privately. Pressed to define who "we" are in what I will have to say, I can only guess that "we" are some people I know, many more whose existence I can only infer, who teach or used to teach English or other subjects loosely called the humanities, who are probably twenty-five to thirty-five years old, middle-class in background, who are generally called converts to radicalism, "radicalized," but who are probably more accurately described as de-converts from liberalism. We are that "junior faculty" who between the press releases of SDS and those of the senior faculty have not got much of a word in edgewise.

Part of the problem, looking at this new year, is the difficulty in teaching just now, even though I am no longer at Columbia and there has been nothing remotely resembling disruption where I am at present. Still, neither the consolations nor the interpretations of literature seem to interest students this year, nor, as other critics have admitted, does the mode of irony through which literature has been approached for at least the last twenty-five years seem to get through to them. But it is clearly not all the students' fault, since neither the consolation nor the interpretation of literature seems to interest me either, not in their public forms anyway, and my remaining fondness for irony is more defensive than aggressive.

What I want to give is one view of what it means to have gone to college in the late '50s and to be trying to teach in college at the end of the '60s, what our suppositions about literature and education were, how founded

"CULTURE" AND "ANARCHY" AND THE PRESENT TIME Reprinted from the *Kenyon Review*, Vol. 31, No. 127, Issue 5 (1969). Copyright © 1969 by James F. Goldberg.

and how changed, and to describe some aspects of the history of the idea of culture which have only now seemed to suggest themselves as relevant to what has happened. It should be obvious that I am not attempting an analysis of the past, present, or future of the University, whether institution or sanctuary (except insofar as a particular idea of culture shores it up). There has been enough, and there promises to be more than enough, written on this matter—nothing that I have seen either advancing or refuting the classic work on the subject, which is 51 years old: Veblen's *The Higher Learning in America*.[1]

Nor am I going to talk about curriculum reform, that diversionary issue that both liberals and conservatives have been able to convince themselves is central. (The only thing in George Kateb's recent defense of the University, published in *Commentary*, that I can wholly agree with is that "the 'liberal' reformers took unseemly advantage of a situation they had no hand in creating," but, after saying this, it is only those reformers that he and others persist in attacking.) What is really needed, to my mind, is not curriculum reform but an intellectual revaluation of some stock notions about the relationship between the idea of culture and education.

If the Veblen of 1918 seems more relevant to the large question of the nature of the University than the recent crisis journalism, that is not the case in the more specific question about the idea of culture and education. In Lionel Trilling's most recent book, relevantly titled *Beyond Culture: Essays on Literature and Learning*, there are two essays that deal with roughly the question I want to consider—the value of literary culture at the present time. The essays, "On the Teaching of Modern Literature" and "The Two Environments: Reflections on the Study of English," ought to be read and considered, but in essence what they argue with different emphases is that Culture has succeeded too well: that the exposure of large numbers of students in the quasi-public forum of the classroom to the corrosive force of modern literature has created in opposition to the old Philistinism a counter- but trivialized-culture, a kind of mass-pop-alienation (this last is my term of course, not his). Writing in 1961 and 1965, he sees this counter-culture as mere stylishness and as a failure of the ideal of Arnoldian culture ("Beyond Culture" is, in both essays, philosophy), but not quite as a danger. Diana Trilling, however, writing about Columbia in the November 1968 issue of *Commentary*, seems to take the idea that further step:

[1] His position can be illustrated by a brief quotation: "While it still remains true that the long-term common-sense judgment of civilized mankind places knowledge above business traffic, as an end to be sought, yet workday habituation under the stress of competitive business *has induced a frame of mind that will tolerate no other method of procedure, and no rule of life that does not approve itself as a faithful travesty of competitive enterprise.* And since the quest of learning cannot be carried on by the methods or with the apparatus and incidents of competitive business, it follows that the only remedial measures that hold any promise of rehabilitation for the higher learning in the universities can not be attempted in the present state of public sentiment.

"All that is required is the abolition of the academic executive and of the governing board [i.e. trustees]. Anything short of this heroic remedy is bound to fail, because the evils sought to be remedied are inherent in these organs, and intrinsic to their functioning." (Italics added)

The teaching of modern subjects in our universities, especially literature, proceeds of course on some unadmitted (because inadmissible) assumption of a drastic discontinuity between art and life. It is as if the professor who sanctions the revolutionary content of the contemporary literary works that he teaches were still speaking from the platform of one hundred years ago, when art was outside the stream of real life, the real life of action and political choice, its influence on public affairs a matter of the slow mysterious interpenetration of the public consciousness by some strange remote thing called culture. Among the many assumptions undermined by the attack on Columbia, not the least important was the illusion that contemporary art is an academic subject like any other, one that is adequately dealt with without doctrinal commitment. It was only the blindest eye that could refuse to see the extent to which the revolutionary scene at the University represented the moral substance of contemporary art brought to actual life, indeed the triumph of culture over politics.

When first I read this, I was struck with the idea, in a rather frivolous way, I admit (and in quite the reverse of the way it was meant). Fleshed out, it had a whimsical irony, characters coming out of books to confront their startled and discomfited readers, and in that spirit I developed the idea. Here, I said, were senior faculty, men who had read, pondered, taught things such as the relationship between Melville and his narrators, and now they were faced with roughly 750 Bartlebies at once. Or, here were Barnard girls shocking everyone with their language, but what if they had buttonholed one of these readers of Yeats on College Walk to insist that "Love has pitched his mansion in / The place of excrement." Or, what if Mark Rudd had emerged from Underground to announce: "I am a sick man. I am a spiteful man. I am an unpleasant man. I think my university is diseased. . . . My university is bad, well then—let it get even worse!" The point I was trying to make with this whimsy—that the faculty over-simplified and over-moralized the Columbia situation in a way that they would never do with literature—still seems broadly valid. But, looking at the students (who are, after all, what Mrs. Trilling is describing), the game I was playing seemed not only frivolous but untrue. The students in the buildings had political demands; their obscenity was not that of Crazy Jane; and Mark Rudd was not Dostoevskian in any sense. If Mrs. Trilling's comment had any validity, and I think it does, it was not in reference to those students but to other people. It was in fact we who were older who could be called culture-ridden. That is, however, a matter to be considered later.

If Mark Rudd was not in all truth the Underground Man come to life, he did manage to shock as well as dismay many faculty. He appeared before the faculty who were trying to mediate to tell them that what they were trying to do was . . . "Bullshit!" The word itself, quite aside from the tone, seemed to set a good many faculty reeling—indeed, every faculty account seems to return to it again and again in shocked fascination. Yet it provides an interesting study in comparative expletives. The night before, when the university announced (prematurely, it turned out) that the police had been called, the faculty, or at least a good number of them, gave vent to *their* emotions. What they cried out was "Shame!" True, of course, the faculty's expletive came from purer, if not necessarily worthier, motives, but I remember that it struck me even at the time, even in the tumult, as a puzzling style of public emotion, an archaism in these men of complex modern mind that seemed a discrepancy.

The point in comparing outcries is not simply to see on which side I range myself, though it might be a nice question of social history to ask why I, twenty-eight years old in 1968, was unbothered by one expression and taken aback by the other. The point is the opportunity given in the face of all the talk about the irrationality and destructiveness of the students, of which saying "bullshit" is taken as the emblem, the opportunity given to see what the rationality affirmed amounted to, if saying "shame" was its epitome. That it derived from British Parliamentarianism was obvious enough, and with the help of a source such as G. M. Young:

> The manners of Parliament in the [eighteen] thirties seem to have been the worst on record. . . . With the windows shut—and the stench of the Thames made it impossible to keep them open—the mooings, cat-calls, and cock-crows, what O'Connell once called the "beastly bellowings," of the faithful Commons, could be heard fifty yards away.

it could be seen that the style was not the timeless usage of rational discourse, but could even be dated. It was the style of the high noon of Victorian prosperity, the 1850s and 1860s, which brought me by another road to the place where the idea of culture was fixed—to Matthew Arnold.

II

As if there were a special magic, or irony, in centennials, 100 years from its publication Matthew Arnold's *Culture and Anarchy* has been infused with new life. It is not, of course, as if the essay had been forgotten. If we add to it "The Function of Criticism at the Present Time" (in effect an earlier version), it is safe to say that there is no essay of the last 100 years that has been more influential in formulating the values of liberal humanism. To be more concrete, there has been no essay more valuable in recruiting college English teachers—not that Arnold is what we all pursue, but he is why we pursue it. Whatever may happen eventually, no one chooses teaching *in order* to impart to seventeen- to twenty-one-year-olds the results of scholarly investigation or *in order* to impose on them the specific weight that some books have in his mind. One chooses teaching for the same bewildering multiplicity of reasons that one does anything, but, in the public, social sector of motivation at least, to devote oneself to teaching literature is to affirm the value of culture, and it is Arnold who has set the terms of this affirmation. If it is to Arnold's heroes, Goethe and Wordsworth, and the testimony of their nineteenth-century readers, that we owe the possibility of literature as a therapeutic agent, it is to Arnold that we owe its introduction into public health (even, one might say, preventive medicine), and the injunction to spread the cure, to "recommend culture," as he says, "as the great help out of our present difficulties." For 100 years, Arnold has provided the moral aesthetic to call a liberal who liked to read to the vocation of teaching literature.

Moreover, for 100 years there has been no essay to replace *Culture and Anarchy,* or rather to place it, as Arnold intended it should be placed, as a document for his own times. If we neglect, as we can for these purposes, their particular contributions to criticism, I. A. Richards and F. R. Leavis are both Arnoldians, Richards giving us in effect Practical Arnoldism and Leavis demonstrating in the main a more embattled form. The special interweaving of the generalizations—culture, liberation, society, education —is the same. It combines a generalized pessimism about society with a qualified optimism about education. It argues that education, specifically literary education, can change a student wholly—not just add to his stock of information, but liberate him from the idols, change the quality of his life, and through him change the quality of society. All this is the legacy of Arnold. As for the more "formal" autotelic criticism, an analogy is too tempting to resist: if Arnold (in a metaphor he would have hated) is the Protestant ethic of culture, Cleanth Brooks and others are its spirit of capitalism. The only serious challenge to Arnold's hegemony comes from T. S. Eliot, not only in his insistence that transcendent religious emotion belongs to religion but also in his argument that the proper home of culture is in the theater, not in the academy. (The war between the theater and the academy, between Dionysus and Apollo, was hardly invented overnight by the Living Theater.) With that exception, however, it seems fair enough to say that in the realm of devotional works that English majors customarily read, and that form the ethos of English departments, *Culture and Anarchy* has never been superseded.

Yet a student of the '50s, or '60s, when he read an essay as important as *Culture and Anarchy,* almost certainly read it in a truncated version. There was one complete modern edition, prepared by J. Dover Wilson, but otherwise, for all the canon of organic form and the work-as-a-whole, in no anthology of English literature, no anthology of nineteenth-century literature, in no anthology even of Matthew Arnold did the essay appear entire.[2] In most cases what was omitted was not even remarked. Lionel Trilling, who did comment on his omissions (which are the customary ones), said in *The Portable Matthew Arnold*:

> The essential matter of *Culture and Anarchy* is to be found in the Introduction and first four chapters, which are printed here. I have omitted the Author's Preface, the last two chapters, and the Conclusion, which are largely topical and local.

---

[2] The construction of what is now known simply as *Culture and Anarchy* is usually unremarked as well. It was put together in 1869 from two separate essays. The introduction and chapter one ("Sweetness and Light") were originally called "Culture and Its Enemies" and formed Arnold's last Oxford lecture. The remaining five chapters were published in the *Cornhill Magazine* starting seven months later, under the title "Anarchy and Authority." The seam shows in places.

What was indeed for various reasons topical and local in the late '40s and in the '50s is not, however, topical and local now. Here is what, among other things, the Conclusion to *Culture and Anarchy* has to say:

But for us,—who believe in right reason, in the duty and possibility of extricating and elevating our best self, in the progress of humanity towards perfection,—for us the framework of society, that theatre on which this august drama has to unroll itself, is sacred; and whoever administers it, and however we may seek to remove them from their tenure of administration, yet, while they administer, we steadily and with undivided heart support them in repressing anarchy and disorder; because without order there can be no society, and without society there can be no human perfection.

And this opinion of the intolerableness of anarchy we can never forsake, however our Liberal friends may think a little rioting, and what they call popular demonstrations, useful. . . . And even when they artfully show us operations which are undoubtedly precious, such as the abolition of the slave-trade, and ask us if, for their sake, foolish and obstinate governments may not wholesomely be frightened by a little disturbance, the good design in view and the difficulty of overcoming opposition to it being considered,—still we say no, and that monster-Processions in the streets and forcible irruptions into the parks, even in professed support of this good design, ought to be unflinchingly forbidden and repressed; and that far more is lost than is gained by permitting them. Because a State in which law is authoritative and sovereign, a firm and settled course of public order, is requisite if man is to bring to maturity anything precious and lasting now, or to found anything precious and lasting for the future.

This then is the Matthew Arnold who was not relevant then. It would be hard to say that he is not relevant now.[3] Though it would be extremely difficult to find any historian who would not think Arnold's response to the Hyde Park riots overwrought, if this same quotation were to be submitted to any group of senior professors, including historians, as a draft resolution on student disorders, there would probably be those who would like to change the wording ("repressed" bears a particular twentieth-century weight and taboo), but otherwise there would be a broad general acceptance.

When classes were disrupted at Columbia and 100 Senior Faculty denounced the disruption (and, obliquely, the disruption of last spring or any other disruption) in a statement titled "The University as a Sanctuary of Academic Freedom," it must have been depressingly clear to those of them

---

[3] It is not my intention to imply anything so shady as a conspiracy of editors and critics to avoid this side of Arnold. The matter is more complex than that, as I hope to indicate. It might, in addition, be argued against any such claim that Arnold says the same thing, in almost the same language, at the end of chapter two, "Doing as One Likes." My rebuttal is that 1) the differences in the language are significant: the word "repress," for example, with its special twentieth-century weight, does not appear in DAOL. 2) The context is different. In DAOL the parallel passage is part of an even-handed attack on all classes at the behest of the Ideal State. 3) In DAOL the passage simply does not have the prominence that it has here in the conclusion. (If this rebuttal is not sufficient, I am willing to concede that editing Arnold had nothing to do with the problem—even that it was my reading of Arnold that was to blame. That one could easily misread *Culture and Anarchy* in the '50s is enough for my argument.)

who knew *Culture and Anarchy* that Arnold had once again to be taken as a whole.

The implications are even larger, however, for those of us to whom this rereading of Arnold comes as a shock. What does a person do who has chosen to teach literature under the spell of Arnold's moral aesthetic, but who also, with Arnold's conclusion not equally firmly in his mind, has himself joined these last few years "monster-Processions in the streets and forcible irruptions into the parks"—or onto the Pentagon steps? If he cannot support "whoever administers" the State "in repressing anarchy and disorder" or even affirm the "University as a Sanctuary of Academic Freedom"?

When the processions and irruptions reach the campus, and it is no longer easy to divide our lives into radical politics and liberal arts, a decent respect for the opinions of mankind and a certain curiosity about our own opinions requires at least an attempt to account for what has happened to the value of culture in our minds.

To begin, I think I must rehearse certain melancholy reminders of America in the '50s which more than any knowledge of Arnold's time or Arnold's England controlled our reading of *Culture and Anarchy*. A reader of Arnold in the '30s would have had to confront the question of Arnold's politics; in the '50s it presented no problem. Arnold seemed to mesh perfectly without the politics. Politics could be subsumed into Culture: Eisenhower was the arch-Philistine who had twice defeated Stevenson, representing Culture. McCarthy had been something worse, but still a Philistine. Arnold's Ideal State, if we thought of it at all, resembled the New Deal, but the besetting ailment of the world outside was Philistinism: suburbia, cars with tailfins and chrome, Madison Avenue, *Time* magazine, Norman Vincent Peale.

But Arnold had written *Culture and Anarchy,* not *Culture and Philistinism.* Did that never cross our minds? Probably not, except as anarchy was in some way the essence of Philistinism—suburban sprawl and Eisenhower's syntax were in *that* way anarchic: they both lacked a central, controlling intelligence (as we used to say, judging novels). Even if we had confronted Arnold's notion of anarchy, mass-action in defiance of law, his "hooting and bawling" populace could have been easily translated into Southern mobs in Clinton, Tennessee, and Little Rock, Arkansas, screaming and attacking Negro children who in ones and twos were lawfully integrating the schools. (None of us could question at that time the liberal procedures that determined that black children, in what seems now a parody of individualism, should "integrate" *in ones and twos*.) As far as I can remember, though, that kind of anarchy, like the peripheral problem of Southern racism, was a minor issue. The real problem was Philistinism: complacency, conformity, banality.

When one looks back on the near-unanimous agreement that this was in fact the problem for the humanities, it is possible to think that the agreement certifies that the issue was actually non-political, but that is not the case. It seemed that way because the politics was unanimous, completely overarching, and therefore, at least for those of us who were growing up then, well-nigh invisible. The '50s in education were also the time of Sputnik, of Why Ivan Can Read and Johnny Can't, but at the end of every call for scientists and engineers came, in monotonous antiphony, a call for more humanists. The politics was the politics of national mobilization, and like any centralized politics it fostered the appearance of local depolitization, and in this sense culture was one locality. A mobilization, moreover, in which individual rights are subordinated to national duty demands that every institution be structured like an army. What that meant in education can be seen clearly in a little pamphlet of 1958, issued over some very big names, called "The Pursuit of Excellence: Education and the Future of America":

It is now widely recognized that our society has given too little attention to the individual of unusual talent or potentialities.

It is crucial to understand this tug of war between equality and excellence in a democracy. When the rewriting of the rules is prompted by the standards of fair play, by elementary considerations of justice, by basic value-judgments as to what sort of a "best man" the society wants [sic!], democracy can have no quarrel with it. . . . But when the rewriting of the rules is designed to banish excellence, to rule out distinguished attainment, to inhibit spirited individuals, then all who have a stake in the continued vitality of democracy must protest.[4]

The pamphlet goes on from there to propose extending the track-system (segregation by ability within high-school classes), discouraging the "non-academically gifted" from crowding the colleges, and so forth—all by indirect means, of course, "for a free society cannot commandeer talent"—in short, everything we have learned to call, from the Selective Service Memo, "Channelling Manpower." The theoretical basis on which this passage rests (see the second sentence) is a travesty of genuine democratic theory in which the essential dialectic or "tug of war" is between *liberty* and equality. To promote the aristocratic critique of democracy in the chummy guise of a "tug of war" *within* democracy is either ignorant or disingenuous, but it is the way to justify an officer-corps. The important thing to remember is that this demand that more attention be paid the elite, "the individual of unusual talent or potentialities," did not limit itself, as is usually assumed, to scientists and engineers. "Humanists" are included:

The trend toward specialization has created among other things an extraordinary demand for gifted generalists—men with enough intellectual and technical com-

[4] *Special Studies Project Report V*, Rockefeller Brothers Fund. The big names include John Gardner, Theodore Hesburgh, David Riesman, Fred Hechinger, James Killian, and Henry Kissinger. Father Hesburgh, at least, still seems to believe that this "tug of war" is an adequate description of education in a democracy; recently, he was quoted as saying, with some resignation, that he guessed the times were calling for equality, not excellence, in education. I have noticed the term "excellence" wielded regularly by opponents of opening up admissions to the City University (such as Max Lerner). This is obviously not the place to discuss the idea of meritocracy or the way in which it tends to replace democracy in the middle-class pantheon, but such a discussion would be very useful.

petence to deal with the specialists and enough breadth to play more versatile roles
—*whether as managers, teachers, interpreters or critics.* (My italics)

One does not need to be Herbert Marcuse to see that when these men,
mobilizing education, can so casually group teachers and critics with managers, teaching and criticism have been redefined, and a rapprochement
between education and society *as it is* is being proposed.

In the "local" area of culture, the same forces were at work. All the attention to culture, particularly in the "thaw" at the end of the '50s, was natural, one can see now. In the American defensive celebration of the time, if
America was the greatest, strongest, richest country when the GNP was
added up, shouldn't she be the most cultured—buy paintings, build cultural
centers, support opera, ballet, repertory theater—increase her Gross Cultural Product? And, importantly, wasn't culture just what all the visitors,
Tocqueville, Dickens, Arnold, had found most lacking in America? Wasn't
the lack of it why Henry James and T. S. Eliot had left? The unanimity
was possible, of course, because the issue was depolitized, patriotic, and was
carried on by those who considered themselves cultured already. With the
"thaw," and the beginning of "the battle for men's minds," we had to have
something grand enough to impress the Russians in Cultural Exchanges, so
all the audible voices decried Philistinism and extolled Culture.

By the end of the '50s, questions about the quality of American life were
a standard feature of magazines such as *Life* and probably even the *Reader's
Digest* (omitting of course the attacks upon themselves); the same objections
informed the popularized sociology from Vance Packard to William F.
Whyte to David Riesman, and became the basis on which academic departments in the humanities rested, or at least the basis on which they lobbied
for their share of increased federal and foundation aid to education. It was
relatively unimportant that, when the chorus arose that America needed
more serious theater, *Life* magazine meant more William Inge, the *New
York Times* meant more Tennessee Williams, and the academy meant more
Pirandello. In the concrete, steel, and money part of the world, Lincoln
Center sprang up in record time. Put another way, to find the dissenters
from this position you would have had to find those few who objected to
the idea, not the particular realization but the *idea,* of Lincoln Center and
its proliferating brethren. Or, in the universities, you would have had to
find the few who would ask what theory of society (not simply theory of
education) lay behind humanities courses (was it in fact the "extraordinary
demand for gifted generalists"?) rather than simply agreeing in varying
tones of piety that college students should take more of them.

Yet, despite all these indications and more—the spectacular increases in
professors' salaries, for example—the illusion that the University was depolitized and critical, that the major problem was Philistinism and the solution was Culture, persisted. Since, under the pressures of the '50s, the
political space diminished to a mild conservatism and a mild liberalism,
expressible in the privacy of the voting booth, there was a rapprochement
on the campus, pleasant words exchanged across the smallish gap to the

effect that, while we may vote differently on election day, we agree on what constitutes the great tradition and what it has to say, and we agree on the theoretic necessity of reconstituting community/*gemeinschaft*. (The publication of early Marx helped there.)

It cannot be forgotten, however, that for many men the University was a haven, literally and directly, from politics, from the betrayals of the '30s, and, if the administration was courageous enough, from the threatening purges of the '50s. But in choosing the University we did not need such a retreat. We were educated into irony and contra-Philistinism, we did not find our weary way there. We had the '50s without the '30s, and we had *Culture and Anarchy* without the conclusion.

With our understanding of the workings of American civilization we chose the University as an alternative to life in society. As an alternative, a place outside, but not, I think, as a community. This is clearly a crucial distinction, and to some readers I will already have convicted myself in making it. Yet, at least provisionally, one may be permitted to doubt the depth of an attachment to community that is formulated only under attack. Any collection of people on the defensive will probably call themselves a community, including the N.A.M., which has long described itself as the representative of the "business community." With all the *gemeinschaftlichkeit* around, one must, I think, look carefully at all assertions of community. There are, I am sure, some professors (particularly those teaching at their own alma maters) who have long believed in an ideal of community, but I doubt that they are fooled by its sudden rediscovery. If one accepted Arnold, if culture was "the great help out of our present difficulties," then the University was not a sanctuary but, to use current student jargon, a liberated zone, or even, to be a trifle grandiose, an Archimedean place to stand.

An objective reader, assuming there is such a thing, and assuming that there are any left, may think by this point that I have been too generous to myself and my generation, have made us appear too noble and too victimized. It is an imbalance I want to redress. But first, with the slightly new perspective forced upon us by rereading Arnold against the background of the last few years, I want to re-examine briefly *Culture and Anarchy*. The usual interpretation of Arnold's call for repression would be that, in the face of a working-class aroused, his deep conservatism asserted itself (as opposed to the true liberalism of John Stuart Mill, who met with the leaders of the planned demonstration to ask them two questions: were things bad enough to desire a revolution? and could they accomplish one?). That interpretation is too simple, though, because Arnold does not use conservative arguments to justify his position. The arguments are not appeals to tradition, as taking the passage I quoted earlier one paragraph further will show:

Thus, in our eyes, the very framework and exterior order of the State, whoever may administer the State, is sacred; and culture is the most resolute enemy of anarchy, because of the great hopes and designs for the State which culture teaches us to nourish. But as . . . we grow to have clearer sight of the ideas of right reason, and of the elements and helps of perfection, and come gradually to *fill the framework of the State with them, to fashion its internal composition and all its laws and institutions conformably to them,* and to make the State more and more the expression, as we say, of our best self, which is not manifold, and vulgar, and unstable, and contentious, and *ever-varying,* but one, and noble, and secure, and peaceful, and *the same for all mankind,*—with what aversion shall we not then regard anarchy, with what firmness shall we not check it, when there is so much that is so precious which it will endanger! (My italics)[5]

Arnold once defined himself as a liberal of the future. He was, and the future was bureaucracy.

Arnold cannot be taxed with the future, however. Bureaucracy is not the same as bureaucratization, just as rationality is not the same as rationalization. Although Arnold had in more than usual measure the English intellectual's fondness for things Prussian, if he was thinking of the framework of the State "filled" with the English equivalent of the bureaucrat, he was on firmer ground than one might otherwise think. There can be little doubt, as even Marx recognized, that men like Kay-Shuttleworth and Richard Horne really were the "best selves" of nineteenth-century England.

On the other hand, Arnold is hardly perfectly clear. He does after all support the State as then constituted in the crisis he sees, and the italics in what he says are after all mine. His inconsistencies in politics are not particularly important, though; Arnold was not an influential political theorist. But if the distinction between Burke and Arnold, between an appeal to traditional authority and a prophecy of bureaucratic authority, is operating in the idea of Culture, it is much more relevant. If we are all more or less Arnoldian in our attachment to the value of culture, we are half-embarrassed but half-pleased when it is said that the Arnoldian idea of Culture represented the religion of literature. We are likely to respond differently to an inkling from other texts that the prospect of Culture was the *administration* of literature. Arnold said the former, while he only implied the latter, but the implications are suggestive. In "The Literary Influence of Academies" he speaks not just of the intrinsic merit of the French Academy but also of how Richelieu saw its usefulness to himself and managed its official establishment over the objections of the French Parliament. More abstractly, English antipathy to an academy comes from the English spirit of energy, since "what that energy . . . demands and insists on, is freedom; entire independence of all authority, *prescription and routine.*" It is not simply authority or standards that an academy represents, but "*central* authority representing high culture and sound judgment." (Arnold, of course, disavows wanting to impose an academy on England, but that does not change the advantages he sees in one. How that political position could spill over into his cultural position is best indicated by the terms of praise and dispraise, more French than English, that he assigns to literature in this essay: "urbanity" and "provinciality.")

What saves Arnold—though not, I think, his successors—from the implications of his position is his own ambivalence on these matters. Politically,

---

[5] Again, it is useful to note that there is no passage in DAOL to parallel this. The emphasis there is on "our best self" which "inspires faith and is capable of affording a serious principle of authority."

with every reason to prefer the Education Commission to the Parliamentary likes of Robert Lowe, he nevertheless maintains an attachment to the idea of the citizen. He takes the time, incredible as it may seem, to analyze the proposals of the Real Estate Intestacy Bill and the policy of free trade by which he thought John Bright and others were stirring up the workers for middle-class purposes. He was always careful to see that his essays got into the hands of key M.P.'s. If he could not accept Shelley's revolutionary idealism—"Poets are the unacknowledged legislators of the world"—he could at least think that legislators ought to be educated, cultivated men, in fact the Guardians of the State.

As far as Culture is concerned, what saves Arnold from his own implications is his tact, his tone, his involvement with literature, what he calls, apologizing to an author who has taken offence, his "vivacity." But as for his successors, what can we say about the tact, the tone, the involvement of the following—I quote from Mark Schorer's essay of 1948, "Technique as Discovery," which was widely anthologized throughout the '50s, as an example of modern criticism at its best:

Modern criticism, through its exacting scrutiny of literary texts, has demonstrated with finality that in art beauty and truth are indivisible and one. The Keatsian overtones of these terms are mitigated and an old dilemma solved if for beauty we substitute form, and for truth content. We may, without risk of loss, narrow them even more, and speak of technique and subject matter. Modern criticism has shown us that to speak of content as such is not to speak of art at all, but of experience; and that it is only when we speak of the *achieved* content, the form of the work of art as a work of art, that we speak as critics.

We are no longer able to regard as seriously intended criticism of poetry which does not assume these generalizations; but the case for fiction has not yet been established. The novel is still read as though its content has some value in itself, as though the subject matter of fiction has greater or lesser value in itself, and as though technique were not a primary but a supplementary element, capable perhaps of not unattractive embellishments upon the surface of the subject, but hardly of its essence.

In drawing connections between the bureaucracy Arnold favors in government and seems to favor in culture, I am leaning on a few metaphors—centrality, impartiality/disinterestedness—which may not bear more weight than I have imposed upon them already, but in this modern example the classic processes of bureaucratization seem to be realized—means swallowing ends/form swallowing content, method as rationality/technique as discovery. Or, applying Mannheim's succinct formulation—"The fundamental tendency of all bureaucratic thought is to turn all problems of politics into problems of administration"—it can be said that the announced intention of all criticism of this sort is to turn all problems of truth into problems of technique. (I do not mean to avoid the supposition that this and other criticism like it is declaring its emancipation from philosophy by an analogy to science. What is being echoed no doubt, in Professor Schorer's opening words, is an imagined rhetoric of scientific statement [modern science has shown . . .], but, unfortunately for the analogy, no modern scientist with any knowledge of the history of science or the process of discovery would ever use that phrase. Statements about what modern science has shown emerge only from salesmen of toothpaste and breakfast food, and from the administrators of scientific funds and programs.)

I am well aware that criticism of the "technique as discovery" variety has been regularly pronounced dead for the last ten years, that its appellation "new" survives solely in ironic usage. But, if it is dead in the critical journals, it remains very much alive in teaching. Professor Trilling, in the course of rejecting it, recognizes the safety that is its attraction:

Very likely it was with the thought of saving myself from the necessity of speaking personally and my students from having to betray the full harsh meaning of a great literature that I first taught my course in as *literary* a way as possible. A couple of decades ago the discovery was made that a literary work is a structure of words: this doesn't seem a surprising thing to have learned except for its polemical tendency, which is to urge us to minimize the amount of attention we give to the poet's social and personal will, to what he wants to happen outside the poem as a result of the poem; it urges us to fix our minds on what is going on inside the poem.

But, Professor Trilling continues, this safety went "against the grain of the authors themselves":

—structures of words they may indeed have created, but these structures were not pyramids or triumphal arches, they were manifestly contrived to be not static and commemorative but mobile and aggressive, and one does not describe a quinquereme or a howitzer or a tank without estimating how much *damage* it can do.

Eventually I had to decide that there was only one way to give the course, which was to give it without strategies and without conscious caution. It was not honorable, either to the students or to the authors, to conceal or disguise my relation to the literature, my commitment to it, my fear of it, my ambivalence toward it. The literature had to be dealt with in the terms it announced for itself.

However much I might want optimistically to add plowshares and pruning-hooks to Professor Trilling's howitzers and tanks, this still seems to me a valuable statement. What Professor Trilling does not say (and cannot say, I think, since his argument depends on what follows from his decision) is that 95 per cent, to pick a figure, of the teaching of literature does not confront the problem as he does, but is content with the notion that a "literary work is a structure of words," or even, as Northrop Frye renders the dogma, "that poetry is primarily (i.e. literally) [sic] an ironic structure." As for the troubling aspects of modern literature, most criticism and teaching, most what I have called polemically "administration" of literature, has not felt Professor Trilling's ambivalence, but has rested content in, for instance, Northrop Frye's theory of modes:

If inferior in power or intelligence to ourselves, so that we have the sense of looking down on a scene of bondage, frustration, or absurdity, the hero belongs to the *ironic* mode. This is still true when the reader feels that he is or might be in the same situation, as the situation is being judged by the norms of a greater freedom. . . . During the last hundred years, most serious fiction has tended increasingly to be ironic in mode.

All the irony is comfortably confined within the walls of the work itself. The reader becomes the spectator, the critic the administrator of Bedlam.

There remains one more essential component to the model of the department of English that I have been constructing, and that is the peculiar sport known as Freshman English. The source of its peculiar philosophy can plainly be seen in comparing two documents of the early 1930s by F. R. Leavis. One is an essay, "Mass Civilization and Minority Culture" (1930); the other is a short book, written with Denys Thompson, with a deceptively similar title, *Culture and Environment* (1933). The earlier essay is directly in the tradition of *Culture and Anarchy*. It takes as its epigraph a quotation from *Culture and Anarchy* and maintains other quotations as almost a running commentary in footnotes. Still, there are differences, and those differences are in the direction of a significant retrenchment. Arnold's minority, his "remnant," is defined by its freedom from class-feeling; Leavis' is explicitly a literary minority. More importantly, Arnold's minority is to be aggressive, " 'to make reason and the will of God prevail' "; Leavis' is essentially passive, the bearer of culture and the tradition through the new dark ages:

Upon this minority depends our power of profiting by the finest human experience of the past; they keep alive the subtlest and most perishable parts of tradition. . . . In their keeping . . . is the language, the changing idiom, upon which fine living depends, and without which distinction of spirit is thwarted and incoherent. By "culture" I mean the use of such a language.

It is the other work of the early '30s, *Culture and Environment,* however, that seems to me more important in its actual consequences:

. . . in a world of this kind—and a world that changes so rapidly—it is on literary tradition that the office of maintaining continuity must rest.
    But literary education, we must not forget, is to a great extent a substitute. What we have lost is the organic community with the living culture it embodied. Folk-songs, folk-dances, Cotswold cottages and handicraft products . . .

It is hardly necessary to continue through Leavis' definition, but it is interesting to note that it is not the Arnoldian tradition but the Cobbett, Carlyle, Ruskin (all three of whom Arnold attacks for their failure in disinterestedness) tradition that holds sway here. What is necessary to note is what Leavis proposes:

We cannot, as we might in a healthy state of culture, leave the citizen to be formed unconsciously by his environment; if anything like a worthy idea of satisfactory living is to be saved, he must be trained to discriminate and resist. It is encouraging that in America, where the process of Western civilization has gone furthest, there should have developed such a reaction as Consumers' Research. We need to exemplify the same reaction in the educational field: a critical habit must be systematically inculcated.

The analogy to Consumers' Research is more than just an analogy; it marks again a significant retrenchment. Students are not seen as future citizens (despite the use of the word), as Arnold might have seen them, nor are they seen as future producers, as Cobbett, Carlyle, Ruskin, Morris did see them, but as consumers. Yet, for all that, what Leavis is proposing for education is a radical departure. Literary education is not put forward to broaden students' concerns, nor to transcend the present civilization, but to *"resist."*

Even though these two essays differ in their traditions and their definitions of culture, they are not in fact contradictory. "Mass Civilization and Minority Culture" addresses itself to the study of literature in the University —eighteen years after its publication Leavis includes it as an appendix to his *Education and the University. Culture and Environment* addresses itself, in its resistance to modern civilization, as a text for use in the schools.

In America the situation is different, but the distinction implicit between Leavis' two versions of literary education still applies. The de-socialization he calls for in the schools is in this country the prime function of the freshman year, and the division of labor in most universities and in many colleges gives the freshman year into the hands of graduate students and junior faculty. The particular job of the freshman English instructor, assumed gladly in the case of many of us, has come to be the purely negative job of scouring off the accretions of thirteen years of what Leavis calls "environment." Successfully cleansed, the student might then pass on to the hierophantic (or technophantic) realm of advanced courses in literature. Put another way, what preserved us in our attachment to the idea of culture as the '60s wore on was our particular role in teaching freshmen, or unteaching them. While many of our friends went directly into community organizing or became lawyers to work for civil rights or civil liberties, it was the possible critical nature of the University that held us there. Even when teaching courses catalogued as "Introductions to Literature," we dealt with not only English majors but all the students, and tried to face the large questions that, asked or unasked, always hover in the air of the classroom—"Why do we have to read this stuff?" "What's this guy trying to say?" "Why is D. H. Lawrence better than Ian Fleming?" We had to face, in short, the Benthamite question, "Is it true?" instead of the equally difficult but more comfortable Coleridgean question, "What is the truth in it?"

If Leavis' call for "resistance" seems to mark an important development, it is nevertheless the case that there are varying forms the resistance can take, and varying ways that the "environment" to be resisted can be perceived. By the environment Leavis means, conventionally enough, industrialism:

The machine has brought us many advantages, but it has destroyed the old ways of life, the old forms, and by reason of the continual rapid change it involves, prevented the growth of new. Moreover, the advantage it brings us in mass-production has turned out to involve standardization and levelling-down outside the realm of mere material goods. Those who in school are offered (perhaps) the beginnings of education in taste are exposed, out of school, to the competing exploitation of the cheapest emotional responses; films, newspapers, publicity in all its forms, commercially-catered fiction—all offer satisfaction at the lowest level, and inculcate the choosing of the most immediate pleasures, got with the least effort.

The connections between machine production and mass-culture here are quite tenuous, and the tone has a lot of what Professor Trilling calls the "pathos" of the counter-culture, but it presents accurately enough the suppositions on which a freshman English program of the '50s rested. It suggests, moreover, though the logic is perhaps more habitual than inevitable, the guise in which literature will be introduced. In this scheme, the literary work is the non-factitious, the real article.

Gradually, without any real change in theory, the focus began to shift from an attack on the blandishments of advertising to an attack on the lies of propaganda. Figuring out just what lay behind this shift would take (and is taking) volumes, but it was not entirely Vietnam (one event among many which seems to have passed out of the ken of the sort of people who investigate "youth in revolt," since it came nine years ago, was the U-2 fiasco of 1960). There is no denying, however, that Vietnam provided the focus for the mid-'60s, that the symbolic center of freshman English for many of us became Orwell's "Politics and the English Language," and that the center of that became "Defenceless villages are bombarded from the air, the inhabitants driven out into the countryside, the cattle machine-gunned, the huts set on fire with incendiary bullets: this is called *pacification*." From there it was a slightly longer step to pass students on, or to pass on oneself, to the consolations (or methodology) of literature. Instead, for example, in the early teach-ins one found a surprising number of young English faculty— beyond the expectation of anyone who looked at their specialities and assumed that they were busy with Shakespeare or Milton or Keats.

Even this was not the final stage in the devolution. To suggest what was, one has to approach the matter in a slightly different way. Teaching freshman composition as a "resistance to the environment" demands by its nature a large umbrella of philosophic idealism: a faith that, in brief, style is honesty, perception not data is at the center of thought and writing, that the self creates the world it inhabits, that consciousness can determine existence—Leavis saying, "we are committed to more consciousness; that way, if any, lies salvation." One chance one takes with that position is, as everyone knows, that someone or something will come along like Marx to turn you upside down. The someone or something took different forms: to some it might have been the realization that those who favored the war had no illusions about words like "pacification," that for example the very men running the program in Vietnam called "Winning Hearts and Minds" could with cheery cynicism refer to it as "WHAM." Consciousness is not enough.

To many of us the realization appeared in the outlandish costume of a Selective Service memo titled "Channelling Manpower" which first saw the light in the spring of 1967: "The psychology of granting wider choice under pressure to take action is the American, or indirect way, of achieving what is done by direction in foreign countries where choice is not permitted." The document was not blandishments, or lies, but policy and power to enforce it. How could we free our students, or ourselves, by showing them the "object as it really is"?—this was the object as it really is.

It was, what seemed worse from our standpoint affirming the life of the mind, psychological (like the man says) control, even, one might say, actuarial control, supremely disinterested as long as the percentages in engineering, teaching, and soldiering came out right. It was this document that crystallized our feelings, that took us that crucial step to believe that the draft (and in widening ripples Vietnam, racism, perhaps the whole drift of the '50s and '60s) was not just an aberration or the stupidity of inadequate men in office, but an aberration being institutionalized. From there our 2-S or 2-A deferments seemed like the outer sign of our inner acquiescence, a successful bureaucratic control that wasn't anything like red tape or forms in triplicate. Seeing this, and ourselves, we had to join "monster-Processions in the streets and forcible irruptions into the parks," and, if we had enough courage, to turn back draft cards or at least support those who did. Had to join, not out of pacifism which is still the faith of scattered saints, but to try, with all the quixoticism that it implies, to free ourselves. If this is what Arnold meant by "anarchy," if this is what "culture is the resolute enemy of," well then, a new definition of culture would have to be found.

III

These reflections are not meant to reduce the teaching of English to one pattern. Of course there were and are freshman English programs taught out of a handbook of standard usage and a brand-new book of essays with the "issues of today" plugged into the same old ideas. Of course there were and are, on the other hand, courses in literature taught with a vivacity and intelligence neither hierophantic nor technophantic, including many that take no stand at all on the value of culture, but assume only that a human being might spend a certain number of hours reading and discussing Milton or Keats. These exceptions on either side may even describe the largest part of the field of literary education, at least undergraduate.

Even a presumed preponderance of these courses does not in itself invalidate what I have suggested as the ethos of the department of English, its public, Arnoldian stance. I have tried to explain how rereading Arnold against the events of the past few years has suggested a kind of revisionist interpretation of Arnoldian culture; that it involved more than a liberal humanism which could substitute for a dying religion.

In sum, Arnold's politics called for repression in the name of a prospective bureaucratic state that has been largely realized in a way that Arnold could not have foreseen, and whose realization has changed for many people the connotations of Arnold's word "anarchy."

Arnold's politics and his culture are not unrelated; they are connected by ideas of centralization and control.

The mainstream of modern critical interpretation of literature, though it would claim for itself an objective, scientific basis, can be reasonably seen as the development of what is only implied in Arnold, the administration of literature.[6]

The teaching of freshman composition as a resistance to the environment derives in large measure from a non-Arnoldian, non-disinterested tradition, and is useful, even radical, in tendency, but it depends on the supposition that the "environment" is factitious and can, like advertising or propaganda, be nullified by pure consciousness.

From here it would be pleasant to conclude that those of us who are, let me say for short, junior faculty are in a good position to evolve a replacement for *Culture and Anarchy*, to find new ways to define the function of criticism at *this* time, but I am not so sure. The process of de-conversion is too dislocating, too apt to drift into a yearning for apocalypse. In his essay on Columbia, "The Unliberated University," Eric Bentley mentions in passing that, when he heard mutterings of the "let it be burned to the ground, destroyed utterly" variety, they were likely to be coming not from SDS or Harlem but from those of us who were white and older. I know that he is right—I may even have been one he heard.

A sober student of democracy, reading this passage from "Channelling":

Delivery of manpower for induction, the process of providing a few thousand men with transportation to a reception center, is not much of an administrative or financial challenge. It is in dealing with the other millions of registrants that the System is heavily occupied, developing more effective human beings in the national interest.

might reasonably conclude that this is bureaucratic totalitarianism (if they have the power they claim) and that the Selective Service System ought to be dismembered. If he were then shown the pamphlet on education I have cited, if it were explained to him who John Gardner, Henry Kissinger, Theodore Hesburgh, and Fred Hechinger were and what they represented and nevertheless how closely, though in more careful language, their pamphlet paralleled the Selective Service one, viz.:

And if [education] is to have vitality both teachers and students must be infused with the values which have shaped the system.

We would not wish to impose upon students a rigidly defined set of values. Each student is free to vary the nature of his commitment. But this freedom must be understood in its true light. . . .

In short, we will wish to allow wide latitude in the choice of values, but we must

---

[6] An interesting partial corroboration of the claims by modern criticism arises from the fact that Arnold's word "disinterested" needs a gloss for the modern student. Professor Trilling accurately gives "impartial," and uses the analogy of, perhaps significantly, a labor arbitrator. The widely used *Norton Anthology of English Literature*, edited by the top names in the critical establishment, gives the misleading and quasi-scientific "objectivity of mind."

assume that education is a process that should be infused with meaning and purpose; that everyone will have deeply held beliefs; that every young American will wish to serve the values which have nurtured him and made possible his education and his freedom as an individual.

reading this, he might still have a question in his mind: Do these doctrines really control education (as "channelling" undeniably has controlled Selective Service policy), or is this just an ordinary public document of the Cold War '50s? Asking *that* question involves one not in revelation but in research: How prevalent did "tracking" become? How are funds allocated to the different tracks? To what extent did high school counselors discourage which students from applying, and how far did the colleges approve? Or, more difficult to answer, to what extent was education turned into propaganda "infusing" students "with the values that have shaped the system"? (How many copies sold to how many schoolboards of J. Edgar Hoover's *Masters of Deceit*?) After these questions, he might conclude that a system considerably more comprehensive than the Selective Service one has traveled far in the same direction.

Our confrontation with the memo on "channelling" was not in sober contemplation, however, and hardly with questions. Instead, we confronted it in a combination of rage, humiliation, and guilt, because we knew everything it said already. The revelation consisted in the discovery that we were implicated: we had not been beating the system, we had been playing the game.

It is not only in guilty nihilism that this yearning expresses itself—there is also a streak of masochism: real, pointless courting of nightsticks, and Mario Savio saying that there comes a time when one must put his body into the machine, when any assembly-line worker could have told him that a monkey-wrench is the traditional device. (And to complete the triad, there is, it seems to me, in some people who are shaken but cannot bring themselves to join, a tinge of sadism: at Columbia they would say that the students' grievances were just, that their tactics may have been necessary, but why won't they take their punishment gladly, the way Martin Luther King used to—as if King had demanded punishment, instead of submitting to the beatings and jailings perforce.)

These are crude pigeonholes, I'm afraid, but what is common to them is the projection of one's inner unregenerate self (formed in another country and long ago) onto the social screen. In an early and relatively benign version it can be seen in the chasm that separates the last from the next-to-last sentence in James Baldwin's *The Fire Next Time*:

If we—and now I mean the relatively conscious whites and the relatively conscious blacks, who must, like lovers, insist on, or create, the consciousness of the others—do not falter in our duty now, we may be able, handful that we are, to end the racial nightmare, and achieve our country, and change the history of the world. If we do not now dare everything, the fulfillment of that prophecy, recreated from the Bible in song by a slave, is upon us: "God gave Noah the rainbow sign, No more water, the fire next time!"

It is not just that Baldwin has no program except "consciousness"; it is the converse—he has no way to describe what will come, only the myth and finality of apocalypse. Compared on the one hand to the resolutely private voice of his own "Notes of a Native Son" and on the other to, say, the public voice of Malcolm X, it is a melange inferior to both.

In the face of the escalating mayhem of this year, it sounds foolish to claim that there is less of this yearning for apocalypse among the current college generation than there is in us, but I think it is true. Not less damage, or less violence, but less apocalypse, less nihilism. Jerry Rubin is thirty-one, and Mark Rudd is twenty-one, and anyone who cannot hear the difference between them isn't listening. Rubin talks apocalypse, and talks it incessantly (Sol Yurick, commenting on the media-assisted predominance of the Yippies —whose leaders are all pushing thirty—refers to the post-Chicago period as the "year of the heroic loudmouth"). In style, Mark Rudd is a reasonably authentic model of a populist, and populists don't talk apocalypse (when he says "bullshit," it sounds almost bucolic). And, more important, there are groups who strike no cultural pose at all, who work hard organizing outside the university, who do research. (Ironically enough, it is these people, and they are not necessarily associated with progressive labor, who would be likely to agree with Professor Trilling that we must go beyond culture to philosophy. Of course, they would say, Hegel, Marx, Lenin, Mao . . .)

Not necessarily less violence, so one cannot expect those who affirm the University as The Sanctuary of Academic Freedom to care much about these distinctions. But for us, who came late, who fell backward one might say into our participation in "monster-Processions" and "forcible irruptions," yet who still believe that literature has a public value, the distinctions need to be kept in mind. If the direction Arnold set for culture, toward centralization, control, and administration, has been precisely what has made literature seem unusable in fighting those tendencies in society, we still need to rid ourselves of the reaction into pseudo-literary apocalypse in order to do some thinking. What we need, beyond a critique of the way literature has been taught, is an idea of culture we can use and a criticism that can reopen the experience that reading a book can be.

THE EXPANDING HUMANITIES AND
THE INDIVIDUAL SCHOLAR [1]

Walter J. Ong, S.J.

A common assumption about the humanities used to be that they were always the same: both their subject matter and the ways of studying them were invariable. "The proper study of mankind is man" was an evident enough truth, and when one got down to the study, one found oneself at best working over again "what oft was thought but ne'er so well express'd."

Such an assumption of utter changelessness in the humanities, however, hardly lingers in informed circles today. In the sector of the humanities of most interest to the Modern Language Association, that concerned with verbal performance, most members of the Association would probably admit that matters are no longer what they were in the time of Alexander Pope. But what would they say if someone were to ask whether there has been a knowledge explosion in the humanities?

KNOWLEDGE EXPLOSION

We should be able to take for granted that everyone knows there has been a knowledge explosion in the humanities which matches, if it does not indeed surpass, that in the sciences. If we cannot take such knowledge for granted, humanists themselves are partly to blame for shying away from their new responsibilities and taking refuge in persecution complexes. But they are not entirely to blame. Knowledge in the humanities has low visibility. The results of the science explosion are, many of them, highly noticeable: radio programs and rocket ships, penicillin and computers. A new insight into intellectual history or a brilliant study in literary criticism has little to package or to broadcast and no hardware to show.

Nevertheless, all we need do to become aware of the humanities knowledge explosion is to glance around and take a little thought. We can glance for example at the 18,852 items in the "1965 MLA International Bibliography of Books and Articles on the Modern Languages and Literatures" in the May 1966 issue of *PMLA*—a limited as well as selective bibliography, we must remind ourselves, restricting itself to Western European languages and literatures with some perfunctory attention to Eastern European, and thus designedly excluding a good many of the most widespread languages and literatures in the world.

THE EXPANDING HUMANITIES AND THE INDIVIDUAL SCHOLAR Reprinted by permission of the Modern Language Association of America from *PMLA*, Vol. 82 (September 1967).

[1] An address delivered at the Plenary Meeting of the MLA Standing Committees in New York. 30 March 1967.

A total of 18,852 books and articles is pretty sizable. We could, of course, at some risk of being cavalier, discount the value of a great many of these studies (remembering always that the bibliographers have excluded countless items of minor significance). But even after a large discount, we must face the question, how much of the knowledge purveyed in the thousands of remaining studies was at all available in 1865? Simply fingering through this bibliography at random turns up items such as George A. Miller and Noam Chomsky on "Finitary Models of Language Users" (No. 679), R. A. Ranald on the degrees of myth in William Faulkner's South (No. 7550—consider the difference between what 1865 and 1965 make of myth), Norman T. Pratt's analysis of relationships between Lear and Oedipus (No. 4150—consider the difference between what 1865 and 1965 make of Oedipus), James J. Murphy on rhetoric in fourteenth-century Oxford (No. 1799—consider what was known of the history of rhetoric in 1865 and what in 1965), and David and Kay Henry on classificatory verbs in the language of the Koyukon Indian tribe (No. 339—ask yourself how many languages had been scientifically described in 1865). These and thousands of other studies like them employ material and techniques and insights which have been made accessible only in the past few decades.

It is true that an increment of such material may not at all indicate a growth in wisdom. But the increment makes wisdom an even more urgent need than before. We cannot abolish the accumulation of knowledge. We are going to have to live with it and face all its implications. The fact is that the number of languages, literatures, and oral traditions accessible to study, the light which these languages, literatures and traditions cast on one another, the emergence of modern linguistics, the introduction of anthropological and psychological insights, and countless other new accumulations of knowledge and new fronts of awareness have made earlier language and literature study in many ways primitive if not obsolete. And in the humanities obsolescence itself does not reduce but adds to the knowledge explosion. For the humanities do best when they carry their past resolutely and sensitively with them, ruminating over it and converting its obsolescence into new relevance—as, for example, Noam Chomsky is undertaking to do with hitherto obsolete approaches to literature and language.[2]

Language and literature studies are not alone in this involuted richness. A comparable state of affairs exists in virtually every humanistic field. An obvious example is history, where instead of a small segment of mankind one must now study the entire human race and where the important but relatively superficial details of military and political history are being woven into a much higher-pile fabric, the history of the development of the human psyche through the evolution of cultures and of their knowledge-and-communication systems. Other complexities exist in sociology and anthropology, which were hardly even known as special subjects a century ago; in psychology, which has been so transformed in the past two centuries as to be virtually a new field or fields of knowledge; in philosophy, where existential-

[2] See Chomsky's recent *Cartesian Linguistics: A Chapter in the History of Rationalist Thought* (New York: Harper and Row, 1966).

ism and personalism (both relatively new) and linguistic analysis (relatively old, but refurbished a bit) have given new contours to thought; in theology, where the ferment, in Christian circles at least, has never been more active and where still more activity promises as the frontiers between theological and other thinking continue to expand; and so on indefinitely. The size of this knowledge explosion in the humanities dizzies us, and it dizzies us even more if we add in, as we quite legitimately can, the sciences themselves. For all of these, too, have their humanistic significance. They emerge from the human life world and have a history. The history of scientific thought and technological inventions, pursued in depth and detail, is as humanistic as anything one can conceive of, for it reflects the structuring and restructuring of man's relationship to his life world in a way which closely parallels and interacts with that of art and literature.

What can the individual scholar do about this situation? The first thing of course is to acknowledge it, not run away from it and pretend that the humanities are being neglected. If they are neglected, how did all this come about? An enterprise which is in fact as active and creative as is that in which we are engaged does no one any service if it projects an image of itself which falsely minimizes its achievements. It is true that not everything is succeeding in humanistic studies generally or in literary studies in particular. But nothing succeeds like success, and to secure the personnel and financial wherewithal for doing better we need to let the community at large know what a massive enterprise humanistic scholarship now is—what its achievements and its promise are as well as its needs.

The knowledge explosion in the humanities is perhaps best brought home to the general public by reference to quantity and variety in research, such as the foregoing recitation details. The explosion, however, in fact involves much more than this, for it involves a new kind of sophistication entailed in our present-day historical sense. Because we have access to so much historical fact, today we know a good deal about changes within the humanities which were not apparent to those in any age much before our own and which the individual scholar must constantly reflect on. Without pretending to exhaustive completeness here, we can consider some of these changes as they affect Modern Language Association interests, grouping them under three heads, namely, the changing cultural relevance of literature, the corresponding changes called for in education, and the shift producing what I have elsewhere styled a sense of "synchronic present." [3] I shall take these up in order.

1. *Cultural relevance.* We should be quite aware by now that imaginative verbal performance—poetry, let us say, in the large sense—does not fill exactly the same role in all cultures or in the same culture at different stages of its development. The work of Albert B. Lord, Eric Havelock,[4] and others has shown, for example, how poetry in oral or nonchirographic cultures

---

[3] Walter J. Ong, *In the Human Grain* (New York: Macmillan, 1967), pp. 17–41.
[4] Albert B. Lord, *The Singer of Tales* (Harvard Studies in Comparative Literature, 24; Cambridge, Mass.: Harvard University Press, 1960); Eric A. Havelock, *Preface to Plato* (Cambridge, Mass.: Belknap Press of Harvard University Press, 1963).

serves a much wider spectrum of purposes than those it serves when a culture takes up the use of writing. In oral cultures, the singing of the bard was simultaneously a narration, a social event, a musical concert, a patriotic celebration, and a course in history, sociology, civics, demography (the list of the ships in the *Iliad* ii.494–875 serves purposes like those of a city directory), cosmology, and various skills such as shipbuilding (the maximum verbalization concerning shipbuilding, the closest thing to a shipbuilding manual of which Homer's Greece was capable, is the sort of thing found in the *Odyssey* v.225–261).

The history of the epic, we are now finding, is intimately connected with the changing fortunes of oral elements in verbalization and in thought itself. We have long known that with writing the epic becomes a different thing. Now we know that a basic reason why it does so is because writing affects the storage and retrieval of knowledge and thus relieves the oral epic of one of its major functions. Later print, too, radically affects knowledge storage and retrieval, and epic enters into still another stage. By Milton's age the relationship of epic poetry to man's life world or his total culture was radically different from that in the ninth century B.C. Now epic was supported in a slowly dissolving Latin matrix and was highly academic in a roundabout way, still residually oratorical, but more consciously programmatic and didactic and remote than before, though, for all that, none the less gorgeous.

The transformation of the epic is matched by similar transformations in other genres, some of which, such as letters, come into being with writing, others, such as tightly plotted long prose narratives, with print, still others, such as nonplotted or deplotted narratives, with our electronic world. What is changing here, we have became increasingly aware, is not merely a literary form but a whole culture and indeed (what comes to the same thing) the personality structures of those who make up the culture.

We are only beginning to understand the restructuring of the psyche entailed or implied in these shifts in the functions of poetry. But we do not have to have much experience to know that the successful teaching of literature depends on having a sense of what the psychological structures are today. This sense of difference does not separate us from the past but rather ties us to it, for it makes the past intelligible. If we have this sense, and some scholarly knowledge of the differences between ourselves and the past, there is nothing more fascinating for a class, undergraduate as well as graduate, than the literature of the past unless it is the literature of the past and the present taken together.

2. *Educational significance of verbal performance.* As the place of imaginative verbal performance evolves with the evolution of cultures, so, too, the way in which verbal performance is utilized in education likewise changes. We are becoming somewhat more aware of this, but perhaps not enough. Before the advent of writing, there was no study of literature or of anything else. Troglodytes were Deweyites. They learned by doing. Writing changed all this, as Havelock has shown in his *Preface to Plato*, but with glacial slowness, so that rhetoric (which is to say the study of oratory) remained in

effective academic charge of literature from antiquity through the eighteenth century to a degree which today even a scholar can hardly believe. Ideas of literature, moreover, were confused by the academic ascendancy of Latin, the symbol of rhetorical culture which had itself paradoxically become a chirographically controlled language whose study, as I have attempted to show elsewhere,[5] constituted a puberty rite. We have never fully enough reflected upon this state of affairs out of which the study of modern vernacular languages and literatures emerged. In our postromantic bisexual academic setting, puberty rites are no longer what they used to be: certainly some of our younger citizens of university age show few external signs of having been through them. Little wonder that they do not think of literature the way Coleridge or Matthew Arnold did.

We sense the differences. But do we understand them? William Riley Parker has started us on our way with his sensitive summary of certain relevant facts in his article on "Where Do English Departments Come From?" [6] But the causes and nature of the changes need still more study in depth.

If we are more fully aware of the resemblances and differences between past and present and thus of the changing roles which verbalization must play as cultures and psychological structures change, we will not be entirely petrified by the complex interaction today between literature proper and other forms of communication, notably the other mass media of movies, radio, and television—I say "other mass media" because print is already a mass medium, as for that matter spoken language itself is once a single language comes to be spoken by millions. One meets all too often with the hold-the-line mentality in the teaching of the written word. What is television doing to literature? The problem posed by a post-Homeric Greek would be: What is all this writing doing to our poetry? Pretty soon our children will even stop talking and simply pass letters to one another. And then where will we be? However, the children did not stop talking. But the writing did change poetry drastically, as we now know. In the sequence of the verbal media, a new medium does not cancel out an earlier medium but interacts with it. Writing changed poetry drastically, but it did not wipe out the oral medium. It is probable enough that after the invention of writing people talked more than ever: they certainly concentrated more in urban centers where talking was perhaps more likely. It is equally certain today that the new oral electronic media of radio and television are not going to wipe out the ability to write. Improved fountain pens are being developed, and there is even some hope for reliable ballpoints. And typography is moving ahead like any other technology, faster than before. But just as the style of speaking changed after the invention of writing—slowly but inevitably it became less formulaic, sparer, more analytic—so the style of literature is changing by interaction with the new media. We need to find out what the changes are in order to do our work better.

[5] Walter J. Ong, *The Barbarian Within* (New York: Macmillan, 1962), pp. 211–216.
[6] *College English*, XXVIII (1967), 339–351.

3. *Synchronic present.* Our accumulation of knowledge in the humanities has not been simply a linear development. That is to say, accumulation is not merely additive, with new facts piled on old. The humanities have always to do with the present in that they afford man his access to his own life world. As Alphonse de Waelhens has so aptly put it, the problem of the humanities is that of man in his present facing his past and his future.[7] But the past is not simply strung out as a line behind us. It enters into us, and it turns us in on ourselves and makes us face the future, which is inside us in a more real sense than it is "ahead" of us on some metaphoric chronological "road."

Our present age is the first age of mankind which has embarked on a serious academic study of itself. Generally speaking, earlier ages studied either abstract sciences or the wisdom of the past as such. Only recently have universities offered courses in contemporary history, contemporary civilization, or contemporary literature, to which have been added now new courses whose subject matter is expressly the future, such as courses concerned with urban problems or economic growth.

To superficial thinkers, this concentration on the present indicates that we are out of contact with the past. The fact is that concentration on the present is possible only because of a contact with the past which is richer than any other age has known. A few generations ago man was looking back over a few thousand years to what he thought was the beginning of the universe. Now we locate its beginning at five to ten billion years ago, and our knowledge of scores of cultures traces each back, in varying amount of detail, over thousands or even tens of thousands of years. Most of the knowledge of the past on our library shelves has accumulated in the last three or four generations.

Once one knows this much about the past, the present takes on a face of its own. It is both like and different from its antecedents. We study it circumstantially in terms of its likenesses and differences, tracing in today's United States culture, for example, romantic influences, rationalist and deistic influences, Renaissance, medieval scholastic, Augustinian, classical, and Hebrew influences all the way back to the elusive American Adam himself. Because he had not our kind of access to the depths of his past, Aristotle was quite unable to do this for the Greece of his day, although he made a brave little attempt at the beginning of his *Metaphysics.* We want to know where we came from in order to know where we are and, so far as possible, to plan where we are going.

The result of our penetration of the past is that our present is synchronic at least in the sense that it catches up all past time into itself. It is, we might put it, historically synchronic. But it is also synchronic in another way— geographically, we might say. In the past, geographic distance fragmented man's sense of the present. When news could travel only thirty miles a day, an event three hundred miles away had its impact in man's consciousness when it was ten days old. Events half way around the globe often had no impact for years. Today events that happen at a given moment are syn-

---

[7] *Existence et signification* (Louvain: Nauwelaerts, 1958), p. 143.

chronic not only in the external world but, more and more, within man's consciousness as well. Gertrude Stein once said that there is one thing everybody is and that is contemporary. But contemporaniety made less difference in the past, when, no matter how much you believed in the simultaneity of your actions with myriads of other events, your experience of simultaneity was pretty well limited to your unaided sensory fields. Simultaneity was bounded by the horizon. Today we are overwhelmed with simultaneity and contemporaneity in our communications media, which short-circuit the rest of the world into our ears every quarter hour.

Our synchronic sense of the present has implications for the individual scholar which as yet we have not faced with sufficient reflection. Its most massive effect is the demand it creates for relevance. A demand for the "real" is always part of the humanities—the great age of humanism in the Renaissance grew out of a conviction that the curriculum was out of touch with man's "real" life world. But never has the demand been more insistent than it is today. More than ever before, the humanist is expected to show the relevance of his work, even when it is concerned with the distant past or with the most arcane minutiae.

The individual scholar in the humanities can get a hearing from the public today more readily than it is fashionable to profess in some learned circles. First of all, no one is campaigning against the humanities. In the ideal order, the cause of the humanities is as incontestable as motherhood. And in the practical order, the humanities as such have in our day at long last commanded direct support from the national government. Although we can regret that full funding of the National Endowment for the Humanities has not yet been accomplished, it is heartening to reflect on the general friendliness with which this new instrument of national policy and the associated National Endowment for the Arts have been received.

When we look to the popular media, although it goes against the accepted mythology to say so, it appears to me that never has society in general been more willing to accord some relevance to almost any kind of cultural pursuit. Magazines for which we might even use Dwight Macdonald's designation "midcult" and which Walker Gibson might class variously as "tough" or "sweet" or "stuffy" [8] have built their circulation in part on this willingness. Such magazines and the slick weekly magazines as well are now doing features which capitalize on the rather widespread persuasion that there must be something of intense human value even in the most bemused intellectual boondoggling.

Humanistic scholarship is not intellectual boondoggling, and it is hardly at its best when it relies on journalistic sensationalism. But we should know how or learn how to make the most of public expectancy. If public opinion is at all disposed to see the humanities as relevant in a variety of ways to modern education and culture, scholars, individually and corporately, should see to it that they are as relevant as possible. One of the most effective means of

---

[8] Walker Gibson, *Tough, Sweet, and Stuffy: An Essay on Modern American Prose Styles* (Bloomington and London: Indiana University Press, 1966).

doing this is to keep the various stages in the educational process in contact with one another, relating the elementary and secondary and higher educational efforts as much as they allow. We can learn here from the scientists who have to an impressive degree succeeded in remodeling mathematics, physics, and chemistry through increased contacts between elementary, secondary, and university personnel. The problem of the humanities is not entirely the same, but it is similar. The 1965 Tufts Seminar to Initiate New Experiments in Undergraduate Instruction found it could not realistically think of undergraduate instruction in the humanities in isolation from graduate instruction on the one hand and elementary and secondary instruction on the other. One of the sequels of the Seminar, the Voice Project at Stanford University under the direction of John Hawkes and Albert Guérard, has both faculty and students in freshman English working with grade school children in the process of improving techniques for teaching freshman English writing in the university.

TECHNOLOGY AND HUMANISM

The problem for individual scholars today in the humanities is not a dearth of material and interest but a surfeit. If we face this fact, we can better develop or strengthen productive attitudes toward the tools which present-day technology has provided for handling masses of material, for we will be aware that we need all the technological helps we can find. We will welcome the computer, for example, which has been invented by present-day man because his unbearable accumulation of knowledge demands this new instrument for storage and retrieval. The more of our grub-work we can push onto the computer, the better. The computer will of course not only lighten but also add to our work. Inventions always do. An instrument devised to serve one more or less explicitly conceived purpose inevitably begins to generate and serve purposes for which it was not consciously contrived. The computer has opened whole new fields of humanistic research—in the study of stylistics, for example, and in lexical organization—which we can welcome, just as the early Renaissance humanists welcomed the great technological invention of their age, the printing press, a lumbering, depersonalizing, grimy, mechanical contrivance, a mammoth artificiality, which made possible modern textual study and all that has come out of it, as well as whole new literary genres such as the novel itself. (Imagine *Finnegans Wake* in a purely scribal culture.) If we can regard the computer as a friend, we should be able to welcome also the use of mathematical and statistical theory, indispensable tools in handling the scholarly and educational problems with which we are faced in the teaching of language and, perhaps to a lesser degree, of literature.

Of course, individual scholars have thousands of problems which technological and statistical methods cannot solve at all. And the computer can become a distraction. The machine is there, and all sorts of useless investigations can be undertaken—and beyond a doubt are already being undertaken—simply because they are mechanically feasible. This, however, is nothing new. Think of all the useless matter put into print over the past five centuries simply because the presses were available. Or, for that matter, of all the idle words flapping around Chaucer's *House of Fame* or Socrates' Athens simply because man could talk.

PRESENT, PAST, AND FUTURE

The pursuit of the humanities is central to the reflectiveness whereby man lays hold on himself in his own history. It is thus an ongoing enterprise, never quite the same in a given age as it was in earlier ages, and yet in its development not at all freakish but continuous and patterned in ways which give rise to always further reflection. As study of the humanities develops, it plunges man farther and father back into his past and at the same time concentrates his knowledge of the past more intensely on his present and forces him to plan for the future. We live today in an age more history-conscious, more self-conscious, and more future-conscious than any previous age of man.

This situation has its rewards but it also has its dangers. The relationships here are dialectical. The past is always approached through questions generated in the present—there is simply no other way to approach it. But to secure worthwhile answers to these same questions we must study the past not as a reflection of the present but on its own terms. This means that we must have serious scholars with the skills and knowledge affording direct contact with the past. There is, I believe, no small danger today that the fruitful relationship of past and present may be disturbed by our failure to foster the skills needed to maintain and develop contact with the past and thus with the present and future—skills needed not to a lesser degree than hitherto but to a greater degree, if only because our humanistic knowledge is expanding on all sides so rapidly.

Probably no studies can live off their own capital. Humanistic studies certainly cannot. We must have continuously new capital if we are to survive. This can be created only in the minds of individual men and women who have the power and the tools and the sensitivity to reinterpret man and his life world once again. For each age must deal afresh with the past. The truer each earlier interpretation has been, the more it has laid the ground for further investigation and understanding in the years to come.

This means that to carry forward our understanding we must make a supreme effort in our elementary, secondary, and higher educational institutions to attract first-rate minds to humanistic studies, and not merely in the colleges and universities but as far as possible very early, in secondary and even elementary schools, when they have the time to build the needed skills —to lay the foundations for mastery of ancient and modern foreign languages, the knowledge of linguistics, literary history, psychology, cultural history of all sorts, including intellectual, philosophical, and religious, which the humanities require. There is danger, it seems to me, that in our necessary focus on the present and the past-in-the-present, on scholarship which is not merely antiquarian but truly relevant, we may lose sight of the fact that relevance is hard to come by, that in the last analysis it demands true learning, that is to say, it demands individual scholars of high intelligence who are truly sensitive because they are equipped with the hard-nosed, demanding skills which imaginative creative learning has always needed and needs now more than ever before.

WHAT WILL BECOME OF THE PAST?

G. Jon Roush

The humanities are not a group of "subjects" or "fields of study." They are a group of disciplines—if by "disciplines" one means a mode of investigating, judging, and acting. It is notoriously difficult to say what those disciplines have in common, but they share at least the task of connecting the past and present as they are manifested in the works and acts of men. As one who preserves the past and continually invigorates it for his contemporaries, the humanist is above all else a teacher, and the problems of humanism are invariably problems of education as well. The objective of a humanistic education is competence in the judgment of human creations, with that judgment informed by an awareness of pertinent historical contexts. It is, however, becoming increasingly difficult to achieve that objective for two reasons. First, the problem of obsolescence is impinging on the humanities in some special ways, and conventional humanistic pedagogy is not designed to meet that problem. Second, it is likely that our man-made environment is the most significant human creation of all time, in that it has the most immediate effect on men's lives and souls, and yet the traditional humanistic education provides little guidance for anyone who would evaluate that complex, changing environment.

The problem of obsolescence and the problem of dealing with our present environment both pose questions about the contemporary relevance of the past and of history itself. It is important that we understand what is at issue. The question is not whether we can still profitably read *The Oresteia* or *Il Principe*; the question is whether we owe them the automatic allegiance due to forebears or whether we are somebody else's children. As a teacher of medieval literature, I would insist that the study of Chaucer is its own reward, that *Troilus and Criseyde* is immediately relevant to anyone who understands it. As a humanist, however, I do not find that argument so easy to make. As a humanist, I should be able to assert, at the very least, a connection between *Troilus and Criseyde* and the present state of the art of verbal expression. I should be able to describe a pertinent tradition, and I should

WHAT WILL BECOME OF THE PAST? Reprinted by permission from *Daedalus*, Journal of the American Academy of Arts and Sciences, Boston, Massachusetts, Volume 98, Number 3.

be able to educate students who will understand that tradition and continue to find it pertinent for the next fifty years. I should be able to assert that in order to understand how we have arrived here, it is *important* to read *Troilus and Criseyde*. To defend that assertion requires new thought about the uses of humanistic learning, for although we know more about the past than we ever have before, we find it harder than ever to say why it is worth the bother. The humanities deal with traditions that are considered intrinsically valuable, because they comprise objects, ideas, and events that embody characteristic and valuable perceptions of human life; yet those traditions do not seem so pertinent as they once did.

The difficulty is revealed clearly in undergraduate education in the humanistic disciplines, which is rarely based on any cogent idea of tradition. Nor is that surprising when one considers that the culture that the conventional course in the humanities "transmits" is in many ways not the one that the students have actually inherited. The problem is not simply that most of the students are being introduced to most of the materials for the first time. The real problem is that the typical curriculum in the humanities, no matter what its official rationale may be, has as its organizing objective the presentation of objects with which "any educated man should be familiar." It is intended as an initiation into the living mysteries, and perhaps it really worked that way when the humanities were the province of an elite, self-conscious class. For most undergraduates now, however, the house of the humanities seems not a sacred temple but a museum. In the anthropological sense of "culture" as a shared set of values, customs, and symbols, the artifacts in the humanities museum come from a culture radically foreign to the one in which the students have been reared and to which most of them are destined to return. That is why the museum had to be built in the first place.

But the teacher still sees the temple, and his role is not only curator but missionary. The teacher in the humanities often finds himself in the position of correcting the errors in his students' culture, and so like other missionaries he behaves toward his charges with a condescension born of frustration. Meanwhile the students, like natives the world over, repeat their catechisms until sundown, after which they are free to go off to their native rites. In short, modern courses in the humanities are usually remedial in intent, even at advanced levels, but the odds against their success are high.

Any undergraduate instructor in the humanities realizes his foreignness and usually takes some pride in it. He has two arguments to explain and justify it. First, the culture that he represents is in some significant sense better than the culture of the typical American. This argument assumes a goodness not culturally determined but intrinsic to objects themselves, so that the degree of goodness in objects from different cultures can be compared. To read Milton or Dante is more rewarding than to read the works of any living author. In fact, he argues that the artifacts of the humanities culture, because of their greater truthfulness or beauty, are actually more relevant to the essential life of the students than is most of contemporary culture—*The Reader's Digest,* United Artists, and Hugh Hefner all lumped together. The second argument runs as follows: The humanities culture is the historical antecedent of the students' culture, and consequently its foreignness is illusory. In this argument, the objects gain their significance from their importance in The History of Western Civilization, and an understanding of them is necessary for any understanding of this age.

These arguments fail, however, because students usually have the good sense not to be taken in by them. They both rely on three common assumptions: the assumption of identifiable and permanent standards and values, the assumption that those values reside in or are exemplified by specific objects, and the assumption of a continuous, sacrosanct past. Those assumptions have been always debatable and often debated, but today they are being challenged with special force. That challenge is one of the chief differences between earlier cultures and this one—the culture that has nourished our students and, to a lesser degree, us. Those three assumptions, which worked so well for Matthew Arnold, have been called into question by a number of changes that seem to have separated us irrevocably from Arnold. The most important of those changes is the growth of a worldwide and culturally pervasive technology, with its attendant democratization of education and power. Traditionally the *studia humanitatis* have been the concern of a select group within the society. It was possible to maintain that situation until after World War I and to pretend to maintain it until after World War II, but the situation has changed with the expansion of education and leisure. In the past, the values of the many seemed inimical to the best judgment of the few in matters intellectual and artistic. We have now assumed responsibility for democratizing that judgment, and it seems unlikely that we can do so without changing the nature of the values.

Apparently one of the changes in values which is ensuing is the acceptance of technology's commitment to change. The idea of progress by revolution and invention has led to the acceptance of the idea of the irrelevance of the past, at least the past that preceded the latest quantum jump. Like the scientific jumps, the artistic jumps seem to be coming closer and closer together, and it is difficult to disagree with Marshall McLuhan's argument that the culture of the present will look more and more like a throw-away culture, without past and without future.

Like culture, man himself has come to be viewed in many ways as an ahistorical phenomenon, although the humanities generally have not been able to cope with this view. Certain disciplines that are essential to a contemporary definition of man—psychology, anthropology, biology, sociology —all offer ways to study man outside his historical setting and all are normally excluded from humanistic curricula. Even when they offer tools for objective historical research and for objective statements about change itself, these disciplines seem to render irrelevant the older historical myths in which the past is a guide to the present. The mythic theme that until recently justified the work of artists and historians is the theme of regeneration, in which the past dies to live again in the present:

> For out of olde feldes, as men seyth,
> Cometh al this newe corn from yer to yere,
> And out of olde bokes, in good feyth,
> Cometh all this newe science that men lere.[1]

In the new studies of man, however, understanding comes not from old books, but from "the data," the here and now.

Moreover, even in the disciplines that are recognized as humanistic, the old certainties about the nature of our past seem increasingly insubstantial as we turn to new sources and create new traditions. Not for centuries have Westerners looked to Asia and Africa for artistic and moral guidance as they now are beginning to. The two generations that produced men like Pablo Picasso, Henry Moore, Ezra Pound, Martin Buber, and Carl Jung have spelled an end to the self-sufficiency of the Greco-Roman tradition. Whatever will replace it will not be so neatly linear as that tradition was once thought to be.

Each of these changes in its own way enforces a new relativism, a sense that values emanate from the perceiver and that each man carries the burden of constructing his own past. Thus each of them contributes to the invalidation of the conventional assumptions justifying the humanities. They do not make the works of the past meaningless or uninteresting; but they do call into question their historical and cultural relevance, the assumption that specific objects exemplify permanent standards that taken together form a continuous tradition behind us.

To understand fully the difficulties that this relativism creates for the humanist-teacher, it is necessary to understand the difficulties that it creates for the humanist-scholar. For the man who accommodates to these changes, it would be easier to describe the structure of something like an event or a society or a language than to evaluate its substance. He could see significant analogies between prehistoric Greece and modern Tibet, between television and communications within African tribes; but he would find it harder to evaluate Greek justice or television drama. Being unwilling to ascribe any certainty to the values of his own age, he would be free to appreciate archaic art in its own terms, but would have difficulty settling the conflicting claims of that art and his own. He would be aware of a wide range of pertinent history, but uncertain about the pertinence of history itself. His view of the past would emphasize discontinuity, and it would be more important that something had happened than that it had happened at a specific time. This discontinuity would also complicate the business of evaluation, because it would call into question the conventional use of the past as a wellspring of wisdom and standards. Finally, even if he were to look to the past for guidance, he would have a confusing array of pasts to choose from and not just those two that seem to descend in a straight line from Greece and Israel.

In such a situation there is no clear historical context to apportion sig-

---

[1] Geoffrey Chaucer, "The Parliament of Fowls," *The Works of Geoffrey Chaucer*, ed. F. N. Robinson (2d ed.; Boston, 1957), p. 311.

nificance among works of the past, and it is all too easy to retreat into Alexandrian pedantry in which all objects of study become equally legitimate, and the only praiseworthy discovery is the cleverness of the scholar himself. With this fragmented vision of the past, the scholar becomes an antiquarian and the teacher a purveyor of bonbons. The dilemma we face, then, is clear: To abandon the ordered house of tradition is to step into what seems an absurd world of superficial flux and profound stagnation; but, on the other hand, the sense of tradition that has sustained humanistic study until now does not seem adequate to this age. If that dilemma is to be resolved, the most important challenge facing humanists now is the reconstruction of the very idea of tradition. Whatever form that reconstruction will take, it will not succeed unless it answers the needs of both scholarship and education, since both of those activities invigorate traditions.

Earlier humanists dealt with two notions of tradition, and one of them will not do—the idea of a syncretic tradition, which posits that truth is a discoverable unity and that when you have the key, you can show that all wise men in the past either have seen the one truth in their own way or else have erred. Syncretic thought shaped the idea of the humanities. The humanities have conventionally been seen as a group of disciplines concerned with the study of a tradition whose character, chief exemplars, and progress are continuous and fairly well defined and whose value is beyond serious question. It is a tradition that accommodates to the differences among its members so that it can assimilate, for example, both Rabelais and Cardinal Newman with a minimum of friction. Yet no matter how eclectic the tradition may be, there will always be certain works or ideas which cannot be accommodated, which are beyond the pale. Consequently, such traditions are defined not only by what they include, but by what they exclude, and critics whose bias is toward the syncretic idea of tradition, like Berenson, Eliot, and Leavis, spend a great deal of effort identifying who is in and who is out. The criteria are usually explicit and assumed to be universal. In all of these respects, the purest Renaissance spokesman for the syncretic view of tradition was perhaps Pico della Mirandola, whose sense of tradition was both widely eclectic and narrowly self-serving: "Taken altogether, there is absolutely no controversy between ourselves and the Hebrews on any matter, with regard to which they cannot be refuted and gainsaid out of cabalistic books, so that there will not be even a corner left in which they may hide themselves." [2]

For the modern man whom I have described, the traditional idea of a syncretic tradition would be of little use. The sense of belonging to a tradition requires that one understand how one got where one is and where one is going, or at least what the next natural step would be. But in a relativistic and divergent age, the old ideas about how we got here no longer seem appropriate; nor do curricula based on the history of the West. In fact, although the

[2] Pico della Mirandola, "Oration on the Dignity of Man," trans. Elizabeth Livermore Forbes, in *The Renaissance Philosophy of Man,* ed. Ernst Cassirer, Paul Oskar Kristeller, John Herman Randall, Jr. (Chicago, 1948), pp. 252–53. For discussion of Pico's syncretism, see Kristeller's "Introduction" to the "Oration."

study of history remains a humanistic discipline, the idea of history as the organizing thread of human endeavor may be a historical accident and an anachronism.[3] If the past does become relevant to a man who lives through the next fifty years, it will happen because he has been able to fashion his own statement of meaning and test it against others, not because he feels heir to one past or another. He will not want or be able to deal in received opinions.

Another type of tradition does seem more promising, however, as a way of giving meaning to the past. Rather than being concerned with accommodation, it is dialectical and personalistic. In this view, one participates in a tradition not as a discoverer but as an artist whose one final truth is his own and for which he is accountable to the past but in his own way. Whereas a syncretic tradition tends to submerge differences, a dialectical tradition seeks out differences, plays with them, and demands that men make choices among them. In literature, the syncretic style is a mixture of judiciousness and self-righteousness; the dialectical style also begins with judiciousness, but moves between irony, familiarity, and confrontation, as in the writing of its clearest Renaissance exponent, Montaigne.

Montaigne's emphasis on self-knowledge seems to lead him to the dialectical view of tradition, and in that also he is typical of those who share that view.[4] Montaigne, like his model, Socrates, insists that his skepticism is consonant with traditional piety, and also like Socrates he regards tradition as a continuing process that thrives on self-assertion followed by correction. He learns by talking to people, so that growth becomes a communal activity. That undercurrent, important throughout his essays, illuminates a characteristic of the idea of a dialectic tradition. "I do not teach, I relate," [5] he says, and Montaigne's relating is a social act of an intensity foreign to most teaching. It assumes the active participation of an audience: "I would have my voice not only reach my listener but perhaps strike him through. . . . A speech belongs half to the speaker, half to him who hears it. The hearer should let the form of its delivery prepare him for its reception; as, with

---

[3] In an interesting discussion of the psychological effects of a rapidly changing environment, Kenneth H. Craik predicts that in the future: "The human organism, as a physical object, will emerge as one of the most durable objects in the surround. For an object having by that date a life expectancy of 80 or possibly 90 years and having the property of maintaining a reasonable degree of identity of shape and form will present a marked contrast to the ever-changing and rapidly changing non-human environment. In terms of durability, the human organism will become the background and the fleet-formed non-human environment the foreground, in contrast to the English village of a century ago, in which the cathedral, shops and houses were the stable background for the brief-spanned entities which inhabited them." Craik, "The Prospects for an Environmental Psychology," *IPAR Research Bulletin* (University of California, Institute of Personality Assessment and Research, 1966), p. 15.

[4] For example: "I would rather understand myself well by self-study than by reading Cicero. In the experience that I have of myself I find enough to make me wise, if I were a good scholar. Anyone who recalls the violence of his past anger, and to what a pitch his excitement carried him, will see its ugliness better than in Aristotle, and will conceive a juster hatred for it." Michel de Montaigne, *Essays,* trans. J. M. Cohen (Baltimore, 1958), p. 354.

[5] *Ibid.,* p. 237.

tennis players, the man who takes the service shifts his position and makes ready according to the movements of the striker and to the nature of the stroke." [6] The image of a game is apt, because it underscores the peculiar social tension essential to the dialectic. Images of fighting and love-making are signs of kinship among men like Montaigne, Blake, and Whitman, who share the ambivalence toward the past characteristic of the dialectic view of tradition and for whom intense human intercourse seems almost a surrogate for the certainty of a satisfactory and instructive past. That intensity may sometimes be an end, but usually it is a means, the prerequisite of knowledge. Here is Montaigne: "I like strong and manly acquaintanceships and society, a friendship that prides itself on the sharpness and vigor of its dealings. I like love that bites and scratches till the blood comes. It is not vigorous and free enough if it is not quarrelsome, if it is polite and artificial, if it is afraid of shocks and is constrained in its ways: 'for there can be no discussion without contradiction.' " [7]

For these men, the past is not unimportant in their search for self-understanding, but it is important in a special way. In a syncretic tradition, the past is important as a linear succession that we should be able to retrace to our roots; in a dialectical tradition, the past is a home for one set of loving antagonists who can inspire, correct, or be corrected or rejected by us. A dialectical tradition is not so much a history as a mode of social behavior, an *agon*. Dialectical traditions, like syncretic ones, are regenerated in the present, but for dialectical traditions, regeneration is much more a communal act. Any notion of tradition assumes an identifiable community that is both the recreator and the audience of the tradition, but in the dialectical much more than in the syncretic, the community *is* the tradition, and the tradition is alive only in the interaction of its participants. This idea of tradition has proved especially congenial to Americans, and Walt Whitman, addressing the poets and philosophers of Europe's past in *Democratic Vistas,* suggests why:

Ye powerful and resplendent ones! Ye were, in your atmospheres, grown not for America but rather for her foes, the feudal and the old—while our genius is democratic and modern. Yet could ye, indeed, but breathe your breath of life into our New World's nostrils—not to enslave us, as now, but, for our needs, to breed a spirit like your own—perhaps (dare we to say it?) to dominate, even destroy, what you yourselves have left! On your plane, and no less, but even higher and wider, must we mete and measure for to-day and here. I demand races of orbic bards, with unconditional uncompromising sway. Come forth, sweet democratic despots of the west! [8]

For Whitman the quality of a tradition is defined by the quality of the community that is living it. Speech belongs half to him who hears it, and a dialectical tradition is the activity of live men talking with and adapting to one another and their predecessors.

[6] *Ibid.,* p. 372.
[7] *Ibid.,* p. 288.
[8] Walt Whitman, *Prose Works, 1892,* ed. Floyd Stovall (New York, 1964), Vol. 2, p. 411.

Not only has this idea of tradition, with its emphasis on communal inter-action, influenced American thought and letters, but it has had some impact on American education, thanks primarily to the brilliant synthesis of John Dewey. Dewey's philosophy of education, as he says in summarizing *Democracy and Education,* "connects the growth of democracy with the development of the experimental method in the sciences, evolutionary ideas in the biological sciences, and the industrial reorganization, and is concerned to point out the changes in subject matter and method of education indicated by these developments." [9] Dewey sees a democratic community as the only defense against the fragmenting force of Western industrial individualism, providing the only context within which men can criticize and alter the very ideas that the community holds dear. Conflict and diversity are not dysfunctional in such a community, but rather are necessary for its vitality. Thus, in a democracy, conflict and diversity should be a *sine qua non* of education.

Despite Dewey's influence, however, much remains unchanged and as we move into a post-industrial, or at least a post-Arnoldian, civilization, a well-fashioned theory of humanistic education based on such a communal dialectic would be very useful. It could provide a systematic way of dealing with the diverse and fluid quality of our pasts and our presents and for preparing students to continue to do so in the future. It may seem strange that anyone feels the need to stand up for diversity and conflict when humanism has always been characterized by a tolerance for differences of opinion, but to take this idea seriously in education could seem threatening to many people. I confess that it sometimes seems so to me. It suggests that the function of teachers and scholars is not to transmit, but to challenge and be challenged. It suggests that their ultimate objective is not a better understanding of their material, but a better understanding of one another, of their students, and of themselves. It suggests that their strategy is to give students opportunities for making significant choices and at the same time holding them responsible for the choices they have made; it would produce educational imperatives for giving students power over matters pertinent to their education.

In short, to take such a theory seriously, one would be forced to ask radical questions about the way matters are normally handled now. I am in love with Chaucer, and love, I know, is a fine thing. I never had much trouble with the question: "Why do I read Chaucer?" Why do I cherish my family or eat oranges? But I have had difficulty answering the question: "Why do I teach Chaucer?" What, in fact, does it mean to say: "I teach Chaucer"? Does it mean simply to be a matchmaker, to bring Chaucer to students so that they, too, can fall in love with him? To be a matchmaker in that way is no small accomplishment, perhaps, but why Chaucer? There are any number of attachments students could form, and who am I to say that they should spend their time falling in love with Chaucer rather than Shakespeare or biophysics or dogs or one another? Such loves are sometimes mutually exclusive.

[9] John Dewey, *Democracy and Education* (New York, 1916), p. v.

The question makes sense only in the present context of the American academy, where *to teach* usually means to act like an inviolable expert whose task is to put his students through his paces. Assuming that definition of teaching, let me rephrase my question: What *right* do I have to teach Chaucer? What right do I have to tell adults past the age of consent what they should know or whom they should love? I refuse to accept the notion that I have the right because Chaucer is good, or because I know more than my students, or because they will be grateful to me subsequently. If I want to work within a dialectical tradition, there seem to be only two conditions under which I have the right to teach anyone anything: when he asks me to or when a community of which he is a member agrees that whatever I am teaching is something he should learn. On most campuses today, neither condition obtains.

Many American colleges were founded on the explicit understanding within the founding community that certain things should be taught, and on the implicit understanding that students did not know enough to ask voluntarily to be taught the right things. The things to be taught were generally dictated by the genteel Christian tradition or by the community's need for mechanical and agricultural skills. These communally shared purposes were important; they clarified a teacher's duties and sanctioned his authority. To the extent that a student was a member of those communities—for example, the son of a Baptist or of a Brahmin or of a farmer—he also gave his implicit assent to his obligation to be taught and to the right of his teachers to teach. Yet the double sword of the knowledge explosion and social mobility is cutting up those communities forever.

To understand what has happened, one need only look at the current isolation of humanistic professions from one another and from the society at large. As a humanist, I have had no recognizable community to guide and sanction my teaching. The "company of learned men," into which one of my diplomas welcomes me, is not really a community that can speak for my students. A community, whatever else it does, provides a microcosm of purpose within which an individual's own purposes play a functional, organic part. A community is a group in which any member of the group can go to any other member and expect that his goals will be accepted as legitimate, that his needs will be considered a matter of mutual concern, and that his identity will be accurately perceived. That idea of community may live in some graduate departments and professional schools, where specific educational goals are shared by most people. Except in a handful of possible exceptions, however, it does not live in whole colleges. The things most faculty members expect from their students are manifestly different from what the students, their parents, and the larger society expect. Those differences are aggravated by all the devices and strategies that keep students and professors separate, even when they share a classroom for a semester.

It is possible, of course, for competent teachers to overcome these barriers. They do so in innumerable ways and in classes that often appear quite conventional. We each have our own style of wrestling. But even when individual teachers live up to these ideals, the cause of humanism can never be fully served until this idea of community finds a central place in our concept of the humanities themselves, until we have developed a non-elitist mode of community to keep the traditions alive. Our students' lives are not spent in our classrooms, nor for the most part do our books play a very durable role in their lives. If our best work as teachers is to be of any use, then as professional scholars we must be working concurrently to revise the concept of the humanities in order to provide contexts outside the classroom within which humanistic learning is appropriate. As teachers and scholars we should be skilled at enhancing the identity of those around us. When someone says, as a black student at San Francisco State College did recently, "We're not looking for a melting pot; we're looking for ourselves," we should be prepared to treat that as an invitation to our kind of conversation.

That skill requires a new methodology. As humanists, we may be good at teaching and even, like Montaigne, good at relating, but we tend to be poor at listening and responding. We do not often hear ourselves being questioned, much less contradicted, by our students and our society; when we do, we generally do not answer, unless with a shrug. Much of that methodology would be transmuted social and behavioral science. On the one hand, we need to find ways to monitor what is going on around us; on the other, we need to frame pertinent alternatives. The humanist's concern should be not simply objects and events of the past, but equally his society's perception of those objects and events. As a teacher and scholar, he should be building utopias, real and imaginary, that are specific responses to the world in which he lives. Consider the man who lives in a modern city and understands what Chaucer has to say on the subject of love. If he is not moved to challege those aspects of his environment that prohibit love, he is not a humanist but a pedant, and he should not be surprised if his society considers him expendable.

It should be clear that some changes are due in our professions. For college faculties, we need a set of academic career patterns that allow the development of a humanities specialist: a man skilled not only in the judgment of human creations, but also in the Socratic art of shaping his information into a specific response to another person's situation. He would need a new kind of graduate training that might, for example, take cognizance of humanistic psychology. We will have to tolerate a system in which each man defines his own specialty with much greater freedom than is now the case, and it should be a system that rewards him for changing specialties as well as for getting better in one specialty. We need to make room on all our faculties for doers as well as thinkers, and we need to devise ways to assimilate them. Such a faculty would engage its students in judging their environment and acting in it and on it. The resulting curriculum would appear problem-oriented but the problems would be set by the students themselves and continually revised and refined as a result of a real dialectic with teachers, with books, and with the world. The problems would certainly not all be "contemporary" in the usual sense of the word, but they would reflect the concerns of living men.

Of course, if no such reforms come about, all will not necessarily be lost. We will probably continue to be tolerated, though ignored, by an indulgent society. We will continue to appear at ceremonial occasions, and our books will have attractive jackets. Our numbers will be replenished every June, and our robes and mortar boards will always fit. And, of course, we will preserve and comment upon our artifacts with increasing skill for the benefit of future humanists.

TWO STYLES:
A Challenge to Higher Education

James S. Ackerman

The two-culture problem that worried us a few years ago seems less serious these days; scientists and humanists are communicating with one another, maybe better than they used to, and surely better than the older members of either "culture" communicate with the younger. The generation gap itself—the characteristic split of the 1960's—is more dramatic and often more violent than its supposed predecessor and cannot be explained or understood simply in terms of the normal pace of cultural change.

The conflict is not so much one of ideologies as of styles. The senior style, Objective Analysis, is the better established; it represents the intellectual achievement and position of the first half of the twentieth century, a period that has been called the Age of Analysis. The upstart is the Engaged Style, the channel through which young people are searching for new sensations and experiences, expressing their mistrust of authority and tradition, and bearing witness to strongly felt convictions. The Engaged Style is more penetrating than the modes of student unrest in earlier times, though it has similar surface characteristics; it is global, and it seems to have powers of survival that will keep its adherents from joining the Establishment as readily as their fathers did. Its intellectual stimuli are variable and inconsistent—Western romanticism, Oriental mysticism, anarchism—but they have in common that they did not exercise much impact on the American intellectual of middle age who now represents the Establishment.[1]

TWO STYLES: A CHALLENGE TO HIGHER EDUCATION Reprinted by permission from *Daedalus*, Journal of the American Academy of Arts and Sciences, Boston, Massachusetts, Volume 98, Number 3.

[1] Political radicals of the two styles are vigorously opposed; members of the older generation who were raised on Marxist idealism are appalled by what appears to them to be the absence of specific goals and by the simply negative or destructive response to existing institutions. Many of the new radicals are as disaffected from Marx and modern Communism as from Capitalism, and look on both as imperialistic machines.

The style of Objective Analysis assumes that the primary responsibility of the individual scientist, scholar, or artist is to his subject and craft. For the researcher and teacher, this implies that one should attempt to examine one's material as objectively, as impersonally as possible in order to minimize the danger that one's own point of view might distort the interpretation of the material. To have a point of view at all is considered to be an unscientific position unless it can be demonstrated to be the result rather than the stimulus of investigation. It is labeled "unscientific" because the educational theory of the last generation was haunted by a scientific image—but not one that would flatter a creative scientist, because it regarded science as preeminently an enterprise of dissecting, measuring, and testing, a laboratory affair concerned not with the making of principles and theories but only with demonstrating their validity. This style forged tools of great sophistication, from psychoanalysis to atomic fission, from analytic cubism to analytic philosophy, from the New Criticism to the digital computer.

In each discipline, the method of Objective Analysis has required the fragmentation of the object of investigation; philosophers put aside the study of the embracing concepts that had occupied their colleagues in preceding centuries to examine the use and interaction of words; psychologists came to see that the personality is not a unit but a complex of conflicting levels, and devised a therapeutic technique on the principle that the integration of a disturbed personality could be achieved almost entirely by analysis of its components; physicists pursued the investigation of matter into its smallest complexes and eventually discovered and unleashed a terrifying power by breaking down even these into unstable subunits. A similar method came to dominate historical and critical studies as well. But properly pursued, the analytic method is not an end in itself; in each field its purpose has been to facilitate the study of the interaction of the analyzed parts with one another and with the observer and to arrive at definitions generally termed operational.

The power that atomic fission gave to those who discovered how to bring it about and how to control it is symbolic of the over-all effectiveness of Objective Analysis. It has facilitated the transmission of data and technique, promoted an incalculable contribution to the sum of knowledge, and brought about an extraordinary refinement of our critical faculties. In addition to its quantitative achievements, it has proved to be the means by which, in the span of only a half century, the American scholar, scientist, and artist have been able to arrive at a level of sophistication that equals or surpasses that of their European colleagues. Though largely a European creation, it is a style that suits American culture.

The Engaged Style cannot be defined clearly in these terms because it opposes not only the method of Objective Analysis, but the concept of an articulated method itself. It invites an existential absorption of experience rather than the channeling of investigation toward particular ends, and it resists the effort of analytic teachers to discipline the expression of feeling for the purpose of communication, persuasion, and achievement. It is individualist, vigorous in its opposition to prevailing systems and to the power that Objective Analysis has given to those who practice it. Its strength is a strength of antithesis, calling to attention the values that were considered irrelevant and damaging to the method of the opposition. In the form of student activism, it is beginning to make itself felt as a force in education through criticism of administrative regulations, of the academic authority and standards of faculties, and of curricula and teaching that lack "relevance" to contemporary life and issues. Its intellectual fuel is said to be provided by a variety of writers including Hermann Hesse, Herbert Marcuse, Norman Brown, Marshall McLuhan, Che Guevara, and the spokesmen of the black revolution, but I believe that these writers are more often referred to than read, and that when they are read, it is not for guidance so much as for the buttressing of attitudes already formed.

Criticism from this source now is forcing a reassessment of the methods of Objective Analysis. It is becoming clear that our attempts to approximate objectivity—a condition that psychologists long ago showed to be unattainable—keep us from recognizing and examining the beliefs and principles by which we work, and promote a professional training primarily devoted to method rather than to the study and formulation of principles. While a search for *principles* may help to reveal useful interconnections among different disciplines (as the theory of evolution or the concept of entropy has been used effectively in cultural history), quite different *methods* are required for studying objects in diverse fields,[2] and an increasing emphasis on "methodology"[3] has isolated and narrowed all the disciplines. The danger of overspecialization so often cited in discussions of education is the inevitable product of a system that discourages generalization, for only through generalization can the common ground between different areas become visible.

Furthermore, the scholar and student trained to suppress their convictions and feelings in order to arrive at an objective statement are unable to establish within the system firm grounds for judgments of value. Consequently, scholars are poorly equipped, regardless how learned they may be, to make judgments where a consensus has not already been established (as with the masterpieces of the past), and rarely have taken positions on contemporary public, moral, and aesthetic issues. The increased political activity of some academicians in recent years, in part stimulated by the Engaged Style, only emphasizes the point, because it has remained extracurricular, divorced from professional attitudes, and consequently no more effective than the public roles of other concerned citizens. The physicists who collaborated in the making of the atomic bomb, appalled by the human consequences of their brilliant achievement, sought expiation in the political arena rather than in a reassessment of the principles and aims of laboratory research.

One of the strongest supports for scholarly disengagement has been the

---

[2] See my paper "On Scientia," *Dædalus,* Vol. 94 (1965), pp. 14–23.
[3] "Methodology" is a characteristic term of Objective Analysis; it means "the science of method" and implies that method can be a learned discipline in itself.

nineteenth-century delusion—applied particularly to the humanities—that the study of great works makes the student not only more versatile but a finer human being. Values residing in the object were believed to have the power to reform the values brought to it by the subject. The falsity of this claim is apparent; apart from the dubious assumption that values exist independent of a recipient, we can find throughout history men of great knowledge and sensibility who have used their skills to evil as well as to virtuous ends;[4] the only claim we are justified in making for analytic education is that it helps the recipient to be more effective, more independent, and harder to trick. I am not convinced that we can devise any system of education that will make men good as well as efficient; but whatever our aims, they cannot be served by the self-deceiving myth that knowledge is synonymous with virtue.

A final limitation of Objective Analysis is its tendency to direct attention only to the kind of object that yields most readily to its method: to verbal rather than to visual and aural compositions (and to aspects of the visual and aural that can best be verbalized); to the products of "high" culture rather than to popular and material culture; to the classical tradition of Western Europe rather than to the more elusive and, to us, mysterious cultures of Asia and Africa; and to the increasingly minute examination of well-established fields rather than to the exploration of uncharted territory.

When the Engaged Style defines a relevant educational experience in terms of a particular subject matter, it is accepting uncritically one of the principles of the opposition. The educated individual is not identified by what he knows, but by how he thinks and acts. The truly relevant experience is the one that helps us to articulate and to communicate our beliefs and to expand the capacities of our imagination and senses; it is a moment in the maturation of human functions, and only incidentally the acquisition of particular data.

The intensely felt convictions of the engaged individual are not gathered from the books and classrooms of analytic professors, but are absorbed, from infancy on, out of the subterranean stream of our democratic and Biblical heritage. An ethic transmitted more by parents—particularly mothers—than by teachers, and concocted of the Constitution, the Ten Commandments, and the Sermon on the Mount continues to hold sufficient emotional power over Americans in the 1960's to provide a passable substitute for religious credos.

The sophisticated generation of objective analysts devised tools to free us from the dark power of such unconsciously acquired beliefs and superstitions, and to subject all simple idealism to scientific scrutiny. But expression and action—if not thought—on the major issues of our time continue to be dominated by underground idealism. Passionate feelings about liberty, equality, freedom, fair play, individuality, and so on affect public affairs more than sober analysis and statistical research. While they hold American society together, they also are the source of intense internal conflict, because

---

[4] This observation was stimulated by George Steiner, one of the participants in our first conference, in *Language and Silence* (New York, 1967), particularly in the essay "To Civilize Our Gentlemen," pp. 55–67.

they can clash among themselves (for example, loyalty to one's country vs. the Brotherhood of Man; individualism vs. the sharing of benefits).

For all of its influence upon the intellectual timbre of this country, the style of Objective Analysis paradoxically nurtured the forces of the opposition by supporting an educational system that was not rigid and exacting, as might have been expected, but permissive or "progressive," emphasizing individual initiative and "creativity." Before the curricular reforms of the 1950's, Americans were not expected to be really serious about their education until they reached graduate school, at which point the curriculum did abruptly become rigid and exacting. The inconsistency is one result of the absence of any philosophical support for the analytic method; educators were eager to adopt the method, but lacked the conviction to organize the system around it.

That the American manifestations of Engagement only partially explain its genesis is proved by the recent explosion of student activism across the world. Huge numbers of young people have ignored physical safety and the protection of the laws to demonstrate in behalf of the oppressed (whether themselves or others) and in opposition to the oppressor. While this may be explained partly as a reaction to the mechanization and depersonalization of modern life, its occurrence in preindustrial societies (for example, India) suggests that the common denominator may rather be awareness of the impermanence of institutions, the threat of overpopulation, and the potential imminence of global annihilation. Facing these terrors, today's students question and resist the traditional fare and style of the humanistic disciplines. Disengaged reexamination of the past offers too little preparation for such a future. For some, drastic action seems to be the only response; a greater number seek the discipline and the content of an education that will prepare them for the special responsibilities that fall to those who have the advantages of advanced learning.

Although it is true that adherents of the Engaged Style constitute a minority, even among university students, the statistic is not relevant; in the competition for dominance in the intellectual spheres, it is the only new force worthy of attention.

The social role of the style of Objective Analysis is to preserve and to refine our processes of thought and action and our institutions; it is a bridge that joins the traditions, the experiences, and the norms of the past to the present. Since it is not itself disposed to normative judgments, it has been able to accommodate innovations that meet its standards of objectivity, but reluctantly: While it is not intentionally conservative, it has great inertia that resists deflections from familiar paths.[5] In some aspects, Objective Analysis could be seen as a communal superego, by contrast to the Engaged Style which, in its explosive drive for expression, would be the societal equivalent of the id. Engaged expression, when it is extreme and violent, is prompted more by feeling than by thought—feeling linked with the basic drives of childhood, which can remain at a child's level of articulation. It has been

---

[5] See Bernard Barber, "Resistance by Scientists to Scientific Discovery," *Science*, Vol. 124 (1961), pp. 596ff.

given little encouragement to more mature development by an analytic mode of education that refuses to confront issues which threaten to become too charged to be resolved by pure scientific method.

If the personality of the educational community is split in this way, it cannot be reintegrated simply by repressing its "id." A more promising therapy would be to encourage the articulation of deeply felt convictions by giving them rational as well as subconscious expression. This responsibility of the teacher and scholar cannot be assumed so long as feelings and values are exiled from the classroom.

In trying to formulate goals for higher education in the coming years, we must preserve the best in both of the styles and find ways of arbitrating their differences. The Analytic Style gives the individual precision tools with which to manipulate his environment. From it, we should preserve the degree of objectivity and rational method required to support intercourse among individuals with different aims and talents, and we should retain the principle that knowledge of what happened in the past and in cultures different from ours is essential to our survival and must not be lost. The Engaged Style demands effective human contact between the individual and the object of his attention; it has shown us that a legitimate function of higher education can be to help people to formulate and actively observe ethical and aesthetic commitments.

GOALS FOR HIGHER EDUCATION

Since the age of Objective Analysis has defined its functions in terms of techniques rather than of principles, the aim of higher education has been simply to train students to perform effectively. What they should perform and why have not been discussed seriously; each individual is expected to decide this for himself. So the growing adolescent is assigned the most crucial decision of all: to determine the purpose of the whole educational enterprise —and without the encouragement of his teachers. No matter how effectively techniques are taught, they cannot help students to make this decision wisely. Educational leaders describe their goals in vaguely articulated expressions of confidence in the educational efficacy of the values presumably transmitted by contact with the great works and thoughts of the past and with the mature scholars who teach and do research on these works and thoughts.

This vacuum of purpose is the inheritance of an earlier period in which the social function of education was to prepare a small number of the sons (and a few daughters) of an economically privileged and powerful class to assume well-defined responsibilities in the community, primarily through the professions and other roles of leadership. The universities were not expected to define the goals of education; figuratively, they contracted to produce graduates equipped to perform the tasks and to reflect the principles defined by the dominant class. The dependent position of the universities in formulating goals was reflected in the menial position of professors in terms of income and status.

Today, the social role of higher education is radically altered.[6] With enormously expanded enrollments, and with a significant shift of sponsorship from private to public support (even for private institutions), a democratic education open to all citizens on the basis of merit rather than privilege is nearer to being realized and provides the base on which an educational philosophy may be constructed. The unrest in the new generation of students is due in part to the failure of educators to redefine their goals in terms of this wholly different function. Because today's student is not being prepared to perform predetermined roles, he wants to be trained not only in how to understand and how to perform, but in how to choose what it is he wants to understand and to perform.

These decisions, which are ethical as well as practical, have come increasingly under the control of educators, as other social institutions, particularly the church and the family, are losing contact with, and normative influence over, young people, and as other professional groups such as lawyers and doctors, because of the increasing specialization and democratization of their services, have had to reduce their role as moral preceptors to individuals. The influence of teachers is increased further by the fact that education is virtually the only path to interesting and remunerative careers; young people can ignore the guidance of ministers and parents, but they must satisfy their teachers or relinquish many of the benefits of our society. The era of the self-made man has passed.

In this situation, educators cannot choose whether or not to assume the responsibility of guidance; it has been assigned to them. If a teacher refuses to face the issue of value decisions and preserves his scholarly neutrality, he is then not socially neutral, but indicates unconcern or incompetence to deal with the implications of what he teaches. This itself is a value decision by default.

The need for individuals in all fields prepared and willing to make decisions on ethical grounds increases as more specialized skills are required in our technological, business, and professional enterprises, and as the specialist controls smaller and smaller segments of larger and larger systems. Inevitably, the impact of the division of labor is to reduce the individual responsibility for the larger decisions in our society. In the professions, a crisis is being caused by tensions between the internal inertia of scientific progress and the well-being of the society as a whole. Characteristic examples from the field of medicine[7] have been such issues as: What proportion of limited human and financial resources should be allotted to advanced research as opposed to community care, particularly of the indigent? When is a heart donor dead, and who decides? How shall the imminent capability of con-

---

[6] This change is intensively examined by David Riesman and Christopher Jencks in *The Academic Revolution* (New York, 1968). Their solution to the problems I am defining, especially in "Reforming the Graduate Schools," pp. 510–23, is close to what I propose here.
[7] See "Ethical Aspects of Experimentation with Human Subjects," *Dædalus* (Spring, 1969). For parallels in architecture and engineering, see the article by Michael O'Hare, pp. 765–77.

trol over the human mind be itself controlled? These questions cannot be solved with technical expertise; they must be referred to a value system developed outside the sphere of science, and because they are so important, the development of that system must be part of professional or pre-professional training.

Educators in the sciences and technologies already are aware of the shortcomings of overspecialization; the cure most frequently prescribed is a larger dose of humanities courses. But the humanities, themselves driven by internal "scientific" imperatives and guilty no less than the sciences of overspecialization, have not been able to respond effectively. The challenge cannot be met simply by introducing the specialist of the future to the arts, literature, and philosophy; though these fields offer unique potentialities for examining values, the study of them is no more assured of being a humane enterprise than the study of the sciences or social sciences.

It is possible for a teacher to present value issues openly—without imposing his convictions—by aiding his students to examine and to articulate the principles by which they live and to investigate the relationships between those principles and the actual situations of life and of scholarship or research. Yet it is not necessary for him to conceal his own convictions; a teacher can himself be a model of the mature and conscious integration of belief and expression or action, while being prepared to entertain from students and colleagues ideas that differ from his own. Occasionally, the values of student and teacher will conflict without an apparent possibility of resolution, as has happened in destructive confrontations during the last two or three years, particularly over the educational goals of racial minorities. These eruptions may have been inevitable, but they probably were made more violent by having to break through the calm crust of academic neutrality. If the classroom were a place for examining feelings and clarifying convictions, it could accommodate divergences of principle more peaceably.

The area of agreement is larger than that of conflict. Diversified as our country is, the ideals of the Constitution and of the system of laws built upon it are generally shared; we tend to disagree on interpretation rather than on principles. The value system is for this reason social and political in character, and it is natural that we should define the goal of our education in social-political terms.

The increasing demand in all the functions of modern life for people with refined skills and with the capacity to adjust to rapid change confers special privileges on educated men and women that are accompanied by special responsibilities toward society. It is therefore a legitimate purpose of higher education to prepare students to assume the responsibilities as well as to practice the skills: Generically, they may be defined as *the making and the maintaining of a humane social and physical environment.*

But the forces impelling the university outward toward the community must be restrained by the centripetal forces of a tradition of cloistered learning undisturbed by immediate social priorities, not just because the university must develop the inner resources as well as the public effectiveness of its scholars and students, but because a portion of the social needs of the future will be met by learning and research the utility and value of which cannot be calculated now. If radical efforts to wholly politicize the university were to succeed, they would restrict its universality, increase its materialism, and, in the end, be more destructive to individual and social freedoms than pedantic academism.

For this reason, the proposed goal does not imply an expansion of college programs in the social sciences; it would be an arid future in which a poet, a historian, or a forester were not thought to be so important a contributor to the public welfare as the social worker and economist. We cannot anticipate in what areas and situations future students will find opportunities to make their contribution; the significant change would be the introduction not of new subjects of study, but of approaches to existing subjects that will make it more possible to realize the potentialities of the educational experience.

A program seeking to prepare young people to assume responsible roles in society must admit ethical and aesthetic judgments into scholarship and teaching; it demands a significant change in the orientation of higher education—a return to traditions abandoned only at the start of this century with the rise of Objective Analysis. The education of the privileged class before 1900 was intended to produce good and pious graduates through grounding in a classical curriculum and in religious principles. To attempt to reintroduce ethical issues today may appear to be a dangerous approach to training a large and diversified student population in a society without generally accepted—or acceptable—religious or philosophical principles. But the violent disruptions that are a recurrent feature of today's university life suggest that the more dangerous decision would be to perpetuate education that does not recognize even the need for ethical and aesthetic commitments.

My attempt to define educational goals on the vague basis of America's liberal social tradition is simply pragmatic; it lacks philosophical justification. It is a device for persuading a vigorously antiphilosophical and diffusely moralistic society to face the need for formulating principles, for making judgments. We may, paradoxically, arrive at a philosophy of education only by making that achievement one of the goals of education.

FUNCTIONS OF THE HUMANITIES

It used to be said of the humanities that they were distinguished from other disciplines in "dealing with values." The statement is meaningless, because it would be impossible to define "values" in a way that would exclude them from the purview of the sciences and social sciences. What does distinguish the humanities is that they are devoted to the study of things that men have made and thought, and on this account they cannot be adequately studied and taught without reference to value systems. The humanities are a constellation of disciplines peculiarly adapted to assist students in the articulation of feelings and beliefs and in the processes of self-realization.

But this distinctiveness has not protected the humanities from the dehumanization of the Objective Analytic method. By subjecting the experience of art, literature, and philosophy to the limitation of a particular alliance of history and criticism, humanistic education has restricted and perverted its potentialities.

The prevailing, historically oriented, methods of criticism promote the suppression of the uniqueness of the individual work or act by a relentless emphasis on the chronological flow of culture, so that the focus of critical attention is on a process rather than on the single object. Virtually all instruction in the arts and literature from secondary through graduate training is offered within the framework of a linear historical sequence; general courses and books "survey a field" from an early date to a recent one; the more advanced follow an identical process within a segment of the chronological span. It is understandable that a society obsessed by process and productivity, one in which individual achievement is progressively demeaned, should sponsor a theory and method of historical criticism so well adapted to its dynamic thrust, but humanists cannot be at the same time critical of that society and loyal to the historical attitude that justifies it. The humane alternative is not the rejection of history, as the style of Engagement suggests, but the formulation of a historical and critical method that sets human achievements in relief, within the context of the events and ideas that make them possible.

Our linear-historical method has also confined the concept of our tradition within the narrow frame of the high culture of Western Europe and its roots in Greek and Roman thought and Hebraic and Christian religion. If a primary purpose of education is to stimulate the creation of a new and healthier social environment, the educational experience cannot be restricted to the study of the traditions that have locked us into our present condition. An understanding by humanists as well as social scientists of the traditions of the East and of Africa, of Islam, and of the cultures we patronizingly call "primitive" and "popular" can help us to achieve the perspective we need to re-examine our own position.

To give curricula the increased intensity and variety that these observations suggest, the quantitative acquisition of information to which the present survey-system of humanistic study is committed will have to be left to the initiative of the student; it is in any case only a preparation for education. The curriculum itself would then concentrate on the intensive examination of material in such a way that the student might come to terms with it as a formative experience. In choosing material, the teacher would be free to select what he finds valuable and stimulating, which may or may not conform to the issues, objects, or ideas previously identified as significant. The choice may alight on small or obscure as well as great and celebrated objects, as the scholar often finds in the unexplored crevices of the distant or recent past something that enlightens and moves him, and he may be able to communicate his response with intensity. Besides, student demand for relevance in teaching is not answered only by subject matter that bears on problems that are most apparent at the moment; the sense of sharing with a devoted preceptor a convincing encounter with unfamiliar or esoteric objects, whether of the past or present, may be a more stimulating experience. The less familiar the material, the more it may extend our horizon, and the more it may reveal aspects of our own culture that we were not prepared to perceive. Indeed, in the humanities, contemporary works prove often to be more foreign than those of the past; even sophisticated undergraduates today seem less at ease with Genet, Boulez, and Olitsky than with Shakespeare, Bach, and Piero della Francesca.

The possibility of intensively examining the material of the humanities in an enlarged cultural context rather than in the linear-historical mode also encourages penetration of the rigid barriers that now separate the fields of the humanities from one another and the humanities as an institution from the sciences and the social sciences. Since all disciplines that bear on man and his work are potential contributors to the understanding of humanistic themes, the healthiest atmosphere for scholarship and teaching is the one that encourages contact and collaboration between specialists in different fields.

The curriculum cannot be uniformly involving because many experiences have to be prepared by hard and often unpleasant work. Students of foreign literatures have to learn verbal languages, and scientific students mathematical ones. Moreover, the technology of our time offers a large variety of new languages—the computer and other electronic systems, the film and television—that not only are new media for the communication of familiar concepts, but stimulate the formulation of concepts beyond the reach of the words and symbols we have used in the past. The discipline involved in acquiring tools and techniques is an important factor in self-realization, particularly within an educational system that demands so little of it at the lower levels. But it can be discipline with a purpose, not an end in itself, and the preparatory tasks can be made more interesting and productive than they have been, as the reformed secondary-school curricula in mathematics and science have demonstrated.

As mathematics and language have been made unnecessarily dreary in the era of Objective Analysis, the performance of art, music, drama, and literary genres has been made demeaningly recreational, as if they were a relaxation from study rather than challenging disciplines. But in spite of this, courses offered in these arts by almost all universities have been preoccupied with technique to the point at which content and meaning are hardly considered, and they rarely have been integrated in conception or in practice into related programs of academic courses. Those who teach them are isolated from others in the faculty, as if the makers of the arts were a threat—not being "objective"—to those who interpret them. Yet a case may be made for the arts on purely academic grounds: The analysis of a poem or a sonata can be done better by a person who tries to make one, regardless of whether he succeeds. Practice opens a realm of criticism that resists the grasp of the library-bound scholar. Beyond this, the disciplined training of the ear and the eye that is one of the aims of workshop training does not occur with the same intensity in the process of criticism. Finally, the physical component in the making of things is a unique experience that is at once elemental and sophisticated, and it is one of which most of us are deprived by a culture that provides everything at hand, ready made, and no longer offers us the casual occasion to dance, sing, build, fix, mime, or recite. An educational system in which expository prose is the only legitimate form of expression not only arbitrarily limits the capacity to communicate and the range of what is communicated, but denies fulfillment to individuals peculiarly gifted in other forms of expression, and at inestimable cost to itself.

In portraying the crisis of higher education in terms of the confrontation of two generations with antithetical aims, I have exaggerated for the sake of emphasis. Many teachers and scholars impart more meaning to their subject than my caricature of the Objective Analyst suggests, and many students attend college passively, without demanding—even without wanting—relevance and intense experience. But the conflicts are threatening even if most or all of our universities can be saved from destruction without substantial reforms, because they are the symptoms of a grave ethical vacuum in our society which institutions of higher education are uniquely qualified to fill.

AUTHOR-TITLE INDEX

A
B
C
D
E
F
G
H
I
J

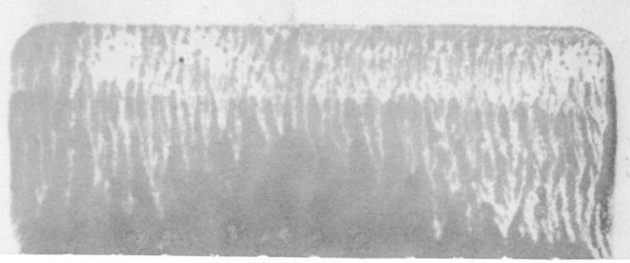

PT
5411
.G 7

Greshoff

Harvest of the Lowlands

HARVEST
of the
LOWLANDS

HARVEST
of the
LOWLANDS

AN ANTHOLOGY IN ENGLISH TRANSLA-
TION OF CREATIVE WRITING IN THE
DUTCH LANGUAGE WITH A HISTORICAL
SURVEY OF THE LITERARY DEVELOPMENT,
COMPILED AND EDITED BY J. GRESHOFF

1945

QUERIDO · NEW YORK

PRINTED IN THE UNITED STATES OF AMERICA
AMERICAN BOOK—STRATFORD PRESS, INC., NEW YORK

PREFACE

THE COMPILING OF AN ANTHOLOGY SUCH AS THIS INVOLVES NUMER-
ous difficulties. The first requirement was to give an adequate
and accurate survey of the development of Dutch prose since
1880; at the same time many limitations had to be observed.
The compiler has endeavored, wherever possible, to include complete stories and essays; fragments of longer works will be found
the exception and have been used only when short prose pieces
by a particular author could not be provided. In addition, the
compiler had to bear in mind that the anthology would be presented to a public which is unfamiliar with the literary environment of the Netherlands. For this reason many pieces which
mean a great deal to Dutch readers are lacking in significance
for American ones and indeed might well be completely unintelligible. Finally, it must be pointed out that when this selection was made the Netherlands was still cut off from us; hence,
certain material which the compiler would gladly have included
was unobtainable, for only a relatively small portion of Dutch
literature in the original is available in the United States.

The compiler has therefore assembled the best that was within
his reach and that he considered appropriate for publication
abroad. Because of limitations of space—and the volume has nevertheless grown larger than was first planned—a number of authors who rightly belong in such an anthology have perforce
been omitted. Consequently, those writers whose principal work
exists in English translation—for instance, the main work of
Frederik van Eeden, Felix Timmermans, and some others—have
been left out. In other instances, the compiler chose an outstanding author to represent a group; thus Top Naeff was selected as
the representative of female writers like Carrie van Bruggen, Ina
Boudier Bakker, etc., who between 1900 and 1930 made valuable
contributions to the Dutch novel. Special attention has been
paid to recent authors, that is, to contemporary literature and to
contemporary writing which indicates possibilities for the future.

The volume concludes with four examples to illustrate the
spread of Dutch thought throughout the world. In this section,
Cola Debrodt represents Curaçao; Albert Helman, Surinam; Bep

Vuyk, the Dutch East Indies; and J. Van Melle, South Africa.

It would have been impossible to accomplish in any proper degree what the compiler set out to do without the assistance of Jan-Albert Goris, whose extensive knowledge of Dutch literature, infallible taste and untiring enthusiasm played an important part in the making of this anthology. The novelist Adriaan van der Veen also rendered valuable service, mainly by his critical comment and suggestion with regard to the volume as a whole and to the introduction in particular.

CONTENTS

PART VIII: *THE DUTCH IN THE WORLD*

INTRODUCTION

NETHERLANDS LITERATURE BEGINS WITH A NAME WHICH REPRESENTS a legend: that of the blind singer Bernlef, who lived in the eighth century in Holwerd near Dokkum, the northern part of the northern province of Friesland. In the biography of the devout Servant of the Lord, Luidger, written by Altfridus, Bishop of Munster, he is offered as an example of a man "loved by his neighbors for his good nature and his ability to relate most poignantly in his harpsongs the stirring deeds of ancestors and the wars of the Kings." But Bernlef also knew higher values than those of feats of arms, for whenever he met Luidger he learned psalms and received heavenly enlightenment, which was imparted to him and remained with him until he died in peace, old and full of days.

No texts by Bernlef have been preserved. The earliest written expression that comes down to us dates from the ninth century, composed in Latin. Milo, a monk from the monastery of Elnon near Doornik (about 872), wrote a biography of Saint Amand in 1800 hexameter lines, and after him countless pious gentlemen went in for a sort of rhyming art devoid of all poetry which is only of value today as historical raw material.

The first poet in the Netherlands language whose works have been at least partly saved was Hendrik van Veldeke, a Limburger and thus a man from the south. In 1171 he wrote his Saint Servaes legend in verse. And from that moment we see flourishing a rich literature in the lands south of the Rhine and west of the Meuse. Rich in more than one respect: the number of lyric, epic, didactic and dramatic poems originating between 1300 and 1600 is large and complex, but even more striking is the endless variegation in feeling and form.

The discovery of the Middle Ages must be considered one of the highest achievements of Romanticism. For a very long, far too long, time, there was in the Netherlands also talk of the "dark Middle Ages," in a disapproving tone, as of a period in which ignorance, force and cruelty ruled. There was no interest in the architecture of those days, which was considered barbaric because it departed from classical order and classical order was holy, the beginning and end of all conceptions of art. The art of painting in the Middle Ages was considered common, not exalted enough, without style, because in this respect too esteem for the classical and imitation classical was unlimited. As for medieval literature, there was refusal to acknowledge the art of poetry in such clumsy efforts, in such language-poor stammering. These prejudices made a thorough and impartial study of medieval intellectual life impossible. At present we view the Middle Ages as one of the happiest and most glorious periods in the intellectual life of the Netherlands.

Gothicism meant, in the Netherlands too, the discovery and glorification of the vertical line in contrast to classical architecture, which is based and executed entirely upon the horizontal. The rather sudden flourishing of Gothicism meant an irresistible breaking-through of lyric feeling, whereas before, reason, governing both chronicle and discourse, had been predominant. The history of intellectual life in the Netherlands or—to confine ourselves to the subject—the history of the literature of that country, reveals an uninterrupted contest between the two elements, feeling and reason, which—like fire and water—by their inherent contrast and latent potentialities rule human existence. When, as in the early Middle Ages, feeling, too long suppressed and ignored, was liberated suddenly with uncommon force, a beautiful period of flourishing resulted, in which poetry pervaded even the humblest expressions of life. However, in the course of years, very gradually and slowly, reason asserted itself again.

The period of the rhetoricians, that is, the period of deterioration which concluded the Middle Ages, noteworthy in many respects, can only be viewed as a victory of reason. Netherlands literature, which was from 1300 to 1400 remarkably spontaneous, rich, fresh, colorful and full of feeling, declines, after 1400, gently and calmly in the strange, ingenious fabrication of the rhetoricians. In such all too reasonable periods, life is lived in one design. There are no more secrets; only one force rules, that of ingenuity, which expresses itself in a formality that comes seriously near to poverty.

But when the people had again accumulated sufficient vitality for a new outburst, the result was—after the transition period which we call the Early Renaissance—the Renaissance, the rehabilitation of real, natural, free feeling. What was Gothicism around 1200 was Baroque around 1600. The forms of expression, both in architecture and in painting as in literature, were very different, but in both cases we were dealing with a rehabilitation of the unlimited superiority of feeling and of inner life.

The intellectual period of prosperity in the Northern Netherlands during the seventeenth century, which we call the Golden Age, in turn tired itself out in the period of the so-called societies of poets: the eighteenth century is again a period of cautious intellectuality and therefore unsuitable for the production of great art.

Liberty came about through Romanticism, the third great outburst of feeling, at the beginning of the nineteenth century. Romanticism has not yet been concluded.

Netherlands literature seen as a whole from 1250 to 1950—thus during seven centuries—has therefore known three enormous revolutions of feeling: the Gothic, the Baroque and the Romantic: the Middle Ages, the Golden Age (seventeenth century) and the New Period.

It goes without saying that these radical revolutions took place not only in Netherlands intellectual life: movements like these are always universal. It is merely that variations of form appear in the various nations.

In the Middle Ages there was as yet no talk of national characteristics. Intellectual life in Western, Central and Southern Europe formed a nearly complete uniformity, with Rome as its center. The Gothic is therefore a conception involving far less differentiation than the Baroque. And the Baroque in its turn is again less differentiated than the Romantic.

THE GOTHIC

In literature the European cohesion of Gothic life shows most strongly in the assimilation of the same themes into the various languages. The idea of plagiarism did not exist, and there was no talk of plagiarism in the strict, modern meaning of the word, that of deliberate literary theft. If we consider our Netherlands dramatic production in the Middle Ages, we discover that *all* subjects and personalities treated appear also in the French and English drama. Only the noble play entitled *Karel ende Elegast* is not known outside the Netherlands; but this does not mean that the play is a Netherlands one: the possibility that the original text has been lost cannot be altogether disregarded. Such a genuine, strictly Netherlands poem as *Reinaert* is adapted from the French *Le Plaid du Reinard.* And here we find two remarkable symptoms, which attract the attention of anyone studying Netherlands literature in the Middle Ages. In the first place, notwithstanding the fact that the themes, and often the details of the subject-matter, have been adapted, the adapters managed to give their adaptations a tone of their own. A mutual alliance exists, which, however, does not exclude personal nuance. And in the second place, though it had only a limited amount of themes available, literature in the Middle Ages gives the impression of wealth and large variety, owing to the fact that authors in those days knew how to arrange and rearrange the available subjects with surprising cleverness. From a comparison of medieval texts in which, in various languages, the same or allied motifs have been assimilated, the influence of idiom upon literary expression is clearly demonstrated. The same play, written in French or in Netherlands, thereby acquires a totally different character. Not only the sound of the language but also the color of the language is involved. And so the clear, guileless, somewhat stammering Netherlands of the Middle Ages determines to an important extent the special poetic character of our medieval literature, including those cases where it was built upon adapted motifs.

Not so very long ago, at about the turn of the nineteenth and twentieth centuries, very shortly after the period of lack of appreciation, it became the custom to make the Middle Ages an example. It was called a great period of intellectual unity and for that reason was able to produce a monumental art with very pronounced character. Catholicism was the inner cohesion, and the feudal system, no matter what injustice was connected with it, had (it was believed) the advantage of creating a strong social structure. And in contrast was indicated our inner conflict, our lack of intellectual solidarity and as a consequence our crumbling society. The unity of religion created, according to this theory, an art of unequaled vitality and especially of an unparalleled grandeur of purpose and structure. Modern man, beset with conflicts, was, on account of these conflicts, incapable of such superhuman performance. And, to go one step further, against natural fellowship was placed our individualism; against the religion, our skepticism. And herewith the road was opened to a conception which reigned for several decades in certain Netherlands circles, that only a new communal sense and a new religion, bound mutually, could save art. Some made a religion out of socialism, others demonstrated that socialism and Christianity were in reality one, but all were looking for the unity lost since the Middle Ages. They tried to conquer in their minds the Renaissance and Romanticism, which they could not undo, for they saw therein symptoms of decay. To these desires for a new social structure based on a new intellectual unity, there was no objection whatsoever. There was objection, however, to the fact that, as soon as reference to the Middle Ages was made, a completely incorrect idea of it was conceived, because little is known about social unity in the Middle Ages. Christianity was the universal religion, without doubt, but Catholicism in those days was not yet the uniform system that it is now, and in practice we see how numerous Roman Catholic forms were disguised or barely disguised expressions of paganism. Paganism in the Netherlands had a tenacious vitality, and it took Christianity centuries to conquer it completely.

Christianity introduced, apart from a number of new dogmas and customs, a completely new conception of existence, created a new relationship between life and death, laid the basis for a new social theory. We should not forget that Christianity meant a complete revolution, compared to which the later revolutions, the violent social and economic changes in England, France and Russia successively, are symptoms with limited meaning. Such a complete and thorough revolution does *not* achieve effect without striking a blow.

The Middle Ages, therefore, could never have been a period of sublime rest, of unity, of balance, because it was ruled by the tragedy of the fall of one form of life and the rise of another. This tragedy explains the impressive violence of expression in the Middle Ages and of the religious in particular. The new religion could only maintain itself through battle and fierce affirmation. Those who were moved by the urgent power of religion had to testify to it vociferously and with emphasis. Violence marks almost all poetry of this period.

We have, therefore, in the Middle Ages an intellectual life that forms no unity and hence is extremely agitated and dramatic. On a social level unity was unknown as well. In the first place, there had been from the earliest times a clear division into nobility, clergy and peasantry. These classes did not live in hierarchic harmony together; on the contrary, they were unceasingly involved in a mutual life-and-death struggle in which the peasants, and the later evolving bourgeois class, proved to be the element with the strongest vitality.

The separation of the classes was so complete that we can speak of three lives on three levels, which only rarely came into contact. The nobility had a mythology completely of its own. Around the worship of woman was built a complicated and charming ritual; out of primitive pugnacity was created a magnificent game, the tournament, in which the initiated spectators enjoyed the colors and the rhythm and also the deftness of the participants and above all the subtle code of honor which was a part.

The clergy created, for their own use and for lay believers, a mythology in which Mary seems to have taken a higher place than her Divine Son, and in which, as we have seen before, numerous heathen after-effects were assimilated in more or less shrewd manner. The third social class had at its disposal two groups of motifs, and these we again find very clearly in literature: the glorification of daily life, earthly love, food and drink—in which a feeling for rough but real humor is never lacking—and satire on nobility and clergy, in which a passionate bitterness is usually expressed. This third social class for the first time brings the element of conscious criticism into literature. Criticism of the landowners, who obstructed the economic development of peasants and bourgeoisie, criticism of the clergy, which did not always succeed in bringing its actions to the level of its words, and also self-criticism in the attractive form of self-mockery.

The endlessly variegated literary richness of the Middle Ages extends over a period of almost three centuries. When the inner power gradually slackened, literature declined into the sometimes foolish, sometimes alarming, but always poetryless fabrications of the rhetoricians.

These rhetoricians usually were well-to-do townsmen, who, as a pastime, composed poems according to highly complicated schemes of verse. When we take offense at their complete lack of insight into the essence of poetry and personal talent, we should not forget that their sometimes clumsy, sometimes far too facile examples of poetry at least prove one thing, the high esteem in which literature was held in their day. The making of poems was considered the noblest and most sublime of occupations, and anyone who wished to show that he was not uncultured devoted himself to it with enthusiasm.

It took some time until Netherlands literature had torn itself free from the influence of the rhetoricians. Even in the great poets of the Golden Age traces are still to be found. The rescue came partly by way of popular poetry, which, though not always of pure quality, possessed the invaluable asset of reality, but chiefly through the influence of the tremendous renovations in the intellectual structure of the Western world, an influence which was felt strongly and permanently in the Netherlands, because the Reformation became an inseparable and gradually predominant part of the movement of renewal.

The transition period, in which the medieval spirit produced strong after-effects and in which the new idea developed with even more force, created in the Netherlands numerous new figures but no one great literary work of art in the Netherlands language. When we speak of important figures, we are thinking of course, in the first place of the universal humanist, Desiderius Erasmus of Rotterdam (1467–1536), who, no matter how valuable as a thinker, not only from the point of view of the Netherlands but also from that of all of Western Europe, may be mentioned in a survey of the Netherlands literature only in an indirect connection, because he wrote in Latin. The same circumstance affects his older and less-known contemporaries, Wessel Gansvoort (1419–1489) and Roelof Huysman (1422–1485), both men of Groningen.

The period of the rhetoricians, which went to pieces as a result of its absurdity and emptiness, allowed scope, in the ensuing period, for the development of folk-songs, which were a natural reaction to the rhetoricians. They are, so far as the period of the Early Renaissance is concerned, very seldom of outstanding beauty, although some few but authentic masterpieces were produced. The bricklayer of Bruges, Anthonie de Roovere, who died in 1482, composed among others a famous dance of death, *Van der Mollenfeeste,* in which there are portions of rare power and originality.

The most important folk-songs (and the Beggars' songs [1] are to be considered as such in the first rank) originated towards the end of the fifteenth and the beginning of the sixteenth centuries. The new popular art developed with cheerful enthusiasm and created the genuine masterpiece—the Wilhelmus—which, around 1572, was the battle- and comfort-song of the Dutch inside and outside the occupied Fatherland.

The text of the Wilhelmus is attributed to Philips Marnix of Saint Aldegonde (1539–1589). Marnix, who excelled as a poet if the Wilhelmus was actually composed by him, was one of the strangest figures of the early Reformation in the Netherlands. He put a flourishing finish to his studies with a course at Geneva, which he left in 1561, "Calvinist to the backbone."

[1] Beggars were the rebels against the Spanish tyrants.

Besides Marnix, Anna Bijns (1494–1575) should be mentioned. She stood for a passionate glorification of the Old Testament, grimly opposed to the not less passionate papist-hater, Marnix. In Bijns and Marnix the medieval accent is still strongest; in the nobleman, Jan van der Noot (1539–1595), and in Karel van Mander (1548–1606) the Renaissance-like Baroque spirit already dominates.

It does not seem necessary to list more authors of the so-called Early Renaissance in the Netherlands in a concise survey such as this. They were remarkable figures, but the works that they left us are unfortunately rarely, perhaps never, more remarkable. And it is this "more" with which literature is concerned.

There might be one other reason why the Early Renaissance did not produce any great writers. The Dutch had just begun their great battle against Spain. The arts, literature and science seldom achieve their highest flowering in times of disturbance and war. The production of art irrevocably demands time, time for reflection, time for slow, thoughtful preparation, time for deliberate work and as to the reader, time to assimilate the work quietly and time to meditate.

Apart from time, art requires the possibility of concentrating upon things beyond this world and upon matters out of the present. All periods of violent action are periods of intellectual poverty. The transitional period between the Middle Ages and the seventeenth century was therefore especially important for the things to come, but it was not the proper time for the "finished piece of work."

Just as ideas and judgment about the Middle Ages, in the course of the nineteenth century in the Netherlands, were subject to a complete revolution, so later historians changed their opinion about the old idea that between the Middle Ages and Renaissance there was a wide gap. In history generally, and in the history of culture most certainly, some rapid changes with alternate slackening or acceleration of rhythm are observed, but the symptom of rupture is unknown. Events always result from one another. If we sometimes do not perceive the connection, that is owing to our limited knowledge. When we sum up the symptoms of Humanism and Renaissance and Reformation and Baroque, we immediately discover that the conditions of their origin were present during the entire Middle Ages. To mention a single example: it is generally stated that the Renaissance meant a revived interest in Greek and Roman antiquity. This is true in so far as that interest was extreme during the Renaissance, but the adjective "revived" is incorrect, because interest in classical antiquity was never dead. During the Middle Ages the old languages (Latin in particular) were taught and kept up with care; in the literature of the Middle Ages classical motifs are to be found; Aristotle was an object of serious study. I should therefore prefer to say that the Renaissance was characterized by a clearer understanding of ancient culture, by a more unbiased study and interpretation of the texts and by a passing beyond accepted limits; what had formerly been the privilege of monks was now brought within the reach of literate laymen. This latter symptom is so typical of the period of transition which we are reviewing that we must pay it special attention: *the breaking of shackles and the surpassing of limits!*

As the medieval class system had in the course of years lost its solidity and thereby much of its sway, during the Renaissance laymen of every rank could obtain admission to the sources of knowledge and science and later also to posts and offices.

In the period of transition we still see the three medieval social classes continue parallel to each other, but the separating walls are no longer completely closed and the accent has been shifted. The nobility no longer dominates, the clergy too has lost of its privileges and the third class has secured a dominant position in society. When a new group of the population rises, we always see the same symptom: a violent thirst for knowledge, because knowledge is power; a no less violent vitality, because the joys which were formerly inaccessible must be enjoyed by taking deep draughts; finally a need for personal liberty, which is likewise obvious, after the economic and social coercion under which the third class lived in the Middle Ages.

Thus we have the three strong passions which characterize the Renaissance: passion for knowledge, passion for life, passion for freedom.

The study of the classics as a basis for every sphere of culture was taken in hand, not only with zeal, but according to new systems, by men who had to face this material new and fresh. The bourgeoisie, who for the first time had money and possibilities for enjoyment, certainly did not pass up this opportunity. And where freedom was concerned, this was not only political freedom but above all intellectual freedom. Political freedom was not very great, according to our present ideas, but in comparison with the condition of slavery and servitude in which a large majority of the people lived during the Middle Ages, this period was assuredly an enormous change for the better.

To be an artist in the Middle Ages did not really differ from being one in the Renaissance, because all that is art and that concerns its origin is not limited by time; but the artists of the Middle Ages were far less conscious of the value, purpose and meaning of art than the people of the Renaissance were. An intellectual pride originated which, in my opinion, is one of the most convincing symptoms and one of the greatest charms of the artist of the Renaissance.

Apart from all the above considerations it should never be forgotten that *all* intellectual currents were and are originated and carried on by man, and that man changes his ideas, preferences, morals, may improve his knowledge and deftness, but that in reality he remains unchanged, and that his existence is defined by his relation to life and to death. All human feelings and thoughts, without exception, are directly or indirectly connected with life or death, heavenly or earthly love, desire for power, richness, pleasure, joy, grief, each movement of intellect or mind being a movement connected with life or death. And this connection with the first and last things is revealed to us most clearly and convincingly in fear, fear of life or fear of death, which fills our entire life and which is our mightiest impulse to all creation.

This fear, in the Middle Ages very strong and directly present, expressed itself in the Renaissance indirectly, in a passion for life. Fear always has a double action: that which makes us fearful both attracts and repels. Death fascinates us and makes itself so desirable that we long for it, or it appears so terrible that we fly for refuge to all the pleasures which earthly life offers us in vain. And it is that irrevocable, fruitless spirit that gives each joy, and particularly the colorful sensual festivities, of the Renaissance the tragic accent.

The fear which in the Middle Ages welled forth unprejudiced, openly and forcefully, assumed in the Renaissance the form of a much more conscious and more concrete desire for eternity. While medieval man consoled himself with the church's promise of eternal life and eternal salvation, man of the Renaissance took certainty for uncertainty and looked for self-perpetuation in form as realized in a piece of art.

In medieval mysticism (and all medieval Netherlands lyricism is mystical) man tries to save himself by losing himself in God; in the Renaissance, he does so by making himself immortal by means of a permanent outline, by means of the miracle of creating form. It goes without saying that from this new idea there also originated a completely new relation between the artist and his work and art generally, and, as a consequence, a new conception about the value of man. In the Middle Ages, mortal, physical man was only a painful obstacle to the spirit's achieving its highest destination; in the Renaissance the worldly man was the means of the superworldly spirit revealing himself. The man who had to be despised by all the faithful of the Middle Ages because he impeded the approach to God, this same man was revered in the Renaissance because he was part of the grand world entity in which God revealed Himself.

THE BAROQUE

Netherlands literature is in its highest and most remarkable expression a lyric literature. Many are astonished to learn that we Netherlanders, known, not entirely without justice, as sober, businesslike, exact and, let us be frank, pedestrian, that we, merchants and seafarers, possess a literature, in which the pure lyrical element strongly dominates. I see in this a natural and necessary reaction to the moralizing quality that characterizes both Netherlands individuals and the Netherlands community. The fervent relation between the traditional national character and accepted Calvinism has created a typical mentality, which we may call typically Netherlandish. And this mental condition still more or less characterizes those who are no longer directly connected with Calvinistic dogmas. I do not know how far this comparison goes, but the picture which Van Wyck Brooks has given of old New England shows here and there striking resemblances to Netherlands life and the Netherlands way of living. The Netherlands lyric is the often pent-up, violent reaction to Netherlands dignity and virtue, which have a tendency to stiffen into dogmatic forms, while a certain theological, Old Testament hairsplitting was not foreign to our ancestors and is still not so today.

Poets in such an old, solid, stiff society cannot be anything but rebels, grumblers, fervent opponents of law and order, because they announce a higher order, that of poetry.

We therefore combine a strong (often painful) urge to moralize with an irresistible need for lyric flight. Our lyric forms the exhaust valve for a life that is dominated by strong moral laws and an almost servile adaptation to traditional habits. Though medieval life did not give much occasion for this, we may see the first indication of the phenomenon already at that time. But it could only acquire its full meaning for us after the victory of the Calvinistic idea, which for centuries has defined the spirit, even of those who believe they have put aside the religion of their fathers. The epic as synthesis of the lyric and didactic we find in the Middle Ages (Van den Vos Reynaerde), when Catholicism did not exclude a strong worldly passion, and we find it again in the twentieth century (in the form of the modern novel), when Protestantism has lost, together with its preponderance, much of its absolutism. In the early Renaissance, in the Golden (seventeenth) Century, and in the period of decay which followed, we find in Netherlands literature, ever close to each other, hostility and, inseparably joined, the irresistible urge towards learning and the enchantments of song.

Both these currents find expression in the work of every important author of those days, and we see these currents most clearly in Joost van den Vondel, who is, perhaps not the most subtle poet in the strict sense of the word, but undoubtedly the most impressive human and literary figure of our literature. Vondel, as a great figure is likely to be, is the complete summary of all the currents and undercurrents that determine the time in which he lived. We have seen how a period of unknown richness and variety, the Middle Ages, passed away into a poetry of the rhetoricians, which could at best be called intelligent and in which there is very little of lasting value. In Vondel we recognize traces of the pure medieval mystic, traces of the meaningless playfulness of the rhetoricians and traces of the new understanding of man and his value, which were put into circulation through Humanism. In addition, above all, Vondel is a man of his time and fervently connected with all expressions of it, but he is also as an individual so strong and powerful that he not only pierces the framework of his society but also the borders of his period and therefore cannot but remain for the Netherlands people even now a living reality. His art is so incomparable and moreover so indestructible that it has saved even his least important occasional verse from transitoriness. Yes, so strong is his personality, still present to us, that we are convinced that circumstances have not influenced Vondel, rather Vondel the circumstances, so that many events of his period take on for us a Vondelian character, while they occur in a Vondelian atmosphere. The Council pensioner, Oldenbarneveldt, is a character with a clearly defined outline for historians, but we, non-historians, see him and recognize him as a contemporary through the verses in which Joost van den Vondel has pictured Oldenbarneveldt's fate for all time.

Vondel's dominating power forms one of the greatest curiosities of our literature. Because, though surrounded by men who were his superiors in many respects, he remained, in his time as in ours, the first one, the only one. Vondel lived long, from 1578 to 1679 (both Marnix van Saint Aldegonde and Jan Luyken were his contemporaries), but he remained himself throughout all changes in conception and taste, the master who stands in the midst of life and yet above it.

The secret of Vondel's irresistible personality and vitality is brought about by his profound mystical alliance with the people from whom he arose. This fact in almost every respect determines his being and also the contact between him and contemporaries like Hooft, Huygens and Cats.

A comparison between Vondel and Cats in this respect is extremely instructive. We should observe, to start with, that such a comparison can only be superficial, because, if we confine ourselves to the real, that is, poetical value of their works, Vondel is a genius and Cats an ordinary paltry rhymer. But Cats was a man of standing, rich, distinguished, a man who held high posts; yet he wrote books filled with didactic poems, filled with coarse, jocular familiarities, while Vondel, first stocking-merchant and, after his bankruptcy, clerk in a pawnbroker's shop, an unimportant citizen, wrote in an exalted tone, not only when he treated of exalted subjects, but also when he stayed close to the ground.

Cats always showed, in all his trivialities, the man of standing; Vondel, in all his sublimity, the man of the people. The secret of this symptom was the fact that Cats wrote *for* the people, while Vondel wrote *from* the people's hearts, that Cats consciously and benevolently "descended" to the masses of his simple countrymen, while Vondel, who belonged to the masses, worked himself "up" and "carried along the masses in his ascent."

Vondel did not possess the refinement and lyric tension of Hooft, but he possessed a number of qualities, which nevertheless made him rise above Hooft and Huygens, both great and important figures in Netherlands intellectual life. He possessed a holy ardor, an untiring passion, a vitality welling up from deep sources, a fervency, a frankness, a freedom of spirit and mind and, above all, the power to renew his vigor time and again.

He was about eighty when he wrote his greatest masterpiece, the most important work of Netherlands literature, the dramatic trilogy, *Lucifer, Adam in Exile* and *Noah*. Not only does this work show no trace of the author's age but, on the contrary, it abounds richly in lyric youth.

In the year 1641, Vondel became a convert to the Roman Catholic faith. This fact in itself, considered in the surroundings and the period—which was fanatical Protestant Holland relatively soon after the Reformation—was a deed of courage. For Vondel there existed only one law, inner conviction, and for that he braved all consequences and danger.

Joost van den Vondel was a respectable, a great, an upright man. For example, he was too honest to be able to be pleasant, and he therefore lived in the midst of the artists of his time as a solitary and he found companionship rather among simple citizens than among his brothers in art.

P. C. Hooft, the master of Muiden, had made his castle there an intellectual and fashionable center. Authors, painters and musicians met there to have serious discussions and to enjoy themselves. In this famous Muiden center, Vondel, the unchallenged master, was a guest only once. He felt completely out of place in the midst of this refinement of intellect, this style of living and the courtly people around. By contrast, Hooft felt uncomfortable in the presence of such a natural power, of such a real and ingenuous man as Vondel.

The real difference between the Baroque man and the Renaissance man is shown by the comparison of Vondel and Hooft (1581-1647). Hooft was a man of refinement, who composed a number of graceful, harmonious and yet emotion-arousing poems (in particular his sonnets), a learned man, an author of dignified and well-considered prose, a person of high standing, a man of the world, an epicurean and above all a pleasant man, obliging, polite and charming. Far less a poet than Hooft, but just as learned, Constantijn Huygens (1596–1687) was the type of the perfect Hollander of the Golden Age, righteous to the backbone, quiet and zealous, liking the good things on earth and blessed with a magnificent human humor.

Jacob Cats (1577–1660) was, we have seen, also a representative of the leading social class. His poetical work, which is far from being poetical, was for centuries the household book of the Netherlands citizen; his pedestrian morality, his coarse realism and his mostly scatological jocularity entitled him to this honor.

Much nearer to Vondel, and thus also nearer to the Middle Ages, was the man who, together with Vondel and Hooft, was the greatest poet of his time, Gerbrand Adriaanszoon Breeroo: like Vondel, a child of the people, a magnificent figure, real through and through, at one time crude, then fervently religious, rebellious, then humble. And consequently he was always driven by a supreme love, in turn for an earthly woman and for his Saviour. Breeroo, the first Bohemian in Dutch literature, is above all the poet of repentance. After he had lived out his unbridled youth with wine and women, he found his most moving poetical accents in self-reproach and in prayers to God for forgiveness.

What a richness there was in the Netherlands of the period! Time was ripe for it. The war for freedom against Spain, though not yet crowned with a peace treaty, had been won. The young republic day by day gained power and respect in the world. And, what is of particular importance, wealth flowed to Amsterdam from all directions and from all continents. After long years of struggle and difficult existence, at last the time had come, and attention to higher things of the mind developed.

Besides the eminent figures which I have named, besides Vondel, Breeroo, Hooft and Huygens, we see poets who, perhaps secondary in rank, have yet without exception enriched the Netherlands lyric with a number of masterpieces, poets who even at present are still read and lived with: Jacob Reefsen (1568–1658); Heiman Dullaert (1636–1684), a painter, Rembrandt's pupil; Johannes Stalpaert van der Wielen (1579–1630), and Jan Luyken (1649–1712) who concludes this great period with dignity. Luyken's profession was that of lithographer, and many hundreds of his works have been preserved. He started his poetical career with a volume of love songs, *Duytsche Lier*, which among many virtues especially possesses that of jauntiness, but which in its laboriousness appears somewhat poor. Later on the poet bought up all copies of this book and destroyed them: as far as we know, only three copies were saved. In 1924, for the first time, a reprint appeared in a very limited edition. Luyken's conversion from a gay, careless, superficial existence to a life of meditation and dedication most probably took place under the influence of the German mystic, Jacob Boehme. In his second period he was inspired to compose a series of the deepest and most beautiful religious poems ever written in the Netherlands language.

THE ROMANTIC

Before we discuss Netherlands Romanticism, we must first establish the fact that two clearly distinguishable meanings are attached to the word Romanticism. Romanticism is the name given to a rather exactly limited movement in the history of literature, which made itself known for the first time toward the end of the eighteenth century, and in the midst of which we still live today. Romanticism, according to an infinitely wider conception, is also the term applied to a form of thought and conduct which has appeared, and will appear, in all ages. We have therefore to deal with a historical definition for professional uses and with the appellation of a state of mind or human disposition. Everyone recognizes that there is a connection between these two applications of the same word, but this connection is not so close that we may identify them. The romantic person is characterized mainly by two qualities; consciously or unconsciously he places the soul above the intellect and thus builds his real life almost exclusively of emotional values. He believes passionately in imagination and inspiration. Consequently he considers the precepts of reason incomprehensible and even a hindrance to his clear and honest development. He recognizes that life can only be inwardly experienced and inwardly justified and thus finds the origin, criterion and purpose of all his thoughts and deeds in himself. He creates for himself a world outside and above reality. In the last instance he bows only before the superior power of his own imaginings.

The romantic life is an uninterrupted movement without absolute laws imposed from above for all time. It is dynamic and it creates, according to its own needs, a complete, changing ethic which, according to the example of the Sophists, quickly leads to the glorification of power and the theory that might is right. Romanticism is not restricted to the fine arts. Now more than ever there is talk of a romantic social doctrine which is founded on the irrational forces which stir the masses and thus exerts a strong influence on political economy. These political romanticists oppose reason and, still more, rationalism. We see them in clear contrast with the classic conceptions concerning society and social classification. The Netherlands philosopher Kohnstamm rightly says: "The conception of the world of Romanticism must be considered first of all as a reaction to the philosophy of the Enlightenment. It therefore places at its center not Reason but

Feeling; it therefore makes, not the separate parts, but the whole that is more primordial than its elements, its most important category. It places oneness above multiplicity, organism above mechanism."

For the Romanticism in present-day thought, new names have been sought. At first vitalism was used; after that, more generally, "philosophy of life." This was characterized by the preponderant significance which its adherents gave to the irrational in the world, in society and in the individual. Inspiration is glorified at the expense of the intellect. The two great romantic influences which have been felt in various spheres in the Netherlands are Henri Bergson and Sigmund Freud. Ludwig Klages went so far as to represent the mind as the enemy of the soul, in which case mind has to be understood exclusively as *ratio* and the soul as the summing up of the unconscious. Romanticism is thus medieval mysticism, Shakespeare, Baroque, psychoanalysis, fascism, surrealism. . . . The entire Netherlands literature from the beginning of the nineteenth century to the present is romantic; the *Camera Obscura* of Nicolaas Beets (the most-read, popular prose book of the Netherlands) is romantic, despite the fact that the romanticist Potgieter put it aside as an expression of the "copying lust of daily life," so rejectable in his opinion; the naturalism following the literary movement of 1880 is also romantic, although it mistakenly considered itself to be objective and thus anti-romantic.

At the beginning of the nineteenth century stands the first absolute and great romanticist, the remarkable figure of Willem Bilderdijk (1756–1831). In his day he was, as human being and as poet, the object of violent disputes and, up to now, posterity has not determined its attitude toward him. Until recently passionate debates were conducted about Bilderdijk as a poet and about his character. He has had defenders through thick and thin and critics who consider no line of his of any worth. From the fact alone that he has been a controversial figure for a century it is to be seen that he possessed special qualities and special faults and was no indifferent, banal figure.

His lyric poetry, according to my personal taste, is careless in construction, over-rich in false, turgid feeling and impotent bragging, but with here and there, suddenly, some flights of true genius. His personality in the world of daily life was not very attractive: Bilderdijk was an example of a cantankerous psychopath who elevated falsehoods to rules of life. Grandson of an innkeeper, he drew up a forged family tree for himself, according to which he was descended from the Counts of Teisterbant and thus from the Knights of the Swan. But what is most difficult to forgive Bilderdijk is the weakness that he showed in public life. He left the country as an adherent of the House of Orange when the French marched in, but as soon as he saw advantage to himself, he returned to Holland, became a "collaborationist," at first degraded himself to accepting a job from the "King," Louis Bonaparte, and finally went so far as to glorify Napoleon in a bragging ode.

There is an utterance of Bilderdijk's in a letter to Tydeman, which is very significant, particularly now:

> I immediately looked upon him [Napoleon] as the man called to establish a new general monarchy. Yes, I looked forward to his coming before he existed.

Bilderdijk believed in the millennium that would be founded according to the Apocalypse and he assumed that Napoleon would be its builder, just as a few years ago some excited, irrational people believed in Hitler's millennium.

But hardly was the House of Orange back in the Netherlands when Willem Bilderdijk executed a right-about and begged at the new address. William I was generous and liberal enough not to punish Bilderdijk for his needless treachery, but it is perfectly natural that he refused to give him a professorship at Leiden. Bilderdijk, however, did not find this so and went away complaining and scoffing. One cannot deny he had poetic passion, a passionate nature. He was a picturesque figure, but he was surely no great poet and behaved like what is called "un villain bonhomme."

The really genuine poet of the beginning of the nineteenth century was A. C. W. Staring (1767–1841). In many respects he is akin to Hooft, both in his attitude toward life and in his pure lyric nature. After having completed his law studies he went, like Hooft, to complete his education at a foreign university and, again like Hooft, he later lived—not in a castle, it is true but in a stately country seat in the Province of Gelderland—the noble life of a poet, a wise, educated, cultivated man. Staring's poetic art is certainly meaner in quality, less penetrating and stately than that of Hooft, but he had the same sensitivity, pointedness, the same preference for a dashing arabesque, and as an artist and personality he is equally lovable. When at the end of the nineteenth century a new critical attitude, with pitiless and not always just severity, rejected almost the entire work of the preceding hundred years, an exception was made for Staring. His exemplary poetic dignity and his gifts of mind and heart appeared incontestable.

What Staring was for poetry, Jacob Geel (1789–1862) was for prose: a witty, clever, careful stylist and a versatile scholar, the man who for the first time in the Netherlands sharply formulated the problems in relation to the conception of romanticism and classicism and treated them in a clarifying manner. Geel is and always will be the greatest essayist, in the strict sense of the word, that the Netherlands has ever produced. He wrote only one volume of prose, but this is still alive and significant for the readers of today, as if it had been written yesterday.

From Bilderdijk and Geel two currents start out, which we can trace a considerable distance into the nineteenth century.

Bilderdijk's fanatical, prophetically inclined Christianity met with response in many disciples. His belief in the apocalyptic millennium had power of attraction, especially for certain Jews who found in it the echo of their expectation of the Messiah. (Bilderdijk himself said: "A Jew who is faithful to God is Christian in his longings.") His followers, the poet Isaac da Costa (1758–1861), the latter's wife, Hanna Belmonte, and Abraham Capadose were baptized with great solemnity at St. Peter's church in Leiden. Round Bilderdijk and these enthusiastic, high-strung disciples a group formed that is called the Reveil: the awakening of a new Christian realization of life. This movement is of inestimable importance in the intellectual history of the Netherlands because from it proceeded a man like Groen van Prinsteren, who exerted a decisive influence on Netherlands politics. But literary works of real and lasting significance did not emanate from it. The work of da Costa, great in design and intention, was not proof against time; its human substance was completely lost in its verbose rhetoric.

Geel's point of view asserted itself indirectly in politics and led to the liberalism of Thorbecke, Groen's great opponent, but can be traced most directly and clearly in literature. One cannot speak of a "school": Geel's personality was too modest and removed from the public eye to found one, but the word "example" fits him excellently. Geel's example, both as regards his conceptions and his manner of writing, affected the three great prose writers of the nineteenth century: R. C. Bakhuizen van der

Brink (1810–1865), E. J. Potgieter (1808–1875) and C. Busken Huet (1826–1886).

Potgieter dominates the entire middle of the nineteenth century. He was the founder and leader of the periodical *De Gids* (The Guide) which, as far as I know, still exists and is in its 107th volume. He was considered a perfect prose writer, an inexorable yet just critic, and a pure poet. In short, Potgieter was the center and personified ideal of all who between 1840 and 1880 were liberal and practised belles lettres or were sincerely interested in them. The significance of Potgieter as leader and as literary figure can hardly be overestimated. But part of his writings is only accessible to us after great self-discipline and exertion. His critical work has been best proof against the years, and after that some of his great poems—*Florence* and *The Inheritance of a Country Squire*—have been able to maintain their position with proud positiveness. Together they form the most monumental poetic work of our literature, pregnant, full of scholarly contemplation, full of human reflections and of a truly great design and structure. Potgieter gives us the maximum that can be achieved with talent, supported by extensive and profound knowledge, a noble purpose and a perfect mastery of technique. What he lacks is a spark of genius.

Beside Bakhuizen van den Brink and Busken Huet, Robert Fruin (1823–1899) must be mentioned here. Bakhuizen and Fruin were primarily historians, but their sense of form and the purity of their language gave their compositions literary as well as scientific value. Huet was a born literary critic who, toward the end of his career, devoted himself to historical work and wrote two compilations of history of art which received great acclaim, *Het Land van Rembrandt* (Rembrandt's Country) and *Het Land van Rubens*.

It is not possible to form a clear idea of our literature in the nineteenth century without including in it the noble, quiet figure and stately, extensive work of A. G. Bosboom-Toussaint (1812–1886), most of which consists of historical novels in which, with a single exception, native material is treated. Mrs. Bosboom-Toussaint, with an undeniable and convincing epic talent, was one of the few genuine, born story-tellers in the Netherlands of the nineteenth century and one of the most richly gifted women that our country has produced.

But however highly one may speak of the many-sided merits of a Potgieter, a Huet, a Toussaint, however gladly and liberally one wants to give them all the praise that is honestly their due, one must, in order to maintain correct proportions, state clearly and emphatically that the nineteenth century in the Netherlands produced, besides many talents, only one artist of real genius: Eduard Douwes Dekker (1820–1887), who became known by the pen-name which characterizes him: Multatuli. In Dekker's nature, and thus also in his uncommonly rich and vivid prose, we see for the first time the complete and harmonious synthesis of the two national qualities which we can perceive as enthralling antitheses throughout the history of Netherlands intellectual life, namely, the inclination to moralize, the old, innate urge and desire to preach and, as the only means of escape, lyric flight. Dekker is now the lyric moralist, now the moralizing lyricist. His life's work consists of dissertations which are really like outpourings, aphorisms, witticisms and fragments, animated without exception by a dark glow and formulated with cutting keenness. Even the two books by Multatuli that are considered novels, *Max Havelaar* and *Woutertje Pieterse,* are composed of a number of fragments frequently very loosely connected. They completely lack the set, traditional structure which characterizes the proper nineteenth-century novel. They are no worse because of that; on the contrary, they derive their value and charm from their freedom and their unconventionality, their whimsicality, their quick, surprising turns and their inexhaustible wealth of ideas and feelings.

Dekker's life was a life of passionate conflict. His vital force, his conviction and interest, were so great and so many-sided that he was unable to remain neutral with regard to a single problem of importance. The best period of his life was entirely dominated by the great problem, like none other in national importance, of the relation between the Netherlands and the Indonesians of our Asiatic territory, for which he invented the melodious name of Insulinde. By his actions as well as by his writings he rang in an entirely new conception of this relationship. This was, in the beginning, sharply and not always honestly opposed. But in the end the ideas defended by Multatuli with much fire were elaborated and generally accepted as basis of an administration of loyal collaboration.

Multatuli's importance for Netherlands Indies politics is outside the limits of this survey and of my competence, but his importance in the Netherlands literature is no less great. For although Dekker would have liked best to continue as reformer and prophet, he was by nature and always, even when he entered the political domain, an artist. He possessed the gift of the seer, the inner passion and the sense of form, without which one cannot imagine an artist. Before him, the Netherlands language had rarely been handled so ardently and fervently, with such tempo and conviction. Multatuli's influence is still felt today, because he rehabilitated the spoken language and not only defended the "ordinary word" against the somewhat ceremonious loftiness which was peculiar to his best contemporaries, but raised it to be a serviceable, concise and penetrating literary means of expression. It is no wonder that in the years round about 1930 Multatuli found among young writers such ready-to-fight admirers (we may mention Menno ter Braak and E. du Perron); they defend the rights of sober language and natural style, as he did in his day.

Of all the writers of the nineteenth century, Multatuli is the only one who has remained alive after more than half a century. On a Potgieter and also a Huet, time has left its mark, and we read their works with a constant realization of living with them in the past. Only Multatuli's quick, lively and deeply penetrating prose makes the impression of having been written today.

It is therefore not absurd for us to consider Multatuli the precursor of the intellectual revival that took place in the Netherlands in every sphere between 1870 and 1880. He was not the only one who heralded this renewal, but he was among those in whom we perceive the first possibilities of a radical change.

THE REVIVAL OF THE EIGHTIES

The Movement of the Eighties represented a general longing for a deepening and purifying of the conception of art on the basis of a glorification of personality. This longing appeared not only in literature but also in painting, architecture and philosophy and was accompanied by a passionate criticism of the immediate past. The character of the new movement was mainly determined by a reflowering of individualism as a conscious ideal. From this it followed logically that criticism had to occupy an important place in it.

Far and away the most important poet, as far as pure lyric potentiality is concerned, was Herman Gorter (1864–1927), the author of *Mei* (May), a symbolic narrative that in a very short time became one of the classic works of our literature. In the same period Gorter wrote a number of short poems which were collected under the title *De School der Poëzie* (The School of

Poetry). In this, poetic individualism finds its richest and most glorious expression. Later, after having joined a then still young socialistic movement, Gorter wrote two philosophical poems, "Een klein Heldendicht" (A Little Epic), and the voluminous work "Pan." These contain a number of fragments of incomparable beauty, but as a whole they no longer satisfy us, because in them the thinker and politician too frequently imposes silence on the poet. The numerous little poems of his later period are also uneven. Beside utterances which represent Gorter at his best, we find uninspired exercises that sometimes strike one painfully as childish. But whatever shortcomings we can discover in Gorter's life-work as it now lies before us, it is on the whole of an unheard-of superabundance and radiant vitality. Of all his contemporaries Gorter exerted the deepest and most lasting influence on younger people.

We quote here the first verses of Gorter's great lyric poem *Mei*, verses which every lettered Netherlander knows by heart, "A new spring and a new musical note." (The translation that follows below is by Professor A. J. Barnouw.)

> A new spring, and a new, musical note!
> May this song sound as the song of the flute
> I heard one summer day, before nightfall,
> In an old town along the hushed canal.
> 'Twas dark indoors, but outside the still street
> Gathered in dusk, and in the sky shone late
> Daylight. A pale and golden glimmer fell
> Across the gables on my window-sill.
> Then a boy blew, clear as an organ pipe.
> The notes shook in the evening air, as ripe
> As tender cherries when a breeze begins
> Among the bush its airy wanderings.
> He strolled across the bridges and along
> The water's edge, going slow, and scattering song
> Like a young bird, and in unconsciousness
> Of his own gladness with that evening peace.
> And many a tired man, sitting at his ale
> And supper, listened as to an ancient tale,
> And smiled. A hand that pulled the window to
> Paused for a moment as the piper blew.

Willem Kloos (1859–1938) was the theorist of the Movement of the Eighties, and he illustrated his principles with a number of truly human, deeply stirring poems. But he did not fulfill the very high expectations that were rightly entertained of him at the beginning. After a period of intense intellectual life, he suddenly collapsed; a serious illness left nothing of his former passion, his former strength and lucidity of mind. He filled his long life with studies upon the history of literature, of secondary significance, wrote many critiques without conviction and without discernment and a series of 1500 absolutely unreadable, mostly ridiculous sonnets under the title, *Binnengedachten* (Inner Thoughts). The young Kloos, however, whom we honor as one of our masters, wrote about a hundred poems that seem to have been proof against time and a volume of theoretical essays that have as yet lost little of their value and nothing of their beauty. In 1883, Kloos established a periodical *De Nieuwe Gids* (The New Guide) which was the center of the intellectual life of the Netherlands for about ten years but which lost all significance after Kloos' collapse.

Besides Kloos the editorial staff was formed by, among others, Albert Verwey (1865–1937) and Frederik van Eeden (1860–1932), two writers who occupied a very important place in the period 1880–1910. Of the two, Verwey made the deepest impression on his younger countrymen, while Van Eeden succeeded in procuring an international audience for himself. Verwey carried on the tradition of Potgieter. In a new time and a new environment he was the representative of intellectual passion. His work consists of a series of voluminous essays of lasting significance and of many poems which do not always correspond to our poetic ideals but, because of their noble content and stately form, rouse our interest and respect. Although himself not academically trained, he was appointed professor in Netherlands literature at the ancient University of Leiden and in this capacity he performed pioneer work by stripping higher education in literature of its all too scholastic constraint and by bringing about harmony between knowledge and insight.

Frederik van Eeden, whose first period was so strongly influenced by Thoreau that he gave the name "Walden" to the countryplace where he made experiments in cooperative cultivation of the ground, was a versatile man: a physician full of interest in psychiatry, poet, novelist, dramatic critic, sociologist and practical reformer. He ended his life and career as a Roman Catholic convert.

Frederik van Eeden was originally richly endowed but he lacked self-criticism, and the indeterminateness of his character was again and again detrimental to his work, which was consequently deficient in outline and stability. During his life he was embroiled in so many theological disputes that public opinion and the critics did not succeed in forming an honest opinion of his character and value. Now that all the storms he raised have abated, it is generally observed that he enriched the Netherlands literature with some substantial works. First of all there is his allegory in three parts, *De Kleine Johannes* (The Little John), the first part of which is the best known and far and away the weakest; further, his drama in verse, *De Broeders* (The Brothers), great in design, rich, and magnificently varied; his psychological novel, *Aan de Koele Meeren des Doods* (By the Cool Lakes of Death); his comedy, *De Heks van Haarlem* (The Witch of Haarlem); several profound philosophical studies and a small number of good poems. And these are only the highlights of his voluminous work.

As a genuine writer of the Eighties, mention must be made of K. J. L. Alberdingk Thijm—who used the nom-de-plume, Lodewijk van Deyssel—born in 1869 and still living. He wrote two novels, *Een liefde* and *De Kleine Republiek* (A Love; The Little Republic), intelligent, painstaking school examples of what is called naturalism. But he is above all a critic, a critic of a particular kind: a lyric critic. He arrives but rarely at a well-considered, quiet, solidly grounded opinion; he damns or glorifies, he reviles or sings songs of praise. The content of practically all his writings has already lost much of its meaning, but the best is nevertheless saved by the unequaled beauty of his language.

In the School of the Eighties we must still reckon three prose writers of importance: first, Jacobus van Looy (1855–1930), who was at the same time a meritorious painter. Van Looy is a man of description, of plastic prose and of this he has produced several small masterpieces, but his real significance as a human being and an artist is seen only from his *Wonderlijke Avonturen van Zebedeus* (Wondrous Adventures of Zebedeus), a book in three volumes that stands entirely alone in our literature and that has no resemblance whatever to any work in foreign literature known to me. If one wants to find a vague similarity, one must compare it with one of the loveliest, most capricious books of the German Romantic Movement, *Kontraste und Paradoxen* (Contrasts and Paradoxes) by Frederich von Sallet. *Zebedeus* is a book full of the most exquisite discoveries, rich in unexpected nuances and changes, poetic, satirical, humorous and, in the true sense of the word, inexhaustible. Anyone who knows the life of Van Looy and his environment again and again discovers entertaining allusions to it, and anyone who studies the history of the Movement of the Eighties and is able to fathom Van Looy's playful symbolism finds rich material in his *Zebedeus*.

The second prose writer alluded to was Louis Couperus (1863–1933), who is one of the few born "narrators" in our country. His work was very uneven. Next to novels of great significance and lasting value, he wrote cursory, entertaining works calculated for a cheap, temporary success. But Couperus at his best forms a steeply rising pinnacle in our new literature. His books have been translated into many languages: the English translation by Teixeira de Mattos became famous. His work consists of "modern" and of "historical" novels. On the whole the first are more personal in tone, stronger in characterization and more profoundly experienced. We may mention *Eline Vere*, a youthful work; *De Boeken der Kleine Zielen* (The Books of the Small Souls), four novels which together form a whole; and indisputably his masterpiece, *Van Oude Menschen, de Dingen die voorbijgaan* (Of Old People, The Things That Pass). In these books lives forever an atmosphere and a mentality which is characteristic of life, especially in The Hague, and in a particular period, namely circa 1900, an atmosphere and a mentality which were largely determined by Indian influences. Of all his contemporaries, of all the so-called Men of the Eighties, Louis Couperus was, in his somewhat mannered and nevertheless genuine refinement, the most picturesque figure and was at the same time as human being surely the most lovable.

Finally, there was Frans Erens (1857–1939). Born in South Limburg, he introduced into the "New Guide" a peculiar tone of his own: in a pagan environment he was and remained a Catholic and he knew, better than any of his young friends, the new literature of France. He published a few novelettes, which were distinguished by a tone of their own, innumerable volumes of essays and an autobiography which is of great importance for the knowledge of the New Guide period in the Netherlands.

Immediately after the first generation of the men of the Eighties, who gradually applied and carried on the principles of the movement, a number of prose writers of significance made their appearance, of whom we mention above all Frans Coenen (1866–1936) and Gerard van Eckeren (1876–).

As a playwright of international fame, Herman Heyermans (1864–1924) should be included here. Besides his plays, which were translated into many languages and played on many stages, he wrote innumerable frequently attractive and witty novelettes and some novels.

It is impossible and furthermore undesirable, when we speak about Netherlands literature, to associate with it the political boundaries of our country. Netherlands literature is not the literature of the Netherlands but of the regions where Dutch is spoken. The Netherlands itself has nine million inhabitants; the language sphere includes more than seventeen million Dutch-speaking people.

The writers who in the lately formed kingdom of Belgium, in the beginning of the nineteenth century, began the strongly romantic movement for the maintenance of their own language knew only Flemish and therefore demanded its recognition. This "Flemish" was a conception difficult to define. For, speaking philologically, no Flemish languages existed. There existed many splendid, rich dialects in the two Flanders (East and West), in Limburg, in Antwerp and in Brabant. Which of these dialects was the Flemish language for which there was such fierce struggle?

Natural development has brought the solution. From 1850 to the present day, but especially after the complete Flemishization of the University of Ghent, the Dutch language asserted itself in the South Netherlands also. With that the word Flemish, in its too wide and therefore incorrect meaning, is disappearing.

Official documents of Belgium authorities speak exclusively of the two vernaculars, Netherlands and French. All educated Flemings speak Dutch and *besides,* as do many of their North Netherlands brothers, one or another dialect. The contributions that the South has made to common inflexion and vocabulary are no less in value and number than those of the North. Those who are not well acquainted with Belgium and the Netherlands—countries which belonged together before the Reformation and are now again growing strongly toward each other—find it difficult to imagine this contrast which does not exclude a close bond. One cannot study the Netherlands without Belgium, nor Belgium without the Netherlands. Perhaps it would be better here to replace the political appellation by the geographical and to speak of North and South. In the past few years the intellectual bonds between South and North Netherlands have so tightened that, while retaining the shading, a philological literary unity is becoming ever more distinct. This phenomenon was made possible by the emancipation of the Catholics in North Netherlands. After that the influence of Catholicism grew steadily. There came about a mental rapprochement between the Roman Catholic South and the mixed (but, according to tradition, Protestant)

North. In the South, meanwhile, the influence of Latinity in its modern form of manifestation, French intellectual life, steadily decreased, facilitating the approach toward the North.

It seems necessary to round off the picture of Netherlands literature by including the works of South African writers. The fact that Afrikaans has developed in a most felicitous manner into an independent language, with a form of its own and above all a very peculiar, rich, enthralling vocabulary, must not blind us to its original oneness with Netherlands. When one surveys the literature in Afrikaans one discovers in it a number of figures of speech and notions derived from African nature and the African way of life, but one also discovers a subjection to Calvinistic traditions, a way of feeling, thinking and acting, which excludes any doubt of an inner relationship with the Netherlands. After all, the Afrikaans language and the still young but already important and rich Afrikaans literature have developed from the Netherlands. Our classics, the masters of the Middle Ages, and Vondel, Hooft and Luyken, are also the classics of the Africans. In some respects the Afrikaans language and conception is even closer to seventeenth century Netherlands than to the modern North Netherlands ways of thought and expression. I believe that Afrikaans and Dutch are equally benefited by the perpetuation of the memory of the common past.

The value of a language cannot be measured according to objective standards. In judging it we must simply go by the results achieved. In Afrikaans there are poems of such intriguing beauty as we possess but few of in Dutch. There are good novelettes, novels, plays; there are scientific, philosophical and religious dissertations written in Afrikaans which are in no single respect inferior to what is produced in this domain in other languages. People sing, pray and teach in Afrikaans, profound conversations are carried on upon every subject in Afrikaans. There is thus no longer any doubt regarding the serviceableness, richness and beauty of this young language.

The Flemings who in the first half of the nineteenth century began the fight against the systematic Gallicizing of the newly formed, independent kingdom of Belgium, immediately realized that they had to draw arguments from two wells: the medieval history of the Flemish provinces and the primitive strength of the people as revealed in folklore. The glorification of the past served to create models for the present; the glorification of the lyric love of life of a firmly rooted country population served to give these models a new possibility of existence.

And right from the beginning these two tendencies have been fully present in the two great figures who completely dominate the Flanders of the nineteenth century: Hendrik Conscience (1812–1883) and Guido Gezelle (1830–1899)—Conscience by his wonderful ability—despite poverty of language and lack of psychological insight and sense of form—to revive the past and make it true and acceptable, and Gezelle by the spell of his sovereign poetship.

Those who judge Conscience according to purely literary standards come to an unfavorable conclusion concerning his work, but they thus do him and young Flemish literature an injustice. For one should not estimate works produced in a time of transition and conflict exclusively according to their artistic value. Indeed, Conscience's language is at the same time commonplace and bombastic, his characters lack the inner truth and vitality to make them people, his field of vision is as limited as his intellectual viaticum; but despite all these shortcomings Hendrik Conscience is able to assert himself, not only as a literary figure in a given period, but even as a writer seen from outside his time. He possessed a natural gift for narrative, for holding the attention of his readers who are really his hearers, and his love for Flanders and the Flemish past and his hope to revive Flanders through this love were so sincere and so great that they were able to save him from his rhetoric.

Gezelle's case is entirely different. Like Conscience he possessed the gift of captivating his readers and of keeping them captivated; he too cherished a love, at the same time human and superhuman, for Flanders; he too hoped to awaken Flanders to a rich, glorious new life, partly by reminding it of the riches and glory of the Flemish Middle Ages. But over and above that he was one of the greatest lyric poets that has ever lived in the two Netherlands. With heart and soul he lived the life of the simple and he elevated this to an unheard-of glory. In him worldly and divine love were not separated. He knew but one necessity: love of God, nature, his fatherland, people, mankind. . . . And in his childlike profundity, God and people and Flanders formed an indissoluble unity. He loved God because He had made people so weak and pitiful and Flanders so radiant with beauty and love of life, and he loved people and Flanders because he recognized in them God's greatness and goodness and purity. Guido Gezelle consecrated the new Flemish literature and immediately raised it to such a level as had hardly been known even in the Middle Ages, which cannot be praised enough.

No revolution in any literature asserts itself unpreparedly and suddenly. The revival we know in North Netherlands as the *Movement of the Eighties* or the *New Guide* movement was, as we have seen in this survey, heralded and rung in by Eduard Douwes Dekker (Multatuli). And the corresponding phenomenon in Flanders, the *Of Now and Presently* movement (from the periodical *Of Now and Presently*) was prepared for, heralded and partly made possible by the poetic work that Gezelle had produced silently and secretly, unconscious of his great destiny.

The writers who made *Of Now and Presently* (later continued under the simple, proud name *Flanders*) a good and important periodical in Flanders, were, to mention only the principal ones, Stijn Streuvels (pseudonym for Frank Lateur) (1871), August Vermeylen (1872–1945), Herman Teirlinck (1879), F. Toussaint van Boelaere (1875) and the youngest, but as an artist the most enthralling, Karel van de Woestijne (1878–1929).

The *Of Now and Presently* writers undoubtedly underwent the influence of the principles which the young North Netherlands writers advocated. They of course knew French Symbolism through and through. They had access also to English and German literature. But all these influences were completely dissolved and assimilated. This was made possible by three factors: the strong personality of the writers concerned, the pronounced Flemish national character and finally the exceptional controversial position into which the Flemish were forced by the systematic suppression of Flemish and the Flemish will-to-live. In this way the *Of Now and Presently* movement acquired a character of its own, with its own aims and own color.

Those who fought for a young, free art had also, in the strict political sense of the word, to join in the fight for a liberated, rejuvenated Flanders. And this double fight was led by the young August Vermeylen. He saw, more clearly than any of his contemporaries, the great truth which he finally formulated and which remained the general directive for many years: "We must be good Flemings to enable us to become good Europeans."

Every intellectual movement is carried on by a few personalities who derive their importance in the movement from their personality more than from their artistic power. This is the case with August Vermeylen. Had he, aloof from the intellectual revolution of his time, written only *De Wandelende Jood* (The Wandering Jew), he would hardly have the right to a place in this survey. The novel, which contains some fine passages written under the influence of Flaubert, had the double disadvantages of being written with a purpose and too "nicely." But in Vermeylen's rich and warlike life "The Wandering Jew" was not much more than an incident. As a whole, his second novel, which appeared in 1943, was not a success either. But the inestimable and immortal significance which he has for his people and for literature is based on his battling articles and his personal fight. Vermeylen's papers, contained in two substantial volumes, form a monument in South Netherlands literature. They are strong in argument, noble, strict and yet colorful in writing and rich in essential content. If one can read with success and pleasure controversial pamphlets and speculations on phenomena and figures of the day about fifty years after they were written, their lasting right of existence, I think, is proven conclusively. Besides this, Vermeylen rendered important services to the Flemish cause as member of the Senate and as professor at Ghent.

Vermeylen was the man who first saw and first formulated: a) that, every political fight, thus the Flemish one too, can end in victory only if one takes into account the mighty economic forces which are involved; b) that every national movement, thus the Flemish one too, attains its full unfolding and significance only in an international association.

The *New Guide* writer, Lodewijk van Deyssel, in North Netherlands and the *Of Now and Presently* writer, August Vermeylen, in South Netherlands set themselves the task of developing national possibilities to the utmost limits because they saw in this procedure, not without reason, the only means of giving their nation a place and a sphere of action in the new Europe.

August Vermeylen belongs among those leaders who have the rare good fortune to see a great part of their ideals realized. Beside and behind him a generation of artists grew up that made it possible and justifiable to speak of a Flemish Renaissance: prose writers, architects and painters.

Stijn Streuvels (1871) created a world of his own with laws and myths of its own, a world without complications and without nuances. Such systematic simplicity always suggests greatness in literature. Both nature and human beings in all their movements and transformations seem above the normal measure. Figures of such unusual dimensions and deeds of such unusual purport fall outside conceptions of time. That is why past and future do not assert themselves in Streuvels' work.

Stijn Streuvels' greatness is evident from the fact that despite his irresistible inclination to simplify and arrest life, he always succeeds in keeping his nature natural and his people human. Though one may not expect penetrating analysis of the soul in novels of this kind, one is never annoyed in Streuvels by the rhetorical systematization which is the great danger for writers of this kind and which turns so much of Jean Giono's work into falsehood. Streuvels is genuine. His childlike surrender to the original facts of life springs from a deep and sincere need; his no less childlike longing to portray nature, animals and people in more than natural size, forms an inalienable part of his being. Thanks to this undeniable and essential genuineness Stijn Streuvels is one of the few who can dare to mix an elementary psychology with a primitive feeling for nature and to season it with folklore, without his characters giving us the impression even for a moment of being invented or affected. It is his absolute honesty that saves him from "literature" and that makes us accept his world unsuspectingly.

Next to Streuvels, who makes a legend of nature and man in their mutual agreement and contradistinction, Cyriel Buysse (1859–1932) is the typical "realist." He has very little disposition to mysticism and he sees nature only as the natural environment of his characters. And these people have the dimensions of the people we daily see around us. Buysse's realism is based entirely on the formula that became famous in the Netherlands literature: lust for copying daily life. Buysse sees people and their actions sharply and pitilessly. His work is rich in striking psychological details. He understands, as no other, the art of describing environment according to the recipe of the French naturalists. And he is the born narrator. He knows the human value of anecdote, he knows how to dramatize it, sometimes wittily, sometimes touchingly. But he lacked entirely Streuvels' cosmic strength and deep love of life. He remains, even when he treats of subjects from rustic life, the homme du monde, clever and skeptical, who knows what his public demands and how it can be captivated.

Next to Streuvels' great conceits, next to Buysse's sharp, critical realism, little or not at all related to one another, rose a Herman Teirlinck (1879), witty, inexhaustibly ingenious, over-refined, lyrical, elegant, constantly changing and in movement. He wrote much, and that much is unequal in value. A novel like *Het Ivoren Aapje* (The Little Ivory Ape) is a mixture of surprising beauties and contemptible posturing. It is alternately original and of a most painful banality; it has elements of a modern city epic poem and of old-fashioned kitchen-maid literature.

His volume of stories, *Mijnheer J. B. Serjanszoon, Orator Didacticus*, grouped round the figure of a shy eighteenth-century epicure, is a sound masterpiece, enchanting from beginning to end, over-rich in sweet, nutty, skittish strokes and written in a Netherlands rich in arabesques but fitting the time and the figure of Serjanszoon in a natural way and therefore extraordinarily irresistible.

But despite this complete success in the domain of prose, the real significance of Teirlinck is in his dramatic work. Because of his plays and his theoretical conceptions, he became the great reviver of the dramatic art in Flanders and exerted a decided influence on the theatre in North Netherlands where his plays, and especially *De Vertraagde Film* (The Slow-Motion Picture), were frequently performed.

Finally we should mention Fernand Toussaint van Boelaere (1875), the writer of short, but in their conciseness and purity of writing, perfect stories. He is one of the few who can write coldly and loftily and nevertheless touch us. He wrote rustic stories in the style of the most refined symbolism and the effect was surprising. His best pieces are *Landelijk Minnespel* (Rural Courting), *Petrushe's Einde* (Petrushe's End), *Lente* (Spring), *De Doode die zich niet verhing* (The Dead Man Who Did Not Hang Himself) and *Turren*.

The word genius is indefinite in purport and scope and yet it is the only one we can use for a person who is undeniably driven by a superhuman force. We have spoken of Gezelle's genius; we must also speak of the genius of Karel van de Woestijne (1878–1929). And what a world lies between these poets!

In the case of Gezelle, life with its infinite riches is yet very simple, because all phenomena and persons may, in the last analysis, be reduced to their origin and final purpose: God. Nature, human beings, animals and things, all come from God and turn to God. And God, the Oneness and All, is supreme simplicity.

Karel van de Woestijne, on the other hand, who was a pious man, though with his whole being attached to the earth, wrestled with God all his life. In his work, worldly and heavenly love are so capriciously mingled that, compared with the Gothic Gezelle, he must be called a school example of the modern Baroque poet.

Although Gezelle's world may not be so simple as one thinks at first and after superficial consideration, it is a quiet, pure world compared with that of Karel van de Woestijne, in which lust and bitterness, joy and sorrow, excess and asceticism alternate with a sometimes bewildering rapidity. If I were asked for a formula to characterize Van de Woestijne's poetry, I should like to suggest "embellished torment." In this poet everything is torment, everything ends in self-reproach, and this constant, silent anguish gives his poems, and especially his love poems, a tone that I have not met in any other poet in any language. He is a masterly player upon a language that generally sounds heavy and somber and complaining but sometimes suddenly lucid, exalted and pure. Karel van de Woestijne is above all and always a poet, even in his heavily written, pregnant prose works and in his criticism.

When the *New Guide* lost its significance and influence, after a highly felicitous existence of ten years, there came about a simultaneous reaction against the slogans proclaimed by this periodical. Impressionism, subjectivism, sensitivism began, together with naturalism and realism, to lose their enchantment and sense for the younger writers.

We now speak of the First Transition and generally mention in this connection four writers, lyric poets who, although originally strongly influenced by the Eighties movement, worked their way to a new attitude toward life and a new style. They are J. H. Leopold (1865–1925), P. C. Boutens (1870–1943), Henriette Roland Holst (1860), and J. A. der Mouw (1863–1919). Of these J. H. Leopold is the most touching poet, refined and at the same time childlike; P. C. Boutens, seen as a whole, created the most impressive lyric ensemble in our literature, noble, pure and cool; Henriette Roland Holst, like Gorter moved and driven on by a deep social passion, wrote a number of enthusiastic, human verses, innumerable theoretical writings and some excellent biographies (among others, of Garibaldi and Tolstoi); the philosopher Der Mouw did not begin to write poetry until suddenly in his fiftieth year, and he published under the pen-name Adwaita three volumes of poems, uneven in value but all, even the less successful ones, bearing the mark of an unusual and impetuous personality.

To this First Transition also belongs Arthur van Schendel (1872), in whose work the contrast to the *New Guide* is certainly most clearly expressed. Arthur van Schendel has never expressed himself critically or theoretically. His absolute rejection of naturalism is evident from the very nature of the voluminous lifework which he built up. In Netherlands textbooks Arthur van Schendel is sometimes called the representative of a neo-

romantic school. I have always contested this classification. Of
all his predecessors and contemporaries, Van Schendel, with his
strong and conscious classic conception, is the least romantic, unless one seeks romanticism not in the spirit and the treatment
but in the choice of subject! It is customary to divide the production of Arthur van Schendel into two periods: the first, embracing the books which use late medieval and mostly Italian material, the second characterized by Netherlands motifs and a greater
interest in the present. Like all grouping, this too has only partial
validity. Despite an undeniable change, which occurred about
1930, Arthur van Schendel's work forms a closed, natural whole.

The most important and certainly the best known of what is
called the first period is the *Roman van de Zwerver*, in two parts,
Een Zwerver verliefd and *Een Zwerver verdwaald* (A Vagabond
in Love, and A Vagabond Astray). The two nuclei of Van Schendel's being, the problem of destiny and the problem of loneliness,
are present already in this early work.

The climax of the second period consists of the trilogy: *Een
Hollandsch Drama* (in the English translation rebaptized "A
House in Haarlem"), *De Rijke Man* (The Rich Man), and
Grauwe Vogels (Grey Birds). Altogether, Van Schendel wrote
about twenty novels, which are all without exception important
and significant. One can discover slight differences in value, but
his work shows no decline or failure. This writer has maintained
an impressively high level for forty years. There is no point in
listing many titles, especially since only a few of Van Schendel's
books have been translated into English. However, mention
must still be made of *De Waterman*, a sound masterpiece, and
one must draw attention to Van Schendel's numerous fantastic
stories, of which five volumes have now appeared. These enable
us to see quite another aspect of his nature and talent; they are
playful, wise, witty, surprising, and give us an impression of
the writer's unlimited ingenuity. Arthur van Schendel is the
greatest *living* prose writer of the Netherlands and one of the
greatest Netherlands writers of all time.

It is customary to group a number of writers who came immediately after the first transition together under the name,
The Generation of 1905, from the year in which they first began
to manifest themselves. They are indeed contemporaries, but
I have not been able to discover a deep inner resemblance between them, except that they are all, though not exclusively,
mainly lyric poets. Epic prose has rarely been cultivated by this

generation. By far the most important figure among them is
A. Roland Holst (1888); along with him there are J. C. Bloem
(1887) and P. N. van Eyck (1887).

Holst is the poet of sea and wind, of dream-islands, of Elysian
passion and cosmic longing; but even in his most unworldly
poems he always maintains an undertone of profound, true humanity. Bloem's work is dominated by bitterness over lost illusions, failure and loneliness. He compares everyday reality with
an idealized youthful glory and feels himself defeated. His three
volumes constitute a touching evidence of human weakness that
is magically changed by the wonder of poetry into greatness and
strength. P. N. van Eyck, Verwey's successor as professor at Leiden, wrote, especially in the last few years before the invasion,
a number of profoundly appealing essays. He built up a rather
voluminous poetic life work, which is not always appreciated at
its real value.

The Second Transition is represented by four poets of undeniable significance: J. W. F. Werumeus Buning (1891) and
Victor E. van Vriesland (1892), M. Nijhoff (1894) and Herman
van den Bergh (1897); of these M. Nijhoff, who wrote very
little, is beyond dispute the greatest. He brought a completely
new accent into our lyric, succeeded in realizing a wonderful
sort of ecstatic objectivity and exerted a decisive influence on
the younger poets. These young poets united in a periodical
De Vrije Bladen, which in its turn produced three lyric poets
of great significance: J. Slauerhoff (1898–1936), H. Marsman
(1899–1940) and Hendrik de Vries (1896).

An intellectual movement derives its value and significance
not from its extent but from its richness and tension. The movement that found its expression in the periodical *Of Now and
Presently* was indeed richly diversified, and the young Flemish
writers certainly did not lack tension. When one considers how
Streuvels and Buysse, Teirlinck and Toussaint, Vermeylen and
van de Woestijne came together here on the basis of one enthusiasm and how they placed their so thoroughly different personalities and talents at the service of one aim, we must come to the
conclusion that those were incomparably beautiful years in
Flanders from 1900 to 1914.

Such a movement never forms a closed whole. One cannot say
exactly where it begins and ends nor ascertain with absolute
sureness who belongs to it and who does not. We suppose, however, for the convenience of compiling manuals and surveys, that

Willem Elsschot, Felix Timmermans, Jan van Nijlen constitute a new generation, a transition from the Of-Now-And-Presently Flanders to the so-called "modern" or "younger" writers.

Timmermans (1886), who perhaps still more, and certainly not less rightly, than these others represents Flemish literature abroad, carries on the tradition of the rustic novel. His *Pallieter* —a rustic guzzler—caused a sensation and made a great hit. But I am of the opinion that this book has been overestimated and that the Flemish people are bitterly wronged if *Pallieter* is considered as the pinnacle, the compendium of the Flemish spirit. *Pallieter* represents, at best, one side of Flanders: good-living, joy in the earth's glories and enthusiasm for the most natural in nature. But here the presentation is exaggerated and too studied to make a real impression. Nevertheless, Timmermans wrote a masterpiece, *Boerenpsalm* (Peasant Psalm). This novel is a complete success because in it he does not let himself go as in *Pallieter,* but, on the contrary, restrains himself with an admirable self-control.

One cannot imagine a greater contrast than that between Felix Timmermans and Willem Elsschot, pseudonym of Alfons de Ridder (1882). Timmermans is inclined by nature to boisterousness, joviality and exaggeration, while Elsschot is frugality personified. His inner sullenness, his soberness and his systematic control characterize him as a man who loves tranquillity. He made his debut before the First World War with a novel about a Paris boarding house, *Villa des Roses.* This book attracted great attention, especially in North Netherlands, but there too almost entirely in literary circles. The general reading public was not attracted by this cynic wit, and in Flanders it was felt instinctively that this new writer possessed and developed a number of qualities of character which did not fit well into the traditional framework of art and society. Elsschot also wrote *Een Ontgoocheling* (A Disillusionment), *De Verlossing* (The Deliverance) and, during the First World War, *Lijmen.* But the indifference of his environment discouraged him so much that he put down his pen. Not until much later, around 1930, did appreciation of him begin and grow slowly, first in the Netherlands and then in Belgium. He then began to write again and published, rather quickly, one after another, *Kaas* (Cheese), *Tsjip en de Leeuwentemmer* (Tsjip and the Lion Tamer), *Pensioen* (Pension) and *Het Been* (The Bone). In these later works it became increasingly clear that cynicism and harshness served Elsschot to shield an almost childlike sensitiveness. This embittered scoffer is in reality a defenseless man who suffers from his split personality.

Jan van Nijlen (1884), who published two detailed critical studies of the French poets Charles Péguy and Francis Jammes, is by nature exclusively a lyric poet, a lyric poet with a limited world but master in this world. In Flanders, where reality holds such great importance, he represents the "absentee," the man who, wherever he may be, knows but one desire—to be elsewhere. But in Van Nijlen this heavenly nostalgia is not a strong passion, which expresses itself in raptures, but a state of silent protest, mostly ironic, sometimes with a touch of bitterness, but always absolutely controlled.

During the First World War and shortly afterwards a double influence asserted itself in Flemish literature and especially in poetry. It was on the one hand that of German expressionism, on the other that of French poets of the school of the *fantaisistes* and of whom P. J. Toulet was far and away the most important.

The German impact is most noticeable in Paul van Ostayen, the French, in the poets who were named after the little periodical they founded, the poets of *Het Fonteintje* (The Little Fountain): Richard Minne, Reimond Herreman, Maurice Roelants and Karel Leroux.

Paul van Ostayen (1896–1928) was a new phenomenon in Flanders and, even if he founded no school, put his stamp on a number of contemporaries and followers. With all his talents he lacked spontaneity. His work (poems, stories and reviews) is intelligent (probably just a little too intelligent), special, full of striking discoveries. But our full appreciation is always withheld because we are disturbed by its deliberateness. In Van Ostayen's work theory is always present as theory and is not absorbed by the flesh and blood of the finished poem or piece of prose. Van Ostayen lacks naturalness. We see that he is constantly doing his best to be modern. Van Ostayen is counted in with a group of writers who came together in the periodical *Ruimte* (Space) and who turned against what they called the aestheticism of *Of Now and Presently*. They desired an ethical-social art, but this demand was difficult to rhyme with "pure poetry," the poetry of exclamation, adjuration and invocation, which Van Ostayen and his supporters cultivated. This whole movement, despite the great talent of several of its adherents, makes an impression of uncertainty and impurity.

The men of *The Little Fountain*—a vivid little periodical—who had set themselves a limited task, were able to express themselves infinitely more clearly within that limitation. In their work, playfulness of mind and feeling found expression in the most enchanting manner, and this work reveals, what is particularly striking, that those who scoff at all big words and all weighty slogans, prove considerably more genuine, warm, purely *human* in their being and their work, than the neo-humanistic poets who proclaimed a new society.

This was a time of hesitating, searching and fighting. It was to be given to a great poet to sum this up in one work, small in extent but great in scope and intent. The first really superior poetic figure after Van de Woestijne is Marnix Gijsen (pseudonym for J. A. Goris), who was to humanize the modernism of *Ruimte* and modernize the humanism of *Het Fonteintje*.

The work of Marnix Gijsen (1899) is the fulfillment of the promises made by both groups, by *Ruimte* and by *Het Fonteintje*, and gives in verse that is strongly personal the *synthesis* of the poetry of revelation and the poetry of confession. One can hardly overestimate the significance of Gijsen's *Het Huis* (The House). It is, considered by itself, a collection of poems almost without fault and it is, besides, a milestone in the development of Flemish poetic art. One rarely finds poetry in which *all elements* and qualities are united in such a happy manner. After *The House,* Marnix Gijsen wrote only a few poems, which appeared in periodicals. These show a change, in so far as they have become much more fervent and darker in tone. Moreover, Marnix Gijsen is, together with Van de Woestijne, the best verse critic that Flanders has ever possessed. His critical writings derive their value from the fact that he is absolutely free from the prejudice of any theory.

Gijsen's important contemporaries, Maurice Roelants (1895) and Gerard Walschap (1898), have devoted themselves mainly and exclusively to the novel.

Of these two—who, though contemporaries, manifest little mutual relationship—Maurice Roelants is the closer to the *Of Now and Presently* writers, as far as his manner of writing is concerned. But he differs from them because of his more subtle psychology and above all of his far stronger feeling for the aesthetic value of moral nuances. Roelants has developed a style of novel all his own: clearly and simply he states his problem, clear and simple are his characters, clear and simple his plots. The whole is enacted in a calm, transparent atmosphere, and yet—this is Roelants' strength and peculiarity—we have constantly, in the midst of all this clarity, the feeling of experiencing a wonder, of participating in untold secrets—a mystery in full daylight. Roelants wrote three novels: *Komen en Gaan* (Coming and Going), *Het leven dat wij Droomden* (The Life We Dreamed) and *Alles Komt Terecht* (Everything Comes Right) and an excellent novelette *De Jazzspeler* (The Jazz Player).

Beside Roelants' purity and modesty, Gerard Walschap's mysterious intensity, his irresistible driving power, his inclination towards extremes, are very striking. The element of good taste, strongly evident in Roelants, is lacking in him. But in its place he offers an urgent power of conviction that never fails to impress. The standard of all Roelants' work is very high; in Walschap's we find the very best, a burning veracity, side by side with the worst, an impetuosity that has became mania. But one important and characteristic quality he has in common with Roelants: his disdain for scenery, for local color, in short, for the accessories, for all that distracts from the psychology and action, that is to say, from the story in its essential meaning.

His great novel, *De Familie Roothoofd* (The Roothoofd Family), a trilogy in three parts, *Adelaide, Carla* and *Eric*, is a masterpiece; *Trouwen* (Marrying), *Sybille* and *Houtekiet* are excellent novels, each with a character of its own, and an autonomous existence in literature. Walschap, a strong, tormented mind, with a splendid, rough and honest temperament, is one of the great figures of Flemish prose.

The literature of South Africa because of its intrinsic value deserves separate and lengthy consideration. Here I can give only a concise survey, merely to round off the picture of Netherlands literature.

South African literature begins shortly after the peace of the Union (1912) with writers like Eugene Marais (1872–1936), J. D. du Toit (Totius) (1877), Jan Celliers (1865–1940) and C. L. Leipoldt (1880). We call these, although two of them are still alive, the "classics," and they form the first "generation."

These writers, appearing shortly after the tragic war, between 1900 and 1910, aroused great interest in the Netherlands as well. And they fully deserved this interest; for, besides their proof that deeply experienced, euphonious poems can be written in Afrikaans, they introduced a new spirit and, above all, a new feeling. Netherlands readers enjoyed both the undeniable relationship and the equally undeniable difference. Above all, the most important critic of the Movement of the Eighties, Albert Verwey, has followed the development of the young Afrikaans literature with love and correct comprehension.

Eugene Marais' poems are collected in a small volume, and this little book stands as a beloved monument at the beginning of modern Afrikaans literary history. It is not great, but pure, noble poetry, which derives its significance, however, from the fact that it originated during precisely those first years and in a South Africa that was struggling upwards with incredible strength of mind. Totius (J. D. du Toit) wrote religious and patriotic songs, among which there are some of great beauty, and he made an excellent Afrikaans rhymed version of the psalms. J. D. Celliers, a kindly narrative talent, will remain famous, above all on account of some lovely nature impressions. Of these four, C. Louis Leipoldt, a physician living in Capetown, is the most remarkable figure because of his versatility, his whimsicality and his vitality.

Modern South African literature is dominated by the mighty figure of N. P. van Wijk Louw (1906), without doubt the greatest writer that South Africa has produced up to now, and beyond that one of the greatest writers of all the domains in which Dutch is spoken. He united in himself all the elements that make a great poet: a strong feeling for form, a sweeping lyric power, the ability to conjure up living characters and an inexhaustible vocabulary. Like none other, he has known South Africa, with all its problems deeply rooted in the past, and suffered there, as none other, and this intimate, indissoluble unity with his country has in no way cut him off from the rest of the world. Van Wijk Louw always sees South Africa as part of the world and the South African man, with his strong peculiarities, in the midst of humanity, and he always considers the intellectual problems of the Union in connection with the intellectual problems of the world. Thus he represents, because of his universal disposition, the classic ideal of the poet, who is above all poet but is at the same time thinker, politician and seer. His work consists of three volumes of poems, the last of which, *Gestaltes en Diere* (Figures and Animals), contains a number of masterworks; a great epic poem *Raka*, which has for the young South African literature the significance of Gorter's *Mei* for the Netherlands, a chorus to be spoken and two volumes of essays. South African literature, which has developed very happily since 1900, reached world standard for the first time in N. P. van Wijk Louw.

For all who have followed the development of South Africa, it is a magnificent, gladdening miracle that, from the original

Netherlands colonists, through years of continual struggle and privation, in a relatively short time, a new people and a new culture with a strong character of its own have been able to develop. African literature, with its variety, its vitality, its vividness and its strong personality, constitutes an important part of the African national existence. This course of events should particularly interest American readers, since they know from their own experience how from a language and literature a new language and literature can develop that differs greatly from its origin and yet remains inwardly connected with it.

LITERATURE BETWEEN THE WARS

Coming to the literature and especially the verse of the period between the two wars, I feel obliged, first, to draw attention to one important point, which is, in my opinion, that the essential changes in Dutch writing are most completely and clearly revealed in poetry. The prose of the years between the wars is of the greatest significance, especially that of Menno ter Braak, E. du Perron and S. Vestdijk, who are represented in this anthology. But the prose does not represent the intellectual life in the Netherlands so completely and convincingly as does verse.

Thus, if in the following pages literature and poetry are for practical purposes identified, it is primarily because this is in keeping with my personal inclination, but at the same time, more consciously, in order to impress readers as much as possible with the value and nature of the new intellectual movements in the Netherlands.

I use the word "new" here, but not without wishing to emphasize that in my opinion poetry is not bound to a period and still less is determined by time or anything temporary. It is necessary to realize that there is no essential difference between old and new poetry, or, in other words, that the miracle that makes a poem poetry was the same in the Middle Ages as it is now and will remain the same to the end of time.

If there are no two kinds of poetry, there are two main variations. And these we see side by side in the Netherlands from the earliest times until today. It is always difficult to apply precise words to a matter so full of mystery and dangers, but, for the sake of comprehensibility, I will use the terms revelation poetry and confession poetry, knowing that in their absoluteness they are incorrect.

Revelation poetry is poetry that is built up (not exclusively, but mainly) of motifs taken from the subconscious life of the poet; confession poetry is poetry that is built up (again not exclusively, but mainly) of motifs taken from the conscious life of the poet.

In the first case inspiration predominates, in the second, experience. But it is necessary to emphasize that the two kinds never occur in perfectly pure form. In revelation poetry there are elements of confession; in confession poetry, revelation breaks through. Conscious and unconscious life, experience, inspiration, memory and supposition are, in *every* poem, closely intermingled.

In the Middle Ages we have already seen, and there very clearly, the difference between revelation and experience, between mysticism and morality. And we can perceive these two currents in our entire literature. They always exist simultaneously. It is only that in a given period more attention is paid to, more preference is shown for, the one than the other. And, to come to our own time, we see side by side at the beginning of the Eighties, equally admired and praised, the typical confession poetry of Kloos and the not less typical revelation poetry of Gorter. Anyone a little informed on this subject immediately observes the difference, the profound difference, between a poem in which Gorter conjures up, with a few simple words, a world of play and light from nothingness and a poem in which Kloos makes us share his despair and his passion. These two forms of poetry we constantly see side by side in the period which occupies us in this section, the period 1920–1940. But before going into details, I must revert to what was said at the beginning: the adjunct of time, especially in this case, is completely arbitrary. On literature in general and on the Netherlands literature in particular, the war of 1914–1918 exerted no real and profound influence.

Strangely enough, the at that time eighty-year-old Penning showed considerably more feeling for actuality than the eighteen-year-old Marsman. Not that I consider this feeling for actuality a special merit of a poet; on the contrary, I am merely pointing out that the older men were more strongly influenced by the circumstances of war than the younger were. I myself lived in the Netherlands from 1915 to 1918 and in the midst of the literary life of those days, and however passionately pro-French we may have been at that time, on the whole the war was and remained an unimportant, that is, small and unessential, element of what was produced in those years. In the period that immediately followed the Armistice, the influence of world events asserted itself more strongly, even if indirectly. For during a short time German expressionism exerted its influence upon the Netherlands too. It was a very transient phenomenon and indeed the expression of a mentality which was closely connected with the facts of the day. The group of the "moderns" in North Netherlands was formed, first, by H. Marsman (1899), J. Slauerhoff (1898–1936) and Hendrik de Vries (1896), to confine myself to the' most important figures.

During or shortly after the war of 1914–1918, Marsman wrote the magnificent poems that constitute the first section of the first part of his Collected Works. He was to exert a strong and lasting influence on his contemporaries. Marsman himself has characterized this youthful phase as his vitalistic period. What this vitalism was he formulated as he took leave of it: it was a longing to be absorbed in a nameless life, in a dynamic community. It was valor and leadership. The poet was seer, supreme example and at the same time one among millions.

This sort of verse, built upon motifs which the subconscious provides, is strongly bound to the personality of the poet. If he, with great inner riches, does not possess a strong sense of form, the work soon declines to formless incomprehensibility or to a most unbearable kind of rhetoric. And so we see that under the influence of Marsman and Hendrik de Vries, the two purest poetic figures of that generation who expressed themselves in the periodical, De Vrije Bladen, a number of Epigones appeared who misused a terminology which was for them an artistic pose.

These Epigones, with their rhetoric that was mockingly called the rhetoric of the angels and of blood because these motifs again and again cropped up, made a strong reaction necessary. This was constituted by the periodical Forum, under the initial leadership of Menno ter Braak, E. du Perron and Maurice Roelants.

The verse that was produced and accepted shortly before and during the existence of Forum is in almost all respects a contrast to the "high" or rather true poetry of a Marsman or De Vries.

There has existed from the beginning of literature until today didactic poems, occasional verse, chronicles in verse and rhymed wisdom. And there is no reason to withdraw these modes of expression entirely from our attention. If in connection with Forum I speak of unpoetic poetry, I must explain its origin as a revulsion after a period of all too poetic poetry; the "over-poetic" means in this connection the far-fetched, the false. Those who imitate always exaggerate, because they lack the inner moving spring that determines and limits action. The protest of *Forum* was thus *not* against a Marsman or a Slauerhoff but against the bustling, inconsiderable writers in their train. As a matter of fact, Marsman and Slauerhoff soon belonged to the trusted collaborators of the review. And *Forum* was not against Anthonie Donker, whose poetic gifts were undisputed, but again against his followers who cultivated a neo-Parnassian, that is to say, impersonal picturesqueness. The men who founded and managed *Forum* knew that their aesthetics, which ended in anti-beauty declarations, was a phenomenon of the time and thus a temporary phenomenon with a definite and limited aim and consequently a definite and equally limited scope. The fairytale of a ter Braak, who was supposed to be insensible to "high" poetry, belonged to the malicious fighting tactics of the expressionists' threatened followers. Ter Braak knew, perhaps better than they, the value of the work of A. Roland Holst, J. C. Bloem, H. Marsman. And E. du Perron as a young boy already defended, when no one in Flanders and the Netherlands dared do so, the *poesie pure* of Paul van Ostayen. But what they all abhorred was the posing parroters of Marsman, Engelman, van Ostayen and Gijsen, who did not know the true meaning of their models and imagined they were equals.

It was not the wish of the *Forum* writers to disparage poetry—just the contrary, to restore to poetry its worth and power of effect by making the bad verse, which throve luxuriantly around it, ridiculous and hence impossible. The slogan of "everyday language" was started. And in 1931 Menno ter Braak wrote in a copy of his first novel for one of his friends: "To the brother-in-arms, for the ordinary word." With this they had come to a stand as unmistakable as possible concerning poetry, for poetry in principle is the *ordinary word*. They believed that this ordinary word should be preferred to lies, that is, to words that were passed off as unusual but were really not so. *Forum's* fight, which forms a closed period, was a fight for sincerity. That poetry was occasionally hard-pressed caused no great concern, because in the last instance the outcome would again benefit true poetry. *Forum* was thus in a certain respect a *reversed* New Guide. The New Guide put genuineness and loftiness in the first place against the false pedestrian poetic art of 1860–1875. *Forum* also demanded genuineness but deliberately made itself "pedestrian" so as to expose as false the current loftiness of the Epigones, in order to be able to fight against them more effectively.

But *Forum* too was followed by a reaction, which was bound

to come. Poetic art in the exalted sense, as this has been understood throughout all ages, cannot be conceived of without revelation from the subconscious, without the wonderful testimonies of a life deeply hidden within us. Reasonable poetry forms a contradiction in terms. So, when the necessary purifying process of *Forum* was completed, the young poets, who were not born to imitate, soon realized that one could not live and work upon this basis. Critical, moralizing poetic art has always a limited task and possibility and never contains nuclei from which a new existence can develop. After the predominance of reason, there came of itself a renewed interest in the irrational. No really great poetry can be built upon a critical foundation. Just as the *Vrije Bladen* tired itself out in exalted rhetoric, *Forum* tired itself out in vulgar rhetoric. This was not the fault of the *Vrije Bladen* or of *Forum*—both periodicals faithfully fulfilled their tasks—but was due to the law of nature, according to which, when the necessary things have been said by the people designated, the parroters know nothing better to do than to distort the original principles into a mocking picture. No one could be so astonished and annoyed as the founders of *Forum* were at the bad influence their concept exerted. The disillusionment, necessary to them through a coincidence of circumstances and in a limited period, withered away to a dishonorable fashion. The proposal of an unpoetic poetic art was accepted as a relief by all who, sometimes, but rarely, equipped with talent, were born unpoetic. Irony, only justifiable as a form of self-defense, became in their hands a bourgeois pedestrianism which both the *Forum* and the youngest generation loathed.

Even while in the Netherlands a small group of disciples, and part of the reading public, was still attracted by a poetic art which, militant and commonplace, had kept no more than a few external forms of poetry, the attention of the younger generation turned to an irrationalistic surrealism. The irrational was declared to be the origin and beginning of every poetic possibility; doubt and inquiry, the cause of all the misery in poetics. It was maintained that as long as consciousness predominates, there can be no question of poetry. He who experiences and recognizes poetry as revelation can hardly do anything but reject every rational objection with force and indignation. For the poets of this surrealist school it was exclusively a question of free and above all uncontrolled expression. This leads irrevocably to the glorification of automatic writing: the absolute can be approached only if we succeed in putting both will and intellect out of action. In this way one achieves Perfect Attention, that is to say, complete absence of interest, with, as a practical result, the possibility, means and purpose of revealing the mysterious powers that come from us but are more than ourselves and use us in order to reveal us to ourselves. One sees how far we are here again from poetic art, from literature in general, which aims at the confirmation and glorification of personality. Poetry is, according to the taste of surrealists, unconditional surrender. Their kind of poetry excludes thought, in the sense that for the poet word and idea are born simultaneously, are equal and interchangeable; the word is idea, the idea is word.

A number of the Dutch poets who belonged to the new irrationalistic movement, opposed to the reasonable and critical *Forum* writers, did not always remember the axiom that the treasures of the subconscious could only become art through form, through a rational arrangement. I still believe that one approaches truth most closely with the concept of a poem in which the everlasting impact between the rational and irrational is crystallized. The poem is thus at the same time rational and irrational and yet something different and something more: a new order in which the word contrast is dissolved.

The African poet, N. P. van Wijk Louw, is convinced that all intellectual occurrences of real importance originate from polar tensions. The poetic is thus neither rational nor irrational but coincides with the tension between the rational and irrational. We can vary the poles: between form and content, between reality and dream, between good and evil, between life and death. Here I see a possibility of dissolving the antithesis between talk poetry and the stammering of the surrealists: poetry is neither sensuous nor transcendental but originates from the tension between sensuous and transcendental.

Dutch writers between the two wars moved then, as we have seen, from expressionism (under German influence) via *Forum* (in which a distant relationship with the group of French "fantaisistes" can be felt) to a surrealism curbed for Netherlands use. Characteristic of the first movement is the glorification of speed, strength, passion (dynamism); of the second, doubt and local association, expressing itself in irony and a popular choice of words; of the third, the diving into the depths, half Freudian and half somnambulistic. The *Forum* movement is thus a short attempt at rational classicism, between two outbursts of romanticism.

In this survey I have tried, by means of a rapid succession of motifs, to create the impression of a living literature. In so doing I was constantly aware that for interested foreigners the indication of general tendencies and ideas will signify more than the characterization of personalities whom they do not know and, if they do not have Dutch at their command, cannot learn to know.

I hope circumstances will permit this book of Netherlands prose to be followed by a translation of the best Netherlands poems of seven centuries: for without that the picture is not complete.

Now that the Netherlands is resuming its independent existence we impatiently await what Netherlands writers have thought and written during the occupation.

J. GRESHOFF

Translated by MAURICE T. GROEN *and* JO MAYO

PART I

THE RENAISSANCE OF 1880

Jacobus van Looy

THE DEATH OF MY CAT

IT WAS FREEZING HARD ENOUGH TO BURST STONES. FROM THE PATH down below came the running conversation of two men who were late. Their talk rose along the smooth surface of my studio window and the beating of the soles of their shoes upon the hard ground froze into the rarified air, sharpened by the cold, and became as pure as the high voices of young boys. I saw how the bitterly cold night frost started to spin her treacherous needlework of frost flowers into the lower corners of my windows and gradu-ally covered them. Before me the fire crackled and the stove spread a delightful glow. I had put my old easy chair as close to it as possible and was thus drenching my body with its heat; I looked straight ahead and watched the fantastic figures develop on the big windows.

Where could my cat have disappeared? She had been gone for three days. I had been looking for her for hours. What pleasures could an animal derive from wandering around on such a bitter-cold night that would murder anything that was delicate and needed protection. In the patch of ground before the door there was nothing to be had. The old grass stood there frozen, white like old hair, dead like the dead soil, and in the garden next door it wasn't any better. Was she at the neighbor's, with the black tomcat? Perhaps she had been killed; the boys along the path used slingshots, training them between latticework on the cats that wandered about. They would sell the skins, and they had such beautiful fur—oh, if those hateful boys had killed her!

Where could she be all this time, just now, when I wanted her here with me, when I felt so lonely, and she was so gay as she played; now that I wanted to hear her walk around in her digni-fied manner in the attic, or as I should see her silently make her way to her favorite spot next to me on the easy chair, carrying her striped tail high like a plume of vanity? I wanted to see her lie down behind the stove, blinking her eyes at the red glow, see her stretch her legs in lazy comfort and then lick her long body, making it glow with her rough red tongue. Look how the black rings in her fur had started to shine happily under the constant application of her elastic tongue in long strokes along the back, cleaning the nimble body! Sometimes she would stop suddenly, still stretched out, lifting her head and pointing her ears, the eyes wide open and glittering like amber, and the thick tail beating furiously on the floor. Did she hear a mouse or perhaps a bird rummaging in its nest on the roof? But her round pupil again narrowed like a curtain to a thin slit; she again lay stretched out to her full length, and her purrs came contentedly from between the white whiskers. How I should love to see her lie again on the red glowing floor made of old wooden boards, luxuriously stretched out, like a miniature royal tiger on a red rock, warming himself, satiated with food, with glowing eyes in his mighty voracious head, yawning and stretching and blinking at the sun!

On my large barred window there was a wir-war, a quick spinning hither and thither of thin threads of ice, advancing and retreating, zigzagging, straight out and curved like a hoop, shrinking and breaking and shooting out like splints of broken glass. On the opaque background of the aqueous precipitation it was like an etching; from all sides the frost flowers would shoot out, putting forth blossoms on pane after pane.

Didn't I hear the mewing of my cat coming out of the frosty night? There was a steel-blue reflection behind the crystals on my window. Around the house I felt the night stiffening in a still greater cold. My tiled roof was surmounted by icicles and rough white stretches as from high up in the sky more blue cold descended and more white frost covered the ground, until the air seemed to shrink with it, and the last bit of life was obliterated pitilessly under the haughty splendor, under the far-off glittering of the severely blinking stars. Didn't I hear the mewing of my cat, plaintive-sounding like a feverish child? . . .

Then I went down and out in the night to look for her on the path; but there was no trace of the cat, there was nobody, there was nothing, nothing but cold darkness and clear cold. There was but icy-blue sky, an endless stretch of glaze, scratched and pinpointed with stars, jeweled sparks, like frozen drops of light, so cold, so tingling around the phosphorus stream of the Milky Way, which like a much used skating rink, devoid of its hard glow, goes straight through the field of heaven. Like the dome of an enormous ice hall the heavens stood over the vast land, above the row of the last houses of the streets of the most recently-built quarters, massive black shadows against the extinguished halo of the city lights, a dull stony darkness, in which two or three illuminated window squares glow with friendly red light. The sky curved more chillily and clear above the dark sheds which disappeared in the entangled masses of the factory buildings, in the midst of which the chimney rose like a gigantic icicle into the sky, also above the houses of the villagers along the now dark and cold, sandy path, with the little windows shut tight, leaning against each other, blunt, puny and pitch-black, the dwellings of Samoyedes in the silent northern night, so lost in this terrifying numbness.

In this great and outside deathliness the street lamps along the path were a shrill child's game in a house in which death has taken place, still, red-glowing candles, put there by fearsome hands next to the body of the dead ruler.

But the warmth I had taken along from upstairs had already long vanished and the clothes had been aired, the cold penetrated my skin like the pricks of a needle deep into the flesh; I felt death by freezing crawling up through the soles of my shoes, up toward my heart, as I stood there; trembling and wishing for heat and light, I retraced my way along the path, called out once more, saw a small red cloud of smoke, which was my breath, heard the echo of my own voice as if returned by steel walls, and then I was inside again in the darkness of the staircase and went unhappily upstairs.

My large lamp hung like a sun from the center of the ceiling, it was reflected in the back of a canvas, which stood turned around on an easel and threw a vague shadow upwards. I filled the stove with coal, because I wanted to keep it glowing, and then I slid down again in my easy chair, with all the pleasure of feeling the heat between my knees. Where could the animal be? If she were still alive, she must freeze to death, because nothing as small as my little cat could withstand cold like this.

But it was impossible to remain quiet; restlessly I began to pace back and forth and every time I came near the window again I saw more ice flowers on it; the mysterious procedure continued without stop. The leaves of the ice flowers now thickened, every leaf was surrounded by a field of white weeds. The night outside was closed out, the light of the lamp sent forth beams, made yellow golden threads shimmer amidst the icy pattern.

That was an exotic flora: there were flowers, complete clusters of crystal flowers and a rich tangle of frosted needles; there were winter tulips with scalloped leaves, striped like summer carna-

tions, with sharp edges and indentations; there were beaker flowers, open like the jaws of a fish, veined morning glories, dry medicinal herbs, white frosted foliage; there was a wild profusion of
worthless weeds and the rich ostentation and contortion of hot-
house orchids; there were pointed thistles and whole bunches of
hairy stinging nettles, and wild chervil. It was all a wild growth,
windblown small stuff, all entangled; it had the appearance of
a rough field crossed by paths made by men with heavy wooden
shoes; denuded and savage was this lush vegetation, flattened out
as are wild plants by a violent wind-storm.

Look, there, way at the top of the window, a pane swept by
the shadows of a growth as I had often seen it in the country,
dark shadows beneath the surface of the water, at the bottom of
a pond; I could watch them grow here, and become the ragged
skeletons of the leaves of trees kept between the pages of an old
book; and lower down, there they became strong stems, streaking
across the glass, or as leaves hanging down, or like plumed reeds,
or waving, floating grass, or the long green swords of the gladioli!
Small flakes, snowdrops, grow hidden amidst them. There was a
growing crystalline metrical system and the sinuosity of plants,
metrical flowers, prisms and octagons forming ferns, the mineral
wealth grown from thousands of pine needles and the fine branch-
ing-out of reindeer moss; there were plumes of proud peacock's
feathers and also the hairy brooms and the stinging of bunches
of cat's whiskers. Oh, it was beautiful, those white frost flowers
in the winter garden of my window-panes, that became a rough
surface of stars and stems, of foliage and crystals.

Was it not possible that my cat might be in the garden next
door? She loved trees and was crazy about being independent, as
indeed she was; she liked to sit in the upper branches to spy upon
birds; she liked to sit high up in the wind, firmly ensconced in
the fork of trunk and branch; once she climbed so high that she
did not dare come down again and stayed there even under a
storm of hailstones that intended to drive her out and then she
had had to be fetched down. I had given her a beating then, and
if she should come back now, I should beat her again and teach
her to give up her mania for always running away, thus leaving
me all by myself.

Bah, that kind of an animal; she was just like the rest of them,
always on the lookout to please herself! Bah! Wasn't that her
nature?

But all this still did not give me power to do anything. I continued pacing back and forth, from the white frosted window to

the red-hot stove and then again to the frost-flower-covered window, up and down, like a bear in its cage. I wanted to read, but alas, on every page appeared a cat's head, and as for work—how can one work when one has lost something precious. Bah! work—wasn't work, drudging away everywhere. Bah, work! Brrr, it was cold here. It became as freezing here as outside. Come, let me put some more coal on the fire and then. . . . Listen! there is the hoarse shriek of the nightboat on the Amstel, it is getting late. How late? I do not hear the ticking of the clock any longer, the clock has stopped; but the ship has to tear the ice asunder, I think it must break up everything in its way. Listen, there it goes again, somewhat nasal; it gurgles from the smokestack; it is as if the noise came through a fog. Was there going to be a fog? Frost and fog, that is weather for haddock, and haddock's heads and food for my cat.

She has already been gone for three days, that Gypsy.

Where, oh where could she be?

How nice it is here, the stove is nice, the heat is nice! It rises pleasantly along the hard steel of the pipes, it goes up in trembling waves, it weaves fantastic figures around the branches of the pipes; it goes up into the low beams under the roof, it gathers into a little smoke in the golden glow of my lamp. Thus it fills the attic, my domain, with lazy dreams, thus it awakens desire for continued existence in sweet comfort, when one rubs one's hands from satisfaction; what do I care about the great death outside, though the winter with its tyranny of ice weaves as a whim of utmost charm a garland of flowers for my home? . . .

Where could she possibly be? . . .

Could she be lying between the trunks of the trees of the next-door garden; or was she lying dead in the dry crackling shrubs underneath, as she had fallen from a high tree; would she be lying there, crooked on the ground or sunk in the half-rotten leaves? Dead, dead, insensible to cold or weather, and deaf to my calls. . . .

Or would she be lying, stretched flat on the empty field, in the white grass, like nothing that anybody could find; stretched out dead in the too cold winds, in a hole which a horse's hoof had made when it was still summer? Murdered. . . . O, my small, royal cat, if you should have died thus, if you have disappeared in such a fashion, I shall build you, out of the treasure of my heart, a broad clean grave, a mausoleum built from ice!

For that the whole heaven is mine, high and cold as it may seem, I will take from it the threads of ice and weave from it a shroud delicate around your smallness. I shall cover you with the flowers of the cold, the leaves of snow, with the down of the frost and the brilliants of ice. I shall stretch you out in my palace of the dead. There is a vault of blue crystals, and there the stars will be your mortuary candles. . . .

But what is that? No, this time I wasn't mistaken.

It was mewing and it came from near by, from behind the door. Jumping up, I tore open the door. Brrr . . . what cold, the walls are white, the street door is ajar. Left open. But there she sat on the mat. So small, so small. Brrr . . . how bitter cold. She no longer stands up. She blinks her eyes at the brilliant light from the attic. Irritated and a little too hurriedly I step over her and give a wee push with the point of my shoe. There, then. Slowly she now goes inside, so thin, all skin and bones. . . . She moves silently, with little jerks of her shoulderblades, just like a poor devil who pushes a heavy handcart. Brrr. . . . Quick, down the stairs, closing the door with a bang, so that the windows rattle in the freezing night.

Upstairs. There she sat, in the middle of the floor, beaten by the cold, terrifying in the light, the two front paws close together on the floor. She sat straight up at the border of the shadow thrown by the canvas on the easel.

Was that my cat, my sweet little cat? No, no, that was a strange animal, gone to seed. Where were her round eyes, her round, childlike eyes, where her beautiful fur with its shimmering markings, where her proud tail, and where the lovely velvet of her ears? No, damn it, that was a strange beast. That one no longer looked straight, but askance; those were the timorous eyes of a pitiful human being transplanted into a strange environment. This one had a sick look, not that of my little fellow . . . damn it.

Miaow! . . . what a distant sound. . . . It came from outside still, from the street; and I had seen already that little mouth inside was no longer red but blue-white, night-white, winter-white, winter-white, dead-white. . . . Miaow! . . . "Cut it out, animal. Cut it out, or I'll kick you out!" . . . in my chair and reasoning with it: "Where have you been? where have you been hiding for such a long time, eh? . . .

"Aren't you hungry? For three days there was your meat and bread and milk. Where have you been in the cold, miserable animal?

"Come here, then. Are you cold—there is the stove. Don't you want to come?"

Then I went to pick her up and put her on my knee. She

weighed almost nothing. She was nothing but cold skin, with a miserable living head attached to it, her fur felt stiff and cold . . . the soft fur under her belly stuck together and was frozen in little tufts. How quiet she was, so quiet! how large was the night and the cold everywhere. . . .

Softly I let my hand slide over the fur of my little animal, and then a great sorrow started welling up in my eyes.

"Come on, Louis, please stand still."

"Yes, Mynheer Ko," he said submissively.

And for a little while it was again quiet in my studio. Under the light which came through the skylight, facing me, the boy posed, with his hands in his pockets, staring straight ahead. Just as I had seen him standing in front of the door of the house, a pedlar of lampglass-wipers and brazier-trays, and immediately struck by his handsome, outdoor appearance, I had persuaded him to earn some money as a model. That had gone on for some time, he was an inexpensive model; but it did not work out.

He was standing there now. With a lazy jerk, without taking his hands out of his pockets, he hoisted up his pants, which hung from his hips by a string. He looked out of the corner of his blue eyes, without effort, out of the window, at the broad sky, into the white glowing sun, where the dry snowflakes passed the window like loose little bits of fluff, which seemed to come from nowhere.

"No, Louis," said I.

The boy looked at my work in the attic, and a cleverly innocent smile split open the red of his sensuous boy's mouth as his cheeks puffed out; but before I really looked up he had contrived to make the smile vanish with a motion of his lips as if he were sucking it in and was again sweetly looking straight ahead. I had already known for a long time that the ragamuffin was laughing at me. In his moods of dissolute indifference he had already told me many times that he thought it was foolish on my part to take so much pains with his mug.

But again his eyes looked around for distraction and he said: "She's in a bad way, ain't she?"

He was speaking of the cat, who sat huddled on the pillows of the reed chair under the window. Yesterday she had been restless all day and had dragged her spoiled stomach and her sick body around in the attic; but now she stayed quiet, she would neither eat nor drink; she was dozing without sleeping and she made herself very small, sometimes following my movements with listless eyes.

"Too bad, she is such a nice little animal."

The villain. But a moment ago he had told me that I ought to beat her to death; he would do it, he knew where he could sell her fur for fifteen stuivers.

"Come, Puss, yawn for me," he said suddenly making a motion, and with the yellow brush of his lamp wiper he began to tickle the animal's nose.

She moved dumbly back, afraid of the contrivance.

"Cut it out, will you!"

He broke out in short, cruel guffaws. He had fallen forward from delight, the curly fair head with its greasy fur cap going down as he burst into uncontrollable laughter, holding his stomach with both hands beneath the blue surface of his almost unwrinkled vest. "I got to laugh when you get mad," he said, when it was finally over. "Still it is too bad, such a nice animal."

"Only the day before yesterday I caught two cats," the boy said, spitting out the words. "I stepped on one's head; they can't bear that."

"No?"

"No, you see, first I threw a stone at them; this one walking around in our yard, near my brother-in-law's car, you see, and he started to go around in circles; well I ran up to him, and there, with my heel on his head. Like this, you see. . . . Well, that way he was out of his misery. What do you say to that?"

His neck had become swollen as he was telling this; his voice had become increasingly moist, as if water were running to the front of his mouth; when he ground his heel he stamped on the ground on the imaginary cat; a flicker of the white of his eye had glowed fiercely, but slowly his eyelids came down again, the arrogant look had disappeared and he stood there again contrite, his head cocked sentimentally sideways.

And when his voice stopped it was again the quiet of a working atmosphere. Outside, underneath the window, the children were tripping by, school was over. I heard their busy squabbles, their excitement in the slowly falling snow. There a boy came running as he shouted; in the back of my laboring brain I heard the fresh noises, the jubilant sound, the high laughter of young innocents. I continued working frantically, struggling to catch the boy's vanishing expression, which had escaped me day after day, which returned and disappeared in his mobile face. Underneath, in the stone masons' place, came blows, the dull report of hammers as they crushed the stone.

What a queerly shaped nose—and it looked as if this vagabond had a hundred mouths; yet a while ago his neck was as slender as a boy's neck and now it was a maw that he filled, a pocket that he stuffed with his bubbling bad inclinations.

But in his sloppy-looking old clothes, spindly legs stuck into threadbare trousers, and too lazy to take his hands out of his pockets, he walked away from his position without saying a word, dragging his feet, and sank down on the small rush-bottomed chair that I had placed for him when he needed a rest.

"You get such a pain in your back from standing up," he said.

"Nonsense. You probably drank too much gin again last night, your head is as red this morning as a red cabbage."

"Oh no, I'm off the stuff."

He sat with his elbows resting on his knees, playing with his fur cap as with a dead animal, quite bent over, heavy, foursquare, like a load on the floor. Thus he let me look at his vicious back, which stuck out under the pile of old clothes that poor people wear to protect themselves from the cold. Under the flood of light this back was like a surface of stubbornness, a tough sounding-board, from which all decent thought would recoil and be beaten to smithereens. There was something so terribly beotial about the preponderance of this rounded back, something so low and down-to-earth about this submissively bent, slave body. How was it possible that in this piece of uncouthness I had every once in a while seen the freshness of an outdoor child, the unconcern of a tramp who goes wherever the spirit impels him?

That is the way I had looked at him and that was how I had started on him, with his roving appearance, tame like a wild summer bird during a difficult winter; but when the money had come regularly, all that had disappeared; he began to come in the morning dragging his feet, yearning for more money, bloated, the dissipations of the night before shining in his eyes, with the guzzling still swelling his cheeks and throat. Should I send him for a while again into the fields? But how should I get hold of him again? He lived with his mother in a caravan, and three times a day he spoke about becoming a soldier or a sailor or something else again. To get away, far away, because here it was misery.

Still he sat in front of me, as I laid my palette away, my cat with collapsed back, with shanks and shoulderblades sticking out from under the skin, in one sad bunch on the muslin chair cushion. She sat on her paws, hidden under the fur, and her tail curled around her as if to protect her from the cold. And she was so quiet, one was hardly aware that she was there, the small head with the pale bloodless nose motionless; and the ears pointing up, dry and withered at the edges, without the slightest motion. She was mortally sick; it was only from behind her half-closed eyes that the fever of life burned and shimmered darkly. I had made her a little resting-place near the stove, thinking that she was cold, but with hesitating steps and mewing sadly she had run away from the heat and had returned to the freshness of the window. Then I had left her to her fate, one can't continuously be preoccupied by a sick cat.

"No! I won't have any more of it!" the boy spat out with his face directed toward the floor.

He sat there, fussing with black, dirty fingers at the small mourning ribbon fastened to the side of his cap, then he lifted his arms, first one and then the other.

"I can stand it all right, you see, but twenty drinks ain't right; don't you think?"

"You rather than I."

"What?" he boasted, sitting up straight again, "Jan's brother drinks at least thirty of them."

"Who is Jan?"

"Why, Jan, he is the boss of the dance hall, you know, where I sometimes play."

"Oh, yes."

"A good fellow that Bram, he cares a lot for me, but he has had two strokes; did you ever hear about it, mynheer, the flame shot out of his throat, on account of the heat inside, of the burning gin."

The skin under his eyes started to tremble and the words came out of his mouth softly and scaredly, when he repeated once more: "No, I won't take any more of it. . . ."

But as his fear quickly subsided, he changed the position of his skinny legs and prattled on: "Oh, we've had a good time together, because he's a good fellow. He likes me. They all like me. Do you know why that is?"—"No? Well you see, that is because I am always cheerful. You see, I'm always cheerful. I make my mother laugh, see? Lately when my father, blessed be his memory, died, I still made her laugh. She said to me, 'Louis, don't you want to say good-by to your father for the last time . . .' and she was crying something awful. . . . I said, 'Yes, mother . . .' and then I went to his bed in her caravan . . . see . . . and I said, 'Well, so long, Pop, hope you make out all right.' Then my mother started to laugh. Hey man, she laughed so hard . . . I thought she'd laugh the old boy back to life. See, that's why they all like me."

I had been sitting patiently next to him, allowing him to indulge in loquaciousness. He was like that on those days after the dissipated nights, such as the night before. He always went on in this way, to get away from work. And he had a knack for telling stories that he could sometimes make me listen to the echoes of his dissolute life. From his untutored brain sometimes sprang yarns that made me forget my studies and my work.

He would tell me how he would leave as soon as the cold weather had passed, with his wagon, his habitation on wheels, and his mother, whom he called *"kokkerol"*, his father *"sterestan"*, and his foal, going from fair to fair, living in the open air, under the big sun. He could tell me about the camping along the paved roads, with his little horse grazing at the border of a canal and he would imitate the "ho-o-o-ho" of the skippers of the barges. He would tell me how during hot summer days full of stolen strawberries he would spend the sultry, misty nights laden with the smell of new-mown hay. And he liked to boast about his fights with boys, and the fights of the grown-up men, emphasizing those which had been the bloodiest and most magnificent. Sometimes his stories were a bit too bold and they were filled with cries for help, shouts in the night of the wooden traveling coaches, coming from under the lowered sails of the field tents and from beneath the protecting coverings of the merry-go-rounds, where in the early morning men with hair rumpled from the night chased each other with knives, seeking to strike and to kill each other in the morning darkness, between the wooden horses and between the stiff swinging of the yellow painted carrousel lions. And he knew how to tell!—and he loved to do it!—of closely observed bacchanalia, of groups of people with coats off. Then he came to life; then he started to step out and did things with his arms; with a jerk he would cock his cap and, looking at me with enlarged eyes, he would shout: "Look, this way!" How he would stride through the red smoking night of the fair, in the wild excitement of music coming from all around him, in the greasy smell of cheap doughnuts!—everywhere the air was full of it!—in a jolly crowd possessed by freedom and gin as he himself; sawing on his concertina, he would send forth his high boy's voice into space, singing: "Oh, what a girl, what a beautiful, lovely girl!" Then I saw him again, as he jumped up and there rose out of his flattened, gin-filled head, out of his winter sleep, his total youth, sometimes springing like a flash from a struck tinder, sometimes in the broadness of his flaming imagination, all around him, coming before the slobbering gait; and there was something unusual, something fresh in his filthy voice, when he then sank again onto the stool and uttered his great desire for the spacious summer: "I wish it was spring again."

But when, as now, he began to tell about his wanderings, of his wild nights and his pickpocket stories from the city, then often there came between his gin-scented tales of thievery, like a stake sticking out from the ground, his deep fear of police; then he became embarrassed, dumb, with his mouth still talking, as if a fist had grabbed him from behind the neck, and would shut up to start again stutteringly, lying so much he convinced himself of it.

He did not even know what lying was; he lied from habit and because he liked to lie; like an artist in the midst of his material, he often stood surrounded by his lies. Then he got caught in his own stories, and before it was over he would have belied himself a dozen times. Then I would pretend that I believed every word of it, that was the best for my work, and he would not feel it but would drool on, carried along by his fantasy. But sometimes I could not withstand the temptation and told him how he lied. Then he became shortspoken and surly or he would laugh right to my face or, most often, strike a sentimental pose, cock his head, begin to complain, uttering hypocrisies, phrasing his biggest lie, the lie of his whole race and kind: "What can a fellow do to earn his bread; what can you say about it?"

The rest period had lasted long enough, and I said: "Do you feel like working?"

"Yes, mynheer." But he remained seated.

"No, stand up. If you do it well I shall give you a cigar."

"Come on, two, then I still got one for tonight."

"Two then."

"I believe that there are few boys that are as well off with you as I am."

"Come on, stand there now."

"You are a nice gentleman."

He got up, with a jerk, as if he were seized by a sudden hacking cough, a short laughter, stood up in his full length and shuffled ahead lazily.

The work was resumed while the boy was yawning loudly, his wide-open yaw turned toward me; this enabled me to look into his mouth with its short, cruel teeth, like the maw of an ape, palely red inside. The opening closed.

"It is a pleasure."

After the struggle, my strength for work returned, life again possessed me, the life-giving power, only the great urge to accomplish deeds.

"Look, look, she wants to get down. Can you do it, puss?" the boy mocked. "Shall I give you a lift from behind."

The cat had gotten up and tried carefully to get down from the cushion, her body stiffly bent forward, her tail slack behind her; did her instinct tell her that tomorrow she would not be able to get down any more? She hesitated, felt with her paws beneath her and so let herself finally go. The claws hooked themselves into the cushion of the chair to break the fall, but she fell softly to the floor; noiselessly she immediately took some steps, but she did not totter, her paws were clawing the floor.

Like a somnambulist, who neither sees nor hears, but walks straight ahead in the security of its dream visions, she went, moving along the floor, between the boy and myself, under my eyes, along by the easel, and made straight for the door.

"She wants to go out," he said.

"No, she is looking for air."

She was already at the door. There stood these two painting boxes made of wooden boards like the coffins of poor people, rough and unpainted. They stood against the wall, with loose covers, leaning against each other. She shoved herself in between them, through the open space until only her tail remained outside, then it also disappeared. Then for a moment her head appeared again, she had turned around, as a cat will do in its basket.

"Leave her alone," I said to the boy.

"Sure, such a nice little animal; it's a pity."

I put a small saucer with water in front of the opening between the boxes, the ill are always thirsty,—but then I went to work again, one cannot busy oneself for ever with a sick cat.

Outside beyond the window the snow had again started whirling, criss-cross, the white flakes floating up and down and the pale shimmering started to spread a shadow in the attic, veiling the window, like a curtain of thin gauze before the light-shy eyes of one mortally ill.

For two days she remained there sitting in the dark, without movement, without a complaint, dying in a corner of her own choosing. I often went to see her, though I knew it would always be the same; the slight hope, the sickly sheen of her fur in the corner between the boxes and mournful expression of her inward-turned eyes, which bore witness to her silent suffering.

Once more, on the third day of her illness, I had disturbed her and taken her up, placing my hand gently under her breast and had put her near the window in her old habitual place. A kind woman neighbor had come to have a look and had shaken her head under the black woolen winter cap; she was of the opinion that perhaps it was the teeth. So many cats and children died from them. She talked about nature, which had to run its course, because one did not know what to do about an animal under such circumstances. But a little later, when she had gone, the cat had gotten up and tried to get down from the cushion, but that she could do no longer, so I had had to lift her down to the ground, very carefully, afraid that I might hurt her. Immediately she started to walk, but with small shaky steps, and stubbornly crawled back to the space between the boxes, huddled together in the corner where she would die, her smallness shut off from her surroundings, but without a complaint, like a strong man who only silently protests against his suffering.

Outside the snow obliterated all noise and the steps of the passers-by had become inaudible. It was Sunday, the fourth day of her illness. When I came downstairs I saw the path, disappearing between the trees and the little houses, with the glistening traces of the soles of the shoes and the wagon wheels, because it was still freezing. There was nobody in the neighborhood; from the further end of the path a peasant woman came tripping along smoothing her Sunday clothes, in her hand the missal with its golden lock. The house gables were covered with snow, and smoke from the dark chimney pots was faintly blue in the warmly white air, still packed with snow. Broadly the land stretched out behind the black picket fence, it bulged away under the new blanket of snow in the white, wintry silence of Sunday. From beside the Amstel one could hear occasionally the clanging of an approaching tram; it came, the pure ringing of the bell into a space, empty of noise, like the sounding of the priest's bell as in a Catholic country he advances bringing the last sacrament to a dying person.

In my home it was still too, still because of the snow, still through the Sunday loneliness of the house, and from my window I looked upon the light blanket, the pall covering a bier.

But toward the night of this silent day, when I again went to see how she was getting along, she had crawled out of her hiding place, her head above the saucer of water. Was she thirsty? I took the saucer up to her, but there was no more any desire in her small body. Was it because it was cool that she huddled that way over the cold water? Was there a deathly fever in her head? What could a large, uncouth man do in his love for such a small object? Perhaps a saucer with snow would be even more refreshing. I went downstairs and scooped up some fresh snow in the stone container. Then I extinguished the stove and left her alone in the cold of the work room.

But the next day the path was a pool; it had stopped freezing; the melted snow leaked and ran around my house, water streamed into small holes in the mess of snow and mud and made grooves between the yellow cobblestones. And inside there were the sucking and sighing noises of the released cold, and on the roof and in the trees there was a springlike life as if there were many cats there. But with a dull noise, with the muffled drop of a shovelful of earth upon a coffin, the clumps of snow slid down the roof and fell onto the ground. There was an air of decomposition and transition about, the tepid odor of a vanishing beauty of winter, the smell of thaw and of rotting and melting ice. The moist light cast a sad reflection inside the house, bluish like the haze around the eyes of a dying man, encompassing the room with its feeble shimmer.

The cat was still alive: she sat huddled in her corner between the boxes, without a peep coming, her head held low, the eyes staring emptily ahead, in mad fear of death, above the saucer full of melted snow.

It was already noon when the boy rang the bell. Breathing life, he said that he had not been able to come earlier, he had had to register with the Army. The water from the thawing snow seeped out of the ragged legs of his trousers as he mounted the stairs behind me; he carried along the mud from his wandering through the streets, everywhere he set his shuffling feet. He swung inside, hands in his pockets as usual, closed the door with a shove of his elbow and shouted at once, seeing me near the boxes: "My goodness, she's still alive; my, ain't she a tough one!"

His fair head swung on his shoulders. He was wearing a new cap, cocked over his right ear. It was a sailor's cap with a shiny visor and a patent leather storm band to which were fastened two copper buttons upon which gleamed two yellow anchors. His tie was new, too, and not fastened like a string around his neck, but tied with loving care into a sailor's knot under his Adam's apple.

He made himself at home and immediately fell down into the small chair.

"Where's your cap?"

"Here."

Like an old skin, and folded fourfold, the thing came out of his pocket. "I ran fast," he started to lie as he hiccoughed, "because it was late; we had a lot of fun, there were at least twenty of us boys . . . eh . . . but those gentlemen have always time on their hands, they made me wait for a long time, well . . . about three hours. They had to verify my records, where I was born, see? Now I know . . . my old lady never wanted to tell me, see . . . but now I know . . . the twenty-seventh of May of the year seventy-one. . . . Do you know my age now? . . . No? . . . Eighteen . . . the gentlemen told me, from the year seventy-one . . . a nice age . . . if the old lady would give her consent, then I'd ship out, to the East . . . but twice they hauled me back . . . my mother always tells them . . . once I was as far as Harderwyk, I can't do anything any more today, what do you say to that? . . . But I'll be rejected, I have a broken blood vessel in my eye . . . here in my right one."

That promised something. The bumming around in the morning, the playing at being heroes of a troop of wild boys, all brave because they had enlisted in the armed forces, the boasting among themselves about the East and the sea and the fine uniforms, the treating all around, always "just one more," the noisy pilgrimage from one gin-mill to another, had loosened him from the grip of winter and had awakened him. He was irresistible that afternoon. Like the foam on the lips of one possessed, life bubbled over his lips; it shone from his eyes, it foamed in his mouth, it lived in his released arms and legs; with his hands, no longer inactive, he made gestures in the air accompanying his vague visions.

And in his puffed-up boasting, in the realization of his own valor he had started to chew tobacco. . . . "A man must be able to chew tobacco, what do you say to that? . . . If you no longer take a drink . . . otherwise he isn't a man. . . ." There he stood, chewing or shoving the hot wad back and forth in his mouth; there was dirty filling-out of the cheeks around the nostrils, because the superfluous juice bothered him and his mouth was running. Then he would leave his place, realizing that it was not nice to spit on a gentleman's floor. He expectorated between his teeth, and the spittle landed hissing in the coal-box, or sometimes, when he did not dare leave his place, he swallowed it with a grimace as his hot throat protested and the bitter juice went down.

In this way the afternoon went by. There was no longer any question of working. I went from time to time to the boxes to find out whether she had yet died. His boisterousness went over my head, my thoughts were not of him.

So he did as he pleased. With his instinct of a wild beast he felt he was the boss again, the few times that I forbade him to continue, he smiled slyly or posed sentimentally. But then his joy again reverberated through the attic and his noisy, gay voice rambled on; he brought forth all his knowledge and tricks, bragging about what he was going to experience in order to attract my attention and to escape work and the necessity for standing still.

He turned the burning end of a cigar butt inside his mouth with his lips and smoked with the fire inside his mouth, and then he flipped it out again with his wet lips, pulled and puffed with a sucking-in of his hollow, elastic cheeks and made the wet and half-extinguished butt flare up again in a red glow. He bit a penny in half, chewing and twisting the copper between the vise of his cruel teeth. He crushed a piece of coal from the stove into fine bits with his teeth, and the black liquid drooled from the corners of his mouth. Oh, there were many other tricks he had up his sleeve. . . . He began to walk on his hands around the attic, with his fingers close together, and hands flat on the floor like a monkey, his legs bent at the knee in the air, his dirty coat hanging about head and hands. After that he took a piece of paper—"there's enough paper around"—and folded it into at least fifty strips, slowly, patiently, as if it were something important and had to be done very precisely, and then started—"Look now,"—and turned it and twisted it, unfolded it and closed it up again, wrinkled it and folded it in all kinds of figures like a full-fledged prestidigitator. In a tedious, whiny voice he began to recite his lesson, immediately falling back in the right tone: "That's for a start, ladies and gentlemen, a little mouth organ music," he drawled and sang with his voice, as if he were at a fair, as if he were standing in the center of the marketplace in the midst of a group of onlookers, or before a fashionable house, surrounded by many children on a wide street. Figure after figure he fashioned from the paper, things which bore some resemblance to the objects they were supposed to represent. "That's a flight of steps for getting upstairs; now I turn it around, and it's a church window . . . and that's a cockade the postilions wear on their hats and that's an emblazoned star for kings and emperors. That's a fan for keeping cool . . . and that an epaulet the officers wear on their shoulders. . . . This is a small sentry box and that the wine glass from which gentlemen like to drink champagne . . . and that a sofa and that the foot rest and that a child's cradle. Shoo . . . shoo . . ."

The stiff paper rattled between his fingers, fumbling and fiddling, pinching and stretching it: "See, the paper is too stiff, I want to make an elephant. . . ." He developed it with much working of his arms and twisting with his fingers, a little untrained in his virtuosity, and made his series of paper likenesses. He let joints of his fingers crack and snap, as with one movement and a lot of hocus-pocus he allowed one finger to produce another, to the delight of the crowd, he imagined around him. The session was nearly over . . . he had reached the letter K, a Spanish cellar became a pulpit with steps . . . then the paddlewheels of a steamer that goes through the water. . . . "That's a summer house," he sang, "and the cap my grandmother wore, blessed be her memory, and if she isn't in heaven she's at least out of the way . . . and that's a spittoon . . . and that a cooper's plane . . . this is a coach lantern . . . and that, ladies and gentlemen, is an English salt cellar and if you now will all be kind enough to give a small contribution I'll have something too."

The folded and thumbed paper had now become grey under his dirty fingers. It achieved the form of two clumsily shaped containers joining at the ends, which he held in the middle between thumb and index finger. He held the container out to collect, and with his other hand took off his fur cap, holding it at the top, pulling it from his head like a plaster, and made the rounds.

"No, that was just in fun, you see," he said somewhat abashed. "But, you see, now you have learned a lot . . . but I know a lot too. . . . Oh, my dear sir, I know still more tricks . . . and you may have seen much in your life, but this you never saw before . . . now give me a swallow of gasoline."

"*What?*"

But before I could prevent him from doing it, he had taken the oil can from its place and uncorked it.

"But no, please give me a match. No, don't be afraid, I will do nothing wrong. Open the door, if you want to. . . . Come on, give it to me . . . oh, you are crazy, it's a fine trick."

And then he set the can to his mouth and drank, pursing his lips, a good swallow of the filthy liquid. His eyes laughed triumphantly above his greasy mouth, he turned his face to the door and lit a match. And slowly, still looking around, he lifted his

arm with the burning stick of wood to just above his chin, and
then he blew, with a blast of his cheeks, slightly bending his
shoulders first forward and then backwards, moistening his lips
with the oil, into the still blue and yellow small flame.

Like a sheaf of fire a red sparkling flame, a plume of burning
spangles more than a meter in length, flew from his mouth. It
looked as if the very fire of life sprang from his gullet; I stood
staring at him as my throat constricted and with my heart beating
faster from fright. I saw how his wild, merry eyes blinked with
pleasure, lit up white in the play of fire above the sparkling gold.
He closed his lips as if he were biting off the flame while it went
out; his almost distant laugh gurgled in his throat, but around
him it was dark for a moment.

But again there was the spray of flaming light, a sheaf of light;
as he gulped, his hot breath seemed to have caught fire, and his
animal-like nature exploded like a fiery arrow, hissing out his
boiling interior.

Had I been mistaken? Didn't I see my cat crawl underneath
the column of fire, out of the corner, where she was dying?
Hadn't I seen her sinuous darkness swinging her way toward the
open outdoors? But the boy continued spitting fire; It flew out
of the door as with a last effort of his lungs and cheeks the little
red flames, scintillating like fiery butterflies in the light heat
which spread like powder in the black smoke rings, winged their
way through the opening into the small hallway.

And then . . . the muffled thud, thud, the dull cadence of a
weak thing, falling and bumping into things along the wooden
staircase.

Flames of death, flames of death . . .

But there was the laughter that started thundering, a crazy
laughter, the hard jerks of an explosive laughter. I saw the boy
standing on the top step, bent forward over the well of the staircase, holding his belly with his hands, bending and twisting and
stamping his feet with insane joy. The blood swelled in his
throat and his ears, and he jerked with his head, his eyes were
cramped in their sockets; but from his oily lips laughter burst
forth his guffaws, it came in spurts and shrieks, raw like the shrill
blaring of a triumphant trumpet.

"Oh, oh!" he said between bursts of laughter. "Oh, oh, look,
mynheer, she has come to life again, but now she is done for.
Look, look, will you . . ."

I looked; she was dead. She lay at the bottom of the stairs, she
had come down sideways after her fall, she had tumbled onto

the dirty yellow crossed rushes of the mat below the stairs; she lay flat on her side, dark, with her tail behind her, as if she had stayed dead after her frightened jump.

Again, as if I were discovering it anew, as one will see something for the first time, as I looked down upon her her smallness impressed me, again I perceived how puny and thin she was.

I went down the stairs, I bent down and picked her up from the mat, while at the top of the stairs the terrible laughter of the boy kept falling down upon her and myself. There he stood on the top step as his fits of laughter broke forth spasmodically.

"You had better go now, Louis," I said as he came down the steps. "There is your money."

"Ain't I coming back tomorrow, mynheer?" he said, his moist face still creased with laughter.

"No."

"Or the day after?"

"No."

"Not any more? Perhaps you will call for me?"

He ran out, rattling his money. In the distance on the path I could still hear him remonstrating with the children in his loud boy's voice; but in the house everything was quiet again.

Then I carried her upstairs and silently took a sheet, a clean one from my bed, and laid her out carefully, smoothly on the muslin of the chair cushion.

Thus she lay stiffly stretched out in death, thus I put her down, her tail in the white folds.

I sat down on my camp chair and bent over her, I gazed at her, as she lay there, sunk into the cushion, but not as small as before. There she lay, looking at me with her eyes wide open, full of reproach, from the white mourning cloth of the poor people's shroud.

Translated by ALFRED VAN AMEYDEN VAN DUYM

Albert Verwey

LEONARD AND JULIAN

AS DAY DAWNED, THE YOUNG BOYS SAT IN THE DAMP, ROCKY CLEFT. The morning before they had left their home on the plain behind the mountains. Playing together they had trotted through the watery valleys. Searching for stones and plants they had clambered up the rocky slopes. And when the sun was at its height, sheltered among fir trees near a silvery brook they sat down to feast on the fruits they had gathered by the way. The heat over, walking was pleasant enough, but both boys had become quieter and when at dusk they descended on the other side of the mountain and got into the bushes and briars of the ravine, courage failed them, in the darkness, to seek their way out of it again.

All the night, shivering in the damp mist, they leaned against each other, now awake, and now asleep, wishing again and again that the day would come. At last they saw light appearing in the sky above them. The vegetation around them became clearer, still dark but less threatening than when, just a moment before, it had seemed a part of the night. A bird uttered a hoarse cry and flew in an oblique line across the space between the two edges of the cleft.

The younger had jumped up, but his feet pained him and he staggered so that the older boy had to catch him and make him lie down again. He then leaned over and took off the other's shoes and rubbed the soles of feet that were both cold and swollen. So occupied, his blond head with round, blue eyes, anxious and kind, was held close to the pale features of the dark child who painfully smiled up at him.

They were obviously brothers, both clad in jacket and cap of the same black velvet. Lost in the mountain woods there was nothing about them that did not appear strange, for one would have imagined them, with bow and arrow, crossing the courtyard to go and shoot at birds in the park, or running up the stairs and through the rooms of a castle in pursuit of a ball that had flown in through some window and rolled underneath a heavy old chest. Parents would certainly inquire for them, and a grumbling steward or huntsman keep an eye on them.

But it was not so. Their parents were dead, the faithful servants dismissed; and over the castle, now deserted, there ruled only the truculent relative who had come from the city and said that he would take the children with him.

The world of childhood had closed behind them, and of the other, the great world beyond, they knew only that it lay open. They had made no plan, for youth's plan lies always in its inner certainty; and only now, with the feet of little Julian before him, Leonard thought of the possibility of going on again.

Of the impossibility he did not think, only of the means. He encouraged his brother and supported him when he stood up again.

The ravine was now all light. There was an opening toward the south where the sun shone on the rocks and bushes. The way was not steep but rough and barren so that the journey for both, now that they were hungry, and thirsty, became the more difficult the longer it continued.

"Leave me alone, Leonard;" said Julian, "and go to see if there is any water yonder."

However unwillingly, Leonard left him. He quickly reached the height and, between the branches of the fir-trees, he saw wood piled up in the distance. A man smoking a pipe was carrying tools toward a clearing. Nearby stood a cart, with a brown horse moping before it.

The world was now altogether different—not alarming and hurtful, but sociable and friendly, so that Leonard did not think at once of his brother but of the landscape. He let his eyes wander about and then walked slowly up to the man. Sometimes hidden behind the trees, then visible again in sunny openings, he went on, but the man did not notice him until he was close by. He appeared astonished when he saw the handsome boy and heard the tale of being lost and of a younger brother who had been left some distance back and who was thirsty.

The wagoner gave him at first no answer, but pulled a tin flask out from under the seat of his wagon and said: "I will come with you." They departed together and, when they approached the cleft, Leonard hurried ahead. He came to the spot where he had left Julian but did not see him. He looked about in dismay, then deeper into the ravine and upward on the mountain, but there was nowhere a trace of Julian. The wagoner had now approached also. He understood that the child had disappeared. He saw the anxiety in Leonard's face and helped him search here and there in the brushwood and clefts; and the boy's treble and the man's heavy voice called out so that the sound reverberated and echoed from the mountainside. But neither search nor shouts availed. Exhausted, Leonard had to return with the man, who gave him food and drink and promised to take him along in his cart to the nearest village.

They followed a hilly path between the tall fir-trees. With the leafy tip of a long switch the wagoner tapped the flies from the horse that jogged along in his harness and only occasionally shook his head impatiently. Now and then the man asked a question: who were Leonard's parents, where was his house, where were his relatives and what was the name of the place he had come from. The boy talked vaguely about the death of his parents, the sale of his house, of having no relatives and of coming from a region that lay far behind the mountains.

The shadows were already lengthening when they rode out of the woods. The road sloped steeply so that the brakes ground at every turn and the horse's bells tinkled harder. On one side the view was cut off by the mountain growth; on the other, the land lay in broad and deep undulations. It was late haying time, and little women with colorful kerchiefs on their heads hurried up the hills with amazing strides and with such huge bundles of hay on their backs that they could scarcely be recognized. Down below, still invisible because it was huddled against the side of the mountain, lay the village. At the end of the road the cart, with one turn, clattered in.

The wagoner jumped down and led the horse by the rein amid cackling hens, dabbling children and low houses over a plank bridge that crossed a half-dry brook. Curious women made for their doors and stared at the blond boy in black velvet who sat alone in the cart and thus made his entrance.

There was silence in one yard where lay filthy straw. Before the stable door stood a tall, broad-shouldered man who was something between a farmer and an alderman. The wagoner, in his bushy beard and blue smock, talked with him while the other kept his eyes fixed upon the boy. He nodded approvingly, beckoned the boy to come down from the cart and told him to follow. He entered a house that stood next to the barn and that was half shop, half inn.

Within, the room was much larger than it seemed from the outside. There were two counters, behind one of them stood the buffet, behind the other, shelves of merchandise, and in front stood casks of provisions, a side of bacon, a barrel of meal, wooden shoes and straw brooms. Through an adjoining passage the man called: "Maria!"; a good-natured, fat creature in a black skirt and purple jacket appeared and was ordered to give the boy something to eat. She looked startled, shook her head and disappeared, to return soon with a supper of beans and boiled beef. In the meanwhile the man had drawn a small glass of beer, which he set before the boy on a little table near the window.

The boy ate and drank sleepily. Then his host led him up to a little room at the top of the house overlooking the stable; there was a bed, and the man told the boy that he ought to have a good sleep.

The following morning, when he awoke, his black clothes had disappeared, and in their place a suit of gray bombazine lay on the chair. It looked comparatively new and fitted him rather loosely. He was now a fair, sturdy youngster and as he went down the stairs he himself realized that he would be worth his keep.

The proprietor of the house—who was waiting for him in the taproom—was in fact everything that a man could be in the village: burgomaster, alderman and town-clerk, farmer, merchant and miller. He looked over his new acquisition and remarked that the boy could work, first in the storeroom that was behind the house and also had an entrance to the stable, and later, perhaps, in the mill, where there was an old workman who was ill and would probably not recover.

Leonard then worked in the storehouse, where he received goods from the carters or handed it to them, or brought it into the shop, arranged and listed it. At times he still felt the loss of his brother Julian as a void, and the thought of where his brother might have strayed could suddenly constrict his throat; but, most of the time he thought only of his work, which had to be done and was at no single moment wholly finished. And gradually he also became one whom people knew in relation to his work; about his origin little was asked. From the wagoner's story they knew that he was without relatives and that he did not come from the neighborhood. Nor did it seem to the patron's advantage that the authorities—which were himself—should make a search for the boy's family. He was loved for his own sake, by Maria, the old housekeeper, as well as by the carters, the women and the children and the people of the district who dealt in the shop.

When, after some time, the old workman died, and Leonard was given the place in the mill, he was known to them all, and no one ever spoke any more of the unusual way he had made his entrance into the village.

The mill was behind the settlement where a stream, which did not dry up even in summer, kept the gigantic paddle-wheel in motion. In that damp, out-of-the-way place, where some broad-leaved trees gave a luxurious shade, Leonard had a comfortable little job. He attached the wheel or unfastened it, he attended to the sluice that could wholly or partly dam up the water and he saw to the necessary repairs—for the rest of the time, he received the grain that was thrown into the hopper and put the meal into the sacks that were loaded on wagons and taken to the shop or, more often, to the town.

In the clatter of the wheel and flying dust of the grain, gentle and powdered white, he became the miller, in that position respected far and wide.

His patron was content, the villagers liked him, the children going to school in the neighboring hamlet always stopped a while to listen to the water and the clattering of the wheel at which they threw pebbles. They paid no attention to him, convinced as they were that he would do them no harm. And every other Sunday he went to listen to the Minister of a little church a good hour further away, and he recognized many a farmer there whom he had seen passing by or whose meal he had ground.

Sometimes he went also to the town. Not toward that side of the mountain where he had lost Julian, but to the opposite side, and the trips there were his only journeys of importance. He went with the wagon laden with sacks of meal, which he carried to the baker on the neatly cobbled town square. And he stopped at the large inn where townspeople and strangers spent their money, at the same time doing business.

He never thought of his youth, only of the years that he had passed in the village where he had become a young man.

Julian, left behind in the ravine, was soon in a condition of stupor from thirst and pain. Thus he was found by the Graybeard of the Mountain, who, by paths known only to himself, took him to his dwelling.

The Graybeard lived in a wondrous mountain world. Closed in on all sides by high walls, it was none the less accessible from all sides. But it seemed that everyone who approached the path from the outside, which was clearly to be seen from within, was struck with blindness. In the center stood the House, hewn from rock, with open galleries overlooking a mass of fantastic crags on which red flowers climbed. There he carried the child, laid him on a restful bed and gave him into the care of little Monica.

She was, in fact, a very young girl, who called him grandfather. She played with and cared for the boy, that was all.

Julian lay in a raving fever that lasted ten days. When he recovered he found before him a life of the greatest simplicity and yet full of wonders. His physical life consisted of meals with the Graybeard and Monica—the servitors were numerous and yet seemed to be absent because nothing of their activity penetrated to the mind—of clothing that remained the same although it was constantly changed. But more than that there was life itself, as Julian became conscious of it. He thought of Leonard, thought of him with all natural feeling, with sorrow for his loss, with melancholy remembrance of his kindness, with loving perception of every small detail of their years of childhood companionship, and their flight of a day—but all these feelings and images were like fish in a stream, freely coming and going, but enveloped in a gleaming, moving, penetrable light from which it was both better and desirable not to separate them.

Julian had forgotten nothing; on the contrary everything lived in him more vividly than he had ever known it, but at the same time he knew, as if by some secret prompting, that it would never move him to action, never bring him back to the actuality from which it sprang.

And just as the past lived within him, the present lived outside him: the Graybeard whom he accepted as a model and to whose words he daily listened, the little girl with whom he ran and played, the whole wonder-filled world of the mountain in which he came to be at home and which let him know its secrets ever more clearly. Inside the house and without, there was order in all natural things: as unchangeable a regularity of meal-times as of seasons, yet in this regularity there was a sensation that he could interpret in no other words than that there was no time. He was captivated from hour to hour, finally from year to year, but when he had lived long enough to recall himself, to wish to recall himself, then he discovered that nothing, absolutely nothing, had happened and that nevertheless the same enthralling fullness still existed. But it existed—and this he now understood—as the stream of his own consciousness. He grasped at every instant the whole living mass of drops which the completeness of life mirrored for him, lost and then gave back again. He felt submerged in a life so fervent and so real that he retained nothing of the casual.

An indefinite sadness developed in him, which he had never before experienced. He had grown older—how much older he did not know. He had once, bathing with Monica in the clear mountain pool with the dark woods standing above them, looked down at his feet and perceived how high above the water his head remained. He had called to her to see how tall he was. He had looked at her, too, as she stooped on the borderline of sunlight and shadow and with a movement of her head tossed back her long, golden hair.

Noticing the curve of her shoulders had released in him one of the great emotions of his life, that of an indescribable grace. Henceforth all that was most moving existed for him in that curve of her shoulders. The dark firs and the blue sky were merely background for that whiteness, to bring it out and illuminate it.

But in that emotion lay a secret that he could not discover in Monica. Nature that surrounded him possessed it neither. The words of the Graybeard, however weighty, lacked it too. In Monica's voice it never reached expression.

He became restless and wandered on the borders of his mountain world. One warm afternoon he lay outstretched behind a thorn bush, with his eyes fixed on the stark blue of the summer sky. Suddenly he heard soft warm sounds, as of clucking. Through an opening in the thorn he saw a young woman, on the edge of a dusty road, suckling a child at the full breast that swelled from her open kerchief. A young fellow lay looking on. He was a tinker, sunburnt and with unruly, curly hair. She was coarse, red and friendly. The color of health and long roads was upon them both. Their eyes beamed as they regarded the child.

Julian remained watching until the woman, who had closed her dress, had fastened the child over her shoulders in a cloth, the man had gathered his tools and they had stood up.

He turned homeward, something less than before and yet greater. He felt slave to the idea that he was richer. The following morning saw him on one of the roads that led to the outside world, an ordinary bachelor in search of the happiness of all men. The world that he came into again was then as it is now and as it always will be. It consisted of the orderly elements, that is, of those who willingly or unwillingly allow themselves to become co-workers with others and of the disorderly, those for whom co-working is impossible. The marvel was that those who called themselves the co-workers had the sword always in hand, contended with each other, and did their work in a state of self-created confusion. The disorderly, on the other hand, were the defenseless, those who had no swords, the peaceful who would gladly have wished to work together but who thought they could not do so otherwise than peaceably.

When Julian had walked half a day he came to a farm. He was hungry and asked a laborer, who on a ladder was driving nails into the cornice of the roof, if there might be work for him. The laborer pointed ot a farmer who, fat and red, was standing near a cesspool. When Julian had repeated his request, he was asked what wages he demanded. "I demand no wage," he answered: "I am hungry." The other gave a short, hard laugh and said: "Good;

then I'll discharge the useless eater: he gets high wages and does little."

Julian went away, for he did not want to deprive the laborer of his bread.

He walked through a town where there were benches in a park on the square. There he dropped down to rest. But a helmeted man came and ordered him away. He complained that he was tired and had walked the whole day. But the warder of the peace became impatient and said sharply: "The bench is not for tramps." At that moment two dandies, who were discussing the light women of the town, approached and, still chatting, settled themselves on the bench and poked the sand with their walking-sticks.

Outside the town Julian found an inn where a marriage was being held. The host smiled, taking him in his velvet suit for a showman, a runner, unhooked a fiddle from the wall and told him to play. That he could do, and when he had eaten and drunk and arranged for a night's lodging he played the merriest dance music for the farmers and farm girls who stamped and clumped on the floor. That evening when the lights were already smoking, two of the farmers drew their knives, and their wives took themselves off with two others to hide in the hay.

The next morning the host made him a present of a large, gray cloak. Clad in this he succeeded in getting a place as runner for the bank that had its granite front with bulging, square, latticed windows on the main street. With his first pay he bought himself other clothing. He ran to and from the various offices of the town and showed himself to all inhabitants who did business with the bank. In the bank itself he appeared only to receive orders or to report. But when he had worked for a year he was called before his employer who proposed that he become a clerk. He accepted the offer and from now on sat on a high stool before a wooden desk with a list of quotations at hand, figuring the prices of stocks and the coupon-interest. He sat there with several other clerks and a bookkeeper. The time was passed mostly in figuring. It was always done by more than one clerk, so that the chance of error would be as small as possible. Letters were written, also, for which the rough draft was given by their employer who sat in the more handsomely furnished front office. Once written, they had to be copied on the press by the youngest clerk. When the employer, smoothing over his narrow, shining cranium with his fine, be-ringed hand and blinking his eyes, called: "Mister, down here!" the bookkeeper propped his pen attentively on the rim of his

desk, whipped off his stool and appeared before his master, who
issued exact questions from his fair beard or gave temperate orders.

A wind of activity swept through the office at that time and at
the Bourse hour, too, when both employer and bookkeeper disappeared and there was more chance for young townfolks'
chatter.

But the liveliest excitement was caused by the calls made at
the bank. Julian had long ago noted how wide was the circle in
which the bank did business. Not only the business of town and
province stood on their accounts or had shares of their stock from
which their own enterprises were fed—as those of certain persons
who, indeed, would have seen no chance to collect interest on the
national debt, to bring about a purchase or sale or even to find
opportunity to place investments in mortgages—not only were the
people of the town and province dependent on the bank, but, as
a result of connections with other banks, so was the whole kingdom and, in still wider relations, a good part of the world.

And Julian observed again that the apparent cooperation was
a mask for war. Seemingly the bank was intended to make easier
the lives and affairs of the people who came to it. Its connections
were like a thousandfold rope stretched as a support across the
world. But the twist of the rope became a net in which not
merely something occasionally was caught but which was purposely laid for the greatest catch. The money entrusted to the
bank was the capital with which it worked. The confidence that
the bank enjoyed was used for recommendations of doubtful
worth.

The calls made at the bank were exciting—and everyone in the
office felt this without expressing it unless by chance—because
though apparently paid for the purpose of cool-tempered business, they were actually made in rage or bleeding heartache. The
practice was for Julian to speak to the customers first at the clerk's
window, subsequently, if they were to be admitted, to show them
in. After that he shut the doors between the front and rear
offices. One glance often told him enough. This one was a captain
from a foreign financial camp; that, a victim. This one wore that
satisfied air of conquest that is always thinking up new approaches. The other bore in his countenance the despair of one
who knows himself irretrievably lost.

It was not Julian's way to sink himself so deeply in the feelings
of others that sympathy gave rise to weakness. But he saw in the
simplest play of a gesture the unending possibility of emotion,
and he knew enough of the world of humanity to perceive the

chaos of strife and suffering that is betrayed in one such ripple.

Behind the closed doors hissed the shameless conquest, shattering desperation seized hold—and the clerks in the office knew it, though they saw the faces but for a moment, though the words scarcely penetrated to them. Sometimes, however, either the bookkeeper or one of the clerks was appointed to deal with a less important customer.

When Julian had filled this position two years, he was ordered to go to a part of the kingdom where rents were to be collected. It was an outlying province. The people there lived on land inherited from father to son. For centuries the kingdom had taken no account of them. They were never called up in the standing army. They paid no taxes. They had their faith which was the same as that of all mankind but without church affiliation. Their land lay apart and safe, and from generation to generation they had grown strong in peaceful cooperation. They recognized the king of the realm. They sent him ambassadors bringing gifts at stated times. They trusted him, as their fathers had done before them. They thought him good and holy, and in the depths of their hearts slumbered the conviction that if ever any evil should befall them it could never be from him, that, on the contrary, he would do everything to ward it off.

But in recent years the powers of the realm had approached as never before. Railroads had come nearer. From these stepped officials who demanded money for the state. Officers appeared who called up sons to be enlisted in the army. Decrees were issued by a synod, which ruled the life of the churches, declaring themselves heretics.

Their communal life once disturbed and weakened, failure of crops and reverses were harder to bear than formerly; to stock up provisions and seeds they were obliged to mortgage their lands, and the time came when, without completely understanding how it had happened, they were destitute and dependent upon powers outside themselves.

So it was that Julian, on his arrival, found a people that had formerly been excellent in all respects, in open war with church, army and financial power, with the whole state and with powers abroad—and trusting still only in the prince, whom they had never seen. Julian observed that not only in their province but also in all the regions between them and the capital discontent was brewing and that faith was still strong. No one believed that life as it was could be borne any longer. Everyone—even if he did not believe—hoped that the prince would help.

Nothing seemed more natural to Julian. He shared the conviction of the people. He was present when they decided to march to the capital. He was at the head of an army that grew and grew, that, as one man, inspired with faith in the prince who would save them, marched along the quays one cold morning and to the square before the palace where it was to halt. Then out of the side streets where they stood hidden and prepared rushed the prince's glittering troops into the morning mist and, without a word, without a warning, men, women and children were shot, trampled and cut down. Julian was taken prisoner.

Soon after he was sent to a smaller town to be tried.

It was the town where the bakery stood on the neatly cobbled square, where Leonard had formerly delivered his meal. Leonard himself was now the owner of that house and a respectable citizen of the little town that had seen him grow in prosperity. He was a member of the church, an advocate of order which was embodied in the town. He was still unmarried, but he had grown one with the world that had accepted him, and he had spoken loudly with his fellow citizens against the rioters who had disturbed the peace and against their leader who was to be tried.

It was permitted to Julian to send for the clothing he had formerly worn. It was a whim of his, but that was the only costume that reminded him of his youth, of an earlier happiness and of one act of human kindness: the suit of black velvet, and the gray cloak which he had received as a gift from the innkeeper.

On a sunny morning he was led to the gallows. The crowd roared. Soldiers kept an open space on the square. He mounted the ladder and the noose was placed around his neck. He flung the cloak from him.

At that moment, as the hangman kicked the ladder away, he heard a scream. He saw Leonard, with hands outstretched, collapse, and next to him Monica, who, with great tears in her eyes, supported him.

Translated by WILHELMINA C. NIEWENHOUS

Frans Erens

BERBKE

SHE WAS BORN IN THE SOUTH OF THE LAND OF LIMBURG, IN A VIL-lage near the Prussian border. Her parents were poor and lived in a clay hut which hung from the flank of a sloping meadow like a white die.

When she grew up she looked like a statue of Mary in a little mountain church along the River Rhine. She was small of body, with a round face, and her eyes were large and blue.

She was in service first as a nursemaid with the notary public of the village in which she was born. She stayed there nearly two years. She played with the children and took good care of them. The notary's wife took pleasure in the good nursemaid, and the notary himself smiled kindly into his long beard whenever he saw her. The children ran around her as chickens round the mother hen and they loved to sleep in her lap.

In the end her thoughts were very rarely with her work and sometimes, when she took the children into the neighboring meadow where cows and other cattle grazed, she fell upon her knees and spelled her rosary in a loud voice.

One afternoon, when the sun was setting, throwing a stream of gold through the appletrees, she sat praying in the meadow while the youngest child played all alone with a little bell that a neighbor had brought back from a fair.

Berbke did not notice that a cow approached the child and touched it with her horns, so that its little head began to bleed and it yelled shrilly.

Quickly she picked up the child and carried it into the house; and a man was sent in a hurry to the doctor who lived in a nearby, larger village. Her mistress scolded her and said it was scandalous to leave a baby to its own devices. She did not want Berbke any longer in the house and dismissed her. Crying, the girl climbed up to her small attic room, and there—below the tiles and among the spiders' webs—she sobbed bitterly.

But soon she found other service as a workmaid on a small farm. Generally she stood in the cowshed or in the window open-ing of the attic, dreaming and looking at the skies and seeing the clouds sail past. When she noticed a bird in its flight she stared after it till it had disappeared, and when a man or a woman came by, her glance followed them as long as possible. She prayed a great deal, and before she got into bed she knelt down next to it for a long time. In this position she sometimes fell fast asleep and in the morning would still be lying there, wrapped around like an old length of cloth.

The maids and the farmhands made fun of her; at night, after working hours, they sat together in the kitchen and laughed about the simpleton. Yet Berbke never failed to answer back and many a time she deeply hurt a maid or man servant by her sharp retort. Then the man would call her names and the smile would fade from his face. He would stop heckling her, but another would take over. And so things went on till bedtime, almost every evening. But whenever she was alone, she did not work but went on dreaming.

One Saturday morning the farmer approached her while she was sweeping with the broom. "We can't keep you any longer, Berbke. You'd better go." She placed her broom against the wall of the barn and went to her attic room where her large wooden chest was standing. She took her clothes, her old broken mirror, her comb full of hair and the hatbox of blue cardboard, and threw them all into the chest: also her missal and rosary and her worn shirts and her red woolen socks which had been darned with black and yellow cotton. She did not cry but merely went away, saying only that she would have her chest fetched that very day by her father who would call for it with a wheelbarrow.

She went back to the home of her father and stepmother. But they became cross when they saw her and said that she would have to leave again the next Monday to find another job. After all, she was twenty-seven and they could not take her in; they had not enough bread for her to eat.

She now roamed from one village to the other, going to this farm and that; she offered to watch the cows in the clover meadows and to sweep the stables—but nobody wanted her. They said they had no need of her. But they would give her a plate of warm potatoes or a chunk of bread with a little butter. On the tenant farms they let her sleep in the stables or in the meadows where the cows were grazing at night; she drank from the water pools along the road, or from the brook she saw before her and whose pure stream, running over the gravel, brought the sudden awareness of an unquenchable thirst. She had herself locked into churches at night and slept in the confessional until in the morning the sexton came and, upon opening the doors of the church, saw Berbke crawling out of the confessional, on hands and feet. He seized her, thinking she had stolen from the offertory box.

When for the first time she saw a bicycle passing, she was greatly shaken. With wide-open eyes she stood as if petrified, staring at the man who on his iron wheels disappeared with speed along a curve of the road. She did not understand it and yet she had seen it. But when, next time, another cyclist passed her, Berbke no longer felt astonishment, and looked as it were disdainfully to the other side.

At night she sometimes sat down near a chapel in one of the large forests surrounding her birthplace. She lay down below the tall oaks and went to sleep on the mossy ground whilst above her the crowns of the heavy trees were swishing softly. The wood-pigeons were frightened and took to the wing with nervous flappings and cooings. But when Berbke woke up, after some hours of deep sleep, and heard the night sounds of the forest, she felt afraid, and she cowered. After a while she sat up straight and listened with fear to the dead branches crackling and falling to the ground. Sometimes a terrifying cry resounded through the woods; she did not know what it was, but it made the birds flutter in the tops of the trees. Then a fox would shoot past; she thought it was a dog. She saw the animal rushing along in the dark, and at times something fumbled with the withered old leaves which the wind had blown into heaps.

It was very alarming. She did not know what it was. She thought she saw things floating past and told herself these were ghosts. They were white; and there between the trunks of the trees they halted. The boughs rustled tremblingly in the heavy night.

At other times Berbke believed she saw a human being sitting. But she remained cringing in the many clothes which hung around her body.

Very quietly a little worm would gnaw at the soil next to her. Perhaps it was a mouse, she did not know. And she prayed an Ave so that the Lord might protect her in that black and desolate life.

An owl screeched under the high dome of the forest and from afar came the soft howling of a dog, full of sobbing pain. Then a gust of wind would rattle with the leaves; it was as if spirits flashed by her.

Through the branches Berbke saw a few stars high up in the blue darkness; she thought those were lamps which had been hung there for her by the Almighty God, whom she imagined as an old man with a long white beard, sitting all by himself somewhere above the clouds.

Sometimes she would hear a carriage in the night slowly winding its way through the forest. At first she was afraid because it seemed as if two lights were coming toward her. But when she knew better she rather liked the thought of poeple coming through the dark. She heard the clatter of horses' hoofs slowly dwindling away, and slept quietly till the early morning.

The chirping of the birds would wake her up. The wood-pigeons began to roocoo loudly high up in the trees, and the finches would twitter fiercely. The morning wind blew fresh through the ocean of leaves and chased the mists away. And high above her the pale blue of the skies would slowly turn into a darker hue.

The sun would rise and strew magnanimously the red patches of early morning over the grey trunks and the dark brown soil. There was a great noise in the boughs and among the leaves, a scraping and scratching, a singing and whistling and shouting of small and larger birds. She liked this very much.

She stood up and, without moving, looked with large eyes at all this happiness above her, and she said to herself, That is beautiful. She then began to pray aloud so that the birds grew frightened and the crows flew off with hasty wing-beats, cawing raucously. She was silent, afraid of her own loud voice and she prayed more softly.

Then she went to the church in the neighboring village, waiting at the door till the sexton came to open it. His eyes were still small with sleep and in a drowsy voice he bade her good morning.

She became dirty and smudgy. She no longer washed herself, and dust and dirt began to collect upon her body. She kept on wearing her old clothes and, if someone on a farm gave her a piece of clothing, she put it on, atop others of a similar kind, so as not to lose it—for she had no home or other storage place.

And so, gradually, she turned into a square bundle of old clothes carried by her small body, wandering along the quiet roads of the district in which she lived. For months she wore the same shirt close to her body, and lice began to march across her sleeves, her back and her chest. She saw them crawl about and looked at them tenderly, her head aslant; they did not frighten her. She let things run their way, around her. Sometimes, if she were alone, she would catch a louse and from a kind of mischief would squeeze it between her fingers. She would look to see whether it was dead and laughed if some passer-by had seen her do so. A woman scolded her once, and Berbke said, "But they are only small animals."

People began to avoid her and crossed to the other side of the road when they saw her coming. Yet they greeted her in a friendly way, calling out from the opposite sidewalk. She never answered much but went along quietly, in her hand an old bag tightly packed with her rubbish. The wife of a tenant farmer had given it to her one evening when dismissing her; and in it she kept her rosary and an old prayerbook, a yellow cotton vest which she had got from the notary's daughter, a few colored pictures and crumpled bits of paper with nothing in them but in which, Berbke thought, she might some day have something to wrap. There also were a spool of cotton and an old shoe; the other one she had lost. That old shoe, not yet worn like the pair she generally used, she put on when she went to church on Sundays.

There she sat, her prayerbook open in her broad and dirty hands, the eyes cast down; around her head a grey woolen scarf which hung down on her back in a triangle. She knelt motionlessly, a very small, hunched figure, and always stared before her, upon her prayerbook. Sometimes her soft large eyes fluttered brightly upwards and around her, but no one saw her look at others. Yet she saw everything and everybody and nothing escaped her.

Timidly she turned the pages of her missal, for she had learned to read and to write too. She was proud of this, for many other women sat about with their rosaries but Berbke knew that this one and that could not read. There was always a wide space around her, for people were anxious not to touch her.

Sometimes she dared not enter; she remained standing at the church door while inside the organ's thunder made the windows tremble and the song of the choir sailed loudly across the arches.

When the Mass was finished and the congregation passed her, she remained immovable, looking down upon her missal which she held in front of her with broad hands. Girls and boys who knew her called out, "Berbke, Berbke!" But she did not look up and remained standing like a statue, quiet and mild—the large, dirty thumbs widely pressed upon the pages of the open prayerbook. Old women and old men looked at her with a smile, said nothing and went on. The sexton, a lover of dry humor and a man of solemn appearance, who left the church last of all, once said to her, *"Good-by Maritsibil."* She opened her eyes, large and wide. She looked up at him and smiled, full of respect for this fine-looking gentleman. He went majestically on his way, satisfied with his little joke and laughing to himself because of the halfwit.

She liked listening to a sermon. She well remembered the words of the priest and at night, in the kitchen of some farm or to the people she met, she talked of the beautiful things he had mentioned, "And above his head a little white dove was painted." Thus her thoughts would suddenly focus upon the painting on the sounding board over the pulpit.

One evening in summertime she came to a farm with her traveling bag, a woolen scarf around her head and a warm, heavy, black winter coat around her body. It had been an oppressive day and the walls still reflected the heat. It was eight o'clock. She set down her bag on the floor and stood quietly before the large carriage portal. The milkmaid came outside, saw her standing there and cried, "Heavens, there is Berbke!" She asked whether she might sleep in the stable that night.

From the stables and the kitchen came the men and the maids, and the tenant farmer and his wife as well. They formed a circle around her and looked at her. She cast down her eyes. Then the tenant's wife said it was all right, she could sleep in the cow stable.

Silently, without thanking them, Berbke passed the dung heap on the way to the cow stable, the bag in her hand, her little head softly shaking whilst she carried it. Quietly the others looked after her, touched by the misery of this creature carrying on its lonely existence. When Berbke entered the stable, a large bat streaked past her head and flew in wide circles round the square which was formed by the farm and its barns. Cautiously she made her way past the cow which stood close to the wall. The animal turned its head with the large astonished eyes and touched her with its horns. Berbke was frightened and went on to where the fodder lay heaped behind the manger; and there in the half dark she stood still. The cows looked with amazement at the quiet creature they did not know; and all of them, Berbke and the cows, stood in quiet contemplation. One snorted very loudly, and Berbke trembled. She now thought of placing her bag next to her, on the ground, and she remained standing in the sultry stable air, still wearing her coat and with the woolen scarf around her head.

After a while she took these off in a corner. She sat down on some bundles of straw, and loudly she repeated the Ave Maria many times, melancholily and tenderly, as if in great sorrow.

The dog in his kennel, chained as it was, barked continuously because of this unusual noise. His yelps were hard and furious and ended on a long-drawn note of pain.

Gradually Berbke's prayers grew quieter and only a few words, some disconnected sounds, drifted along upon the silence, weakly and meltingly. She slept, crumpled up like a parcel of old rags. The cows had lain down and were chewing the cud, snuffling in the thick and sultry stable air, through the darkness.

In the kitchen the farm people no longer thought of Berbke. The maid washed the dishes, and soon the farm lay hushed in a deep slumber. Only the dog howled and barked because of the stranger. In the stable a horse stamped with its feet and in the yard gutter a couple of pigeons were scraping. From an open door came the loud snores of a sleeping groom. Then everything was quiet again, and suddenly there was the clattering of wings and a cock crowed stridently.

It was very warm in the cow house. The air hung mistlike below the beams against which countless flies were crawling. Berbke slept peacefully but when the skies began to pale and the cocks, one by one, started their morning song, she awoke.

She always loved this moment, for it meant the day of light was coming. The nights were full of fears and anxiety, which often made it impossible for her to sleep.

She got up, took her coat and her old apron and hung these out over a thorn hedge, in the meadow. She found a broom and began to sweep the cobblestones of the courtyard. She swept and swept the whole morning and when she had made the round of the court she started all over again. That was her task all day, and throughout many months.

One day it occurred to her that she should no longer sleep in the cow house. Secretly at night she went to a room where the bread was baked. She thought that no one would notice her and lay down upon a sack of potatoes. But late at night, when the tenant farmer made the rounds to make sure that everything was properly locked, he saw Berbke get up from the sack. She said nothing but ran hastily to the window pretending she was afraid it was not well locked. . . . She began to cry.

"Go to the little room upstairs," said the man with compassion. In that room had lived a farmhand who had recently been taken to an institution for the aged. Berbke began to pray aloud and her prayer sounded sadly over the farm, through the night.

But once more the lice came crawling over her clothes and the tenant farmer's daughter found two on her own frock. That was too much. Berbke was sent away.

She took her traveling bag and at night followed the road to a Prussian village close by. There was a farm where she had worked many a time in harvest days. But the farmer's wife did not want her in the house and said that she could sleep in the meadow. It was summer time and the fresh air would do her good.

There she would sit all day and at night she slept somewhere along the thorn hedges, and when it began to rain she stood under a great cherry tree thickly grown with boughs and leaves, and when the thunder rumbled through the clouds and she saw the lightning, she crouched below the deformed trunk of a broad peach tree. Through the darkness she saw the little lamps of fireflies. She was afraid of them. She thought they were ghosts or maybe stars, fallen from the skies.

But to wake up in the meadow was always a festive hour. From across the farm roofs she heard the crowing of the cocks, and the cows were many-colored patches between the trunks of the apple trees. In the clearing, silvery sky she saw the last stars dwindle away, and the blackbirds and titmice flew around her with many other birds. And Berbke wished she had a chunk of bread to make crumbs of for the birds.

She played with the cows, stroking their backs with her broad hands. No longer were the cows afraid of her and they went on grazing when she approached them and tapped them on their backs. But one Sunday when she wanted to go to church, she found her bag bitten to pieces and many of her things as well; a pair of stockings was even missing. The cows had done this during the night, and she complained of it for many days.

The tenant farmer's daughter brought Berbke something to eat: in the morning a slice of bread, at noon some warm potatoes with a flour sauce and in the evening another slice of bread. In the autumn days Berbke ate many apples that fell from the trees. Sometimes she threw a stick at them but this never succeeded; no apple ever fell off. She threw with difficulty after much swaying of the stick above her head; and when at last she had thrown she quickly ran away, afraid that it would fall upon her head.

So she lived on until late autumn. But when the leaves began to wither on the trees and in the hedges and blew across the meadows carried by the wind and rustled over the short grass

Louis Couperus

OLD TROFIME

I AM BORED. AMIDST THE ROSES I AM BORED. IT IS MAY AT NICE, and very beautiful: it is summer, a summer of roses, round me roses blow in ecstasy. They blow round me, they blow on each side of the iron gate of my villa, and they blow climbing round the two old, old palm trees which stand in my front garden next to a very heavy, old magnolia-tree: a magnolia-tree so heavy and so old that it was trimmed and clipped and cut by a Vandal who does some gardening for me and declared that the magnolia kept out the sun. I myself had never presumed to say any such thing, being afraid to offend that fine, old tree in its beauty and vocation to spread shade and coolness.

I am bored. Amidst the roses I am bored and it is impossible for me to admire all those roses which blow around me; I consider the delirium of the roses really overdone, and I am only looking with a certain silent joy at my magnolia, who has availed himself of Spring to blossom everywhere for all he is worth, the dear old rascal, who is without beauty now, because his trunk is too heavy and too muscular for his youthful twigs and delicate green leaves. . . . He is a little ridiculous, my dear old magnolia-tree, but inwardly I sympathise with him and I wink at him and say:

"You go on, old boy . . . blossom again, put on a new coat of leaves to annoy the Vandal, also because it is the only joy left you, since for years past you have not lifted up your alabaster flower-cups in Spring, like vases full of incense, to honour Her. . . . Go on, old boy; and if you have lost your stately beauty, annoy them all by blossoming for all you're worth. . . ."

The magnolia smiles at me, pacified. (Do not believe, you pedant, that a tree cannot smile!) But in spite of the kindly smile of my magnolia, and in spite of the mad ecstasy and wild delirium of my bacchantic roses . . . I am bored. Oh, how I am bored! I am sitting almost *in* the roses, or rather, in a wicker chair I am lying in the roses, and I am bored, and newspapers are spread open around me.

I am bored. My hands are propped against the back of my

head, and my weary eyes follow, without the least interest, the play of Imperia's tail: my puss who, on the lawn, moves her tail up and down in maternal fashion, to amuse her two babies; a jet-black and a grey one, the one a little devil, the other just like a Danish majolica kitten in a china shop. . . . The black and the grey one clutch with gracefully extended paws at the tail of Imperia, which she swishes maternally to and fro.

Still I am bored. My wife is engrossed in mysterious domestic occupations, and my friend left for Italy the day before yesterday. I consider both the occupation of the one and the departure of the other unfair to me, when I have to be so bored as I am this morning, amidst the roses. . . .

But as I have enough of the philosopher in me to bear my martyrdom, I only sigh very deeply with boredom, and . . .

Suddenly I hear a voice . . .

A voice in the street, calling; the voice of an old man who approaches.

I listen, I recognise the voice and the call and the man.

It is Trofime.

It is old Trofime.

He cries solemnly, like an approaching oracle:

"Je raccomode . . . le verre . . . la faïence . . . et la porcelaine . . . je raccomode le cristal . . . le marbre . . . l'albâtre . . . l'or . . . et les bijoux . . . Je raccomode les précieuses antiquités . . . Je raccomode . . . je raccomode. . . ."

Solemnly the oracle's cry is drawing near, rhythmically, full of dignity. The voice sounds like that of a prophet proclaiming unassailable truths. No one would doubt the truth that Trofime, he who approaches yonder, can repair whatever he calls up before you in a vision of costly splendour and brilliant luxury: not only glass, earthenware, and china, but also crystal, marble, alabaster, even gold and jewels, even antiques of fragile material, but still trembling with a soul: the soul of the Past, which trembles in all things antique.

"Je raccomode! Je raccomode le verre . . . le cristal . . . le marbre . . . l'albâtre . . . !"

The voice of Trofime is solemnly drawing nearer, and it seems that Imperia, too, recognises it, for Imperia's tail regulates its maternal swishing to the rhythm of the approaching oracle: the black and the grey kitten clutch at mother's tail to the time of the prophetic call.

I am very much impressed. My boredom has suddenly gone.

However stately and solemn the prophet's call may be, there is gaiety in the air: a gay breeze passes through the thousands of roses, through the youthful leaves of the old magnolia-tree.

I am still lying in the same attitude, my hands supporting the back of my head, but . . . I smile and am bored no longer. On the contrary, I am amused. And without so much as changing my lazy, but now contented attitude, I cry, when the oracle has approached the gate of my villa:

"Trofime!"

"Je raccomode . . . l'or! Les bijoux! Et les précieuses antiquités!"

What a sonorous voice Trofime has! So sonorous that he has not heard my falsetto cry:

"Trofime!" I call in deeper chest-notes.

A prophet's head appears between the bars of the gate. Dark eyes look searchingly round, a white beard is seen to undulate . . .

"Trofime!" I say. "Good morning! come in. I have just broken something."

The gate of my villa is the only thing the roses have spared. The gate is solemnly opened and a prophet's shape steps in. A bronze-coloured old hat overshadows silver locks. A long pale blue smock envelops skinny, gnarled limbs. And upon his back, on a strap, the prophet carries a square black-enamelled box, like a mysterious shrine.

"Bonjour, monsieur le baron," says Trofime, with great reverence. For we are in Nice, and Trofime, however prophetic in exterior and tenderly artistic in mind towards broken objects of art, prefers to work for the aristocracy and generously distributes titles.

"Trofime," I say, amused, "it is a good thing that you happened to come round, for, would you believe it, my cat over there has done something she never did before; she has broken a little image, a dancing terra-cotta faun, and I wish you could see your way to repair it for me. . . ."

"If monsieur le comte would show me the object of art, I shall be honoured to try and repair the Dancing Faun," says old Trofime oracularly.

I rise and walk up the few steps that give access to my room. From a corner I get the Dancing Faun, who by Imperia's clumsy movement was precipitated from the high old frieze over my writing-desk and has, alas, not danced for weeks now. For the Faun is broken at the ankles: on the pedestal still stand his feet in the rhythm of Dionysian gladness, but he himself lies down powerless and with a shattered arm of which I have carefully collected the bits. . . .

So I re-enter the garden, in my tender, careful hands the swooning Faun in pieces.

"Look, Trofime, that horrible cat did this, and she was quite callous about it, too . . ."

Trofime looks sidelong, indulgently and roguishly at the culprit who swings her tail to and fro in all the tender luxury of motherhood.

"Old Trofime is very much obliged to Madame 'Pouce' for having for once put him in the way of earning some money," says my prophet, "especially since Trofime—as you know, monsieur le marquis—repairs everything that is broken . . ."

On a garden-table I have exhibited my limp Faun and Trofime says:

"It's as if he were dead. . . ."

"Yes," I say, "it is as if he were dead, Trofime. . . . You must now, like the magician you are, call him back to life, and make him dance again, with that gay movement of his arms in the air . . ."

"I shall try, monsieur le duc. . . . Where can I work?"

"Shall I instal you over there, under the palm tree?"

"Excellent, but you needn't instal me. You know, I prefer to work on the ground. Then I have everything around me. If only I could have a couple of old newspapers, for the garden is cemented and my 'petite cuisine' might spoil the cement. . . ."

"There are a few newspapers there . . ."

I have not yet read them, but what does it matter? . . . Trofime seizes the open papers and spreads them carefully, weighting them with a few pebbles, to prevent them being blown away.

He lays the limp Faun on the newspapers, and unbuckles the mysterious box from his back.

As for me, well-satisfied and amused, I stretch myself lazily on my long wicker chair, prop my head on my folded hands and look on with a smile. How could one possibly be bored now that so many deliriously blowing roses waft me their odour, and Trofime, who is about to call back my Faun to the dance, is hunched on the ground before me?

I am pleasantly lazy, and, moreover, interested, and so is Imperia, who is looking at Trofime with an air of wisdom and dignity. Though I am convinced that she no longer remembers anything of her clumsiness which precipitated the Faun to the floor. . . .

"I believe that all the pieces are there, even the little arm . . .
even all the little fingers . . . monsieur le prince!" says the elated
Trofime, whose gnarled but tender fingers fumble among the
pieces. "Therefore, I think I shall be able to make the faun
dance again. . . ."

"O Trofime!" I say, "Then I shall be so happy, for I am very
fond of that little image . . ."

"It is antique, is it not, monsieur le prince?"

For, reader, I have obtained my highest title. I cannot get
higher than "prince." Trofime will never, never, to my profound
and silent chagrin, call me "Altesse Sérénissime." Let me not be
ungrateful. To be grateful for what one gets, is the secret of
earthly happiness.

"It is a copy from an antique bronze statue in Naples," I correct him. "And whenever I was sad or gloomy, Trofime, I looked
at that little image, and, I do not know why, but something like
joy and pleasure in life would come over me, in spite of sadness
and gloom, and. . . ."

Trofime smiles somewhat ironically, and while he carefully
fills a spirit-stove—he has produced from his box all kinds of
bottles and pots and arranged them neatly round him on the
outspread newspapers—just like a miniature chemist's shop—he
says:

"But then, what real grief and real sadness could monsieur
le prince possibly have . . . ? He lives in a splendid villa, he is
very rich . . . !"

Why do they all think that I am rich, poor me . . . ?

"He is healthy and young ("Thank you, Trofime") and madame la princesse is adorable . . ." I like that, my wife at once
gets the highest title, without the hierarchical ascent . . . "Come
now! what grief and sadness could monsieur le prince know!
. . . the world's favourites sometimes make themselves believe
that they do, but they don't, we only do, monsieur le prince; we,
poor devils . . . we know grief and sadness . . . for objects of art
can nearly always be repaired, you know, if there are no bits
wanting, but when your life is broken, though you may collect
the bits ever so carefully, you cannot repair it . . . no, monsieur
le prince, that cannot be repaired. . . ."

"Do you think so, Trofime . . . ?" I say, timidly and anxiously.

What has happened to old Trofime, that his life should be
broken? And suddenly while I lie lazily in my long chair amongst
the roses, whose leaves are falling over me, and look at Trofime,
who in a saucer on his spirit-stove makes an alchemistic mixture

of brown and yellow powders, which mixture he continually compares attentively with the tint of my broken faun, and which he stirs with a porcelain staff. . . . I see, I see, though I know nothing, that old Trofime's life is broken . . . ! By whom, by what? I do not know. Perhaps I shall never know, and you, reader, no more than I. His life may have been broken by a woman, by a friend, I know not by whom or what, but broken, broken it certainly is. For look at that man, in his dirty blue old smock . . . His head, while he attentively stirs his mixture in the saucer, is delicate, like an artist's, with its long grey hairs—(the old hat lies on the ground)—with the long grey beard. Only an artist's soul—a painter's, or a sculptor's, anyway, only an artist's soul can look so lovingly on a broken image out of dull, lacklustre eyes. . . . Only an artist's fingers can attempt so lovingly to join the scattered bits of a broken faun . . . And when an artist is very old, with grey hairs and a grey beard, and walks through the town every day, with a black box on his shoulders, in which there are numerous mysterious pots of paint and bottles of glue, and then calls out that he repairs everything that is broken—china and alubaster, earthenware and jewels, gold and valuable antiques—then his life must indeed be broken, irreparably broken, his life the only thing that, irreparable, he cannot join together again into a whole of beauty and joy, a whole of noble line and beautiful colour. . . .

I have become very silent and lie still and motionless, looking at Trofime. Imperia dozes, and the two kittens slumber in her embrace. Around me it is still; the roses smell, the sun is warm and golden, coloured flies buzz about. . . . Everything is still, I am still and Trofime, too, no longer speaks. He manipulates a little brush which he has dipped into his saucer. He daubs with the brush over and along the stumps of the faun's feet, which have remained in a strange rhythmic motion on the square pedestal. And suddenly I start up gladly, despite the melancholy of a moment ago. . . . For Trofime has very, very carefully placed the faun's body on the stumps, lets go his hands—and . . . my faun stands . . . my faun dances . . . though his arm still lies shattered on the newspapers.

"There he stands, monsieur le prince!" says Trofime.

And the thin lips of the old man, compressed with some bitterness under his grey beard, open into a gentle, happy smile. . . . I say nothing. . . . If, a moment ago, after my boredom, I was amused, I am now, after my sadness about Trofime's broken life, touched and moved, and my mood changes and changes. . . . I am moved, and at the same time very glad, because I see my faun dancing again. . . . And I say nothing, and look on, as with his brush Trofime juggles the shattered arm into a whole and sound one.

The arm has to dry a moment, and he lays it in the sunlight on the newspaper. And he looks at me, and says:

"We must wait a moment . . . before we glue the arm to the shoulder, sir . . ."

I am no longer "prince," but I do not mind: I am only too glad that my dancing faun lives again. And Trofime, also rejoiced by his magic art, says radiantly:

"You like art very much, don't you?"

"Indeed, I do, Trofime," I say. "That's why I like Italy so much, with its countless treasures."

"I was never there," says Trofime, "but our country is also rich. . . . Our country, too, has treasures. . . . I was in Paris, I saw the Louvre. . . ."

Recollection lights up his lack-lustre eyes . . .

"It is long . . . very long ago," he says. "I remember, sir, I used to be fond of art (like you), of anything that was beautiful . . . and at the same time I had been very piously brought up by my mother. And because she had told me the legend of my patron, of St. Trofime, I afterwards went to see the Venus of Arles . . . in the Louvre. . . . I was a young man then . . . and I was in Paris . . . and I was very fond of art. . . . She is beautiful, isn't she, but my patron, St. Trofime, did not think so, and . . ."

"What is that legend then, Trofime?" I ask, greatly interested.

"Do you not know it, sir? Well, St. Trofime was a pupil of the Apostle Paul and came from Ephesus, in Asia Minor. . . . He wanted to spread Christianity, and landed here at Nice, and he went on to Arles. . . . And when he came to Arles, it was, as now, in the month of May, the month of roses, and all the people rejoiced at the spring and the roses and life, and they danced, danced in long rows, holding each other by the hand. Women, men and children danced, crowned with roses, as they did in ancient times when they were merry and gay: they danced in long, long rows and assembled singing and dancing round the rose-crowned statue of Venus, who holds in one hand the apple and in the other the mirror: the Venus of Arles; she stood in an open temple, a round temple of columns, you know, sir, and they danced round the temple, and round the Venus, thanking her for the glorious May, for the roses and for life. . . . Then came St. Trofime, with his followers, for he had already converted

many. And when St. Trofime saw the people dancing and singing, crowned with roses, he stretched forth his arms. . . ."

Trofime has risen, his beard and locks are a silvery grey, he is
tall and loose-limbed in his blue smock, and he stretches forth
his arms towards me, where I am still lying on my long chair,
under the roses. . . .

And it is as if I no longer see Trofime . . . but his patron himself . . . the holy Trofime. . . .

"He stretched forth his arms," continued Trofime, "and his
eyes shot lightning; and he cursed . . . he cursed with one im-
precation after another the dancing, singing people. . . . He
cursed them because it was sinful to sing and to dance round the
Venus, who held the apple as she had been the most beautiful
of the three goddesses. . . . He cursed the sinful people with all
the force of his voice and his word, with all the strength of his
new faith . . . and then, then a thunderstorm gathered over the
town and the people went mad with fear and fled in all directions. But St. Trofime continued his curses, which he now directed against the Venus herself, Venus, who, rose-crowned,
looked constantly at her apple with a smile, and then, sir, lightning shot from the dark sky and struck the glorious statue, so
that it fell down and was shattered to pieces . . . and the people
fled, fled in terror, but those who did not flee gathered round
St. Trofime, and knelt down, and begged for mercy, and he converted them all to Christianity: he remained at Arles and was
the first bishop there . . ."

"It is a beautiful legend," I said; "and you have told it beautifully, Trofime. I should only like to know how the statue of the
Venus of Arles, if it was shattered by the imprecations of your
patron who caused her to be struck by lightning . . . was yet
called back to life and beauty again, so that it still stands as an
everlasting joy in the Louvre at Paris . . . could you not tell
me that?"

"No, sir," says Trofime, with a significant smile, "I could not."

And he crouches down again, after his prophetic recital, and I
see that he carefully fits the arm of my faun to the statuette,
which, on the newspapers, seems to revive more and more every
second.

"Then I will tell you, Trofime," I say, glad, lazy and with
numberless rose-leaves blowing about around me, for there is a
breeze now. "Then I will tell you. The white goddess of Arles,
though lightning struck her, revived from her fragments without the repairing art of any of your colleagues, but only because

the gods are immortal, because they are the eternal beauty, which no prophet's word and no stroke of lightning have ever been able to destroy. She has spontaneously risen from her *débris*."

The old Trofime looks at me, and his bitter mouth smiles gently.

"You may be right, sir," he says, reflectively. "I believe that formerly . . . I sometimes thought as you do now. . . . What is beautiful does not perish unless savage barbarism . . . and callous cats destroy it. Fortunately old Trofime is your faithful servant to repair, at least, what Madame la Pouce has knocked over. . . . You see: your little faun dances . . . he dances again . . . with his same gesture . . ."

And Trofime tenderly imitates the gesture with his arms in the blue, dirty sleeves of his smock. . . .

"And if you would allow me now to take him to the place in your room where you put him to look at when you are sad or gloomy, that you may become cheerful again . . . then I should feel much more easy about it, for it is not quite dry yet, and another might destroy my labour. . . ."

Trofime has risen. He shows me in his loving hands my dancing faun. My faun dances again! Only a moist tint is spread over his ankles and shoulder: for the rest my faun dances as before. I am as glad as a child that has a toy given back to him. Trofime climbs on a chair: Trofime himself puts the faun on the point of the frieze dancing airily, airily, with arms uplifted . . .

Imperia has drawn nearer and looks up, inquisitive, wise and yet indifferent.

"Take care, you!" I threaten. "If ever you climb on the frieze again!"

She purrs and rubs herself against my knee. My threat makes no impression. . . .

How glad I am! And how surprised my wife will be when she comes in presently, finished with her mysterious domestic occupations, when she sees the faun dancing again. Look how gaily and gracefully, and yet powerfully, he moves in his immobility!

"Thank you, thank you, Trofime," I say, and squeeze his two gnarled hands, hands of an artist who turned workman.

"This is too much honour, sir," says Trofime, equally rejoiced at what his art has been able to call back to life. . . .

He turns a last look on the faun, and he also threatens the ever-callous Imperia. He puts his "petite cuisine" back into the black box, and he crumples up the stained newspapers into a ball and flings it over my gate. He has fastened his box round his shoulders, and put on his soft hat. And now, contented and gentle, and glad, too, because he has repaired something beautiful that was broken, he thanks me and gives me back my first titles, with that vain weakness of his to work for the aristocracy only.

"Too much honour, monsieur le comte! Et merci, monsieur le baron!"

He lifts his hat with a graceful gesture of his hand. I see his last smile through the roses . . . his undulating beard . . . he vanishes. . . .

And suddenly I hear, sonorous and solemn, like the call of a prophet's voice, like a retreating oracle, Trofime's voice in the street:

"Je raccomode . . . le verre . . . la faïence . . . et la porcelaine . . . l'or . . . les bijoux . . . et les précieuses antiquités . . . je raccomode—"

The call grows weaker, the voice dies away . . .

I lie among the roses and smile and my eye feels moist. Why? I do not know . . .

There my wife appears on the steps of my room. She smiles because she sees me so lazy.

"What have you done?" she says, pleasantly.

"I? nothing . . ." I say, slightly embarrassed. . . . "I have done nothing this morning . . . but Trofime . . . *he* has done something! Look at the frieze."

My wife turns round, and sees the faun: he dances; she is glad, glad as I am . . .

"Trofime is very clever," says my wife; "he repairs everything . . . everything."

Yes, Trofime repairs everything; gold and jewels, marble and alabaster, china and objects of art. . . .

Only his own life, alas . . . his own life, his life that I know not who or what has broken, Trofime has never been able to repair. . . .

Poor, old Trofime . . . !

Translated by J. KOOISTRA

(From Louis Couperus, *Old Trofime,* copyright 1930, F. V. White, London)

Frans Coenen

IMPERSONAL MEMORIES

IT WAS IN HER EIGHTIES THAT SHE NOTICED A SWELLING UNDER HER breast for the first time, a small lump, which hardened quickly, so that she knew almost immediately what disease had showed its symptoms there. And, when there was no longer any possible doubt, she sat down in insane fear. Not because of the threat of death: what more could she expect from life! But, as before, it was disgust at her own body, its secret, autonomous workings, which cruelly dictated her fate and forced her to reveal to people her shocking deviation from the normal. All her life she had struggled against this revelation; she would do it again. Though she knew that there was no social curse attached to this disease, it still had in her ears a dangerous, threatening, contagious sound. She did not give a thought to medical treatment. She had a horror of any medical intimacy, which would unavoidably bring her great failing to light. She could only try to hide her shame.

And this thought, along with the pain gradually added to it, became an obsession with her, a continual worry and distrust, ever increasing in violence and absorbing her more and more. She cut herself off from human contact almost completely, and the people she still chanced to meet were treated in a gruff, almost inimical manner. Old Doctor Ferguson, a family friend of the Le Roys who came to see her occasionally, was warned each time that she only wanted to see him as a friend, certainly not as her doctor. As far as lawyer Schermer was concerned, her suspicion grew with every visit. Wasn't he anticipating her property, about which he knew everything and she so little. Putting his chair so that he would face the light, she watched his face sharply and was gradually convinced that he was cheating her and making away with her money. So she began to flatter him and to buy his honesty by rather plain allusions to making him her heir. Of this she really had not the slightest intention. And, to be at least partially safe, she asked to have certain of her documents. The man did not understand and saw in this nothing but the idiosyncrasy of a rich old lady. . . . But, once she had cut the coupons, she did not dare convert them into cash again and kept them as well as she could in books and under the linen, until she would be able perhaps to turn them in herself.

But she hardly went out any more. She was afraid to be among people. From the large bedroom, with its strangely frivolous furniture, she went into the living-room on the same floor, her tall figure more and more bent, leaning on a cane. And the haughty face with the deep lines along the mouth became flaccid and the skin grey, as her disease became worse and she also neglected herself. This floor was like a menagerie, there were four dogs and three or four cats, with tom cats added, that were no longer let out and that filled the house at times with their howling. The increasing smell of cats, in the bedroom as well as in front of the door, did not seem to be noticed by Louise any more, who now sat at times on the floor, conversing with the animals, who according to the way they behaved, were petted or repulsed by her.

And though she forgot the world of people in deep contact with more simple animal nature, she would become mortally frightened when the impenetrable gaze of the tom cats was bent on her for a long time. Then she would wake up and would chase them away and suddenly become so keenly aware of her loneliness that she almost wanted to cry out.

But she was still able to control herself, for she was afraid of the world of servants downstairs, where she no longer appeared. There was a vague fear in her that they would come storming upstairs and murder her if she made them too much aware of her existence. It was better to let them steal from her a bit here and a bit there. That she could not prevent, could only try to keep as much as possible in safety. Thus she tried to hide a lot of silverware and used only "plate," which would rouse no desire. Yet she could not bear that she should be cheated too boldly and, as anything might happen to her horse-and-carriage now that she no longer went out driving, she ordered the coachman to drive along the canal every afternoon, while she sat at the window and watched the carriage.

The evenings, however, became the hardest to live through. The animals went to sleep early and kept aloof. Then she could no longer stand the congealed silence of the room with its ticking clock, and she would go to bed, but could not sleep. She heard indiscreet noises rise from downstairs and sometimes stiffened with fright as a door was shut with a bang.

Then she would listen attentively, bent over witchlike in her nightgown at the door slightly ajar. . . . When the fun had again died down to a whisper, she was aware of a deep silence exuded from the feebly lit staircase, where the pale statues seemed to listen themselves in their motionless attitudes. Aghast she would close the door, but feel immediately behind her the tenseness of the high hollow space of the room, which she had forgotten. . . . Then she would light all the lights, waken the small dogs, caress a sleeping cat and feel almost at peace, until a stronger attack of pain would distract her from awareness of her fears.

But the time came when at night and also during the daytime she dared no longer stay alone and wanted somebody to sleep near her. But the maids—who changed about every month in spite of their high wages—refused to stay in the company of this weird human being in its pestiferous atmosphere during the night, and they were then dismissed because of their insolence. So finally there remained only a cleaning woman, who was willing to take on the task, a stalwart woman with fiery grey eyes in a bony face and the walk of a queen. Poverty—her husband had lost his job on account of drunkenness—made her ready to accept anything, but at the same time she felt a certain affection for the unfortunate rich being, was vaguely aware of the old woman's situation, though she never alluded to it.

She, and a somewhat simple-minded man, were the only servants that Mrs. Le Roy trusted and with whom she considered herself safe. The others, under the supervision of the powerful cook, she felt creatures in an inimical world, which concerned her as little as possible. Out of this world came also new lady's maids, whom she received with suspicion. They had to take care of her quite extensive wardrobe, but never stayed for any length of time in the queer, bad-smelling house, where the mistress was a witch and the kitchenfolk a rough lot. So Koos, the cleaning woman, also acted as lady's maid from time to time and furnished the little help Mevrouw required personally. But, beyond having her hair done, she would not tolerate anyone's touching her body. Now less than ever, now that there was sometimes bleeding, sometimes terribly painful wounds on her breast, which she hid shyly.

But at night, after she had allowed Koos to go to bed and was convinced that the woman was asleep, she sat down and undressed on the sofa with the flowered designs and began exceedingly carefully to loosen the sticky chemise from the wounds. And Koos, who always pretended to be asleep, saw the feebly lit figure, whose shadow shot out monstrously from the background as she bent forward. She heard the choked moaning, she saw the face distorted by pain as the flames shot up in the fireplace, as the hand silently dabbed at the chest with lukewarm water, and the old lady finally threw the chemise into the fire. And Koos' heart beat with shuddering, superstitious fear and pity.

But she never dared allude to what she had seen, or give advice, after she once had furiously been called down and threatened with immediate dismissal.

It was in this manner that Mrs. Le Roy passed the last years of her life, between pain and delusions, with her animals that nevertheless did not save her from loneliness and could not prevent her anxiety. As to reading, except for the French newspaper she read nothing any longer, because she lay for long periods of time under the influence of drugs which she finally, at her wit's end, had obtained from Doctor Ferguson.

And the only thing that kept her fiercely busy, during the few clear hours in the afternoon, was her will. As comfortable as possible, she sat in the large chair near the window, half turned to the light, so that only her profile was visible. The notary, sitting in the light from the large table, listened patiently to her elaborate explanations and only gave careful and professional advice. The testatrix was particularly obnoxious to him, but she had brought a great deal of money his way. She apparently experienced a vengeful satisfaction by leaving her family, but specially that of Le Roy, out of her will. They had never paid any attention to her, she said. But she really took vengeance upon her whole circle, all of whom she had envied in their shameless health and whose contempt and derision she had felt during her whole life. They had never taken a step toward her, so they would not have any need of her money.

At the same time she wanted to wreak her vengeance upon Le Roy, who had indeed greatly sinned socially. But had not his weakness dealt with him in the same way as she had suffered from her failing? And did not this weakness at the same time denote a refinement of taste, which he had not been able to develop in this dull world? He had possessed gifts that might have lifted him way above the money-making and business circles, if they had been recognized at the time. . . . She then wanted to do him justice and perpetuate his name. Nobody could prevent her from perpetuating his name in and with this house, which he had embellished and filled with artistic treasures. It would be given to the community as a legacy, to be kept eternally in both their names as a museum. Thus the world would accept and recognize, after their death, what had been so cruelly kept from them during their lives.

Trembling with excitement, the old woman had the legal document read and re-read to her. And with it she felt that the principal part of her last task had been fulfilled. She cared little for the rest and she followed her notary's advice with regard to other legacies. The legacy itself she had long ago destined to an acquaintance from Le Vésinet, a former Amsterdam merchant who had retired from business and certainly had never expected her money. What he, as an old man, would do with it in the future was a matter of profound indifference to her.

A little less than a year after Mrs. Le Roy had finished her will, she died.

She was often laid up in bed and sometimes unconscious. The nursing, that is as much of it as she tolerated, was principally done by Koos and by a hunchbacked little seamstress whose face she could bear. They took care of her, after a secret consultation with Doctor Ferguson. It was only a question of washing and easing her pain. More she did not want, because until the end she hid her illness from those around her and, in pain and dizzy weakness, she sat stiffly in her chair at the window. The cats had to be brought to her and she caressed the small dogs, whose playfulness she could hardly endure any more. But after an hour or so she would order the servants to carry her to her bed in the large bedroom and would take a sedative in order not to lie awake all night long in pain. Yet this happened often, when the drug took effect too quickly. But sometimes the pain was not too acute and she would lie quietly listening to the noises of the night. She thought then about her last will and how because of it the house would never again serve as a home. She was the last of a long row of generations whose life had passed within rooms, within these walls.

Nothing had remained of them but this house, which had received them indifferently and had seen them pass away. She had loved the house, the home of her parents and of her marriage. And she had now dedicated it to herself. She had had the power to do it, so that in the future it would only exist about and for itself. A museum is for nobody and belongs to nobody. It only fulfills its own purpose.

She experienced a feeling of satisfaction because she had been able to do this for a double purpose: to perpetuate both their names, spiting the good world, and to make the house into a personality, never again to be devoted to an indifferent posterity.

Louise Diefenbach, Mrs. Le Roy, died during a rough night in January. Nobody was with her. She had been unconscious, and the little seamstress who was watching her had seen no objection to going to the kitchen for a short while, to make herself a cup of coffee. There the cook and another servant were still awake, and her absence had been longer than she had originally intended.

When she came upstairs again into the dimly lit room, everything was over. The little woman had quite a fright when she no longer heard the breathing and saw the relaxed features and broken eyes as she held the lamp high.

Then followed a hurried walking back and forth in the house by the servants, who were made restless by the unexpected, uncontrolled death, as if they might be suspected of all kinds of things. The cook decided that Mrs. Le Roy's most trusted manservant ought to try to awaken the notary, who would decide what was to be done. He ought also to stop at the doctor's. In the meantime nobody was to be allowed to remain in the room of the dead. The cats had to be watched.

Within an hour Doctor Ferguson was there. During his examination he recognized what he had always suspected and he remained for a moment in deep thought. How that woman must have suffered! And, remembering her marriage, he thought how little life had brought her in spite of her riches.

Then he went to the living-room and had some wine brought to him and waited for Mr. Schermer, who came upstairs at dawn, sleepy and shivering.

The last tragedy of the house had come to an end.

Translated by ALFRED VAN AMEYDEN VAN DUYM

Herman Heijermans

CANDY

"DON'T FORGET TO BRING ME A FOOTSTOOL."
The boy sloshed with his bare feet through the wet sand.
"What a beautiful evening! Don't you think so?"
"Yes, ma'am—beautiful."
"And what a lovely sea. . . . There isn't a ripple on it."

"Yes, ma'm, very smooth."

"Thank you, my boy."

They are sitting on the sands, the four of them, very cozily, he with his legs crossed, looking dreamily towards the sea. His wife chats with the guests.

"Uncle, isn't it drafty, where you are?"

"No, Corry."

"You'd better put your collar up, Hank. You catch cold so easily."

"Oh no. Leave me alone. . . . I'm all right. It's fine here."

"Corry, put your feet on the stool. The sand is very damp at night."

"Would you like a candy, Auntie?"

Mrs. Tas dips into the paper bag with her heavily ringed fingers.

"No, you must take one of these fondant centers. They're lovely. See? They're Droste's. Corry . . . want one too? Here . . . take that one in the silver paper."

"Aren't you a sweet tooth, Laura!"

"Huh! as if you don't like candy. Mr. Tas, would you like to have a piece?"

"Thanks, Laura."

"What a lovely evening!"

"Beautiful . . . heavenly."

There is a moment's silence. He smokes his cigar and looks at the pale little clouds that are broken up by the evening wind. His wife is rubbing the tip of her tongue against her teeth, to flatten the not-so-soft center of her candy. Corry chews, and picks at the sand with her parasol; gray particles fly into the water. Laura fumbles with the paper bag and cracks a sugar bean.

"You know who that is?"

"Who . . . ? That lady with the shawl?"

"No, further back."

"No, Auntie, I don't."

"That's the Princess who's staying in our hotel."

"Who? the one over there . . . in black?"

"Mm, mm . . ."

"Gee! Doesn't she dress simply? You wouldn't say she's a princess."

"That's right. At dinner she doesn't wear anything in particular. Yesterday I sat next to her. Well . . . she ate everything and when she got up she said: 'Auf Wiedersehen.' "

"Isn't that nice?"

"Didn't you talk to her?"

"No, because my German is not so good and . . . er . . . I didn't quite know how to address her."

"Well, you say 'Prinzessin,' of course."

"That's not so *of course.* You don't say 'King' to a king, do you? No, it's not so easy."

"She's coming our way again."

"Hank, take off your hat when she passes."

"Uncle is asleep."

"Hank . . ."

"What's up now?"

"Take off your hat to the Princess, will you?"

"Must you wake me up for that?"

"Did you see how sweetly she greeted us in return?"

"She looks high class all right."

"Well, I don't think so. Is that the Prince?"

"No, the Prince will be here tomorrow."

"Would you like to have another candy, Mrs. Tas?"

"I don't mind if I do. . . . Are those brown ones nice? I think I'll take one of them."

"Corry . . ."

"Hold the bag a little closer."

"Mr. Tas . . . have another soft candy. Come on, take another one."

"Uncle's fallen asleep, Laura."

"What . . . ? Again? Hank! Hank!"

"Ah, leave him alone, Auntie. He's sure to be tired."

"Hank, you might at least put your cigar aside. . . . Now look at him making a mess of himself with the ashes!"

With her handkerchief Auntie wipes the ashes from Uncle's trousers. Uncle doesn't stir; his head has sagged away, on a slant against the side of the beach chair. Auntie sees nothing of him but the point of his brown beard, the gleaming of his gold-rimmed eyeglasses and the tip of his nose.

"After dinner, when he falls asleep, he always makes a mess like that with his cigars."

"Is Uncle's health getting any better here, Auntie?"

"Better? He is as strong as a lion. It's all imagination. . . . He's never been sick yet."

"But he wrote Father he felt very weak."

"Nonsense, he is as healthy as I am. One day he's got a weak heart, the next he's got a liver disease and then it's his spinal cord. . . . All imagination, that's what it is."

"He looks pretty well."

"That's right, he does."

"Have another sweet, Auntie."

"Not now, child . . . a little later."

"You, Laura?"

"No, no, not that one. I'd like that toffee."

"Is there a rhyme in it?"

"Just a minute. . . . Yes . . . there it is."

"Let's have a look at it!"

" 'The beat of every loving heart brings . . .' Oh, what a pity!
There the wind blows it away. . . ."

"Is it high tide now?"

"Can't you see that for yourself?"

"Well, then we shouldn't stay here much longer."

"Oh, we can stay at least another ten minutes."

"Isn't the ocean lovely when it gets dark?"

"Mm . . . You see that little white cloud . . . over there?
That's where the sun has set."

"And do you see the lighthouse, far away?"

"What a light! You'd swear it was just next to you."

"Are you getting cold, Auntie?"

"Yes; at night it's always chilly on the beach."

"Look'it . . . how close the water is coming!"

"Won't Uncle catch a cold?"

"Oh, no. He dozes here every night."

"Couldn't his cigar set him afire?"

"His cigar? Where is his cigar?"

"He dropped it."

"No, don't pick it up, Corry. He wouldn't smoke it any more,
anyhow."

"Look, look at that yacht! I wouldn't like sailing at night."

"Hah, the sails almost touch the water. Isn't it terrible? Ooh,
ooh!"

"Ooh, ooh!"

"Ooh!"

Auntie and Corry and Laura jump up and down, with little
cries of fear. Suddenly the tide comes in with such force that
the water spatters their lacquered shoes, but rolls back immediately.

"Shouldn't we go and sit somewhere else?"

"No, Auntie, let's stay here."

"It's so lovely here, Mrs. Tas. Just another minute."

"You're such children."

"This afternoon I saw a man sitting on the beach and he remained where he was till the water had passed him by. Then he had to take off his shoes and socks. You should have seen him, Laura. He looked so funny . . . you'd have died with laughter."

"Was that the fellow with the red whiskers?"

"Yes, that's right. Did you see him too?"

"Won't you have another candy, Mrs. Tas?"

"Well . . . just one more."

"Take that one in the gold paper. That's a glazed chestnut. How do you like it?"

"Look out, Laura, for the wave."

"No, that didn't come that far . . . You, another one, Corry?"

"Are there any more toffees left?"

"Just one."

"Now I'll be more careful. Here's the paper."

"What are you laughing about?"

"Huh, listen to this nonsense. Hah, hah, hah . . . it's good enough to make you faint: *'His eyebrows and his hair are red, he'll love you till he's cold and dead . . .'* "

"That's the man of the beach chair this afternoon."

"Come, girls, don't be so childish! Don't you think we ought to go and sit somewhere else now? C'mon, Hank."

"Heh, Auntie, just one more wave."

"It's getting very chilly, children."

"Oh, oh, hurray!"

"Well, that was touch and go."

"You'd better get up, Auntie. We'll bring your chair along."

"Call Uncle too. His feet will get wet."

"Heh, no. Let him sit in the water for once."

"No, no, no."

"Look, Auntie, this way. . . . A footstool under his feet and he can stay at least another minute. When the water's all around him, we'll call him. Yes?"

They laugh and wait for still higher waves to roll along. Uncle sits high and dry, his feet neatly on the footstool. All they see are his knees and his trouser legs, well pulled up, one sock that has come down and his shoes. The round form of the yellow beach chair contrasts sharply with the almost jet-black expanse of the ocean. It seems as if the little hills of white foam run straight towards it, inexorably. . . . But very close by they slide away, like a knife scraping across a board.

"I've only got three pieces of candy left."

"No, Laura dear, I don't want any more."

"Come on, Mrs. Tas, *that* one is nice."

"This one is for you, Corry. So . . . finished."

"Auntie, look. There's the Princess again."

"She stays late on the beach, don't you think?"

"She spoke to us again; didn't you notice? What a nice woman!"

"Yes, she's not a bit proud—that must be said."

"Hurray, hurray! The water's all around Uncle now."

"Hendrik . . . Hank!"

"Hen . . de . . rik!"

"Uncle . . . , Uncle . . . Uncle!"

"Hah, hah, hah . . . He won't know where he is when he wakes up."

"Hen-de-rik! Hen-de-rik!"

"Mr. Tas! . . . Mr. Tas. . . !"

"Uncle! . . . Uncle!"

"Well, there you are. Now he doesn't hear us because of the noise the water makes."

"It doesn't matter. I don't mind running through the water."

"No, don't you do it. You'll get your feet wet for nothing. . . . Hey, boy . . . , boy! Just run to that gentleman in the beach chair and say he's got to wake up."

"Aw'right, ma'm."

"Such a good boy he is. Does anything you like."

"What's he looking at now?"

"Wake up . . . the gentleman! . . ." Corry shouts against the wind.

"The man . . . is so fast . . . asleep," the boy shouts back.

"Give him a good shake," shouts Mrs. Tas, the fondant melting in her mouth.

The boy shakes him. In the falling dusk they can see the yellow chair, the trouser legs, the pulled-up knees and the boy in his bare feet leaning over the chair, shouting and shaking.

"Hen-de-rik! Hen-de-rik!"

"Uncle!"

The boy comes sloshing back through the water.

"Looks as if the gentleman is dead," he said. "He lies all in a heap in the chair, and he's ever so cold. . . ."

"What's that?" says Auntie, frightened. On her lacquered shoes, still sucking at the tough bit of fondant, she wades through the

foaming, bubbling water and begins to shake her husband who
lies there, staring toward the ocean with great, dead eyes.

"Hen-de-rik! Hen-de-rik . . . Hank . . . Hank!"

Uncle had quietly passed away. . . .

Translated by JOSEPH W. F. STOPPELMAN

Herman Heijermans

GRAN'MA

ANXIOUSLY, WITH SHORT NERVOUS JERKS OF HER BONY SKELETON
hands, she rubbed her knees, which came protruding through
the worn cloth of her blue serge frock. If only he'd come, if only
he would come soon. Such a playful boy! Gertrude might be
back any time now. Then the fat would be in the fire; there
would be another row and plenty of shouting. Where could he
be , , . and she'd told him so to hurry . . .

There was the bell. Was it Gertrude or one of the children?
Now the maid was opening the door. It was he. Only Georgie
bounced up the stairs that way, without even wiping his feet.
. . . Thank God!

"Is it you, Georgie?"

"Yes, Gran'ma."

From his trouser pocket the little fellow pulled a medicine
bottle, half filled. She took it with her trembling old hands and
uncorked it, smelt it, closed it up again and slid it hastily into
her pocket.

"How much have you got left?"

"Fifteen cents."

Carefully he counted out the warm cent pieces upon the
window-sill.

"They're for you, Georgie. Will you say nothing?"

"No, Gran'ma."

"Your mother needn't know of it, you hear?"

"No, Gran'ma."

"Now you go and buy yourself some marbles. No candy, you
hear?"

"Yes, Gran'ma."

She heard him rush down the stairs as he always did—two,
three steps at a time. Now, quick—before anybody came in. The

bottle neck click-clacked against her teeth; her bony hands trembled violently. Umm, umm. . . . No more now. The rest for tonight. Umm . . . that made you a different being. . . .

Ring . . . a . . . ring . . . a . . . ring. . . . That's sure to be Helen; she always pressed the bell so long when she came from school.

"Hello, Helen dear."

"Hello, Gran'ma."

"What time is it?"

"Half-past four . . . Smells sort o' funny here. . . ."

"Funny . . . ? Funny smell . . . ?"

"Yah; I don't quite know like what."

"Maybe it's the flowers."

"Isn't Mommie home? Jane . . . Janie. . . ."

"Yes, miss."

"What are we having for dinner today?"

"Lamb chops."

"With what?"

"With string beans."

"And what have we got for dessert?"

"Strawberry jelly."

"Give me a hand with the tablecloth, will you?"

Jane, with her red hands, held two corners of the cloth, Helen the others.

"Isn't it a scandal, miss, the way Georgie makes the runner dirty?"

"Has he been out?"

Jane nodded.

"Uh-huh . . . he went on an errand for Gran'ma."

"Gran'ma, has Georgie been out for you, Gran'ma?"

"For *me* . . . ? No, nothing for me."

"Jane . . . *don't* you smell something funny?"

"Maybe it's the silver I cleaned this morning. We used gin and chalk."

"Oh? . . . Will you bring the plates in, Janie?"

Helen laid the table. She laid it for seven people; every day seven plates in the same places. Pa sat at the head of the table opposite the window; he had a napkin with a silver ring. Mommie sat next to him with a red velvet napkin ring. Next to Mother was Kees, and Helen sat on his left. On Pa's other side was Mary's place. She always had to have the cut-glass goblet with "For Your Birthday" engraved on it. She'd had it from Georgie and her, together. And next to Mary came George; next to George was

Gran'ma's place. Gran'ma had a brass napkin ring, a beautiful one carried by two little dogs.

"Janie, will you bring in the cruet and the table mats?"

"Helen dear, think of your father's apéritif."

"Yes, Gran'ma, yes . . . I don't forget nothing."

"Don't be so catty."

"Well, I can't help it . . . You're saying the same thing every afternoon. . . . Jane, Janie, where are you now?"

"I'm going to open the front door to your mother, miss."

Mother came in with Mary. They had been shopping—four ounces of Maria cookies for the tea and some trimmings for Helen's new hat.

"Nobody been, Jane?"

"No, ma'm."

"Who made those filthy marks on the white runner? . . . What a shame! . . ."

"Master Georgie, ma'm."

"But his father has forbidden him to go out after school."

"I don't know nothing about that, ma'm."

"Did *you* send him out, Mother?"

"Huh . . . what . . . ? I? . . . I haven't seen him yet."

"There, he's just ringing."

"You bad boy—hasn't your father forbidden you to go out into the street before dinner?"

"Yes, Ma. But I had loaned one of my textbooks to Hendrik and I had to have it back for tonight."

"What've you got in your pockets?"

"Nothin' . . ."

"What nothing. . . . Now look at all those marbles! Where did you get the money for them?"

"I got them for nothing."

"You're lying."

"No . . . I *really* did get them."

"You're *lying.*"

"No, Ma, I'm not."

"Did you go out for Gran'ma?"

"No, Ma."

"On your word of honor?"

"No, Ma. . . ."

"Good afternoon."

Pa and Kees came home together from the office.

"Isn't it nice and cool today? . . . How are you, Mother? . . . Have you got something good for dinner, Jane?"

"Lamb chops, sir."

"Helen, where's my drink?"

"Mother, give me the keys, will you?"

"What is this nonsense? Why're you locking away the gin nowadays?"

"All right, all right. . . . Here it is. . . ."

"Does the maid . . . er . . . try to get at it?"

"No."

"Mother . . . a small glass for you too?"

"Don't give Mother any gin, Charles."

"Aw . . . come on. . . ."

"Really—it isn't so good for her."

"Oh, come. When you'll be ninety, you'll like a drink too."

With glittering eyes the old lady followed every movement of her son who, close to the window, filled a tiny tumbler with the colorless liquid.

"Don't give it her, Charles."

"What's it got to do with you?" old Gran'ma snapped, crossly, and her skeleton hand grabbed the glass.

"Because it isn't good for you . . . that's why."

But already the glass was empty. Gran'ma smacked her lips, in heavenly after-joy. Her dark eyes, shining brightly in the wrinkled yellow face, gleamed with delight. Charles was a good son . . . but her daughter-in-law didn't like her. She knew that all right. . . . However, everything was fine now, just fine.

"Are you all coming to the table?"

Charles shared out the lamb chops. There were eight; the largest for his wife, the smallest for the maid who could not stand meat anyway because she had stomach ulcers.

"Jane, your plate. Mary, hand this on to your Gran'ma. George, keep your fingers out of the gravy."

Then the string beans made the round; the potatoes and the gravy followed. There was a moment's lull, disturbed only by the forks and the smacking sounds the old woman made.

"Kees, you are very quiet today."

"Yes?"

"Uh uh; he's in love, Ma."

"Keep quiet, you."

"Oh, look, look, what's up? Look at Gran'ma . . . !"

"Good God. . . . What's wrong with the old woman?"

She had sagged away in her armchair; of her eyes only the whites were visible. Georgie began to howl, and the women looked on with shocked, white faces.

"Get some water and don't sit there like pillars of salt!" father shouted.

Kees was sprinkling vinegar over Gran'ma's head.

"George, stop bawling at once!"

"If only she isn't going to die! Oooh! . . ."

"Hold your tongue, you good-for-nothing!"

They had lifted the old woman and laid her on the sofa. The gray patches of her hair were like smudgy flakes on the red couch pillow.

"Give her some air at the throat. . . ."

"Cum'on. Cum'on, Helen. Get going."

Helen and Mary opened Gran'ma's frock; Kees held the vinegar bottle under her nose and Charles rubbed her corky, skeleton hands.

"What's that? . . . What are you taking out of her pocket?"

"A bottle."

"Let me smell!"

First the woman smelt and then the man.

"Well, in all the world. . . . How did she get this gi . . . ?" the man asked furiously.

"Keep quiet."

They looked at one another and kept their mouths shut, for the children's sake.

"She is coming to, Pa."

"Shall we lay her on the bed?"

"No, let her first come to completely."

"Feeling better now, Mother?"

Quickly Gran'ma opened her eyes, looking vaguely around, still half conscious, then closed them again and remained inert.

"Come on now, Mother."

"How is it, Gran'ma?"

Slowly life surged back into the old woman. She looked from Charles to Mary and from Mary to George.

"I thought . . . that . . . er . . . I was going . . . to die . . . just now," she mumbled.

Then, suddenly, everything seemed to become clear to her. With her trembling skeleton hands she rubbed her eyes and all at once jerked down to her empty pocket. She fumbled nervously; then with eyes full of hatred she stared at her daughter-in-law who was still holding the medicine bottle in her hand.

Five minutes afterwards they were all at table again, busy with the lamb chops and the string beans which had got rather cold.

Translated by Joseph W. F. Stoppelman

Lodewijk van Deyssel

A NEW LITERATURE

IT IS MY OPINION THAT A GREAT ART IS NOW BEING BORN; I ENTER-tain a strong hope that Holland will contribute some of the best elements to this art. And I shall proceed on my way and collaborate in order to vindicate my hope, but time and again I am hampered by the nasty things that obstruct the road.

I am thinking of Holland and of her art that I want to help create. The road is wide and is bathed in sunlight, but wherever I go I have to get past the filth that I see before me. I cannot escape it, as I at first thought. For when I say and shout that we Hollanders too must try to have a literature, there is an answering growl on all sides: "A literature? But we have one! An ancient one and a seventeenth-century one; the history of both has been written, in honor of both, festivals are held; our book-cases are full of the works representing both!" And that is just our shame and our misery.

The generation of literary men that preceded my generation falsified and spoilt the intellectual capacities of its readers, not only by telling them of old native literature and by dishing up as old native literature what was no literature, no art at all, but even by creating things themselves which they passed out as literature, in public everywhere. A certain number of citizens have had a great mass of sentences printed and distributed in Holland in the last fifty years, some rhyming and some not, contending that it was poetry and prose, although it had nothing to do with either poetry or prose except that it can be called a feeble parody thereof. They produced a pile of works that are obtainable everywhere in the bookshops, that are discussed in the newspapers, that are read and reflected upon and seriously and affectionately talked about by Dutch people. This is a situation that arouses annoyance and disgust. The whole life of the now official Netherlands literature is a constant insult to literature.

We therefore turn against the entire preceding generation of Dutch literary men, except Multatuli and Huet, for I too except them; Multatuli, a lyric artist on the strength of his humanity, Huet, no artist and no great critic, but the only sensible literary man in a whole company of stupid people. But as regards all the rest, we shake off the hands they may place on our shoulders and kick them if they try to touch us and spit on their thoughts and pay no heed to their enthusiasm.

Foolish group of fifty-year-old infants, poor wretches of an age of decay, you who have never been stirred by a great feeling, lame and crooked, leaping in the skittish dances of your glassy souls, boring little fellows of A.D. 1, you loveless, hateless, brainless and heartless beings! You are absolutely nothing, you make no particle of difference; those who fight against you really fight against windmills, but I do not laugh at Don Quixote; we are just as indignant because you are nothing, for we want to destroy you, because you have turned our country into a barren moor, into the laughing-stock of other countries, into the "European China," and our literature into a slough of complacent stupidity, into a sewer of musty banality.

We want to push Holland high up, right into the momentum of the nations. I do not just say it "poetically"; I say it exactly as I mean it. As Greece once was, as Italy in the Renaissance, as we ourselves to a certain extent in the seventeenth century, that is how we want to make our little country. It grieves us always to hear foreigners speak of England, France and Germany; we want to create a splendor that will make their eyes shine with admiration; we want to make them kneel before the glorious-colored vapors rising from the watery land. For, by God, by God, there will be a passion and an intellectual tempest such as even the old in years have never yet seen. We are human beings, do you understand that, you dull-headed youngsters of the preceding generation, we are people with great, deep violent emotions; we shall write our souls on sheets of paper and they will be printed and published; and in all kinds of quiet rooms in narrow streets that you do not even know, we shall be read, and everywhere in the town and in the country admiration will be aroused, and there will be people at tables reading attentively with serious faces.

Then come to us, you herd of buffaloes of mediocrity; you are really no buffaloes, you are patch-work quilts hanging over horizontal bars, filled with the vacant wind of your "self-esteem." We shall take you and hang you up on the strings of our fooling. And there you will hang, sheets without life. Once in a while, when it is dark, we shall look upon you as ghosts, stored in the attics of our minds, but every time day will return and we shall see that we can be without fear.

But there is a festival going on in Netherlands literature; why do I not enjoy myself, why do I not join in the general amenity, conviviality, amiability and merriment? There is always a festival in our literature, it is always kermess.

Yes, look at it, the foolish kermess of Holland's literary life with its congresses like waiters' meetings, its polished, soap-parson societies and associations! Do you see those waffle bakers with their sugary faces? They are our literary artists. Look indeed, they are licking from their fingers the greasy fat with which they have just been baking. Do you see those fat fritter-women? They are our poetesses and novelists. Take care, don't compliment them, for then they will become generous, and their fritters are not very digestible. Do you see all those booths with gaudy glass and tinsel decorations? They are the meeting halls where teachers and pupils drink healths to each other with the insipid lemonade and sugary cookies of their writings. Do you see those heyday merry-go-rounds? That, if you please, is our prose art. Jan ten Brink, the well-known commercial traveler, stands grinding the organ, Vosmaer and the rest are sitting in the little boats, each kissing his girl. Dirty barmaids are their sweethearts, their goddesses, indeed. That is how they go on turning. And then they stop for a moment. The bell rings! And then they go on. And so on, to infinity. There was one who sat on a lion quite alone looking in vain at the people round about for a girl that would please him. He sat gazing angrily at the spattering light and the monotonous jingling. He was sorry he also sat on the merry-go-round. Then the others threw him out because he looked so surly and was not at all jolly. Don't you find all this entertaining? Very entertaining, eh? Yes, I too find it all devilish entertaining.

And then again I don't find it entertaining; no, I find it enough to make one cry, to make one crazy, and I don't understand why it doesn't rain or storm to blot out the whole cursèd show-booth.

But I am not afraid. There will be someone who will pour his grief over this silly literature, who will put an end to all this amiability and crazy pleasure; there will certainly be one who will strike down all the crazy merry-go-rounds with the lightning of his wrath and his woe.

Away with you, out of my thoughts, university potentates who gnaw like mice at great memories or deck them with the bows and ribbons of your veneration, you who dissect corpses and fail to see the living life!

Away with you, little poets, who have minimized and destroyed the strong feeling of men and turned the most beautiful sounds into dissonance in your mouths; now it is finished; you no longer belong to our land with your puppet conceit and silly words.

Away with you, you prose writers; the word was given unto you, and what have you done with it? You have murdered it, botched it into barren dumbness. It was in you, and you did not know. Which of you was a man and spoke up in the land? You puny of soul and puny of language, away, away with you!

Look, there they stand in groups, with their low foreheads, little figures round images of brass, in petty and sham veneration of petty dead; they assemble to eat and drink and laugh, chewing the while, at gruesome insipidness.

Listen, they are talking . . . about what? They are talking, talking about language and about literature. But what are their words? I no longer understand or grasp them. Dead words from dead mouths. No, they have never loved. These people are lunatics, ghosts, dead bodies. O gloomy, laughing corpses, let me whip you out of my thoughts, for the day of my life will be great with sharp clarity and burning heat, unblemished by your pettiness and unadulterated by your dead life!

For the great art has come to us. It has been born and pushed its way upward to the most glorious growth, to the greatest power of our time, to the highest life and the most splendid glory to which humanity has ever risen.

The world has had its prophets of the gods and witnesses of God, and age after age the nations have knelt before the powers that came from above the clouds. People have built upon reality; they have built a road past the palaces of dream and the temples of prayer; and high up on the towers they have seen things of beauty; but after the collapse of civilizations, after the tottering and submersion of the generations, after all the beautiful tempests of the tidal seas, we have been thrown onto the beach, we poor, naked people, alone with each other. And we have looked up; there was the sky, and in front of us, there was the water, and underneath us, there was the sand. And we thought and asked whether there was nothing, nothing. Then suddenly our eyes perceived one another, and in those eyes we saw unknown depths. We understood that we existed, we human beings; we live, with our wretchedness and our bliss.

After India, Egypt, Greece, finally after Rome, after all the great divine visions of our Germanic civilization, after Dante and Milton, after the great kneelers before the unconscious deity, after the idolizers of the Idea and the world-soul, after Goethe,

Shelley and Hugo, come we, witnesses of life, prophets of reality, passionately devoted to facts, enraptured by perception.

O human beings, if you have imagination and, sitting still, peering, in the middle of your loving thoughts, you once feel something coming from on high, twinkling and rustling, infinitely sweet and kind, a supreme delight, oh let that being into you, and look, look at our visions; there, nailed, glowing, to the pinnacle of your thoughts, come live in heaven, come, come and be blissful with us!

If you desire great joy, oh, listen to me. For in me there lives, like a dry, hoarsely rasping thirst, the eternal unquenchable desire. The great infinity, personified and worshipped by preceding peoples who built the earth full of houses the roofs of which point toward the pitiless sky, under whose vaults the burning sacrifices of enthusiasm and veneration climbed in twisting flames up the silent columns, that has enveloped human bodies in golden dream clouds so that they no longer saw each other or anything of all that was about them—this infinity which has raised the passions of mankind to the most glorious heights, which has poured over gasping heads the raging passion poems from the seething souls of the prophets, which in pure lines to the finest point has raised the towers of reason in the holy brains of the thinkers; this infinity has shivered through my consciousness and blown like a scorching wind over my gesticulating actions and through my aspiring thoughts and has remained in me like a kingdom of will, like a stupendous power of desire, to create beauty, to give life, to be capable of the impossible, to be one who, like none before, reached the topmost heights of humanity on the most hazardous journey and remained standing at the edge of madness with satisfied and sure eyes and with the white heat of contented love on his forehead.

What I have wanted is not in the world. I have sought it in the eyes of living people, I have sought it in the books of the dead, I have dreamt of tendernesses standing around me like golden shapes, intangible and alive with whispering, consoling voices and with soothing kisses for my poor grief.

I have sought right and left to catch it in the glances of my mother, to feel it in the smile of a woman, to hear it in the approaching step of a friend.

But then I turned into myself and remained alone with myself, and it descended from the high heaven into me, coming down like dew in shimmering garments of sweet ecstasy, rolling up in large gentle dreams and basking in glorious love.

For what has come streaming from the bowing plains of the ages, glowing from the great and golden passion of loving throngs of people, radiating from the infinite passion and the flaming desire of the few lonely great ones, what they all loved in beautiful gods, what some understood and suffered, has arisen in me to the strength of pure perception, to the power of the immaculate supreme word, for my god is my love and my world is in me. It has been born in clouds of long desire and gentle thoughts and risen slowly from my dark, raging youth, with flowery plains full of fiery colors of splendid passions and silent silvery meditations into the high dawn of the new day.

And the time has come to be introspective and still. The high word of great beauty is at hand. The living sounds ring of silver and crystal. They have spouted up from the sea and fallen sparkling from the skies of love-laughing light and like tears of color gathered up into shining nosegays and strung together into wide garlands of flowers. Because the sun has risen from the highest life, the golden glowing sun of pure love in the spacious heaven of my great day. For the wild watching night was great with the storming of rolling clouds and the whispering rustling of the blinking stars, but greater is the day with the universal light, my own day of white burning love with ages of hours rising heavily from compressed golden growth. For in me is life, and love is in me, and my day shall live, risen so gloriously in hotly burning sounds and hot living golden light.

Translated by JO MAYO

PART II

REVIVAL IN FLANDERS

Cyriel Buysse

PEETJE THE PRUSSIAN

IN 1870, AT THE OUTBREAK OF THE WAR BETWEEN FRANCE AND Germany, the Prussian King Wilhelm was a somewhat unknown character in Flanders, at least in the countryside. The French Emperor, on the other hand, was known as the colored prints depicted him: the thick moustache, the heavy goatee, the dull, rather sad eyes, the brilliant uniform with golden epaulets and, crossing the chest, the wide, red ribbon of the Legion of Honor.

But as soon as the first, brutal battles had been won by the Germans, our land was flooded with pictures of the German generals and princes. Bismarck, Moltke, Prince Friedrich Karl, the Crown Prince, the King—their many portraits filled the illustrated magazines and people looked around for resemblances: this well-known, hardy peasant, from some distant hamlet looked somewhat like Bismarck—that old, bent-down little fellow from the poorhouse like Moltke, that commercial traveler, who every few weeks or so came to the village with his samples, like Prince Friedrich Karl . . . And so there was one in our small community, who was the spitting image of King Wilhelm.

There was a well-to-do retired gentleman who lived on the outskirts of the village with his wife and daughter in an impressive country home. I can still see it as it looked at the time: a high, white building, with a stucco front, beautiful shiny windows and lovely, light-pink Venetian blinds. A fresh, charming little garden, filled with sunny, brilliant colors, was divided into scrupulously tended small flowerbeds behind the iron fence with the gilt-topped spikes, along the street sides. Behind the house stretched a very large and beautiful pleasure garden, with magnificent old trees and velvety, undulating lawns.

He was just a plain, well-to-do retired gentleman. He bore the not unordinary name of Amedeus Fruytier. He liked good food and drink and he met his friends in the village taverns. Every day he read through a couple of newspapers from beginning to end.

He didn't take any part in politics, though he had definite political opinions and wasn't a member of the village council, though he knew exactly how the community should be run. He was very proud of the fact that he was completely independent and therefore stood above and outside of all parties.

"I," he would say, as he pompously inclined his sturdy figure backward, when people asked him why he, who was so rich and intelligent, did not want to concern himself with anything, "I eat my chicken and drink my bottle of wine comfortably at home and in so far as anything else is concerned I do not care a rap."

Neither was he definitely an unfeeling man. He could show himself roughly pleasant. He would then strike an attitude of gruffness and speak curtly, but it was often to hide a deeper emotion. Only he was vain, unbelievably, childishly vain.

When the war broke out he had immediately, definitely and sharply taken the French side. This at least he found it worthwhile to get excited about. "The Germans, bah! What a people! Not worth a damn! Not a sou! They will be beaten to a pulp!" He called them names at night in the tavern with his friends, who rarely dared to contradict him because he was the richest man in the village. And with a grin of satisfaction he would read to them his daily paper, the first news of the war that was favorable to the French. "Yes, but this is only the beginning! Now that the emperor, Louis Napoleon, is going to the battlefield things will change even more, now that he himself is leading the troops!"

He pronounced it "Louie Napoleon" and spoke of the French Emperor with familiarity, as though he knew him personally. Louie Napoleon would do this, Louie Napoleon would do that; Louie Napoleon had his plans all set, though they were known only to a few; and Mr. Fruytier made no secret of the fact that he belonged among those few privileged characters.

Then came the first, bitter blows: Weissenburg, Woerth, Froeschwiller; and our illustrated papers, which at first had shown nothing but the French portraits, were now filled with German pictures. That is how Mr. Fruytier saw the first time the likeness of King Wilhelm, and the resemblance to himself hit him at once, violently.

There was the same forbidding countenance, the surly eyes, the strong jaws, the grey, thick muttonchop whiskers, the heavy moustache. The chin of the Prussian monarch was then clean shaven—that was the only difference—and when Mr. Fruytier for a moment pushed the hair away from his chin and looked into the mirror, the resemblance became so striking that he burst into vainglorious laughter at his own image. He went to his wife and daughter, laid the picture in front of them, pushed his beard away with his hand, gave them a forbidding look and asked:

"Don't you see the likeness?"

"Oh Lordy!" the mother and daughter cried out simultaneously, struck by the resemblance.

"Oh! If you were walking in France now!" They shivered.

"What! . . . What would they do!" he called out proudly, leaning backward.

"Why, shoot you of course!" Madame said with fear in her eyes.

"Bah! . . . do you think that King of Prussia would allow himself to be shot like a sparrow," he said deprecatingly.

That morning he went earlier than usual to his habitual *estaminet* to have his drop of liquor. His eyes were smiling with internal gaiety, his cheeks were red; he approached his friends, took the folded illustrated paper from his pocket, pushed his beard away from his chin and then let them look at the likeness, while he grinned, vain as a child:

"Hmm! Did you notice? My picture in the paper? Hmm? What do you say to that?"

"Oh! I'll be damned! How did you get in there?" the friends showed their surprise, each in turn comparing the picture with Mr. Fruytier's face.

"Hmm! What do you think? See the likeness," he repeated, swollen with pride. And then while shaking with laughter he suddenly unfolded the paper completely and showed them what it said underneath:

William I, King of Prussia.

"What! Peetje the Prussian! Is it the portrait of Peetje the Prussian?" his friends shrieked. "No, really, Mr. Fruytier, it looks as like you as two drops of water! If you shave the beard off your chin, everybody will think that you are Peetje the Prussian!"

From that moment there was a turn in the external political feelings of Mr. Fruytier.

Without actually giving up Louie Napoleon, who certainly was a fine fellow but who alas had a weak character and been dominated by bad influence, he began gradually to criticize and make fun of the French generals and the French army; and it did not take long for the sympathies of Mr. Fruytier (and of course those of his listening friends, who were subjected to the natural influence of success) to be completely reversed. Continually he brought new papers, now all pro-German, and he grinned with pleasure at each new French defeat, because his predictions always came true. More and more he began to talk in a familiar tone about the German army, the German generals and also the Prussian King, whom he pretty soon seemed to know as intimately as he used to be acquainted with Louie Napoleon. Also he more and more began to bear a resemblance to the portraits of the German monarch. His stature became steadily and stiffly martial, his eyes looked forbidding, he was curt of speech, his voice was commanding and clipped; and it seemed too as if the hairs on his chin became shorter and more sparse, while at the same time his grey muttonchops grew broader. His friends noticed this and called his attention to it and with knowing smiles said:

"Damn it all! Mr. Fruytier, your beard is falling out. You're looking more and more like Peetje the Prussian!"

"Yes, do you really think so?" he said, childishly pleased in his vanity. But he knew it very well, just as he knew that everybody in the village now called him Peetje the Prussian. And he told them that he was afraid that there was something amiss with the hair on his chin. His beard sometimes hurt him there; it broke off, and fell out; he thought about consulting a specialist.

"You'd better shave it off, then it won't trouble you any longer," counselled his friends.

I still remember the sensation caused in the village, when Mr. Fruytier one morning, bent backward in his haughty pose, passed by on the street with a shaven chin. The people stood on their thresholds to look after him. I still can see him climbing the stoop of "The House of Commerce," then, turning slightly around to the people like a king, with a stately gesture, stroking his grey muttonchops, disappear into the tavern.

"Oh! Peetje the Prussian! Peetje the Prussian!" shouted the people. A strange shiver of respect and almost of fear went through the crowd.

That was on the day after the battle of Sedan! . . . He had the newspaper with the terrible news in his pocket; he produced it, solemnly unfolded it, and read it to his friends.

"We got there!" he said. "We caught Louie Napoleon! We must now advance in leisurely manner and within a fortnight we shall have put our hands on Paris."

The sensational news swelled to the proportion of a global disaster that would also engulf us. Some people maintained that they heard the thunder of the cannon in the very heart of Flanders; they had felt the tremor of the earth, and in the evening the fear-haunted eyes of the villagers saw giant blood stains in the sky. There was talk of a hundred thousand dead and wounded; and whoever was not too frightened or too horrified, and who had courage and money for it made plans to see this horror of horrors at the very spot where it had occurred.

It goes without saying that Mr. Fruytier was one of the first. He announced it solemnly to his friends, that same night, in the *estaminet*, "The Golden Threshold," and announced excitedly to his wife and daughter when he came home:

"Pack my trunk; tomorrow I leave for Sedan!"

"Oh God, oh God; you don't really mean it!" the mother and daughter flew up startled.

"Don't I mean it! . . . Ha, you'll see!" he said with bravado.

They ran to him, barred his way and clung to his clothes, begging and sobbing.

"Oh no, dear husband; please don't, papa; please, please, please! Don't do it! They'll shoot you there!"

"Shoot me? I'll take my hunting rifle along!" he boasted.

"Oh no, dear husband; please don't go, papa, please, please, please!"

"Let me go!" he shrieked, suddenly furious, all excited and combative. "I must go there!"

"Oh, just wait a day or two, just a day, half a day!" his wife implored him. "Wait at least until tomorrow morning, until we have read what it says in the papers!"

After considerable argument back and forth he agreed to the latter. All right. He would wait until the following morning. But his bag had to be packed, and as soon as he had read the latest news in the papers he would go. He remained adamant; he must go there. He had solemnly promised it to all his friends at "The Golden Threshold."

Disconsolate, his wife and daughter went upstairs to pack his clothes, while he, feverish with excitement, took his hunting rifle from the hook on the wall and filled his bag with ammunition.

The next morning the newspapers were filled from beginning to end with tales of the terrible battle.

Even before breakfast Mr. Fruytier started to read aloud. His wife and daughter, who had not slept all night, were trembling on their chairs. That lasted for hours, in ever-mounting, strained attention. Mr. Fruytier now and then took a hasty bite of bread and a swallow of coffee that had become ice cold. Anais, his daughter, gave now and then signs of fatigue and stared at the door as if she wanted to get up, but every time, her mother with severely knitted brows sent her an imperative glance to make her stay. It meant that much time gained. While he was reading he could not make any preparations for leaving.

At last, when the whole newspaper had been almost finished, Mr. Fruytier read the following sensational item:

"Thousands upon thousands of soldiers of the French army are continuously fleeing over the Belgian border. Many are wounded and all are in a most deplorable state of exhaustion and misery. They are immediately disarmed and are as quickly as possible directed by train to various places in the country. Last night three trains crowded to the limit departed to Liége, two to Namur, two to Brussels and two to Antwerp. Early tomorrow morning two will be sent to Ghent, where they probably will arrive between four and five in the afternoon."

Madame Fruytier suddenly had an inspiration:

"Oh, husband, let's go there all together to see for ourselves!"

Mr. Fruytier put his paper down and stared at his wife motionlessly over his glasses.

"And my trip to Sedan?" he said.

"What will you see there? Nothing any more! Of course, everything there has been closed off by the troops. Tomorrow, there will be much more to see in Ghent!" assured Madame Fruytier.

He hesitated for a moment. She felt that he hesitated.

"Let all of us go there, your friends too. They will also want to see it," she insisted.

There was a fair in Ghent.

The curious had come by the thousands, from all the regions of Flanders, to witness that unique spectacle: the arrival of the refugees and the wounded prisoners of war.

The square before the railroad station was black with people as well as all the streets surrounding it. Carriages could no longer pass through, the police had been crowded out, and only gendarmes on horseback succeeded in more or less maintaining order.

Mr. Fruytier stood in the front row, with his wife and daughter, at all moments pushed, crowded and hustled about. His chin was freshly shaved, his muttonchops stood forth, his eyes had a commanding glare, his figure stiffly bent backwards. He had not doubted for a minute that his appearance alone would create an enormous sensation, but nobody paid particular attention to him, nobody seemed to be struck by the astounding resemblance, and Mr. Fruytier boiled inwardly. What kind of stupid people were they, that they did not notice somebody so striking! He felt humiliated and hurt in the presence of his friends, and he continuously blamed his wife and daughter for having prevented his going to Sedan.

"What is there here? What does it look like? There is nothing to see here!" he growled.

"Be patient, husband. Just have a bit of patience, papa," his wife and daughter implored. The daughter had come against her will and she was almost suffocating in the crowd.

It seemed endless, in the anxiously increasing hustle and bustle.

Then suddenly a wave seemed to sweep over the crowd, and something approached, preceded by a troop of gendarmes on horseback and framed to the right and the left by policemen with drawn sabers.

The French prisoners of war! . . .

Suddenly a solemn, deathly silence, instead of the seething mob. Everybody motionless, without crowding, nailed to the ground by respect and emotion, with wide-open eyes. Some people, on the station square, uncovered their heads, as before a funeral; and mechanically all hats were doffed.

There they came . . . ! Yellow, haggard faces, pale or darkly staring eyes; long, heavily hanging moustaches over unshaven, hollow, sunken cheeks. The red and blue uniforms were discolored and torn, rain-soaked and scorched; the epaulets hung down in rusty shreds; shakos were dented; the naked, dirty, stumbling feet burst forth from reddish-grey, gaping shoes. Arms were supported by dirty grey linen bandages; bloody cloths were wound around carved-up faces; and now and then, carried by four men, there passed on a stretcher a long and flat extended figure, its yellow face with closed eyes on the blue-and-white square pillow, powerless and motionless like a corpse.

The silence, the great, solemn, sudden immobility and stillness of the crowd was still the most impressive and moving thing of all. Those red, healthy faces of the onlookers, those well-fed, jolly fellows who lacked nothing were finally seeing from very close that which they had dreamed of for months and which had excited them; a picture out of the war! . . . This was what had now become, through hunger, through exhaustion, through cruelty, through blood, of all those human beings—their fellow mortals—

who did not know why they had fought and who were chased to their deaths like wild beasts! It was hell by its very torturing injustice, it was like the silent vengeance-shouting threat of the whole of humanity, like a dumb, gigantic attack, that, carried toward the sky, had been powerlessly crushed by a horrible fatality and again fallen down to earth in ruins.

"Oh God, oh God!" Madame Fruytier suddenly sobbed, clutching at her husband's arm.

"Shut up!" he shouted, "shut up!" shaking her off violently. And suddenly, overwhelmed by the spectacle, he could no longer hold himself back, and in the midst of his friends, who glared at him in dumb astonishment, he started to cry and sob like a child. . . .

Some weeks later Mr. Fruytier wore his full beard anew. His eyes had now a softer expression, his carriage was humbler, his words sounded calmer, quieter, without stern authority.

No longer did he look like Peetje the Prussian.

Translated by ALFRED VAN AMEYDEN VAN DUYM

Herman Teirlinck

LITTLE COUSIN

WHEN MISTER SERJANSZOON HEARD THAT HIS UNCLE SOOI PLANNED to spend a day with him, in the company of Petite Cousine, he went about town to buy some playthings for the child.

Though Mister Serjanszoon was by no means young any longer, he actually possessed an uncle who, though a few years his senior, had married a young widow of Antwerp some time before. This woman of wonderful beauty had a child that was lovely as the fresh, young day, and Mister Serjanszoon called her Petite Cousine, my little Cousin. Uncle Sooi's wife died soon after their marriage, but this was not as tragic as one would think at first sight. For she deceived her husband with an officer of the Green Lancers, on barrack days, and with a major domo of the Regents at all other times.

On a Wednesday, in the fullness of summer, Mister Serjanszoon received the tidings that Uncle Sooi was on the way to Paris with Petite Cousine and would stop at his house on Thursday, to rest and enjoy himself. He was very pleased with this unexpected visit. He gave ample instructions to Filmene, the maid, and had a curious conversation with Huplinck, his cat, from which it appeared that he looked forward eagerly to coming events.

He walked around the town with joyful gait and in his thoughts made all sorts of plans which, barely conceived, dissolved into thin air. He had no idea what to buy for Petite Cousine; but it became a festival, which filled the near future like the atmosphere of a summer country fair with multicolored flags. He stood upon the threshold of ten shops in turn, and every time he thought the better of it, smiled innocently and moved on. The show-window of a doll shop brought him to a final decision. He entered.

He became very busy; he wished to see everything so as to make a good choice. He handled the wax puppets with their beautiful clothes of brocade and silk and satin. He nodded at the imperturbable little doll faces and soon enjoyed hugely this little world of clowns and marionettes. The shopkeeper, a fat little fellow with a good natured face, displayed heavenly patience, and it really looked as if Mister Serjanszoon was greatly abusing this tolerance. He asked information on everything. That doll with her yellow curls over there, could she say Papa and Mama? He pulled the gilded string and listened repeatedly, and with joy, to the squeaky little voice. And that other one, could she sleep if one laid her down? Indeed, she could. He tried it out, for his own satisfaction. But the most beautiful of all was, he thought, a large doll with porcelain teeth. She smiled with them to warm your heart. He took the doll in his fingers and went over to the window, into the full light.

Carefully he turned her round and round, in the sunlight. She wore an evening gown after the French fashion, just like grand ladies, a jabot with genuine lace, and a frock of shining taffeta, sprinkled with moss roses, the color of light tea. Her tiny head was crowned with a high pouffe, and across it three purple pumpkins were fastened with blue ribbons. A beauty spot trembled on her left cheek.

And, Mister Serjanszoon asked, what can she do? She can do *something,* I hope?

The shopkeeper blushed with pride. Silently he took the doll, wound up a screechy spring with an invisible key and placed her upon the smooth counter. For a second she remained motionless, then she was moved by a small and jerky sort of life. She took a few perky steps and, making a slow and most respectful bow, said, "Good day, ma'm, how do you do?"

She was a marvel. Mister Serjanszoon declared he would have no other doll, and his decision seemed so irrefutable that the funny little doll man never hesitated to double the price for so resolute an oldster, and as a remuneration for his own great servility. Without a murmur Mister Serjanszoon paid the price. He had the toy placed in a white cardboard box, and while the shopkeeper fastened a red string around it and talked, Mister Serjanszoon looked out into the sunlit street with satisfaction. And thus he saw the eager face of a poor child, pressed against the low window-panes, staring covetously at the feast of so many colors. He thought: You poor thing; your eyes filled with fire have seen the little lady's bow.

He felt unpleasantly moved and turned away. Fearing his feeling of pity, he thought of Petite Cousine, and although in his heart he recognized the rights of the other child, he completed without qualms the preparations for Petite Cousine's enjoyment.

Like a smile he entered his home, together with a ray of sunshine that lay in waiting across the front door till someone should open it. He spent the whole afternoon experimenting with the doll, and after supper Filmene, too, had to see and admire the lovely purchase.

Thursday was a beautiful day. At half-past ten in the morning a hired carriage halted in front of the garden gate, and Mister Serjanszoon himself crossed the hall and went out onto the high stoop where, in his violet house wrap, he waited in friendly fashion and, with cheerful eyes. He saw how Filmene opened the carriage door and how she helped the old uncle with great care; he was, it seemed, suffering more than ever from gout. He jubilated softly: "Welcome . . . please be welcome. . . ."

Uncle Sooi was placed in the golden sunshine like a sagging bushel of clothes. But indescribable is the feeling that came over Mister Serjanszoon when shortly afterwards he saw a sweet lady hop out of the carriage. She wore a light traveling jacket, and her fluttering frocks blew across the most lovely little feet in the world. Her face shone like a peach warmed by the sun and her golden red hair, thick and curly, flowed richly from beneath a little hat with red primulas. She was Petite Cousine. Idiotically, Mister Serjanszoon murmured,

"That is Petite Cousine. . . ."

He was ashamed of his violet dressing gown. He felt ashamed of his entire ludicrous attitude. He felt ashamed of standing upon the stoop like an ancient gout sufferer, incapable of receiving his guests and prevented by flannel, baize or duffel from being gallant. His situation grew completely unbearable when Petite Cousine came gaily tripping along and made the round of the pond in which the clear hues of her robe were reflected in quickly succeeding colors. She called out:

"Oh, cousin . . . how quiet you look . . . !"

She could have said nothing worse. To Mister Serjanszoon the word "quiet" was a palliative, the politeness of which hindered him like the pronouncing of names. He smiled none the less, to hide his disappointment, and opened his arms, as Petite Cousine had fallen around his neck with sweet rustling of her clothes.

During dinner, which was served on the sunny porch next to the dining-room, he could not withstand his desire to hear something about the age of that incredibly beautiful girl. Uncle Sooi allowed her seventeen Mays, and to these—meticulous as he was —he added three months and eleven days. Silently Mister Serjanszoon stared at the blue glycine-bells which jingled over the woodwork of the porch, between the green foliage and the golden skies, and then he remembered that six years had gone by since he had visited Uncle Sooi at Antwerp. He had not expected Petite Cousine to grow like this, like a young filly in the meadow. Thus he said:

"My child, the days have passed me by. I have stayed behind with a little girl, fair of curls and playful. . . . It is the past. *I* am the past, I know it well. Be merciful and allow me to enjoy in abundance what the summer brings to me: flowers sprung from their buds and a young woman, born from the fairy tales of Time. I thank this magician, though already he silvers my head with dangerous threads and compresses my future more and more in the wrinkles of my face. Will you have some more olives, Petite Cousine?"

"Merci-merci, mon cousin."

Mister Serjanszoon did not mention the doll. He was too busy holding a conversation he had not expected and he was, moreover, obliged to show some interest in his uncle's gout. Uncle often busied himself describing diseases and medicines and advising his cousin to beware of both. Mister Serjanszoon accepted the advice with great patience and now and again glanced at Petite Cousine as if to say: "Ha ha . . . there's plenty of time before we shall have to worry about old men's diseases. . . ."

And every moment he felt anew that so young an outlook on life did not harmonize with the quiet homeliness of his purple

dressing gown. The dessert brought him the idea of an outing.
"Brabant," he said, "is the land of fine verdure. You must not
leave it again without having seen the picture of all that tender
and varying green, tones of great clarity interwoven with the
intelligence of the most perfect symphonies. The weather is
lovely. The light is excellent, and I know some walks that are
delicious."

The hint was taken, but Uncle Sooi—who was toying with some
sugared plums on a silver platter—declared that he would not
come along but would be quite happy to stay at home. He had
some letters to write and to fasten a mustard plaster somewhere
which he could well do with Filmene's assistance. Mister Serjanszoon insisted that he should come along on the ride, but Petite
Cousine said,

"Leave him . . . He won't come anyhow. He is so soon exhausted. . . . Poor papa. . . ."

She laughed, threw the brown husk of a hazel-nut over Uncle
Sooi's head and suddenly announced her intention to sing. This
led, first of all, to a quick conversation, in which Mister Serjanszoon learned that Petite Cousine was really on the way to
Paris with very definite ideas. It gave him an involuntary shock
to hear that there she was going to study in the conservatory,
under the musical leadership of a certain Señor Alvarez, and that
Uncle Sooi completely agreed with this plan.

Later, however, when Petite Cousine was seated in the salon,
before the clavichord and sang a song so that the air seemed filled
with the flutterings of crystal birds, he understood that her decision was not a rash one and he even felt inclined to congratulate
her with her strange prospects. He leaned back in his reed chair
and listened with pleasure, his head filled with a world of sounds
that whirled around and sometimes twinkled, like a display of
trickling pearls. The clavichord possessed rare sounds and adorned
with carefully selected and brittle twanging of strings the suspended tones of Petite Cousine's voice.

Later he stood next to Petite Cousine, to turn the pages of her
music. And so, close to her, he softly inhaled the delicious perfume of tuberoses which arose from her red-gold locks. She sang
a short, tinkling aria from Mozart's "Magic Flute";—the sultry
salon, heavy with its tapestries and curtains, was suddenly endowed with the light life of a strange musical box around the gilt
and lacquered panels of the clavichord. It intoxicated Mister
Serjanszoon, and the broad panels of his long dressing gown
trembled against his calves.

"Petite Cousine," he whispered, "you bring into my quiet house a light full of wonders. Your song is like the blinding rays of a many-branched chandelier, set with strings of diamonds and hung with mirrors of emeralds and rubies. Truly you bewitch the air you breathe, and it seems to me as if you are the rosy goddess who, arisen from the abyss of the green-dark ocean, sprays the clear azure with sweet-sounding bells of foam."

She was suddenly silent and looked up at him, astonished. She saw his good-hearted smile and solemnly she arose, to walk slowly to the porch. There she turned around with a quizzical glance; mysteriously she laid a finger across her lips and with her other hand pointed at Uncle Sooi who nodded and slept where he was sitting.

Of this opportunity Mister Serjanszoon made good use to escape to his bedroom so as to exchange his ludicrous violet gown for something more adequate. He rummaged through all his closets and drawers, searched for his best clothes and made much of color harmony when it came to the choice of ties, a flowered waistcoat and socks. Finally, he stood before the high and narrow cheval-glass in gorgeous attire, and addressed himself in a neat little speech.

"Ha ha," he said, stretching out his arms and shaking the lace cuffs of his shirt that peeped from his black-purple sleeves. "Of what caprice of whimsical fate are you, dear sir, the victim? What do you intend to do, now that you are standing here like a Sunday child, your hands full of the richest favors and loaded with the luxuries of blind fortune? I understand, dear sir: you are out to deceive yourself concerning your own principles. You search for an excuse for your difficult confession and a hiding place for your roguish plans. But I tell you, dear sir, you are searching in vain, in vain!"

Mister Serjanszoon became truly arrogant and puffed out his chest. His eyes were shining.

"Sir," he resumed, "you must restrain your egotism and temper the decisions of a philosophy which in later days will prove insufficient to calm your conscience. Remember that the present moment is not everything. Fear that the shadows of a doubtful past will lie broadly across the days which are still to come. Be afraid of yourself in the future, dear sir. . . . The girl is very beautiful. She may be admired with respect; do not forget that. Are you going to abuse the confidence of a defenseless uncle? He has no idea of the recklessness of your desires and he entrusts to your instincts—which he believes honorable—the innocence of a young woman, still a child, the lovely fruit of a careful education. Shame on you, sir, if in your secret thoughts you intend to betray the peace of a graybeard and the guilelessness of a virgin." Extremely satisfied with the tenor of these admonitions he left the room, to display his splendor on the porch.

Mister Serjanszoon sat next to his cousin in the tilbury borrowed of Mr. Daubrecourt-Sart, his friend. Petite Cousine, in the bright sunlight, was the picture of health. She held the reins herself, and the orange-clad groom, on a lower seat with his back towards them, seemed to hang out of the carriage. The daylight glittered powerfully on his brass buttons and on the gold embroidery of his cocked livery hat. He did not speak, he did not move, he did not breathe; he seemed to be a quiescent object of possible usefulness.

None the less, Mister Serjanszoon conversed very cautiously with Petite Cousine, on the rhythm of the jolting wheels and the veering of the springs. He was a guide to her, pointing out the beauty spots of the landscape that stretched away in the abundance of the summer day. He waved slowly with his yellow-clad hands or held the gold knob of his cane over the shining back of the dark-brown horse. They drove to Zeven-Born, via Stalle, Dworp and Rode. Petite Cousine, very dashing on the little box, held the taut reins firmly and at times made the whip whizz lightly through the air.

In Verrewinkel valley Mister Serjanszoon made a peculiar suggestion: the carriage was to be left for a while with the orange groom and the forest of Verrewinkel was to be traversed on foot. Enumerating the excellent reasons supporting his proposal, Mister Serjanszoon was uncertain and shy, and his uneasiness increased when Petite Cousine, suddenly halting the horse, looked at him long and inquiringly. She did not speak but her straight glances continued to stab against his hesitating forehead.

"Indeed, cousin," she said at last, "you are right. Nous ferons à pied le promenade. . . ."

And they went.

The valley was wild and lay bathed in powdery sunshine. The light flowed as the finest dust; like a blue haze it milled around the tops of the trees and settled upon the gray-green meadows like a lazy streamlet. Along the road the silvery, capricious babbling of the Merel Brook was clearly audible, and one could well imagine her firm voice where she struck rocks and heavy tree roots.

Until they reached the entrance of the forest Mr. Serjanszoon remained silent, in shamed meditation. Under the first beech-tree, however, he stopped still, took Petite Cousine's hand and, embracing the entire valley with a beautiful gesture of his eyes and arms, he said,

"You see, my child, this is a picture of our lovely Brabant. How the valley cradle rocks! How truly it possesses an extraordinary cadence within its living loins, and how subtle this movement is. When I see such a spectacle I think of those wonderful German dances in three-quarter time and one accent. That accent throbs in the distance, all along, from beginning to end of every bar, and on it balances a lithe little song, moving softly and bright of tone. Such is the valley in its colors and its being—a waltz of lines and of melodious hues. . . . I am sorry, Petite Cousine, that I cannot express myself better."

They penetrated into the greenly glowing forest. The ancient trees lifted knotty roots from the moss-covered soil and their heavy trunks reached solemnly out towards the lilting dome of boughs and leaves. Here the day had a quieter appearance and the sun, tamed by the foliage, shone upon those rustling giants with a mauve light that seemed to penetrate both objects and beings and turn into an independent, quietly active life. The deep forest glowed green and strangely. It was filled with indefinite sounds that sometimes resembled a faraway choir of human voices.

Petite Cousine said,

"I feel so afraid here, so insignificant. . . ."

Strange vegetation arose on every side, motionless and mysterious. Unusual animals were hidden in the bush.

"Petite Cousine," said Mr. Serjanszoon, "this is a temple full of mysteries and I am not surprised that you feel oppressed. The great practices of nature always frighten, because we little humans, my child, have remodeled nature with our hands and by the means of a conceited art. We have estranged our minds from her, to use it for supernatural purposes. We cannot, therefore, love her any more or respect her. And now she terrifies us as a mother is certain to frighten the children who have forsaken her. In the forest, Petite Cousine, lives the mystery of nature, and nothing can disturb it in its church of silence, so that at once we are merely frightened strangers. Look, a heavy power of love hangs in space! The ferns spread their finely laced leaves and form bouquets in the moss; the smaller vegetation parasites below, and everywhere flowers spring up, the tokens of a lovable ecstasy. Do you hear how under secret domes the ripe seed trickles hither and thither from dry calices? The ivy climbs along the somber columns of this temple of burning sighs and loving delight. But above and below, on the ground and in the tree tops, what teeming life, how splendid a joust of the desires, how mighty a love play is in progress!

"The finches, hedge sparrows and marsh titmice, the robin red breasts, orioles and kinglets—all these little folk, sharp of beak and light of wing, all those warblers of the forest, these jumpers and twig-dancers, with their caroling and whistling . . . do you hear them quarrel and titter, do you hear them proclaim their lusts, each in his own manner, filled with desire and intoxicated with life's abundance? Shortly they will be tired or satisfied, and then, in the peaceful afternoon, arises the duet of two love-lorn blackbirds. Shortly the velvet evening will fall and then the cuckoo, with mysterious double tones, will blow the tattoo for the day. Shortly, Petite Cousine, the stars of night will peep through the richness of the foliage and then, in the stillness around, the High Priest of the magic wood-palace will speak—the nightingale with his crystal tongue and his sweet-voiced poetry. The eyes of the brown owl will shine chimerically, as he sits upon his throne of oak and listens with devotion. And grand, slowly moving, the wind will weave through the dark halls, puffing without wrath his invisible cheeks. . . . Ha . . . Petite Cousine, it is, I assure you, a stirring ceremony.

"But more, more movement, more life is active on every hand. Three squirrels skittle across the branches, jump into space and try to grasp one another's tails. A badger lazies between two hazel-bushes and, in his mind, thinks of some little love story, of no importance to us, but eagerly expected by him. A field-mouse couple sits under a low beech-tree and lovingly rub their muzzles together. What are they saying, Petite Cousine? A whip-poor-will waits in the dusk and in the mirror of a quieted pool makes sure of the gracefulness of his form and the perfection of his summer toilet. Moths and black-shielded drones whirr through the air. Strange spiders brood in brittle webs of most extraordinary rendezvous. Six beetles form a circle and count and count, before they take to the wing. There is a terrible battle in the offing between armies of ants, gnats, worms and scorpions, while a monstrous insect with a brown hood and the timorous eyes of a plagiarist, stands on a little hill and, a wooden monk alike, reads an unthinkable prayer. . . . And that, Petite Cousine, is the awful mystery from which humanity has become estranged. That is the glorious happiness-in-love which men have run away from, like ludicrous fanatics, on the shaking ribs of the Rosinante of a so-called science. And you, my sweet child, are afraid of the dizzying truth of that only happiness because already you have turned your face toward the sad lie of human society. . . . But let us walk, my dearest, and give me your hand."

She did this willingly and now they walked like happy children, their encradled hands dandling up and down with every double step. They hardly spoke any more. Sometimes Mister Serjanszoon gazed long into the radiant face of the young girl, and while they walked an inexplicable feeling oppressed his heart and made his cheeks throb with fever.

"Are you not tired, Petite Cousine," he asked. "Will you not rest for a while?"

"No, mon cousin," she said, quietly and falteringly, and she was afraid that he would insist.

It grew brighter. They were nearing the end of the forest and already they could feel the full splash of the glaring sun. Petite Cousine looked at the open country nearby. Among the tree trunks the golden light of day showed in slanting patterns. Spatters of strong sunbeams flashed fiercely in front. Petite Cousine began to hurry and Mister Serjanszoon became aware that she would like to take her hand out of his. At the edge of the wood she stood still, breathed heavily and seemed filled with unusual anxiety. She blushed deeply.

There, in the gorgeous fire of the summer day, lay the wide landscape of Zeven-Born, the three domed hills crowned with dark fir-trees, the seven pools like seven eyes of a gigantic monster head, the yellow sandy patches and the dirt roads, the rows of poplars and the variety of bushes.

"That is Zeven-Born," Mister Serjanszoon resumed. "This, my child, is the true face of Brabant. Do you notice the fine color nuances, those hundreds of greens and yet *one* green, modulating lithely in a thousand silky shimmerings? Here, Petite Cousine, I have so often watched the battles of Whitebeard-Winter and the golden-locked Lord of Summer! . . . Sit on this soft ledge of the road and quiet the frightened fluttering of your large eyes. Are you afraid? Let me tell you of Zeven-Born."

They both sat down, and the grass was tepid. At a little distance a grasshopper chirped excitedly.

"See how the splendid Lord of Summer now rules the land! You feel the peace of his victory, and in his richness he grows over-lavish. But soon, within a few weeks, the heralds of Whitebeard-Winter will arrive. They will blow their brass trumpets, and the sound will roar across the fields and villages like a storm. Frightened, the swallows will gather over the seven pools, chirping and turning and tossing until, in the wild storm-winds, they will change into a cloud of moving pinpoints.

" 'Hi,' shouts the Lord of Summer, 'it avails thee not to blow thy trumpets, for it will all be in vain. Thy noise can only frighten the birds. . . .' And he sees the cloud of swallows move toward the south and merely shrugs his shoulders. But the pools of Zeven-Born grow dark. He himself, stunned by the hellish trumpet blowing, feels how his eyes grow clouded and each night he goes to rest at an earlier hour. Then the animals, the plants and the waters complain; a great sigh is heaved by the earth itself. The Lord of Summer says, 'Fear not should I sleep a little longer for I shall hang the light across the tree tops. . . .' And he does hang the golden light above the trees, that turn into palaces of the noblest metal, and shine.

" 'Zu . . . e . . . u . . . e . . . ue . . .,' the trumpeters blow; they roam across the forests, shaking the treetops and biting into the foliage with much noise. Space is filled with dying leaves, the storm swishes golden boughs athwart the skies. And then, Petite Cousine, the rain men come. They spread their wet sleeves all over the heavens and empty their vats. The Lord of Summer is drunk with conceit. The grapes from his vineyards he presses out into his mouth, and he winks. 'Never mind . . .,' he says lazily, 'it's bombast, all of it . . . it's idle . . ., idle. . . .' But far away you can already hear the jingling of Whitebeard-Winter's harness. In carriages of the most beautiful purple the bewitched Lord of Summer spreads out his illusions and dozes while, on a wagon made of snow, the mighty enemy makes his entry. He wins with ease, and next morning there is a crust of ice upon the seven pools of Zeven-Born."

In that moment Mister Serjanszoon truly thought that he had witnessed all this, and it was not difficult for Petite Cousine to believe him. She looked out across the summery land.

"For months he rules like this, Petite Cousine," Mister Serjanszoon resumed, "till at a certain moment the disillusioned Lord of Summer comes to his senses. Now the struggle is cruel, for regrets sharpen the fury of the Summer Lord and fear doubles the prowess of Whitebeard-Winter. In March, by way of declaration of war, the Lord of Summer hangs out the silver flags of Spring and the stuffy mantle of snow below which the earth is choking, melts away. 'That shall not be!' Whitebeard shouts; he packs the cold clouds tighter together and rattling hailstorms come slant-

ing down to earth. Once more the horrified heralds blow upon
their trumpets, they storm the land again and shatter the meekly
waiting verdure. Whatever they do, Summer, with quiet force,
warms their breath. Buds swell upon the tree limbs and a curious
movement stirs the water of the creeks.

" 'Damnation!' the Winter swears exhaustedly, 'you are a coward, youngster! You shoot from afar. Hurrah . . . we shall not die
without revenge.' He exerts himself tremendously, jumps across
the fields, his chilly harness rattling and from his hands, in widest
sweep, burst forth the terrifying hurricanes. The light of heaven
is dimmed; it seems as if the Winter will after all be victorious.
A relentless hailstorm clatters upon his back. . . . But, zoom . . . a
golden sword tears through the tightly packed clouds and plants
its hot fire in the land. A long-drawn wail sounds from the wet
horizon and on wheels of slowly dying thunder the broken carriage of Winter runs to the smithy of the North where eight
months will be needed for its repair. Smilingly the mighty Lord
of Summer sits on his throne of Light, and sweet virgins stretch
out against the bright, clear skies the fluttering azure flag of
peace, in token of his conquest. Ha! now the trees grow green
and the primroses peal their bells. Now the clover nods and the
rose sends out her sweet perfume. Now a young people jubilates
and their limbs are intertwined in love's sweet gestures—now,
Petite Cousine, the swift swallows return from their foreign
country of exile."

He was silent, mused a moment and then he whispered slowly,
"It happens there, around the pools of Zeven-Born. The frogs
will tell you of it, and as sure as I speak to you, my child, as
certain have I seen it and watched it with my own eyes. . . ."

Petite Cousine did not answer. She had trembled and her nostrils quivered slightly. Then she closed her lovely lashes halfway,
fell back and her head rested against Mister Serjanszoon's cheek.
Tenderly his arm surrounded her and a warm glow brought tears
to his eyes. Knowing no more, and thinking no longer, he bent
over her and kissed Petite Cousine on her mouth.

"Oh heavens," he whispered in her hair. "Petite Cousine . . .
Petite Cousine. . . ."

And Petite Cousine, against his mouth and with both her
hands upon his chest, said,

"You are very good . . . you are a poet. . . . Next to you I am
so very small. . . ."

"Petite Cousine! Petite Cousine! . . ."

He caressed her, became strangely excited and trembled with emotion.

The eyes of Petite Cousine shivered with green rays of fire. It seemed to Mister Serjanszoon that she arose far above the earth and lived in regions of sublimity. She was in ecstasy. She said, "Now to flee from here. Now to run across the fields, to foreign lands, and to go on . . ., go on . . ., only to live and to go on. . . ."

He hardly recognized her voice. He trembled, did not know where to hold the porcelain bowl of chance. To gain time he clung to her words and chanted after her rapturously,

"To go on . . . oh, to go on, Petite Cousine. . . . Do you know the wonderful intoxication of those trips through the unknown? To march in clothes of freedom, sowing dreams along the roads! . . . To glance into the suns of the Future, hand in hand, on the rhythm of our united hearts and driven by the fever of our blood, Petite Cousine. . . . To go, go, without end, away from all men and their miserable eloquence. . . ."

He felt her breath and the fragrance of tuberoses bewitched his senses. He felt her soft little hand. He felt the mad desire of her flaming lips. . . .

"Ah . . .," stammered Petite Cousine. "I love you . . ., I love you so. . . ."

And he also felt that a scintillating porcelain bowl (what could it be, what could it be? . . .) tired of offering its contents, dissolved its wine-moist edges into mist. . . .

They descended into the valley, found the orange groom and the light tilbury and returned home. Uncle Sooi, in a thousand fears, stood awaiting them and wondered whether the stage coach would meantime have left.

Petite Cousine departed as she had come. She gave her hand to Mister Serjanszoon and with her rosy thumb she lightly flicked his nose. Blithely she laughed in his face, and her parting words were,

"God, weren't we stupid. . . ."

And so she left Mister Serjanszoon behind in his garden, looking down upon his age; and the good man, having driven from his thoughts the picture of a certain Señor Alvarez, began to think of a poor little girl he had seen somewhere, her nose plastered against a show-window, and to whom he wished to present a wonderful doll.

Translated by JOSEPH W. F. STOPPELMAN

Stijn Streuvels

THE END

ZEEN PULLED UP HIS BENT BACK, WIPED THE SWEAT FROM HIS FORE-head with his bare arm and drew a short breath.

Zalia, with her head close to the ground, went on binding her sheaves.

The sun was blazing.

After a while, Zeen took up his sickle again and went on cutting down the corn. With short, even strokes, with a swing of his arm, the sickle rose and with a "d-zin-n-n" fell at the foot of the cornstalks and brought them down in great armfuls. Then they were hooked away and dragged back in little even heaps, ready to be bound up.

It did not last long: he stopped again, looked round over all that power of corn which still had to be cut and beyond, over that swarming plain, which lay scorching, so hugely far, under that merciless sun. He saw Zalia look askant because he did not go on working and, to account for his resting, drew his whetstone from his trouser-pocket and began slowly to sharpen the sickle.

"Zalia, it's so hot."

"Yes, it's that," said Zalia.

He worked on again, but slowly, very slackly.

The sweat ran in great drops down his body; and sometimes he felt as if he would tumble head foremost into the corn. Zalia heard his breath come short and fast; she looked at him and asked what was the matter. His arms dropped feebly to his sides; and the hook and sickle fell from his hands.

"Zalia, I don't know . . . but something's catching my breath like; and my eyes are dim. . . ."

"It's the heat, Zeen, it'll wear off. Take a pull."

She fetched the bottle of gin from the grass edge of the field, poured a sip down his throat and stood looking to see how it worked:

"Well?"

Zeen did not answer, but stood there shivering and staring, with his eyes fixed on a bluebonnet in the cut corn.

"Come, come, Zeen, get it done! Have just another try: it'll get cooler directly and we'll be finished before dark."

"Oh, Zalia, it's so awfully hot here and it'll be long before it's evening!"

"But, Zeen, what do you feel?"

Zeen made no movement.

"Are you ill?"

"Yes, I am, Zalia. No, not ill, but I feel so queer and I think I ought to go home."

Zalia did not know what to do: she was frightened and did not understand his funny talk.

"If you're ill . . . if you can't go on, you'd better get home quick: you're standing there like a booby."

Zeen left his sickle on the ground and went straight off the field. She saw him go slowly, the poor old soul, lurching like a drunken man, and disappear behind the trees. Then she took her straw-band and bundled up all the little heaps of corn, one after the other, and bound them into sheaves. She next took the sickle and the hook and just went cutting away like a man: stubbornly, steadily, with a frenzied determination to get it done. The more the corn fell, the quicker she made the sickle whizz.

The sweat ran down her face; now and then, she jogged back the straw hat from over her eyes to see how much was left standing and then went on cutting, on and on. She panted in the doing of it. . . . She was there alone, on that outstretched field, in that heat which weighed upon her like a heavy load; it was stifling. She heard no sound besides the swish of her steel and the rustling of the falling corn.

When at last she could go on no longer, she took a sip at the bottle and got new strength.

The sun was low in the sky when she stood there alone on the smooth field, with all the corn lying flat at her feet. Then she started binding.

The air grew cooler. When the last sheaf was fastened in its straw-band and they now stood set up in heavy stooks, like black giants in straight rows, it began to grow dark. She wiped the sweat from her face, slipped on her blue striped jacket, put the bottle in her hat, took the sickle and hook on her shoulder and, before going, stood for a while looking at her work. She could now see so very far across that close-shorn plain; she stood there so alone, so tall in that stubble-field, everything lay so flat and, far away over there, the trees stood black and that mill and the fellow walking there: all as though drawn with ink on the sky. It seemed to her as if the summer was now past and that heavy sultriness was a last cramped sigh before the coming of the short days and the cold.

She went home. Zeen was ill and it was so strange to be going back without him. It was all so dreary, so dim and deadly, so awful. Along the edge of the deep sunken path the grasshoppers chirped here and there, all around her: an endless chirping on every side, all over the grass and the field; and it went like a gentle woof of voices softly singing. This singing at last began to chatter in her ears and it became a whining rustle, a deafening tumult and a painful laughter. From behind the pollard her cat jumped on to the path: it had come to the field to meet her and, purring cosily, was now arching its back and loitering between Zalia's legs until she stroked it; then it ran home before her with great bounds. The goat, hearing steps approach, put its head over the stable-door and began to bleat.

The house-door was open; as she went in, Zalia saw not a thing before her eyes, but she heard something creaking on the floor. It was Zeen, trying to scramble to his feet when he heard her come in.

"Zeen!" she cried.

"Yes," moaned Zeen.

"How are you? No better yet? Where are you? . . . Why are you lying flat on the floor like this?"

"Zalia, I'm so ill . . . my stomach and . . ."

"You've never been ill yet, Zeen! It won't be anything this time."

"I'm ill now, Zalia."

"Wait, I'll get a light. Why aren't you in bed?"

"In bed, in bed . . . then it'll be for good, Zalia; I'm afraid of my bed."

She felt along the ceiling for the lamp, then in the corner of the hearth for the tinder-box; she struck fire and lit up.

Zeen looked pale, yellow, deathlike. Zalia was startled by it, but, to comfort him:

"It'll be nothing, Zeen," she said. "I'll give you a little Haarlem oil."

She pulled him on to a chair, fetched the little bottle, put a few drops into a bowl of milk and poured it down his throat.

"Is it doing you good?"

And Zeen, to say something, said:

"Yes, it is, Zalia, but I'd like to go to sleep, I'm feeling cold now and I've got needles sticking into my side . . . here, see?"

And he pressed both his hands on the place.

"Yes, you're better in bed; it'll be gone in the morning and we'll fetch in the corn."

"Is it cut?"

"All done and stooked; if it keeps fine tomorrow, we'll get it all into the barn."

Zalia lifted him under his armpits and they crawled on like that into the other room, where the loom stood with the bed behind it. She helped him take off his jacket and trousers and put him to bed, tucked him nicely under the blanket and put his night-cap on his head.

Then she went and lit the fire in the hearth, hung up the pot with the goat's food, washed the potatoes and sat down to peel them for supper.

She had not peeled three, when she heard Zeen bringing up.

"That's the oil, it'll do him good," she thought and, fetching a can of water from outside, gave him a bowl to drink.

Then she went back to her peeling. A bit later, she sat thinking of other remedies—limeflowers, sunflower-seeds, pearl barley, flowers of sulphur—when suddenly she saw Mite Kornelje go by. She ran out and called:

"Mite!"

"What is it, Zalia?"

"Mite, Zeen is ill."

"What, ill? All at once?"

"Yes, all of a sudden, cutting the corn in the field."

"Is he bad?"

"I don't know, I've given him some Haarlem oil, he's been sick; he's complaining of pains in his side and in his stomach; he's very pale: you wouldn't know him."

They went indoors. Zalia took the lamp and both passed in, between the loom and the wall by Zeen's bed.

He lay staring at the ceiling and catching his breath. Mite stood looking at him.

"You must give him some English salt,[1] Zalia."

"Why, Mite, I never thought of that; yes, he must have some English salt."

And she climbed on to a chair and took from the plank above the bed a dusty calabash full of little paper bags and packets.

She opened them one by one and found canary-seed, blacklead, washing-blue, powdered cloves, cinnamon, sugar-candy, burnt-ash . . . but no English salt.

"I'll run home and fetch some, Zalia."

[1] Epsom salts.

"Yes, Mite, do."

And Mite went off.

"Well, Zeen, no better yet?"

Zeen did not answer. She took a pail of water and a cloth, cleaned away the mess from beside the bed and then went back to peel her potatoes.

Mite came back with the English salt. Treze Wizeur and Stanse Zegers, who had heard the news, also came to see how Zeen was getting on. Mite stirred a handful of the salt in a bowl of water and they all four went to the sick man's bed. Zeen swallowed the draught without blinking. Mite knew of other remedies, Stanse knew of some too and Treze of many more: they asked Zeen questions and babbled to him, made him put out his tongue and felt his pulse, cried out at his gasping for breath and his pale color and his dilated pupils and his burning fever. Zeen did not stir and lay looking at the ceiling. When he was tired of the noise, he said:

"Leave me alone."

And he turned his face to the wall.

Then they all went back to the kitchen. The goat's food was done. Zalia hung the kettle with water on the hook and made coffee; and the four women sat round the table telling one another stories of illness. In the other room there was no sound.

A bit later, Mite's little girl came to see where mother was all this time. She was given a lump of sugar and sat down by her mother.

"Zalia, have you only one lamp?" asked Treze.

"That's all, Treze, but I have the candle."

"What candle?"

"The blessed candle."

"We've not come to that yet: it's only that Zeen has to lie in the dark like this and we have to go to and fro with the lamp to look at him."

"Zeen would rather lie in the dark."

"I'll tell you what: Fietje shall run home and fetch something, won't you, Fietje? And say that mother is going to stay here because Zeen is dying."

Fietje went off. The coffee was ready and when they had gulped down their first bowl, they went to have another look in the room where the sick man lay.

Zeen was worse.

"We must sit up with him," said Stanse.

"For sure," said Treze. "I'll go and tell my man: I'll be back at once."

"Tell Free as you're passing that I'm staying here too," said Stanse.

"We must eat, for all that," said Zalia; and she hung the potatoes over the fire.

Then she went to milk the goat and take it its food. It was bright as day outside and quiet, so very quiet, with still some of the heat of the sun lingering in the air, which weighed sultrily. She crept into the dark goat-house, put down the pot with the food and started milking.

"Betje, Betje, Zeen is so ill; Zeen may be dying, Betje!"

She always clacked to her goat like that. Two streams of milk came clattering in turns into the little pail.

People came: Treze and Mite's little girl, with a lantern, and Barbara Dekkers, who had also come to have a look.

"I'm here," said Zalia, "I've done, I'm coming at once."

They stood talking a bit outside in the moonlight and then went in.

"Perhaps my man'll come on," said Treze. "A man is better than three women in illness; and Virginie's coming too: I've been to tell her."

"Well, well," said Barbara, "who'd ever have thought it of Zeen!"

"Yes, friends, and never been ill in his life; and he turned seventy."

Stanse mashed the potatoes; Zalia poured a dram of milk over them and hung them over the fire again.

"Have you all had your suppers?" she asked.

"Yes," said Treze and Barbara and Mite.

"I haven't," said Stanse.

Zalia turned the steaming potato-mash into an earthen porringer and she and Stanse sat down to it. The others drank a fresh bowl of coffee.

They were silent.

The door opened and from behind the screen came a great big fellow with a black beard:

"What's up here? A whole gathering of people: is it harvest-treat today, Zalia? Why, here's Barbara and Mite and . . ."

"Warten, Zeen is ill."

"Zeen? . . . Ill?"

"Yes, ill, man, and we're sitting up."

Warten opened wide eyes, flung the box which he carried over

his shoulder by a leather strap to the ground and sat down on it:
"Ha! So Zeen's ill . . . he's not one of the youngest either."

"Seventy-five."

They were silent. The womenfolk drank their coffee. Warten
fished out a pipe and tobacco from under his blue smock and sat
looking at the rings of smoke that wound up to the ceiling.

"Well, perhaps I've come at the right time, if that's so."

"You can help sit up."

"Have you had your supper, Warten?"

"Yes, Zalia, at the farm."

"And how's trade?" asked Stanse.

"Quietly, old girl."

They heard a moaning in the other room. Barbara lit the lantern and all went to look. Warten stayed behind, smoking.

Zeen lay there, on a poverty-stricken little bed, low down near
the ground, behind the loom, huddled deep on his bolster under
a dirty blanket: a thin little black chap, leaning against a pillow
in the dancing twilight of the lantern. His eyes were closed and
his bony face half-hidden in the blue night-cap. His breath
rustled; and each puff from his hoarse throat, blowing out the
thin flesh of his cheeks, escaped through a little opening on one
side of his sunken lips, which each time opened and shut.

"Ooh! Ooh! Ooh!" cried Barbara.

"That's bad, that's bad," said Stanse and shook her head.

"His eyes are shut and yet he's not asleep!"

"Zeen! Zeen!" cried Mite and she pushed him back by his forehead to make him look up. "Zeen! Zeen! It's I: don't you know
Mite?"

"Oof!" sighed Zeen; and his head dropped down again without his eyes opening.

"He's got the fever," said Barbara. "Just feel how his forehead's burning and he's as hot as fire."

"Haven't you poulticed him?" asked Stanse. "He wants poul-
tices on his feet: mustard."

"We haven't any mustard and it's far to the village."

"Then he must have a bran bath, Zalia. Stanse, put on the
kettle."

"Have you any bran, Zalia?"

"No, not ready; but there's maize."

"And a sieve?"

"Yes, there's a sieve."

"Hi, Warten, come and sift!"

Warten came in:

"Zeen, how are you, my boy? Oh, how thin he is! And his breath . . . it's spluttering, that's bad. He'll go off quickly, Barbara, it seems to me."

"Not tonight," said Treze.

"Warten, go to the loft, take the lamp and sift out a handful of maize; Zeen must have a bran bath at once."

Warten went up the stair. After a while, they heard above their heads the regular, jogging drag of the sieve over the boarded ceiling and the fine meal-dust snowed down through the cracks, whirling round the lamp, and fell on Zeen's bed and on the women standing round.

Zeen nodded his head. They held a bowl of milk to his mouth; two little white streaks ran down from the corners of his mouth into his shirt-collar.

The sieve went on dragging. The women looked at Zeen, then at one another and then at the lantern. In the kitchen, the kettle sang drearily. . . .

Warten came down from the loft with half a pailful of bran. Barbara poured the steaming water on it and flung in a handful of salt.

They took the clothes off the bed and pulled his feet into the bran-water. Zeen groaned; he opened his eyes wide and looked round wildly at all those people.

He hung there for a very long time, with his lean black legs out of the bed and the bony knees and shrunk thighs in the insipid, sickly-smelling steam of the bran-water. Then they lifted him out and stuck his wet feet under the bedclothes again. Zeen did not stir, but just lay with the rattle in his throat.

"What a sad sick man," said Stanse, softly.

Mite wanted to give him some food, eggs: it might be faintness.

Treze wanted to bring him round with gin: her husband had once . . .

"Is there any, for the night?. . ." asked Stanse.

"There's a whole bottle over there, in the cupboard."

Zeen opened his eyes—two green, glazed eyes, which no longer saw things—and wriggled his arms from under the clothes:

"Why don't you make the goat stop bleating?" he stammered.

They looked at one another.

"Zalia, why won't you speak to me? . . . And what are all these people doing here? . . . I don't want any one to help me die! . . . I and Zalia . . . I and Zalia . . . Look, how beautiful! Zalia, the procession's going up the wall there . . . Why don't you look? . . .

It's so beautiful! . . . And I, I'm the only ugly one in it. . . ."

"He's wandering," whispered Treze.

"And what's that chap doing here, Zalia?"

"It's I, Zeen, I: Warten the spectacle-man."

His eyes fell to again and his cheeks again blew the breath through the little slit of his mouth. It rattled; and the fever rose.

"It'll be tonight," said Treze.

"Where can Virginie be? She'll come too late."

"Virginie is better than three doctors or a priest either," thought Mite.

"Zalia, I think I'd better get out the candle."

Zalia went to the chest and got out the candle.

"Mother, I'm frightened," whined Fietje.

"You mustn't be frightened of dead people, child; you must get used to it."

"Have you any holy water, Zalia?"

"Oh, yes, Barbara: it's in the little pot over the bed!"

"And blessed palm?"

"Behind the crucifix."

There was a creaking in the kitchen and Virginie appeared past the loom: a little old woman huddled in her hooded cloak; in one hand she carried a little lantern and in the other a big prayer-book. She came quietly up to the bed, looked at Zeen for some time, felt his pulse and then, looking up, said, very quietly:

"Zeen's going. . . . Has the priest been?"

"The priest? . . . It's so far and so late and the poor soul's so old. . . ."

"What have you given him?"

"Haarlem oil, English salt . . ."

"And we put his feet in bran-water."

Virginie stood thinking.

"Have you any linseed-meal?" she asked.

"No."

"Then . . . but it's too late now, anyway. . . ."

And she looked into the sick man's eyes again.

"He's very far gone," thought Mite.

"Got worse quickly," said Barbara.

Zalia said nothing; she stood at the foot of the bed, looking at her husband and then at the women who were saying what they thought of him.

"Get the blessed candle; we must pray, good people," said Virginie; and she put on her spectacles and went and stood with her book under the light.

The women knelt on low chairs or on the floor. Warten stood
with his elbows leaning on the rail of the bed, at Zeen's head.
Treze took the blessed candle out of its paper covering and lit
it at the lamp.

Zeen's chest rose and fell and his throat rattled painfully; his
eyes stayed gazing dimly at the rafters of the ceiling; his thin lips
were pale and his face turned blue with the pain; he no longer
looked like a living thing.

Virginie read very slowly, with a dismal, drawling voice,
through her nose, while Treze held Zeen's weak fingers closed
round the candle. It was still as death.

"May the Light of the World, Christ Jesus, Who is symbolized
by this candle, brightly light thy eyes that thou mayest not depart
this life in death everlasting. Our Father . . ."

They softly muttered this Our Father and it remained solemnly
still, with only Warten's rough grunting and Zeen's painful
breathing and the goat which kept ramming its head against the
wall. And then, slower by degrees:

"Depart, O Christian soul, from this sorrowful world; go to
meet thy dear Bridegroom, Christ Jesus, and carry a lighted
candle in thy hands: He Who . . ."

Then Barbara, interrupting her, whispered:

"Look, Virginie, he's getting worse; the rattle's getting fainter:
turn over, you'll be too late."

Treze was tired of holding Zeen's hand round the candle: she
spilt a few drops of wax on the rail of the bed and stuck the
candle on it.

Zeen jerked himself up, put his hands under the clothes and
fumbled with them; then he lay still.

"He's packing up," whispered Barbara.

"He's going," one of the others thought.

Virginie dipped the palm-branch into the holy water and
sprinkled the bed and the bystanders; then she read on:

"Go forth, O Christian soul, out of this world, in the name of
God the Father Almighty, Who created thee, in the name of
Jesus Christ, the Son of the living God, Who suffered for thee;
in the name of the Holy Ghost, Who sanctified thee."

"Hurry, hurry, Virginie: he's almost stopped breathing!"

The cat jumped between Zalia and Treze on to the bed; it
looked surprised at all those people and purred softly. Warten
drove it away with his cap.

"Receive, O Lord, Thy servant Zeen into the place of salvation
which he hopes to obtain through Thy mercy."

"Amen," they all answered.

"Deliver, O Lord, the soul of Thy servant from all danger of hell and from all pain and tribulation."

"Amen."

"Deliver, O Lord, the soul of Thy servant Zeen, as Thou deliveredest Enoch and Elias from the common death of the world."

"Amen."

"Deliver, O Lord, the soul of Thy servant Zeen, as Thou deliveredest . . ."

"I'm on fire! I'm on fire!" howled Warten. "My smock! My smock!"

And he jumped over all the chairs and rushed outside, with the others after him.

"Caught fire at the candle!" he cried, quite out of breath.

They put out the flames, pulled the smock over his head and poured water on his back, where his underclothes were smouldering.

"My smock, my smock!" he went on moaning. "Brand-new! Cost me forty-six stuivers!"

And he stood with his smock in his hands, looking at the huge holes and rents.

They made a great noise, all together, and their sharp voices rang far and wide into the still night.

Virginie alone had remained by the bedside. She picked up the candle, lit it again, put it back on the rail of the bed and then went on reading the prayers. When she saw that Zeen lay very calmly and no longer breathed, she sprinkled him with holy water for the last time and then went outside:

"People . . . he's with the Lord."

It was as if their fright had made them forget what was happening indoors: they rushed in, eager to know . . . and Zeen was dead.

"Stone-dead," said Barbara.

"Hopped the twig!" said Warten.

"Quick! Hurry! The tobacco-seed will be tainted!" screamed Mite; and she snatched down two or three linen bags which hung from the rafters and carried them outside.

First they moaned; then they tried to comfort one another, especially Zalia, who had dropped into a chair and turned very pale.

Then they set to work: Treze filled the little glasses; Barbara hung the water over the fire; and Warten, in his shirt-sleeves, stropped his razor to shave Zeen's beard.

"And the children! The children who are not here!" moaned Zalia. "He ought to have seen the children!"

"First say the prayers," ordered Virginie.

All knelt down and, while Warten shaved the dead man, it went:

"Come to his assistance, all ye saints of God; meet him, all ye angels of God: receiving his soul, offering it in the sight of the Most High. . . .

"To Thee, O Lord, we commend the soul of Thy servant, that being dead to this world, he may live to Thee; and whatever sins he has committed in this life, through human frailty, do Thou, in Thy most merciful goodness, forgive. . . ."

"Amen," they answered.

Virginie shut her book, once more sprinkled holy water on the corpse and went home, praying as she went.

Zalia made the sign of the Cross and closed her husband's eyes; then she laid a white towel on a little table by the bed and put the candle on it and the crucifix and the holy water.

Warten and Barbara took Zeen out of the bed and put him on a chair, washed him all over with luke-warm water, put a clean shirt on him and his Sunday clothes over him; then they laid him on the bed again.

"He'll soon begin to must," said Barbara.

"The weather's warm."

"He's very bent: how'll they get him into the coffin?"

"Crack his back."

Treze looked round for a prayer-book to lay under Zeen's chin and a crucifix and rosary for his hands.

Mite took a red handkerchief and bound it round his head to keep his mouth closed. Fietje was still kneeling and saying Our Fathers.

"It's done now," said Barbara, with a deep sigh. "We'll have just one more glass and then go to bed."

"Oh, dear people, stay a little longer!" whined Zalia. "Don't leave me here alone."

"It's only," said Mite, "that it'll be light early tomorrow and we've had no sleep yet."

"Come, come," said Barbara, to comfort her, "you mustn't take on now. Zeen has lived his span and has died happily in his bed."

"Question is, shall we do as well?" said Mite.

"And Siska and Romenie and Kordula and the boys, who are

not here! They ought to have seen their father die! ... The poor children, they'll cry so!"

"They'll know it in good time," said Warten.

"And where are they living now?" asked Mite.

"In France, the two oldest ... and there's Miel, the soldier ... it's in their letters, behind the glass."

"Give 'em to me," said Treze. "I'll make my boy write tomorrow, before he goes to school."

They were going off.

"And I, who, with this all, don't know where I'm to sleep," said Warten. "My old roost, over the goat-house: you'll be wanting that tonight, Zalia?"

Zalia wavered.

"Zalia could come with me," said Barbara.

"And leave the house alone? And who's to go to the priest tomorrow? And to the carpenter? And my harvest, my harvest! Yes, yes, Warten, do you get into the goat-house and help me a bit tomorrow. I shall sleep: why not?"

"*Alla,*[1] come, Fietje; mother's going home."

They went; and Zalia came a bit of the way with them. Their wooden shoes clattered softly in the powdery sand of the white road; when they had gone very far, their voices still rang loud and their figures looked like wandering pollards.

In the east, a thin golden-red streak hung between two dark clouds. It was very cool.

"Fine weather tomorrow," said Warten; and he trudged off to his goat-house. "Good-night, Zalia."

"Good-night, Warten."

"Sleep well."

"Sleep well too and say another Our Father for Zeen."

"Certainly."

She went in and bolted the door. Inside it all smelt of candle and the musty odor of the corpse. She put out the fire in the hearth, dipped her fingers once more in the holy water and made a cross over Zeen. While her lips muttered the evening prayers, she took off her kerchief, her jacket and her cap and let fall her skirt. Then she straddled across Zeen and lay right against the wall. She twisted her feet in her shift and crept carefully under the bed-clothes. She shuddered. Her thoughts turned like the wind: her daughters were in service in France and were now sleeping quietly and knew of nothing; her eldest, who was mar-

---

[1] A corruption of the French *allez!*

ried, and her husband and the children came only once a year to see their father; and even then . . . And now they would find him dead.

Her harvest . . . and she was alone now, to get it in. Warten would go to the priest early in the morning and to the carpenter: the priest ought to have been here, 'twas a comfort after all; but Zeen had always been good and . . . now to go dying all at once like this, without the sacraments. . . .

Why couldn't she sleep now? She was so tired, so worn out with that reaping; and it was so warm here, so stifling and it smelt queer: what a being could come to, when he was dead!

Had she slept at all? She had been lying there so long . . . and there was that smell! She wished she had sent Warten away and gone herself to lie in the goat-house; here, beside that corpse . . . but, after all, it was Zeen. . . .

The flame of the candle flickered and everything flickered with it—the loom, the black rafters and the crucifix—in dark shadow-stripes upon the wall. 'Twas that that kept her awake. She sat up and blew from where she was, but the flame danced more than ever and kept on burning. Then she carefully stepped across Zeen and nipped out the candle with her fingers. It was dark now. . . . She strode back into bed, stepping on Zeen's leg; and the corpse shook and the stomach rumbled. She held herself tucked against the wall, twisted and turned, pinched her eyes to, but did not sleep. The smell got into her nose and throat and it became very irksome, unbearable. And she got out of bed again, to open the window. A fresh breeze blew into the room; far away beyond, the sky began to brighten; and behind the cornfield she heard the singing beat of a sickle and the whistling of a sad, drawling street-ditty:

"They're at work already."

Now she lay listening to the whizzing beat and the rustle of the falling corn and that drawling, never-changing tune. . . .

The funeral would be the day after tomorrow: already she saw all the troop passing along the road and then in the church and then . . . all alone, home again. Zeen was dead now and she remained . . . and all those children, her children, who still had so long to live, would also grow old, in their turn, and die . . . ever on . . . and all that misery and slaving and then to go . . . and Zeen, her Zeen, the Zeen of yesterday, who was still alive then and not ill. Her Zeen; and she saw him as a young man over forty years ago: a handsome chap he was. She had lived so long with Zeen and had known him so well, better than her own self;

and that he should now be lying there beside her . . . cold . . .
and never again . . . that he should now be dead.

Then she broke down and wept.

F. V. Toussaint van Boelaere

LATE IDYLL

ON THE EASTERN SLOPE OF A HILL ROSE THE RENTED FARM OF FAR-
mer Cies. On the opposite side, on the western slope of another
hill was situated the homestead of Farmer Jan. From each of
the two farms a winding path went down toward a lonely canal
that flowed in the valley between the two hills. A small wooden
bridge over the narrow waterway connected the two paths. Then
from the small bridge a path that was wide enough for a fairly
large wheelbarrow led along the water to the end of the valley
and came out on the main road further on. That path was on
the property of Farmer Cies. It had belonged to the estate for
a long time.

Farmer Cies had a daughter by the name of Joanna, because
Farmer Jan was her godfather. Farmer Jan had a son called
Francies, because Farmer Cies had held him at the baptismal
ceremonies. At the end of the baptismal celebration in honor of
Joanna, Farmer Cies asked her godfather to contribute something toward the upkeep of the path they used in common, as
well as toward that of the small bridge. Farmer Jan, satiated with
heavy courses of good food, gladly consented. The next day
however he regretted his promise.

When Francies also was baptized and every belly had been
fully satisfied, Farmer Jan confidentially tapped Farmer Cies'
shoulder and said:

"Friend, what do you think, shouldn't we widen the path as
well as the small bridge?"

"I won't give no for an answer, godfather," replied Farmer
Cies. "But I'll have to think it over." He was, however, laughing
inwardly. And he never did give an answer. This increased Farmer Jan's resentment.

In the morning, as Joanna was going to school, she would wait at the little bridge for Francies, who had a hard time getting up. She would sit down on the wooden boards, her books in her lap, and let her small legs dangle over the water. Her bright face looked rosy. Her blue eyes, beneath the gold of her sunlit hair, looked straight ahead.

When Francies went to school in the afternoon he tarried on the small bridge until Joanna, who was already helping with dishes, arrived. He rearranged the boards, improved the dyke, threw pebbles at a small fish he saw moving in the water and looked continuously with lifted head toward Farmer Cies' homestead, whence Joanna had as yet not appeared.

Together they would follow the same road. First they would walk silently side by side. Then, as they reached the mainroad, they would break into a run. They were in a hurry to join their companions. On the way back they would dawdle, however. They would look at the herbs, the shrubs and the trees. They followed with their two pairs of eyes the activities of an ant or a beetle in the dust of the little yellow path. They also knew where by the side of the ditch the sparrows or finches were nesting, how many eggs were in the nest of the blackbirds when the young would come out of their eggs. Together they pursued butterflies and would upset the wondrous molehills with their wooden shoes. And sometimes they sat on Thursday afternoons for hours on the small bridge, close together, fishing with rods made by Francies from a lath, a thread and a crooked pin. Often too, taking off their stockings and with pants or skirt rolled up, they would wade through the flowing water to catch fish with a thin box, or just for the fun of it. . . .

When Francies and Joanna were to partake of the Holy Sacrament for the first time, their mothers agreed that common festivities would crown their children's happiness.

Farmer Cies agreed and Farmer Jan did not say no: the feast was to be most elaborate.

Where both orchards reached the waterway, a large bridge was thrown over the ditch with boards and supports. From two young apple trees only the blossoming tops were visible; on either side of the tent there was one, and they looked like giant nosegays, which smelt sweeter than any bouquet ever has smelt. Farther on around the tent over the bridge stood the two orchards also in full bloom.

A mighty ox was slaughtered, three pigs and eleven piglets, forty-three rabbits, fifty-six roosters and one hundred and twelve pigeons. One hundred and sixty-five large cakes and sweet custards were solemnly brought to the tables after forty bowls of rice pudding had been emptied. In front of every man stood five bottles of red wine and before every woman two bottles of white wine. And three boys continually walked back and forth from the large barrels of beer, which were monumentally piled up in a corner of the tent, to the table to fill the empty glasses.

In the place of honor sat Joanna and Francies, behind a beautifully mounted snow-white lamb with a large gilt wooden cross. Joanna was beautifully dressed in a pure white dress, which reached to the ground. She also wore white shoes and stockings, but hid them modestly beneath her dress. On her chest she wore a golden cross and on her fair golden hair was a virginal chaplet of flowers. Her cheeks glowed red, her eyes were a deep blue. She fixed her gaze steadily upon the snow-white lamb. Francies looked fine. He wore a brand new black lounge suit, black socks and black patent-leather shoes with buttons. Around his neck he wore a spotlessly white collar and white tie. And from his breast pocket peered a lace handkerchief. His hair had been curled down to his neck. He was beautiful. He would have liked to run to the small bridge to look at the free play of the little fish in the ditch. But he did not dare. He glanced steadily at the snow-white lamb; otherwise he would look at his plate.

The mothers were very much affected by the seriousness of the occasion and the particular beauty of their children. It was, moreover, a beautiful day: the sun glowed in the blue sky. The grass was green and fresh. All the trees around were covered with white and pink blossoms, and the smell of almonds was wafted by a gentle breeze through the air. Joanna and Francies, what an ideal couple they made!

The fathers were extremely pleased: their faces shone with satisfaction. If both their holdings were gathered into one, there would not be a richer homestead in the whole of Flanders. Then there would be prepared a meal compared to which that of today was but child's play! . . . With that Farmer Jan forgot his intention to obtain from Farmer Cies the understanding that he no longer would have to pay a cent toward the upkeep of the path. And Farmer Cies had forgotten that this time he had decided to force Farmer Jan to widen the common path and bridge. So the next day they felt even worse toward each other and they regretted their neglect.

When Farmer Cies noticed his neighbor first from across the waterway near his land, he would say: "Morning, Farmer Jan." If however Farmer Jan spied his neighbor first he would call out: "Morning, Farmer Cies." Politely each of them would then reply. But otherwise Farmer Cies went alone to High Mass and Farmer Jan did likewise. After church Farmer Jan would go to the "Merlo" and Farmer Cies would drink his schnaps at the "House of Trade." Both, as they had long been accustomed, would go homewards at exactly half-past eleven. But the "Merlo" was closer to the church than "House of Trade," so that all the way home Farmer Jan would see Farmer Cies walking ahead of him without recognizing him, and Farmer Cies would continuously hear the footsteps of Farmer Jan, while stubbornly refusing to see the person who was following him. In the evening Farmer Cies would play cards at the "Crown"; Farmer Jan frequented the "A Few Steps Up." And thus it was that they never met each other any more, neither in the village nor on the common path.

On Sundays, at twenty minutes of nine, Joanna and her mother stepped out of their house; at the same moment Francies and his mother would appear on the threshold of their home. They really met on the little bridge. And all four together, they would go to Mass. They also went in the afternoon together to the church services. And they again would go home together; on one side Joanna would walk next to her mother and on the other side Francies would flank his.

Now that Joanna and Francies had received Holy Communion for the first time and so had come to the age of reason, they began to help with the work. Francies turned the earth with his spade, and he preferred to do this at the border of the waterway, in the neighborhood of the small bridge. And Farmer Jan became proud of his son. Because he noticed very soon how Francies, as he was using the spade, turned over the soil up to the extreme limit of the stream and how every time a clod of loose soil slipped down from the bank into the water, he would drive the water further away: thus the property was gradually being enlarged. Farmer Cies also noticed this after a short while. He saw that this would cost him even more pains to keep the water in its course, so that he would incur no damage; and he became furious with that hypocritical rascal Francies.

Joanna now was allowed to take care of a cow. She preferred to herd it along the side of the water, in the neighborhood of the small bridge, to let it graze. She always went along the small path. And Farmer Cies was very well pleased with it. Because he soon noticed that he would be able to feed another cow with the neglected grass along his path. He therefore let the herbs and the weeds grow and luxuriate: the cow would eventually become aware of it. Farmer Jan soon noticed that the path, toward the upkeep of which he did not contribute, was no longer taken care of, in order that Farmer Cies could feed another cow at his cost. He began to dislike horribly that sneaky Joanna. His hatred mounted. "I won't contribute even a button toward the upkeep any longer," he concluded angrily.

Cordule, the wife of Farmer Cies, died at midsummer. The solemn funeral took place at the eleven o'clock service. The church had been completely covered by black cloth on which glistened silver tears; fifty heavy candles burned on the high altar as well as on the side altars; seven priests in full robes celebrated the Mass. After the funeral, Farmer Cies invited people to his house. He had hired the best cook in the village. The meal was even more copious than at the time of the First Communion. Because Farmer Cies did not want anybody to think that he was a poor louse when Farmer Jan did not contribute. Carloads of fish and fowl, cooked and fried, twenty-seven bowls of rice pudding were scraped clean and ninety-one cakes and custards were enjoyed by the company. Five large barrels of beer were stacked up in the garden and four boys were incessantly walking hither and thither to fill the pots and the beakers. Far, far away on the main road, the poor of the village pursued their jollities.

Farmer Jan had not been invited. But during the whole course of the meal, he would come to stand in his shirtsleeves on the threshold of his house for a few seconds, with a brilliantly white napkin tied under his chin. His face was an uncompromising, shiny red. Every now and then he would noisily uncork a bottle of wine between his knees, sniff the cork and the neck of the bottle and make smacking noises, and would then lift it with the eye of a connoisseur and glare at it happily. At other times he wiped the abundant sweat from his face with the tip of the white, shining napkin, would laboriously loosen his trouser belt and, leaning heavily against the doorpost would gasp for breath: he no longer seemed to be able to talk coherently. But Francies was not to be seen all day.

Three months after Cordule's death, Apolline the wife of Farmer Jan, gave up the ghost. She had succumbed from a linger-

ing ailment that had been undermining her health for a long
time. Her body was not yet cold when Farmer Jan ordered twenty
laborers to build a wide path along his side of the stream. He
had gravel and fine ashes brought from everywhere to cover the
new dirt road like a coating of macadam. It looked like the
driveway to an important castle. Farmer Jan did not want anybody to think that he cared about a day's spading of soil, in
order to be independent of anybody.

The departure of Apolline took place in the morning at the
eleven o'clock service. The parochial clergy came in full vestments to fetch the body from the house of death. Four men bore
the casket. Just as the funeral procession left Farmer Jan's
threshold and wound its way along the path toward the waterway, a cart loaded with manure appeared from Farmer Cies'
courtyard. The wheels shrieked agonizingly because of dryness.
The cart slowly descended the slope toward the small bridge
and made for the old common dirt road. It kept even with the
procession on the side—in step with Farmer Jan and Francies,
behind the casket. Farmer Cies then appeared on the threshold
of his dwelling. He had his working clothes on and his feet stuck
into the heavy wooden shoes amply lined with straw. Over his
jolly countenance was his grey cap, with the visor turned sideways. Thus he stood indifferently leaning against the doorjamb
watching, a long, broad pipe alight in his mouth. But Joanna
remained invisible all day.

Without a woman Farmer Jan could not get along on his
farm. He hired a young thing, known throughout the neighborhood as a work horse, but rather limited in intelligence. She
could not abide Francies. But Farmer Jan thought the most important thing was that everything ran smoothly, and this the
new servant girl did superlatively.

Now that he had such a beautiful driveway, Farmer Jan
bought a stable horse and a light coach. Thus he could save a
lot of time. All day long he rode in and out. Every time he came
or went he let his whip crack deafeningly; he sat straight as a
pole in the carriage and held the reins like a baron. Farmer Cies
might see him or spy upon him, but that was exactly what he
wanted. However, not once when he drove out did he see hide
nor hair of Farmer Cies, nor did he see that pest of a Joanna.
Francies himself never used the coach. He just wandered around
by himself. . . . The day Francies went to draw his number for
conscription in the army, he came back home, very quietly and
disheartened. Farmer Cies, as he saw Francies come by, slowly

approached the door of his homestead, smiling with pleasure. Hardly had Francies disappeared into the parental house or Farmer Jan ran shouting and jubilating down the hill, and behind him ran the new servant girl, swinging her skirts. Farmer Cies realized that he had been mistaken: Francies was out of it! It looked as if he had been born with a caul, that Francies. Enviously he thought of how he was the son of Farmer Jan. Otherwise both the homesteads' together would have celebrated.

For a moment he thought about a reconciliation. Then he suddenly saw the radiant expression on Joanna's face—how but a while ago she had been about to cry her eyes out. And then he heard how Farmer Jan and the new maid were bragging and crying at the small bridge, on the beautiful driveway. That female was waving a bit of paper. And Farmer Cies flew into passion.

In the course of a few years Farmer Jan died. He was buried solemnly, but without ostentation; there was no solemn funeral repast. The new maid left the farm the day after the inhumation. "I have been chased away," she cried everywhere; "I have spent my youth there and worked like a truck horse." Shortly thereafter an old woman moved into Francies' house, and life went on as formerly.

Three months precisely after Farmer Jan's demise, Farmer Cies also exchanged the temporal for the eternal. He was put to rest simply and quietly. Another farmer was found to run Joanna's homestead. And again the seasons followed one another with their different tasks and their same aim.

One Sunday Francies met Joanna at the little bridge. They were both going to Mass. Francies looked at Joanna, his eyes moist like those of a timid dog. But Joanna kept her glance turned earthward and continued on her way. As time passed, she dressed almost like a nun. Always clad in black, the golden fair hair flatly combed back and hidden under a black-brown cloth, as under an unchangeable smooth cap. But she went to church only on Sundays.

She worked as if she had to take care of a whole family. Her farm was getting ahead fine, though only the manservant stiff with years could do the masculine chores. But when sowing time came along, a tall figure would stride over the land to plow and sow. Then with the eternally revolving seasons, the harvest month would come again; and by the silver light from the moon and the countless stars there rustled, with the gleaming of the scythe, the blessed song of the down-cut wheat; the wheelbarrow creaked under the load of golden blades, or there sounded the tireless beating of the flail upon the threshing-floor. Otherwise the whole homestead was plunged into dark quiet.

In the early morning Francies' homestead, which stretched out over the eastern slope of the one hill, rose first from the vanishing night darkness. The white walls shone shrilly; the roof gleamed red as if it had just been varnished. But the doors and the blinds remained closed as if the homestead had just gone to rest. Joanna looked at it every morning from the porch of her house shrouded in darkness. Lovingly, deeply stirred, she felt stirred like an innocent child. But every time she felt her heart throttled again; she knew how Farmer Cies had once appeared in the same spot, in his wide, straw-packed wooden shoes, his cap askew, the smoking, puffing pipe in his mouth in order to sneer at Farmer Jan in the presence of death. And in her own blood that turned cold in her veins she thought to understand that this was an evil deed, which sooner or later must be avenged.

Her dead father suppressed her will. . . .

Francies, however, was now farming behind the house. The beautiful driveway, which Farmer Jan had built and had always specially cared for, had disappeared under a carpet of hardy weeds. But the little bridge, nearby, still looked as before. Nothing seemed to have changed in it: no new beams, not a new nail. Even the mouldering board was there yet. The bridge could still be used at any time.

Daily, as soon as night fell, Francies appeared on the threshold of his already darkened home. Joanna's house would still radiate by itself in the glow of the setting sun. The white walls shone brilliantly, and the red tiled roof blossomed like a sweet-smelling exotic flower. Francies saw that the seasons passed regularly over Joanna's activities and that life was unavoidable and disappeared into the closed circle of the year. He knew his work, the work that came back daily: together with the old housekeeper, he accomplished it listlessly. He realized too what work needed to be done on Joanna's homestead. And only this work could give joy. Once he had wanted to talk to Joanna but she had gone on her way without lifting her eyes. And indeed it was on the same spot where Farmer Jan had behaved so cruelly and as if relishing it, sweating, drooling, puffing contentedly, in order to sneer at Farmer Cies. Past events have no turning.

Joanna died. She had left all her possessions, as a duty, to Francies. They talked about it in the village—thus the wish of Farmer Cies and Farmer Jan had been realized!—then all were silent again. Francies was indifferent to the legacy now that Joanna was no longer there. He labóred on this land as well as on his own and took care of one as well as the other in so far as his strength allowed him. He lived by himself in the homestead. And as the years went by and as he became weaker and weaker, the round of his self-same labors encircled him. The weeds luxuriated everywhere, they grew over field and pasture and road. The unpruned trees of both the orchards grew wild, still producing healthy fruit, however, in turn ripening and then dropping one by one into the growing, sun-bleached hay. But Francies still stood every night on the threshold of his barren house. Resigned and happy, he breathed the well-known air of solitude spreading all around him. He looked over there at Joanna's empty homestead. He thought of how she had let herself grow old on the slope of the other hill, of Joanna in front of her house, of how she had greeted him and sometimes waved at him with her hand. But still he never felt the inclination to go there; the path that led to the little bridge had become invisible, overgrown with grass. And the little bridge itself, useless since Joanna was dead, had shrunk to a mouldering beam covered with green moss. Only the water of the brook still lapped happily and sang its eternal song.

Translated by ALFRED VAN AMEYDEN VAN DUYM

PART III

THE FULFILLMENT

Arthur van Schendel

ANGIOLINO AND SPRINGTIME

A SINFUL MAN IS NEVER WHOLLY SINFUL, JUST AS A POOR MAN, however poor he may be, is never wholly without some possession. How else could there be saints—for, when they were little they also screamed if they were hungry, played in the mud of the street and probably did things that only the angels know. But they had a little spot that was kept white, and when the golden rays fell upon it from day to day evil left them, passion, anger, the inclination to steal or to curse. And when they had become wholly white within they were able to do miraculous deeds so that the other saints saw them and spoke of it before the Throne of Bliss. Then He sent forth one with the loving message that another might enter blessedness. I do not say this because I imagine that I know better than the Fathers, but because I myself have seen how it happens with mankind. We are all born poor, but, as soon as one opens his eyes, he finds all that is necessary, yet for the other, the mother can find no decent cloth in which to wrap him. And then the vicissitudes that follow! Beppe can never waste so much that he does not always receive more; Felice is now rich, now poor; and let Buonaventura smile ever so amiably or complain ever so bitterly, it helps not at all, he cannot number the times that he has had to go without bread. And yet Beppe does not know what Buonaventura has more than he, nor does Felice know what is the best of what he does have. But Buonaventura certainly understands more because he is the poorest. That is the white spot in the poor man, he understands more than another. He knows that the lord who walks along and acts as if he did not see the outstretched hand is neither more nor less than himself. Most passers-by do not look at us, but have they the time, or have they learned to see others as we see them? And some are annoyed and consider it their right to pass unmolested, but have never understood anything that is outside their own profession. And others are annoyed because they think that we are lazy, but however much they may be wearied by their own daily work, they do not know the weariness of waiting. And among them are some who are ashamed; they are poor even as we, though they wear silks and jewels. When they notice us they suddenly see an acquaintance on the opposite side, or they perceive something in the distance to look at, and the hand that they pass by remains empty. These are certainly neither more nor less than we, because they have, at least, shame, a good beginning for every man. Sinfulness is given us to understand the saints, and poverty, so that we may understand ourselves and each other.

How I ranted and cursed, when I was young, against the lot that withheld from me what others had in overabundance! I was prodigal and rich in desires, I believed with burning zeal that all the good things of the world were created for each and every one that was born and I raised my fists against the injustice that thrust me out of the existence of the rich, with their smiles and blushes, their broad chests and free eyes. Hundreds and hundreds of them I saw pass by, yet not so many but that the curses in my mouth were greater in number. And when the pain in my feet forced me to return to the darkness where my parents and the others spent the night, when I had suffered a beating and thrown myself on the ground, then the tears would fall because everything around me was so black with injustice. But thanks to God, I have always been really poor, the reality of it is the best thing that I have. I have never actually believed that in poverty there is injustice, neither of heaven nor of man. I have seen others who take up a weapon to revenge themselves or, by cunning, take what they desire, and of all those who did so when I was young I now see not one left, and the world has not changed for them nor for us. What they called unjust still exists, as it has always existed; can it then be unjust? But others who endured as we remained poor and learned. And there can be no better friendship, no more cordial wish than between us, Beppe, Felice and the others, when we see each other in the mornings or call a good night after a long day in the sun. Inherent in poverty is the beginning of wealth, just as in the blackest sinfulness there must be a beginning of holy life.

What harm does he do who begs? The worst accusation against him is that he lives a useless life. Who so accuses him has never begged, or seen as the beggar sees. Hundreds and hundreds pass us by before one at last stops, his hand trembles as he searches for the coin and as he hands it over there is a look in his eyes as of prayer. Who knows, then, what has stirred in his heart?

The Fathers speak of charity that is one of the virtues, but he who sees it daily can swear that it is more than a virtue that so moves men. It is a glance of more than pity, more than reverence, more than the best one might name. I have met that glance so frequently that I could say: I have seen it there, or there, and they would be holy places that I named, but it would not become me, and rather than that I will be silent and bear the reproach that a beggar is useless. 'Yes, and probably the reproach is just. A beggar is the least of all men, so there must be much of evil in him and he may be thankful if uselessness is his worst sin.

But the worst of the beggar is not his uselessness. He is a creature born little, always thrust into positions where he must forever remain little. But certainly there is truth in the accusation that I sometimes hear made by pious people, that he is immoral. Some of them, I know, steal easily, even though they have not the habit of theft. They carry off something if it lies handy and if they can make use of it. I even know some so unmoral that they will let a thing lie for no other reason than that they have no use for it. That is neither good nor bad, just unmoral. But for such as we it is often difficult to discern the line between good morals and bad. I have seldom stolen and often let a thing lie because I did not know why I should pick it up, but recently in the Corso I was ashamed of myself. I had earned little and given that out again for too little supper. Although it was already late I went home by a roundabout way because I enjoyed the first warm winds and there were many little stars. On the corner of the Corso, just under the lamp that was still burning, lay a strong rope, four or five yards long, I think. I stood and looked at that rope and did not know what to do. One may honestly keep what one finds if the loser does not return to ask for it. The saddler would give me five or six cents for it in the morning. But should I have any need of it in the morning? Then why should I not leave it there for another? Why should I always take what I find? And I thought further that a poor person has no right to pass by a good find, those five cents that I might get for the rope would be five cents that a wealthy man might keep for another tomorrow. But I turned away and, though I was so ashamed that I could feel the warmth in my cheeks, I let it lie. I am not sure, but I think that it was unmoral, San Giuseppe intercede for me; for how can a man know whether to listen to reason or to an inspiration. I walked on and quickly forgot the shame; there were many more stars now, and as I crossed the bridge I smelt the fragrance of flowers in the night. It seemed as though I heard someone say: Angiolino, all things pass, rope, pennies, morals and everything, but if the shining of the stars and the fragrance of flowers delight you, say then an Ave Maria and you possess one thing that remains. And I bent before the blessed Virgin that stands on the other side and said three Aves.

On the following day I returned to the bridge. Buonaventura was already sitting there with a few others at the approach from the street. Now I had never taken my stand at the river, because I prefer to be in the crowd on the Piazza; you receive less there, for everyone is in a hurry, but the place swarms with so many, many people, and all those who came by regularly I knew well, was glad to see some of them although they never gave anything. Now I got the idea that it would be better on the bridge, I do not know why, perhaps because I had had a good inspiration there the evening before. It is not good to break from an old custom if one has profited by it, and here, moreover, there were already so many that the pennies must be scarce. They were all at the entrance to the bridge, near the crucifix on one side or near the niche opposite. And I had heard the voice on the middle of the bridge, there at the arch where you can see the water and the mountains in the distance. Now when I came and saw the sun on the river and heard the rushing of the water beneath, I did not hesitate, but thought: This is my place, heaven bless it. It was not long before Beppe came stumping along in amazement and he tried to convince me that if I was really not going to the Piazza it would be better to join the others because standing over the water never brings good fortune. A foolish superstition; there are some who believe that indeed it brings luck because there is a resemblance between fortune and water. I was of no mind to tell him that for me it was a question of sun and breeze, of the distant mountains and the fragrance, and not of gain. And when he saw that I wanted to stay he left me alone, but all that day I noticed their concern for me and their derision. Three pennies I got that day, one from a mendicant friar who looked poorer than any of us. But it must bore people, if they have already given at the entrance to the bridge, to see an outstretched hand again in the middle. That evening when I was reminded of my stomach and stood before an inn where roasting was going on, I thought of the rope that I had allowed to lie. But before I turned toward home I went back to the bridge and stood for a moment where I had been standing all the day long. There were many, many stars and the moon was just coming up beyond San Frediano. I do not know what made me think of long ago, of my parents, of children with whom I played when I, myself, was a child, of a brother who always touched my cheek when he passed, of one whom I often saw when I was a boy but to whom I never spoke. I heard the plash of the water, I sought the mountains that were hidden in the night, and tears came to my eyes. Why? I do not know, but it was good, after a long day, to be in the darkness undisturbed and I let the tears fall without asking for the reason. On the opposite side someone began to play a guitar and to sing, judging by the voice it must be a boy. I sighed, but I would rather have sung. And all was quiet again, again I felt my empty stomach, and I must get home. And suddenly it seemed as if I heard a voice again, it said: Angiolino, hunger passes, but if tears fall for a time that has passed, if you think of people that you would wish to see again, if you would rather sing than sigh, then say an Ave Maria and you shall sing and hear the people of earlier days. So I went on; I knew that it was good on the middle of the bridge, and on the other side I said three Ave Marias.

On the following day also I received but little, something more, I think, but not enough. It seemed as though fortune had entirely forgotten me, for me there were no more of those many windfalls that we find through our habit of looking at the ground and examining the value of what others throw away. Beppe paid for my bread that evening. But before I went home, when it was quiet and the moon, somewhat larger, shone more clearly on the water, I stood on the bridge again at the midmost arch that looks toward the mountains. The wind was warmer and I heard more sounds. I waited, for the voice might speak again. While waiting I began to think of the boy that I had been, of the years when I laughed at nothing at all and my heart throbbed at nothing at all. Ah, that I have no better word than this "nothing"! For it is still so, at that very moment I could have laughed again, and my heart throbbed as it used to, just let me say at nothing, the same nothing for which, among the many evil things, we sometimes do a thing that we know certainly to be good though we do not understand it. I stood there for a long time, waiting and thinking of those days when so much might have happened that never did happen, until the first bell of morning sounded from San Iacopo. I was not hungry and not sleepy and would rather have stayed longer, but one learns with the years that it is not wise to forget everything, and what age learns is surely no less good than what youth discovers. I should be too tired for the task tomorrow if I did not rest. So I left and naturally said an Ave before the blessed Virgin on the corner, even without being told to do so.

And so the days passed. Ponte Vecchio brought me no prosperity. Friends tried to persuade me to return to the Piazza again or else to come near them, therefore I told Buonaventura that I had had an inspiration which told me that good fortune would come to me in the middle of the river. After that he came each day to ask, although he walks with difficulty. The saints have never been indifferent to me, though I seldom enter a church and pray only when it is necessary, but now it was as if the saints were looking down on me and a prayer often came to me of itself. And I noticed that many a time I forgot to lift my hat when someone approached because I was thinking of other things, and I was not surprised that I received so little, nor did it grieve me, for I was not much tormented by hunger, even though I had less food. In those days a sparkle on the water or a thought of Saint Joseph was more to me than bread.

And one day in the past week, a wonderful day, fortune came, and the way of her coming was strange and amazing. I sat with my back turned to the passers-by, for I was looking at the mountains, when I was called and saw behind me a nobleman on horseback, a count or an ambassador; he had such bright eyes that my heart began to throb, there was something about him that reminded me of long ago. He asked at what I was staring and when I answered: "At the mountains, noble sir," he laughed aloud so that the air resounded with it. The voice, that laugh was more than fortune ever could be, it was a sound of true happiness as if the sun or the wind were to laugh. Then he called out: "Look well, spring comes from the mountains!" I was so amazed that my ears rang, now I knew that his voice resembled one that was dear to me, that this was the sound for which I had waited all those long days. But it was strange and sad, too, however silly it may sound, that he then took a purse from his belt and tossed it to me, as if after the gift he would pass on like any other and never return again. And he did leave, too, before I could say anything. When he had disappeared from the bridge I took up the purse and looked at the mountains yonder in the sun. What had I to do with gold now that the voice and that laugh, which promised everything, had vanished again? And as I stood dully staring with my heart full of grief and my body all weariness and fatigue, without a thought, I heard those words again: Spring comes from the mountains.

Was it spring that I saw coming there? It had been bright and now, suddenly, a mist hung in the distance, the sun over San Miniato became pale. I saw a cloud of dust swirl up from San Niccolo, high above the trees, the river below began to foam from the strong, hot wind. It lasted but a moment and everyone who passed looked at the next man with gleaming eyes and red face, and the cries that were called out had a foolish sound. The water flowed, shimmering, and even the light shimmered. I made the sign of the cross while thinking of the blessed Maria, but I thought also of that nobleman who had gazed on me with eyes like the archangels in the church. I felt that I could stand here no longer this day, that I must walk, walk a great deal, hear and see a great deal.

But first I wanted to give thanks, and the nearest church was San Stefano. Not more than three candles were burning before saints that I did not know, before San Giuseppe there were none. People always give more to the others and forget him, probably because they think that he cannot help as much as the others. But it is all one to me, I know that in heaven he is second to none. So I thanked him for what had happened to me and when I had looked at the money in the purse I asked a brother who was busy there to give me a four-pound candle. He seemed to have left the world not long ago, for he looked from me to the purse in astonishment. But he brought the candle and I lit it myself. This was the second time in my life that I could afford to light a candle; the flame was so pure, so still, that I had to pray: San Giuseppe, pray for us that every heart may go, as quiet and as pure, toward holiness. The crowds and merriment of the street are good to look upon, for the improvidence of man is a lovely gift, but what every one of us most desires is really the stillness and the purity of the most Blessed. In stillness we can hear Him, in purity we begin to comprehend. San Giuseppe, who was a father to the Child, knows well what I mean.

Then I went to walk among men. It was a pleasure to see how they no longer hurried now that they had forgotten their business in the spring, all with flushed faces, or with loose or open clothing; on the corners of the streets the wind fluttered their hair. If you watch them when they are engaged in business there is always a hubbub of vehemence or contention, or you notice that a grudge is kept hidden, and I even have friends who say that there is more evil than we can imagine. But it is certain, as I plainly saw that morning, that there is also more kindliness among men than we can imagine. The greetings of two friends who embraced each other were good to hear: the nonsense, if they were youngsters; old people who nodded with half-shut eyes and now and then clapped someone on the shoulder; the laughter of young women; the quiet words of mothers. Do the doves of Santa Maria make sweeter sounds in the early morning or before they go to sleep? A man cannot be so sinful but that he possesses something from the time before he was created, you can see it and hear it whenever you will.

Two women were standing there with flowers, and again and again I saw someone come up to buy. Why were those flowers plucked and sold? It could not be just a few lovers or the carefree who carried them away for I saw old women, too, trudging along step by step with their flowers firmly clutched to their breasts. And I bought a bunch, too, because spring had come and I too sniffed their fragrance and felt a smile. I thought: I wish that I could take them to my mother's grave, she must have had so much anxiety about me of which I never heard and much sweetness, too, when I was still little and lay in her arms. But I could not do it, because I was in the hospital when she was buried and by the time I was able to leave no one knew any more where she had been laid. I was standing in front of the Santa Maria cloister and I went into the yard and laid a flower here and there on the graves, they who lay beneath understood well that it was for my mother and for them, too, for beyond they do not make the distinctions that we do here. They know that no flower is necessary, nor even a thought, if we but step softly over the ground where their dust lies, as a dove alights. If you stay there long it is as if you heard them: not even your prayer is necessary; but they are no longer in want as we are, that makes it for us a necessity.

I could not stay long in Santa Maria; from outside a song floated over the wall and I wanted to see more of the clear sky. A barber lives there near the market, who sometimes helped me and as I seldom come into this neighborhood I went there now to visit him. I would gladly have given him something or brought sweets to his children, but I remembered that he was certainly one of those who gives rather than receives, he would rather have a word of greeting and my thanks than a gift. He was standing at his door and welcomed me with friendliness. I could hear in his hearty laugh how well pleased he was that I remembered him. He said that I ought to look more tidy, sat me on his stool, clipped my hair and shaved the bristly growth from my cheeks, and, when he had finished, gave me two pennies. I needed neither the clipping nor the shave, the pennies even less, but could I have refused? One must accept even when one thinks one does not need it, for it may be a necessity to the giver to give. And even a beggar may not refuse what is offered to him.

It was approaching midday; I realized that I was getting hungry. It was a long walk to San Frediano, and I knew an eating-house nearby, but on the day of my good fortune I did not want to desert my friends and Gino who sometimes gave more than I paid for. So I walked back and I did not regret it. They received me boisterously. They had already heard of my fortune, how I do not know. The rumor of misfortune spreads quickly, yes, but among us good fortune is so coveted that we feel when it is near, even if it is in another street, and we are glad of it. Whether that is a virtue or just something natural I should not be able to say, but I know very well that it is not only the poor who can rejoice over another's good luck, a child sometimes looks with a lovely blush at a doll that another child is holding, and I have often seen wealthy people stop in admiration of another's furs or jewels. It is because there is joy in every heart over the good gifts of the world.

There were ten of them sitting there, some who never come here otherwise but were called now by the rumor of my good luck, and Buonaventura, who is not miserly but never parts with his wine, let me drink from his cup. I called to Gino that I was giving a feast and that all were invited. Then they began to shout so that I could not say a word, they would not have it, they claimed that I must be their guest in celebration of my fine day. At first it seemed foolish that I, who had more than all of them together, should be their guest instead of their being mine, but they were right, it was their right to celebrate the good fortune of a friend. And Gino did his best, that is certain. After we had examined the purse full of golden ducats and florins, enough to live like a lord, we ate and drank and laughed and sang songs until vespers. Then they all got up, for they had to think of the morrow. And I left, too.

On the river it seemed that sadness took possession of me, a need to be alone or to seek for something tender. I left my friends and went close to the bank. There was a strange fragrance in the air, of flowers, of a church, of a burial. I have thought more than once that there must be a connection between these three. Flowers always bloom at the time when the world is full of joy and love and devotion, and there must surely be a connection between these things and the church and the time after life. I enjoyed the fragrance as much as I could. Where the water falls and flows faster, passing San Niccolo, I stood still to listen to the hissing. It flowed with a great splashing of foam, and then flowed onward faster. Water is indeed the purest substance, it has no form of its own and can have all forms. What is now a drop or a spray is not to be found again the next instant in the stream. But is not the heart that I call my own just like that? Now it is here, the heart of Angiolina standing here, and happy, and where will it be tomorrow and how, and will it truly be a heart? And may I truly pray that heaven which made it will never let it perish? It is better, I thought, to be grateful that this heart can rejoice here in itself that would like to be all things and is nothing.

Behind me stood the heights of San Miniato, there whence the spring had come. I climbed up and, as I felt a heaviness in my legs, sat down upon the grass. Then suddenly I saw the glory of the sky and the splendor of the city. The sun was setting and painted the sky on the other side, a glistening mist hung over the roofs. As the sun set now I had seen it many times, every spring and every summer, year after year, and yet there came from the glow a beatitude I did not know. And it was even so with the city; the haze and glisten were, of course, well known to me, but in them gleamed another light. It seemed as if a warm breath rose from below, from the hundreds of houses and churches, and as if from above a refreshing fragrance fell. And it was true, also, only I had never seen it and therefore it seemed new to me. Am I not one of the many people and am I not a part of the earth? And does not a warm breath rise from me even though I do not speak? The golden haze yonder held the sigh of the smallest child and mine as well. And where there are sighs and longings, comfort certainly falls too. While I stared out where the light was already becoming redder and a star began to sparkle clearly, thoughts of the long ago awakened in me with sometimes a question of the future. I had never loved anyone very dearly, not even myself. But there was one for whom I would willingly have burnt the little that I had and that I was, so that on the last day I should not have had any soul left. And that one never knew me, never even saw me. When I think of it I must fold my hands and pray: Blessed Maria, blessed San Giuseppe, I am poor and weak, I have received little in my heart to cherish the love of others, forgive me. All my life I have been able to do nothing but wait on the street, in truth, not just for pennies, I was too weak to do what I ought to have done. And now that I pray I dare not promise that I shall ever do what I ought, for I know that I am too weak for anything else than waiting. I have not been able to love the many who were my friends because I always looked forward and to you, blessed Maria, to you, San Giuseppe, I dare admit that the hope that it may happen is ever in my heart. For some who in this world have not the happiness of a wife, a child, a home, ah, of all that is best in the world, it is kept for the future, for heaven has placed that happiness in their hearts and what heaven does is truth. All that happiness in their hearts and all the loving-kindness that shall one day come to them is one and the same. The house exists although it has not been built, the child exists though it has not yet been born. I pray thee, protect the wife whose hand I have never touched, the house that is to be built, the child to be born; I pray thee, protect them.

I sat there for a long time, until all the stars sparkled in the night. Possibly I slept or dozed, possibly my soul had even wandered from me. Then I felt a breath over me and I heard words, quite clearly; I dare not think that it was Maria or San Giuseppe, I thought it must be the spring, in passing: Angiolino, every prayer is heard even though it is not spoken. And then again, still more softly, more kindly: Wait, and all your desires shall be given you. My heart was full, I could no longer hold the fragrance of the night.

I stood up and went into the city. It was lonely and quiet, almost all the lamps were out. Below the wall of the prison a woman spoke to me, lamenting and begging. In the darkness she could not see my clothes. Her husband was in there, she said, and could not go free until the fine was paid, she and her children would have to beg. "Oh, noble sir," she wailed, "preserve us from the very worst." I had the purse in my pocket and gave it to her.

It was glorious walking all that night, under the stars, with a song on my lips. A sinful man is never wholly sinful and a poor man sometimes possesses more than he needs, then let him thank the saints and laugh as the wind of spring blows over him.

Translated by WILHELMINA C. NIEWENHOUS

R. N. Roland Holst

DOG AND MAN

WHEN, ADVANCING IN YEARS, YOU ARE GETTING MORE SELF-CONTAINED and apt to turn away from the world; when the autumnal silence within you, though by no means wintry decay, makes you incline to a peace too easily gained; then the moment has come for you to have a dog. I wish you to have one as a companion, partly because you probably need comfort, but more still, because it is good to have a warm-hearted being beside you, who knows nothing of what you have achieved, nor cares what you are trying to achieve, who thinks nothing of what you consider important and, so exacting is he, never spares you, but is victorious on every occasion.

Ever since the dog attached himself to man, he has shared the human lot and has been subject to the same humiliation which threatens man. Estranged from savage nature and freedom of chase, he has, through the centuries, grown more and more dependent. If you are shortsighted, you can easily make him a slave of the bread-basket or force him to a submissiveness which scarcely astonishes us in our fellow-men. You can teach him to cringe or, misusing him, turn him into a policeman, a buffoon or a miserable clown. You can make him vain, lazy, fond of dainties, or change him into a servile fawner. It may be owing to man that dogs become vicious and sullen or deteriorate into bold vagabonds when they find no outlet for their faithfulness. Man may also turn into a calculating, petty-minded creature, and that quite easily, for are there not thousands of such people?

All this you can do by hunger, pain and cunning, not because you are their superior, but because you have the power to humble them and render them contemptible, exactly in the same way that you can humble and render your fellow-men contemptible.

All this you can do.

But you can also, thanks to the dog, become more human, and wiser too, by recognizing nature. You will also be comforted by him, innumerable times, and be enabled, better than by listening to the confusing talk of insistent men, to fortify your faith in mankind, reflecting that men, those other poor dogs, may eventually regain their pride and self-reliance by being nobler and wiser masters to themselves.

But remember that every dog is a character, however pliable his nature may be, and that if, instead of choosing your companion, you buy him haphazardly, you may find yourself deceived. Indeed, it is needless to increase your difficulties by living with and beside a dog who does not fit in with you, who understands you as little as you do him. Believe me, nothing but annoyance and humiliation on both sides will be the result.

You think this exaggeration?

Very well, then buy your dog at random and you will find what it means to be neither loved nor trusted, but constantly jeered at by an animal. Do not take a dog out of pity, either, for really we are sufficiently pleased with ourselves already and quite sentimental enough.

But if you are lucky enough to possess a dog who strengthens the feeling of responsibility in you, you are privileged, for inasmuch as you love you will be changed.

Two primitive instincts appear strongly and distinctly in every dog. Through hundreds of centuries those two instincts have been preserved and they lie intact in every young, unsteady, puling little dog, like two poles between which its consciousness grows—the emotional instinct which urges him to seek man, and the physical instinct which urges him to go roaming and hunting. This is what gives the dog his great charm: his touching need of love and, side by side with it, his obedience to the strong call of nature, luring him to go where he entirely belongs to himself and lives at his own sweet will. But most touching is it to us, divided in nature as we are, to see how those two primitive instincts are at war in him, each fighting for its own rights so that the dog himself has great difficulty in finding the balance between those two compelling, yet clashing desires on which his happiness depends to such a degree. Who does not discern this struggle in the dog has never understood the torturing nostalgia expressing itself in the deep sigh with which he curls himself up in the corner of the room, when he knows that all the doors are shut. Neither can he understand the exuberant joy which the dog shows when he comes home, after a long ramble, to his master, in whom, between ourselves, he has an exaggerated faith. As this exaggeration remains silent, it never becomes, as among men, a public lie.

We are walking to my studio together; the sky is clear, the day fine. He goes along with me or runs on in front carelessly, but at one particular spot there comes a moment when, every day over again, the struggle between his two desires has to be fought. To the right are the woods and rambling and hunting, to the left the studio with snugness and the master. He hesitates, he lingers, he stops—the same struggle recurs every day . . . except when it rains.

"All right, go then, go then," and I close the door of my workshop. After a while he comes back and asks for admittance. He is wet with dew and out of breath, his panting satisfaction reminds one of the exhilaration with which a skater, after a long run, enters the warm inn, so that no one can doubt of the tingling joy outside. He is happy, but now his other urge must quickly be satisfied. It does not matter if he is dripping wet, he leaps to his master and presses close against him. Not till now does he feel completely and entirely satisfied.

What has the master done all this time? Often not yet ploughed a single furrow of his day's work. Might not he too have found happiness in the clear morning outside? We are often uncertain in our desires and but rarely steer our barque in a definite direction.

Certainly dogs are sometimes inconstant in their love, but are not we the same? Sudden moods come upon them as well as upon us. But how soon they turn back to the safe harbor! It seems that the slight menace renders the gained certainty deeper and happier. Whoever raises a wall round his own personality, and keeps his friend a prisoner without, robs himself of the satisfaction of being preferred to every one else and of being, after all, the chosen one.

Coming home, back from the world of men, full of bitterness at the never ending waste of words, your self-confidence maimed and riddled, feeling weary and dull, you are hailed by your silent friend. Touching your heart at once by his gladness, he settles down quietly, leaning heavily against your leg. The animal warmth rises higher and higher, the nothing-demanding, calmly waiting source of love at last softens and thaws the heart.

If, by and by, the master, delivered from pride and irritation, thinks more kindly of men, not after all so very different from himself, it is really not because his bitterness was without cause, not because he has become wiser in such a short time, but because the silent animal has nourished him imperceptibly from the only source which can give relief from all the bitterness of life.

Now and then he slips down and falls asleep across his master's feet. Is he really asleep? Who shall say? You accommodate yourself to him and sit still, waiting till your friend awakes or wants to do something else. Who has not, keeping vigil by a bedside, unexpectedly received illumination? Who has not, when ill, although lying with shut eyes, recognized in the unseen presence of watchful love, a source of safe and blissful calm? Watcher and watched simultaneously, the dog is a weaver of repose, and, while you imagine that you are allowing him to rest, it is really he who forces you to that quiet which brings healing to the tired heart.

Hours have passed. You have sat bent over your work. Following your searching, winging thoughts your glance turns up and aside. There your eyes meet two other eyes which, who shall say how long already or why, have been watching you from the depth of the chair in which your friend lies curled up. No sound, no movement, nothing but two pairs of eyes which in the buzzing silence of the room meet, and in that meeting become aware of unexpected happiness. He wags his tail, scarcely perceptibly, but immovably he keeps looking at you, with persistent gentleness, as if he feared that by and by immeasurable seas will separate him from you again.

But these wide seas! They separate you even now, gulfs of spiritual and bodily differences not to be bridged. You are indeed out of each other's reach and yet, at the same time, touchingly near. You ask for miracles; here is one of the miracles surrounding you which you so carelessly pass by. For is not this a wonder greater than the meeting of two souls who can measure each other's virtues and needs in the depth of their own hearts?

This is the meeting of two souls flying to each other from two worlds which are irrevocably separated, different in kind, in aim and destination. And yet, just as a power that moves the universe rushes through the infinite, incalculable distances, so a small spark of that same power can do away with all distances and separations between two beings and kindle the desire for warmth in their hearts.

I have not tried to draw the picture of a special dog for you, for this would be doing injustice to the kind. To be honest, I must acknowledge that my thoughts have been stimulated by the remembrance of a small, black friend who accompanied me on the road of life for a while. The time was too short certainly, for I assure you that we had not nearly reached the end of our grateful astonishment at each other.

I am now thinking of his coming and departing. I saw him for the first time at my back-door, bright, strong, very young still, out of breath from running behind the bicycle of a grocer's boy. We caressed each other, and a mutual liking at once sprang up. So he stayed with me. Indeed, this was a happy day in our lives. I remember the warm love he gave me, the many-colored joy he brought me, the rest with all its beautiful revelations from which his presence dispelled the too great loneliness. When I saw him as he lay stretched out, the warmth of life ebbing from him, I fully realized that he had been my superior, at least in never-failing honesty. He was my superior also in strong self-completeness.

At last, he pathetically inclined his soft head to the great rest, and I realized that he who had so often overtaken me with wild joy was now irrevocably in front of me on that long, uninterrupted course which we all make through the secrets of inscrutable nature.

Translated by J. F. De Wilde
(From *The World's Best Essays,* copyright 1929, Harper & Brothers, New York)

Aart van der Leeuw

MINIATURES

FREDERICK THE WHISTLER.

During my youth, whistling was considered the exclusive privilege of schoolboys.

What fun it was to wander around with hands in one's pockets, head tilted backwards and lips pursed, to sling one's fanfares into the air! Those who attended the *gymnasium* only seldom indulged in this pastime, and then only by mistake, when they had for instance had an unexpected holiday given them or had been to a party the night before. Students were in no case allowed to do so, and once your clothes were cut to the pattern of a doctor's, a clergyman's, or a captain's, as you promenaded through town, it was equal to having yourself torn to shreds and thrown to the dogs still to indulge in whistling. Yet there was F. N., professor, mind you, at the Polytechnic School within our walls, who daily committed the sin of whistling a given solo on the public thoroughfare.

The result of that was that he received the nickname "Frederick the Whistler."

The story goes that one day he was rebuked for such bad manners by a friend. He looked up surprised, reflected and then said: "I believe that I do it when I see something in the street."

Of course the friend had not been able to keep quiet, and so this extraordinary explanation had been spread abroad, even reaching the school benches. With the result, that we nosy people had to find out what was at the bottom of it all. On the street? Something pleasant?

That was something to be thoroughly investigated.

"Here he comes," we whispered to each other one beautiful spring morning. Right in front of us, F. N. was navigating past the houses next to the canal. Solitary and in deep silence; only a silly little girl tripped close by, a skinny thing on long, skinny spindle-legs, with a ridiculous braid over her shoulder. Nowhere else was there anything in sight, and yet we suddenly had to listen breathlessly; we held a finger into the air. There it was, and not another mortal was in sight but that chit with her music briefcase. On the street? And what was pleasant about it? The spirited whistling lost itself in the distance, because we had stopped in order to submit the housefronts, the windows and the basements to a closer scrutiny. All in vain.

The second time we came upon his track, it was again on the street along the canal, again in the morning; it was a market day, but too early for much traffic. Only a flower boat was sailing through the water, a fat skipper at the rudder. We could hardly withstand the temptation to bombard him with horse apples. And we were sorry that at that moment we couldn't find anything to throw. . . . Moreover, we didn't have the time. . . . We were dogging Frederick's steps. He was walking slowly along, sunk in thought. Suddenly we saw him looking around, as if somebody had called him, to his right at the house, above there he started whistling, as if the world should be witness to it.

"But why?" we asked ourselves, completely at a loss.

And then there was that hot day in August, when I and a little friend were playing marbles. I had scooped out a hole with my five fingers, only there was such a vibrating heat rising from the ground that sweat rolled into our eyes, and all our aims failed to find the mark. Mad, hot and carelessly holding our caps in our fists, we marched homeward, and who should meet us in the middle of the sunniest street of the city but Frederick the Whistler. As usual, he walked sunk in a problem, somewhat bent, frowning with his mouth tightly shut. When he was only a step away from us, he lifted his head, glared at me and, at the same time, like powder that has been touched off by a spark, a triumphant march burst forth from his lips.

"Nonsense!" we mumbled.

Still I could not refrain, as soon as I was at home, from posturing curiously before the mirror. I felt deeply ashamed. I was scarlet, my hair was tousled and apparently I had rubbed the result of my gravedigger's labor over my face, because there was a broad black smudge running from my nose over my chin.

"Is Frederick the Whistler crazy?" I asked that afternoon at the table.

"Quite the contrary," my father said as he laughed.

He remained a riddle to us.

THE MERCHANT WITH THE BLUE FEZ.

I want to warn you against the Oriental merchants, the Persians, who come to your door luring you with their rugs. Mostly they wear a red fez, but the one I will tell you about had a blue one.

I have a friend living here with his wife. Highly respectable, solid and level-headed people; very rich and without children; not old at all, but still, past their youth.

One morning they find this Persian standing in their hallway. After a few dignified salaams he spreads his rug over the floor. A beauty; smouldering in its subdued tints; bronzy green, wine-red, and in between garlands of branches and flowers, motifs of animals. He asks a fabulous price for it.

"Are you crazy, fellow!"

"A prayer rug, two thousand years old."

Solemnly, slowly, he lets himself down onto it, crossing his legs, and then he invites the lady to sit next to him. Heaven knows why, but she does it; she is sitting, however, not on the floor, but on the saddle of a snow-white ambling horse. Separated from the hunting procession, she has lost her way between the bronzy green and the wine red. She sees a horseman approaching, a prince apparently, bejeweled and with a turban, his right hand on the gold leather rein, and in the left hand a hooded falcon. He greets her.

"Will you do me the honor of being my guest? Close by, my palace is awaiting you."

A reception like a fairy tale. Music in the evening.

"Yes, but my husband at home. . . ."

Which does not alter the fact that before a year is gone by she gives birth to a daughter, and after an equal amount of time, to a son. Twelve children one after another. So she lives prosperously and happily. And finally she dies from nostalgia and worry, because the council of the viziers, in which her lover had to participate, lasted an hour longer than had been arranged. With all the twelve children following her bier she is buried.

"Well," says the Persian, as he helps her to her feet. She can't utter a word.

It is my friend's turn now. He obeys also, lets himself sink down with a sigh, has some difficulty in folding his short legs and tries to maintain his balance no, not on the rug, but on the hump of a camel's back. Following him is an endless caravan, bales and boxes piled in between hairy humps. Through luxurious country. . . . For his merchandise he will get tenfold the amount it cost him two weeks ago. New provisions are bought for the money obtained, which he hopes to get rid of at twenty times the purchase price in Bagdad. He is figuring. The ships of the desert swing along lazily and undisturbed, until suddenly, from the side of the bushes a shrill whistling sound pierces the air. Robbers. Clash of arms—the attack—the retinue is hacked to pieces. They spare his life. They chain him in order to sell him in the first village as a slave. He is sold to a miserably poor baker who cannot even afford a horse. He will now have to tread in the mill; and if there is the slightest bit of dirt in the flour or a kernel that has not been completely ground, he receives the only too well-known number of blows with a stick from the Thousand and One Nights. Thus he lives until his beard has become white. And he dies, because the giver of the blows with the stick has lost count and given him one more than the original order entitled him to. He is buried.

"Well?" asks the Persian, as he helps him up.

He, too, is unable to utter a syllable.

And the merchant asks for double the amount he first mentioned.

"Come on, don't you want to, husband?" his wife whispers hastily.

"Get out!" my friend shouts, scarlet of face. And if the rug merchant had not disappeared instantly, as if he had sunk through the floor, he would have left the house in a very untender fashion.

They both told me their adventures, but they did not tell each other. She has become restless: since then she must go to all kinds of places at night to find amusement, and she asks everybody for news about the Persian with the blue fez. My friend has, however, subscribed to still more newspapers and from early morn to late at night he sits there with a dark and worried face and tries to decipher the news about the crisis.

So when a merchant with a carpet under his arm comes ringing your doorbell. . . .

THE STOVE.

Autumn winds, the dance of withered leaves, and the rain pinpointing your window. . . . It is getting cold, and you forgive yourself for having sent somebody out to get it.

"Come in!"

Two pitchblack smith's helpers bring it in and set it down on some part of your carpet, "Je brule tout l'hiver sans m'éteindre" —a Goddess-salamander stove, unwieldy, as tall as a man.

"All right, thank you."

It is impossible to live without some kind of rhythm to give some measure to your getting up, your meals and your going to bed; your thoughts stumble, when they don't run in some kind of verse form, and especially in your surroundings you need some kind of melody. The table. No, it cannot be moved, the closet occupies a definite place, and may the hand wither that takes the picture from its spot; your fireplace—the mantel, mirror and vases—impossible to move. And into the midst of all this comes this cast-iron monster like an animal on four legs, and it opens a maw like a monster in tales for children.

"Ought to make a fire right away," you mumble thoughtfully and you stare anxiously at the shiny black lead. And of course the stink lasts for two days. You retire into a corner of the room, cough, sniff and make a lot of erasures in your writing, and in the meantime your torturer grunts, snores and rattles, sends forth smoke and greets you as you pass with the mocking smile of a falling spark behind the mica. That is the way it starts, and there follows immediately the betrayal of the cat, Theodorus. Day in day out he has lain cozily on the chair next to your desk, rolled into a ball, or awake, straight up, proudly sticking out the white shield of his breast, taking you in with the sphinxlike glare of his yellow green eyes. His calmness made your work restful, and his dignity helped mold your sentences. But now he noiselessly glides from his cushion, slinks in the direction of the Goddess, sniffs the plate, poker and coal-scuttle, and chooses a place right in front of the metal feet of the new master.

"Dorus!" you call severely, but he turns the side of his tail toward you. Disowning you, turning against you. "Desertion," you mumble; in reality he seems more of a mediator between yourself and your enemy.

The wind has changed, and you are prevented from looking through the window at the garden by the flora of frost-flowers. You shove somewhat nearer to where it is warm; first you let a shovelful of anthracite and coke thunder down the dragon's maw, because this gives a more sparkling, effervescent glow; and then Dorus jumps onto your lap.

"Yes, dearest, the three of us."

You have surrendered your sword, and now your scepter follows also. You are dethroned; and the one who makes the laws from now on is the intruder. He shows you a chair: not this one, but the more comfortable one; excellent . . . somewhat closer by, it does not matter . . . and then he sends you to work, weaves dreams around you, and that is the devil of it, puts you even to sleep. He chooses your reading for you. *Treasure Island, Great Expectations, The Moonstone,* adventures, in English, of course, language of the hearth, of winter freshness. You read about the sea, plots, famine, snowdrifts and stolen jewels, while your head is resting comfortably on a down pillow, and you let your legs roast.

That is the degeneration you gradually achieve. Theodorus purrs. Without pangs you hear the wall clock ticking, and when you get up it is only to fill the glowing belly of the moloch with a fresh offering. Months go by, and the famous rhythm you subscribed so heavily to has completely slipped your mind. "Je brule tout l'hiver" has become the focal point of your room.

Until the ice starts to melt, and the breeze from the south acquires a fragrance. Outside you suddenly hear a thrush sing, from a vase on your mantelpiece dangle a few snowdrops, and in front of your window a crocus blooms.

Yes, really . . . but the stove grumbles, rattles and laughs mockingly with the falling sparks. You wipe your moist brow and have to open the windows. And still not before the midsummer sun glows in the blue sky do you dare to come to a decision.

"Yes, come in!"

Theodorus, deathly scared, crawls under the settee.

"Careful now!" and the two pitchblack smith's assistants drag away your comrade—host, guest—into the hallway, one on each side like the carriers of shields.

"So long," you sigh, sadly left alone, button up your coat and again put your chair in front of your desk.

THE TWO SWANS.

They lived in the pond of an old rundown country house. Their owner, who was a character, called them Marceline and Vondel. Marceline in memory of Madame Desbordes-Valmore, because that poetess had passionately sobbed over betrayed love, had prayed most fervently, and because it had been she who, when she lifted her little daughter Ondine from her bed, felt under the armpits there the beginning of growing wings. He too had lost a woman who had been very dear to him.

As far as the other name of the Dutch poet is concerned, comment seems unnecessary.

The owner of the country estate was not rich; he had no car, no telephone and no radio; he only had a son, a small boy. Therefore he often came to look at the swans, in the summer, in the afternoon, when Vondel, its white feathers folded, let itself float with the breeze on the water, like a legendary barque, and Marceline drifted about along the shore and was caught in the golden maze of sun and shade. He came in the evening, too, in the moonlight, when they were dripping with quivering silver foam to see them rise and flap their wings.

Of course, this seems *vieux jeu,* but, for a lonely dreamer who tried to cure his sorrow, not without charm.

Young Richard fed them early every morning. I am sorry but I cannot avoid mentioning, that he wore his hair in long brown curls and also had a lace collar over his green velvet blouse, that he was pale, short and well behaved; yes, well, he looked like a prince. He called the swans by the names whose significance he still did not understand. They approached confidently. Vondel laid his head in Richard's hands, and Marceline, her neck on his knees, while the little master sat on his haunches.

Every spring for a month, Richard transferred his job of chief bread-distributor to his father. Because then Marceline sat on her five or six eggs, the leaves and branches of an island in the center of the pond, while Vondel, all his feathers bulging, stood guard like an angry Turk. The young never remained long in the spot of their birth.

As soon as they had lost their grey down and begun to glow in the light of fall, they rose on their beautiful feathered pinions, and disappeared behind the beech woods. One could hear the report of rifle shots in the neighborhood, and whether somewhere else a new colony was ever started is a question nobody can answer.

The child became ill and died. His strange father went away, and because he had also suffered financial losses he wanted to sell the country estate. Nobody put in a bid; there was no road communicating with it, and though the city was gradually extending its western end day by day, foot by foot, it was still at some distance.

The empty house gradually fell into ruin, and the garden became wild. Vondel and Marceline began to know what loneliness was. Sometimes a little girl, who was taken for an idiot by the villagers, brought them the crumbs of her bread but otherwise they had to collect their food from the mud of the pond. They swam in their stately way with proudly upheld necks through the still brown water, perhaps even more beautiful now that nobody was spying on them.

Then there came a winter when Marceline could not disengage herself from the ice of a frosty night and she had to sing her swan song.

Vondel still lives, still fills the region of slumbering foliage, a thoughtful reflection of the grandiose dream vision of his presence, and seems to want to surpass the almost hundred years of his famous namesake by five years or more.

In the neighborhood there runs the fairy tale that he wanted to wait for a solution, one of two: either that the city would reach the country estate, which would be divided up, a network of roads would be built on it, and the pond filled in, in which case he would perish, and his down would be sold; or that the city itself—by a natural disaster, or it might also be through force of arms—would be destroyed, in which case the limits of the park would be extended, and the kingdom of the swan would be established for ever.

THE DOOR.

One of the greatest wonders of childhood is the life of those things about which everybody says that they are dead, their breath, their heartbeat.

Of course, a closet has a face, and the singing tea-kettle is blessed with a voice. But you never feel things living as vividly around you as when you are in bed at night or have to stay under the covers during the daytime because you are ill. There is nothing which then chooses to remain firmly in its appointed place and does not slink from dusky corners and gather back of where your head rests. The lamp lowers itself like a giant spider along its thread, the flowers of the curtains multiply luxuriously along the walls like the *berceau* of a rococo garden that has grown wild, and covers the edge of your bed.

Everything possesses a soul, but in the whole house there is no presence that turns such a living face upon you as the doors.

There is in the first place the door of the living-room, where you spend a while every day. How many times during the day did you clutch its knob, and that is why the imprint of your nearly unsoiled fingers makes a garland of worship around its keyhole. When it swings creakingly on its hinges, you need not look around to see whom it lets in. The rustling of Mother's skirt you recognize from a thousand other noises, as well as the heavy booted steps of Father.

The porte brisée is more standoffish. White and gilt, it makes one think of a bride, whom you admire from afar, but do not touch. When you pull away its veils and when it opens solemnly, it is the furniture whose company you may enjoy but for a moment. You see somebody get up and nod at you, but before you have been able to make up your mind how you should react toward this unknown smile, and while you plant yourself more firmly on your small legs and stretch out your neck from curiosity, Father and Mother have disappeared and you are left staring again at the snow and gold of the bridal dress.

Then its neighbors, the garden doors. They are more frankly genial. Between the frame that encloses the glass they hold many beautiful promises, and still, when they are rattled open, they give much more than they even promised. In the first place they allow the breeze that is laden with fragrance to blow in, then they make way for the footstep of the sun upon the doormat, and at the same time call in the notes of the finch and the song of the thrush and thus summer steps in with its greens and blues and takes your little hands stretched out in welcoming gesture.

One door only is unmoved by the wish of a child. Stern and forbidding in the dusk, it precedes you into the bedroom and closes with a metallic creaking of its hinges. At the same time it buries the lovely day and buries it irrevocably in the grave from which no dead ever rise. When everything has become dark, it glares at you with the glimmer of a sleepless eye.

Yes, all those doors, but none equals the one of the hundredth gate of the hundred and ninth night of the Arabian tales, I mean the door that you are never allowed to open.

The most fascinating place, wherever you look, is the attic. Like an explorer you wander amid all the secrets of discarded articles of household. From the leaky garden tools you remove the rust; from a tear that is as long as an arm you bring the contents of a mattress to light, you try to climb the moldering rungs of a small stepladder, and on a flagpole you try the giant swing. In the meantime you hear the birds scratching in the gutter and see a spider weave its web between the beams. When you pull the dirty clothes basket aside, and turn an empty box on its side, then you suddenly stand with an accelerated heartbeat before a firmly locked door.

It is simpler than any of those I am in the habit of opening. It is unpainted firwood full of splinters and with a knob of rough iron. How many times did I not climb onto the wobbly little bench and push and pull, without ever being successful. Sometimes Mother surprised me while I was at it. She looked at me frightened, lifted an admonishing finger and shook her head as if she were very worried. Thank God, she had the tact never to disclose to me the secret of what was hidden behind that lock and bolt.

Thus I could imagine behind that forbidden threshold the sleeping princess resting on her bed underneath the thorns, it could hide Ali Baba's forty thieves in their oil vessels, and I could see Bluebeard's wives dangling from their ropes. I sat down on a chair with a broken back and tried to fathom the heart of the silent door. Hours passed that way, apparently aimless, but now I know that I then filled the boxes and trunks with precious things that never lose their value, the jewels of my dreams.

MELODRAMA.

For a short time I had to stay in a foreign city.

One night there, it was already late. . . . I was bored, the noise of the traffic was dying down in the streets. I entered a theater, bought a ticket and purchased a program. I was shown a seat. The first piece, a drama, had already ended; what we were waiting for was the last one, a one-act play by a Russian author, as I read on my program, played by two people, Dimitri and Natasha. They had already raised the large curtain; only two heavy, purple velvet curtains with tassels and fringes at the borders hid the

stage. Three short hard knocks, and the curtains began to separate slowly in a singing sweep. A small part of the stage became
visible; a trunk on the floor—it might represent a hotel room—
and in the background a window through which one could see
high mountain tops that glimmered white as if they were covered
with snow. But then something remarkable happened, yes, almost frightening; a man jumped onto the boards from the front,
grabbed the curtains that were being pulled aside with his two
fists, and tried to pull them toward himself and close them. His
face, a savage Danton head, glowed with the effort.

"Stop! No, I don't want it," he shouted toward the side-wings,
and still louder and more passionately, as if he answered something that was called to him: "That the sun is shining on the
carpet, and that the country people are singing harvest songs as
they are coming down the mountain paths, and that a mighty
love will bloom, what does that matter when every step I take
will bring me closer to the noose, when the gallows is waiting for
my neck. I refuse; I won't." And he planted his nails in the velvet
folds, that tried to loosen themselves from the spasm of his
fright.

Suddenly, the flight of feet, somebody ran toward him who up
until now had remained hidden. My heart started to beat, I had
never seen such a beautiful woman, half undressed, in her white
underthings, a blonde with a braid partially undone on a naked
shoulder.

"Come, quiet down," she said, "it is no good, we have to," and
carefully she tried to disengage his hand. He shook her loose.

"In order to sit together on the edge of the bed," he said in a
choking voice, "and then you say: 'Dearest, my Dimitri, tomorrow
we say goodbye forever,' and I answer: 'That isn't allowed, that is
not possible, Natasha.' Slowly and emphatically you repeat: that
is not possible. And then there will be talk about that trip, the
trip of the three of us, you, I and Vladimir, who is your husband.
Very soon, this morning. And I explain to you, that the path is
steep, even dangerous at one spot. 'Dangerous?' and you look at
me with a glance that chills my blood. And in the next scene we
have really reached the spot—rocks, snow, and solitude, and—
'Vladimir,' I say, 'do you hear the Djiester seething? Bend down
and you will see it breaking down there on the cliffs.' And he
bends down and I grab him by the back of the neck and hurl
him then into the depths. And in the last scene we are again in
that room, and we pack our trunks because we are going to leave.
O freedom, safety; because we do not know, two poor foolish

blind ones, that the dead Vladimir holds a shred of my blouse, or is it a knot, clutched in his fist, and that the imprint of my five fingers is plainly and deeply visible on his throat. We whisper, because we feel a burden weighing on our hearts. There is a knock. Deathly pale, you rise and open. Three men enter the door, each of them with a revolver in his right hand. I tell you, I refuse, I won't do it."

Like a fly caught in a web he stood between the folds and the tassels convulsively clutching at the curtains with his arms.

"Come on," she soothed, "quiet down," while gently she stroked his hair.

Yes, and you saw it, his grip now became weaker, and suddenly, in a quick gust of wind, the curtains flung open. It was the hotelroom, the sun shone on the carpet, and outside you heard that harvest song. They sit down on the elge of the bed— "Dearest, my Dimitri," she said, "tomorrow we must say goodbye forever." "That can't be, that's impossible, Natasha," he mumbled feebly, and as if with endless effort. At the same time the curtain closed, the spectators rose, after weak applause, and the hall began to empty itself. A strange play.

Translated by ALFRED VAN AMEYDEN VAN DUYM

P. H. van Moerkerken

PSAMMETICUS PHILOLOGUS

IN THE FIRST PART OF THE SECOND BOOK OF HIS HISTORIES, HERODOtus relates that once upon a time the great and shrewd king Psammeticus devoted himself to the hoary-venerable science of philology. When this monarch became the absolute ruler of Egypt, about the middle of the seventh century before our Christian era, he turned his mind to various matters of spiritual value, among them the knowledge of bygone centuries, the fates of peoples and kingdoms.

In these times the Egyptians fancied themselves the oldest people in the world. And their mighty monarch, whose mind was searching for a clear truth among the faded traditions, believed this, too, when he rode along the rippling banks of the Nile and beheld on the western horizon the mysterious triangles of the thousand-year-old monuments of kings; he imagined it—

and his people too—his subjects, as he roamed with the priests, through the lane of sphinxes at Thebes or stepped beneath the high pillars of their temples. Never had the Greek seamen and Syrian merchants, whom he had met while living in exile in the marshes close to the sea, told him of graves thirty centuries old or of pyramids or granite statues erected by any other people for their heroes and kings.

Yet Psammeticus was in quest of scientific certainty and, since his wisdom embraced a wealth of unknown sources, he knew how, in this historical problem, to obtain help by an experimental method.

From a farmer's family living on a hill between humid Nile fields, he bought their newborn child and took it, together with the young child of one of his mistresses, to a goat-herd, a three-days' journey away, whose hut was in the arid mountains of the Arabian desert. There, in a little shed near the goat stable, royal baby and villager's offspring would be kept by the lonely man, separated from the world. The king bade him never to speak a word in the children's presence and to forbid entrance to the hut, to everyone, be it ruler of the Persians or high priest of Thebes. He was to feed the children with milk from his goats, but otherwise to leave them to themselves.

In this way sagacious king Psammeticus set out to discover what word the children would pronounce first, after the period of confused stammering. That word, he thought, must be a word from the oldest language of the world, spoken by the most ancient people.

The goat-herd, a silent old man who, like all the slaves of those remote times, knew not even the temptation to disobey, took care of the little ones as prescribed by the king; they grew and prospered in the pure air of the lonely mountains, safe from the contagion of children's diseases. They drank the goat's milk and ate a porridge of brittle cakes that was prepared by the old man in a cave behind the shack.

Two years passed. Then . . . but here I must interrupt the history of Herodotus for a little while.

The thoughtful inquisitive mind of that great historian knew a great deal, it is true; but we, who are living twenty-four centuries later, know far more, even about king Psammeticus, although Herodotus traveled to Egypt less than two hundred years after his reign. It is indeed recognized by all present-day historians as a psychological as well as a common logical fact that the greater the time separating us from an individual or a nation the better we are able to view and understand them. Geerard Brandt in his *Life of Vondel* made errors which have been corrected by our contemporaries. The intimate friends of Rembrandt and Napoleon failed to probe the depths of those titanic souls to such an extent as the history-delvers of our day with the help of old bills and church records, old letters and secret archives. Few poets have given rise to an equally voluminous literature as Shakespeare, of whom we know nothing with reasonable certainty. And should I myself, in all modesty, ever undertake to describe the life of one of my poet friends for the coming generations, I am fully aware that the professor of literature of the twenty-fourth century will condemn and shut away in the stifling narrowness of a nutshell as an unscientific jest or a psychological impossibility many a wondrous anecdote to which I was an eye-witness.

How then could Herodotus have known what were the veritable facts of history—when his spokesmen, the priests of Memphis, Heliopolis, Thebe, were ignorant of them?

A year after Psammeticus had delivered his philological preparation to the lonely goat-herd, a foreign traveler appeared in the midst of the imposing precipices and the scorched-dry desolation of the mountain range. He climbed from granite block to granite block; he found no paths but followed goat tracks, glancing about from ever increasing heights. And many times he stopped to rest. For he was no longer young, and his yellow complexion was not like the tan caused by the burning of the sun or the fierceness of winter-night storms: it was the sallowness of old tallow candles, of soiled parchment, of much unrolled papyrus. He walked with a stooping gait, not like that of a farmer but of a man in search of immaterial things. His right hand grasped a staff—the left held in place a threadbare cloak around his waist; slim were they, these hands, with pallid, pointed fingers. A grizzly beard hung shaggily down over his hollow chest; his unwashed feet shuffled along in dusty sandals.

He came from far off, over sea and over land, from the Phrygian city of Cibyra, which he had never left before. But an Egyptian slave had come to see him in his quiet cell and had shown him the signet-ring of his younger brother who had sailed with Carien pirates to the marshy lands of the Nile estuary. The slave brought back fantastic tales. In the war waged by the pirates in the service of Psammeticus against the eleven other kings of Egypt, the old man's brother had been killed, but a Greek woman, who had followed him from one of the islands, had shortly after given birth to a girl child. This child had been brought up in the royal palace of Memphis. There, four years before the time of which we are speaking, the mighty Psammeticus saw her one evening as she sat staring from the highest arcade over the grey-damp plains to the north. He took her into the women's quarters, where, because of her sparklingly clear mind and intoxicating beauty, she became the monarch's chosen one. A child was born to her, but immediately was taken from its mother's breast by the king himself. After a few months only, Psammeticus, yielding to the girl's constant pleading, had told her of the child's fate. He had taken it, he said, together with a lowly peasant's baby, to the lone mountains where the sun rises, so that he might hear once and for all from these children a word not taught them by human lips but whispered into their deepest being by nature itself, the word which would reveal to the king the language of the oldest people of the world.

The young woman, who still loved the tongue of her Greek parent and, amid the splendor of her surroundings, dreamed of the never beheld country of her ancestors, now sent her most devoted slave to her father's brother, who lived in the town of Cibyra of which a pale youthful recollection still lived on through old tales told by her mother. For a great idea had come to her that night when the king had confessed the purpose of his kidnapping; she wanted the people from which she had sprung glorified as the oldest of the earth, to hear the Phrygian tongue praised as the first spoken by human lips. Therefore she sent the slave to her father's brother, so that he, if still among the living, might carry out the proud though deceitful plan. He must cross the ocean and, in the mountains east of the Nile, search for the lonely hut where the two children were isolated from human language. He must go to them secretly and whisper to them one Phrygian word, which they would learn to stammer as a first greeting and prayer to their keeper and to king Psammeticus. So the old man, at this cry from the heart of a young woman whom he had never seen, started out upon his journey. With moist eyes he closed the little cell in which, among learned scriptures, he had roamed through worlds of beauty and knowledge and wisdom for half a century. The voice of his blood was calling him, the pride of his country's tongue.

He sat down on a rock on the edge of the precipice and his eyes sought a well, for his thirst was great after the long hours of wearisome climbing in the heat of the shadowless slopes. But his gaze found no luscious green of dew-soaked meadows, no waving tree tops; only grey nettles and sun-scorched grasses sprouted out of the thin layer of earth that covered the rocks here and there.

Then he heard from far off the sound of the little herd bells and saw, high up, the goats grazing in the sparse grass. Filled with new hope he continued on his way, craving to drink their milk.

Suddenly, at the foot of a perpendicular wall full of caves he perceived a rustic hut. And he pondered: could it be there? Where else? . . . For here he had found the first glimpse of life after days of roaming through desolate wilderness. . . .

The mouldering door fell open under the pressure of his trembling hand but, blinded by the scorching heat of the barren rocks, he saw nothing but darkness inside.

He listened. Outside sang the far-off bells of the herd; but from a corner of the somber shack came the plaintive wail of a child.

The grey Phrygian stepped back. He feared discovery by the herdman; secretly, with utmost caution, he had to bring his niece's proud plan to reality, he who knew nothing but the deeds of the mind and the contemplative life. He must watch the children's keeper, find out the hours when he drove forth the herds and when he brought them back, so that he might then approach the little creatures undisturbed and teach them the first word of a human tongue.

He hid in a narrow, elevated cave. He lured a goat to him and refreshed himself with her milk; he ate the hard bread which he had brought with him from the last village on the border of the desert. And for three days he remained there, spying from the obscurity of his cave the pursuits of the lonely herdman.

He knew now that the entrance to the hut would be safe from morning to evening. On the fourth day he left the shadow of his rock and entered the hut, feeling his way to where he had heard the vague, childish sounds. His hands were still trembling, for he was about to deceive the mighty ruler of all Egypt.

He offered the children bread covered with sweet dried fruits —and when they grabbed it with their tiny hands, and he thought he recognized in the noble face of the frailest of the two the features of his long-lost brother, tears welled up in the eyes of the lonely scholar.

In a soft voice he spoke a word, the first word that had reached the children's ears: "Bekós."

And he repeated, pointing to the bread: "Bekós, bekós."

They were silent, but stared at him with wondering eyes.

And for days on end, during many weeks he came to them, speaking the same word, always that one word. They tried, still awkward and inept of tongue, to repeat the word as soon as the old sage began to search in the pockets of his cloak for the sweet tid-bit. In those still days spent in meditation, the yearning for the short hours with the children became stronger and stronger. His sallow face lighted up with a smile at the happy gestures and strange cries of the little ones. And the approaching hour of parting filled him with sadness.

Yet the last day came, for he knew that they would soon cry out the strange word to the goat-herd and that he would report it to the king. For the first time in his life the Phrygian scholar kissed a child's face and, for the first time also, children's hands stroked his grizzly, disheveled beard.

Then he wearily descended by the loose rocks northward in the direction of the big cities in the plain.

Two years had passed—thus Herodotus resumes his story—since the lonely goat-herd had received the children from the king's hands.

Then, one morning as he opened the door of the hut, the children crawled over their straw bed to meet him and, their tiny arms outstretched, cried: "Bekós!"

He paid no heed to their sounds for he did not understand them. But when they greeted him with the same sounds for many succeeding mornings, he went off to inform the king, who bade him bring the children to him.

Now Psammeticus heard with his own ears the outlandish word. From the seaport towns at the Nile estuary he summoned to the palace merchants of many foreign lands and questioned them about the significance of those childish sounds. Finally a Phrygian traveler, an old stooped man wrapped in a drab cloak, told him that the word "bekós," in the language of his country, meant bread. And Lydian sailors of King Gyges confirmed this.

Satisfied with this philological research by the outcome of his experiment, King Psammeticus let it be known to his wives and to all his Egyptians, to the priests, the soldiers, the artisans and the merchants, that the Phrygian people was the oldest of the world.

On the following evening, the loveliest and youngest of the

women smiled in a cryptic manner as she folded her arms around
Psammeticus' head. And the grey-headed linguistic scholars of
Alexandria bestowed upon the great king the title of doctor of
etymology, "sagacitatiṣ causa."

Translated by PAULINE BUKOVSKA

Gerard van Eckeren

PAST

THE GLASS REVOLVING DOOR, TURNED BY THE DOORMAN, HAD LANDED
them inside, and she stood for a moment at the entrance to the
lunchroom searching with her eyes over the moving heads of
many eating and talking people for an empty table. Then, resolutely, with a melodious "pardon" to a stout gentleman behind
a wiener schnitzel, she shot across to the window side, laid her
parasol and handbag on the white table cloth and stripped off
her gloves. Following her, more cumbersomely—why were there
suddenly all kinds of legs in his way and why did a little table
of giggling schoolgirls who sat poring over their afternoon lessons, stand across his path?—he felt a smile spreading under his
mustache. That was his sister all over: "the bee line"! She took it
in her marriage, the bringing-up of her children, the training
of her servants, even in the manner in which she steered to a seat
in a tea-room.

Sitting opposite her at the open window overlooking the sunny
shopping street where the loud sounds of rattling carts and trolleys running along rails mixed with the fine tinkling of bicycle
bells clamoured past them, he continued with a broadening smile
to watch her as, with the movements of a spruce little woman,
she made herself more comfortable, unbuttoned her coat, indicated to a passing white-jacketed waiter that he should add two
or three dirty plates from previous customers to his already high
heap of used crockery and then let the pink little nail of her
right forefinger wander hastily down the endless menu from top
to bottom—to Assorted Ices; after which the finger shot up again,
wavered for a moment in the middle of the card like a compass
needle, finally to rest with a very determined pressure on the
paper.

"For me just a small salmon salad. For you too?"

He nodded. Menus were his abomination; despite his bachelor life he still did not know his way about on them any better than in a Hebrew Bible.

"Two coffees?"

He nodded again and stared dreamily out of the window along the bluish smoke of his cigarette, while she gave her orders to the little black and white waitress.

In this street he had walked as a boy with a pile of books under his arm, coming home from the grammar school. Nothing seemed changed; or, yes, the trolleys were electrified, the sociable, jolting vehicle with a horse in front had long disappeared; but look! that hat shop opposite was still the same: the old firm-name still glittered in the same gold block letters on the glass pane, and the little man with the curly head who stepped to the open door with a pile of Borsalinos and let his brush dance over them was the same little man that had sold him his caps and, toward summer—a great event!—his first brand new straw hat. . . .

There it was again, that strange feeling! Something in him sank, a melancholy which did not smart; it rather resembled a sweet, faint pain. And in the crowded room, there was bright reality. She told him in a matter-of-fact voice about Kitty who had met a young man at her dancing lesson. . . .

"You see, you understand. . . . I have talked to Evert about it, and he too finds the child far too young. The boy hasn't a job yet, no prospects. Oh well! fortunately the dancing lessons are now stopping for the summer, and Kitty's tennis club is full; no new members are being admitted there. So I hope that for the time being the danger is over. . . ."

She remained silent, preparing her salmon salad with care.

"Wait a minute. Let me help you. Men do these things so clumsily. . . ."

She exchanged the plates; like an obedient boy he pushed his toward her.

"And how does Kitty feel about it?" he asked in order to say something.

"Well, you know . . . bitter tears. . . . Do you want salt and pepper?"

He nodded slowly, his thoughts with his fair-haired niece who could laugh so boisterously. Well, yes, Emily was right.

Then he asked: "Do you realize that this is the town where we used to live as children? The same houses, the same paving stones. . . ."

She looked up from her plate and glanced round the room for a fleeting moment.

"Eh? What's that? Oh, yes, funny, isn't it? But this place did not exist then. Well, I find it an improvement. . . ."

"No, you girls used to go to an ordinary confectioner's when you had a treat after an exam or something like that. . . ."

"Yes. At the corner of Cock's Alley. There was such a good one there! And we poked our hat pins in to see if there was cream inside!"

She laughed a gay laugh that reminded him of earlier days. She now realized the situation fully. Then, again practical, she asked: "Have you a timetable? I think it would be awfully nice to go for a little walk along the ramparts with you—it happens so rarely that I have my cosmopolitan brother so quietly to myself, doesn't it?—but I don't want to get back to Amsterdam too late. The maids don't do a stroke of work when I am away, and for the children it is so unsociable if I am not at home for tea. The purpose of our trip has been achieved now; I find we have managed very well with that carpet, don't you?"

He turned the pages of the little book and moved his head a little; it was meant as an affirmation.

They had gone to G. together early that morning, as delegates of the brothers and sisters. "William has taste" had been the verdict "and so has Emmy. Besides, a man can't do a thing like that by himself; he only looks at the colors and design; for the quality it is as well if a woman is there too." And that is how it came that they—oh, rare occurrence!—now sat together in G. where was the store for carpets of the kind their mother wanted as a present for her seventieth birthday.

"Strange that they never have so much choice in Amsterdam as here."

"That is because the main store is here. The factory is here, too. What do you think of the 3.05?"

She did not answer. She had pressed the last leaf of lettuce together with the last little piece of pink salmon neatly with her fish-knife onto her fork and made it disappear between her full lips. Then, putting her fork and knife down on her plate, she pulled her chair a little nearer to the table and cupped her cheeks in her small hands. Then she looked at him, resting her elbows on the edge of the table.

"And?" she asked. Her long lashes blinked slowly over her dark eyes.

"And?" He smiled back, not quite comprehending. And yet a

vague uneasiness welled up in him; he gently flapped the time-table on the marble in front of him, then put his hand into his inner pocket to take another cigarette from his case.

"Well, what we talked about last time. How do matters stand now?"

"You mean . . ." he groped, uncertain.

"That short story that you were going to write . . . for the Family Album. Have you got anything yet? It is getting time. . . ."

Immediately he stiffened.

"I have already told you that I must ask to be excused. Really, Emmy, I can't. I have no subject and no inspiration. Whatever you like, but to work to order like that for an occasional album —that is nothing for me. Believe me, I would not be able to produce anything passable."

She continued to look at him from between her hands, an urging, compelling glance.

"Not even if it is for your seventy-year-old mother?"

His glance tried to escape the ban of her compelling eyes by turning to the street.

"Not even then," he said shortly.

She began speaking hastily, whispering, her voice cracking hoarsely occasionally with the strain of keeping her quickly rising indignation within the bounds of a subdued conversation.

"Then I'll tell you what it is: a lot of nonsense. Selfish love of ease and vanity. Yes, even if you are already shaking your head, I insist: it is vanity; you are afraid to compromise your name as a writer in an album in which girl cousins and boy cousins write down their well-meant little inanities. You are afraid that your piece will not show up too well in comparison; that what you write *about* and *for* your mother will be disappointing. They are all contributing. Jimmy has drawn something; Kitty I helped so long with her water-color motto till she . . . till. . . ."

"Till she wept bitter tears," he said sharply, spitefully. Immediately he regretted it.

"Your brother Nout has written a lovely, witty poem, and he is only a notary public. But you, the *famous author*, William Veenhorst! . . ."

"You need not say that so scornfully and emphatically. Besides, I am not famous."

"Well then, well-known. Everyone can do something, and everyone does. Only the well-known author William Veenhorst

can't scrape together even a little sketch or story out of love for
his old mother. I find that . . ."

"I will not and cannot 'scrape something together'! That's just
it, Emmy; please understand!"

His voice was gentle, almost imploring. He laid his hand on
her sleeve. "And hadn't we better go now? I don't find a lunchroom the place . . . outside on the ramparts we can talk much
better. Or shall we first have a whipped cream puff, eh?"

But she pulled her arm away impatiently.

"Thank you. I don't want to start it all over again. When I do
something I finish it all in one go" (the bee line, he thought
sarcastically) "and that is what I want to do in this case too. So
you won't participate. All right, I shall tell them. What they will
think, I don't know. But what I think of it, I'll tell you. In one
word I find it *mean.*"

"Then," he said icily, "we have no more to say to one another
for the moment. I'll go and pay at the buffet. Goodbye. . . ."

Her anger subsided immediately. With something of dismay
in her look, still dark with vexation and regret, she glanced at
him.

"Then, at least, wait till I . . . And we wanted to . . ."

"I no longer feel like a walk along the ramparts under the
circumstances. And you didn't want to get home too late, did
you?"

He stood close to her for a moment and his voice sounded
milder. "Believe me, Emmy, we had better part now. The walk
won't run away, and we'll have a talk another time. I wanted to
call on my friend Termeer. He will probably be at home still.
You can take my timetable along. Kind regards to Evert and the
children. . . ."

He waved a goodbye and walked slowly to the door; looked
round once again, waved again to where she sat at her table, taut
with surprise, fumbling at her handbag. Apparently she did not
notice his farewell.

In the street he sauntered on thoughtlessly for a few moments,
stood still in front of a shop and stared at the articles displayed
there without seeing them. The summer was so sultry around him
at this early hour in the afternoon; above him, the sun was
burning in the blue sky; somewhere at the back of his head was
still his sister's urgent whispering, like the noise of a distant
waterfall. He felt dull and crushed, heavy and sad. Then, while

he walked along the pavement a little more energetically, he caught himself expecting to hear her spruce little steps clattering behind him; he immediately slackened his pace. But although people came up behind him and passed him, his sister was not among them.

And then he suddenly resumed his pace. It was better so. The conversation again stood out clearly in his mind. "Mean" she had said—a word she certainly was already repenting. But had he behaved meanly toward her? Go back, express his regret? Tell her that he would try it after all? . . . Oh no, he had better leave it alone. Should he think it over again, how and what? Now better go on to Termeer. It would distract him a little after this disagreeable business.

It appeared that his old schoolmate was not at home; gone abroad, the maid told him. He walked idly through his native town; a spider-web of narrow streets round the old market square where the St. Jacobus church, gray and weathered by the ages, rose above the irregular roofs of low houses. The lace-work of the ancient spire hung like the petrified beards of grim mountain gods; the bells, green with age, hung in the black holes, and the freshly gilded dial-plates that indicated the time in all four directions shone in the midst of this gray venerability like fair gimcracks in a museum of antiquities. Of course, they were again busy restoring—had he ever seen this tower without the poor cloak of wooden planks? A workman, a little black figure from a toy box, looking very small, moved at the distant heights. He remained standing, while the bells tinkled slowly and laboriously, as if an inexperienced and unsure hand was turning a musical box. Like jingling coins, thoughtlessly scattered, the sounds fell on the patient houses with their stepped gables and dainty festoons, out of a time when builders were still artists.

A large modern dress shop had arrived, brutally hacked into the broad front of old houses on the south side; much brass, French polish and glass. Expressionless wax ladies displayed a crazy coquetry in the somber cast-shadow of the ages.

Through a narrow side street he reached the river with its rattling bustle of unloading and loading. The sun glistened on the water with the cold sharpness of polished steel; a departing freight boat snorted out a cloud of dirty yellow smoke into the blue quivering air. In front of the weighing-house purple-jacketed fellows were throwing greasily shiny cheeses from one to the other, as in a monotonous game of ball; on the slope wagoners cursed as they drove their horses: the cobblestones emitted sparks.

A barrel organ was snoring a whining tune on the other side
under the young green of a row of trees. Dreamily he watched
the dexterous ball-game with the cheeses; sniffed the sour smell
of pigs; looked at where the grocery store once stood that had so
often received the bashful boy with his satchel full of books and
his heart full of fear about the algebra sums which he again did
not know and which the patient fair-haired schoolmate up there
tried again and again in his rather weary, meek voice to explain.
. . . On a sailing trip years later his boat capsized and he was
drowned.

Walking on, he mused on his life as a full-grown man in St.
Petersburg, in Paris, where he had been sent by his newspapers.
For a moment it seemed to him as if he were walking in the
spacious remoteness of the Place de la Concorde, with cars rushing past him at a dangerous pace; then there was the pleasant,
fashionable crowd of the Rue de Rivoli at teatime; voluble
French rattled at his ears; he lunched on the Boul' Mich' at Harcourt's with Bihi, the proper little working girl who seemed so
affectionate and yet deceived him.

Suddenly he stood by the little medieval canal in front of the
House; his feet had carried him there, and he wasn't astonished,
for it had to be so. He smiled as if he had come home from a
long journey and the feeling overcame him as of someone who,
after a tiring trip, does not realize until then how fatigued he is.
He leaned against the iron railing and let his eyes wander over
what was old and familiar to him. He was in a small provincial
town that did not mark the passage of time. The water between
the dusty embankments lay green and nacreous in the depths;
a bridge with white painted balustrades led to the metaphorical
perspective of a little street, like the primitive background of a
vaudeville. He put his foot onto the stone steps of the house and
laid his hand on the brass bell-button. He was a schoolboy, coming home hungry. The door would open and he would sniff the
smell of roast meat and dried apples. His gray father was clattering in the hall closet, about to change his boots.

The door yielded and an old woman looked at him inquiringly.

"Did you ring?"

Yes, he had rung.

"Is . . .," he stammered.

"This is the club-house of pensioned sergeants," the woman
anticipated him, slightly snappy. Then, apparently under the
impression of the cut of his jacket—cut by Jean Délibart from

the Rue Saint Honoré—she inquired more gently: "Have you perhaps a message?"

And suddenly he understood that he really had a message; that he had come here to fulfill a mission.

"Madam," his voice still sounded a little unsure, "I have come to . . . view the house."

"It can't be viewed," she put him off promptly. Then again recovering submission to the cut-Délibart, Rue Saint Honoré, she explained:

"It is not to let, you see."

He nodded meditatively, realizing the strangeness of the situation . . . for her.

"And yet I'd like to see the house," he said, more to himself, "You see, I used to live here; twenty-five years ago."

Still the woman hesitated.

"That's a long time," she nodded, "my late husband used to say: Time, he'd say, does not stand still. He'd say . . ."

"So you understand that I am attached to this house; I should very much like to see it again, if only for five minutes."

Only on one other occasion had such power of persuasion rung in his voice. That somber December noon in the private room of his chief in Rotterdam, who had wanted to transfer him to London at a time when he wanted to stay in Paris at all costs— on account of a woman who deceived him. . . .

But the little woman at the door had already yielded. "Well, all right then, because it's you. . . ."

He crossed the threshold and entered the coolness of the marble passage, slightly astonished not to find the big table in it with the green plants, the pride and care of his mother.

"This," the woman explained opening the room on the right and letting him in, "is so to say the reception room for the majors who play dominoes in the evenings, you understand?"

He nodded absent-mindedly. How could he get rid of her? But she anticipated his wishes. "I should like to show the whole house," she hesitated, "but, you see, it is Friday and washing day." She looked at him uncertainly.

"You just go along," he said hastily, "I'll just walk round, if I may."

Two tooth-stumps became visible in the grinning little mouth. "Of course! There are no pitfalls here. Go right along."

Amiable and grateful, he nodded her out of the room.

He was alone. Through the drawn Holland curtains the summer sun poured a yellowish light on the bare tables and benches that stood where his father's writing table, book-cases and sofa used to stand. He saw a quiet figure in sober black moving in front of the wide rows of classics, and searching white hands moving caressingly along the shelves edged with strips of green flannel.

> My lord, I shall reply amazedly,
> Half asleep, half waking; but as yet, I swear
> I cannot truly say I came here. . . .

Was that not the voice of Shakespeare who spoke there, Shakespeare's Lysander from *Midsummer Night's Dream?*

> We the globe can compass soon
> Swifter than the wandering moon. . . .

What was Time, Space, a human life? Vanity of vanities, all is vanity. And yet . . . was it not as if the atmosphere of this bare room was still peopled with the spirits of all ages: Shakespeare, Tennyson, Homer, and Goethe? With all changes, with all things that grow weary and dull, was it not the spirit that, everlasting and unchanging, remains the same? "I shall be who I shall be. . . ."

He left the room and walked down the long passage; there in the round alcove near the kitchen he used to stand when he was "he," when they played at touch as children. In that little side room he used to drum his lessons and his catechism into his head. He climbed a stair in the back part of the house and wandered through empty lofts, lumber attic, play attic. Here the tin knights errant still gave their childish performances. Surely on this rusty nail the curtain used to be fixed that separated the nervous and often itching artists from the yawning public.

Back in the passage, he opened the door next to his father's wardrobe. (No doubt there now hung the uniform and dress-sword of one or another sergeant-major) and stood at the foot of the steep steps leading upstairs. As he climbed, a step creaked as of old. He wandered through the bedrooms, after a preliminary modest tap at each door; there was some scrapped furniture; somewhere stood an iron shake-down. He climbed still higher to the attic, the loft, and looked out of the dormer window, down to the quiet canal. The old trees carried their fresh green like flowery bouquets. A little girl, a small white figure, was skipping at the water's edge.

Downstairs again he opened the door to the suite at the back of the house. Here was the room overlooking the garden, the heart of the house. There a table used to stand, and there the stove, and over there his mother's little book-case full of old-fashioned writings, among which "Little John" was his first acquaintance with modern literature. And in that corner, the piano. Emily sat in front of it, practising her Heller studies. No, it was his mother, and she was singing. The room was half dark and the golden candlelight flooded her dear face. Her short-sighted eyes stared at the sheet of music and her hands moved a little helplessly over the keys, but her voice sounded like that of a nightingale, so clear and pure in the listening stillness.

He pushed up a window and sat down on one of the wide window-seats, staring into the garden. Not much of it had remained; factory sheds stood where their sand-heap had once been. He folded his hands and sat still a long time. He thought of his mother and of a girl he had loved and watched a little bird that sat rocking itself in a shrub. The sinking sun shone on a piece of weathered wall with ivy upon it, and above in the sky floated the rarefied sounds of the St. Jacobus chimes. Time held its breath, shrank away till it met Eternity and then only the Everlasting survived. They were all as they had always been, and it seemed to him as if he had always known that he would find his dear ones here again. He had known it, in St. Petersburg and in Paris, in the autumns when he had walked along the Champs Elysées under the dying yellow of the autumn trees, in the gay nights on Montmartre and in Montparnasse, with Bibi in St. Cloud, and in the bitter loneliness of his room when she had deserted him. They were all assembled here and awaiting him: his deceased father, his mother, his sisters and brothers, the girl he had loved.

The little bird, tired of rocking, flew up, but another bird immediately took its place. The sun, which lay on the shrubs like golden powder, pierced shining edges along the somber leaves of the ivy. The St. Jacobus chimed again and by degrees he learned to distinguish the feeble little air:

"What God does is done well."

He thought also of the wise man of the Paviljoensgracht, the optician and of his motto: Bene agere et laetari.

Then the door opened and on the threshold stood his sister. Behind her the caretaker's wife made an embarrassed, apologetic gesture.

"You here, William?"

"You here, Emmy? And I thought . . ."

"That I wanted to be home early, eh? And I did, too. But I missed my train, and then . . ."

She walked up to him and put her hands on his shoulders.

"Do you know, I have always longed just once more in this house. . . . But I could not have imagined that . . ."

He had risen and threw his arms round her.

"Emmy, forgive me. . . ."

"Forgive you, boy? I know very well that I . . ."

But he did not let her finish. "And do you know," he whispered kissing her, "I have found my subject."

Translated by Jo Mayo

Top Naeff

THE FRIEND

WHEN I THINK BACK TO THE LITTLE TOWN, I SEE BEFORE ME TWO houses, theirs and ours. All the streets of my memory terminate there, and in my mind's eye rises the façade of their home, monumental and engraved like a memorial plaque. . . . It was a grey, square structure with two windows on either side of the granite steps and a row of five above. The brass trim of the black front door, shining as gold, and the evenly hanging shades whose scalloped borders just touched the lower curtains of linen lace, gave evidence to the outside world of the prosperity and the sense of orderliness of the inhabitants.

Only on Sundays, when the white-capped maid was allowed to look at the passers-by from behind the window of the reception room, was the neatness of these curtains slightly disturbed; and the glow of the open fireplace in the drawing-room on the other side of the front door, where the lady of the house received her visitors, sparkled through the lacework, making the little figures, a knight on the left, a lady on the right, stand out as if modeled by the fire. To those standing on the steps, waiting in the wintry twilight, while the deep sound of the doorbell faded away behind the front door, it gave a feeling of comfort which, on entering, would be enhanced by the delicate fragrance which distinguished Conny's drawing-room from all others in town. That fragrance seemed to radiate from her mild, well-balanced personality and somehow imparted itself to everything that surrounded and belonged to her; the inner warmth of her being filled the room. She did not wait for a visitor to enter; she went to meet him and ushered him in, and each visitor's importance rose by her way of welcome, as she convincingly put her hand into his as though it were a gift. "Come, sit down next to me," she would urge, and her eyes would have the misty gleam of a longing which seemed ever present in them. And, in the conversation that followed, no matter who or what held her attention, she seemed completely absorbed. "Conny," her husband used to say in a jocular way, "shares a secret with each and every one," and that actually meant almost everyone in town, from the proud young lieutenant to old Daatje who was everybody's aunt and slightly given to drink. And it was curious to see that each person seemed to have the feeling of being the special favorite, and nobody felt slighted by the favors given to a predecessor. She found exactly the right tone for everyone, knew how to kindle the tender spark of interest, and I was often astonished at her faculty of remembering all the events and all the relations of those mixed crowds. In her crystal-clear memory every event seemed indelibly engraved; whatever she promised, she fulfilled; no detail escaped her. She had the broad smile of those who understand by intuition; she had eyes that always gave and never requested. . . . And this sympathetic quality was so much a part of her that the thought of special intention or affectation on her part never occurred to anyone.

Even now I still do not believe that she consciously followed a certain pattern of behavior; I believe that Conny, indifferent within, barricaded herself behind conscientious outward efforts, her face a fitting mask. A delicately cut mask it was, unreal like the impression in wax of a dead friend, strangely familiar, aloof and yet glowing, and of a loveliness seen through a veil. It has delighted many people and to me it was a priceless possession. For, although through the many years of our friendship she never allowed me—just as little indeed as her husband—a glimpse into her own inner life, I never felt this to be a shortcoming or an obstacle in our association. Everything about Conny, even the things that sometimes puzzled me, seemed at the time as they should have been and, to be absolutely frank, they appear so even now. At any rate, I have never regretted my, well, somewhat naive devotion to her, to the woman she pretended to be, and I would never think of setting the friendly confidence, which I willingly made to her, against the hostile secret which she, under the disguise of intimacy, kept from me.

There are people who can wear their heart on their tongue as a jewel, while others have to hide it as a treasure. I myself belong to the category called "an open book," and for a long time I considered this a privilege and a tribute. Now that I am fifty years old, in good health and a cheerful companion for my aging mother, I am still praised for this quality. "With Marie you know exactly what's what," is the verdict of my numerous acquaintances, but I for myself see matters in a different light. I believe that frankness may give a certain comfort but that it can never be a luxury . . . and this is perhaps the only conclusion which I, who have always appeared exactly as I am, have decided to keep from my relatives and friends, at least for the time being. That frankness, moreover, resulted in a "simplicity of soul," as our minister calls it, to which everybody as well as myself has become accustomed, and now that I am getting older I do not wish to lose it. It is to this day a part of my vanity, because it goes so well with my appearance, stout as I was to start with and growing definitely heavy with the years. Always straight to the point . . . I look the part!

Constance Grashorst and I were of the same age, that is to say, she was a young woman and I an aging spinster when we both approached forty. Her exact age I learned only recently from the official death notice. She always used to say laughingly, "Une femme de trente ans remains that age. It's just like smuggling over the border." She had a vague dislike for her birthday. On that day, February 12, I was usually the only guest. Her husband wanted no strangers around! From the time that I was called her friend, however, she had urged, Let me ask Marie; because Marie was no stranger. . . . In my memory this date hangs in a flowery wreath. And on each February 12 I see myself and the family gathered at the table, abounding with food and set as if for a banquet: the person whose birthday it was sitting opposite her husband, the boys, white-collared, together at the lower end, myself, in my black and white checkered blouse, broad and talkative, at the upper end . . . a parapet indeed! I can still see the smile and the tender look in her eyes, as she gazed over the heads of the boys, while Grashorst, his glass raised, commemorated their Mama's birthday in a little toast. The words were always the same, arranged slightly different each time, and it seemed to me that even the emphasis, which brought a certain warmth to his voice, was always on the same syllable. He exalted her virtues as a wife and mother, thanked her for her devotion to her household, recalled days of sickness and once more wished her happiness, also on behalf of the children, the relatives, the friends, "represented here by our friend Marie."

The little carillon of clinking glasses set in promptly and, as the tense quiet was broken, I felt that I was taken into the intimacy of this happy family. Tactfully I glanced the other way when Conny rose and offered her cheek to her husband for the official birthday kiss, and without jealousy I looked on while Ewald and Jopje, with their glasses of red-tinted water, tiptoed behind their mother's chair, quickly set down their glasses and put their arms around her neck, both at the same time, with an ardor resembling fury, as if they were storming a fortress. I wanted Conny to have all the joys of this world and thought that they were her rightful due; but towards the end of such a day, when we were sitting together in the living-room, as in a spring garden, I sometimes had to tell her, "You know, Conny; it's really a shame that you, of all people, have the nerve to look down on birthdays." She would nod and look at me with her dream eyes and, though she acknowledged my reproof, suddenly looked tired. . . .

Our friendship—at any rate that's what it was on my part, the only friendship my heart has ever felt—our friendship dated back to a winter when a few children, including Ewald Grashorst, were to give a performance of a fairytale for the benefit of the local Poor Relief. I was then a member of the board of that organization and in that capacity I met Mrs. Grashorst at one of the rehearsals. Hand in hand with her son, who was dressed in a page's costume, she walked up to me. The boy bowed from the waist as he had just learned; the long blue feather on his beret touched my hand and briefly tickled my nose as I bent down. The mother smiled, blushing a little as if she wanted to beg my indulgence for her impetuous cavalier. I stayed with her for the rest of that afternoon and afterwards I often found excuses to sneak off into the rehearsal room, a world in itself and to me a world of marvelous enchantment.

Then it came to pass that she had to take over the role of the fairy, in place of the colonel's daughter, who had fallen ill. I shall never forget how almost supernaturally fair and lovely she was on that night, as she came out from behind the dark chimneypiece, all aglitter with spangles. She was the answer to all that fancy has woven around fairies. The children gazed at her be-

witched as at a genuine apparition, while the mothers and fathers
sat in breathless wonder. She was truly a fairy-godmother. And
how charming, in a different way now, come back to earth, a
happy, sweet human being, she appeared at the end of the performance, as she received flower tributes brought to the stage by
the pages, in the full glow of the footlights. More flowers and still
more: her hands could not hold all the abundance, her feet were
buried in waves of lilacs; Ewald had to take the golden sceptre
from his mother, so flower-laden was she!

Was she overcome by all this homage or only timidly happy?
She buried her head with the imposing sugar-loaf hat in the roses.
Her delicate chin, her quivering, smiling mouth, disappeared.
Only her eyes, all tenderness, still shone above the flowers. They
wandered through the hall over the long rows of people; over my
nodding head and clapping hands, over the many admiring faces,
among which I discovered, in the front row, the bald pate of her
husband, they fixed themselves on one point. Surely, at that moment she must have been filled with happiness. A happiness that
not everyone can approach.

From that night on I grasped every opportunity to meet Constance Grashorst again: even to the point of taking over from
her a complicated and perfectly useless secretaryship. Homely
women are sometimes partial to beautiful ones, and vice-versa,
provided there is enough difference between them to make competition impossible. Thus, in the shadow of a pretty or outstanding woman one may often find an ill-favored friend, such as the
"nurse" in old-time tragedies. And when I recall the old days of
our friendship, it seems to me that we approached this classic
prototype fairly closely.

My admiration, which in the beginning was held within timid
bounds and which I nursed tenderly and adroitly during the
period that followed, led gradually to a relationship which the
outside world called intimate. Although I was fully aware that
Conny, had it not been for a few chance circumstances mostly
brought about by myself, would never have chosen me, I was
careful to make our relationship appear to others as ideal as
the friendship of Castor and Pollux. More enjoyable even than
being in the house with her was taking a walk together, and
when, in the evening, I entered our club room in the wake of her
high heels, I marched like a conqueror.

The Grashorst family was an institution in town, the "beautiful Mrs. Grashorst" almost a celebrity. Whenever the foursome
appeared, the tall, distinguished man—honorary chairman or at

least patron of every organization—his graceful wife, dressed like
no one else, the princely looking boys, a smile of affection went
around. They simply belonged to the town. And until they had
taken their seats in a public hall, restlessness prevailed in the
ranks. Once in a while an envious acquaintance spoke in my
presence of the "royal court," and this increased my self-importance. I have never been able to find out exactly what was
Conny's attitude toward that universal admiration: whether she
accepted it as her birthright, to what extent it flattered her and
how indispensable it became. Nor did I ever get an insight into
the character of her feelings toward myself. I never overestimated
my value and I knew her to be a blind philanthropist. . . . Per-
plexingly good and affectionate she was to me throughout many
years, and never in a way that seemed to me condescending. She
had the talent to be good, to grasp the happiness of the moment
for herself and others. In the upbringing of her children she demanded above all the right to give them pleasure, not the sort
of pleasure that was thought good for them, but the pleasure to
which they clung, with the passionate tenacity of children. Laughingly, against all reason, she would defend that heavenly right.
She would go through a great deal of trouble just to hear them
chuckle. . . . And to think of all the things she invented to keep
up my morale in the years of balance, to fill my empty days, to
turn my heart away from that which passed it by . . . !

I sincerely believe that the day on which my father told me
that he had bought the house next to that of the Grashorsts was
the greatest day of my life. The surprise at this almost incon-
ceivably good fortune, the joy that was like entering a new world,
the excitement which made me ignore all my principles of modesty and run right over to Conny . . . I can still feel them in my
stiff limbs when I think back to that time. The distance in age
between my parents and myself had not been diminished as the
years went by; regardless of my ample shape, I remained in their
eyes the child, the minor, uninitiated into any of life's happenings until Mama and Papa had agreed fully about it. And so I
enjoyed this arrangement with all my heart.

Everything about our new home, even its discomforts, seemed
delightful to me: the little garden with northern exposure where
no rose would bloom was admired by me because of its low fence,
the picturesque remains of a pigeon house on the lawn. . . . And
my own room, painted white, full of fussy furnishings, among
which I walked with resolute steps, arranging all the pieces with
loving care, while humming a tune in falsetto voice. On each

little gilt chair, on the daisy-pattern of my tiny sofa, my mind's
eye saw her sitting down and her face smiling at me so sweetly
from the golden frame of my Louis XVI mirror long before she
actually came. . . . And when at last she was there, the first afternoon, and drank tea from the cup that was different, especially
intended for her, this was to me an apotheosis, a complete fulfillment.

Living so close to her was all I had hoped and expected and
even more. For, by way of exchanging little neighborly courtesies
and services, I had an opportunity to become better acquainted,
in a natural way, with the less accessible, more formal Mr. Grashorst too. And one fine day, the boys started calling me "aunt,"
This became the bridge for the father, leading from Miss van
Drunen by way of Aunt Marie to Marie pure and simple. And I
called him Grashorst, just as Conny did in talking about him.
I came to their house in the morning, the afternoon and evening, under all circumstances, but never on my own initiative.
However, the least encouragement, impatiently looked forward
to and immediately taken up, was sufficient for me. Without this
encouragement I did not have courage. . . . And perhaps it was
my instinct that led me, the same instinct that brings a dog back
to the right track, that keeps a sleepwalker from falling, the so-
called sixth sense which failed me for all other purposes.

Somewhat peculiar and, I should almost call systematic, was
Conny's way of inviting me: the time of coming and going was
regulated by the clock, and I complied intuitively with an equally
strict observance of precision. Taking a walk together at three
o'clock meant that I rang her door bell on the stroke of three.
Conny planned the walk, which was just long enough for the
allotted time. In the evening she invited me either for tea, that
is to say: at eight; or for after tea-time, which meant not before
nine. And when I was asked to come for dinner, which was
usually every other Sunday, the invitation implied that I should
not put in an appearance in the afternoon, as I did on the alternate Sundays when Conny held her reception and I called at four
to pour the tea.

On the dinner Sunday there was usually one other guest at
Conny's table, Mr. Alting Reys, mayor of one of the villages
across the river. He was a boyhood friend of Grashorst's, but their
friendship of many years standing had suffered an interruption
following Alting Reys's ill-advised marriage to a peasant girl.
After some time, however, mostly through Conny's efforts, because she rather liked Alting, the two men patched up their

friendship. But their relationship remained somewhat strained. He came regularly to town without his wife and visited a few friends, among whom were the Grashorsts. This, however, did not prevent Conny from occasionally taking the ferry to pay a visit to the wife and children. Grashorst, who was a director of a large banking house and was kept at his office until five, never accompanied her on those trips. On Alting's visits to their home, his wife was never, the children rarely, mentioned, and it seemed evident that this was arranged by mutual consent. Somehow I never asked Conny about it and I finally arrived at the conclusion that seemed logical in the light of both personalities, namely, that Grashorst was only partly reconciled, while Conny took the whole thing lightly and, in the warmth of her heart, sided with the mayor's rejected wife and their rustic offspring. Through all the years of my extremely shortsighted complacency, the attitude of Mr. Reys remained to me inscrutable and, I must confess, open to reproach. A marriage is a marriage after all, a concept: once the step has been taken, the husband belongs with his wife as the cup with the saucer. In the face of these virtuous principles, however, I took a great delight in sitting next to him at the table, captivated by his lively stories about hunting and fishing, about all the animals on his farm, which he treated as his friends. With his rugged outdoor look, his bachelor air, Reys, though of the same age as Grashorst, seemed ten years younger; he did not appear out of place even among the organdy-clad very young girls. He was tall, broad-shouldered and tanned, and he had a soft, light laugh, deep in his throat, that gave color to everything he said. He talked for the pleasure of talking, without expecting applause or even an answer. Touching on the different approaches to a subject, he always achieved a personal point of view, suddenly developed a slight detail, which he became aware of while talking, into shining significance. His banter was always serious, his seriousness always jocular; awkward people were afraid of him because he thwarted expectation and nobody knew how to take him.

To me he always spoke like a friend, mostly about or in connection with my affectionate admiration for Conny, which he fully shared. Occasionally he called my attention to a book which he had read during the long winter evenings on his isolated place. He would then summarize in a few short phrases, with a halting gesture, the contents of, sometimes, three heavy volumes, at that time occupying his deepest thoughts. Tolstoi was his favorite author; his love, Anna Karenina. He could talk about

her with a subdued passion, with such cold fire, as if his own
blood were at stake. And sometimes, for one fleeting uncontrolled
moment I saw his face glaring, his mouth twisted as in hate.

When I sat on the host's other side, as happened frequently
in small company, I was often tempted to compare the two men:
on the left the pale profile, bent as though in search of something, on the right the dark, eagerly lifted face, the soft, blue-
veined hand, crumbling bread between our plates, and the strong
hairy fist that protruded from the cuff above the table.

Mr. Grashorst, too, in a more emphatic way and always in
search for the unquestionably right word, was an interesting
neighbor, and whatever I still remember in my old age of statesmanship and the rights of nations I owe to his dinner talk. His
thoughtful manner of speaking was in perfect harmony with his
forward-bent figure and the delicate, moistly-pale face above
which the forehead, like a white shell, was prolonged to the fair
fringe of hair marking a half-circle around the skull. A pair of
glasses with ground lenses seemed to cut his eyes in two, and a
fluffy little beard, in which his white hands used to play at
moments of high tension, lengthened the lower part of his face.
Accustomed to making himself understood in public with a naturally low voice, he often finished off a sentence with an eloquent
gesture, as graceful as the gesture of a woman.

When Conny sat opposite us, it seemed to me as if she, too,
was driven to comparing, as though the wide differences of character in these two men, which often came to the fore alarmingly
in casual conversations, secretly worried her. On those occasions
she agreed now with one now with the other, always speaking
in a questioning tone, but when the situation became one of
threatening danger she chose the side of her husband, while I,
without having any convictions except to strike a fair balance,
supported the guest whose inner passion foundered on Grashorst's calm and efficient opposition. Laughingly, disregarding
my own conscience, I would defend his radical ideas which shook
the very foundations of world order. I did this mainly for the
satisfaction of revolting against Grashorst who would, under all
circumstances, uphold existing society, its principles and general
interests. And if we won the battle, Conny, though on the losing
side, would look at me tenderly. "Barbarian," she said once to
Alting, after one of these pitched battles, while taking him up
into the same tender glance, "it's lucky for you that Marie is
so emancipated nowadays. . . ." And then, while the four of us
had a good laugh at my emancipation, since conservatism was

manifest in my entire appearance, culminating in my stiff hair-do, I saw the fist next to me open and close, as though grinding life and its passions to bits.

Our conversation seldom circled around persons, was mostly concerned with ideas which we connected with imaginary persons and, for the sake of the children, we expressed ourselves in words evading the direct issue. If town gossip gave cause for praise or blame in a more personal sense, Conny was silent immediately, while the blood rushed to her cheeks. Occasionally I seemed to notice that, after such excitement, she would, still blushing down to her neck, defend a guilty person. She never condemned anybody or anything. "If one only knew everything," she would say with a face as if she fathomed life's innermost secrets, "if one always knew everything. . . ." Oh, how I loved in her at such moments that open-mindedness and mildness, that natural eagerness always to believe in the best of everybody and everything, that tentacle-sensitive understanding with which she guessed our warped thoughts—and disproved them before they were uttered. She was undoubtedly a good mother to her children, even if she was not strong enough to make the supreme sacrifice for them.

In the town of my past the days were monotonous and long. The friendship with Conny grew to something like a tradition. Twice a week we took a walk together, on three afternoons she made her appearance in the daisy-setting of my boudoir, and we had tea. Some women can read and knit at the same time. In much the same way Conny could float on her own thoughts and meanwhile carry on a regular conversation. In a sense I was her knitting at that time, and she never let a stitch drop. During a walk she talked little, often not at all, and this experience motivated me to chide women who always had to have something to talk about. This—that we could be silent together—seemed to me one of the noblest elements of our friendship. And yet I remember that it was a relief too when, in this exalted state, we met a good friend, Mr. Reys for instance, a sturdy hiker, or someone else who would accompany us part of the way. And what I liked best of all was to go on charity visits with Conny. On those occasions she was like a child: no system, no regulation was sacred to her. She worked like a goblin, laughed at miscalculations and was fond of "surprises." The sight of a worn-out old woman moved her to tears, the dirtiest-looking children she took to her heart. She knew everyone in the street by name, stopped suddenly to inquire of a John or a Mina, of the family, going into all possible detail. As a member of the Aid Society, where I had risen to the post of treasurer, it was often my task to curb her generosity. In this connection I learned to appreciate her husband. Though he had little sympathy for her unbridled helpfulness, he never hesitated when it came to providing her with the means to keep family honor intact.

On Sundays Conny told the three of us about her experiences, gave each event a suitable touch of color and, in recapturing the mood of the moment, her face assumed a childlike, pure expression. Her eyes had an inner light, her mouth opened and the red tip of her tongue moved along her eager lips. . . . We three, the two men and I, each in our own way, how much we loved her!

My fortnightly Sunday—thinking back to it now. . . . On the stroke of six-thirty I stood on the steps and with the doorbell I rang in my holiday. The soft huntsman's hat of Mr. Alting Reys, which he wore winter and summer, on weekdays and on Sundays, already hung on its peg, and in the front room I found them, Conny buried in the many sofa cushions, he in the low tapestry chair by the fire. The shaded lamp behind the sofa, the only source of light in the dreamy room, poured its yellow rays over Conny's neck and hands, over her silken hair, the sofa cushions that seemed to be woven of old gold and priceless damask. I was keenly aware, as Conny's arm pulled me onto this throne beside her, of how sadly my black and white checkered blouse shattered this idyll of Thousand-and-One-Nights, but just then the master of the house, returning from his club, would put his key into the door and the meal would be announced. Conny, tall, slim and supple, preceded us through the wide, white-marble hall. In the dining-room, Ewald and Jopje, in velvet suits, were awaiting us, each behind his high-backed chair, with napkins, little bibs, already tied on. The table with four candles in silver candlesticks, the crystal, soap-bubble thin and reflecting the light; every Sunday we found everything like this. We sat far apart, the chilly, pressed napkins slid along our laps, the fragrance of the linen mingled with the spicy odors of the soup. The memory of a scent has magical powers. . . .

In the evening we sat once more in the drawing-room in front, where now the center light was also lit and the furnishings assumed a simpler appearance. The men read the papers or talked; Conny and I busied ourselves with needlework. And not one glance ever disclosed. . . .

Once I went with Conny across the river. "Come with me, Marie," she said, "they are such a jolly family." I hesitated:

wouldn't Mr. Alting mind the visit of a stranger? But she said that he knew all about it and would be glad if I came. On a fresh autumn day, the waves of the river topped with white crests, we sailed across and found the mayor at the landing place, waving his little hat. He drove us in his carriage through the old village to his place, a more or less tumbledown estate on which, in former times, a castle had stood. After a number of ravages, one of the side wings had later been rebuilt into a residence; it was close to the cow shed and gleaming with ivy up to the rafters. There were still luxuriant woodlands around, and one part, behind the meadows, was called "the mayor's forest." At first I hardly realized that the peasant children, who were playing around the house, among dogs, chickens and rabits, also belonged to the mayor; that the chubby woman who rushed to the scene at the call of "Mother!", wiping her hands, was Mrs. Alting Reys. And inside the house, where handsome old pieces stood amid trash, I sat down next to Conny, who had cheerfully taken the youngest girl, Brechtje, from the carriage outside and was now cuddling her on her lap; I was surprised and slightly indignant. How could a man of good breeding do this to himself! He seemed to take it calmly and good-naturedly; and how almost astonishingly he achieved the right tone towards his awkward wife who called him "Fawther," with a deep "a", as if this were the first title to which her husband had rights. He showed us the peacocks and the angry turkey, the large aviary and the aquarium, and he offered each of us a late red rose which I, because I saw Conny do the same, pinned, somewhat defiantly, on my navy-blue bosom. He also showed us his own quiet room, almost a room of state, with a high wall of books, antlers and trophies. And later, after Mrs. Alting had offered us some lemon-peel brandy and I had yielded to the temptation, he went back to his room with Conny to show her some negatives of photographs of a mare, taken for a show.

He walked us down to the ferry landing. During the long walk, with his left arm in Conny's and his right arm in mine, he tried to adjust his steps to our uneven efforts. He was known in the entire vicinity as the eccentric mayor of M., but from the way the villagers greeted him one could clearly see how popular he was, eccentricity notwithstanding.

As we returned on the ferry, with a stiff breeze whipping our hair into our faces—we stayed close to the funnel to keep warm— I talked incessantly of the problems of love and marriage. That man with that woman!

"She is very good to him," Conny said simply, "very good!"

"Well, perhaps . . . but for heaven's sake. . . ."

"What is wrong with it? . . . All men don't desire the same thing in a wife."

"But can you believe that a man like"—and I yielded to my impulse to throw all the male virtues and attractions of Alting into the balance, and I can still see her smile at this unexpected tribute—"can you believe that such a man can love a woman like her? . . ."

"Love is an enigma, you know," she concluded sagely, with her most charming aplomb, which now contained a note of mysteriousness. . . . And she drew the white veil, which made her appear ethereal and transparent as down, tighter around her chin.

She stood against the blue sky, bold and laughing in the breeze, with her hands like protecting shells closed over the rose on her bosom. And finally, by telling an anecdote about Pieter, the oldest, who so strikingly resembled his mother, she succeeded in breaking my stubborn rebelliousness, which she felt still present although I had stopped talking. After that visit, however, I went over to the side of Grashorst and relegated Mrs. Alting Reys to oblivion.

And so the days of several apparently uneventful years slipped through our fingers; it often seemed to me that I lived from one alternate Sunday to the other. I was happy, for all those small joys, elevated to blissfulness, returned faithfully time after time. Until one Sunday the little felt hat with the grey partridge feather was not in its place and when I entered the drawing room, where Conny sat as always among the cushions on the sofa, I learned that my cavalier, as I liked to call him, was ill.

"Seriously?"

Without concern in her voice she said:

"Yes, pleurisy."

I talked at length, with the compassion peculiar to women who distribute their love over the whole world; I recalled seeing him a few days before, when he was attending the horse fair in town, asked whether we could do anything and predicted that he, such a strong and tough man, would surely recover. She winced, as if suddenly her self-control had left her, and nodded shortly, "Of course."

At the dinner table that day we sat farther apart, but the

conversation, which was kept up by the hostess, was as lively as ever.

On the following morning I hardly dared ask for further news about the patient, because Conny steadfastly evaded the subject, until she suddenly said, of her own accord, "We phoned. He had a quiet night." And so well-trained was my friendship that it was contented with this strange reticence, that not even a thought rose on account of its silent depth. . . .

Because of the reassuring news and because I had not lost my heart to Alting, who, in a sense, was my rival and moreover a man who had chosen his maid for a wife, the incident was of only secondary interest to me.

The next day was Ewald's birthday, and the long promised girl-and-boy party took place in the attic room. For this noble purpose I was to turn the fruits of my many piano lessons into the "Myosotis" and the "Polka with Variations," which I knew by heart. Because of a delay in the purchase of a birthday present I was a little late—which hardly ever happened. I met Grashorst, who had temporarily taken my place, on the stairway and heard from him that the reports from M. were less encouraging again and that the fever had diminished only slightly toward morning.

Upstairs I found Conny surrounded by a crowd of young boys. It was a point of pride with all of Ewald's little friends to have danced with his mother. Because I had kept them waiting, I was received with an ovation that was slightly embarrassing, and a swarm of cotton-gloved hands applauded me to the hired piano in the corner of the room. Now the ball could really begin.

While Conny, bent down behind a hedge of curious people, helped Ewald to unwrap the dog whip and whistle that I had finally been able to buy for him, I planted my foot on the pedal, spread out my hands that could span more than an octave . . . then Ewald blew his whistle with a shrill tone. . . . And as though this were a signal, my fingers descended forcefully; in a trice the light colors whirled past my eyes and the rhythmless shuffling began, skipping against the stately cadence of my one polka.

When I got up courage, after the third Myosotis, to turn around while playing, I saw Conny in her old white frock, selected by the birthday-child for the occasion, saw her dancing, dancing like a young girl, in the flickering glow of candles and the flowery light of a genuine Chinese lantern. Straight through the crowd she led her little cavaliers, a clumsy boy, a hopping little girl; restlessly, to all four winds she set her course. . . . She missed not one dance—everyone got a turn. And when they bumped into each other, there were loud cheers, she herself laughed. . . . I see her before me now. . . . The white dress made her look pale and, above the leaning shoulder of one after the other perspiring lad, her eyes stared dark and wide. . . .

In the intermission, Jop distributed gilt party favors. Mine contained a cap with ribbons, and Conny's a soldier's hat. And later, in a whirl of confetti, we had a snowball fight.

At the end of this glorious evening, when I relieved the tired mother of the task of putting little Jop to bed, Ewald came dancing from the adjoining room in his night clothes, to thank me, too, for my part in the "most wonderful birthday he had ever had."

"How did you like the hats, Aunt Marie?"

"Very nice."

"Mummy always thinks of something funny, something new and different."

"Yes, that Mummy of yours. . . ."

"Only it was too bad that Uncle Hans wasn't there."

Two days after the party she stood unexpectedly, before ten o'clock in the morning, in my room. I felt embarrassed because the slip covers at this inhospitable hour still covered up my little gilt chairs, and now Conny had to see them. I was thinking of a place to hide my dustcloth and so did not pay too much attention to her appearance in the beginning.

She was sitting in the window-seat, with her back to the light, in her wide fur coat, unbuttoning it at first and then again closing it up to her neck. It annoyed me that there was no fire in my little hearth, and I was wondering whether I could, unnoticed, strike a match to the wood shavings. . . . Then I heard her say:

"At the hospital there was not a single nurse available; now Grashorst has phoned to Utrecht. At any rate I am going there. On the ten-thirty ferry. Somebody has to . . . a woman like Maaike hasn't a notion. . . ."

It was the first and the only time I heard Conny's voice burst out in contempt, and I have never forgotten the tone of voice in which she said, "A woman like Maaike. . . ."

"So you are going, . . ." I said hesitantly.

"For a time . . . until help arrives. Hans is very ill." Otherwise she had always called him either Alting or Reys.

"Doctor Smit, who called up this morning, said that it was critical. And when a doctor says critical. . . ." Her hands tightened around her coat collar, pulled it up high.

I nodded, in worried sympathy: "And now you would like me to. . . ?"

She took hold of herself then: "Yes, if you'd do me that favor."

"Of course."

"When Grashorst and the boys come home at noon, it would be so lonesome for them to find nobody. And then the meals. . . . If I may make a suggestion, Marie, come . . . to live with us . . . for a little while. . . . Tonight I may . . . it will all depend . . . that nurse from Utrecht. . . . You see, it would give me greater peace of mind. . . ."

I was only too glad to accept this trusted position!

At ten-thirty I saw her off to the ferry boat. She was calm and, in contrast with her dismay of a little earlier, became finally almost gay, as if by her setting foot on the gangplank all was going to change for the good. She kept me on my toes with little hints about her well-organized household. Each child required special care, the chambermaid had to be reminded . . . and her zealous, "Grashorst is used to this, Grashorst likes it this way," assaulted my flawless illusions about the married state. While the gangplank was pulled in, she called to me from the deck, smiling encouragingly:

"Oh, Marie, I just thought of something. . . . Next week we are going to have the dinner for the bank commissioners at our house. Myntje, the cook, is coming tomorrow morning to talk the menu over. Will you arrange with her. . . ?"

"But, Conny dear. . . !" For attractive culinary arrangements I was certainly the last one to choose! My consternation amused her tremendously.

"You'll be all right," she called out as the boat in taking off drew a long green line through the drab water. "Do a good job, now! Just pick out what you like best!"

Standing in the icy wind among the ferry people at the quay, I followed her with my eyes, thinking, How kind she is! Whoever is in trouble, wherever help is needed, Conny knows no hesitation. All egotism gives way to the dictates of her heart. And I waved to her once more, enthusiastically, when, in the mist-veiled distance, her hand like a little white flag motioned to me from her huge muff.

At noon I made sandwiches for Ewald and Jopje and felt

alternately indispensable and superfluous in the large living-room that was dark in the daytime. I had taken Conny's seat and handled the Meissen coffee service as adroitly as possible. Grashorst was quiet and uncommunicative and extremely formal. I had the impression that, with Conny's parting, all bonds had been disrupted. We exchanged a few words about the patient; he told me the outcome of the telegram sent to the Utrecht hospital and fell in with my admiration for Conny's generous and efficient action.

After dinner he asked me to accompany him and the boys to fetch the Utrecht nurse from the train; the four of us rode in a big cab to the station. On the trip from the station to the ferry I sat in back with the nurse, while he and the boys occupied the front seat. Grashorst and I, who were little informed, more or less evaded the questions the nurse asked us concerning her prospective patient and his family.

"You will find my wife there." I can still hear Grashorst saying, and this was the only definite information he gave her in his own emphatic way. The subject of her return, which I had still thought possible that same evening, he did not touch upon at all. At the ferry he carried the nurse's basket across the gangway, with great care, as if it contained eggs, and he parted with a bow and best wishes for the Alting family.

On the return home, we walked. And after the boys had been put to bed, I poured tea for both of us in the front room where the evening papers were in their usual place. At about ten o'clock Grashorst asked me to play a game of cards with him as he did every evening with his wife. On this first day it struck me how true to his habits this man was, and he gave me the impression that, in his daily grind and in the light relaxation he allowed himself in the evening, he hardly noticed the absence of his wife. To me, who missed her intensely, his easy resignation was so annoying that I constantly tried to bring her name into the conversation, whether appropriately or not, as if to keep the memory of a dead loved one alive.

In order to follow her wishes completely, I stayed overnight in the room next to the children's. She had obviously herself prepared it for me that morning. Nothing was missing; a little vase with three magnificent roses was on the dressing table. And early the next morning I was on hand personally to get Jopje dressed, boil Grashorst's egg—not too soft and not too hard—and to get Ewald, well-fed and properly equipped, off to school. After that, the problem-laden conference with Myntje, the cook, took place.

In the afternoon, Dr. Smit called the house to tell us that the condition of the patient remained critical. The nurse had proved satisfactory. The sick man required much care; Mrs. Grashorst sent word that she could not be dispensed with at the moment. A note from Conny, scribbled in pencil, in which she asked me to take her place a few days longer, followed in the last mail. No approval or disapproval on Grashorst's part; no hesitation, of course, as far as I was concerned. I wrote Conny a long, enthusiastic and reassuring letter, in which I idealized the whole situation, with her doing a work of charity over there, myself replacing her here as well as I knew how, Grashorst agreeable, the boys delightful.

To be truthful, the days in the large house, from which the light seemed to have vanished together with Conny, were long and weighed heavily on me. The feeling that I made myself useful, the inspiration of little duties from which many of us women draw their vital strength, kept my spirits up, but Grashorst's painstaking courtesy, as if he, too, had only duties to perform toward me, depressed me in spite of myself. The children, too well trained to complain, showed in their eyes a longing for their mother all day long and one night, as I tucked Jopje into his blankets, he said—just as if he, too, had been wondering about the emptiness in our friendly relationship and meant to comfort me in his own way—"Why is it, Aunt Marie? Now you know how much I love you, and still I'm so lonesome for my Mummy every night?"

I cannot say that this confession gave me as much comfort as Jopje had perhaps a right to expect. Nevertheless, on that evening, being "lucky at play" and inspired by the great powers that bind and divide, for better and for worse, I played a profitable game of cards.

The news from M. was scarce. Every day I wrote Conny of how well the household was run under my supervision; the boys received postcards with pictures of the "Municipal Building," the "Ferry Landing," the "Sun" inn, with "Love from Mother" written underneath. And every evening I said, only to provoke a protest from Grashorst: "It's good that Conny stays there quietly. We get along all right here, and over there she is worth a million right now."

But he answered readily in the same spirit, thoughtful and contented: "I think you are right. Constance had a lot of experience with sick people when she was younger; she is clever and she has a steady head."

Is it possible that he never, never suspected anything? A hundred times I have asked myself that question, now, afterwards, looking back. . . . I believe not. He, as well as I, as so many others . . . has lived in perfect balance with his life.

In the days of which I speak, however, I was occupied with other problems. They were indeed more or less my initiation into the wedded state, the bound unity, the inviolable companionship. . . . Like a puzzle I studied that card-playing forehead. How could this man, whose finely cut and certainly aristocratic face reminded me more of a fish every day, how could he have had charm in his younger years for Conny; Conny, who could have married any man she wanted. . . . And upon love I meditated, with fervor and indiscretion.

I stayed at the house for five days that seemed five weeks. On the sixth day a telegram arrived, which I opened while Grashorst was absent: "Alting passed away during the night. Coming home tonight, Constance." I telephoned the bank and told Grashorst, and I perceived in the distant voice a little of the dismay that made my knees give way under me. Grashorst said: "I had just wanted to go there this afternoon. . . . Yes . . . now . . . maybe I will . . . is there anything in the telegram about the funeral?"

"No."

"Oh, I see . . . I suppose . . . let me see . . . Thursday. Then . . . now it's all over. . . . I had better wait." At lunch that noon his mood was somewhat livelier. He told about some of his recollections of Reys, who had always been peculiar, a hot-head, from the time they studied together at Leyden University. At that stupid mistake of his marriage—what did he have to marry that girl for!—he was more embittered than ever before. And it seemed as if he still blamed the marriage for their estrangement.

"No," he repeated, "I could never forgive him for that!"

"You?"

"None of his friends could."

"Conny. . . ."

"Well, of course, a woman."

The urge to contradict him tempted me to plead in favor of people who certainly were man enough to take the consequence of their errors, but the maidenly shyness that had always been part of my nature held me back. I vented my feelings by reprimanding Jopje.

The boys, to whom we did not speak about the death of Alting, were boisterously happy at the prospect of their mother's return. All the goodies saved up during the week were put in readiness for her. And then there was a scene in which the fatherly authority had to exert itself and on the basis of which I had to confess to myself that they were not spoiled children, since neither of the boys was allowed to stay up after dinner until she came home.

My arbitrary promise that Mama would surely kiss them good night in their beds finally calmed Ewald down; Jopje, exhausted, had cried himself to sleep.

And after this skirmish I suddenly felt my task cut off, and the thoughts came back again. Returning to the front room downstairs, I, who according to relatives and friends had no nerves at all, became strangely restless. I made tea and revived the fire. Grashorst was at a conference at the bank and from there would call for Conny at the ferry. I felt as if some of the sorrow of death would come with her from the other side of the river. Yet I had no realization of the full extent of this grief. She had lost a friend and was affected by other people's sorrows. That thought was sufficient for me to anticipate her coming home with that vague anxiety which besets awkward persons in the presence of tragedy. That I should have to miss my "cavalier" at the fortnightly Sundays from now on, that our circle had lost its fourth man—all this had not yet taken shape in my head, which was above all filled with Conny; but at the same time my eyes strayed again and again to the low armchair in which he had always sat before the fire, broad, strong, hale and hearty; and then the knowledge of his death was a new shock to me each time. That man . . . Reys . . . dead . . . one moment it seemed true, the next doubtful again. When I heard the ferry whistle from afar over the water, I pushed the chair against the wall next to the chimney and pulled the sofa in front. And after brief consideration I turned off the center light.

They came back at half-past eight. In the dim light of the standing lamp I could not immediately see how Conny looked. She did not seem to see my hand wanting to take off her fur coat, and my kiss went past her veil. And then she stood still in the middle of the room, with her hat still on her head, as if, running at top speed she had suddenly been stopped. She replied calmly, however, to my agitated questions, posed blindly.

He had died early in the morning.

"Was he conscious?"

"Yes."

"Were you . . . there?"

"Yes."

"Dreadfully unexpected still. . . ."

She shook her head in denial.

"It wasn't? Then you did. . . ? But take your things off first, Conny."

She pulled up her veil and automatically loosened a few buttons of her coat, but in the midst of her motions her arms fell to her sides.

"Did he . . . suffer?"

"Not then any more."

"But the days before?"

She nodded, swallowed audibly.

Grashorst, who had heard the story on the way home, unfolded the newspaper while standing and looked through the pages, holding the paper toward the lamp.

"You stayed with him at night too?"

"Yes, we took turns. Last night I . . . it was my turn."

"Aren't you tired out?"

She ignored this and other questions I asked in order to get closer to her.

In the stillness of death which still hovered about her, hauntingly, I groped for words, anything at all:

"It must be a great comfort to you . . . that you went right away that morning."

She stared at me from the low chair against the wall. But she drank the hot tea I handed her.

"And for him," I persisted, while guileless tears choked my whispers, "for him it must have been wonderful . . . you . . . a friend of . . . so many years . . . that you were there."

She returned the empty cup without a word. Only when I asked directly, "How does his wife take it?" she answered again.

"Very well," she said, "very well." And slowly she added, on her own accord:

"Maaike slept in the room next door. Then the nurse saw . . . she wanted to call her . . . but just at that moment. . . ."

The eyes which suddenly looked at me were those of someone in the death throes.

"Just at that moment. . . ." She failed to complete the sentence. Her hands reached out in a wild, gripping gesture, and then she folded them in her lap.

It seemed as if all her strength had been spent in that gesture.

In heartbreaking helplessness she remained seated for a little while, motionless, with those hands pressed together as if in prayer; then she got up, took my arm and said that she would like . . . would rather . . . go to bed.

"I'd do that," her husband agreed. "It's been a shock, naturally. And it is a sad case. The notice is in the paper. She signs herself: On behalf of the family: Mrs. Alting Reys, née Plomp. I'm afraid she is not very well taken care of financially either. Good old Reys was never good in money matters. And with that big family. . . ."

"Good night," Conny said, offering him her cheek.

"Sleep well; Marie will help you, I'm sure. Marie took good care of us while you were away."

Then, in the hall, I noticed how chalk-white, white as the wall, her face was above the dark coat-collar.

While going upstairs I dared not speak a word, until we came to the door of the children's room. . . . There I remembered my promise and, after some hesitation—maybe it would do her good to see the boys—I stopped her.

"No," she countered, "not now."

On the threshold of the bedroom she took my hand and thanked me effusively for my willingness, my help, which had made it possible for her to stay away.

"But, Conny, that was only the normal thing to do."

"Yes," she repeated, and the sacred light that went from her eyes into mine when she looked at me consciously for the first time since she had come home, has warmed me until this very day. "Yes, it was normal. Everything . . . was . . . normal."

During the days that followed this evening, she received no one; nor did she want to see anyone on the day of the funeral. The first time I saw her again was at the dinner of the bank commissioners for which I had planned the delicacies with Myntje. Conny sat between the commissioner-president and the mayor of our town, and she wore a garnet-red satin gown, cut rather low at the neck, the waist trimmed with old, diamond-sprinkled lace. She had powdered her face and, I suspected, put on a touch of rouge. More than ever her face looked like a waxen mask that stands out in my memory. I never saw her lovelier than that evening, at the head of her table, round which the men sat smoking. She and I were the only women, and I saw her from the other end of the table, in the trembling light of the candles, like a flower under water, far off and strange. She was very lively, bending tirelessly towards the hearing device of the grey notary who was rather deaf. With her burning eyes she dominated the serving staff, unnoticed by the guests. I received a glowing tribute

for my successful efforts and she apologized for her evasive attitude during the past few days by saying:

"I was so busy, Marie, and everything went wrong. One of the
waiters sent word that he could not come and before I could
get another one. . . . The dinner for the bank commissioners is
always a point of pride with Grashorst, and nothing should be
missing. . . ."

Nothing was missing indeed that night. And when the commissioner-president started his speech to the "highly respected"
director of the bank with a toast to Madame, his wife, our
charming hostess, *la main invisible* . . . the acknowledging "Constance," with which Grashorst waved his foaming glass towards
his wife, was a tribute earned with her life blood.

After the death of Mr. Alting Reys, who was rarely talked
about any more, I continued to be the dinner guest on alternating Sundays. On Conny's desk stood his portrait; the grey par-
tridge-feather of his hat was stuck between the picture and the
framing glass. It was a youthful portrait and a good likeness, a
face one could forgive much, and when I looked at it I felt an
undefinable pang of regret, as if we had somehow failed to pay
off a debt owed him.

My relationship with Conny gained by her loss; it became
an exception when we did not see each other for a whole day,
and the hours of coming and going were less rigidly controlled.
Her friendship remained my delight, the meaning and the comfort of my existence, in contrast to my difficult and hardly interesting home life. To me as well as to all others, but especially
to me, she was the best of all friends. She shared, as no other
could, the circumstances of my life; she understood my suppressed
loneliness as . . . my wish. The friendship of Constance Grashorst, the beautiful lady, who maintained her former prestige
even now with her prematurely white hair, that friendship elevated Marie van Drunen, who was somewhat of an oddity, to
the foot of the small-town idol.

Because of Conny I loved that forsaken place, because of her
family, the neighborly home; I waited until two years after my
father's death before consenting to my mother's nagging insistence to return to her native village in Gelderland, before I on
my part made the sacrifice that any love asks of us.

In that village we are living now, in the cheerful little cottage
named "Benvenuta," where Conny once came to visit with her
husband and children on a summer vacation trip. The condi-

tion I made for consenting to the removal, namely that I spend a vacation at the Grashorsts once every year, I was able to carry out only during the first few years. My mother became too feeble and could not bear strange hands. . . . But last fall, at Conny's omnipotent request, I spent a day with her at her home, and it was then that she told me what even her husband did not yet know, that she was ill. She gave no name to the illness. But in her parting kiss I felt something that had not been there before.

Every week during that long torture-filled winter I wrote to her with greedy zeal; with mounting anxiety I counted the letters from her. . . .

And at last the end came suddenly.

What her body must have suffered was never mentioned in her letters. But Ewald wrote me: "Mother was a wonder, Aunt Marie. She suffered infernal pains, her sweet face was twisted and still she smiled, told Father and us that it was not so bad, it only seemed so; everything was always so different from what it seemed."

And in the local paper I read that she, a friend of the poor, had been buried under a mountain of flowers, mourned by the whole town.

And now I am sitting in our sun porch, next to a little garden of forget-me-nots, opposite my mother, and with my first secret. And that secret is not even my own. And upstairs, in my room with the Louis XVI furniture, where I hid it like a thief, is the box I received a few days ago, a sealed leather case with my name written on it. Blushing as never before in my life, I took the two bundles of letters from it, and in my awkward hands they lay like live things. . . . Between the ribbons that held them together was a note whose contents I was at great pains to understand; a small ring with a blue stone and a grey feather fell out of it.

"Marie, these are the letters from Hans to me and from me to Hans. I could not part with them. It was not friendship between Hans and myself. I don't want to lie to you any longer after my death. And now I want to ask you to burn the letters for me and to forgive me for having misled you so long. I often misused your friendship and maybe it is that which weighs most heavily on me now that I know that I am incurably ill and have begun to take stock of myself. In friendship one can be honest, in love not always.

"The rest . . . ah, Marie, when it so happens. . . . To me it happened so, and I cannot even say that I have regrets and now repentant. . . . Because the other, the relationship with Hans, that was my whole life. We loved each other beyond all boundaries.

"But, on the other hand, I have given my husband the life that made him happy in his way. I brought up our children with all my devotion and to my best knowledge. Nobody has had to suffer through me. This has always been my fear: that I would give in to the temptation of being myself once more, an honest woman, a mother like other mothers. Confessing seems something so wide and light. A secret is a jail. But now that I am near to death that silence seems not so hard any more. And I am certain now that I shall be able to keep my secret and to leave the memory my husband and my boys deserve. I can at last lay down my head, and I am grateful that the time has come. My dearest Marie, forgive me and, please, I want you to have a good laugh, that frank, guileless laugh, for having been drawn into sin, willy-nilly, through my poor letter. . . ."

When mother rang the bell that evening for tea, I descended the stairs with a less assured step, in fact, with a heavy feeling of sinfulness. And as I sat down opposite her, I found it difficult, for a moment, to look into her eyes. Mother, who had been hard to get along with all her life, but who had always been so correct! And I, straightforward Marie. . . .

"When it so happens, . . ." wrote Conny.

Bending over my game of solitaire, I had to think of it all the time . . . jack, queen, king . . . when it so happens . . . the inexorable.

And in my virginal bed I lay awake that night, an accessory to the crime . . . won, lost, *himmelhoch jauchzend, zum Tode betruebt* . . . on my little finger was the trusty ring from Conny's middle finger, a secret bridal pledge, a pawn of adultery. . . .

Translated by PAULINE BUKOVSKA

PART IV

TWO FLEMISH MASTERS

Karel van de Woestijne

THE WIFE OF CANDAULES

THE WIFE OF CANDAULES, MY BELOVED, MY BELOVED, (THE EVENING is tranquil and you are listless and I am sad and weary); the wife of Candaules, my bitter love, was very beautiful. . . .
Above the high arch of her little feet with toes the color of white-edged peach blossom—and light sandals of red leather, buckled with a red ruby which sparkled upon the arches—were her small tapering ankles, rosy from the blunt, gay little bumps of the bronze rings that encircled them and that sometimes, when she moved her legs, made sounds of heavy metal and caused a pleasant pain by gentle contusion. And like round spools the curved but not muscular calves rose to severely fastened garments that were numerous, thick and remarkably white. For the wife of Candaules understood the art of being demure.
You mustn't laugh; to look demure is the most lovely demonstration of sweet wisdom; and is there not an irrefutable proof? Who doesn't like to find in a painting a fine reproduction of nature, and who, having found it true to life and lovely, still wants to think of canvas and oil? Who does not like to believe that an actor, with the right voice and gestures, is really Agamemnon or Harlequin? The wife of Candaules knew how to conduct herself with great demureness, even though the thick, heavy draperies about her hips and breasts—only the full round throat with the numerous rows of pearls was bare—allowed one to guess at the perfection of a somewhat small figure, which would perhaps have disappointed you, beloved, because the ripeness of its curves that had probably softened them. For, though the wife of Candaules was very beautiful, she had left the years of youth behind her, which one could guess from her broad, flat arms but not from her charming hands which, without a jewel, were ornamented only by dainty, shining nails. Her eyes—under a low, wide brow that curved like an amber haze—were black, but a moist black as of gazing gazelles, and it remains a secret how they could look demure. If found in other women, they would have

passionately aroused either melting, glowing love or pity that was painfully real, yet she kept them open, and one was neither shocked nor did one lose one's courtesy; for she continued to seem blamelessly wise and intangible. And even her mouth, with open and provoking lips between straight white cheeks, was red like bleeding flesh, and indeed as if weary from frenzied biting; but that mouth aroused no desire that it bite you, though you looked with pleasure at the beautiful line from one corner to the other, like a bow not very suitable for shooting but beautiful and well-shaped. And her face with the imperious nose of a queen was framed by a low hairdress of heavy, dark tresses. And it was so perfect—even if it had struck you as lacking your unusual freshness, my beloved—that one thought of nothing except merely looking at it.

Now this woman was very much loved by her husband, Candaules, who was king of the Lydians. He was a fiery and loquacious man, friendly by nature. He was dressed in garments of red and purple and profuse golden opulence, which left bare his arms, in which brown muscles bulged and gleamed, while in the whiter crook of the elbows and on the broad wrists swelled green and blue veins. He wore golden bands and chains wherever he could place and attach them, and about his hair, that hung curly and black and shiny behind his fleshy ears down to his shoulders, he wound fluttering, fire-colored ribbons. His high-heeled, perforated shoes showed his bare toes, the large one separated by a leather strap from the others—on which he wore rings of no mean value. He generally did not gird on a sword, for he was not a warrior, but into his embroidered sash stuck a long, springy cane with which he laughingly beat his slaves and indicated the turns to the lance bearers when they marched before him in dignified manner, making many maneuvers with a swinging gait. Weighty ornaments heaved on his wide-breathing chest that made his silken vest creak. His fattening belly did not prevent his step from being young and faster than majestic. Nor was his bearded face majestic, for it was like the evening sun, and when he laughed he showed milky white teeth between thick, parted lips, his blazing eyes glowed darkly and his nose had quivering nostrils. Candaules was a man of exuberant, shouting manliness, who loved his wife very much and said to all who wished to listen: "I have the most beautiful wife! I have the most beautiful wife!"

Although he had moods in which he wanted to beat her out of sheer joy at possessing such a beautiful wife, he was full of tender, fatherly care for her, and sometimes spoilt her with his excessive care. He made her sleep in the coolest chambers (for in Lydia it was doubtless rather hot) and chose for himself the apartments in the west where the sun burned longest and strongest, which in a man may be considered a fine proof of loving self-sacrifice. And he chose for her a retinue of the most beautiful serving women and yet remained faithful to her, which was surely flattering for her. And though she would never wear the jewels he gave her, he was not angry and had no suspicions; for his love was very great and it continued to burn in his body with a steady warmth, or rather heat. So he frequently visited her in her chambers with ever renewed joy, and he loved her so much that he did not ask whether she loved him. For she was a very beautiful woman—though, for sure, no longer very young. . . .

And outside the palace too, he showed his devotion to her, by proud ostentation. To her were dedicated the numerous festivals of which there was so much talk throughout the kingdom and to attend which people came even from the deserts. Because Candaules, contrary to custom, attached importance to her presence near him so that he could speak to her in whispers, she and her closest retinue of women were conducted to the festivals in closed palanquins, and to the crowd she showed herself in thick white veils for modesty's sake. For in this way (but this she did not admit to herself) she made them more desirous and regretful and eager that she would once come with her face exposed.

And below her the games took place: tigers that writhed under arrows shot from above and roared entertainingly until they dragged themselves to the corner where, with their golden eyes broken, they died; wild boars that, provoked and furious, with all bristles erect and eyes blood-shot, ran straight into multitudinous, severely trained spears—and what laughter when one of the lancers was thrown over by the all too mighty collision with the animal; or leisurely bears that very calmly clawed open human shoulders; or the personified violence of bronze-fisted athletes from Greece—which was also the home of the singers who came full of beautiful tales of struggles; and the sweet-mouthed flute players, who were less esteemed.

And the wife of Candaules did not speak a word at these performances, but her eyes, through the narrow slit in her veils, followed the fighters who were stalwart and beautiful; and then, if she looked down at the king, he thought that she was smiling sweetly at him from behind her thick clothes and was pleased and touched and very happy. And when the feast came to an end in the evening, she was carried back to the palace in the golden palanquin, while the people shouted, making Candaules proud; and then at night, when the moonlight lay green on the verandas, his shadow slid over the echoing marble floors to speak to her and tell her of his great joy. But often she slept, quietly, nobly, below the double-spouted lamp which smoked slightly. And Candaules looked at her and turned back and thought what a beautiful wife he had. . . .

And did the queen really love Candaules? Really, she loved him; really. Had she not bestowed on him the favor of becoming his spouse? Women love the men they favor; and one sees many taken with very ugly men, for it is a bad woman who does not become attached to the man she has given herself to. Now Candaules' wife gladly and deliberately forgot that he had raised her from a slave who dyed and wove the fleece of sheep to be the ruler of his heart and his numerous tribes, and only remembered that she had given him her youth and her beauty; her attachment to him was thus greater than the memory that he had been good to her. And that was almost love, dominating love, which favored the loved one. But not without a certain boredom, as always in cases of domination.

For, you must know, Candaules was very boisterous. He was like an ever crazy, exultant spring wind in young foliage, beating his vivacity against the cool chastity of her white, thick garments. All his movements were like an attack, almost an affront, against her stateliness, and his laugh sounded to her nearly like a very humiliating box on the ears. He used words like pepper, and all in all she found his insistence unpleasant. His skin shone, his lips were moist. He loved her very much, but not with love like hers. She was a very beautiful woman, was she not? And she also had a sense of modesty, did she not? And I do not think that Candaules possessed that in too great measure. . . . He was a strange man; yes, the liberties that his wife allowed him had not estranged him from her. His love had remained passionate, for he was not a man with calmly reasoning brain, nor with nerves like ours, my beloved, full of inherent weariness. He was a beautiful, virile man and strong, without fine manners, noisy in his love and without sentimental modesty.

This bored her, for she felt too much that her love compared with his had become yielding, a disapproving surrender, without regard for a youth that had grown languorous, heavy and ripe. My beloved, my beloved, it must be sad if one thinks sufficiently on the subject of love when one of the partners exists merely on endured passion, and the wife of Candaules was no longer very young in body; she had, not in royal but in womanly fashion, in the manner of those who no longer feel desire, woven a garment of modest, self-belying gentility (about which I have now spoken enough), which suited her well but which in hours like this, beloved, is paralyzing and brimful of grief. . . . She loved Candaules, certainly; but there grew in her a secret like a growing and hardening little coral tree, and she dared not believe it at first, but it soon crushed and jabbed through her love. It branched out in her daily thoughts, and it would have shown even in her gestures if women were not so good at keeping their own secrets, although they are lavish with those of others, differing in this from men, who give themselves away. And this growing secret was that the bodily love of her husband with which she did not yet dare to be disgusted, for she forced herself to love him, constantly made her think of another love, of more unity with the spirit, of finer taste—though this taste bordered on the bitter—of better understanding, yes, of modesty, and of fitting manners; no tumult, no more riot of love, but the same enjoyment out of a long open glance, a quiet and almost indifferent word, and even in the kiss something pious and holy— Candaules' wife was no longer very young. . . .

Yes, she still loved the king; but he could never become womanish enough, meltingly affectionate, not sweet-feeling enough— he had even never understood that his wife's moods should have been for him a healthy measure of her attachment—to prevent her love from turning lingeringly into another less simple but more adorned one, which would not long falter or tarry to flame up out of the ashes if she found her target.

She found her target. Its name was Gyges. Not difficult, this find, by the way; it was offered her by Candaules himself, who thus presented himself with a rival, as so often happens. Vigorous upon his muscular, tense and sinewy calves, he was slim, with sloping shoulders and well-shaped arms, and on a broad neck he had the noblest, curly, narrow and fine-colored head, blue eyes and lips like a cherry which were not yet concealed by a beard; his straight nose and his small shell-like ears were still very young, and his voice was low and pleasant. As a child the king's favorite, and the most beautiful boy of his most beautiful pair of slaves, the king had let him practise games, ride trotting horses and handle weapons, made for his hand, while still quite young. Then, grown to a youth, in the years when his laughing voice broke and became deeper, and terrifying passions began to boil in his brains, he was sent to Greece to learn the noble arts of language and song and become a man of profound scholarship, of great service to the state, as well as popular in society. He went there and knew women, of houses of pleasure and others, and they soon became repulsive to him; for the sweetly smiling wisdom of the Hellenes had influenced him, an immature and moderate Asiatic, in such a way that after a short time the delights of criticism hindered him from noticing the beauty that is in everything. He also learned the sciences, which roused in him a desire for dominance greater than love. He became a man full of rhetoric, who managed all things cleverly and pleasantly and ever to his advantage. He also acquired distinction and the art of veiling his thoughts in elegant words that could be interpreted in different ways. And he returned to Lydia proficient.

He was the object of the king's unreserved admiration, for with his undiminished bodily beauty, which flowed in the lines of his chest and belly under his tight jerkin and rose from narrow knees to massive thighs—and his hands had not become heavy— there shone in his glance and manners and caressing words a refined courtesy; he gave wise counsel and was, at the same time, affectionate. And he wore clothes which, though not splendid, were of a beautiful, characteristic cut; and his sword, not large, was light and mighty. Candaules weighed it in his hand, cut through the air with it, and it increased his admiration for Gyges who became a friend whom he trusted, almost deferentially and as happily as a child, with all his affairs and whom he led to his wife's chambers in order to show her with what excellent and refined people he associated.

Candaules' wife did not please him at all; at least, a certain restraint in his dry and nagging disposition did not permit him more (and that was much) than to find her a beautiful woman, no longer very young. This restraint even hindered him, in truth, from making any compliments. He was one of those people who, having overcome passion, or scornful of all passion, can only flatter with hard and forced arbitrariness, be it in word or in deed. Not yet low enough to be able to lie cynically, but already quite soberly descending the stairway of bitter disillusion, which people call truth because it is very deep, beneath everything that used to be dear to them, so that the little patch of blue sky they still see is too small to be called heaven. That is how things stood with Gyges; but he did not suffer much from it, because he was still very young. He thought that was how it should be, for the Greeks had taught him their life's raillery, which incidentally had grown in him into a grinning caricature; but not being a Greek, he had not mastered their love of beauty or their forgetfulness of all theory when beauty had awakened their admiration. And the most glorious woman, however provocative, was not able to overcome his calculating intellectualization. Was he of a cool nature? By no means; but passion, so easy to create in a little love affair, the highest point that his conception of life admitted, can be reasoned away. Never fooled except deliberately, he thought he could chat with women and found it amusing with his sweet words to make them fall almost in love, although he himself never made false avowals of love; but it seemed ridiculous to him to fall in love himself; there were too many women in the world for that, and after all he was a beautiful youth. . . . And sometimes, if passion got the upper hand, he was ashamed of himself and laughed at his all too vulgar humanity. For alien culture had made him so that he did not consider himself good unless he was the opposite of his countrymen.

This is how he appeared to the wife of Candaules, who saw him, beautiful, serious of face, deeply educated, with appropriate gestures, and, she imagined (what he was not) full of fine feelings —in all modesty, an image, a beautified image of herself.

And, dearest, she loved him, after some resistance to her reason that told her that she loved the king. And, because Gyges apparently did not at first notice her love—although by this time she wore for him an exposed and very readable expression—she loved him still more; and because Candaules did not notice her new love (she wanted to suffer a little from it: that was part of her nature) she began to hate him, with a hatred that grew smartingly like a cancer, day by day, and which she tried to disregard.

See how this passion that had come into existence grew! . . . When Candaules was her first beloved, how she had quivered at the first caress of her limbs that were muscular and hard in those days, raised her wet eyes gratefully and closed them blissfully, and offered her mouth for his kiss, so light, so light—in an atmosphere of love with mild scents, smothering her warm fresh cheeks. Then she was free and such a happy little queen, who enjoyed everything, the days and the clothes and the new jewels, as if she nibbled at these things like a child, her eyes wide and smiling at finding everything so wonderful. And she loved her husband, her real husband, stormily. Her firm, strongly entwined arms were a crown about his head. She belonged to him; she was grateful to him because she could belong to him, be his wife, entirely his wife.

Alas, her arms had untwined; they had become soft and broad. . . . To think that even the best of sauces grows cold, beloved! And still Candaules was unchanged, neither cooler nor less in love. She still received new jewels; she was tired of wearing jewels, and . . .

Then she loved Gyges. . . . It was quite different, and she felt some shame when she thought of earlier days. For now her limbs were soft and listless. Her beauty, which was great, was like that of statues which, not newly hewn, get marly and weathered under the pattering rain and blowing wind yet still retain their beautiful lines; and, frightened, she almost wept when she felt that she no longer had firm flesh and that her body was no longer like that of a youth approaching manhood. And she grieved that she no longer loved as happily as at first.

But she was all the defter, she knew, and since she had to conquer, could show more importunity. And though she had to safeguard her demureness—and she did it without hypocrisy, for it had become part of her—her eyes, ogling with modesty, and her dainty hands and gait, which she showed off, and the inflection of her voice, though no longer freshly enticing with exuberant youth that screamed for love, spoke so that it would be noticed, she hoped. Ah, if only it had not been noticed! She was frightened, thrust out of a proud peace that was not unhappy, to descend into the garden of a new love that would not be wholesome, perhaps. . . . Would boredom give birth to fear as its only daughter? And she had never been so conscious that she was no longer young; now she combed her hair herself to see its black, lustreless length; she herself prepared the perfumes of leaves and chose the dishes for meals that would not fatten her. For she now loved with a love that was giving, not receiving, and her pressing concern was that the gift be appreciated and accepted gratefully according to its value.

On this she concentrated all her attention. If she did not ask Candaules directly, she knew how to arrange conversations with him in such a way that he himself talked about Gyges and exuberantly praised his accomplishments: he had remained as skillful in driving horses over the clouds of golden sand on the race courses, as he had become in speaking with a sweet mouth about the philosophy of Epicurus (or was he then not yet born, beloved?); he was young, but his youth did not impair his wisdom; he was beautiful but his beauty was never affected. And he was such a modest friend; he never answered Candaules' praises of his wife's beauty, except to indicate with modest respect that he shared the king's joy at having such an excellent spouse. All this Candaules told and retold, and when his wife heard it she felt a cold, fearful shudder go through her. And she pitied her husband and was seized by pious horror at the great love she bore unobserved for Gyges. Ah love, so sadly unnoticed, so wretchedly alone and blazing so painfully in her heart that was learning to hate!

So she thought, and sometimes she was quite desperate. But Gyges had seen everything she did with practised gestures where the spontaneity of youth could no longer speak. Her hesitation did not conceal her desire, nor fastening her dress still more tightly that her heart was beating violently under it. And he found it pleasant to be loved so, although he was not flattered: for his vanity exceeded his ambition. He despised all that was transient, of which the earth consisted, and honored only the spirit, exclusively. But it was not unpleasant to him, this passion for him of a woman whose beauty he daily heard praised by her own husband. There even grew in him a concealed, amused sympathy for her, and when she was near him, he no longer looked at her with the first indifference but found it pleasurable to follow her with his eyes. Fortunately he dropped these before she looked round, turning her head slowly, for she could well have imagined. . . . Certainly she grew, if not in his estimation, then in his merciful toleration of her love for him, and the more because, incidentally, Candaules began to appear to Gyges like an old fool, ridiculous in his lewd fat, no match for a woman who, even though a woman, was perhaps worth something better.

Oh—Gyges had no affection for her! But irony teaches one to be patient. And it was with great patience that he allowed this love to grow around him like a wild rose and he derived almost pleasure from the pricking of the little thorns that were in the queen's eye and word every day, to tell him secretly that she was entirely his, entirely his.

For, with his feigned indifference, her daring became more urgent. He received anonymous letters to the effect that a woman was dying for his love; in his chambers he found new garments, which he recognized, having seen the queen embroider them in the long afternoons. And if there was talk of games and festivals, he heard her sigh, and if he praised a steed or a weapon, she turned her head away from him with sadness in her eyes, saying nothing. And she seemed to him very unhappy—and he thought of her with curiosity and astonishment long after he had left her, and he found Candaules very stupid and very lacking in refinement to make his wife so unhappy. For it was his fault that she could no longer love him.

And so the sprouting eglantine of her love grew about him and gradually strangled him, tied his limbs fast and made his will powerless. He now more seriously analyzed the nature of this love, knowing well that it could not be purely passionate, after the manner of a Candaules, and guessed that she was looking for other enjoyment, of the spirit, in so far as a woman can enjoy spiritually. No, well, no, he did not love her. But ought he to sink to the meanness of love-making when the circumstances, perhaps, demanded of him a manly, strengthening friendship? And the fact that she loved him was no hindrance to him; no, her love did not hinder him, not at all. He suffered it, but now he was already a little flattered by it, like a male nurse who is sometimes bored while tending his patient but is grateful, although he may answer him with annoyance, if the latter speaks to him soft words of appreciation. Thus the love of Candaules' wife was somewhat constrainingly unpleasant if he let it affect him more deeply without mental resistance, but nevertheless it was gratifying, and—annoying? No; he liked it very well, although he considered it below his dignity to let this be seen.

Nevertheless he still approached her only as if he were bashful; he had been by nature loquacious. And, while he had formerly been such a master of words, he now hesitated in all he said, apparently really embarrassed lest his words sound inappropriate. Oh, he still had control of himself; but he was afraid to let one of those short, hasty signs escape of a kindly reaching-out disposition—first estranging and then constraining, and finally for a long time, almost troubling, and yet lingeringly blissful, like the scent of a suddenly smelt bouquet of roses that had not been noticed—those little hints which he had seen had such an effect even on those who could joke about themselves. . . . Besides, this kindly disposition surely did not exist! . . .

But it existed, and Candaules' wife no longer doubted it. While he was hesitant, respectful and wary, she became companionable, sweet and winning. In her certainty she chatted naturally with him, leaving out all that might appear to be love-making. It was a pleasant rest, as after a difficult delivery; the mildness of an evening after a fierce afternoon; something, however, with a very importunate indifference, an innocent sweetness after a fierce fire that has quieted down though is not yet extinguished; the coolness of a wine that may yet become heady.

Then, during his more frequent, though timid, visits, she showed Gyges materials that she had had woven, quite two fathoms wide, and then, negligently against the light, the ivory close transparency of the imperceptible mesh. And then she asked whether Greek styles suited Lydian figures; and whether Greek women were beautiful. And Gyges noticed that she did not look at him, and he remarked that he had never looked closely at Greek women, and then she, aside, asked, "Being a Lydian?" which he answered with somewhat offended pride and yet almost shyly, "Oh no, oh no! . . ."

Or she would have some light pastry baked and, Candaules being present, they would all three taste it along with sweet, cool drinks and then, with a serious face, she would praise the happiness of domesticity with the man one loves and with whose every thought one agrees. And then Candaules would laugh without sound, flattered and very much in love. But Gyges would have understood.

Or, for instance, many slave girls passed through the room carrying a great deal of linen to the spring, and beautiful was the line that started from the heel, up the calf and hip, rising to the stretched breast and gracefully curved arm that bent over the load. And, with a meek voice, the queen asked him whether he found one of them beautiful. And Gyges did not dare to answer that he hated the feminine body, hated it with a real fear, as soon as it no longer resembled that of a beautiful youth with sinewy, hard muscles.

This feeling was very genuine in him; like a beloved clump of nettles, it had a sweet taste and left a burning wound. It had become in him feeling, after having been for a long time thought—strange unnaturalness. His brain had made him a soul out of the dregs of many varying arguments. Uprooted from his natural state, he could only obey the acquired conceptions that had perforce given him a new psychic nature. . . .

And that is how we all are, beloved, if we don't degrade ourselves in order to remain near our origin; for men are still more complicated than you women, O my incomprehensible beloved! . . .

That is how it was with Gyges. And, would you believe it, he began to suffer! His youth was a torch that had burned out everything of thought and breeding that he had not brought from Hellas; and he had been stupidly happy because he could laugh about feminine beauty without urgent desire, and had found it inwardly agreeable. But now—he knew Candaules' wife was in love with him; he ought to have hated her, she ought to have annoyed him with her pappy-softening beauty (and every day he saw better that she was no longer very young); he felt somehow filthy because she loved him. And yet he was wretched because he could love this woman only in thought and for the sake of thought. And this annoyance and wretchedness were for him, by way of education, a cruel pleasure and the enjoyment of a feeling of pain.

And nevertheless he realized that she was no longer quite alien to his life, no longer like a statue that one looks at closely and with interest and later thinks over but sheds no tears over because of its absence or feels pity for when musing on its sorrowful expression of face and gesture. Although he really did not love her, it became a bitter thought now and then to resist something like her, something to which he was forced and yet disposed . . . he could not say toward what disposed. Yes, Candaules was really churlish and ridiculous, although Gyges had to admit to himself, naggingly and resentfully, that Candaules and his wife belonged to one another: this satyr forest god and the shy, smirking nymph.

In this way their hesitant relationship lingered on and the silences that gaped in their conversations were long: she, with her love on her lips like a red morning flower and her eyes cast down —he saw the cobweb of fine little blue veins over the lids fluttering like dark shadows—stitched, long-suffering and submissive, with long movements and she told in the linen, with colored silken threads, the events of a boar hunt between the outlines of two beautiful little palm trees (but she did not let her love pass her lips); he, Gyges, with dry mouth, anxious, disgusted with himself, crossed his legs under the seat, afraid of his own reply if she should make an avowal. And so the days passed: Candaules was away, having left his wife to be diverted by Gyges—for at last he had noticed her boredom. And who, he thought, would entertain her better than this refined Gyges?

Until, one morning, the event took place that decided. . . .

Prepared or by accident? But who knows on which side the purity of feeling was greater or smaller? Don't women always row to the farthest bank while men, being cautious, think it over and remain more in the middle of the stream? For women, when perpetrating villainy, act without principles, having no compulsion but immediate sensation, without the sequence of testing and contemplating and ripening to well-weighed thought.

So, when he entered to receive the greeting that every day was like a bath of cold water, though not unpleasant—and he was generally received in orderly daintiness that had been prepared during many hours—Gyges found the queen stretched sobbing on a couch, with her face buried in the cushions, tightly wrapped in night attire and unapproachable in her deep sorrow. Unconsciously he neared her with rapid strides and, tender and anxious, wanted to say, "You are weeping, Madame?" But he recovered himself, said nothing and remained standing at a distance of three long paces. With displeasure he suddenly saw the shocking line of her hips as she sobbed. He was on the point of withdrawing, looking round meanwhile, when she turned her head, her eyes sparkling and burning from hot tears, her dry mouth open, and her cheeks a fiery red. Then he stepped toward her again. A movement of her arms made her wide sleeve fall back to the elbow. He did not like thickening arms. . . . Then she closed her eyes and sighed. . . . On the dull marble pavement he noticed the shadow of a small, trembling leaf. . . . And he had compassion. . . . The day was overcast, one of those days he loved because they did not overwhelm or make him incapable of thinking. He had come easily, in a light mood, through the inner courts. A bird had sung and he thought of and Philomela, without scorn. . . . Then he had found her crying. . . .

And she sighed: "Oh, Gyges, Gyges!" One of her hands clasped the upper edge of her garment and moved it, leaving a part of her breast exposed, and quietly she began, with a convulsive swelling in her throat: "Oh, that we prepare our own undoing like a condemned man his own winding-sheet! Was I not happy? And what had I done wrong that I was no longer happy? And now—entirely alone, entirely alone."

She was silent and looked sideways at Gyges, who was greatly disturbed. And she said, more dully, with staring eyes: "Candaules was here all night. Perhaps he had drunk light, glowing wines. He was very, very much in love. For him I was like his child, and he did not see that I was restive. Why? Oh! . . . He flattered me, said things that almost made me weep. He called me his beautiful, beautiful wife. And I was as if I had death in my limbs and I could not answer or move. He spoke of you with joy, of you, Gyges. Then I burst out crying. . . . Oh, Gyges, Gyges. . . . He wanted to calm me, he lit all the lamps, wanted to be boisterously happy so that I should be too . . . but. . . . And he went away, very regretfully, Gyges. And now I feel so cold. . . ." And modestly she covered her shoulder again and was silent.

Gyges, feeling limp, did not move; he suddenly saw in his mind's eye a disgusting spectacle of the ageing Candaules drawing toward him the fattening queen who turned away a sulky little mouth, shaking her heaving body like an unruly school-child. And then the king, running round, frightened, unable to find fire-flints with which to light the chandeliers. And then, Candaules, going away with great difficulty and yet regretfully . . . And she; she was not so ridiculous as he. . . . And thinking of her Gyges forgot his sudden desire to laugh. He again had pity; and, when she looked at him with eyes full of tears, he half sighed and sat down in painful awkwardness.

He found no words. The situation did not seem so amusing to him as it had in the case of others. Again he half sighed. He moved a little nearer and saw that she had stopped crying. He gave a little cough. Then she started again, very quietly, in a steady voice, first rubbing her eyes and cheek with the back of her hand:

"You know everything; you know everything, Gyges, you understand me so well. And—I know very well that only out of respect. . . ."

And Gyges nodded, seriously, almost sincerely.

"But now—I can't stand it any more. He really hurts me. I used to love him, but now he causes me intense suffering. And his hair is so greasy with perfume. . . . He loves me. He has no other women. And I am ashamed that I must hate him. He does not touch one's wrists without hurting. His kiss burns a stigma on one's brow. . . . Oh Gyges, why do I tell you this, you, who already understand it? But I know: considerateness; he was your friend. . . . He is your friend, you who do not dare to become my friend. . . . But I am unhappy, Gyges and—only because of Candaules? One doesn't leave barrels which contained pure oil empty, or they'll crack and burst. And one who once knew love demands love again. Oh, how I loved him then! But it was so different; I was so young. Forgive me. Only now do I know beautiful deep love, like still pools under dense foliage, and even the moon will not discover. . . ."

Gyges thought: "The woman is like the tubers of the leek plant. They look white but have a pungent taste." But he said nothing.

And she played on with her quiet phrases as with bobbins over a cloth being woven.

"Candaules was beautiful and good. . . . Don't be angry. . . . And I was so young and inexperienced and did not know myself. His love was like a smile for me, and I trusted him. His passion was full of tenderness when he first had me as wife.

He was like a father toward a delicate daughter, proud that she was growing up to be beautiful. He could caress my hand a long time in his like a Cyprian kitten, and I tremble when I think how inexpressibly happy it made me. And I was. . . . But now; yes, Gyges, now? And whose fault? Ah, Gyges! . . ."

She moved closer, ogling. Gyges found her vulgar and remembered that she had been a wool-dyeing slave girl. And then he wondered why she had fallen in love with him.

Again she began to speak: "Gyges, you . . ."

But he, suddenly rising with much courage, said:

"Madame, they are waiting at the stud farm to choose the king's horses." And bowing, he went away, drawn up to his full height with springy step, head up, not turning around. . . . She was at first bewildered; then she shrugged her shoulders. Then bitter tears rose, tasting like gall in her throat. She very nearly wept again. But she called the servant girls and dressed. After that she withdrew to her own rooms and remained alone.

Gyges, having left her, was in thought for a long time. The case no longer seemed so strange to him. But it was as if he were walking in new air, air for him alone; as if a wreath floated round him, or sometimes also on unseen clouds. He now reflected more and more consciously. . . . The day had remained a dull blue, without too much sun or shadow, until toward evening, when the light poured from the sky over the earth like the blazing basalt of which crags are cast, palely glowing in the air and blackish-red like the sheen of a distant burning town.

Then Gyges washed carefully and put on a steel-blue jerkin with gold, which suited him well, and red-leather gauntlet gloves. He left off his sword and chose the newest, narrowest thongs to strap round his calves. The helmet, which he had from a Greek conqueror, shone. He found his face in a silver mirror distinguished, and he stepped, sureness beating in his heart, to the queen's chambers. . . . The light from the high windows lay square and motionless on the surrounding purple marble floor; the darkness was already becoming more impenetrable in the corners and the doorway.

From this darkness stepped the greying paleness of the veiled wife of Candaules. Walking slowly across the long hall, she passed alternately through patches of blazing light and enveloping obscurity. Gyges saw the strange spectacle, and, my beloved, since he was contemplative that evening, he thought: "O, Woman, you are approaching, like the soul of your whole sex, which passes by our male life sometimes as clear as the intensest truth and sometimes as black as the most unfathomable secret." And he was content with himself, but he was not without some restlessness when she, coming very near him, smiled full of sweet reproach and pining forgiveness.

He stood very straight, with his helmet on his left arm. He did not consider it necessary to bow low. His hair waved in a rosy halo of light from the sun behind him. The queen found him beautiful.

He began: "Madame. . . ."

But she motioned him to sit down. She herself lay down on the couch of that morning.

Then he spoke long-considered words, in the best style:

"Madame, I fear I have not misunderstood you. I believe I have noticed that you showed me confidence in expressing a judgment disadvantageous to your husband and his love, increasing it by a surrender which flatters me, but which I do not wish to analyze more deeply, for I am afraid of you, Madame."

She smiled as if saying, "I know better." Her lips curled, showing her teeth. His rhetoric tried to unroll further periods:

"I do not analyze it, Madame, for I am also anxious about my own conceptions. Incidentally, I know you too well not to know how much we think alike about the human feeling that, forgive me, is called love. You have learnt to abominate it through practice, and I, through thinking about it. We are both young, Madame"—he bowed while she closed her eyes—"and how can I help fearing rash and over-hasty, let us say, confidence? For all certainty is relative, although I am convinced I need not fear my own weakness. And yet,—Madame, we must be cautious, not only for our own sakes. One must not be ruthless, although it is good to replace timidity by scepticism. So we must not let Candaules, honored be his name, become suspicious, not out of fear of chastisement for wrong-doing or thinking, but because we stand above a love affair, Madame. You have come to stand above it through experience, have you not, Madame? And I, through upbringing. At most a fine friendship, perhaps? But, even supposing our youth to be armed," he bowed, and she again closed her eyes, "is it not more deceptive even than love which, though despicable beyond measure, stands on the firm ground of animality. But this ground, Madame! Don't let us talk about it! Oh, love! Friendship!" And he felt the blood rush to his cheeks. "Madame, I beg you to believe that I am very flattered and shall remain your loyal servant, a support in all that may overtake you, a protection against anyone who may

disturb you; believe in the devotion of one who no longer believes in duty, the most spiritual of virtues, but who, born of
slaves, puts his pride into being a slave who is better than his
master."

And at these last words he did not bow. He realized that he
had not told half of what he had prepared and he reflected that
there must have been gaps in his speech.

Three times she rolled her black-tressed head from side to side
upon the cushions. And after that, half wrathful, in her distressing boredom, she sighed:

"If only the king were dead."

He shuddered. It was already quite dark—eastern darkness.
The white of her eyes shone like very distant lamps encased in
alabaster. . . .

Then, Gyges, again at ease, after a pause in which he had
realized the disappeaarnce of the evening light and had been
almost amused by his agitation:

"Does not Madame perhaps wish much more than a little
change?"

But now her words sounded dull and deep in the obscurity
that was steadily growing denser:

"I have been thinking of that for a long time. His death,
the wish for it, is perhaps the only thing that lets me strive for
you. If it is mutual. How do I know? But—" and she gave three
hollow sobs. "I have had enough of it." And then: "You would
be a beautiful king, Gyges, and a real one, and not that man of
alms, stick beating and other whims."

She was silent, and so was Gyges. It lasted a long time. Then
he stood up. She saw his tall figure rise against the light of a
window square. She said:

"Now, farewell. Don't think about the fact that I shall have
much grief tonight."

He did not answer, first hesitated, then went, very erect and
noiseless, out of the room. . . .

In the inner court he saw Candaules, surrounded by bronze
and green, and a sharp, short-skirted flute player, who was showing him—bending over it attentively—how one stops up the holes
of a flute in turn to make melody. The king spoke to him generously, looking up, and Gyges guessed at the candid face:

"May the night bring you the dreams I wish myself, O Gyges!"

He answered with a counter solicitude, in a subdued voice. And
—he thought then of the frightful murder it would be, with
blood on his hands, upon an evening like this. Candaules' open

mouth would be black, the fingernails in the torn flesh of the palms, his glowing beard pointing toward heaven, as he lay. . . .

Then Gyges passed with even tread to his room and to sleep. He still heard three flute tones and Candaules' boisterous laugh. And, after undressing carefully, he went to bed.

But he did not sleep. He reflected, though he fought against the thought, that he would be an acceptable king. And Candaules' wife was not too bad. Had he perhaps not drivelled this evening, contrary to his opinion? And then, improvements were very necessary: agriculture. . . . Candaules was a good man, but to learn to play the flute at his age. . . . Drama was little known in Lydia; it would be good to introduce it, to educate the people. And there was especially the army. . . .

For three days he did not see the queen. He remained in his apartments and was surly with his slaves—he had three. The first was tall and stalwart and after all the women and had glittering eyes. He was tractable and cheerful, and Gyges liked him because of his great beauty and feared him somewhat. The two others were shrunken creatures whom he despised and found to be like warts.

On the fourth day the queen sent a message that he was to come to her. Then he was truly afraid, and he went. She had a searching smile to receive him and said, after his bow:

"Three nights Candaules has been here, as far as this bedroom. But could I still receive him, Gyges? So, each time he turned away. You know where his rooms are? In the right wing, yes, in the right wing. . . . They are murmuring in the palace; at the moment he is going about very much with a young fluteplayer, who will certainly be his favorite. And he remains faithful to me, for every night he comes. . . . You see, Gyges, I have no secrets from you, but seriously, I can't stand him any more. Must I still. . . ."

Gyges felt a great, sad boredom. Surely he did not love this woman?

And then, she continued, languishing: "Can he understand me? Oh, if he would only once make a long journey. You would be the master, Gyges. It's astonishing that I can't easily imagine you as king. . . . But you cannot fancy how I detest him! . . ."

Gyges said nothing. And then it was suddenly as if hot water boiled up in her, and she said, passionately:

"But are you stupid after all? Speak, speak! After all, you wish the same!"

And she approached him with her bare arms, their scent being wafted toward him. No veiled fire was in her eyes; her lips were wet. Turning pale, he held her away from him; with his open hand he felt the heaving of her breast. He said, with reproach and with little more:

"Madame, Madame!"

She burst into sobs, sank down into the cushions. Again a laugh bubbled up in him, which he quickly smothered; it was really rather boring! Then he made as if, even hesitatingly, to go away. But he returned and with infinite pity (yes, he thought out of pity for the woman who needed his help), with a sudden trembling and noiseless quivering of his voice, which was at the same time calming:

"Is it tonight that you want him to be. . . ." He felt as if sinking into a pit. She did not answer but her sobs stopped. Silence. She did not look at him. And he went away—like a murderer in a melodrama, beloved. What good manners can achieve!

That was at noon. He did not know how it was possible for him to eat with appetite a leg of mutton served by the beautiful man who was his slave and was called simply "Aner." This Aner told Gyges, during the meal, that the king had asked whether he would go riding with him that afternoon. Gyges answered coolly and without alarm in his voice: "I shall go."

Then he and Candaules rode high, white steeds, through the radiant day that gradually grew red with the saffron evening; and beside them leapt like drawn bows the whippets that panted with tongues out and flanks quivering. So the night approached, but this did not silence Candaules. His voice echoed while he said:

"Gyges, I have the most beautiful wife. But what a caprice, that for days now I may not visit her? She is depressed, Gyges; you must cure her, Gyges."

And he kept coming back to this until it riled Gyges, who no longer dared to answer, for there would certainly have arisen a quarrel of sharp words.

Fortunately, they arrived at the palace; and Gyges had never known a colder evening than this. The air made one shiver. His hands, which he constantly rubbed, became clammy. He thought: "What shall I do now?" His good short sword, which he did not look at, hung on the wall. Its strap was of red leather, richly embroidered, and fell in a heavy coil with reflections of white light upon the curve and with a play of golden points.

He still heard the king's clear voice giving orders to the grooms, after that the king's steps toward the drinking halls while humming. His voice approached like a swarm of quivering gnats and then again became more remote. Gyges thought with annoyance: "He is drinking sultry wines; and tonight. . . ." Then he wanted not to think any more and immediately sat down, dull and benumbed, without emotion. The night came damply through the open window onto his shoulders. Then in his mind's eye he saw again Candaules' wife in the form and shape of the dancer that had become an almost burdensome mental obsession of his, the dancer that twisted round the belly of all Greek vases—the knee of one leg poised on tiptoe, bent, and the head, under a heavy load of hair, turning sideways, and the double flute slanting. Gyges said to himself determinedly: "Surely not for that woman!"

Then it was already very late. The cold was like unseen shadows in the room. His mind suddenly became sharp and cold and as clear as ice. His teeth chattered. As he rose briskly and automatically, the bench fell over, and this made him break out into a sweat of fear. He gripped his sword; the handle was icy. . . .

Then he hastened over the inner courts, dazed and yet very sure of his action, toward the light that shone from Candaules' bedroom. . . . His left hand steadied the sword in his right. He entered by the ever open door and a pleasant scent met him. The king lay snoring on his stomach. He did not see the face that was resting on the bent arm. Then Gyges' heart beat like a sledgehammer, but he chose carefully and well the place where he had to strike: on the left, the third rib, downwards. Then he thought, yes, then he thought that it was incomprehensibly strange that he. . . . And as in a sudden whirling intoxication the sword struck not far from the best place. . . . And Candaules neither cried out nor sighed. But he was dead. . . .

Gyges was now calm, and he left, not looking round, naturally. And on the way he thought over how he was to tell her. "Immediately," he reflected. But then arose a certain boredom on account of an undeniably bad deed. . . . Oh, he detested the woman, really, in a way. She was getting old, she was stout; and tearfulness. . . .

He walked through the dark row of rooms that became lighter and lighter the nearer he came to the queen's. And the air became more full of perfume. There was still one door curtain; should he raise it? He heard hushed voices. . . . Then there was in him such sadness. . . .

He ventured in, and . . . there she stood, naked; she was awaiting him with outstretched arms and sharp, red mouth. All the lights were on, they shone on her white body. One slave girl was washing her, with scented water, hands gliding over the thick limbs. All she still wore, round the pink, bruised ankles were her irremovable, bronze slave rings. . . . And she smiled and turned her bosom and was about to speak.

But Gyges uttered a cry, and shouted, crazily:

"But you are naked!"

And he fled, into the night that was still and full of stars.

You are weeping, my beloved? Oh, don't cry, although the evening is now tranquil and you so listless and I so painfully weary. . . . Be comforted, my beloved, be comforted.

For, when Gyges had reigned three months, having been named king, and had not visited the queen a single time she had him murdered by the beautiful Aner, his valiant slave, who became the very virile husband of Candaules' wife.

Her name is mentioned neither by Plato nor by Herodotus. Have I told you that her name was Gune?

You are weeping, my beloved?

Translated by JO MAYO

Willem Elsschot

THE LITTLE BOY

DEAREST WILLIAM,

I am writing today because I want you to know that your twentieth birthday has not passed by your father unnoticed. Shall I congratulate you? Otherwise there is little that is cheering when the year-clock strikes. As regards the everlasting tie—this time too I could find nothing better—it will be handed to you by your mother personally, and certainly not without comment. But let me tell you in advance that I am almost not to blame and assure you that my conduct is pretty innocent. What one calls in grain, "fair average." The best cannot be expected of me, can it? Your mother will leave on Monday to go and see on the spot whether the six months in Paris that you now have behind you have left you untouched as to body and soul, and whether you are being looked after by her excellent sister as she believes a boy like you should be looked after. You are thus warned and still have time to wash your feet and go to the barber. And every time there is talk of your father, try to exert a soothing influence.

And now to the point. For you must know, William, that your mother will not come alone but that your three-year-old nephew will accompany her on the journey. And Jan, to mention him by name, has undergone an evolution since your departure, I can assure you. I don't mean so much appearance and size, for in half a year that changes little and he has still his curls, you may be sure; I mean the bewilderingly quick development of his thinking faculties and of his oratorical talent. You know that six months ago he still had pleasure in senseless questions, as intermittent as the jug-jug of a nightingale. Well, that time is over and will not return at present, unfortunately. For not only is his interrogation full of pitfalls, but he goes on till I take to flight, and escape is impossible when there is no one at home, for I dare not leave him alone. Now please don't laugh, for I can assure you that you haven't the faintest notion of what awaits you while your mother and aunt do the Paris shops, and you will be thus occasionally sitting alone with the little absurdity.

But dry theory does not convince, and so I cannot do better than send you a true report of a conversation that I had with the young man this afternoon, while your dear mother went to town to try on a dress. It began when the street door closed behind her, and if she had not returned two hours later, probably driven by hunger, I should not have been able to finish this report today.

As always he went straight at it without any consideration for my activities. For the bang of our gate had not died away when he threw his spade into the grass, wiped something away from under his nose, looked at me as if to say, "Now we are ready," and played his first card. He did not actually wink, but there was something like it in his look.

"Is the lion as big as the world?"

If I have to go through with it, I like his lion best, for I myself am not sufficiently sophisticated to have lost all awe of this terror of the desert. So let's go right ahead with that beast. I make short work of it:

"No," I declare as decidedly as if I had really weighed it against the King of the Desert. And with a sigh I close my book.

I have said "no" because it is true and short and because he likes conclusive replies. He can't bear evasion. According to his fundamental law something has to be large or small, strong or weak, hot or cold, heavy or light, for he finds that shades of difference complicate his world unnecessarily. He sees to it that the large dominates, the strong oppresses, the hot burns and the heavy crushes, and the small, weak, cold and light are there merely to make all this enduring. And he himself is the hub round which everything turns.

But however conclusive my "no" was, he looks sour, and it takes some time until I realize that this glorious truth is not to his taste. This time it is really too true, and so I spontaneously correct myself:

"Yes, Jan, the lion *is* as large as the world."

I have used his name confidentially with a slight tremolo, in the hope of getting him into a gracious mood, and this time I give him a mouthful all at once by not simply saying "yes," for after my "no" it would have sounded a little silly. And, above all, he is not to think that I am simply blurting out something, otherwise he will lump me together with the charwoman who gives no answer at all and goes on mopping the floor. I therefore add to that "yes" his whole original question with lion and all, and in a rather exaggerated tone of affirmation, so that he at least gets the impression that this second completely contrary answer is the result of deeper reflection and at the same time prevents him from insisting on confirmation. Lose no time. The less he has to repeat, the sooner he will get to the end of his rosary.

My bumptious sureness apparently does not yet give entire satisfaction.

"Larger?"

He seems to know very well that two things are never equally large and that therefore in this case also one of the two is probably a little larger. I even suppose that his conviction about the relation of lion to world was already fixed before he asked whether one is as large as the other. His first question was simply an introductory allegro. He only acted as if he were in doubt so as not to influence me in the choice of my answer. For an opinion dictated by him, as it were, can never give him as much pleasure as the free expression of my opinion, at least if this does not conflict with his peculiar management of his no less peculiar creation. In any case I know that I may not hesitate now between the positive, well-tried lion and the abstract world, otherwise things will immediately go wrong. After all, his question has something of a summons in it. I hear him thinking: "Just dare, with your nerve, to find that lion only a little smaller!" And to be devoured myself, well, no thank you! For he understands that one can without difficulty give someone who is so easily brought from "no" to "yes" a second kick in the behind.

"Yes, larger," I admit reluctantly.

He enjoys his victory and that of his lion for a moment, so that I already take up my book.

"If Jan puts a lion with the Germans, what then?"

What have they not done with that poor Germany since the Treaty of Versailles! And now, after all those vultures, this lion, too. I should answer that the Germans would put his lion in a cage at Hagenbeck's, but I dare not. That beast's prestige lames me completely.

"Then it's bad, Jan," I assure him with a troubled face.

He finds that "bad" much too vague and altogether inadequate.

"What do the Germans say then?"

"Nothing, Jan. They run away."

Did he think he'd make a fool of me? As if he would ever permit those Germans simply to react with words upon the sudden appearance of his lion! Then they might just as well remain sitting and go on drinking. No, whether I like it or not, I must at least make those people take to their heels, however warlike they otherwise are, or I shall certainly get into hot water with His Majesty. For this "say" of the Germans is only the introduction to a far more difficult ordeal that he has in store for them, but he doesn't let loose at once because he wants first to put me through my paces. One hundred per cent lion-minded, or he will place me on the retired list.

His resentful glance searches the distance. It will not please him if the Germans transform their fate with the help of their legs.

"Why do they run away?"

Without committing himself to anything, he wants to hear it definitely declared that all that running is not just for fun but has a deeper cause. And this must not be sought outside the teeth and claws of that beast. Indeed, I feel tamed and entirely reduced to nothing.

"Because they are afraid," I admit meekly.

He puckers his growing eyebrows slightly, very probably because my discharge is progressing too slowly for him.

"Why are they afraid?"

And almost whispering, as if to give me courage:

"Does the lion eat up the Germans?"

He wants to hear wailing, he wants to see blood, or his lion will be stabled for the rest of his days. But Jan must learn geography later and should know that the global munching of all

Germans is too difficult even for a lion, at least at one meal. I shall risk it, for it is for his good.

"Eat them up? Yes, Jan, a few."

"What's that?"

I have fired it recklessly and now he wants to hear then and there what that suspicious "few" means which according to him does not fit in, and to investigate if it is not a beast or something else that could injure his lion, so that he can, if necessary, immediately intervene.

"What?" I ask back in order to win time, for I really don't know how to pump the conception "few" into him. But he is not in the least served with this counter question.

"You must say it."

I put on a meditative, deeply wrinkled face, like a real Archimedes, and now it turns out unexpectedly that my mimicry in itself gives him satisfaction. Have I something of the grimness of a lion, or does he know in advance that not much is to be expected from my search? At least he does not press the point and just lets me sit with that "few," tongue-tied. The main thing, he probably finds, is that his lion fancies Germans and has started eating them up. And, after having followed the first phase of the devouring:

"And if the lion fights with a horse, who wins?"

"The lion," I declare scornfully, for I find that is a question not worth the asking.

"And the horse?"

He wants the wretched end of that horse to seal for the umpteenth time the victory of his lion.

"And the horse?" he repeats imperatively.

"That loses!"

Yes, I should have foreseen it. He knows better than I that the horse is in for it, but he expected machine-gun fire from my mouth, a torrent of rattling verbs under which that horse would be destroyed then and there. And then a disapproving grimace. For "losing" he finds dull, because he who simply loses can win next time, and that thought alone is nothing less than lèse-majesté. Besides, in the depth of his soul, he has determined that his horse shall have no chance to relapse into crime, at least not today.

"Does not the lion eat up the horse?"

It threatens to become a repetition of what has happened to our Germanic brothers, and that "not" means that I could have said it long ago of my own accord. And again the irritated tone.

"But Jan, he can't any more, because he has all those Germans in him." For I find that an early comprehension of logic will not hurt him, and indeed he seems to realize that there is something in it, without however giving up even for a moment the axiom of the ultimate devouring.

"Does the lion eat the horse up when it is dark?" When the Germans are digested, he means.

The auto-da-fé is postponed for a bit but it will be performed. He just gives his lion a little respite, for it is now only four o'clock and still bright day.

It seems to me that his indulgence deserves a reward. So I shall restore his lion to honor and make a radical end to that boring horse.

"Yes, when it is dark the lion catches hold of the horse, shakes it well, tears it to pieces, eats it up and licks the floor clean."

"Only the tail he leaves," I say further, to soften the gory scene a little, for I fear that pedagogically it is not as it should be. After all, *something* may remain of that poor horse.

He thinks about our tail; it seems to run counter to his wishes; apparently he doesn't at all see why that appendage should remain behind on the clean-licked floor for an indefinite time like an annoying posthumous. Perhaps he finds that the curtain cannot fall on this horse-and-lion scene as long as that tail still lies there. And behind his curtain there are still numerous matadors, stamping.

"Why doesn't the lion eat up the tail?"

Before possibly clearing away this remnant himself, he wants to know whether there is not some acceptable excuse for the incomplete dispatch of our late horse, for he likes to see his lion perfect in all his doings and omissions, especially doings. How much prestige has that animal lost, that is the question.

"Because the hairs would tickle his throat."

As motive it is rather poor, but I can find nothing better for the moment. And I see that he finds it an inferior way of doing things on the part of his lion, an inexplicable shortcoming, a professional neglect of duty, for he decides to straighten out this unsolved question of the tail later in the day, suddenly puts away tail and lion and, by way of distraction, lets some of his steam monsters line up.

"And if the engine of the train fights with the steam-roller?"

Occasionally such a lumbering monster comes jolting over the cobblestones of our street. It spits fire and makes the walls shake violently, I must admit. And yet I don't understand how he

comes to let it suddenly enter the lists against his engine, which
is his first heavy-weight champion. Does the thing seem larger
to him in our narrow street than it really is, or has that ponderous steam-roller built up its prestige out of pure noisiness? So,
if those two fight, he doesn't even ask any more, "Who wins
then?" as if he considers that I have had enough practice to be
able to guess that part of his question.

"Then the train engine wins," I declare airily. For I wouldn't
think of giving that beast of a steam-roller a chance in the first
round.

Unfortunately he is not pleased. Yes, his steam-roller is something new again and will have to serve for a time. And I quickly
realize that this heroic challenger is being treated by me with
too much unceremoniousness. That the roller doesn't explicitly
win may not displease my friend, but someone who is especially
called by him to join issue with that overwhelming engine in
any case deserves consideration as being of a good family. Suddenly I get a brain-wave to bury this ungracious treatment with
marks of honor, then and there. And, as always, I exaggerate.

"No, Jan, then the steam-roller wins." After all, why not, if he
prefers it?

But his face remains surly. The sudden turning of my coat
looks most suspicious to him, and besides he considers it presumption that I permit myself, of my own accord, to pronounce
such an unexpected knockout of his engine. It looks as if he is
getting enough of my self-opinionated judgments, which are too
much subject to ebb and tide. What should I do now? That encounter cannot pass without consequences, can it, I think? Then
sport gives me an idea. Why not a draw or dead-heat? But then
at once, or he will find me ridiculous.

"The engine of the train comes from there and the steam-
roller from over there. Closer and closer. Be careful, for they
bump against each other! Rattle-bang! And they both stop!"

He follows the spectacle of these two monsters attentively, looks
at me sharply as if he weren't sure that I really mean it, is not
dissatisfied and again decides, in God's name, to postpone the
investigation of the true procedure until this evening, for suddenly he stables engine and steam-roller with tail and lion and
throws a searching glance at the lanky silhouette of his great-
grandfather who is making his entrance. He has been for a walk
and dropped in to see whether we are all alive still. At the sight
of his great-grandson he gets tears in his eyes and jovially holds
out his carpenter's hand, a hand to frighten one.

Before this coal shovel Jan makes a few steps backward, for he is not generous with handshakes, looks at his older adversary for a moment and finds he is after all worth a question. In any case he digs his steam-roller up for him again.

"And if Great-grandfather is crushed by the steam-roller?"

Great heavens! The man is hardly in the house and he is in for it already. And he laughs and cries too much. If he hasn't any more to say to us, he had better send out a crackling curse now and again, or something else that can make an impression, for that little monster always sticks handkerchiefs in his hand, even before the tears are really there.

"When Great-grandfather is crushed by the steam-roller, he is dead," I declare bitterly.

"And what do people say then?"

"They say that it is a pity."

"And what does the man of the steam-roller say then?"

Thus he does not count that man among the common crowd and finds that he has the right to make his opinion known separately. And in any case he wants to know how the culprit himself will react to the crushing.

"He says: 'By George! There's someone under my machine again!'"

Now pay attention, William. He will reach his aim by a roundabout way, in two stages.

"*What* does the man say?"

This first question not only has the purpose of hearing me say again "By George," which particularly pleases him and which he has definitely adopted, but at the same time to make me repeat the word "machine," which I do, for how could I assume that I am being led by the nose by something that is hardly higher than our table? So I repeat good-naturedly:

"He says: 'By G-G-George! Someone under my machine again!'"

And, because it gives him pleasure, I let the "By George" roll in with an extra hiss this time.

He receives the hissing unblushingly as one who finds it is his due. And now that I have so foolishly confirmed that "machine," and even in the presence of his grandfather, who just smiles:

"Why does he say 'his' machine?"

"Well, Jan, because he rides on it." For in my innocence I think he wants me to demonstrate the possessive pronoun, furnish evidence of ownership for that man on the machine.

"But it is no machine."

"Then what is it, Jan?" For a lion is in any case still less so, and I don't like to see that someone who is nearly four still makes no distinction between his living and his mechanical champions.

He again looks like gall because he does not at all adjudge me the right to interrogate *him,* as if he were conscious that the glorious time of asking belongs irrevocably to the past for me.

"No," he repeats obstinately, "it is no machine."

I'll agree with him, though the violation of the truth goes against the grain with me too.

"Of course it is no machine." "Obviously" the surviving Germans should say, but they keep quiet. From the fact that my admission is not followed by an elucidation of what it *is,* he concludes that I don't know, for I always spontaneously furnish the maximum.

"What is it then? Don't you know?"

No, confound it, I don't know. And I look into Father's eyes to see if he happens to know, but there I only meet tears. Tears of happiness because Jan asks like that, because I give answers so well and because God allows him to live to see it all.

"It is a steam-roller," says Jan softly, as if he was ashamed for me because the old man is present. And he takes my handkerchief out of my pocket for staunching Great-grandfather's tears in time.

Yes, it is a steam-roller right enough and no machine. If they were all machines, how should we be able to arbitrate without getting into confusion? Indeed, I should have thought of it long ago, that there is only one machine, namely the mighty, shrieking, hurrying machine of the train, the glorious locomotive.

Fortunately he does not let me sit too long in sackcloth and ashes.

"You must say what Jan says when he sees that."

"When he sees what, boy?" For I have entirely lost my bearings and feel as sore as if I had lain under the steam-roller for hours.

"When he sees that the steam-roller has crushed Great-grandfather."

Now that good man will hear his own funeral oration, and who knows whether Jan won't add a few of his new "By George's"?

I shall just think it over, for if he talks about his family I must be doubly careful, pay some regard to ceremony and wrong no one. And I really don't know what he prefers: lamenting at the sad loss or rejoicing at the thoroughness of the crushing. But to the latter I shall not lend myself, for Father's prestige is poor enough. Father himself, who has least to say although it is the question of his hide, has started filling a pipe. He patiently lets things pass him by in the certainty that gin will soon have the last word.

I must present Jan with something valiant—something like a charge of the blue hussars.

"When he sees that the steam-roller has crushed Great-grandfather, Jan says nothing but gets angry. He lets his eyes roll, stops the steam-roller with one hand, with the other drags the fellow from the machine, no, from the steam-roller, squashes him flat, and whirls him over the Eiffel Tower into the Seine. Voilà!" For I am trying to make him gradually acquainted with Paris by occasionally referring to the Eiffel Tower, the Seine, catacombs, your aunt and other curiosities. He already knows that the Seine is fluid, just like the Schelde.

"What are you saying?" Of course it is the strange "voilà" that he finds suspicious.

"Nothing, Jan."

He looks at me sharply as if to say: "Take care!"

"When Jan whirls that man into the Seine, doesn't he drown?"

I believe he is beginning to grow anxious about the fate of the man, not so much on account of the drowning itself, for his victims are legion, but because he doesn't want to see the steam-roller immobilized forever. And it can't move without that fellow. Yes, the man must be helped.

"When he is nearly drowned and comes up for the last time, Jan fishes him out of the water by his hair, makes him promise never to do it again, gives him a kick, puts him back on his steam-roller, blows his trumpet and lets him drive on."

If he doesn't oppose that driving on, the steam-roller is out of the way; we can still have a great deal on hand. But about that trumpet I should have remained silent, for I believe he has one lying about somewhere.

"And Great-grandfather?" he asks hesitantly.

Good boy. As long as Great-grandfather lay invisible under the steam-roller he could stand it. But now that this roller has withdrawn, he doesn't dare to look at the remains. Is it something that still has shape, or simply a spot, a skin, in one word, a second annoying horse-tail, the clearing away of which can again cause a lot of bother? And now that that fellow has been allowed to keep his fated life, he seems to feel inclined to place our crushed father on his feet again. But I'll have to take care with such an operation, and the best thing is probably to consult first. I look concerned. And in a lisp, so that our hard-of-hearing victim cannot understand:

"Shall we cure Great-grandfather, Jan? Then he can have a drink."

Jan hesitates but hasn't the courage to go on sitting near that corpse any longer. He flees from the terrible truth to accept a role in the comedy of this resurrection.

"Uncle Karel?" he suggests in a whisper.

Unforgivable that I did not myself immediately think of that doctor of a brother of mine. Good for you, Jan. And in rapture I take hold of Father's hands, who feels that I want to congratulate him on something or other, for he squeezes back energetically, and I see new tears.

Meanwhile Jan has caught sight of a box the lid of which is ornamented with butterflies.

"What's that?"

"Butterflies."

"Are they also animals?"

"Yes, Jan."

"Are those animals in the zoo?"

"Certainly, Jan."

"Were those animals bitten to death by the lions and tigers long ago?"

"Yes, boy, don't worry."

"What are you saying?"

Again he finds that that "worry" is too much. Those animals are bitten to death, or they are not, and that's all.

"May the lions and tigers cack and piss in the zoo?"

I find this transition astonishing and ask myself anxiously why he suddenly leads his noble lions onto the stage in such a grotesque act. Surely no innate obscenity? And the theory of heredity haunts my mind, for I have a whole lot behind me in all sorts of spheres. And from what has leaked out, my forebears were no better. In any case his vocabulary must be purified. But I resolutely say "yes," for truth before all.

"Who lets them cack and piss?"

"The bosses, Jan."

Slightly deaf and puffing, Father stands looking, waiting for the drink. He has just sauntered as far as our sideboard, but has returned without doing anything, for he wants to receive but not to take.

"Why may Jan not cack and piss in the garden?"

Thank goodness it has nothing to do with obscenity, but with our good neighbor's wife. For he himself has scandalously abused our garden till the lynx eye of Mrs. Peeters, though hindered by a curtain, discovered that it was no pumpkin. And then she immediately took her pen in hand.

"Why?" he insists.

"Because Jan is no lion." For I hate the classic "Because!"

"And if Jan is a lion after all?"

"Then Jan must eat horses up every day, and the tails will tickle his throat." For I don't want to talk about that smutty story any more, especially now that we have started on the good path. Then I'd rather dispatch that tough tail in any possible way.

He seems to feel that I am resolute in contradiction this time, for he again looks attentively at the lid of that box.

"Aren't those sunstrokes?"

"No, Jan."

Now at last I understand why he threw those butterflies to his lions and tigers just now. For when it was very hot, I warned him against the sun and spoke of sunstroke. And a little later he came rushing into the kitchen, moaning: "Sunstroke! Sunstroke!" His mother dropped whatever she was holding and flew to meet him, whereupon he showed her the sunstroke in question, sitting quietly on a white rose.

"Has a sunstroke paws?"

For a sunstroke is, and at present remains, an animal for him, something that has shape, volume, weight and weapons, and can perhaps fight against steam-rollers.

"Will Jan never die?"

Would the bitter fate of Germans, horse and Great-grandfather have brought him to his senses?

"No, boy, never."

I wish it were true.

"And if God fights against a sunstroke?"

I see to my amazement that the Supreme Being is also engaged in his troupe, and ask myself who has let me in for this. Luckily that sunstroke is relatively harmless, for if it must fight against his lion, I am at a loss what to do.

But his feelers have caught something, for he dashes to the street door, opens it, and his mother sails in carrying a neat package, the pink ribbon of which he immediately begins to untie.

"Do lions and tigers eat chocolate too?" I hear him ask.

My ordeal has thus come to an end, and I walk with Father to the bottle of bitters. His hand trembles slightly when we clink glasses and before he sips he lets his misty eye, which has seen more than he will see again, rest like a blessing on his great-grandson.

Now, dearest William, you have some idea what awaits you. Remember that *he* leads the dance. He, and no other, has proclaimed that that lion is larger than the world, that all Germans will be devoured hide and hair, that a little later there is still room for a horse, that its tail does not receive pardon but stay of execution, that Father is reduced to a fig and then blown up again like a balloon, that a steam-roller is a steam-roller and no machine—that the conductor does not drown but will continue riding on cobblestones to the Day of Judgment, that a sunstroke has at least paws, and that he himself will live forever, and down here. And you are no more than the irrational mouthpiece through which he now comes to announce his doctrine also in Paris. See therefore that you are booted and spurred, for he will probably begin before he takes his cap off. You are a pretty reasonable boy and I count on your handling his troupe with tact. If you see a chance of increasing it with local celebrities, all the better. And if I may adjure you, see at least that he brings back his collection, as it is at this moment intact. Above all, treat his lion with the greatest circumspection and temporarily give him Frenchmen to eat. Pass over that cacking and pissing as if you didn't understand it: that is probably the best way. But don't leave him quite unguarded meanwhile, for I don't believe that in principle he would shrink from a practical demonstration in Auntie's Louis XV drawing-room if he comes to the conclusion that your narrow-mindedness cannot do without it. And if the little fellow should not unbend immediately upon entering, then ask him casually whether Great-grandfather wasn't recently crushed by a steam-roller and whether he hasn't by any chance left a horse-tail here. Then you will see.

William, William, do your best with him! And now you write once to your loving father.

Translated by Jo MAYO

PART V

THE GENERATION OF 1910

A. Roland Holst

THE DEATH OF CUCHULAINN OF MURHEVNA

I

MANY SAY THAT HE MET HIS DEATH WHILE COMBATTING COUNTLESS enemies and that finally, exhausted and red with the blood of his wounds, he bound himself to a rock so as to die standing up. After his death—it is told—he should have been seen by the high, royal women, standing in a strange and hazy battle wagon, driving past them swift and wild but inaudibly, across the plains of Emain Macha, along the dark walls of the king Concobar Mac Nessa.

This is the great story of his death.

But there is another still which many have never heard. And those who heard it, denied it, though they narrated it themselves. For it sounds like the dark, wild plaint of the ocean against the cliffs and of the wind across the solitary dusk of the hills. In this tale his death is not an act of limitless heroism midst the oncoming enemy, an epic eulogized by the admiration of his men, but a thing of desolate somberness, a madness that came to him through the hostile fear of his king and his comrades-in-arms, And behind this downfall, mercilessly, is the vengeance of a woman who once was loved by him.

Her name was Aoife and she was much dreaded in Scotland where she lived. It had been seen how the greatest warriors recoiled before her power, wavering and falling through the impact of her spears and her sword. Cuchulainn, when a youth, had been sent to Scotland by his king Concobar to be so trained in the handling of arms that he would be invincible. He had gone, and when Aoife and her warriors marched against the people and the king with whom he lived, he had defeated her and carried her in his arms as a prisoner to them for whom he fought. There he laid her down upon the earth and placed the point of his sword between her breasts until she begged for mercy. He gave her back her liberty and she loved him because of his prowess and magnanimity. And he lived with her in her abode on the wild coast.

But too much of a life with which his youth was as yet unacquainted stood between him and her. His days could not be filled with her. For hours on end he roamed in utter loneliness over the rocks; and when the sun submerged into the western waters and behind him the dark wind of night began to rise, there awoke in him the great longing for his country, for Ireland, and it blew over him like a mighty rain and the rustling of autumns past. And he thought of the beautiful and lovely Emere whom he had left behind. He saw again the sunny pasture in which he had encountered her for the first time, amidst her young girl friends. He had come in his speedy battle wagon, standing high in the colors of his festive cloak, and they had talked together and understood each other in words which remained secret to anyone else who heard them.

But Forgal, her father, was afraid of their love. As an unknown he came to Concobar with costly offerings and, praising the heroic deeds of the youthful Cuchulainn, he had advised the king to send him to Scotland, for the completion of his training as a warrior.

And now, in the desolation of this country and living with the woman Aoife whose dark power loved him because of the light of youth that was slowly extinguishing within herself, he understood that Forgal never hoped to see him back in Ireland. And his desire for the lovely Emere grew in sorrow and loneliness. He stretched out his hands towards the darkening sea, and to the fading light. And above the dashing of the waves his voice could be heard, chanting the songs which once he sang in unison with his brothers-in-arms, in the halls of Concobar, in the evening when the storm roared plaintively across the plateau of Emain Macha. When the night was full he returned to the dark house of Aoife, slowly and with head bowed, and gave way again to the caresses of her who loved him for his strength.

But once—on a bright, quiet morning when he walked along the coast—he saw a ship with sails large and white that slowly came nearer. And soon he heard that from the stern there came the sound of a song. The wind blew the singing voices over the waters and Cuchulainn saw that people were waving at him. A fiery haze of joy and desire surrounded him. And when at last his friends had landed and greeted him with gladness, saying, "Concobar sends us to thee, to bring thee back to Ireland," he stretched out his arms to them but had no words. His eyes looked out over them and they were filled with light. But one of them took his hands and forced him to listen to the good news they carried. Then he understood. Swiftly he went to Aoife's house where his shield hung and his sword. But at the exit of the great hall Aoife came and stood in front of him. She was pale and asked in a smothered voice,

"Where goest thou, Cuchulainn? Who are these strange men that stand outside and spoke to thee?"

He laid his hand upon her shoulder and pushed her aside. Looking straight before him, he said,

"They come from Ireland. They come for me. I must go. I cannot do differently."

And then, glancing at her, he added, "Do no longer place thyself between me and them."

But she did not desist and spoke—her voice was softer than he had ever heard it.

"Cuchulainn, I carry thy child. It will be a son. Shall he not know his father?"

For some time Cuchulainn was silent and when he looked at her again his eyes were pensive; there was a strange distance in his voice when he asked her slowly, "And wilt thou be the mother of my son?" Staring in front of him he said, as if speaking to himself, "And would he be like me?"

But now Aoife's voice sounded certain and proud.

"He shall be like his father. For my love for thee who conceived him was great, Cuchulainn! He shall be high and mighty, and a danger to his enemies."

Thereupon Cuchulainn took from his finger a golden ring and gave it to Aoife, saying, "Let his name be Conloch. When he is a man and can wear this ring, then tell him to go to Ireland. And let the warriors of Concobar be able to witness that the son of Cuchulainn is strong and without fear!"

Then he passed her and went out into the cool morning air. She saw him approach the strange men who were his friends and who walked towards him with rejoicing. Not once did he look back at her and with his friends he disappeared.

She remained where she stood; she did not move but stared out over the ocean. At last she saw a ship that drifted towards the blue horizon with large, smooth sails. She bowed her proud head and turned around. And shiveringly she went back into her empty, dark abode.

Not long afterwards, in her solitude, the son was born whom

she called Conloch. During those first years he grew up into a strong and handsome lad. The desire for a life of action and rejoicings awakened in him like a morning wind, when his mother taught him the handling of his weapons. But though soon he acquired great dexterity, his mother never allowed him to leave her but for the hunt with some of her most trusted warriors. Conloch loved his mother, but respect and an undefined fear were stronger in his affection than tenderness. Too often did he feel his youthfulness placed in the shadow of her high and dark taciturnity. Yet at times she was wistful and tender and spoke to him of his father Cuchulainn. But she stared into the flames and her words seemed hardly meant for him; for if he asked a question she seemed to be startled, and her answer would be vague and indeterminate.

Once it happened that towards the falling of night he came back from the hunt. Approaching the gate of his home he saw his mother standing there, high and still in the dusk. His coming she did not hear; she was looking out across the ocean. And when he had reached her and, leaning upon his spear, gazed at the far horizon across the waters where the sun had set and the last fires of day were slowly extinguishing, she remained silent.

"Whereof thinkest thou, mother?" Conloch asked.

She answered slowly and said,

"This is the light of the great sun, setting. But oh, the light that shone around the head of Cuchulainn when he became a conqueror! I can bear witness to it—for I saw it when his great prowess defeated me and laid me down upon the earth."

But Conloch said, "I understand thee not, mother. What is this light thou speakest of?"

Then Aoife looked at her son and said,

"When Cuchulainn, in the growing heat of the battle, is gifted with the strength of ecstasy that turns him into victor, his enemy sees a flaming light appear around his head. For though his mother was an earthly woman, his father is the Sun God of the Tuatha the Danaan. And when this light becomes visible then his enemy knows—'this is Cuchulainn of Murhevna, and I am lost.'"

Aoife was silent and entered her house. Slowly Conloch followed her, thinking of her words and of the father whom he had never known.

Another year went by. Aoife noticed the strength of her son and the dreamy fire in his eyes, and she thought of his promised voyage to Ireland. And still she could not decide. But one day, when she was alone, a man who had long lived in Ireland and who had only recently returned to Scotland, came to her and he said,

"I have spent long days with Concobar Mac Nessa and his warriors. And I have seen Cuchulainn of Murhevna there, great and revered. He is happy and full of love for the beautiful woman Emere. His great deeds are done in her name; for him there is no one else but she."

After having said this, he left Aoife.

Until the sun had set she walked up and down the great hall of her house. Wide and cold her eyes were opened. Her lips were pale and thin and closed; and the nails of her taut fingers pressed deeply into her breast. She walked up and down, through the stillness between the stone walls—up and down, with long strides. And with every step the certainty became harder and heavier to bear; until suddenly she stood still and she knew and pronounced it through her white, bared teeth: the death of him whom she loved, the death of Cuchulainn of Murhevna.

"He shall die!" she called out through the somber silence of the hall. The sun had set and it was almost night around her. She looked outside and heard a step approaching. "My son," she whispered. And then, in a voice of great decision, she said, "And it shall be through my son's hand."

She went to the other end of the room and sat down upon her high throne that stood completely in the dark. Conloch entered. He stood still in the center, between the four walls and had not as yet noticed his mother. Then her voice arose from the obscurity and reached him.

"My son, thy time has come. Thou art grown into a mighty warrior; thou art the strongest of these lands. It is my wish that thou goest to Ireland. Tomorrow thou shalt leave."

"Is it to find my father that thou sendest me?" asked Conloch, and there was happiness in his voice. She bent down from the dark that veiled her face:

"I know not where Cuchulainn is."

"Is he no longer with Concobar Mac Nessa?"

Again she bowed and said,

"No."

But she continued immediately,

"Instead thou art to go to Emain Macha where Concobar and his warriors are. And two things thou shalt promise me: to ask no one for Cuchulainn of Murhevna nor to divulge thy name to whomsoever it be, except when the power of the sword forces thee to do so."

Conloch, foreseeing an arduous journey and mighty deeds in foreign lands, said without hesitation:

"Thou hast my word. I shall leave tomorrow."

The next morning a misty rain blew around Aoife where she stood upon the rocks, high above the seething ocean and looked for the ship upon which she knew her son was sailing farther and farther away. And she thought of a quiet, bright morning long ago. She lifted her voice to the dark winds:

"Through his son he shall die! He forsook my love. Through the child of my love he shall perish!"

And silently, with slow steps, she returned to her house, her head deeply bent against the wind.

II

Many were gathered in the great hall of King Concobar Mac Nessa. The sweet sounds of a harp trickled through the semi-darkness. An old woman played, lost in dreams, of the lovers of her past. High and mighty men they had been but now forgetfulness was whistling over their graves. And through her playing, monotonously, recurred the theme of life's relentless instability.

Concobar sat pensively upon his throne, his heavy head bent. His golden crown shimmered through the dusk.

Cuchulainn of Murhevna was seated near the fire and at his feet was the beautiful Emere. She looked up at his impassive face and thought of the mighty wonder of his life—and how great deeds were to him like the leaves to an oak tree.

Behind them, in the dusk of the high-ceilinged hall, were many warriors with their wives. They all listened to the harp; but suddenly the playing ceased. For a moment the wind alone was heard; then a hasty step. And below the torch over the entrance to the hall there appeared a young warrior. In a loud voice he announced,

"There is a stranger outside. He wishes not to divulge his name—but by the force of the sword. One who was with me fought him but lies defeated. For although this stranger is young, his sword is powerful. Shall I conduct him into the hall?"

Cuchulainn arose and spoke,

"He shall not come here unless his name be known to us. And to me he shall divulge it."

Without glancing back at Emere he passed through the rows of warriors, beneath the torch and outside the gate. There Conloch was waiting near the body of the man whom he had defeated. He leaned upon his sword.

"Tell me thy name, stranger!"

Conloch looked up. A mighty figure was standing before him. Above the dark shield was the head, proud and serious and the naked sword shone brightly. They faced each other in the dying of the day. Behind his opponent Conloch saw how the sun was setting; already the hills were steeped in black.

"Has not my answer been given for the king and for his warriors? My answer is my weapon!"

And Conloch lifted high his sword. The steel caught the last rays of the sun and was transformed into a line of fire. His adversary retreated a few steps, and certain of his conquest he asked with gentle emphasis,

"Is there not in the country whence thou comest a young woman who loveth thee and looketh forward to thy return?"

But Conloch came nearer whilst he cried,

"Thou knowest my answer!"

The fight began. So loud were the clashes upon the bronze shields that warriors and women alike came forth through the gate of Emain Macha. They saw how Cuchulainn was pressed back by the wild attack of his youthful opponent and did not understand why he recoiled. They knew not the vague tenderness which rendered mighty Cuchulainn uncertain of himself. Until, of a sudden, they heard him cry,

"But tell me—who art thou? Thy face is like that of a woman I once knew."

The stranger did not reply. A new attack, more powerful than the previous ones, followed. Emere appeared upon the wall above the gate. The sun had meantime set and the darkness of evening descended rapidly. The clashes on Cuchulainn's shield became heavier and more menacing. Cuchulainn shrank back further and further, to the place in which a large rock stood solitarily upon the plain. There he must make a stand; but it was as if he hesitated.

Speechless with fear Emere stood upon the wall. She watched the unknown warrior approach and a resounding clash followed. The shield of Cuchulainn came slowly down. But then of a sudden, they all saw the sign of his godliness. Around his head a strange light appeared, the flaming light of the Sun God of the Tuatha the Danaan. It burned before the rock like a heavenly fire. A shout of joy arose from among the group of fighters and women in the dusk. Upon the dark wall Emere stretched out her arms. And they all saw how Cuchulainn's adversary staggered suddenly. A breathless dismay seemed to have overtaken him. His shield was trembling. His sword hung powerlessly from his hand. For Conloch stared into the light and knew that he was facing his father. He wished to cry out, but his voice lay dark and dead within his throat. Now Cuchulainn was held by the force of his divine invincibility. He lifted the spear of Tuatha the Danaan and threw it.

And the many who watched them in the growing dusk saw the young warrior fall and they heard a loud voice crying,

"My father, my father!"

And they saw the head of Cuchulainn bending over the black spot where he had gained his victory and they heard him ask a question to which a dying voice answered. Then the strange light was extinguished and the obscure stillness was torn by the sudden, deep voice of Cuchulainn, crying, "Conloch! Conloch! My son!"

And the many came nearer, a whispering group of anxious people who wished to know. They saw the figure of Cuchulainn kneeling down by the defeated. In his trembling hands he was lifting the pale face and he looked at it with wide-open eyes. And they heard him moan,

"My son—oh my son; how beautiful thou art. And oh, thy strength and thy courage that lie here in the darkness. My son! Conloch! Arise! Stand near thy father! Oh—to go into battle together with thee, and against us all the men of Ireland from ocean to ocean! There would be fear among them all! Oh, thy shield and thy sword now lying in the dark wind, beyond the touch of thy dead hand! Oh, Conloch, my son—but *art* thou dead? I cannot venge myself. Oh, curse upon Aoife who has wanted this to happen. Curse and dark storms upon her head! If a mighty man had done this and he stood here bragging . . . how I would batter him down and break him! But it was *my* arm! It was my spear! And after this tragedy . . . should this land be to me as before? No! No! No!"

And Concobar's warriors saw how Cuchulainn had arisen, swaying the spear of Tuatha the Danaan. And they heard the wild voice of madness calling, "There shall be collapse! Fright and chaos and the thunder of breaking shields! Where are the fighters who dare to live where Conloch lies defeated? Fear and death upon them! Conloch lies upon the dark soil—and should *they* stand and look at me from over their shields? Never! Down, down into the dust and the winds of night! Down!"

They looked at one another and took to flight through the evening—and the women went with them, back through the gate and inside the walls. In loud confusion they rushed into the dark hall where Concobar was still seated upon his throne. And all together, in a medley of voices, they called out to him, telling of Cuchulainn's madness and the storm of his wrath that was on its way and menacing them with death and destruction.

But Emere still stood upon the wall, frozen with fear and horror. She saw how Cuchulainn raved in his grief, and she felt that no life would be safe before the black hurricane of this madness. She stood there, cut off from him forever. The power of a woman whom she had never seen, had separated them irrevocably. In her loneliness she knew that the end was near. She saw it coming, swiftly and inescapably.

For when Cuchulainn, crazed with anger and pain, approached the gate through the night, swaying his mighty weapons and threatening with defeat and death, she heard a song—wild, monotonous and somber—that passed through the gates and went outside. Looking down she saw how Cuchulainn stood still and was silent. It seemed that a long-forgotten dream began to come back to him. And when the singing Druids approached him, he turned and went away while through the evening his voice sang a song of plaints, unbridled and yet so wistful and infinite that human hearts perished in it like small ships in an ominous sea.

And he went in the direction of the ocean, followed by the Druids who chanted wildly and monotonously and somberly and drove him before them by the spell of their fatal will.

And now the warriors and the women came out again, to follow at a distance. And Emere heard them say how Concobar, through the magic power of the Druids would force Cuchulainn to recognize his enemy in the dark, relentless sea, and how he intended to destroy him in a battle against the endless darkness of the waves. And so great and strange her loneliness had grown, and so powerless she felt against the tragic storm of this happening that there was no resistance left in her.

But she saw them all, going across the plain in the evening and long afterwards she heard the singing until this, too, died out. And nothing remained but the cold night and the blowing of the wind that came from afar where the ocean was, the roaring of the wind that was like a call from the dark.

For three days Concobar Mac Nessa remained alone, in the large hall. Sometimes one of those who had followed the Druids appeared before his throne and said that Cuchulainn in his madness was fighting against the waves, and that he penetrated ever further into the seething surf, swaying the mighty spear of the Tuatha the Danaan, and that the Druids continued to place their sorcery between him and the rocks along the coast. On the third day the wind increased. Late in the afternoon Concobar sat by the light of a smoking torch and—while the storm howled over the darkening plains—he thought of the sunny years when Cuchulainn was his friend and the mightiest pillar of his power. And great sadness hung a cloud alike around his kingly head.

Then, towards the coming of the evening, a messenger stood before him and said,

"We have witnessed the end of Cuchulainn's battle against the ocean, oh Concobar! We saw him yield and we heard his mighty voice get lost in the sizzling foam. We saw the swaying of his powerful frame before he disappeared in the dark waters. The waves have left the coast and there is nothing now but darkness, and the voices of the storm and the sea."

Later the warriors and the women returned. They stayed with the king and through the long and somber hours they watched with him, silent under the great sadness of their loss.

Of Emere there was no trace.

In the night the wind subsided. Then at last when the day had come, the king went outside. Still and alone he stood in the calm morning light and his mourning was like a timid child before the strange, exalted peace of this life—until in the end he went back through the gate with a steady stride, to the usual deeds of his day.

Translated by JOSEPH W. F. STOPPELMAN

Dirk Coster

APHORISMS

THERE ARE TWO MOMENTS IN THE LIFE OF MAN WHICH DETERMINE everything: the moment when for the first time he truly loves, and that other moment when he reads the Gospels and for the first time understands them in their higher sense. The one moment is often a bridge to the other.

A man in love wishes to be redeemed by the beloved, and at the same time feels a compulsion toward redeeming his beloved from the guilt of the past, from the weakness of the present, and from the menace of the future. Love is the only feeling in which weakness and strength, the need of help and the impulse to save, self-forgetfulness and self-consciousness, can live united.

The first urge of which man becomes conscious in his love is care for the soul of the beloved, and the first longing of which a woman is conscious is for the beautiful deeds of the man.

Man in his love suddenly realizes with calm serenity that he has come to himself. Man comes to himself by going out to another. Here is the simplest and most palpable proof that man can find himself by losing himself.

Man thinks *about* life; life thinks *in* woman.

It is the law of life that man shall give consciousness to woman, and that woman shall give man strength for deeds.

Love discloses to man a world outside himself, and to woman a world within herself.

The highest love of a life is recognizable by its simplicity and by its simple readiness to overcome at all points the claim of the senses.

Love in its first unconscious beginning is the glorious omen of what it can some time become.

As long as love remains unconscious it betrays its origin as part of the All-Love, as beauty and communion with all souls in an undreamed-of heaven. As soon as love becomes conscious it forgets its origin and believes its beginning and end to be love for one single person.

A single, continuous love does not exist in one human life. But there may be many loves for one single person which follow each other in succession.

Love for one person extended over a whole lifetime, which ever becomes new and yet remains itself, is the most beautiful love of all. Above all else, it bears witness to the freedom of the human soul.

Every period of human life has its own love.

Many men learn only after many experiences and many loves to recognize the wonder of their first love.

The higher a love soars, the more does its revelation savor of sameness. But behind this sameness are hidden limitless riches which are quite withheld from the ordinary eye. This is as true for the love of the holy man as for the noblest earthly love.

In the perfect marriage between man and woman, many dangers arising from the masculine and feminine nature are averted by mutual support.

The danger for the woman is the extinction of the higher intuition; the danger for the man is the wandering away of consciousness into barren logic.

Man seeks himself. Woman seeks others. The danger for man is in becoming hardened within himself; the danger for woman is in losing herself in others.

Women have wonderful discernment in attacking the evil in man at its most vulnerable point. They attack man's evil where it is ridiculous. They intuitively feel that many evils are maintained by the illusion of the greatness of the evil.

To make the child the aim of marriage is one of the logical degeneracies of a period that has gone astray through logic. Man was born for happiness, and happiness is the flowering of his personality. Only he who is happy can give birth to a more beautiful future. Only he who lives for the present lives for the future. Only the man and the woman who live for each other live in the best way for the child. They create a realm of happiness which causes the soul of the child to flower more fully than all willed care and love.

They who make the child the one aim of their marriage make the child the symbol of a joyless resignation.

They who concentrate all their attention on the child take from the child's soul that part of freedom and of its own life that it needs for its development.

For two people to renounce their own human future and to place it in a child—which is often not even their own child but the germ of long-forgotten ancestors come to life again—is the superficial altruistic command of the century of the child. Yet this means nothing more nor less than to burden a new life with the curse of two lost lives, for sooner or later this curse will fulfill itself. The child takes his real experiences from life, but his general conception of life, the key by which he unlocks the meaning of these experiences, he derives from the life of the parents. The child who has seen the life of his parents become lost in his own, lives burdened by the presentiment of the uselessness of all lives, sees his own life stretching toward joyless horizons.

Man desires woman, and woman desires a child; that is the familiar definition of marriage, but only of blind, sensual marriage. If love raises marriage above sensuousness, the man will grasp and possess the world in and through the woman and the dearest and most real child of the woman will be the life work born from the inner embrace of both.

The woman of vital force loves the child more than the man. The woman of soul force loves the man more than the child. For to love the man above the child establishes the triumph of the soul in woman, the triumph of free choice over the necessity of nature.

Love that becomes ever purer becomes ever greater. The lower mother love is continually dividing; the higher mother love divides no longer. The woman of a higher nature already loves the child in the man, just as the highest-minded man loves God in humanity. The one is the feeble antecedent of the other.

He whose heart is joined to a living heart, he only has found, for the first time, true union with life. Only from this moment can his understanding vibrate in unison with life, and this vibrating in unison alone brings forth wisdom.

The dual birth which takes place in every true marriage is the birth of two true natures. Viewed in this light, man and woman are each other's creation.

The greater the number of persons a man can love in turn, the greater has been his love for himself in these loves.

The man who loves sensuously worships himself through others.

Where love is not, the innate hostility of the sexes instantly reveals itself.

Man's sensuousness is egotistical because it seeks to express itself at the cost of the woman's personality. But the woman's urge toward motherhood is no less egotistical because it seeks to realize itself at the cost of the man's personality. As long as these impulses remain in their natural state they are a bitter denial of each other's eternal life principle, of each other's individuality.

Without love woman sees in man merely gluttony of the senses, and man sees in woman merely the agent of procreation. Without love woman feels man's nature merely as a blind devouring force, and man feels in woman's nature merely blind resistance, an ambush placed by nature for his lust. From the conflict of these two only blind hate can arise. Therefore every sensuous, instinctive marriage is the beginning of a tragedy, a covert, endless struggle to the death.

Married love does not fade out in comradeship as is the common opinion of the thoughtless. Married love is either extinguished in the bitter hostility of the sexes (concealed behind the cloak of comradeship) or else the joy of the soul which the first glance promised is found again. These are the only possible outcomes.

There is a moment in every love when the imagination of the lover voluntarily pictures the loved one in ugliness and sickness, in order to greet this image with a more triumphant love. Thus the strength of the soul manifests itself and renders powerless by its light the dark accident of the senses.

There is another work of the imagination which is involuntary and which reveals man to himself. Whenever the image of the beloved appears as sick or ugly, in dream or in fantasy, and the man feels his love suddenly paralyzed and dissolved, his love is still clouded by secret lusts.

Woman's judgment is infallible when passion does not mar her vision. Her judgment can become appalling foolishness when passion governs her. Woman's method of judgment is of a higher order than man's, yet at the same time fraught with much more danger for life.

What makes woman's judgment so dangerous for life is the fact that she listens to no doubt, either in wisdom or in folly.

When her soul is at peace, the judgment of the noble woman can be the infallible guide of man's reason.

Man's reason, man's consciousness, should ally itself with woman's wisdom, just as the loving man naturally allies himself with the woman. Governing and directing her, he must feel himself the servant.

The great malady of the modern world is the dominion of the masculine element over the feminine.

A complete natural love is not conceivable without an absolute jealousy. Jealousy is the supreme proof of the genuineness of a natural love but also the scorching mark of its shame. The fact that man in his jealousy at a given moment or under given circumstances is able to create joy out of the bitterest sorrow, out of the bitterest lashing of the one being to whom he otherwise wishes all good—this fact alone is enough to convince one that man should not remain in a state of natural love but must direct himself towards a higher love—no matter how long the road or how beautiful the naturalness of his present love. For what is a love which is already prepared so that tomorrow it may turn into the deadliest hate?

Translated by BEATRICE M. HINKLE
(From Dirk Coster, *The Living and the Lifeless,* copyright 1929,
Harcourt, Brace & Co., New York)

Just Havelaar

LITTLE THINGS

WE LIE, THE TWELVE OF US, IN THE WHITE WARD WITH ITS EMPTY walls, where nothing arrests the eye. There is not even the shabbiest symptom of that ineradicable urge toward beauty which has brought so much delight and so much ugliness into the world. Empty and neutral are the walls, and along them the iron beds are ranged, with smooth, white spread at the foot of each.

Hands lie motionless on the bed-clothes; the masks of the faces sleep on, though awake. The eyes stare openly, veiling life. Life here has become a staring.

A dark head across the way moves monotonously from side to side on the white pillow, in a mechanized gesture of pain. I try not to look, but again and again my glance is attracted by it: the head goes incessantly from left to right, from right to left, regularly, like the pendulum of a clock.

At the low table in the middle sits a nurse, busy with our "charts."

It is the quiet hour of the afternoon. But there are no hours here, time here has no significance. Each hour is an eternity between eternities. There are the short interruptions: the noon meal, the cup of tea, the sandwiches, the evening porridge. . . . There is the instant at which both electric lights on the high ceiling begin to shine. There is the instant that these are turned out and the little green light governs the dusky space: the little lamp above the table where the night nurse dreams away her hours. There is the endless night, which is just as little a night as the day has been a day.

Time flows on, indolent, faded as a sewer canal. "Das Leben ist ein schmutziger Strom."

Now it is afternoon, the dead time of the afternoon. We wait. For what? The duties have been attended to. The doctor has gone. We have all received treatment, one after the other. We wait.

We wait for the evening, for the night, as we wait at night for the pale dawn.

Each one waits for the hour when he will be delivered and received again into the great, far world. How many weeks now? How many months?

How, indeed, has this all happened to us, and how shall we ever again adjust ourselves to the world?

Many have gone away, many have come. Nothing has changed. Each one waits. Each one thinks his little thoughts, always the same. Each has his cares, each his burdens. Each ponders upon his malady, his pain, his own body. Each one has his pocket mirror in which he uneasily scrutinizes his face.

We live here in frightful solitude. There are times, certainly, when we talk together; there are even moments of gaiety and moments of discussion. Good-nature is possible among us. We feel that we are the room "team." But it is teamwork among ghosts. No one resembles himself any more. We are impersonalized. It is teamwork in a negative world, in a world that waits. Our true self feels completely abandoned.

The differences in position, in class and in education, have flowed away. All has become negative, even this uniformity. Never has anyone been so desperate an individual: at the mercy of his own negation. Never has anyone so consciously concealed himself from his fellow beings, as though he were hiding an unspeakable and shameful secret in his heart.

Each one refuses to live here, to make a life here. Each one clings firmly to that other life, the former life in the world. We did not know each other while we were still living, when we were "I." We only know each other since we have become ghosts. Hence this alarming solitude behind the appearance of comradeship.

Each one is abandoned to himself, to that which still remains of his old self. Each one is ashamed of his disguise.

This is the age-long hour of great melancholy; a melancholy as empty, colorless, endless as we have never known until now; a melancholy that washes over you, in which you are surrendered as a drowned man to the fate of the unfathomable waves. A melancholy that stares at you from the dead eyes of the masks and from the white emptiness of the walls; that buzzes in the vacant space.

In the world, melancholy remains a malady *de luxe* and is mostly an aesthetically decked out boredom. But here it is the misery of hell. Satan's substance must be of melancholy, for the substance of melancholy is negation; the thing common to all of us. One hides it behind his laughter, the other behind his silence. You wrestle with it, in vain. All your energies, all your thoughts and feelings are corroded by it.

When people from the world of living realities come to visit us, they ask us if we aren't bored. No indeed . . . we aren't bored. In order to be bored there must be the possibility of an activity, an unfulfilled possibility. But we are absolutely passive. We lose our way in total apathy. We are tossed about on a gloomy, fatal sea of melancholy. Melancholy is our most deep-seated illness, the shameful sickness of which we do not speak.

Will this sickness ever withdraw from us? When we return

to the great world, shall we ever conquer this sickness? Or will a solitude continue to surround us? Will there be a despair always gnawing at our hearts? Will an estrangement remain between us and those whom we love the most and of whom we think with such hopeless longing the whole day, every moment when we are not thinking of ourselves, of our ills and troubles?

Once we had a certain pride, a certain briskness, even in bitter days. Where has it gone? We still act as though we were brisk, but we know that each day leaves us weaker and more humiliated, each long day, each eternal night.

How still, how enigmatically still. . . . An emptiness rather than a stillness. If only one began to speak again, the nonsense talk of every day, to sing as we sing here, just to make a sound.

I peer through the great empty windows. There is a wall opposite, a wall of the same building in which we are lying. Some dim hall windows break the dullness of the barren prison-like wall. Above the wall, above the gray, ruled-off tile roof I see a long narrow streak of the sky. I stare endlessly at that streak of sky. Sometimes clouds go by; it is a smooth unbroken gray curtain. At night one can sometimes see a star wander across the small space, a frightfully faraway star, solitary and eternal and useless, like everything here.

I stare at the little piece of sky which is now blue, thin blue, luminous and far. This sky radiates over the world in which we lived, acted, moved. People don't notice it; but we know what this sky means.

I stare and think my sluggish thoughts, which take no form. But suddenly my attention is strained, sharp. There, in that small strip of sky, there is something moving, endlessly high and far. A bird? It wheels about and glitters a minute in the sunlight, like silver, and veers in a circle, disappearing diagonally upward: the aeroplane!

An almost unbearable joy has sprung up in my heart, like that of the day when I first saw men soar upward from the earth and drive about in the unending space.

To me this fleeting apparition is like a glorious message from the world. It is as if the world came to deliver me from this forlorn condition. It is as a sign sent out to me by life, to encourage me.

I cannot get over it. I sit up straight. I feel my heart pound as if a miracle had occurred to me.

Fool . . . these trifles! The nurse was right in what she said
to me last night while she came clandestinely to console me
with a cup of tea. She was right when she said that I could be
so excessive, so immoderate in my thankfulness that no one
could tell whether I really meant any of it. Such little things
must remain only trifles, she said. And her black eyes in the pale,
pointed face laughed sorrowfully and mockingly.

But what are trifles? What would life be without them? Perhaps life is nothing more than a succession of trifles.

Whenever I think back, yearning, to my old life, do I think
then of great events, of heroic deeds, of rare experiences?

I think then of little things. What makes life lovable is the
memory of little things. Deeply and intensely to experience little
things—there you have the secret of life. I have never understood
it so well as here. What we miss here is the little things which
are great experiences. Therefore this life is unbearable. Therefore the profound and powerful books which I have read here
have remained trifles. Therefore fine and tender verses become
so insignificant here. Therefore everything that once fascinated
us now tires us. Everything becomes equally indifferent, now
that little things have lost their meaning.

It was not that glistening object which moved me so strangely;
it was not the thought that we, earth-creatures, had conquered
the heavens, as they say. It was something else. It was the symbol
of freedom.

Freedom moves me. Not the romantic freedom which dreams
of heroic deeds, not the freedom youth speaks of; but the freedom to live our lives, to be ourselves in the surroundings which
we ourselves have created. The freedom of daily duties, the freedom of good work, the freedom of one's own home.

My thoughts go there where my heart is. I see the rooms again,
where the light is so beautiful, so beautifully, so gently shining
on all the faithful objects. You can sit still there in the chair
by the window and look around and follow the easy movements
of the exquisite fair child, always busy. You listen to her crystal-
clear little voice and to the quiet ticking of the solemn wall
clock, and you feel satisfied. You can be there, engrossed in a
book, and feel the whole beloved atmosphere, faithful and protecting, around you. Each thing has its own story, everything
awakens memories, everything is woven into your memory. Indifference does not exist there.

I see the room, even more quiet and subdued, where I am

alone with my work. The writing table where the chaos of life is in combat with the order of the spirit; the familiar, faithful books along the wall, the portraits of those who have meant the most in my life. It is sober and frugal, noble and austere, but never gloomy.

In this atmosphere I remember how full of significance the little things are. The daily dinner there takes on the consecration of a communion. Tea-time is a rich little ceremony, not to be celebrated thoughtlessly. When, on holidays in winter, the fire flames in the evening on the hearth, we stare fascinated at the little wonder flame, that small violence of the fire which destroys, purifies and awakes to life. The magic of the fire awakens dreams as great as those caused by the sounds of the music to which I so eagerly listen because it frees my soul.

There are the good friendly people into whose eyes you can look during the conversation which need not be interesting in order to have depth. It is good to be silent here with those who give inspiration to this atmosphere and who make things real. When two people who understand each other draw together in the silence, in speechless tenderness, because their depth is the same and the music of their lives is in the same key, then life has been fulfilled. Then dream and reality are no longer distinguishable.

I think of Verster, the painter who died recently, a passionate man who continually withdrew from the turbulence of the world and its opinions into the narrow compass of his old country house and the things that were nearby. A limited existence apart from the world; an endlessly rich life in the chamber of the soul.

Few could manage to live that way without shriveling up, without evaporating in the egoism of self-sufficiency. I do not know whether I may call his the most beautiful life, but I know that his life was justified. For his relation to things became ever more sincere and deep, the little things became ever greater for him, his soul became ever more independent of the world.

Has tenderness ever expressed itself so firmly? Has repose ever been so tense?

The world became as crystal, so transparent. Each thing became a mirror of the soul, and yet remained but a thing.

What is great and what is small? And if the little things are not great for us, how, then, could the great things ever be so? Eternity spans the distinctions between the small and the great.

A tall form suddenly rises up near me.

"I thought you were asleep," laughed the nurse, offering the thermometer with a gesture not lacking in grace. I look at her thoughtfully.

"On the contrary," I say, "I believe I was quite awake."

Jacob Israel de Haan

HAMAME MARRIES

HAMAME, WHICH MEANS LITTLE DOVE, IS ONE OF THE JEMENITIC servants at the boys' orphanage. And she is going to marry. It is time, too, for Hamame is already over twenty. But she has not been lucky in love. This is her second betrothed, a widower. Hamame let the first marriage go by. And that cost her eight pounds sterling, as had been agreed in the engagement terms. No small thing for a Jemenitic servant girl at a boys' orphanage. Afterwards it turned out that Hamame, which means Little Dove, had made a mistake. She did not really love her second betrothed. But let another marriage go by? It will cost her eight pounds again, and everybody will laugh at her. So it is agreed that Hamame will marry the widower.

And now all the difficulties in the path of love! The money that is needed for a black suit and a new fez. For a white bride's dress with a veil of white and silver. For new shoes and for new handkerchiefs. There are now long conferences with Hamame's mother who is a witch. Small, sunburnt and skinny.

And will Hamame's father, Mr. Mozes Azirie, come over from Egypt for this great day? That he ran away from the witch is a matter of course. Hamame has never seen him. Will he come? And above all, will he send a contribution to the expenses of the unforgettable day? And will Reine, the Jemenitic kitchen maid, be invited? Terrible things have happened between Reine and Hamame. Of course neither of them began it. Hamame very much offended Reine. She said: "Reine, you are a thief. And your sister, who lives at Rischon le Zion and washes for the English soldiers in Ludd, your sister is a bad woman." It is a matter of course that Reine then took counter-measures. She went to the synagogue of the Jemenites. She opened the Holy Ark and she solemnly cursed Hamame with the widower and the two families to the third and fourth generation. It is doubtful if she will be invited now.

We, however, receive a beautiful gold announcement on tissue paper. A branch with birds. The initials of the Little Dove and her widower S and H. Between them in a sweeping curve the proverb: "Voice of happiness and voice of joy! Voice of bridegroom and of bride." Underneath that again a double triangle with "Zion" in it. Then the invitation: "The bridegroom's mother, Mrs. Hamame Jozef Saied, and the bride's father, R. Mozes Azirie and spouse have the honor to invite you to the marriage feast of their children Salomo and Hamame. And those that do us the honor, we shall honor! Church ceremony, so God will, Friday 15 Kislev 5681 at two o'clock European time, punctually in the house of the bride's father in the quarter 'Hut of Peace.'" No wonder we are going!

The festivities begin for the women on Thursday afternoon. We enter the house of the bride's father in the "Hut of Peace" quarter. And we survey the crowd. Reine has not been invited. The witch did not want it. We hear that R. Mozes Azirie has not come. And he has not sent any money either. But a beautiful letter. And so we have to be content with that. The whole room is crammed full of Jemenitic ladies and Jemenitic offspring. Some are already dressed in European style. But most of them in Jemenitic style, in gay colors that clash. They have much gold, well embossed and beaten. For the Jemenites are beautiful goldsmiths. And they sit on the floor, so close to each other that there is hardly room for us. Of course, we get a place of honor, next to Hamame. The bridegroom is not present. That would not be proper. Hamame sits like a doll in white, with veil of white and silver. She may not say a word and she must keep her eyes modestly cast down. It is very difficult, but we trust that after the wedding she will make up for lost time. Next to Hamame sit the bridesmaids equally doll-white, doll-stiff, each with a tall, white candle in her hand. All the ladies smoke. Cigarettes or steadily at a Turkish water-pipe. There is also singing, clapping of hands and some powerful music of kettle-drums and tin cans. And the refreshments! Lavish refreshments! A large washbasin is brought in full of peeled "kersaussies," nuts and almonds. A smaller one with pomegranate pips. Everyone gets a handkerchief full. And then we tuck in. Lucky that this does not cost Hamame any money. For each of the guests pays. Everything is dear here now. Also marriage feasts. The least is now already two shillings. We

have given a pound. But then everybody respects us for it. We
are invited to the midday meal: bread, meat and "hilme," a
Jemenitic dish of pepper with pepper.

It is a very beautiful feast. Hamame's mother beams. She has
on a flowery pink dressing gown with stylish white lace at the
neck and sleeves. And she, the woman, fierce and brown. A witch.
If she is lucky, there will be some left over. All the furniture has
been taken out of the little room. Only a large bedstead has remained. In this a little row of offspring sleeps sweetly and peacefully. Sometimes, when one wakes up—there are nine lying there
—a Jemenitic mother gets up and gives her baby the breast.
There is a very young and very beautiful little Jemenitic mother
to whom belongs a very beautiful little Jemenitic boy. I praise
him like this: "What a nice little boy." But she looks at me,
frightened and indignant. What a dangerous stupidity to praise
a child like that! Do I want the Evil Ear to hear it? The beautiful little Jemenitic mother therefore gives the beautiful little
Jemenitic boy a good shaking and she grumbles at him. "This is
a dreadful child. Bad and ugly. God has indeed punished me.
But what can I do, a poor woman?" The formalities with respect
to the Evil Ear are herewith fulfilled. She now cuddles the dear
little fellow again. And she puts him down to sleep nicely in the
row of little snoozers.

In the evening we go to the men's feast in another little house
in the "Hut of Peace" quarter. It is of course very full. And very
hot. There is music. And there are psalm-singers with loud voices
and dangerous handclapping. There are of course refreshments:
salted peas, nuts, almonds, pomegranates. And there is a substantial bottle of sour, slightly fermented wine. And a devilish
beverage which they distil themselves from dried raisins. There
is also dancing. But not men with women. That would not be
proper. The ladies occasionally come peeping round the corner.
But even that is new-fashioned. A tall, thin man is dancing. A
tall, black youth. Perhaps he is the Devil. But it would not do
to ask him. The one who dances with him—but they do not
touch one another—is a slim, dark Jemenitic boy of fifteen who
is called Jozef and is a shoemaker. But he is also the best dancer
in the community. There goes the music and the clapping of
hands. The man and the boy go devoutly and carefully. Restrained and taut, they look at each other's feet. At each other's
movements. Slowly, little moved at the beginning. But the music
becomes wild. The hands of the assembly go faster. The man

and the boy go faster. Breathless. Music, music, music. The hands beating. The boy, the man. Breathless. Finished, finished, finished. Entire stories are danced in this way by the Jemenites. They dance all through the night.

When the young Jozef has recovered his breath somewhat he naturally receives a present. And I ask what story is depicted in this dance. "Sir," says the youngster Jozef, coloring, "this is a dance to the rebuilding of the Holy Temple." And to think that I have always imagined the rebuilding of the Holy Temple quite differently!

And on Friday afternoon in the little house in the "Hut of Peace" quarter Hamame and her widower acquire each other. This time men and women together. And all the little offspring safe and out of the way again in the big bed. In little rows and heaps. There is again wild music. A Jemenitic boy beats two drums at the same time. One large, dark and somber. And over against that a small, taut one that crows and laughs loudly. They acquire each other amidst a great hubbub. The seven blessings are pronounced, holy one and sensuous one at the same time. Two old men dance the prescribed holy dances in front of the bridal pair. Wondrous twists and turns of the powerless bodies. But exactly as it has to be. Dancing in front of the bridal pair is a holy task with which the oldest and most dignified are honored. The handsome boy Jozef looks on. He dances differently, after all.

In a procession we then bring Hamame and the comforted widower to the conjugal abode. Also in the quarter called "Hut of Peace." Of course with music in front. Then the white bridesmaids with the white candles, the flames flickering in the wind. Then the bridal pair and the guests. According to rank and station. There is the old rabbi who has the seven blessings on his conscience. A purple caftan and a white woven shoulder-shawl. The mild, broken sky. The wind. But no rain yet, although there is already dampness in the air. We walk very slowly and in dignified manner as the music makes us walk. All the people of the "Hut of Peace" come running out. A very little alley and a very little house, into which we dive. I shudder. Tomorrow the slave-life will begin for her. Hamame is married.

Translated by JO MAYO

M. Nijhoff

PEN ON PAPER

BECAUSE I HAVE SPENT THE SUMMER IN A TENT ON THE BEACH CON-
tinually squinting in the sun I have dead-white crow's-feet across
my brown temples on either side of my eyes. Now, in my room
again, when I sometimes cross my legs under the desk they burn
lightly at the spots where they touch each other; and even sitting
on a chair I feel somewhat too high, for I used to remain hour
upon hour, days it seemed, on the sand under the canvas, looking out across the sea through the three-cornered opening of the
tent. From that habit my hands have kept a sort of inclination
to be clasped over my knees and feel strange here on the writing
pad in sudden indetermination, idle, fluttering in endless space,
and like an aimless bird my pen begins to describe vague circles
from ink to paper and over the paper, back and forth. But my
eyes pay no attention to it, no more than to the confused cries
and circlings of one lone sea-mew, for still half-closed in protection against the salt wind they stare along the shore to the first
houses of the bathing place, turning slowly sidewise with the
horizon to the point where the sun stands directly over the sea
and a strip of glancing rays makes the water impossible to view,
are dazzled for a moment and then turn back with a jerk to look
down between my knees at my feet that have burrowed into the
warm sand. Yes, I know certainly that I can recall myself to consciousness a hundred times to fix my attention here on what I
am writing; it will be in vain; I am estranged; my skin has been
too long uncovered; my blood is in all parts too near the surface
and I, aware of it, have neither part nor parcel in this body, in
this figure, half animal, sitting here at my writing desk as if in
a tent. It is this body who writes, who lets my pen flourish and
soar with long, undulating strokes, who dreams a monstrous
dream on which my consciousness has no hold. Formerly, when
my conscious mind wrote with careful strokes up and down, clear
and lucid, noting the results of abstract reveries in which I
sauntered with my tormented, philosopher face through the suburb where I live—what a trouble it cost me then to give my
thoughts something like flesh and blood emotion. Whereas now
that the strange, free swing of my self-motivated hand writes

independently, I begin to perceive that it expresses itself in a trim and tight form, the dreaming beast, and that my alert consciousness can do no better than to measure strength against it, wrestle with it and follow these voluntary movements of the pen on paper to get them into control if possible—in so doing have I not become two opposing elements striving against each other, beyond control of reason, possibly in a struggle to the death?

Because, moreover, of late particularly in this lonely spring after innumerable fruitless nights of bitter effort wherein I failed to drive my soul in its intellectual essence up to what I called a "vision of God," I made up my mind to choose the opposite extreme, to hold it down to my body, and decide to write only that which tended toward physical enjoyment such as an adventure or a contest; for now I know, thought I, the rules of this game and feel myself equal to it. I must refuse to work on anything that, begun with emotional impulse, is carried on with talented study and completed with the conscious daring of speculation. I must require that the subject appear to me as such a strong antagonist that it will set me at work and keep me at work so that I do not give way to it—the psychic, therefore, I shall leave to it, I thought, for my own part the only criterion will be the physical enjoyment in writing, a pleasure so intense that in the last analysis all gloomy literature by its incompleteness must contain something of insincerity, ingratitude in the author who merely suppresses this great pleasure while living through his disheartening sentences. This explains why the dejected realism of some ten years past goes paired with so-called objectivity. The author eliminates himself, for otherwise in his pessimistic view of the world he would have made a laughable discord of himself which would, of course, have spoiled his book. And so this objective realism was actually a perverted romanticism, suffocated to keep a mood in tune, a disguised bovaryism and, written as spectator standing outside of the subject, was actually a critical rather than a creative method of work, which does not shut out feeling, on the contrary objectivates and sterilizes it to a mood in which the writer himself froze fast. This, in my opinion, leads only to mind or characters in a story, never to major characters, which differ precisely in that in them the author writes fully and gives them a share in his utmost perceptions, above all in his creative delight, and thus maintains their superiority over the other figures. To bring this into my own domain, the realm of poets, there have always been two kinds of poets: on the one hand the secretaries to themselves, a little by their own will but not of their own fault, tormented lives, and, on the other hand, the stubborn pioneers of new feelings, themselves the cause of all that happened to them and who, in whatever doubt and weakness, still knew the chief fault to be in themselves. There, on the one hand, is Baudelaire with his matchless clarity and simplicity of expression of the dark wisdom of which he himself was the dupe, without being able to do anything about it, and, on the other, Verlaine, who experienced nothing but what Verlaine wrote, wrote with the left hand or the right, but was ever master and responsible in that world which from top to bottom he himself created. This is all very well, very true and profound, but what am I here but a tool, a seismograph for that which I note down with physical enjoyment while my body does the thinking and my pen scratches great circles over the paper? Shall I join issue with this writer, shall I wrestle with him as did Jacob with the Angel until the break of day? Shall I be able to check his speed with my arms that I fling down in desperation on the paper? Shall I construct a tale to canalize his periods into a higher level? Shall I, in writing, write?

Because, in the third place, it has not bothered me for a long while whether people think me mad, since I know positively that I am not; no, to put it more strongly, since I feel a sort of regret that I am no longer mad enough, not so mad as I was for example some fifteen years ago, when my fancies completely engrossed me, when the reality of their plain force exerted its influence on me here and there with demoniacal threats to rise up above the normal to my heights. To name an instance for you, I remember a certain house in the woods where I chose to ramble in a definite spirit of triumph, but would not willingly have passed at night because of a reed-covered dormer window that stared at me like a wide, somber eye so that I fled screaming or, another time, stood petrified calling God and Saint George to my aid, unconscious with fear of the shadow of a dark dragon which I saw there in that garden lying in wait for me, crouched and prepared to spring—of the shadow, I wrote, for had a flesh and blood dragon sprung at me I should resolutely have defended myself and been killed, believe it or not, with a serene mind; so it was only fear of the shadow; and in later life I became aware of my fear and learned to control it. I was afraid, namely, of all that showed itself ill-defined, imaginary, incorporeal, of everything intangible that haunted my brain, of everything, in short, that had no existence, that announced itself only to disappear without leaving a trace: a footfall and no one walking, an opening door through which no one entered; but like Saint Thomas I was always set at rest as soon as I could experience some real contact or other with the apparition. I recall that in childhood I was never in the least afraid when Saint Nicholas with mitre, crozier and cope (how necessary and "liberating" are the effects of these attributes!) solemnly stepped into the nursery and called me from my mother's side to him. I would give him my hand in confusion, but the confusion, rather, of inexpressible joy, feeling life suddenly take on an improbable proportion in the broad light of reality; but when, fifteen minutes later, my younger brother, who had followed Saint Nicholas out into the hall and there found the hastily discarded masquerade costume, came into the room and walked up to me holding the long, gray beard firmly to his childish face, imitating the apparition in gesture and walk—I recall that as one of the most frightful moments of my boyhood; I dared not stir for fear, naturally not for fear of my brother, but for fear of the invisible graybeard who was present. To give a last example from my present, poet life, I am no longer afraid of a feeling or an idea that passes through me if I cannot separate the idea from the words that I have found for it, if words and image have presented themselves together; often I have stood in terror of the hovering of a wordless poem, powerless to bring about its union with the releasing imagery of words, put it away from me for years, using ostrich-policy, have forgotten it and felt myself plagued meanwhile and secretly persecuted by a sensation of void, as when ancient peoples supposed that barren parents were tormented by the souls of their unborn children, until suddenly a traditional verse form seems to be the incantation by means of which the words, understood in this connection as a sort of body, come to hand of themselves. Now the older I grow the less this fear shows itself so that I often think, and observe too in certain behavior, that only my blood is disturbed while my mental life is wholly free, more and more balanced and has even become cheerful and carefree. With an eye to that fact I called myself, in the opening lines of this paragraph, "not mad enough," for the question worries me whether the vanished frenzy held down in my body lurks in hiding there so that I now feel something like fear of my submerged self, of the dreaming brute here at my desk, a fear that forces me to exert my utmost strength to keep pace with him, to write what he dictates and, if possible, by a sudden stroke of all that remains at my disposal to compel him as a rider does a horse.

For all these reasons, which I have given you so extensively

and, alas, in such ridiculously long and wavering sentences and
which I now pray you above all things not to read again in their
clumsy form but to reconsider in the form in which they rose
up in me, that is to say, in arrow-swift movement and, as I also
surveyed them when all at once they cleft vertically through
my personality, in a bird's-eye view—for all these reasons of
which the horizontal succession must make a plea for your clem-
ent discernment, but which are, at least, the pathological pre-
history, and contain the explanation, of the marvelous and
permanently conclusive experience that I am just about to undergo, here, under this lamp on my desk, in an hour perhaps—I felt
that summer evening, which will always be for me an unforgettable yesterday, in a mood as clear as crystal, as despairing as
a genial sluggard at the end of his days and as inspired with the
mood of that impossible "last attempt" as it is at all possible to
be. This is all you need to remember of the foregoing if you wish
to join me in the strange adventure that I feel is now close by,
that stands behind the door, as it were, and will presently enter
in word form.

After I had killed several hours more at my desk without result I betook myself to the city, on the last tram, and a while
after midnight found myself at the Vijverberg in The Hague, but
without paying the least attention to the most beautiful scene
that has ever been created in any city of the world, although, as
you shall hear, it had kept me particularly occupied for some
time past. I sat down on one of the benches that are ranged
under the trees along the water and began, softly and gently, to
whistle a melody that was probably suggested by the mood of
the hour. I already cursed the decision that had brought me at
such an hour into the city: now, I reflected, I should have to
walk back to the house and would it not have been more sensible
to remain seated quietly at work under my lamp? I could have
looked over my notebook, in which I write down fragments and
opening words of poems as they come to me from time to time,
perhaps I could have made a correction here or there or, who
knows, have completed a verse; and if that did not work I could
have finished off some correspondence and in any case I should
have done better to go quietly to bed, a book in hand, to read
until sleep overtook me, and so on—when the Pied Piper of
Hamlin, whom I recognized at once from Robert Browning's
poem, which at one time I could recite from beginning to end,
he it was, without a doubt, this tall, thin man in a Russian

blouse of red and yellow that was gathered together high at the waist with a scarf and then fell right down to his feet, with the pointed hood of Pinocchio and with the flute, on the end of a red and yellow scarf, stuck into his belt like a dagger, almost hidden under the folds—when the Pied Piper stepped right up to me with the friendliest bow, took a seat next to me on the bench and leaning nearer spoke:

"How can I serve you, Nijhoff, now that you have called for me?"

I assure you—and you will believe me if you will recall the third "because" above or will take another glance at the recollections of my childhood that follow it—I assure you that I was neither astonished nor afraid when I saw the Pied Piper approach and take a seat beside me, nor when he spoke to me. On the contrary, I took the opportunity to observe a few particulars of his appearance, which agreed entirely with the figure that I had imagined him. He had, for example, gray hair cut very short, narrow eyes which were light blue to the very whites, a swarthy, weatherbeaten face that was really much too small for his height and a small head that wagged slowly but regularly to and fro on the long, flexible neck. No, I cannot but say he pleased me; he was much more familiar than I had expected him to be, supposing that one could expect to meet the Pied Piper. But when, after the few words of introduction, he suddenly called me by name, right off, as if in everyday speech, I was thrown into such a state of shock as must befall the suddenly wakened somnambulist. A surprising dizziness, a distressing weakness forced me to clamp both arms firmly to the rail of the bench in order not to collapse. I had the sensation for a moment of being flung into nothingness, I tumbled through a pit, whirled star-swift into space, was dumped head over heels out of the world into the universe, nothing but a kite from which one has suddenly cut the string. The discovery of this comparison, which cost me a superhuman effort, brought me back to my senses, and I knew why the faintness had seized me. By uttering the strange word that my name became in his mouth, the Pied Piper had given me to understand that just as I had recognized him I was to him also no stranger. I already belonged to his world, who knows for how long or in what position he considered me rightly as one of his own kind. What had I to do with him, or ever had had; where, when? The vaguest recollection of it had completely uprooted me for a moment.

He repeated his question: "Were you in need of me that you whistled just then?"

But now I was wholly master of myself and with recovered confidence, relieved, I burst out presumptuously:

"Yes, of course"—with mocking unconcern—"I need you and so I whistled the tune with which you lured me, as a youngster, into the Koppelberg. I remember very well that when the dark grotto was shut fast behind us, and all the children pressed about you in terror, you promised to make up for our irrevocably lost parents by always coming to our aid if we should but whistle or hum the alluring tune. I have forgiven but not forgotten you"— I added laughingly, even clapping him on the shoulder—"for you never hold a grudge against anyone for such a tune, nor do you ever get free of it again!— But now, to business: I have been working this long while on a poem that must have for its setting the Vijverberg which has always attracted me, I do not know why. Every time that I come from Leiden, go through the Haagsche Bosch along the Hertenkamp and Korte Voorhout and approach the corner of the Tournooyveld where the museum is— every time, at sight of the broad sheet of water and the profile of the city around it, I am filled with rapture, deep homesickness and an overmastering urge toward a noble and great deed. As a boy I used to stand there for hours and I planned to describe all this in a great poem: fantastic sham battles were to be staged on the water with ornate tapestry-hung boats, flags were to be draped between the trees, while on the island a festival banquet was set up. Later, during my military service, when I went from the barracks into town, the same deep feeling always flowed through me as I came to this point: it was as if I had to swear an oath, a solemn oath with my hand upon the ensign or on the head of a child. In my brimming heart would sound a masculine music, the Wilhelmus anthem, and there would come again that overwhelming urge toward the great and noble, to die for the fatherland or to look after the affairs of the republic with broad and clear understanding, quite mild and fatherly. And still, to-day, I pass here often and wonder in bitterness why I have not become such a one as he" (and I point to the statue of Willem II) "who stood for his country in Quatrebras or as he" (and I point to Johan de Witt) "who was our best citizen."

I was silent and stared over the pond that rippled under the moon in the silvery reservoir. Over me the trees locked tight the silence that followed my words. On the further side age-old façades, crenelated walls and dungeons reflected a silhouette of our great past in the midst of the city.

The Pied Piper smiled, nodded and turned to me:

"And how far have you advanced on the poem?"

"That is just why I called you," I answered seriously. "Years ago a few lines occurred to me that, in spite of their crudity, contain perfectly for me the idea that I have just described: four wooden verses, which have finally become a frame from which I cannot think myself free. And now I hoped that you"—here I broke down, for what had I actually expected of him?—"that you," I went on, "might be able to make this dead wood bloom as once did Tannhäuser's staff."

Then I selected a strophe from my long poem, which was to become a counterpart of Huygen's *Voorhout*, and I heard myself speak in a voice that seemed as unreal to me as if I were reading something, quite without connection, from a book lying open by chance.

> I know no city of the world does yield
> More beauty than this broad quadrangle field:
> Prague nor Paris—no, nor are there any spots
> Where one strolls from the Tournooyveld to the Plaats.

My voice broke off as if I had shut the book from which I read.

"The question is," said the Pied Piper after a pause, with that peculiar smile that Browning drew with such mastery when he described his lips "where smiles went out and in," "the question is that your whistling was done with the mouth and not with a flute. You are weak from deep emotion, quivering from exertion and gratify your speech rather than your hearing. Moreover, the scale is limited, and through all this you must steel yourself and restrict yourself to a certain matter-of-factness that is in strange conflict with the tenderness of your intentions. But have you any idea of the freedom and power an instrument lends us? The lips can sing only of what the heart is full, but every flute is a magic flute and fills the empty hearts of other men with song. For the rats, I sang of raisins and bacon, of open provender casks, of a land without poison or traps; for the children, I sang of toys and cakes, of boats and gypsy-carts, of a land without school or bedtime." Thoughtfully he stroked the flute of soft, straight reed that stuck in his belt at the end of colorful scarf. "I shall advise you to begin for the present as follows: describe only the experiences of other men. Sympathy is no moral duty, it is an inborn passion and finds its source in the attraction that magnetically binds all flesh. For your own sake develop that passion, make yourself conscious of it and live and think in the feelings of other men. Only in that way will you be free of yourself, that is the aim. If this is too slow, then keep a diary, and every time that you are possessed with the desire to listen to your own feelings write down what occurs to you and that with as much daring as possible, with exaggeration, literary delight and self-pity. If, however, you take up verse form—only the feelings of others. Is there something wanting, for instance, in one relation or other in friendship or in love: jot down your own sentiments in the diary but try to express the attitude and grief of your friend in a poem. You will observe how strong you manage to appear in contrast to her, and for that matter, in contrast to yourself. Be prudent, lest your own voice cry out, be most prudent, lest you begin by losing the whole world and all it is worth for the sake of making verses of your own emotions. Do not willingly do that. Wait until you are free, wait until you have become a stranger to yourself, until you begin to lead a double life, as it were. To everyone there comes a time when he sees himself step out of his own life. But for many that moment comes only late, late in life, as it runs toward the close."

He had risen, and I perceived in his attitude the wish to depart. I asked him to stay a little longer, but he merely said: "I shall just see you home by the shortest way."

With a jerk I was up and mechanically walked on with him.

"Now, as to that Vijverberg poem," he continued after a few steps, "the ancients were not mistaken in giving substance to such natural sentiments and earthly inclinations in local gods. In that way, at least, they released the emotions, and such autochthonic, almost animal sensation must itself be carried out of human nature. But your modern sensibility, egocentric and anthropomorphic, is of no use. You would make a weeping dandy of a water god and a Salome of a wood nymph. Not for nothing, indeed, have saints, kings and poets existed. Go to work in this way: pay attention first of all to what, if you have let yourself go, the diary affords you. Read it over carefully and then seek in history or within your own sphere for a figure that approximately represents such a feeling for the fatherland, the national anthem and the refined republic of seamen and artists, and whoever it may be—Huyghens or Saint Martinus—call his figure up in your poem. He will come, as you will see, and will bring with him all that you need. You have only to sit down and move your fingers over the flute."

We had now come near the Gevangen Poort, where the Pied Piper stopped and, as if we had come to the appointed place, shook my hand in parting. I reminded him that he had promised to accompany me to my house.

"But by the shortest route, I told you," said he smiling, "do you not see that we are already there?"

There is a tea-shop next to the Gevangen Poort, and on the first and second floors above it the proprietor gives you the opportunity to rest a little in a cosily arranged tea-room, to enjoy the view over the Kneuterdijk and to try his tea. There is an inner stairway for the staff, but the public reaches the rooms from the Plaats by a winding stairway in a tower specially constructed for it outside of the shop. This little tower, though it does jut out a bit, forms a whole with the Gevangen Poort and the tea-room; it has always irritated me as a product of bad taste that instead of contrasting strongly and honestly in its modernity assimilates itself fraudulently, like a spurious antique, to the adjacent Gevangen Poort.

We stood on the steps of the tower, at the door that is made of light-colored oak planks cut lengthwise. Once more the magician shook my hand, smiled and left me, gliding like a shadow with long soft strides through the Poort.

Strange: although I was certain, just as I reminded the Pied Piper of his promise to accompany me to my door, that I was not yet home, strange, when I saw the dancing skirt of his colorful tunic disappear and I turned again to the oak door, I was standing without transition on the clinker path in the untidy, dry grass of my garden in the suburb, recognized at once my green-painted front door and, as a matter of course, pulled my key out of my pocket. With it I opened, as the most natural thing in the world, the door of the tower stairs as if it were my own house door. When I began the climb, it occurred to me vaguely that the stairs seemed longer and higher than usual, that above the banisters were narrow windows which I do not have at home, that through these slits I caught distant views of The Hague in the moonlit night: rippling water, the head of De Witt's statue on the Plaats suddenly close by, a little later the garden of the palace where once, as soldier, I had stood on sentry duty, the long gully of the Laan van Meerdervoort, the towers of a new church in Zorgvliet, the thick row of trees on the Ouden Weg, and more such pictures, which actually, to my reassurance, alternated with prints along the wall of my own staircase, an engraving by Redon representing a man balancing an enormous cube on his shoul-

ders, Dürer's "Maria with the Monkey," the inn with a boat near
it by Jan Steen—until at last I reached my own upper apartment,
looked for mail on the little table in the hall and hung my hat
and coat on the rack. Just as I always do when I come home of
an evening I felt my way in the dark along the walls of the hall
without putting on a light, reached the bathroom, ran the comb
through my hair and took a draught of water; things I always do
if I intend to sit down to work again. Then I turned off the light
there and again felt my way along the walls of the dark hall until
my hand found and turned the knob of my study door.

At once, on entering, I perceived through the opening door, by
a vague light on the wall, that I had left my shaded study lamp
lit on the desk. The shade is a large hat, impervious to light, such
as the Chinese use in the rice fields so that the lamp lights only
the table cover and leaves the rest of the room in darkness. I like,
now and then, to lift my head from my work and to look over the
shade into the nightlike room and then, when my eyes have gradually become accustomed to the dusk, to glance down at the white
paper and my hand upon it with the pen in the circle of light on
the table.

I left my lamp burning, thought I in the open doorway, sus-
pecting nothing when suddenly I was frightened by the sound my
chair makes when I shove it back in order to get up. My face became cold; gray death carried me away. Not daring to take another step from the threshold, I stood stock still in terror that
momentarily ran wild in me, clammy with sweat, in the empty
dizziness that had overcome me when the Pied Piper had suddenly called me by name, staring at the apparition that I saw
would have risen from my chair but that was seeking support
with his hands on the arms of the chair into which he had fallen
back, whose eyes, equally stiff with fright, held mine fast in
judgment.

I recognized him: that short, broad-shouldered figure in the
seablue pajama jacket; it was I who sat there. He still held the
pen in his hand and the upper half of the foam-white paper before him was covered with waving lines closely written. He threw
the pen down upon the sheet and grasping with his hands tried
again to rise out of my chair. In vain, he fell back further, so that
the face with its dreadful stare, that never for a moment turned
away from me, hung aslant and became visible under the lamp.
His thin, limp, fair hair, lightly falling out of its part from dryness, had just been combed back and left free a forehead across
which a dark wrinkle was furrowed. I saw the black nostrils in

his not fully matured, boyish face. I saw his clear, white teeth gleam between strangely drawn broad lips and with indescribable sinking of the heart I heard his slow, sucking breath come and go. Suddenly, as I stood in the open doorway, the words of the Pied Piper rang in my head: "Late, late in life does a man step outside of himself," and turning away I leaned my arm against the door frame, hid my head in it and burst into the bitter tears of bottled-up emotion.

I do not know how long this lasted, but I knew as if I had seen it with my eyes that the figure in the chair collapsed still further, that the staring of his open eyes slowly glazed, that his hand hung cold and slack beside the chair; and I heard in the deathly silence that his breath had ceased heaving.

Not so much from fear as from unbearable weariness I did not raise my head when, an immeasurable while later, my shoulder was lightly touched, and I felt someone cautiously push me aside in order to leave the room. For an instant, as he passed the door-post, he stood next to me, at my own height, and spoke with a voice that is mine, I think, in moments of deepest tenderness when my consciousness is on the point of losing itself.

"Do you know that . . . has come home and is upstairs, asleep?" and glided away soundlessly as a shadow in a mirror.

The word I did not write was faintly sighed, a whisper, the name of my little son. With a jerk I stood erect and without casting another glance into the empty room, for I knew there was no longer anyone there, I turned, felt my way through the hall and climbed the attic stair and stopped at the nursery. I stepped in and closed the door after me and locked it as if I were being followed and the pursuers were close on my heels. The narrow room, of which the window took up the whole width of the wall opposite the door, was already dimly lit by the glimmer of dawn over the city. On the left, against the long wall, stood the child's cot and on the table next to it a night-light flickered, a thin and yellow flame in the glimmer of the morning haze. Around this light stood a picture of my wife, a bronze statuette of Saint Anthony and a toy automobile, his dearest possessions. I sat on the edge of the bed and gazed at the sleeping boy. He slept quietly, his head sidewise on the pillow, one little hand, relaxed, stretched toward his two "children," Jan and Kees, a sailor and a teddybear which by day he already neglected but which still accompanied him to bed at night. I was not in control of my emotion, and hot tears streamed down my face. The child, however, was not wakened by my sobs, at which I wondered, for I had frequently noticed that he became restless whenever I looked at him in his sleep. Now, however, he did not stir, his eyelids were not closed to the line of the lashes, and through his open mouth over which I could not resist placing my hand I felt the warm current of his breath. I bent over him and lightly kissed his straw-white hair in which I still detected a trace of the fragrance of the "land of milk and honey" as, in the old days now ten years past, I called his cradle. To be sure, other fragrances were added, too, of "sand in the sun" and of "dried flowers" and "iron and leather" but "the land of milk and honey" had not yet wholly disappeared, and with some astonishment I sought the impression of his body under the covers down to the feet and found it longer than I had thought.

Opposite the bed, in the other long wall, the door of the adjoining room stood open, the guest room. It was quite dark in there, I noticed from where I sat, for the shades were drawn down. I stood up to make sure that my conjecture was right. My wife was home. Looking around the edge of the door I saw her head with its heavy, fair hair on the pillow and heard her regular breathing. I was seized with an overwhelming feeling of gratitude, warmer and fuller than I could comprehend. In order not to waken them I stole back through the nursery, quickly and on tiptoe. I opened the door, hurried down the stairs and finally, at the hall door, leaning against my coat on the rack, gave myself up freely to the overmastering outburst. It was already broad daylight in the hall of the silent house when, passing the door of my study into which I did not look again, I reached my bedroom.

I undressed quickly but found, even as I half suspected, no pajamas on my pillow. I took no further account of it but wrapped myself without hesitation in a large, white sheet, stretched out full length on top of the bed and folded the sheet tightly over me, and so, arms folded across my chest, I lay staring for a while at the crucifix that always stands on my mantelpiece until, unexpectedly, I fell asleep.

The sun was high in the heavens when I awoke. I went at once to my study, where the lamp was still burning. My pen, stretched out like a dead bird, lay obliquely across a pile of paper torn from the writing pad. And I was still standing thoughtfully by the draperies that I had drawn aside, gazing at that object I dared not touch, when I heard voices and laughter outside the window, and my wife walked into the garden holding our son by the hand. They came straight from the station, returning from a long journey; they wanted to surprise me and had not let me know when the train arrived. She was carrying a valise, and he was thrusting Jan and Kees triumphantly up at me. I made the impression, they said afterwards, of having just been awakened by their homecoming.

Translated by WILHELMINA C. NIEWENHOUS

PART VI

NEW FLEMISH PROSE

Marnix Gijsen (Jan-Albert Goris)

ON THE GENIUS OF FLANDERS

IN ACCORDANCE WITH APPROVED SCIENTIFIC PROCEDURE, I DECIDED, before approaching my subject, to find out what the best writers had to say on the question we are about to discuss. In this process, I had a most unfortunate experience.

It so happened that the first book I picked up was by an American writer, whose name I shall charitably withhold. This author painstakingly examines the characteristics of the Belgian people and the factors that distinguish Walloon character from Flemish psychology. In a passage which seems to be the synthesis of this thinking and impressions, he arrives at the following conclusion: "The Walloons have a volatile character but are malicious; the Flemings are well-meaning souls, not too intelligent and even a little bovine." . . .

The perusal of this text plunged me into deep reflection. I decided to abandon my scholarly ethnological research and rely exclusively on my own lights. It is by the vacillating clarity of my own personal observations that I permit myself to lead you.

Let us first examine the title of this discourse and arrive at agreement on its exact meaning. I suggest this in order to avoid what is very accurately called in Flemish an "oeverloos" (a shoreless) subject, that is, a subject without shores, which is at once broad and fluid, and which threatens at any moment to overflow to the right or left.

The subject comprises only two terms: "genius" and "Flanders." The word "genius" may seem a little pretentious, a little pedantic. One might have said: Flemish psychology, Flemish spirit, Flemish substance. And yet, what we are going to deal with is not exactly that. It is that, and, at the same time, something more. Genius is something that is actually a part of a person or a group, that determines his or its individuality, personality, being. Someone once referred to the "invisible genius of the city." This is its meaning. There must be a character of the Bronx and Brooklyn, as there is one of Athens or Rome. The word does not, therefore, necessarily imply superiority of intelligence or of artistic creative power, but it is a sure criterion, a definite landmark.

Since the character of a people cannot be seen, since it can only be sensed empirically through its numerous external manifestations, I could easily enough claim to immobilize it, to materialize it for a moment before your eyes, and you would have the perfect right not to be convinced, not to recognize it, if you so wished. We shall deal, then, with what is exclusively characteristic of Flanders.

There is still the word "Flanders" or "Flemish." Here again, there is nothing precise, except the absolute necessity of circumscribing, of limiting, of being precise. Victor Hugo thought of Mons, in Hainaut, as a Flemish town, and Octave Mirbeau found Liége "an exceedingly pretty city of Flanders." There have been several "Flanders" during the course of the centuries: one has been called "Flemish Flanders," another "French Flanders," which, to our partisan ears has the wee, small sound of a paradox. In the beginning hemmed in between the North Sea and the Scheldt, Flanders stretched eastward to the Meuse, but she has been chopped off at the base. She had conquered Brabant, Antwerp, and Limburg; she had lost Lille, Valenciennes, Tourcoing, and Arras.

When Rubens spoke of *la Fandra la mia carissima patria*, his mind probably did not stop at Enghien or Wavre, but he included in this tender phrase everything that fell within the spiritual orbit of Flanders. Apart from the Principality of Liége, this probably included all of present-day Belgium. When the Canadian poet, John McCrae, wrote his beautiful poem "In Flanders' Fields the Poppies Blow," he certainly did not mean to imply that the poppies on the graves of English soldiers killed in Hainaut had merely strayed there by mistake.

At the beginning of the Flemish literary renaissance of the nineteenth century, there was a slogan used which, like all slogans, was partly false:

"De Taal is gansch het volk"

"The language is the whole people": those who speak Flemish, those who express themselves in Flemish would, therefore, be Flemings, and, of course, no one else would be. This is an obvious error and too easily refuted. Character is revealed in hundreds of different ways, of which language is only one, and, on the other hand, so many men, unquestionably heart and soul of

Flanders, have expressed themselves through the channel of another tongue than Dutch, or used other means of expression than language.

We can conclude, therefore, that in order for a person or a thing to be Flemish, a certain physical contact at least is needed with the region, with its atmosphere, its monuments, its culture, and, above all, with its people.

It follows that the physical appearance, the size of a being or of a group has an influence on the very nature of that being or group, and, inversely, that the size, the quantitative aspect of a thing or group may be determined by the essence itself of the object. In other words, there is a close relationship between the physical and spiritual features of a people.

The fact that there are only 4,500,000 Flemings in the world is of importance. It is of no less importance that this group of modest numbers is surrounded by entities, more powerful and at least as homogeneous, if not more so, than itself.

This was not always the case. In the Middle Ages, and even in the Burgundian period, Flanders, strong and united, was surrounded by a swarm of small states, and her wealth in gold as well as in manpower assured her a preponderant position within the strange European mosaic of that time. This was the moment when she was able to express herself with the greatest freedom, with the fewest restrictions, as equal to equal.

Before burying herself in the penumbra of the Jesuitical mediocrity of the seventeenth century, she produced Rubens. It was necessary to wait until the middle of the nineteenth century for her to wrench herself free, to refind her faith, forget the prudence and false wisdom that the masters of smug mediocrity had lavished upon her during the entire seventeenth and eighteenth centuries. Here then, is a hiatus of two hundred years which will explain many a thing about the real, vital forces of Flanders. Here then, is a halt, a breakdown of the creative faculty, a moral diminishment, which will also tell us something about the basis of that fugitive reality we all pursue.

Those who are too easily discouraged by ancient scripts or who are unable to penetrate the mysteries of an archaic language, say all too easily that the Flemings are people who feel the outside world as an hallucinatory reality, who are powerfully obsessed by it and whose painters and writers express it and interpret it with an intense sensual lyricism. No, everything must be given its proper place, no factor should be neglected in that powerful symphony which expresses the soul of a people—neither the heavy, sumptuous tones of our tapestries, nor the strident cries of Bacchic poetry, nor even the tang and violence of insult and gross popular obscenity. For a work of art is not conceived in a vacuum, painting does not suddenly loosen itself, without warning, from the monotone of history. It springs from the interruptions themselves, from the hesitations, the weaknesses and the mistakes. It is nurtured by time as well as by the masses. In a people, everything holds together.

Paul Valéry, and he is the only witness I shall call to my assistance, described the Flemish character in the following way:

"This race, distinguished by a special alliance of impulsiveness and languor, of violent activity and a tendency toward contemplation, which is passionate and patient, sometimes sensual to the point of fury and again completely detached from the physical world, withdrawn within the mystic castles which the soul secretly builds upon the confines of intelligence and of night."

In other words, Mr. Valéry says, as does everyone else but certainly better than everyone else, that the Flemings are at once sensual and mystic. Is this correct?

In its broad outlines, the portrait is probably true, but it is not very distinctive because, when you come down to it, it must be admitted that the Spanish are "mystic and sensual" too, and the Italians as well, and, to a certain extent anyway, this same dualism, this same mixture of contradictory factors may be found among most of the peoples of the Christian world. Mysticism and sensuality are the very H_2O of the baptismal waters. The only difference is in the amount, the manner, the nuance.

For my part, I believe that the keystone of the Flemish structure is the fact that the Flemings are essentially peasants and inhabitants of small towns: eighty per cent of them live in the country; ten per cent live in towns of from 25,000 to 100,000 inhabitants; and ten per cent reside in what may be called, from a European point of view, large cities.

This is the practically immutable background of Flanders— this solid peasant mass which has held together through the centuries, which was assailed and massacred by the aristocracy in the twelfth century, which was admirably castigated by a great anonymous poet, which suffered all possible outrage, all rapine, all cruelties at the hands of the Burgundians, French, Spaniards, Austrians, and Germans.

The main characteristics of the Flemish peasant are no less repugnant to civilized people than those of any other rural population of Europe. He has the same mixture of craft, rapacity, avarice, heartlessness, physical violence, meanness of spirit, the same absence of civic and military virtues, as are to be found almost anywhere else. Nothing has basically changed since the old days, when the peasants were called—and rightly so—*vilains.*

A peculiarity of Flanders is the extraordinarily unstable climate, which constantly forces them to be crafty with their land, never to put their trust in the morrow or even in the afternoon; nothing is certain in their lives or their production—nothing except absolute uncertainty.

The poetess Hadewych has put it very prettily:

> Seghet die landman; jegen avent
> sal men loven den scoonen dag.
>
> (The peasant says: "Don't praise
> the good weather until the day
> is done.")

This constant calculating, this incessant battle with inclement and brutally capricious elements has taught the Flemish country folk extreme precaution and almost complete skepticism. It has urged them into patient observation and taught them to see the details of Nature rather than her motivating principles. They have developed a cult of shortsighted wisdom, of a fragmentary philosophy, which is no philosophy at all, but rather a system of petty accommodations to life than a solid philosophic structure which would cast light on our problems and give meaning to our existence. And so, there are no, or few, philosophers in Flanders, but a plethora of amusing moralists.

The Flemish climate, which has neither rhyme nor reason, has made the Fleming highly sensitive to color, smell, volume, and all the physical appearances of worldly objects.

The great majority of Flemings are, therefore, realistically minded individuals, easily and constantly moved to tenderness by the smallest details of nature, by the atmosphere, by changes in climate, but too quickly forgetful that the drama of the world is not outside of us, but within ourselves. This is translated into a savory folklore, full of color and abounding with acute, but relatively unimportant, observations.

I have been able to compare certain parts of the early works of the great novelist Stijn Streuvels to brilliant meteorological bulletins. Indeed, on page after page of his early novels, he describes the weather somewhat as the landscapists of the seventeenth century paint for us, but with far too much insistence, the cloudy skies of Flanders. Only at the very end does man make his appearance in this countryside—he, the only living thing that matters and whose grandeur consists precisely in dominating, with a certain arrogance, the pretentious and cumbersome spectacle of elements and climates.

When our lesser masters paint calligraphic still-lifes, when our writers describe, with amusing and picturesque commentary, the various minute aspects of the countryside and its produce, it is always an attentive Flanders which speaks, which examines itself and which, in this contemplation, is sufficient unto itself.

But we know that this naive tenderness, occasioned by the petals and the trees, the insects and the cattle with their smells, their colors, their habits and their manias, is of hardly any importance. It may serve, at most, as an escape from the real problems of man, as a palliative for that ennui which, Pascal tells us, is at the bottom of the human heart. It is an evasion, a cowardice, a flight into the smug and mediocre.

From an artistic point of view, all this would be very discouraging if, from time to time, a miracle were not produced, if, in compensation, something splendid and marvelous did not arise from this mass of mediocrity. This occurred in the figure of the poet Guido Gezelle.

Gezelle was a believer, a Christian. He saw the world only in the light of religious principles. For him, all creation, which he loved and which he saw through a gardener's eyes, was but the image of God, a symbol of future life. Everything mediocre and amusing in the comfortable and savory realism of Flanders, was ennobled by his words.

Nowhere in the European literature of the nineteenth century, except perhaps in the writings of Francis Jammes, was so complete an understanding of nature sustained by so simple and profound a faith.

I will not violate Gezelle by translating him—it is almost impossible—but I shall give you a more modest example of typically Flemish writing.

Georges Chastellain, one of the historians of the Burgundian Court who, though born and educated in Flanders, wrote in French—for which he offers his excuses, incidentally—tells, in a famous passage from his chronicles, of a violent quarrel between the aged Duke Philippe the Good and his son Charles the Bold. The Duke is so troubled in spirit that, toward evening, he departs from Brussels on horseback:

"Les jours pour celle heurre d'alors estoient courts, et estoit jà basse vesprée quant ce prince droit-cy monta à cheval, et ne demandait riens autre fors estre emmy les champs seul et à part luy. Sy porta ainsy l'aventure que ce propre jour là, après un long et âpre gel, il faisoit un releng (dégel), et par une longue épaisse bruyne qui avoit couru tout ce jour là, vesprée tourna en pluie bien menue, mais très-mouillante et laquelle destrempoit les terres et rompoit glaces avecques vent qui s'y entrebouta."

(The days, at that particular time, were short and it was near first vespers when the prince did mount his horse direct, asking only to be left alone amidst the fields and by himself. It so happened that on that very day, after a long and bitter frost, there came a thaw, and through a long and heavy fog, which had prevailed the whole day through, there fell a rain, extremely fine but all pervading and which in intermingling with the wind, did drench the earth and break the ice.)

It is on a level with the best of Gezelle and Timmermans. It combines both Lemonnier and Claus; it is an utterly and superbly Flemish piece of writing.

It is not surprising that the love of the land and the things it produces has given the Flemish people a reputation for exacerbated sensuality. No one will deny that the Flemings tend toward sensuousness, but their supreme wisdom lies in the fact that they do so in a simple and bourgeois fashion. Our poets of the Middle Ages devoted long pages to a summing up of everything which they believed estimable in this world. They listed the fruits, the flowers, the victuals, the drinks—everything that might appeal to the senses—but these enthusiastic inventories hardly ever went beyond the point of a thanksgiving which closely resembles a catalogue. There are a few exceptions. One lucky day, I had the good fortune to discover a poem, buried in oblivion for four centuries, in the Library of Manuscripts at the British Museum—a poem by one of my fellow-citizens, the Antwerp poet Cornelis Crul, a superb poem which begins like this:

Ghij die appelkens, peerkens en nootkens maect,
Sijt ghelooft van uwer goeder chyere,
Van vlees, van visch dat zoo wel smaect
Van broot, van botere, van wijne, van biere.
Ghij cleet ons, ghij licht ons, ghij wermt ons met viere.
Ghij geeft ons ruste, blijscap en ghesonde.
Ghij spaert ons, ghij bewaert ons, heere goedertiere
En leert ons metten woorde van uwen monde.

Tleeft al bij u dat is in swereldts ronde
Tsij zijerken, tsij mierken, tsij vloe, tsij das.
Dies segghen wij u Heere, uut goeden gronde:
Benedicamus Domino, Deo gracias.

(You, who make little apples, pears, and nuts,
Be praised for your good cheer,
For meat and fish which taste so good,
For bread, for butter, for wine, for beer.
You clothe us, you light us, you warm us with fire.
You give us rest and joy and health.
You teach us with the words of your mouth.
All in this world live because of you
Be it a gnat, be it an ant, be it a flea, be it a badger.
Therefore we praise you, Lord, for good reasons:
Benedicamus Domino, Deo gracias.)

It is simple, direct, and touching. It is not perhaps great, but it is admirably pure, warm, and honest. It is the honesty of Saint Francis of Assisi. Reading this poem, one is struck by an innocence of heart and feeling found only among simple, sturdy people.

It has been thought possible, on the strength of Rubens' abundant anatomies, and by isolating this phase of his work from the rest of Flemish artistic and intellectual life, to ascribe to the people of Flanders a tendency toward sensual excess and an immoderate, almost animal, predilection for the pleasures of the flesh. Fromentin and Verhaeren have their share in this, and since their time, practically nothing has been done but repeat and amplify their ideas. However, on closer inspection, it can be seen, here as elsewhere, that the Flemish character is manifested in the same bourgeois forms, with the same lack of dramatic intensity, the same touching simplicity.

The most beautiful Netherlands poem of the Middle Ages—a pure work of art—is the "Beatrijs" legend. The subject is a familiar one. It is the legend of the vergeress. The Sister Vergeress Beatrice summons her childhood sweetheart, a young knight, to her convent and declares her love. They decide to flee together. Under cover of darkness, the knight carries her off on his horse and, as day breaks on a radiant May morning, they reach a sun-drenched glade. The young lover makes to Beatrice a suggestion commonly known as dishonorable. She objects, not from principle, not as a result of any sense of guilt, secret reserve or inner struggle of conscience. She has fully decided to see the adventure through to the end. But certain forms should be observed, everything should be done in order and with proper decorum.

I give you the remarkable translation of Professor Adriaan J. Barnouw:

> He looked at that lovely one
> To whom he bore a steadfast love.
> He said, "Dearest, if thou approve,
> We should dismount and pluck a flower.
> This is a pleasant place and hour.
> Come and let us play love's game."
> She spoke, "What sayest thou, for shame
> Should I lie down in the wood
> Like women who earn a livelihood
> With their body boorishly?
> Then were there little shame in me.
> This wouldn't have come into thy mind
> Wert thou not of boorish kind.
> I have reason to be sad.
> May God curse thee for such bad
> Intentions. Speak of something else.
> Listen to the birds in glens and dells,
> How they carol and make glee.
> Their music will pass the time for thee.
> When I am naked in a bed,
> Neatly made with sheets and spread,
> Then mayst thou do thy will with me,
> To whatever thy heart prompteth thee.
> It maketh me sad and void of cheer
> That thou didst propose it here."

This extraordinary exchange of opinion is one of the few love dialogues in Flemish literature. One will note that there is nothing here reminiscent of the tormented and pathetic cries of Tristan and Yseult. At no point do the lovers involuntarily inflict upon each other those superb wounds upon which the beauty of amorous dialogue rests, and which, to the extent that it is rendered public, constitutes its real justification. At no point do they throw the solemn shadow of death over the traditional exchange of fantasy and affectionate desires. And finally, they make no appeal to the outside world, except as a side-track, a temporary sedative whose only purpose is to allow time to return everything eventually to its proper place.

At first sight, one might be tempted to say that the conception of life and love, as expressed in this brief passage, is not very elevating and—supreme criticism!—without a moral. And indeed, it does not perhaps advance us in an understanding of the human heart or in the study of our passions, for, although the poet tells us that the gods prefer the depth to the tumult of the soul, we know, nonetheless, that only the sight of a wild inner disorder can move our tired consciences and sluggish minds.

There is another, even more pointed example of this solid, bourgeois background which forms the basis of the Flemish nature. Rubens was remarried at 52 to Helen Fourment, a girl of some sixteen or seventeen years. In a letter written to Pereisc, a humanist friend in Aix-en-Provence, he announced his second marriage in this way:

"I am resolved to marry again because I find that I am not yet ready for continence and celibacy; besides, if precedence is supposed to be given to mortification, we can also, in offering thanks to Heaven, enjoy what pleasures are permitted. I have taken a young wife, of honest but middle-class parents, although everyone tried to persuade me to make my choice at Court, but I was afraid of encountering pride, that vice inherent in the nobility, particularly in its women. I want a wife who will not blush when she sees me take up my brushes; in a nutshell, I am too fond of my freedom."

What a magnificent example of that solid harmony, that sense of proportion and prudence, that balance of the flesh and spirit which has always made of the great mass of the Flemish people an element of stability, solidarity and richness!

Perhaps I have given the impression that the spirit does not count for much in Flanders. Nothing could be further from the truth, for beyond that eighty per cent of country- and towns-folk, there is the twenty per cent of the Flemish population which dwells in cities. There is obviously more to being an intellectual than just living in a city, and besides, no one is even sure that it is a particularly desirable state, but in the urban centers it is difficult to escape being contaminated by the printed verb or by the spoken word.

The Flemish character is most clearly perceived within the framework of the community. For, outside of the solid peasant mass, the Flemish people are essentially a bourgeois people.

It is remarkable that the nobility of Flanders has never been an important factor in the life of the people. The Counts of Egmont and of Horne, decent weaklings, were, without any doubt, the pathetic victims, the martyrs, but certainly not the heroes, of liberty. Except in 1830, our nobility, like most nobility in fact, was always essentially preoccupied with serving the Prince, no matter what Prince, believing, and in good faith, that they were thus serving the nation at the same time. The harshest reproach that the Flemings hold against this class of people is that for several centuries they have done everything to create a respectful distance between themselves and the masses of the people, and that rare are those who have tried to raise the population to their own level. History has punished this sin of omission!

Flemish city dwellers created in the thirteenth, fourteenth, and fifteenth centuries a masterpiece: the community, the municipality. They discovered the art of establishing order in the city, convulsed by violent turmoil, conflicting interests, and bloody passions. They accomplished the miracle of social organization—harmony and prosperity.

Like the Greeks, they tried several methods: democracy fought oligarchy, demagogy rent the delicate woof of democratic harmony, until finally they arrived at a middle way, a bourgeois regime. Broad common sense, moderation, had triumphed.

I need not tell you what the bourgeoisie is: in some people's eyes it is an abomination, in others' the salt of the earth. Léon Bloy said that "the bourgeois is a pig that wants to die of old age," but it was none other than the Flemish bourgeois who, according to local custom, inscribed, on the first page, as the first article of their laws:

"In dese stad sijn alle menschen vrij ende gheen slaven." (In this city, all men are free and none shall be slave.)

It is these bourgeois who resisted the knights and who, when it was necessary, defeated the Kings of France; these were the bourgeois who freely concluded treaties, as equal to equal, with the Kings of England. It is they who subsidized the Flemish primitive painters and who, later, accepted with understanding and gratitude the superb lessons in humanism taught them by that great bourgeois genius—Rubens.

Erasmus had already remarked, early in the sixteenth century, that there was nowhere else in Europe "as considerable a number of good average minds" as there were in Flanders.

These are the men who, from the beginning of the fifteenth century up to our days, have made great lawyers, unexcelled administrators, patient scientists. Their writings are forgotten, but let us be honest: What is still living of the numerous writings of Erasmus, apart from his delicious *Eulogy of Folly,* which everyone discusses without having ever read, and a few of his Colloquies? But all the writings of these diligent men, if lacking in brilliance and genius, with the exception, perhaps, of Jansenius, have been absorbed into the body, into the very marrow of our national thought. Among them might be considered the work of Leonardus Lessius, *De Justitia et Jure,* which Archduke Albert had constantly at hand in rendering justice, as well as those innumerable treatises on law, ethics, finance, and administration, and, at the end of this long procession of writers destined for oblivion and today consulted by only a few specialists, might be seen advancing His Eminence, Cardinal Van Roey, son of one of the notables of Vorselaer, with his book *De Justo Auctario Ex Contractu Crediti* (Fair Interest in the Credit Contract). Here, then, is an element of permanence, consistency and continuity which it would be vain to deny.

Eventually so much balance, so much harmony and solidity would be almost painful and certainly irksome to us if we had not before us the charitable warning of Hippolyte Taine: "All this," he says, in his *Philosophy of Art,* in dealing with the Flemish character, "all this makes for rather short common sense and a rather broad happiness. A Frenchman would soon yawn at this, but he would be wrong. This civilization which seems stuffy and vulgar to him has its own unique value: It is healthy. The men who live here have that gift most lacking in us: wisdom and (a recompense which we no longer deserve) contentment." This contentment, whose delights the Touraine printer, an Antwerper by adoption, Christopher Plantin, has described in his *Sonnet du Bonheur de ce Monde,* flows from the extraordinarily home-loving character of the Flemish population. For at least three centuries, there has been no important migration. In the thirteenth and fourteenth centuries there were fairly large population displacements. There were Flemish *treks* to Germany and Hungary. Attempts were made at colonization in the Azores and in other distant territories. There was a large Flemish emigration to England. More than twelve hundred Flemish words were absorbed into the Anglo-Saxon vocabulary at that time. Flemish bankers even succeeded, in the fourteenth century, in driving the Lombards and Jews out of England. Flemish emigration only ceased when the indignant Londoners massacred en masse the entire Flemish colony at the time of Wat Tyler's revolt in 1381. The tables were ironically turned, for they used the technique of the Bruges Matines. In 1302, the French were massacred at Bruges if they could not pronounce without too strong an accent the difficult words *Schild ende vriend.* The Londoners made the Flemings pronounce the words *bread and cheese,* and if their pronun-

ciation was too close to *brood en kaas,* their lot was cast. The
Flemish caught on. They stayed at home.

There is no question but that man most easily betrays himself
by his purposeless gestures, by the things he does when he has
nothing to do, by his amusements, his play. What does he do to
escape the monotony of life, to shatter this contentment which
often must seem like satiety?

Where the Flemish people are concerned, it is almost impossible to answer this question without bringing up for a moment
the question of political history. For several centuries, the Fleming has felt himself humiliated and looked down upon, and this
feeling is heightened to the exact extent that nationalist faith
(one might even say "nationalist mania") has become the corner-
stone of European politics. He has felt himself a second rank Burgundian, a second class Spaniard, Austrian, Frenchman, Dutch-
man, and, finally a second rate Belgian.

I do not say to what extent he is right or wrong. I am simply
stating a fact.

During this long period of humiliation, in which he tenderly
and fervently nourished his inferiority complex, he searched for a
way out, a deliverance which would secretly give him confidence
in himself and raise him in his own eyes. Before long, he began
to make fun of his own misfortune, to brag about his deformities.
He tried to disarm the criticism of his enemies or his masters by
hastening to draw his own caricature. *Reynard the Fox* and the
Legend of Ulenspiegl are both glorifications of the rogue, the
scoundrel, the rascal.

There are hardly any romantic heroes in the Flemish Pantheon.
If Spain is personified in *The Cid* and *Don Quixote,* Flanders is
personified by Reynard, who in spite of more powerful forces,
manages to live as he pleases, and by Ulenspiegl, an unscrupulous
gamin who thumbs his nose at tyrants.

We are told that Louis XIV, when he saw the paintings of
Teniers and Adrien Brauwer, said: "Take these wretches out of
my sight." He could not stand the spectacle of those carousers in
their smoky taverns, the tumbling about of those harlots, those
animal brawls and doltish dances. His reaction is understandable.
As a matter of fact, there was nothing for him to learn from this
elemental humanity whose message was mainly directed to those
who actually lived among these scenes.

In all Flemish painting, in all the literature of Flanders, ancient as well as modern, in short, at the basis of the Flemish character, may be found this will to ugliness, this urge to caricature

nobility of feeling, this obsession to inflict upon one's self the spectacle of a systematic deformation of everything worthy and significant in the social as well as spiritual order. This could be misunderstood; this tendency might well be considered a symptom of collective masochism, were it not almost wholly compensated for by one of the most precious of spiritual gifts—the resilient nature of the Fleming. Those who see in Flemish intellectual and artistic life only its noisiest manifestations, find it difficult to understand the delectabilities of the Flemish spirit in its most refined expression. Herein lies a treasure of vitality, a vivacity of spirit, a gift for verbal pyrotechnics and spiritual choreography which is generally unknown to those who only participate from afar in Flemish life and which becomes ever richer and more abundant, as Flanders again becomes conscious of her own forces.

The finest example, the most magnificent illustration of this youthful spirit, of humor sometimes macabre but always healthy and vigorous, is the painter Bruegel. Bruegel's work is abundant proof of that gracious subtlety of spirit to which I allude.

He is proof not only of a profound consciousness of the individual drama, but, confronted by social and political problems, he knew how to handle them without rhetoric and without recourse to extravagant gesticulations. Thanks to that fundamental optimism which lies at the base of Flemish character, he has remained—as an American critic says—"the most human of all the great painters."

The same spirit may be found in Karel van de Woestijne who is, with R. M. Rilke, the greatest lyric poet of Europe in the nineteenth century, as well as in the authors of the preceding generation and in those of the generation to which I—and very proudly —belong.

It is obvious that the Flemish character whose major outlines I have tried to draw has been subjected to foreign influences and even to violent assaults. If it is true that it resisted triumphantly and that it needed, in sum, only one historical novel to revive it again—*The Lion of Flanders,* written, incidentally, by Henri Conscience whose father was a French émigré—there is also not the slightest doubt but that it bears the imprint of its great neighbors.

Has the Flemish character borrowed from Germany?

I believe that, without being swayed by the circumstances of the moment, I can frankly reply in the negative. One would search in vain for any sort of trace whatsoever, in Flemish spiritual as well as artistic life, of a German influence in Flanders.

None of the masterpieces of mediaeval literature derived their subjects or inspiration from Germany, and if Dürer was able for a moment to influence the formal side of Flemish painting at the beginning of the sixteenth century, Flemish art, on the other hand, completely absorbed Hans Memling.

In modern times, German editors have paid court to certain Flemish authors, trying in vain to win them to their political cause, but the upshot has been that Flemish authors are read in Germany, not that Germany has influenced Flanders.

It is an incontrovertible fact that French influence in Flanders has been very strong, and that the French spirit, which combines moderation, clarity and grace, and, above all, impeccable logic, has considerably attenuated the Gothic sentiments which persisted long after the Middle Ages in Flanders and which, among other things, made the plays of Paul Claudel so popular in the smallest Flemish villages.

One might believe that French influence in Flanders was above all of a rationalist character. It is true that here and there a provincial notary, taking Voltaire for an atheist, announced himself one with the sage of Ferney, thinking thus to secure a lien on elegance and free thinking. In so doing, he demonstrated his stupidity as surely as do those American boys in their teens who purchase a translation of *Candide* in the second-hand book stores of Times Square under the assumption that they are acquiring pornographic literature.

No, one should not talk of French influence in Flanders in terms of Mr. Dekobra's literature. It goes a great deal further. Thank God it is more profound than that. At its best, it is eminently beneficial; it only becomes irritating in its numerous mediocre expressions. It serves as a judicious rein on the Flemish spirit—naturally inclined toward an unbridled romanticism—as a discipline, which it too often lacks.

There is no basic opposition between the French spirit and Flemish psychology. Political preoccupations on the part of each have alone aroused suspicions which a stabilized political harmony can fortunately put to rest.

And finally, there is England. It is strange to think that for a whole century the English were forced to defend themselves against Flemish expansion. There are a number of rhymed pamphlets of the thirteenth and fourteenth centuries which put the English on guard against an imperialist Flanders and against those Flemings who ride too high and have too much money in their purses.

The Flemings have never, since the fifteenth century, feared being absorbed by England, and it should not be forgotten that this danger of absorption is the national nightmare of all small linguistic communities.

They have always felt at ease with England and the English. Jacob of Artevelde gave the first proof of this state of mind. Later Rubens, frankly Francophobe, at least in politics, was much more pro-English than he was pro-Spanish, and we know that Guido Gezelle found far richer spiritual nourishment among the English and American poets than anywhere else.

Herein is an historical trait, a current of sympathy which is sometimes hidden, but which should not be underestimated. It may be said of the majority of Flemings, without any fear of being wrong, what the chronicler Froissart said of Jacob of Artevelde, with pique and a certain astonishment: "His heart was more English than French."

Translated by MARY TAUSSIG

Marnix Gijsen (Jan-Albert Goris)

WHAT TO TELL THE MILKMAID

WHEN THE FRENCH TRIED TO IMPRESS THE NORTH AFRICAN ARABS with the marvels of modern machinery, airplanes and the like, the sons of the desert remained unmoved. When the French had really shown them the final achievement of mechanical ingenuity and asked for comment, the sheiks just nodded politely and said: "Why do you spend your precious time inventing contraptions to amuse people? Life is too short for that."

Do not blame the Arabs for that lack of appreciation of our mechanical age: they dispense with the trimmings around things, they know that you can't change the three basic events of life—birth, love and death. To a certain extent the people of Europe are also like that. We are told that a Normandy milkmaid went on milking her cow while all around her Yanks and Nazis were fighting in the meadow. A seven-year-old American girl, riding over a bridge, asked if it was riveted or welded; the Normandy milkmaid did not ask if the soldiers used bazookas or submachine guns, she went on about her usual business. If the Yanks tell her that the Empire State Building is that high, she will not be interested, but she will listen eagerly if she is told what the milkmaid in Montana does on Sunday afternoon.

The trouble with the world (one of the troubles, of course) is that peoples do not know how to make conversation: as a rule they are boastful. The French say: we have the Eiffel Tower. The English say: we have the crown jewels in the Tower of London. In Baltimore they have the Duchess of Windsor's bathtub, and in Antwerp they have a shoulder bone of the giant who once ruled the city. It is a bone of a whale, but that doesn't matter. Every nation, every city seems to bring forward only those things which are exceptional and therefore not characteristic of its real existence, and the world is presented to us like a curiosity cabinet.

Something should be done about it: some way should be found so that the Americans who are swarming over Europe might forget about skyscrapers, ships built in the wink of an eye and airplanes that go faster than light and gossip. The Europeans should be told how America really lives.

They should know that the United States is an enormous but provincial country. That the *Penasco Valley News* reports not only world events but also informs its readers that Mrs. R. Waters has had her tonsils removed, that Esther Cartwright has the measles and Bobby Burns the mumps. That Joe Stillman was in town Tuesday selling hogs and that Lucius Hartford bought some flowery wallpaper to redecorate his house. They should be told that every well-to-do American family does not have a swimming pool, but that the youngsters go out to the old swimming hole and that every five years at least one of them gets drowned there.

They should hear about the American churches, not so much about the cathedrals and St. John the Divines as about the humble white wooden buildings with which every village is endowed. They should know that a sexton of the Congregational Church of Walla Walla is very much like the sexton of Bouillon. And they should be told that in every one of these houses of worship there is an old maid who plays an asthmatic organ while the dapper congregation remains consistently off-key. They should be informed that the pastor and the clergyman walk around in the village just like the curé, apparently idle and going nowhere in particular, but in fact navigating between the moral coral reefs of their flock and trying to improve whatever can be improved of their habits and morals. They should be told that the Evangelists in Iowa shout and yell at least as loud as the Redemptionists in Belgium, that a clergyman in Columbus is the spiritual replica of the clergyman in Hilversum. If possible, it should be withheld from them that New York policemen filing out of St. Patrick's walk down Fifth Avenue preceded by a majorette whose anatomy cannot be considered a well-guarded secret, but if need be they can always be told that strange lands have strange customs.

They should be told about the American village, about the drugstore, the social rendezvous of youth, about that single soda high-school youngsters sip with two straws, which becomes in their lives the equivalent of the cup Brangäne served Tristan and Isolde. They should know about the way the boy greets his girl friend when he takes her out the first time to a dance—that "Hi!" a masterpiece of understatement which can express as many shades of sentiment as a Chinese syllable is apt to have meanings. They should know about the pink and light blue dresses the girls wear, baring lovely shoulders and still bony backs. They should hear about the chaperons and about the good-night and thank-you-so-much kiss, a mere formality, a receipt and a conclusion. They must hear about the square dances in the barns, not about the acrobatic feats of the Savoy in Harlem, but about the honest "swing-your-partner" procedure where the partner hesitates a little when confronted with a bulky female.

They should know that not all trains in America are manned by lewd Pullman porters ready to strangle girls in the lower berths, but that American trains look much like rolling maternity wards with uncounted thousands of babies who are going to meet their grandmas and grandpas. That in the stations, soldiers, as everywhere else, will whistle at the girl in the window or imitate successfully an appreciative wolf call.

They should know that schoolteachers here, as there, look painfully neat and resigned, that pale and bespectacled (rimless, of course) assistant librarians invariably wear flowery smocks which must prove to the world their tidiness but also their permanent longing for beauty.

They must be informed that all Americans do not play jazz from 8:00 A.M. till 12:00 P.M., although there are some of this kind, but that on summer nights they sit, in silent, devout rapture, thirty thousand of them, in open stadiums and listen to the noblest music man has written.

They should be told that an American park is like a European park, except for the presence of Mr. Baruch. That it is full of lovers, of gentle old folks, of children, of ice-cream vendors and of benevolent cops. That on Sunday afternoon people walk around in the parks in their best clothes, and girl friends photograph each other, standing with a sugary smile next to the biggest rose bush, as if there were any connection between their budding youth and the floral display.

Not all Americans, they should learn, spend their time commuting from Hollywood to Washington; and thousands of Italians in New York assert with pride that they have lived and stayed twenty or thirty years *"in questo blocco."* They should be told that they are not always chasing money, but that many of them stop working when they seem to have enough to subsist for a while and go out simply to enjoy that complete three-feature program the Declaration of Independence promised: life, liberty and a chance to happiness.

They should know that the great symbol of American democracy, the initial step on the road to felicity, the first comfort in all the so many dramas of life is that cup of coffee one offers to those rescued from the sea as well as to those who are saved from sin through the Salvation Army. Frenchmen will offer a glass of wine—it will look suspicious. Belgians will offer a glass of beer —it will be lukewarm. Dutchmen will present tea—it will look like a dark and menacing brew, but nobody will be able to understand without comment what the American cup of coffee means.

They should know about the small American town at night, about the strange howl of the train when it hurries west or east, about the poolroom that is a place of perdition, about the diner where the sleepy waitress keeps up a motherly conversation with the soliloquizing drunk, about the lighted Christmas trees in front of the New England houses in the countryside, about the farmer who comes to town with his skinny wife and a carload of kids and, with muffled curses, repairs a punctured tire before driving home.

They should hear about the Middle West craftsman behind his glasses, as reliable and as conservative as a Dutch watchmaker, about the night watchman in the New Orleans warehouse, as philosophical and inarticulate as the old men who watched over the goods in the European harbors and who could at least report that something had been stolen, even if they were unable to prevent it.

They should hear about a *human* America, not about a race of supermen and glamor girls.

It is said of the Frenchmen that they are unhappy as soon as anybody does not want to kiss them on the lips; they want to be liked and even loved. Americans are a little bit like that, but it is far more difficult for them than for the French to accomplish that ambition. They are handicapped by their own enormous and fantastic achievements. Europeans sometimes have difficulty in discovering the man behind the powerful machine, and after all it is the man who counts. We do not like people for their greatness; we like them for their weaknesses. Caesar used to hide his baldness by wearing his laurels. It would be a good thing if the victorious American on European soil took off his laurels and showed himself as he is: a simple, likable human, the salt of this good, lovely, brave earth.

Gerard Walschap

PEUTRUS

I ONCE SAW PEUTRUS CLIMB UP THE SPIRE, ALONG THE OUTSIDE, UP fifty-two metres. He ran there from his house, caught hold of the lightning conductor and within ten minutes sat on top against the weathercock. From everywhere in the fields—it was about one o'clock—people saw him climb; at the cross he looked no bigger than a cat. The village policeman was busy harvesting, too far from home to fetch his gun; he said: "I had a good mind to shoot him down." When Peutrus was almost down again, he saw his father waiting for him with a strap. Peutrus scrambled up again and then ran along the gutter, all along the nave of the church. That meant risking his life again; if one fell off there, every bone in one's body would be broken, of course. Somewhere near the vestry he slithered down nimbly, crossed the churchyard, went through the hedge and into the fields.

That was the sort of fellow he was; it had never been possible to do anything about it; he had been like that since he was little. At home they continued to call him Peutrus but in the village he soon had his name; "Peut" they said for short, just as they pronounce "put" in Bruges and that neighborhood.

If you had known the old Biezemans, his grandfather—but he is dead now—you would know from whom Peut got it. The grand-father was a squat little fellow, but with broad shoulders, as strong as a horse and as nimble as a cat; a hard worker all his life, and a fierce fighter. A good man, but when he had had a pint he became pigheaded and nagging; he had to fight. His name was Wies, and that is what one had to call him, too. One

could make him raging mad by patting him on the shoulder in a
friendly way and saying, "Hello, Wieske." An innkeeper once
gave him a high-chair on purpose. Wies could not reach the
floor with his feet. They were playing cards. Wies sat hemming
and hawing and did not pay attention to the game. Behind him
they stood smiling and winking. Then someone fetched a bench:
"There, Wieske boy, put your feet on that." But this man got the
bench on his head and if he had not gone out of the door
quickly, Wies would have knocked it to pieces on his back instead of on the door arch. After that he tore his jacket off and
shouted: "Come on, if you are all so big! Come on, damn it."
There were eight of them. "Come two at a time"; then he counted
eight windows in the inn. "I'll throw one into the street through
each window."

Yes, he had guts. If there was any fighting going on anywhere,
he ran up and tore them apart. "What's this?" asked Wies. They
explained the case to him. "Don't both talk at once; first you,
and now you." Then Wies said: "You are right," and if the other
was not content with that, he flew at him himself. If people
fought in a group, he helped the side that was a man short.

For a bet he once raced Joelekens Gust, also a hardy man, to
Lippeloo church and back—two hours. Gust was behind and shot
up a shortcut. He thought he was ahead, but when he stopped
at the big house and was on the point of letting himself down
on the threshold, Wies came out with his second pint, already
half emptied, in his hand, and asked innocently: "It was probably muddy on the shortcut too, eh, Gust?" Gust said he had seen
no shortcut. "You're a good-for-nothing," said Wies irritably;
"but you should not have lied; I don't want that." Gust insisted
that he had seen no shortcut. Thereupon he had to fight again
for the five francs they had bet. "You can still earn them."

For sixty-five consecutive years Wies walked with the procession to Scherpenheuvel. The sixty-third time he could hardly
follow; a man of seventy-seven years, what could you expect? But
he did not give it up; he kept on. Afterwards he complained that
it was no longer so serious as it used to be and that it consisted
entirely of young people. "Next year, I'll go alone." When the
time came, he started off alone in the evening, with his sandwiches in a kerchief and some clogs on his stick. The procession
started as midnight struck; by that time he had already tramped
five hours. At one o'clock the next day he arrived at Scherpenheuvel, two hours before the procession. He performed his de-
votions, lay down to sleep on the grass round the church; at seven

o'clock in the evening he went to eat something with a cup of
hot coffee, bought a fresh loaf and started off again. At half-past
four the next afternoon he arrived home in the village; the procession, half an hour later. But all the people were by then standing outdoors to watch for the procession, and when he saw that,
he suddenly straightened up and held above his head the flag
of Scherpenheuvel, which he had tied to his stick. They all
cheered and cried; not one that did not shout and have to blow
his nose. "Go it, Wies! Bravo, boy! Seventy-eight years and such a
pilgrimage, walking all alone for two days on end!" He felt as if
he were intoxicated with glory and happiness; two men ran to
the church and rang the bell for him as for the whole procession.
He felt a lump in his throat and began to sing: "Oh maid, so
pure and fair!"

But the following year the procession passed him at Leest, still
two hours from home. At Thisselt he remained sitting three
quarters of an hour in the inn, and as night fell he came home
by shortcuts. Everything had gone against him; the leather had
come off his clogs, and so on. "But next year . . ." And the next
year he was dead; he did not have to go again; sixty-five times
had been enough.

In the case of Peut there was more devilishness than had ever
been in the case of Wies. Things like that are often the fault of
the parents; a child that is well brought up does not go wrong
so easily. At Biezemans', it was a strange household. Trien, the
mother, one could hardly make out. Sometimes she was rough
and cross with the children and at other times stood laughing
like a fool at the very same thing. She had large eyes, without
lashes, which always watered. No matter what she was telling
or heard told, she always wiped her eyes with the corner of her
apron. Biezemans himself, the father, was tall and thin, and a
witty wag away from home, but in his house he did not open his
mouth. To his wife not a word; the children could crawl over
his head, he would snarl for a moment and that was all. But
once he was out and with other people, he was the entertainment
of the village. A dry humor. And then there was Karool, Trien's
brother, a giant of a man who squinted and stuttered and was
occupied with all sorts of learning, every two years with something else. With photography he was busy the longest. He would
stick under the black cloth for half an hour, then "Loo-loo-look
up!" and then he would pull. It was not to earn money; he put
money into it; but if you wanted several prints, you had to pay.
Occasionally he went to Brussels, and if he saw anything special,

he did not hesitate to ask: "Ho-ho-how does that work, sir?" He spoke learnedly of Belgian industry, of the distance to the moon and of Italy's abutting on the sea on both sides.

At Biezemans' they did not care for him, neither the little ones nor the big ones; but he just said, "Duffers!" and let them have their way. So nobody was boss, and each did what he wanted. Peut smoked from his sixth year. The pigeon fanciers, who came to have their pigeons entered on Saturday evenings, let him draw at their pipes, drink from their pints, and sometimes gave him a cigarette. He was able to do it and it amused them; nobody forbade it. In the nursery school he swore at the Sister, and once he pulled off her wimple. Her hair was short and badly cut, just as if the rats had been at it at night.

Sometimes Trien knocked the cigarette out of his hands; at other times she laughed with the pigeon fanciers. One evening she came running from the kitchen into the pub, roaring with laughter; Peut, furious, was after her with a poker. It amused her; what a fellow! But the fellow struck, and it hurt pretty badly; she became angry herself and started hitting back. In a powerless rage he lay down on the floor, kicking; that was a habit of his, to be ragingly angry, to scream and upset the whole village while he threw himself on the floor. Then she laughed again. "Just look at that choleric fellow!"

The master at school also did not know how to manage him and as a rule did not shrink from giving him a beating. He had a whip, a ruler and a long beanstick for it. The beanstick suddenly got you on the head when you sat chatting with someone. For the ruler he came up to you; those that sat in the way had to creep under the forms till it was over. For the whip you were dragged out of your form and laid over his knee. The master was a verger from Flanders; he had got into the school during the education conflict.

Peut caught hold of the beanstick before it touched his head and broke a piece off; when he got some of the whip, he bit the master in the calf. Otherwise he was an extraordinary pupil. At home he wrote on a board that was hung on the shutter: "Pigeon-fanciers! Entries for Quiévrain on Saturday evening at 8 o'clock," and how much the prize was and that there were twenty-six regulators for hire. In the left-hand corner he drew on his own initiative two pigeons billing and cooing. The master stopped in front of the board. "Not a single mistake! Oh, that is fine, Petrus!" Karool made him change "Pigeon-fanciers"; it was low Flemish; "In French they don't say it like that. It should be am-am-amateurs." He gave him an old atlas; let him draw the outline of Belgium and put a dot in it for the village and another for Quiévrain-in-de-Walen.

A ferocious heart beat in that Peut; you could not make him out. Trien could do what she wanted with him because she almost always laughed at his tricks. He caught hold of a half-grown pig by the front paws and danced round the dung heap with it. Trien stood leaning against the wall, laughing. "Peutrus, stop it! I shall die of laughter!" He rushed to her and kissed her on both cheeks; but a simple peasant boy does not kiss his mother. He had this wild tenderness, and for the rest he was a ferocious fellow. Once he caught a strange cat on their loft near the dove-cot. He caught hold of it by the neck, went downstairs with it, held it down on a block of wood, and smashed its head with a great big hammer; it made one go cold all over. He had a dog which he loved like a human; he trained it; if you dared approach it you risked disaster. But he seized strange pigeons and pulled their heads off; Jefke the shoemaker lost all his white ones.

As they grew up the children of Lowie Biezemans began to differ more and more, like animals and flowers. At the beginning they had all been alike. Mie, the eldest, remained simple and became ungainly. She did not grow any taller, but spread out in lumps of fat and jelly, and she no longer combed her hair. Gust and Pol shot up tall and thin like their father. Gust was a bright-eyed and quiet rascal. Pol was a dreamer and looked pale. The youngest, Martha, was also on the pale side, an upright and good child.

She gave Biezemans pleasure; he put her on his cart and took her along wherever he went. She sat quietly behind him and he stood with his legs wide apart and the reins in the hand that was in his trouser pocket. The left one he put to his mouth when he called to anyone, generally in rhyme: "Good morning, Marie! Glad you to see!—Sooken, turn to me; on your back is a flea!" One could not understand that at home this gay man was so sour and taciturn and did not even look at his children, except at the youngest. After all, there should be a father in the house; especially Peut should have had one. He now had his foolish mother on his side and tyrannized his brothers and sisters unchecked. For a long time they let him go ahead and get involved in his evil doings. Here they got a drubbing, there the dog was set on them. But when Peut once spoke of a pistol as long as his arm, loaded with six cartridges, and "I won't say who will be shot, but this evening it will be his turn, and the day after tomorrow they will put him in the grave," they gave him away, all three of them at the same time. They were trembling; but Trien laughed at them and immediately went out into the street to tell the neighbors. "What a head that child has! It's strange!"

But one evening a shot was fired in the barn, and they all jumped up and cried: "Bah! our Peutrus!" Biezemans put Martha down from his lap, saying: "If I don't break his bones now . . ." went out, was nearly at the barn, turned round, put his hands into his trouser pockets, went in a leisurely way in at Jefke the shoemaker's and said: "Good evening, family Verstappen; I'll take a chair; I've come for a chat." And the whole evening he made them laugh. But meanwhile Trien and Karool stood in the barn with their lantern, and there sat Peut on the stack with father's double-barrelled gun. He was hunting the rats, just sitting there in the dark, and, at random had shot a tile to pieces. Karool said: "Co-co-come down, you rascal!" Peutrus called: "No-no-no, nu-nu-nuncle Ka-Ka-Karool!" Suddenly the double-barrelled gun fell onto the floor, the shot went off, and Trien, screaming wildly, ran away. Biezemans said to Jefke, the shoemaker: "Stay right there, Jefke boy, it is our Karool trying out my double-barrelled gun." But Karool was running up the ladder; this time Peutrus should be plucked! When Karool was halfway up, Peut seized the ladder at the top and held it straight up. "Go down this minute, or I'll throw it over backwards!" That would have meant death; it was a question of going down or having his spine broken. Karool went down, took a flail from the nail, beat mightily and angrily with it but hit nothing but a thick oak beam. In the dark, Peutrus showed his teeth in mad delight. Here in the dark barn it was a question of life or death; a stutterer who could not spend his rage with his mouth and had to do it with his hands against a ferocious young snotty-nose, half a devil. They both thought of the double-barrelled gun at the same time. Peutrus could not reach it; Karool looked at him for a moment, then went out and locked the barn door. And the pranks got worse as time went on. Those who had not cared began to regret it. His first enemy was Karool; between these two things were never again straightened out. One fine afternoon Peut stood at the church square with Uncle's camera and all the new plates. Some young fellows allowed themselves to be snapped, first seriously; afterwards they pulled faces and put their caps askew. Suddenly Karool stood there. It was his camera; he had put his money into it; the plates were expensive; it was his only love and recreation. He knew for certain that he would stutter; perhaps he would not be able to speak at all; but he just stood there and looked pale. If Peut had run away, or if he had used up more plates, Karool would have been relieved; but Peut simply said: "Hello, Uncle!" and crept under the cloth. Suddenly, while he stood bent forward, Uncle gave him such a furious kick that he was lifted off the ground and uttered a short groan. Then they flew at each other and soon lay on the paving stones, fighting; but not for long. Peut soon sat on top and beat the poor giant wherever he could get him. Karool remained lying with some blood in his graying hair; when he saw the young bandit kick his camera to pieces, he began to howl loudly. It was not exactly howling; it sounded much more final, almost like a donkey, far gone in years, that can no longer bray, if you have ever heard that. Then the people came running; the women cried: "Oh, poor man! You ugly bandit, standing there!" Jefke, the shoemaker, an irritable man, began to speak, but he was too angry to do it well. He made some gestures toward Peut, who stood there panting and pulling up his trousers, and toward Karool. "You . . .," said Jefke. "Your uncle . . .," and Peut got a slap in the face. "What, who do you think you are?" said Jefke. The second eldest of Wannes van Zaelens' boys suddenly pushed through the crowd, crying: "Get away!" and rushed at Peut, caught him by the throat, ran with him to the church and bashed his head against the wall about twenty times. And, oh wonder! Peut let him, and the people shouted: "Give it him hot!" One of them said: "He's lucky that I haven't drunk five or six pints. I would have given him his portion; but, so sober, I can't do it— hit a man!"

Jefke, the shoemaker, pulled Karool up. The latter sat crouching before his camera. Tears ran down his face. The people turned away a little; it touched them, and they shook their heads at one another, full of compassion. "That camera, you'll pay, you bandit. Did you hear what I said or did you not hear it?" said Jefke, and came closer for he felt like giving him another good punch. Then Peut put his hands into his trouser pockets, turned round and walked away. The hostility of the village was upon him. "You've seen the last of me," he thought.

He tramped into the fields, kicking out turnips from pure mischief. Then he walked along the edge of the brook. Somewhere there was a net stretched; he cut it loose and into pieces. Then he went on to the water-mill in another village; along little copses and rows of alders. Toward evening he was back at the

little bridge. Two girls were coming along; they were learning
to sew in the village and in the evenings were always afraid to go
home. Peut turned up his collar, pulled his cap over his eyes
and quickly crossed the road toward them. They began to run.
He ran too, made his voice deep and swore. Then they began to
scream. From both sides of the field some people whistled on
their fingers and shouted: "Hé!" Peut sat down and grinned.
Strange and frightful things were going on in him. He looked at
his hands. Supposing he killed someone here and buried him in
the bed of the brook! After that he heard an old pigeon fancier
say: "If such a boy got his learning, he could easily become a
schoolmaster. With such a handwriting; so quick in the uptake;
and capable! Yes, by God, schoolmaster and more."

Peut again wandered along the bank of the brook; everything
smelt so wild. Suddenly he stood in front of the new forester who
shot out from behind a tree. It was a Fleming; he let Peut walk
along with him and boasted that the fellows would henceforth
have to look out. "You saw how I suddenly stood in front of you.
And I don't hesitate to climb into a tree; I see where the little
lights dance, and then I am there in a jiffy. 'Halt! Who goes
there?' " Peut looked askance at his double-barrelled gun. If that
Flemish braggart would unload it once. . . . "Shoot something,"
said Peut. The other immediately showed him his gun. "Do you
know anything about it?" he asked. "That is a gun, young man."
Peut aimed at the sky, at a tree, then at his forehead. "If you got
one like that on your star," he said, but the other caught hold of
the barrel and took the gun out of his hands. Peut sat down; his
legs were trembling. "What things come into one's head!"

It became dark. The forester told him where he had formerly
served. Peut lit a cigarette and said: "I should have become a
schoolmaster."

For more than two weeks he roamed goodness knows where
and came home only occasionally. Trien wept with joy when she
saw him and threw a big piece of beef into the saucepan. He
looked unkempt. Someone came into the pub and called and
whistled to make someone come forward. Peut jumped up, ready
to run. Gust and Pol looked at him. What did he have on his
conscience?

Peut walked along the vicarage garden. He fiddled a little at
the gate, to see whether it was locked and how one opened it.
"Turn the knob well and lift a little," called the priest. He was a
new one, too. Peut had not seen him sitting there, and he now
had to enter. "What brings you here, boy?" asked the priest. Peut

stood there smiling suspiciously; he had just come to have a look.
"Do you want a pear?" They walked together to a pear tree, full
of juicy fruits, each picked one and stood eating. The priest was
a peculiar man; he said almost nothing and tucked in heartily.
"Just look at those thrushes in that mountain-ash, sir!" "Shall we
shoot them down?" Then they went to another tree and ate more
pears. The priest said: "You did not get so many as I." "Yes, I believe it," said Peut, "not so many, but twice as many." They went
to another tree, stood eating and did not say much. The whole
yard lay full of sun; the abundant fruit hung ripening and some
of it was already dropping. Here it was quiet, the afternoon
passed, and Peut said that he had had enough. "I am going to sit
in my room. Will you come along too?" "But, sir," said Peut
rather touched, "what can I do there?" The priest looked at him
quietly and half surprised. "Sit in an armchair and smoke."

Peut sat in a low, soft chair with a cigar in his mouth. The
ashtray stood near him. The priest acted as if Peut had always
sat there. He wrote some letters; occasionally he said something
to answer a question: where he bought his cigars, and how one
could get at those goldfish. Then said Peut: "Sir, I am not so
bad," and the priest said: "I did not say you were." "Then why
did you ask me to come to your room?" "What a question!" said
the priest quietly. "You are sitting comfortably, you are smoking
a cigar; isn't that enough?" Peut was filled with astonishment
and a strange happiness. His badness went far from him and he
became enthusiastic. "Sir," said Peut, "you are a good man. You
are a real priest." The priest continued to write his letter. "Don't
drivel, boy." "I mean it," said Peut and sat up straight. "You are
a good man, an honest man. You see, only I can't say it—I'll howl
in a minute." He laughed, but the tears were already there. Then
he began to speak of learning; that it was so pleasant if one
understood everything; he boasted a little of his own easy intelligence. "If I have seen a thing once, I remember it. A tune, too.
I hear it sung once, and that is enough. On my way home I realize that I know it and at home I play it on my bugle. And writing, nobody can beat me at that; with a pencil, with a pen, on
the board, it makes no difference. And something for which I also
have a talent—that is, painting. I have painted the whole of our
house, inside and out. And the tiles you see lying on it, as if they
were real!" The priest looked at him sitting there, short, squat,
with a strand of hair in his eyes, a body full of power. "Would
you like a book?" "Sir, I didn't dare ask, because you would perhaps give me something that you would not like to lose." The

priest looked at him and said: "You are also a good man." And Peut felt as if he were being slapped in the face from all sides and that something was being done to his heart with a sharp knife. He could not say anything, blushed, coughed, laughed; everything hurt him inside. He wanted to say: "No, I am bad, I am a bandit," but he could not, and at last he got out something: "Now you are driveling, too." Then they both laughed, the priest and Peut. "Take another cigar—and what book shall it be?" "It must not be a book in which they tell a story; that wouldn't help me; if I had to read that often, I would go crazy; that would play round in my head. But a book from which one can learn something about the sciences. Something simple and stiff, to which one must give all one's attention. I want to study the book seriously. You see, sir, a schoolmaster! If I could only become that!"

In the middle of his studies Peut went to school, laughed a little foolishly at the headmaster, felt embarrassed, scratched his head, hitched up his trousers. It was not so easy. He would have to get permission from home, and for the least fault he would be expelled for good.

Peut went to school, a chap of nineteen years among all those younger fellows. Some courses he attended; for the rest he got lessons and worked separately. In the playground he felt tall and responsible; sent the fighters each into a corner, and "Don't come out or you'll get a beating from me!" He would occasionally take off his clogs and run across the playground on his hands, silently admired by all. A whole heel stuck through his stocking. Once a boy ran away; Peut caught up with him and brought him back to the master. Eagerness made him close his eyes to the fact that the master himself was sometimes wrong. But when they ceased to care for him in the village, when the novelty had worn off for the youngsters and for himself, he would have loved to play a prank occasionally, too. And one day Jefken Spiessens innocently got a beating with the ruler; Fiekens Fons had done it. Peut said: "Master, that boy hasn't done anything wrong." He did not give it up. He stepped out of the form and stood in front of the master. "Don't you hit that child any more." So he was expelled.

Every Thursday they had a free afternoon. Every time the master went to the house of his wife's parents, a little farm. He put into a basket the potato peelings of the whole week, and at the farm the basket was filled with carrots and beans, etc. He always returned at the same hour, except the one time when Peut suddenly stood in front of him in the half dark, saying: "At school you are master, but here we are equals." "Petrus," said the master, "get out of my way." "I'll give you 'Petrus,'" yelled Peut.

The next day the master stood in the classroom with a black eye and a short, deep scratch on his forehead. Nothing else could be seen on him, and the boys wished him joy of what he had got. For thirty years he had beaten children and had never got a single smack for it himself. One of the De Bondt boys behind his back threw a marble at his head. Then the master turned round, stood still, and said: "Go on, De Bondt, throw it, boy"; and went on to say that he had worked thirty-two years for the parish; their fathers had all sat on these forms in front of him; from his school had gone out four priests, one missionary, one Franciscan monk, one high official at a ministry, three teachers, four winners of the first prize at the competition of the diocese. "I wanted to help another along, that big one who still sat on this form last Monday. From the far Congo I get every year a New Year's letter from my beloved former pupil, the Reverend Father Antoon De Scheppe, missionary of Scheut. 'Master,' he writes, 'I thank you for the good example you have given me. Master, I have been teaching at a school here for one year and I already know what it means, and you, master, have been at it for thirty-two years now.' I have contracted rheumatism here. Perhaps a hundred nights out of the three hundred and sixty-five in the year I can close an eye at night. And now that I can no longer defend myself, I am attacked in the dark. Yes, now I get my thanks. Here, De Bondt, here is your marble, boy."

They all sat still; the master had never before spoken like that. At last a boy asked whether he should shut the window. "Why?" "Because there is perhaps a draught for you, master." The master looked at him. That, too, had not happened in thirty-two years, and just as if to excuse himself, he laughed strangely and showed his hands, the fingers of which he could no longer open. "Rheumatism. Yes, when you get old. It is age." He fumbled with his stiff hands; no, they could no longer open. One couldn't see if he was smiling or wincing; nor whether it was with grief or pain.

Peut could not save himself so well. He no longer cared, if only he could return the book. He waited till the priest rode out on his bicycle, and went and laid the little package in front of the door of the room. He put a little note in it: Many thanks, Petrus Biezemans. But suddenly the priest returned. "Will you mend my puncture, boy?" Peut mended the puncture. After that he had to go in with the priest and fetch a cigar, and again he was allowed to sit down, just as if he had not knocked down the master, as if there were no evil in him. But he didn't want to go and sit down, and right inside him he cursed himself. The priest did not hold him back; it seemed all the same to him whether one came or went; it is all right with him if one does what one likes. Peut left.

He stood outside and felt relieved. For weeks he was not seen. It appeared that he was staying in a remote hamlet, a little group of houses in the middle of the woods and meadows. Chicken thieves and suspicious hawkers lived there. The village asked: "Where is that Peut? He has knocked down the master, but he deserved a drubbing. Where is Peut?" "In the meadows," others said.

When Biezemans was asked, he replied that he did not know, "But he can't be suffering from hunger, for then he would have returned." Karool wished tha-tha-that he would remain away. Trien wiped her watery eyes. What anxiety she has already had in the matter! But that example did the children no good. Gust kept at his mother till he got a racing bicycle; then he sat on the wheel the whole day; in the summer he began to take part in the races at the fair, was in the forefront in winning prizes and wanted to become a professional racer. One fine day, Pol, with a collar on, was seen walking to catch the eight-o'clock trolley. In the evening he came back. In this way the work at Biezemans' was left to the three adults; the younger ones tried to pick up a livelihood without work. It is not stupid, but nowadays it rarely succeeds.

Some people saw Peut set a trap in the fields, but, "Just wait, he won't catch his tenth hare, for the new forester soon catches thieves by the scruff of their necks." Another said: "Peut is away again; so many chickens are being stolen just now." A little later there was a rumor that the gendarmes were looking for him. People have to have something to talk about.

It must all have been talk, for on the Sunday of the fair on October 1st, when everybody was talking about him, there was Peut with a sweetheart. It was an ugly little thing with a wide, bloodless mouth, red eyes, and blue veins at her temple. She hung onto his arm and let her head lean blissfully against him. He went and sat in the swing with her and whirled so high that the little boat stood almost erect at either end, but she did not utter a cry. She was from the meadows and accustomed to more. Then he stood at a booth for dolls and toys, aiming boisterously, while she looked at something else. He gave her the four paper roses with two silver leaves which he had won, bought a lottery ticket for fifty centimes, won with the ace of diamonds and chose a silver necklace with a golden horse's head in a ring for her. She put it on, and they went home. Karool was standing leaning against the wall outside, staring at the sky, and he let them pass in front of him beneath his glance. While they were coming in, Biezemans left. "Hello, mother!" and Trien answered indifferently, "Peutrus." The girl said nothing.

There sat Mie, his eldest sister; she had also got a man at last, a coarse, rough workman who was silent and looked just-home-from-work and always asked gruffly, "What is it?" when Mie spoke to him. They were on the point of getting married. Mie was artful no more; she went to sit by the girl: How old she was? Not yet fifteen; that she was so thin, and had our Peutrus lost his head? Meanwhile Peutrus sat alone in the kitchen eating; after that he went back to the meadows with the girl.

That afternoon the village was still sniggering; that evening in the dance hall there was already a scandal. The girl's brother took his sister by the arm, pulled her outdoors, and, "Go home or I'll kick you there." It was a tall stalwart fellow, the only serious one from the meadows who had ever made his way. He had been living in the village for two years and was married; he was a poulterer and was getting on well. Peut stood behind him and asked him what he intended to do. Lewie answered that he had nothing to do with him, but as soon as his sister was round the corner over there, on her way home, he would like to have a talk with him. For a little while it looked as if they would fight, and then Peut decided: "Wiske, go home." She went. Then said Lewie: "If you want to fight, begin; if you want to talk, come home with me."

Peut talked. "Lewie, you don't understand me. With what I am doing, I have a purpose."

"You begin wtih grand words, boy. Talk simply."

"Lewie, you don't understand me. You are mistaken; I know what I am doing. I am protecting your sister. You mustn't laugh before you know everything. You are a serious boy, I want to talk to you; I shall open my heart."

"You mustn't talk so grandly, I say; where did you pick up those words, or are you perhaps already drunk?"

Peut explained his purpose. He wanted to take her away from over there in the meadows; it was time. As surely as there is a God, he hadn't touched her, not yet kissed her. He gave her a box on the ears because she did not want to go with him. He was a thief, he had stolen, but he was well posted on the matter over there, and knew what there is to it: "Well, Lewie, it has done something to me; I am going to become serious. She must get away from there and I'll look after her."

Lewie says that that is his business; he will provide for his sister himself. A great magnanimity makes Peut tender. He has only done it for her good. "I have a soft heart, Lewie, but now it is all right, if you will look after your sister, I'll keep off."

They went off together to play cards. People laughed and did not understand. Lewie and Peut parted at midnight, both a little talkative after the beer. Peut boasted of his good heart, which always held him back; otherwise he would have become a great bandit. It suddenly overwhelmed him, and he then ran and shouted and didn't know what to do with himself. Lewie said: "I didn't know that you had such good stuff in you. You must now improve your position; why don't you begin a poultry business?"

Yes, poultry business! The next day Victor Kiek came running to Biezemans, a poulterer who had grown rich and now lived in a villa with a big nursery garden. "Where is the thief? By God, this time he shall have the gendarmes to contend with; it is the second time, thirty chickens; the thief, the loafer!" Biezemans himself turned pale; there you had it; a thief! "Go in, he's still in bed. Do him in, then I needn't do it myself." He went and harnessed his horse, put his little girl on the cart, rode away and did not speak to anyone.

In the afternoon the chief constable and a gendarme found only Wiske at home in the meadows. They wanted to take her along to prison, but she began to scream and confessed everything. She knew nothing about it; over there in the wood were the chickens in a basket, and Father and Peut had talked about it, but Peut told her that he had not done it. The two men of the law met Biezemans and his wife and only inquired when Peut had come home after playing cards at the pub until twelve o'clock. Biezemans said, "At four o'clock, gentlemen." Trien said that it wasn't anything like as late as that; she had lain awake and, "What do you know about it, you were asleep?"

Peut had certainly gone to bed at twelve o'clock, but to Biezemans it was clear that he had stolen, so he would have to take his punishment. He said to Trien, "You would still take the bandit's part," and persisted that it was four o'clock; he had lain awake. The constable was a severe man with a thick mustache. He had once in another village at night shot down a Walloon clerk who did not understand what he wanted with his, "Who's there?" Three times, "Who's there?" and that Walloon did not understand. Bang! and he was struck, stone dead. Since then the constable had walked with his head down, a lenient man who spoke softly behind his mustache, but inexorable as to the law.

When they came out, Peut was standing on the steps on the other side. The two men walked toward him with their bicycles. Peut also began to walk, looking round to see how far he remained ahead. They jumped on their bicycles, and Peut began to run, but they caught up with him immediately, and Peut jumped into a house. But he went wrong, and instead of running into the fields through a back door, he stayed in a small room from which he could not get out. The gendarme was behind him; Peut hit him on the head with a piece of wood. The constable went quietly outside, pulled a heavy piece of wood out of the pile, stood in the doorway and commanded Petrus Biezemans, in the name of the law, to surrender. He closed the door; and then the fight began. Neither of them could swing their weapons properly; the place was too small; they smashed the lamp and everything that stood on the cupboard. That went on for a while, till the constable, himself grown furious, shouted, "Surrender!" and felled Peut with a last blow. The gendarme tied his legs together and clapped handcuffs on him; a peasant had to harness his horse, and Peut came to again as they were putting him on the cart.

That is how he was driven through the village. His hair was wild and tangled; his left sleeve half torn off; his shirt open in front; blood ran down his face; the cutting handcuffs made him wince. That is how he rode out on Monday of the October Fair. The people stood shuddering. Never will the little chaps that saw him forget it, if they live to be a hundred. So he drove past his home. Biezemans and Karool did not even come out to see him. His mother, brother and sisters stood on the steps, crying, and Trien ran to the constable with a package in a kerchief: "Please take it along; some clothes and food for my boy, sir." And "Goodbye, Peutrus, goodbye, Peutrus!" She went and stood with her face to the wall, crying. The constable hung the package onto the handlebars of his bicycle and walked behind the cart with his head bowed.

Soon after that the trial took place. Peut was acquitted, because he had not committed the theft, but for resisting the police he got eighteen months. He served them at Vorst.

Little Martha fell ill. The people said: "Always on that cart; she has contracted something." And indeed she had had a dry

cough for a long time which it hurt one to hear. It did not last
long with the child; in the spring she died. For two hours on
end Biezemans ran through the house, crying, "Oh! Oh!" with
his two fists at his temples. Then came a letter from Peutrus, in
beautiful handwriting, sixteen large pages, and everybody said
that it was particularly well composed. Everyone was allowed
to read it; one did Trien a favor if one asked to see it.

"Vorst, the. . . . Beloved parents, sister and brothers, I have
just heard of the grievous loss that has come upon us all in the
sad passing of our beloved daughter and youngest sister Martha.
In my lonely cell, where never a ray of sun enters, I sank weeping to my knees and my tears mingled with a fervent prayer
that welled to my lips and rose to the high heaven. Our beloved
Martha, our darling, is no more! She has gone from us, snatched
away from our love, like a delicate flower, crushed under the
foot of the passer-by in the field."

After that he began to describe her life; how, as the youngest,
she had always been the darling and joy of the family. Here he
occasionally lapsed from the high-sounding phrases to tell, simply and vividly, some nice stories from the life of little Martha.
"Do you remember, it was in the winter and there were many
people in the pub, and Broeckers Jan was also there; he loves
children so much and he was always concerned about our Martha.
And Jan, etc. . . ." Then he became solemn again, and described,
falsely and sentimentally, how the child died.

"Beloved parents, sister and brothers . . ." Oh, could he only
be with them in this hour of trial! His heart melted with homesickness. "Mother dear, please come and visit me some day; after
all, I am your son; or don't you want anything more to do with
me? Am I deserted by everyone on earth?" Where could he find
the words of consolation, like sweet balsam for their wounds?
"But take courage; your child is in heaven."

While doing clerical work and glueing bags in the prison, he
thought without interruption from morning till night about the
course of life. They won't hear of his saying that he is innocent;
no, certainly not; he is surely guilty and he sheds hot tears over
it. He thinks of his beloved school fellows; he thinks of his sol-
lemn first Holy Communion. "How are all the boys? Please write
me a word about them. Doubtless most of them are married and
enjoy the happiness of fatherhood at their own hearths." And
when he thinks that he too could sit at home at this moment
with a modest, tender wife, and that there could already be a

little child in the house, beloved parents, sister, brothers, his courage fails him completely. And then he asks himself: Why? and how? He will spare them all the painful memory; in short, now he is sighing in jail, he who could learn so easily and could surely have got ahead and earned a white-collar living.

He sat there as a result of a mistake, for the court had proved that he was not guilty of the theft. His blunder had been not wanting to let himself be seized, being guiltless, and when he was in that little room at Treze's and could not get away, he became like a raging devil and fought for dear life. However, as the Reverend Father Almoner said to him only the day before, he did not consider everything as lost. On the contrary, in eleven months and seventeen days, upon leaving this gloomy prison, a new course of life would begin for him. He was bearing his long punishment with patience and begged the same of them, till at last the hour of his release came and he returned to the bosom of his family as a new man, a worthy son, a good brother. Meantime he was learning and studying as much as possible like a real student; he was also learning French in order to acquire more and more capability which a man needed so much in life, and in order to become something. As he ended, hot tears of repentance and grief fell upon his paper; he implored them on his knees for forgiveness for the disgrace he had brought upon the family, and he promised them solemnly to return one day as "Your loving son and brother, Petrus Biezemans."

Even the masters were speechless at the letter and the priest said to Trien: "Your son is a gifted boy; he has much talent." Then Trien laughed through her tears and said that he had always had it in him; that one could tell from everything; that he knew about everything and immediately understood everything. But he had always been such a smart one and he got these occasional attacks, and then she saw well that he could not get on with himself. And what came out then was often astonishing. She said: "On Sunday, so God will, I'll go there once," and she wept. Every month there came a letter like that, more correct each time, with practically no mistakes, with strange ideas and vehement feelings. "If ever there is a letter for me, I tear it open, and if it comes from home, I could pull the prison down with pleasure." And so on. He described his day, explained his plans, but gradually began to write more things that they didn't understand at Biezemans'. He suddenly began to talk of social problems, justice, order, the encyclical Rerum Novarum, and that such principles were the most important things in life. The two masters read the letters at Biezemans', over a pint, and they talked it over between themselves. Then one of them said loudly, so that the whole pub heard it, that one could feel that Peutrus was studying hard and that he was occupied above all with social problems. Thus he used the same words as Peut, and the people understood no better.

Peut came back. He looked a little paler and was a little stouter. He seemed quite a different fellow. He let his hair grow in a brush and had become contemplative; no longer anything like as wild and boisterous. He talked much on summer evenings in the little groups that sat crouching on the threshold and the steps, and astonished everyone with his knowledge. It mostly came round to the problem of society. "History teaches that there are various systems by which to solve it, but what we know for certain is that there is only one truth. Jef, you are sitting there or you are not sitting there; but you cannot at the same moment sit and not sit there. One or the other. There is only one truth. And with justice it is exactly the same thing. Let us suppose I must pay you five francs; four is too little and six is too much; it must be exactly five francs. That proves that there is only one justice. Just is just, and if it is not just, it is unjust."

But that too lost its novelty; he was told once that he was a liberal or a socialist, one of the two, but certainly not a Catholic. The village life, the work without uplift, the freedom and his own strange nature, all began to torment and irritate him, and it made him writhe that nothing came of all his plans and dreams except virtuousness, which tortured him like a straitjacket.

Suddenly the affair with Wiske, who now lived at Lewie's in the village itself, began again. The child was not yet seventeen, still ugly, quiet and stupid; what Peut saw in her, God only knew. But Lewie would have none of it, and at Biezemans' they were also against it; and again his work suffered. Trien tried to reduce his pocket money; Karool put in a word; Lewie boxed Wiske's ears; it was no joke. One evening Peut came home, sat down, and nobody spoke to him. Biezemans took out of his pocket a letter that Peut had written from the prison and read aloud about the solemn promise, a new course of life, to return to the bosom of his family, a new man, a worthy son, a good brother. Then he laughed scornfully and went out; Karool said with a deep sigh, "Yes, yes."

In the end there were all kinds of rumors, and "Where did the money come from to go to the fairs and to give Wiske a gold bracelet as a present?" Lewie found out where it came from, but he told nobody except the constable, and one fine morning they took Wiske away. It was all done quietly and quickly; Lewie had high friends in Brussels. If he was served a police warrant for driving without a light or on the wrong side, nothing ever came of it. But he didn't mind delivering a couple of chickens; one good turn deserved another. And so Lewie knew what he was doing; he played safe with his sister; it was for her good.

The raging devil again entered Peut; there was no getting on with him; he did wrong for wrong's sake. Suddenly Karool packed his things and said that he had been accepted at the charitable institution at Mechelen. Two weeks later the armory men saw from the train that he had become ferryman. For ten centimes per head he ferried the people across the canal. It was a small raft that he shoved along by a chain that was stretched across the canal. "How much does it cost?" "Te-te-ten centimes."

Before the trial came on Peut went to have a row with Lewie. Plates for a meal were just on the table. With one arm he swept everything onto the floor, and he threw the full soup tureen through the window. Lewie flew at him. Peut managed to escape. He ran straight to the trolley, rode to Brussels and rang at the house of the juvenile judge who wanted to send Wiske to a reformatory.

Mr. Judge, he had not much to tell him; the day after tomorrow the trial of Louisa Teugels would come up. That was his sweetheart. He had come to ask him whether he intended to break up his life by sending that girl to an institution till her twenty-first year. The juvenile judge was a gray man in his fifties with cold steely eyes. He shrugged his shoulders: "My dear man, what is all this talk? Aren't you well?" and he pointed to his forehead. Then Peut began to bang on the table and to shout that one life was as good as another, "My happiness is as good as yours; who do you think you are? Don't look at me like that or I'll jump over the table and on to your head. And the day after tomorrow I'll be at the Court of Justice, and if you dare send her away, you will be dead before you leave the court. Let this be a warning to you! Oh, you probably think that the poor will continue to bow before you, that you can go on doing with us what you like. I repeat, you will be dead if you dare to send her away."

Peut traveled back. At Grimbergen, when changing trolleys, two gendarmes already had hold of him, struggled for a moment and clapped handcuffs on him. With that telephone nowadays one can no longer think of running away. Jump into the train in Brussels; they telephone, and at Antwerp the police stands waiting for you when the train arrives.

No more was heard of Peut.

Years went by; time passes quickly. Biezemans died. Trien died; when the time comes, one is called and has to go. Gust and Pol married into other villages. Of the Biezemans only Mie remained, and she said: "Our Peut, God knows where he is."

Wiske came back; she could sew; she married a workman and it became a household like any other.

Lewie maintained: "As long as the juvenile judge is alive, we shall not see Peut." Once it was said that Peut had studied himself crazy in the prison. "One could hear that already when he spoke with all those grand words here; what was all that leading to?" And that they had transferred him to the lunatic asylum at Doornik. For a time it was said that he had tried to escape and had already swum to the other side, when the guard found out, shot him twice in the back, and he sank like a stone.

So people tell all kinds of things. My idea is that we don't know the ins and outs of it. I am certainly in two minds about the course of life, and, after all, I read such a lot of books.

Translated by Jo MAYO

Maurice Roelants

THE JAZZ PLAYER

Novelette with one person and seven instruments, being a complete battery of percussion instruments.

Yes, certainly, sir, rather great tragedies are enacted in the secrecy of the heart. Who will write for me the novel of one heart, the novel of one person?

J. Schrey.

COME, COME; GENERALLY WE LACK THE TIME. LIFE IS A FLIGHT INTO work, into a vulgar and unproductive occupation which finally leaves us with some paltry pension to be administered, a flight into a few social duties, the reception of a few acquaintances, who are tired of the dishes from their own larder and who follow a heart which no longer dares to know its wishes.

But be still. Here is the sea. Two weeks' vacation. We shall dare the great adventure: not move, but throw ourselves head over heels into a silence in which we hear the secret voices of our longings.

We planted our feet on the dune sand. There was a sweet sinking feeling, a slight dizziness, as when your mouth for the first time touched the cheek of a girl.

Between two rugged dune crests the sea folded licking flames of sun and oil on sheets of shallow water.

Not from the slow-moving crests of the waves—but from the murmuring pits of our secret beings, sirens suddenly sprang up. A breeze, a salty tang passed lightly over our lips—but this did not give that taste of unexplored distances, of earth and grass, which touched our tongue with a strange delight.

We stood like conch shells filled with a loud murmur in which sounded the grating beat of the waters, the rustling of fine gravel along the dune shrubs and a distant droning buoy that shouted its echoes over our heads in hollowed-out sand basins. But did not all that bluster come from us, mingled with the processional jubilation of the awakened sirens?

"The sea, the sea, the sea," I said to my wife, my voice low and quivering and with all the symptoms of suppressed emotion.

She did not answer. She was carrying our little two-year-old son on her arm. But she leaned with her shoulder against me. Immediately there flowed between us a current of warmth, easily penetrating our clothes. We soon glowed together, with the same glow as when we were first engaged ten years before. Only that her one shoulder was weighed down heavily and wearily by our boy. I took him from her and, each foot sinking in deep, quickly climbed to the top of the dune. There, breathless, I raised my son above my head and turned him gradually, facing the entire horizon, as a rapt dedication to the wide world, to that line between cloud and water yonder; there the train of smoke of motionless ships, here the land with slanting trees and in that corner, a cluster of houses belonging to a town sunk in mists.

Beneath us in the dunes, my wife lay back and laughed so that the sand vibrated like metal. I rushed down. Our little boy among the grass stalks, our lips met. Our eyes closed. In us was a great and wonderful rhythm. On the one side the sea quietly lapping the shore. On the other, a mighty breath heaved onto the land. Earth and sea balanced in this kiss. Our hearts thumped as if they would spring out of the slow measure that rocked the whole world with its oscillating beat.

Somewhere this strange happiness touched a still stranger pain, a restlessness—a realm where contradictory forces wrestled with each other, where there was stamping and fighting. No, no, we didn't want to lose this heavenly freedom, we wanted to continue this ascent, this elevation from the rut and from mediocrity. Were the little daily miseries already after us? Fight, fight.

Like young lovers we threw ourselves upon each other. Was this still play? Her shoulders writhed with delightful effort in my hands, in which she twisted like a swift animal. Her entwining arms round my loins clutched me as in a too tender embrace. With my muscles and sinews tense, all cords, I leaned against her; my back thrilled at her all too sweet softness. I turned in the small strength of her grasp. At first, when I overpowered her, she laughed. I don't know whether her laughter and her breath on my lips whipped up or tormented the voluptuous tenseness of my being, but I pressed her so hard against my breast that she creaked like an apple and uttered a sharp yell. I let her go, a little annoyed because my great happiness and animation could not fight it out to the end with an equally strong force. Her weakness had vanquished my violence.

And then, our little boy cried. In the sand his mouth had become a little snout of white emery-paper.

No, I am no poet. I am a manufacturer of furniture. Year in, year out a yearning smoulders in my heart. The fabrication of furniture takes up nearly all my time but does not wear away the mysterious wheels that have been rotating fast and noiselessly in my mind and in my soul ever since my earliest youth. Am I an exception? Can it be that others concentrate their entire personality, their entire play of feelings and thoughts on their business? In my case it is different. I have, so to say, no difficulties, no incidents, no setbacks, except outside my trade. I love my wife and my boy. I hate a half surrender with all the force of my being. Every day I pray to the Lord to let me keep the certainty that I shall die on her faithful heart and that my son will grow out of our united love.

And yet, alarming realization, the sober husband and father who keeps the manufacture of furniture in action in such an exemplary manner, has not killed the young man, particularly the youth, in me, the man. It is perhaps natural that the passions continue to burn and ferment in the heart of the socially domesticated. And yet, can I call passion the youth's purity, his first admiration for life, his expectation of great things, that melting tenderness for a young girl's eyes, that mixture of Platonic dream and first puberty?

But before declaring my trade to be that of manufacturer of furniture, I have often to state that it is that of a tormented human being. For, deep within me, a reasonable and orderly man, I am doing violence to a youth who has always remained sixteen. I am going on to forty-five, and day by day the cleft that separates me from this youth is getting wider. Naturally—or perhaps not naturally. Daily I am getting more ludicrous because I cannot part from this boy I once was and shall always remain. The time will come when I shall be a sixteen-year-old lad with a bald head, a back like a tunnel and a stout walking-stick. I shall look just like those little old men who secretly and sadistically enjoy looking at young girls, but I hope that the pureness of my insight can then be reconciled with my pride, which guides me and prevents me from having to blush before my wife and son.

For I suffer from the joy that the youth secretly gives me. I fight against this young chap who has been leading me, a maturing man, by the nose for twenty-five years. It is he who threw me into the arms of my wife. I praise him and am grateful to him for it. But whatever he may do now, he shall not tear me away from her. What does he whisper in my ear? That I have become bourgeois and am withering with my love and fidelity. That I am despite everything a young poet. No, no, I am a manufacturer of furniture, I am a manufacturer of furniture, I am a manufacturer of furniture, I am a manufacturer of furniture, I am a manufacturer of furniture, I am a manufacturer of furniture, I am a manufacturer of furniture, I am . . ., I am . . ., I am. . . .

Yes, certainly I was always punctual when I was sixteen years old and about to meet a girl. Irene, your mouth is large and the curl of your lips in the corners that expose your far too numerous teeth—Irene, you have a hundred teeth—makes you look like a savage. You are as yellow and brown as those dirty Italians who let go of the handles of their barrel-organs in order to rattle their tin mug. And the white of your eyes gleams blue, their pupils flame, shining darkly like polished chestnuts.

Irene, yes, we are walking along the Leie. We are walking away from the town, which lies behind us in the Saturday afternoon. Bullets crack behind the banks of the rifle range. An oarsman in a red- and white-striped sweater passes on a skiff, sculling rhythmically. The fields open out. Irene, our arms rest crosswise behind our backs. On each side a modest hand lies quietly on a pliant, heaving waist. Irene, behind your ear and under your hair two chaste lips seek the warmth of your neck. And you walk right on, without turning away or fearing.

Between the first sweetness of the senses and untouched purity a world of youthful bliss is balanced on a gossamer. What are we saying? Irene, you have a beautiful voice. Irene, look how that heap of washed carrots lies reflected in the Leie? Irene, how quickly the afternoon is passing! And then, do we feel anything? A wind that, with the scent of grass and clover, and fresh and dewy, has just touched the water, betrays to us the warmth of our cheeks. Where are we going, what do we expect? Around us the meadows loom. We follow the windings of the river. We are afraid that the evening will set in too early and with all our fear hasten its rapid ascent into pollard willows and shrubs. The sky, the clouds, a starling. . . . What is the use of it all? Two eyes subdue their lustre and light, two eyelids quiver and close, a tear flows from between black lashes, a forehead buries itself on a shoulder.

Irene, what strange shame has come over you? Lift up your head and do not be afraid of these wonderful delights; it is our youth taking its first steps; it is our lips that at first pursing retain the taste of a mouth; it is our first tenderness, which gives and takes; it is our first rapture that takes possession of another dream.

It is the first morning in Paradise. All the gloomy heroism that is necessary to lead a simple, ordinary, social life without erring or greatness is still strange to us. We are still flowering, attached with tough bands to our home and our youth. We have sinewy roots in the light of day, like white water-lilies on large leaves. We know nothing as yet of the fatal drifting, the high waters that will soon carry us off. Whither? Whither?

Irene, and you, Clara, and you, Yvonne, and little Anne, you manifold faces of my youth—here I am again. Through you I am always rejuvenated. Through you I always drink again the water of the springs. Through you I always strengthen myself again to remain faithful to the only chosen one, to the mother of my son, not to betray the prosperous manufacturer of furniture, that everyday man, that adversary who has renounced the thousand passions and disturbances of life. You all love me, I love you all. I have chosen you all in my wife. You are all in the one chosen one.

If she would only change, if she would only take on all your faces. But no, she remains herself. I know, through and through, the pleasing smoothness of her skin, all her gestures, all the impulses in her heart, all the workings of her mind. She is as I love her. She tires me. She deadens something in me. She weighs me down. I can't stand her any more. We must fight with one another; bite one another.

Irene, and Clara, and little Anne, and Yvonne, lay me again quietly with my cheek on her breast as on a warm peach. There alone I am well off. There alone I find rest and salvation. There I am every day the prodigal son who returns from the pigsty of the furniture manufacture.

But let me determine still better the positions in this small drama in which I am the only actor—this solo drama, if you like. The Lord has put in me a tragic dose of reasonableness and fantasy and over and beyond that an honesty which I can perhaps betray but to which I always want to return. There are men who are destined to unfold themselves completely as poets, as leaders of peoples and revolutionaries, as benefactors of humanity, as saints. I was marked by nature as young Ariel, as a lad who possessed the highest power of his soul when leading a girl before she became a woman. For Ariel is the poet in me, the general, the revolutionary—my greatness and glory and strength.

But I have also been marked by nature to make Ariel die in me, to deprive myself of this heavenly enjoyment, to part with this enchanting power and inspiration—which incidentally makes more desperate gestures from day to day. And it is my reasonableness to be on the side of the Lord, to accept my role of father and husband from the 15th of July of one year to the 1st of July of the following year with its hiding away in orderly work. And daily I stand at a sharpening wheel which grinds out my soul, my imagination and my sensitiveness. How I love you, my wife and my son. For your sake I cut to pieces within me the heart of Ariel.

Then when the holidays come round, when the manufacturer of furniture, the man of nearly forty-five, gets two weeks' leave, the old boy raises himself, throws a year of habit, a year of holy, heroic barrenness of the soul away, strengthens his adversary for a new campaign of lustreless prosperity and pumps glorious fresh blood into the mummy until it rises and walks again.

Lord, what is it, what is it this year? Never have I run over to

Ariel with so much heart and soul. I know that I am getting too old to do this without danger. In previous vacations it was enough for me that my wife was also rejuvenated, till she was like a girl. But now? But now? The first approach to the sea, the great liberation from the slavery of the every day, has already whipped me up terribly. I even had a vision in which Ariel with a torch and a red flag—ridiculous, ridiculous—revolted against a hideous bourgeois. He carried the fire to the wood piles of his adversary. He splashed and scratched his polished furniture. And what did this madness and this blasphemy mean? The hand that poured petroleum on the foot of the cross on which a bourgeois by turns exchanged his own face for that of Christ? What else than that Ariel revolted against the Lord also?

For don't let me be cowardly but let me recognize that it is the Lord who stands right at the back impassively watching how I shall draw myself out of this trial. I have already experienced it for years. He denies me a certain greatness in my existence as family father, a certain heroism, if need be, that of setbacks and of poverty, with which I could much more easily and with equal weapons resist the young hero Ariel; who knows, perhaps defeat him. I am not mistaken about this: all heroism means joy, intoxication, voluptuousness, and He summons me to renounce it, He demands of me that I carpenter gloomily on one love in this miserable, flourishing furniture business.

Oh, let me pray! Let me separate by means of my prayer this young heathenish hero and this poor, mature man with tears in his first wrinkles.

I chew words in my mouth like lumps of rubber. Round it flows a juice tasting of mastic and benzine. Pray, merely pray. I end by belching forth the prayer. Before long familiar mysteries beckon temptingly. I surrender. No, I am no longer menaced. There bubbles in me a wild enthusiasm. Shall I still fear? Away, you doubt. I shudder with disturbing, dissolving splendors.

My wife is digging a hole for her boy somewhere in the sand. From the terrace of our cottage I see the beach, the dike, a bandstand, a boat on its side, the small bathing machines and cabins. Large clouds are floating across the sun and over the sea with green patches of molten bronze. In gusts the wind brings the smell of shrimps and wet shells, of seaweed and fish, of salt and meagre dune roses.

There is a girl walking on the asphalt. She is carrying a racket under her arm. She smiles at someone out of awkward seriousness. But she does not blush. Then suddenly, she stands still. She lets the whole world come up to her and she laughs.

The whole world, that is, seven girl friends. They walk arm in arm and prattle. The whole horizon full of girls closes in a semi-circle round the one girl with the rackèt. They chatter. All their feet and knees dance, making some Charleston movements.

And I, I too, between the little raffia chairs, let myself go for a moment to the music of an invisible jazz band, of water and wind perhaps. A wonderful bobbing moves my knees rhythmically, my legs kick out sideways, my feet come down softly on the ground that seems elastic and chases a shooting pain quivering through my whole body. Girl with the racket, and you, O all you girls, we are young, young for all time. No one old in years knows how we avow our youth in this Charleston. It is in us, we are in it. This is the rhythm of this time, of our youth.

What was it? What betrayal? Who made this boundless youth suddenly crumble? My heart does not yet fail nor does my breath and, though it is true that I have become corpulent, my belly does not yet hinder me. And it is not the departure of the girls that has left me alone with my forty-four years. Nevertheless, with one blow I am again forty-four, even older, much older, older by all the years that I still have to live. And I sit there with the whole rocking sea in a tear, welled up from a sorrow, a despair, a frenzy, and especially from an unspeakable powerlessness that overwhelms me, I don't know from where, and makes me tremble and shake.

How the love of those who cherish us frequently comes inopportunely. At that moment my wife, back from the beach, laid her hand on my head. It was as if that familiar hand had suddenly crushed together in itself all the weight of the years. Was it shame or annoyance? I could not be honest. I wanted to take her fingers to my lips and explain to my wife how my heart beat and labored in distress. But I was helpless. I had only the strength to ward off her friendly gesture with a ruse. My hair occasionally stands unruly and dry and then hurts me as if at the least touch it would snap off at the root.

"Jo, darling, my hair is again brittle. Take your hand away."

The false tenderness in my words quickly warned and offended her. She pulled her arm back as if she had felt near her the icy flight of a machine-saw. The sea and clouds spun before my eyes, for her glance searched my face. Meanwhile she tormented me with her silence, a silence full of the muffled sound of sand and water. When she had sufficiently taken me in, sufficiently tested "my mood" in terms of former experiences, she again picked up the sweater that she had put down when she came in, moved a chair before going away—in her case a sign of orderliness, which she always makes when she has something still to say. What would it be? Would she again, out of pity, withdraw unasked from the conflict, suppress all reproaches magnanimously to leave me all the more ineluctably to my inner oscillations? If she would only show annoyance! At the first reproach I would be able to snub her, to rush at her, to raise my hand against her, like a brute that has found a tangible form for all the restlessness and frenzy with which he is being belabored. Who knows how I would love her if I could, once and for all, wreak my torments on her for whom I go through all these ridiculous tortures, if I could thrust from me all this ferocity in one unjust chastisement?

"My friend, you have been sitting around the house too much. In the town. And here again. Walk to the end of the dike. The Heuvelmans are there. Drink a glass of beer with them, at the 'Bass.' And go to the 'Abbaye' this evening; there is dancing there. You need some diversion."

If this poor young woman—she is twenty-eight—had given advice indifferently with the superiority of a wise mother, who starts her children at games, certain that a little distraction will drive away all bad tempers, I might have considered myself offended and behaved rudely. But no, she had spoken with barely concealed emotion. She had quivered with a diffident delicacy, in which there was something like fear, something like a prayer—as if she knew that in this tension a higher peace, a love, a happiness was at stake.

Pity, magnanimity, you are the utmost provocation, the nip of pincers to which one can react only with cowardice. I avenged myself as much as I could, although it hurt me more than to yield to despondency and grief.

Sad refuge into smile and tenderness! I laughed at my wife. She did not answer with a tear of relief—her unrest would not be relieved. Did she foresee that the conflict would not pass so quickly or easily? I held her to my breast. No warmth, no fervent current in our embrace. Only from a distance, in the stereotyped gesture of the kiss, boy friend and girl friend waved encouragingly to one another. "There is no fellowship, no bond. But hope, good hope. Persevere!"

And as if we had talked a long time with one another, we, who

without a word fight the conflicts in our own souls—as if the why
had to remain hidden and only the battle plan had importance
and significance, I said with feigned levity, "Fiddlesticks! Don't
give into whims. (Ariel, Ariel, forgive me this denial, of which I
don't believe a word.) We shall go out together this afternoon.
Into the dunes with our boy. What have I to do with the Heuvelmans and the 'Abbaye'?"

Will the struggle be easier when placed under the eyes, and at
the side of my wife? Who will fall in line, my cowardice or
courage? But my wife surveyed the difficulties with great care
and disbelief. Did she fathom the musty smouldering in my heart
more deeply? She shook her head and replied:

"Go out for once. That will be infinitely better."

But Ariel must have incited me to a stubbornness, the consequences of which he foresaw, for it was almost angrily and certainly crossly that I raised my voice in order to speak cuttingly
and firmly, as if my mouth were full of reproaches:

"I don't like this pretended self-sacrifice. Don't carry on as if
your pleasures didn't count. We are going out together. That's
that!"

Poor, good woman. Yet I knew well that she had not thought
for a moment of the pose of self-sacrifice and, being well-meaning, only felt pity for my disturbed mind and its brooding. But
I overflowed with falseness and treachery and I saw without
blushing or repentance that under her self-control her lips were
trembling and her eyes suddenly flamed, as she said:

"Do what you like, my friend, you are old and wise enough."

How would I have rejoiced to know that she tormented me,
to know that, hypocritically and falsely, she let those innocent
words fall, those foul, biting words that laughed caustically into
my face: old and wise enough. I, who go to pieces, right into
degeneration and destruction because despite my years, my wife,
my son, my life—I cannot become old and wise enough. How I
would have offended her love with an avowal, a confession out
of virtue and pleasure and avenging lust of this man in me, because of which she long ago became an old, wrinkled woman!
How I would have mocked her confidence, offended her noblest
attachment by letting the girls pass one by one before her
imagination who, from my bursting youth, from beside the Leie
to here on the beach, have pulled me out of her arms. But no,
you are old and wise enough, she had said, with a nervous
charitableness that sounded like an exorcism of the dark happen-

ings in my being. And I continued to seethe with rage because I found no wrong in my wife.

Round about noon, while we were at table, a thin, light rain fell outdoors. It brought as it were a little truce in the repulsive conflict within me, which I now tried to direct outwards in futile bickering and then with jealous care thrust back, as inescapable, for later. A little rain, a cool bath, and all that inner scorching will pass, I laughed equivocally to myself, and my eyes examined the sky full of water and sun with childish hope. If it continued to rain, nothing could force me to go out alone, as my wife had wisely recommended, but then I should also not need to execute my senseless plan of a family walk. Hide myself behind the sunny rain: that was all I found to reconcile Ariel and the manufacturer of furniture for a little while and let them sit side by side near a spouse without youth or age, O cowardice, O enjoyable cowardice!

But fortunately, soon after noon the rain was taken from my face. And as if to grant me a last chance of reflection, my wife asked with a sweet reserve that left me absolutely free choice:

"What are you going to do, Herman?"

"Go out together, of course!" I blurted out in an uncontrolled voice, and the certainty suddenly threw me into the inward struggle I feared so much. I began to be excessively active. I myself put our boy into the baby carriage, made him laugh by tickling him, and pushed him, before his mother could get ready, outdoors in front of the cottage. It was probably instinctive that I thrust the father in me into the foreground. Should it be called excessive boasting? But from my son's laugh flowed a great cheerfulness into my heart, as I ran with him along the railings.

I had passed perhaps three or four times by the De Kinkankhoorn house when I noticed on a terrace a young man in grey flannel trousers and yellow sweater. He lay on a deck chair doing nothing. In one of the corners of his mouth I saw a sneer, a superiority over me, which I immediately accepted. I walked a little further—how ugly is a man getting on in years who still strains playfully at a baby carriage—but it was so as not to show at once how ashamed I was. Shame, yes, but also regret, and above all jealousy, a tormenting envy of that young man who possessed his youth.

When at last my wife came up to me I snarled at her as if I could by rage shake off my fatherhood:

"How long you always take! And meanwhile I have to play nursemaid!"

She took over my place at the baby carriage without a word, without a gesture of opposition, as if stubbornly determined to endure everything and certain in advance that my anger and vexation would wear out on her patience.

We walked silently side by side. In the unpaved Poppy Lane that leads to the dunes the wheels sank into the sand. I turned the carriage round and pulled it after me. Offended I dragged unspeakable burdens—the whole betrayed family. I sulked and did not want to look aside at the tennis courts where rackets were just driving the balls and making the asphalt bang with rhythmic rubber bouncing. There was the sound of counting voices, bright flashes through the stormy murmur in my head. I pulled like a blind man, with hot blood in my eyes, up the dune. The wet sand and the bundles of grass beat an odor of sick hares against my face. Having struggled onto the top of the dune, I stood still to pant for breath. A hammering flinging of rackets beat in my heart.

Then it was that on the wind that blew cool along my glowing neck and ears my name was called. Who had called, who down there from the valleys? I recognized all the girls' voices from the tennis courts. It sounded like a last call, a call of despair and at the same time of longing, a chorus of fresh voices: "Are we lost for all time? We are lost, lost for you. Lost our laugh. Lost your youth, your inspiration." And then, from the mouths of a thousand girls, my name, nothing but my first name.

Or did no one really call? What is the use if the heart nevertheless turns over, if the mind is inexorably shocked and life and soul begin to ebb? For in the twinkling of an eye there sprang at me like a cat the thought, the inevitable recognition: "I am a man who is at an end. I am even beyond the end. It was childish audacity still to believe that once over the culminating point of the years one might still return." But not even that, not the impossibility of return, placed this glowing band of suffering round my temples. What is a return? one wonders. But I suddenly knew in great alarm that I had always loved something in the Girl, always longed for something, always worshipped something that was greater than the charming figure I pressed to my bosom and kissed, greater than the woman and the human being. Something, something, something— Lord, what is this hankering in the heart, what is the momentum of the spirit that rises above mortals, that heavenly intoxication, that wonderful power that lifts us above ourselves?

And this call from the mouths of a thousand girls, this call of sublimity and of the most beautiful moments of my life, gradually sounded like an agonizing reproach: "You are now smaller, you have always been smaller, than you could have been. You possessed nothing but the promise of a possession, a sweet vertigo —give all promise and vertigo back. And continue your fall into a roaring bottomlessness. . . ."

But, oh, that last resistance, that clutching and hitting about one! I stood, turning pale; my abhorred wife began before me to blush with a strange fear on her cheeks. I turned round—there stood, so it seemed to me, a glowing sun ready to dive into the sea, for all order and all bands were broken. All was abandoned: this woman, this boy, this bourgeois prosperity of a manufacturer of furniture. And with a last scornful word to the mother of the child in the baby carriage who had suddenly become illegitimate, absolutely and entirely freed, heroic, I ran down: "You are right, I must get out!"

But at that moment it had the secret meaning of "Adieu, adieu, forever." And I did not turn round.

As in a dream I pursued a way prescribed to me. To the 'Bass.' I drank, one after another, three glasses of mellow Scotch, which made me a little bloated and heavy but did not harm my regained youth and its ecstasies. I saw from underneath a silk lampshade, beneath which electric light glowed, a sunset fit for a picture postcard of the Italian lakes. As evening fell, innumerable girls came strolling along the dike. I got up and started walking among the dear children. At nine o'clock I found myself at the 'Abbaye' in front of a little table with flowers and lamps, next to a shiny dance floor, a few steps from a Negro jazz band. There I would pour out once more my seventeen years as a challenge. How young I was again and in heavenly expectation! A banjo and percussion drum, saxophone and muttering stopped trumpet played rhythmically a wonderfully sentimental dance of pampas and gold fields. Which of these young children, who silently and solemnly caught the rhythms in their hips, in their knees and little feet, would I presently lead along a nocturnal sea that beat with murmuring shells and foam on the firm sandbanks?

But among the couples there suddenly trotted an old gentleman with a young girl. He danced with a wonderful proficiency, ran from girl to girl, after each dance, and guided them with unbearable sureness through the varying measures. I don't know why a crazy hatred for this old dancer overcame me, a feeling of modesty, perhaps, a recognition of the hopeless ludicrousness and the lies of these old fibres and sinews that still made the gestures of youth. I had ordered champagne. When the waiter placed the ice on my little table, I could not refrain from asking him contemptuously:

"Why don't you throw such old curs off the floor?"

With a short nod he just flicked up the tail of his coat, like a blackbird. Without winking, and most politely and stiffly above his little white tie, he replied:

"Dry wood, sir. Breaks off by itself. I even hope it won't happen here."

Then a fleeting flash of laughing understanding shot into his eyes, whereupon he quickly dropped long lashes. He went away. I sat with a long face before my glass of champagne. I no longer had to decide to refrain from leading away any girl. There suddenly growled in me a pride, a grim pride, a pride without profit or rest, which did not compensate for the sacrifice, nor offer consolation to the victim: Ariel. I really experienced the pains of what is generally called a soul in distress, a soul which does not know to what to cling; Ariel, impossible return; family, wife and child, had become symbols of a defeat. The champagne stood before me and the boom of the dance chased sparks into it of mirrors and light and strange constellations with secret promises of intoxication and torpor. In the same way the shining darkness of a river must promise stupor and peace to the hopeless who envisage death in its soothing eye. But this utter cowardice I scorn from afar with certain opposition. It was as if I spoke aloud to myself:

"Rather a bottle of gall than drown misery in drink. . . ." And in my head I began to rattle off a verse that I had once seen quoted in my daily paper: "Waiter, bring me some gall in a large glass."

"And if still sharper pain should cut through you?" a voice challenged in this crazy conversation with myself.

"It can't become sharper," I replied and in order to answer the challenge I deliberately, although with apparent carelessness so as not to attract attention to myself, threw my glass over.

The waiter who had modestly come up had not yet finished cleaning my little table when my heart was crushed still more caustically: after one accepts suffering, one never knows where the torment will end. The old gentleman was in a corner where there were carpets and low square little seats. Two girls had hold of him by the wrist and tuxedo and restrained him. A third held

up an open book and murmured something, that the old dancer
did not want to hear, for he tried to wrestle himself free. I stood
up, walked by the gay little group, close enough to read askance
at the top of the page of the book: "Your body is yours." All the
disillusionment the ludicrous little gentleman had made Ariel
suffer, three girls, three cherished young figures, now painfully
made the man of years in me go under. The dream of my youth,
which I did not want to renounce, was torn out of my hands, for
perversity had always seemed to me the mask of old age and
weariness.

I went to the wash-room. It was as if the little old dancer stood
next to me, shedding into the basin two tears he could not keep
back, and I could have done so along with him. When I returned
to my little table I found my glass which the waiter had refilled.
I was overcome by disgust. Nevertheless I pushed the champagne
aside.

"In view of the fact that the decay can always go further," I
said to myself in a glowing inner debate, "I am prepared for the
worst. Lord, try me further if you so desire. I shall not flee; I
shall not drink."

Indeed, my exhaustion was complete when a Negro suddenly
cheered me up. In the middle of a fox-trot he gave a violent bang
on the cymbals. He let its clattering drone on. The copper jingling quivered to the last fibres of my whole body. For one moment I no longer felt my misery: it was like a long echoing blow
of the trumpet of archangels, which lifted me out of myself. It
must have been sheer madness, but in the middle of all that
worldly hullabaloo, those lamps, liqueurs, evening dresses and
dancing I was suddenly conscious of a divine presence. Even
more; unconsciously my eyes searched among the Negroes on the
platform for a heavenly face, a heavenly light, love in two eyes.
A thudding pain entered my heart, as if it had just stood still;
my eyes remained fixed on the face of the Negro who controlled
the instruments of percussion.

He was what is generally called a pure Negro: very ugly because of the protruding cheekbones, the brutish thick lips, the
flattened nose, the ears that stuck out from the dusty frizzy hair.
Only once in a while I saw his eyes; he clutched blindly at all the
devices of the battery and handled them in blissful absorption.
His fingers, which had long become red on the inside, let the
drumsticks dribble on the hollow castanet, the little drums, the
cymbals and drum backs with indescribable elegance. When he
opened his eyes, a miracle happened: in the jet, in the middle of

the yellowish white, shot a spark of dull gold. That was not the wonder, though, but a look that was not of this world, the look of a savage, a man completely unconstrained, for whom a raindrop, a grass blade, a forest, a noise, are full of God and for whom each gesture is a sacrifice. When he opened his eyes, his lips at the same time parted over a painfully decayed set of teeth: the smile of the hideous. But he smiled at no one and resumed his play with the instruments of percussion with a touching seriousness, in an ecstasy, like a dedication, a rising beyond the world, a prayer.

I would not have been of my time if I had not fought this emotion with all the scepticism I was capable of. "This Negro wipes his bony structures squarely on all the instruments. He is bored. He earns his living and is resigned to his boredom," I meditated with self-contempt. "And then, then?" I replied to myself, always again surprised by the roll, the rhythm of the beats, the grating friction of steel fan-brushes over drums and cymbals, all sounds that cured me of my endless poisoning of the mind. Meanwhile the ecstasy continued to be clear on the Negro's face; it raised a hope in me which made me tremble.

"If I am not mistaken about this Negro," I finally thought, "who knows if I cannot realize the wonder that I have seen in him? Who knows what plans the Lord has for me? If I could make the great leap into jazz?"

A languishing accordion tango drew sweet rounded lines and movements out of the bodies. I had an urgent desire to pray, there, at that moment. Too averse to all ostentation, I made in thought the sign of the cross and that already gave me strength to suffer only triumphantly in my disillusionment.

When I left the 'Abbaye' it seemed to me as if the sea breeze, full of stars, blew freely through my body and I had undergone a great cleansing. The pits of despair lay, steep and safely crossed, behind me. I felt virile, ready to carry out my simple, my shabby, great plan.

There was no longer anything that still had much immediate importance: not the return to my wife, not the wait for the retreat to town. And nevertheless, how moved, though secretly, we were when we saw each other again after this absolute parting, after this far, somber voyage to inner solitude. My wife was waiting for me, as one roams along the quay and hopes for someone, **not** knowing what boat he has taken: love and patience and anxiety melt together into a yearning cry that only the very sensitive hear.

I too had become sensitive again, having pity for conflicts and emotions other than my own. It was almost midnight. Jo had remained up. When I opened the door of the room, she did not look up from the book that she pretended to be reading. By circles of fatigue round her eyes and by an affected calm I immediately recognized her extreme consideration: she wanted to pretend that her reading had enthralled her so long and was doing so still, in order not to offend me with her anxious vigil, in order not to signify: "You see, my friend, how I sacrifice my night's rest, even more, my peace of mind to your caprices."

I went to her. I kissed her forehead, for I had to behave very nonchalantly so as not to mingle too much formal admiration of her self-denial with my surrender to love. She trembled under my kiss. She jumped up with suppressed over-excitement. A rapid flickering of her eyelashes made her eyes very anxious. That kiss on her forehead, was it still the cool absentmindedness, the estrangement? her glance asked my whole face. Her cheek moved hesitatingly and without asking, especially without entreating, past my mouth as if to know whether no urge from the heart would hold her in a fervent embrace. And it happened. In that vehement embrace coursed the violent alternating current of our rescued love,—a great love without great show. On my cheek I felt a tear that had burst from between her lashes. It is by way of such sensation that one descends to the murmuring depths of the soul, where one has crushed from holy feelings the bitterest happiness, the most blissful sorrows.

The same equilibrium, the same intertwining continued all the remaining days of our vacation, which we spent no more apart. Only at the end I began perhaps to long for the year of work at home. That was the first time that I felt homesick for my ordinary daily task—reconciled to my manufacture of furniture? But I would try to build a support.

Laugh, if you want: there are no small actions, if it means keeping a heart, a life, a love straight. Back at my work, I strengthened my position, for every evening, when the fall came, I became a jazz-player by my stove. I had a gramophone, and in the little mechanism sat my fellow players. It is difficult to make oneself understood, even by the persons with whom we have grown together—that wheel of a thousand reasons and feelings cannot be taken apart, even if no virtuousness or obliging love is mixed up with it. Even my wife, usually so accommodating, protested crustily when I had a perfect battery of percussion instruments brought into the living-room. I laughed her indignation away—it was for me too holy and serious a necessity of life to be disturbed by her opposition.

Undeniably she was right when she sulkily left the sitting-room during my first exercises; the booming of the percussion drum, the roll and clatter of the various drums, the clash of the cymbals, even the tinkling of the triangle, which is after all an instrument full of refined sounds, were at first cannibal noises, the more so as I had great trouble with the syncopated rhythms. Incidentally, I beat out of time, drowned out the gramophone and was not yet able to produce the subtle shading with which a thump is reduced to a murmuring roll. And, of course, she failed to realize behind that grotesque business the laborious effort of soul that was practising for greater flights, the soul that was every day separating itself more surely from Ariel, the soul that was steeling the furniture manufacturer to his only and undying loyalty, the soul that purified itself in the limitation of wife and child, of household and dark death, lost itself and plunged in God.

But after a short time I had the jazz band in my blood. I reached a point where I was able to adjust all the percussion sounds to the volume of the gramophone music. At first it was the angular rhythmic clanking of Charleston and fox-trot, the far too soft melodic patterns of "Javas" and blues. And finally I climbed to the melodious heights of spirituals, sung by full Negro voices. I even went much further: I improvised with percussion instruments on airs by old masters like Palestrina and Bach. It was a day of happiness and temptation when a young composer, whose acquaintance I had made, felt so transported by my jazz performance that he tried to persuade me to perform in the concert hall.

My wife, however, cannot conduct herself in an unprejudiced way toward my so-called "strange mania." My progress has led her from astonishment to sharp annoyance. She understands me less as time goes on because she does not simply surrender to my jazz music. She asks herself: "Whence comes this caprice, whither will it take him?" I see it in her concerned face, when I wake from the inspiration of one of my performances and open my eyes again. Indeed, I already manage easily to ascend into the ecstasy that the jazz band player from the 'Abbaye,' or the Lord

Himself, revealed to me—ecstasy in which I beat my drums like consecrated instruments, from which sings and radiates my whole departed youth, a heroic love and subjection, an offering of all my tears, this whole heart of conflicting humanity. How could my wife understand that I love her and my son in all these percussion instruments, that I pray and sanctify my life through them?

It has therefore neither astonished nor discouraged me very much that every time I tune my beloved instruments an ever growing anger flashes in the eyes of my spouse. I am more obliging to her than ever, I surround her with the clear signs of a rejuvenated, elated love. I give her no single reason to show me smouldering annoyance. But it cannot be denied that she has transferred a strange hatred, which she cannot pile on my head, to my jazz-band battery, as if there was in the instruments a living soul, an evil spirit, responsible instigators of what she labels in me a pathological mania. Who will tell me where jealousy ends in a woman's heart, an inexorable hankering to attach the man to herself alone?

But the conflict between my wife and my jazz-band battery is another little drama of which I shall here merely note the miserable result. In the height of self-excitement, she murdered my big drum. With a violent blow of the pedal, like an explosion echoing through the house, she tore the parchment. Caustically, furious, I stood watching—at first disapproving; but when I saw what misunderstanding disturbed her so, a feeling of extenuation and strange regret came over me; how blind are our sorrows!

There is in this world no constant equilibrium. I had fought out a little drama with myself. The woman of my love, she who has won all by it, has risen in opposition. The harmony of my heart, which I have realized in the jazz band, is unbearable to her. I am an honest man and on the side of the Lord. Let me now search for an intelligible equilibrium between my wife and the equilibrium in myself. Peace to people of good will. But to show good will, always anew, that's a lustreless heroism, without drunkenness or rewarding intoxication, that's a heroism of long breath.

Translated by JO MAYO

Raymond Brulez

THE EIGHTH VOYAGE OF SINBAD
or "Happiness lies elsewhere . . ."

. . . wretched one: go and sail where never the sun rises;
where the grim waves stand on end like towers of
ice, like rocks, and where neither flower nor leaf ever
adorns the belly of Mother Earth!

AFTER SINBAD THE SAILOR HAD COMPLETED THE SEVEN VOYAGES
whose adventurous nature is known to you, he decided to retire
to a countryseat with a few faithful servants, where he intended
to crown his achievements by writing a standard work about the
history of navigation. But the popular hero, who upon his last
return to Bassora had been triumphantly welcomed with a show
of flags fluttering from every mast, the nervous shrieking of
sirens and, above all, the elevating spectacle of thousands of
waving hands, laughing eyes and exulting mouths, was slowly
forgotten in his solitude. The photo services no longer requested
his latest picture, the "Argus of the Press" no longer sent newspaper clippings, and the magazines no longer included him
among the ten leading personalities of Arabia who could be
interviewed during the slack season when it was customary to
hold inquiries concerning disputed subjects such as: "co-educa-
tion", "the wearing of soft or stiff collars" or "the return of art
to a new classicism". Besides, when the time came to renew
Sinbad's honorary chairmanship of the Navigation Society of
Arabia, an unfledged little naval officer was elected in his stead,
a young man who averred to have discovered the source of the
Gulf Stream with a submarine.

Apparently Sinbad had outlived his fame. All this depressed
him very much. Not that he had at the time undertaken his
dangerous peregrinations out of a thirst for glory. It must be
admitted that he always sought " adventure for adventure's sake",
just as the sincere artist pursues "art for art's sake". But who can
view the waning of his own fame with complete equanimity?

My name will surely turn up again some day, mused Sinbad, and that will be precisely on the day of my death. Then
my black-bordered face will appear in the papers, the news reels

will include several yards of film dedicated to my person—between the opening of parliament and the last races. In the cafés and on the benches of the city parks, for just a little while I shall still be "the subject of all conversations". A few days later my funeral occurs "attended by vast crowds". The high dignitaries kick about the difficulty of reaching this remote provincial hole, and while perspiring profusely they stumble on behind my cold body down the dusty country road to "this damnably distant little village mosque", they already begin circulating false legends about my life. Then, as time passes, the little article which the encyclopedias concede to my deeds shrinks more and more. And it presumably ends with: "He also wrote a not undeserving history of navigation. . . ." *Not undeserving!* Do you hear this cautious praise: two negations which are meant to convey a feeble confirmation? And upon this I squander the last years of my life! . . . sighed Sinbad disconsolately, as he gazed at the pile of notes and musty books which created barren disorder on his desk. While out there the world. . . .

For indeed, out yonder the grain billowed toward the horizon like a sea. And a new yearning for the sea which hums like a beehive bubbled up in his adventurous heart. The sea whose surf,—a raging beast, foaming at the mouth,—pounces upon the dunes, while the stormwind chases the helplessly fluttering gulls along the coast like fallen autumn leaves. For there are still seas which he has not traversed, depths which he has not plumbed, forgotten islands concealing enclosed temples dedicated to unknown gods. Sinbad wants to return to the deserts where once his caravans of shaggy camels dotted the unending, barren sandplains like strange shrubs.

The setting sun on the western horizon sweeps over his litter of books with a golden sheaf of light, and suddenly reveals the gleaming full-bellied sails of the silver miniature galleon which had been presented to him by his native city, Bagdad, and whose artfully embossed prow bore the legend: "Navigare necesse est, vivere non necesse! . . ."

So Sinbad decided upon a new voyage. Practical as the fellow was, he knew how to interest various institutions in his new project. For even the most selfish idealism must be built on a sound foundation. Thus the Arabian Academy of Science granted him a substantial federal subsidy on condition that Sinbad, in the course of his voyage, conduct a deep-sea investigation as to the gold content of sea water. Once the matter of finances had been settled, Sinbad went to Bassora and there picked up the little cargo ship *Sea Dog* at a bargain price. A remarkable boat, which already had a hazardous past in its wake, and which had been in the service of various human passions. During the World War it had served as a munitions transport. After that, the C.P.N. wanted to equip it to capture Wielingen. There was, however, a dearth of volunteers for this expedition. Then it was converted into a "yacht for vacation cruises", which as a matter of fact consisted of taking aboard a few dozen "artistes lyriques" at Hamburg now and then, and setting them ashore at South America on foggy mornings and with romantic cautiousness. Some time later, the *Sea Dog* was purchased by American bootleggers, and off and on it had been riddled by the machine-guns of incorruptible revenue cutters. And Neptune and Mercury only know how it came about that this object was now being put up for sale in Bassora by a Jewish ironmonger.

As it lay there, nestled against the wall of the dry-dock, like a drunkard against a curb, its appearance was unsightly. But once the green seaweeds had been scraped off, the pockmarks caused by the muscle plague had been healed with a layer of tar, and the superstructure neatly made up in white and red, it could again pertly display itself upon the great sea lanes. In the meanwhile Sinbad had engaged the crew. A dozen congenial rogues: deserters from the last World War and other fine fellows for whom it was best to remain concealed from the keen-sighted police for several months. Furthermore, as ship's cook, a Frenchman who had become neurasthenic in the subterranean grottos of large cosmopolitan palaces, and had been led to believe that only an extensive sea voyage could restore his impaired health; as wireless operator, in a sparkling uniform, a brave Ephebian who had learned telegraphy from correspondence courses, now wanted some practical experience and at the same time desired to confront a romantic *Weltschmerz* with reality. And finally, as first mate, Stephens, a fellow who felt at home on every ocean and evidently had swum through various waters. Now the day of departure had come. The cargo: paradise wood and a parcel of Persian rugs intended for the wigwams of the last Mohicans had been brought on board. The smoking white stack of the *Sea Dog* resembles a gigantic cigarette advertisement. And up there a sailor is actually hanging a painted sign on the railing with the arrogant warning: "Keep clear of the propeller!" Which arouses sarcastic derision in the loafing idlers on shore belonging to the guild of those excellent helmsmen who are just where they should be, and one of them loudly proclaims to anybody who cares to listen: "He'd better cross the ocean in a bathtub than in that insignificant little freighter . . ."; pessimistic remark which frightens to death the good-natured little mother in her Sunday coat, who now and then secretly presses a white handkerchief against the twitching corners of her mouth, or shyly waves her small, blue-veined hand to the young wireless operator, who does his best to act bold and calm. The annoying cables over which the onlookers stumble as they would over tree roots protruding from forest moss are finally unwound from the bitts, the siren puffs a graceful little white cloud which roars a mighty bellow, as though the ship's entire hull were nothing but an extraordinary, hollow sounding-board. Hereupon, the proprietress of "The Town of Liverpool" has her juke-box ceremoniously play "God Save the King" in honor of Stephens who, besides several pounds, also leaves behind the memory of a tattooed skin which constitutes in crude fashion a complete encyclopedia of nautical symbols, as well as of the names of women of all races and peoples.

The *Sea Dog* glides away from the quay and picks its course among the anchored fishing sloops and sailboats. In the clear channel it makes faster headway. Out of the smooth surface of the water the ship rams a seagull of foam which with its white wings gracefully nestles against the flanks of the prow. They pass the pilot-house whose semaphore waves a whole paternoster of well-meant signals. The two slightly diverging palisades sketch the strokes of a gigantic swimmer practising the overarm crawl; the surf surges against their extremities. Here the *Sea Dog* does not choose the briny deep, but the sea thrusts itself upon it in such a way that a wave gushes into the open porthole where the ship's cook is punctually inhaling salubrious iodine and bromide molecules from the air. And now the turbulent sea like a multitude of thousands on a great city square . . . !

Thus manned by devious, strange ambitions which, however, were bound together by Captain Sinbad's desire for adventure, the *Sea Dog* had for weeks been steaming towards its economic and at the same time esoteric destination. The coast line no longer broke the perfect, surrounding curve of the horizon. However, the ever-shifting circle whose restless center was the ship was, alas, not the famed geometric figure whose circumference lies everywhere and whose center nowhere. It remained a fact: the *Sea Dog* was imprisoned behind the bars of latitude and longitude. And for a heart "yearning for infinite spaces" this was rather discouraging. To be sure, one was diverted by the rotation of approaching and vanishing days. Night froze the constellations upon the dome of heaven like frost-flowers, which the morning sun invariably thawed again. And there, too, between the masts hung the meshless hammock where, at the command of the medium, "Accumulator", the "astral self" of the Ether Muses obediently comes to swing itself. They did not, it is true, present the "music of the spheres", but the choice programs which Hilversum sent out to them via Bandoeng: selections from *Tosca*, the latest jazz songs and interesting observations concerning the attitude of the anti-revolutionary party in reference to the legal status of office clerks. After the ship's progress had for some time been favored by clear weather, benevolent winds and kindly currents, on a certain evening, at twilight, an unexpected storm broke loose. The strong wind scoured the rough-gray soap-clump that was the ocean into a flocky foam which gleamed pale against the dark firmament, where a first flash of lightning briefly betrayed the cracks in the cloud-urns. Heavy seas crashed over the forecastle and hail clattered against the hull and on the zinc decks. The *Sea Dog* bore up bravely. Undismayed, it vaulted over and through the obstacle-hedges of the mighty storm-waves, while its stack tossed a tangled mane of smoke. Fortunately this ordeal did not last long. The squall departed and presently there again on the declouded horizon stood, in perfect roundness, peaceful as a lone, illuminated porthole, the full moon. . . .

Sinbad inspected his ship. A broad smile spread over the stokers' faces, still pale and beaded with the sweat of fear, now that the captain assured them that danger had passed and praised them for having kept up the fires so well. The wireless operator, who had remained magnificently calm, was busy polishing the brass of his instruments; and Stephens insisted with his gum-chewing mouth that he had experienced much beastlier moments in the Straits of Magellan. But when Sinbad entered the map-room, he detected a sailor there who hastily fled and whose surprised Kalmuck face he did not recognize as belonging to one of his own crew. And worse still, the panes there had been shattered by the storm! Heavy seas and showers of hail had soaked all the maps. The colors of land and sea had fused until the maps resembled soiled palettes; the lines of latitude and longitude were erased!

"The only thing that remains legible are the fingerprints of this skunk's filthy paws!" Stephens declared.

"This is great, now we'll have to sail blind, just about like Columbus or Vasco . . ."

A sailor came to report that a vain search had been made for the stowaway in the galley, the hold and the cabins. Only the fugitive's cap had been found in a deserted passageway. He held the dirty object between the tips of his thumb and index-finger as if it were a dead rat. On its sweat-stained band stood: ATOS, but several gilt letters had apparently peeled off.

"That's clear! Must be: H.M.S. ATOS," said Stephens.

"ATOS? If it were ATHOS with an H, it'd remind me of the mountain in Greece where the famous monks' republic is."

". . . Or of the Three Musketeers . . .," suggested the book-loving wireless operator.

"Ship sighted to starboard!" the lookout suddenly warned. They ran up to the bridge again. Indeed, at a short distance, in the pale-blue light of the full moon, they distinguished a strange affair resting motionless and dark upon the calm surface of the sea. It exactly resembled a 16th century Spanish galleon like the silver ship the city of Bagdad had presented to Sinbad. The masts were stripped of their sails, and with their triple yard-arms they formed huge papal crosses. Sinbad had the *Sea Dog's* searchlight turned on the ship, which now assumed the chalky, ghastly white appearance of a pavilion at an exposition. The lofty poop and the bowsprit were decorated with mythological figures, monstrous animals and carved foliage. Sinbad read the name "THALASSA II". "What a queer derelict!" Stephens uttered his surprise; "if the war wasn't over, I'd take it for a mystery ship, a submarine trap!"

"Perhaps a ship for an historical film. For 'Ben Hur' they built a whole fleet of Roman galleons like this," explained the wireless operator. "Signal to the THALASSA II to ask whether it needs anything," requested the captain.

And surely enough, the boy returned at once, astonished, with the answer: "Alpha-omega! . . ."

"A silly joke! And in Greek, too . . .," Stephens exclaimed angrily—as though this detail were especially objectionable; for, since he had left behind three teeth on the basalt blocks of the Piraeus in a nocturnal scuffle, the helmsman's attitude toward the Hellenes was not a friendly one.

Sinbad sensed adventure! Just as unexpectedly and mysteriously his previous wonderful encounters had begun. He ordered them to draw up alongside the other ship. The *Sea Dog* approached carefully, until the sailor who was sounding warned them that the water was beginning to get shallow. Was the THALASSA II perhaps on a shoal? But the distance between them was so short that one could cast a cable whose end was knotted like a lasso around the neck of one of the mermaid statues on the rear of the vessel. Along this, Sinbad began to climb to the galleon. Stephens, who was watching him, remarked: "But damn it all, we made a mistake! The name of the ship isn't THALASSA II, its THANATOS II. Its godfather must have had gruesome ideas. . . ."

A creaking of moldered wood. . . . Through the upper deck rash Sinbad fell into space!—His fall shattered the keel, *which was as thin as an eggshell!* Bruised, he swam back to the *Sea Dog,* but reached out in vain for the life-lines which had been thrown to him. He felt the metal flank of his own ship with its smooth rivet-heads glide past his shoulder. For a moment the horrified face of the cook appeared to him on the medallion of a porthole. The whirling, cleaving screw approached and struck the helpless man between his neck and shoulders like the blow of an ax! . . .

His heart pumped blood through the wound. Euphoria of bleeding to death in water, like that of Petronius when he committed suicide by slashing his wrists in his bath. . . . Now this restless heart is running down. . . . Now it has stopped. . . . He knows it. His eyes no longer receive impressions. In vain his hands blindly try to find each other. Floating. . . . Quiet. . . . Only in his ears still the mighty throbbing of a factory. Then the slow trumpetting of horns in the forest. And now the softer throbbing of a single long-drawn-out cello tone quavering into silence. . . . Was this death . . . ? He has, however, still the consciousness of a remembered existence! What a Sinbad he had been! The Sinbad of eight adventurous voyages, shipwrecks and miraculous rescues. Sinbad for whom the back of a whale had served as an emergency raft; whom the bird Roc had borne through the skies to the valley of diamonds; who had burned out the eye of the cyclop with the spit upon which the latter had roasted his human victims; who had escaped from the tomb where he had been buried alive with his dead wife; who had been attacked by pirates; who had taken the precious gifts of the Calif Haroen-al-Rasjid to the king of the island of Serendib. . . . Sinbad whose life came to an end on his eighth voyage. . . . Physically, at least. His body now drifts somewhere between the surface of the water and the inaccessible bottom of the ocean like a Cartesian diver. And when it is washed ashore, the coroner who has been summoned will examine the lungs to ascertain whether he died from the wound or from the suffocation of drowning. But how little Sinbad bewails the fate of his bodily remains!

However, because of this memory of his life, this memory which perpetually renews itself as long as it continues to exist, Sinbad will not completely vanish into Nothingness! He must not let go of it, he must cling to it with the power which is: his soul!

How often and how fast did the memory of his life's history repeat itself? Time was immeasurable. . . . But one day this purely spiritual process was clouded by a physical sensation. The "ego" of Sinbad reached out like the caressing of water along limbs beginning to feel anew. And what a surprise it was to ascertain that his will, awakened from pure contemplation, could again direct motion! His hand touched his neck and shoulders: the wound was no longer there! Then his palms felt something like an obstacle, a wall. Was this the keel of the *Sea Dog* or of the THANATOS II? But the wall gave way elastically and then surrounded him! It was like the envelope of a balloon divided into squares by its meshes, under which he was going to be buried. Then a strange, powerful motion propelled him out of this confining embrace . . . till a hoarse, rasping, inhuman shriek and the merciless pricking of light through his shut eyelids made him faint! . . .

. . . Air which effervesces through his nose, throat and lungs like bubbles escaping from new wine. . . . At rest, and rocked as though by a ship on gentle waves or by a mother's arms. . . .

"Make sure, Sinbad, open your eyes! . . ." Bent over him he saw three similar, gigantic, earnest faces like those of Buddha statues in Indian forests. And between these figures there appeared a green canopy like that of a translucent forest-dome whose foliage has grown together to form a seamless surface! Was this the sky? A green sky? He feared color-blindness; then one no longer differentiated between red and green, he knew. But he saw the other colors too: the golden blond hair of the giantesses, the red of their lips, the blue of their eyes which bore witness with a friendly smile that they were not idols but living beings. His gaze swerved around their bodies, and then Sinbad discovered that all three of them were reposing upon the water with the scaly, mother-of-pearl colored tails of mermaids! . . .

Your Majesty must not, however, think that with this, my story, I desire to incite you to doubt the authenticity of that which the Koran admonishes us to believe concerning the here-after. But is it not plausible that for a person as eminent as Sin-bad, who had so many illustrious deeds to his credit, Allah should make an exception regarding his otherwise inexorable predestination and just for this once suspend the validity of the banal laws of nature? . . .

The sea-world into which Sinbad was thus reborn as a defective child—for his body ended in two limbs which remained unscaled and finless—extended in dimensions whose mathematical category is not exactly known to us, but which certainly are not those of Einstein's universe. And just as those who believe in relativity, in order to convey a plastic image of their finite cosmos, try "for the sake of convenience" to represent it in the form of "a slightly curved oval watch", thus I beseech Your Majesty to think of this other world as a gigantic phonograph record. Just as the lines engraved in ebony encircle the pole of the steel pivot, thus, concentric, gray, muddy waves rolled around an iceberg of rather unimpressive proportions which the Centaurs had reserved for their own use. The strangest thing of all was that on the emerald dome of heaven, which was apparently self-illuminating, there appeared neither sun nor moon nor stars. Thus there were no directions, no north, south, west or east and —as Sinbad thought at first—also no time.

Work was unknown to this nation of mermaids and tritons. They lived a life of indolence but not of ease, for they had to feed themselves upon that which floated around them: uprooted aquatic plants and a sort of foam-manna. Among them there existed no differences of race or class. A society of integral communism under a sort of "theocratic" supervision by the Centaurs, the "guardians of truth", who could be seen, bald and fat-bellied, walking about on the white shores of the iceberg, with the stately tread of their four horse's legs. To be sure, in the ever intermingling masses of water it would have been impossible to partition off any private property. Absolute brotherhood and equality prevailed, equality which even mirrored itself in their physical appearance, so that all seemed to be of the same age, and could not be distinguished from their "classmates". Tritons and mermaids also bore no personal family or Christian names, but solely and exclusively a number. An individual was nothing else than a "member of a class", "somebody 15" or "27", for example.

In this world where no change of day or night or of seasons occurred, where all atmospheric conditions remained unaltered, sickness was unknown. The tritons and mermaids lived their monotonous life together until the moment of collective death, which seemed to be prescribed by Nature herself. The "Great Whirlpool", an occurrence "which was attended by a certain solemnity", announced itself by causing the green of the sky to change to somber purple veined with innumerable lightnings. These lightnings, however, did not flash briefly, they glowed for a long time, somewhat like a rainbow in our world; so that the sky remained covered with a network of phosphorescent weed-roots, as it were. When the Centaurs signalled with their whelk-horns, the sea people formed a procession which set out from the iceberg to the foaming edge of an enormous whirlpool. The black water-ridges funneled toward a seething center from which a blue haze arose. Here the oldest generation, which was designated by the number 50, sang a last farewell song. Sinbad understood that they "willingly went to their deaths in order to furnish the basic material for waiting life, so that the eternal cycle should not be broken". It was truly a moving Ave morituri! . . . Then the streamer of those voluntarily dedicated to death once more swirled past the onlookers like the last spin of a carrousel, to the mournful blaring of the whelk-horns, in order, hand in hand, to entrust themselves to the revolving water-walls which dragged them along to the boiling deep. . . .

Thus it was death which in this world divided time and lent it rhythm. For all who were born between two "Great Whirlpools" belonged to the same "grade", and after the ceremony everybody's number was increased by one. Only the Centaurs appeared to be immortal and therefore they were also sexless.

After Sinbad, seated on the shoulder of a powerful triton, had for the first time witnessed this essential occurrence, he was old enough to be educated by the Centaurs, who taught school along the edge of the iceberg, where the knowledge-hungry tritons and mermaids were requested to repose.

What the teachers had to relate was probably not very important. The chief consideration was that "things were essentially as they appeared to be". There was no other reality besides that which was directly perceptible. The world was finite and limited to this body of water concentrically situated around the holy iceberg, the "axis of the universe, resting upon the fundament of the sedimentary stratification of primordial being, having sprung from permanent necessity." It was of primary importance to know this little sentence well by heart, for it constituted the core of the Centaurs' whole metaphysics. Matter was without origin and formed an "indispensable counterweight to Nothingness". In it existed two "principles of energetics": "Good", the centripetal force which bound all things together in perfect harmony around the iceberg, and "Evil", the centrifugal force which, were it ever to dominate, would cause the waters to flow asunder and the universe to revert to the "chaos of contradictions" and finally to "the volatilization of Nothingness!" . . .

And you are politely requested to accept this "truth" unhesitatingly and not to formulate any personal interpretations. This the tritons and mermaids did very willingly, so that the results of the final examinations were always uniformly gratifying.

About death: "resolution of the antinomy of freedom and determinsim", the Centaurs taught that, after the "Great Whirlpool", the bodies of the dead returned to "original plasma, the organic pulp where, after having enjoyed a bit of well-deserved rest, at a suitable moment, the biogenetic forces again began to ferment at the summons of the necessary replenishment of life". Between death and rebirth there were 50 stages, which exactly corresponded in duration to the period of 50 "years of life". "Because the complete evolutionary cycle necessarily had to present the mystic total of 100!" One argument was as good as another. Moreover, all this metaphysics struck Sinbad as being too simple to be true. This cyclic materialism naturally left no room for the existence of an individual soul, which would only have been a nuisance in this social community based upon "the firm linking together of the organized and conscious individuals to achieve the higher unity of the group, of the completed circle". And morals also were wholly in accord with integral communism. In order to prevent "the formation of a family-nucleus", the law decreed that sexual life should be promiscuous, but that this promiscuity should be restricted to members of the same "year". And as all tritons and mermaids of the same age were physically and literally alike as two scales—they constituted just so many identical X-es—this regulation was very natural and gave no cause for jealousy. Thus it was only sinful to fall in love with an older or younger mermaid and vice-versa. Many of them thought that Sinbad's monstrous figure was to be blamed on such a relationship. And he alone, besides his "year-number", bore the disgrace of being branded with his own name. The mermaids called him the "scaleless one" and his playmates "the smooth one" (with a pejorative connotation).

And it was perhaps this disapproval which prompted him to preach *his* truth to these children of nature. For, incessantly, while he was growing up, the memory of his former existence on earth remained with him. To anyone who wanted to listen, Sinbad told about our world. It was really a very difficult undertaking to convey a plastic picture of our nature and a conception of our life together to these primitive beings. It was, however, possible for example to compare a lotus flower to their tail-fins, a pine-cone to the scaled tritons' flanks, a crackling fire to the mermaids' red hair fluttering in the wind. At a pinch, he could even suggest the atmosphere of a stock-exchange session by comparing it to the din of the sea. But once the anatomic and other metaphors had been exhausted, not much remained for him to use except the suggestion of beautiful sounds, which permitted each triton and mermaid to form his own ideas. Such was the power of his words to stimulate the imagination! The principal thing, Sinbad correctly surmised, was to conjure up that mysterious aura which surrounds the names of all earthly objects, beings and happenings, and which bestows exquisite happiness upon each one who is readily receptive to it. It cannot be denied that Sinbad possessed certain poetic talents. In masterly fashion he celebrated the play of the sun, the azure sky and the infinitely variegated clouds in the quadrille of the seasons; the star-foaming nocturnal sky; the moon, at noon almost as invisible as a lump of ice thawing in water, but at night gleaming like the full-bellied silver sail of a miniature galleon; the good terrestrial globe wrapped in its domino of black night and white day. He celebrated the separation of land and water, and how, notwithstanding, the ocean penetrates to the heart of a continent through arteries of rivers, streams and brooks. He celebrated the animals: the horses, the cows: Centaurs who do not give one lessons, but serve mankind; seagulls tacking against the wind, swallows whose wing stroke resembles the fluttering of nervous lashes; cobwebs stringing raindrops to form a pearly design. Then the plants of the fields: willows standing up to their chins in the flood of a sea of grain; woods abounding in echoes. And technical marvels: stations at night like lumps of ore in which sparkle topazes, sapphires and rubies. . . .

Sinbad sang the melodious names of nations and cities, and above all else praised our mighty Bagdad. And then he eulogized man—dressed, creative, political man, harnessing the forces of nature to suit his own convenience. He glorified the blessed weariness after work, and the pleasures of relaxation: Friday's surprise in the form of changed motion picture programs. Man's existence was not as colorless and monotonous as that of the tritons, but was full of dramatic emotion. Man tasted happiness:

that of recovering from illness, of being promoted after the punctilious discharge of one's duties, of seeing one's honor restored after having been misjudged. He spoke of various professions: all of them useful and for one reason or another picturesque, besides presenting a thousand opportunities for practising civil, ethical, martial and sportsmanlike virtues. Then the dwellings: the humble cottage of the poor, upon whose whitewashed walls hang newspaper photos of the ruling dynasty, testifying to the loyalty of the occupants; as well as the palaces of the rich, which are decorated with the higher, abstract color-harmony of grouped geometric figures.

And thus Sinbad also got around to contrasting the magnificence of private property with the poverty of the integral communism of the tritons. The greatest joy was property: a little piece of rich earth, neatly surrounded by a fragrant hedge, a fence with gilt-tipped lances, or a wall topped with fragments of glass. And this ideal principle of private property was sublimely crowned with the accepted code of ethics. Love was concentrated upon one person—naturally without, for that reason, withholding well-intentioned sympathy from other fellow-beings— this one person was the faithful companion who always stood by one's side, whose heart and soul vibrated to all sorrow and joy, who presented one with real children which inherited one's features, character and fortune. And the symphony of human life ended in a death which was definitive, blissful rest, glorious quiet from which one would never again be roused by the "Eternal Return"! (Sinbad's own case merely constituted the one exception which was needed to prove the rule.)

It was especially the exaggerated individualism of earthly civilization which impressed these sea-people. This "levelling" equality for which we humans strive so hard (when we belong to those classes which possibly have more to win than to lose) was a common property of which the tritons were heartily sick. It was exactly this "old whirled" stagnation, this "lack of history" which made these people unhappy. For happiness is never what one possesses, but always "lies elsewhere." . . . Thus his listeners quite naturally began to ask the "Smooth One" to lead them to this ideal world. And Sinbad was incautious enough to agree to their request. And he promised them: the Earth, the Sun, the Stars and very emphatically the Moon in its various phases. Now the question may be raised whether this prospective journey to the earth should not be considered to be solely of allegoric significance, and whether Sinbad did not essentially mean that this

Realm was situated in the soul of each triton and mermaid; and thus that they "must develop their personalities", "build up feelings of self-esteem" and other fine ethical projects of this sort.

Though I incline toward abstract, even mythical explanations, I think I must believe that Sinbad was seriously planning an actual expedition. His idealism was always coupled with a generous dose of practical realism. And in his imagination, the brave adventurer probably already saw himself triumphantly swimming up the Euphrates at the head of this new exodus. It would not even surprise us if he had made all kinds of earthly plans. For example: to appear in vaudeville. "Sinbad and his Tritons!"; "The 20 Mermaids". To recreate the scene in a gigantic aquarium. Apotheosis: the fountains of Versailles with tableaus, and he himself as Roi-Soleil!

But how to find one's way on this unending expanse of water, under the green sky in which no constellations beaconed, and where no compass-rose blossomed? The poet, to be sure, contends:

> Ein guter Mensch in seinem dunklen Drange
> Ist sich des rechten Weges wohl bewusst;

but a reliable compass would have stood our new Moses in good stead. One thing was certain: he would depart from the iceberg, and whatever the future held in store, when the unknown presented actual problems to be solved, he was confident that he would not be at a loss.

But now the Centaurs still had to have their say in the matter! . . . As long as the "Smooth One" had limited himself to reciting his little poems about this mythical Utopia, they had bothered very little about him. The Centaurs attributed all these "original, romantic brain-waves" to his physical defects. Apropos of which one coined the phrase: finless—brainless. But when they noticed the fanatic following the prophet was attracting and heard of the exodus which had been planned, their consternation was great! This was understandable: it is never pleasant for the dignitaries of a cult to witness the defection of their followers. And now they were threatened by the danger that thousands of tritons and mermaids would leave the holy iceberg to follow this monster to a destruction which had nothing to do with the "Great Whirlpool".

Their resolution was quickly made. In vigorous formation, the Centaurs plunged into the water, swam toward the rebellion, kicked the gathering apart with their hard hoofs, took the leader prisoner and dragged him along to the iceberg. There he would be tried for his false teachings.

The prosecution hurled all sorts of sophisms at the deformed feet of this "rebel", this "adventurer": that he incorporated "the evil centrifugal principle, and that apparently being afraid of the 'Great Whirlpool,' he wanted to slip away along the tangent from the cycle of Eternal Return"; that he was ruining the young people by preaching "an immoral and unnatural monogamy" which, if it were carried out, would lead to the fatal destruction of all solidarity and would cause the ring of the communistic structure of society to burst asunder into egoistic smithereens!

The Centaurs, however, were magnanimous. They would forgive him all these blasphemies if he were willing solemnly to declare that this heresy, these "disastrous divagations in every sense of the word" about that other Earthly world were nothing more than a figment of the brain, a bit of tritonic deceit which he had invented just to "pass the time away". But above all, he must publicly avow that the iceberg indubitably was the "axis of the universe, resting upon the fundament of the sedimentary stratification of primordial being, having sprung from permanent necessity!"

There stood the accused, both of his legs firmly planted in the truth of his original human existence! He could not do otherwise than remain faithful to his memories! . . .

Sinbad viewed his judges with a melancholy smile. His answer would be succinct. With cold condemnation and the steely emphasis of conscious self-esteem he raised his voice:

"I am not a member of your gang! I am not number so-and-so! I am Sinbad the sailor from Bagdad, and I have experienced more during my eight individualistic voyages than you millions of sleepyheads in your poor, boringly organized community! In no way do I disavow *my* truth. My Earth, with all its bright colors and perfumes unknown to you, revolves in dimensions different from yours. And concerning your 'sedimentary stratification of primordial being' I permit myself, worthy Centaurs, by way of explanation, to say this: The foundations of your famous iceberg, at the very most, extend downward only nine times as far as that part which protrudes above the surface of the sea! I can demonstrate this to you by the laws of physics. A stupid fish can swim under it. And far from being the 'immovable pole of the universe', it is nothing but a rough-hewn, unwieldy mass which floats around trusting to luck. . . ."

Nobody will be surprised to hear that condemnation followed upon such a tactless defense. One can certainly remain objective, can one not, toward all ideologies; but to be offended regarding one's holiest convictions, to be positively insulted is too much even for the most impartial judge! The sentence was as follows: that the guilty one be drawn and quartered. Besides "public disgrace"—and this penalty would have been much too light for such a great crime—one knew no other punishments there.

Four of the strongest Centaurs were tied to Sinbad's wrists and ankles. A whelk-horn trumpeted the signal. The monstrous executioners pulled this rebellious, adventurous body to pieces, dragged its bleeding limbs across the white surface of the iceberg, painting a red cross which perhaps corresponded to the cardinal points of our compass. But at the spot of his execution, Sinbad's warm-blooded heart thawed itself a shaft through the ice, and heavily freighted with its golden cargo of rich memories, it sank to the sediment of eternity.

Translated by JOSEPHINE VAN AS

PART VII

BETWEEN THE TWO WARS

J. Slauerhoff

LARRIOS

WAS IT BY CHANCE THAT I MET YOU, UNEXPECTEDLY, IN PLACES AS far apart as the world is wide? Why should I find you again and again where I must lose you, hopelessly, each time? I cannot believe it was fate, for I never could share your lot, scarcely touch it; nor have I lived long enough to learn whether I changed it in the least.

Was it by chance? What evil destiny caused me to find you four times, under strange circumstances and, almost at once, to lose you again?

It began long ago. Europe was not yet slowly dying, but the land through which I traveled was even then dead. The extremities of a diseased body may begin to mummify while the body lives on in apparent health. I passed over hot, hard plains, as the slopes fell inertly away, where few houses stood and few cattle grazed; where many stones were strewn and the points of rocks stuck out from the soil like knuckles through dry skin. I had left a ship in one of the southern ports, because the food on board was even more rotten than the scoundrelly crew. I hoped to find another in Bordeaux, a better one if possible. First afoot, then by freight train, I came from the southern heat over the sharp, cold ridge of the Sierra Nevada and then downward to the warm plateau and in three days reached Granada. I slept in a park, not venturing my rags or my jaded spirits in the princely Alhambra; but in the early morning I took a train for Madrid and was cooped up for almost three days in a third-class compartment where soldiers slept on the benches, or in blankets on the filthy floor, already exhausted from I know not what expedition against a *pronunciamento* in the South. Neither did I venture into the Plaza de Toros in Madrid, though it was Sunday. I knew indeed that the sight of blood would be unbearable to me. I hurried nervously through the quiet, deserted city and took the train for the North, and in that wandering, strange condition I reached the point of sleeplessness wherein one no longer knows whether one is hungry or revolted by food, exhausted or capable of going much further. With an army in that state it is possible to win battles, or suddenly to lose everything in a panic because of one soldier who has dropped his weapons. At last I slept through every stop, through every station and was finally awakened by a shuddering halt. It was Burgos. The squat cathedral stood in the distance amidst a group of low, gray houses. The end of the long train was halting before a row of city houses of that ugly, barrack-like structure to be found everywhere, even in dead Spain. I turned away and closed my eyes. The train stopped for a long while and was finally set into motion with a jerk, and my heart seemed to stand still in I know not what sudden despair at this departure. What could there be in this city where I had never been, of which I knew nothing but that there was an old cathedral where Columbus lay buried?

I sprang to the window and saw nothing but long verandas of red brick houses, divided by partitions from ground to roof into rows of hutches. I was about to turn aside. Then you appeared on one of the verandas of the last house. Then it began. You leaned over the unpainted balustrade. At first you did not look up while I in one glance took you in from top to toe, from skin to your very core, to myself. Yet you looked like so many Spanish women, a mantilla around your slim shoulders, but betrayed in your attitude the possibility of languorous, graceful motion and, of course, there was a red flower in the all too gleaming hair. I could not see your eyes but guessed their color and expression from your whole appearance. When you lifted them just before the now swiftly passing of the train, a few yards off from the window, I saw that they were full of disturbance, full of a suffering that has endured for centuries, never yielding to pain and subjection but grown great in opposition; and a something indescribable seemed to wait in readiness to become proud and irresistible, as if the long abasement was undergone voluntarily through a strange delight in self-probation.

So you looked up at me, and I forgot everything, even that I was being dragged by. Then I awakened to the torture that overtakes anyone suddenly confronted with a vital decision, which, delayed for a moment, can never be taken again and, taken at once, is irrevocable. This is the true death struggle, though in the midst of life; compared to it the later death is a painless drifting-away; and I stood still and lost you, Larrios. I left you alone among enemies, and perhaps your endurance had come to an end just at that moment, and you fell a prey to them. I lived your life condensed into a moment and suffered and, motionless, was carried on. Then I leaped up and should, perhaps, have jumped but at that instant you placed one quiet hand over your dark brows and waved to me with the other. I could not be mistaken. I was the only one who hung so far out of the moving train, and I knew: you wanted to see me again and called me invitingly to you. Now, no desperate leap; in Vittoria I could get out and walk back, or, if need be, ride the rails; but on the way my old doubts and my doubting self overtook me. Was she any different from the many in this land, pious, stupid, beautiful, who kneel in the dark cathedrals with the same absent devotion whether they be much tried women or much used whores? And if she held a secret within her would she be aware of it herself, living in a trance from which no awakening was possible? Would she not laugh in embarrassment if someone came to her saying:

"Look, my feet are sore: I've walked from Vittoria to Burgos for you."

"Why walked?"

"Because I had no money and wanted to see you again."

"Why want to see me again if you have no money to pay me?"

Why that gesture? Could it have been mere habit? But to one who would never return? I listened to a conversation going on in the train among salesmen who traveled weekly between Bordeaux and Madrid. I did not want to think and I could not sleep. I was staring vacantly out over the arid plains when, suddenly as it grew dark and threatened rain, I saw another old cathedral. It stood alone, under a shadow that narrowed and widened with the sun, like ebb and flood, and never wholly lifted. Flowers stood shaking in the wind, red petals atremble, fluttering against the dark, damp stone. And then I shut my eyes. In Vittoria I got out, but staggered before I was off the platform, dizzy with lack of food. I had no money, the ticket to Bordeaux was my only earthly possession. Larrios, forgive my hesitation, not my suspicions, though they came from the life I led more than from myself; forgive me for going further, for further deserting you. I should only have reached you dying. In Bordeaux I might find a ship, get well again, wait and seek you out from the next port. I did get a ship, but it had orders for Seattle, a long way off—but I thought then that death was still further.

Then came the second time. After ten months of constant shifting from ship to ship I reached Santander and could take a train to Burgos. I walked its streets for days, sat for hours in the cathedrals, visited all the markets, watched the exodus from factories and caught many a mocking word, and in the evenings I tramped the sparsely lit streets; but it became clear to me one evening that I should not find you, for who has found by searching? I could stay no longer in Burgos, but neither could I leave Spain. It was as though in that land I felt myself with you. I turned southward and, one evening, after a long trek over the mountains, I came to the dried bed of a river that by way of old Moorish Malaga flows to the sea. I saw it lying between two hills flecked with the red of sunset; its blocks of houses dingy white with black spots of abandoned ground between them.

At that moment it began to rain. The yellow, uneven bed filled slowly with water that first colored the bottom gray and then began to stream through the numerous gullies. Mule trains that had at first followed the soft river bottom climbed up and struggled on over the stony path on the bank. On their sunken backs the pack animals bore through the melancholy evening the fatigue of the long day. Going faster, I was not able to pass them. When I sat down somewhere on a hayrick the drivers went into an *osteria,* and when I got up they had emptied their glasses and went on, right before me. So, at the end of this dreary procession, I approached the city. It had begun to rain harder. The river now foamed over its full width and swept dry shrubs under the bridges. That day I had had nothing but stale bread, not daring to take a glass of wine which afterwards makes walking so heavy. I was sweating and soaked with rain, my clothing stuck to my skin, and I was seized with a gray sadness that only the wanderer knows when he comes at evening into a city never before visited, where the lights and quiet of evening glow as things apart from him. The suburb began to spread out: low, dark houses with broken windows. The caravan spread itself out on a dark square, and suddenly I was alone and I missed that company at first undesired. I was not thinking of you then. I was cursing myself for trailing out here instead of being on some ship in the offing. I leaned against a bridge. Out of a narrow, dark side street a figure came toward the bank, skirts lifted. Under the umbrella a pale face appeared, a lily with a large, dark calyx hanging over it. She walked with a light step as if released after a hard day's work. Then she came up to me, and I saw that it was you for whom I had almost stopped searching, and with a wonderful, pitying gesture you held the umbrella over both our heads and touched my shivering body with your own. Wordless, I went with you, not knowing what to say. I had waited too long, thought too

much. At last with gentle force I wanted to make you take a glass
of wine in a brightly lit café. But you laughed and took my sleeve
and wrung the water from it and pulled me along. We went
through numerous alleys and up many steps to a small room with
two narrow windows; beyond them, the shallow dusk. There you
lit a lamp that shone on a brown statuette of the Virgin; and I
saw your room: a bed, a table and on it a sewing machine; on the
wall two banal paintings, and on a shelf some crockery, that was
all. Even the Japanese girls who squat, sleep, make up, eat and
give themselves to their clients on one and the same mat, have
more. They have their vase with its branch and a flower curving
outward, a screen with its flight of storks, a graceful fan.

You did not make ready at once, as do they who must earn—
the English who say in harsh voices: "Have you short time"—or
the Japanese who save assiduously for their dowries; and the
Spanish factories also pay far too little. You helped me out of my
leaden clothing and wrapped me in a rough woolen cloak. Did a
monk leave his habit, together with his faith, here with you? In
any case it was warm. For a long while I lay shivering under the
covers while you finished some work on the machine and knelt
before the statuette and then sang in a soft monotone so that,
resting, I kept awake. It was late when you undressed and came
to me. I did not ask much of your love, I was soon asleep, and
when the morning dawned grayish red over the wall, the place
at my side was empty. What was I to do? To spend all day there
was impossible. With all that I still had to say, stored up for
years, it was too much for me. I had only asked:

"Did you know in Burgos that I would come back?"

And you: "Yes, but not here."

I could not hold out any longer, ran through a few streets, and
discovered in a small, noisy square that I had lost my way. From
which street had I come? It struck me with a horrible shock:
found and instantly lost again—and I wandered on in the maze
of narrow streets. Then I returned to the river and tried to find
my way from there, climbed stairs and went down them, not
even knowing whether your room was on the fourth floor or the
fifth; I knocked on many a door and was driven away. At noon
I climbed the blazing Alcazador hoping to recognize from the
height what I could not discover below. I sat there on a pile of
ruins and lost consciousness. I thought I saw a woman with black
hair and a red flower lean from a window and I started up, but
a heavy weight on my shoulder pressed me down. Gypsies stood
all around me, and a girl had set a heavy jar on my shoulder;

they all laughed, but the girl saw the despair in my eyes and lifted the jar from my shoulder to my lips. That evening I walked the streets for hours. Did I hope to meet you, or some other with whom I could forget you? You know how despair confounds all things—hate and love.

I stumbled, exhausted into a public house in some byway and drank to benumb myself; my head sank to the table; a hard slap on the back roused me to face a heavy, potbellied fellow with a flabby red neck and watery eyes.

"What the hell do you want?"

"A man: my quartermaster deserted."

"Where are you going?"

"Everywhere, my ship is a good old tramp."

Ah, Larrios, since I could not find you in Malaga again, why not then everywhere? I agreed, received thirty pesetas down and bought a shabby outfit, and that same night I lay in a pitching forecastle among other offscourings of the sea.

The *Glenmore* was not a bad ship. While on most the hammock is the only bed and must be rolled up at break of day, here we had each a bunk to take refuge in. Three tiers of them, in three rows along the walls of the forecastle, but you could cut off your own by means of a curtain and be alone and unwatched. There was room on the wall for a few photos or prints; everyone seemed to find that most beautiful which he had never seen. A Chinese had adorned his wall with a Dutch mill and a girl from Marken; the boatswain, a Norwegian, lay staring at a geisha, her hair dressed high, with Fiji in the background. My wall remained empty: whose picture should I hang there? I wanted you alone, Larrios, before my eyes and I always saw your face there, every feature, and with my knife I began to cut lines as I lay sleepless in the berth; gradually they began to take shape. The wood lost color and one morning in the early light I clearly saw your face. Perhaps I alone could see it—but I saw it. Only in full light was it obscured again. Yet I was afraid that someone else might see it and when, in an old *London News,* I came across a head that resembled yours a little, I hung that over it so that the place was covered, but I could see you by pushing the picture aside. The day came when the *Glenmore,* after a bad collision, was laid up and we were paid off. That happened in Swansea. We waited in the seaman's house for another ship. The watchman stopped me at first but finally let me by on the mumbled excuse of something forgotten and the shilling I gave him. There in the night, on that dead ship, I cut you from the wall and took

you with me. Two weeks later I managed to become fourth officer on the *Elefanta,* bound for the East and to stay there. I
shared a cabin with the third officer. You lay in a drawer, your
double stood on the table. I saw you only when I came down
from my watch but you had changed, your face seemed more
suffering. It saddened me to see. For a long while I did not look
at it. I was almost never alone. I would have liked your picture
tattooed on my breast to keep you with me always, but who could
do that? I myself branded your name in the flesh under my arm.
I didn't know, didn't hope that you might one day read it yourself. Years passed by in sailing up and down the coast of China.

We lay in Shanghai one time, at the Upper Wharf, two hours
from the city by steam launch that left four times per day. The
very first night we got rid of our advance pay in Russian drinking places and, for the rest, stayed aboard. It was winter, the
cabins were badly heated, at nine-thirty lights were out. Dinner
was eaten in haste and shivering in the chill mess room. Nights
were spent alone in the berth.

Each one lived alone in his cabin as in a cell. No one played
cards. Each drank, secretly, the amount of gin necessary to keep
him going. The amounts varied greatly. I did not need much, I
merely stared at a piece of wood.

One evening, about ten minutes before lights out, an old ship-
mate of the *Glenmore* came to look me up. We grumbled and
complained to each other as seamen do when they visit neighboring ships in port: about the cold, the poor food, the plundering
that awaits us the moment we set foot on shore. There is a certain comfort in this complaining. You hear that it is no better, if
not worse, on other ships. Then the lights blinked their warning,
on and off, another five minutes. Jorgen proposed to go ashore
again. He knew a place in the Chinese town where it was cheap,
yet fairly honest. It was tempting, now that the deathly still
darkness of the ship threatened, to go to a house with lights,
though it was only false, red light. But I knew what the outcome
would be, I had not a cent, and refused. Jorgen offered a loan,
but I held out stubbornly. While talking, he picked up the
London News picture.

"Don't you want to see Dolly again, she came from the St.
George and is there now?"

What was that? I seized my glass, emptied it and collapsed;
and when I came to it seemed to me that I had been gone for
years. But Jorgen still sat there with the picture in his claws and
repeated:

"It is, positively it is."

I tried to laugh: "That was cut out of a magazine a year or more ago, a countess, or something, I think."

"That may be. You know they will use a dancing girl with an attractive face if they can't get a picture of the countess herself. That's probably why these girls all call themselves baroness or countess. Well, a dancing girl can just as well become a sing-song girl. It is Dolly, she used to be in the St. George and is there now," repeated Jorgen stubbornly. "All right, maybe it isn't; let's not go."

But now I had to know. I pulled the woodcut out of the drawer. It was the first time I let anyone else see you. With that the light went out, and then, by the light of a match, it appeared again more clearly than in the full light. Jorgen stood up to stare. He was long silent; then: "The very image, positively she."

I was up the steps, Jorgen after me.

"Wait quietly below, it will be an hour before the last launch goes. A sampan would never make it with this tide."

But I had already called one, the only one that still lay under the landing bridge in the eddying water, and he demanded a dollar for the trip over. The old ferryman sculled us slowly across the broad stream, damp snow whirled into the hutch. Between whiles the lamp threw a fitful gleam on the yellow water. We drifted way down and came in three docks below the city.

Half an hour's walk; a half hour in the tram; a rickshaw through the concessions, and a chair through the Chinese town. It took hours. I suffered years. One behind the other we went through the alleys in the swishing chairs, to the grunts of the bearers and the screaming of the crowds that swarmed out of the houses into the streets. And all the way I asked myself: Could it be you? And would we cross the bridge? No, in God's name, not that.

But we crossed the bridge.

(White women, once in a house across the bridge, never return to European ground except to be buried there.)

We crossed the zigzag bridge, and Jorgen hurried the coolies. Through one or two more crooked, filthy alleys we came to a dark little square, unlighted but for a dull red transom in a blind wall. Beneath it was a low door, unpainted, the lettering half obliterated. The snow beat against the wall and slowly buried the beggars that crouched there with hands thrust out toward the late-comers.

We pushed in at the door. A gray-haired boy dozed on a chair.

Up four steep steps. A cold parlor, devilishly poor. On the rickety table was an album. Like one possessed I flung through the pages. One, two, three, twenty, thirty; you were not there.

"What's wrong?" cried Jorgen, seeing me slump down in my chair. Yes, what? I came to again. Was I sorry or glad that you were not there? Oh, Larrios, sorry; I wanted to find you and had waited for years. What difference could it make, whatever the place might be?

"She is not among them," I said, hoarsely.

"Just hand me that book," said Jorgen. "Here, you passed it by. There she is, look."

Then I had to find you! My hand shook over thirty-nine: "Here, this one"; and the old boy shuffled off.

We waited some time. Now and again I started up to run away, only to sink back in my chair. Jorgen saw my uneasiness. He said anxiously: "If only she is free. She has numerous clients. And it's the Chinese New Year."

My hand went to my right pocket.

"Here, give me that thing!" A struggle followed, and the boy came down. "Number thirty-nine can do."

I made an effort to go up, but could not get past the door. Jorgen helped me, hushing me, not understanding at all.

"Don't be a fool. Take it easy. I'll come for you in an hour."

I pushed open a door, stumbled over a screen, and there you lay, Larrios, in a kimono which you threw open as I came in.

I pulled it close and sat beside you, caressing your blue-black hair, muttering your name. Possibly you had forgotten your name and thought me drunk, so you sat and stared. Then I said: "Larrios, Burgos, Malaga . . ." but you began to laugh and recite a list of places: "Marseilles, Port Said, Colombo. Debt, sickness, work." Then again that hard, affected laugh. But I did not laugh. You nudged me. Still I sat there. Then came tears, a long fit of weeping. What for? Were you offended—in your calling, Larrios? I must almost believe it, because when I started to undress your face cleared. Did you think that I would use and then desert you? Why should I first have taken so much trouble to distress you?

It was very difficult. But it was still more difficult to make you understand that you must now take my clothes, my money, and leave. Take passage and wait for me in Manila. There you would be safe under American government. And when finally you understood and agreed, more amazed than ever I saw any other creature, then you thought I should still take you and I believe that you were angry and abashed that I would not, that

I hurried you on to dress, nor would you go without the solemn promise that I should have you, without cost, for a year in Manila. A thought did come over me that you had less in common with the old Larrios than the crude woodcut picture I had made of you. But I would find you again, Larrios, even if I had to do as you asked. A year—for nothing—I would teach you, gradually, to love again. I would surely unearth you again. How was it possible for a man to be so hopeful after eight years of wandering after a woman, after eight years of that life!

You were nearly ready and I was about to put on your kimono when there was a knock. You shrank back and seized my arm: "Don't open, don't open it."

Oh, Larrios, it was nothing; stranger things happen than this game of exchanging clothes. But you were afraid, afraid that you might not get away. I was glad of your fear; forgive me.

It was Jorgen who came to see what was keeping me.

He took it in at a glance, but was worried about me.

But I said: "I'll get out of it all right, go away quickly. Leave me your overcoat, Jorgen."

And they went. Such was the third time: a hurried, harried hour. The first was a glimpse from a train; the second, a night of exhausted sleep. And on these three meetings hung my wretched life like a broken bridge on unsound piles. Years long. I lay on that divan full of imaginings: now Jorgen is paying while she goes out ahead; now they are getting into chairs; now they are out of the Chinese district, thank God.

The door opened. An Irish sailor was let in. He did not betray me. A splendid joke, he called it, when I gave him some explanation, and he went on a door further.

But almost immediately afterwards came a Chinaman who found it no joke and raised a row, with so much noise that it brought the keeper and two servants to find me there. In place of a lotus of the house, an offscouring of the sea. The two servants caught me by the neck and the elbows. The keeper went out and returned with two coolies who carried bamboos, a brazier and tongs. Glowing coals were put into the brazier. Me, they bound. The keeper said I was under Chinese law here. He heated the tongs himself. I determined not to utter a sound, but when the tongs struck my flesh I let out a scream, repressed it for a moment but could not hold out, could not keep my jaws together.

Then the door was kicked open, the Irishman, two other white men and all the women of the house pressed in. One, two slashes with a knife and I was free. The Irishman shoved me out of the door, the keeper and his helpers were jammed in by the press of women. Behind us we heard: "Banzaai, evviva, hurrah!" The outer door slammed, the Irishman had the idea to shove in front of it a heavy stone pulled down from the wall. We ran on, thrusting coolies aside, turning all the corners that we could. Behind us alarm gongs sounded; we tore on amid grinning, yellow faces and swinging lanterns. There seemed to be no end. Would we ever get out of it? The whole Chinese city was aroused for an hour. But we had to get out of it. We stood still behind a dunghill, no one was there as yet. Morning began to dawn. Three rickshaws came along, they had unloaded late callers at one of the houses. When they saw us they hurried over and dropped the bars at our feet. Thank God, they knew nothing of the hunt.

"To the Bund," the Irishman ordered the leader, and in an incredibly short time, through a couple of alleys, we were out of the gate and riding up the Avenue Edward, another world.

Where was I to find Jorgen? First of all I had to go into a pub with the Irishman for a drink, a drink to this mad joke, this narrow escape. Finally he had enough, half choked between laughter and whiskey. I saw him to his launch, my rescuer whom I shall never lay eyes on again.

Now to find Jorgen. Where would he wait for me? All the next day I strode up and down The Bund, resting now and then in a Russian tea-house in the narrow wayside park where the flotsam of the great city and of the ships is gathered: beachcombers, starved Russians, prostitutes who can no longer find work, and rickshaw coolies who can no longer run.

There I sat and waited. Would Jorgen never come along? "Larrios is off, out of it," I mumbled, to keep up my courage. Toward midnight I got up and went with a sudden certainty to the Alcazar to find him. He was there, sitting in a corner with other Norwegians. He saw me, got up and, pushing me into a chair, shoved a glass across to me. I drank. He said something to the others. They laughed and nodded approvingly. Finally I plucked up courage:

"Where did you leave her?"

Jorgen grinned: "At first she didn't want to go. But she's on board already. The *Susanna.* I know the captain. She has a good cabin. Sixty dollars. She may have to pay something more."

Now, for the first time, I remembered that she would have been fairly safe in European Shanghai. Why the mad haste? Now we are parted again. Why? I had wanted to get her away, far away from there.

Jorgen stared at me. "Cheerio, in a few days she will be among her countrymen. That's where you want her to be, she must surely have someone there."

How good it was to hear Jorgen say that! For now I knew why I wanted it. As long as she remained in Shanghai she was a prostitute. In Manila she would once more be a Spanish woman from Burgos, from Malaga.

"Do you know of any ship going that way, Jorgen?" I asked. Just as the first time, I had no money left with which to follow you. I gave it all to pay for your ticket.

Jorgen stared into his glass. Finally: "The *Long Shan* touches there sometimes, I don't know of any other."

I returned to my ship in the dark and kept the sampan waiting. In a few minutes my chest was packed. I gave the watchman a dollar, slept that night on Broadway, signed up on the *Long Shan* as quartermaster.

At noon we sailed out of the Yang-Tse. I stood on the deck, passed by the *Glenmore* with Jorgen on board, the *Elefanta* still lying in the harbor, paintless, half dismantled. I saw no one; no one saw me, standing on the deck of the *Long Shan,* sailing out the river to meet Larrios. We passed the cruisers lying in midstream: the Spanish, a small and dirty ship, with the flag at halfmast. It saddened me. Why?

Larrios, we sail to meet again. It will be months before we come into Manila. We did touch at Cebu, Mindanao, never at Manila, never at Luzon at all, or I should have attempted a trek overland from any port. Why was there never a cargo for Manila? Once we were under way but struck a typhoon, had to make shelter, and the load was dumped overboard.

And then I gave it up and became what I had never in my life been, a passenger, deck passenger at that, and sat for three days among Chinese and Filipinos on a hatch cover, staring toward Manila like a hadji toward Mecca. It stank, the food was revolting, the crew looked with contempt upon me sitting there. What did that matter? In my belt I carried one hundred dollars, which I would rather have given to Larrios than to some ship company. And as we sailed into the bay I felt like the governor, like Columbus.

Larrios, I had my own ideas of where to find you. Live you must; but I took it for granted that you would not live in the same way, on my account, on account of your wonderful escape. What remained? You could not sew here and you would have forgotten how. Tap at a machine, or sit behind a desk—you could not do that, either. What else is there for a girl who has no one and will not give herself to everyone? I should find you on the dance floor, of that I was firmly convinced.

I started with Santa Anna, where there is a floor for three hundred couples at a time. For three nights I sat there behind whiskey. But I never saw you among the Filipinos who hold their mantillas while dancing, their arms, in wide sleeves, turned out from their bodies.

I sought further, in more and more obscure places, where it was more international.

During the day I rambled in the Intramuros and took shelter from the glaring light in the gray dusk of the cathedrals.

One Friday, after walking about for a long while, I went into the San Pedro to rest in a corner. And there, in the distance, in the tinted light near an altar I saw you kneeling close to a pillar and hastened along to embrace you, disregarding church and veil. But I looked into the frightened face of a stranger and fled from the cavernous church as if I had seen a ghost. For days I dared not enter a church; fortunately there are streets so narrow that a shadow hangs over them almost all day. The Intramuros is large, but I passed through the same streets as often as ten times. What else did I seek? Were you, all this long while, shut up here in some place from which I could not easily get you out? The days went by. I tramped the streets, muttering, demented, stared after, feeling my way with a stick. Or I lay against the side of a wharf, dozing, among beggars covered with ulcers that drew the flies, and discharged sailors who would never get another ship. Had I come to that? I did not know, would not try any more. Here I should stay, even if I rotted. At night I slept between bags of tobacco or rice—I don't know. Out of pity the coolies let me lie there.

One morning, hustled out early, I wandered through Manila in the early dawn toward that section of low hills where are villas, not seeing them, my eyes bent upon the ground, following the path. At a turn of the road I looked up to see a green terrace with beautiful flower beds, a pink and white house against the blue sky. I stood staring at it.

After a while some dogs barked. Had they been set upon me? No, they were held on leash by a woman, slender, in a dark dress, toying with the whip in her hand; in attitude and face, you.

It was almost fearfully quiet: we, in the open morning, the grass between us, the blue sky overhead. No train rushing me onward, no ship to which I belonged, no house imprisoning you.

I had no need to hurry. This is the one moment, the place to which I have come over almost all the seas.

Slowly I went up the path, you remained standing above, looking elsewhere, not at me. Did you not recognize me, Larrios? But we were always masked!

You were about to turn back to the house but a gesture from me as I advanced stopped you. You let the dogs go, but they hardly stirred. One lay down immediately, the other padded around you. But at the moment I came close enough to see your eyes, you were even further away from me than when I followed you from sea to sea.

"Larrios, don't you know me any more?"

"Don't you see that I have changed, that things are . . ."

"You had changed every time. What is there in that? I expected that. Let me rest." And I wanted to come near her. Yet I had seen her eyes!

She took a step back.

"Don't you understand, you can't stay here like that."

I saw: in that house was another owner, more powerful than the poor Chinese keeper; he let her move about freely.

"Come back this evening, then I will return the passage money to you, get dressed, come back, perhaps . . ."

In two minutes it was over, with a few words Larrios died to me. Larrios who had lived in me for years. How can one outlive it, passing so swiftly? Truly, I had aged all those years as I went down the hill again. She, behind me, called out something more, but it was all over. I did not look back again.

I do not have to take my life. If tonight or a few nights later I lie in the forecastle of some nameless ship, a bit of filth amidst more filth, and the night and the sea surround the ship, is it not just the same, above all if I never land again, but lie under low beams, in a narrow bunk, mouldering wood at my head and feet, and above me, is not that the same thing as . . . ?

And if, the first night out, I bind a stone to a piece of wood that has been a part of me for years and let it fall from the half-deck—one, two, three, forever—is not that just the same thing as a rope for my neck or a bar of iron for my feet?

Let everything stay the same. What, actually, has been changed?

Translated by WILHELMINA C. NIEWENHOUS

H. Marsman

TERESA IMMACULATA

ON THE SECOND DAY OF MY STAY IN ROME I WAS ALREADY SPENDING the evening with Serra. I had first met him half a year before in a little village on the Lago di Garda. He was a lawyer just as I, but fortunately this did not remain our sole point of contact; a mutual predilection for the writings of Burckhardt supplied us with material for more than three days of endless conversation. Serra was older than I; I took him to be about fifty, a celibate possessed of a very un-Italian amount of circumspection. Even his gait was a bit dragging; he was heavy, his figure seemed to have sagged a trifle, and the weary monotone in which he spoke made one surmise that life had spared him very little.

As I entered, he led me through his study, which appeared to be higher and lighter than I had expected, to a balcony that looked down upon neglected gardens with ghostly cypresses, motionless and black in the autumn night. To reach Serra's house, I had had to climb the long flight of steps at the Piazza di Spagna and, as I entered his door, I reflected that he must enjoy a wide view of Rome from his dwelling. But his study and the balcony lay at the rear. On the far side of the gardens rose the dusky façades of supposedly empty palaces.

Serra guessed my thoughts.

"This Rome no longer exists," he said in his dragging voice; "and of what avail is impressive architecture when life is continually getting poorer and more oppressive, when there are no more people to live in the palaces."

I knew this tune. In Torri we had already more than sufficiently ascertained our points of view regarding the so-called decline of the times; to his romantic pessimism, my hope for the future had stubbornly replied with perspectives that had merely elicited a compassionate smile from him. The game of being able automatically to foretell his reactions had soon made me impatient, and I did not feel like spoiling our reunion. What prompted Serra to touch upon this subject again? I examined him more closely. He seemed to have grown older and wearier since the spring, and again I felt my youthful resilience to be almost inconsiderate. He leaned over the railing of the balcony and stared out into the night.

After a moment he spoke.

"Tomorrow I have a difficult case to plead. It is an extraordinary case, which, alas, took a fateful turn several days ago, so that I expect a judgment that, to say the least, will be ruinous for my client."

It was the first time that legal matters had been alluded to between Serra and myself. So this was the question that even after my arrival had been occupying his thoughts! I begged him to tell me about the case. He continued immediately, as though he were rehearsing it all for his own benefit point by point.

"As to the facts of the case, they are very simple, and juridically too the case is of little interest, but morally it is of the greatest importance, of the very greatest importance.

"My client is a boy of not yet twenty-five, a lad of the people. He comes from a stonemason's in Rome, better say, in Trastevere. When he was three or four years old his parents died and he was brought up by his uncle, a smith, in Amalfi. His little sister, two years younger than he, stayed with her grandmother in Rome. I have received the impression that the boy spent an untroubled youth with his foster-parents. His uncle allowed him much free time and plenty of pocket-money. He fished and swam, rowed to Capri in calm weather, had his own garden on the hill, was a choirboy at the wonderful Norman cathedral of Amalfi and read whatever he could. But a special treat was always an excursion by way of Salerno to Paestum, where for hours he would in solitude enjoy the temples. I find him very appealing, a reflective and at the same time a generous nature, but with the scholastic obstinacy of the self-taught, who will not budge an inch in discussion and yet are receptive to every aspect of life."

"A fervent Catholic?"

"No, not fervent, but Catholic through and through, despite many doubts and in such an harmonious way that one is almost tempted to believe in the famous thesis that man is Christian by nature. And Gino, as the boy is called, really has still something of the fusion of heathen and Christian elements, such as one finds on the old murals of Orpheus and the lamb in the catacombs. Moreover, in his culture also he has completely remained the boy from Amalfi, simple and rustic.

"The strangest thing about him is his eyes, which usually search the world attentively, but sometimes in the course of a conversation become of a sudden defenceless, though if possible still superior, and his gaze turns inward to escape to that irrational terrain which he certainly feels to be quicksand, but which nevertheless serves him as a last refuge. His voice has a very subdued quality, and his movements are so controlled that they possess an almost feminine coquettishness, yet at times they shift suddenly to an overburdened baroque. Nevertheless, if I did not know more about him, I should look upon him as a well-balanced person; but life has once again taught me how prone to change such an equilibrium is. And who knows with how much trouble he acquired it, with how much exertion of his stubborn will? For years he remained master of himself in this way, by modulating his passions and even suppressing them, still they unexpectedly revenged themselves upon this beautiful training and simply burned all the decrees of his will like scraps of paper. What can we do," he sighed in conclusion, "against the animal that we are?"

"Little," I said tersely. (Why did he always employ these generalizations?)

Serra was silent for a moment: disapproving or perhaps hurt. "Shall we drop ethics and philosophy, Serra?" I asked a moment later, "and continue with Gino? He interests me."

"He interests me no less," Serra went on calmly, "and not only because he arouses my sympathy and threatens my career, but because his life, despite your aversion to this sort of representative case, once again shows how powerless we are.

"When Gino was twenty-three, both his foster-parents died in quick succession, and at the same time the grandmother with whom Teresa had lived all these years passed away. The children wrote to each other; Gino had inherited a few thousand lire, felt no desire to continue the smithy and wanted to go to Rome. Teresa gave lessons in history and Spanish. They decided to live together and rented a few rooms in the oldest part of the city.

"Teresa's nature was completely different from that of her brother. In her grandmother's shadow she had led a religious and introspective life, but now, 'in the spring sun of my presence,' to quote Gino, she thawed a bit. But even after they had been living together for some time, and he teased her about the regularity with which she fulfilled her duties, she still went to church every day and often, while he was reading the paper or his dear 'Chroniques Italiennes' she would sit silently opposite him at the table all evening, engrossed with austere passion in her Spanish mystics, especially in her namesake, Santa Teresa de Avila, whose work she read over and over again with such concentration and rapture that she seemed to be discovering herself, and in San Juan de La Cruz. Gino tells that at such moments she herself resembled a Spanish nun.

"I have seen a picture of Teresa, a very good likeness according to him; an oval, handsome face which wears a mixture of diffidence and concealed spirituality as a mask for a turbulent temperament: in her eyes something of subdued ecstasy. During the years from which the picture dates, all her passion was still focused on her saints, but already one feels that it would not have taken much to make the flame strike outwards. It is possible that I now discover things in this photograph which I should not have seen were I less well informed, but unless I am very much mistaken, even without this knowledge I should have noticed that Teresa had a fierce nature which she conquered with difficulty. I have little sympathy with the theory that religious feelings are merely sublimated eroticism, and in the case of Teresa I have the impression that both eroticism and mystic inclinations were the desires of a nature thirsting for complete surrender. Her mouth is somewhat thin, not to say pinched, and all in all I am continually reminded of a bird that, afraid of its stormy desires for space and freedom, at first recalcitrant, but finally of its own free will, out of fear, locks itself up behind the bars of religious belief.

"Between Teresa and Gino there sprang up a love that was perhaps their greatest happiness but, in any case, also their fateful destiny. I really do not know whether people like us, who are free-thinkers in regard to morality too, can sufficiently imagine ourselves in their position; rather as far as I am concerned, I know very well that it is impossible for me. Completely imagine myself in the state of mind of a young woman who had a strictly Catholic upbringing, a reserved, passionate nature focused on the absolute, who was saturated with Catholic morality, and raised by a gruff, bigoted grandmother and no less bigoted nuns; who from her cradle had delivered up the secrets of her soul to priests; who ever since she could read had grown up with the lives of the saints and later with the mystics . . . and who then, with the awakening of love, must realize that for her this love would be inescapably bound up with a mortal sin because it was cherished for her brother? No, I cannot imagine it. But one thing is certain: she had to carry on a struggle which taxed her to the limit; and it was all the worse because at the same time she too remained convinced of the purity of her feelings. 'Before our innermost consciences we were innocent,' this sentence recurs again and again in Gino's account of the matter; and still they doubted whether they should obey their consciences in the face of such a despicable inclination, whether they did not assume too readily that such consciences were a reliable compass. 'We deceived ourselves,' said Teresa repeatedly, 'that we might possess a sanction for our behavior,' but although she realized that the evil had already begun with desire, she clung to the notorious precept as to a straw, that they would not be completely guilty as long as they avoided the final act. These conversations, however, began only after it had happened. Gino himself calls them a labyrinth of sophisms and evasions; and how weak all this was compared with the silent struggle at the start, after they had discovered each other's feelings!

"For, as I have already told you, they combatted for a while their fateful desire. They avoided each other as much as possible. Gino arose early in the morning, roamed through the city, very seldom ate a meal with Teresa and came home when she was already in bed. But she would not yet be asleep, for hours she had been waiting to hear his footsteps. Only when he had gone to bed, could she hope to be safe. Once she noticed that he stood still in front of her door, hesitating as to whether he should enter her room, and with closed eyes and a pounding heart she had felt herself dizzily faint away with him.

"This tension lasted a month; resistance wore them down and intensified their feelings; through the endless weighings of pros and cons, moral control had lost its hold on their emotions and slipped away like a defective screw. One evening Gino, trembling with restrained tension, entered his sister's room and embraced her. After a weak show of resistance she allowed it.

" 'I myself,' said Gino, 'had become so profoundly familiar with the thought of it, I had already made her body such an integral part of my imagination, that even the first time was like a recognition: I also noticed nothing of the antipathy which one is apparently supposed to feel toward one's own blood. Neither did Teresa; no matter what she may later have said in desperation about the depravity in which we were living, she never denied the integrity of her physical feelings. But remorse obsessed her. Poor Teresa, she struggled, filled with despair, but she struggled in vain. She no longer recognized herself, and this was perhaps her most bewildering experience. Where was her tranquillity, her faith? At an enervating tempo she was torn between the most conflicting emotions. Sometimes she locked her room, and when I came home I found letters halfway up the stairs in which she implored me to break off our relationship, but through the most horrible reproaches, against herself, again and again there glimmered something like desperate supplication and the fear of losing me entirely. After a few days her room would be open again and it began anew, more mysterious and seductive than before. For the more passion is satisfied, the more it desires.'

"Then Teresa became pregnant—several times they had feared it, but the fear always appeared to be unfounded—and just as, for her, the embrace had been the decisive step in the evil, so her pregnancy was the first earthly punishment for the evil. Now there was something much stronger within her than the feeling of remorse and self-accusation, which with all its intensity and all the physical agony it had caused still retained something abstract; now there was a little devil inside her, a goblin that had ensconced itself in her like a bloodsucker and that slowly grew and made her nauseated like a throbbing tumor. The somber visions in which she had seen herself and Gino condemned, sentenced to eternal damnation, faded away in the presence of the living being within her womb, that being which was the personification of the evil and which all its life would have to bear the curse of its creation as a stigma on its existence.

"The nights became unbearable, she hardly slept any longer. She had placed Gino's bed next to hers in her room, and when toward morning he finally fell asleep after perpetually the same hopeless conversations, she still remained awake and thought about the child: it would be an idiot or cripple and shunned by everyone because of its origin. Gino's proposal to have it removed she resisted with a sudden fierceness which reminded one of the old Teresa, a wild, desperate protest, in which, despite everything, her maternal instinct mingled with a desire to keep alive that which already lived, even if it were a cursed monster, and with a last remnant of moral strength to endure the full punishment. 'But the child will suffer no less than we,' Gino had once said; she, however, referred him to the Old Testament conception of vengeance, which visits the sins of the fathers upon their children, to the third and fourth generations. To interfere was to combat the evil with a greater evil. For that reason she also rejected Gino's urgent wish to leave Rome and set out for a distant country where they would live with the child like ordinary parents; and she was unyielding in her resistance; it was cowardice, after all that had happened, to want to escape from their fate and to make an idyll of that which already on earth was to be their curse.

"Their cup, however, was not yet full. Through Teresa's condition their secret, which had been suspected and slandered for some time, became an undeniable fact. Withdrawn into the twofold isolation of their joy and the approaching indignity, they proceeded to pay less and less attention to their neighbors, and this now avenged itself: like a running fire the dark secret spread through the street. And no matter how proudly Teresa tried to bear her disgrace, she sometimes felt as though she were being stoned. The women especially were without pity and flung the cruellest jokes at her.

"One evening when heavy and tired she had climbed the steps to her apartment, she saw a caricature of herself on the door (a halo around the head and with a monstrously swollen belly) with the inscription, Teresa Immaculata. These words so upset her that she seemed for the first time to realize the hopelessness of their position. That her name could be used to insult Maria proved to her how far she had gone astray. They were lost. Until now, despite everything, they had still hoped for salvation, but now she understood that her doom was irrevocable.

"That evening she threw her crucifix in the fire, with the books which had so long been her favorite literature. She no longer had a right to them, and besides, they had shown themselves to be impotent against the devil. 'I understood,' said Gino, 'that this signified the end for her, that life had now lost all its purpose and its value. But I could not comfort her, I did not want to restrain her, I could not do anything for her. The flames cast a reddish glow on her face while aghast she watched them slowly turn to ashes, as though she had burned them alive. But again I was powerless, I could do nothing for her. Slowly we began to drift apart, yes, almost to hate each other. Sometimes it even seemed to us that there was nothing left of our love except a strange, inimical emptiness. They say that misfortune deepens and strengthens love and unites estranged lovers. I did not observe this at all. No, on the contrary, misfortune at times as good as destroyed our love. But this happened, I now think, because fundamentally our natures were too divergent and especially because we had completely different ideas about the matters connected with our misfortune; and we were inclined—I at least was inclined—to blame the other more than myself. It seemed senseless that what had begun as, and what once had been, a mysterious joy now seemed a corrupt adventure. We were alone, each with a different despair and with a different accusation. We no longer understood each other. But when she did *this,* I realized that for her the last stage must have begun, a condition of despair and misery that was beyond even my comprehension. How terrible to be alone, just in these matters, and after what we had lived through—alone in the same house. Sometimes when I saw her wild-eyed expression I even feared for her sanity; and now she sat there really like a dazed person, lifelessly staring into the fire. Thus our days passed by. I could not leave her alone; she had canceled all her lessons; our money slowly dwindled away. We no longer did anything: now and then she would review the whole matter again.

" 'The root of everything had naturally been her pride. She had refused to confess her dark desire, partly because it would not be completely true as long as she had not confessed it, partly because she did not want to have such a despicable feeling known. But this new sin of not confessing also turned against her; she had had the feeling, even before she was pregnant, that she was poisoned, physically too, because she no longer cleansed herself in the confessional and by repentance: she lived in a cesspool and suffocated in her own filth. Moreover, her belief had shriveled, it could no longer renew itself, now that it remained deprived of the Body of Christ.'

"To you and to me," continued Serra, "such a reaction naturally seems absurd, just as every belief resembles a primitive superstition for one who does not share it. But all the same there is enormous force in the conception that one does not have to attach a symbolic meaning to the Sacrament, that it is a real presence. However, let us not discuss theology; the condition of the poor children was already sad enough without this sort of complication. Yes, that was how they now lived, cut off from the springs of life, cast out by their environment, in revolt against themselves and each other.

"Finally the torture became so great that one evening they decided to end their lives: and now that the thought which had been pursuing them so long had once been expressed, any delay would have meant protracted agony. Teresa was no longer able to realize the sinfulness of the deed, or perhaps her realization of sin was suppressed by the tardy happiness of a joint undertaking.

"Toward dark they dressed themselves; mechanically she threw her short jacket over her shoulders and arranged her hair—'Why in God's name does a person, a woman like Teresa, still stand in front of the mirror an hour before her death?' thought Gino—and after they had closed the door as carefully as that of a sick-room, they quickly left the house.

"It was evening; they left the city; Gino carried a revolver, Teresa, the child. They walked apart and did not speak a word. On the Via Appia, close to the grave of Cecilia Metella, Gino took her by the hand, gently led her into the shade of a few old trees and kissed her. Teresa was pale but controlled. All the courage and pride she had possessed returned and steeled her. She went to stand opposite him like a royal lamb. 'Close your eyes, Teresa,' he said; and she shut her eyes and opened her mouth as though she wanted to receive the Host. He embraced her with his left arm, pressed her against him, put the barrel into her mouth and discharged the pistol. She fell backwards and dragged him down with her. He lay on her as though he had taken her in a struggle. Dazed by the shock, while his body covered hers, he pointed the barrel at his temples and fired. But his hand trembled and the browning missed. When he awoke, he lay in a hospital and slowly remembered what had happened. But Teresa was dead."

"And now?"

"Now he is going to be tried tomorrow. Only today I received a letter from him about the fatal turn his case threatens to take. If you will wait a moment I will read it to you:

" 'I must write you once more before the trial. I hope that my letter will not annoy you, but everything that you have done for me would prove to be ill-fated if the rumor which reached me the other day were true: to be precise, I have heard that there is a possibility of acquittal, or pardon, which amounts to the same thing for me. Despite my threefold misdeed, an atmosphere of sympathy and forgiveness toward me seems to have come into being, which wants to present me with a new life. As if this were not just the one thing which I find unacceptable, impossible.

" 'This aspect of the case has never been spoken of between us, and for this too I am grateful to you. I understood that you also silently accepted the fact that nothing else but death would follow. I counted the days, not expecting a reunion, the possibility of which I doubted, but because then at least something would be decided. Death with all its terror was my only mainstay in the nightmare in which I lived. If death had held no terror for me I naturally should not have missed my aim, even if I had not missed on purpose. An instinctive fear must have guided the bullet in this way. I often think that in my last seconds everything will be different from what I imagined—easier perhaps— but I find myself continually engrossed in this. In this respect my nature is searching and restless. I am not so much thinking of infernal punishment as I am thinking of the death struggle; aside from the pain, it must be terrible when the soul is torn from the body. In my case it will be a long struggle, even if the execution lasts one second, because my soul is entirely interwoven with my body, and my will was concentrated on a long life. But after what has happened, I cannot and no longer want to live. I lack courage for a second attempt at suicide. I must therefore be condemned. I should still have been able to conquer my remorse if I had only killed her, because death in itself might have meant deliverance, but I had first driven her to mortal sin and then killed her in that state.

" 'Despite everything that I have told you about the last period of our life together, I know for certain, and now that I am alone I am more certain than ever, that for me life with her, even in the greatest depravity, is the only life. For it is not happiness that matters, but the strength of love; and although one half of my soul, in accord with the world and, what is more important, also with the church, unconditionally condemns the life I led with her, the other half of my soul knows that I can live a life of love only with her—and does not love justify everything? This is my dilemma, but in this dilemma I should like to live, I should like to bear it until the very end.

" 'Do you understand how much the news of a possible pardon has alarmed me? First came the warden, then the doctor, then the priest—each one wanted to be the bearer of the message of salvation, and every word was new agony for me, new fear. Is it not enough that I, after what I have gone through, have had to discuss my life with an investigating judge who considers himself a paragon of broad-mindedness, but, who just for this reason, thought he could at least demand a decisive answer concerning my "motives." (As though one lives according to motives!) Is it not enough that everything is going to be enlarged upon again the day after tomorrow at the session; by a tribunal which, God knows why, has made up its mind that I must be "saved"? I have often thought about this session, always with disgust. My only consolation is that it will all be so unreal in comparison with what I have lived through that I cannot become essentially involved in the matter. When I imagine how I will stand there and you will finally speak, forgive me, then I hear in advance that it will be different from our talks, that it will be falsified to make an impression upon a jury which oozes satisfaction with the magnanimity it will soon display. I shall not recognize you in this.

" 'In any case, I am at the mercy of my fellow-men—and this humiliation is perhaps the worst punishment of all. I shall try to resign myself, but you can understand that sometimes I pace my cell for hours like a hunted animal and ask myself: what *devil* had this idea?

" 'I hope very much that you will forgive this letter. The only reason why I write you is this: please frustrate this criminal plan if it is still possible to do so; assure me of the death penalty. I know that it is not easy, but only if you advocate it do you remain till the end the friend who has risked his subsistence by defending me.' "

When Serra had put away the letter, I asked him hesitantly what he intended to do.

"I have decided," he said with circumspect conviction, "to comply with Gino's request. Let us not stop to reflect upon the duties of a legal counsel. Gino's wish seems so justified to me, I am so completely on his side, that I shall endeavor with all my might to convince the jury of the mistaken humanity inherent in such a pardon. But it is plain that I shall thereby gain for good the reputation of being an impious cynic and that this case ushers in the end of my career. The public, the whole city, is following the trial with the greatest suspense, and the disgust and consternation which will break out when I oppose an acquittal will not be small. People cannot well endure it when someone distrusts and thwarts their idealism, and in this case they are in advance so touched by their own humanity that their jury makes them swell with pride. Tomorrow a flood of holy enthusiasm and benevolent joy must pass through the streets of Rome, so that one may wallow in blood or in humanity, just as one used to do when the Christians were torn asunder by the lions."

Toward midnight I said goodbye and wished him luck.

"I fear the worst," he said with his sceptical smile, "when our enemies think they have to love us, we are usually lost. Will you call me up tomorrow evening? Ten to one he will be condemned to live."

Translated by JOSEPHINE VAN AS

E. du Perron

THE INDONESIAN CHILD GROWS UP QUICKLY [1]

I

MY GOVERNESS' NAME WAS KITTY WAHL, BUT TO ME SHE WAS "NONNA Dobleh": the lady with the hanging-lip. She had kinky hair and small black eyes and she was very temperamental and she preferred playing rough games with us—that is with Flora, myself and the native children in our own "yard." She would collapse in our midst, and then we would have to pull her up or walk on her until she came to. A pronounced Javanese accent caused her to speak Dutch with accentuated h's, as with a "blow on the gong," as it was called. Her mother, moreover, was Javanese and sometimes came to call on her. Out of respect for her, the governess asked leave twice a week to meet her in the waroeng of Po Sen, because in our house the woman would have felt rather embarrassed. My mother could do nothing but give in to such a delicate form of childish affection; but in the waroeng the timid Javanese woman would resolutely take the shape of a European sergeant. I was already acquainted with the picture of this sergeant, because my governess had shown it to me with some pride; because of my admiration for the military, I was the obvious confidant in this case. But when the servants told my mother about this metamorphosis, the governess was immediately dismissed. I have never understood why my mother was so fussy about the lack of sexual abstinence in those in whose care I was put; the only explanation she gave for it was that it would bring *sial* (bad luck). Shortly before Kitty Wahl left something strange happened within me: I thought, or perhaps I was only dreaming, that as we were playing she suddenly fell between us, that she sent all the native children away and then asked Flora and me to massage her, during which performance she was completely naked.

Of my sexual precociousness there was no doubt. A long time before this I had made friends with an Ambonese woman who had been married to a European and was therefore addressed as

[1] Fragment from the novel: "Land of Origin."

Mevrouw. She gave me the chromos of princes and Boer generals that hung in her house, every time I called on her, but that was not the principal attraction. She was no longer young and was as black as a Negro, but beneath her kabaja, which always was carelessly left open, hung two enormous black breasts. One day when she personally brought me back to my mother she said: "It is funny, Mevrouw, but do you believe it, that child has only eyes for my *teteh.*" Grown-up people are in the habit of laughing with superior secretiveness at that kind of innocence. Perhaps a year later, a real European lady was staying with us, a stately fair woman who read a lot and walked with me in the garden. I lied to her about all sorts of childish fantasies, among other things that I always crossed the river swimming; she seemed to listen attentively to my stories and did not tell my parents about my lies, but called herself my "lady friend," which filled me with pride and was something no other grown-up person had done before. One day she was going shopping with my mother; the carriage was brought in front of the house, and my mother sent me to tell the lady that we were ready to go. She was not ready and, probably in order not to tell my mother about it but to return with me, she called me in and let me sit on a chair. As a knightly servant I witnessed the rest of her toilet. She went to sit in front of the mirror and soon she was naked to the waist; when she bent over I saw her in two different ways, that is, from the front in the mirror and from the side in reality. I had often seen my mother undressed, but I held my breath, did not say a word and took it all in, and up to this day I do not think I have forgotten the impression. She was pinkish white and must have been about thirty-five years old at the time; her high coiffure, black hair, the whiteness of her body and especially her breasts, and the complete naturalness with which she finished her toilet in my presence—how little perhaps does such a woman know what she gives in passing to a boy of perhaps seven or eight? I thought of her naked body when she had already been sitting for a long time next to my mother, in a smart dress. That same day she bought me a book, in which she wrote in tall characters: *For Arthur Ducroo from his big friend Mevrouw O——.* I never saw her again, at least not from nearby. Much later, when I was perhaps eighteen, she passed in a car, while I was standing with guests on the front verandah; there were two ladies in the open car, one was she, but both waved. What I caught in passing of her face did not correspond with my remembrance of her, but it was as if her waving was particularly directed at me. I had forgotten that other people were standing next to me. If she had then stepped out of the car and I had pressed her hand, I would certainly have tried to retrieve the memory of my "big friend" and the secret of a past time. I really had everything necessary in order to be initiated by a "friend of my mother." Then it would not have happened as on that dismal evening, because the other was not there, and out of pride before my friends I accomplished the first amorous game with a native night beauty with a face like the back of a shoe.

If the theory is really correct that all our inclinations towards the other sex are based upon our first impressions, I was perhaps the dupe of the older women whom I continually saw around me during my childhood. A woman with small, high breasts always seemed ridiculous and unreal to me while, as a child, I experienced a sexual thrill at the tale of the *kelong wewe,* a female spirit with enormous breasts, who kidnaps children that are often later discovered sleeping in or under a tree and whom she has kept all this time as if under her wings, caressing and hiding them. In my imagination this spirit was not repulsive to me. Later on Catherine the Great of Russia seemed more desirable to me, as pictured in a historical book, than all the young women. These cerebral inclinations I have never followed in reality, but perhaps rather out of discretion than on account of sound reactions; an older woman who has some charm left seems even today in principle more attractive and engaging to me than a young one. The truth is, however, that few past a certain age still keep the necessary charm.

Yet when I was still very young I was already falling in love with young women. In Soekaboemi, near Wa Gedah, I met a girl, perhaps sixteen years old, who was called Den Boewah (Fruit). I have completely forgotten her, but the old Wa Gedah later on teased me that I had really been in love with her. I stayed around her, did not dare look at her when she looked at me and, when they drove me to her, I was supposed to have said with a great deal of coquetry: "No, I won't go with something called 'fruit,'" —plain marks of amorousness indeed. But at the same time I was mostly a quiet and serious child. My parents took me along on a visit to my uncle the general. He was a robust man with a deep voice, pouches under his eyes and grey, flowing whiskers, the type of the old growler; for me his uniform was an object of the greatest admiration. His wife, my father's sister, was an example of a sweet lady and gave me much lemonade while she quarrelled with my parents about the foolishness of teaching me to recite "Our Father." Their daughter, then twenty-three years old was as pretty as a picture and played the piano holding me on her lap. My aunt said: "I never dare to talk simply to the child; he looks at me out of his big black eyes and then gives me an ironical smile, I tell you." "And when you grow up," she would ask, "what do you want to be?" "A naval officer." "And what will you do?" "I'll sink Uncle Jan." He was told about it and called out in a thunderous voice: "Then you want to sink *me?*" And I would hide behind a chair, scared to death and had to be comforted again with lemonade. The daughter walked through my room one afternoon and, as it was very warm, she simply undressed me and let me lie quite naked on the counterpane for health's sake. She really had less knowledge of human beings than my aunt. I hardly dared nor could protest, but as soon as she had left I called for Alima to dress me again as quickly as possible. Not ten minutes had passed before my big niece passed through the room again. "What? Is that child dressed again?" she asked. "Yes, nonna," said Alima timidly, "but leave him that way; he isn't accustomed to the other way, you see." Perhaps I was in love with the beautiful niece; the more reason for my prudish reaction.

Before we went back to Sand Bay, I would go to school again for a while. I must have been eight years old at the time, because I was too old to be a beginner and as the son of a gentleman I had to be guarded against bad company. I was sent to an institution run by Ursulines, where little boys of over ten were considered too masculine to stay or to be admitted. I was therefore already one of the oldest boys, but I felt very miserable when I was put in a class with the other children. My mother had told me that she would stay outside to talk with the sisters. At the first recreation period I realized that I had been fooled: I kept quiet and sat down on a bench; immediately a little blond boy with a sugary expression on his face came up to me and said in a bleating tone (I do not think that he meant to tease me): "Oh, what a sweet little boy!" These completely unexpected words robbed me of what remained of my dignity; I jumped up, and two sisters tried in vain to seize me. I ran out of the garden, across the street and into the barracks that were on the other side. The soldiers received me with cheers and laughter, and the sisters, who had followed me out into the street, quickly retreated. When I no longer saw them I called a sado and let myself be driven home. My return home filled the family with consternation and I was immediately taken back to school.

I stayed but a few months with the Ursuline sisters. I remember only a few things: that I said "Jah" in the clipped way that my father had, and that this was allowed when I explained that it was my father's way; and again that I spun stories for my preferred sister, Mother Jozefa, namely, that every morning I wrestled in the stable with my little native friends and that as true wrestlers they only wore trunks. In order to show her precisely what I meant, I drew the picture of a little man on my slate, about as I had seen it in a book. "But that is a grown-up man," said the sister, knowing the difference. "Yes," I said, "but that's the way I am." I was not punished on account of my fibbing, probably because the sister was enough of an educator to classify my lying as fantasy. I was, moreover, considered a hero in school and always chased the whole class in front of me on the playground. A little girl with fair tresses, whose pretty face I only then learned to appreciate, looked admiringly and dreamily at me from a bench. A sister suddenly grasped her by the shoulders and said: "Do you think it is right, what he's doing?" and she nodded with something like ecstasy in her eyes.

But soon our family would have to return to the wilderness, and so I acquired a new governess, who took me to school in the morning. I do not know why, but one morning I had the feeling that I had lost her. Quite upset I ran along the street in the hope of overtaking her and passed the "real" school not far from the Ursulines. A number of older boys stood at the gate; they shouted something at me and as I was running by I called out anxiously: "Have you seen my governess?"—at which the whole group burst out laughing. I was humiliated and at the same time I felt sharply that I would not be able to become a hero in that school.

The new governess' name was Bertha Hessing. She was tall and white and the only pure-blooded Hollander among all my governesses. At first she made quite an impression on me and when I became familiar with her, I liked her in a different way from the other governesses. She talked much more with me. I also looked upon her as the "big friend" and we had the feeling that we always had something to say to each other. She told Flora and me marvelous stories, which she invented herself, she said. In reality, they came out of her favorite book, "Adam Bede," with its characters disguised as princes and princesses: there was Prince Adam, a bad Prince Arthur, a Princess Hetty, etc.—that there was such rivalry between the two princes that it made the fairy tale more fascinating to me than all the others. Through Governess Hessing (who was not called by her Christian name like the other governesses) I almost lost my belief in Santa Claus, about whose existence I had never thought much until then or whom I perhaps thought of as one Santa Claus among thousands of existing Santa Clauses. He now suddenly wrote to me a letter in purple ink, wherein I was told that this year I would still get presents but next year no longer, "if the little boy persisted in swearing so badly." The purple ink on the letter exuded a disagreeable smell, absolutely identical with the little bottle of purple ink with which Governess Hessing wrote her letters. But I solved the riddle by believing that the presents came from Santa Claus and the note from her in order to frighten me.

She went with us to Sand Bay and walked with me along the beach. In the direction of Tjimarindjoeng our walks were quiet and dark, as if we were going through a magic land. The other way was more populated; in the first place one passed the winged praus, the most primitive model of a boat, a small, roughly hollowed-out tree-trunk with wings of bamboo on both sides to prevent it from tipping over: the whole thing reminded one of a see-saw on dry land. Fish scales, and in places a small dead fish, lay here on the sand, and at set times the fishers would push their boats into the sea. When my father had brought over some of his Batavian sailors, I had looked with disdain upon these fishermen of Balekambang. Now, however, my governess and I were fascinated by their activities, while we gathered shells on the beach. She taught me to gather the beautiful ones and leave the ugly ones alone, let me listen to the roar of the sea in some of them and continued chatting with me. She told me about her fiancé who was in Singapore and showed me his picture: a very fine gentleman, I thought, with his hand upon his side and his small turned-up mustaches, and I had to call him "Uncle Edwin." "And what are you going to give me when I marry Uncle Edwin?" I promised her a box filled with shells, but those she could gather herself; then a box with postage stamps because she had to write so often. But if she did not write to Uncle Edwin, who then would be with her? By arousing my interest in Uncle Edwin and her marriage, she increased my jealousy. I cared so much for her that I neglected my mother. "You don't care for your mother any longer, you are in love with your governess," mother would say. And, with a kind of hatred perhaps against all "intellectuals," "And she is such a real *totoh;* she never brushes her teeth."

Miss Hessing left and was replaced again by an unadulterated daughter of the native soil, with a broad face, unbelievably long hair and again a strong Javanese accent. Her name was Fientje Flikkenschild, and I right away took a dislike to her; she followed me everywhere as if I were a baby and she answered all my questions with her gong-beat accent: "That may be known to Joost van Vondhel." One day I emptied the half-filled chamberpot over her hands; my father, who saw this, gave me the worst beating I had ever received. He beat me with the flat of his hand; he was so furious that my governess thought he was going to murder me. From that day on every close contact with him was a thing of the past: I ran away when I but heard his voice or saw him approach from a distance. I had always been afraid of him, but from that moment on I considered him as an evil spirit. My mother told me later that sometimes I would beg her on my knees not to tell something or other to my father; I don't remember that, but it may very well have been true. He beat me perhaps because of righteous anger, perhaps because of hidden anger against his coolies, perhaps out of chivalrousness towards my governess, whose hair was so long that it must have been a joy to his eyes. That, at least, was my mother's interpretation; she angrily took my part and did not rest until the governess had departed on a prau. She left probably the next day, after a stormy evening session between my parents, very poorly handled by my strong father. In order not to have to bid her goodbye, I had hidden in a new place, where the praus were stored away, near the Tjikanteh.

I discovered a new friend in the aristocratic Ading, a rather light-hued native of about twenty-four who wore his hair in a knot atop his head. He was the greatest rival of Moenta in the whole of Balekambang; less shrewd and articulate, but finer in appearance and lighter of color: from him I received at the age of nine my first lessons in sexology, in the same building where the praus were put away and where I had hidden myself when my most detested governess had departed. He explained to me what a man and a woman did (as an example he rather took a boy and a girl) who wanted "to form one body." When I finally understood what he meant, though I still looked at him unbelievingly, he said: "All the small boys in the village who go bathing do it with their little sisters." Then he enlarged upon the subject by comparing both of our persons; the difference was really startling in many respects. "But can't two men ever do anything together?" I asked, and it was surely less from an evil inclination than from the fact that I had never given up the idea that my mother was like a man in this respect. "Yes," he said, "but it is very difficult and would be very painful." I did not at all have the personal friendship for Ading that I felt for Moenta, and it was quite by chance that I sat that afternoon with him in that building. One day the rivalry between him and Moenta took on such proportions that both drew their knives; their fathers came running, Isnan, I think, with a rifle, and perhaps it was this that prevented a disaster. Ading was the oldest of four or five brothers, some good-looking, some ugly, their faces pockmarked. After his instructions, I understood what my father meant when he called him one day to tell him that he and all his brothers would have to leave the premises, because they only knew how to work with one instrument (and he named it).

I do not believe that there was much perversion in Ading's opinion that I should know about certain things; his answer on the last question proved that, unless it was that he was afraid "to injure a child of white parents." But I found another teacher in Kiping, the foreman of the Batavian sailors; Kiping told me fairy tales in which such matters were treated in the simplest manner. A fairy tale would start for instance: "Once upon a time there were a man and a woman who liked to form one body together [*la bête à deux dos* of Rabelais] and who had many children in consequence." When sexual matters shocked me, it was usually not the natives who were responsible; in their teaching, absence of tact was excellently replaced by complete naturalness.

II

From now on I received instruction from my father. The governesses were no good; he would do it himself. He had therefore gone to a teacher who had given him a list of all the books that were used in his school. The rice-hulling works were now active, and every morning before he went there he gave me a lesson. It was my good fortune that I was not mentally lazy, because in that case he might have mistreated me and then left me to my fate. He instructed me in everything: Dutch, history, geography, arithmetic—and while he was in the factory he let me do a lot of work by myself, and in the evening when he came home, no matter how tired, he would go over what I had learned, looked into what I had accomplished. Because of this persistence alone he deserves my gratitude; as I got to know him later on, with his hatred for schoolteachers, his anger and his pent-up irritation with the Sundanese, I am surprised that he gave himself so much trouble. Sometimes he would throw books at my head and called me a triple ass, but he kept at it, and for him it must have been worse than for me, though I considered him a tyrant and a schoolteacher and as a teacher, a tyrant too. My mother sometimes tried to intercede and asked him to give me less work; he should not forget that he was giving me private lessons, etc., etc. As a reward he lent me books, most of which I had already read in private. Two or three of Walter Scott, those that were less chaste than the others, he eliminated; I read them in the same way I had the others. I searched all the boxes and closets, when I could no longer find any books of my own to read, and one day discovered a catalogue of semipornographic literature with illustrations; in one of them a farm boy tried to overpower a girl on the grass and beneath it it read: *Oh, Tony, if your mother only knew!—Don't worry, she knows more about it than you do!*—This illustration remained a mystery to me, in spite of all the natives' revelations. What did mother know better? I asked myself. Why did that boy struggle with that girl, and on what occasion would my mother have had to struggle like that?

Sometimes my father called me to him outside of lessons, as formerly when I was allowed to play with his watch chain. But it was no longer the same; since he had given me the beating, he remained my enemy. Once I sang what I had to read, a little verse from a reader, because I happened to know the tune. My mother heard it and said: "You must read it." To my surprise he said: "No, let him sing it." I did not trust this either; I felt that my mother was right and that I was betraying something when I sang for my father's pleasure.

During my free time I organized a troupe of native playmates. The most important ones remained the children of the stable boy, Enih and Entjih, a boy and a girl. The girl was very imaginative and played "house" with my books; we could even construct houses of several stories; cut-out dolls were ladies and gentlemen calling on each other. Enih made up great stories of what happened between the Ducroo family and the Rengers family whom her father had served before. My imagination soon excelled hers, I thought that I had really been acquainted with the Rengers family, especially "sinjo Rentie," the son, who was at least ten years older than I and whom I only knew from Enih's descriptions. I told her in all seriousness that I had had all kinds of adventures with him, that I had even once been with him hunting for *tjoeliks* (kidnappers). "And did you shoot too?" Enih asked, sneering. "No, but I walked behind him and was allowed to carry his gun."

When I became older and began to awaken sexually, I imagined that I was in love with Enih; this too started with dolls; she had to be a doll herself now, though it might have been a lady from a fashion catalogue, and the other doll was myself, and these two dolls I married in spite of her laughing protestations. One day I proposed to her to marry her really; she understood immediately what I meant but remarked that there was nowhere a place to perform the ceremony. I proposed all kinds of places, including a pit on the beach; she told me then that it was impossible because I was not circumcised and therefore was on the level of a Chinese to her. The great contempt in which the natives held the Chinese convinced me right away, but also the contempt I meant myself to have for the Chinese: that Enih did not want me as if I were a Chinese to her seemed irrefutable to me in logic.

That I was in love was self-evident: all the knights in Walter Scott were so and ended by marrying. I was even violently in love with an illustration, showing Isabelle of Troyes who held out her hand to be kissed by Quentin Durward; the presence of the kneeling Durward did not interfere with my love in the least, for I identified myself with him. Perhaps I felt myself in this manner represented by one of the heroes in every book I read. But sometimes the choice was difficult: in "Ivanhoe" and "The Talisman" but not because of the presence of Richard the Lionhearted, since without hesitation I chose Ivanhoe and Sir Kenneth as the younger ones, who did marry in the end; in "Guy Mannering" I was in a quandary because the hero of this tale became old and I had to wait for young Bertram who showed up for the first time in the middle of the book and whom I considered the real hero. In "The Fair Maid of Perth" (one of the books I was not allowed to read) the choice was the most difficult: Henry Gow, the smith, was without doubt the hero and did indeed marry the beautiful girl, but he had a full-grown beard and was thirty and that made him old to me; I felt already much more attracted by the illustrations of the two beardless young men, Conaghar and Robert of Rothsay, but the first had been beaten by Gow as a child and the second did not fight at all. From Walter Scott I derived a manner of looking at life which I wanted to be confirmed in each volume; before I started one, I would ask my father: "Who is the hero? Who is his friend? Who is his enemy?" Even the finding of a real friend or a real enemy was sometimes rather difficult.

In Soekaboemi, where I had cried over a book for the first

time, when I read "A Schoolboy" by Farrar, which my father himself called a "magnificent book," he said to me: "And don't you think that somebody must have suffered a lot, to be a good author?" I was completed bowled over by the idea; that there was some relation between the author, probably a gentleman like others, and his heroes had never occurred to me, but such a sensitive remark, coming from my father, made me think. From that time on I began to look for the author's suffering to appear through the book; I even found it in a book about Indians: the death of an old beaver hunter, a passage which I read to my mother with a lump in my throat but which left her to my great surprise and chagrin unmoved. Even Scott gave me little satisfaction in this direction, as little as my other favorite author, Captain Marryat; but another "magnificent book" which I received on my birthday, "Uncle Tom's Cabin," reaped a rich harvest. Strangely enough, whether because of my father's sympathy with Uncle Tom and his antipathy for Legree, I did not for a moment compare him to the slave driver.

When Enih had rejected me, I felt I had to look for love elsewhere. I remembered the European girls I had known at school in Soekaboemi; I hesitated between a girl who was a few years older than I was, who was skinny but who had magnificent black curls as some of the heroines of Walter Scott or another who was about my age and with whom I had played hide-and-seek in my father's club. I chose the latter as the better possibility because she was about my age and her name was Polly. I told Enih about her and tried to convince myself, by pronouncing her name with a great deal of emotion when I was along. But two *koetjiahs* (professional actors) who came to live in Balekampang, and each of whom had a wife, offered me greater reality: I again fell in love, this time in deep secret, with a living woman, starting with one whom I thought better looking at first, but her chewing of betelnut repulsed me: then with the other, who attracted me on account of her white and unfiled teeth.

With the native boys I played tag, but I always identified knights' tales with the names we called each other—Ivanhoe, Kenneth and Richard, something the native boys considered rather odd; later as I was reading a book about lion hunters I wanted to change the names and wanted them to call me Marandon, but they protested, because they found the old names easier and had become used to them. In reality their names were Entjih, Hatim, Snoeb, Ahim, etc. Ahim was a fleet-footed, dark boy, who was on a footing of greater equality with me than the others. His father had given him instruction in Pentjah, which was a mixture of fighting and dancing; one day I proposed to him to try his skill on me. At first he refused discreetly, but I forced him and took hold of him. Within five minutes perhaps he threw me down twenty-one times on the sand, but once I half pulled him along. Every time I fell, all the other children, boys and girls, would jump up and down and about. Finally I was dead tired and bathed in perspiration, but more surprised than humiliated; I never lost the idea that all would change when we fought seriously and that then I would beat him instead of only pulling at him. But my personal prestige had suffered with the others, I was now only their superior as the son of a blanda. Later, when Ahim had gone, Entjih told me maliciously that he had said I was a real blanda, because all the time I had smelled like a *andjing basah* (wet dog).

The father of this Ahim was called Pa Sahim and was probably crazy. Once three coolies ran away but were caught by Isnan on horseback and brought back. They sat on their haunches in our yard, all three next to each other; my father scolded them and afterwards beat them up separately: the first two, who did not resist, each received a few blows and nothing more, but the third, who jumped up, was beaten in a manner that looked rather like a wrestling match. I had seen all this ever since I was a baby, but now that I saw my father on top of a native who had lost his headcloth and was pushed against the ground, I experienced a sexual manifestation to which I did not pay any attention. My feeling at the same time seemed to come from fear and exaltation. While my father was beating the third, Pa Sahim came running out of his house and suddenly gave one of the two other coolies, who were again sitting on their haunches, a blow in his neck from behind. My father immediately let go of his victim and shouted to Pa Sahim that he must go away; the man stood facing him, strong and thick-set, and looked with his red eyes into my father's. I thought later on that the scene might have ended in a murder; if my father had not controlled the other with his greater will power, if the other had pulled out a knife, my mother and I might have seen him murdered in a few seconds by the four natives; it is not impossible that they might have thrown themselves upon us afterwards—such things have happened in just this way. But the men left, and the three beaten ones followed him; my father went to lie down on a couch where my mother brought him some tea, uttering soothing words. What would I have done, I then thought, if I had seen my father being murdered? I think that I would have immediately run away, through the kampong, straight to the spot of the Tjiletoeh, to hide away with Kiping and the Batavian sailors. Or would I have defended my mother?

Another time, when Ahim did not want to play with me, I went to call for him at his home. He was busy eating, facing his father and with his back towards the door; half angry, but partly too in joke, I pulled him from the bale to the floor, before he had seen me. He refused to come along, and his father began to roar as I had never heard a native do before; I left in order to tell my father. While I crossed the bridge over the Tjikanteh, because the coolies' habitations were on the other side, I could still hear the man plainly shout: "Go ahead! I'm not afraid! I'm not afraid!" When I had come back to our own house and had told my parents the story, I was called down, but for a moment my father seemed inclined to go towards the upheaval which could be heard in our house also. Perhaps he might also have been murdered that time. But my mother kept him back with the argument that the man must be insane, that one could see it in his eyes. Some days later he was sent away and thus I lost my comrade Ahim Foo.

In spite of these things, my father's behavior towards the natives did not please me at all: I experienced it like fate, but I shivered as soon as something of the kind reoccurred. My mother sometimes warned me that I ought to go away, that one would surely get a beating again. My friend Moenta, Don Juan that he was, was given a beating too, after which he ran away; this caused me to hate my father anew. Once he beat an already aged, rather fat man from the village, who fetched our mail from Pelaboean with the winged prau. Probably the man deserved it, because he had probably opened a registered letter to see whether there was any money in it, but that afternoon I seethed with pity and indignation. Like a reflex movement I ran back to my room and broke open the penny bank wherein my mother sometimes put a dime: the result was about one guilder. I knew for sure that my mother would not scold me, but I was mortally afraid that my father would see me: bending myself up double behind the *djarak* hedge I had to run hard to catch up with the man. He was stumbling along, busy putting on his sarong and fastening his headcloth. When I had caught up with him—it was already between the two hedges in the kampong—I hastily gave him the money and then slunk back with beating heart along the shrubs that were to hide me. I buried this "noble deed" as well as my feelings of vengeance, almost like unreasoned impulses and nothing else. I had again experienced such an impulse ten years later when I was a young reporter on the *Nieuwsbode* at the Kali Beasar at Batavia: on a suffocatingly hot day, as I was waiting for a street car to take me home, a native came to stand in front of me with an unpainted table which he offered me for sale. I asked him whether he perhaps thought I could take the thing along in the street car; he looked at me beseechingly and said in an almost toneless voice: "For one guilder, sir, for whatever you think it is worth"—and with a gesture indicating his mouth: "I am so hungry." There was famine at that time in the Buitenzorg region. I had hardly half a guilder in my pocket and the same reflex motion occurred; I shouted at him to wait and ran as fast as I could over the bridge of the Kali Besar, back to my paper, because I might still find the chief copy-reader. I found him there and asked him for a guilder; then I ran back and found the native, who was waiting. All that time I had one fear: that he would have left because he did not trust me. When I sat in the street car, which luckily was just passing by, I felt myself unutterably happy and yet I was astonished at myself.

Later on, like all Indian boys, I beat the natives myself; especially the *sado* coachmen whose backs I have often poked with my fist so that they might drive on when they refused. But all this came from a misunderstood conception of sportsmanlike behavior, following the example of others, without much conviction, and once even, after I had boxed a native's ear and sent the man away without another word, with a strong feeling of humiliation and pity, furious with myself because I only had one urge: to find the man again and apologize to him. On the contrary, at Tjitlengka, when I was seventeen, I fought with the house boy Piin who refused to obey me while my parents were away. He was unusually tall for a native and had manifested a sneering laziness towards me for a period of weeks; I now jumped up from the table where I was eating and followed him into the hall to give him a slap; he turned around and seized me and we rolled over each other in the hall until we bumped into the wall. I put a scissor-hold on him exactly as I had seen my father do, his headcloth came off, and I would have been able to beat him because he had suddenly ceased defending himself. But I did not do so; I pushed his head against the wall, got up, smiled and let him get up; because I had not given him a beating I went with a pleasant feeling back to the table again. He continued serving me, and when my parents came back home neither he nor I spoke about what had happened. Since that time he flew to exe-cute my orders and paid all kinds of attention to my wants. One day I cut my ankle to the bone with a sort of short saber and limped inside with my slipper dripping with blood and he ran towards me, his face ash-grey, to support me. It was a short saber attached to a stick; I had just purchased the weapon and he had sharpened it to a keen edge for me, which was perhaps the reason, but that sort of pang of conscience seemed too subtle for me in a native. What a magnificent subject for the Freudians: the "link" between master and servant after the beating. I should have liked to have seen my father's face if I had asked him for his thoughts upon feelings of this sort.

I shall come back to the subject of Pa Sahim and Balekambang. The man was perhaps not insane, but certainly cruel. One day Isnan shot a *binjawak* (small alligator) in the Tjinkanteh. It was still alive when brought ashore. Pa Sahim put his hunting knife between the jaws and split it apart like a piece of firewood utter-ing a sonorous "Ha!" at every new blow, and with every new blow the mouth of the animal continued to open, though it had already been split open to its stomach. That sort of thing seems amusing to the natives. When Otto came to us in Balekampang, he shot a *loetoeng* (black monkey) for his collection; the animal was brought home while it was still alive. Moenta came to me and said: "Go and look at the *loentoeng* your brother has shot, a *loentoeng* is like a human being, when he is in pain, he cries." I went to look at the animal, which was lying down; it moaned like a human being and had indeed tears in the remarkably human eyes. I became very upset and went with tears in my eyes to my mother, asking whether the animal might be kept alive. She was afraid not; moreover, Otto wanted the skin for his collection. During the night the moaning body was brought to the adjoining buildings. The next day, as soon as I had gotten up, I went there; the animal was still alive, I scratched its head cautiously, I gave it my hand, which it clutched anxiously. Isnan appeared in order to skin it. I protested, saying that perhaps it could be kept alive.—Nothing doing, he said; he had received orders to skin it, and he let it be taken away. I went everywhere to find my mother, but she had gone for a walk with Otto and my father. When they came back the *loentoeng* had been skinned. All day long I did not speak to them; I would have despised my-self if I had spoken to such people. But the most painful thing was told me by my playmates: the *loentoeng* had been skinned alive; when he was without skin, he was still moaning, and only then, said either Enih or Entjih, their father the stable boy had cracked his skull with his hunting knife.

I am trying to discover the old pain while I am writing this; but there is nothing . . . it is past or the action of writing it down has replaced it. Years later I thought back upon these things and found again the same intensity within me the feelings of pity and hatred; I have sometimes dug up the story for my mother in order to punish her because she did not prevent it. The *loentoeng* hide hung for less than a year in Otto's collection; he himself was sorry that he had shot the animal, but perhaps only because he had not hit it in a better spot.

This incident drew me away from Isnan. I really did fight at Balekambang with two adult servants when I was a child, namely with Isnan and Pieng, the cook. Pieng was perhaps merely hysterical; she gave vent to this in abundant shrieking when I had done something wrong to her daughter, my playmate Amsah. This wrong was never of a serious nature: she received a ball against her foot as we were playing nine-pins or I would say that she looked a sight (she had then been chewing betelnut, something I could not bear), having prettified herself for the benefit of one of the Batavian sailors, Normin. When my parents were at the factory at the time, Pieng came to bawl me out. I felt the urge to fly at her, though she was an old woman, but soon I succeeded in wounding her by words and that was much better: she would again escape into the kitchen, and there between her pots and pans she would shriek and in the mean time beat her breast and not quite but almost pull out her hair. I then opened the small door leading to the adjoining room, where Isnan was busy sharpening the knives, and said: "Look at this foolish woman." His facial expression remained indifferent, but in reality he enjoyed the spectacle. I do not know in the least any more all that I said, because my childish psychology may have taken a strange turn. Isnan said to me: "Allah, but you have a sharp tongue!" as if I were battling him. It was a good thing that I was able to use my tongue against this man whom I could not touch in any other way. He was the great animal destroyer in our house; he shot cats and dogs considered dangerous to the hen roost, and one day when he caught a dog in the chicken coop, he broke its back with a bamboo stick. The animal howled horribly; I heard it and ran up: there was a mix-up between the animal that lay howling but powerless in a corner on the ground, Isnan with his bamboo stick, and I who ran between Isnan's legs, flew at him and pushed and pulled wherever I could, all this happening in the small enclosure full of chicken manure and feathers and with the door locked. That the dog did not bite both of us is a wonder. Isnan pushed me aside, almost knocked me down, as he finished the dog with his bamboo stick. I shouted: "Wait, Isnan, when I am grown up I'll treat you in the same way!" I hated him at that moment more than I ever hated Bapa Tjing.

Those animal stories are in my memory the most moving episodes of the time we stayed in Balekambang. In the back yard was the chicken coop, so that the chickens were everywhere, even sometimes in the house; nowhere could one be absolutely sure that one would not step in some chicken manure. But they furnished meat and eggs, the only variation from fish, because the cattle were seldom slaughtered here. The rare times we were given buffalo meat we had to be very careful to find out whether or not the buffalo had perhaps been sick. We had buffaloes ourselves; they were common grey ones with a few albinos mixed in, on whom I preferred to ride after my little friend Sanoeb had taught me how to climb onto them. My mother's favorite cow, Sajati, had no horns and had pushed me into the mud of the river, but the buffaloes with their large thick horns went on dumbly and placidly with Sanoeb and me on their backs. At home I had a chick that ran around peeping, even over my books, but it was one day stepped on by a mysterious stranger; with unutterable sorrow I buried it in the garden next to the place where they weighed the grass. One day my little friend Hatim gave me a *perkoetoet* that had been reared in the coolies' house of his parents; I proudly put it in a cage and asked Amsah to feed it at the same time as my parents' birds, but a week later it had perished from hunger because Amsah had forgotten about it. It was at the time when my father had overwhelmed me with work so that I had no longer paid any attention to it; when I saw it dying and my mother discovered the reason, I was furious with Amsah but also with myself. The fact that the animal had grown up in Hatim's poor surroundings, that he had fed it from his mouth, and that it had to die in this manner in our well-to-do house, gave it the melancholy quality of a fairy tale, but this aesthetic consideration sharpened my pain instead of lessening it. I could have let Hatim beat me if he had consented to do so. But he took it quietly; he had a stupid face with large protruding teeth. After the death of the chick my mother gave me a large yellow rooster who would not have been in any danger of being trampled to death. He was only mine in name, because that is the only way I could claim him, only rarely could I carry

him around for a moment. But from this rooster I derived nothing but pleasure: at one time Otto had sent my mother half a
dozen fighting cocks, all with shaven combs, and mine, who still
possessed his comb, chased them all away. I had vague plans for
declaring him a fighting cock and winning bets with him, and
the *koetjiahs* even made me the proposition, but this right away
showed that he was only mine in name.

The one that really belonged to me, though in name he was
my father's, was the fox terrier Loulou. He was, on account of
his race and color in the midst of managarie, a real white man's
dog, domineering, energetic and unafraid. As his mate Lili had
died, he lived in our yard with his daughters, which did not prevent him from exercising his *droit de seigneur* in the kampong
among the more common canine breed. He fought ceaselessly
and was always the winner; the villagers respected him because
he was an *ardjoena* among dogs. Sometimes, however, he came
home with damaged skin, once in the middle of his forehead; it
was so neat, so deep and so round a hole, that I could not understand that it had not run into his brain. My mother dressed his
wound and nursed him with *kojoepetih* and iodine just as she
did with the wounds of the natives. When we played tag, Loulou
was always present: though he obeyed my father implicitly, he
would go around in circles when my father and I whistled for him
at the same time and would end up by coming to me, though with
a shrinking-back in fear of my father. My father would sometimes
beat him with the whip; not I, I wrestled with him, pulled his
ears and would lift him high and then drop him to the ground,
but it was all in fun. A childish cruelty towards animals did
exist in me, but it did not go very far; I teased the animal in
order to pity it afterwards. We also had many cats, almost every
one of them tri-colored, whom I took to bed with me in turn. My
way of teasing cats consisted of throwing them softly against the
rug that hung from the wall, so that they would fasten themselves to it with their claws high above the ground; they would
hang there mewing pitifully and not daring to drop down, and
as soon as they would risk it I would renew the game. When they
tired out, I had the feeling that now I could spoil them. I only
remember this naive kind of sadism from the time we were in
Balekambang, though later too I always took cats to bed with me.

The fox terrier had a furious dislike of monkeys. A little past
the cow stable was a pond covered densely with green, dark
green, behind a curtain of lianas with white flowers; when he
came here Loulou would start to bark as he trembled all after-

noon, because he smelled the monkeys behind it, whose presence we only noticed by the soft creaking and swinging of the branches. One afternoon I went to one of the coolies to look at a monkey just caught. The animal sat on a stick, making fearsome little sounds like the chirping of a bird. I had forgotten Loulou, who stood behind me looking up at the stick while trembling; the small monkey saw him and clung to me for protection like a child, but with one jump Loulou caught it around the middle and dragged it along through the garden. It happened so fast that nobody realized it, but I quickly got a hold of Loulou, beat with my fists with all my might on his ribs and tried to pry his jaws apart. But he stood as if rooted to the floor, until he had become sure that he had bitten the monkey to death; then he dropped it disdainfully. It was dead; a little bit of blood ran out of its nostrils. I took the little corpse along, with Loulou suspended from his collar in my other arm, and when I came home I tied him, put the little monkey down on the floor in front of him and beat him mercilessly with the whip until he whimpered softly. Still afterwards I went in a desperate state to the beach: if I had wanted to balance my sorrow at the time by a deed, I should have hung Loulou.

He died of hydrophobia. For a few days he had been wandering around grumbling and had become listless, and I had sometimes pulled his ears, taken him up and dropped him. He would go away then, somewhat uncertain on his feet; my father noticed that he was not well and let him lie down in a cool spot on a chain; there he lived for two more days. I was not allowed to come near him, but my father went to look at him daily and patted his head. When he left, Loulou looked at him with glassy eyes. "A harmless hydrophobia," said my father; "good dog, he did not even think about biting any of us."

I still ran a few more dangers from animals, not only danger from cockroaches and centipedes, at the thought of which Dutch women shiver when they think of the Indies. Every day I saw cockroaches at Balekambang. Some snakes had even been slain in our yard. But one day when we were playing at hiding our handkerchiefs, I reached with my hand into an empty birdcage, when Enih suddenly gave a yell. Like a green arrow a *boengka laoet* shot out from under the tin roof of the cage, a snake whose bite is mortal. Another time when the bridge over the Tjikanteh had collapsed, Entjih and I rowed people across in a small prau. As we came back, we were attacked by wasps at precisely the spot where there was a crocodile *kidoeng*. We beat around us with our paddles, but the crocodiles attacked us so furiously that our little vessel was upset and we lay in the dark water above the *kidoeng*. Otto had already taught me to swim; I was therefore not afraid of drowning, but more afraid that time than when the snake had shot out of the cage. Entjih and I swam to the shore, leaving the boat and the paddles. I thought of the woman Djassilem and already felt the crocodile's teeth in my leg: afterwards I was often obsessed with the idea of what one would feel exactly if one were dragged along under water by a crocodile; henceforth I included the following in my evening prayer: Especially do not let me be killed by a crocodile.

And then there was the glorious day when father came home with a tiger—but he had not shot it himself. The animal had been lured in the usual manner with a goat that had been half eaten; a lantern was hung at the spot, and my father and the Loerah *preman* (a freeman, ex-village head) sat in a tree until it would come. My father had taken along the newest rifle of his arsenal, a double-barreled gun, the Loerah *preman* his own old rifle, perhaps one of the first breech-loaders that had been imported to the Indies. When the tiger came hesitating into the circle of light, the native nudged my father; he twice released the catch and both his cartridges missed fire. The other, who had politely waited for his turn, then shot, and the tiger fell without further ado. He was skinned and this time I went to the prau shed to look at his skinned body. He looked strange but still like a tiger. The villagers came in groups, each to buy a bit of tiger meat; according to what Isnan said, not to eat but to use as medicine. The head through which the bullet had passed was boiled in a large kettle in order to be able to give my father a clean skull, and the water became a strong brew with large circles of fat floating on top. The skin was stretched along the back wall of the back verandah, smelling foul for months.

The only time that my father and mother were away and left me in the care of Alima, I had the feeling of being king. I let the *gamelan* be brought in at night in the living room and Moenta had to give a *wajang* presentation for my benefit; I let Enih dance with flowers in her hair, and I, who later on never wanted to learn European dances, shamelessly danced along with my native friends. I almost emptied my father's book box on the sofa and during the day I read until I got a bursting headache; Alima, Ma Oemih or somebody else had to massage it away. During the early morning I was called from my bed because a giant turtle, such as had never been seen here before, had been caught on the beach right in front of our house. I hurried there in my nightgown and on naked feet; the sun had hardly risen and it was cold on the beach and a large number of fishermen stood around the caught animal. It was really enormous, and a little bit beyond, it had laid a number of eggs which also seemed three times as large as the turtle eggs I had seen before. The natives spoke about dragging the animal to the village and butchering it there. At the moment I thought that this was what would happen, when a boy with a stick injured the animal's eye. I then immediately ordered the rope to which it was tied to be cut. The turtle slowly crawled towards the surf and then went in a stately manner into the water. For a moment it disappeared in the foam, but when it had passed the surf it swam away from us in a straight line, towards the center of the bay, and rather above than below the waves. Until it was far away one could see it lift its head, and the natives followed it with their eyes as if they were witnessing a sea serpent swimming away. I had them bring the eggs into the house and I felt wonderful. In the afternoon one of the notables of the kampong came to shout at the gate that I never should have let the animal go, that he would have even given eight guilders for it.

I must have been about eleven years old at that time, it was perhaps during the last half-year of our stay in Sand Bay. I do not remember much about the last days there except the atmosphere. A young European came to live at the other side of Tjiletoeh; he had a gramophone, and we rowed over to listen to the music, which was much better than our symphonium. The waltz from *Coppelia, Tesoro mio,* Rodolphe's song from *La Bohème,* remind me of this period. We sometimes rowed up the Tjiletoeh until we reached an old farmer Pa Sain, who had the reputation of being able to *teloeh* (make people waste away through magic), which according to my father meant that he knew how to get rid of people by poison. He was a very small and skinny, beardless old man with smiling eyes. We had to get out of the boat and climb a steep wall, with steps dug out of the earth, which usually caused my mother great efforts, but once in the garden one was transplanted into a paradise; one sat, walked or crouched under the leaves; one ate fruits and all kinds of tuberous plants: oebi, talles, ketella, as much as one could eat. It was the jungle in all its loveliness; his house stood in the midst of the greenery, fish nets, fishing rods and farm implements stuck out from everywhere, and everywhere the bamboo had been colored with betel stripes. When it became dark we went back, my parents were quiet, the oars creaked, the voice of Kiping at the rudder related a joke, and the sailors hummed a rowing chant. The setting sun on the broad Tjiletoeh, the shadows that fell quickly over the water and melted the lianas and rattan stalks on both shores with the foliage, the hollow, dry sound of the bird that was called *toekang kajoe* (woodpecker), and my hand gliding through the water, feebly gives me, as I think back to it, the atmosphere of those happy days when I was free of school books. We also went to the *sero,* a kind of labyrinth for fish, planted in the sea, with successive rooms out of which the fish did not dare escape because the openings through which they swam would end in a point in their direction. My mother always considered this way of catching fish a pleasure; for me a slight touch of seasickness spoiled the fun.

When my father gave up the work in the factory and specialized in the renting of plots in the interior, we made journeys to other regions and we again slept in native huts. My mother and I in sedan chairs, my father, Isnan and some village head on horseback, we would go through the woods, sometimes over swinging bamboo bridges; and at night we slept on mattresses on the floor, with my mother's sarongs put up by herself like mosquito curtains around us. I would have to write for pages and pages in order properly to picture these journeys, the enjoyment of having a breakfast consisting of weak coffee prepared in the native fashion and turtle eggs that had to be torn apart like parchment bags, the joy of entering a "small town" hardly as large as Pelaboean Ratoe, with a *passanggrahan,* where unexpectedly we would find a stack of torn European magazines, and a market where one might buy all sorts of baubles like great treasures, such as red-lacquered Japanese boxes and for Alima a kabaja pin with glass instead of diamonds.

In all this I have forgotten to mention my foster-sister Sylvia. Because they had no daughter my parents participated in the custom of many Indonesian families of adopting an *anak mas* (literally "golden child," foster-child).

One day my mother came home with a little girl that had been given her by a coolie, a child perhaps a year old, with a pretty round face and large dark eyes. It was called Bettina, after the operetta *La Mascotte,* because it had to be a mascot itself; my father played with it even more than my mother, but after a fortnight the parents came to fetch it back, the mother was continually crying for it and she was not able to separate herself from it. My parents sadly gave it back and let it be known in the kampongs that they would like to adopt a child. From a village high above the Tjikanteh a woman came with a child nine months old, still carried in her *slendang*, with closed eyes, a flat face and feverish cheeks. It had, moreover, a wound in its forehead, because when its mother had gone into the rice field she had put it down somewhere on a rice block, and one day it had fallen from it. The child was less attractive than the one we had given back, but it was pathetic because of its situation: the mother was already an older woman, the father, a young man, was not married to her and had not been willing to recognize it. It came to live with us and in a few days my mother had cured it, the fever had disappeared, the wound was healed, only its flat features remained unchanged. The name given this child was no less classical, in the *anak mas* tradition, it was called Sylvia. I was about nine when it came, and it must have been almost three when we took it along from Sand Bay; still I do not remember anything about its first years but that it called me "pappy."

Neither do I remember how or when precisely we left; my parents and I had recently suffered from malaria, nevertheless it was their intention to return as soon as possible. But in Batavia itself my father found buyers for his renting plots; with the money he earned from this he had a small villa built on the land around Gedong Lami. We could live on the rents; the adventure of Balekambang had cost much energy and good humor but the financial losses suffered were thus made good. The factory there was neglected, and one day it burned down and the house where we had lived fell apart; nothing remained but the cocoanut trees grown wild. Some years later we went back for a visit: everything had changed, even the journey was different, because we went from Soekaboemi to Pelaboean in a car and from Pelaboean to Balekambang in a motor boat. Enih was married to a *koetjiah*, much older than she, and had gone away with him; the villagers called me *djoeragan anom* (young gentleman) instead of the familiar *neng* of before. I remember no more about this visit than that I stood alone under a large tree—the famous fig tree and looked towards Tjimarindjoeng, listening for sounds. There I had walked on bare feet, hidden behind the shrubs when we played Richard the Lionhearted and Ivanhoe. When we were afterwards in Europe, I thought back sometimes about this region as an ideal place to end a turbulent life; with just a few books, I imagined then, and making great friends of the villagers.

Translated by Alfred van Ameyden van Duym

Menno Ter Braak

THE INSTINCT OF THE INTELLECTUALS

WHEN I ASK MYSELF WHY DURING A NUMBER OF YEARS I INSTINC-
tively ranked a man like Spengler above the average intellectuals, I can find only one answer; Spengler cast aside the élite-
principle of "spiritual" man and forced him without further ado
to justify himself under the, to him completely foreign, aspect of
power. The word "power" once seemed to me so superior to the
phrases about a loftier life and advancing science, that it was
easy for me to put Spengler's fatalism against the naked psychiatric work of Fedor Vergin, *Das Unbewusste Europa,* an
argument filled with the typical sagacity of a scholar and with abstract optimism beneath the skin of an exactly as dogmatic pessimism. In the person of this Vergin was represented, so I thought
at the time, the intellectual as counterfeiter, whose instinct of
"little" man drives him to confuse the issue of might through
something like a "soziale Vernunftreligion" as the fairy tale of
the future after the psycho-analytical repast.

Since I wrote the essay, *A Study in Shadow* (1932), the intellectuals of Europe have had ample occasion to think deeply about
the problem of power, which has become more plain than ever to
them after Hitler's victory. If anything has contributed toward
lessening the value of Spengler's words concerning power, it is
most certainly the triumph of this fraud; and our mistake was,
when we admired Spengler too eagerly, that, living under a
democratic form of government, which respects the intellect up
to a certain degree, we had only academically considered the expansion of power of those who not only despise the intellect but
(what is worse) force it into servile malpractice. Whoever is put
in the position of academically debating on the question whether
power, and Hitler's betrayal of the people are two expressions for
the same thing, might perhaps easily say yes, because an academic
answer is after all as futile as an academic debate. I am convinced
that one can only seriously consider such questions if one accepts
responsibility. Most Europeans lack the imagination to guarantee
at the price of their lives the answer to theoretical questions. Just
as little as we wish to subject ourselves to the hellish pains which
Philip II once suffered, so are we inclined to take a purely the-

oretical problem seriously. I do not claim exemption for myself; my admiration for Spengler always had an aesthetic, academic character, just as much in fact as my depreciation of the medicine man Vergin. As long as we profit from the advantages that democracy brings to the intellect, it is not hard for us to be antidemocratic fatalists and submit ourselves to the fact that history only exists as the struggle of one deceiver of the people against another. It was for that reason that a little fellow like Vergin, who resisted with all his might such fatalism and who did not even fight shy of a very cheap mythology as a final morality, seemed a rather reprehensible being to me. The Prussian Spengler, on the contrary, became a soldier from Pompeii, who is willing to die at his post, buried under the lava of vulgarity. It is a frequent phenomenon that intellectuals, who profit by nothing so much as by the democratic way of life, spare themselves no pain to do damage to democracy, because this democracy is founded on false principles and, moreover, does not recognize the beauty of dying at one's post.

Apparently one must have seen from nearby the triumph of power in the shape of a vulgar betrayal of the people to understand that the problem of power is not always only an academic and aesthetic problem. For to argue about power (and this is especially true about someone like Spengler), to write about power in the fatalistic style of the philosopher who stoically submits to the course of events, is already a proof of antagonism toward the existing powers; it is an attempt to reduce everything that is brutal and bestial in the display of power to an intellectual game and thus to bring within the power of the intellect. It is therefore not very astonishing that Spengler, immediately after the official recognition of National Socialism, ranked himself among its antagonists, though with not quite the Pompeian heroism one had been led to expect by his previous pronouncements. In his *Jahre der Entscheidung,* which for the greater part is a violent polemic against the new rulers, against their fusty autarchy and their noisy swindle about races, the name of Hitler does not occur. Apparently Spengler preferred not to identify the post at which he would have so willingly died with the prosaic latrine in which Erich Mühsam was hung. But however that may be, Spengler did not officially become a tool of the political gangsters; though his taking sides against National Socialism was of course in a quite correct manner morphologically and fatalistically made accountable, I am convinced that (like every decent intellectual who watches power function separated from the intellect) he was first of all disgusted by the brawling of the power bad boys, whom he theoretically would have loved to have served . . . theoretically, that is. . . .

The problem of power and the intellectuals has since the advent of National Socialism, which also boasts of intellectuals to justify its power, changed color for us, just because it can no longer be called a theoretical problem. When we at this moment, in the year 1935, speak about *our* power problem, then we have let the all too obvious Spenglerian tone go by the board, because we have become aware that in the future we would rather be "illegal" intellectuals listening to hedge-sermons than numbered heroes with a skull added to our body. We must take into account that before long, perhaps, an intellectual will be talked about as one now talks about a professional criminal. Probably the intellectual will only exist in the greater part of Europe as a clever evader of the legal directives to think only as the leader thinks. It is possible that the once so much respected intellectual will be on the same level as the bootlegger and that official morals will judge him accordingly. Whatever power instinct we have within us protests against this. Rightly or wrongly? With or without a chance of success? It matters little, so long as we resist. Nobody enjoys living like a pariah among his fellow beings, not even the intellectual, though he once might have championed the cause of bohemianism at a time when the liberal citizens (in spite of moral objections) financially supported them. No intellectual who possesses anything like instinct can enjoy the idea that an original thought, uttered in public, may now carry the death sentence with it. The living condition for "thought" is "liberty": two words that twenty years ago sounded like platitudes and that achieve again today terrible actuality, because we are forced through "the revolt of the masses" to take into account in what a Yellowstone Park for intellectuals the nineteenth-century "thinker" really lived. Compared with the Hitler régime even the "curtailment of intellectual freedom" by the Czarist or the Kaiser's government gives us the impression of an impossible and very dilettantish effort to improve through pedagogical correction the work of scholars. As, moreover, the nineteenth century was considered "la vérité en marche," the intellect was able to allow itself the luxury of such opposition. There was no system at the base of it, and in the history books, which educate liberal youth, censure and Siberia are treated as the last manifestations of Metternich's Holy Alliance policy.

A beautiful illusion, originating in the blind self-satisfaction of the Western European schoolmaster, who thought himself superior to the mammals on account of a couple of liberal and Darwinian phrases! The son of that schoolmaster became a Marxist, that is to say, he set the idea of evolution on its head in order to be able to admire it in a position more complimentary to this earth. ("Ganz im Gegensatz zur deutschen Philosophie, welche vom Himmel auf die Erde herabsteigt, wird hier von der Erde zum Himmel gestiegen"—Karl Marx in *Die Deutsche Ideologie*.) He yet remained a schoolmaster, more than ever full of "laws" and "improvements." Now the grandson stands again in Germany, as a schoolmaster before his class; from standing the ideal on its head he has now also taken away the head, so that finally (and one may at least congratulate oneself on the candor) the moment has come when the teacher shows himself openly as the enemy of thinking. The situation has been "clarified"; the schoolmaster, that is, the intellectual, who was by mistake so named, we see at this historical moment as the swindler pictured in his masterly invention, the Aryan. One may see from this development, foreseen by neither Hegel nor Marx, what conclusion may be drawn. The first conclusion is that for the intellectuals-by-mistake, the schoolmasters, there is no proper problem of power, because they make power subservient to the form of the state under which they have to live. They are satisfied with it in the liberal, as well as the Marxian and Fascist stadium, as long as the régime allows them to give up publicly a quantum of relatively sincerely meant word combinations. They do not want any more "liberty" for their "thought." The principal matter for them is that they can give up something in public, because that is how they retain a modicum of self-esteem; nothing therefore is easier for them than to "make a link" from one to the other phrase "acceleration." That is exactly what the German schoolteachers have done. It is therefore above all necessary to dissociate our problem of intellectuality and power completely from this schoolmaster's élite. For, apt in the art of compromise or harmless objectivity, they are ready at any time to fall in with the political ideology that makes their phrases adaptable to today as well as to tomorrow. The objectivity of the schoolmasters allows them always to be in time to welcome with gentle historical sounding of the trumpets the power constellation of the ruling or "coming" party, and to make it theoretically acceptable to the multitude who need the moral justification of schoolmasters in order to idolize a power constellation as the righteous one.

From the first conclusion follows the second: the intellectuals for whom the power problem exists are rare. By far more numerous are the industrious academicians, the harmless commentators, the sonorous ideologists, whose greatest pleasure consists in bellowing again and again through the fallacies of phrases all that through the fallacies of practical politics had already been accomplished. (This is often done in complete sincerity.) And the third conclusion: that the intellectuals have their own power problem, does not mean that we go back to the "soziale Vernunft-religion," to the end of the days of Fedor Vergin, who really only attempted to prove the "Vernunft" of the schoolmaster. When one has gone through Spengler, one *has* learned something—though in some respects perhaps—from a schoolmaster.

The schoolmaster, in all his dimensions, has not in vain been so long identified with *the* intellectual; he *was* indeed during the nineteenth and the beginning of the twentith century the representative intellectual. By "schoolmaster" I mean in this case the cultured person who in order to maintain his prestige appeals to a "higher instance": Evolution, Spirit, the Word, Art, Objectivity, and whatever else one calls to mind. The schoolmaster is someone, who exists only by the grace of the authorities outside the schoolroom, and, when this authority fails, his authority also disappears. In the year 1935, the majority of the intellectuals are still under the spell of the belief in the authority of the schoolmaster. They do not dare play their role of intellectuals without borrowing the responsibility from no matter how minor a deity. That is the cause, among others, of their blessed belief in the little sun of reason, which is but temporarily obscured by the clouds of medieval superstition (the optimism of intellectuals), or their being permanently downcast on account of the clouds which have always obscured the sun and will continue to do so (pessimism of the intellectuals). One can see that in both cases the sun is the "higher instance." That is why the intellectuals in their attitude toward what they believe to be the man of the masses show a schoolmasterish naiveté, which is only exceeded by their schoolmaster's conceit. Depending on whether they belong to the optimistic or pessimistic faction, they make it appear as if their élite humanity must triumph some time (though a lot of confusion will precede it) or is perhaps too good ever to triumph in this miserable world. These are two poses which may today cause loud laughter, but which nevertheless dominate the behavior of the schoolmasters. For these intellectuals the growing barbarism of the masses is but an interlude on the road to a fate which makes their own superiority appear to that much greater advantage.

It follows therefore that, from everything at present being done in intellectual circles, the intellect has become only in exceptional cases *instinct*. Most intellectuals show derision for such an instinct and would rather camouflage themselves as women-chasers or Balkan travelers than admit freely that they are neither one nor the other without the intermediary of literature. They have doubtlessly instinct enough; they have their vanities, they have the desire to rule over some portion of the world in one way or another by wielding their pen. It is evident that their intellectual function renders them a valuable service. But when they are asked to relinquish their authority, the "higher instance," one sees them retreat and hide themselves behind the cheapest taboos. They dare not approach the intellect as instinct; preferably they justify themselves by contrasting instinct and intellect, so that on the one hand they can proudly elevate the intellect as the standard of humanity and on the other can still play their instinctive roles; because the average intellectual wants to be a thinking human being, but by all means not an intellectualist! This interpretation of intellect and instinct is still dominated by the (mostly not even clearly realized) supposition that instinct is something original, animalistic, paradisical and impenetrable, that intellect on the contrary is something derivative, human, abstract and fixed; as if hunger and love were not just as much disciplined by civilization as the intellect, as if our hunger and our love were not just as much phenomena of a definite period of life! The use of the word instinct in contrast to the intellect betrays the schoolmaster who for centuries has accentuated this contrast as a guarantee of human dignity; by human dignity the schoolmaster means the dignity of a small group of "civilized people," who borrow from this contrast the right to consider themselves an élite. The intellect guarantees culture, and culture guarantees the instincts a cultural name; that is why the schoolmaster wants instinct and intellect to remain separate conceptions.

This interpretation of the relation between the intellect and instinct has been current since the Renaissance, and one may deduce from its currency that it was needed to make European culture possible. Among other things it gave to culture authority not only for the masses, who hardly took part in any cultural preoccupations, but also vis-a-vis the culture-carriers themselves;

by clothing this play of culture with the responsibility of "higher" aims, by putting the aim outside itself, it enabled the culture-carriers to look at the particular instinct which drove them to the stylization of their expression of life, as being not an instinct at all. Culture remained "the higher," the authoritative, the *urge* for culture was not admitted among the instincts. Now, after the dismal mess the intellectuals made in Germany, this is more than ever obvious, because as long as the cultural game is continuously considered under the aspect of authority and is therefore placed above the instincts, the player remains a *bad* player, without the true intimacy which there should be between player and game. The sort of intimacy which used to exist between culture and the intellectuals (and still exists), was (and is still) often the intimacy between a lion-tamer and his circus lions. Only the innocent public, who have come one evening to admire a harmonious performance, actually see a unity of "thought and feeling," but one need only let the well-informed keeper, the cynic, tell something about his experiences "behind the scenes," to know that the illusion in this instance only serves the desired appearance.

So when the intellectuals, in order to defend their position, call upon an authority, a "higher instance," they call upon the lion-tamer. One observes immediately from the cultural movements of the lions through the coercion of a whip, how they "inwardly" stand for the tricks which they must perform to give "sense" to their circus existence! If schoolmasters could be born among these circus lions, they would surely be lions that have become conceited because of the fact that they (thanks to the whip, which however is never mentioned among nice lions) have become superior to desert lions by their far-famed pyramid number. . . .

When I am told that there is not much news in all this and that, since Freud, the "better" intellectuals have fewer pretensions, I am not immediately ready to agree. Indeed, it is not especially typical of modern intellectuals to draw attention to the contrast between intellect and instinct; when they still do this, psychoanalysis is immediately invoked, while the efforts of Adler and all the little Adlers to sabotage Freud through a new religious urge too obviously betray their preconceived Jesuitism. However, one must not tackle the schoolmaster on his theory only, that is, under his most unreal mask; there especially the schoolmaster becomes a piquant phenomenon because he is quite ready to give up everything *theoretically,* when in reality he firmly holds on. Freud himself is one of the best examples of a schoolmaster, who committed suicide in theory and nevertheless stays alive as the "sublimated schoolmaster." Instinctively, that is, in all its manifold forms, the schoolmasterish intellectual sticks to his interpretation of the relation between intellect and instinct, because its abandonment would force him either to let go of the whole cultural hierarchy or to admit, without any reservation, that he defends himself as an intellectual *because he cannot do otherwise.* This last admission, the most honest an intellectual is capable of, implies that he admits defending himself with nothing but his instinct.

When one considers the words, "truth," "justice," "spirit," "liberty," and others which are used to death by the schoolmasters, as the instinctive words of intellectuals, then they suddenly achieve a new color. They become the terms in which intellectuals put their power problem aggressively and in this aggressiveness, purely. After having lived a long and once upon a time undoubtedly fruitful existence as terms of justification, they have arrived at the state of instinctive innocence. They may even, as soon as the circumstances have altered, be exchanged for their opposites, without thereby harming the intentions of their users. Terms like "truth" and "freedom" have sense for those who love truth and freedom only, when they realize that as soon as they are spelled with a capital they are already falsified and that without *un*-truth and *un*-freedom they represent nothing. They are our "power words," now in attack and now in defense, and their effect is to be judged by their offensive or defensive positions. Under certain circumstances it may even be quite desirable for an intellectual to fight for un-truth and un-freedom; not *always* are the Nazi swindlers of the "folkish" symbols on the other side of the fence. Our phraseology at present is again in accordance with the slogans of the French Revolution, though as little as five years ago we were disgusted with "liberté, égalité, fraternité." For the same reason barricades are only raised when the situation requires it.

Let us, however, be careful in making the schoolmaster absolute. An absolute schoolmaster, outside ourselves, who acts "in the name of civilization,"—not to speak of even cheaper slogans— is easily recognized, because one cannot mistake his tone. Much more dangerous and problematic is the schoolmaster that every intellectual carries within himself because of his past. We are not being created out of nothing; we are the products of the carefully nurtured schoolmaster discipline of centuries. Even without having been seduced by the swindle of the "Erbmasse," everybody, merely by listening to himself, may be caught by an inherited burden of schoolmaster's conclusions. The intellectual who justifies himself only by his instinct is a relatively new phenomenon, because in past periods of culture he could only lead an officious existence. One may see him for instance in the sceptic or vitalist, who rebelled against the schoolmaster and yet was often in a sense his dupe. By doubting he tried to wear out the intellect (the extreme consequence of this was Pascal); by vitalistic slogans he tried to orientate it toward the power problems of generals and Huns; so is pessimism on the one hand a forced attempt at conformity, on the other hand often the masquerading of people whose strongest instinct was the intellect itself. Nietzsche too, above all man of intellectual instinct or of the instinct which has become the intellect, had at the time of his *Der Wille zur Macht* a distinct inclination to force himself to participate in society as during his Wagnerian period he was inclined to interpret pessimistically his predestination to be a typical intellectual. The intellectual then, and this should not be overlooked, was always "protected" by the schoolmaster and his authority and thereby motivated as a human being. As soon as he is limited to his instinct, he must find the means to maintain and justify himself, that is, to live according to his possibilities. The merchant, the diplomat and the laborer, the miser, the Don Juan and the gastronome, have therefore more assuredness in their acts than the intellectual abandoned by the schoolmaster. The merchant calls upon his affairs, the diplomat upon the interest of the state, the laborer on the proletariat, and such pretexts are generally sufficient to act, to transact and to act together. The schoolmaster allowed the intellectual to act under the pretext of the evolution of another "higher instance." What can the intellectual do without this authority for acting of the schoolmaster, when he encounters stagnation and his instinct asks for the truehearted security of words? It seems to me that his first reaction would thus be to recall the schoolmaster. For he is often a comforter; moreover, he is waiting at the door and he does not bear any grudges; for an authority that has become unfashionable since the intellectual got rid of it in order to trust to his own instinct, he gives lovingly a new authority in exchange which may even be masked deceivingly as a duplicate of the instinct. Just because we cannot afford to miss the word as a means to power, we are also exposed to the schoolmaster's vengeance by the word. As soon as we have used it in a sentence, the sentence threatens us with a false responsibility, the responsibility of "what has once been said." What I repeatedly admire in Nietzsche is above all the readiness to overcome this crafty responsibility; no stagnation of the instinct, nor the hussar's contours of the "Uebermensch" have been able to make him a vassal of the grammarians, no matter how much he too (and he especially) could guarantee that "what has once been said." If Nietzsche sometimes called back the schoolmaster, he was never the man to take advantage of it; he dismissed him again with a new phrase and remained what he dared to be: an intellectual.

They have tried to tell us that this independence based on the intellectual instinct is nothing but the flattering formula for a social stroke of luck. They have tried to interpret Nietzsche, the lonely and asocial intellectual, in the light of historical materialism as the more or less unsuccessful bourgeois professor, who was able to be independent and courageous because he had a little money. And indeed, the Marxist is right, when he considers independence and a pension as the two sides of a same question. The intellectual unfolding of Nietzsche's "spirit" is as little to be dissociated from his potentialities as a *rentier* as the pamphlets filled with platitudes of so many Marxist apologists from their lack of inherited capital. We cannot better show the cheapness of this kind of incontrovertible facts than to obey our intellectual instinct in the middle of the large cities of Europe, without a pension and far away from Nietzsche's home in the solitude of Sils-Maria. The establishing of these "truths" serves exclusively to give those who utter them an opportunity to free themselves from the "truths" that Nietzsche has formulated in his *rentier's* segregation. In this manner too does the schoolmaster attempt to maintain his authority.

The intellectual instinct is not a miracle, neither is it a panacea, nor is it possible to think of it independent of the society in which it manifests itself. Probably it will have disappeared after five days of starvation and a week or two of concentration camp; it is possible, it is even probable. But when we are confronted with this fact, as if it would mean a lessening of the intellectual instinct, then we know that here again speaks "objectivity," which can no longer unconditionally obey any single strong instinct. We really do not belong among those who doubt instinct because it has "been developed" and the story of its source can still be followed by proofs at hand! Neither do we believe in the intellectual instinct because there always has been one and there always will be one; perhaps it has seldom been there, perhaps it has never been there in that form; perhaps in fifty years it will only exist illicitly. I accept the fact that Erasmus, who is looked upon as the typical intellectual, was a schoolmaster to a high degree, simply because a schoolmaster at the time represented and resumed within himself civilization, and even the man with the habits of a born polemist could not have missed the schoolmasterly justification. One would have to mix Erasmus with Machiavelli to obtain a substance that would make us think of "our" intellectual with his own power problem; but it is certain that Erasmus and Machiavelli, if they had known each other, would have passed each other by, probably as sworn enemies.

Considerations about the past and the future of intellectuals are in the last instance intellectual considerations; in many cases they are, moreover, a sign of intellectual weakness in the intellectual instinct, which needs the affirmation of a curve to believe in its right of existence. A Machiavellian Erasmus, an Erasmic Machiavelli: even from this synthesis of two names as the symbol of intellectual instinct one can realize why it is so difficult for the intellectual to be intellectual without the schoolmaster's protective covering. In so far as he has an "Erasmus" in him he wishes not to give up the intellect as a principle of the élite; at any price he wants to remain a humanist and to preach the crusade against the "revolt of the masses" under the motto of "lofty historical duties" (Ortega y Gasset, Julien Benda). In so far as he has a "Machiavelli" within him, he is ready to put himself on the same level as the beast of prey and to roar louder about power relations than the human voice is really allowed to roar on paper (Spengler, Julius Evola). But "Erasmus" and "Machiavelli" cannot any longer be separated in the intellectual; the countermelody in Ortega y Gasset is Machiavellian, and Spengler in the professor's chair at the University of Leyden is rather a fat Erasmus than the celebrated two-in-one of the lion and the fox of *Il Principe*.

"The person who lives another life than his own, who has falsified himself, must try to justify himself in his own eyes," said Ortega y Gasset in an excellent essay about Goethe, in which he tries to explain the Weimar double of Goethe. One should like to apply the quotation much more broadly; in the first place to all intellectuals who twist themselves into the most elegant and objective poses in order to remain faithful to "Erasmus" and "Machiavelli," which means in both cases to their schoolmasters. What the "other" and their "own" life is, even a virtuoso like Ortega y Gasset will find hard to decide, without calling upon his "own" instinct, when the whole play of culture is pointed to make the other one's "own," and to objectivate one's own so much into the other that at times it seems to "sing itself loose." Whether in the future we shall play the part of the intellectual or the pariah can no longer be predicted with any certainty; but as long as a strong instinct dares talk about barbarians and swindlers, where it concerns those who waste the terms of the intellect for a race theory, the intellect of Europe will still be more than an academic curiosity and an objective perfume.

Translated by Alfred van Ameyden van Duym

S. Vestdijk

THE WATCHMAKER VANISHES

With a little exaggeration one might say that albertus Cockange became a watchmaker the moment his great-grandfather established the watch business. He was what he was before he existed and was at that time already a watchmaker, a remarkable craftsman. The only thing his great-grandfather, his grandfather and his father could do was to beget him, in this form, with this future career. Incidentally, his most precious heritage was not the watch business but his ability to identify himself completely with the clockworks that were submitted to him. Not infrequently he performed the most complicated repairs without paying the slightest attention to the customer who stood waiting in front of the counter.

One rainy morning he was about to pry open the lid of an unusually thick, old-fashioned watch, which he had been told was slow, when he saw, lying a little to the left but at the same distance from the edge of the counter, a pale hand opening and closing as if to attract attention or to give a sign. He looked at it with half an eye. That this hand belonged to the man who had just come into the shop hardly entered his head, although he vaguely remembered an ungainly figure in a loose dark raincoat with collar turned up above the ears. But the man had no sooner handed over the watch and stated the complaint, than he vanished out of Cockange's circle of vision, and even now the pale hand, pushed so far, so impertinently far forward, seemed more a part of the rows of clockworks under the plate glass, on which it lay, than part of a human body. Working away mechanically, he determined, more out of habit than fear of wasting time, not to let himself be distracted. This resolve was really nothing but a further confirmation that once again he would not allow himself to be distracted, and this gave him satisfaction.

Meanwhile the opening and closing continued regularly, dully, almost pathologically; it looked like the symptom of a grave nervous disorder, the convulsions of which a competent physician had provisionally regulated before achieving a complete cure. While working, Cockange had again to take notice of it. It did not enter his head that he might be being made a fool of; he did not think of the possibility that the man wished to furnish some more particulars about the bulky watch by means of this monotonous gesture language; not for a second did his fingers cease their insect-like movements. He was not frightened; he was hardly disturbed. But perhaps, he thought, it would be better if the hand were taken away.

He was on the point of mumbling something about it when his efforts were crowned with success and he succeeded in opening the lid. Without doubt the inside of the watch would now have drawn his entire attention away from the pale hand, if his eye had fallen on an ordinary brass interior instead of on what really filled the watch: a piece of thick paper folded together, crumpled at the four corners where it had conformed to the roundness of the case. While the hand went on uninterruptedly with its finger gymnastics, the watchmaker suddenly thought of the students to whom his wife rented rooms and who had once hoisted a chair on the flag-pole. These annoying rowdies, three in number, supplied in turn by his wife and two daughters with tea and food and suits cleaned after being bespattered on a drinking bout, were one of the reasons why Cockange shut himself up more and more with his work and did not leave the shop for days; sometimes he even had his dinner brought to the workshop or behind the counter, and then had to be on the lookout for greasy fingers on the watchglasses, while after matrimonial quarrels he often slept on a camp bed which he had had put up in this same workshop. He frequently had disputes about these students with his stout, surly wife and he trusted his daughters, especially the youngest, less since he had seen her late one evening walking arm in arm under an umbrella with one of the three, or perhaps a fourth student, for enough of them came to smoke and carry on in the rooms upstairs, shouting down with affected voices for fresh tea. His old father, blind and half-childish, often asked whether it was thundering when the students were at it upstairs. But, because they had a separate entrance, Cockange had thus far never been bothered by them in the shop.

In order to ascertain whether one of them had now after all entered the shop in disguise to play this trick upon him, he slowly raised his head. Then he heard the voice of the visitor, and it was certainly not that of a student.

"You had better look at the hand."

"What do you mean, sir?" asked Albertus Cockange, the awl in one hand, the deceptive watch in the other, and his eyes turned searchingly to the face opposite him, which was just as pale, fleshy and sickly as the hand that made the movements, and at the same time absolutely vacant, without explanatory mimicry. That the man had said "the hand" and not "my hand" underlined the independent life that Cockange thought he had already noticed in it.

"I have nothing to do with the hand," he said, "I am a watchmaker and not a salesman for joke articles and surprises."

"That is not necessary, either," the man asserted, his eyes sliding over his right sleeve to the hand and back again. "Just as a watchmaker you had better look at the hand instead of trying to start business conversations."

"But I don't want to look at the hand," said Albertus Cockange.

"If you look or not, it will happen all the same," remarked the man, who stopped sweeping his arm with his glance. He looked at the wall behind Cockange, where about forty clocks were ticking, and continued: "Only you will still have to say what you choose: write or make sounds."

"Now look," said Cockange, forcing himself to a vicious affability, "I can ring up anyone from here. Kindly take that watch with the paper in it away with you immediately, and the hand too."

The man began to laugh. "I knew that watchmakers were against themselves, but . . ." Suddenly he again stared at the hand so immovably and significantly that the watchmaker had willy-nilly to look too, and he then said with something triumphant in his voice:

"Now you must look! Now look! Now look what is happening to the hand."

"I don't want to look at the hand," repeated the watchmaker dully, as if under compulsion, already entirely engrossed by the new performances of the part of the body indicated. Meanwhile the man looked on, beyond his outstretched arm, as absorbed as the other whom he kept egging on to miss nothing of the spectacle. Behind the watchmaker ticked the clocks; their forty-fold rhythm made him dizzy; one was just striking three despite the fact, also neglected by the other clocks, that it was about half-past ten in the morning; it confused him to think of this difference while he had to look, and he really looked, yes, looked and listened; he did not notice how the awl slipped from his fingers to the counter and that the watch had been pushed to the edge with the bulging paper now only half in it. What he saw was this: the pale hand that lay on the plate glass with the palm up was now only half a hand. Nothing of the fingers could be seen except an indistinct swaying, floating like an X-ray photo over the glass, while the palm of the hand, the three or four sutures of which ran diagonally or crosswise and were alternately brought together in folds and separated from each other, was eaten away on the little finger side. This process was now completed with considerable rapidity. The regular movement of the fingers stopped, the palm of the hand took on a wedge-shaped appearance and then melted away to a little notched triangle next to which the stump of the thumb continued the movement longest. Would it now be the turn of the wrist, the arm, the trunk, the whole body to disappear? But before it had gone that far the man pulled his arm back and put the invisible hand into his coat pocket. Albertus Cockange's legs were trembling.

"Now, you will begin too," said the man, who apparently did not take much notice of the disappearance of his hand. "Only tell me first what you want. For a thinking man, writing seems preferable to making sounds, especially if you are contemplating continuing to live in this clock shop. There are already enough noises here, yet the time is not properly indicated, so that I must now assume at random that it is half-past ten. Besides, you will have to reckon that, in case you prefer making sounds, speaking is not included."

When he noticed that the watchmaker continued to stare at him with open mouth, the man approached and stood close to the counter. In a more confidential tone he gave further particulars.

"You would have become blind as a bat. But your father's blindness was enough reason for you to choose the other way. And then you will have to admit that you are tired, dead tired, less from seeing than from being seen. Think of all those spying eyes: the brass wheels, the everlasting, restless blinking, your own eyes staring at you from watchglasses and the smoothly polished insides of watches whose owners watch your fingers. I could explain all this to you. What I mean is: gradually you have acquired in common with all these objects the fact that you can only be looked at," and he threw a glance around the shop, sparing none of the things that indicated time. "Your body has gradually become a mechanism, something amusing for the village fair, a deplorable adjustment to the thing which I tried to make you realize by means of the behavior of my hand, which has meanwhile become invisible. You are a watchmaker, are you? You *were* a watchmaker! You have gone too far, Albertus Cockange. You have served your time; now you will be thrust through space. You must go back to the many different kinds of interchangeable possibilities and impossibilities. . . ." He was interrupted by a weak cry. In an outburst of anger Albertus Cockange was trying to check the visitor's flow of words by hurling, if not the thick watch, then its paper contents like a pellet at his head, when he noticed that he was subject to the same process as the pale hand just now on the counter. Half of his right arm had already dissolved. The left one was wasting away more irregularly, with a frothy bubbling and little clouds of steam. His clothes were going the same way. His whole suit was going—but if that had been all! He looked down and no longer saw his feet. Was it imagination that all over his body a soft hissing could be heard, as if a lump of sodium were oxydizing in the air? No wonder he staggered and closed his eyes and could give no reply to the question that was now being asked for the third time:

"So what do you want? To write or make sounds?"

"Write . . . or . . .," stammered the watchmaker, merely repeating the question with sickly lips thåt were dissolving into a soft jelly. But the man stuck to the first word and brought out a dirty notebook from which he drew a little note block and put it down on the counter. With his invisible hand he scribbled a few words. Albertus Cockange was now invisible except for the left thigh, but he could still see perfectly how the little pad, a silver pencil and the notebook were put aside again and how the man turned away without a word, intending to leave the shop. At this moment footsteps were heard from the sitting room.

A square-shouldered woman with a boxer's chin stepped in maliciously, with awkward, lounging movements. She looked behind the counter, then at the visitor at the door.

"Isn't my husband here?" she asked; whereupon, turning to the door of the workshop, she called: "Ab! Ab!" "Ab isn't here," said the man not unkindly, pressing his invisible hand stiffly against his body. Albertus in a panic had almost collided with his wife, who was dashing up and down behind the counter and in an outburst of impatience threw first the little sheet of paper, then the contents of the watch under the counter into a corner. Albertus did not know what would happen if he ran into his wife; it seemed to him that she would probably suffer most; he therefore shot round the counter, the point of the plate glass cutting him through the hip, by chance the one that had not yet become absolutely invisible. It hurt him, but not badly. As he wanted on no account to let the man get away, there was nothing to do but run, or float to the shop door, for running was so easy that it hardly deserved the name. He was afraid to call out, because of his wife, but if it came to the worst, he would even do this.

"Is this your watch?" asked Albertus Cockange's wife. The man had opened the door. "No, it's Ab's," he said, mealy-mouthed and facing her.

"Aren't you taking it along, sir?" asked the woman.

"It's Ab's, I told you," said the man.

"Ab's? . . . My husband's name is Cockange," she said suspiciously; then, after a moment's thought she held up the watch. "You'd better take it along; we don't buy old gold."

"Old gold doesn't rust," said the man, grasping the doorknob, "and work ennobles." He opened the door in order to run up the street. At that moment the watchmaker wanted to start shouting something like, "Stop thief!" but to his dismay—far greater than when he was becoming invisible—he noticed that he could not utter a word. Hurrying to the door, he saw the man already on the steps in front of the window. When he too wanted to grasp the doorknob his hand slipped right through it, fell through it, without a trace of pain. And then he realized that he would not be able to stop the man even if he caught up with him. That finished him. He yelled noiselessly, raised his hands to his throat as if to press out the sound that did not come; he crouched down, straightened himself in despair, jumped up with a feeling in his feet as if he were treading on a soft balloon and knocked his forehead against a clock on the top shelf without feeling anything of the bump. He was only aware of, "The clock! if I go to pot, a clock too," but nothing happened. The clock pointed to ten minutes to eight and continued ticking, although Cockange's forehead had also been near the spring, right inside. Elastically he came down again upon his invisible toes. And like a cat in its death struggle he repeated the useless jumps, always with his hands at his throat, two or three metres high in all directions, against clocks, passing through strings of watches, thick plate glass and wood, but always within the walls of the shop. When he was beginning to realize that he would go mad if it went on like that, he fainted and remained lying motionless near the floor mat for a quarter of an hour. Three customers waded through him during this time.

His first thought, after he had dragged himself out of the shop and halfway up the stairs to the first floor (where he sat with his head in his hands or half through his hands just as it happened to be), was pretty foolish and entirely unreasoning: that now he could no longer die. What had come over him was indeed much worse than death, although he felt fairly quiet, without the despair of before his swoon and even fairly comfortable, apart from the slight twitch in his left hip which had remained after contact with the plate glass. This hip, in which the process of becoming invisible was apparently arrested, remained a place of greater density in his body for some time, like a knot in a plank; perhaps if one looked carefully one would even discover some shadowy bundles of muscles, but in a few hours that would be over and no sensitive plate would have recorded anything of his body floating by, or a hand passing through him feel any resistance. On account of the hip, Albertus Cockange compared himself not irreligiously with Jacob who had fought with the angel.

Although he was safe everywhere and could, so to speak, have hung over the electric chandelier in the sitting-room, he went to the loft in order to be able to think better. Little rooms were partitioned off, a servant's bedroom and two for guests: and he now tried to get accustomed to his new existence by walking through the walls from one to the other or by standing in such a way that his body was in three rooms at the same time. He also jumped a great deal and at one moment even pushed his head between the roofing tiles; as it was still raining, he pulled it in again, although the drops naturally fell through his head without making it wet in the same way as his head penetrated solid objects. What impressed him was that the force of gravity still had a hold upon him. He could get through everything, through wood, almost as easily through iron—he tried it with an old bedstead—and by applying himself he could float wherever he wanted to. But if he then relaxed, which was not very difficult after a little practice, he came down again on the spot from which he had risen, unless an unusually thick sheet of iron was between him and that spot.

Although all this gave him a childlike pleasure, at which he caught greedily as at a compensation for what had come over him, he determined not to commit any stupidities and not to abuse his new powers. On the following days he therefore followed the normal way of getting from one room to another, except when all the doors were closed, and then he went right through them. The sight of a crack where he could just squeeze through pleased him; he then made himself quite narrow and acted as much as possible as the former Albertus Cockange would have done, deliberately overlooking the fact that frequently large pieces of his body, whose measurements had remained unchanged, still cut through the wood of the door and doorpost. He could not see this, of course, but he noticed it by an extremely delicate, swift, crunching feeling which he from now on called the "wood-worm tingling." Only of woolen and linen materials he felt nothing; he once danced round his wife's wardrobe in order to confirm this once and for all. He saw all these things like every mortal; to his eyes there was no difference between one material or another as regards their transmission of light rays. If he was inside, it was simply dark round him. The fact that he could not speak or make any other sound fitted in with the announcement of the man in the shop. He breathed ordinarily, although this was apparently not necessary, any more than was sleeping, which, owing to the general relaxation of the muscles, could also have had strange consequences. The taking of food and what belonged to it no longer existed. To his former existence there testified, besides his memories which had not faded, only an occasional unbearable itch in his fingers for the movements of gimlet, chisel and file, and the longing of his eyes for diminutive brass objects.

As he was unable to think of the shop without horror and worried so much about the fate of the watch business that he preferred avoiding his wife's and daughters' conversations on the subject, he at first remained in the loft the greater part of the day. When he had once become accustomed to the new conditions of life, had learnt to move about without being astonished that he never knocked himself against anything and could say to himself without a trace of inner protest: "I am invisible, I am no longer a watchmaker, but I am invisible," as if the main thing about it all was not so much his unusual condition as the incompatibility of the conceptions "invisible" and "watchmaker"

—he settled down for hours to brood on the beginning of his adventure: the man in the shop, the watch, the paper, the hand and the little note pad. He had wanted to find the man again, not to ask him for an explanation of something so strange, but to call him to account. He would like to seize that fellow by the collar and bring him back to the shop, as if then everything could be undone on the spot. Where was he and who was he? Would he, Albertus Cockange, ever be able to be visible again with or without the intermediary of this man? What was written on the torn-off little paper, and what on the thick paper in the watch? But under no circumstances would he have gone to the shop to ascertain these things.

Before one of these questions could entirely preoccupy him, however, a new perspective was opened by the reflection that though he could not seize the man by the collar, he could track him down, no matter what thereupon happened. Nothing prevented him from leaving the house, he had only to walk through the roofing tiles and he would be in the open; and if he, out of respect for the former Albertus Cockange and his habits, definitely wanted to go out by a door to reach the street, there was available the door used by the students instead of the shunned shop door, to permit his leaving. Cockange's house had rather a complicated construction, mainly because it really consisted of two houses. It was a strange world of rooms which he could cross at will in all directions, so that passages seemed like rooms too because one entered them in the same way from the top left-hand corner, or by putting one's head through a skirting board; ordinary people never enter or leave a passage, they go through a passage. The two houses stood behind one another, which was made clear to visitors by a double scar in the form of a little staircase in the two enormously long passages; the first floor of the house formerly in front was occupied by the students: this part was connected with the street door by means of a stair. Besides that, there was a middle stairway leading from the sitting-room to the back part of the first floor and through a passage door also to the students; this functioned especially as a servants' stairway; his daughters and sometimes his wife tripped or stumbled up it with steaming dishes on a tray, but in the evenings they went more stealthily to their bedrooms, not so much in order not to disturb the students, who generally began to kick up a row at that time, as not to be heard by them and run the risk of another request for tea or grog. The blind, half-childish father was generally put to bed at eight o'clock.

Strange that Albertus Cockange, devising plans to leave the house, was more and more intrigued by its intricacy. And not only that; he seemed attached to the house. Although of course he would always be able to return, it is questionable whether he would still possess the strength, after the experiences that awaited him outside. For that is what was occupying his mind more and more; not the man he wanted to find, but the paths he would follow to find the man, paths to freedom, unknown paths. . . . After all, the man was nothing more than a pretext. The outside world, and the incredible adventures an invisible man, even an invisible watchmaker, was capable of, were beckoning. What a watchmaker! Watchmaker is what he had been; now he could do everything and be everybody, everybody and nobody. He could keep an eye on everybody from as close by as he wished, first the watchmakers, his former competitors, then the others, as they had formerly done in regard to him; everything they said and did and wrote, how they plotted—the statesmen, politicians—how they loved and hated and all the rest of it; in short it was too much for him. And then, finally—then he remembered for the first time the choice he had had to make quickly—would he perhaps be able to write down all that he came to know, what he saw and overheard?

Animated by this thought he hastened to the wall of the servant's bedroom, near which he was sitting, and scraped his right first finger over it, obeying an impulse, a contraction and urge in the invisible muscles, which had suddenly replaced the craving for subtle fingering, Cockange's worst torment since the change. And he was able to—he wrote. Letters as if in pencil, not very black but pretty thick and clear-cut, grew before his eyes, and as his sense of feeling indicated, from his fingers. He wrote with pleasure, not too much at a time, but drawing handsomely with a vain complacency. He wrote: "Albertus Cockange, watchmaker, Albertus Cockange, formerly watchmaker, was overcome by something in the shop—in the shop—in the shop, Albertus Cockange" —and more such words that signified nothing. Then he sighed deeply and wanted to rub it out with his fingers, but this of course he could not do; once written down they were beyond his power. He had not reckoned with that. The pattering of the rain —again the rain—attracted his attention. He shuddered a little, although there could be no question of real cold. He shuddered on account of the world outside, of the things in the great space on which he appeared to have so little hold. This writing exercise did more than anything else to tie him to the house during the first few weeks.

Insensibly he overcame all diffidence as to what could be discussed about the watch business and often he spent half an hour at a time with his family, mostly squatting in a corner of the large, irregularly built sitting-room, which opened by means of a garden door into a dark little courtyard. The reasons he gave himself for this aloofness—he could just as well have moved up to the family circle, he could have sat on the table with his behind in the soup tureen, although that would never have entered his head—were that he could get a better general view in this way: there his wife with her jaw and sallow skin, often scolding, there his daughters, the youngest despite her spectacles not uncomely, with a particularly pretty figure that had often made him think of her with good-natured chaste consolation, since she had reached maturity, as of a woman that would make a man happier than he had ever been, finally the old grandfather with his gray spectacles, his bald head with irregular tufts of hair and his trembling chin, whose childishness expressed itself especially in the incoherent manner in which he, as initiate, spoke of watches. By observing this circle as a whole, he imagined, he would be able to study how things stood more easily than by a more individualized spying. In reality quite different reasons made him remain in the corner of the room.

Soon he noticed that his going had not caused the least disturbance, except perhaps for the first few days. Everything went on as before. People rang up about repairs, bills were presented and made out, and his wife kept the cash; the amounts that were concerned showed clearly that the business was flourishing despite the invisibility of its owner. How could this be explained? Neither his wife nor his daughters knew anything about clocks and watches, while his father was at a stage at which he needed winding up himself, so to speak, in order to be able to make another step. From several utterances it seemed, and he was surprised that he had not thought of it earlier, that they had taken an assistant or substitute, probably a competent craftsman and surely an industrious one, for all those weeks Albertus Cockange had not caught sight of him. Following the example of the former master he not only spent all his working hours in the shop and the workroom but probably ate and slept there too. The only thing that made Cockange doubt the existence of an assistant was the circumstance that he never saw his wife, otherwise a great meddler and keen on money, check the actual shop books; she displayed great confidence, which would have astonished him with regard to himself, let alone a hired hand. Also in the following respect nothing had changed: his wife and daughters concentrated entirely on preparing what the gentlemen students desired; they cooked, brought home bottles, made these bottles disappear again; then a bespattered suit came along and the youngest daughter or the eldest went to work at it, singing. Conversation at table also turned upon the students. They raised their pranks, or at least excused them, and even his wife, otherwise so imperious, was indulgent toward the students, the racket they made and the dirt on the stairs. It was true, they paid well. Sometimes the old man looked suspiciously at the ceiling; but that was nonsense; the bedrooms were up there; the students lived in the front part of the house and only if they went jigging and singing could one hear them. The old man trembled and spilt his cereal; for him there were many things not right in this house; not infrequently he suspected during the meal that a student, an overgrown young gentleman, stood behind his shoulders; they would tie his napkin round him in a minute, he had better make them laugh; he could do it very well. Then he would turn round spitting a fine streak of pap, so fine that the bothersome daughter-in-law did not notice it and say with a bleating sound: "I too was often drunk." If one of the daughters then came to help, he recognized her by the smell of toilet soap instead of the already expected cigarette smell, this toilet soap that was more familiar to him than the one with which he himself was occasionally washed. For it was the girls during the last few years who brought him to and from his bedroom and let him get a breath of fresh air on very hot summer nights on the canal in front of the house. And he smelt their hands and faces, large invisible flowers, which had been brought close enough but not too close to his.

Now, was there a substitute or wasn't there? It sometimes happened that his daughters or his wife used expressions like: "He isn't in," or "Isn't he coming?" or "Go and give him that, will you?" At first Cockange thought that this referred to one of the boarders, the tall student with the finely chiseled nose, who had found most favor with the ladies despite his ridiculous exactingness, which trotting about from morning till night could hardly satisfy. But then there were some remarks in connection with a broken spring, a time-piece glass-bell, that left no doubt. Here at first his own name was used, probably—he came into the room just too late to be sure—as a hint of how things used to be done. They seemed to have forgotten him very quickly; but his relation to his wife had been cool of late, and the girls were superficial creatures. Perhaps the whole affair, in which doubtless the police had interfered in the beginning, was too painful to them.

A short time after that he saw his successor in the flesh, in the half dark, so that he had to guess, but it could not very well have been anyone else. It was a strange meeting; he was more curious than suspicious, although his suspicion had been fed the last few days by something that should really have prepossessed him in the man's favor as a worker: his obstinate preference for workroom and shop. In this way, however, he escaped all control; would he not be able to idle with impunity, appropriate valuables, embezzle money? Here it should be mentioned that the invisible man did not feel inclined to play the role of supervisor, not only because the shop was still a place of hellish horrors for him—a place where watchmakers were so to say razed to the ground—but because if he discovered any cheating, he would not be able to do much about it, at most, write his findings up somewhere and then still have to see whether they were taken account of. But, all in all, he did not think that the business was in bad hands.

It was already late, past eleven, when he saw the dark figure with bowed head climb the servant's stair. The electric lights in the passage were particularly dim, one of them was even broken. He himself was standing in front of the door of the loft stairs, which he had reached by a somewhat irregular route up between two beams of the sitting-room ceiling and then by a few swimming strokes in the wood to the left; he knew from experience that in this way he would come out exactly at the loft door with the least possible loss of time, and on some evenings he amused himself by barring the girls' way as they went off to bed, to look once more into their faces in the uncertain light, as if it were a lonely goodnight kiss, when his wife, usually still downstairs, was not present. But he was too late, the girls were already in the back bedroom which he did not wish to enter because they always immediately began to undress; then there was a whirlwind of arms and legs and white clothes, finally one or the other came flying off over their heads, and then they flopped into bed, cackling—all habits from the time they were little girls. So he stood in front of the loft door and looked at the door of his wife's bedroom—formerly his also and now his still if he had wished, although he promised himself wretchedly little of it—and heard the stairs creak under a man's slow step. The assistant appeared, turned the corner of the passage, shuffling, his hands in his pockets, apparently deep in thought; he was clearly not a talkative man; no longer young, not much shorter than the watchmaker and with clothes that seemed strangely familiar to Albertus Cockange. He stood looking for a moment like someone who is just about to call down over his shoulder; then he steered toward the first bedroom door, opened it and entered the room, leaving the door ajar. He turned on the light, sighed, blew out his breath. A chair creaked. All this was extremely strange, even frightening, for what did the man intend, and were there no valuables or even money locked away in the bedroom? Cockange lacked the courage to peep in; and then his attention was already drawn to the continuation of this unexpected scene. It was his wife who now came upstairs, stumping as usual. When she stood in the passage, a loud tinkling of cups could be heard from the students' rooms, whereupon she listened for a moment at the partition door, automatically fumbling open some snaps on her skirt; the watchmaker guessed at the conflict between her coarse fingers, her thick nails and the sharp-edged little buttons that ought rather to have been in a watch than on such a skirt. And he guessed more when she steered resolutely toward the lighted door crack. He guessed an astonishing amount as he stood in front of the closed door, a few moments later. He suppressed the thought of entering and having a peep, and he departed to the loft where he belonged.

He did not much mind. Perhaps they were right; marriage plans would only increase the assistant's devotion; and his wife seemed to him too sensible not to have seen to it that he had marriage plans. It was perhaps a little shameless so near the girls. The occurrence, which was not repeated for some time, as if the man had taken over not only the work and perhaps the business but also the conjugal rhythm of his predecessor, brought the advantage for Cockange that he began to feel much less guilty toward his wife and his whole family. By his disappearance he had harmed or could harm them; now they were all quits. The fact that the man wore one of his suits, even his best suit, could indicate that he would not be taken into the business as a partner well provided with capital; it also indicated the presence of certain feelings in his wife who had never been very ready to help, that is to say, feelings toward the newcomer. Reverence in the matter of worn clothes might have played a somewhat larger role, he thought bitterly, but he was quickly reconciled by the reflection that the solution was also the best for the girls. He determined to leave the house for ever before the wedding took place.

Albertus Cockange did not again see the assistant, who slept on the camp bed in the workshop every night now, and as the suit was the only thing he had been able to place, he had no clear-cut impression of the man. Besides this, he began to pay more and more attention to other things, which were going on in the sitting-room and which touched him more than a watch business that flourished or not and a conjugal fidelity that was preserved or not. The fact that he still remained sitting in the corner of the room had a different reason from the one he had deluded himself into believing in the beginning. He did not keep aloof in order to have a better survey but because he feared nothing so much as bodily contact with people, especially with these people, his own flesh and blood. If he came close to them he might not be able to resist making use of his new capacity and simply float and fall through them, which seemed unbearable to him in the case of his father, indecent in that of his daughters and repugnant in that of his wife, although his brain told him that they would know as little of such passing of the invisible as he himself. His feeling forbade him to approach them closer than about four paces. Instead of solid bodies against which one could bump and which one had to evade, it was human abysses that one had to avoid for opposite reasons. It would also, for instance, have been indecent in the eyes of the watchmaker, who apparently had many more scruples than when he was still visible, to stare at them from close by; perhaps it was precisely to resist this temptation that he always stayed as short a time as possible in the sitting-room and quickly withdrew again after gathering some data or information, or what he considered as such. While falling down human abysses would not have been much more than clumsiness or a defiance of the laws of nature, looking long and searchingly from so close that he could imagine he was breathing with their breath, seeing with their visible eyes, represented something that he longed for violently and at the same time feared as an enslavement from which he would not be able to free himself again, a morbid but overwhelming desire. Stare so long that they had to look back and yet see nothing! And then think: they don't see me; they don't see anything; they are stupid and fat and grasp nothing; there are places where they can't go, even with their glances, places as close to them as I am now.

That seemed to him amends for much; but he would remain clinging to them as with suckers, because the feeling after the parting, when the one who was stared at regained his former preponderance, seemed worse to him than anything else in the world.

But how great was his terror, his horror, when he noticed that this vampire-like staring had long been practised in this house. Formerly Bible evenings used to be held regularly in the circle of Cockange's acquaintances; he himself was sufficiently versed in the Scripture to consider this a pleasure, but on the other hand there was his wife in her dull ignorance who seized these evenings to ridicule him or to expose his ignorance, which was very simple for her as she had the book in front of her and then heard the lesson. The atmosphere of an assembly of elders, of which the little evenings were a free imitation, then turnd into that of a fairly vulgar confirmation class. Preferably Albertus' wife hurled prophets and sequences at him and then when he did not answer, remained reasonably content for the rest of the evening. The blind old father was always present and was allowed to stay up late, as he was on the occasion of the first resumption of the time-honored custom after Cockange's accident, the first at least in their house. First he went down to see whether everything was in order and whether his father was sitting comfortably in the big armchair with some hot wine in front of him; it also interested him whether the visitors would speak about him, but in this he was disappointed. The assistant was not there; possibly the man was irreligious—the matter of entering the bedroom also seemed to point to a lack of scruples. At nine o'clock he came again to look. They were occupied with Ruth, and everything was going splendidly. His wife interrupted nobody, neither during the reading aloud nor during the interpretation, and improvised little sermons that everyone was allowed to offer at will. He then remained in the loft until a quarter past eleven, listening to whether the girls came home from a party to which they had been invited and listening to the students just beneath him, who seemed also to be busy discussing, even if other subjects. By the sound of voices and banging of doors he heard that the guests were leaving; he waited, because he thought he could hear by the conduct of the students that the girls had by chance come home: pushing up a window and calling down. But if they were drunk they might also have the impertinence to call after the departing guests. No, it had not been the girls. Everything was quiet again. A little later he went down for the third time, suddenly worried about his father who had now to be put to bed by his wife, so worried and even impatient that to save time he entered the sitting-room between the two beams and thus caught full sight, at an angle from above, of what was going on at that moment. The two people were sitting opposite each other at a table, his wife behind the Bible, her hands supported on either side of it like a pulpit orator, her eyes fixed on the blind eyes of the old man, whose right hand was groping for his wine glass. Cockange knew that on such evenings, once over his sleepiness, he needed wine, or thought he did. But as soon as his hand neared the glass, the woman bent forward and put it a little farther away. Apparently thinking he was alone in the room, the old man, mumbling, again began his search. But then the terrible thing happened. The woman rose slowly, still with her hands on the table, still staring at the blind eyes with a burning hatred, so unbearable, so obstinate and complacently convinced of her own right, so scathing, that it seemed to the watchmaker witnessing this scene with beating heart not far from his father, that she could at any moment strangle the old man across the table without a trace of remorse or even of fear of punishment. Never had he known that she was possessed of such hatred, even if the old man did give a lot of trouble. Bent far over the table, she pressed against the Bible with her fat belly, just staring as if her eyes would come out again at the other side of the old head where there were a few foolish, yellowish wisps of hair that Albertus could well see. She could go no further. But now she began to make faces, to threaten with lips and teeth and with her jaw, while the old man mumbled and looked for his glass and missed it and stared into the emptiness in front of him. She seized the glass, put it to her lips to empty it and then—this too belonged to the derision—replaced it on the table just in front of his chest between his arms while his right hand was still groping much further forward to the left and right.

Without realizing what he was doing, Albertus ran round the table and stood next to her. He extended his invisible right arm, which was trembling much more than that of the childish old man on the other side, and wrote as large as possible on the open page of the Bible that was now almost entirely under the woman's belly: "Stop that confounded nagging!" This approach cost him an enormous self-conquest. I'll have my hand in her in a minute, he thought, and then there'll be letters inside her. Even for such pestering, this struck him as too cruel a retribution. He would have preferred to choose for this purpose the chapter about the writing on the wall, but there was no question of choice, for he could no more turn over pages than box his wife's ears, kick or scold her; it was Ruth, and Ruth it remained, and after all the place made no difference. He waited tensely to see what the consequences might be. With a grin full of malicious joy, which tried to become coarsely, maternally teasing when she heard the street door bang, she snapped her first finger at the old man's ear without touching him. For this movement she had to bend so far over that the Bible shifted and came to lie at a slant, and when she raised herself to resume her former position, she lost her balance for a moment and with her body turned over at least a hundred pages, which happened easily, for the book, still fairly new, did not stay open very well. Suddenly the girls came in, and Albertus Cockange hastily got out of the way while they moved toward his wife, flushed, chattering, fresh from the night air.

So this was his house. No house, indeed, for a man who had the world before him and the place to himself if he wished. Again the old plans raised their heads, and the following evening, very early, wantonly neglecting the natural style of the architecture and sally-ports, he set off at a great pace, cut through clothes-lines, beams, tie-beams and roofing tiles, touching everything he could, and raised himself in the sunny air above the roof with birds round or through him, and a solitary butterfly. Spring! Now what? Quickly his feeling of power grew, making him forget all humiliation by assistants, devilish daughters-in-law, refractory Bible pages. After all, what he was doing now no one could imitate. Rising still higher, he obtained a general view of the canal, the young green that almost completely filled the gully. Then the water appeared and through the hazy branches he saw the cobblestones and the butcher and baker. Perhaps this was beautiful. The sun stood quietly at the end of the row of houses, of which he saw more and more roofs, red mountains of rocks with moss and the glacial grottoes of dripping kennels and over everything, doves and crows and a single sea-gull moving off to sea. Courtyards came into view, gardens became square, outer walls, in perspective, impossibly narrow. He had no plan, merely enjoyed the power and the movement and his own crystal transparency. More and more roofs; then the town lay before him, girded by the green of boulevards, the blue of distant hills. He made a quarter turn in the air and observed the towers of the cathedral above which he began to rise.

But then an unpleasant empty feeling tore through him. He suddenly realized that he must on no account lose sight of the roof of his house if he wanted to go further. Had he not lost sight of it already? Probably he had strayed too far to the right; the foolish thought even stole over him that the wind had hold of him, blowing from the west, judging by the trees and the smoke. By making himself limp, he descended some tens of metres and again caught sight of the canal gully, remembering some details of it that he had just noticed. As the roofs were all alike, there was nothing left to do but to let himself drop further and to investigate one roof after another or, as a last resource, to go down to the canal and upstairs through the students' door, his eyes rigidly turned from the shop. Just when he had begun to carry out this plan, holding his breath the while and thus probably aiding the relaxation of his muscles, he discovered on a roof some little human figures, little men waving their arms. He steered a bit nearer but, before recognizing their faces, realized that he had found his house. Then he also saw who it was: the tall student with the superior air and the most affected voice of the three, and the short, fat one who always posed as the tall one's satellite. Although something told him that here danger threatened his peace of mind and that it was not for nothing that until now he had avoided the students and their rooms as carefully as the shop and the workroom and that he ought to use this warning to float further, never to return, he paid close attention to their demeanor, wondering at their quick movements, as of young animals, bears for instance, which had at the same time, something indescribably scoundrelly—a knavery of the species, not especially of these young gentlemen, an innocent but therefore all the more dangerous knavery.

In spite of this, he thought it would amuse him, at least if he did not have to reckon with a loosened tile. Up the slanting roof with gymnastic shoes, then feats with one leg in the air and, meanwhile, shady little songs; but that was nothing; that was even comical. But after these more or less unimportant stunts, they became wanton. They let themselves down, beating the tiles with their fists, sang down the gutter, kicking viciously to destroy it. In this way they approached the back of the house where the tall one a few minutes later lay down on his stomach in order to stare down over the gutter pipe. Just below him was the little courtyard. Behind him stood his satellite, yelling and dancing like an old woman. But the tall one kept still and, when the other nudged him, made signs with his hand that he did not wish to be disturbed.

Albertus Cockange on the ridge of the roof, now also moved to the back gable and immediately saw what had attracted the attention of the student. It was nothing in the little courtyard or in the neighbors' gardens. It was just between the courtyard and the gutter, it was on the first floor, by the bedroom window where at that moment his youngest daughter was putting her head out and looking up. She was quite flushed, blinking behind her spectacles in the strong light; but the eyes themselves were turned to the student obliquely above her; immovable, appealing and in love, those blue eyes looked through the curtain of blinks like a ray of light through restless waves. And this look was answered; there was no possible doubt! What a play of eyes, what a shameless exposure of the pupils; it made Albertus Cockange turn hot and cold and above all anxious, more anxious than angry. After such looks one could expect anything. There was no longer a question of wantonness or playfulness, although the fat student still stood carrying on behind the love-maker; and this was no first sly attempt at approach; no, it was, with this spring weather, a sealing of countless meetings of eyes and hands that had preceded it. The student who was otherwise so cocksure was almost as flushed as the girl. By God, in a minute the two faces would become detached and unite in one red glowing globe, shooting rays. If after such looks one pushed such a young man into hell and the girl into heaven, they would still be able to come together. And he was powerless. As father powerless, and as invisible father still more so. This staring, though it did not last longer than twenty seconds, was much more painful than what he had witnessed the previous evening.

Like a harpy he fluttered through the house that morning. He went to places where he had never before been and especially again and again into the rooms of the students with the significant disorder: cigarette ends and scholarly exercise books. They had gone out. Wherever he came in the house, except in the shop and the workroom, something could go wrong or was just going wrong. The business, the money, the childishness of his father, his wife's debauched cruelty that would burst out one day, the assistant who would desert her, the foot-warmer over which his father could fall, what the neighbors said of the students, what the students said of his daughters—an endless torment for Albertus Cockange's spirit to which all serenity had become foreign since the happenings on the roof. If he could only express himself! That was the worst: to be the conscience of a whole household and not to be able to pronounce the word that would hold back from destruction the people assembled there. He came upon things that made the heart in his body, his invisible heart in his invisible body, turn. Unutterable forms of distress. Dead flies in places where nobody ever came, but which were there all the same. Cigarette ashes in food, absolute and infallible. Holes as large as fists in his father's socks. And everything connected with the girls. He found out, and an unbearable remorse harassed him because he had let this custom become deeply rooted, that the girls did the students' rooms and made their beds. Now that he accounted for it he realized that this was after all no work for his wife, but what sins, what horrors were there that could not be explained away? The more one spied, the more one discovered.

Finally, two days later, again in the morning, he discovered what he wanted to discover. He had let himself down into the students' room in the front part of the house at this special hour, the hour of doing the rooms. For he had made up his mind not to miss it for a single day. At first the students' rooms seemed deserted—his daughter was not yet there, everything was in disorder and he was annoyed by this provoking slovenliness that really seemed to have no other purpose than to be unpleasant to less slovenly people. Then, suddenly, he heard whispering behind him. He wanted to ignore it by first looking in the other two students' rooms; finally it seemed the best plan to move in their direction with his back to them and then to turn round with a jerk. Indescribable moments followed. From very close by, closer than he had dared to come to any human being in his new life, he spied, in horrible self-torment, the student and the girl, leaning toward each other in a corner of the old sofa. Without any other wish than to see, to see all, he was, in the most abnormal way—the short distance particularly was something insane, as if one sat with one's nose on a panorama—witness of an amorous play that was perhaps new to the two, but that looked as if it would lead quickly to an irreparable end. The student, at least, was kissing as if his life depended on it. Cockange's daughter pulled herself to him and pushed him away with almost the same movement of the arm. For half a minute she sank into the sleep of a thousand years' of the fairy tale, tender, lonely, willing to die. The student said she was sweet, whereupon she acted brusquely and wildly, taking off her spectacles, while the student looked at the window as if he wanted to pull down the blind. And at all this the father looked with a taste in his mouth as if, although invisible, he was about to decompose. For it was death in life that he was experiencing, the death of old, long-cherished feelings, the sinking away of all support, and that was so not because the panting piece of shamming there was his daughter whom he had to protect, but because he desired consummation of himself with all his soul. There would have to be an end, somehow, an end to the tormenting doubt and the care for others —the visible ones would have to fend for themselves. His daughter was the sacrifice on the altar of his peace of mind and like every sacrifice, her approaching downfall gave enjoyment, and this enjoyment shamed him, and this shame increased his powerlessness, which in its turn made him long for peace of mind.

At last Albertus Cockange awoke from his ill-fated trance. This must on no account continue! It was his duty as a father to interfere. He hastened to the wall, the papered part above the more and more suspiciously rocking sofa, he bent halfway over the couple, taking every precaution not to touch them, and wrote with trembling but huge letters: "Hilda! Take care! Your father." Running through the room, he scribbled exercise books, and the young gentleman's letters lying about, full of the same warning. "Hilda, don't do that to me! Your father," or "He will make you unhappy, Hilda. Think of your mother." Hereupon he scratched two more walls full of huge letters, but it did not help. Like a caged bird he flew round struggling with ebullitions as ridiculous as they were inappropriate: to write on their hands, on her skirt, to throw himself upon them, to run through them in the hope that they would notice it. Bah! then perhaps they would kiss each other in the place where his liver was! He was powerless. In an attack of desperate fury he struck the back of a chair with his hand, and struck through it. Would the boy be such a brute as to seduce this girl in front of his eyes? My God, what should he do?

But then he realized what was his only chance and his daughter's too. He would have to try and become visible again! At any price! As visible father he would storm avengingly into this room and throw the young scoundrel out. It had to be done. As he had become invisible by a hand and a watch with a piece of paper in it, so could he now try the opposite by means of the same objects which might probably be found in the shop; only too well did he remember where his wife had thrown the thick paper and the sheet on which formulas were perhaps written or hints to invisible watchmakers who had had enough of it. To see the shop again would be terrible, contact with the assistant probably disagreeable. But his child was worth it. Without further hesitation he calculated at which place he would pass through the floor; he let himself go limp, felt the "wood-worm tingling" rise higher and higher like water round a bather's legs, while his legs were already sprawling into the shop. He closed his eyes in order not to have to see anything more of the sofa. With closed eyes, now for other reasons, he fell into the shop and landed gently on his feet, immediately stiffening so that he should not sink further. He opened his eyes.

He found himself in the shop, so long shunned, so little changed. Rows of clocks, with the stupidity of their dial plates and the safety of their mahogany cases, ticked frantically, a cuckoo clock that would choke in the entire nature and the kingdom of the birds, if one didn't take care; watches that did not indicate a smaller time but the same time, which was after all strange. Wrist watches! A wide bundle of sun rays on the alarm clocks for bedside tables with radium stripes. Albertus Cockange took all this in at one glance, for he wanted or his soul wanted to know whether this shop had remained the same, not less dangerous but also not more dangerous than at first. After this glance, which embraced all and decided nothing, he turned to the counter. Behind it stood a figure in a long, gray dust coat repairing a watch, slightly bent forward, with steady skilled hands and a completely rigid forehead between his eyebrows, a forehead that looked like the figure XII on a dial plate and that immediately showed Cockange what this man was not and would never be able to be, even if God jumbled all professions and their representatives and subrepresentatives together. For this man was not the assistant whom he had expected in the shop. Why was he not the assistant? Because it was himself.

Indeed, the invisible Albertus Cockange who had just tumbled down from the student's room stood there looking as into a mirror. With this difference: the man opposite him not only was visible, unlike himself, but worked and showed no trace of the bottomless astonishment to which he himself was a prey. They were the same but behaved differently. Attentively, with the attention of a child that sees something for the first time, he watched how he himself, or his image, or the real Albertus Cockange, or however one wants to call the figure behind the counter, picked up a little wheel with an extremely fine pair of tweezers, held it against the light and very gravely blew through it, through all the tiny teeth. That was formerly his work! This mouth had been his mouth, this nose his nose and that pepper-and-salt mustache had often reminded him of approaching old age. The hollows in the cheeks, the wart on the left of the forehead—everything was there. And the same wooden movements. There

could be no doubt; it was the living—even if also a little dead—
it was the plain, living watchmaker Albertus Cockange, deprived
of nothing, standing there before him and making the movements that belonged to his trade and that he would continue to
make until his death.

A feeling of respect overcame him as he slowly approached the
counter, a feeling almost of pity. He felt a desire to salute. For
the first time he understood everything about his life and why it
had undergone this change—especially this new change, which
was as if he had become invisible once again, still more invisible,
now not chemically affected by witchcraft but terminated by one
blow. What was this man there, absorbed in himself, how had
he put all his soul into that watch, into one little wheel of it,
into one little tooth of the wheel and the dust that stuck to it? A
slightly foolish, a slightly inanimate man, this Albertus Cockange, who would remain behind alone and from whom he must
now take his leave.

For that was the decision he had made: not a minute longer,
not a minute on any one of those ever ticking clocks, would he
remain in this house. He had nothing more to do here. He had
become detached from everything. As the clock ticks at home, so
it fortunately ticks nowhere else, nowhere would things hang
over his head as here, ridiculous duties and responsibilities of
which nobody on earth could acquit himself, duties that one had
best transfer to some figure, a puppet with a striking likeness
to one.

Though the feeling of respect and pity had not grown less, he
ran close to the counter, picked up a made-out bill, which lay
there under the eyes of his double, stuck out a finger and wrote:
"Sir, your daughter is being seduced upstairs." While writing he
had some difficulty in imagining that this warning concerned
the youngest daughter of Albertus Cockange who was so absorbed in watches. Was it really the youngest? No, he must not
start doubting that—it was a certain youngest daughter of a certain Albertus Cockange. Then he took a little run, flew through
the pane of the show-case, through the shop window, between the
green branches of the trees and disappeared into space.

Translated by JO MAYO

F. C. Terborgh

EL GRAN CAÑON

IN 1527, SIX YEARS AFTER THE CONQUEST OF MEXICO, A HANDFUL OF
adventurers left the Spanish settlement, which was then already
flourishing, and set out to a new Mexico, in search of the seven
northerly towns and of new gold. The troop consisted of forty-
eight foot-soldiers, seven horsemen, ten harquebusiers and an
almost equal number of Indians. The route went north-west; a
message that the twenty-ninth degree of latitude had been crossed
reached the Governor; after that there were no further reports,
and not a single member of the expedition was ever seen again.
The west coast was never reached, and the Commission, later
charged with an investigation, expressed the surmise that the
marching route had been changed, contrary to instructions, to
north-east, upon rumors of gold and the proximity of the seven
towns.

The expedition had met no opposition; the terrain was easy
and it was possible to lengthen the stages. The journey went
through wide, steadily rising valleys, to high plateaux, through
steppes to new valleys, sometimes through forests. One of these
forests was particularly dense and extensive. After two days it
became lighter; through tree-trunks and brushwood gleamed an
endless steppe and the soft glow of bluish-pink evening light; on
the horizon, mountains. Diego Perez, the captain, rode ahead
with Don Huarte Padura to look for a suitable camping place.
Near the last trees the horsemen stopped, impressed by the wide
plain stretching to the horizon. The captain took off his hat,
passed his hand over forehead and hair and looked long at the
last rays of the sun on the mountains. He had never spoken
much—nothing superfluous—but this distant view made him almost loquacious. "It reminds one of Estremadura, Huarte; sunset at home. It is as large as Spain." Then he twisted his body,
uttered a short cry and slipped from his horse. The other stared.
A snake was hanging down from a branch, its head where the
captain's neck must have been. The creature had bitten. Its head
was not an arm's length from Huarte's face. He grabbed at it
with his mailed hand, but the creature was quicker and stronger.
It slid along the steel arm, along the shoulder plate, wound itself

lithely round his neck and bit him in the temple before he was able to strangle the monster in his iron grip.

When the foot-soldiers arrived at the edge of the forest, they found only two corpses: one with his face down, convulsed, his right hand on his neck which was bent backwards; the other on his back, clenching a still living snake in his hands. The troop had lost its leaders.

Half a mile further, they pitched camp on the plain. Night fell; nobody spoke. They placed the dead in the middle of the camp and began throwing up earth-walls as if they had to defend themselves against a still invisible enemy. The priest tried to make the hands of the dead grasp wooden crosses upon their chests, but each time the dead hands let the crucifix go. One seemed to be wanting to grab at his neck, the other at a snake that had long been beaten into an unrecognizable mass in the dust. Two candles were lit at each head in the dead-calm night. The priest prayed; sometimes the yellow flames flickered. He had come along with the others to convert heathens, thousands of them. They remained out of sight. God gave no profit, only loss. Fires burned in a large circle; the men sat round them, silent; occasionally one spat into the flames, the spittle hissing for a moment. A one-eyed man with decayed teeth suddenly raised his riding-crop and flogged two Indians who had been talking softly to one another and would not repeat their words. Everywhere there was the smell of betrayal. Three men ran a little way into the darkness in order to listen better, but heard nothing: the rustling of a thistle, the cry of an animal at the edge of the forest. It remained quiet all night. The stars sparkled; no wind rose. In the gray of the morning most of them rolled themselves into their cloaks for a short, restless sleep.

A stone's throw from the camp a grave was dug the next morning, deep, so that wild animals should not grub it up. A rough cross was carpentered, two names upon it, and a hurried mass was said. Then they again waited for the night; but the second night, too, everything remained quiet. When nothing had changed on the empty horizon by the fourth morning, they saw that nothing threatened them. The danger was gone, and so was discipline.

Conflict arose about the route to be chosen; conflict about the succession in command. Nothing had been foreseen; no opportunity had offered itself to show generalship, and lack of experience allowed dispute and vanity to grow rank. Two camps had formed; one chose the one-eyed sergeant who claimed experience in earlier expeditions and found cursing and lashing the most

useful virtues; the other backed a runaway student, Don Pedro
Carvajal de Susa, young, not strong and without experience, but
calm and with the often unfounded authority of taciturn people.
The majority declared itself for experience. Susa remained silent.
It was decided to continue the journey to the north-east under
the blustering leadership of the sergeant.

The steppe turned out to be more extensive than was originally thought. The mountains rose very slowly. The daily
marches grew shorter and slower; discipline had relaxed altogether. It was not a compact column that marched over the plain
but a thin line of scattered groups, some further apart than a
voice could carry.

Susa was among the foremost. He had started walking to spare
his horse and walked slowly behind three archers. The animal
pulled at its reins and wanted to graze; sometimes he allowed it
to do so for a moment. The priest caught up with him, said
something, but received no answer. He did not persevere, but
walked on silently for half an hour, sweating in his greasy brown
cowl. Then he began again:

"What do you think? When can we reach the towns? Will they
be large? Densely populated? Larger than in the South?"

"Did you think, priest," Susa snarled at him, "that they would
be kneeling in the market-place there, waiting for you, dying for
your gospel?"

The other considered it advisable to pay no attention to the
affront.

"God's word can only bring them joy, when once they have
heard it."

The sun burned on constricting breastplates; tough steppe-
grass and thistles, sticking to their boots, vexed the foot-soldiers.
Sometimes one of them would lose his balance under the heavy
armor, stumble and rise again, cursing. Rarely a word was said.
Thirst, and the uncertainty regarding the distance to the next
water-course, began to torment the men. Again suspicion about
threatening betrayal developed, as it had in the night after the
disaster, but now hidden, gnawing at their inmost souls, inciting
them to accuse each other blindly at the approach of the first
vague danger. Weariness, exertion provoked spite; dully the spirit
of rebellion rose. But nothing happened. At sunset the heat diminished; cool winds brought relaxation, and in the nightly en-
campment there again reigned unconcerned quiet.

On the fifth day they found clear, cool water in a fairly shallow

ravine. They resolved to stay there for two days. Indians and
foot-soldiers had gone hunting; they had been lucky. The booty
was roasted over a crackling fire at night. The rations were am-
pler than usual; there was even excess. The sergeant's immediate
circle played dice; future booty was played away, and one of the
men had got a guitar from goodness knows where. Melancholy,
raucous songs died away into the night. Forbearance had come
over the men; hardly anyone cursed. Even the grumblers grew
talkative. It was no longer a handful of adventurers, greedy for
gold, who were bivouacking. They had become peasants again,
resting after a hard, monotonous day. Their thoughts strayed to
their homes, their fields, their poverty and their parents, to misery and to long-forgotten faces grown friendlier and more attractive with the passing of time. They made plans and dreamed.
At the bottom of all the dreams lay gold. The priest sat on a
stone, sunk in thought. His zeal to convert had waned; he was
back in his youth, in his village. He mused on the sacraments of
marriage and baptism, on work for a new family, the dream of a
new happiness, and was in a mood of conciliation, even toward
the baleful metal. The student lay in the grass on the other side
of the fire, with his legs drawn up, his hands clasped under his
head, and chewing a grass stalk. He let others do the talking,
but after a time the priest asked him also, the youngest:

"And you—what are you going to do with the gold?"

The other did not turn round.

"With the gold?" he said slowly. "One can't do anything with
gold. It dragged the men from the bridges of Tenochtitlan into
the water and drowned them like cats. Those that remained
squandered it. It passed through their hands, rolled on. Nothing
were they able to retain. The first to find it were murdered, or
died, forgotten. There is no blessing on that gold, as little as
there is on a stolen heritage."

"And yet it is worth setting out for, and risking one's life,"
mocked the priest.

Susa half sat up and looked at him. "Why, man, have you
never, at home in your stuffy cell, looked out of the window in
the evening over the empty fields where the sun sets in the distance and thought that behind that there are more fields, hundreds of miles away, and behind that the sea and still farther,
other plains and mountains? Inconceivable immensities to who
knows what limits? And did you never feel a longing then to set
out for them, further and further, not in order to win or rob, but
for the journey itself, till an end is reached? A wall or a vaporous

abyss without light, or an unexpected glorious death?" He spat
contemptuously into the fire, rose and walked a little way into
the darkness. The priest smiled at the other's extreme youth.
Hardly one of the men had listened; each was busy with his own
approaching, great, exceptional good fortune. The cry of an
animal came from the distance; the fire had died down to a mere
glow. One after another rolled himself into his cloak; then there
was nothing but the great, wide night.

They reached the mountains; the steppe came to an end. The
trees that were scattered at first soon stood closer together, forming a forest that hid the mountain-tops from sight. Beyond that
the rocks diminished, a fertile valley followed; soon it branched
out into several valleys. It was again decided to rest for a time
and to send scouts ahead to look for the best way. Five men were
picked by lot. Three men returned after a few days, worn out,
perspiring, covered with blood, and reported a town; blocks of
gray houses, built in the shape of terraces on the slopes of the
mountain, fortress-like towers and rickety wooden bridges, wall
behind wall, and a maze of winding roads. In the background a
pyramid temple, just as in the south in Mexico. They had seen
everything from a hill, had been attacked by Indians and had
beaten their retreat with difficulty. Two comrades had been lost
sight of.

A feverish suspense took possession of the men. The end of the
expedition was in sight, the first of the gold towns reached. One
more day they waited for those who had gone astray, but who
did not return. In the plain before them everything remained
quiet. Then the troop slowly began to move. Discipline had returned. Thirst for gold, and danger, again made each conscious
of what was expected of him. They were again first-rate soldiers,
quiet and hard, Spaniards with that almost incredible contempt
for death and a courage which was nothing but a mixture of
healthy peasant obstinacy and boundless pride.

Toward evening scouts saw the first Indians. They spent the
night on a hill where a surprise attack would have been difficult,
listening and waiting in the penetrating cold of mountain mists.
The following afternoon, as they approached the edge of the
forest, the long-expected war-cry broke out. In the twinkling of
an eye the plain was full of feather-tufts and naked bodies. The
fight was short. A living wall of shields was formed between the
rocks and tree trunks, the harquebusiers at the back, the horsemen in the middle of the ring. The first torrential wave of arrows
and darts was caught by the shields. Covered with spikes like

porcupines they were dragged down by the new weight, leaving the bodies exposed. They answered with a thundering volley, and horror spread among the savages. Then the horsemen broke into the confusion and rushed, mowing down like raving demons such as had never been seen before, right through the groups of howling Indians. In a flash everything was over. Desperately the crowd fled back to the edge of the forest, followed by horsemen and foot-soldiers. The groaning wounded and the dead remained on the field.

The war council, held on the spot, resolved to move on, to lose no time, but to break down all resistance in one fast, wild march. The one wounded man was carefully concealed. The legend of invulnerability had to be maintained at all costs.

The forest was not deep. The troop found a wide valley behind it; foliage trees in steppe grass and fleeing game in the distance. They remained encamped in the field by great fires. No one thought of sleep. The next day, when the troop had long been under way, five Indians were seen near a clump of trees. They were making signs, apparently wanting to negotiate. Interpreters were sent ahead, and soon soldiers had encircled the group. The dead and wounded had already been searched in vain for gold; nothing was found on the state robes of the negotiators either. The men asked about gold, but the Indians apparently did not understand the interpreter. One pointed to the south-west with a vague gesture. Their evasion was considered a ruse.

The sergeant pushed his way through the quarreling soldiers, stood in front of the negotiators in martial posture, his mailed fist on his hip, and asked for an explanation. His men drew back, and the oldest of the Indians understood; he knelt down, caught hold of the sergeant's foot and placed it on his own bowed neck. A triumphant murmur rose from the crowd; festive salutes were fired right beside the ears of the terrified savages, and immediately a marching column was formed, the sergeant, the harquebusiers and the priest in front.

The valley became narrower; it seemed endlessly long between the more densely wooded hillsides. Indians bobbed out of the brushwood, even women and children, and an ever lengthening train followed the conquerors. The sun already stood low over the mountain-tops when the town was seen on the left hillside. The shadows lengthened in the valley, the sky grew a darker blue, steeped in a pale pink light, the color of the feather headdress of the Indians. On the towers and temples lay a ruddy glow like the reflection of a fire. The troop marched faster and faster, their desire for gold driving them forward; no one thought of danger. The path grew steeper and wound over bridges, along empty terraces and deserted defences, between rocklike walls, and then unexpectedly widened into a spacious square.

The goal had been reached; for a short span of time authority revived. The troop formed ranks, knelt down bareheaded during the priest's prayer of thanksgiving; but the men soon ceased to listen and suspiciously followed the Indians' movements with their eyes. The sergeant took possession of the town in the name of the King of Castille and Aragon; and below the black cross, hastily erected in the middle of the square, the priest began his first sermon. The interpreter translated, but he did not understand the meaning himself; an ever denser crowd, packed at the edge of the square, listened in silence. The exhortations of the priest became more and more fiery, almost threatening. Slowly night fell in the square, and the stillness round about it became oppressive. Finally an old *cacique* stepped forward, white, with bent figure, supported by two young men. Then shots rang out in the approaches, and wild confusion spread in the throng of people.

Soldiers had found the heads of their two missing comrades, still dripping blood, planted on poles in front of a temple. The slaughter began. A roaring din arose; cries of distress from women and children, gunpowder smoke and soon the thick smoke of conflagration filled the square. The ruddy glow leapt from every corner, lugubriously illuminating the valley and the endless procession of Indians fleeing to the forests. In the drab morning only smoke rose from the charred ruins. Occasionally a shot was fired. The town was dead. But no gold had been found.

When it was day, the heaps of ruins were thoroughly searched. The result was frightening. In as far as the houses were not burnt down, they were miserable huts, gray and empty; even the temples were empty. All that was found were idols of roughly hewn stone and poor furniture. The food that was collected did not suffice for two days, and a deep dismay came over the troop. Charred beams, and corpses piled in the narrow alleys, was all that the laborious journey of many weeks had yielded. The shrill cry of a bird sometimes came from the edge of the forest, above the men, and was answered from the other side. The men feared betrayal and decided to march on.

Not far above the town the valley turned into a ravine. A path led up through the dry bed of a river to more, denser forests;

beyond that again, a wide barren prairie. But this time there were no mountains to be seen on the horizon. Again quarrels ensued. The majority of the group wanted to stay at the edge of the forest in the hope of hunting quarry and not risk the hot journey over the steppe. The region was apparently growing wilder and more barren. They had better wait; some even wanted to return.

In the growing confusion, the student finally spoke:

"Men! What was the purpose of the expedition? To find the way to the west, the way to the sea. Then why not march on? Is this steppe the first we have seen? Have not others already been crossed? Does so little frighten off a Spaniard? The forest behind us is full of savages. We have heard the cry of a bird and the answer in the distance. They will come back with tenfold supremacy. Tomorrow; perhaps already tonight. Does anyone really believe in safety here, in front of a forest teeming with Indians? Forward, men! Santiago! Viva el Rey!"

He drew his sword and stormed ahead, straight into the empty steppe. But in the troop nobody moved. Outside, in the waving lyme-grass, he turned round and saw that he had remained alone. Shouts of laughter rose from the crowd. At that moment the fate of the expedition was sealed. Don Pedro Carvajal de Susa raised himself high in the saddle, cast a long, contemptuous glance at the troop and rode on, slowly and gravely as if in a procession. An embarrassed silence fell upon the men; then two horsemen and a harquebusier separated themselves from the group and followed the student; later, three Indians. None of them looked round. In the distance they melted into a thin line; then they disappeared among the thistles or into a fold of the earth. The sergeant spat when he had lost sight of them, but remained silent.

The account of those that remained behind is soon told. They wandered along the edge of the forest in an easterly direction for two days, until they thought they were safe. In the third night, Indians as innumerable as a suffocating swarm of grasshoppers stole upon them and cut them down to the last man.

Does our fate really lie in the circular course of the stars? Does our futile existence really follow their eternal orbit? Or does the heart only lift itself to their chill remotenesss shortly before the transition? Is that dully crying bird a messenger?

But does not the body still feel the caressing warmth of the earth? Does not the hand greedily grasp the bumpy sand, and does not the ear listen intently to the song of the cricket and the dying wind through long dried grass-stalks?

From the grass comes the sound of three men sleeping heavily. The student found no rest. He had lain down and then sat up again. Between his fingers ran warm, gray sand; his face was raised to the firmament where the stars sparkled in the almost tangible darkness and the great constellations ran their eternal orbits, moving on irrevocably, hour after hour, like the hands of a gigantic all-dominating clockwork. Never had this sky been so close to him, never had he experienced its depth and intoxicating infinity in such a hard and direct way. And for the first time the thought came to him that this black remoteness was more dizzy, more overwhelming than his breath-taking dreams of journeys to a shadowy distance sinking into vaporous abysses. Could they not have led his thoughts into other channels at home, in his bare study? Could they not have changed his path? The rigid irrevocability of the firmament up there only shows the emptiness of such resistance; nobody escapes his fate; all return is senseless; there is no return, for it only leads to the same end by another route.

A drowsy wind has risen again; it wafts the smell of heat and dust from still unknown distant places. Sand rustles through the prickly stalks. Susa has jumped up, stretches his strong young limbs and stares into the black void from where it must come. But there is nothing to be seen in the night. Nothing looms up in the endless darkness. He lies down again beside his comrades and after a time he too is overcome by a deep, healthy sleep.

The next morning there was again the same barren steppe and nothing reminiscent of the night. Heat and a burning sky above sulphurous sand, greenish-white; couch-grass turned yellow, and soon also limestone. The animals, tired and thirsty, began to walk unsteadily. Sometimes their hoofs knocked against hidden stones overgrown with grass; sometimes they sank into an invisible hole. Nothing bothered the troop as much as the slowly increasing thirst. On the third and the fourth day still no water was found, and nothing indicated the direction in which one should look for it. Shapes loomed in the distance. At first they looked like tree-trunks, bare and snapped off by the gale; then human shapes, adjuring, with arms uplifted. Fear and hope filled the men, hankering after change and afraid of each new disillusionment. But on drawing nearer they turned out to be cacti often higher than a man, hard and prickly. No trace of moisture. Between the stumps rattlesnakes rose menacingly, making the horses rear and, sweating with fear, gallop on wildly for a while, till they stopped again, panting and exhausted. The sun burned intensely upon the blinding, glaring sand; the men's heads grew light; they became giddy and at the end of the fourth day they came across their own tracks again. Of the day before? Of the day before that? Who could tell? From the water bags trickled a thin stream of dreggy moisture, brown and tasting of leather. In dull despair the men decided to walk on at night in order to be able to keep their direction by the constellations. In the pale light of the waxing moon, shadows moved round them in wide circles. Foxes? Jackals? They remained too far away to be shot at. Shortly before the gray dawn, resting by a piece of rock all were overcome by a feverish sleep that did not refresh. Pale daylight spread in leaps and bounds over their camp in this desolate wilderness; their last, perhaps; perhaps already their grave.

At noon the horses had to be killed. They had collapsed, exhausted, and lay panting, foaming at the mouth and bathed in sweat, the agony of death in their bulging eyes. From their emaciated flanks, the Indians cut strips of stringy meat, hoping in this way to eke out their provisions; but the supply became spoilt on the way. Moving on, toward evening, they still saw the carcasses lying in the distance, black against the yellow sky, and vultures above them. Vultures had followed them all day.

At night the landscape changed. In the moonlight silhouettes at the horizon looked like castles, walled towns rising steeply from the plain; but on coming nearer they turned out to be limestone plateaux, erosion islands of primeval ages, purple in the pale morning light, with jet-black shadows in the crevices. The troop moved past them, futile as toys in a realm of giants. In one of the folds of the earth they found some brackish water.

In the evening of the sixth day they saw the miraculous. The terrain was again flat and in the distance gleamed a line of mountains through the hazy air. But there was something strange about these mountains. They soon looked hardly higher than the ground on which the men were walking and not far off. They rose out of a void, out of an invisible depth, as if the earth were torn in two and, in the mists on the other side, a new continent was beginning. With their eyes still turned to this strange reflection, they suddenly stood at the edge of a dizzy precipice: steep rocks, ruddy, yellowish-green and brown, and in the depths below, some water that looked like a brooklet but was surely a wide river; birds of prey hovered over the rocks below, and everywhere there was a deathlike, unearthly silence.

The man who reached the edge first, crossed himself; nobody spoke. Something like horror seized them, a hellish fear of this superhuman spectacle, more magnificent and terrible than the wildest imagination of painters, now flooded with flaming evening light that seemed to spread over the end of the world with waning bundles of refracted rays.

The men camped on the edge of the abyss. Their exhaustion was greater than their terror. The night blotted out the picture, and sleep soon enveloped them all.

On the seventh morning, rested and sobered by a current of cool air that came from the ravines, the spectacle no longer appalled them. The light was different; the sun rose behind them, and mist blurred the distance. They would have to climb down the rocky side to reach the river, and follow the watercourse that would end somewhere at a coast, perhaps hundreds of miles away, but with certainty. Their salvation seemed assured.

The most necessary things were tied together into bundles, and straps and cords knotted into a rope, half the length of which easily reached down to the first rocky ledge below. What lay beyond that, one step deeper, was apparently no more than the same distance away. They would let themselves down, one by one, the Indians first with the bundles, then the harquebusier and the horsemen, and finally the student. They would descend, from ledge to ledge, down to the water; the work of half a day, perhaps.

The first ledge was easily reached. The second was large enough for them all, but the rope had got caught somewhere in a cleft in the rocks. An Indian pulled himself up by it in order to free it. When he was halfway up, the stone gave way. The man tried to cling to the rocks, but, struck by a stone, fell down upon his comrades. Rocks followed, first slowly, then faster, and with a thundering roar dragged six of the men along into the abyss.

Susa, pressed against the wall under a protruding lump of rock, was bruised on the shoulder by a falling piece. The greater part of the ledge on which he stood had been struck off; comrades, bundles and rope had disappeared into the abyss; not one remained alive. Two he saw, covered with blood, on a lower ledge; the others could no longer be seen.

Trembling, with a throbbing pain in his arm, he sat down, leaning against the wall, his eyes turned to the wide depths below him. So this was the end that was intended for him! This was the picture that had never loomed up completely in his daydreams but had guided his actions and his life! Horror and, at the same time, contentment filled him. Then the pain overpowered him and he lost consciousness.

In the evening he awoke. A level light lay on the sulphurous green rocks about him; they seemed alive in the falling dusk. They moved and took on the shapes of the wild rock formations near his native town. They looked to him like the old acquaintances of his boyhood, the vast, hopeless emptiness that had dominated the first beginnings of his thought, that had made him set out to find a still vaster one. He was tired but content; he was at home again. And, as in the days of his boyhood, he inscribed irregular letters with his knife into the chalk wall beside him. They formed the name of his native town: CALATAYUD.

Translated by Jo Mayo

Adriaan van der Veen

POVERTY AND YOUTH

I. Bread and Work

Once i dreamed: i awoke one morning and saw the fire across the way. I knew then that the long-expected was near. I woke my wife and called my sons. Outdoors we joined the leading group and ran along the street with all the others. When we got to the end, we heard shouts of joy and, round the corner, we saw the great fire. I looked at the shining faces of the younger ones. Then began the great dance. I had no fear. Three times we jigged round the fire, the fourth time we leaped into it. I felt it especially about my belly and thighs. I wallowed and stumbled around. My sons came towards me with outstretched arms. They clung to my sides. And there stood my wife, with body erect and arms outstretched. We strode solemnly towards her. Round us sounded songs of praise and happiness. All the people whirled in a wild dance. The fire was like an exciting caress and a liberating bath. Suddenly there were cries of abhorrence and fury. Slimy toads and cowardly frogs had been found and dragged from their hiding places. They were thrown into the fire and torn asunder. Dancing people by the thousands jumped on their slushy bodies. The fire licked at them and shriveled them up. As far as we could see there was a great dancing fire, with golden bodies. We walked for days and joined other groups with different-colored skins and sang songs together. Finally there was nothing but fire and people. All hiding-places, with their vermin, had been devoured.

And one day we all stood motionless in interminable rows. We took into ourselves as much of the fire as possible and the rest we placed as a sun above us. And we turned our eyes to the earth and understood our task.

I knew when I had put down the first sentence that it would be nonsense, stupid nonsense. It is apparently impossible for me to think of anything good; because I once had the spark of a new idea and wrote a parable with success, vanity spurs me on to write. To write, spasmodically and without content, about fire, fire and once again fire. What have I to do with it? All that does not concern me. I am not a convinced Communist and I am not impressed by anarchism. And perhaps I cannot really write. My egoism clings to a poor talent for writing as an expedient for getting out of the mess. I live solely on the thought of fleeing, rending the ties and forgetting faces.

I know, of course, that this too is all idle talk. True, I am resentful; perhaps I really want to get away, but I shall never be able to do so. I am no longer capable of anything, anyway. My little room is 2 x 2 x 2 metres, and next to it is the sitting-room. And my father is so heavy, so stout, so large; and how can I write when he gets up and walks through the room, up and down, down and up? He is walking: now his body is inclining to the left, now to the right. Sometimes I catch myself staring at the wallpaper; then my mouth drops open and I move my finger in time to his heavy footsteps. And that is how it has been going on for a long time—every day. I listen, and must write. Where is my mother? She has gone out. To X or Z. And why? For money, of course. I am choking, choking with fury, choking with compassion. There I sit. I must write, for I must get out of it. Forward! You are a Communist! It is the fashion nowadays. Write an essay about the Artist and Communism. But I am sitting here in my little room 2 x 2 x 2. It is hot and a quarter to three. The sun is helping to crush me to death. Oh, I do not only listen. My sports shirt is open and I amuse myself scraping my nails along my sweating back and then picking the dirt out of them. For that matter, my hair is also too long. If I scratch hard, my nails are full of dandruff, and I throw that on my notebook instead of letters.

How long has this been going on? For three months we got eighty per cent of the salary from the union. That was three months ago. So that makes six months and two weeks. We should of course have cut our coat according to the cloth and then we should have had a little savings-bank account. That would have been enough for two months. But we have six children (I am the eldest but one), and my father was always so heavy and good-natured, and until then he always worked and had always worked, and it looked as if he would still work for a long time; but suddenly it came to an end. We were sitting in the room. We were laughing, and talking about something. Then came the mail with a letter from the office. Oh, yes, I remember now; we were teasing Jan, whom we had seen with a girl, and he was squirming and turning red. My father was laughing heartily. When he laughs, he half lies in his armchair and throws his mouth wide open in his fat, kind-hearted way. And that is how he opened the letter. Every day letters used to come from the office with instructions and such things, and so we merely went on talking. My father was still laughing. Then he read the letter. And his face had still the grin from which he could not quickly part.

Then he sat up, creaking helplessly in his armchair, and said: "Listen to this." He said this to my mother, who was standing by the tea-table. My mother came towards us with the tea. My father was again staring at the letter. "What do they say?" my mother asked. And he read aloud: "Dear Mr. de Beer: On account of a general reorganization of our business, we regret to inform you, etc.," and this he read slowly and emphatically. He likes putting it on a bit; you should hear him on family evenings! And this pompousness could not vanish quite suddenly, however surprising the news might be. "But how can that be? But no, how is it possible!" cried my mother. My father, with astonished, naive eyes in his thick face, looked first at the letter (which he folded neatly and put into the envelope and then fetched out again), then at my mother: "Can you make that out?" And they looked at one another with faces as if, instead of a clear statement, a puzzle had been laid before them. My brothers were already taking part in the general astonishment, and there was no more need for my younger brother Jan to blush. The subject of girls was dead and buried.

At that moment I had already the same feeling with which I am sitting now in my little room. Only then it was new, and now it has been stinking for a long time. A feeling of crabbedness, of discontent, more than anything. Was it really so astonishing and strange? How many people were being sacked every week?

And at the same time, I felt a tender but fast-growing pity for that big head, that heavy body, which suddenly saw its justification for existence disappear, and for that small woman always tripping about diligently with an anxious face and wrinkled forehead. I should like to be above this sentimentality a thousand times. If you reflect, all these things are of no importance. And yet I know, know now, especially this afternoon, that this is a lie. I am bound, hopelessly bound. Our family is one body, and that body is wounded and suffering pain. And even for me I hate the idea of calling all these feelings together: filial love.

I know that freedom won by flight is impossible for me. Enjoyment of it would be out of the question. I am in for it now. And I simply sit here, I stand up and I crawl in here and remain sitting, brooding, mooning away my time—drying up. Now my mother is out to find money, which is needed. The stout landlord downstairs, who used to be affability personified, is turning out to be a greater cad than I thought he was. (My father even tries to muffle his footsteps when he goes downstairs, so convinced is he of his own uselessness.) And all that for the forty guilders he gets! His fat paunch at the bottom of the stairs, and my mother at the top— "But I can't do it, don't you see? Such a beautiful house in such a fine location, for such a low price! I can rent it to someone who *can* pay the rent, hi, hi, hi!" Mind you! I am in my little room, my father in the living-room, and my mother on the stairs. But that fellow is not downstairs; that fellow is sitting on us; he is driveling his words into me. What shall I do now? Run out and go from house to house, asking for money? Or kick that fat fellow to death? Which would better serve my parents?

But apparently I do not understand that for my father it is not the question of money. The fact that he no longer feels that he is the leader, that there is no longer reason for him to be pompous (which always struck me as comical, but with which he was happy in his good-natured way) is probably getting him down. He suddenly feels like a piece of useless furniture that is pushed aside. Hence his soft, affectionate, awkward bearing toward us and, sometimes, his sudden outbursts against my brothers about some slightly ill-chosen word. That is all quite usual, almost hackneyed. Seen soberly: the normal human being cannot live without the fixed norms on which he leans. But, now that it concerns my father, I cannot stand it.

Once shortly after my father was fired, there was a ridiculous quarrel between my parents. My mother thought that my father should call personally on people who might help him with connections and should not simply apply for jobs in writing. At first my father tried to pacify her with the kindly, patronizing jokes of his working days, which he forgot to omit and which, in his opinion too, befitted only a useful, thus money-earning, member of society. This false tone irritated my mother still more and provoked violent and unmotivated reproaches. Then my father became angry. My brother, who is two years older than I, interfered in a voice that was quarrelsome from the start and took the side of my mother. The whole thing made me think of the slums, where we should infallibly land, so that I suddenly joined in shrilly with, "Shut up, God damn it!" thus showing myself to be the worst of the lot. And why this quarrel? Because my mother had been frightened by nothing the night before.

My father said that he was going to the Public Library to look through the advertisements. Usually he returned at half-past nine. At ten o'clock the Public Library closes, and at half-past ten he was not yet home. My mother had already remarked: "He is very late tonight." When he was not yet back at half-past ten, my mother, who had been looking out of the window for quite a time, made the idiotic remark that I had already expected: "You don't think he has laid hands on himself?" I was annoyed and answered roughly: "Of course; he has jumped into the water." My mother said: "He is such a strange man." My father is not a strange man, and my mother did not mean that. She meant: the situation is strange. And why did I anticipate my mother's supposition? Because I, although annoyed and ashamed, had thought the same and knew, pushing away the thought as far as I could, that my mother would express it.

After eleven my father came. He had gone to see the union secretary to settle about relief and had been detained for a long time. Then my mother, apparently unintentionally, went and stood close to my father. At first I did not know why, but then I understood suddenly the fear that my mother no doubt entertained day and night; that the family would go wrong altogether. And what fears existed? Unemployment, drunkenness and infidelity. She smelt his breath. There my father stood, a little pale, a little drooping like an old man, and, above all, uncomprehending; next to him, my mother. I almost groaned with horror at the ludicrous side of this second-rate melodramatic situation. But who will contend that a boil hurts less than a wound heroically gotten?

Not until the three months of the dole payments were over did I realize how little is needed to ruin a family financially. For us it took only the lack of 100 guilders, my father's monthly salary. Six children are enough to prevent anything of this salary from being left over, especially if one marries on the installment system, as so many do; for years the mysterious messenger from the reliable store comes to claim his share (which becomes greater with each child). But then—how go on living without the 100 guilders? This problem we had to solve like thousands of others before us.

At the very beginning there was pity; an uncle lent money; my father's mother and family lent money, money that soon disappeared and could not be repaid, as everyone had expected. But one gets used to everything, and those who first had pity were later sick of the whining. Then the landlord could not be paid. All right, he put up with the promise of "next week, double." After that the messenger could not be paid. All right, but he would have to speak to the manager about it. And after that they and the baker and the greengrocer could not be paid. All right, then bread was bought from a strange baker, and food from strange tradespeople. And then came the electric light and the gas. And then the rent had to be skipped again, because we could not be without light and gas. And then the landlord did not put up with it any more, and there came a letter from the installment store, and the tradesmen became rude, and the health insurance crossed us off the list. We satisfied them for the time being with the proceeds of the sale of the pension insurance, which every nice family has. But that merely caused a short pause and then everything started again, hungrier than ever. And that is how it went on, for three months and three weeks. The installment company will now place the matter in the hands of its lawyer and probably have us adjudged bankrupt. My father does not say much. My mother says, "Let them have their way," and discusses with me whether they could sell the furniture. I do not know, but I am afraid. The old tradespeople are often abusive. My mother tries to appease them with fifty cents a week.

My little sister buys bread at a cheap baker's; eleven cents a loaf. He does not sell on credit; our old baker has warned him. Formerly desired as customers, now it is signaled everywhere, "Be careful!" when we approach. That's three months without 100 guilders.

As regards clothes, I once looked in the closet for my brown suit. It was at the pawnbroker's with my plus-fours. I did not say anything about it, though clothes mean much to me. My brother, whose suit (like my father's wintercoat) had also disappeared, *did* scold and loudly. I hit him and got a beating from him. He was much stronger. There was a terrible hullabaloo, partly because my mother acted so strangely. This quarrel cost her another illusion: peace in the family.

We shall have to leave the house. Although the owner knows that he will not be able to collect his debt for the time being, he wants to get rid of us anyway. That is why my mother is looking for something else.

I remember a painful story about my mother, which I want to write down too. Our former milkman did not supply us any more, and that is why my mother bought from a hunchback man who was passing by the door with a little cart. Sometimes he gave a week's credit, and once there was no money for him: so many people had already come for money. My mother got a fright when she saw his little cart through the window. I was annoyed by her guilty look; it was a question of a few guilders. My mother did not dare invent some pretext and sent my little sister to say that she was not at home. We listened and expected, as usual with put-off creditors, protesting grumbles and the closing of the door, but instead the man began to shout, pushed the door open and yelled in the passage that he had to have his money and that he did not believe that my mother was not at home.

My little sister remained silent and naturally looked anxiously toward the living-room door. The man continued, while he stepped out into the street and let the neighbors enjoy it too. (We lived in a poor street, but at the "nice end.") I saw my mother turn pale and understood how intently the neighbors would listen. I was disgusted by this tradesman, who knew so well how to take revenge when one failed to pay, and I sprang up furiously, even seizing a bread knife, although it is a question whether I should have done more than slam the door. But my mother came and stood in front of me and prevented me from opening the door of the room. Meanwhile the fellow made a game of it and ran several times into the middle of the street. My mother still stood in front of the door. Her face was white and her eyes stared fixedly into the distance. Now he jumped into the passage and, amidst general hilarity, took the mat along, as we saw from the window. After that he spoke to a little group of women and pointed to our house. My mother stood at the window and said nothing. She only put her hand up to her forehead and rubbed it. Then she said: "I'll go there." Now it was my turn to prevent her, but she said: "Go away! They don't know that he is making all this fuss over three guilders." I heard the cart drive away and saw my mother going toward the neighbors in front of the window. They were a baker's wife, a printer's wife, a policeman's wife and some others I did not know. My mother had not yet reached them when they turned towards each other with their backs to her. I saw it clearly through the window. My mother hesitated, but said something to their backs. They did not answer. Then she stood silent. Some of the women went up to a greengrocer's cart. Others went into their houses. My mother turned round. She came into the house, said nothing, sat down and wept. I do not believe that she will quickly forget that. The necessity to justify herself to the neighbors had made her forget the instinctive feelings of revenge which the "inferior" neighbors feel for the neighbors at the "nice end."

This afternoon the moving van is coming. My mother has found an apartment in Station Street. That is a narrow, winding street with two-floor apartment houses. We live on the second floor; room and suite, kitchen and two bedrooms. So now I have no longer even a little room 2 x 2 x 2. If I want seclusion, I can choose between the toilet and the coal shed. But there is one advantage, my mother will not have to whisper with the creditors any more. In that street every one has debts.

But in God's name what must I do? I am still writing quietly as if nothing were happening. Late today we shall be moving in, and then I can go and sit with the whole family. In my little room I could not get away from them, but now they will sit almost on top of me. I had better give up even the appearance of working and go on relief, arm in arm with my father. And why not? I am learning to be resigned.

The tone of my writing is getting false again. My mother has a tear-stained face and hasn't begun to pack, although the cases are standing ready and the moving van will be here in a few hours. I hear my father talking occasionally. If only they would act normally and, above all, not make a drama of it!

II. The Shadow of the Mill Sails

On Saturday, when the sun shone into the room smelling of tea, our cotton suits were ironed. My mother was busy with it for a long time, pressing her lips together and holding the iron in her hand convulsively. On Sunday, when the church bells had ceased ringing, we put them on; they were tight at the waist and the white shirts felt cool against our necks. The footsteps of the walkers rang in the streets that lay arched in the quiet Sunday sun. We knew that we were being watched from the upstairs window as we walked away but we pretended not to notice it. The crease in our pants stood out sharply over our bare knees. Our shoes shone, but the holes in the soles felt cold on the paving stones.

Two rows of trees with young leaves stood bolt upright along the lane that led to the woods. First there was the park with the mounds and fountains laid out in a rough circle, with a board at the entrance as a warning: "No admission after sunset", and a monument of the Queen Mother with a face that had turned out too severe. We followed the road alongside the park and ducking under some gnarled trees that felt left out by the spring, we came to the path with the bumpy cobblestones and a bridlepath that led directly to the tennis courts. With as much indifference as our tight little suits would permit, we put our hands in our pockets and, unruffled and whistling, we approached the Bench, the quarters of the tennis caddies. They stood in a bunch, shouting, cutting sticks or sitting nonchalantly at one end of the Bench. As we went by, they became silent, watching our movements with suspicion. One of the biggest of them walked towards us menacingly, swaying his hips. But we kept our eyes glued to the pointed cobblestones hurting our feet and disappeared into the woods. There was a winding path with hawthorn in the distance and the twittering of birds and other sounds, buzzing and warm as if it were already summer.

We looked through the trees intently toward the beginning of the tennis caddies' path. Cor jumped up and pointed to the cyclists coming around the corner. With our heads bent forward we ran along the bridle-path like a flash, past the Bench. There was mostly dust to be seen at the quarters by the time we reached the cyclists, the players on the Red Court. We followed them running close to the bicycles. At the Bench the caddies were all standing in a heap ready to drag us away, but the leader in a turtle-neck sweater just shook his fists and sent three of the boys after the bicycles. They trotted along too, at the same time trying to tread on our heels. We got closer to the bicycles, moving our arms and legs rhythmically. At the path where the cyclists had to get off, the boys whined, but the tennis players decided to take the cotton suits. A stone hit Rik through the trellis-work, a beginning of what was awaiting us.

But the sun was already low on the horizon when the players on the Red Court stopped, and we sauntered along the road each holding forty cents in our moist hands. Our knees were trembling and the crease had disappeared from our pants. Everybody had gone home, only one early couple was already walking into the woods, where the birds were chirruping their loudest just before the sun disappeared entirely. The little tent where the caddies spent their money was still open. Klaas and Leentje were waiting for the evening strollers. They revived when we came. When we were licking our ice-cream cones, Klaas asked, "Are you new?" and Leentje said, with two big wrinkles in her freckled face, "To-morrow they will bring knives and waylay you." And, muffling her voice, she told us about the ways of the tennis caddies from Friendship Street; how they had followed her one evening and thrown her to the ground. Klaas listened disdainfully, raising his shoulders higher and higher till they left no room for his neck. He knew everything and therefore gave Leentje a sign to go away for a minute while he called us behind the curtains of the tent and told us what we had to do. When we ran home after that, I was already seeing Rik lying in the dust at the side of the bridle-path bleeding from the stomach. They ought not to punch any-one in the stomach. Not below the belt, we had been taught.

The windows were open when we came home and we smelt fresh fried potatoes and salad. In exchange we were able to give ninety cents. With the tea after supper we had cookies, and sit-ting on the closed veranda I heard every movement of the cane chair in which my father sat. From the garden came the sounds of cats nearing each other and miaowing. The wind played with some neglected rose garlands over our neighbor's gate. My mother stroked my hair, staring vacantly into the distance. Rik and Cor were in the street with Wout and Lange Jaap.

We felt it our duty to go to the tennis courts the following eve-ning, but first we walked along the dike and the ditches, gazing at the weeping willows through which the white crosses of the churchyard gleamed. Rik listened attentively to the frogs that were croaking at the side of the ditch, but Cor gave him a push, and without further roundabout ways we came to the bumpy road and approached the Bench. We had white sweaters on, with the sleeves pushed up. There was a hubbub and hissing as we came near. Pebbles clattered on the cobblestones quite near us. One of the boys whose name was Tinus came toward us. He danced out in front of us, distorting his wrinkled face and curs-ing uninterruptedly without perceptibly opening his mouth. I looked at his feet that hardly touched the ground, like those of a marionette held too high. Rik walked very straight, Cor swung his arms, and I felt my knees tremble. At the Bench they then performed a screeching Indian war dance and one, two and then three figures broke away and rushed toward us with heads bent, howling like factory sirens. We stood still, our bodies tense, when suddenly the signal of the leader sounded: "The bicycles!" The group drew up in order of march and swarmed round the cyclists from Court A, sending shrieks into the air. We remained behind and then ran along too, pushing and kicking as the others were doing to us. All found something to do on Courts A and B and the Red Court. Cor and Rik were busy too, and for a moment I looked bewildered at the caddies deftly unrolling the nets and putting the balls in their places. Cor and Rik waved to me, and the others cursed at me whenever they got a chance. I stood leaning against the trellis-work when I felt something wet from behind. I looked round and saw Tinus standing with his legs widespread. The water was coming in a wide arch, now watering the flowers. "Beat him up," I heard my brothers shout and slowly, my legs still trembling, I approached Tinus. He pressed himself against a tree and for a moment his face was still. I saw the warts on his hands and his thin legs through the holes in his pants. His throat contracted nervously. "Beat him up", I repeated to myself, but he was already giving me vicious punches. I felt them land on my shoulders and come lower to my stomach, and I turned red. My hands grabbed at his body, at his neck, but couldn't find them until I had raised my arms in front of my face; going toward him in this way I seized him and twined my left arm round his hot neck. He yelled but I pressed against him and pulled my other arm around his neck like a vice, bending his head down. His long legs trampled to and fro, kicking my ankles, but his neck glowed against my arms till I threw him to the ground with a jerk. It seemed unnatural, to find myself so empty, without his neck. But I had no time to think. He had already jumped up and, encouraged by the caddies who pressed their faces against the trellis, he hit me on the lip with a trembling paw. But he recoiled and bounced back when I approached. His arms were beating and churning as if a giant were after him. I felt myself breathing more deeply and my chest expanding. Then I seized him, this time easily, and while he yelled and his parchment face glowed as if I were lighting mysterious little lights, I bent his body almost coaxingly and pushed his head between my knees. I pressed his seat against the fence and beat him, the more vigorously the harder he tried to wriggle. When I stopped my hands

were smarting. Rik and Cor were dancing on the court, the others
were hissing at Tinus who opened his mouth wide, showing decayed teeth, and yelled.

Pretending I did not care about my victory I sauntered away,
my hands in my pockets. As I came near the Bench, Menten, the
well-known Jewish dealer in old iron, stepped out of his car and
said, "I need you." The day before, although I had not been
working on his court, I had handed him a ball, and he had not
forgotten me. His trousers had a sharp crease and covered a fat,
squat body. His pale face with horn-rimmed spectacles was serious. His forelock through which cream-colored skin could be
seen was stuck to his skull. I followed him as he opened the door
to his court. I fetched the balls out of a dark shed smelling of
showers and perfume. Menten did not move while I stretched the
net. The copper-colored light of the sun twinkled on his spectacles while he indicated to me to stand on the other side and
throw the balls to him. We went on till the light had gone. All
the tennis courts were empty. The noise had died away. Menten
looked at me seriously when he gave me my pay, and nodded.
Cor and Rik were waiting for me at the exit, and we celebrated
the victory over Tinus and the Bench with ice-cream.

The Christian schools had a day off, and Cor and Rik went
fishing as soon as the sun was visible on the horizon. I got up
later and first did some gymnastics. My body was smooth, with
very fair little hairs and a three-cornered birth mark. My arms
were thin, but yesterday I had tried them on Klaas when he inquired after Tinus, and he had not been able to throw me off.

I walked to the Bench where, to my disappointment, I found
only one boy with fat white legs, short pants, a receding forehead,
large watery blue eyes and a small mouth that stood open. I sat
down next to him on the dewdrops that were still on the Bench.
We both remained silent, and I drew little figures on the sandy
path. In the distance I heard hammering at the dockyard, steam
whistles on the river and sometimes the bicycle bell of someone
still on the way to the office.

"Tinus would have beaten you up if you hadn't thrashed him,"
said the boy.

"But I did thrash him," I answered, suddenly restless and
thinking over how I had done it.

"Why are you caddies?" (I said nothing.) "Tinus and Govert
call you poor lice, and Hein knows from the grocer that you have
debts everywhere." I stood up and bending over the hedge cut

off a stick with soft green bark which I cautiously peeled off,
sniffing up the smell of the pale wet wood.

"Have you finished school?" asked the boy.

"No." Then, remembering in a flash how strong I was, "Say,
do you want a beating. Poor lice!" But I had no desire to get up.
He said, "I could stab you in the shoulders with my knife, and
then your arms would hang limp." Slowly I swished the stick
through the air, but the boy paid no attention.

"I wanted to stab my father with my knife," he resumed, "but
he threw me down the stairs."

"Where do you live?"

"In Friendship Street; all tennis caddies live there."

"My father never hits us. He just grins and threatens with a
stick."

"My father is a lunatic. He shouts so loudly that my mother
wakes up. She is ill."

"What's your name?"

"Lambert."

In the distance some cyclists were approaching, fat De Hoed,
his wife, son and daughter, of the Red Court. We got up and,
without arranging anything, trotted along. We stretched the net
and ran after the balls for hours while the sun stood above us
setting Lambert's head afire.

When we were free we bought apples and wandered off to a
grass field; it was one o'clock. I looked at Lambert who could
only eat his apple in small pieces. "How did you get such a big
head and small mouth?"

"I am like my mother. You should see her."

"How long has she been sick?"

"Twelve years; she is paralyzed and lies in the cupboard-bed
in the dark so that sometimes I only see her forehead and eyes.
It smells of old apples in the bed, when the sewer doesn't stink."

"What's your father?"

"He is a machine fitter but he has been on the dole for the last
five years."

"Have you any brothers?"

"No, a sister who has been living with an aunt in Gelderland
for a long time. She doesn't want to come home any more."

We ate the apples and Lambert asked, "Do you give the
money you earn to your mother?"

"No," I lied.

"We all do, except Tinus who lives with an uncle who works
at the gin distillery." Before we went home Lambert warned:

"They'll beat your brothers up tonight." I walked alone through our street musing on that egg-shaped head that would bend over a white forehead and large eyes in a cupboard-bed with old apples. Rotten apples, perhaps.

It rained the next day and the day after, and both evenings I was alone by the river where green lights winked. There wasn't a single couple in the Privé, the lovers' lanes behind the river. The rain from the branches dripped cool on my eyes as I lay stretched out on a seat with my raincoat over my legs.

But on Saturday evening, after a hot day, there was fighting at the Bench. Cor stood panting by a tree, and his victim crawled on his feet for the last time. Rik was still fighting, and I admired his body that advanced and recoiled while his arms and fists moved steadily, warding off, pushing forward, high and low; punching the bulldog boy's nose to right and left, a movement that made blood flow. Rik's forehead was grazed, blood ran from his lips, but then he shot forward and pummeled the bulldog, who closed his eyes and moved his mouth foolishly.

Rik stopped, and we stood side by side waiting to see if anything else would happen. We had seen no knives. Opposite us stood the group: Tinus leering over the heads of the others, Lambert a little offside. Janus, the chief, had let the others fight so far, but now he ran forward, hitching up his pants, waddling as he ran as if we were three ninepins desirous of being overthrown.

Something else did happen. Just in front of us a cat shot past, black, with a tail that stuck into the air like a quivering arrow. After her came a big dog, his head to the ground. For a moment everybody watched the chase; then, without signal, we ran after the animals. Tinus in front and Rik next to him, Lambert and I behind them, through the lanes, along the tennis courts, over the grass fields. We heard the cat spit before she disappeared into the woods. Breaking branches, bumping into each other, we followed in the dark until we lost both animals. Panting we stood facing each other, not knowing whether to thrash each other. But finally we walked, somewhat self-consciously with our hands in our pockets, back to the tennis caddies' path.

After the chase we were welcome on the Bench, where Janus explained the rules to us and where Lambert and I considered ourselves partners. Being official caddies meant that now we could no longer follow the bicycles as freely as before. Now we had to sit on the seat and wait for our turn. When Menten sent Tinus back and wanted me instead, there was fighting again, and Janus said that we didn't belong there. But we had captured our places for good by the time Janus had left to work in a factory.

Everybody knew us. On hot afternoons we fetched ginger ale for the players, and the girl whose black hair fell over her pale face gave us a drink, even when I accidentally kicked her glass over. Rik was greeted smilingly by a worthy lady whose clothes rustled and who lived in a big house with chestnut trees. Menten, when helping a lady into a car, had turned round and smiled at me. We were asked who we were and what we generally did. We felt we were the center of interest and sometimes we talked about how we had come into power.

The son of the baker in our neighborhood formed a tennis club with some friends and they occasionally succeeded in hiring one of the courts. They did not use caddies and the sons of the notables joked about these poor devils. We stood near them and glowed with enthusiasm at giving information. "The one is a baker in our neighborhood," I remarked, and one of the tennis players said, "Say, that is the fellow who brought tartlets to the party on Saturday." They laughed about the fellows who dared to play tennis, and we joined in before we began our task. Not until I was on my way home did I try to find an explanation why I, a little slave, laughed with the masters at the baker and his companions. Did I hate them because they had bad rackets and their pants were too short and because they laughed too loud? After all, everyone could play tennis, everyone, we too and even the tramp who picked up cigar ends. Picking up balls, running after bicycles and fighting for power with Tinus and Janus was an adventure. If I wanted to I could have fought the notables and exterminated them, preferably together with the bakers who laughed too loudly. All the tennis courts should be for the tramps with cigar-ends in their pockets and for girls with fair hair and pink dresses with flared skirts.

Lambert and I were late the following evening. Near the Bench we watched the swallows against the turbid sky. It was so quiet that near the forester's house we heard a leaking tap dripping. All the courts were occupied by tennis players and caddies and we walked into the woods. Lambert's white knees sometimes gave way as if he were on the point of abandoning walking as useless. We skimmed past loving couples who seemed to be outgrowths of the trees along the lane.

"Would you like to play tennis?" I asked Lambert. He did not look at me when he answered. "No, I wish my father would die.

Yesterday he came home and tried to lift the blankets from my mother's bed. She was afraid of him; I listened."

Three birch trees stood on the grass field at the side of the lane. We dropped into the grass and looked at the sky. The swallows had disappeared. In the distance we heard rumbling.

"I have tried to stab him. I followed him to Noordmolen Street near the gin distilleries. I jumped into the cellar just by the grain shutes and I saw him go by. I ran after him as far as the gin shop and I waited there for hours. He recognized me when he swayed out of the door and I supported him and led him close by the water not knowing what to do. I had no knife, but near the pipes I had picked up a file, rusty but with sharp edges. A policeman walked by and I quickly stuck the file into my father's pocket. After that he leaned heavily on me, his hands on my neck. At home I left him lying in the hall and went upstairs, stepping over his body. My mother lay in bed with open eyes, but I know that then she is asleep, and I played with her hair. The next morning he kicked me out of bed and asked how he had come by the file."

Then big drops fell, but we lay motionless in the grass with our heads down. I closed my eyes, and tried to comfort Lambert. "Can't you flee with your mother? Can't you take her on your back instead of leaving her in the cupboard-bed with rotten apples? You are strong. Take one of those boats in the Maas, row to the other side. Go to Vlaardingen and hide her in one of the barges that smell of fish. Sail far away from Friendship Street. Stay alone with your mother somewhere in the sun where you can stroke her hair as long as you like without having to fear kicks from your father and to think of files to which dust from the gin distilleries is sticking."

Lambert turned round, his face wet from the rain that was now splashing on us. He came close to me and whispered, "You are a stinking fool, a stupid idiot. Go to hell and back to where you belong." Long after he had gone I still lay in the grass feeling the rain on my body.

That evening Rik and I walked in the woods. We watched the glowing cigar-ends that came flying, sometimes right across the path, until the figures of the smokers came out of the dark.

I told Rik that I didn't want to pick up balls any more and he said I was crazy. "Mother needs the money."

"Then I must do something else, there is so much one can do." Rik remained silent and in the dark I couldn't see his face. We walked on, past the glowing cigar-ends, numerous as fireflies. I said, "In a little while Lambert won't be picking up balls any more either, he will stab his father to death." Rik laughed. "Nobody stabs his father to death."

"But Lambert is not a liar. He told me how he would do it. One night when his father is drunk and beats his mother and gets him out of bed. Then he will jump on him—and you know how strong he can be—and take a rusty file out of his father's pocket where he stuck it long ago. He knows exactly where a throat is most tender. He will first cover his mother and then he will take his father on his back and carry him to the canal. You know near the little bridge there is a boat with a hole in it. He'll stuff his father into that hole and let the boat sink half under water. Then he will go back to his mother and flee with her."

"And where to?"

"You can go anywhere. Everything is open to everyone. And in Friendship Street she is lying in a dark cupboard-bed with rotten apples. You will see, Lambert is capable of anything. He hasn't got a big head for nothing. He won't be seen in the streets any more. He will row to one of the big ships where everyone speaks English, French or Italian and where they throw oranges overboard, they have so many. And we'll never see Lambert again, unless perhaps we pass one of the islands where palms grow."

"Lambert will probably land in the rope factory," said Rik, "he's pale enough for it."

"And his mother?"

"She will keep lying and waiting for Lambert and Lambert's father."

"Do you think they will stay together and set the place on fire on New Year's Eve to begin another New Year?" Rik did not answer but when we came out of the woods he said, "I shouldn't read so many fairy tales. What you talk about never happens."

When I walked to the tennis courts, a few days later, Menten was just stepping out of his car and he asked why I didn't pick up balls any more. When I explained, he told me to come and see him the following evening. Why, I asked myself when I saw him walking slowly to the court, and in bed I imagined that he wanted to take me along to his house in the mountains in Switzerland or that he wanted to undertake a cruise to an island in the South Seas. Perhaps he had heard of Lambert and his file. It was also possible that he wanted to teach me to play tennis in the garden with the fountain and the tortoises behind his house.

Nobody could enter his house with the austere double windows, until he had banged the knocker that awakened a brassy sound which echoed all over the house and over the canal, so that a policeman, whose helmet I could see gleaming in the distance, stood still and looked round. A maid with a stiffly starched cap showed me into a room with dark paintings and red velvet, where it smelled of dust until Menten's perfume came wafting in. He took my hand and held it while he asked me to take a seat. Sitting opposite me and looking at the palms of his hands he said that the house would be pulled down stone by stone and that no painting would remain in its place and that the tortoises would be placed in Blazers Zoological Gardens to everybody's pleasure. He was starting for France the following month and so he would not come to the tennis courts any more. He had been pleased with the way I had always thrown the balls to him and therefore he would like to do something for me. The word "do" got all the emphasis of the carelessly spoken sentences and for the first time his eyes, behind the glistening spectacles, looked at me. What did I want to be, he asked me. What would I like to be? I didn't know. Everything, nothing, only not a tennis caddie.

"Then begin in an office," he said, "don't go in for old iron, that presses too hard, but keep yourself busy with buying and selling. My broker needs a junior clerk. Report to him on Wednesday morning."

He stood up and I stood up and he put a hand on my shoulder and nodded. With the other hand he rang the bell and a butler came to lead me to the hall whence I got a last glimpse of Menten's round and serious head. On the steps in front of the house I stood still. I felt empty. How much I wanted to ask him! Why had he wanted to throw balls with me and not with the notables? Did he mean by pulling down stone by stone that he would make a bonfire of his house? Lost in thought, I sauntered along the water. The conversation with Menten seemed simple enough. But the way he talked made me curious. It seemed as if behind his words a completely different, baffling meaning was hidden.

Over the Kippebridge, high up in the mill, cries had been heard in the afternoon. Lambert's mother had died unexpectedly and quietly that morning. Lambert had come home, had scarcely looked and only stretched out a hand as if he wanted to touch her. After that he had been seen running to the mill where his father was working for a few days. One of the neighbors ran after him and asked him what had happened, why he was running.

And he had answered, "My mother is stiff, she is dead." Perhaps he ran to stab his father to death at last, perhaps to seek consolation. But when Lambert hastily climbed the ladder high up the mill, his father, who had seen him stand by his bed one evening, took a certainty for an uncertainty. He kicked with his boot against his chest and then watched him fall. The boss and his men heard Lambert yelling and came running up. When they had attended to him and at last rushed upstairs, the father was still tugging at the bars of the window, perhaps in order to be able to jump into the water, perhaps merely to be doing something. In the cell at the police station, he stared straight in front of him as if the stains on the dirty walls would offer him the solution of how to make everything undone.

Lambert had broken ribs and there was something not in order with his brain. He didn't recognize me when I went to visit him. But the nurses said that he roared when he was brought in until his mouth could no longer pronounce the word "mother." Now he groaned softly with pain. There was not much left for him without the woman who had the same mouth as he, for whom he picked up balls and who lay in the cupboard-bed so that he could bend over her.

On Tuesday evening I walked on the Westvest by the mill that creaked and threw long shadows over the crooked houses that leaned over to the Orange market. I thought of the mother who had been buried that day at the expense of Friendship Street. Lambert would probably go to a rush-and-mat asylum and later to a Poorhouse where he would gradually turn yellow.

And my cotton suit lay ready ironed for me to present myself at the broker's office the next day. My life would have to be like the shadow of the mill sails that flashed by ever more quickly until one could no longer follow them with the eye. Everything could happen, everything would happen.

Translated by Jo Mayo

L. Vroman

THE BREATH OF MARS

EVEN AT THE BEGINNING OF MAY THE WAR ABROAD STILL ADDED TO the intimacy of Dutch home life, as a storm outside will heighten the coziness of the living-room and the warmth of friendship.

For myself, in Utrecht I had a girl, my studies and some kindly disposed people; in short, something to hold on to. The talk about an impending invasion only led to the utterance of heroic phrases and projects, after which we separated in good spirits and with faces expressing elegant cynicism, hardly imagining the bitterness—should the Dutch border spring a leak—with which they would be repeated subsequently.

One morning, when the sky had a milky texture and the sun shone brightly, I awoke, because all around me, from nearby and far away, doors seemed to shut with a bang, and I gradually recognized anti-aircraft gunfire. The violence of the explosions was greater than ever before, but when a little later it became calm and the starlings could again be heard chirping, only peace and the spring morning remained. . . .

But again and again and again the gunfire sounded. It was as if one woke up in pain that at first appeared to be casual but that returned to develop into a malignant disease. I still did not want to get up and admit thereby that something was out of the ordinary—and what else but the worst?—had happened. A little later, however, the advance radio news announced that which was no longer a surprise. The first sounds coming out of the loud-speaker in my living-room obliterated all other sounds in the house; everybody was listening. I had on my shirt and one sock, the other, which I held in my hand, I examined minutely while I listened; it was gray with red dots in groups of three, which were arranged in rows and were somewhat discolored at the sole. "Rejected with indignation, unprecedented violation," the radio announced officially but with great bitterness. I thought: How troublesome are socks and how silly are garters, while I felt confused and deep indignation and an irreparable and incalculable loss as I drew on my second sock.

I had two landladies well up in years, spinsters. They said that this was quite a situation and with anxiety shining in their eyes and worried voices they set about their daily tasks and conversations. I ate my usual breakfast with new thoughts in my head, especially about the front, which I tried to picture as a field of fatal casualties—luckily so far away that the blood could not yet trickle into Utrecht. I thought also, but not quite convinced of my sincerity, of sweethearts who had been separated by death. On the wall of my living-room I had hung a large map of Europe and stuck little flags into it; in Finland, right across Poland, some in Luxemburg. I took one of them and stuck it at the border, in in the direction of Germany, as if it came rushing from that direction.

On the street everything was normal and quiet; soon a few more house doors stood ajar, suggesting neighborly calls. I went to my girl. There reigned an almost spasmodic everyday atmosphere, which made us laugh. My girl and her elder brother left for college, and I went on my way to the botanical laboratory where I worked at the time. Here there was a kind of feverish activity; apparatus was carried from the upper stories to the cellars, new acquisitions of which we were all proud, ancient models often treated with respectful amusement, fragments of framework which had still functioned the day before, like detached but still recognizable limbs of good friends. Our professor descended the stone steps, bent under a massive metal X-ray apparatus, which was more than a metre high. It was painful to see how the veins on his temples and neck were swollen and how his hands had become claws, he whose profession had never called for heavy physical labor. One of our assistants arrived in uniform and was surrounded by others. "This telescope belongs in the former undergraduates' room, these are the keys of the closets upstairs. Six airplanes have already been shot down in the neighborhood of Utrecht. I still don't know where they are sending me— Ann is . . . I wish you all the best of luck!" His voice and his gait had already become heavier, and his eyes seemed to have acquired the isolated enthusiasm of one who is about to make a speech. We all wished him courage, followed him with our eyes as though he were leaving for a long voyage, and I felt that the war had begun.

Books were brought downstairs from the library. The older ones were stacked in piles and on them the shelves of the empty bookcases, which in turn bore the newer volumes. It was hard work, but the physical fatigue served to explain away the inner anxiety. After that was over I erected my apparatus; I worked in the cellar, so that my work did not have to be moved away. Next weekend would be the Whitsun holiday. I therefore stopped the experiment, opened the ventilator, so that the thermostat, in spite of the warm spring weather, could maintain a temperature of 20° C., extinguished the white light in the room and the red one in the hallway and again went into the daylight. I had taken along the results of my work—many columns of figures, which required simple but tedious calculations, in order to work them out during the following days. These days I would spend as a guest at the home of my girl and her family, which was situated about a quarter of an hour's walk from my rooms. It seemed that there had been no question of classes at the college. My girl and her brother had helped bring the alcoholic preparations of the medico-anatomical laboratory from the building into the inner court, where in case of bombardment the inflammable fluid would run out before it could catch fire. Because we all felt to have participated so actively in the war, the circumstances seemed much more real than in the morning, and we actually went to lunch in high spirits. From time to time airplanes approached. At first one felt a few indefinite impacts of far distant cannon fire, as if the wind was passing by windows, then a short silence, after which the high humming of motors could be heard. Then immediately followed the explosions of the cannons at Baarn and Soesterberg and, a moment later, the booming reports of the anti-aircraft batteries of Croeselaan. As soon as this started we ran to the balcony of the apartment house, hoping to see a few airplanes hit and falling, but we were always disappointed.

The planes were very high; their noise and appearance were irritatingly mosquito-like. Little black clouds became suddenly visible, disappeared from sight and often vaguely took on the shape of airplanes, which stood still as if in fear and then fell apart and made one think of stricken machines. However, they soon became completely transparent and no longer fell; the real airplanes had in the meantime disappeared undamaged. Then we again looked up to the high sky at other planes which acted likewise, and we went back inside where our suspense was accentuated by the unfinished, abandoned lunch.

I went to my rooms during the afternoon to fill a very small valise with necessities for the coming holiday; a blackout torch, pajamas, toilet articles and a change of underwear.

Back in the flat I found the family already busy with the blackout. We got out the black paper, kept inside since the last air-raid drill, fastened the upper corners above the windows, temporarily rolled up the loose hanging part and attached it. It hung somewhat crooked and low and gave the room a crazy twilit appearance. We arranged the same funeral decoration at the home of Mevrouw Smit, a neighbor and block leader, whose house was occupied by the air-raid protection unit. In her house we struggled between the crowded furnishings with large sheets of paper, which we pasted together from long strips. Thus we immediately darkened the room. We turned on the light, fastened the paper and lifted it halfway up—again that faint malicious daylight, which penetrated. After we were through we ate, with our fingers still sticky from the paste and the effort. In the meantime it had become dark, so we let the paper down and pinned it over the half-open windòw. Every breeze stirred it, and it made disquieting creaky noises. Sometimes it bulged like a full sail, and we had to shut the windows.

Only the living-room had been blacked out, so that the home life was crowded into it. In the empty corner a divan was placed for those who had worked the hardest, which caused many expressions of altruism and offered diversion. The evening was spent in looking at pictures in magazines and doing in the Germans and listening to the confused news that interrupted the radio music. Finally we decided to go to bed, for we were tired. My bed seemed unfamiliar, it was a camp bed. I fell asleep empty of thought.

The anti-aircraft guns started early in the morning. The early sunlight caught the new houses on the other side of the street; the rooms were airy, and a gentle, cool wind moved the curtains. Peacefully cradled by the noises of housekeeping, I sat at the table to make an illustration for a child's story; it would appear next Wednesday in Rotterdam. At first the explosions of the anti-aircraft batteries interrupted the lines I was drawing, but finally I succeeded in moving my hand continuously during the loudest explosions. I was very proud of myself and secretly saw myself in the company of undaunted spirits who were inspired by their greatest thoughts during the turmoil of battle.

This day also and the following were spent in peaceful, trifling occupations. The windows were plastered with pieces of white paper, which divided the scene into triangular sections; we read, listened to the news about air-raid protection and followed the cited aircraft over tne map. They went in an unindicated direction like ants on the wall, with alarming uncomprehensibility.

Those among us who came home from running errands, always brought news and cast it in bold form, but it was so chaotic and incoherent that all opinions, even the most sombre ones, vanished and left us finally indifferent.

The following morning, Monday, was somewhat more lively. Windows had to remain shut, and cars drove through the city, carrying men with bayonets which were directed at everything and everyone, like a bad conscience. Towards the afternoon the dusty troops approached. We saw them sit down against our walls; some lay down. A little later the civilians mixed among them. They seemed to be a different kind of animal, delicate and variegated, distributing victuals; then the soldiers mounted our stairs. They looked large and heavy, as if they could not turn their heads or spread their fingers. But they were quite whole, one could look at them without fear. They came from the Grebbe defense line. One of them sat down to change his socks, but fell asleep with his ruddy face turned up and his mouth wide open— we had to wake him when the troops left. There came still more, who were fed and disappeared. Later we heard that the Grebbe defenses had surrendered.

Firing sounded in the city, but there were no front-line noises, only separate reports of shots, which did not get closer. In the neighborhood there was a house that had aroused suspicion. Soldiers filled it, and it stared out stupidly from its shattered windows as if it had been arrested.

There was a hospital right across from us; Red Cross cars rushed out and re-entered slowly. It fascinated us like something forbidden; we were uncertain about the healthiness of our curiosity. We also felt the need of amusement in proportion to the approaching stench of corpses, and we looked for it. The Burgomaster made an encouraging speech over the radio; thinking that the microphone had already been disconnected, he finished with a sigh of relief; and the news broadcaster once started his report by slowly counting to five. All this made us laugh out loud, and we repeated it several times.

In the evening of this day, joy reached its apex. The daughter of the neighbors downstairs, Puck Sachs, who worked for the L.B.D. (Dutch Air Protection Service), was tireless and wanted gaiety. We all gathered in their living-room and after tea-time we played a game; sheets of paper were folded three times and the first player would draw a head, the second a rump and the third legs on the last folded section. Thus strange figures were created; a vague elephant with the sharp head of a stork, or Hitler with the perplexed body of a dog and frog's legs. When we had laughed ourselves out, we took our leave, and one of the ladies began to cry, which hastened my departure.

The next day we prepared ourselves for eventual evacuation. Around a briefcase we would roll two blankets; over that we would tie an old raincoat with a rope that fastened onto a handle made from towels. Everyone received such a bundle, which measured about a metre. The work became more and more realistic: to my luggage I added Goethe's *Faust*. We dragged preserves, typewriters and a dictionary to the cellar, ate hastily as laborers and heard that in the afternoon we should really have to leave.

At half-past four we waited with our bundles and trunks on the sidewalk in the sun. From other streets were already streaming people loaded with blankets, sheets and household goods. All of them walked as slowly as if it were a funeral procession, and many of us uttered pitying remarks, forgetting that we shared their fate. Mevrouw Smit, with the proper spirit but weak in body, unsteadily carried a sign bearing our evacuation number. She was very restless, often looked at the sky and said that it was about time. At five o'clock a city bus approached to take us; it was moving to see how this goodly conveyance, breaking its former itinerary, cheerfully came to our aid.

We drove to the outskirts of the city, always passing évacués, through a bobbing sea of luggage. We were housed in the Evangelical Community house, in a stone room with wooden benches, shared our bread with strangers in another room, and had the appearance of a conducted tour, jovial in our common adventure. There was a small garden behind the building, surrounded by high walls, where we could relax. There we found our heads covered by slowly descending ashes and saw large pieces of burnt stuff, twirling high and quickly in the approaching twilight. From this unfamiliar building all Utrecht seemed foreign to us, and everything spoken seemed to be in a strange language.

Beds were made on the benches, the women were to sleep apart on the gallery. This caused a great deal of hilarity. Puck Sachs entered in the midst of the jokes and said that Holland had surrendered.

"Then we might as well have slept at home," I still thought, as I was running outside into the street; I saw how quickly the pavement moved from under me and that I was not alone; feet ran behind me. We reached others, who stood still, as did we in turn, to listen. We heard the loudspeaker admonishing us to behave in a dignified manner and forbidding resistance. This was enough; we ran back with the news. When there was no longer any reason to run, I was gripped by a strange fear. I saw lights being turned on in the city, and a woman cried as she ran; disarmed soldiers hiding their inactivity behind a grin, and others inside, who moved mechanically, arranged their pillows and remained silent. Did they want to go to sleep at the approach of the black, bloody thunder of wheels? The East burst forth into light that I felt in the right half of my body, the might which surveys everything would find me faultless and tear me apart. Now already I knew how shamelessly my mortal fear was being exposed, I saw it in the eyes that observed me curiously, heard their pity humiliate me audibly.

This would remain. There would always be the shame of my fear, when it would appear groundless, for my submissiveness when I was caught. Bodily contact with the enemy already seemed to end in death for me, afterwards there would only be ridicule as he would fold my limp body into preposterous positions—at sports I had always appeared ridiculous—but this would make my loved ones lose all respect for me . . . this I must avoid. Away from the East . . . the railroad map of Holland was a straight line leading to the West, from Utrecht, over Gouda, where my parents lived, to Scheveningen, to the sea, to sailing boats and England.

Thus a resolution was formed which obliterated all fear. I was drinking tea as I told of my plan and felt it grow under the protests of those who listened to it. I asked for a taxi; it was fetched by the religious teacher of the community. When I said I still wanted to have a walk with my girl, he indicated how I could do this, while his eyes expressed fear.

We decided that I should go first to Gouda and only after at least a day of consideration to England. I agreed, because I already knew then that I would go and that nothing could stop me any more. I took my small bag and overcoat and then many hands grasped mine. I counted the tearstained eyes and there were six. My girl took me to the taxi; before I drove away I saw her reliable back as she went into the house; I should not have looked.

I sat next to the silent, fat chauffeur. We drove through illuminated Utrecht and the empty suburb into the lonely polder. "This is going to be some trip, sir," he then remarked. In the light of the streetlamps the white ashes whirled down again; all around it was dark. A cold, fitful wind was blowing. It was half-past eight.

I was enjoying the westward movement and the uneventful

race with the enemy. The chauffeur used his brakes; a long column of military cars was on the road and the first ones stood at
an angle. I heard someone call in the silence, a motor was started,
and I saw the car turn slowly. My man got out, and the gravel
crunched under his shoes; he moved into the headlight, talking,
and returned. The military ordered us to extinguish our headlights. "But the war is over," we said; they had heard nothing
about it. Where did we come from? The news had not come to
Woerden yet, so we could only leave on the sidelamps. By the
dim light we followed our way, the chauffeur protesting like an
expert. In the distance to the left was a fire—Gouda?—but it
stayed along the horizon. In the town I pointed out the way to a
quiet avenue on which my parents lived.

Here I got out. It seemed like summer, so sweet and fragrant
was the air, and the elm trees were in full leaf. Some army cars
were parked in the black night; our house was dark too. I let
myself in with a key by the light of my blue torch. Nobody was
in the living-room, only the loneliness of familiar objects. I went
upstairs—the way which formerly led to my bedroom—and knocked
at the bedroom door, but I did not hear anything. The knock
still reverberated in my brain, but I erased it with another one.
Then something creaked, the voices of my father and mother
called, "Yes?", "No!" and "Who is there?" It was I.

Mother had already laid out my passport. Haste made the telling of my plan easy, but I thought I could depart without money,
because it sounded very unreal. No, I should take something
along, something like two hundred guilders. Often repeated farewells, two often, often touched hands, one soft, the other hard.
When I drove away I had forgotten my torch.

We were just outside the city when our lights failed. Two soldiers passed by, helped us and rode along. One of them took the
steering wheel. "It's hell there," he said, indicating the conflagration with the back of his head. He had been there, been
taken a prisoner, escaped, been caught, put into a bus, driven
away with nine other prisoners, shot at, but not touched. We
were now driving very fast along a new road, passing the regular
obstructions made by cement sewer pipes, and we looked entranced at the orange-yellow blazing line along the horizon,
which was enormous and far away like a natural phenomenon,
an endless, shrieking death scene from which sometimes anguished flames shot up in different places; then we sighed as if
we had been stabbed. Later on the spectacle became reduced,
because separate houses nearby interrupted it, and as the houses

stood closer together they altogether obstructed our view.

The wide streets of The Hague seemed unconscious and forsaken, but with a shock I discovered the dark masses of people that covered all the sidewalks and mid-street shelters. They stood motionless, like nocturnal animals, waiting for the men who were to come back from the front.

We took the soldiers to their homes in the city and drove to Scheveningen. I was to visit a friend of my mother's, to ask for her advice about my escape. In front of the house I paid for the taxi, bade the driver goodbye, rang the doorbell and was immediately let in by the woman who lived there. Her voice showed no surprise, she spoke quietly and her tone was business-like, but her face was contorted by horror. Perhaps she had been waiting thus for hours, or was my unexpected appearance—did I look strange, bewildered?—an alarming revelation? She did not give me much of a chance, she said; but I could not weigh her words, I only thought: Those eyes, that voice, perhaps she is going to sing—I must get away.

And I left. The way to the harbor was straight; along it my legs moved. I respected them, because they seemed indefatigable under the strain and they bore me along like a vehicle, as I counted the streetlamps that I passed. The limits of the world were reached, the painful silence of the city subsided and became more natural and unfolded itself finally in the pure, placid sound of the wide sea.

I stood at the shore, with my small bag—containing one change of linen—in my hand. To the left, in front of me, I heard voices, and I walked in that direction. Even from close by the talkers looked like silhouettes. There was some cursing and the rest was incomprehensible. "Are you looking for a boat?" somebody said and asked me how much I wanted to pay. "Two hundred?" I queried, because that was all I had and my voice was too low to participate in the debate. The man laughed derisively. "Why, mister," he said noticeably proud of his bad news, "some have offered as much as ten thousand and could not get anything!" He continued talking to the others. Apparently they wanted to chip in to buy a sailing-boat from him for four thousand guilders, but suspicion was aroused and there was fear of treachery. Sometimes one would detach himself from the group in despair, or walk away whistling. At other times a loudly preferred remark made it sound as if the group had been tickled.

It gradually grew lighter, the sky became paler and the faces more gray. The man who offered the boat for sale had a long

face, a flat, formless cap and wide trousers; others had jackets on.
One small fellow, bald and without eyebrows, had thrown a thin
blanket around his shoulders.

Above the still motionless sea the faintly green sky shot out
and threw an unreal light upon the quay and some boats in the
open. A little further off stood a small car; its motor was suddenly started and it made off hastily. Somebody cursed, because
it was his car that was being stolen. Many spoke with an accent:
German Jews who were already familiar with the procedure of
flight. A young fellow from Scheveningen took me aside and
asked me in a friendly tone for twenty-five guilders in return for
helping me. I gave him the money. But later on it was said that
nothing would come of it; they thought it was too bad about us,
my helper said, almost sadistically. It was almost half-past three;
we had been expecting the German soldiers for a long time. How
would they come—first a few, firing from armored cars, or in a
large gray mass, which would approach like the shadow of a
cloud? "They are there now!" someone shouted, but it was only
the racket caused by the little stolen car, which hurried along the
deserted quay. Finally an agreement was reached, suddenly at
four o'clock. We all walked towards the barbed-wire obstruction,
the entrance to which was near; a motionless sentry was posted
there; we were not allowed to pass. Somebody tried to go underneath it and got caught like a fly in a spider's web. He looked
at us from between his legs, as he had fallen forward, and asked
us in a flat voice to help him. Somebody said that he would never
be able to extricate himself from it, but that was not true. After
some pulling back and forth, the wire soon let its victim go, and
we climbed over it. We found more soldiers; a long army car
without doors was started. "Pay first," somebody said. We all
gave ten guilders, jumped into the car, piled together like a
human dunghill, and drove away. I hung on with one hand, balancing myself with my knee against the dashboard and knew
that I looked ridiculous. Thus we reached the other side of the
harbor, where our boat was supposed to be. Nothing was there;
we had to return and found the fishermen busy with an un-
rigged ship, which was to become ours. Sails were lowered and
hoisted. At half-past four the now completely visible boat was
ready. It was painted white, its name was *Emma,* and though it
was not built for seafaring, it was sturdy and watertight. We were
all proud of our possession, in whose fate we should share. We
jumped aboard, examined the sails, the mast and one another's
happiness. The man who sold us the boat had received the money,

he fingered a note for a thousand guilders, which he held for a long time against the light in an unprofessional manner. He would have preferred silver, he said. In the meantime, and as we were paying off his helpers, a gentleman with a briefcase made his way through the crowd on the quay. There was some shouting. He wanted to go along, but a small girl followed him and threw herself against the wall gate, all the while sobbing and mumbling to herself. Her mother, also talking, approached: Dad must go away on business; Dad would come back soon. When the gentleman asked whether she could come along, they at first refused. Women aboard, where there were no accommodations and much danger—that seemed in contradiction with our manliness. But they gave in because of the little girl, so we took them on.

The cables were cast off; the two Scheveningen fishermen would steer. For a moment the boat rocked, then it moved away from the quay. At the end of the pier stood two coast-guards, who shouted at us that the wind was in our favor and that we must follow a westward course. As if they had waited for this, our sailors began to offer objections, steered towards the quay again and sprang from the boat; we must fend for ourselves. One of us, whom I had taken for a fisherman because he wore a blue jersey, took the rudder. He had sailed before, he said, and we all eagerly accepted.

We were now really in the open sea, a world apart, which moved through empty space, with only the creaking of the wood as a sound in the midst of our forlornness. The jersey-clad fellow, with only Scheveningen as a background, beamed confidence and gave instructions. We must lie down in the forward part; if enemy planes circled above us, they would take us for cargo above deck, and I must lie prone in the bow, taking turns with others, on the lookout for mines. Stretched out along the cool boards, I heard the murmur of voices from behind me and the noise of the small waves lapping underneath me. The sun rose fiery red, barely covered by brown-yellow skeins of clouds. The ashes were still falling. In the early morning light the last vestiges of cold and discomfort disappeared. I looked for the separation between air and water, it was really summer already. The sea shimmered, sparkled, and was patched with light and shadow. The little things that bobbed up and down and disappeared were not mines, but waves; but how far away were they? The bow of the ship had an iron ring, which was eaten away and flaky; it looked appetizing; what was its name again . . . feuilleté? . . .

I was almost asleep, but the thoughts of mines awakened me. The sea was empty; I reported a small white stripe. One of us had a piece of bread. Half of it was for the man in the jersey, on account of his steering; who as we now learned had not slept for three days. He had been a sergeant at the Grebbe defense line; he was pale and friendly. The remainder of the piece of bread was cut into small squares, of which each of us received one. We played with our hunger and thought of ways to make it last longer, some chewed it but others thought that to suck it was better.

Three times we saw airplanes circling over us, and we hunched down like people saying their prayers. Towards afternoon, when the heat became suffocating, we heard the thunder of the cannonading from Zeeland. Above the coast we saw pointed columns, too high for towers; they must be columns of smoke. A motionless yellow steamer lay on its side in the misty distance.

We had a small hold in the forward part of the boat, in which stood a bucket attached to a rope; this served as a toilet. It was shallow and whoever stood in it showed his head, looking straight ahead with an intense expression. But it served its purpose. In the same hold somebody found a ship's compass.

We became thirsty and started to argue whether we should go first to Belgium or straight to England. At half-past two someone saw a freighter moving along the coast. The man with the jersey steered towards the ship, which now came in our direction and aggressively showed its red, white and blue bow.

Soon it was alongside, rather large, with one man on deck, who shouted that he was sailing for England and asked whether we wanted to come along. One of its sailors grabbed our mast, we lowered the sail in a heap and climbed aboard. The sail-boat looked skimpy as we left it behind in the sun.

This new world had four inhabitants, two skippers, a cabin boy and a passenger, a major. We were given coffee and remained on deck until it got dark and cold outside. Then most of us went down to the cabin; I, however, remained in the steering cabin. The night pressed against its windows and a biting wind blew up. The boat with its empty holds bobbed up and down, then straightened out drowsily, and the people in the cabin made horrible retching noises. Subsequently a foul air came up, it got thicker and penetrated my mouth like a greasy, decomposing substance. We in the steering cabin did not get sick, but were beside ourselves from this stench. At times some one struggles through the small door to the outside; as I was dozing off, I

would be awakened by the cool draught and I would see somebody standing faintly outlined against the darkness, his hair
blowing with the direction of the wind as he leaned over.

Far below I saw the foamy crests of the waves; then I felt as if
suspended in mid-air, and suddenly the sea would tower above
us. I could not understand the few words the sailors spoke, they
did not seem to make sense. After many hours, however, one of
them explained to me that we were circling a buoy; thus we
waited until daybreak. We had now passed the mine fields.

It was three o'clock. I looked out into the distance for a long
time, following the light lines in the dark, then I looked at my
watch again. It was one minute after three.

I must have slept. It was daylight when I was awakened by happy
voices. Some people were already on deck, waving and pointing
out the coast of England to each other.

Two mighty, silent shadows slid by close to us; English destroyers, which behaved as if they did not notice us, but which
watched us out of the corner of their eye.

Harwich looked near, as a small boat signaled to us: "Drop
your anchor."

> *Translated by* ALFRED VAN AMEYDEN VAN DUYM

M. Vasalis

THUNDERSTORM

THE MEETING OF TWO ECCENTRICS IS ALWAYS LESS EXCITING THAN
one is led to expect. The guests had watched tensely to see how
the meeting would go off between old Redhurst and Pole, who
to a certain degree could have become the former's rival, since
he possessed a legendary amount of knowledge and lived as
strangely and as much in retirement as Redhurst. But nothing
happened.

The two men shook hands, Pole looking away in the meantime, trying to find a chair. Redhurst contemplated him for the
first and last time, conceived a vague dislike for him and forgot
him. Mrs. Northcraft, who competently and with great cheer
managed the small hotel, poured tea, standing at the table covered with a white cloth. She was a sturdy, very blonde woman, of

great joy in living and a motherly nature, which extended to all
sickly or suppressed people. With it, however, she had a strong
sense of humor and little taste for dramatics. Into her concern
for her guests she never mixed a condescending pity, and she
herself did not feel called upon to comfort the unfortunate. She
was tender and wise and full of laughter. Here perhaps lay the
reason for the success the hotel had enjoyed from its very first
year.

The hotel was situated on an extensive sheep ranch, a wild,
apparently abandoned high plateau. Surrounding it were a few
other houses and a charming small grove of trees, ponds and
meadows. It was here by preference that the guests liked to center
their activities, playing tennis, chatting and carrying on social
life as they had brought it from the city.

Outside of this small oasis, the veldt stretched out so far under
the vast sky that at first one saw nothing but the horizon and the
great changing play of light, and only afterwards, very small, the
huts of the Kaffirs, and the Kaffir boys riding their ponies behind
the white swarming herds of sheep.

Besides healthy tourists on vacation, ill people and convales-
cents often came to the small hotel and sometimes stayed for
years.

Mrs. Northcraft knew all their life stories, and in her attitude
when she stood as now on the lawn at her tea table, there was
something of a mother as well as of a general. Her husband stood
next to her and passed out the cups. It was a quiet and rather
warm afternoon. The guests sat on the grass under a large cedar,
in whose upper branches there always seemed to be a rustling.
Some desultory conversation was going on. Mr. Northcraft did
not listen to anyone; he cast an ironic glance at one after the
other in turn, but a somewhat longer glance at Pole, whose shyness and exactitude irritated him every year anew. Mr. Northcraft stood with his feet wide apart, as he slightly teetered back
and forth. His untidy trousers had a surprisingly low crotch, he
held his pipe in his brown, wooden-looking hand. It always produced a slight gurgle, which he could never get rid of. His light,
old man's eyes were sharp and open, and he often laughed inwardly. He felt again, as he stood next to his wife waiting for
his cup of tea, the same irritated urge to shock Pole, to upset his
room, where everything was in its appointed place.

"He is no man," he mumbled to himself. A new thought occurred to him, he took in Pole from top to toe and again laughed
softly to himself.

Pole in the meantime was suffering unutterably. He sat in an uncomfortable chair and dared not get up again. He was used to having his tea served in his room, but Mrs. Northcraft had resolved to make him more human and had induced him under a pretext to come to the lawn among the other guests. He could not sneak away and he had not taken a book along, the greatest disaster that could occur to him.

He sat besides Mrs. Copper, a very articulate and fat little woman who, cramped by her own bodily form, sat back in a chair partly buried by herself and kept up a steady chattering, gurgling like a shallow small brook. She was here with her son, who suffered from asthma and who now sat alone a little further away, looking at the sky and in a continuous struggle with his breathing.

Leaning back in his chair with his legs on another sat Redhurst. His trouser legs were drawn up high and his naked, hairy calves were exposed to everyone's view. Every once in a while he would glance at himself with satisfaction. He was having a devilish lot of fun, because he had just attacked the Reverend James about *The Miracle* and everybody was listening.

He could stand a crowd like this only when it comprised an audience. Usually he avoided all company and sat reading, either on the front stoop or in his room. But sometimes, in a sudden urge to test his strength, he would go among the guests, who were all a bit scared of him, and hold forth in a monologue, which was meant to shock as many of those present as possible. Patriotism, mother love and religion, and sometimes as an added dish, morals, were his favorite subjects. Then he would retire again, licking his chops like a satiated lion.

Even Mr. Northcraft had some respect for Redhurst, who had led a life filled with adventure. He came of a good old family, had inherited a great deal of money, gambled it away, earned and lost it, and had a humble passion for the arts and sciences. One would say that in every respect he was different from Pole; nevertheless they had a lot in common.

They were both in bad health and did not want to admit it. Redhurst was a sickly, fat, loosely jointed old man, with powerful bone structure. His face was large and yellowish, and he had deep pockets under his darting, cold, grey eyes. His lips were blue-tinted, his teeth were regular and yellow. As he stood there, his hairy hands were thick and slate-colored, as if they belonged to a body that had floated for a long time in the water. He walked heavily, with an impaired swagger, and he breathed hard after he had taken a few steps. He never wore socks and his naked feet were stuck into old-fashioned high boots, without laces or buttons, which made them appear blind and inexorable. He dressed like a French peasant and still gave an impression of smartness.

Pole, on the other hand, was almost a clothed, disembodied spirit, who only seemed visible by what he wore. His clothes were always spotless and trim and, though they had been made by a good tailor, they flapped around him as he walked. He spoke with a hollow, strangled voice, as if he were deaf, and walked lightly and quickly, all the while gesticulating with his arms as if they were tentacles. His breath simmered and whistled continually in his hollow chest, and he was ashamed of it.

Both men liked to be blasphemous, Redhurst taunting and laughing loudly; fundamentally he did not much care whether God existed or not, but he drew pleasure from the painful silences and from the protestations that followed his blaspheming. Pole reacted fiercely and vengefully; the problem was not at all a matter of indifference to him.

Both were passionate readers, but strangely enough Redhurst had an aversion to all novels, except old French ones. He preferred to read sociological, ethnological and philosophical books and knew a great deal about astronomy and physics. He felt the urge to know everything, preferably backed up by figures. He had never been a student, but he was educated as only a non-student can be.

Pole was an amateur archaeologist and a teacher of English. He read during meals, in bed and all day long, and when he was not reading he looked for fossils and prehistoric tools. He felt no desire to taste his food, to carry on a conversation, to be aware of his bed, or to know his fellow humans, except those who had been dead for thousands of years. When he was walking by himself in the hot sun, bending down or erect, looking around and talking softly and touching the stone in his hand, he would live again the fantasy of his childhood: all people on earth were dead but his mother and he. They wandered together over a deserted world; she found all kinds of remains; they were able to use everything. He stopped to play everywhere, and she waited until he got tired and then she would carry him home. Thus he was walking around now and his little old black car waited; his little car, which he loved very much, for which he cared as it cared for him, when dead tired and, his head buzzing with ideas, he drove home.

Neither Redhurst nor Pole had any friends; they were engrossed in themselves and would allow no one to intrude. Redhurst did not want it otherwise. He enjoyed many things. He lived royally and abundantly and was afraid of dying. Pole on the contrary was afraid of sundry small difficulties; he lived a careful and worried life and believed that he would not die before many unpleasant things had happened to him. He was familiar with the image of death and thought about it as an important, good event.

Mary, Mrs. Northcraft's daughter, was a nurse and had come home a few days before on a vacation. She noticed Pole's suffering expression, went into the house and came back with a book.

"I've finished it," she said, "but I found it most difficult. Could you explain it to me again? . . . This passage, where he speaks of all those races . . ."

Pole almost cried with relief and gratitude. He got up, excused himself to Mrs. Copper and walked with Mary out of the sun and into the darkened house. Mrs. Northcraft went into the kitchen and found, to her despair, Miriam the cook sleeping in a ring of grease, her brown countenance turned into a stone image and the stove cold and black.

Miriam awoke with a start, so self-conscious that she immediately went to the attack and asked to be dismissed in a shrill voice. Her face was smooth and youthful, her hair was in stiff, short curls; her long skull was nicely shaped, her eyes were golden and somewhat protuberant, so that light sometimes shone through them from the side.

Mrs. Northcraft paid no attention to her and called through the back door to another Kaffir servant, who sat on his haunches, splitting kindling while he sang psalms slowly and with propriety.

"Light the fire, old Jan," said Mrs. Northcraft. Proudly, sticking out his chest, he passed Miriam on his way in. As soon as he had done his task, he left the kitchen, in which he had never been allowed before and, once outside, burst into soft, happy laughter.

Mrs. Northcraft continued to work with Miriam, who felt insulted because she had an unshakable conception of hierarchy: old Jan belonged outside and her job was to make the fire! The servants ate beforehand, a staff of six men, all differing in race and color.

Miriam had to take them their food every day. She did it under protest, because she thought it below her dignity to serve "black folk," because she was a Basuta woman, of a pure and unmixed race. The other servants had, besides their Kaffir forefathers, Hottentots, Bushmen, Indians and whites in their family tree, and she considered them inferior.

As soon as Miriam had left the kitchen, she called out in a commanding and threatening tone to old Jan, "Come here, you old baboon, grab this food, I am tired of fetching your food, do you hear? Hurry up, boy!"

Old Jan, unwillingly took the tray and carried it to the servants, all of whom lay on their backs in the shade, softly humming in many tones. They received him with laughing derision and called him Miriam.

"Miriam, what did you do with your fat, how did you get those legs? Come over here!"

Miriam, who had remained to peep around the corner, went back to her kitchen shaking with laughter, her self-respect completely rehabilitated. She sounded the second gong for dinner as if it were a war drum. Outside it had grown almost cold. In the dining-room the fire had been lit. Two old dogs baked their sore spots before it; little old Grandma Northcraft sat quietly and hunch-backed in a corner and nodded and smiled whenever anybody looked at her. She had already eaten; she ate before the others, because she spilled her food badly.

With a solemn, slightly hesitating voice the Reverend James said grace before the meal. The prayer took quite a time. The clergyman had been continually contradicted that day by Redhurst and now pronounced a somewhat irritated, long and stiff prayer, while all those seated around the table looked into their plates. One of the dogs audibly and slowly licked his belly under a mangy, lifted paw, and little Grandma laughed gaily like a child.

A servant then brought in the dishes. He was a tiny Bushman with a wrinkled, small, embryonic face; who moved with a swinging of hips in a coquettish manner. Other servants said that he was neither a man nor a woman; he lived by himself in a clean hut and had adopted a Kaffir baby. He took it along wherever he went and put it down in the shade, where it crawled about on its naked, velvety limbs and played contentedly.

Pole had leaned his book against a glass of water. Redhurst ate greedily and in silence, so that the conversation was led by Doctor Coleman, who had waited for this opportunity and kept it going in an authoritative manner. He had a dictator's exterior. He was a good surgeon, but in his daily occupations he retained the commanding look and clipped tone which he should have reserved for the operating-room. He was devoid of any interest in culture and self-criticism, which heightened his assuredness. Still it was considered a privilege to have such a capable man at hand. "A real doctor," opined Mrs. Copper.

Mary, who knew many doctors and saw through his pose, nevertheless became restless under his steady glare; she laughed too much and blushed too often. He was good to look at—and she need never be afraid that he would understand and criticize her with any subtlety.

Cutting through all conversations, not interested in any audience, sixty-year old Mr. Northcraft held forth untiringly, never waiting to clear his throat. He talked about his old hunting adventures and of how he, with his brothers, had frightened the servants, as they were smoking opium, by previously filling their pipes with dynamite. He laughed over his own stories, his laughter often ending in a coughing spell.

At the end of the table sat the two eight-year-old Pette twins, a slip-up of the old Pette couple, who in their forty-fourth year, after a childless marriage of twenty years, were suddenly surprised by this event. They were delicate, fair-complexioned girls, fleet as water, always secretly excited; they lisped and giggled simultaneously and looked into each other's face, as if into a mirror.

Pole in spite of his book, observed how the doctor and Mary had developed common interest. He held himself aloof, but his eyes at times carefully looked up from his book, as if he were slowly stirring poison. He was very much upset. During his previous stay at the quiet hotel he had become friendly with Mary; that is, he was no longer afraid of her and he could look at her without having an unpleasant feeling.

He thought her beautiful and he had even allowed her to come along in his car, which so far as he was concerned was something like being extravagantly accommodating. He had so much familiarized himself with her and conducted so many conversations with her during her absence, that the meeting again that morning had been very disturbing. And now he interpreted her smile and amused interest in the doctor as flagrant infidelity. She remained friendly, respectful toward him and at the same time deeply concerned, as a nurse for her patient. She had the same warmth of heart as her mother. He tolerated this attitude, because he did not know how to alter it and he could make use of it.

"I should like to go for a ride presently," said Mary to the doctor. After the meal they walked silently to the stables, where the saddle horses were feeding in the semi-darkness. The horses looked up uneasily and snorted as Mary entered; the white of their eyes shone in the darkness.

She patted their warm, strong necks and put the saddles on. They backed up and still unwillingly shook their heads protestingly at the unusual hour. In the open arena beside the stable the work horses walked around freely, they came now running with their long, uncut manes and looked at the shiny, well-groomed saddle horses, snorted and disappeared again in a free gallop.

The sun was setting, half of the endless plain was dark under the yellow, glowing sky; in the other direction heaven and veldt were hazy and blue. Then the sun suddenly dissolved, its light suffused the sky, which became yellow as honey and translucent.

They rode over a red sandy road, then across the veldt. The horses were fresh and happy; the twilight did not last long and soon the sandy places between the low, dark, wooded groves looked like water, through which they galloped dangerously.

The evening star rose, alone in an empty sky. The breeze was clean and gentle and blew against the cheeks of Mary and the doctor. They stopped now and then to look around. Mary looked like an Indian with her black eyes and high cheekbones. She belonged so much to this cool emptiness, high on her horse, that Coleman felt something like respect rising in him and he almost gave up his plans of seduction. He was, to tell the truth, not a very good rider and not accustomed to the sudden wheeling round of the horses in the increasing darkness in order to avoid pits and bushes. His greatest fear was that he would fall and make himself ridiculous.

Mary noticed that he was quiet, but she misunderstood the reason. The thought that he enjoyed the ride and the loveliness of the evening tempered her own delight until she became as still and serious as he.

So they returned, riding at a foot pace, to let the horses cool off, the only sound the clumping of the hooves and the soft creaking of the saddles.

In the hotel they found Pole who, with a face contorted by disgust, was trying to chase the moths out of his room. He had already put on his housecoat, looked pale and self-absorbed and was apparently occupied with endless preparations for going to bed.

"I'll just take you to your room," said the doctor firmly and without embarrassment to Mary. "It occurs to me, that I have

never seen it." His dictator's countenance remained undisturbed.
He left her no time to think things over; now that he was off his
horse his confidence in himself rose with every worthy surgeon's
step he took.

Pole now stood before the open window, staying a while contrary to his custom, after he had carefully folded his clothes and
had draped the mosquito net around his bed. Through the finely
woven screen he saw the large stars caught in the mazes of a
spider's web, shimmering and glittering like drops of water. The
night was filled with awesome silence. He rubbed the palm of his
hand along his narrow chest and stroked his lean hips. He could
not get rid of the memory of the day: the doctor's dashing appearance, Mary's glowing eyes.

> "Tired of all these, from these would I be gone,
> Save that to die I leave my love alone . . ."

Tired . . . and disgusted, yes. But he did not leave any love behind. He had never considered suicide, not even in his periods
of greatest depression. And about a woman, a loved one, whom
he would have at his side all his life, he had no longer thought
after his illness, until today when he had read Coleman's intentions so plainly in the other's too clear eyes.

The hotel was quiet now. The little Bushman with his small
son lay wrapped in a blanket before the annex, the boy still
clutching an orange; his small mouth was open and the moon
shone on his two wide little teeth.

The horses sometimes stamped the hard ground of the veldt,
and a shivering, damp snort came now and again out of the
neighboring stable.

Mary was restless; she could not get to sleep and whispered
now and then "no" and savagely shook her dark head. On her
dressing-table, multiplied through the double mirrors to a triple
unity, stood the portrait of a friend smiling stiffly in the direction
of the disorderly bed.

Pole lay open-eyed on his bed and lectured: "The interest
which of late has been manifested in Donne, is for the greater
part due to his eroticism, though many of you do not realize
this. It is not a coincidence that at a period when Lawrence is
worshipped . . ." He cleared his throat, took a lozenge and closed
his eyes. Everyone was asleep now, the sufferer from asthma sitting up straight-backed against his pillow, the couple Pette who

had gone to sleep quarreling, the couple Northcraft, hand in hand and still smiling because of one of his stories; the eight-year-old twins, freckles on their delicate little noses, more alike than two white mice, straight on their backs and breathing quietly; and Redhurst, a glass of whisky next to his bed as well as a book about the economic development of Japan.

Next day was an unhappy one for Pole. He wanted to look for stones with Mary, but she was already on her way with Coleman, a rifle over his shoulder, to hunt wild duck at one of the artificial lakes near the oasis. Pole went out by himself and did not find anything worthwhile. Coming back he saw Redhurst spread out like a lonely plateau on the lawn; he was drinking and reading and intermittently teasing Mrs. Northcraft by telling her that it still was not established that women had a soul.

"I really don't care, you know," he said, winking his large parrot-like eyelid, "provided they have a body."

"Hear, hear," said Mr. Northcraft, lifting his hand to slap his wife's generous thighs, but he scratched the back of his head instead.

Pole was jealous of Redhurst. He envied his isolation, so easily obtained by strength and self-confidence. He himself had to acquire solitude and rest by withdrawing himself and making himself small. Redhurst made a large space for himself by obliterating everything in close proximity and then enthroning himself proudly in the empty space.

Pole also took up a book, but after a few moments the print became blurred.

That evening, after the children had been put to bed and none of them knew what to do with themselves, they decided to play a game, the game called "Murderer." A jury had to be chosen from the company. Mrs. Northcraft, with her white healthy face, sparkling eyes and strong chin, would make up the jury with Mr. Pette. Mr. Pette had "had a couple" before and after the meal, and while he usually spoke in a soft and muffled voice, as if he were lying in a closet bed, he was now his old-fashioned, courteous self and almost boisterous. Mary looked around and missed Pole; she went to fetch him from his room, where he lay on his bed inside the muslin screen knees pulled up and sharply outstretched arms like a giant mosquito. Mary put an arm under his body, lifted him with ease from the bed and took him, blinking at the light, to the other guests.

Mr. Northcraft had taken Redhurst out of his isolation by

other means. "I know a joke," said Northcraft. "Come along, the women mustn't hear it."

"Is everybody really acquainted with the 'Murderer' game?" asked Mary. "The jury, mother and Mr. Pette, will allow us all to take a card from the deck. We agree that the one who has the ace of spades is the murderer. Nobody must let on what kind of card he has. Afterwards everybody hides in the house. All lights must be put out, you may enter all rooms except the children's room, of course. And after five minutes the murderer, who is hiding, must steal about and attack somebody. The victim must cry out, the murderer escape, all lights will be put on and then everybody must prove his alibi to the jury. You must tell the truth, only the murderer may lie. Let's start; you'll understand as you go along."

Mrs. Northcraft and Mr. Pette then allowed the guests to draw a card; they all disappeared, laughing and anxiously whispering in the dark halls and rooms, looking for hiding places.

Pole had drawn the ace of spades; he was the murderer. He had never played this strange game, he had never played any game. He walked around nervously, thoroughly confused, and was about to put on all the lights, to give up and go quietly to his room.

But then he saw, in the faint shimmering of light that penetrated through the crack of a door, that, very near him, the doctor was pulling Mary along and that she looked around.

Noiselessly, with beating heart he ran along the dark hall, into an open door. He heard a faint shriek; Mrs. Copper, squatting behind an easy chair, shouted at every noise she heard: "Oh! the murderer!"

Pole ran disdainfully out of the door, he was now really looking for his victim. He thought he heard the hated voice close by, vaguely he distinguished a broad back disappearing behind a door. He jumped and grasped a large soft neck, in which his skinny fingers sank almost completely. Horror seized him, but his fingers seemed to have acquired a life of their own. All his anguish, his love, his humiliation and his hatred streamed with cold rapture into his fingers, he pulled and pinched, and a sort of daze, akin to love, mastered him.

The cry of the victim was so natural that the guests, who had run toward the sound, admired and praised him.

"Lights" was the call. Solemn and swinging hips, the jury entered, Mr. Pette arm in arm with Mrs. Northcraft. They had both put on beards to appear imposing and were full of laughter.

From all the rooms the guests now gathered, to prove their alibis. There was general laughter, which, however, stopped suddenly.

For on the murder spot stood Pole, looking palely at Redhurst; Redhurst groaning, lying half in and half out of the room. His face was blue, his eyes were closed and blood came from his open mouth.

The doctor knelt at his side, felt his pulse and lifted an eyelid. But Redhurst had already sat up straight and had to vomit. There was one big broken yellow tooth.

"The shock," said the doctor to the bystanders. "He has a weak heart, he has been frightened and he fell down, isn't that so, eh, Mr. Redhurst?"

"Go to blazes!" said Redhurst. "And help me get up."

On the threshold the twins appeared in long pajama legs, their shining heads glistening in the lamplight. Intermittently they exchanged glances and then looked at Redhurst and his yellow tooth.

Mary had eyes only for Pole; she took his hand in an unobtrusive manner and led him to his room. He was as in a dream, but he still acted in a pitifully dignified manner. Mary felt curiously guilty.

"It will be all right with Mr. Redhurst," she said.

"Yes," said Pole speaking in a muffled tone. "But I wanted to murder him." He smoothed his hair and talked through the window, through the sparkling screen, "I thought at first that it was the doctor . . . but then I thought: It is Redhurst, and I could no longer stop. But he was afraid . . . he thought he was dying. I never do anything like that, I don't touch anybody. Sometimes in thought . . . I am fighting, I . . ." He sat down; it became oppressively still in the room, on the ceiling a large black beetle walked slowly, like a funeral coach. The faucet of the washbowl dripped persistently, everything seemed in suspense and to last for a century.

Mary fled to her mother, who, like herself, understood what had happened better than did the doctor and the other guests.

Redhurst lay on his bed. He was no longer angry, but still frightened and in pain. He did not think of Pole. The attacker had made no impression whatever upon him; he thought only of the occurrence itself.

He, Redhurst, had been attacked, he had been choked. His self-confidence was shaken, he had been left by himself, he had not put up any resistance. He was afraid and terribly lonely; he was aware that he was an old man and that he must die some day, that some day that would happen irrevocably. He was moist with sweat, there were smarting tears in his eyes. "Mother," he called.

Next day Pole was up before daybreak. He carefully packed his trunks, put on his traveling suit and after a half-distracted, half-ignored breakfast he took leave of Mrs. Northcraft, who warmly held his hand in both of hers and shook it. For a moment he looked at her with his wary, disillusioned eyes. She smiled and threw back her head with the carefree, ironic gesture of a French woman when she says, "Fiche-t'en!"

"So long," she said, "hurry back, Mary and I like to have you here."

His car was ready. He gave the servant a small tip, he tested all the straps to see that the trunks were well secured, he checked his gasoline supply, the oil, the water, even the knotted white handkerchief on his head, put on his goggles and stepped inside. He pulled his legs in like long weeds; when he was ready and seated, Mr. Northcraft, who was looking on from a distance, spat on the ground. "An old young lady," he remarked. Pole's car disappeared at great speed between the trees and, when it was again in sight on the bare road, it was going with the inflexible purpose of an industrious insect.

The sun was already beating down fiercely and there was no wind. The red soil was soaked by the narrow, larger beds of little dried-up streams along which moved vividly green, tall herbs.

Pole looked around and as he did so, there was of a sudden a faint rustling coming from all sides, which increased and became stronger and louder. Everywhere around him on the veldt eddies of sand stood up high and straight in the air, to the right and to the left. The wind was as yet not strong.

He halted and put up the top; as he heaved at it quickly, two slate-colored thunder-clouds showed on the horizon. Looking around he had still in view the small oasis, in which the hotel was situated, in quiet sunshine, a perspective as beautiful and unreal as if it were a vision—a past, to which he would never return.

He got into the car again. Far in front of him blue rays from the sky stood out like hair combed straight up from the ground. Enormous shadows flew over the far distant mountains, some were as yellow as sulphur, others deep blue and black. A herd of sheep spread like flakes of foam in a long wave over the plain through the wild shadows and remained standing in a large island of light. Slowly and broadly the rain edged up closer, hiding the mountains. The rustling increased. The air became, even in the sunlight in which he still drove, cool and open, like a theater when the curtain is raised.

Then a terrible thunder-clap resounded through the violet sky, after which the rain increased its patter. Pole continued driving. He was alone in the universe; the beauty and the violence, the great breaking-loose of the elements, made him feel beside himself with ecstasy. He shouted at the thunder in a loud voice.

The parched veldt began to glisten near and far; he drove straight through the level pools that were in his way; from all sides rivulets began to stream. He was wet and cold, and he had not been so happy since he had left Europe. Rain and thunder and the streaming of the water against his car window. . . . The road became impassable; he drove beside it, on its bank, but finally he stopped and deliberated whether he had not better turn back.

Redhurst got up somewhat later. He was still in a somber mood and decided to stay for a few days in a neighboring city, where he had acquaintances who lived in comfort and security. He wanted to read, to go to the theater and to have his tooth repaired.

He did not say goodbye, and his room remained untouched. He packed his small trunk and sat heavily back in the car. He did not pay any attention to the road, for the chauffeur knew it by heart. He remained dreaming for quite some time, but suddenly sat up with a start upon observing the pouring rain. They drove more slowly and then stopped. In vain the chauffeur tried to start the car, it would not turn over. Redhurst cursed and looked around.

He found himself, to his horror, in a décor of Judgement Day. There was still one spot of the somberly violent sky penetrated by a bundle of apocalyptic light, which flamed like a pool of fire on the plain. Thunder and lightning raged directly above his head and, in the somnambulistic state in which he found himself the circumstance fitted in remarkably well with his misfortune of the previous evening. Never before in his extremely eventful life had he been afraid of a thunder-storm, nature had never made any particular impression on him. But last night he had died many deaths, he had called for "mother," and in this lonely and dangerous situation a long-forgotten symbolism imposed itself; he was dead and still not safe. His soul was now being judged, he might suffer eternal damnation. He pronounced the second forgotten word and whispered, "God . . ." and he prayed for help.

At that moment he noticed Pole's car, which was moving by jerks and starts like a frightened lobster. He had been bogged down, got loose with a great deal of difficulty and had now turned back from sheer necessity.

Redhurst felt insanely grateful when he recognized him. "Good fellow!" he thought. "Hey, can you take me back? This car is out of commission," he shouted.

Pole opened his car door without comment, and heavy Redhurst sat down on the hard front seat against Pole, who was slowly warmed by his contact. The chauffeur climbed into the back. For a quarter of an hour they drove along in silence and then, as suddenly and majestically as it had started, the storm ceased.

The wind subsided, and one could hear in the otherwise arid plain all around the rushing of water. Blue rivulets ran through the red sand, in the suddenly cleared sky now drifted great coral reefs and glowing shells. They drove along a swamp where a thousand little birds boiled and seethed and the bushes swarmed with white butterflies. Storks and herons drifted in the almost white and glittering sky. They were near the hotel, when Redhurst started to speak.

"It is funny that the whole dried-out caboodle does not catch fire through the lightning," he said. He glanced at Pole from the side. Pole's face was relaxed and boyish, almost carefree. He drove with great ease.

"What!" exploded Pole. "But, my good fellow, they find traces of fire everywhere, even in the stone tools. Probably all their wooden objects had been consumed by fire."

"Or rotted away," said Redhurst.

"Not rotted away," said Pole, "it doesn't rain enough for that, it's as dry here as in hell."

They had arrived and climbed out stiffly.

"Come with me," said Redhurst, "I've got a brochure about it." He took Pole's arm.

Mary and Mrs. Northcraft looked on, greatly perplexed to see Redhurst disappearing into the house, arm in arm, and absorbed in hot debate, with his murderer.

Translated by ALFRED VAN AMEYDEN VAN DUYM

PART VIII

THE DUTCH IN THE WORLD

Beb Vuijk

WAY BAROE

THE HOUSE STOOD ON THE HILLSIDE, FIFTEEN METRES ABOVE THE
sea; the crowns of the old cocoanut plantation reached almost
to the same height. In the evenings these tops looked like dark
birds sleeping, while their feathers moved in the wind. The
glistening, white beach formed a path along the edge of the
plantations, almost disappearing at high tide and many fathoms
wide at low tide; it looked still wider because of the brown coral
reefs that smelt of seaweed and putrid fish. Higher up, the coast-
line curved out into a little spit of land. There the crocodiles
kept their kill among the spreading mangrove trees. The cadav-
erous smell and the aerial roots resembling fleshless bones were
reminiscent of death.

The house was large but primitive—thatch walls and a corru-
gated iron roof. Furniture was scarce, but the children numerous.
In the evenings a little oil-lamp was lit, and shadows quivered in
the corners. Sometimes a dreaming child would cry out in terror;
outdoors, leaves, night animals and the monsoon rain rustled. To
the older children this life was familiar, it warmed their hearts;
their desires barely reached out beyond the landing-stage.

There was always rice in the larder and chutney—crushed
chilli mashed with sugar and salt. Sometimes there were remains
of highly seasoned meat, salted eggs or fried fish. They ate when
they were hungry, all day long; there were no regular meals. At
one o'clock, father came in from the plantations and ate while his
wife passed him the side-dishes. By that time the children had
eaten, with their fingers, their fill of the warm white rice from a
chipped enamel plate, with all kinds of sharp side-dishes; broiled
chicken, vegetables boiled in cocoanut milk and fried bananas.
They slept in their beds or on a mat under the verandah or in
the shade of the lime trees in the back compound.

At the evening meal at eight o'clock, the two eldest were occasionally present, and there was always a loudly squealing baby.
Onno Bouvier had long ceased to demand regularity of his fam-

ily. Resignation, submission without struggle and a chronic sapping of the will and conscience made life bearable for one who had taken a girl from these islands to wife and had begotten foreigners for children.

In the mornings he would go to the plantations: the cocoanut plantation between the beach and the hill, and the little coffee plantation on the slopes beside the house. In the afternoons and evenings he would lie stretched on the old ratan chair and read. Books were the only thing the mail brought him. He chose them according to weight: thrillers in periodical form, Lord Lister, Buffalo Bill, detective stories, but also antiquated romance— Hugo, Dumas and Eugène Sue—in cheap editions. Reading was a substitute for the activity he had lost. Literary enjoyment he did not know, he was never struck by a happy, figure of speech, descriptions he skipped, the development of a character escaped him. He read for the sake of the story, for fights, murders, ghosts and thrilling adventures.

He had been an inert, taciturn child, in a small town with silted-up harbors where the activity of three centuries had run aground with the old boats on the river banks. There he had lived in the last house at the corner of the harbor and the quay along the river. His father, the notary public, had lived there for years before marriage. His mother had aged early in childless wedlock, when, in the last year of her summer, his life sprang from her death.

The stones of the house had turned brown and the stepped gable leaned forward a little. The freestone steps in front of the house gleamed brightly in the sunlight—a small patch of light between the row of dark houses and the battered green foliage of the elms. The harbor-water was stale and still and of an opaque green like old bottles. It rose and fell with the tide and fed the profuse moss on the weathered quay walls. On the other side stood a mill, its sails turning like flashing swords in the air and, infinitely more appalling in the dark water, distorted by the current and unreal. As the sails stirred the water, the boy screamed. It was an irrational fear—perhaps a horror of death, or a memory of the terrors of his birth—stifled by life. People laughed at his timorousness, but the doctor advised keeping him in the room overlooking the garden on the days the mill operated. Later the sails were brought to a standstill for good.

At school he was a mediocre pupil, not stupid, but slow and absolutely passive. He had no friends, but his schoolmates ceased teasing him because he never defended himself.

From the moment he could spell he read during every free hour. Reading became the only form of activity in his life, a means of substitution for the deeds he himself was unable to perform. He was too tired, too apathetic, too slow of movement and thought, but at the same time he longed for the rapidity, liveliness and tension of a perfect adventure.

When he had passed through three classes of secondary school, for which he took five years, his father kept him at home and made him sit in the office among the clerks. But the doctor prescribed a different mode of life, and so he attended the horticultural school. His movements remained slow but his body grew strong and he became interested in his work.

A year later his father died. The old, unknown man was buried by weeping aunts and an uncle in black clothes. Onno did not join in the weeping; he felt strange, almost hostile, but after a time the former security was restored in part. The notary candidate took over the notariate and looked after his affairs. Four houses in a row, from the blind alley to the quay, were Onno's property. The new notary rented the lower part of the house, and Onno climbed a floor higher, moving into the large corner room. It had double windows that looked out onto the deserted harbor; through the two others the evening sun shone red from the sky and, redder still, was reflected by the broken river water.

After his final examination the notary enquired regarding his plans.

"I don't yet know," answered the boy. He went slowly up to his room where he slept and read. He was restless. The work at the gardens had accustomed him to regular exercise; he could no longer read all day; he could no longer breathe in a closed room. Before he went to bed he threw wide open both the windows overlooking the river. There was little traffic; sometimes he was awakened by a small motor boat which, puffing heavily and steadily, towed a few barges full of vegetables and fruits to the public market in the town.

He was bored without work, yet every job seemed tedious to him, and the free adventures of his books fictitious. Summer faded into autumn. He had to close his window to a mere crack because of the first storms that blew from the north-west. Night fell earlier. The old maid-servant lit the lamp when she brought up the newspaper. He never read the papers—reality seemed to him so unimportant—but in the local paper he followed an enthralling serial.

It was blowing hard. In the harbor a discolored boat splashed

with regular jerks against the half-decayed embankment, but out
on the river the water was black and throbbing, breathing rapidly, and there were dashes of white foam like a herd of dark,
fleeing animals. Leaving the window, he returned to the table
and fingered the newspaper.

"Employee wanted for a cocoanut estate in the Moluccas."

He sat bent over the small advertisement, re-read the words
and felt a rising excitement.

The Moluccas, lonely islands in a distant blue sea!

Moluccas! The strange false romantic world of his books distorted the sound of this word into a name out of a story. Islands
outside reality, in a zone apart! He was holding his thumb between the most exciting pages of this new book, for there life
would become more thrilling than the most thrilling novel! For
weeks he had fearfully pushed aside the thought that his life
would have to change. This was the change!

All of a sudden he became very active, wrote the letter and
went out to post it. With the wind behind him, he ran home
with long, awkward strides.

He had lived for twenty-two years but had never thought about
anything; and because he did not think, his life was limited to
the mechanical things that keep existence going. That evening he
tore loose and drifted off with the current. He felt freed and at
one with the wind, the rain and the water. He ran along the
water's edge with great strides at an unusually quick pace.

Back in his room he could not sleep, so he opened his window
and leaned out; the wind and rain stung his face with cold.

The Lanspijckers were an old Molucca family. Having come
to these regions in the seventeenth century as ensign and copyist,
they grew rich, during the corrupt eighteenth century, in goods
and lands which they began to develop at the end of the nineteenth century. In the twentieth the children went to Holland to
study, and Egbert Lanspijcker had to find strangers to administer
his lands. Gerard, his eldest, had settled down for good as a
lawyer in Amsterdam and looked after his father's affairs. He
asked Onno Bouvier to come over, in order to make his acquaintance, and he furnished him with all particulars.

The Way Baroe estate was situated on the south coast of
Ceram; 62 hectares of cocoanut which would be harvested for the
first time the following year, 124 hectares of old plantations in
full production and another 62 hectares of clearing. Besides these
there was a small coffee plantation on the side of the hill. The

work was done by people from Kei and Boetoeng; the Chinese
bookkeeper at the same time looked after the estate shop. Once
in two months the K.P.M. Steamship Company called at Way
Baroe, and three times a year the owner came to inspect the
plantations and to visit his nephew Roel, an eccentric person
who helped a little here and there but whose working capacity
could not be relied upon.

All these details meant nothing to Bouvier, but he was fully
resolved to accept whatever was offered.

He was the only applicant. In Java and Sumatra a well-paid
job could always be found, the backward Moluccas, where life
was as monotonous and primitive as it had been a hundred years
before, attracted nobody. Gerard Lanspijcker thought of his
father, a little old man, hesitant in his deportment with strangers
though well-spoken and fond of laughter in the circle of his
friends. With this quiet, retiring young man he would get on
well.

Without further questioning, Onno was accepted.

One month later Onno Bouvier embarked on a German
freighter, which was sailing from Antwerp via Port Said and
Singapore to Macassar. He was the only passenger besides two
nuns who walked the deck or read prayers from small books and
merely said: "Good morning" and "Good evening." The broad-
shouldered, boisterous captain had tried for three days to keep
up a conversation at table; after this he had meals served in his
cabin.

Onno lay on his deck chair and started on a new supply of tales
of horror. They passed mountains in the distance and sailed close
to islands, carelessly strewn in a deserted sea, but called at few
ports. Very early one morning they arrived at Macassar, and that
same afternoon Onno had to go on to Amboyna with the K.P.M.
. . . It was the change of the monsoons. The little ship pitched up
and down and from left to right. He was traveling second class
with three Chinese traders whose language he did not understand. In the evening the second mate joined them at table and
after dinner they smoked a cigarette together at the railing. The
mate had sailed on various Molucca lines for four years. He knew
the people of Ternate and Hollandia, Fakfak, Banda and Amboyna; he also knew the Lanspijckers and Way Baroe. "And you
are going to join Little Roel, the inventor! He makes the most
startling discoveries in the most varying fields. He is the most
talked-of man in the Moluccas. There are some wonderful stories
about him in circulation! He is apparently in the habit of giving

his visitors a choice between two drinks: tea planted and made by himself and so bitter that one feels one's innards contract—but drink this tea by all means, for the other drink is chocolate liqueur which he obtains by chewing cocoa beans, spitting them out and letting them ferment."

Bouvier laughed. It was a joke in keeping with the barbarous history of these islands.

Lanspijcker came on board at Amboyna. The little old man took Onno along to his house outside the town, on the other side of the inner bay. They crossed in a small outrigger proa, two men paddling so fast that the proa's nose got stuck in the white beach. The large open house stood behind a row of cocoanut trees; it had brown thatch walls and a brown thatch roof. But the floor was of red flagstones and it was pleasantly cool in the half-dark inside.

Mother Lanspijcker was supervising her foster-children, who were kneading bread and shoving cookies into the oven. The *Boeroeng Laoet* was to be ready to sail in two days' time, and there was still much baking to be done, cookies, coco and sagae, coffee roasted and ground, and coco pips mashed with spices and red pepper to make chutney. When she heard her husband's voice she came out to meet them—a little brown woman in a white cabaya with batik sarong. To her husband and foster-children she generally spoke the rapid Malay of Amboyna; in honor of the guest she tried to be genteel and jabbered a Dutch that Onno could not understand either.

Coffee, "boebinka" and spiced cake were brought. Lanspijcker lit a pipe with home-grown tobacco and began a lengthy story about a trip with a schooner, full of reverses.

Onno stayed for two days while the *Boeroeng Laoet* took in cargo for her trip round Ceram. He ate and drank with the two old people; he slept in a wide, white bed and, when he opened his eyes, he looked at the green feathery crown of a small dwarf cocoanut tree.

After breakfast he sauntered round the large compound in the shade of the fruit trees on the wide sunny lawns where the dogs rolled over and over lazily and a small deer was being suckled by its mother.

On both sides, the length of the house, were the kitchens, bathrooms and old slave quarters built side by side, connected with each other and enclosed by a low white wall. In the middle of the grass in this spacious inner court was a large well, where girls laughingly did the washing under a green shrub with long, bright red flowers. There was a small pond with ducks diving in it, and on the wall sat a gorgeous peacock letting his flashing tail hang down carelessly. And over everything the sky was golden and blue and cloudless, and between the trees the water of the bay could be seen, glowing like a blue fire.

On the second day came a large canoe; everything was packed into it: bread, sugar, cookies and coffee in petroleum cans, a dinner carrier with freshly fried fish and many spices, and big baskets of fruit. Evangelina sat on the middle hatch surrounded by her boxes. She was the brightest of Mother Lanspijcker's foster-children and spoke a little Dutch and could cook very well. The old woman had generously handed her over to the stranger.

An hour before sunset they embarked on the *Boeroeng Laoet,* a large native proa rigged like a schooner, with an auxiliary motor. They sat on the poop deck under the awning, and the birds chirped in the evening breeze. For three hours they drifted, the sails hoisted and a man at the helm; then they heard the wind come sighing from the slopes of the mountains; the sails grew taut and the water began to gurgle past them noisily. That night Onno slept out-of-doors for the first time between the dark water and the dark sky in which the stars came out after midnight. In the morning they sailed close to the coast of Ceram. The mountains looked green, the water white over the reefs. Behind the gleaming beach mangrove woods fenced off the land. A wooded cape jutted out into the sea; a small bay receded landward; sometimes a mountain as steep as a wall came down to the water's edge.

Lanspijcker lay stretched on his old ratan chair, his shirt open to the navel. He called for drinks, and a small Papuan boy brought some young cocoanuts.

He passed one to Onno; the milk was cool and sweet.

Lanspijcker began to speak of his nephew, knocking out his pipe on the deck the while.

"Little Roel they call him because I don't want them to say 'Crazy Roel.' He isn't crazy; he is smarter than most people, but he lacks the knack to achieve success. I don't know if I am making myself sufficiently clear; perhaps I'd better give you an example. Last year he made some soap of cocoanut oil, but it was twice the price of imported soap. He is now working at reducing the cost price. He never lets failure discourage him; sometimes, in the excitement of a new discovery, he forgets that his previous work has not yet achieved results. But he looks after the vegetable garden and he will want to help you with everything." "Yes," said Bouvier vaguely for he could think of no other answer.

And Lanspijcker seemed to consider this sufficient.

When, steering carefully between the reefs, they came to Way Baroe at about six o'clock, Little Roel was standing at the jetty, waiting for them.

He had a very dark face, long black hair and restless gray eyes. The most striking thing about him were his clothes—a dark blue shirt and green- and red-checked trousers. Later Onno discovered that he possessed a whole piece of this checked material and had a pair of new trousers made of it every six months.

Lanspijcker remained at Way Baroe for a month to show Bouvier the ropes, and after that he went on to Amahei on the schooner.

Every morning Onno went into the plantations where the lithe Kei Islanders casually clasped a high cocoanut tree with their hands, placed a foot between their arms against the trunk and ran up to the crown of leaves twenty metres above the ground. They threw the nuts down to where other coolies picked them up, split them open and laid the hard, white kernels on the cement floor in the sun to dry. The producing plantations required little upkeep; most of his time he spent on the clearings near the boundaries, two hours' walk away. The cocoanut trees there had been planted the year before and the first feathery leaves were coming out between the smooth cotyledons. A few had been attacked by cocoanut beetles and had to be looked over every week; the young green manure had withered on account of the premature drought, and at the edge of the plantations Onno one morning found ten young cocoanut trees uprooted by a herd of boars. Little Roel built a small hut of bamboo and thatch and shot seven boars in three nights, after which the animals did not show up again. Ina cut the meat into thin slices, smeared it with salt and salpetre and dried it in the sun.

In the mornings, before the sun grew hot, Roel worked in the little kitchen garden, gathering beans and cucumbers and picking caterpillars off the cabbages. Later he worked at a cement tank in which he wanted to keep fish, an absolutely superfluous job in a country where every child with a pin on a wire could catch fish. Roel ordered two barrels of cement from Amboyna and used one for his fish tank. The other remained lying in the back compound for a year and hardened in the rain and sun.

For Onno the days became monotonous, like a tune too frequently repeated. In the mornings the walk through the plantations and the trip back in the bright, hot noontide light; after the meal and afternoon nap he checked the copra on the drying floors and the germinating nuts in the nursery beds behind the vegetable garden. In the evenings he read, lying on the long ratan chair, while Little Roel worked at an intricate design under the hissing oil lamp. At night he slept in a big bed with Ina.

"Be good to her," Lanspijcker had said. "Perhaps you might marry her when there is a little one."

One hundred, two hundred, three hundred days, one year. No change but the rain in the west monsoon and the scorching days during the season of the east winds. The rush of weighing and finishing the sacks of copra three days before the K.P.M. boat called, and two or three times a year a visit of Lanspijcker with tins full of food and many stories.

Onno had long since returned to the excitement of his books. While turning a page he would look languorously at the blue water that sparkled between the crowns of the old cocoanut trees. On the other side of the bay lay the village of Way Baroe, where the Administrative Officer and the missionary lived. Onno never went there.

The view over the cocoanut trees and the strip of white foam over the reefs, the screech of a bird of prey and the cry of a pig overtaken by a crocodile, had violently excited him in the first few months, but after that they had become part of the ordinary stuff of the landscape. The old decay, temporarily halted, had started to spread again; a listlessness like an illness, a sort of numbness of the mind, paralyzed his energy. Once he had stood erect, and the landscape of those days, Lanspijcker's house at Amboyna, the trip on the *Boeroeng Laoet,* and the first months on Way Baroe stood out sharply in his memory. They were very clear days, transparent and raised out of reality in a bright, feverish dream. But after that the light that burnt brightly behind things flickered out; a mist rose, a fatigue of body and weariness of mind. He had made an attempt to escape the cobweb and damp of an old house, but in this new country, under a brighter light and in a spacious room, he lay befuddled and listless, incapable of fresh deeds and too tired to attempt complicated thought.

Roel worked on steadily. He had taken over two cows from the missionary, and in the evenings he designed a churn of a very special construction; it was provided with little wings so that the wind could churn it. He needed wood for the construction, but since by chance there was no hewn wood on hand and since his genius burned within him, he took one of the wooden corbels from under the house and put the barrel of hardened cement in its place. It fitted exactly and withstood the great earthquake of '28. The story of the exchanged corbel circulated all over the Moluccas. The churn was a complete success, but for the time being the buttermilk tasted of the tar of the corbel, and the butter remained too soft to spread.

Shortly after that, Onno's first son was born. Lanspijcker came over from Amboyna with a trunk full of children's clothes and some stout for the mother, and a message from his wife that they would now have to marry. And, because there was no reason whatever not to do so, they married, first before the Administrative Officer and afterwards before the missionary. It was the first time in two years that he had gone to the village of Way Baroe.

This child died, probably owing to an over-measure of good care; but another was born, again a son, and after that the children came every year, as regularly as the monsoon rain; and most of them remained alive. Occasionally Onno was vaguely surprised by their number—he was easily tired and not very sensual, but Ina bore a child every year of her youth, fruitful as a cocoanut tree.

Roel's death had nothing to do with his inventions. He was fishing with dynamite and the cartridge exploded in his hand, about the height of his face. Some Boegoengese fishermen brought him to Bouvier. His hand was entirely blown off and his head partly so, but the red- and green-checked trousers made an exact identification superfluous. He was buried in the cocoanut plantation next to Onno's children, who had not yet been christened.

In the year that his first clearing began to produce, copra dropped below cost price. Lanspijcker came over, and together they talked about the retrenchments to be made. The workmen whose contracts had expired were not replaced; less weeding was done and a stop was put to clearing. On her way home the *Boeroeng Laoet* ran aground on a reef off Amahei and sprang a leak. It was Lanspijcker's last trip, for he felt too old to get accustomed to a new boat.

A year later Bouvier unexpectedly received forty thousand guilders. In Holland a wide highroad was being constructed from North to South, and the old houses on the quiet harbor had to be pulled down in order to lay the foundation of a bridge. His father's successor, who had looked after his affairs for years, asked him in what to invest this free money. Without this problem Onno would probably never have thought of buying Way Baroe, but now he wrote to Lanspijcker for advice, and the old man, glad that his property would not pass into the hands of strangers, let him have the house and plantations for a fairly low price. It became still quieter on Way Baroe now that the work had almost stopped and the old man did not come any more. Times were bad; despite all retrenchments copra fetched barely more than cost price. But these worries scarcely touched Onno. Ina looked after his clothes, his food, all his bodily requirements without ever inviting attention to herself in any way. His children tumbled about him, learned to walk, grew up and had to attend school on Amboyna. He never missed them. He was never particularly unhappy or particularly happy. He had escaped for good the storms and lulls of life in this last bay. At noon he lay on his chair, listened to the breakers beating against the reefs like a distant thunderstorm and read. This reading became an increasingly parasitic form of life; only in this way did he take part in the existence of people. As others lived for alcohol or opium, so Onno Bouvier lived for the stimulus of his books.

There are many half and many completely crazy people on the Moluccas, confused by the might and the loneliness and the terrible monotony of their days. But Bouvier, fleeing from the land of the living, found a refuge there, unerringly led to the secure house and blue bay of dreams from which one need never return.

Translated by JO MAYO

Cola Debrot

MY SISTER THE NEGRO

FRITS RUPRECHT PEERED INTO THE IMPENETRABLE DARKNESS. GRADU-ally his eyes grew accustomed to the night, but it was so dark that objects could only be distinguished by a smaller or larger degree of blackness, or rather by their rustling. It was only in the distance that he saw some fluttering lines of light upon the sea, between the dark, looming rock masses of the rocky coast. The northern coast of the island was so inaccessible that the narrow light, which he saw from here, had formerly served only as a playground for Frits and his white and colored little boy and girl companions. Among them was Karel, who later on used to go hunting with him. To them also belonged his niece, of whom he carried a painful memory from that afternoon in town; she stood between the pillars of her spare body, with her rather large feet, but also with her clear blue eyes and her golden hair; they laughed at him. Even as they played on the plantation they always laughed at him. All the games that Karel, with his light forget-me-not-blue eyes, invented, she thought marvelous. She only contemptuously curled up her lips at the lovely shells with their pink insides, which Frits found on the beach, as with a caustic movement of her hand she threw back her hair, which blew across her forehead. No, she had not cared particularly for him.

Over there they had played too. Over there, the large leaves of the cocoa and the date palms rustled. A single glimmer of light, of a heaven knew how many centuries distant star struck the metal leaves. The rustling of the sea mixed with the rustling of the leaves, then again each separated from the other, so that two motifs were distinguishable by themselves. . . . The rustling music awoke in him the memory of another fourteen-year-old girl. . . . A feeling of gratitude arose in the heart of Frits Ruprecht for his small Negro friend, Maria, who always took his side against that of his small niece and who in turn found all Karel's games tiresome and preferred the more innocuous ones of Frits.

In the garden, where the cocoa and date palms rose above the clustered groups of mango and medlar trees, moss-grown stone benches were scattered; built in the times of slavery, they had no other purpose than to allow one to listen to the rustling of the palm grove: the rhythmic scrubbing of the leaves against each other, the periods of breathless stillness, the distant creaking of a branch or a twig.

Little Frits had then invented the game of climbing on the stone benches and of simply sitting close together. His little niece, of course, thought it a silly game and would go off with Karel. For long minutes Frits would sit there with Maria and they would both count how many times they could hear the wood pigeons coo in the distance. A heartfelt cooing, which came from deep in the breast.

Frits vividly remembered the young colored girl. Among the fairly well-mixed Negroes of the island hardly any were as black as she. But there was something remarkable about her: the shape of her skull, her nose, her lips were those of white people, they had almost nothing negroid. Even her movements were typical of white folk, with the angularity of movements in the joints, the quadrocento-like quality of her gait, which the supple Negroes do not have and which among the whites often degenerates into woodenness. Maria did not create the impression of being a mulatto, but a pure-race Negro girl in whom certain characteristics of some far-distant forefather were again manifesting themselves. Ruprecht had felt the urge later on, while he was already traveling in Europe, to obtain some information about the girl in the days of his youth. Gradually a continuous story developed from what he heard about her, which however he had again forgotten years ago. She was the child of the eldest daughter of a rent collector. The mother had not survived her birth. Her father had cared little about her. He was one of those men about whom it can be said that they did not "behave." His name was Theodore. As Frits Ruprecht had done, he had got lost in Europe. Frits had met him as a waiter in The Hague and also as a doorman of an establishment in Paris, which Frits principally frequented in order to see lesbians dancing together. Their faces were so tragic that they looked like drowned people who had just been pulled out of the water.

That was father Theodore. The daughter Maria had, with the help of Ruprecht's parents, been enabled to study as a teacher, third class, at the normal school in the only city in the island. There she was qualified to stand day in, day out, with somewhat astonished eyes before the poor Negro children, who with their arms neatly folded upon their breasts monotonously and in chorus repeated the following in a row: ab, bc, cd . . . three, four, five; one, two, three. . . . That afternoon in the city the chorus had reached him from one of the buildings, but he had hardly paid any attention to it. Perhaps it was she who directed the chorus. At any rate he resolved to look her up before he took the boat again and left the island behind him. But in spite of anticipation of strange adventure he knew he would not remain here for long and that his short stay would be limited to talks with the old notary. He took a few steps backward until his heels touched the threshold.

He was teetering on the narrow threshold. He now felt a smile spread over his face; he was not a bit happy, but he felt as if he had been taken into a sphere of well-being. In front of him lay the night, which he had peopled with tender images from his youth. Behind him in the living-room he heard the tinkling of knives and forks and the sound of plates as they were put upon the table. It was the housekeeper preparing his meal.

"How dark it is tonight! In Europe they think that there is always either a bright moon or starlit night in the tropics."

The housekeeper did not answer.

"When does the moon rise?"

"There is no moon tonight," she answered in such a clear voice that he was almost tempted to turn around and look at the woman to whom this voice belonged. But he did not turn around. He still wanted to stand that way for a while: teetering back and forth, behind him the light of the lamp suspended from the ceiling, the tinkling and the noise of crockery, the woman's sandals shuffling over the cement.

It gave him a safe and almost caressing feeling that the housekeeper was continually moving around him, like a cat that one can hardly see but of whose presence one is continuously conscious. He was quite satisfied that he had not turned around; it was exactly right that way, to know her to be around him without having looked at her.

The housekeeper, a small Negro woman, stood bent over the suspended lamp, which through the reflection on the white tablecloth seemed to increase its light many times; carefully she fixed something on the table. When she was ready, she took up the tray on which she had brought in the plates and the food, and walked slowly through the arcade to the kitchen, where she put the empty tray on a table. As she left the room, she had looked out of the corner of her eye at Frits Ruprecht, who was still standing with his back towards her. In the kitchen she blew up the fire in the stove, then sat at the table and thoughtfully rubbed her forehead with her fingers. Then she got up, lit the lantern and went outside. The wind blew against her skirt, which barely reached her knees. Slowly she walked along the terrace in the dark. The lantern swung gently like an incense burner. The light fell occasionally on a cactus stem, which would suddenly spring out of the dark and reach up to the sky. In the shrubs the lizards would wake and rustle along the leaves. The light swung over the bare soil, and even the smallest piece of gravel would throw a shadow. At a luxuriously overgrown piece of ground which was in sharp contrast to its surroundings, she put down her lantern and crouched. Patches of light and dark interchanged between the leaves and stems. The body of the woman too was fragmentarily struck by light: her neck, her face, her legs. A single beam of light struck the point of her sandal. She saw now that a snail shell tottered over a few lumps of earth. On a heart-shaped leaf a caterpillar was upset by the unsteady light and stuck half its body into the air. A flower bud thrust up out of the darkness, where it was separated from its stem which had just received the light from underneath. The woman dug with both hands between the leaves and the tendrils of the melons, pulled and plucked one of the melons as her lips pressed together from the effort.

In the meantime Frits sat down at the table with a smile on his face. A contented, indifferent smile, now that the chewing of the food brought him back to reality and to distrust of more or less complicated stories through which one human being tries to fool another. He had been told that Maria was Theodore's daughter. That might be so. But it could also be different. He interrupted his meal and put down his knife and fork. Jaws closed, eyes peering, he followed his malicious train of thought. He himself came from the island, he knew the circumstances, he could look through fabrications. So he would not have been astonished to come to the conclusion some day that the unkempt Theodore was not the father, but that Alexander Ruprecht, his own father, *was.* He knew that men like Theodore, who ended up in Europe's bars, were often chosen to cover up for the sins of white gentlemen. But there remained one thing through which these white sinners betrayed themselves; they gave their hidden children an education which made the children and, themselves too, suspect in the eyes of others. What betrays man mostly is his own heart with its irrepressible feelings. . . .

Frits turned his head. He heard the shuffling sandals in the back of the house. He would have liked to have talked with someone, but she had already disappeared into the room to the right at the back of the house, where she probably slept. Frits smiled and repeated significantly, almost obscenely to himself: "Where she is probably sleeping." Talking half aloud to himself as he raised his index finger and threatened an imaginary person opposite him: "Yes, my little papa, what I don't know about your doings. We here on the plantation are perhaps all your children, O father who art in heaven."

His face became clouded immediately thereafter, the uncalled-for observation and lightheartedness of the voice seemed to belong to somebody older than himself. He pursued his meal as quietly as a mouse, corrected by his own childhood conscience. Then he got up. From a chair nearby he took a briefcase, in which he had brought the most essential material. He went into the room to the right, in which he used to sleep, opposite the door which he had closed because two glowing eyes came towards him. He left the door open, until he found an oil-lamp on a table with a copper plate as reflector. He fussed around with the lamp, lit the wick and put the chimney over it again. The room had no windows, but a second door, which led on to the terrace. There was a sort of camp bed. He remembered how he had yearned in Europe to sleep on just such a bed, principally because one used no blankets, merely two sheets. On the wall was a framed print, which he also remembered, representing a very young girl kneeling in her nightgown, with folded hands: pre-Raphaelite. He had seen the original in the Tate Gallery; that is, unless he was mistaken. There he had remained in front of it for a long time, because it looked like a copy of the print on the faraway plantation, just as the face, which he was now probing in the round mirror above the table, seemed a crushed copy of his former childhood face. He remembered now how he had had to have his hair cut quite short, because even the slightest length meant something incredibly dirty to his father. Therefore the parting on his brow became a lock like Napoleon's, which he himself had always found ridiculous. Brusquely he opened the table. There were many shells in it. He remembered how his father, who had enjoyed few things, sometimes showed great enthusiasm over the shells: "Give your father that shell, Frits."

Did the shells he had given his father still exist? Then they must be in one of the drawers of his father's desk. He would find out. Quickly he walked out of the room. He had already jerked open the door. He wanted to see the three-master in a bottle and the hooded typewriter and the rifles and the pistols; it was from the study, too, that in the absence of his father he would climb up the ladder and lift the trapdoor and see the bats, swaying like flakes of black cotton. The memory of these spooky animals did not cause him fear when, thinking himself safe, as a small boy he chased into one room and out of another and went busily back and forth through the parental home. He recognized the dent in the doorknob; it felt familiar in his grasp. He had already entered the living-room and was crossing towards the entrance of the house, when he stopped involuntarily.

In the furthest arch, on the side of the kitchen, he had seen the face, the face of Maria. The shock made the blood course irregularly through his body. The tips of his fingers tingled, almost hurt him. He stood there like a ninny, both of his hands stretched out in front of him, and there was empty surprise in his eyes and face. Slowly the shock subsided, he heard the ticking of the mahogany wall clock, which was in back of the house; he had noticed its ticking before during the evening. The quietness of the living-room, illuminated by the light of the oil-lamp, caused a stream of well-being to flow through his body. It was remarkable how the aspect of things can modify one's state of mind. The same room which before that night had made him feel uneasy with its aura of circular light, into which he had plunged himself as if into something immaterial, now calmed him by the harmlessness of its countrified illumination. For a long time Ruprecht had not stood in its peaceful light. He looked up at the oil-lamp. His glance followed around the bowl the metal band from which it was suspended by three chains attached from the ceiling above the table. The minute clamps, through which the wick pressed closer to the glass, even mellowed him, because the little details again evoked the past. It seemed almost impossible that in this peaceful atmosphere he would be pursued by images forced upon his mind. Was it reality or just hallucination? No matter how peaceful the light in the living-room appeared to be, the double shadows along the arches of the arcade continued to conjure up the adored picture: the face of Maria. Or rather, as he imagined the face of Maria as it had developed from girlhood into maturity. Framed by the arch it looked like the pious enlargement of the familiar photograph of a woman who had died young. She had on a white linen blouse, which was tucked into a black skirt. It was a European profile; her hair too stood out further than was usually the case with Negro women. . . . But it was not impossible. . . . He also heard the shuffling of the housekeeper's sandals. And Maria could not possibly be housekeeper here. She was a teacher in the city, with the monks and nuns who brought religion and religious education to the small Negroes of the island. Mere coincidence. The housekeeper bore some resemblance to Maria, which was not surprising; she was perhaps—no, even most probably—a relative of Maria's. . . . Despite this, he hurried, almost ran, to the kitchen. As he sped along the arcade his own shadow floated like a black cloak from his shoulders. He found no one in the kitchen. The fire in the brazier had already been put out, in the semi-darkness he saw a cat curled up on the cane seat of a chair.

He retraced his steps. First the glowing eyes and now the face of Maria. What would all this lead to? Why did this woman move so invisibly around him? She had cleared the table, while he was dreaming in his bedroom over pictures in the Tate Gallery. Why this invisible prowling about him? In the study he opened one of the desk drawers. The drawer was empty, only one of the boards had been stained by ink spots. In the other drawer was a browning, next to a yellow ruler and an electric torch which he tried out; the browning and the torch he put on the table; then he closed the drawer. In the next drawer were only a few wads of paper upon an opened package of candles. It was only in the fourth drawer that he found the shells which he had gathered for his father on the white sand near the sea. Frits turned the shells over and over in his hand; with his fingers he felt the protuberances of the shells, but he had no longer any interest in the multicoloredness of the shells and their nacreous texture, which he had formerly so much admired. He stared vaguely ahead, he saw the face framed by the arcade; for just a moment he had seen the eyes glance sideways, frightened, as if Frits meant disaster. Had he ever signified disaster to Maria? Again his thought wandered back to the young girl with whom he had once sat on the moss-grown stone benches in the palm garden. His heart flinched with pity. . . . He remembered how he had once scolded Maria. He had then seen her lips tremble, but she had immediately and resolutely pressed them together, as a brave girl who did not want to cry. . . . Before the first tear had been shed, he had kissed her, somewhere on her cheek. . . .

Who knows how unhappy she might have felt later on? . . . When a colored boy became a teacher, then it was plain what made him do so, what he had in view. He wanted to get on in the world, to be a servant no longer. A girl like Maria, on the contrary, became a teacher because she wanted to do what was expected of her, nothing more. . . . Who had demanded of her that she become a teacher? . . . A girl like Maria was apt to return to her former origin, as Frits had done. . . . Who knows whether she had not exchanged her teacher's position in a girl's school in the city because of an inner urge for life on a plantation, compelled from within by her origin, she had taken off her stockings as well as her high-heeled slippers?

Frits was letting his fancy run wild as he handled the shell. Finally he dropped it among the others in the drawer; he chose another, to which he gave more attention than the first. In his fancy he became convinced that it was really Maria whom he had seen. And into his fancy gradually crept a strange jubilation.

She had taken off her stockings as well as her high-heeled slippers. Again she stood in her sandals, just as she had when playing with Frits in different places in the plantation, the beach and the palm garden; perhaps too in the small garden, which they had both made, directly behind the house; they had sown some bean and melon seeds and also mysterious seeds filched from the drawers which would develop from something unknown into something familiar in the future. Who knows but that Maria had enlarged that garden patch and that she would still attentively sit on her haunches next to a blade with two seed pods, or next to the tendrils of the melons, which are hazy and hairy like the legs of an insect? Perhaps she even cultivated those useless things called flowers: the rose, the dahlia, the camellia. . . . But who or what could have persuaded her to give up her teaching and return here to the plantation? It might have happened like this: She might have fallen ill in the arid lifeless city. Not only that the slippers with the high heels pinched her. . . . No. The nuns and the monks must not have neglected to exercise their dreadful pressure upon her. She must have been taken ill and therefore have spent a few weeks with her grandfather, the rent collector. Then she must have gone back. Then returned, ill again. And on a certain day the thought must have taken root in her mind: never to go back again, never to wear those shoes again with high heels, never to climb on the bus again which passed there twice a day, never to wait again upon Mother Superior. . . . To stay here . . . amidst the melons, the roses, the palm trees. . . . The northern Trade wind blew in her hair. . . . Life became melancholy again, but filled with the significance that she missed elsewhere.

Frits Ruprecht smiled tenderly. In order to achieve this she must have told the rent collector a story. He must have shown surprise in his faraway, staring eyes when a girl made up her mind to exchange her genteel teacher's position for that of a common servant girl on a plantation.

But perhaps she had not told the rent collector any stories. Perhaps she had never come back to the plantation and it was purely Frits' imagination. But he also found it impossible to tear himself away from the almost frightening charm of the other possibility, that only a few meters separated him from her, that he needed only to push the door open to experience again the sweetness of her presence. Frits felt the irresistible urge to go to Maria's room, to awaken her, to question her thoroughly as to why she had done this. And whether his father had assisted her in doing this. . . . And whether she wanted to stay here always.

. . . And to stay here without a man . . . and wither away slowly. . . . And fade out like an autumn leaf which sinks deeper towards the bottom and dies.

Frits put away the shells, gathered them in a group, as he had found them. Slowly he closed the drawer; it hardly moved. Frits thought: Why shouldn't I go to her and comfort her who really is my sister; the Negro? It could be pretty well established that she really was his sister, that she was not the daughter of Theodore who turned revolving doors for lesbian drowned souls, but of Alexander Ruprecht, Frits' father, who one night as unexpectedly as the inner rosiness of a shell had been enraptured by the daughter of his rent collector.

With a violent shove Frits closed the drawer and ran out to the study. In the hall he noticed that the woman had again wandered through the house, while he was thinking of Maria in the study. She had extinguished the lights in the hall and the back of the house; only in the living-room the light burned low. A woman was wandering around him in ever narrowing circles, or was it he who moved around her and came ever closer? As he was approaching her room, once more but now for the last time, a doubt assailed him: whether she was Maria and whether Maria was really his sister? But then he dropped all doubt, because he no longer cared for mental calculations, he was in another world. He had already reached the door of her room. He opened it, took one step and still another, but did not let go of the doorknob and did not close the door. In the darkness he noticed that she lay there without breathing. An unexpected change in his feelings for Maria took place. He listened to the buzz of the silence, he heard the coursing of his own blood. The fragrance of a woman hung in the room. It was as if the unexpected, the shining newness met him. It was no longer the child Maria which made him feel mellow, but the woman who wholly enraptured him. . . . Maria, or that other one, who resembled her and could be none but Maria this very night. . . . He thought about it; how they both so strangely happened to meet this night. . . . Here, where everything was so faraway from Asia, America, Europe with all its somber strivings, in which, unless he were mistaken, he had participated for a very short time. How trifling their two powerless slowly breathing bodies seemed to him—like the animals in the compound—in this white house on the hill, where every glimmer of light and every noise in the night was absorbed by the rustling of palms and sea. It was not only the mollifying loneliness that drove him to her. In his vivid imagination he saw the sweet little sister grown into a young woman. He looked on enraptured. And this enraptured consideration of her familiar girl's body awakened in him the desire for feminine completeness, for her embrace, for the curves of her body. His hand was still resting on the doorknob. He still heard that she lay there, still, breathless. With his heart beating in his throat he closed the door. He could not see his hand as he put it in front of his eyes, it was so dark. . . .

Maria, or the other one, did not offer any resistance; she did not even make a feeble attempt. The arms that wound around his neck embraced him ever more closely; then she let him go and, keeping at an arm's length, told him: Do you know, Frits, how you always stayed in my memory? As a small boy, apart from the others, with your two crowns, that lock, that bitter little mouth. . . .

For a moment he had been startled, because it was now undeniably established that it was Maria. But laughingly he closed her arms around him: little hateful Frits. His body relaxed in her embrace until it was he that embraced and her body that relaxed. Already his hand caressed her hip, already the fervor of his heart changed into the desire for her body, when suddenly a violent rattling at the door penetrated his consciousness. Suddenly Frits stood straight up beside the bed. Tears of fury sprang into his eyes. And in his mouth he tasted bitterness. He snarled at her:

"Have you a man in the neighborhood?"

"A man, Frits?"

"No jokes now. Have you a man? Yes or no?"

"No. What is the matter, Frits? Let me open the door."

"No. You stay here."

They shouldn't get him. It was not that easy to get at Frits Ruprecht. He locked her door; he still heard her voice, "But Frits, why are you doing that? . . ." In the room he extinguished the lamp, so that the house was completely dark. He went to his father's study, caught up the browning, took out the cartridge slip; it was empty. He opened the drawers two at a time; there were no bullets to be found anywhere. He found the cartridges for the hunting rifle in the corner of the room. He slung the browning and the cartridge clip over the table. He grabbed the hunting rifle, loaded it. He put the remaining cartridges as well as the electric torch into his pocket. He closed the door behind him; from here no light could penetrate into the house. Through the dark hallway he walked to the front door. Again it rattled.

The rattle made him beside himself with fury. At the door he stood still, held his breath and listened. Just as the rattling started again, he jerked the door open. At the same time he directed the light of the torch upon the visitor and the faraway staring eyes of the rent collector.

"What do you want here at this hour, Wantsjo? I thought you all still went to bed at eight o'clock. This is the third time today that you've bothered me. Couldn't you wait until morning?"

"Mister Frits . . ."

"Never mind Mister Frits. Get out and go to bed. Tomorrow we can talk again."

"Mister Frits . . ."

"I remember how you were. In the middle of the night you disturb people and this way you think you can have your way."

"I don't want anything, Mister Frits."

"We know all about that. A goat for the feast of Aunt Carolina. Or a rabbit for the feast of Aunt Esmeralda. You'll get it all. All right. But tomorrow. Not tonight. And now off to bed, Wantsjo. I do not want to hear any more rattling at the door. Sleep well."

At the moment that he wanted to slam the door in Wantsjo's face, he heard a shriek which was as unreal as when, some time before, he had opened the door of his mother's bedroom.

"Maria is your father's daughter!!"

With a jerk he opened the door anew. He did not know exactly what happened then. He had probably slipped on the worn threshold, fallen as his arms clutched the air, on account of which the barrel of the rifle hit Wantsjo in the chest. When he had straightened himself out and stood straight up again, his first thought was: "It's lucky that the cock was not released, in addition to all that has happened." He helped up old Wantsjo, who had fallen down as he was struck and was softly moaning. He had to do this as he felt his way along. It was pitch dark; he did not see any stars, the sky was heavily overcast. Ruprecht had difficulty hiding his emotions from the other, who still had not overcome his fright and whose teeth were audibly chattering.

"Nothing has happened, Wantsjo. I just slipped, so that the gun hit your chest. It was your chest, wasn't it?"

"Yes, my breast. . . ." He could barely utter the words.

"Shall I make a light and see what's happened to it?"

"No, not inside. Maria must not know anything about this. I only got a shock, I am not hurt."

"Well, all right then, Wantsjo. Let me lead you away until you have overcome your fright."

Wantsjo allowed himself to be led by the arm, as Ruprecht soothed him.

"I only slipped. You must not think any more about it. You must also know that I had a faint suspicion that Theodore was used as a cloak. It was easy for me to guess as much when my father sent Maria to a school to become a teacher. I need keep nothing from you. You are an old man; to my father your life was more valuable than mine, you have a right to know everything."

The gravel on the drive crunched under their feet. A glow-worm shone and disappeared, the only point of light in the night. Along the way the old man rested his arm on Ruprecht's; the latter realized that he must accompany him a little way further.

"I admit, Wantsjo, that your granddaughter is a beautiful girl. You are black, but comely, you daughters of Jerusalem. Do you remember that from the Song of Songs? I suspect that you know the Bible better than I. If I hadn't had the slightest doubt about it, then perhaps there might have been something to be afraid of. But, Wantsjo, my good Wantsjo, why should I have been in such a hurry?"

Ruprecht felt that the arm which he supported was beginning to disengage itself from him.

"Wantsjo, I believe that you think that I am worse than I am."

He heard Wantsjo shuffle at his side. He could have walked that way for hours beside the old man, silently and thoughtlessly. But he did not want to be a burden to him; as soon as he saw that the other no longer needed his support, he took leave.

"Well, Wantsjo. Let's shake hands. Sleep well."

"Sleep well, Mister Frits. Don't blame me. I have seen so much unhappiness. Unhappiness to others which I could have prevented."

For a moment, the old Negro's hand rested in the hand of the young white man.

"Sleep well, Wantsjo."

The two separated. Wantsjo continued on his way. Ruprecht looked in the direction in which the other had disappeared, until he could hear the steps no longer. Irresolutely he remained standing in the quietness, but turned around abruptly as he heard some rustling behind his back. He listened. It sounded as if people were whispering. For a moment he even imagined that he heard muffled footsteps and giggling. He held himself prepared, was sharply on his guard; it sounded like the whispering and laughing of people. But it must have come to him from the gusts of wind in the palm grove, as the trees swayed back and forth, creaked and rustled. For some reason it reminded him of Karel, who, as a child, could not laugh without malice. But Karel was now reading *Othello,* with his mysterious smile, which was part will-power and part enmity. This rather unpleasant memory of Karel passed as quickly as the breeze which blew through his hair. . . . Frits turned around. The road back was hard, but he had found a sister, where he had lost a sweetheart. He was so tired that only for a moment did he look for excuses to offer Maria, so tired that he wanted to give up immediately.

Come what may! When, however, he unlocked the door and found her room lighted, he understood immediately that the cry of anguish of Wantsjo had also penetrated here. She was half sitting up in bed, her wide, open eyes were looking down. He sat next to her, but did not know what to say and also gazed at the floor. Finally he put an arm around her shoulder. He pressed his face against hers. She allowed him to do as he wanted, but her face, unlike his mother's formerly, did not answer his pressure. Thus they sat next to each other and began to rock slowly back and forth. Doing this he made, as he used to do with his mother, the humming sound that came deep out of his chest and he did not unclench his teeth. Tears streamed from her eyes. . . . Life became sad, but it became filled with a significance which was nowhere else. And this is the only thing which cannot be taken away from the children of this earth.

Translated by ALFRED VAN AMEYDEN VAN DUYM

Albert Helman

SOUTH-SOUTH-WEST

HE WHO IS AFRAID WILL NEVER BE ABLE TO PENETRATE INTO THE interior of my country. The journey there is so long that all links must be broken, that one must give up all things. The heart of my country is a swampy forest, impenetrable with climbing plants and lianas. A forest completely isolated. Who goes there rides in a canoe with grinning death; therefore strangers are afraid to journey into the interior; they do not go any further than where the railroad stops in the woods. But what child of this country is afraid to see the beauty of its own home? No animal harms him and no evil vapors. He threads down the moist leaves until they become a path and the lianas are woven into a fence. Quietly he looks over the black swamps and finds a spot where he can wade through.

To reach the heart of my country a voyage is required, more difficult, than the most exhausting pilgrimage. The journey through the forests brings mortal danger; the navigation of the undulating river, above the falls where the water churns foaming downwards between the rocks, means the cool-blooded challenge of death. Its hand is that of the long stick of the Negro who steers it at the end of the canoe. On the bank downstream one can still see the splintered wood of a previous boat, which was smashed to pieces.

But whoever is once able to overcome it, crosses over the high thresholds of these pitfalls into the mystery of the back country, there where there are steep, bare mountains with enormous, strange inscriptions, geometrical patterns which must have the deep meaning of unknown words.

There are also the fertile, fat mountains, solidly forested with precious wood: purple and bronze-green wood, brown mahogany and yellow cedar, hard as steel or brittle as kindling wood. At their feet grow medicinal herbs and plants that produce paralyzing poisons.

There are no valleys. For tens of centuries they have been overgrown and the mountain brooks have gathered their water in the forests. At the foot of the mountains are the endless swamps, stretching as far as do the lowlands. In those valleys grow mushrooms more than a metre in circumference and insects build their own towering nests; there wasps make their multi-colored honeycombs. There humming birds and large silvery-colored butterflies and golden-green bees gather; a monkey vanishes between the branches, and in the distance one hears a tiger crossing a creek.

There are large, velvety wood spiders and the big, brown poisonous snake that is called the mother of the forest, and the snake with the scorpion's tail that is called the "father snake." Here reigns the undisputed hierarchy of the beast and the Negro, who is at home in the woods, calls all animals "brother," with the exception of the tiger, whom he addresses as "little father" and the snake, whom he dare not address in familiar terms.

Here also lives the good-natured anteater with his pointed snout, from whose embrace nobody escapes, and the opossum with its musky odor, and the skunk, whom everybody avoids. Here, also, from the low branches the sloths with their long rusty fur are suspended, who only move a few metres in seven years, and the black tapirs who dully break the branches which are in their way. There, and there alone, exists a zoological garden.

Throughout this sort of forest and along these untrodden paths human beings risk themselves on their way to the high plateaux where they will look for gold. But mostly the forests close down over them for eternity. The sultry vapors of the forest, treacherously mingled with the fine odors of musk and tonkas, befog their thought, and the hypnotic stares of the animals paralyze their limbs; the poisonous sweetness of the water disturbs their bloodstream and dulls their vision. The hot dream of gold leads them into the labyrinth of tough lianas. The metre-high petals of the carnivorous flowers enclose them. They never return. In the forest the country avenges itself upon the thirst for gold of the city dwellers. Only a few reach the gold fields. Do they find there the gold dust at the bottom of the creeks or in small gold fragments deep in the soil, or in small flakes in the red granite? Emaciated they return to the city, and their treasure has become a dream after one day. The color of gold has blinded their eyes, and they have seen nothing of the luxury and the beauty, there where even the condor is astounded at so much green.

Once a year the family came from the camp to the city; Captain George and three or four men and women. Then they would be busy in the house with rifles and game bags, quivers of arrows, hammocks and colorful materials. Everybody brought along a little of the air of the forest. They only came to the city when there was some trouble with the government, or when the gold seekers had trampled upon their rights. Then the father had to tell their long story—long because it was told in short, slowly made-up sentences—with much head shaking, and everything had to be written down, so that the Governor, who was the chief forester of the mysterious Woman on the other side of the sea, would realize the injustice and correct it. George looked like his father; they might have been brothers, and they acted as brothers and called each other by first name. The other men and women were mostly silent during the time they stayed with us. How magnificently brown-red they were painted with the sap of the koesoewe, how gracefully their strong legs were hung with rope ornaments, the amulets of the tiger's teeth shining whitely around their bare throats! Their hair knots were brilliant black, and the older people had a protruding lower lip in which a pin was coquettishly stuck. Magnificent people of the Caribbean, small but solidly built, with broad shoulders, strong legs that had trod the savannahs for centuries, strong arms which tautly stretched the bows and ended almost conically in their small, graceful wrists! Had ever a dying people had such strong offspring?

The light of the sun shone like metal over their smooth heads, over their smooth chests. The women carried their quiet, almost timorous babies upon their backs, never separating from them as long as they were still dependent. With one movement of the arm they shove the baby under the armpit, whence it happily partakes of the motherly fare; with one movement it is again hoisted up on their backs, where it sleeps as they travel, as if in its own hammock. They wear few clothes; the sultry wind of the savannahs, the sunlight itself, covers them with a warm cloak which does not fall in false folds. They are all tanned to a soft brown through sun and sap. But, coming to the city, the women have thrown a gay cloth over their shoulders—black, red, yellow and blue—which half covers their breasts.

With a few words Captain George extended another already oft-repeated invitation: when would we finally visit the camp at Matta? But this time Father said: "All right, I'll come in three weeks; in as many days as a man has fingers and toes, after that I'll be on my way." It was agreed upon and it happened, too.

From the village that could still be reached by boat there ran a path straight through the forest, to the point where the savannah started. It ran past pina palm trees and fragrant shrubs, over rotting tree-trunks and thick moss. It was cool there and dark, and one had to thread one's way carefully through thorn-covered trunks and exposed roots. Once in a while a snake would slither away, or one would just perceive a monkey fleeing; and there was always the slow noise of heavy, falling drops, but at wide intervals and in between the trees hung a heavy, muggy stillness. Nowhere was the smell of the earth and of growing things more pungent.

The light between the trees was toned down to gold by all the deep green, but gradually it became whiter, a diaphanous white, which indicated that the savannah was not far distant. The shrubs and the undergrowth became less dense; the palms became taller and no longer stood so close together. Soon one could see over the brush and perceived a plain of low and coarse grass that became lighter and whiter towards the horizon, with here and there a solitary palm.

How can one describe the palm trees in this country! There are very small ones, with almost circular, edgy leaves, and others whose leaves hang down in streamers to the height of a man. There are magnificent, wavy palm trees under which one can take shelter from sun and rain, and there are dark palms, whose featherlike branches are laid upon graves as a gesture of farewell. And there are also the youthful, glad branches which welcomed a lonely king to Jerusalem, and small ones which Zacchaeus agitated in his boundless joy. There are the large heavy cocoa palms and the slender maurice palms, high and airy with a swinging top, the stately royal palm with its polished trunk, and the fruitladen obé palm compared to which even the proud date palm looks dwarfed. The palm trees are our ferns, the palms dominate our streets; under the fan palms sit the evening lovers in a corner of a garden, and in the crown of the royal palm hides the tiny little bird of God.

A palm tree grows up like a human being—and may a human being be as straight as a palm. They are the riches of the country: they give cocoanuts and their clear sap, oil and white meat from the tops, the fragrant obé and the brew of the koemboe, just as they nourish other peoples with dates, others again with pure sago and still others with sweet wine. Every palm tree is the story of the integrity of the country, and thus is the slender maurici—like a tall blade of grass it bends over the plain—the story of the utter loneliness of the savannah.

What wind has carried the small seed, when not a single plant was growing on the white, crumbly soil above which the whole air vibrates with heat? Were these palms here already when the first men of my people—they came from the cold dark mountains towards the west—beheld for the first time the openness, greater than that of the sea? Did they then already willingly bend their slender shadow over a crying woman and an ailing child?

Blessed palms, blessed palms, under which on a sad flight the saddest of all mothers rested, as well as the most languishing child. Does not your blessing sway any longer over the people who fled past your trunks—driven by what fate?—into the open gateways of a city, behind the fences of the houses, a city made up of houses in which the old folk had to perish . . .

Still my palms stretch their frizzy tops towards the metal sky and the glowing disk which indicates the days and eradicated them on this empty stage.

And as to ourselves. . . . How small and lonely we wander through the savannah. The grass disappears too. And now comes the bare, glassy sand which glows purely white in the strong, stinging sun. The palms have disappeared. Openly, endlessly the burning plain stretches out. Nowhere is there shelter in this plain, which goes on in terrifying and lazy waves as a skin under the hot breath of the sun. The powerful rays hit the earth; the vibrating air above the burning plain frightens me.

As a small boy, I cried violently when I was for the first time on the savannah and saw, materially saw, what loneliness was. Air and land, and a man who had to find his way through all this to the secret behind the horizon. . . . Narrow, mortally narrow, the world closes in about one. The earth is a bowl, a tight shell from all sides, and the sky a shell above it. Inescapably we are enclosed in this tight space.

And fright would paralyze my small feet that ached from the hot earth, and my eyes burned from the hot light and the fearful staring, wondering whether that horizon would open upon a better region. But to the left, to the right, everywhere the same vacant emptiness. Then I thought, for the first time I thought: to stand there motionless and die there; then for the first time I felt the anxiety for my entire people— O courageous Caribbeans, all your spirits stood in battle array around me with clenched teeth, and I did not see it!—all your fear for this empty, vacuous plain, which is the lonely life, which we must follow, straight through until the last rim of the horizon. . . .

But did the father suddenly live again in the sun of the savannah more strongly than ever? Without a word he set me upon his shoulder and carried me for hours to the camp. I felt his springy, strong gait under my shaking body; and his daring, his strength, no, all the old strength of my people, O brave Caribbeans, I sucked in; a swelling fruit of an old twig . . . It was Christopher in the sea of sand when Christ's name had barely reverberated in the white light of the savannah. He brought me back to the people to whom I belonged; may once his name as a watchword on my paling lips make a stranger recognizable among my forefathers, when I once enter upon the eternal hunting grounds, carried along by an immortal instinct. . . .

Captain George met us and, a man of few words as usual, he invited us to his tent which had been prepared for visitors, or really for the true children of his tribe, who were always irresistibly drawn back to the savannah. The camp was situated at the edge of the wood, where the savannah ended and where at a few minutes' distance the quiet brook lost itself amidst the trees.

The camp was decimated. There were about twenty huts, pitched tents, covered with the entwined leaves of the pina. Most of them came as slanted roofs down to the soil and had an opening in front. In George's hut, as in the others, there were few household effects; three hammocks, a few benches, arrows in the corner and a few baskets in which must have been all the worldly goods of the chief.

In former days, oh indeed, in former days! Always when I visit the camp I must think of the glorious former days. And I think that it is so with every man of the tribe; but who dares to think about it aloud? Who still dares to evoke the picture of the time when a mighty chief led thousands to new forests and new hunting grounds, to ever new and open savannahs where strange animals still fled through the high grass, animals whose name only exists now in old legends. . . .

Sitting on their haunches around the camp fire, does not every one see in the slender white smoke the play of the warriors, does not everyone hear the whirring of an arrow? Expressing himself slowly, mysteriously, the sage explains the nature of the world: I am one, every object is one. Seeing outside myself originates duality; and from duality comes life.

Oh, the wise men of the land do not write any books, but their pronouncements are deep enough to meditate upon forever. Little knots in a rope are the signs and symbols of their wisdom, better and deeper of meaning than corrupting words. Around the lonely campfire at the edge of the savannah sit the last males of the old tribe, the ancient people of golden masks, who built tall temples on the shores of an unknown sea. The ancient people that, despoiling itself, was hospitable to the wanton Spanish conquistadores and to a man who was a leader in Christ's name. A people who were hunted down. . . . But I promised not to blame you. . . .

Around the campfire there is no longer anyone who utters evil words. Everybody lives in the most profound loneliness and is seeking for an old way. Everybody is crouched to an old, old sorrow, which slowly emerges and then submerges again like a serpent with the playing of its master's flute.

A youthful hunter sits next to me, staring into the flames. His thoughts seek a way amidst the undulating, burning wood. Slowly his mouth opens, and his thoughts suddenly take the form of this hymn:

"On the heights of life I have climbed to sing this song for you, because you do not come nearer over the pale year-long paths; not yet. . . . Therefore I call to you; come to me out of your rosy tents, O fowler. I call you from land to land, come then, my impalpable friend. You live in the twilight of eyes, you know a song and pipe it so sweetly. . . . You are a desire; an abyss between the embraced Loved One and myself. . . . O Death, do not wait for the incompleteness of every smile and the unfulfilled day. To the mountain, whence I can tell you, the Satan of Beauty has seduced me. . . . Come then, O flame, O fire. . . . Here it is that the wood will burn, one with you, one with the inextinguishable fire. Does the eternal flame of death burn deep in the earth?"

The young hunter thinks of death as a welcome danger. He knows himself to be a tiger on the hunting grounds of a strange Orpheus and looks around watchfully for his prey. He sings in a soft, almost inaudible voice, and the melody is barely perceptible; it is almost a tune, hesitating, slow and dreamlike. . . . The song itself does not know where it has vanished, and, suddenly aware of the silence, you know that this group of humanity is lost, perhaps lost forever in the endless plain. Motionless (but also silently), they all sob, these brave hunters, who know of the town of houses like a narrow prison, and the women who know the city like a strange and fearful fairy tale, beckoning, but who still feel this earth, the gray, obscure savannah closer to their bodies. Immersed in thought the young hunter looks up at the large star. . . .

Then I listened to the story of the great father of the tribe, how every father of a strong tribe leaves his small children behind and moves himself to a further region. Homage, homage to the father of my tribe! Okamé felt with his fat little hand the smooth trunk of the goyave before he fastened his hammock to it. How his hand trembled as he tied the knot; six times he had to strike the tinder before the dry wood caught fire. When, however, the smoke rose in heavy clouds it drove the nocturnal animals into the woods, and he climbed calmly into his hammock and as he lay down waited for nightfall.

Okamé was already old, very old to be the chief of an Indian tribe; more than sixty years ago he had become captain, and his son had succeeded him and his son's son, who had now become a Christian and also was named Captain George. But Okamé did not want to think about all those things right now. For several days quite a different thought had occupied his mind. And it was really an ancient thought, one with which he was quite familiar, but now it occurred again to him with renewed force. Now the boys prepared to break camp and to wander further, much further up north, where there would be trading of wood and skins for knives and shotguns. Okamé had an aversion to all this, but he could keep quiet about it, because he had lived so many days, days of much greater danger, of exhaustion and hunger and strife. Did he not know now that he was near the end of his days and that soon now he would close his eyes for good? . . . His spirit would mount the ghost of a horse, and he would ride away to the eternal fields. With childish, blissful anticipation he waited for this, as for a feast. In the evening, in the circle of the council he had told all the men that he would remain behind, to die alone in his hammock, so that his spirit might depart undisturbed to the better regions. Silently they nodded their approval, and George his grandchild, who had too weak a heart to be a captain of the Caribbeans, had tried in vain that morning to drag him along. He remained behind all by himself to die, as everyone should die who does not die in battle; all alone, all alone.

It had become very quiet on the savannah, as Okamé peered over his toes at the horizon. The sun that had disappeared behind the horizon colored the sky above the savannah with a faint red, which suddenly melted into carmine. Okamé looked steadily in that direction. A large bird flew along the even cloudless sky. The light on the earth became vague with shadows, the white sand of the savannah attained a violet hue. No breeze disturbed the pointed leaves of the arrawé palms, which loomed large against the far heavens. The smoke of the early evening hour rose hazy and motionless. The thick, wrinkled hand of Okamé played with the wooden tassels of his hammock.

From the fire the smell of freshly running blood was wafted towards him. It caused a pricking sensation in his head, and for a moment he became excited. He clenched his fist, then he felt tremblingly for the quiver at his side. But his arm fell lifelessly. And the smoke now smelt like the blossoming branch of an oleander. A butterfly flew along his cheek and brushed his sleek white hair. Thus the Great Spirit approaches us, like Okamé. He is all powerful, we only behold him in the shape of a minute animal. Okamé knew that his life had been righteous, as must be the life of a great warrior who can be wise in council and conciliatory in the shadow of the tents. All lines smoothed out on his old face.

He kept his eye steadily on the horizon, as if he were looking for a new way. The carmine dissolved into violet and spilt out over the horizon. How is it that suddenly, as night falls by degrees, the sandy savannah becomes covered with young green grass? Okamé already saw the first star as a silver decoration on an endless carpet. All this was on the other side of the smoke. At this side the savannah had become a creek. Whence the water came he did not know, but for one who has lived so many days there is no longer any wonder.

Okamé wanted to rise in his canoe, but he saw how calmly and safely the stream took him along peaceful shores; he leaned back again, and through his half-closed eyelids he saw many stars appear, large, like lighted cocoanuts suspended in a gigantic cluster and others playful and agitated like a myriad glowworms all around and above the canoe. He saw them reflected in the water.

From the forest came soft noises, far, far away. It was the trembling growling of a baboon, and above it, a choir of bird-song, delicate and high. The sickle moon was like a golden horn, on which an invisible man blew muffled, deep tunes, which trembled against Okamé's chest. The music came in detached small scales from his heart, but the boat took him further and further in a strange cadence. Okamé shut his eyes and no longer saw anything; but he felt as if he were shot forward like an arrow from a bow. . . .

Now Okamé stood leaning against his strong, white horse. It was trembling on its legs, while Okamé counted the arrows in his quiver. Then he jumped astride, the horse's mane fluttered in the wind as flags in the sunshine, and high up his dark head flew along the light sky. Okamé whistled shrilly, drew his bow, and the arrow shot away over the green plain, carried by wide white wings. He laughed uproariously and his horse stopped next to the dying tiger. To the depth of an arm his arrow stuck in the yellow spotted neck. So the days passed and the nights had become days.

In the morning a gray stork on its tall legs stood staring at the body of Okamé. The fire had gone out; only a few sparks remained, and the sun came out across the savannah. A striped serpent crawled near. It was beady-eyed and slung itself around the goyave tree, pointing its split tongue towards the stony face of Okamé. The sun made his body look shrivelled and bony. But his spirit was aloft; with dizzy speed and boundless joy his spirit wandered over the Eternal Hunting Grounds.

During the day it is even more quiet in the camp than at night when the fires are lit. But when the feasts begin all gestures are faster and everyone dresses up with multicolored ornaments and red feathers. Crouched around an empty boat the members enjoyed their peace drink. They all spit a finely chewed root into the empty boat; this brew is covered with palm leaves and from it comes a white fermented potion which goes to the head and drives away all sorrow. Tapana is the ancient peace drink, which is passed from mouth to mouth and is kept in a whitely polished calabash; the drink through which are exchanged all the life ferments of guests and tribe members alike, so that there will be peace and no treason. It is the symbol of the ancient communion of this small congregation, because is not the loneliness of this soil, even the open savannah, a dark catacomb? With a solemn expression on his face George passed around the tapana to his guests, and Father drinks, I drink. . . . This gulp coursed burning through my throat, my chest, my entrails, and through my arms and legs. I jumped up and shouted: "Ohé, ohé, let's dance as of old!" This drink had kindled my bloodstream.

And George had passed the cigars, rolled from mabo bark; what a prickly aroma was wafted towards one from the intensely blue smoke. Slowly and seriously the captain inhaled this smoke. He held his hand in front of his mouth and the mabo bark between his fingers; with a deep draught he absorbed its burning life. Then it was my father's turn. But they skipped me because I was not yet a man, but George smiled encouragingly at me, his strong yellow face breaking into fine wrinkles.

Many more times the tapana was passed around, so that all faces shone with serene happiness. Then, when the afternoon was gone and coolness spread over the land, the dances and festivities of manhood began.

Great is the wisdom of a dying people; it gives its thought to the deepest things, because it knows that its task will soon be achieved, and the last man, "O terror, am I the last of my people?", must answer the question: Why has this tribe lived and has the sorrow been carried from child to child? And it is the last ones especially who think all this over, because they have been left by themselves and led into a lonely plain; there they can reflect.

The sage of this tribe says: man is born to sorrow and to bear his sorrow in solitude. Therefore we will prepare a feast, O those among you who have attained manhood and wish to be accepted in the ancient circle of warriors, who want to draw a bow and plant your life in a woman's body! therefore we will prepare a feast, so that we may judge your courage and see that you are no longer children and no longer complain as if you were a sick woman. That no pain can be so great that it makes you cry out in anguish, because physical pain is small compared to what you will suffer from loneliness. Dance then so that you may think through the intoxication caused by the divine rhythm.

The kettle-drums and the flutes drown out all thought; the rhythmic song of the women lures the dancers out of their tents. One by one they come to the captain, who hangs the Koenana, the significant symbol of life, around their necks. It is made of woven reed ornamented with colored bird feathers; but between the rushes vicious wasps are fastened, with the back part of their bodies turned inside. And the dancers are hung with this kind of living ornament. High sounds the song of the women, higher go the flames of the fires; the music grows faster, the dancers pipe a shrill tune and the rhythm makes them bob up and down, it throws them against the earth and lifts them high in the sky. The smoke curls fantastically around the dancers in slender columns. New ones arrive, clad in long woolen tassels, and with arrows fastened to their backs and arms. A high headgear made of blue and green feathers flutters above them. "Ohé, ohé!" the children shout, and with the swinging of their arms the spectators urge them on to the dance and the music until it becomes a savage whirl.

Then the bearers of the wasps step out one by one from the ruddy circle. Their faces are pale, not a muscle twitches in pain. Indifferently they allow themselves to be rubbed with herbs and oil by the old women. Now a circle of warriors is formed around another fire, and the youngest hunter makes room for his new brothers. In this circle they will learn the secret words of their tribe for evenings on end, the real names of every tribe member and the totems of every family.

Presently, when everybody has returned to their own tent, he will find his new weapons, a thicker bow and heavier arrows; the new warrior then considers which girl of the tribe he prefers, and how long he will have to work to buy a rifle, like those of the captain and the city dwellers. . . . They are already estranged . . . already different; there remains only the wisdom of a dying people and the lessons of its last sage; life is born from duality. Will a new life spring from this dying people?

You, who are reading this, remember the soul of the very righteous Fray Bartholomé Las Casas who, his whole life long, fought the injustice of the conquerors. Through prayer and offerings, through words, deeds and writing he asked for mercy for the defenseless victims of the white man's hunger for land. His voice sounded as that of one possessed and, still misunderstood after centuries, his name is barely remembered among the last children of the exterminated race.

You, who think about peace and ask about man's injustice towards his fellow man, remember him, because wherever your path may lead in these lands, his name will be your watchword, the only magic word that will unlock their hearts for you.

The day after the feast everything is again serene and quiet at the camp. The men go out early, hunting or fishing in the forest creek between the winding, exposed roots. Sometimes they pursue a fleet fish in their canoe and shoot him with an arrow which floats above the water; the loose point sticks in the back of the fish and is attached to the drifting shaft with a piece of string. Thus the fish betrays itself.

At other times they build dams in the forest creeks and throw small pieces of nekoe reed into it, and after a few hours all the fishes float to the top, paralyzed. In the woods they set traps for the deer, then lianas are attached to the rifles; in the water they lay large fish traps made of wariembo rushes. No animal is shrewd enough to escape from the triangular arrow of the Indian; and he kills birds with a small arrow ending in a heavy head. He spits on the soil to catch snakes, because he has potions and powders that paralyze all reptiles and make snake-bites as harmless as a scratch.

When all men have left the camp, the women have already toiled for a long time. Some sit at looms and make hammocks from the filaments of wood agave or palm rope and ornament the borders with woolly fringes. They also make small pieces of cloth from raw cotton and weave lovely figures into these, as lovely as women's dreams can be. . . . Others again sit on their haunches moulding slender crocks from gray loam, sometimes too they make crude lizards and crocodiles from it. This material is baked dry and colored with red sap. And these crocks give to the water the pure taste of the soil and the fresh aroma that is the rose oil of my country. Some women cultivate the soil, others go to look for the eggs of turtles and leguanas. But the children patiently keep a watchful eye on the traps set in the nearby wood to catch the swift robin redbreasts.

Few words are heard during the daytime in the camp: only the wind which rustles through the leaves, and the mother who calls her young ones home with a long shout. In the furthest interior théy live undisturbed in their own loneliness. The elders are tolerant of the recklessness of the young huntsmen; the boys listen with respect to the words of the elders and their impatience subsides at the campfire. In smiling humility the women drift through the stillness; the children stare out of large black eyes at the ever changing wonders of life. The beautiful wonder which always renews itself in all hearts, but with what anguish. . . .

Gradually they all became Christians; they settled at the bend of the river, far away from the savannah. They built a church there for the missionary, who visited them every month for a few days.

And as the tribe has procceded, further, yet still closer to the end, then the rainy season comes finally over the land, the short season wherein everything blooms anew. In the innermost part of the country life begins anew. The savannah is empty, and in a few years at not a single edge of the wood will there be any longer the ancient tribe's campfire.

The soil becomes moist, all the trees in the forest drip, large brown drops; long tears of resin ooze from some trees, and the forest exudes a somber chill, which makes one sleepy and feverish. The toads stretch themselves croaking out of the swamps; the bitterns paddle dully through the wet leaves. The sun disappears for days, the sky becomes dark gray, and the low clouds drift by in a haze. On every branch a foolish bird calls, tarata, once every minute. A little bird of God flutters by frightened, in the distance a chirp responds. Then nothing; it becomes dead still.

But now a soft buzzing is heard from far away, like a distant wagon over a hard road, which gradually comes nearer and nearer. The rain rushes over the forest, swishes through the trees. Thousands of leaves and twigs fall, but before the rain starts there is the buzzing of swarms of insects. The wood is a pond, the rain streams along the thick trunks and drifts along to the mountains, to the savannah. A bolt of lightning strikes straight down the plain and divides the land in two. The thunder subdues to a weak rumbling in this endless space. But nothing is any longer to be seen, for the rain falls in thick, gray curtains.

Hide yourself, hide yourself then, because this is the time that my country expels all intruders, to be empty and bring new life to everything, to plants, to beasts, to human beings! Especially human beings. The sky mixes with the earth, the water with the soil; strange fires are lit, where heaven and earth meet. Chaos rolls all into one, and then again water and sky, land and sea, disentangle themselves.

And suddenly the rain has stopped, a ray of sunshine has swept it all away, and the greedy soil absorbs all the new sap. The forest still drips, but the drops fall slowly, as a taut memory. The tiger comes out of his hiding place and peers now to the right, and now to the left. The bird starts calling again with a sad cooing, first soft, then louder and louder.

But the savannah remains empty. . . .

The bird flies away over the many forests and settles on a new tree, near a small village on the river, a new hamlet with a church. Once more he calls; then silence. . . . I have heard him . . . he called the name of a people, an ancient people, which was the loneliest of all, because it died out in a short period of time, and only its name remained. All the birds call its name from the furthest interior on the country.

Come back.

Translated by ALFRED VAN AMEYDEN VAN DUYM

J. van Melle

REVENGE

BEFORE THE THREE YEARS' WAR, UNCLE BEREND VIVIERS, A TRANS-vaal farmer, had a tenant farmer named Strydom. In the course of the war Strydom was captured, with a few other members of the commando, and he was persuaded by the English to join them. He helped them in all sorts of ways; led them where he knew the road, provided them with useful information; and he was often present where they burnt down houses and carted the women and children off to the camps. He was also present when this happened to the house and family of Uncle Berend. There was nobody at the house then except Uncle Berend's wife, their little daughter Susarie, and Andries, a boy of fifteen. The boy refused to be taken prisoner and, while the soldiers were busy searching the house, he raced away on one of the English horses. Strydom then fired upon him and shot him dead.

Uncle Berend was a religious man and, from the day he received news of this, he wrestled with the question of whether it was right for him to hate Strydom for that act or whether it was demanded of him to forgive in his heart the man who had murdered his child. Thoughts about this continually tortured him, until finally he found a certain calmness in the conclusion that one must forgive one's fellow-man everything if he comes and asks for forgiveness, but that if he does not do so, if he shows no remorse over his act, one is not called upon to forgive him.

Thus it was that, when peace came, he hoped that he would not meet Strydom again, that Strydom would never come and ask for forgiveness, so that he might keep cherishing his hatred against the man.

It was a Sunday afternoon, about a year after peace. Instead of the big house which they had before, there was now a much smaller one. The living-room was much smaller too. Everything spoke of diminished prosperity, even if it was not really poverty. The furniture consisted of cheap cases and chairs in the place of the firm and attractive Boer furniture of former days. The walls were not papered but simply plastered, and on the floor there was, true, a carpet, but the floor itself was earthen. Uncle Berend, still drowsy from the afternoon nap which he had just enjoyed, came in: a powerfully built man of medium height with graying hair but red beard. His small blue eyes were as keen as steel. His face was burnt red, contrasting sharply with his white forehead. A courageous face, which would almost have been noble had it not been for the nose, which was too small and coarse in shape. He carried his hat in his hand, and as he sat down he placed this on the ground next to him. He yawned once or twice and then stood up lazily to reach for the newspaper lying on the table. He read with little interest. After a little while his wife came in, Aunt Hannie, a typical farmer's wife of good family, a woman cultivated without being soft, who could appreciate luxuries and had also learned to suffer deprivations. She still looked bright and spirited, although her black hair was almost gray; in her gray eyes there was a serious, almost sad, expression. She sat down at the table, and with her hand to her face she pensively stared outside. They did not speak.

After a little while she said: "Shall we presently go to the graves?"

"That is good," he said.

A little girl of about fifteen, bearing a strong resemblance to Aunt Hannie, came in with coffee and Boer biscuits.

"Oh, you have already made the coffee, Susarie; you are quick," said her mother.

A youth of twenty or twenty-two years of age entered also; he paused and said: "I am riding over for a while, Father, to Vye-fontein, to Uncle John's."

"Yes."

"I may be back a little late."

"Yes, it is well; give them all our greetings."

Martiens went out and the two old people again sat silently together. Susarie, who had gone out, returned. "May I go over to Katrina, Mother? I shall be back at five o'clock."

"Very well," said Aunt Hannie.

Susarie prepared to go, but it appeared that she was hesitating about saying something. Uncle Berend and Aunt Hannie looked at her questioningly.

"Father, Kaatjie says Mina says that Uncle Willem has seen Strydom in the village. Uncle Willem says he is looking dreadful. Uncle Willem says he pretended not to see him, but he says Strydom slunk by like a dog afraid of a kick." Uncle Berend said nothing, but Aunt Hannie said: "I do hope we shall not run across that wretched dog. What should he be doing in the village now? I am surprised that he dares to come here where everyone knows him."

"It is good, eh, Father, that he looks so?" said Susarie. "He is suffering, says Uncle Willem, one can see that in him. That is good, eh, Father? The more he suffers the better, eh?"

"The worst for him is still not bad enough," said Aunt Hannie.

"No, wife, no, after all we are Christians; let us not execrate. Let the Lord judge; let the Lord punish, but let us, if it is possible for us, remain quiet."

His wife made no answer, but her face and her whole attitude spoke of vindictiveness.

"Then I'm going now, Mother."

For a while neither said anything. Finally Aunt Hannie said: "What should that beast of a man be doing here? If I met him, I don't know what I should do; I'd be capable of doing something dreadful."

"Yes, if one followed the dictates of one's heart." Then they sank deeply into thought again.

"Shall we leave now?" asked Aunt Hannie.

"Good, we shall go now." But he remained sitting, and Aunt Hannie too; she had lost herself again in bitter thoughts.

A native appeared in the doorway. He stood hesitating as if he were afraid to talk.

"What is it, Kameel?" asked Uncle Berend.

"Baas, here comes Baas Strydom."

Aunt Hannie jumped up from her chair. "What?" she asked angrily. "Where?" Uncle Berend, with his two hands pressing upon the arms of his chair, slowly rose to his feet. He looked at Kameel furiously. "What are you saying?"

"Yes, Baas," said Kameel, afraid of the anger his words had created and at the same time, also angry with Strydom who had dared to come there. "Yes, Baas, it is he that is coming there, Baas Strydom, Baas." He waited a few minutes and then left. Uncle Berend peered through the window. Aunt Hannie hastily came to his side and so for a few moments they stared silently at the approaching man. It was clearly he. They knew him too well to make a mistake; because Strydom, their former tenant farmer, the "Joiner," was the man who had shot their child dead. He rode his horse at a walking pace, straight for the house, not looking about him, but staring straight in front of him. Near the house he dismounted, and tethered his horse to the branch of a tree. Then he approached slowly. His attitude was depressed. He was a tall, muscular and still young man, but his walk and his attitude were so downcast that, from afar, one would take him for an old man.

"It is he," said Uncle Berend. Aunt Hannie turned round and walked through the room, her fist at her mouth. She cried with rage. Uncle Berend also turned away from the window and stood with his clenched hands pressed together, his head bowed. There was a soft, hesitating knock at the door. Uncle Berend opened it. In the doorway stood Strydom in a dejected attitude. Uncle Berend stepped a pace backward, and Aunt Hannie blazed with hostility.

"You here?" asked Uncle Berend angrily. "What are you doing here? How dare you come here?"

Strydom took his hat off and spoke in a soft voice, very humbly. "Uncle Berend must chase me away from Uncle's porch, if Uncle Berend wishes; I have only come because I cannot do otherwise; because I want to ask Uncle Berend and Aunt Hannie for forgiveness and then Uncle Berend can do what Uncle Berend wishes."

Uncle Berend hesitated. What ought he to do? But, after all, it was quite clear; he knew well what he should do. He had long since decided within himself that if Strydom should come to ask forgiveness then he could not refuse it. Therefore, he said, though it was with distaste: "Come in."

"What?" cried Aunt Hannie, astounded and angry, but he took no heed and stood aside to let Strydom enter.

"Just as Uncle Berend wishes," he said as he slowly came in. "I have only come to ask your forgiveness."

"Sit down, then," said Uncle Berend roughly. Strydom sat down, in a bent attitude, a picture of dejection. Then, after a few moments of silence, he started to speak. He spoke in a low, almost monotonous tone. "I came to ask Uncle Berend and Aunt Hannie for forgiveness for the great evil which I have done on this farm. I have not come to make excuses for myself, I have come only to ask for forgiveness. My conscience plagues me; my heart is always sore; I am as one who has no faith left in anything. Life is a torture to me because the memory of my misdeed is with me day and night. I want only Uncle and Aunt's forgiveness. I ask no more. I do not wish to be in Uncle Berend's and Aunt Hannie's sight more than I can help, but I ask if Uncle Berend and Aunt Hannie can forgive me."

"Do you know that you are asking us something that is almost impossible?" said Uncle Berend more calmly.

"I know, Uncle," said Strydom humbly. "It is impossible, but I had to come and ask. We are all human beings, Uncle, and each in his time requires forgiveness."

Uncle Berend sat down. Then he said with emotion in his voice: "Cousin Pieter, God's Word says: If your brother sins against you, and he says he feels remorse, then you shall forgive him. That I will try and do although I do not know whether I shall be able to, whether it will indeed be possible for me, because the grief you have caused us is so bitter and your deed so cowardly that it is almost impossible for flesh and blood to forgive it. However, God is judge and His is the vengeance, but we must forgive. I want to try if I can. More I cannot say."

Strydom stood up. "Thank you, Uncle." For a few moments he remained standing there on the floor as if he was turning over in his mind whether he should say anything else. Then he turned slowly towards the door. In a humble and depressed voice but, at the same time, with gratitude in his tone he took his leave. "Good day, Uncle Berend; good day, Aunt Hannie."

"Good day, Cousin Pieter," said Uncle Berend, though with distaste, but Aunt Hannie did not answer his greeting. Strydom went out and himself closed the door behind him.

When he had gone Aunt Hannie said angrily: "I cannot forgive the murderer of my child." Then she asked accusingly:
"How is it possible, Berend, that you allow this man into your
house? He does not deserve that any person on earth speaks to
him. He is the lowest human there is." She started to cry. "Oh,
when I think of the day when he shot our dear Andries dead,
and that he now dares to come into our house." She dropped her
head on her arms and began weeping aloud. Uncle Berend went
to her and placed his hand on her shoulder.

"It is hard to be a Christian, Hannie, but this man comes to
ask forgiveness and we may not spurn him. The Bible teaches
us that so emphatically that I have not the courage to refuse him
forgiveness." Aunt Hannie stood up and dried her tears. She
went to the window and stood there looking out.

"Since we have been married we have done our Christian
duty," he continued. "Our home has always been a home where
the Lord has been served, and do not let us stop now. Let us,
however hard it may be, try to forgive this man."

"He will come and ask for work again; I am sure of it," she
said.

"I hope not. I hope that the Lord will spare me this trial. But
if the Lord demand it of me, then I shall do it."

Not more than ten minutes away from them lived Gert, their
eldest son, on the portion of the farm that would one day be his;
a quiet man who worked hard during the week and stayed at
home on Sundays to rest. His wife Koba was different; she liked
company. That afternoon she said: "Won't you walk across with
me? You need not come, if you do not wish," she continued
when she saw him hesitating. "If you would rather stay here, I'll
go over by myself."

"If it is all the same to you, then I think I will stay," he said.
"I am feeling rather too lazy to walk."

"Anna," she called to the servant-girl, "come, I'd like you to
walk across with me."

Along the road they met Susarie with a little maid with her.

"Do you think Katrina and the others are at home, Sister?"
asked Susarie.

"I think so, Susarie, we did not see them driving away. Were
you going there?"

"Yes."

"Are your father and mother at home?"

"Yes, Sister."

"Were they perhaps not driving somewhere?"

"No, I don't think so. But perhaps they are going to the graves. Father and Mother often do that on Sunday afternoons when there are no visitors."

"Do you know, Sister, that Uncle Willem has seen Strydom in the village."

"Strydom? What should he be seeking here? From whom did you hear it?"

"From the servant-girl, Kaatjie. She heard it from Mina."

"I do hope he will not be coming here."

"Oh no, Sister, he will never dare do that."

"One never knows," said Koba thoughtfully. "One never knows what a person will do or won't do."

"If he does, then something terrible will happen."

"Yes," sighed Koba, "I don't know what will happen then."

She was near Uncle Berend's house when she saw a man on horseback stopping at the house and walking towards the porch. She stopped in fright. "Strydom," she thought, and then she doubted it again. Hesitantly she walked on, afraid to go to the house. A servant-girl hastily came to meet her, half-terrified, half-excited. "Missie," she said as one glad to have something exceptional to say and, at the same time, indignant: "Missie, Baas Strydom is here. Baas Berend allowed him into the house."

"Are you sure?"

"Yes, Missie, I know him well. It is he, Baas Strydom, who shot the little master Andries dead."

Koba said nothing, wondering greatly. "How on earth is such a thing possible?" she thought. She walked to where, from behind a hedge, she could see the front of the house and there she waited until she saw Strydom coming out and riding away again. Then she approached the house. All this time she had expected something or other to happen, loud voices charged with accusation, or a fight perhaps; she feared that she would hear shots. But nothing happened; Strydom had come out and ridden away after a while as if no great tragedy had taken place within.

"I cannot understand it," she said, "I cannot understand it," and she walked to the house and went in. Uncle Berend and Aunt Hannie were sitting in silence in the living-room in an agitated and, at the same time, melancholy attitude.

"Good afternoon, Mother; good afternoon, Father," she said, and immediately afterwards: "Was Strydom here?"

"Yes, he was here," said Aunt Hannie.

"And so?" asked Koba.

"He came to ask forgiveness," said her mother-in-law bitterly.

"And what did Father say? Did Father let him come in?"

"Yes, Koba," said Uncle Berend dejectedly. "What would you do? The man came to ask forgiveness; as a Christian, one cannot do otherwise."

"This is going too far, Father," said Koba indignantly. "I would have driven him off like a dog. And I don't think he is honest about it either. He is such a low beast. He will just say so in order to come and live here again."

"That is what I say, too," said Aunt Hannie.

"I do hope he will not come and ask for a place again," said Uncle Berend in a weary tone. "Because it would be the greatest trial of my life to see the murderer of my child before me every day."

"Where is Martiens?" asked Koba.

"He has gone to Vyefontein," said Aunt Hannie.

"I wonder what he will say there," said Koba.

Susarie came in. "Katrina was not there," she said, "and so I just turned back again." She paused suddenly, looked from one to the other, became aware of their gloom. Then she went up to her mother. "Did Mother go to the graves?" she asked.

"No, my child, we did not go to the graves."

"But Mother has been crying. Why did you cry, Mother?"

"I was sad, Susarie. We were talking of little brother, who is dead."

Susarie placed her cheek against her mother's. "Mother will surely never forget our little brother. But Mother must just think that little brother is in heaven, not so, Father?"

"Yes, my child, I certainly think so," he said.

Susarie kissed her mother on her forehead and went out. After an interval of silence Aunt Hannie said: "I wonder what Andries would say of this if he knew?"

"If he is in heaven now, I know well what he would say," said Uncle Berend.

When Koba reached home and told it all to Gert, he said: "I can understand that of Father. With him, his faith goes before everything else."

"But everything has a limit, Gert."

"Everything has a limit, but each one must decide for himself where that limit is. For me the limit may perhaps lie here; for Father, the limit lies much further away. But perhaps it was a good thing that I or Martiens was not there."

"What would you have done?"

"I don't know. You never know what you would do in such a case. But if one day I should meet Strydom and shoot or strike him dead, then I would not call it murder."

"In any event he will probably never come here again," she said to reassure herself.

There were many joiners (traitors) at the place Strydom had moved to after the war. The man who gave him a place to live in was also a joiner. He had learnt to know this man during the war and this man had told him that he could come and stay with him after the war if he wished. This man had also heard of the shooting of the son of the very man with whom Strydom had been staying, but this did not affect his intention of taking Strydom on his farm. He knew he would get on well with Strydom, a hard worker, as he had learnt, and an honest man to boot; besides they shared the same political feelings and that helped a lot towards getting on well together in times such as these. He had never revealed to Strydom that he knew anything about the shooting of the boy. And he never spoke to anybody about it, yet, by some means or other, the matter became known in their neighbourhood. The joiners, in fact, associated only with other joiners, because other people avoided them as far as possible. So in the first years after the war Strydom and his wife were very much thrown together and sought among each other the necessary company and friendship. But when Strydom had lived in the neighbourhood for a little while, the attitude of the people with whom they associated underwent a sudden change. The visits of neighbours and of acquaintances, few in any case, came practically to a stop. Even when they mingled with the others, in houses, or at celebrations or at the church, they felt that there was something about them the people did not like. They were always being left alone. When they addressed an acquaintance, he was in a hurry to be on his way and had little to say. When they joined a group talking together the circle immediately diminished until they were alone again. When one of them entered a room full of people, the conversation stopped and everybody regarded them curiously.

For Strydom this was nothing strange; he realized that the crime he had committed there on Uncle Berend's farm had leaked out in this neighbourhood, but his wife knew nothing of it, did not even know that he was present when the people were taken from the farm to the concentration camp.

"What possesses these people?" she asked in despair one day.

"They avoid us as though we were lepers. And just see how strangely they look at us."

"You imagine it," he said.

"No, I am not imagining it. No, good heavens, Pieter, I am beginning to hate the people here. What have they against us? They do not come to visit us and when you go anywhere they avoid you. Are we then so contemptible because we are tenant farmers, because we are poor?"

"But there are other tenant farmers among us."

"That is what I say too. But they are not always left alone as we are."

"Perhaps they are, too. Perhaps they are only more thick-skinned."

So far as he was concerned, it was of no consequence. He did not hanker after visiting places to seek pleasure and company. He would rather not go anywhere nor visit anybody. For her sake, he now and then drove somewhere for diversion, but even this he did not desire. It was of little concern to him that people avoided him. He knew why it was. Could one blame them? Could you blame anyone because he did not wish to associate with such a low fellow? No, he did not hate them for this. But he preferred not to meet them. If now and again he forgot about the affair then there was probably somebody who by his attitude, by his look alone reminded him of it. It was better for him to see nobody except the people of the farm. They were accustomed to him. They knew everything but had surely almost forgotten it again. With them he could associate without being reminded of the shooting of Andries.

The affair tortured him a good deal. Some days it seemed as if he would go mad. There were days when he would not speak a word, when he would see nobody, when he fled from his wife and his house. For hours at a time he just sat. If then, unexpectedly, she asked him what he was sitting and thinking about, he started. Then he mentioned something about the farming and she believed it. She was also getting used to it that he was so taciturn. She accommodated herself to it although it was no pleasant thing. She had her two children and this helped a good deal to pass the time. She chatted to them and played with them. To the future she gave no thought. She thought no further than the day itself. But sometimes she longed for the old farm and for Aunt Hannie and the others; but she supposed that they would not want a joiner on their farm; it was no use even thinking about it.

One day Strydom said to her that it would be necessary to go to Uncle Berend to fix up certain things. There were perhaps still some cattle of his, and possibly sheep. He had also buried a little money there and a few other things. Perhaps these were all still there. One could not dispose of all these things by letter, one had to go in person. He had always been afraid to go but the people in general were quieting down; the hatred against those who had joined was no longer so strong. He would not stay away long; at the most a few days.

When he came back he was for a while more cheerful. He spoke again and there were no more days when he avoided her altogether.

"How were they all at Uncle Berend's?"

"Friendly," he said, "not at all antagonistic."

"I am so glad," she said. "And the goods we buried there, with the little money?"

"Gone."

"Oh, what a pity."

"And the few head of stock?"

"The English took them."

Then she asked: "Do you think they would have you there again if you asked?" But he shook his head: "That we must not attempt," he said. "They will not do it." When later she again mentioned the matter, he answered discouragingly. Then for hours he did not speak again. The little spell of cheerfulness which he brought with him from his visit to Uncle Berend's passed and his silence and taciturnity and his need to be alone gradually got a grip on him again. He was never unpleasant or easily angered, but so very morose. She could not understand that he still retained his health in the circumstances. She assumed that it was the war that oppressed him; the hatred and the contempt of the people, his mental torture that he had betrayed his people. He never spoke about the war; he avoided it completely. She only hoped that time would heal it all.

It was about six months after the visit to Uncle Berend that a letter arrived from Strydom. Uncle Berend was sitting alone in the living room, resting, when Martiens came in with the mail. Uncle Berend looked at the letter and then gave it to Martiens. "Please read the letter for me," he said, "I have not got my glasses here at the moment."

Martiens tore the envelope open, looked through the letter, but said nothing.

"Who is it from?" asked Uncle Berend.

"It is Strydom writing, Father."

"From Strydom?"

"Yes, Father. He asks if he can come and live here again."

"What?" said Uncle Berend, rising angrily. But he at once controlled himself and sat down again. Then he said: "Read what he is writing." Martiens read. He read haltingly, with short pauses, as if he did not grasp everything immediately, but it was only due to his internal anger and agitation:

"Dear Uncle Berend,

"By God's grace, it is still well with us, and we hope we may hear the same from Uncle. Uncle, I want to ask if Uncle will again give me a place. We would like again to come and live with Uncle. Not that it is not well here with us, because we have not got a bad place here, Uncle, but I am longing to be back at our old dwellingplace. On Uncle's farm I had the happiest years of my life, and on Uncle's farm I committed my greatest sin. That is the place where I fell so deeply. I am longing to go back there, Uncle. Uncle may find this strange, but that is just how it is, Uncle. The place where I fell, Uncle, will, I hope, be the place where I shall arise again. My thoughts are strange, Uncle, but I imagine that God will forgive me my sin the sooner there where I committed the sin than here. If Uncle Berend has truly forgiven me, then I want to ask Uncle please to give me a place again. Please, Uncle. Uncle can give me just what Uncle wishes. I shall be satisfied with what Uncle thinks is good. Perhaps the Lord will so dispose that I may still sometime be able to do something good for Uncle Berend. I do not ask it because of poverty, Uncle, but only because my thoughts are always turning back to Uncle Berend and the others and to the old farm.

"I close my letter now, Uncle. If Uncle Berend does not see his way clear, then it is also good, Uncle. I can understand it.

"Marya knows of nothing, Uncle. I shall still tell her, but so far I have not had the courage. She is the only person who still thinks something of me, and what will she say if she knows everything?

"With greetings from myself and Marya,

Pieter Strydom."

There was a long silence. "Father will surely not let him come here again?" asked Martiens.

"I don't know, Martiens, I first want to speak with your Mother. This man is fighting for his soul, I feel it." Martiens was angrily silent. "Please see where your Mother is."

Martiens went out and Uncle Berend walked to and fro in the

room. A little while later Aunt Hannie came in, furious and excited.

"Did a letter come from Strydom?" she asked.

"Yes," answered Uncle Berend as he sat down.

"What does he write?" she asked. She took up the letter lying on the table and read it. Then she angrily flung the letter on the table. "That he should still dare think that we will give him a place again." Uncle Berend remained silent.

"You are surely not thinking of taking him again?" asked Aunt Hannie uneasily.

"I do not know myself yet, Hannie," he said despondently. He stood up again and walked backwards and forwards. "I have no wish to, Hannie, but it almost seems to me as if we must. It is as if the Lord wishes it of us. It is as if the Lord would test us in this way. Why should this man now insist in coming back here? It is really strange. And if the Lord tells me I must, yes, then we must, however bitter it might be. It seems to me that this man is seeking. He is seeking relief. It is a man who feels remorse and who cannot find rest. Now he seeks it here, here with us. If it is the Lord who sends him, is it then for me to spurn him?"

"It may also be the Devil urging him on."

"No, Hannie, I do not believe it. This man is praying, that I can see. He is suffering. He is being sorely tried."

"And now he comes to us to help him, to those who hate him."

"Yes, it seems so inexplicable. And yet it is perhaps only human."

"But you are not going to give him a place again, Berend. I do not wish to see this low beast again every day."

"I do not wish it either, wife," replied Uncle Berend, reflectively. "It will be just as hard for me; but I am afraid to go against the will of the Lord."

"The Lord cannot wish it."

"The Word says if we do not forgive then the Lord will not forgive us either."

"You can forgive him if you wish, but you can refuse to give him a place to live in."

"You now wish to travel two roads at the same time; you want to forgive and yet not to forgive. You know that if we forgive him in our hearts then we shall also allow him to come back. We must not run away from the truth. If we face the matter honestly, then it is like this: We keep nursing thoughts of revenge and we do not wish to see him again, not to help him in his soul struggle, or we forgive him and then we forgive him out and out."

Aunt Hannie spoke up angrily: "I cannot understand how you can talk like this, Berend; how for one moment you can think of having him back with you here."

"I am speaking against my own feelings. I only do not want to deceive myself; I am placing the matter open and above board. Thus it is now. It is dreadful to have to do it but yet, it seems to me, this is God's command."

"And then, what about the children? They will be furious."

"This thing is between you and me, Hannie. The children have very much less to do with it. How they will treat him is their affair. This thing is between you and me."

"We shall see this man every day," she wept.

"I do not think we shall see much of him. He will want to keep to himself. His house is not near us either, and he will seldom show himself here, of that I am convinced."

"As if you knew him, now."

"I also know what it is to suffer. The hardest is when you feel remorse for your deed. In any case, we need not immediately come to a decision."

Uncle Berend stood up. He lingered as if he wished to say more and then went out. Aunt Hannie went to sit at the table with her head on her hands. Martiens came in.

"Mother," said Martiens.

"Yes, Martiens?" asked Aunt Hannie dully.

"I heard what Mother was talking about with Father." Aunt Hannie remained silent, she waited for him to continue. Martiens put his arms out aggressively. "Mother, please do not let Father allow that man to come back here again. I hate him so dreadfully; and so do we all. I would be capable of shooting him dead."

"Yes, child, I understand. I feel it even more than you all do. But if your father wishes it, then we must. He is your father, Martiens. And your father believes it is his Christian duty. We must not prevent him from doing what he believes is his duty. He believes that the Lord expects it of him. We must not do anything that would burden his soul."

Martiens was silent. Aunt Hannie began to cry. "Oh, but it is dreadful to think of it. How shall I endure it?"

On Vyefontein there dwelt a man by the name of Uncle Jannie. He was an old friend of Uncle Berend's, already an old man, of wise disposition. When he heard that Strydom had been at Uncle Berend's and that Uncle Berend had forgiven him, he said: "Yes, that I can believe of Berend. He is like that. Everything for his

Christian religion. But I wonder how he feels deep in his heart."
When afterwards he heard that Strydom would get his old place
back again as Uncle Berend's tenant farmer, the old man disapproved. "Some people want to be more Christian than is possible for a normal human being," he said. "It will never do. Berend
wants to do it now, but I do not believe for a moment that his
heart is in it. He is doing it because he thinks he must do it,
but within himself he will rebel against it. I know him well. He
is very proud, this old friend of mine. He believes that he is more
of a Christian than other people. He imagines now that he can
do this big thing, a joiner, your old tenant and one who deliberately shot your son, to forgive him, and to give him a place on
your farm, next to you where you saw him every day! Good
heavens, he will no more be able to do it than I could do it. I
must ride over there and try and persuade him to change his
mind." But Uncle Jannie was no man of prompt action and
while he was still planning to go and talk to Uncle Berend about
the matter he heard that Strydom had already moved in.

"Now we shall just have to wait and see how things go," he
thought.

One day after Strydom had been there for a little while, he
rode over. He saw at once that Uncle Berend was no longer the
same man. It was some time since they had last met each other
and Uncle Jannie could at once see a difference. It was as if a
suppressed rage smouldered in his friend's eyes.

"Like a dangerous bull," he thought. After they had sat talking a while, Uncle Jannie asked: "How are you getting on with
Strydom?" At these words Uncle Berend looked at him as if he
thought: "Uncle Jannie, please keep yourself out of this. Concern
yourself with your own affairs. This is my concern, and I am
fighting it out and I do not want anyone else to interfere."

"Oh, so-so," he said brusquely. And there was a long silence.

"There is evil brewing here," thought Uncle Jannie. "There is
evil brewing here. But every man must fight for himself. In matters like this, one man cannot help another. There are times
when a man has to go through hell alone, and nobody is able to
help him. Berend is now going through such a hell, I see it. What
will come of it, nobody can say. But things are not looking too
good to me."

In their small, poor but decent home Mrs. Strydom was engaged in all sorts of small tasks. She was now in the living-room.

A tall, dark woman, energetic by nature, but now weighed down under a deep depression. She was possibly thirty years old; not unattractive in appearance. It was raining and therefore the light in the room was gray and cold. There was nobody else in the house. All at once, sad and agitated, she started speaking aloud: "Now what is he doing outside in the rain?" She fluttered her hands as she spoke. She stood in front of the window and impatiently wiped off the moisture in order to see better. "There he is again, on the same spot. What is he seeking there? Always on the same spot. Look at him standing there now." She walked nervously through the room. "He is losing his mind. We must move away. We must move away from this place." She went into the kitchen and started working there. Strydom came in. He had on a long raincoat from which the water was dripping. Outside he first kicked the mud off his shoes and then hung the coat on a peg. With his hat on, he sat staring at the ground. Mrs. Strydom came out of the kitchen and looked at him questioningly.

"Where are the children?" asked Strydom.

"They are playing in the wagon-shed," she said. Strydom spoke in a dull voice as if what he had to say was of little importance. "It is really raining now. I wish it would stop so that we can go on with the work again, for one can do nothing; the yokes hurt the necks of the oxen too much. But it is necessary for us to start weeding, because the fields are really overgrown; the weeds are quite overtaking the corn. And I am so tired of doing nothing; I cannot sit the whole day. I want to work and be active. Sit still I cannot."

"I can see that," she said. "You scarcely sit for five minutes before you're off again. You walk in and out of the house apparently without knowing what to do."

"That is just so; I do not know how to pass the day with these continuous rains."

"But before the war it was not like this. You were then only too glad when it rained, in order to rest. We sat and talked the whole day and you didn't complain of boredom."

"Yes, then."

"Why cannot you be like that again, and sit and talk a little? Do you think this is pleasant for me? You come in and scarcely speak a word and when you do say something, you only express dissatisfaction. I sit the whole long day without being spoken to, for hardly anybody comes here, and when you come in and I think of talking a little, then you say nothing and you sit as if you have a hatred against everything. And it is not long before you are off again, goodness only knows what to go and do. Before the war, you were never like that."

"Yes, before the war," he said morosely.

"I had longed so much to be in my house again with you and the children, and what have I now? Since we have been together again, I have never once seen a smile on your face."

"What is there to laugh about?" he asked angrily. "There is reason enough to curse, yes, or to cry, yes; but to laugh? Ah! and I am the one to laugh."

She asked hesitantly: "Is it because you joined?"

"I am always prepared to defend the fact that I joined the English. It was hopeless for us to continue fighting, it was just pure foolishness, and the sooner the war came to an end, the better. Had some of us not joined the English, then the war would only have lasted longer and the end would in any event have been the same. Only more people would have been killed, and many more women and children would have died in the camps. And you must certainly not hold that against me, for what would have become of you if they had sent me overseas with the rest of the prisoners of war? When I joined, I could provide for you and you had everything you needed. No, I do not reproach myself for it. I did it with open eyes. I would not do it a second time, that is very true; if I were faced with the decision again, I would not do it again, yet I did it with a certain purpose, with the thought that this was perhaps the best thing to do. But that other thing that happened here, for that I feel deep remorse. It is breaking me; it is draining my blood; it is smothering my soul. If I could undo it, I would let myself be shot ten times over. It is always with me. I cannot drag my thoughts away from it. Especially in such weather when we cannot work. I wished that I could drink myself to death or that the whole damned world would blow up."

"What do you mean, Pieter?" she asked in fright. "What is this other thing that you are talking about?"

"That I shot Andries dead."

"You shot Andries dead?" she screamed. "But, Pieter, what you are saying is surely not true. Of course, the English shot him dead, as you always told me. Pieter, Pieter, speak, man! Did you shoot Andries?"

"Yes," he said sombrely, "I never wanted to tell you. I was afraid you also would despise me like the others. But so it is. Not the English, but I, I," said he, and struck himself furiously on the chest. "I committed this murder. Because it *was* murder. The cowardly murder of a child."

She made no answer and suddenly ran out of the house. She looked around agitatedly as if seeking a place whither she could fly, and then hurried away from the house to a poplar grove and entered it. There she burst out crying. She beat her fists against the branches, she struck her forehead against a tree trunk, she forced her pinafore into her mouth until she nearly choked, until finally she fell exhausted to the ground, her face in the rotting leaves. After a long time, she became calmer and stood up. She flicked the earth and the leaves from her clothes, wiped her face and found her way out through the thick undergrowth of young poplars. Strydom stood there waiting for her and silently they walked back to the house. She now felt a deadly weariness. After they had walked a little distance, she asked: "Oh, Pieter, how could you do it?" Despairingly, he answered her: "I do not know myself. Aunt Hannie first insulted me, and I was angry, and when the Tommies were shooting so badly, I wanted to show them how a Boer could shoot. The devil himself made me do it. As soon as I had fired the shot, I wanted to kill myself." Then they spoke no more. They entered the house, and Strydom sat on a chair, staring out over the veld. Marya stood about as if she wanted to do something but could not concentrate her thoughts on anything. Then she said: "But that is all past; nothing more can be done about it; try and get it out of your thoughts, and let us move away from here, far away from here, where nobody knows us, where you will never again see anything or anyone reminding you of this thing. Let us go to German West or to German East, or to the Mines, just anywhere you wish; but I want to get away from here. You are so peculiar, you are always walking to that spot. Sometimes you look so strange; you look so sad. I am becoming so frightened, and I have become so nervous. Oh, let us please move. I would go anywhere, even if I suffered poverty and privation, but I want to move from here; I want to get away from here as soon as possible."

"I don't know; I am attached to this farm."

"Attached to this farm?" she asked in utter amazement. There was a knock at the door and Strydom opened it. It was Uncle Berend.

"Come in, Uncle," said Strydom. "Sit down, Uncle." Uncle Berend sat down. He looked worried, and his thoughts were confused. He looked restless. He continually fidgeted on his chair; he was smoking, but his pipe kept going out. Strydom was calmer;

he spoke in a subdued voice, but without strain, and he showed no nervousness when there was a silence.

"The rain is really coming down now," said Uncle Berend.

"Yes, it is really raining a lot, Uncle."

"The fields are now so overgrown that you can scarcely see the corn," continued Uncle Berend.

"Yes, Uncle. I was just saying to Marya that I am longing to go into the fields to weed them, but that it is impossible while it rains like this."

"No, it is no use even thinking of it; the fields are too wet, but when the rain stops it only takes two days and then one can make a start."

"The corn will be swamped if this goes on," said Strydom.

"Part of it is already swamped. The corn is turning yellow."

"Yes, Uncle."

Mrs. Strydom had gone to the kitchen and returned with coffee. Uncle Berend and Strydom drank.

"The wind has veered somewhat," said Uncle Berend. "It is now almost due North. I expect this weather will now pass. You will see it clearing this afternoon. I should not be surprised if that is so. If it does not rain tomorrow, can you go to the mine to fetch coal? Then we can start weeding the day after tomorrow."

"Yes, Uncle; very well, Uncle. I shall warn the Kaffirs this afternoon that they must all be in readiness early the day after tomorrow."

"And your Communion dress, is that ready yet?" Uncle Berend asked Mrs. Strydom. His attitude was at once easier and more friendly.

"No, Uncle, I still have to make a start with it, but I am not sure whether I shall be making one; I don't really need a new one, and I am not sure that I want to go to church."

"No? Why not?"

"One does not always feel like driving to church, Uncle," she said casually. There was a silence.

"I think I shall be going again," said Uncle Berend.

"Uncle Berend is in a hurry," said Strydom.

"I want to ride to see the sheep; the poor things are having a bad time in this wet." Uncle Berend walked out but turned to Mrs. Strydom in the doorway. "I think I should have that dress made if I were you; you may still feel inclined to go." Mrs. Strydom did not answer and when Uncle Berend had gone she walked into the kitchen. Strydom was once more sitting in his former dejected attitude. Mrs. Strydom returned from the kitchen. "I am quickly going to see what the children are doing," she said as she went out.

"That man is to be envied," spoke Strydom sullenly. He pointed to the door. He spoke with brief pauses. "He feels grief, but he has no struggle of the soul. He is still trying to forgive, even though he cannot. He is a Christian. But what am I? A cowardly murderer." He laid his head on his hands. Suddenly he rose impulsively. He spoke loudly. "But I shall not move. I want to stay here and always think of my sins. I want these people and this place before my eyes, day after day, and thus punish myself till the day of my death." Agitatedly he walked to and fro. "Here I wish to be tortured by always seeing the place where I shot this poor boy. Some day God will take pity on me and take me away from here. But I do not want to go of my own accord. Some day the Lord will say: 'This man has suffered enough; it is sufficient; take him away there.' But I shall await my time. I shall not run away: I shall stay here and I shall endure my punishment till the end." He put on his coat again. Just then Mrs. Strydom came in.

"Are you off again?" she asked.

"Yes, I am just going to see where the horses are grazing."

"But the food is nearly ready: can you not wait until we have eaten?"

"I shall be back presently." Mrs. Strydom sat down hopelessly and rested her head on her hand. "Oh, God, God." She covered her face in her hands and began weeping bitterly.

It was a few weeks later and Uncle Berend entered the dining room. He looked careworn: he was not so erect and he was thinner. He sat down with a sigh and rubbed his hand across his forehead. Then he jerked his head as if he wanted to shake something off, a dreamy vacancy of mind that worried him. Then he remained without moving for a while, with his head backwards, as if he was sleeping with his eyes open. For a long time he sat thus. Then it was as if he suddenly awoke. He rubbed his forehead again and spoke aloud: "What is the matter with me these days? Just as if there is a great emptiness here!" He stood up and shook his fist: "The thing is working on my nerves." Again he started pacing to and fro. "If only he would go away of his own accord."

Aunt Hannie came in and sat down. Uncle Berend also sat down and tried to act normally. He filled his pipe while Aunt Hannie sat looking at him anxiously.

"You must give Strydom his marching orders," she said. "I do not want him here any longer. It is driving you crazy and me too. My nerves are giving in; I cannot endure it any more. Tell him he must move and then we shall have peace again."

"It is easy for you to talk about it," he said. "It is not so simple. I can send the man away, but what then? Will that dispose of the matter? Did I not tell him that he could live here and can I now send him away without breaking my word? Did I not relinquish revenge as an offering to God, and can I now take it back? Can I rob the Lord? Vengeance is the Lord's.

"God loved Andries more than you or I and therefore His the vengeance," he said in a quivering voice. "It is the Lord's right. He shall punish this man. He is punishing him now. Do you not see that He is already punishing him?"

"But if you tell him he must move, then that is surely not taking revenge. You do not want him with you, that is all, that does not mean that you are taking revenge."

"Yes, and yet it is so. If I send him away it is like saying: Man, I am still hating you all this time, even though I said that I want to forgive you. You are the murderer of my child and therefore I am chasing you away; I can no longer endure you before my eyes—and in this way I would take back everything I first gave." There was a silence.

"It is hard, bitterly hard," he continued. "Never in my life have I suffered so; but it will pass. Leave it in the hands of the Lord. He will in His time dispose of it."

"This is a trial, I feel it. To me it is as if the Lord thinks: I shall see if this man will be faithful and obedient."

Aunt Hannie sighed, stood up and went away. Uncle Berend remained immersed in his thoughts, and gradually the staring, vacant expression returned to his face and the tautness to his attitude. Suddenly he rose. He walked through the room, then stopped to look outside for a while, motionless as a statue. He spoke: "What is he always seeking at that spot? The worst of it all is that the fellow always goes and stands where Andries was shot. Now he is pretending that he is looking for his horse when he knows very well that his horse is up on the hill."

Angrily he shook his fist. "If it was still war, then I would shoot him dead on the spot." After a while he turned away and sat down, but after a few moments he stood up again and walked hesitantly through the room; then he turned to the wall where the rifle was hanging. He remained standing there. He moved like one in a dull fog. He took the rifle from the wall and stood with it in his hands for a while, then went to the window and stood there motionless. He saw Strydom moving off again. After a few minutes he turned away and laid the rifle on the table. Then he slowly went outside. A few moments later Aunt Hannie came in, and immediately saw the rifle lying there. She looked around and picked up the rifle.

"What is this rifle doing on the table?" she asked herself. She replaced it on the wall. She sat down at the table, her head on her hand. Koba came in. "Father is looking very poorly these days," she said after a few moments.

"And it is no wonder," answered Aunt Hannie. "Who can endure it. This thing is preying on him and on me. But your father will not listen to reason. I have so often spoken to him, but he will not listen to me. I tell him: Let this man move away or otherwise give me a dwelling-place on one of our other properties, but let us not continually meet him. But he will not listen. It has now become a matter of conscience with him. Oh, Koba, you do not know how I am suffering. May the Lord cause this man to go away."

"Father looks so preoccupied these days. One can see that he is suffering deeply. I just met Father here outside the gate. I said: Good morning, Father, but he did not even answer me. It was almost as if Father did not see me. I doubt whether Father heard that I said good morning to him."

"I am getting so anxious about him," said Aunt Hannie. "I am so afraid that one of these days something terrible is going to happen." She leaned over to Koba and whispered anxiously: "You know, Koba, your father does not always know any more what he is doing. There are moments when he acts as though he were in a dream."

Koba commiseratingly shook her head but said nothing. Aunt Hannie pressed her clenched hand to her mouth and gave a half suppressed sob.

"I do not know what to do. He will not listen to me."

Outside they heard Uncle Berend's step. He came in slowly and remained standing near the door.

"I am going to lie down for a while, Hannie, I do not feel quite well. Perhaps it will pass over if I rest a little."

"Did you take the rifle from the wall, Berend? When I came in the rifle was lying on the table."

"No," he answered, feebly astonished. "No, I did not take the rifle down—not that I can remember." He stood waiting for a few moments, but Aunt Hannie said no more and he slowly turned away.

"Don't you want your powders?" asked Aunt Hannie.

"No, thank you, wife, I am not really ill; only tired, very tired."

"I wonder, then, who took the rifle down?" Martiens entered the room. "Have you been in this room, Martiens?" asked Aunt Hannie.

"No, Mother, I have just returned from seeing to the sheep."

"Martiens, we must tell Strydom that he must move away from here," she said passionately. "You must tell him. Your Father need not know about it. Tell him it is best for him to move away. Speak nicely to him. And I shall pay him. Tell him I'd rather he left here. Tell him you feel that it is the best thing to do, but don't say Father wants him to move. He will understand. In some ways he is, after all, also a human being."

"Yes, Mother."

"You must make him understand that we want your father to think that he went of his own accord, do you hear, Martiens. Your father must never find out that we have done this."

"Yes, Mother, I shall explain it to him."

"It is dreadful to have to do a thing behind your father's back, but we cannot do otherwise. This affair is driving your father to exhaustion. I had thought that it would be harder for me than for him, but now I see it is affecting him far more than it does me."

"Yes, Mother, I can see that too."

"Martiens, we must wait no longer. Please speak today. I shall not rest before I know that he will be leaving here shortly."

"Yes, Mother."

"Do you know, Martiens," she said half hesitantly, "I am afraid that your father will still be driven crazy by this. Sometimes he is so strange, so absent-minded, sometimes not himself at all."

"Oh, no, Mother, now you are exaggerating, Mother."

"I tell you, Martiens, it is serious."

"Very well, Mother, I shall speak to Strydom, this very day. If I do not happen to come across him, I shall go to his house."

"I do hope he will move," said Aunt Hannie.

"If he won't, Mother, then I shall make him understand that he must," said Martiens decidedly.

"No, I think he will understand, Mother," said Koba.

"Oh, yes, he will," said Martiens. "It is not pleasant for him

here either. Everyone avoids him. It is only Father who sometimes visits him."

"Then things will right themselves again," said Aunt Hannie,
relieved. "As soon as he has gone away again."

Without saying another word, Martiens went outside.

"Where is Susarie?" asked Koba.

"She is sitting in the small room working on her dress. I would
rather not have gone to church, but your father wishes it. I don't
know whether Strydom will be going. I do not see my way clear
to sitting with that man at one Communion table. But Berend
will. One cannot talk sensibly to him about it, Koba. In this
matter he is so obstinate. He says we must drain the cup of
bitterness to its very dregs. But perhaps Strydom will not drive
to church. Marya has said that she has no wish to go. And if
they do go, he will perhaps not go to the Communion table.
Perhaps he will have enough good feeling not to do that—but
one never knows. One does not know what that man is capable
of. In any case, Martiens will now talk to him."

"Yes, Mother, perhaps everything will still come right. I am
going to see Susarie for a while."

Martiens first walked to the house of his brother Gert, but he
was busy ploughing in the fields. Then Martiens walked across
to the fields.

When Gert saw him, he ploughed to the end of the strip and
then waited to hear what his brother wished of him.

"May I see you a moment?" asked Martiens, and Gert walked
a short distance with him so that the driver and the leader could
not hear what they were saying. "We must try and get Strydom
away from here as quickly as possible," said Martiens.

"I see that too," said Gert, "but how?"

"Mother wants me to talk to the wretch."

"Yes? And what will Father say about it?"

"Father must not know about it."

"But he will not hide it from Father. If Father asks him why
he is trekking then he will, of course, say what you have told
him."

"We must ask him not to do that."

"We? Do you want me to go with you."

"Yes, Brother. You must come with me. I fear for myself. If I
must talk to the man about these things then I do not know
whether I shall be able to control myself. If we two are together,
then the one can control the other."

"That is true," said Gert.

"What are you going to tell him?" he then asked.

"I simply want to tell him the truth, tell him that Father's thoughts are dwelling too much on those old things and that he is losing his health."

"And if he does not want to?"

"Then," said Martiens with suppressed fury in his voice, "then I shall tell him that his life is in danger here, that he must clear off or else I shall kill him."

"We must only take care that we do not kill him there on the spot," said Gert.

"Are you coming with me?"

"Immediately?"

"Yes, the sooner the better."

"Unhook and let the oxen graze," Gert instructed the Kaffirs and together they walked to Strydom's house. They spoke no word along the way, each gripped in a maelstrom of thoughts.

When they arrived at the house Strydom was not there. With fear on her face, his wife awaited them at the door. Neither of them had ever been there and now that they were both approaching, silent and ominous, now that she knew what a dreadful thing had taken place here, she feared new evil. Her face was pale. She awaited what was coming.

"Is your husband here?" asked Martiens.

"No, he is not here."

"Where is he?"

"I do not know. He has not been away long, but he did not say where he was going." The two brothers looked at each other questioningly, irresolute.

"Do you want to come in?"

"We will wait outside," said Gert. She looked at them for a few minutes in silence and then went inside. Martiens and Gert walked away a little distance from the house and sat down to wait for Strydom.

After twenty minutes there was the crack of a rifle shot. Startled, they rose to their feet.

"It sounded to me as if it came from Father's house," said Gert. It did happen sometimes that somebody fired a weapon, perhaps at a hawk, or when they killed a pig or an ox, but now this shot startled them. They saw a servant girl standing transfixed at the homestead as if she had also taken fright, and some distance from the house, near the blue-gum trees, was a Kaffir hastily approaching a spot.

All at once Martiens started running towards the house, while Gert hurriedly walked after him.

Half an hour after Martiens had left, Uncle Berend had again entered the living room.

He sat down on a chair in a corner of the room in a bent attitude. Then he looked through the window. He jerked as if he would get up, but remained sitting again, leaning backwards. First there came a vicious and then gradually an absent expression on his face. "Yes?"

He got up and stood next to the table. Then he went to the wall, where the rifle was hanging. His attitude was peculiar. It was evident that he did not quite know what he was doing. His movements were slow and irresolute. Suddenly he raised his head and listened intently. He spoke hastily: "What is that? Common shots, the English are here! I must quickly saddle my horse!" He moved to the window, put his head out and called aloud: "Wilde-bees, Wildebees, fetch the horses and saddle up quickly. Hurry, the English will soon be here." He withdrew his head and again stood for a few minutes staring out. A tremor ran over him. He pointed with his hand at something outside and mumbled, then put his head through the window again and shouted: "Wilde-bees, wait, there is something I must put right first." He stood as if thinking. "What is it that I must do first? O, yes." He went up to the wall and took the rifle. He knelt at the window and took aim. His movements were now hurried, almost furious. The rifle cracked.

He stood up and replaced the rifle. For a few minutes he stood again as if thinking. He spoke half aloud: "Is everything all right now? Yes, everything is now in order." He went out and immediately afterwards Susarie came in. She was surprised to see that there was nobody in the room. She looked at the rifle. Aunt Hannie also came in, frightened, deathly pale, and trembling. She also looked at the rifle, and spoke with a note of relief in her voice: "O—who fired? Do you know?" she asked Susarie.

"I don't know, Mother; I thought it was Father who fired the shot."

"Your father had gone to sleep."

"I heard Father getting up. Perhaps Father was simply firing at something through the window."

"What would your father be firing at?" asked Aunt Hannie doubtfully.

"At a hawk, perhaps, Mother." Just then Martiens also entered the room.

"Who fired a little while ago?" he asked.

"We thought it was here in the room," said Aunt Hannie.

"Here, in this room, Mother?"

"Yes, so it sounded, but there was nobody here. I got a terrible fright. Susarie, please go and see where your father is."

Martiens went to the window and looked out. "What is that?" he asked anxiously.

Aunt Hannie came to his side. "What are they doing there?" For a while they stood looking. "I shall quickly go and see," said Martiens. Aunt Hannie wanted to go with them, but changed her mind and returned to the window. Susarie rushed in, terrified: "Oh, Mother, Strydom has been shot dead."

Aunt Hannie turned deathly pale, and almost collapsed, but then she sank into a chair. "What are you saying?" she asked.

"Strydom has been shot dead, Mother. He is lying there at the fence," said Susarie, more softly.

"Who shot him dead?"

"I don't know, Mother, but he is lying there near the big blue-gum tree at the same spot where little brother fell. Geelbooi found him there. He says the bullet has gone through his heart. Who could have shot him, Mother? How could the accident have happened? Mother, how pale you are, shall I fetch you a little water?"

Susarie hastily went to the kitchen and Aunt Hannie walked to the wall, took down the rifle and looked at the breech. The safety catch was not on. She plucked open the slot and an empty cartridge case fell on the ground. The rifle slid out of her hands and in despair she struck her hand against her forehead. "Berend shot him. It's Berend! It is Berend!" she wailed hopelessly. She sank into a chair; with her head in her hands, she rocked to and fro in distress. Susarie came in with a cup of water. "Oh, Mammie, Mammie," she screamed in fright and knelt next to her mother.

"Susarie, it was your father. I knew it; it was bound to happen. We had waited too long to do anything. If Martiens had had time to talk to Strydom then everything might perhaps have come right. I was just one day too late. Oh, Berend, oh, oh!" She stood up, staggering, and walked out, anxiously followed by Susarie. Martiens entered the room. He picked up the rifle and the cartridge case and looked through the window. He replaced the rifle and put the cartridge case in his pocket. His movements

were hurried, like one trying to hide something. Then he suddenly stood still. He clenched his fists, his face shadowed with
grief and hatred. "The swine," he said furiously. For a few moments he stood thinking, anger and doubt in his attitude.

Uncle Jannie rode over from Vyefontein to see Aunt Hannie.
It had just become known that Uncle Berend had been acquitted and he was now riding over to congratulate her. It was
possible that she was away from home and then his trip would
be to no purpose, but he would take a chance. He had his youngest child with him, a boy of about twelve, because Uncle Jannie
had married a second time and his wife was younger than he.
The child had learned not to talk when his father was immersed in thought. Then in any event he received no answer, or
answers which conveyed nothing. Uncle Jannie was thinking
about the affair of Uncle Berend. It was something one did not
readily stop thinking about. Not the court case, but the affair
itself. That Uncle Berend would be acquitted was a foregone
conclusion. It would have been an odd jury to have found him
guilty. Everyone could surely see that the man had committed
the act in a moment of insanity. But the deed itself? What was it
that had forced him against his will to commit the act? It was
quite clear. Hatred was always there, suppressed, it was true, but
not conquered. It had to break out in some way or other, and
then it happened thus. Thus it happened if a person attempted
more than he could do. Then something gave way. It was as had
happened with Saul and David. It was a precisely similar case.
Hatred, suppressed hatred, that boiled up against one's will. A
suppressed desire, but too strong to keep under. So he sat and
mused, the same view which since then he had so often reached
himself and had explained to others. . . . Saul wanted to kill
David, but his sense of duty restrained him. But the desire to do
so was too strong and, at times, maddened him and made it impossible for him to control himself; it caused him to be like one
possessed.

When they arrived at Uncle Berend's house, Susarie let them
in. "I shall tell Mother that you are here," she said. "Please take a
seat meanwhile, Uncle." Oom Jannie and the boy looked about
the room. They kept turning their heads to look at everything,
but said nothing.

"That is where the rifle was hanging," whispered Uncle Jannie
and pointed to the wall whence the rifle had been removed.

"Yes, Father."

"Through that window he fired the shot."

"Yes, Father," whispered the boy. At that moment Aunt Hannie came in.

"I have come to express my joy that cousin Berend has been acquitted," said Uncle Jannie.

"Thank you, Uncle."

"When do you expect him back?"

"We expect him back with the three-thirty train this afternoon. Martiens has gone to fetch his father in Pretoria."

"Yes."

"Go and see if the horses are still standing, my son." The boy went out and Uncle Jannie said: "We are all truly delighted that the decision was so favourable, but then nobody expected anything else."

"I, too, Uncle. From the outset I was convinced that the Lord would not impose on us even heavier trials. I did not doubt the outcome for a moment." There was a pause. Then Aunt Hannie said: "The statements of the two Kaffirs, Geelbooi and Kameel, helped a great deal. You see, Uncle, they heard him crying out that the English were coming and he had called for Wildebees who was his servant in the war and who has long been dead. Added to the other evidence the judge and the jury accepted this as proof that, at that moment, he was not quite in his right senses."

"Yes."

"A great help was, of course, also the statement of the doctor. He said it sometimes happened that a man who had always been normal momentarily quite lost his sanity." She looked at the door and said more softly: "He says it can happen like this: If a person has a great desire with which his thoughts are always busy and he suppresses that desire, then it is possible that that struggle will temporarily cloud his mind. And thus it was the case with Berend according to him."

Uncle Jannie became loquacious. "I understand. To me it seemed very much like the case of Saul. Saul also had such a struggle between his conscience and his desire to be rid of David."

Aunt Hannie nodded.

"To me the case is strikingly similar. Saul feared and hated in his heart, but he could not bring himself so far as to have David done to death, at least not at first. His sense of right restrained him. But then came times when the evil spirit was in him and at such moments desire got the upper hand and he twice attempted to stab David to death."

"Yes, Uncle."

"You see, Cousin Hannie, this, to my mind, was the case with Cousin Berend. He wanted to forgive Strydom, but could not. It was too difficult. He wanted to do something which not one of us could find it possible to do. It was superhuman. But he wanted to, because he felt that he must. There was, so to say, a continuous strife in him between these two desires, and it began to affect him and in the end it broke him. He had moments when he was out of his mind. He had thought: If I had come across this man in the war, then I would have shot him dead. And there was a moment when he believed that it really was war, and at that moment he saw Strydom. Then he had to shoot. It could be nothing else. I have thought a great deal about the matter."

"Yes, Uncle," said Aunt Hannie, somberly, "that is more or less what the doctor said."

"It was the Lord's will," said Uncle Jannie.

Aunt Hannie made no reply to this.

"We were really concerned about you, Cousin Hannie. Berend and I have always been friends. He was my old companion-in-arms. I am really grateful that he has been acquitted."

"Yes, Uncle."

"Now everything will come right again," said Uncle Jannie. "You must keep up your courage. Nobody will blame him for this deed. On the contrary we rather admire him. He had attempted to do what none of us would try to do."

"Yes, Uncle."

"Martiens went to fetch him, you say?"

"Yes, Uncle, I had wanted to go but Berend sent word that I should not come too."

"That is right, I think. It is better that you meet him here at home."

"Well, I think I shall go now," said Uncle Jannie. "I shall then rather come and visit Berend later."

"Yes, Uncle, perhaps that is better." Uncle Jannie stood up and said goodbye. "Good day, Cousin Hannie. May the Lord still be with you." He started to leave. Aunt Hannie accompanied him to the porch. She returned inside and sat down at the table in a depressed mood, at once nervous and agitated. She looked at the clock which showed a quarter of five. "They can be here presently," she said to herself. Susarie came in and sat down. They did not speak.

"Mother, I am afraid," said Susarie.

"Don't be afraid, my child. Your father is quite recovered

again. He was just confused for that little while. You need not
be anxious at all. Your father will now again be just as he has
always been. And, Susarie, don't give your father an inkling of
your thoughts, do you hear."

"No, Mother, of course not," said Susarie decidedly and half
impatiently. They sat in silence for a few more moments and
then Susarie left again. Aunt Hannie went to stand before the
window and looked out. She felt nervous and ill at ease. Suddenly she pressed her hand to her breast. "Here they are." She
glanced sharply through the window and after a few moments
went outside. A little later Uncle Berend came in, followed by
Aunt Hannie, Martiens and Susarie. Uncle Berend walked slowly,
less erect. He had become much greyer. His face was somber,
yet at the same time solemn. He sat down in his chair. He looked
around and his eyes kept turning to the window through which
he had fired and then to the place where his rifle had been hanging. He sighed deeply. He spoke in a somewhat dull and lifeless
tone, yet with much of the old strength in it. "And how are
things here, Hannie?"

"Well, Berend. How are you feeling now?"

"So-so. Reasonably well."

"Go and pour coffee for your father," she said to Susarie.
Aunt Hannie signalled with her eyes to Martiens, who got up
and walked out. She stood up and drew a chair next to Uncle
Berend. She stroked his hand lying on the arm of the chair. "I
am so grateful that you are back, Berend," she said. "The Lord
has helped us wonderfully."

"The Lord has helped me wonderfully. But the Lord has also
caused me to go through deep waters, through great terrors."
Aunt Hannie rested her head against his shoulder. She kept on
stroking his big, strong hand. Every now and then she wiped her
tears. "The Lord has caused me to see how small and insignificant
man is," he proceeded, "of how little worth he is. I had thought
that I was a good Christian, that I could do much, that I could
forgive as the Lord would have it. But I could not. My heart rebelled against it."

"It was too hard, Berend. It would have been too much for
any man. No man with human feelings could have carried a
thing like that. Please do not worry yourself about it any more. It
is past. The Lord willed it thus. You could not do otherwise."

Uncle Berend rested his head on his hand, and gesticulated
with the other: "I could help it. It was because of my sinful heart
that this happened. But how deeply have I not fallen! I had said:

Vengeance is the Lord's. And yet I wanted to take revenge myself. Until eventually God said: Very well then, if you want to take back what you have given unto Me, then take it back. I took back my offering which I had brought to God. I have robbed His altar." He groaned.

"You could not help it," said Aunt Hannie, beseechingly. "You did not know what you were doing."

"Not at that moment. But the desire was always there. I had thirsted for this man's blood until the desire overcame me. I know that so well, better than the doctor knows it." There was a silence.

Susarie came in with coffee and a plate of rusks. She handed coffee to her father, who accepted it silently, and placed the plate of rusks on the table. And then she went outside. "Will you not eat anything?" asked Aunt Hannie.

"No." He drank. Aunt Hannie took the empty cup from his hand and placed it on the table. She sat down next to him on the arm of his chair and placed her cheek against his hair. "The Lord has forgiven you, Berend," she said. "Take new courage, my man. The Lord will help you again. He has forgiven you everything. Look how merciful the Lord has been in bringing you back home."

"Yes, the Lord is merciful—but I? Who am I . . ."

Aunt Hannie drew his head towards her, and her face worked spasmodically in the effort not to burst out weeping.

BIOGRAPHICAL NOTES

BIOGRAPHICAL NOTES

GRESHOFF, J; born in Nieuw Helvoet, 1888.

Until the outbreak of the war he was co-editor of the literary monthly *Groot Nederland* (Great Netherlands). From 1927 to 1939 he lived in Brussels, from 1939 to 1942 in Cape Town, from 1942 to 1945 in New York; he recently returned to South Africa.

A poet and essayist, his principal poems are collected in *Verzamelde Gedichten* (Collected Poems) (1939); his prose is represented by *Rebuten* (Cullings), *In Alle Ernst* (In All Seriousness), *Steenen voor Brood* (Stones for Bread) and *Rariteiten* (Rarities). He also published four volumes of aphorisms: *Mimosa Pudica, Kalender Zonder Dagen* (Calendar Without Days), *Bitter-zoet* (Bitter-Sweet) and *Voor Volwassenen* (For Grown-ups).

LOOY, Jacobus van; born in Haarlem, 1855; died there in 1930.

Van Looy began his artistic career as a painter. While traveling in Italy, Spain, Tunisia, etc., he began to write sketches, which are collected in his volumes of prose I and II. For many years he belonged to the editorial staff of the literary monthly *De Nieuwe Gids* (The New Guide).

He is one of the most typical authors of *De Beweging van Tachtig* (The Movement of the 1880's). He idolizes words, especially in his travel books; he is an epicurean and writes with imagination about the outward appearance of our every-day life. Not until later does he reveal an epic talent. There is something majestic, sometimes even overwhelming about van Looy. Moreover one finds in the short story, *De Dood van mijn Poes* (The Death of My Cat) and in his autobiography, *Jaapje* (Jimmy), a tender humanity and a gentle wisdom. As a painter van Looy also revealed himself to be a witty and dignified craftsman. Many of his paintings are to be found in Holland's leading museums.

Among his best literary works are: *Proza* (Prose), *Gekken* (Madmen), *Feesten* (Festivals), *De Wonderlijke Avonturen van Zebedeus* (The Strange Adventures of Zebedeus) (3 volumes), *Jaapje* (Jimmy) and *Jaap* (James).

VERWEY, Albert; born in Amsterdam, 1865; died in Noordwijk-aan-Zee, 1937.

In 1881 Verwey made the acquaintance of Willem Kloos, founder of the literary monthly *De Nieuwe Gids* (The New Guide), who at first became his teacher; together they finally became the leaders of *De Beweging van Tachtig* (The Movement of the 1880's). He belonged to the editorial staff of *De Nieuwe Gids* from 1885 to 1890. Disputes of a literary nature caused his resignation and led to the founding of a new literary bi-monthly magazine *Twee-maandelijksch Tijdschrift* (Bi-monthly Magazine), later of *De Beweging* (The Movement). Verwey was the leader of a generation of young authors who—especially in his magazine *De Beweging*—opened and paved a new way.

Verwey was a poet and essayist. His first poems were written under English influence, but he eventually developed more individualistically and became a great poet and prose writer, craftsman and philosopher.

His most important work is *Verzamelde Gedichten* (Collected Poems) (2 volumes), Prose, Volume I to X. His three dramas in verse, of which *Cola Rienzi* is the best known, were inserted in the *Verzamelde Gedichten*.

ERENS, Frans; born in Schaesberg, 1857; died 1942.

This author of sketches and short stories belonged to the founders of the literary monthly *De Nieuwe Gids* (The New Guide), in which he represented the Roman Catholic element. His best-known volumes of sketches are: *Dansen en Rhythmen* (Dances and Rhythms) and *Gangen en Wegen* (Alleys and Paths). He translated St. Augustine's *Belijdenissen* (Confessions) and Thomas à Kempis' *Imitatio Christi* into the Dutch language.

COUPERUS, Louis; born in The Hague, 1863; died in De Steeg, 1923.

Couperus never took part in any literary movement, although it is undeniable that he was influenced by *De Beweging van Tachtig* (The Movement of the 1880's). From his tenth to his fifteenth year he lived in the Dutch East Indies and then went back to the Netherlands. In 1893 he began to travel and lived in Italy and the South of France for many years. He also spent some time in Africa and Asia.

His first novel *Eline Vere* (1889) was widely read and appreciated; it is the story of a young girl of one of The Hague's decadent upper-class families and her life ends tragically. His works on all subjects reveal two tendencies: a naturalistic realism; imagination and symbolism.

Of his many works the principal are: *Eline Vere, De Stille Kracht* (The Silent Strength), *De Boeken der Kleine Zielen* (The Books of the Little Souls), *De Dingen die Voorbijgaan* (The Things That Pass), *Komedianten* (Comedians) and *Het Zwevend Schaakbord* (The Floating Chessboard).

COENEN, Frans; born in Amsterdam, 1866; died there, 1936.

Coenen was one of the most interesting prose-writers to come to the fore immediately after the leaders of *De Beweging van Tachtig* (The Movement of the 1880's). He wrote several novels and volumes of short stories and toward the end of his life a more or less historical novel *Onpersoonlijke Herinneringen* (Impersonal Reminiscences) which rates among his best. Coenen was co-editor of the literary monthly *Groot Nederland* (Great Netherlands) until his death. His most significant works are his critical essays, not only about literature, but also dealing mockingly and ironically with politics and current topics. His *Studies van de Tachtiger Beweging* (Studies of the Movement of the 1880's) is of great and lasting significance.

HEYERMANS, Herman; born in Rotterdam, 1864; died in Zandvoort, 1924.

As a playwright Heyermans gained world fame. His plays generally revolve around some rebellious thought, wittily interpreted and with a more or less popular sense of humor. He obtained his greatest success with *Op Hoop van Zegen* (approximate translation: Let's Hope for the Best) which, however, from a literary point of view cannot be counted among his best works. For many years Heyermans wrote, under the pen-name of Samuel Falkland, short, often very sensitive, stories about the trifling events in the life of the "little man," which were widely read, especially in the period following their publication.

His principal plays are: *Ghetto, Op Hoop van Zegen* (Let's Hope for the Best), *De Meid* (The Servant), *De Wijze Kater* (The Wise Tomcat). Of his prose should be mentioned the 18-volume *Schetsen* (Sketches) and the novels *Droomkoninkje* (The Little Dream King) and *Vuurvlindertje* (The Little Firefly).

DEYSSEL, Lodewijk van (pen-name of Dr. K. J. L. Alberdingk Thijm); born in Amsterdam, 1864.

Van Deyssel is one of the leaders and principal spokesmen of the literary monthly *De Nieuwe Gids* (The New Guide), of which he was a co-founder. He wrote a great number of essays on literature, dramatics and the art of painting, expressing his opinions in a, for those days, new and often ruthless manner. These were collected in *Verzamelde Opstellen* (Collected Compositions). As a piece of narrative prose, his novel *Een Liefde* (A Love) created quite a sensation and was branded "immoral" because of a few indelicate words and expressions. His love of detail is clearly demonstrated in his lyrical, aphoristic collection, *Uit Het Leven van Frank Rozelaar* (From the Life of Frank Rozelaar).

BUYSSE, Cyriel; born in Ghent, 1859; died 1932.

A well-to-do industrialist, Buysse was at the same time one of the most captivating Flemish novelists, co-founder of the Flemish periodical *Van Nu en Straks* (Of Present and Future) and later co-editor of the Dutch-Flemish literary monthly *Groot Nederland* (Great Netherlands), which he remained until his death. Buysse gives a very true and complete picture of the Flemish people as they live between the rivers Leie and Schelde.

The best-known among his numerous works are: *Het Leven van Rozeke van Dalen* (The Life of Rozeke van Dalen), *Het Ezelken* (The Little Donkey) and *De Tantes* (The Aunts).

TEIRLINCK, Herman; born in Brussels, 1879.

A Flemish author and co-editor from 1903 to 1907 of the Flemish monthly publication *Vlaanderen* (Flanders), the best examples of his beautiful, rather exact prose, are *Mijnheer Serjanszoon* (Mr. Serjanszoon) and *Zon* (Sun). His novel *Het Ivoren Aapje* (The Ivory Monkey) is excellent in detail but as a whole its structure lacks sufficient "backbone." After the First World War he devoted himself primarily to the stage revival. He wrote several plays, among which *De Vertraagde Film* (The Slow Motion Picture), *Ik Dien* (I Serve) and *De Ekster op de Galg* (The Magpie on the Gallows) are the best known.

Teirlinck is director of the Higher Institute for Arts and Crafts, and was formerly personal advisor to King Albert and King Leopold III.

STREUVELS, Stijn (pen-name of Frank Lateur); born in Kortrijk, 1871.

He was originally a baker at Avelghem; in his numerous novels and novelettes he describes especially the farmer's life in West

Flanders. He is more lyrical than his compatriot Buysse and is a master of the art of creating a particular atmosphere. *Minnehandel* (The Business of Love), *Langs de Wegen* (Along the Ways), *Dorpsgeheimen* (Village Secrets) and *De Vlaschaard* are among his greatest works, the last book being by many considered his best.

TOUSSAINT VAN BOELAERE, Fernand Victor; born in Anderlecht-Brussels, 1875.

This Flemish author attracts attention by his dignified and pure style and the peculiar manner in which he combines realism, imagination and character analysis.

His principal works are: *Landelijk Minnespel* (Rural Courting), *Turren* and *De Doode Die Zich Niet Verhing* (The Corpse That Did Not Hang Itself).

SCHENDEL, Arthur van; born in Batavia (N.E.I.), 1874.

Van Schendel's first work immediately assumed a special place in Netherlands literature because it was completely different from that of his contemporaries of the naturalistic school. In his youth he gained his greatest success with a short novel *Een Zwerver Verliefd* (A Wanderer in Love). In his stories he shows great preference for Italy where he has been living for many years. The early stories are about imaginary figures, incarnations of an elementary longing for love and wisdom in idealized, historic surroundings. In 1930 Van Schendel's talent revealed itself in another aspect with *Het Fregatschip 'Johanna Maria'* (The Frigate 'Johanna Maria').

His principal works are: *Een Zwerver Verliefd* (A Wanderer in Love), *De Berg van Droomen* (Mountain of Dreams), *Angiolino en de Lente* (Angiolino and the Spring), *Het Fregatschip 'Johanna Maria'* (The Frigate 'Johanna Maria'), *De Waterman* (The Waterman) and a trilogy, I. *Een Hollandsch Drama* (A House in Haarlem), II. *De Rijke Man* (The Wealthy Man), and III. *De Grauwe Vogels* (Grey Birds). I and III have been translated into English. During the occupation he wrote among other things *Mijnheer Oberon en Mevrouw* (Mr. Oberon and Mrs. Oberon).

HOLST, R. N. Roland; born in Amsterdam, 1868; died in Laren, 1938.

R. N. Roland Holst, first professor, later director of the Academy of Fine Arts in Amsterdam, was known primarily for his decorative art, murals and stained glass windows. He was also an excellent prose-writer with a particular style of his own. His two volumes of collected essays *Over Kunst en Kunstenaars* (About Art and Artists) I and II belong to the representative works of his time. His only purely literary work is a little volume of philosophical sketches, *Overpeinzingen van een Bramenzoeker* (Meditations of a Blackberry Picker). For several years R. N. Roland Holst was on the editorial staff of the monthly *De Gids.* (The Guide).

LEEUW, Aart van der; born in Delft, 1876; died in Voorburg, 1931.

Van der Leeuw wrote beautiful, quiet and tender poems and novelettes. His art drifts away from reality and is dreamy and poetical.

His principal prose works are: *Kinderland* (Children's Land), *Ik en Mijn Speelman* (I and My Fiddler) and *De Kleine Rudolf* (Little Rudolf).

MOERKERKEN, P. H. van; born 1877.

Van Moerkerken became known through his book *De Dans des Levens* (The Dance of Life). His best-known works include a series of ten novels under the collective title *Gedachten der Tijden* (Thoughts of the Times), in which he uses historical material and gives a true picture of certain periods or currents. He has also published poetry.

ECKEREN, Gerard van (pen-name of Maurits Esser); born in Haarlem, 1876.

For many years he was director of a large publishing firm. As an author he became known through a number of novels, most of which are considered to belong to the naturalistic school. Among his principal works of that period are *Ida Westerman* and *Annie Hada.* He later changed his style and wrote *Oogen In De Spiegel* (Eyes in the Mirror) and *De Parade Gaat Door* (The Parade Takes Place). As a contemplative critic van Eckeren has done excellent work, especially in *Den Gulden Winckel* (The Gilt Shop), a monthly for book-lovers which he edited, and later in the literary monthly *Groot Nederland* (Great Netherlands).

NAEFF, Top (Antonia Naeff-van Rhijn); born in Dordrecht, 1878.

Top Naeff gained her initial success with a book for adolescents,

Schoolidyllen (School Idylls), which has been reprinted many times since its publication in 1900 and is still widely read. After this, followed novels, plays and several volumes of short stories. In the novelette and short story only a few Netherlands authors are her equals.

Her best-known books are: *De Dochter* (The Daughter), *Voor de Poort* (In Front of the Gate) and *Een Huis in de Rij* (One House in the Row).

VAN DE WOESTIJNE, Karel; born 1878 at Ghent; died 1929 at Zwijnaarde, near Ghent.

Van de Woestijne studied at the University of Ghent. He then lived at Latem and identified himself with the Latem School of Flemish artists. He was still very young when he began to write poetry; he contributed from time to time to the periodicals *Van Nu en Straks* and *Vlaanderen*. He was correspondent of the *Nieuwe Rotterdamsche Courant*, for which he wrote a number of literary reviews. In 1921 he was appointed Professor in the Netherlands Literature at the University of Ghent. Van de Woestijne is considered one of the greatest Flemish poets. His work comprises critical essays and some romantic novels—mostly symbolic tales—and verse that is profoundly imaginative and subtle. Van de Woestijne has revealed a many-sided, complex personality, refined and high-strung, and an endless conflict between sensuality and the purely spiritual.

ELSSCHOT, Willem (pen-name of Alfons de Ridder); born in Antwerp, 1882.

After finishing his studies at the Trade School in his native town, Elsschot was employed for many years at Schiedam (South Holland). He then started a publicity agency in Antwerp. His first novel *Villa des Roses* (1913) immediately achieved a great success, greater in Holland, however, than in Belgium. His second novel *De Verlossing* (The Deliverance), appeared before the outbreak of the First World War; during the German occupation of Belgium his *Lijmen* (Glues) was published by a small, unknown publisher in Antwerp. Circumstances prevented this work from receiving much attention, a fact that discouraged Elsschot so much that from 1917 until 1932 he did not write at all. In 1933 *Kaas* (Cheese) appeared, and from then on *Tsjip* (1934), *Pensioen* (Pension) (1935), *Het Been* (The Leg) (a sequel of *Lijmen*) (1938), *De Leeuwentemmer* (The Lion Tamer). *Tsjip*

en de Leeuwentemmer (Tsjip and the Liontamer), a reprint, was published in 1943 by Querido Inc. in New York.

HOLST, A. Roland; born in Amsterdam, 1888.

Considered a poet of great importance in Netherlands literature during the period following the 1880's, his poems express a metaphysical longing, a desire to be detached from this earth, hovering between time and eternity. His prose is either philosophically contemplative or inspired by the Celtic mythical world.

His principal poetic works are: *Verzen* (Poems), *Voorbij de Wegen* (Beyond the Roads) and *De Wilde Kim* (The Wild Horizon). Prose: *Deirdre en de Zonen van Usnach* (Deirdre and the Sons of Usna) and *De Afspraak* (The Appointment).

COSTER, Dirk; born in Delft, 1887.

Coster gained great fame as an essayist and critic. In 1921 he founded, together with Just Havelaar, the literary monthly *De Stem* (The Voice), of which he became the managing director. His best-known book is *Marginalia,* a volume of aphorisms. Some time later appeared two critical essays *Verzameld Proza* (Collected Prose) which should be considered the most valuable contribution to the understanding of literary conceptions in our time. He has also published a drama with William the Silent as the principal figure.

HAVELAAR, Just; born in Rotterdam, 1880; died in Amersfoort, 1930.

Besides being a painter, Havelaar wrote essays on literature and the fine arts, expressing his opinion about arts and primarily in connection with religion, ethics and society. Together with Coster he founded the literary monthly *De Stem* (The Voice).

His chief works are: *De Religie der Ziel* (The Religion of the Soul), *De Nieuwe Mensch* (The New Man) and *De Weg tot de Werkelijkheid* (The Road to Reality).

HAAN, Jacob Israel de; born in Smilde, 1881; died in Jerusalem, 1924.

In Amsterdam de Haan was a well-known lawyer and private tutor. He first published some novels and many short stories but drew attention more particularly as a Jewish poet after publication of *Het Joodsche Lied* (The Jewish Song). As a Zionist, de Haan went to Palestine in 1919, where he became a lecturer at

the Government Law School. After having turned slowly but definitely away from Zionism, he was murdered in Jerusalem in 1924.

His principal works are: *Libertijnsche Liederen* (Libertine Songs), *Het Joodsche Lied* (The Jewish Song) and *Kwatrijnen* (Quatrains).

NIJHOFF, M.; born in The Hague, 1894.

Nijhoff studied law and, after receiving his doctor's degree, devoted himself to Netherlands philology and literature at Utrecht. He published lyrical and critical studies, showing a keen intellect in writing witty and sprightly speculative pieces. His lyrics are among the best of their kind that Netherlands literature has produced. In these he seems to cling to a happiness, past yet never completely disappeared, which is very typical of his work. For many years Nijhoff was co-editor of the leading monthly *De Gids* (The Guide).

His principal poetic works are: *De Wandelaar* (The Walker), *Pierrot aan de Lantaarn* (Pierrot at the Lantern), *Vormen* (Forms), *Nieuwe Gedichten* (New Poems); in prose: *De Pen op Papier* (The Pen on Paper), *Gedachten op Dinsdag* (Thoughts on Tuesday).

MARNIX GIJSEN (pen-name of J. A. Goris); born in Antwerp, 1899.

Goris studied at Leuven, where he was promoted to doctor in history in 1925. He was, successively, professor at that university, chief of the cabinet of the Mayor of Antwerp, director of Fine Arts of the municipality of Antwerp, chief of the cabinet of the Minister of Economic Affairs, High Commissar of Tourism in Belgium and finally director of the Belgian Information Bureau in New York.

After spending a few years as a young man in the United States, where he studied in Seattle among other places, he paid many visits to this country and in 1927 wrote *Ontdek Amerika* (Discover America). Goris' poetic work, collected in one volume *Het Huis* (The House), is small in quantity but great in value and significance.

During the Second World War, Goris published in New York *Belgium in Bondage* (L. B. Fischer, New York, 1943), written in the English language, and *Le Genie Flamand* (The Flemish Genius) (Editions du Roseau Pensant, New York, 1943), written in French. His anthology of Flemish lyric poetry appeared in Pretoria (South Africa) in 1944.

WALSCHAP, Gerard; born in Londerzeel, 1898.

This Flemish writer, first a journalist, later a library-inspector, is one of the most original and powerful authors in young Flemish literature. He deserves the great prestige he enjoys for his talent of keen observation, the courage with which he analyzes pathological cases in his direct, sober style.

His chief works are: *De Familie Roodhooft* (The Family Roodhooft), *Celibaat* (Celibacy), *Trouwen* (Marrying), *Sybille, Een Mensch Van Goeden Wil* (A Person of Good Will), *De Dood In Het Dorp* (Death in the Village) and *Het Volk* (The People).

ROELANTS, Maurice; born in Ghent, 1895.

This Flemish author began his literary career as a poet; he afterwards published a novel, *Komen en Gaan* (Coming and Going). His prose is moving because of a subtle, analytical and sensitive style. He later published: *De Jazzspeler* (The Jazz Player), *Het Leven dat Wij Droomden* (The Life We Dreamed), *Alles Komt Terecht* (All's Well That Ends Well) and *Gebed om een Goed Einde* (Prayer for a Good End).

BRULEZ, Raymond; born in 1895.

This author's important work is *Scheherezade,* a series of short stories. His writing is marked by its philosophical quality, as well as its cultural background; and "his delightful prose," says one critic, "is of an epicurean skepticism."

SLAUERHOFF, J. J.; born in Leeuwarden, 1898; died in Hilversum, 1936.

Slauerhoff studied medicine in Amsterdam and then made countless trips to China, South America and Africa as ship's surgeon. Slauerhoff published lyrics, prose and plays, and should be counted among the most important representatives of the young author's generation. In his work we sense the nature of a restless wanderer, with a contempt for life, seeking quiet and solitude, a subtle and over-sensitive artist. Although he died at an early age he left numerous works.

His principal poetic works are: *Archipel* (Archipelago), *Soleares, Eerlijk Zeemansgraf* (An Honest Seaman's Grave); in prose: a volume of novelettes, *Schuim en Asch* (Froth and Ashes); two novels *Het Verboden Rijk* (The Forbidden Kingdom) and *Leven op Aarde* (Life on Earth).

MARSMAN, Hendrik; born 1899 at Zeist; died 1940.

Primarily a lyric poet, Marsman was the author of novels and short stories. His verse is modern in form and significance, courageously independent, often strikingly and aggressively intense. His work is for the most part more a reflection of feeling and sense of appreciation than it is purely literary. In his critical essays, Marsman is more impressionistic than contemplative, but always clear, sharp and hard-hitting. His novel, *De dood van Angele Degroux* (The Death of Angele Degroux), was widely appreciated as a literary experiment. In 1936 he received the Van der Hoogt Prize of the Netherlands Society for Literature for his collection of poems *Porta Nigra*. Marsman was drowned in the sinking of a ship carrying him to England.

DU PERRON, Charles Edgar; born in Meester Cornelis (Java), 1900; died in Bergen-Binnen (N.H.) 1940.

He came from an old distinguished Netherlands East Indies family and spent his entire youth in Java. As a young man he came to Europe where he lived mostly in Brussels and Paris. In 1938 he returned to Java and stayed there until 1940 when he came back to Holland. There he died a few days after the German invasion as a result of angina pectoris.

Du Perron is one of the most remarkable and important figures in modern Dutch literature. His life-work comprises a volume of collected poems *Parlando,* two volumes of short stories, three novels, of which *Het Land van Herkomst* (The Country of Origin) —his masterpiece—is of incredible richness and variety, four volumes of essays, a literary diary *(Blocnote Klein Formaat—*Little Notebook) and four studies on Multatuli.

BRAAK, Menno ter; born in Eibergen, 1902; died in The Hague, 1940.

Historian and philosopher, he received his doctor's degree on a thesis called *Kaiser Otto III, Ideal und Praxis im fruehen Mittelalter* (Emperor Otto III, Ideal and Practice in the Early Middle Ages). Ter Braak was the most militant and powerful spirit among young Dutch authors. He originally expressed himself in essayform and concentrated mainly on general cultural problems. His fierce and bold critical attacks on the spiritual life of Catholics and ecclesiastical Protestants were expressed in his book, *Afscheid van Domineesland* (Farewell to the Pastor's Territory).

Ter Braak was one of the founders of the periodical *Forum* introducing new thoughts and new ideas into Dutch literary life. From 1936 until his untimely death—a few days after the German invasion of the Netherlands—he was the soul of Dutch anti-fascism.

His chief philosophical work is the trilogy: *Carnaval der Burgers* (The Citizens' Carnival), *Politicus Zonder Partij* (Politician Without Party), *Van Oude en Nieuwe Christenen* (Of Old and Modern Christians).

VESTDIJK, S.; born in Harlingen, 1898.

After studying medicine in Amsterdam and traveling as a ship's surgeon to the Netherlands East Indies, Vestdijk gave up practice. Only much later did he begin to write. He was co-editor of the literary monthly *Forum* and, after its discontinuance, of *Groot Nederland* (Great Netherlands). He wrote six volumes of poetry, three volumes of short stories, four volumes of essays and critical studies, and ten novels of which *Het Vijfde Zegel* (The Fifth Seal) (with El Greco as its principal figure) is the best—one of the masterpieces of Netherlands prose. His prose is distinguished by ironical scepticism and subtle psychological discernment.

TERBORGH, F. C.; this pen-name conceals a Dutch diplomat on active service.

VEEN, Adriaan van der; born in Venray, 1916.

This writer made his debut with a number of sketches dealing with the life of the unemployed, *Geld Speelt de Groote Rol* (It's Money That Counts), in which the people take stock of their poverty. He was immediately recognized by critics as the most powerful and vivid author of his generation. He has also published a volume of fantastic poems and prose called *Oefeningen* (Exercises).

VROMAN, Leo; born 1916.

He studied biology in Utrecht; he managed to escape from Holland during the German invasion in May 1940. He visited South Africa and from there went to Java where he became an assistant at an Indies university.

Vroman has illustrated comic strips in Dutch East Indies newspapers, has written poetry and short stories.

VASALIS, M.; (pen-name of M. Leenmans).

A woman physician in practice in Amsterdam. She has written two volumes of poetry and a few short stories of which that in this book is a reminiscence of her stay in South Africa in 1938.

VUIJK, Beb; born and brought up in the Dutch East Indies.

For many years she lived on the lonely island of Boeroe where her husband owned a kajapoeti-oil distillery. She has written two novels and a volume of short stories.

DEBROT, Cola; born in Willemstad (Curaçao, N.W.I.), 1906.

Debrot first studied law in Amsterdam and after receiving his degree went on to the study of medicine. He published two long short stories, *De Mapen* and *Mijn Zuster De Negerin* (My Sister the Negro). He is editor of *Criterium*, a literary magazine of the younger generation.

HELMAN, Albert (pen-name of Lou Lichtveld); born in Paramaribo (Surinam), 1903.

Helman spent his entire youth in Surinam. The scene of his first work is laid in the tropics and his novel *Zuid Zuid-West* (South South-West) expresses his love for the tropics with charm and purity. The scene of *De Stille Plantage* (The Quiet Plantation) of a later date is also laid in his native country.

MELLE, J. van; born in Goes, 1887.

In 1906 this author went as a teacher to Transvaal (South Africa). After a visit to Holland three years later, he returned to South Africa to settle permanently. The greater part of his prose is written in Afrikaans; some of his books are published in Netherlands. In most of his short stories he renders perfectly the atmosphere of the typical South African farmer's existence, the peculiar rhythm, so characteristic of life in the vast fields and plains.

Among his principal works published in Netherlands are: *Zuid Afrikaansche Schetsen* (South African Sketches) and *Bart Nel, de Opstandeling* (Bart Nel, the Rebel). Of his stories published in Afrikaans we mention: *Oom Daan en die Dood* (Uncle Daan and Death), and of his novels *Dawid Booijsen.*

ALPHABETICAL LIST OF AUTHORS

ALPHABETICAL LIST OF AUTHORS